EAST OF
THE SUNRISE

The National Library of Poetry

Cynthia A. Stevens, Editor
Nicole Walstrum, Associate Editor

East of the Sunrise

Library of Congress
Cataloging in Publication Data

ISBN 1-56167-268-8

Manufactured in The United States of America by
Watermark Press
11419 Cronridge Dr., Suite 10
Owings Mills, MD 21117

Editor's Note

The artistry within this anthology, *East of the Sunrise*, will take you upon an intimate journey of emotional enlightenment. The broad assortment of poems presented here is wonderfully enthralling. Each of the poets featured within this anthology has succeeded in crafting a true work of art. As one of the editors and judges of the contributing entries, I had the rewarding opportunity to review and ponder the many pieces presented within this anthology. There are several poems, however, I wish to honor with special recognition.

Achieving grand prize was Frank Morris with "Awaking from a Dream" (p. 1). Morris utilizes some unique, surreal images to represent the conflicts in today's society. In the onset of his piece, he tells the reader to: *"**Go and bedevil** organ grinder monkeys - needle their gypsy blood... /aboiling with rotten bananas - **skedaddle them shrieking** ...."* In these first two lines, Morris seems to be satirizing the current political policy on American social problems. He later goes on to describe the relationship between the lower classes and authority in contemporary culture. *"Call out the olive drab National Guard rolling down freeways -/ ...to feed the poor in your dreams/ who lick milk and honey off their bayonets..."* as if you are to harass the lower-class, drug-addicted, and homeless -- make them run away.

Morris continues to sarcastically portray how wonderful our society and government appear to be, *"Release white doves/ for every prisoner free...."* In actuality, it is not wonderful at all. He explains that although we may view the ways of society and government as wrong, few of us really do anything about it. *" ...when the good sense of love/ comes knocking at your door -/ **both barrels blazing gold dust and champagne corks -/You'd better open up**..."*

Morris is taunting the reader by suggesting that when things are going our way and we have an opportunity to be all we wish to be, then there is no need for lawful regulations. Open up: *"Let the monkeys swing about/ without their leg irons,/ the doves dance with their/ white silk top hats/ tilted back **cooing...**"*

In addressing the objectivity of moral conduct in society, Morris asks the question why should we dispute what is wrong or right in society -- it's not going to get you anywhere, *"...you're just spinning your wheels in sand, **Honeybones**."* Morris ends with the word Honeybones as if to say "make no bones about it." We will have no direct objection to the overall situation as long as everything is sweet on our end. Overall, after sorting through the provoking images and implied sarcasm, I believe Morris wants us all to take a look at our society and really do something. Wake UP!

Another piece touching upon the impressions of life is "On Pushing Sixty," by Frank Bayer. Bayer speaks of the repetitious acts of giving and taking involved in everyone's life. He conveys the concept that no matter how much we try to give away, we are always collecting. And perhaps the older you get as in "on pushing sixty," the things you collect and distribute seem all the more valuable. Bayer compares the giving of material things to the giving of ideals and morals -- that no matter how much you give away, there will always be more. And that everyone may not accept what you contribute to life, but each and every one of us has a lot to offer.

On a more chilling degree, Laura Sperry offers us "Grave Interruption" (p. 103). Although her piece is short and concise, it is quite profound. A relationship which is in the midst of flourishing is quickly buried because of a "grave interruption." There are a few other melancholy poems full of wonderful images and depth: "All that is Left" by Elaine Emmett (p. 194); "Heritage" by Paula Alexandra Fernandes (p. 272); "Statue of Ambiguity" by Brian J. Lawson (p. 80); and "Worn Gloves" by Ryan W. Shaw (p. 424).

Several other prominent poems you won't want to miss: "mitigated endearment" by Peter J. Dahlstrand (p. 586); "Forked Tongue" by Richard P. Fernandez (p. 146); "Night Shift" by Valerie J. Rosenfeld (p. 410); and "Contributions" by Mark Cristopher Whitmore (p. 120).

Although I do not have the time or space to individually critique every eminent poem appearing within *East of the Sunrise,* you will notice that each piece of artistry is an admirable contribution. May all of the artists within this anthology be renowned for their talents and efforts in creative writing.

Cynthia A. Stevens,
Senior Editor

Acknowledgments

East of the Sunrise is a culmination of the efforts of many individuals. The editors are grateful for the contributions of these fine people: Elizabeth Barnes, Jeffrey Bryan, Chris Bussey, Kim Cohn, Amy Dezseran, Joy Esterby, Aundrea Felder, Ardie L. Freeman, Hope Freeman, Kathy Hudson-Frey, Paula Jones, Steve Miksek, Diane Mills, Eric Mueck, Lamont Robinson, Rich Schaub, Michelle Shavitz, Jacqueline Spiwak, Caroline Sullivan, Nicole Walstrum, Ira Westreich, Tiffany Wilson, and Diana Zeiger.

Howard Ely,
Managing Editor

Winners of the North American Open Poetry Contest

Grand Prize
Frank Morris / Gunbarrel, CO

Second Prize

Frank Bayer /The Woodlands, TX
Peter J. Dahlstrand / Villanova, PA
Elaine Emmett / Pittsburg, KS
Paula Alexandra Fernandes / Kearny, NJ
Richard P. Fernandez / Bayport, NY

Brian J. Lawson / Rutland, MA
Valerie J. Rosenfeld / Albany, NY
Ryan W. Shaw / Monroeville, OH
Laura M. Sperry / Mentor, OH
Mark Cristopher Whitmore / Corpus Christi, TX

Third Prize

Robert Aikins / Parsons, KS
Phil Ballbach / Lansing, MI
C. H. Barry / Yale, OK
Ida Bithell / Santa Clara, CA
Lillian Bosworth / La Mesa, CA
Catherine G. Bratton / East Palo Alto, CA
Jennifer L. Brunk / Overland Park, KS
Jo Santoro Cialkowski / Lincoln Park, MI
J. E. Coakley / Spring, TX
Fern K. Cullom / Lexington, MO
Mike Day / Phoenix, AZ
Jeff DelaVergne / Denver, CO
Amanda Dershem / San Diego, CA
Brian Elliott / Mount Laurel, NJ
Philip David Forsyth / Providence, RI
Sunny Franson / Upper Lake, CA
B. Green / Southfield, MI
William Brown Hanford / Howell, MI
M. Michele Hardy / Laurel, MD
Rick Kachigian / Garden City, MI
James Kohfeld / Santa Monica, CA
Robert Christopher Lenoir / Birmingham, AL
Mary T. Linder / Wood Haven, NY
Herschel Wayne Lucas / Savannah, GA
Mathew Karl McKenna / Cleveland, OH
Terrin "Bones" Martin / Estes Park, CO
Micah Mesler / Leawood, KS
Madeline Moore / San Francisco, CA
Randy T. Nelson / Taylor, MI
Debo Richards Obawole / Austin, TX

Rebecca R. Odom / Franklin, TN
Lora Passetti / Bloomington, IL
M. Kathleen Phillips / College Station, TX
Michael A. Pinkelman / Northville, MI
Calvin R. Pollard II / Bellaire, TX
John J. Quirk / Lees Summit, MO
Michelle Rambo / Orange, CA
Chad Reimann / Rolla, MO
David A. Robinson / Glendale, AZ
Kevin B. Robinson / Arlington, VA
Amanda J. Rutledge / Guthrie, OK
Margaret A. Ryan / West Long Branch, NJ
Jean Older Scott / Ypsilanti, MI
John P. Shields / San Francisco, CA
S. Marie Shuman / Frederick, MD
John P. Smith / Albrightsville, PA
Kimberly Soloman / Charlevoix, MI
Beverly Stanczyk / Country Club Hills, IL
Jeanette Strack / Edgewater, FL
Marvin Tanenhaus / Binghamton, NY
Barbara M. Thomas / Lula, GA
Phebe Alden Tisdale / Winchester, MA
Carmina Amezcua Towe / Everett, WA
Rebecca Van De Voort / Mountain Iron, MN
Justin David Wade / Arlington, TX
E. Carol Walker / Shrewsbury, PA
Mary G. Walters / Loves Park, IL
Kerry Wilson / Garden City, MI
Yolanda Wysocki / Lihue, HI

Congratulations also to all semi-finalists.

Grand Prize Winner

Awaking from a Dream

Go and bedevil organ grinder monkeys - needle their gypsy blood
aboiling with rotten bananas - *skedaddle them shrieking -*

Call out the olive drab National Guard rolling down freeways -
Old Glories whipping from radio antennas on faded canvas-covered trucks
to feed the poor in your dreams
who lick milk and honey off their bayonets...

Release white doves
for every prisoner free...

But when the good sense of love
comes knocking at your door -
both barrels blazing gold dust and champagne corks -

You'd better open up -

Let the monkeys swing about
without their leg irons,
the doves dance with their
white silk top hats
tilted back *cooing...*

Otherwise you're just
spinning your wheels in sand,
Honeybones.
Frank Morris

A Wonderful Death

Eyebrows pointed up
Lips smiling.
Wind as still as glass
Arms open wide
Earth moving farther and farther away

Old relatives waiting to see me
Sky like a cloudy red fire
Encountering a perfect life
Into his arms I jump with tears of happiness
Leaving my earthly possessions behind,
I arise to the one place were "sin" has no existence.

David Paul Miller

Take Time

Take time to smell the roses,
take time to look and see,
at all of God's creation,
on earth for you and me.

The palm tree stands so straight and tall,
waiting for God's beck and call,
to cool us in the summer's heat
when bumble bee we chance to meet.
In flower he will busy be,
busy as a bumble bee.

The humming bird so small and swift,
like helicopter he will lift,
his body from a flower shaken,
from some nectar he has taken.

The colors of the world we see,
put on this earth for you and me,
by God who loves us tenderly.
If we would only look and see.

Genevieve Deering

Felicidad- The Return To Happiness

Happiness is a definite possi-proba-reality in my life again!
Having been beyond depression, beyond despondency, beyond hope
  and dreams
and even the most remote thought of the future was replete with
bleakness, barrenness, sterility, negativity, emptiness, and hopelessness-
a future of emotional impotence;
Having been ready to negate and cancel the being that was no longer
capable of grasping at even the most infinitesimal shred of hope;
Having felt the horrible totality of despair in every quadrant of life
and the inner self feeling deeply that the quality of life to be
endured would be totally unacceptable in any and all ways.

Fortunately, for this being, the intrinsic desire to be was stronger
than all the potent forces that allowed it to be tempted into non-being.
This being will most definitely survive, live, enjoy, be and be happy!
Viva Felicidad!
Know that happiness- felicity- is a state of mind and being.
Happiness might slip through one's sphere, be elusive, seem to disappear
for what might feel like forever and at times, its very existence is
doubted but Happiness is cosmic and my being and I are happy again!

Janette B. Aufrichtig

"Sadness"

Sadness is a lonely man, a child without a home, a fallen tear,
we all must journey through sadness, without sadness happiness
cannot exist and wisdom cannot be attained, sadness is a river
and we must learn to swim or we will all drown in despair,
nothing can compare when you're not there, a child is crying,
while man drinks his sorrow away, another one dying, I read
the news yesterday and I thought of you... Sadness

Fareed B. Abdallah

Education

"What is education, Mom, the teacher says we must get it
To read and write and surely never to forget it
So, what is education, Mom, she says it's worth the strife."
"Why education, sonny boy, is learning,
  The rest of your life."

Emma Randolph

An Oeuvre

The movement of the artists hand writes creative tales of the painting.
With exaggerated marks in the medium images of turbulence are conjured.
Tangled brush strokes give a sense of lost emotions, equally obtrusive
are the distorted shapes in the midst forming areas of tension.
Icy vermilion red, viridian greens, cutting blues are the piercing
colors creating a distressing mood.
Above a feeling of isolation forms as the haze of smoky colors interweave.
Is it all an art of illusion?
For the rich painting can not hide its deeper resonances.
Concealed in its depth are quaint qualities, a belief of the soothe,
calmness that lays reflected in the turmoil.
Light delicate touches of an intriguing ultramarine, azure.
A hint of yellow ochre, and red earth that can be rarely captured.
Underneath the mirage the abstract has a simpleness to it.
The painting interpreted in several ways by the observer.
A rare occurrence of how the artist wants it interpreted.
Alas!

Anu Sharma

Just A Moment

A moment of silence, a moment of peace
A break in the chaos, for a moment at least
Please have patience and don't get mad
I need just a moment is that really so bad?
Children crying, people dying
Giving up without even trying
People living with constant pain
Values and morals going down the drain
My head is spinning, my body is worn
I need just a moment to mend what is torn
Thoughts just keep coming, but rarely complete
I need just a moment to get back on my feet
People lying, cheating, killing, beating, destroying all that is pure
These people need help, we must find a cure
I can't change the world, but my mind feels the strain
I need just a moment, so I won't go insane

Christle Marie Ross

"What Next Lord"

Oh Lord, from just a chrysalis,
  a butterfly comes forth.
While one small seed becomes a tree,
  to beautify the earth.

From one small egg there comes a bird,
  to sing its lovely song.
And each small drop of rain that falls,
  to the ocean runs along.

A sudden rain will fall, and then
  perhaps the sun will shine,
And like a miracle there will be
  a rainbow in the sky.

If you can do so much Dear Lord,
  with simple things like these
A flower, butterfly, bird, rainbow, and a tree.

What may you even yet do Lord,
  with such a human being like me.
I pray it will be good like you Lord.

Bertice Lee Merritt

The Child And The Clown

I stand there in my disguise.
A clown.

A clown wanting desperately to bring a smile.
My heart aching for the child.
My heart wanting to hold and love the Child.

The suffering Child lays in bed.
Each breath a painful struggle.
A cough so painful, the Child's eyes are sad.
A whisper to talk. Effort more than the Child can handle.

I kneel there in my disguise. A clown.
Praying for the child. Groping for words.

The Child doesn't know the heart behind the disguise.
The Child is open, exposed. The pain and suffering evident.

The clown is hidden, disguised. Hoping to help in some small way.

The child is exposed to needles, tests, and whims of others.
Others who forget or avoid the dignity of the Child.

The clown can take off the costume, the paint, and the mask.

The Child cannot take off the suffering, the pain, the disease.

I stand there in my disguise.
A clown.

Glenda J. Windham

The Fate Of The Flower

A bud opens up to welcome the morn
A creation of God has just been born
As life starts afresh with this flower to sweet
Another will die as the cycle repeats

For all live to die, though there is a way out
You just need to learn what life is about
We all have this chance though the flower does not
We can live for eternity, while the flower will rot

We were given free will, we were given a choice
We've the ability to speak, how will we use our voice
He gave us this freedom to find him on our own
and the one way to find him is through his son alone

So remember the flower, remember its fate
remember that Jesus Christ opened the gate
think about the life the truth will provide
unlike the flower with God you'll survive.

Craig Phillips

Clouds

Soft wind blows
A dandelion fluff
Blanket over me
As I lay, sun numbed,
On rain soaked grass.

I can not move!

Only my eyes flow upward where
Miles above green cotton candy
Makes grinding noises as the wind
Bends and straightens, bends and straightens.

I ache! To Be!
Against the linen white clouds.

Diana Federl

A Time To Worry

The Bible say's the time will come,
    A disease will take us, one by one.
A friend, a relative, we just don't know,
    "Who" might be the next to go.

The scare of "aids" has hit us hard,
    Could it be in your back yard?
It's not just gay's, or casual sex,
    Needles, drugs, could you be next?

In the still of the night, a friend lays there,
    No hope for life just utter despair.
They ask "why me?" - no answer comes -
    A mother disowns her only son.

Well I pray for you, I pray for me -
    An answer to this that we may see.
A new vaccine - that's all you hear,
    Still today, there's constant fear...

Judith A. Collier

A Biological Father's Love

Pressed between the pages of an old and tattered book,
a few surviving photographs upon which we can look,
to recall the angelic face of a baby as she smiled,
in a long ago, distant time, when she was her father's child.

Nursery rhymes she must have sang, when she was at play,
bedtime prayers she might have said, once in a long ago day,
rhymes and prayers we never heard, at least not with our own ears,
but they echoed in our minds, as we drifted through the years.

Like shadows cast, from the east, by the morning sun at dawn,
as surely as the night's tears dry, when the morning dew is gone,
one's childhood is so fleeting, just a fraction of our time,
and so quickly her's was gone, we missed her uphill climb.

And as the days turn into weeks, and the weeks turn into months,
after all those years he proudly recalls, he was her daddy once,
and though her name is different, their blood and cells are one,
and there will remain through time and change, a bond that won't
be undone.

Dixie Harden

Love

A fire burns bright inside,
A flame that is strong,
A bond we cannot hide,
An outrageous feeling that we belong,

Love is something we cannot explain,
A secret deep and true,
A sense your heart will claim,
Knowing that someone loves you,

Love is something precious from the heart,
A fortune money cannot buy,
An inspiration that cannot be taken apart,
A treasure that will not die,

Love is a pain without sorrow,
To cry without a tear,
A gift your heart will follow,
For love is special and dear.

Angela Arsenault

A Distant Call

A distant call one seemed to hear
A gentle voice but persistently clear
It spoke of heritage an ancient dream
From a grandparents' home having never been seen

This call had grown stronger over the years
Over all hesitation and scorn from one's peers
An old country was visited above all concern
Of personal safety in a quest to but learn

As third generation a transition complete
The loss of old culture was cut very neat
But the instinct remained quite simple and true
That this country was home and a place to renew

Language and customs barely shown as a child
Came alive like escaping to some mythological isle
Castles and cathedrals were each viewed with awe
But a strong bond with the people was felt most of all

The new world returned a new sense was perceived
The nuance of culture of how life is received
It would have been easy to ignore this old call
And to live in a bottle a world safe and small

David B. Kobus

"Confusion"

Did you ever ponder what's right or wrong,
a hole that's so deep and dark and long.
Did you ever have numbers that you couldn't add,
you try so hard and it makes you so mad.
Did you ever have thoughts you couldn't hope to combine,
your thoughts seem tangled like an ever-growing vine.
Did you ever have thoughts you couldn't put into motion,
giving up is reality - not just a notion.
Did you ever feel that life is a maze,
running in a circle - walking in a haze.
One of these days I think things will get clear,
as the end of our lives grow ever near.

Janet L. Hysell

Who I Am Inside

I walked slowly down the street without a care,
A homeless man greeted me with a crooked smile,
My instinct told me to walk away quick,
But I could not resist helping,
It pained me to see another human being in this situation,
Especially if it were not of his own making,
If he would take it,
I would give him a job,
Some are too proud,
Some will take only money,
To blow on beer and drugs,
I approached him slowly,
"Would you like a job, sir?, "I asked kindly"
He lifted his head and said "Yes, thank you!"
I was glad to help,
That's just who I am inside

Dustin Stevens

Snowflakes

Snowflakes are a beautiful sight
When observed on paper as black as night
The intricate patterns and designs
Make identical snowflakes impossible to find
In strong wind they show furious rage
In a breeze they dance as if on a stage
All angles of snowflakes reflect the light
And they're very beautiful; beautiful and bright

Gretchen Begley

Stormy Night

I awake to see a steak of lightning dancing in the sky.
To hear the wind as it rushes through the trees.

I hear the thunder shaking the earth;
I start to hide my head under my pillow.
No.....Stop.....Listen.....
It is spring come at last.

Barb Strode

The Phantom

Across the street there is a light
A light, a life that no one likes
no one dares go out at night
for fear of the one who makes this light
Those of those who love the night
and are ignorant to the phantom's bite
Will walk about without fright
until they're charmed by the light
the phantom's kiss is so light
It's never felt until the bite

The phantom smiles and flashes teeth
Then pierces skin and sinks beneath
leaving the victim without relief
dropping the victim in the street
The phantom licks his lips and sucks his teeth

Only one thing will satisfy the elegant beast
The blood of a mortal is its feast

You can't run or escape the power that's acquired
You can't run or escape the being of vampire

David Gale

A Mother's Joy - My Son

A little smile - a little tear,
A little finger - a cry of fear,
A little boo-boo - a kiss to heal,
A little boy - not a doll - but real.
Little blue eyes, so big so bright,
A little hug - a kiss goodnight.
broken wrists - two skinned knees,
Unconscious falls - climbing trees,
measles, mumps - chicken pox too
Bee stings, scrapes and black and blue
Skates, sleds - toboggans and such
Falls, stitches - this is too much
Can I stand dirty towels thrown down in the tub?
And those muddy shoes means I must scrub.
How can one little boy do all of these things?
But when I see him asleep-how my heart sings.
But all of these things wrapped into one,
Let's me know I'm his "Mother"
And this is my "Son".

Ed Lewis

Hoping For The Spirit Of Restoration

Dead, for nothing
A little lamb lay face down
   Looking almost dead
      While people walked the other way,
      Although he moaned and bled

All they had to do
   Was stop and go for help
      But all were busy doing things,
      To benefit themselves

A little lamb lay motionless
   While friends just walked on by
      For those that should have helped him,
      Instead have let him die

Diane B. Jackson

My Love For You

I have this special love for you,
A love that grows from day to day.
A love as fresh as the morning dew,
A love that will never fade away.

Sometimes I find it hard to express,
This love I have for you.
But it's a love, I must confess,
That is only shared by few.

This love of mine that I feel for you,
Is one I have never felt before.
I guess it's all the nice things you do,
That make me love you that much more.

So just remember this one thing;
I love you with all my heart.
And as long as you wear that diamond ring,
Nothing can draw us apart.

Bob Sanders

Martin Luther King

A man with a dream, and full of esteem.
A man with the power, as tall as a tower.
A man who could lead a peaceful march.
With the strength of peace and God's
heavenly watch.

A man with a desire for his people to be free.
Not only for the white man's eye to see.
He only wanted me to be me
To be free of bonds with such a grip,
And to have peace of mind on our daily trip.

The freedom to eat, drink, and be known.
The freedom to work and be left alone.
The freedom to walk and talk with ease,
And not to worry who we please.

I sit and think of his days in jail.
With only the hope of God, to pay his bail.
The strength of this man was oh "so great"
I often wonder if he was sent by fate.

The image of this great man will linger on.
In our hearts, mind, bodies and song.
He lived out the words he preached so well.
And continued on, till the toll of the bell.

Dorothy Ashley

Cathedral Of Pine

Anticipation fills the soul as you begin
A maple bowered trail which leaves
Yesterday, today, and always as
Voices dwindle down in fading sound,
Steps along the path begin to slow
Beneath the hush that's just been found.
Branches high above bow and caress
While sunlight and dust seem to dance around
Dark knotted trunks enveloped with stillness
That whispers within your soul.
A smooth fallen timber invites you rest
And ponder what for you this place will hold;
And soon the sense of being blest
Here in this space that was foretold.

June Stout Bradley

Celebration

It was about the middle of October;
A most beautiful time of year.
There was going to be a celebration,
Because - my birthday was near.

But this particular birthday, was to be quite different;
Not just because I "lost" my church, and my best friend,
But - because, there was soon to be another end.

This particular year had been, so very, very trying;
Among a lot of reasons, my mother was dying.

We all made many visits, to her bedside every day;
We all said hello, talked, and we prayed.

Yes, there was a celebration, but not the one for me;
This celebration, was made on bended knee.

As we entered the church, to pray for our mother;
We all talked quietly, among one another.

Yes, there was a celebration, on a beautiful October day;
We thanked Our God for what Mom gave;
As we all knelt down to pray.

Dianne Faubert

A Losing Battle

He was just a youth and alone on the street,
a pair of worn sneakers covered his feet.
He wore a shirt a couple of sizes too small,
a pair of pants for which he was much too tall;
that was all.
Down the alley he walked on this cold winter night,
a place where you or I would shiver from fright.
Suddenly, he clenched his fists and his eyes oh so tight,
For a scream was let out on this cold winter night.
A noise as loud as a hundred drums,
but this was no parade; this was no fun.
He ducked and dropped to the ground,
frozen with fear that he would be found.
He lay that way,
until he realized, night had turned to day.
He rose to his feet to face the reality,
another of his friends had been lost to the streets.

Jennifer Israel

A Mother's Love

Like the fresh dew on a rose of garnet,
A pastel palette, the remains of a shower of crystals
A fiery ball of tiger's eyes sets into the horizon,
A mother's love is a treasured jewel for all to behold.

Like a single dove flying carelessly into the clear sky,
embracing its refreshing currents,
A dolphin emerging out of the crystalline Pacific,
A doe bounding out of a clearing in the lush and vibrant forest,
it's hooves melodically pounding gracefully like a ballerina,
A mother's love is forever enduring.

Like the satiny clouds that adorn the heavens,
The broad ocean of water,
The true friendships that are etched in your heart,
A mother's love is simply, and purely everlasting.

Davina Waikar Lam

Fantasy Roadhouse

There is a roadhouse in a distant galaxy,
a place of magic and wonder for all the creatures to see.
A place for the its, the that's and them, even you and me.
A place of such pleasure that all intelligent beings seek;
take a flight path to nowhere and when all magnetic gauges freak....

You will go blind as your molecules fade away, as you disappear;
when you begin to see something, it utters welcome into your ear,
greetings, glad to have you, welcome back,relax, you are here!
You've never been here before in the life you just ended, yet
some place in time you find all these creatures you've befriended.

Life like the parking meter of time had just clicked away;
our physical lives ended, but our imaginations had more to say
what we called fantasy, a dream world, that's where we'll stay.
It is the other dimension of which we all spoke,
so in the end we find reality is but a joke!

Fred Nicolai

"Afrikka"

Do I know of AFRIKKA...
A place where the moon lies on it's stomach.
Where people sweat in the days sun...as they
travel for hours in search of the water-hole.
With a pail, and hours back to the Village...
in the distant Setting-Sun.

See Lions and Zebras participating in their
role of life...there's dancing and singing,
Children playing.

A place where language differs, But, the cry
is the same... same as yesteryear "Come home
My Brothahs and Sistahs, come home, your Mothah
(AFRIKKA) awaits you"

So I ask myself...Do I know of AFRIKKA?...
Does AFRIKKA know of me?!!

"Sweet Jesus' (the boat) take me home"
Derrick Lowery

The Seasons Of Life

Spring leaves of shimmering green,
A prettier sight, I've never seen.
So like the bundles of living joy,
Of a baby girl or a baby boy.

Summer brings growth and healthy foliage
Blossom grow and multiply in marriage.
So like the children we have been given
Molded and cared for reaching for heaven.

The season of autumn now in here
Adorned in full splendor they now appear.
So like the lives trusted to us from above
At the height of success, wealth and love.

Winter descends in all its fury
The leaves drop withered and dreary.
Just like our lives, once lived so free,
We return, oh God, to be with thee.

Dee Myers

Untitled

lines crossing like sticks in the wind
we imagined ourselves new words in the vocabulary
and fought to keep the smiles from falling
but the sight of one soon fell upon the other
until the atmosphere that let us breathe closed in tighter
and made a harsh whistling sound like crying

Jeremy Jusay

Cold Spring

Everything should be sequential, a dream,
a puddle of rum. The green walnut
is no different than the unidentifiable apple
which has escaped the wasps. Look and see.
The walnut jumps off the page. The junkyard
of planetary debris litters the predawn August
sky. It is cool beyond the terrestris and
terranova - the great meridian breaking
the back of the waxy pine night.
East Mountain heads North in serpentine waves
transsecting the sunrise. The hemlocks,
Clove Creek, Denny's Mine, Odelltown,
Davenport Corners, all the references
of hawks charting the eastern boundaries
of the highlands, the migration lines
like ancient genetic contrails
hovering, like the land itself
in suspension along the spine
of the great river.

Allan Cox

It's A Long Way

It's a pipeline straight to hell,
A real social call.
To the object, of intense curiosity, disciplined with rugged
features.
But polite am I, in the answering of my distaste.
In the corner, all alone, in the rain and snow.

Still, in its foul repair, it made an impression to the
family tradition.
Knowing, she had developed a strong friendship, with the
devil himself.
And now, loyalties lay burning at my feet.
And it's all window dressing, in the coming attempt of a
serious religion!

It's all a complex course, for humanity to evolve to.
While eons ago, we lost the understanding to be patient.
It's such a simple attitude, knowing the goals of our
satisfaction.
But blinded are we all, robots to a dark passion.

Gary Lilley

Forever Love

When I look into your eyes I see,
A river of dreams,
Overflowing with peace.
One touch...love returns again.
One world...how can we help but win?

I love you with the life,
In the depths of my heart,
And to see you weep,
Tears me apart.
One hundred times,
I would return again.
One love...how could you have helped but win?

Forever like the stars,
In a clear night sky,
Is my love for you,
That should never die.
Infinity times,
I will prove it to you.
One living heart,
Beats with my love for you.

Jedediah Lack

Slumber

There is a slumber that stays in my heart; that always seems
to tear me apart; with life's ups and downs, that always seem
to be around; with a little happiness here and there, it's
hard to share; the little joy that comes my way and, sometimes,
I do pay with loneliness and despair, for this slumber that
stays in my heart; Dear God, stop letting it tear me apart.

Annie Curry

A Boy's Black Eye

A boy of twelve, came in from outside, with a black eye
A sight to be seen, no tears a streaming from his cheek,
But a jolly good yell, mama guess what?
"Oh no, now what is it," came the usual reply.
A football player and a boys elbow
Just came too close together,
Turning his brown eye to black.
We called the doc, in case the insurance banged
Then on went cracked ice to his head
Early to bed as black eye needs a rest;
Morning came with eye all swollen, but,
The doc gave it a clear wash out and mixed a little
Green liquid and little, to swallow
Keeping smiles across his loving face.
Playing hooky from school, a great idea
With a patch on his eye, a pirate he is and
Ready to meet his ball playing friend again.

Beulah McCaston Sawyer

Neighbor

...And the horn man played
A silent darkening blue sky with
piercing stars scattered about
And the far off sounds of silence as back up.
Each sigh of the horn carried his
blues to the height of explanation
to depths far below.
Relief being only that of a tear.

The horn let his misunderstandings
let his mistakes, his anger be carried
far away to be buried deep
not to be judged
not to be seen.
The horn was good.
It was good to let the horn man know he was
worth the sound of silence
worth the darkening blue sky
worth the beautiful piercing stars
worth just knowing.
And the horn man played...

Christopher John Fay

He the Master

Terror pierces my fingertips;
A slave bound tightly by my master.
He tears me apart, his pulsing testosterone
unyielding.
Desire drives out reason; Id abounds-
Slithering, groping, lusting a chance to strike;
Controlled by no law.
He passes to it, chained by its waning.
Those damn Christians, calling on a God
To fulfill their emptiness, their inability to
control.
Spare me you meek slug.
Philanthropy is your prayer, strength mine!
Desire is my God. I run with Jesus' brother; such a
wild pack of
gods. He the master, he is me.

Gene Edmiston

The Scattering

Farewell, my love. We give you to the deep,
A softer bed than most, for your last sleep.

Sleep? No, not likely, as we know you well.
You will ride joyous on the ocean swell,

Tasting the tang of the salt, foamy crests,
Twining among the sea kelp's leafy nests.

Unbound, you'll float upon the manta's sails;
Race with the dolphins; clutch the slippery whales

With hands unhampered by the pain you knew
When earthbound. In the endless miles of blue

Space that an artist's hand has yet to limn
You will see marvels, eyes no longer dim;

Ears newly-wakened to the murmuring strand
And voice now strong, you'll shout toward the land

A last adieu: "I'm free, I'm young and strong!
Gone is the weariness I knew so long.

Think of me now as one with life and motion,
Until you join me in this peaceful ocean."

And thus we leave you now, as, growing late,
The low sun fastens firm the Golden Gate.

Bette V. Levine

Thoughts On My Mind

As I await my child's entrance into this world
A thousand thoughts cross through my mind
From the depth of my inner being I already hear my baby's cry
Why oh why Mother did that man die?
My answer to him is muffled by my own cries
As I race to hold him and shelter him from this drug filled world
I look at him face full of expression
Acknowledging the pain that we both feel
Yet daring not to speak not at this moment
Mother and child embrace full of love
Shutting out the outside world for today
Hoping and praying that tomorrow will bring a better way!

DeLois Franks

In My Dream

In my dream you came to me,
a troubadour with a song to sing.

We loved then, it was both joyful and tragic.
You had to leave; there was only brief magic.

  In that lifetime, I was the only one for you

The castle was cold and you were far away,
now in England, two hundred years astray.

Only together briefly, though our love was old,
it broke my heart deeply to die on my own.

  In that lifetime, you were the only one for me

We met again in the 20s in an anti-prohibition club.
We were rebels in that time, and yes, we loved.

That was the time when our loved lasted the longest
and our love, we thought, was at its strongest.

  In that lifetime, I was the only one for you

Now I have been waiting for you to answer my thoughts;
I feel if I think hard enough it won't be lost.

My prince, I will await for you to come into view
This time it is now, so the story will wait to continue.

  In this lifetime, you are the only one for me

Cami Kidwell

A Mature Love

There exists a mature love that grows stronger each day
A unique couple who live in separate worlds in the cruelest of ways,

They met unprepared for this fairy tale romance
How would they know it would blossom by chance,

A long-distance affair consumed with laughter and promises to
   help us cope
No one would dare touch such dreams of hope,

Each memorable rendezvous remains unique and dear
Trying hard every departure to hold back the tears,

Traveling together all over the globe is natural and secure
Two lovers together, safe and unblurred,

Supportive family and friends say ours is a first-class
   book to unfold
So we endure with trust, patience and this love story to be told,

Sooner or maybe later, we can unite as a solid pair
Until then, our destiny is still in doubt and unfair,

Determination, fate or perhaps blind love is the key
That will open the closed tunnel for Simon and me,

I know there's a bright light and a colorful rainbow
Heart filled memories and endless love keep telling me so.

Denise Dowd

Hope

Space is the last unknown
A vast darkness
Never-ending

A faint light in the distance
Brighter than the sun yet dimmer than the faintest reflection
Never dying

I feel an uncontrollable urge to feel it
I continue to try knowing I never can
Never giving up

Every time I get close
It seems to move farther away
Yet never moving

Eric Charlson

Mamuka

You stand upon a sepulcher of ashes,
A veil of lace encompassing your body,
Metal rose pinned to your heart,
And a spider plant's tentacles caressing you.

Dusty roses on an old wooden table,
Prayer beads hanging into a bed of dry flowers,
An embroidered tapestry sings,
"I love you, Grandma".

We danced to gypsy violins
But now you've become
A stocking head with braided yarn
And button eyes.

On a bed of prayer
I look out the window above your altar.
A black tree stands with naked arms
Waiting for spring.

Ida Bithell

The Beauty In Her Patterns

Such beauty has thee which from nature is made,
A willow or maple we take cover in their shade.
What patterns of symmetry are the wings of the butterfly,
Such color and flicker, looking wet but is dry.
And so be the changes which her cycle of seasons doth portray,
From the blue skies of July to her December gray.
For the beauty found in she so visible to the eye,
So is the love of nature,
How wondrous and mystical to thy.

Donna Esposito Di Salvia

Perhaps

She is just a wisp-
A wisp deep into the darkness.
And yet she lives.
She has a force-

A force that allows her to stay here.
Perhaps you feed this wisp-
Perhaps you love her.
What will happen to this wisp when your love dies?

Perhaps she will leave.
Perhaps she will take your soul with her-
Leaving behind an empty shell.
An empty shell that is you.

Bradley Coyote Martens

Untitled

Fetus in conception...?
A wonder of life?
The mystique of yonder...
What strength do thy possess...?
The formulation of a path.
A true pleasure of life...yes!!!
Is it an organism or an instrument of a
manifest
Your growth is but a pulse your movement
excites thy parents what is your message?
Open our minds, eyes and grant our perception of thy
conception, for you were conceived in love, for love is
thy
Way but surely what is thy answer to this question oh!
The unborn fetus silence is surely not thy say or thy
way...

Joseph E. Boakye-Asante

Mother Nature's World

The morning air smells so sweet. The only sound is of my heart beat.
The wind moves so harsh yet true. The only sight is of the morning dew.
The light is still yet to come. The darkness is like a low, brisk hum.
The child like cries of the sunshine near for it not knows it will bring great cheer.
As day moves on the sun begins to fall yet it seems it tries to stall.
Soon the darkness over bares and the dark, sleepy night is full of stares.
This process seems to happen so much yet to Mother Nature it's just one touch.

Catherine Hunter

A Little Girl's Story

I may be black, and fat and maybe old, but I have a story to be told.
About a girl who lost a part of herself.
When no one knew what she hid way back on the shelf.

Lies were told and promises not kept. Whom should she
Trust or who should she let. Maybe God can see and hear her cry.
Doesn't matter though everyone else says by.

Someone told her because Jesus lives, her pains will be no more.
Someone lied so she shut the door.
Church Folks giggled behind her back.
Wondering what happened when will she be back.

Mother fears that her child had gone,
but little did she know about what had been done.
Grandma suspected the worst she could.
Not knowing a single thing, knowing that she should.

Sister and brothers bragging in her face
about a man they called father; who obviously never knew his
place.

Is life worth living for the girl in this tale,
as she lives a life that smells?
There's more pain than joy In the road up ahead,
maybe this little girl would be better off dead!!!!!

Bevie Louis

He Cares

I should not worry
 about each day -
For the Lord has told
 me to pray;
Then have the faith, for what He said
 He will do,-

And look to him fully - Not fret and stew!
 He feeds the sparrow small -
Even knows, when one doth fall.
My Lord is watching over all -
And I know;
He cares!

Jeannie Marie Lewis

Fifteen

Fifteen and not a clue
About love, about life, or about you.
My mind says yes
While my heart must confess
It's too young to tell
Whether or not being with you is heaven or hell
My eyes are in lust
But are my feelings in love?
Indeed I don't know.

The ecstasy within me when you are there
Is just too much to bear.
Do I love you?
I cannot say
But give me a chance
And maybe one day
I will then have a clue
About love, about life
And about you.

Charlotte Canedy

Love Song

When day breaks forth and casts its splendor
Above the eastern rim,
And song birds greet the opalescent dawn,
I think of you.

And when the tempo of the day creates
A symphony of sight and sound,
There comes a pause, and thru the mists of time
I see your face.

And when the lingering shadows fall
And night winds murmur softly thru the trees,
Like the haunting melody of a half-remembered song
I feel you near.

Alice Powers

Power Pole Kachinas

Giant 20th Century Kachinas marching in metallic lockstep
Across the barren vastness of the Reservation.
Only in stark outline do you vaguely resemble
The warm sacred spirits of the people you emulate.
Your cold hard shoulders carry unseen power captured by man
Across dry windswept sun-baked miles to a distant civilization.
You do not transmit invisible memories
From ancient generations to those yet to come.
Your mission is utilitarian.
No individualized loving carving of wood, painting with color,
Decorating with fur, feathers and cloth,
One of a kind.
No, you are mass produced,
Uniform,
Not for soul
Or dreams
Or past
Or future:
Only now.

Annette Richards Parent

Oasis

Brown sugar sand being sifted
Across the scorching hot dunes of the desert
The days' moon throwing blazing spears of fire
Upon the object of it's fury - the tortured sand.
They walk, they search, parched throats emit cries of longing
Where is it? Does it exist, This Fountain of Eros?
Searching, searching ..... when suddenly it appears.
Lush gardens blossoming with flora
Trees offering their wine-sweet fruit, shade beckoning.
But even enticing - The Fountain! In their haste they stumble.
With muscles stretching and fingers groping,
they reach, reach, reach in vain.
They have learned it is just - an illusion
So, I have walked these burning plains
I have reached the blazing sands for the Fountain
for the Fountain and one day I came upon lush garden
blossoming with flora, trees offering their wine-sweet fruit
shade beckoning me to enter and drink from the Fountain.
And I did, and what I found, was not an illusion
I found you, and, You are my Oasis!

Aleksandra Wasylyk

"This Old World"

 This world in which we live,
Where life goes on as usual.
 As we see it right now,
That seems to look a bit lost.
 By only helping ourselves and one another
This world will be a pleasant place to live in.

Blase M. Nocella

My Solitary Rose (In My Garden)

You stand so graceful and so tall,
Against the briskly chill of fall.
But soon you must return to earth,
Until the Spring and your rebirth.

I gaze your crimson face,
So soft and smooth and full of grace.
Your lovely petals fold - unfold,
Indeed a beauty to behold.

You're there to greet me everyday,
I'll miss you when you fade away.
But as our God would have it so,
Come Spring, once more I'll watch your grow,
Into my Solitary Rose!

Caroline M. Orlandi

A Cry From Within

From the agony in the garden to the
agony in the womb I was unwanted
unloved like the manger there was simply no room.
Please tell me why, was it a
moment of passion or a moment of lust.
You are my parents; in you I placed my trust.
Here comes the doctor to take me
away. We can't afford you, we have
too many - you simply just can't stay.
In just an instant the warmth turns
to cold my heart ceases to beat that
doctor was sore bold.
Was it for the money or the time I was going to consume,
I never had a chance at life just one of doom.
No Funeral no flowers no chance to grow old.
No chance to give smiles to hug or to hold.

So away they take me to that
big red bin they call me medical waste and toss me in.
What a waste of human life, what a sin. I wish they
could have heard the cry that came from within.

Edward Madejek Jr.

"I Am Life"

I'm all the joys you'll hear coming from a baby's voice
All the right or wrong turns at the end of a lonely road
As well as all decisions that you will ever make by choice
I am also those burdens on your shoulders you call a load...

I bring tears with the hurt that you will have in your eyes
Whenever there was a love you had and it went wrong someway
For what it's worth I'm a song that sings hello and goodbye
And I'm a challenge to those who don't know of my ways...

I'm knowledge you must learn in order to make your plans
Also I'm old age I start the very first day you are born
The rivers mountains and meadows you see in this great land
Belong to me but I will share until your welcome has worn...

I'm the evil that sometimes lurks down deep in some minds
I cause the cool feeling at night that you call a chill
I'm a soldier marching onward to battle when it is my time
Also I am death watching over from the top of a barren hill...

You'll see that I am the tide coming in from across the bay
I'm all the reasons why a man needs a woman for his wife
Dare to ask who or what are you? And you'll hear me say
Listen close as to who and what I am for my friend...I am life...

Bill Brooks

From Without/Within

Everyday is trying to symbolize,
all the truth stored inside
Happiness, sadness, the world continues
get on - get off life isn't simple

Do what needs to be done
sunshine and darkness keep going on
Hurt, shame, sickness prevails . .
also, light, happiness and success may curtail

Blackness breeds sorrows
Killing love and happiness for tomorrow

Yet I will continue to say
get on up and make it a happy day
your way.

Georgianna Maxwell

Harvest Moon

Hello harvest moon
All yellow, orange and red
On this night which belongs to the dead.
My breath, like the smoke from a candle,
Rises and swirls,
As the wind, your breath, blows
Coming to chill.
Shall sing for you Moon? Shall I howl?
As the nightbird stirs the wolf and the owl.
Or shall I curse you and your night
It's blackness which has seeped into my heart
No hope of dawn.

No. I will sit quietly
Denying you any pleasure out of my protest or praise.
Finally, the knowledge is bestowed!
The salty pools are my own!
You have no hold on me.

Heather Edwards

Beauty

Said the moth to the flower
"Am I beautiful?"
"The rainbow did not paint my wings;
Like it did the butterfly.
The midnight sky did not baptize me with its color;
like it did the raven.
And the rain sprinkled your petals, and made you smell beautiful;
where I smell of nothing."
Said the flower to the moth...
"What do you see when you look at a rainbow?"
"What do you hear when you listen to the sky?"
"And what do you feel when the rain falls on your wings?"
The moth replied slowly.
"I see a miracle when I look at a rainbow."
"I hear peace when I listen to the sky."
"I feel life when the rain falls on my wings."
The flower stretched its head to the glowing sun, and smiled.
"Then yes, you are beautiful."

Heather MacDonald

Untitled

Another rainy night I'm spending alone
Wishing, my love, for you to come home.
I would snuggle up with you all night long
Safe in the knowledge our love always will be this strong.

Instead, I sit here alone and sad,
Thinking of all the good times we have had.
I love you, my darling, with all of my heart,
And anxiously await the day we will never have to be apart!

Cynthia Dawn Helton

Miss Liberty

Alone she sat by the fireplace
  an endless frown lay etched in her face.
The smile had long since gone away
  and now alone she sat on that cold, miserable day.
She dreamt of the days of old
  but never did she forget the days of today, miserable and cold.
She dreamt of the past, the good old days
  when things were accomplished in simpler ways.
No guns, no knives, no senseless killing
  to simply talk things out, many more were willing.
She wondered why this world could be so cruel
  killing one another like a stupid fool.

Christopher J. Long

The Ocean

The ocean....like me...
An entire galaxy unto itself..constantly on the move.
Pulsating with intense strength and truth,
The knowledge of the universe inside its chest.
Full of treasures that swim with a beat in the night.
This rhythm..evolved through epochs of time.
Deep in the currents...the magic of life.
Crescendoing songs from ages gone by,
Sung from the chamber, immersed in the soul,
Ensuing thoughts of survival that juxtapose
Symbiotic composure—balance—control.
Control of the turbulence that rocks the terrain,
Challenged by the impetus energized by the brain,
Seeking cohesion with each pulse in the vein.

Barbara Peck

Beach Glass

Chipped off...from the whole...
An entity, unique, with its own curves
With its own color, texture, feel
Beautiful in its own right

To look at, to admire, to wonder at
Oh the waves it has traveled the storms it has survived
And still it remains, remolded, reshaped, smoother here
Sharper there, yet strong, resilient, beautiful

Such a simple thing yet..such a marvel
How did it get to be this way?
With time, with patience
By tumbling with the storms
By riding softly in the waves
By flowing in whatever comes, whatever's there

And someday landing softly on a beach
To be found, admired, valued, cherished and even loved
And maybe being placed in a pocket
Where it witnesses the journey of a new entity
Riding new waves, new storms, floating along
In whatever comes

Emily Marsden

Seashore

What is it I adore
About this wonderful seashore?
There has to be a reason I prefer
This lovely seashore as a comforter.
Looking out at its everlasting sea
Can make you feel sweet harmony.
Come to the seashore and look at the view
When you need something to comfort you.
As for now I bid adieu
To all who enjoy a seashore view.

Jill Hulber

Winter Whale

Winter comes like
an unexpected flu
like a giant whale
about to swallow you.

It has no mercy
and has no choice.
Don't try to make a deal
or you'll be its next meal
for it'd rather not hear your voice.

Some people say you can't get away,
They say there's not even a chance.
If I were you I'd just head south
Before I was caught in the winter whales mouth.

John Tate Higgins

Wildflowers

The wildflowers are dying,
And a part of me is dying with them.
The vibrant colors fading,
The softness of their petals becoming dry,
Shrivelled and lifeless.
Soon the snow will come
And bury them with it's weight.
Part of me will be buried too.
The happiness, the love, the life,
Gone.
When spring shines it's fresh new face upon us,
The wildflowers will bloom again.
But with this abundance of new life,
Will part of me be resurrected as well?
I fear that it won't,
That I'll never see that vibrance,
That softness, that life.
I'll know when the wildflowers
Greet me again in the spring.
Only then will I know.

Aimee M. Perrin

My Grandfather

With a heart of gold,
And a smile that shone like the sun,
That's how my grandfather lived.

Into the land of darkness he brought light,
Teaching that happiness helps and sorrow makes you suffer,
That's how my grandfather taught.

Hearing children's happy shouts,
And adult's thanks at the end of each day was rich enough reward
That's how my grandfather thought.

Smiling serenely while telling us of fishing trips,
Magic wonders, and things of a seemingly by gone age,
That's how my grandfather loved.

Bryan Middlebrook

Decision

She lies deep into the mattress
The weight of two quilts forms a nest of hibernation
Morning light makes the room appear in shades of gray
Two floors below she hears the furnace rattle
The house is cold after a frosty night
Mother is up an hour before the rest
To make the heat and the bread rise
She lies deep into the mattress
Swearing she will never get married and have children.

Carol Carlson

"Weeping Willow Tree"

All is fair in love and war!
And all is fair to me!
And if I don't fight
With all my might.
I'll be like a weeping willow tree.
I stepped aside.
Too many times
For someone else to be.
And now I'll fight with all my might!
Not to become a weeping willow tree.
Weep no more
Weep my Lord.
Weep no more for me.
For there's a time and place for everyone.
And now's the time for me!

Judy A. Boyett

Mistaken Love

Love, 'tis a happy day!
And all the wooing and swooning do sway,
In favor of the blissful couple who meet.
Who take their vows of honor and marriage to union complete.

Lord, help them now to o'er come the destiny that fate doth throw,
When reality deals a terrible swift blow.
And man and woman do not recall,
Love of a genuine heart at all.

Now, time after time this story has been told,
Love, long ago so bright, now turned cold.
"It was all a mistake!" between the two, they shout.
All they can see is that they want out.
So, do they part? What must be, must be,
Only time will tell, you see.

Alison Lanham-Gaskamp

The Search

The earth returns to peasant fears,
And all you want seems very clear.
You dream about it night and day
You harbor it, you put it away.
Until the time you seek to find
A body enhanced in soul and mind.
To take these dreams, these fears, these wants
Passion filled he then taunts
Your every move, your every whim.
Until you wake up one morn
To look back upon your plan
As you saw it and now at hand.
To your surprise it all has changed
Your want to love, and your need, secure
And ever shall you dream some more?
He stares across a crowded room
Captivates and tries to ruin
Those dreams you have
And instead replace, for all it's worth
Reality of the finished search.

Danielle Signorelli

My Man

The man to be my husband has to be very sweet and kind.
The man to be my lover has to be so fine.
The man to be my friend has to care enough to share...
every thought that would help us grow,
every feeling that would show,
We were made for each other;
Destine to be husband - wife, lover and friend.

Denice Sheffield

Morning Prayer

I drove my car on a clear, crisp day, God -
And as the warm sun shone through my windshield, my eyes swept over
Your Glorious Heavens.

What reason and conclusion have shaped this man-made mind?
What thought and what illusion have I let be instilled inside?

I knew You once, perhaps only as a child -
Sweet innocence now wears a Mona Lisa smile.

Evolution, Revolution, and the Scientific Method -
God, I did well - straight A's in all my lessons.

Some say ignorance is bliss -
I say, not to question, would be remiss.

Too many questions and no answers have thwarted my blind faith -
Today, I See - Too many answers - There is no question and precious
    little time to waste.

Beverly Vigil

For Everything Lost

For everything we've lost, what has been gained?
And at what cost your evil spirits tamed?
We are alive and doing lonely well.
In solitude we count our blessings, for these you can't control.

But meager few they are and tainted with bad memories.
Who fights a fight with demons and wins?
Who gains by losing home and friends?
And if you've gained... can you count it anything but blooded coin?
Ill gotten gains are just but that..and sadly. I wish you well.

For you will need my wishes. God only can forgive the wrongs you've
done me, the malice with which you manipulated lives.
Perhaps you've learned from this, but I dare say not,
For fools love folly and power the same,
And chase it in a nervous game. I hope you get it before it gets you.
For me, the pedestrian on life's road,
it was a hit and run from which I have
survived, scarred. Yes, haunted some. But moving still.
Beware of someone greedier than you...or more wanton, perhaps.
Beware because just as you didn't look back for me...
He won't look back for you.

Georgine Dickens

"Aye!"

It's "Aye!" to the lass and "Aye!" to the land,
And "Aye!' to the fairy love.
It's "Aye!" to the crags in Scotland's heights,
and "Aye!" to the Laird above.

It's "Aye!" to the kilts and "Aye!" to the pipes,
And "Aye!" to the Highland Fling.
It's "Aye!" to the crags in Scotland's heights,
and "Aye!" to the rhymes that ring.

It's "Aye!" to the kith and "Aye!" to the kin,
And "Aye!" to the fighting Bruce.
It's "Aye!" to the crags in Scotland's heights,
and "Aye!" to the English truce.

It's "Aye!" to the braes and "Aye!" to the vales,
And "Aye!" to the meads of hay.
It's "Aye!" to the crags in Scotland's heights,
and "Aye!" to the clan Mac Kay.

It's "Aye!" to the lass and "Aye!" to the land,
and "Aye!" to the fairy love.
It's "Aye!" to the crags in Scotland's heights,
and "Aye!" to the Laird above.

Benford Walker

The Door

I stood upon the green grass
And breathed in the air.
I ran to the edge of the cliff
And before me I could see
The world unfold like a scenic map.
I looked up and the sky was as clear
As a looking glass
With a few clouds passing through
Like a sweet memory.
Down below a light fog filled the valley.
A mountain stream twisted it's way
Through the boulders.
The sun cast it's mighty beams
Upon the surface of the water
And it sparkled like diamonds and crystals,
As it flowed toward the falls.
I looked back towards the rolling fields
And smiled, for I knew, I had found
The doorway to eternal peace.

Danette Lee

Night Blues

Stars are spontaneous
And fade out of the night
Like love that flows from the light
Pale moon cascading brightly
Caresses the rocks by the brook
And the shadows are ever veiling
With the melodious tempo of the crickets
Played through the night
Echoes ringing through the dark hues
How empty a heart
A bellowing sigh
That repeats through my mind
Shadows hide reality's side
Only your faith that hopes that feels what is real
Unplanned picturesque
Splattered view of golden light
A dark canvas of dark hues from
Fading blues...

Jennifer Poulson

To A Child - Grown

And I see your face
and feel the loss
and wonder
it will be this way every time I see your face

And I feel the loss
and wonder
who lost
and who is lost

And I wonder
why you had to tear
away again
a part of me

Do you need
a part of me for you
to be free?

From what are you free?
from love? from me?

And I see your face
and feel the love and I knew
It will be this way every time I see your face.

Claire Lobel

Prayer For New Year, 1995

My Lord, I kneel before your Holy Cross
And finger furrowed seeds of agony.
I ponder piercing pain, the selfless loss
That promised saving grace and harmony.

My Lord, what gift to You may I return
That You may cancel out the debt I owe?
I'd give You all that in this life I earn,
But Lord, what need have You of paltry show?

You Who direct the stars and anxious seas
And orchestrate the movement of an ant,
Or fire comets into ancient galaxies,
You need not me except as penitent.

A gift to You I am obliged to give,
What more than this: I take this life and live!

Elizabeth McCarthy

Untitled

I looked to love for Gentle nurture
    and found but cunning deceit.
I embraced my anger for it's sustaining virtue
    and hastened my own defeat.
I sought out God to extract an answer
    Brazen questions casting to skies of brass
Resounding silence is my answer
    Pain belongs to those who ask.
Survival borne by howling mistral
    Death devoid of rest.
Invisible wings of pain slave only to blind reality.
    Having lost the hope of love's leading.

Jonathan Hampton

A Friend

Remember the day you came to me, not so long ago,
and gave a hand to help me through a trying time or so.
You gave me bread, fed me meat and even gave me drink.
You didn't ask for anything, but kept me "in the pink."
You stuck it out through thick and thin when times were good and bad.
You shared with me the joys I knew and stayed when I got sad.
You gave me more than bread, my friend...You gave me so much more.
You gave me love and happiness when you knocked upon my door.
I know you're moving on to give this gift to others now;
But, I'll always remember that you showed me how...
To be a faithful friend, not once, but every day,
When you came to me and showed a loving kind of way.
I'm sure that it was Christ that stopped that day, not so long ago,
for only God could make a plan that worked so well, you know.

Elaine Diot

Untitled

Merry winters
    And have a warm upcoming season!

A poem to you from all of us here
filled with one wish, we wish you were near;

Since you are there, then do as we may
we decided to write this our very own way;

The Yuletide Spirit has given us the blues
things aren't the same till we celebrate with you;

So we'll all hold tight, close our eyes and pretend
Dreaming of good thoughts that this
    nightmare will soon end;

We love you our Father, my Husband
    Our Friend
Filled with wishes, dreams and love to you
    this poem we send!

Christina Cain

The Ball of Life

I am born with anticipated breath.

I grow quickly into the lives
and hearts of those around me.

We share laughter as well as heartache.

As time passes, the scars of everyday life
show greatly on my worn skin.

Still I am there for them, dependable, yet exciting.

Year pass. I find myself becoming less important
to those who once loved me dearly.

Suddenly, life is cold and lonely.

A strong and bitter wind pushes me away
from the place I once called home.

The happy squeal of a child is what I long to hear.

Instead, it's the familiar squeal of tires
rushing towards my body.

With no one to save me; the sudden impact
tells me that death is near.

The once anticipated breath is now exhausted.

Only the flood of memories of happy times gone by
allow me to slip peacefully away.

Donna Mottola

The Boy Who Ate The Sun

Once upon a time there lived a little kid
And I am going to tell you just what this boy did.
This boy was real and this story's true.
Sit back, relax because I'm going to tell you
About the little boy who, when he was only one
Opened up his tiny mouth and swallowed the whole sun.
The little boy was hungry, but his mom said, "not before lunch"
So he walked around looking for something he could munch.
He ate up all the flowers, but still he wasn't full
So he gobbled all the trees, which tasted rather dull
The boy was very hungry and though he was very small
He looked at all the buildings and said, "I'll eat them all."
He ate up the whole world and when he was done
He craned his neck, opened up his mouth and swallowed the whole sun.
He was finally satisfied and he was done by noon
So he said to all the stars in the sky. "Tomorrow I'll eat the moon!"

Jennifer Dillman

The Land of the Dead

When you want to see blood
And maybe a rolling head,
Just think of this place—
The Land of the Dead.
When lightning streaks across the sky,
And your boat is ready to row,
And it feels just like a sad goodbye,
Then and only then are you ready to go.
You sail along a sea of disaster
Until you see a pool of blood, bones, and hair.
Soon you hear some loud, deep laughter,
And right then you know you're there.
You step upon the land,
Then fall into a well.
There's fire anywhere you stand
In this heated place called Hell.
You know that death is soon to find,
When you see the land's keeper.
He'll scare you out of your mind—
He's the Grim Reaper.

Heidi Neu

Definition

I look forward to death in my way
And I'll have no fear when it comes
A waking state of grace is on the "other side"
A place to ponder my souls travels, past and future ones

I will contemplate all I have done
And mourn for all I could have become
For I know I must grow spiritually
To reach a higher sense of peace

Yet I will not stay in that heaven
Though I may do so if I please
But will choose another path
Another life to help me achieve that higher sense of peace

A rebirth into earth's sunlight
Another chance to be all I can be
I will travel another lifetime
With it's pain and ecstasy

And I hope that with each new experience
I will fulfil a higher decree
One that someone pure and almighty
Has had in mind for me

Jerri J. Mohr

Friendships

As people go through the years, as they grow
and mature, it is only the future they fear.

Being afraid of what to do, of what to say,
what to think, and of what the outcome will be,
it shall ever be unclear.

The responsibility of taking the news, and how
to react-if it is bad-you shall act like a leader,
and have courage, and shall be strong in emotion.

Even though your emotions are full of hurt, sadness,
and sorrow, the feelings of the joyfulness and happiness
shall all come back soon!

It is that, you should never forget your friendships
when they are down, because the memories of the fun times
you had together shall never keep you apart.

Cristina Estrella

Thoughts

My eyes gently close...
And my mind wonders off...
I hear your tender voice breaking through the
silence...
The quiet storm magnifies the beauty of your tone...
Your sensitive laugh takes my fears away... Your
understanding gratefulness reaches out to dry my
tears... The tears I cry of longing to be near you...
I hear a hideous thunder pounding, only I know It's
our hearts...
I hear bolts of lightning nearing closer to the
ground... I imagined it as our lips meeting...
I felt a raindrop fall upon my forehead.

...It awakened me...

My mind had overflowed with thoughts of you.

Clarissa Carriger

If I Should Lay Me Down To Sleep

If I should lay me down to sleep
And not awake, again.
If I should leave you, quietly,
With no goodbye to send.

Please, do not think this thing I've done
Was one of my own mind.
I could not, willingly, agree
To leaving you behind.

And if the pain of parting, thus,
Is hard for you to bear,
Remember, dear, the parting time
Was not our choice to share.

So, if you waken and you find
I, still, am fast asleep,
Know this, in truth, 'til we are one,
My love a watch will keep.

Gerald Gentry

The Heralding Breeze

The finger of a breeze draws a picture in watery lace,
And obliterates the reflections on the glass-like face,
Of the reservoir——,
Shadows deepen and grow——,
And the cold comes crawling with clammy claws,
Bringing forth the diamond sky with perfections and flaws,
As it has forever more——,
Night birds call——, And insects chirp——,
As they crawl from their hiding place,
No longer needed, now that darkness baths their ugly face,
And fits their feet with seven league boots——,
The artistic breeze now wafts nights smells to an unseeing nose,
And brings forth sounds of fabrication to the ears of those,
Who find fear in the heralding of darkness——,
By the wind's trumpets and the breeze's flutes——.

Ace C. Young

God's Gift Of Love

As I stop and look around I see Him in the tree's the skies
and on the ground. The flowers all dressed in colors so
bright, the grass that is oh so green and the beauty in a
butterfly's wing.

The pretty little birds as they sing their songs of joy. Just
in reach for each of us to enjoy. The awesome display of the
rising of the sun. The brightness of the moon when the day is
all done.

So I'm pleased for all to see, a craftsman's work indeed my
"Master" is HE! While all things from above truly show us
we are blessed with "God's Gift Of Love!"

Dianne Elgin

The Crown Of Thorns

Some things we are given on the day we are born,
And only because, of the crown made of thorns.
So ease on the pressure you put on yourself,
You were already forgiven so you could be yourself.
Just think as you struggle through the trials of this life,
They could have been worse if he hadn't given His life
So as you make choices and choose what you'll do,
Remember that God sends love to you.
And try and remember as you open your heart,
God's already proven He'll hold up His part.

Billy Vaughn

The Diabolists

Anger is a short madness
And our hearts are the asylums in which it lives
It transforms a placid soul into a crazed caitiff
And takes away from its victim as it gives

It fuels the fire of an irascible temper
For the wicked it's an eternal flame
It is the heat from the flare-up of an argument
It burns its victims and leaves them in pain

Hate is the son of this monster
In the soul of the scorned is its place
Together these two fiendish emotions
Are committing genocide of the human race.

Jill MacDonald

Absent Ulysses

I shall come back to our bedroom,
and push aside the empty years,
and see you there sitting at the ancient loom,
the whistling echo of the shuttle hear
as threads of hope, time and sorrow laid—
dream patterns for the knowing eye—
by resolute fingers made.
You, for our dreams, defy
the empty hours and their tender needs,
which breed doubts and discontent
that hobble love's intent.
You withstood the empathy of friends,
and would not to their pleasures bend
or to nature's urging heed.
We are of a different breed.
I, too, for those missing years grieve—
my mind's eye sees your patterns weaved—
soon hope's end will be achieved.

Jerome I. Kahn

Woman

From the tent's opening, as I rose,
  and rested upon my arm,
    I saw her,
Amid the dawn and desert sand,
  Standing. The dawn's breeze bellowing
    her garment.

There she stood, veiled in earthy colours;
  the gauze of her linen wrapped snugly and
    draped about her, head to calf.

A sculptor's dream;
  feet barely sandaled, planted upon
    the knoll's crest.
    Still.

Her rapture held my heart through my eyes.
  In a sigh, a single utterance escaped,
    "Woman."

Cynthia G. Usher

Firefly

The mind is a firefly,
Piloting through the darkness,
Shedding light on what is to come.

Deceived is he who tries to contain it;
For humanity will set it adrift,
Venturing into the unknown.

It's persistence determines its vividness.
The beauty within overcomes its exterior,
Forcing the identity to come forth.

Andrea Davis

Say Goodbye

I cried as I held you in my arms
And said my goodbyes as you died.
The angels swooped down to greet your soul,
And I could feel the beating of their wings
Following the rhythmic pounding of my heart.

And I kissed you farewell
While the tears of the day
Washed me to the present.

And now my words of love
May fall on others-
As the rich pitch of pines
Falls on shade seekers in summer-

But you never need ask
If my love for you has passed-
I grieve for both of us.
I taste the salty memories.

And though I live for today
I know my love will reach beyond tomorrow-
Until I see you at the end of my sorrow.

Cindi Baldi

Remember I Love You!

It seems such a long time 'til I see your face again,
and see the way your eyes shine the moment I walk in;
It makes me feel so proud to see you look that way,
And you know there's only one thing I really want to say;
There's something in my heart, it feels oh so true,
I love you more than you'll ever know, so please don't be blue;
When I have to leave you, I know it can be tough,
And facing the days ahead almost always seems rough,
But our love is never ending and hopelessly true,
So always remember, I love you!

John Thomas Stephens

Last Shot

She beat the boys in the mud, tackling hard
And seeing the black drip down their faces.
Cold water was thrown on her victory joy
When she walked into Mama's spotless kitchen.
Instead of love, came the blast that girls should be
Little ladies, not bellowing boys.
Mother led the way down the feminine path
Where Tom was a man and boy a follower,
Together defining the girl as a Tomboy.
Grace and charm and the proper word need strength
Which thrived in the growing female body.
Sport followed sport and mother was glad
That in the struggle feminine was clear
And rather than victory, beauty was won.
Each eye makes its own world and lives in it.
The statistician measured her by points.
"High School" was clear to mother but not "basketball"
Since she followed the ball but not the basket.
Beauty was present in daughter's last shot,
But others saw it as the new girls' record.

Frank A. Langer

Sometimes...

Some times it is better to walk away from
Some things that are giving us trouble because
Some where we were with the wrong people at the worst time but
Some how all our problems are solved when the ONE
Some body walks every where with us and takes care of not
Some things but every thing not just
Some times but every time.

Cynthia P. Roddey

Untitled

You give it all, You take it back,
You try your best to make life the best it can be.
You love with all your heart and soul,
You want that special person to love you as you love them.
But sometimes it just doesn't happen,
So you have to start pulling yourself away.
For some crazy reason when you start pulling away,
They start showing some kind affection.

Donna Hatt

The Good Old Days

We dressed up as monsters, giggled through our dates
and shared our most intimate secrets with each other
We cried, we sang and danced together and nothing
or no one dared come between us
We learned from each other, sharing our cultures,
languages and our dreams, we served as the support
system each of us so desperately needed . . .
Separated by the conventionalism of a mere blood line
We were closer than Siamese Twins

and then one day . . .
like the ruthless and ferocious hurricane which attacks
without warning, taking all . . . you were gone

and I no longer giggle.

Gloria E. Perez-Ramos

Untitled

I awoke to the scent of you
and smiled
it was as though you were next to me
and I remembered
fondly
the events of the evening before
Still smiling
I covered my eyes with my hands to keep the picture longer
and realized
it was I who smelled like you
It was my pillow, my bed sheets, my hair, my skin
I sighed
thank you for filling me with the scent of you last night

Annette Aben

Moon Glow Reflections

The astronauts sped up toward heaven,
And star dust encircled the three,
As Armstrong landed the "Eagle"
On the Sea of Tranquility.

With Aldrin he stepped on the surface
Of our distant, mysterious moon.
They went for a stroll while Collins
Was in Orbit up there all alone.

With courage and endurance, the first
To walk weightless in the bright moonglow,
They worked 'midst rocks and moondust,
While earthlings watched TV below.

Apollo II's mission near completed,
After a thrilling journey through space,
They carried the American flag
And left it on Tranquility Base.

Our world has problems and troubles;
We long for peace and brotherhood.
May our lives and work be a blessing,
Then God can say, "It is good."

Astrid A. Swanson

Snow Birds and Breakers

Believers come to Paradise for the first wine
and stay, or clear the way to return
The curious follow
But they bring too little and make many excuses
for it that are all the same when they leave

Often when the breaker's influx swells at Easter
young life is sacrificed before the resurrection
They are silenced, still in heaven for all it alters
Franciscan friars, evangelists appear organized to
end the mishaps
Civic minds bar off balconies to protect them from
their unbearable freedom

Beach driving tolls infringe inciting protest, clamor
But nothing will stop them from coming,
The beach seduces them as it does the tides through a
higher power that is in them and gives them the same
right to trespass as those who live in the mansions
line the sea
Bonnie Jean O'Lone

Reflections

Another melancholy day has come to me awake,
and streams of dull reality, they cling, I cannot shake,
so switch on the tube, the tube that makes you fester,
mirror of our ethics, all corruption comes to nest here,
reflections of our morals, our hopes are laid to rest here,
outstretched on the couch he lay a shapeless, lifeless clump of clay,
molded by the media, it's work is all the same
planting seeds of ignorance flowering greed and shame,
some say it's human nature, for we never take the blame,
always looking elsewhere excuses old and lame.
Christopher Edwards

My Father - My Friend

He walked with me when I was young.
And taught me songs that he had sung.
I would listen to his stories with rapture of joy

Of the things he did when he was a young boy
Always there with words of cheer
Held me tight, kept away my fear

Even though at times, we don't always agree
One thing for certain, he always will be

My Father, My Friend
Jeanine M. Serwatka

Did You Burn Dinner?

I'm the clock on the wall that beats the hours away,
And the beater that beats the eggs.
Time is my enemy,
And I am the frying pan that it will burn in.

I have no more ingredients to give,
My mind is a bare as the cupboard overhead.
The stringy spaghetti hands of time
Are nothing without the sauce of one's desire.

Can the sticky, grainy sugar of our lives
Hold together the fragile egg-shell of our being?
Is out bland cauliflower face the messenger of our fate,
Or do we have the peachy smile to melt the frothy foam
Of time's transparent cling wrap form?

Time is the dish that we prepare.
To scorch it we simply reject it,
But to make it into a gourmet feast
We add the garnishes of our dreams.
Ellen Edwards

The Tales They Tell

The gentle creases of your skin cradle tired eyes.
And tell a thousand tales of joy and pain.
They show how time has weathered you and journeys you have made
Once smiling of stories still untold, they now cry of confusion and fear.

Time has taken from you the strength to tell of times of past
Of the love and joy and freedom of youth now disappeared.
Those gentle creases now funnel tears of hope turned bleak
Of pity so unwanted and pain too strong to fight.

Those tired eyes, they tell me, it's time for you to journey home
You are not what once you used to be or ever wished at all
Don't look to me for answers, for the choice is yours alone
I only know that your leaving can't hurt more than I hurt now.

I watched you leave this earth as your soul leapt through my heart
On the way to heaven, to new journeys, new life.
What lay left was simply a shell that no longer told the story of who
  you were.
And as I stood there weeping, I could not help but feel the joy of you.

And it was then I prayed; Let your memory not be what you were when
  you left me
But what you came to be in my heart along the road we travelled.
And when time's cruel clock strikes midnight on me, let those who
  love me
See not the gentle creases that cradle tired eyes, but the new found
  freedom and joy of moving on.
Jennifer L. Brunk

Greatness

And they say that time is of the essence,
and that everything matters. And they feel
with their glass hearts and see through
their clouded eyes and plastic faces, and
they are not real. You run away from their
demented sense of morality to escape their
ignorance and embrace the truth. Your comfort:
the simplicity of nature and innocence of tranquility
where you run,
  fly,
  soar.
Free from their oppressive clutches
and their lies. All their lies
  you are different
  you are great
you believe that with age comes grace
and that time is irrelevant and you -
  you can fly
Erin Gutierrez

"Ode To An Oosik"

Strange things have been done in the midnight sun,
and the story books are full-
But the strangest tale concerns the male-
Magnificent walrus bull!

How can this be, this clandestine glee
That exudes from the walrus like music?
He knows, there inside, beneath blubber and hide,
Lies a splendid contrivance the oosik!

Oosik you say - and quite well you may,
I'll explain if you keep it between us,
In simplest truth, thought rather uncouth-
Oosik is, in fact, his penis!

Added to this, is a smile you might miss
Though the bull is entitled to bow
The one to out-smile our bull by a mile
Is the satisfied walrus cow.
Buddy Hartman

On The Chesapeake

The air is thick with mist,
and the ever present smell of the bay.
Deep in the darkness a fog horn sings,
answered by another further out.

The Town of Tilghman is still, this early morning.
The skipjacks and work boats sit idle,
in the still black water,
waiting in silence for the watermen.
Their ropes pulled taunt and neatly coiled,
riding securely, near weather worn docks.

The lights of the local cafe,
shine like a lighthouse beacon,
for those who are up out of habit,
and have no place else to go.

"The sun should burn through by midmorning."
One man says to the next.
They both drink their coffee,
and wonder how to pay the bills,
or where to use their tongs.
Things change slowly, here on the Chesapeake.
        David J. Binder

The Flower of My Childhood

It is spring, the time of lengthening daylight hours
And the fine mist of April showers.

It is spring and time for the flower of my childhood
Memories the pansy brings that make me feel so good.

The memory of a little girls love for the flower beside the door
And the wonder that of all flowers it was the pansy that I did adore.

The feeling of love came out of the air and into the now
Without my knowing why or how.

It may have been because I, a child, had dug the hole
And helped to plant this balm for a beauty hungry soul.

It may have been because of the colors so bright
That shone into the heart like a beam of light.

It may have been all the pansies laughing faces
As they pranced and danced in their places.

Then again, it may have been the joy I knew
In having a nosegay all my own when my possessions were so few.

The reasons why I may never understand
But the feelings are a part of memories wonderland.

They can be recalled with each springs maidenhood
The joyful recollections of the pansy, the flower of my childhood.
        Annabel Lynn Freeman

The Sounds Of Autumn

As the chilling breeze blows
and the gentle creek flows
The leaves of different hues of red, yellow and brown
They rustle and fall to the ground.

The birds all singing their tunes
know that winter will be here soon.

Autumn is a gentle season to us all
For soon the snow will fall.

Enjoy the sights and the sounds
before old man winter pounds.
        Amy R. Karper

God's Christmas Gift

(Submitted by Esther Wenzel)

The moon was full in the eastern sky
    And the sheep were asleep on the hills.
A "No Vacancy "sign hung on the Bethlehem door,
    While only the stable had room for more.

Joseph arranged the hay in the stall,
    And rolled out his sleeping bags, that was all;
And then it happened, that dark cold night,
    A baby was born beneath the star light.

Jesus grew to be wise, honest and strong,
    Pleasing his Father and helping the throng.
he taught on the hillside the lessons of life
    That deal with faith, hope, love and Eternal Life.

And then one night when the moon was full,
    And soldiers were plotting their plans to fulfill,
He prayed alone in the garden still,
    "Not mine but thine" is my purpose still.

He died the next day on a cross on a hill,
    For your sins and mine, tho we walk in them still.
He arose the third day, to comfort the sad
    God's Christmas gift, Rejoice and be glad!
        Sterling Wenzel

At The End Of The Rainbow

When things go wrong and you are feeling blue
And the sun refuses to shine
When folk's keep saying "How are you?"
Tell them you're feeling fine.

Just look the whole world in the face
And smile your biggest smile,
The cobwebs will become as lace
And you'll know it was all worthwhile.

If you will scatter your seeds of love
To the weak and those who are low,
You will find your reward up above
Somewhere at the end of the bow.

As you climb up on the satin lanes
Of those colors side by side,
You will ride horses with silver reigns
And a star will be your guide.

You will walk on streets of purest gold
And sit in a diamond chair,
You will always be young and never grow old
When you meet your friends up There.
        Frances McNish

The Boy

He's a poor boy, say the old beat up clothes
and the worn out boots hanging from a rusty
nail in the wall. A smart boy too, say the
stacks of books on the table near the cracked
window and the file of straight "A" report cards
next to the rusty bed. "What a friendly boy",
say the town folk. Yea, A friendly boy with a deadly
secret, says his diary. He used to live with
his father, say the pipe and cigars on the shelf
near the door, but one day he disappeared; and no
one knows where he went says Father's old bed.
"The police are coming", whispers the wind. "RUN!!!"
"The boy's hiding something", says the school
teacher, "something huge and mysterious!"
"RUN!!!" Whispers the wind, "RUN!!!"
        Ashleigh Brooks-Izer

Past, Present And Future

The past can be lived, many times that is clear,
And the times I remember, are the ones with you dear,

The past has its pain, and its happiness too,
But my greatest memories, are memories of you,

But the past is long over, there's no more to find,
Sit it up on the bookshelf, and leave it behind,

The present I know, is where you want to be,
The past has its sadness, and that includes me,

The present is here, there's nowhere to go,
I stare at your picture, yes, I still love you so,

The present is new, and there's so much to see,
You can trust and believe, but you still don't know me,

But now of the future, what does it hold,
All our thoughts and our dreams, but we're never told,

The future is ours, but at times looks so lonely,
All my hopes and my prayers, are thoughts of you only,

The future won't tell me, what I need to know,
Will we be together, or should I let go,

Past, Present or Future, no matter the time,
I'll still love you forever, you will always be mine.

James W. Brown

Life In A Wheelchair

I look out my window as the world goes by,
And think of earlier days with a long sigh.

To a time when I was king of my hill,
And could work at my dreams, almost at will.

Then life said, whoa, let's test you a bit,
To see what you're made of, see if you're fit.

Because for your life, God, has a plan,
See what you're made of and change if you can.

He told me, there's something I must know
Life is no game, no more one big show.

So everyday I sit here in my chair,
My life is not over, to dream I still dare.

It has given me a wife, whose life I can share,
And shows me how much she really does care.

My life is not over, my spirit is strong,
And with the Lords help my life will be long.

As I look out my window I'm not bitter,
For the Lord showed me how not to be a quitter.

When life is over and deaths work is finally done,
May the devil say he lost, my soul God has won.

James Hoogland

The Best Friend

If ever you are depressed or lonely,
there is always one person who will
listen to you no matter what -
his name is Jesus Christ.

When you feel like the world is rejecting
you -
Just Remember You are accepted by Him.

May you confide in Him for everything you need,
For He is always there to listen
to your problems - big or small.

Angela Youtz

Friendship

We started out as the best of friends
And though the years, we have diminished
 to nothing more than strangers
Our lives went in different directions,
 and we choose to forget one another
We found new friends, not remembering the old
Some of us moved away, and some stayed
No matter how close we were, we became no more
We can't just blame one of us for letting go,
We all had our part
Some of us choose to remain,
 although none of us will forget the ones we lost
We might talk to each other when passing in the street,
 but we know we will never be the same friends we used to be
The friends we were cared for one another
Now we would not know if one of us were dead or alive
We knew life would lead us down different paths
Although we never dreamed our friendships wouldn't last

Amanda Moorshead

Me Too

I cried too when it happened
And thought of all my old stereotypes
That reminded me of myself
Your pain is mine

I tried to think of something wise to say
To make it easier I'd hoped
But I couldn't it was all wrong and dumb
And I'm suppose to be good at that

I could tell you not to cry, to forget it
But you will, and sometimes you won't
It would be pretending, and to pretend is so unpredictable
I wouldn't want that for you

I could tell you it hurts not but won't always
And I'd true in part, you'd remember
And remembering not bad if the lesson's learned
Your lesson is mine

But because I love you, I can only say
Cry now, and hurt now
Tomorrow's almost here
Your pain is mine.

Hazel N. Evans

The Gift I Could Not Give

My mother will be ninety one tomorrow
 And today I am buying her a gift.
I wander around the shop
 Seeing all the things she once enjoyed -
A fragile china cup, a book, a puzzle -
 What shall it be?

Not the cup. It is too fragile - too hard to hold,
 And where would she keep it?
A book then - I'll get her a book!
 But she says she can no longer read,
She who all her life loved so much to read.
 The puzzle - but no, even a small one
Is too hard - too frustrating.

Tears fill my eyes
 Not because I cannot find her a gift,
But because she has lost so much
 Of who she is,
And I cannot give her back
 The gift of herself.

Edith Zimmerly

Things Will Melt Away

The Bible tells of scoffers that will come in the last day
And try to keep people from believing in God's way
They will say things haven't changed since creation began
But its not true for it is there in God's plan

In Noah's time the world was destroyed by water
It's there in the Bible for all to see
The next time it will be destroyed by fire
What a terrible sight that will be

In the second epistle of Peter it warns of a day
When the earth shall burn and the heavens pass away
That day will come as a thief in the night
And with such a noise everyone will have a great fright

It will be a very intense heat
For even the elements will melt that day
If we grow in grace and knowledge of our Lord
We will be ready when its time to fly away

To the Lord one day is as a thousand years
And a thousand years are as one day
It is not his will that any should perish
But all should come to repentance and learn His way

Allen Claude Carter

A Kinder Light

The old man stood on his front porch
And urinated on the ground
It did not seem to matter that, his
House was in the heart of town.
A neighbor watched from her window, in
Anger and disgust
He should be put away, she said, then
Slammed her window shut.
Come on in, I called. Come on inside
Sit down in your easy chair, and rest a while.
My heart bled for the old man, who now lived
In the days of out houses, bathing in rivers
And running away. My biggest fear was that
He might succeed one day.
I'm just a few steps behind, so I understand
Him just fine.
Everybody knows, that youth won't stay, you can
Grasp and hold, but it'll break away, only
To return blind, some dark weary night
Begging to be seen in a kinder light.

Berlene Howard

My Dad

He had always been ill in one way or the other
    and was not Apollo I wanted to see in a father.
His glasses, slow moves and short height
    made him a philosopher by day and a poet by night.
Great in dentistry and vet. surgery, by the trade
    optimism, patience and humor perfected his rate.
We have never been close, I did not know why...
    He was always low key while I was quite high.
Helping others rather than his family, was his habit.
    He was an Aesopian turtle; I was a show-off rabbit.
Our tastes were different but pride was the same
    but "love" had never been the name of the game.
It seemed that I could not know him somehow...
    I say, it is a quite bit late to say it now:
I wish he would be sticking around a little more
    enough to tell him I loved him; couldn't do before.

Fuat Ulus

Iridescent Soul

Echoing silent warning, radiant and majestic color wanes
and withers in subjection to its deprivation.
In repetitious cycle, Sol-warmth enthusiasm slowly ebbs-
    no sustained energy now for arborous arms or
        contented constellations or
            white dancing damsels waltzing on air.
Benign breezes dissent, sirening a cacophony of churning confusion
- a foreboding dervishness, brooding what must be
    coursing a reign of terror in one seemingly insignificant day
        disturbing the gentleness
        paralyzing the life-dance
        stealing the joy-warmth
        daring to imprison radiance
        silencing words, quelling laughter
        rendering lifelessness to life

    leaving a wake of seeming barrenness.

Death: Deliberate, Difficult, Delicate.

But in one small Peace of the Soul nothing disturbs
    the Resurrection Garden!

Joan P. Smith

Times, Times, And Ages

Behind the wrinkled, aging face
    And within this shapeless form,
Resides the child that once was I
    And the youth who battled the storm.

Centuries of life have passed through this mind,
    Legends of civilization lives in books,
Experiences of eternities walk through time;
    Who has reason to speculate on looks?

We pass on the streets and the eyes perceives
    The ages of mankind walking in steps
Of those whose lives have passed on to other pastures —
    Who alone know they have reached the heights and depths
Of their own existence and their capabilities
    That have stretched their souls.
The eagles seek the skies and their eyes are keen,
    The blind of all species burrow the ground — as moles.

The choices were mine as the child became the youth,
    And the adult grew from the young,
But life that still lingers in this frame desires more.
    Like words added to a song that's been sung.

Glorietta King

Melody Of Love

Oh Lord, My God, Your words
Are like a melody of love to me.
They make me want to sing sweet praises to Thee.

Oh, how wonderful love can be when it comes from Thee.
No matter what life will be
Or what the future might hold
As long as it is controlled by Thee
It will be alright for me.

I keep on singing, making joyful noises of love to Thee.
Your words will always guide me
To be in harmony with Thee.

I will dance for joy.
Praises will be on my lips to worship you.
You are a wonderful God,
My Saviour and Redeemer, My Lord, My All.

Your words will always be
A sweet melody of Love to me
Now and throughout eternity.

    Amen!

Irene Laube White

The Wall

Take a wall and present a form of art
Wash a white cloud hanging from a far window
Stir the paint to form a rainbow
Let the paint cool to a haze
Then watch the art raise.

Jon McVeigh

Vows Ready For Filled Is Our Cup

Our Body is present in the land of paradise
    And yes, our life is painted with new avenues...
But you mustn't overlook, our Father's Holy Book
    Because our love is more apparent than clues.

It's an emotion-ripping experience
    When the love must travel to and around...
But without any wonder, though perplexities and thunder
    Because our love is in no need of sound.

The obtaining of our spiritual goal
    Essentially, the feeding foundation of all...
But one must comprehend, the immensity and understand
    Because our love is woven with Christ's sacrificing fall.

Through God we have chosen our path
    This sacramental day to be united as one...
Vows Ready for Filled is Our Cup
    Because our love, undying, reflects God's Holy Son.

"My Heart is for you," too
    And the dreams of ours are blessed forever more...
Today, our vows are fulfilled for filled is our cup
    And our love can live like never before.

Desa Marie Mandarino

Eric At Two

Today you are two, and what a little man! You've gotten so tall,
and you can talk and we understand.
You arrive on our doorstep each Saturday as planned, with your
diaper bag, stroller and Barney video in hand.
We have such fun with your tools, blocks, balls and bat, you can
even play golf, climb a ladder and chase MEW, the cat.
GUMP-PA makes pancakes, and GRAMMIE makes lunch, Baked
potatoes,
melons, carrots, and broccoli are your favorites to munch.
With your barbershop haircut, Oshkosh jeans and designer socks -
you are such a doll, every little girl we meet at the park for
you does fall, after lunch you take a long nap in your magic pen, and
GRAMMIE, MAGGIE and DJ nap too and wait for you to call.
At your birthday party, we all had such fun - As you sat by your
Barney cake and blew the candles out, one and one.
We had such good news on Mother's Day - a new baby to welcome on
next Valentine's Day -
We'll have to learn to share and care for a new tot, And teach
you to say "yes" instead of "no", "no way" and "will not."
Just one little man has taught us all so much love, as we thank
God for bringing us this miracle from above.

Connie Peterson

A Gift And A Letter To A Wife

I give you these flowers because I love you.
And you mean so much to me.
You are my wife, the love of my life,
the mother of my children, my best friend
and most of all you are my only true love.
You done so much for me I love you for it.
I only wish I can give you more besides flowers
to show you how much I love you.

And I do love very much.

Chris Coffman

In The Dwelling Place Of Our Dreams

There was this dream
And you were there
The joy just happened
The joy just dared

Our faces beaming
Our souls careening
down to the end of the pier
Where you held me high
Above your head

I wasn't afraid
As I stretched out far above you
The fingers of your hand supporting me
The fingers of your one hand imploring me
To trust you

The sun joined in and worshiped us
Divine Love came and spoke us

This sweet, intangible thing
Called love... ers

Bri MJS-Held

Grandma's Delight

A beautiful grandson so soft and warm. A dazzling
angel, cheeks like rose petals. His picture perfect
irresistible happy face, there is no one that could take
his place. So adorable, his twinkling captivating eyes
win him the hearts of everyone that's wise. He holds a
special place in my heart, that's treasured, he is so
smart. He is caring, sharing his exquisite face as lovely
as an angel, warm as the afternoon sun and he loves to
run. With his spirit wild and free he could melt me.
The button nose and precious smile, his sweet ways and
joyous expressions are like a breeze on a warm day. His
hand of an angel so small but firm, soon grandma hopes
he'll return. An innocent baby's cry we hear, I go in and
kiss away the tears and he hugs and kisses me, and that
gives me precious moments. The image of him I'll cherish,
This memory will never perish. I could spend endless
hours in the stillness of the tranquil mountain setting
watching him tilt his head in wonderment. I watch with
delight my grandson Mike. When he goes in his diaper, it's
such a sight, I give back to mama and say
"good night." For sure he is grandma's delight!!

Janey Crowley

Hyacinths

Last night. At my door. Mystical.

In bleak April's gale... where lonely stars hid...
Angel wings fluffed a mystical apron of diamonded snow flakes.
Drifting down into scintillating star buds of satin.
Pearl. Azure. And rose.

Last night at my door.
Nestled in snow glitter, crystallized star eyes blinked
in scented satin. Pearl. Azure. And rose...
Warmed by morning's sunrise splashing petal tips in emerald glow.

Last night. At my door.
The fierce chill wafted. May's radiant gown lilted where star blooms
heralded fragrant new life in satin. Pearl. Azure. And rose.

Last night. At my door. Mystical. Hyacinths.

Jo Santoro Cialkowski

A Mind Is A Terrible Thing To Waste

Seek and you will find, a world as beautiful as mine, release your
anger and let stress slip away, come join me on this beautiful autumn
day, wind breakers on sale, all throughout the town, beautiful brown
leaves falling gently on the ground. Kids in a huddle,
playing loudly in the park. The wind blowing a top the trees,
because its almost dark, can you feel the temperature, drop so calmly
and splendor, come all and catch this ride to winter, the lawn is
white while the sky is so alive with a glow, it's the time of our
first taste of snow. Mother nature is on course doing her thing
do you see the beautiful waterfalls, taking us to spring? Do you
hear it, the birds by the window, singing early in the dawn,
Beautiful ducks and swans swaying gracefully on the ponds.
Bands on the circuits, concerts and fun, people sun bathing using
up the sun. I remember the little boy wanting to be a
drummer, making soft notes, that sounds like summer, so much
To meditate on all about seasons, let your mind be
free and have a dream, forget skin color, and learn to love not to
hate, because a mind is a terrible thing to waste

Darryl V. Roberts

Untitled

You filled my cup with love; it will not hold
Another drop more than you gave to me
That short weekend we shared. And when you told
Your love, and questioned me, so laughingly,
Yet filled with awe, at Love's expression gained,
Denied the question asked, nor need to know,
Because our love had answered you. No pained
Or saddened heart could stop that warming glow
Of sated love, of joyous bodies locked
In love's embrace, nor blot the anguished bliss
Of that sweet afternoon. We have but blocked
With warmth of body, hands, and the sweet kiss
Of love the years of longing, sorrow, pain,
Until these treasured hours shall come again.

Francis Russell West

Snowbound 1995

The calendar proves its 1995
    Another year just took a dive
The year joins others, our history
    What lies ahead, unsolved mystery

A day dawn so bright new year
    Wherever it leads ears to hear
Try doing good in helpful way
    Make your life count, in productive way

Count your blessing everyone
    Sandwiched between work, a lot of fun
Choose your friends, take your time
    True friends are a gold not silver mine

Exchange with friends tit for tat,
    Strike a hit when up at bat,
Give to life more than your best
    And don't forget to feather your nest.

Janet Dole

What Is Love?

Love is something you cherish each day.
Love is something you keep in your heart.
Love is something you can count on.
Love is something where you treat people the same.
Love Is something when where ever you go you can
    take it with you.
It really seems like LOVE is nothing,
    but you know what, LOVE is everything.

Connie Kim

Unbearable Pain

I sat in the doctor's office and waited,
Anxious and in pain my name I anticipated
While doors keep opening and closing
Everyone seem to be just musing.

The pain ripped under my rib cage
As I bit my lips and sigh with rage.
My stomach's empty and it roars,
It felt like an open piercing sore.

Tears start welling up in my eyes
As I painfully watched people go by
No one seems to notice as I groan,
So up to the receptionist desk I bemoan.

"Hello" I said "what happened to my name?"
"Oh Lord," she beckoned "the same story again?"
"Story," I cried, "a story I never tell,
My only aim here is to get well."

Back to my seat I stumbled in pain
My short visit seems almost in vain
Then in my head a familiar name spells
Then I realize it was my name she yells

Eula Graham

The Body And It's Dangers

After these days of passion and play
Anxious at the passing of each new day
Unspoken the loss of lovers and friends

Now we must talk about the body and it's dangers.

Revolver-like passion, perhaps:
Kills the ones we love. Loves the ones we kill.

The one empty chamber is not for us meant.

Death's face, familiar to me now as the palm of my hand,
I know as universal certainty.

But, all the knowing of sex, disease, life and death
Can't protect us from the body and it's dangers.

Chris Karnes

Sunsetting Dreams

The memories that were once so clear,
Are now just like icicles on a sunny day.
Slowly melting away.
Diminishing into the beauty of the clear blue sky...
Never to be seen again.
The harder you try to hold on to the past,
The faster it slips through your hands.
Dreams become reality.
Reality fades to black.
Wanting things you do not have.
Having things you do not want.
But still, you keep hoping.
Your hope, though, only leads into a tunnel of desolation.
Confusion, loneliness, a deranged obsession.
An obsession with the way things used to be.
Before the pain,
The hurt, the tears,
The sin.
It must all be stopped!
Before vicious fate can cast it's deadly curse.

Amy Hartman

What Is Truth, What Is Real

What is truth and what is real
Are these items to buy, to cheat for, to steal
Some seek for these things in riches and fame
And in worldly possessions they stake their claim
What price will they pay for these objects so dear
For many, the path to these treasures is unclear.

What is truth and what is real
Are these things we can see or things that we feel
And where can we look in order to find
These things that exist only in heart and in mind
Which way to proceed the question may be
When searching for truth and reality.

What is truth and what is real
The answer to this Jesus Christ will reveal
By increasing our faith and accepting the light
By closing off darkness and doing what's right
The Lord will reveal all the things we wish to know
Simply stay by his side and he'll never let you go

Gregory Alan Hunt

Little Rabbit Blue Eyes

Dedicated to my first Granddaughter
"Katelynn Nichole Connolly"
Little rabbit blue eyes
Are you telling little lies
Hoping that your tale flies
So you can have an alibi
For all the mischief that rays
With your cute little ways
Sparkling like a shooting star
Dancing circles around your Pa
What a darling little sight
For all who watch your delightful flight

Ida Sugrue

Tell Me, Love

Will you tell me, love, where you're heading tonight?
Are you walking the path of the lonely?
By yourself with a thought, of the things you've been taught,
And the dreams known to you only?

Can you hear me, love, or am I like the rest?
Cast aside in the cold without warning;
Perhaps caught in the night, without shadow or light,
There to stay 'till the break of the morning.

Do you see me, love? I'm wandering, too,
I've got no place to focus my eyes on,
Yet I'm pulled by the tow, of a wave creeping slow,
To a shore you're longing to lie on.

Oh, feel me, love, if your fingers desire,
My body to hold and to borrow,
Then will both of us know, do we part or soon go,
Down the road to a single tomorrow.

Bo Links

Untitled

Roaring thunder, mighty wind, flashing
lightning and it shall begin.

A dance of beauty that has always 'round
A dance of beauty between the sky and the ground.

Drops of life forever beating upon the earth
Who is receiving

Receiving what she already gave to create
The clouds and water cascade.

David L. Kiser

The Angel of Icarus

My head rests softly on a snowflake pillow.
Arms and legs sweep the snow as I dream of
      soaring in the sky.
I fly higher, and feel the sun burning the
      edges of my wings like flame on paper.
I glance at my father, he too trying to become
      an angel in the snow.
But he is slower and older than I and doesn't
      dare touch the sun.
Speeding, I feel rays burning me deep in the
      snow, boring a grave in the ground.
I look at my father who slowly rises to examine
      his work.
Proud, he smiles and tells me with his eyes that
      flight is within.
I look at his angel, noticing the arms never
      moved an inch.

Jennifer Cerritelli

Story Of Christmas Tree

Oh Shining Tree
Arrayed in all your glory
So strong and straight and green
Your branches laden with silver and gold
Shimmering under the lights so bold
Her majesty and all her glory
Could not display the colors of your story

Oh Shining Tree
Time has gone and so have thee
Your branches bowed and colorless
From life's weight of tarnished adornments
Bright lights have now grown dim
And you that was once a proud beauty
Becomes only a sad tree

Florence M. Wise

The Cross Did Not Kill Jesus

"It is finished!", cried the Saviour,
As He hung upon the cross,
The work He came to do was done;
He had covered sin and dross.

Majestically, He bowed His head
And to His Father spake,
"To Thee my life and spirit give,
No man could ever take."

Oh, He walked and talked and prayed,
But ere His teaching men have strayed.
Even so, completed was His Redemption Plan,
Acceptance or rejection, now it's up to man.

The cross did not kill Jesus
Neither did the soldiers standing by.
He freely chose His life to give
That we, thru eternity, might live.

Dena Archer

My Love

You are my true vision of love
      of a sweet storm as wind soars to a whisper.
I dream of a symphony moon and music
And pounding seas.
I smell rain as mist falls from you.
We together shine with beauty it is love.
A moment only to see roses.
My skin and breast ache enormously for you.
Flooding through me there is light
sky life love death.

Betty Stewart

Woe Is Me Though I Say

Woe is me though I say.
As I lay in the dark.
A vision runs through my mind.
But I can only seem to find.
One thing that really matters.

As I hear the pitter patters and
    clatters of your feet in my mind,
    I know I'll be able to find
    the path to your heart in no time.

Soon enough we'll begin to find each other.
And when we do, neither one of us will feel scared.
As I grab your hand and place
    it in mine, then we begin to
    find each other's soul
You reach out for me as I reach out for you.
Then I know I really do
    love you.

    Jacquelyn D. Mangual

"My Dream"

Now that the day is over and the night draws near, It's
As if I can hear your sultry, sweet voice whispering in my
ear.

I can feel the warmth from your soft hand placed gently
upon my thigh. The sparkle in your eyes and your radiant
smile beams for miles across the carolina skies.

Your voluptuous body has the scent of a freshly cut
rose. You place a passionate kiss upon my forehead, and my
eyelids close.

As I am sleeping the agony and pain of not being with
you cease. Love shall pass throughout my entire body, and my
heart will find it's hours of peace.

But, as the night begins to end loneliness creeps upon
me once again. However; I know that this loneliness and
daylight can't last long, because dusk will soon be
approaching and the light will be gone. Then we can be
together again, once more like before, in My Dreams.

    John W. Lewis

Heart Beat

The mysterious sound of a heart beat.
As it pumps the blood from head to feet
So comforting to a newborn baby
Yet so deadly to a psycho like me it starts out smooth and slow
While I search for the next victim to go.
SHHHH!.... listen, over here, Her heart beat is loud and clear
THUMP! THUMP! as she struts past, It's so calm until I grab her fast
With one unexpected touch of fear
Switched from calm to a dangerously fast gear
The noise is driving me mad
When this murder is through I'll surely be glad
The beat interests me like an unexperienced drug
But then irritates like an annoying bug
Shredding the flesh, and piercing the heart with a splintered stick.
Stopping the unwelcome sound so quick
While her lifeless corpse falls to my feet
I no longer will have to hear her heart beat
A heartbeat is evilness lurking inside
You have to kill the eerie sound to feel relief
But that's just my psychotic belief..

    Joe Conklin

Goodbye (For Becky)

She was numb at the funeral—the shocked nerves reeling,
As it wore off after time and she regained feeling,
She began expecting him to come walking in any moment.

Where have all those friends from March gone that were supporting?
Now that the nerves are tingling, and the tears are trickling,
And she keeps expecting him when she's in the living room.

Who's going to watch over her while she's watching over Her?
When She's saying, "Why now?" and asking stinging questions—
"And yet She's expecting him to come walking in just as I am.

I couldn't describe this pain if I began trying.
It's hollow and it's burning—it's numb and it's testing,
And keep expecting him to come walking in by the front door."

She was numb at the funeral—tears running unchecked,
having races down her cheeks. Can someone please tell him
that she's been expecting him to come walking in any moment?

    Jennifer Hopkins

My Teacher, My Friend

You're more than a good friend to me.
As my teacher, you gave me the key
to unlock Heaven's door, where tears flow no more,
Yes, you're more than a good friend to me.

As my teacher, you opened the book
called the Bible and told me to look,
read a portion a day, and remember to pray;
Yes, you're more than a good friend to me.

As my mentor, you seized my hand,
advised me to speak and to stand
before others and say, "God's love is the way,
to sustain you with peace every day."

Many times you have dried my tears,
explained away my foolish fears;
You're my everything, I can smile, laugh, and sing;
Yes, you're more than a good friend to me.

    Dorothy Morris

In Spite of Taboo

I run my fingers through his coarse hair
As our lips meet.
His are melons,
Mine are paper thin.

His lips envelop mine
And we blend to make gray.
I love him, in spite of taboo

But he thinks I'm curious.
He loosens my hand as we confront stares
And mutters of outrage
He tells me why we should not be together,
As I battle with tears.

He talks gibberish,
Saying his world is a jungle and
My word is a country.
He does not belong in my country
Nor I in his jungle.

He say that zebras and penguins are ugly
And so is our love.
But I love him, in spite of taboo.

    Atonio Littleton

Nature As I Wish It Is

Misty green cloud hovers above the fading orange sunset
as peacocks fly in the distance flapping their beautiful
wings and happily singing melodies which ring and echo
through the air loudly and clearly with a wavering pitch

Down between the massive mountains of rock and dirt lies
a narrow brown valley which has no life nor vitality yet
looks so alive for within it are myriads of rushing
streams full of cool water flowing around in a circle

Rose growing and blossoming among fields of wheat and
corn while horses graze upon the grass and sheep roam
across the pasture landscape searching for the flower of
their dreams that will feed them for a fleeting instant

By the cragged edge of the cliff a duckling lost and
lonely whimpers softly until the warm breeze arrives to
lift her up and take her back home to the pond where her
mother anxiously waits to once again cuddle her child

Andrew Olson

The Kiss Of Death

Our love is bliss
As soft as a gentle kiss
A gentle breeze combing through my hair
Nothing really matters as long as you're there
We slowly walk through the shadows of night
you hold me close and whisper "everything will be alright"
As long as we're together I fear not loneliness
I wait, craving for your kiss
Your love is true to your death
I inhale and feel your breath
The kiss of death

Audrey Tench

Filipino Heroes Galore

Filipinos abandoned their families to bear arms.
As soldiers of World War II, they had to leave their farms.
American General MacArthur had many charms.
As commander-in-chief, the Pacific won't have harms.

But Japan was prepared for war for a very long time
And America thought its war arsenals were prime.
On December seven, Pearl Harbor was Japan's first crime,
It was nineteen forty-one, damage costs, more than a dime.

Americans and Filipinos fought as real allies;
When the war ended, soldiers thought how fleeting time flies.
And briskly, Filipinos began to wail in loud cries,
"Soldiers' equity, American Congress denies."

In fairness to Filipino World War II veterans,
"Congress: do away with discriminatory bans!"
On American soil, heroes galore have many plans,
Because they are accustomed to hard work with honest clans.

Alberto S. Navarro

In Memory of a Rose

Time stood still as I watched life awaken.
As water nurtures a rose,
The bloom began to open,
Then time stopped forever.

Now there are only the petals that fell,
They are the precious memories others trample,
Feverishly I struggle to dust them off,
There will be no bloom as beautiful.

The tears will fall from time to time,
As if to nourish a rose,
Somewhere in the corner of my mind,
There is that one bloom forever.

Chanda May

The Song Of The Old Track

In the lonely night of coldness,
As the air itself does crack;
I alert my ear with boldness,
And listen to the Song of the Old Track.

Listening to the whistle moan,
As the wheels churn "click-ity clack";
My boyhood mind is like a drone,
Carrying me to the porch out back.

Into the distance the whistle cries,
Bouncing across the snow laden fields;
Great cities I behold with eyes
Focussing only as my wandering mind wills.

On those cold and bitter nights,
As song would sing beyond mountain far,
Ears strained with all their might,
Then sleep lifted me through door ajar.

The years have turned my hair to gray,
And the old coal train has gone its way;
Yet, on a cold night, lonely and black,
I still hear the Song Of The Old Track.

Ed M. Elliott

The Bully And The Flunky

Everybody hates the bully, because nobody wants to be the flunky.
As the bully speaks oh flunky, flunky, flunky how do I see you
slap, slap, slap, that's how I greet you the flunky starts to
cry I thought you was my friend as the flunky sobs an pout,
oh I am your friend and your bully o pall, so stop being s sissy.
Here, I bought you a piece of candy. The flunky happily grabs the
candy as he starts to scream and shout. I knew it, I knew it, I
knew you was my friend o bully o pal, you don't have to worry I
won't tattle-tale on you as long as you give me the candy, and
you promise not to tell my mommy that you turned me into a
flunky.
Ha, ha, haa, the bully slaps him five.

Daniel Horn

Signs Of Winter

The sleeping trees shiver
as the cold wind blows.
People on the streets rush
to find some warmth.
Chimney stacks hold lengthy conversations
with the sky above.
The once clear windows are covered
by frost and snow.
Snowmen greet guests visiting their homes.
No one complains about the summer past,
Instead they dream of the summer yet to come.

Cherie Smollek

Ocean Dreams

The salty waves splash along the shore.
As the creamy blue currents twist and turn.
As they have thousands of times before.
My young feet stand in the age old sand.
Salty waves hit my feet a place where sand and ocean meet,
Sends a cold chill up my spine and
    I dream of another place in time.
The bright sunset slips away the sky darkens ending another day.

Amanda Larsen

A Sunrise Atop a Crystal Morning

The night no longer seems so dark, laying upon this foggy morn',
as the first rays of clear crystal sunlight ponder along the way
through the filmy mist,
taking flight atop the dark v of the geese,
traveling swiftly along the current of the breeze.
Rising from the greatest depths of the Earth,
a fiery glow of the brightest of suns,
shedding its crystalline colors with the gentle breeze,
fluttering through the willow blossoms, silhouette at the far edge
of the horizon.
Streaks of pearl pink and luminous gold rolling across the clouds
and into the night,
turning the sky into an artist's easel, of beautiful color splattered
rhythmically across a page.
As the sun rises over the willows.
Two lone geese fly gently across the sky,
now knowing the flock to be long gone.
They fly in a loop, caught in the translucent light,
and fly onward toward the towering mountains in the distance,
the sun gleaming atop their wings.

Holly Zindulis

"This Gloomy Day"

A tear drop falls from her eye
As the rain drops fall from the sky
Outside her window the clouds are gray
Her mood sure matches this gloomy day.

The lightening throws shadows on the floor
As the thunder comes knocking at the door
She wants to leave, she knows she can't stay
But she wouldn't get far on this gloomy day.

Last night the sky was clear and bright
But there's no moon or stars out tonight
She has many debts she needs to pay
But she can't find the will on this gloomy day.

She thinks her whole world has fallen apart
Because where there was love, is emptiness in her heart
Somehow, someday she hopes the pain will go away
But the future looks bleak on this gloomy day

She lets the tears fall freely now
Stopping them is useless, she doesn't know how
Outside her window the clouds are gray
Her mood sure matches this gloomy day.

Jennifer Massey

Lasting Love

The snow came down so soft and light
As they stood gazing into the night
The flakes just fell upon their face
While their hearts were warmed by deep embrace.

The love they shared could not be told
Some day the feelings will just unfold
Our love no longer we must hide
The journey of fears we'll take in stride.

The love we have it has not bounds
Like the falling snow that covers the ground.

As we stare out into the night
The love we feel we can never fight.
I'll love you till the end of time
For in my heart you'll always be mine.

Eugene C. Haskell

A Christmas Poem

The other night I was tired
As tired as I could be I left my playthings on the
    floor and climbed on Daddy's knee
And he rocked and rocked and sang to me
About the Bethlehem star and the Christmas Tree.

And while I was thinking of that beautiful land
Some shepherds came by and took my hand saying,
"Come walk with us for we've come from afar
And all night long we followed a star."
An angel told us on the way we would find our Savior in a manger
    on a bed of hay.

When we reached that lowly bed the shepherds bent their knee and
    bowed their head
And took their gifts of spices sweet and laid them at the Savior's
    feet.
And all around it was so bright, It didn't seem that it was night.
And angels were singing on every hand, peace on earth good will
    to man.

And as I was listening to that music sweet, I heard my Daddy say,
"Why Doris dear you've been asleep."

Doris Schaller

Slash Me

Ripping my heart with a ferocious force
As violence piercing razor- like through my veins
Holding my boiling growling anger
Moving like poisonous venom through my mind.
Like sleeping dangling death inside killing my mind
Entrancing my soul with every droop of vengeance
Viciously seething from your mouth
Squeezing my life with your rough dirty hands
Scratching my insides with such precision until they bleed.
And my pain explodes through bloody teardrops flowing
From my eyes like pools of blood covering my tattered mind.
Finally protecting myself with every layer added to my soul
As my intestines scream pulsating with intense hate for you.

Ginta Rae

"One"

You are me
As we do not seem to be
Our colors blend
Leaving contrast between us
We are alone, but only together
Your mind reads my thoughts
Only to realize my thoughts are of yours
My heart is mine, but only for yours
Is it longing to beat at your speed
We are one!
Only in the eyes of the blind are we two
Our blood is warm to each others touch
Only to leave someone else's touch unfeeling
We cannot make love with each other
Only as one, together, in pleasure and pain
You are my sun!
As I am your everlasting light
Why are we separate?
When closeness is our means of life and love
You and me as one, seeming as two.

Elizabeth Zaremba

The Sea

The sea, the sea, I see the sea, what a beautiful shade of blue,
So deep is the hue, that it calls to you,
Like diamonds spun under the sun,
To come in and have some fun.

Anne Gallant-Bowman

Christmas Cheer

This Christmas season should be filled with cheer,
As we set our hearts and minds,
For the upcoming year.
Remember all the vast memories,
Which will always stay close to the heart,
The many friends and laughters shared with all,
Will help and enable us to look forward
To the upcoming surprises that lie ahead,
Let all the feelings of despair be uplifted
Into the heavenly sky above.
And let the joy of the angels descend on
Us with the wonderful gift of Love.

God gave us life and presented us with nature.
On this glorious holiday a savior was brought forth,
To help bring happiness through our tough journey.
May the upcoming years be enjoyable and fruitful.
One of the best gifts of all time,
Is being blessed with a friend like you.
My friend, You mean so very much to me,
That May your life be Merry.

Jonathan Chew

Untitled

Dance allows the spirit to soar with movement
as wild as the wind lashed trees
or as gentle as a dandelion
floating on the breeze

The dancer is the moonlight
the stage is the sea
and all who view the partnership
are taken by its grace.

The costumes, the lights, the audience
the music to enhance...
a body can learn the steps,
but only the soul can truly dance.

Casey Renz

Wildflower

I was like a wildflower blowing in the wind.
As you passed by,
I posed against my grassy field.
You looked toward me longingly.
You knelt down beside me,
Touched me.
I bent toward the warmth of your hand,
As the days went by I grew from your love.
If I began to wilt,
You embraced a cloud until its' drops
Soothed my thirst.
You shaded me, you warmed me;
But you never picked me
Or confined me to a vase.
You trusted I would be there
And enjoyed my freedom with me.
For you knew my fragrance and beauty
Was for you
And from you.
I love you.

Dina Marie Ayala

Prayer

I don't feel that I ask for much, but I fear that what I
ask for may be forbidden. A key is a tiny object to all
but the imprisoned. I beseech thee for the Vision that
was torn from my innocent eyes; the nebulous but real sense
of purpose that once guided my heart. My struggle to retain
your stolen gift has led me down subterranean corridors of
madness lit by reason, restraint, and denial. The shadows
these cast distort you beyond Belief, twist you into shapes
of abandonment and betrayal. I know this is my fault, not
yours. My wings were lovingly singed. But I cannot leave
until my simple chalice is filled.
   I do not have the white flag of faith.
   I do not have the salve of amnesia.
   I will not present to you the arrogance
   And insult of a wallet
If my request is forbidden, or impossible to fulfill, then
I ask you for one symbolic representation/manifestation of
your gift to be restored to its former majesty. I ask this
so I may leave my labyrinth and return to the world of men.
   I will look for you there.

Chris Adams

Heartcry

Lord, I lift my heart to you,
asking you to fill it new;
to look beyond my feeble tries
and hear my humble, fervent cries;

This soul is torn mid life's storms,
its' tossed and battered, weary and worn;
the devil shouts his taunts of defeat
yet over his cries, a voice so sweet;

"Come and lean upon my breast,
you who are weary, I'll give you rest;
my fainting heart beats with courage renewed
I recognized the voice - Lord it's you!

Your promises were made to keep,
even if I'm in the murky deep;
within my soul I'm touched by your hand
and I'm uplifted, victorious once again.

Betty Brown

"Feeling Of Love's Tragedy"

A time of fortunate memories, a tragedy of sorrow. Two birds play
at foolish love, match made by Eros. Life was but a sweet Sunday
afternoon, full of sounds of cheerfulness. Obstacles were invisible
and petty, every moment was luscious. Everyday's amorous feeling
become monotonous, as one become worthy of love. The evolution of
their love was inevitable, for playing at foolish love come to its
maximum development. For this caused a petty annoyance, a candle
was still burning, weakening by the breeze. One could overlook
this, however, a love-knot formed a sense of being pressured by the
other. Finally a gust of wind became apparent to both, the birds
were no longer able to soar freely. The one's, whose love became
weakened, will was diminishing, and was carried by the gust in a
negative direction. The other bird reached out to grasp her in
solicitude, but she slipped into oblivion. She flew backwards
further away out of reachable sight, leaving only relics in his
mind. Unaware of this vicissitude, the birds were force to wonder
aimlessly once again. The malediction took its toll, signifying
only the contemplating of the amorous relationship's future coarse
of events. Left by a tragedy of sorrow, yesterdays are long but
forgotten. The mortal candle eternally smoldering...

Christopher N. Eisenhauer

Remember

There at your feet a mound of earth.
At it's head, a small white cross.
Beneath the earth a soldier lies.
His countries greatest loss.

He may not have been a hero.
Wore no medals on his chest.
But, when he heard his duty call.
You can see, he gave his best.

He died and lies beneath the earth.
On which he shed the blood you see.
He died so that flag could fly.
You and I, We could stay free.

You ask his Church, His Creed, or the color of his face?
We need not know to reply.
He believe in God and Country.
He believed in You and I.

So, stand tall when that flag goes past.
Bow your, head when you enter here.
Read his name, the dates, Remember!
He asks but once each year.

David L. Wetherspoon

Anger

Liveth in the mind as a thought unprovoked
  awaiting the call from beyond

It searches in silence, its wrath is defiance
  of all that is meant to be

Like the hermit marooned on an island
  he who forgets his own name
This violence inside us, it lingers behind us
  our conscious has gone astray

The prey it does taunt, with the shield of naive
  not realizing they stir the potion
This beast in which we change, we let out of the cage
  into the zoo of human emotion

Beating and tearing at human sensibility unchecked
  until we must oblige

An altered state, we recreate
  in order to appease our pride

And even with this Malebranche lurking the inferno
  of the mind
'Tis love we fear the most

Sibley O'Bhraonain

Pulse

All's lost in sleeping I drift back
Back to a divine time where grapes ripen into a sweet wine
So sweet and savory the bees take its sweet nectar;
Thus feeding their hungering babes

And these babes grow
Into workers enslaved by the day
And driver mad in the heat;
They bring a sweet, salty sting

But in the heat the sting burns and pulses
Pulses then quickens
Taken aback to a real alarm;
Lost no more I awaken

Anthony J. Jensen

Promises

He tried to get the little girl's sweet round face
Back to life, but when it went unmoving, the heart
of him was falling powerfully and strongly through his
body, it was falling, falling, falling until it had
fallen dead. He knew his destination, he knew where
he must go. Then, he was falling, falling in slow
motion until he hit the ground from the high ridge.
This wasn't the only time it had happened. Two years
ago, his five year old daughter died. He had promised
her too, he just couldn't make anymore heart breaking,
promises.

Charlotte Ebert

Friendship

Friendship... a delicate thing. Yet the strength of it should
be compared to that of a strong substance. As the strength
of Spring is compared to the delicate flowers it produces,
so is the strength of friendship measured by the delicacies
it produces.
Time does not hinder nor alter it's course... Neither can
distance separate it.
Wherever we go, friendship shall find us.

Chester H. Miller

"Beware"

I wrote this poem to make you aware.
Be real careful, It's a jungle out there.
Smoking kills and AIDS kills too.
Gotta be real careful, whatever you do.
Stay away from booze, drugs and sin.
All these things can do you in.
Beware of salt, sugar and fat.
They're all killers, you can bet on that.
Whatever you're doing that feels real good.
You're doing more than you really should.
If all I've said is getting you low.
Forget about it and go with the flow.
Life can be hard and sometimes unfair.
I was just trying to make you aware.
So do what you want, come what may.
You're the one who will have to pay.
The Piper will come, demanding his due.
Your life is what he'll ask of you.
He doesn't care that life's unfair.
He curses those that became aware.

John W. Goetz

Memories

Memories...
  Be them good or be them bad
  The Memories that we hold on to and cherish
  Are a wonderful treasure
    Without them we would be nothing
Memories...
  they make up our lives
  They bring back pride,
    happiness,
      success, sadness, failure...
It's such a big part of our lives
  that what feelings would we have
  without Memories
Memories...
  May they bring a smile to your face
    or a tear to your eye... Memories...

Audrey Lynn Roemhildt

And The Child Sleeps

A very young couple they decide to wed, and a
beautiful child is conceived in their bed, and the
child sleeps. And as the days go by they argue and
fight until the father decides to leave one night
and the child sleeps. The daddy kisses the child as
he leaves and wipes the big rolling tears on his

sleeve and the child sleeps. Mom stands at the window
alone in the dark the child in her arms, she's got a
broken heart and the child sleeps. A girl of twenty,
a mother so young, she looks in the mirror and asks
what went wrong? And the child sleeps. Why is he gone?
What will I do? The child is growing, soon he'll be
two! And the child sleeps The child he doesn't
remember his Dad, only the loneliness that's made him
so sad and the child sleeps. The child grows up and
he just can't cope, so he runs with the gangs and he
tries a little dope and the child sleeps. The night
comes when he rides with the gang, a gun in his hand
he dies with a bang and the child sleeps.

Catherine L. Holder

"Put 'Em Up Pam"

"Put 'em up Pam" is the name that we gave her
Because she does for everyone the very best favor.
She loves everyone like sisters and brothers
She has a fun game she plays - she "puts up" others.
She helps people believe that they are all right.
She says, "You look good!" not "you look like a fright."
When someone feels dumb she doesn't make them feel dumber,
But makes their day lighter
By showing the way that they are much brighter.
She puts people up, does put 'em up Pam,
It just isn't in her to put people down.
She spreads her up putting all over the town,
And her up putted friends would never put down
A wonderful friend like put 'em up Pam.
If you want to be great, don't work on your greatness
But help others find theirs
And soon you'll have found - you are great!
Like put 'em up Pam.

Frank Pollard

Crying

I often find myself crying,
because you are always in my head.
Through my tears, I see a future without you.
This outcome I cannot help but dread.

In front of me past the blur of tears,
I see your beautiful face,
and when the blur clears when I clear my tears,
your image is suddenly erased.

I feel like bursting out to tears again,
because, I know I can see you once more.
That is often why, with you I let myself cry,
so, that when you're gone, I can see you like before.

Even when I don't cry, I imagine seeing your face,
but, the image is just not as real.
For, when I cry, I would see you more clearly,
as if your hand in mine I could feel.

So I guess I'll have to keep on crying,
so that I could always see you close to me.
I just hope that you would actually be here,
so that your face would be easier to see.

Alfonso J. Galvan

Watching Destiny

Impressions stark and real
Beckoning
Like ever-spinning memories
With the bridging force of steel,
Whether up touching-close or far,
Distant as the first Beginning
Or the moon or even a star.

From a Source vivid and deep
The moon and sky and flowers,
Impressions that lively leap
With sharing forms of will;
Images shaping images
Urging discoveries to their fill.

Ages old, the moon, yet never again the same;
Once so far, unreachable
Then the curators came
As we watched with electric eyes
Trying to grasp reality's game
And hold its fleeting moments
While seeing an image share its fame.

Carl Joseph Davey

My Grandsons

My grandsons are very young,
Being with them is lots of fun.
When I am deep in though or very still,
One will ask, "Granny, do you need a pill?"
I'll perk myself up and then I will say,
I am feeling very fine today.
We pick up a book that I have read,
"Granny, I am glad you are not dead."
They settle down and I start to read,
One will say, "This book is great indeed."
Then they start to play with their toys—
You can guess how it is with boys.
Trucks here and cars there,
Toys, Toys everywhere.
Some are in jars, boxes and chests,
From morning until night there is little rest.
They are as busy as bees, they walk, walk, walk.
When I ask them to sit they talk, talk, talk.
When the day is over and there is little to do,
The most precious words are, "Granny, I Love You."

Callie W. Lawson

Those Who Sleep Not In Flanders Field

Weep not for those who sleep in flanders field.
Beneath the poppies, row on row.
They sleep 'neath deaths' sweet kiss of peace,
Oh God: 'twas better so.

Pity those who bled and passed old liberty twice,
shell torn and weary, broken in their prime.
Condemned to live in idleness and pain.
Three long-long eons of time.

For those men, old now before their time.
Let your eyes with tear-drops dim,
could they have found rest in flanders field,
would lift thankful hearts to him.

Hillard Allen

· True Love

True love is of God; it flows from the heart.
Beyond selfish greed, it seeks those in need.
Like the flower that blooms in spring,
is true love that God brings.
Sharing its fragrance of joy and peace;
It is always a sweet release.
It is God's amazing focal sound
that stabilizes the soul when it is around.
It is God's reliable source,
that steady the nerves when you feel the loss.
It is the benevolence of the impeccable
character of the Creator to the created;
Which is never flimsy or shaky and cannot be sedated
Because it is built upon the unselfish sacrifice,
and magnanimous life and death of our Lord and Savior Jesus
Christ.
It is the impulse that reverberate through every fiber of our being;
Acquainting us with God's light which keeps us seeing.
Yes, true love, that's what we need:
The path where hate dares not impede.

Adwell Hawley

The Dreams Of My Soul

Gazing out the window of my soul to dreams
blanketed
in a misty gauze of white, are
aspirations
not shrouded by a bitter chill,
but lie glistening with fondness' light.
Fresh and new as the stillness of a warm summers day,
with bugs lazing and hazing along woven bough arched paths
they play.
Sun drenched filigreed fingers of finest lace
beckoning
come closer.
And as the warmth starts to chill
and a lambs wool covering clouds this scene from sight.
tiny blades of green, I see
slumbering, waiting
for springs breezy song to awaken them
and set them to flight.

Amy J. Davidson

White Raven

I am the white raven
Blazing blue eyes
Laser piercing beak
Flying in the night to speak
No one can see me and the landscape I use
Often brings happiness yet sometimes the blues
My wings are strong and supple
I can fly anywhere
Preferring the ocean depths
Creatures who live there
I am the white raven
Blazing blue eyes
Laser piercing beak
Have you seen where I've come from
Do you know what I seek
I am the white raven
Blazing blue eyes
Laser piercing beak
I am a lover, lover's I keep.

Christopher Bryan

"Blessings"

Blessings here Blessings there
Blessings, Blessings everywhere.
If we would take the time to share
We'd see the Blessings that are there;

When everything around us flow
And there's no one young or old,
Then we would truly, truly know
Are these the Blessings that were of or told?

Just think about how things would be
If there wouldn't he any Blessings to see
To go along from day to day
Not knowing what to do or when to pray

But because we do have a Friend each day
One who hasth really showed us the way
That when we are down and on our knees
It is His Blessings that mean the most to me.

Gwynneth White

On The Death Of My Mother

Come, lend me all the flowers of faith,
blossoms intertwining, tendrils of green winding.

Lo, there my dear brave soul waits
long down the seaside calming.
There she waits for no other save her lover.

Quicken sounds of wave length beating
heart to heart upon the shore of love entreating.

Go, for fast the leaves go floating
o'er her bier and she is gone
and none can find her.

Before the sea tide quickens
and the flow of ebb tide ceases.

Go, hearken to the call of deepening.
Twilight glows for those now leaving.

Tender be thy journey for the place of joining.
Out to sea, out to sea and out to stars.

The mourning world depart
and leave thy trace of eternity's shining dust
among the hearts that knew thee.

Carol Poss

Time Will Heal

Bluebird, bluebird why a face so long,
Bluebird, bluebird is there something wrong?
Is your heart hollow?
Have you lost the path you follow,
Or does life have you down?
Tell me bluebird, why the long frown?
Have you lost the one you love?
Tell me, are you a lonesome dove?
Does your heart ache, do you want to cry?
If so tell me bluebird, I will no longer pry.
But dear bluebird, I leave you with this,
And listen, oh bluebird this is not one you should miss.
If your heart's hollow, then pray, God will fill it.
If you've lost the path you follow, I will help you find it.
And if you have lost the one you love,
Then remember they watch you from heaven above.
Dear bluebird, I have tried my best to console;
And if I have not healed you, time will heal your soul.

Genny Chacon

The Welfare Widow

Old mother hubbard went to the cubbart to get her old dog a
bone; But when she got there the cubbart was bare because she had
not gotten her check from the welfare.

Oh my!, what shall I do she cried in despair; because my check
is late from the welfare?

There is no gravy train she told her dog kits; and you have
eaten all your kibbles and bits.

My children will have to go to bed with food; and to be
without booze and cigarettes puts me in a bad mood. I tell you dog
my cubbart is bare, and if you want to blame someone blame the
welfare.

I've used all my food stamps, she said in despair, and that is
why my cubbart is bare. So out of my way dog if you don't want
hit. I'm all out of coffee and having a nicotine fit.

So she went to her neighbor to tell of her strife. Oh my! she
said that will never do you must have the necessities of life.
Here is a pack of Camels and some Miller Lite.

Bob Goins

Hawaiian Blues

I was born in Hawaii walked through the mud,
Born brown in Hawaii walked through the mud.
But when I reached the age of two I left that place for good,
My Daddy he drove big cats and drank his liquor straight.
When I left that Sunday morning he was leaning on the barnyard gate.
I left my Momma standing with the sun shinning in her eyes.

Left her standing in the yard and I headed north as straight
  as a wild goose flies.
I've been to Oregon and Hawaii been to New York City too.
I'm still the same old brown girl with the same old blues.
Going back to Hawaii this time to stay for good.
Gonna be free in Hawaii,
Or dead in the Hawaiian mud.

Chelsea Alionar

Chances

Reaching the crossroads I look both ways,
Both ways darkly lit it seems.
I've walked here before in past, gone days,
In this land of broken dreams.

I can't go back, the corners I've turned,
Chances lost, decisions made.
I can't recross the bridges I've burned,
It's time all my debts be paid.

Is there a gleam in this forest gloom?
Is there a way to be light,
Where I can escape the dire doom,
And start it over, do it right?

There's hope for me yet, if I escape
The land where my hopes turned black,
Back to the light, with chances to take,
Get back on the winning track.

Jennifer Geibel

Untitled

My soul will never blossom
Let the sun shine, let the moon appear!
You're the only one I love in the whole world,
Innumerable are men in love with you.
I tolerate my sweetheart's pranks
Even if she is unfaithful - I won't stop loving
But if she makes fun of me — I'll order my passionate heart to cool.

Deena Muhamedhan

Backroads

I see the traffic constantly speeding by me
Breaking any violations they see fit
As they hurry effortlessly to their individual destinations
I'd like to join in that race, as I'm also in a hurry
And my journey's end is just as urgent
But I am not allowed access to the faster interstate
So, I am forced to travel by the backroads

Now, I travel by the backroads, to get where I need to go
These roads are bumpy, and go on in a roundabout way
Full of potholes and sometimes they even just dead end
And sometimes the journey is lonely and desolate
But they do take you through the small friendly towns
Where there is generally a word or two of encouragement
And someone willing to tell
Of the pitfalls that lie on the road ahead

So, right now, I'll take the backroads, that is if I must
It is strength and endurance, on these backroads that I gain
You can deny my access to the faster paced interstate
It may be slower, but I'll reach my destination just the same.

Herman Wilson II

Dancing Class

Happily they arrive....little feet pattering...voices chattering
Bright eyed and flushed with anticipation
Long stemmed bunches of rosy cheeked children
So eager to begin.
Rolling little heaps of cuddlesome innocence
Struggling to pull on the soft shoes
Which identify them as prospective ballet dancers
Taking their first step along the hard road of success.
The soles of tender little feet beat in intricate rhythm
Repeatedly correcting each mistake...to achieve perfection.
Tiny hearts sing at the marriage of music and motivation,
Happiness pirouettes across the room,
Moist curls bouncing, petal faces flushed,
A lesson learned...and praise is earned
Are they not the very signature of God?

Cielle Lord Osbourn

December '94 Ice Storm

Mother nature rained an icy world all night,
Brittle and crackling with each mother sigh.
Handblown masterpieces greet dawn sight
As sunfire in the golden ice ignites.

Fragile frozen fans of ferns
Glitter glass bathed in sunrise.
Delicate crystal works of art
Fan a frozen countryside.

A spidery swaying golden spray
Of shivery gleaming glassy ice
Becomes a beautiful bathing blight
On every plant and tree in sight.

The infant limbs of a chinese elm
Shiver under the burden of ice,
Shedding broken limbs and twigs,
Glittering like falling starlight.

Bending heavy on their stems,
The bent and bowing evergreen mourn
Like beaten soldiers grieving
At a broken limb graveyard.

Jody Anne Bresch

Renaissance

This year... a large, blackbird
brought pear-shaped wisdom,
a happy catechism,
and the candle-lit nest
to prepare my wings upon.
I am learning to speak
to find my mouth wet
with unspeakable ghosts.
I awake now with talons to replace tears,
    and feathers where fins used to be.
Last year, I was a gold-flecked fish
A dragon swallowed the gray water, swimming in my own guiltless
demons
cooing to pat its belly.
With a grumble and a roar, I wobble downhill.
I rest for a moment-reflect on the karmic lesson,
somersault in my fluidity, alive, raw, and newfound.
I tap at the circular wall of my world,
I crack the red, red eggshell...
- I am born.

Andrea E. Jackman

The Earth

The earth is full of mighty blues
Burgundy, reds, and cloudy whites too
There are animals of hide, of fur, and feather
Of scales and skin
With claws and feet and fin

There are exquisite plants like flowers and trees
With pretty animals swinging from their knees
There are hawks that swoop tigers
That sneak up on prey
Run, run, run away
There are coral reefs with fish so bright
With sharks and otters that always fight

So keep it clean
Don't be mean
Our beautiful earth
Is the universe's only sign of birth

Adam J. Kaphan

Images

Ocean...temple for the soul,
Burial ground for the heart.
Where I washed my broken heart, healed my
    wounds, and drown my sorrow.

Stood drowning in tears from the sky.
The walls of my glass box were closing in.
The child's fingers touched the pond, and I watched
    the moons image shimmer away.
Happiness comes at dawn.

My head was swimming, as I began to fall... crazy!
Crying, curled in the fetal position, rocking...
I became a child again...

And you still think you own me!

Jennifer Lynn Beam

"Waiting Till Death In Tranquility"

A traveler who's longing for death roams around a shore
Not knowing what he wants to live for.
He roams around in the ocean's tides.
Not knowing when to end his life the sooner he wants to die.
The last time he watched the ocean he never felt rejoice.
Drowning in the ocean, death was his only choice.

Denise Nunez

Music Of The Spheres, Off-Key

Those cold fires in outer space
burn me nonetheless. I must confess
their place and pace in time
are greater far than mine.
I only mark a moment of their span.

What consumes me then?
It's not their flames but knowledge
of our complicity: coeval, they exist
and burn with me, their cruel light speaks
of duplicity, beginning alone before my birth,
so what we see happening happened long ago.
Our existence cannot be contemporary
with some lie of harmony.

Gerald A. Somers

Hold Me Against the Night

Quickly, before the sun's first rays
burn the last Moondrops
from the window sill.
I want to see you body in soft morning light.
We chase the dawn!
Hold me against the night
because darkness scares me
and tomorrow scares me
but when we are together
times evaporates
and darkness — our darkness, our depth
we drink to the dregs and celebrate
Hold me against the night;
your body shimmers in the light
of a red candle
and beckons to mine.
Your beauty illuminates
my darkness and sets the night on fire.
Let's melt into each other.

John Grimes

With Or Without A Painting

Today I have no inspiration,
but a dark silent night on the ocean or the light of day at sea.
Yet I keep thinking of how nice,
it would be to be on the cool ocean or breezy sea.
I'm within the shadow of no food or water.
Yet I linger for a single drop of water,
or a morsel of food.
I wonder shall my painting be imagined or resumed.
I think I will imagine the ocean with its big, and beautiful white
    clouds.
The rest is the beautiful blue shattered skies,
and a flock of sea gulls gracefully flying above.
"Shall you please hand me my dry,
but soon to be beautifully colored paintbrush,"
I said to my assistant. Then I began to paint.

Heather Dawn Gibson

Untitled

Your smell on my hands like a warm spring day
  blows through the air
A cool breeze as dusk sets upon us,
  and a chill races through my bones

And your embrace as gentle as two young lovers
  bound by eternal love
Our souls one forever
And a flower grows upon the laden snow
  reminding me of you

Cathy Hetfleisch

A Lasting Look

Desperation may be a key to open a door
but can it open the door inside
if a candle can burn all night
can it melt away the despair of wax
that abides

in a look there is so much light that can
be reflected back
but of much of the light you can't see
if the eyes use feelings to touch
can they reveal the agony

when hands are numb and eyes are blinded
does a looking glass have a view
when my eyes were opened and hands could heal
I saw myself in you.

David J. Heim

The Battle Within

In my heart of hearts I want to stay,
But deep inside I'm beckoned away.
The calling seems far but oh so near,
As I try to sense the voice that I hear.
I'm in a place where my mind goes freely
Against the flow of time and reality.
Is it all in my mind or is there more there,
I try to reason but just more despair.
My soul keeps calling to listen within,
Though my earthy body still enjoys the sin.
I'm tattered and torn at this fight I must face,
For its the battle within us the human race.
So why am I here on this earthly plateau,
And where do I go when its my time to go.
The questions elude my mere mortal mind,
Yet the knowledge is here just awaiting the find.
Why is it so difficult for me to conceive,
That when I die only my body will leave.

Christina Storch

The Dream Lover

He comes to me in the night
But disappears with each morning light
To him my soul I do surrender
In memory of his kiss so soft and tender
And in the inevitable light of day
I beg my lover "Please, please stay!
I can't stand another minute without your touch,
Or those whisper soft kisses I love so much.
Please don't leave me! Please, please stay!"
But on a cloud of mist he floats away........

Cheryl Walker

The Girl With The Black Hair

Her beauty is before me everyday.
But I can't approach her and say what I want to say.

As I look, she passes me by.
I say nothing-to scared to say Hi.

Why can't I talk to her I start to scream.
The only time we are together is in a dream.

It is in a dream where I know her love is there for me.
But, then I wake up and enter back into reality.

One part of me says speak, you can be with her if you try.
Another part says that is foolish, you are telling yourself a lie.

Maybe my feelings for her will some day fade and I won't care.
But, until that happens, I still can't approach the girl with the black
  hair.

Damon Wadley

Forgiving To Heal

My body was wracking with Pain
But I continued to work in order to gain
Everyday I hurt so bad I could hardly take it
My Kids said "mama don't keep falling to the floor"
So I left my job early and went through the doctors door
He had constantly told me "there is nothing wrong with you"
I said "doctor, please help, I don't know what to do"
Doctor was tired and wanted no more patients that day
But his nurse said "come on, but you may have a long stay"
When he did emerge, he said "tell her to go away"
I definitely will not see her today
I cried and I cried because I was rejected
But thank God my cries were detected
One of his colleagues who was standing nearby said "don't you cry
I'll get you some help; just standby"
Soon the cancer in my body was discovered
And with help from God and the doctors, I am almost recovered
Thank you Lord for ending my hate
I hope that person who wronged me will go through your gate

Freda M. Mays

To Catch a Thought

I had the urge to write today,
But, I know not what to say,
Like writers of old, inspired and fueled,
Waiting for the unraveling, prophetic word.

Perhaps, we're to let our thoughts flow out,
And linger midst our heads,
But when they do, as in a twinkling of an eye,
They vanish quickly stead.

Inspiration, you may say, is a word not well defined.
It surfaces on an instant,
And when you turn around, it's gone.

So, how to tap that urge, I wonder,
What is the secret key?
A game of wits with the beyond,
Is making this a trickery.

Sue Martindale

The Waif

You don't know me, Sir!
But I live next door to you.
for that is where
your garbage bin resides.
Your fat tabby cat came last night
So slow so sleek
To meow me out of
The luxury of beating the rats at their game
You don't know me, sir!
But I am a constant companion at your table
For I get to eat
What you had for dinner
When it gets to the garbage bin.
Pray Sir! Can you have me
Your kitchen boy be? For my hands are so
Calloused and hard
To make your kitchen floor
Clean and shining
And your cooking pots
licked clean and empty.

Aimee Okenwa

"Mary Called From Far Away"

Mary called from far away: She finally made the call,
but I was not there to hear what she had to say.
You see I was out in the street trying to put to
an end the battles that happen when we do meet.
Now it is no physical conflict I hereby describe,
but a raw, emotion-filled one that leaves me crying inside.
Our passion together is real; full of pleasure and promise.
We abandon our 'other' lives for moments as one.
At the end, there is a sweetness and ardor that dismisses
the brooding for a time.
Her life is exciting, it's true.
But the white powder and white crystals that command it
won't ever let this beautiful creature rest her form.
She owns not a minute, each second, day and night is
controlled by the demonic foe.
It prevails.
I know I must retreat again and again, though my heart and
being cry out at the delicate love lost—forever.

James Charles Putz

Love

Love comes and goes like money and friends,
but if you really love someone it doesn't go away,
you can say it does sometimes you can feel it does,
but when you think about it everything's the same,
you're still in love with that things that gone away,
so don't be shy and don't be afraid everyone has feelings,
for one thing or another that they can't let go ,
whatever's on your mind let it go,
I have a story to tell ya listen carefully cause I'll only say it
once, I have little cousin who I love so much,
he was such a cute little boy, his favorite toy was a truck,
then the day came when he left I was terrified
and I miss him till this day,
sometimes I wish I could disappear from the world
and see him I'll still cry with pain,
I'd leave loved ones behind and think about them,
the world can come to an end,
but it can't change one thing it's just too powerful,
no one can change the wonderful thing,
it's a wonderful thing, I call it LOVE.

Helen Rosner

Friendship

At times you'll feel encircled by darkness
But know I'm still here for you
At times you'll feel you can't stand tall
But know I'm still here for you
At times you'll hurt over a broken heart
But know I'm still here for you
At times you'll fear the world
But know I'm still here for you
Although you may stumble through the paths of life
Be assured you will never fall
Because friendship is the biggest
And most powerful love of all

Jennifer Manis

Perfect Union

Thriving in the inclinations of man
is a deficiency,
A deficiency which can only be quenched
through an exclusive union,
A union which lures two hearts to surge into
an alliance of perfected passion,
a passion void of restraints.

Don Robinson

Life

Life is a beautiful word,
But love is sweet because of the way it sounds.

Don't take life for granted,
Not as a toy.

Life is full of passion the way we
Would want to be.

You can find someone special to share it
With and make the best of it as much as you can.

Life is the key to your heart, enjoy
My thoughts and enjoy our love as one.

Life is something good,
But love is real and also beautiful.

Audrey Sinclair

To Enjoy Nature

Nature's creations should be enjoyed by all;
But lovers of nature are a minority — small.
Nature is better appreciated by two;
And my choice, by nature, is none other than you.

Like a child with a toy, how many enjoy —

The bark of a squirrel, the gentle green plain,
The black bass's swirl, the soft falling rain;

The full of the moon, the wild canna's blossom,
The mockingbird's tune, the grinning o' possum;

The impenetrable thicket, the snort of a buck,
The chirp of a cricket, the flight of a duck;

The bob-white's whistle, the sunset's hue,
The dandelion's thistle, the early morning dew;

The wild violets bloom, the twinkling starlight,
The cloudy sky's gloom, the still of the night;

But nature's creatures are not enjoyed by all;
I'm proud to be in that minority — small.
You in my arms, nature's magnificent view,
A lover of nature — a lover of you.

Carl Darden

Sparkling Treasure

Diamonds and gold I always wish I had
But my fortunes had always been bad
Then I met you and now I realize
I have found a much greater prize
Glistening diamonds could never replace
The brilliant gleam of your pretty face
And golden nuggets with their radiant glow
Could never glitter like your shiny soul
A sparkling treasure is what I have found
A heavenly angel who flew to the ground
And brought to me a most glorious day
Heavenly angel don't you fly away
Fascinated and delighted is the way I feel
The pleasure that you bring me is for real
The light that you give illuminates my day
Heavenly angel please always stay

Carlos Lizarraga

Four Letter Word

Often mistaken as loyalty to the Brotherhood
but not referred to as what it really is.

Hate.
Who could imagine that a word so small
could bring about powerful feelings that run as deep as an ocean.

Hate.
It looks so harmless
yet the anguish it brings is so massive.

Hate.
It has been masked for so long,
many do not recognize it when they confront it.

Hate.
Man's way of concealing his fear.
Man's way of cowardice.

Hate.
Who would have thought that so much pain could be caused by a
four letter word.
Hate.

Ernestine Lucas

That Beautiful Old Rugged Cross

'Twas only a tree in a forest
But oh what a treasure in store
To be singled out for a special task
And be remembered for-ever-more.

'Twas a thing of beauty with leaves galore
And the birds to nest on it's limbs;
And then to become that old rugged cross
To be used to crucify HIM.

But once again it's beauty will shine
Because of that special day;
To be a part of the treasure of Calvary
Calling people to know the TRUE way.

It means a lot to most of us
But to those who don't it's a loss;
Jesus died that we all may live
On that Beautify Old Rugged Cross.

Helen G. Wilcox

Time Oh Time

Christmas comes and the year would end.
But the joy goes on till New Year's Day.
Then think what you forgot to buy and send.
To friends and families to be merry and gay.
So off you go to stores and malls.
To exchange return and buy some more.
Surprised you will be to view the halls.
Jammed with gifts for Valentines, galore.
Then when you are ready for Valentine's Day.
Malls are ready for Good Friday.
Then comes Mother's Day and Father's Day.
In between there are Birthdays and Labour Day.
So quickly decorate for Halloween and Thanksgiving Day.
Now where did the time go??
December 25th is Christmas Day.
Christmas comes and the Year would End.

Asha B. Aikat

Interaction

It lets you in
but then closes you out:
A new, tightly bound book that has to be broken in.
The glue is still wet and the pages still hot.
But as time goes on and the glue dries, it becomes more rigid.
It takes time. Go gently.
If you try too hard you'll break it, then nothing will suffice.
Your favorite edition, an original that cannot be replaced:
Reading it gives you a knowledge and an acquired insight.
You are enraptured by the plot, the twists and corners.
It just can't be put down.
You are always anxious to enjoy its beauty.
As the span gets shorter and the pages thin out,
the story comes to an understandable close.
The intrigue, the past:
There is nothing left to sort through.
Let it end and do not reread it
but remember it for its enjoyment in your hands.
It is time for another book.

Danielle Porcelli

The Writer

I got up this morning determined to write
but try with my heart and try with my might,
the thoughts in my head seemed to take flight;
I couldn't put words on the paper just right.
I scribbled and crumpled until it was night
And the floor all around me looked quite a sight.
With fingers grown sore and muscles gone tight,
I rose from my seat and stretched to my height.
Then I sat down and turned on the light,
but the paper before me stayed perfectly white.
My pen had run dry to add to my plight!
So I checked in the drawer in the twilight,
but only a pencil popped into sight.
My lips started twitching on words impolite
though I clamped the lower in a lingering bite.
When I was too tired and weary to fight,
sleep overtook me like a deadening blight;
or, perhaps more aptly, like some parasite.
Suddenly I awakened with a flash of insight,
and wrote this poem with that stick of graphite.

Delphia Danner

What You Mean

  I can't begin to tell you how much I care.
but want you to know I'll always be there.
I may not always see eye to eye, but
I want you to know that I do try.
  The times you are there when I need you most,
are the greatest times, because you are close.
You wipe the tears from my face, and
hold me with you're warm embrace.
  The things we share I will treasure,
for there's no one who will ever care as much as
you do. So I thank you for the great times we
have, and for that I am glad.
  I hope you know what you have given me,
because I want you to see no one can ever
give that much love to me. For the many things
you've given me, I give you my heart and soul forever.

Cyndi Devore

Last Good-bye's

You've moved on from here, where we still are
But we've not yet recovered from your death
Memories are all we have of you now
And the last good-bye is all that's left

I feel I could've helped somehow
Like maybe it would've changed things
But then maybe you're watching over us
Like the distant bird that always sings

You touched the heart, mind, and soul
Of everyone you ever met
It's why you were taken
That I just do not get

Dear Colleen, I'm sorry, no more can I write
For if I did, forever I would cry
There is simply no more I wish to share
In this, our last good—bye

Danielle McCann

As He Wanders...He Thinks....

I must not seek too much, but be the one who is sought after.
But who am I to forget that time of sadness, and those of laughter?
Was I but a fool that fell all for just one look?
Is my heart so foolish that an emotion it mistook?
I must not beseech those who openly seek for I-
Because of their thick hearts and thin minds, I must pass them by.
And those who can not appreciate-I totally despise.
For one who takes for granted, by myself, is never wise.
Who is not wise is clearly a fool, lost within their self.
What have they become? Do they seek just for outer wealth?
Truly it is sad what this world has become.
While people sit in shame I have escaped with a work that God has done.
He has brought forth into mind a world all my own-
A place where happiness and love in depth have grown-
A place of untamed beauty and passion, to a common man unknown-
A place you've dreamed of, and all this time you didn't know it....
It all lies, not in this world or any other,
only in the mind of a poet.
Seek after this poet lost, and thou shall only find,
But mere is displeasure and the remains of a boggled mind.

Jeffrey Armando Vasquez

People Need People, But Also Need Themselves

There's a time in life that's rough,
But you can always get through.
There's a time in life where all the fingers point at you.
You sit up in your bed drinking it up, letting the steam go to your
    head.
Someone comes in trying to kill the pain in you.
All throughout, you're kicking, screaming, throwing them out.
You're left there helplessly,
With enough pain inside to breakdown and pout.
Even when someone else comes in you haven't learned your lesson yet.
You turn around, point your fingers at them.
Yet still you scream and shout.
Your pain is out, left in someone else's hands.
They say no pain, no gain, but what did you gain?
Now what can you say?
I'll bet you know what you lost;
It's what you needed the most.

Elisa M. Kvitky

Riding High

I'm on a rocket ship in the sky.
But you can only see the flames
    I shoot behind .
And sometimes I ride too high.
But you can only know the difference
    if you'll give it a try.
Sometimes I fly and fly to the top
    of the sky, with little need to wonder why.
I'm just cruising the outer limits
    of space and time, a frontiersman
    of new order, the Knight of a better rhyme.
Sometimes, I ride too high
    new frequencies flood my mind.
When I ride too low I feel
    like I'm blind.
Speed me up at the end of the sky.
Slow me down when I ride too high.

Brian Abramson

Wishing And Dreaming

Today I felt so beautiful, I wanted to share it with you
But you weren't there or within reach to talk to.
The sky was so clear and the grass so green
The only thing missing — was you and me.

I hope that you also felt the same way,
It could've been the most perfect day
Of course - I only wish you the best
To share all good things, is all that I wish.

I heard the birds sing and looked to the sky
And thought of us — only you and I.
On the wings of a butterfly my mind did float,
Remembering our "secrets"...I smiled, you know.

Though our lives are short and time flies so fast
Your life is your own-but I'm glad that we met.
I wish I could give you everything that I'd like,
But I'll keep on dreaming-as this day turns to night.

Barbara Stolzmann

The Stars In Myth And Fact

THE STARS IN MYTH AND FACT is a book
By Oral Scott—1947—an Idaho imprint
So important are the stories of "Stars"
As known to the Ancients and Miss Emily

To fully understand "Her" Signs—Symbols
And Emblems she used and used many times
She—"Virgin Queen"—"Emperor King"—He
"Arcturus" of Poem 70 is Sam Bowles—SB

Ms. Dickinson was a "Druid" Princess—by
Her own admission—Poem 44 She sent to Sam
"Since I am of the Druid"—She says of self
And Mary—Sam's wife—is of that other life

She called Herself His "Rose"—even early
On—in this earliest of "late 1858" poems
Remember to remember He published Her Rose
In His SDR that same year—in His buttonhole

In 1866—Her famous "Snow" poem celebrates
"A Druidic Difference Enhances Nature now"
"Summer—Birds"—acrostic—stanza ends with
An anagram-verso—So Believe—"Mass"—SSAM!

Bill Arnold

Just Another Line

Like those who "live day to day," I exist
by the line. English sonnets and compact
discs usually have fourteen to consist.
Immemorial lyrics coenact
presidential election, covertly
decided, with no collaboration.
Invent aphorism or analogy,
and sonnets conceive you education.
Shakespeare engendered forms called "conversions"
when there were no classics but Greek, Latin.
Will is our poet, makes English no tin,
aurally speaking. Sonnets to begin
a duel of our springing language then.
Sir Philip Sidney, Marlowe, Ben Jonson
vied with tongues as professional teams, men.
Sonnets bore most sensationally, fun-
minded folks, but love poems form operas
and operas, soaps.

Amy Hammerand

I

I
can
not
endure
the pain
during those
endless moments
each day when I
feel my peers' eyes
boring into the back of my skull
as they brutally pass judgment on me
by critiquing my cherished convictions
or scoffing at those whom I have befriended
or secretly gossiping about my "odd" behavior
or offering me lessons of quaint, ideal mannerism
or jeering at my expectations of personal grandeur
or believing I am too selfish to notice anything other than
the self-made wall of my own obstacles...

Brennan Thomas

The Woman On The Bed

She often sits alone on the age'd wooden bed
by window overlooking the field for the dead.
   Without a stir but for cry in the night,
   as darkness awaits the arrival of first light.

Time unwinds without lonely form
rising from seat while soul becomes torn.
   Though recognizing pain as only in head,
   she prays in solitude to be like lover dead.

And she reflects alone upon days of old
when she once wore a smile or so I am told.
   She survives only by heartbeat and breath,
   patiently awaiting her anticipated death.

He will bring her spirit love
and engulf her world like hand inside glove.
   For he'll make a small pitch to be easily sold
   for a life and some memories — more valued than gold.

Bradley Allen

Eternal Happiness Is Not Lottery

   Winning numbers in lottery can be one, two, seventeen,
Can be also six, nine, sixteen...
Sometimes happy numbers are...
Seventy seven or fifteen, but (b-u-u-u t);
   Always in lottery a blind venture decides
Who is a winner and who is not (n-o-o-o t)!

   No winning numbers are very important in our life,
No thousand dollars, no even million five...
Sometimes poverty lives...
In the best friendship with happiness, but (b-u-u-u t):
   Always love in our life and only love decides
Who is really happy and who is not (n-o-o-o t)!

   We love Lord who is "the way, and the truth, and the Life,"
Holy God, Holy Immortal One...
Sometimes suffering because of our sins...
With all His Heart loving us, but (b-u-u-u t):
   Always we ourselves - being free God's children - decide
Who will enter God's Kingdom and who will not (n-o-o-o t)!

Benjamin Witold Marczewski

A Time Remembered

The hollow ring of a distant bell
Calls upon a time untold.
And as the breath stops suddenly still
An ache pours out forever old.

A time of demanded memory loss, derived
With those who bore the reproach.
And on whose watch they could not hide
A rage and pain that nothing could broach.

As broken pieces are fit together
A somewhat blurred picture comes forth.
Out of kilter voices, motions without measures,
Becoming renewed hope, healing, and birth.

No sense is made of primitive intent
By the rememberer who has come to learn:
The acts no kind soul could begin to invent,
Which left scars like a branding iron burn.

Flames of empowerment begin to fan,
As this quaking memory's no longer bridled.
And the despicable abuse of molesting man,
Shan't claim victory over this innocent child.

Amanda Dershem

The Gift of Love

A little something from the heart
Can be worth much more than the greatest piece of art.

From showers of flowers,
To love poems for hours,
I had no idea what would win your heart.

From Teddy bears,
To cuddly white hares,
I thought until my head hurt, on what you would love.

And I began to think, Innocent as a dove,
From pieces of art,
To writing something from the heart.

Although it would have to fit like a glove,
It would have to be something sweet,
Like a big candy treat;
So I decided to give you this next time we meet.

Eric W. Nickelson

"Rescuing Heavenly Angels"

The 'world' here below says, "there is nothing we
  can do."
We servants of the Lord on high- 'Prayed,' —
Dear Jesus, help us please.
And Jesus brought the angels back -
  to us freely.
One angel came to the foggy darkened —
  window at unawares,
Uttered not even one amazing word —
Without even one spoken mutter,
  started miraculously too work;
Thank you endearingly, Jesus Christ —
  we were delivered.
  Hallelujah! "Praise the Lord-"
The one mighty and bright, mystery-angel,
—like for Daniel and David -
  speaking at last, I love you -

    Bert Rivett

Untitled

If you look then I'm sure you
can find the person you will always
love. They may hurt you and may
break your heart but still you
will find yourself loving them.
As you deeply stare into their eyes
you can almost see the love you
feel. As you hear his voice you want
to cry, as you feel him standing by
your side you want to die, because
you still cannot have him. You
fantasize and wish it were real, but
you will always know that it's not. As
he leads you on which he always does, you
wish it were for real. As he talks to you,
And he always does, you wish you could tell him
how you feel. You just want to die as you remember
the night when you saw them together holding hands.
And you know that the memory is proof that there is nothing there.
But still you can't move on, because you love him.

    Caiti Lavoie

A Different Kind Of Love

To love someone with all your heart,
  can make it easy to be apart.
Yet when together our love is shown,
  through things that are so called unknown.

Although the unseen which lies ahead,
  can bring a tear of joy you said.
Through time our lives will be affected,
  it still may bring the unexpected.

To you I pledge my life to spend,
  from now until the very end.
Our love will hold our souls complete,
  not like the others, but ours will keep!

Beyond a death we must go on,
  and realize that we have won.
Because of this which we believe,
  others will know what we perceive.

Our love is not the same as them,
  because we are so close to Him.
But when our lives of truth are o'er,
  then we shall live forevermore.

    Dawn D. Kouf

The Message

Teacher, do you see me as I sit before your desk?
Can you hear me screaming silently?
Have you noticed my red streaked, tear-filled eyes
which unbidden blink so violently?

Teacher, read the message I so desperately send!
Look pass the roll you're taking!
Let your mind probe into mine
So you will know my heart is breaking.

Teacher, you're looking thoughtfully at me,
And, Oh, Thank God! You see, you see!

    Betty Hazen Brooks Brown

The Dream

I'm running through a tunnel,
Can't seen to find the light,
I feel I'm being funneled,
In the darkest of the night.
I close my eyes to hide my fears,
I don't know where to run,
My cheeks are cold, from trickling tears,
Oh, when will there be sun?
And when my eyes begin to awake,
There is a twinkling of light,
The dampness upon my skin, I shake,
In the darkest of the night.
I begin running with all my might,
Hoping to find the way,
At the end of the tunnel there is a light,
For the dammed, I do so pray,
The sweat is dripping from my soul,
I can hear the people scream,
Life can really take it's toll.
Even though it was a dream.

    Carol Landes

Redemption

Must I always be the almost was,
Can't you just like me - just because?
I've done some things, but I was younger then,
I'm better now, you just tell me when.
Before, I didn't think - I'd see and I'd act,
To keep your affection now - I've learned how to use tact.
Patience is a virtue, I've learned that now,
Adoration is a learned behavior - let me show you how.
Tomorrow is a question, the answer escapes us both.
With you and me and our creator - the outlook is full of hope.
So, therefore my dear,
I speak very clear.
Must I always be the almost was,
Can't you just like me - just because.....?

    George Franklin Arterberry

The Forbidden Wall

A nation divided where East meets West
By a wall, some wire. Rifles at rest

The wall stood for years for honor, distrust
Not to mention the political stuff

Stained red with blood, washed white with tears
Disgracing this nation through the years

So they tore down the wall. If we study we see
That people everywhere just want to be free.

    Eugene L. Seprish

Untitled

Christmas is coming, Christmas is coming,
  can't you see it everywhere.
Sleigh bells are ringing, children are singing
  can't you see it everywhere.
Soon night will be falling, and they will be
  crawling, in their beds so snug and warm.

Oh! can't you see them on that morning dancing then
  around the tree so bright.
There is a dolly Nancy wanted with all her
  might.
There is a train with so many tracks,johnny
  will be proud to show, a pipe for daddy to sit
  around the fire and smoke.
Gloves and scarf for granny to wear upon her
  trips where every she may go.
Pink and white show for Granny to wear upon a
  cold winters night.
Grandpa is getting old to you see a pair of
  house shoes to put upon his feet.
We must not forget the most important thing
  of all to tell the children of how Christ was born this day.

Florine Fisher

Guidelines For A Christian Life

Praise the Lord each day you live;
Care and share with others;
Treat each one you meet along life's way
As a close friend or a brother.
Read the Bible; it is God's word;
Pray and have faith in Him;
Witness of His steadfast love,
That others you might win.
Thank Him for your blessings, whether large or small;
Listen, that you might hear His voice
And answer when He calls.
Keep the commandments as best you can;
If you stumble, ask Him to forgive
for He is there to help you
Every day that you shall live.
These are the guidelines for a Christian's life
Amid moments of happiness, turmoil, toil and strife.
When you reach your final days and life on earth will end,
He'll meet you with arms outstretched;
Your Saviour and your Friend.

Elsie Armington

Colors

Man has made himself separate, placing each into
  Categories of dark, light, black, white.

Life is a blend of races working together in a world where
  It's wrong to hang with that color of marry this color.

I know in my heart like I know my name,
  God likes variety, He created it.

If everyone had the same color, same mind, same likes or dislikes,
  Same goals and dreams, it would be a boring world.

The world needs to wake up,
  To laugh, to smile, to cry, to feel,

We can't begin to end prejudice without these,
  If someone is different,

Respect that,
Learn from it.

Life is short.
Live it.

Jamal Gibran Sterling

Untitled

Please don't be late
cause we live in such a beautiful state.
I never thought a guy could cry
but seeing you walk by
proved me wrong
so let me play you a love song.
My lady called me a clown
but that is how it goes in my hometown.
I like my gals so very charming
cause beauty is only skin deep
and the hills of home so very steep.
So climb a mountain to it's peek
and there you will find the true love you seek.
Are friends like fortune cookies?
I say they are because it's what's inside that counts
whether it be a heart so true or just your fortune
A prince charming or a Rhinestone Romeo I am not.

Bill Cornell

Untitled

I saw this girl, so frightened and alone,
chewing her fingernails down to a bone.

She was just a little girl of eight or nine.
Being so frightened, it seemed out of line.

I tried to be friendly and offered her gum,
She shied away and tried to run.

What was she doing in this local dance hall?
Where so many were drunk and often a brawl.

She was clean and neat, but oh so frail,
with big brown eyes in a face so pale.

Where was her mother, out on the floor,
forgetting her daughter there by the door?

Did she come with a brother, who shouldn't be there?
Was the guarding her secret so terrified there?

The answer to it, I'll probably never unfurl,
But I'll never forget that frightened little girl.

Alice Koch

Grandfather

Just a reminder to say I love you Pop,
and to say thanks for loving me nonstop.
Together we make a pretty good pair,
it's a great relationship the two of us share.
We should be proud of the way we are bound,
it's a special kind of love in you that I've found.
I am grateful that I know someone like you,
for truly great men are but a few.
Your love for me is strong and true,
I want you to know I will always love you.
Thanks for doing all things that you've done,
when it comes to buddies, me and you are number one.

Jamie Stuart

"A Miraculous Invention"

Nine months before light comes into focus...
But perfection takes patience.
Innocent as an Angel, precious like a rainbow...
Oh, what an embryo, oh, what an embryo.
To take a journey through a warm tender canal,
Not yet born, the unborn child.
What a blessed event to participate in,
Without malice, without sin.
The outcome is a miraculous invention!

Alisa Nolden

Who Are We?

Who are we and what have we become? We call ourselves Americans,
and were proud to say were number one.

We will travel across the world to help a fallen foe, but when
trouble comes to our own backyard we'll turn our backs and go.

We are proud of our heritage each and everyone, but look at us the
wrong way and you'll be staring at our gun.

We have a reputation of supporting those in need, that is why we pay
our professional athletes for there greed.

Who are we and what we become? We call ourselves Americans, and were
proud to say were number one.

Our children are much more educated than we were back then, they learn
early about drugs, sex and killing a friend.

We say our justice system is the finest in the land, but how can this
be when the criminals are the richest of the clan.

We cannot understand why are children are in such despair, it is very
simple I tell you the values are just not there.

Who are we and what have we become? We call ourselves Americans, and
were proud to say were number one.
        David A. Midcap

Living

I remember a time when I was a kid; just a boy and I didn't need drugs
as a toy. I remember dreaming of a magic place were dragons were your
friend. We did not slay them; we rode them to fly. Now that was a
natural high! A cerebral hemorrhage of your brain.
Mixed up which side is right and what is wrong. Creativity does not
come from a drug made of chemicals in a lab. Have you just been had?
Images in the head, hey it will really make you dead. Or just flip
over to stay on the other side of brain. Which hemisphere though, the
right or the left? The left to calculate numbers for the rest of your
life thinking you're a genius, only to come up with an equation; or
the right to see those creative images for which you took the drug.
Which will it be? Images of heaven or images of hell? What if the
dragon bites you on the neck to leave you in a pool of blood to stay.
What if the unicorn flew away in the sky to stay. You could not get
back down cause you ruined your head. Just because you thought you
would gain the secrets of life and not pain. I took drugs to tap into
the right side of my brain, to get more in touch with my emotions, not
to let them over flow to control my life. Life is hard. I'm not
going to lie, but the secrets to life are not going to come from
L.S.D. The secrets to life lie in the sky, so don't get high.
        Christian Eugene Beats

Passage

There before me looms the threatening storm so fierce, groaning,
    churning, darkening the very light that shines so clearly.
I had emerged, I thought, from brooding clouds and mists, and now
    again they herald forth this day.
Why now, I ask, staring deep into the streaking, murky blackness,
    for I passed this way before, in a different age,
And now I face the darkness, frozen, waiting, expectant, shaking,
    wondering what comes this hour.
I turn, glancing back in time, believing that I paid my debt
    in earlier storms, a beaten passage, pale and ragged.
Fresh light shown in the aftermath and I sighed, wiping away the
    tears, wet, burning...staining.
Another came and still another, rumbling, screaming, striking out
    as not before...and yet the same.
I plead for strength and calm, passing one more time through
    endless void, to this arena of golden brilliance.
Refreshed, I whisper to myself, how much more to bear in running
    once again, cringing, crying, trembling in fear?
No, not now I say, my passage paid before, standing tall and steady,
    renewal comes and strength dissolves the trial.
        Don F. Blayney

Rebirth

Naked in the chill of wintry December,
Cloak of sanctuary on the ground
Stripped of protection, raped by the wind,
Left to survive the frozen mound

Pounding, icy pellets paralyzed movement,
Reaching skyward for the grace
of warmth, concealed by brooding clouds,
Refusing its tender embrace

But when springtime brings rebirth—
A new cloak will transform the limbs,
Branches will be rewarded by the sun
For the unending patience of them

I will enjoy soothing favors, come summer,
When the feverish earth begs for shade
And the sun - quarantined in winter -
Will burn incessantly the long day
        J. Newberry

Fascinations

Some see beauty in the sky!
Clouds galore, they gasp and sigh!
And oh, say I, it's justified!
For to my mind, they magnify!

For just to visualize these glories,
Search would I, to find such stories
Elsewhere, such as those the clouds provide
As they roll by.

Form as do they fascinations
Venting my imagination
Darkening so my mortal mind
To all, except the tales told there.

So while I'm gazing tentatively
The clouds disclose identities
Impressing visions endlessly
To all who seek them there.
        Carol Kieffner

Endangered Species

A desolate, old oak stands alone weeping.
Chattering squirrels gather its nuts no more;
birds no longer come to sit and sing their songs.
The murky brook beside it holds no fish or frogs.

Gone are the animals, said the old tree,
industry has killed them all, you see.
Among littered forests, fields and streams,
the helpless creatures could not exist.

Like the flowers, I too will wither and wilt,
for the sun is blocked by thick, dark smog.
The air and water are heavily polluted;
certainly not fit to breathe nor drink.

I cry not for myself, nor beautiful days gone by.
The tears I shed are for you, mankind.
For now that all the nature is gone,
you're the next endangered species.
        Carole A. Kveen

Illusions

Can you see beyond my eyes? Can you hear beyond my mind?
Can you feel my heart beat, with every lonely sign?
These are all illusions from the soul of my very beings.
My illusions of the day are my illusions of the night.

If you could see, feel, hear my world as I do, would you understand?
Would you shy away in a very Polite Manner.My dreams are of flowers
Blowing freely with every passing Breeze, Mountains Green and Lovely,
Seas blue and calm, with waves as white as snow.
My world is untouched my human beings, filled with creatures now
extinct, they walk through mountains green untouched, playing in
flowers with a loving tenderness, careful as not to disturb the
beauty they hold, the seas they swim and play within, without the
threat of mortal man.

Now can you see beyond my eyes? Or hear beyond my mind? Can you feel
my heart beat as time goes slowly by? Look beyond my world for my
fantasy is Reality. For the reality now should never exist.
Escape now, go beyond the world you live, for you will find the
beauty it holds, the reality of life, love and freedom, the happiness
that once was still stare you in the eyes.
You will hear, see, feel the reality beyond, the reality you live now
Pick out your world and live it, for it's there deep inside your
mind's eyes.

Joyce Johnson

Key World

It is time to leave once again, and go to the place that
know one knows, cover my trail leave no evidence behind.

I found a rhythm of my own and can keep the same beat,
I have arrived at my destination,

The wind has magic, the trees have wizards, the shells have
elves, to guide me along.

Black skies, red sun keep the border of this land, rain is
its only way of crying away the hurt.

Joseph Stouch

Unrequited Love

It often happens in an empty room when there's not a sound nor a soul
around. Time seems to stop for an eternity and you're back with me
like you used to be. The same old careless curl across your brow, the
same enchanting smile, the same od thrill. I must confess I loved you
then and guess I always will.

It often happens on a sunny day, about the time that I begin to tell
Somebody new I think they're really swell - and then I think of you!
What else to do but slowly walk away. There's nothing more I can
say. I can't forget you - and sunny skies turn gray...

It often happens in crowded room while the party swings and its
laughter rings. No matter where I go you follow me. Why deny what's
true? I belong to you. I must confess I miss your tender kiss, your
hands enfolding mine, I feel them still. I must confess I loved you
then and maybe always will.

I never dreamed that we might end like this. I can't decide the real
reason why someone so loved would choose to say goodbye and seek a
life alone. It plunged my mind into a deep abyss, just knowing things
went amiss. Your heart turned to stone, forgetting early bliss.

It often happens when I try to sleep but I see your face darkness
can't replace. I'm sure we both will muddle through somehow, taking
life in stride but not side by side. I pray each night that you are
safe and well and to accept my fate despite its chill. I must confess
I love you now and fear I always will...

Frank Spitzig

Untitled

Van Gogh landscape lemon yellow fields
cobalt blue sky a colorist
taste the brush strokes a white hot
heat of cloud regard it does work
Russian olive in a New Mexico desert
cottonwood gone silvering the sound reaching
in my bones
yours was the sunflower for me heavy
blocking trunks with ants crawling
for me the morning glory and white
white daisy with lemon yellow center and
four o'clock blossoms early early morning
different natures same fears and madness
you offered her your ear but kept
both hands and a brush and canvas
and thick tubes of color ground
out by those two hands
it is you I hear rustling in
the cottonwood planning yet another
study of sunflowers

Ann Haltom

Discredit The Innocent

Today is now, tomorrow will come;
    Cold hearted people the kind are some:

Here's America the land of free;
    murderous, robbers, rapist we see:

Know time given for crimes like these;
    they've worked hard, they hold a degree:

Petty little crimes our America see's;
    discredit the innocent with an honest degree:

Has our Law gone completely blind;
    it's all mixed up that's what I find:

The innocent sent behind closed doors;
    murderous, robbers, rapist the law ignores:

Deborah Liparote

I Imagine

In my imagination, I see the world below.
Come and imagine with me, a world of peace and love,
Where every soul is sovereign, where each one has a place,
A place to live in dignity, a place to be as one
With nature and Akua, mana within us all.

In my imagination, the world's a better place.
A lei of love surrounds it, uniting all within.
The brown man and the black, the yellow, red, and white,
The plants and all the animals, our lives are intertwined.
All life upon the planet deserving of respect.

Imagine, if you can, the family of man.
The hue of skin or color of eye matters not at all.
What matters is the simple fact that we all have a place,
A place upon this earth of ours to thrive and to be free,
To live in nature's true accord with peace and aloha

'Ilima Kauka Stern

War

On the field lay hundreds of men
Some lay wounded - Some lay dead.

The odds of their victory was somewhat slim,
but their leader was a man that would fight to the end.

The final victory came somewhat late,
but the battle they fought had united a state.

Carrie Bachrach

Books

What stately things Books can be,
Come, read these lines and you shall see.
This Book has poems running across the page.
And this one speaks of elders, its about age.
Why! This one has soldiers marching through and through,
Its about war and liberty true.
Well look at this, would you believe,
Its all about paintings, so beautiful to see.
Here is one after my own heart,
All about love, marriage and best not to part.
This one is about children running and playing,
Tells you what they are learning and saying.
Don't forget this one, about stars, planets and galaxies,
Its about the universe, making the mind soar to heights of ecstasy.
There is no end to the things Books proclaim,
There is no end to what the mind can attain.
Oh beautiful stately Books setting upon the shelves,
Waiting to be read by us, for joy or to improve ourselves.

Eva K. Holbrook

"Baby's Creed"

I was sent here by my Father, From the heavens above,
    Comforted by the glow, Of my parents love.
That glow will be the key, That unlocks that heavy door,
So I can cross that threshold, And be held down by sin no more.

    To pay back my parents, The love they gave to me,
Will be to raise my children, As a part of God's family.
And when my day is over, And I cross that threshold once more.
I will give to my children, The key that unlocks that door.

    When I'm finally gone, And my children's children read this poem.
They will raise their children, In God's gracious home.

Raise your children wisely, And keep them in your heart,
    Then you will see them again in Heaven, And you shall
    never be apart.

Josef Alexander

Common Sense Is A Precious Jewel

Common sense is where life started,
Common sense is how life begin,
Common sense, teach us about love and hate,
Common sense teach us how to control our feeling.
The words common sense mean so much to me,
It give me strength and courage, wisdom and understanding.

Common sense teach me about the past, it help me with the
Present and it prepare me for the future.
Common sense, teach us that there is a higher power,
We must listen to and talk to and believe in trust in a higher
Power, if we listen to our common sense,
We will be able to achieve our spiritual power that
We have been bless with.
Just open your mind and let common sense in,
It will give you love, hope and fulfill your dream.
Just open your mind and let common sense come in.

Julia P. Brown

The Seed

I plant this seed today in hope that one day it will grow.
I will nourish it with my love.
I will water it with the tears that flow from life's understanding.
I will cultivate it with all of my experiences and learning.
And carefully guiding it with structure and freedom to define itself,
I will send it out to bask in its glory, as it learns to stand on
    its own.

Carmen A. Vazqueztell

The Way Out

A state of manic depression
Complicated by aggressive agitation
This is our psychological evaluation
They still don't understand the complete situation
Suicidal tendencies are in our possession
Members of the X generation
It's time to play Kurt Cobain, the musician

Pull the trigger, fall to the floor
Leave the public asking forever more
Why we left in such bloody gore
Tired of living life, the eternal bore
To suicide the answer, someone opened up the door
Now that our time is o'er
We gladly cling to life no more

Anthony Harmon

The State Of...

In my next chapter, the villain,
    confronted, confounded
        Relents
At the hands of those who have nothing
Who eagerly take up their tents.
They lead him, in bondage, through desolate regions,
They learn from the turn of events.

"Vision"
Once a man followed
And once a man fled.
Through fields of disfunction
Where challenge lay dead

On the hills where the platforms,
Success and dismay
overlook wasted valleys
of death and decay

Lived the king of this country
(Where, once men would flee)
Who abandoned his throne,
For a seat, by the sea.

John Lee Stockard

My Mind's Better Half

I have one mind, it has two parts
Conscious demands, subconscious has the smarts
Subconscious never sleeps night or day
Always receptive to what conscious may say

My subconscious from birth until now
Keeps my body functioning with infinite know how
It heals my wounds and keeps me well
Hears my prayers and does everything I tell

Subconscious knows neither right nor wrong
Whatever I desire it will go-a-long
My demands must be positive and true
So pleasant results will follow through

Therefore anything I want is mine I find
If I use the power of my subconscious mind
Belief in its infinite wisdom and power is the key
This is the part that belongs to me

The great discoveries and works of mankind
Were developed by the subconscious mind
What a wonderful place the earth could be
If each of us would solve the problems we see.

Dewey I. Jones

The Mist

There is a silent mist
consuming much of me.
An obscure and unknown tryst
to be kept, that my mind cannot fully see.
Forgotten are all recent facts and thoughts.
Yet for all of this, my heart besought
dimmed passages dreamed outgrown.
People and happenings long forgot
struggle in my heart to be known.
I fight the silent fog and fear not aught
for God is here and Heaven near
safe my soul from any onslaught.
So, gentle mist, consume all fear
and take me gently from here.

Joyce Presley Davis

Untitled

Up to the ends of night
Conversation, Tobacco, substance, and Ideas.
Shapes form in creation and mold
Through metamorphosis and reflection.
Live to experience
Where? Here.
When? Now.
A feather in the street.
Paper in the wind.
Tomorrow's dream.
People of coincidence.
Confirmation of thought.
Radio talk. Listen....A new sound.
A blissful stupor of love wrecked lives
Burn in the tragic candle of romance
Young orchids with withered souls
Loose dry petals into moist winds
Take care.
The inevitable happens.

Jeff DelaVergne

Saturdays Past

I awake to the smell of Bacon, Eggs and Toast, Moma in the kitchen
cooking breakfast for all us folks.

I particularly love those mornings when there's no place to go, just laying around doing nothing like most folks I know.

Girlfriends come over, gossiping about this and that, day dreaming about that special boy, who you just saw last. "Moma say I'm so fast and I better watch out," she don't know nothing, I know what it's all about!

Time to go to the movies to watch the latest show, straight to the balcony, that's where we belonged you know.

Got to be home by 3:00 to help prepare the evening feast, peeling those potatoes, snapping those beans, and watching Moma fry that chicken, crisp as crisp can be.

Papa blessing the meal, while Moma watched us out the corner of her eye, letting us know we better not touch a parcel of that food, until we gave the Lord his do.

Dinner was delicious as it always is, time for that peach cobbler to bring it all to an end.

As I turn on the radio to hear my favorite tune, I think Oh how I love Saturdays, Saturdays that past too soon.

Jean Weathers

Coming of Age

Androgenous me-
cotton hair and noserings,
combat boots and lipstick stains,
all these things have loved you.
everything in me has loved you.
tough and fragile inadequate me,
all my fears and strengths have love you.
in the summertime hanging off the balcony
where your words and fingers first suspended me,
I married you with my heart and my hands
and in one deep lung collapsing breath
I grew up as we had planned
and unplanned you left me.
and now I already know-
how it feels to grow old alone.
I press my face against the glass
and drink the air here
with you.

Heather Rosson

Double Dream

Last night I dreamed of you. It was an incredible dream, I
Could even touch with my fingers that gorgeous naked body of
My dreams.

It was the blossoming of my desires, that body shaped like
An harp playing a sweet melody gave me all the
Satisfaction I could ever dream of.

In my dream, our love was shared beautifully when we united
To discover a world of mystery. We were getting sweet love
Like a flower that yields its honey to a bee.

For the bee a flower is a fountain of life, and to the
Flower a bee is a messenger of love, and to both, bee and
Flower, the giving and receiving of pleasure is a need and
An Ecstasy.

Dalmy Onofre

The Finale Whale Song

The soft lull of the sea gull,
Could put me to sleep,
Yet my heart is still awake,
Awake to the call of death
That waits for me upon the shore.

My young body years to swim
Further out to sea but the earth
Has got me in its grasp,
The pull of the moon is far stronger
Than my will to live.

The tidal swells seem to be beckoning to me,
The lost love of its youth.
As I lay upon the shore and listen to
This final whale song offered
Up from my friends of the deep.
Though I know I shall be known only as
  beached whale

Joyce A. Bair

Love You Forever

Because I am woman, mother to all
I must think; I must cry; work my hands to the bone
I'm not asking for rest, and I wish you the best
You show me your best, or equal; you should
Now that I'm old and my work should be done
You wish I continue, the things I've begun
I've showed you my best, taught you well
Don't make my pass heaven, unworthy of rest.

John G. Daniel

Untitled

May your feet touch many mounds of worth upon the earth.
May you live a life of pleasure,
one that can't be measured.
May love travel with the winds to all ends,
to reach all across the planet.
Only to touch those who desire it.

Daniel E. Willingham

Beautiful Rain

When the waves wash up upon the shore
Could you ask for anything more?
And if you ever feel any pain
What is better than the beautiful rain.

The rain makes the flowers grow
And it makes the rivers flow
But you never know
When the rains will come, when the winds will blow.

I look sometimes out into the trees
And see the branches waving in the breeze.
So when I walk out into the wood
It seems so peaceful, it seems so good.

When rain makes you appreciate what is here
You realize what is far and what is near
But nobody should ever fear
After the pretty rain, the sky will clear.

So why don't more people go for a walk
It's so refreshing and better than talk
And ever if they are in pain
Maybe they'll feel better because of the rain.

Elliott B. Elfrink, Jr.

Unto A Pearl

I've watched the sun rise from the east and the clouds converge and
cover its ferocity;
I've seen Roman soldiers pass by;
A mermaid with her golden hair and piercing blue eyes once stood in
my presence and kissed the crest of the wave as it dipped;
I saw and touched the Leprechaun's pot of gold at the end of his rainbow;
A peeress without rank or stature am I;
Through the years I have known the pioneers of medicine and science;
Though tough at times, I have held steadfast to society's rules
and declined my own passions;
Time passed, ideas changed, the earth changed and I too with them;
Once I was caught and held captive for many years;
While captive my being succumbed to passivity and amour;
I assumed the likeness of a sphere
I am.

Zhan

Feedlot Cattle

Just look at 'em stand there with muck on their body
covered in stuff that I'll call potty.

Lookin' cold and humpy backed
they want to die and that's a fact.

What they don't know is that it'll come true
in about ninety days their life will be through.

They'll end up as a fine cuisine
whether they are Hereford, Angus, or Limousine.

Us humans will eat them hopefully well done
there is no other way to eat it not even one.

As they digest in our bellies we don't even think
of the muck that they stood in that made 'em stink.

Cy W. Ricker

Our Trees

Take a look around you at the lovely trees
Covered with so many shimmering leaves

There are orange, red, yellow and green
Such vivid shades ever to be seen

With their many limbs stretching here and there
Twisting and turning, up, down and everywhere

Attached to the trunks with roots so deep
Support for these beauties they do keep

Then winter comes and they become so bare
But their beauty is still there to share

The snow and ice on their limbs so bright
A scene that still brings such a delight

And with spring comes a brand new start
New shapes and colors, a joy to our heart

They can be found all over the world
With so very much beauty unfurled

So take a look at God's wonderful gift
This alone should your spirits lift.

Charles E. Fink Jr.

Little Circus Clown

I wished to swing on the high trapeze
  Crack whips at the wild jungle cat,
Ride on the head of the elephant;
  I knew even I could do that.

The tent boss said, "You are much too small
  To do all those hazardous things,
Come, you can sell this bunch of balloons,
  But, mind you hang on to the strings."

I did as the man told me to do
  And now I am floating with ease,
Having such fun up here in the air
  Looking down on his old trapeze

Alice Rockwell

Ride The Tiger

As I close my eyes, I see him coming toward me,
Crashing through the wild wet of the wood,
Baring long white teeth —
The tiger.
Fierce, black and orange, now black and white —
The tiger.
Two colors coming closer, closer
To me, through me, to the other side.
Then I walk right up to him and say, "Sit!"
And obediently he folds his legs, looks at me and yawns,
Look at me and licks his lips
As if he'd had his meal, his satisfaction.
I lie beside him then to show him that I'm not frightened.
We roll over and over together
In the small green meadow of mossy grass.
And when he stands up, I stand up too,
Mount his back, and ride the tiger out of the forest,
Ride the tiger out of the night of that darkness.
And as I open my eyes
I see that he is all one color now.

Carol Sheldon

3:22 A.M.

It haunts me still.
Creeping like a
Specter in the night
Crippling my conscious

I see it still
HIS F
   A
    L
     L
I mean.
As if I were once again young and staring
Out the pane glass window that
Cold wintry day.

Strange how some memories linger,
Begging to be reckoned with
But making few strides
Toward understanding.

And all that is really left
Is only the pain and confusion
And the mental replay of HIS F
        A
        L
         L.

Jeneece Bishop

If I Could

If I could but paint a picture it would be
crimson red pooling at the foot of calvary.
I would take my brush and touch my palette
and tip it in gold, with a stroke of
My brush I would paint a face full
of mercy and grace.

Etched with a trace of sorrow and pain
crushed to produce a glorious refrain.
...If I were to paint a picture of me
You would see one who abides in mercy and grace.
Full of joy, being held in the Father's embrace
One who with laughter and tears that has
stained her face... would be looking into
her Saviour's Face.

There would be the two of us you would see,
The Holy Spirit and me. Together we walk and
talk as he guides and directs me.
...If I could paint a picture you would
see only Jesus who abides in me.

Diana Lynn Rogers

Candle Burning Through The Night

Candle burning yellow light,
curling wax, droplets take flight,
racing to the cradle-plate
to embrace their loving mate.

Candle burning through the night,
casting off dawn's early might.
Steady, Roman, pillar frame -
a simple torch, an eternal flame.

Candle burning giving sight.
Cupid aiming just and right
through the eaves to human hearts
unaroused by passion darts.

For when the sleeping heart awakes
and the candle's light flickers and shakes,
a flame ignites within a soul
to keep alive Love's precious hold.

Eugenie Juliet Theall

Nothing Ever Mattered

I watch from aside,
Cringing at every action,
Taken further away with
Each passing sorrow.
The rain falls in a disheartened state,
In a not quite constant stream.
They ebb their way along.
The sun finally comes out,
Making my body hot and
Just when I feel good all over
The clouds subsume the rays
And it is cold once again.
It is then that a
Bolt of lightning begins to shock me,
Until my body can convulse no longer.
I am just a lying heap on the ground,
And no one seems to notice as they
Step by to reach their destination.
It's as if nothing ever mattered,
And nothing ever will.

Jennifer Boatwright

Caribbean Cruise — The Greatest

I can't begin to tell you, what this trip has meant to me,
   Cruising on the Nordic Prince, way out to sea.
Captain Skjerve and all his crew, couldn't have done
   better for you and me.
The excellence of service from cook, waiter, bus boy
   and Maitre D.

I can't begin to tell you, how wonderful all of you are,
Cruise director, members of his staff, and entertainers
   from near and afar.

The cruise and shopping in San Juan and St. Thomas too,
   Was everything they promised for me and you.

I can't begin to tell you, at the gala buffet, the food
and treats were to beautiful to eat, all the magnificent
ice sculptures that would eventually melt at your feet.

I can't begin to tell you, that I'd like to go again,
cause the cabin crew and all are just like a good old friend.

Charlotte A. McGraw

"The Sickness"

It swoops over the night sky in misty space.
Cry's of pain don't cruse.
Smells of death, sickness soar through blackened air.
Children-adults do nothing, just stare.
Eternal blackness comes with its kiss.
It lets out a taste of a sour kiss.
A shrill of horror shrieks out from below.
Death strikes full power with its strongest blow.
People die left and right.
It's too fast,
No to fight.
The town lies still and silent.
Sickness has gone.
Left are the bones of the young.
Remains of the old.
Once were bold,
Roaming with a dignified grace.
Now Struck down.
"Aids takes their place."

Adrienne Houser

Diamonds In The Blackest Mine

Beneath the blackest coal a diamond shines.
Crystal clear, pure, and fine.
Its beauty stands the test of time,
dug out from the deepest mine,
to the surface brought to shine,
like the brightest light you'll find.

Sometimes face value makes you blind,
judging covers is unkind.
So look beneath and you will find,
the diamond in the blackest mine.

April Masotti

Close

Like the beauty of an eagle in flight, wings spread full,
cutting through the clouds as it soars ever so
gracefully

Like the serenity of a trickling stream flowing over the
jagged rocks down the mountainside

Like the stillness of midnight, with only the stars
twinkling as they fill the sky with their array of
astrological arrangements

Like the softness of the moon as it lightly caresses your
face

Like the roar that comes from within the depths of
your soul in the form of motivating, tantalizing
sounds, when one is aroused with that tender final
touch that takes them over the edge and you explode
with edifying ecstasy from the intimacy, when the
spirit of love and the two souls evolve and you become
as one.

Love is Magic
Abdul Sunni Ghani

Prisoner of Conscience

I desire in my dreams to fly away on feathered wings
Darkness of night betrays the tortured screams
In the center of my soul, bars of steel shroud clouds of grey
Might makes right in the victor's power play
Inside information has arrested my development
Freedoms lifted at the whim of the establishment
Felonies from the ID, never informed of what I did
Mere words spoken, bonds are broken
Hostages are taken when elections are forsaken
Semper Fi, do or die, another mother's wailful cry
Only in the end we regret, never having said goodbye
Speak out now and walk foundation's edge
Feel the icy stares rumors do allege
Who bears strength to say what must be said
Courage of convictions despite what lies ahead
Carry the message to the edge of the community
Unite and organize to challenge this infirmity
Seek not the amulet resting in the ivory tower
For he who gains the knowledge, in the end holds all the power.

Brian M. Warshawsky

The Dead

The dead make no sound.
Yet you can hear there spirits all around.
The dead make no noise.
They have no structure they have no poise.
The dead have no life.
They do not hear us fight.
The dead does not live,
The dead cannot die.

Diana Keller

Precious Brother

The space you once filled in my life
Is now filled with love and happy memories
We shared together.
The pain and sorrow of your absence slowly fade.
As the Lord had told me that you and I will
be together in heavenly peace in time to come.

Allen Louis Yates

Articulate Vacuum

Marvin McQuestion, when he was ten,
Decided to be a leader of men
And started to study immediately
To express himself fluently.
Very soon he conquered conjugation..
A master of articulation.
He used nouns and pronouns in such a manner
That he won for himself an excellence banner.
At Yale, on perfection he did insist,
And earned a spot on the dean's honor list.
Soon, foreign language became his goal
And he could converse from pole to pole.
For Marvin, expression became an obsession...
His dictionary his prized possession.
He took a course in public speaking..
Pure enunciation he was seeking.
You'll pardon me now if I hesitate
(The result I almost hate to relate!)...
Poor Marvin McQuestion awoke one day
And found, to his sorrow, he had nothing to say!!

Ethel M. Chaput

"them"

In the land of the free—home of the brave.
Deficit reduction, prison construction, the
jobless, homeless, which to save? They're
everywhere and nowhere, mere shadows on the
walls, silent footfalls. Standing with signs
in place, no names, no face, life such a
busy pace. Looking yet failing to see, their
presence but a transparency. Tattered legions
growing, carts filled with memories overflowing,
where are they all going? Victimized, traumatized
and forever ostracized, their road is
paved. In the land of the free—home of the
brave.

John J. Moore

Believe

Feed me not, wicked temptations,
Deliver me from evil.
Free my soul so I can believe,
In love,
And your love, for all your people.

Give me strength and self control,
help me define wrong from right.
Guide my way through anger and pain,
Shine on me your holy light.

Believe in me as I believe in you,
let us walk hand in hand.
You've given me life and your precious words,
So I shall always know where I stand.

Allow me to wander, but keep my direction,
Down the paths that I have paved.
Bless my soul within my faith,
In my life to which you gave.

Charles Muse

The Grain and Me

Sitting there, the water glides in around me and leaves the
deposits of a thousand lands;
Made up of one tiny grain.
A grain that seems as insignificant as I am in the world, the ocean
and the sky around me.
Was it that grain that was under the foot of my forefathers.
Did the early explorers and settlers rejoice at its sight, and
empty it from their boots before they lay down to rest.
Did a tiny crab deep on the ocean floor burrow itself under it and
many others like it to protect its fragile being from the cruel
realities of the underworld.
It has seen the beauty of paradise and the violence of storm.
Lands of different worlds and times.
One tiny insignificant grain has seen the birth of existence.
One tiny grain, that with the help of nature, becomes the beauty
of a pearl.

John Demeo

The Street

Rachel someone like Laurie
Determined, dedicated, thriving on glory
So brand new
On a street so slew
That God has given up on it
Cops would arrest it, but, the straight jacket won't fit
New and evil
Old and feeble
Both will mix for new and evil are not opposite
Can God help us
Will He, will He
Maybe not cause God would bill me

Christa M. Garress

Jesus Wept

I stood beside her grave and asked,
    "Did Jesus weep for me?"
He took back the child that
    He had loaned me for just a little while.
To watch her grow,
    Hear her laugh
And see her pretty smile.
    Didn't seem much longer than a day
When He decided to take her far away.

Did Jesus weep for me?
    I stood upon a mountain top
In the softly falling rain.
    The sun was peeking through the clouds,
As if to ease my pain.
    And in the pain of my distress.
I felt His tears of gentleness.
    Oh, yes He wept,
My Jesus wept,
    Jesus wept for me!

Brooxie Williams

Garden Angels

Were there angels in my garden, last night as I lay sleeping?
Did they slide in on a moon beam, and quietly come a peeping?
Did they dance above the bird bath, with songs upon the wind?
Did they kiss the tiny rosebuds, and teach the fish to swim?
Where they playing with the creatures, in the starlight in my garden?
Did they tell them it was safe, and nothing there would harm them?
Did they kiss the fruit for sweetness. And touch the daisy's faces?
Were they planting new surprises, in funny little places?
Are those angel tears or dew drops on the roses and the leaves?
Were there angels in my garden? What do you believe?

Arlene Brittingham

You, You

How come we're not who we were?
Did time grab our old?
Or did time leave us out in the cold?
Life with you was at one time intregeful
And at the same time a river.
We rolled through all of the downs
That always made us high as we hit the up's.
Change to us was a word not spoken
Because... Ah! that's when.
That was as far as we had made it,
Just at that point we thought:
What about - me - you - and change?
Why didn't we realize
That time doesn't care.

Jonathan Capps

September Fourth, 1993

My Ann, my best beloved, gently died this day
Died without pain, it seemed, and quietly
Died unafraid and gallantly, lovingly,
The soft pressure of her hand in mine
Remembered well; the suggestion of her smile
Left there for me on her so dear countenance.

You who grant her peace deserved
Gave her laughter, that gay defiant challenge
To days of stress and nights of sleeplessness
Gave her constant thoughts of others
Rarely of her own afflictions
In a life lived full and strong.

Grant her too what you know to be
Her due.
So much of You there was
In her
That love is close to worship
And thus remains to me.

Charles Foltz

Cathedral Of Tears

Angel-like sea gulls o'er the ocean skies were
    dipping and gliding
and moaning like a new born babe, they met
    their time abiding
Amidst the waters, tall waves soared and
    as in a moonlight madness
they met the sky and kissed the sands
    and showed a grateful gladness.
Oh waters blue in this atmosphere of heat
    and soaring light
resisting in the emotions of the poets,
    with heart strings pumping trite.
Waves shining like a night that possesses
    many thousand eyes
that pierces the darkness and like a bird,
    flies through the starry skies.
Oh ocean mine, a cathedral of tears
    that fights with all its might
to make its tide, its sands to hide
    to roar on through the night.

Emily Ann Ogden

Untitled

A blue eyed devil
Disguised with angelic looks
Curiosity sparkles haunted by the mocking laughter of
unseen demons, flies in the night
Distanced by the knowledge

Masked by the appearance of innocence
Hidden fears grow, nurtured by voices
The charade of normality crumpled
The pieces of this intricate puzzle
Shattered, delusion, illusion with
no sense of reality runs
Unable to hide from the tormentor.

Numbness, complete isolation then fire burns
The flames enveloping shadows
of the tormentor, scorched beyond recognition

A blue eyed angel disguised with devilish looks
Peers from beneath the eyes
A grown soul, aged beyond
comprehension, soars without wings
Into complete darkness unable to escape the knowledge.

Andrea Montpas

Unanswered Questions

Have you ever made a wish upon a falling star?
Do you accept things always, exactly as they are?
Are you always satisfied, do you never seek?
When questions are unanswered, do you never speak?

Are you ever happy, are you ever sad?
Are there ever good days, are there ever bad?
Do you ever shout for joy, do you ever weep?
Are there ever any dreams you would like to seek?

Are you never angry, are you never blue?
Are you always satisfied with what life brings to you?
Have you ever searched for rainbows with their hidden pots of gold?
Do you ever wish for memories to cherish when you're old?

If everyone accepted things exactly as they are,
And no one ever made a wish upon a falling star:
And everyone accepted, without question, what is said,
We'd be no more than robots, or worse, the living dead!

Byrona Lee Wadsworth

Old House

I wonder as I see you there, old house.
Do you contain a loving family, a dog, a cat,
And, perhaps (unnoticed by them all) a mouse,
And a chair where a Grandpa often sat?
Are your floors all clean and polished "till they shine,"
Or do they contain a little dust here and there,
And scuff marks (lots of scuff marks) just like mine?
Do children run up and down your stair?
Are there pencil marks lined up along your door
To mark, each year, the number of inches grown
By the children who played upon the floor?
Is the nest empty because the birds have flown?
Did you ever hear the sound of lullabies,
Or the creaking of a much-used rocking chair?
Does your kitchen smell like cinnamon and apple pies?
Could a loving Grandmother be living there?
Was there ever perched high in your apple tree
A little barefoot girl in overalls,
A little tomboy like I used to be?
I wonder as I watch you and recall.

Angeline Maine

Acceptance

Walking down
    down
        paths
of fall's final flowers,
I stop to seek one last butterfly, or green beetle,
struggling through fading leaves of summer.

With chill wind,
and surrounding sounds as clear as the cold air,
I stop and stoop among the browning mass,
with fleeting wish, for things to be the way they were.

Yet, with promises of autumn's painted hues,
and crystal quiet nights of winter,
I move forward as the seasons,
looking back only for remembrance.
       l o o k i n g
        b a c k
only for remembrance.

Cynthia A. Conciatu

All Gone

It seemed so far to Grandmother's home,
down a long dusty road at the end of a lane.
The straw stack gleamed golden in the morning sun.
The only sound, cow bells in the field beyond.
All around as far as you could see,
the ducks and chickens roamed there free.
A pansie bordered path led to the front door.
Oh! that I could hold those moments once more.
No perfume like hers I've ever known,
as to grandmother's bosom I was drawn.
A hug, a kiss, that took my breath away.
The aroma of fresh baked bread
mingled with new mown hay.
With the corner of her big apron
she wiped away a tear.
Was it happiness or did she the future fear?
My grandparents are gone, the house torn down.
The once quiet farm replaced by a town.
Only time is to blame,
That nothing ever stays the same.

Darlene Azar Rubinoff

Flower

Over in the meadow,
down by the deer,
there lived a tiny little flower
in all it's cheer.
It rose up through air,
misty and calm,
like a dainty woman, the wind through her hair.
The petals like velvet,
the stem curving, and swerving
with the greatest of care.
When nightfall came,
it closed all it's glory,
to sleep until morning

Courtney McGrath

Gift

True vision must extend beyond the self
For understanding that this life's true wealth
Abides in hearts which hold us each most dear
And sacrifice their oneness to be near
To see the one is lost without the whole
The whole without the one is less a soul
To understand that we may share the pain
And share the love which make us whole again.

David W. Sjoberg

The Passage Of The Pummeled Pomegranates

From Puerto Rico, Past The...

The pomegranate testing site,
    Down in Puerto Rico,
Is very, very quiet tonight
    you can even hear your echo.

Very late, a mad chemist
    Awakes from a bad dream;
But not before he hits his fist
    On the sensitive machine.

A mighty blast and loud KA-BOOM!
    Send those pomegranates flying.
Out of the atmosphere they zoom
    And leave that chemist crying.

Quiet lay the little town,
    The town of Pensacola —
But soon - the noise! - it did abound
    When those 'granates splattered like granola.

So that is the way it was,
    Or the way it should have been.
But never count your fruit because
    They could blow up in the end!

   Christa Mackey

Thru the Glass

as the rain rhythmically falls
downward, against the window,
tapping to the beat of my heart,
my mind composes a new song
    with a recycled melody.

looking thru tears on a translucent glass,
i see her standing alone in the rain.
she seems to be looking right at me;
but i know she doesn't see.
    (man, i wish she could see me!)

but the hourglass runs out,
and times fades without warning
as she slips away in silence
as quickly as she had appeared,
    leaving me with my tears.

and once again the poet writes
a song of recycled emotions,
as i gaze out thru the many
glorious prisms in motion,
    the drops of dancing light.

   Edward Keels

Thoughts By The Sea

He stands alone on the sea shore,
    drawn by the waves as they crash against,
    then caress the cold sands.

Frozen by a fear he cannot name,
    he stares out over the empty expanse.

The last embers of sunset die,
    taking with them the last feelings of warmth.
    A bleak wind blows through his bones.

His reverie is broken by the cry of a lone gull,
    silhouetted in moonlight, as it hunts the surf.

Alienated, he turns to go.

   John Schneider

The Silver Ribbon

A silver ribbon crystal clear winds and ties itself thru a forest drear, where shadows dark as ebony lie waiting to be touched with silver glow and colors like the rainbow.

On and on it winds and moans over things forever gone waiting to shine like a crystal ball over the rippling waterfall. Everywhere in its path come beautiful sounds, gurgles and gasps.

Light reflects from this silver crystal ribbon through morning mist of fog, waiting to touch trees, flowers, butterflies and frogs.

The deer dip their heads to taste silver crystal deep because you see this is a sparkling creek.

The ribbon floats to and fro over rocks, toes, meadows over hills and dales it floats and twines, teasing every creature over and over again

It winds and ties itself silvery bright through misty morning sunlight and comes to tie itself in a big bow outside my window, but it does not stop here this silver ribbon crystal clear.

   Joan Sluder

The Dance

Tattered, torn rags replace the ruffled
dresses, curled tresses of days past.
Open doors, warm floors are dreams
gone by, to pass through her mind.
Once a dance, easy and graceful,
life became marching through a snowy blizzard.

Thoughts pierce her soul as the
wind whistles, striking her heart yet deeper.
One dance, dusty and far away,
waltzes in circles around and around.
Ivory hands clenched in soft embrace,
sweet melody, harmony, life-giving echoes.

Life ceases, lost in the dance,
preceding the rising sun.
It ends as the rain falls, kissing
the morning, beginning the day.
Her place unsure, the faded, worn shoes
go on, a tear streams down her face.

   Jennifer Bonck

Song Of The Homeless

I walked the street of silent apathy
    dried the eyes of tears
That was my bed where my clothes have lain
    I said, "Thank God,
    it didn't rain."
My hands are shaking more now,
    the lady said, "We're not
    to blame"
It didn't quite seem not so long ago
    the government had
    said the same.

The man in a suit, avoided my street,
    and whispered,
"These destitutes just have no shame!"

    The law said, "No panhandling!"
    My stomach disagreed,
        But my mind, he understands.
    So, I stretched my empty hand
Into the mist, and caught the falling rain.

   Alexis Balunsat

Love Is

Love is everything when I'm with you.
Love is when the only thing that matters is you.
Its when you have faith in all that I do.
Love is everything when I'm only loving you.

Donna Mathews

Drugs

Most of the sins and crimes of the world are drugs related.
Drugs can take a brilliant mind and make it dilapidated.
Drugs are the instrument of the devil for our soul he does compete.
Drugs transfers our conscience to the classification of obsolete.

Drugs bring wealth and luxuries to those whom of the sales do
    partake.
When they leave this world with them the sins of the addicted
    they do take.
Because satan is sitting back taking surveillances of the scenes.
For the drugs participants are doing his will and on them he leans.

Just as sure as there is a heaven there is also a hell
And the people dealing in drugs know that very well
Someday when they will look into the eyes of God what will they
see?
The almighty says "Whatsoever you do to one of mine you do also
    unto me."

Dante Gramolini

Untitled

Seated in... silence
    dwarfed am I
    by a herd of Wild, Silent Giants....

    We are alone...
    The Woods and I

but for the Fleeting Chatter of Unseen Birds
but for the Distant Wave of Wind's Bough Calling
but for the Healing Touch of Sun's Warm Rays and

    I am peaceful and free and
    The Power that I feel Is GOD AND LOVE—
    THE LIFE FORCE—ART—
    A LANGUAGE I CAN'T SPEAK....
    for I am only human.
The how's and why's, I can't identify
all I know is.... The Magic
        is.... The Moment
    and I must keep this part of me alive lest I
    perish with the tribe in
Civilization.

Barbara G. Ayers

Secret Lover

For me you are the meaning of my life
each day is filled with love from you to me
I only wish for you to be my wife
But I my love wish you could only see.

Your hair flows on your shoulders like spun gold
when I caress your hair it feels like silk.
My love you are more fair than I was told.
Your skin to me is fair and smooth as milk.

Your lips are red like roses in the spring,
they seem to call to me and speak out loud.
If they could only touch mine I would sing.
If you were on my arm I could be proud.
You are as gorgeous as a turtle dove,
I wish to be with you forever love.

Blake Began

Reflections

My daughters reflect four sides of myself
Each every different from the other
When I try and understand one of their tactics
I have to remind myself "its' from their "Mother."
One is as sweet as can be...most of the time
She's full of energy and wit, she also has a stubborn side
That's a side of me I'd like to forget.
The next is industrious and independent
and sympathetic too; but at times she uses not tact
and this too is a fact She's a lot like you know who.
My other daughter is a free spirit as free as the birds and the wind,
She never takes anything serious,
She's all about laughter and "wrap."
With her I can never lose patience.
This as me as a teen. But one day, when I grew up
My free-spirit was gone in a snap.
My youngest daughter is spoiled rotten.
A real daddy's girl is she; looking back on when I was her age,
She's the exact replica of me.
And then...there's my son!

Johnetta Love

Point Of View

A girl in a tower, a small golden flower,
Each has a beauty beheld.
A free flowing stream, a galloping steed,
Each with a power to move you.
A spider in web, the tide at its ebb,
Both in their manner receive you.

The beauty we see
Is the beauty we find,
The beauty that we all are kin to.
Perceptions decide
What to show, what to hide.
Of ourselves.
In a world full of beauty.

Who's to say that a face,
Lines all over the place,
Morning breath,
And a head full of dreams,
Is any less pleasant
Than a wandering pheasant
Feathers wet, dew from the leaves?

Ellen G. Gunther-Keith

The Night

The night is peaceful and calm,
    Each little star twinkles in its place.
No more is the brightness of dawn,
    For the moon shows its glowing face.

We can hear the cool wind as it blows,
    Through the mighty tree tops so high.
We can see each leaf as it glows
    In the brightness of the sky.

The summer night brings us a wonderful feeling,
    As we lay on the grass so smooth.
We look up to God's great ceiling,
    And feel its every move.

Blackness has covered our part of the earth,
    As our minds are deep in thought.
We dream of the new night and its birth,
    And of the future that will be sought.

Danny E. Kingsley

A Vessel Of Honor

Each man is a world unto himself, and each man must stand alone.
Each man must make his own way in this world,
    He must stand or fall on his own.

Some men might say that this is asking too much, after all,
    I was made out of clay.
I'm dirt, I'm mud, nothing more, and I'll return to dust someday.

But a wise man might say, yes, I too am clay and
    I'm made from the soil of this earth.
But I have found a sparkle in me,
    there is something in me of great worth.

There are rubies and diamonds and silver and gold,
    and all kinds of expensive things.
That spring from the soil, and the dust of this earth,
    the same from which I came.

So now I know that it was not by luck,
    that God decided to make us from dust.
But it was wisdom that only God could know, the extent of each us.

And though we try to destroy ourselves, with drink, drugs and lust.
We've only ourselves to blame for the mess we make,
    because blessings are ours if we'd trust.

So we did not spring from the dust of the earth,
    but we were designed and cuddled by God.
And in each one He put enough ores and gems,
    to make a bright shining vessel for Him.

Frances F. Jones

The Ever Tightening Vice

A plane full of boys took off for a place called Vietnam.
Each on their hearts, without a qualm.
For they were going to fight for old Red White and Blue.
Why can't the people of America look back and see what was true.
These boys turned to men, ever so fast.
And oh would the memories forever last.
Upon arriving in Vietnam, I feet every man had attached to their head
A squeezing vice, of which you must wear for the rest of your life.
People say forget, it's in the past.
    They just can't understand why it still must last.
When you came back you were shunned away like infested with lice
All it was, was the over tightening vice.
Few will understand, except those when were there.
Some will not even probably care. So Be it!
For we are still all free, and you cannot forget those who died
So that this can always be.
And don't forget those with the invisible vice,
For we all paid one hellava price.

Allen D. Daley

Tapestry of Life

Our lives are tapestry. We are a thread among many.
Each thread represents someone we touch or are touched
by during our lifetime. We are woven in and out of so
many lives. Sometimes side by side throughout the tapestry
of life; and other times crossing paths but once.

Some threads are dark and ominous while others, colorful
and cheerful. Without the contrast, our tapestry would
be uninteresting and we would be bland.
Let us be thankful for all the people woven intricately
into our life, for they are the pattern of our tapestry
and we are the theme...

Star Lin

The Lever Of Levity

It is you and I who pull the handle that causes all our pain.
Each time we commit the same foolish act while saying "Never again."
It is we who place our fate for years in the hands of just a few,
And it always turns out that these few folks have it in for me and you

It is we who usher in the people who are supposed to be our leaders,
But the odds are better than even that all turn out to be bleeders.
One solid statesman that we all chose uttered the famous
    "Read my lips."
Then our money flew away at a rapid rate from the wallets on our hips.

There's only one lever in the world that could cause us each more
    grief,
But even the finality of this lever would at least bring us relief.
This lever of which I speak can deliver us from continuing despair;
It's the lever they pull when they light up the state's
    electric chair.

Gary Newton

Who Can Fly Higher

Who can fly higher, eagle or man,
Eagle said, "Fool you know I can."
Man bet his soul for the eagle to keep,
"I'll beat your height with a single leap."

The bet was on and the eagle was ready,
He flew his best and he flew very steady.
The man said, "Eagle you know I can beat you."
Without hesitation he jumped and he flew.

Up, up into the sky he went,
He beat the eagle, but his life was spent.
He had hit heaven, he knew he was there,
The man felt foolish to have made the dare.

The Lord appeared before him and said,
"You did your best, but now you are dead."
"Why did I die Lord, please tell me why."
"Because when you jumped, you jumped too high."

"You flew, with the angels and flew through the sky,
You wouldn't have won if I hadn't made you fly.
The eagle was the devil and he would have won,
But I am your creator and you are my son."

Anthony Lester

Wild-Flower

Of all the worlds we could have chosen
Earth was by far the most beautiful
But now like a rebel child we are cast out of Eden
driven within by a stolen taste of knowledge
on a quest for precious freedom
We came; we saw; we move along
Peace tonight; we leave at dawn
Perhaps something different will satisfy our soul
Tomorrow: another day; another test
A journey to the ends of the world
or just to the end we're still not sure
Wandering far, and wondering why
Too old to go home, yet too young to die
Of all the friends we could have chosen
you were by far the most noble
Remember us then when we're no longer around
Cast a shadow for us when our sun goes down; we still love you
We didn't mean to hurt you weeping Willow, Flower Child
And though we quarrel amongst ourselves
our bond remains unbroken for we are One

Jean-Louis Blackburn

Free Me

Wind - Breaking down the doors of love.
Emotions all mixed up.
Set them free, Set them free.
For I will crumble and blow away
If you don't set them free.
Feelings of sorrow and despair need to be released.
I am losing touch of it all,
Free me.

Finally free - Out in the desert on a clear,
Mystifying night.
Twinkling stars light the dark sky.
Sleeping and dreaming;
You're riding through the sky on a gold-covered star.
Swiftly you move through the light,
Mysterious air.
Finally, you land, and the dream is over.
Wasn't it a wonderful experience?
I am finally free of it all.

Joanna M. Kniep

Shattered Asylum

The poignant stillness of the night
Engulfs the vast enigmatic skies
Carefully portraying the serenity.

Subtle winds blow optimistically
Swaying the luminous figures of life
Together with the euphony of the nocturnals.

Moon beaming light falls upon the city
Casting reflections of the lighted buildings
On the smooth calming surface of the river.

This tranquil asylum is now shattered.

Envious feelings finally ruptured
Causing an ominous amount of chaos
Transforming happy memories into despondent ones.

Bringing forth unwanted feelings of contentment...
....this tranquil asylum is now shattered.

Irene Frangos

Unparalleled

When in your good company I reside,
Enrapt to look upon your handsome face;
Compelling emotions well up inside,
Which I endeavor to handle with grace.
But I find it difficult to respire
When held utterly spellbound by your gaze.
And I, so moved from within by desire,
Am confounded into a silent daze.
And all the thoughts I so wish to express
Remain unvoiced in the depths of my mind,
And the ardent love I long to confess
Will lie in my heart forever enshrined.
No one will know of the love unbeheld;
Steadfast in my heart and unparalleled.

Jennifer Orsenigo

Playing Chess With Dad

I'm going to play chess with Dad.
He really makes me mad.
It takes him till dawn, to move his pawn.
I had to hassle for dad to move his castle.
If I didn't read him a book, he wouldn't move his rook.
I had to force, for dad to move his horse.
I had to give him a bean, for him to move his queen.
I had to sing! "Dad move your king"

Daniel John Beacher

The Walk

Today my walk was a motion picture of limbs,
Entwining as they passed before me
And beyond my vision.
Dusted with the sparkle of frost,
Against the blue of sky and mountain,
Sloping valley,
Red-roofed barn,
They stood stationary
As my mind's eye saw them criss-cross
With their interplay.
So still
In fact,
Dancing within me.

Carolyn Spelt

Pope Wrote Only Prose While

Johnson Was Surely No Botanist,

My..... Dear Candide
Wisdom breaks forth from a particular seed and curves upward
   espaliered.
Let no skeletons interpose their differences.
Renaissance Man's been buried long ago.
Let not his bones rattle the boards—
Neither his, nor Mozart's nor Shakespeare's.
Give me private, peculiar worlds:
Scenes framed by prosceniums suitable for theater-loving ants which
   take a break from work:
Give me mole crickets at their dismal tunneling; spiders at their
   crystal netting.
If PELLEAS ET MELISANDE be blur, I'm charmed, and should
   come to harm to snuff that taper's tip.
(Papa Haydn scraped no cradle songs for me.)
The palette's not the rainbow, nor should it be.
Paint monochromatic Corots; carve miniatures of smoky jade
   cupolas and top them with spires and crocket's
Confusing East with West.
These bulbs of green shall suffice, and they shall seed
   your private garden, Candide.

Frank Pellecchia

Untitled

WHO painted the picture
   etched this morning in golden frost
      here on my bedroom window pane?

Who worked the long, cold night-time through,
   with stars thousands of light years away
      the only eyes to witness
         and inspire
      the patient creation
         of this frosty work of art?

What spritely artist sketched the lacy
   tracery of leaf and bud and branch —
      and graceful trailing vine —
   a ghostly wintry garden scene —

Using for pigment
   the ebb and flow
      of my mortal breath
   as I lay sleeping,
      unconsciously dreaming,
   in my bleak, unheated, lonely room?

Dorothy J. Mock

The Sea Is Mine

As it rolls to the shore
ever changing its form
to wind its way up to the beach
for an instant
then off it goes once more
to gather its ripples
as a mother gathers up her children
repeating its pattern time and again
first backward then forward sending its pounding
blue-green waves farther into the
unknown horizon where white-winged gulls
float upon a puff of air
lazily turning and dipping
ever deeper down to some sea life
that makes its home untouched by the world
coming up and going down into the depths
deeper and deeper to mingle with the
coral floor brightly colored; the swaying sea grasses keeping
their rhythmic beat in communion with the Creator who fashions
all things. The Sea is mine a gift of beauty for the soul.

Emma K. Moeckel

"Fear?"

Laugh at fear, cry, confront, defy....
Ever present, foreboding FEAR?
Why is humanity subject to fear?
 A nuclear war, Violence on TV which so many adore.
  A gun at the face? A total disgrace!
  A bad dream, or friends who scheme,
  Loneliness when one doesn't make the team.
Trembling FEAR: Who can allay perhaps only an audience can say.
 The dreams are gone; yet fear still belongs.
Its absence nothing and its presence something
Or are we making something out of nothing,
Or am I nothing without fear and "something" when it's very near?
How much fear should one endure
Before it makes life insecure....?

Awesome FEAR. It's not the end... Share it with a caring friend.

Fear prompts caution with an intelligent mind,
Courage and confidence one will find.
Respect fear, give it its due.... It has its place alerts us too!
Do not suppress fear: it can create internal strife,
 But do not let FEAR interfere with LIFE!

Geoff Smith

Angels Of God

Angels of God - walk with man as he runs life's paths.
      Ever with us,
      Ever close to us,
      Within hand's grasp.
      Within a prayerful whisper.
   What do angels do as they run with us?
   They sing and praise God in all His glory.
We who seek our angel's help also give praise to God,
  For we who believe in God's gift to man
  Sing praise to God with every angel prayer.
      Angels are beautiful
      In their dress of angel finery
      And sweet words of praise.
They never sleep and never leave our sides to weep.
      They go with us as companions,
         Sent by God
      To help us through life's maze.
   So, never be sad or feel helpless,
  For such a friend you'll never earn on Earth
      As the friend God gifted to you!!
      Praise to God on angel's wings.

James R. Collignon Jr.

Paths Laid Out

Is the path I walk mine to choose,
Every choice determined kindling a new trail,
That at the conclusion of the life I may look back,
To resound my successes and retort where I failed?

Or am I but one of many pawns,
In the game that the eternal play,
Nary aware as they plant ambitions in my head,
To urge me through their intricate maze?

Have I been used all along to further their schemes?
Are my thoughts of my own accord or even my dreams?
Is my destiny laid out, defined in detail?
Can I change its course if backwards I sail?
Do the end and the beginning converge when they're near?
Even with death this question will I fear...

Dan Weber

"Green Eyes"

Whenever it rains...
Every drip is a kiss from somebody,
that loves you each night.

When the Autumn comes...
Everything looks like a beautiful thick rug.
You are blue, because of the fog!

In the winter time...
The hills are covered by snow.
It's cold, but your soul is covered with love.

Whenever the sun comes...
You can see the light, that you were waiting for!
And everything looks...

Green!
Very green!
Like your beautiful eyes!
Green!
Very green!
Like your beautiful eyes!

Jose Luis Castillo Garcia

Untitled

Shades of glass
Every piece a mistake
That I had made
But as each piece I broke;
A new one replaced it.
For each time I made a mistake
God gave me another chance.
As I learned the less glass broke.
So the glass made a mirror
A picture of my full grown life.
Each piece that was left
was a little picture of my lesson in life.
So that now I know what its all about.

Carrie R. Brown

In My heart

You're in my heart always
Ever since you walked in my life and walked out.
Sitting here in total darkness thinking are you coming home?
Why do I think?
Why do I cry all night waiting for you?
You broke my heart, why do I want you?
I love you, I keep telling myself I don't.
But, I do.

Denise A. Garcia

Thinking Of You

Even though you're not around I still think about you.
Even though you're not mine I still think about you.
Every time you enter my mind my heart pounds a little bit heavier.
Whenever I think about you, I get confused & don't
  know what to do.
If this isn't love please tell me what is.
What did I do to lose you.
    Jason Waldemer

Passionate Desire

When love comes for the first time,
Everything even a lonely withering
flower seems just fine,
When I see those beautiful eyes
Those eyes full of deep passionate love,
I feel a warmth in my heart
even my soul rejoices in a way
That I have never known before,
Your kisses, oh heavenly sweet kisses
feed the fire burning in my soul,
I know your love belongs to me and only me,
I caress you in my arms
As I feel the burning fire in my soul,
The loving ever lasting fire
my soul needs,
For you my love are all I desire.
    Beatriz V. Carrillo

"An Everlasting Change!"

From the moment I heard his name,
  everything in my life has changed.
My thoughts were more clear,
  as he drew me near...
    with the love that he showed to me.
I prayed for a while,
  and then it got old...
    there were so many things I should have been told!
But no one took the time to see,
  my Jesus was drifting far away from me.
I went back to my old selfish self,
  that's when I could think of no one else.
And one day it hit me,
  how blind could I be?
All along Christ was walking beside me.
Now this is the day to be happy for living,
  time to spread the word...and time for giving,
  it's time to help others who were once like me.
For those who choose to follow...
  will forever be free!
    Crystal Boyd Adams

Winter

My flowers have all died; the yard is bare
Everything is so lifeless as I gaze out there
And look, there's a squirrel scampering around
Gathering food, where it can be found
He knows the winter can be long and hard
So he's looking for nuts all over the yard
Neighbors closing storm windows; to keep out the cold
Getting ready for winter; they don't have to be told
Ground soon will be frozen and then will come snow
One could easily get depressed if he didn't know
That after the harshness of winter is past
Spring will come again, at last
And flowers will bloom, and birds will sing
For there is new life to everything.
    Hazel B. Turkington

Who's There

The gentle peaceful silence reigned throughout my ear
Everything was quiet-the silence was all I could hear
Suddenly I heard something tromping, tromping up the stair
But when I went to look, there was nothing there

The sound was growing louder, it was coming straight for me
I hid under the blankets for I knew not what I would see
My heart started pounding, pounding fierce and hard
My body was petrified and I feared I'd drop my guard

And now the tromping clamor was heard so strong and clear
The thought that I might be attacked was my awesome fear
"Who is in my room, I really want to know,"
But this question could not be asked for my mouth still
quivered so

This tromping made more noise but there was nothing to see
And I figured out not one body was ever close to me
Instead it was the spirit, the spirit of my friend
I guess his love and thankfulness was all he wanted to send

The gentle peaceful silence reigned throughout my ear
Everything else was quiet-the silence was all I could hear
    Audrey Ronquillo

Let's Try A Little Harder To Agree

There's no escape from this "worldly prison"
except oblivion. That's obvious,
so we had better in what's nearby trust.
We should conform, simply because we must.

The soul is kept within the body's walls.
It operates in things both large and small.
He was the man who was expandable,
because he seldom was dependable.

There always should be one who "pays the piper,"
and always one prepared to snipe the sniper.
So let us all agree we should agree
and take dissensions much more cheerfully.
Let's put a new lens in our blurry eye,
then we will better see until the day we die.
    David P. Boyd

Hollow

I found God today, he's living in my fridge
Excuse my ignorance
I'm on a mission of id
If I were to call you to me would you come?
Never mind...leave me be
I'll be fine on my own

My arrogance rots like a bowl of fruit
Go ahead and pull the trigger...
I DARE you to shoot
The light of the moon outshines my soul
I realize it now
I'm filled with a hole

Ignorance is bliss...or so they say
These thoughts in my brain are darker than most
When I die I'll be a ghost
Unable to reside in a heaven or hell
Just left for an eternity
On a familiar plain to dwell
    Jason Philo

A Thought

I listened to the mild-mannered grandmother
explain in a gentle tone of how she hated to
see Halloween come.

Stupidly, I asked because of so many trick or
treaters —No, she sighed because of how the
older kids act.

I said nothing but thought that age should mean
peace instead of fear.

Then I wondered what generations didn't do that
now we don't respect the past.

When women/young girls protrude their tongues to
show what they like/do without discretion.

Where men/young boys gang rape and use "freaky", etc.
to describe females.

Somehow, we have to return to our roots-of-respect for
one day we will be grands.

Antoinette M. Smith

Woodlands

Down the woodland path I trod
    exploring the marvelous creation of God

An atmosphere of sight and sound
    where balance and harmony of life abound

Enraptured I became spellbound
    in awe of the mysterious world I'd found

A never ending abundant display
    of magic and beauty along the way

Majestic trees so proudly stood
    protecting, shading the deep, dark wood

Delicate flowers with fragrance sweet
    formed a downy carpet beneath my feet

A chipmunk here, a lizard there
    the sound of songbirds everywhere

A world of life, both great and small
    and me — in the midst of it all

Jean Bowles

An Inventory Of Self

There are times when I take a little inventory of myself through my
eyes and others, and I have found that...

Though I lack a generous amount of hair upon my head,
My generosity lies within my heart
Overflowing unto my mind, forever giving, always forgiving
Yet never obtaining that ultimate peace.

Though I may lack that perfection of body,
I have perfected the art of love
That dash of naivete, a touch of shyness
The baring of a passionate soul;
The loneliness and emptiness when used or neglected.

Though I may lack fair skin and blatant beauty,
I find that beauty is truly in the eyes of the beholder
My beauty is within my character;
That uncanny ability to go with the flow
Fit in wherever necessary, be there whenever needed.

And once I have disengaged myself from my own self pity,
I discover that all in all, I'll do just fine.

Jacqueline D. Jackson

"Let The Stars Shine"

Let the stars shine upon your
face to show you the way;
Let the stars shine thru the darkness,
to show you night from day.
Let the stars shine in the sky,
to separate the moon from the sun,
Let the stars shine on you darling,
to show me you're the one.
Yet this one big star that shines
for you through darkness and in light,
tells me that my love for you,
will always be in sight.
We see one now, shining there way over the sea,
a special star for a special love,
a love like you and me.
We see another, its so bright,
our heads are in a whirl,
It doesn't matter as long as I know,
that this will always be our world.

Andrew L. Jones

Our Intimate Night

Alone in the night
far from sound and sight
we kissed, we touched
we shared so much
In the darkness, two people united as one
two people aware of what they had done
but would show no shame for this night they shared
for they had the never to show they cared.
Dusk, lighted into a new day
we parted, you went on your way
Our lives will be lived so far apart
but our intimate night will remain in our hearts.

Billie J. Klemser

Tears and Pain

A glass teeters, a breeze ruffles the leaves of an ancient oak.
Far off an ominous rumble of thunder echoes.
The drizzling rain patters on the roof and the sweet smell it brings
wafts throughout the humble abode.
But a cottage, it stands firm and majestic atop a rolling hill.

A rustle, and out peers a woman from the oaken bed.
A face as beautiful as the rays of sun.
Awake now she ponders the night.
She stands, her slim body angelic in the moonlight.

An owl in the distance sings it's questioning verse.
The glow of the moon radiates shadows of trees bent and crooked
    with time.

Such a beautiful night, the figure sighs.
She sits in the window listening to the rustle of leaves.
A crash of waves not so far off, the feel of the breeze.

The gray clouds above shift aimlessly.
Reminders of people and feelings once known.

Life so beautiful, yet full of such pain.
She lays a shape in the oak bed, quivering as she weeps.

It is silent now, the rush of the wind the patter of rain.
Nothing left now except tears and pain.

Eric Barnett

Fatherless-Motherless Children

Fatherless-motherless children on the street,
fatherless-motherless children in their homes,
adults with things they must do
did they ever take time for me or you?

Did you know you counted?
Did you know they cared?
Did they help you learn about a world that is unfair?

Did they shelter you in their arms?
Or explain the things we feared?
Did they tuck you in at night?
or
Wipe away your tears?
  Della Koster

Freedom With Chains

I walk feeling the presence of someone,
fearing that it might be something;
I run faster, trying to escape its grasp,
it comes closer, I run faster;
Its almost upon me, my fear grows greater, greater,
consuming me with every step as I run faster, faster,
I hear its breath,
I touch its mass,
I smell its odor,
I taste its fumes,
I feel its triumph over me,
Then, I wake realizing it's a dream;
But, as I struggle to get up,
sweat pouring off my brow,
I realize that it was a struggle to get free of it,
The World.
  Gabriel J. Thibodeau

Sunshine

I've never felt a more wonderful
feeling than the feeling
felt through the sun.
Predictable, everyday.
That it opens up to each to the sky,
to you, and me,
slow and easy.
Like a rose given to me,
and by the next day its petals have opened.
Beyond the trees, above the birds
and up into the clouds.
Until it slides through again,
to meet the blackness,
the night.
Only to think, on the other side of the world
it is rising.
Such a foreign, unspeakable rush that fills me,
as the sun reaches out to greet me.
  Caryn Anne Cavoto

Widow

No longer is my life complete
Each day I wake up, dress and eat
But all the while my heart curls tight inside
Drawing me in smaller and smaller
Trying to shut out the pain,
The feeling of alone against the world.
Buy clothes, join clubs they say
Come back to life, to civilization!
But everyday I move away
Farther into the jungle.
  Beth Megrail

Reality Lies O'er Yonder

"Have the new potatoes been brought in from the
field, child... the turnips weeded?"
"Fear not pa, all is well, 'tis but March, a tad
too soon."

His mind flutters back upon the wings of time,
today's dreams not remembered.
"What is this place, why are we here, is it May,
child, or December?"

Come back to us, pa, from that place where you
roam, so alone, so far from home.
"No, not that way, pa... o'er yonder lies the
roan."

Nervous laughter bubbles up to stem quaking fear
that threatens to destroy... can't cry now...
no relief for tears. "No, pa, you are not crazy.
Your mind is simply a wee bit hazy."

"Follow me, pa, our ma has prepared a feast... so
what if she has forgotten the yeast. We'll give
thanks on these good days as well as the grey.
Tomorrow, we will take time to play in the hay."
  Avalon C. McGann

Chasing the Sun

It seems so loving and so bright, I can only imagine it
Filling my heart with light.
I have chased it today and I will chase it tomorrow just
Hoping that touching the sun will heal my sorrow.
I see it there in all its warm glory, like my mother's love when
Reading me a story.
I look outside at the sun in the sky, only in its beams will
Its beauty lie.
With its love in its light it shines over all, even in the
Night darkness shall not fall.
It brings joy to all it will see, why God why is there a
Shadow over me?
I can only hope in my wildest dreams that someday my life
Will be as it seems.
I try so hard, if only you could see, how much it hurts,
It's killing me.
I will chase the sun with all my might, hoping that sometime
My days will be bright.
I have faith in God that my someday will come, but just for now
I will chase the sun.
  Breanne Clifton

The Shepherd

Your presence so near — Your presence so dear
Filling my soul with calmness — never fear
To know that you live in my heart each day
Your rod — your staff leading — I will never stray

To know still waters — and stay by your side
Praises be to my Master you will always abide
Paths of righteousness — I will always know
For your namesake — you restoreth my soul

The enemy knows thou preparest for me
A table of love — anxieties must flee
The oil of gladness you freely give
My soul is restored — and I truly live!
  Donnadee Baxter

Where Has My Life Gone?

I feel my life slipping away with each passing day.
First, my kindergarten years were gone.
Next, Time came and stole ALL my grammar school years.
Before I could stop him-Father Time stole my teenage years;
Never to be seen again-
But in a passing remembrance.
Now, here I stand trying to make a memory of the time I have left
  on this earth.

My Life is slipping by so fast.
I hardly have the time to enjoy ALL it has to offer me.
If only I could suspend time for one day-
I would share ALL the love I have inside with the world-
The Whole World!!
I long to See Life;
Touch Life; Feel Life; Enjoy Life; Live Life;
LOVE LIFE.....
Time: Please stop, if only for a moment,
So that I may!!

   Jennifer Wehry

Enlightening Thunder And Lightning

Heavy, dark blue-green clouds rolling in lower,
Flashes of fire, seen coming from their core,
High winds howling and swirling as the rain pours,
With a fire ball explosion, - then tornado like roar.

Now the spear pointed streak of lightning's might,
Pierce and cracks—* around the center of thunder,
Fragments of sound, small and magnum, roll and rumble,
Against that stagnant, heart-shock-impact of . . . fright.

Eerie blazes from magnetic ion waves so very fine,
Mock those weird echoes, blending in the season of time,
As strong as the powers above agglomerating we find,
Hills and trees trembling, felt up and down our spine.

Our thoughts as in prison caught in wonder,
At that vast strength and power of God's might,
This proud vanity with bold egotism, cast asunder,
In reverence bow low, and plead our humble plight.

Still!— there is no need to fear or be moved,
If we but keep faith, — knowing will so prove,
Also showing how his greatness and true love
Flowing, reaches out, homing like a dove.

   Harold C. Schoessel

"Desert Description"

The air shimmers; you look across the sand and see a flat horizon,
flat sky, flat color.
You can feel it sucking the life from you, leeching your skin of
moisture until you feel like a dry husk ready to blow into millions
of particles on the first desert breeze.
But the breeze never comes and you pray it doesn't. If it does,
it brings with it the wind, and the deadly sand sharp as shark's
teeth as it slices at your flesh.
When the night finally comes, it feels like home: peaceful,
quiet, solemn. Someday, someday, you dream.
And someday we will be home.

   Dan Millhouse

Friends

Friends can make happy.
Friends can make you sad.
When you get in trouble
Friends have a helping hand.
Friends are forever.
Friends go through and through.
You can make a friendship just by being you.

   Ashley Snick

Freedom Flight

Love of life
Flies on the wings of freedom,
Cherishing every moment
Of its freedom flight.
Spreading its wings wide open
And soaring up to the sun
Absorbing all its wonderful rays of energy.
For it's need to be stronger and fly higher
With it's illuminate light of love
Rejoicing over and over
How wonderful it is to be free.

   Donna M. Phillips

Untitled

I'm waiting for you, to come on through
fly with me and make it new
When the heights don't scare you and you
think you belong, I'll say
Let's fall in love for an hour, an hour
is all that we'll need, the healing it
brings, and Heaven does sing, break through
this heavenly seed.
I'll go it alone if I have to, fly through
the clouds learning secrets.
Fall to this earth when it's time for my birth.
And pay once again for my crimes, but let's fall in
Love for an hour, and hour is all that I have
for night is the whore, that wants more and more,
and screams at all that is bright.
And if an hour is all that we
had it would be more than enough.
For silence is death and to hear from your
breath three words outs the light of 'morrow on hold

   Jack Rodriguez

Ghostly Face

Certain I'm
For ever, you'll be mine
I created you from my desires and dreams,
and you become real with time.

No matter where I go and do,
You're on my mind,
walking by my side,
alive in my view.

I've made my heart
your dwelling place,
never again, I will fear loneliness
as I hold in my closed eyes your ghostly face.

All love cells of mine,
those tiny breaths of time
stretching out to reach you
your helping hand will get them through.

   Hind Salameh

We Have A Dream

We ride the Crest of our Wave,
Building Energy, our Gift that God gave.
Our Time; Our Life; Our Love;
Building to a Glory we can only Dream of.
We are ready to Travel our Dream,
To reach the Heights; Together a Team.
We have set about to Create our own Reality;
Hand in Hand, Heart in Heart, Life in Life;
WE.

   Barbara Hyde

The Hallowed Oak

Behold the Grand Oak adorned in winter white;
For hundreds of years it has remained upright.
When my vision is graced by such a sight,
My soul embarks on a heavenly flight.
Thoughts and senses dissolving into one,
A journey into peace has just begun.
All disquietude and sorrows evanesced,
By the Creator of this ideal have I been blessed.
The roots of the Oak give rise to angels,
While the roots of evil are choked with tangles.
I could spend eternity in this celestial state;
Oh, how I dream of a similar fate!
In each and every moment of my days,
I see truth in life's glorious displays.
A wondrous ethic in the Grand Oak I have found
Which the awesome virtues of life will unbound.

Alicia Elmer

Gary

Don't cry for me dear family and friends,
for I am in a better place, you see.

My time of suffering is at an end,
my limbs are no longer bent, I'm free!

Now I know why I was born this way,
as you will come to understand one day.

And so to you this final wish I send;
love one another, as you have loved me.

For you will no longer have me to tend,
but you have each other, and my memory.

And in the Lord's kingdom at your life's end,
we will be seeing each other again.

Carol Stecher

A Holiday

When I woke up this morning I started to pray.
For I knew today was a very special day.
But what today was I could not recall.
It's not Easter, Halloween, or Christmas at all!

Relatives come over and we give thanks
for God's blessings.
We have a big feast with turkey and dressings
Oh what is today, why don't I know?
This day was very special to people long ago.

To make peace, the Indians and Pilgrims
had decided to meet.
And ended up sharing everything they had to eat.
On this day I share what is mine........
Now I remember...it's Thanksgiving time!

Beth Foley

Blue

Blue is the color of a crystal-clear lake;
Blue is the color of a blueberry cake.

Blue is the color of a cloudless sky;
Blue is the color of a baby's eye.

Blue is the color of some cars;
Blue is the color before scars.

Blue is the color in the middle of fires;
Blue is the color of beautiful sapphires.

Amanda Shaul

Fireweed

Pine trees standing tall and proud no more
Lacy fern covering not the forest floor
Homes for eagles and squirrels no longer there
No hiding places for moose or bear
All that is growing is the fireweed
A fitting tribute to man's sad deed!

Carole East

Untitled

This day has impressed upon my soul the severity of my condition
For in as much I have loved you, I have fought the contagion
I have feared for my heart that it should feel faint or vulnerable
Today love grips my heart and my soul is seized in your embrace

Love comes to me not as a threat upon my life or my existence
Rather as deliciously as a kiss of rain upon a barren land
Bringing to this a beauty and richness beyond any measure
Love, a word so small fills this heart to immensity

Shelter I no longer seek but to drench my self in this downpour
I fly into this storm of passion soaking my wings with desire
No more do I meditate on destruction or adversity, my spirit rests
I have in this love a new birth of freedom, I fly unrestricted

My wings feel strong enough to face the fierce winds of emotion
Flying above the clouds of doubt and uncertainty to touch the sun
I will not look back and regret the distance that lies between us
For no space in time or in present shall distance you from my heart

You are there watching me soar and cheering me to greater heights
If danger is eminent my heart will hear your warning cry
You do not hover over me but share the vast sky as we explore
Our horizons may vary but our souls remain companions in flight

Danni Dawson

Things

You can lose people with brief concern
for it is not always comfort that they bring.
To seek to acquire cocoons without conflict,
you would rather acquire the security of things.

Then would you not be viewed as
foolishly emotionless and inhumane.
To think that one can live one's life,
only for inanimate objects and material gain.

You cannot ask a thing for advice and help.
It cannot soothe your deep and nameless fears.
To whom will you turn when you have
carelessly lost your souvenirs?

Harold K. Kimelberg

A Tribute To Mother (Ida Kahler)

I cannot pin a flower upon my mother's breast
For it's eventide for mother, and she has gone to rest;
But I can wear flower just o'er aching heart
To show the world I love her still, even though we are apart.

I miss her love, her tender care,
Her gentle touch, her guiding prayer,
Her words of hope, I hear them yet;
I know I never shall forget.

And although for her I sometimes weep,
I know that's mother's just asleep;
And some day on that golden shore
I'll be with her forever more.

Then in that land of fadeless day,
With all earth's sorrow wiped away,
We'll live a life supreme to this,
A life of everlasting bliss.

Francis Kahler

The Willow

The willow does not weep to the stream
but extends her branches downward
in humble gratitude of the life she brings

Gwendolyn Robertson Urick

Unopened Doors

This fleeting night the moon is clouded over
For most,
Who are taught by cold experience
To keep their doors locked at all times,
Especially on nights like this,
As they huddle alone in a corner
Trying to keep warm,
Seeking the warmth of another, but unable to open the door,
As they hear the windstorm loudly beating against the window
And they think that they are safe,
As they see shadows flicker across the window plane
They faintly hear a knocking, but maybe it's only the wind,
Stepping to peek outside the window
They think they see an outstretched hand,
Unable to trust it, they realize it's gone,
And as the windstorm flees like the shadows
They just keep staring out the window,
Wondering for a moment if it could have been different,
Never knowing they turn, returning to the corner
Alone.

Echo Jablonski

Dare To Discover

Dare to discover things you do not know,
For new-found knowledge will make your mind grow,
I always like to learn things new or old,
It helps to listen to what you're being told.

I can do most anything, if I learn all the right stuff.
Everyday is an adventure, there is never enough,
And for life's tough problems, nothing beats the truth.
When you're really in a jam, it's the beat way to get loose.

When we learn about others, why and how they act,
Sympathy and reason come with all the facts,
With love and understanding we can get along
that's why you should listen, you're friendships will be strong.

I dare to discover. How about you?

Ashley Ernst

A Housewife

A housewife is someone who lives her life
  for others. She cleans, she cooks,
  she takes care of their laundry

A housewife shouldn't be treated as a maid,
  she should be treated with respect,
  yes, she's human just the same.

A housewife should not be taken for granted
  because of what she does just maybe
  a word of thanks and concern would
  help to unload the burdens. After
  running the errands for everyone else,
  Never time to unwind and care for herself.
  She's always busy keeping up her home
  guess why she would be missed if she ever left home?

A housewife should be taken as serious as can be.
  She never gives up because
  she believes in the end it will all pay off,
  with the reward from God saying
  my child that's enough.

Delisa Phillips

Grandma

Today should be a joyous day as the gates of heaven expands.
For this loving and caring lady now rests in our Lord's hands.
She was the spark that lit our life.
From being the best mother, grandmother, and wife.

In our hearts and in our souls there's no one that compares.
Through the love, joy, and caring that through many lives she shares.
We will never forget her for the inspiration she has passed.
Through the years and many lives that forever in our hears will last.

The hardest words are to say goodbye to someone that is so dear.
But we will all meet again with peace and joy,that we will never fear.
We know now you are happy with grandpa and the rest.
You will always be in our hearts for you are truly the best.

Love is the only feeling that comes to mind
When we all think of you.
So rest and be at peace Maw-Maw,
For now the loneliness and pain is through.
So as I said two years ago
To Grandpa as he laid in peace,
Close your eyes Maw-Maw,
Close your eyes and sleep.

Aimee Marie Levron

Traveling By Plane

Have you ever flown in a plane?
For those who haven't -it's a shame.
So many people say FEAR is to blame!

Some say, having many drinks should calm the fearing pain.
But a headache is what you'll gain,
And feeling tipsy wouldn't be the same.

It's much more thrilling-being sane,
Cause an exciting flight is what you want to claim.

Boarding for trip, fills your heart with a flame
Waiting for the ascending and descending "theme game."
Gratitude goes to the PILOT who later gives his name.

The STEWARDESS, so politely trained
Thinking of comforting words for those who complain.
"Restrooms straight back, then enter right lane."

OOPS, almost missed-grabbing onto rails as if it were a cane!
(Must of hit a storming pocket of rain.)

Variety of drinks-1st Class meals fancy-Coach, tasteful but plain.
Such comfort then snoozing with head against the window pane.

"We'll prepare for landing after our movie, FAME."
"Hope you enjoyed our AIRLINES and we're glad that you came!"

Joann Knapp

Sami's Memory

"I will not forget you, little one," said the mother to her child.
"For though you were only with me for a little while,
Your joy will stay within my heart until the day I die.
Everything I see and feel will make me think of you.
From the evening glow to the noontime heart to the early
morning dew.
I'll feel your touch when the warm wind blows,
Your kiss will caress my face.
The laughter I hear is the bird that sings, though it cannot
take your place.
I'll see you when the flower bloom;
You're with me every day.
I'll not forget you, little one, I'll be with you again one day."

Joanne S. C. Schotthoefer

A Gardeners' Lament

On the old oak tree, the leaves are red
For today
And they're turning brown, as they're falling down
And away
Dried and lifeless on the ground
Casting "ugly" all around
'Till the brittle boughs are hanging bare
By all their leaves forsaken
Some like me will always be, rakin'
Rakin' in frustration
For every breeze, just blows more leaves
Blowing leaves, from distant trees
Soon spring will come, as buds appear
In marvel, as they waken
And I wonder, as I always do, in my anticipation
"Will I forget," as seasons change,
"How soon I will be rakin'?"

Joy Pursifull Green

Music To Us Known

You've touched my heart with love and love I must
For you are harmony with life sublime
That plays my soul's triumphant song till time
Is slave when I am in your arms. I trust
My inmost self to you and hopes, unhushed
By fear of loss, teach love felt here is mime,
Mere shadow of closeness beyond our time
With endless joy to spring from mortal dust.
Now come to me in love and me enfold;
Entwine your heart securely in my own.
Our symphony of love may be an old
And well-worn tune for which there's no renown,
But we shall live within its notes and hold
Each one as sacred, music to us known.

Christine D. Wahlquist

A Friend Of Mine

A word of praise to one of the best.
For you make me laugh more than the rest
You always come with a joke and a smile
To brighten my day and make it worth while
The days are long where you're not here
But when you return you bring back the cheer
You make the sun in my life to shine
And that is why you are a friend of mine

Donna B. Yell

Cities Asleep

Went out tonight with so much to see
Found the party over, time was the thief
They said I'd matured but meant grown old
Living with dreams growing colder

Warm July laughter, youth's delite
Soft summer Cindys and others her type
Every day was all Fool's Day ———-
Didn't know it would end that way

Up and down and in and out I danced a masquerade
I danced so fast I had no time to say hellogoodbye
Then after the music the piper was paid . . .
Who ever said grown men don't cry

So what's left? Nothing maybe
Amphetamine dreams? Self pity?
The gentle rumble of a sleeping city
Grinding on without hope? Yet . . . maybe?

Gary E. Locker

Lily

Lily swinging flowers in the air;
Free as a butterfly and no one cares.
Dancing and praying to the melody in her mind;
Leaving all of civilization's troubles behind.
Lily swinging flowers in the air;
completely naked and no one stares.
Singing all playing her song all the time;
Leaving all of civilization's troubles behind.
Fields covered with flowers in bloom;
From sunrise till first glimpse of the moon.
Forest and moor is where she dwells;
For it 'tis pine and maple she loves to smell.
Lily swinging flowers in the air;
Free as dove and no one cares.
Dancing and spinning to the melody in her mind;
Leaving all of civilization's troubles behind.

Angel T. Brown

What's Wrong With Our Country?

"What's wrong with our country?", the plaintive voices cry. Where freedom rang, and people sang, and blue the color of the sky. Miss Liberty's torch held so high, beside the golden door. Promises to keep, opportunity to seek, yes once, but nevermore. "What's wrong with our country?", the ghostly voices sigh. Our country's fathers ask us, expecting a reply. We gave you freedom's treasures, a legacy so dear. Now we watch you squander all, and waste them year by year. "What's wrong with our country?", politicians always know. Telling us so often, like flakes of driven snow. Big brother this, and tax you that, all programs are a must. An endless search for magic answers, mostly all a bust. "What's wrong with our country?", the preachers know too well. People used to pray a lot, love God and, yes, fear hell. Family used to mean much more, right was right and wrong was not. Man's name, his word, and honor measured worth, his wealth did not. "What's wrong with our country?", teachers ask each day. For now we're teaching things in school, that should be left alone. Of, if they must be taught at all, should surely stay at home. "What's wrong with our country?", the answer rings so true. To be so bold, the truth is old: There's nothing wrong with the USA, the problem's me and you!

John N. P. Reisbick

Dear One

What comes to mind most often, is the friendship in my dreams. A friendship so divine, it fails to feel real to me. These days, I often wonder why I miss you so much, for my Dreams sometimes turn into nightmares. You gave me the strength to conquer my hardest problems. I felt secure walking beside you. You never were the smarter one, you were my friend, though. Fate pushed us together, just as it tore us apart. I didn't get the chance to ask you who you really were, or why you came looking for me when you did. Even when I hurt you, you still wanted me there, as your "Friend till the end." Oh, I'm sorry dear friend! Why did it ever have to end? You never know how good you have it until that good is gone. Even though I don't blame you, I can't seem to blame myself either. Maybe you were sent to me for specific reasons, or maybe it truly was fate. If not for you, I imagine myself as a different person, maybe even a better one. Still, thinking of you doesn't seem so bad these days. I never did understand you, but because of you, I was better able to understand myself. From my heart, thank you dear one.

Brandi Fry

Time

Time flies by when you least expect it.
The hands can spin, and the years will pass.
The minutes go slow, But the hours go fast.
Nobody knows exactly what it is.
But it controls our lives each day as we live.

Anna Martinelli

Stranger

He barreled and grunted as he made his decent
From a top a great horse ten years past spent
He looked as though he'd been riding for months
Running from God and the Devil all at once
His skin was like leather weathered by rain
And his eyes told a story of torture and pain.
The stranger swaggered past the saloon
Stood in the road, it struck high noon
Another man stepped into the road, trailing dust from heel to toe
He brushed back his coat exposing his gun
It gleamed with a brightness blessed by the sun
The stranger drew, with a smooth even action
As he fired the shot he smiled with a passion
For the life he had lived and the death he'd escaped
Not by cunning or quickness maybe only by fate
But he left the road the same way he came
Head held high no remorse or shame
He spoke only once in a low surly tone
As he mounted his horse and headed for home
He said "It's not a matter of quickness but whether you're willin'
    to die."
Then he turned the great horse and rode into the sky.

Jacob M. R. Adkins

The Devil's Pyramid

He built a pyramid of flesh and blood
From countless souls of lost humanity
Who serve him well, and feed the rising flood
That fills the world with sin and misery

The mighty dollar bears its evil seal
With Satin watching all who serve below
And gives them all the riches they can steal
From all the good, the humble, and the low

They do the will of Satin with a smile
And heap the wealth of nations in his name
But he who gives them pleasure for awhile
Will take their souls, for power, wealth, and fame.

Curtis L. Atchley

Message To My Inner Child

Weep, weep, my inner child. Let the sorrow flow from your heart,
    from deep within.

Release the pain, feel my embrace. Allow the tears to flow from
    your eyes, so that you may see what your future beholds.

Grieve, grieve, grieve, my inner child, for now you must
    begin to grow....

Stand up, stand tall, my inner child, for you must go on.
Know that love is within, it still exist....

Walk, walk, walk, my inner child, for a path of happiness awaits.

Say goodbye to yesterday, move on....for it is gone in time,
Greet your moments of today, my child, for it is here and now.

Julia A. Briggs-Kidd

Festival

Spring has tatted it's tender lace of leaves.
Fresh new dogwood petticoats peep coyly
from under winter's long-leaf dress.
Hillsides display their panorama of delicate greens.
Azaleas open hungrily
as forsythias leave sleepily;
tulips frolic at the feet of tired jonquils—
each part expectant, patient, forbearing,
making way for the next.

Beth Cartwright

My Phone Call To "Mom"

I wish there was a phone, that reached
from earth to heaven's door,
If only I could pick it up and hear her,
lovely voice once more.
I would tell her how much she's missed.
everyday, all year round.
It doesn't seem that moms been
gone six years
and laid to rest near a place she loved best.

I would tell her of her grandchildren,
How they're grown up so tall.
I would tell her of her handsome
little great grandsons, and how they
would love her so.
I would tell her of the sadness within my heart.
That never seems to go away.
I would ask her how she's feeling,
and then just gab on as we did before.

I'd think of anything, to hear my moms voice
on the phone at heavens door.

Barbara A. Stewart

Beloved

I love thee more than words portray,
From shadowed eve till sunbathed day,
In my thoughts, my every sigh,
If I should lose thee; I should die.

In yonder garden, silk gowns flowing,
A whisper of breeze softly blowing,
Caresses thy cheek with invisible fingers,
The very thought of thee still lingers.

Since that moonlit eve whence I saw thee first,
I've longed for thee with hunger and thirst.
Take my soul, my love, my life,
And say that thou wilt become my wife.

I give thee my wit, my self, my heart,
And promise to love thee till death do us part.
Take my hand, my beloved, and follow me,
Through life's portal till eternity.

Gloria Ott Warczak

A Soldier's Fright

Light is protection,
    from someone here to there.
Darkness is preventable,
    when a shadow Isn't there

I suffer in the morning
    I cry at night.
I pray to myself,
    and do what's right.

The evils taken over me,
    I try to let it go.
It stays within me.
    It just flows and flows.

It's lifting me, possessing me, taking my mind.
    I can't hold on anymore.
Soon I will die.

Is this a new life?
    Is this a new beginning?
How will I know? What is this understanding?

I can not explain, I can not control
It is over, It is over. It has taken my soul.

Jacqueline V. Stanton

An Inspiration

Gaze up at the brilliance of light emanating
From stars-each slightly different.
Take a good look.
This same brilliance is reflected in your eyes reaching,
Depths 20,000 leagues under my skin.
You are an old chest in the attic, full
Of hidden treasures that one will discover
On a rainy day while looking for those old photographs.
Remember the walks at night, the times at the cafes-
Time together - Time stopped.
Your embrace is a warm fireplace,
Each of us adding a log of trust, passion, and faith
To the pile. A fire which last all day and all night.
Eat of me. Drink of me.
Let me flow through your veins as you flow
Through my mind
Giving nourishment to my soul.
Take hold of the key and open the door. The door to my heart
To which only you know the way.
Come in, sit down, take your shoes off and stay awhile.

Danielle Gromosaik

My Daddy's Hands

My Daddy's hands were creased and bent
from the coal he dug and the hours he spent.
Working the mines and working the soil
for the family he loved it was ceaseless toil.

Dad's coal mine work took its toll. It took his leg but not his soul.
He never showed it got him down,
He bought a farm and worked the ground.

To make ends meet in them days meant raisin' cows and bailn' hay.
Tendin' hogs and chickens too... barely makin' out and makin' do!

Dad's hands hunted squirrel and rabbit meat it sure tasted good when
took our seat. He also trapped furs for a fair price... scrapin' and
stretchin' far in the night.

When Santa couldn't come one year... Dad's hands got busy makin'
gifts so dear. A cradle, a windmill, toys and chairs on the shelf...
Our Daddy came through, a true Santa's elf!!

Daddy's hands could play the guitar and he sang us all to sleep.
He would pray to the Lord at night for all our souls to keep.

Our Daddy's hands put down his hoe and plow and he's up in Heaven
with Mama now. We know as he met the Almighty One, God said,
"Come in my son, job well done!"

Betty Burns Lawrence

To My Mom

You loved me so as if your own
From the start I wished I'd known
You brought me up and gave to me,
Those gifts of life I thus received.
Honoring and cherishing all I portrayed,
regret those times I disobeyed.
Forgiving me and once more friends
Continued on those loving trends.
As days past on I loved you more
That parent glow I finally saw.
Supporting me through times of sorrow
pass on your courage I need to borrow.
with you gone I hope I'll learn
to love as you or then thus burn.

David C. Lew

"Wonder Of Winter Forever"

Winter has shown her biting chills;
Frost has painted the once green hills;
The limbs of the pines are swaying in dance,
As the love birds proudly proclaim their romance.
Where in all the world is beauty so vast,
So I look outside my window remembering winters passed.
She always provides a blanket of fresh white snow,
and brings life to the leafless trees, with an icy glow.
To climb that snow capped hill is my endeavor,
To ride that sled down through
the wonders of winter forever.

Judith D. Collins

Puny Mind

Oh, puny mind, you cannot fathom the depths of God's love...
Full-known only to Him Who richly sheds from above.
Moving with compassion... His tears flowed as a flood!
And grace has none matched... to that of His blood!

But ah! puny mind, you can through the eyes of faith see
The shadow of the Godhead crucified to set you free;
And raised again to life on that glorious third day...
To give victory complete: today, tomorrow and always!

So rejoice puny mind! Overcome by what you know in your heart,
As it rests in the peace He did so wondrously impart
When He said, "Alone you'll not be. A Comforter I give.
And you may be certain of this: by My Word you will live!"

Harold V. Trumble

If You Would Wonder

When you wonder, your heart is pure
Full of joy and happiness, your foot steps leads
you into another world...
When you wonder into the sight of love
You go beyond another dimension into a
world, full of wisdom and knowledge.
If you would go deeper into your heart
You would find a greater gift than love...
If you would wonder far enough into your spiritual mind...

You would find your soul and spiritual self...
If you would wonder into the sight of love
You would find that love is one of
The greater powers of God Almighty above.
If you would wonder....

Alfanso Joshua

The Eyes of Beauty

Eyes are said to be one of the most glorified features of the face.
Glory, drama, and dimension displayed with unlimited space.
Some grand some small, but beauty found within them all.

In youth your eyes are easily deceived,
decisions and concepts to be perceived.
So few times are the eyes linked to the mind,
is it a power or force from behind?
Is it not true that what is brought to sight is
relevant to all powerful decisions?
Do we not feed on its wonder, thoughts, and provisions?

When you look into my eyes what do you see?
Are you willing to pay the price the precedent fee?
Can you see the hurt that my heart retrieves?
Or the range that my brain defies?
The feelings that presents themselves as a surprise.
Are my intentions revealed in the color of my eyes?

The things brought to light are not always a pleasure,
yet the gift has a purpose and possesses a treasure.

Tenise Austin

Go Away

Vanish from my mind and leave my soul
　go away, go away
　　Memory of the love, I'm ever known

Disappear from my heart and begone for good
　go away, go away
　　Memory of the love, I've ever understood

Memories run and leave quickly if you can
　go away, go away
　　The hurt is more than I can stand

Feelings that were once shared and not to be known again
　go away, go away
　　So that my new future can begin

Leave me now and escape from my mind
　go away, go away
　　Leaving only the scars that will heal with time
　　　JoAnn Wheatley

Undying Love

He is gone, his grave has set.
God has taken his soul to rest.
She is sad, but smiles yet.
Her love is gone, only traces left.

But she is strong, a faithful thing,
Memories left, and one last dream.
The wind still blows, the birds still sing
Storms still fall, rain they bring.

She runs away, into the night.
To his grave, containing fright.
She bows her head, she sheds some tears.
Left alone with only fear.

For he was loved with all her heart.
He took from her a cherished part.
She is left, mourning alone.
For he has left her royal throne.

One last tear, falls from her face.
She stands and leaves, with peaceful grace
She looks back and sees a dove,
A symbol of, undying love.
　　Abigail Hall

Brother To Brother

I know in my mind
God's love is not blind
So listen to God's rhyme
And feel his love begin to unwind.

As the mountains are settled so high
I know we're the light and the glory in his eyes.

He picks us up
Through trouble and strife
The Lord thy God even sent us Jesus Christ.
Is there anyone who can say, "This was not nice!"

Let nothing but love flow from heart to heart
Let's use our God given mind
To change these troubling times.

Give heed to your lives
Throw away those guns and knives.
Let nothing that simple
Take away our lives
Kill your spirit and your God given mind.

Always give love to one another
And hold fast and uplift your spiritual brother.
　　Donald R. Vance

The Father's Love

The Father's Love, is so infinite we can not phantom its depth.
God's Love, is so vast we can not comprehend its height.
The Father's Love, is so precious we can not receive its fullness.

It was This Love, that Kept His only Son, Jesus, on the cross for you and I.
It was This Love, that caused His Only Son, to go down into Hell,
To break the spell, Satan, thought he held;
To keep the captives, from being set free.

This is why, Satan, tries to Kill you and I, so that we will
never tell others; W H Y, our Lord and Saviour died.
But, it was God's Love, on that cross, when Jesus cried;
"Father, take This Pain, of all those whom been deceived and slain."

For, when He realized the Intensity of The Love and the Sacrifice
"no one else," could pay;
He vowed, "not my wish Father, but thy desire;" For it is This Love,
The Father's Love, that has redeemed us, from an eternal fire.

Now, can you see! God's Love, lifted you and me, so that we
can also fulfill the destiny; that is meant to be.
Always remember, my friend, "The Father's Love," is forever
and always there;
Because, He actually C A R E, and knows how much we can B A R E.
　　Debra Marcelle-Coney

Tender Is The Night

Tender is the night, breezy and warm.
Golden is the moon, low and calm.
A perfect night for loving; a perfect night
for setting the future right.
I look at you and see a wonderful possibility in your eyes.

Wondering if the gleam in your eyes is from the
moon or from the knowledge that I love you.
Stars slowly appear two by two as couples should do;
filling the sky with a beauty that seems meant only for
me and you.

Sent from above, we select a pair to guide us
through our future together, knowing that with
God's guidance we're guaranteed a lifetime together.

Yes, tender is the night, breezy and warm.

The most perfect place for lovers to be: Feeling
arms wrapped around you in total serenity, gentleness,
and abandonment can't help but make one
feel happy to know that the night can be tender after all.
　　Darline Beck

Down Home

"We're going down home," Mom used to say, "We'll see how Grandpa's
doing today." Down home, you know, was that little farm that Grandpa
kept with all its charm. An' Grandpa was that great big guy with a
heart of gold named Zenas Fry. On the farm, Grandpa had a pigs, an'
chickens and a horse; he had bees in the orchard and a cow, of course.
In the barn were two buggies, in the front a stack, on the side was a
chicken house with melons growin' in back. A creek ran though where
we used to play, an' just east of the creek Grandpa made his hay. I
remember the wooden pump and the big grapevine near the large tree Mom
planted when nine. I remember the crackling on the butcherin' day,
the making of sausage and hams smoking away. I remember the fried
chicken, and that we never broke bread, until Grandpa's prayer of
thanks was said. Oh the memories are great from that little old farm
that Grandpa kept with all his charm.
And it all started out in about 1880 when Grandpa
built the house and married his lady. Nine girls and two boys God
blessed them raise and they never forgot to give God all the praise.
So don't let us forget what this family's about, out heritage is
great, so let us all shout: "Hurrah for Grandpa and Grandma too,
their prayers and their lessons have carried us through."
　　Donald G. Henkel

Golden Moments

As days go by - some good, some bad,
Golden moments have you ever had?
Golden moments spent with a friend,
Golden moments sometimes hard to end.

It's a simple smile on a loving face,
Smiles that make two hearts embrace,
It's a look in eyes that talk to you,
Then silence is golden between two friends too.

It's a hug that says, "How is your day?
Good or bad - hug me anyway,
Just because we're friends, it means so much,
To keep our friendships close in touch.

Laughter that's shared - personalities blend,
When hearts both hurt your tears are friends,
Care and concern when troubles run high,
They are golden moments that will let you cry.

As days go by - some good, some bad,
Golden moments always try to have,
And when those moments come to their end,
Cherish them in memory with your golden friend.

Cynthia L. Smith

Untitled

Look at that big black woman standing in line at the grocery store
Got her bedroom shoes on and curlers in her hair
  think she dresses up like that to go everywhere?
Holding up the line making a fuss over things on the counter that
  don't matter much
Saying if she was white she wouldn't be treated that way -
  Everybody's looking now what do you say?

Look at that skinny young red-neck standing in line at the grocery
  store
Got his cowboy boots on and his cap backwards over his hair
  think he dresses up like that to go everywhere?
Holding up the line and making a fuss-says taxes are so high the price
  of beer is too much
Saying if there weren't so many free-loading niggers it wouldn't be
  that way -
  Everybody's looking now what do you say?

Look at my little son standing in line at the grocery store
Got a curious grin and is surrounded by innocence in the air
  all little boys dress like that to go everywhere
He don't hold up the line he don't make a fuss
  before today seemed like nothing mattered much
Saying nothing tears rolling down his face as he frightenedly turns my
  way
  Everybody's looking now what do I say?

Jeff Stilwell

Green

Green makes you think of meadows and plains.
Green is sometimes the color of a candy cane.
At Christmas, green befriends red and white
And is a color on a traffic light.
Green is the color of slime.
Green tastes sour like a lime.
Green is yuck and green is minty.
Green is pine needles that smell leafy.
Green makes you think of an alien from space
With nine eyes all over its face.
Green is a tree that is all mossy.
Green is greed and being bossy.
Green feels good, yet some what bad.
Green is happy, yet some what sad.
Green is a color second to none
Which makes it one of the best ones.

Bucky Franzen

Red

Tender cherub faces hidden by a masque of
  grey
Depression a foot
Boys that wanted to lead the pack find it's
  more enjoyable to stay with the rest
But they play the game
cold bodies
wet feet
Live or die
Lying on the ground unwashed as time slowly passes
Slow hours quick weeks fast years
All thoughts watch the same channel; Home
Starting in a mother's arms
Ending in an enemy's hands
To each a different enemy
Looking down the sights from the wrong end of
  the rifle
Reality is too real
And blood is too red.

Gerald A. Inglesby III

Warped Floorboards

Piles of junk strewn about the room:
grimy spoons, photo albums, browned dental floss,
a chair whose legs are coming loose,
an old tuxedo from someone's prom

or marriage. A mustiness is carried by a stealthy breeze
through faded books and postcards, into an ashen fire
place that had flourished until now. I fear
that someone has left me this unpleasant surprise.

In a corner, clothes lay tattered and torn
filthy and listless where none have wept
or even pretended sorrow. On warped
floorboards, the memorials lay forgotten.

Daniel Vu

"One Who Honors God"

An emissary's tiny fingers
Gripped our hearts today.
Grief and sorrow's fragrance lingers
As we bow our heads to pray.

Buckets of tears bathed every face
That looked on "Timothy David."
Warmed by a covering of blue and white lace,
His resting was calm and placid.

A host of love flanked the room,
Precious parents gave God their son.
A lovely white rose flourished in bloom;
Timothy's life in eternity had begun.

We commend his spirit into your keeping
And claim the promises sweet.
"John 3:16", a place of no more weeping;
Again, . . . we will meet.

Colleen Capes Jackson

"King Won't Be King Anymore"

Oh! Prince Charles won't be king anymore,
As Princess Di put a look on her door.
He thought, that he'd be her lover, for life,
Now he's only, the sweet pea rolling of her knife,
Princes Di looked in her pockets and saw
Camilla's stocking, she always wore.
It was then Princess Di smacked Charley in eye.
Oh The King, Won't Be King Anymore.

George E. Neubauer

Squeeze Play

Shackles of flesh surround my head
Hand upon hand down by the sandlot
Baseball daze who would rule Camelot
Trumpets blared announcing the king
Triumphant I entered the square flanked
By soldiers in diamond formation fluffed
Like peacocks dancing "matily" in the grass
Worms slicing gracefully through blades
Shackles of memories till I'm dead
Playing fields ruled by enslaved children
Driven to follow evolution dust-cloud pleasure
Body and soul lust in bound treasure
Found near the moisture of morning dew
Drowning in all that is worshipped
Shackles of faith fill my bed

Gregory S. Patrell

Wherever

Christmas of 1992 brings a new state of mind;
"Happy Sad" is definitely my new find.
Happiness comes first, with life so full;
Sadness slips in, with a quiet lull;

My soul resides this Christmas season
In the land of ancient Indian ruins,
Where "the old ones" are guided by spirit - not reason.
But survive they will, for eons.

My heart soars up over the High Plains,
Where "the little one" searches the books.
The mountaintop is close by, if one looks.
But life has so many different lanes.

My spirit dwells just down the road,
Where "the wise one" forges a code.
Life and survival all take time.
But never forget to enjoy the climb.

My soul, my heart, my spirit - all three.
Forever - they will always be.
Wherever - they remain within me.

Dee Vincent

The Majestic Mountain

The majestic mountain standing so tall
Has beautiful trees showing splendor in the fall
    And the tops covered in snow
    With a lake down below
Is a magnificent sight to each one and all

The sunlight streams off the mountain peak
As if it were playing hide-and-go seek
    The moon beams a light
    On a dark starry night
That makes the coyotes send out a shriek

The fluffy white clouds that float in the sky
Are a delight to behold o'er the mountain top high
    And purple shadows creep
    Down crevices deep
Painting a picture I can not deny.

Barbara Drouillard

Nite Time

The moon lighting the path for the creatures of the nite.
Crickets chirping their soft lullabies.
The frogs harmonizing in the moist night air.
The stars decorating the nite sky and giving
you wishes of hope, joy and love.
Nite time comforting, peaceful.....beautiful.

Bridget Mundth

Yesterday, Today And Tomorrow

Yesterday is full of sorrows and joys, laughter and tears, love and hate.
Things that cannot be changed.
Yesterday has memories and mistakes we will cry over now and laugh
about later.
Perhaps we will regret them or love them all our lives,
But yesterday has tiptoed away on silent feet and we cannot bring it back.

Today is full of merry pleasures held out to be loved and enjoyed
Along with these, come frightful horrors and melancholy happenings.
We cry and cower away from these
Burying ourselves in joys
Until they leave us in our meadow of delight.

Tomorrow is there without bliss or mistakes.
Nothing has stirred this day yet.
It is like a cup of happiness not yet drained. It is not disturbed.
Tomorrow is waiting for us to come repent our sins and correct our errors of today.

Whether you are in yesterday, today or tomorrow
You have had and will have your laughter and tears,
But always remember yesterday, today, and tomorrow
Are often among your dearest of friends and rarely your enemies.
They are there to comfort and to love.

Ashley Costello

"Ode To Lynn"

Her hair's as dark as the black of night.
    Haunting is her face, never out of sight.
Be it lust or love I know I'll never be free,
    From these chains that bind and torment me.

I sit deep in thought; questioning in solitude:
    Is she a player of hearts? Am I such a prude?
She has stolen my heart and weakened my defenses,
    With her beauty and my own numbed senses.

Chains of love can never be severed or broken.
    A fire in my heart she masterly awoken.
On this her birthday I picture her face.
    I know now, no one can ever take her place.

At times I fear she will make me look like a fool.
    For her emotions I may be a mere buffing tool.
But if love makes me a fool, a fool I shall be,
    From now, tomorrow, next year to eternity.
Happy Birthday Lynn, I'll see you in the morrow.
    And for today, may you have joy not sorrow.
May God protect you and forsake you never
    You'll be in my heart, forever and ever.

Joseph T. Kane

Forbidden Thoughts

To go against my mother's wishes and
    have him as my own.
And to sneak out late to see him so I won't
    feel all alone.
Or to make love all night long, on a
    sofa at his home.
Or let his lips and tongue find
    somewhere on my body to roam.
To wander through the depths of love
    with thoughts of ecstasy,
And fulfill all my expectations that
    include you and me.
But these, my mind shall not
    sought,
Because they are forbidden thoughts.

Courtney Lane Holladay

My Doctor, My Husband, And My God

My doctor told me I would die.
He diagrammed the way I'd go.
I didn't let him see me cry,
But out of there the tears would flow.

The man I chose at twenty - three,
The man who thought he'd won a prize,
Has spent these many years with me
Trying to whittle me down to size.

My God will do what's right by me.
As long as I shall draw a breath,
I'm as happy as I choose to be
Though trimmed to size and doomed to death.

Of leafy trees by breezes blown
Enjoy the fruits, throw out the rinds.
The kids are great and they have their own.
I'll dream and sing and quote my lines.

And when I gaze up at the skies,
I'll praise the Lord upon my knees
For though I'll have dab my eyes
I'm crying at my ease!

Gladys James

Age: 17

As he arose from bed
he eagerly jumped up
and went outside.

He look up and saw
something as beautiful as
a budding rose.

He saw an array of yellows,
reds, oranges, and golds.
That defined his eyes and rattled his soul.

Then he turns around and
sees a lake as of crystal
which quiets his soul.

Then he looked right
into the eyes of God
and began crying out of excitement.

Then he looks up beyond
the defying colors and asks, "Why?"
and a voice proclaimed, "Because I
Love You," and a teardrop falls
because he has waited so long for him to come.

David M. Parran

Free

From a small ripple in the ocean,
He floated with resolve;
Toward an un-molested island of dense forest
And clear, flowing brooks.

Ashore he crawled, scratching and struggling
Free from the tide's vigorous grip.
Driven, guided by an unknown force
Ignited in blind regions.

Alone, he was broken-
Divided to become complete.
Then into the forest they trudged, and were
Fattened and nourished from its fruits.

Back to the shore, they
Kneeled at day's end-Isolated.
Prostrate, set facing the drowning spirit
From which they came.

Gary W. Donohue

A Boy Called James

A boy grows into a man
He has finished his final journey
Through the intricate networks and webs of education.
We stand with gratifying envy as we watch him receive,
The paper that is so called graduation.
We laugh to ourselves for we know he is not finished with schooling
He will not be finished with education for many years
At the moment he is flying high
Higher than an eagle anyone has ever seen
We are all watching the little boy we once knew
   With never ending Spirits.
Once before he was the wind in the shadow of the wing but now
He is that shadow with those magnificent wings out stretched
With many winds in his shadow now he soars over all.
Not willing to land, but for now that is alright, he is happy.
And as I speak I feel I speak for all in saying
I hope you stay happy.
God bless you James!

Jon Huckestein

Ask Him

Ask Him anything...Praise His Holy Name.
He is Alpha and Omega, forever the same.
Ask Him anything... Kneel before Him in prayer.
He is always available, He knows your every care.
Ask Him anything... Simply trust and obey.
He is your security, your strength day by day.
Ask Him anything... Claim the gift of amazing grace.
He is Jesus, your Lord and Savior, seek His gentle face.
Ask Him anything... The Holy Spirit, who will intercede.
He is The Counselor, The Helper who knows your every need.
Ask him anything... Abide in his eternal love.
He is your Heavenly Father, God Almighty above.

Judith M. Perkins

I Am

Humility and sovereignty, together in one man.
He is like no other, He is the "Great I Am."
With a voice as loud as thunder or as subtle as a breeze
His message is carried throughout nations - across the seas.

He prevails and says "I Am!" with words and so much more
The I am stands and calls, "Please open your hearts door."

The Before and the After, The Beginning and The End.
Lord, Master, Savior, and Understanding Friend.
He is the Great I Am, who came down from heav'n above,
To teach us Gods great promise and save us with his Love.

"Please take Me as I Am," He calls, "For I died that day for you.
There will be no other, who loves you as I do."
"I love you as you are, my life for you I give,
So you too may join the Father - Eternally to live,
 - and say I am."

Cynthia J. Mason

One Man

There is one man in my life.
He is more than worth the price.
I don't know what I did to deserve someone like him.
He makes me feel loved whenever I'm around him.
There is a certain thing about him.
That makes me want to love him.
He has that certain touch,
That makes me love him very much.
He's a real nice guy,
And well worth the buy.
I love him more then I can say.
And no one can take those feelings away.

Diedre Hays

The "Jumping Jack" Man

There once was a man called the "Jumping Jack" man.
He jumped every place, never walked, never ran.

He jumped over silos and jumped over each farm,
'Till the cows and the horses ran with alarm.

He jumped over houses and even a steeple
And you can be assured, it scared all of the people.

He rattled the windows, dishes bounced off the shelf
All this making him very pleased with himself.

At the edge of town on a hill oh so high
Stood a magnificent tree reaching up to the sky.

He announced to the townsfolk that on Saturday night
He would jump over that tree, using all of his might.

And that night all of the people gathered with glee
To witness the "Jumping Jack" man jump over the tree.

In hushed silence he approached, the people did freeze
As higher he went, branches swaying in the breeze.

Suddenly his suspenders caught in the tree on the hill
And as far as I know, he's hanging there still.

Ginny McCauley

Sonnet To A Child—My Son

A small boy worships at a shrine;
He kneels, his eyes aglow with adoration.
In steady flow comes forth his supplication:
"Dear father, who art ever mine. . ."

Command rings clear from every plea,
As he entreats for daily ministration,
His thirst for love beyond all satiation—
Unhindered by humility.

But even when, as needs must be,
The father's voice speaks reprimands,
He sulks and pouts, unclasps his hands:
"I do not pray for homily."

Not long away, ardor rekindles faith—I am brave;
I ask his pardon—I, his shrine, his God, his slave.

John E. Driemen

My Friend

He was my friend
  He said.
I was his ONLY friend, he said.
A moment did my feeble Pride distend
  (Here Ole Skepti lif his hed)
That such as HE should call me friend
And add "You are my ONLY Friend"

But to deflate and to amend
My wits were stirred to apprehend
Why such as HE should have apprehend
But simple me as ONLY Friend (Ole Skepti ope an eye)
  What did portend?
  Did he intend
To wangle me his ONLY Friend
To breach the faith of every other Friend
By tempting me in answer to commend
That he was MY only Friend?
  (I see Ole Skepti's face turn red)
I could not so dishonestly pretend
And contemplating comprehend why now I say 'he WAS my friend!

Gretchen Buendia

Temptation Came From Every Side

The Devil came and lied to me the way he always does.
He said, "How can you trust in God?" I said to him, "Because
He's done so much for me thus far my tongue cannot express,
Nor words enough to give Him thanks, His faithfulness to bless."

But Lucifer would not give up, intent was he to win.
He said, "You really don't need God, I'll give you more than Him.
Why should you miss so much of life, there's so much fun in sin."
He showed me then the things he'd give to trust and follow him.

I felt my heart begin to lust, my flesh was getting weak.
I cried to God, "Please help me, Lord!", and I began to weep.
His Spirit came just like a wave, I was weak no longer.
As Satan tried to tempt me sore, God sent Power stronger.

Then I began to quote the Word, much to his surprise;
He'd thought he had me there for sure, but God said otherwise.
Not once or twice, but thrice he came to tempt me on that day;
But God gave me the words to speak to drive him straight away.

The Devil comes and tempts me still, he'll not give up the fight;
But Jesus is my strength and shield, His name makes him take flight.
Get thee then behind me Satan, you cannot prevail;
Greater is He in me than thee and He can never fail!

Garry Belizaire

Ode to My Brother-In-Law

He came to the house and stood in the drive
He said, "I know that rumor is rife.
I want to ask you each one and all,
To avoid any family strife.

As you all know I've been paying court,
Keeping company with your older sister,
I want to make it clear from the start
I was moonstruck when I kissed her.

I'm asking you all if you object
If I take Rebecca to wife?"
"Thank God," we cried, "we won't be stuck
With her for the rest of our life."

So Ed married Becky years ago
And somehow I just feel
He got himself a darn good wife
But we got the best of the deal.

Janet M. Parker

He's Just A Dog

People say he's just a dog, but I don't think that's true.
He seems to know your every thought and always stands by you.

He can't talk the way we do, but still he has his way. His
pleading eyes and wagging tail says all he needs to say.

When days are long an things go wrong, your dog is always
there. If you're a king or just a bum, he doesn't really care.

So who cares what people say. Their mind is in a fog. They'll
never know a real true friend, until they have a dog.

Earle N. Williams

Don't Give Up

When you have a child it's time
for happiness and a time for loving.
You will always remember them in
your heart when they grow up, but
its not the time to give them up.
There the only thing in your heart that can
make your life so happy.
So make it possible and please don't give them UP!

Christine Desautels

Through Open Eyes

He came into my life as if he owned it
He talked to me, laughed with me, cried with me
my eyes were closed
I could not see.

He was so charming with his smile
He wrote me poems, He told me stories
He played with me.
My eyes were closed
I could not see

Times got hard and life changed
He changed or I changed
My love was still there
But his couldn't be
My eyes were closed
I could not see

He held my heart
He broke my heart
One sided love can never be
With my eyes wide open
This I see!

Dawn R. McCowan

My New Home

He took his clothes and he took his books
He took his humor and his funny looks
He took his T.V. and his remote controls
He took his clock and his fishing poles
He took his car and he took his gun
He took his mounted trout that he kept for fun
He took the pictures of me and my brother
He left the ones of him and my mother
He left his couch and he left his bed
He left the hats he wore on his head
He left the mower and the gasoline
He left me a note to keep the yard clean
He left all the things that had grown into place
I hope he'll be back to show them his face
Things need to change or so my Mother says
Or the love they once had will forever be dead

Jon English Walker

"To More Than One Friend"

It was a long time ago when I first met my friend.
He was loving and good yet a strong and brave man.

Whenever I needed him, there he would be.
Like a knight in fine armor, there just for me.

As time passed on, my friend started to change.
I did not see him much, When I did, it was strange.

My friend found a new friend he liked called cocaine.
And from that moment on things would not be the same.

I told him a few times, "That stuff takes its toll".
But he assured me it was under control.

Over the years he became an old man.
He met his match over and over again.

It made him do things he would never have done.
Making his mother ashamed of her son.

Today I said bye to the one I can't save.
Tears fell as they lowered him into his grave.

Debby Pary

Why

In Loving Memory of Jeremy Dodgen 1977-1994
Why did you take him
he was so young
Why did you take him
his life had just begun
Why did you take him
why did you make him leave
Why did you take him
when you could of took me

Joyce Lea Flesher

The Fork

We met at the Fork, many years before.
He was standing outside, I was holding the door.
I distinctly remember him calling me by name,
And recoiled with embarrassment when I couldn't do the same.

We sat. He in the grass, my back against the brick,
I spotlighted my struggles and his crux was victory.
(A comforting aura lingered at the Fork that cool afternoon,
As the answers to my questions were beginning to loom.)

My hunger and thirst grew as the aroma of a meal
Floated through my senses. The warmth of his voice helped me feel
Satisfied in knowing him. The soothing conversation quenched
My appetite, so we arose and sat side-by-side on a bench.

Intrigued, I probed him to continue sharing his life.
I was amazed at the similarities and saw myself striding
Over my earlier struggles. The longer we talked, I learned
How much we had in common. However, I became concerned

Of the imminent darkness. Not wishing my acquaintance to leave,
I invited him in. I was nervous at first but I believe
That I made the right decision. We've quickly become the best
Of friends and I treasure our intimate quest.

Brett Rachel

Don't Look Back

Don't look back when you
Head for the door,
Because baby I love you no more.
And if you do,
I'll hurt much, much more.

Don't stop to explain,
Don't tell me why,
If you're going to leave,
Just kiss me good-bye.

I love, and I miss you
But I can make it on my own,
Remember because your mistake,
I'll be all alone.
I still want you to be mine,
But sometimes people like you,
Need to be left behind.

Just kiss me good-bye
If this is the end.
And If I feel better
You can be my friend.

Jennievy D. Martin

"Just A Thought..."

Imagine all the world at peace,
Tell me then, where would we be?
Sitting at home, staring at our TV?
Tell me then,
WHERE WOULD WE BE?

Erica Lynette Edwards

Only Within

The mystical, beauty of faith,
heartfelt warmth,
no human touch nor earthly reward can replace.
To be blindfolded and led on a journey,
and know in your heart, your safe.

To hear whispered words, Trust Me,
and follow at God speed pace.
To have Divine presence always near thee,
without ever seeing a face.

An everlasting hand to hold as trying times
do unfold.
A guidance set just for you,
To fulfill your mission as journeymen do.

So be true to your spirit as it urges you thru
the next turning page of life's book for you.

Barbara McCormick

Journey Through My Heaven

As fate could take the soul of thee to a divine and glorious sight.
Heaven that is so heavenly I follow the shimmering light.
Comforted by my known deceased their love I shall devour.
A feeling that I am at peace. I savor the Almighty Power.
Brought before a gallant God I felt his healing hand.
I was greeted with a nod welcomed to His land.
When softly an angel sings. A woman in white veil.
Before I am received my wings I'm directed to a trail.
"The Trail Of Life" all in awe. I see my wrongs and rights.
Won't believe the things I saw the future in my sights.
Clouds of cotton, sky's of blue my body wrapped in leather
Though my corps is kept with you my soul's light as a feather.
Sins no more, I am free I peer down at the earth.
No one can begin to see the value life is worth.
Forever I am seen no more for me you begin to pray
Happy as I was before on my Judgment Day.

Augusta Dawn Gooley

On Pushing Sixty

Everything that would not fit in the U-haul we gave away:
Heirlooms back to the family that treasured them
Clothing, furniture, and kitchen tools to needy students,
Model airplanes and stereo equipment
To neighbor kids (who quickly destroyed them, no doubt)
And garbage bags of the rest
To the American Rescue Mission on Court Street which accepts anything.
Freed from the years of gathering
We moved from the rocky Pennsylvania hills
To the piney woods of Texas and effortlessly amassed anew.

Once again we are giving away our possessions
Social positions to the family which treasures it
Culture, civil, rights, and the aspirations of youth to needy students
The quality of daily life
To neighbor kids (who will quickly destroy it, no doubt)
And garbage bags of the rest to our children who accept anything.
Freed from years of gathering
We move from the rocky hills of aspiration
To the piney woods of seasoned experience
And begin effortlessly to amass anew.

Frank Bayer

Jay's Ode To Helen's Chicken Soup

When Pastor Shawn was sick, couldn't make the scene,
   Helen brought him her magical cuisine.
The ingredients include friendship, love and lots of prayer,
   And the milk of human kindness - it's all in there.
Pastor Shawn was sick and getting sicker,
   When Helen brought her magical elixir.
On Sunday night he was flat on his back,
   By Tuesday he was up and back on track,
He had eaten two bowls that night for supper,
   This turned out to be his fixer-upper.
Impossible? You think I'm leading you on?
   If you don't believe me - just ask Pastor Shawn.
We know Pastor Shawn - he wouldn't prevaricate,
   Or Saint Peter wouldn't let him through the Pearly Gate.
As you can see, her chicken soup is exotic,
   Some folks say it is also erotic.
After having one bowl at night with their meal
   They say they have feelings they don't usually feel.
Ridiculous you say? It just can't be?
   But I'm going on 80 and it works for me.

Argie Jay Miller

"My Brother Stan"

My brother, Stan, is quite a man,
   He'll help you whenever he can.

I was going away for just one week,
   I asked him to repair a plumbing leak.

He changed the fixtures all just right,
   Only thing is, he bolted them too tight.

The house was old, the pipes were weak,
   Oh my Gosh, they sprung a leak.

The ceilings dripped from the waterfall,
   Over the rugs and down the hall.

Buckets and buckets he mopped and mopped,
   My brother, Stan, he almost dropped.

To "Home Sweet Home" I then returned,
   My heart stood still, my stomach churned.

My brother, Stan, he felt so bad,
   How could I ever be so mad?

A plasterman did smooth and plaster
   No one could tell there was ever a disaster.

Now the rugs are new, the house is dried,
   I'm sorry now I ever cried.

Catherine Mihalic

Trinity

Jesus help me to walk in the way,
Help me Lord to watch what I say,
Jesus fill my heart from within
with Love - that's where I shall begin.

I sing the song of penance oh Lord,
The sin of envy, of bitterness and of being bored.
I pray that I shall walk closer to thee
for thee alone knows what I ought to be.
I pray for knowledge, wisdom and for love
not only the kind for a mate but for all of mankind
and creatures thereof.
Please Lord rid my heart of fear, jealousy and hate
and fill it with contentment, peace and let love
permeate my being and let love be my fate.

I love thee Lord, I love thee Jesus,
I love thee Holy Spirit,
fill my heart with thee all!

Jeanette Emelia Gotay

"With Angels' Hair"

Tears blur my lonely eyes
Her angels' hair; so long, too lovely
I watch her walk on by
She smiles, I turn shy.

Dreams crash inside my head
Reality turns into nightmare
Heaven won't send to me
The love that's meant to be.

Days drag on, dragging
Each second lasts forever
Alternating gray & blue
Day-dream wishes don't come true.

Life takes its' lonesome course
& Foolishly I choose to follow
Love, still she sees' me blind
Her life has no need for mine.

Hurt fills up my senses
This shattered heart falls to pieces
Crumbling hopeless, helplessly to the ground
As tears drop, emptiness is the only sound.

Donald A. Ankofski

Her Face

She had a deep look in her eyes,
    her glace was on a faraway place.
And when I saw her close her eyes,
    a tear trickled down her face.

With that one tear I saw,
    the hurt and pain etched on her cheek.
And then I saw her lips quiver,
    but through it all, she did not speak.

Beads of sweat clotted the tip of her nose,
    as some strands of hair swept through her face.
And when she opened up her eyes,
    the faraway land still hovered in her gaze.

I looked at her and tried to ask what was wrong,
    and then her eyes blinked once as though.
They spaced to me and meekly replied,
    that she did not even know.

Engulfed with sadness, I shook my head
    and to my surprise so did she.
It was then that I realized,
    that the girl I was looking at, was a reflection of me.

Andrea Y. Ruminer

Battered Will

Reverence preferred, hospitality accepted
Her grace that of a swam
Beneath beauty protected a heart cold and torn
Tasseled by greed and the green monster that separates us all.
How flaunting does sway the evils in even wisest men
Why does this now in time of need come upon me?
I will for strength to carry alone, yet find none.
Can beauty help, knowing of its masquerade?
In perspective it may save for a while
But as does all, the swam will die, leaving hearts colder.
If to find a bird whose heart was full of joy
Fly in chaos, create our own order,
Hearts would need no protection glowing bright.

Jason Prine

The Last Good Bye

She knew it was coming, but didn't expect it so soon
Her happy love filled days now will be filled with dark gloom
Nothing could have prepared her for the strong pain inside
That stabbed her so hard when she said the last good bye

Tears stream out and drop down like rain
Leaving small salty puddles created by pain
Never before has her heart ached so much
Whenever she thinks of his warm gentle touch

How can one person have so much control
Over someone else's affections deep in the soul
He held all her love she gave him to hold
And carries it with him to warm him when cold

Oceans apart and hours away
They look in the sky each different day
Remembering the times they once shared together
And hoping their love will stay there forever.

Aimee R. Moore

Ororo

Her hair is lightning, her garments a cloud.
Her skin is earth, her thunder loud.
She glides on wind and soars on lightning.
Sending rain to restore withered and dying.
She scatters lightning from her hand,
Striking it down upon the land.
Her winds blow wild across the globe,
Causing trees to bow down low.
She's fierce and mighty, yet graceful in form.
She's Ororo, Goddess of the Storm.

Dennis M. Heath

Life In The Sky

If you would like to visit a zoo,
Here's a simple thing you can do.
Whenever you start on your beat,
Board a bus or a car for a ringside seat.

Mother Nature invites you to look and stare,
At the odd things you can see in the air.
With blue sky as the background and silver clouds
as the screen, watch for the show picturing all types of scenes.
Out steps a tiger, a lion and a duck.
Here comes a monkey with his head sticking up.
Brother Rabbit and the tortoise are in for a race
With a blink of the eye, they are about
to change place. Well here's Abe Lincoln, what's he doing there.
It looks as if he's being chased by a bear.
There's the Cro-Magnon man the rarest type
In this modern age, he's a frightful sight.

A duck, an alligator, a boy with a bat
A wingless chicken and a maltese cat.
I must stop right here, but take this tip.
Look for life in the sky on your next zoo trip.

Bernice A. Duckett

The Papa

Once upon a time there was a man name Bert Swift.
He was married to the Nanny. He was like the Nanny.
He's not that bad, he was really nice to me and
my sister, Leah. After a while I started to love
him very much. He was really cool and nice, I like
him very much. On Christmas Day he got me a lot of
presents. That day it was really special to me.
One day he had to leave then I started to cry, I
miss him very much.

Florence Howard

My Father

My father's a man, true and wise,
He's all of joy, a mountain wide,
He walks upright and full of pride,
He's a man who's always by my side.

My father comforts me when I'm sad,
And holds me when I cry.
He laughs with me in times of joy,
My father and me I've come to enjoy.

My father holds me and scolds me,
Comforts me, loves me, tells me I'm his joy.
He's my father, whom I love and adore,
There's no better man in this life of mine,
No man truer or wiser than this father of mine.

Diane Wright

To Adria

Did you know daddy's watching,
He's sitting on a cloud,

So when you do gymnastic's,
You don't have to look around,
Just stretch your hands straight to the sky,
And smile, Oh, so big!!!

'Cuz daddy's watching from above,
Just like he always did,

He'll see you while your swimming,
And at your brownie troop,

Why, daddy, can even see you...
While your at school,

So when your on the playground,
And running all around,

He wants you to be happy,
And to have a lot of fun,

Although he's gone to heaven,
He watches from above,

'Cuz you're his little "angel"
That he made with all his love...

Darlene Girroir

Promoted To Glory

The Lord says, precious in the sight of the Lord is the death of
  His Saints,
To grieve and sorrow for this brother is very faint.
Paul says, for me to be absent from the body is with the Lord to be,
How we should rejoice as we think of what he now sees.

Yes, I fully realize that we would desire to keep him around.
Aren't we selfish for wanting to keep a loved one down?
And I know it is so hard to give our loved ones up,
But just think of him with Christ and him filling his cup.

God says, eye hasn't seen nor ear heard what God has prepared for
  those that love him.
When we meditate on what heaven has to offer our vision must be dim.
So as we come to the end of this life's story,
He would remind us now, don't grieve, I'm promoted to glory.

Harry Masters

All Systems Go

Traffic lights are all green today
I can go as far as my mind will carry me
Stop signs all are turned the other way
Their harsh command I cannot see
Now is there time and space to play
I find I like this running free.

Gail Garner

Angels

"In speaking of the angels he says,'He makes His angels winds,
    His servants flames of fire."   Hebrews 1:8

A brief storm falls as I wait for my slumber.
On this lazy, wistful, thoughtful afternoon
our Heavenly Father reminds me of what's important
in a booming voice of wet streaks in the sky
crashing upon the ground, creating puddles
in the man made crevices of dried cement.

He who created all life and all things on Earth,
blessed is He who can take all our troubles away
as I lie here and ponder my frustrated world.
I look up and see the birds whom He provides for
gracefully take flight among their wet surroundings,
He who creates life and at any time can take it away.

O ye of little faith, take hope, see light.
Ponder the flowers, the trees and the leaves,
the birds without worry and the wet of the sky
How obtrusive the brick and cement seem
especially when drowned beneath the puddles of rain
Take hope, see light — I look up and see, angels.

Brian Howes

"Silenced"

Move, I could not, for I was frozen
His silver front fender stared me in the face
Blowing its hot breath, panting

The driver spoke naught
And neither did I
I just put my hand to my heart as he drove
on by

I kept on going, and I didn't look back
As a single tear of fear and remembrance
crawled down my cheek
Not a soul I did tell of the night
I fell

Bettina L. Davis

Rain

God must be crying because
his tears are falling heavily
onto the pavement
Why is he crying? You ask.

Is it because of the children who
are lost in the garden with no where to go?
I think it is
Look at them now His own children
that were made of His own image
Are now lost souls of the world

Where do we go when everyone has
turned their backs on us? they shouted with fear
In my arms which are always open
to any and everyone

You may become the worst person to
be born in this world but one thing
never changes and that is that
God loves you!

Dorayley Ramses

Snowstorm

Waiting in the night for the snow to fall
Hoping for a prolific shower
  of the stuff that seems to clear the earth
    of all unpleasantness and clean that which is hidden

The dawn creates crystal flecks of magical light
The prisms that have awakened from the sleep
  are eager to glisten towards its source, the sun,
    whose power is providing the warmth of the cold

The quietness pervades all that is a part of nature
Only the creak of the trees and the call of the birds
  signal that all is still alive but yet asleep
    under the blanket of the restfulness

The winds and flurries of the afternoon warn of the approaching night
Time for all living creatures to attend to the needs
  which will provide comfort for the dark and chill
    of the time when light and warmth of the sun must be aided

Unassisted by the services of earth and given technology we plan
Just as the other animals take shelter and food
  to cover and nourish our frailties against the universe
    we huddle together and share our power to survive

    Jan K. Adams

Falling Love

How do I know when our love isn't right
How do I know when I need to fight
Our relationship is important to me
Next to you is where I want to be
When we talk and make love everything's OK
Then the next time we speak you push me away
My emotions and love are something you tease
You treat them like they are blowing in a breeze
I understand your need for space
After you I will not chase
My heart needs to know the score of this game
Is your heart feeling the same
I need to know just where I stand
For you my heart beats like a marching band
I would go to great lengths to hang on to you
What the problem is I have no clue
How do I know when our love isn't right
How do I know when I need to fight
I have one thing to say I don't know what to do
I Love You

    Diane Jensen

Elmer

He spoke of planting impatiens in his Hampton garden—
how he felt alive with his old hands in the dirt,
smelling the spring - earth broken for the first time.
"It is not extraordinary—I've done it always."
He smiled.

A silent moment between generations.
"I just wrote my friends and told them I planted impatience,
I dug the earth, I heard the birds sing."
He bowed his head shyly, almost apologetically.
"I soaked the paper with my tears because I'd just had a stroke—

and I was so happy to plant impatiens again."
My heart stopped for a second.
"Well—say something!" he demanded.
I caught my breathe and wiped my cheek.
What could I say of more importance
than his admission of joy at planting impatience again?

    Jaymie Meyer

For Only A Time

Weren't you just here a minute ago?
How I wish you I did know;
As a bird, you're ever elusive,
Yet like a pig, so passive.

Your marks are seen on all men's faces,
Vividly sketched across natures laces,
Starting unnoticed and slow,
But quickly do they show.

To each has been given the same,
Though having regard for no name;
You're a friend to any,
But enemy of many.

Of all man's gifts most treasured,
You're by far one of the best,
Though most your value not measured,
Until the nearness of appointed rest.

Just as all who have, will or be,
Must reckon themselves with thee,
So you too will face your time,
Though eternally ceasing to chime!

    Joel Holm

Thoughts of Truth

Jesus,
How many times have we reached our hands out
to receive your hands divine
Only to withdraw them for a thought or
deed unkind.
Let our thoughts be guided "Lord" by your
words of truth
So when we reach our hands out again they
will be grasped by you.

    Doug Henning

For My Husband On Valentine's Day

Valentine's day is here at last and it gives me a chance to say,
how much the love I have for you gets bigger each and every day.

You mean so much to me and I just want you to know,
each day that passes makes my love for you grow and grow.

So many times we forget to tell someone we love so dear,
just how happy they make us year after year.

Valentine's day is one of the times to say how much we care,
and our happy life together is a wonderful thing to share.

I am so glad you are my husband and I am your wife,
I am looking forward to being with you for the rest of my life.

    Christine R. Pease

My Husband

Husband, you really light up my life
I am blessed, proud and lucky to be your wife,
We have been through a lot of stormy weather
But god has blessed us to stay together,
After all of the things we've been through
My love has not changed for you,
I know there is a god up above
Because he blessed me with your precious love,
Each and every night on my knees I pray
Thanking god for your love each and everyday,
Love, caring and kindness you give to me
I am as happy as any woman can possibly be,
From way down deep within my heart
God bless us and keep us so we will never part.

    Bertha Redwine

"Simple Happiness"

When I think of all my kin,
How we lived dodging daily sin.

We were happy most all the time,
Laughter and fun we had without crime.

Mamma's seven children 'twas fine,
Papa worked hard nearly all the time.

How we made life so good I'll never know,
We danced, sang and played in the snow.

We all married and made life our own,
Four boys served America, got to roam.

Three girls like Mamma, made happy homes,
Meals and doing for children was condoned.

Loving Mamma and working Papa was proud of all,
God, Jesus and Holy Spirit guided us all with our happy call.

Dorothy Gemes

Panama's Dawn

Dawn, a reminder of renewal, greets mankind.
However, this deadly dawn favored nothing but an untimely, bitter end,
As my lover's decision left my soul like a forlorn traveler in a
    blizzard storm.
Shivering, I imagined the listless spirit of the sea's movement;
In reality, her waves glistened with silvery, pale pinks and gold.
As they chased one another playfully,
My heart scolded their frolicking behavior.
How could they...in time of such hostility and war?
For this deadly dawn stood moments still,
As the waves freely danced their tune to the rhythm of my love's end.

Diana C. Penner

Untitled

I believe in the integrity of man, and in the eternity of the
human spirit.

I believe that dying is not unlike being born. Dying is a
process that is made less frightening with sharing. The sharing of
dying's stages can even bring on uncanny peace especially when
shared with someone you love.

I believe in the comforting of the dying spirit. The body
must be as comfortable as possible before the spirit and emotions
can have opportunity to seek their peace.

I believe in using all of my knowledge and expertise to gain
these ends for the dying. May my path through deaths tunnel be so
lovingly guided.

Ella Mullens

Leopard

Leopard, leopard in the night,
hunts without a cowardly fear of any
man who carries a spear.
For a mortal hand may not touch thy head,
and if they scare away thy keep your fiery
wrath they shall reap.

For you hunt with great skill, and speed, and
to disturb you all men do heed.
For you are a hunter in this savage land, and
may not be touched by a mortal hand.

Chris Tonick

Solari

My friend
    hurts.
Today she has said goodbye to a loved one
For today she buries him.
And I hurt:
    For her, with her.
I, too, have buried a loved one. Frozen in time is that day.
A little one so innocent, so loving.
My sweet little one,
    my precious child.
Never let her memory dull, Lord;
Prick my heart!
I gently welcome the bittersweet pangs
For then I still have her—
Here, with me.

My friend hurts.
Will she embrace her grief, her deep pain?
I hope so, for then we can hurt
    and heal
        together.

Donna Forrest

I Always Succeed

No matter whether it's night or day,
I always manage to push evil out of my way.
    I always succeed!

My friends treat me wrong,
But I remain strong.
    I always succeed!

When nothing seems to go my way,
I kneel down and pray.
    I always succeed!

When I was faced by problems that I didn't understand,
God solved them and took my hand.
    I always succeed!

As a child, my parents used to fight;
But now, I am my family's glorifying light.
    I always succeed!

When no one was there to help me,
God came to my rescue and made me see.
    I always succeed!

Of all the times that I have cried,
God blessed me and stood by side. I always succeed!

Clarence Easter

Iridis

I wrap myself in night's silken cloak;
I breathe the air of secrecy that surrounds me.
With eyes of fire I watch the world go by;
It runs from me, like death and time unchanging.
I swallow the light that filters from the moon;
To breathe my joy where dark things seldom crawl.
I listen as screams fill my mind at every turn;
Screams I cause in my everlasting thirst.
I soothe and take, and time becomes me;
Like a fine cloak, it wraps itself around my soul.

So come with me, my little one;
I'll show you pleasures that never end.
I'll soothe your soul and calm your lusts,
And wrap my nighted cloak about you.
I'll taste your life and hold you tight;
And day will pass us by unnoticed.

Christian Aldridge

Obituary

My solitude is of crucial concern to the dispossessed,
I am a reservoir of their dreams — A flawed avatar shifting moods
between patches of memory,
Here is the island of rooms where my lovers had lain,
Sweat pouring from bodies as we shared kisses that tasted like hope,
Here was the echo of an embrace as I reached for the city — extending
my arms toward an obituary of thrills, here a man child
shudders beneath a whores kiss creating a collapse of years,
Here the harlem river was a womb of indifference until an image of
vengeance stirred the dying tide and there is the smell of blood,
Here a flood of red interrupts a pimp making the sign of the cross
while winters sour ice reflects the scars of a whores welcome, the
uptown 4:17 meanders along a tunnel of knives — my dead are on
    schedule,
I sing to them — give sustenance to their reality — slice their dreams
with wet kisses and a thousand warm words, the distilled hopes of
futures fractured by probability do not dissuade me,
I am relentless, this wound of solitude seems to encourage advances,
I cut the throat of sanity — spread fire upon false hopes and embrace
the inferno, the burning shrivels the tongue,
Here I have no voice — yet I sing to my dead and bellow in triumph

David A. Robinson

"I Am"

I am just one person, I am a simple beam of light.
I am the towering mountains, with their majestic height.
I am the silver moon, that shines up in the sky.
I am the 3 year old who's always asking why.
I am the seasons as they slowly change.
I am animals roaming on a range.
I am every single question, I am every hidden fear,
I am the reflection, that's seen in a mirror.
I am the falling leaves of an old/Ancient tree.
I am every single person I am me.

Beth Parlow

Untitled

I am the background music of the mountains
I am transparent in sunlight
and you can see my bed lined with satin smooth earth-hued stones.

Clouds color me opaque.
In the wind I ripple like a dune.
Rain makes dimples.
Then we become one.

In winter I forge my way through fields of frozen diamonds.
In spring the sun releases me into liquid life
and I joyously rush down the rock staircase of my mountain home.
My energy is a rolling boil; a gentle simmer. Sometimes I even go
    backwards.

In summer people love to loll along my flanks
    to cool feet in my flow
    to listen to my whoosh and whirl
If you concentrate, you can hear my heartbeats.

In the autumn of mustard-colored Aspens, I prepare for winter -
    Reassured by my seasonal routine,
    counting on mankind not to betray me —

I am a mountain stream
I am forever —

Dena Kaye

Hey, Mr. Monkey! Wait For My Lullaby!

Mr. Monkey, if you jump on trees,
I am with you.
Mr. Monkey, if you walk on grass,
I am with you.

Mr. Monkey, if only you will give me a toy,
So I can give my baby some joy.
Or even a jingle bell,
So I can put him to bed.

Then he will cease to cry.
And I can bid you goodbye.
Mr. Monkey oblige me, I beg you.
Please Mr. Monkey, before you go through.

Buchi F. Offodile

Sonnet For The New Year

I watch the sullen hours shuffling past,
I beckon and I coax them on their way,
For every hour is longer than the last
And every moment dawdles in the day.

The plodding weeks that know not when they're spent
But dangle like the last dried autumn leaf.
Tenaciously they cling, and weary, bent,
Eke out the last full moment of their grief.

The lumbering months that wait upon the moon
Like mournful dancers, each in clinging robe
With heavy steps to a lugubrious tune
Mark out the pivot of the slowly turning globe.

Then why do I sit, and with nostalgic tears
Mourn the swift passing of the years?

Florence Young

Dancing In Her Heart

She won't come in out of the rain.
I beg and plead with her,
but all she hears is the thunder.
All she sees is a better time in her life,
dancing in the rain on the bridge over the river.
She sees his smiling face
and his laughter echoes in her memory.
Quickly it becomes the worst time in her life.
He dances closer to the edge.
He is waltzing on the brink of death.
He danced too close.
He taunted the devil,
rocks forty feet below and rapids rushing over them.
She watched the waters pick him up,
and carry him downstream.
Now the rain dances in her eyes,
and he dances in her heart.

Christina Godfrey

I Believe

I believe in sun even when it's not shining.
I believe in darkness even when light is blinding.
I believe in beauty although standing in a barren dessert.
I believe in horror although beholding a beautiful red blossom.

I believe in happiness even when eyes are full of doubt.
I believe in tears even when the cease to fall.
I believe in falling when standing on steadfast ground.
I believe in standing although I get pushed down.

I believe in past even when memories are forgot.
I believe in the future although there fails to be a present.
I believe in missing someone even when next to you the stand.
And even when I'm alone, I believe in love.

Gerrick Stanton

Confused

You told me that you loved me
I believed every loving words you said to me
Then you go on your own trying to get
    something out of life.
You left me for just a little while,
I thought that you were doing it for us.
But later, I found out that
    you had your heart set on someone else.
You really hurt my feelings.
I stop believing in the word, "Love"
I will never forgive you but I love you
    too much to hold a grudge on you.
Now I'm confused, I want to love you
    and at the same time I hate you
    for what you have done to me.
I will never forget how much you
    hurt my feelings.
From now on, I just have to live
    with it as long as I'm with you.

    Ella Mae Henry

Never Climb Walls

I saw a nightingale that sang very sadly;
I came up and asked the reason of sadness.
There was no answer, but only surprise
In the bird's widely open eyes.

I dared to ask for the second time
Rejecting the thought that stuck in my brain,
And was telling me something in me was wrong;
The bird did not stop the song.

"A very strange bird," I thought to myself
Annoyed by the silly and stupid creature,
"Why has he to sing so sadly at night
When days are so bright?"

"You're odd, poor bird, you're enormously queer;
Just notice the joy of the life that surrounds you.
The life is so wonderful, the sky's always blue;
Look at the world around you.

Hey, tell me what troubles you, makes you unhappy;
I don't see anything that can cause sorrow!"
I cried out in anger seeing just sad surprise in the bird's
widely open eyes looking at me through the bars of the cage.

    Andrey Nedilko

Willow

As one day I wondered through the wood
I came upon an essence thought of as existence never could.
And as I was fatigued and ready to fall,
this marvel still winded me of my breath and all.
Thoughts raced through my mind of it's old age and wisdom of
time.
As my elementary eyes studied it's infinite shape
I could feel it's powerful stillness and the art of it's masculine
drape.
It's arms revealed the sorcery over the land
and love for it's survivors as it held out it's hand:
upon which to nest, and to feed, and to grow;
to swing and to play, and to climb, and to discover what you know.
This native keeper of control.
This constant giver of all, but it's soul.
The ruler of strength and ongoing might,
who for it's defenders will fight, through past and future decades
of night.
This warrior that stands proud, but loves even though
left me praising and pondering so over how it was once to tiny to
show, but grew to be the majestic willow.

    Emilie Belanger

Separation

I'll stand on my feet to see you next to me.
I cannot go before you. I want to gaze at you forever and a day.
If forever was a minute, by God I would not waste it.

What is life without you? Do not leave me! Do not let me go!
Do not let me stand in sorrow, like a naked tree wrestling
against the Winter's frozen days.

Oh, I want to see you. Let me see you!
Let me be the Ocean in your eyes,
For I shall dive in them and drown my last breath.
I'll fly like a breeze to steal a nightingale's note
and savor your love in its scented melody.
I'll steal the glorious Sun for you my love
and melt it in my arms for you to drink its sunshine with your eyes.

Open your wings my child, open your wings!
You are me and I am you; A body of two directions
and a soul of one love, that holds our thread of life that never breaks.

I'll stand on my feet to see next to me.
To heal my scorned and wounded honor,
    and pray for the nightmare to melt away
which for a day's moment had crippled my destiny.
I'll always stand on my feet.

    Amy Kaskadami

The Encounter

One day while walking in my garden,
I chanced to meet a little sparrow
  Who hopped onto my path.
We stared at each other and I said, "Hello!"
He looked at me quizzically and seemed to say,
"You know, I live here too. Let's share
    This world together."
As we go to and fro, we will encounter many people.
May we always accept and love them
As we share this world together.

    Edna Zimmerman Prentis

The Song That Never Dies

Everything I look upon is the sun within your eyes,
I cling to my usual bearing though my endless Spirit cries,
I fancy myself a warrior, whose time has long since past,
Living only for Love, which I think I've found at last,
My Spirit belongs to an ancient age, troubled by these times,
I console myself with bits of romance and helpless little rhymes,
Though my time has passed my Essence over, my Destiny concealed,
I know that with you beside me, a path would be revealed,
You could give me your understanding of this detailed modern stage,
I would show you the righteous way, custom to my age,
Life and Love forever, as the Songbird cries,
The melody in my Heart for you, the Song that never dies.

    EB

With Love

I can't imagine life without you
I close my eyes and hope it's not true
I just want to hear your voice once again
I never dreamed I'd lose my best friend
Too many memories in my brain
I know nothing can ease my pain
So sad and empty I am inside
I feel like all I've done is cry
But now you're in a better place up above
Looking down on us with all your love
And even though we were torn apart
Your memory will always live in my heart.

    Diana Carroll

Magical Thinking

When I want to go to a place that's serene
I close my eyes and set the scene.
When I want someone to be what I think
My thoughts create in less than a wink.
The magical thinking that takes me there
Covering up the truth I'm aware.
Sometimes I do it feeling better just then
Away from the truth with my magical pen.
I rewrite the person color in the place
Change all the stuff I need to replace.
It's really quite easy I avoid any pain.
Nothing to lose and nothing to gain.
My magical mind journeys wherever it need be
Controlling thoughts in my head when I choose not to see.
I don't change a person nor a thing or a place
I keep it real simple with my mental erase.
Magical thinking a fantasy ride
How often we choose that truth be denied.
Rose colored glasses one size fits all
There when I need them to feel ten feet tall!

Barbara P. Fields

One Single Touch

He placed his hand upon my cheek.
I could not move nor could I speak.
And I instantly knew that a single touch
Would never again mean so much.
Like the shifting sands beneath the ocean
I was so moved by this gentle motion.
It was an act of God in its purest form.
Now I have naught but a memory to keep me warm.
And as I remember his touch I look for the rose
That beyond my bedroom faithfully grows
Throughout the seasons of my life
Reflecting our years as man and wife.
Now the rose and I will both grow strong
As his voice becomes the wind that whispers our song.
And it is his breath that will now caress my cheek.
Yet, again, I will not be able to speak
For my soulmate no longer shares my bed
As the autumn of my life looms ahead.
So 'til I am touched by the wings of a snow white dove
I know I will not feel such complete love.

Donna H. Martin

The Touch

As I walked down the shady lane one quiet and peaceful day
I could smell the many flower as I walked along the way
From the fragrance I could tell which flower it belong
For God has given me a special gift
To name each flower from it's fragrance as I walk along

The grass felt just like a quilt with it's many shades of green
This brings to mind the beauty of things I've never seen

I heard someone approaching as I walked along my way
A hand rested on my shoulder this quiet and peaceful day
From the touch I can't explain the feeling that I had
For God was leading me as I walked down the shady lane

The sun did shine through the clouds
Its rays did shine on me
One wonders how I can see much beauty
Even though I cannot see

Carl B. Mosier

Mumps

I had a feeling on my neck, on the side were two big bumps
I couldn't swallow anything at all because it was mumps mother tied
it with a piece and then Rufus, Junior and no one else but mart
was left because he didn't have a mumps rag on.
He teased at us and laughed and said whenever
he went by its vinegar and lemon drops and pickles,
just to make us cry but on Tuesday mart was very sad and cried
because he got the mumps and not a one said sortings to
anybody any more.

Beckie Cunningham

Untitled

I cried last night
I cried for you
I cried for me
I cried for all the pain you had endured
I cried last night
I miss you so
I long to hear your dear voice say my name
I want to hold your hand in mine
I feel the magic of the love we shared so many years
I loved you so
I love you still
I miss you so
I cried last night

Geraldine R. Smith

Forever Us

Sweetheart, before I met you
I did not know what love was
Then you came along and started something...
You set my soul a fire
With heat so intense
It melted the sun like ice
There's more than enough heat for a lifetime
of love.... and passion....
I would burn a thousand years in hell for you
I want you to forever be my flame
And roam the depths of the earth with me
And to have you never leave my side....

Allen Bednarski

Unconditional Love

When I look at Jesus, I do not see nail scarred hands,
I do not see the scars from the crown or the pierce in his side,
I cannot see the pain brought to him by man.

Instead, I see a vision of his body whole and white,
unpierced and untouched by man, wrapped in such a great light,
so pure, so white, a man with out-stretched arms, calling us
to his light, giving unconditional love for you and I, he
reaches out for us, begging us to see and understand, the
love within that's wholesome and pure. The love within this
is our cure.

A love that's in everyone's heart, if you would just seek and
find. How you might ask? Jesus it rattles my mind. How do I
find a love of this kind?

Then Jesus answers. Stand by my side, listen with your heart,
Not the mind. It is important to use the heart, not the mind, for
the mind can be fearful and drenched with sin, but the heart is dealt
with deep within, it wishes not to be broken or filled with hate and
sin. Trust in your heart and hear what it has to say.

So open your heart then your mind, then let Jesus show you.
LOVE TRULY ISN'T BLIND.

Frances Stovall

Love Hurts

Everybody said that life will go on.
I don't know if I can live with you gone.

I have to live with all my fears.
Never talking to you, never making it clear.

Now my eyes swell up with rain.
My heart is exploding with all this pain.

I felt the answer in my heart.
Knowing from this day on we would be apart.

Now I sit here feeling all alone.
Hoping and praying that you will phone.

I wonder why I feel this way.
I still love you what can I say.

All the feelings I try to hide.
I keep them locked up deep down inside.

I never want to say goodbye.
You have hurt me I can not lie.

Does my pain show, can you see?
You say you love me and then you leave...

Billie Wade

The Image In The Mirror

Who is that dreadful image as I gazed into the mirror
I don't like the way she looks... I wish she'd disappear

She's old and she looks tired and there are wrinkles on her face
The time has sped by so fast, I feel I'm out of place

What happened to the dark brown hair, the figure that once was trim
The youth that once stood before you now looks very grim

Why is this happening to me, is life playing some cruel game
Maybe something is wrong with the mirror, I'll give it total blame

I once was very pretty, I once had all the stares
The lovely brown flock on my head is now covered with grey hairs

My eyes no longer glisten...they are full of tears inside
I can't stand what I'm seeing, I want to run...I want to hide

I thought getting older was more graceful, am I running out of time
I wish I could go back to those happy days when I still was in my prime
There is nothing left to show for, I feel I'm losing my mind
I'm all alone and miserable.....the year's were never kind!

Gloria Sanders

Sweet Appeal

Here we are, just me and you,
I got something to say, I wanna make love to you.
So baby take my hand, hold me close,
I'll pour the wine slowly baby, make a toast.
I glance in your eyes, you return my stare,
Put your arms around me baby, let me know you're there.
True the definition of a kiss no doubt,
If you don't know it, let's find out.
This sweet feeling, I feel inside,
My emotions are free, I cannot hide.
My heart is here for you ten fold,
Feelings for each other, together we hold.
Love at first sight is my fate,
But wait, recuperate, then contemplate.
Your heart and your love make me feel,
The real deal, love appeal.
My feelings for you are oh so strong,
I'll keep you in my arms where you belong.
My affection so strong, my emotions so deep,
A dreamland of togetherness, so please let me sleep.

Daryl Watkins

My Awakening

I dreamed of fame and fortune once, so many years ago.
I don't recall the name I'd chosen, something elegant I do suppose.
To be known, respected, even envied and very much adored.
I would make an everlasting mark, a peer of the most renown.

Somehow I lost sight of my goals, letting the tide of life sweep me along.
Suddenly I awoke in a frightening, dark and unfamiliar place - alone.
I seemed to be struggling to find my way - not home, but to a light.
Doing things then, not of my heart, but simply to survive.

The course of my life forever altered, not quite glad to be alive.
No medals or worthy recognition, just living a life.
Daily doing what I must, the endlessness of routine.
What kind of an example have I set, who looks up to me?

Deep inside where the waters are still, the gnaw of regret lingers.
Not that I have accomplished nothing, there was mothering to be done,
But with the gifts I had been given, I never really tried.
The passion and the fire, now a smoldering ember that has all but died.

There are memories of raising two sons I cherish, and yes -
    knowing love.
I'm sure I did my best for them, but what if I had stayed my course?
Could I have done so much more, touched so many other lives?
I do not want to leave this world, a disappointment to myself,
    my sons and God.

Cynthia French

God The Mother

I the unborn,
I don't see my mother, but I sense what she provides.
I sense the warmth,
I sense the nourishment she provides,
I sense the nurturing, the environment in which I grow,
until I die to the womb and see my mother.

As we, our lives entwined, can't see our God,
but through others,
and through the actions that we do,
and the creation that we see.
We are nourished and nurtured,
until we die to this womb and see our God.

James Vorbach

Alone, With Love

Searching, searching, oh love be there for me;
    I don't want to be alone with love.
My heart is filled, I search, I want to give;
    I don't want to be alone with love.
So many people looking for love, wanting love;
    Why, why must I be alone with love.
Eyes meet, hearts open, souls reaching out;
    Love, come to me!
Let your eyes see, let your heart feel, your soul
    desire, love, beautiful love.
Love must be shared, love is two. Come to me.
    I don't want to be alone with love.

Dolores Bryl

Passion

As I gaze up at the stars
I dream of only you,
holding me close;
kissing, caressing.
I look into your eyes, I like what I see:
Come closer,
Together with me to see
the moon, the stars,
and the sky;
For they are fore us
if we wish it to be.

Cherie Courtney

Untitled

I had a dream the other night
I dreamed you held me: Oh so very tight
You told me not to worry
You told me not to fear
You even told me not to shed one tiny tear
And daddy dear you did
What you always did best
You have laid all my fears to rest
It's been so very hard
Since you left us that day
I think about you often
And each day I pray
That you won't forget us
Even though our lives are in disarray
Yes: I had a dream the other night
Thanks for holding me so very tight
And giving me the foresight
To do things mostly right.

Barbara Barcomb

Alone At Last!

Alone is how I want to be and alone
I feel I can achieve my goals, my dreams
But always when alone I feel, it seems
As though the world is not real.

I search and search for someone who will
Bring to me the kinds of things that I want
In life. I face each day with renewed hope
That today is when my life will change.

Sometimes I sit and think that while
I live in happy and contented bliss there is no one
Who shares in all that makes me smile or even weep
Although I feel ok, It seems to everyone I'm incomplete.

I know there is someone waiting out there for me,
But in my busy state, It's very difficult to see
That special someone who will bring to me
The satisfaction that I get from being alone and just me.

Delia M. Diaz

Mercury

I am, silvery white, "water silver," watch me at night.
I glow all alone, for I prefer myself over radon.
I walk on the table number eighty, periodic that is, as if
you were debating.
You see me a lot, in many forms, I'll be liquid if you're in the norm.
But I also produce light, vapor, sun and florescent seen at night.
I am highly resistant to corrosion, too bad your body can't
consist of my poison.
I lurk you everyday on vegetables promised to be safe.
I reach your mouth a lot, usually when you're feeling hot.
I'm what tells you you're sick, or find you're lying a bit.
I've been around awhile, prehistoric times, but someone lost my file.
I am fairly heavy at 200.59, that's me, my atomic weight.
Me my chemical family metal, Hg, me, my chemical symbol
though we don't sound alike, comes from Latin Hydrargyrus, right.
You'll find me in a friend, mineral cinnabar but that's the end.

Jammie Sidley

Prescription

I told you I needed to do something uplifting
And you let me help fix the barn roof.
I lost nothing but a bucket of nails
And it hit no one as it slid to the ground.
Invigorated by the sun and wind
And my unique view of the world,
I did come away uplifted and soothed,
Feeling bright as the tin's reflection.

Brenda Whitten

Driftin'

I'm a drifter on the high plains of life.
I go from one place to another,
From one friend to another.
Like a piece of dust blowin' on the wind.
Like a piece of driftwood
Floatin' on the sea.
Driftin' from shore to shore, from friend to friend.
Not knowing
Where I'll be or who I'll be.
Driftin' out there alone.
Just to come ashore.
Just to be thrown out again.
Just to be alone.
Just to find a new shore.
Just to find a new friend.
Will I drift back to an old shore, to an old friend.
Or
Will I keep on driftin' AWAY?

Julie L. Van Fosson-Robinson

Boy With His Thoughts

When a man is fighting his way out in the gloom,
I guess he is always thinking of home.
And when he sees an awful sight -
something in side of him gives him fright.

But then he thinks of his mother and dad.
Then the things aren't so sad.
Suddenly he looks up in the sky and sees
the stars up in the heavens so high with his
eyes filled with glee and wonders when he can
come home to a land that is clean and free.

Betty Jane Selhorst-Leanen

"I Miss You"

Ever since you moved away
I have been missing you from faraway
I still remember through the good and bad times
We have laughed and cried
But I don't have much more pride

You have broken my heart in tiny little pieces
I don't know what else to say, except
What happened to all those kisses

Till now I sit and think
But I don't know a single thing
I always thought that you were my king

I will never forget
But I know that you'll regret
I might as well not say anything
'bout the ring that you gave

I thought we had started a relationship
But I knew I was wrong
I will never forget
the day you sang me a song

Chantal Kianoun

The Corner; The Hole

Walk around the corner fall in a hole, walk around the
corner where did it all go?...
A dark lonely place full of anger and pain. Walk around
the corner fall in a hole. A cold empty boage seeming
endless and grey. Walk around in circles drifting down
drifting fast. Walk around with nothing, walk around alone.
Walk around the corner fall in a hole. Walk around the
corner, where did it all go?...

Edna McClellan

Top Shelf

I have many memories of our times.
I have many sad times of our life.
When you and I had parted for all the good
and bad of it, I put it upon a top shelf.
There are so many times, I wish I could just
clear that top shelf, not to remember any
of those memories which still bond us together.

Hoping they break like fine China.
Too be able to sweep them up and too
Dispose of them, never to be able too creep
into my mind, and soul again.
If things we're different, which they aren't,
I would never have had a top shelf——
to be cluttered with memories and
sad times, so it can be dusted off when
you creep into my mind, my soul.

Cassandra Lee

I Am Dead Now!

I am dead now; my life is through.
I have no more places to go, or things to do.
So forget my life; it's best for me and you.
It's so hard to see the sorrow and pain your going through.

Everywhere you go, I see you. I see the stuff of mine
Being packed and locked, never to look through;
And I see all the pain your going through.
I feel the guilt as I look upon you.

Yet there is no way that I can help you.
I have had a great life,
and I want you to have one too!

Bronwyn Simbeck

Forever

    When it is my time to leave
I have not really gone, I will
still live in each Birds Song.
I will still see through each
sunrise, and grow still each night
when it closes its eyes.
The wind is my voice, hear me whisper to you?
And know I am smiling when a
flower starts to bloom.
Hear my sighs with each falling leaf,
for when it is cold, only then I'll Sleep.
But do not Be sad, for I will Come again,
you will hear my laughter, "Forever", on the wind.

Judy L. Killen

Walking On History

I have borne the years of life's journey
I have walked along the history of life's past
As I enter slowly the days of my autumn
I savor the moments, these precious moments
As I live my life's treasures
And as the passion within my heart,
Still yearns for life's pleasures:
Forming warm memories within the pages of life's book
That others may walk on my history
To form their life's past.

Bernadette Kolpacki

Statue of Ambiguity

Mother cries and sleeps without you; incompletion in her eyes
Honestly she tries to play your part but she's only half of me
    Not self conscious; just insecurity
Crossed arms restrain the guilt within and simulate feign fenders
Resuscitating anger and save me from the hands of apathy
    Am I who I am; who am I to be; Statue of Ambiguity

Mother said I looked like you today; then I said something, she said, you'd say
Do you ever think what I've become; do you realize you're probably wrong?
The saboteur of chastity, reflecting my aggressions at me
Don't know how else to say; like the clouds, ashes to ashes blow over and away
    I can smell the coming storm rage; dead sensitivity

And the wind will burn my face; while eyes have grown so pale
What are my means of escape if I go down in flames; let me burn
In this maddened fairy tale where no one comes in; no one gets hurt
Oh no color; no more pages to turn; with no footsteps to follow or heed
I planted my roots in bad soil and grit my teeth at the sight I see
My blood rolls off all the broken glass; am I to be the bad seed

    Everything that grows must die; makin' my way despite
Ya can't learn to care; daddy you don't care where your child goes at night
    Father.....why do I hate?

Brian J. Lawson

"Children"

One day the Lord looked upon His paradise and to His eyes came a tear
For in all His wonder, He forgot Adam needed a child to be near
So He commanded that forever that children's smiles be for all to see
And He whispered to Adam to be as a child for that is how He wonted
    mankind to be.

From the unity between Man and woman the Lord provided for the making
of a little girl or boy. He only asked that whatever seed grew, would
be welcome as a great joy. Each day a new child comes upon the earth,
the angels whisper and I know what they say. Today, in his mercy He
has given mankind another chance to understand a better way.

Lord thank you for the children they make the world hope for it to be
a better place. Let us all try to love another with a love as pure as
a child's trusting face. Children they say belong only to the father
and loving Mother. But I believe children belong to all for we are the
same as one another.

Children are born and they are innocent of prejudice against creed or
race. Their happy hearts only know love, for it makes the world a
better place. When children gather they laugh and play, and to each
other they let each have their say. Why can't grown ups teach the
children God's chosen way?

John N. Adam

A Room For God

I would like to ask You God to be my lifetime Guest; to stay at my
Home and be the Head of my Household. You can have the top Floor. I
would like your advice on all of my Problems because you are a problem
solver. And God, I would like for You to be my Interior Decorator
because I love the job You did on Your World. How You gave us Four
Seasons, and dressed each Season to Perfection. How You put Your
trees to Sleep in the Winter with Your white snow and then You wake
them up with Your Spring Raindrops. Then in the Summer You bring the
Flowers and Plants to Life. But "Oh" what a beautiful sight to see,
how You decorate Your Fall with all of the many colors of your leaves,
so I know that I could never pay You for what You are worth. So I
would like to be Your Walking Witness giving You the Glory for all
things.

Holy Spirit and Evelyn Clayborn

"Uncertainty"

My child, how do I help you understand:
You're young and so carefree
Tossed to and fro: in life's flow
By this age of uncertainty

Still so frail and fragile
Like a newly planted tree
And every 'ill wind that blows
Shakes your roots with uncertainty

I brace you with reassurance
Straighten you true and tall
Praying that a most destructive one
won't come and cause you, my
twig, to fall

Lord give me strength to encourage you
Until wisdom lets you clearly see
That faith enables us to live our lives
With less uncertainty

But when there's times you need someone
You can always count on me
For I've walked a lot of miles
In the footsteps of uncertainty

Linda H. Willingham

Death Of A Loved One

Six years have passed, it's been awhile
your memories on my mind
I was young and didn't know
but time has helped me find
the hurt I feel, for you each day
will be there all my life
No matter how I fight to win
My heart is full of strife
Your memories linger on
There's nothing I can do
each chapter in my life
Leads me back to thoughts of you
No matter what I say or do
I cannot turn back time
The way I feel, the hurt I show
Keeps your memories on my mind.

Larry L. Hardig Jr.

Aging

Like honey to a bee
your life is love to me
As time erases passion strong
The depth of our caring moves along
Becoming an invisible protective cloak
That blocks the pains aging hurls
against we two
Still we cling together happily facing
life anew
For forty years are but a day
When precious love is here to stay!

Bev Palef

Family Ties

When mom and dad left this world
For a better place to roam.
It made me feel so very much alone.
But when I look into your eyes,
I know that they are home.
Now we are together with a bond
of love forever, for I know we'll
never be alone.

Mary Ellen Trine

The Center

Enthusiasm, Happiness, and Joy you see
Do give opportunity for us to be
What truly we can achieve in Life
To set us free from our strife
Take the meaning to your heart
As all things from this do start.

Irwin B. Sower

Baby

Baby,
your first kick,
your first touch,
cannot escape my memory.
That feeling forever lingers on.
But in your own way,
that first kick,
that first touch,
was a sweet, sad, goodbye,
Mother.

Mary Ellen DeCosta

Love

I love to watch you sleep at night
your beauty I behold.

I love it when you laugh aloud
your smile uncontrolled.

I even love to care for you
when something gets you down.

I love it when your all dressed up
and were out on the town.

I love it when your holding me
for everyone around to see.

I love to watch you horse around
and even when you act a clown.

I love to watch the sun on you
I love all that you do.

I'll never get enough of you
this vow I do hold true.

Patricia Walkins

For

For the months
you waddled around,
For the mood swings
that got you down.

For the days
you spent at my school,
For the times
I acted a fool.

For the heat
cast from a stove,
For all the lies
that you were told.

For the years
that I did not,
For all the thanks
that I forgot.

For the confidence
You've given me,
My Love to You MOTHER
God Bless Thee...

Michael Earl Ellington

Drugs

You life is a mess,
you think drugs are the only way to
relieve your stress.
In your mind you think the
drugs are working,
yet in your mind the
problems are still lurking.
All you want is to forget,
however you can't hide it your
still upset.
The people around you fade
away.
And that is the price you have
to pay.
So please don't do drugs!

Loren Barrie

School Year

Dawn
You see me
tall, menacing teacher.
I see you
small, frightened child.

Midday
toys, ABCs, finger paint, snack.
You see me
tall, familiar friend.
I see you
small, calm student.

Sunset
goodbyes, hugs, tears.
You see me
tall, familiar father.
I see you
bigger, confident son.

Jason Gorbel

"Life"

Life is like a book.
You never know what will
happen next.
For everyday is like a page
a page of wonder.
What will that wonder be?
Will it be good or will it
be bad?
But till we find out lets
Take it step by step
day by day or
page by page.

Jessica Jacques

Loving Him

You can't stop talking about him.
You can't stop thinking about him.
You can't stop dreaming about him.
You can't stop loving him.

You can't help shedding tears over him
You can't help looking at him
You can't help wanting to be with him.
You can't help loving him.

You try to stop obsessing over him.
You try to keep yourself alive.
You try to go on.
But you never stop loving him.

Nicole Arana

You, Alone

You make me feel ugly
You make me feel unwanted
You look at me like I don't exist

You do not understand my feelings
you really don't want to.

You live for you, you look only at you,
you want only you.

Well;

I am not ugly
I am not unwanted
I do exist.

And I am sorry for you.
For when you die,
only you will remember you.

Lynn Doud

Giving

Give of yourself,
You know you can
You're loaded with talent
Someone is waiting
For your helping hand.
Your smile, your touch
Your words can heal,
Can't you see
How they can feel?
Of course, you can
Keep giving, if ever so small,
Some talent, some help
to that special pal
You'll be happy for life
to know you cared,
If only one
person with which you shared,
A smile, a touch, a helping hand,
keep giving to someone
And make them feel GRAND.

Paul P. Hedlund

"The Rose"

Love is like a rose
you handle it with care
and the color and the beauty!
is all that it will bare.

At first you stand alone
then eventually side by side
Now, we become as one
With this I can not hide.

Love is something special
true love is hard to find
My love for you is pure
In my heart and in my mind.

Now that this is pledged to you
my love, my life, my man
I can honestly say to you
"Together we will stand."

With this poem I give to you
my all and everything,
and with this key I give to you
my "heart" is in your "hands"

Jean McMillan

Shattered

I am out of chances.
You gave me many,
I took none.
I regret that now
As you tell me of your love
for her.
You'll never know how I hurt.
I gave you my heart
And for a time I had yours.
Suddenly mine is shattered
As it falls to the ground,
Dropped by you
To make room for hers.

Meredith Grether

Still Of The Morning

Still of the morning
you couldn't hear me say
that I'll always love you,
but I needed to get away.

No wind was blowing
everything was standing still,
but still when I walked out the door
I felt that morning chill.

Please try and understand
as I turn away,
I will never come back to you
cause it was never meant to be.

Still of the morning
you could hear my tear drops falling,
I know I will always regret
but I most try to forget.

No one will know how much I suffered so
but the still of the morning -
you will feel the morning chill for my tears
were falling
when, that day, I disappeared.

Nancy Robinson

The Forest

The forest is wide and dark and deep
You can see from where you are
Shaded grass covering the earth
Trees that touch the stars

But look from where I call my place
And things seem not the same
The eerie, mystical sight it becomes
Can make you forget your name

The soaring trees that touch the sky
Become menacing towers of pain
They strike the clouds in the sky
Forcing down the bitter rain

The once green and flowing grass
Now stands brown and dormant
Weeds are overgrown and strangling
Serving as a living torment

Deeper still amidst the dark and death
Somehow living and able to cope
Grows one lonely, budding flower
Which almost gives the forest hope

Joey Cupp

Love Letter

For the joyful elation
You brought that bright morn
When you arrived
Our waited firstborn.

Daughter, I love you!

For the daily delight
Of your childhood days.
Your first words, first steps,
Your dear little ways.

Daughter, I love you!

For the pleasure and pride
In your growing-up years,
With talents unfolding,
Shared laughter and tears.

Daughter, I love you!

For the closeness we feel,
Since you are a wife and mother,
For the friendship we enjoy
As we pray for each other.
Donna, I love you!

Lynadese Calhoun

"Death"

What is my destination,
  you ask.
Does it really matter,
  I retort.
We are all in such a hurry.
And for what reason,
  I ask.
So we may all reach the same point.
Sure, we may all take a different path.
But somehow we all end up there.
  Where, you ask.
With a sadness in my voice, and eyes,
  I reply.
Death.

Pamela Marie Percle

Dare To Discover... Who You Are

You are the one that is my friend,
You are the one that helps,
You are the one who is nice,
You are the one that is good in class.

You are the one that can win,
You are the one who gets checks,
You are the one who's not a brat,
You are the color of light brown.

You are the one who is the best,
You are the one who is the pest,
You are the one who is the boss
And you are my class.

Madison Claire Roach

Something Of Yourself

Something of yourself, dear God,
You have put in the seed
and the seed in its pod,
and, oh, what a wondrous mystery,
You have put your Spirit
like a seed in me.
May I bear fruit
to honor Thee.

Marjorie L. Turner

My Friend

My friend, my friend,
You are so special to me.
How was it that we came to be
to meet by chance, a twist of destiny.

You make me search my inward thoughts.
I put before you all my doubts,
and together we try to figure them out.

When I think of friend,
I think of you.
Please let me be the same for you.

I know you need my strength and logic.
They are gifts that we can share.
But a friend like you is beyond compare.

If it weren't for you.
These times of trial
Would leave me helpless as a child.

My friend, my friend
you are so special to me.
How was it that we came to be?
It was the hand of God that sent me thee.

Linda Smith Coggins

My Sister My Friend

You are my sister.
You are my friend.
How can you leave?
You'll make it all end.

You have to go.
I know that it's true,
But when you're gone
I'll really miss you.

I've helped you to pack.
You're ready to go.
I'll always be here.
I want you to know.

We've been through a lot.
Now we start something new.
I'll always remember
My time spent with you.

I'll talk to you often,
And letters I'll send
I'll love you forever
My sister, my friend.

Michelle Zearing

Weekends

Adventuresome are my weekends
Without a moment to spare
Committing no great sins
And having not a care

Secret are my weekends
My parents don't have a clue
Spending them with my friends
They really know what I do

Risky are my weekends
But escaping trouble by far
Different mixes and different blends
Making my eyes see only stars

Endless are my weekends
But now they've come to a close
Left with only my very true friends
And the weekends that we've known

Kendra Sester

The Valley

You are close to God in the valley.
 You are close to God on a hill
You are close to HIM in sunshine,
 And when the wind is still,

And in the hush of evening
 You look all around and see.
The evidence that God is
 still with thee,

You pause alone at sunset,
 And lift up thine eyes
To thank HIM for HIS help
 That has guided you since sunrise,

The valley now is quiet.
 Except for woodland trills.
Of night birds call that
 echo over the hills,

Each day a moment of silent thanks you give,
TO HIM for this place on which you live,

And realize you have come to rest
In the valley of quietness,

Naomi Lehnhoff

Friends Forever

Whenever I need an ear to listen
 you always have on there.
You give me advice in tough times
 and help me all the way through.
We just became friends a couple
 months ago but I feel as if
 we've been friends for years.
I can tell you just about anything
 and you'll still stay my friend.
When we're all grown-up, married
 and moved away,
I'll always be just a phone call away.
Writing letter is okay but, just
 hearing your voice over the phone
 will take all my blues away.
As we grow old we'll still remain
 friends because of how we learned
 to know and trust each other those
 so many years ago.

M. K. Essary

A Tribute to Michael Landon

Hi I'm in heaven
You all, don't be sad
Though I'd love to be with you
Still up here I'm glad!

Thought I was going to BONANZA
Cuz at first, do you know?
When I first came to heaven
God called me Little Joe!

Well the spot he's prepared me
Is such a beautiful place
If you all could just see me
There's such a smile to my face!

Yes my place is so lovely!
God says "Michael don't fret!
your place here is permanent
Because it isn't a set!

Pam Johnson

For Patricia's Love

We live and love by the light
Yet frightened of the heart
A place, a time without words
Sometimes risking to fall apart
A place secluded and passion burns
A time eluded in the mist
Someday soon my lovely wife
Right now darkness embraced to kiss

I know the Lord is watching all
If this is sin in which we fall
I pray forgiveness for us both
This heart of love and my betrothed
We live and love by true light
Only human's holding tight

Lonny Dean Flaharty

Life Is But A Memory

My life is but a memory
written on the sands of time,
shared by countless others
but ultimately it is mine.

So when life here is over,
this body known as me is gone-
look at what I leave behind
my memory to pass on.

Family, friends and enemies
my memory they all well share,
some with love and tenderness,
but only a few who care.

So I'll live each day to its fullest
and with deeds both good and kind,
I hope to leave only good memories
forever in their mind.

Linda L. Workman

"Nothingness"

I sit alone,
wondering what will become of me.
My life seems so meaningless,
as if it were all some sort of a game.

People try to toy with my mind,
take my innocence away.
They are successful,
and I am left behind,
with nothing to show for myself.
Nothing to show for my life.

Monica Kim

God Cares

I sat beneath the pine tree
Wondering, does God remember me?
Does He even care that I am here?
Then I heard behind me the steps of a
timid deer
A squirrel scampered by—
A sparrow flew through the sky.
They made me remember that each one
of God's creatures
Have their own special and individual
features.
God created us and loves us through it all
Spreading his arms and reaching out to
pick us up when we fall.

Linda Nelson

"The Hard Step Forward"

I sit beside my window
wondering about my life.

Shall I go left or shall
I go to my right?

Before me sits a decision of
a destiny unknown.

I have but one mind yet,
I must grieve so long.
I stand in the doorway.
Shall I stay or leave? Is it me?

I see you ahead but, don't know the way.
I yell, but for another day.
You do not hear and keep on your way.

Is this it, the chapter is over?
On to the next
I put my foot forward upon the path.
The step is taken no more decision making.
I dare not look behind.
For I know there is less
then forward to find.

Katherine Allman

Winds Of Time

Combined with yellow sands
With the greatest of land. There's
a little lay with no joy. He
speak not one zone he stands alone.
His bones are weak he can hardly speak
his cheek are blue he can hardly chew
a scrap of meat people laugh as they
go by as a tear rolled down his eye

Kids throw stick at him his parents
hit at him then one day he dies
now people cry as they go by
because all the hate has caused
his fate now he has met a true saint

Joel Simpson

Change

I change. I start out light
with simple, conservative colors.
But it won't last. Eventually
I'll become dark and black.
This is my cycle of change.

You can not claim that I am
good or evil because I am both.

You may look at me, smile, and
begin to daydream. Or perhaps you'll
stare at me and become overwhelmed.
Time will decide which.

Will the shine that I behold bring
back your forgotten past, or foretell
your unknown future?

Either way, I will always be
above you.

Always.

For I am the sky.

Jessica Felder

My Friend

Darkness used to scare me
with shadows in the night.
It lasted from the dusk of day
until the morning light.

Shapes and sounds were all around
with shadows in the night.
But the best of all protection
was my blanket, Snow White.

For when she lay upon me,
the darkness could not stay.
For the comfort of her brightness,
cast all my fears away.

Now when darkness creeps into
my bedroom down the hall,
I throw my blanket on my head —
the best protection of all!

I no more fear the darkness
or shadows in the night.
I get my friend, who is within,
my blanket named Snow White.

Janice Tackett

Lullaby For A Homeless Puppy

Hello, I'm a newly-dumped pup,
with no guarantee where to sup.
I see a man walking toward me,
followed by his dog full of glee.

Might as well join them, go their way;
at least I was dumped on nice day!
Mister, why do we walk so long?
can't you see I'm little, not strong?

Finally, we are slowing down;
here's some kids, one fun as a clown!
He takes me to his house to live;
his Mom shakes head, "No, positive."

That man with dog has a sick cat;
turns me away, with friendly pat.
I know I'd love this country road;
but sad future I do forebode.

Hey, people, I don't understand;
you say, "Pups and kittens are grand!"
Yet too many in world you bring;
death's lullaby for me you sing?

Lowell "Ted" DaVee

Beautiful Nebraska

If, you want to see Nebraska
where the land is fertile green
you have to go in the Summer
where the life is just a dream.

Buffaloes roaring in the pastures,
cows, horses, everywhere.
Barley, corn, and good alfalfa
pretty life is just right there.

I want to return someday,
and see the Indian reservation,
and smell the clean hay
see the forts in restoration.

You don't know how much I miss you
my beautiful Nebraska state.
Where the life is just so peaceful,
and the people are so great.

Oscar Fuxa Balarezo

Female Judas

Female Judas
with bleached blonde hair
and faded blue eyes,
you swore to know more
while having learned less.

You deceived yourself,
and others,
as you carried out
your cruel plot.

Did you not know?
Deeds shaped in darkness
always demand light.

The darkness of your lies
and the light of the truth
murdered both me and you.

Your serpent's tongue,
with its kiss of lies,
intended to kill once
but killed twice.

Phyllis J. Dales Davis

Untitled

What if I touched you
with a line of love?
Wrote words from my
heart
Telling how I would
set you beside me...
Walk, run, laugh, cry, fly
with you at my side,
Wrote words from my
soul
Of perfect trust.

Would you come with me
to live,
Would you take my hand
and let me be with you,
Would you touch my neck
and smile?

John Branath

Live And Let Live

Husband is five feet ten and skinny;
Wife is five feet two and plump;
Now this can create problems
And make blood pressures jump.

"Wifey dear, I feel a breeze
Please let that window down;"
But wifey who is ironing
Takes this suggestion with a frown.

"Go put on your winter underwear
If you're so cold and freezing,
I'm sweating up a storm;
To me the breeze is pleasing."

To solve this thorny problem,
Here's the answer that I choose;
Hubby needs to gain some weight,
And wifey needs to lose.

T. W. Powell Jr.

Demise Of A Daisy

Red red daisy
why were you crying -
the reign of your skies
object to your dying?
your colors uncommon
reluctantly bared
shamed by your brilliance
electrically aired
yet your cease to survive
despite scanty grace
(but sorrow obscures
one's submissive face)
now no more red daisy
whose view will be missed
no more red daisy
whom fairies once kissed
red jewels descend downward
for my earth to contain
lament for a daisy
for no petals remain.

Meagan Amber McCluer

My Reason

Some people ask
Why I'm obsessed
With this door
And to be the best
But I'm not here to out do any
Nor to lead you to your grave
I'm here to show you the way
And to keep you from being a slave
Beyond the door
Is the ideal life
There is no war
There is no strife
In all the good
You will see
That I am one
One of the free
This is why I show you all
The way of life and peace
Now is when you must go to church
And listen to the priest

Keith Alan Fusinski

Grandma's Love

To my darling grandchild
whom I'll never know
my daughter had you
so very long ago.

She was oh so young
and foolish too
the choice we made
we made for you!

I wish you much love
you deserve the best
a happy home, a mom, a dad
brothers, sisters and all the rest.

I still shed tears
I still feel the pain
there's no guarantee
I'll ever be a grandma again.

To my darling grandchild
I don't even know your name
I imagine that someday you'll know
I love you just the same!

E. Edlund

Our Mother

My heart goes out to our Mother
Who was a beautiful woman
The time has come too soon to say
Good-bye to her on her special day.

It's very hard for those so dear
To leave us here both far and near
Her life has been lived
Her children have grown.

She's seen all her grandchildren
Although they're still small
She had the chance
To visit them all.

Remember we love you
This we know is true
Thank you for loving us
It was the best you could do.

Thank you for being our Mother
A wonderful Mother is what you were
You have done all you could do
We will always love you.

Peggy Gilley

A Father's Fright

A father's query,
Who has daughters delightful;
As you approach their teenage years
More than a little bit frightful;

With my son I was always,
Almost always, In sight
Of his day-up to sun-down
Nigh-to-night flight;

With my girls
My experience seems irrelevant;
I'm a fish out of water;
A man out of his element;

So, I'll sing to them,
Cling to them;
These lovely, dear ladies;
And, concurrently fall
To my knees as I'm praying.

Mark O. Decker

My Father's Prayer

Our Heavenly Father
Who dwells above
Bless my Soul
With Eternal Love.
I Pray to Thee
With all my might
Brighten my path
With Thy guiding light,
And then Dear Lord
May my loved ones be
Safe in Your Heart
And at Peace with Thee.

Lloyd T. Dixon

Intimations On Revelations

Like children with pleading arms,
  Hope reaches up to me.
I lift it-embrace it
  For without it,
  I die.

W. Faye Lanier

"Dark Nights"

Looking over the sea of blood
which seems to run for miles,
I stare into the midnight sky
and the Gods begin to smile.

The land starts to shake and tremble
while the rain begins to shutter down,
the Gods commence to show their wrath
as I stand and watch the world around.

Now the earth is cold and barren
the sun has set the Gods to sleep,
I glace at the sky, upon the clouds
and see the angels weep.

Keith Lemmermann

Another Life

Green leaves vine crawl up into the sun
Where the roses stay down below.
Trees grow taller
But the flowers stay the same
As it were months ago.

Rocks tend to fall
And the ocean makes the way for nature,
Where it is often unattended,
But we all know what lies below,
The night, the shine and the glow.

Could it be we've just forgotten
Or is it we just don't care,
But whatever goes on
It's sure to be noticed
For there is "ANOTHER LIFE" out there.

Kristy Duplantis

Snowflakes

Snowflake, snowflake
Where have you been?
  Snowflake, snowflake
  cold on my chin.
Snowflake, snowflake
So beautifully shaped
  Snowflake, snowflake
  On my window you draped.
Snowflake, snowflake
It's been a long time.
  Snowflake, snowflake
  One of a kind
Snowflake, snowflake
Where are you going?
  Snowflake, snowflake....
  Standing there hoping.

Heidi Marks

"Meeting Your Love Again"

Way up in the heavens
  where eternity lies
Exist those who left their beloved
  and said their last goodbyes
Only 'til they find again
  the ones they have so dear
When once again there's unity
  and find their love so near
Together they'll create a world
  others would love to see
'Til then we'll wait and wonder
  when forever reaches you and me.

Kristine Alfaro

America The Beautiful

America the Beautiful
Where do we find such a place?
Our world is in chaos,
All our own human race!

With Wars, poverty, and hunger,
Children crying in the street,
Bag people in Washington,
Theirs no food for us to eat!

People dying all over,
Fever, killings, and of aids,
What a wonderful world this is,
A place to expose all our rage!

We never seem to grow-up,
Set an example for our world,
Our minds are always filled up,
Our lip is always curled!

America the Beautiful
Where do we find such a place?
Our world is in Chaos,
All because of our own human race!!

Pam Horton

"That's Life"

What do you do,
When your panty hose
slips down to your knees
and you have the urge to
sneeze?
Do you grab your hose,
or cover your nose?
Its hard to decide what to do.
So find your sense of humor
Give a yank and a wipe
Laugh is off. "That's life."

Hilda Horton

Who Cares?

Does anyone really care
When your heart is beating,
From the workload that's hard to bear,
And your mind is bounding.

Does anyone really care
After you've made another mistake,
And things appear so unfair
That life seems hard to take.

Who really cares
About you racing against the clock,
To have a minute to spare,
Or a minute to darn a sock?

Is there one who cares
That a fever attacks your being,
Or your nose is a bruised pear
And dampened eyes are no longer seeing?

Yes, there is one to care,
Beyond all earthly measure.
Talk with Jesus now, to share,
Because He's your greatest treasure.

Patricia Cruzan

"The Time Has Come"

It seems just like yesterday,
When we first fell in love.
I was blessed with your beauty,
Blessed by God above.

You picked me up off the ground,
You gave me a helping hand.
You told me that you love me,
You helped me up so I could stand.

And as time went by, we married,
We both became as one.
Together we were so happy,
As you bore my only son.

Together we had everything,
You was a perfect wife.
Darling, you gave me all you could,
Things like love and life.

But now the time has come to say goodbye,
And I must be so brave.
For the hardest thing for me to do,
Is walk away from your grave.

Jeffrey A. Davis

Thanks Mom

Thanks mom for your loving;
when no one seems to care;
I look through the clouds;
and see you standing there.
I know that God has asked you;
to help me through the day;
to hold me and to hug me
until everything's O.K.
You see I don't always realize
just how much you really do;
You are always there when I need you
and bring me up when I'm feeling blue.
As I go down life's lonely highway
with so much more to learn
Not knowing where I'm going
you tell me where to turn.
I know I'm going to make it as I wait for
the sun to rise;
it helps to know you are there to wipe my
crying eyes.
Thank you for everything you've done.
I thought my life was ending when it's only
just begun.

James E. Anna

Father To Son

In the past,
When I was young,
I used to think
That wrong was fun.

There came a time,
As it passed by,
That I would remember
And begin to cry.

As an adult I should say,
That these things you
should shy away.
But also remember
as you grow,
I've gained the wisdom,
to say I know.

John R. Penta

Tomorrow's Yesterday

Tomorrow's yesterday
When hope ran dry;
When blue colors ran against
A pearl pink sky.

When loved withered
Like a rose in the sun;
When I dreamed of
Adulthood fun.

Tomorrow's yesterday
I can't explain
The feelings I felt against
A cold blooded rain.

In the womb I slept
Among crying stars;
Dreaming of tomorrow
With festering scars.

She wakes unto thee
The light is so blind
And leaves tomorrow
For others to find.

Kiara Rankin

Friends

God gives us a wonderful blessing
When he give us friends to love,

The times we spend together
Are truly a gift from above,

So cherish your friends forever,
And keep them in your prayers,

For God knows there's nothing better,
Than to have a friend who cares.

June Thomas

Still There

Some times
When evening bedtime comes
Your name keeps me
From my sleep I keep thinking
Are you still there?

When will
the morning come?
when will
the sun rise?
Honey child, you know that
you drive me wild.

Reassure me
Rock me asleep
Take my hand
Let me know that
You're still there with me.

I can see
Its time to rise now,
I can feel better now 'cause
you're still there, with me.

Herbert Baker

Sun Beam

As the sun rises in a
different path no longer can
it be seen, as the shadows
limp across the field then
and only then the sun will
start to beam.

Natalie Lopez

Spring

Spring is when everything blooms,
When Easter comes,
And longer days begin to loom.

When leaves return to their trees,
And when young buds blossom into
Beautiful, colorful flowers.

Spring is the only season of the year,
When the World transforms,
And is born anew.

Kristin Arndt

Untitled

Christmas is the time of year
When all the world is full of cheer
By rich and poor, old and young
The Christmas carols will be sung

The Christmas tree, all bright and gay
The symbol of a lovely day
Santa And his reindeer, too
Bringing joy for me and you

Christmas is the time to give
With open hearts and hands
Reminding one and all to live
To live in peace through out the land

F. Abed

My "Doggerel"

This is my poem to Spring....
   What's "that thing?"
A spring is a well;
A spring is swell
   on a pogo stick;
A spring helps us to walk along;
A spring is to sleep upon —
   [No Peas Allowed]
One can get a spring from jail...
... many answers will not fail.

And, most of all-"That Thing"
   is a state of mind
And that state is hard to find
   in the Northeast Spring!

So — My doggerel —
   My dog-gurr-All!

Marion A. Congdon

Thank-You

How do I prepare myself for
What heavens cards have dealt?
Inside my body I have grown
A little blessing I call my own

He has tiny little hands and
tiny little feet a very round face
And big chubby cheeks

He is God's child as well as mine
For He has granted my wish for
a brief period of time,
So when angels are ready and his time
on earth is up, I will know
How it is to truly love; Lord
How can I ever thank-you enough?

Joanna Frantz

When Jesus Calls

Sometimes we wonder
What will it be,
When Jesus calls
For you and me.

As we here on earth
Do toil and labor,
May our actions and words
Show love for our Saviour.

God's promises are true

In the Bible He does say,
Fear not, my child
I've gone to prepare the way.

Some have gone on before
Other there to meet,
Happy and smiling again
At our Saviour's feet.

They can't return to us
But we can go to see,
Our loved ones once more
When Jesus calls you and me.

Helen Kruse

Woven Words

People rarely say
what they mean;
they say things
that only hint to
what they really
mean -
Knitting sweaters
of woven words,
hiding -themselves
from the coldness
of the world.

McGuffy Ann Morris

"Up From The Ashes"

Quite coziness, flicking lights,
What tales my heart is telling,
Thoughts enter in,
Of the main core of the dwelling.

Can one ever explain,
What bless they feel,
Watching embers dance back and forth!

Can this passionate beauty dare to die,
As the embers take their course??

Or can dreamers like I,
Light the fire again,
Throughout eternity?
Oh, yes I'll light it,
For all its ashes,
That died so willingly.

Will rekindle the stone cold ashes,
To the flame that burned before,
It separates the darkness,
That holds us from its core.

Michael D. Shaffer

Silent Colors

Shadows of dawn appear to me,
What lovely colors do I see?
A sky so blue, with clouds like milk.
A smooth horizon, just like silk.

A stream of water, cool and clear.
With fish of gold, that seem so near.
Trees so full, and grass so green.
What lovely colors, have I seen?

Shades of dusk, do I see.
What colors then appear to me?
A sun of bronze, with streaks of red.
What lovely colors, fill my head?

Shades of night, come into view.
The colors aren't many, just a few.
The moon looks like a cotton ball,
And oh the trees, they look so tall.

The stars are like diamonds, up in the sky.
With streaks of gray clouds, passing by.
What wondrous colors, I've seen today!!
It's God's way of saying, It's all O.K.!!!

Patricia L. Smith

The Key

Open the door, I'd like to see
What life has put in store for me.
Stepping in slowly, taking a peek,
Moving about, starting to weep,
For all I can see is sad and bleak.
Wondering if time has sprung a leak,
Dull and dim I started to seek
For a ray of light to shine on me.
Giving me hope and faith to be
Strong enough to hold the key.

Marion Karam

The Cold?

Many forms are there.
Weather, with no shelter or clothes.
Alone, and no one to share.
Someone who has nothing left.
Their eyes are gone, they only stare.
From a life lived, where no one cared,
For some life was gentle.
Some had help along the way.
And for some all alone.
Rejected in despair.
Why can't we find,
More people to care?

Kastberg Jehan Twedt

Untitled

Another time-Another Place
we were lovers.
Now when we pass
on the street we are
strangers.
Our lives have
changed to meet our needs.
We are no more.
Still deep inside
I hold our love.

Mary Lee Richter

My Brother

We shove, we smash, we push, we bash,
We turn priceless antiques into trash.
He kicks, I yell, we punch, we hit.
I call him "jerk", he calls me "it."
He will bite and I will scratch.
It gets bloodier than a boxing match.
And with my arm he'll twist and bend,
But he's my brother, he's my friend.

Laura Milton

Freetime

Lazy in thought
  we run away

To the farthest edge
  of this glistening day

Alone and ourselves
  the company of our keeping

Bridges of laughter
  willingly reaching

Paths of our minds
  gently exploring

Friends with the sun
  quietly smiling

The green in your eyes
  seductively leading

The day is at hand
  and peacefully leaving

Judging to follow
  the forest remains

Lets leave for an hour
  and spend the whole day

Poetry by Ronnie

Christmas Wreath

Thirteen Christmases
We have hurried to her grave site,
Our mending hearts not quite healed.

This Nativity past,
Under the snow
And thrust within the wreath,
We found a red rose—
Frozen in time
Just like their friendship—
With a loving note
From a loyal friend
Who now hugs a daughter
Of her own.

Thirteen Christmases,
Yes!
Sweet Jesus,
Where would we have been
Without you?

Olivia McFadden

Thanks For Being Our Father

F - is for the firm hand you raised us
A - is for always being there for us
T - is for all the things you taught us
H - is for all the help you gave us
E - is for your eyes so bright and clear
R - is for the respect you gave us
This is the best way to spell Father

Joel Vaccaro

"A Tablet"

A tablet can be many colors
  We can color of draw
  We can write letters
  We can write an-I.O.U.
A receipt book
A tablet can be a
Good hand exerciser
I would like, one
A tablet.

Laverne Moore

Parents Prayer

Forgive us, God..... if we hesitate.
We are trying to understand.
Hearts still ache with grief,
Tears just will not cease.
She seemed so young to die,
Forgive our question "why."
Help us to live without her,
Teach us how.
We long to live for Thee,
Show us the way.
Lead us away from sin.
Grant that we may, someday,
Be with her again.

Marjorie M. Bertlett

Because We Are Friends

We see ourselves in one another.
We are not perfect, but we suit
  each other perfectly.
We are friends because we see into
  one another's heart and what
  we see is not a black or white
  person, fat or thin, tall or
  short. What we see is a
  beautiful, loving person.
We see ourselves.

Lenora Price

Harvest Time

Lonely child, silent child
Watching for someone to say
By not one
Not even one
Will you be betrayed this day.

Angry youth, hopeless youth
High on sex, no time to play
Lost in transit
Death one exit
By whom were you betrayed this day?

Tired man, father man
Watching for a dawn each day
Democracy? Polity?
By what were you betrayed this way?

Bewildered woman, bent with grief
Stripped of face, but not belief
Jesus, lift us up we pray
Come into our hearts to stay.

Jeannette B. Rynd

Their Gift

Mother, afraid of wasps,
watched the busy hornets
create their round house.

"Look at these architects
making layers of hornet paper!
They shape it into a globe
as they hang it on a limb!"
Amazing - what hornets knew.

Father said, "Children look!
Be quick! This iris bud
is unfolding into a flower!"

"See! That robin returns
with a beak full of straw
to weave into its nest."

The words - Look! See! Watch!
Listen to miracles of nature —
gave us the gift of awe.

Awe grew for oceans, earthquakes,
lightning, sunsets, and mountains.
For us, it all began with "Look!"

Mary Evans Priestley

Compassion

Compassion is a yellow sun
warm, powerful, uncontrollable,
fiery hot in the soul
bright in the heart,
huge, round, comforting,
always present,
but when it's gone,
compassion of the yellow sun
lingers on

Lisa Mathews

Unseen Ghost

The ghost of my past
walks with me,
Memories and emotions
not set free

My constant companion
each step that I take
Heeding its counsel
in the decisions I make

Wisdom and knowledge
acquired by time
Disappointments and pleasures
guiding my mind

All the moments gone by
I can not change
Only the present
can I rearrange

Penny Lane

The Ancient One

Who bars my path
With measured contemplation
And somber gaze arrests
My stride inviting meditation
Two equals, we, in quiet glen
Amid the shadows broken.
Companions sharing weighty thoughts
'Though not a word is spoken...

Marie Knowlton

Lullaby

Little boys
wake up and taste little girls
it is your duty
and I can tell that you're hungry
Little boys
wake up and fight for your country
it is your duty
and I can tell that you're strong
Little boys
wake up and pray to your gods
it is your duty
and I can tell that you're faithful
Little boys
wake up and put on a brave face
it is your duty
and I can tell that you need one

Luiza Dini

Diva

Face like an angel,
Voice like a lyre,
Singing her song,
Higher and higher.

Messenger heavenward,
Singing his praise,
Minute to minute,
Days upon days.

Trusting in hope,
Living by faith,
Keeping her mission,
On his love to wait.

Norma Van Brunt

A Baby's Journey

The look of innocence,
very first smile.

Just melts your heart,
longer than awhile.

A heavenly first laugh,
rings a bell.

Doctor, lawyer, or surgeon,
time will tell.

A gift from God,
makes you whole.

This little baby girl,
bless her soul.

God watch over her,
as she grows.

May she be happy,
her love flows.
Soon she'll be gone,
on her own.
Not a baby anymore,
she is grown.

Patrick Patterson Cullia

A Soldier's Silence

Somewhere on a distant hill,
Upon the highest peak,
Strives a heart that barely fills,
A soldier with its beat.

Deep inside there's something else,
Than duty on his mind,
It's his heart which hasn't felt,
The love he's longed to find.

Rules for love he wants to meet,
Yet something holds him still,
The heart he has, has no feet,
Has kept him on that hill.

When the day's relieved by night,
And stars patrol the sky,
He'll reflect on what life's like,
And ask the reason why.

Such a life he can not stop,
No cries of his are heard,
When silence owns a mountain top,
There's not a spoken word.

Jerry Capka

Death of August N

This humble man be nominate
Unto posterity as great.
August he in thought and deed
Though not in ostentatious need.

His light be lifted back on high
His load was borne with grace each day.
Courageous in adversity
Exhorted us along the way

And tempted us to reasoned thought
Engagingly with candid talk.
Tended both his fields with care
This farmer and philosopher.

Gently place his frame to rest
There to slumber with the blest
Where we who loved him may restore
For strength, as pilgrims, yet once more.

R. Garner Brasseur

Silent Heart

Alone I sit in silence
unknown of what's ahead
My shadow unmotionless
Reminds me of the dead

The darkness is a symbol
of my emptiness inside
Lurking all around me
is my loneliness I hide

I wonder how I'll make it
Now that I'm alone
The pain in my heart
is a pain that can't be shown

Forever it will be hidden
Until he's by my side
The fear I have released
is for my lonely heart has died

Kimberlee Nye

Friends Indeed

Together we have met
under circumstances we might regret.
In some ways were all different
in other ways were all the same.
All in all were living and
playing the same games.
Were not sure why were here
were not sure of when we'll leave.
Hopefully for the better at our
own pace, ar our own speed.
Every time you'll read this
you can always think of me.
Forever my friends you will always be.

Jackie Owen

"Bloom Field"

A passing field
under a golden veil,
Flowers in bloom
Arise from the gloom.
A half-days ride
Rolling with the tide,
Before you know it
You are beside,
A full moons field
On a river tides heel.

Keith Allan Lonon

Untitled

Did you ever see
   two butterflies kiss?
Did you ever walk
   thru the morning mist?

Did you ever feel
   the sun's rays?
Did you ever feel
   the ocean's spray?

Did you ever touch
   the moon's silver beam?
Did you ever touch
   a love song's theme?

Did you ever hold
   a warm summer's breeze?
Did you ever hold
   an evergreen's wheeze?

Did you ever see
   two butterflies kiss?
Did you ever guess
   my heart's fond wish?

Paul Wittenberg

Snowflakes

Splendid, dancing, shining
Twirling, floating, shimmering
Oh! Watching them is so much fun.
It makes me want to run.
Soft, fluffy, flight
Gentle, fragile, light
My eyes see a toy.
Filling my heart with joy.
Pure, clean, white
Pleasing, joyful, bright
My mind filled with peace.
I share it all with my friend Louis.

Nureen Haq

The Ties That Bind

If only I could reach out and
touch you again.

I long to remind you that
friends are forever
if...
you will just let them be.

No one said that the ties that
bind,
once broken,
could ever be mended.

I don't think they can,
my dear.

Leslie Farnsworth

The Dream

Listen to the voice of the whale
Touch a distant star
Dream a dream that never was
Of worlds both near and far
Stand apart from where you are
Rising as you fall
Looking back upon yourself
In the maelstrom of it all
Embrace the thunder as you drown
Love the fear you feel
Stand alone in a crowd
Immortal and surreal
Journey thru the mystery
Void of face and rhyme
Wash ashore upon a beach
Apart from space and time
Quicken now to consciousness
That shines above the deep
And marvel at the tide of thought
Lost within your sleep.

Joseph R. Hartley

The Breath of Life

Her pale, dainty, ghost-like hand
took mine—lightly,
uplifting me inside
as she bade me walk beside her . . .
and it felt so natural, so loving,

I went willingly — unafraid;
not wondering where we were going,
not wondering why;
just going along for the adventure!

And my eyes were opened . . .
She took me places I'd never been,
she showed me things I'd never seen,
and she breathed the meaning of life
for all mankind inside of me.

When I awoke—all at once—
I knew . . .and still believe
with all my heart and soul,
with every fiber of my being,
that I walked with an Angel last night!

Kenneth Rea Berry

Holocaust Museum

I saw shoes
too many shoes
empty shoes
homeless shoes
silent shoes
they lay in a pile
still, hushed, sad
one shoe caught my eye
a lady's sandal
white straps rimmed with gold
an open buckle
a delicate heel
party shoes
dancing shoes
happy shoes
tears trickle down my cheeks
as I mourn for its owner
for her unjust end
and for what might have been

Marlene Klotz

Untitled

Sometimes the world spins around us
Too fast for us to hang on.
Fall turns into winter
And hearts become cold.
Emotions twist and turn
But are never understood.
Secrets are kept and never told
While souls search their hearts.
The world changes and
I am left to wonder.

Irish Faye V. Rivera

What pleasured rapture
tonight
were I
lying so easy
at your breast,

with your arms
holding me
so close,
and so softly,
in Eden.

Michael M. Waller

Before Its Too Late

Yesterday has come and gone
Tomorrow may never dawn
Live for today
  before it's too late
See and touch
  not only with your eyes
  and hands, but
From deep inside
  for tonight they may die
Live for today
Dream of tomorrow
Remember yesterday
  before its too late

Kimberly Marks

A Precious Gift

On the day when you were born
God sent an angle to adorn
A precious gift from up above
For all of us to cherish and
to love.

Pearl A. Brown

Vigil

I saw your sadness
Today.
It fell from you
Gently
Like soft, summer rain.
It collected in puddles
Until they became
Full, then rivulets
Gathered, trickled;
Slowly tracing a path
Across your soul. . .
Beginning a bed
For the River of
Grief
Yet to come.

C. Suzanne Bailey

Flight To Life

Fly on the wings of your angel
To your heavenly home above
Where your Lord and Savior Jesus Christ
Will greet you with His Love
His arms will be extended
Reaching out to you
His warm and tender welcome
His love so strong and true
Will surely let you feel secure
No matter what you do
For He did give His life
To free us from our sin
He promised eternal life
To all who follow Him
So when our life on earth
Has finally reached it's end
Our eternal life in heaven
Will lovingly begin.

Mary H. Dichiara

Vision

I listen
  (to words, that you preach)
save me and mine
  (Gods scripture, teach.)
I shouldn't doubt
  (my heart, does cry,)
above
  (On your alter)
a cross
  (gets my eye.)
worship
  (the weapon)
a symbol
  (you say,)
where is the memory
  (for blood shed, that day?)
please don't (condemn me)
for all rights (I stand.)
I pray not (to Crosses)
I bow (to the man.)

Jacqueline Albert

Warrior's Prayer

As I go off
To war this day
I hope our foes
Come not this way

To burn our homes
And kill our wives
To loot for joy
To sustain their lives

Though my redemption
Is bandits' gore
I kill so they
May kill no more

Though die I might
I shall not think
To where I'll go
At the light's brink

If not to heaven
Or the fiery lake
I pray my soul
The sword shall take.

John Grodis

My Footsteps

For I was put upon this earth,
to wander here and there.

With each and every footstep,
I knew not exactly where.

I have walked in the dark,
and have walked in the light.

But when I take my last walk,
I will be walking out of sight.

Remember how I looked,
When upon this earth I did smile.

For that is how I want to be
remembered all the while.

Mary Lou Graham

Phraseology?

If I were rhetorical in dialogue....
To verse some lovely muse.... To waken
the ear in sheer delight.... To ignite
the heart to fuse.... I'd surely
sit day in and out.... And put to use
my art.... Expressing to you, my very
soul.... That pours out through my
heart.

Mark S. Teachnor

Let Me

Let me take you with me,
to the never ending sea.
Let me take you far away,
to see the water tides sway;
Let me take you to the promised land,
you and me hand in hand.
Let me take you to the deep blue skies,
Where I can look into your eyes.
Let me whisper in you ear,
all of the things you want to hear.
Let me take you for a ride,
to see the ocean tide.
Will you give me a chance?
for a romance?
Will you let me?

Lyle W. Tryon

Rebirth

The blue sky is falling
To the crimson earth
The black night is calling.
A world's rebirth
An ocean of feelings
A sea of despair
Can't shield us from the torture
And pain that is there.

Peggy Bancroft

All I Need

The rain outside it pitters and patters
To me your love it is all that matters
The sun may shine the moon may glow
To me your love is all I need know
The tides may rise and then recede
To me your love is all I need
I'll love you till the rivers run dry
There will always be your love and I

Kevin J. Whitcher

A Prayer

Lord, as I serve you now,
To me impart your faith,
And give me understanding,
Each morning that I wake.
And help me know that as I serve,
You're there to lend a hand,
That never alone, or by myself,
Will you ever let me stand.
To learn that what I do to others,
Is as if I do to you,
And never are there too many,
But always are too few.
Help me Lord to seek your face,
To teach this also, now,
And talk to you all the time,
My heart to humbly bow.
Make me learn that all I do,
Is full and not part time,
To want to serve you daily,
So please Lord, help me shine.

Linda R. Kurtz

Untitled

The psyche predator starves the soul
    to kill or lay dying.
The soul searches for nourishment
    through doors with complex locks.
Locks only opened in unison
    when the soul finds the keys.
Keys hidden by obscurity,
    need illumination.
Then the soul will flow
    through spaces where doors once were.
Embracing with wisdom and gratitude,
    all that existence offers.

Karen Sotile

Soccer

When I play soccer.
I kick the ball.
I'm scoring, blocking and
    having a ball.

It feels good to win a game,
We go home in fame,
And sometimes in shame.

Liam O'Toole

Baby's Prerogative

All I have to do is gurgle and coo
To get my way with you know who,
    My Grandma.

To her I'm precious and so grand
I'll grow up to be a little man,
    My Grandma.

In these hands the power have I
To make her laugh until she cries,
    My Grandma.

I reach out for more and more
Of abundant love she has in store,
    My Grandma.

Where else am I King of Kings
Other than when mother brings me,
    My Grandma.

A baby's life is really great
It's growing up I'm going to hate
    Right!, Grandma?

Pearl Wheeler

"Beware Of The Spell Of Adam"

Beware of the spell of Adam,
To Eves near and far,
Deceiving eyes will cheat you,
And your heart will have a scar.

Beware of the spell of Adam,
Never trust his lust for love.
For he only intends to use you,
So his pride will rise above.

I may be young and innocent,
But I have one thing to say,
"Beware of the spell of Adam.
Save your blessing for another day."

Kathryn Ganime

Yesterday's Feats

Somehow it's not important now
To dwell upon the past
And all those feats that seemed so great,
The plans one hoped would last.

It doesn't mean that much today
To score the winning goal,
And rub a "crucial" victory in
That it might sear a soul.

The thrill for sure's no longer there
To bag a trophy deer,
Or limit out on trout or dove
Like back in yesteryear.

No, it's not knowing what we've done
That helps to set us straight,
But rather what we need to do
Before we reach God's gate.

Phil Dinan

Here I Am!

Out in the open
I'm not hiding, I know it's the end
I don't care, why should I?

They're All against me now
I think
I'll disappear
Or maybe cry

Katherine E. Wheatley

Forever And Always

You'll be the one,
to bring me joy and happiness,
to keep me from crying,
to help me through the hard times,
just to look in my eyes and
make me wonder.
    Forever and always
I could never forget,
how much I care for you,
how much I trust you,
how much I could never forget you,
but most of all
    Forever and always,
I'll always love you,
I'll always hold you in my heart,
I'll always be here for you,
    Forever is what
you are to me no matter where you are.

Paula Whalen

Untitled

Which is best, 'tis hard to say
To be numbing cold or lonely,
But loneliness has hope for day
Cold has darkness only.
Behold, a heart is lonely.

With memories of Autumn leaves
Now buried 'neath the ice and snow,
Of coldness deep and 'ere within
Behind a wall of chilling stone.
Behold, a heart's last warming glow.

And better 'tis to think of death
As nought but endless sleeping,
And thus a lonely heart in glass
Imprisoned for safe keeping.
Behold, a heart lies weeping.

Jason Fosso

Growing In Joy

Changing our hearts
    to be more like him.

Giving up carnal
    and worldly sins.

Restoring this old earth
    to fery and laughter.

Joining the redeemed
    In heaven's
        high rafters.
            Amen.
A dream for us all.
May it come, true.
Just out of an azure blue.

Joy Pakko Kellogg

Fear

In the death of night it creeps,
waiting for its prey,
for it is at light it sleeps,
at the break of day,
a sign of death, the feared one,
it is people's FRIGHT,
as it comes unexpectedly,
at the break of night....

John Thomas Ensell

I Feel So Small

I feel so small
    to be immersed.
In the wonders of
    God's universe.
The mountain so high
    the star sprinkled sky.
All human power
    His works defy.
And surpassing all
    my eyes can see.
Is one great gift
    He's given to me.
The gift of life
    In my human frame.
That His own image
    I may contain.

O. John Perrello

Untitled

This is my favorite time of day;
    to be holding you this way,
    and rocking you to sleep,
these are the memories I will keep.

It feels so good when you snuggle,
    the day is done-no more struggle;
    just off to dream land you go,
        your Mommy loves you so.

A kiss good night and then sweet dreams;
    these are the best times it seems,
To watch your tiny eyelids close,
    and to admire your button nose.

That a tiny part of Daddy
    and a tiny part of me
    with the help of God's love
    made the baby that I see.

You were a miracle so small, only just a
year ago
Already growing up, and having Mommy
let go.
So on your first birthday I just wanted to say
How much that I love you — even more
than yesterday.

Neisa Hodge

Untitled

Moral
    to appreciate death
Moral
    to appreciate darkness
Is it moral to appreciate
    death
    and
    darkness
Who decides
Who's to say
    Moral
    or
    unmoral
What does it mean anyway
    the word
    Moral

Lanea Naylor-Murphy

When

To conquer love is a journey,
to achieve love is a chore.
To experience love is a blessing,
the searcher of love explores.

To truly experience love,
is to love deep within.
To feel what you seek,
You must look from the outside in.

That's what we are taught,
when we read hearing the spirit.
The gift of love is from God,
you'll know it when you feel it.

To love another is to know,
that God is on your side.
with God, you share all your feelings,
because you'll have nothing to hide.

Patrick L. German

To a Place

To a place that's free.
To a place of beauty.
Happiness is glorious,
love is forever.
To the one you love
he is in perfect harmony.
The sorrow and the heartache
is not for always.
Your heart will remember the
true Love you shared.
Take day by day,
step by step.
The one you love is just a
glance away...

Kimberly Collins

Adjusted Again

I   Ode to a life gone past
        To a life once tasted
        To giving and being left
        To try and try again
        To being stopped

II Ode to this life past gone
        To the bounce defunct
        To hunger toyed
        To 84,000 miles unnoticed
        To trying

III Ode to the shine doused
        To sparkle scratched
        To dance tripped
        To wanting wilted
        To flowers

Karin R. Staples

Disguise

Look into my eyes
this is what you will see
Your every own reflection
staring hopelessly at me.
Behind them there's nothing
only sorrow and pain,
a soul with nothing to loose
a heart with nothing to gain.

No hope of lasting love
no vision of future dreams,
just empty lonely echoes
and tormented silent screams.

Nadine Taylor

Look Beyond The Morrow

Look beyond the morrow, far
Tis through the clouds
We see the sun
In all its' glory,
Shining hues of pinks
And blues and
Bright orange reds
Bringing color to our lives.

Look beyond the morrow and
Bringing gladness to our hearts
E'en though we'd thought
it'd fled.
Surely peace and beauty lie o'er
the hills
of our despair,
Takes only time, to find it there.

Mary Crebo

"My Poems"

My poems are my diary of happy
times, sad times, and sometimes
being just content.
Without my poems, the words
would pour out everywhere,
disorganized, with no real intent.

My poems are my other world,
My hide-a-way from things
We deal with in everyday life.

In poetry I find a fantasy
world, beautiful, quiet and
serene, and not a sign of strife.

Real life is also great with many
rewards. Live it with zest and
appreciate all we take for granted.
But sometimes write a poem
sweet or sad and for a moment find
that other world so enchanted.

Peggy Wirtz

The Lady Soil

She works alone in the garden
Tilling the soil
She works long and hard and tediously
Alone with the sun to her back
And her life ahead of her
Her heart beats
Solemn and plaintive
She reflects on those she bore before
And nourished in her richness
She is the earth
She is one creation
One passage of time
Until she tills no more.

Lawrie Ann Ignacio

Moonlight

The spotlight in the sky
illuminates the darkness.
It baths the earth in its
glow of peace.
It brings a promise of tomorrow
for all those yet to be.
And gives those now the romantic
promise of love.

Marilyn Bunk

"Direct Tap Line To God"

Direct tap line to God above,
  Through Jesus Christ our King.
Our Lord and Saviour, Son of God
  Of whom the Angel's Sing.

The Holy Ghost Our Comforter
  Will keep the channel clear.
If we will but let Him have control
  Of us throughout the year.

Direct tap line to God is free
  To those that will receive
Eternal life the gift of God,
  If they will but believe.

How strange but yet how true it is.
  How simple and complete
The Peace that comes into our Heart
  When sins become delete.

Direct tap line to God above?
  Ah! Yes, Indeed it's true.
No secret I have heard it said,
  The things that God can do.

Melvin L. Shumate

Insanity

We wander as slaves
through a garden
with no flowers.
For where did you go
my sweet womb of paradise?
My furious muse of slumber?
Do you remember how we painted
those murals of ecstasy
against the red forgotten sky?
No one warmed me
of losing faith in the dream
or the wonder of knowing you.
I fear that my brothers
have forgotten
the myths of our woven being.
Yet knowing so little,
I shall likely again travel with them
into these illusions of chaos and desire
that move us onward
like statues beneath the sun.

Jon Bidwell

You Deserve (For Shannon)

You deserve everything wonderful
This space and plane have to give,
You deserve a life that's magical
With every positive reason to live.

You deserve roses and verse
To embrace you each day,
You deserve music and mirth
To chase sadness away.

You deserve to be admired
(A woman such as you is so rare),
You deserve to be desired
By one you trust to always be there.

You deserve time and space
To develop every potential,
You deserve comfort and grace
And the balance that's essential.

You deserve moonlit beachside walks
With a companion who's always kind,
You deserve the space between thoughts
Where there is ultimate peace of mind.

Marshall Reissman

Remember

It's time I told you how I feel,
This love in me is very real.

I think about you night and day,
And dream your love would come my way.

I'd quickly give up my last chance,
Just to feel your sweet romance.

For time has past and I'm still here,
Through every smile and every tear.

Good times-bad times, I don't care,
Just so you know, I'll be there.

And when it's time to say goodbye,
I won't let you see me cry.

So when I'm low and feeling sad,
I'll just think of what we had.

I hope someday you'll look back and see,
Who really loved you—that was me!

Kaci Purtle

Becoming "Mother"

Here comes new life,
  This is such great news.
Here comes new life,
  Will it change any of my views?

Here comes new life,
  This time seems so slow.
Here comes new life,
  Oh my, how I seem to grow and grow.

Here comes new life,
  So much to learn and do.
Here comes new life,
  Am I yet ready for you?

Her comes new life,
  A precious bundle of joy.
Here comes new life,
  Is it a girl, or is it a boy?

Here comes new life,
  Finally, it's so tiny, pink, and bared.
Here comes new life,
  Oh, Dear Lord, I am so very scared.

D. L. Henderson

As I Sit Here

As I sit here
Thinking of you,
The lovely scenery
Reminds me of you.

As I sit here
Missing your touch,
Seeing your face
Loving you so much.

As I sit here.
Watching you smile,
You're next to me
Not so many miles.

As I sit here
Seeing a rose,
I know you're near
As our love grows.

Paul M. Dornberger

What He Did

She stands upon a cliff
  Thinking of what he did
She thought that she had loved him
  Not knowing the monster he hid
When she had found that thing
  She became so frightfully mad
Because he had done it
  And this made her sisters sad
"I wish that I could push him off,
  And watch him fall into the sea.
But no they wouldn't understand.
  They'd lock me away," thought she.
"I'll fight this never ending war
  Against this undying pain.
But in the end there is nothing.
  No peace for me to gain."
So she made her way home
  Thinking of what he did
No longer did she love him
  Such pain for a nine year old kid

Jennifer Cross

Untitled

As years go by
Things in our life can change
People come into our lives
And people leave our lives
Perhaps the hardest parting of all
Is the one with those we love
When the time comes for them to leave
All we can do
Is set their souls free
We can keep their spirits alive
By keeping them in our hearts
The difficult time
Comes after the parting
When life must go on
Without the one we love
During this time
Our true strength comes through
This is the time
We must bind together
And be there for each other

Karen M. Cahill

Passing Through

People come and people go,
  they're only passing through.
And so it is with life we know,
  we're only passing through.

Our days on Earth are an unknown, so
  each one who is passing through
Should take the time to let Love show;
  they're only passing through.

Norma Jones Chambers

Urgency

The class is still,
Their studies doing.
The course of knowledge their
Thoughts pursuing.
When to the teacher's desk a tread
A small boy of strained intent
His voice a husky murmured strength,
"May I go?" That look! It's life or?
A whispered "Yes", his breath escapes,
The ordeal's won, his goal achieved.
He's gone.

W. Walter Greene

Pain and Glory

In each dawn of sadness one yesteryear,
they came across rolling meadows and
wooded land, with glory in their
hearts, and muskets in their hands.

In each dawn of sadness one yesteryear,
they came across rolling meadows and
wooded land, some too young, some too
old, yet they fought in pain and glory,
only to step into the fading pages of
life's story.

In each dawn of sadness one yesteryear,
they came across rolling meadows and
wooded land, many a Lad, now a man,
and they died in pain and glory,
with their muskets, in their hands.

Robert C. Pardoe

Looking Forward

I'd like to remember
These days
These carefree, happy days.
No longer clinging to the past.
Looking forward.

I wish to remember him
In many little ways.
The twinkling eyes.
And funny laugh.
And forever present smile.

His easy manner
In everything he does.
His willingness to love and learn
To share and be shared
Will make him ever present in my heart.

Melissa Michaud

"Stranded In Time"

My time is at an end,
There is no one to fend.
Please let me go,
I love you so much,
Please let me go,
I have waited so long,
But you still won't let me go,
I did all that was right,
According to your might,
Please let me go,
I know that I was wrong,
According—to my song,
Please, Please let me go.
"Can I go home."

Nazim A. Gorib

"Forfeitures Of Life"

A lonely bud in the spring,
  there for all to see.
Blooming into a summer flower
  and smiling happy cheers.
But as the year rolls by,
  I become exposed in the autumn air.
As the wind laughs at me
  and leaves me naked in the fields,
I am stripped of all I earned.
My fears of loneliness have returned.

Jennifer Masscotte

Missing Someone Special

I look up and see his face.
  Then look away.
I try to remember what he meant to me.
  But it's all gone.
My heart is alone and afraid.
  I feel for him.
But there is nothing to touch.
  I call for him.
But there is no answer.
  I wish he was near.
But he had to go and leave.
  I asked him to stay.
But he said in another lifetime.
  I look out the window.
But no one walks by to say hello.
  I scream for him.
But all I hear is my own echo.
  Then when I feel tears of my own.
There he is my true love standing in the
door alone.

Laura Murrer

Untitled

If all men are created equal
Then explain such boundaries
Between friends and foe
Black and White ; Red and Yellow

Where's the sequel
Does it lay within cemeteries
Forgetting the skyline glow
After the star light show

If all men are created equal
Then what's the weapons for
Why can't we live in Xanadu
Filled with desire and ecstasy

Paul Domanski

Cry No More Tears

I only spoke from my heart...
  The words I longed to say...
Words that comforted...
  Words that would not fade...

Your eyes...
  Stared deeply into mine...
Hoping I couldn't see...
  The secrets you had to hide...

A tear...
  It fell from your face...
A tear...
  I could embrace...
Understanding them all...
  Yes...
I've been in your place...

Soon, I hope, tears...
  They will cease...
So cry no more tears love...
  Together...
We will find peace...

Larry Holmack

Untitled

Come friend, trace with me,
  the wild field of memory -

Where flowers in rows
  or tumbling askew

Suggest moods of the past
  and faces come through -

Where in the wind
  petals fall back

Revealing a core
  then as now, intact.

Passion remains
  in full power

Under the present,
  in the heart of the flower.

Phyllis Grilikhes

Hypnotic Gaze

To watch the pages flutter by;
The type set pica greets the eye
Transfixed in hypnotic gaze
Mind entranced to search a phrase

Hours drifting quickly by
As night descends on weary eye;
    As covers close
    And lovers doze
You peer into the glimmering sky

Soon engulfed by numbing sleep
The focus fades
as dreams now creep
Into subconscious,
Mesmerized
You drift afar
With sleep-sealed eyes

Michael Kuzmitz

School Memories

The days have passed so quickly,
The time is almost gone,
But all the memories we've shared
Will still live on and on.

The clubs we once belonged too
The friends that we have made,
The fun we've had together
With the parts that we have played.

Activities like our dances,
Homecoming, and Powderpuff, too,
Have made this a year to remember
At my high school.

Joseph Paul Morelli

A Bird's Call

When I'm outside with nature I hear
The song of a bird - it is clear
To sing a song so dear.

The song of a bird is the best
When it sings to you like a guest
Upon the building of it's nest.

Once again I hear the song
And is most forever long
For a bird's call is always strong.

Marissa Pepple

Untitled

Every year with Christmas near
The thought of Friends becomes more dear
The memories that fill the mind
Are those rare "one-of-a-kind"
Can any human being know
Just how much friendship will grow?
Allowed to take its proper place
In the world's ever uncertain pace
When our lives are filled with
  JOY AND SORROW
Friendship will lead us onto
  TOMORROW
And bring us round another time
To share a MERRY CHRISTMAS rhyme

Lee Hogberg

Imagination

I dwell in imagination-
The things that may happen-
The things that are not possible-
Will happen where I am-

The things to think-
Huge realms unexplored-
The things that can't happen-
The opposite of the way things are-

Of travelers and warriors-
And animated dragons-
The way things aren't supposed to be-
The way I think when I am free-

Kevin R. Glandon

Our Child

When I went back
The tall hedges had grown
At least four inches.
The olive tree looked down
Upon our bedroom window.
The pear tree was in full bloom
For the first time
Since we planted it.
I took it all in stride
But when I stumbled upon
The one lone rose blossoming
Between two dead stems
I cried.

Patricia W. Hiscock

Do Not Weep

Do not weep my child
the sun will greet you
Do not weep my child
the moon shall guide you
Do not weep my child
the animals protect you
Do not weep my child
all is safe
Do laugh my child
the world is your oyster
Do laugh my child
G-d does dance
Do laugh my child
the sun has welcomed you
Do laugh my child
I kept you safe

Mercedes Melton

The Castaway

Stars by night.
The sun by day.
Hopelessly lost,
I, the castaway.

Wind-chapped skin.
Exposure day after day.
Dreams that dearly cost,
I, the castaway.

Bonded to self.
Slave to what I say.
The elements weather my resistance.
I, the castaway.

Please rescue me,
Or let me die today!
Eternity with every flip of the coin.
I, the castaway.

Solitude is my lot.
Harshness is my stay.
Silence is not golden,
When you are the castaway.

John M. McClung

Where Dreams Are
Only Hidden Hope

Your eyes are very beautiful
The stars do really shine
And how I wish upon this earth
That one of them was mine
Your cheers are sort of rosy
Like lips of scarlet wine
And how I love to kiss your lips
From the lips that's really mine
They say that love is wonderful
But need less for me to say
For has love really come
Or will it go away
I planted some petunias
Red, white, pink, and blue
And then I had to lose my head
And fall in love with you
I took and grew a pretty rose
And seem it from the street
Where dreams are only hidden hope
That lays beyond the seas

Leroy-James Hendershot

That Sweet Spot

It's only a game.
The soft grass that
gives beneath my feet,
the summer smells
of a lazy afternoon
where men play
at being boys
and fathers,
sons.
There'll always be
an innocence about it
that's timeless
and though it's only a game
when today
is less than a memory
boys will still take
the green fields
bats in hand
and try to hit
that sweet spot.

Michael LoCurto

Summer's Lament

Winter comes-
The snow is so sweet
It blankets the land
Like a white linen sheet

All of the colors
Are buried so deep
God gave us rainbows, yes,
But none to keep

I look out my window,
All covered with frost
My memories of summer
Are now all but lost

I look to the sun
With a hope in my heart:
Waiting for God
To let a new season start.

E. J. Wilowski, Jr.

Sea Treasures

Beautiful in the morning sun
The sea is sparkling bright,
So very cool and pleasing
With foam that's glistening white.
It is such fun to gather shells
So early in the day,
Barefoot on the cool wet sand,
Feeling the ocean spray.
The sand is smooth, ironed by the tide,
Sprinkled with shells galore,
Jewels from the sea, so deep,
Treasures along the shore,
Waiting there for those to come
And gather all they may,
Before the tide comes in again
And carries them away.

Jean Fleming Blitch

Separation

I sit, I wait,
The sandman rarely comes.
I hear devils and angels,
neither one is done.
I lift up, I sink down
I pray that I'll be found.
But you, your wondering, your weary,
the story yet to be told.
It's not in your heart to be so cold.
Your hunger for joy,
Your hunger for life,
Will all be yours
If you'll be my wife.

Kenneth J. Hagen

Untitled

The hand goes up once.
The light is coming to an end.
Hope is fading fast.
The water is suffocating the soul.

The hand comes up a second time.
The aloneness grows stronger.
The hurt grows deeper.
The hand comes up for the third time.

Still there is no one.
There is no trust.
There is no pressure.
The hand comes up no more.

Kevin Lawton

Walking Up The Mountain

Walking up the mountain
The pathway turns and twist
Thick trees evoke darkness
And morning dew provides a mist

Unfamiliar sightings
Uncharted land
Wondering what will happen
When we reach the top and stand

The walk is never easy
Struggles to overcome
The pathway never clear
And there is always more than one

Inner strength is the driving force
Sometimes raw guts alone
Something deep inside
Makes us continue on

Until we reach the mountain top
The battle rages on
And we continue to climb
Because our destiny is unknown

Pam Mashburn

Untitled

What strange and wonderful things
the passage of endless time brings
The many new horizons
The days of many suns.
From the first new days of spring
When flowers bloom and birds sing
Through the warm fresh days of summer
When the days are long, the winds murmur
And the ever changing days of fall
When the cool winds begin to call
To the crisp white days of winter
When the ice floes crack and splinter
All is ever changing
Across this world wide ranging

Mark K. Camper

Blind Love

I didn't ask for this!
The pain was not on my mind.
All I wanted was love,
but that love I didn't find.
The smile was always tender
and I thought you would care
I guess I thought wrong
and from me, my heart you did tear.
Your words were always kind or
At least that's now they seemed
but that day your words became a storm
and blew away all I had dreamed.
My heart has been burned
and I'm the one to blame
It was not your fault
I put my heart in a flame
I should not have tried
for I had no right
But that love I still desire
and for it, I will fight!

Osiris Bejarano

Wonder

Have you ever wondered why
the ocean is so deep
Why God created the waves or tides
Was it to be a sign
all must come and go
Some more intensely than others
Have you ever wondered why
birds fly so high
almost untouchable
Only to be seen with the eye
could your heart have wings
only to be seen by the soul
Could your love set you free
think of the joy that would be
Only maybe will the tides of
the wind bring them back again
each time taking more
of you with him when he goes
Will it ever be known?
Why was one so faint? And the other so
intense?

Kristey Harrington

Environment

The ocean licks the oily beach
The mushroom cloud blocks out the sun
The reactor waste eats at its tomb
The polluted water soaks the soil
The fluorocarbon foils the sky
Oh sweet mother earth
Kiss your ass goodbye

S. G. Johnson

Flow of Love

The ocean flows tide high tide low.
The mountains high the valleys low.
Our lives they travel sometimes so.
And through this journey we seem to know.

To try and keep an even flow.
For love is what we seek to know.
We know not what our future holds.
Our daily lives they go untold
And then one day your heart unfolds.
The hidden treasure in your soul.

Mark E. Young

Darkness

She is left standing in the darkness
The mist surrounds
Her tears fall and join the dewdrops
That adorn the ground.

Her love is now shattered
Like crystal that has been thrown
Never will she recapture
The happiness once known.

She stands alone in darkness—
The blackness of night.
Her vulnerable heart shuns
the presence of light.

The light of hope, the light of love
Keep calling her near.
The blackness holds her distant
That blackness is fear.

Jeanne M. Humphrey

Storms Of My Life

I hear the storms, there all around
   the lightning crashing to the ground
So like my life these storms I feel
   the crashing of my dreams are real
The pounding of the torrent rains
   so like the tears my heart contains
The thunder rolling loud and clear
   reminds me of the things I fear
About the beatings and abuse
   the pills, the alcohol, misuse
The winds are howling loud outside
   reaching in to where my soul abides
My heart is yearning for the day
   when all the storms will so away
And all the rain that rains on me
   will just bring rainbows, to set me free.

    Lora Emery

The Storm At Midnight

The thunder boomed,
The lightning cracked.
The sky was gray,
The clouds were black.
The wind was cold,
The black sky bold.
Then died down with
a sprinkle.

    Katie M. Breckel

"Fall In The Mountains"

I fly from tree to tree,
The leaves falling under my wings,
A little wooden bird house,
Waiting just for me.

   Down below are children,
   In their scarves and hats,
   Raking and piling they play,
   As they end the windy day.

Flying under the canopied lane,
Of oranges, reds, and yellows,
I see the vast horizons of mountains,
As it lightly begins to rain.

   The colors seem to run together,
   As do the ice cold creeks,
   I swoop down to the moistened ground,
   a big juicy worm I found.

The loving touch of mother nature,
I'd seen today,
Made me feel a warmth,
On this chilly fall day.

    Kelly Moody

Untitled

Lo and Behold!
The King and Queen,
   Donned with Diamonds,
   Scrutinize their Subjects.

Low and begrimed,
   The minor and his spade,
   Robed in rags of blood red,
   Channel for coal
Underneath the alluvial earth.

    Matthew Evans Arkin

"The Hands Of Time"

Seeing things that were said
The hands of time hold you.
The winds of change blow away
As your destiny does too.
Time is of the essence
Short, as it may be.
Vapors in the wind
I'm sure that you'll see
Though it always seems the same
The days, months, and years
Time flies when you have fun
Though I always hear
Time is the only barricade.
That blocks us from perfection
Time is the reason
That we have recollections.

    Michael Gardner

My Prayer

God, grant me common sense to see
The good in folks of Thy creation —
Help me to overlook the flaws
And see divine the soul of all.

Let me find joy in simple tasks
Which ease the burdens of another.
Give me the patience to await
The guidance for my daily life.

Grant me the wisdom to remember
That others too have plans and dreams.
And when chaotic our world seems
That The Great Plan shall be fulfilled!

Give to my restless wandering heart
The calm assurance Thou dost care!
Spread over me Thy boundless love
Which ever conquers doubt and fear.

    Nellie Crabb Batt

Warm Embrace

Raging fire burning
The flame tall and bright
Oh, this sensation
Holds me tonight

Let me wrap myself around you
Hold you like the flame
Fill you with my endless love
Then we can feel the same.

Show me your warm love
So tenderly and true
And I will show you ecstasy
When I make love to you.

And as the flame die down to embers
Romantic as the stars
And the night fulfills itself of dreams
Tomorrow will be ours.

    Monica Blackman

Tonight

Tonight, tonight,
the moon is so bright.
The air is just right.
The stars are shining bright,
tonight.
All that I have to say is
good night!

    Kandis Belback

Make Believe

My heart grew wings and fluttered
   the first time you looked my way.
When you spoke my name out loud,
   I did not know what to say.

When you stepped into my world,
   felt like I could walk on air.
I knew that I was dreaming
   as you gently touched my hair.

Thought I'd wished upon a star
   and you were my dream-come-true.
My whole world turned upside down
   every time I peeked at you.

Summer nights and rainy days,
   they all seemed the same to me.
Full of fun and love and warmth,
   I was happy as could be.

And now the spell is broken,
   like the fragments of my heart.
Guess the dream was make believe;
   your "goodbye" tears me apart.

    Karen Holt-Spickerman

The Truth

Everyone around us all
The disconcerned of mankind
Non involvement from the careless
Hatred's gonna make us fall

The earth has shed tears
For the plight it has seen
And with our fears
It cannot be keen

As I transcend through eternity
One thing keeps coming to mind
That we need to stay kind
Maybe then we can live in serenity

    Ken Guy

The Play

You broke my heart a thousand times
   The day you walked away
For when you left, you also took
   The cast within the play
Along with you, my lover went
   My best friend at her side
My partner in the game of life
   As well, my future bride
My show-mate of the theater
   My dinner-mate went too
Little did you seem to think
   They all would leave with you
And then, of course, my traveler
   Who traveled when she could
My critic and my conscience once
   Were standing where you stood
So many more within the cast
   Have left and gone away
The curtain's down, the lights are dim
   Alone on stage, I play

    Matthew Lyson

"Best Friend"

Do you remember-
The day-

In our little girl lives-
That you and I...

Happen to realize
That we were Almost...
Just alike...

Back then the same
Hair and size...

The laughter I know...
you still can hear-
a little giggle...

A whisper in our ear...
oh, how precious...
The time has been-
Since we became...
"Best Friends"

Lisa Cameron

Sitting In Darkness

Kyle sat in
The darkness, wondering
If Delilah would
Come back home.

Kyle sat in
The darkness, pondering
The reasons why
She left him.

Kyle sat in
The darkness, furious
Because Delilah never
Told kyle what
Was really wrong.

Kyle sat in
The darkness, praying
For their differences
To be reconciled.

James V. Scarpace

A Way to the Light

The crushing depression
The crippling fear
Stones of darkness weigh heavy
His power is strength

A dark place to live in
The child needs more
I'm buried beneath it
The darkness to strong

She held out her hands
Pushed the darkness away
Her light pulls me up
Her love helps me stand

We start over now
The fear is still here
It lessens as time goes
And cripples no more.

Linda M. Jewell

Spring Storm

The roar of wind, a flash of light,
The crash of thunder in the night,
And Springtime's own fireworks display
Will soon be getting underway.

The storm is near; no time to sleep,
I slip out of my bed and creep
To my window sill to see
The storm's primeval majesty.

Phyllis Cooper Pace

The Liberty Bell

In time of war
The church ring the bell
And the people
Were ready for attack,

In time of peace
The church ring the bell
For any celebration
People are happy.

During a working day
The bell ring for time
And its song
Is beautiful.

In Philadelphia hall
Is hangs a liberty bell
This bell remind us
The independence war.

In July 4 of Independence Day
The bell ring
For historic events
Where the declaration was adopted.

Lazar Maria

"The Herald Of The Great King"

Hurry, the Dawn!
The Christ child is Born!
Golden is the Gospel Scene!
That St. Francis looked upon.

Sandelled Soft!
Thy Treading Feet.
The Sleeping Infant ...
And St. Francis meet.

Umbrian Hills ...
Echo a Holy Song,
Along the Scented Pines,
A Christmas scene enshrined!

Holy is the Song!
That Franciscan Footsteps,
Roam, Roam, Along!
Holy is the Christmas Song!!

Mary L. Kenneally

Cancer....

I wake with it every morning.
The days are never dull or boring
with appointments to make
and doctors to see
wonder why it had to be me.
Chemotherapy isn't a blast, with shots,
drugs and side effects I wish would pass.
But it's needed to survive
the Leukemia I'll still have in '95.

Leigh Ludban

From When In Beach

The Cage Is Laid

From when in beach
The cage is laid
And sparrow driven
Wide of green in song-fields
Nests of sorry child
With breasted amber smile
Lurching from orange beat
Clasps with longing paws
Nails ripped and bone withdrawn
Orange beat in flames release
Which to one reels
And rents of two-way drum
Wakes in tears
Loss in rotting pull-away shores
Let-blood and shrivel catatonic
Severed from sun
Paper tear in amplify
Throat shortens, shoulders weep
Sight is seared
And pain crackles in shards.

Philip David Forsyth

The Soul Alive

And when I think about him
The beauty that remains
The laugh that came so easily
The smile to ease the pain

And when I turn around
His shining eyes I see
They seem to look into my soul
Into my memory

And when I remember him
The friendship that I find
Will stay with me forever
Alive within my mind

And when I think about him
I smile within myself
To have known him for an instant
Is my greatest wealth

Mary Kolar-DeNunzio

Untitled

You are a perfect masterpiece,
The awe I feel with never cease.
Your skin has such a soft warm tone,
It's smoother than I've ever known.
The way you look sets me afire,
With a special deep, burning desire.
To hold you in my arms so tight,
To keep you safe, away from fright.
You've moved me like I've never been,
It feels so good, should be a sin.
And when I see your body bare,
My heart it skips, I have to stare.
You have such class, grace and charm,
I'm proud to have you on my arm.
For all the world to see us go,
Wherever our love wants to flow.

Joseph Vergilio

90's People

People of the 90's,
the American dream come true.
People keeping busy,
so many things to do.

Kitchens filled with gadgets,
hi-tech all around.
Microwaves, cuisinarts,
gourmet delights abound.

A stereo in the family room,
the computer and TV set.
Trivial Pursuit and the VCR,
entertainment needs are met.

Bodies fit from workouts,
the Nautilus is a must.
And for the mind the latest books
on finance—how-to—lust!

Upwardly mobile people
needing to be the best.
Hiding what's real with make-believe,
no feelings, no love, no rest.

Norma Ketzis Bernstock

What Is Christmas About

Christmas is a day of cheer.
The absolutely best time of year.
Christmas isn't about Santa or
    nice little toys.

It is about a little boy, Son of a King
    born in a manger.

Have you heard of anything
    stranger?

His name was Jesus,
Savior of the world, who was to
    die for every boy and girl.

The Wise men brought him gifts
    from afar.

What should we give him?
Give him our hearts.
That would be a good start.

Lauren Jones

A Friend Forever

Dedicated to Melissa Darcy

A friend forever
That's what you are
A friend forever
Is a golden star
A friend forever
Means friendship won't cease
A friend forever
Means friendship will please
A friend forever
Is the guiding light
That gives you the strength
To face your fright
A friend forever
Is the one that will stay
With you through night
And with you through day
A friend forever
Is on whom you depend
A friend forever
Is really a FRIEND

Leanora Regan

The Cove

There is a cove
That we all know.
There children play
Each and every day.
There lovers meet
To be discreet.

But no one knows
It's where I go,
Just before night
When it's very quiet;
To be by myself
With no one else.

Mahalia Flippo

Solstice

Yesterday I was the anger
That someone else needs.
Until tomorrow disappears
I'll be the one who feeds.
Off the poise in my burning soul
Where the broken voice leads.

My clouded heart is now a storm
Waiting for some release.
On angel wings so thin
I can't find any peace.

Whispering into the faded light
"I tear the angels out."
So I let them attack again
Eden withers about.
Purity was killed so solemn
Enter the binding doubt.

The flowers bloom in the solstice
Where the water turns to ice.
In the garden disillusion
Even love has a price.

Michael Andrew Balasa

This Poet

This poet cannot speak but ought
That she herself has known;
She testifies to pique and ache
And contests left unwon.

She builds upon the basis of
Byways she has tread;
In process suffered, 'ere the grief,
And through it, sundry bled.

She speaks of God all laud with praise,
Through all He's by her side;
Of joy and laughter, love and hate,
As she rides upon life's tide.

This poet writes of what she knows,
And places she has been;
And that to pull from mind and soul,
Long engraved within.

From 'ere it comes, all blessed inmost,
As pen she puts to page withal
Until the day she hears the shout
That heralds her final call.

Lou Hensley-Parks

Love And Fear

Love and fear! The greatest attributes
    that makes man mortal.
Fear: a strong influence
    that keeps man's existence.
If we control fear,
    we can accomplish miracles.
Love: the greatest miracle among man.
    with love, you can defeat
    Fear and overcome death.
While fear can be temporary,
Love can last for eternity.

Kalani C. Boyer

Life

What is age but a number
That labels a lover,
Age in our society
Is today's child yelling "Poverty."

We the masses are listed by classes,
But for rich or poor
Our hearts are our core!

Our signature through life
Must not be one's age
It cannot by evil, hatred or rage!

Love must be our (Moni Ker) in life,
For our society is filled
With disarray and strife,

God in our life can settle us down
Make good out of evil
And our decisions sound!

A life full of love
Is our only solution
We must try our best
To silence life's pollution.

James M. DeStefano

Regrets

You once made me believe
that I was the only one,
how could you deceive me
oh, what harm you've done.

You always said you Loved me
I proved to you I did,
you said that it was nothing
when she crawled into your bed.

How could you say
that what you did don't mean a thing,
you can cry all you want
but it don't change the tune I sing.

I want to know the total truth
don't try to spare my pain,
because no matter what you say
I'll always feel the same.

Someday I'll forgive you
but never will forget,
of the time you lost me
to something you'll always regret!

Nichole Johnston

Easter Time

Easter is the time of year
That I always love
Every thing is shining
Even heaven above

I love to see the children
With smiles on all their face
It's a time to thank Jesus
For his amazing grace

It is a time to thank Jesus
For he died on the cross
So this sinful world
Would not be lost

Now when this day is over
We can all bow our head
And give thanks to him
For he is not dead

We may not see another
But in our heart it will always be
Knowing our Heavenly father
Will keep us always close to thee.

Margaret Brown

December Delight

I'm just a little fir tree
    that did not have a chance,
Until you came into my life
    and 'round me did your dance.

All those hanging bag worms
    that you have plucked away,
Gave rhythm to my branches
    as they began to sway.

Since you trimmed and cut away
    those nasty little burls,
Fruit can be provided
    for the friendly hungry squirrels.

Now that I have rid myself
    of all that fear and care,
I hope someday you'll find
    a nest of robins in my hair.

I want to thank you for
    the many things that you have done.
Together let us celebrate
    the birth of God's own son.

Martha Penney Butler

Untitled

Out of millions, there were but
    ten to work with
That's all he choose
Looking, examining where the tide left
That color, that shape
Buried in a box almost twenty years
I fancied what lay in that box
Today I glued them to the top
Now I see what he touched
Before the tide went out.

Margaret Robertson

She

Smiling, at the door, she stands,
Teddy wrapped in fragile hands,
Standing, smiling there.

Her cheek as smooth as innocence,
Life new to experience
Yet she knows of all.

She sees something I cannot,
Gentle eyes in silent thought,
Standing, watching me.

She whispers words in youthful shrill
Though tender lips sleep soft and still,
I hear but cannot guess.

With my voice she calls to me
And shows me what I cannot see,
But my eyes remain at loss.

Patiently, she closes hers
And points with heart in hand.
I look at her and see myself
And now I understand.

Mary Schindler

Love of Dares

Love is like a knife
taking a way ones life
Love to some, sounds real dumb
but to others it sound like fun
Love is someone who cares
by living life on a bunch of dares
Love is a dare in its self
just by opening your mouth
Love is to let someone know
how you feel about them
Love is learning from your mistakes
because every rule will break
Love is with your heart
take a dare, by letting it have a start.
Love seems like a game of death
it steals your every breath.

Rachel Martinez

Command

Come on babe Let's make peace
Take your hand off me you beast!
I command the God in me let you die
As you have always made me cry
Than when you lay on your bed
To rot! To rot!
I shall laugh O'laugh
Deep down inside my lot! my lot!
I wont be able to help as help
I have for many year my dear
Your soul shall know how you
Have always bent my ear
My dear your peace is fear
And death is near
Ossify! stagnify! O blood will still
My command is at your will
Go death go! go! gone
As the sorrow of tomorrow dawn.

Helen Sherwin

Helping Others In Need

Let some body know you are caring
Take the time to listen, to what
    they want so much to tell you.

For kind people are only a few,
    you are not so occupied
That you cannot spare a smile.
    for you never know why you might
    need somebody after a while.
Let somebody know, they are wanted
    Do not turn and look away
You will someday have to answer
    For the things you do today.
Never be in such a hurry
That you have no time to do.
    A kindly deed, for some one else
So in turn, some help you might need
    may come to you.

Nettie Katz

Tired Of The Same Old Thing

Relax before eating
Take a walk
Talk on the phone
Take a shower
Invite a friend over
Go out on a date
Try not to eat alone
Listen to some music
Go to see a movie
Go shopping after a shower
Go to the Library
Ride your bike
Play your violin
Start a new novel
How about house work
Go window shopping
How about church sometime
Volunteer once a week
Take a trip or a
Small Vacation!!!

Ola M. Peete

The Mind

Looks at
sunrise,
Heart
hears it.

Day
gradually
moves.
Light
comes.

Clouds
aligned,
colors
assigned,
I see
how
Morning
starts.

I hear night
breaking
Apart.

Myrna L. Baldwin

Untitled

Tomorrow's Christmas
Sugar plums dancing,
presents glistening,
children squealing.
Everyone's hearts
filled with Joy.

Christmas is soon to be here!

Ding, Ding, Ding, Ding
Twelve o'clock
Christmas is no longer near;
It's here!

Christmas morning
and the children
are laughing and talking
as if they are monkeys.
With all the wonderful presents
surrounding them
Everyone is having a ball.
For Christmas is here!!

Michelle Kinley

Friendship

When you're with me friendship is
such any easy word to say...
My memories bring back the days
in May....

We played in the beach day, and
night....Everyone was right, that
we have fright, when we are apart....

We just can't live without each other...
When I'm with you, and I come
home I have hard times with my
mother....

I tell her I can't live without
you....So that's why I go out with
you....
Friendship

Linda Moya

Untitled

Vines intertwined on a cobble -
    stone cottage.
Animated and breathing.
A song of years past
Two aged souls living pacifically
    in their honorable cove
A distant voice calls to them
Is it a God?
Beckoning them to come
    home
To a new life.
One without pain.
"A final wish before we depart"
To grow again on the earth
    in which we lived.
Two more vines intertwined
    on a cobble stone cottage
Together for eternity on
    earth in which we lived.

Michael W. Thomas

Power to Create

With each new
step down a lighted path,
ones eyes are presented with
a new wonder.
With each new
wonder that ones eyes vision,
ones mind is presented with
a new imagination.
With each new
image that one imagines,
ones thoughts are presented with
a new idea.
With each new
idea that one thinks,
ones hands are presented with
a new task.
And with each new
task that one takes,
that one holds
The power to create.

Melissa O'Brien

Two-Fold Thanks Are Due To Thee

Upon a Magic Hill
Standing still'd a Lonely Sun
A painted cow gazed her fill
A raptured tree embraced us One
All England's virtue did adorn
A true and gentle Lady Born -
And a weary flight-jacket, torn . . . .

I wish'd that I might be
The truest Knight of Chivalry
The First to wave and gaze upon
That Singing Sword from Britain's Stone

Then, perhaps I could proper share
A mite of the worth
Of the Lady there.
And give thanks for that veil
O'er what would be -
A true love e'er wed
To Our Divinity . . . .

Henning Meriwether

Stack And Visocki

Tweedledum and Tweedledee
Sound a lot like you and me
Always fighting, yet ever friends
When one rifts, the other mends

Plus, Tweedledum looks just like you
Well, Tweedledee looks like you, too!
For shortened names for you and me
You be "Dum" and I'll be "Dee"

That's better for us both, you know
Should there be people, friend or foe
That want to call us (What a bummer!)
Tweedledum and Tweedledummer!

So, "Dum" and "Dee" we'll be, my friend
Yes, friends forever to the end
Wherever we go, whatever we do
We'll always be friends, me and you!

Nancy G. Visocki

My Cat

I eye him napping in my seat,
Soon hear the tap of tiptoe feet;
Caress his fur as he strolls by
And call his name (there's no reply).
Precocious purr with flawless feature -
There is no more exquisite creature.

Through the yard and up a tree -
He'll get stuck, just wait and see.
Get the firemen on the phone -
I'm sure he feels he's all alone.
Give him a week, he'll try again;
The squad's becoming real close friends.

Move aside if he spots mice,
No hiding place will long suffice
These mismatched game for feline zeal;
He'll claim a toy, if not a meal.
But now he's tired - he's claimed my seat -
The sweetest thing you'll ever meet.

Melody Williams

Heart Strings

Sometimes played in harmony
Sometimes strummed off-key
Sometimes all tied up in the knots
Sometimes soaring free.

Often moved by kindness
Often wrapped in silence
Often warmed by memories
Often touched by loneliness.

Feelings play this heart of mine
Chords of notes in time
Written by those around me
Sharing life's encircled rhyme.

Love can make my heart sing
Love can make it sting
How empty it would have been
Had love never meant a thing.

Caress the heart strings with tender love
As gracefully melodious as the wings of a dove
For each song takes flight within my soul
The soulful symphony orchestrated from above.

Pat Tonelli

Believe

When I was a child,
someone said to me,
believe in your dreams,
and your dreams will be.

It took me these years,
I now understand,
listen to your dreams,
follow their command.

If you want to sing,
get up and do it,
if you just believe,
there's nothing to it.

If you are told no,
you'll never make it,
you search for your chance,
and then you take it.

Listen to your heart,
for your eyes won't see,
believe in your dreams,
and your dreams will be.

Mary Lisa Bonner

The Way We Care

Some of us care, but not enough
Some of us love, much too much
Some of us care, only to the cusp
Some of us love, beyond life, as such

Some of us never seem to open up
Some of us go all the way
Some of us never fill our cup
Some of us, the love will never stray

Some of us share love, but only part
Some of us give it all we got
Some of us hold feelings, from the start
Some of us love no matter what

This poem is difficult to finish
Because it really has no end
True love can never ever diminish
That love need not ever mend.

James M. Pinelli

Sweetest Kiss

Sweetest kiss;
softly friends.
Fingertips touch,
eyes always meet.

Music tells a story,
souls sing together,
a oneness takes hold.
People wrapped in sound.

The charm is subdued,
a shyness slips out,
neither a facade,
both are truth.

So far apart,
spirits keep in touch.
A simple symbol,
Talisman for soul.

Two people close,
yet barely friends,
apart, but also together.

Lynda Ferrell

Misty White

Misty white, snowy delight
Softly falls, painting walls
of pure tranquility!

Beauty grand, God's lovely hand
Touching earth with the birth
of a rare tapestry!

Peaceful mind, moment sublime
Touch my heart with a start
of deep humility!

Marie S. Williams

To Fit In

To fit in
That's the thing
The very key
Blunt out your sharpness
Refine your bluntness
Grate, peel and polish
Until something shines
And something fades.

Manjula Malimath

Soaring with the Wind

Two knowledgeable, free souls are we,
Soaring with the wind
In its gusts and breezes,
Forever looking for that day
When we should meet.
On that day,
the gusts have settled us together
on a limb of an old oak tree,
So there we may grow, together,
as one soul
Soaring with the Wind.

Paula M. Tuzziano

Wondering

Have you ever loved someone
So much that it hurts inside?
When you finally find the one you love,
he turns around and
stabs you in the back.

You buy him stuff,
and all you want in return is his love.
Well, I found someone who
means everything in the
world to me and he won't
even stand still.

When I look into his eyes all my
troubles disappear.
I gave him a hug and I never
wanted to leave his arms.

His touch felt so warm and
If only I knew what this would lead to,
wondering
why he went out with me wondering if he
truly loves me,
wondering if all he said was true.

Someone told me if you be true to your
heart, it'll be true to you.

Kelly Hodgdon

Life's Not Fair!

Life's not fair
so I've been told.
It matters not
if you're young or old.

When fate decides to deal a blow
Age has no bearing
This, I know.

You try to be just and fair
and you hope that maybe
someone will care.

Life goes on, this is true
but it makes it harder
when things start affecting you.

You work real hard to do your best
But you have to realize
that you're being put to the test.

Can you survive the hard knocks everyday?
Is there some sort of magic to make the pain
go away?

Whatever happens don't despair
just remember that LIFE'S NOT FAIR!

Myrtle Rosenblatt

An Artist In The Making

Art is wonderful, art is great
So I decided to celebrate.
I painted pictures wide and narrow
I even painted a tiny brown sparrow

I had a great time; I had a ball
I painted pictures all over the wall
I painted my books, I painted my fish
I even painted their fishy-fish dish

I painted the carpet, I painted my bed
I painted my toes, I painted my head
I painted my dolls, I painted my clock
I painted every house on my block

I painted the bottom, I painted the top
I thought that I'd never ever stop
Until my mom yelled, "No, no, no!"
"Put down that brush; you are not
VanGogh!"

Melinda Joleen Hernandez

Blanket

Happiness is fleeting
So grab hold
And ride it long

It's the very essence
Of what makes us all grow strong

Happiness is our blanket
It shields us from the cold

It keeps us all young at heart
While sorrow makes us old

Happiness is a fountain
That sometimes over flows

As tears of young lovers
Who may never even know

That happiness is fleeting
And one day your grasp won't hold

Jason M. Campello

A Gift

Life is a gift
so gentle it is,

Like the foam on your pop
or is it called fizz?

God holds you like a vase
never to be dropped,

For if he were to let you go
my life too would be dropped.

The gift is given only once
so handle it with care,

I only have one life to live
sorry - I don't have a spare.

For if the gift is dropped
or wasn't meant to be,

Remember in the end
God gave it to you and me.

Nicci Maher

The Jolly Old Man

There's a jolly old man,
So far and gay.
Once a year he comes your way.
With a jingle, jingle, jingle
And a hi ho ho,
As he goes dashing through the snow.

He comes with a leap,
He comes with a bound,
Churning the snow upside down.
From the north in a sleigh
To the south in a jeep,
I tell you now, you must not peep.

A bag of toys so bright and new,
He'll have gifts for me and you.
For he sees so far,
Knows what you do.
So, be good the whole year through.
Have lots of fun, run and play,
Santa will be here Christmas Day.

Jane Bearden

The Love I Once Knew

I love you;
So deep and true
my heart still
aches for the
love I once knew.
I look up at the moon
all I can do; Is
Think of the little
things we used to do.
Now my heart still
beats for you.
I hope all your dreams
have come true,
I pray one day
I'll get over you

Kimberly K. Lovett

Grave Interruption

We parked at the roadside and I
snapped shots of late winter
headstones, gray pieces
on the alabaster ground.
You, the digger, brought me to meet
those sleepers, witness life's absence
against our vital mood.
Images recorded, I turned to your lips,
wanted you to bury my darkening
apprehensions right there

But a car sped past us, cold
March melt was thrown in our faces.
I forgot young misgivings and you swore
we'd never get dry standing so close.

Laura M. Sperry

Plea of an Unborn Fetus

Please
Let me live
That honor and glory
To God I may give
Please
Let me live!

Priscilla M. Davenport

A Bit Of Fluff

Soft
  Smooth
    Soothing
      Tender
        Sentimental

Delicate
  Rosy
    Gentle
      Feminine
        Kissable
And just sixteen.

Peggy Schmalleger

Fall 1991

I loved the smell of Bristol Lights
Smoking up the warmth of your
Silver Subaru on cool evenings.

One crisp October night
We drove up Kingston Pike,
Restaurant and nightclub signs
Glowing in red and purple sunset,
Shopping for a range hood.

We held hands in your lap
But I couldn't stop squeezing
The muscle of your thigh
Or the softness of your groin
Through worn maroon sweatpants.

You grinned at me cockeyed
Like you always did,
Called me honey
And said you wanted
To spend your life with me.

Landon C. Harless

Smile, But Not Today

Some days, we really don't have to
smile.
Can't
won't
don't
want to smile today.

And if they make us,
we'll
pout,
shout
and carry on.

A smile is good,
but some days
are meant for
frowns.
So for today,
no smile.
Maybe tomorrow.

S. Brownstein

A Poem

The sky is blue,
and the air is crisp,
the grass is covered by
dew,
but these beauties I
can not enjoy,
for my heart does ache for
you.

Leia Guccione

Just For Now

You're someone very special
Sixteen years mark this day
With all the kind and thoughtful things
You often do and say.

A baby — a child
A young lady at last
Too fast — Too fast
The years have past.

We know you want to spread your wings
So much to do — So many things.

We know you want to rush with the wind
And in due time we will rescind.

But—JUST FOR NOW wrap up that smile
Tie it with ribbons and keep it awhile.

JUST FOR NOW we want to hold
More precious memories yet to unfold.

Please God— She's only sixteen
Let her spirit be free
Let our daughter
Be all that she can be.

Mary Brower

Autumn

Like a child
sitting on the harbor at sunrise
waiting for the wind
or some sign to appear
on the horizon,
she remains still.....
Awaiting tomorrow, the summer sky
now fades to grey
as the seasons ready
for Autumn.....
One final warm breeze
brushes her hair
leaving traces of salt spray,
and days gone by.
Deep blue waters grow restless
in anticipation - strengthening by night,
exercising their power upon the shore.
Like her dreams the changes come,
departing uneventful, and unforgiving,
inevitable though they remain.

T. Dianne Strasser

A Tugboat Christmas

Saturday night and all alone,
sitting by the telephone,
Work is done and kids asleep,
glad to stop and rest my feet,
You are in another town,
pushing barges up and down,
It's Christmas time and I miss you so,
I wish you didn't have to go,
I guess I'll have some tea and bread,
take my bath and go to bed.

Mary Cornwall

A Bonfire Is Blazing

It is the bonfire of recent loves
It discharges a load of the forgotten,
All love is in the beginning dry fire
abstruse game
A sword that opens a wound in the stone.

Hector Ruiz Diaz

"Infinity"

It was the night when we saw the eye's
Singing silent lullabies,
Crying softly to themselves
I heard the weeping of it myself.

It was the night when we saw the wind
Singing whispers constantly again,
Chiming off particles of grass
You came walking to me at least.

It was the night when we saw the dew
Was it whispering a song to me and you?
Calling it the time of day
It had to end this very way.

Katina Rice

Thinking Of Angels

From the corner of my eye
silver wings brush by
gentle winds awaken
sleeping spirits listen

In darkest moments
wings out spread
words of truth listen - listen

Clouds of doubt are left behind
swift moving wings of change
soaring past fear past pain
living in the moment

Golden music pours from heaven
clearing pathways in my mind
distant echoes from the garden
sound harmonies I've yet find.

Wings caress faith renews
souls bathed in rainbow hues
cords lead past strife
balancing the dance of life!

Nancy Murphy

Stone Walls

Wandering through the forest
Silent sentinels of time.
Long toiling hands that laid them
Now forgotten from the mind.
Gray guardians of New England
Tumbling granite now at ease.
Once warmed beneath the sunshine
Caressed by a timeless breeze.
Here canopied in cooling shade
Dozing under a blanket of moss.
Hushed watchmen standing ready
Enduring border, friendly force.

Phyllis M. Brown

When

When I am old
I will live alone
Beside white walls
Lilac and hyacinth
Scrambling through my windows
The grass will grow
Too tall
And small children will share the pebbles
Along my walk

Anne Whiting Miller

Night Storm

The thunder rumbles
Signaling
The light show
About to begin.

A jagged finger
Leaps to the heavens.
Then another one
Skitters across the sky.

An electric jolt
Sizzles along the horizon,
Cracking
A crooked smile.

Laser bolts
Shatter the sky
Like a hammer
On a piece of window glass.

Suddenly,
The whole sky is afire.
It's the Fourth of July
In monochrome.

Melanie G. Flanders

A Christian's Love

A true christian
Should have a love,
That isn't fake
But comes from above.

This love should stand out
From all the rest,
And it should withstand
The hardest test.

It's always patient
And very kind,
And if you will let it
This love will shine.

Just remember
When Jesus died,
The love that he had
Came from inside.

Because Jesus died
For you and me,
We should let our love shine
For all to see.

Lucas Binkerd

Untitled

Big, small
  short, tall,
    love, hate
      on time, late
        happy, sad
          joyful, mad
black, white
  prejudice?
    What's it's opposite?
Monica Oliver

Hearts River -

Passion flows through streams of winding
Currents pulling drifts of pain.
The winds add waves frustration blinding
In hearts river made of rain.

Keriba Gormley

Dazzling Darkness

The beautiful night sky
Shines in Godly darkness.
As the ebony rays float over
the dreams and brief calmness.

A celestial face glows
in the dazzling darkness.
Its radiant brightness shows no
feeling, thoughts, or distress.

While the darkness has many eyes.
The day has only one.
But the light of the jeweled sky
fades with the rising sun.

Laura Howell

The Clouds

Come fly with me and
    Share my love;
Of the wonderful world
    In the clouds above.

To look below at
    The earth and land;
These feelings are
    So very grand.

To fly with eagles
    To touch the stars;
To escape the earth
    And all its bars.

To touch an angel
    With wings of lace;
Time has stopped
    There is only space.

We'll dance upon the clouds
    And race with the wind;
Then tumble back to earth
    And have the dream end.

Lynda Logan

Open Up

Open up your eyes,
    see the beauty
    that nature has to offer.

Open up your ears,
    hear the whispering
    winds as they move
    through the trees.

Open up your mind,
    realizing it has always
    been here for you to enjoy.

Open up your heart.
    please give your heart to
    preserve what God
    has made.

Mary Bates

In A Little Town

In a little town where nobody cared,
Nobody begged, nobody shared.

There lived a man of many things.
Cats and octopus, lions with rings.

But only a little bit belonged to he,
The rest of it belonged to ......ME.

Kathryn E. Edgar

Spontaneous Combustion

One deceitful word,
searing from the lips,
scorching the ears,
sparks another.
Quickly an innocent lie is ignited and
begins to dance around the truth.
It blazes on,
charring the words it surrounds,
growing uncontrollably,
until an entire trust
has to be extinguished.

Matt Lehman

The Mannequin

The Mannequin...so real yet very fragile,
scars, bruises
And tragic memories,
Were now his blessings,
Each day his
Conquest,
In the midst of distress,
But serenity is defiant
To exist,
It must because he wants to live,
His purpose is
A mist,
An oddity is a myth,
For we all wonder,
When will I
Know?
And reality simply answers,
At the last show.

Lonny Boivin

Farewell To Thee My Love

Lovers who must say farewell
Say good-bye to heartfelt dreams
They give so much of themselves
And never learn what true love means
Lovers who must say farewell
Traverse a path that parts midway
And when that fork appears ahead
Lovers don't know what to say
Lovers who must say farewell
Cry when fate tears them apart
They cry and fight and rant and rave
But violence heals no broken heart
Lovers who must say farewell
Say farewell with tear filled eyes
For lovers who have said farewell
No word hurts so as does good-bye

Joshua P. Milner

The Green-Eyed Cat

The green-eyed cat
sat and watched and
swished anger in its tail.
How dare another have
what it wants
The other one should fail.
The green-eyed cat
looked long and hard and
meowed a warning to spring.
Took out its claws to threaten
But then —
Just sat on the fence to sing.

Mayhugh Palmer Tees

Desert Release:
Thoughtforms of Peace

Cosmic silence
Sands eternal
Ever-stretching crystal earth
Mother Father God maternal
Constance

Blue shadows
Cool thoughts
Remaining in the air
Peace pervading oneness
Silence

Transparent wall
Spiraling and hiding
Distant dance
Unending
Grace

K. J. Laramie

Sailing

Gone today,
sailing,
upon the great blue sea.

Remembering the way
the wind and the sun's warmth felt,
the coolness of the water droplets
splashing tenderly on my face.

Who would have thought,
that day,
those very water droplets
drowned by happiness
would want more than their share.
They took you from me.

Jerene Koenig

The Proposal

Will you be my valentine?
Said a little voice.
Will you be my lovely bride?
Can I be your choice?
Will you dearest marry me
and live in my tree house?
Even though I'm only three,
Grammy will you marry me?!

Mary G. Harvey

Wash

The mouth of a soul
sacred to all but
the caring one.

If you say it, I care.

Knowing is what I do
understanding I don't.

I say and it goes
through a storm for you.

Call it what you want.

It's only as far
as you see it.

Wash.

Heidi Streit

In Morning

East
rose its usual dawn
of
orange atmosphere,
black coffee
and
newspapers
left
for
dead
in
yellow plastic bags.

Patrick John Mittig

Visions

Crystal clear visions
Roads never crossed
Fogged by man's pride
Time that was lost

People are stealing
Crying for more
Realizing not
They'd had it before

Dim light is coming
Seeking are we
Lost in a world
Never to see

My life is ending
One last clear thought
All the money I've spent
All the wars that were fought

What does it matter?
This is the end
Up a new ladder
My spirit I send

Phillip M. Batchelor

Immortality?

Oh what dreams ye mortals keep
Of Heaven, Hell, eternal bliss,
A promise of eternal sleep,
Your Paradise is only this.

Paul Noble Jr.

Real Love?

What is this thing that they call love?
I hear that it's just great
is it two people like hand and glove?
Who make love, not war or hate?

How do you feel when you know it's right?
I hear that you can just tell.
Is it two people who laugh, not fight?
Who never scream or yell?

How do we know if love even exists?
I think the word is abused
how can it be if everyone resists
because we always get used?

I hear stories of love that make me dream,
but I just can't understand
things are never as they seem,
but I hear that there's only one man.

Deepa Madhavan

My Mother

My mother has always been there for me since the moment I was
born.
When I was ill, she held me in her arms until the eve turned morn.
If I'd fall asleep on her lap, she'd carry me to my bed for a nap.
She taught me how to tie my shoes and gave me love that I'd never
abuse.
When I was upset, she'd rock me to sleep.
Upon her breast no more did I weep.
I love to hear her laughter and see her care-worn smile,
because when it came to me being happy...she'd go the extra mile.
It her hurt me when I saw her cry, so I approached and asked her
"Why?".
She looked at me and wiped her tears, and said,
"You've grown so much in so few years".
As I walked out the door, I gave her a kiss.
I proceeded to tell her what I'd most miss....
you, my mother.

Kristy J. Fernandez

A Sight To Behold

Moonlight dances off of the rolling waves,
A baby duckling hides among the swaying seaweed,
And in the distance, a wolf howls upon a cliff high
Above the glowing lights of the city.
It is a sight to behold by any wandering soul.

Flashing across the night sky at a great speed is a
Shooting star, leaving streaks of glittering star dust in its wake,
A mother holds her newborn daughter close to her breast,
And a farmer watches as yet another year's harvest
Is accomplished.
It is a sight to behold by any amazing being.

Running down a sloping hill with arms open wide,
You let out a shout of pure joy,
A middle-aged man finds love once more,
And in the aftermath of a downpour, a single red
Rose blossoms to life.
It is a sight to behold by anyone young at heart.

Katherine Brown

To Know Such Love As Your Holding Your Own Child

Oh, how you carried love all along
A baby from heaven above
like carrying in your womb a beautiful song
How the baby breaths with such love

What's it like to carry your own child
Feel such love within you
To know the Blessed baby is your own child

How the Blessed Mary and Joseph
Prepared the way
For the Blessed child to be born that day

To have such joy in your own soul
To know the child is a part of you
To hold in your arms such a beautiful soul
Baby breaths of love so true

To know heavens love is not far
As you hold your own child
Like looking at the most beautiful, the brightest star
To know such love as your holding your own child

Like looking at the most beautiful, the brightest star
To know such love as your holding your own child

Karen Sobek

Your Child

Dedicated to Samuel Keith Wilson - Born 2/13/94

Fresh and new. Precious and delicate
A baby's birth brings hope of a
better life.

Beginning with a joyful scream
during the first breath.
Within that scream the little
child's lungs are being filled with
the spirit of God.

The purity and innocents of a
baby, changes the meaning of
life and death.
The wrinkled little body
reaches out for your touch, is
dependent on you, and loves you
unconditionally. He or She is a part
of you through trust and friendship.

It is an unbreakable bond.

Kellie R. Wilson

World War

The first was thought to be the last,
A black moment in history,
But not forgotten in the past,
A triumph of democracy.

The next more deadly than the first.
Won't we ever learn,
That death and war won't quench the thirst.
For the power that we burn.

The third will be the worst of all,
The coming day of judgment,
To show us all that we are small,
The ultimate mass movement.

The third world war won't be the last,
The destruction will maintain,
A tribal struggle like the past,
But never more humane.

James Karnes

Emotions

I trembling pulse. A painful fear.
A broken heart. A jerking tear.
Waiting on the edge,
not knowing when you'll fall.
Crying, screaming, can't help but feeling lost.
Like a sweet passion in your soul,
you don't know which way to go.
Unnecessary, unreal, you don't know how to feel.
Burning, bleeding, helpless, needing.
Is it the truth you seek?
Or is it the terror from beneath?
A partial form of reality shattered into tiny pieces
off into the heartbeat of the immortal thoughts
that dance inside your head.

Laurie Williams

Beauty

Beauty is in the eye of the beholder
and beauty doesn't always appear on
the outside of the surfaces.
Beauty comes from within yourself
and beauty is also another word to
describe your attitudes toward others.
such as: kindness, love, honesty, and etc.

Danette S. Atkins

Alone In The Cold

I stand here alone. Alone in the cold.
A broken heart with no-where to go.
Alone in this world of misery and pain,
somehow, some way I have to escape.

Wondering if this, will last my life
stuck in the capsule of eternal fright.
Living in sorrow day by day,
watching my life just break away.

As the leaves that fall from a tree,
is the same way my heart is falling beneath.
Not all at once, but slowly and surely,
I will soon be left weak and weary.

But to piece it together, I cannot alone,
I need someone beside me to hold.
So until that person comes along
I stand here alone. Alone in the cold.

Maylin Y. De Leon

Anne's Teen-Age Lament

At what age in my life shall I cease to be
A child in my thinking and in your thinking of me?
I know that I'm a problem and may never cease to be
But please try to understand and have patience with me.
Oh, why must one go through this adolescence age?
Oh, if only I knew, then I would be a sage.
Perhaps some not too for off day we'll understand each other
Then there will be no conflict between parents and daughters.
I have this mixed feeling what I'd rather be
Is it a grown up or a child? Both I want, but this cannot be.
So please someone tell me, at what age in my life will I cease to be
A child in my thinking and in your thinking and in your thinking of me

H. W. MacMillan

A Cry For Help

Somewhere in the night
A child is running
Passersby see the child
A kid no more than 15
These passersby take no notice
The child's just another
Street Urchin.

They do not see
The heartache within
The reason that this child
Runs away in the night.
For the few who feel some pity
Have no fear for this child
For already their feelings have died inside.

A nameless, faceless child
No longer is a child
An unknown street Urchin
Has died this very night.

Kim Wagner

Minding Your Heart

Relationships shall come and go,
But the mind, you see, ultimately is the compelling foe.
With each union that passes away, the mind becomes distraught,
And bitterly torn.
Only in time will the heart rule the mind.
For only the heart has the capacity and the willingness to
Allow unconditional love to make one feel,
Reborn.

Edward McNamara

Mother

Her face was happiness to look upon.
A child, young and eager.
The tiny body that would run, jump and leap for joy,
    Now stood.

Her face was tenderness to look upon.
In her youth, a body that knew.
A new life was hers to behold.
    She loved.

Her face was compassion to look upon.
Strong and able—yet, the lines were there.
    She held.

Her face was weariness to look upon.
Old from life and its toils,
    She lay.

Her face was quietness to look upon.
One who could no longer respond was still.
    She died.

Her memory is joy to look upon.
The life she once knew now reflected in the eyes of her child.
    She lives!

Lavinia R. Hopfe

Jenny Wren

Little wren so small and fragile
a child's stone could stop your travel
your wing damaged but you do not despair
as you try to climb into the air

The ground is your runway
but in the sky you are home
won't you let me help you
why must you get there alone

    In you I see such a strong soul
    and there's no other heart so brave
    you continue to try to fly on
    not waiting to be saved

What would others do
if caught in your plight
most would drown in self-pity
never again to take flight

    I wish others could see
    the inspiration you have been
    you've taught me so much
    oh thank you, little Jenny Wren.

Mary A. Coulby

Journey Of Fools

A spear flashes against the sky
A city disappears in a burst of light
Superior to the animals we rule
We use the traits that make them beasts
Our moments of brilliance are far between
We spend our time rolling in the slime
Reaching out for all we can
Never really ever satisfied
We hurt the ones we love and hate
Never stopping to identify
We pound our heads against the bricks
While searching for the truth
But the answers are locked in Eden
For which we have no key
One day the veil will fall from our eyes
And then we will see far too late
For all our apparent intelligence
We have made ourselves extinct

Philip C. Carlson Jr.

The Broken-Off Song

Bright song was in the summer air;
A common catbird cried somewhere
Behind the wall and thicket-green
Although the bird could not be seen.

The small boy listened to many a note
Plaintive from the grey bird's throat.
To him it was only a summer sound;
He had not yet felt nature's joy around.

Close by his feet lay one round stone;
In half a moment he'd seized it and thrown,
Stilled the bird and stopped the song,
Broken the round of the Creator's song.

The boy was a statue with beating heart;
Sweet day and he seemed far apart.
His earth-caught mind had not foreseen
What throwing a stone at the bird would mean.

It was in the breaking off of song
That a man came into the small boy strong.
Where the boy would praise the arm's fine aim
The man would give the song acclaim.

Maxwell Millard Welch

A Reflection On A Foreshadowing Of Spring

All is at peace.
A dormant spring
awaits within
for His touch.

I trust in Your
incomprehensive Wisdom.
You, who fashion
a universe,
can make a spring in me.

Miriam Fidelis Pinchot, O.S.U.

Why?

I have this feeling of heartache,
A feeling I can't explain,
I'm not for sure what it is,
But I think it's called pain.
The pain that she left me,
When she pulled that trigger of dreams,
Oh, how my mind is in a whirl,
And I don't know what it means,
But when she pulled that trigger of dreams,
The trigger to my daddy's soul,
And the pain that I felt, when I woke
Up that morning, and heard him
Holler "no", why she ever did it,
Will always wonder in my head,
And I pray for her every night,
When I lay down for bed,
I will always love her,
Even though she stole my heart,
But, I will have to accept what she did,
I guess today will be a start.

Keila Perry

Life's Test

When we watch the sands of time descend each day
Alone, we glimpse our tracks made along life's way.
Deep into the soul we must search and reflect,
Past deeds might point to some character defect.
We shun those thoughts which tarnish our perception.
Simply be guided by this for reflection —
What we do for and to others is the test,
Only then can we know if we did our best.

Frances C. McGarry

Lessons Along Life's Way

On a day like any other, around the first of May
A friend of mine stopped by, with things he needed to say
But by learning the things of knowledge
Or so the scholars say
I did not listen close enough, and sent my friend upon his way
As I tried to study, it began to impart
How much more I could have learned had I only opened my heart
The things that seemed to torment him came from the bowels of hell
And again and again I asked myself of which of these I dwell
I have always tried with the compassion of my heart
But the trappings of this world are those that hell calls to depart
So Lord I ask you to understand
For I am a mere and mortal man
Help me with your kindness
As you have from the start
To change the things in which I must
That dwell within my heart.

Michael D. Johnson

Gentle Breeze

So long ago, yet like yesterday
   a gentle breeze touched my life-
Amazing, so soft but strong free but sharing
   cool during the heat of the day
   warmth in the night-
Still like a dream
   yet - I know it was real -

That breeze - awakes the sun and
   there is sunrise - swishes it's broom
   scattering clouds in the sky -
   chases the sun to the horizon and brings
   on the sunset - lights the stars
   and tows the moon thru the night

Where did it go - and yes why?
The trees are motionless
   or blown to the ground -

Sad, the breeze can't kiss the sapling
   and not try to topple the oak -

Gentle breeze, where did you go —-

H. T. Burton

Renewal

Yellow lie the leaves beneath the tree,
A golden blanket for its special place.
At first they fell like tear drops, one by one,
And then in torrents until all were gone.

Were those tears of sorrow for the summer past?
Or tears of joy that they, at last,
Could succor Mother Earth, that she might bring
A bounty of renewal in the spring?

Mildred E. Hooper

For Only A While

My baby for a while.
God let you into my life.
For only a little while.
We nurtured you
and watched you grow
until your mother could show
she could handle you.
God let you into my life
for only a little while.
I'm thankful it was me.
To see your sweet baby smile.
Even if it is was - for only a little while.

Ethel Duran

Untitled

I look in the mirror and what do I see?
A grown women where a girl used to be.
The little girls eyes seemed to sparkle and shine.
It's hard now to believe they were actually mine.
The little girl's world seemed so colorful, so bright.
And now the world seems as pitch black as night.
The little girl had no fears in her head.
Except maybe the little monster under her bed.
Now I don't have the courage to walk outside.
I conceal myself in my bedroom to hide.
The world's a lot scarier than it used to be.
Everyone seems more heartless than when I
was three.
Nikki Wieder

In Dot's Backyard

What a quiet serene place,
A little gazebo surrounded in lace.

Sitting at the table, just me and God,
Such a calming place, waiting 'til I nod.

Wake up and listen a little more,
The frog band playing a little score,

Lily pods and goldfish, a pleasant sight,
Trickling waterfall, soft breezes in the night,

Come see my garden, where an arched bridge stands,
There is none so beautiful in all the lands.

My own little Paradise here on earth,
Pleasures the soul, with each moment a new birth.

Precious time fully enjoyed it seems,
Fond memories pass sparking plenty of dreams.

Each setting in my garden, seems so new,
Different thoughts, good ideas, and sky so blue.

Flowers a plenty with neat little bugs,
Everyday my garden gives me loving hugs.

Listen to the animals, the birds and such,
This enchanted garden is all mine to touch!
Linda D. White

Smile

If you should meet
A man on the street
Smile, smile, smile.
He may look down or up at the sky.
No matter the reason why.
Smile, smile, smile.

As he goes along on his way.
He may meet some lonely gal, and stop to say.
Aren't you happy dear? Please tell your face.
For an ugly look, there is no place.
Smile, smile, smile.

She smiles at him and away she goes.
And where she's headed, no one knows.
She has a message, she too, has learned
That the face tells all, to those concerned.
Smile, smile, smile.
Mrs. E. R. Palmer

Hidden Valley

A bronzed mesa wrapped in a sunset flame;
 a melting horizon pressed in a fiery frame,
Forever secure in my own meditations,
 never straying from my dreamy contemplations.

Gliding through lush, green fields;
 natures domain where nothing yields,
Lies a foal with her coat a gleaming;
 she slowly awakes from her gentle dreaming.

Queen of the forest, tall in her place;
 a spiral tower of crystallized lace,
Reaches from her forehead, proud in its height,
 she spreads her wings for an afternoon flight.

Wind through her mane as she gathers her speed,
 joined by the company of a jet black steed,
Together they rise, synchronized as they were;
 then he leads, to make a cloud path for her.

Dancing through the sky with heavenly grace;
 enjoying the bounty of the infinite space,
Eventually they seem to be only a spot,
 sparkling in the distance with a rhythmic trot.

Then they land on the marsh; plush in its feel;
 they slow to a walk, bow, and then kneel;
At the end of this day, fatigued from their ride,
 the imaginary creatures retire to my mind.
Laurie Brazil

Mom

A mom is someone who cares and who always shares.
A mom is someone who will be there and will try to be fair.
A mom does stuff for you and will be with you when you have the flu.
A mom is the heart of the home and will never leave you alone.
A mom is always willing to take a walk and will listen when you talk.
A mom is someone who will supply love and is kind of like a turtle dove.
A mom is someone who will stick up for you and help through hard times, too.
A mom will give you confidence when you're not sure and be there with the cure.
A mom is someone who will tuck you in, and she will pack your lunch tin.
A mom is someone who does good deeds and will try to fulfill your needs.
A mom will take you to the mall and fix your knee when you fall.
A mom will encourage through the years and when made fun of by your peers.
A mom is someone who will ask about your day and will help lead the way.
A mom is someone who will believe in you and will always be ready to help, too.
A mom is someone you will not embarrass and one you should always cherish.
Nicole J. Skelton

What Is Love?

The years I spent in waste and want, my soul crying out for affection.
The heartfelt longing for someone to share, my joy and comfort affliction.
 I knoweth not, for I've ne'er had, a true love nor yet a companion.
Those empty years near at an end, along with its dominion — was this love?

Long I've craved, by necessity saved, my heart bursting with longing,
For mate to share this love I bear, with all the tender loving care
 stored long within my being; and how I cried, nearly died, when
someone callously turned aside my need to love, and of giving.
 Is this love?

I only know, since first we met, a joy when you're near, and better
yet, a vision of beauty to thrill my soul, a spirit of gladness, delightful, bold.
 An empty void when we're apart, a touch of sadness in my heart, and
an impatient longing on my part, 'till next my eyes behold thee — This is Love!

But genuine love, real, with utmost potential,
Needs mutual giving, and a love that's reciprocal.
 When mutuality exists, equally, each to the other,
With time grows and grows, growth lasting forever. That's true love!
Charles E. Watson

Untitled

The heat bears down like a blanket of hell
smoke
wind
They say you can hear the trees scream
The ashes of moonscape envelope me
why?

Erik Sveum

A Mother's Love

A Mother's love is deeper than oceans
A Mother's love is higher than mountains
It's majestic beauty is so amazing
Each time her hand reaches out to comfort
Her love is felt to be so caring
Her love is forgiving, healing and freeing
It's a love no human can take away
It's a gentle love that lives through time
It's a love that brings cheer though sadness may come
It's a love which believes when believing seems hard
And all the world remains in disbelief
It's a love which glows like a precious jewel
This kind of love is worth more than all gold
It's a Mother's love which loves beyond measure
A Mother's love is a miracle of joy
It's a sign of God's special gift of love.

Mabel Su

"The Wisdom Of The Tree"

Looking out the window I see a magnificent tree.
A parasol of swaying branches as nature meant.
Playfully dancing in harmony to some secret tune.

Providing homes for bountiful birds
Listening to their beautiful melodies
Attentively bent to the sounds of nature.
Delighting in children's gleeful laughter
Or listening to the calls of pain and despair
To wonder of life's secret treasures.

Patiently awaits the blossoming of your being.
From seedling to death it fulfills its destiny
Never striving to be more than was intended.
Oh! Why can't I be like a tree?

Marie I. Knarr

Life's Miraculous Flight

There is a place where everyone's been,
a place all golden and bright,
where people come and people go,
on life's miraculous flight.

The place I know, has stairs that go,
from the earth up to the sky,
And whether you climb, or whether you fly,
The shell you have must die.

It's sad sometimes to leave behind,
the people that you love,
But always remember and never forget,
that special place above.

Don't think that life is over,
once you've passed away,
for this is just the beginning,
and the start of a whole new day.

And when at last he comes to you,
and tells you of your birth,
He'll send you here where you'll be loved,
on a miraculous flight to earth.

Kathryn Thurman

Loves Remembrance

A shooting star amidst heavens grace,
A subtle kiss, a soft embrace.
A gentle rainfall, and a rainbows surprise,
The beauty in your face, the care in your eyes.

The miracle of life in a newborns cry,
A gentle touch, a soulful sigh.
Seraphic sounds of spring riddle their tune.
A star studded sky, an enlightening moon.

This soft light shines for few.
A gift of love, a chance to renew.
I envision your eyes, and the care in your face,
I long for your love, and your healing embrace.

Michael T. Conser

The Still Figure

Filled deep with sadness as innocent eyes stare into the black night,
A sudden fear builds up with her aching heart,
While she momentarily catches a glimpse of someone's pain and
    suffering,
Dancing out of reach inside the darkness.

She sees herself kneeling above it all, looking down,
Teardrops falling to the lifeless grass below,
Finding she doesn't know the still figure of a girl before her.
And staring into the eyes of sorrow she understands she never will.

Does pain have a name or does suffering have a soul?
She silently cries out to the night.... to the world,
But as no answer will come she gives in to the emptiness,
And dances one last dance... inside the darkness.

Melissa Melton

America

Sweet land of Liberty, hold her standards high,
a symbol of freedom where the brave gave their lives.
America...founded upon the knowledge that all people
are equal in God's sight, yet often our forefathers
prayed to be led by The Holy Spirit exceedingly bright.

The bells of justice ring each day anyone enters
a church to worship Jesus King of Kings, and
missionaries are sent forth from this nation
to spread the Gospel on Angels wings.

This country has been so blessed by the Father above,
in abundance like the land of Canaan our needs
are supplied in love.

Americas greatest treasure is The Bible worth
more than the finest gold, what a privilege to
be a citizen of the greatest land in the world.

Kathryn J. Smith

Giving

Oh here it is that time of year
A time of joy, a time of cheer.
Treats and gifts and love abound
Many fond memories are once again found.

There are bows and lighted evergreens,
But is this all that Christmas means?
So few of us will realize
This Day is no different in some eyes!

No homes or friends or even a meal,
Unbearable the sadness these precious ones feel..
I hope that some day we will learn to give
To those who ask, "just help me to live".

Linda M. Collins

Non-Directed Direction

A man of non-directed thought stood at the point of
    a thousand endless roads.
Grave steady eyes of concealment clouding an
    unknown living past.
Mused by tenderness, frightened by poise, and
    never an aim he sought did offer
        fire for his coal.

Shed of duty, emotions loosen, revealing even
    less of the past.
Asking more of the future, needing badly a conclusion.
Choices unending, callings unnoticed, seeking
    the first of the last, finding only the
        agony of his own fault.

Cemented worries pave ruts in the mind.
Skipping records of thought, scratches needled
    over popping out loud.
Massive unskilledness, numbered measured means.
Pits of worldly misfortune, problems created in fun.
Make all of the thousand endless roads all seem as one.

Kevin S. Amstead

Reflections

As the rosy glow of the morning sun rises to greet a new day.
A thousand sounds and shadows flit across the beginning of a new day.
    Busy hum of bees, birds singing their songs.
Smells of the new mown hay.
    Heat rising from the glow of a new day,
Sun on the azure blue of a stream of water lying between great
    mountains.
    Whispers, of the evening, and breezes close the door of another day
As evening pulls her curtains and pins them with a star.
    As the sun sinks into the vast world of the beyond to rise again
Another day.

Millie Mullen

Untitled

Words, desire, despair, compare.
A time to die, a time to choose.
Four are found, yet ten bound.
You choose, you loose.
Prepare to repair, your tripe little life;
    the image of one, seen as another.
My brother, sister, a trapped tornado twister.
Life, Death; you flirt with fingernail dirt,
I rhyme with time, crime pays for the days of confusion,
diffusion, thoughts of the dream scene.
I ream and bask in thoughts of streams,
movement, stillness, till eternity do connect.
A line is stressed, bent, wrecked.
On top of space time does sit, triply viewed as Earthen king,
yet, the peasant of the Universe
we dwell, so, those rare, dare to stare,
clouds, mountains, sky, puddles alike, life abound do you care?
Poignant passion, plucking flower.
Frolicking thoughts, wondering why.
Hurricane chains, thundering rains, we complain.

Jason Benny

Jim

The lights turned on to begin the show,
Yet darkness remained in his mind.
THERE WAS DARKNESS.
Darkness fills all spaces of time and matter.
Darkness that of which we don't speak unless...
WE TAKE THE TRIP.

Joel Koch

Men

Why is it men must never cry,
Why must we keep our emotions deep inside?
Why can't I find the key to unlock the
feelings inside of me,
    As I sit and wonder why
    A tear falls from my eye.

Brad Thompson

Autumn Splendor

Autumn is a season of gatherings and reflections,
A time to thank God for His divine protection.
Scenes of pumpkins, Indian corn, and bales of hay
All lure us on to the splendor of an autumn day.

Like the display of a colorful quilt, the autumn leaves
Of gold, scarlet, orange, and brown drift from the trees.
They come tumbling, swirling, and dancing down,
Swiftly making a patchwork over countryside and town.

Yes, it's Indian Summer days,
Early mornings are filled with haze.
The nights are crisp and clear with brilliantly twinkling stars;
One can easily view the little Dipper and Mars.

Wildlife—deer, ducks, and pheasants abound;
They're fleeing from hunters in the woods and fields around.
Wild geese in their V-formations southward fly,
Bidding forthcoming icy winds and snow good-bye.

The days are gradually growing shorter,
In keeping with nature's plan and amazing order.
Autumn splendor is great to behold;
It is a time of mellowness etched in gold.

Nancy Grady Wilson

tiny as an ant

a single man:
a tiny ant:
working and toiling blindly
tiny and minuscule.

an ant builds a mound
with great labor
a single step from a
human brings it down.

a man builds a life
money and power
comfort and a family
it takes so little and they are gone.

and like an ant in a field,
killed in a flash unknowing death's arrival
by a single step, little missed by the world,
so too a man is gone
with the slightest brush of God's hand.

Matis Shulman

Untitled

On the top of a stump what a sight to behold
A tiny city of orange and gold

Ivory towers some tall others squat
Their turrets all rounded like kettles and pots

The inhabitants here both wriggle and squirm
And in the main thoroughfare a centipede worm

You've guessed it by now
As our small city booms

On top our stump
A bunch of mushrooms.

Peter B. Felts

This World Of Mine

My world is like a hollow sphere
A vast and empty space;
Like a vacuum, yet dense with doubt,
And shadows every place.

I dreamed I stood at the edge of this world
And searched it far and wide;
Although it was dark I could faintly see
A silhouette on the opposite side.

So I started to walk, alone and afraid
Like a stranger in a foreign land;
The silhouette became a familiar face,
Like a mirage on the desert sand.

I quickened my pace and hurried on;
I must have walked for a day;
And when I'd think I was almost there
The mirage had slipped away.

Always just out of reach it was,
No matter how I tried;
Then I woke, and you were gone,
And I hung my head and cried.

Juanita M. Manning

Summer Of Her Seventeenth Year

The summer of her seventeenth year
   A woman in the mirror
In a gown gauzy and sheer.

The summer of her seventeenth year
   On the rose fell a tear,
As she stood waving farewell on the pier.

The summer of her eighteenth year
   Her knight on a Harley appeared.
She hesitated between delight and fear.

The fall of her thirtieth year
   On his hand fell a tear,
As he lay in his bier.

J. Pierritz

Moving Day

There was once a beautiful bottle
A wonderful genie lived there
Her voice was filled with laughter
Her love was everywhere.

This lovely spirit touched others
Her smile was always returned
She was held in the highest respect
A respect she'd quietly earned.

After her earthly work was complete
It was time for the genie to go,
Tears were shed and hearts broke in two
As prayers were offered from heads bent low.

She smiled a sweet smile
And sighed a soft sigh
And gently closed her bottle home
She raised her eyes and her soul
   took flight the bottle was left alone

Here lies that lovely vessel
No less beautiful to see
But it's only an empty bottle
For the spirit is set free.

Kim Blevins Stiltner

Ghosts At Thanksgiving

There are ghosts at Thanksgiving, but how can that be?
Aaah, I screamed-one just landed on my knee.
No one can sleep, not even a mouse
with the ghosts running all over the house.
When I start to fall asleep,
a ghost takes a leap across the room and on my bed.
"'Tis a fine house," he said.
So, when I get up I'm in a bad mood.
At the breakfast table the ghosts are so rude.
When I went to school, they went in the pool and sat on my stool.
One ghost tried to act cool so he took my Dad's tool.
Finally, I couldn't stand it any longer. "Get out of my house,"
I said. "Get out of the house, get out of the house," said the mouse.
"Get out of my house," said my Dad and boy was he mad!
"Get out of my house," said my Mom and she wasn't calm.
"Get out of my house," said my sister. "You hurt my blister."
"Get out of my house," said my brother as he slapped one and then another.
The ghosts went away. So you may be thankful on Thanksgiving Day.
Hurray, hurray.

Jennifer Sawayda

Holding On

When I think about yesterdays gone past, remembering the dreams I've had, it all makes me feel so glad I took a stand, I'm holding on.

Learning not to fear that which I don't understand, overcoming that which can't be changed, just making the best of everything, I'll just keep holding on.

It seems like magic, time goes and time comes, changing our lives, you know it all seems strange like chasing after rainbows, its amazing, I'm still holding on.

So reach for the sky, climb your mountain, live your dreams, learn the unknown, overcome all your fears, just reach out and keep holding on.

Alvin L. Giles, Sr.

Wisconsin Eschatology

Maple leaves explode in crimson, scarlet, gold of truest hue.
Green kin, awaiting miracle, give lively background.
Stately unchanging fir smile soft boughs of accent.
Total radiance-fit for grandest King-but never wasted seen or unseen;
Noiseless-yet welcoming the gathering fowl, whose strong wings whisper yet another seasons end.
Silent, with awe, we revel in the beauty, until overwhelmed we exclaim praise and wonder-
What will Heaven be?

Charles D. Wright

A World In Need

The community is drugged. The people are rabid and violent.
All of society is at a loss.
The family is weak. The unity is destroyed and the future generations will pay the cost.

The vows are broken. The altar is forgotten. The rings are no longer a token.
The congregation's restless and the preacher is upset and the Holy Word is no longer spoken.

Oh but things can be better, yes so much better if we would only build on strong foundations of love.
And stop trusting and modeling after man, but our Heavenly Father who looks from above.

Keith McLendon

The Invisible Enemy

An Anonymous Incident of Death Spreading
Across our once strong, and powerful nation.
Conceived from nowhere, and lingers everywhere.
Silently he whispers but no one hears him until
   he screams.

The enemy, built of solid stone, unable to be penetrated.
Nothing can defeat it.
And we are frail, fragile and weak.
Breaking with every mere breath, easily defeated.

The day of ribbons where the oceans meet the shores,
   without resistance.
The day of the dead and the living combined.

A palm flexes,
Inside the hand of hope lies an arched red ribbon, and a pin.
A single injection threw the center, and into one's heart.
The men that died, the women that cried, trapped forever,
Contained within the walls of this blood stained ribbon.

Some discard it, recognizing it as just a ribbon.
Loosing respect and gaining a disease.
They marry the enemy.
Till death do they part.
    Kelley M. Brine

Old Friends

The good times shared were all forgotten.
After that night, life was so rotten.
Words were spoken that weren't easy to bare,
tears were shed, but no one cared.
It once was forever, now it's for never.
We shared so much, you now would never know.
She treats me like dirt for what she only knows.
She gives reasons, but they don't matter now.
The friendship is gone, never to be found.
    Lindsay Verone

Mom and Me

Just my mother and me
All alone by the sea
That's the way I wish it could be
Just so I could show her and make her see - the real me

With the waves crashing on the sand
I'd ask her to hold my hand
And tell her that I understand
More than she thinks I can.

As we walk through the faint mist
I'd hold up my palm and clench my fist
And finally have the guts and the courage to let her know
That now is the time for me to let her go
And once I got done saying what I had to say
I'd open my fist and let the wind take it away
All the old - past and present pain.

And although I know that somewhere in time
Our roads are bound to cross again
It doesn't really matter when
Because I now know my heart has come to see
That she doesn't belong to me...
    Leslee Renee Nance

Whispers

A whisper can be beautiful.... as a breeze upon a tree.
A whisper can be beautiful between my love and me.
But a whisper can turn ugly when it falls on neighbors' ears.
It can wreck one's self esteem and drive one close to tears.
"So when you consider whispering," as told by one wee elf,
"If you don't intend for all to hear, then keep it to yourself."
    Joan M. Miracle

Treasured Love

I remember when our love was new,
   All the things we treasured too.
Sharing one another's feelings helped us walk the line,
   Into the commitment of caring for a lifetime.
I rejoice in sharing the love that brings us close today,
   And through out all that life has brought our way.
A love built on trust and understanding,
   Forever hopeful, strong and everlasting.
Dreams of our future I treasure too,
   Filled with tender moments of loving you.
All the wonderful things that are yet to be,
   I am now awaiting to see.
For I have found my lucky charm,
   The love of a lifetime wrapped in your arms.
Just wanted to say,
   I love you in every kind of way.
And to thank you now for everything you've done,
   In making our life together such a warm and special one.
    Karla Griner

Fool Of Love

I remember all those nights I spent alone
All those nights you were out and gone
Those nights I walked the floor with tear
filled eye's.

Now you sit there and ask me why
Why is my love for you gone you ask
look back over your past
you've cheated and you've lied
I've hurt and I've cried
well you thought you had it made
but look who's sitting there begging me to stay
you're the one who tore our love apart
you're the one who broke my heart
A fool I was before but never again
I'll walk out the door and never remember when
I was fool enough to walk in!
    Karen Woods

God's Bouquet In Heaven

God has picked beautiful flowers with his
   Almighty powers
He picks the babies that's never breathed
   Sometimes the withered as they sneeze
Look at you flower bouquet on the table, now
   tell me our God isn't able
To put us all in a bouquet in heaven. Just now
   my Johnnie is fading
In heaven, he's shining bright, being dad
   and grandfathers light
Also, there's Moms and Grandmothers, these
   Gals are like no others
He picks the young and tender, our hearts,
   He is the mender
God's bouquet includes all ages, our lives
   are like turning pages
Beautiful sight, heaven, we are told, God's
   love for us can't be sold
Fulfilling the bible everyday, soon he's coming to say—
"You, too, can be in my bouquet"
    Patricia J. Stoufer

Ode To A Tree

So strong, so brave do you stand
Alone on the far away hill.
So many have been touched
By your stately grandeur
Your never ending solitude
Your comfort from life's storms.
You bring freshness with your emerald greens
You bring coolness with your heavy boughs
You bring loneliness with your cold nakedness
Yet, you bring eternal hope
With your budding limbs.
None can compare to your ever-changing beauty
Your place in Nature's plan.

Patricia Stephens

"I Walk In Sorrow"

I walk in sorrow
Along the streets where you and I once used to roam,
A sad tomorrow I know will greet me,
When I choose to journey home.
So dark the night, so empty is the thoroughfare,
That only the echo of my footsteps fills the air.

Could I but borrow
One shining moment of those happy days we knew,
I know my sorrow would disappear
Until I'm once again with you,
Tho' stilled your heart and cold your lovely brow so fair,
The memory of you, lives in beauty, everywhere.

Margaret Maene

Untitled

I went to a wedding the other day
along with a friend who is also my fiance
We met new folks and got along fine
The best man did a toast with some very good wine
The ceremony was truly very moving
At the reception several of us started grooving
We got up to various sounds
All of us were dancing in rounds
But do you know what the best thing that happened was?
It's something only the most blessed lady does
When we went to the wedding reception the other day,
I reached right out and caught the bouquet!
Now that means my fiance and I shall be next one day!

Mary D. Martin

Lost Brother

In darkness, I see whom I despise:
An ugly coward with bulging eyes,
A bully who deals self-serving lies.
He's not the man I'd hoped to see.

And yet, somehow, he resembles me.
Twisted twin in a darkling mirror,
Ebon, wrong-handed, a foot that's queer,
The one my parents would not rear.

Oh twisted brother whom I must know
If in this life I would deign to grow,
Open to me please, if need be, slow,
That old wounds might heal and trust be sown.

A peace with Shadow it requires
To breach the gates where self respires.

James C. Daly

We'll Meet Again

Water running cold and deep,
Although they're tears from when we weep.
Shouldn't they be smooth and warm?
Unlike the harshness of the storm?

They should be gentle,
They should be soft,
Like angels flying,
And children playing in a barn loft.

And when we rest,
We'll meet in Heaven,
Until we die, we'll be together.

And after that,
We soon will see,
That it won't be so long
For you and me.

We'll meet again,
And we will see,
Not much has changed,
And happiness will never cease,
If you are there with me.

Kate Inglett

No Place To Run, No Place To Hide

I was their first born
Always considered number one
When I was younger
I had so much fun.

Though through the years
I jumped through different cages
With seeing eyes, and listening ears
To all my many changes.

I had so much fear
That my father would destroy me
With just a drink of beer
I never had no joys
Always my fear of making noise.

To them, they never knew I grew up
I was always know as their little one
Who wanted to have her own world
But now the past will never be undone.

Nadine L. Ostlund

Ode To Mike

We will remember him as the family jester -
Always provoking laughter.
There was never a clue.
We never knew
That he was crying and slowly dying inside.
We couldn't alter the way he died - SUICIDE!
To question and wonder why will serve no earthly gain.
'Twill only increase the pain.
We must now be content with the knowledge he is
currently God's angel of mirth and glee -
Now home safe ... and eternally free.

Pauline A. Agan

So Real

My feelings for you are so real they pierce my very soul
and when I'm not with you I just don't feel quite whole.
When we argue my pain is real enough to make me cry
It's even more so real now that we have to say goodbye.
I am a real person and I do feel real pain but soon on
the other side I will see you once again.

Alison N. Parham

Blessings

I count my many blessings
Among them are wonderful friends
I'm thankful that God has bestowed upon me
The many bounties he sends.

In thinking back upon my youth
I hear my grandfather say
Treat others as you'd like to be treated
You'll never go wrong that way.

I hear my gentle pastor
His voice so soft and kind
Urging his members to take the high road
And make use of their God-given mind.

I hear the bird's sweet voices
Each one is different, you see
Their songs are like a melody
Oh, how happy they make me.

Lonnie H. McLain

Hope's Resurrection

As Life weighs down upon my weary soul
And all I have is stripped from 'neath my feet
I stare into an endless, clinging hole.
Sour tears are torn from eyes that dare to weep
And wail at Life's unfair, intrusive hand.
He reaches in to where the flesh is pink,
Unsheathes His blade and makes His harsh command:
All ships must sail to His foul winds or sink.
But my salvation dangles like a rope
From Heav'n. A sweet and still, refreshing breath.
Enfolding arms renew my trampled hope.
The brightest star steers me from darkest death.
Life beckons from the grave to all who'll hear.
To he who listens not, God eases fear.

John H. Woodard

Untitled

I thought of you tonight
    and all my sorrows
melted into gentle pools of happiness.
Like the tides of the omni-present sea
    you are near me.
You are life itself, and into life's hands do I
    commit my soul.

I thought of you tonight,
    and all my troubles faded.
My joy surmounted the highest peaks.
    Like the rains of the heavens
you are sent to refresh me.....
I thought of you tonight
and became intoxicated with the presence of your mind.

Janet Crance

To You In A Lighter Mood

A little bird flew round my ear
And buzzed a story I waited to hear
About a lad across the way
Who when he had something to say
Did it in an unusual way
Especially on St. Valentine's Day.
He sent some sweets to a little bird
Who is sometimes blue, that's what I heard.
She burst with joy, and what do you think?
She's no longer a Blue Bird, —now— she is Pink!

Norma S. Tyburski

Saying Good-Bye

One day the sky turned black,
And an old fool thought how smooth the lake was.
When lightening flashed and thunder crashed,
He saw lovely flowers and listened to the birds sing.
The wind hit his face with an icy slap,
And he said, "Ahh, what a great day, the sun is shining!"
The sand tried fiercely to sting his hide,
But the old man looked straight ahead.
With a spring to his stride,
He said with much pride,
"My son never loose sight of love."
He stopped, shoulders squared and turned to stare.
A little boy watched as the old man waved to him.
The little boy stood in the middle of the street,
And then he began to weep.
As the little boy wiped his tears and waved back,
A smile started to crack,
And his face glowed with a bright light,
For, the little boy remembered something he once heard,
"Good-bye is not forever."

Karina Davis

Nature, At Her Best

Day is done. The heavenly streetlights, stars, blaze,
And below, in this fuzzy haze,
I get a slight glimpse of golden angel wings.
You can tell it is twilight by the peace it brings.
The lovely blue-carpeted sky has pictures nature drew.
And the gentle light shines through.
If you see it all in this view,
No fear of night will overcome you.
A silver piece glows in the midnight sky.
Oh, to see where angels fly!
Don't you ever feel the sensation of a mid night rest,
When you know nature, at her best?

Marita La Palm

Grandpas

Grandpas are good for planting seeds,
And doing all sorts of good deeds.

They're always here for you,
In whatever you do.

But then one day they're gone,
And so you're left with none.
You know they're in a better place,
And don't have problems that we face.

Where the sun shines everyday,
And happiness never goes away.

They suffer and have no strength to gain,
And even though they hurt, they won't let you
see their pain.

You're gone forever,
But you'll lose us never.

Mandy Dean

After

After we die, where do we go?
Do we go up to heaven where the clouds are like snow?
Do we come back for more? Or forget all our past?
It just makes you realize that life moves so fast.
Do you come back a cat? Or maybe a bird?
If this is true will your voice be heard?
How can we know what will be next?
Is it written in a card, a novel, a text?
After you die where will you be?
For that simple answer, we'll just have to see.

Kristen Watland

Alpaca

'Said good-bye to all we knew
  and drifted to the west.
Traveled days on dusty trails
  and thought that we were blessed
  when the sun went down behind a cloud
  or breezes moved the air.
But time was never on the side
  of that old milk wagon mare.
Alpaca, Alpaca
  a tried and true old four leg'd pioneer.
  'carried my weight and moved my soul
  and whispered in my ear.
Memories of days gone by fill me with remorse
  cause I can't bear the losing of that old gray talking horse.
Twenty one years of endless days
  and nights beneath the stars
Pannin' for gold to turn to cash, then spend it in the bars.
The wisdom old my gray friend I quickly cast aside.
Horses ain't to listen to, they's only just to ride.

  Mark Keillor

Together In Love

When the wind blew, and the stars danced,
and dusk fell over quite romance.

When the moon was a spotlight on a tender love,
two hearts came together and joined as one.

When peace joined peace, and hearts did collide,
he longed to be the one by her side.

She longed for him too, their love was so strong,
yet, in elder's eyes their involvement was wrong.

He swore to her someday, that they would be together,
and she pledged her love to him only, forever.

They carried the burden of love in their hearts,
and dreamt of the day they'd no longer be apart.

Till at last came the day that they could be together,
a ceremony of happiness which would last forever.

With smiles on their faces, they had wanted this for years,
and the eyes of the guests slowly filled with tears.

Time had taken away their chance to be married,
so together in love that day they were buried.

  Kim Minter

Running Like A Fool

Everybody knows that babies got no clothes
and everybody sees she's a victim of disease
it's the same old story our endless fight for glory
when it's all said and done... you'll answer to one

There's a stranger among us, there's a fire down below
let's burn down his property because his color doesn't show
he's his own worst enemy, she is the face sin
the devil's on the other side, don't let him in

I heard it on the radio, I saw it on the news
the lines were drawn in the sand and their prayin' in the pews
It's time we end this blood fight
it's time we end this feud
I really can't believe your running like a fool
There's danger all around us, it's the sign of the times
he's got the perfect alibi, it's the nature of his crimes
for vengeance is mine he said, I hold the only key
I'll shed a tear for all mankind on my quest to be free....

  Michael A. Lopez Sr.

The Wondrous Rainbow

It comes across the sky,
And everybody wonders why.

It is a covenant with the Lord above
To show us how great is His love

It colors the sky after a very long rain
And all searches for it's gold is in vain

No one knows where it comes from
And no one knows where it may go
But we thank you Lord our God,
for you wondrous rainbow!

  Jeff Taylor

Untitled

Rip my heart apart
And feed it to the ground
Take away my soul
and slaughter it in cold-blood
I am made from the fire of the earth
Burning white-hot passion burning
Control me if you dare it will only destroy me
Believe me if you will of little comfort that is
Tread on me if you desire I cannot fight back
You will never feel my raging spite
You will never touch my scalding mind
You will never dance with the joy that beats painfully within my heart
You can try to look into my eyes
  Through the so-called window to the soul
What you see will only frighten you
I have no humanity left in the tips of my fingers
I have no pity for myself all I feel if the fire
The fire that rampages through my mind invisible from mortals' eyes.
I am too numb to feel I am too dead to kiss
The ground will envelop me but the fire will still burn on.

  Josh Walker

I've Known Life

I've walked through the valley of dry bones
and felt the hunger
I've stood and watched as the sky
filled with thunder.

I've seen a child take its first step
and soon stumble
and I've seen the hand of God
that made me humble.

I've stood at the crossroads of life
and chosen well,
Sometimes fallen blinded by truths
I could not tell.

I've touched a flower
and had it crumble to the sand
and I've known the heartbeat
worn of a wedding band.

I've felt the cold steel
of a sharp tongued knife
so truly I can say
I have known life....

  D. S. Shanon

Love

To love someone is to touch someone,
In your feelings and tears.
Trust and faithfulness,
Lies before your eyes.
The feeling that is in your heart,
Is the one that steers you through it all.

Ali Trimble

First Kiss

For years I had waited so long and patiently,
And finally found the person I wanted it to be,
There in the dark I could barely see,
Suddenly you leaned in closer to me,
My heart started pounding, could this be real?
Was this the way that it's supposed to feel?
Just as a spark you ignited a flame
Never would my life again be the same.
Something in the atmosphere made it just right,
My spirit floated high like an eagle in flight,
Though only seconds, eternity seemed to past,
Forever I wished that moment would last,
My emotions took over and almost burst,
And I realized I picked the best to be my first.

Kevin Thetford

Heavenly Home

I sat in a field of wildflowers
And gazed at a cloud filled sky.
While butterflies fluttered above my head,
With wings of transparent blue and red
Delicately trimmed with golden thread,
And tiny diamond-like eyes.

A heavenly valley surrounded me,
And fear gave way to delight.
The misery and pain of this world below,
Along with the heartaches, trouble and woe,
Suddenly faded in a mystical glow,
And was replaced by a glorious sight.

My soul was lifted from me
To a place beyond the skies.
Angles were flying through the air,
With snow white garments and golden hair.
There were big bright mansions everywhere,
I'd reached heaven, where no one dies.

Loveta Mullican

So Is...

As fields of flourishing flowers
And grass upon hills of green
So Is God's Grace toward me

As sands on supple seashores
And stars in silent skies
So Is God's Mercy toward me

As succulent sweetness of honeycombs
And songbird's ballads of beauty
So Is God's Goodness toward me

As first flights of butterflies
And whispers of whistling winds
So Is God's Gentleness toward me

As the sun shines upon morning dew
And the moon pierces through midnight darkness
So Is God's Faithfulness toward me

As His hands were nailed, His side pierced
And as His scars and wounds remain
So Is God's Love toward me

Lena Ford

"To A Friend"

A dear friend I have found in you,
And hope you feel the same way too.

You're an inspiration to all whose lives you touch.
You're an angel on earth, who we adore so much.

You have a quality that is Oh so rare;
For others, you are always there.

Your faith in God will now sustain you
and also bring you comfort too!

Here is a thought I wish to convey,
Sunbeams and rainbows are on their way.

So clutch "God" close to your heart;
His love for you he's set apart.

For though you've suffered here on earth,
God's been with you since your birth.

The crosses that you've had to bear,
will someday bring you to his land so fair.

A place of beauty without pain,
sunshine everlasting will replace the rain.

God will be forever at your side; fear not,
In his glory you will abide.

Pauline Tretock

"Four"

I'm headed out the door
and I am only "four".
I got me a new cap pistol,
that I will shoot some more!
Here I go and I'm "fourteen",
across the fields and a nearby creek.
Shotgun in hand, some quail I'll seek.
And here I lie in a faraway land,
I'm "nineteen", grasping an "M16."
The mud is deep and the fields are bare,
and somehow another I just don't care.
Over there is my buddy, and he's no more...
I guess somebody forgot - "to tell him the score..."
The sky is dark except for the flashes.
In the distance I can hear thunderous clashes.
LORD, just one day more....
What I wouldn't give...
Just to be "FOUR"!

Martha Manning

Knowing Of Sin

I do not like to see your eyes frown
and I do not like to give you this grief.
Maybe I should turn the page
or take a walk.
There must be another path.
There must be another way.

I keep hurting you,
Stabbing you with another lie day after day.
And you will not walk away
And I cannot tell you good-bye.

As only us,
we lay in silence,
a lonely woman and a worn man.
We lay naked under a sheet of darkness.
I think sin never felt so pure,
as I trace tiny hearts with my finger
through the dew on your back.
I wonder if all those hearts can break.
And I am sad,
I know I will only bring you more pain.

Jamie Lawson

The Sea Of Life

My name is "Captain" Sam and I am six
And I have tasted Heaven,
'Cause Daddy lets me watch the ships I'll sail
When I'm a MAN of seven.

Eleven years have passed
As I sail the ocean's crest,
Loving all my childish dreams,
And living them, the best.

At seventy years I'm still aglow
With the wonder of the sea,
With the ups and downs of the ocean waves,
And what they mean to me.

Why not stroll down to the sea with me
And liken it's magic ways
To the storms of life, and the peaceful calm
That follows the stormy days.

It matters not our age in years;
The sea plays an ageless game.
The storms and strifes of sea, as life,
Are one and each the same.

Margaret G. Joseph

A Letter to My Friend

I know you are hurting because of someone you love
And I know how many times a day you cry to God above
And say, give me a reason, and Lord why can't you see
What you're doing to my family and how you're hurting me
They say you are a loving God, in my heart I know it's true
But it sure don't make it easy to understand the things you do
But Shar, just take a minute to look at things this way
We know God has a reason that we'll find out some day
Could be He needs a gardener to sow the seeds of love
And tend each precious petal He showers from above
Or maybe there's some old folks sitting around up there
And God needs someone able to rock their rocking chair
Or what about the babies that he has got to share
Could be my little brother needs some loving care
So when the time does come for you to finally let him go
Oh, you'll still cry and wonder why, but in your heart you'll know
That God does have a purpose and what will be will be
And nothing we can do can change the course of history
And through it all treasure each sweet memory
You're still Walt's daughter, show the love that you could see.

Marsha Witek

No Answers

It's almost been a month now, since you've left us behind
And instead of concentrating on other things,
I still find you on my mind.
Your laughter, your smile, all your funny little lines;
Why aren't you here with us
Making our lives shine?
You were so young and full of life
So why was it so suddenly taken?
No matter how much time passes,
Your memory will not be forsaken.
You will always be with us, forever in our hearts.
At any unexpected moment
The thought of you starts.
Although this may seem a little selfish
Because you're in such a better place,
I wish you could still be here
And I could say, I love you, face to face.
I'm glad I got to tell you that
Before this nightmare began
And I'll never forget you Bradley Aaron Shively. Never!

Mary Smith

Missing You!

I know I don't see you much,
And it's horrible to know,
That when I don't,
I miss you so.
You are my sister,
My best friend, too,
If we could be together,
I'd show you.
I'd show you that no matter how far apart we'd be,
My love for you, won't leave me.
I miss you so,
I don't want you to go.
I hope to see you soon
If I don't, I'll see you in the moon.
Your face will shine,
As far as can be,
And you'd see, how happy it'd make me.
So, until I see you,
Good-bye for now,
And, I'll try not to be blue.

Krystal Murphy

A Growing Love

I see your face among the fields.
And know that in my heart you are sealed.
For though I have many fears and many doubts.
Which to the fields creates many droughts,
Your smiling face comes shining through,
Making the fields come green anew,
A stunning reminder of just how much I love you!

I see your hand come close to mine.
The fields grow more and all will be fine.
We hold each other and forget the rest;
In the fall we know we'll reap a rich harvest.
We speak of the future and all we'll see—
Our fields are no longer full of debris,
For in all our plans we include you and me.

So whatever it is or whatever I see,
You are the seed and I the soil for planting
A love that will grow in perfect harmony.

Mandy Kristine Corbitt

Our Hope Is In God

If you can rise above the pain and sorrow
and make it to find a new tomorrow
waiting beyond this mortal fight
beyond the wrong, towards the right

If your eyes are set upon the goal
of giving in to God's control
then all the things you thought were lost
was only by our Lord's life, he paid the cost

The temptations, the trials seem to never end
and you come up short of a mortal friend
until you bow your head to pray
and God's peace descends upon your day

He is love, and truth and light
his hope eternal, freedom flight
to which we look and plant our hope
beyond this planet's mortal scope.

Linda L. Marrotte-Jones

A Panama City View

The beach explodes with scarlet, orange, gold
And melts away like ancient myths retold;
A string of small pearls soon soar to touch fire
And turns to black when brushed by strong desire
To race the wind. These gulls unite our days
And nights. The sandy beach and rippling rays
Fall head over heels into salty waves;
A heartbeat is heard over docks and piers
The warmth and the rhythm echo for years.
As light forbids dark the sun blazes on;
The people, like memories, soon will be gone.
As for my crimson beach, it will remain
Brilliant as always untouched by the pain.
Sweet colors now hide, the night lives in vain.

Lisa R. Garrett

If Only...

My heart aches, my soul is weary,
And my strength is diminishing.
So much time has been wasted.
So much could have been done.

Helplessly watching opportunities pass me by,
I am plagued not only by unnecessary failures,
But haunted also by memories of good times-
Moments lost forever.

Silent prayers for courage, are but thin shreds
of hope to which I desperately cling.
Shattered dreams, and an uncertain future.
Make even the brightest of days seem dim.

I am a prisoner of mind-
Enslaved by my own thinking
The shackles that bind my soul,
Seem to be gouging at the very core of my being.

My heart is filled with so much pain.
My days are days of sorrow.
But worst of all is knowing I have only myself to blame
For if only I had done things differently.

Nicola Tugwell

Fond Memories

Sweet memories of a very young boy
And the cousins of this young boys past
Spent time together and laughed together
These things will forever last

Vacations spent together with our families
At good old resort town Pismo beach
Spent collecting bottles and star fish
Nothing was out of their reach

He grew up to be a smart young man
A very hard worker he became
And what he accomplished in his life
Made his mother and family proud of his name

But the Lord wanted him for himself
And though its so very hard to bear
We have to give him up to heaven
Because now he's in God's care.

Isabelle Mattos

Life After Death

As she watched him slip away,
    and the day came to an end,
She wandered what life would be like,
    and how she could begin again.

With no more "I Love You",
    and "How was your day today"?
Her life would be so empty,
    without those words to say.

How could she start over,
    when her life was such a mess?
Many years were spent with him,
    and now only memories are left.

She can never go back in time,
    except to Remember When...
By the grace of the Lord, and the brain he gave,
    She can Re-live those memories again.

Kimberly Eilers

The Future

I look to the future
    and the future seems grim,
I look to the past
    and the past grows dim,
Will happiness always escape me
    and sadness there will be
I look to the future
    and the future looks bad,
I look to the past
    and the past is sad,
Will there never be wealth
    and always a concern for health?
I look to the future and curse
    and finally realize others have it worse.

Karen K. Yoggerst

For My Teacher

Sun is rising high
And the grass is green.
I can see the tracks,
Where you have been.
Dear Teacher mine,
You are like a star...
Where can I find you?
Where can I see you?
On your table lie little notebooks,
Kids are playing in your holy room,
And the little birds flying in the sky,
And the bell is calling for the early time...

Kitty Dudina

The Place

When I think of happiness, I think of being free.
And the place is deep inside myself, where I can be just me.
No nasty words, or disrespect can ever enter in.
Its a place that's deep inside myself, where only I, can enter in.
Now I don't go their very often, for there isn't always time,
but the times that I have spent in their,
are the ones that I can call, all mine.
Now wouldn't it be wonderful if, the outside was the same?
No nasty words or disrespect, and other causing pain.
Yes when I think of happiness, I think of being free.
And I crawl deep down inside myself, where I can be just me.

Marilyn Simonie

The Silver Sea

At the dawning of the morning
And the rising of the fog
The wind and sun dance upon the waters

Lonely beaches stretch endlessly
As the tides caress the shores
Washing up their bounty from the deep

Gulls maneuver gracefully as a cloud
As an ancient cypress
Stands guard over all

The skies slowly darken
As Orion stalks the heavens and
Fog horns disturb the darkness
Where light-houses put forth their beacons

As morning dawns again
The golden sunrise
Meets the silver of the sea.

Mary L. Fox

Storm

Wind blew like a hurricane,
And the snow fell like an angry God.
Blackness was everywhere,
The night stars screaming
To break through ghostly clouds.
The people of the town could go nowhere
like those trapped on an island;
The snow poured in sheets
Blanketing the ground with a white carpet.
The wind still howled
A wolf's cry
As the eye of the storm passed,
Laughing at those who dared,
Who dared to try escape.

Natalie Cozzi

Peace Of Mind

When you're down in the dumps and feeling blue
and the world has nothing in store for you
Your troubles pile up like a mountain so high
They're stacked one by one clear up to the sky
You wonder how long you can stand the strain
For each difficulty brings more pain.

Then it's time to sit down and recall again
All the blessings you've had since your time began
And the chances are you've had millions more
And that many more for you are in store

So meet every worry with a prayer and a smile
And ask God to guide you down each long mile
You'll see all your troubles just vanish away
And be able to conquer new worries today.

Helen Blake Curtis

Sights and Sounds of Late Summer

The roar of trucks on the freeway
    Driven by people accompanied by their CB radios
Crickets singing their hearts out to anyone
    who will listen
A full harvest moon casting shadows through
    leaves that know their final curtain is about to fall -
A soft warm breeze, rather unexpected this
late in the season, makes us think that -
Could some of these things, be served
to be eaten with a spoon
Would only be served as dessert

Marion C. Johnson

Contributions

It was blood that gave logic its belly
And then boiled over onto the brain
Hate enabled evil to sprout a head
But kept it from thinking clearly
Jealousy gave doubt its hands
Which try desperately to cleanse that spot on its damned soul
With trust came the lips
That sit moistened, untouched
Love is the heart of the matter
Simply waiting, ever so patiently
The bosom came from desire
That yearns to be pulled ever closer
Need gave the gift of the opposable thumbs
So as to acquire things like you and I
And pride swelled up so big inside
That the whole thing blew up leaving only emptiness
Who had nothing to offer

Mark Cristopher Whitmore

Everything Changed

Joyous anticipation, an eager wait, agonizing moments,
and then you were here;
Squirming, wincing, full of life: you touched us
and everything changed.

Tiny fingers clasped our hands, as wondrous eyes gazed our face
with a touch so tender and a look full of trust.
Relief and happiness flooded our hearts;
as overwhelming, uncontrollable - the tears flowed.

Tears of joy, grateful tears, cleansing tears of cheerful hope,
for wishes realized, dreams fulfilled.
Tears of pride, tears of relief, all flowed freely,
so fulfilling the gift, precious, unique: and a promise was made.

A promise of nurture, a promise of trust,
Being there for you, coming through for you.
A promise of faith, of love unconditional
Letting you grow free, towards the goals you see.

Because everything changed that wonderful summer day,
When a gift of happiness enriched our lives;
With the treasure of love, trust and faith.
An affirmation of life, a touch of immortality.

Prasad Prabhu

Friendship

'Tis true the clock of life is wound but once
And this we can't deny
But He who made the clock of life
Can'st hear our every cry.

He knew along this path of life
A friend I'd need to care
So gracious has He been to me
Your friendship for to share.

I know not when the clock may stop
But this I am for sure
A friendship based on His great love
Will ever more endure.

And in this World we know as "HIS"
Are new friends in the making
May you and I be faithful ever
In the bread that we are breaking.

For surely as the clock ticks on
Christ looks to you and me
To introduce them to our "Friend"
The Stranger of Galilee.

Opal Carter

That Certain Age

That certain age has crept on
And time crowds and must be stayed
Beset as it is with the end of things.
Finalities alter definition and overtake
The simplest breath like the setting of the sun
In its rising, the dry stalk in the seed,
Autumn in spring. The more the mind adjusts,
The more aware it is of our getting there,
Although our bones know and cannot beguile.
Ticking off calendars
Is pernicious arithmetic
Which makes that certain age
More certain of its end.
Even good-byes presume in their assumptions.
Perhaps deception can stem this rush
And recall that immortality
Long ended and gone
When getting there was all
Wherever there might be.

   O. A. Lopes

Summer's Leaving

Summer's leaving and I'll miss the hot days
and time out of school when we went out to play
Visiting the family on a daily basis.
Or having lots of fun with bicycle races.
Going to the movies,
staying up late,
going to the rollerway learning how to skate.
During the day we had lots of fun
playing basketball until the day is done.
We played tricks on everyone,
but now we're even.
I can't believe that the Summer's leaving.

   Jason D. Butler

It's a Small Thing

Animal insane
And walks like it's lame
Grabs it's crotch and shakes with that same
Can't complain about it's own pain
Killed education but skilled in profane

Life for it ain't been no crystal thang
I heard that somewhere somebody sang
It's get - up - and - go and in - come - drained
Objection to living... sustained.

Nothing to lose so it chooses big bang
What is wrong?
What it is to gain?

Check it's eyes realize it's strain
Vision is perfect it's living is vain
Before birth was stripped of fame
Trained that way...
Trained shame.

Ignorant, dumb animal insane
A man eating beast
That's how it hangs.

(godlike Yabach UAC of Peace of Mind)
   Lee Harvey Stone

Blessed

   If I could have stepped out-side of my body,
and watched my-self grow, to contemplate all of the
thing's that I have come to know, to reaffirm faith,
when I have lacked endurance, putting all trust in
God, for he is my true insurance. Crossing each bridge
with life, like tomorrow was already mine's, living my
life, instead of dying for time. To claim my life as
my own and enjoy the world, while it last; to create
as many beautiful memories, instead of dwelling on a
lost past. But through time I have gained wisdom, and
with wisdom I have come to know, that I am truly
blessed, for God had made it so; for God is with-in my
body, and he also watches me grow, he give's me the
opportunity to do what I want, but he never let's me
go. This is why, I thank God; - for I am truly blessed.

   Joseph D. Dinkins

Untitled

We are seventy now- things are winding down
   and we are living on the very edge

On the edge of that mystic line just above
   and a step or two from that deep abyss
   into which one topples and is seen
   no more on earth forever.

Before the disappearance unwelcome surprises
   keep springing upon us.

It's pretty late to be rushing around
   no time for crowed agenda
   no time for to grumble
   and fuss over minor matters

Yes, there are consolations
   in doing small chores already late
   and cherishing whatever big
   or tiny favor each day grants.

There are still stars above
   and a great good beautiful earth
   with many good people
   and spring and sunshine all around us.

   J. L. Hartz

Great Grandma

(Author - age 10)
My Great Grandma gave me some money today,
   And when she did, I didn't know what to say.
It's more money than I've ever seen.
   I'll probably save it until I'm a teen.

I wish I could buy a car or a horse,
   But Mom and Dad won't let me, of course.

Instead I will use it to go away to school,
   So when I grow up, I won't act like a fool.

I'll spend it on music my Grandma adores,
   And when I play the piano, it might shake the floors.
I'd like to give Great Grandma a kiss on the cheek,
   And give her a hug that lasts for a week!

Thank you Great Grandma, I love you so,
   And thank you more than you'll ever know.

   Kayci Herron

Life's Little Joys

Life's little joys are sometimes rare.
And when they appear out of the blue,
You suddenly realize why you care,
A little joy is well overdue.

Life may be filled with despair and gloom.
Suddenly you see a star lighting up the night,
or a rhododendron bush in bloom,
and life for a moment seems bright.

You look into the face of a trusting child,
or feel the warmth of a glowing fireplace.
You see flowers around you growing wild,
or take a peek at a tablecloth of Chantilly lace.

You witness the cleansing beauty of the first winter snow.
Or see a little red robin light upon your window sill,
and in your heart you will truly know,
that life's little joys are real.

When these precious moments are all tucked away,
and reality hits you again in the face.
Whisper to yourself, where can I find joy today,
and right under your nose you will find a place.

Marjorie Y. Dickens

The Ebbing Tide

I sit in the sand, moist with salty tears.
And wonder.
I ponder upon life.
Why am I here?
The future holds only foreboding,
And the present, only timelessness.
I do not wish to be scared, or infinite
So I look to the past.
It is comforting in it's sereneness.
In it, I can foretell no change.
In this thought, this strange image,
I realize that the past lies dormant,
A memory inside my mind
I realize that I must face the change
That I so abhor,
And the timelessness that I hold no desire for,
So that I may live.
The water ebbs,
No longer wetting my feet with it's dampness.
Now, it is only a memory.

Katie Lynn

Friendly Love

Symbols of hearts, as too, flowers
And words which solely be true
Are @ what be pledged this day to you
For the tenderness you show
As the beauty, you I see
Be why there's so much of love,.. FRIENDLY, from me
For in one's heart beats many feelings
As do flowers express such to be
That words host, the carriage, INTENTIONS
Of how one wishes one e'er to be
So in appreciation of you being, woman
Relating @ of me, thus,.. the man
This day shall be like s'veral celebrations
For whereto we hold LOVE, friendly, and in hand

M.C. Rhodes

Reply to Love

I was looking for someone who would take my hand
   and you were there - - and you weren't square.
You fulfilled every dream I had and I thought I had it all
in the palm of my hand but, now that you're gone...I must go on
and I'm doing everything I can, yes I'm looking everywhere I am
for someone who can fulfill may new found list of Requirements.

I've been looking all around, in and out of town, and so far —
there's no one who can fulfill my new found list or requirements.
I keep thinking that it's all in my mind — That I'm looking
for someone I won't find... but I'm stubborn, and,
   I Won't Settle For Less
And I'm looking at my list of requirements.
And there's no one who can tell me he/she's not here
And there's no one who can tell me he/she's not there for me
   To care fore me, have faith in me
   To live for me, be there for me
And there's no one who can tell me he/she's not there
   And there's no one who can tell me she/he's not there
And there is no one in this world who can tell me
That there's no one who can fulfill my new found list of requirements.

Joan M. West

To Those Who Bled And Died For Us

Your heart no longer beats, but hark,
Another poet speaks for you; the spark,
Ignited by a fellow poet's pen
Inflames my soul and words spill forth again.

Your eyes no longer see, and yet
Your spirit lives and we cannot forget
The tears you shed, or shallow grave
wherein you dear heart bled.

Your skin no longer feels, but how
You suffered and you died is now
And will forever be revealed
In hallowed verse,
Upon our sad lips sealed.

Your voice no longer speaks, but we,
Your spokesmen will forever be.
Destiny chose you to bear our guns,
No one shall call you our forgotten sons.

Jean Leonard

Good Morning

I look out my window what do I see?
Apple tree blossoms, lilacs, green grass, and yellow dandelions.
Our birds are back, Robin is busy building a nest on my Patio.
All this reminds me the garden must be worked for home grown
Tomatoes, carrots and Lettuce.
Will I drop a worm in the Rifle River to catch my breakfast or
will it be McDonald's for coffee and to tell Grandpa how big one
got away.
Will I look for wildflowers today or just sit on my Louis the 16th
couch potato chair with remote control T.V.?
Don't count me out of this game yet
My boiler still has steam to blow it's whistle
Maybe even drive a piston like it used to
After three score and ten. It's fun to dream of things
you did and maybe didn't.

Lew Fields

Choices

Are there more ups than downs?
Are there more downs than ups?

    The heart is on a merry-go-round,
    each passing scene you ponder, some
    of those moments you wish you could honor.

Is it right? Is it wrong?
Will I be weak or can I be strong?

    The emotion is like a steady rain,
    the voice you recall is like soothing
    snow mixed therein that comes to
    make its claim.
       Linda D. Myers

"Freedom"

Peace of mind and freedom from all worry,
Are two major things all of us curry;
'Tis sad we permit obstacles to appear,
When the peace and freedom become near.

We often ponder and procrastinate for awhile,
Even foster a suspicion of guile;
We look at the world as a grain of sand
And hold tomorrow in the palm of our hand.

Opportunity never keeps knocking on a closed door,
Often it knocks once and then no more;
So it behooves each of us to accept that fact,
And to meet each new day with tact.
    Marian Jean Fletcher

Children And Adults

Are we children acting as adults, or
Are we adults acting as children?
Children have fights, then they're friends.
Adults have fights, then they're enemies.
Children have something to share; they give.
Adults have something to share; they keep.
Children respect the old and life.
Adults avoid the old and life.
Are we children acting as adults, or
Are we adults acting as children?
As adults, maybe we should copy the children,
Before the children copy us.
    Nancy E. Wellington-Coffey

Mother

The still of the night, so quiet and peaceful,
as a busy world lies waiting to be reborn
So many things to do...
So many seeds to sow...
How much time we have no one can know.
So many songs to sing...
So many rain drops to fall...
The keeper of life shall come for us all.
This life is a blessing for our goals it may seen
But it is just a passing like out of a dream
And if I am blessed with one cherished day
I shall be ever humble to have passed by this way.
As I sit and I watch the stars in the sky.
the mood brings a trickle of tear to my eye.
For I have been chosen to sit here tonight.
to draw in Gods Glory to live in this life.
    Timothy J. Gostlin

Seasons

Autumns breath has caressed my cheek,
as a lovers kiss warm and sweet
I find the time for life's refrain
of seasons passed in joy and pain.

Now it seems so long ago
springs promise of life, a wisdom ho
that time is a parade of rain and shine
its debris, the yesterdays we leave behind.

Eternal tomorrow is one more day
but as a winter laughing; come who may
yet memories of summer none shall take
like the April blossom never more to make.

Seasoned hearth from change in weather
as sunrise and twilight come together
for in this winter my days grow short
midst the promise of life in deaths retort.
    Michael Brandon

Childhood Glance

A final glance through the tower window,
As day blends with dusk.
The little princess sighs as she recalls;
The memories of just,
How it was to fly away on a winged horse.

The light begins to waver, ere, she tries to focus on
Some elusive image of grandma's dress, dolls, and friends.
She shivers slightly-hugs herself tight;
Not quite understanding the closing of an era,
Where all things seemed just right.

A silent tear drop glistens on a rose-kissed cheek.
For left behind are all the dreams that make life unique!
Tears of uncertainty cling to a last pale shred of hope;
That tomorrow will dawn bright
Putting an end to this dreamless sleep.

The window fades, as do the elves and unicorns.
A time has come, as oft it does,
To step off her merry-go-round.
Looking back; she tries to hold on,
But, alas the rainbows have all gone.
    Laura Hatton

As Days Go On

As days go on I wonder what's to come,
As days go on will I have any or some.
As days go on will there be rain or snow,
As days go on will I ever really know.
As days go on I wonder will I find a way,
As days go on will I make it from day to day.
As days go on will I grow stronger.
As days go on will time span be longer.
As days go on I wonder if life will be as one,
As days go on will I be cherished with a wife and
    my own son.
As days go on will I have better years
As days go on will I have a lot of fears
As days go on can I ask you in a simple way,
As days go on help me find a better day.
    Luis Santiago

A Father Knows

A father knows the burden he must bear
As first he looks upon his baby's face
And feels the great force of his love and care
Rise up within his heart and take its place.
He anticipates the joy that he will know
As he looks upon his newborn child this night,
And feels the glory of his creation grow
Carrying his soul up to a wondrous height.
He feels the burden of the years to come,
Holds out his hands to accept this newborn child,
Gathers him closely to his breast — his son,
And suddenly he feels his heart gone wild!

Only a father knows he can conceive
This greatest gift of all that man receives.

Lucille M. Kroner

Rain's Miracle

The world's locked out by the blinding rain,
As I sit at my window and ponder;
The lightings flash and the thunders roar,
And I cannot see out yonder.

After the storm there is sacred calm,
The sun again shines clear;
The clean washed earth has known re-birth,
And lies respondent far and near.

When all the storms of life have passed,
And I again can see my way.
Will I have weathered my trials and woes?
Will I reflect His glory that day?

Lula V. Moody

My Eyes Are Right

Sun shining on my face
As I slow my normal pace
And what do I see
But a perfect beauty in front on me

Of all the ladies, never have I seen one like her
To all my pains and bitterness she is the cure
A happy smile I give
Watching all she does to live

Come live and be my love
Cause I want to you prove
That I am the one for you
And not those other few

I am prisoner to your gentle peace
And I beg you not to release
I know my eyes are right
That you are beautiful in every light.

Michael D. Stewart

If Chance We Meet

If chance we meet along the way
And stop to pass the time of day,

Let's speak of warmth and summer things
And not the cold that winter brings.

Let's look at birds with rainbowed tails
And bees, and flowers, and garden snails.

Let's watch the grass grow blade by blade
And listen as the trees make shade.

And as we wave our last goodbye,
Please smile! But one of us should cry.

Inez M. Kirby

My Boys

I'll draw my sword.
As I take my two boys through their journey of life.
I hope I can be strong, but gentle when needed.

There isn't nothing I wouldn't do for these boys of mine.
If they are hurt, I'll pick them up.
I'll draw my sword

If someone hurts them
I'll draw my sword.
I hope I'll be strong, but gentle when needed.

I'm their security and rock
Don't hurt my boys
I'll draw my sword

If you hurt my boys, I'll be the knight
Putting the sword through the dragons heart
I hope I'll be strong, but gentle when needed.
I'll draw my sword!

Marsha (McGillis) Gunnerson

Oh, How I Hunger

Amidst the moonbeams she doth gleam
As if the goddess of a dream;
To see such beauty by moonlight,
Oh, how I hunger for this night.
Her moonlit mouth glows with desire,
Enough to set my soul afire;
That our warm lips should meet in bliss,
Oh, how I hunger for a kiss.
Through sheer black lace her smooth skin shows,
Soft as the petals of a rose;
To feel her flesh, I ache so much;
Oh, how I hunger for her touch.
If she'd but come to bed me soon,
We'd be as one beneath the moon
And stars would shake and burst above;
Oh, how I hunger for our love.

Mitchell Coleman

To Ron With Love

In the quiet nights of summer
As my thoughts turn to you,
I reach out to touch the beauty around me
And I feel the music start to swell in my heart.

Watching the shimmering stars above me,
Feeling the wind breezing through my hair,
Hearing the crickets kissing the night,
And the fireflies lighting my mind...
There you are...And the music begins.

As the sweet sounds echo through the air
I can feel your tender smile,
And as I listen,
I see your sparkling eyes playing a rhapsody of light
With the earth all around me.

I'm in a beautiful world when you sing your song,
Listening to the softness of your love,
Feeling the music of your soul,
And knowing that the melody is you...

Marie G. Landis

Scout

The sun was hot, the trail was rough
As scout picked his way along.
I dropped the reins, let him have his head
For I knew He'd not go wrong.

We came upon a little glen,
Beside a real clear pool.
"We'll stop right here and have our lunch
In the shade where it's nice and cool".

The pace it quickened after lunch
Trail smoother, the sun went down.
I just sat back and enjoyed the ride
Scout knew we were "Homeward Bound".

Then came to the day when Scout took sick
And in lots of pain, I know
The vet said: "The's not a thing that I can do,
I'm afraid he's got to go".

I look now at his empty stall
As teardrops fill my eyes.
But I rejoice as I think about
Our future trail rides in the sky.

Larry Felt

Silhouettes

Sun is almost set and I see glassy silhouettes
As the last of it reflects in corners off the water
And dims my vision.

Faint sounds of children's laughter at destinations
Down the shore.

A little boy, my son,
jumping off the end
of the old wooden dock,
at the precise moment a flock of ducks
float gracefully by.

My daughters lean body riding the waves
as if she were a mermaid or some other
beautiful water creature.

Sea gulls perch themselves on mooring boats
and the rustle of the waves
brings treasures to the shoreline.

This is what it is like, here by the water
on gentle summer days.

Mary Coleen Clewley

The Sad Truth

The morning comes, ever slowly,
As the sun takes its time to arise;
Dawn is here, and night is over,
It's time to open up your eyes.
It is early, and yet, it was planned that way,
Someone figured, the earlier, the better;
All the information had been sent out weeks ago,
By an invitation, or by a letter.
You get dressed, and open up your jewelry box,
To put on your wedding ring;
Walk out to the car, pull away,
And roll down the windows to hear the birds sing.
You are at the designated area,
With flowers and tissue in hand;
You walk over to the crowd of people,
Around your husband to which they all stand,
You look at him, and take your seat,
The thought of him gone tears you apart;
The ceremony ends, but the pain continues,
For you will always love him in your heart.

Lorie McClelland

Then As Now

"Into the castle," the villagers cried
As the onslaught of warriors drove them to hide.

The kings in the lead of the raging charge
Were destined to rule over kingdoms large.

Knights on great horses rode through the fray
Wielding sharp weapons on that woeful day.

Many great men fell in the battle,
Slain by their foes, slumped in their saddle.

But heroes were found who are sung about still;
Knights who died bravely or lived by their skill.

After the battle, the vanquished slip away
To plan their revenge for another day.

And the victor's celebration in the Great Hall
Is one of great cheer and food for all

Until the sated soldiers sleep.
Yet, in the night, the peasants weep.

Some things never change, it seems;
Still soldiers fight to fulfill their dreams,

And kings still seek more lands to keep
While the villagers are left to weep.

Matt Cohen

Dreams...

The longing to be held so gently
As the rain hits the soft rose petals
Hoping the touch will last forever
Not wanting to awaken from the dreams
I have chosen to hide under.

Remembering the first time he held me
So close to his body I could feel his heart beat
Holding my head in his powerful hands
As his lips so gently touched mine
The feeling of contentment rested within my soul.

Our bodies moved in unison
To the rhythmic beat of the music
The silence broken by sounds of bass drums
As the desire to love invades our thoughts
Our reason for existing is now realized.

Mary D. James

Indian-Anglo Races

Bare feet barely touch her
As they dance a race to Mother Earth,
   Bless her, caress her, return the beat to her heart.
Elders gently prod the young with spruce boughs
And mingle their wisdom with the falling snow.
   "We cannot take forever and never return."

Steel feet harshly stab her
As they prance a rape of Mother Earth,
   Scar her, mar her, wrest the beat from her heart.
Rogues hawk her breast by day and by night
And chain down her tresses with a familiar creed:
   "If you see one tree, you've seen 'em all."

"Yiya, yiya, I yearn to hear the songs of your feathered friends,
The sounds of your waters, the sighs of your winter winds."

"Hell, world, why do your waters continue to play tricks
When we repeatedly tell them where to flow and when to mix."

Which race will win the race and save the earth?
Which feels her heart fail? Which can nourish her rebirth?

Liz Barnes

Swans

The pretty swans are so very graceful
As they swim about in a way that's peaceful.

Their image casting over the cool waters.
Giving the world a brand new outlook on life.

The wings splash the water when they bathe each other.
As the young ones play and love their Mother.

Their beauty shown as the moon shines.
At night the stars twinkle really bright.

The trees give them lots of shade all the time
So they don't get too hot and stay cool, and feel fine

The swans teach us a valuable lesson, of being
peaceful all the time towards others.

Kara K. McEuen

What Makes The Difference?

Oh how emotions rise and fall
as we progress through life's stages.
Passion, enthusiasm, high hopes for the future
in our youth
Concern, exhaustion, excitement
mid years of raising families
Pride, professional motivation, letting go
as children leave home, establish themselves
Self doubts, successfulness, ambivalence, confusion
as grandchildren arrive, retirement looms, travel beckons
Gratitude, solitude, regretfulness, fulfillment
the last years
Then peace, acceptance, understanding, love
Why do we wait so long?

Margaret Wright

As The Day Passes

The new clock beats time to the morning shadowed frost,
as winter will not relent.
The season changes thickets from green where life was a flurry,
now to a soft, barren brown.

The birds pass descending from flight every so often;
the smaller alight upon the fencing,
while the larger choose the branches.
Watching the yard as a field of terrain, they have attuned
themselves to the brisk season of their existence,
for which they have prepared.

May life not linger to waste,
but be filled with what is sought or destined;
just as the sparrow seeks the new day.

Kathryn Momcilovich

The Saying

There's someone above, the all mighty to say.
Asking for the love, of the children today.
With peace your to make, come together you call.
Your never to take, love is given to all.
For all it is worth, that's between you and me.
Loving for the earth, a passion for the sea.
Wanting the earth clean, pulling together would.
Do away with mean, leaving only the good.
Unity to seek, if needed give a hand.
For when you come weak, others will come to stand.
No worries of why, and never to measure.
Your always to try, to spread about pleasure.
As long as you live, with the soul to enhance.
With all your to give, try giving peace a chance.
Together at heart, everyone will be.
Even when apart, peace and tranquility.

Jason E. Lee

Scot The Cop

S — is for Special,
  as you are to me.

C — is for Confident,
  as you can be.

O — is for Organized,
  as we know you are.

T — is for Talented,
  I feel you will go far.

  THE

C — is for Caring,
  as we know you do.

O — is for Observant,
  as you are — and have to be.

P — is for Polite,
  just be yourself and everyone will see.

Karen M. Vaver

Thank God It's Friday

Most Friday evenings I join two couples, each with a young son,
At the Baldwin home of Debbie and Bob Berardi.
We talk over the week's tensions, troubles and triumphs.
Then, with the work-week behind us, we party!

Someone, usually Bob, will shout "Thank God it's Friday!"
"Another week of dealing with "people." You know. Morons,
  cutthroats and slobs."
To escape from such people I begin my weekends in Baldwin.
Together with Diana, Wayne, Debbie and Bob.

Diana and Wayne, who live just a few houses away,
Have a young son named Lance, who I'm guessing to be about five.
He, and the Berardi's son Matthew, have all the energy we adults don't
And each Friday they have the time of their lives.

These two sets of parents, each with a sensational young son,
Share in whatever life brings their victories, and their defeats.
They combine kindness, courtesy, and an unselfish nature.
It's this combination that makes our Fridays so sweet.

Some future Friday, when maybe my life isn't so sweet,
Should I find myself heartbroken and wanting to sob.
I'll find comfort in my memories of the many fabulous Fridays
Spent together with Diana, Wayne, Debbie and Bob.

Mike Wall

Silence

  Silence.
At times one of the loudest noises there is is silence.
For all the yelling and screaming and crying, none can top
  the deafening sounds of silence.
Surrounded by this is be caught in the trap of one's own
  consciousness.
Running can only avoid - but there will always be silence.
We can never run away, we can only run toward.
Running toward can only result from facing that which we ran from.
It is in these silent times we argue most passionately and
try most desperately to understand, forgive, accept.
We may learn to accept but we never forget.
I look forward to the day silence is golden.

Maria Fulgieri

Voyeurs Lament

I use to look in windows
at what people had to show.
Sometimes it would be art
and other times furniture and Tsatskes
and when I was lucky,
living art would show itself to me,
Now,
more and more, it's hard to see anything
through the hospital bed rails, IV bags, and walkers.
I use to look in windows
at things alive and pretty
Now, all I see is sadness
reminders of illness, and approaching death.
I now look into windows
and think of days gone by
and hope that someday
I'll once again see art.

Kevin Woodward

"Because"

Some folks say I'm crazy, a bit teched in the head
Because I go out walking when they're gettin' into bed,
Because I like to wander on some far distant hill
And see the world a-sleepin' in the black night, deep and still.

Because I'd rather listen to the bull-frog's throaty croak
And see the stars a-twinklin' in a midnight velvet cloak,
Than to lie and hear them snorin' underneath the counterpane
And hear the bed a-creakin', crying out against the strain.

Because I'd rather listen to the songs that robin brings
Than to sit and writhe in torture while a mighty Diva sings.
Because I like to ponder not on great affairs of State
But on just how many rose-buds there are on my garden gate.

Because I like to sit and dream down by the river's bend
Those gossips wag their heads and bleat, "she'll come to no good end"
Those folks think they're a-dyin' if a raindrop hits their coats
So they grab the antiseptic and start sprayin' at their throats.

They're scared to death of animals, they say they carry germs,
And if you want to see them run, just show them a few worms.
They think they're mighty capable of judgin' the domain,
But if that's called being sensible, I'm glad that I'm insane.

Muriel A. Davey

Dear God, I Hope That You Are Listening

Dear God, I hope that you are listening,
because I need a friendly ear.
I have so much to tell you, I hope that you can hear.
What's happening to our world or is it just me.
Everywhere I look I see poverty. There's so much hurt and suffering.
We need you Lord, to heal these needs. The sickness, the hunger,
the homeless living in the cold. No jobs, no money, no place to go.
No food in their stomach's, just pain in their souls.
The violence, the drugs, this all has to stop.
We want good lives, should we roll back the clock
To the beginning of time. We're moving to fast, to remember our past.
Let this be a clue, what we all need to do.
We all need to be thankful, and start talking to you.
We all know you are there, and we all really do care.
We all take for granted our everyday lives.
For we only live once, never twice.
Let us all pray for everything good.
Let the hunger and the pain, go away for good.
Let the homeless have a place to stay.
And let us all promise to take the time to pray every day.

Kathy Griffith

"Meaning Of Christmas"

The meaning of Christmas is plain to me,
because of a Christ child I believe.
Born in a stable with straw for a bed,
while all the other kids slept in brand new beds.
Now where were the Christians when they turned Mary
away? How many of us are doing the same today?
No one offered her a place to stay.
I can see Joseph and Mary afar, how happy
they are holding their child.
No worries of shopping, or how much they can
spend, just enjoying each other and rejoicing within.
While we're rushing about, trying to buy the best.
Spending all of our money and charging the rest.
Then I stop to think is this the real test?
The real meaning of Christmas is by far the best
I think of the Christ child and the wonder of myrrh
What would've happened to us, if there had
been no Christ's birth!..........

Marie Perry

World of Ignorance

I cry when I see innocent children dying, and why
Because we didn't want to help;
Because it's a different country, or
We think, what can we do?...

I cry when I see people fighting because of different beliefs...
I cry when people hate,
Without knowing why;
Except the person is of different color or culture...

I cry when I see this,
Because it hurts to see people hurting each other over nothing;
What kind of world is this?
When the simplest thing can cause a war;
And people live in fear,
What are we teaching our children?
And why, because we're scared?;
Of things and people that are different...
Why!?

Mandy Weinert

Death

Death is a part of us now
Because you no longer live
And I feel I don't either.
I could tell you anything
And you would always listen.
You knew when I was in trouble
Even before I did.
You could feel my pain
Even before I could
You understood me
When nobody else did.
When I was confused or down
You helped me understand and brought me up.
Even though you are gone and away,
I still talk to you
And tell you everything.
I only hope, that you still listen.

Katherine Moser

A Tribute to K.J.

Here's to the little duckling who has
become the lovely swan.
Oh no! You were never ugly
just a bit awkward and stepped upon.
But with this past year of self knowledge
you know that you are full of grace.
And that you have much more to offer to others
Than just a warm smile and pretty face.
So blossom my lovely swan - spread your
wings and fill your space.
Use your brain as well as your
good looks to find your rightful place.

Pam Taylor

Dandelions

I catch a glimpse, but blink my eyes
Before the sun, on my doubts, can rise
The friendly breeze has now turned chilly
Blowing dandelions that look so silly
Bent, not breaking, all the same
Thoughtlessly playing the living game
Some in the sunshine! Open, and light
Some in the shadow... closed as the night.
The same rain falls, keeps falling down
And both the dandelions
will drown
The sun may come to quite the rain
the Dandelion will feel no pain
but if it could, it just seems right
that the rain should spare the ones in the light.
Move into the sun! It's cold where I stay
But why move when I'm comfortable, too? I say
Sure, though it's cold and I'd like to be thawed
How do I know that the warmness is God?

Kayla Jolene Walker

Untitled

Before there was land,
Before time started,
The world was deep,
Black and departed.

There were two forces that disgusted each other,
One was good,
Evil the other.

Lord, grant me the gift
to accept things I cannot change,
Courage to change things that I can change,
And wisdom to know the difference.

Leah Kogen

Of Life And Death

It's late in the night and I feel tired, tired as never
before, tired of dying each day, 'cause we all die each day we
live... We all die! Each day something of us die, and something
new is born. That's the way of life... and death! Those kids once
we were, dead in the past remain. Something new is there instead.
We die everyday and I'm tired, not of living, but of dying. I'm
tired of fighting each day and stand day by day, but I know I have
to, because stop fighting means only death, and I'm tired of dying,
not of living. So, to live is to die, and we were born to die, but
if to die means to live, let's die to live one more day.

Luis A. Garrues

Unbreakable

The last thing you did
before you made my heart
sleep was create a hole in
the wall which surrounds our

hopes and dreams of the future we
had together. You made me feel
lonely and lost when we were apart,
yet relieved of all the pain you put me

through. Hate and disrespect flowed
from your spirit; you were none of these
things to me. I hate your life-style, your lies, your
jealousy. I hate your attitude about others.

Your attitude toward me was always different,
you loved me. Our bond seemed unbreakable. Even though
I am tired of you and sometimes hate you, I
love you with more of my self than I want to.

Michele J. Giddens

Nature's Empathy

Down softly laden paths behind the hearth,
behind sanctity
a child's hidden escapade twists and turns
like the delicate stream she is chasing

She is leaving for a little while, they are calling
Stand still in your tracks, stand still and listen
They are whispering in the sway of limbs,
beckoning upswept arms rising and falling

She is mistress of God's creation
The smells of green she boldly snaps open
and carries them, bound forever in her heart
There they are abiding, there a consolation

Death's fence lies between her and hearth
The child's steps will never be retraced,
and in her grief they carry her
the secrets of the earth.

Mary Ann Coniglio

The Tree

In amazement I consider the tree.
Behold, it's branches so many I see.
Extending toward the sky.
My! such glamorous trim
A curve in the trunk, a twist in a limb.
Nothing seems to matter at all,
As it grows sinewy strong and tall.
Dazzlingly it stands dignified
It's alluring beauty magnifies.
While taking in life and bringing forth joy.
The leaves in the wind seem so happy and gay,
It's as though I knew just what they say.
You too can be as happy and free,
For you have dominion over me.

Margaret Williams

Did You Hear

As you stood by the river,
Did you hear the water whisper your name?
As you pressed your ear to the ground,
Did you hear the deep throated language of a distant train?
As you raised your face to the summer sky,
Did you hear the breeze as it passed you by?
As the darkness wrapped around you and held you tight,
Did you hear the stillness of the night?
As you look at the wonder around you, and above,
Did you hear the sound of God's love?

Lewis Greene

"A Full Bucket"

I am lovable, as we grow in his power
Being sweet as self esteems hover
Put on love, bear and forgive
Clothe with compassion and live
Get out of the way of relationships
Take care and please people equips
Less growing up and responsibilities
Exhausts your supply and mars possibilities.
For others to achieve your martyr controlled
Shows perfectionist itself, not spirit enrolled.
The workaholic does not have the time
To develop intimacy and trust, we find
Lets build relationships close to our maker
Richer, rewarding makes prize partakers
A bucket full of positive achievements
Full and overflowing focuses intimates
Family, friends draw closer and deeper
Forgiveness, openness not the cheaper
Forgiveness at night is a must for all
To open up and share, cry, forgive-no wall.

E. Lenore Miller

Rare Is The Beauty Of Our Love

Loving you is a beautiful thing I will share with you
beyond the end of time
Loving you is glancing up and see you watching me,
your love radiating deep within to warm my heart.
Loving you is hearing your soft mellow voice flow through me
Love you has made me realize there is a God and He's deemed
us worthy to make us one in love.
Like two tall timbers in a forest of many we stand side by
side, our limbs touching gently but never crowning,
our roots entwined caressingly but never choking our
love, so we may drink from it and thrive.
Loving you makes the sun's morning rays even
warmer thus, loving you had allowed me to feel
love so intense no other love can compare.

Paulette Gough

June 3rd, 1993, Gotta Meet

Work is pressurized, Gotta Sell, Gotta Produce
Big presentation tomorrow - is the price right? Gotta Know
Dave the owner, me the V.P. - Gotta meet, gotta meet
He'll be back in a 1/2 hour - Gotta meet, gotta meet
The day is ending - Gotta meet, Here read this -
"Dear Employees, turning out to be a tough year, Gotta cut overhead
Gotta cut overhead, the following people no longer will be employed..."
June 4th, no presentation today, Don't Gotta meet -
Got dropped off in the driveway yesterday evening, cardboard box in
    hand -
My wife with neighbors chatting, looks bewildered as my little boy
    asks -
"Daddy where's that guy going with your car?
The pressure has changed - Gotta find a job, Gotta get a car
"Dear God, Gotta help..."
Gotta, Gotta meet, Gotta find a job, gotta meet...

Paul J. Seeling

Reincarnation

I've finally escaped now to my eternity, my neverending life
beyond hatred and anger, guilt and sin; but more than that,
imaging beautiful gardens and floating water made from spirits
of faith and joy, sorrow and depression, half-stricken the mind
but never so close, kill thee for beauty, never really so,
but for death beyond death, living as I wake up and appear in
white light, not speaking, not able to, scream is the only way,
frustrated with such menace I lay, people watch and I be reborn,
not for the liking, everything dawns; now I forget, forget,
forget, blank.

Joseph Zimmerer

Little Bird

At the beginning of your endeavor you epitomized a young
bird just setting out from the nest
Trying to accomplish what seemed to be beyond your reach,
trying just to fly at best
Uncertain of what lie ahead, you reluctantly tested your
wings and began to fly
Isn't it amazing what you can achieve if only you'd just try?

Knowledge is Power — it is the only of many possessions that
has a lifetime guarantee
Once acquired it undeniably belongs to you, it's how you become free
Knowledge is Freedom — freedom to know, to think, to do, to see
With your new found freedom, I dare you, I challenge you,
I believe in you to be all you ever aspired to be

You have risen and you are shining, you have escaped
the hands of defeat
Obstacles may have accompanied you, but now they're just
dust beneath your feet
So go on and fly little bird, but remember it's a little
different than before
Because now you not only fly, Little Bird, now you SOAR!

Muriel Tracey Watts

Tomorrow For You

Tomorrow for you can only bring
Birds of song who love to sing

Sunny days with skies of clear blue
A colorful rainbow with a golden hue

Water so clear, you can see your reflection
Memories so sweet for your recollection

Stars so bright, like diamonds they glow
A sparkling blue river, running peaceful and slow

A glorious dawn to start each day
A bed of flowers on which to lay

A gentle breeze running through your hair
Angels singing a soothing prayer

Fragrant budding roses, holding drops of dew
Moon beams casting shadows on the ocean blue

A little brown church in the dale, in a humble parish
A memory I know we all will cherish

A state of mind so peaceful and true
A smile on your lips because you know we love you.

Kathleen Ann Murphy

Soul Friend

Every step a more agonizing ache
blackened inside, she still wanted joy
No sorrowness, what could I write
I want to feel you in my arms again
The laughs and good times we both shared
Will only be memories in my heart
The vision of her nearly struck me down,
yellow and bloated as she lay in bed
She fought the tubes, she wanted to hold me
With her eyes into mine, we both felt the bond
Her blood boiling, she could fight no more
As she lay withered, her battle was over
She went thru me, I finally held her,
She was not a vision, but an awakening
She was in peace as was I
And I will be with her again when I die.

Michele Nowitzke

The Flowers

I remember the flowers that he would
Bring, each night as he came home to me;
I never knew from whence they came, each
Special and beautiful to see.

So pure and delicate, as I fondly recall,
And he always put one in my hair; that fresh
Sweet fragrance of babes in the prime, or
Pine cones fresh in the air.

I remember his face as he entered the
Room, just like a little boy at his best;
Always striving to let me know that his actions
would pass every test.

I still can not believe he's gone, from
The happy times we shared, we had our little
Squabbles and spats, but I always knew he cared.

The limbs of the trees eternally wait, and
The flowers no longer smile; the ominous
Clouds are always there, as if waiting for one to beguile.

My plans, hopes and aspirations are gone, just as the fleeting
wind; but I will never release my dreams of eternity with him.

Nancy Calhoun-Medlock

The New Year

The cold silence of each new morning,
Brings rain, fog or snow with its dawning,
A blue sky alive with white fluffy clouds.
Every day wears its winter shrouds.

Then slowly the rain begins to fall,
And quietly the blossoms come to call.
The grass grows green, the winds begin to blow,
Spring is here, with its glorious show.

Summer has come, seems like overnight,
Warm and aloud with pleasures in sight.
Camping and swimming and new sights to see,
With my mom, dad, my brother and me.

The leaves are turning to red and brown,
The year is wearing its farewell crown.
The thanksgiving feast, the holiday bells,
Lets "Old Man Time" know, that all is well.

Now who is this? What do we have here?
Its that brand new baby, "Happy New Year"!

Marta Thirion

Caroline

Innocence is so adored,
But it's hard to find in this cold face world.
    Where everyone is hurting,
and wanting more.

    And, through all my travels,
and all the sights I have seen,
    All the discouragement that has been on my hands,
And giving up is as easy as it seems,
    With all the disappointment
that has brought me to my knees.

    There is still a place were hope lies.
Just look into the face of Caroline.

On your worst day, she can smile.
She doesn't know any better.
    Let your spirit float like a feather.
Past the reasons that made you cry.
    Behind the scenes of the tear filled eyes,
    Beyond the petty of our lives,
to find, there is still a place where hope lies.
    In the face of Caroline.

Michael Gibbons

Snowy Owl

On a stump deep in the undergrowth...

A great owl waits.
Broad wings lay protective
Over a powerful body.
Black-night talons flex
As they emerge through heavy feathered boots.
Marble-balled yellow eyes miss nothing
As they scan from within that huge, plumed, white head.

A great owl waits ..hungry ..ready to strike.
Wings which carried this tundra bird to the south
Press closer upon the magnificent body.
A dagger-sharp seal-brown bill opens and closes
As if to practice the death pierce.
Finely-honed talons emerge further
From within their downed protection;
And cold, purpose-filled eyes focus with greater intensity.
Perhaps a hare or a mouse will still the gnawing ache.

Ah! There! A brief flight, a lunge, a strike, a hold ... a kill,
And the full-bellied bird will go on
To carry out its life's ritual.

Persia Straub

Bliss

I am a ray of sunlight
Bursting from the Great Star
Reaching out and stretching over the world You created
Bathing it in my warmth.

I am a blossoming flower
Perfect and delicate
I feel the warmth of Your Sun
And lift my petals in praise.

I am a great mountain of stone
Still and silent
Solid and unmoving I remain
For all to see what You have done.

I am a mighty river
Thundering and powerful
Flowing freely, over mountain paths
Glistening and reflecting Your Glory.

I am but a humble servant
Trying so hard to repay all that You have given
Forgetting so easily what joy can be found in simplicity
What happiness, what Bliss.

Mary Laura Kludy

Cold And Cloudy?

Today, the weather report is dreary - "Cold and cloudy" they say,
But crime dropped significantly so the sunshine should be out to stay.
The Hubble mission goes brightly - the telescope's vision may be
    20-20 soon,
As the astronauts take their longest walk past the moon.

Today, the weather report is dreary - "Cold and cloudy" they say,
But nuclear warheads could soon be pointing at the Atlantic and
    Pacific,
Not towards people, so coldness gradually fades away.

As we approach each day can we say,
"Today is going to be `cold and cloudy'"
Without looking at it closely?
"Can't judge a book by its cover" I'd say!

Leslie A. Githens

Untitled

A little drink is fine at times, when toil has you down.
But getting drunk and out of sorts, proves the demon wears the crown.
You can't let up and feel so sick but push that out of your way
And take another lethal drink that's your habit day by day.
Soon you find you cannot change and really can't control
You throw all caution to the winds, the devil has your soul.
What started as a tranquil balm has turned into despair
It neither calms nor rests your soul its more than you can bear.
The reason for your sorry plight no longer is the cause
You've thrown away all caution nor given time to pause.
But after several months of this, you'll find you can't return
To make a decent living or friends with much concern.
The demon in the bottle has you tightly in his fist
He knows you are a weakling and too besotted to resist.
You assume the demon was invented by old ancient scribes
But truth remains in tales of woe, he's ruined many lives
So my friend if you persist on going in your way
Don't ask for pity from your friends get on your knees and pray
You need much more than we could give and its a trying task
But God is willing to help you now if only you would ask.

Lillian M. Parent

"Love Hurts"

You told me that you loved me,
But I was blind I could not see,
That all you were doing was hurting me,
You used and abused me,
But through thick and thin
Day out and day in I was still with you,

I loved you with all my heart,
But we slowly moved farther and farther apart.
I should of knew right from the start you didn't love me,
But I met some one new, who loves me who's true and after
nights of hearing our favorite love song, now I'm glad
that your gone.

LaDenishelle Robinson

"God's Grace"

Up ahead is a beautiful light,
but I will not go without a fight.
They push, I pull, and I fall through
the door, when I open my eyes I'm
flat on the floor.
Just then I feel someone pulling
my hand, and he pulls so gentle
to help me to stand.
Just then I knew I was in "God's Grace,"
and never again would I fall on
my face.

Leanne Darrell

Untitled

We look out the window
As the tears seem to flow
We watch the people as they come and go
Traveling through life's trials, so to say
Wondering how to live each moment, day-by-day
Yes, people can fill our hearts with happiness
But, they can also fill our hearts with sadness
Life is but a mystery, so it does seem
Why do the people appear to be so mean?
As we turn our heads and look the other way
We wish and pray that someone will ease the day.

Lori L. Groves

Second Shot At Love?

Yesterday was perfect for I didn't have a care,
but I'm dead today because two boys agreed on a dare.

I was never given the time to kiss my love good-bye,
and now I can not console her when she cries.

I watch over her daily and listen to her pleas,
she asks for her love back while kneeling on her knees.

She knows that her prayer is one that God can't fulfill,
but the emptiness in her heart needs to be filled.

She finally finds someone who she loves as much as me,
but she wonders daily if this love was meant to be.

She looks towards the heavens asking me for a clue,
she says she's confused and doesn't know what to do.

I put my arms around her even though she doesn't know,
she starts to cry and tells God "this just isn't so!"

She finds the courage to ask him how he feels,
and he tells her that his feelings for her are real.

She knows now that this love was meant to be,
but it will never be the same as the love she had for me.

Nanci-Lee Roias

I'll Be Smiling Just For You

You asked me to smile, and not to cry.
But it's hard when someone you love dies.
You try to believe that it's not the end,
And someday we will all see him again.

But there are times when we all have doubts
And we wonder what life is all about.
Why must we lose the ones we love?
Is there really someone looking down from above?

Will we meet again Someday?
I think so, and every night I pray.
For there must be somewhere we go when we die.
Somewhere up above that big blue sky.

So look down on me from heaven, and when you do
You'll see I'll be looking back up at you.
And I'll remember what you asked of me.
So don't be disappointed with what you see.

You may see tears in my eyes, but look close if you do.
I'll be smiling just for you!

Mary Beth Young

Pen Or Pencil

Do you prefer to do things in pen or pencil,
But let's describe them by giving them life.
If you are the pen you are permanent,
But if you are the pencil you are erasable.

Then from that I must be a pencil,
For I have been erased and written over a great deal.
No things are for sure anymore in my mind,
But then again maybe I NEED HELP FROM A PEN.

I could also be a pen, because of the marks I leave,
They are permanent and are not changeable.
Oh how I wish those marks could be erased,
But then again maybe I NEED HELP FROM A PENCIL.

Are you the pen or are you the pencil,
The choice is yours to decide,
Just don't hide your feelings inside,
Write them down, but what will you use... pen or pencil.

Jared Zalewski

X-ray Vision

The difference between you and I are not within
But merely the only element is skin:

The feelings inside are all quite the same.
The passion, hurt, love and the pain.

But when the tears start to swell in the corner of our eyes.
Therein lies the vast difference between you and I.

Because the tears flow down an unlike color face,
the tears and the pain we can easily erase.

Someday when we wipe every tear away
We can stand tall and say

I was there child the day it was done!
We were all united and stood as one!

And I hope in the future our children will forgive
This terrible injustice we used to live.

Meanwhile we have to live in this present hell
Here is the legacy we'll have to tell.
I know this is difficult for you to understand

But you see; we used to judge
by the COLOR our fellowman
Linda Wells

Her Signature

I watched from a distance as intricate rose petals melted,
but not forever;
they emerged again in another time drifting like a blue vail
from beyond the fog that descends and silently
frames her signature ——-
Her creation will endure.

I watched from a distance as new life delicately pushed inside;
and from an infinite trace of peacefulness
shines a light that reaches out to surround but a few.
Suddenly she signs her name ——-
Her hour is not pure.

I watched from a distance as sand filtered the gold dust,
before it could rest
then with great strength she tipped the rock over;
disturbing the birds nest.
She walks from the water and ascends to the top, framing her
certificate and as I watched she slowly escapes making her way;
existing from the outside within
knowing that somewhere in her space ——-
The cactus becomes a rose.....
Lisa Wooddell

One Time

She barely knew him, they've never really met,
but now it's all over, all done, but still yet.

She'll never have a husband, she'll never be a wife
because starting last night she's losing her life.

The tears will fall, the pain will come,
all because she acted so dumb.

But the bad news is still to come,
she's pregnant with her first son.

She'll have no life ahead of her,
the road ahead will soon end,
although it never really did begin.

Things seemed pretty calm
until she acted so dumb
on the night of her senior prom.
Melanie Perniciaro

"She's Gone"

She use to sit up in that window where you could see her head
But she's gone now forever to the city of the dead
She waited just to see you, but you had always "just forgot!
She's gone now forever buried in that sacred lot
She use to sit up by the window until the early evening shade
Always looking just for you with something she had made
So here you are with memories, some good some bad more or less
She's there now neath her headstone where gentle winds caress
Still, flowers bloom there in her garden just below her window sill
She always waited just for you just making time stand still
But now she's gone forever to that great beyond
If you would take it back today would you able to respond?
To give her just a little love like some she gave to you
If she were there this moment would you be able to?
If you could take it back today when you were busy and knee deep
Would you share with her a moment, now that she's asleep?
Kelly Cotterill

In My Life.....

I wanted you in my life
but someone always got in the way
a certain complicated strife,
but my feelings for you always
seemed to stay.

I know I have caused a certain
type of confusion
and maybe a struggle to try and figure out.
I'm sorry for this delusion
but struggles are what relationship are all about.

I guess what I am trying to say
is that I still do want you there....
To give me those reassuring smiles,
and to tell me that you still care.
I think that the thing I regret the
most is the things that I never got to say....
Krista Brooke Lloyd

The Gate

A darkened sky is broken by dawn,
But still the demons wish to linger on.
These demons realize with much anger,
That daylight brings to them many a danger.

Ahead they hear their master's
  beckoning call,
And recalling the punishment,
  they dare not to stall.
The demons pick up the pace
  and travel away from town,
Their faces full of mischievous
  smiles or gruesome frowns.

When dusk comes once more
  they will try again,
To make all humans suffer,
  to make them sin.
But now the demons would
  be forced to wait,
Behind the doors of their home,
  the place called the Gate.
Nicole Woodard

Alone

I'm lonely.
  But tender saplings, children of the forest, slowly bend
  and softly whisper to me.
I'm lonely.
  But delicate flowers with nature washed faces, curtsey and
  sway, smiling at me.
I'm lonely.
  But seasonal gentle winds, caressing the sky, touch, tease,
  and smooth my cheek.
I'm lonely.
  But piercing rays of sunshine, entering the day, bath and
  warm my body.
I'm lonely.
  But sudden unruly noises, created by street and city,
  energize my senses.
I'm lonely.
  But strangers passing by, pause to speak or nod, and lift
  my spirits.
I'm lonely.
  But a stable pampered home offers challenge, comfort and
  solitude for me.
I'm lonely.
  But I smile, my feelings charged with the sights and sounds
  surrounding me.
  I'm not lonely...... I'm just.....alone.
  Louise B. Ostrander

"Aging"

The doctor said I had a good heart,
But the rest of me is falling apart.
Now with colitis and arthritis
I've just found out I've got 'Bronchitis'
I've also got nerves of steel
  and a great disposition -
But half the people I meet, just
  doesn't listen (deafness?)
Just when I think I'm feeling great.
My husband comes home with a prostrate!

So the other day I got into my ear
  and was feeling fine.
When some kid decides to race and
  miss a stop sign!
Well now I'm lying here in traction,
Why can't we age without aggravation.

So if you think your feeling old -
It's not age - it's your rolling
  panty hose.
  Lillian Hill

The World Is Getting Old

The world is getting old and forgetting lots of things.
But there's one thing I remember my Lord, my God, my King.

He made the pretty flowers;
He made the birds that sing;
He made boy and girl;
He made the bells that ring.
He made these perfect things for you and for me
But the world is getting old and forgetting lots of things.

Now the world is ended;
And I'm with my God, my King.
He made my world in heaven;
He made these perfect things.
He made these perfect things for you and for me
But the world was getting old and forgetting lots of things

Now lets forget the world.
Forget the worldly things.
For there's nothing that compares to my Lord, my God my King.
  Marjorie L. Christle

Our Children

We are the parents, the voice and heart of creating
But to out children we have stopped relating
The family life of being together had disappeared
And in it's place we now have children of fear
We love our children, this is true
They need our guiding hand, this they are due
But we are too busy just making a living
And we have so little time for giving
What ever happened to the family dinners
Where we talked about life and being a winner
Now it's T.V. dinners, we're late always on the go
Or we just have to get to that new show
It's time now to stop, to talk, contribute and take stock
Listen you your children, so you won't be shocked
That they are in trouble or committed some crime
That could have been avoided with just a little more of your time
  M. E. Snuggs

True Love

I loved you dear more than I could say.
But to play second fiddle was not my way.
I have to be first or not at all.
If you want me to come at your back and call.
As humans we have so much pride,
and our true feelings, we try to hide.
But even tho we are far apart.
I'll survive my broken heart.
If I but know that you're all right,
and haven't done something foolish in your flight.
Please stand still and think about your life,
and know that without me you can still survive.
Maybe as time goes passing by.
We'll meet again, you and I.
And life will be good, just wait and see.
Because I once knew you and you once knew me.
  Mary Kohler

The Desert Wind

It was only an old shack on the desert,
But to someone, it was once called home.
It seemed you could almost hear laughter
of the happy days long ago.
Weeds had grown up around the old place
And a tree stood close by the door
Where wild flowers had once been blooming
Had now withered up and were gone.
While peacefully enjoying this beauty
of life in this colorful land,
Coyotes could be heard in the distance
And sheep that had strayed from their band.
When the sun had gone down at long last
And the stars could be seen in the sky
Where they held all of the secrets
In the breeze of that starry night.
  Marian Brown Wikoff

Mistake

When I first met you, I didn't want anything
but a friendship.
As our friendship grew, I wanted much more
than I knew I could have.
As I wanted a relationship, our friendship died down.
And now that you're gone all I can do is wish
to start over.
  Kim Brener

More Than A Word

Love is a powerful emotion,
But to thrive it needs devotion.
It's a tear, a smile, and a soft gentle touch,
And nothing else can hurt so much.

Love can give you happiness that's so deep,
That your heart overflows and causes you to weep.
It's expressed with a tender kiss,
And can take you to a paradise filled with bliss.

It's compassionate, it reaches out to those in need,
But it can be as sharp as a razor,
    and can make your heart bleed.
Love is the morning sunshine, free and shining bright,
But it can leave you in darkness that's blacker that the night.

Love is patient and giving, it's purpose is to please,
A powerful emotion that can bring you to your knees.
It's a blessing and a curse, but there really is no doubt,
That love is more than just a word, and so hard to live without.

Paulette Seniff DiTizio

Mother

I felt a slight touch on my shoulder,
but when I turned, there was no one there.
I sensed a presence surrounding me,
a familiar and comfortable feeling of care.

I wondered throughout the day
exactly what this feeling could be.
Then I suddenly realized it was you, Mother,
In heaven, lovingly watching over me.

It was the feeling I'd had all my life;
A feeling I'd known since before birth.
The loving bond between mother and child
is not just restricted to this earth.

You have been there for me always
through the bad times and the good.
You encouraged me to accomplish the things
in which you had the faith that I could.

I do not know how many times I thanked you
for giving me life, so this I do now.
And even though you are no longer here with me
I'm sure you feel loved and missed somehow.

LeiAnn Pate

Teen Support

Sometimes your burdens are more than you can bear,
But you do have parents that want you to share.
Why drudge on when the load becomes too heavy?
Your parents are there; use them for a levy.

"Leave me alone! Get out!" you shout,
When pushed away, they still reach out.

Consideration is a mighty thing
For peace and great contentment it does bring.
A note when you go out;
A phone call when you're late.
If you plant worry and cause fears,
They can haunt and harass for years.

You may face hills and mountains, and you may have steps to climb;
Sometimes you may need a push before reaching heights sublime.
Parents may seem to be your foe, but in truth really are your friend:
Sometimes they already know what you might encounter in the end.
Stop! Look! Listen! Don't cross the track!
Parents are there for you. Just look back!

Kathy Blankenship

The Gain Of Death

It's hard to lose someone you love,
but you know their just as happy up above.
Where there is no crime, and there is no time.
Where man is treated fair, and fear is very rare.
Why did he leave? What did I do wrong?
So many questions I want to put into a song!
Once he was as cheerful as a flower,
but now, he has no power.
Sometimes I think, sometimes I wonder,
and maybe I'll just ponder.
It's hard to believe - but you'll think they deceived.
But soon tomorrow, all you'll have is glee,
and the most of memory!

Jill Eagan

My Magic Button

To-day I was a silver magic
button,
Much, to my delight."
I will always keep my magic button
as a symbol of "What is Right."

I'm at the cross-roads of my life
"Perhaps my silver button, can put
things into a different light.
I sure hope it will; as all I
want to-do, "is write and write and write."

To-day I'm on a Ferris Wheel
"My head just" "spins around."
"I feel I'm on a different planet"
But I know, my feet are firmly
on the ground: -

I know my silver button will
help to pave the way. So that
Peace, will reign once more, I
know my magic button, is really
here to-stay-

Prunella Stack

Love

Love they say is a four letter word, that can be expressed
by a human, a bee, and even a bird.

Love is great and love is grand, love is best with someone
special holding your hand.

Love shines down on all like the moon on a lake, and being
without love is like a birthday without a cake.

Love to them might be a four letter word. But to me its a
three letter word: that spells Y-O-U!

Melissa Stebbins

Thoughts

Tears fall like rain while I wait, sitting
    by the window
My heart pounds against my chest like
    heavy boots against the floor
Still, no answer
What happened to our souls?
Why does love hurt when it should not?
Without you life is unexplainable
Empty like a field without flowers
Time goes by slow as the wind hits my face
    so cold, so breathtaking
As you

Meshelle Mangum

To Honor Beethoven's Sixth

Like water,
Calm, serene with insinuations of eternal peace
Then the wind, whipped up by the unknown force,
Causes powerful waves to crash, beat against the rocks and shore.
Drums march upon me like rain clouds, heavy and dark
As violins mount endless stairs, so the spirit soars with them.
Transported to another world, emotion filled,
   descended upon by waves of sound, enveloped.
Currents of his mind, soul,
   driven by his genius to express, God -given.
Even when you have stopped, I will think of you too much,
And leave reality to speak again with you.

Lauren Allison-Fisher

The Death of a Friend

No longer in the calm of night,
   Can peaceful slumber claim me.
As sad memories will always bring to light,
   The tragedy and grief which now contains me.

The hopes and plans we shared for years,
   A devoted friendship broken.
My eyes once gleamed, now dim with tears,
   At the thought of those words unspoken.

Our friendship had us linked together,
   Like two pillars in the schoolhouse hall.
And as leaves are tossed in the wintry weather,
   An act of cruelty made one fall.

I feel like one who walks alone,
   On my path of life deserted.
But in my heart of hearts my friend lives on,
   Until my life on this cold earth has departed.

Mary J. Spivey

As I Rock Her

Dear Lord of faith and love divine
Can this child really be mine?
No greater peace hath this world
Than the soft, closed eyes of the one I hold.
But to capture this time forever,
Babe and I in motion together.
Back and forth slow and fast,
I long for this moment to last and last.
We come to a stop, my heart knows when,
It's so hard to let go, I don't want it to end.
I stand and I cradle her tiny head,
And slowly I lower this angel to bed.
I cover her and watch with a tear in my eye,
And prepare to make my tip-toe goodbye.
"Good night little one" as I close the door,
God's preparing me for the time, we won't rock anymore.

C. Price

The Ordeal

You know the time is here.
Cautiously you open the door and enter.
Nervously you approach the counter and sign in.
You wait for your name to be called.
Will things turn out the way you want?
There it is, your name is called.
You rise and approach the chair.
She greets you with a smile that relaxes you.
A cloth is draped over you, and fastened.
The appropriate tools are brought forth.
With smiles, conversation, and skill she
   brings you through the ordeal.
And, your new haircut is perfect.

Mike Stephenson

A Christmas Daydream

In your imagination —
Can you picture it — if maybe
We could have lived long, long ago
When Jesus was a baby?

We might have lived in Bethlehem
And on a sunny day,
Filled a basket with some goodies
And walked over to see him, on the way.

And there he'd lay in Mary's arms
And he'd look around and smile
And Mary'd look at you and say,
"Would you like to hold Him for a while?"

You'd cuddle him and rock him
And even sing him a little song.
Then you'd gently give him back to her.
Saying "I'd better be getting along."

Today we stand before him
Our love and praises we impart.
Saying "Thank you, dear Jesus, for all you have done,
You will always live in my heart."

Margaret L. Glins

Final Touches

I chase my dreams as the artist with the brush stroking the face of a canvas.

I am as the face of the canvas, patiently waiting to the completed by the dreams becoming reality.

Reality is a step ahead with my hand grasped tightly as a strangle hold on life waiting to be released.

I dream dreams of truth; I see myself whole and good inside with the willingness to share all I have to give.

My inner strengths are starting to surface, and my deepest feelings are being brushed on the canvas to complete the person I am.

For I am as I am and what I am to be.
I am the final touches to the masterpiece;

I am the artist behind the brush;
I am the best I can be for all the world to see, especially those dear to me.
I am me—just me; God's handiwork for eternity.

Kay Moore

The Shadow

Sunlight fingers through open blinds
Casting stretched shadows on the wall.
The play of light and dark can trick us all,
Lengthening shadows lengthen in our minds.

The sunlight, attracted to your face
Put its hand upon your cheek and lets it rest,
Affectionately lingering from its journey West.
Its etched shadows fills a slightly larger space.

Although the sun's most ardent hour's passed,
Honeyed fingers trace your smiling lips.
Shafts of light explore like fingertips,
Each moment passing magnifies its cast.

I am your sun, shining love on thee,
My youthful vigor hence I once pursued
Has riven deep and now rests more subdued.
You are, thus lightly loved; reflect it back to me.

Each day that passes deepens loves light,
And magnifies the quiet kind of caring,
A tender love tied to lifelong sharing.
That makes you such perfection in my sight.

Prentis Hall

The Machine

Bent wheels and burred cogs
Cause the slow stopping of a great machine
    That rolled and purred a hundred years
Unfettered by the mindless tinkering
    Of stolid workers and the
Revisionist with the fevered glare.

    And as wheels grind to their final stop
The engineers all blame each other
    And point to the other.
"'Twas his responsibility!"
They say as they shake
Their nervous heads.

    The machine stands still
Silent with the dull accusation
    Of cold, hard steel
That will either run or rust.
        Mike Dunklin

Skin Deep

Beauty,
    Certain as a sun rise
    Yet essence masked beyond skin deep
Tears shed like streams
    While eyes of rivers weep
Two lives full controlled by hearts incomplete
    Minds once full of laughter now show signs of sleep
Nurturing hungers fed of thirst
    Quenched by beauty unrehearsed
Creatures unfolding as darkness is pulled to light
Behold!
    True beauty without sight
Surely as day shall become night.
        Patricia A. Jones

African Sky

Skip the rock
chance on a happening
the day races the night
jump rope with an African tribesman
see the union take flight
elephant stomps down the brush
zebra sense the fierce lion
taking off in a rush
waterfalls stumble down in the imagination
a child is born in the fields of a silent hush
listen to the calls of the wild
whisper fore not to disturb such tranquility
sip moist droplets of water off the leaves of life
see the antelope gallop off into the rich sun
the tribe migrates the renewed perspective
to harvest a new crop of the ever-changing
as the reptile sheds the skin of old
skip the rock
see how the ripples fold
into the African sky
        James Hoeft

Breakfast Solo

4 a.m.
Breakfast alone again
Jazz in my head
and java in hand
and ham on my plate
Spinning
dim
chords
below
crisp notes covered in broken yolk and slathers of ham
        Jeff Caruana

Life Is A Journey

What we touch as we move in our many worlds
changes forever as we gather its soils.
The changes we make are what we leave behind;
the changes in us are what make up our mind.

We're making the world an image of us.
All that we are is left when we're dust.

When we tread unpolitely we injure our home
and leave to our children a desert to roam.
When we do not take notice of what we pass by
we live unenlightened and then we just die.

We're moving along a path of our choice.
As long as one hurts we should all raise our voice.

As children we see the true wonder of things,
but rush by it chasing the power age brings.
Then as we grow older we see the child lost -
each path not chosen has its own special cost.

We're here together on this spinning mudball.
What you do to another you do to us all.

Life is a journey if you know it or not.
What seems just a trifle could mean a lot.
        John C. Bohannon

Inner Sides; Inner Signs

Changing times
Changing tides
Inner voices
Inner rhymes
Magical scenes of inevitable dreams
Magical scenes of irreversible schemes
Patterned shapes of fears
Patterned pieces of emotions gone by
Intricate fragments of hearts and visions gone awry
Memories vivid amongst the battered winds
Memories apparent in the middle of the sun and it's heated sins
Emotions we may hide to protect the ghost in us all
Emotions we disguise to prevent reality from surfacing be it
    big or small
Masks we wear to protect our faces have us going to unheard
    of places
Masks we wear to protect our shells of many shapes and colors
Be it fragile or strong; right or wrong
        Maria Picar

Tomorrow

Standing on a cracked and dusty road
Chariot tracks permanently embedded within,
Pillars cracked and broken along the roadside.
To each side I see the ruins of ancient monuments;
The bath house with its broken mosaic floors
    and murals pealing from the walls,
Temples who's ceilings and alters have disappeared
    along with their Gods,
The market place empty, no caravans left to stop there,
The amphitheater will never again hear the laughter or sobs
    from an audience watching forgotten plays.

My city will one day mirror this city
Roads full of potholes and tire tracks,
Stores and malls empty and crumbling,
Churches and libraries forgotten and abandoned,

We do as we have always done
Leave monuments to prove our existence
And hope there will be someone to remember us.
We are a link....
    Apart of all that was and all that will come.
        Kari Naso

Abuse

Beaten, battered and so often abused,
Children of this world are so often used.
Too often they grow up without love, but instead hate,
A living hell so often these days becomes their fate.

Children so young and so very impressionable,
Often grow up in a hell that is unimaginable,
They deal with being beaten and to often molested,
Their frail bodies and minds wrongfully tested.

Instead of sanctuary in their "loving mothers arms,"
They are often laced with a torment that only harms.
I can only hope they will someday find a cure,
So that the children will have a safe world instead
of one so unsure.

Our children need to learn love and trust,
Instead of learning abuse and hate,
For with these values instilled in them they stand
A chance at a better fate.
Children can be taught without physical or mental abuse.
But it is up to us to put love and understanding into use.

Mark A. Naylor

Pandora's Gift

Out of the gift box
Claim the coveted treasure,
A package of beauty and motion together.
Where is the source of the energy found?
Science and logic will try for the answer.
So, disassemble the workings, inside and out;
Disconnection, disorder, disaster result.
Something is missing.
Directions are needed.
Lift up the box lid.
Look underneath.
See the small printing -
Read it aloud, "Chernobyl."

Grace B. Miller

Choices

A sea-bound ship floating on the water
Clear blue ocean all around, yet it's hard to see.
The ship stranded, going no where
The star - lit sky looking at me.

The Captain's choice of which way to go,
His confusion as clear as glass
One wrong move could bring death at sea,
His stubbornness not willing to ask.

Stars all around him, giving him advice
Stars are not caring or knowing what's right.
Darkness surrounding the deserted ship
Not able to tell the difference between black and white.

Panic flowing through the Captain's body
Almost giving in to the treacherous waves,
Realizing the danger, trying to stay away
Not wanting to put anyone here in a early grave.

Trying my hardest to do what's right
Not knowing which direction to take.
Hoping the ocean will shrink with time
And turn into a small, clear lake.

Kara M. Cravens

Memory of Tears

Hours move by my eyes - when only minutes move by the hands of
the clock.

Dreaming, I fear its delusive splendor, so the simple sweetness of
sleep takes my mind prisoner and my body finally lays free from the
grip of tension.

Your darkness is blurry, a few words exchanged-My thoughts awaken,
clouded with a dry pallet by the early murky waters of memory.

And then comes the rain,
Swelling inside the clouds, its
Moist hands clapping the rooftop, continually
Cooling the concrete as it pours down its sides,
And begins to flood the heart of the soil.

Your pillow holds with it the proof that the rain had already come
even before we had wished for it.

Quinci S. Boos

Christmas Every Day

Tradition compels us to pay attention to our immediate family and
close friends during the week of December twenty fifth.

We mail dozens of greeting cards proclaiming good will to all.

We greet strangers with a hearty Merry Christmas and provide
Santa Claus for the children.

This is truly a pleasant time, with the enjoyment of feasting
and spicy exotic beverages.

Charity during this time is much more prevalent in our thoughts.
There is no question that the atmosphere contains a positive force,
created by the optimism of the multitudes during this interlude.

As this is my belief may I offer you this Christmas ode.

Tolerance, patience, and brotherly love, have come more to the fore.
More smiles coupled with tenderness, are shining from every door.
If I could leave you with one gift, understand me when I say.
I wish, I wish, oh how I wish, it was Christmas every day.

H. Dale Walker

The Experience

Loosen your soul oh do not weep
Close your eyes for now you shall sleep
Become as one for that's what's right
Follow the tunnel at the end's a bright light
You're at the end it's all so peaceful
But in your mind before it was so dreadful
Your happy now but want to go back
The love of your family is what you now lack
You wake up in a harsh snap
You had just fallen into a deep trap
Should you tell what you saw when you were asleep
Or know something no one knows
A secret for you to keep

Kristy Yeager

"The Artist And The Poet"

An artist has many mediums he can work with at his command,
Compared to the poet with pad and pen in hand.
The artist paints the blue sky and white clouds with his brush,
The poet uses quiet words, serenely, in no rush.
Both artist and poet have talent to spare.
Each uses the medium they're most comfortable with care.
The artist paints the huge pin oak in every season's shades,
The poet writes of it as one more miracle God made.
The artist quickly takes his brush to catch a bird in flight,
The poet thinks which words best describe the lonely sight.

Lewis Lembo

My Passageway To Tomorrow

The constant turbulence my mind endures due to the
continual thrashing of my body from side to side
is more than one can comprehend. Promising the mind
tranquility as the body requests rest. Close the
eyes, rest the soul, serenity close. My mind an
abundant clutter of endless thoughts, refusing to
shut down. Continuously fighting myself as I understand
the need to shut out the world, yet full of
unquieting queries. Relaxation ebbing away as dawn
begins to unfold out of the darkness. My body somewhat
rested but the mind still jumbled with antagonizing
idioms. The passageway to tomorrow smothered
with wrinkles of yesterday. Hoping for a freshness
of the new dawn that's drowning in ruffled
night shadows. So begins the day—still connected
to the twilight. The morning sun setting the precedence
of hours to come.

Mary M. Blessington

Haunted Halloween

Spiders, wolves, ghosts, and bats,
Costumes, candy, kids, and cats.
Watch out for the witch's spell,
Ghouls and goblins down in Hell.
Burning in devil's delight,
Caught in a web as black as night.
The werewolf's howl is eerie and mean,
Ghosts in the graveyard don't want to be seen.
Weaving through the bleak tombstones,
Scaring kids as monster clones.
Haunted houses, spooky masks,
Trick-or-treating is quite a task.
The full moon in the graveyard shows,
Where the spirit hides and goes.
This is how Halloween was,
And always be, just because....

Karie Yanick

Sounds Of Love

Listen...listen to the earth voices
    crackling brooks
    exploding waves of the ocean
The Dolphins Song, croaking of frogs
    clapping leaves, as the wind whistles gently
creatures of the earth speak...the bugling elk
the butterfly as it emerges from the cocoon
creatures....large and small, seen and unseen
    The soil...yielding forth her
    fruits as if giving birth

As the voices travel full circle...
    ashes to ashes, dust to dust
    they return to live again...to replenish
Listen...listen to the earth voices
you will hear the sounds of love

Melissa Ashley

Creation Undone

A seed unplanted and Faith unfound
Creation undone and the trickster unbound.
Unthinking children for one days play
have chosen the price we all must pay.

The cut of the knife and the cauldron of blood
regrets then a wash like a river in flood.
Blessed were we and so were our sons
Now we must pay for creation undone.

Mark D. Kurtz

Eyes

Arteries of the archaic.
Dappled light couriers casting
Soliloquy shadows through the fronds of foresight.
Misty, veiled, juxtaposed medleys of
Winking, blinking, fluttering and, crow's feet.
Shielded by mini-framed, stained-glass panes,
Or crescent-shaped, paper-thin jello slivers.
Anointed with war paint; transfixed on lucid illusions.
In polarized pageants, a cadence of color
Animates the soul of the pupil we know and,
Deciphers the gradient, jaded pallor of our peers.
Granulated, teardrop amulets,
Awakening from twilight sleep,
With memories of a horsefly's
Honeycomb, mosaic eye.
Aesthetic infusions of crystalline marrow.
Refracting and reflecting afterimages of blind spots,
To screen unwanted light from Earthen eyes.
Luminous prisms into the convex abyss
Of countenance.

Pennie McGlothlin

Moon And The Sun

When night falls,
darkness invades the light,
and the moon takes over the sky.

As it shines over the vast land and water,
it waits for the arrival of the sun
to carry out the dawn of a new day.

Then the moon sets
and the sun rises;
life begins to awaken.

The bright of day continues till the evening comes;
the sun sets
and the darkness takes over the light.

Nicolle E. Lundeen

The Exodus (The Book Of Exodus 13:20 - 14:31)

Darkness.
Darkness that could be felt.
Thick darkness that night, despite the Fiery Pillar.
"We're for it now!" I said. "Pharaoh will get us!"
It was bound to happen.

Hear the chariots? Hear the armies?
Hear the people shouting and yelling?
Blaming Moses....

Then dawn at last.
See the chariots? See the armies?
See the blood about to be shed?

O Pillar of Cloud - Have mercy on us.
O Pillar of Fire - Save us.

Raise your arm, Moses. Divide the Waters. Take us across.
Get us out of here!
Lead us to the land you promised.
The Land of Milk and Honey.

So he did!

And God brought us here.
And God brought you here.

F. Anthony Cayless

The Survivors

They stand naked between earth and sky,
Dazed and bewildered, wondering "why?"
How to prepare for a thunderous rain
That ripped through a path called a hurricane?

Out of the rubble and the dust,
They clenched their fists, sworn to new trust.
Out of the mist and mystery
Came a new cry that made history.

Look forward, not back
There's a happier landing
Where new seeds grow, love and understanding
Let's gather the mood, spirit and mind.
For try we must to better mankind.
Gather our people on how to survive
Giving our thanks for those kept alive.

Muriel Pravda

Death, On That Judgment Day

Death hits hand
Death hits tough
Death hits in away you're unspoken
When she or he will be missed.
Death comes at day
Death comes at night
Death hits young and death hits old,
Death will hit your mother, sometimes
Your sister or brother.
Death can make you cry or, death can make you die.
Death will come upon us day or night,
Young or old.
When the time is near, you will hear, your
time is up, time to leave us and face
another place where, there won't be know
fear or long time suffering just a peaceful
Place to rest are faith until are date
on that Judgment Day.

Navaline Smith

Mother

Sweet brown walls the eighteenth century wood cut paintings
Decorative iron the lead glass window...
65,000 flowers paint the ceiling:
This is my mother's house, she sits in the lion-back chair
Mourning the loss of her son.
Grey hair falling over the collar
of her black dress, and Father cannot move her
She refuses to eat, sleeps disturbed and prays Oh God,
Does she pray...
For one last supper one long moment with her boy
Who left a daughter with all his traits she
Bounces with his rhythm sings lullabies to herself.

Darby Lane...my son's baby (don't leave me that young)
Don't forget your daddy...child, he wasn't well at the time
And I know how much he loved you, still does...love you.
It's going to be a while yet, she says, before the family comes.

Lay here on my chest let's think about your daddy
And blow kisses to the sky...

Mitchell Michieli

Beyond Imagination

Deep in a room, enclosed in no walls,
deep in a world where the night spirit calls.
falling 'round the table high,
on it the fears of the world lie.

Memory fades into shallow pools,
the wisest men are the laymen's fools
shadows hide inside the light
nature mounts, prepare to fight.

Cities are vanished, people are gone
the only ones left are the weak and the strong.
The sunset goes down, heading due south,
this backward world tastes sweet in my mouth.

Falling ever upward, rising ever down.
The lonely tree crumbles, producing a sound
all action stops, time has just froze,
killing the blossom of the last bloody rose

Took to his heart, how full a sensation
For this is my world, beyond imagination.

Michael Devon Donaldson

Ways

Ever been to a place
Deep into night how you guess your fear
Highest upon the hill surround misty willow
As close your eyes to imagine your deep real
As know stars always there make of sure
See trees sway in every motion of Heaven Breath
Nothing shadow upon your naked eyes
How counted every stars ream turn of your years
Hear sweet music of river pushing their tears
As touched of soil of tough the made of man
Every once dream of dreams how you want be wanted
Spared your feel by lip of wine
Will find yourself swaying with tree of every trees
Singing your child song with river of tears
As gather all your feel so strong made to cry
Upmost of your now time as open your eyes
Feel every touch of cold as you gather for home
As shed your tears to trace your fair
Knowing somebody found ways
As know you will be back someday

Marvin Coffin

Confidence

Be self confident today
Despite what others do or say
We're all born equal in God's eyes
It's up to you to form your size.

Discouragements will come to you
Don't let them stop you - go and do
Friends of both sexes will flock to your side
Just live as though you have nothing to hide.

If you are making a speech
Think of what you want to teach
If a favor you wish, go on and ask
The answer shouldn't take you to task.

Be brave, decent, honest and true
The only real way to see you through
Thank God for the life He gave you to live
You'll always be confident of what you can give.

Opal H. Lazar

Just A Memory

I made a mistake,
Did what I shouldn't have done.
I can't erase my past,
I can't dwell upon it either.

The problem is, I've been hurt.
The pain I've gone through,
has left constant reminders,
permanent scars, never ending tears.

I have wounds that have not yet healed,
Nor will a few ever.
I try to move on, and halfway succeed,
Other times I fall into a hole.
I once again
Cry myself to sleep.

There are many strange powers in the world;
But no matter what I do,
The truth hurts most of all.
The truth is...
    You're just a memory.
    Melissa Hansen

Did You Remember?

I woke up early this morning to say my prayers.
Did you remember, that we have a GOD who cares?

Life seems so tiresome, seems like morning won't come.
Did you remember GOD as you saw the morning sun?

The sun was shining; I could even feel the wind.
Did you remember to thank HIM for being your friend?
I thought I was important; I thought I knew how to win.

JESUS asked me, "Did you remember I always was your friend?"
Remember there is someone who will love you until the end.

"Greater love has no man than this, that he lay down his life for his
friends." JOHN 15:13
    Pauline Mixon Brown

Aerial Ballet

Feather-weight,
Diminutive,
Spark of joy!
Sipping sweetness from full-blown blossoms,
Dancing on tail-feathers to wing-pulse rhythm,
Hovering gently o'er crimson corolla—
Daintily stealing from willing victim,
Probing for nectar with sip-stabbing darts,
Humming and singing —
Diving, flitting in wanton abandon.

From where comes your ruby-throat
Suddenly splitting the pale colored feathers?

Blood-colored,
Scarlet, spilled from mid-summer vessels,
Leaving
A throbbing memoir
Matching
Gift .
    to
      Given.
    Miriam Saumweber, S.S.N.D.

QUIT QUI dOC

WARREN A. SCHRAGE
Doc Yarnspinner
Panther Badger almost she boy again Redskin

Forward ho
catcher in the cornfield he will become
hurdler of tall buildings in a single bounce

UNCLE CHAMPION
of breakfasts
before
photos

Drag raced PT-109 and won

Calculated the precise distances between stars births deaths
and
AUNT DELORES

Who now can that up to live
    Katrina Yabash

Little Zachary

A small sweet boy was swept away, and now it's just another day.
Does anyone care what he was like, he couldn't even ride a bike.
When you looked at him, he would get a bashful smile.
Oh, if we could have him back, just for a while.
Wings of snow, a halo of gold, he is an angel of God now don't
      you know.
We can't understand why you took his hand and took him away to the
Promised Land.
You know what's best, it's time he rest from the pain of life itself.
It's painful to say goodbye, but he will always be remembered and
loved, and we will meet again in the sky.
    Pamela J. Lambert

Untitled

A star shines bright out in the darkish night.
Does anyone know why it shines and glows?
Does anyone know why it burns so bright?
Does anyone know why it even shows?
I often wonder how it was place there;
Was it placed there by some God who was great,
Or was it placed there by someone who cares?
Could it be placed there by some trick of fate?
What value has this star that brightly shines,
Like millions of fireflies it does burn,
With all the glitter of emerald filled mines;
Turns wisemen from those who could never learn.
Who owns this star that twinkles in the sky;
It is owned by all, not just you or I.
    Joseph Smith

Lemmings

Run, I did, at his bequest
Down to the beach with all the rest.
Why we were there I could not be sure
Except for some undeniable lure.

I hit the water at full stride
And realized then it was low tide.
I thrashed and fought with all my might
Until the surface was gone from sight.

So I settled myself to accept my fate
Watched my decent, ignored the rate.
The depths enveloped me like the night
As the world I'd known disappeared from sight.
    Jeff Forker

"The Little Voice Inside Me"

The little voice inside me
Does not know what to say
Because the number of problems far exceed
The number of answers today
The voice tries hard to comfort me
As it attempts to work things out
But it comes up empty-handed
And makes me want to shout
Soon it places all its effort
On trying to keep my head cool
To control the bad feelings that I have
And keep me from acting like a fool
Luckily it overpowers
The ugliness there is inside
But these feelings aren't gone forever
They just temporarily hide
So an important thing to remember
Is always keep your little voice strong
Cause sometimes its the only thing
That keeps you from doing wrong.

John Krejnus

"Drop Out"

"Drop out"
don't pout
you're exiting the nonsense system
just another worn out piston

"Hey you", we always knew
that you wouldn't make it through
A talker and a dealer, you were the leader
but you never became the learned reader

Best friends at one time
once your mime
then I stayed out of trouble
in the nonsense system, boy in the bubble

In class, I could see your point of view
being told what to do, regimentally, like military school
You fought Big Brother tooth and nail
We all watched as you would finally fail

I'm not saying you were wrong or right
But judging me differently was wrong, when you wanted to fight
As you angrily approached malice
I only said, "we'll both find new wonderlands", "Alice"

Paul Szymanski

The Discovery

I watched Mary race
down to the water's edge
and play chase with the waves.
She bent and inspected
shells, then carefully chose
those she wanted to save.
She placed them in her bucket
and watched the salty water
cover up her sand-buried feet.
Her dark hair glinted red-gold
where the sun-rays met the
tangled locks as she skipped
and sauntered, unaware I was there.
Then, she turned, saw me, and pointed out to sea.
I looked to where she was pointing and saw fins
from a school of dolphins.
She melted, chapping her hands,
jumping up and down.
She never noticed the sand, shells, and ocean
water spill from the bucket to their home, the water's edge.

Nancy Kerr

Untitled

Come dance with me won't you
down where the dead lie
we can celebrate life there before sightless eyes
we can laugh at our wisdom
we can laugh at the stars
we can dodge between the markers just like dogs between cars
'cause if we can find pleasure
where most kids won't play
we may be in tune to what the dead say
to live life to the fullest
at least while we're here
for once we reside with them there's only sorrow no cheer
I'm gonna heed their warnings
and live for the moment
so I don't wind up wondering where my youth had been spent
so won't you come dance
down where the dead lie
you'll find many reasons to live for and none to die

d.e. stadnik

Winter In Suburbia

Little snowflake, mask promoter, sugar coater, north wind rider
driving down, driving down, not from on high do you drop
nor confront stiffly head on, but subtly floating, drifting
angling in, fancily deceiving, warily curling, truly believing
yet coming on down, down, down
the harmony of your ideal shape belying
the wretched sound of your host crying
all the while you keep on streaming, joining comrades already fallen
still veiling, still dreaming, a cozy fairyland, bright and gleaming
dust to ashes, now cream all over, where green pines and tinsel
    crinkle
everywhere jingle bells tinkle, and gaily colored halos hover
over the cold earth down under and the gray grime, rubble and plunder
that deeper and deeper you cover
as want and blackness pale, whiteness and purity to prevail
always and forever, as does the snowflake
with the warmth of ice and the strength of crystal

Phil Ballbach

Autumn Sunday

The clouds crowd in—suffocating,
drowning the struggling sun
beneath a sea of gray.

My little cat takes small, shallow breaths.
Feigning death,
she reveals her vitality through an unintentional twist of the tail.
She will awaken soon, and leave—
her shiny fur coat no longer reflecting any warmth.

I longing absorb every drop of sunlight that warms my paling skin.
But the shadows are fading quickly...

Glancing Northward,
I mournfully accept that today,
the clouds will win.

Katee Czarnowski

The End

Boy you were good, I'd say
Even great
All of the music you made was so up to date.
The feats you accomplished with your
Likeable songs, made
Everyone love you, I'm
Sorry you're gone.

Leo J. McGuigan III

The Struggle

Life is hard in this day and age,
drugs and disease, and heart's full of rage;
follow a leader and a leader will fall,
to be replaced by another who will beckon the call.
Disaster and murder; blood stains our great cities;
the rich or the poor,
which ones should we pity?
The old act too young and the young seem too old,
and the ones in between bare secrets untold.
A day is an hour, a year is a day;
the hands' of time are running away.
I believe we all have the power to see,
the dark demons that keep us from our destiny;
so lets all look inside our own tortured souls,
and bring forth the courage to reach our goals.
Life is hard in this day and age,
there's a great need for peace in all hearts full
     of rage.

Kevin Moore

The Afterlife

In the afterlife it is cold as stones
Drying like grey chalk
On that beach you only half-remember
From the other life, the first life,
Where in mornings crowds of fishermen would gather
Winding their nets in like webs
Silvering and ripe in the early light
Where now no touch cools your skin
But once the hands of one man burned it
And if he still lived he would not know you
Remembering only the salt of your flesh
And the scent of hibiscus.

In the afterlife of volcanos you remember the fire
And your own color when you began to burn
The way you ran down that shingle beach
Possessing for once every life, that man,
The hands that once held you.

Now, in the afterlife,
Do you feel beneath your skin
The fire as it quickens?

Kelley Hollis

God's Wonders

Here I stand, a small insignificant being,
embracing thoughts of majestic mountains.
Spectacular formations reaching to heaven;
touching the sky with white snow-capped peaks.

And, imagining the vast life-filled oceans
with its abundance of unique creatures.
Harboring illusions of rhythmic waves
enveloping me in its serene restful movement.

Visions come of beautiful multi-colored rainbows
enhanced by sunlight following a storm.
An arch of color gracing the sky,
bringing delightfully refreshing hues to the heart.

And while pondering on the awe inspiring splendors
of God's wondrous creations,
an affirming voice within whispers
"I also made you my child!"

Linda L. Susiene

Untitled

The Moon is the Sun's parasite,
Employing the fuel
It provides.

And so long as the Sun does set at night,
The Moon
Shall always rise.

Stealing rays to furnish its own,
The Moon does not repent;
Nor does the Sun refuse to shine
To keep its mate absent.

Should darkness bring the Sun's demise
And give the Moon command,
Stolen beams would rekindle the dying source
That shed its light so grand.

But so long as the Sun does share its grace
To give the Moon
     A life,

The Moon shall neither fade away
Nor vanish
From the night.

Kurt Knaus

First Words

By the window I found you weeping in sorrow
Erasing the memories of another
All I could do was watch you suffer
Urged to make you laugh
Tried to comfort you
I wanted only a simple
Friendship
Until the day I fell in
Love with you

Caring for me, like no one has ever done before
However, another has returned
Reaching foolishly to try and touch your heart
Inside where it is so warm to be
Silently I sing my song of love for you
Together we would live perfectly
If only you could see
No, it would never be because there is
Another

Manan Shah

Dreamscape

My mind unravels like a ball of yarn and
     drifts like a cloud in the sky.
It drifts to the special place, the dreamscape
     only I can reach.
I reach the ultimate state of Nirvana. I'm 2,000
     light years away from everything I knew.
My mind experiences a state of euphoria, and I
     see the depths of my soul.
I act no role here, I am in the purest form.
I climb to my highest aspirations, and sink to
     my deepest fears.
No barriers hold me back, and no person passes
     judgement.
In my dreamscape I am me, I'm not the person
     everybody sees.
I'm so far gone into my soul It's kind of nice here.
I like just being me.
I think I'll stay inside my dreamscape.

Henry Jerome Stockard V

I'll Walk With Pride

Please don't stare, then turn away, as I am retarded, can't you see?
And there are many children just like me. Our minds may not think as
fast as yours. Also, there are many things we cannot do, but we will
still walk with pride.

So please don't stare at us, without feelings. Or don't laugh at us
without caring, when you know we are hurting inside. But we will
still walk with pride.

So please accept us for the way we are as we are God's children too.
And we have feelings just like yours.
But we will still walk with pride.

So please take our hands, don't turn away, let us share our love with
you to show others that you care — that our lives are real. But we
will still walk with pride.

So please don't weep for us when we are gone if you can't show us that
you love us too. You say you love us but then you don't. But we will
still walk with pride.

In God's hands we will find our peace.
There will be no more stares and no more laughter.
There will be just love and happiness forever after.
And we will walk with pride.

Patricia Jenkins

A Brides Gift

As I think of the day I met you, a smile caresses my face.
And though it seems so long ago, no time shall ever erase.

The first time that I saw you, how could I have known,
That before too long I'd understand that my heart was no longer my own

That first kiss was the beginning, of a love I could never replace,
And I've never felt a more loving touch than your warm and gentle embrace.

From that moment on, I was inspired by the love bestowed upon my soul.
And it was then that I knew,
that if ever without you, I would never again be whole.

You've been my salvation, my inspiration, my ever impassioned love.
And until the end, my lifelong friend, it's you I'll be thinking of.

And now we'll begin our new life together,
We've attained that wealth at last.
And the longing to be not two, but one,
Lay silently in the past.

Heather Castleberry

Keep Wondering Why

Looking out at the stars, the universe above, keep wondering why I'm here
and wondering why I love you, keep wondering does it matter anymore,
In the world why can't I see you,all the answers become questions,
and mysteries still seem unsolved, and the mystery of you,
and the mystery of you, has been there, been there for a while,
The universe above, and me down, here, so many mysteries, on this earth
we may never know, keep wondering why, just got to believe,
love is somewhere here, but keep searching for something to hold near,
something that will solve, this feeling I have inside,
Somewhere here, gonna be next to me, somewhere here, gonna be just right
people keep saying, love don't matter anymore, but maybe that's why
we're lost, in a universe of desire, deep down I still want to care,
and I know its mystery, that makes us more, than just a candle in the night
Something from up above, let me know, I can see you,
nothing can stop this journey we call love. There's
always hope in this mystery called life.

Nicholas Bochain Jr.

Profile Of A Madman

Every statement begins with "I"
Even if the "I" factor does not compute

He clears his throat
Bellows a story-line then gloats

He boast on his prison sentence
From junior to high to Defense

"I've been there, done that...
I'm glad to have my life back."

With thunder in his hand he clinches
A dastardly deed in mind as his eyes glisten

Hatred fortified by insecurity
Respect reflects cowardliness

"I'm in charge." He proclaims
His life at a glance suggest failure's frame

He's stern with a harsh tongue
He's unaware whence his so-called position stems

It's nothing more than a label
Used ineffectively labels cripple and disable

How many will he captivate with his tactics?
How many will disregard the Madman's antics?

Kaloa Illana Hearne

Joust

Sometimes the expression on your
face is taunting and still sends a
twinge through my spirit.
I feel as though we have begun an
emotional joust; we the knights
with our lances, and today no different
than some medieval time long ago.
You piercing my soul and I piercing
yours; still twisting the knives in
each others back.
We have managed to contaminate each others
beings with our swords and now it seems
time to let go. If you feel the need
to win the game, then I give you
my consent to be the victor, or maybe
you will just have to play the
game alone.

Memory Ferguson

Autumn

The breath of summers over
    fall is in the air
A gentle breeze - cups golden leaves
    and scatters everywhere
Trees - standing bare and lonely
    appear so very few
Yet - full and green, somehow they seemed
    a lovely forest grew
Daisies and forget me nots
    that only summer brings
Have gently bowed their heads in sleep
    until the coming spring
My eyes - drink in the beauty
    of such a lovely view
God's creation for ALL men
    yet - witnessed by so few
AH! said I hear the call of birds
    sing their departing song
Reminding me that winters near
    and all this beauty gone

LaVoyce Dickerson

Songs

Once there was a time when the world was young.
Every child was a song and the songs were all different.
The children kept their songs with them all their lives.

But as the world grew older the children forgot their songs,
forgot their childhoods. They grew up to leave their childhood
behind and raise more children, more songs for the world to love.
They say that with this joy, they don't need to be children again.

But every child in the world knows that their parents long to be
children once more. They wish that it is possible to return
to a world of bliss, but it is not.

Before you forget YOUR SONG and leave your childhood somewhere
unknowing, remember the good times. Think of them often and pass
them on to your children. Play your song on the piano,
hum it at night or sing it out loud, but never... forget them.

Lindsay Moody

Anyways

And you keep talking about it to anyone,
Everyone;

Hoping and believing that one of the times you'll
find someone that can say or do something,
Anything;

Taking the pain away a little or a lot or,
Completely;

You realize; it never happens.

And you keep talking about it to anyone,
Everyone....

Lisa A. Szlag-Hoye

Who Are You

I look at you
Everything is there
Anger, love betrayal, trust and dreams
Who are you?
Are you the future?
I am afraid
When I look back there appears to be no past
But when I turn around and see you I reach out
Hoping to find a beginning, a tomorrow

Kim Eileen Thompson

Fearful Tears

Rainfall sprinkles over the house;
Evening pulls its hands around her tears
Her heart cries tears that douse,
Night is a lonely time she always fears.

The house dark and gray with brown boxes
Cold and damp the lonely women.
The sleep that will not come without toxins
Her heart is as cold as tin.

Past time in her soul and heart
Lonely visions from her sorrow,
Songs from the past playing on heavens harp,
Mornings light shines on the sparrow.

In the tree he sings on high—
She awakes taking in life's breath and sighs.

Judi Hotsinpiller

Finding Yourself From Within - Fly Sky High -

Break your limits!
Extend your reach.
Shake your brain,
Bake your soul.
Make your game.
No name, no blame,
No fame, no shame.
Discover yourself and the world.
Fear not what you see,
Express what you believe.
Hate nobody, but love everybody.
Take to your wings and set yourself free.
Fly high and wide as far as you can see.
Think wise long before you die.
Make your dreams come true, the best they can be,
You'll leave the crowd but still live in the clouds.
Your spirit reflects the rainbow of diversity.
We all become one and we are part of God.
The concept that all human kind accepts.
Then humanity reaches Eternity.

Light, Love and Luck,

Ngo Dong

Feathers

Feathers,
Falling,
Always falling,
Floating down below,
Into the frozen snow,
Tickling the faces who get in its falling path,
Feathers.

Feathers,
Falling from birds up high,
Landing right below,
Falling, like parachutists,
Slow, very slow,
All the way down below,
Feathers.

Feathers,
Twirling, enjoying the air,
Falling down to land,
Drifting, down in the air,
Playing, playing on its way down,
Feathers.

Matt Schwaab

"Sonnet"

Wondering, wondering... in your eyes.
Falling in love with you.
Mentally, Physically, Emotionally.
No, for I cannot lie:
For, it is our souls which fall in love.
Or souls which ride together through time and time again.
Yes...our souls.
The same souls from another life.
Falling in love over and over again.
Souls which knew each other before.
Souls which fell in love a time before.
Time and Time again.
Somehow destined to find each other,
Through time and space.
Searching and Searching...
Until one day, finding each other's souls.
Or was it... just the fact that you were always there?
Just waiting, waiting for time and space
To bring us together again.

Paul John Siwek

Untitled

Its getting time to see Kris Kringle
Families sit around to sing a jingle
Now's the time to be happy and give
Do the right thing you only got one life to live
Lots have family members to turn to
Others are poor and live on the avenue
They have no home and that isn't their fault
Nothing to give, no one to consult
This is the time to give to the needy
Don't be like scrooge and act like your greedy
So this Christmas give some of your wealth
Think of others, not just yourself

Liz Stacey

"Life Goes On"

You can blame it on the man who made you or the one who held
your hand
Father, brother, sister. They all had a hand
You can blame it on the school yard children, how they ridiculed you.
Blame it on the teacher, the minister, and your marriage too.
You can blame your marriage,
But Life Goes On, Life Goes On.

You've taken all I've given, Yet you have given too.
I know its been a roller coaster from New York to Malibu.
So lets hang up the boxing gloves, in exchange for something new.
As you know, Life Goes On, Life Goes On...

I've walked through many ghettos, along sandy beaches too.
Now I sit here watching the old day become new.
My thanks to psalms and proverbs for all that you do

It's just a passing moment that we all must go through.
Life has many treasures, some joyful and some blue.
There is no happy ending, except that god loves you.
Yes, life goes on, life goes on.

Michael Lovy

If Crying Is Made For Fools (I'm A Fool For Loving You)

Since you went away, all I do is mope around
feeling sorry for myself. Thinking things would be
different. Blaming myself over your mistake.

This can't go on forever all I do is cry over you.

If crying is made for fools. I guess I'm a fool
for loving you. I was a fool to believe you could love
me. When no part of you had any love to give.

Saying it's over is just a phrase you use to hurt me
you just want to see if I'll beg you not to go. I knew all
along your intentions were not real.

Why did I think I was getting somewhere
with you. When all you did was treat me like a fool.

Nikki Guiseppe

Home For The Holidays

Your memories bring you back,
Even when "life" keeps you away.
The smells; the tastes; and all of those old feelings....
Traces of youth, from days gone by.
Home made cards, tin foil stars, and a child, somehow entranced by
    the lights on a tree.
The gathering of loved ones, from far and near;
To share a laugh, and a cup of cheer.
A time to worship, and reflect upon the past year.
So, come all ye believers;
Come home;
Home;
Home for the holidays!

Natalie Rose Freeman

Untitled

Today I walked on familiar ground;
Felt a presence much to close:
Remembered tears of sad and joy:
One by one they come around;
Sought to touch a sweeter time:
To give a smile for that I've known;
But like a spirit that comes to life:
The heart caress's a hidden wrong;
Greater by far the memories stand to judge:
And endless cry of words my thoughts have found;
Yet reflections thrown like seeds, that
surely meant so much;
To turn aside my heart has failed;
And walk beyond this familiar ground;
For the many have crossed this place I stand;
With driven force and great of mind;
Together we've met in symbols of time;
The swollen heart and gifted hand;
Spread the wings of memories abound;
That dwell all here, oh familiar ground:

B. J. Jones

Body Of Young Woman Discovered Along Interstate

Slippery Dawn
felt her way up my thigh
and rested knees down
inside my heartfelt darkness.
I had imagined you a brutal angel,
cloaked in scars and crimson, a beckoning menace—
anything but this timid waif,
this slumbering bride of newborn moss
having me bleed through
hasty Reservations.
She weaves; my doubts thread through twilight.
Fear leaks the last of its red courage.
The night is velvet milk; I would drink.
Crow gather in ceremony.
Yes, oh, yes...
I already see it...
a randy landscape carved
on Mother Earth's belly,
my eyes a silver lake
mirroring the sky.

Jennifer L. Scott

We Need Heroes!

The teenagers go through the whole gamut of
Filas, Nikes, L. A. Gear shoes.
The Girbauds, Guess and Fila pants,
The long, bald, shaved or dyed hair.
Some put earrings in their ears and
Some in their nose!
Some even wear gold necklaces!
Oh, yes. The music! Some listen to it for hours at a time,
They go from Sega to Super Nintendo for playing games.
Thank God for sports! Baseball, football, basketball,
golf and tennis!
When the uniforms and shorts are worn, it's like the good old days!
Its time for real heroes!
The teenagers need to look up to them.
Such as Lindbergh, Eisenhower, Babe Ruth, Joe Louis and
Jessie Owens.
Maybe some teenagers, now, will become the next heroes,
For the next generation of teenagers.
We need heroes! Please heed! We need them for a better future!

Mary Coats

Untitled

Christmas is a time of joy
   filled with holiday cheer
A special time we all enjoy
   that passes every year
We get so frantic buying gifts
   and sometimes lose our heads
We forget the meaning of Christmas
   and commercialize it instead
Christmas is not about the money
   or how many or how much our presents are worth
It is a special time of praise to our saviour
   because of his birth
It is a time of love and joy
   to loved ones far and near
To bring the separated close again
   to see the ones you hold dear
So with all the light and presents
   with all the hustle of the time
Remember the true meaning of Christmas
   keep HIM in your mind

Kimberly Minton

Beneath Many Smiling Faces

Beneath many smiling faces there lie a life that's bleak.
Filled with many pains and sorrows that sometimes will
not be reached. Tossing and turning day by day seeking which
way to go, hidden beneath a smiling face so that others
may never know. Some are given good foundations to help
them in years to come.

Others are given shallow starts that's bound to do them harm. But!
Whether good or shallow, all are required to be: that good and
faithful servant God has created them to be.

Although life seems unfair and frivolous to those on
shallow ground. But somehow they must weather the storm
and be released from things that bounds. Beneath

Many smiling faces there lie a life that's bleak. But
there is hope for those who know that Jesus saves and
keep. So keep on smiling despite the test for surely
you will see a life invested in God is bound to bring
victory.

Odessa Thomas

Forked Tongue

The striker's lips are as hard as a swift sucker punch,
Filling the room with words that trail stagnant smoke clouds;
Piercing the heart like a burning cigarette
Jabbed over and over into a fresh, styrofoam cup.

A window is opened,
But it just won't clear away,
Spinning about the eardrums,
Swishing throughout the blood.

It eats at you,
Feeding on resistance,
And defensive thoughts,
And hexes,
And screams that shatter
Dazzling irises.

The damn bursts,
And cold streams flow forever.

Hearts, thus, drop like rocks.

It's inescapable.
It's harsh.
It's human.

Richard P. Fernandez

Now

The ultimate strength was in my decision to move.
Finally, consciously deciding to move on!
Now I am at a decision more monumental than my move.
Now I am at a fork in my life's road that will decide
my ultimate destiny.

Now I am at a time when my will is being tested
and my backbone will prevail if I so choose.

I will not ask for strength because I feel I possess it.
I will not ask for a decision for it is solely mine.

I will ask for forgiveness and understanding.
I will beg you to see through my bleak and
feeble communication.
I truly care - more now than I ever have.
I do.

Melinda Taylor-Brown

For The Children

As you travel life with all its twists and turns,
Find something for the children and teach them
   what you've learned.
Give your knowledge to the eager, and the ones
   that will resist,
So when they face a challenge they'll know how to persist,

As you dream the music and hear the language of the harps.
Write something for the children to stir within their hearts
If you take a little when you need a lot,
You'll leave something for the children,
Because we are all they've got.

Mary A. Burnett

Imagine!

   The General gave it the
first utterances and the tragic reality
of it started their imaginations—-

   Very few of them were left after
they had fought and bled and died
all over that country; and so did they try
to control their imaginations—-

   The rowdiness, glee, sense of who
they really were, the thought that history would
tell of them only served to more
fuel their imaginations.

   And so it happened that the world
did applaud them for posterity- it eventually
bound them together into a kind of nobility-
and this was not a figment of their imaginations.

Mary Ann Mitchell

MISCOMMUNICATION

Friendly fire, that's what it's called,
For acts so horrendous, you're really appalled,
When people mistakenly kill those on their side,
It gives you the chills, you just want to hide.

The no-fly zone over northern Iraq was the spot,
Where twenty-six peacemakers were wrongfully shot.
Was this miscommunication or just human error
That resulted in such unspeakable terror?

An investigation will aid us in finding the cause
Of the death of the twenty-six wiped out without pause
To discover the identity of the two UN choppers,
Regrets sincerely offered; the mistake was a whopper!!

Miriam Moskoff

Old Shoes

Old shoes standing in the corner, among
fishing poles, and old hats covered with dust.
Memories of long walks down shaded lanes,
with a good old dog, you could trust.

Old shoes standing in the corner, now
many a passing year, you often wonder
how you missed them, someone must have
placed them there, by the stair.

You must have forgotten, just for a little while
you thought, until you found them once again
today, standing in the corner among fishing
poles, and old hats covered with dust.
After all, you're sure you wore them it
seems, just yesterday, walking down a
shaded lane, with a good old dog, you
could trust.

Robert C. Pardoe

Fire Within Yourself

The flames of intense heat await your touch. Fire upon
flames swirling in a circle of red, orange, and yellow. Burning
fierce is a light that protects and sets you free upon the earth.
The feeling of intense desire burns with in you as you roam with
out a destination or rope to tie you down. Nothing stands in
your way now. Fly to the stars, join them if you must. Fly over
the sea and lose yourself in your beauty. For everyone is a flame
and whether you kill yourself with pity or drown in sorrow, or
let your flame burn bright with happiness and joy. It's your flame
and no one can extinguish your dreams except for you. There's a
whirlwind of fire just waiting to be freed. Let it go, PLEASE!

Miranda Beaulieu

autumn reflections

i watched the leaves falling from the trees today
floating to the ground a thousand at a time
as the tears that trickle down my cheeks

i watched the sun and the moon today
both affixed in the sky simultaneously
as the nights grow longer drowning out the daylight

i watched the thermometer drop a few degrees today
old jack frost will be arriving any day now
but death is already tapping on the window

i watched the children playing outside today
running around in their warm little wind-breakers
as Saint Peter waits patiently at the gates of dawn

i watched the geese flying toward the south today
migrating to a more tranquil climate
as the spirits who are approaching heaven

Lawrence Roy Younge Pete

The Orphan

I watch the world through teary eyes
For I as a child, learned how to cry.
Abandoned by family, left with shattered hopes
I as a child learned how to cope.
Lost in the darkness, alone and afraid,
I wondered to myself why had I been betrayed?
I reached out a hand that no one would hold
and thought how could people be so cold?
Again I reached out, hoping someone would hold,
then there was someone who took me in from the cold.
Someone who loved me and showed me they cared;
someone who's warmth and happiness we both shared
and so I tell you, more important then the above,
I as a child learned how to love.

Kelly Henry

Mama's Prayers

Lawd dis is ole black Maria getting down on her knees. I want to pray
foe my fambly if you please. First there's pappy, skin like leather,
that ole goose still drives his model T Ford, broke down ole thang,
huh, got seats o plank an run on tabakey juice! bless that ole fool
Laws foe he kill his self in that contraption. Then theres these
chilren, they ain't the best
    tramping thru my vegetable garden, theys a mess. I whops
um when theys bad, and hugs um up when theys sad. I makes um kiss
each other when theys fightin mad.

When they mama died, an left um all alone, I took them chilrens into
my po home. I got down on my knees, all my life and axed you Lawd
to make me a mother an a wife, well at 70 Lawd ain't it kind of
late in life? I'll not dispute your choices Lawd, cause you
know best, but do they has to get the croup together I caint get
no ress. My bones is achin both day an night I done shelled so many
peas, I caint ebon write. Lawd I'm axin foe a little mo
    time to grow up these chilren and see um doin fine.
    They may run me plum ragged from dawn to dusk, but
      I thanks you Lawd foe puttin um in my trust.
      So bless these here chilren and pappy an ole Blue.
    I got to pray foe that ole dog foe they kill him, too.
    Maria Ligons Isola

The Forest Jamboree

They met one day in the forest deep
For a free-for-all grand Jamboree.
Sly Reddy Fox, so cunning and sleek,
The first to arrive at the old oak tree.
Then came Peter Rabbit so fuzzy and gay,
And lazy John Woodchuck awake from his nap.
Gruff old man Wolf and saucy Blue Jay,
And Timmy Black-Crow with a loud wing flap.

In the grand Jamboree, all began their song,
Some soft and low, some loud and long.
They danced and sailed round the old oak tree,
As all joined in the grand Forest Jamboree.
The rabbit, wolf, fox and Timmy Crow
With a silly tee-hee and gruffy ho-ho!
Old Mr. Owl form his oak perch high,
Sang not a word, but winked an eye.
Then all again began in glee
The song of the grand Forest Jamboree.

Dicy Hall Byerly

Through It All

How could I be sorry,
For everything we share;
How can I help myself,
When all I do is care.

Your love has seen me through some times,
I could have never faced alone;
When my days seemed toughest,
Our love has somehow grown.

There were those days it would have seemed,
Easier to give up;
But something wouldn't let us do it,
Love was stronger than we thought.

So don't you ever wonder,
If I'm sorry that we met;
Because through all the years of loving you,
I have not had a single regret.

Kelly Curry

The Stuff Life's Made Of — "Time"

Today I write, it never stops, a thing all know as TIME
For ev'ry tick, that precious stuff I'd wish to have a dime

It waits not for the swift or slow, it waits not for the fair
It waits not for the one who has to brush or comb her hair

We go to work, to school, to shop, we base our very life
To cook, to sew, to wash the clothes, in doubt just ask your wife

This stuff called time, it's here to stay, there's nothing you can
    change
Before you came, before you go, still here! It is quite strange

Who made this thing, when did it start? I guess you'll never know
Go back in time, let's say 10 years, it had to watch you grow

Still miffed about it's constancy, in awe about it's length
To try, I dare, to try you may, our quest, we'll have no strength

Dost thou love life, who asked of such? I think his name was Ben
It tells not where or even how, it tells not why just when

This stuff called time, I'm on its side, with it you'll only win
It's bigger than an inch, a yard, 10 feet a thousand hin

I hope my so few simple words did not commit a crime
I choose to write, I hope you like the stuff life's made of — TIME.

Myron Frye

Rules Of Life

What was spoken unto thee: The words barely heard.
For I am the powerless with needs of life.

For those who say; Speak only unto those who will listen.
Be with only those who want you; want only those whom you can't
have; cry to only those; who try to understand; trust only those;
who are willing to trust you; show only those; who ask to see.
For you are the powerless: You can not do without request or
permission.

But remember: You must always watch, wait and listen; be true; but
never show if your feeling blue; think quietly; never aloud.
Because you have your soul and for that you are proud.

Remember what happens: When you don't do any of these.
Life was not at all a breeze; for all those things have brought
satisfaction for some around; As for me it's the best way; I
have found.

My purpose on earth is not for me.
It is for those around me: To be happy, healthy in what some
call harmony.

Kelly B. Fairfield

Feelings

When I come upon the scene, your eyes sparkle with a gleam.
For if in doubt, in how you felt, one look is all I need to make
    my heart melt.

I need your love both day and night, but other times will be alright.
We laugh and sway to all our needs, hoping to capture sometimes
will lose.

When it time to say goodbye, tears come into my eyes
But oh' to think of all the fun, I know that life has just begun.

For it took all my life to find you, It takes the rest of my life to
    keep you.
For you are my first, my last, and my everything.

Naomi Briscoe

Love

Love is a beauty and cherished to see,
For lovers, love will have you on a knee,
For love goes far beyond the body,
You should not pay for or be naughty;
Instead you have a connection for real,
Your heart wildly pounding you feel,
For nothing else matters but the one you
    care for,
Whether he or she be rich or poor.

For friends, love is all seeing,
You share everything even forgiving
Through times of good and bad,
The emotions like happy and sad,
There is a real strong bond between the two,
If it ever dies, it will be broken by you.

When one mate leaves another here,
Part of you dies and you shed more than a tear,
It really hits hard for the survivor,
Until there comes another.

Patricia Manix

A Birthday Sonnet

I searched birthday cards by other bards
For messages sweet and sincere
But what plight, I found the words too trite
For a person I hold so dear

A poet myself, I put the cards back on the shelf
Knowing I could do better than that
Opening the lexicon, soon I was done
Exhibiting my heart's habitat

Then I looked in your eyes and soon realized
Silliness is not always trite
It is not a crime to make silly rhymes
If it's aimed at your friend's delight

Only to you this belongs and it lasts all year long
To entertain and make you aware
How I've tried to show what you may already know
That is, I truly care

Mark Fennell

The Farewell

From this old world now I must go.
For pain, sorrow, joy,
all have I known;
I've tasted, touched,
smelled and felt,
Saw and did it all
that this world holds:
Now it is over— and I must go.

No helping hand guiding my steps,
Like an infant unsure of where they'll land,
sad, yet frightened,
To face that alone what lays beyond;
Still I am glad,
Now It is over — and I must go.

Weep not for me nor of pity hold,
For happy I be, my journey to finish,
I lived it whole, there's no regrets
For nothing I done or left behind;
Now its time — and I must go.

M. B. Conley

Staying Power

I sometimes wonder what it takes
For people who are down and out;
To get off their knees, regardless of breaks
Standing for the next bloody bout.

Their bodies are battered, their clothes maybe torn,
but you can see it in their eyes.
That drive to succeed for which they were born;
Their expression is just a disguise.

Never underestimate the power of their will
Because the stronger the adversity is,
The more reason they have to find a way, still
Their stamina just reinforces.

Not many have this power—this strength
But you can learn this skill—
It takes guts and persistence and a
belief in yourself that no one can ever kill.

Mimi Feliciano

Festival

I cut a white sheet to fashion a hide
    for reveling on the eve of all holy...
        two holes for the eyes,
        some liquor, inside empty air;
    a disguise sets a soul free.
With devils ascent, we went to raise cain;
    all evil,
        to steal graves and eat corpses.
Joy of the fear!
Man, delicious of pain,
    abandon to excess
        that usurps his brain.
I forget how I got to my bed.
My head must invent the sins to undo...
    guilt the air over;
    awake for the dead;
    repent to the fathers-providing,
who have penance waiting to even the score.
Lifeless, my sheet is spent there of the floor.

Marie Allen

The Open Heart

Hear! O'Heart, the call to love
For the blooming is yet to come
The meadow lies unfolded
Nourished by the seasons and promises of life
Seen through the window of the heart

Hear! O'heart, the call to love
Of a cherished love wounded, with tears
Of a cherished love grateful, with smile
Of a cherished dream, that must be shared
Seen through the window of the heart

Hear! O Heart the call to love
Accepting the richness of the years
Warming in the fire of life
Giving what we have given
Seen through the window of the heart

Hear! O Heart the call to love
Greet the past, welcoming
Accept the awakening, seeing
Offering the future, being
Seen through the window of the heart.

Philip N. Papaccio

A Dastardly Deed

Unlatch the closet door, the searchers pled
For these old bones have long been dead
Let deceit and betrayal there lie
Hidden from the pure powdery sky
These old skeletons must be freed
From the Valley of a Dastardly Deed
Then release the Skeleton Brigade
So they may wither in the grave
Let the guilty atone for a deed so ill
That all those damaged may be healed
And the innocent by Truth be shield
Let the mystery of this deed be known
For it is concealed in the title of this poem

Marjorie Guess Hall

My Beautiful Ponies

But lo, in the distance there's hoof beats I trow,
For they do not answer by voice you know.
Now the thundering is closer and in thru the gate
Comes beautiful Bonnie,
Yes, my Bonnie lass with her head held high,

Full speed she is traveling all beauty and grace.
Then trotting behind at a much slower pace,
Comes the gentle and steady most predictable Betty.

They're a team of pure beauty these ponies of mine.
Mother Nature has blessed them with all of her charm.
Welch Pony's, dapple grey
Creatures of beauty are they.

Margaret Keigley

Walls

Be wary of building cellophane walls
For time will make them opaque
And block the window
That leads to your heart.

Some build their shelters of mortar and brick
To hide from the world for a while.
But mortar hardens,
Their jail is complete.
A while becomes forever.

Break down your walls of fear and disguise.
Reach out and touch those around.
Be happy and savor being alive:
Love is worth the risk.

Nancy Skolnik

Babies Are Fun!

Babies are fun for Mommies and Daddies,
For Uncles and Aunts, Paw Paws and Nannies.

They're soft and cuddly and loveable as well,
And the smiles they give you are really swell.

Precious little baby we love you so much,
That we just can't wait for that first little touch.

So keep on growing just a little bit longer,
We really want to see you but you need to be stronger.

When you are stronger and ready to be here,
You'll see lots of love and probably some tears.

From Mommy and Daddy and even big Sister,
We love you baby brother ... Our Little Mister!

Patty E. George

A Boy Who Died A Man

It was sometime ago today, my son you disappeared.
For when they send a young boy to war your mother said that's not fair.
Holidays come and holidays go we wish that you were here,
your picture hangs upon the wall a young man in battle gear.
When new friends come for a night of cheer,
they always ask who's that there I proudly stand up
and with a tear I tell them that's my son, a boy who died a man.

Joseph Morton

Mirrors

Mirrors are tools
For you and me
A thing to test our vanity
They tell the truth
To you and I
There is nothing a person can ever hide
See yourself happy
Or watch yourself cry
For some they're erotic
A sexual high
Some see beauty
Some see plain
Some see truth which causes great pain
But one thing is for sure
What you see in a mirror is real and true
There is no hiding the real you

John M. Osborne

The Power Within

When reading this poem must wear nothing but joy
for you are going to take miraculous ride through the depths of life
you must absorb the power of this poem
and breathe in the scented air emotions.
You are trapped now in blackness;
your cries will only ring in the ears of pain
Do not cry; your cries are brought out from fury
and only the silence of love can overcome fury
You can now hear the beating of your heart
joy, laughter and kindness lie within each beat
Absorb the joy of life and withdraw from the obstacle of hatred
The power within this poem is also in your heart
and the love in your heart has added to the power of this
poem.

Luke Mogelson

Candle In Your Window

I see the candle in your window
From a million miles away
I reach out to touch it
But it's gone as night turns to day

I know that you are lonely
That you are scared and unaware
But fear not for I am with you
Even though I am not there

Remember that I love you
And carry you deep inside
My shoulders are still stained with your tears
From the feelings you could not hide

Even though the candle may fade
The flame will never die
I will always know you are with me
In the corner of my sky

Michael Sell

"Leave Your Mark"

Live each moment as you find it; take each day as it is,
　For you life can be take; tallies run on what you did.

Leave your mark upon the moment; don't let it slip by you,
　Take time out to spend with loved ones; say the words "I love you".

Memories are but cherished moments; smiles, a touch or loving words,
　They leave their mark on all that know us; and thus, our mark
　upon the world.

So as you hurry through you life; doing what must be done,
　Take a break from all that strife; and schedule in some love.

Take an hour from every day; a day from every week,
　Pull close your family to your heart; turn off that old T.V.!

Get to know your family more; ask them of their day,
　Share their hurts, their trials, their dreams; support them
　each always.

Communicate and you will find; less troubles come your way,
　With family, boss and even friends; and in the end they'll say:

'He showed us that he cared for us; buy things he said and did,
　His memory lives on in us; because of how he lived.

He left his mark upon us all; and taught us how to love,
　By taking time from busy days; his mark's upon our world.'

Linda K. Purvis

Moonspun

He walks in the shimmering light of the moon...
Forever dazzling, causing me to swoon.

Incense embers glow surging with oxygen's power
Life tones creating a beauteous, tremulous flower.

A woman I am, though a child I sometimes be;
I listen to you as a master, as we make love under the tree.

Woman-child. Woman-child. No longer a child I want to be;
The child is mute; the woman now, you alone, fully see.

Master of my heart! You know I love you as no one else ever will.
Make love to me as we hear the once lonely bird sing on this hill.

Joan S. Beck

Holding On, Ten Years Gone

Ten years gone, as you sang of your first love, the one you never
forget.
Ten years gone, and my passion is living on.
Ten years gone, your presence still strong.
Ten years gone, I doubted my love could last this long.
My flame has simmered from time to time and I've asked, "Where
　do I belong"?
Ten years gone, I know my love wasn't wrong
Just that one song, it's now ten years gone.
I love you now, I loved you then even though you were ten years gone.
I still sing each song.
It's only now after ten years gone. I finally feel it in my heart.
Where you're at, is where I belong.
Because ten years is so long, doesn't mean that you're only ten years
　gone.

Never go, Never leave.
Ten more years to hang on.
before too long, once again you'll be ten years gone.

Karac Chantell Moore

The Lord

The Lord is merciful,
Forgiving and saving anyone who believes.

The Lord is faithful
To those who call upon His holy name.

The Lord is powerful,
Performing unbelievable miracles.

The Lord is loving,
Giving up His own Son
    for the lives of
        His people.

Marilane Mesler

Ode to Immigrants

You who crossed the seas in search of,
Freedom, work, and happy pursuit,
Rejoice...Here you are better off,
In this land of honey and fruit.

Shoot in roots, grow, flourish, expand;
Honor the laws that shelter you,
For they are your shield and your friend,
When adversities boil and brew.

Put to rest your past and your flags.
Follow this one with Stripes and Stars.
We all are pioneers and stags,
In the same good Old West town bars.

Washington, Lincoln, Grant, Einstein,
Are your role models and your lights.
What made them great is yours and mine.
It is there in the Bill Of Rights.

To you, America, I toast.
I love, honor, and cherish Thee—
A humane and welcoming host—
"The Land of the Brave and the Free."

Nakley A. Risk

The Friendly House

A friendly house you might say.
Friendlier than most people -
People who pass and never speak.
But it seems to welcome everyone.
A worn old couch
With sagging springs,
A tattered rocking chair
Reeking of cigarette smoke,
And a coffee table,
Rarely changing its flowered dress,
All seem to be calling.
So at home do they make you feel,
That you quite forget that you're not.
But even so, they aren't even real,
Yet can be much more company than the lot.

Michelle Johnson

A Moment...

A night to remember, a moment never to forget.
Finally, the question was asked.
He was mine, I was his.
A feeling of love took over what once was confusion and fear.
To be in his arms was to live again.
All sorrow and pain was washed away by one kiss.
To gaze into his eyes was one step closer to heaven.
The refreshing crash of the waves filled my ears with joy.
The moment went so quickly, but will last forever!

Lacey Marcks

Here Nor There

The summer was the time before
Friends and memories in familiar halls
But now summer is no more
Her golden leaves have turned to fall.
I watched their transitions one by one
In a sudden gust, mine first blew 'way
Caught unaware, torn toward some
Unknown. Instantly from gold to gray,
Welcomed by the hard, cold ground
Crushed, swiftly among the brown. A sea
Of empty faces, no memories when I look 'round
Confused. Gold? Brown? They are not me.
Where do I belong? Home is - where?
Surely, neither here nor there.

Jon D. Farr

Untitled

Red flows through my veins again
From a heart pounding to the rhythm of sand
Swept shores under a sky of fire
While dimly lit spaces echo with serenity.

The meeting of lions is fierce and gentle all within a
Single moment.

As the moon hugs the earth as it always has
and the rain falls and all things grow and nature's
orchestra fills the air with music for each season.

I see that all these things so unchanged with
Each passing tick are so different
Because my eyes no longer see just black and white...
Thank you for bringing color back to my world.

Keith Fricke

Child

This child doesn't feel drool crawling
from corners of his smile, stretching to his
hairy chest. Doesn't care.
This child emerges from a tent at three a.m.
bound not by clothing or social norms, sputtering
broken phrases in a deep voice to
the darkness. Calls to a squirrel he named
earlier. Calls to anything that wants to laugh.
This child stares out the car window with alien
eyes, mouth agape, tongue in
the way. Doesn't see freeway or even the Grand
Canyon, but focuses only on his ghost reflection
smudged with fingerprints and sun.
This child says he's Elvis sometimes, says I
know after everything, says his birthday is tomorrow
every day, says he's been there.
Probably has.
This child is thirty-four and somewhere within
his uncluttered mind, decided five is a fine age.
This child stayed there.

Michelle Rambo

The Master

He played my body like a fine violin
fingering and bowing with skill.
The master's hand kneaded my skin
evoking my music at will.
The perfect match of that special pair
never escaped the audience's eye.
And the silence deafened their attentive ear
when he let the melody die.

Peggy Garvin

Remembering

I know you, my friend ... we've journeyed far
From past lives to this one ... from star to star
Across the galaxy ... pathways we've known
Riding on the wind ... gentle breezes we've flown

I feel you, my friend ... inside my soul
Familiar your presence as my memory unfolds
We have walked hand in hand ... together we have stood
There's no mistake why it feels so good

Star so bright ... beauty and light
Shine from above ... illuminate the night
Grant me this wish that I'm dreaming of
Send me your warmth ... peace and love

I see you, my friend... in all that I do
Thinking of you helps to get me through
The vision of what I know it could be
Fills up my senses ... it's setting me free

But ...I've yet to recall the sweet smell and taste
For fear takes a hold of my actions in haste
If I begin to open my heart up to you
I can remember once more ... what my soul knows is true ....

Kate Stead

Seal Rock

Grey, dim, misted air hovering above
Frothy, whispering waves that roll onto beach and shore.
The cold western sea behind echoes loudly in chorus
As it descends from dike-like line high up and distant
Where clouded sky and black/green waters merge.
There silhouetted tankers sit alone and wait,
Weightless, dreamy, eerie phantoms, puppets
Who perform and vanish into space around the bend.
Nearby, roaring, angry, constant currents mingle,
Pellet, pierce and pound the pock-marked cliffs
Creating stone-holed arched-rock islands, grotesque guards
Who stand as shields against the cutting winds
Providing safe way/solace to the tiny bay and busy cove.
Here fish of all kind flourish, seals cavort and bark,
Humpback whales feed, frolic, spume and slap the gentled sea.
Suddenly into view, thick-petalled brilliant flowers
Blanket cliffside, invade, explode the mind and senses
Perfume the air and titillate the eye with vibrant scent and color.
I know the place, I have been there.
I call it "solace to the soul."

Clara M. Frieder

My Life

My life is like a rainbow.
Full of colors and a pot of gold at the end.
My life is like a car.
Always on the go or going nowhere.
My life is like a child
No worries at all just
playing and singing all over the world.
My life is like a roaring forest fire.
Trying to spread out all over the world.
My life is like a bomb.
Dropping and hurting the ones
I love and care for.
My life is mine, nobody else's.
My life is all I have right now.
My life is just the way I want it to be.
My life is mine, nobody else's.

Melissa Clingan

Christmas Shopping

I felt like a child in wonderland
Gaping, stumbling through the mall.
   Brash sounds in festive beat
   Mixed smells, pungent and sweet.
   Searching masses milling to and fro
   Joyful registers ringing the toll,
Caught a-whirl as in a Princess Ball.

A forgotten toddler amusing his new toy,
   sits unfettered, idling by
Oblivious, as the world about, the gift from God,
Unheralded, unsought cry.

Paul L. Mogyordy

Salvation

The eternal God, the great Creator of heaven and earth
gave us his only begotten son Jesus, SAVIOR at birth.
I pray for forgiveness of all my sins to you father above,
please forgive me of my sins with your mercy and love.
Jesus, who died on the cross to be our savior is your son.
I believe this and in him and that he is the risen one.
After being dead three days in the tomb,
you Heavenly Father brought him to life to leave that room
to preach some more to the chosen men
and send them though out the world seeking souls to win.
Now seated at your right hand is the ruler of heaven and earth
the one three kings gave gold, frankincense, and myrrh at birth.
Heavenly father, please prepare a heavenly mansion for me
so that after death I can live with you and Jesus for eternity.
Please write my name in the book in heaven above,
because that is where, after death, I will find abundant Love.

James E. Jackson

Too Much Information

I've been told fortune's key is to create a better me.
Get my body into gear, no flaw is tolerated here.
My brain is full of clutter from all the knowledge THEY do utter.
Whom to believe I can't conceive; each expert has a new gyration.
IT'S TOO MUCH INFORMATION!

If I am to be fit and strong I must avoid all that's wrong.
No fat, no stress, no sun, even water's under the gun.
But facts today as stated tomorrow will be vacated.
What is true, wish I knew; always some new revelation.
IT'S TOO MUCH INFORMATION!

My self esteem takes a whacking for I always seem to come up lacking.
In the view of should and ought, I dare not risk being caught
Sloughing any recent finding so on myself I keep grinding.
An endless relay, of not okay; all I get is more frustration.
IT'S TOO MUCH INFORMATION!

Conflicting advice abounds from authority all around.
Rules for living and loving to obey, be correct in what you say.
Colliding prophecies of doom in fads and fears that boom.
I am not amused, I'm just confused; absurd levels of expectation.
IT'S TOO MUCH INFORMATION!

Linda Kramer

The Simple Things In Life

I like the simple things in life.
Give me a rainbow or a smile, and it makes my life worthwhile.
Give me a butterfly and I will rejoice to the man in the sky.
Give me a dove and I know I'm in love with life.
Give me flowers and I'll look for hours
   and be in his everlasting powers.
Give me a ray of light and I will pray with all my might.
Give me time and I know he's mine.
Give me a hug and I'll tug on the simple things in life.

Linda Kay Bird

Things I Promise

Give me your fears — So that I may calm and reassure you
Give me your hurt — So that I may bear the burden of your pain
Give me your despair — So that I may lift you up
Give me your troubles — So that I may give you piece of mind
Give me your grief — So that I may bring you happiness

Give to me things I ask here
So that I may give to you
These things I've promised

Give me your dreams — So that I may make them come true
Give me your hopes — So that I may fulfill your wishes
Give me your arms — So that we may hold one another
Give me your heart — So that I may hold it next to mine
Give me your love — So that we may grow as one

Give to me things I ask here
So that I may give to you
These things I've promised

Give to me your self
So that I may give myself to you

M. Anthony Williams

Fear

Fear is something we discover when we take our eyes off of our
goals.
Therefore we should not look any farther
than our own goals.
Because we might discover something we don't
want to explore.
Fear.
Fear itself is the only thing that can take our
minds off of our goals.
And Goals are the only things that
can take our minds off of our fears.
Goals shall always win
over fears.

Mandi Salzman

Circles

Most of my life has been constant circles
going from strong to weak
instead of an even parallel
I go from sublime to bleak.
I can be bold as a lion
and dare the unknown or shy as a kitten
frightened to be alone.
I can glare as a hawk
all emotional control in my ability
or fall like a sparrow
unveiling my vulnerability.
Hard as steel cold as ice
bending like a willow sweet as spice.
I can be an absolute bore or a person you adore.
My mood can be rude
if I conclude to only solitude.
So love me or hate me
at this point I can not say
what I will be like tomorrow
much less the rest of today.

Lin Clark

Hasn't the Fear of Flowers, Gone from You?

Hasn't the fear of flowers,
gone from you.
the selfishness, in the gathering of them.
from me.

I make love with myself,
and with your ghost,
grasping distractions otherwise
aware to the bone of my loss -

If I cry your name out loud
can we just go home? -
Sick, silent, fear of an echo

Hasn't the fear of flowers -
gone from you
the selfishness in the gathering of them -
from me.

Raquel Patton

Untitled

So many years of history
Good and bad memories
They say time heals, pain will subside
Don't know how I feel, tears I cry inside

So there's a reason for all that goes on
God's new season, a bigger plan
Guess I have to start again
Even though I've lost my very best friend

Things interfere, come in between
Love means more than those trivial things
Pick myself up, start living again
Depend on myself, make my heart mend

Have to go on and make my own way
Someday I'll look forward to each new day

Karen E. Caudle

The Maze

Through the long corridors I wander,
Grabbing the sides as I go,
The darkness almost blinding,
Have I really lost control?

Round and round I turn,
Harder and harder I stare,
But confused I remain—
Have I really lost my way?

Which way did I come from?

Exactly where was I going?
Nothing feels or looks familiar anymore—
Who am I again?

Everything once so bright, now quite clouded over,
Basic shapes stay the same,
But their meanings have all changed.
Am I dreaming?

I can't understand anymore the logic and sense of it all.
Pieces which once fit so perfectly together still work,
But not the same way—
Now the picture is different — or is it?

Leah Hall Langsdorf

Positive/Negative

Absolutely positive! decrees the notary.
Greedy beast, a fiend, breeds inside of me.
Empathetic healer offers trauma anodyne.
Moldy scourge must be abscised
Like leaf from wintery limb.

Dear ones, stunned by brutal truth
and burdened by their love
Keep silent vigil filled with hope
And faith in One Above.

Splendid troopers dice with death,
Excise the outlaw cells-
Fixer's face relaxes, says
"We think we got it all."

Life is nothing much to lose,
And who am I to live?
Suspenseful agony awaits
The final valedictory.
Positively negative! decrees the notary.
Born again, I will not die.
But yet, I ask "why me?"

Mildred A. Smeby

The Night Snow

The silent rush of snowflakes crush
Green pines with soft white lather;
Whispering winds whisk past tree limbs
Leaving crystal beads to gather.

On ponds of ice melt glowing lights
From street lamps softly beaming;
The earth lay still against the chill
Of night and winter's dreaming.

Up chimneys steep circling smoke rings creep
Through a haze of fires burning,
Which wend their way with winds to stray
To take their heavenly journey.

In moonlit hues of gentle blues
The starry skyscape hovers;
The ground aglow in satin snow
Lawn wrapped in winter's covers.

Linda Louise Greene

"Christmas In The South"

Decorations shining in all the stores
Green wreaths with red ribbons on the doors
There's a holiday spirit that comes once a year
For Christmas in the South is almost here.

The trees are standing with their lights so bright
They seem to be just waiting for Christmas night
All the children hoping for the snow to fall
But here in the South we don't get much a tall.

Christmas in the South it's a time for joy and smiles
For celebrating the birth of one small child
It's a time to remember the things that use to be
Now it's Christmas in the South again for me.

Now we all know that Christmas is a time for giving
It's a time for laughter it's a holiday for joy
But we need to remember those we can help
For they won't have much to eat or shoes on their feet
Or that little child that would hug one simple toy.

Yes it's a time for memories of days that use to be
Now it's Christmas in the South Again for me
Merry Christmas to you all- from the South

Phares Parsons

Just A Name

A Beautiful individual (without spirit),
Guarded; behind a wall to difficult to destroy.
You were a Challenge - a Need. I offered myself
to you - good times, bad times, in between times
I was there for you - I believe you, I did not question your
answers (even when you were lying), you offered nothing - I accepted.
I knew I was, only one of many - I have no meaning - I am nothing to
You, Just a person you know just a Name...

We had no special bonding no special meaning,
no special anything. Soft sensus mouth, kissable
Lips and a nice smile, made me loose my senses.
Being physically and sexually attracted to you
your lack of consideration and common courtesy were
intentionally over looked, I admired yourself
assurance - until I realized it was a conceit.
(Being a dreamer I played along).
Forced to regain my senses - "getting you out of my system"
- eliminate you from my life - fade out unnoticed by you.

You were not a friend nor lover - Just a person
I knew - Just a Name To be Forgotten in Time....

Margaret Luna

Untitled

Winter storms have come and gone and
guess what's around the corner,
that's right I think you've got it, of course
it's spring. And we all know what follows
spring, that's summer. Along with summer
we have the clear blue oceans that sparkle
like a diamond in the rough when the sun
hits it just right. And we can't forget the
sandy, white beaches that are as soft as a
brand new babies butt.
The oceans, the beaches, the fun, and the
sun are all great in a sense, but the best thing
about summer is the peace and quiet, and having
the friends around that you love.

Jaime Keplinger

Untitled

Mmm, mmmh, humm.
Guilty love,
guilty of love and it is crying softly.
Love is guilty so it cries sweetly, serenely.
Dry your eyes, warm yourself, warn yourself.

The lost and found yesterday's tomorrows
And love are so sorry, so very sorry.
Guilty love and no hurry to virtue I am very sorry too.
So love let us stop crying softly and we may gently laugh.
The courting bird is flying.
Let us have clear eyes and passions
And feelings so our hearts and minds
Are healing, winter change to spring.

Saints of guilty love don't worry
Pray and kneel but guilty
Just come on love, stop crying.

Love, please love stop.
Come on love stop crying,
Love stop
Guilty love stop, hmmm.

Henry J. Oughton III

Rose

Can you hear me rose?
You stand in a perfect pose.
I think you're like a diamond ring.
But most people think you're just a thing.
You're so pretty in the vase.
You really feel like silky lace.

Erin Martin

Sixth Game, World Series

Seven days since Thomson's shot
Had pinned me to the sofa's spot,
Dad fanned two tickets to the game.
Could World Series 6 soothe some pain?

So a Brooklyn boy in upper left
In girders' shadows still bereft
Touched shoulders with his Dad and stretched.
Bauer tripled over Irvin's head.

Years later Yvars' letter said
Keen knowledge of Kuzava led
To that line drive which cut the light
And sped to sliding Hank in right.

When sudden outs end highest hopes
Remembered clouts are frozen ropes,
Bauer's shoulders germination
Framed with Yvars' termination.

Only when the eighties came
We saw it as Joe's final game.

Lawrence S. Groff

Campsite 16

A majestic heron flies through the sunset
Haloed by the tangerine of an evening sky.
It scoops down on the sandy rivershore
With the precision of a surgeon
    and grace of a ballerina.

The son has been replaced by the moon, now
Black shadows of a mighty forest
    line the river.
The rotting limestone holds within
    the mystery of night.
Kissed by a moonbeam a vein of
    diamond like granite appears.

Shimmering stars peek through
    our personal canopy.
The waits, with their brown and
    gold bonnets sleep,
Swaying in the summer breeze,
    as they wait for the sun.
It will rise to wake us all, tomorrow.

Michelle Phillips

Forgive And Try To Forget

Forgive and try to forget.
Hanging on to old resentments won't help a bit.

When you hang on to the past how can you have a future.
Mistakes were meant to be made, from them we should mature.

Try to forget what someone has done.
Learn to deal with your problems then and there, don't run.

Life can be so much fun.
Maybe there's something to tragic to forget,
Pray for strength from the Lord, this you won't regret.

My brothers and sisters around the world let's love each
others and just forget.

Lena Elizabeth Davis

Inside the Self

In an unseen place,
Harbored by a meager existence,
The sun is bright.

Brooding at times,
But birds still sing soothing melodies,
While laughing shadows dance about in wildflowers delight.

Inside,
Evil is only one step away,
From snatching what is right.
Locked-away memories don't dare escape,
Escape from their home which they share,
With love and hate.

Kasey Doshier

The Cat

The cat is a most mysterious creature, but its independence
Has got to be its most maddening feature.
He meows and nags his owner to be let outside
And when the door is finally opened, he sits down and
    looks inside and out and cannot decide
The owner gives him a nudge and he finally goes,
Yet that is only the beginning of her woes,
Five minutes later as she is dressing for work
He paws at the door, while his face produces a tiny smirk
So she accommodates him, knowing she will have no peace
And hoping that his selfish behavior will cease.
She proceeds to the kitchen to pour a hot cup of coffee
And sees the cat sitting beaming with glee,
Having dropped a dead mouse right on the table
And acting ready, willing, and able
To accept for his efforts a positive report card,
When instead he spends the whole day shut out in the yard.
Keep a sharp eye on your cats, or someday they will turn into
    childish brats
Taking care of a cat is frustrating responsibility
And probably why most cat owners lose their sanity.

Kristen Neville

Once More

What seems to me an eternity
has passed and I see you again
a surge of emotions
overwhelms me like a sickness
that touch that gives me textured skin
my body is suddenly alive
every chilling drop of the
rain stings my face,
my blood scampering through my vessels.
Reaching out for you,
I reach out for nothing.
You are only an imagine, an outline,
intangible dreams of calcified sea-fronts,
eggshell blue and
wine-united sunsets.
It has been too long. I ache to feel
your body pressed upon me once more
as a child puts his hands on a window
and exhales heavily,
leaving tiny circles of fog.

Jennifer N. Brown

Pegasus In Us

This winged wonder like love is truly a miracle
Every breath, every movement resplendent and purely lyrical
And within a twinkling of the eye can transplant the heart
To an enchanted moment unruffled by the dark
Undisturbed with the coming of the happy solitary tear
Coaxed forth from being lost in the rapture of being ever so near.

Cynthia Schult

Untitled

Dad left me after many years of suffering with cancer.

I can't believe he's gone.
He fought for more than 13 years.
The cancer didn't take him, it was his heart.

He never gave up, and he never stopped living.
He lived each day to its fullest, as if it was his last.

He wasn't the perfect dad, he made his mistakes.
But I loved him.

I wish I could have said goodby.
I wanted to be by his side, but the Lord had his own plans.

He always told me, "Never give up, never stop trying."
"Losers stop trying, its easier to quit, its harder to go on."

So now I must go on.
Never giving up, never stop trying.
Living each day to its fullest, as if its my last.

Don't take for granted you have tomorrow.
There only is now the moment, don't waste it.

No one know's how much I'll miss him.
No one know's how much I loved him.
But I feel in my heart, he knew.

Lou Ann Uyeda

Son Of God, Son Of Man

He comforts and guards me in my valleys.
He gives His joy and shares my peaks.
He guides me in my walk through this world,
And holds me tenderly in my sleep.

He is in my every waking moment
And even tho' my feet should stray,
I only need to ask forgiveness.
He smiles and points the better way.

So even in my deepest sorrow
And always in my darkest pain,
I lift my hand. He firmly grasps it
And sets my world aright again.

And so my Shepherd leads me onward
With still small voice and gentle hand,
Until I share that last tomorrow
With the Son of God, the Son of Man.

Isabel Ruble

The Shore

We stood on the shore, in the light of the full moon,
he holding my back to his chest,
While looking at the full moon.

A light breeze blowing in the air.
We talked of sweet things to come for us,
And felt our love grow more.
We watched the waves roll gently upon
The shore.

He turned me around very gently,
Then we knelt together face to face upon
The shore.
To pledge our undying love, to each other for forever more.
Looking into each others eyes, to see each others souls.

To give our love freely to one another on, the shore
Open hearted, no holding our feelings back.
One heart to the other,
In hopes our love will last,
Like the waves, that very gently touch,
The shore.

Lailani Luna

The Worth Of A Soul

As he made his way up to the stage, a hush descended on the crowd.
He introduced himself as, "David", very confident, quite proud.
He spoke of obligations, of commitments to mankind;
Of the hours he'd invested; and how his life was intertwined
With disabled vets and homeless children; illiterates and drug abused;
The jobless and the elderly - no cause had he refused.
He was living life on purpose - he strived to share his
gifts from birth.
Though war had robbed his arms and legs - he'd never lost
his own self worth!
He pleaded with the silent crowd to see him with new light;
To understand his loss - however grave - had not deprived
him of his plight.
He asked for their acceptance and compassion for his peers;
Vowing love and human kindness would help pacify their fears.
Emotions ran high through the silent crowd - some were speechless,
while others cried.
For the good in this humble, limbless man could never be denied!
His presence was strong and his story touched deep - to make
closed minds open wide;
And realize that beauty and power don't count - it's our
faith that determines our stride!
For, it's not what we lack, but with what we are blessed
that enhances the worth of our soul.
It's our love for ourselves, our belief in mankind that, in
God's eyes, makes us whole!

Nancy B. Rudasill

Just A Dream

He hasn't really gone away, I see him everywhere.
He is walking in his garden in the fresh morning air.
I see him among the flowers as he selects the perfect one
To bring to me so proudly. "Look what God and I have done!"?

I hear him talking to the children making everything alright
Or writing letters to his loved ones far into the night.
I still hear the organ playing, Oh be still my heart!
Ten thousand times I hear the song, "My God How Great thou Art."

I hear him singing in the shower, although he gets off key.
I hear the song. "Somewhere My love" and I know it's just for me.
I hear him whistling to the birds perched high upon a limb.
They keep drawing ever closer thinking he is one of them.

His Spirit is still with us though his body has gone away
His hand is on my shoulder as he guides me through the day.
Deep within the caverns of my mind, I chanced upon a stream
It's serene waters whispered, "Death is just a dream."

Leoda Maye McMurtry

The Ship I Can Not Sail

He's left me alone with her again.
He says she'll be good company, good conversation.
She is my burden, my problem.
I punish her for his absence,
for my loneliness.
She asks for good meals.
I feed her only bread.
She asks for friendship.
I lock her in a hidden shanty.
I deprive her of happiness, since she has stolen mine.
If I see satisfaction in those dark eyes,
I tear her down.
She's not worthy, she doesn't deserve peace of heart and mind,
I can not find.
I'll show him she can't be happy when he is gone.
I'll show him she's not good company, good conversation.
She is my burden, my problem.

Krista Beller-Collins

The Path

The season upon us brings darkness to light,
he sends his message fast to the young that last.

Sadly there are not many chiefs left understanding the way,
each family floats alone to find a path.

The winds of change are forever blowing,
hold fast to the winds of goodness.

Move away, move away.
Hear not the young warriors with no hunting under their feet
but the chanting of those that trod before you.

Young warriors tie not your fate to one another.
Each young warrior follow the opened path
or be looking for an opening along your way.

Take heed to follow and improve the path for your brother
to find his way.

Bitterness swells as warriors tell a path
trod by young warriors only.
The chiefs dance and shake to awake,
to awake the way of the path.

Softness lost to a cruel world where there's been no chiefs.
Turn around; see deeply into the heart of softness once there.
But now a chief dancing and shaking.

The blessings abound for those that have found
their way to the path and improve it.

Mitzi Mascio

The Light Of One Candle

We are no different
He stands with a cardboard sign in his hands
The sign reads "Will Work for Food"
We roll up our windows and stare at the stoplight

He stands with a cardboard sign in his hands
An Army issue duffel bag of wishes at his feet
We roll up our windows and stare at the stoplight
Green light means go and don't look back

An Army issue duffel bag of wishes at his feet
Wishes made, wide-eyed, blowing out birthday candles
Green light means go and don't look back
His dark weathered face has fragile blue eyes

Wishes made, wide-eyed, blowing out birthday candles
"Your wish won't come true, if you can't blow them all out"
His dark weathered face has fragile blue eyes
and the light of one candle flickers within

"Your wish won't come true, if you can't blow them all out"
The sign reads "Will Work for Food"
And the light of one candle flickers within
We are no different

Kimberly A. Holliday

The Ocean Speaks

The mighty ocean speaks to me!
He tells me young boys dreams,
  Blue skies
  Love lost
  Passion
  Death
and
  Life!
The mighty ocean whispers poetry in my ear,
And I laugh like a child!
On a cool summers day,
I fling my naked form into its vastness,
And feel the cold power that never rests.

Jesse Rupp

The Tree

As He stood alone in the desolate fog,
He thought of how things had changed
from the happy laughter of yesterday,
to the sorrowful mourning of the present.
What had happened to those carefree days?
When happy smiles surrounded him intoxicating him
with their very laughter.
Now the only comfort left was the lost voice of
the wind as it mercilessly ripped at his weary soul.

This voice would be the very same that would undoubtedly
haunt him for all his days to come.
Finally, as the last of his many tears fell silently into the
dark abyss of eternity, he stole one more forbidden glance
into the hole left in his fallen heart and swore,
as he had many times before, that it would be the last.
Although, in the depths of his tortured soul,
he knew it could never be.

Melissa Santanello

A Tiny Bird

A tiny bird came to our boat, and rested on the boom;
He was tired and not afraid—and took but little room.
We offered him a ride and crumbs, but he didn't understand,
And a scant few inches above the sea—again flew—
    though miles from land.

His strength near gone, he altered course, and headed for our sail—
In a desperate flight to save his life—he tried to reach the rail.
The rail to big for tiny feet, his strength now all but gone,
He fell into a wave below—the tiny bird was gone!

Too slow to act and slow the boat, I denied help I could afford,
And felt like I had caused the loss of the tiny little bird.
God help the little bird I prayed—I failed my only chance!
And after two, three miles or so, the rail again caught my glance;
And there the tiny bird was perched, my plea answered to His word—
That God loves all His creatures—even a tiny little bird!

Lewis H. Roberts

"Beyond The Reach Of God's Hand"

Beyond the reach of God's divine hand
He will not let me go
Through sin and sorrow of this present land
He'll keep me pure and whiter than snow.

I dare not wander beyond the reach of his hand
There's danger and destruction lurking there.
We must not venture on forbidden land,
For away from his hand, is sorrow beyond compare.

Beyond the steps of his sacred feet
I dare not walk alone
Each step I take He'll surely keep me
For I am one of his very own.

His guiding eye both direct my path
He'll not let me wander too far from the fold.
In his loving hand, all power he hath
To hold me, never let me do.

Minnie Breeding Everidge

"Peace"

Why do people go about killing each other
Everyone wants to smother
The next man with a nuclear bomb
We should get rid of games like "Corncob"

In this game you fly around killing
Why can't we be friends with farming and milling?
If people would try to show some peace
Then maybe the world wouldn't need police.

Martin Zahra

Man's Way

Is it man's destination to see the world in violence?
Hear the children cry?
Mother earth is being raped by man's thirst for power.
Look around. See what's happening?
See the signs of time of Satan's rule over man?
Evil is prevailing.
Do you see your future melting away in a genocide before you?
We are so far away from what is really happening. Why?
It is because we cannot see? Or is it we choose not to see?
The answers seem to live in what man chooses to ignore.
The hate spreads so fast, ricocheting and crushing every beautiful
creature, hope, thought, dream and the freedom of this earthly realm.
Man will not be doing this for much longer; for one day he will
be on his knees, answering for everything he has done.

Michelle Minnis

"Here I Am"

One day I awoke and said here I am; no one
heard me. Am I just another statistic, another
teenage girl with problems, hopes, fears, another
drop out society just wants to forget or to
stash away in the title "Generation X". Here I
am; love me, educate me, help me, don't forget me,
don't categorize me, don't tell me it will
be all right. Why should I fear for my life I am
a child in your eyes but yet I am adult enough
to know something is wrong. Here I am; hug me,
hold me, show me what's right. Don't fear me,
show me you need me, show me I'm worth it. One
day I awoke and realized that someday, somewhere,
someone can help me, Here I am.

Michelle Newell

Untitled

Sorrow, Tears, Pain
Heart breaks, Fear, Heartaches
What more again
To much I have been through
So what must I do
I searched and looked everywhere
Until, a stranger told me about this friend
A name that's above and unlike all names
His name is JESUS
The son of the only Living God
A great deal I have been told and learned
of Him.
Jesus delivers, heal and restores
And as of this day forth - I can truly
Say he is Lord, chief and savior of my
Life
He did it for me, I know he will for you
So do today what I should of done
Yesterday: Accept Jesus for all he is
I crown Him King

Jerneal Edmund

Untitled

This is my world, my domain
Forever in life I shall remain,
in a world of fantasies I made from scratch,
I was like a god making up a batch,
a batch of dragons, gnomes and such;
But soon I awake and it wasn't much,
back down to life and a mundane earth,
At least I still get to dream of my planet
next to a nice warm hearth.

Michael Gray

I Hope For Tomorrow

Into the realms of wonder, we all delve deep
Heeding no other voices, but the ones that fill our sleep
Over mountains of possibilities, into oceans of dreams
Prayers become reality, for nothing is what it seems
Everyone asks for more, if only they would give
Forever fighting nightmares, afraid to wake and live
Only hope can survive, the chance of becoming true
Racing the beat of time, for nothing is forever new
Toast to the future, while you weep for the past
Offer your sacrifice now, for tomorrow is coming fast
Maybe you'll find the answers, to the problems you seem to bear
Or if you finally find them, will all have ceased to care
Reap the wild winds, and sow the seeds of pain
Roll the clouds of hatred, as your tears form the rain
Only pause for a moment, to think what could be
Were it not for useless despair, like me you could still believe

Patricia M. Crawford

An Ode To Betty Jo

There once was a rose, flaming red 'twas to the sky that it
held it's head.
There once was a cloud, the sky for it was a shroud

Then there was a man in his eyes rose, sky, cloud couldn't
hold a candle to his love so proud.

His love was a wee thing no bigger than a mite his love was
a good thing though somewhat of a riot.

The things that we call life his love joked about his love
though a mite was bigger than life

His love was life in his eyes his love is you my love and
this I shout no man could ask for more, and no man could
pray for more.

This I say my love your love is my love and I am yours.
What more could I give, what more could you ask what more is
there Love it's the same only with you it's alive with the
flame of the rose, it's above the cloud it's over the sky,
it's my love my wee mite Betty Jo....

Michael Gamble

She's Hot

It's cold.
Her body quivers, longing for shelter within the realms
of warmth. Yet her chattering teeth can't seem
to conjure up a single cry for help.
She ponders within the mist of darkness; lost. It's cold.
Nothing but frosty icicles leering above her head;
jagged and evil, yet some how, comforting in her time of pain.
Her shaking hands reach out to a love; which is now lost.
It's cold. Her fear quickly turns to fury.
Sadness is lost in the storms of forgetfulness.
Her passion calls her to a dimension of wickedness.
And warmth rises up from her toes. It's hot.
A look on her face shows anger. The sorrow has disappeared.
And a frozen smile wipes away the misery and the tears.
A transparent form takes over her soul; and she laughs. It's hot.
Unforgiving shadows race before her eyes;
as a demon Lord reaches out, and pulls her away.
She follows her new Lord, to dwell amongst the night;
for mischief and madness,
to catch some poor soul; in the cold. She's hot.

Lorie Anne Dowd

A Mother's Tears

She is mother to many children, her name is Nature
Her children are dying from starvation and decay
The seas that once danced upon her skin like silk have become
hardened by pollution and now harsh to the touch
The hillsides where she used to play with her children have
all burned or have become barren.
The animals for which she used to care look scared and discontent
The sun that shown against her face in now too hot for her tolerance
Her favorite son has turned his back on her, how will she cope?
Our mother needs love
Her son must find compassion and his name is MAN.

John Weaver

My Grandma

Twenty years ago, my grandma and I sat at
  her kitchen table sharing coffee.

She stuck out her foot, turning it from side to side
  and said, "I used to be quite a dancer."

She said her ankles were thin and small
  and all the young men used to look at her legs.

I was only seventeen, and with the clarity of youth
  I saw only a foot and ankle swollen and knobby with age.

I felt some sort of sadness for her need to remember
  but I said, "I bet you were a looker."
I am now close to forty years old.
  I look at my hands and think,
    "I used to wear a size three ring."

Now my hands are swollen and my rings
  are hard to get off.
    They used to be thin and soft.

I remember my grandma's feet.
  Now I can see them fine and trim - a dancers feet.
    I wish I could have then.

Meribeth P. Mattson

That Rascal Jack Frost

'Tis a mid winter night
High in the vermont hills.
I snuggle deeper beneath the musty antique quilt.
No heat flows up to the attic bedroom
Under the slanting roof of the old farmhouse.
The blankets are heavy.
But they don't keep out the penetrating cold.
That strengthens as the days begin to lengthen.
Just before dawn the temperature zeros down.
Then that rascal jack frost creeps in.
He pinches my toes and nips my nose!
He plasters the window with layer on layer of frost.
Lacy images appear.
A crystal winter wonderland emerges.
With one last sweep of his magic brush
And a farewell nip to my nose.
Away he scampers!

Lois A. Pratte

Fannie

Each time your name is spoken, it brings on pleasant thoughts.
For all of us remember the happiness you have brought.
When you leave, please remember, you take with you our blessings.
Just to show how we care, enjoy today's dinner with all the dressin's!

Should you look back and think of us, we wish that you would smile.
Because for one who brought much laughter, we'd gladly walk a mile.
We wish you every success in the job that you have taken.
And, also, that you remember the souvenirs on your vacation!

Pauline E. Maxey

Appalachia

Oh, appalachia, your dusty, orange
hills do pierce the distance.
I have looked out upon you.
I perceive your timeless truth.
How great is the heritage within your belly.
So many are the days you have talked to men's hearts.
I have heard your words.
Your amber, autumn hue has caught my heart's thought
and reverberated it back to my mind.
Your seasons remind me of the seasons in my own life.
With shadowy stillness you show your dignity.
You are weathered to rounded cliffs;
and I see your wise character, for you have watched over time.
Wisdom you gave to the early people;
and the Lord makes you
to content my heart with your essence.

Mary Brookes

The Refugee

The old man plodded weary and slow,
  His back was bent his head bowed low.
Alone, he thought, on this road of sorrow,
  Hating today — dreading tomorrow.

Behind him the past horrible and grim,
  What lies ahead? - Nothing for him.
My home destroyed - My loved ones slain,
  O why must I alone remain?

Then suddenly he felt a presence there,
  He saw a boy so young and fair.
"Are you all alone?" The little lad said,
  Slowly the old man bowed his head.

"I am too — my parents died",
  then the poor little fellow broke down and cried.
Gently the old man gathered him in,
  laid that golden head under his chin.

Then those tired old eyes were raised above,
  with a gleam of hope - a newfound love.
"A reason to live, at last", said he,
  "God has sent a son to me".

Max W. Churchill

My Little T-Ball Boy

The day is here, he grabs his gear
His eyes shine bright, his grin just right
He's ready for the teams next win.
Oh, My Little T-Ball Boy!

His turn is up, he swings his bat.
His eyes shine bright, his little legs run fast.
He's safe at first, he grins just right.
Oh, My Little T-Ball Boy!

The next one bats, they run quite fast.
He's made it home and scored a run,
With bright shiny eyes, and that just right grin.
Oh, My Little T-Ball Boy!

The game is played and won, he's all tired
And smudged, with his bright shiny eyes
And that just right grin.
I shine with pride and love, just as happy as can be,
To share that day, and that just right grin.
Oh, My Little T-Ball Boy!

N. Lillian Picard

"Angel Boy"

An angel was born upon the earth, he stayed with us awhile.
His face more precious than gems or gold, he
could melt any heart with a smile.
A face so small and innocent yet his eyes
looked old and wise.
There seemed to be vast knowledge there
despite his small size.
His parents gazed upon him with love their
hearts so full of joy.
Lucky were all the people who got to love
the angel boy.
For some reason still unknown he was not
allowed to stay.
All the angels rejoiced when he returned to
heaven that day.
Now our angel is complete with his halo and
his wings.
All we have left are memories and a few of his little things.
As the years pass slowly by our hearts still hold his love.
I'm sure he's smiling down on us from his place with God above.

Nina Henry

A Tragic Romance

He waits, watches, and listens
His face sparkles, his eyes glisten.
He sees her beauty in his minds eye
He feels if he waits much longer he'll die.

Alas! Here she comes, from top 'o' the hill
He is sure his love for her will spill
She spots him, he runs to her
He is drawn by her exotic lure.

They clasp each other and hold tight
Her skin is as soft as a ray of moonlight
Tonight is the night they say goodbye
But! Not to each other! to their past lives.

They know what they must do now
But, can they do it somehow?
He takes her hand and a knife
He kisses the hand, and says "Bye" to his wife.

The knife plunges deep. Deep into her heart
For a very short time, the two lovers part
He first kills her, then himself
Now they are together, forever, in the afterlife.

Marie Christopherson

My Son - Through A Mother's Eyes

When my son was a baby he would rest,
his head against my breast.

It seems like only yesterday
that my son was a little boy,
playing with his favorite toy.

Soon my son was a grown man
Walking out the door,
going off to war.

In my eyes there is a tear,
and the fears, because he is no longer near.

My son is grown,
and out in the world on his own.

Karen Dobson

Untitled

The professor knew the subject, he studied it quite well.
His lecture was well prepared, but his discourse was hell.
"Uh," he said and I giggled. "Uh," he said and I writhed.
"Uh," he said and I bit my tongue and held the air I breathed.
"Uh," he said and I turned red as I slowly lost control.
And my friends sitting next to me were just about to blow.
I glanced at them and lost it; my friends had lost it too.
We tried to disguise our outbursts with cries of "a-choo."
The professor was persistent, he kept, "Uh"-ing on.
I sat there and bit my tongue until the hour was gone.
The professor finished satisfied that he filled our heads;
But as for me, aside from "Uh," I don't know what was said.

Kent Thurston

His Eternal Love

I see my Lord Jesus hanging on the tree,
　　His regal head bent low.
He died there for my sin, and yours,
　　How can I thank Him who loved me so?

Three days and three nights He spent
　　In the grave alone,
Because of my sin, and yours.
　　How can I thank the King upon the throne?

He arose triumphant over death,
　　And lives with the Father in glory.
He reigns victorious over my sin, and yours,
　　I'll thank Him with praise, and tell His story.

Praise God for His great eternal love,
　　The measure unmatched among the living.
Praise God He is Lord of my life,
　　His love I claim with thanksgiving.

Grace M. Fox

"Two Years Of Regret"

Calmly he speaks of it, deprived he now feels,
Holding back his lip, his tears that he kills,
To shy to show his heart, this man who cannot bare,
To be so far apart and feel no one would care,
He remembers her when they slept side by side,
Her skin so soft, so pure, their love which had abide,
Their home was poisoned too, their lives all drained away,
She died, her life was new, on a cold rainy day,
He sat to dry his eyes, through tears he could not see,
He felt no man should cry, he would not look at me,
Finally, he glanced up, and I could see his pain,
A storm bound to erupt, he speaks of her once again,
He spoke of the times they've had and feelings they had worn,
Of memories gone bad and the day that I was born,
And now he can't remember a day he'd shown her love,
Before that day in December when she had rose above.

Kristi McCormick

Father

My heart is so humbled by an example so giving.
How can I measure out to Him that which He has
measured out to me?
I was not yet, and yet He loved me...And loves me still
I hurt Him: I hurt all I love, but especially Him.
For He knows what I can be - But I make excuses,
Only to apologize and try again
Try harder for he demands nothing, and asks little.
Who can deny Him?
Who can love Him?
Only the child who owes his life to Him.

P. M. Force

"Evening Walk Along The River"

Outside. Lone goose calls, and flies on.
Hollow breathing (blowing their throats)
Brother and sister dog, mates to my soul, GREET the night with me.
They pad quietly almost silently:
  Missing nothing. Taking in everything.

The river. Whispers. Flowing gently.
Scores of water bugs scoot along the top.
Owl — across the shore — plaintive hoots. No reply.
First frogs of the night. Two
  Croak and recroak, chirp and call: Celebrate!
Goose's flock — honks and wings overhead —
  echoes linger on a breeze.

Gibbos waxing glows: ... Eerie distant firelight.
The dipper — leaps out of darkness into form. Jupiter shines.

Dusk magnifies everything: Sound intensifies. Sight diminishes.

Spring (although fledgling) is here.
Arise! Awake! Take back the life from darkness.
Take back my life from sleep, from winter's confines,
  recesses, denials:

Come out and live! Spring beckons me. This time... I dare.
    Martha B. Hickey

The Donkey

The donkey reluctantly obeys.
Hoof after sure footed hoof.
Bobbing head down, doleful,
cradling on worn shoulders
two large wicker baskets of potatoes.

Commanded over hillside by a
trailing weathered man,
clicking praise to his burdened friend,
offering snaps from his willowy stick
as encouragement along the dusty, stony path.

A day's wages unearthed and earned
when sold by his wife
at her front door in Almocageme.
Three souls
working together.
    Paul Sheckler

Hope Is

Hope is - something we should never despair
Hope is - think of success and never stop - until you get there.
Hope is - that all country's disagreements would fade away
      and be safe for children to work and play.
Hope is - that someday cures for all illnesses will be found
      and everyone would be free of pain - the world around.
Hope is - that we will be safe all our lives
      and the world would be free of war and strife.
Hope is - for our loved ones that we hold dear
      and that their dreams will find the success
      they want year after year.
My wish is - I hope we all will find happiness and peace of mind
      and look forward to the future and leave the
      past behind.
    Minnie Kelsch

Woke Up Cold
Reaching for something to drink-think
Colorless, odorless, trying to kiss-another chance at this? Bliss
Wish you well-overload of monetary gains and hunger pangs...
Reading the times, record, or something with words...
Can you remember what was said?
Alone, diluted dead....
    P.J. Frain

How Is It... How Can It Be?

Something 'bout life I just don't see.
How a little twig grows into a mighty oak tree!
I don't understand the beginning of time, the end sign
or how human beings stagger around drunk on vintage wine.
The way aging pyramids rise up so majestically,
While the sun rises and sets babies get born miraculously.
I don't understand how stars stay up in the sky and eagles fly.
Why is it broken hearted men aren't supposed to cry?
I don't understand how jilted poets chase lost love so foolishly,
Beyond the Milky Way lies Andromeda, another heavenly galaxy.
Why in the world would Wonderful care for one so unworthy?
How does raging war bring peace when trouble's already in the land?
How does a man born truly free enslave his own fellow man?
How does the Sears Tower, skyscraper bricks and all stand so tall?
Even strong winds blow up against it don't make it fall.
Some like drinking black coffee; others sip steaming hot tea.
Oh, the answers like mysteries keep on puzzlin' me,
Yet, the river still flows willingly into the arms of the sea.
Guess there're so many things I'll never see,
Tell me, how is it... how can be?
    Fanon

What My Mother Is Made Of

When I think of you mother,
How could there be no other.
Always there in time of need,
To take my hand and always lead.

My debts are a long time past due,
You know I'll repay them because I love you.

Many times I look back on the past,
Of all the good times that went by to fast.
Together we've spent over twenty years,
Having to listen to my laughter and see my tears.
Even through all of the hardships we've had,
Rough times never turned out to be sad.

I love you mother, I'm sure you know that,
So as you read this, just try and look back.

Mother, how can I repay back to you,
All of the wonderful things that you do?
Did you ever think how wonderful you are?
Ever so beautiful, like a shining star!

Often I think of what our future will be,
For I want us to be friends, just you and me.
    Linda Gregory

To: Ronnie

It was hard for us to understand
how everything could happen so fast,
and how many people have put you in their past.
But your many loved ones are still
in deep pain.
In deep pain, most will remain.
Although we all realize you're
in a better place,
the happiness you brought us, we
cannot replace.
Your face still stands out in our minds,
and your words are still
in our hearts.
Never, until we meet you in heaven, will your
memory from us part.
    Katie Hatch

Ah Love

Ah love
How I thought it was mine to keep
I thought it was mine to hold

I did not know it was holding me
The strength that gave me Joy
The Joy that gave me Laughter
The Laughter that made me Free

I felt so very full, now I am nearly empty
But the years of living formed me
The Me that can now hold on
The love that taught me to hold fast the day

Though the love is no longer here
I remember and gain Strength from the Memory
Memories that hold me like the Love

So I will hold fast and "Remember"
The Laughter and the Joy and the Love
One day God will take the Memory
But that day He will give me back the Love.

Margaret Huffman

"I'll Miss You Too"

Visions of my Mother fill my mind
How she suffered to make me shine.
The times she called, I was not there
The times she yelled but still she cared.
The times I was punished, so easy I say
I was so lucky to have her till this day.
She has raised me truthful and fair
That is why I could never compare.
God will now take her to Heavens space
But visions in my mind are what's left in her place.
Now I have a six month old son to love
And his Grandma will love him from up above.
Why, I wonder, what went wrong
She laid in pain for so long.
I remember giving her water and shots
But still I'm here mourning my loss.
The last few days she lay in her bed
Her voice so soft as she said, "I'll miss you."

Krysta Lowell

All I Want For Christmas Is You

My love for you is so deep and yet my knowledge of
  How to show my affection is so shallow.
I love you; I love you with all my heart and all my soul.
I love you in the deepest, most precious, and
  Most concealed part of my heart.
Darling, it's all because of love is such a beautiful thing
  And yet it could be ruined by common soul with such ease.
I have all that I ever needed and yet I still feel empty inside.
You are the only one who could satisfy this emptiness.
Michelle, all I want for christmas is you.

Paul Huang

The Beach

As I sleep on the beach,
I can feel the waves crash upon the sand.
I can hear the mourning whispers of the wind
over the sea.
I awaken to see the dolphins leap from
the ocean in unison.
And, I go back to sleep at the bubbly
touch of ocean water on my feet.

Laura L. Haynes

Fateless Love

Solitude is silence and lonesome is the breeze;
Hunger craves inside me and plays games like a tease.
Decisions leave my soul and mind bare;
My fate's confusion I can not bear.
Dreamless is the sleeper whose pillow is of stone;
Even beasts can not protect against my shrieking moan.
Danger is my shadow, for in the dark I can not hide;
Drowning in a teardrop deeper than the tide.
Careless is the soul whose heart has been broken;
Lips are sealed with a kiss, a timeless token.
Silver moonlight reflects memories of the past;
Of this curse I can't be rid for the evil spells been cast.
Mindless philosophers close door to our lives;
Entering the shallow waters with a daring dive.
Summer's sun can not bring snow;
I can not make you love me, this I know.
For a hunter can not love the deer or the doe;
Now that time has moved on with nowhere to go.

Lauren Pugliese

What Am I?

I am an ADORATION to the human body
I am an AFFECTION to the human needs
I am an ATTACHMENT to the human mind and soul
I am a DEVOTION of free will to the human heart
I am an INFATUATION that the human conscience thrives on
I am a deep PASSION that involves blistering body chemistry
I am RAPTURE to the human species
I am YEARNING for human lust
What Am I?
"LOVE"

Patricia Alcala

Shadow

Who are you?
I am but a shadow of who I wish I were.

What are you?
I am but a shadow of what I wish I were.

How are you?
I am saddened by my portrayer's problems.

Is this all I am destined to be?
A shadow, a follower,
No! I will find the key,

The key that will let me be me.

Melissa Allen

Inside Of Me

I am who you want me to be.
I cannot bear to see inside of me,
  to what is reality.

So I hide behind a smile,
  and maybe for a while
    you think you know me.

But how can you?
I am only a composite
  of others' expectations.

I hide the fears, and hold back my tears;
  though my heart races, no one must see
    how much I tremble deep inside of me.

Olga Lozano

"Where Is The Balm In Gilead?"

I am before you like a blade of grass blown by the wind.

A strong puff and
I am gone.

I am a tinkle on timbrel sounded once in joy,
A gift to welcome,
Now silenced by Vow.
A muted melody in Mizpah.

My tear becomes a flame,
A primordial Holocaust on Gilead's plain.

I feel the fragility of this body.
Yes,
"The Lord gives, the Lord takes away."
Blessed be Hashem.

Without Your sustaining power, EL Shaddai,
Your comforting Presence,
I am nothing.

I am a breath, Adonoi,
in frosty mountain air.
Even now I disappear.

Miriam Fidelis Pinchot

The Poet

Unlike the norm
I am part of the unknown
One of the few
On the quest for truth

I've realized confusion is a great
    part of my truth.
Regret, suffering, loneliness,
All part of the world of the poet.

I imagine all those before me
have felt the same
Little by little, they've all made their claim
I have yet to reach this pinnacle of success.
Yet I hope to accomplish this before my
    final and most treasured last breath.

Paul E. Cano

I Am The Earth

I am the earth. Treat me with care.
I am the deer and the grizzly bear.

I am the eagle that soars through the sky.
I am the wind and the butterfly.

I am the song birds sing in the trees.
I am the buzz of the bumblebees.

I am the seed from which all men were bred,
The black, the yellow, the white, and the red.

I am trees reaching high and grass swaying low.
I am the rain that helps everything grow.

I am the glaciers, the rivers and seas.
I am the waterfall's symphonies.

I am the rain forest, untouched and pristine,
Where the air is still pure and the water still clean.

I am the Earth. Treat me with care.
For if you do not, I'll have no more to share.

Martin Thompson

Thus Saith The Lord

Thus saith the Lord to all man kind, upon this sinful world
I am the way, the truth and life, I am the gate of pearl.

Thus saith the Lord to all man kind, I come to you again,
I am the door there's no other way, you can enter in.

Thus saith the Lord to all man kind, I am the street of Gold,
Turn back to me my dear friends, let not your hearts grow cold.

Thus saith the Lord to all man kind, just seek my face and pray,
I'll go unto my Father for you, it's almost redemption day.

Thus saith the Lord to all man kind, hide my word in your heart,
And live by it each day, and we shall never part.

Thus saith the Lord to all man kind, this might be the day,
I'll send a messenger by, in a very special way.

Thus saith the Lord to all man kind, look what's come upon
Your land, the soon returning of the Lord, is at hand.

Thus saith the Lord to all man kind, this might be your special day,
That I have sent a messenger by, please turn me not away.

Maude Little

A Pause For Love

When you said those words that cut deep in my heart,
I bowed my head, nodded once, playing out my part.

I could not tell you not to go or hold you back.
I kept my peace as all around me slowly turned to black.

Now I watch you from afar with silent tears,
letting myself cry only when you cannot hear.

Why did I let you go your way without a fight,
leaving me to cry to sleep every lonely night?

My love for you has led me to this choice I made,
this love that grows despite my silence and can never fade.

Just as love has brought our hearts to beat as one,
love also let's me let you go when the time has come.

Yet as you go my love keeps alive the dream
that someday love will help you find your way back to me.

So now I sit alone to watch the stars above
and wish this time apart is just a moment's pause for love.

Kimberly S. Barber

Society Vamps

Lost in a world overloaded with judgmental people,
I cannot express my feelings
Of anger and curiosity
With happy-go-lucky beings
Who never think about dying others
But of their very own selves
And occasionally their high-and-mighty brothers.
They only care for people with shelves
Of society awards but not the ominous
Other worlds that try to provoke
Our pathetic way of life.

Ingrid Mitchell

Alone In My Room

As I sit alone in my room my mind is wandering
My tears of hurt become cries of fear
As the blade comes closer and closer to my wrist
My life gets closer and closer to its end
My hands are trembling with fear
As I cut a bloody smile on my wrist
I know the end of my life is near.

Maria Clark

"Disenchanted"

I dig down deeper,
for something to spoil my intuition
for what is unknown,
I suppose for something simple and true
not in regards to what is expected or understood
but instead for what exists,
and is still labeled as unexplored

Jessica Shannon Lowe

Relative Reverberation

Dreams of pain and twisted hope.
I cannot see the way your heart sparkles in the sun.
Running away from the monsters in your closet.
Beyond the sun and the moon there is just you and I.
Rusty nails and splitboard fences.
I jumped to save my own life. Not yours.
Maybe you have her but she is my friend. Not yours.
Shiny tears on the tips of roses shimmer like broken glass.
I never said it was fair, but I live for myself.
I am not selfish, but I want myself and not you.
Space and time one in the same. Yelling from a mountain top.
I scream at you, but it all falls upon deaf ears.
Glitter and stars. Love and the hope you shattered for me.
I will color the sky purple and the grass yellow if I want.
You say I can not. You think you rule me.
I live my own life and cry my own tears. You can not do that.
Spinning away around the isolation you sent me as a gift.
Take it back. I do not care for the pain, the jealousy, the hate.
Take it all back and bury it beneath the thorns of your heart.
Keep it locked deep within you and hate yourself. Not me.

Loryn Hild

Final Sunset

As I see the beauty of the sky
I can't help ask, why God why,
As I remember my life's past
I know on earth we do not last,
I think of fond family ties
I can see the beauty of birth in the eyes,
I know the warmth of love I have felt
I know life as good as it was dealt,
I can feel sunshine on my face
Because I feel the love in Gods grace,
I feel the awe of an eagle in the sky
The joy I now feel you cannot bye,
In Gods arms I will rest
My life has been the best,
My heart no more will fret
As I view my final sunset.

J. M. Nordstrom

"You'll Never Even Notice"

You'll never even notice, how much I need your smile,
I can't relive the moments, you gave to me awhile,
I'll gaze upon your picture, it's what I have for now
I'm grateful for the memory, it please's me somehow
No, I'm thinking it won't last, now I'll have to stray,
You'll never even notice, how much I wanna stay,
I'll pass your way real gently, don't look me in the eye
I'll love you in the midnight, as stars do in the sky.
No you can't regive the moments,
Still they're written in my soul
You'll never even notice
just how you've made me whole
So I'll pass your way real gently, don't look me in the eye
I'll love you in the midnight, as stars do in the sky
Yes, I'll love you all the night, as stars do in the sky!

Leah K. Wiley

Only Because I Love Him

It was a Friday night and one thing led to another
I couldn't resist myself and now I'm to be a mother
I've thought about every option
From abortion to adoption
I've decided to give up my baby ....
Is this a must or a maybe?

I'm only sixteen I want so much in life
I'm too young to become a mother and wife
I hope someday my baby understands
Why I gave him up into a strangers hands

And if he wonders why
Or what he did that was so wrong
Tell my baby that I love him
And I've loved him all along.

Patricia Hoskins

The Things That Mother Said

There was a time when I was young and careless as could be
I didn't think about the things that Mother said to me
But now I'm wise and realize the things she said were true
That's why I'm passing on the things that Mother said, to you.

Mother said it doesn't matter if you're not a millionaire
You will find the things you need the most around you everywhere
The mountain high, the desert dry, the valley, or the sea
Yes, these are just the little things that Mother said to me.

The time has come I'm not so young and thinking quite a lot
About the things that Mother said about the things we've got
There's water when I'm thirsty, when I'm hungry there is bread
There's peace and satisfaction in the things that Mother said.

Mother said there'll be a judgement day when we must face the Lord
He will hand us down our punishment or give us our reward
I think about the things to come and as I look ahead
I thank the Lord and Mother for THE THINGS THAT MOTHER SAID

Lela Danley

Suicide

People think I was crazy
I don't think no more
I didn't do anything stupid
Just let the gun drop to the floor
People think I made the wrong choice
It was not their decision
I decided to take my life to make all the pain vanish.
It vanished all night into darkness bleak and dim.
I was put into the ground like it was a sin.
No one will ever know how much pain had to go through.
Screaming and crying myself to
Sleep, it just went on and on
Until I went in deep.
People must of thought of me
Because seeping into the ground
Where tear after tear of the love I so profound.
I now regret it, but I know its still within
Because now I feel the love I dreamt for deep
Inside them.

Nicole Powers

The Tall Little Lily

Down below, stands a tall, proud vermilion lily.
Its petals, striking blood red.
Its green sherbet leaves widens toward the yellow star
And its stem stands high with the Lady of
Liberty.

Mai H. Phan

Untitled

Wishing on a star and holding on to love,
I dream of having you in my life -
With help from above.
The fire burns deep within your eyes,
Of hopes and dreams you have yet to realize.

Your strength is remarkable - you seem invincible.
Nothing seems to hurt you - do you even love?
The wall around your heart seems impenetrable;
Just let me in and trust that you will always have my love.
I promise I will never hurt you, or ever let you down.
What can I do to convince you that I'll always be around?

You lost your mother as a child - that I understand;
The pain and loneliness that you feel, I can't begin to comprehend.
I only know this - I love you more each passing day;
I hope you can understand, the only thing I want from you:
Let me inside of your heart - I will never leave you in the dark!

Lisa Pyatte

Thinking Of You

When I think of you
  I feel a spot in my heart
  That I could only feel for you.

You mean the world to me
  I can't live without
  your friendship and love.

You are as special as any holiday
  or anything many could buy,
  and if I ever last you, I think I'd die.

So when I think of you
  I think of all the things in love and life
  and I see them all in you.

Keira R. Warren

A Cry For Help

My life is so messed up right now
I feel like well, I don't know what
Or how I really feel.
I feel empty, shallow with a life that
  I want to end.
Sometimes I wonder "Why me?"
What did I do to deserve this life?
Why all the pain and suffering?

Life is so tragic,Is it because
I'm making it that way or is somebody
  making it this way for me?
If I was somebody else would I have to go
  through this?
So many things go wrong for me.
If I was gone just how many people would
  truly miss me?
How many people would really care?
In my eyes not very many, Maybe my life
  would be better in another world.
I don't know, maybe I should just find out...

Melinda Rodriguez

Sunrise

The sun peeked over the horizon
It was like a huge golden ball pouring over
the earth
The sun had so many colors through the big blue
Sky
I could hear bees buzzing and birds chirping
I knew it was going to be a beautiful day.

Crystal Contreras

Definition Of Love

Love was once a passionate dream
Swiftly soaring into the tiny gleam,
Of hope, light, and infinite glory.

Love is shared by more than one,
Like a river that always comes,
Flowing deeply in the heart of only some
I knew this wonderful thing was yet to come.

Paola Nichole Lau

"Lonely Thoughts"

I feel down because I can't be with you.
I feel up when I know that you care.
I feel happy when my friends are near.
I feel sad when my heart is so weak.
I feel like a roller coaster that has
  so many turns and hills to climb.
It seems that I'm climbing and climbing,
  but I can never reach the goal.
Every turn I make always seem like a dead end.

I wish, I wish you would be waiting for me at the end,
I don't know what will happen
I think I'm blind.
I think I'm afraid of the truth.
The truth that lies beneath my heart, but I can
  never say that I didn't try.
I can never say that I didn't try to understand.
I never did say, I wouldn't always be there for you.

Prima Rouse

Special Day

Today's a special day for me
I found a poetry contest in the P.D. (Plain Dealer)
Poems have always come easy to me,
Just rhyme the words in harmony.

A special day is feeling good
Being happy as a lark,
Although sometimes it's very dark,
When darkness rises, the world's still here
Open your heart and spread that cheer.

Although our lives are short in years
We must not dwell on all the tears.
The past is gone, the present is here
The future's tomorrow and tomorrow is near.
Special days come every day,
It's you, yourself, who makes them dear.

Patricia A. Perram

Atlanta

On Peach Tree street
I found you
running, rushing, passing by magnolia trees that shimmy
winnowing velvet pedals about you
across vast waters and confederate bridges that separate
our spirits travel through wires of mabell
we share secrets air mail
gather inspiration that fed us well
we are but gluttons
full of ourselves
lying blissfully drunk on canvas
exposing narcissistic nymphs
fondling the desire to seduce
visions of surrealistic soothsayers
we wait for our manmade bird
to carry us across oceans going north so lovers can become
quilted comforters
for each one's soul

Lydia E. Percy

Where Am I Bleeding?

I get sad. For unknown reasons, I'm feeling alone.
I get angry. No one understands my fear...I've lost my brother.
Here's the hole.
My heart misses you. Things aren't the way I planned.
I'm getting by. Songs make my eyes fill with tears.
This wasn't supposed to happen...
It did.
God needed you. I feel the knife, but where do I bleed?
My family is strong, stronger now. We're getting by.
I'm sorry for sometimes feeling sad. This never used to happen.
Death has never been this close.
It's affected me but I can hold onto memories forever.
Goodbye, brother...
When it's my turn, I'll see you. Give me your strength.
I want to carry your love through life.
I'll hurt always because you were my brother.
But, nowhere do I bleed.

Kurt Hoffman

Deer Poem

Grass leaders,
I have killed the buck
whose fawns will devour me.

For three seasons
I watched the six point buck
drink my spring water,
eat my summering grass and fall sweetcorn;

Dancing down sunstreaks
he came in early winter
I shot him.

He moves,
and is not lost.

I pulled the steaming paunch
from his frame,
and knew the traditional
first-kill meal of fresh liver
and garden onions.

When I die
and move to the earth,
my bones will sprout more summer grass.

Martin Thompson

Carrying The Sorrow

I have seen her when she has carried bliss and love
I have see her with tears in her eyes
I have been there when she has been enlightened with new ideas
I know her as an impassioned young woman
But today, she carries a sorrow which is so deep I can't understand
This feeling is so deep that I can't even reach out to her
I see it and also see that she wishes someone could touch her, and heal her
I am no healer
But she is
She has helped so many
Unfortunately, she can not find someone to heal her sorrow
No one has the power it seems
If they do, they do not have the ambition for its use or the sight of it
This in turn, brings sorrow to me

Jill C. Pyle

Untitled

Darkness frightens me as I walk alone
I hear footsteps and find no one around
My heart beats fast as animals groan
There is not a living soul to be found

With hate and violence, I feel unsafe
The world is suffering from the human race
This crazy world haunts me, I've lost my faith
The "Land of the Free" has become a disgrace

Whispering winds sing the songs of the night
The only calm of the present
Dreams that people will look toward the light
And make living an even that's pleasant

We need to make a difference today
Because life is not a game we play

Michelle Sadley

The Thunderstorm

I hide. I feel alone.
I hear the thunder roar, deafening my ears.
I feel the wind blow so hard it appears the
trees are angry with one another.
The lightening strikes, and for one short
moment, the earth is ablaze with light.
And then quiet. Oh, so quiet.
Soon, I know it will end.
It only seems to last forever.
Now it is dawn. Another beautiful day.
All my fears of the night before have vanished.
As I look out, I see the flowers, still wet,
have been kissed by the rain.
And the trees, no longer noisy, are just
as strong as ever.
And I am not alone.
I need not hide any longer.

Kathryn Mann

Earth

Earth, oh why do you rattle at my door!
I hear you slumber no more -
I feel your pain rumble under my bed -
Are you hurt and talking instead -?
The Reciter scale shows your off
you head. It may read seven I dread -
Our waste we dump into your
veins below. It must be hurting you so -
O Bombs explode all over the place -
Our fighting in many lands a disgrace -
We send rockets with men into the sky -
With dreams someday we may live by -
What are we doing to our planet below
There'll be no place else to go-
There will be no human with a smile on his face -
We will all be flying in outer space -

Linda Daly

Untitled

I hope what we have will last forever.
When I'm with you I'm light as a feather.
When we are together I have no blue days.
You make me happy all different ways.
When my head is cloudy, you wipe my tears.
You hold me close and ease my fears.
You make me feel safe and secure
I have you. I need nothing more

Karen Reynolds Sausville

Untitled

Seek to find the undying love of your heart
For the one who holds its key
He shall remain its keeper throughout eternity
Keeping the flame burning year after year
When the body is gone, thoughts are lost
But the heart shall always be true.

Pamela J. Jacobs

"A Key To No Lock...?"

Early one morning while day was still night
I heard a rap at the door and a voice like the Killer of Light...

He came in with a quickness with a "key-to-no-lock"
Saying, "Take this and ride for the answer's where I stop..."

He drove into a darkness past shadows that moaned
And said, "I AM LOUIS CIPHER and they are NEVER
ALONE..."

Curious I asked, "So,...where do these wheels burn?"
He smiled as he mentioned a night club called "NO-RETURN"

With the Fury-of-Fire light broke-sky, Amidst a roar of thunder I heard
"LO IT IS I...STOP IN THE NAME OF JESUS...OR YOU WILL
SURELY DIE...!!"

Words from above descended upon me
"...CONFESS CHRIST AS SAVIOR...AND YOU'LL BE SET
FREE..."

True to the light its wisdom I did say
Lou was gone as My Night Turned to Day...

You search with a key that has no lock,
But a key that opens no door doesn't offer a lot...

As for your future, it has been deciphered
If you don't change you too will fall for LOUIS CIPHER

And when you're gone there's nothing you can do to deter
For he's the fallen Dark Angel whose true name is LUCIFER...

Roderick B. Dillard

Plan Two

As I lay there dreaming:
I heard the God's screaming
"Kill all the people who are poor or sick
Clean up this planet for the well and rich
Kill all the people who are drunk or whine
also the ones who are deaf, old or blind.
— There's no one left
— What shall I do?"
"Turn back the clock, we'll go to PLAN-TWO."
Then I said, "what did you say?"
They replied, "Go brush your teeth now
and have a NICE DAY."

Lorelei P. Allan

From the Womb

In the days before my borning;
I heard you while I was lying quiescent in my sea.
Singing softly the songs of love
To your child as yet unborn.
Man - child, Woman - child, it didn't matter.
The song was the same, singing of your love.

And now that we have parted
Still your song haunts me
At odd times, waking, dreaming.
It comes to me as a hidden breeze;
Enters my soul and your song of love
The happiness in its lilt brings me peace.

Milton Reich

Realizing He Is With You

It is morning and as I awake I have an exciting feeling
I hurry from my bed and look out of my window to see
The first snowfall laying upon the ground.
The sun is beginning to awake also and as it arises it
Yawns with brilliant rays of light
And the snow comes to life glistening as though a shower
Of diamonds have fallen to the earth.
The snow untouched except for the footprints of a rabbit
And you can see him standing as if like a statue.
The woods looking airily with her white towers of branches
But underneath guarding her animals.
The fields are covered and the farmer knows that under this
White blanket is laying the wheat of spring.
In the quiet distance, you can see the church steeple and
Hear the faint ringing of the bells knowing that the priest
is preparing for Mass.
And in this precious moment, you have a feeling
In your heart that God is with you
Looking upon the countryside with peace.

Kathleen Bergman

A Lament

I haven't quite finished yet,
I know I'm not done,
I haven't picked apples
Red and yellow, one by one,
I haven't stood at the top of a hill
And shouted so loud
That the woods became still,
I haven't made snow ice cream since I was ten,
Surely, there's time to try it again.
These weathered hands can not be my own,
Why, just a short time ago
They held a new son.
Oh, reflection in the mirror
Your grey hair is unkind,
Somehow, you've left me behind.

I haven't quite finished yet,
No, I've just begun, to pick apples red and yellow, one by one.

Leanne Gibson

My Greatest Fear

I can feel it, see it, taste it.
I know that it is yet I use it
    loosely and abuse it.
Just when I think I caught it by the throat it slips away easily.
I fell as if I abuse it, yet it abuses me, taunts me,
Shows me it's boundaries and lets me experience them yet I
    cannot scale its walls inward...
I escape freely, at my own will.
I can see its core clearly yet it is still a great distance away.
It taunts me only to educate me.
I never lose hope even when it hurts me the most.
Just when I think I understand it shows me I know nothing.
I am still ignorant of the power love possess
The clearer I see it the close it draws me,
away and from one close to another.
Why is my greatest fear such a beautiful thing?

Mark Huffman

"My Michelle"

My heart hangs low, because I miss you so,
My love will never die.
It may take my lifetime to win you again,
but my heart will not cease to try.

Taylor

167

A Letter to My Love

Dear Love,
I know that you may have doubts,
but I'm writing you this letter to let you know
that my love you will not be without.

Through some hard days we have been,
and I feel that we will never go through them again.

You may wonder why I am so sure,
but I am confident that these hard times,
we can endure.

Be assured that the love I show you
is for you and only you.

I promise to dedicate my life to making you content,
Making sure that the days on our relationship
have been time worth being spent.

I hope you believe me when I say,
"I love you, I love you, and it can't be no other way."

Marcia Terry

Untitled

We've been together for so long
I know this love cannot be wrong

All the times we shared
I never knew how much I cared

But now your gone and I'm all alone
With nobody, nobody to call my own

I'll always remember how I used to be
The way I was, you and me

These feelings I'll always have for you
I am so alone I'm so confused

But now your with somebody new
I ask myself how could you

I just don't understand why
How quickly you said goodbye

My thoughts return to you often and I begin to cry
Asking the question why, why
For you would I die

Well maybe I want work, maybe it wont come true.
But I'll always have one wish
And that wish will be for you

Jolene Fralick

The Night

The sky has darkened
I know what is happening
The night is coming
Soon the light was completely gone
The dark has taken over
I can not see
Which way am I going
Where is home
I ask myself as I feel my way around
The street lights soon come on
The dark has fled and the light has returned
What a relief to finally get home

Matthew Williams

One Hundred Nineteen Plus (119+)

On April 4th, 1970, a son was born to us.
I later came to know him as one hundred nineteen plus.
A boy of early talents was reading by the age of three.
At two years old was counting while horseback on my knee.
Reciting all the numbers in his own special way,
From one just past one hundred, progressing more each day.
Oh, how I love his gestures as his arms flowed with the air.
Although I knew there wasn't, could an audience be there?
The same year came my birthday; a gift awaited me.
An angel came a-running and jumped upon my knee.
All dressed up so handsome with every hair in place,
Gleaming eyes did greet me, a big smile on his face.
"Daddy, here's your present. I will count for you."
A kiss on twenty-seven, big hug at sixty-two.
Tiring at one hundred, I knew he's soon be through.
Then he reached a number and said "Is that enough?"
"Dad, I'll always love you ... one hundred nineteen plus."

D. Granville Ivy

The Sound Of The Meadowlark

Reminds me of my mother-
I listen carefully to the sound-
Trying to memorize the sequences

Other Bird calls can be whistled frequently-
But not the sound of the Meadowlark

Oklahoman Meadowlark's sound different
From Northern Species
It is all in a Dialect, or so they Say

The little things in life-
Are what we should Cherish
Like the red clay squished
Between your feet on an
Oklahoma man-made lake

Where I come from is like this
The Meadowlarks sing a Sacred
Song on the Wind as you drive down
A South Dakota highway listening to the Spirits
As they praise the Day

Some Day the Meadowlark
Will Call My Name

Kelly Morgan

Who?

It was early one mourning when I began to wake
I looked in the mirror and my reflection looked fake
His lips were my lips and our faces were the same
But I knew nothing of this man not even his name
They say the eyes are the keys to the soul
I looked in his eyes and I saw they were cold
I saw the terrible and horrible death that awaits us all
Within his eyes I saw our rise and fall
I saw the doom of a world with no heart
A world that let the color of a person's skin tear us apart
Because of fear Hell came to Earth
It made me ask what's it all worth
In whose best interest is racism the answer
For years it's been eating away at us like a form of cancer
It has no cure except for education
Teach the children that we can be one nation
For right now I fear what I saw in his eyes will come true
And if we don't try to change it, then who?

Nathan King

Picture Frame

In the photograph in an antique shop
I meet a young man in a rumpled suit.
His deep piercing eyes reach out and touch me.

They are filled with pain of a life now past
with secrets, mystery and adventures of another time.
He takes my hand and we walk together.
He whispers unknown confidences
of life on the prairie in the 1860's.

A priceless treasure,
distilled now to only a trace of his original essence,
the tag says,
"picture frame, $48."
I take him home in my arms
and we dance.

Mary K. Martin

I Never Thought

I never thought I could feel this way
I never thought love would come my way
And when I look into your eyes I'm more than only hypnotized
And when I am within your arms all I see is your loving charm
I never thought I could be here with you
I never thought I would say "I do"
And when I lie beside you I know I can't deny that I love you
And when I see your smile I know my life will be worth while
I never thought I would be this happy
I never thought I could be this lucky
And when we found you in our lives we were more than glorified
And when we felt you in our hearts we were more than gratified
We never thought we could feel this way
We never thought love would come our way
But now this love is here to stay

Kara Young

A Secret

There's a secret that I keep from you and all the rest
I nod absently, falling asleep, burnt-down days like cigarettes

While you show your feelings, I have to hold my hailstorm back
Like a retired clown cries but sings, they'll never reach me
    on the track

Yet there's no sign of shame in them, and whenever my eyes meet yours
Just a common tragedy again, I gaze dumbfounded at your source

And now I think I'd better go, as though you were never real
I've done too much, you know, painful memories are all I can feel

But the time I spent with you was every way one of my greatest days
Something different, something new, how I hate this omnipresent maze

Still what keeps me going on my way is that I never see anything
That there will come the day when I see every one and every thing

Well, but today never comes at all, how superficial, my shout in vain
I must make no noise as I fall, even if I'm down and wholly in pain
Burnt-down days like cigarettes, I nod absently, falling asleep
From you and all the rest there's a secret that I keep

Katja Dolinschek

Pardon

As I wander through my tiny garden,
I humbly beg the flower's pardon,
for spilling the dew the night placed there,
as they nod and whisper in the morn's fresh air,
but later, as twilight falls, I see
each flower forgives, and waves at me.

Jan Buffington

The President of the United States of America

W-orld renowned political figure
I-ntellectual person, a vigorous leader
L-eadership is the key to your success
L-oving, caring, generous, a religious man
I-ndustrious, incredibly lucky, great ability, a
    glorious victory
A-lways a devoted man to your family and country
M-an with guts, your dreams came true

J-ust, only a man of integrity can make this nation great again

C-ommander-in-Chief of the Armed Forces of the United States,
    the most powerful nation in the world
L-oyalty to your native land, may God bless you
I-nspiration of the younger generations
N-othing is impossible for a man of high caliber like you
T-oday, tomorrow and forever your name one of the great
    men in history
O-utgoing personality, open and accessible one of the most
    extraordinary persons in American history
N-ever to forget a gentleman, trustworthy, with a Christian
    heart.

Leonides S. Sales

Can You See Me?

Is it odd to wonder if you care?
I often notice your distance stare.
You sit and act like I am not there,

But I'm here....
Can't you see me?
You talk to me when no-ones around,
but when you are busy,
I here not a sound.

Some people say you are stuck in this world,
where people are looking for diamonds and pearls.
If you look in my eyes and talk to my soul,
There are riches that people consider my gold.
I am here...
Can't you see me?
I defend your heart-and look past your dead,
I love what you are and hope I'm somewhere in your head.
Everyone knows that I'll stay true,
They can look to me,
Why can't you?

Katie James

A Teachers' First Day

Stomach flipping over and over.
I organize the room before school starts.
The first day of school, I stand at the door, waiting.
The bell rings while the students walk in.
From the roll I call the student's names.
Each time I mess up,
    my face begins to look like a very ripe strawberry.
"My name is Miss. Swain,
    I'm your English teacher for the year."
"By opening the doorway of English,
    you and I can change your future together.
I hope you enjoy your year, I want you
    to learn as much as you can, but also
    have fun at the same time."

Laura Swain

"Without Me"

As I sit and think alone,
I regard I have no home.
Left there is no empty chair,
There is no one whoever cared.
Alone I stand in a darkened room,
Pondering my thoughts, creating my doom.
By myself on that chair, lose my support and live nowhere.
Life is but a mere part of living.
I feel there is no one whose giving.
Lifeless I hang, anxiously I wait,
Piercing pain 'bout my throat seals my fate.
Without me I feel no change, without me everything is the same.
No one missed me, No one cared. Open my eyes to see nowhere.
Upon the heavens I am alive but not living.
I've done no taking, but I have given.
Given my heart and given my soul. No one cries down below.
Death is but a pause in life,
For others but not for my own eyes.
Stir no thoughts about my head.
Stir no thoughts for I am DEAD.

Matthew Fella

I Remember

I remember being together, walking hand and hand;
I remember being together, laughing out loud;
I remember being together, holding each other;
I remember being together, always wanting more,
I remember being together, making love;
I remember you and me loving each other;
I remember wanting to be with you forever;
Now that your gone, I remember how much Love hurts.

Rebecca Abbott-Vetter

Grandma

How quickly the time seems to have passed
I remember the nights as a little girl
Lying in bed, eagerly awaiting your arrival
When you would read to me of grand adventures
And stories of old from that treasured family Bible;

I remember the summers spent with you in New York
Running from place to place, eager to take it all in
You were always by my side ready with a smile
If you were tired, you never showed it
Just gave a young girl a taste of her own grand adventure;

I remember as a young woman, ready to take on the world
You were there as well with a calm and steady hand
To gently guide me through life's ups and downs
From first loves and broken hearts, to dreams of the future
You gave me a firm and solid foundation from which to grow;

Now you are gone and all I have left are the sweet memories
Of yesterday, and the hollow rings of what might have been
But knowing that you will always remain in my heart
Gives me hope that you will continue to live in the lessons
That I will pass along, to those who will call me Grandma.

Melody Ritchie

The Star

One star by the moon shone,
While the others all run.
One star dares to peek,
While the others play a game of Hide and Go Seek.
That one lonely has to seek,
While the others don't dare to talk or peek.
All of a sudden they all appear,
And the sky glistens with great amounts of cheer.

Elizabeth M. Henley

Yesteryear

Thinking back on yesteryear
I remember you standing, so full of cheer
How I left you so all alone
You not knowing I was heading home

Thinking back on yesteryear
Our first hello, was our last goodbye
The smile on your face that said it all
Perhaps, this was the Greatest night of all

Thinking back on yesteryear
Knowing The end of the night was growing near
haven to end and say Goodbye or speak and see you cry
Not wanting to put pain in your heart
When it finally came time for us to part
So I turned and walk away saying nothing
Because I had nothing to say

Thinking back on yesteryear
Got me wishing that you were here
Remembering your smile so perfect and bright
And being with you was such a Delight.

Kevin Powell

Now I Can See

O-mother whom I love;
I return to thee as a dove.
I was once a beautiful child;
But I turned into an animal running wild.

I have done things to put you and I to shame;
And I'm the only one to blame.
I have come to see;
Only God, will set this child free.

No words can say;
That I have found a new way.
Today I know;
Only my actions will show.
As long as I remain true;
There is nothing that I cannot do.

The gift I have to give;
Love and prayer for you to live.
I hope you sleep good at night;
Knowing your little boy is all right.

Today you should know;
That your little boy has started to grow.

Kelvin E. Woods

The End Of It

The sky was like a golden lake
I sat back and let it take
The sum...the total...of what was there
Along with acceptance, the need to compare
Here, the gentle brilliance of our love
Standing unsteady - not willing - no ready
Above, the radiance from day meeting night
Volatile light, explosive and bright
Both scenes unfolding, reckless, yet holding
Our lives, our time, captured
Frame by frame, a visual game
Just as quickly the images fade
The sameness, the differences all cascade
And in the end, enchantment pervades

F. V. Wight

Natural Art

The changing seasons are the ubiquitous art
That result from the paintbrush of time.
A message of nature is painted each day;
Be it gloom, light or beauty sublime.
  Marilyn R. Strayer

Shooting Star

Last night in the heavens afar
  I saw a shooting star.

It lit the sky so bright
  With its wondrous trail of light.

I watched in wonder and awe,
  Then pondered what I saw.

I remembered two things I was once told,
  That A "Shooting Star" is a meteorite dark and cold.

The other I cherished from the start,
  And to this day hold dear in my heart.

That a shooting star is an angel sent to earth,
  Too watch over a child's birth.
  Orest Panashchuk

A Prayer

Each night before I go to sleep
I say a little prayer to the mighty God
Hoping that he will hear my prayer for peace
I'm grappled by fear, trembling with horror
I wish I had wings like an eagle
So I would fly away soaring into the midnight sky

I see violence and riots in the city
Surrounding it day and night
Like melting candle wax under a luminous flame
There is evil in people's homes and in their hearts

I beg for the mercy of God to save these people
  from their prejudice and fears
I pray that someday that we will live together in
  open arms no matter how different each person is

Through my simple prayers
God hears my pleas for brotherhood between us all
As I look up at the evening light
I feel the refreshing sense on conversion
  from blasphemy to salvation
  Michelle L. Synowiecki

Country Beauty

As I walk down the country road
I see so many wonderful sights.
Beautiful tall trees and pretty wild flowers
And colorful birds in flight
Clear blue water rippling over rocks
In a small creek bed
Sunbeams dancing down through
The tall trees overhead.
Little animals scurrying through the tall green grass
Chasing each other and running so very fast.
Cool breezes blowing softly overhead
Causing the water to ripple in the creek bed.
I stopped and clasped my hands in prayer
Thanking God far all the beauty I saw out there.
So thank you dear God
For all your gifts from above
And the showers of blessings
You send with your love.
  Lou Beltz

Black Days

As I sit here encased in my theatre of pain,
I sip my hemlock quietly, amused by thoughts of the sane,

Sweet melodies of sad songs roll out of paper,
Reminding me of past, not so distant, not to savor,

A heart that has never known love, looks out of glass,
Never to escape the ill fate of the past,

An angel awaits...For even those damned,
And the hourglass will soon, run out of sand,

The courtroom fills with laughter, as the King silently weeps,
The Jester comforts him, for he knows where the Queen sleeps,

Pain is not of flesh, it is a sense of the soul,
Ignore it, it builds, and the strong surely fold,

They say revenge is a dish best served cold,
But to do Satan's bidding, a soul must be sold,

Darkness turns to light, as day turns to night,
Dreams aren't just shadows, that disappear in the light,

When morality is immoral, dignity falls short,
Deception is reality...No good news to report,

Struggling through Life, making my way through this Maze,
I have acquired the gift of embracing BLACK DAYS...
  James L. Harbin III

Understand

Tears streaming down my face, heart wrenched from my chest,
I sit alone in a dark hallway. I can't even remember how I got here.
I still see all the faces laughing at me, thinking I must be crazy.
What do they know! I am me and no one else, I act on my feelings
and do as I please. I will not be changed or molded into something
I'm not. So why must people judge me and tell me what to do?
Yes, people are cruel and unkind, just once I wanted someone
to see me as I am, not as what you want me to be. I once knew a
person like this, he was understanding and never laughed at me for
my thoughts or feelings, I could always go to him for anything.
And now he is gone. So to my best friend and only love I would
like to say, thank you and I will always miss you.
  Madelynn A. Malloy

Homeless In Miami

Rest your heads upon these stones...
I sleep a thousand souls...
The dead and the living dead
Who curse the wicked
As day melts night.
Run..Jesse..run!
Carmen..scream! SCREAM!
Crawl, Anton.. into safe sleep..
In broken tombs.
Lost children who ask not to be 'born again'
Rest your heads upon these mounds
Search empty skies
And find a star
That dares to shine.
  R. Claire Goodgame

Place Of Birth

There is nothing as miraculous as the rising or setting of the sun.
There is nothing as miraculous as the scintillating glow of the moon.
There is nothing as miraculous as the changing of the seasons.
There is nothing as miraculous as the twinkle in the stars.
But, when it is all said and done, there is nothing as miraculous as
a woman's womb.
  Jagnarine Sumrah

Perception

Underneath the exterior, are things the way they seem to be?
  I tell you, no, without a doubt;
We see what we want to see.

We listen with unhearing ears and see with unseeing eyes,
  And the deep things remain hidden as if in a disguise.

But, sometimes the veil is lifted and we really see and hear,
  And the things which oft' are hidden from us
  Come through then loud and clear!

At these rare moments in life, Our finite minds and hearts
  are feeling, seeing, and comprehending realities so deep
That its like walking thru the mystical fragrance
  of some unknown flower.

Then we perceive that the unknown fragrance is Love,
  And the Garden we are walking thru is Life;
The Truth half hidden from our eyes is Eternity,
  And the Music we hear inside is Heaven's melodies,
Playing within our hearts the unspoken and intangible
  Truths of Life, God and Reality.....

Frances Marie Bass

Think About Love

When I think about love,
I think about a single white dove,
who can communicate from far above,
feeling the warmth and security,
allowing oneself to let the other become free,
giving the ability of trust,
knowing the relation ship will never rust,
always showing complete respect,
in return feeling no neglect,
every day showing a feeling,
never needing any heeling,
never seeing any hesitation,
each day improving our relation.

Mark Kammerer

Your Voice Is Love

As the wind blows thru the trees,
I think about you
The wind is your voice
That whispers to me

It whispers, I love you, I love you, I love you,
It whispers comforting love
It whispers the mood of tranquil.

Your voice in the wind sends peace to my heart
That our spirits are still entwined
Thru storms that rage
Thru winds that swirl
Our spirits flow calmly

Hand in hand, we drift thru the winds and storms
Fighting foes who besiege us,
Who battle to defeat us,
Who vow to separate our love

Love that was once cold
Love that now surges forth
To bind us forever,
Forever in its circle of peace.

Marjorie Harvey Chambers

Hold On To Autumn

Looking in the mirror today,
I think if only the hand of time would stay.
So in the beautiful, easy days of autumn I could lay:

Safe, well past the wild storms of spring,
That forever in my heart will ring.
And the swear and toil of summer days,
That my best did take and pay:

But time seems faster now that I would have it slow,
With what's left of life in sure tow.
Time now for thoughtful reflection,
And questions of past direction:

Now with each autumn leaf that falls,
Time trudges onward toward the call,
Of cold and winter days,
When it finally drags me on no more,
My body sore,
And leaves me here to stay:

Norma J. Ramsey

Joy of Mary Magdalene

Your knock upon my door was quick, but quiet—
I thought You just another man without a face.
Somehow, I knew Your name, but could not tie it
To sweet tomorrows in a better place.

How could I have known You'd be so vital
To any existing self-respect in me—
That I would shed those demons for a noble title,
And become a princess in Your royal family?

Oh, I'd heard talk of You—they called You "rebel"
In things that You would say and do.
But You were only on a different level,
And pride kept them from looking up to You.

I recall the hour You hung from that tree
With nothing but compassion in Your eyes—
When, the one beside You, unfit for their society,
You took with You to paradise.

Oh, sweet Redeemer, how I love You
For falling so low for me 'neath angry sky.
You are Lord! No other stands above You—
Only the Son could reach so high!

Kathryn Anne Howell

Hello Mommie

Today I saw you, you were looking so sad.
I wanted to hug you, kiss you and tell you
that I Love You.

I wanted so much to tell you that I miss you
but I was too high in the sky.
The other kids here are so happy, they call
this heaven.

Today I met God all mighty, the one you taught
me so much about.
I told him I was sad too, he already knew why
he told me that one day we will meet again.

"Oh, how happy I was to hear that".
So mommie don't cry, God has promised that
I will see you in heaven.

Mommie it's so beautiful up here and peaceful
I don't have to worry anymore, because
God has taken care of everything.

So mommie until we meet again in heaven
I just wanted you to know, how beautiful
it is up here in heaven.

Linda Bundrage

"Legacy of a Loving Mother"

I gave birth to my daughter the other day
I vowed to love and protect her without tiring,
To teach her and provide for her without faltering,
And she would cry out into the night and I would comfort her.

There were days of swimming and days of snow,
And the childhood diseases would come and go,
And she would cry out into the night and I would comfort her.

Through her, I could feel the sunshine and the rain,
I could feel her laughter and I could feel her pain,
And she would cry out into the night and I would comfort her.

The years went by - oh so fast!
Pre-teen years of hugs, kisses, and obedience without question,
Adolescent years of bewilderment and determination - mine and hers,
And she would cry out into the night and I would comfort her.

We shopped for months for the perfect gown,
She was, without a doubt, the most beautiful bride to be found.
She was radiant when she became his wife - beginning a new life.
And she would cry out into the night and I would comfort her.

My granddaughter was born yesterday, and looks like her mother
    they say,
And she would cry out into the night and she would comfort her...

Linda Hurt Brown

Life, As It Should Be

I close my eyes:
    I walk with the wind
    I play with the sounds of the creeks
        and the colors of the flowers

A sigh...and laughter comes out
I laugh...and a song fills the clouds
I sing...and the moon sings with me,
    the stars murmur with a chant of love,
    and the world dances on its melody

I open my eyes:
    I see life opening its arms wide
    saying:
        "Hello for a lover who shines again
        "Hello for the destroyer of the storm and rain"

At last,
    I feel alive
        Mamoun Ahram

Bless Me

Bless my body and soul
I want God to be in control
I know life is not a bowl of cherries
God will find the one I will marry
God will bless me with a child
He will stop me from being wild
He will tell me when, where and how
God bless me, NOW!
I know when God blesses me it will be a wonderful delight
It will be so true and out of sight
I will be so happy when God will bless me
One day I can't wait to see
I'll be one of the angels in the heaven skies
I'll be looking at God eye to eye

Michele Pancoast

Not Long Ago

Not long ago, when I felt ready to learn everything,
I went to the city that was the best teacher for a human being.
My age at that time might have been around... I think... twenty-two;
Yes!, I have little doubts now, I believe that's true.
While living and dreaming under New York's glow,
I was quite amazed with all that I saw,
and... nothing has changed since that long ago.
When I became richer in mind and possessions,
I jotted down novels with the best intentions,
I wrote many poems that I spread like collars,
and saved a few dollars...
till not long ago.
Now, I write for children of many an upbringing,
stories or tales that mainly are beginning
with three words I love,
and amuse me so,
because I always start them by saying so:

    Not long ago...
        Jairo H. Nemocon

Forever Love

Forever you'll stay in my heart. You say you need to know that
I will forever love you. I need to know the same thing too.
Everything you want from me, I need the same from you. I need
someone to stand by me, to feel my heart with sweet sensation.
I need someone to give my heart and soul undying inspiration.
I need someone who will never leave and someone who won't try
to deceive me. I need to know when I'm down and out, can I
count on you to be around? Forever love! I'm willing to give
as long as we both live. Can you promise you're willing to
do the same or is this love to you a game? I really need to
know how far are you willing to go. Forever Love! My Forever
Love. Life isn't always fair, but through the hardship I need
to know that someone will be there. I can't take a chance on
a sometime thing. I need a love that's going to be everlasting.
You say you want the same things too. But are you willing to
do for me as I've done for you? Forever Love! My Forever Love.

Mary Louise Craig

This Next Year

This next year when new blossoms are in bloom,
I will take you by the hand, and we will walk
together into the many memories of life's carefree
ways, and now fading days.

This next year when new blossoms are in bloom,
I will take you by the hand, and we will walk
together across the rolling meadows of passing time,
into the newness of spring, and look upon the
many wildflowers, it may bring.

This next year when new blossoms are in bloom,
I will take you by the hand, and we will walk
together, as we, have always been but one. Then
suddenly some quiet autumn eve, when the
twilight falls to night, and the golden leaves
have gone from sight, we may step into life's
stolen picture from the past, and fly away at last.

Robert C. Pardoe

All In Me

When I cross a mirror, I see the image of you in me
The destiny of your stares, the movement of your body all in me
The sweetness of your voice, all in me
All these things I see in me, come from the vision of you

Michelle Goolsby

Freedom

A dove is as free as free can be,
I wish I could be free and the real me.
But I hide my face in such disgrace.
I hide my caring, that I should be sharing.
I hide my fears, behind all these tears.
Everything in my life seems to go wrong,
Every time I try, I can never be strong.
I'm not sure what life has in store for me.
But I wish I would be left alone,
To be what I was intended to be.
But people are always telling me the best way,
I guess they think I'm not old enough to have a say.
For once in my life I would like to be free,
So I can experience and be the real me.

Ann L. Shuster

October And June

I wish I were pretty and young once again
I wish I were still in my spring.
Cause then I could love him and feel all the joy
Loving him freely could bring.

But I am a "citizen senior," mature
My black hair already turned gray
And I am approaching the sunset
While he's in the summer of day.

I'm not so old that, I see his smile
As it dances across his gray eyes
His mouth, his brow, his yet springtime soul
I'm not filled with delight and surprise.

I'm trapped in my body, full two-score and ten
I've children of almost his age
His book is close to just half-way read,
While mine is now on its last page,

So daydreams and fairy tales, just go away
Though his presence can rock my old heart
And a school girls' feelings won't sing in me,
Our seasons are too far apart.

T. Human

A Poor Man's Confession

I'm here, but I don't know why.
I wish sometimes I could even die.
Food all gone-No money to spend,
Just my reputation I got to defend.
I left Grammar school some years back.
Didn't learn to count, so I can't keep track.
Learned to put an "X" where the letters should be.
Lord, have mercy on poor old me.
I got a little job but it don't pay much.
I just buy cigarettes, bacon, bread, and such.
Sleeping in a shack-wet and cold all the time.
What happened to me? No wish of mine.

Lillian Y. Haile

"Mother"

Mother you are so special in my life
You are there to catch me when I fall,
To hold me when I cry.

Mother I will always need you by my side

Mother's like you are one in a million,
And I am proud that you are mine

Mother I thank you for all you have alone, and
For all of your advice

Lizzette Lemaitre

If I Should Leave You

Should this be the last time I shall look upon your face
I wish to leave a memory that time will not erase
Not one to haunt you everyday, nor one filled with regret
But one to make you thankful, for the day when first we met

Think not of things you should've done, things you could've said
Be thankful for the good times, that we have shared instead
Although we had our bad times, sometimes lived as peasants
We worked hard to get this far, from when we wed, 'till present

We were blessed with our dear children, of which we're very proud
We've always clung together, as we originally vowed
You've always been my "one love," that no one can replace
If I must ever leave you, my last memory shall be your face

A precious face, that's come to mean so very much to me
And one I'll cherish through my time spent in eternity
So don't be sad, or mourn for me, for 'twould be such a shame
But remember me with kindness, when someone speaks my name

O. Jeanne Miller

The Fawn

As I look out my window, pondering the moment
I wonder at all that I see
The gentle sway of evergreens, softly blowing snow
The imposing mountain peaks above me

Winter has crested itself, as in days gone by
All about me glistens in white
The steady fall of snow, adding to the mounds
The brook slowly turning to ice

A steady fire warms me, logs blazing in the pit
The wind whistles gently outside
Coals gleam brightly, drawing me closer
Safe from the chill of the night

Just then a movement, ever so slow
Compels me to turn from the fire
A fawn struggling against the drifts, shivers and falls
Hungry, hurt, and dying

In a few short steps, I'm at its side
It enjoys the warmth of my features
And the glow of my fire, leaps and bounds
As it warms another of God's creatures.

Norma Jean Joiner

I Am

I am a believer.
I wonder if all countries will be free.
I hear the cries of help and pain.
I want the world to be free.
I am a believer.

I pretend to be a peacemaker.
I feel the pain and anger in me.
I touch the hearts of the homeless.
I worry that there will be no peace.
I cry when blacks and whites don't get along.
I am a believer.

I understand the difference between blacks and whites.
I say that Martin Luther King's dream will come true.
I try to believe.
I hope for worldwide unity.
I am a believer.

Krista Nicole Byers

I've Had It All

Surrounding me from days gone by, the lonely hours fall.
I wonder where the laughter is. I listen for my children's call.
I hold my breath to hear a voice or hear a footstep fall.
But silence greets me at the door. Dark silence, that is all.

I flick a switch and softly there the light around me glows.
Mementos from the days gone by are scattered like the petals of a
   rose.
A vase she made in second grade; a silver cat to hold my rings.
A pretty porcelain girl he gave on Mothers' Day.
The things around me show - the love they gave me long ago.

A trinket box of pearly pink, a crystal clock; a silver vase.
My Mom and Dad their 50th year - framed in golden lace.
The man I loved, who stands so tall, in picture there amongst it all
Beside my precious Stars and Stripes. The silence of a house so
   still.
And yet I know I've had it all.

Just one more thing, and not the least, my Holy Bible lay.
And on my knees in silent thanks, I look unto my God and Pray
And thank Him for this blessed gift
That for a little while I had it all.
Maxine Faktor

Beach

Rickety stairs to descend. Wood. But, my bare feet.
I worry about splinters. The air. A slight smell
Of fish. Fried, coming from the pier.

The Mighty Bluffs tower, jagged and
Permanent. Tufts, that are trees and dirt, cling
And tell of mountains chopped by raging storms
And seas. Peanut butter cliffs, the knife spread the
Design. Gigantic. To see from the beach.

My foot touches sand. Warm. Soft. Comfort.
Restful, this stretch of beige. Glistening sand
Shows off fragments of worn down things.
Ocean. Glacier blue. A trim of foam at the edge, the Grand
Sea reaches and brushes the tide pools. Life living there.

Distant. Fog. A soft line divides sea and sky,
Crisp. Cerulean and clean. Sea gulls screech,
Dive. Born from a backdrop of blue eternity.

I lay down on the welcoming sand. The tide
Licking my toes, Red toenails shimmer sea life.
My body sinks into it. Sand. Water.
The sky, my cover. I am where I began.
Mary Jo Olsen

If I Were A Dictator

If I were a dictator
I would call the United States my own.

I would turn her into what I wanted her to be
in the name of goodness and reform.

I would plant my weeds everywhere
so they could grow big and strong.

I would tell them to act incompetent and inept
so no American could catch on.

I would establish my battlefields
place by place.

I would attack the true Americans
and make laws that would erase.

I would slowly capture the people, one by one
health care, education, wildlife, and guns.

The Americans will not notice
they are too busy having fun.
Mitzi Waters

The Gift

If I could give the world a gift,
I would give the gift of life.

I would give my heart,
so they could feel the love and joy
of the heartbeats inside.

I would give my lungs,
so they could breath without having to fight.
They could breath the sweetness
of the world waiting for them outside.

I would give my eyes,
so they could see the wonders
that their world could bring.

If I could give the world a gift
I would give the gift of life.
Megan Rae Lucas

The Lady Lex

Oh! if I could bring to mind all the thoughts that arise in me,
I would write a beautiful poem about the Lady by the sea.
As she is anchored there by the docks, so calm and unchanged today,
The mighty deep is no place for her.
Her place is by the sparkling sea.

The blue ghost as she once was called was no correct name for her.
A ghost but only a shadow, and she proved without a doubt that
She was alive and well, and knew what it was all about.
A job to do was her desire and she proved that could be done.
And by her efforts and will to aid, you know the was war won.

Her decks were once alive with all sorts of activity.
She proudly plowed the ocean and flew the flag of Liberty.
Her job was to launch the planes that protected our country.
America the beautiful is the home of the brave and free.

And if you have ever visited the Lexington,
what a beautiful sight to see! With the job well done
and the war well won,
She still stands for all the world to see.
Never unbending, never unending is that beautiful
Lady by the sparkling sea!
Pansy M. Frazier

"To My Sister - Life Gets Even"

When we were young and life so bright,
I'd make a face and start a big fight.
I'd hold you out at arms full length
And smack you hard with all my strength.
You'd stamp your feet and yell for Mommy,
"Sister's making faces and hitting on me.

When we grew older - the hitting ended,
But I stole your clothes cause mine weren't mended.
I'd throw on my coat in 90 degrees
To hide your shirt and blue dungarees.

Then we both married and got oh so busy
Bearing our children - so many I'm dizzy.
Now I have daughters who fight and make faces,
Steal from each other from barrettes to shoelaces.
I've thought and I've thought to see what this means
I've finally concluded - Its all in their genes!!
Maggie Magee Molino

Flying High

If I could give the world a gift, it's clear to you and me.
I'd make the world a big green ball in the lap of luxury.

I'd be like an eagle getting ready to fly.
Take off like a plane soaring straight to the sky.

On my way to the ground I'd take happiness and joy.
And introduce them to every girl and every boy.

Crime and poverty would no longer be.
So people of all races could live in harmony.

So come and see this grand new place.
And remember bring only a smile on your loving face.

Of course life can't be full of just games and fun;
But it will be good enough for everyone.

This world is really a great one as you can truly see.
But if I could give the world a gift, that's what my gift would be.

Mitzi Payne

God's Artwork, Childhood View

The evening sky now has billowy clouds flitting overhead.
If I could I'd fly up to the fleecy clouds and snugly
    pillow my head;
To watch the sun rays streaming through the crowded sky
And see the clouds changing form as they go fleeting by.
I'd dreamily relax as if on Grandma's featherbed,
Seeing as in days of youth, where only dreamers tread;
Laying aside the cares and stress of the passing day
I'd watch God artistically paint the sky in only His own way
The faces, the animals, the clowns and forms of different kinds
Come and go as I see them in the windmills of my mind.
The wind sweeps the clouds steadily through the azure sky
Hiding the sun, temporarily chilling me as the clouds go drifting by.
As warmth returns and dreams live on and continue
My childhood eyes now see yet another form that's new.
On and on I'd watch and wait, dreaming, until suddenly
I'm beckoned by my mother dear, back into reality.

Margaret Good

To Know The Lord

What a wonderful blessing it would be
If I knew the LORD, as he knows me!

To finally relinquish the hurt, pain and sorrow
And never worry about the untrue promise of tomorrow.

To be free of a sinful circle that holds so much complexion
I hope for the day where my life flows in a righteous direction.

I'll pray that I don't make the mistake or the delay
By putting it in my own hands and doing it my own way.

To know the Lord as he knows me..
Your faith and his spiritual guidance must be the key.

So, as I end this poem..
It doesn't matter if I have to beg and plead.

I just want to know my Lord and savior as he knows me!!

Leonard Lipscomb

Untitled

Drugs are bad
The worst thing you ever had
They make you have less friends
You get less grades
At school then nobody thinks you're cool

Nichole Mealey

North Carolina Wildflowers

North Carolina is the place to be
If it's wildflowers you wish to see!
Wildflowers dance in sparkling array
Along roadsides and centers of major highways.
From the mountains to the shore, the flowers mesh and fuse,
Reminiscent of rainbows in glorious hues.
Spring, summer and fall, there's wonder and delight,
As you travel amidst the spectacular sight.
Corn flowers of blue, ox-eye daisies of white
Glisten and shine, and reflect the sunlight.
Carolina phlox and pink catch-fly
Nod in the breezes as drivers pass by.
Cosmos, sunflowers, black-eyed Susan's too
Add to the beauty of this magnificent view.
Toadflax, goldenrod, and Queen Anne's lace
Are a joy to see and bring a smile to your face.
For the wonder and charm of this delightful creation,
Thanks be to God, our Garden Club and the
North Carolina Department of Transportation!

Mae Murray

Reflection

Would it not be nice
If the world stood still
For just a moment
So I could see the setting sun
Watch a mother bird
As she feeds her young
See the children as they
laugh and play
watch the clouds as
They roll away
with hustle and bustle
around today
I am sorry to say
that time has passed me by for yet another day

A. Thweatt

Cycle

From the moment of conception, we absorb our surroundings.
If we are surrounded by love, then life is good.
We revere the sources of love and they become our Gods-
It is beginning of religion as we put down our roots.
Thusly tended and showered, we reach up toward the heavens,
Learning lessons we're empowered and with evil we are even.
And we blossom and are flowers as we wear our haloes proudly,
Never dreaming we are the Gods to those who sleep soundly.

Kathryn Estes

"Revelation"

If you knew Pain,

If you could hear her howling on moonless nights,
If you could feel her needles piercing your side,
You would see me in a different light.

Pale green and glowing,
Coming from my head and magnifying

Hope for you.

If you understood my plight,
At once for all things trying to strive,
You would no longer pass me by,

Rather, you could see
That hope for you is me.

And no one else.

Justin Weaver

Wrong - Doer

Don't dig a hole for anyone
If you do, don't dig it deep
cause you may be the one
who'll fall in it for keeps
Wrong - doer it doesn't pay
It will get to you someday
For every wrong there is a right
To crush it with equal might

To rise with the sun up bright
Try to make your doing right
Cause it take so little to spoil your day
And so much hard work to pay
Wrong doer your action attracts few
That have been blinded by your news
But aren't willing to pay the dues
Wrong - doer it will catch up with you.

Mike J. Peters

For My Angel, Larry

Will there ever come a day
I'll find someway to say, "I truly understand?"

I'm waiting on the time
I'll feel your hand in mine, and smile 'cause you're my man.

I cherish all those hours
I was sure our love empowered everything under the sun!

Maybe in later years
Tears will wash away my fears but for now it's just begun.

There's really no one to blame
But nothing seems the same since the day that I lost you.

The pain is empty but not weak
As your face is all it seeks and pictures just won't do.

How could you really do it
And put all of us through it? Was it all on trial for you?

Comfort and prayers our friends will bring
But if I could have anything, I'd ask for just awhile with you.

Paula Mariola-Gill

"Family Memories"

Our baby brother arrived one day, one fine April morn;
I'll never forget when Dad climbed the stairs and told us he was born.

He was big and healthy in every way, except for a tiny broken arm.
But that soon healed and we were immediately captivated
By his dimpled smile and charm.

He was Mom's pride and joy, her little bundle from heaven.
She beamed as if he was her first, even though he was number eleven.

Bob was her first son and Mark was her last.
But they have the same qualities of being strong and steadfast.

Their brown eyes twinkle as if lit from within.
And there is a radiance about them that is obvious to all men.

Mark called me "Sissy" and I called him "Bubby."
And we were great pals right from the start.
It didn't take long for this chubby brown-eyed lad
To win this sister's heart.

He has been a lot of places and seen a lot of things.
Yet he has always remained the same. He can go anywhere;
North, South, East, or West and people smile and call him by name.

Some of our good times are gone and so are Mom, Dad and Bob
But just for a while, you see. When the Lord returns to claim us for
His own, we'll all be part of his family.

Linda K. Niner

A 1936 Bouquet

Though I sit and while away the hours,
I'll revisit old memories
And put them with my bouquets of flowers,
For none were quite so sweet as these.

Most of them were grown in childhood,
Some by the little girl next door.
We always wished as hard as we could
That our dear young Daddies were not so poor.

Those time were very hard, lean and bare,
And oft we stared at our scruffy shoes,
And wished for a ribbon for her hair,
(A red, red ribbon, if she could but choose.)

Somehow, rainbows always seem to end,
But lingering long are yesterdays,
So, I'll buy a ribbon for my friend
To tie her flowers with my bouquets.

Mary A. A. Morse

The Consciousness Epic

Hey everyone, look at me!
I'm all of a sudden so very alien,
because now self-inflicted wounds come my way
through the smile I display.
Maybe they're common scratches of a progressive existence,
felt by all who grow and live.
Anyway... my once throbbing brain has bestowed upon itself a plate,
a plate made especially for torture pie; torture pie
flourishing oh so plentifully on my new found field of consciousness.
Yes, a daily slice of pie, made with five regrettable layers,
to choke down in solitude and wash down with a glass full of her.
The meal grows in the grass, like the flower she probably once was,
Who among you can smash my plate, burn the hillside and pour her out?
Who will grant me starvation and bless me with the ecstasy of
stupidity?
I'm going to be here awhile, I've no wish nor strength to climb
higher. Perhaps the land will erupt, violently rejecting me,
And eventually puking me onto a limb of blind acceptance
on the tree of normality, home to so many far below...
And I'll worship God and be a liar, just like you.

Josh McBee

I Told God

I told God- the way I wanted things for me to be, God told me,
I'm in control, you just wait and see how things are going to be.
I told God- things are taking too long so long,
God told me, hold on be strong, be strong.
I told God- things getting so hard- so tough, I just can't seem to hold
on cause I'm taking too much.
I cried out "Oh help me Lord", I seem to be losing me.
God said its ok, reach out, extend, take hold and lean on me.
I told God - babies dying everyday, God told me new life always being
created, and on its way.
I told God - walls of darkness surrounding and overshadowing me
The darkened hours of despair overcoming and consuming me.
The Lord said, allow me to be the strength that protects and comforts
  you.
I told God- how empty I would be without a joyful spirit;
  the Lord said,
not if you keep my words near it.
I told God- I don't know what or where to go - come he said, trust and
go with me, through the gates of life and you will see.

Linda Betts Watson

"What I Am"

I'm not a colored man,
I'm not a black man,
I'm not asiatic,
I'm not an afro ameriKKKan,
I'm not an afrikan ameriKKKan...
    I'm an ameriKKKan born, afrikan, who's been stolen from the
motherland, stripped of my language and victimized to white
supremacy.
    I've been cheated on, lied to, lied on, spit on, stepped on,
hoodwinked, wrongly incarcerated, stereo-typed and oppressed.
    But through all the pain and strain, through all the suffering...
...I'm still 100% afrikan man! You still with me? 100%....
...no chemicals, no contacts, no face lift, no implants, no jungle
fever, no make up, no nose job, no self hate, no shame, no skin,
bleach, no weave and no sellout!
    Those who, do need to get the hell out!

Kalan Jay Holt

Getting Old

I really don't like getting old.
I'm suppose to be wiser at least that's what I've been told.
My once blond and bouncy and shiny hair too
has now become frizzy and gray soon to be blue.
At age 40 your life is at half
and that once muscular derriere is now down
to the calf.
    Those age spots, big veins and
so called character lines, increased
showing, hot flashes and there goes the minds.
    Tougher prescription for the failing
eyes oh how did this happen time surely flies!
You start watching your diet or
surely you'll die. I'm getting
older, gotta go so I can cry.

Pam Arsenault

The Future

Success is unclear to me,
    I'm uncertain of future plans,
    I pray to God for only happiness,
    and leave it in his hands.

I wish to become strong enough,
    to be all that I can,
    to have determination to follow through.
    or the courage to take a stand.

I only want to prevail,
    in all I do and say,
    to make those who love me proud,
    and live my life day by day.

I want people to admire me,
    to think of me and smile,
    I hope to do all these things,
    only then my life will be worthwhile.

For this is all I hope for,
    and all I'll ever need,
    money should not matter,
    for we are all judged by our deeds.

Patricia Marie Marshall

My Christmas Prayer

I'm spending this Christmas in a foxhole
In a place I can't even pronounce.
But I'm fighting for a worthy cause
And that's what really counts.

This rifle is my Christmas gift.
My snow is the falling debris.
This foxhole is my living room,
The camouflage, my Christmas tree.

The whining shells are Christmas carols,
Singing as they fly past.
The candles burning here and there
Are machine gun muzzle blasts.

The mocking, savage, kiss of death
Is my wreath of mistletoe.
And hangs suspended in no-man's land
Between my foxhole and the foe.

Soon we shall rise and attack
Through that kiss of death out there,
But now I kneel in reverence
To whisper my Christmas prayer.

Melvin C. Walthall

On The Bridge Of Wishes

On a long meadow brook
In a small quiet town
I walked upon a bridge
And made a wish
I wished for things I had never had
And for things I could not forget
Under the bridge was a small tapping sound
Some trap from a fisherman's lure
The sound on the rock had a harmony
So silent...so still...yet still heard
It made thought easier somehow
That light rap-tapping sound
On the bridge with my wish and the creeks and the stone
With the fabric worn wood and the pillars of oak
They would stand on the bridge with others of dreams
The dreams yet to come so unheard
In a small quiet town
By a brook on a bridge
Where I once...once
Made a wish

Nicole R. Bartok

The Poet

    The poet speaks of tomorrow and erases yesterdays sorrow.
In evening's quiet sphere, no rest with thought's to inspire.
as if there's nothing to borrow, with freedom to say, I loved
yesterday, today and tomorrow.

    I tell the world that fear is sorrow, which stands still
till morrow.

    No heart shall bleed with sorrow, for I fail not to hope.
like flowers blooming, sun glowing and stars shinning, all with
God's heavenly powers.

    Memories of sadness shall pass and healing heart, bright
days will come.

    With hope comes strength, so fear not tomorrow's end new
life begins. With our heart's each moment spent is precious
time lent.

    Each poet then must write with heart's content, to reveal
what life has meant.

Mary M. Perretta

"Trying"

No more had the devil cried-
in her dream. Far more intense
as she may seem. Dreadful in
thought and body was she. But
inside was someone trying to be
freed. As the devil tried to lead.
But she trudged an in melancholy,
in death, in sin, in a cry. And the
more pleads for help she heard
afar, the more she had tried.
As she crept along on her empty
path - the sidewalk of wrath,
she heard outer voices carry her
away, desperate cries to stay.
But she was her own and listened not to them
but only to her, and the choice of death made her
sure. She strike herself and wounded to deep.
And this memory she wanted to keep.
the dark stream crawled down her face.
And in happiness, she died in grace.

Katie O'Brien

"Garden Of Roses"

I was sitting alone in my old rocking chair,
In my garden filled with roses,
That puts perfume in the air.

I look all around to see what I'll see
When a large yellow butterfly, lands on my knee.
I pick him up gently, and then let him fly,
As I know he's going to head for the sky.

There are daffodils, and puppies galore,
Pansies growing out of the wood floor.
You can see my morning glory, climbing,
   up the window sill -
It gives you the feeling of spring, with out the
   winters chill.

I turned my head, and what did I see?
The biggest gold and black humble bee.
It looked like velvet, I so wanted to touch,
But changes my mind,
When, a big pink rose, I did clutch.

I took a deep breath of my "Garden of Roses",
Which God, gave us the privilege now and always.
So think of me, in my old rocking chair.

Helen I. Snow

A Gentle Man

This man was so great in the time he was here;
In my heart he was so very dear.

He wasn't someone important or high on a ladder;
But, of course, to me that didn't matter.

My time with him was so special to me;
What I saw in him others could not see.

To others he may have looked ruff and old;
But not to me he was someone brave and bold.

The days were bright, and I was safe with this man;
And when I needed him, he was there to hold my hand.

He was kind and gentle in his own way;
But I never thought that he'd go away.

Now he's far away and lies quietly upon a hill;
And when he died my heart stood still.

Mary Ann Witt

First Born

You are our first born and special to us
In oh! So many ways
You have been like a breath of spring
Brightening up all of our days

It was you who first called us mom and dad
It was you who could make us smile
Even when we were sad
It was you who could make exciting a trip to the zoo
It was you who made many of our dreams come true

It was through you that we learned how to be parents
And because of you we became first time grandparents
It was you with your love who stood loyally by your
Mom and Dad
Sharing our good times as well as the bad

Is it any wonder we are so proud and eternally glad
That God chose to send us the very best that he had

Philomena Paris

Moonlight Morning

Life was good this morning.
In spite of the alarm sounding off at 6:00 as usual to announce
the daily regimen- bathroom, breakfast, drive to work....
Life was good this morning.

The living room was bathed in a soft, angelic light and out of the window
I saw the huge full moon beaming down, streaming onto the armchair.
I sat down and basked in its moon rays, warm and awakening.
Life was good this morning.
I lay down next to you and held you, your body so warm from sleep.
Life was good this morning
and I knew I could seize the day.

Martha Graham

Untitled

The sun was still low in the cloudy sky
In the cold winter morning by the sea

Trails of wheels on the dead beach
Warm air from the dashboard
Dry smoke from a cigarette

You were there with me
In the moment too unreal to be
Watching the loose sand blown by the wind
And travelling parallel to the ground

So they say life sometimes is so tart
Our days together are now in the past
Our paths someday are to go apart
Across the wild ocean so vast

What could we have done
Where could we have run
To exist in an eternal bond
Like a pair of carps in a peaceful pond

I guess it doesn't matter now
And our lives should move on

You can not love me.

Miwako Tokugawa

Seeds Of Rage

Strong vines of rage grow within me deep,
each day a new seed is born as others ..... continue to grow,
pushing violently through my mind wanting to be free,
to stretch their black buds of poison and prick.
All those who dare come near with a thorn so sharp, so painful
come closer, and you, maybe its first prey.

Kate Smith

The Drought Of A Sunset

The wolves bark out a love song to the approaching moon.
In the distance, their voices sound smooth, and serene,
but their motives lack innocence.

Perched on branch, two squirrels act as art critics.
Chattering with displeasure at the orange
and blues hues of the western sky, but pleased with
the dreary grays that have recently appeared on the canvas.

The robust oaks anticipate a cool nighttime shower.
Less for themselves than the saplings gathered at their feet.
The pines stand emotionless, ignorant of any changes in the breeze.

The lazy catfish have already settled to the bottom
of the shrunken ponds.
They are mired in their beds early on this evening.
Each night their beds are moved closer, and closer together.

The owls peer through half closed eye lids,
debating the worth of awakening.
For them it will be a quick hunt, and a short night.

Corn stalks, dry and thin, humbly stand at attention.
Their roots have grown deep. Perhaps they, more than others,
are aware that the long wait is nearly over.

Joe Skahill

The Passage Through Time

Her eyes are like fire burning
In the flames of passion,
Deep within her soul I penetrated her
heart and showed her my love.
But Alas, will she take me in her
Arms to hold forever, or will she
Banish me to the Black Hole which
Lay beyond her thoughts and in her heart.
Now I ask her if my love will make her
Happy, she pulls me towards her chest
And kisses me all over, and I know our love is true.

Paul Rogers

The Rosebud

She sits almost a silhouette
In the shadows of her room.
Her hands are folded in her lap;
Her concealing hair is caressed
By the sympathetic moon —
Light peering through the window blinds.
Her lips, quite young, are sealed in thought,
And her eyes, half-dimmed, reflect upon
Another place where a lady walks and
Laughs with the grace of a summer breeze
As it softly drapes its fingers
Across the emerald trees
Under the golden sun.
But there are no laughs as she speaks no words
As she sits alone in her room.
There are no laughs as there are no words
To the song of a rose afraid to bloom.

Matt Garcia

"Wake Up and Smell the Coffee"

Be proud of who you are!!!
I'm tired of seeing the worse in us
The killing!!
The black on black crime
Following the crowd and disrespect fullness
It's time to think and face reality
Make a change and bring out the
best in you and us!!

Mabunty Manneh

Star

The heartbroken star forfeited his place
in the sky. Coasted quietly past the
Milky way and fell into the arms of
Green Sweet Earth. Waited for resurrection

The universe cried an ultra violet moan.
Stars sang flat notes, minor harmonies
of soulful sadness, meteor showered
the galaxy with an elegy song

The heart of the earth rang with great alarm
Heeded the tone of the sorrowful sky

She raised her sight to the firmament and
gazed at the empty slot her star used to
inhabit. Opened her heart, found a patch
of love, placed it in the dormant heart of
the celestial body- RENEWED THE DEAD
SOUL HURLED THE STAR ACROSS THE PRETTY
BLUE EMPYREAN, BACK INTO THE WOMB
OF THE UNIVERSAL, TO LIVE again.

Michelle Caples

The Vision Of Michelangelo

(Before The Pieta In St. Peter's)

Three times he strove with stone until it bore
    In three dread forms the vision of his youth,
Each trial more terrible than the one before,
    That beauty might appear in mortal truth.
This was the first, and though the others match
    The poignancy, the passion and the rage
Of time and sin, he sculpted this to catch
    The inner drama, freed from earth and age.
What are these bright epiphanies of the soul,
    These haunting forms to which pure feeling flows?
And when and where and how is beauty truth?
    Lost paradise, or glimpse of distant goal,
It seems to capture all that yearning knows
    Of love and beauty and eternal youth.

Kevin Rai

Profound Moment

The sun warmed the moment of this
Indian summer Autumn day

Nestled between two neatly pruned
little bushes were his mother and father

Her parents and brother only a few feet away
surrounded by their forbearers:
Other German, other Scandinavian families

They settled as good hardy stock now
Nurture the land called America, Gladys
Koberstine and Lawrence Melin in quiet dignity

Their son beside me, my tears welled,
His hand tightened in mine

We placed Gladys' rust colored flowers
between them - it said something

We walked a few steps - he turned his arms
around me, my arms circled his warm
kindness, he gently wept and remembered -

For a moment I shared his youth,
his family, his vulnerability.

Kim Atkinson-Melin

Hades Beckons

St. Peter is judging and denied Cobain
Indifferent to living - we chose death in lieu
Apathetic to sweltering, albeit insane
My son was born that makes us two

Flatlining on time the cadaver will form
Epitaph poets engrave on my stone
Invitation is nixed by familia swarm
All but damned if He's not your own

Hell shouldn't be bad, I've plenty of friends
Accepted as my final stop
I've got Satan on hold this is my end
But what about the plea I've copped?

Don't want not to go - but f— my reasons
Stay composed and save the face
Hades beckons guess 'tis the season
At least you'll know where to reach me. Grace.

Askia A. Farrell

"Is This What Life Is All About?"

Life is filled with joy and pain, promises of making it or either go insane. We can choose to sit idol as we watch the time go by, or we can get caught up in this race of do or die. Life is what you make it; or that's what one may say, but do we have the powers to change our destiny. Opportunity still comes to those who are wise enough to grasp it, but what happens to the ones whose always seeking but some how always passes. Are we traveling in a world seeming to go place to place, or are we really somewhat lost in space. We must believe in someone other than ourselves, perhaps could there be that Creator that created my internal cells. Is life really that short that we can't find time for a quick lunch, or are we killing ourselves with that 24 hour brunch. Our children are coming and going before we can say goodbye, was this in the plan of life- to live and to die. I guest there is a time for everything under sun, but does this time include all the bodies being lowered by the gun. I really need to know and without a shadow of a doubt, is this a mere sample or is this what life is all about.

Linda G. Toms

In Darkness

In Darkness,
Into the woods on a trail whose dangerous past
We have chosen to disregard.
Not the ashen dark of a city street
But a deep, vast darkness.
Obfuscating the decayed fishing cabin from the stately colonial.

In Darkness
A shawl of ambiguity, of altered vision.
Imagination replenishes perception's diminished reality.
The fear of the unknown or the known?
What is seen or not seen?
Heard or unheard?

In darkness,
Stillness of time and sound tempering the journey's anxious heartbeats.
Tranquility of the glitter washed sky.
Persistent rebirth of muted ripples crossing the lake,
Illuminated softly by the pallid, crescent moon hovering low in the sky.
Only to disappear into the darkness once more.

Kenneth B. Jeffery

A River

A river as far as the eye can see,
is a strong as our hearts,
A powerful force that runs through our lives.
A spirit high in the mountains
is carried down the mountain side
by this powerful river that is
a part of our lives.
The spirit in which has brought us to a new beginning.
This is how our new lives began in this world,
the world in which we live in.
The place where we were born
and the place where we will be reborn.
In our hearts and in our minds,
we have asked the question of what a river is.
I guess you could say we are
pretty blind because the whole time the answer
was right in front of us.

Kristen Gillon

Mortal's Love

The fate of Mortal's Love,
Is ever to unsure.
It flickers about uncertainly,
As a candle flame buffeted by a breeze.
An unstable affair,
With nothing to grasp as it falls.
Only once in a lifetime, it is said,
Will Love ever truly be found.
Such a sad, sad condition,
For the lonely and longing heart to endure.
Waiting and yearning,
Hoping that the Fates will be kind.
Trusting that when true Love is finally found,
The strings tangle not.
The Love will not slip from one's grasp,
And the search need begin again.

Margaret M. Russell

Beauty

What is beauty?
Is it something your are born with?
Is it on the outside?
Or is it deeper than that?
Can anyone acquire it?
If you try hard enough, will you get it?
Every time you smile, can people see it?
Is it the twinkle in your eyes?
Is it the way you walk down the street?
Is it the glistening of the sun in your hair?
Or is it all of these?
Or none at all?
Is it the way you treat people with kindness?
Is it the way you treat yourself with respect?
Is it your personality that shines through?
Who can see true beauty?
A plastic surgeon?
A priest?
A poet?
Only the ones who can see deep enough.

Kelly Wolfe

Untitled

I asked God to give her, snow on Christmas Eve
But the next day was normal,
The snow she didn't receive
I questioned the reason, why He didn't care
Behold! Two days later the snow came
Because it was a long distance prayer

C. R. Lewis

I Write Novels and I
Would Like My Due

An author by desire
Age seven ignited the fire
I prefer to write novels
But I don't want to grovel

To get published is my aim
But the business is a game
It's not what you do or how
It's who you know and take a bow

This is an old-fashioned rhyme
Certainly not before its time
Although I hope to get published here
The outcome won't be quite as dear

Maybe an agent or a publisher will see
That among the best I'm all I can be
To be recognized as a writer of books
Is - as they say- that's all it took

Diane Fisher - J

A Christmas Dream

I was taking a trip on a mystic ship
Ahead lay an endless realm.
Surrounded by friends on every side
With the Christ Child at the helm.

Over vast fields of silver clouds,
Through banks of glistening stars,
Seems I rode through endless space
That showed no earthly scars.

Surrounded by family and neighbors
I could feel they were different than I,
I'd go back to the world I came from
To my friends, I'd say goodbye.

From my dream I now have awakened,
All is dark, but I don't feel alone.
The one at the helm of the mystic ship
Is the one that will bring me home.

Henry Byrne

The Race

The race went off, the pace was fast,
And my horse started second last.

"But not to worry," said the form,
"He starts out slowly; that's his norm."

At the half and no one passed,
The horse I bet - still second last.

Onto the stretch they're in the groove,
And seven trotters make their move.

Ponies everywhere try their best,
They're moving up to eight abreast.

And at the wire they're nose to nose,
Eight strong horses at the close.

The crowd stoop up, a mutual sigh,
The photo flag was raised on high.

Even the judges didn't know,
Of who would win - and place - and show.

They took their time, the race was scored,
Excitement grew among the horde.

The toteboard lit, the dye was cast,
The horse I bet - was second last.

Eugene V. Bianchi

On The Inside

When I look at myself I think of a room and everything that's within,
I see in my eyes the windows of life that greet me when I grin.
I can tell there's someone home, they look out at me at times,
and I wonder if I should disturb the resident and if the resident minds.
The room of my soul takes up little space, except for all the things that fill it,
all the things that sometimes entertain, but sometimes can interrupt it.
The little room is cluttered at times with worry, pity and shame,
but I plan to take out extra time to make it a pleasant place to be again.
Whenever I enter the room, I want to turn out the lights,
because I don't want to see it all; it all seems pleasant, less less intimidating at night.
At times I've closed the doors to the room and locked out all the world
so that I can spend some time alone to think like a child, an innocent, and young girl.
When visitors come to the door or tap at the window pane,
I look away and draw the shades at which time it sometimes rains.
Then just when the rain has dried and the day is blessed with sun,
I can then realize that after all a little company may be fun.
Welcome! "Come on in," I'd say. "Join me in my little room,"
now that I've thought it over a bit, company does help remove the gloom.
One of these day's I'll clean out my little room and I won't be afraid to share.
'Cause when the excess baggage is removed there'll be plenty good room in there.

Lynnetta B. Floyd

My life is at a standstill at this moment. I don't know where I am
going or where I have gone. I see my life before me, a long stretch
of images depicting all my rights and all my wrongs. Reflections in a
looking glass, memories on a patchwork quilt strung together like
notes to a song. The past and present have merged, and this haunting
melody goes on and on. In the midst of this sea of confusion, I see
your face. And I remember. Oh, how I remember. You came with the
wind; and with the wind you left without a trace. Now that my guide
has left me; I have no one to lead the way. And I shall wander this
lifetime hoping to find you again someday. With all that I am and all
that I have become, I have found the strength that sustains me. My
hopes, my dreams and these memories I carry with me along a lonely
path that has become my destiny. And forever I will remember
everything that you are: your essence, your strength, your smile, the
sometimes frown on your forehead, the disappointments, the sorrows,
the wisdom, the joys, the pain, popcorn and leaded coke, coffee in the
mornings, peanut butter cups made for two, Santana and dancing, a
necktie and a tearstained handkerchief, the timbre of your voice, the
sound of your footsteps, your hands, your walk, and the light in your
eyes. But most of all I will remember the good-byes.

Marie Navarrete

The Last Goodbye

The sun was shining, but the air was cool. Everything grew quiet all
around the school. The flag was flown at half mast. For happy
memories long since past.

That night the sky was filled with stars. As they took off, racing
their cars. It did not take them all that long. Because by then,
something went wrong.

They were having fun, just playing games. Then they crashed and there
were flames. The ambulance came, at a pretty fast rate. But, for one
boy it was already to late.

His parents dreams were shattered, they were full of fear. He was
their only son, they loved him so dear. They went to the cemetery on
that cool spring day. And listened to what the minister had to say.

His girlfriend stood there with tears in her eyes. She bent over the
casket and kissed him goodbye. She turned to say something, but
started to hesitate. She whispered she loved him, but it was too late.

She walked out of the chapel on that cool spring day. Then turned
around as if she had something to say. She turned toward the casket
and started to cry. She dropped to her Knees, and said The Last
Goodbye.

Michelle Mientek Solocinski

Look for Me

With my spirit free you may look for me, deep within your heart for that's where I'll be.
In my husband so frail and old, you may look for me with a heart of gold.
In my children's every grin, you may look for me from deep within.
In my grandchildren's smiling faces, you may look for me with some small grace.
In my great grandchildren's every tear, you may look for me for I am near.
On the mountains and in the skies, you may look for me with gentle eyes.
In the twinkling of star light, you may look for me for I'm in you sight.
On the land in the seas, look for me that where I'll be.
On the plains and in the streams, look for me in your every dream.
Look for me in the night or day, I'll be their in many ways.
Look for me amongst the birds that fly, for flying free that is I.
Look for me at Christmas time, I'll be in church serving bread and wine.
Look for me in the spring of the year, for you know that's the season I hold so dear.
Look for me on Mother's Day for I will not be far away.
Look for me when you see a shooting star, for I am with you no matter where you are.
And when your faith starts to glow and you think of thee, look for me for with him I'll be.
And when your day comes and the heavens you'll roam, look for me for that's my new home.

James Walser

Lover's Lament

Alone in the shadow of yesterday's dreams, remembering what should be forgotten—the hopes, the schemes. Facing the twilight with agony and disgust, robbed of the bliss of loving, of lust.

Put out the fire, the longing the wants, only to replace them with teasing and taunts.
Where is the morning, with sunshine with light? Take away this everlasting night.

Let me dream, let me love, let me be me; to smell spring's scents—to hear the roaring sea.
Let me feel a lover's arms, a gentle kiss and joy in sharing a moment's bliss.

Erase this loneliness which robs me of sleep and fills the rivers with tears that I weep.
Love, you have forsaken me, cheated and lied, robbed me of happiness, stripped me of pride.

Where can I go to escape this spell? Much taller than a mountain, much deeper than a well.
Escape from this misery that you have nursed, escape from all that you have cursed.

No! Not into the night for the darkness can see and sings sweet songs reminding me; and not into the sunlight, for my eyes cannot bear the sweet kiss of lovers, to know that they care.

I beg you to take away torture and pain, and let me rejoice in living again.

Heiderose Groves

Friends

Friends are people who listen to your problems
Friends do a lot for you
They help you through difficult times and are always there for you
Whenever your down, happy about something, or just whenever you feel
like saying something, your friend listens
Friends are patient, kind, loving, and very caring
The world wouldn't be the same without friends

Patti Gonzales

The Politician

There was a governor of a renowned state. Born to riches, only the finest foods he ate.
A well dressed man who wasn't too old, with a tuxedo, a top hat and buttons of gold.
His hair was dark brown, and his eyes a deep blue. The grin on his face was as real as he knew.
Being an educated man, for he went to Yale, he was a man that all people would hail.
His tongue was like fire, for he knew just what to say. The people all loved him, never neglecting to pay.
An honest person, whose conscience was his guide, he stretched the truth a bit, but he never lied.
A man of compromise whom the law could not touch. He could talk his way out if it didn't cost too much.
He was a churchgoer, a man of God, though the religion he practiced seemed somewhat odd.
The churches he went to were different each year, but wherever he went, the press would be near.
The man was a leader, who always took charge, but his advisors would handle it if it wasn't too large.
His minions would all listen, and do as he desired. If they did not agree with him, they would be fired.
Prestigious was he, a man with fame. People everywhere would remember his name.
Taking both sides to please people more, he was a politician down to the core.
His army was strong and ready to fight, and all of their foes would shake at their sight.
He had lots of missiles, and he still wanted more, but peace was his goal; he hated war.
His taxes were high and his laws were unfair, but he need not adjust them since his paycheck was there.
Crime rate was high, and employment was low, but his checks were all good, unlike his foe.
His opposition was weak, and they had lost face. He had ruined their reputations to win the race.
He promised a better life, just as he must. His promise wasn't possible, but he won their trust.
He lead all the polls with the people's affection, so it must have been fate that he won re-election.

Peter Cozmyk

"Special Friend"

Soft and gentle,
Beautifully fair,
The sweetest laughter,
Floating on air.

Playing games,
Exchanging wit,
Sharing with friends,
Comfortably fit.

Special Friend,
Lover of life,
Unworthy of suffering,
Pain and strife.

And so we grieve,
For life past,
But haloes become her,
and peace at last.

Angel forever,
Beautifully fair,
The sweetest of laughter,
Still floats on air.

Dwanda Wright

Lingering

You are gone,
    driving.
I am here with
    memories,
and your smell.
Cigarette butts lay
    abandoned,
and I lie almost
    spent.
Aglow with the
    warmth,
our love has left
    in the room.

Jo Pat Scanlan

Distilled Spirit

Fragrant leaf
    If I could taste your color
    Pomegranate wine!

Jane Bergman

Untitled

Up high in the sky
A little star
He's not judgmental
But accepts who you are.
Can you teach me
How to smile
Need an inch
Take a mile
Help me find
My little light
Show me how
I've lost my sight
Need more time
Far away
Have to find
Another way
Happiness
I have not
Another year
I do not want

David Nunn

Tether Me Gently

Tether me
Tether me gently
To the meaning of life
For my infant understanding
Cannot yet grasp the ocean's span
Or the vastness of our universe
Speak in whispers to me softly
Of the wisdom which abides
In the rare tombs of truth
For my precocious wit
Cannot yet perceive
The ultimate
Destiny One
You one
Me we I
I
I
I
I
I

Jeanne H. Lanier

A
Tree
Who's green
Branches spread
Aloft beyond the trunk
Who sleeps sound in winter
Wakes and blooms again in spring
Won -
Der -
Ful.

Creda Stanczak

Dimensions

Moon
glittering, flowing
sliding softly
she holds me
moon

Stars
shimmering, shining
in and out
scattered through time
stars

Time
hopeful, causeless
hurriedly, wandering
ceaseless, never-ending
helping me to grow
time

Bayla Parkoff

Time As I Know It

We all know it as time
always moving and
not always nice it
is friendless, and
endless, this is time.

Lila Coleman

Hologram

The Crisis
Between
Person and Image
Reaches into the
Fundamental
Angst:

The Perception that
Image
Dissipates
And
Is not Replaced by
Mass.

The only Certainty
Is
That
There
Is
No
Substance.

Jean M. Hendrickson

generations

bulbs
brown with dirt
memories of grandma's dahlias
towering over me to reach the sky
colors of sunset
pink, yellow, and orange
now grandma is gone
father continuing on
bulbs growing strong
time passes
grandma's dahlias
father's dahlias
now my dahlias
generations old
memories of sunsets
dreams in the sky
live on in
bulbs
brown with dirt

Ginger J. Buffington

"Let My Heart Float Free"

My heart floats above me,
A balloon on a string
Filled with the air of my fantasies.

His smiles are the wind
tugging on my balloon,
Come, be free, play with me.

His touches are fingers
trying to untie the knot
holding my heart in place.

I know that soon
the fantasies will fade
and my balloon will deflate.

I know if I untie the string
my balloon will float away
and be lost forever.

But now, at this moment,
I yearn to see my balloon
soaring free on the wind.

Barbara Levine

Bar Of Soap

My love for you is
a bar of perfumed soap
Over the years, after
each hurt or
disappointment

I run the soap under water
to wash away
the top layer of pain
or disappointment

The soap's sweet smell
of perfume has already
evaporated
Two or three more washings...

Cynthia C. Chagois

The Fife And Drum

Down the dusty road we hear
a battered fife and drum,
It sounds so sweet and meaningful
in the soldier's ear.
The men behind are stiff and strong
and glad they won the day.
The fife and drum are ringing still
the song of liberty.

Down the dusty road we hear
a battered fife and drum,
The men who gave their lives for us
honored be their names.
The flag that passes by the dead
shall see the men who died
For country and for liberty
they faced the old death call.

Oh! Proud am I to be an American,
the land of the fife and drum.

Deborah Alfaro

Searching Spirits

Dreams as a young one
A beach walk
At first light
The wonder ever present

Two hearts meet
Crisscross under a pier
A mutual discovery
Shared feeling unmeasured.

The encounter mere magic
One special eve
Each silently staring
Adventure upon them.

Each soul drawn by sight
Moonlight was their dance
And now years later
Shared words doth bind them.

That need for another
Long ago known
Has come to fruition
To endure for all time

Barry Edward Sessoms

Free Land

She's stood now for 200 years,
  a beacon in the night,
Holding out her loving arms,
  a glimmer of free light.
To all the people in the world,
  She's stood a mighty rock.
A place they could find refuge,
  and to her shores the millions flocked.
A place to raise their families,
  a place to worship God,
They spread out among her rolling hills,
  and upon her lush green sod.
There are people of all religions,
  and from every walk of life,
Who are working altogether,
  to fuel her freedom's light.
America, they call her,
  And Freedom is her cry.
For 200 years now it's been ringing,
  And it's never going to die.

James H. Walker

"Find Your Heart "

A beat here
A beat there,
So goes the heart all thru life.

It works, it takes,
And gives so much, and
Love as well, that lives
In each of us,

A kind of heart
That God controls
In everything we do
Or say, and yet, what
I can, I give to God
My heart and soul
To use and do for him.

Frankie K. Richardson

Conception

A starlit night my father's age ago.
A cone fell to earth with no one to know.
Its outer shell soon decayed,
Its inner life with struggle saved.
Who are the skeptics who say!
life from above just no way!
I have the proof!
Look out my window high above the roof.
A lofty pine
When you again view this tree,
Think of it as you and me.
For we as humans have lost our sight
Of a long ago star lit night.

Dennis F. Slomba Sr.

Who Am I?

I am kind and
nice and always think twice.

Witty and sweet and
always discrete.

Helpful towards others
whenever I can.

That is the That
I am.

Theresa Ann Arana

Mama's Hungry Babe

A babe in arms cries out in pain
a cry with so little to gain.
Mama holds him close
giving love in a strong dose.

He cries with great strain
his tiny stomach hurts with pain.
A tender touch of mama's hand
still it's hard for babe to understand.

A cry of pain pierces her heart
that just tears mama apart.
She sings those special lullabies
hoping babe will soon close his eyes.

A babe in arms cries out in pain
still with nothing to gain.
Mama holds him close
and still only giving love in a strong dose.

Denise M. Gotimer

Disturbance

An eruption of one mind,
A demolition of two sides,
Bound together by a hostility,
A morbid discrete laugh,
The fight of purity and sanity,
Is only a joke,
You hear the abnormal,
You fear the unusual,
Yet some to forward to it,
The unbalanced beat,
Some hear it, many don't,
From the birthdate on it is considered,
A disturbance to most....

Christine Chiren

Time

Grandfather's clock is ticking
A drum beat to your grave.
Always forward, never backward
The course of time is laid.
The days are long, the years are short,
Time keeps racing by
You are a boy, then a man
Suddenly you die.
Time is happiness, time is strife
Time is the very essence of life.
So live your life to the fullest
Use the time you have
Time is for the living
Eternity for the dead.

Don Schau

My Dog - Little Anne

My dog is a hog.
She sleeps like a log.
She follows a frog,
She is a hog, but I still
Love her because she is
Still my dog.

Laura Meinhardt

Love

Love,
A gift from the heart
Meant to be shared
Priceless like a piece of art.
We are the sculptor

And like an artist
We give a part of ourselves away
Shaping other lives
A return of equal compare.

If we let it
It can consume our being
We give it all away
Only to become more whole.

Love is a mystery
A precious gift
Given from a lover
To another.

Angela Sellen

Desire

When I look into your eyes,
A lingering warmth I see.
Suppressed though it be from the world,
Your heart from then I read.
I see the burning desire
Hidden, yet manifest-
That prying eyes and wagging tongues
May not be set agog.

When I look into your eyes,
My heart is set afire.
For the tenderness and love therein,
Can melt a will of metal.
Your touch on my flesh
And your lips on my bosom,
Encompasses my soul,
Electrifying my body.

Debo Richards Obawole

A Cloth

If I could weave a cloth for you
A magic cloth it would be

It would not be of silk or wool
or any tangible material
It would be of the fabric
of life
Truth, Sincerity, Trust
Honor, Love and Compassion
Bound together with
the threads of hope and time

It would be as rich as I
have the power within me
to make it.

It would be for you
to wrap around yourself
and know
This cloth
is the fabric
of my soul.

James Norman Craig

Death Of One

A book without a cover,
A mask without a face,
A love without a lover,
A man without a race...

How can you be so narrow?
You'll never understand
How it feels to be a sparrow
Searching for a place to land.

I seem to fit in no where.
I can never have a piece.
Why does no one care?
Will you try for me at least?

Look beyond the outer visage
And meet what's trapped inside.
I'm a messenger who has lost the message,
A soldier who has lost his pride.

We are running out of time you know?
It will all soon come to end.
Encourage yourself now to grow,
The times not ours to spend!!!

Catherine Fisher

New Beginnings

With the coming of dawn,
a new day begins.

Bringing with it
an array of
new possibilities.

With the coming of spring,
life is reborn.

Renewal of the physical
and the spiritual.

With each new beginning
we are given, the
opportunity to create,
to love,
to live....

Cassandra Conyers

Being A Grandma

Your daughter's in the labor room
A new life's about to start
You pray and walk and worry
It's enough to break your heart.

For your mind is full of pity
And you'd love to ease her pain
And you know as you are sitting
That she'll do this again.

But how quickly it all passes
As you see that tiny one
And thru your mind it flashes
Being grandma is such fun!

Then your mind goes to your daughter
Oh, pray God that she's alright.
And you're glad to see her smiling
Tho' you've nearly died of fright.

Agnes E. Paul

"Time Shared Alone"

Inside, a feeling of pain, distraught,
   A shattered dream a love that's not;
A hope, a dream, a love untrue.
   Alone, afraid, a heart of blue;
Inside, you search for reasons why,
   You, yourself the only lie;
Close your eyes and hold them tight,
   Hold her close with all your might;
And in a whisper, say goodbye,
   Two lovers lost,
      Two lovers cry....

Clayton McCowan

My Verses

My verses?
A shy
And a melancholy cry
Of dead leaves at dawn,
Crushed underfoot,
Off and on
By the passer - by.

Slender life I put inside,
And my sap didn't offer the force
Of the trees ramified,
With their branches towards the high,
Darkening the path
And my starry sky.

If I would have had ahead
A more lasting fate,
I don't know
What I could have been,
but my seed turned green
A moment too late.

Constantin Stoicescu

Son

The babe - perfect, beautiful
a smile so sweet and contagious like
"no other"
A wonderful love is in the bright
blue eyes of babe and those of father
and mother

The boy - intelligent, warm eager,
filling the home with joy and laughter
Leaving a family bewildered at the
sadness to come there after

The man - eyes sly, greedy,
shallow, cruel an empty heart.
Deceiving all around him now,
except those he chose to depart

The father - gone to his rest
The mother - doing her best
to remember the smile like "no other"

Helen Tuohey

Untitled

Death walks in unannounced.
Refusing to be dismissed
it captures attention and
pulls the rest of us
a little closer
to the firing line.

Lynn Halper Rosen

The Tree

Some ask will there be
A sound in the forest when
A tree falls and there is
No one to hear it

The answer was told to me
By an old man who had no home
But walked and walked till
He dropped and rested until refreshed

"I was in the woods when the
Oak tree buffeted by
Clamoring winds, its power
To resist diminished by age-fell"

"I listened," the ancient wanderer
said, "and what I heard was not
The crashing of venerable timber
But the pensive lament of a dying creature"

Elliott Caplin

Fate

A taste of love
A taste of hate
The murderers glove
Creates ones fate

Taste a smile
Taste a frown
Walk your miles
From town to town

A hint of fear
A hint of anger
No more cheer
Everyone's a stranger

A bit of pleasure
A bit of pain
No one can measure
How much the world's insane!

Donald W. Brown

Until We Meet Again, My Friend

Blue this morning was the sky,
   A thought of you.
Someone smiled as they passed by,
   A thought of you.
Flowers dance against the winds,
   A thought of you.
Laughter rings out amongst friends,
   A thought of you.
A glimpse of sunshine through the storm,
   A thought of you.
A place within my heart forever warm,
   A thought of you.

Cathy Riley Lawing

Youths

A time to think
A time to dream
A time to grow and wonder
A time when everything begins
   to come together.
Our hopes our dream's
   and all of our tomorrows.
Our tomorrows are made
   in the yester year
With time to think
With time to dream
With time to grow and wonder.

Alene M. Anderson

To Conquer Your Dreams

I may look small,
A weakling in most eyes,
But I'm a dreamer
Strong in God's light.

I don't act with violence,
But I'm peaceful and kind,
Because I am a conqueror,
I battle the mind.

I dream to conquer
I conquer to dream.
I reach for the stars
I do my own thing.

If I am small
And if I don't lean
I am still the stronger
Because I conquer the dream.

Alicia S. Maloney

"Safe"

Is how you feel
    about what you have
    when you know it's real
Like a sock around a foot
Like a glove around a hand
Like the sun warming your body
    as you lay motionless in the sand
Like a baby in her mother's arms
Like a soldier when out of harm
Like the leaves around a tree
Like the feeling I have
    when you are with me...

Bill Enderley

"Destiny"

Life is a puzzle
about you and me
it's all in God's plans
called "destiny."

There are roads and pathways
going left and right
some are short, some show long life.

Mountains so high
with valleys so low
but those seem to be the ones
that make us grow.

Days of sunshine, yet days of rain
storms move in
you can feel the pain.

With all our faith
and God's guiding light
he'll help us continue
this journey of life.

So live each day to the fullest it can be
for it could be the end of your "Destiny."

Barbara Collins

Untitled

The skier zig zags through the snow,
slush, slush, slush.
the surfers wipe out on the waves,
splash, splash, splash
and I sit and write this poem,
scribble, scribble, scratch.

Michael A. Rose

The Night

The moon is shining so bright
above my head this breezy night.
The geese are flying away
as the sky begins to turn gray.
The homes are lit with sparkling lights,
with colors of such beauteous sights.
The stars begin to twinkle above
like a single white dove.
The clouds are turning fluffy
like a lamb all soft and puffy.
It's time to go to my house
where it's so quiet you can hear a mouse.

Cathy Richards

Untitled

The memory of a smiling face
Across a table spread
How was anyone to know
That soon she would be dead?

A speeding car came over the curb
Upon a lush green lawn
Where little Mary was at play
With her rag dolls, Doe and Fawn

A tombstone stands on a lonely grave
With rosebuds now unfurled
Who knows how much this happy face
May have brightened up our world

The driver was taken into the court
Where he had been before
When the judge had set him free
To drink and drive once more

This time behind the prison walls
Things were not the same
For the little girl who died that day
Bore that judge's name

Alvin E. Anderson

Indecent Thoughts

In our lives we often come,
across our own indecent
thoughts about life.
We soon underestimate the important
values of our own,
Indecent thoughts.
Coming to realization of society,
as how it relates to,
what we think.
We render our own mind,
to bring together collective
indecent thoughts about,
what really is important.
Indecent thoughts comes and
goes, but we suffer the aftermath
of what is said.

Edwin McKinney, Jr.

Bouquet, Of Joy

I am some flowers as you can see,
so full off joy, I laugh with glee.
In many colours so bright and gay,
I'm sent to you to brighten your day.
Look at me for just awhile, and I
will glow and make you smile

John R. Iley

Rainy Day

It rains
all day
grayness abounds
sadness astounds
wind gusts
sway trees
twist boughs
bend flowers
weaken knees
who knows
when will
sun again
glare still
hot rays
bake bodies
not rain
all day

Helga Cramer

The Reflection I See

I took a look into the mirror
All I saw was a person,
A person full of pain and fear.

I slowly turn away,
Hoping that she'll just go away.

Thus,...I take a glance once more,
To find that she was there no more.

But, what I did see was a person,
A person very happy.
It was the kind of person
    that was full of joy and grace,
She was the one who took her place.
Once more I take a look to see
    and all I found...was me!

Heather Savolainen

Weathered Pages

The story of a commoner,
Plain as it may be,
Is the heart, the roots, the origin
Of persons much like me.

Its existence is but history,
A sequence of events,
That passed from father to son
As the years came and went.

Thank God for the quiet man
Who took the occasion to write
About his ordinary days
By the dim candlelight.

His hardships and joys,
Expressed on weathered pages,
Reveal a host of occurrences
Passed down through the ages.

Through the leaves of a journal,
We walk his steps a mile;
Feel his heartbeat, touch his hand,
Spend time with him awhile.

Janet Lux

You

When I look into your eyes
All I see are
The lies
Lies that came from your mouth
The pain
Pain that came from your hand
Pain that will never go away
I will never forget how you hurt me
I remember every sweet kiss
Every soft touch
I also remember the sadness
The manipulation
The scare of my life
You took something from me
That you can't give back
You took my heart
Broke it
And left me to fit the pieces back together
You hurt me
Why do I still love you?

Beth Cali

Love Travels

Love comes and goes.
All the people want it to stay.
It fills your life,
upsets the pain.
On it goes to another day.

Reflections in life's window.
A call from the past.
Love is there again,
it goes to fast.

I don't believe in magic.
I don't believe in the fool.
I believe in wanting love.
I know it can be cruel.

Fame and fortune
money and power.
They mean nothing
in a lonely hour.

Come back love where did you rome?
Threw the mind, threw the soul.
Come back please into my home.

Chris Campanozzi

Our Little Dream Come True

I have waited for so long for you,
almost all my life.

You're the most important thing to me,
aside from being a wife.

Your Daddy is so special,
he will love us both forever.

I know he is at work a lot but,
to leave us he will never.

We'll be a happy family,
for now we'll start anew.

This family will begin in perfection.
'Cause the beginning starts with you.

Christine E. Butler

Irony

The young woman sits
Alone.
The water of the fish tank
Bubbles with life.
The cat prances by
On a secret mission.
Her husband's soft breathing
Comes from the next room.
The cars woosh by
So many places to go.

She seeks comfort and love.
She knows where to find it
And goes there.
At the church:
Condemnation and hypocrisy.
In the "believers":
"I understand." Hug. "Gotta go."
In the unbelievers:
Acceptance.
There she is not alone.

Faith Spivey

Hologram

My life is like a hologram
An image set in space;
Dimensional,
Illusional;
A vague elusive place.

From every angle, every view
And every sideways glance,
I pause outside;
I long to hide
But yet resume the dance.

I think it's real, it beckons me;
I slip into the scene
Of fantasy
And make-believe
Existence so pristine.

Suspended in a frame of time
Captured infinity;
Perpetual,
Conceptual
Etched for eternity.

Josephine Findley

The Mountain Man

When the sun sets on the mountain,
And a breeze gently whips the pine,
And the world is quiet and peaceful,
I've a picture in my mind.

I've a picture of a mountain man
Trudging home across the hill,
As the singing of a songbird
Rings out and breaks the still.

The plaid-blue shirt is strained
Across his shoulders hard and strong.
On straight, strong, muscled legs
He walks, in haste; his strides are long.

With a twinkle in those sky-blue eyes,
And a smile on his bearded face,
Like a king with a scepter and a throne,
The mountain man fits this place.

In the valley spread out before him,
The cozy little cabin stands;
With strength and determination,
Built with love and his powerful hands.

Catherine Ross

"To Jennifer"

The days are getting shorter
And a little cooler too
This is the time of year
To notice a little sky that's blue

Another thing to notice
And truly must remember
Is Jenny was born
In the month of September

She makes our hearts go lighter
As she brushes her red-gold hair
It truly is so beautiful
With curls here and there

This year she'll be three
About thirty-six inches tall
She'll help us all to remember
We have another precious fall

HAPPY BIRTHDAY!

Genevieve Rowland

My Dad, My Sunshine

You have left this world,
And are now at peace

You are up in heaven
At God's retreat

You and Mom
Are together once more

And the love you have
Will flow once more

You treated me
As your own from the start

And I will always love you
From the bottom of my heart

Sunshine you brought to my life
Just by being you

And I know there were many people
You made not blue

The world lost sunshine
But it's heaven's gain

Because with you in heaven
It will never rain

Debbie Bond

I Am Shy

To Steve Ilten

I want to be a Rain
And caress you tenderly
Without telling you it's me...
I want to be an Ocean wave
And play with you carefree
Without telling you it's me...
I want to be a Wind
Looking straight in your eyes
Without telling you it's me...
I want to be a Dream
Snuggled lovably in your heart
Without telling you it's me...
I wonder if you meet me after all
Will you recognize that's me?

Danielle Nicol

Untitled

The sun kissed her flesh
And danced along it with a lovers caress
It touched lightly along her thighs
The curve of her breast
The Mona Lisa lips

She warmed under its touch
Lovers sweat slowly, sensuously
Made her flesh shimmer

She shifted, turned
Offered more of herself
To this branding touch

Her first and only
Faithful lover

Denise Mentzer

Mother

Your illness creeps along the wall
And day by day, I see it fall
With no more laughter, no more smiles
Oh, how I pray - you'll last awhile
But I see this change come over you
How sad it is that you're so blue
NOW! I must pray, for a better way
Oh GOD, MY GOD - Take her away.

Coletta M. Hines

Silence Screams

Silence screams within this house
And destroys our happy home.
Three broken hearts reside here.
Each person, all alone.

A man, too strong and angry
To let his feelings show,
Has a deep abiding love
No one will ever know.

A woman, scared of being hurt,
Builds walls as thick as steel.
No one can get past them
To see the way she feels.

A child hides within her room,
Afraid to show her fear.
She pushes everyone away;
No one gets too near.

Silence screams within this house,
A mournful, deafening moan.
Three broken hearts reside here.
Each person, all alone.

Jeannie Nillen

Alone

The trees walked along the mountainside.
Against the sunset,
I see them dancing with one another.
I run after them -
But they run faster.
I dance by myself against the sunset.
Exhausted - I fall.
The trees trample me.
The sun sets.
The trees walk on.

Jill Alison Kent

The Best Leaf

Sleep, beautiful leaf, sleep!
Swiftly come down into your
cozy autumn bed.
Dream of the sparkle light stars.
Sleep, beautiful leaf, sleep!

Natasha Lynn Kurtz

To Andrea:

So small - so sweet
and eyes so blue
A gift from God
just an hour new...

Your hair was light
with a hint of curl
I knew from his smile
you were Grandpa's girl...

You had little white hands
and a darling little nose
You were so freshly "picked"
and no sign of clothes...

Your mom was tired,
your daddy high.
I understand them
'Cause so was I...

From Grandma

Ines Hahs

Crack

Crack for fun,
and for its thrills.
The thought consumes
my heart with chills.

An instant addict
on our streets.
This driving force
their soul defeat.

All crime mounting
in its wake.
They sell their bodies
for its sake.

Disease and murder,
one step behind,
and forever lost,
this great young mind.

Grant L. Bascom

"Some Weak"

Once again the year has come
and gone. It left some weak
and some strong.
Children are wrapping some
cracking, some are weak others
are strong.
Hundreds lose their life to streets
alone.
We Prance and Pray, walk the
floor all night, let our kids come
home tonight. And when the morn
has come and they are not around
to hide our tears and brace
our fears, for we know some
are weak others are strong.

Bertha Griffin

A Mother's Love

To my beautiful daughter,
And handsome son;
A more precious gift,
of course there's none.
The gift of life,
the two of you;
Gave me hope, and
dreams come true.
I watch you sleep,
and dream away;
Of life you'll have,
your own one day.
To watch you grow,
to laugh, and love;
A wonderful gift,
from God above.

Darlene Brown-Keith

Remember

When friendships blossom
and happiness abounds
when you feel warm inside
and there is love all around

These are the memories you remember
the ones you never forget
no matter how far away you move
no matter how bad times get

Just send us a letter
a telephone call will do
all of your friends will be there
to say "We miss you!"

Friendships never fade
no they never do
I know this for a fact
because I will never forget you

Brandy Neal

Someday

There's the man that I love,
And he worships me...
We share the miracle of life,
We belong together... a family.

Except... as in all fairy tales...
Something stands in the way.
An obstacle... to be surmounted...
Only I can overcome it.

They're waiting...
My family... my fairy tale.
But I have to overcome it...
Only I can bring us together.

Someday... we'll be,
together.
Never say never...
together...forever.

Amber Dietrich

"The Poet"

Good night...
Sleep tight
Wake up. Bright
In the morning light
To do what's right
With all your might
Good night...

Kevin Cook

A Lesson In High Finance

When I was just a little lad
And heard the old folks chatter
A bit more knowledge I could add
But thought - What did it matter?
A few short years soon rolled around
And what they'd said seemed more profound
I learned a lesson - sorely taught
For what in my opinion rated naught
By the time I'd almost reached the roof
I'd skinned up both my knees
And had indeed quite ample proof
That money doesn't grow on trees!

Bernice Sherry

Rose Petal

Take this petal,
and hold it close.
Thou now dead,
it still lives,
for during the past,
it brought joy and happiness,
to two who were together.
Although its death was saddening,
it's seed,
will bring a new rose,
that's beauty will be of its ancestor.
To tie the past with the present.
into a new form of happiness,
that takes the two who were together,
and brings them closer,
than ever.

Angelica Hurtado

Untitled

I Love you very much, I do
And I don't want you to go.
I want you to stick around awhile
And help me as I grow

I know one day you'll die.
This I understand
And when I die I'll meet up with you
And take you by the hand

We'll walk along in silence
For words need not be spoken
Our love will bond us forever
For it cannot be broken

Barbara Smith

Hidden Love

   I dream of you sometimes
And I find it hard to forget
The moments I shared with you
Are forever etched on my mind
I can't get rid of them,
No matter how hard I try.

   You are a part of my past
A memory that won't die.
No matter the times I love,
You will always be the first
That I love completely.

   After you love someone
The way that I loved you
With all my heart
I don't think it's possible
To ever love that way again.

Crystal M. Thomas

If You Were Mine

Destined to be are you
and I, for if my heart
had eye's it would cry.
to seek another love
that's is just like you.
would be an impossible
task for me to do.

A broken heart and lost
lonely eye's is the way
you shall leave me if my
love for you was to die.

So please don't leave me
and if so not yet, for the
love we could have between
us I will not soon forget.

David Dudley Jr.

Light Years Away

I hear your name
and I see you for
the first time and
the sadness covers
me again
And the lies said again
While naked
Life is wicked and divine
You will always serve yourself
Don't you!
Hate is the factor you
always take
You put is away, but
it will return.

Heather Janelle Secrest

Emotions

The days go by
And I want to cry
But the tears
Just don't come out
I want to scream and pout
Why does the anger
Bottle up in me
Just waiting
To be let free
Why can't I just
Be happy or glad
Why must I always
Feel so sad?

Julie A. Zimmer

Child of God

Come follow me child of God,
And I will show you the way,
To truth and love and all good things,
If you will learn to pray.

Obey my laws, be good and kind
As good as you can be,
For as you do to others,
You also to do Me.

Beth Holobowski

The Greatest Mom

I'd like to write this poem to you
and in a very special way
to tell you that I love you
on this very special day.

I'd like to start by thanking you
for simply being you
and helping me to meet each day
with a happy point of view.

And now I want to ask you Mom
to please forgive your son
for very seldom thanking you
for all the things you've done.

To make me strong and very proud
to say to all my friends
that I've the greatest Mom around
and now I'd like to send.

This poem to you with sincere words
and in a very thoughtful way
again to say, I love you
on this, your Mother's Day.

Danny Knoff

Lord, That I May Hear

I hear You in the thunderstorm
and in the patter of the rain.
I hear You in the soft Spring breeze
and in the hurricane.

I hear You in the whispering wind
and in the swaying trees.
I hear You in the rippling brook
and in the surging seas.

I hear You in the kitten's purr
and in the puppy's growl.
I hear You in the baying sheep
and in the wolf's night howl.

I hear You in the bird's soft twill
and in the geese's flight.
I hear You in the hum of bees
and in the mosquito's bite.

I hear You in the children's laughter
and in each baby's cry.
Grant, Lord, that I may hear You
in every neighbor's sigh.

Helen E. Haky

Do You Believe?

As the Bible says, The earth shall end.
And Jesus shall come, once again.

He shall come in glory, In loving
grace. To take His children, To the
holiest place. As place called heaven
With streets of gold, were told it's
given, to the righteous soul.

Oh how we long, for this beautiful day,
when the lord shall come, to take us
away, and the sinners shall know,

My Lord is true, that he came for me,
and I hope for you. Oh how I pray,
you change your ways, for the lord is
at hand. In these days. I praise the
Lord, For these lines I've wrote,

And to the Lord Jesus, this
poems I devote! Amen

Arlon Myers Jr.

"Jesus And The Judgement"

The world is up for judgement,
And Jesus will be judge.
And the man will give account that day,
For all that He has done.
Every one who's ever lived.
Will be on trial that day.
The rich will be judged with the poor,
No one will get away.
God the Father, on His throne,
Will over see it all.
And justice will be Godly served,
To all the great and small.
Jesus Christ gave up His life,
To save this world from sin.
But He'll return to earth one day,
To claim this world again,.
Jesus and the judgement,
Will not be put on hold.
So why don't you give Christ your life,
And let God save your soul?

Earl Jones

My Colors

My colors; a tree with a purple trunk
And leaves of gold,
A river that gleams of the deepest,
Darkest black, reaching unknown depths.

My sky, a galaxy of color to hold
Your very eye; to the mirror of a
Mind undreamt of
Yet as clear as day to I.

The picture so true to others is
Pure delight, but naught to me.
For to the depths of my soul
I reach to see.

To reveal my inner most thoughts
Is what I must try.
To convey the thoughts I
Feel every day!

George M. James

A Song

If short enough, isn't long enough,
And long enough is wrong.
How you gonna get the long enough,
Short enough, or the short enough,
long enough, to make a gosh darned song.
To please a public throng?
Now 'fore I die I'm gonna try to get
the long enough, short enough and
the short enough, long enough to make
A gosh darned song,
To please a public throng.

Annie R. Forrester

To All Of You

To you who fought and died
To you who fought and returned
To you who gave of yourself
During times of strife and peace
To all of you
I salute thee

John R. Wheeler

The Memory

I wandered through a second hand store
And Memories filled my mind
Of yesterdays and loved ones
That have all been left behind.

There stood a rickety rocking chair
A fan hand painted with gold.
A China doll with a blue eyed stare.
Red satin dancing shoes wrinkled and old.

And then I found my special it.
A garnet studded tortoise shell comb,
I knew it was impractical,
But I had to take it home,
"What did you buy"? My husband asked
And he smiled tenderly at me.
"I think", I softly said to him
"I've bought a memory."

Hilary Thompson Thorne

The Battle Is Won

My axe, red with blood
and my battle is won
A thousand men dead
since we begun
I'm sorry my Lord!
what have I done?
killed like a mad man
killed my own son
tears line my eyes
my pride all but gone
no need to be happy
no need to sing songs
my first born is dead
killed by my swing
I need no golden medals
from the almighty king
just one thing to do
my life's torn apart
bring honor again
a sword through my heart.

Carlos Resto

Winter On The Salmon River

Bright flashing water up ahead
and noise of gravity and granite
the hush of lichen on decaying giants
lying silent on the forest floor.
Bitter is the cold upon her heights
where open sky the howling
winds unhinder their fierce bite
and mighty Hood's peak pierces
the blue of winter's heaven.
This cascade of melting snow
and sprightly springs arisen
from earth's mystic depths
become transfixed upon
the leeward face of rocks
thrown down from ancient furies.
The prize for walking forth
in such frigid landscape
is to know that nature owns
a winter face worth viewing
if but for one brief shivering moment.

Frank Stovall

The Agate Vision

Serpents of hope, crawling into
And out of boiling waves of time,
Press their indolent egos
Against the bulky ship
Of forgiveness.

Cringing beneath the mold-rotted wood
Of a mountainous vessel,
Afraid to strike, and afraid to hide,
Beady eyes, half-lidded with evil,
Blink as the iceberg looms.

Cold mass that shatters nothing
Pulls the shutter
Down, over the serpent's eyes
And ends the agate vision
Of the slimy, despicable reptile.

Barbara R. Reid

Peace 1995

One seed drifts across a weeded city lot
and plants a flower.
Small drops of rain fall into the sea
and form a universe of plankton.
Two hearts, multiplied...
link a chain of cultures.
Two brave hands, one black, one white...
....worlds unto themselves...
Reach across the world, with hope,
and hold a weighted globe
in palms of love.

Ellen Ziegler

The Summer Solstice

You showed me my mammogram
and pointed to a white star
in the dark sky of my breast-
how innocent and far away it seemed,
a sparkle on the horizon,
but I could tell that you, stargazer,
had seen that heavenly sign many times.
When you excised the cancer,
no bigger than my fingertip,
I saw the red glare of my incision,
a half moon reflected in your glasses.
No need to remove my breast, you said-
had you done so how could I have filled
the emptiness, the darkness of space?
Heal my wound the way Heracles
had his charioteer, Iolaus,
seal the gashes of Hydra-
I need your magic,
not your strength.

John Manesis

Home Sweet Home

If you were an animal,
what would you be?
Where would you go?
And what would you see?

When you make your home,
where would you be?
On the ground, by the pond
or up in the tree?

Lindsay Heintz

Childhood Springs

I saw a bird grab chunks of sky
and pull itself into the sun
Daisies, shed their midnight dew
and open, brown eyes one by one
I saw a lazy butterfly stretch
silken wings of golden corn
And watched the world roll over once
to welcome in the morn

I saw these things in childhood springs
and I haven't seen them since
But I wake each day and listen close
and hope that just by chance
I'd hear the morning sing the song
that made a boy's heart dance

John C. Tomlinson

Lonesome Star

Let's hitch our wagon to a lonesome Star
and roll around a million, stars or more

Slide down the Milky Way,
past the big dipper,
and the Three Bears.
Play with tag with,
The Northern Lights,
And set our wagon down,
In the Land of The Midnight Sun.

Frank J. Jameson

No Safe Haven

I looked about me in the night
    and saw that I was filled with fright

For in the darkness bleak and cold
    I found I had no one to hold

I heard myself begin to cry
    "Oh Lord, No safe Haven have I"

Although the days were long and gray
    They always kept the night away

I ran around from place to place
    and always tried to hide my face

My world was falling down around me
    Wherever I went I could not feel free

I asked the Lord to take me in
    and thru his grace I began to win

For now I have his heaven in sight
    and I no longer fear the night

Ida Mae Fairgrieve

What's Important

As I sit at home
And wait for three

I think
What is today going to bring to me.

As I wait
I think

What it may be
When they walk in

I thank God for why
He brought me to thee.

Julie Kathryn Johnston

'The Bride'

She sings songs about angels
And she holds on to the cross
She'll never feel the pain you give her
And she won't ever feel the loss

As the blood drips off her pillow
And onto the braided rug
You can't save her from this madness
You can't hold her with a hug

The tears she cries are yours
Drink them in and hold a smile
They will quench your thirst forever
Or maybe only for a while

She dances in the darkness
And holds the day at hand
She runs with the breeze
The starlight helps her stand
You can cry for her forever
Or you can just let go,
She hides he secrets never
Her love you cannot know

Darcie Adams

The Air Of Christmas

The ring-a-linging of the bells
    And shouts of glee I hear;
The smells of fancy baking
    Mean Christmas Day is near.

Sounds of carols in the air—
    Songs that are heavenly,
The glory of the Christ Child
    Reigns here for all to see.

Stories of His Holy Birth
    Go 'round the world again;
Truths of our Holy Christ Child
    Are part of our Masters plan.

The very air is Holy
    As again we hear His Word
On Christmas from our Bibles,
    The sweetest ever heard!

Claudia D. Ward

Just Say A Little Prayer

When worries all but swallow you
    and skies are never fair,
For consolation that is real,
    just say a little prayer.
When heartaches mount and
    dreams take wing,
Don't sit around and stare,
try talking to your God above
and; of your troubles, air.
Then you will find your pain
    will ease,
Dark clouds will pass away.
    And just as if by magic,
    you will find the happy way.
So when all other helpers fail
    and friends are very rare,
You'll gain a wealth of comfort
    If you say a little prayer.

Anne Cooley

The Lord's Bouquet

Flowers, flowers, how plentiful they are
And so are we, blooming from everywhere-
Some are big, some are small
Some are straight, some nearly fall,
Some are useful, some are not
Some are pretty, the rest look "flat"-
But the Lord above looks down on us
And one by one we must vanish -
And so we leave this earth; maybe today
To become a flower in God's bouquet.

Jacob J. Kaiser

If

"If" has caused much sorrow
And some of gladness yet.
The word has shocked us lots of times,
But we'd sooner just forget.
"If" has been the only hope
And often just a prayer.
But "if" is often over-used
When hard, true facts are there.

Adeline Wance

Untitled

The wheel will spin.
And the day will begin.
This is life and you will win.
If you have fortitude
And spin the wheel.
This is a good deal.
And this will have appeal.
For the wheel will spin.

Angela Putnam

Apology

I've watched the spinning worlds of space
    And the light years in between;
One alone was blessed with grace;
    One alone was green.

That one had a special birth;
    I chose it for my own.
Someone chose to call it "Earth".
    A strange name for my throne.

I gave it air and gave it life
    And sent it on its way.
I hoped it would be free from strife;
    I gave it night and day.

I blessed it with a shining star;
    I sent it gentle rain;
With love I watched it from afar
    From Heaven's window pane.

I made the dust of Heaven shake;
    I had a master plan.
But I made one small mistake;
    I created Man.

Charles T. Sweeny

"My Feelings For Jesus"

You're a fuel of my faith
    You're the fighter of evil
You're the father of my love
    You're the freedom of justice
You're in my heart forever.

Nancy Massaro

The "Lord"

I love the "Lord"
And the "Lord" loves me.
How do I know;
Because, he has increased my tree.

I live for the "Lord";
And the "Lord" lives in me.
If I didn't.
He wouldn't bless me.

Where do I go?
What shall I do?
I have no idea;
But, the "Lord" do.

The "Lord" is sweet;
The "Lord" is kind;
To those who can see
And to those who are blind.

Gwendolyn Young

My Love For You

As the midnight stars begin to fade,
And the moon becomes a shadowy hue,
I awake from my restful slumber,
Remembering my dreams of you.
The birds outside are singing,
Their beautiful song, I'd say,
Is the reason I get out of bed,
And face the lonely day.
For without you, my only love,
My heart begins to ache,
I pray that we will be together,
Until our wedding vows, we take.
Every time that we're apart,
The day seems so much longer,
When I'm alone, I think of you,
And my love for you grows stronger
I love a lonely day,
It turns my thoughts toward you,
All alone, I can easily find,
Your precious love so true.

Adrienne Sopher

"At Heaven's Gate"

I held your hand and stroked your brow,
And the night dimmed the room.
There was no more I could do now,
For death would be here soon.

The wrinkles faded from your face,
Time seemed to stand still.
Silence took it's place,
As you accepted his will.

I stood there in wonder and awe,
As you watched a glorious scene unfold.
'Thou I couldn't see what you saw,
I knew it was something to behold.

There was a quiet and peaceful perfection,
And like a child, fascination glowed.
For I saw in your eyes the reflection,
Of those heavenly streets of gold.

Arlene J. Johnson

The Sea At Dusk

When the night falls
And the sun begins its rest,
When the breeze from the sea
Lends its gentle caress,
Then is my soul set free.

Give in to your senses,
And reel in the splendor.
The melancholy melody
Seems to hang in the air;
Then is my soul set free.

Only the wondrous stars
Along with the glorious moon,
To offer their company;
I feel as if in a swoon.
Then is my soul set free!

Amanda Sander

A Community Prayer

Tell me what to do Lord.

A major war, can we endure
and the White House is it secure?

Tell me what to do Lord.

Now, we rid the unborn.
The live young we mourn.

Tell me what to do Lord.

We keep our doors lock,
but crimes do not knock.

Tell me what to do Lord.

Yes, I have a job today
or will this be my last day?

Tell me what to do Lord.

Why cancer is no longer a sign
and sex is no longer benign?

Tell me what to do Lord.

They're called ice, water and rock.
Soon, these may be on our block.

Please, Lord tell me what to do.

Donna Murff

One Day

One day I was here
   and then there
   and slowly faded away
away to a land
   with tears and fears
away to a land
   with guns and bums
away to a land
   with drugs and thugs
only to know
   no dreams
   no hope
just away to a land
   of life

Jana Carlo

"Leaves"

Leaves are falling, falling, falling,
And twirling around.
Leaves are falling to the ground,
Spinning around.
Leaves are falling down, down, down,
Spinning around and touching the ground.
Leaves are falling on the daisies
Waiting for me to come.

Audrey Kon

Alone

It's hot at home 98 they say
And warmer on the morrow

Here at the beach it's 68
And breezes blow a sorrow

For she's at home with just a pet
and I alone cannot forget

Einor Staples

Who has revered providence,
and who has pondered fate?

Who has delivered the oppressed,
and who has found the lost?

Who has directed the wise,
and who has betrayed the fool?

Who has deciphered knowledge,
and who has perceived truth?

Who has slept with hatred,
and who has laid with contempt?

Who has sought vanity,
and who has brought futility?

Who has established misery,
and who has determined sorrow?

Who has feigned ignorance,
and who has professed wisdom?

Who has remembered the ancient days,
and who has foretold of days yet seen?

Who has considered many things,
and who has resolved not one?

Brian Allan Morse

Untitled

Four months have passed away this day
   And winter is upon you.
So stoke your fires and chase away
   the icy winds that haunt you.

For spring will come. My day is done,
   And yours has yet to find you.

Give flight to fears and dry your tears.
   this time of weeping's past,
And with my love - as it always was -
   this gift of life I pass.

Denise Ayers

Walk With Firm Feet

When days seem like years
and years seem like days.
When time passes too quickly
and you run out of time.
When life seems to hectic
to go another day.
You can get through it
if you walk with firm feet.

Plan your actions
one then another.
When you accomplish one
proceed in order.
Live each day to the fullest
and do not rush.
Remember, my child,
To walk with firm feet.

Jeffrey McCoy

"The Man To My Left"

I feel so alone
And yet someone's there
I only now see
His body is bare

His presence is strong
I can't turn away
He gives me His hand
And then we both pray

Only I see Him
The others are blind
He makes me believe Him
And this is my time

We walk out together
I now feel okay
We leave the waiting room
Of Satan's young prey.

Eric Sawey

"Lucky Little Darling"

Baby dear, I have a secret,
And you should hear it too:
They've planned a shower for your Mommy,
But the gifts are all for you;

You lucky little darling,
You'll get the sweetest things;
And they'll all be waiting here for you
When old Storkie flaps his wings.

Baby clothes are cuddly:
And I'll never miss my guess,
You'll look sweet in what you get
regardless of your sex.

And there'll be some anxious ladies,
To watch your Mommy's eyes
As they glow with utmost happiness
When she opens each surprise.

Now please don't tell our secret,
It's between just you and me,
And should you wonder how I know,
Baby, I can see: Mommy's pregnant as can be.

Dorothy E. Newton

The Phoenix Calling

When you know that you are falling
and you think you'd rather not,
listen for the Phoenix calling
"Death ain't all that hot."

That mystical bird from ashes arose
to keep our wings from melting,
to save our souls from choices chose
and pain we would have felt.

Listen closely to the wind
when you feel that you are falling,
it will whisper, "I'm your friend"
and you can hear the Phoenix calling.

Ashes to ashes and dust to dust
will you be the same tomorrow?
Live your life, do what you must
experience the joy and sorrow.

And soar, my love, on magic wings
fear not you may be falling.
A cushion below that bird will bring
if you can hear the Phoenix calling.

Charlette Goodyear

Another Day

Momma hit my Dad today
Another hit, another day
I'm prompted to just run away
I hate it when she gets this way

Daddy drank too much today
Another drink, another day
I'm prompted to just run away
I hate it when he drinks this way

My brother played his game today
Another game, another day
I'm prompted to just run away
He shouldn't make me play that way

Uncontrolled rage and anger
Uncontrolled thirst for booze
Uncontrolled sexual desires
Either way I turn, I loose

I'm just a child can't you see
But don't you dare feel sorry for me
I know one day I'll get away
For now it's just another day.

Eric H. Hollaway Sr.

Friends

You would do
Anything for one,
Many people don't
have one,
Some have a lot,
Some think they
have a lot.
But they aren't
real friends.
Real friends
would be there
till the end
They don't just
leave you hangin'
Real friends would do
Almost anything for you.
If you have one
you are lucky
There's not many out there.

Amanda Brandle

All That Is Left

When all that's left of day
are tarnished silver bands
of western light, when a rush of night
stirs thoughts with cool hands
and a last bird calls,
we follow ourselves
through a dimly lighted hall
to a childhood porch
where Cracker-Jack treasures were lost
between worn boards.
The swing's creak and screen door's sigh
send a man's silhouette
to hover in our memory
with his glowing cigarette and low voice.
He never grew old or fumbled words.
He fell away, a lost star
our upturned faces tried to wish upon.
As we feel the robe of sleep enfold us,
we go to our beds
groping our way, no father to hold us.

Elaine Emmett

"Words"

The words not spoken...
Are tearing us apart...
Breaking up our hearts...
Keeping us apart.
Each tear is shed...
Is a tear unheard...
Not a word is said...
Yet, each of us is broken.
No matter how we try...
We must not lie...
Cause surely we'd die.
We must let each other know...
What's hidden deep inside.
The love we have is so strong...
It's worth one more try...
For you and I.

Dawn L. Ball

Inside-Out

Inner peace and solitude
Are what I'm searching for.
Some time to be all by myself,
To pad along the shore.
Breathing in the salt sea air,
Spying birds that soar.
Kicking shells I ask myself,
"What am I here for?"
"Just, what am I here for?"

I think I want to be alone.
"Just leave me be," I shout.
The brisk salt breeze picks up my cry,
As soon as it is out.
I spot a friend along the beach.
This jars me from my pout.
To share with someone, all of this.
That's what it's all about.
Yes, that's what it's all about.

Julie E. Colyer

Untitled

I float...
arms outstretched in supplication
Suspended...
between heaven and earth

Hovering....
motionless against the sky

As if...
I am already crucified

Time bleeds away...
... Abandoned hopes

The distance is too great...
... empty space in my heart

I...

Daniel C. Awkward Jr.

UMIandIRU

A flush of the cheek
As a thought dances through

(IMI
and
URU)

Your smell, skin does reek
Your hair something soft too

(UMI
and
URU)

Body fluids leak
Sweet moans utter anew

(UMI
and
IRU)

Debra Angeline Walkush

"Experience"

Regina danced when she was two
As buttercups and daffodils do,
Spirited, frail, naively bold.
Her hair a ruffled crest of gold,
And whenever she spoke,
Her voice went singing,
Like water up from a fountain springing,
But now her step is quiet and slow.
She walks the way the prim roses go,
Her hair is yellow instead of guilt
Her voice is losing its lovely lilt
And in place of her wild delightful ways
A quaint precision rules her days,
For Regina now is three, and oh,
She knows so much she did not know.

Dorothea McGee

Untitled

There once was a clown
who lived in this town
with a big furry wig
and a potbelly pig
she scurried all around

Megan E. Way

Vengeance Is Mine

If I was a bird
   I'd sit in a tree
And nest on the folks
   Who mess with me.

Madeleine Sophie

Lakeland

Golden sands embrace these shores
as crystalline seas open up to infinity
Magnificent barren mounds
ancient, blazed bronze
Duneland love lore;
Carl Sandburg did saunter here,
"The Birthplace of Ecology"
Senator Paul Douglas of Illinois;
circa late 1930's, on a moonlit eve,
"took an oath" to save Indiana's
Duneland coastline from the
pollution of progress,
Industrial regression passed.
Wooded Pines, paths, trails endure
A Piper skips it's graceful prance
Peaceful spirits come here to rest,
A Cardinal chirps loud atop a Sycamore;
Forevermore revere these shores
sands lost in time.

John Vincent Brozman

Marriage

Lives often combine,
as golden strands on the loom,
twisting and twining,
with God the Father as the weaver.
His hands shaping the pattern,
that is love.

Threads are added,
various colors of the friends and times.
What once was a beginning
now assumes a new shape
and changed by sharing
grows stronger.

Then it is done,
this labor of love and holiness.
He holds up his handiwork,
admires it and cherishes it.
For He sees the cloth is beautiful,
and now it is whole.

Brian D. Baumgard

The Sage And The Sparrow

He watches the boy run
as he tries to catch the sun
'tis only he
that can set the sun free

And he,
an old man
stares into the still valley
barely walking when he can
and always dreaming of being free

Dreaming of chasing the sun
He knows
that one day
again
He will run!

James L. Nash

Of Dreams And Nightmares

Once upon a summers night
As I lay sleeping in my bed
I woke up suddenly with fright
And an awful throbbing in my head

I don't know the reason why
Was it a nightmare or a dream
I felt as if I wanted to cry
Or let out a big scream

As I lay there thinking
And trying to forget
I felt like my life was sinking
And full of regret

I don't know what was on my mind
Or what was going through it
Was the dream sorry or kind
I can't remember it one bit

Dreams and nightmares can be very bad
They can also be very good
Dream and nightmares can be very sad
They can also put you in a happy mood

Daniel McNeill

Untitled

The murky water laps against the dock
as I try to see my reflection;
try to find myself.
I am greeted by only the misty
darkness of the river below.
To think of leaving is ever so easy.
But then I think of him.
If I left, he too would have water,
However, not murky,
only salty.
Salty tears to fall from his eyes
if I were to leave, he said.
My options are before me.
If I choose the murky water,
he will have water that is salty.
Slowly I turn and head towards home,
realizing both of our lives would be better
with a little less water.

Jennifer Butler

The End

The silence thundered in my head
   as I watched you walk away,
While the echo of your voice
   bounced off the chamber of my thoughts.

And a great expanse of emptiness
   replaced the throbbing heartbeat
   of the love we'd shared.

I feel dead inside as my body
   attempts the motions of the living.
But you'll never be aware of these
   feelings of mine—-

I won't let you see my pain.

Barbara R. McDonald

"Bunny Under A Blanket"

I feel toasty and warm,
as if I were a caterpillar in a cocoon,
awaiting for the magic moment of time,
When I turn into a beautiful, colorful
butterfly.

The blanket holds my ears up in the air,
As they sway back and forth,
like a bee moving from side to side,
and flower to flower.

I close my eyes,
in peaceful and stillness.
I lay there asleep in the dark,
like a raccoon in it's den,
all alone,
and no one to turn to.

Danielle Forshee

Untitled

Shadows have passed
   As shadows shall fall
Dreams to come true
   Flow to rivers of pain
Yesterdays sorrows
   As raindrops on rose petals
A precious secret
   A precious place
Earned by a tear
Tender struggles
   Now gentle sunsets
A touch, a look
   Known only through one
A strength found
   Only in love
      Only in You.

Cassie DeMonde

The Race Track

The fumes and smoke
As the car flies past
Racing around
With the smell of gas

Engines roaring
Tires blowing out
With excitement and energy
The crowd will shout.

Screeching and screaming
The brakes will cry
Once it hits the guard rail
The pieces will fly.

Round and around
In circles it goes
Who will win?
Nobody knows!

Jennifer Teschner

Untitled

Peace, nobility, liberty.
War, fear, hostility.
Change, revolution, rearrange.
Our world - how strange.

Natasha Stewart

Chance

I met you before
as the sun was going down.
I searched for my heart
and in your arms, I found...

The warmth of a hug
or a passionate kiss.
As we leave alone
I already do miss.

I look forward for night
and forget the day.
Just to see your face
that very same way.

I cry for your love
but you don't for me
What did I do wrong?
Cause, I just can't see.

You turn away
at that final glance.
But I ask you again
for that one last chance.

Colleen Christensen

When Children Pray

Angel's wings lay so silent,
As the voice of one dear child,
Prays to God up in heaven,
Sweet gesture, meek and mild.
The child ask for guidance,
Love and blessings for his friends,
Food for all starving people,
And broken homes to be mend.
Angels shake their heads confused,
For the future they have seen,
How children grow into adults,
No longer on God, they lean.
How many times they've seen it,
Hatred, pillage, mocking sore,
Because adults no longer pray,
Or believe in God anymore.
But now the angels linger near,
Guarding this precious soul,
Learning of this selfless love,
And wishing it would never go.

Debra L. Savrtka

There Comes The Snow

Here comes the snow
As the winds blow
Although there is no storm
It sure isn't warm!

The birds fly south
As I put hot cocoa in my mouth
Oh how I wish it were summer
Winter is such a bummer!

I'm going to freeze
From the winter breeze
Get me inside
So I can hide
From the snow
And the winds blow

Jessy N. Reed

One Breathless Night

The full moon is ascending
As the winter descends.
The night is all but breathless
As I stand watching the
Shadows of the trees in the moonlight.
Seemingly deaf, I listen to the
Silence of the wintering forest.
Thoughtful, I catch my breath
To find myself
One closer to my last!
Then I pray to myself,
Trying to hide from sin in the
Darkness of fear, to live my life alone,
Without you!

Brian Stellinga

Broken Love

My world fell apart tonight,
As these words he spoke to me.
"All good things must end tonight,
We must go our separate ways."
"This is not easy for me,
For I know not what to say,
I know what we have said my dear,
And yes they stand the same."

I knew not what to say to him,
Nor did I say a word.
But that was not enough for him,
For he had to say some more.
"I only need a little while,
Just time to think things through."

"Please don't get me wrong tonight,
for you are not to blame."
"I know you will cry my dear, for I will do
the same."
"I know this is not easy for you,
Nor is it easy for me, but that's all I know to do."

Bridget Lynn Cheek

A Home

A home is a place we treasure
as we meander along life's way,
and for some a thankful measure
of joy at the end of each day.

For 'tis here we find devotion
by family and friends alike,
with love and genuine emotion
which no hearty man could dislike.

But for those without relations
and love to nourish their souls,
poor homes can lead to temptations
with grief that may thwart life's goals.

So build your haven with great care
as you chart your course ahead,
and the rewards will far out-share
the miseries we all so dread.

Glenn A. Swanson

Wake Up

A morning star shines
Aside the great maple tree,
Azure sky background
Grace snowy mountain peaks...
The buzz of the human hive
Has not yet begun
The riot unfolds
At the light of the sun.

Busy in the flight
All our daily routines
Scar the nature
Of the entire theme.

Bred to progress,
Bred to compete...
Synthetic tradition,
Nothing unique.

In what direction are we going,
In all reality?
I rise early to worship
Each star that I see.

Catherine Mary Wolford

April

As our body wakes refreshed
At the dawning of each day
Looking forward to our duties
And the pleasures of our play
So the earth shakes off it's slumber
At the spring time of the year
Spreading myriad mariposas
Bringing people heart-felt cheer

Cleansing rains, like needle-showers
Drench and drive the film a-far.
Rays of sunshine warm earth's mantle
Urging plants to rise and star
On the stage of mother nature
It's the show time of the year
And for each of us who view it
We thank God that we are here.

James E. Martin

Red River Vision

I gaze out over the vastness
at the edge of Red River Canyon
and I watch the clouds embrace
and the eagle dance with the sky.

I see the wind run quickly
and the tumble weeds follow
as the grass waves hello
to the river on it's merry way

I stand and watch
as the sun bows to the moon
and the stars begin to sparkle
and the night wakes from the day.

The creatures of the night
frolic and play
as water talks to stone
and the wind makes love to the coming rain.

And as I think of her
my heart dances
like trees in the wind
under the Moon of Strawberries

Jason Nation

Untitled

I Look
At the World
Through a
Clear Glass
Cracked in
The Corner
I View
My Life
Through
Brown Eyes
Opened
By Pain
I Breathe
With Lungs
Constricted
By the Air
Of Oppression
I Speak
With Words
Covering Anger

Diane C. Thompson

The Fairies Of The Moon And Stars

The fairies of the midnight hours
Awaken from their sleeping flowers

They hang the moon up in the skies
And put to bed the butterflies

Sprightly dancing, they will sprinkle
Diamond dust to make stars twinkle

The laughter of the fairy throngs
Combines with chirping cricket songs

When the horizon dawns deep reds
The fairies nestle in their beds

They lay their heads upon their pillows
Of queen Anne's lace and pussy willows

Alongside the cradle they will keep
Dream-dust to help their babies sleep

Until the moon glows in the night
When fairy wings again take flight

Eileen Emily Chollet

Jesus Came To Me Today

Jesus came to me today, and wiped
away my tears, he said to me why
do you cry you have nothing to fear,

There is not a problem nor to big or
small, tell all the one's that love me
I am your all in all. You may not
understand my works, or all of my
great power, just see me as a rosebud
or even a beautiful flower.

I'm your light in darkness, the star
that shine so bright, look up my child
don't look so sad just follow the guided
light.

He ask what do you think of me? I said
I think you're swell, he said my child
go on now, I think you've done quite well.

So hold your head up high my child, and
do not walk in fear, just hold on to my
hands and know I'm always near.

Cherie C. Hamilton

Mexico

With a pretty little lass I know
Away we go to the gulf
Down to the gulf of Mexico
Where the warm breezes blow it's fiesta:
Singing, laughter, fun time
And dancing in the street
With each and everyone you meet

Then—back to the little lass
Waiting on the gulf
Down on the gulf of Mexico
I depart with the girl of my heart

Come another day for sun, fun and play
Down on the gulf
Down on the gulf of Mexico

Gladys L. Cooley

October Moment

Alone in space guided by the wind,
basking in the sun.
Watching, waiting, listening
for a signal to dive.

Images of grey and white and black
go drifting by
taking up the space
only for a moment.

Take-off is smooth, the sun on my back
the skies clear
the winds strong.

Sitting alone,
taking glimpses of you
inside myself.
Calling out to you
screeching, crying, screaming,
your name.

Images of you
here in a solitary moment.

Anne Richards

Joyful Mystery

Mary, Angel Gabriel,
"Be not afraid!"
The Annunciation.
Prepare in joy and hope and wonder.

Mary and Elizabeth,
"Be not afraid."
The Visitation!
Prepare in joy and hope and wonder.

Angels, Shepherds, Kings,
"Be not afraid."
He's born in Bethlehem!
Rejoice in faith and love and splendor.

Jesus, Mary, Joseph,
"Be not afraid."
Presentation in the temple!
Love is faith and joy and splendor.

Jesus, priests and scribes,
"Be not afraid."
He teaches in the temple!
Love in faith and joy and splendor.

Grace Dupuis Hunt

Music

Music - jovial, delightful, happy,
　Beautiful and harmonious.
Flowing from the lips of many,
　Entering the ears of the open.
Listen to the rhythm.
　It meanders and pervades through
　our interminable minds.
It soothes us.
　It frees us from our stressful lives.
It is our daily incentive.
　We thrive to keep music alive,
In body, mind, soul, and heart.
　What would the world be like
　without music?
Our lives would be dull and despondent.
　We'd be in a state of turmoil and
　seclusion,
And eventually wilt as flowers do
　When deprived of their crucial need -
water,
And us - music.
　　　　Jonelle Baker

I Am Black And Beautiful

Black and beautiful
Beautiful I stand
Proud and healthy
It is all in my skin
I am beautiful and
Black smiling I stand
Thank God I am
Black and beautiful that
Is what I am.
　　　Chauntell Lanee Pullman

Tassajara

You can tell it is summer
because the roar of the spring melt
has been shushed to a babble.

Dry mountain air
parches your throat
and no amount of water
seems to quench your thirst.

Sandled feet trudge
silently to and fro
dusting your limbs.

All is soft and mellow here—
sulfurous pool in which to plunge
shadows against kerosene lit walls
cushions on which to sit and meditate
breeze wafting cooking sounds and smells
sauna opening pores
rocks on which nudes sprawl
your kisses bedding me down.
　　　Carissa Schlosser

Sands of Time

A perfect moment....
　At the beach
The sun sets colored..
　In amber hue
The sand tingles silkily...
　Upon touch,
A kiss so soft, so right...
　So sweet.
A perfect moment...
　In my heart.
　　　Angela L. Henry

Ignition

Spark ignites spark and
becomes flame.

Flame folds into flame and
becomes fire.

The fire burns and rises dancing
against the dark, raging against
the cold.

Only thru such seething intensity
can your spirit finally unfold.

Fire goes back to flame, flame goes
back to spark leaving your glowing
embers shining through the dark.
　　　Catherine Oram

Daybreak

Bodies melting in the sweat
Being one is coming yet

Sexy smells throughout the space
Looking at each other's face

Parts assemble inside out
Passions pleading, murmured shouts

Hands use fingers to linger on
Pleasing circles that mesh till dawn

Daybreak brings a glistening steam
From the heart for feelings mean

Love conceives a new born child
Life from love fulfills the while

Hearts beat wild to syncopate
Another session to copulate

Love me now while I can't seem
To understand it was all a dream.
　　　Jamal Wells

The Shaking

With the ground shaking
Beneath my feet
Where can I go
To make my dreams complete

With polarized thinking
Playing tug or war
Leaving little hope
For peace in the core

Is there no place
In the heart, mind and land
Where truth calms the tension
And love quells the shaking man
　　　Frank E. Robinson Jr.

Halloween

(Written at age 7)
On the midnight hour
Things have the power
To devour.
　　　Paul Lewis

Bob

The yearbook says
"Best friends to the end."
"Best friends to the end."
But that was all then.

It's hard to believe
A friendship so strong,
Which could never go wrong
Is long since gone.

The question remains—
When a friendship dies,
What severs the ties?
The lies...the lies.

What's one more girl?
To him they're the same.
They all feel the pain.
For him, none remains.

I want to warn them
And tell them beware.
But they wouldn't care.
They wouldn't dare.
　　　Jeff Sandler

No Fear

Devil's arithmetic, pure poison,
beware of the danger,
a thief of time.

Heart, never say die.
Fly with wings,
never fear, trial by fire.

Hate, recipe for murder,
may take you over the edge,
into the shadows.

Heart, never say die.
　　　Dominic R. Johnson

A Credit to Honor

(Home: A Loan)
Once, the stage was set
　beyond Two Presidents and a King —
(Where GOODWILL, TRUST and HONOR cast
　the common character.)
Anyone could buy a ticket to
　the daily matinee,
Including the local assassin...

Now, the assassin
　owns the well-connected theatre —
(He traded one of many guns
　for the new projector.)
No one's selling tickets, but the show
　is all sold-out, they say,
Despite the bullet holes in the screen...
　　　Daniel C. Meadows

Journey

a false horizon...upon it
brilliant light descending
upon green fertility
consuming first the heart
then the soul

within lies
one-ness with nature's eternity
creating a pinnacle...a-top
it you lie
consumed by ecstasy
　　　David J. Spiess

Winds

On the wings of the wind
Birds float and glide,
Soaring gleefully ever so high.

On the wings of the wind
Leaves dance down,
Softly, gently to the ground.

On the wings of the wind
Winter came,
Bringing a cold and icy rain.

On the wings of the wind
I hear a sigh.
Life is over, the earth must die.

On the wings of the wind
Spring blew in,
Life renewed, once again.

Carole Ranney

"Red"

Burns like fire
Bleeds like blood
Crimson Tide
Flowing over me
Feeding my desire
Setting me free
Kiss me - kill me
What will it be?
Red is total power
And it's devouring me
feel the heat - let it
Soak your skin
Fueling the desire
Deep within
Close your eyes
And try to hide
But there is no denying
We are all red
Inside-

Gwendolyn Janine Davis

Feeling Color

The gray sky matched the mood
Blue sky smile
And the sun is a path
Gold and free
And suppress desire
Things just happen
He pushes me
The gray is the feeling
Reasons we will never see
We throw the gray at each other
Because feeling is too strong
Clouds cover the blue
And perhaps always will

Aimee Raffiani

Dogs

White, black, brown, gray,
Every day dogs will play.
Huskies, terriers, poodles, hounds,
Don't let any of them go to the pound.
Sweet and cuddly, playful too,
They also whine when they are blue.
Different sizes, different shapes,
I think all of them are very great!

Alexandra Edgar

Knowing The Difference

Drugs cure, drugs kill
Take care, be aware
To know the difference.

Marsha Blyth

Persimmons

Soft and lush
Browning brush
Chamber waiting on the ground.
Plump and prime
Destined time
Jewels drop without a sound.

Small and fair
Answered prayer
Ocher treasures now abound.
Wild and sweet
Tangy treat
Autumn's beauty God has crowned.

Harolyn Pinson

This Land, Dark, Desolate, And Dead

The world has now expired,
Burned and destroyed in eternal fire,
Everyone's death and funeral pyre,
This Land, Dark, Desolate, and Dead.

Moans, shouts, screams of pain,
The air is filled with death and decay,
Many bodies burnt but still remain,
This Land, Dark, Desolate, and Dead.

Is there hope, is there faith,
No one can say on this morbid day,
All is thrashed, all is blown away,
This Land, Dark, Desolate, and Dead.

The Apocalypse has now occurred,
Visions of the past are just a blur,
The land is still, not a stir,
This Land, Dark, Desolate, and Dead.

Brent W. Sanders

"Dedicated To A Memory"

The words written on this page are only
but a few, for life with all its ups
and downs has much to offer you. For
if you seek the inner things that money
cannot buy, you'll find a step on
which to build a stairway to the sky.
Your dreams are one of many that life
will offer you, remember though, that
all the time your dreams may not come
true. Yet don't give up or turn away
keep moving toward your goal and life
will always offer you a gift worth more
than gold. And also seek that inner
love that all of us possess, for it can
always help you rise and soar above
the rest. Believe in you thru thick
and thin and always keep in mind.
In "you" will be no greater "Love" or
"Friend" in which to find.

Iris Williams

No End

People come and go
but a friend never says no
In the end
Everyone needs a friend
If ever you do
Say me
and I'll say you
Together we'll say we
and our relationship will survive
with life to strive
Fate will take you away
and cause many tears on that day
But forever I'll be there
no matter what...I swear
People come and go
but a friend will never say no
We will be friends
even if there's an end

David Shannon

The Moon And Me

I look for the moon,
But all I see is
A cloudy sky.
I can barely make
Out the shape of the moon.
It's as if the clouds
Have imprisoned it,
And it's trying so hard
To be seen.
I feel one with the moon,
For I am imprisoned too;
Not by clouds, but by myself.
I want to be seen,
I want to be heard,
But my evil self won't let that be.
I need to free myself
Of these invisible bonds,
So I can shine like
The Moon.

Emily Sue Clifton

Angels

Perhaps you cannot see them
But believe me, they are there
We often entertain them
Though we may be unaware.

They join us in our laughter
They whisper words of cheer
In our darkest hour they are there
To wipe away our tears.

Warriors of the highest realm
They fight our unseen foe
Guarding the hearts entrusted to them
We, his children, here below.

They tend our bedside while we sleep
They watch, they wait, they care
From God's hands they shower blessings
When we bow our heads in prayer.

Mighty beings that protect us
Reaching out to us in love
Ministering spirits of gentleness
Messengers sent down from above.

Glenna McDaniel

"Love Versus Evil"

Evil oft' comes cloaked in beauty fair,
but beware,
love be not there.

Evil thrusts its greedy hand
to pillage and plunder
throughout the land,
without a care,
so just beware,
love be not there.

Evil casts out love,
and givith hate and despair,
beyond compare,
so please beware,
love be not there.

Evil and love cannot co-exist
so beware, and take care,
spread love everywhere.

Joan Reego Gully

But....

Life seems brief
    But can be eternal
Death appears final
    But begins the beyond
Sight seems precious
    But wisdom is divine
Hearing is desirable
    But knowing is supreme
Speaking is artful
    But silence is virtuous
Singing is stirring
    But laughter binds it all.

Billy Abrams

Uncover

My fears,
But dreams,
Have stayed,
But have gone,
For all of too long.

My smiles,
Are lies,
That have got to end,
Sometime,
But not anytime soon.

To be gone,
Is all I ask,
But I have no say,
Of what's yet to be,
Of my yesterday.

Emily-Jo Bembenek

From Deep Inside

For he can't explain why he knows
    but he knows
Something he can't see
    but he hears
Something he can't touch
    but he feels
For he searches
Not knowing what for
Knowing he must search
Finding what he must find

Duane D. Slaski

Ties That Bind

It was a tiny crack
But I slipped out
Free
To reconstruct
My version of me
Sans family tree
Or so I thought
But dragged the
Whole redoubt
Behind me
To dismantle
Stone by stone
Tone by tone
All my life
Walls of judgment
That bound me.

Hallie Burton

Love

Love: Can be great,
    But it can break;
Love: will be strong,
    And last how long;
Love: will be kind,
    But play with the mind;
Love: is in the heart,
    Why does it smart;
Love: will go deep,
    Knock you off your feet;
Love: is so tender,
    But watch the danger;
Love: can take your breath away,
    And also go astray;
Love: shall be gentle,
    How much is mental;
Love: may turn into hate,
    Should we call this fate;
Love: good or bad,
    We have to have.

Carol L. Avery

Angels

There are so many angels
But none so dear to me,
As love that cast the sunshine
And lights so well the sea,
An angel with a special love
To spread throughout the seas
And care for all the lonely ones,
Who can't be here with me.

"I saw a lonely angel child
She cried 'til her tears ran dry,
She cared so much....
Her heart could break;
For the one she loved, had died!"

The sunshine came, dried all her tears
Rainbows brightened up her life,
She cries no more, for her lost seas,
She has found happiness...
"In being your wife!"

Char M. Hare

Someone To Turn To

Someone to turn to,
but nowhere to go.
By now, you know
my life's a joke.

Someone to turn to,
but I don't know when.

Someone to turn to,
is my last real friend.

Someone to turn to,
their life's the same
for the love she gave
was done in vain.

Someone to turn to,
with all my wrongs.
Knowing she'll be by me
to help me along

Someone to turn to
without thinking twice
I'm just glad
God brought her into my life.

Elizabeth Horton

People

People have many faces and names. Oh,
But people play so many games. They
Have troubles and they have fears.
When people cry, You'll usually see
Tears.

Whom can they turn to when their skies
Are grey and other people have gone
Their own way? Pick up the phone,
That'll do the trick. Then comes the
Hard part, Which person do they pick?

If a person is deaf and cannot hear,
Will people speak to them and make
themselves clear? If they cannot
Speak and their face looks grim, Will
People read their lips and listen to
Them?

Well, whom can they turn to if they
Cannot see? Except for different
People, Like you or me.

Donald Elton Hatcher

A Treasure

He's a man,
but really a little boy inside.
When I was down,
he made me so happy that I cried.

When feelings of despair
came over me,
he made a change so desperately.

Across my path
inadvertently he crossed —-
making my life significantly so.

There's no other like him;
I hope he knows it well,
because he saved me from doubting hell.

May God have him a special corner
in heaven to rest,
as gratitude for helping me to pass life's
test.

Eunice Negron

Christmas

Who would have known
but the poor and needy.
What it is like
without family or friends,
presents or gifts.
Who would have known
what is really going on.
Who would have known
people are dying while we sing of joy.
Who would have known
that one day
you could be that person
waiting in that line for
food.

Christopher A. Saikus

True Love

I drifted away from reality
But your words were so convincing
True love sounded so good until I learned
That love brings pain
Both inside and out
When it isn't taken seriously
You said it was love
But I only felt pain
Trying to save you from destroying
All that you were
I let you destroy me and spare yourself
It was true love, right?
Now that we have parted
I try with all my deepest feelings
To hate you
And everything we've shared
But I know I never can
Because you were the one who showed me
The pain and sorrow of my only
True love

Jennifer Odum

Sadness Of The Heart

Rain starts drop
by drop
Then flows more
freely.

Thunder crashes and
shakes the earth
Lightning flashes
in the sky.

Rain ends as it came
then soft stripes of
color show gently
in the sky.

Andrea L. Ward

The Beauty Will Show

How does one grow without love?
Can anyone answer that!
Do you grow or die. You grow,
but also die many times
What type of person do you
become, very strong but angry.
And later, lost and alone.
Compare the person with a cactus,
little love, little water,
no nurturing, no weeding,
the rains came, the love came,
BEHOLD THE CACTUS FLOWER

Geraldine W. King

Behind These Eyes

People show or tell what they are
By the look in their eyes.

A man may be inspired by his
Intelligent mind.

Another man shows that he is
Soft and tender.

Behind other eyes you see
A face that is drawn
And looks much older than she is.

Some eyes are filled with tears
And the face is bronzed
From their sting.

You may see a glow
As bright as the light of the sun.
Behind these are emotions of
Love, faith, admiration and tenderness

Sometimes these eyes show that
They want to talk to others,
And, sometimes, after talking
This person feels better.

Gretchen L. Josephson

The Measure Of A Man

What does it take for a man to be
    called a man?
Is it his wealth or position that
    determines this plan?
Or is it his will to achieve his dream
    that's worth seeing?
That man is eventually measured as to his
    worth as a being.

Is man measured in worth by his
    ability to get a job?
Or can we weigh his merits by
    friends gathered 'round in a mob?
Are pleasantries of value to anyone
    whose life he touches?
Or do we perceive measurement as the
    amount of possessions he clutches?

When all is said and done what will this
    creature be remembered for?
Will the sum total of his equity be
    the measure of his very core?

Joey Kelly

The Dearest Time Of All

Descending slowly
From love's
Dizzying heights
We cling
Together still
The frenzied emotions
Turning now
To peaceful ones
The dearest time
Of all
Between two lovers
When souls are bared
And trust is
At a premium
Such lovely talks
And laughter
Weaving enduring
Love ties
Between us.

Barbara A. Evans

Wind

The wind
can be
a moaning ghost,
or a
joyous angel
singing.

The wind
is ferocious
and unfeeling;
the wind
is gentle
and soothing.

It seems
that the
wind is a
creature
whose feelings
are always
hidden.

Carrie Louise Higley

Life

Life with no reason;
Can end in any season.
    Life with no gain;
    Is continuously full of pain.

Life with no love;
Has no meaning from above.
    Life with no trust;
    Will eventually make you lust.

What is life without all this?
    No life can survive without a reason;

Without gain, without love,
And life surely can't survive;
    With just fortune and fame.

Life has many reasons;
It has been for many seasons.
    Life is what you make of it;
    And I know that is for sure.

Life can be beautiful; and life can be sad; but,
Life with a lot of worldly things,
    Is just as good as none.

Even Mae Mathis

Fading

Can I just cry?
Can I shed a tear?
Why do I hold back?
What do I fear?
You'll never notice
You don't care
Why do I worry?
I see your blank stare
Something's missing
The love we had
I can't find it
And I want it so bad
The music plays softly
And I think of you
My spirit drowns
I don't know what to do
I fear the future
Live in the past
Let me shed a tear
For all that's fading fast.

Ayanna Widner

Losing The Battle

In the casket her best friend lay,
cause all the feelings she couldn't
display;

Many of her feelings were shared
with a friend, but none of them
seemed to come to an end;

Weeks dragged on like months and
years, though every night she cried
with tears;

She felt as if she had no one, still
searching desperately for someone;

Bearing the feelings deep inside,
she knew no longer could she hide;

So with a knife she laid in bed, and
decided to take her life instead;

Now you must take one day at a time,
and leave the grief far behind;

Then go on with your life, never to
forget her sacrifice.

Gwen Hobbs

Woke Up Crying

Woke up crying again this morning
'cause I went to sleep dreaming of you

It's been over for a long time
But I can't get you off my mind
Your face and voice still haunt me
chasing my soul cross the night sea

Why can't I cut you loose
or at least call a truce
over the battle raging inside
But I can't, I know, I've tried

Woke up crying again this morning
'cause I went to sleep dreaming of you

I love you, I hate you
Sometimes it's both — what's new
I can't get you out of my head
so I kick and squirm in my bed

Now I'm afraid to go to sleep
and let you get into me deep
If I dare to close my eyes,
will you come and tantalize.

David C. Isgur

Perspective

Perspective, it always seems to me,
Causes us to disagree;
I think one way and think I'm right,
You think another and start a fight.
But, if you really think it through,
I am right and so are you.
Just because we see things differently,
Need not mean our discontent.
Perspective isn't right or wrong;
Nor a sign of weak or strong;
Only that your mind can't see
What I know the truth to be.

Angeline Bender

Your Funny Facade

Genuine simplicity
clashing with conformity
in understated attire
like an unspoken satire
your resolute stance
lends just a whisper of a chance
just like the idea of you and me
things are seldom what they seem to be
never only what we see

the nonchalance that carried you through
when silence sought a word or two
caught me off guard
then a few seconds past
at least it didn't last

with a smitten kiss
too charming to dismiss
a poem fades
our gem is restless

Jennifer Rich

Our Recipe...

First you take both you and I
combining both our souls.
Then you add a little warmth
so neither would be cold.

Take five cups of happiness
and fill up both our hearts.
But add a dash of loneliness
to feel when we're apart.

Then you add a scoop of trust
so we wouldn't be afraid.
To follow through any plans
that either of us made.

Finally add a bunch of love
and now your mixture's done.
Let it simmer through the years
as two hearts form as one.

Christopher J. Harbeck

Life So Precious

Life is just a flickering moment
Compared to eternity,
We cannot put a price on it
The value we cannot see.

When we start each morning,
Be thankful for every breath,
We must make each day count
Get going and do our best.

We must be kind to each other
Whomever we may meet,
For they may not be having a good day,
Instead a bad defeat.

We should strive to meet our goals
And encourage others too,
It won't be an easy road
But we don't have to sing the blues.

We should try to be joyful
In all that we say and do,
Remembering life is just a flickering
moment
Our best we should strive to do.

Elaine Benchoff

Untitled

Overcast above me.
Cool breeze passing by,
On a summers day in May.
Little voices laughing all around.

Birds in the trees
Singing so gay.
Children playing, having fun
Mothers eyes watching out,
Families together reaching out.

Now the sun shines on me
Puts a glow in mine eyes,
What a peaceful afternoon
A wonderful feeling inside.

Some people don't realize
Sometimes, how nature can be so kind
Boys walking dogs
Teenagers playing ball.
The life around us we take for granted day
to day.
The best things in life are free, we just don't
accept them.

Judy Martin

The World Is Fake

Look Around You

Pink skies, black oceans, white air
crayon green grass
reflects off my shades
at the man-made stadium
fluorescent fish
bait the fisherman's hook
machines wonder
how your day went
children remain indoors
forest's pathways, untouched,
pure under fresh snow
trees shiver off dead bark
surrogate mother
gives birth to grandson
granddad's retired now
running marathons
uncle ned is still in Leavenworth
awaiting parole
as aunt edna visits
bringing gifts of Lucky Strikes

Carmina Amezcua Towe

Special One

Did you know God above
created you for me to love.
He picked you out from
all the rest, because he knew
I would love you best.
If I should go to heaven
before you do. I will write
your name upon the golden stairs.
So the angels they
can see how much you
mean to me.

Annette Feichko

I Am

People of Earth I am your God.
Creator of all things unto all
ages. I gave your fathers my
laws of life in ages past.
They will endure for ever.
Remember people of earth from
dust I fashioned you and to the
bowels of the earth you will
return. My laws are for ever.
Do not transgress them. They are
over and above the laws of your
finite nature. You who turns and
twists my laws to your own ends
be fore-warned these transgressions
will not go un-answered as you
pass from life to death. Remember
my people, I AM

Arthur L. Andre

Afraid

Fading promises. Dirtied dreams.
Cursed fear of the other man.
He screams at the one man.
He puts his mind in disarray.

Beaten, head down. Drenched
In rains of doubt.
Shamed. Guild. Blinded by the clout
Of the other man.

Bitter cries. Bleeding heart.
Unheard calls for help. Seeds
Of incertitude. The other man feeds
To the one man death.

Touches and caresses. Little and
Little, he takes his guard away.
Tosses and teases. Soon done with sway,
He leaves him to the mud.

He crawls. He runs.
He thinks out loud.
Feared reared head in the crowd,
And breaking from making.

Christian Kunle Awogbade

Untitled

Was I Rocking?
Daddy's not crying.
His brother won't stop.
His sister repeats,
I should have been here,
I should have come sooner,
It's my fault.
Don't cry, calm down.
Take deep breaths.
My chest hurts,
I can't breathe.
Am I rocking?
Do you want to kiss
grandma goodbye?
NO.
I can't.

Erica Williams

Forever Free

Velvet beneath me,
Dark sky above me,
How could he be,
Although he takes me,

To wondrous places,
I have never seen,
To places a heart,
Thought never had been?

We run together,
Across starry plains,
But when I tire,
He never complains,

He is tonight,
And forever will be,
A bright, wild unicorn,
Forever free.

Abigail Darcey

Jessica

She ran free with somber thoughts
darker than night.

Passing time through the present
with little reserve.

Tempted for happiness that surpasses
one's right.

Taking in excess beyond most
courage and nerve.

Her stir felt upon each whose
paths by chance unite.

She was Jessica, her love to
many would serve.

Dan Snook

School Of Our Happy Childhood

O school of our happy childhood!
Dear friends of each youthful heart!
We pause awhile on Life's threshold
As the tears unbidden start —

For truly the years have woven
Among us love's magic spell,
Since first we entered your portal
And now bid you fond farewell.

May life bring joys, with sorrows few,
And to all success and fame.
When my hair has turned to silver
I will love you just the same.

Our class sang my poem above
High School graduation day.
Though my hair has now turned silver
I still feel that love today.

Hulda Sellingsloh

Flowers Grow in Spring

Flowers grow in spring
like a colorful rainbow
in the cloudy sky

Nichole Garcia

Snow

Snow drops to the ground
   as soft as a child's dream...
      with whispers and wonders
         so pleasant the gleam
Kelli Latchem

Life

Life before Death?
Death after Life.
It seems not that way to me!
Death has come.
Death has gone.
He has not yet taken my soul!
He has tried.
He has lost.
Over my soul he has no control.
God favors me in this one,
Just till my mission is done.
Until then sorry Death,
I'm stayin' right here, at home.

Emily Atkeison

Grandpa Loved Christmas

Grandpa loved Christmas
Decorating was his specialty
Thousands of lights and his
Personal touches made Grandpa's
House the place to be.

Grandpa loved Christmas
'Twas always plain to see
With angels on the awnings and
Christmas Village under the tree.

Grandpa loved Christmas
And giving presents to all he'd see
From the youngest to the oldest
There was always two or three.

Yes, Grandpa loved Christmas
And tho he's not with us here today
His spirit still lives on
In that Christmas Village far away.

Jaime L. Ingram

The Darkened Soul

The black cape of night
descends upon me swiftly...
The hour when I become alive
approaches, oh so quickly.
Gone, will be all of my
harsh feelings of despair.
And once again I'll know
what it means to care.
I know this for a fact,
for I have done so in the past.
I will prey on the innocent
for I have no control.
You see, it is an evil thing
which possesses my darkened soul.
My suffering is quite horrible,
though I suffer, I go on; I must.
And I shall go on until daylight
arrives and makes its final thrust.
May 5, 1988

Cheryl Ann Grimes

Nostalgia

The sight of an old barn
  Deserted and alone
In winter's sleet and snow,
  Stirs memories of a barn
I knew long ago.
  Our childish laughter
Filled the rafters
  As we played and jumped
In fragrant sun-dried hay -
  Then down the chute we went
Into the stalls below.
  So vivid are the memories
My nose begins to twitch
  With the musty barn odors
Of feed - grains in their bins -
  Of old leather tack -
Harnesses hanging on wooden pegs.
  Now I hear the jingle of their bells
As old Ned pulls the sleigh.
  Those happy days - Sweet are the
memories.

Aletha Rappaport

Definitions

A lie is linear,
direct,
pointed as far
as can be
away.

Truth's faceted,
subtle,
rich in variation,
infinitely reinterpretable.

Lies are simplistic.
They lack dimension,
vitality. Scope.

Truth
is serene.
Even terrible
truths lead
nowhere
else.

Ellen Peckham

Mommy Dreams

Sitting here alone,
dirty laundry 'round my feet.
Thanking God I finally got
my babies asleep.

Years of school and college, too.
All behind me now
as I sit and wonder
what to do.

How did all the love and dreams fade,
into the lonely place I live today?
I'm told I'm still young and pretty, too.
Sometimes it doesn't seem so,
with so many Mommy jobs to do.

I was going to change the world
and make a difference in this place.
Maybe, I will
starting with the promise in my child's face.

Jessica Clifford Farmer

Tender Journey

If myriad monarch butterflies can wing
Distances untold, fulfilling destiny...
Or a lone meteor, sustained in space
Through eons, can reach the earth;
Surely a loving thought can journey
Far, through night-misted skies
Or sun-edged clouds at dawn.

If, now and then, some fleeting sense
Comes like a stray breeze,
Elusive as moonlight on water,
Be still, my child. Receive it
Wherever you are; let it caress you
Like tendrils of fog close to shore
Enfolding you gently. Have peace...
Know, at that moment,
Love reached its journey's end.

Helen Mann Sanborn

Dreams

Are these dreams I'm having real?
  Do they express how I really feel?

What will happen when I wake?
  Will I realize that it was all fake?

Or will there be more to dream of?
  This is a question for up above.

Soon these dreams will be gone,
  I wish I knew what was
    going on!

Jennifer Bryson

Growing Old

You think birthdays are bad?
  Don't believe what you're told.
Just take it from me.
  It's great to be old!

Go to bed, or get up,
  You don't need to be told.
You can do as you please
  Now that you are old!

You can say what you think,
  You've a right to be bold.
They will listen to you,
  Because you are old!

Stay up North when its warm,
  And down South when its cold.
Have the best of both worlds,
  Because you are old!

When you see a rainbow
  Go look for the gold.
Good things often come
  To those who are old!

Esther Jensen

I Love

I love my Mom
I love my Dad
And they love me
Or I'd be sad

Jaclyn Maynard

"I Wanna Be"

I wanna be an artist, but I
  don't know how to paint.
I wanna be an actress, but I
  don't know how to faint.
I wanna be a famous author and,
  some day write a book.
I wanna be a great American chef, but
  I'll be darn if I can cook.
I wanna be a singer, but
  I can't even carry a tune.
I wanna be old enough to retire, but
  I know it's too soon.
I guess it's mighty late for all my
  dreams to come true.
So there's only one thing
  that's left for me to do.
For of all the things
  I could ever hope to be.
I'll just be happy being
  the same ole me.

June Carol Ellis

A Tear

A tear runs down my cheek
down my chin into a sea
of tears that have passed
my cheek.

I find myself drowning
in a sea of tears with no
hope, of rescue.
So I close my eyes, and give up
my long hard struggle on life.
As that last and final tear
runs down my cheek into the sea
of so many salty and lonely tears.

Ivory Jazz Mitchell

Deceit

You walk in smiling laughing
Dressed in a glimmering gold gown.
Like rays of sunshine
Coming through undressed windows
Still smiling still laughing
you turned away
Walking toward a place, I never
knew existed
I turned to look
But all I could see was blackness
Backing away, I was horrified
At the realization that I
looked deep within your soul.

Anna Pascarella

My Life Failed Twice

In my life, I failed twice
Due to the fun things in Life.
And yet it remains to be seen
In which direction my life will beam.
If I don't follow my dream.
I will never know what's on
the other side of the rainbow.
I have to reach out and not let go.
I won't let anybody tell me what
I cannot do.
Potentiality is mine.
All I have to do is exert my
energy and not waste time.

Alfreida Kay Cansler

Ice Storm

Crystal trees & diamond bushes,
Each buds & blade & branch,
Frozen into a symphony of ice,
Whose sparkling beauty
Awed us into glassy silence

An unforgettable vision,
Transient,
But transcendent in its power.
Imprisoned in the icy splendor
of our thoughts.

Arlene Cohen

Jeweled Children

My children are my jewels
Each set apart and so,
None shine more bright than others
All set my heart aglow.

As I kneel before my children
They are kings and queens I know
And rule the hearts of many
Ever high or ever low.

So I wear my crown most humbly
Love, adoration and pride
And my children can see their reflections,
On my face when their by my side.

Evelyn Hicks Antle

The Vagabond Heart

The mournful whistle of a train
Echoing across the valley of the night
pierces my heart
With a sharp, sweet pain
Of longing
For distant places I have never seen
And lovely, lonely people
I have never known
And likely never shall
Ever.

Jean McGuffey

Good-Bye, My Love

Good-bye is hard to say
especially to you.
I don't want to say the word
I don't want us to be through.
It's going to hurt me
It's gonna cause me pain.
All I want, all I wish
is that my love was not in vain.
You lifted me up,
You set me right back down.
And through it all
I thought you wore a crown.
I crowned you king,
I believed I was your queen.
Now I realize that through my eyes
the truth is hard to be seen.
Now I can see the truth
And I realize what I have to say.
This is my good-bye
Even though I love you in every single way.

Jessica Ann Johnson

Reunion

"Oh passionate moon, don't hesitate!
Eternally for you I wait
To share once more our destined date.
As one, we'll slowly nestle down
Upon Lake George's western crown."

"Tonight you're passionate with me.
Tomorrow, Jupiter you'll see,
And then with someone else you'll be...
Saturn, Uranus, Neptune, Mars,
Or one of several thousand stars."

"Your return to me is nature's will
Decided eons ago. And still,
Within yourself, could you fulfill
A love for me, as mine for you...
Inspired, undimmed, eternally true?"

"You're not to blame for what you are.
Fate might have taken you afar,
To orbit 'round a distant star.
And I, my life left unresolved,
Would never have, or have been loved."

Harry Haigh

Voices

A face calls out my name
Even now the same
As lightning struck
And thunder shook
   My world and heart asunder.

A moonbeam falls to place
A teardrop on my face
The wind rips through my hair
And weaves a golden lair
   To capture me unknowing.

The rain begins to fall
But I feel nothing at all
As I struggle through the dark
To find the secrets of my heart
   And unlock the chains that bind me.

I fall to the ground in shame
Forgotten, alone in the rain
I wait for the voice once again
And wonder at my silent friend
   Then, a face calls out my name.

Jamie Anissa Summers

In Memory Of Jeremy

You memory I keep
Even though I weep
The look in your eye
As you whispered goodbye
Good times we had
They now turn sad
You'd take me places
We'd meet new faces
Your witty charm
You did no harm
I wish I knew
Why he took you
I see your smile
I look for a while
I love you J
Why couldn't you stay

Courtney Harris

Untitled

Mother you're always near me
Even though I'm far away
You're my constant inspiration
You're my guide from day to day
God blessed our little family
When he united you and Dad.
Because you're the finest Mother
A yankee boy ever had.
The things you taught me as a child
Are with me these many years
I see your face before me
You're quickened steps are in my ears
St. Patrick chose the seventeenth
To set all Ireland free.
But the seventeenth of March
will always mean much more to me
God bless and spare you mother
May this day be filled with joy.
You're always in my thoughts and deeds
All my love from your little boy.

Edward A. Borkoski Jr.

Midwinter

Now comes the deadliest time of year
Evenings come early — morn is drear.
The brief hiatus of each day
'Twixt dark and dark, soon fades away.

But hope - remember - springs eternal:
Soon we awake to mornings vernal.

We lift our heads and feel the sun -
Acknowledge winter's course has run.
One day - indeed - we find green shoots,
And toss aside our winter boots.

Then search for flowers in the grass,
To offer them to those who pass.
While He who lights the Evening Star,
Will praise our efforts from afar.
Gently insisting we remember
That after August comes September.

Catherine D. Grafflin

About Ricky

Everyday I live my life
Everyday I have the same scare.
When I go to school
He will not be there.

As I sit here watching
The days go by,
I try real hard
Not to cry.

He had a smile
One you couldn't resist.
His jokes and laughter
I will always miss.

Everyone loved him,
Everyone cared.
He was everyone's friend
So many memories were shared.

I loved him dearly
He was one of my bestest friends.
His memory will be with me
Till the end.

Erin Durkee

Aunt Tina

An Aunt is a wonderful thing in life
Extension of our family to new Heights
Very special woman never going away
Yet a support system any day.
Learning much wisdom from her life
to make ours right
Like a shinning star
Sometimes going dim
Sadness and heartache
Comes within.
Strength enough to fight back
not taking any thing but a laugh.
Life, such a funny thing
Auntie, what a miraculous ring
small word meaning so much
Auntie on God's wings
(clutches hard to every touch)
never to fall only to achieve
Harmony in her life for Eternity.

Andrea Moritzky

The Cry Of Nowhere

The bitterness of the cold wind on his
face
He walks slowly down the street to
nowhere
No particular place
He whimpers to himself as he sees
others of his kind
Card board boxes and bonfires
keep them warm
Another baby born, but no
place to go
No where away from the
snow
Innocent children parted from
families
Nothing but cries

Elizabeth Lotito

Untitled

In a world of daydreams,
Fantasy cannot intrude.
Nature takes control and
glides you through the forbidden side.
A side where wisdom never meets reality.
As I stand in awe
Meandering across the riverside,
Tenderly running my feet through
The long green whipping grass.
When all cannot be supreme
I see you gingerly walk straight up
to me and smile.
As if the whole world intended
us to meet...
And you were my chosen angel.

Corey Zubia

The Tree

The tree is all green
Screaming for the bright sun
Peaceful nourishment

Melissa Walker

Growing Tall

Cacti growing tall
like the giraffe in the zoo
feeding off the trees

A. J. Dickinson

Fear

Sitting here watching the rain,
Feeling so, so much pain.
Why can't I see
That people care about me?
I hear what they say
I feel love coming my way,
But I remember the hurt well,
As if it had been, my turn in hell.
I feel that love now
For a voice spoke somehow.
Yet I question that voice,
As if I fear out of choice,
As if distrust was my friend,
Please, please my heart will you mend?
I feel love and caring
But my past leers a glaring.
Will that love still be there
When I wake from sleep so fair?
That, my friend, is my fear,
To you my friend, I shed a tear.

Bob Armintrout

...Of Time

Edges of time—hedges of time
Fences, walls—barriers of time
Depths of time—limits of time
The clutch, the touch of time.

Suffocates, liberates, impersonates
Mystic, but precise—gives yet takes.
Strokes, escapes—validates
The grip, the squeeze of time.

Almost, but not quite—
A fleeting without greeting
Elusive, yet to be grasped
Lost in hours—pressured by minutes.

Longing for moments—even seconds
On and on in endless cycles
Interval to interval—era to era
Synchronized in precise chasms.

Waiting—devoid of wanting
Feeling—beyond reaching
Besought on the edges—
Caught in the hedges of time.

Donna L. Bayse

Songs of Yesterday

Eagles fly. Spread wings.
Child cries. Child sings.
In the woods. On the plains.
Land destroyed. Land regained.
Open heart. Open mind.
White man came. White man blind.
People danced. People loved.
Now they fight and go above.
Songs of days past fill the night,
longing to make what went wrong—right.

Emily Jane Carroll

Mothers

We must stand tall in times of adversity
Fight for the rights of our children

Love them through their failures
Bring our hearts close to theirs

Walk in their shadows
to find we are so much alike

Let us not forget, they are children of
God with so much love to give

Only if mother's learn to forgive and
nurture that love so they may live

Without fear of redeeming themselves to
the world

Mothers need love and security
along with respect and dignity

Society must do its share to help
mothers learn to teach children well

Remember to serve our mothers of today
so they may help their children grow

And flourish into a bed of roses and
not a bush of poison ivy.

Elizabeth Fontaine-Grieco

Rebellion

Going against the grain
Fighting for recognition
As a separate human being
Looking for an answer
In all the wrong places
The need for acceptance
Flowing through youthful veins
It's all so close
A seemingly bright future
Where we will show them all
A guiding hand holds us back
And pushes us down
Beneath this hand we kick and scream
The creative human mind
Has the need to be free
To fly unyielded
Amongst individual dreams
Once placed into the morals
Of a singular society
All exhilaration of rebellion is lost.

Allene Jones

"Clean Up Our Act"

There is a time near
filled with fear,
and then,
it will strike again,
because of crime
there will be no time
to patch up the past
so it will kill us fast,
but as we go along
and keep friendship strong
we will all be saved
from that horrible, horrible day.

Jennifer Johnson

206

Embers

There are times when the
fires of life burn as embers
within my heart and I feel
I've nothing more of myself
to give

At these times
when life feels unfair
and I've lost control
of myself, my dreams
my goals

It's at these times when
I feel this way
I take a look at life
and realize I have love
to give, to receive and
as long as, there is an
ember within my heart
a fire is but a breath away

Alton Curtis

Angels In White

As a fresh white uniform
    Flashes by the door
I know she's going to comfort
    Another patient on her floor
With a needle or thermometer
    Bed pan or chart
The kindness she offers
    Comes from the heart
The hardships of schooling
    To some, like a curse
Still they gained the title
    The proud title of NURSE
The right hand of doctors
    They should be known
And while you're in the hospital
    They make you feel at home
The husband of one patient
    As he worried through the night
Didn't see any nurses
    He saw ANGELS IN WHITE.

Jerrell Rowell

Bubble Of Life

Effervescent, shiny new,
Floating rainbows pink and blue.

Shifting form, erratic speed,
Evading fate, noble deed.

Fragile in conditions fair,
Briefest journey, no compare.

Bubbles, laughter, life so dear,
Encroaching boundaries, golden sphere.

Spinning, peaking to the top,
Searing beauty always—Pop!

Christine Babb

Though Of You

We are alone in this world
flooded with the tears of more
broken hearts.
filled with the haunting music
of destroyed hopes and dreams
painted with the blood of
so many tortured souls
yet, our world is empty
void of any compassion,
warmth, Love
as I take my last breath,
my last look, I wish that
I had received
one last kiss.

Bailee Martin

Untitled

I walked the path in darkness
following the endless glow
what was out there in the distance
the answer I didn't know
with every step I got a little closer
and new expectations filled my heart

I wasn't sure if I should go on
till I heard a whisper in the dark
it said, "If you come, I swear to you
I'll never let you down,
and anytime you need me there
I promise I'll be around"
so I continued walking
towards the glow that was so bright
and finally I came upon
the world's most beautiful sight
the thing that I now realize
is that heaven on earth is true
for what I saw that glorious night
was a heavenly angel — I saw you.

Brad Martin

God's Seed

The seed that grew inside you
For just a little while
Brought such happiness and sunshine
One your face it brought a smile

For reasons we don't understand
And never will I guess
The Lord He took the seed away
Left you with emptiness

You know it's not for you to question
Though you'll question Him today
"Lord why did you forsake me?
Took this child I loved away."

Yes, the seed that grew inside you
Lives with Jesus now instead
A blanket of stars to cover Him
A soft white cloud beneath His head

God feels your pain and sorrow
Hears each tear as they do fall
But you will find such comfort
If you'll listen as He calls

Charlotte Fowler

Untitled

Thank you, Dear God
For my friendship of old.
Precious are they
For the memories they hold.
Like a rose in a garden,
A bud at first sight;
Yet, grows to blossom, despite
Harsh rains that have fallen
On those whom we love.
In faith we take flight
Like the wings of a dove,
To be by their side.
Letting petals unfold
Allowing them freedom,
Glorious colors behold.
A gift from a gracious God, he
Who can guarantee,
The rose becomes beauty
As it was meant to be.

Diana Weber

My Journey's End

When looking back, I thank you Lord
    For my journey's end
With all the stormy winds that blew
    You have really carried me through

Some valleys deep I had to cross
    Before my journey's end
things were hard to understand
Until you took me by the hand

You gave me time to receive peace
    At my journey's end
Even to pause and rest awhile
To gain new strength, for another mile

I knew I have a while to go
    To approach my journey's end
To share this priceless treasure
That joy no scale can measure

Let me hear the harps of God
    within my journey's end
Secure me both night and day
So I can be with you all the way

Bernadine Pesicka

Bronze Statue

I am like a bronze statue
Beautiful in form;
Yet frozen, lifeless
Dead in spirit.

Hold me, stroke me,
Whirl me, twirl me
Around and around
Until the facade melts

And you find
My heart and my soul,
Trapped for so long

Eager to burst open
Like a geyser
To show off its splendor,

Ready to love again
And be loved again.
But afraid.

Don't put me back
On the pedestal!
Dance with me.

Corinne L. Frazier

Karalee's Secret

I'm taking a moment
  for my valentine.

My heart,
  I can't ignore anymore.

It whispers to my soul of love,
  and tender times.

And of promises
  that God couldn't cherish more.

Let there be no doubt
  in the path we walk
Or the choices we make together.

You've taken me to places
  where to others have been locked.

My devotion will last forever.
So I'm out on a limb,
  with these feelings for you.

My eyes couldn't lie to see.

I'm a man in your heart
  with so much to do.
I pray for your love to me.

James Clark

Time And A Smile

A smile is like the time of day.
For these treasures we do not pay.
One of the few things you get free.
Given only once to you and me.
Do what you ought.
Time and a smile cannot be bought.

Remember you must use it.
No return not one bit.
Start with a smile and then a double.
Natures best antidote for trouble.

A smile is quick to pass
But the memory will forever last.
Both have no value unless given away.
Have a great day - What do you say.

Jean Scott

How Long Shall I Wait.

How long must I wait.
For you to call, write or speak.
How long must I go on feeling,
Lonely, depressed and unloved.

I wrote, oh so many letters.
No reply, no answer.
In them I cry to you.
Where I can be free.
Free to love, feel and express myself.

Vaguely you come to me in a dream,
Where it is so good to hear your voice.
But, in the dreams,
You're always angry with me.
Not kind and gentle,
Like I know you to be.

So forever shall I long.
And forever I shall wait.
Until once again we realize,
The relationship we have or had,
Is or was nothing but fate.

Adrienne Snow

A Prayer To God

Precious little baby hands
  four of them in all
A little girl, a tiny boy
  a doll, a book, a ball.

Fingerprints and diapers
  that irked me to no end.
Now, dear God, I'd give the world
  to have them back again.

Oh Lord, please give them back to me
  to have, to hold, to own.
Please give me one more chance to make
  a holy, christian home.

Each day that they're away from me
  seems a hundred years.
My broken heart, my empty arms,
  the hundred thousand tears.

Forgive me for the wrong I did
  and all the pain I caused.
Give me back the life I love,
  the life I fear I've lost.

Clarice M. Gebeau

Priest

Let loose the lion.
Free yourself from his jaws.
Let loose your fears.
Speak your word not theirs.
Hear your call to be free.
Loose the lion.
Run toward the sun.
Feel the cool breeze.
Hear the sea gulls squawk.
See the waves crash.
Loose the lion.
Keep on trying to set it
free.

Eliott C. Willis

Love

  New like warm blood,
Fresh like fallen rain.
  It brings little comfort,
As it enhances the pain.
  A light in the sun,
A shadow in the dark.
  Says not a whisper,
While leaving its mark.
  At peace in the silence,
Alive through life's lies.
  Thrives on the innocence,
In the heart where truth dies.

Amanda Lang

(To My Kids) Understand

To make your children
fully understand
The love you have for them
can never be replaced nor
stopped in any way
A mother will love

Till the day she dies
Yet I know I'll love
You all beyond my grave
And never leave your side

Haydee Silva

Sometimes

Friendships last
Friendships die
Sometimes they make you cry.
Love is there
Love is not
Sometimes love's all you've got.
Hearts break
Hearts mend
Sometimes they lend a hand.
Beauty's blind
Beauty can see
Sometimes beauty comes naturally.
Sadness comes
Sadness goes
Sometimes only certain people know.
Time lasts forever
Time's running out
Sometimes that's what life's about.

Erin Wachenheim

I See You

I see you in the distance, near
From here, I gaze intently
Across the water, blue and clear
That flows with time so gently

I see you walk along the shore
And I see you smile contently
I see reflections of times before
Deep waters flow with memories

My view of you-without obstruction
I see you standing there
Nurtured in the Savior's blessings
I see you, oh so clear

I see the path - where God had placed me
Winds far beyond my view
And without His hand to part the waters
I cannot cross to you.

I see me traveling to do as He bids me
Loving others and wearing His name
I see you dwelling in God's homeland
And I long to do the same.

Andrea J. Ciora

Earth

The earth is beautiful with it's animals,
from the crawling ant,
to its mammals.
The birds fly free,
in harmony with the bee.
The fish swims,
as the frog skims.
The earth is for everyone to share
with the bear, lizard, and hare.
The earth is meant to share,
with the elephant, snake, and boar,
and many, many more.

Erika Fulton

Untitled

The past grips tightly
Not allowing the future
To evolve from the present

Leah Grant

Mother's Love

A mother's love is like a rock, which is strong and does not break easily.
A mother's love is like a breeze, soothing, on a hot summer day.
A mother's love is like afire, offering warmth and comfort on a winter day.
A mother's love is like a teacher, who teaches right from wrong.
A mother's love is like a compass, giving direction when you are lost.
A mother's love is like a temple, offering a place to find peace.
A mother's love is like the sun, shining equally on every child.
A mother's love is like a medicine, sometimes bitter but cures the disease.
A mother's love is like a tree, providing needed shade on hot summer days.
A mother's love is like a flower, whose sweet fragrance softly lingers.
A mother's love is like a full moon, that everyone admires and looks at.
A mother's love is like the sea, which absorbs the waters of roaring rivers.
A mother's love is like a puzzle, which can not be solved.
A mother's love is like the law, offering punishment and reward.
A mother's love is like a smile, which is always welcomed.
A mother's love is like delicious food, that you don't want to stop eating.
A mother's love is like a comfortable bed, allowing a good night's rest.
A mother's love is like a true friend, who is loyal during troubled times.
A mother's love is like a pure diamond, precious and a value for ever.
A mother's love is priceless, yet free to all!!

Shiv Saxena

Do You Remember The 70's?

Do you remember the cars the styles, the dudes, the clothes,
    even the afros, that you pick with the picks with one flick of the wrist?
Do you remember the bell bottoms that everyone use to wear, with
    colorful striped underwear?
Do you remember when Emit was O.J., when Jordan was Dr. J, that
    everyone loved to watch them play?
Do you remember the black and white TV's, Eight Tracks and no CD's?
Do you remember the time when Jackson 5 sang live, when little Mike
    rocked the house with ABC-123?
Do you remember the mac daddies, the pimp walkers, the jivers and
    even the sweet talkers?
Do you remember the times, when everybody put up the peace signs?
Do you remember the cultures, the spirit, the peace dove, and
    most of all do you remember the LOVE?

Jabari A. Oliver

To My Daughter

Daughter, this one is for you who has written many, but received only
a few, this one with my love, is meant especially just for you.

As you walk across the graduation stage, I'd like for you to, perhaps,
think about these thoughts from me to you, a little wiser, and of
course, a little older sage.

You may have figured out by now, life is but a riddle, and success and
happiness depends on finding the key,
the same for truth, honor and integrity.

As you take your steps through life, and as you have experienced
already, there is a little strife. Just in case you do forget,
remember always, I'll be there to help you through,
for if He wills it, at least most of your life.

Yes, life is a game it has been said, and if my experiences have been
true, it does take hard work, determination, and at times a little
patience to get ahead. Self-confidence and esteem also play a part,
in those that finish and those that really never seem to start.

These words I've spoken to you seem to rhyme, but as you have taught
me, along with other things, some not all the time.

Remember, my daughter, as you take your walk across life's stage,
these words I've spoken to you, are from your father's heart. And
one last thing before I part, congratulations! your life is about
to start!

Robert J. Brooks

Smelly Jungle

Lion's wet jungle
smells like pickle juice puddles
on a sunny day.

Preston Bull

Rain Music

Soft sounds drifting freely
From the lustrous, silver shaft.
Horizontal hummings
Fading slowly as they're flowing past.

Sweet night whispers chanting
Hushly singing as they fly
Sorrowful mementos
Shouting softly, sousing withered eyes.

Short staccato wind tones
Sundered by legato rain.
Sudden silence echoes
Then the flutist births a new refrain.

Daniel Drew Butterworth

The Mighty Gun

More killed this week,
From the mighty gun,
No one had a chance to run.
No one had a chance to say,
Please spare me this day.
No one had a chance to be,
No one had a chance to see,
Another day go by,
And still we cry.
The mighty gun rules,
It's one of many tools.
But this pen meets it head on,
Until we can say we won.
It will never relent,
It's like God sent,
It a mission to do,
For me and you.
For if it can save just one life,
it will be worth the strife.

Charles Strickland

As I Dream...

I see a wondrous land
Full of health and love
Free of hatred and evil
Home of the happy and honest.

Many a time the evil
Try to interrupt the peace
But the power of love and truthfulness
Overrides that of hate.

All mighty and powerful rulers
Yearn to take over that spectacular place
Change it to a sinful place
To rule forever more.

Even as they try their hardest
Many more pure and phenomenal things
Try to regain what's rightfully theirs
And they succeed.

A dream
A helpless and far away dream
Is all that is there
While reality breaks the silence.

Allyson Torres

The Beauty Of Winter

Is the cold snap in the air,
For people have to dress warm and take care?

The beauty of winter is when the tree branches
show against the sky.
The sun filters through the trees
and gets in your eyes.

The snow softly falls.
Come little snow flakes, one and all,
This is the time of year you must fall.

Covering the roof tops, trees and ground
The beauty of winter is all around
Majestically holding you spell-bound.
Shirley A. McCann

My Friend

At the start it was fun,
4th through 12th grade, I reminisced what we had done;
It made each day exciting to have a special friend,
I could let my inner feelings escape to no end;
Our deepest hopes, dreams, and secrets where held
in each other's hearts;
I liked that, I felt secure until we started to part;
She left her friend and family to try to find something,
I couldn't figure it out, I think she was looking for anything;
It made her sad to find nothing was to be found;
She realized she was alone cold and without a friend;
Now I see her in her own little boat,
sailing in the worldly ocean without a reason to float!
I can't help my friend, She says she is fine,
I hope she will acknowledge life before she goes to THE END!
Roxanne M. Anderson

What Is Silver?

Silver is a coffee can
A 25th anniversary watchband.
It smells like clean, shiny air,
Or can be polished silverware.
A high-pitched whistle may be its sound,
A silver studded collar on a very rich hound.
Silver is coins in a pocket,
A little rich girl with a silver locket.
Silver is guitar strings, Tinfoil or wedding rings.
In the Olympics the 2nd place medal,
The silver boiling water in a silver tea kettle.
It's the feeling of a filling in a tooth,
The outside edging on a telephone booth.
Silver is the buttons on an expensive suit,
The color of a toe on a steel-toed boot.
They make silver dollars and cents,
Silver, the color of a chain-link fence.
It glistens and shines in dark or light,
Silver is the color of the stars at night.
That's what silver is.....
Ryan D. Hollingsworth

Butterfly

A flash of color in the sky.
A faint movement in the corner of the eye.
Rainbow of colors, soft and divine,
Memories of beauty mine.

Fields of flowers, dewdrops on,
Butterflies, come and gone,
Fragrance of roses, strong and sweet,
Dampened by the summer heat.
Tamara Salas-Tull

Sands

The sands of time slip softly by,
while children build castles and bridges.
Autumn's rust leaves blow freely the vision
proud birds cresting sharp, broken ridges.

The sun's golden haze lights the end of our days,
unnoticed 'til twilight has risen.
The child's gaze reaches high up to a star,
silver blaze splitting wide the horizon.
Maria Holden

Memories Of Nana

The memories are clear in my mind
A better Nana I couldn't find
Camp meeting and bathing in the sink
My baby brother so tiny and pink
The thunderstorms and being afraid
And through it all beside me you stayed
So many things I wanted to say
Like how special you were to me in every way
When I married my husband, you and Grandpa were here
And when my son was born, you hid your fear
You didn't want us to know you were ill
So you smiled and said you were proud of us still
We'll tell our son of the person you were
Of the love that you gave from far and near
Nana, I'll miss you more than I can say
And your memories we will start sharing today.
Shyla Lamb

An Elegy To Alzheimers

What could be said of fifty-two years—A tree, root system laid deep.
A blight has set in. A terrible sin. No way to recoup or redeem.
The struggle: How long? No one really knows.
Who wants to? Yes, who wants to know?
Too little. Too late. The gradual movement now slipping and sliding.
No braking. No wheel blocks. No chains or upbraiding
Can halt the progressive insidious raiding.
I lie here beside you. This body long strong
Now wasting away, a diminishing song. Slightly off key.
Yet there comes to me the image of all you once used to be.
They like to recall, "I remember him when...."
Some tears, consolations from many, but then
Most distance themselves, understandably, though.
Afraid of what? They don't want to know.
At times, guiltily, I long for completeness.
The rest, peace and quiet. For myself? Or for him?
I'll wait, watch and grieve, seek help from above.
"Faith, hope, and love....and the greatest of these is love."
Dear Tree. Dear Rock. Dear Love of my life. Amen. Your wife.
Vergie E. Gabbard

Jacob's Smile

Jacob's smile is so grand,
A cuter face could never be planned.
Dimples deep in each cheek,
Eyes that gleam and make me weak.

A laugh, a giggle and a trill,
My heart of love he does fill.
He's granny's pride, and papa's joy,
God couldn't have sent us a sweeter boy.

Jake runs and plays and sings a song,
He claps and snaps and hops along.
Jake throws his fits and stomps his feet,
When we say no or won't give a treat.

But soon he is happy and his smile is back
Without our Jacob - our lives and hearts would lack.
Susan K. Newberry

Midnight Sky

When the dark peaceful night appears
A dream of a moon that fears
Not to be shared by the two who cares
A noble moon hunter and his mistress of the stars who must
    share the midnight skies from a far
Separated by the Ruler of the mistress of the stars
The Ruler who keeps the mistress from moon hunter's love
All from the darkness of the skies above for it's the Ruler
    who wants to have the mistress's love
The love of the hunter and his mistress will always be
For the stars are the ones who holds the key
So their love will always be free
Look to the sky when the moon is full and stars are bright
    for this is the hunter and his mistress while in flight
So they may meet to share their love this very night

Robinlee Payne

Dream

On a crisp night, the moon a sphere,
a force unexplained draws us near.
Complete strangers, yet best of friends,
walking in the garden, silence descends.
The mystery in his eyes unsolved,
my steps haunted by pain unresolved.
His lips brush against mine as I turn,
I feel a strange fire start to burn.
No thoughts or concerns, hurt recesses,
my skin so alive where he caresses.
He draws away with groan, I feel so cold, so alone.
He says this is a bad decision,
we'll only end up in collision.
Am I so close to the end,
that I may not comprehend?
My mind won't listen, due to my fiery condition.
He draws closer and we unite,
Our passion burns under the moonlight.
I wake alone to see a moon beam,
was it all but a dream?

Wendy Lynne Hayes

Winning Is Losing

Winning is not two pair ace high
A full house that really only is a sultry pair
Settling like thickened dust
Satisfied with complacent straights
Compel the white unknown to stay a blackened pit
The piercing notes!
The shameful shrinking!
The purple pleasure!

Is it not the splashing red flush
Breathful bliss
Not the best!
The ego wins!
Slippery suits pass by so close we do not look
But seethe and grab not welcoming the warm exchange
Taking second best
Hoping others find third or fourth
We win!
The familiar lonely straight
Not the grinning flush.

Susan Cangurel

Friends For A Lifetime! Only In My Mind...

"Catch Ya' later!" The last phrase he spoke,
A gentle, caring man drifted from my life.

"Life is a circle!" He said.
"Put inside your circle things that make you happy".

Each morning I was greeted with
Sparkling eyes and a soft smile.

"How are you today? I hope everything's okay!"
"Great," I'd say, sometimes trying to hide sadness.

"Are you okay today? You seem kind of down."
    He always knew...

"Be happy!" He said, and quietly walked away.

Friends come and go...
    This friend will linger a lifetime,
        Struggling only in my mind.

Sally Hearne

Untitled

    A tree once stood with branch out flung,
a home to birds and creatures small.

    A welcome refuge from the storm, a shelter
safe to one and all.

    And yet we humans pick and choose, the ones
with friendship we would have.

    God made the tree without a heart, and yet
it pays its dues.

    God blessed our body with a soul and spirit,
for others gave us love to use.

    Remember all the love for you, be like the
tree, spread out your love to all.

Ruth Vivian

"I Love You Because"

I love you because you are a gentle man.
A man of compassion and tears.
A man who has learned through the years
What life is all about,
And there can be no doubt
That deep in my heart I love you because.

I love you because you are strong.
You have a strength strong like steel.
A power from within that is real.
Energy going through you.
A love that is true,
A heart of pure gold is why I love you because.

I love you because you are you.
You take risks you live, you share.
You play, you laugh, you care.
You smile, you struggle, you wait.
You confront, you pray, you create.
But most of all, you love, when I love you because.

Vicki Jung

Bus Stop

To wait a bus out in the cold was too much to endure.
The children were not ready for the drop in temperature.

Then one day their mother had a brainstorm you might say.
She talked to Dad and he agreed there surely was a way.

It took a little plotting to perform the clever stunt;
But move they did that out house from the backyard to the front.

Peggy Braddock

Precious Sight

As I went into surgery that day
A mere routine a tumor to excise
The diagnosis, though, was grim and grey
How bad it was, the doctors realized.

So after surgery and some weeks past
The doctors told me I had lost my sight
They said the tumor was growing fast
But I was grateful I could see some light.

One thing that never changed was my belief
That God would always be at my side
Whatever happened, God would never leave
Because he would be right there as my guide.

A lesson to be learned from all this fright
Is never lose your gratitude for sight.

Travis Lee Hendrix

Gorillas

A staring contest; you and I, destined to test the other's power.
A mussed back pressed against a wall, without you it would fall for
   sure.

You sit there in your salad bowl, embarrassed that you have become
A vegetable, just like the rest, whose urine was the only dressing.

(Am I the one who's behind bars in those lost eyes of yellow film?)
You pick out from your web of black a bug, who's used as his home.

I see you have not aged real well, your fingers are so worn and
   cracked.
A head flops over to one side and tells why hair on your neck thinned.

Your size is a contradiction to what weak power you possess.
You tell me that you'll be right back while you weigh yourself for all
   your "fans".

(Are we the ones that should belong behind those bars of rusty death?)
You return tired, out of breath. Your stare tells me to walk away.

I came to visit you last week and found new life put in your cell.
A beautiful black coat that shined just like the newly-painted bars.

Fresh vegetables were tossed his way and leather gloves would pick
   them up.
His mighty body held the wall which drained you of the strength to
   live.

(I wish the bars were taken down instead of you, old memory!)
And as he stared me in the eye, I saw his head begin to lean.

Robin C. Drew

Parents

It seems we were given whatever they had,
A part of their best mixed with some of their bad
It's not like we chose all we seem to possess
We just came to be some with more, some with less.

We all have our problems in living each day,
And all of them different - it's fate you might say.
But I know the root of it lies with our start,
The way we were raised, what's instilled in your heart.

And I say you can't be no more than you are
You'll not climb that mountain, you'll not touch that star,
If they did not give us the tools to succeed
The road up ahead will be rocky indeed.

So I as a parent have one thought in mind
To make sure my children are not left behind
By letting them know they are precious to me,
And loving them always is where I will be.

Robin Phillips

Two Hearts

When I was young, I dreamed fairy tale dreams.
A prince on his steed, a castle on high,
And a love that would never die. Now that I
have felt the pain that love can bring, I know
there is more than just happiness and a golden ring.
It takes two hearts beating as one to create a reality
from the dream. We can spend every day of life
together, yet things may not be as they seem.
The two hearts begin to drift apart as the days pass by.
The prince and the princess become just two people
who cannot look each other in the eye.
They hurt each other without even knowing, and the
two hearts, further and further apart they are growing.
If they'd only remember the love that bound them from the start
They would again feel the joyous rhythm of two hearts.
Then a fairy tale it would no longer be - the castle would
be a happy home, the prince would be a wonderful man,
loving and true, and the two hearts that once beat
so separately will again beat as one, not two.

Tracy L. Thomas

Picking Up the Pieces

It seems to me there use to be,
A purpose to my life,
But now it's hard to have a goal,
I seem to have only strife.
The days go by one by one,
I have no ambition,
I know I must do something,
About this condition.
Things seem to be a little better,
I don't cry as much,
I do get out and see my friends,
And with them have some lunch,
I know I can't live in a shell,
That's not the thing to do.
I must go on, and become a part of this life too.
So, with Gods help, I'll put on a smile,
Pick up the pieces and go the last mile.

Virginia Wurm

Free

If I had one wish away from reality
A sea gull for a day is what I'd like to be

Descending low and soaring high
Upon glistening waters, amidst livid blue skies

The rapture of my beauty suspended in the air
The sounds of my voice like music to the ear

Cascades of colors of a rainbow you see
But upon my back are the reflections to be

To witness a sunrise that begins each new day
With a tip of my wings, I can fly any way

The sky is the limit in this my vast kingdom
For the one thing I value, and that is my freedom

My day has no worries, no problems to project
Only breathless journeys from sunrise to sunset

As I look up to the heavens, God's light shines down to be
Remindful of the blessings given a creature like me

Through me can be shown, as an example alone
Of all God has given in the world that we live in

Wish not to be something you are trying to seek
For in his likeness, God created each one of us as unique

Virginia Kiraly

Cycles of Life

An old oak tree stands in the meadow.
A sentinel to time and weather,
Its branches reaching heavenward,
Its gnarled knees bowed to the earth;
Attest to its ancient age
When long ago the acorn was buried
By some hapless creature or winged jay.

Each season clothes it in new array.
Spring hails, bursting forth its swollen buds
Pregnant with life;
Until a shaded silhouette catches every
Languorous breeze and hurls it through the
Balmy morn, drying drops of sparkling dew.

The autumn air whispers through the golden leaves
As they wait in respite for the wind
To sail them to the dank humus below.
The old oak tree shivers as it stands unclothed
And barren; stripped of its bowered beauty,
Silently it waits for its blanket of snow.

Rebecca R. Odom

The Memory Soul

Your face suddenly dark and arrogant
A shield against my heart, eyes, mind
And the hunger in you that only feeds me
Rails against all that you've been taught

Seeking shelter in a crowd
And yet more alone than before,
It is surface and nothing more
The sand before our tide

Would anyone pretend to know
How a glance can fire a rage or cool a tenderness,
Can be a gift or a curse
It can require an eternity to decide which

I now recall that it was long ago
And this is just another mental haunt
No dagger I could dream
Could cut you from my mind

Who can take the soul of a memory
But the Nature who allows you it
So I resign to live with and without
Until this journey of ours is done.

Randy Clear

Silence (Autism)

My eyes are open . . .
A sunny day . . .
Will this be the time . ..
What will I say? . . .

I hear so many voices . . .
Someone is calling my name . . .
But I don't know how to answer . . .
To tell them of all the pain . . .

What should I do? . . .
Should I reach out and touch? . . .
Or would they truly understand . . .
I'm not reaching out in anger . . .
Just the touch of another's hand . . .

There are so many things here inside me . . .
Things I want so much to say . . .
But my lips just won't form the words ..
So I'll just be silent today . . .

Rose Daniels Gleaton

"Unconditional Love"

The time to write is from the heart
A thought comes in, that's where you start,
No sentences needed, a thought will do
Our life in present, child hoods gone through,
An occurrence of past, of sadness or joy
These that stay with us, values employ,
My poems come flowing, my life time till now
People who surround me, happiness they allow,
The thoughts of family, blessings from above
With rhyme and reasons, unconditional love,
My poems disclose in a general way
As love grows stronger with each passing day,
The strength that I show you, must always be known
It came from your heart, then to me it was shown.

Randi S. Friedman

"Marriage"

Marriage is sacred
A union both should cherish,
Guard it as though it were a pot of gold
Never let it perish.
Try to remember the preachers words,
"Until Death Do You Part",
Always be happy as two little birds,
Plan your life right from the start.
Above all try to agree, although your ideas may differ,
Just remember those sacred words,
Then you will never be bitter
Do your best, look your sweetest
Keep your home the very neatest,
Take those words seriously, for they were not said in jest
For only then can you be sure your marriage is blessed.

Rose De Santis

What Is Forgiveness?

To err is human, To forgive divine,
A universal principle contemporary for all time!
To give up a deep-seeded resentment against,
Free's oneself in a Godly sense!
Being angry with another only hurts oneself,
Bringing disillusion regardless of power, place or pelf!
Forgiveness is to let up, then let go,
Realizing the peace of mind you'll always know!
Effacing the affront from memory's recall,
Passes the forget to forgive as everyone's pitfall!
Apologizing for releases the mind's tensions,
Exempting from, then dispensing with our own apprehensions!
So relaxing, wiping the slate clean, scot free,
Excuses the apology for the release from, we clearly see.
So let bygones be bygones, bear us no malice,
Toasting forgiveness' wine from Life's silver chalice!

Roger Pique

Communication

The language of the heart is easy to understand.
A special look, a touch of the hand.
A universal language, without a spoken word!
The message clearly heard.
It transcends age or color of the skin.
When an emotion springs from within
And you don't what to say,
Let the language of your heart
Your thoughts or feeling share,
No matter who you are, or where.

Virginia T. Christofferson

A Certain Time

I have a memory of another place and time:
a warmer place;
a younger time.

In the evenings, to the ringing of bells
the oil was poured, the lamps were brought to life.
Patterns emerged from nowhere;
from heat and blistering light,
from mists
and cow dung cakes that had baked all day in the sun,
from dust
and the scent
of lime-trees.

But now the screen door creaks, and
a UPS parcel clunks onto my step.
Suddenly,

Uma Krishnaswami

My Son

A son; what Glory, my heart sings and beats with joy
A warmth upon my heart and a light into my soul
He'll carry my name and hold it high
be what I could not, to shine and glow
He'll do the things put off and know why
I hold him close and help him grow
As tall as a tree, strong and proud
Through years of triumphs I swell with pride
Investing him with hopes and dreams.
And through his tears and pain I too have cried
Watch him as he walks away, tall and straight
into life, finding his way, seizing his day
Then with quick time past so unfair
with aged hand I reach for him
and he is there, with hope and love on a smiling face
As we wander, hand in hand, through rememberings,
I know he understands, in his heart of hearts and his soul of souls
What Glory a son brings.

Robert A. Bimson

Untitled

Many different shades of green, all of which can be seen scattered across the country side; it's beauty you cannot hide.

Motherhood is a sacred call-she's a friend, a teacher and that's not all lack of sleep for many nights worrying, waiting, settling fights For all the blessings Mom will get she gives much more I will bet-so thank you Mom for all you've done my love and respect you've surely won.I know I'll never be able to pay the debts I owe you, but I'll say I love you Dear Mother of mine I will be grateful for all time.

Fatherhood is a thankless job he usually feels like the head of the mob.Dad is a provider, leader, comforter and friend not to mention all the money he's asked to lend.How does he do it? I've often asked does he expect to accomplished every task? Pushing himself beyond all limits in each day there aren't enough minutes So, keep on striving is what I say-in your debt I'll always stay. You gave me life on God's green earth-how can I thank you for my birth? Without your guidance I would not have found the happiness I have sought. I honor you dear father of mine. I will love you until the end of time.

Rashelle Udall

Field of Snow

Do you remember that one snowy day!
We played in a field and were joyous and gay.

But then the clouds moved past
the sun, and the snow melted
and ended all our fun.
On that one day I really loved you.
But that day is gone, and now so are you.

Karen Metz

The Nestegg

When they met she was a widow,
After devoting years to caring for her family
She was left with the two youngest of her four
   children still in school
And no career to fall back on.
He was a widower with his youngest son
   still in school
And devastating medical bills.
Now they are retired.
Between them they have raised nine children,
With the physical, emotional, and financial
   burdens this entails.
These things left little opportunity to build a nest egg;
Or did it - - in its place they built a family.

Wynona S. Tavernier

After

After decades
After frightened deer sitting in the sixty back seats of a Florida bus
After the separate ladies rooms
After rotwood shacks with last strands on the line
   and new white washing machines branding their porches
After the no vacancy sign has been removed from an off-season motel
After Mississippi
After bussing
After the black boy on your Kellogg's cereal box
   moved into your Westchester kitchen
After blacks are blending into your white buildings
After black is beautiful
After soul is where it's at
After black Miss America
After blacks are making it
After swimming with blacks in $42.00 a day pools
After Beverly Johnson superstar
After Roots
After Martin Luther King

Debbie cannot play with niggers on Northern Boulevard

Sofia Lederer

The Lady

Realizing that she is free for the wind
all I can think of is the storm
calling my name and reaching
here to grab my soul
else I die and be seen no more
likening to a swirling pool of despair
lusting for the energies of my life
even though I sing with false hope

My love cannot sit upon the mountain
under the spell of the lady
reason why I cannot resist the beauty
power and forces of the temptation
hallowed ground is the earth upon which she walks
yet evil draws her into itself while I stand and watch

Warren Vincent Bost

His Looks

I have no idea what you look like,
All I know is your voice,
But I wish I knew more about you.
I wish I had a picture in my mind,
So I can see this man who I've been talking to.
So many times I've heard your voice,
But I can't put a face with it,
How I wish I knew this man I've been talking to.

Shandylinn Kelly Maynard

Strangulation

The sun rises, golden and sparkling
All knowing against the darkness of the city mountains
Who stand untouched by the light,
Made only into a lesser shade of evil
By the golden rays given freely from the glowing globe
Who always rises on que, bringing joy into the world.
However, to the receding hairline of nature
So small and meek, the sun provides the life
Sought for and priceless to the thing the steel mountains,
Cold and cruel, try to cover up and steal for their own warmth:
Smothering out the life of a loved member of nature
Whose brothers and sisters are bowing,
Dropping the occasional leaf, seeming to be a tear
Of sorrow and remorse at the senseless suffocation
And the constant laughter of the cold buildings
Reaching toward heaven and robbing the life
Of a shrinking population of the little bit of nature left
That is fighting and struggling to remain a power in the world,
And is crying, screaming, and begging to be set free
Of the darkness of the prison they are slowly being confined to.

Robert Dale Smith

Roses And Hearts

Roses and hearts and wings all a flutter,
all spread together like smooth white butter;
Music and joy and happiness flow,
although the wind and rain will blow;
Lace and silk and jewelry gold,
tell of treasures we long to hold;
Bears, puppies and cats galore,
make me want to hold you more;
Evening time rain or shine,
and candle light dinners made with wine;
Memories of joy and love with you,
are like nothing that I've ever knew;
Wild am I calm are you,
the memories we have are few;
Dozens of roses in red, white and yellow,
come to mind when I dream of this fellow;
I love him sweetly and I love him dear,
but now he is no longer here;
He was mine but now he's gone,
and still even now my love lingers on.

Rachel Diane Jackson

The Ultimate Price

Human is what we are.
All that trouble over a yellow star.
A star came between the nations and in a place.
Hitler tried to destroy the Jewish race.
So if you think the government is a leaking boat,
remember Hitler came to power by one extra vote.
And if you believe your thoughts do not matter,
try to hear the dying chatter;
of the millions of Jews that were
killed by this man and paid the
ultimate price to reach the Promised Land.

Texee Brewer

Heaven's Door

Heaven's door is beautiful in sight
All the glowing bright white light
It's time to go to my peace and eternal rest
Wish you and yours all the best
So I say good bye to you
But please always remain true
I love you forever more
So go inside Heaven's Door

Yianice Hernandez

December 25

December first it has arrived
All the hustle and bustle has just started
Will I make it to the twenty fifth?
Oh, Dear Santa help me along
Just to find that special gift.

Fourteen days I have left to go
Hurry and scurry to make it right
Toys or clothes, which will it be
Santa is coming with a ho, ho, ho

My chest is full of Christmas stress
I cry, I laugh lets get it over with
I want to look nice on Christmas day
Will I be able to wear that dress?

Only seven days left till that special Birthday
In all the hustle we sometimes forget
The Christ child was born December 25
The gifts are bought, the house is clean
It's time to settle down by the Christmas tree
Just like the wise men and little shepherd boy
We'll give our gifts of love and joy.

Sharon G. Voorhis

Dream Come True

I feel drops of rain from the sky,
All the pain is the reason why.
So I launch my mind to the stars,
To a place beyond the moon and Mars,
Where millions of people are face to face,
United together in one embrace
I say things I don't really mean
About people who I have never seen
One minute I carry their pain as well as mine
The next, I'm stepping out with Saturn's danceline
I'm awakened to what is real
And have completely forgotten how to feel
Millions of people torn apart
When the answer to their pain
Is in their heart

Ron Buss

Lonely Prelude

All is void, all is void
All the sweet things I've enjoyed
Past and present now collide
Future heartaches coincide

Can you find me? Can you find me?
Love is like a chain that binds me
In it's arms it holds me tight
Cannot struggle, cannot fight

Can you here me? Can you here me?
Let not your soothing words come near me
While I rest on clouds of sorrow
I curse the night and dread the "morrow"

Bells are pealing, bells are pealing
Cannot hide this lonely feeling
Goes the summer, comes the winter
Into this lonely void I enter

No more talking, no more talking
Guess I'll be forever walking
Searching, seeking for a meaning
On my heartaches safely leaning

Robert C. Taylor

Lady Liberty

She stands in the harbor with her ever present light
All through the day, and all through the night
And to all who seek her a very welcome sight.
She's a highly sought after lady, for you see
She stands for freedom and opportunity.
She's oh so special I would say, a gift from the French to the
U.S.A.
And so she stands there come what may.
All through the night and on into day.
With her ever present light that seems to say
Come! Come unto me! If you desire to be free
If you have hopes and dreams you want to see.
I stand in this land of opportunity with its red, white, and blue and
Stars and Stripes too! The Bald Eagle and "sea to shining sea"
The Constitution and the Bill of Rights you see.
And last but not least of course there's me.
I stand in the harbor with my ever present light all through the
day and all through the night giving a ray of
hope to all who seek me.
For my name is Lady Liberty.

Talice Burks Biggs

Looking Back

I look back on my life and see it as an
Allegory.
When I'm day dreaming my whole life
Passes through my mind,
As though I was looking back at old movies.
But these events are acted out on the
stage of life.
History repeats itself through the young;
I now see what happened then, that I did
Not understand at the time.
It clears a lot of tangled webs away.
I'm grateful for this gift of sight.
Though I wasn't perfect; nor was my
oppressor or I would still be in the dark.
I still may not be completely free, but I
Know what's happening to me.
The world records all we say and do, and
I want to share that with you, knowing
God will make ado, and right the wrong
Done to you and me.

Ray O'Neal

Already! (A Day Of Life)

As quickly as the sun wakes the summer morn,
　Already, I was born.

And dries the early morning dew,
　Already, I was two.

And rises rapidly towards heaven,
　Already, I was seven.

And fills the sky with a great, bright sheen,
　Already, I was sixteen.

And hastens the bee to and from his hive,
　Already, I was twenty-five.

And lengthens the shadow of the eastern tree,
　Already, I was fifty-three.

And as bright and dim begin to mix,
　Already, I was eighty-six.
And as the setting sun turns the blue sky red,
　Already!

Richard J. Dailey

Lovers

Lovers are two people who are willing to share.
Also two people that care.
Just as me and you.
And two people that tells the truth.

Lovers are people that are willing to give.
If I didn't have your love,
I wouldn't have a reason to live.

Lovers don't run over one another.
Because they have to look out for each other.

Lovers think of each other as a song to remember.
Just as I think of you when I hear secrete lovers.
And others!

Sherrie Hill

Moving Onward And Upward

We are the class of nineteen hundred and ninety eight.
Although we are not yet ready to graduate,
　In four short years we will be .
Then, the world will be waiting for us just through that open door.
　Think about this no more.
Concentrate on this last year.
　Think hard, and you might shed a tear.
We lost a face in the eighth grade crowd.
　I think all of us thought hard about this, some even cried out loud.
We have sweet memories to cherish and hold,
　As well as others that are bitter and cold.
They are mine, and they are yours, forever.
　I know I will not forget any of them, ever.
If you however, do forget a few memories of this last year,
　Remember all of us, sitting here.
Of everything, just remember this night.
　Remember to always keep a hold on your dreams, and never lose
sight.

Shannon Smith

Trapped Within

A two way mirror, of what you and I see,
an image distorted, not of you, but of me.

The picture of a person lost and unfound,
afraid and confused with her head pointed down.

Thoughts of changing so many things,
my looks, my words, my thoughts -my dreams.

I starve to fill the emptiness and pain,
I exercise to purge my fear and shame.

Reaching out to a hand nearby,
but falling short by saying good-bye.

Refusing the truth, believing all my lying,
of what could keep me from dying.

A time to open, admit to myself,
I'm not as strong as I thought,
I may need some help.

Shari McLaughlin

A Dreamer

A dreamer listens but does not hear,
In circles he run; pushed by fear,
Quietly he screams in search of truth,
Only to find; it was lost in his youth,
When he is older a day will come,
His dream is finished, it's over, it's done,
Always looking back his mind tries to relate,
All the time lost his dream's very fate.

Lewis Ralstin

"This World"

Come to me poor naive one, I'll tell you of my dream.
And all about this cruel cruel word and exactly what it means.
   Although you think you understand, I beg you not to try,
for every time that someone's born, a thousand people die.
   Diseases and hate, and war among the races, if you
look around you will see the starving faces.
   Humans are the cruelest animal God put on this earth,
they will destroy there own families, and kill babies at birth.
   They will watch there brothers and sisters blood spilled
upon the ground, and though many eyes are watching no one will
make a sound.

   It is too late to save the world, there is destruction all around
and until there's no more life to live, peace can never be found.
   Mankind will destroy itself, and innocent people will die,
and if you ask them to tell the truth, they will answer with a lie.
   Why is this world so cruel and inhumane, why is it the
rules of life will never change.

   I hope that I am dead and gone before there's a story
to tell, and I'll prey for all the cruel ones who will never
rest in hell.

Tina Smith

Rainbow Heroes

They are touched by gentle breezes
and blossom in the golden sun
But no words do they speak
Yet, one day each will voice the emotions
For someone
Who cannot think what to say

They'll be there in times of gladness
Or when it's time to say goodbye
They'll bring a moment of happiness
Or maybe a tear to the eye

They live only for that moment
But through their beauty
They touch the heart and soul
And to me they are the rainbow heroes
With hearts trimmed in gold

Vicki S. Parks

Your World

Come and sit and talk with me again
   and bring me into your happy world
      to let me view the often dismal one
         through the glints of amber
            in your hazel eyes.

Your unusual view allows me to see the same scene
   at a slightly different angle,
      think the same thoughts
         in a somewhat different way,
            hear the same sounds
               on a new and different level.

Your special left-handed vision
   flows into me
      through your eyes
         by way of your own
            expression of your happy world.

You bring out of me
   a different part of me
      and I am more than
         the person I was before you.

Teresa Baker Kelly

Of Life, Love, Laughter And Hope

We are born into this world, unsuspecting of what life holds,
And by parental love, guided into right directions, we are told.
So now we have the life, we have the love - the laughter comes
   and goes.
And as we trod the path of life hope begins to grow.
Hope for a beautiful, wonderful world, in many ways, now gone
   astray-
But already having love, laughter and hope, we have a
   loving God to help us on our way.

Ruth Hannaford

Mother

You gave my life one summer's day
and cared for me in your gentle way.

You taught me it all - from A to Z;
but best of all, you believed in me.

You said I was special - one of a kind.
I seldom thanked you, but you didn't mind.

You opened me up and tore down my wall.
You're the only one who knew me at all.

You've been there for me my whole life through,
so in my own way, I'm saying thank you...

Tracy Single

Lonely and Despair

   I woke up this morning feeling lonely
and despair. Lonely because I couldn't
find any one there in the house I call
despair. This house use to have plenty of
voices and furniture of all choices. I used
to say "Good Morning Grandma Dear," Get
coffee and read the newspaper, while sitting
in a comfortable chair. Now that Grandma
and Granddaddy are gone I sit here pondering,
Here I am, so all a lone! Today, I pray
that I find true happiness and peace of mind
But, right now I sit lonely and despair
Pondering for happiness while sitting
on the living room chair.

Tyrone Ellis

Morning Dismay

She is artless with her addictions,
and has depression from feeling perfect.
She is a queen in an expressionless castle -
Except her shadows, they exhibit her every gesture,
and jail her from the sinful cries she desperately wants to answer.
The cement walls punish her hunger -
Craving the dark through her bedroom window,
chambers eyes gaze, seducing her with guilt...
Still he comes with the sundown,
and she makes love to the Nightfall
howling in her utmost bliss.
Nevertheless .... Dawn escorts her dusk away,
and she is left again, resentful of the sun.
Covering her skin in sable robes
to mask her from the morning kill,
she sits graceful like death on her throne
and overdoses her last remaining pill -
Giving her hope to drown in demise
and to relish forever within the night's eyes.

Rondalee Munson

Riding The Rails

The boots on his feet were tied with rags
   And he carried his world in a grocery store bag
He walked down the road with sadness and pain
   His bags he had with him and a broken old cane.

As he sat by the tracks to wait for a train
   He looked at the sky and the big silver plane.
His mind returned to his brothers and sisters
   While he powdered his feet to tend to his blisters.

Then watching some bee's making honey
   He pulled out his wallet to count all his money.
Four Washington's, one Hamilton and one torn Lincoln
   Enough to buy some food today, is what he was a thinking.

He heard a noise and looked around
   Then laughed out loud at what he found
There, sat a mutt with one bad eye
   And looked as tho he soon would die

Reaching into his bag, stale bread was all he had
   "Come on old mutt and eat some bread!"
"Cause if you don't, you'll soon be dead!"
I think I'll call you, "Wonder boy," It's the bread that gave you joy.

Sheila Skelley

Sweet Memories

Lately my dreams are filled with your sweet memories
And I'm feeling your heart
I never knew that I'd be finding love so right
You walked into my life and took my heart
My love, it means forever, or I'll never fall in love

So, I'll keep your sweet memories
As though you were here
And as I wander through the darkness
I'll keep crying one last tear
No more bruising my mind

Now your heart is gone
As time goes by
I'll keep telling myself
No more bruising my mind

A letter signed "Good-by-Love"
But I'll cherish the your sweet memories
As though you were here

Oh, my sweet memories
Sweet memory of you
"Good-by my Love"

Ryuji Iwazaki

Love Poem

As the music stops I continue to sway
and in the smokey bar I smile
though I am being shoved against a sweaty back.
I have arrived.
My Paradise is regained.
I stumble but I do not fall
because I clutch a stool and I hold on.
I do not leave when propositioned by that ugly
pimpled man. I only smile and nod
I am sorry for him now, now
when I am not sorry for myself.
tears fill my eyes as always in this desperate
throbbing room.
But my smile does not go away.
I lift the wineglass to my lips,
but set it down again distracted slightly by the
white sparkle on my hand.
I use it to autograph the
check and wave goodbye to Pimples.
He smiles back and I turn to leave the bar.

Stacie Lents

Morning People

They wake up bright and early, ready to start their day
And I'm punching the snooze, hoping for Saturday.

The covers are heavy. They must weigh a ton.
I'm too weak to lift them. I'm comfortably numb.

They're up bathing and ironing and such.
Singing and humming, way, way too much.

My cat keeps me warm like a mom and her pup.
I'd better stay still so I don't wake him up.

I'll get up, get motivated and have some caffeine.
Make myself beautiful instead of just mean.

I still don't feel pretty. I must shower again.
For I feel all dirty 'cause my coffee kicked in.

They skip out the door. Oh, I wish they'd trip.
'Cause my hose have a run right up to my hip.

Finally at work, "Good Morning!", they shout.
I give half a smile, reply and then pout.
Boy these morning people. They just make me sick.
They burn like a candle with an extra long wick.
Get used to these people. Get used to their style.
Like it or not...They may make you smile.

Tiffany Furrow

Legacy

Bury my heart at Wounded Knee
and let the earth reclaim this body, long bruised and battered;
long tortured and defiled.
Let Mother Earth soothe my pain and let my spirit
remain to soar high and true to fly among the clouds.
Let my soul roam free to walk the earth;
to stand tall and proud;
to regain in death what so many tried to take from me in life.
Thus rests my heart at Wounded Knee — buried, but not forgotten.
Bury my body at the Old Plantation
and the dirt will cover this shell, long flailed and flogged
long tortured and defiled.
Let the Lord dry my tears
and let my spirit escape the chains and shackles
to fly among the clouds.
Let my soul roam free to walk the earth;
to stand tall and proud;
to regain in death what so many thought they took from me in life.
So my body rots in the soil of the Old Plantation — buried,
but not forgotten.

Vanessa Crouther

Making Happiness

I would love to lie on a bed with you,
and let you take control of my body, and you
let me take control of yours too.
I can feel your strong hands moving up my high,
arousing me gentle on the bed which I lie.
touch me forever and never stop giving.
because without you life isn't worth living.
I can feel your lips on my neck, with your
tongue circling,
you are so perfect and so in your love making.
your hot mouth reaches my chest,
on my darling! you rare the best.
I respond to your touch because it feels so good,
more than I ever though it would.
I wrap my legs around you and begin to feel
you touch,
Darling I've never wanted anyone quite so much.
Don't ever leave me say you won't go,
Because darling to your I'll never say no.

Tara Leesa Sawh

A Poem To My Bride To Be

Oh my darling dry your eyes
   and lift your thoughts up to the skies.
No more doubts and no more fears
   there's no reason for your tears.
Our wedding day is coming soon
   the one we first had set for June.
The vows we make will then endure
   because they're based on love that's pure.

I never thought that you could bring
   this love that makes of me a king.
So till your standing by my side
   my love, my happiness, my bride.
Just think how wonderful it will be
   the two of us just you and me.

    Richard Nixon

What Price Our Love

Now autumn leaves are falling, I want you so,
And 'mid winters white journey, when bleak winds blow.
Into my willing veins you've poured
   The sweetest urge, desire —
A disease, almost a fire;
   Of loving you I'll never tire.
When Spring rolls round another year,
   When Summer's come once more, my dear,
Each season following season,
I'll need you beyond all reason.

Last night I dreamt
   A midsummer's dream;
We lived here, you and I,
   A cozy nest next to the sky,
Impervious to the world of men
We loved and loved and loved again.
Oh, the days and years, they pass so fast,
Let's seal our love and make it last!

    Virginia Holden Williams

You Cared

When you were here, we never talked too much.
And now that you are gone.
How I wished we would have spend more time
Talking.
About the weather, your aches, your pains, your
Joys.
But you were a quiet man.
Words did not come easy to you.
Is silence not communicating?
Does it not have a language of
Its own?
Does it say you are here.
You are near, how comforting.

    Rose Milavec

Mind Games

He came to me in the wee hours of the night
and held me 'til my hearts content
Like a startled bird, he took flight
and I know not where he went.
I searched for him in my memory-
my lover, I could not find.
Then I realized he's just a fantasy
and exists only in my mind.

    Rachel Ann Beshears

Winning Is My Natural Habitat!

I won again,
I did, I did
I won, I did
I did!

    Max Gregory Parker

"Brotherhood"

Two brothers play tennis; one smiles at the other;
And on a nearby park bench watches their mother;
A volley here, a laugh there as they play in the sun,
And I get a little tickled just watching their fun.

And on and on they frolic; first deuce court, then ad;
But wait! For some reason, their mother is sad.
She is sad I am certain, but what can she rue?
The older son seems happy, and the younger does, too.

So does the weather sadden the mother? No, that cannot be right;
For it's rarely this pleasant, and never this bright!
But still, she looks troubled, her face filled with woe;
I decide I must ask her if I'm ever to know,

"Why in your eyes do I see such regret?"
She said, "I just hate to see them on opposite sides
   of the net."

    Vincent Hicks

Mother's Autumn's

1993: The leaves are changing, The brilliant reds, yellows,
   and oranges are "breathtaking!" The days are shorter,
   what a waste, less time to enjoy the splendid beauty.
   The color's reflect on the rippling waves, as a warm pleasant
   breeze guides across the water. The sun reflects, as it sets,
   behind the lake. We walk hand-in-hand. Life is grand! Yes;
   growing old together will be heavenly!
1994: The leaves are changing again. The color's aren't as brilliant
   this year, Rusty Reds! dull yellows! Brown Oranges! The rain
   falls more often, than not. The dampness chills me to the
   bone. The days are longer, dreadfully, dragging out, the
   nights are worse. The windows are drawn in darkness, as I lay
   a bed. Alone! Sorrow fills my soul! The leaves fall silently
   to the ground, waiting for an icy blanket of snow, to cover
   them; to cover you! Emptiness, echo's in the rooms we shared
   for so long. My heart is heavy, with the dull throbbing
   pain of knowing, you can never return to me. Wishing
   my life could end with yours. Knowing it can't!
1995: The leaves are changing again. There not as dull as
   last year, but not as brilliant as the year before!

    Regina K. Perales

Through Eyes Of Love

'Twas toward the heavens I gazed last night
And saw the moon in all its' light.
I watched the stars go drifting by
Their steadfast path across the sky.
Their patterns weave as on a loom
Enhanced the beauty of that room.
I saw the lights of northern air,
Their beauty radiant, rich, and fair.
The pureness of the blue above
Was as the whiteness of a dove,
In that there were no flaws or mars
Except the ever stealing stars.
No thoughtlessness, faithlessness, hate or lie
Is found contained within that sky.
The beauties of these sights above
I see more clear in you, my love.

    Ralph M. Snyder

Living A Lie?

At one time I could look into your eyes,
And see paradise throughout the skies.

But now I don't even have your face,
As my body breaks down at a very rapid pace.

At one time it was hello but now its goodbye,
As I sit here and wonder have we been living a lie?

I never thought so,
But it seems I've taken a very hard blow.

As I sit and stare at my wedding band,
I wait for the news to see if I can hold your hand.

This time when I look into your eyes,
Will they be filled with rain and saying good-bye?

Theresa A. Brown

My Grandmother

She's warm and beautiful and sensitive and kind.
And she's God's special gift to me.
She's got a heart of gold, and the will of steel
I love her more and more everyday.
Because I know for sure she's God's special gift to me.
She may be tall, she may be blind but she,
can see and hear more than anyone else can.
I know for sure that my Grandmother was
a special angel sent from heaven.

Sharon Appell

Soul Mates

Life's never easy, it gets harder each day
And sometimes it's people that get in the way
Opinions and theories on how we should cope.
Our minds get all full of confusion, not hope.

Christ talks of love forgiveness and faith.
Something in this world most people won't embrace.
What keeps us so distant from God's simple words?
Our stubborn convictions, our inward concerns?

So what is the answer to this unGodly trend?
It's simply a Soul Mate, a companion, a friend.

The message is clear, you can't do it alone.
You need someone open and honest and prone,
To be there is good times and bad times as well,
To love and support you through heaven and hell.

For a Soul Mate is someone you must give your heart.
And when you do, suddenly life's problems depart.

The Bible says what must I do to be free?
Love your neighbor, just as you do me.

Steve Wasko

Compensating Factors

A mortal man lives only unto death,
And take from life whate'er he may, he cannot stay the doom
That hovers nearer with his ev'ry breath -
There is no greater certainty than that there is the tomb.

Immortal man dies only unto life,
And in this paradox he finds the essence of his goal;
Why quail at thought of that inevitable knife,
When death is but the birthing of his undying soul?

Roger L. Van Dorpe

My Soul, My Life!

My soul has become my counsel
and taught me to give ear to
the voices which are created
neither by tongues nor uttered by throats.

Before my soul became my counsel,
I was dull, and weak of hearing,
reflecting only upon the tumult and the cry.

But now, I can listen to silence
with serenity.

I can hear in the silence the hymns
of angels chanting exaltation unto
   the Throne revealing the
   secrets of all eternity:
Forever I am thankful that
my soul has became my counsel
and inner wisdom has become my life!
   "My Soul, my Life!"

Rodney A. Graves-Bey

"The True Meaning Of Christmas"

   Christmas comes but once a year
and that's okay with me.
   It brings lots of joy and laughter
for all of us to see.
   I always think that it's going to snow,
because it's Christmas once again.

   You know, it really doesn't need to snow,
to enjoy this Christmas Cheer.
   For this Special Holiday,
there are lots of questions I ask myself, like:

   What is the true meaning of Christmas?
Does any know today?
   Oh, yes, I know!
In the word Christmas, it's there for all to see!!

C-H-R-I-S-T is there for you and me!
   So I hope you all enjoy your Christmas
this year and many more years to come.
   It's very nice to know that Christ will
always be with us, each and everyone!!
"Merry Christmas"

Sandra Pickney

The Sound Of Silence

The sun slowly rises in the sky up above,
And the fresh morning air just radiates love.
To my left is a woman so sweet and divine
Her dazzling beauty just won't be outshined.
I look in her eyes and get lost in their splendor
The touch of her hand seems so soft and so tender.
Nature has made this beautiful creature
Her lips, her hair and every last feature;
She sits there in silence and speaks not a phrase
Her thoughts she makes public in her own special ways:
A smile, a touch or the wink of an eye
Says more than my words and I know not why.
I want to reach out and speak to this queen
But I can't for I do not belong in this scene.
She touches my hand and kisses my cheek,
I open my mouth but I cannot speak.
The words in my head just swim in confusion
Her glorious beauty is more than illusion.
I know what to say but I can't say it right,
So for now I'll just sit there while holding her tight.

Raymond Suarez

Kansas Sunset

As the beauty of the sunset flares across the western sky
And the scarlet spreading upward as the day is loath to die.

The sun a ball of crimson, sends out its sparkling rays
If perchance some clouds are present - then more beauty is displayed,
For they saturate the color that blazes 'cross the blue
Until the sky is radiant with a brilliant fiery hue.

Now the lustrous rays withdrawing toward that glittering orb of flame
As it dips ever lower all this color it will claim.

The display is not over, tho the sun has sunk from view.
And for a few brief moments, the sky's a washed out blue.
Then up comes a flash of color that will expand and grow
Till the western sky is blazing with the sunset's afterglow.

Once more the clouds, the heavens reflect the transient scene
As if they could capture it, and all its richness glean.

The horizon is illumined by a deepest blush
That gradually will lighten into the softest flush.
The evening star is twinkling in the ever changing light
And another Kansas sunset, slowly — fades away to night.

Velda Transue

Even Now

Even now, though the things in life I've strived to do have changed,
And the times we once had are no more,

I write these words which to you must mean so little,
But to me, mean the world.

I never really knew why I let you go,
Nor do I know now either.
I just hope someday you'll understand.

Even now, as tears fill my eyes and the memories of you
drip from my face,
I realize that there's no more.

And sitting here with your picture in my hand,
And old letters that you once wrote,
I realize I still love you...even now.

Robert M. Browning

God's Hand

Sometimes the future may not seem clear,
And the unexpectedness of life is something we fear.
But, yesterday's fears are written in sand,
Washed away by God's own hand.
By God's hand we've learned to cry,
When we hurt or when someone dies.
By God's hand we've learned to smile,
When we're happy or during the birth of a child.
By God's hand we've learned to grow,
And there's one thing he wants us all to know,
In everything beautiful God has His hand,
You're beautiful and God says you can.
And wherever you go and whatever you do,
Just remember that God has His hand on you.

Robin M. Carroll

For Little Tears In The Night

What is this?, What do I hear?
Why does my little one have such tears?
Why are you so lonely? What do you fear?
You are not alone little child, I'll always be near.
You are my treasure, a love more than I can measure.
Now sleep in peace, forget the darkness and the sounds in the night.
For I shall be guarding you with all my might.

Michael Andrew Cubstead

A Name

Something was hurting her inside
And though she has such a beautiful name
It changed how she looked at the outside world
And was difficult for her to tame.
I don't know when it started
Or from which direction it came
But it tugged at her heart with its teeth
And it ripped at her soul causing pain.
The first time I listened and saw it
Fear twisted my heart into chain
Instead of helping the girl in kindness and love
I ran away from her problem with blame
It was easier then not to notice
And if I should notice, to shame,
Than to helpfully have faith in protection
And hope for both our souls gain
Though my own growth did not prepare me
To show her her beautiful name
One day she will see it inside her
And only light that it grows will remain
And she'll say goodbye to the pain...

Wendy Jo Jensen

Celestial Home

On that cold, icy winter's day, you left me
And went to that heavenly home far away,
That beautiful place where you went, it
Is said "The streets are paved with gold, everyone
There is free with a happy soul,"
A bright kingdom is now your home land,
It's the house for the soul of mortal man,
This was our Master's divine plan, but being
Humans this hard to understand,
You traveled to a peaceful, serene abode
That's above the stars and the moon,
Someday I'll make that journey too,
Or it could be soon,
I saw you sail away on a silver chariot,
"Please don't leave me, I need you to stay,"
You said "I can't I have to go today."

Sarah Elizabeth Phillips

Birthdays

Birthdays can be a lot of fun
Do you admit you still have one?

The gifts, the cards, the congratulations
Are all part of this celebration.

No matter the month, no matter the day
Mondays in March or Fridays in May.

Enjoy it fully - spare no expense
Do as you please - you need no defense.

Eat what you like - have a drink or two
You can't go wrong, in whatever you do.

You'll get plenty of special attention
Birthdays are such a great invention!

A time to let it all hang out
Fun time is what it's all about.

For me, it's the best day of the year
With memories which I'll hold so dear.

So, cherish each birthday, celebrate! Have a blast!
For you don't know, which one will be the last

Helen V. Burton

221

A New Day

Did you ever wake up in the morning,
And you felt you couldn't make it through the day?
and then on the second thought,
You remembered you forgot to pray.
Once your prayer was finished,
You could hear the Master say,
"Bless you my child, spread sunshine along the way."

Then you start visiting the lonely and the sad.
Meeting all the new friends you never knew you had.
With all the joy and pleasure you forgot you ever felt bad.
Nothing in this world to compare with
God's precious lad.

Don't waste your time complaining,
God has given us a brand new day.
Fill it with love and laughter
Helping others along the way.
This blessing is ours I'm sure you will agree.
Let's not let the devil cheat us
He's after you and me.

Wade through these dark storms of life
Reach out a helping hand
There's someone waiting on you
Over in the Promise Land
No trial is too hard for God to understand
He's right there waiting to give you a helping hand.

Ruby Henson

The Children are the Memories of the Future

Today some people say, "The children
Are our future, we should teach them
What they will need to know about their future."

Once upon a time the children had a future
To look forward to and today all they have
To look forward to is defeat and misery and war.

They used to learn what they needed
By being who and what they were and
by trying to show us what we had left behind.
Today, I say, we should put the future away
Until tomorrow comes.
For the children of the present should be allowed to be
the children that we need,
And show what they are,
And bring back the child in us that we have forgotten,
So that we may bring back to the children today
The future that so many of us
have lost and left behind.

Tina E. Merrigan

We Ask Why?

Often times we ask why?
Are the good ones, First to Die?
There is no one here to answer our cries,
There is no one around to hear our sighs.
But someday when this troubled life ceases,
And our knowledge of God's Plan increases.
We will understand far more,
When we reach the other shore
Our pain and sorrow will be erased,
As we meet Jesus Face to Face.

Susan Purcella

Threads

The threads of love and life
Are woven by lovers and dreamers alike.
Forming a delicate fabric of intricate and
    fascinating pattern.

Enhanced by the creative touch of romantic eloquence
    and endearing tenderness.
All too often a nearly completed design loses its
    quality of enchantment.

The weaver seeking to unravel and start anew.
But alas the weave is all too permanent and can but be
    altered by additions to what is.

Each unique tapestry a life of torment, passion, love
    desire and hope.
Seeking to be displayed in the celestial palace of
    our Lord.

I am now transiting from the anguish of attempts
    to unravel.
Into a euphoric state of design recast
To rebeautify the efforts of this weaver's dreams.

Ted E. Kapus

Nobody

Day breaks over the hills,
as humans awaken and animals
begin their daily routines.
The brightness blinds all:
the dew is glistening,
pine scents fill the air.
The mountains shine with confections sugar
and pleasantness and joy fill the atmosphere.
A day begins and people go about,
cars start and babies cry.
Soon, the cold air becomes crisper,
the lights start to dim in the mighty sky,
as night shall take forth.
It approaches and children go home,
the faint smell of pollution rises,
cars are arriving home
and nobody cares.
Nobody sees the beauty in a day,
nobody but I.

Tara Mihailin

Going Back

As I walked down the tracks toward the trestle
as I did in my Childhood days,
happy memories engulfed me -
I was going where yester-year stays.

The stream flowed ever so gently -
it's hypnotic effect lingered still.
Time had not changed the "blue magic",
just to absorb the beauty, a thrill!

The rumbling roar and the whistle
of a train thundering 'round the bend
changed the mood to a livelier tempo -
it's place in my past to defend.

My hill still loomed in the distance
I ran to my own special place
to survey the landscape with pleasure -
the wind blowing soft in my face.
as I sat in the tranquil surrounding
- for a moment-time's race I had won -
I was back in my childhood of fancy
enjoying the setting of sun.

Sandra M. Morse

A Time, To Say Farewell

The time has come, to say Good-bye,
As I leave, with my Fears Inside,
And my confusion, which I cannot Hide.

I'll have to journey, down another Road.
New adventures, will be left, to be told.
My fears and doubts, inside I'll Hold.

New days, will be Left In Store,
The unknown, I'll greet once More,
What awaits, I'm not Sure.

I'll pack my bags and say my Farewells,
I'll have mixed emotions, hard to tell,
Thus, I'll hide, within my Shell.

My Good-byes, will be hard to Say,
As I'll turn and walk away,
My thoughts and fears of future Days,
All Good-byes, are hard to Say.

Mixed emotions, hard to Tell,
I'll turn my back and say Farewell.

William F. DeSimone

When March Winds Blow

When March winds blow, a mystic breeze unfolds.
As I plan for tea, setting places for three;
-a familiar giggle I recall.
Chasing firefly's in the night; building sand castles;
smelling buttercups at daylight; laughing at yellow noses.
Serving tea with my dollies delight;
Only, when March winds blow.
When March winds blow, melting moments away;
visiting shadows display; reflections in my teacup invite
images of enchanted princess, white stallions, and bold knights.
Allies reanimated; defeating dragons, dungeons,
-and lonely afternoons.
Defining paths of a finer tune; only, when March winds blow.
When March winds blow, revealing fairy tales unwind;
Migrating, escaping time.
Who would ever know- the miles I traveled afar.
chasing rainbows to Neverland; watching children play;
catching raindrops in my hand.
Venturing forth to dream- absorbing moonbeams;
Only, when March winds blow.

Virginia Martone

Seeing Through Clear Eyes

My Black brother -
As I step close to you, I can see we've become distant.
And as I move a little bit closer, I can see
That I'm no good without your aid in tearing
down the barriers that keep us divided.
My Black brother -
Two halves make a whole only when they come together as one.
But wait, there's a brightness about you
that keeps my eyes focused, And I
can see "The Beloved Son in whom
His father is well pleased!"
I can become one with this Son because
I fit so perfectly.
I love you. My Black brother.

Sheila Adams

The First Fall

It all began with a soft white flake,
as it lands slowly, a new form it takes.
A bead of wet water quietly sets there,
and soon it is seen to have moistened the hair
of a small innocent child.

Consistently it falls and brightens the ground,
quicker and quicker, yet it makes not a sound.
The sky is a blur, a large gray cloud,
the shrieks of the children are angelic and loud
as they play among the whited bliss.

The rosy cheeks and the runny noses,
the snow angels molded in various poses.
The sleigh bells ringing strong and clear,
the warmth and excitement of this time of year
the joyous holiday season.

Their wet boots and mittens thawing in the hall,
sharing hot chocolate and egg nog as they wait for night to fall.
The snow draws on an emotion that is found within us all,
the thrill of amazement at winter's first call
glistening in the moonlight.

Rebecca Burkdorf

I've Never Hopped A Freight Train

I've never hopped a freight train
As its lonesome whistles whined.
But I've felt the empty loneliness,
Like the tracks it leaves behind.

I've never flown an airplane,
In the blue majestic sky.
But I have seen an eagle soar,
Over mountain ranges high.

I've never seen the flowers bloom,
In deserts hot and dry.
But I've been captured by the innocence,
In a newborn baby's eyes.

I've never sailed the deep blue seas,
Or felt a sailor's lure.
But I've quenched my thirst, from spring-fed streams,
Of water sweet and pure.

No, I've never hopped a freight train,
And perhaps I never will.
But I have lived and loved and laughed.
I have hopes and dreams......still.

Rachel Sidebottom

Song Of Winter

How gently they dance on hands of the breeze
  As they scatter their crystal 'among limbs of the trees.
   Silently now, they waft toward the earth,
  Enjoying the ride in quiet mirth.

All creatures are sleeping, awaiting the day,
  As the beauty of winter is well on its way.
Snowflakes are gath'ring on bare-headed trees,
  Building white crowns, protecting from freeze.

Never again do I think there shall be
  A scene of such peace as that I now see!
The earth is all white in the quiet of morn,
  As snowflakes so gently on wind's breath are born.

As they settle to earth true beauty they bring,
  And the song of winter they silently sing.
I, too, sing their song as I utter this prayer,
  With thanks to our maker for a blanket so fair!

William P. Jacobs

How Much Shall I Give

How much shall I give? Where there is need,
As long as I live? I must give and free my soul, share my love,
understanding and wisdom when I'm old.
How many times shall I forgive? As many times as my Father
    forgives me,
Yesterday, today and as long as I live.
I must let my voice be heard as I soothe some lonely heart,
With a kind and friendly word, while I'm here until I depart.
Really, how much shall I give? I must always lend a helping hand,
Never thinking I can't, but believing I can.
Telling somebody regardless of how hard things might seem,
I have a goal, I shall accomplish my dream.
How much shall I give? Let someone know that whatever road you
take, there are others on that road too, but whether you make it, is
    entirely
up to you. How much shall I give? As much as God has given me, I
must respond to the needs of others, whatever they may be, for I'm
responsible for whatever I do, so I must help someone on life's
journey as I pass through.
How much shall I give? I must render compassion, never overly
criticize and complain, for usually when things don't go well you'll
find old self is the blame. How much shall I give? How much is
required as long as I live? This is how much I shall give, a listening
ear to someone's cry, a welcomed friendship or a tearful goodbye, stop
and listen to someone's call, save a life, prevent a fall, let someone
know I really care, with my giving or with my prayer. How much shall
I give? I really can't say, because I never run out. I guess I'll
keep on giving, that's what life is all about.

Thelma J. Carter

"Last Days"

By his bed she paused to stand,
as she bent over and kissed him
on the hand.
All were watching did not speak,
as a silent tear ran down her cheek.
In her mind the memories ran
of the times they laughed while
she lingered by his bed.
Now his eyes are very cold,
she will never again have him to hold.
The doors opened and they carried him away,
just a week before Thanksgiving day.

Sherry Green

Rhapsody Of Nonexistence

Do I exist only to myself?
As soon as they flutter out of my mouth
worlds travel to the oblivion
where they instantly vanish like they never were.

Please, tell me I'm real
I beg the mirror to say something to me
when everything inside of me
is like the whispered memory of a dream.

The Black Hole
In the place of my heart there lies a black hole
because once forgotten love
results in forgetting that I exist too.

Sarah Mirza

A Portrait Of Hate

Peering through the window, darkness resides.
As the harsh lightning pierces the sky,
You catch a glimpse of the wretched furnishings
And the horrid red demon running amok.

This odious emotion originates through anger or disgust.
More often than not, it plagues the soul
And can readily be likened to a disease.
Hate is a hurtful feeling that has nothing good to say.

The object is the wood precariously piled.
Hatred is the embers burning bright.
Anger feeds and actions fan the flame.
The result is a scarred ground scattered with ashes,
  — as the lingering smoke slowly fades away.

Sonja C. Smith

A Summer's Evening

The evening sun had melted down over the purple mountain
    as the water in the creek babbled with the fury of a fountain;
As you could hear and feel the warm summer air whisper through the
pines and in a faint distance, the calls of nature's lonesome whines.

At first you may be lonesome and scared and feel all alone,
    but you then might feel like a king sitting on a throne.
For all of nature is now in your own control
    and the feeling of greatness reaps down in your soul.

For just to be out here with all that God made
    should you now know you're foolish to be so afraid;
For all night's creatures close in for the night
    and the stars and the moon make it all just right.

So no matter how you see it, in your single eyes
    the vastness of nature is the perfect of tries
That God made it perfect and could not go wrong
    when he added little touches like the Nightingale's song.

This may be how I see it, or my way to fit in,
    but to experience this nature, I can only grin,
To think in my mind of all the beauty at hand
    I think we might just be here, in the Promised Land.

Tony Dale Shelton

"My Girl"

In all the world's great riches none could be so sweet
As the wonderful girl God has lead me to meet
Our hearts have joined into one love surrounded by joy
My feelings remains fresh like a child with a new toy
As long as you are in my life and still holding my hand
I could fly to any destination anywhere across the land
Your caressing touch comforts my every need to the bank
Your heart keeps us together like a common link.
With eyes of a crystal sea with a soft glare
The way you look at me shows me how much you care
I don't need someone to tell me how to feel about you
My heart is all I need to remind me, how much I love you

Randall Dewayne Collins

Creative Process

Time for thought, inner observation, for gratitude and speculation,
for sensing all that is around me, stretching...stretching my
imagination.

This kind of time is not wasted though some might think it so.
I spend such time in rumination waiting with expectation for
some great insight...some inspiration.
Then...I write it down.

Laura Robertson

"A Cruel Reality"

   Standing a top of the world gazing at the stars
as they shined upon us as diamonds in an endless sea
of night. A warm summer evening breeze touched us
with fingers of contentment and we stood embraced with
love. Our souls locked together in our own little
world we made the promise for better or worse, as we
conspired under the moon. In a distance a howl cried
out as a prophecy of what was to come. Just then a
chill of fear was sparked into the depths of our minds
which led to our departure back to the cruel world of
reality...

Stephanie Lynn Toth

"It's Christmas Time"

The air is cold, stars twinkle bright
As winter blows on through the night.
It's Christmas time, It's Christmas time

A time of friends and family too,
And love that sends me back to you.
It's Christmas time, It's Christmas time.

A gift of love so long ago,
We sing and worship as it snows.
It's Christmas time, It's Christmas time.

Sweet memories of days gone by,
We lift our voices to the sky.
It's Christmas time, Sweet Christmas time.

Tim W. Davis

Silent Abuse

They wanted a puppy, so they chose me.
At first it was fun, I had so much room to run and play.
Then it got dark and they all went away.

Don't they understand I need love and three meals a day?
Not just a few scraps of leftovers once a day.
I also need a warm place to stay.
I get so thirsty and it never goes away.

Now that winter is here it is even worse.
The food they give me is just not enough.

On a cold and snowy night a big man in blue came in the fence.
With the light he held he saw I had no food, water or shelter.
   but he just turned and walked away.

Sometimes I wake up with ice on my coat. Winter seems so long and
   cold.

My only companions are the toys I find in those plastic bags.
Tin cans are fun but the sharp edges can hurt.
Empty milk jugs are so much fun, you can toss them in the air and
   chase them for hours.

What will the spring and the summer bring?
Rainy days and nights with no dry place to go.
When it gets really hot, will there still be no water or place in the
   shade?

Sharon Snavley

Love

Isn't love a wondrous thing?
A thing that only God could bring.
Love as a rule, is a virtue itself.
Kept Clean and pure, it is greater than wealth.

Without it, there is fear and hate.
With it, there is the joy of fate.
Isn't love a wondrous thing.

Leon J. Dutkiewicz

A Civilized World

We live in a civilized world today.
At least
That is what we are told.
But do children kill children
In a civilized world?
Do people hate and oppress other people
In a civilized world?
Who, in their isolated and secure little fortress
With all its convenience, decided we are better
Than those who've come before?
It's not that progress has not been made.
But to ignore any decline
Is to increase the speed of the demise
Of our "civilized world."

Todd A. Campbell

"The Light"

There is a light at the end of the tunnel,
At least, that is what some people say.
At times we do not take the time to look,
And our decisions go astray.
May our days for this year be optimistic and bright,
And by letting go of all that's past,
We all might just see that light.
But if by chance we go amiss,
And look for all the bad,
We'll only end up with a bad case of the "sad's".
So let's keep our chins up and look for the bright,
God only knows we just might find the end of the tunnel light.

Rose-Anne Blake

The Hyphen Of Life

I looked at the gravestone cold and bare
at the dates of the life represented there
and I pondered in my mind
all that was kind
and I thought of all that was bad
and I was just a bit sad

I was struck like a brick
the light came on with a flick
the hyphen separating the numbers signified a life
it cut cleaner than a knife
everything accomplished or not accomplished by the individual in time
   on earth
has happened until death from the time of birth

We may pass this way but once
but we treat this life like we were a dunce
give unto others to receive the crown
but we reach to take then we sink and drown
and living thus we die and leave to others and this time
the thoughts they say which mark our stay on earth with words
sublime

Robert C. Appel Jr.

"Sad But True"

A window to a house as a book is to a mind because;
The wound it seemed both sore and sad
To every christian eye.
And while they swore the man would die
That showed the rogues they lied
The man recovered of the bite
The dog it was that died......

Vincent L. Poindexter

The Night The Manatee Cried

I sat one night on an old battered dock
At the edge of a small lagoon,
And watched the manatees in their watery world
'Neath the light of the August moon.

Like giant gray bubbles they floated along
Just out of reach of my touch,
And time moved as slowly as those great gentle rocks
In a world so peaceful and hushed.

A particularly large bubble broke the surface nearby
With a swish and a whoosh of air,
And uttered a low and plaintive wail
Filled with sorrow and despair.

I eased myself off of that battered old dock
Taking one last peek o'er the side,
And spent many an hour in the subsequent years
Wondering why that manatee cried.

Susan Napier

My Heart

"Come" says my heart to me "and let me give you rest."
"Aye, but my journey is not yet over and many battles
lay ahead of me to fight I reply, but my heart rebukes
me on the grounds that "I have no feelings towards her."
"Oh, my heart think never thoughts as these, my most
prized possession come walk with me and me with you and
listen to my words."
"It is because of these battles that you are still very
tender and pure. It is you, I live and die." "If I show affection
to any persons on my travels, isn't it solely because of you?"
Never think that I don't love you not for surely, as I breathe
every breath is for you.
Then my heart rose crying from my side and said
"fight! and I will never forsaken your journey again
because truly love rules all things."

Wayne Ladd Vazquez

Ever Want To Go Back

Have you ever wished you could go back home.
Back to the warmth and comfort of never being alone.
Did you ever want to go back to mom and dad.
Back to the people that made you happy when you were sad.
Did you ever want to go back to the age of innocence.
Back to the time when it didn't matter and made little sense.
Did you ever want to go back.
I do.
Back to the memories that warm the heart every time I think of you.

Ron E. Shelton

The Fence

Two are as one while green leaves part, allowing the sun's
beams to stream toward the forest floor...

Ancient, rusty strands of wire separate those who have
fought life's battles and lost,
from those who seek love and can battle life together...

Love flows generously, free from this day's commitments, while
remembering those who no longer can love on this life's earth...

Sad thoughts occur as we realize life is temporary.
Why can we not enjoy these days, these times, these loves, as we
can?

We realize now that only a fence is all that separates us from
life's termination...

Lets not allow a fence to divide our existence, nor our lives.

Ron Sullivan

The Man In Me

Time scares a man like myself!
Because, I really don't know what lies ahead for me.

My beliefs tell me I will live! My situation tells me I will die!
Tell me;
    What shall be my destiny?

Shall I always live alone in a world that hates me?
Or, will I share what I have your kind is gentle heart?

Will my part deeds always prevent you from accepting me?
Or, will your fear of my "Trivial death"
Forever keep us apart?
Princess; speak to my soul!

I would be that friend for you! I will do what no other friend
Will do for you!
Surely, a friend like me is worth more than any man's "pot of
gold."

A man like myself could be your guide.
But, he can also follow your lead.

Because, the man in me possess the gifts of love.
And that is the simple man indeed....

William S. Jones

Silence

I'm afraid of your silence
    because of what it could mean.
I suspect your silence of meaning your are getting bored-
    or losing interest
    or making up your mind about me
    without my guidance.
I believe as long as I keep you talking
    I can know what you are thinking.

But silence can also mean confidence
    and mutual respect.
Silence can mean live and let live.
The appreciation that I am I
    and you are you.

Can this silence mean that it's an affirmation
    that we are already together -
    as two people?

Words can mean
    that I want to make you into a friend,
And silence can mean
    that I accept your already being one.

Santo Joseph Cala

Expressions of Love

I wish you were a sheet of paper
Because that's where I express myself best
I'd take my pen in hand and pour out my emotions
Giving you only a short time for rest
Writing about my love, all over you
First finding the place representing your heart
Then taking the time to fill your mind
Never stopping once I get a start
I only wish it was so easy
Just like holding your hand
There would be nothing about my love
That you would not be able to understand
Once my love was written upon you
It would stand the testament of time
A display for all to see
A reminder that you are mine
A living memorial
Of my love's endeavor
Not just a tribute to fleeting love
But a pronouncement of love forever

William F. Holder

"Changes"

I keep thinking about changes in you,
because when we were together it was just us two-
  But now I've seen things that I know
were bound to happen, and those are called changes.
  Changes in you not in me, I treated you
like a king, and loved you everyday, but what you gave
me in return was not you.
  It was the feeling that you had after
you've found someone new, a stranger cannot give you
what I have already given you.
  That will be the change you didn't want
to experience in me.
  Star Hernandez

Years

As you
Become more than just a Child,
Deep inside everything
Feels worried. You're going to have to worry about
Guys, having fun and joking a lot.
If you think it gets better your
Joking yourself. You can
Keep dreaming of Love, Money,
Nothing matters when you're a teen.
Otherwise you'd listen to
People like me. Don't
Question how you feel. I
Respect you being Scared.
Tons of people get scared. It's not
Unique, you'll go through a
Valuable time in your life.
Wondering what you'll do next,
Excited about your new school,
Your new boyfriends, yes,
Something special. Something new.
  Rochelle Livingston

Sounds

  Sounds of darkness, visions of light, things that have
been, and things that still might.
  Valleys and mountains, rivers and seas, I can view
all these things in my memory.
  Sounds of laughter, children at play, to feel the sun's
warmth, on a new spring day.
  All of my hopes, and all of my dreams, I woke cold
and lonely, thinking what do they mean?
  Sounds of the forest, the birds on their wings, the
voices of choirs and the songs they sing.
  The world is a shelter, for greed and despair, people
look for what's not, instead for what's there.
  Sounds of the ocean, the wind and the waves, and
old man watching, from the beach where he stays.
  Watching and seeing, feeling and being a boy fills
a needle, when he'd be better off reading.
  Sounds of nature, the thunder the storm.
In the midst of confusion, a child is born.
  People in chaos, they struggle they fight,
They just can't understand the magic of life.
  Robert L. Miller

Carved

Trees press against an orange oil paint sky.
Motionless, calm.
From where I stand it seems the setting of a
  cardboard puppet box.
Carved by hands young and imaginative.
Are Gods hands young?
  Terry Vaughn

"Thinking Of You"

  The thought of you runs through my mind;
like the flow of blood through my heart;
  My heart beats; beats for you
when they cease so shall I.
  Wilfredo Matthew Lopez

Untitled

My poet's are gone
been shoved out by fame
sought shelter in others
couldn't even trust their mothers

Their pain brought me songs
poems and novels
but is it right to enjoy
do I treat them like toys

They give me emotion, direction in life
will I end up with them
could I be so blessed
do they know how their missed

I tell myself
I'll never be that fragile
those people can't get me if I have no feelings
yet I cry for them every night, as I fall asleep just staring at
the ceiling
  Sean Reichert

"Stream Of Life"

In the beginning,
Before man, woman had loved....
There amongst the mighty waves
That mists the air above,
With its power and motion....
Had started with a stream;
And throughout the ages
As rock corroded, and gave way....
The stream developed to a bay;
As the rain poured, creating more;
Drew water from all sides around....
And the streams became an ocean!
As like a stream..a dream is found;
And within the mind, a desire is born....
So with the idea, and plan, that I can speak....
So that it will touch every human I meet;
In time, my dream today, that lies in my mind,
Will blossom my desire....
That will move me to succeed;
Though my duty to myself.... "My stream of life"
  Sanford Potiker

Family

F is for fun, not feuding
Being caring, loving and kind.
A is for all togetherness and happiness.
For I am yours, and you are mine.

M is for making peace at all times,
Do all the you can, while you can.
I is for I do... I must, I will... I can,
I'll try to do good every woman and man

L is for the love that is in our hearts,
That we share wherever we go.
Y is for you and me... me and you,
For we are one big happy family you know.
  Silver Lee Nears

"Eyes of the Deer"

Imagine
   Being one with the deer
   Feeling its anger and pride,
   That is how the deer feels inside.

Going
   To roam the forest and woods
   Seeing the predators and allies,
   Watching the graceful birds soar
   Wishing someday you can leave the forest floor.

Wanting
   To just be free,
   Being a target for skilled marksman
   Never knowing when danger arrives
   Not knowing if they will come at night
   Just waiting all in fright.

Realistically
   Reality strikes,
   Are you glad at what you are?
     Vincent Nguyen

'Lovelorn Angel'

Lo! Behold a spiteful mistress,
   Beware of her baneful caress,
A lovelorn angel with repulsive admiration,
   Her spiteful sympathy disguises odious affection,
This insidious beauty brings loathing thirst,
   A malicious hunger many hath cursed,
Her wretched love induces odious fervor,
   Jilting all gallantry, oh sweet whore!
A detesting fancy sleeps in her venomous kiss,
   Innocuous hate, oh disgusting bliss!
Bitter keenness hollows revering bane,
   Oh this love reeks insane!
But still her affections I do crave,
   Blessed am I to rant and rave.

     Seth Barrows

"Sour Dream"

How many times have I looked at your face?
Bold and strong but with infinite grace.

How many times have I looked in your eyes?
And seeing within them where my soul now lies.

How many years have I wandered to you?
The journey seems so long yet hardly through.

How many years till the journey ends?
Shall we be enemies or more than friends?

I long to see your face
'Round every corner, in every hallway, near every crowd.
And when I find nothing, my heart turns cold as stone
When I reach for you...I reach for you and find I'm all alone.

My dreams do play such jokes on me
The cruelest it may seem.
For when I wake I find
That it was only a sour dream.

So that's the tale of love once lost
To my own dismay.
The lovers being star-crossed
Will have to part their ways.

     Terri Moser

The Journey

At the end of darkness a passage way of light;
   brilliant, wondrous, frightening, light.

The provenance of aspirations
   progressing on through countless nights.

Demanding endurance, strenuous, beauteous
   journey of delight.

Terminating earthliness, slowly rising,
   to a passage way of light.
Brilliant, wondrous, welcoming light.
     Roberta M. Willhite

The African

I come from soils of gold, silver, and diamonds,
Brought to bondage to fertilize another's land....
My sweat nourished the crops, and my hands waxed hard....

But I hear the drums of Africa, deep within...Boom, boom, boom...
I come from kings and queens of GREATNESS....Tut, SHAKA,
NEFERTITI, AND SHEBA.....

My family shaken by winds of greed, hatred and change.....
My blood, joined with scars, scattered through the land...
I, THE AFRICAN, often not understood.....
     Tonya F. Greene

Remember Me

This is a day that I'll no longer be here
But for me, please don't shed a tear
Because in your heart, I'll always be
Just please always remember me,
Remember the things that made me laugh and cry,
Remember my smile, remember my sigh,
Remember me for who I was, not what I did
There was no way out, that's why I hid
I never thought it would happen this fast
But I didn't quite know how long I'd last
I have to leave so many friends behind
each and every one of them caring and kind
I hope they forgive me in their hearts
Knowing I never wanted to be apart
As they realize their fault
That my life has come to a screeching halt
It is now my time to say good-bye
The time has come for me to die
As I take my last breath
I must complete my death.
     Shiloh Becker

Love

Love is something that you can't measure
But its something you should treasure
Love has its joys and some pain
It starts at the heart and runs thru your veins

Love is something you can deny
And it's definitely something you can't buy
Love is sometimes used in the wrong way
And it's not just something that you can say

Love is something that you must feel
And when you do you will know it is real
Love's something you feel when you hold them tight
Love's something you mean nothing you kiss them good night
     Robert Lee Edwards

Will I Forget My Once Hidden Cry?

The rent is high,
but I'm not poor.
The bills are rising, rising, to the sky,
but I'm not poor.
Sometimes I feel life is, is to live, so you could die.

Daily I cry,
I often wonder whether survival and success is worth the try.
I really, really — try — to hide my cry;
but the tears of dismay which are inside me, will let me try.

They all think I have everything to gain.
But no one knows my pain.
Should I! Should I to them— explain my pain?
Should I! Should I to them — complain of my pain?

You say knowledge is power.
So why do I ponder by the hour of my knowledge being sour?
You have long known —of my quest for knowledge and power;
But you fear I will forget you.
Therefore, do you feel I should not have that power?
Dear:
    Mother...
Sharon L. Giffard

Liberated Viewpoint

A working woman, I, the soul of liberation
But my neighbor on this point has no such inclination.
Contrary to modern sentiment, she looks at me with scorn,
And I can understand her view at each six a.m. alarm.
When I scamper out the door and down the steps I caper,
I see her walking leisurely to get the morning paper.
Again when I lag in at night she looks sedate and calm,
Playing with her kiddies or watering her lawn.
I no longer spurn her life or view her with disdain,
Especially on these mornings when I wake to pouring rain!
I wonder if the Women's Lib should need a delegation,
Who would best epitomize the Joy of Liberation?

Sharon Hawkins

Entropy

The sound of a scream is one that can forever live in the world.
but, not just any scream, mind you;
agony, shame, torture; elements of purity.

If you listen very closely on a clear night
you can hear the screams of everyone
who has ever known pain
in the very spot on which you stand.

The beheading of an innocent bystander,
the burning body of a young "witch,"
the silent suffering of a dying matriarch,
the pain of a child caught beneath the wheels of a train.

Tears may have been shed in countless agonies.
Deranged thoughts may have led to suicidal instincts.
Sweat may have once and again poured off the mind of a doomed soul,
but, it is the screams that will live forever in the world.

Can you hear them? I can.
Sherrie Nichole Duggins

My Love For You

From the minute that I saw you, I knew nothing could part us,
but now I'm just another face in this lonely world.
My love for you grows every day, hour, minute, and second.
You have left me to live but not to love.
I have been wishing upon a star in the sky above
to feel your embrace me with your love, I can't wait any longer.
How can you see me, how can you know me? How can you say you hate me
when you have no heart for me?
I have been mourning for you in this horrible pain.
You have left me to live but not to love.
Who have you given your dear heart to or have you saved it?
Oh I love you so and I will save my heart, my purity,
and yes even my love for you until this deep hole in my heart is
filled with your love.
You have already made a wound and now a scar to come.
I love you with a passion. I love you with a hate.
I have been living in this world of darkness and hate, but yet I can
close my eyes and see your face and it brightens my world from a
distance of space. I have cried for you during the rains,
I have loved you by the sun and in the snow my love for you grows.
Sabina Catarina Boggess

The Colorless Road

Can my heart feel? Am I real?
But on my heart I bear such pain. Alas, I cry alone in vain.
Never could mere mortals know. The pain of poets like me or Poe.

What cursed things plague my mind. They put my thoughts in such
    a bind.
I'm left in the dark, no light to be found. Sadly, sorrowfully, by
convictions I am bound.

The flower is cut, its beauty short-lived. It withers and dies,
    beauty now hid.
My thoughts are empty. My emotions are gone. Without love,
    there's no
rhyme in the song. Sadness will give you no abode.
On this long and dismal colorless road.

On my journey, I have found not a friend. I am a windless person,
    no love to expend.
A passion for music is all that is left. I play my notes in treble
    clef. I am
summoned home by the sound of the gong. Through this misery I
    trudge along.
The fire of love no longer burns. That very thought and my stomach
    churns. My life has no meaning, no reason, no rhyme.
        Am I condemned to be alone till the end of time?
William E. Wilson

In Memory....

It seems too soon for a year to have passed,
but our love and memories will forever last.
You brought joy and happiness that will live on and on,
with memories so real it's hard to believe you're gone.
For it was you who taught love, laughter, and how to cry.
We grow from your love as each day passes by.
Your hands have touched many and none will forget,
the smiles you brought that wiped away the regret.
To us, children and grandchildren, you did not die,
your spirit just knew it was time to fly.
Terri L. Konz

When Obstacles Befront Me

I ask not for the mountain to be moved
But, rather, that I'm given strength to climb it.
I am willing and determined, therefore,
I only ask for guidance.

I possess the capability bestowed upon me at birth -
To grasp an infinite scope of knowledge -
I am strong, yet, weak
Therefore, if I stumble, catch me.

Steady my fall and encourage my climb
For I must move onward toward the zenith
The zenith of my being - The zenith of my goals
Where the beauty of fruition awaits me.

Not for show or for praise
But for a sense of accomplishment
The blossom of my ideals
The reality of a dream -

Therefore, if I stumble catch me
Encourage my climb
For the zenith of my being awaits me.

Tobitha R. Moran

She Left

We were happy at first,
  but she began to thirst, for more.
    Then there was a fight,
  one with screaming and shouting, then finally
  this began; the bad flight to a strange place for
    her.
    She was elated but of course not he.
He was not happy that her plight to flee was carried
    out.
  He and his children lay wondering of their future
    with their lost sibling
She then awoke and rang to her children who were
  amazed to hear of and from her.

  Then a date for the battle,
    and it soon began, but ended in misfortune
  for her but not him.
  She and he carried on their lives with
    the new and the old.

Sara Manwiller

New Sonnet XLV

You can't remember even how it started,
But somewhere, nightmares overcome your dreams.
The happy-after died it seems,
And left you hollow, fearful, broken hearted.
He's split your lip to match your swelling eyes.
Just like the last time, and the time before.
And still, you pick yourself up from the floor.
believing in your self deluding lies.
Take no more blows. Just take yourself away.
Disrupt the violence of this loveliness act.
Reject your victimhood and seized the day,
With head erect and spirit yet intact,
Alive, with mind and body well preserved.
Embrace the self respect that you've deserved!

Vern Golden

Hawaii Nei

The distant orbs stand vigil yet
o'er island crests their subtle powers have wrought
from fiery ocean mounts, with rainbows blest
and endless patience bought.

Richard S. Grigsby

Alcoholism

I know you don't understand, my thinking is so unclear.
But you didn't grow up living with abuse and fear.
Alcoholism is so much more than just unfair
It takes a child's life and turns it into total despair.

You grow up covering things up, trying not to cry
When all you really want to do is scream and ask why

Why did I have to have this life so empty and cruel
Why did he leave memories of black and blue
He never once asked how it made me feel
I guess he didn't want to hear what was so real
He hurt me when he hit my Mom like he would
Everything he did I never believed he should
The time he hit her so hard she bled
He just left her there and went to bed.

I can't forget his drunken rages, still clear to me even now
I don't believe I truly could, I don't see how
The hurt is so deep and strong inside
I wish I could leave it, just run and hide
But it always follows me wherever I go
Showing me how it has the ability to grow.

Robyn Dandar

Emptiness

You tore our relationship apart,
But you didn't realize you broke my heart.
You sat and listened to the Judge, all heartless and cold,
You didn't stop to think I might have a hold.
Will someone please stop this storm of rain,
That keeps pouring from my brain.
A few more years,
A thousands tears.
When will this bitterness end,
So I can see my next of kin.
You don't know how I long to see,
The mother who means nothing to me.

Stephanie Hughes

It's Okay - Don't Throw Your Life Away

It's okay to do what you want
But you don't have to do what you don't
It's okay to say what you feel
Just make sure everything you say is real
It's okay to try to make a change
But not everything should be rearranged
It's okay to follow some one's footsteps
Just make sure he has enough left
Make sure he has enough left to guide you all the way
'Cause if they stop that's where you're going to stay
It's okay to make your own path and go your own way
Because some one will walk in your footsteps someday
It's okay to make many changes with your life.
As long as it doesn't involve using a gun or a knife
It's okay to try to make it in the world today
But no matter how hard times are....
  Don't throw your life away

Tameka Martin

Mona

Mona, you mean the world to me, you really do
I'm sure my feelings will always be, I love you!
All the memories we've made and the new ones I'll treasure
Being your friend will always be a pleasure!

I write all of these poems to let you know
With you in my life there is always a glow!
With an official document we gave a part of our heart
With that being done we will never be apart!

Trudy L. Colucci

Everything's Going To Be Alright

I know that times are hard now and then
but you have to remember that God made man
not only to suffer but to lead the way
by showing People that you're going to heaven on Judgement Day

Some people don't understand what you're going through
but God know the right thing to do
it seems like things only happen to you
don't worry because on that day or night
you'll find out that Everything's Going To Be Alright

Tangenicka Williams

My Angel Amongst Us

I knew he was special from day one,
By the aura surrounding him, my first son.
He was — My angel amongst us.

As he grew in body and in mind,
He became Angelic, this child of mine.
He was — My angel amongst us.

As a man, he sacrificed for others by his deed,
He spoke, heard, did no evil, take heed.
He was — My angel amongst us.

He was 26 when he died Christmas Eve,
To join heaven's choir, from us he did leave.
The newest star — My angel amongst us.

We remember his smile, his perfection, my son,
Good to all, hurtful to no one.
He was — My angel amongst us.

When the pain is too much, and I cry,
A gentle Breeze whispers, here am I.
He is — My angel amongst us.

Sharon J. Boan

The Will Of The Wind

A Northeast wind draws sharply for the old man's hooded parka,
calling him to wince, therefore imposing on his graciousness towards
the warming sun. His face is pleasantly weathered, thoughtfully
handsome. Boyish features bestow it, despite the incessant passage
of time. The bench, upon which rests a man bemused, stings with
callousness. A songbird speaks a few feet away, finding solace in a
twisted maple.

This place, grey stoned, is not home. The feeling of abandonment,
he muses, has aged him more than time itself. Inside, resentful
hallways appear itchy and yellowed. They harbor lifetimes
seemingly
spent. So deeply in thought, he fails to notice a young woman slump
down beside him. She weeps terribly.

"I have lost my mother," she murmurs. "She passed away before I
could tell her I loved her."

"I am sorry," he replies, reaching for her hand. "When she was of
life, did your love for her show?"

"How shall I know?," she questions, "for there were times of much
sadness and times of great joy."

He rises from his seat, sending the beautiful bird into the crisp
autumn sky. "My dear," he tells her, "today she has set you free of
that sorrow, for by her passing you will see that she already knew."
Sporting the color of rich, red satin, the maple leaves crumple
underfoot.

Steven Nohr

Oh Youth! Why Must You Go?

Oh youth! How I loath to see you flee, leaping steadily into the past.
Can it be that you have gone so quickly? How can I make you last?
So much did I seek. So much did I desire.
How quickly you are gone, that burning youthful fire.

Why do I find no patience in the years that past?
Oh youth, why must you depart, leaving me so fast?
Oh youth! Why can't you stay another day?
Oh youth! Someday will you return my way?

Oh sweet impatient youth, why must you leave,
    when I've only just begun?
Oh youth, why must you turn and run?
Must so soon you go, leaving me to flee?

Oh creeping mantle of wisdom that comes with age,
    why does your presence fill me so with rage?
Oh youth, if you're so impatient, foolish and brash,
    why do I cling to you and let you have your say?
Oh age, if you're so patient, wise and worthy,
    why do I dread your day?
Somehow I feel no different, but it's a feeling untrue,
    for feelings aren't enough, and youth has slipped away.

William C. McDonald

Paradise

As you sleep I watch you and
can only wonder what you are thinking.
Your face is a smooth flawless
one and your eyes are ocean blue,
your hands are soft and caress
me and touch me in a way I only dreamed about.

Hold me throughout the night,
You are so gentle with me
that I had forgotten how
love felt until I met you.

Let us fly and be free from society,
As we journey through nature
I find myself waiting to stay here forever,
Just you and me.

As we bathe in the stream under
the waterfall I feel fish nibbling at my toes.
As we hug and hold one another by the fire as night falls,
I wish that this could be our home,
But as dawn nears I remember
we must return to the city of dismay

Rebecca Schraut

Halloween

Halloween what a treat give me something good to eat.
Candy sprinkles every where candy sprinkles in your hair.
Scary stories are quite fun when they scare everyone.
Bats and goblins ghost and ghouls.
Grandma grady looking down people jumping all around.
Candy gun chocolate drinks these are things that make
you thinks. Halloween orange all green candy treats that
you eat man o man it's kind of neat.
High o high in the sky is where a witch will fly a cat
is screaming kind of loud people looking on the ground.

Zollie Davis

Dark

It was dark, like a summer's night.
No one even in sight,
If they were they wouldn't be near
To me they would be probably a smear.
Cause there's nothing that you can see in the dark,
Nothing!

Sabrina Brown

Thanks Be To God

I thank you God for the morning dew
Cast down heads are lifted up
They look to the sky and find hope
Fears within vanish like fog, that surround mountains

I thank you God for the freshness of spring
At sunset flowers bow down
Like magic at dawn, show inward affection
Toward human hearts

I thank you God for the snow
The snowflakes like crystals, fall to the ground
To capture your creation for human hearts
Children mould snowman to be a friend
To tickle you to smile

I thank you God for the prevailing wind
The fog, the snow the frozen droplets of ice
Bring sensuous pleasures to the beauty of your creation
As I desire the warmth of the cloud
The freezing touch of the air
Energize my children to activity

Ruth J. Moyo (Chimbumu)

Understanding

It really is hard, I know you can't see
Cause right now you don't feel, the same as me
I know I have to, I know I should,
I have to get over you,
I wish I could, thinking of being with you.
It's such a nice thought.
Then I come back to reality,
and see what it really has brought.
Being strangers, I will not be fair.
No, that just can't be
Cause I know you care
Maybe the future will hold something new.
But during this time you will be you.
Right now, the only way for me to be happy,
and mend my broken heart.
If I can have you for more than just
A "One-Night-Thought!"

Shirley M. Hewes

Scolding The Wind

My reverie was safe, serene and free.
Cavorting wanton whirling winds
Penetrated none of the containment within,
Until a raucous throaty high-pitched
Cawing pierced the walls with a powerful continuous din.

At the window I beheld a huge black crow
Perched on the head of a shaking, badly bent
and frightened adolescent maple tree.
A bold black force of fury bravely berating
His careless and powerful adversary.

Pandemonium had disturbed my orbit;
I opened the window and shouted at
this astonishing creature, "Stop that racket!"
"What is the matter with you?"

He turned his head and stared disdainfully
For only a moment, then fanned his wings.
But, as he flew away, I thought I heard him say,
    "Who did you protect or defend today?"
My day dream had become shallow, I was truly contrite.
Scolding the wind was his sacred right.

Rose Marie English

Besieging Blackness

Blackness besieges the world in my eyes
Changing the truth to ever present lies
Life in itself continues to die
Wars are started without asking why
Men fall to the ground with bullets in their chest
The nation is put to the supreme and ultimate test
Small and large children fall to burning evil
As they load their bodies with drugs that are lethal
The world is falling through the pits of hell
Acts of horror that men cannot tell
The number rises to horrible highs
As blackness besieges the world in my eyes.

Richard W. Curry Jr.

Night Life

Sirens blare from the car
Children crying from the pain
The fire crackles and swallows the house
Neighbors watch in awe and shame

One man stands alone—the father
He shot his wife and his mother
The children stand with their aunt
Crying for mama, but she is gone

Policemen and firemen shake their heads slowly
Guilt ripples through the Doctor
For he knew the father was ill
But he never did bother to tell

The night life was shattered
In a small family house
No more laughter and tears would come
From a family full of hope and fun

Slowly the sirens start to fade
No more children crying from the pain
There's no fire—just water and soot
And the neighbors go home mourning and gloom

Rachelle Rivera

Violent Piece

In these violent times, peace is cheap.
Churning potion allows release of my inner calm.
Abuse is famous in its ashed ways —
Burning away love and life into a black-grey
And white.
Colors exist as intoxicated blurs of fuzzy,
Euphoric, relaxing pleasures.
Home made multi-personal lifestyle smolts in
a glass medicated with death.
Misery turned its back and fled from my
pathetic, holocaustic corpse.
I live only for peace — minute by minute and
seconds after.
Destructive measures are required to survive my peace.
My peace is possessive.
It clings for support in a vice of anguish and
suffering.
In these peaceful times, violence is cheap.

Robert Aikins

Untitled

Look not at my eyes when I pass,
You need not know them.
Know not my sorrows from my breath I sigh.
The bags are parcels of the weak.
Do not listen to my words for they may change you.
Count the clouds in the sky, the birds in the trees,
While you still effortlessly watch my shadow pass by.

Ryan Ellis

English Sky

Revolution man sitting in the garden
Clasped hands with the soil starting to harden.
He looks up towards an English sky
Trying to figure out if he can reach that high?

Revolution man waiting for the sun
Eyes closed with the rainbow surprising ev'ryone.
He hears the birds flying through air
Wondering if he would be able to follow there?

Revolution man writing in his mind
Thought control with the words counting time.
He feels it's all wrong to him
Explaining to himself that he could never get in.

Revolution man smelling the flowers scent
Elapsed time in between each one that he meant.
He touches the outside of a rose
Thinking to himself how an English sky knows?

How does it feel to be one of the lucky ones around?
A never ending story with opinions turned glory.
How does it feel to be one of the lucky ones around?

Scott Peterman

"Crazy Grandma"

Jennifer, just 5 years old; saying what she has been told.
Climbed upon my lap one day, here's what she had to say.
"YOU CRAZY GRANDMA, you know that? NO, she's not a little Brat;
asking why she calls me thus, causing heartaches and a fuss.

"Mommy told me, it is true, and says I must hate you too;
you can't see us like before, we won't let you anymore.
Mommy's very very mad, says that daddy is so bad;
she divorced him yesterday, CRAZY GRANDMA, stay away.

Jenny and Lisa moved away, broke our hearts too, I must say;
we can't visit, IS THIS TRUE? for we will still LOVE you.
Sing for Jesus like you've done, when you lived here, little ones;
Pray for mommy, both of you, God loves "CRAZY GRANDMA" too.

Violet Holt

Fantasy of Dreams

A whispering romance and pieces of time.
  Collect all moments to bring two worlds together.

  The story has been told before,
  and although the pages of time are short,
the dreams and memories will always be never ending.

Take a look to each passing star.
A fine tuned illusion that only two will share.
  Thoughts so distant.
Only to be brought together by hearts that beat as one.

Time the familiar enemy has kept us from holding each other.
But it has allowed us the chance to see the realism of fantasy.
  A fantasy made of past and present lives.
    All with a common purpose.
  To bring the gift of emotion to new and everlasting heights.

Take with you all of your dreams.
Hold them as if tomorrow another will come true.

For me,
I search for new dreams.
  When I met you
    all the old ones came true.

Scott Reindel

Lead On My Pen As You Must

Lead on my pen as you must
Commanding scribe of nature
For you alone are the instrument to my soul
You alone verify my inner oneness

Transmit the ideas from on high
The spirit of truth shall guide you
He shall give you the words to bring to life
All that is in the sanctuary of mind

There's corners and rooms yet undiscovered
There's millions of words and ideas
All waiting for you to ponder and arrange
In the order that best benefits you

Lead on my pen as you must
This is your dedication to this life's art
These are your words put before me
That your usefulness was not in vain.

Timothy E. Pilant

A Tear Of Rust From An Ancient Warrior

Drifting across the fields of snow and ice
Conquering the hills of brush and rock
Thunderous footprints quietly placed
Parting the cold air as the cut of a knife
Heaved these primitive tools of demise
Stained and torn from history's past fight
Feared by all a pilfer of the open light

There a countryside with a valley in view a different time a similar
Place paused for a glimpse overwhelmed by memories of past
Overtaken and absorbed were the feelings
Cased in iron this heart full of trust but lost in life

Piercing the snow and frozen soil thrust the chipped bloodstained
sword forgotten and tossed was the shield against all thunder and
lightning separated by a lash the beast and iron man
Solemnly standing tombed in misery

Through the open slits through the holes of light
The eyes of steel that beheld the horror and hate
Gazed upon the light to life with a new perception
Reflected that day that moment for all to see
A tear of unwanted trust a tear eternally held in rust

Stuart L. Brown

Contending For The Faith

Praise God from whom all blessings flow,
Contending for the faith is the only way to go.

If you choose not to contend,
The rod of God on your back will bend.

For God does love all His sons,
And wants you in the race to run.

So run the race by means of grace
Where faith causes us to seek His face.

There we receive His peace of mind,
That allows us to put worldliness behind.

Then love to others is expressed around,
And blessings from God flows on down.

Which encourages us to contend some more,
For God gives back what we laid up in store.

And when we come to the heavenly bank,
We will have much for which to give thanks.

Reuel Barnes

He Wept

I watched the small child lie there
covered in blood and soaked rags
a halo gathering of onlookers trembled
bewildered by this unfortunate everyday tragedy
a small boy, tossing baseball in the street
engulfed by the first summer that he would remember
was struck down by an innocent driver caught unaware
I'll never forget the crowd
whispering like serpent tongues at the man's long hair
he was in shock
the driver crouched over the boy - convulsing as if in a
seizure bleeding tears
his screams attached to failing appendages would not suffice
the boy had slipped into irreversible subconsciousness
An ambulance descended like a mass of tattered angels
navy blue coverings helped distance them from the reality
instantly the child was swept away both by flashing lights
and the everlasting death
The driver remained
weeping.

Tony Lowe

The Box

A child's secret box lies untouched.
Covered with dust from years gone by.
Inside a rock pleasing to the eyes of a small curious child.
A string of beads found under the porch
A tiny china doll that looked lonely on a mercantile shelf.
Beside the doll a beautiful ring given
by a mother who so loved her little girl.
Also in the old wooden box was a leather tobacco pouch
filled with marbles bits of string and other special little things.

A child enters an attic filled with cobwebs.
She searches through old boxes and
clutter finally finding what she seeks!
A small wooden box filled with memories she had nearly forgotten.
Carefully she retrieves it from where it had been hidden.
Tenderly lifting the lid, she places inside a pretty
piece of colored glass she had found down by the well,
where years ago a little girl had died.
Then with one last look inside, she closes the box
with a sigh of contentment and turns to leave.
The box complete...

Roxann Dentlinger

Deep Convictions Of Passion

With ashy eyes an a tattoo of PERDURABO, an Ancient Daemon,
crawling up her shapely thigh,
Your look turned to a stare-as she glances, her fiery violet eyes;
make your blood bubble and boil with a wicked chill.

For, your heart drips with Age Old love which is encased in
Shadows Of Illusions,
The sparkle in her eyes and sassy smirk is just for you;
But when she looks deep into your Onyx toned eyes-she feels the
  unknown
Love, the Temptation of Tricks and the Sweet Sleek Spell of
Seductiveness; which entrances her like a wolf to rare meat or the
taste of a coppery raging red, red—Vampyre Kiss...

Therefore, Star-Crossed Loves meet in every lifetime and Century,
To share a Love that they can only have and understand.

Valerie F. Jacques

"Good-Bye Lilly"

A spot lay on the ground where my Lilly came down,
crimson red, blood let till dead,
I killed my beloved, I murdered my love.

Driving on through the night searching for light,
my eyes grow weary, my outlook is dreary,
I killed my beloved, I murdered my love.

I cannot be caught, sweet patience be sought,
oh, but she was only a child, why did I grow wild?
I killed my beloved, I murdered my love.

And now I smell the fragrance of Lilly, but I must not
get silly, I'll turn off at the next exit and perhaps there
I can fix it, I killed my beloved, I murdered my love.

While looking down in my bag my emotions now sag,
Lilly's poor head has been severed, so I must now be clever,
I killed my beloved, I murdered my love.

In the distance I see a trash bin perhaps ideal for me to
put her in, quick now the coast is clear, one last kiss and
Good-bye my dear, I killed my beloved, I murdered my love.

Whew! Now that was close, and is the heat on in this car?
I'm beginning to roast!

Shawn Martin

Untitled

Moonbeams whisper a gentle rain's lament.
Crumpled, tortured grass wiggles from pure earth.
Quiet my child.
Ubiquitous clouds gathering around my bed.
Shading my dreams, muffling the sun's lurid screams.

I find brutal grandeur under my fingertips...
Contemptuous dirt flirting with the worm's remorse.

Moonbeams whisper a wind's solemn secret
As the lilies hush the daisies
And the rose drowns in her own vanity.
Stare into a laughing stream
And flow with the minnow's dream.

The lips of a child fall silent.
In the dream - - clouds disappear
And the sun reclaims its throne in the valley.

Robert Christopher Lenoir

A Precious Farewell

Thrilled with excitement pleasure and joy,
Curiosity overwhelming whether you were a girl or a boy.
My heart skipped a beat to know you were there,
Forever together our lives we would share.
Continually guessing your weight and your size,
The color of your hair and your twinkling eyes.
Wondering about the first words you would say,
Would your spirit and nature be bright and gay?
The wonder and amazement of becoming a mother,
Created new sensations quite like no other.
Just when all was prepared and ready for your birth,
A higher power decided to remove you from earth.
Wanting to give up and just lay down and die,
I struggled to move on with tear filled eyes.
Never to connect or touch, your tiny spirit and mine,
The only thing to heal this loss was an enormous span of time.
You'll never be forgotten, a reminder in all I see,
Like the stars up in the heavens or the Angel on top of my tree.
May your spirit be protected in the heavens up above,
Until we once more are united someday, My Precious Little Love.

Sharon R. Frank

The Freedom Of My Soul

Like the sun's reflections, suffused with its own light,
dancing spiritedly across the ripples of the ever expansive sea,

And like the wind which blows, with both force and subtlety,
passing through the open arms of myriads of trees,

So must my soul, the very essence of my being, my connection
with the universe, be allowed to roam free.

For with this freedom of my soul, my unique essence will
shine through, with a golden shower of creativity, so please
just let it be.

This freedom comes not without its price, for others often
want to stifle me.

It would do well for me to see that most others do not
understand my unique quintessence, and even fewer hold the key.

I will thankfully pay the price for this joyous opportunity,
for I know that I will be graced with the freedom to be me.

Sandra L. Smith

Death to the Traitors

Death.
Death, I say.
Death to the traitors.
Death to the soul, the village, the knoll.
Death near and far.
Death is here at the door.
Death is love, hate, anguish of the soul.

So death.
Death, I say.
Death to the traitors of the heart, mind, body, and soul.
Death is everywhere, near and far,
Even at the door.
A shadow here,
A cupboard there.
See the flicker of life to death.

So death.
Everlasting death.
Death, I say,
Death to the traitors of life.

Robynn Lynn

I Wish It Would Rain So Deeply, Deeply Inside Me

I wish it would rain so
deeply, deeply inside me
But rain is just water drops
It's something special
When I see the clouds gather
around,
I know it will rain deeply
inside of me.
Most of the time I wish it
will rain so deeply, deeply
inside me,
To wash my sins away,
After, when the rain is over
I have to see deeply down
to my soul,
How I wish it would shine
so deeply, deeply inside of me
To remind me it will shine
deeply down into my soul.

Sheng Vang

The Awakening

You awakened and enticed me with an overwhelming and uncon-
trollable
desire. My entire body now quivers at the sight of you!
Then when I look into your hypnotic eyes,
I am stunned by their radiance. At this
point the necessity to touch you, is greater, than the need for
discretion. And when we kiss, the world ceases to exist, my only
focus is you. You could never kiss me that way and not feel it too!
There is nothing that I can do to disguise the way I already feel
about you. What I'm afraid of is, how deeply I could feel about you,
if you let me or, if I let myself. I am aware of what you can do to
me mentally and physically. But it doesn't stop me from wanting you,
or the need I have to be with you. I am totally perplexed by these
feelings, so early in the game. I don't know where this is going
or where it will end. But at this time in my life I must take a
risk. So I will start as your friend, hopefully progress to someone
you love, and then into someone you can't live without. So, allow
yourself to experience extreme happiness, it's as close as your
imagination, and me. Oh, and one more thing, thanks for breathing
life back into me, I forgot how nice it could be. You are a friend
to the end.

Sarah J. Elio

And Still I Smile

What was that news I heard today!
Did someone predict the end was near in sight
With gangs and drugs and moral decay;
And the quest for power propelling the way?

And, so, I smile when I stop and think...
When was the last time you said hello
to your neighbor across the way,
Or took the time to watch a little child at play,
Or shared one brief moment with a
Lonely, sad, and forgotten soul?

And still I smile when I look and see
faces of facade and beguile,
And hear words insensitively spoken by
those who wish to determine the ultimate
destiny of my sisters and my brothers.

So listen well, for have you not heard
That justice shall reign and the judge nor
the jury will be man? But HE, Who is All Powerful,
Will Hear, and Know, and Reward....And Still I smile.

Rubye Doss Peach

The Pyramid

I see myself in a thousand images
distorted and confused
The void surrounds them all
The blackness surrounds me
We're trapped
inside the pyramid

The steeplechase has begun
Wire walls enclose the killer
The soul and mind have no walls, only doorways
Enter the pyramid

Does the mirror lie? What do you see?
The demons dance, the angels fall
The door is under your feet
Escape from the pyramid

We must fall before mankind can rise
The stars will follow the laughter
I was pulled through the void
Everything is clear
I surround you
Become the pyramid

Steven C. Price

Stand Fast

Never back down.
Don't let them push you back
into the pit from which you just rose.
Stand fast on your new ground.

Don't turn back;
advance.
Never give up;
stand fast.

Retreating is the coward's way
to justify his actions.
Don't back down or you
will give your life to different factions.

If you are knocked down;
get up.
Do not give in or
give up.
Shannon Drake

A Breath

Descending deep into the Grand Canyon I inhaled...

air

filling every corner, deeper and deeper, reaching
down into my toes, up
beyond my head, airing out stale
dead spaces, filling, filling
FILLING
(How much longer can I keep inhaling?)
Like helium-stretched rubber I
become larger and lighter with each step.
Like a sponge soaking up a spill,
like a starving beggar sitting
down to a banquet,
like an addict, crazed
with craving, putting the needle
into his vein

every corner, every dark
empty space every cell of me
sucked in
silence and space.
Yolanda Wysocki

Feeling of Serenity

Going for a walk through a meadow of flowers
  Down to a rolling brook,
    Listening to the cool, clear water
      As it ripples over the rocks.

Looking up at a spectacular view of a mountain
  Slanted from the earth to the sky,
    Inviting me to come climb it
      Just like a stack of blocks.

Enjoying the breathtaking beauty of a rose
  Laden with dew in the morning,
    For soon the sun will rise
      And dry away it's tears not of sorrow.

Waiting for an awesome sunset of an evening sun
  Dying only when the day is ending,
    Resting for awhile during darkness
      Only to show up again as brilliant tomorrow.
Sybil F. Gallier

Shame Of Reality

Look in the mirror honest or fake
Dreams surrender, reality takes its
place. You always talk of honey
but to me it's a bad taste. You always
act like somebody, I've seen the
photo, I know the first take.

No more endless lying
No more confrontational embrace
No more blunt decisions
Reality knows your name, oh we're all the same.
Don't question who you are.
Hearts always feel pain always the same,
  always the same
Too many suns and moons have rested in the
west, you're moving east now, but no one
No one cheats death. No deserved answers.
  No commands in vain
  No, all through your life you denied your soul was
  caged, no shell to escape
  All the same hearts and pain whispering everyone's name.
William Bret Buck

In Vino Veritas

The spirit is in the wine.
Drink up says Blake.
Holding tight to something that's not there
gives the illusion truth.
Makes me feel like life is real, life is real.

Day after day you go to work
put your heart on the line for an idea
that doesn't pan out.
Love remains out of reach.
The spirit is in the wine.
We're running short of time.
Let me go to where the concrete's hot
and the hills are brown.
Home to where I've never seen the sun.
Home to find the one who needs me.
She needs me but she can't admit it.

Patience is a virtue
I have no time to wait.
Temperance is essential
That's just not my fate.
Scott Lettieri

Life

The human race is like a corn field
Each ear has its' season
Then it grows old and sheds its' grace
And dies without cause or reason
Each ear struggles through weathered times
And awaits that last moment of gold
It seems they work so hard in life
To have just one moment to hold
But when that moment of gold is reached
It seems as though life is so great
But when comes the hand of the harvester
It seems they hesitate
Because they've realized that life does have a reason
But now it's too late
For the whole field knows
That death has no certain date
But the reason of life is inside
Each ear has a reason of its' own
So hurry, find it, live golden
Because the day of the harvester is not known
Taylor Kastner

"Prayer For The Hurting Child"

Oh Lord I'm young and fragile, my will I cannot hide,
Each night I'm more frightened, and this I can't deny,
Dear Lord please let him sleep tonight, so I can enjoy
  morning light,
I'm very tired and full of pain, for his acts I can't
  explain,
With each hurt Lord, make me stronger, till he's to weak
  to hurt no longer.
    Susan Carlyle

Selene

She lives in shadow of the night,
  Endless hunger of blood and life,
A fetish of the undead,
  She drank of blood,
She drank of the soul of the damned.
  Still she lies all covered in lace,
A trickle of blood on a milk white face,
  I watch her sleeping so peaceful and calm.
A blood red rose open her breast,
  A ruby of blood wells upon her finger,
I lick it away, her kiss still lingers away.
  I can feel her fingers like ice down my spine,
I feel her tremble as her souls bound in mine,
  She hears the whispers on the wind,
Mine and hers three fates we bend.
  I taste her tears they fall down her cheek,
In sorrow she mourns the death she has cheat.
  I look in her eyes and I see pain,
Then I see love they are much in the same.
    Tony Peirce

To My Loving Wife...

God's given glimpse of life is but a fleeting span
endured, enjoyed and wasted by butterfly and man.
With true exotic being emerged from rawest earth
they free themselves from shackles inherent to their birth.
Both start a lifelong search to maybe never find
the prize of love and beauty with one of like and kind.
The gift of love is beauty, the truest form of art
Its gentle touch comes swiftly to linger in the heart.
Soft stolen sips of nectar, in fragile fleeting flight
make lasting scars of sweetness, best seen in dark of night.
Hearts that come together to flutter in the sun
Appear as two in passage, but they are really one...
    Walter Ivey

This Man

Helpless as a crew of a small vessel we sit,
Enduring the fierce storm.
Waiting, hoping for the calm.
The sails torn,
The mast broken like matchsticks.
Still, we remain.
The life we cling to so dearly has served its purpose,
And now must go to from which it came:
The ultimate and final just reward.

It is said, "A man who helps a stranger is surely a man of
  heart, a man of deeds."
Deeds, all but forgotten to most,
Shan't be overlooked by the keeper.
May the gates swing wide to let this proud man pass,
And be reunited with those who have gone on before.
He is not gone,
For there is a spark of him in all those he touched.
I am truly fortunate to have known and learned from
This man I call DADDY.
    William Byrd Haynes

Stands for liberty
Enough taxes! We say
In lusty language of Boston's bay
We have our rights and the King his tea
Whatever the price to be free!

We know our chances,
In view of the circumstances,
Seems folly to smile the royalty.
But there comes a time in human events
When things must be shaken - sides be taken
We take the stand for liberty!

Weary cold and hungry troops
Wearing rags in painful stoops;
Long, dark, somber faces
Shadowed by a death that chases
Those of courage enough to pay
The price of freedom here today.

Now on that coast, a perpetual toast,
In the hand of the symbol of freedom
Inscribed to the lowly, her message is solely,
That she stands for liberty!
    Ron Nellermoe

Love And Torture

I love and keep on loving,
even though he is taken.
I keep on loving
with the hope that he will someday be mine.
For love is really the only torture we have in this
world,
Even though love makes this wretched world go
'round.
And this is why
I love and keep on loving
this boy
who is taken by another girl.
    Sherry Lynn Beattie

In You

(for S.P. - dedicated to his Mother)
In you, I've found love....
Even though we're miles apart,
I think about you night and day;
This precious gift you've given me,
I know, comes straight from the heart.

In you, I've found hope....
In all of the smiles and all of the tears,
I see a silhouette of you;
The courage to go on alone,
Through good and bad times over the years.

In you, I've found life....
Somehow, somewhere the years have passed,
I miss you more than words can say,
The tears I can't hold back;
But, the memories I hold in my heart,
Like our Love, will always last.
    Shawn-Marie Billick

"My Son"

We will always be together...
Even when there is no more...
We have taught each other,
How to forgive and what love is.

There are always todays, and,
Tomorrows... but, there is never total...
Except with you and me.

My friend... my son...
I will always be there.
In whatever time.

I always cry when I'm happy.
I'm crying.
Wallace J. Gunderson

A Gift

Life was ordered, it seemed complete.
Events came and went, nothing different.
Everything the same, till there was you.

Days were scheduled, each ran together.
Actions taken were routine, outcomes measured,
results obtained, till there was you.

It happened, before I knew.
I wasn't looking, it happened.
Lost love, unfounded, till there was you.

Feeling, sensing, touching, loving,
finding ways were never easy.
Experiences forgotten, till there was you.
William C. Snauffer

Inner Strength

It controls the mind, the heart.
Every thought, every problem, every
solution. It makes war and peace.
It controls only to be controlled, and
it only controls the weak. It's a
mind twisting work of art within
everyone waiting to be explored.
The more you sacrifice, the more
you gain control. It's not so overwhelming,
all the let downs, and in the
confusion, through the sorrow,
you'll know it won't last. You'll
be able to appreciate the pain,
and the strength. In the
morning when you rise, and through
the midnight hour, or after breakfast,
in between lunch, it might hit you,
then hit you again, and you'll be
stronger than you ever were then,
when all the pain began.
Tiffany Tilley

Me, Myself

I have no claim to fame, for I am only me.
I am what I say, what I do, and who you see.
I've tried to copy styles, hoped to be like others.
Tried to follow footsteps of my sisters and my brother.

I've changed my mind, put on new faces,
Searched for approval, fought for your good graces,
But I am only me, And what courage that took!
Balk if you want to. Don't like it? Don't look!
Rebecca Ledder

Cristina

There are times when words alone can not
express my thoughts for you.

When I hold you tightly in my arms; your
warmth and desires overpower my senses, and
I find myself wanting to be in your arms
forever.

Stroking your hair in my fingers, as if they
were pearls, really makes me warm. Your lips
set my passion aflame, and making love to you
is an adventure I wish would never end.

I am so glad that you reached into my life and
whatever may come of it, I know that I am a better
person for having met you.
Ray Dean Mason Jr.

Endurance

I have painted this picture in my mind's
   eye

Of a beautiful brown pebbled rose who refused to
   die

I saw her bud blossomed proudly early in the
   spring

The rain storms and heart of summer enhanced her it
   seemed

I notice the trees changed its colors, and watched the leaves
   fall

But not one of her beautiful brown pebbles dropped or dropped at
   all

When winter came, I put on my hat, my coat, and my
   boots

The ice had frozen her beauty ever so stiff, and caused her to
   droop

I dug her up by the roots, and brought her in where it was
   warm

She blossomed ever so brightly, and weathered all seasons and
   storms
Robert E. Franklin

Bureaucrat Lament

Up at dawn, walk the dog to pee
Eyes aglare, in traffic's snare
Only to work in a bureaucracy.

Days are steady and long
Complaints and continual calls
Barren friends singing same songs.

Distinguished and disguised
The act of nothing
Unduly interested in other's affairs.

The pension is good
Days off understood
Outside beltway, diametrically opposed.

We continue and grow old
Eager beaver, burn-out, rebirth, indisposed
Then suddenly it's time to go!
Rebekah V. Pearson

A Tribute To Richard M. Nixon

He looked far into the future
   farther than the human eye could see
caught a vision of the world of Tennyson or
   what it was mankind could hope to be
glanced rearward, too, towards the store of Time
   recognized some misery in America's past
Then let himself down on his very own ground
   but not before saying: 'I must forge a WAY that lasts!'
And he did. With Pat.
   Not once!
    Not twice!
     But thrice, and more
   He forged a universal lease
That tapped God's Eternal Stream of consciousness
   His vision: A world at peace.
Five living U.S.A. Presidents, past and present,
   along with their wives, agreed; and
countless millions, in addition, watched
   as he left this world in peace: To who knows what?
Could it be to a more 'Perfect Judgment'? For now, let's wait and see!

   Tennyson Jenkins

No One's Wife (A Widow's Awakening)

As she walks the dreary path of life
Feeling alone cause she's no one wife,
Depressed and down for the bills are due
She sits and withers, she feels so blue.

She feels so helpless, so full of strife
Searching for light in her darkened life,
One step forward, can she feel some hope?
But ten steps backwards, she cannot cope.

Her tears are streaming, her mood depressed
Her problems many, she feels so stressed,
She feels her struggle may be in vain
For the darkened clouds just bring more pain.

Though her problems many and she feels so stressed
She can not deny that her life is blessed,
The sun has risen, now her eyes can see
Others worse off than she could ever be.

Who cares if she is nobody's wife!
Her family, her friends illuminate her life,
The problems, the bills, she leaves them to fate,
Her mood now more peaceful, priorities straight!

   Roe Schrock

Remember You

I know you are leaving for an exciting life
Filled with both joy and strife
And my head keeps saying it's what you have to do
But that doesn't keep my heart from breaking into
When I was lost and looking for friends
You found me and took me in
You will never know how much you mean to me
Or how different, without you, my life would be
And now as your time to leave grows near
Our time together becomes so dear
I hope you won't forget us, those you leave behind
But will always keep us in your hearts and in your minds
So goodbye my friends and remember, too
That I will always remember you.

   Tami Tanner

Fall of Man

This world is a crazy place-
filled with hatred and anger,
all caused by the human race

Millions of years ago was when it all began
To be exact, at the beginning
when Eve committed the first sin
An thus began the fall of man

Incest and adultery were both part of the game
People selling their bodies,
degrading both man and woman's name

Jealousy and rage for one's own's personal gain
We each remember the story of Abel and his brother Cain

And still today it's still the same
The same old song, with a different beat, nothing has changed

Everyone has their own idea of the right way
Never ever stopping to listen to what God has to say

Love the Lord, Almighty with your heart, soul, and mind
And true, eternal, rewards you will truly find

   Tiffany M. Lacey

Song

Into this vast and endless
Fit of stars
You might never have come,
Nor I;
Or come too soon, or in a black year hence,
Or issued from a far country
Whose paths
I would not chance to travel.

And so now I sing in praise
Of the God whose grand mathematic
Brought us, after long and careful testing,
Ever nearer until we touched
And sparked our hearts
Into unending song.

   Robert Lee

Fear Of Sleep, Daylight Flash

Home from school, I hated the most
Flesh torn and body beat in, not a child but a ghost,
As my blood flows upon the floor,
My brothers and sisters watch, eyes of horror,
Screaming in silence, turning and running thru the door.

Ran away and wanted to be free,
All I could do was hide in the tallest tree.
Sometime my bed was under the house,
To sleep with the roaches and a mouse.
Locked up like an animal in a cage,
Only I could hear my silent rage.

   Richard J. Wilkerson

You Showed Me Love

You gave me confidence; you showed me love
I saw things big and bold in a whole other color
You walked me up to things that I could never get to before
You gave joy; you showed me love.

You gave me a future; you showed me love.
I learned things that no one could teach me.
You showed me the world from sea to shining sea.
You gave me life; you showed me love.

   Sarah Turner

The Matrix Of Our Lives*

The matrix of our lives flows around us
  Fluid always
And changing as it flows
  Brings us joys and sorrows
Hopes and fears

Paths cross, entwine, and separate
  Yet the fluid marks of one upon the other
Long endure
  Always adding to the impact of others
Moving into the matrix

Thus there is no separation
  Once mixed the fluid can't be filtered out
But only move along
  As one, together, enriched by contacts
That last forever
*Published in Attain magazine, July-August 1985
Published as Introduction to Victoria's Story—
Reincarnation—God's Love Returned, Vantage Press 1992*

  Victoria Schmidt

Saturday Sonnet

The rain, like an omen, enters the night.
For as the stars twinkle, I'm filled with despair.
With whom this great burden will I ever share?
If only my heart could find pure delight.
Happiness is a privilege and never a right.
Where is it written that things will be fair?
Dismay and regret are things we must bear,
Why all the battles must I alone fight?

Say you'll stand beside me and help me along
And keep all my fears an arm's length away.
I'm not asking more the someone to trust
Sometimes the cold wind that blows is so strong,
I let the cold hands of darkness lead me astray.
If you travel with me, I'll do as I must.

  Sarah E. Medley

On My Mind

Do you talk to me for closure or
for comfort?
For vengeance?
For glory?

I only wanted to know you — again,
I wanted to speak on the terms of a friend.

Do you hate me or loathe me?
Does your lover disagree?

Is there peace in this time
In your heart
In my mind?

Do you need my rejection to find life
in today?
Or will my arms always haunt you into
making you stay?

Will I cross you again like an ocean unbound
Or hold tight to your love — knowing just
what I've found? — I pray!

  Rebecca D. Helms

The Hardest Elimination

Thunder had sounded, but the night was still,
For everyone knew, it was God's will.
The time was right, but completely wrong,
"Time's up," God said, "there's no way to prolong".

Mankind had not yet finished, dinner was not yet done,
The plates were snatched up before the course had begun.
Refusal to obey God, so great was their thirst,
Thirst for knowledge, the pain was reversed.

So there a hand came down from above,
To take away all that they loved.
First went the earth, the first he had made,
Then gone was the sun, so quickly did it fade.

As God reached up to wipe away a tear,
What he had to do was painfully clear.
To destroy the human race, his greatest creation,
For now it becomes, his hardest elimination.

  Joseph L. Sindhu

Betrayal

Fancy me not as blissful
For I hide my anger
With a surprising touch of authenticity.
I wear upon my face
The countenance of a jovial wife
Yet, in my heart,
I need not drag on this charade any longer.
I feel that expressing myself in words
Uplifts the burden revenge
Has put upon my shoulders.
And so, I will write
Until my darkest depression
Changes itself to gleeful laughter.
My novel speaks of dreams I have
Of driving a stake through
My lover's deceitful heart.
And, in the books end,
I shall wear the genuine smile
Of a blissful widow.

  Shelby Thayer

Faith

Life has no meaning
For I shall live and die
For the love that I have given
Yet I just sat and cry

The wind that blows my spirit
For yet the heart is still known to whisper
My mind is still in the dream, that I've inherit
For my life is just a picture.

Everybody believes in fear
But I just see in what's far and near
I have no reason for living
My heart still not to be weaving

I believe in what I see
I believe in what I hear
Yet I still seem not to be free
For the falling of my tears

  Vanessa K. Rash

Eternally Yours

Lord, I want to thank you for all you've done
For in my life you are Number One
The love you give is forever and true
It comes from Heaven, straight from you.

Each day you show me how much you care
By answering each and every prayer
And when I start to lose my faith,
You take over, and renew my strength.

I personally witnessed your love for me,
The day you brought me to Heaven you see.
I wanted to stay in The Light with you,
But I knew that I still had a job to do.
Since that day ten years ago,
I've shared my testimony so people will know
To have faith in you, and confess their sins.
For, whoever gives his life to you always wins.

"Eternity Yours" The Lord will be
When you let Him in your heart Faithfully.
Just pray to GOD, and he'll be there,
To keep you safe and without fear.

Robbin L. Rogers

You are the Title of My Life

Tell me today the moments I lost with you
For the moments that never came
And I will give now what I can of me.

Tell me now what dreams you had dreamt
What goals you had set
so that I can weave my goals around you.

Tell me O'dear about the happiness that was yours
and I looked away
Since my happiness is you my dream come true.
I would like to give it all back to you.

Wasima E. Alvi

Feelings

FEELINGS...overwhelming and scary
Foreign to me and yet daring
To slice into my solitude
My isolation to rudely intrude.

HURRY...dull the pain - medicate
Alcohol, drugs, or even chocolate cake
Anything to stuff those feelings down
Stifle the fear that in my emotions I'll drown.

WANTING...so much to recover
Learn how to deal with life and discover
That feelings are not really something to dread
Just feel them, have them, without them I'm dead.

LEARNING...to live life one day at a time
Hoping serenity soon I'll find
Trusting in God more and more every day
To help me deal with my feelings in a positive way.

Sherrie Jackson

"God's Miracles"

What! You have never seen a miracle?
Have you ever seen a child?
Have you ever seen the flowers in a meadow, growing wild?
Have you ever seen a sunset turn from pink to gold?
Have you ever seen your loved ones change from young to old?
Oh yes! We take them all for granted, as we go along life's way,
But God performs miracles each and every day!

VaDella Burris

You're Entitled

You walked toward sanctuary,
found that you'd been turned away and felt betrayed.

You were surrounded by hostility,
anger and violent thoughts and felt attacked.

You looked for friendship and understanding,
instead you found enmity and were confused.

You sought out the person who professed to love you
and encountered a cold emptiness and were hurt.

Your rise out of the devastation of your spirit led you
painfully, inexorably away from your security and you were angry.

Your fight for the restoration of your sanctuary,
your security, your spirit is all that matters.

Your feelings about your loss are true
and your anger seeks a victim.

Your heart knows its true target and aims for the bull's eye.
On your mark, set your sights, and let fly.

You're entitled.

Sheena Carey Gransberry

Bodyguard

He watches over me
From place to place
When he is around I know I am safe
He is my guide my comfort my shield
I can be in no harm
For I'm at his will
He is my master; my companion; my soul
He keeps me from danger
He makes me feel whole
When he is around my nights turn to day
He makes everything alright
In every sort of way
He does most things; other men can't do I'm so afraid
I've fallen for him too
For him; nothing is to hard
For he is so special
My bodyguard

Trish L. Carr

Rainforest

It is damp and hot
Full of growth and rot
Leaves that drip with wet
Tangled together to form a vast green net
Plants and animals of many a hue
Red, yellow, green and blue
Everything is all so alive
A place where in profusion everything does thrive
Ultimately working as one like bees in a hive
Plants, animals, and native peoples woven together
Claw, hand, foot, paw, and feather
Within its green border cures and knowledge yet untold
Benefits to us all as yet to unfold
All things within its continues are more valuable than gold
Things we should leave alone
Not seek to reduce to cinder, ash and bone.
Greed and shortsightedness destroy things that are interlaced
Things that can never be replaced
A closeness to nature, the land, and God that may be lost
Disappearance of these things will be greeds greatest cost.

Todd Heiler

My Own Little Word

I am full of laugher, full of love
   full of pride, full of joy
I am full of energy and free as a dove,
   yet rather pent up, and sometimes coy.

Some people say I'm weird,
   I say just different
I'm hardly ever feared,
   sometimes I feel a bit belligerent.

For no one knows what goes on in my head,
   it's only at home when I'm in my own world.
I lay my head down in my own little crib,
   where all my thoughts are locked and said.

Alone, in my tiny dimly lit be bedroom
   I pour out my discombobulated thoughts.
Writing them down on paper, telling of my doom,
   changing the phrases until delicately wrought.

    Shekinah Rogers

Ghostly Conversation

Whispering words carry on the wind,
Gentle voices secrets from within,
Sighs of confusion,
Tears of hate,
Mystifying dreams transfixed state,
Ghosts all in white take a terrifying flight,
All is unknown,
Emotions are shown,
All to be dealt with alone.

    Wendy Copp

Daybreak

An unseen Hand, in the predawn hours
Gently took hold of mine
And bid me awake; though I knew not why,
I took the Hand in kind.

After the sleep was brushed from my eyes,
I wondered if this were a dream.
I longed for the slumber I now had missed,
But something beckoned me, it seemed.

I started the day while the darkness prevailed
And tried to make sense of the night.
Then, all of a sudden, the puzzle was solved
When I met the most beautiful Sight.

There in the distance, beyond thought and time,
The light of the new day appeared.
As it quietly rose to reveal all of life,
I felt a soft Presence draw near.

Proud and majestic, silent and strong;
A powerful message of Love.
The sunrise proclaimed the beauty of life
As hope filled my heart from above.

    Shelley Ferrito

Life's Way

Put everything into everyday
Get all your troubles out of the way
Don't let fear occupy your mind
Then we can make good use of our time
Erase all thoughts of selfishness and greed
Help someone in despair and in need
Love one another as time goes on
Let God come into your heart and mind
Love and peace you're bound to find.

    Wynona Hurley

Dusk After Rain

Gentle rain ending, a silky star glimmers,
Glistens in moist dusky sky
World being newborn, atmosphere shimmers,
Sheen of fog-clouds whiffles by.

Sphere held in cobwebs, realm of the spider,
Lustrous in glittering angles,
Silver ray centered, arachnid a glider
Through spectrum of prismatic bangles.

Fields rolling richly, verdant and vital,
Moonbeam within each fresh blade.
Spongy earth yielding, each step a portal
To sensuous feast newly laid.

Stillness is broken, hordes of frogs greeting
The night, alive with its wealth.
Sorcery present, obligingly meeting
The mind, in moment of stealth.

    Sunny Franson

Lucky Me!!

I love to get up early in the morning
Go outside to hear the birds a singing,
And feel the warm sun on me
Knowing I am as lucky as can be!

To go to the woods in the middle of the day
And see the squirrels all at play,
And listen to the breeze in the trees
as it rustles through all the leaves.

Go fishing at the rivers, lakes or streams
With the ducks and geese swimming around,
It all seems almost like a dream
The beautiful sight and peace all around.

I love to go out on a very dark night
And see the moon and stars shinning so bright
Look around at the big vast space
Wonder how all stay in their place.

One knows that God has a hand in this
He made it all just for us
To show us the best if yet to come
When God calls us all to come home.

    Raymond Wiesenmayer

The Hunt

As the precise movements of the lion,
Golden in the sun, cease,
The gaze of the hunter moves quickly to sight his prey,
Idling closer, wading through the fresh cut lawn,
Now ankle deep as it brushes against
The fur of this ferocious feline.
The gentle breeze of summer compels the leaves to whisper quietly.
My glass of lemonade is sweating from the heat;
I take a sip, savoring the cool sweet taste on my tongue.
Just then, he pounces, missing by a fraction of an inch;
The feline does not accept defeat
With so little a struggle.
As his prey turns and darts
For the protection of a hollow tree, he is cut off,
And the hunter, tossing the terrified creature into the air,
Juggles it with his paws and with a silent growl
The cat smashes his victim to the ground,
TRIUMPHANT!

    Samuel R. Kniffen

Ete Adieu

The
  fallen
    leaves
      lay
like smoldering embers of the summer past.
   Shelley A. Topham

Lost In Vietnam

Bullets flying over his head.
Groping in the dark among the dead.
Frightened by the sound of the wind.
Now he's remembering all his sins.

At home his mother is sick at heart.
Worried because they're so far apart.
1,500 killed in a week.
For months his mother has had no sleep.

Two days later a letter she receives.
Her son gave his life for his country's pleas.
1,500 killed in a week.
How many mothers worry?
How many get no sleep?
   Vicki M. Harris

Flowers In The Wind

A seed that gets planted so solemn and few,
grows with the music of wind blowing through.
A sprinkle of light and condensation to grow,
makes the seed germinate allowing it to show.
Dainty and figged the root starts to deepen,
making the stem heighten and stretchingly steepen.
With time by her side the bloom starts to open,
wind pushing the petals and making commotion.
In moments of minutes it erupts into showing,
a spectacular site to all of the knowing.
So delicate and beautiful is the bloom that we witness,
like a virgin so brilliant with all of her pureness.
The bloom expands powerfully with all her boldness,
everything respecting her and giving her greatness.
With autumn arriving its time for her calling,
she opens for the wind to escort her falling.
He powerfully blows and the petals diffuse,
until next year he calls her and awakes her deep snooze.
   Randall Steel

Poems And Songs

Pens and papers are the tools of my trade,
Guitars and pianos and notes scribbled on paper.

Poems and songs are the light of my life.
Thoughts in my head that are dying to come out.
Artistry and music are the way of my life.

Poems and songs live deep in my soul
Pens and paper are the only way I live.
Songs about life are the only way I give.
Songs and poetry hold the meaning of my life
Pens and paper help me express joy and strife.

Happiness is there in notes and in poems.
Joy is found on tiny scribbles of paper
Poems about life and music and God
Are like songs to me that live in my heart.

Pens and songs, guitars and poems are the force
that drive my life forward.
Poems and songs on scribbles of paper are powerful
meanings in the notes of my heart.
   Kerry Boone

To Her On Our First Year

With all the trials that we've been through,
has proved to me that I love you.
  Onward we press and this I know,
my love for you will always grow.
  The love I see deep in your eyes,
By far transcends the starry skies.
  As sure as the waves caress the shore,
I'll love you always and ever more.
  For loving you has been so easy.
Yes loving you is truly pleasing.
  Our years ahead appear smooth and bright,
Filled with love, and laughter, and pure delight.
  For now I close but must impart,
That I love my wife with all my heart.
   Robert A. Wheeling

The Pimp

I'm better than the pimp, standing on the street, What I
have can't be beat.
I got love, hope, charity, can the pimp give you prosperity
The pimp have your mind, filled with smoke, puffing, coughing,
almost choked,
But look at me, I have your soul, I'm the only one, who can
make you whole.
Do you think the pimp can raise the dead, Make the sick get
out of bed.
All these things I can do, their is no fee, or charge to you.
When you want a puff, puff on me, Will it be death or victory.
The pimp will leave, he won't stay, But I'm with you, every
step of the way.
I can get you high, won't cost a cent, take a dip in the pool
(IT'S CALLED REPENT) Which road would you take, the pimp or
me, Death or life expectancy.
Once you've tried me, you will find, I'm the best drug, I'm
one of a kind.
The pimp will make you kill and steal, but what I have it's for real.
I don't get paid for what I do, It's my job to save sinners like you.
   Rosie Lee Carruthers

But, It Was Cold

How could I know that he would be the love of my life?
He came to me like the soft breeze on a summer night,
but it was cold - so many things going 'round in my head.
I was afraid. I didn't want to live.
He was warm like the sun and I felt life again,
but it was cold - my heart began to reach out.
I had never felt this way before.
I wanted to feel this forever. I grasped.
Could I be falling? Yes!
I knew where I looked in his eyes, but it was cold -
time passed by, so many things going 'round in my head.
A tornado swept through my soul.
My heart cried out like the roar of thunder.
I knew I couldn't and wouldn't feel this way again,
but it was cold - Oh love of my life,
you slipped away like the soft breeze on a summer night.
Not knowing that you hold the hole from my heart,
but it was cold -
   Rajonda E. Parrish

Sachiko means Happiness

The irony,
The hellish contradiction
You imposed — existential blackmail!
   Patricia Best

"City Boy"

Though he grew up in the city
He dreamed of clear blue skies.
Of honesty and freedom of love that never dies.

He swore that someday he would move,
To a place down by the sea,
Or to a farmhouse in the fields,
Someday he'd be free.

He'd marry and have children,
And all his love he'd give
His wife and he would raise them.
In the country they would live.

But before he could grow,
To live out his dream,
He meet a mugger in the park,
There was a wild struggle,
And a switchblade pierced his heart.

We buried him just yesterday,
In fields down by the sea.
He had to die to earn his dream,
But now his soul is free....

Tonya Hornung

Ode To My Dad

My dad passed away last night
He finally gave up the fight

To say I'll miss him is an understatement
For this loss there will be no replacement

No matter what crisis in life I had
I knew I could always turn to my dad

Whether it was a broken toy
Or a fight with that special boy
I knew my dad would always be there
To say "Don't cry! Dad loves you Shar"

And though I know he's with the Lord
My heart feels as though it's been pierced
with a sword

I'm crying dad, why aren't you here
To hug me close and hold me near?

I miss you dad! I always will
And so will Mom and Barb and Bill

Sharon Seckel

"I Was Here"

Everybody has his own way
He has a purpose for living
Whatever he does or doesn't do,
He should try
He can build a monument,
Write a song, a book,
Leave memories in loved ones
But do something to show you were here on this earth
That whatever your ideas or ideals are; are your own
That you have a foundation for being - existing
And by the grace of God
You can carry them out.

Renee S. McIntyre

He Lies...

He lies when he smiles
He lies when he cries
His whole life is a lie and if you ask him "why?"
He will tell you that there is a lie
In this life everywhere
And if you wanna survive
He will tell you that you have to lie
In this ruthless life out there

He feels strong enough to hurt someone

But is he strong enough not to
He has to care about someone before it's too late

His life goes on he lies to everyone
His whole life is a lie and if you ask him "hey!"
Do you know the truth about you and your life
And the people 'round you you can ask him 'bout
Anything you want he will tell you a lie that is his response

He has to learn how to love
He has to learn how to trust
He has to care about someone
Before it's too late

Svetlana N. Romanov

Love's Different Ways

A child falls and hurts himself while at play,
He runs to his mother, who loves the hurt away.
This is an enduring love between mother and child;
It keeps on loving, regardless of each trial.

The bride smiles at the groom, as she says, "I Do"
The groom smiles back, meaning, "I Love You Too."
This is a love between husband and wife,
It will endure through struggle and strife.

The most enduring love that I know,
Is when God sent his son to earth long ago.
God's love was so strong for the people below,
He looked through heaven and asked, "Who will go?"

Jesus' love was wonderful and true.
He came, suffered and died for me and you.
He arose, and is seated at the father's right hand.
This is the greatest love ever known to man.

Ruby W. Taylor

Broken Dreams

Sometimes, late at night
he stares into the infinite space
above his bed,
in his room full of broken dreams —
and wonders - when it is all finally
going to come together, like it was
supposed to so many times before, but
was cut off so abruptly and cruelly...
FINALLY... the pieces are coming together,
and the opportunity is right in front of
his eyes...
there is a choice...
he can relive

Robert Porto

Who Are We

He was dead but not quite dead
He was alive but not quite alive
He had lived alone but not quite alone
A few thought they knew him
But they did not quite know him
He had lived a long time
But not quite so long
He was every man and he was no man
He was my father and I thought I knew him
But I did not quite know him for we are all him
But we do not quite know it

    Rudy Rubin

I Wish I Would Have Listened

I wish I could put my wise aged
  head on your youthful shoulders-
I could lead you to paths that are unfamiliar
  And never been tapped by you
You listen with your mind, but your heart
  beats a different tune-
Oh why do you not hear or see that I
have traveled that way long before you where born-
That l am trying to protect you from all the
  pit falls I have fallen into - you are experiencing
What I have experienced many times over
I too would not listen to a sage I called Mother -
  My path would have been entirely different -
It is now that I realize that it was a
  strong love who was advising me -
I wish I would have listened.

    Rose Antelis

Hurricane Sonnet

The fog covered the ground like a sheet.
Heavy rain fell throughout the humid land.
Water was so high it covered my feet.
The pounding hard rain washed away the sand.

The strong, driving wind gusted all around.
Saturated clouds hung high in the sky.
The wind blew the mighty oaks to the ground.
The great storm had finally reached its eye.

We anxiously waited for it to end,
And hoped that it was beginning to cease.
There were many hearts and houses to mend.
At last our wish came true and we gained peace.

Like a stranger unwelcomed by its host,
Hurricane Frederick destroyed the Gulf Coast.

    Samuel P. Di Benedetto

Thanksgiving Day Prayer

Thank you, God , for all your blessings on this Thanksgiving Day.
Help us when we stumble and forget to live your way.
How good it is to be alive; we thank you for our birth,
Allowing us ever to enjoy the blessings of this earth.
Let us see the rainbows when our lives have floods of rain,
For when we're looking upward, it helps to ease the pain.
And now we want to praise you for your great power and might;
And thank you that you love us through every day and night.

    Ruth Burleson

Ode To Mother Earth

Ode to mother earth, from whom's womb we came bursting forth to rule
  her and subject her to our power.
Yet babes, we take from her and revolt against her when she fails to
  give more.
She nurses us until we perish and return to her womb;
  Never disowning us,
  Never turning her back on us,
  Never denying or punishing us.
She provides our life's sustenance,
  Even though she is starving.
  Once her breasts swelled with nourishment,
  Now they have collapsed through years of abuse.
From her self-made beauty we form objects of
  ugliness to please our distorted sense of pulchritude.
When our "creations" no longer serve us, we
  return them as discarded toys upon her lap.
A loving mother, she gives until there is no
  more to give, and takes until her heart is full of sorrow.
Alas, we have succeeded in contaminating her soul,
  and the course we have plotted leads to annihilation.

    Yvonne D. Inman

The Doe

From her fetal sleep, she stands
  Her ears vibrate, aware of danger
Soft eyes furiously darting back and forth.
  searching,
She crouches, ready to flee.

From his fetal position, he stands
  Hands of stone grasping the cold steel;
  he is the danger
The eyes, he aims at his prey
  Fury flies, cutting the air red.

    Trenton Gabriel

The Watch

Her coat is white, her carriage majestic,
Her eyes sparkle black
They walked and played in mutual joy
Till the day he didn't come back
Each day she ran about the yard
The queen of her domain
Watching and waiting for his return
But the waiting was in vain.
The new place had no fence, this was very strange
But beautiful walks and places to search
In case he came back again.

Hours of waiting turn to years
The sparkle in the eyes grow dim
But the walk is brisk, the tail still wags
As she still watches for him.
As I see the question in her eyes
I hold her close and feel the pain
Neither of us wants to say good-bye
But he won't be back again.

    Reba W. Sowell

A Friend In Jesus

I was lost in the world, but now things seem to be so clear;
He's changed my thinking, and now my salvation's near;
All those years living in sin, have really taken a toll,
Now I feel a big weight being lifted off my soul;
Why was I so blind, not to see,
How much He really loves and cares for me;
So now I'm going to try to live His Word until the end,
Because I think, in JESUS, I've finally found a Friend.

    Thomas Jordan

He's "The Answer"

He's the strong and mighty rushing wind;
  He's the calming breeze when we cling to HIM.
HE'S THE GROUND WE SHOULD BUILD ALL FOUNDA-TIONS ON;
  He's "The Rock" God said He'd build His church upon.
He's THE ONE with the ANSWER for all mankind.

He's the King of Kings and the Prince of Peace;
  With our hand in His, our joys will never cease.
When we pray in faith and we truly believe,
  In the strength He gives and the courage we receive,
Then our life here on earth can't help but be
  One in which our God would be pleased and,
We can say each day, as it comes to an end,
  "I'm a child of The King on which He can depend."

He gave His very life, shedding His perfect blood:
  Upon that rugged cross, He showed his boundless love.
The price He paid I will forever tell,
  To all who will listen 'til He returns for us,
When we'll go up to Heaven and eternally dwell.

    Ruth Lucile Hampton

Home Again, Home

A salty dog went out to sea
His bonnie lass stayed behind
This dog got saltier, I think you'll agree
As his maiden was on his mind.
Fair maiden, supple, round, and white
She was true to her man on the water
She thought of him, and he of her each night
Their bodies grew hot, and then hotter.
He wrote her that he was headed for shore
She happily readied their place
He made it home, she was at the door
They couldn't wait, and pardoned grace.
He was less salty after giving his best
She was more round beneath her breasts.

    Robert Barnett

A Place On Earth I Love To Be

A place on earth I love to be
Home, my retreat, where there's peace and harmony
A place humble with simple comforts all about
Where I can sit and gaze without
"Look at me," signals a single white camellia
Bushes painted with pink, speckled azaleas
High on a treetop a bird to his mate, in exultation
Twitters, and flits from branch to branch, in salutation
My cheeks caressed, the gentle breeze
Has blown to yonder where I faintly hear the sighing trees
The rain has stopped and from the leaves
Drop-by-drop, raindrops drip into a puddle on the ground
And splash, to form tiny, sparkling, jeweled crowns.

    Yoshiyuki Otoshi

Scene From A Window

The pristine whiteness of the snow
Covers our back yard and
Smothers the icy crust on the lake beyond.

As I gaze from my window
Enjoying its shimmering beauty,
I am alerted to a skittering thereon.

Is it some critter exploring that vast expanse?
Nay — 'tis just a leaf
Belly-flopping across the frozen surface.

    Violet L. Mueller

Sitting On This Launch Pad

I've been sitting on this launch pad waiting to shoot into space.
Hoping and praying my dreams take me to that special place.
I've postponed my launch so often, I can't take it anymore!
My repairs appear to be ready... But I'll never know for sure.
My mind has kept me wondering to where I'm supposed to go.
When I have my liftoff, it's then I believe I'll know...
I pray to go as high as any star!
Never looking back, but always remembering just who you are...
I know my journey will end somewhere in this beautiful sky.
But that will be my Lord's will, I need not wonder why.
My ship has finally become of age,
My time has come to turn the page.
The time has come for me at last,
To look to the future, to forget the past.
The countdown has now begun,
It's time to enjoy life and have some fun.
I'm ready now, I'm about to leave the ground,
As strange as this may seem to be, I can hear a voice, a special sound.
It's someone crying out to me!
Your destiny is about to be found.

    Thomas Murphy

The Message From The Star

Did you ever wonder about a Star?
How did it get out there so very far?
Why does it twinkle and shine so bright?
Why can you see it only at night?

It is so beautiful to our eye,
as we turn our head toward the sky.
Here I am again, it seems to say,
but you won't see me during the day.

There is a message there, you can be sure.
To get it your thoughts must be pure.
It only takes a small amount of time,
before the answer will come to your mind.

During the night the Star will do its best,
to watch over you while you get your rest.
During the day you must shine bright,
and be like a Star with a shining light.

Some people you meet are that way.
They give you a smile and wish you a good day.
You can tell these people without a doubt,
because like a Star their light shines from inside out.

    Roy E. Donaldson

You're Very Special To Me

How do I thank you for caring?
How do I repay your sharing?
For raising my hope when life looks bleak,
For giving me strength when I feel weak,
You're very special to me.

You have helped me to belong,
Your love has made me strong,
You have guided me along the way
Your sweet kindness I can't repay,
You're very special to me.

How can I repay you?
But with a love that's true.
What can I give you in return?
Except all my love and concern.
You're very special to me.

As the night turns to day,
And the stars fade away,
I greet the day by showing
That with this love that's growing
YOU'RE VERY SPECIAL TO ME.

    Shirlie Sark Fournier Mac Indian

"Carry My Love"

Dear Most Gracious Phenomena,
How elaborate your grace to my world of amazing.
Angels to higher thrones — you rose to be placed among God's
greatest universal Queens.
The royalty celebrations possessed by our spirit can never go
unrecognized.

For you truest love are the birth to all continents in making
touches and desires caress the most sensitive secretive elegance
of the unborn child.

Of the complete utmost upmost of worlds, understanding may be in
habit of keeping confident manner classifications of diligent
statute, surety of obligation,and salvation fulfillment being
supremely in love with knowledge.

Freedom shall be advancement to carry our love most gracious and
ultimate, as in angel of love's life.

Even when peace in hearts are forgotten, hope prevails appreciated
and most dear.

For opportunities of yesterday, availability of perpetual promises,
and echoes of the word wonderful — achievement of reality comes
inevitably love's law...

   Carey Russ Love

All A Sad Refrain

How long is your road, wending through the hills?
How heavy is the load? I know how it feels.

You have walked far alone.
Your shoulders are bowed.
I wish I had known,
but you wouldn't have allowed.

You will let none help you; you have pushed us away.
all but a few. Help given, any day.

You hide it all behind a smile,
Painted, like a piece of art.
You are in pain, all the while
all in pain, in your heart.

You seem so happy in this state.
I must warm you, do not wait.
Soon, too soon, it will be late
to save you from unhappy fate.

I want to know if you will be There.
I know that this is asked in vain.
Do you know that I really care?
Is this all but a sad refrain?

   Rachel Parrott

Such A Little Guy

The weekend's gone, the days flew by,
   How we'll miss that little guy.
His cheery smile, his beautiful eyes,
   Soft and precious by our side.

A busy week lies ahead,
   But many times we'll picture his little face.
We'll think of all fun we had,
   And of all the precious moments in the past.

How it hurts to say goodbye,
   But we have to force a smile.
No matter what the circumstance,
   For a change right now, we haven't a chance.

He seems to be happy and copes with such things,
   Shuffled and tossed like a puppet on a string.
What a man he'll one day be,
   If he's able to cope now with such uncertainty.

   Teri Johnson

"Wolf"

Hungry is the wolf within,
Hungry for the blood and skin.
The wilderness stands still,
As he howls upon the highest hill.
He's waiting till the end of day,
So he can secretly hunt his prey.
The thought of blood makes his lips foam,
Until he eats he won't go home.
He stays low but his hopes are high,
Then he spots game caught by his eye.
Knowing what lies ahead,
The victim starts to fill with dread.
Then with his eyes open wide,
The animal's fear becomes fierce inside...
With his stomach full, and his eyes set deep,
The wolf enters his cave and falls asleep.

   Sonni Manning

Now And Then

I have walked with you though the doors of your mind
I am like Michael, and as I turn the pages of your books
You take me to places I long to find.

I tour the rooms that you have decorated
And I see the art that you have seen
I've been to the gardens that whisper great secrets
You have shown me these places, even though I have never been.

I have felt the wind of the desert
And I have stood at the Sphinxes feet
I've dined with the king who slept in the tomb
I would know his blue eyes should ever we meet.

I have felt the pain of your hero, lost and all alone
When from the sun he would have to hide
As over the world he roamed.

You are my inspiration each time I pick up the pen
Thank you for sharing your gift with me
For taking me from the reality of now
To the magic and beauty of then.

   Vonda Grubb

Be Not Alone

The winds blew and tides were high,
I arose to listen and heard a sigh.

Your words true and your heart divine
Enlightened by your presence I needed no sign.

Be not alone you spoke, it was heaven sent,
A companion true that was meant

I say to you be as one
Look at my life its just begun.
Inspired by the book of Genesis.

   Tina L. Barry

A New Day

As the sun rises above my house
   I awake to a new start of life
   Ready and able to meet today's challenges
I will place my faith in God and my feet on the ground.
My little girl's smile will get me through
   The rough road that I must walk.
If the day becomes to much to handle
   I'll simply sing a song and think about the hug
I get when I'm home.
And when it time to retire whatever
The day has become I will fall to my knees and thank
   God for being with me this day.

   Thomas Paul Sanborn

Hair And Overalls

Monkey men climbing walls
  nappy hair and overalls

I stamp you all, as my brothers
  they mark us as untouchable others

We sit here, in our peace
  smoking Mother Nature
  loving in poetic verse
  and ashing on your furniture

We've learned no manners
  for Mother's gone,
  paying Sam of personal greed

So yes I lie out of place
  broken and shunned in a drunkard state

There's nothing left for me to do
  to sit here silent next to you?

I voice my way, scream it loud
  "I like my hair and overalls!"

    Meg Paxton

Past...

  I am gone forever
never again on the scene will I peek,
  but I can be found in memories...
some, on pages of history books seek
  although, once found out
no life to me can you bring
  for I am lost in thought
on the other side of eternity.

  Sometimes when I like lazarus,
I bring some of my kin
  for they too are suppressed
on pages deep within.
  Sometimes bringing tears and pain
with rivers and spears
  once put away, present comes to reign.

    Patrick McGrew

Getting Old

When I was just a young girl
Full of vinegar and spit,
I conquered every challenge
For I was strong and fit.

There was nothing that could stop me
And no job I couldn't do.
No boundaries could hold me.
The world was bright and new.

But then I started getting old
And reached a smaller goal.
Familiar roads were safer.
Smaller towns lived in my soul.

I don't have to show bravado
And don't want to run the race.
I can walk a little slower
And admire the runner's pace.

I love my home with aging walls.
I'm master of my lair.
And I find that I am most content
While sitting in my chair.

    Dorothy Turner

Untitled

As I stare into the eyes of discontent
I become aware of all the time that I have spent,
Aimlessly wandering from place to place,
Barely recognizing a single face.

I think of the many paths I have crossed,
  and all the memories I have lost.
And for a brief moment I can see,
  a world of emptiness surrounding me.

If only I could do it once again .
Please, Lord, just now I need a friend.
Won't you walk with me a while,
As I journey through this life, mile after mile.

Guide me down the path and set me free
  to walk a lifetime next to thee.
Help me to determine wrong from right,
Grant me the strength I'll need to fight.

Give me the tools that teach me to pray,
Upon the chance we'll meet some day.

    Sharon Cramer-Bratton

Open Casket

Once, I too was, and counted among the living.
I cared, loved and was loved, and for life there was thanks given.
Now, those times seen as the epistasis of my life;
How catastrophic their lack, and how welcomed was the knife. View me.

Don't listen to the words when they're used to elegize;
They misinterpret the motive, and ask me to apologize.
I am only what I became, just more honestly represented,
And would do the deed again if the situation again presented. View me.

Please, don't take from me the only gift that I have left.
Death's purpose nullified, the result of such a theft.
I need for you to see, not close your eyes and pretend.
I want a new beginning, not to verify the end. View me.

Understand what was lost when we, so sure, gave up the fight;
Waived claim to our future while still believing ourselves right.
It was then we picked up the blade that cut deep into my veins,
And the blood flowed so freely life could not sustain. View me.

Pull back the cuffs, see the scars of my final act of contrition,
But to fully understand there must be one condition.
Don't view them as the final act of one who gave in to despair,
But rather as a measure of how much I used to care. View me, and
  remember.

    Timothy R. McBride

City Scapes

When you walk the streets of the city, don't forget to admire the
elements that make this place special.
Don't forget any of the faces you should encounter in and around the
Parks and nooks, up and down the gray sidewalk's that make; City Scapes.

I'll walk with you along the Esplanade and smell the sour odor of the Charles.
We can stop and listen to the sounds of Roller Blades that whoosh on
by...... they carry their hosts as there must be someplace they have
to be right away; what can be more important than a pause?
I think they just missed how the sunlight strikes the gray and gold of Beacon Hill!

In that microsecond that we turned to them, the City Scapes changed again.
Look how the river flows against the Cat's Paw's on a liquid pallet;
Mirrored images flow and flow as apparitions grow.
We can almost see Adams, Franklin and Kennedy in the misty show;
Without a sound they seem to say; "Tut, Tut, Tut; shame for the time that is lost".
Do not merely sip from life; Drink, Drink and most of all; pause.

    Thomas J. Maimoni

Child Of My Working Years

He is mine, this child of my working years. I soothed his hurts and calmed his fears. I told him why the sky was blue and taught him always be true. He was mine, this child of my working years. I wondered with him "Does a frog have ears?" Together we listened in a quiet wood to a hooting owl beneath it's hood. I taught him to hold a pencil right and to LOVE- not fear-the silent night. I held him close when the fever rose and taught him why the North wind blows. "Stay within the lines" I'd say as busily he would crayon away. We splashed in the rain and rolled in the snow we shared popcorn at the movie show I felt his little hands hold tight as I went to hug him and say "Good Night." We talked about so many things like colors of people and butterfly wings. His Grandpa never had time...or so it seems to share in his father's childhood dreams. I know how he felt...I feel it each day as faithfully "I must go to work son" I'd say. He started to school for the first time today as I held his mom's hand as the bus pulled away. He was mine this child of my working years. I bit my lip to hold back the TEARS. As he pressed his face to the school bus door, it hit me he's really not mine anymore. He belongs to the world of books and such, but he's already learned so much...so much. Oh, they'll
teach him to read they'll teach him to write but I've tried to teach him what's wrong and what's right. I've taught him of puppies, ponies and bees, flowers, and blossoms and buds on the trees, lakes, oceans, beaches and skies and heartbeats and how to say "love" with your eyes. He was mine, the child of my working years and peace for my soul as each evening nears, now as I work I can truly take rest for I know I have taught him what I feel is the best. The adventures of learning upon which he will start will bring untold joy to his father's heart for that's what he's been only joy never tears. This loving Young child of my working years.

Scott Joseph Mauro

The Presence Of The Lord

Have you ever looked around you and seen the beauty of nature?
Look up at the blue sky and feel my Lord, I know you are here.

The smile on a child's face when he gets a good report card.
The blessings from a passerby with his warm good morning.

For God works in mysterious ways, sending you inner strength to grow whether planted by beauty of a friendly hello you know his presence is ever near!

Rosette Mines

A Message To My Brothers

Back in the day, I worked from sun up to sun down like you black man and while You tossed and turned in your sleep, I tossed and turned unwillingly with master.

When you were beaten and lynched I still respected you and encouraged you to keep the faith.

When you wanted out of slavery, it was a black women named harriet who helped you reach the promise land.

After slavery, I went out and got job just like you. I cooked and cleaned for those who despised me, then I cooked and cleaned for you the man I loved.

I worked long dreadful days to pay the bills when you couldn't get a job and I never made you feel like less than a man.

But you took out your frustrations on me, you yelled, you beat me, and you even walked out on me. And I still loved and respected you black man.

When you were in the pulpit, I amend for you black man.
When you ran for office, I voted for you black man.
When you were incarcerated, I never missed a holiday black man.

Whatever life brought you, it was me who was right by your side.
Me a black women. The person who holds the key to your very existence.

And now, everyday you tell the entire world through your music and your songs that I'm a ho and bitch......you ungrateful human being.

Valerie B. Joyner

A Loving Touch

As I hold her frail hand in mine,
my thoughts go back to a distant time
when that hand was firm and wide,
and always kept me by her side.

The hand that was so tender and warm
yet managed to shield me from any harm;
The hand that fed me and tended my needs
and was faithfully there to do good deeds.

The hand that knew when to let go
so I could become independent and grow
into the person that I am today,
and here, by her side, I shall stay.

My hand will give her strength and love
and she will know what I am thinking of.
Spoken words need not be expressed
as a loving touch is still the best.

Patricia A. Halk

To Cry

I hide in the shadows thinking
no one can see me cry.
Then somebody turns on the light
and I'm spotted by every eye.
So next I find refuge in an
abandoned four wall room.
But, I can't cry there either;
someone is bound to find me soon.
Then the thunder crashes
and the lightning strikes.
My eyes are filled with
greedy delight.
For when the sky rumbled I knew
what was in store.
A rain that would rain and then it would rain
and again rain some more.
Droplets fall down like tears
from the sky.
And then and only then will no one
see me cry.

Kimberly Brook Thomas

Good Ole Summertime

Summer has arrived; hot days and warm
nights; very few days of rain.
Children swimming in rivers, creeks, or
pools, climbing out to dive again.

Multi-hued rainbows after a shower, too
far to look for the pot of gold.
Beautiful sunrises, gorgeous sunsets, to
have memories as you grow old.

The flowers from spring a riot of colors,
butterflies flutter to each.
Bees flying among them to gather nectar,
pollinate all within reach.

Going to the beach for a swim, a picnic,
and lying in the hot sun.
Playing volleyball, running, chasing and
catching, having fun.

One morning you awake to find the cool
of a new season has arrived.
Summer ends; the children have returned
to school; you have survived.

Margaret Thornburgh

Everyday Hunter

Everyday hunter blends exquisitely into the crowd,
is the crowd.
Smile turned on, up.
Makes small talk,
notices big things.
Vulnerabilities, opportunities,
false kinship.
Forms friendships quick as lightning, and as dazzling,
but never quite achieves
crucial touch.
In the bedroom, love games,
fierce, hungry, always the same woman,
face, dream, fantasy, sweet impossibility,
nothing.
Forever searching, bittersweet end in itself,
reason for existence; vigorous, mechanical.
Handsome, charming, wonderful to talk to.
Extraordinary!
Otherwise:
blank.

Peter Smernoff

Workings

Inside yourself, inside your mind
Is the worst place to be at solemn times.
In times of need
Times you need to express yourself,
The weak and strong a like need a place to rest themselves.
Is that why sorrow is always the subject of sad songs,
Of loves lost, of loves gone wrong?
Is that why it's so hard for a man to shed tears,
Express his joys, express his fears?

I'll never know, I'll never understand,
The complicated workings of man.

Michael B. Dees

In Memory Of You

I close my eyes and all I see,
  is visions of how you used to be
And when you would smile at all my jokes
  even though you had nothing to laugh at
In a dark cold place is where you would lay alone,
  with only your thoughts to call your own
But the darkness slowly took over your mind,
  A lifeless child is all they could find
The roar of the bullet filled your head,
  "Life Sucks" that's what you said
Now you are gone with the blink of an eye,
  people everywhere began to cry
In memory of you is where this poem starts
  and the memories of you are forever in
  our hearts.

Karla Iacona

First Born

The miracle of life is a joyous one.
It brings tears of joy to everyone.
On that day when he was born,
Our lives were changed forevermore.
This miracle we saw on that day,
Brought love in our hearts needless to say.
Though my heart went out to my wife in pain,
To bring life to our son, she would do it again.
Our love is much stronger now that he has come,
For by the grace of God our love is one.

Monty Tubesing

Unforgettable

You are so real in front of me even when you're gone all I see
is you're face.
In my dreams It's only you because you are unforgettable,
like a butterfly on my heart who doesn't know how to fly away,
like a rose upon my shoulders that has
screeched my skin, but still unforgettable. It's only began
yesterday and you already hate me today. I know you think of
me a lot, just hate to tell me, where are we in an
unforgettable dream. If you look at me you turn away, just
when I'm about to look at you, because you're afraid to admit
you love me. Even though I just come to tell you I'm leaving, you
just ignore me, but at the same time you just wane hold me
and not let me go for a second or two. It's over I say, I
guess I'll always love you because you're unforgettable.

Orsolya Karlosak

Paper

Paper is like prizes
  It comes in different sizes.
It is also light,
  and it comes in colors like white.
Paper is good when it rains,
  Because inside you can make paper airplanes.
Paper is really for poodles,
  Because they draw doodles.
Not just humans use paper,
  Animals use it like goats and alligators.
They probably eat it for breakfast,
  Lunch or dinner,
It probably makes them look thinner.
  Paper tastes like a drag,
Because it is made out of old rag.
Paper! Paper! for everyone,
Paper! Paper! it is fun.

Marlon Christie

"City Of Salt"

People of the morning, people of the night
It comes without a warning, and you lose your daily fight.
Oh, people of the mountains, Oh, people of the plains
I'll tell you all that I know, just to ease your daily pains.

But you, people of the city, you're a special kind of breed
You wake up in the morning, and live for that mouth you feed.
You're always in a hurry, and you rush from day to day
You may know where you're going, but when you get there, you
  can stay.

In this so called new world, we're supposed to see the light.
We still walk the streets in darkness, we still walk the streets to
  to fight.

But you people of the city, you're a special kind of breed.
You wake up in the morning, and take all that you need.

Your minds are made of hard times
And there's too fast of a cure
You may know where you're going
But when you get there -
  You're not sure

Kenneth Paresi

Song

Inside everyone is a song;
A song that plays throughout their lives.
Two may form discordant beats,
As each holds their own the melody.
But allowing fate its chance to conduct,
A symphony may form,
As the harmonies of two people
Blend to form a silent song.

Tory E. Scharrer

250

Time Immemorial

I stop in wonder, The Millennium is so close, so near,
It excites, and amazes me, we have coming, a '1000 New Years'
In these 'New Years', it can mean Justice, Happiness, and Peace,
After all the degradation of Wars and Violence, we have a 'New Lease.'

In these coming years, many of us will be Elsewhere,
But for our Children, and theirs, a Panacea will remedy all cares,
At least, that is what we want for this Planet, and all in it,
Because, in the Future, Man and Woman, will still be Pairs.

Looking Forward, gives cause to look in the Past,
Remembering Relatives and Friends, and my 'Love, I Held Last'.
I reminisce about my Childhood, and the happiness I had,
I look at my Scrapbook, filled with Pictures, and I feel Glad.

Once you have passed the 'Halfway Mark',
Not all the things' You Face', can be a Lark,
But, most of us, have had more 'Good Years' than 'Bad',
So, be Grateful and Give Thanks' for the 'Life' you have had.

V. G. Bouret

The Gift

The scent of baby lingers for more than a day.
It filters the air and sneaks up when least prepared.
Eyes, small and fingers tiny, closed laying upon
the breast of mother. Focused eyes trying to find
something to hide the feeling inside. Empty emotions
now hollow drift to a sadness only the lonely
will know. Recalling times when the mind finds
the little ones that has done the lingering inside.
Wishing away many a day wanting to experience
the gift that never may be within. Like baby dreaming
I close my eyes and wish that the baby that lays
is in some way a baby of mine. Over and over defining
what mother means to me. Mother-a gift of love
to share with one sent from above. A life to watch
grow, to love for a life time.

Kimberly I. Gilgen

Awareness

One life touches another, enters it and takes hold,
It holds on so tightly, watches new love unfold,
Spends years together, growing together not apart,
Learning and storing memories, deep in its heart.
Draws in the outsiders, and loves them as well.
Then opens all eyes, to the lies made in hell.

Dumps out the secrets, into an endless pile,
What was once held close to heart, is now ugly and vile,
While all of us heal, from the wounds left so deep.
Out of the darkness, the light seems to creep
Our visions are clear now, love never did exist,
A new life to touch now, a Fresh heart to twist.

Leslie Renee Stinehelfer Jones

Love's Ride

Tears fall from the eyes like drops of rain
Crying out a lover who's now in pain.

A broken heart's left behind from love's cruel game
This person now never being one in the same.

Once happy, now torn apart
Left in pieces is their heart.

Confused, alone, and hurting inside,
One risked it all for this thing called, love's ride.

Ricki Patton

Crying For Help

The sun doesn't shine in my room anymore.
It is as dark as can be.
I block it with curtains, the world is horrible.
The world today is not what I hoped.
It's polluted and ugly.

Most fish and animals are gone, or dying.
We were too selfish to hear their cries for help.
We cared for nothing, but ourselves.

The birds don't sing near my house anymore.
They hide from everything around.
I can't hear them sing, they are sick, and dying.

I don't like to sit under the tree anymore.
I hate the shade of the polluted tree.
It traps me in its arms and takes away my energy.
It hates everything, for all near it is dead.

I don't like to walk outside anymore.
The people are crazy, they love only themselves.
The world is dying because of these things.
People need to work together, to do what they can
to save the world, and the future.

Nashana Reding

What Is Friendship

It is never to condemn him or her
It is being there no matter what the out come is
It is when you lend a shoulder to cry on
It is a person to share your secret with
It is a person, who loves you like a sister, but
    sometimes isn't a sister
A friend will tell you the truth when you ask
    for an answer!
A friend will know just the right thing to say when
    you are at a low point in your life!
A friend can sometime be more closer than family
She or he can become part of the family
Friends never ask more of you than you can give
A friend never ask you to do something he or she
    would never do!
A friend never talks against you
But most of all a friend will be there with you to
    the end!!!

Philbert Anderson

My Healing — His Will

God has brought me to this place for my healing.
It is not for me to say who He uses or what He chooses.
In Him shall I trust.
His Will shall be done.

Would my burdens be lifted?
Would my wounds be healed?
Would my spirit be freed?
Would His truth be withheld?
Would His hand be removed?
Would His love be withdrawn?

His Sacrifice bears my burdens.
His Blood covers my transgressions.
His Love brings me through.
His Grace leaves me never lacking.
His Power restores my strength.

In Him will I trust
His will Shall be done!

A. Denita Gadson

A Walk on the Beach

The sea always calms me
It made my mother restless, but it calms me
It broadens my perspective
Pulls me out of myself

The sea always calms me
It washes away my foolish dreams
It gives me strength to dream again
Gives me hope that these dreams aren't so foolish

The sea always calms me
It takes from me the things I cannot hold
It empties my arms for someday
makes me count my blessings—in case someday never comes

The sea always calms me
It draws a clear line between what matters and what doesn't
It fills my heart with hope
Soothes my troubled soul
I walk next to it for hours
Let it wash over my feet.

J. Scott Blankenship

Healing Lime

Love can play games in a persons mind,
it makes you weak and leaves you blind.
You open your heart to let someone in,
feeling the strength to love again.
Willing to dedicate a part of your life,
to spend time together night after night.
But when one is care less for the other,
a heart is broken the minds in a flutter.
What did I do, what's wrong with me,
what do you see that I cannot see?
I loved you so but you threw me away,
you cared only for yourself day after day.
Your selfish acts brought hatred in me,
that I will proudly display for everyone to see.
Have fun in your world and stay out of mine,
life will go on it will just take time.

Leigh Ann Bolon

Love

Love is very much like tomorrow,
it may bring joy or sorrow.
Love full of surprises,
bought forth in all different shapes and sizes
Some never know the joy that it brings,
Some never forget the wonderful things,
that love has brought them over the years
Though it may have caused them many tears.
If ones love is long enough to last,
You should be able to forget the past.
It can leave you lonely and hurt,
While it last you will be lively and pert.
So if by someone special you are selected,
as long as you love them they will be protected.
If you find someone to love and cherish,
love them always and they will never perish.

Lisa Marie Schram

"The Memories"

I had extreme problems when I was a child.
It seemed so sad that I had to live extreme denial.

The memories of his hands seem so strong.
It took many tears to see it was wrong.

I knew that inside my heart it hurt, but
my soul already seemed torched and burnt.

I did so many things to myself. I didn't understand
because who did it to me was a man.

My heart was so torn with many feelings, I had
trouble dealing. I was only a child with such
overwhelming dismay and feelings.

At times I sit and cry. And wish to die.
I wonder is my whole life a lie and wonder why.

Sometimes things seem so out of reach.
I still have to hide because I can't confide
With feelings that are so hard to express
With other lives.

There will always be obstacles of memories
In my way, but my past childhood is gone.

Some feelings are overbearing, but I still have my life to live.

Karlo Antonio Kumar

Feelings Of Love

When a knife goes through your heart,
It usually means two loved ones part.
But when your heart itself divides,
A person you loved has just recently died.
Your days and nights grow dark and cold,
The crowded street is now a lonely road.
The feeling of joy is nothing now,
You try to understand, but just don't know how
A lovely tear rolls down your face,
Your quick-stepped walk has dropped it's pace.
These days of yours that are ahead,
Are the ones that you will mostly dread.

Jamie Smith

Escape

The phone rings in the dead of night
It wakes the young girl with a strange fright
She answers it only to hear
Someone whispering in her ear
She seems to know the deep sinister voice, but
Still it leaves an uneasy feeling in her gut
She wants to hang up the phone
But she's enchanted by the tone
Into a deep trance she has fallen
The enchanting voice has callin'
Now she will follow the word
Of the voice so absurd
When she comes out of her trance
She doesn't stand a chance
She is at the mercy of a Vampire
Who has held, for her, so much desire
Will she fall victim to his power
Will she become locked in his tower
Will she take shelter under his cape
Or will she be able to escape -

Kelli Nixon

Mother

I had a dream, early this morning or late last night.
It was a special dream - I woke up happy.

I saw my mother sitting in the living room of my parents' old home.
It was some sort of celebration.

And I remember asking her why she didn't come back to stay.
She just smiled and replied that she liked where she was very much.

I was concerned, and asked her if she had enough money for all her
 needs.
She smiled again, and said that she had been "saving up" for a long
 time.

I asked her to please come back and visit again, it had been so long.
She just smiled - I'll always remember that smile.

And I thought to myself... how rested she looks!
She must be happy with her new life.

I haven't seen my mother for over two years now.
She died that March day, when things were so cold.

She loved the spring, that was her favorite time.
Time to take walks in the woods and collect pussy willows.

Spring always makes me think...
You never know how much you'll miss someone until they are gone.
And the parting is final.
At least until they choose to visit you, once again - in a dream.

   Lyn Manera

The End

No one knew it was coming.
It was a surprise to all of us.
It all happened so quickly, his life passing away in front of me
 and I couldn't do anything to stop it.
His cries and moans for help made me realize I might never
 see him again.
He was almost lifeless and I couldn't help in any way.
 I felt so useless.
We all tried our hardest, but we weren't getting anywhere.
Standing there, waiting, wondering and hoping was all we could do.
Being unable to help him was the worst feeling I had ever felt.
When the ambulance arrived it was a total chaos.
When we arrived at the hospital they told us it was too late
 he was already gone.
When I realized what they just told me, it felt like a part of me
 had died with him.
I will never understand totally why he died.
Stories go untold, questions go unanswered.
He will always be in my heart, my mind and my prayers.
I love you daddy!!

   Jennifer Kester

"She"

I ripened as the sun grew strong,
it was midday.
I was sweet and warm as the
sun grew stronger.
As sweet as Grandma's marmalade,
I was a tasty fruit.
The fruit was filled with
knowledge of the world that
had passed by,
I kept my passion of yesterday,
I ventured into a pasture of grazing grass.
The sun set at a golden gleam,
I gathered my thoughts
about a place beyond the moon.

   Leticia P. Johnson

That Kid

That one school day I made a friend,
It was the best day,
We laughed, and we cried,
Most of all we had pride.
It was the day,
His dad has died,
We became the best of friends,
Until that day he moved away.
It's been nine years, and to this day,
I will never forget him!

I ask myself will I see him again?
Will he remember me?
Will things be the same?
Only I can make these questions come true.
The day he moved away,
I was only a little girl.
I still had feelings,
Just the same as any older person.
To this day there has been apart missing.
That part that's missing is that friend I once knew.

   Loretta Evans

The Robin

The Robin was pulling this rope in the air.
It was tied to the apple tree,
to keep my cat there.
She pulled and she yanked it, way to the west.
I guessed that she wanted it, for her nest.

No wonder my clothes lines fall apart.
I guess, for her nest, it's a good start.
The little ones come, and feed on the bread
I put on the ground, for rabbits, instead.

They're all God's creatures,
and come in the night,
stalking for food
no matter their plight.

He sees that they're kept,
in all their missions,
just as we are,
with all our transgressions.

   Marama Kenney

The Kite

A kite riding in the wind
It's black and white tail flowing with each new gust
Soaring and dipping, laughing and crying
Yearning to go higher, farther into the sea of blue
But held by a string
One that will break if pulled hard enough

The kite doesn't pull free
Afraid of losing touch with the hand that gave it birth
Trusting, obeying
But unsuccessfully forgetting what is barely beyond reach
Still wanting to explore.

Suddenly clouds above turn dark, loud and angry
The tight string becomes shorter
The kite fighting, not wanting to go home
Tearing the delicate material, breaking the heart,
trying not to lose control
The strings snaps, a seldom taken chance
Free at last
As teardrops begin to fall.

   Mary Spanton

In My Hand

I hold in my hand, a life near death.
It's hard to believe, she's taking her last breath.

As I watch her now, I can touch her soul.
This poor small creature will never grow old.

I start to wonder, how can it be
That a God so great could do this to me.

While I was thinking of frivolous things,
she passed away, her souls' in the wind.

Tears stream from my eyes, I can barely see.
She lies still now, I hear her voice in the breeze.

As long as we remember, she will never truly leave.
Even though she is gone she's forever a part of me.

Pamela Kiser

Dear Son,

Had you been 4 years old last night I would have said,
  "It's late; go home,"
    But you are 24.
Had you been 4 years old last night I would have said,
  "You are hurting Holly even though you love her,"
    But you are 24.
Had you been 4 years old last night I would have said,
  "Friends are fine, but family should be first."
    But you are 24.
Had you been 4 years old last night I would have said,
  "You are making a mistake; please rethink this whole thing."
    But you are 24.
Had you been 4 years old last night I would have told you
  these things as I put my arms around you;
    But you are 24.

Helen S. Nickolaus

Imagined...

Two moons of sour lips pierced
It's opens after dawn's break.
Before closed to three light shades of
Forever ways into entrances of sealed gates.
Till folded four pages from stories of
Books from an old maid's shelf of dust
And piled upon seasoning dirt.
From which comes five plays of mules
In shadows of disturbing everlasting peace.
Onto steaks of forbidden eyes,
Flies six tells of lies to deceasing bribes,
Convincing to every sound of cries.
Seven sagacious fools tremble in eight
Pools of salt and oriental spices of blood.
To ravel nine strokes of wind into foul distilled
Airs of wondrous fantasies and opulent gems.
Comes ten flakes of drifted snows onto the
Buried solids of earth and known,
To which I laid under,
Dead, like the rest.

Kidd Yang

Dreams

In the middle of the night
Dreams come forth with fright or delight
Make us pause to wonder
Some will cause us loss of slumber.

Upon awakening we rise to see
This couldn't be happening not to me
It's just a dream, a horrible dream
Another mystery in life's scheme.

Sandra S. Jack

Untitled

I'm looking through eternity
its showering on my world to lose someone
to be lost in your heart you just left
but I've been gone for many years
the clowns are crying in my dreams
the Sandman's laughing
my flower is dead
my vision is blue.
I realize
I'm the only clown
in my world of blue
and the sadman
in my dreams is you.

Melinda Sue Roger

Fear

Fear is something we posses deep inside.
It's something we express or sometimes may hide.
It's there before an event, such as a play.
It may go, or sometimes will stay.
Sometimes it's just all in our head
It's so unrealistic, it can't even be said.

Fear is something we posses deep inside.
Sometimes we just want to ignore it.
Often 'cause of pride.
Fear is always there.
It's in me, you and everywhere

Fear is the cause of prejudice and hate.
Many people question that theory and some will
  always debate.
It may cause us to act stupid, and
  sometimes act shy.
We may never express it and always deny.
Some will always wonder, and forever question why?

But, in my head there is definitely no debate.
For to me fear is the root cause of hate.

Katie Leigh Palmer

Make A Difference

How can I make a difference? I ask myself each day.
I've been the victim of this world, as I was learning to pray.
Though sometimes it was scary, a nightmare de ja vu.
I always knew someone was there, showing me what to do.
I searched and read all kinds of literature, hoping I would find
The perfect road where sinners go, to find the Great divine.
I found when times were hard, when I couldn't find a door
I'd feel his love surround me, I wasn't alone anymore.
I see him in the mountains, I see him in the trees.
I see him in the rivers, that flow into the seas.
I see him in the peoples red, black, yellow and white.
I see him in their smiles and little children's eyes.
I see where it would be so very easy, to fall into the hole.
I also see the glorious rainbow, and there is a pot of gold.
You ask me if I stand with the Baptist, the Muslim,
the Catholic, the Jew.
I say to you, I love them all," for my God is their God too!
When I searched my soul, surprised by what I'd seen
I found that I could make a difference,
and that it starts with me.

Kelly O. Bond

A Lost Eagle

I reached out, only to touch a feather, that's fallen from a bird
I've grasped onto something that has disappeared into the sea
The waves roared endlessly with love, knowing you were there somewhere
My hair blew into the wind, as if you touched it.
The songs and chants were for you as I walked down a lonely street
As I heard drums beating in the distance, sounded like
My heart pounding harder for your love.
I held out my hands for a hug
Into the empty air without a prayer
The moon shining on the mountain streams
My love continuously streaming down; like
the falls of winter. You could see it in
my eyes; an eagle that's been wounded.
As straight as an arrow; I want to mend that hurt
when I find the fulfillment in my arms I've been longing for.
Touch me once again, as the sun touches the horizon.

Lorraine Colon

Rainbows

My children are the rainbows in my daily life.
I've shared with them the laughter, joys and pain and strife.

Through the years I've watched them grow to the adults they are today.
Guided them, loved them and struggled all along the way.

Now they're giving gifts to me as I feel myself grow old.
Gifts of love and strength and joy-far more precious than gold.

And when I thought it could get no better, my emotions really went wild.
The greatest of gifts was given to me-my very first grandchild.

Maureen P. Dewey

The Dreamer

'Tis I who dream, the visions are clear.
Ivory towers are constructed upon air.
A hill of multicolored flowers blossom,
propagating with the sun. Grow as I grow.
The stream of my mind flows crystal clear.
I behold Kings and Queens of royalty spreading their law
upon the land, others send their praise.
'Tis I who dream upon every hour.
Opening numerous doors. Images emerge from within,
A knight in sparkling armor warding
Off the evils of life, a minstrel creating
with the voice of his pen, and a
gentle fair princes content in her throne.
I will soon encounter my destination by the path I drift.
Through valleys, and whirling storms.
My visions lie deep in the ocean. As the diamond waves hit the
shore with azure thought. The sea gull soars to all latitudes
Striving with the silent wind of desperation.
Yes, 'tis I who dream.

Natalie Kappes

Love

Roses are red
Just like your soft silky skin

Violets are blue
Just like those beautiful eyes you have

Out of all things, I would want you
I would trade in my old yellow horse
and my saddle too,

But all because I LOVE YOU

Those three little words I mean that,
I would die if I had to live without you
Now do you see what I mean when I say

I REALLY DO LOVE YOU
Neal L. Thomas

Creation

Ocean and seas, rivers and lakes.
Just with one blink it took God to make.
Mountains and valleys, deserts and plains.
All need a drink so He made the rains.
Then came animal, fish, insects and birds.
Who took to the sky with His awesome words.
Finally mankind was put on the earth.
Made in God's image gave them great worth.
Placing them far above all that He'd made.
Giving each choice to die to be saved.
How God must weep when souls go astray.
Knowing the minute, hour and day.
The devils work will soon be done.
But God on the other hand, has already won.

Margaret L. Yannayon

A Statement

As you reach your hand to mine,
    Know that I treasure your trust,
That I will never judge,
    Nor, proclaim I know what's
Best for all of us.

As I clasp your hand to shake
    Know that I will try not to show fear,
Nor puffed-up intimidation.
    But, only care and trust.

As we walk through this world,
    As we argue our differences,
Know that I will look to resolve
    In peace-not war
    In care and understanding-not
Judgmental condemnation,
But, in completeness in all relations.

'A moderate conclusion
...With satisfaction for all'
Loretta Holmblad

Save And Restore The Beauty

    Can this piece of land be real?
Knowing modern society cannot reveal
such splendor at such an inexpensive cost.
Maybe the natural beauty is not completely lost.

    Look at those mountains over there.
They seem to protect and care
for the land the way that they
surround the peacefulness of the Lord's holy day.

    One single tree stands high and accompanies
hundreds of tulips, roses, and pansies.
They grow all around the land,
but have never been touched by a human hand.

    The bright orange, the brilliant red of the sunset
fills me with peace in a world full of upset.
The unlimited range of sky relaxes my soul
and makes me realize I am in control.

    For in this world, you can make dreams come true
if you let God's love and His teachings guide you.
And in your journey, try to realize
that our Earth and future need to be pasteurized.

Melanie Valint

Grey Peacocks

So deft delivery, deaf to knowing,
knowing not that which serviced lips
  do not orate.

Mirrors biased to his iris Peception,
rose window performing acts of transformation,
turning up the ends of doubtful mouths
from the conscience, from the crowds.

Brilliant Chameleon Leader of Power
  (yet stagnant are the eyes)
Great by paper-minded reptilian friends,
Great by your rose iris, growing tall,
  roots and stems.

Grey peacock! Is your back green as if
manifesting intent?

Mouths you may transform, my hand will not.
Your six inch band will not lullaby
this young Justice cry.

Chad Reimann

Untitled

I'd hate to have to dig a grave for you;
  Knowing that your heart had ceased to beat;
Knowing you had left an empty seat;
  Knowing I had bid a last adieu.

But digging for someone I hardly knew;
  One with whom I hadn't drunk or eat;
One to whom I'd never lost or beat;
  I'd feel the task would only be what's due.

'Twould be so hard to do this for a friend;
To know that he'd be covered up forever;
  One to whom I'd give my last regards.
To one I did not know 'twould only be the end,
But it would turn gray skies to lovely weather
  To dig for one who had cheated me at cards.

L. Dwight Parker

Call for Liberty

Only two parties rule.
Large government schools.
Children killing children.
Tax money being spent with no end.
No choice for the poor,
except through a welfare door.
Socialistic ideals are not the answer,
ask any defected Russian dancer.
Everyday more rights are lost.
Apathy is making our young the cost.
The only way to stop the government institution,
is to know your bill of rights and the constitution.
1776 - Don't tread on me.
1996 - Fight for liberty.

Mark Norris

Why?

A question asked down thru the ages.
An answer that we'll never know.
Neither in the beauty of heaven.
Or here on this earth below.

For when you meet you're loved one in heaven.
With the cares of this world in the past.
You will be so happy to see them.
You will never remember to ask.

Stillman F. Webb

Let People Know

Let people know what it's like to be you,
Let them see your side that's true.

Let them see what it's like and how you feel,
Let people know that you're near and that you're real.

Lift up your voice to let them know that you're here,
Let them see all your hopes and all your fears.

So let people know what it's like to be you,
Let them see your side that's true.

Sunshine Menefee

Ode To A Mighty Oak

You stretched out flaming arms in welcome
  last October long ago
You were warm animated, our friend and protector
But then your dead leaves lagged our eaves
You turned defector,
You squirrels were noisy and messy and warm
Inside our attic
While outside a winter storm

Hurled snow on you.
You were cold, supercilious, unfeeling as your
  icicle earnings
But then you liked leafless arms to pray
Confessing, asking forgiveness.
Next though, you put on pale snow sea-
  through lace leaves
Inviting our spring embrace.
And dark green satin leaves for summer flirtation
You give us tempestuous, four
  season fashion show
continents of God, who planted one small cocoon

Hildegarde M. Snow

The Curse

The moon moves slowly in palest sky;
Later the rocks cast shadows on the shore.
And I think,
Do you see it?
And me?

Snow settles on unwrinkled hills;
White and clean and simple as a hymn,
And I think,
Do you see it?
And me?

No beauty passes that we shared.
What one forgot, the next recalled.
Magnified by two.
Now, never see it
Without me.

Mardy Wheeler

"Little Face"

Love is...a little face smiling and
  laughing in the morning sun.

Happiness is...a little face saying "I love you"
  with hugs and kisses

Hate is..that little face crying and never
  saying "I love you".

Anger is...that little face looking away and
  trying to hide the hurt and pain.

Freedom is...when that little face can smile
  and laugh in the morning sun again.

Linda M. Herget

Bloody Peace (A Look At Bosnia/Croatia)

Caught in the silence of the crossfire,
Leaders of the world meet
Waiting for the first move;
Death for hire: won't admit defeat
  People wait for the end of it all,
  For the last final fight
  Cornered behind walls of vanity
  Lost in a blinding light
Children trapped in a world of adults,
Cry out in silent streets,
Lost inside the fears of their parents;
With death they compete
  What will this world come to before we have gone?
  What will this place be like before the last dawn?
Bloody peace, a war in hell, silent battle,
God help us now.
    Michele A. Terwilliger

Lifetime Journey

Sometimes God guides us in ways we don't understand.
Leading us through joy, happiness, struggles and strife.
With faith in our hearts; our lives in his hands,
We journey on our chosen paths of life.

But there is one path which I was meant to travel.
Leading through different lands, but always to you.
As I follow the road God has placed before me,
I learn something that my heart always knew...

God separately shaped us to be paired as one,
Blessing us with a love that is known by few.
You are the greatest gift of my life,
And I pray that we never again walk as two.

May Heaven's angels watch over you.
Their light showing you the way,
On our golden path of promise
Extending to forever and a day.

And as we travel, may you always know...
That God has so beautifully answered my prayer.
It is in you that I have found my forever.
On this lifetime journey that you and I will share.
    Lisa Shroyer

Biology

Biology is boring - my head it fogs
Learn about lakes, marshes and bogs
Read of rabbits, spiders and frogs
Jumping on the ground then hopping on logs.

Biology is boring - I'm very sincere
The baby's the fawn, the father's the deer
The sun goes away, then will appear
You never know then the end is near

Biology is boring with all its junk
Weasels, chipmunks, squirrels and skunks
Of course if I fail it I am sunk
The thought of this puts me down in the dump

Biology is boring- I'm telling you!
Learn about organisms found in a zoo
Koalas, elephants, a kangaroo
Are you confused? I am too!

Biology is boring I say with a sigh
Populations change because people die
They fall asleep in class - do you know why?
'Cause biology is boring and that's no lie!
    Lori M. Dinnella

A Walk Through The Woods

As I walk through the woods,
leaves crunch under my feet,
an owl screeches in the distance,
pine cones let off a sweet but musty smell,
a river flows toward the south,
a lowly raccoon scans the ground,
some deer drink from a rushing stream,
as the sun starts to set,
darkness sweeps over the woods,
as the mountains create large and eerie shadows,
I walk quickly through the almost never-ending woods,
"I'm trapped" I think,
beady yellow eyes stare me down,
a few leaves rustle beneath my feet,
quickly, I run as fast as I can,
I came out of the woods and look back,
the woods are all gone.
    Kelly Park

The Symphony Of Life

Nightfall ends another day
leaving just a memory.
Harmonic notes of joy and pain
in life's melodic symphony.

Some hear a melody of loneliness
when night time shadows arrive.
Reliving the heartaches of days gone by,
'til they lose the will to survive.

But see the beauty that nightfall brings
there is no need for sadness there.
Look beyond the darkened skies
for starlight glistens everywhere.

The twilight hours softly sing
saying put your troubles away.
Allow the echoes of yesterday's pain
to be silenced in the dawning of tomorrow's new day.

Each sunrise brings a new refrain
a song of hope for glad tomorrows.
The chance to learn from past mistakes
and recall no more our bygone sorrows.
    Michelle L. Jacoby

Daddy

Daddy died and went to Heaven,
Leaving me and Mom and seven.

Now and then I see my friend,
He comes back to help our hearts to mend.

In someone's smile or a wink of the eye,
You can see him, if you'll only try.

A gentle breeze,
A simple sneeze.

Listen, you'll hear him by and by,
For you see - spirits never die.

Death is just a cloud away,
Where we'll all go and stay one day.

Another Heavenly being,
We'll be seeing.

We'll be a family again,
As soon as we can.

We'll meet daddy in Heaven,
Me and Mom, and the other Seven.
    Margaret H. Scott

Worth

The petals of the dogwood float gently to the ground
  Leaving on branches above them many a golden crown.
Lazily floating and drifting, like so much summer snow,
  They've had their time of splendor and what a beautiful way to go!

When our days are numbered and time is fleeting fast;
  When earthly works are ceasing and gliding into the past;
Will we, like the lovely dogwood, hold golden crowns to the sky
  That our gracious Heavenly Father will see and bless us by?
    Mary Yates Hall

The Journey

It's a blind admiral's voyage, a journey uncharted
Leaving port on a night with no stars.
A passage uncertain with abyssal foreboding,
Portals covered with drapes sewn from fog.

The ghost crew performs its maritime duties
As though the blind admiral could see the far shore,
The haunting spills out on the decks of confusion,
The masts full with wind but the helm uncontrolled.

This perilous vessel that we call Existence
Takes us its prisoner at the moment of birth.
We sail, yet in bondage, with no map, no angels,
Till the day that the shovels toss earth on our grave.

The madness is shrieking its hideous laughter
Cavorting because of the knowledge it hides.
As we search for dignity, pursue life's elation,
We're forced to be players in this comedy staged.

The ship's log reflects only yesterday's history
There's no compass to show our direction or fate.
The most ghastly component of this spectral voyage
Is that we never know when it will all end.
    Laura Woodward Waddell

"Lines Addressed To Time"

Turn backwards, oh Time, turn backwards for me
Let me wander down the halls of memory
Let the mist rise and the curtain fall away
The dark, heavy curtain between me and yesterday
And let me turn the pages
Now yellowed by the years
Unmarred by passing ages
Not yet scarred by sins and fears
Let me pick the roses
Whose petals still gleam with April's dew
And the brightly blooming wildflowers
Still vivid with their sublime hue
And let me hear the mocking bird
Whose song rings sweet, yet far away

And as the twilight settles, let the whip-or-will still sing
The ancient song that echoes
From the ashes of another day
    Lindsay Paisley

A Look from the Field

Generals plot their strategies
as zebras prance about the grid iron
observing every move of the battling glory-boys.

Drooling spectators watch their gladiators
with voices calling out as if a single entity.

In the air,
a wrinkled, brown pigskin
spins alone.
    Shawn Khol

Romance Me

Romance me my love
Let us have an affair with love that we may find us anew.
Inspired by love songs and flowers,
Let us stroll midst robin birds that sing
And hide behind their blossomed trees and kiss.
Let us climb green covered hills.
Let us run and roll down and fall in each others arms.
Then on your arm let my head rest
With your lips against my face
And your other arm around my waist.
Romance me my love
With simple things to taste to God's country let us go,
Away from everything away from all.
Where love can again be learned.
Where silent prayers are heard.
Where I can hear God's voice telling me you still love me.
Then with trust in each other restored,
Let us go and close the door.
Feed me my love with words sweet as tender grapes
As the moonlight witnesses our intimate embrace.
    Maria Cline

Prophetic Eye

Try'n to find the rhythm: Try'n to find the rhyme
Life in a prism—Reflections of mankind
Socrates and Aristotle oracles who've spoken
Walls of Pompeii—Edifice of Pliny's day

Try'n to find the rhythm: Try'n to find the rhyme
Curiosity can lead to peril—Temptation can be like wine
Ulysses had a vendetta; Troy was to pay the price
A wooden horse of beauty—Vengeance dressed in a guise

Try'n to find the rhythm: Try'n to find the rhyme
Puffballs and rapture tantalize the mind
Babylon a fortress whose end was inscribed
Many failed to believe—Their cries have since died

Try'n to find the rhythm: Try'n to find the rhyme
Watch'n the years go by as stars extinguish from the sky
Rome built as an empire never to collapse
Even her government succumbed to what must pass

Try'n to find the rhythm: Try'n to find the rhyme
The Alpha and the Omega clearly transcribed
Cloud of Harmony; Sphere in divinity
Jury of One—Voice of three—rendering death: Granting eternity
    Madeleine Graham

"The Echo Of Life's Problems"

The world is shouting and we can hear nothing but the echoes of
life's problem.
We have come to a time when we can not hear, hear, hear
Peace, peace, peace...
Joy, joy, joy...
Love, love, love...
because they are overshadowed by the echoes of
Crime, crime, crime..
Violence, violence, violence.
Unemployment, unemployment, unemployment...
Homelessness, homelessness, homelessness...
Hunger, hunger, hunger...
Racism, racism, racism...
Individuals from the far stretches of earth need to unite with
Harmony, harmony, harmony in a strong whisper, whisper,
whisper.
This will conquer, conquer, conquer... all of life's
  Problems,
    Problems,
      Problems.
    Myron Walker

Love, Life, And Death

When you feel the emotion of Love,
Lift your head, and look to heaven above,
For Love with it's symbol the heart,
Is the reason for life getting it's start,
From the act of Love, a baby is born,
Hopefully to be loved, not forlorn,
It is sometimes slapped, to bring out a cry,
Which means the Soul has arrived,
Something nothing on earth can buy,
The Body and Soul which are then combined,
Begin to grow, with the help of a mind,
And to live a full life, till a point in time,
When there is no longer a beat of the Heart,
So where does the Soul go, O Soul of Mine,
When from Life on Earth, we eventually depart.

Marvin Zelman

El Paso

It whispers his name through her heart...
    like a gentle evening breeze.
It slips his shadow into her soul...
    leaving her breathless.

Afraid of being overwhelmed...
    caught up in the emotion.
Wanting it, but fearing it just the same...
    driven by past memories that bring
        tears to her eyes.

The words she can not, will not, allow...
    her mind to say, her heart to believe.
She built walls around herself, sealed out the world;
    and left no opening for LOVE, the unknown,
to enter and capture what was left of
    her heart,
        her soul,
            her very existence.

K.E. Mitchell

Clouds

White, soft and fluffy,
Like a lamb's fur coat,
Gliding across the sky without a care in the world,
These beauteous things,
So soft, so soft,
As a passage to the sky
And heaven.

Katharine Rose Clapham

To Have A Friend

To have a friend is to posses a treasure
Like a rare and priceless gem
Once a friend has been found try not to lose them
A friend takes away the pain of loneliness
They make happiness a reality instead of an illusion
A good friend makes life worth living
They are there for you - through the good and the bad
A friend is someone to talk to
Someone to eat with
A true friend is worth more than a precious gem
worth more than money can buy.

Julie Pierson

A Devouring Heart

How the air is cold and strengthening by moments
Like my feelings in-ward lie, devouring emotions passing by,
Keeping all within and deep inside
Never taking time to cry, or choosing how to ever thaw
The love we have inside us all,
Yet we eat and drink and sleep the same,
In spite the enduring this increasing pain.
Should we let it pass or not
These feeling that cannot be forgotten
And how they made us cold to bare,
This hurt inside, we all do share
So please do try now turning from
And Send to, from whence it come
This grudge you hold like stubborn foe.
Never need his foolish glow
Cause it may seem as though he care
But his love is deceit and not to share
So turn away this do tell, a frozen heart warned in hell
Never learn this to dwell and when you die all is well.

Nicholas Sheda

Bells

Listen to the ringing.
Listen to the chimes.
Each one different in it's own way.
Each one ringing out it's own song.
A warning!
FREEDOM
A cool breeze.
In a life time we hear many different bells.
Warning us of danger.
Reminding us of freedom.
Making us smile.
Many times the chimes of a bell has calmed my tormented soul.
May you always have the peace of mind
that a bell can bring.
The safety and security it gives.
And may you always have a song in your heart
that a bell can sing.

Rowie

Indian Love

On the banks of the Ohio near Hanging Rock
Little Dove and Running Bear used to walk

In the spring when the flowering dogwood came alive
She became his Cherokee bride

When harvest was past and winter was come
As the old year was ended and the new year begun

While the starlight glistened on the new fallen snow
Their child was born more precious than gold

Then Running Bear went away
And left them at the break of day

Little Dove stood beside the tall cotton wood Tree
And looked toward the river running wild and free

She stood with pride as she waited for him
An Indian Princess in white buck skin,

Running Bear was at war on the other side
Fighting for the freedom of his Cherokee tribe

Little Dove's heart was filled with faith so great
And the love for her brave shone on her face
She knew he'd come home to her and his son
When his great battle he'd fought and won.

Helen Molleh Haynes

The Visitor

Once upon a time, far far away
Lived an old man, who had nothing to say
He sat on the porch, humming a song
Until one summer day
A visitor came along
He was a young looking man
Carrying a large suitcase
He said nothing to the old man
No expression on his face
The old man got up slowly
Smiling he walked toward the young man
As their eyes met they each extended a hand
At the moment they touched
Their bodies filled with light
It was all over
It was alright
For in everyday, there ia a night
And we must all sit on the porch of life
Watching over others
Our sisters and our brothers
Kathleen Gautier

Waiting...

They sit on their haunches -
 loneliness, sorrow, and despair -
 waiting.

Why does no one help?
 At one instant, agreement;
 next time, contradiction.

Trying! Trying!
 Better upon leaving;
 not so good upon return.

What should have been done
 differently?
 Maybe spending more time there?

They raise themselves from their haunches -
 loneliness, sorrow, and despair -
 and slowly move closer.
Joan Gallagher

A Man Named June. Cleveland. Winter. Heavy Fuel.

Hollow Howls the midnight wind twixt towering concrete walls.
Lonely arms it wraps in cold embrace about a figure
 streaking through the night with besotted grace.

Mournful wailing keens the dark;
 memories of Summer's warmth and winter's life
 as dying Autumn gasps its chilling breath
 upon a pixilated form who sings and runs with Death.

Moisture fills the air as winter cries its cold white breath
 harsh upon June's warm pink chilling flesh.

Yet on zips June oblivious to winter's cry
 in his betankered mode

Loaded lips croon June's triumphant tune as his pink feet go
 teal and his riches shrink to tiny globes.

At last, as winter's cry howls its throb he stumbles once
 and shudders on a frozen plod.
And on he passes to that esoteric other side-
 his lips warbling that triumphant strain
 as Death's icy vice
 clamps

 with freezing pain.
Lukas Eisermann

A Word Not Spoken In Time

Like dew drops off a wilted rose;
Lonely as a shadow in a colorless corner;
I walk in these days a perfunctory wonderer;
 There is a time, after the victory of night, minutes before the
changing of the stars.
Where silence seizes the cacophony.
When the world is as empty as my heart;
 The echo of my tears create a sorrowful stream reflecting
a longing, yearning thought;
 A stone is tossed, with a ripple of love;
 Waves of feelings cascading a remembrance of;
Like a word not spoken in time;
I fall to my buckled knees;
Cry out my love for thee;
Yet, these earnest words fall but at my feet;
Our love bounds us by one heart;
While still miles between, worlds apart;
Like a humming bird finds a flower becomes a fern;
I will miss the sweetness never to return.
Kyle W. Moselle

"Lonely"

Lonely is down where the bottom is bare,
Lonely is down where you don't even care.
I have no direction, my mind's in a blur,
All the thoughts that I'm thinkin',
Are only of her.

The weeds in the back yard, knee deep have
grown, and I'm standing knee deep in wild
oats that I've sown. My sweetheart is gone
and I'm livin' alone, in a house full of
empty, and a yard full of home.

I'm standin' here lookin' at nothin' in sight,
And the things that I'm doin', I ain't doin'
right. Every time that I start, I go back
where I've been, to a spot without nothin',
to start with again.

Lonely is down where the bottom is bare,
Lonely is down where you don't even care.
I have no direction, my mind's in a blur,
All the thoughts that I'm thinkin',
Are only of her.
Phil Hugenroth

Sonnet

You found me at the end of given time
Long after all my innocence was gone.
You helped my soul from vacant depths to climb
Towards the pulsing light of a new god.
With all the naive zeal of newborn faith
I cast away all earthly things I'd seized,
But could I ever know I'd be the taker
Of holy bread by your hand diseased?
Its guilty past shows my sweet god to be
No more than one warm carnal incarnation
Of all those tempting things I see
Blocking the light of my salvation.
But better to be now with pagan gods
Than to the depths of mortality gone.
Kelly Doyle

"Faithful"

Death should not be too sad,
Look at the good life you have had.

The bible says three score and ten,
At 72 years you don't know when,

Brought up in a good Christian way,
We still belong to the church today.

Life is not a bed of roses you know,
Even the Bible will tell you so.

Just take each day at a time,
With Christ everything will be fine.

People will be people as you will see,
We all hope that the eternal life will be.

Christ died on the cross for us all,
The devil will rule and must fall.

In your life, you will have suffering and despair.
Be faithful with the Lord, and saved with a prayer.

Paul Skinner

An Ode To A Dreamer

Travel is the name of your game
Look through brochures and scan the National Geographic
Make phone calls, read travel magazines before being specific
Study the calendar and ensure when your holidays fall
Buy travellers checks, prepare for a shortfall
When you come back your wallet won't weigh the same.

Have fun and always be merry even when facing an adversary
Remember not everyone can whip up a travel itinerary
It takes patience to make a coherent arrangement
And act your best if confronted by a "B" management
Some hotels and some Inns may shower you with decor
Some Pubs and some B and Bs may serve you with fine liquor.

Travelling can be achieved by air, rail, ship or VHS
Expenses can vary from a minute amount to much
Whatever you owe you'll have to pay or be in a mess
If your wanders run your budget too high then skip lunch.

On your return, check the mailbox, and retrieve the cat from the VET
Place all your bills on the dining room table and utter "NOT YET!"
Pour yourself a toast for a trip luckily completed
And thank your lucky stars it has ended.

Mary Jane Thomas Day

Summer Venturing Around

Summer venturing around,
    Looking for sensational warming of our souls.

I looked over spring and what did I see,
Looking for sensational warming of our souls?
A jet stream of wind ramming right at me,
Looking for sensational warming of our souls.

Turn around off goes spring into thin air,
Looking for sensational warming of our souls,
Compared to summer, it is thin as a human hair,
Looking for sensational warming of our souls.

So big, bright and beautiful like the sun,
Looking for sensational warming of our souls,
So wonderfully, soft, and edible as a bun,
Looking for sensational warming of our souls.

It's sometimes up and sometimes down,
Looking for sensational warming of our souls,
But still its soothes the human soul kindly-bound,
Looking for sensational warming of our souls.

Quadir Hussain

Looking at Me

Looking into the eyes of a person who is confused and afraid
Looking into the eyes of someone for whom I've prayed.

Seeing an image of a person who is out of control with nowhere to turn
Visualizing this person as one who is teachable and is willing to learn.

Looking at an individual who is scared and filled with despair
Feeling that this same person has been running, but has gotten
    nowhere.

Watching someone struggle back and forth with what's right and
    what's wrong
Getting the sense that wherever they are, they feel as if they don't
    belong.

Running, running just to stay ahead of what's in store
Fading in and out of fantasy to reality - but it's time to stop running
Enough - No more!

Looking into the eyes of a person who is longing to be free
You see, I'm standing in front of a mirror and the person looking
    back is me.

Pamela V. Grimm

Game Of Love

Love is a fire that burns in the night.
Love is holding on when it's so hard to fight.
They can say that they love you, but can they prove it?
Some have the love, but don't know what to do with it.
Some will deny it and put up a fight;
But, if they truly love you, they'll see the light.
If the love is not there, you may have to let go.
Just hold onto your pride, do not sink too low.
I know this can hurt. It is called the game of love.
Just look for guidance in the good Lord above.

Kim McMichens

Love Is Not

Love is not a hunger, no food could bear its name.
Love is not just pleasure, as the child is born in pain.
Love is not a sunset, for it passes into night.
And love is not enslaving, it serves both wrong and right.

Love is not a woman, her vanity it does not keep.
Love is not a life-time, thus, in death it cannot sleep.
Love is not an ocean, a puddle would seem as small
And love is not a valley, nor a pit for man to fall.

Love is not moment, as time will forever pass.
Love is not a number, to be counted first or last.
Love is not a flower, to bloom alone in spring,
And love is not the church bell, a wedding nor a ring.

No, Love is not just one of these, let a poet now be bold.
Love; the eternal image, and man, its living mold.

Lucian Stewart

A Lark

Black rabbits, the dog barks,
    And goes upon a lark.
He thinks of rabbits,
    Chasing after, faster and faster.
He runs unaware of the shifting movements of the hare;
    Over, under, listening to the thunder.
Foiled,
    The dog goes home to his master.

Shannon May

"Poor Of Love"

I am poor, of love.
Love is still in my broken heart.
Clipped wings, are my empty hands.
Cut off claws, are my barbed feet.
Dropping, down, down, are my red tears.
Crying, loud, loud, are my fearful fears.
Crawling, out, out, of jails, was my journey.
Flying, high, high, over the oceans of blood, was my foray.
Landing on the top of the statue, in New York,
And reciting, liberty, liberty, is my need.
I am needy, poor, poor of love.
Lighting the sun, up, up, up, by my loving flame, was my deeds.
Falling down, down, at your feet was my climax.
Loving you, you, is the beginning, and the end of my destiny in my life.
Admiring, praising, loving you only you,
Caring, touching, tasting yours, only yours,
Are the first, and the last jobs,
of my dried, and barbed tongue, to do.
I am poor, poor of loving you, only you.

Mammo Golli

In the Name of Love

This heart is a true fact of growing
love out of the days of love.
A true love of all. A hand of tenderness-
A voice of love.
Our sky asserts, the truth of love and we
accept them all as done.
There are more loves and loves that I can understand.
In how is our love late in the night
as God has thought us to love, but our love is eternal.
And yet today I know nothing about love,
That those are curious facts of life that I do not understand.
As the flower of love is in my heart or
drips of heaven into my love.
Or most of love is true as the wind that goes true.
That I love thee as thee love me eternally.

Edgardo Rivera Cruz

Untitled

Love is free,
Love will let what is, be,
Love does not force, push, or retain,
Love is not jealous, bitter, or strained,
Love is patient, and humble,
Love firmly grows, and does not tumble,
Love supports and backs-up,
Love never allows the wrongs to stack-up,
Love always listens, willing to hear,
Love is kind, always there to care,
Love is feeling, believing, and sharing,
Love is always giving,
        Forever bearing.

Karen Sater-Black

The Shadow

It's a cold dark night when a shadow steps into the light.
It is a tall woman.
She walks toward you and lays her hand on you heart.
Then she whispers something softly into your ear.
Then she disappears into the shadows.
But the words that she whispered will echo in your mind and heart forever.
"I WILL ALWAYS LOVE YOU, I AM YOUR MOTHER."

LaTosha Ferguson

Why Do You Treat Me This Way?............

I tried to come home each and every night to a loving home and a loving wife. The JOY I have i GOD GIVEN that know one can ever take away, but that same feeling you did not display.
WHY DO YOU TREAT ME THIS WAY.......
I tried to come up with a million as how many ways a MAN should LOVE his wife, but each time I'm denied because YOU did not share the same feeling inside.
WHY DO YOU TREAT ME THIS WAY?.......
I called you on the phone from work hoping we could talk, I told you how much I LOVE and CARE for you, but to my dismay, you just
    hung up the phone.
WHY DO YOU THAT ME THIS WAY?......
I bowed to my knees asking GOD, "IS IT ME?" I heard a voice saying, "DON'T GIVE UP HOPE", I'LL ALWAYS BE THERE.
WHY DO YOU TREAT ME THIS WAY?......
HOW MUCH CAN A MAN TAKE!!!!! IT'S BURNING INSIDE!!!
No where to
run, no where to hide. JUST A GLIMPSE OF HOPES THAT GOD WILL BE
STANDING BY.

Melvin E. Jenkins

Our World

A world created from time and space.
Made like the patterns of old lace
A world born of volcanic lava flow
Cooled by an era of ice and snow

Mountains created in rough beauty
Rivers rushing with cool, sweet water
Our home, Earth

New, untouched, unspoiled
Ever changing, molding, shaping
The completion of the birth
Now to be cared for, looked after, loved

But alas, look what we have done
War, pollution, hatred, crime

These the evils we leave our
    sons and daughters

Alas, our home, Earth

Mary Watson

"Surviving"

Try to live in the present, not the past.
Make each day count, like it is the last.
Celebrate each birthday, showing delight.
Face the dawn tomorrow, with new insight.

Commemorate every holiday, while you can.
Share the excitement, with a definite plan.
Find a support group, there is a lot to gain.
Get professional counseling, to ease the pain.

Lose the fallacy of perfection, it is unreal.
Forget acting out, tell how you really feel.
Forgive yourself, then everyone else too.
Surviving is not easy, but it is up to you!

Kathleen Wood Doran

Insight

I saw the teardrop rolling off the rose
Heard the whisper rose saying to tear drop
What is the hurry, you want to mix with the dust
Slow down, don't you see we compliment each other
The tear smiled and said, my dear friend
It is my moisture that gave you the chance
To bloom in the desert of my lonely heart

Shahid Maqsood

Sleep Gently

Sleep gently, Love.....
May angels' wings enfold you and soothe thy rest,
Bring peace at last to thy troubled breast.

May rain and snow fall softly,
Upon the dear place where you lie,

May all the winds blow sweetly,
The sun shine brightly from the sky.

Now all your pain and stress is gone,
But you left us all to carry on,

Until we see that longed-for day,
For which we now must wait and pray,

Until the time we'll meet again,
We keep our memories.........Till then,
Sleep gently, Love.........

Mary C. Gaspar

Vacation

No school today, hooray!
Me and Jr. excited for our hotel room.
Mom and dad not noticing mischief,
Daddy looking out the window
Without his face.
Mother sitting on the bed,
Eyes filled with wet;
Oh, why won't mother play?
Father quickly from the window pane.
Too hurried for fun.
A knock at the door; company.
A quiet round man enters the room,
A small card and papers for daddy.
What daddy mean, "Not enough, Not enough?"
Company gone, Mommy weeping,
Daddy rubbing eyes with bandaged hand.
Me and Jr. quiet now.
Remember my secret black room?
Can make light with fire sticks;
Like yesterday, before our vacation.

Phillip D. Kamm

Why Now?

   Why now, after so long do you want to shelter
me with your arms when for so long it was your fists that
put me to sleep at night?
   Forgive and forget are the only words that I can hear
murmured from your lips, even they don't sound sincere.
But for how long do I forget, until I meet your dark
side once again when the world seems to give you the could
shoulder?
How long will this be? You make me fear my own presence,
how dare you make me fear what is inside longing to be free
from the hatred that is within you.
   Unable to let another close to me, I sit here alone.
I will someday repay the favor.

Kelly Stein

The Storm

Screams of laughter rip through your soul
Hands gripping your neck forward to the ground
Darkness fills the space around you
Your eyes swarm the room for coldness
Chills escape through the nails of your mind
Dripping down beneath the ceiling
Painless fear follows your shadow
Before the storm surrounds the evil

Victoria Barragan

Hidden

Vietnam is a dark and gloomy place
all tropical sun and leaves of green.
Sometimes in the mirror is not my face
reflecting what I have seen.
I don't think I will find God's grace
but maybe the love a good woman and time
will ease the screaming night's pain.
Remember not all is what it seems in all places.

William E. Bradley

Untitled

My angel softly whispered to me,
"Michelle there is someone I want you to see"
And I heard his voice so I turned my chair
before I knew it I was gasping for air.
My stomach turned and my chest felt tight
and I thought of him for the rest of the night.
The smile has since not left my face, the
tenderness in his eyes as he looks at
me with grace.
He whispers in my ear, "Are you in danger
of falling?"
I smile, I am silent and I feel myself stalling.
Part of my heart no longer belongs to me,
so I guess I am in danger you see.
But once again I hear the voice of my
beautiful angel, "My dear don't be scared,
just let it be."

Michelle German

Untitled

They said it was something the pills
might not take away;
And that's OK, really,
I didn't want it to be, I even
told them to say it
it can't all be chemicals these days, can it?
I'd rather stand here, body-
guard for the sacred, I'd rather not
practice first
I'd rather admit the unspeakable, that
no one's in charge, that
just this once there'd be no panel of experts;
I'd rather not eat my breakfast in bed
and leave it for the next, untouched and
unmessed, asylum from
the disgrace of order.

Pete Sayles

Grandfather

He once told me, when I was young, to do what I was told.
"Mind your manners! Wash your hands in water warm, not cold!"
At dinner time, we'd gather 'round, and granddad, he'd say grace.
I prayed to be a lady fair, as I gazed down at my plate.
But time and again I found myself at his table there,
With fork in my lap, spoon on the floor, and roast beef in my hair.
Hard as I tried, it seemed as if my granddad I could not please;
and it seemed more so that I was doomed,
when my milk spilled in the peas.
The tears came slow, my gaze shifted down,
I knew I could never be that someone special who wasn't there;
I could never be anyone but me.
As I looked up, my granddad knelt near and took my hand in his.
He wiped my tears and kissed my cheek; oh so tender was his kiss.
He helped me down from the chair so high and stood me on the floor.
We both now felt a special love; I could never have asked for more.
So children of mine, please listen to me when I say I am so glad
that someone took the time to teach me right.
That someone was your wonderful Granddad.

Michelle Diane Byrne

Music Without No Beat

Can't see the signs your nervous
mind's a video tape
Symptoms of a normal soul
increasing heart rate
All your pains are lifted
every time you contact it's
command power faith can't
forsaken power alone you
stand without warning your world shatters bad seed
from the very start situation that's not compatible
yet you can't convince your heart relationship built
on misery confused, you can't let go
Find your self unspirited depressed, uncontrolled deranged
your thoughts are neutered unexplained communication
cease all the trumpets are playing music without no beat
in the dark, as your mind lay naked
whole life a complete confusion
realize you chased a dream with no mercy
dream with love and illusion.

Michael Bard

Thanks to a Friend

(10-19-94)

This world we live in is a ball of confusion
Misery at its best. But unlike all the rest
I have been blessed because I knew you.

You made my life plentiful, with laughter so true
We always confirmed, what's right old and new

You never changed your disposition and you
Never worried about the opposition.
But it was important to keep things in
the same condition.

Yet you, shared your joy and pain throughout
Your journey. Something many wished
they could do and still feel worthy.
I thank God for a friend like you

So I grant your love, peace and joy
and thank you, thank you, thank you.

Mickey West

Look Up

Can't get past the sorrow.
Missing today, tomorrow.
Look up little one and see
  A warm smile from a passerby - bright blue sky
  Sunset orange, pink and blue - all for you
Eyes so sweet and innocent
Truly you're magnificent
Look up little one to see
  Blowing leaves whistle on trees - flowers grand
  A cool clear stream...dream
Your pain and sadness deep
Fearful to hope
Look up little one and wonder
  At ocean waves - birds in flight
  A cats eye moon on a starry night.
Lifting now and lightening too
The burden that encompass you
  All is right
  All is good
Dream the dreams, I knew you could...look up.

Nancy Daeley

True Blue Love

Summer mists caress my body in waves,
More often than my man these days,

Radiant sun unleashes my love starved soul,
My man requests room, board, and toll,

Eyes come in smiling,
In an hour, Baby, see you!

My friend the sun so patient and strong,
Waits as my man and I dance sad and long,

I awaken wondering where has my man gone?

By my side my sun still dances slowly,
Off the remains of loves sad reflected glow,
My love, the sun extracts hurt deep and low,

Without this! Oh were would I be?
No sun drying tears of what will never be,
No sympathetic trees to blow my fears away,
High into the heavens, hear the echoes as I pray,

The earth sings with me sweet and low,

It may sound strange, it may seem untrue,
Nature wonders are my true lovers
Faithful, loyal and true blue.

Leslie Maxwell Cook

Home

Bacon, eggs and coffee stewing on a early
morning stove, the apple grove, hound dogs,
the bird feeder and bull frogs...
  Early morning fog, the howl of a distant dog...
  Gurgling creeks, dewy grass and dusty roads,
these are home.
  Home is a full table with Poppa saying
Grace, or Momma working in the garden with
a smile upon her face.
  Home is a family gathering on Saturday,
church on Sunday and work on Monday.
  Home is security, love and understanding,
compassion, forgiveness, nonbranding.
  Home is a place where the master dwells,
tending his flock as their number swells,
building foundations against tribulations,
preparing his sheep for Godly relations
so that home might be found in all of his nations.

Paul Hettinger

The Dominion Act

*Then God said, "Let man have control over the fish of the sea,
birds of the air, and all the animals."*
Come vitalize the fury in the early
Morning where flesh breeding souls roam the earth.
And poor gulls from the sea synchronize the birth
Of a new day filled with what is to be.

Come vilify the fury with determination.
Where their transparent wings of hope fly to calm
The acrid wave while descending into bombs,
The air into compromise and retribution.

Come viscerate the fury and reason
Why quadrants exist for all kinds of creatures.
And why man must be cautious, uphold and tell,
Those who poison the earth commit dissension.
The animals ask, "Will there be green grass and bleachers
For us to watch man descent into hell?"

Paget Jones

Our Friend, Don

I remember Don from where I sit,
mostly for his endearing wit.
He knew how to make you smile,
to read his poems I'd walk a mile.
Recalling his greeting takes me back,
I still hear him say, "Hello, Jack."
From the day when he first came,
he always seemed to remember your name.
With regret I think of him and say in rhyme,
he was with us so short a time.

Jack Maw

The Gathering of Love

Amid lace and flowers and long curling hair
My daughter waits poised at the top of the stairs.
Her future awaits her in the face of her groom.

He stands so erect, expectant and waiting
Eyes shining brightly with unspoken love.
She slowly descends as the music calls her.
She sees only him in the gathering of love.

But wait! She is stopping just now beside me.
Through tears on my eyelashes I see her come closer.
She hugs me to her as she whispers goodbye.

It is so very hard not to weep or to cry.
As I let her go toward her new life ahead,
The words I'll say to her form in my head.

I love you, Heather.

Nancy K. Walker

"My Dog Rudy"

My dogs name is Rudy. He is the most handsome dog I have ever seen in my entire life. His eyes are a dazzling shade of jade green. His nose is as red as a rose. His coat is a shimmering shade of chestnut brown. Whenever he runs his elongated legs stretch before him and you can see his muscles ripple in the sunlight. Excitement causes his tail to wag enthusiastically. Sometimes I open the front door and Rudy sprints out in pursuit of any puny, helpless creature in his path. On one occasion he stole a chunk of locks from a flabbergasted cat! When Rudy barks the sound emanates across the neighborhood so thunderously it distresses my ears! After a strenuous days exertion, Rudy collapses into a deep slumber. His lips always droop like a saggy, sopping sock. He slobbers all over you leaving slimy trails like a wet snail! If you're not careful Rudy can clear a room in no time at all - he can pass some of the most offensive, odiferous gas!!! But all in all, Rudy is the most lovable, frisky dog in the whole wide world. But burglars beware because if you dare to enter my home, Rudy will greet you at the door with gnashing white teeth and a ferocious growl!

Jaclyn Freehauf-Adams

A Mother

A picture memory brings to me
Nestled on my mothers knee.

Her tender voice so sweet and mild
Calmed the hurt of this Tearful Child.

A mothers Love is like a Scroll
That fills the heart and Soothes The Soul.

She's Something Special above all others
They're God's Gift to us, a mother.

The best laid plans for every man
Is from a mothers benediction,

A simple Gift right from the heart
With pure love and affection.

Mildred D. Windham

To You I Vow

The first day of school I remember watching you walk
my eyes laid upon you and love was my fault.

The tight blue jeans, the wiggle in your walk
you strode into my life with not even any small talk.

To sit beside me in class which we both shared
to learn education, and feel my first love affair.

The shape of your body, the waves in your hair
from the very beginning I knew some kind of
feeling was there.

The rush of excitement, my blood runs through my veins,
I needed to take some time out to see clear once again.

Your talk, your games, you sly little fox,
you lured me into your tower of so called Fort Knox.

My first kiss, to my love, which sent me into bliss,
the departure of my love I new I would miss.

From the day we reunited, I knew I would fall
into the day of our marriage if I may recall.

I vowed, and I cried that happiness struck me again
to the man that I love, I married my Friend.

Maria Batista

Absolution

With hopeful crawl and faltered step,
my firstborn heard repeated, "Be careful!"
The words revolved in natural cycles
of wheels, wavering or powerful,
that propelled him into eager mobility.
He seemed vaguely to hear.
"Be careful!" I implored,
through skies of flimsy wings
and whirling blades that simply
lifted him beyond maternal fear.
The phrase spanned space and years,
to acquit myself of mother guilt.
Do rolls reverse?
Last night, I phoned that all was well,
as I continued my journey west.
This offspring had listened well.
"Have a good trip!"
The magic words were stressed.
"Be careful!"

Patricia Shirley

To Be My Guide

Pressure is building, taking over
my mind can no longer function
I feel locked in, ready to explode
one single step could set me free
the air is thin up here, but peaceful
my choice becomes clear.

Hands guiding me till the end
reaching out, falling, falling
faster I go
there can be no way back
the end is close, but it hides far in the distance
my arms spread apart like a hawk
could it be it is not my time to die?

Wind shooting into my eyes
tears, jetting off my face
I look, but no longer can see
my hands reach out, maybe to break my fall
maybe to change my mind
for whatever reason
it was too late.

Michael Duckman

For Michael

Five years I've searched for you.
My quest was long and
Darkness filled many of my hours.
Somewhere in time I've lost pieces of my heart

And what is left
My tears have frozen it.
Your love for me can now heal my wounds
and dissolve my scars.
At times you seem too perfect to be real.

You squeeze my hand;
No longer are you fantasy.
My journey alone is over;
You are the one I've longed
To share my God with.

Five years of pain—
I looked for you
and began to think
You didn't exist.
My hopes were not so high
Into my life you walked.

Kimm Walls

Falling Leaves

Leaves come furling, swirling, twirling - golden, red and brown
My soul can hear their laughter as they reach to touch the ground
Their beauty's overwhelming falling like a golden rain
Saturating the dry earth below with their splashing gorgeous stain

Then tears from inner person spring for I can just almost hear
One leaf conversing solemnly with other leaf so dear
I heard him whisper quietly "Is that all there is down here

We have lived life without purpose, tell me, why Lord were we here"

And I think I heard my Lords reply with soft voice so filled with Love
"Listen closely now my little leaf, lift thy eyes and heart above
Your life was not in vain dear one - you fit well in my great plan
You have shaded and protected both my animals and man

Tho no-one spoke a thank you and no-one spoke your worth
Your worth was gold and rubies - you were splendid on the earth
Each one of you is one small leaf, but listen now to me
When I look down on the whole of you, I see - a mighty tree!"

M. L. Bean

Always To Be With You

If only you knew how much I care.
My thoughts I express to you, and the feelings I cannot hide.
I would do anything for you my dear, even to the highest extent.
I love you...
You may not see it or know, but I do, believe me.
I often wonder if you know how special you are to me,
and how big of an influence you have on my life.
You have always given me a lift, so high I touched the sky,
when I was scared out of my wits, lost like the wind,
and someone to hear my pains and cries.
Tell me, what can I do without you?
Tell me. What will it be like?
I'm crazed out of my mind.
Tell me, who will be there, I need you by my side.
You are a fascination, my inspiration, one who is unique in every way.
I appreciate you, and thought what it would be like if we never
    knew one another.
I'll always be happy, when you're happy, and you know I am.
I always want what is best for you, through our thick and thin,
    together...
I wish you happiness and joy, and I give you all my love.
We may not always be physically together but, always in my heart
you will be my role model, my mentor, most of all my hero.....

Natalie S. Raghunath

A Revolutionary Discovery

While visiting Paris - "City of Lights"
    My wife and I viewed its world-famous sights

We savored the French cuisine and pleasures
    And admired historic and cultural treasures

It happened one day - close to the Seine
    We strayed, in error - though not in vain

When good fortune led us, luckily
    To our arcane, off beat discovery

There, a plaque on a building was carelessly hung
    Its historic value - neglected, unsung

But its message spoke "volumes" - loud and clear
    "The Treaty of Paris was signed right here
        By Franklin, Adams and Jay - September 3, 1783."
        (Ending the American Revolution, in victory)

France - please make right this oversight
    With an apologetic correction
So guides can point to this great site
    And boast of its French connection.

Manuel Laub

Nasty Nannies

Nannies are nasty, Nannies are mean,
Nannies are cunning. Clever and keen.

Nannies make you nap,
And boy, can they slap!

If you tell them they're a dope
They'll wash your mouth out with soap.

They watch all kinds of soap operas like "Days of Our Lives"
And all those kinds of stories they know that I despise.

They eat everything they see
Except for tasteless little me.

They make you go to bed at four
They kiss you good-night, and close the door.
I dream of beautiful dolls with skirts made out of lace
Then wake up to see my ugly nanny's face.
Such a disgrace
My nanny's face.

Jennifer Maney

Season Contemplation

Autumn
Nature's time to throw a wild party
Dressing in brilliant, outlandish colors
Dancing with the wind
Spilling colors like confetti to the ground

Winter
Moonlight illuminance on newly fallen snow
Hollow howls of night winds racing through barren branches
Icicles clinging steadfast to frozen landscapes
Pine trees laced with powdered sugar

Spring
Sweet, soft rain leaving rainbow footprints in the sky
Scents of soil giving newly sprouted life
Great energy emerging from the earth
Colors added to the earth tones once again

Summer
Scents of freshly cut grass
The feel of a popsicle, cool, sticky. sweetness
Fireflies free nightly entertainment
Soft warm breezes under a cotton shirt

Lee Ann Ludwiczak Sheehy

Giving

Do I believe in Santa Claus...?
Naw...I don't think that I do.
I have tried and tried to believe in him.
But somehow he don't ring true.

I know that Momma made my dress
On the 'singer' in the hall.
Yet there it is, under the Christmas tree,
From Santa Claus?...Naw.

Well I went ahead and played their game,
And pretended I never knew,
That my new doll came in a box from 'wards',
Instead of you know who.

Christmas made everyone so happy.
And we acted all surprised.
"Did you like your beads?" "Did you like your truck?"
I was young, but I realized.

The joy is in the giving,
I'm older and this fact I know is true.
And...maybe there is a Santa Claus...
Its you, and you, and you!

Lillie M. Myers

To Lyall — Enlightened "Lily"

A "Lily" grew...
   near Pontchatrain,
Young, red-crested, tan speckled...
   firmly rooted

"Let's see a sunset."
   To the south bank, Lily turns
This - to a reed, quivering in the
   winds of life, trembling in the
Murk of unspoken gloom

"Look...the colors, the brilliance of shine!
   It's mine." said Lily "And yours,
Tomorrow you'll bloom."

Reed stiffens, rejects. RIGID.
   "It isn't that dark." pleads Lily
"Remember... it rises on the morrow;
   Your hurt, your pain, is also my sorrow."

Reed bends, askance; questions,
   "Is it true?"
Lily caresses the tender reed—
   "Look for tomorrow and taste of the DO!"

   K. Lyall

Ignoramus

Sanity for the enlightened, as the wind, cannot be captured;
never predictable.
Often I have tried to place this elusive label upon my troubled
brow.
It escapes and I reject its definite rejection.
Why do I question?
Why must I incessantly reject the circumstance in which I stand?
Am I to love, to hate, to pulse a constant catharsis which courses
through my veins?
The resolution is simple: Insanity by necessity must be gauged
with clouded reason.
This formula must be coupled with the impulsive urge to learn,
explore, and experience the precious nectar near all dare not
taste.
Ahh! Once let loose freedom exudes and the normal conform.
The self-aware-insane live, experience and suck the marrow
dry of what it truly means to thrive on existence.
The matter is of not. I choose this vibe all else is useless!

Jason Harris Bowen

If Children Were Statues

If children were statues and never a pain.
No cause to worry if they're out in the rain
They'd stay where you put them no trouble at all
And parents would say "having children's a ball".

We could sleep in the morning, no worry for food
No little runny noses, no reason to brood
No yelling no screaming no small tears to wipe
Yes; if children were statues no parent would gripe.

We'd do all our housework and after that's done
We'd sit by our T.V. for an evening of fun
We'd read all the books that should have been read
No one to undress or tuck into bed.

But one thing is missing, alas and alac
When you hug them and kiss them
They don't do it back.

   Michael Caputo

He (Monster)

Eats at my soul, my limbs, vitality, sex knowing
No difference in taste or texture of the physical-spiritual me
Hungry, caring not whether it's legs or
the curve of my smile, He only eats
and eats and ingests some more
Hands tingling, my pelvis aching, dry lips belching
breaths of art, beauty and my too-loud laugh
All this He devours very, very slowly, gently
deliberately digging, those crucifying teeth
I wonder if He'll ever grow weary of me
When there's nothing left, when I can no longer feed Him
Tossed aside like unwanted eggshells

   M. Michele Hardy

Losing The One You Love

Sinking in a pool of tears,
no longer fearing all your fears.
Just thinking 'bout the one for you,
and how your love was always true.
you pledged your love into his eyes,
but now his left you good and bye.
The love you had has drifted away,
and all the loneliness is here to stay.
your hoping one day the hurt will leave,
but the memories of him drift into your mind,
and you know that he was one of a kind
You try to tell yourself life goes on but,
What is life when the one you love is gone?

   Laurie Johnson

The Bread of Life

I'm weary, weary, Lord, please hold out your hand for me
No longer will I tarry, Lord, on that road so far from thee.
I looked everywhere for what I thought my need
When all the while you were there my hungry soul to feed
Not the husk of human kindness, but a banquet before me spread
With streams of living waters my hungry soul you fed
And now when I grow weary, I look within each day
And find that which satisfies in every possible kind of way.

   Lorraine Vollmer

I Am You

I am something you can never forget,
no matter how hard you try.
You can never change me,
even when you die.
I can be the dimmest memory,
or like the sun, a bright reminder in a clear blue sky.
Sometimes I make you happy,
at other times, I make you sad.
You can never capture me,
because I am an elusive spirit, forever running free.
I can be your most cherished moment,
or your worst nightmare.
Sometimes you close your eyes and try to undo me but you know
it's impossible,
for I cannot be altered and I always stay.
You can never elude me, for I am your constant companion.
I can be your closest friend,
or become your deadliest enemy.
And who am I, you might ask?
I am the biggest part of you, I am you, your past.

Peter George

Giving

When I was growing up from a tot,
  No money to buy gifts made me sad a lot,
Until my grandfather helped me to sustain
  By showing me my sadness was in vain.

He said, "The best gifts aren't what seems to be
  The best presents are the things you don't see
Give of your heart, give of your mind,
  Give of your talents, give of your time.

Make your goals to become earthbound,
  Ply intellect and humor the year around.
Develop your skills for a profession,
  Use your talents in the right direction.

Being accountable in the things you do
  Makes you feel good and others too.
Grow to be helpful, honest and kind,
  Boost others to join you up the line.

Then some day you will have the funds
  To buy gifts for yourself, family and friends.
You'll forever feel grateful about what you gave
  When you were growing up and trying to save."

Leona M. Pearson

He and She

He wants to be an island sufficient unto himself...
No one
Is allowed in his territorial waters or on his beach.

She seeks the comfort of his love and approval...
But finds
His ever-changing boundaries impossible to comprehend.

He repels all emotional invasion...
His guns primed; His beaches mined; His nets deployed—
No beachhead can be established here.

She tries to navigate through his defenses...
Only to be dashed, time and again, on the jagged rocks
Of his cold silence, or bombarded by his cutting anger.

He seems unconcerned, even gleeful...
When his verbal volleys rend her fragile ego to emotional shreds,
Leaving her battered, bleeding, broken—litter on his shore.

She slips away, not understanding his need to wound...
Hiding her shame, her failure, she binds her shattered psyche,
Then begs leave to return, again and always...

She loves him more than she loves herself.

A. J. Hunt

"Alone"

She stood there alone, with no one to comfort her.
No one to say "It's all right" or "Don't worry about it"
No one at all.

She wept her tears until they longer came
She wept into her own hands, for there was no on there to
    comfort her.
No one there to hold her hand
No one at all.

She cried for someone to help her.
She pleaded for sympathy and understanding
But no one came to her aid to help her live.
No one at all.

Finally, she crawled into a dark corner.
There she lay down on the cold cement floor,
instead of some one's warm lap.
There she took her final breath,
But no one was there
No one at all.

Lisa Peretz

Question

A boulder stands alone in the field;
No other rocks are with him.
Rain gently washes over him-
Each caress carries part of him away...

After aeons of kindred gentleness-
He will be no more.

And how can man survive,
When the rains of savage new times
Beat at him like madness on an asylum door?

Jason Brock

The Wedding

She walked down the aisle ...
No, she floated down the aisle on her father's arm.
Her white dress ...
Hang on. Her beautiful, snow white (almost virginal) gown of
    pure silk,
(Spun by rare, practically extinct silkworms from some far
flung corner of the globe),
Was liberally decorated with pearls (the real thing, of course),
Delicately embroidered with flowers,
A fifteen foot train (only fifteen? Surely twenty).
The whole effect was topped with a diamond tiara (family
heirloom, don't you know).
At the altar her husband-to-be awaited her, that handsome,
debonair chappy.
Love at first sight and all that.
She stood beside him, he of the balding head, the first few
grey hairs sprouting, the faint lines around his eyes, sweat
pouring in rivulets from his temples to his chin.
(He later denied nerves).
And she took off her rose-coloured glasses, and knew he was
the one, the right one to be her husband.

Nicola J. A. Davies

Desert Seas

If there were no seas
as it seems to be
when you live in the dusty desert like me
it seems like you can't go down to where
the golden sand meets the deep blue sea
so instead you imagine your troubles being washed
away by the waves in your own non-existent desert
sea.

Tiffany Roques

Hunters

They're up and gone before the crack of dawn,
  No thought of food, yet plenty of clothes to keep warm.
They clomp for miles through the woods,
  In search of game for to slay.

They stand for hours in one spot,
  Nor do they blink, nor turn about.
For even a sneeze is a mistake
  Breathing slow and watching close.

No they dare not move, but only stare.
  They move their heads like owls in search of meat,
Not a sound will they dare make
  For the game will become aware.

Yet the game knows they are near,
  For their smell is unique.
They quietly laugh as the sneak,
  Behind the hunter who's fast asleep.

  Linda R. Houston

The Nuclear Amusement Park

Walking along nervous avenues,
nobody loiters.

SPEED DEMONS————— pass you by in cars buses trucks and shoes
going somewhere, elsewhere, the same place, daily.

TWENTIETH CENTURY TRANSIENT criss-cross countries as hurriedly
as telephoned sentimentality streaks hellos on holidays.
The new improve RAPID TRANSIT MIND raises its' fare and everybody
rides it.

And where do we ride it
to...?
Ignited terminals into the TWENTY - FIRST CENTURY,
Nuclear Nations catapulting us into NUCLEAR CONFUSION
  Roller Coasting us into NUCLEAR AMUSEMENT
  THEIR   —————NUCLEAR AMUSEMENT PARK
a park with no benches
a park where only memories exist of extinct children

feeding pigeons.......................................!

  Jack Carnright

Memories of a Sunset

The lake.
Not a wave or ripple was to be seen
Like a mercurial body with a simmering sheen;
The water shone with the light:
For miles and miles the surface was flat,
We stood on the shore in this peaceful habitat.
A view of the serenity of nature.

The sunset.
Birds chirped and the wind was slow
The atmosphere lit with an orange glow;
A radiant ball descended through the clouds;
It lingered in the sky for a little while,
Long enough to make us smile.
Such are the treasures of life.

Memories.
We tried to deny it but now I know
Nostalgia is haunting, it refuses to let go;
Even though we wanted it go slow:
The sun vanished beneath the horizon.
These feelings inside me will continue to grow.

  Puneet Sharma

The Beginning

Fire in the mind, buried deep in the soul
Not knowing of any strong goals

For lost time, I hold in my arms a life unfair
Caught-up in coldness as the plays of an instrument

Comical, yet serious about what should have happened
Spinning in circles; confused about my landing place
Disappearance of sand suddenly thrown at my feet

The nursing of my mother's milk, tells me who I am
And I am strong in the forces of my nature

Yelling and screaming pushed to the limits of no knowledge I have
Chilled heart, black as coal, resting on the warmth of her bosom
Gold soul; solid stone; rock as heavy as love
Diamond eyes broken by tears of seeing nothing I knew was me.

  Lyneise R. Coakley

Stand Up On Your Feet

There was a time not long ago when Black folks moaned and wailed,
Not knowing whether Mother or Father had been offered up 'for sale.'
Out there in those spacious fields... a blisterin' in the heat
''Til Massa said 'enough today...y'all come on in and eat!'

The scraps of God's creation were given to prepare
But, based on God's own wisdom, we made it and, we shared!
Lynchings too often to mention... to keep us in our place
'Look here boy...you bow your head...don't look me in my face!'

A hundred years, or better, didn't bring us anything
'Til bad feet and a strong heart...brought Martin Luther King
To lead us up the highway to freedom's rugged peak
To tell the world of kindness in the wake of oppression steep!

Today we take advantage of the bullet in his brain.
For his own personal effort...the net result was gain!
What happened to our fervor to meet with life's cruel snares?
Is it that we've lost our hearts being confronted with too many dares?

There is but one solution...and we dare not often meet...
But, when your life is threatened...STAND UP ON YOUR FEET!!

  G. R. La Sure

"Each Day Is A Little Life"

Schopenhauer
Birthdays are celebrations
  Not of the day of our birth
But of today, the day of our life,
  An affirmation of existence, of continuation.

The slumberers sun rises, and we rouse
  To breathe each new breath,
See this day as a new incarnation,
  A beginning, the miracle renewed.

Greetings exchanged with friends, lovers,
  Sons and daughters; candles lit,
Song sung, presents presented, all are
  Reflections of profound awareness of Now.

Legends of birthdays past,
  Past times, past lives, all shadows,
Imbue this birth-day with life,
  Appreciation for this gift of being.

Tomorrow is a dream, yesterday gone glimmering.
  The fledgling universe, in its brand-newness
Exists for the moment in its nowness
  A celebration of the wonder of today.

  Peg Hubbard

Goodnight

Instead of goodnight, lets say goodbye.
  not one tear shed from my eye.
Maybe it's best if we leave this way.
Guess you know what I'm trying to say.
The time we spent together was good, but now we must
  move on.
The memories I have of you, will always be fond.
Shakespeare said it the best: "parting is such
  sweet sorrow".
That's why I must say goodbye today and not tomorrow.
Friends? We can try to be
But to my heart you no longer hold the key.
The things you taught me, will always be in my
  heart.
That's why it's time for us to part
So when I say goodbye just look the other way.
Now I'm left with nothing to say!

Michelle Blasie

I Don't See

You're good for nothing. You're such a waste.
Now go to your room and get out of my face.

You're so stupid, what do you know?
You'll be an old man, with nothing to show.

You know you're killing me, making your mother die.
You're going to go to Hell, you're going to fry.

That didn't hurt. I hate seeing you beg.
The best part of you ran down my leg.

Who are you telling to stop? Why do you cry?
It's for your own good, Stop asking why.

You're just like your sister, You both hate me.
I really love you, You just don't see.

H. S. Fix

A Mother's Tear

Where did I fail? I ask
now that my son is gone
if we went to Church each Sunday
and I gave him so much love.

Is there where I failed, my Lord
loving him, I didn't see
that the son I thought I knew
had a criminal within.

I didn't see in his eyes,
now that I think, lately he won't look at me
How could I miss that my son
had a soul in desperate need.

Now, is late, there is no time
to fix what I know is wrong...
he killed a young kid, just like him
stealing away from a mother, her most beloved son.

It seems now I lost the trail
with the everyday routine
now I see my son in jail
and I asked God every night ... Where did I fail?

Norma Acevedo

Haiku

Walking up mountains
High above the fluffy clouds
Silent bird flies over

Jared Higgins

To Live

Forty years does seem like quite a hunk of years
now that we've turned sixty two and take a long look back.
We were only kids when we began this oozing spread of life.
Life better seen through the glow which holidays create
when all, including those who stray, sing away the day
and we join in, letting shadows slip away.

When we are alone again we sometimes spend some time
fumbling through the things we did and didn't do.
Like two old prospectors, we pan each day for hope,
a greeting card, a child reads, some special kindness shown.
I hear the guns, see the drugged, know the prejudice and greed
which rumble through the L.A. basin with greater disregard
than all the earthquakes which have shaken at our roots.
There is the pain. Yet as I watched my wife last night
smiling over treasures gathered from a thrift-shop bin,
I knew that she will always warm my heart enough
to make me want to live.

Patricio Rojas

"Good-Bye"

The years have gone by so fast,
  now these moments are in the past.
Nothing will ever be the same
  We both have our own futures to claim.
What lies ahead remains to be seen,
  And may resemble something like a dream.
Together we were as strong as an ocean wave,
  the triumphs we've shared, I shall always save.
Now that we must go our separate ways,
  We are both at a loss for words to say.
May we remember and never forget,
  that we were friends, and that we met.
We showed one another to be true,
  and helped each other when we were blue.
We've dried away one another's tears,
  and scared away each other's fears.
We've shared with one another our big hearts,
  and we swore that we would never part.
Now the time has come, and I'll try not to cry;
  as we share, one final good-bye.

Nancylyn Hartmetz

Fishing

Up by three, out by five,
Now we have an hour long drive.
"Watch out, Winnisquam, here we come!"
This is going to be so much fun.
There by six, on the water by seven,
Fishing with Dad is like I'm in heaven.
Sometimes the mountains are as clear as can be.
They are so high, strong, and mighty to me.
When I catch a fish, Dad is so proud.
He shouts, "Yahoo," ever so loud.
I think he is more excited than I.
But, when I don't catch a fish I say, "Next time."
I don't cry.
I go home; lay down, and say,
"Don't wake me up. I've had a tiring day!"

Kelly O'Neil

A Lesson...

I tried to love you yet you remained as ice
Now you're grievin' inside for an arrogant price.
What goes around does come back around - that surely has been proven.
Your mental anguish tormented me for most of the time; yet
I ignored the hurt 'cuz I loved you as if it were a crime.
I always wondered why you needed to abuse me - but I see now
it was your insecurity.
As I move ahead, it was a lesson that has been well read.
You see, God has placed another into my life which it turns
out knew how much I loved you and saw the hurt. He waited
until I had enough of your pain then showed me how to press
on and find my way.
It has always been said, "It's more blessed to give willingly
and your abundance will come back many times over..."
All that I gave to you has now been returned with care, joy
and peace—now, isn't that a great receipt?

Piilara-V

Power

As if for fuel, these far, clean bulbs
of autumn hills harvest late-day light.

Cradling this moment — hoarding it
for what's ahead, bundling columbine,
jewel-weed, this timothy, these dirty sheep,
the drying silver vein of a creek.

Even the highway-yellow metal and acrid reek
of gasoline busy tearing
filament of pin-oak and poplar
to this road from their dimming summit.

Seam — splitting with hickory nuts...
where I'll watch them drop,
one by one — go out,
and make for the other side...

Mark De Nitto

Altegarten

There are many gardens full
 of buds, blooms:
  Delight of all who see,
   and smell, and touch-
    sharing
     spring and summer.

Special are autumnal-winter gardens:
 Full of fading blooms,
  tired but true-
 soft of fragrance, frail
   (past, almost)
     touching, yet
 vibrant at the tenderest touch - emotion.

By day, month, year the petals fall, still
 each withered one cannot but be
  a special incense on God's altar.

At last the blossom fades,
 reclines, gives up
 its last strength-
  And joins
    the angel choir.

R. John Nelson

Fahrenheit

You speak to me with the darkest eyes
of eternal life.
You hold the experience I crave
Raven Beauty.
Help me in to the water lover,
cold, deep, and foreboding as I wait with anticipation
as the waves crash up the stairs.
Just as the tide goes out, so do my fears, and uncertainties
as I feel your lips, and hear your voice.
I realize I'm there.
Destiny has had her way again.
I have no more questions,
yet I'm left with an undefinable hunger deep within the
center of my soul that leaves me breathless
waiting for more...

J. Gagliardo

Clouds

I saw the vast unending way
Of flocks, spread out in densely patterned whims;
I saw the streaks of dark array
The velvet shadows, crowned with sunlit brims.
Beyond the mountains, cliffs and winding coast
Winds carried forth, the floating swanlike host.

A world within a world was born
From air and water, merging shade and light.
Abrupt from their foundations torn,
Infinite castles, roaring into sight...
Rotating, bulge-constructed mastodon
On windswept skies, moved fast and faster on.

I knew that once, my eager soul
Spread out, had soared over the open sea
And witnessed scale fulfillment of its goal
To be horizonless immensity;
And recognizing, comprehended why
Among the clouds and stars I long to fly!

Peter H. Katz (A.K.A. Micheal Orogo)

What Make - "True Friends"

Is someone who is patient in listening and with the understanding
 of giving moral support.

It is also a person that would take time, no matter how long
 it takes to build a solid foundation of our friendship and
 assure a better understanding in relationship between each
 other.

But, now there is honesty and loyalty for these two words,
 they walk a fine line of love and hate. But, the knowledge
 to the meaning and values of it, requires great deals of
 compassion and understanding of each other.

When we experience the values of friendship, it will deepen
 itself in our mind and heart.

But, for those that haven't experience it, they are riding on
 years of pains, feeling and loving care "To gain the values
 of friendship". But, then it only take matter of minutes
 to destroy it too.

When you do experience it, your heart will begin to fill with
 joy and happiness. And that is what it takes to make (TRUE
 FRIENDS.)

Paul M. Rook

A Heart's Treasure

Glimpses of memories pass through my mind
Of laughter and love which was so hard to find
They are treasured and stored deep in my heart
And brought back so fondly when I'm falling apart

Tears filled with sorrows come once in a while
It hurts for a moment, then turns to a smile

To sit and dream of days to come
And add to my memories filled with more love than none
Happiness will find it's way deep down inside
And fill up the spaces of the memories that died
Patricia L. Clark

Falling

Raise me. Send me higher. Let the sun burn the truth into my soul
of lost evermores and new nows. With hope rising, silence dying and
Spring propping its wobbling head with a weak wrist, it strengthens
with the weightlessness of truth. I will rise, all will rise to meet
what should have been; rewrite the history of long waywardness and
random impression.

We will learn of richness and sated breath and willing givers who make
us hover above hypocrisy and despicable derision, letting neither
touch even our slightest hair.

Take these eyes. See love and draw it into thyself and stare fear-
lessly at the next soul, transforming it into what needs to be.
Let all crowd into a complete circle, each pair of eyes orbiting until
the madness ceases to have meaning.
Margaret Gaubatz

Those Fields of Cannon

The guns are now silent but the fields tell the story
Of our American heritage - that long march to glory
The valleys are now peaceful where the brave gave their all
To give birth to a nation and a meaning to their call

Lord, it's sad to me the price they paid for liberty
They shared your creed but here they followed a different need
And those fields were crimson red with the dying and the dead
Then with flags at half mast, we turned a page upon our past

But now at Gettysburg our flag and our hopes will fly high
Was a sacrifice for all but now memories make you cry
Those cannons are now a tribute - one nation under God
We'll carry our banner together - seek peace and spare the rod

Rest in our God's peace, Johnny Reb, my lad
This nation respects you for the task you had
And our hearts go out to that yank in blue
'Tis a better nation now - may God keep it true

Those acres of monuments are an awesome sight to see
The stories etched in stone bring tears with the history
It's a valley of forget-me-nots where that granite stands tall
Symbols of our yesteryear's - a whispering voice, don't let it fall
LLewelyn Ellsworth Dahlen

Secret Love

In fields and streams
newts romance naiades.

In whirling winds
the dancing dryads.

When one plus one, plus one, becomes one,
and gentle whispers heard;

Soul-mates are forever,
in the shadows...never seen.
Karen Levesque

War or Peace

War!...war!...war!...the dreaded thought
of peace loving people.

God in heaven, our ultimate power,
with infinite wisdom from above...

Should remind us...any hour...of
the wisdom of his love.

Yes!...there could be less war....
.....If nations' mutual love were given;
In some way that did implore.....
....That, future wars be forbidden!!

Yes!...we've strived for peace,
in our complex world,
Oh, we've tried with endless zeal;
For common ground, with flags unfurled,
to meet demands that seemed unreal.

The ultimate aims not one of ease...
...To yield enough to all...to please;
Yes! "to end all wars!"...but how? "Yes, how?.."
Let's pray to God to help us now!
Whatever our faith...at any hour!..trust "His total power!"
Nicholas Stashenko

Heritage

You dreamed for fifteen days across the Mediterranean
of picking sweet green bananas and ripe mangos on the other side
In the eternal summers of sugar canes, pineapple plantations and brown
skins you forgot what you had lost and never had
You watched John Wayne films at the new movie theatre
not too far from the village where in the early evening natives
boiled water for the pirao
You sold cheap things to those who called you sir and ma'am
in the years before the war
Watered-down wine, twelve-packs of pencils, yards of brown fabric
made you capitalists
But sometimes looking beyond the red roofs of the captured jungle
you remember Portugal in your youth
the church bells ringing in your village at dawn
the nesting hens on your grandfather's farm on the banks of the River
Minho. Your daughter, the one born so many years before me, she did
not know that I, her sister, was already in her laugh, the reaching
forth of her slender hands grew from the dry heat of this African soil
She remained close to it and long after you left, she continued to
scoop grasshoppers into the palms of her hands offering them to her
friends, those who lived in the huts of their ancestors
Paula Alexandra Fernandes

My Mother

I think of my mother with never a thought
of store things like diamonds and jewels bought.
I think of her smile seen way down the road
For she never betrayed her heaviest load.

My mother —the sweetest on earth, I declare!
Clear down to her last days with soft graying hair.
Her ideals for daughter and son were alike
Instilled in each one of us from morning 'til night.

Perseverance, endurance, honesty, truth
Kindliness, selflessness—even to the uncouth.
A smile, a good word, courage, and strong
fine christian character, whatever went wrong.

A beautiful mother, a lady so fair
That mother of mine with soft graying hair.
A delight to her family, never a foe
I see her bright face—yes I do—all a low!
Lila Meyerkorth

Family Values

In the blissful good old days:
Of the toiling fore-fathers,
The family had but only one face,
With one goal as sprouting feathers.

In those good old days of puritanical redemption,
Of mutual talk and dialogue quite un-litigated,
All rustic Moon's brilliant phase without exemption,
Existed no digitals the paradox of Science so mitigated.

The family values of child-ruled equality,
Was that of fair parental mutuality:
Proportionate to roles of espousal individuality,
For father's rib was of much mother equality —

The children of blossoming breast-milk seeds
Have to every right humanly claimed,
Corresponding responsibility that precedes
It and meted out gun-lessly un-flamed —

Mother's creation below that tenderful rib,
Was to have her securely and closely
Loved in tender masculine caressing grip;
For absolute equality fits but only loosely.

  Kawsu S. Touray

Fantasy

I had a fantasy, you see
Of you and me and flying free
Above the earth and all the trees
And we could see for miles

We saw the young and very old
Too old to live but they were there
In worlds their own with minds of the young
Too young to comprehend the old

We saw the givers walking along
The takers were standing in line
About to receive their daily bread
When the givers all went dry

And fields were filled with no hope sand
The sky too cluttered with fumes
To give a damn about the land,
The young, the old, the giver and receiver

The oceans slid from shore to shore
Delivering its dark blanket to the earth
Taking no more than what it brought
But leaving no less than it should have

  Karen Ingold

Substitution

Oh Joy that gives us life
Oh life that loves the grace
That God abundantly supplied for us
When Jesus took our place
The agony, the sin and sickness
That was meant for me
Was absorbed by Jesus when they nailed him to a tree
We that love Jesus know how much it means
To pause and recollect our thoughts
And Praise his Holy Name !!!

  Lloyd H. Thomas Sr.

As I Lay Asleep

I close my eyes to sleep at night,
"Oh no I didn't turn of my light"
I wrestled up to turn it off,
Laying back down on my soft cloth.

Suddenly I felt a weird drift,
All of a sudden I felt my soul lift.
I was going up to the heavens,
To throw away all my sins.

"Oh Lord please let me come in,
For now oh how could I sin.
I'm here at the temple of your love,
I'm here where I won't to be, here up above."

"I've looked forward to this for all these years,
Now it just started to appear.
I am your servant, I will praise you,
You'll come first, I'll never say shhhooo."

I woke up the next day to look up to the sky,
I seen the future, I was there I seen it with both my eyes.
"Thank you Jesus, the main thing I had to say,
Now to go pay my respects, because I have to pay.

  Lailoni Lewis

The Sea...The Sea

The sea, the sea the endless sea
oh what you mean to me.

Afar in the horizon you cover the earth like a blue shroud
Oh such a beautiful sight where the water meets the clouds.

The waves beat against the merciless shore
ceasing never bringing always more.

Billows of foamy white crash against the sand
cold to the touch as they slip through my hand.

Beyond your coast I gaze upon hues of blue,
what realms of secrets are kept beneath you.

Your anger and furry shown in stages of plight
as waves smash and pound the sand in an endless fight.

Yet as the tide resides and water glazes the shore
there seems a quiet peacefulness one can't ignore.

The sea, the sea, the endless sea
oh what you mean to me.

  Noelle Howe

Land of Milk and Honey

Little boy looking into a half empty bowl
Old woman lying in bed sick with a cold
Roaches crawling on the wall
Trash lying in the hall

Land of milk and honey

Old junk cars parked in the street
Cop and his dog patrolling the beat
Sidewalk cracked and falling apart
Old man walking and pushing a cart

Land of milk and honey

People standing in a line to eat
Kids playing ball in the street
City hall filled with gray
 white smoke of promises
 politicians spoke

Land of milk and honey

  Lynn F. Miller

"The Truth Unveiled"

A demented woman,
Once a star.
Oh Madam, do we tell you?
You are nothing, in this time.

I know you think you're still loved by the theatre.
But who is to tell you you're living a lie?
A lie with no happiness,
No one to love, but only yourself.

Long ago, the brilliance of a star,
In the limelight with adoring fans.
Beautiful, Elegant, Young;
Titles of your past.

The sad truth now,
You're fame has all vanished.
You sit - a prisoner in your own world.
The truth unveiled.

Marisa Ialongo

Night

Night sings quietly
One by one the stars ears attune
To listen

Night captures the stars
Holding them fast in his net in accordance
To his wish

Alabaster fishes flailing
Aloft in the shiny anhydrous sea
In night's aquarium

They look at night's velvet face
His loving daughters, satellites
Swim in obeisance

Lyssa Aja

Robbed

I was in a park,
one cold night.
It was dark,
not a person in sight.

Before I knew it I was robbed,
I was black, and blue and thought I would die.
I cried and screamed for I had been robbed,
how could this happen, am I going to die.

I waited and waited and no one came,
I laid there cried and prayed.
But still no one came,
I lay there cold and afraid.

I didn't know what was happening,
but before to long I was dead.
Finally someone came and saw me there lying,
but it was to late.

I had been bashed in the head,
kicked and abused.
No one came before I was dead,
they just left me there cold and confused.

Leslie Ratcliffe

Besiege

Drifting through the hall of darkness, with
one eye closed. Anticipating the vision of
the being, the life which once existed here!
The fear and intrigue keeps me drifting. Feeling
my way through, my hand becomes the eye
of which is closed. The silence is ringing at
the midnight hour! The hour of which the hallway
calls!!!

Jessica A. Camarillo

The Sheik Al-Rashid

You are my dear friend.
One of a kind therefore,
Unique loving and
Sensitive.
Sweet but, more than anything an
Extraordinary, loyal
Friend.

At the beginning I could understand you.
Love was the clue.

Real love, patience with wisdom.
Always work.
Suave aroma for me in your name.
Heaven, pray, God helped me
Immortal beloved, your name
Dearest friend, become a poem in my heart.

Marina R. Mendez

Island to Explore

The few times I have looked into your eyes I have seen an island.
One that I would wish to come ashore on.
For I know that this "island" is but the tip of a great continent,
full of many wonderful places and treasures that have yet to be
    discovered.
As that explorer, I am painfully aware as you are too of the risks,
raging storms, rocks that would dash you to pieces, and times adrift
without wind at all, lost longing for food and the sight of land.
If coming ashore with my burdens of the journey would result
in the pollution and deforestation of this wild land.
I swear to you that I would never make an attempt to chart a course.
Colonization; divide and conquer are not strategies of this humble
    explorer.
I carry no flag and establish no capital.
I come as a visitor, I come as a friend.
As a stranger, I am forever intrigued by this strange land....
that smile... those eyes...Hmmm...Do you know this beautiful
woman?

Paul Lang

Forever Growing Flowers

The flowers that she gave me are now wilting away.
Oh, if I could only keep them alive for just one more day.

The flowers are white, red, violet, and blue.
If you only knew how much I love you.

Even though with the flowers I will soon have to part,
they will always be alive right here in my heart.

But there in my heart I want you to know,
that the flowers, like my love for you, will forever continue to grow.

Ken Mason

The Beauty Within

Go ye as if a herd of wild stallions;
One that is trying to kiss The Rose of Grief.
Miss ye the morning dew as it caresseth the green of life,
And the song of the birds as they calleth His name.
Never take the time to listen as He tells of His love.
Miss ye the great adventure known as life.

As for me, I shall not hurry;
For I know that my days are but like a speck of sand,
That cannot withstand the duration of time.
Still, I shall savor each precious moment as if it were my last.
I shall take the time to live the beauty,
The beauty that is the pink petal of life.
I will feel the brisk early morning air as it caresseth my check.
The birds speak, and I hear their song of faith.
When He calleth my name,
I feel Him tenderly brushing against my very soul.
As if to say, "I shall never forsake thee."
No, I shall not hurry.
For when He calleth me home,
I shall be prepared to accept the beauty within.

Marsha R. Keefer

A Daughter's Precious Gift Is Her Mother

A daughter's precious gift is her mother.
  One who will bring her into this world.
One who raises her like her very own.
  One who adorns her with unconditional love.
One who she will play with day after day.
  One who will prepare her for school.

A daughter's precious gift is her mother.
  One who is always there for her.
One who will be her constant support
  And her best friend.
One who will always be with her,
  During the good times and the bad times.

A daughter's precious gift is her mother.
  One who will pass away,
Knowing that she served her daughter well.
  One who, the daughter will miss dearly.
Her mother may die, but the memories
  Will never fade away.

Miriam Ouellette

My Mom

My mother is so special, I love her so much
Only the good Lord might have a sweeter touch
She has always been kind to me
I don't know how to say thanks
If money were kindness I couldn't put yours
In 5,000 banks I wrote this to let you know
That I really care, if you ever need anything
I'll always be there
I wrote this for you for Christmas
Because money could not buy
The kind of gift that you deserve I hope you can comply
I know this isn't the greatest gift
Or even one that's good but this is directly from
My heart's neighborhood
I don't know how to repay you
For all your care and love
There's only one person that know's how
And that's the man above I hope you like this present
From me to you, I don't know if you'll like this
But everything in this poem is true!!

Matthew Nixon

Memories

Did you ever have the urge to hug an old griddle?
Or cling to a rag doll with holes in her middle?
Do you still wear a necklace that's from your first love?
Maybe in your drawer you keep grandma's old lace glove.
The flowers from your prom are still pressed in a book,
The photos of days gone by, how different you look.
When you hear a certain song, tears fill your eyes,
A teddy bear reminds you of your baby's first cries.
It's funny what triggers a thought from the past,
But reassuring to know that these memories will last.
We each have a lifetime of special things to remember,
These wonderful memories will always spark an ember
For the things we love and hold dear to our heart,
A lasting treasure that will never part.

Nancy Staubs

Love

Is love meant to hurt;
  or is it not really love?

Is love meant to break hearts;
  or was it never really whole?

Is love meant to make you cry;
  or is there nothing left to make you cry?

Is love meant to make you unsure of who you really are;
  or did you never really know?

Is love meant to forget;
  or was it always by your side?

Is love meant to make you happy;
  or did that feeling not stay very long?

Is love meant to love then leave;
  or didn't it stay long enough?

Is love meant to teach lessons;
  or didn't you learn anything;
    or did you learn too much?

Laura Link

Heaven Or Earth

Where have you gone? To the heavens above?
Or to the earth below? I look to find you,
but you have gone. I see your face before
butterflies alight on a breeze.
The gentle smile, and heart full of good things.
I watched you fade. Wondering.
Wondering where you will go.
To the heavens above or the earth below?
What will happen to the soul?
Will the heart break when I can
no longer hear your voice? I only see you in my
dreams. Happy face, gentle smile. You did
love me as a mother
does a child. And now, it is lost. Where
did you go? To the heavens above or the
earth below? Only the tears abound. Not
a bit of understanding.
Why were you taken? And where did you go?
To the heavens above
Or the earth below?

Jeanine Bender

In Memory of Lane Frost

Behind the chutes while I get ready to ride,
Our American flag circles with pride.
We hear the anthem so loud and so clear,
While I sit and wait for my time to appear.
The thoughts of rodeo run round in my head,
Some men have won million, and some men are dead
I very well know I may be the next one to fall,
But the rodeo I know has yet cease to call.
They pull my rope tight and I wrap it around,
The suicide grip is the one I have found.
I tell them "Lets go" and they jump to the side,
On the back of this bull for an eight second ride.
He jumps and he turns and I only ride four,
In the back of my mind I know he wants more.
I watch him turn and paw at the ground,
He charges at me and I hear no more sound.
His horn pierces my back and then he runs on,
As if to say you soon will be gone.
A rib through my heart had taken my life,
Now the only Frost left is Kelly my wife.

Martin Belshause

A Treasure of Unequal Measure

My Sister is a rare and precious jewel, it's true
our lives are linked together with love and fond memories, too
time or distance cannot destroy the closeness that we feel
or the love, we share, that is so deep, true and real
It will always be there, as long as our memory lives, and we
will share the pleasure and joy that, sisterhood gives.
For our happy memories cannot be bought or sold and to us,
they are more precious than silver and gold
Yes, my sister is truly, a precious and great treasure and
there are no scales, large enough to measure, the generosity
and kindness, she has bestowed on me, For the will to share
is there, and it always will be, along with the good, we
also share the pain.
For in each of our lives, there is always sunshine and rain
But our love for each other, is a strong and blessed tie
That binds our lives together, as the years go marching by.

Patsy Thomas

"Mother's Faith"

Our Mother's faith has helped us live,
Our lives for Christ, the King!
Eternal Praise to God we give
And of his love, we sing!

When as a child, Jesus' love, I was taught
Oft times at Mother's Knee!
She lived her life by the golden rule
And lives eternally

Lord give us Mothers great and strong
Who teach us right from wrong
Who spreads Christ's love
In word and deed,
And often with a song

Of all the blessings that I've known,
Our Mother's love was sure
And because of her love for Christ the Lord;
Her heart was true and pure.

M. Alvin Latham

The Love Of A Daughter

Mother, you've gone to heaven, we forgot to say good-bye.

Can't get over the pain you suffered, makes one wonder why!

A breeze from heaven whispered through
    our thoughts so still.

You were wished away by dad, as he
    met you on the hill!

He wrapped his arms around you, held you and said
    we're glad you came, Jim and I.

With some sadness, you smiled, waved back
    walked ahead, after winking your eye!

Saw your mom, sisters and others through that extraordinary glow.

Know you're happy, pain free and living in that pure white soul!

A sense of peace engulfed you as heaven came into view,
With love, togetherness and joy, away for all flew!

In life, three generations, love you deeply, miss you,
    will always cherish our many memories.

Death has taken you, and from within our hearts, we reach
    to the stars, waiting for your touch!

Mary Anne Drummond

Anna

She would tell me some things, some way
out far fetched things about life and
its daily routines.
    Why me I would say as I wondered away,
for you see I do not understand.
In time she'd reply if you live long enough
they'll surely unfold one by one.
    Oh goodness I'd think for this could not
be so, far life does not deal you such blows.
    But the time has arrived I can see those
keen eyes piercing deep down to my very soul.
    Everything that she said has came true and
I dread the last wisdom she'd always bestow.
    You will come to my grave and call
out my name, if I answer you'll never know.
    For I've done my best to prepare you
for the test of life and its unforeseen woes.

Margaret C. Ray

Jimmy

Little one, little one, where have you been,
Out to play and back again?
Dirty hands, pant cuff torn,
Tear stained face, so forlorn.

    Scold him I did, and punished him too.
    For clothes cost money, and these were new.
    "Now stay in the house and out of my way,
    No! you can't go out anymore today."

The boy was little, just turned four,
But all these things had happened before.
And though it was hard to treat him so,
I had to, these were lessons he needed to know.

    The years sped past and now he's grown,
    He's far, far away in a place of his own,
    Oh dear Lord, could you grant me a wish?
    Let me have him again to hold and kiss.

Not for long, just for awhile,
I'd dry his tears and coax a smile.
I still know life's trials are sore.
But it's only once, a boy is four.

James C. Coates

The Journey Home

I soar like the eagle, effortlessly.
Pain, loneliness and despair fall below.
Stretching my wings I climb higher and higher over mountains,
through rainbows and cloudbursts. Fields of flowers,
wheat and corn reach up - only I can fly so high.

But I grow tired - reality, pain, suffering weigh me down.
Leaden wings pull me to the ground.
Loneliness, fear and despair overwhelm me.
Darkness, sadness, grief-consumed with pain - I cry.
I hide in the shadows - tired, frail, disillusioned, isolated.
No one should see my misery - I am afraid.

Glistening tears begin to melt the darkness.
Sadness, grief, despair, loneliness, and fear begin to fade.

The promise is mine. My wings are light.
I climb higher and higher, soaring over mountains,
through rainbows and cloudbursts.

I find my friends and I am no longer alone. Freedom is mine.
Flowers smile at me, showing the way.

He waits for me with outstretched arms, calling.
He cradles me in His arms. I am home.

      Karen R. Carpenter

Minutes Before Daybreak

Doth the cock's crow draw near?
Peter, you are the forbearer of the slave to society,
One who is false to your own self piety.
The sorrowful master commanding the least of humanity's ilk,
Men weak as paper, and flimsy as silk.
Once standing a man molded, true faith's receiver,
Refuted goodness and descended, closet believer.
Missed you transcendence from life's dark half?
Do you also deny Exodus by serpent staff?
Glory be a King born a soft martyr,
For blazing the trail, in comparison, is extremely much harder.
His path is an urgent example, understand its pith,
Choose a day, harvest a dream...Create a Myth.

      Kenneth Lee Norman

Tribute To Rina

A musty smell in the air, the smell of old.
Pictures surround me, taped to the walls.
Objects scattered all about, on every surface.
Always a story behind the pictures,
Behind her simple possessions.
Her soft voice, bringing the pictures and objects to life
Of foreign people and faraway lands,
Of lovely flowers and fascinating animals,
Small trinkets and interesting rocks,
Beautiful sea shells and exotic plants.
Memories collected from this earth
Displayed in the room where I sit with her.
Now this always strong, blessed woman,
Quick with a chuckle and a smile lies quiet and still.
Though her love for God is strong,
Her mortal body fails
And her mind drifts away
As her soul longs for His hand
To reach down from heaven
And carry her home.

      Katrina Cox

The Creature

Make me bleed:
Plant the seed:
There is a vision of the next room
In which you sweep me like a broom.
We have seen our Shaman,
he is gonna leave you now,
You may have made us see-
This must be;
No more clinging support,
These pleasures you must abort;
In our prime-there was no power; got to get it going.

Soon you shall change the thought:
I just wait and watch the rising sun and the breaking clouds.

When the snow falls—she calls;
Not of this life:
She waits with a red soaked knife,
This is so strange,
The Creature is all deranged.
Take us please,
Do it with ease.

      Kevin J. Marcial

"Trampoline"

A seed grows in side of me
Planted, a few months now and people will see
A seed has been planted
Punishment for the crime of having a good time.

There was no real love from me
So you couldn't call it a love child.
All it was, was having a good time for awhile
For a few moments, I had a smile
That quickly turned to tears.

A seed has been planted
Punishment for the crime of having a good time.
Because of the miserable life I've lead
I trampoline, I don't care if I've been seen
Bouncing from bed to bed.

All is done, all is lost, nothings left to be said.
A seed has been planted
Punishment for the crime of having a good time.

      John F. Porter

The Weed In The Style Of Sylvia Plath

An object of scorn
Plucked and pulled out of society
Like an outcast.
Plain
in appearance
no special attributes.

But the inner beauty was mystifying
to the other vines and bouquets of "flowers"
a desire and need to be accepted
and not singled out or excluded.

Ostracized by the other members
of the garden
Be pretty like the others.

In the garden.
But what's the point
acceptance may not be granted anyway.

      Molly O'Conor

These Strong Hands

These strong hands, comfort, carry, and rebuild a life
poisoned by Alcohol. Trying to break a viscous
cycle, picking up the pieces, moving on through the
years.

These hands, once strong, are weakened by
instability, twisted with the pain of heartbreak brought
on by unfaithfulness; yet they move on, starting from
nothing, leaving everything behind.

These strong hands become frail with age, suffer
an unbearable loss and work once again to rebuild;
but now the loss is too great, the hands are tired,
angry and have no will to go on.

These strong hands will always be strong in the
eyes of family for only family can make these hands
feel strong once again.

Patty Estvold

Three Wishes

If I were to be granted three wishes and they were
promised to be fulfilled I'd ask for things that
money can't buy things that never again could people steal

I'd ask to have back the trust of a child so I could taste
the innocence of time gone by where once again I could
enjoy a rainbow and not have to fight the urge to cry

I'll also ask for the sound of laughter to ring true with
every beat just once more this would ensure me a sense
of humor and help prepare me for whatever is in store

And my last wish to be granted would be to set right all
the wrong that has been done to replace in the child the
love, strength and hope where once before there had been none.

Kathleen Meader

Untitled

Sweet persimmoned gales
Propound lulling mysticities to thine self;
Dreams of flight, beholding white sails,
Ever so forcibly within me they dwell.

Thrush at sunset, the color of wine
Escape from society, my constraint, my bound,
An earth of reality and of time
Where passion is deplete and indifference sound.

I yearn intensely to forever break the bind
Live in thoughts, heaven of mine own;
Engulfed in splendor, radiance, shine
Apart from emptiness, apart from home.

Benevolent will, break thy chains!
Let me free thee self, follow my soul;
Reside not here with these pains
Endure not society's barbarous toll.

S. Triple II

Dreams

Dreams are little clouds of hope and fear, love and hate,
pain and denial,
    Dreams can mean everything and at the same time nothing,
    Dreams are baby birds just hatched to grown birds at the
peaks of their lives to older birds no longer to fly,
    Dreams are blooming flowers in the Spring to dead, wilted
flowers stuck in the snow that the Winter brings,
    Dreams can love and be loved and at the same time be loathed
and despised.

Heather Brousell

Land Of Mind

Once ago, in a Land of Mind - Raise the
question, answer to find... noble man, princess
wise — darkened halls, laughter cries... king
once, clown once more - open the door, bury the
whore... In the mind, chains untangled —
broken again, now just mangled... Raise the
question, answer to find — once ago, in a Land of
Mind. 5/9-78 ... 16 years ago I raised
the question, answer to find - long ago - in the
Land of my Mind... Chains were untangled — broken,
then mangled — What's the use of all time?... Love
is the answer - the answer to find — tho' no one to
listen, as they're all so unkind. - If we'd all just accept
to be who we are - the answer to questions would not
be afar. - Maybe someday we all will believe, peace,
love and true understanding is all that we need...
So raise your own question - and you just might
find - the answer there - in the land of your mind.

Marty Smith

This Is Now... That Was Then

Uncertain tomorrows are beckoning me.
Questionable sorrows make it hard to see.
Reliable companions leave thoughts in my mind.
And answers to questions are so hard to find.

Twisted and contorted are my feelings inside.
Left screaming in objection and running to hide.
Arising such doubts that should not appear.
Who am I? Where am I? Why am I here?

Temptation knocks silently on my back door.
To walk to a place that I've been before.
Although deep inside such wrongness burns.
A curious heart will eternally yearn.

Why must these old feelings still haunt me again?
Things have all changed; this is now, that was then.
Unquenchable desire keeps me wondering still.
When all vows are said, how much void will they fill?

Thoughts of desperation are all that I think.
Sailing on a rotting ship; ready to sink.
Fate holds your future in the palm of it's hand.
And sprinkles your days like tiny grains of sand.

Lisa Rae Sindyla

God's Teachers

Inside a child's heart a potpourri of emotions,
    questions, fears and love.
As a teacher we need to be able to respond to
    each and every one of those needs as they arise.
We need to be a listening ear for when the cries of a
    child need to be shared.
We need to be a set of encyclopedias and a bible
    concordance when a child questions why.

We need to be a comforter for when a child feels the
    world on their shoulders.
We need to be a light for them when the fears within
    make their world dark and lonely.
With God's love, His wisdom and His grace we can become
    all these things to those we teach and care for.

Through the eyes of a child may they see God's love and
    all that He has for each of them as I give my life to
    teach them.
Let me never shorten the wonderful gifts God uses through
    me and may I never cut short the things God wants to give,
Just because there wasn't enough time.

Patricia F. Galford

Rain

Rain is a surprising gift once in a while from God.
Rain is a feeling. Really it takes away the
bad, painful feelings and gives you energy.
But the thing is that if rain is water than when we
cry, we rain all over ourselves. See I told you
it was a feeling. When it rains I suddenly feel
good about myself and that I'm living. But what
I think rain is. I think God is crying. Not a sorrow cry.
But a happy cry. He must say to us
in a way "My people you will drink my
tears, and when I cry, I support your food."
But you know what. Rain is nothing but
a good feeling to me. I love it...

Melissa Snell

Currents

Nature flows within it's surroundings
  Rather than against them;
People sometimes resist the currents of their lives
  Rather than sharing the journey;
Not all currents bring happiness
  Not all currents bring sadness;
Some will relax you, some will excite you
  Still others will bring you peace of mind;
Our lives would be enriched if only we could flow
  With these currents;
Regardless of their destinations,
  More often than not.

Mark F. Vetere

Ave, Anima

I'm awake friend, protector, guide,
Ready for Time's daily ride.
And very aware you really care;
For somehow I sense that you are there.
As I see from a corner of my eye
A sudden light like a mist nearby,
A shadow at a place where no shadow should be,
A sound for no reason, it seems to me.

As time goes rushing through night and day,
I sometimes insist on having my way.
When instinct told me I'm doing wrong
I'm imbued with a feeling so very strong.
I know because then I'm in pain
From willfully going against the grain
Of what was truly expected of me
And what was really meant to be.
I quietly and readily admit my sorrow
And hope and pray for a better tomorrow.

Phyllis Robbley

Sisters

Sisters are kind and very sweet,
Ones like you are hard to beat.
You're growing up in many ways,
You remind me of beautiful sun rays.
Sometimes you're mean and a little cross,
But I never ever think you are a big boss.
You're yearning and learning about the Lord,
With God in your life, you just can't get bored.
You have many talents as I can see,
You're always there when I need you to be.
Amy, you've helped me in many ways,
To name them all would take a lot of days.
If they had a sisters' top ten list,
I know you'd be #1, sis.

Laura Jones

A Dream

The thoughts in my dream are so real.
Real as any one can imagine.
It can be as you dream.
As if you could wake up and believe the phrase of desire.

Sacred and yet, all the most desirable.
Chances to unveil the most inter thoughts of the mindless
dream.
Does not make sense to others if explained.
Only a dream to one-self is understandable.
To any other, it is not.

To others, they chance there own meaning of your dream.
To thyself, your dream is sacred.
Your sacred real dream is your desirable thoughts of oneself.
A dream, that can become true in a life time,
And yet, it just become a dream of all dreams.
But only you can really believe in your own dream.

Live out your dream, with the wisdom that you have.
Desire the thoughts that becomes with in you.
A dream is yours and yours only.

Olga Woolard

The Anatomy of Love

The roots of courtship romantic
Really lie in evolution genetic
We share with gorillas, moles and arachnids
Behaviors bizarre and frenetic.

Are people who feel so high and away
That long term attachments seek
Underdosed on PEA,
With endorphinic response weak?

Has her role as ethnologist cold
No room for silly romantic love
To make commitment in move so bold
As to reject her theses said above?

And could this question cloud her mind
If so, she's not alone
"He needs me very much I know:
But is it love or testosterone?"

Marvin Tanenhaus

Eternity of Sight

  Eternity of Sight
Reflections of light are given off
Causing a shine to blind one's eyes
  The sight is marvelous

Details of life slowly come out
Giving birth to new and interesting things
  A horizon of discovery

Rays fill the air with peace
Bringing hope to conquer darkness
  The bright light remains

Visions beyond sore eyes.
Causing blindness to be the way;
  A sight drawing one's eyes
  Into one's heart!

Marie Di Presso

Midnight Dreams

Transpire our dreams
relate a conspiration for undue
endulation.
Besides a G- perfect reason
Reasoning 'all' a triumphant
    sound.

The symphony plays
    and movement creates
I thought we believed,
We've had all romantic love-making and tomorrow
still sustained,
I think, 'I love you.'

Cavalier outburst of thought
    interspersed
We resemble and reassemble
    gratitude;
Forever, forbearing our own
    fruit.
The enchantment .. ... triangular crystallized a
    Doily.

        Jennifer A. Lee

From Z To A

Suspended in my mind
religious practice is a crime
disposal of opponents to prove one's loyalty
appears not only senseless but what kind of God is He?
They devote their life to worship
claiming their beliefs are best, ignored alternatives
so the mystery soul may rest
its purpose engulfed in irony
a disease without a cure wasting non-believers
and resulting in a war
the victors gather in the streets
and proclaim their holy rights
confusion led by icons
and too blind to see the light
the attempt to rescue spirits
by those who assume and cleanse the earth
will be doomed to nonexistence
and too numb to feel the wrath
whatever they want they're not to give up hope
a medium for Nausea they just consult the Pope

        James J. Unwin

Friends of Sapphire

Familiar and I made blue boxes into hang gliders to sail away from
relocation. She notices I have a thin threshold for pain.
Wander-wander away-wander away from you-Stop Stop speaking.
I smell familiar in my hair, on my clothes, in my bed, but I haven't
    seen familiar for years.
Didn't you notice I tried to dislocate my legs but they still walked.
I dial my line but strangers answer.
I feel at home when I take showers in the middle of the night and
never know why. Connections connections to empty houses
wrapped into
a little body with pigtails. I will not hear that knock on my door.
I will not hear "Lucky you" or see jackets jumping through
windows.
I will only carry the feel of a physical tear. Familiar shows herself
to me in shadows of trees. She has good intuitions-tell me if this
will be my last Christmas at home?
Will this be the last house with a room unused but labeled as my own?
Alone alone I do not have to prove myself.
The mystery of the universe answered with one statement "it will work
out for the best." A day of happiness a month of unrest.
Loto-Michigan Lottery-Lottery of tenderness-familiar come play with me
All I want is for you to know I'm out here, out here by you, out
    here sending a dream, a dream to you, so you can sleep.

        Karen Reed

Untitled

I can't help but cry as I think of him
Remembering all the fun times we shared,
And the nights that we made love.
Looking out my window as time passes by.
Knowing the more that passes the less I have.
Not sure how much is left,
But knowing I need to see him.
Hearing footsteps I turn and look.
There he stands with tears in his eyes.
He holds me and says, "I'll always love you."
I look into his eyes and with a teary voice.
    "I'll love you always."
As he holds my lifeless body he looks at the clock.
The clock stopped running when my heart stopped beating.
But he knew our love would live forever.

        Karen Reynolds-Sausville

The Circle

It traps me with its twisted ways,
Reminding me of those distant happier days.
Forcing a confused, dazed feeling
To creep into my heart and mind.
It whirls about me - tightening, choking slowly...
as
the
tears
-fall-
-tumble-.
-rush down.
Frustrating my memory.
Was I ever happy?
-Or was I just naive?
Is it formed by those I know?
Are they reaching through to help?
No.
It's only me.
This never-ending circle-
is empty.

        Kathleen Dempsey

Safe 'Til Eternity

As I sit here, writing this poem,
Rhyming words, I just can't find.
The thought of losing you, my love,
Just can't escape my mind.
I love you, I trust you, I need you.
How much you'll never know.
If for some reason, you no longer love me,
God help you, wherever you go.
May God help you find, what you are looking for,
And help me to set you free.
And may God forever keep you,
Safe 'til eternity.

        Mary Gragert

The Reed

My love is like a pond, and I a reed
Rooted by his side is the place I take.
A glance am I given not, though I plead.
By wind am I bruised, but I shall not break.

The wind, my voice, quiet it can never be.
I profess through the breeze my affections.
The door is locked, my words are not the key
So I must be content with all my imperfections.

My very being is determined by,
The pond, my love, together with the star.
Shining solar rays give me strength, as I
Struggle to gain the love of one so far.

        Molly Ellen Cooper

The Screaming Woman

Out the door she came, screaming
Screaming louder than sirens on ambulances
and fire trucks
Her hair waving in the wind, swirling around
her face
Her hands waving wildly at some unseen force
She kept running, running without a backward
glance
Everyone who saw her were quite sure
She was mad with despair
But what they didn't know was that she
had just left a madman behind
And she kept on running until she could
run no more.

B. Marie D. P. Williams

P.T.

She combed my hair and washed my face
scrubbed my teeth with undying grace,
   because she was an angel.

She taught me lessons when I was young
to watch my actions and mind my tongue,
   because she was an angel.

She spanked my hide and punished me well
I wish I knew then what time would tell,
   because she was an angel.

When she nearly died she read her Psalm
I cried for days but she was calm,
   because she was an angel.

She smiled to heaven then gave me a grin
I know now what I did not then,
   because she was my angel,
      she still is
      and will always be...
                  my P.T.

Kaija Langley

A Feeling

There's a feeling I have growing strong,
Searching for a place to really belong,
This feeling is peaceful and calming too,
It's at its strongest, when there's thought of you.
A feeling direct straight from my heart,
Trying to reach you, while we're apart.

There's a feeling of passion, excitement, and joy,
It's like a child with a brand new toy.
This feeling I carry all through the day,
I cherish and want it, it won't go away
A feeling of pleasure, not sadness or pain,
I'll share it with you, with nothing to gain.

This feeling is shared by many I'm sure,
But does this feeling have a cure?
For this feeling I have, has nowhere to go,
So I'll set it free, like the winds that blow.
This feeling, oh yes it has a name,
And my life will never be the same.
Because a feeling of love entered my heart,
I'll have it always, if we're together or apart!

Mary K. Preston

Dreams

Electrifying visions from the spirit world,
Secret language of the subconscious,
Runic messages from the labyrinthine caverns
Of our reptilian brain,
Haunting images dancing to circadian rhythms
Along the synapses,
Undiscovered subterranean rivers of arcane symbols
Darkly flowing among the neurons
Surfacing as iridescent bubbles
Snared in the dream catcher
Of astounded consciousness
Where they terrify and tantalize us
With the primitive fears
And unrequited longings
Of our solitary silent selves.

Lillian Bosworth

Eyes of Innocence

Who am I? I wonder as I
see my reflection in a puddle.
We come in so many sizes, colors,
nationalities and religions.
I watch the children in the park.
To them they are all the same.
Not one cares that they are different,
just happy to be playing their games.
When they grow up they will not be so lucky,
Cursed with the close-mindedness of adults.
Shackled by their own prejudices and beliefs,
forgetting the games in the park.
Everyone is a color now; black, white, red, yellow or brown.
Or a nationality not your own.
I wonder who I am, wishing we could use
the eyes of the innocent young to see again.

As I turn away an old woman in front of
me loses her hat in the gusty wind.
I see its a struggle for her to pick it up, so I
help her, deciding I belong to the human race.

Kevin Badillo

Walk On!

Walk on! Walk on! Up this pathway of life
seek not the turn ways of strife
each step with courage -
Each arm swing with full confidence
Each solid footprint firm and fearless.

Walk on! Walk on! Up this pathway of life
Let not thistles or thorns halt your journey
Let not rock slides or fallen trees become
your stumbling blocks
Put on the robe of faith
Hold on tightly to your staff of hope
Walk on! Walk on! Up this pathway of life!

Kathleen R. Phelps

Grandfather

I see the old man,
His frame is silhouetted against the wall,
The wind blows him over,
He struggles to rise,
He is up,
For awhile,
A breeze blows him over,
He is gone, gone forever

Sara Smith

Novocaine

Numbness creeping into my body
seeping into my soul
it's taken away a part of me
no longer will I feel whole

Staining my thoughts, breaking the walls
that have held back my hurt for so long
concreting in, never to leave
replacing that which was wrong

Novocaine.......the rush, the feeling is gone
a shot in the dark, through my mouth to inside
the drugs of the devil to drive you insane
goddam this noise, there's nowhere to hide

Screaming.......no pain, no feelings, just numb
inside I hurt, with pain I scream
unconsciousness is welcome, but stays out of touch
the devil is in me, controlling my dream

The bridge to reality.......now shattered, misshapen
resembling my soul, trashed by rejection
the numbness takes over, the voice of the devil
the feeling of pain, another injection.....

Michael Freeman

Seeping Moments

My mind is exploding
Sending splinters to space.
Ideas spurting, spewing
Awaiting an attachment, a function
That which is unattainable, intangible.

Around me all is anarchy
As the seed of influence attempts to sprout
Looking for fertile soul.
Awaiting the nourishment that was lacking
A dormancy, stagnated in turmoil.

Inspiration floats on air
The gentle breeze blowing forever
No rush as before, no needs
Patience is the mainstay to which I grasp.
Yet all that is grabbed slips through my fingers

Michael A. Pinkelman

I Have To Take It

Experiencing AIDS from the HIV Negative Side
Yosemite — the snapshots of '85
Seven vacationing somewhere else now and they're not sending
postcards

A cousin had an accident with a needle trying to help him
Friends didn't know that sharing love meant sharing death

Another phone call:
"You were on his list — he wanted you to know it's over."
Framed pictures — "us together" — side by side by side in my living
    room

And those who go to work and visit and always I ask,
"How are you?" and I mean it
Always end the phone call with "I love you."

I told Ron last week, "Please don't leave."
He said he's trying to stay
I bite my lip I hesitate take my time
to draw that "X" in my address book
My admittance that it's done
I won't forget you no way
In waves they leave in waves
This is what is
and
I have to take it

Lucy Roucis

A River of Tears

Shut your mouth child I heard enuff outta you,
Set your a** on that stool, child,
Whilst I figure what I'm gonna do!

Don't roll dem eyes at me, girl,
I'm fixin to smack 'em right outta your head,
You best keep to yourself right now, or you be wishin' you was stone
    cold dead!

What's this ruckus I'm hearin? You two goin at it s'more?
The big man rumbled as he entered the room and slammed the rickety
    screened door.

It's just Miss Fancy-Pants here says she be too SMART to lift a broom,
Thinks she can lollygag all day, layin' around thinkin' and readin'
    books in her room!

She thinks we be poorer than trash and dumb 'cause I works for dem
    uptown whites,
Gettin' HER UPPITY A** to help me out, well, that's what be causin
    this fight!

Take her to the shed out back, Man, strap her 'til she can't set on
    that lazy a** no more,
Then put her on her knees, Man, to scrub this dirty linoleum floor.

Get your a** up, girl!
You think you better than us? Is what your mother be bitchin' true?
Answer me, NOW GIRL, cause you know what I'm 'bout to do!

Her braided head was yanked up, the stool kicked away,
Then, from the depths of her brown eyes spilled a river of tears,
Flowing silently, they followed the path worn by others-these hundreds
    of years.

J. F. Wennerstrom

The Love Of Mother

Only a mother can give the special love you need
She is there for you when all others turn and leave
When help is needed you know she'll be there
She is here for you now because she was there for you then
A mother is here for the bad times just as well as the good times
Because her child is not only in her heart, but also in her mind
A mother has an important part in a girl's life,
because she is not only there to lend a hand as our mother,
but also as our friend
But some mother's still have another part to play,
it too has been since birth to present day,
and that is the role of a father
And this is the reason I look up to you today
because I know you never put it on as a show!
"But did you ever know that you are my hero?"

Marla Zaffuto Macaluso

A Certain Sadness

There's a certain sadness in her eyes.
She's lost someone very dear to her heart.
She wonders alone- stumbling into a
world of darkness all of her own.

There's a certain sadness in her eyes.
The love of a friend she's been denied.
In a state of confusion she runs and
tries to hide her muffled cries.

There's a certain sadness in her eyes.
If only you knew what she's lived through,
what she feels, what she has lost...
Then you wouldn't have to ask why.
Why? There's a certain sadness in her eyes.

Karen C. Swett

Celebration Poem

My woman called me like Eden,
She named me in my youth,
In my youth when the lands were flowing,
In my youth when the lands were mine.
My woman called me like Eden
From the circle of her grace;
In my youth the days were flowing
And the lands were hers, and mine.

Eden always the same place and time,
The lost continent at the same frequency,
Eden not quite of this world.
Since we remembered time
It runs through our hands,
Our world is at once sealed
And divided, opened upon itself
In the sudden anguish of this space.

Morning plagues me like a gleam
upon the face of persons now remote.

P. L. Bebee

A Baby's Breath

She gave to me a baby's breath,
She said it would tell me everything,
It would whisper it in my ear

In it were many secrets,
And in it were many rhymes,
And from every petal arose a song.

It sang of love,
It sang of care,
It sang of gentle kisses from a lovers' mouth

And thru all the words,
I could here what was meant for me,
"When I give you this flower, I give you my heart.
Be careful with it's blooms, It can fall apart.

Take care of this flower my love,
Promise me, before you start,
For this little flower is me, my heart."

She gave to me a baby's' breath
And when I listened,
It told me everything.

Kenrick Buchanan

Ebony And Aged

Ebony skinned, dried and cracked with age
she stood and leaned on hickory cane, bent from use
Legs bowed, toes toed, back long since slanted
her eyes dimmed, teeth now gone from much abuse

Did you know her back then when dark eyes flashed
and sinewy legs danced, they of strength and grace
Or when she walked with swinging, willowy stride
blowing hair, rubied lips, and smiling, painted face

The beaus of early years remember back in time
when sun shined hot, rows were long, and tassels silked
They looked at long and lovely stalks of corn
and dreamed of her, and night, and skies, soft and milked

They can recall the grace and easy way of move
still feel the heat and pulse of every meloned curve
On scent of rose on night there flashes there
in minds recess, a pulse of every nerve

And do you think that broken body there
stooped over wash tub and board and soap of lye
Remembers not those days of passioned joys
and knows not how to quell her fears of time to die

John Allen Medford

Excuse Me Please

"Excuse me please," my daughter said.
She was very young, at least four.
"Not now sweetheart," I answered back.
"I'm having lunch with a friend," then I ran out the door.
  "Excuse me please," she wanted to talk.
I think she was fourteen or so.
"Not now sweetheart," I answered back,
"I'm so late now, I really have to go,"
  "Excuse me please," my young lady said.
By now she was eighteen years old.
"Not now sweetheart," I answered back,
"I have things to do places to go,
How many times do you have to be told?"
The minister pronounced them, "Man and Wife."
My daughter the beautiful bride.
  "Excuse me please," I said to her,
As I tried to be by her side.
"Not now sweet mother," she answered to me,
There are so many other guests I have to see.

Kathryn Sunday-Davis

Winter is a Time of These

Winter is a time of these; chilly mornings when the warm flannel
sheets are so inviting and the cold, wood floors are so dreaded;
frosty window panes and draughty doors...
Skies of gray, swift moving clouds and fiery-orange sunsets;
bare-limbed trees being tossed by the wind...
tit-mice, chickadees, finches and sparrows;
Brilliant cardinals peeping from branches of boxwood; glorious
hollies with waxy-green leaves and show-stopping scarlet
berries; crackling fires and woodsmoke; bubbling soups and
crusty breads... blankets wrapped around one's shoulders
and books by one's side; the coming of nightfall much too quickly;
Shadows creeping into nooks and crannies and becoming much larger
by the illumination of candlelight; a cozy feeling of being close
to family, drawn to the hearth, and wrapped in the security of home.

Karen Hazlett

Shining Eyes

Well I see your eyes
Shining in the dark

As I take my nightly walk
Through the park

I watch your shadow move in the night
I must decide, to flee or fight

No need to run, because I know
It's just my buddy, in the snow

Sam and I played like this, just last year
Romping in the snow, we both had no fear

But Sam was getting old, he was almost fifteen
And this past fall, two Angels were seen

So now I walk alone, through the park
Sam's shining eyes, are gone from the dark

Larry H. Zimmerman

Ideas

Ideas float around in your head
Some you will love, some you will dread
If you pick the wrong idea, you may be dead
That's how ideas float in your head
Your mind could be blind to many ideas
Or it could be ready to explode
And your brain could be hopping as fast as a toad
As you see, there are many ideas for you and me.

Karim Smither

MacBeth

Silent, as the Moon climbs, leaving behind the Sea,
Silent, reigns the King of Time, of night-entangled trees.
Silent, as the winter land
of gardens made of stone,
Silent, comes the weary hand,
For one not old, nor grown.
"For love, nor life: for Man Oh God
Your deathly harvest sate,
To gather all that springs to birth
With many-venomed hate.
And poisoned meat and poisoned drink
His feast of life to make.
And morning sun nor dawning sky
come never to awake."
Silent, as the Moon climbs, leaving behind the Sea,
Silent, reigns the King of Time, of night-entangled trees.
Silent, as the winter lands
of gardens made of stone,
Silent, comes the weary hand,
For one not old, nor grown.

Nicholas Osburn

There were Birds in the Air

Do you remember the song you taught me
    sitting on campus under the large oak?
I do.
It all comes back as I look out of the window at the tall,
    lush maple—swaying and bowing in the breeze,
    like a ballerina.
This bright, sunny day reminds me of another.
The clearest azure, without a cloud.

Do you remember the long, quiet walks?
"The two of us against the world"—you said.
I do.
We were young and so in love.
The kisses long and hard — yet so tender.
It was so innocent...the bond we formed.
You loved me with your eyes, your smile, your arms—
    and your sweet, sweet lips.
You loved me with your mind as I loved you.
Do you remember?
I do.

Maxine A. Browne

"A Taste Of Home"

I went out today and climbed to the top of a mountain.
Sitting there with myself and the stillness, I pondered...
And, as I sat there such...
I hummed with the late afternoon wind;
and the valley's song below.
The sun sank into the topaz smoke and flames.
And, with the hills and sky on fire, and
the valley settling to slumber behind me...
I went home and ate my mother's
apple dumplings and milk.

H. Gwinn Peck

Untitled

Snow,
Skiing and skates.
Hot chocolate with marshmallows,
The steam that it makes.
It seems a good reason to button our coats.
And then there's Jack Frost who teases the nose.
Add log to the fire and foot to the hearth,
The calling of family,
Brings Christmas to heart.

Michael P. Morris

"Missing You"

It started long ago but it feels just like yesterday. We exchanged smiles, laughs, and words in an innocent way. Maybe there is no innocence when intrigue is involved. This was one mystery I knew I should solve. The very first night it was linked with a kiss. Suddenly I realized all in the past I had missed. It brought me more joy than I could ever express. I knew that these feelings I'd never suppress. I felt I'd found love in the rarest of form. At the age of 28 I was finally born. You blessed me with life and I'll never forget. The best of times angel are still to come yet. I know there've been problems I can't take away. But if I could I'd gladly do it today. At times it has seemed like a long rocky road. Take me back in your arms and I'll lighten the load. I understand there've been things that were hard to endure. Another chance at your love is my hope and our cure. So badly I want you it hurts me inside. The meaning of loyalty I will always abide. A pleasure it's been in receiving your charm. The honor was being on your mind and your arm. I've allowed you to slip through my fingers I know. Grab a hold of me baby and places we'll go. My love for you I know I've given reason to doubt. But look in my heart darlin' and the truth will come out. It's magic I feel when I'm kissing you. but despair I now feel because I'm "Missing you!"

Nanette R. Asher

An Episode Of War

The barking of the guns; the call to death
Smoke fills the air as I draw another breath
As I grab my gun, I see my best friend die
Out here at the sight of death there's no time to cry

The sound draws closer, tanks heading our way
I pause for a moment, please God, not today
A slit second later they launch certain death
Once again I'm forced to see a comrade take his last breath

My foes muzzle flashes; my turn to die
As the round destroys my chest, I cannot cry
As I lie I can feel my life draining away
I realize I won't live to see another day

James R. LaFleur

The Ice Realm

I stare across the arctic kingdom, laden with a white cloak;
Snowy knolls piled high — so great they reach the sky!
Old trees dancing in the swirling breaths of God! —
Frolicking children at play on the fluffy dunes!

Far to the South there lies the Mountains of Crystal! —
their snow—capped towers like hands to the heavens;
Grey to their earthly flesh, they smile onto the world!—
at their feet lay the lands of happiness and music!

The icy plain stretches into the aurora- touched distance,
sprinkled with the tiny villages of beast and Mortal Man —
Burning within them orange lights! —fires blazing brightly!—
for upon their hearths were passion and love to brethren,
For beast and Mortal Man were unified without care in yore!

I am chilled by a sudden wind of the West—o'er the hills,
and I look to the shifting sky resounding soft rose,
Swirling greatly with the talons of the clouds so amber!

In the East, the red sun is rising!—
in the West, the blue moon is dying!

Kevin W. Roberts

Intruder

At a time when no one offered it grace, it entered quietly and
snuggled in place
So quiet, so gentle, with the innocence of a dove,
How could it be a tragedy, it was created of love
Without welcome, without invitation, it began to expand
Soon the knowledge of its existence was doomed at hand
An invader, a trespasser, it was torn apart
Along with its destruction departed a segment of my heart

Jennifer Coleman

Passion

You
so close as
Darkness crowds the stuffy rooms
dulls our perception
The imaginary fusing of spirits
Haunted by images:
I know you think you love me
but I do not know how long it will last
for this love lives only as long as your memory
and you are still a child

but I shall entertain your fancy

Leah Hoffmann

The Human Drum

What is the rhythm that I hear
So faint - and yet doubtless so near
It dwells on spirit, mind and thought
The human drum cannot be bought
Unyielding is the toughness of its skin
Yet, it is sensitive like a string on a violin

It can be cut by tongue or knife
Both deadly weapons in its life
A jolt - a blast, but mostly a word
Will increase the beat if overheard
Tremendous is it's power of expansion
Tested by the art of tension

You live in greatness, sickness and health
You live in ignorance, poverty and wealth
You live high, low and wild
You live in man, woman and child

You human drum
Who are you that we cannot part
It is I, poor soul, your beating heart

Mara Lysova-Newman

A Special Friendship

We have a friendship that is so rare,
So many people really couldn't care.
We give to each what few people share,
Friendship like life; sometimes it seems so unfair.

Friendship is having to say something kind,
For from other it's so hard to find.
We give to each some rare and previous time,
Making sure know ones without ever a dime.

We have a friendship that is so true,
Trying to keep each other from being so blue.
Being there for each other needs is for sure,
For God as our guide is really a sure cure.

Honesty, loyalty and acceptance comes from a very few,
I'm desiring God's best for you.
Making sure through hard times and good times,
I'm that special friend that is so rarely found.

Phyllis G. Moore

The Ripe Old Age (Or Thoughts On Age And Dirt)

"Dust barely ages!"
So say the weathered sages,
who ponder the Hidden Rages,
while growing old and thoughtful and wise.

How old can a human truly be?
(When dust and dirt are free),
thinkers understand that aging is the key-
in gaining wisdom lies our demise.

J. M. Ritchie

"If I Could Give The World A Gift..."

If I could give the world a gift, I would give it love;
so that no one thought of themselves as being below someone or above.

The world needs love (especially today) to help stop the pain; caused
by war and hatred-all this fighting is insane!
Love is wanted all over the earth; more with every single birth.

Therefore I would give Earth love, as much as I could and more.
So long as Earth has love she can't possibly be poor.

Margaret K. Battcher

Tina

Little Lisa, so very sweet,
so very kind
At age ten is sometimes
hard to find
With such a small voice
yet such a big smile
To lend a helping hand,
you would travel a mile
When you're thought of a
ray of sunshine appears
When at times we are doubtful,
you're memories dry the tears
Little Lisa, you'll always be in our hearts
We'll remember you forever
with the greatest of thoughts.

Love,
Patience Faulkner

The Storm

Some lives aren't destined for smooth seas,
Some are placed in the storm.
They don't rely on comfort and ease,
And their eyes may look a little worn.

But do not pity these souls,
They are stronger in the end;
For whether the waves lap or violently roll,
They will never bend.

They may come into port a little weary,
But they will come in alive.
Those who have only lived seeing clearly
When darkness comes may not survive.

Yes, do not pity these:
The hardened and weather-worn;
Haughty knowledge thrives on tranquil seas,
But wisdom lives in the storm.

Leah White

Faces In A Crowd

A faceless person in a crowd of friends,
some are strangers who do not give a damn.
The faces were once ignored,
but now they are touching our souls.
Faces of the past were thought of as
being dirty and old,
but the new faces are an unknown foe.
Women and children fill the streets
of despair,
with no hope for tomorrow anywhere.
Men, women and their families are out
on the street,
while politicians try to figure the
economy's bad streak.
People's hands are cold and bare,
but many do not seem to care.
Remember that face ignored on your way,
for it may be a reflection of reality
someday.

Pedro J. Vigil

The Gift Of Sight

Some take for granted the gift of sight,
Some do not miss it till its gone.
I so desired to see the sunrise,
The beautiful sunset across the horizon.
The gift of sight cannot be measured,
because God created all without a price.
To see the colors with no sight;
I made my patterns without a fight.
I envy those with sight and cannot see,
But if I had a second chance.
I'd see the flowers in the spring,
The morning walks without a stop.
To say the gift of sight is not so great;
The gift of sight is eternal light.
I'm in a world without a light and
Yet as bright as rainbow sight.
God made us tender and yet so rough.
For we are perfect in his sight.

A. Jack Joseph

A Poem

Words all have meanings, each has its own,
some of these words belong in a poem.
The subjects are many, the choices are too,
I'll try to rhyme some words for you.
Life is vast from beginning to end and
a poem can be said for the time that we spend.
Our beginning is slight, our youth is a joy,
as we grow adults, our concerns become more.
A poem is needed for all of us, to keep life in balance,
our thoughts always clear, and always remind us that life is
so dear.
Remember your poem as you go through life, it will help you
ease your struggle and strife.
Be always thankful for all that you have,
cherish your time,
And be part of the rhyme.

Pasquale Santucci

In This Final Moment

It seems that each person I know, has a special effect on me.
Some right from the very start and others increasingly.
But you have touched my life so dearly,
and showed me what happiness is meant to be
That in this final moment, it all comes back to me.

I guess I've taken you for granted, since I'd see you every day.
I guess I really did not express to you, what I wanted to say.
But in this final moment, when I know that now we part—
I have to tell you, oh, just what's in my heart.
Because you've changed my life completely from the start.

Yes, in this final moment, my soul begins to cry,
My heart takes one last picture, as I look you in the eye,
Oh, will the light you gave me—fade—when you're not by my
side???

Well, I guess that in this final moment only in God we can confide,
That someday, somewhere—again—we will reunite.

Jason Steadman

Life

A tree is like life.
Some strong and tall
Others grow small and weak.
I touch a strong branch
it wont bend or break.
I pull and try,
but the branch stays strong.
The small weak branches bend and break
That is life.
Some can take the sorrow and hurt,
the meanness, self-interest of people around
Still they stay strong.
Some sit and dwell at all gone wrong
Whether within, at all life's wrongs.
they sink in self pity and hate to all
In the end they break and fall.

Mary Plant

The Greatest Gift

So many things have come my way for which there is no pay.
Some through toil, others free, circling, surrounding me.

It's time today to look inside and know why, where, I am.
The why's a fact no one can hide. The where's no slight of hand.

In childhood years a base was laid by one you know quite well.
Through life I sail, of naught afraid. Rough seas I strongly quell.

I must admit I'm proud of me, for who I am today.
And as I ride my changing sea, it's you that guides my way.

When things get rough and I get tough, I often hear your voice,
"Just do your best and then be proud. Your future is your choice."

In days when people choose to blame, instead os standing proud,
it's time to thank you, Mother, for a gift I'll shout loud loud.

The gift of life is easily given, and not a parent's goal.
The hardest gift, a base for living, takes apart your soul.

A piece of you is handed down with love and deep concern:
A wish for them, a life full round, expect naught in return.

Some parents have no knack from what I have been told.
But you, dear Mom, are cherished here, for all you've given me.

I make mistakes, but that's OK. I'll learn from them each day,
and go thru life as wished by you, the best that I can be.

Shaun Murphy Steward

You Can Win

Over and over again and again
Someone in this country proved you can win
You may be stricken with poverty, not having a place
But you can be a winner regardless of race

All can be winners, not just a few
If you will work at what you do
There is no short cuts in this race
For someone will take your place

The problems that get in your way
Are not solved at the bar on your pay day
And you never reach the top
If in the beginning you are willing to stop

I have watched the winner all my life
And every one had to pay a big price
But if you won't settle for nothing but champagne
You must work much harder at the game

America is the country offering more than the rest
If you are only willing to put out your very best
And it is for sure you'll drive a Lincoln Town Car
If you are the best at whatever you are

James Taylor

Singing

In a circle, we sit around on the green grass,
someone starts, and everyone follows —
We sing, because we have so much to say.
Although strangers yesterday,
we are brought close together today, like dear old friends.
Do not ask where we come from:
city, countryside, or border area?
Far from home, far from the beloved,
We are here, only because we are carrying on the same dream.

Accompanied by the sound of flowing spring water stream passing
    around us,
breathed in the scent of wild flowers carried by the warm evening
    breeze — We sing, loudly and without constraint,
not realizing our songs have caught many amazed eyes.
Although none of us are professional singers,
and some words are barely remembered, because we have not sung
    for a long time, we sing, keeping singing,
only for the strong impulse deep from our heart,
and for the thousand pieces of awakened reminiscence that we can't
    keep away from...

Jing Li

"Lucky Lindy"

Lindbergh flew the atlantic,-
Over water, waves and foam.
He was flying, flying, flying
For the glory of his country at home.
Nungessor and Coli attempted it,-
It, the wonderful flight
To fly from Paris to New York;-
But met disaster, - disaster's plight.
Lindy had a wonderful plane-'tis true.
Now he's flying everywhere,
And has gained great glory for the U.S.A.
Our "Lone Eagle of the Air"!

Ken L. Cummings

Silent Memories

All I feel is loneliness since you went away.
Sometimes I feel angry God wouldn't
    let you stay.
Why did he take you, and leave me all alone?
no-one can replace you. My heart has
turned to stone.

You were my only love, one I can never
forget. I wish I could tell you there's
not a thing I regret.

Silent memories of you dance in my
head, I feel sad, and lonely knowing
you are really dead.

Holly Junkins

The Right To Fly

Everybody loves to do things their own way.
Sometimes people do not understand the freedom of this.
We should not take this for granted. We can do whatever we
Please. The entire world practices it. God gave us
The right to fly in order to learn.

We fly in different directions to go places we want to go.
If it is Love, we fly onwards and upwards.
But it is just as easy to fall down.
The right to fly allows us to get up
And join in with the rest of the flock.
When your pathway is near, and you are ready
To leave your support, fly.

If it is crazy pathway, just think that,
Wind is all what you need to,
Carry you up and above the call of nature.
This wind might be a stepping stone, but others are flying
Right beside you on the same path called life.

The right to fly is a gift,
We can use it anytime we want to, when it is time.
We all use this right to go to God, that is why he created this gift.

Kevin Williams

Tears of Grief

Tears of joy and tears of sorrow
Soothe my aching heart on fire.
Fools lit fire in burning desire
Sooth the flesh with ice cold shower.
Brilliant stars on moonlit night
Guide my spirit to rest by your side.
Years, that have gone long ago
Meet sky, earth and a night to go.
Memories, that froze in time
Engraved on tombstone, polished bright,
With tales, - that two lovers shared!
Falling snow flakes on this brilliant night
Cover my sorrow in blanket of white.

Kathleen Pentek

Sorrow, Sorrow

Sorrow, Sorrow for all walks of life.
Sorrow tearing into our hearts and breaking them.
Sorrow making the worlds beauties look like ordinary visions.
Sorrow making us change into miserable beings.
Sorrow, sorrow what is the reason? What have we done?
Sorrow for I have the answer. The answer the tinniest of nothing.
Sorrow but still you come into our lives and try to wreck them.
And most of the time you succeed.
Sorrow you succeed to make us bellow out in anguish.
Sorrow for you and I both know why you cause such sadness.
Sorrow, you want to be happy.

Kimberly Linman

Confusion

Spirals of colors circle around me,
Sounds of excitement surround the air.
Dreams flood my thoughts,
never is my mind bare.

Mathematical equations fill my mind,
English and pronunciation trap my brain.
"Everything in its place" is what they say,
well not in my case, trust me it's a pain!

Mindy Krovontka

Special Thoughts

Happy are the times when we walk by a stream and see the sparkling water there.

Happy are the days when at the end, the sunsets mesmerize us, and chase away our cares.

It is in seeing the natural beauty around us that comes from above, that our hearts are lighter, and happiness abounds with love.

Life is precious all around us, it is a treasure to protect.
And happiness exists in each one of us, when we try to do our best.

So put a smile on your face as you awake each day.
And remember, happiness is ours, if we are better to one another every day.

Kathleen Maxine Kane

My Sorrow

Gazing through a glazed charade
Spectacled as life,
Volcanoes of glowing pain
Burrow my soul,
Finding succor in nothing and no one.

The sky, though contoured
By glittering diamonds
Proffer no solutions in a silent, unsettling,
Contemptuous gaze,
Dar'ing an answer to my sorrow...
Sorrow so thick,
I choke on the fumes, triggering piercing
Darts to my eyes.
I cry. But no one sees, no one hears, because
No one understands.

Relentless, I journey for answers... for meaning
Each trudge fuelled
By a conviction of time induced solutions
To the folds and creases
Created alongside life's joys.

Leticia Onyenyeonwu

On Julian Jayne's Bicameral Mind

In ancient days it seems you loved us more,
Spoke with us often, exhorted and prevailed,
But now in silent darkness we have failed
To walk on water or to find a shore.

Do you not wish to lead us any more?
Or has the dawn of history really paled
And we by blanching noonday are assailed
And desiccated to our piteous core?

Can you be calling, straining to be heard
Above our clamor? For our untrained ear
Can scarcely its own contemplations hear
Much less be tuned to gathering in your word.

But you must know how radiant I would be
If from your whirlwind you would answer me.

Mary Burton McKenzie

Life As Living

The mountains that
stand so high
The clouds mixed with a beautiful
blue sky.

The flatlands with
it's crop of corn and wheat
The farmers working hard
against defeat.

The city with its
hustle and runaround
awakening and
bouncing back on the rebound

The Christian church becoming refound and
the religion and preachers so profound.
The bible folk running around so quick.
Saving and preaching, the bible to the wick.

Mitch Payne

Henry V At Agincourt

The king in shining armor stately
   stands,
While round him throng his soldiers, bows
   in hands,
Whose mighty muscles glisten in
   the sun,
Reflecting strength and courage
   everyone,
And yet lest heartless death in
   battle wins,
These knights to holy monks,
   confess their sins.

T. Richard Fahey

The Great Barrier Reef

The Great Barrier Reef-a whole new world
Stiff, straight coral, and sea cucumbers curled.
Different fish all shapes and sizes,
They swim away when tide rises.

The Great Barrier Reef-what a wonderful place.
You can see the wonder in one's face.
Beautiful coral, colorful fish,
To go there is what I wish.

Rebecca Yost

"Tears And Memories"

Loving words you used to say,
Still ringing in my ears,
My thoughts keep drifting back to that day,
Drifting back through all these tears.
Wondering if it's all worth it,
All the pain I'm going through,
Asking myself just where I fit,
Where I fit when it comes to you.
Day after day we grow apart,
Never knowing what to say,
Further and further away from my heart,
Away from my heart you seem to stray.
My heart is filled with so much love,
So much it wants to give,
I find myself looking above,
Looking above to let us live.
Tears are falling,
My heart is calling,
Your face is all I see.
Hoping we are more than just a memory...

Kristi L. Pokorny

Riders Of Evil

You have heard them the riders of hate
Storming through the world
Causing havoc, pain, death
Triumphant they ride
Flashing their swords for evil
As once they did for good.
A weeping world moans letting its anguish out
Praying hopelessly for surcease
From the terrible riding men
Yes, deplorable as it is
Sad beyond compare but tell me, did you not
Put them there did you not summon them forth
From their hidden lair
Are they not obeying your commands
When the Power was yours
Had you mercy, Kindness, love
Your ears were deaf, your tongues silent
Your eyes dry, when others cried
What a pity, that you do not know
That the riders of evil are yourself.

Norma M. Selvi

Entangled Fate of Love

Love Shadowed by guilt and quelled by fear is locked within
Stray not the confines of my mind to behold this love
Nor savor the smell of your whispers while caressing your skin
may never be Nor live the life we were destined makes my soul
yearn for thy hearts caresses yet to express this special love
a love so vast would smother thee.

I fear that what once was a minds treasure has been unsheathed
How to expose this unshared love that burns within me
And lose the fear of rejection for a unity that isn't perfection
lest this be successful then a life in seclusion with stolen
moments will this life bear in despair

I shan't fear the choice to stay alone with a memory of one
and steal not these memories from the confines of my mind
which are kept safe from ridicule and judgment alike
As this my life will be for the gift from my one and only
was and is that my heart will never again be lonely

No better gift you gave to me then a memory of we

W. Padgett

Determination

Power, power, power.
Strength, admiration, determination.
pursuing, reaching, patient.
Endurance, restoration, love, guidance, truth.
Yes I'm destined to win.
Yes I'm reaching for my goals.
I'm coming out. I'm breaking through.
Those barriers are tearing down.
It's really me.
Those stars, oh bright and shining.
clamoring over me.
Rescuing. Not being afraid.

Take me spirit, tenderly up lift me.
Connect my world to yours.
Let's be free. So free we fly so high.
Touching emptiness. Fulfilling.
Conquering, binding, accomplishing.
Connecting, wiring, electrifying.
Believing, receiving, producing.
And fear! Oh fear - faint is your reward.

Marcia Morris

Find Me

Cause of night, course of light, cause of force in all that might,
Strength of fear, pour from veins, in search for my dark heart.
Black as hell, and hard as stone, bleed a blood that sears the mind,
Bakes the air, burns the water, and kills my tears.
Angel water, sadness in joy, or does it freeze in thoughts of right
    and just?
Courage in your curiosity, that look of thought on your face.
Find me, find my place, my world of black, only of hope.
Help the mirror, cast a stone, break the image, snap the bone.
End the pain, or is it the fear, exit of in.
My id or my conscious life, destroyer of the worlds of my own
    dreams,
crying slowly, face to face, for help for right, or nightly might.
Help the mirror, cast a stone, break the image, snap the bone.

Matthew F. Wolf

Stress for Less

Spit Spat, Oh what a rat.
Stress for less, when you put it last.

Find out who's the best stress or the mess,
tired of the old, just get really bold,

And bring in the new so fair and so true,
time for this, and time for that,

Why? Am I always last,
Talk and talk, But what does it mean,

No one acts as tho they can see,
Hope is for now, so don't have a cow.

Madonna Pierce

In My Dreams

Looking across the Columbia River
    stretching my eyes.
I see the Indian village and many cars.
RV's travelling along the freeway.

Sometimes I wish I could be there!
The even clear, haunting, drums and
    music from the Celilo Indian festivals.
And the freeway just gleaming with travellers
My heart wants to travel to unknown
    places and yet, at the same time,
    I love my sanctuary here!
High on the cliff, I can see everything!
    Cruise ships-up and down the Columbia and I dream!
Someday, I will be on a ship like that!
From my home in Wishram high
    on the cliffs, I hear, I see and in my mind I travel!
I can live in the past and now present.
I can have my mind go everywhere
    and still stay in the quiet beauty of my home!
And it is breathtaking and wonderful!

Paula A. Brooks

Alone

The night surrounds me.
Somehow I exist
My life so every changing
Alone to think and feel
The streets so quite

So Alone
A smile on my face
A tear in m eyes
Reflections of the past
I think we all feel that way sometimes alone.

Paul Harris

Simplification

Once a seeker
  studied the world he never made,
  and learned there's no Creator.

Many times he'd knocked.
At first, politely, very politely.
Then he positively banged.
It even seemed as though he'd beat his
  head upon that dumb door, in despair.

If God fails to reveal Self, he reasoned,
Why should I affirm that being?

Liberated he was.
How brave he felt.
No more, what would God think?
From here on, he would judge.

Henceforth, this lonely, puzzled creature
Need only believe in self.

  L. A. King

Turn On The T.V.

Turn on the T.V. and watch the news
Submit yourself to someone else's views
Go to work and just sit at your desk
What to do simply follow the rest
Driving through traffic in your new car
Forty minutes and nine miles so far
Back at the house and you walk right in
No one there asks just how have you been.
Turn on the T.V. and watch the game
Fall asleep until you hear your name
Have some dinner and maybe a drink
Gone are the days when a man would think.

  Jerry L. Gray

The Christmas Star

So distant the star; so shiny, so bright.....
Such beautiful rays, a most purest light.....
Always it will shine, for me and for you.....
An everlasting glow that will always be true.....

Even though we are apart, I am ever so near.....
You are forever in my heart and ever so dear.....
So like the star that shines, in the night and by day.....
I am not very far, not really far away.....

I will be there for you, just think of me.....
It is my love for you, which will always be......
A special love from the very start.....
So special a love which will never part.....

In remembering me on this Christmas Day.....
I love you all in my own special way.....
The star that shines, it will always be.....
You see, the star that shines, it is really me.....

  D. Stephen Spinks

Sunset And Dark

Sunset and dark
  Such quiet eventide
    Settles upon my heart;
The weary sigh, the troubling care,
  Each daily task I bear,
Caravan-like they steal away
My thoughts, from trembling disarray,
And drifting down, down down,
  Come to rest upon the threshold of time;
As whispering sands lie still
Beneath a shimmering sea.

  Joanne Less

Fallen Leaves

Each leaf lives such a brief life to come outside and play
Suddenly a cool wind blows and takes each one away.
The hand of fate is branches of mangled twists and turns
As each leaf is taken we each quietly yearn —
For the beautiful summer with us to stay
Never to falter and turn us away —
To the cold, lonely winter of hurt and despair
We all know could come, but we never prepare.
With the first snow, all beauty is reborn
To rescue us all from our hearts so forlorn.
As we look to the sky and the wind gently blows
We reach into ourselves for what we each know —
We'd just like one more day in the sun.

  Meghan Williams

God's Will

He carried the cross tied tightly to his back
Sweating, stumbling, the weight greater than his own
No helping hand was found-only his peers
The hypocrites were there
He heard their laughter, jeers and curses
Stones stinging his frail body
With all this he struggled toward calvary
The cross became the crucifixion
Nails pierced into his feet-wrists
Head hung in agony
Blood spent-strength gone-his cries weak
My God! My God! He wailed
The end was near — his body grew limp
The torment over
His death for our sins lest we forget

  Marian Harson

Tearing Down The Walls

I'm tearing down the walls of our bedroom
Taking out the studding one by one
  Trying hard to see
  From where you've been haunting me
Since the day my heart ache begun
You can call me crazy if you want to
But I thought your love would always last
  So I begin to run
  Looking for some fun
In which to cover up our past
I was hit on the head with a hammer
Struck by a blow called reality
  When I saw the light
  Of what you said that night
That you would always be with me
Now I look back sometimes with humor
In spite of all the tears I have cried
  Now I truly see
You are always with me
Like you told me on the night you died

  Melvin R. Kehrer

Awareness

Awareness is like standing tall
  surrounded by stones of the tomb.
Any answer received is wind,
  twigs and leaves scraped
  along their walls.
Yet the great spirit, and I know not why,
  may give life to one, two or three
  who lay beneath the materialistic stone.
I wait, I pray.... for awareness not shared
  is love, laughter, tears incomplete.

  B C. King

A Gift For Andrew

The rain drops outside are the heavens crying
  Teardrops on me are from my efforts in trying.
The mother of eight puppies developed mastitis,
  But this was only the beginning of what was to fight us.
She became very ill and looked to be dying,
  She rejected her puppies - now it's my turn at trying.
From 18 days old, I kept them from crying,
  They began to run and jump - it was like they were flying!
They were well on their way to being healthy and strong;
  I had no way of knowing all was to go wrong.
Something called "Parvo" has wiped them all out;
  So all that is left is to scream, cry and shout.
But it happened, and with joy
  I spoke to my sister who told me of a boy,
A boy named Andrew who was taken from this earth
  Before he had a chance at trying.
So now I know why it looked like they flew,
  For they were to fly off to heaven to be with Andrew.

Joe Richard Sneiderman

"It's Not Really Good-bye"

Ten chubby-little fingers
Ten itty-bitty toes
Two piercing blues eyes
One turned-up button nose

Oh, thank-you God, everything's there
Just one more thing...
Please let her know how much I care

Three wonderful days; bless these nights
Amber Nicole, I've held you so tight
Tomorrow I have to find a way to say good-bye
Please help me Lord, explain to her why

Baby, I love you...but I'm all alone
I want you to have more than a single-parent home
Honey, I'm poor...
When I leave you tomorrow it's because you deserve so much more

Right now I'll just rock you and sing you to sleep
It's not really good-bye; we'll once again meet
It's time now Amber, I must go
Sweet dreams my baby...sweet Amber Nicole

Janice Galbreath

Forbidden

Many have been the days and nights
That cool autumn hath brought forth,
The stirring of Primitive passion and rites
From which new love might be born;
The autumn hue of your silken hair,
The sensuousness of your sounds,
The soft radiance of your smile so fair,
An ethereal beauty seldom found;
The lust of men's souls take sanctuary in their lair
Some fearing never to impart,
Yet, you know not, for those who would dare
To journey that path to your heart;
None more than I, seek truth's bittersweet
  decree,
In conquest, my love, I shall never tire
  of thee

James Steven Sloan

Love That Never Dies

It seems so long ago,
That I had you on my mind.
I never thought you could show,
That you had an interest in me inside.
Maybe it's my imagination,
But I feel that you might love me.
I know it's my imagination,
And it's getting the best of me.
I wish I knew who you really are,
Then I'd know how you feel about me.
I hope I'm your wish granted by the stars,
And it's me you wish it to be.
I've known you forever,
And you've known me that long.
May our ties of friendship never sever,
May our love, if you allow, grow strong.
If you have no interest in me at all,
And what I thought was true is denied,
Back inside my romance will crawl,
Within my heart it will cry.

Laura Simon

Untitled

  A place beyond a distant star, a plain in your mind
that is too far. There is no sky, there is no sea, could
there be a heaven above life's tree?
No one could know, no one could tell, is there a white vista,
is there a hell?
  Purple moon hear my cry, I am the anguish of the blood red
sky. Turquoise wind listen now, and you will know the pain upon
my brow, how gray the earth, how black our time, can't you hear
the
pounding rhyme?
  See the hills, the golden plains rolling with the violet
waves. Hear the dove, it's morning cry, know the feeling of
goodbye.
  Rushing in the evening dusk, smell the mystical nightly
musk. Hear the waking of the night, the silent growl of distant
might.
  Total blackness spotted by points of light, this is not
the earthly night. Whirling strokes of iridescent paint swirl
around the illuminated saint. Crystalline spheres float round
and round never nearing the mortal ground.

Nicole Messina

No One Will Ever See Forever

No one will ever see forever,
that magical place where everything goes.
Our tomorrows turn into todays
and our pasts flow behind us,
leaving tiny ripples in the river of time.

No one will ever see forever.
Everyone and everything you've ever known
will be swept away in time.
Even memories of loves and laughs,
of knowledge and experience,
can only softly echo their presence in the vastness of time.

No one will ever see forever.
We try to keep time by hanging it on walls
and strapping it to our wrists, but this is only illusion.
Time is free, never kept, never slowed, nor hurried,
never started, nor stopped.

No one will ever see forever.
Time flows through battlefields flows past lovers, and thieves,
past spring time castles and winter wonderlands.
Always flowing, never slowing

Joe Spada

Laugh And The World Wants To Sleep With You

Eat the lizards
That make your skin crawl

Devour the wolves
That make you shriek in your sleep

Entreat the hideousness of the face you hide
And humor the devil when she
Places her stakes on your soul

And dance with the fat b**ch

Save the whole f***ing world in your sleep
And control the planet with your snooze button

And dance with the lonely waitress

Ignore as if you love her
Courts
Creatures
Corvettes

B***hes
Beds
The blues

And dance with yourself

Lauren Sonoma

Happy Birthday Pop

Life begins at 40, so they say,
That makes you 9 years old, this bright sunny day,
I don't know how you do it, but for gosh sakes
You don't look a bit over 48.
You are always energetic and you sure look fine
I bet on your next birthday, you will look like 49.
There are not many men, who with trouble like yours,
Can hide all their sorrows, and show only their joys.
So may I take this privilege to express my care and
wish you a "Very Happy Birthday, Father Dear."
Oh, yes, all great men were born in May,
as you well know,
You, the President, and of course "Vito."

Lydia Abbatintuono

Lost And Found

Are our saintly souls so lost
  that they must now harvest gifts
  as testimony to our beliefs at the season;
Whereas we pretentiously pronounce
  our faith in love, in joy, in peace
Yet to all in deeds announce
  our insincerity and selfish reason?

For it is clear to one and all
  whose vision is not blurred by xmas sale
  that his is not a moment of community
But, indeed, a bleak ritual of selfish scurrying
  to gather the gifts,
All hurrying before the fields of shelves are bare.

Who among us lingers on the thought
  that all this trampling and scrambling
  ought instead reflect on the message:
We need not ransom our joy and love,
  for to love one the other is not spelled gifts
  but rather is the breath we inhale from above?

Phil Kaufman

Silent Conversations

I hold silent conversations with you in my sleep,
That wake me they're so real.
I can feel your closeness, the sweet warmth your body gives.
Bringing me quiet joy.
Winds howl their deep dark sound, outside my open window,
Cool air washes over my face now in repose.
My slumber has gone by.

A restlessness now started, my thoughts do run away.
They all belong to you.
And throughout the day, I go to you. My mind alive
With poetic homage.
To place my wreath of love, words that speak alone to you.
Dress you in this garment, woven with serenity.
For the love you give.

J. C. Smith

Decide For Yourself

"Live for yourself, and not for other people,"
  "that's the motto I live by,
But many people don't, and refuse to even try.
They live by the standards society has set for them,
They are the leaves, ... and society's the stem.

Be daring, be different, do what you feel in your heart;
For to truly live, this is the only way to start.
Don't let others wrongly influence the choices you make,
If you do, your life is not real, ... but fake.

Time goes by so quickly, soon the future will be the past,
So live each day as if it were your last.
Make your decisions based on what you truly feel,
And in the end you will know exactly what is real.

The choice is yours, don't let anyone take it away,
Decide for yourself, and you will not be led astray.
Strive for what you seek, and in the end you'll see,
Happiness is all you'll get when spending time with me.

Matt Spidle

The Whispers Of The Prairie

Swish, whish,
That's the prairie grass -
Rolling in and out like ocean waves.

Boing! Hop!
Hear that?
It's a rabbit bringing food home for its family.

Whoo! Whoo!
The winds are arguing,
About who blew more things away.

Slither, slither...hiss!
Two grass snakes are bragging,
About what? I do not know.

Slap! Achoo! Slap!
Listen! Do you hear the pioneer woman
Sneezing while shaking rugs?

In the distance,
An Indian drum is beating -
Adding to the whispers,
The whispers of the prairie.

Kaelly Mahlstedt

Skin And Bones

Youth is just a trick
That's turned,
Then washed up
When the pain exceeds the beauty.

Youth is only a guise
For something much deeper-
It feels so intensely
When half the world believes it has no feelings.

Youth is a knowing,
Instinctive yet ignored
In the frustrating
Cycles of life in the "real world".

Youth is not insatiable energy.
It is the will to give,
Enough to share and meet
Its frenzied fantasies.

Youth is not so wonderful-
It flits its fruits
Just to remind you that,
In the end, all things are sour.

Heather McMunn Hill

Enlightenment

Standing on a mountain high...Wondering...Who am I!
The answer came from way down low...From deep within my very
Soul.
The song was rather strange to hear,
And yet, I knew, that help was near
In rearranging my thinking, to bring about the linking
With my Higher Self!
Waking from the deeper slumber
And taking my ticket with the proper number,
I found the joy of life flowing and realized, how much I was
growing.
In all things passing, there are whispers of yesterdays intention.
They Waltz into your mind and dreams to bring about,
Some kind of intervention.
Standing there upon the peak, I wondered what all I should seek.
Once again, the answer came. It sounded just about the same...
You must Run the Race...And pay the Price...
Be even willing to sacrifice,
In gaining your Rightful Place.
The only limitations, I can see,
Are the Ones that I give to me!

Nan Lyon

Window Of My Soul

I look out my window and what do I see
The beautiful world God created for me
I look out my window and what do I hear
Beautiful music that sounds in my ear
I look out my window and what do I taste
The fruits of His glory and His saving grace
I look out my window and what do I feel
Trials and tribulations of which I must deal
I look out my window and what do I smell
Aroma of flowers from valleys and dell
I see I hear I taste and feel and smell
Through the window of my soul
And know all is well-

L. L. Allison

Night Bird

The darkness was like a blanket.
The call of the night bird,
within the depth of time,
as one lies still, listening.
It reminded me of a lone feeling,
so peaceful and quiet it was.
The sudden burst of laughter from her,
calling to anyone to hear.
"Come and sing with me!
I will bring you sunshine and life."
The strong rush of wind,
the rustling of the leaves,
and again the silence.
I thought of what it must be like,
to be free, to laugh and sing, and to call on the night.
Is this the peace for which we strive?
Can it be life or is it just a song,
crying out in the night,
for love, for a companion, with which to fly?
Maybe, she sings to me, to fly, to be free.

Mary K. Hart

Joy

All is pink
The color and sound and smell of joy

The blushing heart of a rose, revealed
     when its creamy outer petals unfold.

A two-year old in a fluffy pinafore
     humming as she strums a guitar
     with her enormous hair ribbon bobbing
     to the rhythm of her song.

A strawberry soda shared with love in
     and old-fashioned drug store,
     sitting on wire-backed chairs.
The almost imperceptible fragrance of the
     ice cream mingling with the clean.
     Pungent aroma on potions to ease
     pain and suffering.

My heart and mind are free
     and my body weight less
drifting on a rosy cloud of memory.

Karwyn Rigan

Love So Supreme

The cross of guilt, the cross of shame,
The cross of lust of every name,
The endless sins of every one
Hung on that cross with God's only Son.

His was the life with no spot found,
Yet, His was the blood that stained the ground.
Hands and feet pierced, spear in His side,
"Father, forgive them," this Hallowed One cried.

Ours were the sins for which He died,
For you, for me was He crucified.
Love so supreme no one can repay,
But...try we must to make His will our way!

Marion de Sarro

Reality

As I look out the window
The day breaking in its light
Will the winds begin to bellow
Or will the sun hold tight

As the world decays in front of me
The people losing faith in all
An unbelievable sight to see
The uncontrolled as a rolling ball

The children walking as men
Growing old and dying before their time
Carrying their arsenals with them
Losing our next generation to useless crime

The world so cold a place
No love or brotherhood
As they throw the dirt of your final resting place
The sadness of those in motherhood

Jeff Higgins

Wonderful Love I've Known

He's gone but forever in my heart and mind,
   the days have now become years;
The pain of remembering doesn't come as often now;
   nor the tears.
And yet at times it seems like yesterday when God called
   him home;
I wish I could have gone with him; oh, the heartache of
   being alone.
It's sometimes more than I feel a person should have to bear;
When you're loved and love so much and now there's no
   one to care.
Certain songs, people and places bring sweet memories
   flooding back;
And then my whole world without him seems ever so black
And yet at times I feel so good to have known that much love;
And I thank God in his wisdom from above.
For no one on earth can take away this wonderful love I've known.

Judith A. Gardner

Both in the Same Boat!

My wife keeps on reminding me, that my memory's fadin' fast;
The days she can trust me to do things, are now a thing of the past!

She's had to remind me to pick up feed, like mineral, salt or grain;
Or get some unfinished projects done, before we get snow or rain.

Well, someone gave us some apples, if I'd peel them, she'd bake a pie;
She came home to find out I didn't, and angrily questioned, why?

The following day I promised results but you know how things
   always go
Things pop up that you never planned, and I never got to it, so....

She came home to find out again, that I never got them all peeled,
But I got out my knife and went to work, when disgusted she turned
   and wheeled.

"I'll bake it in the morning", she said, "Be sure to check it at ten;
I'll put it in before I leave, and it may be ready by then".

So I stayed in the house all morning, I sure didn't want to forget;
'Cause if by chance I'd goof again, I'd be in the dog-house, you bet!

So come ten o'clock, I'm at the stove, you can bet your boots I was there,
I opened the door and what I do I see, just a bunch of hot air!

She'd left the pie on the counter, she forgot it, I've got a clue.
And I didn't have to remind her, that her memories fadin' too!!

E. W. Miller

Sleepless Night

The dreams I have I see only with my eyes opened.
The different colors, I see, is drawn only to me.
I roll around, blinking my eyes.
These are the sleepless night.
The cracks on the walls, I only see during the nights.
The pains that I feel is only felt during the night.
I hear only the sound of silence.
The image I see is fainted and haunted.
I touch my childhood only in my sleep.
In my dreams, I could only see the other side.
My deepest fear is that I may wake up
And see that I will never be.
The shadow of darkness fills my eyes.
I see my life reflected only through the eyes of the moonlight.
I wonder where my life has gone.
Life has gone so fast as night turns into day.

John Soohoo

Through Human Eyes

In my minds eye I see,
The earth, sun, and moon joined in harmony.
The suns golden glow crossing the land,
stretching over oceans and glittering sand.
The earth with its glorious blues and greens,
no other place like it to be seen.

The moon with its silver, white glow,
In eyes of lovers does its magic show.
Though these scenes are ordinary to the human eye,
I feel they are extraordinary,
from the shining oceans to the arid sky.

Michelle Fanelli

Winter Magic

Lazy snowflakes softly, slowly gliding to
   the earth with all the world at rest
The air so crisp and cold with a silent
   stillness that makes winter at its best

All the earth is white with snow
   and has a magic all it's own
For there are many lands we know
   where this magic is unknown

The paintings on the window panes
   are the rarest form of art
And is Nature's way of saying
   that she wants to do her part

Tree branches bent with snow
   and bowing to the earth
It is a rare majestic sight to see
   and fills our hearts with mirth

We see children building snowmen
   and hear laughter in the air
It is that time of year when
   there is magic everywhere!

Mary Alice Warwick

A Mother's Love

Tentacles reach out to enfold
Suction cups touch, grasp, and catch hold
So many arms that can embrace
Their touch can reach you any place
They twist and tangle in their art
And create the shape of a heart
But as the sea turns inky black
It feels more like a heart attack

Marilyn Burton

Celebrate

The New Year's baby adds eye of newt to the black pot
The Easter bunny goes down the chimney, believe it or not.
The little green men with the turned up shoes
held a feast for the indians, they had nothing to lose.

You blow out the stocking on the cake, and hang an egg on the candle
The turkey with a sleigh full of toys, land on they mantle
The white bearded man with a suit of red, hollers "trick or treat."
The witch brings fine presents that are so neat.
The fairies fly on a broom that's first rate.
Someone is mixed up, what the heck Celebrate.

May Messenger

The End

As I wait by the shore for the darkness to fall,
The endless horizon pales, glowing soft red,
Laying warm golden clouds on the vast silver sea,
Fluffing salty white foam for the sun's tired head.

As I wait by the shore, I imagine I see
His tears in the wind as he runs back to me
With his arms opened, waiting to hold me once more
But I know that he's gone...like the waves from the shore...

Irene Mateevici

Learning To Love

The first glimpse of a beautiful person,
the first eye contact seals the beginning,
A starting point for love to be inspired,
and developed with feelings of caring;
from this abbreviation of time, eternity begins.
Conversations start, feeling are expressed,
ideas are exchanged and decisions begin.
Give your hearts, but not into each others keeping,
for only love of one's life safeguards your heart.
Compromise not yourself, morals or ideals,
for this is the beginning.
If compromise is needed now, stop; don't deny yourself.
This will not work, your spirit speaks; listen.
Can you accept the other as is, without change.
If so continue, the seed of love is planted.
Now awake at dawn with a rejoicing heart,
giving thanks for another day of loving.

Michael Lynnan

The Gift Of Love

The first day of life brought joy for all.
The first week of life—the walls began to fall.
After the first month in this world, she was merely forgotten.
After the first year, her life was purely rotten.

For the next ten years, things looked dim.
For the next decade, she only heard about "him".
She was tossed from here to there,
And to ask why, she would not dare.
She kept quiet,
But in her heart, there was always a riot.
Why was she left alone?
Would she live to be grown?
She soon found the answers and a home.
Her heart was finally free to roam.
She gave love, and she got love in return.
Not everyone is cruel, she would learn,
With these new people, she found trust,
And the ties that held them together would never rust.
She had been granted security, peace and wisdom by a power from
    above,
But best of all, she had been given the gift of love.

Melissa Fort

Untitled

She dreams, as sleep slowly takes over her.
The future lies in the days ahead
waiting to be discovered.
She wonders what it will hold.
Life seems so hard, always testing her strength.
She's afraid and weary, tired of being alone, and
not being able to share her dreams.
Images of later creep from the
corners of her imagination.
Will she become a star,
shining into the hearts and lives
of people she will never meet?
Or, will she leave still alone,
with few knowing that she had left?
Can her dreams come true,
or will they crumble like the bricks
of an ancient building?
These questions tumbled in her mind,
refusing to let her rest.
The future waits... to relieve the pain.

Monica Shriver

My Three Best Friends

My three best friends have so many talents.
The greatest is keeping each other in balance.
One gathers data, and gleaning out the logic,
Turns it to wisdom as though she were magic.
They call her MIND. She is much like their mother.
But each and every one consults with the other.

My three friends help each other so much.
With structure, they never get out of touch.
One is always there to lend a helping hand,
Strongly responding to each ones demand.
Her name is BODY, for she moves about so.
She positively nurtures and makes things grow.

My three friends are so harmonious.
One is always very sanctimonious.
She talks with God each and every day,
In her effort to always stay that way.
We call her SOUL, it's her proper name.
We all think that she's destined for fame.

Each in balance, they are a perfect whole,
My three friends MIND, BODY, AND SOUL.

Marilyn Collins Ivy

"How Life Gets Boring"

The old sun comes up, and the sun goes down,
The hands on the clock, keep going around,
I no more get up, and it's time to lay down.
  "Life gets boring, don't it."

My shoe's untied, but I don't care,
I ain't planin' on going no where,
I'd have to wash and comb my hair
And that's just a waste of effort.

Mouse chewin' on the pantry door
He's been at it, oh! About a month or more
When he get's done, he'll sure be sore
Cause there ain't a darn thing in there.

The tin roof leaks, and the chimney leans,
You know there's a hole in the seat of my old blue jeans,
I've at the last of the Pork and Beans
Just can't depend on nothing.

My cow's gone dry, and the Hens won't lay,
Fish quiet biting last Saturday,
Troubles piling up, day by day,
  "Life gets boring, don't it"

Patricia Clark

God's Gift To Us

Our family is our greatest gift, and it comes from God alone.
The hardest thing for us to bear, is that we're only here on loan.

There comes a time we're all aware, when our time here is done.
The way to grace was paved by God, when He loaned us His son.

Yet there are times it seems, the pain is more than we can stand.
It's then we must remember, the story of footprints in the sand.

Perhaps the hardships are only tests, to keep us from straying too far.
How can we doubt when we see the beauty of a sunset, the magic of a
    falling star.

Look deep to find the beauty, for there's beauty in all things.
Believe that when we hear a bell ring, He gives an angel wings.

If we believe He created us, from a tiny speck of dust,
Why can we not believe, that He knows what's best for us.

It takes a true believer, not to be afraid.
When you stand before your Lord, He'll mark your debt-PAID.

Linda Dismukes

"Anticipations"

Life filled full of wonders -
    the heart consumed with hope,
It can not learn to be content -
    all the hurt makes it hard to cope.

As a child, you wish upon a star
    waiting for your dream to come true,
If only it were that easy now -
    life's problems would be few.

We look at things always asking "what if?"
    to know the answers forever haunts us,
We can't be happy with what's before us-
    Why do we always make such a fuss!

Very few of us experience that lifetime chance-
    to be truly loved,
The rest of us just have to imagine-
    "When will it come?"

The future awaits-
    and all it's fascinations,
Reality becomes a game-
    full of anticipations.

Kathy Gillmore

"Never See Me"

Ribbons running through my mind—
    the hopes and dreams I'll never find;
Slip through my fingers as withered leaves
    ripped away by wind-like thieves.

I can never hope you'd see
    what you wish you had—in me;
But everything I wish I knew
    I see each time that I see you.

I know that you will never care
    if I am here, or if I'm there.
And every time I see you smile
    I know each inch is still a mile.

You're my future and my past;
    the dream that's just too good to last.
The fantasy that will never end.
    the Valentine card I'll never send.
The roses that I won't receive,
    the graduation I can't grieve.
The laughter that I'll never share
    because you'll never see me there.

Nikki Wyckoff

Life

I feel empty, I have no substance
The hurt I see so clearly
The joy has been dissolved
People all around tell me to move on
Those words are my anger

My scream never heard

My body floats through life
With feelings constantly drowning
Beginning to taste the water
Not of salt or dirt
The taste is one unable to describe

Only I know

Finally, something in life only for myself
Not only will it take away sorrow
Only I can feel the wealth.

Niki Morrill

So Easy

It seemed so easy.
The insight into the hereafter.
Looking forward to the peace and tranquility.
The freedom from life's pains and fears.

It seemed so easy.
To just sit back and let it come.
Ignore the precautions, all the warning signs.
Dying was such a sensible route to take.

It seemed so easy.
Then the angel's shadow appears.
The long awaited moment is here.
Portions of my life pass before me.

It seemed so easy.
Until the reality of my life's parade.
The sign of all I would never be.
The premature end to future fulfillment of dreams.

It isn't easy.
At the final moments the fight begins.
The struggle to regain what should never have been waived.
Please don't let it be too late.

KathleneAnne J. Reilly

Visions of Fall

A soft wind blows them here and there,
The leaves float softly through the air.

The summer breeze turns slightly brisk.
Trees turns crimson, gold and crisp.

Fall is a beautiful time of year,
The season I've always held most dear.

Cornstalks and pumpkins will be festive soon,
You'll see halloween witches fly past the moon.

Indian corn will decorate doors,
And trick or treaters will come as before.

The mirage of colors will be gone before long,
And the last of the robins will give us his song.

The trees will look bare, all their leaves on the ground,
They'll be a blanket of colors and a crisp crunchy sound.

Maureen McCoy

The Category of Me

The masculine or feminine,
The lightness or darkness,
The short or tall,
The thickness or thinness of me.

The availability or unavailability,
The professional or joblessness,
The richness or poorness,
The knowledge or ignorance could be me.

The childless or proliferation,
The religiousness or atheisticness,
The shyness or boldness,
The helpfulness or uselessness could be you.

The happiness or sadness,
The truthfulness or falsity,
The strength or weakness,
The hopefulness or despondency is us.

Lynn Y. Phelps

Heartfelt

Look inside and you will seek
The love you feel is so very deep

Love is a feeling from the heart
Sometimes knowing from the start

Other times it may take so very long
You begin to think something wrong

It may surprise you when the feeling strikes
When it does you'll know its right

From the heart you will know
A special feeling will start to grow

No matter what if it is real
Nothing will stop that appeal

Heartfelt love will really show
Never wanting to let go

No one can feel the love for you
Follow your heart and let your dreams come true

Mary Ozell

The Middle Brother Quiz

What is older and younger?
The Middle Brother!

What gets hand-me-downs and gives hand-me downs?
The middle brother!

What's the cheese of the sandwich?
The middle brother!

Who is never first and never last?
The middle brother!

Who is not the tallest or the smallest?
The middle brother!

Who gets the old bicycle but the new helmet?
The middle brother!

Who is the even when the other two are the odds?
The middle brother!

Who is the best of the trio, in my opinion...
The middle brother!!!!!

Jordan Windham

That Time Of Year Again

I look at the calendar and what do I see.
The month of December, how fast it crept upon me.
The planning begins for the holidays ahead.
The shopping for presents is something I dread.
What to get Aunt Wilma and my sister Sue.
The paperboy, Uncle Bob and what about you?
I look through magazines and many stores for hours.
To get some ideas, but they all seem to sour.

When the planning is over and the decorating done.
I just sit back and think, "Boy that was fun."
Each year I dread the beginning of December.
But when it's all over I like to remember.
The happy times and the pleasure we bring.
The laughter, the joy and the carols we sing.
I guess all in all it wasn't that bad.
To make someone happy, it sure makes me glad.

Norma J. Anderson

Untitled

When night arrives and darkness prevails
The moon aglow or even when clouds appear
The feeling swells inside as daylight pales
That the time approaches to be with my dear.

Conversely, there are times my dear
When we are closer in daylight hours
When we travel - we shop - and you are near
No matter whether good weather or even showers.

The climate does not really matter
Nor does the time of day or night
And even were I asked which I'd rather
I'd say - no matter - as long as you're in sight.

On the road - in a show - or in the shops
A tender hand squeeze keeps us in tune
And though time continues and doesn't stop
We make every moment one that's very opportune.

Max Gelfound

The Lone Wolf

In the dark, dense forest
The mystical night lingers.
The moon rays are protruding
Through gray drifting clouds:
Shafting luminescence in the clearing.

The rustling of the forest is barely there....
All is silent.

In an enchanted moment,
At the edge of the woods,
Amidst the lush of the trees:
The wolf stands alone.

His eyes with a gleaming aura
Perceive and penetrate.
His hard muscled body
Bears the tokens of life's struggles.
In perfect balance: Unmoving he stands.

The deep cry rings out...
His presence now known
Proof of strength, of triumph
Proof that only the strong survive.

Monica H. Ruzmir

A Day At The Beach

Roaring, tough and sometimes rough
The ocean waves would roar.
Sometimes calm and smooth as a lamb
The ocean waves would flow right over the sand.
Up in the sky are Blue Jays and Larks
Down in the water are fishes and sharks.
Once in a while a ship would go by,
Sometimes smooth as ever like the deep blue sky,
But when the wind was blowing and the waves were tough,
The ship would go by ever so rough.
Then rainbows would appear so merrily and pretty,
Then the ship would go by so happily and witty.
At dawn the sun would always come up,
It would spread over the beach like a big puffalump.
Then at dusk the sun would retreat,
Slowly it would fade then it would soon go to sleep.
Then the day would be over and the night would be calm,
And in the silent night you could hear the wind whistle songs.

Keisha Tarr

A Princess Battle

In my mind I built a castle
The only kind two suitors would raffle

Off a princess, that would be Me
In whose arms will I be

In a war they tug and fight
For only one will win the fight

They say the strongest man will win
But in my heart I hope it's him

Solitaire my heart with laughter
For it's you my heart is after

The essence of blood and sweat fill the air
For it's solitaire I want the affair

Now that the battle is over far from gone
I sit alone and look at old bones

For neither one has won the fight
You see they fought to death with all their might

Solitaire come to me in a dream tonight
Now and Forever our Hearts will unite......

LaShonda Yearby

Pillars of Pain

Darkness fell on my days, trying to face
The pain, anger, pain the feel of disgrace,
The tears fell across my face

Scared, confused, betrayed and used, is
All I have to say. A second came, a second
Gone, never free, the fear prolongs

Can never go back, to change the odds of
It ever happening. The scars are just a
Mark of life, always thinking of it twice

Out of sight means out of mind, all it's
Gonna take is time. To heal the wounds
You dug so deep and forget what happened
As I fall asleep

I never thought it would happen to me
The pillars of pain have captured me

Linda Christine Fiore

"Splinter In My Soul"

There's a splinter in my Soul, a thorn stuck in my side
The pain blooms like a rose and tears me up inside
It's something deep within, something I can't deny
I cannot pull it out no matter how I try

    And sometimes in the night I lie in bed awake,
    And pray for morning's light to soothe this restless ache
    The fever's flame burns bright, I turn from hot to cold
    Nothing feels quite right with a splinter in my Soul.

There's a splinter in my Soul, its driven in so deep
It rips apart my dreams and robs me of my sleep
Sometimes I think I'm healed, the splinter's pain all gone
I never get too far before I know I'm wrong

    And sometimes in the night I lie in bed awake,
    And pray for morning's light to soothe this restless ache
    The fever's flame burns bright, I turn from hot to cold
    Nothing feels quite right with a splinter in my Soul.

There's a splinter in my Soul, a shadow in my heart
It bleeds away the warmth and leaves me cold and dark
There's nowhere I can go 'cause nothing feels like home
So I drift into the night to wander all alone

Jason M. Manhoff

Whispers

The dust of dying memories may blur your eyes with tears.
The painful sorrows of the past may fill your heart with fears.

The abruptness of a sudden loss may encompass your mind in doubt
The tragedies of the past cause wonder of what the future is about.

The heartaches of this life are so difficult to endure.
The events from the past can make one feel so insecure.

And during the hard times when strength should prevail
Our weakness overpowers and in our tasks we fail.

You must awaken all the whispers of the passing time.
Put your mind to conquering the mountains you must climb.

Awaken all the whispers of the real and the reflection
Learn to act from the heart without the mind's protection.

Michelle Lynn Rusnak

Graduation Blues

So where do I go from hear?
The past too distant, the future too near,
the path's not golden as I head out on my way,
too many twists and turns leading me astray,
its not all as simple as it used to be,
no ones at the other end waiting just for me,
no ones there to catch me if I happen to fall,
no handsome prince or glowing ball,
oh if I'm brave and if I try,
I'm sure somehow I will get by,
but education is not enough,
too much competition - way too rough,
can't get a job - experience non-existent,
can't continue school - no room for admittance,
4.0 means nothing anymore,
they fall off trees now - practically pour,
and so everyone scowls with a disapproving glance,
and so I smile and do my song and dance,
but there are a million mes,
each one of us saying; "I'm perfect, so why can't they see?"

Lisa Green

Color Me Happy

Color me happy, a soft shade of blue
The peace and closeness I feel with you
Color me happy a bright shade of yellow, the starkness of white
It lets me know everything's alright
Color me red, passionate and bold
A smooth shade of brown the mysteries untold
Color me peach, the sweet taste of nectar
Color me lavender to keep it together
A fresh shade of green, a shocking shade of pink
The silver lining around this cloud of thoughts I often think.
Color me gold. Impressive and bright or the vibrant
orange of early morning sunlight
Never color me gray, Misty and cold
And please never black so dead and old
I don't want to be beige not knowing where I stand
But color me the warmness I feel in your hands
Just color me happy the way it should be,
Color me happy for the world to see.

Marlena R. Castile

Secrets Victims Hide

What's wrong with the world, all the hurt and pain
The people who are lowly hide their sorrow and shame
For downcast are the ones who are beat down upon
And if no one will speak out, they will soon all be gone
What causes others to lash out to the ones they say they care for
They first start out as yelling and then a little more
A sting across the face leads to a push into a wall
The victims cold an lonely forced to stop and can't stand tall
The anger found in others is uncomprehendible to some
But they only start to care when to the funerals they come
The hurt is not always outward its sometimes stuck inside
And no one ever knows the deep dark secrets victims hide
The secrets of misunderstandings that to the hits
and harsh words it led
Women and children keep it in, until they're taken away or dead
So speak out for those who fear the ones who do physical
and mental harm
And don't let the chance ever come where there needs to be an alarm
Don't risk the situation for people to take their anger out on you
Help stop the growing problem of the violence and abuse.

Katylyn T. Hope

So Gently Tend the Bud

While working in my garden, I knelt to tend a rose,
The petals of each single bud I held beneath my nose.
The shades of color graded 'cross the petals where they curled,
And often differed greatly as the buds became unfurled.
The leaves and buds were dotted with tiny gems of dew,
That brought the rainbow's colors and beauty into view.
And as I pruned the branches that were wont to wander wild,
It seemed to me that roses should be treated like a child;
With balanced, timely feedings and pruning as they go,
A child will tend to run and climb, to flourish as it grows.
And just as roses will respond to water, care and light,
With healthy limbs that have the strength to shun unhealthy blight,
The child who's nurtured with respect and love as they are due,
Can greet the world with blossoms that reflect the care they knew.

M. Kathleen Phillips

The Silent Voice

This I learned from the shadow of a tree
That to and fro did it sway upon the wall
Never give up; there are chances and changes
Helping the hopeful, a hundred to one;
We have not wings, we cannot soar,
By slow degrees, by more and more
And, through the chaos, high wisdom arranges
Ever success, If you'll only hold on.

Mackenzie Nicolaus

Von Leesen's

Quarter till twelve, midnight
The phone rings, startling me
The ringing fills my head, nothing else is heard
A feeling of doom comes over me, scaring me
I answer, somehow knowing what is to come
She is crying, full of sadness and despair
Shocked, I put the phone down
Moving about, almost mechanically
Before I realize it, I am there
The blazing inferno, rises up before me
Literally seconds, between salvation and total destruction
What can be done, nothing
There wasn't enough time, now everything's gone
I see the seven, standing there, crying
What once housed their second family, is gone
Something they once cared about, demolished
A passing stranger would think, just an old building
Not knowing what was felt, by those who cared
But I know, and will always remember
Because I have the last ice cream sundae, in my freezer

Lorraine Pirozzi

Hunter Of The Wild

The lion slowly stalks his prey
the prey won't live another day
the lion slowly leaps from the ground
and moves toward the prey without a sound
the prey suddenly senses that something's
not right
so he bounds off into the night
the lion chases in hot pursuit
and somewhere an owl gives a lonesome hoot
the lion chases the prey into the thick
brush
and suddenly all of the animals hush
and from the brush comes a tearful scream
and once again victorious, is the King.

Miranda Payne

The Life Of A Raindrop

I travel with friends above the ground
The same characteristics are always found
I drift awhile and then I fall
I never carry a heavy hall
I land with a peck and continue on
I slither down through the lawn
I always find others just like me
We stay a little because we're free
But this time I didn't go back to the sky
Though pollutants seemed to be quite high
I found myself being bottled up
I was later poured into a cup
That creature was clumsy and knocked me out
I regained my freedom without a doubt
I was gathered and released
I found the sewer a sickening feast
I reached my goal
And escaped the hole
I drifted up into the air
To relive a life that's no longer fair.

Michelle D. Clark

Love

The golden glow of sunset bathes the land;
The shadows lengthen and merge into twilight—
And here, my love, beside me you stand
Anticipating the joys of a love-filled night.

When youth has faded, and life grows dim,
Will we still feel the same?
Will love still bloom, or will it die
And be consumed by the flame?

Can love endure the ravages of time?
Will it be rekindled in a new and gentler way-
Will the closing years be as sublime
As those we know today?

And when we part, at the end of the road,
And go our separate way,
Will our love be a burden, an added load
For the one who has to stay?

Louise E. Young

Dreams

As I lie awake, I think of the world outside.
The sinful and shameful rules in which we abide.

But as I sleep I dream sweet dreams.
Ones in which I can go any where and be anyone - so it seems.

I dream of walking down imaginary halls.
And bumping into imaginary walls.

Or I can lie beside the ocean.
And forget the rest of the world's bitter commotion.

But mostly I dream of a peaceful mother earth.
One in which our children will someday be brought into at birth.

So hold onto your dreams.
Because they are not always what they seem.

They are fantasies you should not doubt.
So tell me, what do you dream about?

Mary Keys

Life As A Bird

I would like to be a free as a bird -
The sky as my home-a song as my word.
To sway with the trees, to fly with the breeze.
I would be part of nature - each hour of the day
Be close to the flowers, early in May.
In winter, I would find a warm little nest -
Enjoy the peace of white snow at its very best!
No worries, no pressures fly as high as I can -
Be closer to "God" - how peaceful I'd be.
"Life as a bird" would feel me with glee!

Lee Catania

Day's End

A golden sun turns orange at day's end.
The sky in the West is a pastel blend
Of pinks, lavenders and golden blush
As the Master Painter wields his brush,
And creates another masterpiece to frame,
Like a snowflake, not one the same.

Streaks of scarlet etched with gold,
Splashes of violet to behold.
As the fiery crescent drops from sight,
I sit enraptured in the fading light,
And feel the stillness of dusk; there is a hush
As the Master Painter lays aside his brush.

Janice Moore

The Lonely Professor

In a cold northern city he drops by a bar,
The snow and the wind and the dusk settling in,
And asks the bartender for hard scotch and soda
For the long walk home he soon needs to begin.

He looks out the window, and outside the bar
A beggar is asking for his daily bread.
He takes one more drink from the man with the bottle.
He walks to the doorway and covers his head.

A blinding cafe light, a cold darkened alley
And another day ends as he moves toward home
A damp half-lit stairway, a lonely old keyhole
A pair of warm stockings, a sad radio.

Time certainly passes, and youth gasps for air,
And forty comes like an expected old shadow
A book not quite finished, some papers to mark
And no time for love with so much left to do.

Love's not for old bachelors—he surmises sternly,
A professor who studies and seldom remembers
That life is for living and youth is for trying.
Perhaps next time there will be fire, not just embers.

Michael Tod Outlaw

The Song Of Nature

The song of the sparrow,
the song of the lonely willow, are music to me.
They show natures beauty
in sights and sounds unknown to man.
As a sparrow flies on clouds a high,
it shows the beauty of gracefulness.
As a willow sits in a forest alone,
you can hear the sounds of a soft moan.
As the wind whistles, as a squirrel scurries from here to there, as
the leaves rustle and flowers sway to the sounds of the lonely willow,
people realize,
there is more to nature than meets the eye.
The song of the sparrow,
the song of the lonely willow, the swaying of a single flower,
is a picture of beauty in itself.
The spider web,
early morning dew, the amazement just might surprise you.
For beauty may only be skin deep,
but nature lets it shine through.

Melissa Bennett

Open Window

My heart sings.
The song soars on bended wing.
It falls beyond the deep blue sky
Until settled in time destined to fly.

The elegant heart song sighs.
I can't believe my eyes.
With wings spread wide
Love above nearby treetops flies.

I feel the touch of her body beside mine.
I see love light upon the tallest pine.
The rainy morning sun
Casts our dreams as one.

Phillip Brian Hitchings

Moonlight Fantasy

Moonlight embraces the earth erasing
the sorrows of pain and hurt.

Silvery shadows prancing over the ground
Lightens the heart with echoes of musical sounds.

The fierce wind carries the music of flight, and
ancient chimes throughout the night.

The cloak of moonlight masks all things a rue, and weaves
a new mantle of moonbeam blue.

Moon lovers gentle drift down to play
children's game 'til the dawn of day.

Lovers free from their prison in space
Finding solace in our place.

Moonlight vanishes much to soon
Beaming moonlight Lovers back to the moon.

The milky way lingered to see playmates
in love Floating heavenly

The Big dipper and little Sister; Smiled
gentle when the men in the moon kissed her

The lovers will visit our planet again; when
moonlight fantasy needs a friend.

Luella Ganahl

Untitled

If there were a God
The sun would shine,
The sea would roar, the rivers twine

If there were a God
The grass would grow
The forests thrive, the winds would blow

If there were a God
The birds would fly
The fish would swim, the infant cry

If there were a God
The ground would yield
Crops to cover, the fertile field

If there were no God.
I fear alas
None of these things, would come to pass

G. Bartlett Seavey

Granddaughter's

There is nothing like a granddaughter, with her smile she's like
  the sunshine,
That brightens your day.

Her love is pure as the snow that falls on a beautiful
  winter day.
Granddaughter's are one the most precious person in our lives,
  When she puts her little arms around you and say
"I love you" that is one of the most wonderful sounds you can
  hear.

They are little angels that God sent down for us to love,
  I just want my little granddaughter's to know they are
my little angels from heaven.
  And to let them know my love for them is deep in my heart.

Liz Swift

Far Apart and Alone

Far apart and alone,
the tears fall down my face, as
my mind starts to race
thinking of all the times we spent
together, hoping that each
one would last forever...
Yet, it seems somehow we keep
getting torn apart, knowing
only that you will be in my heart.
Happiness can only stay so long
and then I look back and you
are gone.
I never wanted to say goodbye because,
I knew in the end it would only make me cry
I will not see you for a long time, for it is known.
Now and again, I will be alone.

Malissa Smith

Something I Did

As the music plays
The tears start rolling down my pale face to
  fall on the ground, to shatter like broken
  glass.

As I sit and wonder, what to do.
No way I could run from what has happened.
For now I know that he's gone, and won't return.
I feel so bad for what I've done, not knowing what it is.
But I blame myself for what has happened.
I must continue my life, in pain or not.
The sorrow must come to an end.
Wish I could turn back time.
But its impossible.
Got to stop the pain that you've caused, before it's too late.
I wish I knew what it was that I did.

Melissa Rose

Laboratory Lament

I hope that someday I will see
The things I should in Biology.
Some things with tails are flagellates;
Those with spines are vertebrates.
Blood cells are both red and white
But find them, no! try as I might
I clean the stage, the lens, and then
I light, I place, then turn again.
The plasma streams, or so they say
But mine stand still, or dries away.
The fibers thicken, stretch, and pop.
What do I see? A dirty glop!
I get elated—oh, what a find!
You say it's the cord on the venetian blind?
Not all is lost, not gone all hope!
At least I see the microscope.

Lee Fleming Reese

Last Watch

Tyrian purples cover an ultra masculine czar.
The power of his lament grasps our light filled entrails,
  lifting us into this massive unliberated cell of great
bondage.

    Can you fell this long lustful pull of an
unimaginable grip?
I can
Now that you can, come visit my world,
Your crucified pride be ever thanking.

Jake Jones

Far From The Zodiac

This worry that I have is gradually getting stronger
The time has arrived, can't put it off any longer
This lump I can feel, I'm sure's getting worse
So a call to the doctor, then thoughts of a hearse.

My appointment's at ten and now it's nine, I'm just pacing in my room
Positiveness has still not arrived, my room is scented with gloom
So I leave my home and crawl around, I'm oblivious to what's around
And think back to the day... hour... minute, of when the lump was found.

Destroyed nails as I sway in my chair, as the patients arrive and
    leave
Another name is called out, and inside I shake and heave
And then my name is mentioned, and there's a thumping in my chest
One last chance to chicken-out, and stay home like the rest.

I'm rigid in my chair, as my rehearsed words rush out
And the look on the doctor's face, leaves me in no doubt
I tell myself to calm down, I've come here for the answer
But I again land on the fact, the fact that I have cancer.

Paul Conchie

The Last Word

"What brash, un-matched ego-centricity?
The time has come to end the myth with mind:
How could man be himself eternally?"
They said, and thus embraced faith redefined.

"That we should walk and talk again, what need,
When, adding their blessings to our best endeavor,
All memory, influence, even our very seed:
What need that we ourselves should live forever?"

And so they laughed, and loved, and lived their day,
And then one died. I heard the other pray,
Shaking the bars of his enlightenment,
He cried, "Can this be all? All glory spent?"
Beating his head against the wall of grief,
"Speak, speak, O lost Word to my unbelief!"

LauraGrace Eisenhower

A Sonnet to Childhood

Hello old friend whose grace has left my side.
The time's been rough since last we did abide.
The days still pass, I wonder why you went,
so suddenly, without the slightest hint.
I still recall all of the times we played.
With you I'd laugh, I never was dismayed.
The worries of the world were none for me
Content was I, my mind and heart were free.
But still you left, and with me so confused.
I stood alone to be hurt and abused.
I tried my best to learn the ways of life,
without your refuge from its sharpened knife.
Why did you leave, my childhood, my friend?
I long for your protection once again.

Peter R. Baker

Where We Meet

Walking down the street
That is where we will meet.
Touching with our eyes
Looking for a way not to say our goodbyes.
Holding hands for a moment
Wondering if it will become a commitment.
Then realizing that the time has come
When our love will build a strong home.
With each other on our own feet
Finding ways not to come to defeat.

Michelle F. Kinard

To My Love On Christmas Day

The tree is all aglow with light
The tinsel sparkles, warm and bright
The presents lie beneath the glow
All wrapped in beauty and tied with bow.

Our savior in the manger lies
With Mary near to still his cries
The angels sing of peace on earth
And shepherds marvel at his birth.

The holly wreath, the mistletoe
The sparkling windows, the glistening snow
The carolers voices sweet and clear
Singing the songs we hold so dear.

This surge of love for all mankind
Reflects the love of our Father's mind
And because our love is of the Father born
I love you more this Christmas morn.

Peg Grogan

Untitled

A bright fire crackles in the distance
The trees explode into rich, radiant shades
Of auburn, scarlet, and lemon yellow
Light breezes bend tender limbs
While leaves quiver at the strengthening wind
A single ruby leaf, the first of the season,
Begins the long flight to the ground
It floats through the branches
Where songs of birds ring loud and clear
Then the leaf ceases its dance
Till it finds another breeze
And rides it to the ground
Where the emerald grass is glistening with dew.
Fall has begun.

Kara Fischer

The One You Love

I sit among the babbling brook and
the trees, in the distance beyond the
willow tree I do see, a thing of beauty
and eternal grace. For what has appeared
to me but an Angels face.

I turn for what seems but a moment
and the beauty is gone, for this I
now know I must be strong, to
carry forward and to carry on, my search
for the beauty that I have seen, just
to find that the beauty is just an
image of me.

The one you love and the one you need
is the image of you.... that not all
can see.

Kelly J. McCabe

Wonders

In the misty forest green, a shadow swept discreetly,
The leafy floor rustled whispering so sweetly.
Within the clouded eyes, a mystical image appeared,
The bolting lightning scattered, with a strike the land it speared.
Flowing fields of open hills, rolling a river to the end,
The expanding sky churned slowly and silently overhead.
A blink swept away the painful heartache,
With a powerful roll the thunder did quake.
An ever soft snort rippled the flowers,
For not a soul will ever know his powers.

Michelle Jakovac

Is This Just A Dream?

One morning I was so bored I decided to take a walk.
The walkers that I passed were in no mood to talk.
I chanced a look at everyone as they walked on by,
Their noses turned up and their eyes toward the sky.

I never expected anyone to stop and chat awhile.
But I asked myself "What's wrong with a smile?"
Being new in town, I could just be on trial.
We'll I will show them, that's just not my style.

So I started singing as I turned about face,
And started walking back home at a faster pace.
I hope they were listening to the tune, Love Lifted Me
Tra la la la la, still no friendly one to see.

I wondered how it will be if I meet them another day.
Will they still be unfriendly, with nothing to say?
Or are they hoping that I'll just move away?
I guess what I am really thinking is, "Am I living in the U.S.A?"

Joie L. Bullock

The Calling

The ship was being tossed and turned.
The waves knocking passenger and crew.
The relentless sea, boarding the ship,
Wave by Wave.
Tossing and turning forever that hell,
Till one ray of light, one ray of hope,
Comes shining through.
Only then will the sea surrender it's waves.
Only then will the ocean beckon,
"Come all ye, come."
And then we will count the scars
Of the tattered and bruised.
The pain and the sadness of the defenseless,
Punished by the unforgiving sea.
Life after life, soul after soul,
Unforgiving madness.

Mary Rachael Peacock

Set Aside A Day

My life has not turned out
the way I thought it would be,
Somewhere along the way,
I lost track of me

I married very young,
became a wife and a mother,
forgot about myself,
gave all to so many others.

Through the years this became my way,
forgetting that for me, I should set aside a day;
a day to go for a walk or read a good book,
or even whip up a new dish, I love to cook.

But I didn't set aside a day
and now many years later,
I find there is Hell to pay;
My mind is full and confused,
I feel that by others I know, I am being used.

So stop and set aside your own day,
for the price, if you don't, is too high to pay.

Naomi L. Linderman

For Michael

His presence quite surprised me, a calm and gentle heart,
The wells were rich and young, yet weary, worn and wise;

Radiating from his speaking, the wind brought forth his name
Whispering in dove's wings flurry, "Michele" sweet and tranquil;

In silence window's gaze met mine
An utterance of amity passed, through silence once again;

"Again" I say, because we two knew long ago and not so, too,
The strong and binding kinship that draws us nigh once more;

In euphony and laughter, agony and tears
A bond transcending time and place welding us,
Adhering friends, soul to soul, with happenstance and years;

The paths we walk are parting, farewells again are spoken;
Remember this if nothing else I am with you always
And I will ever be your friend.

Lynda-Jean Filipek

In The Canyon

Where distance melts like ice beneath the snow,
The winding road climbs higher t'ward the sky,
Tall pines of richest green are standing guard,
Above the valley where the river flows.
While foaming water spills o'er jagged rocks,
I stroll beside the rushing river's edge.

Like ghosts in flight the swollen clouds move on,
Across the azure sky they dance and sway,
Allowing sunbeams warm to touch my soul,
And fill my aching heart with dreams anew.

Spring's bright new flowers scent the air so fresh,
As gentle breezes whisper through the trees,
And as I listen to the Robin's song,
I'm filled with sweet contentment and I know,
All nature is in tune this wondrous day.

Margery Peterson

The Words I Love You

The words "I love you" mean so much.
The words "I have you" gives your conversation a
    special touch.
The words "I love you" can heal a rift in your
    heart.
The words "I have you" means that we will never part.
As long as there is love in my heart.

Michelle Ray

Alone

I feel immeasurably alone.
The world is a silent pool of darkness.
I look around, and see nothing.
I wait for a sign, a sound,
anything that tells me I am not alone.
I wonder if others are waiting too,
waiting to be saved.
I envy any who have escaped my fate.
I try to think, but my mind is a blank.
Am I the same being I was before?
The darkness surrounding me has seeped inside, blurring my vision.
I lean back, struggling for one last breath.
Now I recall last night I dreamt of heaven.

Linda Skalski

Mud Pies

I remember a place that seems so far away,
The yard was huge, so many acres, where I would run and play.

The tiny little green house had an enormous gravel yard,
And a velvet lawn of green where I would play so hard.

My favorite time of all was spent making muddy pies,
All sticky, black and gooey, often filled with a surprise.

Shavings from Dad's workshop made them a special treat,
It was my imagination that made them taste so sweet.

I gave them to my friends as soon as they would dry,
I shared with all of them, I didn't want to make them cry.

All hard and lumpy and as black as dirt could be,
I made them all real special, but the best one was for me.

Wood shavings on the top, metal shavings in the middle
How could I have eaten them? I guess 'cause I was little.

I can still recall the taste of dirt upon my lips,
Now I can't but wonder: does dirt go to your hips?

Those were the days, those carefree days, those days so filled with
laughter.
Then there comes the days of now, and then the great hereafter.

The moral of my story is to tell you true
Enjoy yourself, make mud pies, grow up just being you.
Nina A. Hurley

The Wounded

Morning, noon or night, it matters not to the wounded.
Their eyes can only see the hole that's been ripped in their lives.
The well intended solace of friends
is nothing more than stabbing reminders to the soul.

You are lost. You are empty. Your world is wrapped
in the fog that grips your heart. Rarely, and briefly,
you remember days when the sun still shone.
The sensations of when you were whole rushes over you.
It leaves a taste in you mouth that you cherish and curse.

The days turn into lifetime. God, will I never heal?
Standing in the ashes and watching others take so lightly
the treasure they've been granted - this threatens to drive you to
either madness or an understanding reserved for the wise.

The heavens cup their hand over you, doing their best to keep
you confined to earth. Observe the spectacle of a billion
worlds oblivious to your plight.
When comes the day when the wounded are again able to stand
with the light of living in our eyes, may we be able to say
with burning conviction, "My heart is of worth. Into the fray
once more. Be not a fool. Time is short"
Lance White

My Grandchildren

I love my grandchildren very much
they melt my heart with a smile or touch
each one is different in their own special way
whenever I see them it just makes my day
beginning with Aubrey my first grandchild
next comes Mikey who's a little wild
then petite Heather with hair of red
while Kelly's the one not easily led
sweet little Lauren is such a dear
and a new baby girl is expected next year
all in all I am truly blessed
for when I lay my head to rest
I thank the good Lord up above
for sending these grandchildren for me to love.
Mary Lou Cassady

Angelic Hope

Facing hope, I am quiet... surrounded by peaceful, serene mountains,
their silence speaks
We—silently speak together and become one
I hear the mountains inhale—they sigh peace
I am complete—I take in all spiritual peace
Immense mountains remind me of my insignificance
Coated with green fir trees, choirs of birds, free-living animals
Running fountains of clear, fresh waters tell me how unimportant my
anxiety and worries are
I am tiny, lost in the grandeur—I am a free-spirit, a member of
peaceful existence
The wind occasionally lifts strands of my hair, freely comforting all
it touches
My muscles are massaged with its loving breath, my nerves soothed
Hope shines brightly, air is filled with quiet happiness...
We all rest in the presence of the Spirit
Moon reminds our oneness—grandeur—of our tiny place on
earth—It
spreads its powerful hope
All one, we quietly breathe hope from God, from one another
We all share this presence and give thanks
Night air is misted with peace and hope
At the peak I see how unimportant my worries are on land
My peace and hope is rejuvenated
I live quietly, thankfully in hope
I long to rest on this peak and peacefully re-charge my heart with
love and hope
Maria J. Juarez

Motherhood

Mother don't punch time clocks or get paid by the hour;
Their work is never done and they never seem to tire

With many sleepless nights and many endless days,
They reap the rewards that Motherhood pays

Like the child's first time he slept through the night
To the time he sang the alphabet just right

Like the first day of school when you knew he was scared
To the note in his lunch box that showed that you cared.

Like the games that were played, like hide-n-go seek;
To the flowers, I love you, and a kiss on the cheek.

Like the day that you watch them walk down the aisle;
They look over at you with a wink and a smile

Like the time that you realize your children are grown;
Is the time that they have children of their own.

You watch and wonder if your job is all done,
That's when you realize your love and work has just been passed on.
Michelle M. Barnabe

"I Stood By You"

When we were going through tough times, I stood by you.
There wasn't anything I wouldn't do.
Now our lives are in a turmoil, and I need you
here to stay.
But I see you slowly slipping away.

Things always look the darkest, just before dawn.
You just have to promise that you'll carry on.
Things will get better, I know without a doubt
It doesn't have to be this way, our past means a lot.

Don't throw our love away after all we've been through.
Everything will work out for me and you.
Give our love just this one more chance
If for nothing else, do it for romance.
Louise Paresi

October

Now comes October, crossing the hills of the valley, changing
them into shadowed shades of golden flame

The sight of her arouses and quickens my blood, and then she
calls to me by name

Come, come, she says, join me in a carefree last frolicsome
fling, drink deep of my beauty, brilliant crimson, russet and gold

I bring you wild asters, goldenrod and fringed gentians,
her voice with the sweetness of sound said, "Look behold"

By my command, the nights will be cool, clear and star-dropped,
the days full of warm, hazy sunshine with refreshing autumn tang

Oh! It is indeed an enchanting song that lovely October, so
enticing and fragrant of aroma, cosmos and calendulas
entwined in her hair, sang and sang

I weaken, and then, yes, I will go to join her for a little
while and be merry within the excitement of the harvest season
that she brings, but I must not linger....no, I must not linger

For beautiful October who flashes with colors, rich and warm,
who gives love and happiness, can and does slip quietly
and quickly through your fingers

Martha S. Hedstrom

In Question

If struggle here is all it is
Then let the cold combat begin,
From bottomed-pit stairway climb
Till light floods the deep, dark abyss.

Maybe sword, or gun, this weapon's choice
Must penetrate the dragon's hide,
Fire and blood blanket truth's cause
Screams of anger swell from pained voice.

Passion and pride competing for space
So play by rules righteous game,
Shadows remain across bent back
Letting rain's dew smoothen lined face force.

To study, to cook, to clean till day's end
Wiping mistakes from smudged chalky board,
Toss scattered scraps toward snarling mouths
That question, attest and avenge.

Mary T. Linder

Jamie's Last Look

Jamie said goodbye as she cocked the gun,
Then she took one last glance at the sun.
Her mind shuttled back to the day she'd met James,
The days of a teenager's fun and games.

Jamie let a single tear slide down her cheek,
She'd never had so much fun as she'd had that last week.
He'd held her hand as they walked along the sand,
On those sunlit days, she'd felt she could conquer the land.

She gave him all she could give and still live her days,
But he took and hurt in a thousand painful ways.
Now, as she raised the gun again, a sob came from behind,
She turned to see James staring at his gruesome find.

As James started closer, the cocked hammer fell,
The last look in her eyes he later would tell.
Jamie's blood spattered as he looked away,
But the memory, forever in his mind, would stay.

NiKi Harrison

Fragile Defense

Sending you kisses through my fingertips,
    there is no more to say
except my heart pleads for me to whisper
    words of love to you
as we stand quietly on the beach.

You hold my hand,
    your enchanting eyes pour desire into me.
An orange sun rides the horizon;
    waves thunder like Arabian stallions,
galloping near, nipping our ankles, then racing home.
My feet touch the cool sand
    but they do not participate in the steps of walking.
Do you feel me in your thoughts
    the way I imagine you to feel in mine?

A breath of life shudders from within my soul
    when your lips sweetly caress mine, and woe
my defending shield is destroyed
    by a defenseless, warring knight.

Karen Fisher-Biggs

What You Wouldn't Do

What you wouldn't do for the love of someone
There isn't much
I would do just about anything for the one I love
He's my everything
Always has been
Always will be
What you wouldn't do
That is an undetermined question that only one person can answer
That person is you
You make the sacrifice
You pay the consequences
The one you love you should be with forever
Love is a very powerful thing
That should never be taken lightly
If you say you love someone
You better be willing to make the sacrifice
And you better be willing to pay the consequences
For the one I love I would do just about anything
That's how it's always been
That's how it'll always be.

Jennifer Lynn Craig

People Must Know

We all struggle along living day by day.
    There must be some reason for this,
But for what purpose, you may say.

We go on living life.
    What do we hope to accomplish?
There must be some meaning, without all this strife.

There must be some kinds of goals to reach.
    Can this life really mean anything?
When we find what life means, strangers we will teach.

There are answers for all of us, you know.
    They lie within Jehovah God's word, the Bible
These truths that we find, to friends and neighbors we must show.

We will discover goals that are easily met.
    To all we will speak these realities,
Without any worry, fear, or fret.

For then we will be pleasing to God.
    By telling people we do what He wants.
This makes Him happy, for in His ways we have trod.

Karen Reed

The Hole In My Heart Is Mended

In her heart she never left me, she was with me all those years
There were heartaches and much sadness as she dried her many tears,
But the painful time is over because of a God above,
The hole in my heart is mended by a mother's constant love.

Sister Carrie wrote and told me of the times they prayed for me,
Of that mother and the children and their never ending plea.
As they gathered round the throne room, they believed in a God above,
The hole in my heart is mended by a family's tested love.

Sister Mary planned a party, the gathering of the clan,
It was she who arranged the meeting according to God's plan.
They all drove for miles to see me, bringing food and gifts galore,
Then we sang and cried and shouted, how much more could we ask for?

One day we'll all be in heaven, the absent ones we will meet.
Then we'll shout the alleluias as we sit Jesus' feet.
We'll remember how He helped us through the intervening years,
Holes in all hearts will be mended as He wipes away the tears.

Maggie Clift

Untitled

In the confusion of the times and its spiritual upheaval
There's a campaign about to whitewash the evil
Of totalitarian tyranny with a never-ending litany
Of excuse socio/economic and conspiratorial.
Their methods were necessary so the apologists say,
And the millions processed in the camps? Why, that was just a
small price to pay. They had to close their hearts to find an
absolute and final cure: To build the workers' paradise
And to keep the race pure. Reality was blurred. The alienated of the
Age followed wildly any psychopathic avatar.
A bargain with the Devil was arraigned:
The nation's soul for the hakenkreuz and red star.
And the new terminology so simplistically applied
Demonstrated to everyone that everything was cut and dried.
The perverted phraseology so painstakingly used
Made it possible for every citizens to be fused
To the party/State apparatus, or branded and tattooed, Jude!
Or bourgeois, useless eater, cosmopolitan, reactionary, un-person,
politically unreliable, and, of course, it was true, undeniable.
Didn't they all confess at their impartial trials?

Wayne F. Cunningham

To Write?

I have no muse, I cannot think
There's nothing here, I've drawn a blank

Inspiration where are you?!?!?!?
I feel the need, compelled to write
might it be my hair's too tight?

I hold to hope that thought will come
Then this pen will scribble some

Sitting here, grasping straws
Trying to end this thinking pause

So frustrated, wanting to scream
I'll never break through or so it seems

Finally, a glimmer of light in all this dark
The dam is breaking, it's not so hard

I'm writing now, may need more ink
It just took a moment to stop and think.

Kellie Dawn Arrowood

A Love Not To Be Forgotten

A part of you given up
These things must be remembered
As a large part of our lives.

Feelings of love so deep
Such a part of our everyday lives
But those around us, our children, need us,
And can help us through this.
Be a part of our future; we will never forget
For love lives on inside of us.

Gather strength my friend
From memories we hold dear;
Will be a part of life everlasting
In our minds and in our hearts.
Hold her close to your heart
Never let your thoughts waiver
For this too will move us forward, into a thing called life.
And let those around you in; to your mind and your heart.
You are loved by many
Let them help you start anew.

Joel Atkeisson

'Me'

'Me' although simple is a very big word.
These two letters contain everything
I will ever do, say and accomplish.
Everything I can and cannot be.

'Me' refers to my mind, my body and my heart.
It is how people see me,
but more importantly it is how I see myself.

'Me' is all of my hopes and my dreams
wrapped up into two tiny letters.

'Me' is my life, my love and my pride...
and I am proud of me.

Nickole Green

His Hands

When I look at his hand's this is what I see
They are strong when I am at my weakest,
When I felt as if life had forgotten about me,
I remember his hands reaching out to me.
When I am tired, his hands soothes me;
and when I can't seem to go on, its his hands
That pick me up and leads me on.
When I need love, his hands caress me
And make me feel wanted.
His hands play beautiful music
That helps my mind to rest.
Sometimes his hands are old
And sometimes they are very young
But most of the time they are
Kind and loving
Because he is my man
And these are his hands.

Lynda S. Malone

Untitled

Down by the river where my boat is tied
There's a little pond where the fish go hide.
I am the only one who knows it's there
And I go there often to smell the air.
If you take your time you will surely see
That its the first place of the turning leave.
There ain't no road for a car to travel
If you go there your problems unravel.
The song of the birds and the waters rage
Helped ease my spirit and I turned the page.

Morgan Koon

Twenty Years Too Late

They could have burned their draft cards, like so many others did.
They could have crossed the border, where so many others hid.
But willingly they went away,
for that their souls were damned,
to fight a war like none before,
in a land called Vietnam.

Our country parted through those years, for reasons I don't know,
from protest rallies to mother's tears, a hatred seemed to grow.
But now you feel you've made things right,
with all that you have done.
But everyday they still must fight-
your forgotten American son.

You tell me time will heal all wounds,
that's where I make my stand.
You cursed the pride of those who died,
in a land called Vietnam.

So you can keep your movies and your documentaries too,
you'll never understand the hell that you have put them through.
This country that they loved before has turned that love to hate,
Don't do no more, forget the score, it's twenty years too late.

Michael D. McDonald

Only One Mistake

Only one mistake,
they did it too late.
All our men who fought for our country
we're seen and we were proud of
for what they were fighting for.
But, only one mistake.
Our men who fought for Vietnam
were not sure of what they were fighting for,
they didn't want to fight for something they didn't believe in.
Only one mistake.
They did it anyhow, for which for some was a mistake.
When they came back and we were not proud
of them for what they were fighting for.
Which the things they have seen with their eyes,
the tears, the pain, the lost.
They went through fighting this war.
Only one mistake
they did it too late.

Melody Hause

Nurses Care

Nurses are special people
They do so many things
Giving medicine to the sick
And comfort, they hope to bring.

Nurses document patient care activity
With pens or use of computers
But they still find the time
To say that patients are beautiful.

Nurses may feed, bathe and dress
Helping patients to look their best
To maintain their dignity and self-esteem
While they are eating, walking or at rest.

Nurses are good listeners
To whatever patients have to say
About expressing their joys and sorrows
Or reminiscing about their yesterday.

Nurses are special people
They will care about patients for days
They will care about patients tomorrow
Nurses will care about patients always.

Otelia Crawley Hendrick

The Christmas Dream

The parents go shopping, while the children stay home to dream
They dream long and hard, about all the things they wish they had
Not of the usual plum pudding and gingerbread men (women)
But of power rangers and face changers and things of that sort
Why do these four and five years old dream so hard, we all know
   we used to do it
Are they more spoiled than we were, or do they just have bigger dreams
By the way, what are dreams
Are they figments of our imagination, that can only seem real in
   this format
Maybe they're just our wishes granted for what seems like a single
   second
With that, I leave you to ponder the translation of what dreams are

Henry Lee Mitchell IV

My Parents

They came to Ellis Island, their belongings were very scant.
They had no place to live, so they lived with my father's aunt.
Soon they had two children, they struggled day and night,
they wanted everything for their kids so they never gave up the fight.
My father worked three jobs at a time, he had no time to play.
My mother did the woman jobs, but she also worked during the day.
She'd come home from work with blisters on her hands
from sewing all day long,
but she still had time to teach us an old Italian song.
She never was very happy, she missed her home land so,
She thought she was coming to a country where she would prosper
and grow.
I can't remember my parents laughing, I only remember the tears,
and that's burned in my memory even after all of these years.
But we grew up and we survived and I never will forget,
the parents that gave up their youth for us, without even one regret.

Mary C. Dukat

The Ballroom Ladies

They walk with a special beauty and grace
They have a white toothy smile upon their face
They wear satin gowns that shimmer in the moonlight
As they walk through the garden at night
They are as beautiful as can be
I wish I could be as dignified as the
They are the ballroom ladies
Yes they are
When they dance they shine like a star
They dance and dance all night long
They can dance to any song
The Tango, the Waltz, the Virginia Reel
Sometimes they wear down their elegant shoe heel
They are the ballroom ladies
Yes they are
And in a crowd they shine like a star

Paige Mefferd

"The Japanese"

The Japanese are very neat.
They take their shoes from off their feet,
When into the house they go,
To keep from tracking dirt you know.

Their houses are mostly made of straw,
Without a hammer or a saw,
Their meals are mostly made of rice
Now, I don't think that is so nice.

And when some very dear one dies,
On their grave they place cherry pies,
Now I don't think that is quite right,
Because only the living have an appetite.

Neva Thom

Demolition Man

The demolition crew stood face to face
They weren't about to leave
Still one more building to push over
Another topic left to cover
All wondering who gave the order
Each one debating on where stood the border
Soon the reminder of what to do
Took over the minds of the crew
The wrecking ball swung hard and fierce
All ears around the sound could pierce
When it was done
Not one part of the building stood in the sun
A single soul was killed in whole
Now I am building with the promise of gold
And in that spot lies what is left of the old

Lacey Johnson

No Matter What People Say Or Do

No matter what people say or do,
they won't understand what I've been through.
I have to say, yes I do, because I myself have been there too.
I was so lost, I could not feel, all I knew was that this was real.

There is a place for people who die; yes, it is above the sky,
He is not dead if he knew God; yes, his soul is still alive!
He can see you, he knows your sorrow my dear, there's always
tomorrow.

Remember I am always with you, what I taught you, it's within you.
Remember our times, remember our moments;
this will bring great joy to you always.
I know it's hard for you right now, and for those I left behind.
But you must go on with your own life.

Remember my dear, life does not end here; yes, my loved one,
I will always be near.
I have no fear, I have no pain; it is so very peaceful here.
I just went to sleep; I have so great a peace;
it was just my time to see above the night.

It's great to be alive; please enjoy your life, as I enjoyed mine.
Please go on, I'll see you soon, not right now but at another time,
in this place you won't need a dime.
Please don't cry, I'll see you soon; all I want to say is I love you.

Marilyn Rosario

Warm Fuzzies

Warm fuzzies are things inside of us
Things that keep us warm.
Found deep inside of us
Beneath the clothes that are worn.

They keep us nice and warm
when the world around us is being torn.

No matter the hurt of pain we feel
Our warm fuzzies are there to help us heal.

A warm fuzzy may be a shiny penny,
or just a smile extended to a friend.
But no matter what they are, real or pretend
Warm Fuzzies are always there, to put a smile on your face.
All you have to do is look in the right place.

So next time you are feeling funny
don't go out and waste your money,
rather look deep inside
and find the warm fuzzies that you hide.

Melissa Wysocki

My Love-My Other Love

Not a day or night goes by that I don't
think of you in some way
All these years have come and gone
and your still so clear in my mind.
One day I hope to look into your eyes again.
I hope to hold your hand
and tell you that you've always
been my love - my other love.
It's always been my biggest regret.
not letting you know.
My love - forgive me...

Kathleen Jaszczak

The General Sherman Tree Sequoia National Park

Magnificent seems weak to reverent lips;
This sun-gilt giant must support the sky!
Those mammoth branches rooted deep in blue
Absorb the light of life, bring Heaven nigh.
Oh fire victor, largest living thing,
Yet humbled by pert fearless chickaree
Who climbs to nibble cones and scatters seeds,
What wisdom comes from all your centuries?
"Three thousand winters hushed with silent snow,
Wind-cleansed since Moses walked the Holy Mount,
I've learned through all creation moves a flow
Of loving gifts between the thoughts of God
My seeds so scattered by each tiny friend
To million unborn hearts their healing send."

John K. Saville

Point Of No Return

Watching you, in the dim half-light,
Those mysterious moments,
  twixt day and night,
I wonder, remote there in sleep,
What secrets do you keep
  in your wild tossing?
Where once was warmth and tenderness,
Nothing is there
Little by little we have ceased to care.
Soon, the sun's first rays,
  will light the sky,
And a new day will start,
A day full of promise,
  but not for you, and I.
We shall drift, further,
  and further apart,
To a gulf - there's no crossing.

H. Crummette

Why Did You Go?

Sitting, just sitting
Things come to my mind - they remind me of you
That car that just went by - wasn't it yours?
Someone just said your name - I think?
I used to wish that these thoughts would stop
But now I don't
We had a short but great time
And you have changed me in positive ways
When you were with me and even now that you're not
I have very special memories of us
And I will treasure them forever
With the tears flowing over my smiles
I still love you!!!

Jennifer L. Smink

Restless

May I rest upon this eve?
Though my thoughts, they do conceive
The safety in her arms, I seek
As heartfelt tears roll from my cheek...

Upon the breeze, a whis'pring song
To only her, I do belong.
Has love itself, known love this strong?
This constant yearning, for so long?

I wonder how things might have been,
As I unfold the days since then
Haunted, by what I can't dismiss,
The longing for her passions' kiss...

Is she my soulmate? I cannot say.
But to my Father, I do pray,
That He will somewhere, find a way,
To make these hearts as one someday...

And though I'm weary, I mustn't sleep,
A promise to my heart to keep.
To wish until the wish comes true,
When one is made, from once was two.

Michael J. Vernetti

Verbal Efflorescence

LOVE — you bet it's a four letter word!
Thought about continuously.
Written about perhaps more than any other topic.
Sometimes misused; often abused!
Spoken in haste for lack of something to say,
Only to be replace by nothing said at all!
Lost when paid no attention,
Taken for granted more than it should be.
Given for no reason at all...or
Removed for the same.
Expected from some who have no idea how to give it.
Confused for so many; severed by a few.
Guarded by those too scared to be hurt,
Discarded by those who have been.
Accused and blamed for too many reasons.
Torn by the indecisive,
Shattered — sometimes along with dreams.
Walked over, stomped on, crushed by false hopes,
Pushed deep until it appears dead.
Only to spring up the next time ready to blossom again.

Marti L. Burch

Love and Lies

Silent words unspoken
Thoughts and feelings too
Strong mind
True wisdom
Thinking of you

Soft whispers echo through my mind
True feelings hard to find
Paper words and midnight dreams
Are they really what they seem

Look deeper and deeper into the eyes
Pass over the body and through the mind
Into the soul, surprised at what you'll find

Passion and desire held deep within
This selfish want - a sin
My heart aches constantly for you
Is wrong, but undeniably true

Are my feelings reality
Or is this just a game
Or are they both intertwined
One and one the same

Nancy Green

Turbulent Teens

I am so restless, why no sleep?
Thoughts of future mind and body peace.
All life's plans in one, so much to be done!

Mood slightly bent
today's the 10th.
Towards the depressing side, I'm afraid!
In sadness, I wade.
Smiles impossible.
Asking too much for a person of such
A call or smile from friend or foe
Lend me your hand, so I can stand again.
At a world, I hope someday to understand?

D. Langbeen

"Do I Love You"

The timeless void of an acquitted crime.
Through a shapeless hourglass of a wasted life
With a rancid taste of a bittersweet love
Engulfed by a shapeless mist of a careless moment
  Do I love you?

In a panacea of forlorn days of loneliness by your side
To a still beating heart of a newborn thought
For a barren womb of moments shared
  To my soul,
  Do I love you?

By the chilling heat of a racy expression
On the trodden back of beasts intermingled
Until the complete spectrum of life runs anew
  To have the words
  To tell
  I love you.

Michael Sprigler

Dreamland

Twinkle, twinkle, star shire bright
Through, and through, throughout the night
Shadows dark and dim do fright,
So shimmer star for your a beautiful sight.
  Dreamland awaits us, so let ut go.
What is out there, I don't know.
What could it be, a far away land?
Or maybe a beach filled with golden sand?
Puppies, kittens, or little bunnies?
It could be something sad or fumy.
Anything we dream, it can come true,
And that is one thing that I knew.
If you will wish upon a star, it will
twinkle in that land afar.
  So twinkle, twinkle, star shine bright.
Through and through, throughout the night.

Misty Gleason

"Transparent"

  I am a transparent wall constantly being looked through, but never seen.
  Though I am able to witness what is going on around me; I can never be part of it.
  Sadness consumes me as I watch them with my invisible eyes, and they walk through me as though I'm not there.
  With a sigh I close my eyes to the reality of my existence, and go day by day ignoring the facts of my life.
  My heart still prays that one day I will be seen, and people will notice me for what I am, and not what they wish me to be.

Heather Crook

The Line

There once was a line which connected us two
Through that line I told all to you.
I told you my dreams and all of my sorrows.
My triumphs of today, my hopes of tomorrow
Like became love though you didn't care,
And though my feelings you tried to spare,
It hurt all over; every where.
You didn't believe in my loving care.
After a while it came to pass.
I had gotten over you at last
I soon liked another, then loved her a lot,
But you and her just fought and fought.
The line grew frayed as time went on.
After while the line was gone.
Time marches on and leaves its track.
I hoped and prayed for the line to come back
Then e talked everything out,
About the fighting and all about,
Problems and troubles buried in the past.
Has our line return at last?

Mike Lambert

Winter

Blustery and cold winds blow
Through the trees and bushes they sing.
All species of birds flock together in the snow;
Then all in a sudden they decide to go.
Vacation toward the south
For they all know it's time to leave the north.
Snow soon covers the houses and earth
No place for them to survive and make birth.
Shiny crystal and white just like fairyland.
This makes all humans and creatures happy for their winter plans.
People usually go skiing, skating all out sports.
Nature creatures seek for food and shelter which is their resort.
Only God knows what is best, at this time for pleasure.
Only God will show us how bells chime for everybody treasure.

Mary Ann Petito

Untitled

I have no children, yet I
   tie shoe laces when they are loose,
   zip zippers on jackets when they get stuck,
   discuss the difference between right and wrong,
   praise, congratulate, and wish good luck.
I have no children, yet I
   educate them about the world,
   read stories everyday,
   greet them bright and early,
   create smiles, laugh, and play.
I have no children, yet I
   know each one's personality,
   weakness and strengths,
   assist in setting goals,
   to be reached at any length.
As far as starting a family of my own,
   I have not yet begun.
   A second grade teacher is what I am,
   and as for children,
   I've thirty one.

Kelly A. Nakielny

"The Wait"

After many months, the wait is almost over.
Time has been both, fast and slow.
Nights were the longest. Days the shortest.
Yet, I wait.
More time passes.
The Death Rattles start.
All hope is gone.
Yet, I wait.
I sink lower into despair.
The bringer of sorrow is near.
Death must wait, also.
Sensing that the wait is almost over,
I take my mother's hand and look on her sweet face.
We all wait now.
Her eyes open for the last time
She looks to Heaven.
We wait
She takes her final breath, she is gone
I whisper in her ear "Mother I love you."
The wait is over.

Hiram W. Conway

Sadness

Emotions lost, caught up in moments,
time will wash away the pain,
Bittersweet love lost in commotion,
Will my heart be cleansed by rain?
Hatred, strong, wells up inside me,
lost and lonely thoughts combined,
All my tears lost in tomorrow,
sorrow so strong my heart has cried
With falling leaves, the wind comes 'round,
Its pain cries out, so much like mine,
I'll wait to see the sun tomorrow,
and my soul, set free, will finally fly.

Misti Devlin Card

Love Of My Youth

Love of my youth, my golden years,
   'tis fair to say;
Just like a spider weaves its web,
   or like a weaverbird its elaborate nest;
Our love, like thread, like twigs, we have woven,
   strand by strand, into a web.
'Tis an intricate set of patterns
   woven in colors of red and white
Our love so true and pure.
   Of blue and green, the colors we love so dear
which only our hearts can comprehend...
   This intimate, this extraordinary
entanglement of ours.

Lade M. Warsaw

Harbinger

The crocus slowly pokes its way
   through snow's last crystalline remains
And in the warming sunlight of
   a chilly end-of-winter day
I watch it open to become
   a brilliant patch of liquid gold.
And in that gold I see and feel
   the summer sun. It warms my soul.
From this day on I know there is
   no turning back, that spring will come.
This lovely flower has told me so.

Mary L. Pruyn

Dear Benjamin

My dear little Benjamin, what do I say,
To a brand new baby born today?
There's so much to tell, so much to see,
So much to wonder and so much to be.
But I seem to think the best place to start
Is way down deep at the bottom of my heart.
Where I've saved a few thoughts all my life through
for a day such as this when I would meet you.
These are just a few tips that have gotten me by,
Like, green is the grass and blue is the sky.
You see with your eyes and you wiggle with your hips,
You hear with your ears and you kiss with your lips.
Angels have wings, four leaf clovers bring luck,
Moo says a cow and quack goes a duck.
Apples are for eating and swings are for swinging,
Tears are for crying and joy is for bringing.
But, most important of all, love is for giving
Children are for loving and life is for living.
So, with the wind at your back and the sun on your face,
I welcome you, Ben, to a wonderful place.

Lori Wilkinson

Little Horsey

The little Horse is sad now his little Boy has moved away
To a much larger home and hopefully more room to play.
'Tis sad to see the Horsey in the gentle breezes sway
    remembering the happy times when little Boy came out to play.
And Oh! The squeals of delight, the days were never long
    enough but ended with the night.
The little Boy was heard to say swinging from the Bars, 'one
    last time Horsey then you are no longer ours',
How could he leave him thus such a pleasurable friend -
    Horsey will surely remember him till the very end.
Gentle little Horsey swaying in the breeze -
    how could your master leave you - tell me please
Or will there be another child - one so sweet -
    that a ride on your back will be such a treat.
Surely there will be more than one to vie for
    your favor and restore the glint in your eyes just to
    please an old neighbor.

Kunigunda Di Manuele

A Would-Be Love Villanelle

I say I don't care about the state of my hair
To act vulnerable through these endless winter days
Cynically feeding on the bluest air.

When the birds are flown and the beauty trees bare,
I sit with my head like a carving in space,
A little sad and frowning, with my filth of hair.

Wild body and shy soul, which art moves everywhere,
If the long-with-love acquainted heart lost its case,
They still seem to catch the breezy air.

Perhaps till the mourning pieces their witness bear,
Till all her love reaches and ends in an open space,
Maybe till I have the filth in my hair.

To me, she's already dead, gone far away there,
Silently turning away my disgusted face
From the psychedelic clouds highest up in air.

No, frankly, she never wanted me to share,
Yet I feel like dying in the faith haze,
I say I don't care about the state of my hair,
As there's the beautiful and terrible thing, needful to man as air.

Libor Soural

Ron And Diane's Baby Ali Marie

She will bring know a happy smile
To all who know she and love her
Your princess she will always be
God entrusted this wonderful human
Being to thee. How lucky is she.
With people like you this world
Is a better place. No pretense, no sham
or farce, just loving hearts

Maria R. Kowalehyk

A Fit of Sun

A fit of warm rend the garment chill
to bare the damp breast of earth
by fickle sun upon this hill
unheralded unseasoned mirth

Discard unwieldy heavy blouse
leave me bare as the huddled trees
lest forever winter house
a frosted soul against this breeze

Bark and limbs, their scant scarves of brown
scarce accept the fleeting pause
for it is they, not I, who frown
at this breaking of the laws

A taunt, a jest, what is now here
my looming moon in place of dawn
I spread bare arms, I smile, I fear
the moving window will be gone

Kevin B. Robinson

Discipline

I wanted my life
To be an alter
A lifetime, of pilgrimage
A testament of timeless love.
An inspiration to soul's desperation
Motivation toward final ascension.
The heart of wanting my test of humiliation.
A fire brimstone passing oblivion
Spent naked heart beating
Last supplication
I am a discipline you my religion.

Holly Dawn Hewlett

Full Circle

God gave me the honor and privilege, it's true
To be the mother of daughters, two.
Healthy and happy - only sixteen months apart,
Our home was very lively from the start.
The months and years flew by so fast,
Kindergarten, high school and college all past.
Now they have moved away and have lives of their own.
We are left, just us two, husband and wife all alone,
Soon to begin a new phase of our lives together
With a grandchild and our child will be the mother.
The cycle starts anew with this gift from above,
God gives us a baby to cherish and love.
Our first grandchild - what a joy to behold,
Help us, Father above, in your ways to mold.
Our family has been blessed in so many ways
Thank you, dear Lord, for all of our days.

Marianne K. Saylor

Look Back In Sweet Remembrance

Look back in sweet remembrance
To everyone who loved you.
To everyone who ever held you close.
Look back and be grateful
For precious mem'ries such as those
Spring and Summer lie far behind you
and the autumn of your life is just around the bend

So look back and be grateful
For everyone whoever called you friend -
The years pass swiftly time slips away
and you'll find mem'ries are all that stay.
Smile and remember those no longer in sight -
The friends who helped you through a lonely night.

Lena L. Murphy

Ecstasy For All Eternity

My dearest love, I ask of thee
To gently take my hand, my heart, for all eternity
Before you answer, please take thought
Most people dream, but have they fought
To truly love only one and never stray
So blatantly explained, they've been betrayed
But I will state with all my heart
I shall love only you, I won't be caught
By eyes and gestures, soiled flirts
My heart knows you, you'll never hurt
Except you'll tear, your loving heart so full
Only our pure love shall forever rule
Two lives so starved for warmth and love
We shall grow as one, please a God so far above
And time will pass so rapidly
When the curtains draw, conclusions freed
That you said, "yes," and I agreed
To love, to birth, feel age and still ecstasy.

Michael "G" Giovacchini

Dear Mother

I've thought and I've thought of what I could do
    To give my thanks and love to you
When suddenly it occurred to me
    Of what better way could there be
Than to write it down and give to you
    My feelings Mom, so that's what I'll do
Thanks don't hardly seem enough
    Nor to say; I love you very much
But it seems to be the only way
    that I can tell you on this special day.
You're worked so hard, you've cared so much
    And did your best in raising us
That I thank God for blessing me
    With you mom, you're special, as can be
I love you Mom, and thank you much
    Even though this hardly seems enough.

Jeff D. Eggers

"The Sounds Of Joy"

    To hear a child laugh,
to hear I love you from your better half.
    To hear the birds chirp and sing,
to hear nature and all it brings.
    To hear little feet go pitter-pat,
just to be able to hear this and that.
    To hear a heart go thump, thump, thump,
or does it go ba-bump, bump, bump?
    These are only a few of the things
that the sounds of joy can always bring.

Kim Peters

How Sweet It Is

How sweet it is to wake and feel the sunshine on my face.
To hear the children at play outside my window
as the day begins its journey.
I look within my heart and soul
searching for the needed guidance
from who and where I don't know,
But I feel the power inside me.
My mind often wonders to places of the past
settling into my comfort zone,
But realizing that I can not stay
for there is today awaiting.
How sweet it is to look above and see the stars gleaming
The day is done and another breath awaits my call.
I lay to rest my peaceful mind
The power does surround me
soft-spoken words of wisdom
speaking to the air
with feelings of serenity
I sleep into sweet slumber.

Nicolette R. Cortez

Friends

Friends are the ones you count on most
To hear your troubles or to let you boast
They pull together, they fall apart
Some are forever, others are not
The ones who help you when
you are down are the ones you
Know are always around.
When you need to cry - to shed a tear
Over fallen friends, who were so dear
They will be there, you know for sure
For an aching heart, friends are the cure
When I am troubled and feeling sad
My friends are there, for this I'm glad.

Leonard Angelini

Never To Love But One

A heart so young and tender, untouched by the world thus far.
To innocent to know the pain, of things as they really are.
The came the one whose love was true, and to her did impart,
His gentleness, his very soul, the first to touch that fragile heart.
Now having known that special love, created before by none,
She made to him a special vow, never to love but one.
And then one day the hand of fate, reached out in cruel embrace,
And gone was the one she loved, never again to see his face.
Now having lost that special love, created before by none,
She made again that special vow, never to love but one.
But time went on and she did try, to love again once more,
And tried to make it special, as it was the time before.
But the years of pain and memory, etched their way into her face,
And an old and much worn body, showed the years of rapid pace.
And now her life is ending, and time is almost done,
And she was never able, never to love but one.

Kay Adams

Watch Out

Watch out for men dressed in black
Watch out for tooth plaque
Watch out for killer bees
And watch out for people who like to tease

Watch out for people who snore
Watch out for things that are a big bore
Watch out for witches who go "Hee Hee Hee"
And please, oh, please watch out for me.

Laura Masch

Untitled

Horizons appear with each idea - in part or as a goal
To lead us into atmospheres, to seek the fortune- they may hold
The fountain then is now, vast, deep and now.
Each a root, unto one's self of various form and hue -
Bearing fruit, sharing reason, thru vision, voice and view,
To serve the palate of one's taste, in thought, flesh and deep
Cultivating fare we deem -
Essential to our need.
Endless to wonder, destined, we pursue, the path
With the heart, the way that leads us thru, the
Illusion, confusion and deja vus, till depth find favor
In the maze and to the breast, staid motive raise
On buoyant waves of here and now, that smooth the furrows at the
Brow, giving sense to why and how the chosen quest is acquiesced
The fountain then, is now.

Paul J. Smith

Parents And Children Of Our Future!

Our children need lots of encouragement,
To learn and continually learn.
They are our future statement,
Something each generation yearns.
Parents—don't stop educating yourself!
Broaden your horizons and skills.
Keep away from them drugs (it helps),
Because learning is a good enough thrill.
Again, drugs is not any key to wealth,
Refresh your own memory on English and Math,
Teach your children and let them lead the path.
If they do not learn, what will they know?
Parents—that's why you're there, to help them grow.
Children—listen and learn from every experience,
Because if you don't, you will never know.
How to take really good care of yourself,
When you get real old.

Janae Hausback

Four Seasons

Mr. Green has come once more
To let the puppy out the door
He comes to let people know
There's no more white, there's no more snow
Mr. Green loves to tease
So he sends a gentle breeze
During spring, he's always seen.

Summer comes with many lies
Some grass will shrivel up and die!
But actually there's lots of rain
Basically plants just gain
Lightning, thunder, many clouds
These summer storms are often loud.

The fall brings down all the leaves
Except those on evergreen trees

Mr. Jack Frost comes to visit the land
Covering everything seen at hand
Snow comes down, oh so white!
Stealing away dead leaves at night
Covering by morning, glistening, glossy and adorning.

Neela Swaminathan

Portraits

In my search for a woman to join in my life,
To live out our dreams as one, man and wife,
I painted a portrait of whom I might find,
It's a woman who's special - both pretty and kind.
I painted a woman with eyes so sincere,
Mysterious, yet innocent, with no room for tears.
I painted a woman with a breathtaking smile.
Compassionate, confident, reflecting her style.
I painted a woman with hair silky smooth.
Stunning, arousing, yet able to sooth.
I painted a woman fit to be queen.
Elegant, graceful with beauty unseen.
But this girl has beauty both inside and out.
A mind strong and clear, a mind with no doubt.
When the painting was finished, and starting to dry,
I took a step back, gazing into her eyes,
I asked, "Who is my princess?", I had seen her before ...
Perhaps in a dream on some tropical shore?
While pacing I marveled, "Is it just deja vu?"
It was then that I realized, it's a painting of you.

Michael Leedberg

The Boundless Abyss

Slowly, ever so slowly did I come
To my present condition
By minute degrees did I slide down
Into the fathomless abyss of despair
At length, I commenced groping
Attempting to discover someone, even something
But how could I find anything
Without having first found myself
I relinquished my futile search
And yet slipped even further
Into the bottomless chasm so alone
Without even the faintest of light from above
I raised my eyes upward yet it was all in vain
The schism was far-reaching and I was beyond reach
A prisoner of myself I am forever trapped

Janet L. McGinn

The Visit

She was coming home again after a long time away
to places that were memories in her heart.

We all wanted her company and a chance to share
some time, because we knew how soon we'd have to part.

It was as though no time at all had passed as we sat together
and talked. We reminisced and laughed and cried
but time was on the clock

Our history together as precious as can be
the intertwining of our lives & dreams,
ever loving friends are we.

We took our glasses off to see each other's face
I honestly couldn't see a change, of aging not a trace.

We talked of pain and love and loss, and all the roads
we'd had to cross. Our kids are grown our lives still turning,
our feet are tired, but our fires still burning.

On the day she left it was hard to say good-bye
We held each other close trying so hard not to cry.
But the sadness was short as I thought about my friend
she will always be a thought away, a kindred spirit till the end.

Kate D. Bolender

Help Wanted

The Savior is looking for soul's to fill this job.
To preach and witness the Gospel of the Holy Book.
Tell people to be getting ready to leave this world.
Hour's are 24 his a day, every minute every second.
No time off no paid vacation, no paid Holiday's.
A lots of praying and keeping the faith.
Benfit's-To meet our Lord and Savior.
Have everlasting life.
There will be no more tear's, sorrow's or sadness.
All peace, To see all of our loved ones who have
    already gone on.
Are you willing to give your Life to God?
He's looking for Angel's to fill his need's.

Jewel Knutson

Love

If love is tender and so true then why when I see you I feel so blue.
To remember when you walked me home or all the time spent
talking on
the phone.
I especially remember the feeling of loneliness
in my heart for all those times we were apart
and that funny looking cookie that was suppose to be a heart.
Those times are gone and in the past and you telling me we'll it
last.
Last forever you once said and you threw it
all away on that could February 14th day.
My heart is in pain as I stand in this cold February rain,
saying "the love has died and now is gone.
Love can not be tender nor be true because I loved you.

Michelle Smith

The Spirit of '76

Not a few, but many, even all it will take
To restore America as great
Not because of its power, pelf or material wealth
But because of its people regaining spiritual health
Not only those already within its shore
But others of many cultures, races, even creeds
With varied talents, even more
To help bring forth what the Almighty Spirit
Has in store..........
For all citizens of our land!
That once again we may sing
In an atmosphere of reality
From the depth of our hearts ———
"My country 'tis of thee, sweet land liberty
Setting us free of every extreme,
So, let them ring! The bells of freedom...let them ring!
Not just outwardly piercing the etheric air
But within!...if true greatness and freedom
Are to be restored
The new beginning...it is there!

Lee R. Geldmeier

Paradise For You And Me

From the highest mountains,
    to the distant seas.
To where the crystal-like waterfall flows.
To where the lilies bloom,
    and the roses blossom.
And the white doves sing.
All is peaceful,
    like a halcyon calming the waves at sea.
Together we have found paradise,
    for I have found it in you,
    and you have found it in me.

Molly Dube

The Family

We gathered together from far and near
To see Dad and Mon, two old dears,
Dad was ready to go to heaven,
Leaving Mom and all the seven.

In order we took our stand
While Dad blessed us, raising his hand,
His smile was so sweet,
As he went off forever to sleep.

We enjoyed life with Mom for many a year
Until death claimed her, our good old dear.
Then we were left the sorrowing seven
To live good lives, till we meet them in heaven.

But death the mightily caller came
One by one, they were snatched away
No more with me to stay.
The youngest of the seven must live until the day
She is bidden to join the family band,
In the better land.

Myrtle May Scott

Broken Wings

I remember the time I flew high enough
To see over all the rest
My wings were my life, they gave me pride
A pair of the very best

They'd let me down, they'd bring me up
They'd help me when in need
Flying was like a miracle
I thought I'd always succeed

Then, one day my wings began to break
Without a reason why
My courage, my pride, my love, my life
All quickly said good-bye.

So, there I sat, alone on Earth
Remembering many things
That was when I realized ...
You can't fly with broken wings.

Natalie J. Pratico

Looking Through Her Eyes

How I wish I could look through her eyes, just once
    to see the world with her loving smile
    to know what she's feeling when she laughs for awhile
    and to feel her tears of joy and pain, when she cries

How I would love to look through her eyes, into a mirror
    to be familiar with the curves of her face and to see
    her life just a little bit clearer
    to embrace her sorrow and realize her fears
    and to behold a reflection of beauty and love that I've
    cherished for years

How it would be great to look through her eyes, as she sleeps
    to visit the worlds where she may go in her dreams
    to protect her in a monstrous nightmare filled with screams
    to learn of her fantasies that she holds in her mind
    and to be the lover that she always seems to find

But most of all; how I wish I could look through her eyes,
    when she's looking at me
    oh what a sight that would be
    when her eyes wrap around me like a glove
    to be looking through her eyes - the eyes of love!

Michelle Rogers

I Sometimes Did Wonder

I sometimes did wonder, if I had the will,
To take someone's life - to actually kill.
It wasn't my choice, it was his life or mine,
I did not think - there was no time.
He threatened my life, but I could tell,
He was just like me - as scared as hell.

I had a knife, he had a gun.
We couldn't decide, to fight or to run.
He heard a sound and turned to see,
Now was my chance to fight or to flee.
I used my foot to kick the gun to the air,
Then looked at his chest - my knife was buried there.

Blood slowly drips, from off my hands.
The air coldly sits, where a man once did stand.
He breathed his last breath, his last word was, "Why?"
I know not the reason, but he did have to die.
The Spirit of Death hangs in the air,
Making me wonder why I'm still there.

Mary Davis

Earthly Angels

Life is a mystery to us one and all,
to the big as to the small;
The reason for your suffering is not known,
just take the love that we have shown;
Know that hope abides in earthly angels such as thee,
to struggle and endure, to survive, just to be.

Blessed with your little life so new,
knowing your pain is hard to do;
Courage can carry both the young and the old,
according to the wisdom of legends still told;
So be patient a little more,
be brave a little longer;
You'll get a little better,
you'll get a little stronger;
By and by child, by and by.

Mary Colleen Connelly

Changing Tides

From the serenity of the sound...
to the bustle of the Great South Bay
to the rhythm of the ocean...
Long Islanders enjoy
changing times with changing tides.

The Autumn hues, together
with the splash of the ocean breezes,
restore a vigor to us all
to help endure the challenges afforded by our
"paved waterways and seas of traffic".

The landscape of Long Island offers us much -
from rough seas,
to tranquil streams,
the journey is always adventurous,
and we take great pleasure in sharing in the
Sail-ebration!

Michael J. Opisso

The Forgotten

A hard park bench offers small comfort
  to our bodies swollen with tranquilizers
  or emaciated by hunger, as ill or uncaring
  we neglect the essential demands of life.
When the demand becomes too strong from pain,
  we'll forage for food in a trash can.
Our hands, mis-shapened from cold and pain,
  reach out to you, hoping you'll understand.

Pearl E. Badaloni

Peace

I possess the great freedom of lifting my face
to the sun - owned by God - gives me
warmth as its light floods the deepest part of my being
and heals my weary thoughts and body.
A crisp breeze from the heart of the wind
passes an amen to the warning sun -
God is love - brings peace - is everywhere -
always has been - always will be
and so never am I ever all alone with
the Shadow's of God's peace - my very own.

Marilyn Harberts

A Wish a Dream a Reality

Beginning with a wish and what we hope for,
To want for the future to open every door.
Next there is a dream that you would hope to see,
To think of or just something you want to be.
If you strive hard enough, you and others will see,
What you dream and wish for will become reality.
No matter how hard life may seem,
There's a time for everything.
Time to worry, time to cry,
Time to live, time to die,
Time to dance, time to sing,
Time to wish, time to dream,
Time to want, time to be,
Time to hear, time to see.
Time for heartache, time for lies,
But there's also time to fall and time to rise.

L. Bernadette Carter

Beyond the Horizon

Su Ping loves to walk by the shore,
  To watch the waves-
    To feel the mist-
There are so many, many, things to explore.

Su Ping loves to see the boats,
  To watch the sails-
    To see them glide-
Oh! How do they stay afloat?

Su Ping loves to feel the sand,
  To watch the crabs-
    To build a castle-
There, beyond the horizon, is my China land.

Marylou Haselton

Dreams:

To whom I know: I sit and think
To whom I know: I watch moon dust falling from above
To many things I love
To many things I cherish,
To many things I know
And too many things I would like to know
I would like to dance unto the rain
And prance into the crystal white snow
Swim into a moonlit pond
And plant beautiful flowers to grow
Life is a big test
You either fail or pass, in many different odd ways!
There is to many things to know, and to many things to learn
I just live freely and let my soul go
All I really know is I have to live until I die
Until then I just let my soul fly....

Kelly Leigh

Midwest Wood

Once a greek man who dreamed of the land,
"To work" he did say, "the dirt in my hands"
and a wife who he did meet only after a brief meeting
said "I do, yours for the keeping".
Afar from theirs friends, family they stood
and settled in the heart of Midwest Wood.

In the heart of Midwest Wood came season of fortune and fall
A farm they did marry, four children they did share,
"a good family we come from", Ma and Pa said.

Harvest brought golden days, winter, purple blue and ice sickle caves.
Through sunlight and moonlight work carried on.

In the heart of Midwest Wood came season of fortune and fall.
As surely would, destiny did call.

Ma counted days past and prayed to Mother Mary,
giving her strength on days she felt weary.
Pa dried his tears from eyes that once did see,
his land stretching miles and trees shady green.

A greek man and woman who dreamed of the land, "to work" they
  did say,
"the dirt in our hands". Afar from their friends and family they stood
peacefully buried in the heart of Midwest Wood.

Pauline Robin Piano

An Ode To Jonnie Katherine

With joy we heard the news from your mother,
  To your four grand-children will be added another.
Later she exclaimed in an excited whisper,
  "Jarrod is going to have a baby sister."

The moon was full, the hour was selected,
  The last day of summer was the time elected.
The day was doubly special, I must say,
  For you and I share the same birthday!

Your name was determined, it would be none other,
  You bear the name of your great-grandmother.
You could not know her, for her life had been spent,
  But we note in God's word that to heaven she went,

What joy, what delight, what ecstasy, what cheer,
  To hear your dad shout, "Our baby is here!"
With dimples, round cheeks, and hair with no part,
  With a smile and a blink you captured our heart.

A little girl to cherish, to hug, and to hold,
  With love and caresses, a new life to mold.
We thank God who has graciously given you to us,
  His blessings have come with a great big plus!

Jerry W. Lee

Jesse The Monster Horse

Jesse the monster, head tossing at will
Twisting and turning - he just won't stand still.
Evading the halter, he does a spin
I follow up - quickly - lead shank - I'm in!

Now for the bridle. His head's in the air
I guide the snaffle - but it goes nowhere.
Somehow the snaffle gets caught on his chin
Everything's cock-eyed, and I am done in!

Wait 'til I saddle - impossible mount!
Side-stepping, side-winding, for no account.
Saddle's in place - how do I tighten girth?
Jesse the monster is kicking up earth.

Tussle not over, he fusses and trots.
Left foot finds stirrup. At last I'm on top.
I'm prepared for the worst; what will be next?
Out strides a gentleman - I am perplexed!

Joy Barteski

Sand In Your Dresser Drawers

Sand in your dresser drawers. Enlarged drawers or little feet with
toes unpolished? Lipstick on the mirrors? Getting lonely these
days? Try some Windex. Footprints, too many to count. Was there
a party..no you just ran around a lot. Is there a banana in your
ear? Can't you hear me? Try the rabbit, pig nose! Pull your
shorts up dear they look like socks. I'll drown you baby, better
watch your bubbles. Daddy's home sweet pea come give him a hug
around his knees, kiss his elbows. Run downstairs and hide because
you know you'll be blamed for the cats misfortune. Go to bed and
try to stay awake we know what could happen. Watch out! You
weren't prepared were you? I warned you puppy toes, leave the
scissors in the drawer with the sand. No more beach, no more
burn, you're getting whiter. Try the window sill. Sleep in the
bathtub with the water running then clean the floor in the morning.
Want some sour cream little girl? Better refuse, your face will break
out...well you know what I mean. Does it look pinkish to you
sweetheart? Look again, take the shades off and lay off the acid.
No more orange juice it's a bad influence on you. Stick to the
whiskey, you don't need your liver. Ever happened to someone you
know? Do you think you know this person?...definitely hopeless!

Melissa Santoni

You Show Me America And I Say "Big Deal!"

I came here for the shock and found it was stale
Too full of caution, no sting in the tail.
Safely Nazis stole the spirit away
In search of protection and a good lawyer's pay.

You used to blaze trails and be truly fee
Now you hide behind disclaimers and say "It wasn't me!"
You complain of the others who are seeking your place
But you're too fat and lazy to compete in this race.

You sit and you eat and you take and you take
Where once you stood hungry and striving to make.
Now it's just rot and confusion and fake indignation
As the inner cities become a new third world nation.

You rest on your laurels, calling others unclean
Self righteous words where once actions had been.
But your military solutions are too little too late
This empire of hot air crashes head on with fate.

Paul Spencer

"Yesterday"

Often something will
  touch your life;
And years later it will appear before you,
And with it will come
The removal of all strife.

Only time gone by will allow you to see,
  this glamour which will allow you to be.
More than adequate is this moment
  of the past gone by,
Years later on when you can only
  recall it with a sigh.

This time gone away
Will leap out for your attention
  in one form or another,
But one thing it will not do
  is smother.

Instead, it will only carry itself
Before you to dig in;
And it will always just go away
  with a grin.

Kathleen Guenther

Lauren...

You came to us in a bundle of joy, hardly big enough to play with a
toy. We watched you turn over and crawl and walk-
and then we listened to your happy talk..

We remember little quips and things you did,
and giving you your bottle with the rubber lid..
We long to see and touch your hand and watch
you play in the box of sand...

To grab you and squeeze you with all our might-
to know you're here and things were right..
We celebrated your birthdays with joy and love-
because you were such a sweet little dove..

We see your little legs go running through the house -
looking for Pluto, Minnie, and Mickey Mouse...
We look out the window and see Dad show up-
to pick you up like a little pup..

Our relationship is over and the story ends-
but let us be happy and still be friends..

You're still our hearts and very near-
and we love you little Lauren Dear..
Because today makes a year and we smile through a tear-
Since you went away, Lauren Dear!

Merle Edmunds Jr.

Untitled

I have never been here before.
Trembling mermaids bathe the tangerine.
Peculiar blue paints the stones...the path to my destiny.
Mossy fields massage my reluctant toes.
   But everything awaits...
Increasing walls of unconsciousness dash the breakwall.
I have definitely not been here before.
The serene mermaid, a siren of sort, tries to speak.
I cannot help but notice her.
My brow drips with anxiety.
Finally, she utters words.
One.
Repeated millions of times.
What does she mean with all this?
All that is meant is interpreted from her yellow mermaid eyes.
   [What an oddity for a creature so beautiful to have lizard's eyes.]
There is a feeling of sensational birth an inevitable death.
As she moves away, she is no longer a mermaid
   but a...mirror.
And I am myself...once again.

Mathew Karl McKenna

Through Mother's Eyes

Well my child, I love you, although my hair is turning gray,
Try to think of yesterday, before time slipped away,
"For time is quickly passing, fading before my eyes
And the mom and dad of my childhood,
Has lived and has died.
Through mother's eyes I see you," some day reflecting me
Always remember mother, although her hair is turning gray
"Always remember mother," I'm just a phone call away,
So many things I should have said and done, "I REGRET
NOW THAT THERE GONE," "I understand now mother"
How you felt so alone.
Through mother's eyes I see you, someday reflecting me!
Through mothers eyes I see you, someday reflecting me.
Well my child I love you, "although my hair is turning gray
Try to think of yesterday before time slipped away"
For time is quickly passing, fading before my eyes
And the mom and dad of your childhood-has lived and has died
Through mothers eyes I see you "someday reflecting me"
Through mothers eyes I see you, someday reflecting me.

Loretta Solon

The Harlequin

The harlequin, without a sound
tries to make the king laugh in jest,
behind a costumed diamond frame
he juggles his life in test.

He's the King's buffoon
that always answers soon
with a hardihood of comedy.
Then the wave of a hand
causes the royal command;
for the harlequin "To be off or Be Off with his head!"

The trick of a clown goes continuously around,
as he side steps out of sight.
Then to trip at will
he keeps the balls circling, still
bows, much to the King's delight.

Then a smirk appears under his painted face
while he pantomimes the fool,
for, knowing he's not,
he likes playing the part
of a comer in a harlequin suit.

Mitchell Ross Abrahams

The Bricklayer

Just beyond the horizon, lies the foundation for happiness.
Trudging through the tiresome trials of life, the distance decreases.

Ever closing, our anticipated arrival looms. But what's this? The
horizon is becoming smaller, diminishing, disappearing. A brick
blockade appears to be rising with every approaching step. Like a
screaming siren, as silver spade scrapes over the bricks.

Who is this with the silver spade slapping cement on bricks; impeding
our path? Who is this bricklayer?

The distance diminishes; the elusive bricklayer is almost visible.
As the bricklayer prepares to set the last brick into the wall, we
pound, plead, promise anything to have one last glance at the horizon.

As the bricklayer withdraws the brick, horror claws at our very soul,
for the bricklayer has shown himself. Ludicrous laughter leaps from
our throat. The dread realization is known as we glance down and find
in our cement encrusted hand, the silver spade.

Kerry Wilson

A New Year's Resolution

Starting a fresh with a new plan
Trying hard not to break it again
Hoping tomorrow will be much better
I'll start by writing you this letter

With God to help and be my guide
I'll succeed with him by my side
When you understand, I'll be so glad
And no longer will I be sad
And as I start a brand new year
I'll not falter or will I fear

If a nursing homes where he wants me to be
I'll be content quite willingly
Until I reach my home above
And am surrounded by God's love

Mary Weaver

Christmas Continuum

Looking back through the haze of nostalgia,
Turning to glimpse the potential excitement
    of the future,
I stand in the middle of all the generations
    I will know
Sensing the continuum that is embroidered by the variations.

There are constants:
    Remembering the reason for the season;
    The aroma of a feast in preparation;
    The sparkle of lights;
    The squeals of joy.

There are unique differences serving as
    markers of social change:
    Popcorn and cranberries to gold beads;
    Candles to blinking lights;
    Home made toys to Nintendo;
    A laden table and party dresses
        to convenience food and blue jeans.

Constants - differences
A package of contentment tied with the ribbon of love.

Priscilla Eitel

Once Learned Twice

Dabbled once, she tossed me a cross,
Two steps forward, one step back.
But I find, one step extra is needed of me.
The lesson learned, twice as hard.

So I dabbled twice, she tossed no cross.
Three steps forward, two steps back.
Seems so long since no times gone by.
But now I see, what is needed of me.
Once learn twice, a third has been seen.

Try expanding the foresights, minded still of a cross.
Once steps are taken, they are evermore.
So a "long ago" time appears twice as far.
But for once, learned twice, my needs are of me.
A third well learned, forevermore.

Paige Masiak

Guernica 1936-1966

A Short History Of The Nuclear War
Guernica - and still it burns
Two thousand people killed, a village was wiped out
But the memory lingers on in the Museum of Modern Art
Whose sign is sidewards.

Carthage must be destroyed, and Guernica must burn
And must America burn too?
Ban the Bomb and Save the Cities!

The bull is slaughtered from above, just bombed away
The sword is broken, too; not peace, but a sword.
The peace is broken, too; the piece is broken more
O broken Guernica, and must America break, too?
(Ban the Bomb and Save our Cities)

And after Guernica, what?
Dresden and Monte Cassino and London and Hanoi and New York too?
And the Museum of Modern Art, whose sign is sidewards,
Where there's a mural borrowed of a village burned.
That was in the beginning
When the world began to turn upside down
And a piano began to play "This is the beginning of the end."

Patricia D. Olley

Pearl Eyes

Gleams of light that always guide a riddle lover.
Ubiquitous image always haunting my days.
Ending my sufferings by curing my fever.
Transcend my heart of your magic and soothing rays.
Tang so sweet that deeply penetrates my soul.
Invading, without stopping, my entire body.
Elusive feelings awakening my eager goal.

Trepidations draw from source of scarlet beauty.
Reminiscences of a concert so perturbing.
Eternal thoughts that sound like my unfinished rap.
Shiny star of a frantic dreamer, in trance, being.
O confounded the time be, if it does not stop!
Reveal, muse, the hidden secret of your essence?

Splendor of life that carries along a rare
Apricot tree, so fine; "halo of quintessence,"
Nestling quietly in the livid pinkish, and fair
Sunny flowers basting of silver cracks of moon.

Pearl emerged from a stake, ungodly paradise.
Rekindle this sacred fire of your eyes, soon.
Impetus of heart and passion gradually rise.

Marc Arthur Lamothe Jr.

Blossom of the Night

Once upon a beautiful star-lit night
Under skies of sparkling ebony.
A new blossom grew enchantingly bright
For one and all to see.

Its silky petals reached into the sky
To grasp the glowing moon.
It grew so quick and grew so high
In a shade of deep maroon.

Its roots grew deep into the ground
Searching for new life.
They spread out everywhere and all around
Through pain, angst, and strife.

No one ever saw this glorious flower
It was completely out of sight.
No one ever felt the sweet power
Of the blossom of the night.

Keith Adams

Awake and Remember

Awake my love
unfold your petals to the breath that was shared
Come claim me
envision the subsistence found only in embracing
Cloak your eyes
that you may know my face and the path that will guide you
Search your heart
for a love born in time's first radiance
fire burning through eternity's final day
Know I await
envelop what has always existed
My soul your soul complete

Catherine Morgan

Hold Your Tongue

Hold your tongue, don't speak the words
That can sear a soul with shame.
If you do, don't you know
Nothing will be the same.

Once words are spoken, they can't be unsaid,
So be careful what you say,
For words have a way of coming back
To haunt you some future day.

Marie Anderson Robbins

Yesterday's Winds

Yesterday winds blew softly as strangers sat
unknowingly in the shop. Strangling their friends with
lifelong problems as if to help their agony. Nowhere
to turn but the old broken corner. Going far beyond in
directions unseen. Over hills comforted by the crescent moon.
They lie in the fields and wonder. Worlds around them have
painful hearts, yet no pity. Hands held out but never seem to
hold on. Carrying a barrier of guilt and shame. Sitting up, cast
in a daze. Stars cloud their thoughts and sky overbears
them. True colors cover the plain as a dark blue haze.
Into the light of that wonderful place.

Michele Joseph

Flame

At first, it flickers and dances,
unsure of itself, and where to go.
As it burns, slowly finding its place,
there is a peaceful, calming effect that it has.
Comforting

Gently
Swaying back and forth, side to side,
holding steady to the destination that it has found.
Swelling tall with pride.
Cowering with fear of going out.

Burning
Filling the air with a sweet scent.
Giving off radiant light,
for all to see.

Quickly
Going out
Flickering and dancing

Joy Shears

The Bandit

He slunk through the dark Alley
Until he reached the house of Halley
I won't let him hurt my friend
I will chase him around the bend
I'll pounce on him
I will bounce on him
Who is he?
I will soon see
Wait don't move he's closer and now he's in the trash
His eyes look a small sash
Maybe oh maybe he is wearing a mask.
Oh my gosh he's carrying a sack.
I wonder what is in it.
If I don't find out I'll have a fit
Look he's dumping it out.
Now I will not have to pout
Out comes a plate, cup, knife, and spoon
Now I know what he is he's a comical raccoon.

Lena Herman

Bird In Distress

I heard the screeching of a bird,
The likes of which is seldom heard.
I looked up in the air to see.
It hanging in a great big tree.
Wound in string from a little boys kite.
So it was screeching with all it's might.
I climbed up there and set it free,
Now it was grateful as could be.
It did not say so in our words,
But I could hear it telling the birds.

Nellie Alders

Alone

Her life is dark, but she is bright,
to some people she puts on a spotlight,
To others that laugh and make her hurt,
It feels like your stuck in a deep hole with
nothing but dirt, she feels she needs a new
life, but that life to her is only a knife,
The sharp feeling of cutting her vain,
is why all of her friends put her in this pain,
She closed her eyes and fell on the bed,
her life was dark and the she was dead.

Lindsay Ioerger

The Companion Came Late But Not Too Late

The sandblaster kept pointing the blast toward me
Until the lifeless, external shells of the past were removed.
I had forgotten the softness of the natural wood;
Its lines and character had become more hidden each year.
The wood that had been hidden still had beauty of its own,
once forgotten but now so evident that no one could escape.
The pithy blast that kept stinging was not welcomed at first
but now the constant peppering has become a numbing companion that
waited with me as the grain began to surface and breathe again.
What a wonder that stripping off one's masks can bring freedom?
What sadness it is to discover that while coverings may be in vogue,
the most precious is the hand rubbed and oiled surface
that lays bare the nature of a being with all its peculiarities,
its strong lines, deep grooves and its fragility in sacred space.

Nancy Draves

Paradise

Before the garden there was the land, primeval,
untouched by human hand,
But the work of God had already begun.
God shaped the vale, and raised the hill.
God stacked the mountains, row on row,
And left the valley floor just so,
A pine tree there, two oaks beyond,
A cedar bent by winter's ice,
And maples scattered here and there,
It was a slice of paradise.
We were given such a place
To tend, to mend, to manage for a while,
A bed of tulips where the rise begins,
And where it ends, some summer flower to catch the breeze
as it plays hide and seek among the trees.
In the evening, as the sun just sets,
We walk with God in eden.

B. J. Carter

November Brother

I would dig you
up
brother
out of that damn Houston hole
and we would race back together
then you could leap like a dolphin
like the rest of them
off Streamer's Lane
in the dove-colored dawn.
then even November
with its battle ship clouds
would burst with the sun's raucous laughter
rising up now in the Santa Cruz hills.

What were you dreaming that November afternoon
when the rain beat against your
endless pain?
Did our daddy come back
offer you his money?
Nothing I do brings you back alive.

Madeline Moore

That Kind Of Love

This kind of love, soars like a dove,
Up high in the air, the perfect pair.
When you love him so much, you wilt at his touch,
It was love at first sight, and really it might,
seem strange in a way, since every single day,
It seems as if the love grows more.
This love comes from within the heart,
The living, beating one inside.
I'll always be there for him, through both thick and thin.
Whatever he desires, my love burns like fires.
Whatever he needs, my open heart bleeds.
As deep as the love goes,
As shallow as the blood flows, strongly, our love grows.
Standing free with open arms, outstretched widely to embrace,
The love that's known to me as true.
For nothing can replace, this jewel; this sacred jewel,
This jewel is the heart. And why is it so very treasured?
For deep inside, under lock and key,
You'll find the greatest blessing of all: LOVE.
It's that kind of love.
Keli Thomason

A Desolate Mountain's Beauty

A mountain stands so desolate
Upon the arid plains,
And moans as though the hot winds caused
Her agonizing pain.

She milks the rain clouds seldom by
To cool her mammoth sides,
Then lets the burning sun release
Its rays hung in the skies.

Yet, she has a twisted beauty from
Large holes hewn in her sides,
That housed the nomads years ago
Exiled from their tribes.

Still merchant laden caravans
Enriched with all their ware,
Seek her shelter from the wind
When sand storms sift the air.

And against the blue her spiraled top
Is burnished by the sun,
Transpiring all the beauty
Nature gave her one by one.
Louise Fogell

New Love

Late afternoon in the warm country air,
Walking through sun rays, sensing God being there.
Listening to sounds of rustling leaves,
I followed a path between the trees.

Proudly performing upon a small hill,
A rare beauty made my heart stand still.
While birds sang their favorite chorus,
New love came to me in this forest.

Among golden hues of bright sunlight,
I marveled at this precious sight.
Standing alone in her favorite place,
She flirted with awesome style and grace.

Watching her limbs move to and fro,
My resistance had begun to run low.
Adorned in her brightest fall colors,
More majestic than all the others.

Older than I,-breathtakingly tall,—
My new love was all I saw.
I knew then she would always be,
My special own lovely Oak Tree.
Phyllis Marie King

"The Gift"

He gave the gift so easily,
    very generously,
    unconditionally,
    whole heartedly.

One only had to know him to receive this ultimate gift.
To young and old alike it was a constant lift, and
as it made the rounds it absolutely knew no bounds.

It ran deep like the oceans, and much higher than our skies.
You always felt it in his presence,
and could see it in his eyes.

No matter your wealth,
you can not buy it.
It can not be wrapped,
so don't even try it.
although he is now gone,
we all must strive to carry it on.

"What can this gift be?"
you ask of me.
The gift was his love,
abundant and free.
Marilyn Hayes

My City Lights

Feeding time came late that evening,
waiting on the snow to quiet,
but it's persistence conquers
mine as I buckle my boots and wonder
if a dollar is enough for chores after dark,
but the thought leaves me as the barn takes my sight,
causing my hands and feet to throb in
search of the outside arena lights.
A switch delivers a vision so pure, it warms me — a sky
of glistening prisms harnessing light to fall upon
a herd of horses — backs powdered like sugar
manes flowing as they fight to nourish the
foals growing inside them. Warning each other with
flattened ears, open lips,squealing through their teeth.
I cut the bales open, watching the slices of hay
fall around me like a Chinese fan. A mare moves toward me,
legs dipped in mud, begging. I brush the snow from
her blazed face, leaving dingy wet fur
and eyes that seem to reflect a warmer snow.
Kristine Cox

Full Circle

Once more the promise of timeless beauty is whispered as she
wakes and pushes back the coverlet of snow that was so lovingly
placed upon her. As it melts away she bathes in gentle showers
and then drapes her budding trees and tender flowers in pastels.

As the days grow warm and smoky song birds serenade her and
fireflies light her way at night. Now her trees are fully
leafed, she wears all the colors to be had, and when she walks
the fragrance from her flowers fill the air.

Time passes and she drapes herself in red and gold as her soft
features and flowing curves become sharply etched. Now her scent
is earthy as her trees drop their leaves and her flowers fade
away. But even as her eyes close, beneath fallen leaves the ever
constant lover tenderly embraces her hills and valleys in green
velvet arms.

And she smiles when gentle fingers lovingly brush a snowy
coverlet over her sleeping form for her dreams are peaceful
beneath its whiteness. She knows he patiently waits and so, when
she hears his whispered promise, she wakes...
C. M. Inman

The Last Petal

Walk to the light and you might see what I see,
Walk to the light so you might see all that you can be.

There's a thousand rays of light shining down upon us,
But none shine so brightly or so warmly as the light you give
    which pierces my soul.

Let me taste of your light, let me see it if only I might!

Let me go where you go and let me ride upon the flow of your wings...
Your wings which stretch the span of the oceans.

Let me rise up upon the beat of your heart

But if nothing else, let me reach for your light
So that I may touch the colors of your soul.

Given the chance I could teach you to be pleased
With the endless rainbows that circle my heart.

Each caress, my God, each look you give me blossoms into yet a new,
self-same spectrum as the colors in an endless meadow of roses.

You bloom more still with every petal that falls...
Let them fall, yes let them fall, because with them
I'll make a spice of life.

Let them fall so that I may touch the true beauty
of the truest rose ... the core ... which is your soul.

Paige Pelok

"The Task"

Do you remember that dark and stormy night
Walking together stealing time for you and I
Feeling the cold wind bringing tears into our eyes
Autumn leaves, friends and lovers
Hearts and dreams one another
Watching clouds pass deep into the night

Recalling the good times can still make us laugh
Forgiving the bad times, putting friendship to the task
Memories worth sharing with a glance from me and you
Holding tight fires burning
Healing wounds distant yearnings
In my mind there's a place that we can last

Lost in our memories the lies we told each night
Feeling this feeling I tried but can't deny
Having to share you but needing to survive
Stick together being denied
Random pain left way behind
Finding a way of being satisfied
Maybe someday you will miss me, someday maybe I can say
goodbye.

James H. Smith

Christmas

A long time ago on Christmas night
Was a large star shining ever so bright
People saw the star in east
but over
Bethlehem about which people could say the least

Three wise men knew the star was rare
And so they followed it until found a baby there
Three wise men with ages of old
Brought gifts frankincense, myrrh, and gold

Many worshipped the baby boy
Him being born such a joy
For the child christ was the Lord's son
The battle of evil and wickedness in the world
Has now begun

Karen Pickard

Daddy God

'Twas a normal day in Heaven and all through the streets
Was heard the pattering of little one's feet
It was a curious sound to the stranger standing there
As he watched all the children with their little feet bare
Where did they come from?
Where are they going?
There seemed to be hundreds, no thousands, a million?
All sizes and shapes, too many to count them
In a hurry they ran with smiles and laughter
With the stranger deciding to follow close after
So excited they scurried down the streets in a hurry
Up to the Mansion in Heaven was the center
They filed in quickly, one by one they all entered
Then grabbing a boy before entering the door
"What's happening here?" the stranger then implored
Smiling real big his answer seemed odd
As he innocently said,
    "We're going to see Daddy God!"

Martha Jean Sanderford

Faith

On a leaky ship floor I'd awoken today,
    waves of the ocean; coarse skies colored gray.
A flowery coast far distant from me;
    the flowing river mouth I can no longer see.

Come spare my soul I ask mercifully,
    for my tired arms long more for God's harmony.
Help for this ship faced such peril last night,
    as a harvest of field might wither for light.

My Lord who is kind, with his hand, calms my mind,
    good-natured, pure beauty and a heart that is rhyme.
Who'd spoken most often warning lost I may be,
    if I ventured a challenge of uncharted seas.

Poor of men always do follow their hearts,
    and by all that's inherit carry on in each part.
How cursed are the treasures that lie down beneath,
    beside the murky ocean floors that grasp at ones feet.

Listen once my dear Lord for no silence will do,
    what I've lost all along I'd long lost in you.
Truthfully all that I am is all that I lacked,
    and before my life's ended please God take me back.

Michael Lippi

Hope

    "So, how's the family?"
we all have the flu
    "Good, good. Glad to hear it."

i can't breathe...
kneecaps pushing, pushing, separating, severing my throat...
my chest...sticks? no...legs....no no NO!
please   get   OFF!
    "It sounds like you have an ulcer or perhaps, indigestion."

perhaps

screaming inside double-panes
        slapping the glass
            squealing down the wall
                scratching on the wood
                    sobbing on the floor
                        dying without death
                    I HEAR YOU.
            I AM ALWAYS LISTENING TO YOU.
        I AM ALWAYS HOLDING YOU.
            I AM ALWAYS LOVING YOU.
I AM.

K. M. Schmidt

We Are Free!

We are men, we are women and we are children.
We are father's, we are mother's and brother's and sister's,
   as well as friend's and neighbor's...

And we are free.

We are black, we are white, we are all colors.
We are Irish, we are Italian, we are Hispanic and Chinese, as
   well as every other ethnic background...

And we are free.

We are doctor's, we are lawyer's and we are teacher's.
We are printer's, we are president's and CEO's, as well as
   sanitation worker's, foremen, policemen and firemen...

And we are free.

We are employed, we are unemployed and under employed.
We live in houses, large and small; we also live on the streets,
   long and narrow...

And we are free.

We are free to speak our minds, we are free to pray to our own
   Gods as we wish, and we are free to petition our government.

We are, after all, FREE...that is how we live and nobody can
   deny us of that!
   Michael Burke

Love In Death

Acceptable loss,
We call fallen soldiers or strangers,
unless Father, Mother, Friend, or kin they be;
Then, we do not accept.

Atheist question God;
Believers renounce him.
Death burns its ugly pyre within.
Forever scared, the ashes build in our soul,
Outrun in tears to cleanse inside,
but memories turned to ash and run again.

How long until the heat is good,
'Til thoughts of love push warmth inside
for only flesh dies.
Love keeps the fallen alive
and gives the live reason to live.
   Joseph Snively

We Find Strength

We begin as a child, no recall of fear
we grow and mature, great wisdom we hear.
Sorrow, suffering, hardships and tears
we all experience throughout the years
Be not for God our hearts would despair
our burdens and grief to painful to bear.
God holds our life in the palm of His hand,
we are His children, this is His land!
His love and forgiveness we can't comprehend
for sin in our life and those we offend.
God will never leave us, He is hereby our side,
we are the ones who run and hide.
When we surrender our heart and our pride,
God uses our sacrifice to open our eyes.
Our life is transformed, our transgressions He hides,
we are now filled with the grace he provides.
Our life and our suffering is never in vein,
God is strengthening us, give glory to His name.
We are His chosen, the children of light,
in Him we find strength, in us He delights.
   Lois J. Shaw

Hand Of Fate

Our paths crossed once on that lonely beach,
We had the sense to hold out our hands and reach.
That late night talk has founded a rock,
Our friendship and love cannot be bought.
You reached out to me like no - one before,
And soon in my heart it was you I adored.

Our bliss together, the sea the sun and....
Those days of happiness, marred by some trouble.
I can honestly say I love you like no other.
The days became weeks, we became so close,
Our love for each other blossoming like a rose,
But time like flowers comes to an end.

The tears rolled down when that time had come.
Parting lovers find that words are hard to say
But I find my love for you, grows stronger everyday.
My thoughts for you night and day will not be kept away.
Parted by distance, Life must go on,
When the time is right like the hand of fate
It is to you my love that I will relate-locate.
   Paul Kennedy

Look Behind You

We have lived enough many a good times along with the bad.
We have been happy, we have been sad.
Many a year have come and gone;
What has happened from dusk to dawn?
Day after day what did you do?
Turn around look behind you,
Where are all the years gone by?
My! Oh! My! How time does fly.
The past we can not keep, the future comes yet while we sleep.
Try to remember what we did before!
Each day that passes closes one more door.
So to the future we must look, our past is a closed book.
How long our lives will be, only God knows you see.
So we must live day by day, Tell someone all about our
Gods love along the way.
While on this earth, we can live and love as we wait to be with
God above.
   Pansie Swinney

America In Travail

How I weep for mankind in it's travail,
We sing, "God Bless America" that it might prevail.

O how hard and rough man must feel,
Cold, sick and dead in it's own zeal.

What keeps you from striking out from your mercy seat?
Why should man refuse to fall at your holy feet?

How can I be filled with your joy and loving grace,
And look upon man's hardened, pain filled face.

"What" and "why" can't be asked in one line so brief,
Or answered with a heart throbbing call in grief.

When does this cry out of darkness see your light?
What keeps it moving rampant within your sight?

How can I see you in this evil nightmare of creation,
And not weep with you, pleading, God, please save this nation.
   P. Sue Johnson

Untitled

The sky... An endless stage of lights, dark and strange
Unseen creatures scream and cry, their bodies flying through the air
The wind whips violently at the horizon; Clouds moved swiftly by

There... In the middle of the vast darkness unable to reach the lights
To brighten the eternal gloom of night; To frighten the dreaded evils away
To touch hope

Somewhere... Floating through empty space, passing within my grasp
The seas so serene; The land so lush
The earth so brilliant

Another place... The wind whipping uncontrollably, forever forcing me
Away from all that I've known; Away from all that I've done
Away from all that I've loved

Far away... The clouds ever darkening with time, existing only for me
A place I cannot exist; A place I am destined to reach
A place I will never leave

The sky... Deeper with sorrow, darker, and more evil than ever before
Overcome by violent obscurity
Unmasking the depths of my soul... Helpless

Jennifer Li

And The Face Came

As I was traveling through life's trials and tribulations, A mystical
phenomenon occurred. I was able to visualize the women of my dreams,
and I was happy. It may seem, We would laugh, and dance and have
plenty of fun, but Her face was a mystery yet to come. I shared with
this Mystery women all my hopes, dreams, thoughts and even my past,
but her face never came. I soon gave up hope because I was tired of
this game. The ocean and the sand several miles away, would add more
mystic to this game I played. Why can't I see her face, was it even
meant to be? Why won't this mystery be solved for me? As time past
on and the sand but a faint memory, mystery's face became visible to
me. With this face came happiness, joy and love. This face was from
the heavens above. As I opened my eyes and really looked at this
mysterious treat, I realized that the face That came was none other
than my princess sweet. I am so thankful for the face that came. It
solved a lot of mysteries In my life so plain, and brought an end to
lots of misery and pain. It answered that inner desire to know if I
would ever love I owe a debt of thanks to the heavens above, and it's
all for You and me my love!!

Kenneth Burton

"Fragile! Handle With Prayer!"

Placid, serene, and so composed...often aloof, your guise;
Did mask a heart and soul so frail; and a keenly observant mind.
Your perpetual smile could light up a room..contagious to all present.
What could it be, was in your thoughts - those secrets never shared?

To those few souls whom you embraced, it was painfully apparent;
That glorious smile did cover well, your deeply troubled heart.
Inattentive to your own silent screams; it's said, "Still waters run deep."
That truth manifest in you, my son; recoiled inside yourself.

You donned a message not discernible to all, tho acutely familiar to me
I too bear this insufferable tiding; "Fragile! Handle with care!"
You came back as you'd intended, from your new home so far away;
But not at all how we had planned it; your body lifeless...your soul moved on.

What was it did convince you son, to take such desperate measures?...
That anguished night one year ago when to your torment you did succumb.
I've hurt with others who've endured the same grief; "Was their agony so unbearable?"
Now I can tell you first hand, dear friend; "My Lord! Oh yes! It's much worse!"

I gathered you up in my arms once more, and stroked your soft curly hair;
Then kissed your face for the very last time, "goodbye, sweet son... goodbye.
Your tragic death, a senseless loss; "Why did you have that gun?!"
"Please, I implore you tell me! Why did you take your life, my son?"

Susan Lee Hughes

Hope In Question

Our hope in God is easy when the
Waters around us are quiet,
When the trip undertaken finds
Our hope and dreams gratified.

But holding on to God is hard
When fighting with our questions,
And when the storms are fiercest,
And our boat is tossed about.

It's then our hope is shaken,
When the Creator's sound asleep,
Not knowing we are sinking, and
The waters around are deep.

Then we wonder how he, who's Creator
Of all the sea and land,
Could seem to be so unaware
Of our calamity.

Then when our hope seems weakest, God
Will calm the soul and sea,
And when we are most troubled
He'll touch, and make us complete.

Joseph B. Good Jr.

Friendship

We share a special friendship
We really care about
Each other's love and feelings
That's what friendship is all about.

We laugh together when we are happy
We cry when we are sad
But most of all we are there for each other
When things we cannot control go bad.

We only see each other
Once in a blue moon
But we are only a telephone call away
When we do get in the mood.

Friendship is a pure relationship
That all of us will need
Because without a friend to talk to
What would life on this earth mean?

Mary Collins

Ode To The Boda

Upon the sun washed deck, he used to lie,
watching through one slit eye.
Tolerating little fuss,
he was an independent cuss!

Through the howling gale, and ranging seas,
nonchalant he'd scratch his pleas.
Or, from the boom he'd hang by claw
an audience, for his circus act, to draw

Dockside, he would room ashore.
There to leave his mark and spore,
At dogs and rats and 'biens he spat,
and many kittens he begat.

But, 'er held the land in scorn,
so he'd return aboard by dawn,
and sneak a little Scotch and Soda.
No 'lubber cat was he, THE BODA!

Ian P. McFall

Reflections

We had our wars and our social ills
We had our drugs of smoke and pills

We let them know of the things we'd change
We'd make things right just rearrange

They worked so hard to give us much more
At their office or factory floor

When we took over they would heed our cry
Of peace and love until you die

As we began with decades of tries
To each other we closed our eyes

With greed and hate we built our castles
Friends and neighbors gave us hassles

Values, morals and biblical guides
All forsaken some never tried

Our world crumbles and some of us die
Of strange diseases some wonder why

Disgraced and humbled yet we still have time
To give unto others be so sublime

To those that will come to take our place
Tell them it's hard this human race

Kenneth T. Ferris

A Painter Paints

In his own room random sketches
His brush draws large moon wedges
His stroke designs a wiggly man
And in the man's hand a beer can.

"I must paint art," he whispers now
As he thinks and scratches his brow
His paint designs a hilltop afar
On the moon with a radiant star

That shines luminously then dies
As the mother of the moon cries
As her son pulls his pants on down.
He moons the world with a small frown.

A tear falls down the painter's cheek
"It's true," he says trying to seek
Inside himself to tell the world
Through art, its problem; creation's pearl.

He then makes a purple flower
Thinking of the colors power
A purple flower on the moon?
"For hope," he insists. To heal all soon.

E. M. Zacapa

Attorney At Flimflam

I got an attorney at flimflam. Who I thought
was an attorney at law. He flimflam me out
of what I had in practically no time at all.
He went to jail for a short while, and I am
sure he came out with a smile.
He must have known the law was on his side, and
that I had no chance of recovering the things
that I once had.
I will never get another attorney at flimflam,
for I will check an attorney out before he has
a chance to flimflam me out of all my ham and
bread.

Paul E. Honeycutt

The Dragon Still

He turned quite casually and asked, "Did you know the dragon well?" I looked away pretending not to notice. Feeling the dragon's breath among us.

He asked slowly again, "Did you know the dragon well?" I turned away, wanting to scream. The dragon very near, hovering over him.

He said quite plainly, "Didn't you hear me?" "Did you know the dragon well?" Well, I thought, ah yes, I knew it well. The dragon lingering still closer. I saw the flash of the tail.

He asked again, this time there was pain in his voice, "Did you know the dragon well?" I turned to answer, wondering, how should I tell? The dragon's eyes pleading, "No, please no!"

He persisted still, "Did you know the dragon well?" I started to answer, the words crushed in my throat. The dragon between us, pleading "No!"

And still he pushed on and asked, "Did you know the dragon well?" I cry out, "Yes, I knew the dragon well!" The dragon heaved a heavy sigh, knowing the truth could kill.

He pushed me farther still and asked once more, "Did you know the dragon well?" "Yes! Damn you, yes I knew the dragon well! Can't you see, it's me, the dragon, THE BEAST IS IN ME!"

He asked so very gently then, as if not to speak crushed, "So you knew this dragon well?" I turned to flee. My eyes caught in the reflection in the mirror. I could only whisper, "Yes, I knew the drag.., know that dragon well."

Linda Clifton

Desolation

The Raven remains motionless,
    perched atop the sunny cliff's side. Waiting.

Far below scuttles a mouse,
making her way across the scorching desert to the shelter
of the shady cliff.

The Raven swoops down silently, approaching His prey in a rhythmical
dance; drawing close enough to be seen and the dancing away gracefully

The mouse looks up just in time to see the Raven's piercing beak
    approaching.
    She ducks and begins to run,
    The Raven watches her try to get away,
    laughing with pleasure as the power fills Him.

He begins teasing her cruelly; darting in, screaming, and finally when
she is inches from safety - He lands in front of her.
    He looks her in the eyes, and then, quick as lightning,
    darts for her neck.

Seconds before death she raises her head and cries out his name.

He looks at the dead, crumpled body and slowly licks the blood off
    his beak.
She loved me.

The Raven waits, motionless huddled next to the small decaying body.
    Lonely.

Lisa Sweeney

The "Night"

Nobody knows from where she comes
    We see her infinite beauty blanketed with clusters of
dazzling snowflake shaped objects.
    She slowly becomes a part of our daily lives
dancing so gracefully-lingering
    Her beauty is unchanging.
Her stillness unfolds into the breaking of a new day,
    and she disappears
Only to reappear again — tomorrow.

Mary M. Gillam

Untitled

The music flows through my mind as the gentle breeze plays with the trees tossing their bows back and forth, up and down. I watch the birds flying from limb to limb, then gently settling to the ground. A squirrel appears, ever careful, always on guard, it's okay, no one else around.

As I watch, I very carefully call my memories down. As if cleaning house I take the bad ones and toss them away. The good ones I look at tenderly, dust them off and put them back gently for another day.

You my love are my newest memory and need no dusting because I call upon you all the time. When I'm afraid, or lonely, or wanting, I simply call your name and through some miracle of time or space I hear your voice telling me it's okay. I can feel your arms around me holding me in your loving embrace. Your lips kissing all my fears away.

Now as I watch the stars, I know in my heart you'll be my only love until it's time to part, or time to go on to the wondrous future that only each of us can know.

We are like the Eagles that fly through the early morning sky. We know what we're doing, and we know exactly why.

So my love, if it is written in the book to see, may we travel the currents, soar with the Eagles, finally settle to the Earth, and become one for all to see.

Patricia Irene Johnson

Destiny

A princess under her father's rule thought she was to marry a fool.
She had not met him nor knew his name, but to her, they were all the same.
To marry a fair princess was their only goal,
They would never gaze into her soul.
Knowing she must run away to be exempt, she only had but one attempt.
Late one night she left her castle and hid away
for the next morning was to be her wedding day.
She took with her not a single possession, she had but only one
intention - to come upon that little shack, without ever looking back.
In her new found dwelling place, she came upon a caring face;
He hadn't been there very long, but her questions, she did not prolong.
Alas, he was a poor man without a goal yet, he dared to gaze deep into her soul.
And within a day, or two, perhaps three, they fell in love and lived happily.
Their love for each other would forever last yet, never once did they discuss the past.
And to share the memories they did carry
would have shown he was the prince she was to marry.

Nicolina Marra

We So Cool

Sometimes we all act a fool, but we think we so cool.
We don't even know our ABC's
The only letters we know is B.B.D.
We cut class, some smoke grass.
Some hate school, but all in all
We so cool.
We buy name brand, because we can.
We don't wear Lee cause it affects Popularity.
We don't know math or even a little band,
We do all that is easy and at hand.
Some don't like to follow rules, but in our heads we so cool.
We buy guns and sell drugs, we steal, lie and cheat,
Even steal sneakers off people feet.
Being stupid makes us look like fools,
But to our selves we so cool.

Natasha L. Walker

A Friend Is Dead

A friend of mine died today.
His life of talent never tested.
No canvas will tell of his life
Nor song to play his deed.
Poets no rhyme will write.

His speech was of a better time
when youth was free.
Constant search for a purpose
angered by waste that was to be.

Life is for meaning
Yet no meaning was his.
Emptiness only, loneliness always.
Still my life felt his impact.
My purpose found by his dream.

A friend of mine died today.
His passing simply on paper.
His death just in my mind.
The waste of his life spilling from my pen.

Bottles lying in the corner will tell of his role.
Murdering his spirit killing his soul.

George Phillips

Carpenters Of The House Of Love

In the beginning we came together as inexperienced carpenters anxious to construct our house of love.
So, we began building aimlessly; each of us erecting a need, raising a want and binding them together with emotional commitment. The desire existed, but the framework was shaky, lacking something that we were incapable of seeing and feeling.

And finally at your unrelenting insistence we abandoned our project to search for meaning elsewhere, but our structure remains, gently touched by our visits, swayed by the other's decisions. These are not nicks to the wood nor blows to the frame. They serve as reinforcing beams eventually making "us" and this relationship stronger, and encouraging a sense of willingness.

So now I see, perhaps as you do, that this abandonment was only an illusion. We came together as lovers to build a structure lacking a foundation. And though painful, we set our tools aside only to find those necessary to lay the foundation of friendship. Again there is love, but its form and function are more clearly defined and less threatening.

Through the abiding love of friendship our house becomes a home. It's construction is sound with security and still bound by emotions and commitment. It encourages acceptance, offers comfort and radiates love. We are carpenters of the house of love, building upon today rather than the uncertainty of tomorrow. And with continued effort perhaps ours will one day be a home of love with a foundation of friendship.

Marty Weems

Eighty-Seventh Street

The man sits there
Gazing, into the dirty streets
None notice —
Dirt and grime cover
his rough and rigid face.
His clothes torn and worn
he wonders where he will get
his next meal.
Hours pass ....
he hasn't shaved or
showered in years.
As night comes he sleeps,
to relive the same day.

Curtis Anschutz

A Child's Plea to Jesus

God is good
God is great!
Please don't let me kill or hate.
If I do,
I'll get sued.
In your way,
I will pay.
I love you Jesus and God
Amen!

Donnell Britt

Winter

Your love was turning colder
Golden leaves came on the trees.
Both were gone by winter
by choice and with the breeze.

You weren't here to see the snow fall
Or to see the flood of tears
the season was so lonely
the coldest one in years.

But as the sun was melting
the very last trace of snow
it uncovered some understanding
now, I think I know.

Its spring my heart is thawing
the leaves are shining green
I realize the only ice princess
was the one that I have been

To you I was always the winter
everything shaded with frost
but now your storm has ended
I'm here, alone, I'm lost.

Erin Prestage

My All In All

He's my guide each day
He directs ALL my way's.
He's my strength when I am weak
He's my joy when I am sad
When satan makes me feel bad
He's the "Lily" in my valley's
He's my bright and morning star!
He's with our children near and far
There's many of "His" angel band
That protect my family daily
And helps them to stand
In "EVERY" situation
Thank you God!

Bea Woods

Lifetimes

The sun rises,
graceful, natural, beautiful,
full of expectation.
In the young day,
the gentle, glowing warmth
shows promise.
Rising constant,
reaching disappointments,
cold winds blow,
countering the warmth.
The sun, victorious,
outshines the cold
and the day grows old.
Descending gently and slowly
upon the earth,
glowing brightly,
differently than before.
Eyes close,
the day closes,
the death of the sun.

Christina Ostroff

Doll

I am a doll, my face porcelain, my
hair made from the hair of a horse's
mane, and my clothes made of cloth.

I am a doll worn from the hands
of many generations, surviving the
torture each had to give.

I am a doll, once that was charming and
beautiful, but now ragged and ugly.
Yet my keepers adore me as if I
were a flower whose petals never
wilted.

To them I am a doll of great age
and beauty and that is why they
keep me.

Annie Keen

Half Filled Reason

Half filled darkness
Half filled light,
Half filled promises
are just not right

Why do we blame ourselves?
Why do we try?
Why do we sit and wait
as time goes by?

And again I ask you,
And again the question is why?
And again the answer is
there's no reason to try.

Half filled days
Half filled nights,
Half of being blind
is seeing the light.

Crystal Eckhart

Beauty

Beauty is a word
but mostly its a vision
it lies in your head
and not in your diction

Mike Allen

Tennis Pro

Soft hands
hard thighs
muscles cough
like twisted wires

Unnatural curves
a searing stretch
a shattering surge

Wiping the sweat
on the arm of a shirt
poised like an egret
before his great flight

winning or losing
dusty and wet
quietly telling
what went wrong
what went right
and why.

Bernice Statman

The Old Steel Lady

The weaving trails of steel ribbons
Have fallen silent and still
Bathed in the mist of dawn
And touched by autumn's chill
The sounds of the night voices
Which once filled the midnight air
Are now but faint echoes
Floating in the dark somewhere
The trains have long since gone
And the silence has taken hold
As they follow their glistening light
Under a blanket of dark and cold
Now the hours pass by so slowly
As the old steel lady silently weeps
For until the coming dawn awakens her
Wrapped in her splendor she sleeps

John R. Shiers

The Love Of Life

There is something we all
have to eventually deal with
and it's called death.

Nobody wants a loved one or
a good friend to die

But sometimes we just have
to say farewell or just a
simple easy goodbye.

We all should love life as
it comes and understand it's
ups and downs.

Life is precious we should
hold on to it as tight as
we can.

Because we won't always
have a lending hand.

Jennifer Laubacker

"The Blind Beggar"

A beggar sits blind as can be,
He asks the Son - mercy on me.
No noise they shout - do not come near,
Jesus himself said, "Call him here."

Take heart they called and up he came,
Jesus asked him - his want to name.
He threw his cloak and then began,
My Teacher let me see again.

Jesus received the beggar's prayers.
He moves us out beyond our cares.
The word is out. The world to tell.
Now go, your faith has made you well.

Edgar P. Roosa

God's Love

For every trial, God has relief,
He has a comfort for every grief.
For every pain, God has a balm,
And for every storm, he has a calm.

For every sickness, God has a cure,
He has a solution for what we endure.
For every circumstance, God has a way,
And for every need, he provides each day.

For every disease, God has a healing,
And for every burden, go to him kneeling.
God has unending love for everyone,
He showed how much by sending his son.

Delta McLauchlin

Christmas Present

Santa has a heavy sack.
He likes to eat sweet snacks.
With his long beard,
Ho! Ho! You can hear.
He walks softly on his boot,
When an owl goes hoot
See him come from the North,
Presents coming forth ,
Is he nice in such a flight?
Merry Christmas! What a beautiful sight!

Charles Won

Loving Laughter

Laughter gazing is loving me-
He lunges for my palm,
To kiss and taste its Tropic scent,
while shivers shake my arm.

His words do tremble in my heart.
Like fire, he lights my soul.
When gone, I dance to feel him near,
To sing his heart I stole.

Laughter whispers while flowers frown.
Tickling with whiffs, He smiles.
I, with envy, grab his whimsies
and throw them to my fists.

Their scathing cries are vile,
while Living Chaos chases me,
Down seas where sins have fought,
Roaring for me to leave.

Two days, trills of thunder...
Trickling Trouble taps on my door.
Inmost, he seizes me,
Vowing Laughter forever more...

Cynthia Medina

Mary Had A Little Lamb

Mary had a little Lamb
  He was born the Son of God
He left His home in Heaven
  Here on Earth to trod.

He walked among the sinners
  To the saints He gave bread
And preaching free Salvation
  Through His blood to be shed.

He said to follow Him always
  Regardless of the cost
He would always be near you
  To help you bear your cross.

So, seek Jesus and Salvation
  Before your soul is dammed
For Jesus is the Holy One
  He is Mary's Little Lamb.

Henry Pierce

Tsunami

Listen,
Hear the rolling thunder sound,
Coming closer and closer,
Screaming a call of death.
Run,
Run away from your land,
It's coming,
Coming yet closer and closer,
It crashes,
Like the world was destroyed,
A bang,
Houses and land destroyed
Water crushes and grinds them
To the ground.
Death,
People losing their lives to water,
It's alive,
And it lives for disaster.

Allison Van Hof

"What Is Love?"

Love is a feeling that is in your
heart
It is a great feeling that also
brings sorrow.
It is dangerous but sweet.
Love is when too people see eye
to eye.
Love is a passion that they
feel.
Love is heat between too lovers.
Love is hope that brings
happiness.
Love hurts when your heart is
broken.
Love can be for ever if you
want it to be.
Love is special when you want
it to be.

Bobbie Jo Wetzel

A Virgin's Fantasy

Twisted throbbing mounds of flesh,
  hearts to hearts, mouths to breast.
Fluids rushing temperatures rise,
  moans of pleasure, hips rub thighs.
Beads of sweat jerking about,
  screams of mercy, bursting out.
Tongues go searching eyes just stare,
  nostrils sniffing, dampen hair.
Hands tingling holding tight,
  taste buds swelling, teeth that bite.
Time seems endless love so pure,
  place so perfect, choice so sure.
Slumber takes you world of peace,
  hunger wakes you, holy feast.
Skins glowing no one knowing,
  head spinning, happy ending.

Barbara Wright-Overstreet

Rural Scenery

Baby possum
Here you lie ...
Struck at night
Doomed to die!

Lovely fawn
Eyes of brown
What clown chose
To mow you down?

Deadly trucks
Speeding cars
Motorcycle men
  from Mars ...

Wander into any road,
Toddler, colt,
  Big old toad...

Racing engines
thoughtless driver
Who will be
the lone survivor?

Gloria McMahan

"Christmas Is Jesus"

The sinless child in a manger lay,
He's bed was just a pile of hay.
Christmas is Jesus!,
Into this world of sin,
He came from Heaven the lost to win,
Christmas is Jesus!
One terrible day He hung on a tree,
So give salvation to you and I to me.
Christmas is Jesus!
May we take the time,
To get Hid Gospel to all mankind.
Christmas is Jesus!

Betty B. Angel

If We Would Care

"If we would care like
HE would have us care,"
"If we would share like
HE would have us share."

Judge our self forget self
We would have spiritual wealth,
Better health
Joy and peace sweet relief
"If we would care."

Arlene Wiley

Buddy

I have a dog named Buddy,
He's really, really black.
I love him because he's cuddly,
And he always scratches my back.

We always get into fights,
Because he thinks he's so cool.
He really loves to bite,
And he sometimes leaves drool.

He's not very big,
And he's not very small.
He likes to chew on twigs,
And he likes to play with balls.

My Buddy's very smart,
He can jump really high.
He'd probably eat Poptarts,
And one day he'll probably die.

Josh Montanaro

Statistics

Watch where they are
    hiding in the dark,
    lurking in the corners.
You can point them out a mile away,
    so stay away.

No you're wrong, you can't
    really tell.
It's probably a friend or someone
    you know.
Thinking it's power or it's right
    to do.

One of the statistics - that's all it is
    to you.
One to three for women;
    one to seven for men.
So count; one, two, three, dear God
    it could be you or me.
So don't be the third or even the seventh.
Because you'll just end up another statistic
    in the book of rape.

Bree Lynn Johnson

Through His Eyes

Cup in hand, outstretched wide,
His glasses black, white cane tipped red,
A torn, gray suit, dog by his side,
He is that which we all dread.

A vase of pencils does he sell
For whatever he can make;
While busses leap and people yell,
The Lord's protection does he take.

As the day turns into night,
And to his small flat he does drift,
He, without a ray of light,
Still gives thanks for his great gift:

That of LIFE.

Gerald M. Warkans

Anna Marie

The winter wind blows bitter
and her goddess chants
to a bare white moon.
I will dream of her
and cry in my sleep.

Cindy Clark

Lodestone

The tighter you try to
hold on to a memory, the
further it drifts away
So just lie still, and
it will come
Floating back to the
center of your mind
And although the temptation
to reach out and touch it
is very great,
Don't - for the memory
will again evade your grasp
and disperse into now
And won't come back again
until it catches you unaware.

Amy Chenier

Freedom Flight

Uncertain eyes, untried wings.
Hopes and fears and countless things
Invade your mind and pierce your soul,
But high above, the sky's your goal.
Spirits rise...
And start to soar.
A burning heart
And an opened door.
No looking back
Your time has come.
Direct your path up to the sun.
Your freedom flight has just begun.

Julie Ilkanic-Butler

Omnipotent One, How Can It Be

Be patient O Lord with my prying
How can it possibly be
Certainly you can't be implying
You nailed your son to a tree

It was not mine, But your complaint
The requirement that he die
He could have lived without constraint
To murder another I do not buy

Omnipotence is your claim to fame
To murder was your decree
This just brings shame to your name
Worse yet, to claim it for me

No matter the length of his days
To take away his life
What you say is "Mysterious ways"
I call wrong, not right

If you had supernatural power
And I'm sure that by now you'll agree
You need not to have made him cower
We could have lived right by your decree

Dillard (Dill) Henderson

Dancing

Dancing it is really neat,
because I dance upon my feet.
Swirling, twirling, jumping high,
It seems my feet begin to fly.

Irish music fills the air,
costumes of color are everywhere.
Judges stare with solemn eyes,
choosing who will win first prize.

Caitlin Stewart

Appreciated

I failed to let you know
    how good you were to me.
How special, kind and caring
    you really could be.
You thought I over looked
    the things you did for me.
The extra time you spent
    so I'd have more time free.
The hours of your time
    you spent in helping me.
This was a special gift you gave
    but thought I didn't see.
Oh, how truly wrong you were
    I only forgot to say.
What was genuinely in my heart
    on any special day.
Sometimes, I'm surely slow
    it takes awhile to see.
But I always appreciated
    the things you did for me.

Douglas Duane Ware Henry

His Almighty Hand

The power of God is tremendous,
how he makes the heavens roar.
And with his almighty hand he
makes the rain to pour.
The rain pours out of the gutters
onto the earth.
Giving God's creation a new birth.
The day was hot the humidity high
Now God shows his love from
way up in the sky.
It chills my spine to witness
such a feat.
That there's not a soul out on
the street.
I'll say my prayers tonight,
tomorrow watch things grow.
And later on watch his almighty
hand make it snow.

Bill Stamper

"Would You"

If I told you
how much I care,
would you be there?

If I told you
you're always on my mind,
would you never leave me behind?

If I held you
a place in my heart,
would we never part?

If I asked you
to show me the way,
what would you say?

Jennifer Ouellette

Spring

Dead
Cold, Stiff
Sleeping, buried, nothing
Dark, black, sun, bright
Moving, jumping, walking
Warm, awake
Alive

Joshua Kuelper

Child's Hand

Small hand of a small child
How much pleasure it gives
To your heart
When it is offered to lead you
Across the crossing spot.

When your eyes are failing
And the years stop counting,
When you need love and help
The child's hand is always there.

You sweet little people
The small hand you give
Is treasure,
So innocent, so true, not false,
Thanks to you we love you more.

Give me your hand and lead me
I feel so proud to know you,
I hope you know and feel
The love I have for you.

Hedy Wolf Formanek

How Precious Are The Children

How precious are their faces
How soft and gentle their touch
How their arms reach out to hold you
It's something you cherish so much

How loving are their little hands
How sweetly they stroke your face
How they look up to you with admiration
It's a feeling you just can't replace

How wide their eyes with wonder
How full their hearts with love.
How simple and pure their thoughts
It's something you think a lot of

How they look to you for guidance
How you keep them safe and warm
How you shield them from life dangers
It's to keep them free from harm

It's love unlike any other
How powerful yet so mild
How wonderful and gratifying
How precious is a child

Jennifer Moseley

Guardian Angel

How soft you flutter
How strong the light
Your wings hold me
all through the night

I do not always see you
But your presence I can feel
Your thoughts guide me
I know you are real.

Without you to carry my prayer
I could not face the day
Without you I would
Lose my way.

Donna M. Spencer

Snowy Christmas

Snow is lots of stars
coming down from the blue sky
on a Christmas night

Christen Squillaro

Promises

Ah, these snowflakes
how they dance, how they play
with the wind
coquettishly and seductively.
They lie down on the bare branches,
hug them, fall in love,
melt
and turn into water and blood,
fill the veins of the earth,
become flowers and resin
and clusters of grapes.

"I'll come back", he said.

Yet he remains here
enchanted by the snowflakes
still dancing around him.

George C. Chryssis

Behold! The Lamb Of God

Christ, Begotten, Incarnate,
Humankind to recreate.
Salvation to impart,
From sin to depart.

Pain and passion,
Overflow into compassion.
Your love to include,
None need to exclude.

Teach me Your way,
Your truth to stay.
Your light overcomes darkness,
Let me be its constant witness.

Though Satan may desecrate,
Your Spirit to consecrate.
Pour out Your enabling grace,
By faith to run this race.

Salvation achieved,
Your saints to receive.
May Your triumphant glory,
Ever be my story.

Jerry S. H. Eng

Fat Chance

None of life's awards
hung from his neck.
Like burnt toast
he was
done over
and overdone,
heartlessly singed,
emotionally crusted.

As if just beyond chance,
she came along.
Like a butter knife
she was
scraping
his deep blues
to sky bright.
spreading warmth,
then love
upon her caringly
nurtured
sustenance.

Bill Burnette

"Forest Vision"

Rumble of silence,
falling streams and rustling leaves
play nature's music,
to cries of soaring eagles
hidden within green valleys.

Gregg Matsushima

Lullaby For Jesus

Sleep, sleep,
Hush, little baby.
God dressed in diapers
Cute as can be,

Coos with the dove
Resting in moon light,
Suckling of Mary,
Messiah is He.

Busily absorbing
The world he created
The human adventure,
Lies at his feet.

So sleep now.
Follow tomorrow
The plan God created,
But now you must sleep.

Cynthia Eddinger

Storm

As I watch the raindrops splatter,
I also hear the thunder shatter,
The tempo of the falling rain,
Hitting upon my window pane.

As the thunder roars through the night,
Lighting lends its bolt of light.
The wind is whistling a lonely tune,
Hoping it will be over soon.

In my room I sit and wonder,
Where Mother Nature finds her thunder.
Is it woven on Thor's loom?
And can it be found up passed the moon?

Faster and Faster Thor sends his thunder,
on down to Earth to do its plunder.
Let the rain and thunder ROAR!
It stops . . .it ceases . . .
It is NO MORE!

Joseph D. Padilla

"The End"

The end is drawing nigh
I can feel it in the air
We could try to stop it
But no one seems to care

Some day it will happen
The earth will start to shake
The sky will turn to black
And the seas will start to bake

Survivors building homes
Bodies every where
People can't find food
Death is in the air

It may come today
Or it may wait a hundred years
But the end is coming
I can feel it drawing near

Carl Hanson

Foreign

To know true unconditional love
Is a gift once in a lifetime
To know true unbridled passion
Is a gift once in a lifetime
To know both is truly a blessing
To lose both is truly a curse.

Charles V. McClain III

Exclusively Halloween

I'm neither ghost nor goblin.
I come from their homes every
Thirty-first of October a-hobbin'.

My dead body walks live,
Thus, I am a zombie,
In some sense of the word.

"Thick or Treat" is absurd—
I knock at their doors and,
Like loser-boy Charlie Brown
They drop rocks in my bag.

Other children are wolves in sheep's
Clothing and mother's a hag.
I receive candy I cannot eat
Because my blood's filthy sweet.

All the candy has pins in it
And jack-o'lanterns laugh
Behind candle-lit smiles.

Occasionally I'm given the
"Thunk!" of a shiny red apple.
The rest is a sack full of stones.

Silence Speaks

Untitled

One day when I had nothing to do,
I decided to write a poem for you.
I didn't know where to start.
so I searched the bottom of my heart.

When the mountains no longer stand,
when the ocean is no longer blue,
that is when I will no longer love you.
My love for you is strong.
my love for you is true,
I will always love you.

I wanna hold you night and day,
because I love you in every way,
I wouldn't know what to do,
if I didn't have you.

Barry M. Davis

Little One

Do we see?
I don't think so...
A little fellow told me so.

For with his simplest way
  to say
I want some love
  in the worst way.

Afraid he'd harm
  himself or others,
I held on tight to calm him...

And with angelic big blue eyes,
He looked up at me and said,
"Tie me up AGAIN."

Jane Gawne

I Want To Live

I want to live to help someone in life
I don't want to be lazy,
selfish not doing what's right.
Life is so precious, no words
can find to tell, how each
part of our bodies precisely
works so well.
Our wonderful heart, no
bigger than our fist, yet
works so efficiently and
does not miss,
To pump the blood into
each delicate part. That's
our wonderful, magnificent heart.
I want to live.

Barbara Ann Bady

Yesterday

Only yesterday
I drove down
this road of green trees
and rolling hills;
of fragrant flowers...
daffodils.

But, today
a snow crown lay
on bare trees' limbs
and motionless hills,
leaving no sign
of the flowers it kills
and no signs
of yesterday.

Jeannette Church

To Hear, Or Not To!

I like my little quiet world,
I feel secure and I have peace.
It seems to banish all my fears
And stressful moments cease!

But when my ears need extra help
To hear what others have to say,
I'm glad that I have help at hand
To assist me in this way.
So into my ears my helpers go
To trap the sound waves,high and low.

There's nothing perfect in this world,
  (I learned this years ago!)
But if you set your sight
On the side that is bright,
It will downgrade lots of woe!

Arleen McMahon

Silk Horse

The horse is like silk
as he runs through the
fields you feel like a leaf
as he runs real fast
the breeze feels so good
as you ride far away
and as you lay down
to rest he lays down
as well.

Jeffery Whitaker

A Date With Neal

He was so neat!
Incredible hair!
Immaculate and could kiss!
Really, he had such a Dirty Mind.

Anne Englert

The Mighty Oak

When I was young and in my prime,
I filled my house with kids.
I never cared to do the things,
That other women did.

I never yearned for riches,
Or to gad about, be "free",
A liberated woman,
Worrying about "identity".

I never felt discontented,
Or stifled in my home.
I felt I was a might oak,
And mighty oaks don't roam.

After all, I had my family,
Who needed lots of care.
Who upon arriving home each day,
Looked to find me there.

My family made me what I am.
I'm happy for it all.
Now the mighty oak can rest in peace,
As her leaves begin to fall.

Janet Russell

I Have Love

I was drained of life and soul
I had no one,
I had no one to love
No one to hold

There was no one that I could trust
There was no one that cared
They said love is a must
But I was too scared

Then you came along
Ready to give all your love,
You came along
And showed me how to love.

You took your time
And showed me you cared,
You took me into your life,
Now I am no longer scared

I have trust
And I have Faith
I have love
And I am not afraid

Cecelia Maser

Santa's Misfortune

On Christmas Eve as I lay in bed
I heard a noise up over head
The clattering of the reindeer feet
For they had come thru rain and sleet
Then in the chimney came a noise
Of santa and his bag of toys
I'm stuck I heard him softly say
Then a big loud thump much to my dismay
With a face of black and a nose of red
I took one look and ran back to bed

Hazel Heins

"Where Did He Go"

As I look for him to and fro,
I just "wonder," where did he go?
As I sat by his side, little
did I realize it was his time
    to die.

He did not die for God was by
    his side.
He just took him to a better home
    in the sky.
Where did he go? to reside by
    God's side!

Carolyn M. Barton

The Stars of the Night

The stars shine gently through the night
I lie here wondering is the
World going to be alright.
The stars of the night have
Great power and light.
They make you dream and
Wish you can take a flight.
The magic of the stars comes
Out only through the night.

Eric Collins

My Little Brother

When my little brother was born,
I liked to hold him in my arms
We would laugh and play, us two,
Just like most kids like to do
My brother was always there for me,
And always kept me company
As we grew up through the years,
I wiped away all his tears
I am thankful for my little brother,
I wouldn't pick any other.

Rebecca L. Mize

"Pictures On The Wall"

As I walked slowly down the hall
I looked up at the pictures on the wall
They all seemed to look back at me
As If to say, stop and remember
We are all here with you
They were of my children of years past
No longer with me, all gone so fast
Each seem to say remember
Oh! How I did as my eyes filled
A tear I shed as I looked
Up again at the wall
It seemed my life stood still in the hall
While looking at the pictures on the wall.

Betty E. Davis

My Love

I love my husband,
I love my sons;
I love my daughters
Every one;
But most of all
I love my God
Who made this earth,
on which I trod;
And gave his son
To die for me,
That by his love
I am set free.

Elveda Smith

What I Miss

I miss the banging of the front door
I miss the trips to the toy store,
I miss our cookies and milk times
I miss your words, "It's mine,"
I miss you curled up in my lap
I miss you telling me, "I'm not fat,"
I miss your miss matched clothes
I miss you funny little poise,
but what I miss the most of all
now that you are a man, a telephone call.

Anita Kyratzis

Dear Sweet Heart

When I was.....LITTLE,
I needed a Mom and Dad.

When I was....SMALL,
I needed a pony.

When I was....MEDIUM,
I needed a friend.

When I was....LARGE,
I needed to be whole.

You have made my life EXTRA LARGE,
And all I need is LITTLE again.
A "LITTLE Love" only you can give.

Christine Moore

Untitled

To me, love is like a seed
I plant one in everyone I meet.
Some take root and grow
While in others, they die.
In some people, it grows like a weed
    that needs to go.
In others, it blooms into a garden
    of flowers
Still in one other, it becomes
    a perfect rose that never dies.

Anthony McDonald

I Miss You

I rise with the sun, missing you,
I pretend to have fun, missing you,
I run to the phone, missing you,
I sleep alone, missing you,
I watch the rain, missing you,
I deal with the pain, missing you,
I hear a love song, missing you,
I can't go on, missing you.

Aishia Roberts

Phantom

With my mind's eye
I reach to trace
The planes and contours
of your face;
I pause to place
My fingertips
Upon the memory
of your lips...
And sigh and weep
Once more to find
That you live only
In my mind.

Joy Allbritton

The Time I Tell You Why

I wear a mask
I refuse to be me
Please don't ask
And don't try to see

I refuse to be real
And let out my true side
I can't tell you how I feel
It's too hard for me to confide

I have been hurt in the past
By those I loved most of all
It may have been the last
But how shall I upon you call

Will you always be around
Or like the rest depart
However this may sound
I love you with all my heart

Please understand me
And always listen when I cry
The next time may be
The time I tell you why

Claudette L. Watson

No More Tears

As a baby you loved and held me all night
I remember when you used to sing while
holding me so tight.
You never stopped working for us it put
blister on your hands
We never heard you say I couldn't
I can't you've always said I can.
Now that we've grown older and each
one of us moved away
It's time to let you know in our hearts
you'll always stay.
Everyone makes mistakes lord knows I've
made mine
But you've always been there for me and
everything turned out fine.
I wish I could give you what you've
given me through the years.
So hold me tight, let me see a smile
and please mama no more tears.

Anita Borrel

Fantasy

Carried by the gentle breeze,
I ride on wings of love.
The open valleys and green hills
are my home;
The sweet nectar of the flowers
my hearts delight.

In the stillness of the night,
I whisper my love,
And burn the flame of passion
in your heart.

With the dawn I awaken,
and drink the sweet mountain dew.

My Love...
I am your hearts delight...
your fantasy...

Frances Falk

Growing Closer

As I stood looking at the sky
I saw two clouds go drifting by.
They drifted closer as they went
And seemed to have but one intent,
To merge completely into one
As they approached the setting sun.

Then as I sat beneath a tree
I saw two birds fly over me.
They too seemed closer as they flew,
And as they faded from my view,
They also seemed to blend as one
As they flew towards the setting sun.

And I thought, how like you and me,
We're just as happy as can be.
In every hour, in every way
We grow closer every day,
And we too become as one
As we approach the setting sun.

John Riedel

Friendships

My friendships are the seeds of my life
I scatter them recklessly
Some blossom and branch out with
little care.
Some are in need of tender and constant
care.
My friendships are food for my
heart, my mind, my soul.

Anne Henry O'Brien

You and Me Now and Forever

Through the darkness
I see a shadow
a shadow of you
when you were here.

I miss the good times
when we were happy
I got to know you
more and more each year.

Now forever seems
like one day
I finally realize how much I miss you
I have so much I needed to say.

Please don't leave me
be by my side
you'll never leave me
You are my guide.

What you've done for me
will always be
This is forever
for you and me.

Angie Auman

Love Displayed

The lovely roses I behold
displayed in odd array
Remembrance of our love once new
and growing every day.
Not fancy by a florists' hand
a message clearly sent
Most importantly about this gift
is the love it represents.

Amy Carden

Love Will Bring Us Back

Here I am again;
I see the end is near;
I try to hang on;
In my eyes, lies a tear.

Oh, my sweet lady;
For all my love's for you;
Realize that I'm sorry;
For all the pain I've given you.

In my heart is the dream;
In my mind are the memories;
Of the days we were happy;
Of the time we shared dreams.

I know I need you, lady;
But the truth has settled in;
You deserve to be happy;
So a new life you'll begin.

Carry on and don't look back;
I'll simply fade away;
The love that we carry;
Will bring us back together... someday.

Glenn Zimmerman

Untitled

When I look into your eyes
I see what I once had,
I had my time of cries
And wondering how it went bad.

Then I realize at least we're friends
And I get to talk to you,
And then I see that around the bend
You and I are not yet through.

So we'll just keep on talking
And on the road of life,
We will continue walking
As friends or husband and wife.

Don't forget yesterday
And remember me tomorrow,
Think about me today
And lets throw away our sorrow.

David Nist

You Are My Day

When I see the sunrise
I see your smile
When I smell the morning air
I smell your sweet scent
When the sun touches me
I feel your warmth
When it gently starts to rain
I think of your gentleness
When the light fails
I see you lying next to me
When I dream at night
I feel my arms holding you tight
When I see you
My heart trembles

Justin Neil Jones

Lightning

Lightning strikes a tree
blue light falling from the sky
and scattered on the ground

Jeff Bemrich

Inner Feelings

As each day passes
I started to think
Wondering about something
As my eyes blink
You feel a sharp pain
Like a knife
It's sad that someone
Just loose a life
Thinking about life
As it smears
Seeing someone you love
Disappears.

Arthur Weathers

God's Sweet Gift

It seems like only yesterday
I stood in silent prayer
Awaiting God's sweet gift of life
My baby, sweet and fair.

And when I saw that precious child
My every fibre glowed
With all the joy and pride and love
A father's soul could know.

And now I wait again in prayer
This little child, to me,
Is bravely fighting pain and fear
To bear her child to be.

So if it's true, as all believe,
Death's shadow passes near
I'll stand, sweetheart, beside your bed
And whisper prayers sincere.

So give that little baby life
And nurture her with love
For you, my precious little girl,
Came here from up above.

Charles E. Kunz

"Sleepless"

Why Me?
I struggle and struggle
But am unable to sleep
I do this to myself
The reasons are clear
My fears of reality are unbearable
My problems are numerous
As many my age do
Some trivial some complex
Complex outweighing trivial
Sleeping is diminished with each one
Day after day
I hide this truth
No more now its out
To you in the same situation
I release this knowledge
Now you know you're not the only one.

Andrew Pounds

Untitled

Winter's lifeless sight of love
brings warmth of a fireplace
set for fall when you
fall in love once
again to springs new life and
creation that warms a heart
filling it with all the warm
feelings of summer...

Elizabeth Gutierrez

Why Didn't I

You the eldest.
I the youngest.
Why didn't I write.
Why didn't I call.

You went to war.
I was not there.
You came home.
Then I was there.

The days gone by.
The nights long gone.
Twenty-one years,
Was given the chance.
Why didn't I write.
Why didn't I call.

But now its to late.
For life is to short.
And time is no more.
Why didn't I write.
Why didn't I call.
O God, Why didn't I care.

Carol J. Hess

Why?

When I think of you,
I think of what we had.
You made me feel special,
you made me feel so glad.

All the times that you were near,
you'd comfort me, and take away my fears.

But now that you're gone,
I have such sorrow,
For I now know, that there is no tomorrow.
No tomorrow with you, makes my life
sad and blue, I still cannot see,
why God took you from me.
Why God? Why?
Why did this have to be?

Catie Wire

You And Me

As the wind blows through the trees,
I think of you.
As the rain falls to the earth,
I long of you.
As the world spins around the sun,
I want you.
As I sleep alone at night,
I need you.
Take me, I am yours to hold,
don't drop me.
Take me as I am to you,
Don't change me.
You, you are my life,
I love you.
You, you are the songs of love,
I hear you.
You, you have a life of love,
I live for you !!!!!!!!

Jackie L. Harrelson

Untitled

Peace,
    the echo of love
    the sound of silence.

Mary R. Wictor

To Mother, With Love

When I was young I gave you dandelions.
I thought they were flowers.
I didn't know they were weeds.
Roses are what you really earned
For the devotion you gave to me.

But you deserve so much more than that
And I find it hard to describe.
You have given so much of yourself
Yet have asked so little in return.

On this day I wish to show
My thankfulness and pride,
That you have been my friend
For these few years gone by.

I wish to give you roses,
But you would not understand,
Because what you are used to
Are dandelions in my hand.

Erin Curry

"Memories"

I thought you really loved me
I thought you really cared
I thought you really cherished
the moments that we shared.

The time that we're together
the time that we're apart
I always think about you
you're locked inside my heart.

I know we've had some trouble
We can try to make a mend,
but please don't let this happen
don't just let it end.

Carole Morgan

Introspect

When I think about the past
I try hard to forget
Yet it seems that I relive it
Everyday of my life

I want my past to be past
And my future happier
But the tapes keep replaying
Those things that I want dead

How long will this go on?
How much can I endure?
Don't I deserve a happier life?
Why should it be me?

I've tried hard as hard as I could
To make things right for most
The harder I try, the worse it becomes
Should I just stop trying?

I know there's happiness for me somewhere
For I feel it in my bones
Before I leave this world someday,
I'll find the happiness I deserve.

Julien K. Boayue

Wants

I want to be a part of two.
I want to learn to move with the rhythms
    of another life near me.
To feel the beating of another's
    love for me close.
I want to know what it is like
To live in the presence of someone
    Who wants to tend to me.
In warm and nurturing ways.
I want to feel the sweetness
    of loves ways in my life.
I want to share space in someone's heart
    with the other things they love.
I want to be a part of two.

Jennifer L. Johnson

Jeff

Your senses are bare
I want to pad you with poems
Give you skins of verse
from hearts gone by

All opened up
Who knew the hurt
didn't stop with time
and changed
what made them cry

The tear they shed
for injustice done
gave forth another
as they turned

from the misery
of a harm imposed
to the ache
that na horizon could be so clean.

Janet Rutherford

Untitled

There was a poem
I wanted you to hear
it had colors and rhythm
and a story most dear
But I kept it to myself
out of sorrow and fear
that you'd hear it too soon
and never again come near
But you read it anyway
and it made you laugh
you saw me too soon
and it cut me in half
But I laugh too
and want the hurt to end
as I sit here alone
with a broken heart to mend
We don't know where we are
we don't know the way
we can't see tomorrow
all we have is today.

Cari Stamper

Untitled

Sanctified Holy Union
Ceaseless Aching
Sanctioned by the word of man
True Stagnates
Anarchic Energy Nullified
Love Waits

Alison Stateman

Penny Candy

Long ago when I was three
I went out on a shopping spree.
I headed for the candy store
With just four pennies, nothing more.
Behind the counter stood Grandma Brown
Who had the best candy in the town;
She also had patience, sweet and mild
For this frisky, energetic child.

Jelly beans and lemon drops
Licorice whips and Tootsie pops,
As I teetered happily from toe to heel
I tried to coax a special deal.

With eager eyes and hopeful mirth
I said, "I'll take penny's worth."
"One of these and two of those,
A chocolate kiss, a sugar rose."
With given time I had a hefty snack
Inside my penny candy sack;
And with given time I learned to know
How sweet was my candy of long ago.

Helen Ann Heath

To Clara

Why? Am I still alive today?
I went to sleep last night, wishing
that death would come to me.
I've grown ever so old and lonely
but my wish was not to be.

I never dreamed,
I'd live to be
so very old and sad.
Maybe, if I lay very still
and think of the past,
of the love and happiness, I once had,
death, will come at last.

I am lonely, oh so lonely,
can't you see?
I can bear it no longer.
My mind cries out in the light
of this new day,
death, please, come to me
take me away in flight.

Gay Lynne Wells

Understand Why?

That I don't understand,
I will never understand.
That I know, I may not
Know later. Why does
That have to be like that!!
I just don't understand,

Why, say why? I just
Don't know it all!
But will anyone ever understand all?
If so, help me to understand all too!

Denise Croom

A Wish For The Children

In time of trouble, when all is bad
I think of the children who are so sad,
To all the children that are so sad
A wish to you to soon be glad.

To have courage, and don't stay mad
To share the experiences you've all had,
To your children as Mom and Dad.

Christine Strange

A Chance

How often have you said.
"I wish I could start anew"
The many things you'd change...
All the different things you'd do

If you're given the chance
And everything you need
You would soon begin to tire
Of the monotonous life you lead

I'm sure you've also often heard
"Life is what you make it"
Everyday's a brand new start
But first you have to wake it

The sun begins each morning
Cleansing the world with dew
And offering a chance to grasp
The things you want for you

And tomorrow will bring you
Yet another day...
For you to start and build
And end it as you may

Christine May

To Molly (I, XIV)

I'm in love for many reasons
I wish the world knew
The endless number of reasons
Why I'm in love with you

My hopes had begun to crumble
I no longer could be strong
My fears were becoming reality
Then an angel came along

You danced your way into my heart
And showed me that you cared
You rescued a lonely, crying soul
A soul that was always scared

You turned the fear to happiness
You turned the tears to joy
You gave strength and confidence
To a helpless, little boy

You rescued me from my lonely world
Like only an angel could do
These are just a few more of the reasons
Why I'm in love with you.

Jeffery Post

When You're Lonely

When you're lonely
  I wish you love
When you're down
  I wish you joy
When you're troubled
  I wish you peace
When things are Complicated
  I wish you simple beauty
When things are chaotic
  I wish you inner silence
When things look empty
  I wish you hope.

Deborah Jean Parks

You Like Her More

Too bad you like her more than me,
I would have really liked you,
could have truly loved you,
  but you like her more.

Your brown eyes,
your long hair,
things I love to look at,
touch,
  but you like her more.

I really wish you liked me more,
but you don't, and I can only wish,
it makes a nice dream,
for a while,
  but, you like her more.

Carmen Pardel

I'd Like To Know

I'd like to know
I'd like to know the why's
The why's of life's deceiving ways
Which seem so smooth but are so tortuous.

I look for answers
And seek in vain for there are none.
I look for rest and peace
But only find strife.

I have to find a tranquil spot
And then stop to think
To give my soul a moment of repose.

Joseph F. Velez

Untitled

Do you want to go to Heaven?
If so, catch that train today.
With Jesus as your engineer,
  you won't get lost along the way.

You see, He knows all the crossings,
  and all the rough spots too!
He will get you there safely,
I'm going, How about You?

When we get to heaven,
  we will walk those streets of gold.
Jesus will tell us stories
  that have never before been told.

So catch that train to heaven,
  catch that train today.
Jesus will get you there safely,
  and for sure you won't get lost along the
way.

Jesus runs that train on a golden track,
  and that train is heaven bound.
So take that trip with Jesus,
  a truer friend you have never found.

Bud McKenzie

Love Forever

Love is love forever
It will not ever end,
  When you have a broken heart,
Love will always mend-

  You always need some love
No matter who it is from,
  Always give some love
And love will always come.

Andrea Conner

Lost in a Daydream

The ocean is beautiful and so
is the sea. I wish I had the beaches,
for then I'd be free.

John Sclafani

Doors

Some doors would have a lot to say
   if they could only speak
They'd talk about their broken locks
   and how their hinges squeak

They'd boast about their super weight
   that holds them tight as glue
While others seem to glide on air
   no trouble walking through

Some doors are made of wood and steel
   and others made of glass
That turn in circles all day long
   they watch us as we pass

So many stories they could tell
   a spot where no one looks
The back side of the bathroom door
   of things left on their hooks

Helen Benskin

Untitled

When you need someone to listen
I'll give you my ear,

When you need someone to run to
I'll be near,

When you need someone to cling to
I'll give you my hand,

When you think no one knows
I'll understand,

When it looks like its all over
I'll be there 'til the end

When you think that you have no one
I'll always be your friend.

Caroline Henley

Untitled

Once upon a time
In a house far away
Lived the Anderson Family
Of Chesterfield Bay

Living there is a mother
A father, a little boy too
His father will come home drunk
But that's nothing new

He comes home at six
After a day at the bar
Screeching and honking
In his little red car

The little boy is scared
The mother is too
They're scared of being hit
By you-know-who

The nights never change
They probably never will
For the boy and the man
With the backhand skill

Christine Williams

Untitled

Among crystal flowers blooming
In a meadow green and fair
Simone plays with Scruffy and Sundance
In that far off immortal land

Where dreams are never broken
And teardrops never flow
Waiting there for us to join them
And never say goodbye again

Jean Nessmith

Untitled

The Sound of Caramel Corn
in a tin barrel Mesmerizes me
It is the most soothingly
bizarre Commingling that pieces
of matter can produce
Better than a big Fat pink
bubble popping better than Bach
or Chopin better than hearing
I love you for the first time
and feeling the Same way
I cannot Imagine many people
calling Hark to this symphony
of Solitude
But Me I have a Different take
on Life and Caramel Corn

Andrea Avant

Proposition

Late autumn is a harlot
In a worn, brocaded gown
Turning tricks and hustling
On every street in town.

She shakes her tattered shoulders
   at every passing breeze
And flaunts her flowered hemline
   to tantalize and tease
The waning sun to take her,
   enticing him to stay
And warm her aging body
   With one more summer day -

Jean Older Scott

My Everlasting Love

He is perfect
in every way
He is always there
to save my day
I only have one regret
about the day that we met
My eyes were too blind with anger
to realize that this stranger
that stood before me
was soon to be
My every thought and dream
He is my everlasting love
He was sent to me
from heaven up above
but that love has turn to sorrow
and there is no tomorrow
That I will see
him with me
for fate has turned against us
and our love was never meant to be

Cammie Laws

M.S.A.C.

We like to call us MSAC.
In fact, that's what we are;
We might even be your neighbors,
We don't live very far.

The M, of course, is Marysville
And Seniors, sure we are;
Against crime, oh, you betcha'
We even have a car!

You may see us in the morning
As we drive around a school;
If we see a sign of trouble
We call in; that's the rule.

You'll see us doing crowd control
At the strawberry Parade;
We may sometimes find a lost child
Who's crying and afraid.

We'll help you start a Block Watch
If you'll just give us a call;
We may be only volunteers
But we're good guys, one and all!

Bonnie Marriott

For The Children

Some of the most meaningful things
in life, are the smallest things.
Which mostly are taken for granted.
The things that are most important,
aren't always first.
It's different for every one,
but the same for most.
We over look their needs and feelings
so easily.
Their the ones that hurt the most.
We have to take care of them,
listen to their thoughts, and be
mindful of their needs and feelings.
For the children of today, are the
hope for the future of tomorrow.
Without them there is no future.

Darlene K. Dulong

True Love

His heart was pounding
in my head,
As we lay there
in his water bed.

My head was on his chest
his arm was around me.
This was so very special
that I wished it to last for eternity.

He is my one and only
real true love,
And I hope we last forever
like two turtle doves.

This is the one
I can surely tell,
Pretty soon we'll hear
the chime of wedding bells.

The white flowing gown is soon forgotten
amongst all the chatter.
Because the next to come along
is the sound of little pitter-patter.

Darla Comunale

A Day At Universal

As I wake up in the morn,
In my soft and comfy bed,
I have to warn myself not
    to hit my head.
And I go on all the rides,
And walk and walk and walk,
And then go into earthquake
But don't even stop to talk!
There's Jaws and Kong and
    E. T. galore,
Though it never rains there,
    it sometimes does pour!
Then we go back to the house,
And crawl into our beds,
And our mom whispers softly,
"Go to bed you sleepy heads."

Alicia Reese

Many Faces

The "not so pretty" recompense
In one way or another
How she's brought up, in which tense?
Does she love her mother?

Since she's not the "pretty one"
Graceful and alluring
She must find a path in life
Something more enduring.

All her drawbacks
have drawn themselves out
No man today says
"You look cute... when you pout."

She looks in the mirror
Eyes see crease upon crease
Why look for the beauty
Until she finds Peace?

No amount of make up
Will camouflage the traces
Left within beneath her skin
She's seen her many faces.

Diane Evans

The Good Life

Have we lost the love of living
In our reckless rush of life,
And feel we that, midst much misgiving,
Life's great goal is selfish strife?

Selfish strife for still more mammon—
Heaping, hoarding as though we,
Prepared for more than Pharaoh's famine,
Should survive eternally.

Not with wisdom have we dreamed thus—
Man whose life is but a breath—
Though it may have never seemed thus,
Life today may turn to death.

Vanity and vast vexation
And a striving after wind—
For man, the crown of God's creation,
Has what God gives, in the end.

Eat and drink, in work find pleasure,
Find enjoyment with your wife—
Under God, these fill the measure
Of what makes a happy life.

Gilbert Greathouse

Thinking

Sitting here I think,
    In peace
About war in the streets
and of mankind
    going blind
As a raisin in the sun

I crumble into one
Nature lives on
Now that I am gone
The destruction I've created
Is now being debated

The massacre in store
Has waited for me before
This time I mustn't hesitate
For now nothing can change my fate
For I sit here and think
    In peace.

Claire Fancett

November

Crispness
In the air remarks the change
That turns the grass to dry
And flowers to whither.

Drawn shadows
From an amber sun
Respond to nature's altered mood
With easy reticence.

Dimmer light
To evening falls in step
To wait for dawn with wearier eyes
And longer dreams.

To winter
Creeps in evergreen
Denied the vivid orange hues and gold
Of colder skies.

In reverence
Nature saves her softer fires
For comfort as the year expires.

Denise Thompson-Bonnett

The Mountain

Has a mountain ever beckoned you
in the early Spring?
To see the flowers blooming
or listen to a Robin sing?

And then go back in Summer
and you can plainly tell.
That the flowers are all different
they even have a different smell.

Then along comes Autumn
to that mountain side.
The birds are all leaving now
and the flowers have all died.

Then Winter comes a howling
and covers it with snow.
Then you sit and wonder
where did the other seasons go?

But in spring or summertime
or autumn and winter too.
That mountain is always beautiful
and it always beckons you.

Jerry Running Foxe

The Jewel

It sits like a jewel
In the nearly autumn night
Peering through an almost cloudy sky
Casting off a most eerie light
The clouds pass beneath it
Not staying in any one place too long
The wind whispers through the trees
Singing it's ancient and weary song
The stars give off
Their year's distant light
Part of nature's cast of thousands
In their performance each night
Like a tear that rolls down
The cheek of someone we love
The night ends and the jewel
Must leave it crown above

Daniel C. Alber

Fresh raindrops fall together,
In the pitter patter sound,
Of tiny little drum beats,
As they hit the ground.
Drum beats, heart beats,
Faster 'til,
Shining light and happiness,
Let youth stand oh so still.

Diana Jabbour

Fulfillment

I need not search for happiness
In vague and distant lands.
The calm content I long have sought
Is here within my hands.

The diamond slippered snow lies on
Our emerald woods of pine;
And solace comes on velvet feet,
Unto this heart of mine.

Frost, studding placid window panes,
A teardrop and a star.
God-given comfort to each man
Who sees them as they are.

Casey Jacobs

Poison Ivy

In the Fall my poison ivy
is a shade of color so bold,
with scarce leaves of green
and a few of gold.
And red.
Like wildfire it spreads
over the hills
and meadows green,
hardly anything else
can be seen.
Bowing their red
wine colored leaves,
Dripping red blood
like a sieve.
Like red bloody fingers
they draw in their claws,
patiently waiting
nature's applause.

Jessica Koenig

Freckles

Freckles, freckles on my nose!
Freckles, freckles on my toes!
Freckles, freckles in my hair!
Freckles, freckles everywhere!
Freckles, freckles go away!
Freckles, freckles always stay!

Christy Byrd

Breathe

Every breath you breathe
is an opportunity to improve
on who you are
and what you inevitably become.

Yes, to breathe is an opportunity
to change your direction.

Yes, breathing is an oasis
of untapped possibilities.

Every breath is a journey
an eclipse
a mission
a liberation
a prize.

Breathe on, breathe deep,
breathe assuredly,
inhaling great possibilities
and exhaling doubts and fears.

Clothilde Belk

The Pen That Writes

The poem that lies upon the page,
Is cold as death at any age,
Until the moment that it's read,
And awakened from the dead.

The symphony is nothing more,
Than notes and lines, a soundless score,
Until the oboe, strings, and brass,
Find the music waiting there,
And come together in their quest,
To touch the ear, and fill the air.

The playwright with his script in hand,
Has nothing more than words on hold,
No love, or hate, or reckless rage,
Until the actor takes the stage,
And gives life to his character,
When he lifts him from the page.

Betty Ann McKenzie

Humanity's Fingerprint

Auschwitz
Is humanity's fingerprint
On time
And time
Is God's fingerprint
On existence!

The past
Is Auschwitz
The present
Is Auschwitz
The future
Is Auschwitz!

So long as existence
Is distrusted
By co-existence
Auschwitz shall be!

Dom Martin

An Angel

What is an angel?
Is it just a myth?
Or is an angel
Up in heaven adrift?

Have you ever seen an angel
That has come down from above?
with halo and wings
Bringing a lot of love

There are many angels
That you can really see
With no halo and wings
And they will always be-

Bringing joy and happiness
To young and old alike
For they are little children
That you hold day and night

So as you go through life
And enter God's domain
You could see an angel
That just may have your name

Harold Gregg Jr.

Reaper's Cause

Life is ended, good or ill?
Is it murder? Is it sane?
Out of what does angel kill?
Does it serve some long lost bane?
Darkness blankets helpless sheep
With comforting and gentle hands
Binding children in their sleep
All across deserted lands.
Is it evil to lay rest
The weary, trembling, saddened soul?
Is true peace a welcomed guest
Or is longed slumber sent to roll?
Life is ended, good or ill?
Out of what does angel kill?

Aaron Miller

Love?

What is love?
Is it that feeling you get,
when you wake up in cold sweat?

Love for me is only a dream.
It might or might not come true.
But for the remaining time,
I feel like the color blue.
Its not he color of the sky,
its the kind that makes you want to die.

What is love?
Do we really know?
Is it all just some big show?

People come,
people go.
If they loved us,
we'll never know.

Love is torture,
and it doesn't pay.
You end up going your separate way.

Amy Brown

Wish

My solitary wish,
Is peace within my life,
The fighting and the anger,
Cuts through me like a knife,
My saddened heart's one desire,
To quit the flow of tears,
The look upon my face,
Shows strain of all the years,
The one gnawing need,
Chewing at my soul,
My whole life crammed into,
A small hell-ridden hole,
The rudeness and the insults,
Like a battle waging along,
I am so growing weary,
I fear I can't go on,
Star light, star bright,
Only star I see tonight,
Oh, where is my wishing star,
Upon the darkened night.

Dawn Simpson

Late Spring Snowfall

Mother Nature
Is shaking her featherbed.
Daffodils
Raise their heads in disbelief.
Forsythia raise golden arms
To catch the downy flakes.
Redbuds dare
The white onslaught
And magnolias
Bow in meek submission.

Fern K. Cullom

Speed

Life at 35 miles an hour
is slow
and obnoxious
Safe
Emotion at 65 miles an hour
is a million sparks
of the cigarette
Splashed on the freeway
Sex at 95
is a runaway freight train
slicing through the darkness
caught by the sparkle of candlelight
Love at 120 miles an hour
is the open window
and the wind rushing into your face
Listening for sirens
but me
I like to walk

Eric Rhodes

Come Together

The eagle that soars freely
Guns that kill the thought
Mountains that come without the thought,

A cry in the night
In the shadow of the moon
Softly turning into the wolf,

One face to the earth
All creations come together
Making peace and love.

Courtney Red-Horse Mohl

Why

Why am I here.
Is this my life?
Not knowing why.
It's not fair!
Doesn't make sense.
Are the blind truly blind?
Can the seeing truly see?
What's behind this mystery curtain?
Or should I say mental block.
The truth maybe.
Is it too painful to know?
How much worse can it get?
Not much worse.
"Ouch-help-why-me?"
Is all that comes to mind.
Maybe I'm exaggerating at times, maybe not.

Annette Iovino

A Grandchild's Smile

There is nothing else to take its place,
It brings such Joy - no matter
girl or boy -
Your whole day seems brighter -
Your cares get lighter -
And life again becomes worthwhile -
When that knock at the door
Brings one, two or more -
of God's most precious gifts,
a grandchild's smile

Annette Schmidt

My Love For You

Love can be deep as the ocean,
it can also run untrue, but I've never
really knew love until I meet you.

My love for you is forever burning
deep with in my soul, like raging fire
burning out of control.

The feeling of comfort to have you
by my side to sooth my sorrow's, as you
wipe the tears from my eyes.

My love for you grows stronger
with each passing day, here in my
heart my love for you will always
remain.

Cynthia A. Rook

Love and Roses

Love is so much like the Rose.
It can be so beautiful, yet
fragile and like the petals
that fall from the Rose, so
shall my tears fall from my eyes,
because I always seem to Love in
vain.

As the Rose blossoms anew, so
shall my Love because you have
found me and I have found you.
And like the roots of a Rose bush
burrows deep in the ground and
grows stronger as time goes by,
so shall our Love grow and live
in God's loving sight.

Effie Butler

Friendship

Friendship is a funny thing
It can make you sad
Or make you sing
It can bring out a smile or a frown
It can pick you up
Or bring you down.
It can hold honesty and trust
And these two things are a must
TRUE friendship is rare
So treat it well
It is not something
You can buy or sell.

Heather R. Black

Scarlet

Her touch was the night
it caressed me
Her kiss was kindness
and understanding

Her lips spoke only truths
and they blessed mine
Her eyes held passion
and so much pain

What was I to do
She tempted me
And all I needed
was an excuse

Forbidden or sought
Right or wrong
Love or Sin
Who's to say they're not the same

Time stands still
Heart runs cold
Life loses meaning
When you have no one to love

Christopher Larsen

A Single Tear

I cried a single tear.
It could have been a thousand,
For the intensity.
The lone drop slid along my cheek,
To leave a path of memories.

I caught it on the tip of my tongue.
It reminded me,
Of a new beginning.
The tiny drop disappeared,
To leave a taste of the past.

I carried a flame in my heart.
It could have been a fire,
For the passion.
The blue flame burned,
To leave a blackened lust.

I squelched it with reality.
It insisted that,
The desire be released.
The tiny flame flickered,
To leave the warmth of love.

Bette Matzas

A Short Philosophy

I think reality is false,
It doesn't really exist.
It's all a matter of point of view,
What you believe and wish.

Some things are fact,
Like color, shape and sound.
But emotional coloring changes
The way we see the total act.

Brenda Jumper

My Little Trumpet

I have a little trumpet
It goes where'er I go
It tags along on balmy days
Winter, ice and snow

After eating beans or cabbage
My trumpet's sure to blow
In musical succession
Rapidly or slow

Often when in bed at night
My trumpet sounds a blast
I then recall the day's events
'till I'm asleep at last.

Albert Dillof

Untitled

Sometimes
it hurts to open my eyes
and face another day.
Sometimes
I can't find peace of mind
or feeling in my limbs
sometimes
the pain goes past tears
to fear
that life is all there is
sometimes
the fear consumes me
and I can not move or see
sometimes
I care
sometimes
I don't
sometimes
sometimes
sometimes

Andrea N. Mosley

I Am Because He is

There is a seed inside of me,
It is a seed of destiny,
And what this seed will produce in me,
is what You have ordained to be,
You have the ultimate authority,
to cause things unseen to be,
and whether its fruits are
love, joy or agility
I know they will cause me to be
more like Thee,
What You have said will be,
Let thy will be established in me,
For it is not in my ability,
But by your grace I will find
My destiny.

Cynthia L. Mozingo

The Long Night

The harmonious quiet night.
It is calm and I am thinking
about our past.
The bashful love wants to reveal
our secrets.
But my heart is speechless,
so my heart shuts down.
The warm silent night which is
sincere and it is far from a distance
of day light.
I will let the night perceive.
As the night perceives, I will
leave my memory in a deep dream.

Domenico Longo

Loaned Land

The land is not ours
It is loaned to us to use
Not abuse
Loaned to a people so many years ago
And taken from a people up until today
To build concrete buildings
and cold monumental things
and deprive them of many things!

Becky Hill

Just Do It

Yes, of course I do it daily
It isn't such a chore
Once you really start doing it
You want to do it more.

There was a time I didn't
I was innocent and naive
The benefits of doing it
I didn't quite believe.

I remember when she first showed me
I've been doing it the same way since
Oh, those wasted years I can't get back
Sometimes can make me wince.

It's kept me young and frisky
And always ready to roll
Actually, two times a day
Has become my long-term goal.

I hope I can keep doing it
Even when I'm old and gray
I'm not ashamed to admit it...
...I'm flossing everyday.

Carissima Aloe

Untitled

Always fill your heart with love,
it will set your mind at ease.
Love makes and breaks the most
impossible dreams.
For it only takes a moment to love,
but a lifetime to build without.
Be careful and cautious,
move forward into the present.
Never look back, for love is the answer
found only in your soul.
You can only give others
what you have within.
Live your life for love.
Always aiming into the hearts of others.

Brenda Davis

Falling Star

I saw the most beautiful star,
It looked so close, yet was so
   far,
I tried to catch it as it went
   by,
I missed and it vanished into
   the midnight sky,
I keep a picture of it in my
   mind,
And I see a face so loving and
   kind,
Too burning and too quick to
   hold,
Too lovely to be bought or
   sold,
Good only to make wishes on,
Then forever to be gone.

Audrey Waller

Simple Things

Lord, thank you for today
It started just like any other
But the sunshine of life
Beamed through like no other
I saw a flower by the road
I usually pass by without a glance
Today I slowed to look
I gave its beauty a chance
Life passes by so fast
That I forget the simple things
The peaceful sound of rain
The joy a smile brings
The touch of someone you love
Wind blowing in the trees
A playful little puppy
The happy tickle of a sneeze
Lord, help me to remember
Help me stop and see
The small wonders of life
And how beautiful they can be

Jodi J. Jacobs

The Doll House

In the doll house I saw,
it was a magical thing.
A little porcelain doll
that could dance and sing!

In the doll house I saw,
it was a miracle.
The porcelain doll was drinking tea.
That moment was magical.

In the doll house I saw,
it was late at night.
The porcelain doll was limp.
What a sight!

In the doll house I saw,
it was something to see.
The porcelain doll was lying there
accusing me.

Those beady eyes,
half closed, half opened,
a reddish, somewhat white color.
Death had happened.

Ashley Revay Mace

The High Chair

I cleaned the baby's high chair
It was really quite a mess
It only makes me wonder
How much food does he digest?

Four jars of jam, some peas and stuff
I really can't describe
It's amazing the places
These foodstuffs found to hide.

We have a well fed baby
From his toes up to his hair,
But it's obvious to me now
He's not as well fed as his chair.

Charlotte A. Noyd

The Pain

The pain will never go away.
It will leave a scar for life.
A sacred that hurts with a purpose.
A purpose of pain and hatred,
That was meant for death.
And the pain will never go away.

Future generations will know of this,
And be angered.
Not because of the knowledge,
But they too will feel the pain.
Everyone will feel it.
And the pain will never go away.

It's amazing to see this.
History tells us of these scars.
Scars of civil wars and violent battles.
And now people want all races to live
together,
But the pain never went away.

Amanda Perkins

People I'm Not Kiddin'

People I'm not kiddin'
it won't be your religion
that opens up heaven's door
And I'm not foolin'
it won't be your schoolin'
that gets you in good with the Lord
you know it may sound funny
But He don't need your money
it's your faith that He's lookin' for
so if you want the solution
to all of this pollution
just give it up and turn to the Lord
You know that He loves you
where He's living above you
And He sees everything that you do
so do yourself a favour
And try to love your neighbor
And let the Love of God shine through

Charles Coxe

A Poet's Poem

It flickers as it sparks.
In my heart is where it starts.
It spreads to my head,
Then flows through my fingers.
I paint my life in a portrait of words.
Looking away,
The feeling I portray
Remains in my heart and lingers.

Gregory G. Druchniak

My Friend Mr. Snowman

Hi! Mr. Snowman
Its a beautiful day
Wait Mr. Snowman
I'm coming out to play
See Mr. Snowman
I've got a brand new sleigh
Look Mr. Snowman
The sun is coming out to play
Oh! Mr. snowman
Please don't melt away.

Charles Dumberger

Just Old Age

I hate to complain - but
It's all so plain.

Everything was great until
I reached ninety-eight!

I was busy as a bee
Until I couldn't see.

I can't look forward, I can't look back.
I can't do this and I can't do that.

I try to be pleasant,
But often lose control.
There's no way to fight the fact...
I'm just getting old.

Waves of depression cross over my brain
That are much worse than physical pain.

I never accepted the word defeat...
At the present time I'm still on my feet.

In the year to come
I hope to see...one-hundred-one!

Georgia Bradfield

Untitled

I look out the window and see a fire
It's flames are forever growing higher
Killing life, killing trees,
Killing things that used to be
Why people are careless
I don't know
But I watch late at night
And I see the flames glow
Higher and higher,
To the sky
Still, it makes me
Wonder why
Why the death, why the pain
Of watching life start again
Much too old to enjoy the fun
Of watching the trees grow one by one
I look out the window and see a fire
And still it's flames are growing higher

Gary Ducharme

The Drop Of Water

The drop of water I
have found in lakes,
Sea and ocean, if seems like
forever my little droplet.
The sky is your home
leave me alone and
go home that's where
you belong.

Amanda Whitsett

Untold Magic

After a rain
It's fun to remain
Silent
And feel refreshed.
Words spoken would only be in vain.

After a rain
Life, itself, seems plain.
Colors are bright.
Friendships feel right.
Nighttime's full moon is on the wane.

After a rain
Who can complain
About the feeling
Of
Beginning again?
Fall on this earth. Let untold magic rain!

Bettye G. Majesty

A Poem For My Angel

What's a rose with out a scent
It's like a day that wasn't meant

Yet I feel better knowing you're there
Being close by me in the air

You are with me my whole life
Even when it is filled with strife

When days are hard and long
You protect me from all that is wrong

Knowing you are by my side
I will never be afraid and hide

When it is time for me to leave
If you are with me I will not grieve

Everyday I thank God above
That you share with me your love

Charlene M. Smith

Our River

Come with me to tranquility
It's not very far - you shall see
Here, come lie with me
You too shall feel tranquility
See the river flow so gracefully
She flows so slow and oh so peacefully
Now close your eyes and listen to her
You can hear her gentle laughter
If you listen oh so closely
You will want to hold her closely
Feel her friend, sunshine upon your face
Can you feel the slower pace
Cob webs hanging from the trees
See them dancing in the breeze
Hold my hand and let us go
Let us go where she may flow
We know this shall never end
We have her as our forever friend
She's inviting us to embrace
She wants us to stay and call it our place.

Jo Ann Shepherd

Thinking About You

Pictures fade away, but memories
last forever, just like sand on a
beach that the tide takes away,
true love may die, but never fade away.

Daniel M. Luongo

A Leaf

A leaf, so like mine
Its pathways of life
mesh artistically
as the dancing edges fill my voids
to form something different
something better
than I ever was before.

My autumnness is
more brilliant with fire and my descent
is no longer solitary.

Not one isolated leaf
tumbling to the unknown below.
But now I am joined in descent,
never plummeting only downward
but drifting upon the breath of winds,
being lifted up and twirling about
as if in some enchanting, entangled dance
that laughs clear bell like laughter
as it carries us until our dance slows to the
to and fro
that settles us within the earth.

Elsa Kaufmann

Our Future Is A Secret

Many want to know their future
I've heard so by and by
And sitting down to think it over
I've often wondered why.

How boring and unexciting
Our lives would surely be
Without the surprises of what will come;
The future's not ours to see.

God forbid I were to die
Some time in the coming year
I would not want to know before
And live my life in fear.

And who I'm going to marry
Whether short or tall
Right now I do not want to know
I'd kill the magic of it all.

So why find out ahead of time
Something only time will show?
Our future is a secret
For only God to know.

Andria Mamolo

The Partnership Of Marriage

It began man and wife,
Join hands and hearts together,
And start to share a life,
But through the years that follow.

Though they be very sweet,
Without the Lord blessings,
Somehow life's in complete,
For he's the unseen partner,
Who makes a marriage strong,
Who renew's hope and brings,
Love and faith;
When things go right or wrong.

A marriage bonds are strengthened
As with a golden cord,
When two can build there marriage.
As partners of the Lord.

Connie Biddle

Unwritten Verse Or Procrastination

Fragments of scattered notes
Jotted down on paper napkins,
On the back od "already sent" envelopes
All hoarded for tomorrow's Future prose.
Lonely words, fragile words
Embossed on perishable scrapes
And too easily forgotten.

Just moments of past events
Soon lost by procrastination
And too easily forgotten
Such unwritten ideas never brought
To fruition. Unprinted verses
Swallowed in the swamp of tomorrows.
And finally lost and forgotten
In the "might have been."

June Vanleer Williams

Toys For Christmas

I got a box of toys for Christmas
Just like the toys on christmas day
I got a box of toys for christmas
Had to give them all away
I got a box of toys for christmas
Up in the attic, stashed away
When santa brings me toys for christmas
He never has the time to stay.

I got a box of toys for christmas
From uncle george and aunty mae
I got a box of toys for christmas
Wonder what they have to say
I got a box of toys for christmas
Another box is on its way
Oh! Santa, please! Bring me a daddy
The kind that shows ya' how to play.

Anne B. Currier

The Me In Me

The little cup of softened butter
just under my navel.

The warm smell of sleep
in the crease of my neck.

The soundless noise of
my distrust and disapproval.

The certainty of my step and
confidence in color.

The electric resistance in
the texture of my hair.

The sharpness of my bits.
The seriousness of my hugs.

The ever present frown, I work
to produce...

And the all to hesitant smile,
that cancels out it all.

Gerris Farris

Little Girl

A baby cute and tan
Long hair as fine as sand
Eyes that twinkle from the light
Checkered dress orange blue and white
Dimples that highlight a tiny smile
A face that glows all the while
a pretty girl, that you can see
that little girl grew up to be me

Beverly Masters

Must Children Die

Why, oh why
Must children die
When I turn on the news
It seems there are quite a few
I wish there was something to do
For I hate when children die

Deanna Hope Kirsch

The Gardener

No one will ever know
Just what it means to me.
To plant a seed into the ground
And wait for it to be...

A something or a whatever
That comes up healthy and strong,
To give the world some beauty
And fragrance from now on.

To watch it grow and harvest
Or see it multiply.
To have it gather creatures
And birds out of the sky...

To know that in its cycle
Of life here on this earth.
I had my hand upon it
From the moment of its birth.

Ed H. Woolsey

God You Answered Me

God I called.
Just when my hope we're low,
and out of the heaven I saw a glow
I cried Jesus
I couldn't believe this
I heard Jesus
God was I surprised when I knew what was
happening to me inside.
I knew Jesus
I felt good to be One
with God and his son.
All my prayers has been
answered
I believe...
I believe...
I believe...

in him... The one I call
my God Lord Jesus...

Jeanette Jackson

Run

Run faster little one,
keep busy...
Burn out each day
behind you.
For if you don't
and find yourself
What will you do?

Who will you use
to run to...
to hide the ugliness
you know is there?
Who will you find
to help you
little one?
Who will you find to care?

Elig Kay

For Jennifer

Don't fret don't cry
Keep the faith
you'll be safe

What life has in store
you can be sure
just wait and see
if it's meant, it will be

Your life such a struggle
you feel so very troubled
Feel yourself blessed
You are a divine guest

All will take place
At it's own pace
take a step back
give yourself space

You have so much light
so always hold very tight
to yourself be so true
that's really the meaning of you

Gayle T. Peters

Daniel and the Lion

Anger tempered with conscience,
kept at bay by the keepers whip.
A muffled growl, a mumbled roar:
a desire for freedom speaks out.
A scolding glance commands
obedience to temperance.

Frustrated in its confinement,
it claws at the walls,
tearing it's prison limb from limb
easing the burning rage
till all is spent.

The lion's den is it's sanctuary.
Few who enter ever return.
Daniel give me strength,
for tonight we meet;
face to fanged face.

Jeff Poole

Tracy Marie

Come and sit upon my
Knee - you're only three
    my Tracy Marie.

Locks of curls on your head.
Eyes so big and bright.
    read me a story nana
Then I'll say good-night.

As I watch you run and
    jump and play all through
    the day singing, swinging,
Never know where you're going.
And with each passing day
You're growing and growing

Oh my Tracy Marie you're
    as pretty as a little white dove.
Do I love you?
Yes I do and your mommy, too.

Donna Smith

Ode to Orphy

Legs bowed in front -
  Knock - kneed behind.
White bib flowing down
  his breast, now mauled and broken,
  he is laid to rest.
A crazy cat, racing up and down
  the stairs, or lying on the top tread,
  with forelegs hanging down.
Too brave for his own good-
A misfit, made up of spare parts,
  but such a character, he
    stole our hearts.

Jeanette T. Gillette

Paranoia

The wind sounds like a stranger
Knocking at my door
My heart pounds like a stranger's knock,
Though I'd locked it out before.
The clock ticks like a stranger's voice
Whispering to me,
Reminding me of forgotten souls
That time will not set free.
The crickets chirping in the woods
Are calling out my name
My name is ringing in my ears.
Reminding me of shame.
The grey dust in the air
Is spinning 'round my head,
Telling me of all the things
I never should have said.
The night's twisted fingers
Reach through cracks in the floor
I suppose I'll let it enter,
Though I'd shoved it out before.

Elisa Dallas

Endless Echo

As I sit and ponder
knowing what is
But not wanting to know
what will be

The thoughts of freedom
cry out
in my mind
As my limitations
engulf me

I recognize the external beings
endless echo
As the pitter - patter
dances with my thoughts

But as I drift
away
Something hinders my ride
leaving me

In the grasp
of life
Trying once again
to sit and ponder.....

James M. Vivolo

Roaring at the Moon

A lion roaring
like my dog Thunder crying
at the moonlit night

Jasen Justesen

Queen Of Space

Earth, walk tall, walk proud,
Knowing you're fairest of fair;
Waving your hanky of cloud;
Shaking your sunshine of hair.
Walking in slippers of rain —
Wearing the moon on your finger —
Swishing your sashes of green —
Letting your perfume linger!
Walk like a heavenly queen,
With the light of the sun on your face;
Earth, walk tall, walk beautiful,
Over the pathways of space.

Helene Grouse

January Time

Silver-toned season of time,
Lake turned blue pearl.
North wind flapping icy wings,
Lucid icicles in a frozen whirl
Nature raising up her fist.

Fossil fingerprints snowbound now
Frosted yule log and tree of holly
Drawing the night like a shade
break a stars whisper melancholy,
barren in the blizzard downpour.

January time, curfew running out.
Stringent earth in fetal coil,
Surfacing, praying, seedtime soon
Give me back my warm soil.
My sweet fruit.

Florence Fiorvante

The Rose

The rose you gave me
last June is gone.
It shriveled and Died
right before my eyes.
What a beautiful Rose,
What a beauty it was.
I Do not want to realize
What we have is now gone.
Holding on to the Past,
hoping it would last.
Though realizing too late
what we have is now gone.
Before is gone and
we must move on.

Elizabeth Garcia

"Redwood Tree"

So tall I stand
like a giant
among the others trees
Even when the breeze
is blowing hard upon me,
it hardly moves me,
for I like to stand strong and tall
If I could talk,
I could tell you many tales
for I have look down on others
for a long time!
When God created me
He really must have like me -
for I can survive
longer than the life time
of any living person!!

Edward Lee Collins

Tree House

The engulfing forest
Laughs with each blind turn
Trail of crumbs eaten
Another traveller cheated

Bastard twigs snicker
A brook points and giggles

Panic spears my fears
Memory betrays
Moss watches me as I timidly
Tear sister bark away
Dead compass rose
Guardians tower over me
I scream
A crow screams back
I run into the trees
A tree runs into me
I bleed
Nobody hears me plead
Home is a dying concept

Greg Wilkovich

Ghost

I like to watch you
lay in the sun.

How neatly you
spread your claws.

How cunningly you
pounce on the string
and then you toy with it
for a while.

Then, when you get tired,
you yawn and walk away.

Justin K. McCoy

The Worshipers

Pyramided at the feet of the god
Lay pounds of human flesh
No Shylock ever dared demand.
Proudly forth the donors surge
Adding, ever adding.

Pleasured by their sacrifice
Yet lusting to swell their faith,
Shout "Down with disbelievers!"
Weapon-words soaked in venom
or pity's marinade
Splattered my outer self;
Then ravaged my skinny soul
Cowering beneath its blubbered shell.
As they — protected by
Their security god —
Preened their reeded pride;
And pranced victory's narrow margin
Before my swollen, shattered I.

Abby Stitt

Loneliness

Loneliness is like an empty cold cell.
It can sometimes turn your heart to stone
it is a past and present reminder
of how no one shows you they care.
Loneliness is painful like a sharp knife
penetrating your heart.
Loneliness is a shadow in the night
scarring your self-esteem forever.

Christine Chaffey

"Madame Butterfly"

She flies,
leading her children
high above the aqua blue waters,
fast and true.
Island to island
rest in sunlight.

Queen of the sky
she sings the blues,
her world slowly dying around her,
her faithful followers shimmering
in her majestic path.
High on the magic dust,
they sing and dance
to this reckless song feeling
helpless and beautiful
Our Madame soaks in
the sorrows
till her wings are black.

Erin Olson

Snow

Snow falls at the quiet time of night
Leaving everything so pretty white
Snow is falling to the ground
A big white blanket is coming down

I watch the snow fall
In the middle of the night
It sure is a pretty sight

When it stops snowing
The land is covered
The world is so pretty and peaceful.

Jacinda Bumgarner

On The Eve Of The Millennium

Round off the rectangular table,
Let no divisions remain.
Titans for earth care, assemble!
Seek only agreements humane.

Alas, can't you trust one another
On the eve of the millennium?

You stem from a whore's bitter stable
Where violence was bred in the womb,
And life threads are woven so thinly
That social injustice spells doom.

Alas, can't you throw away violence
On the eve of the millennium?

How you lack the courageous resolve
To reach out to the beautiful dove.
Beware that all peace will be lost
Without simple forgiveness and love.

Alas, will you titans destroy us
On the eve of the millennium?

Charlene Helgesen

Insomniac Scene

With sleepless eyes
I wander midnight rooms,
spy through darkened windows
at gaunt sentinels casting
leafless lonesome shadows
on backyard snow,
guarding nearby houses
sleeping the moon bright
silent night away.

Elayne Clipper Hanson

The River

Yonder through the fields of reality,
Lie the river of passion and time.
Though time cannot change the river,
For it fills as it takes away.
Humanity tries to fill it,
By flooding it with selfish love.
But the river maintains its level,
When the drought of sorrow takes its hold.
Don't attempt to change this river,
Though life may seem unfair.
Let time take its toll,
For you don't walk through the fields
Of reality alone.

John R. Wilce

To My Daughter Maureen

My first experience with new
life and real love.

From her curly dark brown hair
to her curled up toes I
would learn to love in a
different world.

The world of innocence
untouched and unspoiled.
The world of childhood.

I would be a child with a child
growing to womanhood.

And still, not lost, the love
still grows and I thank you
for your gift to life and love to me.

Christine H. Mann

Love Always

Let me walk in the
Light of your love
And use the word forever
A man can't find his
Love and beauty always
A man acquires lost treasures
To beautified his loved ones

We need no wealth to
Share our love always
The one that I hold dear

Known as faith and hope
On the very land we live
We should welcome a new day

One who loves you most of all
Who's there to see you through

And let's be thankful
That's what love is
Share alike and share
Till our hearts are contented

Joseph Matunas

Untitled

love is tongues
hate is teeth
and lips are
2 huge earthworms
crawling across
a face

Phrancklyn

Love

Love,
like a flower
sometimes blooming
into beautiful love
sometimes withering
leaving broken hearts

Love,
like a bird
sometimes captured
and cherished
other times it flies away
too far to reach

Love
is an object
a chance you have
cherish it
hold it
few have the chance

Hannah Link

Memories

They do haunt you sometimes
Like dust in the wind
you turn them out so quickly
Then you wish you had them back again
Life is all to short
It passes by so very fast
You'll never go back again
you wish they'd always last
Some are so sweet
other all so sad
But once you stop and think
They're the best you ever had.
Some dwell too long on memories
While others choose to forget
Some have no control
they do what their mind will let
So lets live for today
Let tomorrow be what it will be
with one thing in mind
don't live your life for a memory

Ricky Clunan

Visions

You are a vision of beauty
Like I've never seen before
Are you a dream?
Or just my imagination...
If you are a dream
Let me
Never wake
If you are my imagination
Let me wonder
On...
And on...
And on...

Allan Gerard Wickham

Here I Am

Here I am
Holding on
Thinking of you
Wishing you were here.
This feeling will never change
I'll love you forever and ever.

Alta Olesen

For A Friend

Your garments fall
like the robes of an
angel as you crawl
into my arms of silk
kisses.

Your voice forms the
shapeless muse that comes
forth upon staircases
of red.

Your arms lift up
this burdened heart
that gazes to see what
it has become.

Your tears wash away
a poet's debt that can
only lie in cupped hands
of unspoken silence.

Justin David Wade

Untitled

Came.
Lingered.
Saw,
Conquered.
Left,
And returned.
Claimed,
Staked,
And owned.

Barbara Bazerque

Like the Rose

She has eyes of emeralds;
Lips of satin wine.
Her skin is silky soft,
Slender fingers caressing.
Her scent is captivating;
She takes your breath
    away...
Like the rose, she is
Fragile - yet strong
She is sweet -
    yet pure.
Like the rose -
She is lovely.

Doreen C. Green

Outside Colors

Some days I'm bright forest green.
    Lively and awake,
    Loud and exciting;
Standing tall —-
    like a tree —
    among all my friends.

Somewhere deep down, though.
    I'm black inside.
    Depressed and quiet,
    Abused and snappy.

Stay out of my way today
    because I feel forest green.

Erin Cox

Loners

Loners playing games remain the same
    living their life within.
Growing old sometimes cold
    when will their love begin?
Feelings for one had begun
    only to soon run out.
Don't get too near for they fear
    what their life is about.
Picking their friends wherever at
    so few they may choose.
In the role of one no matter what comes
    how can they lose?
No commitments no obligations
    no strings to be tied.
Are they happy? Will they change?
    Have they ever cried?

Beverly Lynn Head

Look At The World

Look at our world
Look at what we did to it
It went through many battles.

There are more roads than trees
We have animals caged up to be
To be away from harm
But they're not.......

Look at what we did...

The world is turning worse not better
Our water use to be pure
But it's not....

Look at our world....

Carrie Yelra

I Love You Lord Jesus

"I love you, Lord Jesus,
look down from above,
and stay beside me,
and show me your love.

I need you so Lord,
without you I die.
Stay with me, Lord Jesus,
live in me I cry.

Look not to my sins,
but cleanse me I pray.
Stay by me, Lord Jesus,
do come into me and stay.

Thank you, Lord Jesus,
for hearing my prayer!
You are so good, Lord Jesus,
to think that you do care!"

Betty Jean Midyett

A New Beginning

A lot of unspoken feelings
Left to rot away.
I wish that I could let them out
But I just don't know what to say.
Wishing you had told me then
The words I longed to hear.
But the words came too late
and now it is a new year
Time to start a new life
to forget about the past.
Time to give up the love
that we knew just could not last...

Dorothea T. Foster

I Stood By Your Side

I stood by your side
Looking into the future
And remembering the past,
And realized how much
You meant to me.

No one realizes the agony
Of your soul, not even me.
No one realizes the agony
Of my soul, not even you.
Two agonies, yet so different.

I won't forget you, no matter
How hard I try to.
I won't forget the laughter,
The tears, and the shared
Times between us.

I stand looking into your face
For the last time,
Wishing you were here,
But I realize you aren't in pain,
God help me to understand...

Bonita D. Whitmire

Waiting For Death

Standing by my window
Looking out on a cold dark world
Alone, lonely and friendless
Watching the feathery white swirl
I am waiting for death.

No hand to hold
No sweet love left in my heart
All faith has left my soul
Eager and ready this world to depart
I am waiting for death.

On golden wings of gossamer
My destiny I can foresee
Sweet angels hovering
Readily loving - Now coming for me
I am waiting for death.

Fearsome and bold he is here
Drawing close to carry me away
Death - The hand of God
Came for me at last today
And I no longer wait.

Donna B. Moore

Meet Me Tonight

Kisses, sweet kisses
Love, sweet love
All I ask is to be
    near you again.
To touch you softly
    and whisper in your ear
    the words you long to hear
Meet me tonight -
Meet me in your dreams
    if I'm not there.
Touch me, hold me, kiss me
    if I am.
And I'll tell you the words
    you long to hear.
I love you.

Don Nabors

It's Such A Long Time

It's been such a long time
Lord since we sit down and talked
It's no fault of yours
I was the one that balked

It seems time gets away
Never again for us to enjoy
Why do we waste the hour
When there is so much to employ

We look upon the troubled times
Forgetting happiness we have in store
We let Satan beat us down
Working us over as in a war

Dear Lord give us a shield
Stand firmly by our side
We are tired of the battle
Lift us in our saddle so we can ride

We know you are with us
But forget to call upon you
Give us strength, wisdom and knowledge
Help us, to you, to always stay true

Elnora Watters

The Infinite

Happiness and anger
Love and Hate, Yin and Yang
Why I just can't wait

The fall breezes, the spring scents
The chill of winter
It is all so infinite

Day after day, night after night
Week after week
Just tell me what is right

Finding Happiness
Losing a friend so stressed out
The rules need to bend

All my life every hour
I search for truth
Like the fruit, life is sour

Forever or now
Sometimes you need it
Love is what finite or infinite

There is no end
For love is the infinite

Eric Masters

Continuity of Personality

Do the rhymes of reason
Make sense in your case
Are you telling the truth
Can I see your face
Are your actions predictable
Is your sentiment divine
Have you disregarded
The intended demeanor
Do your past experiences
Influence present lure
How often do you attain glory
On missions of blur
In recognition of resemblance
Instincts frequently unchange
Continue spontaneous indulgence
Express your inner being
Pretentious reflectionist
Live forever in dream.

David G. Hayes

My Dad

What does my Dad mean to me?
Love and honesty for all to see-
He taught us all we should know-
Then off to Heaven he would go-
I ask God, "Why did you take
    him from me"?
He answered, "My child he is with
me, where he should be."
Oh God, I miss him so- The
Grandkids he will never know-
God answered- "Don't fret my child"-
Your Dad is looking down at you
    with a smile.
I miss you Daddy with all my heart-
Someday we'll never be apart-
I know your love is here for me
The Greatest of love ever to be-
May the gift of love you left me-
Always shine brightly for all to see-

Joyce N. Nielson

Untitled

Peace is in the mind;
Love is in the heart;
People working together,
is how harmony starts.

Music is the language;
Rhythm is the response;
Bodies moving rapidly,
reciting poetic taunts.

From deep felt emotions;
we create the lyrical art;
And with our voices,
we tame the savage heart.

While I have your attention;
Please make a mental note;
We are reaching out to you
With our prayers, dreams, and
    hopes.

Anthony Mason

Departure

Curious creatures that we are -
    mad gazers upon the star,
Craving a glimpse of God.

Instead, we draw in dark caves,
    Run in circles before we sleep
In a vague vision of pathos
    Of the shorn - of -sails lamb.

Ancient shadows lurk over our shoulders.
    The shimmer-down sun
Dogs us to hide in modern caves.

Too much time is spent
    On fantasies we cannot keep.
The bankrupt soul departs,
    Leaving a bed of bones.

Get this time force from behind us,
Let big bells ring in the new century.
Let years spin off the road like tears.
Let my wing, yours fly to distant shores.

Herschel Wayne Lucas

Running

All this talk about running-
makes me want to hide.
I'd rather sit and read a book.
Or get in a car and ride.

Hasn't anyone ever run before?
Frankly, it has become a bore
I've done my share with little to spare
I just don't want to run anymore.

Even now...
I run to the Post Office
I run to the store
I run to the phone
I run to the door.

I'll watch you put on your sneakers
I'll help you count your laps-
But, let me do my running
In my dreams...
    While I take my naps.

Bette Anderson

The Grandma Poem

*Dedicated to my third granddaughter
"Autumn Nichole Sugrue"*
Smile little baby don't you cry
Mama loves you and so do I
You're Grandpa's little sweetie pie
And Daddy's apple of his eye
So all that love will make you smile
And keep you warm all the while
So sh sh baby smile

Ida Sugrue

Untitled

Years have come and years have gone.
Many memories linger on.

Some are good and some are bad.
Making one, feel great and also sad.
Wishing to bring back those wonderful
    years.
Only creates frustration and tears.
Thinking of things that could have been.
With strangers-friends and kin.
The mistakes have taken it's toll.
But with God's help, you're PROTECTED
    from losing you're soul.

Life, itself is a mystery and a game.
Even though you don't get rich or
    have fame.
You're blessed with fond memories
    and many rough miles.
Making you're past years worthwhile.

June Rose Perry

Gone

Kiss me daisies kiss me feet
Kiss me next e'er we meet
Corn me over roll me shucks
Bells the wedding you're in tucks
I'm for grazing other fields
Yon bells for me not peals
So kiss me daisies kiss me feet
Gone's me chances we'll ever meet
So kiss me pinkies kiss me posies
There is me chances I'll rub other noses

Doris Lightfoot

Freedom Flight

By the fields or open shore
Many sounds I do ignore
Yet there's one so soft and dull
This the sound of the sea gull

In the huge blue-gray sky
Often flocks of birds fly by
They fly so light never stoppin'
My favorite one the little robin

In the trees we hear a howl
This the sound of the night owl
Up above the trees so high
These little birds they love to fly

They fly by from day to day
Yet they know not where to stay
Oh these little birds so free
How I wish it could be me
Beverly Perry

Vietnam War Memorial

Row after row of names
March in one last drill
Names of the dead or missing

Silence

Heroes of war in a battle
This Country wanted
But its People didn't
Names carved into black marble
Repose in silent

Dignity

Flowers wilt raggedly against the slab
Turning a memory into

A Tombstone
Name after name

A Silent Dignified Tombstone
Amy Schneider

Counting the Days' 'Til Christmas

Just as a child I am counting
Marking the days one by one
With a heart full of cheer
And loved ones so dear

I'm counting the days 'til Christmas
I'm sure I'll see mama and daddy
My brothers and sisters will be there
With a fire burning bright

on this Holy night
And grandma in her rockin' chair
I'm counting the days 'til Christmas
I'm marking the days one by one

With a heart full of cheer
And loved ones so dear
I'm counting the days 'til Christmas
Joyce Setzer

War

Why did I fight?
Now I will die!
Is it for right?
Why, oh God, why?
Dewey E. Williamson

My Favorite Things

The things I like best,
May seem sort of dim.,
I like lots of things,
But most, I like to swim.
I also like pickles,
They taste just right,
Nice and sour,
I also like to write.
I also like boys,
And pencils and pens,
And junky old toys,
And exploring dens,
I love to dance,
And I love shoes,
I like to prance,
To rock'n blues!
Brooke Malcom

I Miss You So!

You were the one who taught
me to ride a bike
The one who told me to be home
at night.
Now you have gone to be with
Our Father above.
I miss you so, but I send you
my love.
Cynthia Pressley

The Homecoming

You welcomed
me with a sunrise
Presented with such intensity
I sat watching in awe...
A sea gull took flight
at that moment,
Silhouette against the horizon
An inspiration
I would recapture
In my mind's eye
A hundred times over
when I would long
For distant shores...
Cindi Hall

Bye

Sometimes when your beautiful blues
Meet my warm brown
A spark begins with you
And glides o'er to glow
In me

Your precious face;
That dimple placed just so —
A handsome beauty there
In your always-tousled hair

My heart grew a little bigger
My eyes each grew a new tear
When your first word
Embarked upon my ear

"Bye" is a word
Mommies never want to hear
Jennifer M. Oelsner

Hidden Love

Where is it...
Miles away,
No where to be found.
Longing to be shared,

Deep down in the hearts.
Will it ever...
Shine about,

Only the one...
Who shares,
Will ever find out.
Amanda E. Reis

Terpsichore

Cast of water
mixed with dust
a teraph made of clay
with earthen chains
is bound in place
confined to night and day

But then, a note,
a chord, a song
of seraphs stirs the air
and breaks the mold
Behold! Behold!
the breath of God laid bare

And in that nave
of fluid space
a grace transcending time
suspends in air
the mortal flesh
transformed to the divine
Cathleen G. Cuppett

No Lili'u

White Mystic fragrance rare
morning divas everywhere
in my garden

Reds, pinks, orange stools
peacock tails carnations rule
in my garden

Pakalana creeping crawling
Hina's hair gently falling
round the gardenia in my garden

Fragile ilima unscented, entwined
palapalai unfolding, sentinel of time
in my garden

Maili liilii stately serene
Mokihana berries volatile when green
in my garden

Lehua blossoms sparkling in the mist
reaching to the heavens
praising our bliss in my garden

Graceful pandanus dancing in the wind
calling all Divas our day doth begin in my
garden
Angeline Locey

47th Anniversary Waltz

I dance in my head
Much better
Than ever my feet
Could tread a measure.
My muscles remember
And twitch with pleasure.
I'm Leslie Caron,
You Fred or Gene.
Picture the scene?
"My very dear,
Our love is here to stay."
We're gliding and twirling,
Floating and swirling,
My hair matching my feet.
It is too sweet to bear.
Inside my head
We danced that way
Are dancing still
And will — always
Inside my head.

Faye S. Hortenstine

No One At All

It's fifteen below
My ass is cold
Booze is my choice
One of the few I still make
For in my life there's been many mistakes
My mind is strong, my body weak
At times I eat only twice a week.
There's holes in my shoes
Hell holes in my feet
A little what it's like
My life on the streets

Cathy Stitt

Saying Good Bye

I feel my heart breaking slowly inside
   my chest
But I can't help crying, though I try
   my best
You touched my life in so many
   ways
So naturally I wanted you to
   stay
But you said you couldn't and it was
   time to go
I gave you a kiss as we walked
   through the snow
Finally you turned and looked me
   straight in the face
And quickly drew me close in a warm
   embrace
You pulled away slowly and said
"don't cry"
So I looked at you and said
"goodbye."

Amy K. Turner

The Cat

See the cat
Moving swiftly without a sound
Its eyes glowing
Yet the sky is midnight black
I see it and it stares back
Moving slowly I walk to it
Its eyes wide and searching
I reach to touch its velvet fur
And it is gone

Adrian Foster

The World is Bent

The world is bent
My energy spent
On making sense of nonsense.
The more I try
To let go by
The more seeps in my conscience.

So much has changed
Been rearranged
And as the world keeps turning,
Every thought
That's ever been taught
Is now in need of relearning.

So facing the plight
Between wrong and right
While wondering where up or down is,
Makes being insane
Not nearly the strain
That trying to stay mentally sound is.

Joy L. Dominguez

"Awake at Dawn"

Awake at dawn
My eyes became drawn
To the resurrected sun
That yawned yellow fire
That swiped from the
Darkness daring endeavors.
And with night lifted off my lids
I was then free to see again
I was free to observe the
Common occurrence again
To which the blind man once raved

Eight thousand suns
And I could not remember one
Until today.
Eight thousand days of beauty
Had passed,
But this moment will last
When I think what life is full of
—Chances at redemption
When you least expect it.

Eric M. Dennison

The Other Side Of Darkness

Fear surrounds my soul tonight
   my fields are misty grey,
Flowers on the road I climbed
   have all been blown away.

I cannot trace the winners path
   or wear the victors crown.
Nights rest heavy on my head
   the days come spinning down.

Within the corners of my mind
   the walls begin to tremble,
A thief that steals the night away
   my peace to ashes crumble.

There is no meaning on this earth
   my dreams have been a abandoned,
Lonely stars are silent scars
.   that drift down distant canyons.

I cannot laugh with children small
   or sing a prayerful tune,
Until I turn the surging tide
   and ride the wayward moon.

Glen Tustin

In My Heart

Close your eyes and go to sleep, in
my heart your love I'll keep.
The time has come to say good-bye,
this day I've dreaded I cannot lie.
Promises were made and things
discussed, but I can't help thinking
what about us? This may sound
selfish and In sincere, I need you
close, I need you near.
Our life was wonderful and
so complete, In my heart your
love I'll keep, so close your eyes
and let it begin, this journey
I've heard with never end. I'll
sit beside you and help you through
to the warmth and love
awaiting to embrace you.
The time has come to say
Good-bye, your heart is
happy, I must not cry.

Cindi Thornton

Life In Years

Why do I feel so low
my life has changed
it's not the same
bring me back to years before
when I had no worries
nothing to be scared of
my childhood is gone
only of memories
which seem so long ago

Now I think more of my future
so many decisions to make
so many things left undone
still yet to challenge

I never knew a childhood
was so precious
the years went by without knowing
life in years can be complicated
something I wish I knew before

But without knowing then
here I am now

Amy Morrissette

Promised Dance

I will dance for you all,
my mother and grandmother
and great grandmother.
I will dance for your sins unredeemed
and your dreams unfulfilled,
your words unspoken
and your tears not shed
and your joy not felt.

I will dance for your childhoods lost
and your peace not found.
They will know you when I dance;
your stories will be told
and your memories will live on
with dignity.

Franchette Conseillant

"Living Dead"

My eyes are as red as blood
My smile has been fractured
My face is like pieces
    of broken glass
My heart has grown cold
My dreams have been scattered
My love forsaken
My mind is in a whirl
My soul burns like hell's fire
And my spirit is dead

Gwendolyn Shannon

Cross Currents

Simple things - simplify
Never feeling - never needing to
Emptying out, regressing again
Turning inward, hearing nothing
Refusing to hear the silence
Content, content to hear the noise
Trying to be, instead of being
Wanting to own the world
But longing for the infinite.

Jane Johnson

Outside, Inside

Happy, clean.
Never mean.
Laughs and smiles.
All the while.
Alive, excited.
Never worry about it.
Outside.
But inside?
Cold and lost,
As in a deep winter frost.
Hollow and scared,
My thoughts never shared.
Sad and crying,
As if I were dying...
Please look inside.

Itzaida Rivera

Avarice

Nutria mid their bread munching
Nibbling, nibbling, never stopping
While the little birds keep hopping
Round peripheral edges hopping

Quickly to assuage hunger snatching
Stomach pinched to backbone starving
While the nutria are munching
Little Birds are sadly standing

Growing, all the more thinner growing
Munching, crunching, no more hopping
As I lay a sighing, dying
Is there no one, for me crying
I see the nutria a munching.

Anita Ramirez

Am I?

A wisp of whiteness am I,
Neither concrete form nor mass.
The earth that is below. Or above?
How might I grasp?

Perhaps the lightness of a dove
Will bring the power of love.
Then, never again need I ask.

Eldred E. Bunch

Velvet Days and Satin Nights

O, how I long for velvet days and satin
    nights
To see the days and nights ruled by
    their silver lights
To see the tranquil sunset with it's
    crimson hue
To see clear skies made of crystal
    blue
But alas, it is no more than a
    myth
It's worth nothing, with out you to
    share it with
For you are the sunshine that brightens
    my day
You are the star that helps guide
    my way
My love, you are both the satin and the
    velvet which enhances my life
That's why I chose you, to be my woman,
    my love,—and my wife!

Donald R. Vanlue

Like Stone

I sit like a statue,
No feeling leaves my body,
I don't care,
But, neither does anyone else,
They pass on by,
No matter how many tears,
falls from my eyes,
They pass on by,
like I'm not there.

Amanda Lemaire

In This Living Darkness

Surviving in the darkness
No light shines ahead
Easy to get turned around
In this pulsing darkness

No future
No past
Only now
In this oozing darkness

Just existing
Barely breathing
Hardly daring to move
In this suffocating darkness

Alive in the darkness
Anger, pain, fear
Alone with this anguish
In this living darkness

Deanna Redhawk

Joyful Sorrow/Sorrowful Joy

He came into my life
Not to destroy
But to bring love
Bring mutual joy.
I will not focus
On the tragic
Nor even focus
On the magic
But know somehow -
Outside my head -
A hint, a vision
Of the unsaid.

Jo Moore

Shower Tree Butterflies

Shower Tree petals.....
Riding the wind........
Like miniature butterflies.

Jacquelyne Ingledue

Our Love

Our love will always be,
no matter how near or far we are.

If I'm far away,
my love is always near you.

If you are far away,
your love I will always feel.

But when we are together,
and we hold each other close,
that's when I feel your love the most.

So remember, far away,
or close to hand. . .

Our love will always be the same,
in the wind, like the rain,
or growing like the flowers on the land.

Our love never stops...

It just keeps growing

Chris Malcolm

Love (And Villanelle) Practice

The feelings all go down so deep.
No sidestep here, don't make me wait.
Tell me now so I can sleep.

Why is it you alone should keep,
our thoughts from hearts inebriate?
The feelings all go down so deep.

Confusion forces time to creep,
and you say it must be fate.
Tell me now so I can sleep.

Understanding's not so steep,
round in circles cares relate.
The feelings all go down so deep.

You can let the trust ensweep.
Relax the rules so obstinate.
Tell me now so I can sleep.

Steady up, and take the leap.
This love I know will not abate.
The feelings all go down so deep.
Tell me now so I can sleep.

Crista S. Carroll

Hoosier Winter

I marvel at the serenity of the night.
No stars are needed with the icy jewels
on the tree.
It glistens by the night's light.
The snow shines like diamonds around me.
I'm overcome by the wonder that I see.

So bright is the morning dawn.
The snow changes by day to jewels of
pink, red, and gray.
O, the beauty of our lawn,
my hearts beats with glee.
At the loveliness of God's icy tree.

Ilena Buckley

Mr. EverReady

My battery is run down
None can be found.
I find no Energizers
Anywhere in town.

Come running fast
Mr. EverReady man,
Recharge me
You can, you can.

Plug into me.
Create a spark.
I lie awaiting
In the dark.

Full of voltage
Let out a yell,
You have recharged
My Dur-A-Cell.

Job well done!
There's joy in knowing
This lady now
Keeps going...and going...and going.

Janice Wilson

Acid Rain

There sits no robin on my sill
Nor hummingbird or whippoorwill
The butterflies I used to chase
Are gone forever from this place.

As child, I romped the fields in May
Capturing pretty things in Play
We watched them in pure delight
Then set them free to seek flight.

Such wonders of my childhood days
Are gone forever from life's ways
Yet I shall scatter seeds each day
For sparrow or dove and hope they stay.

Alyce Gehrling

To Be Young Again

To be young again, running free,
Not a problem in the world,
To trouble me

I remember the summers, they were all
So bright,
The crickets would sing, in the still
Of the night,

The roosters would crow, at the break
Of dawn,
A day full of adventures, sure to bring
Fun,

Yes to be young again, if only in the
Twinkle of an eye,
I would savor every second, as time
Passed by,

Don't rush it, enjoy it, it will be
Your best friend,
Nothing left but memories, "To be Young
Again"!

Debra A. Daniels

A Moonlit Night

On a moonlit night I sit.
Not a single lamp is lit.
This night is mine,
A gift from time.

Search thousands of years,
You'll find no place like here.
I am quiet and content
In this night that time has lent.

But soon I'll fall asleep,
With just memories to keep.
I will hold them dear,
And wish to be near.

Christine Mathias

Untitled

One more hill to climb
Not far ahead
It's hard to listen
To all that's been said

One more path to conquer
Though it seems long
Head held high
Trying to be strong

One more river to cross
Though it seems hard
Don't give up
It's in your cards

One more battle to fight
Defeat seems so rough
You stood for yourself
You strived to be tough

Your goals were accomplished
Whatever the cost
You stood by your morals
No values were lost

Heather Duff

"The End"

I love you but maybe
Not like I should
If you would just understand
I've done all I could.

I don't deserve this pain
I suffered all these years
It should have been a happy time
But it was full of tears.

The bad times out number the good
I can't control my heart
All the punches and pain
Has torn my love apart.

I care about you
But love isn't there
I've searched for an answer
But it's just not there.

Cathy C. Grundy

One Day Of My Life

Took a step into space with a landing
on an Island. With such beauty and
brilliance, what a view with waves
breaking against the surface and the
friendliness of all! Was like saying
you have been blessed by the Island
of Cyprus and Aphrodite!

Clara Gange

Visions

I thought of you,
not only in this eve,
but on countless ones before.
It was only last night that you
came to visit me in a dream.
You stood there, like a mighty oak.
Straight, and tall, and strong.
You gazed into my eyes,
yet said not a word.
I was certain you could see into my soul,
and knew every thought.
My heart pounded fiercely,
as I reached out to you.
I stroked your hand with mine.
Then ever so gently,
I touched your cheek with my warm
wanting lips.
You smiled,
and in that very moment,
I knew perfection.

Elizabeth Steinhilber

"Separation"

I think of you every day
not with romantic vision
nor with an ache of missing
nor with impassioned wishing,
But with sadness and submission
to the reality of losing
what would have been forever
had our spirits done the choosing.

No different is this kiss
upon your silent soul in sleeping
than the kiss upon your lips
when my love was in your keeping.

You cannot see my face in vision
nor mirrored behind you in reflection.

I am with you just the same
I am within you....just a dream.

Connie Lewis

Fear

Scared, timid, shy, Alone.
Nothing to do, no where to go.
    My world swallowed in darkness,
    All I feel is cold and harshness.
Do the best; fear of failing.
No succeeding; fear of wailing.
    Must overcome this pain,
    just as quickly as it came.
I face my fears; I succeed.
I conquer my fears; I am freed.

Alissa Blair

Love In Full Circle

Into this life I looked for you.
Now, at last, my search is through.
Touch me, love, for time is gone.
Shades of night will fade to dawn.
Infinity calls out our names,
We two are gone....
One remains.

Time marches on.
Transition heals pain.
You memory lives on
Until we meet again.

Colleen J. McClain & Todd Crawford

The Dream

I just had a dream
now, I'm scared to go to sleep.
Cause, though you left me long ago,
your memories are mine to keep.
I dreamt you came into my room
and kissed me on the cheek.
You said that you still loved me,
at this point I was weak.
You started to undress me
I could feel your hands.
You put your arms around me,
and held me like a man.
Then you gave me a kiss
it all seemed so real.
Your breath I could taste.
Your lips I could feel.
We started making love
I could hear your little moan
That must have been what woke me.
Because, now I'm all alone.

Darin Young

Nowhere

Down this road to
Nowhere,
I feel all alone,
on a road as bumpy as
stone,
Did I make a wrong
turn?
When will I learn,
this is the road to
Nowhere,
No one will even care,
on the road to nowhere,
I am the only one
who knows, who sees,
who hears, and who fears.
I'm on my way to Nowhere,
I left without a care.

Holly Carter

My Prayer

Where are the holy women
of I Peter Chapter 3
with a meek and quiet spirit
Lord let me be
a wife who's in subjection
to her husband as the Lord
a heart that's not corruptible
a wife that's not adorned
with plaited hair or gold
or apparel of great cost
but a chaste conversation
to win a husband if he's lost
Sara called her husband Lord
whose daughters we are too
dear God I want to be
a holy wife with great virtue.

Gail Neal

Free

With wings, but unable to fly
With voice, yet unable to sing
My eyes blinded by tears
My thoughts dimmed by fears.

My hands forbidden to touch
My heart banned from love
But in dreams I found the key
To unleash the soul, so it'll be free.

Free to cry,
Free to sing,
Free to fly,
Free to think.

Free to kiss,
Free to touch,
Free to give him
All my love.

When in my dreams I surrender all
My love unfolds so free
That not even him
Is allowed to know.

Aurora Muñoz

My New England

I've been away from you so long
that I can hardly bear it
Your beaches and your ocean waves
I listen and I hear it.

The changing of the seasons
are something to behold
the autumn with its changing leaves
I would not trade for gold.

The winter with its crisp sharp air
and dress of Snow White
pointed there by God's own hand
are such a lustrous sight.

Some day soon I shall return
and never more will roam -
because at last I shall be back
to the place that I call home.

Irene D. Boulé

Outlived It All

Growin' belly.
nutten inside den,
'cept hunger and pain.

Swellin' heart!
Everyting inside!
Tanks be fe me man!

Growin' belly!
Everyting inside.
Sweet yams, callaloo, and pickney.

Shrinkin' heart.
nutten outside now.
no pickney.
no man.
nutten.

Gary A. Negin

Or Else

Life and
Eternity is worth
The wait.

The beginning of time
Has never
Ended and never will.
Remember
Everything you can.

Beware of the
End.

Please cherish the
Earth, be careful,
And always remember everything you
Can
Everything.

Martine Barnes

in - ev - i - ta - ble,

di - ag - no - sis,

Insanity, my disease
Knowledge, its germ.
Infecting, my nervous system
with the speed and agility
of white rapids
That will not cease
Until I can fly!!

Brent W. Foster

Flower Show

I told
my Florist/Psychiatrist
all about you
all about my infatuation
with you

the florist said send flowers
the doctor said let her know
show her

so I send you
some flowers
so that to show
I want you
to know

these are the flowers
You are the Show
You are the Show

Charles Krencicki

Christmas

With these thoughts and feelings;
of Christmas emotion
keep them stowed in your heart;
for strength to keep in motion -
For although there are so many things;
Christmas may represent
The true meaning is faith and love;
and hope though repent -
It's not about repentance, to a preacher,
or an Idol
It is simply, you and God;
a personal recital

David A. Ballard

Dear Mom

Dear Mom, I love you so, so if you I go to war, there is a few things
I want you to know.
Dear Mom, remember the good times, in my youth and in my prime.
Dear Mom, I miss you so much, so please write letters and keep in touch.
Dear Mom, please don't hate the enemy, he too will suffer the pain and agony.
Dear Mom, I can tell you not to worry, but in our hearts we'll all feel the fury.
Dear Mom, you were always there, thanks for the love, thanks for the care.
Dear Mom, when I kissed you good-bye, I could see your love thru the tears in your eyes.
Dear Mom, you'll worry the most, but we must defend this land from coast to coast.
Dear Mom, you must stay strong, with your love and understanding it will help us get along.
Dear Mom, don't spend all your time worrying about me, and don't forget the rest of the family.
Dear Mom, this time will pass, so please hang in there 'til I see you at last.
Dear Mom, remember this, I love you so much I'll see you soon, and look forward to your touch.

> *Jay Keck*

The Recruit

Take a walk with me if you will through insanity's labrynthine halls,
Where the Rats, devouring logic and life, scurry within the walls,
Take my hand and I'll guide you along, I know this place all too well,
There is no other realm as free as this, it has been called both heaven and hell;
Take care and watch your step, the ground is patchwork of minds,
More than a few are known to play games, their tricks have seldom been kind,
Take no notice of your terror, the electric impulses of fear.
Or the darkness shall take you in your panic and hold you so very near,
Take all that you may have been taught and put every little bit of it aside,
If you attempt to rationalize you can never enjoy the ride,
Take not what the residents offer, they all want to lead you astray,
To be imprisoned for eternity, within a single thought locked away,
Take a little advice and scream only when it feels good,
Although it all can sometimes hurt quite a bit more than it should,
Take a hero's stance and defy despair's freezing hand,
Will versus weakness are on the scales, at stake in this alien land,
Take time to study the surroundings, you might possibly comprehend,
The scent of emotions, the feel of the future, chaos without end,
Take a look now at these bits of yourself, at the hole into which you've been hurled,
And know that forever, in heart, mind, and soul, you are part of Insanity's world.

> *Terrin "Bones" Martin*

"Gift From A Friend"

It was getting late in the day, I remember it vividly,
I was waiting for something that a friend had promised me.

I didn't know what he could have that he would want to send to me,
I hadn't ask for anything special, I wondered, what could it be.

As I sat and waited, each minute seemed to turn into hours,
Could it be something precious, or maybe a bouquet of flowers.

Maybe he sent me one of those new tools I was telling him about,
I remember telling him a couple days ago how mine had wore out.

Or it might be something that I really don't care about at all,
We talked about so much that day, maybe I could give him a call.

He knows of all the things I like to do to keep busy,
If it doesn't show up soon I'll go into a tizzy.

Gosh, maybe something happened, maybe it got lost or something,
Maybe, I should make a call to see if he has sent me that thing.

I picked up the phone and dialed the number he gave me the other day,
I couldn't believe what I heard when they answered the phone this
  way.

"PEACE, LOVE, AND GOD BLESS YOU ON THIS BEAUTIFUL DAY"
"Hold on a millisecond, GOD will be with you right away!?

When I heard whose number I had dialed I though, now what do I say?
I guess I'll just thank HIM for the gift of life he gives me
  everyday.

> *george gurney*

Increase The Peace

Stop all the fighting, man
Increase the Peace
Show your brotherhood
from sea to sea.

Stop all the fighting, man
Show your smile around the world
Open your mouth
let the words be heard.

Show everyone
that a smile has no eyes
Color means nothing
to a grin.

Tell everyone
to open up their hearts
and let the peace
flow in.

Stop all the fighting, man
spread the love around.
Stop all the fighting, man
Peace will be found.

> *Bobbi Jo Thomas*

My Prayer

God forgive me
for all the wrong I've done
Show me the way
to become someone

Once these words I had spoken
my soul was filled with love
the comfort I began to feel inside
had come from the Lord above

By asking that He take control
when I realized I truly had none
Peace had come, I felt at ease
from fears no longer would I run

On that day I came to know
at no time alone had I been
the Lord was always there for me
my heart just never let Him in

> *Dale E. Firmin*

The Swamp

The swamp is deep,
do not go near.
Pay attention now
so you can hear.

The terrible swamp
is very dark too.
If you get too close
it might swallow you.

Stay away I say,
The swamp is bad.
Listen to me!
Don't make me mad.

But now come closer,
closer to me.
Chomp, munch, gulp.
I am The swamp you see.

> *Alexander Sluk*

The Maze

When I breath the autumn's air
I hear the chant of spring.
Unknowing what will come to me
I merely have to sing.

There is an echo in the woods
So deep and hollow you see
But tone of it's sound brings mystical music to me.

I see dark I see light there has to be a way
to finally escape you see from this
impure confusing maze.

Dorian Dale McWain Jr.

A Distant Shore

As I walk along a distant shore, my feet sink in the sand.
I hear the waves of the ocean, I reach out to take your hand.

I realize I'm just imagining you aren't here with me.
But I feel your presence so close, so I feel that we both watch the sea.

I'm in search for a perfect gift, something I can't buy.
So I walk along this distant shore, in search as the sea gulls fly by.

I found my gift to give to you, it's perfect in every way.
It's for my friend on another shore, whom I think about everyday.

I've found a beautiful pink sea shell, that I've filled with the
    beach's sand.
I have sent it with the poem, in hopes you'll keep it and hold it in
    your hand.

This is for my friend on the opposite shore, I just wish it could've
    been more.
I can't wait to see you again, for we are far, but we'll be together
    again.

Once again I'm on this distant shore, thinking only of you my friend.
We have a bond, nothing more, and we are going to stay that way till
    the end.

Joe Murray

You

I think of you so often.
I hurt so deep inside.
Why did you have to leave me, never to return.
Everyone had told me that time would Heal my Pain.
But it just keeps hurting, like the falling rain,
It subsides for a while, then comes another cloud.
I miss your hugs and comfort and all of the advice.
Right now I sure could use it;
My thoughts are so confused.
If you were here I'd know just what to do.
You were always there for me no matter what.
I wish you could have stayed.
I know it wasn't your fault you had to go away.
Daddy I'll still continue to miss you everyday.
My Love Now and Always,
Your Daughter.

Anita Burnett

Autumn Magic

The tree was full
of butterflies fluttering in the sun,
I saw the glow through their
wings and longed to capture some.

They floated down to where
I stood and landed on my
Sleeves, but Autumn Magic
Turned them into
Golden leaves.

Blair Stone

Those Banjos

When I heard those Banjos playing and the sound of tappin' feet,
I knew there was a parade a comin', down good ole basin street.
The black folks were a marchin', the melody, oh, so sweet,
The tune that they were playin', had magic in it's beat.
The drums were rolling softly and the trumpets muted sound,
With trombones blending sweetly and the Banjos all around.
I didn't see the saxophones, until they passed me by,
The rhythm they were whispering, just drifted through the sky.
Oh what a day for music and the blackman's happy feet,
The day I heard the Banjos comin', down good ole basin street.

James R. Smith

A Prayer to God

Give me her strength, dear Lord, I pray
I know you blessed her in a special way.
For she was brave and strong and true
And kept her faith deeply rooted in you.

I'm so weak, dear Lord, you know
I cry, I plead for her special glow.
I know she lives within my heart
And the values she taught me will never depart.

You make no mistakes, Lord, and we're not to question
We thank you, dear God for her lasting impression.
You created us all, Lord, so you must know
How our hearts are breaking and that we miss her so.

Help me to live in such a way
That pleases you from day to day.
Let me not forget how she persevered
Even in the face of death—her stronghold was You, she never
feared.

So this is my humble prayer today
God, help me to be like you each day.
Let the love of Christ be my one true Guide
'Til I meet you, Mom and Dad at eventide.

Catherine M. Leaird

Clipped Wings

When I set off in existence
I left your love behind
I tried to scratch the past
From my simple mind

The black and white photographs
Flashed in my head
Beautiful fossils left impressions
Lying in my bed

I felt stark naked
In the spirit of death
With an audience of zombies
All staring at my head

Now I sit in the attic of my mind with closed doors
Peeking out a small window of my past
Sewing my thoughts together
Making a quilt of chains

Holding keys I don't need or believe
Always a bridge to my dreams
Avenues to dead end streets
I'd fly but I have clipped wings.

Brett Neilan

"Sweet Memories"

As I sit by my window in peace
I listen to the wind blow.
I start to let my mind wonder
why the time seems to move so slow.

As I lay my head back, to relax my mind
I listen to the radio play our favorite tune.
Keeping my inner thoughts and emotions to myself
I believe happiness will come, if not too soon.

I hold so many thoughts deep inside
for then will I awake.
I seem to dream on and on
with the memories of our strolls by the lake.

I often wonder what is to become of me
Will I ever leave the past behind.
I drift and I linger on
trying to keep a clear mind.

And once again as I let my mind wonder.
Still remembering the past.
Reminding myself of sweet memories
I now realize I'm happy at last.

Jacqueline Whaley

Reflections

Back in my younger days, when mirrors held no truth,
I lived long with a lady who mirrored all my youth.
She led me through the dance of life; she'd whirl away my hours.
On rainy days, I still recall the pleasure that was ours.

She always loved flowers; she kept them in a vase.
She loved the little bird she had; she kept him in a cage.
She loved me and the songs I sang; she kept me by her side.
But more she loved her memories, and she'd often cry.

She said, "Sing me a sad song of a love that had to die —
Of nevermore memories, reflected in a lie.
Sing to me of dreams holding back the morning sun,
And I'll play you with a passion that keeps the night forever
young."

Sometimes life's a silly game, a mocking manic jest.
It let's us think that where we are is only second best.
So I wonder what might have been if she ever could let go.
But though she's there and I still care, I'll never ever know.

She said, "Sing me a sad song, but this time sing no lies.
My memories are fading and soon, my love, must die.
No more songs of dreams, just one quarter note of truth,
And then I will leave you, Love, what is left of your youth."

Jon Barron

Forever

I mourn you like my own child born
I long for you to wake me in the morn,
as you did so often do.
Your warm soft comfort I can no longer find.
You are gone from my life, yet I love you still.
Once, you were my most coveted friend on Earth,
now are my guidance from afar.
I had not a chance to prepare you for death, as
I was unprepared
You took my life long secrets with you;
and shall keep them until I join thee
You are my one true confidant, past,
present and future.
You, my beloved friend and teacher, forever.

Julie K. Blecker

First Time On A Glacier

Gingerly, I place my foot on the ice,
I look around me.
Shining blue puddles in my path.
like little swimming pools turning into miniature
        rivers.
Waterfalls plunge down towering mountains in the distance,
like cold water flowing from an overflowing cup.
surrounded by an icy wonderland.
soft, cool winds blow gently across my cheek
as I walk on slippery ice.

Adrianne Guerra

Endless Reminders

Sometimes when I'm out at night and
I look at the pale moonlight, I in visualize
the color of your tender face, and the twinkling
stars reminds me of the glimmer in your eyes,
but the chirping of the birds reminds me of
your unique smile across your face when
you laugh your musical laugh.

The touch of the grass, as I walk on my bare feet,
reminds me of your soft touch, and the hot temperature of the
night reminds me of the security I feel when your arms are
tightly holding me close, but the feeling of a flower touching
my lips remind me of your sweet, sweet lips.

But the smell, the smell of the midnight
air reminds me of the scent of your cologne,
and the warm breeze against my neck, as
I stand on the soft grass, reminds me of your
warm moist breath, but most of all the
shining light, for I know not where it comes
from, reminds me of our new beginning
whenever I hear you say: "I Love You"

Jessica Schroeder

Your Child's Role Model

Ever think to see the world thru my eyes and learn what it is I see?
I look to you to be my role model to see what I will someday be
You build a lifetime by making choices in hundreds of separate acts
Sometimes the acts are done by impulse, sometimes by learning facts
It is by being honest in the many little things you do every day
That you reveal the inner values coming out in what you do and say
Do I learn to condemn those whose skin or faith are strange to us?
Can I learn that the same dreams are in all persons building trust?
Remember me when you make remarks about that neighbor moving in
Think of something positive to say and we will all then win
Cheating on your taxes may seem the necessary thing for you to do
Please render unto Caesar the money the government says is due
Help me to turn to hope and turn away from our society's fears
Isn't learning laughter better than to face the world with tears?
If you can stay away from the dangers of drugs, cigarettes and drinks
Than I can be strong in my mind and not go by what my peers think
A childhood's turning kaleidoscope of years will quickly fade away
The values that you personify that thru the years with me will stay

Betty Miller

The Candle Of Love

My heart is like a candle
barely been lit up before,
and then that special someone
comes and lights it up some more.
  It grows bigger and
bigger like a fire in the sky.
All because that special
someone has lit me up inside.

Jennifer Grasty-Todd

As This Night Does

As the final toll comes to me this night
I look upon a dismal sight
Memories, for me, are like a knife
They cut through me before taking my life this night does.

If they were full, enriched, and worthwhile things
Then comfort would surround this earthly king
But they are, for me, like a knife
They cut through me before taking my life this night does.

The darkness, the hatred, the life of sin
They are killing me from within
For they are, for me, like a knife
They cut through me before taking my life this night does.

There's no love or compassion, which brings no friends
There is no life to be taken then
But still, they are like a knife
They cut through me before taking my life this night does.

I think I'll go now to my resting place
Death is coming to this face
No more memories, no more knives
Just a soul, who sits and cries, as this night does.

Daniel E. Richards

My Brother

My brother
I Love you so
I find it hard to let you go

While you're up there
And I'm down here
All I can do now is cry my tears

I can still see your big brown eyes
    with excitement and fear
But you're in a better place than down here

A son, a brother and a great uncle too.
All your nephews and niece will dearly miss you.

A Heart of gold and full of love
Something this family needs more of.

I can honestly tell the world and everyone else
    that your big brother will love you for ever yet.

I still have several things I want to say
    but you're not here for me to say
I Love You, I Love You Kevin I say.
Now I lay you down and pray
    that I will see you another day.

Jim Taylor

Don't Wonder Why

In the early dark hours of Christmas Day,
I often wonder and often pray-
A question plagues my inner soul,
why did my child so quickly come and go.

His body was tiny behind that glass wall,
I longed to hold him, but went numb when I saw-
those tiny fingers and body struggling for life,
as the ambulance swept him away after night.

Though he was in one place and I in another,
I could feel his struggle, I wanted to shutter-
I love this baby, this stranger in glass,
even years later the feeling hasn't passed.

But because of this angel born that cold Christmas Day,
I've a beautiful daughter who warms each day.
She's beautiful and caring and shines in his light,
She's a reminder each Christmas that things turned out right.

Gloria Wessely

Where Do I Go From Here?

What will happen to me?
I mean, when there is no one to watch me grow and take pride in
    what I do?
What happened to the people who said they cared so much about me?
Where are they now?
I call out their names and they're not there.
Every night as I go to bed, I pray to God: "Please God, make them
    come back for me. Why don't they care anymore?"
Where do I go from here?

Every morning when I wake up, I race to the window...
    "Are there any familiar cars? Maybe someone..."
I live with a wonderful family, I really do. But they are not mine, I
    want my own.
Please tell me, where do I go from here?

People tell me that they are there for me if I need them, to talk to,
    to listen, to love me... But, how can I love them back? I may
    have to leave tomorrow. I can not bear losing another person I
    care for.
"God, do they understand?" I hope they do.
People tell me that they will do what is best for me. I don't really
    know what that is.
I just want to know... "Where do I go from here?"

Amy Lecklitner

Midnight Stroll

One cold winter night when the wind was blowing
I met a women that made me forget.
So many have past by but only stopped
I wish it was for more than a second.
I wonder if someone has ever felt that way about me.
I wonder if she did.
What are the chances?
I had a dream - it was icy cold windy and black
Someone was holding my hand.
It was my only hope.
It was what made me win.
The difference between nothing and everything!
It was too dark to see her face.
(I wanted to light a match but instead
I let go of her hand and walked away.)
I started singing so that she knew where I was.
I hope she finds me because my hands are cold.
Maybe she is cold too.

Bruce C. Kopp

"I Met God"

I met God on a mountain where I had gone to pray:
I met Him at the sea shore, as I watched the ocean's spray.

I met God in a valley where sang the honey bee:
I met Him in a forest in the beauty of a tree.

I met God in a chapel where people's heads were bowed:
I met Him on a side walk in the midst of a busy crowd:

I met God on my knees one night where refuge I did seek:
I met Him in the death of a friend while He my soul did keep.

I met God in the summer rain, while answered prayer fell down"
I met Him in the starry night where His glory did abound.

I met God everywhere I went and my soul with joy would start:
He's with me every where I go for He lives within my heart.
So let God's good love be your start.

Judy Charlene Covington

My Son

I miss him, but I must let him go
I miss him, like no one can know.
I miss his bustle and hustle each time he came in
I miss the questions on where he'd been.

I miss waking him up each day
I miss him doing things his way.
I miss him - making messes in the bathroom.
I miss him, watching him comb and getting groom.

But the Lord lent him to me eighteen years ago
And I've tried hard to teach him things he should know.
Now he's a man and on his own and my work is done
But I miss him — he's still my son

Jo Money

Spring's On Its Way

Winter's a hard time! Everything's grey.
I need you, my Darlin'. Oh, don't go away!
I know we'll get thru it but not in a day
Look over the mountain. Spring's on its way.

I've had a bad winter most all of my life
I'm tired of the labor, tired of the strife
But, with you here beside me I'll make it I know
There are sweet blossoms under the snow

There must have been a springtime and I missed it somewhere
'Cause the most I remember is troubles and cares
Somebody told me if I'd just hang in there
We'd have another Springtime, the sky would be fair

They say 'springtime's a fine time with flowers everywhere
Oh how I long to be with you there
I think the winter's over and Springtime is near
Stay close beside me for you bring me cheer!

Oh yes! Winter's a hard time. Everything's grey.
I need you, My darlin'. Oh! don't go away!
I know we'll get thru it but not in a day
Look over the mountain. Spring's on its way

Blanche Phillips

I'm Sorry

I never meant to hurt you,
I never meant to make you cry
I didn't mean the things I said

I know you loved me,
I know you cared,
I know your feelings were so deep
I never meant to leave,
But it was all like a fairy tale that went bad.
I'm sorry!
I don't know how many times
I have to say I'm sorry,
But I'm telling you now.
I'm sorry for everything that went bad

I didn't mean to run away, but
I didn't want to be a slave
I'm sorry I never told you I love you,
I'm sorry I didn't say goodbye
I'm sorry, that's all. I'm sorry!

Andrea Turner

The Unfulfilled Dream

In my dream, I smell the soft of the roses
I never received.

In my dream, I feel the kiss that was
never placed upon my lips.

In my dream, I feel warmth of a hand that
never touched my face.
In my dream, I hear a voice that
never spoke my name.
In my dream, I feel the love you never gave to me,
and never will.

Crystal Ormand

The Mandrake

One day while I was sitting, sitting
I noticed my world was spinning, spinning
Figures dancing all around
People talking but not a sound
I noticed the sky was laughing, laughing
But strangest of all this passing, passing
Was a very odd plant, a hand-shaped green
definitely the strangest thing I'd seen
But stranger than, I do mean
- I thought I heard it scream!

Adam J. Logan

The Wind And I

Each night, before I sleep
I open wide my window
My friend, I ask the wind,
to tell you that I am thinking of you.
And beg him please, to tell you that
I love you.
Each night, before you sleep
He sneaks in through your window
and tells of my thoughts and love,
then gently does he kiss you.
The wind is jealous of my love,
this he has often told me.
Each night, my friend will tell you of
my love, and close his eyes and kiss you.
Each night, before I sleep
I ask myself this question,
who could truly love you more than I.
My friend the Wind, blowing in my face,
will say, I am quite sure my friend, I do.

David R. Walker

"A Prayer For A Loved One"

Great spirit that circles mother earth.
I pray that the eagle spirit will watch,
the path of the one I love.
I pray to your great spirit,
that you may touch her with your blessings,
for she is special to me, us mother earth, is special to you.
I have felt the skies at my felt because of her.
My spirit is as one with hers,
as the universe is at one with your great spirit.
Great spirit that soars as high,
you have touched my heart many times,
and now you have given me someone to love,
someone to touch my heart, as you have great spirit.
I pray that you know,
that I am honored to receive your blessing once again.
My spirit knows that you are great,
and my spirit is forever thankful.
May you always remain true, as you are great.

Amone Camp

Visions From Afar

Images of desire invade my persona.
I pray they will never deceive.
I'm frozen in time by your alluring gaze.
Your heart I stand ready to receive.
Shadows of doubt test my faith.
They pierce my soul with ease.
Although I try to stand firmly on solid ground,
I fall helplessly to my knees.
Your eyes hold the key to undiscovered treasures
That no man deserves to behold.
An illustrious world beyond imagination.
My destiny is forever sold.
Some may speculate that this is all a dream.
If so, I shall never wake.
From this day forth, I proclaim my love
With each deep breath that I take.
Emotions increase with each timeless glance.
They destroy my peace of mind.
For the day that our eyes depart from one another,
This fool will surely go blind.

Detrick L. Sligh

"All That"

I know I'm fly
I pull all the men
Could it be my truthful lies?
Or is it behind my loving disguise?
Is it something that lies in my long, silky braids?
Or is it because I've got you in a daze?
Or maybe it's just my whip appeal
That everyone near me just happens to feel.
Some say it's my walk
Some say it's my talk
I just know I am all that.

Is it my smarts?
My brawn and brains
I'll trap you with my mind
And you'll fall for my game
Try hard to resist me,
But the result is still the same
What could it be?
I truly don't know
I just know I am all that.

Adrienne Mauney

The Apple Tree

I ran
I ran to the apple tree
The apple tree - it knew everything about me

The bark scraped my face
As I hugged the apple tree,
I tried to forget all the people, who had forgotten me

I felt so light
The tear glistened on my cheek
I knew my heart would be forever weak

I closed my eyes
I began to fall
Far, far away - away from it all

The noises were lost
I laid in a sweet darkness
No longer did I feel the sense of hopelessness

There I was buried
Underneath the apple tree
Because the apple tree - knew everything about me

Joy Becker

The Wall

Why must you hide behind your imaginary wall?
I reach out to you and bare my soul...
But all I feel is that barrier you've put between us.
Why must you fight so with your feelings for me?
I know you care
I've seen it there...
In your eyes
In your touch.
Are you afraid of tomorrow?
Or the changes that come when a promise is made?
I, too, am afraid.
So, take my hand, my heart, and my soul
And we shall walk together through life.
We shall look behind us only once,
Just long enough to watch your imaginary wall crumble to the
ground.
And I promise I shall never leave you,
For then, our destiny will be clear, and forever before us.

Janet Pelland

I Wanna Fly

I wanna fly.
I refuse to accept a life of bondage by gravity.
So one day, when I'm older and stronger,
I'm gonna spread my wings and fly.
I'll never have to land for I'll get my food
From the tops of trees,
So non-existent feet never again will desire to
Touch the ground,
For I will be great and admired by all
As that one who soared with the birds
Who overcame all obstacles
And took off on the horizon, escaping a life
Of immobility
To the ultimate freedom.

Channel Brown

Earth Sounz

I call the wind and water,
I ride upon the wings of the eagle.
Speak through the voice of the wind among the trees.
I travel with the great gray wolf when the moon is high.
I learn through eyes of the mighty horned owl that prowls in
twilight.
I bring fright with a roar of the powerful grisly, and I run
Within great herds of buffalo.
I am everywhere the free remain,
Within there my tribes, my dying
Blood Shall Stain.

Christopher S. Krause

Untitled

Hushing to a crowd of unknown destinies,
I run swiftly, but I move by slight fraction.
Large breaths for minor itches.
I seek comforting touch, boisterous chuckle, meaningful mingle.
Tangible happiness seems unrational.
I still look to see my goblet quite full.
Furrows formed in my brow. I remain concerned.
Softly stepping I do not destroy the green. I care.
Morose expressions for joyous moments.
Dread the cause which will end it all.
I fear my shadow will some day not follow the tracks I leave.
I shall not tread on any heals.
Bye, bye worldly ants goodbye.

Christina Spellman

The Stairs That Stood Alone

Hurrying to catch my plane, as I was running late,
I said goodbye on the run as I left the gate.
As I ran for the ramp, I thought it strange,
I guess everyone else must be on the plane.

As I climbed the ramp, I turned to wave,
not sure if I wanted to go stay.
So I figured I'd go, but not be gone long,
As soon as I get there I'll give them a call.

I threw a kiss and, as I turned around
I noticed this terminal down on the ground.
People in headsets were waving weird signs,

but I couldn't make out what they had on their minds.

I knew they were trying to attract my attention,
but couldn't hear a thing for the revved up engines.
As they motioned me down, they caught their breath,
I saw where I'd been and it scared me to death.

Stairs so high with no airplane attached.
One more goodbye could have been my last.
So I boarded could have been and went on my way
but first said "Thank You" what else could I say.

Elizabeth C. Wickersham

Carriage To The Throne

Dancing on the rushing sounds of thunder storms,
I saw her ride the ocean waves,
A whisper in the heart of the little Indian dressed in French.

Our eyes touched, a spoken element garnished with fragrance.
Divine crowns sent jewels of sight
And she came to the garden in a carriage to the throne.

Tomara held in her heart, petals of tears thrown to the wind.
Given to the power of love, she spoke to a man with pearls in hand.

Wings of sorrow dropped her upon a fireburst mirage.
Brightened, lights of mercury and chambers of orange
Became sacred Marietta.

She spoke to the earth and the heavens above.
Radiance of joy surpassed, in the cradle of love we exist,
In God who makes us one with him.

Shallow ends of the earth cried to be held
And water embraced feelings of depth.
Torch of magic tongues, embellished pleasure.

Tunics of blue, silhouetted flamboyance in altars made white.
Almighty power sends us in a carriage to the throne of delight.
All of time, a circle of what is right.

Bonnie Peter

Nature's Beauty

I looked up in the sky one day to see what I could see.
I saw the sky, I saw the sun, I saw the galaxies.
Sun beams played upon the clouds, raindrops on the leaves.
Windmills in the distant skies whirled
While dust danced in the breeze.

Bellowing clouds went swiftly by.
Hiding jet streams in the sky.
Bees were humming in the trees,
Birds were hoping from twigs to leaves.
Time was passing, too fast to please.

Fire flies began to show their light.
When stars and moon came into sight.
The shadows stretched into the night
And gave me such an eerie fright
As I watched the wonders of the night
And felt the power of Nature's might.

Christy L. Wallace

Pride In The Cross

You say she stands for evil,
I say you just don't understand,
For each star and bar across her face
Holds the lifeblood of ten thousand men.

I remember hearing Grandpa talk about his Papa,
Of how gallantly he had fought,
And when he lost a leg on the field of battle
He never once let himself get distraught.

He lived on for forty years more,
Always reminded of his cost,
And when the old warrior finally passed on,
He was shrouded in that tattered old St. Andrew's Cross.

So, each time I see, that old Rebel flag unfurl,
My southern heart beats a little prouder
For I know, I'm a small part of her world.

You say, she stands for evil,
I say, you just don't understand,
For each star and bar across her face
Holds the lifeblood of one very special man.

Harold Cleveland Sullins

Window To The Past

As I sit here and look thru my window to the past——
I see so much pain and heartache.

I dare not open the door— if I did— surely my heart
would burst.
My heart is torn and bleeding, from being hit with so
many stones and arrows of the past.

So, I sit here looking thru my window with such a tiny crack.

I've heard said "time heals all wounds", but surely the
person saying this never looked thru my window.

I can only wish some all-consuming flame, of love, will
enter my house, and I will never again worry about opening
my door to the past.

Bertha Gonzalez

The Question

As I look out across the land,
I see the fields touched by Gods hand,
Some believe its in science, some believe its in man,
I tell you now its easy to understand
One day there was a roar and then there came a voice,
in a kind and gentle way the voice said.
"One day they will wonder if all this is real,
So I bestow upon you this chance to be still,
To record the progress of man and time and report to me
when I come for mine."
I was proud of the duty he had gave and
stood my post and do to this day.
For a while I thought 'man', what a terrible idea
He was given this earth and what did he do?
He stripped my trees and plowed my land,
and now all that's left are the stumps in my hands
But he said "You see, when your chores are through you will
go with me to the greenest of lands." So the mountain stands
high on top of the world fulfilling his duties and doing
Gods will.

Brandie Radigan

Ode To A New Year

As One would shed an old, worn, shapeless coat,
I shed my disillusionment and fear
And turn my face into the raw, cold weightless wind
And drift ahead into a fresh New Year.

I walk into the black and lawless night.
Watch the psychedelic leaves complete their dance
And know that time is really mine to claim,
That I will surely have another chance.

I glide along in darkness...oh, so black...
And see ahead a shining, bright, clean slate.
And hopes arise that love of man can quell
The ever growing parasite of hate.

My prayer that God will give to me the knowledge
That peace-on-earth and love of all mankind,
Can be achieved through careful understanding
As the bridges of the past are burned behind.

Then as the New Year makes itself the past
And all good things borne out of it survive,
I can look myself full in the face and say
"THOSE WERE A GREAT THREE HUNDRED SIXTY FIVE!!!"

Anne Paschal

Rain Blessing

The next time it rains I dare not look toward the clouded sky.
I should hold my head down and pray and thank God for the rain.
I will not hold out my hand and try to capture not even a single
drop, Nor bend down and try to rescue any from the tiny puddles
that form there. I'll only stand still and enjoy the moment. Let
the cool crisp water embrace my crown and rest upon my shoulders.
I would hope to be carried far away to a place beside an endless
sea where I may cast in all of my troubles. Then let go a mighty
Cry for at that moment I will be truly blessed by the power of
the rain, just as I hope to some day be blessed with unending love.

James Bennit Tomlin

"Meditation"

The world has gone to sleep now. I'm the only one awake.
I sit here in the silence while I wait for dawn to break.
I think about decisions that I've had to make today.
Did I help or hurt the people, that I've met along the way?
Did I withhold a kindness or uplift a sinking soul?
Was yesterday a blessing or a loss of self control?
Did I give without expecting, a return of what I shared?
Was selfishness my motive or was it because I cared?
Did I offend my Lord today; or did I betray his trust?
In spite of human failings, were my motives kind and just?
Each night I ask these questions in a silent form of prayer.
Knowing God will answer me and enfold me in his care.
"Sleep my child." He seems to say as the moonlight bathes my face.
A Gardenias scent on summer air, He sends as a sign of grace.
I close my eyes and join the world as my heart and soul take rest.
I have no fear. I'm sure He knows, that today I gave Him my best.

Johnathan McNeil

Love

Love is a gift precious and rare
Love is a gift meant to be shared
Love is all things that are good
A touch, a smile, being understood
Love has no reason, and it is strong
When love is real, it is never wrong
Love can bring joy, happiness, and pain
But when love is true, it always remains
Love is something we all need to live
So don't be afraid to let your heart give.

Donna O'Neill

My Name Is Alcoholic

My name is Alcoholic, I drank too much too long,
I sit here sick and broken...Singing my sad song,

I used to thing I had it all, then booze became my friend,
He took me down to the bottomless pit, that hasn't any end,

He used me and abused me, and made a joke of me,
people said get rid of him, but I couldn't, or I wouldn't see,

There were times he made me feel so good, there were times I felt so
bad, when the bad times overshadowed everything,
he was the only friend I had,

But now the day of dread is here,
I'm broken and alone, my friend no longer helps me,
I sit in pain and moan,

I know I have not long to go, the end I feel is near,
Please, oh please have pity, a pint of wine, a beer,

Please I beg you, help me, before I reach the end,
one more drink is all I need, so I can find my friend,

Harold T. Costello

"Letting Go"

I'm getting older now; I guess she knows
I still don't understand why she won't let go
I give her no reason to worry or fret
I try to prove to her I've grown up quite a bit
I don't think she sees my point of view
The world is changing; so, why can't I change too

I appreciate her more than she will ever know
but still she will have to let me go

It's not that hard to do; just let me crawl
and soon I'll walk; it's Ok if I fall
Cause I'll get up and do it all over again
Even though she wants to help; she has to let go

People let flowers bloom; look at me as a flower
let me bloom too; letting go is what it's all about
all you have to do is give me room so I can sprout
Letting go can be hard; but you'll have to trust me
and keep me always in your heart *

Amber Fairlamb

Why?

Day after day
I struggle to say
the words that could change.
Anger is not the way.
Ignorance cannot slay
the demons that pang.

Why?
Can they not see or try to believe?
I am here to help.
I extend myself—
my hand, my knowledge, my time, my heart.

How can I help
someone who wants my head on a shelf
or teach that special one just out of reach,
or reach him who despises my race?

Why can't I act cold?
Why must I care for people
who can't even share?

Don't they know that they are the reason why?

Brenda Goode

Firefight I

Upon my feet had not been long
I stumbled from rest, my confusion was strong.
Within my eyes the seeds of sorrow,
And in my mind, an absence of tomorrow.

I stepped as feather, that path so shallow,
Afraid to fear but still did follow.
Within my mind my thoughts did lack,
And in a second kak, kak, kak, kak!

To my knees not prayer, my heart did cease,
My skin afire, would death __ be peace?
Those seconds passed as days be long,
With thoughts of death, now here, now strong,

For not I knew which life be lost,
Afraid to wonder, afraid the cost.
But death did pass before this pawn,
Red and green, not christmas, 'twas nearly dawn.

Then out of the mist of gray and pitch,
Red rivers did run life and death did switch.
And weeps were sent towards the ground,
Then, __ the quiet __ not even a sound.

John A. Hradil Jr.

Big Campground In The Sky

I wonder what life hereafter for campers may be
I suspect the campgrounds will be more than we can hope to see.

Will we pull or drive our rigs as we do now
It might be easier to go camping than we can allow.

There won't be water, electricity or sewer to hook up to
Our needs and life styles will be so simple there won't be much to do.

Our campers won't need repair and won't go up in smoke,
Because all will be perfect and things never broke.

Our sites won't require reservations or so I am told
But our names will be on them and the streets paved with gold.
Now this campground is special and not for everyone
But reserved for those who come by the Father, Holy Ghost and His Son.

Our friends and loved ones who have gone on before
Will all be waiting at the campgrounds front door.

We can fellowship all night and give glory to God
Our new immortal body can go forever without even a nod.

This year the Lord needed campers so he took from us an extra share
But they are all better off and do not want us to despair.

Let us continue to live right until its our turn to say goodbye,
And we make that final rally in the big campground in the sky.

Billy Sims

Pure

The purest love is that of a newborn.
Its eyes open wide, ready to learn and be loved.
It knows no spite or hate.

My love for you is like that.
It is innocent & regardless of the trials and
tribulations, it remains constant.

You are my friend, my love, and my heart.
And beyond my last breath my love for you
will remain ... Pure!

Glenn E. Donaldson, Jr.

Memories

When I think of time that's past,
I think of love that didn't last.
Friends I loved and now have lost,
Bridges I burned and ones I've crossed.

My mind has a door that is never locked.
It holds a clock that now has stopped.
I like to open that door now and then,
My memories are pictures that lie within.

The girl I see has grown much older.
The world as she knew it has grown much colder.

I yearn to be that girl so young,
To sing the songs that are now unsung.
To play the games I used to play,
To run in the rain on a summer day.

Reality strikes like a lightning bolt.
I'm not that girl anymore.
I guess it's time to lock that door.

Glenda Hodson

A Rose For A Life

As the red petals fall to the soft sullen ground,
I think of my loved ones whom I know have drowned.
The suffering of my loss with which I am cursed,
Has, I do greatly fear, put me at my worst.
I no longer smile at what one would call pretty,
Nor do I laugh when one's actions are witty.
I have no friends with which I take the time to mingle,
I have no lover to make my heart tingle.
I spend my days morning for what is no longer with me,
I have no respect for the black, roaring life-taking sea.
It took a part of me which I can't place,
It left a memory in my mind which can not be erased.
Now I am holding a dead rose in my hand.
I buried the petals way deep in the sand.
Just like my dear children, if you comprehend,
I took the red roses and their lives I did end.

Diana Wilson

"The Victim"

Last night I dreamed that I was a victim of a crime,
I thought, how foolish of me, as I lay in fear of dying.
I said, "I'm just too smart, oh no, oh no not me,"
I know it's just a dream, or that movie I went to see,
Wake up, wake up; It's all in your head,
Wake up, wake up; you just can't be dead.
But then I saw myself sitting on the witness stand,
"Yes," I said, "I recognize the defendant, it's that man."
Oh dear, I thought, Oh dear, could I be right?
Is he the one who injured me? Is he the one that night?
Wake up, wake up; this just can't be true,
I know, it wasn't me, I must be thinking of you.
Not guilty, not guilty you say, you mean he goes free?
But why doesn't' he have to pay, what about what he did to me?
You say there's not enough evidence to convict beyond a reasonable
    doubt,
A technically of some sort and his confession was tossed out!
Oh, I see, his confession can't be used you say,
We need corroboration, more evidence to put him away.
Oh, good, I am awake, it was not what it seemed,
Thank God, it was just a silly dream.

Brenda Mason

"Indian Burial Mound"

As I stared across the river at the Indian burial mound-
I thought I saw a brave with his face turned to the ground-
He wore an eagle's feather-bound tight upon his head-
This true American warrior was praying for the dead-

The words that he was saying I could not comprehend-
Chanting simple verses - throwing dust in the wind-
A cloud of village smoke went floating through the air-
The lights of many campfires - that really wasn't there-

The sound of ancient voices spoken sorely out of tune-
Gave rhythm to the drums and the rising of the moon-
A tribe of painted people preparing for a fight-
Dancing in a circle and talking to the night-

A hundred bows and arrows lay neatly in a row-
Waiting for the rays of the morning sun to glow-
And a journey into battle that never could be won-
The chances of survival and returning would be none-

The image of an owl calling softly from a tree-
That evil deathly omen sent to set a lost soul free-
And carry off to heaven - to that happy hunting ground-
To sleep eternal peaceful - at the Indian burial mound-

Allen Holloway

Untitled

My heart speaks of things for which
I touch with my tongue, use by my lips.

I love to meditate for it makes me wiser.
For I have learned from my teachers, their
wisdom and knowledge, that I kept deep
down inside of me.

As I leave with truth, courage, and the
Lord on my side. For I have seen my enemies
fall before me, until I can rise again.

I'm the one who walks in darkness,
As I grow old my body is surrounded in
darkness. I can not escape with these
chains that weigh me down.

James Galliher

Ask, And It Shall Be Given To You

With bills piled high, and funds so low
I turned to God in prayer.

I asked for help to see me through,
Then a voice whispered in my ear.
"Someone has asked of you, as you have asked of me.
What will you do for them, so I can do for thee?"

I asked for guidance to accomplish my goal
When a gentle tinge reached my soul.
"Imagine yourself to be, in place as he or she.
Then do unto them, as you would expect of me."

"How can I do this service? For, money I have none."
"Money is a just reward, when the service is done."
"That's the way it's been, that's the way it will be.
Serve first with love, if blessings are to come to thee."

I paused to think, "How blessed I am, his spirit is here."
Yet, I am careless with this gift, when I resort to fear.
I must strive to share love, that I may hear him say:
"You have one more tomorrow, from the works you did today."

Betty David

Planet Earth

Hey, look over there, its planet Earth!
I visited there once, it has no worth.
I grew up there: It made me selfish,
It was my nature, that to be.
I tried to be happy, but from
Unhappiness I could not get free.

It is a sad ole place and full of sorrow,
There is no future, no tomorrow.
I could not leave fast enough.
I tell you for sure that place is rough!
There are so few there you can trust,
So few there who are just.

I knew I was selfish and it was wrong,
But I couldn't change, it's was just too strong!
Man O' man, that place made me sad!
Only the thought of leaving made me glad!

Bill Kline

My Place In This World

I dream of fleeing from my mother's nest.
I want to soar on wings my own,
To paradise high, to learn things unknown.
Yet, there are fears in my mind that won't rest.
I feel fear as I consider this quest;
The questions in my mind through the night drone.
Can I truly survive this world alone?
Can I honestly pass life's major tests?
Yet, I do have hope, a friend and a love,
That I know in my heart will hold my hand.
He's a strength and guide God sent from the above,
And by my side I know he'll always stand.
I will face the real world, a newborn dove,
Pure wonder, I seek a place on the land.

Jennifer Ramming

Happiness Using God's Strength H.U.G.S.

I thought nobody loved me, I thought nobody cared
I wanted what my new friends had, I wanted what they shared
They told me that God loves us, each and every one
His work is never finished, his work is never done
My new friends saw me hurting, way down deep inside
I thought I'd never be happy, no matter how I tried
I wanted what they had, the handshakes and a smile
Please God keep me sober, just for a little while
Then something wonderful happened, I did not drink today
I listened to my new family, I was finally on my way
Oh! Please God hold me close, please don't let me go
I can't do it alone, I need you people so
I've accepted my addiction, no drinking or no drugs
Please don't stop giving, those wonderful God filled hugs
I know my friends will help me, they'll go to any length
Hold me tighter please, for there's happiness using God's strength

John Lingenfelter

Heavenly Father

Heavenly father, please hear me tonight,
I need your guidance to live my life right.
Sometimes the pressure is so hard to bare,
I often wonder if anyone really cares.
How can I wake up and face a new day,
Knowing I have to live my life this crazy way.
Heavenly father, please forgive me of all my sins,
I want to change, but where do I begin.
Heavenly father, please hear me tonight,
I need someone to understand me so I can
live my life right.

Jackie Kidd

I Once Kissed Death

I once kissed death for only a while,
I was given a sentence without even a trial.
There was an accident with metal against metal.
With most of the metal lying heavy upon my chest,
I should have welcomed death and it's peaceful rest.
But in the background of my mind, I could hear my
Little ones called me back from the light.
So I didn't look behind me at the devil's door, but
ahead without any fright.
So I smiled at the heavens and took a welcomed
breath,
It wasn't my time to take a walk with death.
I had things to do and loved ones to hold and
Now time to say "have a good day."
To take time to smell the roses and watch my
children at play.
So now when I have to face the small problems,
I try to remember and welcome a smile.
Because I once kissed death, even though it was
just for a while.

Donna R. Poole

Lost And Forgotten

I was once a little boy.
I was once standing by the shore
the shore of a river,
a river that seemed to cry
come, come sit by my side
for you have no need to hide.
I have many golden tales to spend.
For no one can be content
always lapping at stones and pebbles that lay
ahead of you,
and constantly flowing beneath the trees
with your queer beauty hidden,
well hidden,
and forgotten.

Daniel S. Cohn

Well Worth The Pain

Oh what a hard day this is going to be.
I will be beaten and spit on and nailed to a tree.
The people will mock me - crucify they'll say,
Oh Father, do I really have to go through with this day?

This cross is too heavy, I'm not very strong
Oh why Father, why is this journey so long.
The thorns from the crown that they gave as a gift
Are cutting my flesh - there is blood on my lip.

Why do they hate so, is there no love around?
Oh no! Now they're placing the cross on the ground.
Oh how can I stand it, they're tearing my skin,
How long will it take for the nails to go in.

My hands and my feet - such agony and pain.
"I'm thirsty", "Please help me", - they're mocking again.
Yet I've always known that this day must come.
How else could I show them that I am your son.

At last it is over, it's finished, I'm done.
I'm coming home Father, please welcome your son.
Was it worth, you may ask, all the anguish and pain?
For the plan of salvation, I'd do it again and again.

Diane Goold

"More Than You'll Ever See"

There is this guy that I love, who's name
I will not state.
I miss him very badly, for he has moved away.
I care about him deeply, more than he'll ever know.
I'm not pretty or any of that, but my love can only grow.
I've thought about this long & hard, hoping that he'd see,
    that I will always love him faithfully.
So if you're out there listening, & ever need a friend, I'll
    be here, on your side until the living end.
But for you, the guy that I love who's name I will not state.
I miss you very badly, for you have moved away.
So, while you're meeting all those girls, just please think of me.
Because I love you...more than you'll ever see.

Alyson M. Drake

I Am

I am a good guy who loves sports
I wonder what lies ahead of me in life
I hear nature crying for HELP
I see people settling their differences
I want peace on Earth
I am a good guy who loves sports.

I pretend that life is a test if I fail a test I fail in life
I feel that the walls are caving in on the future
I touch the hearts of my peers
I worry about the end of the world
I cry when people are living on the streets dying
I am a good guy who loves sports

I understand that no one is perfect
I say you only have one life to live so make the best of it
I dream of succeeding in life
I try to be the best I can be
I hope people respect me for that
I am a good guy who loves sports.

Brent DeWolfe

My Child

Because my child needs to be understood
I would go back in time if I could
I would relive my youthful days
My childlike manners, carefree ways
Since I cannot do this, I will keep in mind
Towards you I'll need to be patient and kind
When you whimper and cry over things that are senseless,
I'll remember you're so frightened and defenseless
I'll need to forgive the bad you do
I must remember I did that too.
When you do good, it is praise you need
I remember that great feeling indeed
I'll need to make time to listen and care
On those days when life seems so unfair.
And on those joyous days which seem so precious and few
I will make them seem better by being there with you
I will put myself in your young frame of mind
This is how our love and lives will bind
Yes my child needs to be understood
If I do not do it, who else would?

Diane Lindner

Memories

Gray-golden sands of remembrance
Sift silently through mind's fingers.
Illusive little grains of
Reflective recollections.

Charles G. Cromwell

Untitled

If I had the devil in my brain
I would never dance again or sing or smile
For all the while, I'd wonder if around the room
The devil watched me in the gloom.

If the devil were around
I would never go to town afraid that
He would follow me and somehow cause me misery
I'd look behind me all the time
Around the corner up a tree in an attic
Perhaps I'd see the two horned devil watching me.
If I had the devil in my brain

I'd never want to sleep at night
Especially by candle light
I'd keep the window shut real tight
The devils his meanest late at night
And I'd know for sure that he'd be there
Hiding under the bed
I'd try to sleep but I could not breathe
With the covers pulled over my head-
   If I had the devil in my brain.
   Dorothy J. Krohn

Your Last Day

If I had known it was your last day,
I would not have washed your sheets,
And hung them out to dry
If I had known it was your last day,
I would not have swept the floors,
Or cooked the evening meal,
Would not have wasted time on mundane chores,
If I had known it was your last day,
I would have held your hand in reminiscence,
Recalling 25 years in the Warrensburg house,
Life with three special sons.

If I had known it was your last day,
We would have taken a vicarious journey,
Where you could have walked the sandy shores,
And basked in the Southern Sun.

But all of a sudden, it was your last hour,
I held you close saying it was time to go,
That I would survive, that loved ones waited
On a distant shore.

And on your last day, I kissed your soul goodbye.
   Jeanette Strack

A Horse With Wings

If I was a horse with wings
I would spread them out and even sing
Fly to the sky at night
Touch the moon and stars so bright

And look for a mate some were in the land
Fly over the beach and reach down and touch the sand
Flying so free
Filling the summer and winter breeze

I could go to any land
To Rome even Japan
My wings I would spread them wide
And fly, fly, fly.
   Judy Lee Moon De Moreno

Long Distance Call

Long distance please, to God up above
I'd like him to tell me how to find love.
I know that it's late and he's probably asleep
But this is a matter that just won't keep.

I need his advise, even though I have tried
By his help I will surely abide.
Tell him Charlotte, he'll remember the name
We've spoken before on a matter that's the same.

"Hi God it's me, so sorry to bother you
But I can't find a love that is true."
"My child it's no bother, you calling me
I've been watching you, I'll tell you what I see.

My young one searching for a love that is true
Simply quit looking and it will surely find you.
Now go back to bed and get some rest
Tomorrow I'll send you the very best."

I woke to the morning and felt a little blue
Went on thru breakfast and then I found you.
I knew God had worked all thru the night
To find someone for me that was just right!
   Charlotte Richardson

"Mother's Swing"

If I a child again could be
I'd rest my head on Mama's knee
And we would swing -
Just she and me.

I'd touch again her blue-black hair
And twist a temple curl so fair
And we would swing -
On the front porch there.

   She'd brush my hair, check out my ears,
   She'd tell me of her childhood years,
   Sometimes she'd wipe away my tears,
   With tender voice she'd calm my fears.

Oh, if I a child again could be
I'd rest my head on Mama's knee
And we would swing -
Just she and me.
   Evelyn Handy

If Ever

If ever I am found not giving all I have to give
If ever it seems I am not living the life I should live
Then fall on your knees and for my soul please pray
For I am not loving or respecting God's gift from day to day

If ever I am found lusting for any worldly thing
If ever I am found coveting my neighbors for their songs to sing
Tell me quick don't wait until it is too late
For lusting turns into envy and envy will turn into hate

If ever I me and my becomes the only conversation I can stand
If ever I cannot seem to lend anyone a helping hand
Please find it in your heart to stop me right away
Because my soul will be headed in the wrong direction
   on Judgement Day

If ever I forget to give my Father in Heaven all of the praise
If ever you see my head huffed-up and puffed-up in pride raised
Please call my attention to it as soon as you can
Because I am not the one God is looking for
That ordinary man!
   Lady Rap

If God Is Forever

If God is forever, let us love Him!
If God is forever, stamp out sin!
If God is forever, then let us remember,
To open our hearts, let Him come in!

He loves children playing in the valley,
The babes cuddled close in mother's arms,
The teens walking tall beside their Daddy,
The family's His treasured charm!

He loves our aged people and their wisdom,
The poor and infirmed are hard to bear;
The rich, - the good, - and the wicked,
His cross is for all to share!

So if God is forever, let us love Him!
If God is forever, stamp out sin!
If God is forever, then let us remember,
To open our hearts, let Him come in!

Betty Pierron

"Second Half"

I am he, he is me,
if he's to die, so must I.
For we, are one in the same, called by the same name.
Though our minds run their pace, we share the identical space.
Some may not understand, how we're the same man,
but I assure you by this odyssey, that we do indeed share the
    same body
on this quest for knowledge I held fast, seeking disparately
to know my second half.
Who might this be, some may ponder, am I mad, some may wonder,
if you don't know by now to whom I refer too, then you don't
know yourself quite like I do.
To give a clue in the right direction, it's really a matter of introspection.
I've looked inside viscerally, there I found the real me.
Covered up like a little girl, scared to death to face the world
Putting on faces everyday, so it would be little I'd have to pay.
My second half directs the show, by inflating and deflating my ego
I've learned that life is but vicissitudes, dealt with by attitudes
All this taught by my second half, while discovering who I am.
Well who are you, you might ask, I'm the subconscious, your
    second half.

Anthony U. Ashley

The Emerald City

Seattle always sparkles true to its nickname,
If you haven't been there before, it is quite a shame.
The space needle stands in the city proud and tall,
You can go to Pike's Place Market, or just go to the mall.
The University of Washington is a fun and exciting place,
The campus landscape is incredible, as sea gulls fly above
    it with amazing grace.
Seattle is a city where opportunity knocks,
It is also the home of the Sonics, the Mariners, and the Sea Hawks.
The Kingdome is a huge sports facility where people
    gather to cheer for their team,
After the game is over, people flow out of there like a stream.
Some people drive to their homes on Lake Washington and Elliott Bay,
The view looking over the water is breathtaking,
    you can see it on any day.
On a clear afternoon you can see Mt. Rainier as the sunlight
    beams from the sky,
The Emerald City we call Seattle is beautiful and special,
    this I will not deny.

Brent Oenning

Way Yonder; My Love

When the Sun comes over the Mountains every morning
I'll be there with happy greetings from a far,
And I shall steal a kiss from you, without a warning
While the Sleepiness still lingers in your eyes.

And when the Sun goes down each evening in the yonder
And I find you with your welcome door a-jar,
I'll be there and tuck you in bed before I wander
On my way to be back when the Sun arise.

And I shall tuck you in my dreams and not the lonely
On my journey in the starlight on the way;
For I am happiest when you are with me only
You mean more to me than all the world and gold.

And I must tell you, so you always will remember
When the winds are blowing Cold and Sky is gray,
That the Sun shines brightly above in mid-December
And my Love for you is never ever Cold.

Ingebret Kyllingstad

Stop The Political Parties!

Vote for me! Vote for me!
I'll give you democracy.
Raise taxes, lower minimum wage,
Till the common man becomes enraged.
Get the rich out of taxes,
Let your kids play with matches.
I'm for my raise and rights for gays.
I'll make my birthday a holiday.
Forget the flag and the pledge.
Let's push my opponents off a ledge.
Keep abortions, legalize drugs,
As long as my money is safe and snug.
What? By 99%? That's how I lost?
I just now realized my campaign costs.
I better write this down so I'll remember
What not to use for next November.

Brian Thomas Garrett

Backyard Farmer

Folks,
I'm a backyard farmer now, no spread, no cow, no duds.
I've just a few half-barrels with boughten dirt an' sproutin' buds.
Cause I live here in town now, an' I'm a woman of few means,
But friends, they tell me daily, farmin' still flows through my genes.

I guess it just don't matter, if it's acres, gardens or pots,
As long as I plant somethin', even a few forget-me-nots.
Cause at heart I'm still a farm-girl, and well, you all should know,
Farm-girls, just aren't happy, 'till we plant an' somethin' grows.

I can live without some horses, without chickens, a duck or pig,
But I can't live without that sod - cause my fingers need to dig.
I need to sink them in some earth, I crave to smell that soil -
An' it seems that almost every day, in my barrels I must toil.

I guess that farmin's in my blood, an' so it must be true,
Genetic traits may play a apart, no matter what you do.
Oh, you may travel near and far, or settle East or West,
But somehow you'll end up doin', what your family loved the best.

Ann Blair

A Gift

Gift giving gives glimpses of goodness,
Lets loving linger longer,
Nicely notes nurtured needs,
Properly promotes precious people,
Favors feelings for fostering fondness,
Says sweetly something special,
Kindly keeps caring candid,
Remedies remaining reminders of rifts.

Judith Corthell

But Not Always

Sometimes the rain is warmer than the sun
  I'm often sad on sunny days
Sometimes the wind brings calm
  I feel like crying standing in the middle of a park
Sometimes being alone supplies more companionship than crowds
  I feel alone in the largest room full of friends
Sometimes the night brings a new light on things
  I can't stop laughing at a wedding
Sometimes answers come during sleep
  I saw her smile at me in a dream last night
Sometimes adults are worse than children
  I laugh when I see kids pull the same dumb stunts I did
Sometimes death means life
  I can't help smiling at funerals

  Joel Todd

Dottie's Christmas Poem

'Twas the night before Christmas and all through my shack,
I'm scrubbing and cooking and breaking my back.
The presents are wrapped, I forgot names and sizes,
The kids will be getting some cracker jack prizes.
The gang is all here, they all eat like horses,
And I know they're expecting five or six courses.
They brought two ugly dogs that bark, scratch and fight.
One just peed on my tree, I may kill them tonight.
But miracles do happen, do I see what I see?
They did bring a present for pooped little me!
And what to my wondering eyes did appear,
A rag map, some soap and a six-pack of beer.
Thank goodness it's over and now I confess,
I'm moving and leaving no forward address!

  Dotty Valley

Marjorie Valentine

Marjorie Valentine
I'm so glad that you are mine
Eyes of blue and lips like wine
Dad and I, we think you're fine

When you're older, we'll run and play
We'll sing and dance throughout the day
We'll hug and kiss your tears away
And in our hearts you will stay

I am yours dear and you are mine
That's why we called you Marjorie Valentine
Voices sing and hearts do shine
When they all know that you are mine

  Jane M. Goodrich-Card

Invictus

Far from Erin's green and lapped shore
In darkness waits for sweet Aurora's smile,
A lonely barque which now deserted, bore
A once and precious cargo to beguile
Such Gaelic charms as ne'er were put to trial.
From love's tribunal sweeter penance drew,
And Ero's bow pierced deep the precious while.
And lips that could not stay the bitter yew
Which stung the heart that felt no more as thru
The anodyne of tears, my bootless cries
Thru heaven's vault arise, Alas, perdu!
The lie has found the truth that love denies.
So sleep my love upon thy verdant bed,
While fair Adonis palms thy fustian head.

  James W. Hutchison

What's It Take

What's it take to be by your side?
I'm sure there's nothing I have not tried.
There's nothing that I would not do,
I'd give it all to be with you.

What's it take to win your heart?
I have no clue, I'm falling apart.
Your the one that can put me together,
Could heal my hurts and pains forever.

What's it take to hold you tight,
To hold you close all day and night?
Tell me please, I want to know.
Look in my eyes, doesn't it show?

What's it take to make you see,
The only person I need is thee.
Believe what I say, because it's true,
My heart desires only you.

I want to give this love I make.
I'll ask again, what does it take.

  Bob Wilson Jr.

Standing on the Threshold

I'm standing on the threshold of hardships that just past,
I'm thinking of the friendships and things that didn't last.
Reminiscent of the lying and people with deceit,
The waste of tears in crying,
And goals I didn't meet,

I'm standing on the threshold of things put forth today,
The things that I have lived with,
The things that I gave away,
I'm thinking of the violence the world has pressed on me,

The way we live in silence,
The things we do not see,

I'm standing on the threshold of time put forth to live,
I'm thinking of the future and things that I can give
If standing on the threshold and watching time go by,
Can make us grow yet stronger,
It gives us cause to try.

  Erika L. Neitzel

Set Me Free

Lord, please help me find my way back home.
I'm tired, and I'm scared, and I'm so all alone.
This wheelchair takes me now
Where my legs used to roam.
I don't mean to sound ungrateful, Lord.
I know you care for me.
I've known you have seen me through
When my life has been off key.
You know, the last few years have been pure misery,
and I know only you can set me free.
I'm glad you're faithful, Lord,
'Cause I ain't always been.
You know I'm sorry for all of my sin.
I've tried to be a good soldier,
I've taken it on the chin.
I hope you're proud of me —
I hope you'll call me kin,
When you come back to claim your world again.

  Cecil R. Traweek Jr.

The Portrait

Abandoned, dusty, there you sit,
In a corner, forgotten,
My Great, Great, Great Grandfather.
Your eyes are serious and round,
Like a hawk, watching.
What is the matter?
Did something go wrong in your life?
Is that why your face is so intense,
Like a tiger?
Do you remember anything?
Like where you lived, exactly?
You may have been gone for a long time,
But your portrait is alive with feelings and memories.
You lie there in a dusty corner,
In a tattered frame.
Thinking, waiting, trying to remember,
   Your Time.
   Erica Andersen

The River of Humanity

The water droplets move along
in a lonely, still silence,
As I watch them make their way downstream,
I ponder the question of humanity.

Are those tiny molecules of water lonely?
They just keep rolling along thru the once-forest.
Are they imitating human beings, or do we imitate
Them - drifting in loneliness until eternity?

We hope for the occasional fork in the stream,
so that we may possibly pursue another facet of living
These droplets sense no urgency, rather they are helped
along their journey by the new young batch of droplets
who push them forward into territory that has not yet been seen.

The individual molecules know not what they will encounter,
but that mighty river that keeps flowing seems
to know its destination. It pursues its destination
with a force like no other.

How can that river be so sure, so confident that it will
find happiness at the end of its marvelous journey?
Perhaps the journey is never-ending...the adventure everlasting.
   Cynthia Sue Winkley

Despairing Waters

I cry. I despair. I flounder helplessly
In a sea of confusion.

I sail the waters with determination,
But there comes a storm upon me.

Quickly, without warning, a boiling turmoil
From within.

What shall I do? Which way to turn?

How to know the proper direction and course
Is beyond my realm.

A whirlpool of emotions pulls me in
Deeper and deeper. Drowning, I choke,
"Someone please save me!" as my head swirls in pain.

This oceanic trauma encompasses me, engulfs me wholly.
I start to swim for shore;

Alas, the tide grips me, washing me back out to sea.

There is no solution but the eddy of time.
   Erin L. Taylor

My Fair-Faced Child

My fair-faced child has gone to stay
   in a world that's not her own.
I can't force her to come back home.
My fair-faced child is grown.

She was my first one, this child of fun.
With "sunshine" in her eyes.
Believed in unicorns and wished on stars.
Dear God, where is my fair-faced girl tonite?

We grew up together, this girl and me.
I always did the best I could.
We were the best of friends or so I thought.
She left although she said she never would.

She broke my heart and betrayed my trust.
But I love her even still.
I pray for my child to return.
But I don't think she ever will.

Dear God, my fair-faced girl is out tonite.
Please watch over her for me.
Help her understand right from wrong.
I don't want to lose my baby.
   Carol Holland

The Sweetness Of Roses

A rose garden grows a variety
   in colors, in sizes, and in beauty.

Some are named for countries,
   for title people, and for their abilities.

The rose symbolizes love and loyalty.
   Its exquisite elegance depict royalty.

Oh, what a holiday flora of fidelity!
   The God of love rose from the grave giving bliss for eternity.

Then the rose became a special occasion flower.
   So, baby cupid should shoot roses in lieu of arrows for sweeter
   power.

Its chosen petals on the bridal path lead in integrity.
   In the bridal bouquet, roses pledge honesty.

In renown recognition roses have arrived in society,
   in herbal remedies, in potpourri, and in the eyes of every devotee.
   Ethel Marie Chisholm

Colors

God created all of us, from the sands of the earth.
In every color with every birth.
There's a new generation, a special creation.
A blend, like the colors of a rainbow, that never ends.
We must start to make a place for them,
Before there's no hope, only the end.
God sent His only son, to open the gates of heaven.
Now its up to us, to unite as one.
So our children's children may live on
Long after were gone.
With hope, faith, and the love of God.
All mankind must start, to do their part.
As it was planned long before
{God created all of us}
From the sands of the earth
"In every color, with every birth"
   Catherine P. Carpenter

The Only One

I've seen him many times,
In life he doesn't really belong.
Those gorgeous green eyes,
How they haunt my dreams.
I drowned in his every immortal word.
I feel an uncontained love for him that is so divine.
To the world he just a speck on their shoes.
To me he is an ornament of beauty,
a bird that flies in heavens sweetest air.
To the world he is a corpse which has no life.
But to me even a corpse has beauty.

Deanna Uutela

Camelot 2000/Memphis Revisited

The years are strangely catalogued
In little miraculous boxes of
light and metallic digital CD's
Macintosh
red apple computers faxed our personalities

Floral fields in dresses of disguises
Faded jeans, forbidden colors
Stripped, streaded
and child abused by nature

Around or heads are
Robotic dances
Ear plugged to MTV
multicolored
Isaac Newtonian
Evolution:
and the sound of plutonian
Blues dispersed itself
into a jazz up tempo
Brought to you by a
1/4 million dollar deluxe TV commercial

Everett Charles Yates

Majestic America

I came to this land
In love, full of dreams
To be free
But hate, anger and heartache is all I can see.
We thought our Children the good from the bad,
the wrong from the right
Bad Elements took over and thought them to fight
What is right fully ours we must take back
Restore love, honor and respect
Lets work hand in hand make good what is bad
So all of us are free again
in this majestic land

Gerda Rose

It's Christmas Time

It's Christmas time the world around,
In many tongues the words resound;
It's peace to all, to all goodwill,
Me thinks I hear the angels still
Proclaim the coming to the earth
Of Christ our Lord by lowly birth.

It's nineteen hundred ninety four
And choirs once more repeat the score
Of peace, goodwill to all mankind,
A song, when shared, our hearts doth bind.
My wish again for everyone
Is that we'll honor God's own Son.

Iris S. Nelson

Mother "O" Mother

How you alone gave me yourself
In many ways you put your
heart in mine

Father, Father, Father
How you alone gave me your
insight of life and of man

Father, Father, Father
You told me these things I look for
in life are Man made.
It's a way for me to have as long as I play man's game.

Mother, Oh Mother
My heart "Bleeds" for the
stupidity I see in this life
Oh Mother, how glad I am of my daddy's insight
and for the love of life
I kiss you! My Mother

Cassell Richmond Jr.

Seasons

Now is the time for glistening snow and ice,
In my comfy abode of home, how nice;

To reminisce of the beauty of daffodils
in spring,
As through the breezes the robins, blue jays,
and wrens sing;

Then on to the beauty of lush greens;
Lettuce, cabbage, tomatoes and beans,
Summer lilacs, roses and dreams,

Then comes September with mums all aglow,
Soon pears; and leaves the winds will blow,

Into retirement of another year,
Thank God for creations we all hold so dear!

Bernice M. Helfrich

Carry On

It was just a long and senseless fight
    In my memory now - it's a nasty sight
You were her but now you're gone
    Didn't know how I'd carry on

I though you were the best I ever had
    But now I realize you only treated me bad
You took away my will ya know
    but now I'm making it on my own

I believed
    You were there for me
But now it's known
    I was just your stepping stone

But now I'm strong
    and the pain has gone
No longer the need to run
    I've got what it takes to carry on

Jes Castillo

The Bouquet

Fragrance filled the room so crowded,
Mums, Roses, a touch of Baby's Breath -
the Bridal Bouquet.
A blushing Bride, a handsome Groom,
soon to share a life, but first to toss -
the Bridal Bouquet.
Thrown to someone, but who; only she
will know as she catches -
the Bridal Bouquet.

Cathy Hamill

Phantasm

Is it a person in my dreams?
In reality the person it portrays is human
Phantasm... it has a million emotions
Reality... I've only seen two
The seemingly painless, cloudless, ecstatic side
And the "Why me?" side
How many emotions does "Why me?" portray? only a million
Betrayal? Not betrayal
The infliction of a tragic plight better sums it up
Still, there is no one word for that
The magnitude of a new lifestyle adds to the tragedy
Causing a certain idiocy and delirium to attach itself
To its pure, true, natural personality...
Or may be that's just human; in the illusionary sense it is cultured
Much more than it's somewhat selfish real self
It feels for others... a symptom of traveling all walks of life
It wants to be none other than itself ...
A result of seeing itself as beautiful, a definite
Rarity, a result of seeing world as beautiful
Phantasm...it understands...No one is ugly, just misunderstood.

Christina Holley

Grandmother

I call you grandma cyclops, the one eyed monster.
In the blink of your one eye you gather all of your wisdom.

You say you would eat me like a little taco
but you never do instead you support me.
I've taken your counseling through the years,
gracefully surrendering the things of youth

Cyclops, you give me energy and strength to my spirit,
which shields me from the horrible misfortunes of life.

Just when I think I know you, you come up with something new.
You say, "Speak the truth clearly and quietly,
and listen to others, even the boring and ignorant.

You tell me not to lie, not to cheat, and not to steal.
These are the poison of life.
You said once I'm one of the special kids of
the galaxy no less than the moon and the sun.

I know you'll always be their
for me guarding and guiding all the way
Even if I can't see you, I can always feel you in my heart

And now I know that there is no escaping my cyclops,
my one eyed monster

Nero

Liberty And Freedom

The word freedom is expressed in so many ways
In words and deeds in what we do and say
To be thankful for this land that's free
To see our flag flying her colors of red, white, and blue
So beautiful to look at indeed

Giving thanks for our freedom that's ours to share
To enjoy freedom of worship and feel God's presence there
To enjoy liberty and freedom around everywhere
As we guide and teach our children to care

To believe and keep the freedom as we trust in God in a spiritual way
To know what freedom means that's ours today
As we celebrate our country's freedom as we gather far and near
As we hear the bells of freedom ring out loud and clear

As the Statue of Liberty torch burns day and night
To always believe and have faith in what we think is right
To know nothing is impossible for God is our Guiding Light

Catherine Richey

The Sip

I sit here in my lonely state
In the coffee shop
One I have thirsted to go to for many years

In anticipation of the future and fear of the unknown
I wait patiently for the perfect time
I place the order from between my praying hands
The order that will change my life forever

I am overwhelmed with anxiety
Why must it take so long
It is a special brew of a special blend
But why must it take so long

The long awaited order arrives
I don't rush to take the first sip
No, I stare at this divine cup
I stare at every flawless detail with admiration and desire

Slowly, cautiously, I move my insecure hand
I grasp the cup hesitantly
The warm cup fills my heart's soul completely
I raise the cup to my craving lips
And kiss the brim of eternity

Jeremiah David Duke

When It Comes To Sweethearts

When it comes to sweethearts - I love you most of all,
In the dark of night - YOU, I sometimes want to call.

Just to hear you sweet voice - just to recall,
All those lovely phrases - left lingering in the hall.

In the hall of memories - when I am alone,
I even hear them - just looking at the phone.

All the bright tomorrows - just borrowed for awhile,
Lost somewhere in sorrows - some day, no more your smile.

My special sweetheart - the best that can be,
Holding me so tightly - understanding my plea.

My plea of just wanting - love that is so true,
Oh, just what will I do - when I no longer have you.

I already feel lonely - even though you are still near,
That pain of loneliness - that sometimes lingers here.

That fear of departing time - when I no longer see,
My special precious sweetheart - still just holding me.

When it comes to sweethearts - the best that can be,
'Cause you are my little pal - made especially for me.

Evelyn Ruth Taute

Southeast Light

There's a beacon that sits in silence, unaware of its demise
In the distance you can hear the sound of sea gulls' cries

Mother nature comes beating down the front door
Soon the light will end up on the ocean floor

No matter what tantrums mother nature commands
Bit by bit the cliffs loose its sands

Sadness surrounds the tall beacon as it's guarding the sea
Many wonder and worry how to prevent this catastrophe

Gifts of love helped save the light
Now Southeast's future looks safe and bright

While standing in silence, feeling the wind blow
Peaceful gentle breezes tell tales of long ago

Visitors see what ancestors have before
Southeast light stands tall and proud once more.

Anita Henke

Farewell

Once I found a rose,
in the early part of spring.
It was red and at full bloom.
A truly wondrous thing.

Everyday I would visit that spot,
the home of what I called "my" rose.
And even though I never picked I always sniffed,
because the fragrance tickled "my" nose.

But spring came and went,
and soon was no more.
I went to the spot of "my" rose
Only to have my heart cut to the core.

My rose had wilted and died
never to be seen again.
And even though I knew new ones would grow,
It didn't help ease my pain.

Maybe if I'd kept "my" rose close to me,
it would still be here to smell.
Maybe if I'd shown "my" rose more attention,
I wouldn't be in this spot saying farewell.

Eddie J. Jacobs

Prophecy

When the rays of sunlight shine through the trees
In the forest, which lines the way,
And the world seems complete and perfect,
Then shall we know that mankind
Has achieved true peace of mind.
And the earth will stand still as if in a trance,
While the animals live long and plentifully.
As the air becomes clean and the grass green once more,
We will know we have reached the ultimate level,
Lost since man first walked this planet,
When the earth was new and bountiful,
Undamaged, pure, and whole,
And when waters were blue and fresh.
Perhaps it will return to that state
In the end.

Amrita Mallik

Denizens Of The Deep

Somewhere, deep down below you'll find
In the inner, darkest recesses of your mind,
One personal voice, a friend. One that's true.
It sends a message that's sure to guide you.
Please believe me. The pain you're going through
You see, it is the same pain. The one I'm feeling too.
If we can stay the course, the one we know that's right,
Through the twisted labyrinth of day following night,
Then we'll win the struggle that many have yet to face.
Don't fear these denizens in your personal space.
Take solace and some comfort that through the years
The solution is in your head. It is all between your ears.
Be strong. Take time for yourself and get a hold.
Or the denizens will claim you before you're old.

Christopher Wilkins

Sanctum

I saw my eyes opening, closing,
King Neptune was beckoning,
Seaweed cradle rocking me to sleep.
Quiet darkness, the light blinds me.
My eyes open, I see a kaleidoscope of
faces blending, changing, spinning,
calling to me, why? Why? A haunting echo.
I am running fast! Faster!
Soon I will be safe once more under the porch.

Bettye M. Ellis

Stars

Stars are bright
In the night.
Pretty as mars.
Yellow as stars.
There in the sky so high.
I wonder "Do They ever fly?"
Can they get in your eye?
If so can they go back to the sky?
"Yes," 'cause this is their home.
And here they are never never alone.
Are the stars hard as stone
Or are they soft as fur?
Do they ever have to say; sir?
"No," 'cause they are stars up in the sky.
And they are way up too high.

Brenda Aday

Day at the Beach

Night; black and mysterious like a cat prowling
in the pale moon light.
Then the stars peep out from their bright cover.

Then the sun rises from its gentle slumber.
Outrageous rays of orange and red light make
the sky glow like a ball of fire.

Cool ocean slowly crawling upon the sandy
beaches.
Gentle roar of the waves crashing upon the
rocks.

Miniature dolphins hurdle the humongous waves.
Sea gulls dancing in the breath of Mother Earth.

Sun radiantly covering the sea, glistening off the
white sand.

Everything in the water, air and beach awakes.
Day, bright and glorious begins again.

Ellen Drzewiecki

A Beat Within My Heart

Something special and unique that you hold within your heart.

Something that lasts forever, the two shall never part.

You look into his eyes and a tear runs down your face.

He begins to hold you in his arms with a warm embrace.

He kisses you with his gentle lips and wipes away your tears.

And you think about your love for him that will strengthen
in the years.

You sit there in amazement of how he makes you feel; like a perfect
man from up above so gentle and so real.

You think about him day and night and even in your dreams.
He's just what you've needed for all your life it seems.

This relationship is filled with love that will last forever;
A feeling held within my heart; a beat that I will treasure.

Brandy McEvers

Rainbow

Rainbow, Rainbow, in the sky,
  How long 'twill thee be passing by?
After a rain, you seem to unfold,
  And hang at your end, a pot of gold.

The story of this pot of gold,
  Still seems to be untold
Proudly it produces its colors
  Like a proud new mother.

Amy Yoder

Roses For The Lord

In my earthly garden there are roses with thorns you'll see,
in wintertime they're dormant.. in due season they bloom for me.

But I found a Spiritual Rose that blooms the whole year round,
she led me to the Savior that I would in Him abound.

In God's Grace He sent her in my distressing, darkest hours,
she taught me how to live in His wonderful working Power.

With the passing of the years a faithful friend is Rose to me,
and I sought within my heart another Rose for God I'd be.

For each and every life that's lived there's joy and there are tears,
In prayer we shared them all, the Spirit of God drew near.

Now walking together in Jesus, caring that others know the Savior too,
and for Him gathering a Bouquet of Roses that they be made anew.

Written for my dear friend, Rose Brown
Berthe N. Welch

The Silence Is Too Loud

Shrill notes pierce the silent air.
Incessant wailing everywhere.

Are these the shrieks of people being slaughtered?
Are these the screams of youngsters struck
By bullets in crime-filled streets
Who cry, "I haven't lived yet! Give me back my youth!"

Are these the sounds of growling, swollen
Bellies of children, weak with hunger
Pleading for a bowl of gruel?

Are these the urgent cries of the homeless
Needy and embittered, "I want to live, too!"

Are these sharp sounds the echoes of
Cannon bursting over fellow countrymen
Who war and kill each other in ethnic strife?

Are these the echoes of the six million
Stifled voices, whose only crime was being Jews?

I clap my hands upon my ears to drown them out.
Too loud are the sounds, too many echoes all around.
Time to cease! Time for peace!

Belle Kurman

One Dance With The Purple Rose

Some don't or won't show you
Inside living visions that caress.
Naked without the ram of wilderness
Laughing demons, horde our cell and nest

Erase my reactions words of hurt
Together we stood like tall summer trees
Time seems slow when your planet doesn't pass
Hourglass of patience makes the strong last.

Paint a beautiful picture you must set free
Soft and tender like a purple rose I've seen
She sleeps in my heart and takes
One slow dance with my dreams.

I can't see you, I can't hear you
But I feel you, like a million stars dancing.
They say eyes are the windows to the soul
If we never had eyes would we've of met.

If we never had each other feelings we kept.
Feels so amazing when you know
And sense the smell of a dance
With a purple rose!

Jeff Stewart

Pain

The pain and sorrow eats away the
insides of her body and seems to be
completely unstoppable

She wants to be so close but the
distance seems so far away
He feels the same way only towards
someone new

No ones to blame it's life twisted game
So she holds on only praying for her
dreams to come true.

At times she feels happy, happy but then
She's blown away by life's gloom and sorrow
She feels down and blue

She struggles fights for what she wants
to last more than just one night

Forever he'll be there for her
but also for another.
Even if her dreams never come true
at least there was that one night
anyone could only wish for!

Heidi Wade

Inspiration And Intelligence

To a lady who's smile and beauty
inspires and invigorates a feeling of appreciation.
To look at you, your beauty so
intimately that it reminds me of a
string instrument; to be play'd so
soft and delicate that it defines your intelligence.
The intimately of your quiet smile
that I see tell's me you are a
woman of great quality, and the look in
your eye's inspires deep appreciation to
have met a lady like you in this situation,
and your passion it looks to me that it run's as
deep as the sea.
A sure sign you are a true woman of quality.

Calvin Robinson

Nightmare

I wandered alone in a cave on the mountain.
Interested was I to find, just what
lurked in the darkness, as I wandered deeper
inside.
The black cave beckoned as a magnet, though I
knew that I shouldn't be there
Trudging for minutes that seemed like hours
dirty, cold, and in despair.
MY flashlight made shadowy gargoyles dance
in horrible shapes.
A claustrophobic fear gripped my breathing
as I collapsed upon the floor in a heap.
Suddenly I heard voices around me, anxious to
know what was wrong.
I sat up in bed with a sigh of relief.
Thank God, I was still on the farm.
Fear drained out of my body, as I flopped
back onto the bed.
I breathed a sigh of contentment as the pillow
cradled my head.

Dorothy Beck

Spirits Of The Conscience

Spirits in the mind they roam,
Into corners of a darker past.
Oh silent lips that keep them unknown,
But how long can secrets last?

To get away with evil play, it's true,
It happens all the time.
But, you see, there's such a thing as guilt too,
Those spirits keep this locked inside, to remind you of your crime.

The crime unknown to those all around,
Your dark secret is a silent prey,
An evil deed that may never be known or found.
To be sure these spirits will find away.
To creep into the corners of that dark, stained past.
These spirits have a life long sentence that forever last.

Alison Lanham-Gaskamp

Life

   Life is so damn aggravating, and watching it waste is irritating.
Irritating to every fiber in my soul, we live
and learn in order to grow.

   Yes I know that life isn't fair, and when it is,
it's very rare. It can be intensely frustrating,
and definitely time taking, but try to comprehend to live life
and be your own man.

   Don't lose your self to inhumanity.
Try to forget the world and its vanity.
Yes I know it's hard to believe
when it's far to dark for you to see.
Just remember to be strong,
because life shall get better as you go on.

Heather Pfeifer

"Special Ones"

The child whom we call Wednesday's Child
is a child of special love and hope,
A tiny person whom we care for
with special needs and troubles to cope.

The child is a Special One
one with love and grace,
To make the grownups laugh a lot
and help fill an empty space.

They open our hearts to see
just what we have inside,
And see all our love
flowing like and endless tide.

For Wednesday's child is the Special Ones
who give us love and laughter,
But most of all they give us happiness
and joy for everafter.

For they are the Special Ones.

Edward R. Rhodes

Glory

Dear God, what wanders you have wrought.
In your awesome power you spoke the word,
And made the oceans blue.
You turned the tides to waves of thunder and
gave us joys untold.

Dear God, what powers came to bear when
you opened up the heavens and all the
stars shown through.
You unfolded space where every planet dwells
and gave us a glimpse of you.

Evelyn Ireland

"Look Away"

Why do you look away from me?
Is it because my eyes tell the truth?
Or, is it because you have already judged me?
Why don't you give me a chance to be judged?

Old customs and traditions are so hard to break!
Do they make you look away?
If you look away, you will miss the true
Meaning of peace and love!

There was a time when I was made to look away!
But, Oh how times have changed!
Don't look away to avoid me!
I am only a man who has the same hopes and dreams as you!
Also, I want to forgive and be forgiven!

Struggles within yourself make you look away!
But, hope is not all lost!
Because I had one person today who didn't
TURN AND LOOK AWAY!

Ivory L. Scott

How Do You Define A Friend?

How do you define a friend?
   Is it someone you know,
Who says their with you to the end,
   Or a person who says hello,
   You describe as you know.
   One who means more than so and so,
   Or a kid on the block who moved long-ago.
   One who will give you half of what he's got,
   Or one who rides you on his yacht.
   One who remembers forget-me-nots,
   Or one who plays big-shot?
   You can tell how a friend should be if,
   Less attention is paid to what one says that you might hear,
      And more to watching what a person does.
         This shall remove all the doubts,
         And make the meaning of friend quite clear!

Bozana Belokosa

Misery and Ecstasy

Falling in love
is like a beautiful flower blooming.
It is a feeling I have never felt before.
It has cost me my whole life to be with this one person
and I have done everything to get him.

Like a million stars coming into the sky at once,
my life is in heaven.
Love is a wonderful thing paint a picture of two people
sitting in a meadow.

When falling in love makes vision blurry
a thin layer of water on the eyes.
To find you haven't thought that the person loves you
you will give your friends, family, money
and take away your life to be with him
and live your life day to day
on their love for you and drift off into the sun.

Bria Cheek

Earthly Farewell

Death is but a breath away
Our lungs refuse to play,
This game of living any longer
Our eyes tired and weary
Close forever at ends day.
Lifeless at peace with our inner soul,
we afloat to heavenly clouds.

Beulah McKee

Marriage

The start of a brand new family,
Is like the dawn of a brand new day,
With hopes and dreams and promises,
Of what may come your way.

Some problems in life will give you trouble,
And make you very sad,
But bare them together,
Share them together,
And you will see they're not so bad.

Now you've stood before the Lord,
Took your vows hand in hand,
And became of one heart,
One mind, and one soul,
In God's union of woman and man.

Now start your walk through life together,
Walk it side by side,
And always remember,
A home of love,
Is a home where GOD abides.

Calvin E. Hart

For I Am One With You.....

The feeling of your love for me
   is overwhelming.
It encompasses my whole being
   as a feeling of complete loving passion.
I cannot resist these desires
   of your spirit and flesh.
For existence without you
   is something I cannot imagine.

The spring of my lifetime
   was when I became one with you.
And together we shall share
   so many more wondrous springtimes.
For I am one with you ...
   forever.

Janice A. Caliri

Stability

My hope
is pinned to the wall
and flutters in the window like a curtain.
There is no trickery
my devious heart
could not entertain as a certainty.

Whatever travels ends.
It is my stillness,
reaching out and grabbing at light
as it passes,
clutching the wind in its fingers
and digging in
only to fold back and fall,
sliding through its own grasp in its grasping —
my stillness,
hooked immovably to my stale frame,
that is the keeper of my shallow heart,
that is keeping my reckless heart
doubtful.

Carroll W. Boswell

Alone

Love; a world of confusion and disbelief,
Is sinking deep into the depths of his mind.
Showing not a hint of fear,
Hiding only where no one can find.

How can he possibly smile at night,
Alone and free of affection.
When everyone seems to be uptight,
He's absorbing their pain in injections.

Hatred flowing in his blood and tears,
Poisoning his brain and heart
Yet not reflecting dreams and fears,
Alone as he was from the start.

Selling his life through artificial truth,
Living his lies over and over again.
Causing pain no drugs could soothe,
Slowly he begins to feel insane.

A prisoner to the feeling of need,
A junkie in society's bloodshot eyes.
Addiction growing from it's shiny black seed,
No one caring when he dies.

Heather Cada

Love

Love,
   is the warmth your touch provides
   the safeness your arms protect me with
   the gentleness of your kisses
   the softness your words are spoken with

Love,
   is the trust within you
   the honesty you behold
   your weaknesses and strengths you possess
   the kindness your heart shows

Love,
   is the respect for each other
   the friendship we share
   the beauty within your soul
   a certain closeness we provide for one another

Love,
   is your ability to care for me,
   as I care for you
   the guidance our hearts long for from each other
   the unbreakable bond between us.

Erica Sellers

Up To The Top

Tenderness, kindness, love
Is there no place for these emotions?
The rush and roar of our world
Is slowly killing us.

Climbing up to the top
Stepping callously on the heads of humanity;
Brothers, sisters, lovers, friends.
Where does it end?

When some stranger in a dark alley
Pulls his gun and takes his step—
A step on your head
In his race up to the top.

Brycie F. Klein

Sympathy To You

Perhaps you've heard the words,
Is there something I can do?
I pray God's precious light,
Is shining over you.
If I could make your dark days brighter,
I would turn my lights on too.
As I share your loss of a loving father, (mother)
So dear and kind and true.
For he (she) has joined our heavenly father,
Both watching over you.

Gloria M. Hollingsworth

Living Well With Diabetes

Diabetes is no fun that my friend
Is true at least there are some things
   that you should do
Visit your doctor every 6 months,
He or she will test you for any complications in your body.
If not hurry!!!
Today will be another survival day.
Make sure you take your pills or shots
Once or twice a day
Check your blood sugar everyday
And pray to the spirit above
That you have family and friends to support your love.
Sure your heart can stop any day,
You'll have high and low blood sugar everyday
Only you can control diabetes your way.

Josip Drozdek

The Diet Riot

For some to watch their calories
Is what is called a diet.
But watch 'em when they're unaware
You'll find it's quite a riot.

The doctor's orders are well fulfilled
All measured carefully.
Then to the scales to check results
Look down so prayerfully.

"I've gained!" they cry, with eyes so wide.
"These scales just can't be right."
"I did just what he told me to.
I tried with all my might."

They did what they were told alright.
They did it and some more -
With cakes, and pies, and cookies too.
Enough to fill a store.

And this they give a name, my friends,
"Scientific Reducing Diet".
And we who've watched are so amused
Till we decide to try it.

Berniece I. Wilson

More Than Remains

   One strife of one dive of one life
In the river with a crocodile, you seem to grin, you go to water,
You sink and yet in, in the whirlpool of the Nile.

How neatly spread its claws, you are fed up with it, your brain reels,
You agree a little bit, how gently smiling its jaws.

And yet no more narrow escape, you join the river, adoring yourself
You jar with the quiver, there's something on the tape.

   Deep sympathy, funeral tomorrow
   Black coffin, tears, sorrow

Andre Martin

A Cry For Help

Their desperate cries for help were clear; what happened
is what the nation feared. Their youth had lost all
hope, and surrendered their lives to dope. The nation
grew weary, and heavily burdened—and so she cried. She
cried out in pain from her drive by shootings. She
cried out in anguish from her birth pains to drug
addicted babies. She cried out in sorrow for her
homeless family.
Can you hear the nation crying? They are cries she
can't keep silent. They are cries for help.
One special ruler heard the cries and answered. But for
many, he could not be heard. Yet, he continued to reach
out: Come to me, give up your shame, on your heart let
me write my name. Give up your guns; give up your drugs
let me take away your pain and bless you with prosperous
gains. Let me carry you through the rest of your years,
I promise to answer each of your prayers, for it is I
who truly cares. Oh come to me you great nation, cry no
more, for I am the Lord of all.

June A. Rogers

Golden Wedding Day

When ever I thought about this day,
It always seamed so far away.
But time goes by so fast you see.
And now you have been married fifty years to me.

We've had a lot of good times and some sad times too.
And I owe all that I am to you;
You have always loved and protected and taken care of me,
And that's the way a loving marriage, should be.
You have always been my sweetheart and my lover,
My protector and my best friend.
And I wish that would never end.
We have always been able to laugh together
And talk together and sometimes we cried together
And sometimes we just sit quietly together.
Your first thoughts are always of me
And that's the way a loving marriage, should be
I love you with all my heart on this golden day
And our love will last, forever and a day.
And on this golden anniversary I can only say
a loving marriage should be that way.

Della Harrison Kromer

Man Versus Nature

I stood out side
It could've been in the middle of nowhere
But, it wasn't.
I heard the cricket sound as the wind blew
the colored leaves beyond my reach
and up my spine.
The powdered snow fell gently
as mother nature was ready
to make her rounds again with her touch,
and I challenged all that was around me.
"Come on," I shouted
"Come down on me now!," I raised my fist in anger.
Nothing happened.
My will was strong, but my clothes thin.
My words forced me back in side.

Brandon Russ

Fire Storm

A single smoldering cigarette in a wooded area.....

A night's terror for the forest....

The fire moves slowly but once under the leaves
  it explodes into a world none like it....

Black is everywhere...everything in its path...
  the unsettling black haze thru the forest....

The wall of blazing uncertainty spread thru the
  forest....

Animals run for their lives....

The sound of crackling branches and the smell of
  burning bushes....
The intense heat shot thru the sky and melted all
  the blue clouds away....
The ash and little spots of green left by mercy or by
  rare consequence....

Now it's out....

All is dead in its path....
All is dark and gloomy....
All is still and quiet....
All is gone for ONE CARELESS MISTAKE.

  Elaine Carpenter

Sonnet

The deep, dark hate hotly boils in my blood.
It is drowning my body through and through.
'Tis overflowing my heart like a flood;
I want to cringe every time I see you.
But then I hear you laugh and my heart melts,
Your smile brings sun upon my darkest nights
And it clears from my face the rain that pelts
And makes my eyes to shine like bright lights.
But then again you come to forget me,
And then the lights in my eyes go away
The rain begins again too pour on me.
'Tis the price for loving you I must pay;
  And shall until I find another
  For now in my life there is no other.

  Hattie James

"Writing Is..."

  Writing is intense, focused, passionate.
It is personally revealing, introspective.
  It exposes you and leaves you vulnerable.
It draws you in and won't release you.
You become intimate.
  You cherish the feeling it gives you so you stay faithful to it.
It is time consuming, all encompassing.
  It is emotionally satisfying, sensually stimulating.
You like the way it looks and the way it sounds, when you say the
  words aloud.
It is arousing. It relaxes you and invigorates you.
When it is frustrating you don't give up on it.
You love it so you fight for it.
  And it gives you a purpose, a direction.
You feel accomplishment.
You love it so you fight for it.
  It is always improving, maturing, evolving.
You can lose yourself in it and discover something new about
yourself.
  You discover you made a commitment, to writing.
Writing is a relationship, a love affair.
Embrace it. Don't ever let it go.

  Cindy Streur

Bedtime

"Dad ,three stories" is what he will always say,
It is the perfect ending to my very stressed filled day.
I sit down on the bed, its the only time I rest,
He finds his place between my legs, his head rests on my chest.

He opens up the book and knows the story by heart,
He is pretending to read and I tell him that he's smart.
Then he looks up at me and his eyes are filled with joy.
"I love you, Dad" are the words spoken by my little boy.

When sitting on his bed we can look into the mirror
He sits by his Dad with no sadness or fear
When the stories are done and it's time to go to sleep
The thoughts of him staying four are now mine to keep.

I lay back on the bed with his head on my arm,
I want time to stand still, it will cause no harm.
"Sleep with me Dad" he now whispers in my ear,
He then snuggles in closer so his prayers I can hear.

These are the times that should last forever
To love and to cherish should be our main endeavor
For my son will grow up and these moments will end,
But the memories last forever, I'll just remember when.

  Curt R. VandeVorde

Without Prejudice

My eyes hold a steady gaze I look up into the quiet sea of darkness
It is there that I often wonder from where the human spirit comes
Sliding down the crescent of the moon, like a child in a vast
playground,
the clouds break our fall as we descend from the heavens, without
face, without name,
landing in this magnificent place we call home
It is the ultimate masquerade, for who we are and what we will become
is left to chance
Fate shines through, scattering light in many directions; it is up to
the spirit within us to choose the path to a fulfilling life
Everyone wears a different mask, our true selves hidden behind our
flesh and blood
For beyond this facade lies a brilliant glow, it is warm like the sun,
flowing with energy, it is every breath
It is how I wish everyone could see themselves, out of the darkness
and into the light; only then would life truly be grand, each without
prejudice hand in hand

  Carla Nelson

Hi Neighbor!

There is a special purpose, that this verse has in mind.
It is to thank our neighbors, so loving and so kind.
For the caring things you do, nice things that you say.
Making life more pleasant, by the week or by the day.

Love thy neighbor as thyself, the Bible does us tell.
And you seem, as a family, to do that very well.
Sure, it is a comfort, to know you're always there.
Whether it's an egg we need, or just a word of prayer.

And in this world of hurry-up, and going many places.
It is good for us to see, all of your smiling faces.
Having you for neighbors, has always been a plus.
For our hearts smile hearing, "HI NEIGHBOR", said to us!

  Gaynel Calvird

Life's Lonely Trail

The trail is long and lonely.
It leads me all the way.
Decisions of direction are always there to make.
Which way to turn is most important,
For that journey's end may not be a way back home.
My decisions, upon which I must abide,
Become my actions, which are carried upon the tide.
Each wave of emotion must find its rest upon a solid shore,
Where another sees its action, and continues upon its way.
As my lonely trail continues, I must live emotions,
For only then will I know where I have been,
And where I am, and who I am.
And when my trail draws near the end,
For which I know not where or when,
My life will have served some purpose
For my fellow man.....now and then.
Meanwhile, I will continue upon my lonely trail.

Betty M. O'Hanlon

Insincerity

Her smile lacked spontaneity,
it looked contrived
His words lacked candor,
they sounded hollow and meaningless
The expression of love was empty of genuineness,
its artificial sounds rang hollow to the ear
The invitation was casual and had no real meaning,
its triviality was easily recognizable.
The laugh was forced and lacked humor,
to the one hearing it and to whom it was directed.
Insincerity beguiles, it is unworthy, it lacks
warmth and reality
Insincerity destroys real love and kills friendship,
it flourishes in selfish, self-centered people
Its expressions are best left undone and best ignored.
Its a waste of time and energy,It kills love and respect.
It must be avoided and replaced with SINCERITY.

Ben C. Franczok

A Passionate Color

Passion and anger aren't quite alike.
It must be that sign of love that brings out the color again.
Whatever to do without red never knows.
Without red how would we ever make orange?
What about pink?
How would we ever have Valentines day?
Or how would that fire look on that cold Christmas day
    with only warmth colorless and gray,
    as a bright red cardinal flies on by.
To wonder what Snow White would have eaten
    if not for the red poisonous apple;
    to even have the name
    if not for the wine - red, glossy lips.
Raspberry, strawberry, cherry picking
    as the hot sun burns our skin,
    to look as if we were a raspberry ourselves.
Stop once although you're at a stop sign
    and try to realize by thinking of a rose . . .
The loving feeling red gives us to know it's by our side whenever,
    needed through the sign of life.

Andrea Lohrke

The Artist

White light on white clapboard walls
it needs the scene
pigments of blue diminish to red
images form before words
a night shrouded pool
smooth as ice in the instant before the breeze stirs
with a tinge of autumn in the air
and one moon hanging full in the sky
another reflected so perfectly on the water
it's difficult to say which is real
essence exposed
paint gone
the form falls
as the white light on white clapboard walls
holds the shadow upon the scene

Chris Hatem

The Only One Who Cares

The wall is always there for me.
It never tells me to stop asking so many questions.
It always looks at me while I'm talking to it.
The wall loves me.

The wall doesn't want me to shut my mouth or shave.
It doesn't tell me about its boring life.
It always listens as I tell it about mine.
The wall supports me.

The wall doesn't make fun of my clothes or speech.
It stands there in silence.
It knows all of my secrets.
The wall will never tell.

Aaron Killian

The Language of Life

I have mastered this art we call life.
It no longer threatens my thoughts.
I am happy I have no more worries,
    but what of my dreams — are they lost?
What of my hopes, and what will await me there?
What will become of all I represent?
Who will be responsible for my care?
Who will worry about me when I become sick?
Who will search for me when I get lost?
Who will sit with me when I cry out at night?
Who will pay that cost?

I have earned my right of care.
I deserve what will be given to me there.
No man can justify taking a part of me, unless it
    is given and shared equally.

Perhaps this game that we call life
    is more pronounced and wrought with
    strife than one old lady can be made to see.
It doesn't matter, however, for me.
I am too old, and you are too young to understand
    what cannot be undone.

Jennifer Garnet

The Song In The Creek

Song you are water on my body
In the creek with glistening stone
Seducing me in green shadows
Near trees bending low over the water
I rise wet from my bath
I am the current, the creek.
Trickle through my drifting body, wet lover
Take me into your swirling depths
Friend in the singing creek

Ives Templeton

The Cat

The cat walks slowly through the darkened night;
it pads on and on, restlessly.

It seems to be searching for something it can't quite find;
Its' emerald eyes gaze around endlessly.

The cat fears nothing; it gives ground to no one;
Not dog nor beast nor man.

It knows what it must do in order to survive,
Whatever it takes, however it can.

It can be aloof, or it can be friendly;
It really depends on its' mood.

But the cat is not foolish; it is street-wise,
It knows what it must do to get available food.

Yet the cat is not happy, it is not content;
It yearns to be held, and stroked by someone.
But the cat was abandoned; now it roams the streets-
Striving to survive, trusting no one.

The cat moves on, determinedly-
All it can cherish are its memories.

James Branch

Prayer For A Lost Nephew

Dear Farther in heaven I have a request to make,
It probably isn't possible but it's for a child's sake.
I've been well protected by love all my life,
But this little baby boy has known only strife.

I wish I could say his life will get better,
But I'm not yet sure, so I'll write you this letter.
Please listen dear Lord, I know you are busy.
When I think of all you do and see, it makes me crazy.

I'd like to ask please God since I made it through o.k.
Would you assign my angels to look after him each day?
He's just a little baby Father, living a life he didn't choose;
If you let him share my angels, I know he just can't lose.

He's in your hands Lord, and has been all along;
But with my angels too, he just can't go wrong.
With my angels holding my hand and holding his tiny hand too,
He and I can go through life, holding hands through you.

Cory Potter

A Home Poem

As I wander through my home looking all about,
it reminds me of my home when I was a sprout.

With a porch, and backyard having room galore,
it makes me feel at home once more.

Now as a young wife there are chores to be done,
no longer as a child in my home shall I run.

As life goes on, and children are raised,
in my new home where I once gazed.

I will always remember the feelings I once had,
leaving my folks home for life good or bad.

I'm sure they will all feel the way I once did,
there isn't any place like your own home when you are a kid.

Families will be raised for years to come,
they will all have this feeling ... at least for some!

Joan H. Long

Difficult Situations

Why does life have to be so difficult?
It seems like there are more negative emotions than there are positive
When you were a kid and special moments
happened in special places. They disappear like days and days.
Sometimes we forget about them and the way life should be.
I sometimes find myself into difficult situations,
In which I think my world is
going to come to an end, But there is always
someone or something to lift you up.
I think that the rough times are to prepare us for the future and
the cheerful times give us the confidence and happiness
we need to get through rough situations.
No matter how tough the problem may be,
Keep trying and you will succeed,
For life is a challenge that no one can't overcome.

Crystal Day

Grandpa

You held me in your arms
it seems not very long ago.
You taught us all to be strong
and to stick together no matter what
You gave us laughters, you gave us tears
but most of all you gave us love
that we'll always feel.
The tears roll down to remember
the last time we saw your face
peaceful you laid as we bowed our heads and prayed
The time has come to live the present
and only look back with a smile
this may be hard to do
but we must remember
God loves and needs you too
The day will come when we'll all unite again
but until then we ask,
"Please look upon us and our safety"
So until we meet again
"Please be our Guardian Angel."

Ami Suzanne Krueger

My Shiny Star

A star was born today, with sparkles all around,
It shines so strong, it's going to make a difference
in somebody's life
It had a reason to exist, to show me the value of
life and that love is never too far.
It's so special in my heart that I could reach
it, even if is high up in the sky.
It taught me to fight for love, honesty and trust.
The day I reach to it, it will be all mine; and
today that is your birthday the whole universe
has to applaud, cause you're that shiny star
born today, with a reason in mind.

Anna L. Ortiz

Biological Father

My biological father once loved me.
My biological father once cared about me.
My biological father once kidnapped me.
My biological father also deserted me.
Now he wants another chance with me.
Well he isn't getting another chance from me.
He never called, wrote, or came to see me.
What does he think I am?, a carpet?
He walked all over me and my heart.
He expects me to forget every thing he did.
What a joke! No one can forget that much.

Brenda M. Abeytia

The Trip

Dope and crime are part of me, we all go hand in hand
It started out five years ago, down on the surfing sand
Some kids and I were smoking pot, we thought that it was smart
But now my life is ruined and, I broke my parent's hearts.

Now come all you teenagers, listen to my story true
I haven't long to live, and I must pass this on to you
I was a hardened dope addict, when I reached twenty-one
That is the age for decent kids, when life has just begun

I first smoked pot at seventeen, Just did it for a kick
At eighteen I'd become involved, In crimes that never click
At nineteen came the LSD, then came the needle fast
The doctor's say at twenty-two, I've not a chance to last

Now please don't make the same mistake and sacrifice your life
Instead just tell my story to, each husband, child and wife
And if it helps to save someone, From ending just as I
My life will not have been in vain, Upon the day I die.

Donald W. Murray

Rainy Day

It's cold and rainy on the outside,
It warm and cozy in here,
I wander what my creature friends are doing,
That traps in the rain out there.

The birds are singing sweetly,
In the tree that dripping wet,
They seem to be so happy
I like one for a pet.

I wonder what the insect are doing,
Far down in the ground,
The way that it has been raining
It's a wonder they didn't drown.

Some where there a sneaky old snake
Lying in a coil.
I bet he haven't felt a drop of rain,
Waiting to sneak through the world.

Rain, Rain, Rain
There nothing about it we can do,
So let's be like the little birds singing
Be merry and don't be blue.

Hattie McDowell

"Farewell My Love, Good-Bye"

The morning after was all I remember.
It was a night on the town with laughter
we were two stranger who met in the night.
No one to care or to hold us back.
Your name I did not know.
Your words was link to my mind.
When we dance you held me tight.
I remember your whispers in the night.
We only saw what was in each other's eyes.
The longing and the waiting was no surprise.
We kissed and said good-bye.
Promising never too see each other.
We both thought that was fair.
I'll never forget the passion we shared.
One night will fill a Lifetime.
I only Remember the wave good-bye.
The tears in my eyes, that made me cry.

Alice Evans

Wordmusic

It was a light that sometimes flickered.
It was not always strong, but it was always there.
It was a light that lit around a corner
with the same ease that makes life flow
when daylight follows night.

It was a light of warmth, a light of truth.
It was a light that could create abysmal darkness
in the name of a well intentioned fool;
or make the world flourish and smile in the name of a dreamer.
It was the light of facts, the light of lies,
the light that turns thoughts into weapons
and turns tears into songs.
It was a word.

One day this word was festive and it felt like smiling.
It felt like brandishing its light
and painting the sky with music,
so it molded its glow, and the result was happy.
It was then light with melody.
It was words on a canvas.
It was poetry.

Fernando Vazquez

My True Friend

On the day when I was blue
It was oh-so-thoughtful of you
To comfort me from all my worries
By reading me that one nice story
Because of that, you've proved to me
Just how nice a friend can be
Thank you for that (and everything, too)
It's nice to know I can count on you
My heart was once empty, but now it is full
It's filled with a treasure, like a chest full of jewels
You are my diamond; you are my gold
You will always come first - I won't put you on hold
If you ever need help or if you're ever blue
I want you to know I'll be there for you
Because you're so special, I want you to see
Your friendship means the world to me

Ann Nguyen

My First Time

The mood was set, and the time was right.
It would mean more, than any day or night.

The music was playing. The lights were low.
The touch was soft, and the moves were slow.

Am I ready for this? Was the question I asked.
Could this be a mistake? A scar that will last.

My feeling of uncertainty, kept me from moving on.
But I had to move quick, before the moment was gone.

Our eyes met, and the feelings were strong.
We were together forever, and we could never go wrong.

My heart was racing. My pulse at a rise.
How far could this go? The limit was the skies.

To me it was a dream, that I thought would never end.
A moment of passion, between me and a friend.

The first time for me, is hard to forget.
It was the best of my life.
It was my first kiss.

Julie Pannell

One Size Fits All

Something fell off your face, let me try it back on
It's an unfamiliar face since that smile is gone
I carry extra around for times like this
Let me try to put it on and see if it fits

I understand just what you're feelin'
You think it past you by and now it's leavin'
And I understand just what you're thinking
That this can't be true, I must be dreamin'

Put your hands in my hands I won't stealem'
And your head on my shoulder for comfort and feelin'
I'll just hold you for awhile till your hearts starts beatin'
And try to give you someone you can believe in

I understand just what you're feelin'
You think it past you by and now it's leavin'
And I understand just what you're thinking
That this can't be true, I must be dreamin'

I am always here for you, I will never leave
I am someone you can always believe
Look at me, ...let me try that smile back on
It's an unfamiliar face since that smile is gone

Andrew T. Corbett aka Randy Corbett

Plastic Plants

I looked at the cyclamen daily
it's condition worsened. The plant's life
was up decided by
an ice cream cone clock
melting away. Until
no more green was seen.
In the past plant had flowered. No longer
did it have strength to stand. It looked
more like a pond scum colored octopus
begging for water. I fed it
plenty to stand again. And it did,
but not as a living plant. This time
plastic stems unfurled from
the dirt gave forth a synthetic cyclamen
mimicking the fake flowers
which sit in unattractive vases collecting
dust in grandmothers' houses.

Amy Elizabeth Webber

Dancing

I saw a spirit -shadowed- in the early morning light,
It's hurried footsteps silent, on it's hurried, silent flight,
It's siren song of madness sang the setting of the moon,
I thought I saw you dancing, did you see me too?

Your lovely face was mocking as you whirled across the floor
Unbidden, lonely passions rose to match the haunting score
Soundings, silent poundings, of my foolish heart on fire,
Remembering you loved me, remembering, you're a liar...

Dimly-lit, the dance hall floor glowed with eerie gleaming
Down the corridors of time, I looked but found no meaning;
Up the hallway, once again you danced in full abandon,
A partner for you newer steps, a partner chose at random...

Half-lit, shrouded longings of the half-thoughts of my dreams,
I am the one who sends you, floating softly on the seams
Of the fabric of my reverie from old and worn out days,
Still turning, still returning, for love's familiar ways...

I saw a ghost from youth, long years gone by, the other night,
It's hurried footsteps silent on it's hurried ghostly flight,
And as it passed me by, I heard it's old, familiar, tune
I thought I saw you dancing, did you see me too?

John R. Morrow

World Of Fear

Be not afraid of hell, my friend, for I have found it here.
It's in your world of torment, it's in your world of fear.
You hear but never listen, HE speaks but you don't hear,
You walk past the signs HE sends, HE stands so very near.
You talk but say nothing, your words are insincere.
Such a place you live in — such a place of fear.
Children holding treasures die from a gunshot wound.
Perhaps, they only came outside to see God's glorious moon.
The schools, a place of learning with teaching to be done
but, first we must secure them, there can be no guns.
Something makes it happen, to stop it, there must be a way,
but, the child, dead on the step will see no other day.
What will we leave behind for others to learn our way?
Guns in churches, guns in schools, is this a Judgement Day?
They die in vain, a mistake, a drive-by show.
God must build a bridge for us to let this violence go.
Be not afraid of hell my friend, for you have lived it here.
It's in your world of torment, it's in your world of fear.

Clair Chaplin

Not

It's not that we speak, but speak so untruthfully.
It's not that we act, but act so foolishly.
It's not that we live, but live without thought.
It's not that we work, but work for naught.
It's not that we feel, but don't share feelings with others.
It's not that we fight, but kill our own brothers.
It's not that we see, but keep our eyes covered.
It's not that we hear, but keep what we hear smothered.
It's not that we care, but don't let it be known.
It's not that we love, but don't let it be shown.
It's not that we cry, but cry with tears.
It's not that we die, but die in fear.

Dustin Koehler

Time In Time

Who can tell when time began, or its destiny to end;
It's said there's a power that knows, and he's our greatest friend.

Like the ocean wave that begins its flow:
Who knows where it began, and what end it will go.

To measure time great men have tried, their efforts were in vain:
For he who captures time in time, is certain for great fame.

Our time is measured in segments of life, where humans come and go,
The time of birth to death, is a measure that we know.

Time is not certain for us all, for some comes an early fall:
For others the seasons may extend, but eventually their time will
    also end.

Whichever way we use our time, by the second, hour, day or year;
Use it carefully, spread it well, and leave a legacy fine and
    clear.

Benjamin Franklin Paiz

Untitled

I love rain.
It blurs the lines of the trees in the distance
as in an impressionistic painting.
It's drum beat on the grass, window sill and roof
makes a steady cadence that feels secure.
It's rich, clean, pure odors and are almost sensual.
It makes ever-moving, ever-living pictures
in the puddles and streams.
And for those who cannot relate to each other
on any other level,
it makes for conversation.
I love rain.

Geraldine Kessler

When Will The Madness End

When will the madness end in the city
It's taking its relentless toll
Oh God-what a shameful pity
Is there no peace for our soul?

When will the madness end?
How can we save our youth
On whom can we depend?
As we seek to find the truth.

There seems to be no solution, yet
We know a change must be
It's imperative, we teach our younger set
What it really means to be free.

Free from the drugs that destroys them
And causes havoc in the land,
Their chances of survival are very slim
Why don't they understand?

This madness must come to an end
Or the whole universe will die
We must unite together and make amend
And not wallow in the much and the mire.

Esther B. Thompson

The Stone

The stone was gnarled, broken, scarred.
Its tortured life had made it hard.

What fearsome heat could bend and mold
A rock so hard, a rock so old?

How mean a wind to wear away
The rock we could have held today!
What caused the earth to tremble, shake?
What caused the rock to crack and break?

What river tossed it to and fro,
Upon a whim to watch it go?

I hold a stone, a mystery.
I hold a piece of history.

Through constant heat and force and change,
The puzzle pieces rearrange.

The silent rock will never speak
The foolish words we humans seek.

In eloquence, the stone withholds
Reality within its folds.

I hold a stone, yet it holds me,
Transfixed by pure reality.

Christine Davidson

Memory Row

If I live to be a hundred my life is half begun,
I've built a lot memories, treasure every special one,
Sometimes I let my mind take a leisurely stroll,
Down the winding road of life, down memory row,

The sound of springs first bubbling brook dancing merrily along,
Reminds me of the laughter of my children grown and gone,
The color of a summer sky, the only blue that's true,
Summons thoughts of my darlings eyes I love to look into,

The cool caressing breeze of autumns sleepy days,
Brings up pleasant thoughts of Grandmothers gentle ways,
On a clear winter night every jewel like star,
Draws thoughts of friends old and new, near and far,

As I sit beside my fire, wrapped in its warmth and glow,
I think of past and present but the future I don't know,
I've lots of memories to build, each one a special one,
If I live to be a hundred, my life is half begun.

Cheryle R. Conklin

Untitled

I've seen summer come and winter go.
I've seen the signs of age we all must show.
I've seen life and death and beauty and pain,
But I know I'll never see again
The brightness of our youth.

I've heard every symphony known to man —
Bach, Beethoven, Brahms, Chopin:
I listen to their melodies and find the proof
of the harmony of our lives
Soaring, Swelling, Lilting,
Lifting to the skies!

And I know when these eyes no longer see,
These ears no longer hear,
Your love for me will never disappear
But remain constant through every passing year.

And as I think of you tonight
I revel in the joy we've had,
The intimacy...The tears...
And I face our unknown future
With the comfort of the past.

Edwin H. Yager Jr.

The Healing

I know your spirit, I know your pain
I've stood in your shoes, I've stood in the rain
You think you're broken, battered and bruised
A broken body, that cannot move

But walk with me, my worried friend
We'll walk through the mist, the illusions within
We'll walk together, as children of God
We'll see you as whole, an image of him

Depression is fleeting, a state of the mind
Look past the image, your eyes are not blind
See yourself as a reflection of God
Lean into his love, lean into his side

His arms will encircle you, with comfort and strength
Surrender your fears, let a healing take place

You are not a body, of flesh and skin
You're a reflection of God, a child within

This prayer is a gift, something to keep
Something to help you, get a good nights sleep

You're healing is shared, your never alone
A brotherhood responds, you've found a home

Chip LaMarre

Works And Days

The birds' world is a green world, a treetop world,
just above our own, visible only to those who will look up.
Shadows of clouds are playing over the trees, darkening
first one, then the other, in changing moods little noticed
in the World Below.

Flights of pigeons, wheeling, reeling in great circles
in the sunshine. Bird glee clubs, singing for joy in the
trees. Bird travellers, following air lanes laid out without
regard for our earthbound channels of hurry and care. Oh,
to be free, if only for a little while, from our tedious
rounds of duty and care!

Free as a bird? No, my friend: there are bird seasons
to observe, food to find, nests to build, families to raise,
migrations to join — there is never a moment to lose: always
pressing onward toward the goal.

So, in warbling semaphore, the birds' message comes
clear: work for what you get: and so taste freedom's tang !

David Fields

My Wife

As I sail to some foreign shore
Just as others have before;
'Twill take me to some lonely spot,
But I ask of you dear, forget me not.

As I leave my home, the states I love
I place my hope in Heaven above,
I think I speak for all, when I say
There's no place like the U.S.A.

As I watch the starry sky,
I think of the days and years gone by
The days and years that were so full of cheer,
I pray to God, for a bright new year.

Now, dear, I ask these things of you,
Be faithful, honest, also true,
Take it with a grin, keep smiling, never frown,
Cause dear, I'd never let you down.

When this terrible war is over
Each man starts looking for new life,
I'll come home to you, my darling,
Yes you, my wife.

Alonzo Essick

Crushed Dreams

My dreams are not dead
Just crushed for the moment
Like flowers under foot
In my time of discontent.
Dreams were not meant to be trampled upon
Tossed aside forgotten like old shoes
For like plants after a weeding out survive
And weak ones straggling in growth dare
To bloom anew under tender loving care
Dreams too, come alive once more
With a love true and stronger than before
Crushed dreams are not the end of hope
I will not let mine gather dust to die
Unfulfilled and buried in arid ground lie
Nor water them with tears to drown
And miss the joy happiness brings
In new flowering of heart's desires
And better dreams that live on
Now that my moments of discontent are gone.

Hazel S. Moore

In Loving Memory of My "Guardian Angels"

On Christmas Eve, the holiday of angels,
Kitchens taste like heaven and spill forth
Laughter that heals. Open the door....

Grandpa is here! "Tell me a story," I cheer.
"Welcome home Little John! I've heard so much about you!"
"Uncle Cal, have I got a joke for you!", I giggle.
"Darcy! Julie! Bonnie! April! You're all so beautiful!"
"Uncle Merle, your smile is a sight for sore eyes!"
Grandpa and Grandma! It's grand to see you together again!'
"Uncle Ray, you've never looked better!"
"Dad", I gush, "it's a pleasure to meet you. Your son's a
chip off the ol'block. I've never enjoyed anything as
much as I enjoy being his wife."
"Great-Grandma, tell me, how are you?"

If you're hungry and your body feels the labor pains
of this "Silent Night"...
Be still in your warm kitchen,
You'll hear (their wings in flight)
The laughter that heals on this birthday of birthdays!
Happy birthday Jesus! Thank you for our guardian angels!

Jennifer O'Neal

That Wind

When you walked into my life from out of no where you were
just someone in the wind, but suddenly I was introduced to
you and you became another face with a name and a friend.

With the wind of the introductions and the times we began to
share, made you into a special friend that I can't seem to
remove from my heart.

With all of the disasters and roller coaster rides, I seem to
have fallen into a state of needing passion, warmth, and love.
That was when I let myself go into your arms.

At that point I realized you were still the same person but
now with my heart in your hands. That with a name, a friend,
and someone who became my lover.

With your embrace, warmth, and smile, I would just like to
let you know that this is how I'd like our friendship to grow.
With a touch of softness if either of us need it or
maybe a "HI" or "HELLO" as we pass over each others' path.

Truly I just wanted you to know that you have given me
myself, passion for life, and a great deal more....

With just that gust of wind.

Thank you, From a Friend
Christine Hulsey

"Not Forever"

TIME flew by, deceiving us all.
Just when we finally get
there, oftentimes
there is no
call.
So
take heed,
not greed, explore
every store, every means,
but please BEWARE, care, do not
exceed or endure when the obvious is no
cure, holding on to false hopes, when no way,
it is the day when TIME beckons and runs out.....

Christine L. Pratt

Kite, Kitty, and Me

Crystal clear sky
Kite flying high

Wind blowing through my hair
Jasmine scent upon the air

Tabby cat running in the meadow
Sun shining bright, it casts his feline shadow

Birds singing lullabies
To the cat below, who meows and cries

Calm breeze sweeps in
Kite once soaring, now in tailspin

Cat in my arms
Kite in my hand

We head back to the farm
Across the luscious, green, prairie land

Debra Ann Gutheil

Alive, Not Living

I watched you lie there, alive but not living.
Knowing how active you were and how giving.
Unable to really express to us your feelings
And us, unable to help no matter how willing.

You told your daughter, the world owed you nothing.
Your outlook, a song that we all should sing.
Enjoy life, but don't mistreat others,
You also told me to look after my mother.

You told me you were dead, "I'm in his world", you said.
And my reply was, "You're talking to me, you're not dead".
But, your body was dying yet your soul shall live on
In a better place God has somewhere around his throne.

So is living more than just being alive?
This question I ask to those of you who struggle and strive
with the thought of a loved one who's Not Living, But
Alive.

Gwendolyn Freeman

The Song Of The Singing Whip

Fire-haired lady of the singing whip,
  leading the sleek horses with a sweep and a dip.
Whirling and prancing to the amazement of all,
  she is mistress and master of the beautiful animal ball.
With fire-red hair and ruby-red lips,
  she takes away my breath with her song of the singing whip.
Fire-haired princess why can you not see,
  the mark of the lash that you've put on me.
Strike me, mark me, whip me to a tee,
  but do not pretend that you do not see.
I am he of the shadows,
  who listens to the song of the singing whip.

James Williamson

Yesterday

Just Yesterday I was standing on my porch watching my son
  learn to throw, then climbing on a tree . . .

Then Yesterday turned into a string of time gone by . . .

Just Yesterday I helped my son learn his lessons in math,
  then riding bikes with friends come by . . .

Then Yesterday turned into a string of time gone by . . .

Just Yesterday I was watching my son get a driver's permit,
  then calling to tell all his friends . . .

Then Yesterday turned into a string of time gone by . . .

Just Yesterday I was watching my son climbing the stairs
  of a plane, then leaving for a war . . .

Then Yesterday...

Deborah L. Cook

Here Today - Gone Tomorrow

Here today - gone tomorrow
  Leavin' behind a lot of sorrow
'cause if you drink and then you drive
  there's a good chance you won't make it alive

It'll hurt your mom, dad, sisters, and brothers
  but the tragedy is you might kill some others
So protect yourself and the whole world too
  Don't drink and drive or it might kill you!

Don't do it!!!!

Georgia Brown Wedekind

Untitled

There was a rose
that got squirted with a hose
It wasn't very funny
Because the water changed to hurry
And it hurt the pull little girls nose

Camille Beam

Now...Here In Your Presence

Now three score and then he was born in this land
Less than a score later he chose his wife and that union
That commitment gave most of us life.

Now here in your presence, a proud woman 'tis true
She nurtured and guided and did what women do with
Compassion and foresight and magic plainly seen
Breath of life to ten children, sits calm and serene.

Now here in your presence, two bodies one soul
Two sides if a coin, two halves of one whole
Because of God's blessing and guidance; his will
They now view life's wonder...the top of the hill

An ascent made together with lighted path from above,
Now here in your presence...fifty years of love!

Anthony P. Laws

A Typical Work Day

Getting up in the wee little hours
Let yourself jump right into the shower
Stepping out to be on your way
Thinking about why you want to start this day
Walking right in through the door
When you think your absolutely sore
Doing your job without any regrets
And trying not to become your boss's pet
Sitting down and relaxing while you eat
Just thinking how you're miserably beat
Carry on so you can do some more
While you think of something you adore
Getting to the point where you can leave
After waiting for the pay you may receive
Think about the thing's you've done
Dismiss all of this so you can have some fun
Going to bed so that you can rest
Just like the birds do in their nest
Dreaming of the things that has been
Just to wake back up and start over again

Gerald R. Smurphat III

A New Year's Prayer

Another New Year and the old's slipped away.
Let's make the resolution to live for today.
We've lived out the past and that we can't undo.
This is a new day and He will see us through.

Our God is our Champion and on Him we will call.
He'll guide our footsteps lest we should fall.
Our friends and families we're glad are so near.
Yet He is the One whom we hold so dear.

Valentine, St. Patrick, Independence, and Labor,
Days of the years with a distinctive flavor.
Easter, Thanksgiving and Christmas by far
Remind us to all ways follow His star.

If on this New Year you're about to set sail
Remember in the old year that He did not fail,
Pray He will bring you a glorious New Year.
Trust him for He gives comfort and cheer.

Ivan E. Cousins

"Sometimes"

Sometimes when I was from, three to fifteen - I'd
lie awake afraid to speak.
   Sometimes even tho I was pretending to sleep, the
monster, would up to me sneak.
   Sometimes the nightmare would come every night. And
I'd shiver and shake and run with fright, to see the monster
run and chase me with no where to hide. It took years to
have a home of my own to safely abide.
   Sometimes now even tho I'm grown and have children
and a grandchild of my own, I close my eyes and then I'm
afraid, I just have to open my eyes to see where I am.

   Sometimes I THANK GOD that I am away, from the
monster, that did not know how to LOVE me the right way.
   Sometimes I ask God, "Why did I have to live this
way." And he seems to tell me, "Child that's why you are the
good person, you are today."
SOMETIMES — SOMETIMES — SOMETIMES.

   Freda M. Arnold

Life

Sobs, tears, music, flowers.
Life gone before your teary eyes.
   Why?
Grandchildren with confused faces.
Children weeping to themselves.
Her body, her comforting, pale, gentle body.
   Why?

As I walk through the grave yard
every step feels like eternity.
So many tombstones.
Each one special to someone.
All of them special to god.
I come upon the tombstone that is special to me.
   Why?

When I read her name off of the marble stone,
it sounds like music coming from the harp of an angel.
   Why?

I remember her smile, she smiled all the time.
I loved her smile, when she smiled her whole body shined.
I Know Why.

   Alexis Hileman

Sorrowful Memories

My sorrows run deep.
Like a dagger piercing my soul, I ache from within.
This is my battle. No one can help me. I will get through this on
   my own.
Though mountains they may be,
The obstacles that lie ahead shall be conquered.
At times, my rage overwhelms me.
The blood rushes through my body.
Anxiety takes over. My control is lost.
Weak from internal attack,
I slowly regain consciousness. Reality is back.
The struggle to get my life back
Is like that of one lost in the blackhole,
Trying to find the way out. The violation is done.
Every part of me has gone with it.
Where is my youth? My pride? My confidence? GONE.
To love. To have fun. Memories of these I cannot remember.
The end of my "madness" is an eternity.
When the time for judgment arrives,
Those who have destroyed will suffer forever.
And those who have suffered will find peace.

   Candice Vonasek

"Equilibrium's Peace"

Swimming in the sea, I am playful and alive
Like a fish who just lives to be free
Until the resistance of weight and air
Begins taking its toll on me
When the dawning morn reflects a bright day
I begin with that hope in my heart
Yet as strings get pulled and even walls cry my name
I wish there were never a start
Bodies scrambling for help in each hole
Yet my arms only reach through my space
For each new chore places links in a chain
Which wraps my soul in disgrace
Sinking, drowning, begging
For a world holding unconditional joy
But seeing that dream makes a striking reality
And comparing the two, I avoid
Living each day like tomorrow brings spring
Will keep my mind open to hope
And until that time of equilibrium's peace
I will ravish my sleep to cope

   Holly Davies

The Hunter Of Sarajevo

Behind stone wall the hunter lay
Like a fox from his den on the hill,
Dark netting concealed his pitiful soul
As he watched and prepared for the kill.

Had an eagle's eye, a smooth calloused pull
Curled finger stroked the trigger of death,
His scope brought faces now clouded with fear
So close he could see their breath.

Sarajevo once proud, now a trampled flower
Held hostage by an enemy's yolk,
Her soul cries out 'midst rubble and stone
While peace-makers pound tables of oak.

A mother and child dashing for bread
No sound of children at play,
She doesn't understand the trembling hand
That hurries her along the way.

Ah, the vulture's slow spiral against morning sun
The world yawns-another day,
From his den the fox, he TOO stirs awake
Behind stone wall the hunter lay.

   Grant Halsne

A Rose And Life

A rose bud so unique, so fragile
Like a new born baby...
The rose bud begins to open one petal at a time
Like a baby nursing...sleeping...growing.
The rose bursts forth suddenly, opening many
   petals.
A baby is now a child...curious and learning
   many things.
Suddenly...the rose opens to it's maximum,
   giving beauty and fragrance in abundance.
The child is now a youth full of life!
His exuberance for living continues to
   adulthood.
Soon the petals begin to fade.
The adult becomes a senior citizen.
The petals become wilted and the rose
   is gone.
Life is like a rose...so full of beauty
   and fragrance...
But all too soon fades away.

   Esther Gordineer

Friendship Is Forever

Friendship is forever like a cloud in the sky,
Like a rainbow burning bright, and a bird learning to fly.

It follows you wherever you go,
It's something you learn and will always know.

Like a flower blooming in your heart,
Or two lovebugs that can't be torn apart.

It feels like being crowned with gold,
Like a new born baby to cherish and hold.

Like a breeze on a sunny day,
Or being joyful and feeling gay.

Like a hug and a kiss when your day's all wrong,
Like feeling down and singing a song.

Like running through a meadow when a deer passes by,
You want to say hello, and only your best friend is there to
   hear your cry.

Like laying down at night and dreaming of one another,
To awaken in the morning and play with each other.

   Alexa Krieger

There Is Only One You

You are a wonderfully made creation of the universe
Like a snowflake you will not find any exactly alike
For you are unique
You have all the potential under the stars to be
Whatever you set out to be, never give up !!!
Never deprive your body the respect
And kindness it deserves, be good to yourself!!!
Keep your mind stimulated so that it may stay alert
To set new goals for yourself so that
You will not experience too many dull moments
Live life to its fullest!!!
Keep in touch with your soul! Honor it!!!
For your soul can live on forever!!!
Never waste precious time dwelling on yesterday's mistakes
You can not undo the past, learn from it and go on to
Strive for a better tomorrow!!!
Be the best that you can be, no more, no less!!!
For there will never be another you!!!
   Love yourself!!!
   You are special!!!

   Diane E. Yeager

"I Am! I Am!"

No one can bake like me; I am the best!
Like an artist who, with a sweep of his brush
Puts on canvas what his eyes behold
I, too, put in my cakes what dreams are made of.
Mounds of whipped cream; swirls of chocolate;
Strawberries and maraschino cherries
Float by on soft clouds.
Mountains of yellow batter dance in their pans.
What magic I perform with my utensils of artistry!
I carve out a cat, a dog, a toy, a clown.
Decorated with jelly beans, licorice and gum drops.
Voila, a creation is born!
Lucky are they who taste these delights!
No one, nothing can surpass me.
I reign supreme
Goddess of the cakes, I am! I am!

   Dorothy R. Gratz

A Stationary Tear

I've left my mistakes lying around
like footprints fading into the horizon
I've left my tears dying on the sidewalk,
where people are free to kill them off.
I've left my mind in a strangers pocket,
and, perhaps, one day it'll be discovered
I've lost my pride many, many times,
but each time it was waiting in my heart
I've lost my heart to my one and only,
but I've learned to create a new one
I've lost my hope when dreams were dead,
but they've returned millions of times. I've left my
soul to all who need, except those who have already
taken and all the liars who have stolen. Just yesterday,
I felt a tear, pausing to fall on the corner of my eye
I gave it help but it ignored me and now I know why
All the time I was ignoring that tear
and it longed to drift away
But only now did it dare to become noticed
And when I tried to help, it decided to stay.

   Elizabeth J. Lynn

Requiem

Tears sliding silently down my cheeks
Like raindrops on the windowpane
Only tonight, the storm rages inside
Anger, pain, disbelief, sorrow
Escalating the grief into a tornado in my soul
Wishing I could bring you back again

This doesn't make sense
It's simply not fair
It wasn't your time yet
But still, you've gone

I feel so lost here, alone...
As if part of me died alongside you.
Yet the legacy you left behind
Will play on in my memory forever
You touched my insignificant life
And that will always be in my heart.

Though you were torn from us so abruptly
I believe you knew we all cared for you
And you will live on in our hearts and minds
A friend like you can never be forgotten.

   Jodi Lyn Turchin

Thank - You

   There is a newness within me.
Like that of spring...
   Offering a subtle, yet undeniable
   Freshness.
   Simplicity.
The unconditionally given concerto of
   the blue bird.
   A bird needs not recognition for his
long practiced song.
The flowers peeking from their
   patient silence,
   Must we kill them to love them?
The introduction of the sun...
   A God to spring,
   Bathe in it.
   Grow from it.
Newness is not really new,
   Just undiscovered you.
   Thank - You

   Darcy L. Mondragon

My Existence With You

I came to you with arms stretched wide,
Like the wings of an eagle as it soars the empty skies.

The gentleness of your touch warmed my soul,
Like the sun warms the earth each day of our lives.

The kiss placed softly on my lips was soothing,
Like the hot earth as it soaks in the falling rain.

The whisper of your tender voice was gentle,
Like the night as it creeps upon my window pane.

It was moments like those that often blinded my thoughts,
So that I sometimes believed things that were not true.

It was that mixture of emotions clouding my existence,
That forced me to expect too much from you.

So now when I come to you with arms stretched wide,
Full of yesterday's dreams to be converted into a reality.

I humbly accept all that you can give,
And what you can't will simply be.

Cynthia Deleveaux

"The Mystifying Firefly"

The flickering lights of fireflies - dancing in the night.
Like tiny glowing candles - what a truly beautiful sight!
We sit in the dark and watch them maneuver all around,
They are here - and there - and everywhere - making not a sound!

If you are ever lucky enough to hold one in your hand,
You'll see the luminous body, the coloring so grand!
A mystery surrounds them as they flit here and there,
You find you sit, watch them with a mesmerizing stare!

What is their purpose here, in the insect life we know?
Is it simply to flutter around - sending out their glow?
Or is there something else? See - we think we know everything!
These tiny creatures are mystifying when they take to the wing.

Hovering for seconds - then zip - away they go —
Their movements are erratic as they move to and fro!
Some nights they don't appear at all - where are they then?
We will just have to wait - and know - they will return again!

Agnes M. Dobias

You And Me

You and me:
Listening to a soft breeze
   whisper through the air;
Seeing the sun dance over grasses fair;
Knowing these things tell of a wondrous care
Given by God for those he holds dear;
Everything is so simple and clear.

You and me:
Knowing we should thank God
   for supplying each need,
And being near enough to help and to lead,
And loving enough to make season and seed;
And always ready to help and be near,
And close enough to chase away darkness and fear.

You and me:
Seeing the wind as it lingers in tall trees,
And knowing God's care saves and frees;
He helps the man who stops, and then heeds;
Then begins walking the Heavenly way;
Going toward a never ending day.

Evelyn J. Lewis

The Waiting Lamp

Who awaits my return, with the lamp a burning low
In the dark hours rocking, softly to softly fro.
Many, many years have gone, and out of sight
Since I saw her sitting, sitting by the waiting light.
And well she knows that in my heart there is a yearning so
To return to the awaiter, sitting by the burning glow.
Then in the door and by her side, stands the long lost son,
Blow out the lamp, it's duty's O'er, the waiting done.

Charles G. Tripp

His Light

Sometimes, the hustle and bustle of daily life,
living, gets to me, wears me down.
Then I'll take a drive down a quiet road.
Thoughts of light bills, housenotes, car notes,
insurance, groceries, children, relationship gone
sour, tumble through my head.
Much-like a clothes dryer spinning.
Not really because it wants to,
but because its button was pushed.
And just as tears start to fall down my face
God shows me hope.
"Look," He says," see my light shining
through the shadowed trees?
And you don't have to
get to the end of the road."

Bessie Williams Simmons

Time's Child

It's coming near,
living off only fear.

The girl with the silent scream,
slipping through dream to dream.

Awakened in the blackened night,
she sees the frightening sight.

Evil in it's highest power,
A dead rose, death in the form of a flower.

Memories of others,
nightmares and murders.

She still dreams the good thoughts of others
but she won't wake up if the world doesn't get better.

She's the one who sleeps forever.

Felicity Flensburg

Weeping Willows

Weeping willows.
Long, droopy branches bending to the wind,
Dancing with the rain.
Blue skies backdrop the mighty, swaying branches;
Wispy hair flying in the wind.
These stout trees
Sit like kings upon their powerful thrones.
Allies with the mighty elms,
In ruling nature and providing shade.
Refuge to frail animals and tiny birds,
Providing safety and shelter
From Mother Nature's battling sword.
Full of grace and beauty,
Many wonder why they weep.
Perhaps it's only rain
Falling from their branches,
Or dew sliding from their leaves.
It matters not.
They're strong and so lively,
So full of grace and beauty.

Donna Dissauer

No Tomorrows
(The Ballad of Kurt Cobain)
Look in my eyes and you'll see no tomorrows
Look in my words,
Read my sighs, you'll feel only sorrows
No heroes to be found, in these phrases that I've wound
Into your consciousness, like a thread
Admitting all the secrets that sanity does dread
Spelling out in braille what we're all to blind to see
Selling everything inside me, the cost completely free

The frozen paths I've tread alone are marked in tracks of blood
To follow all you need is nothing,
If you've more then stay at home
For all you'll find is what you've lost, and expect a raging flood,
To take the rest except, the tracks of frozen blood

Joe Gladden

"Look To God On High!"
Lift thine eyes to the Lord-
look to him on high,
seek his strength, read his word-
unto him draw nigh!

Look to him for your answer-
he alone can fill each need,
you will always find him there-
to nurture your spiritual seed!

And he too, can take care of earthly strife,
for he was sent unto this world, to bring abundant life.
So trust as a person, to walk as a child of God-
he is everlasting, let him come in, wherever in life you trod!

Jody Raelene Hodge

Bright-Eyed Little Girl
And then there was a little girl
looking bright-eyed at the world
sitting on a front porch swing
listening to the red birds sing

Off the porch swing, she went her merry way
it was hopscotch and jump rope, she wanted to play
with pigtails and ribbons bouncing through the air
like it should be, childhood games were her only care

The night was nearing, she must get ready for bed
but, not before her two goldfish are fed
so, to her bedroom and up the stairs
now she's on her knees, saying her prayers

she's climbed into bed, waiting for the goodnight kiss
this is something, her parents would never miss
she is the darling of their world, their pigtailed,
bright-eyed little girl

JoAnn Wheatley

"Our Hopeless World"
The love we have has no color. Our love hurts, "it" has no feelings.
Love, Peace, and Happiness we are suppose to have in
our world, but we don't. We have Drugs, Violence, and a hopeless
world. But everything can't be a perfect fairy tale, cause our
world is far from being a perfect fairy tale. Which is sad but we
can't do anything about it. Why must our world be so
imperfect, why must our children be so afraid, why must everyone
have a shield over them? Will the world end like "this?" I know I
don't know... do you? Everyone has to give up something in this
world. You shouldn't have to pay to live in our world, this planet.
Your life should be free, you shouldn't have to pay for your life
with someone else's, but that is "OUR HOPELESS WORLD."

Jessica Camino

My Little Man
He ran up to the barn and grabbed his puppy by the tail,
looking down with excitement at the treetoad in his pail.

His little feet were muddy and his hands were dirty too,
"See what I found Mama? I caught him just for you!"

"Oh what a nice surprise!" I said, giving him a grin—
Disappointing the child would be just short of a sin.

"See that big puddle Ma? I'm going to catch a fish."
"I don't think so little man, but you can try if you wish."

He padded off with his eyes shining, looking ever so sweet
Leaving perfect little tracks with his perfect little feet.

And watching him go with his fishing pole in hand,
I thanked the Lord for giving me something so little yet so grand.

Colleen L. Konieczny

A Time To Let Go
A baby's cry, a little girls tear
Love, family, faith and prayers,
Life's most precious years.
Mother how hard it must of been,
To leave that little girl go,
On to become a women of her own.
Now in the darkness,
I hear your prayers,
I wipe away your tears.
Your soul is reaching for that faraway light,
A soul that fulfill, a beautiful life.
How can my heart leave go
Do I have the wisdom and strength,
To accept the parting of our souls
My spirit tells me, time has come
Go-go mother into that light
Where you'll suffer no more,
Yet begin a new life
For the Lord knows, your heart, your spirit,
Will forever live in that little girl.

Beverly Vest

Instructions To My Physician
I have loved life too well to settle for death in life,
Loved thought too well to decline into gibberish,
Worked too hard for identity to reenter childhood.
I fear too much the loss I will not recognize.

I know I have fiber, tough as beef jerky,
Which will last too long, past when I
Can let go on my own; do not prolong
Me. It will not be me but a stranger
Endlessly folding a napkin, remembering
Fragments of events long over and done,
Betrayed by our very civilization; for

We are no longer forced to do kindness
By necessity, leaving behind the old
And infirm to die when we change camp.

Do I have to teach you your trade?!
Do whatever it takes; give me the dignity
Of a decent death. For God's sake, man!
Put me on the ice floe and let me drift away!

Fred Steiner Jr.

Tomorrow Today Will Be Yesterday

Jumping in the water on a cool still night,
Loving the water and you holding me tight.
Flowing peace all through the air,
Two people knowing they'll always care.
Beautiful, flowing, intimate thoughts,
Passionate love I've always sought.

Floating away on a cloud in the sky,
Unitedly having a natural high.
Ocean waves playing a sweet melody,
Tuning in rhythm with you and me.
Breathless emotions are moving wild,
Perennial love fragrant and mild.

Blossoming love in our springtime years,
Tender youth repressing our fears.
Sharing together peace of mind,
Sensuous thoughts soft and kind.
Walking, talking, hand in hand,
Running, laughing, kicking the sand.
Fulfilling each moment every day,
For tomorrow today will be yesterday.

Debra Anderson

A Father's Love

Fathers are special things,
made by God's own hand.
He lent them his love, his joy, and his hope,
so that they could take their stand.

The joy they use to watch their children grow,
The hope they carry for their children,
to learn, prosper, and know.

The love the fathers carry with them for all time.
Whether their children do good, or bad; become rich or poor.

A father's love holds out strong,
in good times, or in bad times,
whether they're right or wrong.

My father's love holds out till this day.
And this is my way to say,
Dad I love you.

Delbert E. Horne

Six Seed Sauce

Say it in eggplant. Tell her in fondue.
Make marinara romance with just the right explosion of cayenne.
Do tempura dancing and open fortune cookie love,
Stew in Rocky Mountain secrets with Juniper flavor lines,
using Grey Owl etiquette.
Recite malachite, jasper, agate.
Express a cricket mind. And go jungle.
Mix up your tigers. Let your gnat attack.
Take one vine daily.

Meet her off continent.
Show her the eel in you, then slither in her plankton sauce.
Teach yourselves seaweed basketry.
And remember to push the otter cookies.
Become waves of poetry:
rhyming mollusk, granite, and jade gone squid.

Think of sharing Islands.
Black Pelican Sands.
Watch for swimming Unicorns,
spouting Whale curried thoughts.
Imagine Eskimos in bikinis and Warm Waters.

Jeff November

A Texas Prayer

God looked down upon man, man—whom He had created,
man—with little vision and often little hope,
man—stumbling and struggling.

God gave man the beauty of nature
to cheer man and encourage his weary soul
that he might inhale a little
of the love and glory of God Almighty.

God does nothing in a small way, so
He flung His paintbrush across Texas
giving man acres and acres of bluebonnets.

His painting reflects the image of God,
God, who paints in abundance also loves abundantly.
So much does God love man that He gave
His only Son; gave His son not only to die
for man's sins, but to live before dying,
on this earth, which is full of sin and sorrow.

God gave freely and generously,
God gives man the free will to reject the love He offers.
God would not will that any should turn away from Him.

Elaine McKee

Systems Analyst's Prayer

Oh maker of the one big overall system, of which I am attempting to
manipulate just an infinitesimal part, as the solar system races
toward its predicted heat death, which must surely come in nine
billion years, I pray that I may in the meantime create efficiency
in all that I do. I realize that thou didst not make things to
work with that perfection of motion which thou desirest for me to
bring about on this earth before its final everlasting oblivion. I
am ever aware that thou hast left it to experts like me to figure
out how to put contrivances and people together so that both may go
faster and ever faster. In completing your work of bringing all
earthly happenings into one completely synchronized rapid sequence
of events I ask that thou wouldst help me to make machines operate
more humanly, and humans perform more mechanically so that both may
work together in uninterrupted harmony until their ultimate extinction.

Ed James

The Beloved Dance

Music is heard - an intriguing melody.
Many hearts dance - if not all... mine.
It dances, carefully watching its steps,
Trying not to step on anyone's feet.
In this new dance...this strange dance.

Gradually the timidity escapes
My heart dances - freer...faster...higher!
Spinning circles of delight, leaping without a look or care.
But then...

The dance slows down, allowing time for a glance down
Stumbling doubts attacks
Fear swallows the passion of the dance.
Sinking in the water which, moments ago, had been walked on.
Other music blares in confusing the melody.
My heart longs for the simple harmony it heard before.

A smile, a word - brings the dance back with ease
Once again, high above the air.
A new courage - with more love
   Unafraid...faster...higher!
Just wanting to remain in the arms of the dance - forever.

Christina Saltzman

The Resurrection

It was now the first day of the week as the sun began to rise
Mary and Mary came to look upon the tomb where he did lie.
"Who will roll the stone away?" they were heard to say
And no sooner said than done there came a great earthquake!
Now looking up they saw the stone was no longer in the way
Blocking their entrance to the tomb and they were surely amazed.
Then the angel of the Lord appeared, the guards shook with fear
"Do not be afraid," he said, "but Jesus is not here!"

They entered the tomb but did not find the body of the Lord
"What have you done with him?" they asked on one accord.
"Remember when he was in Galilee he spoke to you and said
"The SON OF MAN must be delivered into the hands of sinful man.
I shall be crucified and buried in the grave
But after three days I'll rise again with all power in my hands!"

Now They were Mary Magdalene and Mary the mother of James
Solome and Joanna who witnessed all these things.
They ran to tell his disciples they were eager to proclaim

"The Lord is risen, he is alive" they proceeded to exclaim.
Now these words were nonsense to the apostles in their pride
But Peter arose and ran to the tomb stooping to look inside
He saw the linen wrappings, the face cloth for his head
Yet understood him not that Jesus had risen from the dead.

Felix Lewis Jr.

"Angel In Disguise"

Angel In Disguise or White Knight call him what you
may call him what you might. He appeared when
you needed a kind word. He listened when you
had a bad day, a sad day, a glad day,
at least he did to me.

He had much and he did share it. He gave
to those who felt despair or just because
he cared. I know I was there.

I'll miss his smile, his tasteful dress, so
many things about him will be missed.
The Devil lived within his eyes, but, I know
he was an "Angel In Disguise".

He helped me when I was down and out, his heart
so big and kind, how he was and what he
did will live forever in my heart and mind.

He lives with you now God, this special man.
I ask you please to take his hand set him gently
upon the wings of my "Golden Eagle". We have spoke
and he agreed to share his never ending skies with
my "White Knight and Angel In Disguise"

Ellie Hetman

Clockwork

There once was a boy named Clockwork.
    Maybe because of the ticking of his heart.

    I think his heart was made of brass -
        never built to love.
    Built? You ask - yes built.
    Built by a man who knew no more
    about love than about God.

        A science man

        It's known to us that a man who has forgotten
    how to dream cannot create a dream -

        The Science man made Clockwork anyhow

        Then Clockwork met Lorry,
            and Lorry broke Clockworks brass ticker.

There once was a boy named Clockwork.
    Now he's dead.

Chris Harris

A Father's Prayer

In the puzzle of your life
may I be but a lesser piece
not at the center but down in a corner
where infants and old men sleep in peace

In the rainbow of your life
may I be a pastel hue
not at the apex where red meets green
but in some unobtrusive place where gray meets blue

In the formula of your life
may I add a fraction of me
nothing heavy like a quarter or half
just some binary dust the weight of a flea

In the journey of your life
may I be but a trail
not an x-mark or shortcut or road on a map
just a straightforward path the breadth of a snail

In the cathedral of your life
may I leave a light hopeful prayer
not a long heavy chant that vibrates your soul
but a message of love that floats in the air

Charles Sedita

The Importance Of Friends

As I guard this bit of earth I daily call home
May I look beyond, what I often call my own
So friends won't slip through my fingers like sand
May I try to be first, to offer a helping hand.

In life, many will enter my circle of friends
Some leave slowly, while some stay to the end.
In a fury of words, some will surely part
Others fade slowly, with love still in their heart.

Now if I can just learn to forget the word "I"
Then replace it with "we", mixed gently with pride.
And I'll try to remember, the importance of friends
For without them, empty, is the world in the end.

Jesse L. Markle

Ode To An Impending Storm

Only one spot of blue left.
Memories of blue skies, hopes of rain.

Lightning bolts, thunder roars,
Torrents of rain wreak havoc
With creek mirror's surface.

In an instant, the world transforms
into the drama of a storm born anew.

The blue spot of sky disappears.
Shadows hug the earth.
The creek turns dark, thunder blasts.

Lightening bolts hit,
First from afar,
Then thunder and lightening join in concert.
Crash! The symbols anoint the newly born distant storm.

The drops begin to fall
And then, in torrents, they continue,
Shedding pock marks on the glassy creek below.

The storm is here!
It has arrived to nourish the earth once more
On an August canyon afternoon!

Florencia Riegelhaupt

"Bridges"

Distant drifting visions-
Memories of the way we used to be,
Hand-in-hand, eye-to-eye, passion never seen.
   Where did you go?
   What don't I know?
Caught between us and reality.
   No one ever wondered.
     Not even me.
   No one ever questioned.
     We would always be.
The pain came:
   Washed over me these oceans of red,
   Dead and gone, wasted days race about my head.
   Why with him? Why at all?
   Rage unbound the past few days.
   Until I lost control.
   What did I say? What did I do?
   Take this breath, my final words-
     My God, I still love you.

    Daniel Fettig

Untitled

Women teaching logic? — Unthinkable!
Men could teach logic —
Men who see things as black and white, here and now —
   Strict rigidity —
   Unchangeable durability . . .
Foregone conclusions reaching into impenetrable dimensions.

But women see with overtones of color —
A mesmerizing enchantment of ideas . . .
The soft edges blurring into imperceptibility —
The blossoming of the universe into what might be
Or into that which cannot be seen with the clarity of eyes,
Merely felt with the nobility of heart.

Women will never teach logic.

    Cheryl Austen

In Your Arms I Am Complete

The sun sets the sky on fire with red,
Mirrored in the Autumn leaves.
Memories come drifting back: Of wood smoke,
Of the warmth of the blaze.
The warmth of our bodies in the chill autumn air,
And in your arms I felt complete.

In dreams we're together, and together forever.
Your beauty and pureness will inspire me,
Enrich me, and tempt me.
In my eyes you will be perfection.
And in your arms I'll be complete.

But for now, between the memories: between the dreams,
My heart still bursts with joy;
My brains addled with love.
For now I'll scream your praises to the world,
Anticipating to whisper them softly, sweetly in your ear.
Because in the warmth of the blaze and the warmth of our bodies,
In your arms and in your perfection,
In our happiness, all the world will be justified,
And in your arms I am complete.

    Brian D. Griffiths

Do You Hear My Words?

   Laughter and happiness are no
more. For you have left not just
My heart, but my world a shambles.

   Now you are gone and always you
will be. You have left my world like
a falling shadow. Not giving me a
chance to tell you just how
sweet your love was to me. But still
I sit upon my sill. Talking to the heavens.

Hoping, wishing, dreaming that maybe...
just maybe you're listening to my words.

    Briana Shields

Old Glory

I see you fly,
More now that there is a war going on.
I know that you have seen many wars,
and I hope that there won't be many more.
I hope that we will fly you all the time,
Not just when there is a war.
I hope we will make you proud so I say this,
"fly old glory fly"
Forever more in times of peace
as well as times of war,
fly old glory fly forever more.

    Debbie Knight

Given the Chance

   You gave me something means a lot even
more than romance. Though I was a stranger
true, you gave to me the chance.
   Chance is overlooked by mostly everyone though
an important must. Chance is the foundation in building
the vital force of trust.
   Within the chance are the seeds of love and hope,
both strong powers to hold. The more chances given to
anyone, paths to success and healing soon unfold.
   Without the chance none could overcome oppositions of
human doubt. The forces of all that's evil must flee.
when chance is about.
   Those who stop giving and taking the chance soon
become captives of fear. But, blessed is the one never
losing faith in the chance for by it many blessings appear.
   Thanks for the chance of opportunity given to one
as me. In the heart of all who give true chance dwells
God's mystery. He gave us all THE CHANCE called Yahshua
and Given The Chance we are free.

    James E. Smith

Long Road

Here we are.
More than thirty years
Down the road.
Talking on the telephone.
My, my, who would have known.

That the door to the unknown
Had finally opened up.
No. It is not.
Like the princess who
Kissed the frog.

It is incredible grief for the years lost.
It is the pain of distance;
Which separated loving souls.
It is deep flowing sorrow for having travelled
A long road alone.

    Gilda Serrano

The Leaf Raker

Fathered by a smoldering fire
Mothered by a wisp of air, of this day I am born.
Tossed, I rise gleefully
My graying life edges burning.

Wafted higher and higher swirling, twirling
Above the leaf rakers, above the houses above the trees.

I am vibrant, giddy, alive,
Up, up, and up, I see the western sun
The eye of God piercing the grey billowing blanket.
I become inflamed in its gaze.
I care not if the next instant cinderizes me.
I am a part of now and forever.

My sculptured flame is a mote of ash to the leaf rakers below.
But wait, See!
I sear into their unconsciousness,
For my truth is their truth
And I lie but a step beyond eternity.

Charles T. Armstrong

Piano

I watch your long slim fingers on the keys
Moving swiftly, surely, as they free
A captive song, a half-forgotten melody.

Black and white, in quietude serene,
Now leap, now rill, now leap again unless
They miss the softest whisper of your brief caress.

I watch your restless fingers on the keys
Stroking, thrilling, tantalizing; sweet control
Which frees that haunting melody and sears my soul.

Black and white, so mute, so lonely in repose,
Unnoticed. Like my heart, aloof. Yet such
Concealed desire bides for that capricious touch.

I watch your long slim fingers, and I pray
That they will touch me as they touch each key,
And free at last my heart's long-hidden melody.

Elizabeth Ann Brandt

My Grandparents

There's a little white house at the foot of the nile
My beloved grandparents live there still.
They aren't very well but yet, all the some
You very, very seldom hear them complain.

They have see lots of friends come an go
Watched their own large family be born and grow
Granddad used to tell us such wonderful stories
of little Orphan Annie in all of her glory.

Grandmother made cookies cooked food by the score
was happy and witty who could ask for more.
Things have come to pass since I started this rhyme
Which has made a difference like the beginning of time.

Granddad passed on during the spring
Grandmother followed before Christmas come
Their love lingers on makes no difference the change
They will live on and on In the hearts of their offsprings

Billie Goodwin

Gold

The flames they burn all through the night
my body thus knows its sleep it must fight.
As my eyes gaze out to the golden dawn
my sight bestows the beauty of a fawn
out in the wild where freedom reigns,
it's the grace and the beauty my heart retains.
Onward we must soar like eagles in flight
to yet once again surpass the night.
The silence and the darkness
for lovers, I am told
is a precious as the wild
and it's color I call Gold.

Derrice Fuller

Arita Eyo

Nestled close against
My breast
Heart beats blend
Breathing matches mine she sleeps peacefully
Curly black hair
Soft as cotton
Dark brown skin contrasts
Sharply with my
Pale white hand
Long tiny fingers
Circle around my thumb.
Her nose wrinkles
She stretches, squirms
Deep within her quilt
Beauty in its
Purest form
Touches me.

Joanne Engnell

"I Remember The Times."

The Birds are singing a pleasant sweet song,
My dad use to say, "Now spring won't be long."
I remember the times we spent were so special,
I ask myself, "Why?" Then I remember, "Be Faithful."

We'd sit neath the trees and throw buckeyes in his shoes,
Its some things that we did, It's things we would do.
He got so excited one day neath the tree,
As a beautiful young deer we saw starting to flee.

Across the valley and over the hill,
As we sat so quiet, so quietly still.
It was a joyous sight as it crossed in front of our eyes,
And these are a few things that deepen my family ties.

Now he's sleeping, he knows nothing, he's silently still,
Where we once roamed the valleys, the mountains and hills.
He lays there sleeping beneath the cold clay,
And I soberly realize how much I miss him each day.

So now as I ride through the fields and the clover,
In a life without my dad, but it's only temporarily over.
You see, I pray for the time in God's holy paradise,
We'll be together, forever, never leaving each others side.

Janie Briggs Poole

Untitled

If you haven't heard this message
then here's everyone a tip
Jesus Christ is coming soon
and Has the trumpet to his lip

John M. Hartzell

Finally at Rest

As I laid my tired flesh to rest,
I closed mine eyes from life.
I awakened with wings to
Lift me from the body I borrowed from the earth.

As I rose
I brushed off the sickness,
I pulled off the pain
and I rubbed off the sorrow.

I glided into the wind
making a right turn into the bright.

While faith directed me,
Love carried me, and at the golden gate
He met me.
I knew then, I was finally at rest.
Thomas E. Valentine Jr.

Forever My Friend

To me your Friendship was like a rough Diamond
I didn't know through all the dirt was a precious gem
So I threw it away and someone else found it.
They shined it all up, they put it in gold.
They treasured it like I failed to do
You like to shine with them because they make you shine
And every once in a while, I get to try on the ring,
but I always have to return it
I wish I could go back, I'd love to change it all
I'm so sad and terribly lonely, I miss you forever my friend.
Tiffany Miller

Untitled

I soar on eagle's wings to a destiny
I do not understand
To pluck me from the sky for safety's sake
Lends credence to the inhumanity of man

The wind is my love
It holds me gently in its arms
Always free — soothing deeply, deeply into me
It asks nothing more of me than simply
But to be

It lifts my spirit
And saves me from the carrions below
For demons live only amid the ashes of the soul
And feed upon the seeds
Left lying on the barren floor
Of all that I might be
Sherry Kranys

Shouldn't Have

You work is necessary there's no doubt
I don't know if anything can be done
Especially since building caskets
For children is no fun

Whilst the spectre of death visits
And eventually takes us all
The event is that much sadder
When a casket's occupant is young and small

And never had the chance
To experience the many joys and wonders
   time cut short
By a death that shouldn't have
   occurred at all
Seon O'Neill

"Life's Angry Pawn"

Sometimes I really am confused,
I feel like I'm just being used, as a pawn in life's
wondrous game.

Someone who just helps other players advance,
Someone who really doesn't have a chance, to advance on their own.

In life's great game, pawns are sacrificed easily,
When they die they go peaceably,
And usually are forgotten all too soon!
But not this pawn, this pawn is going to make it to the other side,
Its going to beat life's great game in stride,
Then its gonna turn and laugh at all the other players.

For when I reach the other side, its like a sweet dream,
My pawn's shell is removed, and replaced with a gracious Queen.

Then I'll advance for my own sake,
I'll give nothing, yet I'll take, take, take,
For I feel life's game owes me a great deal.

Now I'm getting closer, soon I'll be the best,
For I alone have captured the king and outsmarted all the rest

For I was a nothing pawn, but I beat life's great game,
By my own sweat and tears, I have gained all of my fame.
Teresa Bushek

"The Mask"

Dear Lord,

   I see this mask and I want to cry.
I feel so sad. I guess it's because I see all
of us, including me, with so many masks!

   We put on one mask to be the perfect wife...
another to be the perfect mother...
another for the body of Christ...still
another to show the world.

   Lord, help us to remove all the masks,
including the one we sometimes put on for you.
Let us be transparent that you can begin to
heal us, and mold us into the image of your Son.

   As long as we insist on putting on our masks,
we tie your hands to do your perfect will. Lord,
I pray, that you remind me and show me each time
I put on a mask, that there might be nothing at
all between you and me.

Written in love, without a mask,
Sylvia Villarreal

The Crash at Pope AFB

(Author - Wife of a Paratrooper)
I see your tears
I feel your pain
Lives will never be the same
Loved ones lost
Such a high cost
the price we pay for freedom
I say a prayer each night
Please God make it right
The sorrow I bear is too great
Was it destiny or was it fate
That lives were lost on this date - March 23, 1994
Toni McGhee

The Calendar

The year had ended, the calendar was no longer good.
I had meticulously created it, combining sequins,
Beads and spangles as artistically as ever I could.
Sequins, beads and threads of gold had proclaimed 1971.
The hours of sewing, bead threading and needle-eye
Hunting had all been such fun.

Sadly, now I took it down and lightly berated
myself for the hours of labor spent.
As I walked to the wastebasket, it was hard to believe
This masterpiece of mine was not worth one cent.

"Don't throw it away, Grandmother dear,"
My little Heather cried.
"In eleven years it will be good — I read it in a book —
And the beaded 71 with 82 you can hide."

We folded the calendar as gently as a wedding gown
And stored it in a box.

As I closed the lid my granddaughter yelled, "No, no,
Grandmother, you must make a wish if you want a paradox.
The story said to make a wish before you close the lid.
And all your dreams and wishes will come true
If you keep the calendar hid."

Just like a prayer, I thought. It's no good unless you act.
As I closed the lid and kissed her cheek, I mumbled,
"A child shall lead them is indeed a fact."

Tahlma Outlaw

Age

With my back to the world
I have my own mental joy.
   Owning the sun with the moon
as my toy.
   My life down on paper and my mind
in the sky, my wings are clipped
but I still know how to fly.
   Now I'm old and life's a chore,
I see the exit sign but can't find the door.
   Running around till I can't search no more,
drop down dead, but still alive . . .
by the breath in me I will survive.

Travis W. Nines

The Man I Love

I love him with all my heart
I have never loved anyone as I love him
The only problem is that he doesn't know I am alive
I have never officially met him

Yet I feel as if I've known him all my life
I will never forget what he did for me
He cheered me up when I was down
He doesn't realize how much his one gesture of kindness meant to
   me

He is the nicest guy I have ever met
I know that I must find the courage to approach him
To at least meet him formally
But I can't find the courage to do that

I am afraid to risk a broken heart
I honestly believe that he would never to anything to hurt me
   intentionally
Yet I am afraid of his reaction when he finds out that I am in love
   with him

I really do love him
Maybe one day I will find the courage, or the strength
Right now I am only able to admire him from afar.

Robyn Brillman

Untitled

In the morning I wake with my eyes closed.
I have visions of the day not good.
There is fear and death all around me.
I see children playing in the streets,
with cars driving by.
Where are their parents - off getting high?
I see walls of graffiti and sex everywhere
young and old.
Haven't they been told that AIDS is here?
Do we just not care?
When will it end? When will we wake in the
morning with our eyes wide open?

Roberta Pratt

I Hear My Heart

In the evening, when all is still
I hear my heart, it has a will.

It will not be silenced, it must speak out
Sometimes it's beat is like a shout.

People, people everywhere - why must you fight
Why do you despair
Find a goal, find the light.

It is here, it is there
Look about you
Everywhere.

There it is - Your ray of hope
All is beautiful - you can cope.

Rita H. Parker

Echo

Every time I feel content
I hear spoken so long ago
The words I thought were heaven sent
In a sweet, haunting echo - I love you

Left in mental comatose
I thought the right one I could see
Yet I only feel morose
As the echo reminds me - I love you

As I look into her eyes
I begin to realize
My nights have no starry skies
Only a faint echo that cries - I love you

The words that dance in my head
The words that speak insanity
Perhaps the words should not have said
Still the echo speaks loud and free - I love you

I cannot love you
I will not love you
Yet the echo speaks
Words so painfully true - I love you

Rick Wiener

"The Skies"

Another day is gone and with it the light,
Night comes silently with its beaming moon light.
Darkness comes in sudden haste,
While flickering moon beams dance about the silent space.
The echoes of silence are in the woodland's heart,
While reaching beyond in silence to its human counter part.
This is the stillness that will move all solemn and forlorn,
In this empty place, until the break of a new morn.
Then the day will dawn with heaven's peace in sight,
Under God's never ending skies of promise and light.

Rosemary F. Schiavi

Spring Morning

As I sit here in the sweet morning breeze
I hear the birds chirp and sing
They sing of the joy that the new day brings

Then I look about at the Peaceful trees
Their putting on their new dresses of green
Trying to impress anyone that see's

Oh look! There goes a butterfly
With it's multi-colored wings, it's as weightless
   as the air on which it glides
It, takes time to smell each flower as it passes by

But as the city awakens with all it's noise
The beautiful scene begins to fade
Who here still cares what God has made?

One day they'll really regret
For they'll finally see what they have done
So paint a picture in your mind...
Before the spring morning is left behind.

   Tabatha L. Kight

My Mind

I see visions in my mind of dark and evil thoughts,
I know it's not right, but it just won't stop.

Sometimes I'm glad, because if it leaves,
I'll have to grasp reality, and then I'd lose me.

So I'll welcome it in, and shut the people out,
For they don't care, they don't know what I'm about.

I want to die, but I don't want friends to hurt,
So I will lie, and cover my feelings with a metal dirt.

So I write these poems, as a type of escape.
It doesn't work, it fills my heart and mind with hate.

People read these poems, and say there's nothing wrong.
So, why do I feel this way, and why for so long?

   Stacy Laub

Day's End

Each night after five o'clock
I listen for your step along the hall
And the rattle of your key in the lock
That lets you in, my all in all...
I listen to every street car
That stops with wheels a-squeak,
And I whisper 'there you are'
My knees shake and I grow weak...
And when you turn the latch
That bring you into view,
My throat stops with a sudden catch
Because I've been waiting so long for you...
Every night I say a grateful word
In thanks to whatever gods may be...
That somehow they have heard
And brought you home to me!

P.S. Such waiting seems a sort of curse,
But image a sorrier kind of fix...
Just suppose, to make it worse,
You had to work 'til six!

   Wilma Shirley Stafford

The Homeless

I sit here in this large deserted area,
I listen, I hear you muffled voices,
I look at the woods, but see through them, I can't,
I try so hard to see you on the other side.

I've looked about you, I've heard about you,
I hear: "Why, why has God put them there? Who's fault is this?"
And to this I say: "Fault, no, it's no one's fault."

I wish there was something I could do;
Give you riches with my words?
Give you warmth with my thoughts? Give you faith with my prayers?

As I get up from the grass, from where in which this poem I wrote,
I feel the cold, cold air against my burning face,
I think about you and how I was only outside for a moment and got so
   cold,
And you, how you stay outside because you have no inside for days
   at a time.

Then I look across to the woods;
I hear you, but I can't yet see you.
I understand you, but I can't yet know you,
And then I ask: Who's fault are you?"
But I quickly answer: "Fault? ... No, you're no one's fault"

   Victoria Lavanga

Lonely Memories

As I walk down this lonely road,
I look to the sky above.

What do I see? But a lonely star,
A lonely star of love.

It makes me think of years gone by,
And the worry I caused the ones I hold dear.

I want to bow my head and cry,
For the burden is so hard to bare.

Oh, lonely star how I wish you would be my friend.

Give me a chance to redeem myself and,
show my loved ones once again.

Lonely star your growing dim and,
a new day is almost here.

I pray to God my loved ones will be where they
belong and have the love we share.

   Rufus J. Burns

Death

   A fog rolled up from the deep blue sea.
I looked around but couldn't see.
I knew you've soon be missing me so I wasn't
Scared at first you see

   Then I felt a cold and chilling breeze.
And the hand of death was lifting me.
I looked at death and said "let go"
You know that I'm not ready to go.
He put me down again you see, but
said that he'd be back for me.

   And now I lay and wonder
still was that a dream or
was It real?

   Sharon E. Talley

"Spring"

Lips of splendor, eyes that glisten, please look at me and listen,
I love you more now than then, fallen to arrow, but not knowest when,

For last a thought I could not feel, into my heart, your love did steal,
Where does thou love take my heart, to be thrown to savage to be
torn apart,

Or is thou love holy and true, does my heart beat next to you,
Fear is present, emotions arise, could it be that my heart lies,

Ache in chest, I do despise, Suppress, suppress these painful cries,
woe to the one who's heart is stolen by love, but then there is
peace, gentle as a dove,

Heart beats and love flows, awaken for it now knows
that love in the truest form is not wrong, it is a bond that is
stronger than strong,

I speak not a word, fear is not found, you gaze into mine eyes,
there is no sound
what you see I cannot say, only that you love me this day,

What lips of splendor and eyes that glisten...

Shane W. Kroger

I Need You!

I need you my Darling to live once again,
I need you endlessly to see the "Heralds of a Spring"
And feel your kisses brought from the Sun Valley
By the wings peak of life resurrecting wind.

I need you, my Love, to go through my life
Whispering our love e secrets from lips to lips,
To hold your hands and drown in your azure eyes,
And listen to our hearts' music from our dreams.

Then dance with me my treasure,
Let me feel our hearts same beat,
Open the gates of paradise forever,
Because forever each other we do need!

Victor W. Sawicki

Love/Hate

As a child I wanted love, but love always had strings attached.
I never learned to love, only to control love by manipulation.
I knew that God never loved me!
Dysfunctional was my family.
So now I dress sexy and men pay for love.
The more love the more money.
I did find love, the love for money.
Now dying of AIDS at the age of twenty,
All that money I loved, can't even buy me a future.
As my pain grows with this fatal disease, so does my hate for you God!
Why didn't you give me loving, caring, and giving parents?
Just then the room got dark, I must of passed out!
For when I opened my eyes,
This sexy brown haired, blue eyed man was standing over me.
He asked if I was all right?
Pushing back my long blond hair, I replied "I'm ok"
Then he said: "My child please don't hate me, I love you.
 I've never meant for any of my children to be hurt.
 Come take my hand, I am taking you home"

Sara C. Koczur

The Beautiful Thing

Moon moon, Sun sun.
The moon is so beautiful,
The sun is so bright.
The planets are so colorful.
I love night.

Amanda Grey Martin

Upon My Head

My life is a series of bungee jumps unplanned,
I plunge head long without farewells, Short of impact,
I am snatched upward with a jolt that confuses my senses
and causes me to be tall and straight as I am.

Wind rushes past my ears as I plunge downward then upward.
There is no rightness or wrongness when senses mix and perceptions
blur, causing reason to be folly and logic a child's game.

Except for the tether, that binds too tightly for walking,
but scarcely tight enough to break the fall that breaks the neck;
that is confining to willful gait,
 but insuring for continued feats of death defiance;

 I fly free.
 Clinging to my humanness, I long to stand upright, to walk within
clovered fields observing brooks that babble and birds that fly.
Leaving the wind that rushes past my ears to be in a horizontal
direction to the solid ground; my senses unwound and rightness and
wrongness in stationary places.

 I rue the weightlessness;
I fear the fall and I trust the cord less and less.
I prefer the draw of gravity upon my feet rather than upon my head.

Velva Boles

Gathering Dust

When you finally left me,
I pretended it just didn't happen.
Preparing supper and tending garden,
waiting... I whittled precious time away
while my journals lay unopened... gathering dust.
And now-now that I'm dead-
I awaken each morning in anger-
as the sun bakes my soul
steamily-in thick, dark earth.
I command these once-nimble fingers
-Move-but to no avail, they rest
I will my placid body
-Rise-greet a beautiful new day-
For there is much to live, to write...
The heaviness of silence is lifted by the whistling wind
dancing through the gravestones overhead.
I can almost hear it rustling
between the pages of my old journals
as they still, and now I
lie motionless-gathering dust-

Susan Pastorius

By His Side Forevermore

I just can't walk away.
I really want to stay.
By his side forevermore.
Yet he turns walks out the door.
I think he thinks my love is true.
When I whisper I Love You.
I've not felt this feeling yet before
By his side forevermore.
He used to talk to me.
Try to make me see that our love could never be.
Could never be because of her.
The one who left him for another.
The one who loved him and ran away.
She found another a different day.
She new he was free all but his heart.
For there the memories of him, her, together would never part.
He would always love her so,
He could never let her go.
Now he wishes he could be
By her side forevermore.

Shannon M. Robbins

The Seasons of Life

The spring of my life like a beautiful dream
I recall with such vividness tonight
From the seeds that were sown, I reaped a harvest supreme
Before I entered the summer of life.

When I entered this time, I became quite alarmed
By the challenging tasks I must meet
But love conquered all, my fears were disarmed
And I survived without feeling defeat.

Now the autumn of life is approaching with speed
And the colors are changing for fall
It's a time of reflection upon seasons and deeds
In preparation for my heavenly call.

The winter's white blanket will warm my earthly remains
When my spirit moves forth to the heavens again.

Vera Thomas Stern

Be Not Sad

Into this life I came,
I remember not from where I started.

I chose this body to remain;
But now I must be departed.

Be not sad, for in your heart I stay,
I'm in another world now, a better one I'm told;
No pain, no sorrow, only joy they say
Into the light I've gone, now you must be bold.

We'll be together once again, when this physical
life you depart.

I'll be waiting on the other side, I'll take your
hand when it's time.

Remember me with the love we had, as each
day you start.

I'm beginning anew, once again I'll be in
my prime.

Sharon L. Nettleton

"Every Now And Then"

Every now and then when I search my heart,
I remember that I am missing a very special part,
you touched my life in a very special way,
that left me without the words to really say,
how much I loved you or how much I cared,
about everything we had and all that we shared,

Every now and then my lost love, I start to miss you,
it seems like the days we shared were too short and too few,
I find you when I walk through the corridors of my mind,
where our love is endless and it knows no space or time,
there we run across the landscape of my hopes and dreams,
where we want or need for nothing because we are all things,

Every now and then I feel lonely and all alone,
because now you are gone and I am on my own,
you meant so very much to me my love, back then,
and I never knew that our love would come to an end,
if I had the chance to do it all over again,
I really wonder if I would, every now and then.

Tina Klinkhammer

Stitches Of Hope

With cancer ripping me apart
I sat to sew this bright quilt.
Stitching, stitching, shaking hands,
Tear-filled eyes, stitch at a time.
Each breath I hoped and prayed
My life be spared another day.
Week after week, month after month
My children's constant vigil and fervent prayers
This quilt I kept stitching.
Tonight it is finished.
Now I can enjoy my remission.
Thank you Lord for all my yesterdays.
For today, and any tomorrows I may share.

Velma Lipe Brown

The Woman of My Dreams

One night as I was lying still
I saw a woman standing on a hill
Her long black hair it glistened so
As the stars around her put on a show

For me this was time of peace and content
Although exactly I knew not what it meant
For this woman with the long black hair
Was a gift from God sent to me there

As the night went on and the cool wind blew
I finally realized what I had to do.
This woman of beauty and full of grace
A kiss I must place upon her face

As I approached her, and the closer I got
Her vision of loveliness in my mind would not stop.
And finally in front of this Goddess I stood
Scared to death asked her to marry me,
The best way that I could.

When I awoke the next morning and looked
At my wife I knew I knew that my journey was not just a dream.
For the woman I saw was my wife so it seems.

Timothy Paul Ferrell

A Field Of Dandelions

In mid spring, along a village street
I saw dandelions not a few.
I slowed my mind and moving feet,
To look at how they grew.

Each was a family of young and old -
From buds to granny's gray hairs,
Some wore faces of pure gold,
Others showed the worries of life's cares.

I thought, which faces are the best,
The ones colored in gold or gray,
Those not yet put to the test,
Or those ready to fly away?

I preferred those ready for flight -
Each waiting to lift its wing.
They will survive the winter's night,
They will greet another spring.

Russell Abata

Some People

Some people laugh and
Some people cry.

Some people make it feel
Like the days just pass by....

And some people are very true.

Cassie Heinz

July 25, 1987

As the dew of Hermon,
I saw it from afar.
Like a crystal of ice
it froze my soul.

Like the mystic breezes from the East
I felt the love, the compassion, the power,
or was it the rage, the evil, the wrath,
of the creator that monsooned over my family.

As the weeping virgin,
my mother leaned on the doorpost calling my name.
Without a word, I knew the call came...
I knew my father was dead.
I saw the dam of my mother's eyes cracking.

Like a martyr, I alone threw the burden of my family's suffering
　　on my back.
Through the ages, I still remain the rock.
Through the misery, the pain, the loneliness, I Stand Strong!
Like the pillars of Solomon's Temple, I Stand Strong!

It's been seven years since mine eyes have seen the glory.
Many sad memories cluster my heavy heart, and the pain and loss
　　remains clear.
But nothing is more painful, or as vivid, as the day I saw that
　　small diamond fall...
the small diamond that was my mother's first tear.

　　Richard Robertson

Road Kill

Sometimes, when I walk down the street,
I see a bird, laying dead at my feet.
And I say "Hey Mr. Birdie, laying dead at my feet,
　　looks like your having a bad day!"
And birdie says to me "No man, I'm having a good day,
many wonderful things have happened, I met grandpas
grill, got a massage from Sam's 4x4.
My head ache's gone,

But I have yet, to meet Cindy for a soda,
Oh yeah, I got caught in Kari's spokes,
　　and that is why the rest of me is over there!
Other than that, it has been a slow day."
　　"Well I've got to go now Mr. Birdie," I said
with a smile, "maybe I'll see you on Sunday."
"Okay," Mr. Birdie said,

　　Noticing the dullness in his voice,
I left Mr. Birdie there in the street,
　　dead at my feet,
　　little guy,
Road kill....

　　Shawn Hampton

Mankind

Founded by love, filled with life;
Made for peace, surrounded by strife;
Architectural feats of the most awesome kind.
An equal creation— who can find?

With power to decide and freedom to choose,
The ability to win, the possibility to lose.
Self sufficiency desired, dependence inborn
Possessing life — is it flower or thorn?

Given a chance to run like the wind
Making every effort not to break or bend
From what will keep the soul alive
Without God, how can man survive?

　　Jeremy Scott Paige

A Cry For Justice

I hear my people cry
I see my people die
While others just stand by
And say goodbye, goodbye, goodbye

I sigh tonight and sigh
to see how they all die
To see them all cry
For justice long gone by

It hurts me to see my people plea
For mercy from afar
Instead they are forced to seek
The ocean and the stars

My people are in an island called "Cuba"
Cuba used to be considered communist and with no freedom
This is no longer true in the political arena
For Cubans are no longer seen to be seeking freedom
Now they are economic refugees from the island of CUBA

Why is the embargo on CUBA still executed?
How can the U.S. still justify it?
Remember, we are no longer considered politically persecuted!

　　Rosa Michelena

Love Everlasting

As I open my eyes and I look outside,
I see the beauty that lies in every sunrise,
I see the lightning strike, I feel the wind and the rain,
I think of why you came, I want to praise your name,
A love so deep, so hard to understand,
Can only be explained through the blood of the lamb,
At the end of each day I think of all of your grace,
Knowing we will be together forever in that wonderful place,
When I grow weary you always come near me,
I call on your name and see things much more clearly,
Often I fall short and lose sight of the plan,
You take me back to where it began, the nail-scarred hand,
I have so little to give, I struggle with how I should live,
But you always find it in your heart to forgive,
Take me as I am, forgive me where I fail you,
I love you, though I seldom tell you,
Cover me, wash me white as snow,
Help me be a beacon of light to a world that doesn't know,
The pain you felt, it cuts me like a knife,
JESUS, your blood frees us, I owe you my life.

　　Rocky Thomas

You

I see the moon and that is you by the pool
I see the stars and I can see the stars in your eyes
I feel the wind and I can hear you speaking
I see the waves coming to shore and I see you
Walking like the waves, so strong but so soft
I see the sun and I see you as you warm up each bright day
I see your smile and it is like each morning sun

But then I look farther out to sea, and
I see the darkness and I feel the deepness of the sea
I can see tomorrow you will be like the white caps of
Each waves as it reaches shore, but
I still have my memories...
Each night I see the moon and the stars, and
I feel the wind
Each day I see the waves moving to shore, and
I will see you...

　　Troy L. Hunley

A New Hope!

As I walk through the dark pathway
I see you, face so bright, like the shining sun;
Waiting for me to come to you.

Arms open wide and I see the final
light of the darkness, and your face
of light shining on to my heart.

A heart so full of light just like your face.
And I wish I were nearer to you;
So I could feel your arms wrapped
around me in a great hug.

As the ocean hugs the shore, so tight
and reaching for the light, that is
uncommonly bright.

As I draw closer to your face so full
of light like the sun, and your arms
wishing to hug me as tight as the
ocean does the shore.
I awake with a new hope of what's to come.

Rachel Deirdre Sadler

Glass

Reminded every day,
I sit alone, emptiness inside
that is wanting to break free.
To dwell on the fictitious fact of life,
yet so scared of the outer core.
Always enchanted by fascination,
the crucifixion, never once scared,
but somehow seen clearly
through the eye.
I'm left to let go of the swinging rope,
and fall clumsily to the ground,
letting go I drift off into
the world I call my own,
which seems to be filled with many.
Only to enter with an injection of thrill.

Shannon Littlefield

Heart Of Ice

Under the endless gaze of the night,
I sit by my fire and wonder
Why am I alone?

The bridge of love that linked my parents to me
Across the vast gorge of loneliness
Has been shattered by my bitterness.

The majestic tree from which grew my friends,
Has since withered and died under the onslaught
Of the frigid bite of my harsh words.

And under the endless gaze of the night,
As I sit by the fire, my heart of ice
Melts into tears, as I realize why I am alone.

Ryan Moore

The Smiling Strange

He smiling at me,
I was smiling at him.
Next thing he was, wrinkling at me.
I was studding him out. He sneak up too me,
asking me out. I gladly excepted.
We went to a show.
I was stepping all over his toes.
He was stepping over my toes.
Oh! What a date that was!
He my kind of guy.

Diana Greegor

Waiting

Smoke fills my eyes as my soul vanishes,
I sit through the lonely, dark hours of the
night - waiting
for this emptiness inside to go.
But as the dawn approaches,
the emptiness still remains
and the pain I feel deep in my soul
is a scorching flame
that burns all I'd ever had.
And more.
I look into the mirror and see a face.
But the face caught in the
reflection does not belong to me.
Or does it? For caught through
the glass, is a face burned beyond
recognition by the everlasting
flames of time and pain.

Valerie Collins

Twilight

Walking toward the lake,
I spot another empty candy wrapper,
Discarded, its protection needed no longer,
The candy gone,
Tossed aside to blow—aimlessly—in the wind.
Aged and brittled by the sun,
Torn and ragged, snagged by rocks and weeds,
Alone.

I am an empty candy wrapper,
Discarded, my protection needed no longer,
Children grown and gone,
Left to wander—aimlessly—in the wind.
Aged and brittled by the sun,
Torn ragged by the snags of living,
Alone.

Wait! I pick it up-
A hint of chocolate endures
Memories flood
  Happy tears flow
    My spirit is refreshed.

Ruth Heldreth

"The Feeding Time"

I slowly trail my elusive prey.
I stalk it silently and with great care.
With any movement, I am ready to strike
And capture it as my prize.
It could be truth, but the shadows hide it.
My sight is clear but sometimes too short.
It could be beauty, but it moves too quickly.
I have been fooled many times before this.
Without a weapon, I face this danger.
I am naked and alone.
It is how it was meant to be
As I stare eye to eye with my subtle target.
My life can be called a great many things;
But for now, it will be captured.
Very soon, it will be my greatest prize

Robert William Nowark

Living Life

Dry, cracking lips,
rough, brittle skin,
wrinkles engraved deep,
shining, shimmering eyes,
slight, soft, tender smile.
This life was lived.

Christian Wanglund

Homesick For Yesterday

As I look out across the sea,
I think of things that trouble me;
Of all the friends I used to know,
And childhood dreams lost long ago.

I wonder back to times since gone,
To a magic place where I belong,
Of friendly faces and happy times,
Of fairy tales and nursery rhymes.

Of ancient castles far and wide,
Fields of green and countryside;
Of clotted cream and tasty scones,
The quaint thatched roofs that top the homes.

The farmers market full of life,
The fields of hay cut with the scythe,
Of summer eves spent under stars,
Of pints of beer and Roses jars.

Perhaps one day I'll fly away,
And leave behind this feeling grey;
To settle down in a memory,
And put behind what troubles me.

Richard P. Nixon

My Love

The world is never quite how it seems,
I thought I'd never find the man of my dreams.
Then one day, along he came,
From that point on my life would never be the same!
He stole my heart so gracefully,
I never thought this could happen to me.
The time we spent together, I never wanted to end,
If he were to leave me now my heart would never mend!
I gave myself solely to him,
The rest of my life, that's where I'd spend.
I could talk about anything or anyone with him.
That's why he made such a great best friend!
I never wanted him to leave my side.
I couldn't wait for the day that I became his bride!
He made the love we shared feel so right.
I wanted to be the one to hold him when he slept at night.
You'll never find a more kinder, gentler, sweeter man.
Than the one I promised I would give my hand.
I swear he came from the heavens above.
Because he's the man I will always LOVE!

Stephanie Fry

A Father's Unfulfilled Wish

Since you were born,
I wanted to spend more time with you,
but somehow I never had the time.

Many times,
I stood by your bedroom door
wanting to come in to say
how much I love you, and how proud I am
of you, but I didn't know how.

Time, however, went by so fast
that those things were left unsaid.

You grew up, got married, and had children,
and although I was hardly ever there for you,
you were there for me when I needed you.

Then just when we were getting close,
I got called,
It was my time to go.
How sorry I am
to have missed all those precious years,
because now it is too late.

Sonia L. Graniela

Lady Snowbird Remembered

As I was out walking today;
I thought of you Lady, as I went along my way.
You were one of three little Pomeranians;
All of you were colored in reds and creams and tans.

The breeder got Angela, flower stayed behind;
You my little dog, soon became mine.
I remember how you used to play.
With your little black ball in your funny little way.

I remember how our evening walk, was your favorite time of day.
I remember compliments given to your, as we went along our way.
Your blindness was not a handicap for me;
I had my eyes, and could help you see.

I'll try not to think of the last walk for you and me;
When a large dog attacked you, so violently.
I'll keep your memory inside me, of all our happy days;
I'll always remember your beauty Lady, and your mischievous little ways.

When I follow you to that great valley in the sun;
We'll go walking again and have a lot of fun.
Farewell my Lady Snowbird - your life has met its end;
I'll be seeing you; till then, I'm your lonesome friend.

Sharon G. Lewis

The Last Day

Reflection.

The last day of every year, I reflect upon the past.
I used to dwell on the negatives, beating myself about all
    the mistakes...the character defects...the regrets.
This year, it's different for me.

Oh, I'm very aware of events I would change if I could,
    relationships I would nurture,
    confrontations I might reprocess if I could erase the slate.
But for the first time in my life, on this Day of Reflection,
    I celebrate the achievements...the growth.
I embrace the Serenity...the Joy...the newfound Happiness.
How powerful, how new, how confusing this change in thinking!

I choose not to analyze, dissect, or obsess about it.
I gratefully embrace the feeling of worth and smile that I
    look FORWARD...that I want to LIVE.

1995...empowerment, hope, anticipation!

Rebecca L. Miller

Repose

I want to be your savoir
I want to dry your tears
    yet the conscience-laden skies
    weep a sad lullaby the wan meadow dreams
    the droughted streams meander here
    about the famished fields of dying daisies
And still the sullen dirges
    of the mourning skies shadow your eyes
I have tried
    tried and died crucified
I want to be your savior
I want to soothe your fears
    yet the gaunt furrows bear only
    the scrub of your woes after the many years
Eden has withered
    under the sky's gray-hued breath
the hymns sung high now reek of death
dolesome are your eyes
I have tried
    tried and died crucified

Zachary King

Our First House

As we start out our adventures anew.
I want to express my love for you.
As I sit here unable to sleep,
Into our house I'll take a peak.

I see two lovers spread on the floor.
I see two cats, wanting food and begging for more.
I see a large dog, all fluffy and happy,
I see your own room for when your feeling "crappy."
I see my targets set up in the yard.
I see us playing life, with this our first card.
And so to make good memories out of this day,
I write this rhyme in order to say,
"Break open the bottle and pour the wine"
We two are ripening like grapes on the vine.
And like grapes, we have not rhyme nor reason,
But merely to grow for one more season.
But we have desires and mine is true,
I have a need to entwine my life with you.
And so much like the vine all twisted and bent,
I ask for God blessing in this our first tent!

Scott Hawks

Mom

You are the one that brought me into this world
With the love like no other
You cared for me as if I were a priceless pearl
You showed me the difference between right and wrong
And with patience and understanding
You have been able to help me along
Through all of my senseless undertakings you were there
With your caring and guidance
To cushion my falls with soft pillows of care
My life has not been easy and you have always stood by me
With your generosity and kindness
To pick me up and place me back in reality
I have done so much and have little to show
But with your warmth and compassion
You have been able to help me grow
Now that I am grown I can see what you have done
With the love in your heart
You are the most precious thing to me under the sun
No matter where I go and no matter what I do
I want you to know that I will always love you.

Steve Brooks

I Am A Penguin Who Likes Fish

I am a penguin who likes fish
I wonder why I can not fly
I hear the ocean every day
I see ice on every shore
I want some friend, two or three...
I am a penguin who likes fish

I pretend to fly in the sky
I feel the water cold and deep
I touch the sand bar way below
I worry if I can come up in time
I cry when some leopard seal's around
I am a penguin who likes fish

I understand there are different penguins
I say I'm the best
I dream about flying in planes
I try sometimes to fly
I hope I make it, but I don't succeed
I am a penguin who likes fish

Trystan Bennett

Tom Hankin's Day

When I was young and in my prime,
I worked all the time in the old coal mine,
Trying to make a dime.

A lot has happened since that time,
I'm old and don't work anymore.
But something has happened that never happened before;

The Veedersburg State Bank had a "Tom Hankin's" day,
And the date was November the 19th, 1994!!!

Thomas V. Hankins

The Taste Of Your Wine, The Sound Of Your Song

If I should never see you again
I would always miss you,
the taste of your wine,
the sound of your song.

I would miss us
Lying together in the warm embrace
of a cool earthen carpet
Standing together in the brilliant light
of evening stars.

The tune of you is the sound of music
beating in the rhythm of my heart,
Washing away the sadness in my soul,
filling my empty cup.

I'll sing while the song is here
and dance while the tune is new.

These sweet, brief moments created you and me.
Though time should end tomorrow,
we are now written.
We will always be.

Sheryl Schadt

Better By Far

As I look back on the things that I've done
I'd been on my own, committed to none.
I found myself happy, at work and at play
No one got to my heart, no one would I would say.

I went through life, having fun, self assured,
of this thing called love, I was finally cured,
My motives were selfish, my reasons were good,
no one got to my heart, and I knew no one would.

I've stayed away from love for the past few years
I wanted to avoid any hurt any tears.
But lo and behold my life's taken a turn
The embers of emotion have started to burn

What a beautiful feeling, what a pleasant surprise.
I was falling in love, as I looked in her eyes.

How she is, things she says, got right to my heart
And although many thing must keep us apart
Now that I see how we feel, how we are.
I think being in love is better by far.

Thomas Grogan

Home Port

The course is set and now I see
Life is but a ship that's put to sea
I've seen the storms, the billows roll
The treacherous rocks, the dangerous shoal
But now I see HIM on the dock
To guide me past the final rock
he reaches out for the mooring line
The anchor is down, the lines is fast
He takes my hand, I'm home at last.

Woody Faw

The Story Of The Wooden Bell

There is a story behind this bell of wood,
I'd like to tell you if I could.
I found a piece of wood with fine grain,
I put upon it too much strain.
It cracked and snapped and broke apart,
Along with it took my heart.
Should I forget it or start anew,
I didn't know just what to do.
Inspired by the Lord above,
I'd make a gift to show my love.
So it was I began anew, this gift of love from me to you.
Twice more it would break and fall,
Somehow I got through it all.
I finished sanding it by hand, not exactly what I planned.
As the stain and varnish made it shine,
I knew in my heart I'd done just fine.
This symbol, it's meaning, it's beauty untold,
More precious than diamonds or silver or gold.
And though it doesn't really chime,
It's a music forever, your's and mine.

Steven J. Kroll

Whistler's Walk

I'm not a bad man My fate's not deserved
I'd love most to change it and be the one served

But what can I do in this strange land
Where black men are ruled by the white man's hand

I cook all his meals but what do I get
Maybe the leftovers, No, not one bit

I don't get paid when I do a good job
But if I make a mistake I'll likely get flogged

I am not a thief I don't like to steal
It still wouldn't matter the path would reveal

If I tasted his food He'd know right away
He would here no whistle This black man would pay

So for the rest of my days like my father before me
I'll serve the white man 'till I become free

He won't let me go but I'm not discouraged. I'll be free one day
With the last of my courage. I can't fight my foe but there's
something I can do. The meal I prepared I'll consider my own food.

I'll east all I like As I walk down that path. The white man will
know And he'll show me his wrath. I know what will happen but
it's my time to steal. The whistler's walk will be my last meal

Reggie Beckham

My Brother

My brother was never born but
if he was he would be 15...I
miss him very much if he was born
he would have light blonde hair like
my mom and brown eyes like my dad.
One day I was a wishin' upon a star I would meet
him in a dream and I did.
He looked just like
I thought he would.
My brother was never born but
if he was I would love him a lot.......

Tara Hill

Child's Society

A young child shouldn't have to worry
if he'll live another day,
the things happening to society, would make
any person shy away.
His only worry should really just be,
whether or not he'll find a swing that is free.
There are vultures out there who prey
on our young, and parents who protect them
with the use of a gun.
No one is a winner here because of the misery
it will cost, a vulture his life, and a father's
love which is forever lost.
There's so much evil in society today,
that it's not safe to let a child go out to play.
There's no quick solution to this horrible crime,
and it's really a crying shame, because it happens
time after time.

Ted Flores

Why Do You Smile?

If I do bad, and I am mad, why do you smile?
If I mention I have detention, why do you smile?

If you have a flue, and I do what I want to do, why do you smile?
If I come home in rags and I don't bring back the bags, why do you
smile?

If I have a fight and I don't talk right, why do you smile?
If I do what I want to do and I don't do what I'm supposed to do,
why do you smile?

If I sin and I do it again, why do you smile?
If I say something wrong in the AstroDome, why do you smile?
If I can only hide the paddle for a while then I may get a smile.

Shameka Donato

Christmas

Our Christmas Club check came in the mail
If we start early, we may hit a sale
We spread good cheer to one and all
As we do our shopping at the mall
The stores are bright with their Christmas lights
I'm going to finish if it takes all night
Let's go over here and look at the ties
For Dad we never know what to buy
He would like to have some new golf clubs
But, can we afford them, that's the rub
Sister Susie wants this new perfume
She'll spray it in the morning and we'll smell it till noon
We need Christmas cards and paper too
It's a week before Christmas and there's so much to do
This is the season to warm our hearts
As family and friends gather round the hearth
It's December 24th, I hear nary a sound
The family has hidden while I run around
I made the cookies and all the treats
So hurry up Santa - I want off my feet!

Shirley Amistade

"Nikole"

My daughter has died.
Seven months I have cried,
Her hair was as yellow as the sunshine,
I'll always have memories of her,
Always staying in my mind,
Every baby girl reminds me of Nikole,
She fills me with happiness and comforts my soul,
She gives you a feeling you'll never forget,
because you know her place in heaven is set.

Sasha Djordjevic

Moving On

I'm standing here my twelve strings' on my back
I'm leaving this town I don't think I'll be back
I couldn't stand the pain that I went through again
So I'm saying goodbye to all my friends

I'll travel this world and I'll sing all my songs
I'll see everything and I'll know everyone
I'll see all the things I've never seen before
But I'll feel all the pain that I felt yesterday

When I return to this town one more time
The people there will say hey where have you been
We've heard all your songs and we've cried with a few
Hey would you stay and have a brew

I'm moving on I can tell that it's best
I'm leaving this town and I'll see all the rest
Spend all of my life as I planned all alone
Never have to cry only in my song

Robert F. Reddick

Over The Hill

I look in the mirror and suddenly see
I'm not as young as I used to be.
It seems last week I was seventeen.
Now it appears I'm not too keen.

Did it really happen just overnight?
My jaws began sagging, my skirt got too tight?
I used to look good in a bathing suit.
I'm no longer pretty. I'm not even cute!

Maybe if I could lose some weight.
Oh, but I fear it may be too late.
I'll give it a try anyway,
But wait till tomorrow, I can't start today.

And what about all those gray hairs?
Good grief! Do they all come in pairs?
I can fix that up with a little dye.
It may not look natural, but why not try?

What happened to those sparkling eyes?
Perhaps too many late night cries.
The wrinkled brow, the double chin.
My goodness, where should I begin?

Tomi Carpenter

Not How I Planned

When I was young
Immature and unaware
I couldn't see the love you wanted to share

We came together like river and stream
Happy and content is how I would seem
But something inside told me to pull away
I had to leave you alone, together we could not stay

Now looking at a picture
A future come and gone
A fool that I was
You were the one

Now sitting in a valley trying to fill empty spaces
With curious and unaware faces
And now I am the damned
For it turned out not how I planned

Stefania Paniccia

We Are All God's Flowers

We are all God's flowers, I am told.
In all colors we majestically unfold.
Yellow, white, red, and brown.
Multicolored we abound.
In his splendor, we do thrive and continue to
survive.
Urban landscapes of exquisite tints, as far as
the eye can see.
A heavenly bouquet of glistening radiance, with
limbs out reaching towards the heavens.
Yes, indeed.
We are all God's flowers, one and all!

Sheree J. Leo

Evil

Evil lives on,
In every human being for now on,
Beauty is obsessive,
Great fortune is a sin to God,
Praying for the wrongness of our souls,
Hearts being filled with pity for each other,

Satan lives in each of us,
We have a part in our mind which only thinks evil,
It's seen by Gods eyes,
Satan laughs at the pure,
Preaches the pressures of evil

When we give in,
He locks us in a dark cave,
Leaves us with a blood thirsty lion to fight off ourselves,
He rips all our goodness from limb to limb,
Leaving us with a life which we live in sin,
Or a death that is a mystery to all mankind,
On the Devils Earth.

Xanthipi Klados

Poetry Contest

"Poetry Contest..." the headline read
In one month's publication.
After some searching to myself I said,
"Surely my showmanship's more than a shred;
That prize could be mine!" Thoughts raced through my head.

Lyrical lines of ladies and lords
Scribbled and scrawled in my script,
Legacies, legends of magical swords,
Good and evil, both loved and abhorred —
Still nothing worthy to win an award.

Page after page I patiently penned
Verses of deep verity.
Persistent, perhaps too much to the end
That joy was lost to desire to win,
But since there was hope, I tried again.

Frantically fishing for phrases just right
The prize seemed hard to obtain.
I wrote all the day and versed until night,
Then I realized the prize had made me lose sight
Of writing for love — but still winning's alright!

Talana Jessie

Emotions

Climbing a tall mountain,
You keep trying to get to the top,
You drop into a valley of daffodils.
They turn into thorns.
You are on the tall mountain again,
You try to master it.
But you cannot.

Amy Lakin

I Love You Mother

In spite of your misfortune
In spite of your nine months
during pregnancy's suffering
You live in poorness and serene
I will never forget your tears
It's enormously too good to your son
who waits for the hope of morning

He will come
In spite of the disappointment of a
nasty husband a ugly man who wanders through the world
The love for all your children is an endless love
That you always offered to us
That you offer again to us

In spite of those quarrels between you
In spite of those tears without a end
You knew to bring up men and women of the world

You are the best mom among the women
The Lord is watching your goodness
He will reward you in the paradise

I love you mom and I always think to you.

Richard Mata

Flares And Beacon Lights

It's easy to keep our way
In the bright light of day.
But when the shadows fall
Our troubles seem like an endless wall.
Then, only the flares and beacon lights
Can guide us safely through the night.

That beacon light of Mother's love
Is like a lamp from heaven above.
It reflects her loyalty, and remains
A watchful vigil, like constant flames.
Like twin shepherds from the flock
Her goodness and mercy never rock.

She fashions the key that unlocks the soul
And finds our talents and treasures whole.
She tells her sons and daughters, too
The golden gospel and love anew.
May the grace of God and His abiding peace
Be with our Mother's and never cease.

Velva M. Chancey

The Crossroads

The day is gray, no trees upon the heath.
In the distance, hills and forest
a drab sad day, no peace.
Out of grass and sky all color washed
no place is seen which has a hearth.

I stand upon the crossing
and look in all directions
yet see nothing with a heart.
The only sign, a giant question mark.

Do I return the way I came?
Or, toward the site
that's been my aim?
Turn to the left or to the right
all looks to me the same.

In the middle of the crossroads,
caught firmly by the question,
the gallows of the intersection.
Hung there twisting, turning in the wind
railing on the gibbet,
Indecision.

William B. Turner

The House Upon The Hill

Lights still on upon the hill,
In the house that stands so still,
In the pale moonlight, it frightens me-
To see a silhouette in the tree
Of a strange phenomenon-
What can it be?
I awake to find its nothing more than an apparition-
The phantom of a wolf that befriended me,
It appeared so real-
In nothing more than a fantasy.

Vera M. Goodale

New England Weather

What will the weather be
In the morning when we open our eyes?
Will it be what we expected
Or be a complete surprise?
I guess it will depend
On where you will be
According to the weather-man
As the weather is announced each night on TV
If a picnic or a wedding, you plan on this day
You better pay attention to what the weatherman has to say
To some people, it really doesn't matter
What the weather will be
Some old-timers will say, "this is New England
You will just have to wait and see."

Wilma L. Wilson

Children of Bosnia

Do you hear their cry O Lord
In the valley, hill and mountain top
Do you see their hungry faces,
The children who have naught
But empty bellies, pain and fear?
O Lord tell me you are near.
I hear their cry of anguish
Hands reach out in hope, in vain.
Pleading with those who have plenty
Ignored as their cries rise up again.
My heart whispers a prayer for children sweet.
Who kneel in supplication hoping for enough to eat,
Again walking forward in faith and you to meet.
Only you Lord can still the crying
Only you can heal the pain
Heaped upon our children's shoulders
By generations sin and shame.
Only you can stop the suffering
Heal humanity, take the blame.

Twyla M. Lubben

Pear Tree

Pear tree, pear tree blooming bright,
Like so many stars at night.

All though the winter and now,
Lovely with each turning bough.

Bright blossoms lifted to the heavens,
How could you grow so old, your decades seven.

And be so bright and shining in the spring,
Faithful friend of earth and loving things.

Jacqueline Wagner

A Glimpse?

A breeze bad kept my ear one day,
In whispers passing through sun rays,
In smiles stretched through grass fields long,
It sang to me its omen song.
It gouged my heart and calmed my nerves.
It slowed my trodden mental swerves.
It bade me look; I saw the world
Give in to fate surrendered burls.
Give in to it, the breeze of time.
Its grabbing shudder so sublime.

It chained me to the begging dance
With warming chills that swayed my stance.
Then, on the weight of its won sigh,
It streamed into the changing sky.

And I am a leaf undone and blown
And shackled to the wind so free.
And it was a glimpse, a flash, just shown:
A pinpoint of eternity.

Rex Charles Baker

Hills and Leaves

The choice is presented but I do not decide,
In whom can I confide but a red book about the hills in a swirling
maelstrom of humor and opinions, acting on impulse over my head.
Or the mellifluous yawning in quiet, sweet smiles, soft designs
to enshroud, partially, the beauty in a pillowed soul, one cloaked
in long-hill-wild-grass, the other in raven's silk, a waterfall of
a starless night, chocolate gaze and one I know not of, I kiss
silence, a tortuous touch, but floods are loud and they surely spread,
so I cannot go where my words have led before, for rumors spread like
humorous plagues, diseases of pleasure and confusion, I wish I knew
the measure of gazes won or perhaps the arms embraced, around the sun
turns the weight because adoration is not ruled by fate, only the soul
that breeds neon and opaque within the mind and blood, attractive dark
green or long oaken dress, words are so sweet from both mouths, silky
lips I know not of, Caress adumbrating a closer tie, bows of
candy-apple and night's crystal silk, I watch over there while the
past is in close proximity and my thoughts drift to laughs and jokes,
telephone conversations, Merry Complications, For the wind sings
through the mellifluous leaves yawning, but the trees stand on the
hills of wild and smiling grass, the walk on the plains is dreamily
dilatory, warm and lost, but I see where to go, all I need to know is
whether it be Hills in a crimson-lips-stained-glass bottle of ocean,
Or mellifluous leaves yawning to a bright day.

Ward Crockett

The One

Once upon a time there were two young,
incomplete Heart
A drift among a sea of young Others,
Always seeking, never quite knowing
for what They searched,
Happy, and yet, unfulfilled.

Then, a moment in time that was meant to be,
Put Them in each other's existence,
and all Others disappeared.
Realizing that in their separateness,
They had been incomplete,
They knew now They were meant to be One.

Each Heart with a single purpose for itself and the Other,
To share hopes and dreams—family and Love.
And Others returned to share in their joy,
to start them on their new togetherness,
and incomplete Others,
But in Love—and traveling on the path to Forever.

Sandy Chismark

The Seeds

Rage,
Indifference,
Hope!

Hate,
Ignorance,
Love!

Pride,
Strife,
Friendship!

Jealousy,
Loneliness,
Hope!

What was once begot by our forefathers
Was born a legacy many years before;
And whatever challenges are sown in the fields,
The seeds of the circle live on.

Tracy Reynolds

My Child's Eyes

Reflections of the future filled with infinite possibilities
Innocence personified
Love alive
Hope rests there waiting to rise and take flight
There is meaning, all is not lost
Second chances await
Forgiveness for all mistakes
Miracles
The reason for my existence
I see it there
I carry it with me
Inspiration overflowing
There is a God
Angels do exist
Heaven awaits, my friend for I have seen it there
The power to warm my soul and make me cry
All this lies
In my child's eyes.

Scott Crawford

The Seed

Although I'm no bigger than a pin I'm alive
Inside here I know no sin I'm alive
Can't hear, see or even speak I'm alive
Keep that wire hanger away from me I'm alive.

Let me grow and develop just like you
Let me smell flowers hear birds see it all
Let me nurse my mother
Let me grow tall

Love is what I want
Love is what I need
Love is why I'm here
Love me protect me I'm your seed.

William Davies

A Special Place

I know a place that is special and true,
It will always be reserved just for you!

This place was hidden away but continued to grow;
And how you found it, we may never know.

It was built so strong and built with such care;
Always remember that your welcome their.

With the exception of you, I could never impart;
With that special place you've built in my heart.

Craig A. Miller

Poetry In Motion

Surrounded by people, I still feel alone.
Inspired by loneliness, I turn to my poems.
There I travel, to worlds unknown,
A place I'm fulfilled, as I write my poems.

I'm touched by the music, I feel in my heart-
my words flow together, like I'm reading a part.
A part of a play, that's in my mind;
Sometimes the feelings, are grossly mankind.

I feel inspired, by the oddest things-
sometimes I'm in a trance
At times my words, sound like music,
enticing my thoughts to dance.

As my words come together, I see nothing else.
Than a way of releasing, and revealing myself.
If you're touched by my poems, than I know I've succeeded,
in conveying some comfort, in a place where its needed.

Sheryl Schlieman

Sacred Spiral

Out of the formless Void we spring
Into these earthbound dreams
Spiraling through these days and nights
We search for the timeless truth

Dancing along the twilight shore
We shake our rattles and hiss through grotesque masks
After the evil spirits flee
We laugh in the ashen moonlight

But that was many dreams ago
Now we're here—we think we're here

Gavels pound, anarchy explodes
We grimace in our business suits
Fascism is a bald eagle
That plucks the eyes of angry youths

Spiraling through the Void
We fall...
Trapped in our earthbound dreams
Spiraling through the Void
We rise...

Spiraling in dreams

Rob La Follette

Being a Kid

Being a kid all through the day
is a hard thing to do in a special way.
We always try to do our best,
that's when we know we've reached success.
When we're down or feeling alone,
we just wanna cruise or talk on the phone
Some of us wonder "is this really life"
and others say "I wish you weren't right"
we try to ignore the problems in this world,
and realize then that we're not alone
It's very hard being this age,
you feel confused and you feel a lot of rage.
So you get my point and know what to do,
that kids aren't stupid, they're people too!

Stephanie Gardner

Final End

In a faraway place that is often spoken of,
Is a place called heaven many miles above.
We hear familiar stories and echoes of yesterday,
Reminding us of the things our forefathers had to say.
Then at the edge of twilight, we find a river of dreams,
Of beautiful stones and a sea of glass in colorful hues and
Schemes.
There, we no longer find morning, night, or noon,
Our trials and tribulations end on this dark side of the Moon.
The day shall come when mercy of God, He will no longer lend,
And Jesus will appear, finally at day's end.

Velma Taylor Williams

To Penetrate a Heart

To penetrate a heart
Is from other things apart
How can you help to ease her pain
To make it easy for her to love again
How do you tell her how you feel
How do you tell her only time will heal
The answer is a burning love one that's real
Not make believe one that she can feel
For the torch this love will hold
Will melt the ice and penetrate the cold
You'll share a special intimacy one that in her eyes sets you apart
She'll see into your soul you'll reach into her heart
When you feel the fire start
You'll know you've penetrated her heart.

Stan Schoolcraft

Procedures For The Snow

Warming up after going in the snow,
Is hard to do without cocoa.

When you are out it seems like fun,
Rolling about, under the sun.

"Getting cold yet? Maybe so,
Only twenty more minutes and we have to go"

"Come in, Come in" my mother said,
Your twenty minutes are up without a dread.

When we came in we were fed,
We brushed our teeth and tucked ourselves
into bed.

I dreamed about snowflakes falling on my nose,
and drinking hot cocoa to warm my toes.

There was no hesitating when we had to go to sleep,
because the snow would be falling all of next week!

Stephanie Selvaggio

Love

Love, can you tell me what it means?
Is there someone out there waiting for me.
I have often wondered what would I do if someone said "I love you."
Love can mean a lot of things,
but to me it means you care.
I often need to hear it, so I won't doubt you love no more.
So don't walk away when I need you so much
Don't leave me behind with no hope or care.
Just say you love me, that you care and I will always be there.
I won't ever let you down.
If you want me to, I'll stay forever with you
All you need to say are three words.
That mean so much to me.
They can be hard to say or easy, but that is up to you.
I'll try to understand if you can not say the words.
But those words mean so much
Those words are "I love you!"

Sara Faith Smith

Thoughts And Dreams

What is this feeling that I'm having right now,
Is it a feeling that I can allow,
To enter my mind, it is not love or hate,
I'm being pulled apart by the wiles of fate,
How can I deal with this, how can I find,
Peace to my troubles, I'm going out of my mind,
It is loneliness and depression that is inside my head,
Will all of my troubles die, if I am dead?

A darkness covers my existence, as time passes away,
Isn't life supposed to be bright as day,
My life is as dark as my soul, a void in the night,
My spirit is defeated, my actions have no might,
Does my existence have a purpose, this I do not know,
Will my life become better, I doubt it will be so,
Is anything real to me, I cannot differ between,
Reality and my imagination, they mesh in a dream,
That becomes my life.

Rajesh Chopdekar

Life

At times I sit and wonder what is life really all about?
Is it just what we see around us, what we hear
when others shout?

Or could it be the feelings that overtake our
thoughts when we are pondering what life is all about?

We think of all the wonders that we have yet to
feel, the beauty all around us...but our eyes
have yet to see.

Do we notice the tiny creatures that lie so quietly
in the grass? Do we see the beautiful clouds that
are high in the sky?

Maybe! Is it the sun that sinks so slowly in the
West? If ever I find the answer to my question
perhaps my life will be dull. For, as I can see it
now,.."life itself" is the wonderment of it all.

Verna May Stagg

Redemption

The branch of reason on the tree
Is making careless habits vanish
    Into the wind.
A tree in which we cannot cut down
Is needed in our nightly reverie
    To retrogress our sin.

I am climbing this tree of reason
And I detest this because it is true
    To my own thoughts.
I am here, but did I ever know how
The world would turn to cause a season
    That I sought?

I'm running too far into the essence
That lurks in my head full of the misgiving
    Lies that surround the meaning.
The meanings that envelop my brain with obsessions
That overcrowd my emotional well being
    To help all of my redeeming.

Timothy Cunningham

And you are sad...

The joy of being raped when you are two
is that it opens up a new realm of feeling;
the horizons of which are vast and unseen by the ordinary, unfortunate
    individual.
There is something to having the filaments of your soul shattered,
each cell in your body raked by the sharp edge of raw pain,
and your mind consumed with a jumbled fog of nothing,
that when you can finally think and see again,
the world take on a new-found wonder.

And you are sad for those people who can not see, feel, and
comprehend
these things.
And you are sad because you are once again alone.
And you are sad because you can only partially understand others,
and they can only partially understand you.

Shelley Freirich

Never To Leave Me Alone

Never to leave me alone; always to be by my side, this
is the everlasting promise of my Master and my Guide!
To be with me in times of trouble when things are good
or bad; He lifts me up when I am down, makes me happy
when I am sad.

Never to leave me alone the truth of this promise I
know. For it is within my
God abides and how I love Him so. May I ever thank Him
daily thru the eons and eons of time. May I ever be
humble and grateful and give to Thee what is Thine.

Never to leave me alone, even in my darkest hour; His
wondrous love comes pouring down, oh what a Blessed
Shower! He is the strength and power of life, the
essence of daily living. Though our ways be sometimes
thoughtless, God keeps right on giving!

He gives to us one and all precisely our exact due. So
do not ask why is this or why is that, God has given us
the cue. He shall never leave me alone, thus I shall
abide in Him. He fills my cup it runneth over it
spilleth over the brim.

Ulysses Grimes

Journey

In my youth, whenever I dreamed of Africa
    it appeared as a mystery ... but it was there..Africa..where
    I longed to be

Now..the years swiftly go, the struggle..here..in the diaspora
    on hold; the 500 years journey to the homeland laden with
    dangers untold

So.. promise me that if I should die in my toil before reaching
    those shores..cut out my heart and bury it in the sacred soil..
    beneath the majestic Baobab tree

Only then... will I be free
    Yakubu Gabas

Love Is

Love is a very splendid thing.
It could be a man for his wife,
a mother for her child
or even
a young child for his or her pet.
A person's love can only be judged
by what is in your own heart and soul.
Not by any material things, such as money.
Love as very cherished by so many people in the world.

Steve Bayko

Miracle Of Love

There's a miracle that some have yet to find.
It could be part of your past, it could be lost in your mind.
It could knock at your door and you never know.
It could be as close as your touch or as far as you can see, you never know it could be me.
You can love someone or you could love something, but a miracle is
said to be as beautiful as the flowers in spring.
People fall out of like often and fast, but when you fall out of love it haunts each day pass.
It happens once in a life time and you will know it's for sure.
It's the one thing in life that is usually pure.
Remember a Miracle of Love most feel compassion, it's the one distraction that is full of satisfaction that is forever an attraction.

Tanyce Jones

God Don't Have To Use You And Me!

If man chooses not to serve the Lord and follow His commands.
It doesn't hinder God, the least, from fulfilling His plans.

He will use something else, to do whatever He needs.
God Don't Have To Use You And Me!

He used a "rooster as a clock," to mark the hour.
He used "dry bones" in the valley, just to show his power

He used a "whale as a ship," to give Jonah a ride.
He used a "ram in the bush," just to save a boy's hide.

He used a "rod, as a snake," to offer a plea.
He used "locust and frogs," to bring a king to his knees.

He used a "dove as a scout," to find dry land.
He used manna from heaven, just to feed a "hungry man."

He will choose something else to do whatever He needs.
God Don't Have To Use You And Me!

Shirley Collins

Fate?

There is a disease that hurts and kills,
it is not racist so it does as it feels.

You can have good health, but then you make your mistake,
by going out on the fatal date.

Things go smooth but then it increases,
wanting to make love but not thinking of the diseases.

That is the last time you see that boy or girl,
but as you know things can come a whirl.

You go to the doctor because you're weak,
hoping and praying it's nothing to keep.

You take a test and find out soon
that your worst fear has come abloom.

When you made love you thought it was fun.
Now think of the life that you now have to run.

As your remember that fatal date you think to yourself,
is having Aids my fate?

Trudi Chavez

Untitled

For Joyce Kilmer
Poetry, Poetry;
What!?
Do you know a tree?

Judy Brown

Twinkle

Wow! you must twinkle all night
It must be such a beautiful sight.

You twinkle as bright as the full moon,
I only wish I could see it real soon.

I wish I could take your heart,
But I just don't know where to start;

Would you please tell me where to begin
Because I dare not try to sin.

I wish to take your hand and kiss it passionately
Yet you must guide me rationally.

Oh yes we will meet soon
And until then, you are my full moon.

Steve Dempsey

Like A Flower

And love is, like a flower it always produces
it own kind from just a little seed.
And love is, like a flower even the smelling
of it is a wonderful experience that keeps
coming back to you, makes you feel glad
when you are feeling blue.
And love is, like a flower there is pleasure
in just watching it grow.
And love is, like a flower you want to share it,
so you can keep it forever more.
And love is, like a flower you have to take care
of it so it will grow.
And love is, like a flower that has gone through
the storm even the strong wind could not destroy its beauty.
And love is, like a flower it comes in many shades.
And love is, like a flower it looks good on you.
And love is, like a flower the world would
be lost without it.

Victor Cecil Ballard

Love Is...

Love is strong.
It reaches you through different ways
maybe after someone is gone
or while they are here to stay.

Love is weak.
Sometimes it is overcome by hatred
for someone we may have met on the street,
or by having to do something we dreaded.

Love is Love.
Maybe for nature
like pure white dove,
or like your mother.

Love is here on this date,
don't realize it when it's too late.

Yvonne Oliver

Love

Love - is like waking up to hugs and
kisses... Love is like a beautiful red
Rose blossoming in the spring... Love is
like beautiful white swans swimming on
a crystal clear lake with the rays of the
sun splashing upon it and making it
glisten like silver glitter... Love is like so
many things, so many things I can't even
say all of them, love is a gift from God...
and we will express it all of our lives...
It will always be in our hearts and souls!

Chloe J. Kelsch

"The Web Of Time"

The brown leaf lay beside death on the cold ground.
  It remembers the life which honors a defender's weapon as truth.
It is the only leaf left to tell the true story...
  Who shall listen?
What started with roots grew to a beautiful tree,
  at sight's length,
But, to those leaves which inhabited the tree,
  sight's length measured short of the truth.
The Sun of age made some of the leaves brown.
  Some died, mostly in the instigated fall. More to grow.
The Wind thrashes the leaves to-and-fro; perhaps, as a divine test.
  They fail.
Several are killed. Love?
  Is there one that knows such a word?
Oh, how they get tangled in the web of time,
  just as their ancestors!
Now, the last leaf withers with a final look
  at a blooming bud.
It's story ends... the tape rewinds.

  Tami Padilla

Freedom

The world around us is shredded and torn,
It reminds me of something old and worn.
It's suppose to have freedom in this place,
But it discriminates against every race.
Each of its stars for our equal states,
But our freedom's gone, it's too late.
Part of our freedom is say of speech,.

That's where they get us, that's why they teach.
That's when we're blinded by the justice of our time.
They start to change us when our life is prime.
I used to stand tall with pride in our flag,
And now that I look at it, it's just a rag.
I want to say I'm proud I'm here,
But how can I say that when there's all this year.

  Tanah Mays

Snow Magic

There is something magic, as it begins to snow,
It seems that God, really want us to know,
He is still in charge and loves us so,
We can have serenity in loving friend and foe.

Quietly falling down, so clean and white,
The snow makes a lovely winter's sight;
The tree branches glisten, with silvery light,
As snow blankets the ground, stilling the night.

Snow is a sign of God's vast plan,
To make us aware of our fellow-man
Taking a look at this snow-filled land,
We must know, that God, has our hand.

The laughter of youngsters, playing on a hill,
As they slip and slide, getting their thrill.
No car in motion, the air so still,
All of life's pleasures, God's greatness fulfill.

The snow brings solace, so quietly it falls,
As it covers the streets, and shopping malls.
Children build snow men and throw snow balls,
Snow brings pleasure, but there's danger, it calls.

  Ramona M. Seay

Interlude

Sun kissed a rose, and gave it birth.
It stood so proudly on this earth.
It's petals soft in merriment,
It's stem was towards the firmament,
It budded and blossomed and grew to bloom,
It's fragrance was of mild perfume.

But all too soon it's pedals shed,
It paused but briefly... then was dead.

The sun it's rays that gave it breath,
And interlude from birth till death.

  Sandra L. Armstrong

Our Favorite Lady Has Turned Eighty

So, to your party they came,
  It was catered by Catherine's Cafe.
You knew all of your guests there by name,
  Their presence made your whole day!

And God had answered a prayer,
  As sometimes He's wont to do.
They came to show you they care.
  They came to say "we love you."

The speeches made by your loved ones,
  Touched the hearts of all who were there,
You thought, "Boy, this is such fun!"
  There was lots of love in the air.

For three most wonderful hours,
  They visited with you and your kids.
There were cards, and pictures and flowers,
  Some cried, and some almost did.

The day, the weather and your friends,
  Were perfect, to the "Nth" degree.
Showing life doesn't come to an end,
  When you reach the age of eighty!

  Richard E. Nickel

Twenty Years

Twenty years from now...
It will not matter how you dressed.
It will not matter who you "hung" with,
It will not matter how much money you had,
It will not matter twenty years from now.

Twenty years from now...
No one will care how much money you spent on that outfit,
No one will care that your hair fell down the night of the
  Prom because it rained,
No one will care that you messed up once on a big test,
No one will care twenty years from now.

It won't matter twenty years from now...
That you still rode the bus when you were seventeen even
  though everyone else had cars,
That you had a different taste in music than everyone else did,
That you bought your Levi's from the Vintage Store rather
  than the Gap.
It won't matter twenty years from now.

And if no one cares twenty years from now...
That you wore two different color socks to school one day,
That the soles of your shoes were always worn thin because
  they were so old,
That you tripped and fell in the hallway on your way to third hour,
Tell me, why should they care today?

  Sara E. Boren

Life

Nobody knows why the most innocent people leave this earth,
It's a question left blank in everyone's head,
It's hard to understand the value of life
but when you loose a loved one you can almost see clearer
what it means to live.

Death feels like a piece of your heart is taken away
You can cry if you want
to get all of the frustration, sadness and anger
out from inside.

You will never forget this special someone who left you
but every one leaves when its time
that is the best time.

Staci Waterman

Second Chances

There's something I've been wanting to say
it's been buried deep within my heart
ever since we both went our separate way
I should've never let it tear us apart,

Fear somehow got a hold of me
casting its' dark shadows on my foolish pride
blinding my heart so that I couldn't see
that all this was hurting you so deep inside,

For days' haven't gone by
nor nights' I've not seen your smiling face
in my dreams' trying not to cry
wishing only to feel your warm embrace,

Listen to what my heart has to say
don't let all of your pain shut me out
for I truly didn't want to push you away
cause 'Second Chances' are what Love is all about.

Rodolfo S. Arellano Jr.

Build Or Bye

He wants to build and I want to buy,
It's causing heated discussions of discourse.
Guess we'll have to hire a builder
Who can also handle the divorce.

I want a house that already exists,
To furnish and wall paper and we'll
Keep the marital bliss.

But he has vision of saws and lumber,
cement and brick.
Vision I would just as soon dismiss.

I want to decorate and move in right now.
He wants to clear, build, fence, and plow.
I want neighbors right next door,
He wants five acres and a general store.

If I didn't love him so much,
I'd run away.
He's my best friend, my pal,
And that's why I stay.

Sandra Bryant Weaver

Entity

Oh sweet and gentle soul
Whose pure love flows like a stream
With a light that comes from within
Show me the beauty and grace of life.

Teach me to be gracious and giving
To know that all life is worth living.
That I may be the better for it
And learn to appreciate that I am.

Julia T. Hertz

To My Nightingale

To thee, my love, do I compare the nightingale.
Its intricate melody, so precious to my ear;
The symbol so sweet will never fail,
To be a token of my love to thee, my dear.

Undying, immortal, ceaseless, in sweet harmony,
Its song, so saintly and divine, continues to fascinate,
Transfixed, spellbound; thy voice to me,
Like the nightingale's doth duplicate.

No uproar or tumult touch my ear,
Tones of love's flavor fill my heart,
Blissful melodies sing there is no fear,
Melodic strains tell me we will never part!

Undying, immortal symbols and tokens from above,
Forbearing songs of your tender and delicate love.

Richard L. Merila

Why I Write

It doesn't have to rhyme at all, or even make any sense,
it's just a way to demonstrate my God-given talents.
I write about my feelings, I write what's in my heart,
I'm not writing to be funny, or to prove that I am smart.
I write about my feelings, I write what's in my head,
sometimes I write of life and love, sometimes I write of dread.
Sometimes I write to lighten up, sometimes I write to smile.
Sometimes I write just to escape, to get away for awhile.
'Cause when I have my pen in hand, and thoughts are on my mind,
it doesn't matter where I am, I lose all track of time.
Yes writing helps me to relax, if just a little bit,
and it doesn't have to rhyme at all, but somehow this all did!

Verdi E. Mathis

Delusion

He reached for her, pulled her close, whispered in her ear
It's not the only time; He's reached for her before.
This time it's different, she's not scared of him ... this time.
At least not like before, the other times he's drawn her close
But those time, he looked into her eyes; His hot, fiery eyes
searing hers and his grip on her fleshy arms not the least bit timid.
Something about him made his embrace unwelcomed.
We'll just forget about it; Pretend it never happened.
He instructs her.
She nods knowing very well she'll never be able to lay it to rest.
Knowing very well it will haunt her everyday, every time she sees him.
Knowing it will be in every thought and everything she does.
But she agrees, what other choice is there for her to make, feeling
that her life is already in shambles and his the only goodness she'll
ever find. She is shamed by her weakness, she lost her strength and
cannot win against him. He'll never feel the defeat she does because
of her inability to control him. Something deep inside her
beats on for him, Throbs for him, Wants him and only him.
His warm breath moistening the soft place between her cheek and
ear lobe - We'll just forget about it; Pretend it never happened.

Rebekka Woodley

Innervision

I looked upon the waters searching for the coolness within.
Not realizing that the love I was holding so close
To me, died right from under me. I only felt it, not really
Knowing or understanding; but just thinking that all along
It was just my girlish mind playing with my subconscious again.

But when the smoke cleared, and the waves rolled back out to
The sea; I realized that I was again-lost, alone, and
Empty again — Love had died.
Now I am craving for a burning desire that I can only see,
And only image-but will never be felt.

Valerie Morrison

"The World Ain't What It Used To Be"

The world ain't what it used to be,
it's suppose to be the home of the brave,
and the land of the free.
Things have changed over time;
the violence in our society is corrupting
our hearts, and mind.
Brother against brother,
mother against daughter,
father against son,
will families ever become one.
Racism, hunger, AIDS, wife and child abuse;
is a plague that is running lose.
Why must the world go on this way;
everyday hope is constantly snatched away.
This is suppose to be a happy place,
might life be better in outer space.
Everybody say's this phrase time and time again;
the world ain't what it used to be,
if the world is to change the labor lies on the
backs of we.

Roslyn M. Gatewood

...Fly By

Mother Nature, set your time-piece
  It's that time of year
Spring is here, Spring is here;
  When the Humming birds appear.

'Little Hummer' I sit and stare,
  Into the air.
I look and you're not there,
I look again and there you are, so serene with feathered beauty flair.

I anxiously await;
  That dip in, visit, short.
Sunlight is your colors,
  Stirred, into a rainbow o'er my heart.

'Little Hummer' I sit and stare
  Into the air.
I look and you're not there.
I look again and there you are, so serene with feathered beauty flair.

I must hurry, to catch a glimpse,
  As you go zipping by my eyes.
I'll hold you in my memories
  Till we meet on your next 'fly by'...

Wanda J. Wilson

Wintertime Is On It's Way Around

Wintertime comes once a year,
It's time for the trees to be bear,
Wintertime it is very cold outside,
Wintertime some people are still in
peeping out window on the inside.
It's time to get warm around the fire.
It's wintertime for you and me.
Lets enjoy our life doing all we can
do and be. Our love is like the
flaming fire and lots of desire.
My every romance is to reach out today
It's time to remember wintertime I say,
Wintertime is special to me always.
Wintertime is like by some people
in lots of ways. Wintertime means a lot with
so many things to do, whenever wintertime
come it will be with us all everywhere we go.
Wintertime brings snow.
I love wintertime it part of me anyhow.

Shirley Ann Ebron

The Cross at Calvary

There's a tree that's like no other,
It's very dear to me. It's on that tree
I lost a friend, one I'll cherish to the end.

There's a hill that's like no other,
A special place indeed,
It was on that hill one rainy day,
that my friend passed away.

But don't you worry don't you fret,
because, my friend is alive still yet.

He lives in glory, and I can't wait
Until on that wondrous day.
I finally get the chance to say.

Thanks my friend.
For the price you paid.

Tammy Faulkner

Bound

In serfdom and servitude, I am bound.
I've known no pain that's so profound.
In bondage, I begin to drown,
Because the color of my skin is brown.

Bound; I am not free to dance; my legs are not my own.
Bound; can't even take a chance. Can't even cry or moan.

Bound, I cannot sing aloud; my voice has been bestilled.
Bound; inside, an angry cloud, and faith that won't be killed.
Bound; I can not show this wrath; Yet I can not hide my pain.
Still bound, I walk the righteous path, with glory as my cane.

Bound; they took my child away, as Satin held their hand.
Bound; I kneel down, and I pray, and then they took my man.

Bound; my God has heard my pleas, as I feel my time is near.
Bound; the ground beneath my knees mingle my last tears.

Shilda D. Pitre

Kids...

Gifts from God that keep on giving,
Joys that make our lives worth living.
Teaching us that life is more
than paying bills and mopping floors!

That worms are fun and bugs are neat
And mudpies might be good to eat.
That monsters live in closets deep
And come to scare us in our sleep.

See, kids are more than mouths to feed,
beds to change and rooms to clean.
Kids are also joys to hold, friends to lean on,
Minds to mold.

From a union born of love
Come the sons and daughters of
Men and women who desire....
  ...Kids!

Timothy W. Ryan

Untitled

I saw a flower on my bed
I said that is just what I dread
It was a poisonous one
It was as dangerous as a gun
It was scared to death
And I was out of breath.
I screamed as loud as I could
But it was like I was talking to a wall of wood.
Finally someone said
There is nothing to dread about that flower on my bed.

Jill Feinman

Just Because

Felt at first that I knew you.
Just because I liked your style.
Sometimes I'd stop and think about us.
Day dreaming with a sigh and a smile.

Just because we sometimes argue.
It's only because I really care.
I know "sorry" sometimes means so little.
But baby, I will always be there.

I know you're wondering what I'm trying to say.
I wanted to share with you how I feel.
Just because I really need someone like you.
Full of life, love, and sex appeal.
>   *Victor R. Rodriguez*

Untitled

You made love to me in a way I had never known.
Just by the gestures of your hands...
your polite stance; a simple glance into my eyes.

I could never see what others wanted me to see.
I guess it was the God in me that saw
the God in ye.

You wrote me songs of love; songs that made
love by the tone of your voice.
Yes! A Love I've never known before.

When our faith began to doubt...our lives
became shadow; as without the love I've never
known before. We grew as strangers...so far
apart...yet side by side.

Once we wed in the name of the Divine Spirit;
the infinity which is one. The truth was fed into our hearts.
Times of challenges through times
of change; yet the truth still remains.

You make love to me in a way I've never known before.
Just the warmth of your hands;
the touch of your smile, makes me to know...
that I'm in love with God's child.
>   *Shirley York*

Untitled

The river flows through the valley
Just like life comes to an end

It flows freely down the path hitting
All the consequences of life

The rocks of beauty gets splashed into the
Air by the red, evil waves of pain

And they fall down on the tears of cement
Like hatred enters a sorrow body

The red, evil waves continue crashing up and
Over the valley like a king taking charge

It then enters death and dives into the
Red sea ready to face the evilness of hell
>   *Sara Vestal*

The Soundless Wonder

As I sit
and wonder...
I hear the thunder
and the rain go under...
Under what?
The soundless wonder.
>   *Christina D. Felipe*

A Straw In The Wind

I was a little piece of straw
    Just lying on the ground,

Along came a gust of wind
    And now I am airbound,

Across the fields and through the trees
    I traveled so swift in the summer breeze,

I don't know where I will land for good
    If I could help myself, I surely would,

My hope will be and I will pray
    That I land in a yard with children at play,

One will pick me up and they will say,
    Let's keep this straw from blowing away,

If the wind had kept blowing
    And I had not landed this way,

The good Lord only knows
    Where I would be this day,
>   *William K. Braund*

Light Blue

Light Blue, Let's Daydream
    Just Me and You
Listen to the Silence, Hear the Laughter
    Just Me and You
Light Blue, Watch the
    Fog Roll In, Smell the Freshness
    Just Me and You
Oh Soft Innocent, Light Blue
    Me and You
Relax in the Immense Joy
    Let the Harsh, But Yet So Calming Wind
    Touch You
Watch Reality Drift Away
    Just Me and You
>   *Ryan Brewer*

Untitled

Together, we have stared up at a star filled evening sky,
Just waiting for a falling star to wish upon.
But we have never really wished upon a star together.

Together, we have walked hand in hand along a sparkling moonlit beach
Just watching the waves dance upon the shore.
But we have never really walked along a moonlit beach together.

Together, we have ridden horseback through a crisp springtime forest,
Just searching for a small, secluded highway.
But we have never really rode horseback through a forest together.

Together, we have tasted the sweetness of our lips,
Felt the tenderness of our kiss.
But we have never really kissed each other.

Together, we have felt the heat of our passion,
Languished in the power of our love.
But we have never really made love to each other.

Together, we have done all these things and more.
But we have never really done any of these things together,
Because we are only really together, in my dreams.
>   *Steven J. Cohen*

Yes Lord...

Oh Lord please hold me tight
  Keep out the rain, keep out the night
  Wait for the sun, wait for the light
I am the rain, I am the night
I am the sun, I am the light
  Oh Lord please hold me tight
  Keep out the rain, keep out the night
  Wait for the sun, wait for the light
In the rain your soul is fed, in the night your mind finds rest
In the sun your soul does grow, in the light My love you sow
  Thank you Lord
  In the rain my soul finds drink, in the night my mind is freed
  In the sun my soul does shine, in the light sweet life is mine
I am the rain, I am the night
I am the sun, I am the light
  Yes Lord please hold me tight
  You are the rain, You are the night
  You are the sun, You are the light

    Stacy Mabus

Torment

Lightning strikes like a dry haze,
leaving imperious minds astray,
carrying on like restless children,
we seem to adhere.

Dissipating thoughts,
stare blamefully at us with accusing eyes,
as thunder hits.

Some count,
some strive,
wishing never hear,
like the cries of a newborn.

Fences drive us,
we brake into,
forbidden though they may seem,
into somewhere were kicked out,
for taking space emptied,
although we crave only,
acceptance.

    Scott Marson

The Woman That Never Should Not Have Been

She was just ten years old, when her Mother died
left alone for Dad, to care for and guide.
The things he should do, all the neighbors did say
to give her a life, is to give her away.

No! said the Father as tear filled his lonely eye
I am her Father and, I will keep my child.
Foolish! whispered the neighbors, he's out of his mind
that child needs a Mother, during these perilous times.

With alcohol, drugs, prostitution, running rampage everywhere
that child needs the firmness, of a woman's care.
They sneered they sniggled and, poked fun at her dress
but Daddy kept working hard, gave her his best.

He took her to school, on his way to work
collected her evenings from the home of teacher first.
They went to church on Sundays, walking hand and hand
they singed the hymns together, with the heavenly band.

The weeks turned to months, the months into years
faced the world with laughter, sorrow and with tears.
She went away to college, and found many friends
now she's the woman that, never should not have been.

    Rufus S. Hill

Abused

Please don't let it be an other night of empty tears, there's nothing
  left to cry
The sun is long gone as midnight nears and I must live another lie

It doesn't even hurt now because there's nothing left to feel
I'm tired, bruised and scared, and I know my fears are real

Will tomorrow be the same, will I make it through the day
Will I offer him an empty hand or try to run away

Please don't let it be this way, each hour as evening nears
Don't let him hurt me as he does and strengthen all my fears

Please don't let him be this way, it's so hard to say goodbye
Don't let it be a night of empty tears for there's nothing left to cry

    Wendy B. Lubbers

The Lasting Joy Of Christmas

Let Christmas last the whole year through
Let love and joy abound.
For God sent down His Son to show,
His love, the whole year round.

How soon the magic disappears,
And love is turned away.
The carols stop, the joy subsides,
And days are all turned gray.

No bells, no wreaths, no Christmas cards,
No angels from high,
That tiny babe from long ago,
A tale of times gone by?

Why no! you say, it was the Lord,
Who lived and died for me.
Who changed the world forever,
By His death upon the tree.

Let love and joy abide with you,
This day and all the rest.
For with this wondrous act of love,
Forever we are blessed.

    Rebecca R. Ennis

The Lovers

"Shh..." breathed the man, into his lover's ear.
"Let me tell you of the loves that bring us together here.

I was standing on a crag, above the ocean high
When moments before I took the step, I heard a weighty sigh.

With that I heard the ocean's voice, in all it's majestic grace
'My child this choice is but one answer, for the questions that
  you face.

The night of many lovers, is coming to close
And the fire that burns within you, has wilted like a rose.

True love is sought by the simple one, as well as the very wise
While pure and in it's truest form, seems often in disguise.

It's the kiss of the ballerina's slipper, against the walnut floor.
It's the dew upon it's flower, always willing to give more.
It's phantom touch and angel tears and ones we cherished no longer
  here.

And yes the cold will come, to stare you in the face.
It seems it's devastation will shake you from your place.
But remember what I've told you, and your will surely be set free
When you find in another, the peace you seek in me.'"

    Robin L. Albert

In early morning hours
I savor the essence of you.
The warmth from your hands
And taste of your kiss linger still.
Precious remembrances,
Tangible and steadfast Rodin's marble.

Amy Norton

The Prism

The beauty of a crystal prism
Lies not in an untouched surface,
But comes from the hard cuts
That form facets
Of exquisite patterns.

Some lives are like these prisms:
Cut deep by hard experience,
They dangle by strong threads of faith
In the window of God's love —
Reflecting the spectrum of His blessings,
They shine rainbows of hope
Into dark corners,
Lighting the world with their special sparkle.

Yvonne Clinton

I Met You

The moment I met your eyes I saw
Life in all its glory.
Two beautiful pools of liquid sunshine,
That would set the oceans ablaze with
Dancing waves of joy.
I swim in those eyes of light, without
getting wet from gloom. I'll have no
Fear of reaching the edge, for if I drown
In those eyes, my being would be complete.

I met a smile full of warmth that would
Scare ice into a mist to be forever gone.
I met skin so smooth to put silkworms
To shame, so gentle and warm to the
Touch, that my finger tips dance with
Excitement, without any guilt or disgrace
   I met you

Steve Reynolds

Night Shift

Fallen once more, blanket of night
Light and life tucked in tight

Hospital corners seam-in dreams
Show life of the light isn't life as it seems

Comforts of down mask comforts of dawn
Dark is the cover that black shines upon

Nestled all snug in our nocturnal beds
With eve's dusking covers domed over our heads.

Sky darkly speckled with other-world suns
Sprays muted white freckles on the face of day's done

Burning bright through the light years
like far away fires
Glow the stars — frozen God's tears
   or alien's pyres

Deep down in the well of moon's domination
Through heaven, through hell, through vision's cessation
Breaks a line o'er the trees, melts the blanket away
Dawn shatters glass evening and showers the day.

Valerie J. Rosenfeld

Untitled

Your eyes like a fire
light my soul
once darkened hallways
that criss-crossed my mind
come aglow
doors that were once slammed shut
by a cold wind
now open by a soft breeze
dreams that held no one
now have a hand to hold
all this the moment you lay down beside me
without any rehearsals-
   theme or plot
as I fall into a deep dream
of how this once evasive
thing called love
is now here to stay

Thomas Tisserand

Sky

Cloud and sky, color and light,
like art and music, changing ever
   passing might
A ragged sky, a squall lines advance,
Over wind and wave, field and rain dance

Moving constant, never to yield,
earth underfoot, it's movement slow,
the speed of it's moments, continue so
A frame bent and level, empty and full,
give place to shape, movement and pull

Our gaze upward, ever does rise,
to visit a time, with our eyes
the light and color, of cloud and sky.

Stephen Vickers

"American Indian"

With eyes burning red
   Like that red of blood,
      With hatred and contempt
         They search for an end
            To their discontent.

Swallowed up by
   The hatred and fear of others;
      Yet the young red child
         Is too proud to cry out for his mother.

For loss of country,
   Rights and freedom;
      The red they come
         Old and young.
            They appear beaten.

Oh, My Lord! why is their downfall ignored.
   Worse yet, it continues to grow.
      Oh, my Lord... please,
         Let my people go!

Ray E. Newman

Between The Lines

Do not judge, until thou knowest
because someone may feel their
lowest
and if you look deep inside
you may find the happiness they
hide

Alma Maria Palacios

Blank Paper

Inspiration comes from the soul.
Like the glow from a midnight moon.
A melody of descriptive thoughts
Sing out like a cardinals tune.

Envision a rainbow, colors so bright, so soft,
Caressing the cloudy sky.
Beauty that's beholding,
Not only to the naked eye. Yet it's blank paper.

He writes to his true love,
Your heart is forever mine.
Although in ebony,
A guiding path you'll shine.

He can describe to you her laughter,
But not her smile,
He can recite to you her whispers,
In poetic style.

How frustrating it must be?
For a blind man who can only see, blank paper.
        Ron Green

And For Now...

Open rapture, strike starkly thy pose,
long love of meaning for full ventures show...
To see the morrow leaving its void a flashing darkness
the cold surround both soul and mind, with numbing, painful,
sharpness.

And now to morning's shining light,
its presence felt not known,
we try to keep our mortal feet
and long for cosmic home.

For morning has no body,
aside, above, below,
a need for love and meaning grips
though life's great blinding snows...
For nothing is forever, tomorrow never comes,
we long for sleep, tomorrow meet, for basking in its sun
        Reginald R. Owens

Through The Father's Eyes

When you take her hand today and start your life together,
Look into her eyes and say I'll be with you forever.
Treat her very gentle, for I made her just for you;
Consider her in everything that you will ever do.

When you take his hand today, please give him all your love;
I know it's there inside your heart; for it's sent from up above.
You do not know the joy that this day brings to me;
The marriage of My children,
and the life that you two will bring.

As I watch the both of you take this wondrous step;
I hope you do not hesitate to ask me for my help.
So if you ever need me
you know where I will be;
Forever in your hearts,
for all the world to see.
        Robert Jason Stewart

Arion

Sharing spaces,
Warm embraces,
Souls that inter-twine.
Feeling love's eternal graces,
Mingle I with thine.
        Catherine Stewart

Terminal Velocity

Hal Baxter on his back
looking at the sky,
at Popocatepetl receding
beyond his feet.
Down the face of sheet ice accelerating,
his head aimed at the heart of Mexico.

At eighteen thousand feet
the friction coefficient
becomes negligible and
he reached terminal velocity at a hundred miles
per hour among elusive molecules.

They say he slid for more than a mile
on his back, his face to the sky,
no longer accelerating

Because when you reach terminal velocity
you cannot go any faster.
        Stephen G. Maurer

Lonely Butterfly

The butterfly flutters gracefully
Looking beautiful against the bright blue sky...
But she is alone...

Why must this beauty be admired from afar?
Some dare to catch her
But she dies in captivity
Only those who know her best
Know how fragile she really is
And even they don't understand her fully.

The smaller and less beautiful insects
All envy her and would love to be her
But what wouldn't she give
To be an ant or a bee?
To be with many others like herself?
To be part of a group?
A member of a team?
But she will always be a butterfly
And she will always fly alone.
        Tricia Lynn Jolly

Love Is Around

Early in the morning
Love will come to you,
When green grass sparkles with dew
When roses lift their heads, how do you do?
Birds sing their song,
Their breakfast fees are prolonged.
The coffee is bubbling in the spout,
Time for you to be up and out!

The door — a heavy slam.
Do hope he caught the train.

My arms go limp
and big tears roll
as if my heart would break.

The sun is rising in sky
The day has begun
and —-
so have I.
        Virginia L. Crandle

"Silent Thunder"

Dancing down the dimly, lamplit street, the
man and his woman raise a rhythmic cadence
on the misty-damp cobblestones.
Not a sound can be heard except their run,
leap, turn, and sway; time standing still
all along their way, as amazed pedestrians
are frozen in ridiculous postures, mouths
agape.
No music, not a sound, not a wind's whisper,
just the rapture of that moment when two
people discover that their hearts have
awakened and ache with the same dreams.
Only this silent thunder roaring through
each this princess and this poet as, faces
flushed, they run hand-in-hand through the
night.

William R. Suda

New Year For Contentnea

Roll on Contentnea, roll,
Meander in still summer
Around gargantuan rock,
And Sugar Loaf, high as a house.

Provide for men with cane poles
And corks that bob and bob.
Let the spring freshet
Gush and push beyond the banks,
Ruin to fields and garden plot.

Let your rush of bronze and gold
Presage the change of tree and air.
To winter ash and bitter cold.
Let your serene keep faith with rock and tree.

Private and remote
As Indian lore that notes,
The site of earth and sky
And leafy home on Quotankny.

Ruby Shackleford

Hope's Light

From Death to life, I sing the breeze
Melting senses and enhancing dreams
My eyes, my heart, my soul; all of these
Is from which hope gleams

The rays of hope are endlessly bright
They seem to envelope the night
Its luminescence is a beautiful sight
Containing dreams, hope, and love in its light

The light seems to flicker in mist
Due to an unknown catalyst
Thought to be true by the theorist
Made untrue by the realist

The strength of the light is more than known
It will never fall from its throne
No matter how hard the wind has blown
The light it emits has never flown

Though many look at it in different ways
It will always stay
Bright and then flickering for days
Nothing can ever stop its rays

Sharon-Lyn Rogoski

New Years Day

As I Stand Here in the Cold
Memories of a day in the Warm Sun
I remember the one I only loved
While the snow shimmers in the light
I can only see the dull gray faded into white
As the New Year comes around
Memories of your voice surround
My head in desolate agony
I felt you once in my arms on a warm summers day
But just as the snow
It all melts away.

Steve Campbell

Today Is Mine

Today is mine, each shining golden hour,
Mine to meet the everyday problems of life.
To enjoy the beauty of God's handiwork
Letting calmness and order overcome strife.

Today is mine, each second of every minute,
Mine to explore deeply the depths of my mind;
To seek out and destroy any unpleasantness
And ignore any rumor that could be unkind.

Today is mine, to drink of the cup of kindness
To give credit where credit is due,
To listen and lend a helping hand,
And to my conscience be true.

Today is mine, it's now and it's precious.
It must not be wasted in idleness and sin
But every moment bring about some good
As this day will not come again.

Today is mine, to gaze at the broad horizon
And choose one of the shining goals for mine;
One to fill my life with worthwhile labor
And be rewarding until the end of time.

Viola M. Brault

The Rainbow's Promise

Though valleys loom low and mountains rise high,
My aspirations undaunted can reach the sky,
Nightmares of yesterday I leave behind,
Dreams of tomorrow I search to find.

Courageous to try, with courage to fail,
Determined to win, my spirits prevail,
Rock of Ages, a cleft for me,
His Word of Hope guides today's destiny.

A candle in my heart shall light my path,
As love melts away the frustration and wrath,
Tears I may cry to soothe the pain,
Faith have I now; the struggle's not in vain.

The storms of life I'll challenge today,
And in opening my eyes I'll successfully say,
That the ribbon of promise has arched on high,
My symbol of victory from valley to sky.

Scott Biggs

The Shadow Man

The shadow man creeps
    at night
He scares everyone in sight
He takes little children
    that aren't in bed
And he steals them and
    cooks them to eat.

Dana Dixon-Miller

My Father

It all began, though it wasn't the plan,
My father wasn't ready for his little man.
He'd planned on waiting for his first child,
Instead, new responsibilities quickly compiled.

With love for my mother, it wasn't wrong,
My father stood both brave and strong.
He gave me his name, his life in a whirl,
Surprise or disappointment, I wasn't a girl.

From that baby boy, a man has grown,
Years have passed, I've a life of my own.
Wishing sometimes my father had been there,
With a hug, or something that we could share.

He's worked hard over all these years,
And recently learned how to shed tears.
A man of power, strong and wise,
Would I ever be good enough in his eyes?

Maybe now as changes take place,
His life slows down, he's won the race.
He's ended his job, his life's just begun,
I only hope he can be proud of his son.

Robert A. Klotz

"Please..."

I can't seem to release the pain.
My heart clinches when my thoughts turn too.
If I could turn back time and gain
a moment's peace of knowing that I had saved you.

Your hair so soft and grey, I would run my fingers through.
I long to hear you softly cry
and I would know just what to do.
How will I ever say good-bye.

Your nails would softly pierce my skin
when you always had that look of content.
A nape the first priority, a request for special food.
You always listened casually when I needed my emotions spent.

Does the person know they took you away?
as they sped past the house?
Do they care that my dreams replay
and never give relief, no not one ounce?

My soul struggles refusing to let go
as I end up on my knees.
Our long talks are over, my feline friend.
Just one more moment with you.......please!

Summer L. Sims

The Window

Looking through an immaculate window,
  my life has become all too clear.
Perhaps I should not have so much knowledge,
  about myself.

But I do.
  I know that I am a loner, independent and strong.
But it is what I do not know,
  that hurts.

I do not know where I am going,
  I barely know where I have been.
Maybe I was wrong,
  the window does not hold all the answers.

Valerie Harper

Guinevere In Love

She dreams of flowering hearts
bleeding like rosebud on white knight,
the jousting of love in sheeting rain
lost in gusts of tease and capture,
wandering through steamy fog
and moats of cream and cloud,
storming the castles in ecstasy.

Susan E. MacPhee

Without Him

Alone and as I lie in my room,
My record player playing, a sad lonely tune.
With him on my mind, the tears
Kept falling as thought of good times I was recalling.
The wonderful days that we shared together
Which I had thought would last forever
Now were gone.
They are all just the past
Those fun, crazy days,that were supposed to last.
That night he said he still loved me,
And always would, I awoke the next morning
And he was dead.
He said he would take me with him
Where ever he went.
He left and I was still standing there.
Now the happiest day in my life will be when I die.

Roberta J. Richardson

Thoughts

Crickets hum through the twilight,
my reflection stares up at me,
as the wind ruffles the starlight,
I sit on a branch in a tree.

The creek sits in perfect stillness,
yet the current rushes strong,
I wonder about this poem,
yet my thoughts are gone..

The sunset is still iridescent,
as it shines through the Willow tree too,
the leafy light from the streambed,
and to the shadow from you.

Pine trees grow through the Ivy,
Honeysuckle climbs up the wall,
and although I do hold it strongly,
my poem it dose fall.
-Stacy Boore
Influenced by a stream and it's surroundings.

Stacy Boore

One Of The Flock Beseeches

Be swift the dark
My shutter eye
captures camera life in dusk
Saving a paper face to touch tomorrow
To speak of what will not be again

Be swift the dark
These books bind no clues
this ease of birth turning my life autumn
and the hellish hours that fester I lead

Be swift the dark
The spotted body that counts the sores
counts the days is a calendar worn

Be swift the dark
and swifter still a heart reconciled
For pariah often die alone

Shane Griffiths

Cupid's Bow

The last time that I saw you,
my soul was left to fall,
I watched your eyes drift downward,
my heart then bled to raw.
The courage you had shown,
that you had told me all the truth,
inside my dreams were spying on a nightmare
now come true.
You came to say it's over,
this chemistry now bare,
out the door went friendship,
and a feeling you don't share,
So as my knees do bend, as salty water runs, I cry,
from night above the arrow shot,
and I watched Cupid die.

Sarah Bailey

Pure Gold

Like the Sun shining through the smile so bright
My soul was warmed with mild, soothing delight.

Magnificence, charm, elegance and grace
Draped her supple shoulders like find linen and lace

Lavishly endowed with handsome mortal splendor
A gift to eyes that see, my mind will always remember

It was the beginning of a Spring
Angels sang at the blessing of the ring

Together we walked through the door of our tomorrow
A holy union born from sanctity and morals

As fresh morning dew births the new from the old
Us two joined as one springs forth as pure gold

Birds fly high above singing songs of cheer and glee
My heart soars my spirit shouts joy for God has smiled on me.

Samuel Wheeler

"It's Just Not Fair"

When I was young and started school,
    my studies taught me this.
Four seasons came in every year,
    and not by hit and miss.

But now I find a season,
    that arrives in just four years.
It's called the political season,
    and covers t.v. with their jeers.

Now we all will surely suffer,
    some time their money will buy.
The luster of all my programs are gone,
    with commercials that make me cry.

The mud that they sling at each other,
    would cause D.N.R. much alarm.
I think they'd do better to help one another,
    leave that fertilizer back on the farm.

Reuben H. Elandt

The Love Of Christmas

The leaves have fallen the sky is cold and clear.
It must be time for old Saint Nick to get here.
The children are glowing and full of joy,
just hoping they will get that one special Toy!
Some have been naughty some have been nice but
all said and done their still our sugar and spice.
So with the birth of our children we feel so blessed,
that's why we try so hard to fill their request!
So with big toys little toys and all of the above,
the best gift of all is, our LOVE!

Robert J. Funk

Living A Lie

To those of you who chose to lie,
    My sympathy now must die;

Days and days have gone by,
    Waiting... hoping you'd realize;

The secret you protect,
    I no longer dare forget;

The greater pain I was not spared,
    It was only the truth I hoped you'd share;

The crime committed and magnitude of the sin,
    Deserves my view of you to be dim;

But even lower on my list,
    Is to be so damn dishonest.

The guilt that causes you such grief,
    That from which there's no relief;

The feeling that gnaws and rots within,
    The pain you feel is from trying to pretend.

It twists and distorts the way you're thinking,
    And has taught you to lie without even blinking.

Terry Bennett

The Water

The vast shadowy water rages silently from a distance.

My bare feet etch memories of my existence in the cooling sand.

The closer the footprints come to connecting with the
mysterious water, the louder I hear the raging fury's screams.

The bounding waves of darkness pounce upon my feet - yearning
to touch my hand.

I cup with my hands the chilled, dark liquid only to
discover truth.

Seeping through my fingers the water runs clear,
the darkness lost.

My feet welcome the warm sprinkle that severed their chill.

The friendly water spoke sweetly of hidden treasures:
tropical fish, healthy moss.

The vast, shadowy water rages at my feet.

My footprints of existence are washed away by the hungry tide.

My feet cast my body away from the intruding water,
the further I get away the more closed I feel.

The unrelinquishing darkness enthralls a tear of fear I need
not hide.

Shannon Nelson

Destination Unknown

I had this dream
I was walking along the road of loneliness
when a figure appeared
The figure pointed the direction
I had peace within myself
I now knew the answer
Upon awaking I did not remember the direction
Then I realized
Now, I had the answer

Sara Manis

Camelot

In distant lights of Camelot. A rage began that's not forgot.
Myth or reality. Peasants dream of what could be.
On horseback into the sun. Daggers met. A war begun.
Wizards and Dark Knights. Flashing swords in mortal fights.

Kingdom ripped to shreds. Drenched in blood from the dead.
Bitter tears in hidden caves. All the souls they couldn't save.
A travesty of Justice. A mockery of truth.
Fighting for survival. Destruction of the troops.

Carnage of the weakest. Longings for the strong.
Death won't deceive them. Hungry for so long.
Ravage of the homeland. Stories for the young,
No where to hide. The message has been sung.

Castle on the hillside. Tower in the sun.
Hidden deep within, Lies the golden one.
Child in the darkness, The road is clear ahead.
Feel the powers of Heaven in your head.

Run to the future. Jump into the light.
No time to hide. You have to learn to fight.
Fight for your freedom. Fight for your right.
It won't defeat you standing in the light.

Tracey L. Whiting

Cocker Talks

Berni, a cocker???
Named Berni because he is part St. Bernard?

No, B U R N I for burnish gold.

But no cocker is so big—
Look at those big feet—looks like he has on slippers.

Feeding him growth hormone?
No, but he eats everything.
Fellows found out; took him for a ride.
Came back with beer breath; pizza around his mouth.

A pony maybe?
No, but kids pull his ears; grab his tail—
Even ride this lovable male!

What is this pet therapy he does?
Burni goes to nursing homes
Repeats each name into syllable barks—
Yes and S, a sneeze; no, a shake of the body.
Stroke victims talk again—
A man was silent for ten years.
Nurses love Burni and cheer.

Rose Marie Pace Barone

Untitled

Draves all wrapped in sprickly broam gramble in the klime
Nervish clantor wrackles forth
as hunkered hordes with glimey prills await the monkish sign
A vemid howl finds wreckled hands all grasping glided brades
to stab each shining epitar regardless of their age;
regardless of their age.
A single breaming mendendure with kinlin close benigh
is all that brates between the horde
with mackled tarse and gethered gash, its hamdled doss held high
into the klime among the draves, the mendendure doth bret
It brenches every kell it finds and tucks them in its fret
snogging Lats all sween away who know the cush be tar
for every drave who skreels its last
whose brade grows cold, whose feen falls nast, another brands anar
For draves have many giles you see, the mendendure but one
and yet the cush be krat each grey, within each lanesome trun
within each lanesome trun.

Rick Goodnight

The Sound of Solitude

Following black coffee and typical melancholy
newspapers the outdoors shout beautiful hymns
    where a spacious azure sky proves to be heroic
and the yellow egg of a sun over easy
    fulfills the required nourishment
and guarantees energetic aplomb
    as my soul like a mythological warrior
wanders throughout the yard's expansive depth

    chasing butterflies which cannot be gathered
but induce warmth of spring and time
    where the living promote rambunctious buds
with extraordinary intricate petals
    and for one second
I am a new born who has attained
    the certain growth factor
        all because I have consumed
The sound of solitude.

Randy T. Nelson

College Greets

Young men and women leave high schools
No having a sense of the right tools
Choose college, not a job
Society doesn't need another mob.

Day after day you come the streets
Wondering when your mission will be complete
Here is a treat,
Arise! my friend, college greets.

It might be four years, sometimes six,
Don't be frustrated, this is better than a fix
So get in the mood
Young people, college is food.

There will be sleepless nights,
But books are all right.
Aching feet, sometimes you can't even eat
But look over into the horizon
Alas! the strides are over
Education is your cover
Under its wings you shall hide
Now reap, my friend, reap.

Una Smalls

Visions Of The Pioneers

There comes a day when aspirations
    no longer correlate with needs.

There comes a time when the future must
    be projected from the present.

We must smell the salt from distant seas,
    feel the breeze from a far away shore.

We need to head for the sunset to
    experience a new sunrise.

Some may say we are dreamers,
    doomed for failure.

But, they are unaware of our inner feelings,
    they cannot see our visions.

We must say goodbye to yesterday,
    and answer the call from tomorrow.

Randy Crowder

Christina

I will always come back to you Christina
no matter how far you have gone.

I will search the world over for you Christina
from dusk to early morning dawn..

It is my memories of you that keep me going
and that smile upon your face.

When we finally live together
I will cherish those happy days.

I know that you really love me
why is it so hard for you to see.

Running away from me Christina
Is truly not your destiny.

Oh my beautiful Christina
Please, Please come back to me.

Our love is like Galilee
the magnificent fresh water sea.

Sometimes rough and sometimes calm
endurable passion like a golden Pond.

I will always come back to you Christina
no matter how far you have gone.

Thomas Zoe

Takin' It Straight

When you're ready to give I'll take it straight
no touchup no tuck or disguise
spare me the armor of self hate
come naked to the prize

Give me your traumatized your oppressed
the fragrance of your fears
the sputter of doubt the load off your chest
the taste of bewildered tears

Give me your blemishes farts and zits
your unabashed skin and hair
your secret badlands unmown pits
your cares my love not your care

It's you I've waited for you I'll have
not a centerfold or a tv stew
I want you heelless sweaty and brave
nobody's bunny with nothing to shave
no mask no filter no chemical dew
when you do come woman make them sure it's you

Tom Reveille

"Window Emotions"

The glowing light of the sign is the light my
life is missing.
The shine from the headlights glisten the tears
rolling down my cheek.
Like the tracks up the road, in my time of life
I too should start laying my ties down, the sound
of the train is like the yearning beat of my
heart, but the track is missing that special tie.
The gutters along side the road are over flowing
with my dreams pouring in.
Every night is the same routine, wishing and
wanting on stars and with prayers, but my eyes still
release these lonely tears.

Sherry Fry

The Snore

Of all the pain that I have bore
None is as horrible as the snore.
I lie there and silently try to sleep;
When a snore disturbs my peace.

I toss-I turn-I cover my ears;
And then I fight to hold back the tears,
I lie there and I reach a decision-
I'll wake him.

I shake him, I nudge him; I hate to be rude.
But the sound of that snore is so
  awesome and crude.
When he awakes-he yells;
And my story he will not believe.

So I silently again try to sleep,
When another snore disturbs my peace
And another-And another.

So if you have a mate who constantly snores;
You know the pain I have bore,
We would be better off to sleep atop an old oak tree;
But I wonder do owls snore.

Sandra B. Martin

My Hero

Not in the pages of same exciting book;
Nor down the aisles of history for him look.

He does not wield, for the moment, any political power.
But he's always been there for me in my neediest hour.

With his name there is no title; no "SIR" or "ESQUIRE";
Nor is he the head over some great empire.

He's not big on the screen, like some Leonard Nimoy;
Deep down in his heart, He's a good old southern boy.

Not to say my hero isn't sharp; he's capable as well as smart.
Honesty and hard work were examples he set from his heart.

Some things in my life haven't been done exactly right,
But my hero's always been my stabilizing light.

Many tests in my life I have all but failed,
But my hero's always been my ship that straightly sailed.

If anything wonderful at all I accomplish, as long as I live,
To my hero, my dad, I'd most of the credit give.

Rhonda Green Dees

A New Beginning

We come to you, injured, afraid, and empty,
not knowing just what our future holds,
We place ourselves in your care, hoping to be free,
free of feeling useless in this world.

Most of our hopes have been shattered by injury,
or a job no longer there,
We look to you to aid us on this uncertain journey,
still afraid, yet still believing in hope.

We have come to you, injured, afraid, void of hope,
we found, hope here, strength, light,
We leave here stronger, hopeful, certain to cope,
with this new path before us.

Thank you all for believing in me, in us all,
as we now believe in ourselves,
We shall go out, empowered, ready, standing tall.

Rose Gomez

Death Of The Nothing

Silence reeked throughout the house,
Not a sound from the crickets or even the mouse,
A chill of blackness came through the walls,
As the nothing no longer stalked the halls.

All was quiet here, and not a sound,
A creak or a whistle had not I found,
And the owl stared in silence outside the frosted window,
Not a drop of the rain or the great winds blow.

The eerie sound of emptiness hung on the ears of my mind,
As I knew not a sound 'round here I would find,
And the noise no longer filled my head,
As I realized now, the nothing was dead.

His footsteps on the stairs I no longer heard,
Not a whisper or a cackle, not a single word,
Long awaited this night I had thought,
The quiet of my house for years I had sought.

And nights before as it resounded through my sleep,
A scream or a howl or a moaning weep,
Those restless nights no longer ring,
Driving me mad with no sound for the Death of the Nothing.

Reanna Stout

My Trip

Take a trip with me.
Not by land, air or sea.
Close your eyes, clear your mind.
We shall then see what we can find.

There is no disease, there is no pain.
Everyone is happy, no one is vain.

There is shelter for all man kind.
Food isn't scarce, it's something all can find.

Gums are not carried.
So no one gets buried.
People working together as one.
Violence, there is none.

Can't everyone stop and see,
this is the way life was meant to be.

Tonya Vannatter

The Shadow

By night and day there lies a shadow above his bed.
Not the shadow of love or happiness but a dark
gloomy shadow that is not there by any other means
than to remove the breath from his body. The once,
strong body is now worn and tired for the shadow is
ready to resume his soul and take it to its final
resting place. For death knows no name or purpose,
just the fact that there is a soul to be claimed.
At last the shadow has taken its soul to its final
resting place. Exclusively to leave behind his
mother with a mournful heart and tear filled eyes.
For the warm, joyful baby boy that drifted so
delicately and sweetly into her arms has now been
therefore taken away. Never to be replaced by another.

Winter K. McCadney

Molested

Shattered innocence of a child,
Agony in a mother's heart.
Pain flows in salty streams;
Evaporating trails,
Scalding eternally
Creating silent scars.

Rebecca Lee Bradish

Existence

The past is the future, Present only in a time where before builds
  now and after,
Where life creates creation, And one man's tears invokes another
  man's laughter.

Drenched by crying eyes because of wrong steps taken in living...
Quenched by drying eyes because of mistakes forgiven....

Pass the toll onto the next man. Let him take his stand.
  It's only in his past, a future for his children.
  It's only his dreams, and only he can fulfill them.
    If creation dies, wherein then, will the treasures of life lie?

    As you wander back, looking at the many roads in life you took,
Did you ever arrive, at others' hearts and minds?
    Even when these precious lives are gone and no longer,
Will you still survive, when merely memories are left behind?

Let it rain. Let Heavens' waters feed you...
Let every name on every tombstone wake up to greet you...
  When you journey through unto your eternal rest,
  Realizing you're a forefather after your death.

Make your existence a duration that will last. Make your future
  appreciate your past.
It's the past that drags the future along for others will still be
  here after you're gone.

The past is the future, Present only in a time where before builds
  now and after,
Where life creates creation, And one man's tears invokes another
  man's laughter.

Waldemar Kornahrens

Gunshots

I wake up at 2 a.m. to the sounds
of gunshots ripping through them.

I get up out of bed to look outside,
I see kids lying on the ground in puddles of pride.

Except it is not pride, it is stupidity,
I bet they wish they had a 2nd chance to get right up and flee.

So as they lay in their puddles of stupidity,
they think of all of the things they'll no longer see,
and the person they'll never have a chance to be.

While the kids that shot them run off down the street,
the ambulance arrives, puts them on a stretcher and
covers them with sheets.

Their families behind them all filled up with tears,
I bet they never imagined this- it was only in their fears.

I think all of this while I'm looking outside,
and think of all the kids who got shot up and died.

So the message I'm trying to get across to you,
is don't get a gun, if you do, trust me,
your worst nightmares will come true.

Tracy Schoedinger

My Friends

All my friends have deserted me
Left me to face my loneliness and miseries
When I was riding high and standing tall
All my friends would not let me fall
But now I am down in monetary reasons
My friends don't come in any seasons
I shall return, this I know
Then all my friends shall come once more
But if I should fall once again
Then this time I will know my friends

Terrell Jones Sr.

Of End I Dream...

Of end I dream...
Of sand,
rushing out of my measure of time and space.
Of the final rhyme.
Of the last ace I'll pull out of my sleeve.
Of the leave I'll take,
the bow I'll make at the end of play.
Of the grey which becomes when all colours are mixed.
Of the sixth seal broken and the seventh cracking,
when spoken already are all lies,
thrown all dice,
and over is all checking.
Of the peace and stillness of the never-land,
soul's wounds and bruises quickly on the mend.
Of nothing else left but the end itself.
Life's weft pulled out slowly by a naughty elf.

Sima Simic

Revival of Light

Gazing upon the billowy landscape
Of the ethereal heights
which are impervious to mankind's touch,
the soul begins its incipient journey
on those tenuous whispers of reality
that glide effortlessly on the naked air.

Wave upon wave,
the red glow of dawn's calling
lines their transparent crests
as the translucent blue complexion of the Sea
stretches into infinite space.

And now the burning embers of the day's fire
lie smoldering in the grey ashes of Vesta's hearth
to give birth to the dawn of a new era
of human consciousness.

Rachel Cox

Lime Lite; Stereoscope

Daydreams, goals, and fame, taps at the door
of the golden gate of conservatory wonderments,
and unfoldments.

Fortunes slip the grasp of many. Listen to the
whisper of lust, and know the pain of defeat.

Reaping the harvest of challenges, peering through
the key hole of success, floating like a penny
in a wishing well.

Like a new breed of idealist we ponder the brinks
of insanity, since an even swap is no swindle!

Samuel Weatherspoon

To Mother With Love

Dear Mother, I shall always remember the stories so clearly
Of the hardships that you endured most of your life.
The memories of all the years you held so dearly;
They were all filled with poverty, struggle and strife.

It was not against humans - but fate as life dealt it.
You fought it so fiercely, so bravely - with all of your strength.
To your dear ones you would never in any way show it,
To keep those problems from us, you would go to great lengths.

Just as it seemed there might be a change for the better,
Fate stepped in again and made a young widow of you.
Mother, we learned the truth then; that you could not be a quitter,
So we all pulled together and together we pulled through.

Sarah S. Schneider

A Cry For Help

Alas the dawn brings another day.
Off to the rat race, the children to play.
Open the store to be faced with a gun.
One man's working day, forever, is done.
Laughter on the playground, screams of delight.
One smile erased in the crossfire of fight.
Around the neighborhood lurks the indescript van,
On the hunt for a boy to be made a man.
A mother's search for a better life
Cut short and found in the end of a pipe.
Corporate sales are up and the profits are high.
Forget the lost waste, mother earth cannot die.
Ignorance has become the killer of man;
Brother against brother and raping the land.
Children look up to us for guidance with grace,
To get pushed away and slapped in the face.
Love amongst man is a treasure so rare,
With none to be found and little to spare.
The fate of our existence hangs on the thread of a rope.
Can somebody out there give us some hope?

Susan Butler

Tippy Canoe

Life is like a Tippy Canoe,
Often rosy, but never blue.

Sometimes it is bottom-side up,
so hang in there, "don't give up"!

In a day or so it is up-right again,
all is well, "the rains never came".

So climb into your Canoe and sail away,
God is with you all the way.

And as you approach the age of 82,
Remember the "good times" in your Tippy Canoe.

Theresa Wolkenberg

Calvary

Oh where would I be without CALVARY
Oh were would I be without you beside me
Wishin' and hopin' in this world, you see
is empty and doomed for misery.

The old rugged cross, a dog wood tree
a touch of love God sent for me
He hung on a hill in humility
To save my soul my life, for ETERNITY

So I give thanks to CHRIST
For he's the one for me,
The Saviour for all Humanity

Sandy Salter

My Raging Madman

I know what fuels a hunger for the desire
    of evil, twisted as it is.
Quite simple to me the Madman is.
His burning flame grows and sears over
    his living years,
    growing greater with the masses of tears.
These pangs and extremities snap him in two,
Now an angry puppet in him will bloom,
    for no container could contain or medicine
    could heal his doom.
Now he is wild, insane but somehow is free.
I know this because the Madman is me.

Vanessa Hammond

Lenten Reflection

A salmon and an oyster
On a table in a cloister,
Were thinking solitary thoughts replete;
But their experience monastery,
Would soon be culinary,
They'd become incendiary lunch to eat.

Overhearing consecration
Each assumed he'd be the ration,
That a convent may not be a place sublime;
It's one thing to be blessed,
Quite another - they confessed -
To be eaten and digested in your prime.

So they trundled 'cross the plaza,
Then through an arched piazza,
Taking little time to analyze their fate;
Both knew something was amiss
When a voice cried, "Nun of this!"
And they went to seafood heaven celebrate.

Steve Hill

I Remember...

Just as we arrived I saw the white bricked building,
On that unforgettable autumn.
He lie there not moving,
Not even blinking.

My mom and her dad were crying aloud.
Can you tell me what's going on I asked my mom.
Bill tried to calm me down. I was crying loud.
Recalling that October day always chokes me up.
I could not decide whether to cry or not.
Do not try to calm me down. I don't think it will work.
Emily was as confused as me; not knowing why all the
    tears and sadness.

Thomas McNamara

Early Watch

The sun rose this morning
on the starboard bow
'tween Thunder's halyard and mast she came
sensuous in her palette of reds
with a passionate caress
she sealed my soul to the sea
and with fingers
aflame
upon the clouds
upon Odin's ledger
she entered forever
my name.

Susan OMalley Wade

"My Husband"

My husband is very attractive,
    No, he is more radioactive.

He is quite charming,
    At times it's alarming.

Oh yes, he is very kind,
    And he has a nice behind.

He say's he is not strong,
    But I say he's wrong.

My husband, he is my one and only,
    Which, by the way, I'll never be lonely.

Sheleegh McDonough

"Shaft 9"

The coal formed a window's vale
On the young miner's hot face
Articles of ashes cast a unique network
And leap desperate in front of the miner's hat light
Suffocation awaits, next in line
He thinks
Does it always happen this way if you're poor
The men and their jobs
The graphic deaths on a cork bulletin board
Six thousand feet up
Bobby Kennedy slain in vain
Likewise King
All America for that matter
But what meaning would come from his ending
The fact that seventy had died with him
That no one out of West Virginia
Would hear of the explosion in Shaft Nine
He bet his steel pick on that
The boulder crushed his rib
Death vanquished the light in his miner's helmet.

Thomas Spencer Colton

At Home in the Ear of the Buddha

I haven't always lived in this bell pepper.
Once, a burnished pot on a piano top
Afforded, in a forced detente, a simile for me.
By chance released from judge-edged eyes,
I shrank myself to line the space
Of volume deflected by curve.

Dark-coiled in smoothness, quiet there,
I stayed my breath, absorbed the view,
Cajoled the vase to hold me
Like the lavender taffeta stole I rolled up in
At eight or mine, to dream.

But a kaolin bowl can grow boring.
And, like anyone holed up in a globe,
So soon deprived of vista, I was only seeing round.
Then I switched to shining green.

Inside, a nightshade offers texture pleasure,
Tissued undulations I can lean and slide on. More,
Its soaring inner scaffold vaunts a polished outer cover
That, un-cut, won't rot or wither, and can keep me,
Ever god-bolt-shy, gourded in gothic peace.

Susan Robinson

It's A New Yesterday

Once again-dawn appear.
Once again- I awake.
To start the day again-only
to start the day again as yesterday.
Off, to school children goes.
Yes! It's the same as the day before.
Here again alone, only to start the day again as yesterday before.
Loneliness is creeping to claim me as his own,
I must fight to be my own,
Or else creeping loneliness will own me,
As a statue of yesterday.
For I am aware of yesterday past-
Creeping loneliness knows no past.
I have won once again.
Yes! The same as yesterday before.
Now I sleep the same as yesterday before,
Only to be woken by the dawn.
That lets me know, it's a new-yesterday.

Rebecca B. Anderson

The China Tea Cup

A china cup sits upon my kitchen shelf
Once beautiful, now is cracked with age, stained by many uses.
Through the years this cup was shared by loved-ones,
life-long friends, and as often as one desired.

Molded into its delicate clay and ruptured lines
are the many memories of those treasured, and
I love this cup so very much.

Looking upon the aged lines, my pondering heart whispers to
remind me
of unkind words or unpaid deeds -totally unaware to me at the time-
that may have offended a dear one.
Words and deeds of this sort slivered
and exploded my beautiful cup, and
this makes me very sad.

Oh! One can glue all pieces together, unnoticeable even by eagle
eyes,
but cracks remain in mortal hearts.
Friendships are our earthly treasures - take extra care -
to clutch and hold tight to your china cup, as
character and friendship skip hand-in-hand as lifetime builders,
One stumble can shatter and demolish both in a second.

A tribute to Friendship
Rosie Lene Carpenter

Hope

AIDS, Cancer
One day there will be a complete cure.
Carjacking, murder
One day there will be no crime, I'm sure.
Rwanda, Bosnia
One day there will be no mass slaughter.
NATO, Russia
Cold peace will be warm friendship hereafter.
Filibuster, confrontation
One day there will be progress.
Pessimism, frustration
One day there will be success.
Sabyasachi Gupta

A Rose

One rose, many petals
One stem, many thorns
One heart, I have to give
To you
Take me for I will give you
All that I am
One rose signifies the
Beauty of our love
Many petals, the good and joyous
Memories we will share together
One stem, we bring each other
Strength and security
Many thorns represent the troubled time we
Weather together
One love, one partnership
For a lifetime to share with you
Tammy R. Lipa

What Is Peace?

What is peace?
But a child
who knows no right or wrong
asleep
in your arms.
Robert Patrick Young

"The Invisible Scar"

This scar, this scar,
Only a rape victim knows who you are.
You can not touch or see it,
But it's there just like the air.
This wound left this scar that will never completely heal,
But you hope and you pray someday it will.
You're there day and night and you're hard to describe,
And this feeling you give is so deep down inside.
The days turn to months and the months into years,
And this scar that's still there still brings on the tears.
You're still there like you were part of me.
If a doctor could find you I'd let him cut you out and make me free.
You bring me fear, despair, and pain.
You are never a rainbow; only the rain.
Shirley Ann Danesi

Of A Reverie

The room was dim, the room was silent. It was dim like a church when
only a soft glow of light filters through the stained glass window
now that she was gone. The air was heavy from the drawn curtains
against the afternoon sun, stifling, choking; everything was the way
it had been before. Abandoned, limp, a dressing gown hung behind the
door, and dust had left a fine mantle over all. Haphazardly , a fly
buzzed. The bed was covered in soft green chenille; the walls shone
pale cream; the curtained windows matched the counterpane; the frail
cushion on the chair had traced her sitting there. The book by the
bed was marked unfinished; terrycloth slippers peeked out beneath the
spread; medicine vials stood half filled of their contents; while the
sound of a clock, just down the hall, could be heard softly ticking.
Raphael Obermann

Sophia The Cat

Sophia peers from under the bed,
only her furry face and
her wise green eyes visible.

She chooses to be under the bed.
Later she will choose
to lie on the sill and gaze through the screen,
sniffing the morning outdoors.

Sophia is choosy
not only about where she is
but also about who she is.

Hissing or purring
playful or quiet
cowering or heroic,
she is always wise.
She chooses to be
who she is,
which means that all of her
is equally Sophia.
Susan Mihalic

"He Said"

He said our love was over.
He couldn't have been more bolder.
But the look on his face.
Only turned to disgrace.
For he could not look me in the eyes.
I was shocked and surprised
For I did not realize,
That there was even a problem!
Vickie Joswick Komaromy

Winter

When winter comes I always know,
I shall see Ice and snow,
Sliding down a hill so white,
I wonder, if it will snow tonight?

William Soper

I Wonder

I wonder why people won't understand
or at least try to understand what she's going
through. All she needs is someone who cares
to comfort through the years. I wonder why no one
seems to know what she's going through.
I wonder why she's always feeling down and out.
I wonder why the birds stop singing and the sun stops shining.
But soon very soon I won't have to wonder anymore.
I wonder as I see her cry who caused the tears to roll from her
eyes. Who caused her so much pain and to feel all alone.
I wonder why the trees stop growing and the noises of ocean's
waves stop flowing. I wonder why do people cry and why do people
die. I wonder when will people wake up and start understanding each
other. I wonder why can't we all get along with one another.
As I look across the dreamy blue sky I lay back and I wonder why...

Syretta K. Ward

Only Once

Only once will we see the sky so blue
or the water so at peace—so calm.
No other chance to live through today,
No more room to run.

Only once will we yearn for companionship
Not fully aware of our needs;
and regretfully throw away true friendship
out of carelessness and greed.

And only once will we see the moon
with tears or the sun with a grin;
or the leaves of the trees blowing
peacefully—in the wind.

Yet, only once, when it's too late,
will we feel within our heart
Like we have lost our souls to the world.

Sharon Peoples

Handicapped?

You may call me "handicapped"
    or view me as "disabled"
but, if you can't see my qualities
your handicap outshines mine!

I don't care what you call me -
    but, please look beneath!
We all have something that doesn't work,
    doesn't function as well as we'd like;
    but let's try to look beyond those faults
    to see the beauty that's underneath!

My abilities will make you pause
    and ask if I'm handicapped at all.
    Am I really disabled
    when you can see what I can do,
    and not ridicule what I can't?

    Try not to put me down
    for what I just can't help...
    Don't try to find my faults;
please don't look for what's wrong with me,
    but, simply enjoy what's right!

Rennie

Do You Know?

Do you know why there are four leaf clovers,
or why the moon is not there for cows to jump over?

Why there are flowers, mice, butterflies,
or why can birds fly so very high?

So many rocks big and small,
in your life, could you see them all?

Dinosaurs, fishes, bugs and you,
he loves creating, you know who!

Puppies, teddy bears, and kitty cats,
just think, the Lord made all that.

His love he sends to you each day,
each ones, sent in a very special way.

With such bright colors, rainbows fills the sky,
and all we have to do is look up and stand-by.

These thing and much more, says he is there,
just stop and look you'll see him, everywhere.

Mice love flowers, pigs love mud,
and all these things come from above.

Bears love honey and fishes love the sea.
Do you know that God loves you and he loves me?

Shirley J. Kroll

"The Honor Belongs To The Poets"

You may be a poet and don't know it
Or you may be a poet and know it
But you should know old poets like Shakespeare have this
Oh the honor belongs to the poets.

Now you may get no pay as some poet
But you may realize it and know it
Uh you should know those poets like great Poe have it
Oh the honor belongs to the poets.

And in ancient days Chaucer had it, and was paid
The king ordered him paid a glass of wine a day
But if you earn no glass of wine a day
Or other pay, don't be fazed or dismayed.

Though you may get no pay as some poet
Still you should realize it and know it
That you just like old poets, find that you have it
Oh the honor belongs to the poets
Gold? The honor belongs to the poets.

Sam J. Alcorn

No Lullabies

There were no lullabies for the
orphan. He had no one to sing for him, no
one to tuck him in.

He's just a small boy who's scared
in the dark. Wanting a place to go, some
where to call home.

As he cries in the dark of night,
wondering why he has no home.
Somewhere he hears a distant
lullaby.

Hoping someone will take him
home, he stands by the door and
waits. As night falls he'll say
tomorrow's another day, but tonight
There'll be no lullabies.

Tina Quinton

"Love's Circle"

Some people say love comes to those who wait
Others never find love for they hesitate
    Beware you who hold shut the gates to your heart
For one day you may find it to late to start
    Aware of the danger it may possess, you could
be content with nothing less.
    Racing from the middle and not the start, you
will caress it close to your heart.
    Crippling emotions the venom runs thru your veins,
and only now you will realize that love is to blame
    For to live without love, is not to live
Just the same.
    Without innocence or a trust of heart,
your only desire will be to once again start.

Ted Maker

Dear Jennie

We are sure you always did know
    Our family thought of you with a glow
An inward beauty of rarity
    A gem of clarity
Whether near or afar
    You were "Our shining Star"

One who cared not for center stage
    Exemplified life as a sage
You asked for little
    But gave so much

Our "Golden Days" together to treasure
    Never to be forgotten
        To cherish without measure

So "Queen of our roost" - "Our family dove "
    Everything did not end
You permeated us with your love
    To transcend life and meet you around the bend
We hope at the "Pearly gates"
    For us you will intercede
        For we sinners are in desperate need!

Walter Darocha

Untitled

There was a fiery eruption inside my heart
Painfully scorching, white-hot and blistering.
Boiling the blood in my inner recesses.
Searing and feeling that I may have left.

Dull now melancholy eyes stare out from an expressionless face.
A body, lifeless, from times of toil,
awaits the soul-seekers.

Never knowing the unexplainable joy of passion,
euphoric and ecstatic.
I had given up on love,
ceased believing in such a thing.

I don't believe I'll ever discover this value,
precious and priceless.
This idea taken from a fairy tale,
romantic and mysterious.

Shannon Young

Waves

Waves forming gently
High, rising, curling, blue tubes
Breaking forever

Haiku Cocosoi

What is the Day?

Christmas, is it cookies, huge and small gifts, wrapped in shiny
    paper? No, it is not, it is about the marvelous birth of the
Christ Child, and it was December 25, the day wrongly
    celebrated by cookies, huge and small gifts, wrapped in
shiny paper. He was wrapped in rags, and lay in a rude stable;
    A gift given of Mary and Joseph, Mother, and Father. And
Santa, with a suit so red, as Christs blood, when he was put to
    death, and said, I thirst, as we thirst for things secular,
and none of true spirit, and we sadden if what we request is
    not received. Request Christ, receive, and be filled with
joy.

Scott Davis

Another Place In Time

There was a time when a man sat upon the beach
peering out over the ocean...
his wandering eye roaming from water, to observe
the land behind him.

No buildings, or hotels met his vision...
quiet palm trees waved their fronds,
in time with the gentle breeze.
The air was fresh and salty... The sky uncluttered
by jets, or other clever inventions.
the man was content... His thoughts peaceful.

Wendy N. Henderson

How Do We See Ourselves?

As merely....
        People touching
            people??
                Yet

Valiantly we, the unknown heroes
    advance the cause of caring and concern
        loving life, relieving pain, and supporting each other

Ever mindful of the strength of illness,
    the depth of despair,
        and the pain of loneliness.

Never giving in, but pushing forward
    to render our contribution
        in our corner of the world.

Neither for the recognition nor reward
    but to extend a helpful hand
        toward the betterment of mankind.

Sandra L. Staggs

Oh - Why?

Wondering why oh why are you leaving me,
Please just help me to see,
to understand just why you're leaving me,
Please I plea?
I wish you could stay,
But I understand there's no way.
I just wish there was,
Well you know... because!
In my heart deep down, there's a frown.
I'll tell you why,
but you have to understand this is no lie!
I still love you, if only you had a clue.
To the way I truly feel,
there'd definitely be a peal.
Please just stay in touch,
because I love you very much!
So, now I let out a sigh,
and for now say Good-bye!

Victoria Goff

Outside

Snow is hurled towards his window in a
playful gesture.
He ducks behind the Christmas tree
to avoid being noticed by the children
outside.

Through the window he is able to hear their
laughter.
His breath which steams the window
is not enough to protect him from watching
as their smiling faces are chapped by the cold.

He imagines what it would be like
to have fun again.
Isolated inside this house
he feels nothing except the
turning of his stomach
and the aching of his head.

One week seems so long
not being able to go
outside.

Tanya M. Sullivan

The Shell

The shell I hold in my hand with all its prickly
"points of interests" reminds me of myself.
"How so?" you might ask.

Armor. Protective shield. The longer the point,
the longer the distance away from my heart.
The shorter points—sharper, tougher—closer
to my "very being" plentiful.

The slight opening allowing one to see
that it's not as rough and tough as it would appear.
But smooth and refined—refreshing, welcoming, ever flowing.

This shell I hold in my hand so evidently seen
but much more than it really appears to be.
The shell I hold in my hand. Life.

Wanda Hugger

Heidi's Gift

On a warm day in March, God answered my
prayer. He sent me a son and lifted me
from my despair.

No greater gift can I ever imagine,
than my sweet baby boy sent to me
from heaven.

Born to another, she set him free, free
so the angels could bring him to me.

You see, my son has two Mothers he can
be proud of, one Mother gave him life,
the other gave him love.

Each playing different roles, the
boundaries well defined, intimate strangers,
our lives forever entwined.

Her act, so unselfish, made my dream
come true, in the boy I call son
in this life we travel through.

Jeanna K. Eckert

Ryker

He may be just one, though he's not even old, a life is so
precious, more special than gold.

His life is so innocent and his heart is so kind, that the
faith that he shows is true love from his mind.

He may not talk and he's anxious to walk. If there's a tear
in his eye, you ask yourself why?

A child only learns by what they are taught, a parent must
guide them and give them pure thoughts.

This world is so cruel and there is so much hate, but we can
all choose our destiny and even our fate.

Don't take life for granted we're all going to die, don't
ever give up and lose all your pride.

He depends on you with each passing day. It's all up to you
to show him the right way.

Tammi Annette Peltz

Legacy

The muddy plaque in God's own land
Proclaims the solid sturdy man
His name is carved in faulty hand
His legacy in mother's tears it ran

Falsehoods on dark December nights
With fears and anger all entwined
Are all remembered sounds and sights
Of tempers raging and apologies ensigned

Now the nights are chorused with ensanguined cries
The silent house, a belated shrine
The lonely tedium of sleep to despise
A litter of shattered dreams in line

They clutch one another in desolate pain
Of remembered warmth and hearts enclaved
One holds another in the distant rain
The flowers in the vase are themselves enslaved

In years to come the tears will cease
They say in confident tones near hushed
But will their souls find endless peace
From a grief suppressed and shorn and rushed

Sunny Singh

Brothers

B - Brave
R - Radiant Flux
O - Observer
T - Teacher
H - Hail
E - Equal
R - Reasonable
S - Serious
The brave observer became a teacher of sorts,
to understand the true meaning of reasonable
and serious.
He was hailed wherever he went.
He could be seen for miles, because of a
equal amount of radiant flux was there.

Shirley Cooke

God

God is nice
God is good
God has always understood
If we pray and have faith
God will always keep us
safe.

Tiffany Verneer

Forever Gone

I think about you constantly,
Rachel, Chris, and John,
Remembering all the moments we used to share
That seem forever gone.

When I think of all the trouble I've caused
Our gradually losing touch
I can think of nothing else to say except
I miss you all so much.

Although I know I've hurt you
Each day I watch the clock
Waiting, hoping you'll give me one more chance
And stop by so we can talk.

I didn't realize the consequences
Involved with doing drugs
Why didn't I listen to you, my friends,
And stay safely in your hugs.

Ronda Christine Dixon

Dream Of Essence

Sunlight peeps through the clouds on stormy, dreary days;
Rays of impeccable endurance, hunt down every shadow mask;
Rain drops off of roses, causing no harm, as thought they may;
Taking away the grief of sorrow, poison in their grasp.
Clear skies with birds soaring high over head;
Clouds floating by wishing where to be; tiny baby chicks are nestled
in their twigged beds; children laughing and playing in a field full
of glee. Welcome the laughter of children at play;
Lazy days have not, yet, come to this glorious land;
Peering out of windows, ordering teachers to keep away;
Umbrellas and swimming can't wait to happen on a beach full of sand.
More rainy days will come and hunt the clear skies down;
Hiding will wait till tomorrow or later;
Hidden treasures of spring will cherish another day to be found;
Flowing so fresh, so clear, so pure-journeys forever dear water.
Journeys for me are fresh and daring without disappointment in fear;
Tomorrow and every tomorrow after, we'll all get rid of
Our evilness, to which we in fear, desperately cling;
Happiness wipes away every last drop of a tear;
So welcome all who, in return, come to join my journey of spring.

Tres Johnson

Unlimited Realities And Dimensions

Infinite vibrations thrumming
Realization of constant flow and change
As a thread to strangle any weave
I am spread across the all
Loosing singularity or solidarity
For love of life and service to all

To unite, to bond, to link
One man to his origin and destiny
The duality of complexity
With pure thought of simplicity

See the presents of short physical life
And eternity of unimagined service beyond
This mortal boundary we all share
Coming to know dreams, to understand oneself

Head still spins in pure light
And heart shivers with the cold of darkness
The blade, however broad is still sharp
I hope that I am not an ineffectual prototype
But a model warrior to be ever improved and refined
Without losing origin of all its beginnings

The Dragon and the Dove

Time Preserved

To experience—
Reliving a moment
catching my breath
a warm thought, a cold chill
seeing through one set of eyes.
To capture such perfection
in a flash of time
takes me back.
The sweet memory of a lost time
fleeting—
time knows no bounds
and we venture forth to the next adventure.
To know is to live and to share is divine
To lose, to gain
are joy and pain
The calm settles in and once again
I smile.
If our paths never cross again
to say that we have shared a time
would be just fine

Shari Lynn Rothstein

"Victims Of Selfishness"

Hearing the news I thought I would cry,
remembering the time as it had passed by.
Contemplating the future, the past, and the present,
thoughts of you filled with resentment.

What right did I have to this thing called choice?
What about this innocent being who was given no voice?
I kept my appointment and tried not to think,
and as they proceeded my heart began to sink.

They tore out his limbs from head to toe.
They seemed most hateful, no feelings did they show!
They neither cared about my child nor me,
their only concern was the money they were about to receive.

My flesh and my blood I could truly call my own,
by watching the procedure I could see how much he'd grown.
His fingers so tiny, his head, oh so small,
and at this moment I could have killed them all.

I pray for you every night my dear,
and hope that you are safe.
I pray that this anguish will somehow escape, yet grows only deeper
as I try to forget, the day I put you in your grave
I will always regret!

Tiffany A. Bronson

Worn Gloves

The pale glow of nighttime stars,
Replaced by this eternal orange light,
Eclipsed only when the cranes pass over,
Casting shadows on the workers in the night.
Reminiscent of a hawk searching amongst the clover,
Memories from a childhood so sweet,
When once he wandered those same fields of green,
But now is a slave to this damned machine,
That must be fed the cold, hurting steel
That cuts the flesh he no longer feels,
Blackened oil-covered cement beneath the feet,
Of a body and soul covered with scars.

Late at night, when he begins to stare,
Remembers an eager youth, putting on his first pair.
Worn out so many since then
Waiting for his final release,
But the time has run out on life's lease.
Years spent - what could have been?
Dad always said, "Son, life ain't fair."
Thrown away gloves, thrown away men.

Ryan W. Shaw

Ocean

Like a bluegreen silk dress
  Rippling gracefully day and night,
She is so nice and gentle on the surface;
  But underneath she is filled with weird
    And dangerous things.

Although she has no feelings when touched,
  You can touch the things inside her.
She smells and tastes of salt.
The sea gulls fly above her,
  Waiting to eat the fish
    That she has stored in her waters.

Sometimes, the stormy wind will force her waves
  Against the rocky ledge with clashing, hypnotic sounds.
The ocean is filled with wonders.
Experience a new life,
  And dive into her challenging world.

    Vanessa Gail Sewell

A Possible Dream

I have a vision of children,
Rising up, all over the world,
Out of war and poverty,
Out of inner city violence,
Out of suppression of spirits,
Out of drugs and abuse,
And attempted murder of the soul.

Children realizing their worth.
Children of all colors playing together,
The reasons for war forgotten.
Children who have survived,
Against unbeatable odds, whole and complete.
Glorious children with newly unfurled wings,
Angels with slight limps.
Only a memory of past crimes against innocence.
Children transformed.
Children of the Earth.
A vision, a hope, a possible future.

    Rita G. Tupin

Trees

  We have the wind, the water, the air. So why can't we spare some
room for the trees? Before we came the forests were full and flush,
and we cut them down so we can use the bus. We treat them bad and
I don't know why for when they're gone we all will die.

  They give us so much, from a pencil, a pipe, to a beautiful carved
duck. So we abuse them cut them down so fast there is no way this
small supply can last. I'll give you something to think about, when
the trees are gone the air will run out. When the air is gone we
can't breathe, and without the air we're dead in our sleeves.

    Shawn Wilson

"All In A Day"

Tomorrow is another day, to watch the children
run and play
I'll show them how to brush their hair and sit up
straight in a chair
I'll show them how to make their beds and put
good thoughts in their heads
I'll try to teach them right from wrong and feed
them well to make them strong
So when I tuck them in at night I know I did my
job just right.

    Vicki Browne Lopez

Friend

My love, joy, pain, sorrow, laughter, fear, hope, anger,
  sadness, excitement ... shared.
A connection of souls through which words, emotions,
  thoughts ... flow uninhibited.
A friend provides a protected place
  to be known, to grow, to simply be.
Understanding quiets all threat of judgment.
  In a friend is found calm acceptance.
trust encircles all.
  And from this safe place blossoms the most pure
of relationships, in celebration of life.
  My senses strain to absorb the riches discovered.

    Sharon Gutwin

US/Paris File

O death is beautiful, so beautiful
Said Zelda, tutu clad, rising on toes
To her majority in art, to fill
Her role as invalid in dancing shoes.
Zelda and Scottie, from a book their life,
Their hectic romance, from Montgomery
To Paris via New York; Hemingway,
A heavy rival, writer with a wife,
Stories and baby, turns to Gertrude Stein
For friendship, criticism, bread and wine.

    Russ Nash

Soul Migration

Geese fly south for the winter,
  Salmon journey upstream to spawn,
And Wildebeests' pilgrimage miles across the plains
  Each one driven by an unknown magical force.

We, too, are driven by that mysterious force
  Of migration to complete our souls' cycle.
It is something we may not understand
  Yet it is the only thing we are here to do.

You may call it a knowing,
  Or perhaps a secret map to your life.
What it is was well defined in your makeup
  And drives the unconscious.

The soul migration is a movement of your energy
  From one level to the next.
On the journey, you gain from the experiences
  That are placed in front of you.

There are many roads to take
  For you to complete your migration.
Although, for you to enjoy it most
  Do it consciously with and through love.

    Richard Aiple

Me

I wish I knew what life held for me
In the hands of God I know he knows my destiny
But in my hands, a mortal hands
I am unsure
To be alive is wonderfully sweet
To know the Lord is a tasteful treat
But what I really want to know
And what my heart needs to hear
Is that God has someone very special
And she is standing very near.

    Robert Lilley

Drummers Of Rage

Rusted hulks lie sea-buried,
Salt and barnacle-bathed.
Mast, bridge, and stacks, grotesque flowers,
From seeds pandered by drummers of rage
Sown into Europe's fierce tempest,
First sight of eager fledgling troops.

Marseille! Port of old world soil
Arid for want of blood and bone,
To be soaked by strangers, man-children,
Delayed from nature's task to breed.
Generations to come, to be
Choked by cannon's ugly breath.

Cityward sweat-soaked, they climb steep alleys,
Passing blue-smocked boys who cry,
Cigarette for Papa? Cigarette for Papa?"
Ship and boy, residue of rape
By drummers of rage,
The salesforce of hate.

William Brown Hanford

A Beach Of Dreams

Dreams carried out at the beach for a day,
Sand castles line the shore.
Everything you need you'll find.
Within your mind is where it's stored.

Dreams carried out at the beach for a day,
As all the children play what they feel.
Singing songs of make-believe,
In hopes of them becoming real.

Dreams carried out at the beach for a day,
The sunnier days make more.
The old and young combine as one,
And so do the rich and the poor.

Dreams carried out at the beach for a day,
Just come once and you'll see,
That they all don't have to be fantasies,
Whatever you wish can be.

Valerie L. Bednar

Innocence

The innocent child hurting,
scared, afraid to move, even exist.
That innocent child is grown now.
But that fear and pain still hide behind
those fragile green eyes.
That young girl has thoughts of being someone else.
Not being alone. She needs to scream out, while
nobody listens. She can only blame herself is what she feels.
That naive girl sits alone.
No one jealous of her for she's helpless.
Paranoia builds inside her
Afraid of everything
Her life fading away.

Therese Thomas

Full Circle

When I was a child, enjoying my play
I lived for the moment, from each day to day
As time went by and the world became real
there wasn't much playtime person could steal.
So much to be done- so many to please
not many moments for just taking ease.
But time marches on, if we're ready or not,
whether winter or summer - cold or hot
I realize now we are not here to stay,
so I live for the moment from each day to day.

Tressa Hancox

"The Dark"

As she walks through the dark,
scared of what may be found,
she turns on the light to
block out the sound.

Lurking in the shadows,
is the horror she fears to find.
She does not look to her safe light,
she is confined.
She fears many creatures;
all images within her mind.

A creature comes out,
it calls out to her in a deep harsh voice.
Then laughs at her fear as it closes
in from behind.
She turns on her light,
to her safe light, she is confined.

Sandi Y. Schlegel

School, Spring, the Moon and You

The crescent is waxing, filling up again.
School days are waning, coming to an end.
When I look at the crescent, I see the brows of your eyes.
When I think about school days, I feel the blue skies.

A fortnight I'll wait for the crescent to grow.
As the sliver gets full, soon a circle will show.
Then it's back to waning, the moon melts away.
School's long over, warm summer days.

From new to full back to new again.
The moon, like my heart, searches but never gains.
Like the tides that change with lunar control,
My emotions swell, then empty. I never know.

The moon is like a clock, a twenty-eight day phase
It's a cycle, a circle, I love to watch it change.
When it's new I'm like it, with love, admiration too.
When it's full I look at it, am dearly reminded of you.

Timothy Lee Cochran

Untitled

- The heat enwraps in threads of flame,
- seductively embraces everything in the vicinage of its claim,
- the sweltering glow all of misconceptions,
- amorous glances, the lure of contradicting obsessions,
- the assumption of passion through a tranquiled mind,
- the restless wavering of a mysterious bind,
- passages of wax to render a new mold,
- envious destruction, infinite times told,
- destroying all acclaimed to what it sees,
- innocence lost as its fee,
- revolted secrets reversing to a new face,
- somehow still full of suspicion, the mystifying glow still
a safe place,
- too many risings of the unrepresented stirred,
- its all to deep rooted to be left unheard.

Tiffany Terlaje

Morning

As I look at the stream, ferns surround me.
Lily pads are scattered all along the water.
Birds chirp as dragon flies dance amongst the wind.
As a deer drinks the water, my joy is overfilled.
Wind flying through the trees,
Water of a recent rain runs off leaves,
But yet the stream is calm as the sun
Peeks out of the dark clouds.
It fills the forest with light.
A butterfly awakens. A new day is coming.

Benjamin A. Hovatter

Meditations

Who made the earth so firm and round,
Setting the oceans in their bounds?
Who made the winds to blow so hard,
While hanging the sun, moon, and stars?

Who made the creatures great and small,
Planting the trees so straight and tall?
Who made the birds to fly so high,
Dipping and skimming over the sky?

Who made the flowers to grow and die,
Answering the babies as they cry?
Who made majestic mountains peaks,
Climbing from plains that speak?

Some always take a chance and rely
    on the big bang,
While others prefer to say nature
    grew us all.
But there are men who pride themselves
    with boastful clang, proclaiming
    a flat plane, no God, and no earthly ball.

        Ruth Higgins

Shadow Rider

A midst the valley of the sun, native tribes fall to white man's guns.
Shadows walk over forsaken lands, united within each others hands.

Proud, free, and once strong, extinction follows just beyond.
Stallions and madmen rule the night, calvary fight the native light.

Many lives have come to pass, red men shall never last.
Pride for death-death for life, spirits roam free through skies.

The more the white men devour souls, insane minds have no control.
Crucified, defending their dreams history retraces dreadful things.

Captured heart and mournful pasts, white man's hunger shall always
    last.
Perish all to white pride, discrimination shall never die.

        Tim Seaver

Talking To Joscelynne

I spend all day talking to Joscelynne.
She doesn't hear. She's nowhere near.
She's made it quite clear I'm rejected.
I spend each day, sad and dejected, talking to Joscelynne.

She has eyes that could light up the skies,
a smile that just beams. Just as sweet as she seems,
she graces my dreams with her laughter.
From here on, through the hereafter, I'll always love Joscelynne.
I'd been searching for her for all of my life.
I prayed that someday we'd be husband and wife.
The answer was no, and it cut like a knife deep inside me.

I wonder why she doesn't want me.
What type does she go for? I'd rather not know, for
my feelings would grow more resentful.
This love has become monumental, I'm so filled with Joscelynne!

No other can match her, she's clearly the best.
I meet other women but I'm not impressed.
So I'll keep on searching for her for the rest of my days,
and I'll keep on spending each one of the rest of my days
talking to Joscelynne.

        Robert Jackson Brown

My Other Mother

I see her as an angel of guidance
She nurtures me when I'm sad

Her long, light brown hair frames her slender
face with tints of silver

You can see her smile for a mile
for it is brighter than the sun

Her dancing is full of fun and style
Her laugh is full of happiness and charm

We talk about the good times the bad times
the sad and the happy times

I can tell her anything and in return
I get a positive response that is full of concern

She is my godmother
        Reann Theis

Untitled

Running with wolves through the night, laughing at the cold
She remembers the pleasures from so long ago
Then blinks her eyes in confusion as the alarm goes off
What happened to her animal skins just a few moments before?

Hearing the clack of chairs, the cold metal or skin
Dancing to the music of ancient Babylon, Greece or Tyre
She grabs her synthetics and hurries out to the modern world
Steps on a bus as thoughts of litters and bearers fade

Hanging gardens, pyramids and sand, swords and cross bows
Are more familiar than this new native land
Old words are spoken with new strange meanings
As she tries to ride the circle within a circle again

Riding a wild horse through harsh canyons
Deer skin and bison adorn her form.
Her husband of a few days was by her side
Until she woke in this crazy mixed up world

Is life a circle in a circle, with mother earth and father sky
Or is she more mixed up then she ever dreamed?
As she starts another day on the merry-go-round
And misses her pet unicorn and the sword at her side

        Tami Bethke

My Mom

She wrapped me in my blankets, cuddling me tight.
She sent me off to Preschool with sorrow and delight.
Kindergarten time she put me on the bus,
Gulping back the tears as I threw a fuss.
White dress and a veil she looked at me and cried,
Said I reminded her of a future bride.
Through glasses and a mouthpiece and kids making fun
She looked at me and said, "You're still my pretty one."
Now she'll glance at me and give a little moan,
Because once again I'm on the telephone.
Eighth grade graduation she's sure to be a sight.
And on through the future, helping me choose right.
Through high school and college I know that she'll be there,
Because you see she is a mom and moms always care.
Mother of the bride someday she will be,
Then a proud grandma teaching the new mommy.

        Tamara Hegedus

Cold Words

She sits there in the dark, her dreams are in her mind.
She sits there in the dark; he sits far behind.

Don't leave! She cries out loud, anxiously waiting for him to
    earnestly answer back.
But, he never does--just leaves her waiting in the cold; her heart
    dripping cold tears.
Her heart slowly sinking amongst her back, she waits and waits.

She sits there in the dark; will it ever be quenched
With the desire she yearns for and the dreams she'll never forgot.
She's strong, yet fading hope she desperately has.

Pray for me, she tells the onwalkers
Pray for me, for my heart has died and I am cold inside.
My heart is not warm yet icy cold icy dark cold yet bold.
Pray for me, for my hope has failed me and my patience is not to be
    found.
Pray for me for the last candle is about to go down.

Susanna Schneider

Dead End Job

Tic, tic, tic, goes the numbered square on the wall
She stares at it intently,
The scissor hands slowly open and close
She gazes out the pale white window, unknowingly her and drifts...

Gray mist covers the forest's softened ground
Patches of ghostly white mounds disappear into the pillowed sky
into the distance, water reaches for the top of its captive dirt
barrier crashing abruptly against the naturally carved harden wall.

She has found a secure spot
By a tall fathering oak tree.
Her ragged clothes were musty and damp,
She rests briefly, the questions consume her empty consciousness.

Had she been lost for days or was it weeks?
Is this comforting spot really safe?
Dense old trees control her ambitious decisions,
She blames herself for this barless prison...

Tic, tic, tic, goes the numbered square on the wall
For in a moment it seemed she had almost escaped,
The scissor hands move closer to cutting,
It's almost time to go...

Wendy Marston

Untitled

This is a story of a little stray cat
She will find refuge wherever she's at
She'll lie in the sun or the shade of a tree
And roam all around as long as she's free
Curiously prowling from place to place
Trying to find a familiar face
Often finding herself in distress
Trying to find someone to impress
One thing I know she's surely to find
A certain someone that's loving and kind
Hoping to find a child so sweet
That loves to have her sleep by her feet
Minding her manners this is a must
Even though she has to adjust
This would make for a long loving home
And ever again will she have to roam

Sue Stuhr

Mother

She's a wondrous woman, a treasured friend.
She'll stand beside you to the very end.

A priceless gift sent from above.
An unconditional endless love.

A heart felt smile, a warm embrace.
A look of pride upon her face.

She'll walk beside you on rugged land.
And guide you with her loving hand.

She's a rare jewel like diamonds and rubies.
A soft spoken angel unique in her beauty.

A shining star of shimmering gold.
With a strength of determination strong, willful, and bold.

A twinkling glimmer of light in her eyes.
Of knowing a bond of unbreakable ties.

A trusted confident of which there's none other.
For there is no greater gift then a love of a mother.

Shelley K. Boyd

"The Light"

Heaven above come to me.
Shine your light so bright, let it shine on me.
Take my hand and walk me home.
Through the light I live now,
I lived for grace, I lived for God.
But now I lived through the grace of God.
He walked me through the light which shines so bright
That now in His home I live by His light.

Tonight as you pray, pray what you see the light.
The light which shines so bright.
It will come and as it does, don't be afraid my child.
Because it will bring you warmth and loven memories
You once had forget about.
This light I talk about is the light of our all night God
    God Himself

Roger Dale Applewhite Jr.

The Crystal Chime

Clear as the deep blue seas,
Shining like dewdrops on a summer day.
Hidden worlds reflecting through day after day.
Beautiful illusions of rainbows to thee,
Transcending into the heavens above.
In the sunlight, always glistening, always glistening, inside the
    window.
Never to lose its sparkle, summer, fall, or spring.
Sounding of the bells hear them ting,
Bringing Forth lost memories of yesterday.
Listen, listen, hear the chimes play,
Their sweet soft melodies of love.
Striking the musical chords in you.
Spreading deep feelings of warmth.
Leaving thee with peaceful thoughts and sweet dreams.
So bright, so bright it shines as the stars in the sky at night.
Like a diamond it shines with great joy.
Casting its spell over you, as a lovely charm around one's neck.
Given off its brilliance that,
Can dazzle you through the night.
A mirror revealing one's soul, one's past, one's present, and future.

Rosaland White

You Left

Ships of destruction
Shores of deceit
Sailed across the ocean
Walked the desert sands on my bare feet
Looking the world just for you
Only ending in defeat
Saw your face up in the clouds today
I fell to my knees and started to cry
The day you left, sadness filled the air
Looking at everyone's face
I knew you were no longer here
Never to hear your laughter again
Never to see your sweet and gentle smile
I wasn't ready for you to leave
Punished for the words I had spoken the day before
Hearing your name whispered in the trees
Explain to me why this is how it has to be

Stacy Walker

If You Believe

If you believe you have more than I have,
    Show it not in bragging or haughtiness,
    In arrogance or just pure hatefulness,
    But in caring and neighborly kindness,

If you have more schooling than the next man,
    Then show it with the refinement you have,
    Politeness and courtesy and not snob,
    Fair dealing with your fellow men with love.

If the Lord has endowed you more blessings,
    Than your neighbor or the next behind you -
    Much more luxuries and comfort to show,
    Then be thankful and humble like the low.

If you believe that there is a Giver,
    Then, if He gives, there must be a reason.
    Things that happen, happen not just by chance;
    All these had been proven not just but once.

But the Giver will take back what He gives,
    If one, not worthy of what he receives.
    So, be humble if you've more than I have,
    Show it with kindness and brotherly love.

Teodulfo T. Yerro

Time

Where does time go, in it's never ending flight
Since the day turns to darkness,
And darkness into light?

As we sit back and reflect on what each day might bring
Quietly in the background
I can hear the birds sing.

While we only hear the melody,
The tune is always new
And with each new day comes a new song
Leaving us with just a tune.

I guess as time passes,
We are left with just one thing
A feeling that this moment
Has brought my life music
A very happy melody.
So I guess with each new day,
As darkness becomes light,
We'll often sit and wonder always
Now, where does time take this beauty
In its never ending flight?

Shardel Threats

No Tears In Heaven

It's been oh, so long
Since my Momma has been gone

The years have so quickly passed by
Sometimes I think of her and I cry

This ole house is not the same
Since the Death Angel came

Why did Momma have to die
our father in heaven knows why

Momma's journey is complete
Her place is at the Savior's feet

A robe of white she now does wear
Angels all about her everywhere

If Momma were here today
I know exactly what she'd say

Trust in the Lord and you will see
Together we shall spend eternity

Momma's in heaven, she is waiting for me
My Lord stands besides her, what a sight I shall see

No tears for Momma, the Lord has wiped them dry
No tears in Heaven and now I know why

Rita A. Stout

Standing Tall

Have you ever seen a child so small
Sit down and began to crawl.
While all the time inside of him
A voice says "stand up". you want fall!
And so is life with all its whelms
Someone has to take the helm.
Stand up, oh soul of mine!
And fight the battle of the mind
That rules and conquers all our foe
That enemy of our soul.
Stand up, oh soul of mine!
You've made it just in time.
To hear the conqueror of all
Say, "you'll make it, only when you call!

Sue Barnett

Reality of Winter

The cold wind blows, all during the night
Smoke from the chimney, can be seen by first light
As we emerge from our home, like a butterfly from a cocoon
Our thoughts turn to spring, which we hope will be soon
The cattle amble lazily, over the snow-covered fields
Realizing and wanting, the grass the snow conceals
The snowplow clears a road, which stretches so far
But, the blackness of the road, resembles a scar
The sun shines so brightly, but the warmth is not felt
For the strong north wind, won't let the snow melt
Frosty, the snowman, who the children made last night
Seems to feel the cold and clenches Grandpa's pipe
The snapping of tree limbs can be heard in the still
The weight of the snow, makes the tree limbs yield
Dusk enters slowly and brings forth the night
We all say to each other, God Bless and good night.

Sharon L. Pierce

Chance

Sweet little angel sent from above, created as a result of your love.
So brief was your stay, we will cherish each and every day.
He came for you one morning, without any warning.
Now you are gone, our precious baby son.
So very deep is the pain, to hold you again.
To see your sweet face, to be able to embrace.
To feel your hair, and skin so fair.
To rub your little feet, so tiny and sweet.
To grasp your small hand, I just can't understand.
The deep loneliness within, from losing our twin.
The aching in our heart, is tearing us apart.
The burning in the tears, will burn for all our years.
The constant sorrow, will be here tomorrow.
Each day seems so long, filled with pain so very strong.
Each and every minute, are filled with you in it.
Though you have eternal peace, our sorrow will never cease.
Your spirit is with us everywhere, with every breathe of air.
Down here we will grieve, yet we sincerely believe.
You now have wings, and all God's blessings.
Our little angel in heaven, Chance

Terri D. Jacques

"Mystical Fantasy"

I remember a place with a trickling stream,
So clean and so clear it could have only been a dream.
It was as clear as crystal dancing in the sun,
And shone like diamonds when the day was done.
Each blade of grass was a green as fresh paint,
And the flowers stood out boldly, colors neither dull nor faint.
A place quite unharmed by our world's revolution,
And also unharmed by smog and pollution.
A place of only peace, only love, not war,
In a cavern of trees with a lush green floor.
Where waterfalls played upon rocks set up high,
Creating mystical rainbows illuminating the sky.
A place where unicorns frolicked with gold tipped horns,
And all of the rosebuds bloomed without thorns.
A place where the hummingbirds fed on multi-colored flowers,
And mother earth and father time were the only powers.
Where mothers gave birth and newborns learned to stand,
And all animals played and rejoiced in the land.
I remember a place with a trickling stream,
So clean and so clear it could have only been a dream.

Sara Samczyk

A Friend

A friend is someone special
Someone that you would do anything for.

A friend is someone who understands you,
Someone you can trust with all your feelings
And emotions, your heart and soul.

A friend is someone you can count on
When you need a helping hand.

Someone full of Love and Laughter,
Never of hate and betrayal.

A friend is someone that needs you
as much as you need them.
And is never greedy, rude, or selfish.
They make you happy and comfort you
When you are sad.

But a true friend thinks of you
When all others are thinking of themselves.

Stephanie Ness

I Wish The Boys Wouldn't Jump On The Bed

Today we had visitors, friends from in town,
  so I carefully made up the bed.
I tucked in the corners and smoothed out the top,
  and evenly straightened the spread.
But I might as well whistle a tune to the stars
  as to keep a made bed free of boys.
From the moment they see it, a lust fills their eyes,
  regardless of whom it annoys.
A bed that is built with a structure beneath
  can withstand the odd onslaught of boys.
Though the mattress and pillows will suffer a lot,
  it's generally nothing but noise.
It's their father who adds all the weight to the game
  as he falls in a flying attack;
Throwing the covers up over the boys, he forces the enemy back.
But they howl in their fury, and flailing the sky,
  they charge with abandon untender,
As Father plows blankets up under the rush,
  and gasps out his terms of surrender.
Then suddenly, everyone dashes away to a theatre far from the scene,
And the bed settles down to a rubble of cloth
  where the chaos of battle has been.
Then Mother gets up and puts fists on her hips,
  gives a couple of shakes of her head;
And quietly pulling the wrinkles out, wishes
  the boys wouldn't jump on the bed.

Steve Waters

Some Children Cry Forever

Children, children everywhere.
So sick, so tiny, some blind, some crippled, starving.
Who cares, me or you?
No they do, they will cry forever.

I've traveled around this great big world.
I've seen so much, some good, some bad.
But I've never seen so much sorrow, like I've seen in all
those children's eyes. Looking for something to eat,
clothes, and maybe a pair of shoes for their feet.
Makes my heart break apart.
I've cried as a child, but never cried like those children.

Some children cry forever.

Filled with false hopes, bad intentions.
Hopes that care will come someday.
Wait and wait, that's all those children can do.

Their Prayers seem to be no substance,
God has given his fury.

But it's up to us to pray,
to find favor in God's eyes for the children.
Because it not, these children will cry forever.

Robert Marshal Lamb

Remember

Remember yesterday so light and free?
So why did God take you away from me?

Remember when you were a little boy?
We'd go to the store and buy you a toy.

Remember when you and Sissy would play?
Was it so bad that you couldn't stay?

Remember when you and Sissy would drive?
God how we wish you were still alive.

Remember when death came to our door?
Can't hold you or kiss you, not anymore.

Vickie L. Zastrow

My Friend

* At time we were sisters, two eggs that laid in the womb of one society.
* As we grew and stretched our limbs, we became two entities entering one world but from different sides.
* We walked a path of life and joined each other for a journey, Oh the lessons we learned-
* We learned of prejudice of skin, skin that was given at birth.
* We learned of barriers, tall walls built to hold us back from our dreams.
* We learned of clicks, secret societies that yield only sorrow and alienation.
* We learned of ourselves, that we could unlearn all those lessons and become prejudice, stare at walls and not charge at them and alienate others causing great pain if we let ourselves.
* We lost the intimate children we once were, we grew into young women.
* Our path split and once again we walked apart, but I still walked with you-you had become part of my soul.
* No matter what side of the world we walk, we will always be sisters from another, better world.

Richele Ferrara

Speaking Eyes

When I look in your brown eyes they speak to me.
Softly whispering - This can't be.

Things are happening I don't understand,
This was not a part of my plan.

I only wish there was something I could do,
to let me know this isn't true.

How did I get in this situation?
This is nothing but one big frustration.

I'm trapped, with no control;
My God, My God, when are you going to get
me out of this "hole"?

I'm still young with plenty to do,
Sitting around here makes me blue,
I'm tired of people telling me what to do.

It's hard to believe this has happened to me;
I'll just have to keep faith that
God will set me FREE!!

Sheila M. Barnes

Once In A While

Once in a while someone comes along.
Someone who sings a different song,
A song of joy when others frown,
One that'll lift you up, not drag you down.

These special folks don't stay too long.
They visit us, then move along,
And when they go, we're left with tears,
Did we cherish all their years?

We want them back, we want to show,
How much we loved them - Did they know?
They gave so much - Did we give back?
We're left alone with such a lack.

But is that so? Now think again,
He let his smile, remember when,
He made us feel so very strong,
He left his love, he left his song.

Tameka Bines

Happiness

Something always longed for
Something everyone spends their lives striving for
But also something that very few people ever truly find
Myself, I wonder does true happiness really exist
Or am I wasting my life in search of a fairy tale
Wishing on the stars, trying with all of my might,
Giving all of myself, wanting happiness
So much in my life
But in reality what I want so much in my
Life is nothing but a lie
Stories told to me as a kid
My question is:
Did happiness ever really exist?!

Tina L. Black

Special Moments

Days come and go.
Sometimes we don't even kiss goodbye.
We solve our daily problems,
Take care of our never ending responsibilities.
We work our work.....and life goes on.
Then one night, you whisper "I love you"
As you pull me close into your lean strong arms
And I remember why I fell in love with you.
Times flies back to years ago, and it is yesterday once more.
Totally consumed with each other, insecure with how the other felt.
Now we know, and still care.
Stronger than ever, secure with time.
We know the good and the bad about one another
and accept each other unconditionally.
Excitement has not gone, it is just put away for special moments.

Victoria Nielsen

Summer Lullaby

The lap of water 'gainst the weathered bank
soothes a coppered sky.
A delicious stretch and the hammock swings
to the river's lullaby.

A July breeze lifts my hair
like the fingers of a lover.
Buzz and hum, they simmer there
Hummingbirds dart and hover.

With one foot propped upon the bank,
eyes closed, the soul adrift.
Bare toes slap the soft, cool mud,
Tousled leaves above whisper down the gift.

A wordless melody, long and low
softly sweetened by the heat.
Feel its thrumming, seasoned slow
It breathes a lullaby to me.

Sabrina Baker

Princess Of Night

As the Princess of Night slowly flew over head;
Silver stars fell from her silky hair.
Then the Princess of Night blew a kiss to the Prince of
day to wish him good night and tell him it was a
lovely day.

The animals of night howled, chirped, and danced and the
wind whispered softly to the trees.
As the hours went by the shiny, shimmering stars slowly
began to fade.

It seemed to be an eternity since she had seen her
beloved Prince of day.

Rebecca Seeley

Helpless

God's tears fall today blending with mine. Despair and
sorrow pound in my heart. Make me function, and go on. I feel
life, yet there is none; such doom destiny brings. Hopeless
beyond hope! What should I do?

Heavy is my heart lost within myself drowning in
discontent. Plain are the days now, no color just a hazy gray
that hangs and shadows out all the colors.

Round and round I go always moving, yet going nowhere.
Heavy laden are my feet, like an oak planted to stay and
observe yet go nowhere.

Life is so fragile so out of our control. We take for
granted the wonder of it all. Till faced with tragedy then we
must decide. It isn't always easy, but God is by our side.

Oh dear God who makes all things; do what's right I will
believe. Ease my soul from pain and hurt, bring my life back
down to earth.

Susan Speakes

Good Comes From Pain (Sometimes)

Sometimes good things come from pain! I know I may not
   sound quite sane!
Just think of what your folks went through.
Now they can give advice to you.
Remember when you had your child?

Now that pain was far from mild!
Yes! The pain of that first tooth! That was the start
   of all your youth.

Remember the pain of exercise?
You were worried about your thighs!
Remember the pain of your first broken heart? See!
You learned from that, you didn't fall apart!

Remember the pain when Scruffy ran away?
He returned with a friend. It was the same day.

There's a time for everything! And sure, we'll complain!
But sometimes good can come from pain!

Sharon Anita Jackson

Starlight And You

At night, I dream about the two of us alone, riding a star through
space; stopping at the moon for a refill, then on our way again.
I feel your slender brown frame next to me as we hurl past Mars.
Lovingly, you turn to me, a smile of joy about your face and we
glide beyond the colorful rings of Saturn. (Actually, I don't
care for astronomy, just having you around makes my whole world
heavenly).
Hey, there are Uranus and Neptune or is it Neptune and Uranus?
(No wonder they're called the twin planets).
I can feel love rising now, but so is the sun, therefore, I too
must rise to meet the oncoming day. When the day is done,
night falls all over again and I dream; I dream about you and
me sharing love; there's not much more I could ask for. God
I love dream!
Sorrow. Knowing that you and me may never be in reality as we are
in my nightly visions. So sad, depressed, love crazy.
Here comes the moon again! Can I please pretend?

Willie Murry Jr.

Our Tree

Our tree is wet in February.
It is wet in February
I hear thunder in my class.
Outside I can see puddles on the ground.
I can see lightning in the sky.
The rain is falling today.

Selisa Rollins

My Memories Of Mother

You are the prism of dew in the morning,
sparkling in the sunshine.
You are the ripples of the stream talking to
me; its rhythm mixing with mine
You are my sunshine, you're the reflection
in the stream.
And even if you can't be near, you visit
in my dreams.
The wind that whispers in my ear, a child
crying in the park - shedding a single tear.
You'll be there, always and forever, year
after year, we'll be together.
Don't be afraid if I forget you someday.
Don't be scared if I should go away.
I missed you but I found you,
In the dew and in the stream, the sun, the park
and in my dreams.

Terrell Rutherford

End Of The Dream World

Walking hand in had along a beach in the moonlight with someone
special that is sweet and caring. As the waves of the ocean wash over
their feet, there is a feeling of love and well-being. As the couple
gaze into each others eyes glimmering from the moonlight they
can see a sign of honesty and self-worth flow out of them. When the
dawn arises they feel a feeling of warmth and love cascade over
them, but as every good thing can never last this feeling also
ends. The beautiful sun light gives way to the dark clouds of reality
and all turns black and cold. Just as the sun can be swallowed up by
the stormy overcast then can be dream be invaded by reality and
and the peaceful world can be thrown into disharmony.
The world turns dark and cold as the feelings of self-worth are
replaced with feelings of self-doubt.
In the real world the eyes of people are replaced with dishonesty
and you realize just how unimportant and worthless you are in life.
The real world is cold and you one day realize that with all the
people around you, just how alone that you really are and just
how worthless and unimportant your life is.
You know that love will only bring heartache and misery to your life.
As you get older in the real world you begin to think about your life
and if you did anything worthwhile or if everything you worked for
was wasted time and your life was worthless and meaningless. There
is no pain like realizing that you are unwanted and alone in life.

William Lingg

Reality

Reality comes into being like a sleek, black jungle panther.
Stalking into depths of greenery
and then turning a corner into a slouching, scheming city.
Alley cat searching through trash
for something good -
like the end of a hazy summer
warming the earth in blissful ignorance,
only to fall to a cruel fate
when winter kills
a fatal, frozen death once more.
And on a cloudy day
when the breakthrough of the sun
is blinding, blinding
Truth hurts screaming, screaming
And Reality
  walks off
    laughing
      laughing.

Wanda Howard

Reminisce

When time has flown and years have left
Its mem'ry etched upon my face,
I shall recall, remember all
And speak of it with simple grace.
Tanya Tipton

A Self-Realized Soul

I am a bit of protoplasmic being
Standing, sitting, lying in space.
I have returned to Mother Earth
But with a different human face.

I lived before in another time
With a body perhaps less sophisticated than before.
As man I traveled in many a clime
Healthy, unhealthy, rich or poor.

With consciousness slowly dawning
To repeated birth, growth and death.
I sensed the light of a new morning
The joy of living without regret.

Slowly the feeling of a greater love
Moved me from the inside out.
A growing sense of universal compassion
Expressed through a heart more lovingly stout.

The colors and fragrance mixed without separation
Of a universe both personal and whole.
And I died to the ignorance of separation
In the glory of a self-realized soul.
William J. Kellaher Jr.

To Be A Tree In Stepping Stone Park

What would I be, perhaps a tree
Standing slim and tall
With arms of leaves throughout the spring
A carpet of them in the fall

I'd like to stand by waters edge
My branches hanging low
So in the summer they could be
A shelter from the sun' strong glow.

And come the winter, when it snows
And all my limbs are bare
I'd like to think some hardy birds
Would help me keep my vigil there.
Sheila Penn

"Trees On A Summer Eve"

Trees on a summer's eve, glistening in the sunlight for all to see.
Standing tall, green, and beautiful - So proud, so high into the sky.

Trees radiate a strength and powerful since of all that's pass,
eternal growth and the perseverance to last.

In the mist of Trees, there's a peace of mind, this feeling is
within this Time!

To enjoy looking at the beautiful, bountiful green upon their vines
and watch them sway in a peaceful breeze is more then enough to
please

God created a beauty that is everlasting on Earth.

Take time to enjoy, lay back, look, Dream among the Trees. Their
Peace and Beauty where put here to please.

Enjoy the Bliss of Trees on a Summer's Eve.
Stella Princess Holmes

For Valerie, Who Was Black,
When All The World Was White

When the thread-bare jeans and band-aid mini-skirt
started tattooing my face and arms with felt tips,
While their two tobacco-smelling leather jackets,
greased down and touting chain belts, held me firm,
and cheered them on as the cement cut into my shoulders,
and the day's class notes scattered away in shame—
It was you alone on that crowded bus ramp who broke forth
calling: "Let that girl 'lone!"

When the bus lurched around the corner, it was you who took
a welted, sobbing Easter egg back into the school.
"Were there any witnesses?"
After the nurse cleaned the blood away, the principal quipped,
"Kids will be kids. Go on home, and try to stay out of trouble."
You drew up all six feet of yourself in righteous indignation,
not even for yourself, but for me; but you were black,
when all the school was white. His vacuous eyes looked through you.

When I invited all my friends for a school's-out picnic
(all the "rednecks," A-students, non-jocks and journalists,
the one's who tutored little kids and didn't wear jeans to school),
all the faces were white, Mother said that you were black.
Tonya Huber

"Raindrops"

Raindrops falling; continuous crowded
Steady, solid, echoes of a calling
Only to fall on ears of society
Unwilling to listen, too busy to hear

Life endures raindrops falling
Protecting the beauty with false umbrellas
Fearing it's purity, separating God's gift
Damaging the soul, hiding from grace

Raindrops falling, nourishing the land
With scents of freshness, yet annoying to man
With inconveniences, interruptions to the routine
Of a life so blind not to see, the other side of a spiritual gift

Raindrops falling, singing, talking
Cleansing, feeding; or maybe to some
Crying, screaming; unable to transcend, unwilling to accept
The creator's shower of love has a reason
To cleanse our soul and be closer to God!
Robert W. Odegaard

Body Logic

Ears don't listen, not a word he said,
Stop the words, from entering my head.

Mouth don't open, you won't be heard,
Don't say anything, say not a word.

Nose don't smell, his masculine scent,
You know the mind it will torment.

Hand don't touch his masculine chest,
Stop what you're doing I must protest.

Eyes don't look, close so not to see,
That beautiful smile, he has given to me.

Heart don't leap, stop where you are,
You know this time, you've gone to far.

Mind don't think, stop all thought,
Now, what was I saying

.... I forgot.
Synthia

I Walk Alone

The beach glistened with the setting sun.
Such a beautiful backdrop to be shared by just one.

The ocean breeze softly swirled through my hair.
Its scent was sweet, like you, so young, so fair.

Clouds shot out in jet streams as light gave way
To a star and moon filled night called heaven's day.

My feet are cold as I pace the moisten sand.
Yet I realize that each grain was formed by the Makers hand.

Lonely is my journey for I continue to play this game of solitaire.
For I will continue to wait for you, someone so precious, so rare.

I walk alone and yet you will always be in my heart.
For I pray for the second pair of footprints when were no longer apart.

As night falls along this pretty shore
My thoughts turn to you, the love of my life, once more.

Thomas W. Albert

The Fan

A fan came into my hands a few years ago.
Such a beauty and so very old.
With floral pink and gray on a dark background,
There were gentlemen's names in the folds all around.
If only this fan could tell it's tale!
So many questions would be unveiled.
It was back in the early nineteen hundreds
when a young girl wrote,
The names and dates for beaus she had hopes.
What was the occasion, a Cotillion, a Ball?
Or maybe nothing like that at all.
The young girl grew old to age ninety-nine.
She died with her secret and the fan is now mine.
I think of the girl, her life from spring into fall.
All those names hanging on my wall!

Sharon M. Barrett

"Obstacles To Love"

There are certain obstacles to love
such obstacles created by the Lord above
we get distracted with other people and things
Distracted with what temptations might bring
Another obstacle to love might be
Not having enough time to spend with you or me
But no matter how tough of an obstacle we face
We'll tough it out with our love as base

Rosie Yarnell

Side By Side

Side by side we started out with no space in between;
sun and rain, together, our wrong-doings gone unseen.
Love is not blind, rather the human heart discriminates;
sight, sound, and heart, our soulful mind emanates.
A story not unlike other's, yet painful it is still;
the flooding memories of me beautiful and him genteel.
One day these memories will not hurt and sense they will make,
but realization must be made that time is what it will take.

Take it did, forever and day it seems,
and in that time my ill thoughts were emancipated by dreams.
Side by side we are not, and much space between us remains;
in our hearts a change was made and much thought it contains.
His-reasons, mine-regrets, our age was not a friend of time.
In memories we are together; the future will be even more kind.

Samantha Collins

Haircut Hassle (or Barber Chop)

I sat in a seat high above the floor
Surrounded by hair clumps by the score.
Razor-sharp scissors clipped the air
As the barber prepared to cut my hair.

Sharpened silver scissors sang snip, snip, snip,
As showers of hair coated nose and lip.
Since my hands were under an apron's embrace,
I couldn't reach itches on my tortured face!

Soon irritations on the tip of my nose
Made me so tense that my heartbeat froze.
With little warning an explosive sneeze,
Lurched my head downward between my knees!

The startled barber then lost his command
And scalped me clean with one swipe of the hand!
My head was clear-cut right down the center,
And I looked like an eccentric inventor.

After some thinking I chose to have finished
What volcanic sneezing only diminished.
I had my head shaved so that I could start over,
And raise a new crop like alfalfa or clover!

Robert C. Zawalski

My Mirror Knows Me...

Looking beyond my Mirror... who do I see.
Talk to me Mirror... who can I be.
My Mirror knows my struggle each and everyday day.
My Mirror knows the things that I may say.
My Mirror knows the fears I keep abyss inside.
My Mirror knows the tears that are tucked away.
My Mirror knows all my pain; let me go my mirror...
or I will go insane....

William V. Howell

Concluding Tears

The meaning is unclear and not understanding brings on the tears.
Experience leaves merely enough with which but to conclude.
With time comes belief, but just as the wind grabs hold and
carries away a leaf, the pacifying conclusion is soon robbed
of its once possessed belief.
As answers these conclusions will no longer do.
The meaning is still unclear through each year,
and through each and every tear.
Time is a decider of fact and theory.
We continue to lie and pacify ourselves with theory.
We play with pain by putting belief in a mere conclusion.
Reality eventually breaks through proving it an illusion;
leaving the meaning still unclear and bringing yet another tear.

Theresa M. Dollison

The Tapestry

A tapestry, exquisite in design
I weave with you, my special one. Each year
We share is woven in, becomes a part
Of its uniqueness and its permanence.
I view its elegance and find a line
Of golden thread, encircling to combine
To add stability — distinctiveness.
I am aware this is the love we share
The glowing portion of the plan that made
A tapestry, exquisite in design.

Dorothy Alta Jordan

Untitled

Lay down on my bearskin rug, alongside a fire and chat with me
Tell me of the far and distant places that you have always
longed to see

Share a kiss at the peak of a double ferris wheel at the county fair
Grow wings of silver and fly to Australia to dance with Koala bears

Enjoy a warm summer day watching turtles sunbathing on a log
As we sit together on a lily pad, alongside a friendly frog

Hold each others hands as together we wait to take our turn
To ride magic unicorns around and around the rings of Saturn

Kiss each others lips while we pledge our love underneath a
cascading waterfall
Have the honor of the first waltz at the ancient God's Ball

Sit on the edge of an erupting volcano and drop in coins of gold
To preserve the happiness we have found as together we grow old

Reach out and grab a falling star as it hurls through the sky
Skip it across a pond and wish to be together until the day we die

Rodney Reid

"God's Hand Prints"

Leave God's Hand Prints, right on the walls of my life,
Telling the many ways, how He moved away the strife.
I don't mind his Hand Prints being there, on all my walls.
They simply show the world, that He answers when I call.

His Hand Prints tell a story, how they kept me through the years,
When things were not going well, and I had cried so many tears.
Those Prints number my Blessings, of all He's done for me.
So you cannot see the walls; just His Prints that left me free.

When I think of confusing times; in stress, my mind would lay;
There's His Hand Prints, that kept my mind from going astray.
When I had so many bills, with a child and food to buy.
I see His Prints again, and I am so filled, that I can cry.

When I remember the sickness, and surgeries gone through.
I see His Healing Hands, and His Hand Prints show up too.
When I look at my child, and her true love for God's Word;
I only see His Hand Prints, and His voice I have heard.

When I think of God's goodness, and the Prints I can't see;
The Prints that were made, when they hung Him on Calvary.
His Prints line my life, from the baby crib up to this day.
My life is full of Hand Prints, with Blessings in each way.

Val J. Randle

Sperm Whales

The sperm whale is odontoceti,
  that contains one or more tons of spermaceti.
They usually live in groups under leadership of a male,
  which compared to its body has a rather small tail.
In it's intestines is a substance called ambergris.
  It is also sometimes found floating in tropical seas.

Anywhere from sixteen to fifty five tons is how much
  a sperm whale weights.
Does it not you, too, amaze?
The whale is thirteen to twenty meters long.
  Although never attaining the size of a
  blue whale, don't get me wrong.
Most sperm whales live in temperate waters,
  although fatter males travel to the arctic ocean,
  and back in a circular motion.
Now that you know about the giant sperm whales
  please... help save their tails!

RaeLynn Van Ornum

"Richard"

I think of you so often, hardly a day goes by
That I don't ask myself... why.... why
Why are you gone, was it because of you?
Was it because of the lifestyle you chose to pursue?
But, I saw you try, try so hard to change
Only to fail, over and over again
I think of how I felt, over those years
What would people think, those were my fears
Then you told me you were sick, I couldn't believe...
There would be a cure, you wouldn't leave
But you did.
Now there are days, when it just pops in my head
I just can't conceive, that Richard you're dead
Was it your fault? Is it something you started?
Probably not, but we're still broken hearted
Of this I am sure, you are now in heaven
But it just doesn't seem right, you were only 37.

Vicki R. Marshall

As I Go

Lord as I go, correct my path in the right direction.
That my life may be kindled with love and perfection.
And as I go, give me grace to withstand all evil
Because without Your help, I am feeble.

Lord as I go, may I do Your will each day
May I be watchful and helpful and always pray
I want to always help those in need
That I may always be helpful and sew good seed.

Lord give me the wisdom to know right from wrong
That my heart may be joyful and full of song
As I go, may Thy word be hidden in my heart
And I will hold it a treasure that will never depart.

And Lord as I go, may my traveling be a delight
To do Your will and let my life be bright.
Let all my days Lord, be lived unto Thee
That others may hear as well as see - The Christ in me.

Viola Blackwell

The Sea

The sea was calm thou it heard of the storm
that raged about, not to far
As if to say don't come my way
Yes without a chance it knew it would have to dance
to a tune too rough that could last for days
Then and there out of nowhere, came rushing in to defend
The sun with its help
Yet the sea still wept
For the storm knew it's course
Powerless with no choice
The sea stood in it's way, as the storm began to play
Swaying out of control
Reaching out for something to hold
No, not even air would dare
to lend a hand to stop the noise of this band
It played for days until it was tired of tossing the sea about
As though there was no tomorrow
When it was done
The sea looked up at the sun
And with a smile, said thanks, we made through another one

Vernon S. Booker

Untitled

I bet you thought a rainbow was just something in the sky,
    That shows its colorful beauty just after a storm passes by.
But there are many rainbows just as beautiful to the eye,
    You can see them every day if you'll only try.
They're in the smile of a friend who will stand by you till the end,
    Or a friendly word a message even a stranger can send.
These very special rainbows are rainbows of love,
    And are far more precious than storm rainbows in the sky above.
For these rainbows calm the storm of loneliness and hurt,
    And they begin to form a path to a pot of gold able to weather any
Storm, a heart full of love, and the peace of a dove.

Steven J. Kolf

Kisses

Kisses are so soft and sweet.
That special feeling when our lips meet.
Some are sad and some are glad.
Sometimes we kiss even when we're still mad.
Some kisses are so demanding and hard.
Others are ones that take you off guard.
You have the kisses between two lovers.
There are the kisses children give their dads and mothers.
But no matter which kiss you kiss.
They all carry a message you can't miss.

Sherley J. Smith

The Magic of a Christmas Tree

What is it about a Christmas tree
that still seems so magical to me?

Is it the bright and shiny ornaments
that are hung just right?
Or is it the hand crocheted angel on top,
who watches over us at night.

Each ornament, whether handmade or a gift,
holds a special memory, that gives my heart
a lift.

So I guess, even when I'm ninety-three,
you'll still find me on Christmas Eve,
staring at the Christmas Tree.

Rhonda Welch

"Thoughts Of You In Interim"

Someone told me (or maybe I read it somewhere)
that when you lay down with someone you leave part
or your soul with that person. Well, I want you
to know that I am a walking shell because you
took not a part but, all my soul. I'm asking
no — I'm begging for it back. I've never
begged for anything in my life. And now I'm
begging you for it...

You are apart of everything I say
everywhere I lay, and everyone I know.

I dreamt of you last night, and when I woke up you
weren't there, but you were, because you always are...

You are in everything I do, everywhere I go,
and everyone I see.

At times I just want to forget all about you, but if I
did I would erase all memory of past and present,
because I can't remember my life before you
and can't imagine it without you.

You are my everything, my everyone and my everywhere...

Sophia Fossett

With God Your Troubles Will Pass

There is no trouble here on earth,
That will ever stay for good,
Because sooner or later everything will,
Turn out the way it should,
And with the help of a good friend
That lives high above,
You will find out that your troubles will pass,
With His help and love,
Please don't ever give up hope,
Because he'll always be there for you,
No matter how long your troubles last,
He will help you through,
And no matter how hard life gets,
Or how bad you are treated,
When you know Him and accept Him,
You will never be defeated,
So I just wanted you to know,
That whatever's wrong won't last,
And with His help and his love.
Your troubles will soon pass.

Sara Perez

The Greatest Sacrifice

How many men in this world do you know?
That would give up their lives to save many lost souls.
That were headed for hell and the devils own way
now thanks to Lord Jesus all can be saved.
He walked here on earth, like you and like me
used his God given powers to calm a raging sea.

Healing the sick, the crippled and the blind
for all to see His love was true and kind.
But they mocked and rejected each thing that He done
they would not believe he was God's only son.

They made a crown of thorns and placed it on his head
he paid for our sins by the blood that he shed.

I can see Him there now, with his Nail scarred hands
He was sent here on earth to be a Saviour to man.

Oh thank you Lord Jesus for taking my place
that I may have eternal life after the grave.

Now you may think there's no way to repay Him for His deed
asking forgiveness of your sins is all that you need.

He will take you in His arms and cradle you in His love
for there is only one Saviour, that's Jesus above.

Wayne Lambert

A Night To Yell

At night I lay within my cell.
That's when it starts, they being to yell.
The sounds of torture, you can tell.

At night I lay upon my bunk.
Unable to sleep, ready to jump.
Who'll be the next they'll thump!

I try to pretend, I'm out of sight.
But when they come, I'll have to fight.
There is nowhere to hide, in a prison night.

At night I lay within my cell.
I begin to pray, I begin to yell.
Dear god please, can't you tell?
I've already spent my time in hell!

Sharron Grinder Boyer

Two - Too Afraid

How can two people be too afraid to fall in love?
The answer is simple:
One has been too hurt too often to try again—
The other is afraid of being hurt!
Yet love is a natural progression of events in any relationship
If the two would just let it happen and let go.
But the past is still too strong for each of them,
To let this love really grow and grow!
One has been living too long independently
And really needs no one's love!
The other has shared this love with one other too deeply
To allow another to enter his heart!
However, if their real feelings would ever be known to each,
Their love would soar like an eagle!
And their love would know no bounds!

Thomas E. Yurek

An Autumn Tree Apology

Was I so young I couldn't see
The beauty in an Autumn Tree
Ten years and eight I spent with thee
And never saw you there with me
I depended on you for the season call
Yet missed your beauty in the fall
How could I have missed you standing there
Your beauty outstretched up in the air
You were so many I was but one
Who burned so badly in the sun
I looked for you with great concern
For without you I'd surely burn
Just as sure as I knew you were everywhere
I never noticed you were there
And now that twenty and eight years have passed
It's been a long time since I saw you last
I apologize to the Artist who gave me the purpose
Why I was to be to notice the beauty in an Autumn Tree
And to share it with you so that you might see
The beauty of art in an Autumn Tree.

Sharon J. Boldvich

In Praise Of Women

Of all the people on this imperfect earth,
The best of all is Woman, in my belief,
While purblind men ignore the Woman's worth,
And plunge the nation into war and grief.

The wisdom of the Woman is profound,
Her values rest on love, the home, and peace,
Opposed to war. With both feet on the ground
She calls for sanity, for stupid war to cease.

The old men send the young to fight and die,
While mothers, sisters, sweet-hearts sadly weep.
Let's send the old war-mongers out to try
Their battle skills, we know their talk is cheap.

So ladies, arise, and start a revolution.
We men are hopeless. You are the only solution!

Tom McGuire

Redondo G

I couldn't have loved you more
    that night.
The pier was dark, except where you stood
    it was light.
We danced in the wind as the spray from
    crashing waves licked our face.
I didn't want to let go.
Storms don't always cause damage.

Stephen Johnson

Natures Weather

As I sit and watch the sky, and feel
the breezes of the four winds blowing by.
    Oh the sounds of all the nature,
my soul is peaceful, knowing there
was such a powerful creator.
    When we're down and feel there's
nothing more, we need to climb out of
that shell, and open the door.
    Walk outside, look what's at hand
it can all be found in this great land.
    It's the sky, it's the earth, we're
all a part of it, since before our birth.
    So ever if you feel alone, sad,
depressed and not quiet all together,
step outside into the wonderful world
and be a part of natures weather.

Wanda Spriggs

Galleon So Tall

The wood of the forest, cedar indeed.
The close of the timber strong indeed.
The mark of the craftsman, carpenter metal in all.
The look of a boat, three stories tall.
The curve of the board gracious in all.
The brown of the hull paint and all.
The paint of the varnish, in brownish hugh.
The tall of 3 masts slender and tall.
The engraved railing on rear deck house.
The white of the sail, rolled tight to mast span.
The look of a stallion the, treasure of the seven sea's.
It plies.
Of vintage 1490, a beauty. A treasure, a ship,
A Galleon so tall.

Raymond Draghi

"Comparison"

The fragrance now dying, petals fall,
the color now fading, the aging is now
present to all...

Once brilliant in color, fragrance
alluring, seemingly untouched by time, this
grandmother of mine...

She's compared to a flower, which may
be at spring till fall, both loved and cherished,
both have sentimental meaning to all....

A rose has many meanings to all, love,
friendship, forgiveness, and more, a grandmother
has these rather rich or poor...

But one thing cannot be compared, though
similar, a flower cannot show feelings, think,
or act on impulse, I thank God grandmothers
are meant to be shared.

Samantha Cooper

Roses

Roses are red like the fire that burns
The beauty of a rose makes the coldest
heart yearn
Roses can die like you and I
But the plant lives on to give new birth at
dawn
Roses are beautiful in so many ways
That the beauty of the rose will always
stay

Richelle Harkins

The Dance Of Never

Across the bar, I touched your fine, bartenders hand,
the dance began.

Love, as I had never known it, soul mates forever,
the dance of never.

Twice, when I was younger, I tried to change my course,
I left you for another, another dance began.

Only to discover, I was not meant for any other, I
returned to our dance of never.

You were very clever, assuring me, you would always be
there for me. Content with seeing you now and then, so
dazzled that I could not see,

that you were leaving me alone, most of the time,
playing, our old song to keep me in line,
the dance of never.

Now, years later, it is I, my love, who must end the
dance, free at last, from this "Dance of Never" - forever.

Sandy Stevens

Peace - Contentment

Her steps a bit short, as she went down the walk,
The Doctor had said, "that's what she needed".
If she met someone, she would stop and talk,
To inform them, the Doctor's orders, she's heeded.

She watched all the children at play in their yard,
She head their cry's and their laughter.
If they ran toward her, she was on guard,
To make sure they got the toy they ran after.

It delighted her so, to watch children's grow,
Into pretty girls and handsome young men.
They didn't realize, - how did they know,
Just how much she loved, watching them.

Her children were grown, - and out on their own,
Each one of them had their own place.
She never complained, content, though alone,
You could tell by the smile on her face.

She had God by her side - That you couldn't deny,
'Cause she lived for her Lord, every minute.
Great peace she did have every day that went by,
'Cause she made "good" everything that was in it.

Verbie J. Harper

Dreams

When deep at night in darkness we sleep
The dream makers enter our minds and peep
They wander through our lives in depth
When sleeping sound we lie in bed
Some people looking on in haste
May believe we've left this harsh life's race
We linger on in dreams so deep
Lily fields we run and leap
With those we love or have before
Experiencing those feelings we all adore
But when the mornings harshness comes
Alarm clock ringing in our ears
Our mind awakens back to today
Where again we experience reality
Why are we split come night and day
As if our spirits our far away
Someday we'll know right where we've been
But as of now we'll wander through
As humans always seem to do.

William F. Miska

Decision

Standing on a precipice
The edge of time calls out to me
There's a part of me that really wants to go
To step into eternity
Let its darkness me enfold
But darkness is part of what I want to leave
Now I feel the numbing cold
As a chilling wind from my own past
Reveals to me all my open wounds
I think the feeling cannot last
When it does I start to cry
The tears of a bitter hope so lately gone
And so I ask the question, "why?"
But just hear it echo in the air
The sound leaves me cold and hollow deep inside
Then the fear I have of what's out there
Is overcome by my despair
And so at last I take my final step into the night

Robert Pettit

The Family Of The Dying Patient

As a patient slowly slips away
The family wants to stay all day.
You'll often feel they're in your way
As you try to do your work
Try to understand their plight
As they slowly lose a hopeless fight
They hope and pray with all their might
As their loved one slips away.
They remember Mom standing over her stove,
Creating for them tokens of love.
Or maybe it's Dad, playing ball and
Laughing with them when he took a fall.
Now all they see is a body so weak
As it slowly slips away.
Support this family as much as you can.
Show them that you do understand
And hope and pray as you do
That if and when you lose someone too
There will be a nurse there who is just like you.

Trendle Cady

He Is Gone

I notice something a little special now that
   the father is gone from the house.
Where has he gone, where is he now?
   Into a new life; he was tired of the old.
No one enters his room, to see the empty closet
   hangers swinging into silence
The closed drawers, the odd coin and pressed handkerchief
left behind.
   Only the small breeze coming in the window
   stirs his old scent.
No one enters the room..it is empty of him
   he is gone.

Sally Douglass Campbell

My Daughter

You entered my life one frosty morn;
That was the day you picked to be born.
More precious than diamonds,rubies or gold;
A sweet baby girl, so I was told.
Down through the years, as I've watched you grow;
I've loved you far more than you'll ever know.
My daughter you're rarer than the rarest black pearl;
I'll always be grateful for my sweet baby girl.

Sharon J. Boyd

City Limits (To Grandfather)

Laboring here, you and our country is what I miss.
The gray fog, this dim city, the rude people,
I'm so sick of this.

I miss the harvest and the use of my hands.
A lighter brown now, I miss the hot sun
and my coal black tan.

I miss the chickens, the horses, and the milling of our cows.
I miss Spot, Old Blue,
and the annual killing of the sow.

I miss the cool country air and how it whistles as it blows.
Here, too many tall buildings.. those sounds I'll never know.

I miss playing in the old corn shack.
I miss my old glove and wooden baseball bat.
I miss the way brother and I used to play
with our trucks and toy soldiers
around grandmother's rosebushes all day.

But most of all I miss you and me
sitting outside under that old shade tree.
I miss us spending time together.
Yes, the blue sky, the mockingbirds, you and me.

Rodney C. Wallace

Sweet Remembrance

I peer into the windows of your soul and find
The laughter and tears of loves left behind.
I search the fragments of a heart that is bare
And question if there will ever be room for me there.

I remember the times of freedom and fire
When your kisses were once laced with the sweetest desire
Those times are past - gone is the game
Gone as the winter winds whisper your name.

The touch of your hand - the warmth of your smile
Bring no promises - only happiness for a while.
I ask no questions - scared of the truth
Scared of my fragile heart broken in two.

I long to hold you, to touch you, to trust you
But feelings so strong must be held by two.
Reach out to me - share with me - shed no tears
Maybe just realize that I'll always be here.

Stacey Lapinski

Dancing Trees

The trees dancing mysteriously in the moonlight
The leaves making eerie whispering sounds
With the branches as arms they reach out to you
Grabbing at your hair, your arms, your legs....

The wind howls loudly through the leaves
In melody with the wolf on the rise
As you walk the sounds seem to follow
And the bushes and trees seem to have eyes

The moonlight now playing with the moving shadows
Making them come to life with just one touch
Dancing and swaying with the melody of the wind
Floating on the air without the slightest sound

The sounds now surround you like a cage
With nowhere for you to go and hide
Trapping you with not objects, but with sounds
The darkness a heavy weight in your stomach

Closing your eyes the trees surround you
Coming closer and closer, cutting off your breath
Opening your eyes wide realizing you are safe
With the cool breeze blowing through your window

Teresa Henderson

In This World

Waking up in this world out on your own
The life that you'll lead will now become known
A life full of hope, love and despair
What will happen to you in this world? Does anyone care?
People laughing and crying, they seem so sincere
A world of unknown, but it seems very clear.
To wake up in this world, unsure of life's roads
Roads that will lead to places untold
Waking up in this world, it sometimes seem rough
And yet all the time, you've learned to be tough
The life you now lead has a glimmer of light
What happens in this world sometimes is worth the fight.

Vickie Renee Jones

A Mothers Soliloquy

Silently I peek into her room;
The light is dim, coming in from the moon.
Gently I stroll over to her side;
Gazing through the covers where she sometimes hides.
Watching her chest rising and falling with the nights air,
I say a short prayer while she lies there.
Then, tiptoeing to the door-
I wonder,
Could I ever want for anything more?

Wendy Ungari

Reflections

My life is but a remnant of time;
The long attachment I once had is now
An unlit flame; the branch which gave me life
Lies barren in the snow. No longer will
I wave my banner in the air or feel
The wind uplift my soul, nor will I gaze
Into another early dawn - for time
Suspends my glory in the waiting skies.
Released in silence through infinity,
I'll journey from this realm and find myself
A silhouette against the sky; amidst
A tapestry of woven threads, casting
Shadows far beyond, to a land of
Endless beauty to greet the morning sun.

Rebecca I. Bratcher

Springtime Optimism

A bomb explodes under the Yucca flats
The loony world is controlled by rats.
But optimism rules the earthly scene
As baseball fields turn emerald green.

Marcos and family con Philippines of billions.
Taking art, many pesos and shoes worth millions.
But spring is here for one and all
As youth comes forth with bat and ball.

Nicaragua is in a state of constant strife
In El Salvador the poor are destitute for life.
But look out the window! It is clear
Children have gathered with baseball gear.

Saddam takes control of the Persian Gulf
'Til the U.N. sanctions said, "'tis enough".
But throughout the land with catcher's mitt
Hordes of small fry learn how to spit.

Everywhere the human race fines added stress
Man battles man from Seoul to Budapest.
But out there only optimism is the call
As burly, blue clad umpires shout, "PLAY BALL".

Wayne Stenson

Of Things Great And Small

The whole word turns for the Lord watches over
The man in the city, the bees in the clover
He watches and thinks of the day He shall reign
To make good His promise, reap the worth of His pain
And reject as some do we must wonder why
He should even be bothered to hurt and to cry
Yet as the pages of ages slowly turn over
He still watches over the bees in the clover.
And tho many high minded man may say
My God's too great and tall to be bothered by
A creature so insignificant and small
But as for me I say He is my savior and my God
And the toil His little bees endure
Produce such sweet reward
Which is why I am convinced
And I will say it over and over
He's watching you and me and His honey bee
And even all His clover
His little bees are in the clover
Still pulling honey from the clover

Rick J. Yoder

"Happiness For Me"

A postponed test, having exact change, a fluffy new towel,
The one rose that lives much longer than the other eleven,
An accidental hair-do that looks great, Rosewood Silk lipstick
from Clarion, waking up to the sound of rain on my window,
falling asleep to the sound of rain on my window, finding
money in my pocket that I didn't know was there...

Shaving my legs without leaving an entire section unshaven,
Shaving my legs without cutting myself every five seconds,
The first day of school, the last day of school, drinking a
cold glass of water after having taken a hot shower,
finding the other sock in the dryer, having someone to think about,
having someone to think about me, the remote control, flipping
the channels and finding something that I actually want to watch,
ShoeBox Greetings, canvas Keds...

The smell of fresh brewed coffee, a black turtleneck sweater,
Wintergreen Lifesavers, carpeting, inhaling helium from a
balloon and talking like one of the chipmunks, popping those
little air filled plastic bubbles that come in boxes marked
FRAGILE, hearing the Star Spangled Banner while in a foreign
country.

Sandra P. Bazzarelli

Cry For The Children

Cry for the child with no one who cares.
The pain and sadness no one shares.
Cry, cry for the children.

Cry for the child with spirits so down
Seldom a smile but always a frown.
Cry, cry for the children.

Cry for the child always abused
The parents need help but always refuse.
Cry, cry for the children.

Cry for the child out walking the streets
Always hungry no shoes on his feet.
Cry, cry for the children.

Cry for this child, this child now grown.
Still hungry so down, abused and alone.
Cry, cry for the children.

Sheila E. Bohall

Dance Macabre

An actor on the stage, in my mind;
The powerful play, a performance in time.
Endless audience of dull stares,
Reflecting apathy from uninspired glares.
Curtains part revealing a child.
Abandoned orphan spirit, fallen victim beguiled.
Dying in the spotlight, I see,
Our ancient inspiration in mock soliloquy.
Final breath, delivered applause,
Conquered child spirit acquiescent to thoughts
Of mortal dreams and immortal fears,
Imprisoned by our pride, escaping in our tears.
Tragic is our program, "the dance macabre", you'd say.
An orchestra of madness, your requiem we play.

Shannon Petrick

Pretty Christmas Tree

There once was a pretty Christmas tree
The prettiest one I ever did see.
When Santa came through the
    snow so white,
He saw the Christmas tree so bright
And when the Angels came through
    the sky a snowing,
They saw the Christmas Tree aglowing
Then I looked on the living room floor
And saw presents, presents, presents galore.

Vincent J. Tutino Jr.

The Savior

Many, many years ago
The Prophets did foretell;
A Savior would appear one day,
And with men, He would dwell.

They said, "He would be the Greatest King
The world had ever known!"
Naturally, they expected Him
To sit upon a throne.

Instead, a tiny baby came,
And, as He grew in years,
He taught us how we are to live,
To conquer all our fears.

His message was a simple one,
"To love God and each other."
We did not learn our lesson well;
We often fail to love our brother!

We're all so proud, we find it hard
To admit we've been wrong in the past.
When we do, we'll find it true,
That peace will come at last!

Rosemary Radant

"Untitled"

The windswept smile of memories so far gone,
The remembrance of long torn feelings,
Forever lost to better days,
When life began anew.

Under lost keys and forgotten letters,
Amongst the torn dress and broken cups,
Next to the unpainted masterpiece and unplayed violin,
Feelings stir.

Like a flower broke at the stem,
Like a song that's never been begun,
Like a tear that's never reached the ground,
So is my love that has never come to be.

Rebecca Waldron

In the Garden of the Blind

In the garden of the blind there are no weeds.
The rose holds no greater majesty than the dandelion.

You work behind your wheelbarrow pushing another load
Of compost toward the flower beds of the front yard;
Orange and red buds of this and that are suddenly technicolor
Against the black enriched soil you've worked so hard to create.

All year we saved coffee grounds and leaves. Where once it took
A pick and axe to pierce the hardpan,
Now with just my bare fingers I can tug a strand of buttercup
With its roots tied to the volcanic center of the earth
At least that's what it feels like sometimes.

The next door neighbor and I have noticed that more and more
The yard you labor so faithfully in is a little
Tattered around the edges.

You can tell me. I can handle it. I know that
You are gradually losing your sight. And that the odors of
The garden guide your hand in your gardener's art.

When I come home from work I guess I wouldn't be surprised
To see a bouquet of dandelion, pigweed, and clover.

Roses are not all in the garden of the blind.

Teresa White

The Deceased Is Survived By

The reclining green chair, worn out.
The smell of beer from, the empty cans.
The bathroom covered in yellow, from the cigarette smoke.
The odor of cigarettes through-out, the house.
The oxygen tank and the hospital bed, left behind.
The laughter stills lingers in the air, of all the
    funny things he said.
The El Camino left in the driveway undriven.
The tears that still linger, in peoples eyes.
Remembered by all that knew him,
    loved by all that knew him,
        cried over day after day.

Tanya Ann Reinke

Daddy's Snow Flake

Snow Flake Snow Flake come to me
The snow is cold under that tree

Jump up here on Daddy's bed
Let me rub that little head

Snow Flake Snow Flake
I am for you you are for me
I will let you lick my feet

Snow Flake Snow Flake
I can see those big black eyes looking at me

Snow Flake Snow Flake
How could it be
O how much you comfort me
No one will take you from me
We are going home you see
No sickness no more pain

Snow Flake Snow Flake
Look for the light
We will go home tonight
I see a light shining so bright
Snow Flake Snow Flake home at last

Shirley A. Laux

Untitled

Standing, Waiting, Watching
The summer haze like a clouded mind,
Blurs the details of reality.
The roar of fire propels a person to his destiny.
We shall see what lies ahead beyond the realm of known horizons
The quickening pace of pounding desire
Aligned...the time it wanders
through clouded skies...hidden in disguise
Like a child alone, in a world of strangers.
All who despise the thought through him
Of a day long since gone.
To see a vision in a rippling wave...so as I've seen
Ripples never come back. They've gone to the other side.
Their point of purpose may never to be known.
A simple seed to be sown...like a tree grown,
From a thought to a temple whistling in a swift wind.
A song always played
To but a few who can but not only listen
But can hear
The song of the Soul.

Thomas M. Hall

Untitled

Stop! The moon has turned to blood,
the sun has melted,
the earth is empty, creation's dead.
But wait...
I feel footsteps of life.
Somewhere deep within my heart.
All is not lost from Judgements knife.
For look! Coming from the blaze
is a shadow of a memory
that at one time held me prisoner in a haze.
Shh...
Listen for his voice slices the stillness.
Taking hold of my sight,
he asks for forgiveness.
My eyes drown in tears of disbelief
for I have been spared. Why?
When life beside me has much to grieve.
Silence! Forget the pain of your heartache,
leave behind those painful yesterdays'
and build on this unity awake.

Shamma Pacquing

The Freeway

Driving home at twilight
the sun has nearly set.
The western sky a brilliant flamingo
its cobalt wings expanding on the distant horizon
I speed down the Freeway,
a sense of freedom I never knew washes over me
like the Ocean's cleansing tide.
I'm blinded to everything
but those white flashing lines.
The smooth concrete of the Freeway
stretches before me in a long, black ribbon.
Escaping the prison of my job,
I rush farther and farther away
from the relentless drone of faceless voices.
My eyes are focused only on that infinite ribbon.
My car and I have become one
most faithful companion
will stay true to the end of the Freeway.

Suzanne R. Brennan

Winter's Child

It's cold with a dampness.
The sun is only warm a few hours.
Fog and chill settle around the feet.
Extra fires are set .... still there is a chill.
This is the time of the Sweet Baby God's birth.
Rays of light reach with hope.
Darkest corners are warmed.
No one is alone in the night.
The Sweet Baby God is born to give hope,
To renew belief.
The darkest time is past.
Just as we are about to be too cold,
He extends his warm, new born hands to us all.
He reaches to us from every crib.
He trusts us to care for him.
Sweet Babies of God
Reborn in every infant.
Sweet Baby of God
How shall we shape you?

Ruth Chambers

Memories Of Miami

I feel her lips touching mine. Intense and hot, like
the sun on my skin. My body is filled with warmth.

I hear the ocean in the distance, waves softly break
at the shore below us. My eyes close. What a sound,
her breath next to me, I am swept away.

Reaching for her, I slowly cover her soft skin with oil.
I watch my hand glide down her back. Together, we
feel the sand that has gathered between my fingers.

As the sun sets, I open my eyes to discover something as
vast and deep as the passion I have for her and something
as blue as the eyes that will engulf her forever.

Yvette Pinazza

Jezebel

There was always a soft, flickering sparkle in her gorgeous eyes like
the sunset's last dying rays reflecting off the tranquil ocean her
friendly, compassionate smile was always glistening like fresh dew on
morning's emerald lawn I long to caress her silky smooth skin once
more I long to tenderly kiss her luscious, vintage wine
lips—passionately and let her gentle kiss intoxicate my vivid,
colorful mind if I could only hear her melodic, telephone operator
voice just one last time more than the desert craves to be touched by
the soothing, fallin' rain I crave for her healing, mystical,
magical, loving touch upon my brow she was always smiling and
illuminating my way through a sea of darkness the black wind had so
elusively taken away her last warm breath I stare coldly at the pale,
marble stone in front of my tear-stained face the dusty, engraved
scripture reads—"always smiling...Jezebel" her name is now only a
mere memory lost in the abyss of forgotten dreams I cry out her name
amidst the harmony of nightingales sweetly singing

her lively spirit still travels with me, like a shadow in the night
although I cannot see it, I know it's still there
Jezebel...I loved you
Jezebel...

Thom Gladden

Spring's Love

Has there ever been a brighter day
Than to see young lovers, stroll and sway
The sun is warm, the breeze is to
Only in spring, is life anew
People laughing, birds singing
The sky's so blue
It's time for lovers, winter is through

Robert K. Tracy

Man's Life

I see your earth alive once more
The trees in bud, the birds that soar.
The time has come to bloom anew
The winters gone, the coldness too.
Just like a preview of one's life
That memories wrote its book an
    placed the pages by a brook,
that glistened with a thousand rays of
    sunshine from your heavenly gaze.
Perhaps I see in your earth
the pattern of myself.
And what lies ahead and what I've left behind.
If in my heart, I understand the birth,
    the life, the death of man —
Then in this place within my spirit,
I can truly live again.

Sandra Lee Golca

Best Friends

Why are friends so hard to find
the truthful ones
and the ones that don't lie
I guess that's because there are only few
look how long it took me to find you
we've been threw some good
and we've been throw some bad
but always made it threw hand in hand
you've been there for me
I've been there for you,
and now as we sit and look back
we can say we've made it threw
as days go by and life goes one
I know now you are one person
I can really count on though thick and thin
we've both pulled threw
even on those days neither of us knew what to do
friends are forever and hard to find
so please let's stick together
so neither of us lose our minds

Tina Marie Flynn

Untitled

"Hey, Spook! What's up, Spook?" they said,
the two last night,
who followed me.
Who followed me seven blocks
in their green pick-up truck.
"So how does it feel to be a nigger in public?" he said,
Flicking his cigarette at me,
Flicking his glaring red cigarette at me.
"SO HOW DOES IT FEEL TO BE A NIGGER IN PUBLIC
    I SAID?"
I stopped and glared and began to move on;
"Come here, nigger!
"Come here nigger, I said!"
No need to second his ignorance
so I moved on;

I have never been so
Intimidated
Insulted
Insecure
IN ALL MY LIFE.

Thomas Matos

"MAN"

I am God's creation   man
The very image of God I am
He gives me guidance and blessings
I thank him for my life's plan
He is my blessed savior my one and truly friend
Whenever I get lonely reach out for his hand
He bids me cheer and dries my tear
yet no man understands
Dammed is the man that denies God and confides in man
If I live   I'll live for him
If I die   I'll die for him
God he is
Man I am
I am the work of his precious hands
To him the glory and the praise
All honor from the whole human race
For I am God's creation   man

Rebecca Castellano

Merjeme

Her eyes do sparkle like the North star at night,
The way she moves keeps the blue skies bright.
And within her heart a treasure of gold,
The pureness of which can never be sold.
She has the hair of the leaves of September,
Her loving touch is gentle and tender.
The taste of her lips are sweet and not tart.
Her beautiful face is a true work of art.
The sound of her voice is like song to the ear.
The strength of her soul will shield me from fear.
Now she appears like a shot in the sky,
Much do I miss to be, the love in her eye.

Rob Duffy Jr.

Sound And Silence

The Roaring of the water, as it Crashes against the shore,
The Whisper of a raindrop, as it falls against the door.

The Thunder of the Cannon, as it belches out the flame,
The Ripple of a brook, as it murmurs out your name.

The Flashing bolt of lightning, as it shoots across the sky,
The Silent sound of time, as it quietly moves by.

And when these things are happening, just where are you my friend,
Amid the Glory of the rainbow, or some dark and dreary end?

If you'll turn your Life on over, to your God who is above,
Then the Roaring and the Thunder and the Lightning filled with love,

Will echo forth your Blessings, to all who care to hear,
And open up a Heart, which might never dare to hear,

The Whisper, Ripple, Murmur, of a Happy Soul so Sweet,
As it moves between the spans of Time, to rest at our Lord's feet.

And say, Oh' take me Master, I'm Yours, I'm Yours today.
Until The Angels call me, on that Not so Final Day...

William K. Sherman

Peace

The sea washes green the rocks
The sun, blue the sky
A tired hand and heavy heart
A worried mind speaks in each crest
And breaks against the stony cliffs

But heart and mind are troubles no more
As on the sleepless banks I lie,
Hidden on the shore
The white sand sun-bleached, before me lie
The sea rushes out to where it meets the sky

Robert A. Mills

Snowman

Pine was the perfume this cold winter's night
the wind was the music that howled for the light
and one stood alone in his torment and ruins
and watched as the stars did hatch from cocoons.

The old man recalls when his thoughts were like doves
and they'd soar in their joy over so many loves
but nothing is fair in the overall mass
for the pain in his heart is just frail broken glass.

Now the rocking chair ghosts sit so very close by
and wait for a hint of a tear in his eye
and he sips at his tea and remembers his wife
of the wonderful years that she shared her life.

Takes a step, maybe two with the help of his cane
still vows to himself that he won't go insane
and he'll settle in bed and does not invite dreams
for the walk of the Snowman is not as it seems.

For he is the Snowman that he made as a boy
and the first sign of sunlight can only destroy
but close your eyes, this death is brief
the child deep inside you shall carry your grief.

Ronald P. Levy

Let Me Talk To You!

Let me talk to you, for a minute or two.
The words I'm throwing down, they're desperately true.

You've got this life to live see, and that ain't all.
If you don't take a stand, you will definitely fall.

Check yourself out, take a look in the mirror.
The changes in you become clearer and clearer.

Don't you love yourself, God I hope you do,
cause if you don't, your whole life is through.

Stop you all, think for awhile,
What you're doing for yourself, it'll sure enough make you smile.

What are drugs, but a stupid false illusion.
They will mess up your life, bring it to a quick conclusion.

How can you love anyone else,
When you're walking with a zombie with your life on the shelf.

This is not you, you know that too.
So clean up your life, it's the best you can do, for you!

Tyrone Heim Sr.

Fool's Eternity

Did you ever write your feelings so
The world could know
How lonely alone is
Or want people to say how smart
Alone is ... and how much they need me?

Life is people and people are together love
Isn't that what we are looking for ...
isn't that what I am?

Yet, like the sun each day I send forth
My rays or warmth to everyone, but still
I'm alone in the sky ....
Each evening I hide on the other side of
Mother earth wishing I could share the
Romance of the moonlight.
I wish.... I wish .... wishing ....
How can you blot out the sun? .... alone....
What are the stars, where are the stars?
Me?

Roy Larioni

Angel's Wings

I once floated on Angel's Wing's
Their voices in splendor unison sings
Graceful in a downward flow
We drifted to the Earth below

We drifted downward graceful flowing
The mighty DOVE, He is all knowing
He knew exactly what I needed
And for my soul He strongly pleaded

My mind was not so clear you see
Yet the DOVE watched over me
A HAND reached out from within the clouds
And wrapped me in a safety shroud

Then gently on the Earth I sat
Feelings of Love and warmth from all around begat
I live and breathe because HE cared
And sent Angels where no human dared

Sandra Evelyn Thompson

Poem to A

When you're tired of being sick of me
Then I could see you which means I could be with you
Still asking myself why do I care
From Germany to L.A - from England to K.C. to L.A.
Found your way into my heart
Shards of glass - a mass of reactions looking for satisfactions
Searching in all directions for the switch that turns you on
Telling truths I wish were lies
Settling for a kiss when I prayed for so much more
Kicking down the door of resistance
Your laughing eyes and smile take me to where you've been
Your voice surrounds me like a glove
When I find your fancy - I'll tickle it love
Finally starting to understand why I care
Even though what I need is not always there
I swear to the heavens above don't need a push or a shove
Daring me to show I care enough for you
Not wanting too much too soon
Falling down drunk letting go of the trunk
That held everything we were

Terry Dawson

Just So I Could Be With You

If angels are allowed to roam on land,
Then that was you, floating upon the sand.

If angels are seen in white and purity,
Then that was you, I saw glowing brilliantly.

As you touched the moist soil, your toes,
Would curl inside, strickened by the cold.

As you stood silent, facing the ocean,
The moonlight danced around the upon,

Your rose pedal face,
Such fullness and grace!

I saw your footprints etched so firm,
I wanted to follow them with every turn,

Just so I could be with you...
Oh! Just so I could be with you!

As I hold you upon the sunset's smile,
I wish how this could last more than a while.

But forever is how long I want to be with you.
But forever is not long enough, I always knew.

If I could capture such a picture in my grasp,
And keep it forever, for I know it will always last.

Steven Kubpatrick Mudge

Love All Over The World

Love begins in the soul,
    then travels to your heart.
Your heart pumps it to your lips,
    and to each arm some part.
Love travels to your feet,
    a little dance, with a little beat.

If we could teach LOVE across our land,
    and extend it to the land of sand.
Instead of sending arms to fight,
    we'd send flowers through the night.
The only thing that they might see,
    is the petals falling oh so free!

This world is a beautiful place to be,
    every race should cherish the land, the sea.
If hatred kills LOVE from the start,
    then the enemy reigns right in your heart.
Don't let the enemy live in your soul,
    think of LOVE and it will control.....
You, your land, and all others too,
    to live in PEACE ......what a break through!!!!

Verna Dermott

The Beauty of the Pearl

When you gather the oyster shells at the beach
There are always hundreds within easy reach.
But if you are the one of the lucky ones you will open the shell and
    find the pearl inside.
You will observe the opulent beauty of the pearl which no one can
    deny.
The rarity of finding the pearl is like my mother.
In all the world there is no other.
Her grace and inner beauty still amazes me.
She had the strength and courage to stand by her family.
To observe her from afar she probably looks like all the others.
But as I look into the empty oyster shell I think of that pearl which
    is my mother
I was one of the truly lucky ones.
When I opened my shell I knew I had won.

Regina Holton-Muller

The Night Poet

I am the Night Poet when I clean this building that I'm assigned
There are many things going on in my mind
I think about justice and I think about the poor and I think that this
job should pay more
While cleaning the sinks I'm thinking about my old friend Hal who fell
by the way-side with his old gal
Didn't he know that if he would have held on for one more day that
light would have struck him in a favorable way
As I dust I'm thinking about a child that lives around the way
You see she's having trouble everyday
She spends her nights at a gas station hose begging with a runny nose
While mopping I'm thinking about the city in which I live
You see its busy building arenas and stadiums and forgot its people to
    give
What really bothers me through Sin-tax a wine-head just gave
He doesn't have a place to stay not even a cave
Wow! its getting late I have to rush and run to get this building
    straight
I AM! The Night Poet when I clean this building that I'm assigned
There are many things that are going on in my mind
I think about justice and I think about the poor and I would like to
do a lot more

Roosevelt Smith Jr.

To Be Free

Through my window
There is much to see
The changing of seasons,
The aging of trees,
A butterfly floating,
Beautifully towards me.
An eagle soaring
so high and free these things I see,
but I cannot feel for I stand here waiting
from in my cell.

Robert D. Wagner

Lost Love

It seeps all through me, in my blood.
There is no one to help me stop this flood.
Part of me is full of this angry feeling,
The rest is hurt, a pain that fills my being.
No matter how hard I try, to kill this hold,
My soul feels empty, my body feels cold.

The pain rips through me, without rest,
Like some unholy torture, some in human test.
As my world tumbles down around my feet,
My spirit desert me, falling in defeat.
I feel hollow, empty of life in my veins.
My voice sounds shallow, echoing in my brains.

My dreams are vanishing, one by one.
My heart sinking, like the setting sun.
My entire being trembles from this pain.
My soul sheds the tears of a pouring rain.
My spirit falls from the world it shaped,
My body feels empty... My love feels raped.

Starla Bell

I Am A Masterpiece

After God made me, he threw away the mold.
There is no other person like me.
Each person is special to God, we are told.
Some people are fat, thin, short or tall, you see.

A masterpiece created by God am I
so unique and beautiful in every way.
God knows my every thoughts and acts until I die.
He is hoping that I will follow him day by day.

God gives me choices for the way I act,
things that I do, say and to see.
I have only one life to live, that is a fact.
What I decide to do with it is up to only me.

For who I am, God, I thank you
for your guidance and all you love.
I ask forgiveness for the sins that I do,
knowing that you are watching over me from above.

Sharron Maline

Memories

An amiable smile, a playful shake of a fist,
There was spirit in her that couldn't be missed.
Eyes that sparkled like dew on the grass,
A soul that was soft but occasionally crass.
With wrinkles patterned like a spider's web,
And lips from which swear words were intermittently said.
I loved her each and every wrinkle,
And her eyes with their soft twinkle.
As I looked at her for the last time,
I couldn't see the grandma that was mine.
Her soul had gone to Heaven to dwell,
And all that was left was her outer shell.

Susan Lackey

If I Were God

If I were God and this world were mine,
There would be no pain or loss of time.
No lightning or thunder or a cloudy dark day.
No need to get down on your knees to pray.

No fights or wars, no need for a gun;
Each day would be harmony, laughter, and fun.
We would all be sympathetic, with a big helping hand,
And we would spread peace and love all over the land.

We could pick our age, whether young or old.
We would have cars and jewels and wealth untold.
Our loved ones would be here, no such word as die.
We would all be happy and well satisfied.

If I were God, how confused life would be;
We must play a part in our destiny.
We need the rain and the snow on the ground;
Troubles and tears bring us closer I've found.

God gave us such wonders, just look closer and see,
That beauty surrounds us now, you don't need me.
Appreciate life and each wonderful season,
Whatever God does, He must have a reason.

Terese Heckenstaller

'Life's Sunset'

As I approach my golden years,
These things, I wish, could be,
The colors of sunset, at days end
Could linger a little longer for me.

The lilting laughter of a child
As he romps and plays with his friends,
The vibrant hues of a summer rainbow,
That follows a refreshing rain.

The sound of birds in the morning mist,
As they awaken the world, so drear,
The fragrance of flowers, outside my window,
That tells me Springtime is here.

These things that I cherish, and hold on to
Make my life happy, and enjoyable anew,
So at last, when my golden years come to a close,
I can say, "It is well, with my soul" -

Wynona McDaniel

The Cup

Is the cup half empty or half full?
These thoughts pull at the mind
The broken cross was one of these
After the black cloud of death had retreated
The cup of jewishness was half empty
But the cup of hatred for a wandering nation
Was at least near the brim

One man's ideals sent a message of destruction
Another man's dreams were turned to ashes
One man's was centered on illusion
Another man's peace was found in the furnace
But what was learned from this behavior
The broken cross is still a message of blood
But two triangles speak louder
They have a history of overcoming

Is the cup empty or half full?
Can you measure blood bones and ashes
Can they rise again and point to an answer
When the cup is poured out
There will be an answer.

Tom Bellacosa

Eternally Yours

To love, honor and cherish; in sickness and in health.
These vows we pledged each other were words of so much wealth.
So many years together, so many things we shared;
Always doing for each other to show how much we cared.

We started out just two of us and soon we added four,
A tribute to our love to live on forever more.
Our children how they love you, they talk of you each day.
So many wonderful memories-no one will ever take away.

My days are long and lonely,my nights are oh so cold.
What I wouldn't give to have your hand once more to hold.
I miss your warmth and closeness; would love to see your smile.
How I wish we could sit and talk once more-if only for a while.

So rest my loving husband; in God's arms may you sleep.
Until we meet again, your soul may He keep
And when we meet again someday, I know deep in my heart,
That you and I will never-ever be apart.

Yvonne Ortega

"Innocence"

A little girl invites her friends
They come to have some tea.
She talks so grown-up
all about what all soon will be.
It's all too clean and innocent
to every truly be.
Remember how it was then, so many years ago.
When we would sit and laugh and think,
of how it's going to be.
Then the world crashed around our heads
with a roar that all but hushed
the whispered word of innocence.
And drained our hearts of blush.

Robert A. Campoli

Kristen-At Twelve

"Thank heaven for little girls-
they grow up in the most delightful ways"
(Popular song-circa 1950)
Our Kristen at twelve is growing just right,
from "little girl" to "little lady" almost over night!
We're proud of you, darling,
Stay as sweet as you are.
With your personality shining
You're our bright rising star!
May year number twelve be full
Of love and good cheer,
Mind your studies, keep smiling,
We all love you dear!

William F. Aimone ("Grandpa")

My World

Welcome to my world.
Thanks for coming.
Here is the pain, the tears,
the lies, and the sorrow that you gave me.
It isn't much, but it's all I have.
In my world, I make nothing myself.
Except for my love, my pride,
my life and my happiness that you took from me.

I'm glad you could stay for as long as you did.
But please don't come back.
And enjoy the love, the pride, the life,
and the happiness that was once mine.

Sarah Metoxen

Guilty

Some people are just guilty until proven innocent
They need not do or say anything to be guilty
The guilty verdict simply comes with the territory
of who they are
Everyone in this doomed species knows the feeling well
Mere appearance provokes heightened anxiety in others
It is indeed a powerful presence
Some have tried to find genetic explanations to justify the
guilty until proven innocent verdict
Others tried religion to validate the all so pervasive
intolerance of otherness
Others yet attempt to neutralize this painful reality by seeking
to be other than what they are
They spend a lifetime trying to prove that they are just like
everybody else
Others have despaired
They have assumed the responsibility of proving the stereotype right
How come blackness seems to complicate life so much?
This question remains yet to be answered
Does somebody know the answer

Susan Tsambo

The Message

Seven little men dressed in gold came slowly marching out of my
soul,
They turned and looked, their eyes full of sorrow,
They said to me, maybe tomorrow.

The melody of their flutes played to and fro,
The star dust from them held a soft glow.
I stood in the shadows, saying softly, 'don't go!'

They looked at me with eyes of old, they said to me,
All that glitters is not gold! We've told you that time and again!
You remember for awhile then forget what we sent.

You'll follow that path over and over until, when, the message
Is clear and you know where you've been.

The lessons will haunt you, so you know,
But the gold you receive will be worth the blows.
For the message within holds all that glitters and glows,
And he who holds that message just smiles and knows.

They turned from my eyes with a smile on their faces,
They're flutes played softly, all the left were their traces
Of star dust and music and suits of gold, and the reason for
Being still untold.

Susan Girard

Eyes

Look into eyes there is much to see
They will tell a story of what was, will be
May be sad filled with fears, tears
Might be closed to hide away the years
If they are bloodshot, swollen, or weak
Open them slowly to take a peek
When they are tired let them gently rest
So tomorrow they will see at their best
If they are glad, open wide
You may be able to see inside
When they have aged like wine, are old
I'm sure quite a story will be told
When they have seen all they can see
When they are everything that they can be
Now when you look into someone's eyes
Search for true wonder and surprise
If you know someone alone in the dark
Show them the way to open their eyes, heart
They will see the sunshine, can begin
To let the love flow from within

Suzanne Krystosek

Illusions

Those eyes, so sparkling, mesmerize my heart.
They're magical, enchanting as the sea
That comes to greet the shore then must depart
Since time began, until eternity.
Their depth reminds me of an ocean green
Where far below the bells of mermen toll,
So silent and tranquil, and yet unseen
Opaque emotions mystify my soul.
Reflections glitter as the sunlight falls
Upon them, like a glacial scape, a lake
That echoes through the scene, a quiet call...
With crystal images of love, I wake.
    From deep within illusions I arise;
    Exquisite was the nature of those eyes.

Sanober Khattak

"Wake Me I Fell Asleep"

Wake me, I fell asleep. This place I fear.
This awful place makes me weep.
This is the place I come to when I go to sleep.
A dreary place with broken promises and empty souls
covered by shattered faces in cold dark places.
I feel sick, I feel fake, it's like my soul is gone
there's nothing left to take.
Here the walls are too high, and the sounds are too thick.
The sun is Dark, the moon is bright and in the light
This bewithered man appears in my sight.
I grasp his hand and say to the man do not let yourself weep.
He tells me I am not weeping, it's just that my heart feels
so weak. Don't be afraid my friend; this is the end.
Your heart feels weak
Because we both fell asleep.
We are only sleeping.

Sharleena Antunez

I Hate

I hate, I hate the ocean wide
    this thing they call the sea
It lifts you up, it sets you down
    until you cannot see
I hate, I hate this home of mine
    This thing they call a ship
I hate it more when above the roar
    The bo'sun shouts "A Trip."
For it is then when you will see
    A sailor lad, which may be me
The food within my being rebel
    why, I really could not tell
With hands clutched to myself I run
    I seemingly to weigh A ton
A century passes, I have reached the rail
My head is reeling, I am deathly pale.

Ramon Limon

Untitled

Dear Joey,

On this Mother's Day, thought I would write a little rhyme, to mark
the passage of time.

Your jeans are much too short, haircuts you now design, clothes must
be chosen, very carefully, regardless of time, smell the cookies you
just baked, girls are fun here of late and ah, Music—you have
found.

I hope to help you, as you grow, even knowing, it means you'll too
soon go.
It's fun to watch you change Beau—please, just try to make it slow.
Why? Because I love you So!!

Rebecca Marlow

Journeys Into the Shadow Side

When I'm alone inside the dark,
—Though it floods my soul with pain,
I feel the pang of blessed peace
I've drenched with mortal rain.
Then I ponder the reasoning
Of coming full circle, and knowing
That once I reach circumference,
I am alone....again
I push their images from my mind
For inside I have changed
Their ethereal essence distracts me from my purpose
My course was preordained
Victim...am I no more
Baptized nightly with prey's own blood
I dance in the shadows of fears' own God
I am redemption's whore....

Shannon Morgan Kirby

The Journey

Our souls journey together
Through life's experiences.
Our minds function as one—soul mates:
You fit into me like a hook into an eye.
We view life together; with open eyes we face
reality.
We cast our lots on the sea of life.
We catch the view of eternity.
Like a fish hook cast into the vast sea.

Shirley M. Beard

Ocean Of Dreams

Slip with me now into Oceans of Mind
Through mystical waters, such wonders we'll find
Spiritual cleansing, we bathe in the light
Of galaxies spinning cartwheels in the night.

Vortex is forming within the Mind's Eye
It's shifting is lifting the Spirit to fly
Over illusions of matter and form
A radiant body of energy borne.

Trusting your being to Angels of Peace
We're guided to soulscapes of Passion's release
Rusting aggressions, like iron, decompose
As minerals needed to nourish the rose.

Roots are extracting their fragrance to share
From under the surface, now into the air
Such beauty created then cast on the wind
While globally holding this mem'ry within:

Everything beautiful lives in the Heart
So perfect, the balance of All from the start
Flowers and rainbows and fishes and streams
Are drawn from this Ocean of Wishes and Dreams.

Robert Walmsley

Hold Fast

Hold fast to your dreams for
they could be gone in just one blink.
Don't let go of a love that is true.
Don't turn away from the soul within you.
Don't look away from face you see in the moon.
Don't close your ears to the voice of the wind.
Don't be afraid of your life passing by you,
For we have all sinned and you will be forgiven.

Stephanie Stone

Untitled

Suffer the children, for they must endure,
Through the jungles of blood and war,
The moon bleeds white light into their eyes,
Flushed cheeks and small bodies; a clever disguise

Suffer the children, for they must stand tall,
Though like ashes, ashes, one by one they all fall,
Hear the birds sing their newly formed song,
Or is it enlightenment they knew all along,

Suffer the children, for they are all knowing,
Having to reap what their parents' been sowing,
And darkness will cut out their eyes once they're old,
To the highest bidder their souls have been sold.

Robyn Citizen

All Around Cowboy

My all around cowboy:
Throws as a loop to catch a calf,
    dallies up to hold the "little poop" fast
Bounds off his horse and down the rope in a quick five
    gently holding him down cause he need medicine to survive
Lives where there are cattle to feed and fences to ride
    every job finished with dignity and pride
Says "I'm going for a long trot to check the herd"
    just wants to be alone and not say a word
Sleeps beneath a star filled sky this Wyoming night
    thinks there's one up there with his name on it, he's right
Grins as he leaves "treat them like they were your own
    Don't break my feed truck before I get home."
Bellows out a "YAHOO" at his horse JACK and dog tip
    So they'll know he's home from his trip.
I'm trying to tell you the deepest feelings in my heart
    My friend, love, partner, hero we will never part.
You try to make me believe you never hurt by pretending to be tough
But my hero, my all around man, you are far more than
    "COWBOY" enough.

Rose Mary Gabriel

A Fairy Tale Called Reality

As we lay there together,
Time goes by as if it's been forever.
I could stay there and stare at you all day,
But then I'd feel as if I were in the way.
I love the way you show me affection and that you care,
I love the way you lay next to me and let me know
you're there.
I adore your sweet and gentle touch,
I adore everything about you so very much.
I tingle inside and feel like I'm in a fairy tale,
Or maybe on a ship that's just set sail.
Nothing like this has ever happened to me before,
But I'm not worried about that anymore.
For no one could ever make me stop feeling the way I feel,
But everything that's happened seems too good to be real.

Stephanie Hobbs

Our World

In our world today, we fear for our lives
While kids walk around carrying guns or knives
We walk down the streets hoping we wont get killed
As we painfully watch another blood be spilled
Everyday we see a new fight
Sometimes it's just the colors of black and white
In our painful and angry world today
We can only sit at home and pray
That one day we won't kill and decease
And maybe then we'll increase the peace!

Christina Halseth

"The Gift"

If there was a way I could purchase time,
    to be with you always.
I'd be the one beginning the line, with all the
    pennies I'd saved.
I'd be willing to stand for as long as it takes,
    from now until the last minute.
My place in line I'd not forsake,
    to be given that special ticket.
I'd hold up my hands with my shining treasure,
    and pray He would accept it.
"Instead", He said, "not coins, but the heart
    do I measure, and the love reflected in it."
"This special gift I give you, to share
    and hold always."
"The hands of time, nor the stillness
    of death will never part your ways."

Regina C. Whitehurst

A Man

Here stands a man so strong and agile

He looks upon himself with great pride,
to conquer all that he is after

He is forever changing like the butterfly
we all know

The proud lion he is

For he knows he is pure and bold,
as he watches over all that is before his eyes

Life is complex in his eyes
But he looks to the future, for it will be the
greatest one for him

Stephanie Kyriacou

Smiles

I really have been lucky
    to have visited far off places.
And the thing that I remember most,
    is the smiles upon the faces.

Some had teeth - some did not.
    Some reached from ear to ear.
Some were old and wrinkled.
    Some were full of cheer.

Some were pretty phony,
    but most were from the heart.
Doesn't take and expert,
    to tell the two apart.

How odd it seems, some how you see,
    when you look in a stranger's direction.
The smile you find looking back at you,
    is simply your reflection.

Robert E. Daugherty

Untitled

What do I beseech of you?
To experience the voluptuousness in the energy of your spirit
To sensually know the actuality of your carnal virtue
Beautiful creature, the smile on your lips...warm, luscious,
    alive with the light
I possess an appetite for the passionate luxuriousness of
    your angelic mouth
Permit me to taste your mouth, so pretty -
    Gently writhe in the cocoon of your embrace
    Inhale the life emanating from your body
    Touch the lush heat of your soul
If only for a fleeting wisp of infinite time -

Robin G. Perez

All I Want (From Patricia)

To hold what you have touched
To kiss where you have walked
To destroy what you have feared
And then wipe away your tears

To never let you be harmed
To hold you forever in my arms
To make love to you with sincerity
And become your fondest memory

To keep the tears from when you've wept
   in a jar below my bed
To lay my head where you have slept
   and always know just what you've dreamt

To know how sweet your mouth will taste
   before I even kiss it
And to always know what you will say or do
   before you even think it

William Jason Mashak

Feelings

How do you think it feels to be left on your own,
   to lose your spirit, your love, your heart?

How do you think it feels to believe that you've tried
   to love at your best, to feel things you've never felt?

How do you think it feels to want to be loved
   to want to love someone so much, to want forever to never end?

How do you think it feels to be empty, to be afraid,
   to want to go back in time when you were happy, and content,
   and loved?
      it hurts so much

That waking up is an effort, smiling is an effort,
   holding on is an effort, living is an effort.

How do you think it feels to know that you can't give up
   because people expect you to survive.
   that your children need you and need to know
   that life throws stones in your path and though you trip and fall,
   you must get up again?

So you try again but it still hurts.
   but one day it won't

Ronda Wolk Gulko

With Wings

With wings, I fly away in my dreams
to places no other has ever seen
With wings, I can take whomever I please
to these faraway places to make memories
With wings, I can venture into my own mind
to meet people who are part of me....
and people who I might wish to be
With wings, I can visit my Dad up in Heaven
and talk with him, it seems
if only for the while that I dream
With wings, we know joy, forget pain
and just share love forever and again
With wings, we can have our own Heaven
and enjoy being like new together
With wings, I'll always be with you and you will be with me.
With wings, though but a mortal I can fly in my dreams
With wings, I can hear the Angels as they sing
sweet songs for my ears to enjoy in my dreams
and though I awaken, quite human it seems
I know that I'll fly again in my dreams....

Robert Morris

The Perfect Stone

I went to the mountains today to take in the quiet,
To search for the peace that being in God's world can bring.
I listened to the whisper of the evergreens.
I looked into the clear, rushing stream.

As I stare into a crystal pool beside the boulder I sit upon,
Memories of my childhood slip gently into my mind.
I can see Daddy and me by a creek
Playing the skipping stone game.

How patient he was as he taught me the ways
To skip those small round stones on the glassy water.
I'd pick up this stone and then the next.
Daddy would say, "Too fat; Too heavy."

We'd laugh and inspect every small stone on the bank
Looking for the "perfect skipping stone."
Daddy could make any stone the "perfect stone"
That would jump playfully across the water.

Reality splashes cold and wet on my face
Bringing me out of my heartwarming dream.
No matter what stream or creek I find myself
I still search for the "perfect stone."

Sandra Farlow

Questions

How can a good man leave his gentle, loving, wife
To seek his pleasure, to escape the cares of life?
Does he not know the grief and anguish that he brings?
Can he not hear the song of sorrow that she sings?

How can he take a stranger's body to his own, while he
knows someone lies awake, and all alone?
And when he's finished, does he ever think, "its wrong,
I should go back to her, back home, where I belong?"

Why can't the good man see the errors of his ways?
Why can't he see, for what it is, the game he plays?
How can he take the precious moments they have shared
To other places, and just toss them in the air?

Why can't she just accept the fact that he is gone?
Convince her aching, bleeding, heart to carry on?
Why do the days turn into weeks, and months, and years?
Why do the thoughts of him still bring his wife to tears?

How can the one he left behind begin anew, and know
That somewhere there's a man who can be true?
Will questions like these ever cease to haunt the heart
Of those who sadly watch their marriage fall apart?

Sharon Rose

Just An Old White Stone

Three went out for an afternoon walk
'Twas a good chance for fresh air and talk
Two were only youthful lads
The other a stately granddad
They noticed on the ground a gleam that shone
One said, "It's nothing, just an old white stone."
But the patriarch of the three knelt down
On his face you could see a somber frown
"Don't ever call this just an old white stone!
For under this slab lies a brave man's bones
He gave his best, yes even his life
To protect us here from war's dread strife
Though forgotten his grave may be
He's still a great hero to folks like me
If it wasn't for this old white stone
Freedom would have flickered and its last light shone."
The three stooped down to clear the weeds
A hero should be remembered for his deeds.

Thomas W. Vann

449

Light Of Day

It is — 'In'
To tell all
Open the closets

Don't worry about — repercussions
Just shed some light
Then stand back gleefully
Let the shadows scatter

Hesitation - Thought - Consideration - only interferes
The investigation is what's important
If you are an impediment
Are you hiding something — Innocence?
I decry your sentence — Guilty?

The tabloids hunt innuendo
Gossip gloats, bloated jealousy
Passersby warm their ears
Heated by the passion

Mar the story
No! Not I
Truth only confuses

S. J. Bailey

"God's Will"

DEAR God - all the people in the world should pray.
To Thank You-for ending the war this way.
YOU know what's right for each of us,
YOU'RE OUR GOD - and YOU - we trust.

Some Forgot - that YOU ARE GOD, and wanted just to rule the crowd.
YOU gave them Time and Watched them so,
When YOU stepped in-they had to go.

Wars are Bitter, Bloody and Sad,
It's a pity the Good have to pay for the bad,
Let's pray for our Dead in this Great Fight.
They paid the Supreme Price for what is right.

Praying to YOU-I know all do, praying is what-we all should do.
But now Dear God-there are lots who pray,
and try to cause trouble in their small way.

Some say, "I'm mighty fine-I pray to god all the time."
They should stop and Think "Are they in line?"
Are these prayers from my heart-not from my mind?

I'm sure all the people want to pray,
We got to Thank You God-EVERY DAY. Don't forget We licked the Foe-
But - it was GOD'S WILL for us - to strike the mighty BLOW

Sue Dicker

My Twilight Years

I sit and I ponder in my
twilight years,
Where have they gone, where are the
tears,
Was I too happy, or was I too sad,
did I do good or did I do bad,
I sit and I ponder in my
twilight years.
Was I caring and daring, was I helpful
and gay, did I stop, did I listen to
what folks had to say, I sit and I
ponder in my twilight years.
Casting aside all moments of fear, to
face the future, to be unafraid, my
debt to Society will finally be paid,
As I sit and I ponder my
twilight years.

Virginia Warner

To Play In The Sand

I remember when it was a big deal to play in the sand.
To walk the beach barefoot...,
As a child hand-in hand;
Forever on the escape from the sandman.

I remember when it was a big deal play in the sand.
As an adolescent with hands free...,
Watching footprints vanish as if not even present.
Timing and changing with the waves,
Influenced the tides, and waving to its authors.

I remember when it was deal to play in the sand.
As an adult hand-in-hand, hand in hand and hand-in-hand again...
Courting time and polishing the hourglass, watching the sands of time.
In an Out..., Over and Over..., Time and Time again...

I remember and now realize it is a gift to play in the sand.
To play in the sand is to play with time itself.
Loose, granular, gritty particles, finer than gravel, and courser than dust.
A part of all of us, worn and disintegrated from rock.
I sense sand an intrinsic part of all the elements, the past,
the present and the future.
And I wonder, if these sands are really numbered,
Which are the ones that make up our lives.

Thomas M. Phillip

Darkness Through The Eyes

As we travel through the depths of
today and the hours of tomorrow,
We look through tangled and twisted eyes forever.
The hair falls down in the face to
protect from the horrid evil we face together.
People wonder if it can see
yes it can see, but doesn't want to.
People look but cannot see
the face, the face of evil, of Death
Only she, and it is she who knows
it is coming soon maybe for her.
She lives this nightmare every day and night.
She wants to take it away, she wants to feel
free and safe, but in this terrible world only
she faces the darkness and only she can see it.
She lies awake at night maybe for hours she
knows it's watching her from below and waiting for
her to make her move, it thinks it will win. It
might, maybe good won't overpower evil this time.
Only time will tell.

Tiffany Weidman

Today

Today was ours,
Together we faced the wind and rode the clouds of our
imagination through the boundless skies,
Together we laughed as the sun warmed us with its gold,
We heard natures symphony surrounding us,
We walked on a carpet of green,
Sat and listened to time standing still,
For a few moments today...
All the world stopped as we tasted life's sweetness,
Hands entwined,
Hearts touched,
Eyes spoke as souls met,
Today... was a day well lived... and I'm looking forward
to another today.

Sarah Dianne Collins

How She Loved Me!!

She read me stories and sang to me her very special song. She always
   told me were I belonged.

I loved her dear as far as I can remember. She took a picture of me
   my first day of school in September.

Always so happy, her eyes always dry, until the day I saw her cry.
I did not quite understand, then she told me as she held my hand.

She told me she would not always be there. Just the thought I
   could hardly bare. Now I am older and I know why...
   My heart broke and I began to cry.

All of her love I know I will miss. Then on her cheek I left a kiss.
   Sarah Czajka

"Our Time"

No fault, we had no choice, our lives took different directions,
Too much planted to uproot, too many wrongs to make corrections.
Friends passing in the day, while quietly loving you nitely,
Knowing we had to let go, just made us hold on more tightly.
Here we are, back to normal, our lives go on, it seems,
While you're locked away in my heart; in my thoughts, my hopes,
   my dreams.
We still have our special places, though we no longer have our time,
So sometimes I go there alone, to keep us fresh on my mind.
We still have all our songs, though no more moonlite dances,
I play them sometimes and hope; while knowing how slim the chance is
In truth we still have us, though time would not let us be,
'Cause I've kept so much of you, and with you is so much of me.
We still have all our memories, planted so deeply within,
And we still have all our love - if our time ever comes again.
   William Rice III

"Once Touched"

I've been down the road,
Traveled a few miles,
Seen worlds afar,
Age causes no trouble for the memories,
Once I was loved,
Several times I loved,
Many times I shared love,
Only once, "Once Touched"
I've seen sights of the past
I thought of future dreams
I've given ideas of life,
The time I've had and the time I have, give me joy
Once I give my heart,
The night and day do not part,
I give of the soul
All or not at all
Only once, "Once touched."
   Stephen L. Dean

Forever More

It seems I'm lost inside my heart.
True love is keeping us apart.
I thought I was in love once again.
But I know how he's just a friend.
I fell in love or so I thought.
My mixed emotions are now so lost.
I had true love like the story books say
but the fool in me let it slip away.
I had it all in the palm of my hand.
True love means forever but mine had to end.
I say goodbye as you walk out the door.
I'll remember our love forever more.
   Shawna Lipper

Crying

Tears that fall from an angelic face,
trying to wash away
the sadness and fear of a broken heart,
like rain from the heavens
that try to wash away
the unwanted dirt and filth.
   I realize he does not love me anymore,
as my wet face glistens in the sun,
like a frosty pool on a spring day.
   Looking out, everything is foggy and misty,
like walking through clouds
that have come down to earth.
   Forgiving and accepting, I stop.
   Relief washes over me like a wave.
   People notice that I'm over him,
as I become happier and friendlier.
   I'm ready for, and wondering
what the next,
mysterious day will bring.
   Rachel Strom

Two Souls

Two souls walking in darkness,
Two souls fighting the pain.
In love they found themselves beaten,
In strength they are one and the same.

As friends they found oneness, compassion
and light.
And for this above all they are willing
to fight.
Their eyes are like windows that can see
thru the blind,
Two souls that have found they are one
of a kind.
The words go unsaid but the feelings
are there,
Two souls that have found there is
someone who cares.......
   Wendy Pacheco

My First Hunt

Into the woods I silently walked
Up the ladder into the chair
My first successful hunt I sought
Hunched down in my seat and started to stare.
Through the trees came the early morning sun
Slowly moving, away goes the fog.
Through the piercing light I loaded my gun
To see two squirrels playing on a log.
As the dew began to glimmer and glisten
Gently raising my gun what did I hear.
Waiting patiently I continued to listen
What I heard just might be a deer.
It seemed time had flown by as I was ready to depart
When I saw the deer and slowly aimed for his heart.
   Timothy Jason Iannarino

Roots

Lost in a field, so wild and free
Trying to grasp onto reality
Darkness caged it as a result of weed
Until a light shined on that seed

A beautiful flower then rose from the soil
The scent so extraordinary, never to spoil.
Even though storms have come, it won't die -
The roots only grow deeper as time goes by.
   Shannon Rhodes Kloek

The World

Hunger, pestilence, fighting and war,
Violence is rising, do you know the score?

Pollution is destruction of our environment
Big companies don't care, it's less money they've spent.

Ecology should be there on every bodies mind,
There's only one earth, not another we'll find.

This is your world, this is my world, this is our world,
   This is the world

Economic recovery will not be in sight,
Our banks are now dying, while their presidents take flight.

Jesus is coming, so you'd better repent,
Take heed of these words, for they are heaven sent.
The beast will head us toward total genocide
In a nuclear war there's no place to hide

Promiscuity is still one the rise,
Aids is the virus that plans your demise.

Rodger H. Keeling

Hymn Of The Eagle

Living flight on sunlit currents,
   Wafted serenely into blue skies.
Piercing orbs that scan horizons,
   Master of the crags am I.

Miles of earth range out beneath me,
   With sparkling stream and turning road.
Encountered by the incessant ocean,
   Flaunting sequinned waves of white and gold.

Kingdoms sprawling lush with verdure,
   I reach and withdraw as I please.
Heedful, not too long to tarry,
   Lest night's shadows still the breeze.

Of all creatures noble and mighty,
   I am blessed beyond compare.
Stolid in my lefty eyrie,
   Where the winds sing, I am there.

Monarch of preeminent summits
   Fearless rapture of land and sea.
Regard my dance upon the sunbeams
   As grateful rejoicing that I am free.

Zane R. Bollom

My Eternal Love

I'm sitting here all alone,
waiting to hear the ring of my phone.
All I can hear are the voices in my head,
telling me to love someone else instead.
I try to listen, it's hard to do.
All I can do is keep on loving you.
I wish I could stop, rid myself of the pain
get into the sunshine and out of the rain.
I know that you will never love me
so I'll walk away and leave you be.
Maybe I'll see you again someday
and you will regret not loving me in some way
I'm leaving now, don't say goodbye
I won't look back because I don't want to cry.
I'm leaving you with a few thoughts in mind
you were the best love I could ever find.
I'll love you always and forever
but forget you "my eternal love", never.

Trina Koep

To Get To Tomorrow

Sometimes you have to do things you don't
want to, sometimes you have to say things you
don't want to, But the hardest is to remember
something you don't want to, Maybe the shock and
hurt of the strike of the hand, Maybe the harsh
words said, but why you don't understand, Maybe
the blow to the ribs that leave you no breath
Maybe the cut that once lead you to and back from
death. Sometimes it takes love to get through
things, Sometimes it takes hate to get through things
But sometimes it takes a different personality
to get through things. Maybe the meanness of the strong
to get past the pain Maybe the laughter of the happy
to keep sane, Maybe the sound of the silence to get past
the sorrow Maybe the words of the strong
to give tomorrow. Sometimes life can be sad, painful,
wrong But to get to tomorrow we have to have
courage, we have to be strong.

Tabitha Lucero

Wondering

Always in search of one to care,
Wanting someone's life to share.
Always the fear never again,
Always hoping but wondering when.

Is there hope beyond despair?
Desolate thoughts are always there.
Living lonely wondering why,
Is there more than a tear or sigh?

Trying to function and hide what you feel,
Envying those that have what's real.
Living on memories of times that were,
Long time passed and only a blur.

Having a heart that longs to know,
The joys it lost long ago.
Always pondering what you feel,
Always searching for what is real.

Happiness seems so far away,
Always wondering is it today?
Is there a time when God will send,
An answer to this journey's end?

Sharon Reisedge

Visions Through A Needle's Eye

Man speaks in many tongues, but how often is he heard?
War: Flaming masses of matter suddenly destroyed
The shrill blasting of an instant killer
   The loud cries of hate and
   the soft cries of peace
Scheming plans and devious minds plot sudden death
The sharp echoing blast of an air raid siren
Bombs that explode to slash the body in two
Heated peace talks in a neutral town.
War! Peace! Are the words that present a new obstacle.
Disagreement is an action that dispels the solitude of a nation
When will war cease? is the question
The answer? Man must first learn to live with himself.

Terry Skowronski

The Oak

My brother has a coat of red
My sister's coat is gold
Hurry, Lord, and paint me too
You've painted all the sky a blue
The grass a lovely green, I see
What color painteth thou me?

Wilma Ray Luster

An Eternal Dream

An Eternal Dream is being alone,
Warned by the sun
Yet cooled by a passing breeze.
Alone is love.
Love within the self.
Solitude is but self transformation
The change of one mental body to another.

If one chooses to live,
Live by the rules of alone,
Then one must die alone
And not a signal stone,
Must tell where they lie.
And forevermore
The soul within
Will live in
An Eternal Dream.

Nicole M. Shammas

War Cry

The still calm of the cold winter morning
   was shattered by the loud concussions of cannon fire,
   as death and destruction rained down upon our
   once peaceful village, the revile of charge could
   be heard over the cries of our wounded and dying
   as your pony soldiers washed through our village
   like a wave of death...killing indiscriminately,
No war cry was cried forth from our people nor one
   weapon raised in defense, ours was not a village
   of warriors...it was a defenseless village of
   women, children and old men, gone were our warriors,
   slain in battle by the blue coats, gone were our
   weapons, gone was our will...
So we died there that day, on that cold winter
   morning, as our blood drained from our bodies back
   into the land, not our sacred tribal land, but the
   land where we were forced to live...given to
   us by your government.

Walter E. Kirby II

Mama's Wood Stove

The house that I was born in
was torn down last fall.
The only thing they left behind
was a stove too worthless to haul.

Porcelain top with chrome design
I can still see the joy in mama's eyes.
When daddy brought it home that day
so proud of his surprise.

In the winter mama and her stove
got along so well.
Come summer time that stove
was some kind of hell.

That stove would get red hot and screeching
you would think it would burst at the seams.
Many a night I wake up reaching
to dry mama's brow in my dreams.

The same stove that boiled the water
Doc Brown used when I was born.
Will rust away and be forgotten
along with a way of life as we transform.

Tony Azevedo

Untitled

In the shade of the old oak tree I sat,
watching the clouds carelessly dance across the may sky.
Alone I sat, aimless thoughts crossed my mind,
all the while time was passing me by.
In my thoughts, I asked myself "Where Am I Going",
and, "What will I have for the showing"?
These questions may seem to some, a bit trife,
But are important in everyone's life.
But as it seems, one warm evening toward the end of may,
A wonderful letter happened to come my way,
Out the door all my troubles seemed to have went,
Ah, this wonderful letter, so beautiful, it was heaven sent.
As quick and refreshing as a spring shower,
Our friendship bloomed as beautifully as a flower.
As time went, our friendship blossomed into love, and I knew,
The rest of my days were to be spent loving you!!!

Tony Cirillo

Pebbles On The Shore

I took a walk along the shore tonight.
Watching the waves lap the shore and the rocks glisten in the
pale moon light.

I was touched by the extraordinary beauty of the land,
And I bent down to hold some pebbles in my hand.

I loved the beauty of each and every stone.
The more I looked the more I picked up and I could not leave one
alone.

All the pebbles, stones, or rocks were different yet very much
the same. And with my pockets tugging on my hips, I realized in that
time frame.

That people are exactly like those pebbles on the sand.
As I held those pebbles in my palm, God holds us all in his hand.

Each and everyone of us is our own special mix.
And even if we have a few scrapes or nicks,

And no matter what color black, white, or brown
God loves us all and could never put one of us down.

I smiled at the rocks I held in my hand and looked at the rest
along the sea. I closed my eyes and promised the rest I would take
them too when I returned to this place by the sea.

Sarah Volk

The Investor

Cross-legged in the sand facing shoreward,
waves lapping at his sun-warmed back,
he confronts a timeless engineering feat:
a sand castle with water-filling moat
and battlements crenelated by tiny fingers.
The engineer, Miss two-year blonde pony tail
  in brief blue suit,
digs and pats and digs again and smiles,
looks up for approbation, which he gives,
And he looks at her for approbation, which she gives
from shining eyes which tell the world
Daddy has been hers all day long.

Robert F. Hemphill

The Warmth Of Love

The quiet thoughts of two people a long time in love
  touch lightly
Like birds nesting in each other warmth
You will know them by their laughter, but to each other they
  speak mostly through their solitude
If they find themselves apart they may dream of setting
Undisturbed in each other pleasure and wrapping them self
Warmly in each other ease

Tony Rossi Jr.

Ecstasy Of Love

I feel ecstasy with the girl I love
The romance thrills and permeates my body whole
What more essence can fill my joy
The girl is ecstasy to my soul
The warmth of her body and softness too
Send calls of love stimulating my emotions
This I feel is ecstasy, because we are enjoying love.

Wycliffe E. Tyson

"My Family"

I'm so happy with my family
We all get along just dandy.
To this family, I gave birth to a son and a daughter
at two years of age-the second child came to me by his Father
of this-we all are very proud.
It's just what the Lord allowed.
Since I married his Father, our last name is the same-
To me-the thought of adoption never occurred
From that moment on-there was never a word
Into our family-He has grown, and as he has grown, a grand
daughter he has given me. A sweeter little girl. I have never known.
Who is so much like my very own. She loves Grand-ma as only a
little-one can. And thru it all-we have a plan. This son and
daughter, who were birthed by me.
She claims them as her family.- And truly they are-since she belongs
to us-of this-we make quite a fuss.
I thank the Lord-for all of this with our
Faith in Him. We can't miss.

Vera I. Urban

Life Of Their Own

   Our parents are moving and we feel bad,
We are going to miss are mom and our dad.
They have been there for us all of these years,
Now its our turn to try and hide back the tears.
Since they have raised us and we are all grown,
They are entitled to live a life of their own.
They took care of us all of this time,
How can we doubt they will be just fine?
They taught us to stand up tall and with pride
When things don't go right just take it in stride
Be kind to others and when you are thru,
Sit back and watch it will come back to you.
Take time with your children and watch them play,
Life goes by so fast they will be grown one day.
We are good people and for that we are glad,
We owe all of that to our mom and our dad.
One day when our children are grown,
We may leave to for a life of our own.
Although we will miss then and sometimes feel sad,
We wish only the best for our mom and our dad.

Sherry A. Helton

One's Injustice

We are the ones who've seen the morrow,
we are the ones who dream of the day,
we are the ones who've felt the sorrow,
and we understand the pain.
We are the ones you say will lead the future,
we are the ones who learn today,
we are the ones who suffer your selfishness,
we are the ones to pay.
Just remember we are always watching and learning,
So always be weary of the day and your way.
We've seen the world today,
and understand its way.
Does that mean we are the ones who must
follow its injustice?

Sarah Weikel

High Tide

Who's watching the moon with me.
We can all see it all over the world
My past lovers I never see.
The ones I don't agree with, the ones I cannot see.
Are there ones up in the skies, whose eyes I may have wandered into.
Can I call on you with the moon lit full?
Do you know I'm watching with you?
Who's watching the moon with me?
The strength I gain when it lights up the sky compares to no feeling
   I could feel before death, when I die.
Could I see in your house,
Could I see in your eyes, I believe.
I just wish you knew we're both looking, in the same sky.
You may be far away,
A young child,
One I don't speak with,
One I may not know,
But if for a second could we meet there and be free...
Are you, are you watching the moon with me...

Shannon C. Shimer

Jennifer

Jennifer is my best friend. We met four years ago.
We had two seats together. That's how we began to grow.
We did sorts of things together,
until the year I moved.
My school was changed, and so was hers.
We were in an awkward mood.
Yet we're still in touch with phone calls and notes,
until one year came to approach.
It was her turn to move away,
to St. Charles she fled today.
But in despair, we kept together,
we're best friends forever and ever.

Tiffanie Kroll

The Gathering

   We all came together on a bright sunny day
We kissed and we hugged and had so much to say
   For some of the travelers, the trip had been slow
What with traffic delays and much stop and go
   But the effort was worth it, because at trip's end
Was a special welcome for those who would attend
   Friends and family joined in the fun
And joined in the laughter as the good times begun
   Happy times were remembered and relived once more
This times they seemed funnier than ever before
   Some people sat and chattered, water sports attracted some
New stories were created for reunions yet to come
   And as the gathering came to a close and some started to depart
The mood became quite somber, with a pulling on the heart
The thing that brought us all together, that bond that we call love
   Was given a special blessing by our family up above
      For the young and the old we bade goodby
         as they went along their way
      God bless you all and keep in touch
         'til next we meet one day

Sheila Rooney

"A Child's Growth"

A flower is like a child's growth
needing warmth
surrounding
and flow
A flower is like a child's growth

Rob Hernandez

Sea Power

The majestic ship sets sail
We leave our loved ones behind
We patrol the high sea
In hopes to keep our children free

Our ship mimics the predator
Stealthily stalking any prey it may find
Upon locating a worthy subject
All sensors are focused on conquering the inferior beast

When everything seems peaceful alarms sound
Personnel scramble like frightened mice
Guns are brought to bear
Missiles point skyward taunting those who dare

As we approach the enemy
Strategies and weaknesses are analyzed
The strike focuses on all vital organs
The attack is quick and fierce

When the smoke clears
Only the worthy will come back to fight another day
The defeated will be mocked
In an unselfish way.

Ray Roberge

"Feeling All Alone"

As my husband and I sit on our deck in the swing.
We listen to the beautiful birds sing.
Over looking the mountains, and the trees,
Enjoying the beautiful country breeze.
Things are quiet, peaceful, and still, as my
husband and I sit in our new house we
built on the hill.
No sound of airplanes, trucks or trains,
as we set on the deck in the swing.
We get sad, and feel all along,
While our children, and grand children
live for away in their own home.
But we always keep in touch, because
We love, and miss them so much,
Some day we all hope to be together again,
When God calls us all home at the end.

Virginia C. Bolton

The Esther Bible Class

We're eighteen in number and hope to have more.
  We probably will, it's almost '94.
Our Sunday School Teacher is Clara, by name.
  She's such a good teacher, we adore her fame.
We gave her a new Bible for a birthday gift.
  She was so happy, it gave her a lift!
Some have gray hair, some are blondes, some brunettes.
  We only have one auburn as yet.
They're all dressed so pretty in blues, greens, and pink.
  If you watch closely, they might give you a wink.
Some have had surgery recently, one is handicapped.
  But we don't worry. One even needs a wrap.
If a member is in need of hospital care,
  We buy them slippers or a robe to wear.
We love to help others who are in need,
  Like the couple in Addis with twin boys, indeed!
We send greeting cards to the sick and the sad.
  It makes them feel good when they're feeling bad.
We meet once a quarter, a covered dish we all bring.
  And we have a good time! Sometimes we even sing.

Stella Diez

Lasting Treasures

   I prayed the Lord world give me treasures and a little wealth, I would not mind.

   He gave me riches far unmeasured, more of a lasting kind.

   He gave me strength throughout the day, and gave me wisdom to know the way.

   He gave me the sunrise in a quiet way; its beauty gave me hope for a fresh new day.

   He gave me the moon in the darkened sky, and the twinkling stars which catch my eye.

   He gave me His Son to die for me, and opened my eyes for me to see.

   He gave me happiness in all things, and gave me joy as the birds sing.

   He gave me so many treasures still untold, he gave to us all, for us to hold.

   Don't look for treasures such as wealth or fame, but rather for lasting treasures that would bring no shame.

Todd Fliehman

The Diver

Five meters, ten meters, platform, spring
Weightless lovely grab the ring
Reach for sunbeams, make it clear
Why Neptune calls you His bombardier.

Guilessform, breathless moves
Let nothing go to chance
Orchestrate; your muscles croon
While you dance your airy dance

A fireball of somersaults
Ignites your show of shows
In pike position you plummet: thirsty
For the wetness just below

In like a knife, curtain down
Performance now complete
Rave reviews, standing O
No one in their seat

Breaking through the waterline
You see the judges' den
And get exactly what you deserve
Another perfect ten!

Tom Cahill

Prayer For A Parent

Where are you going?
What is it that you do?
Be careful my friend
For there is one who follows you.
His eyes filled with love
And a devotion that's true.
He can see no wrong
In anything you do.
He questions nothing in the choices you make.
The road that you travel, he will blindly take.

So measure your footsteps.
Keep your path straight and true.
That this child will find Jesus
Through the things that you do.
And if you should stumble
Or fall in great despair,
Lift your eyes, touch His hand
Feel His presence ever there.

Susan Talkington

November 4th - 13 Years

My Daddy died today.
Weren't this afternoon nor night.
'Cause it wasn't on this day,
and it wasn't on this night,
but many years ago my daddy left my sight.
But he never left my mind,
'cause Daddy was that kind.
Daddy was a man, a kind and gentle soul,
a man that touched the world with
a heart filled with gold.
A shy and sincere man who in his life did his best.
He left this world thinking he was just like the rest.
But he wasn't at all, he was special indeed!
He was truly unusual and was actually in the lead!
He was one hell of a father
and an incredible provider.
He was a good man which is a rare find today
and I spend my life ready and able to say —
I'm proud to carry on my father's way!
'Cause he was the best and a "find" any day!

Robbie Daly

To My Son

Tiny little bundle, soft and precious wonder
What a blessed joy you are to me
Baby teeth and first words, toddling steps get bigger
Laughter as I bounce you on my knee
Growing fast, fast from me

Insects in your pockets, dirty face and fingers
Muddy sneakers in my living room
Peanut butter, jelly, triple decker sandwiches
Balls and bats, and what am I to do?
Tell me do, do with you.

Standing at the mirror, pretty girls are calling
Can't believe you washed behind your ears
Flowers for your first date, mother I can't be late
Tell me why I'm fighting back the tears
Where'd they go, all the years?

Fine and handsome young man, tall and strong when he stands
Doesn't know how glad I am to be
Proud and doting mother, trying not to smother
Thankful prayers because of what I see
Seeing, the best of me

Wanna Eugenia Richardson

To My Mother

To my mother
What can I say
I really love you in every way

From the time we were young
You never walked out
Even though you had a doubt

When it seemed the world would end
You were always there
Just like an old friend

You went without
So we could have
Now it's your turn to let the good times be had

Sometimes it was hard for you to let go
But you knew
You had to let us grow

You're mothering days will never be through
But always know
You're the best mother I ever knew

Rachel A. Johnston

Gaja

If there was only one butterfly,
what colour would you give her
Can she choose her own colour(s),
the colour of nature.

If there was only one dolphin,
In which ocean will you let it swim in.
Can he choose its own ocean, the ocean of blue water.

If there was only one horse,
which meadow can it gallop through.
Can it choose its own meadow,
the meadow of green, green grass.

But then there is only one Mother Earth,
one planet with these treasures. Can she choose her own faith
No, because her destiny lies in the hands of mankind,
some who cherish it, some who will destroy.

Tell me if I am right and don't be selfish,
make sure that you can teach your children how lucky we are,
that Mother Earth will let us live on her planet.
Because she too has her plans ready for us.
And in the end we might be destroyed by her, if not by our own hands.

Susan van Zandbeek

"Years End"

The end is near, not of my life, but of another year.
What have I done to leave a mark on everyone's that's dear.
My husband, who is everything an earthy mate could be.
I've given him extra time and more space to be free.
My children, I've shared wisdom I have gathered thru the years.
I've tried to save them heartaches by shedding of my tears.
I've kept pain hidden deep inside, so as not to give them grief.
Maybe when they are older my heart will free relief.
I pray that I've done something that I can now proclaim
I've lived, loved, learned, and shared,
this year's not been in vain.

Shirley Marsh

Hurt Is Your Friend

How can Hurt be my friend?
When all it leaves in me is a hollow space...filled with loneliness

I ask myself again, how can Hurt be a friend?
When all I feel is a draining sewage of emotional pain,
A rage that internally burns.
A dagger that is constantly piercing my heart.

Since this terminal disease accompanies me daily,
turning and twisting through every corner of my being.
I call it my companion...cause I'm still not convinced it's my friend.

A FRIEND WOULD NEVER, flee me like a thief in the night
leaving me feeling helpless and emotionally raped.
Yet...hurt! My proclaimed friend has done all of these things.

Again I Ask You Hurt, How Could You Be A Friend?

I turn inward for insight...Pain ignites a wick setting off an
   implosion
...crumbling and demoralizing ALL emotions in me.
Now! I'm faced with TRUTH and REALITY

In spite of Hurt's unorthodox methods of cleansing
I realize...Hurt has always been my friend.
If it wasn't for Hurt, I wouldn't have had the strength to change.

God! Thank you for my hurt...thank you for my pain.

Sylvia M. Wheeler

Michael

When ever I see you, I hear birds singing.
When ever I see your face, I pick up my pace.
Your voice is like the sounding sea,
Always a trail ahead of me.

I adore you in every way,
You brighten up my everyday.
You have the most beautiful eyes,
It's like the watching the sun rise.
Your smart and very wise!
I hope you like this poem
Of course it didn't take me long.
I just wanted you to know,
That I love you, and now I better go.
So, Dear Michael, I love you a lot!

Stephanie Henry

Untitled

Cold is the day and bleak the night,
When hope and faith have gone.
How dim the glow of a love that burned bright,
In a heart that was once so strong.

Gone are the visions of true happiness,
I'm the fool of yesterday's dreams.
Security has changed to heart's duress,
And nothing is quite what it seems.

What will it take for you to see,
That I am where I feel I belong.
And if you refuse to face today's reality.
Where's tomorrow's hope when it's gone?

If you are unsure of what love really means,
Closed are your eyes as well as your mind.
It has lived all around you for all of your days,
Is satisfaction so much harder to find?

I've heard of such people that live on this earth,
That are never quite satisfied.
If you can't count your blessings as your life's worth,
How can you say that you tried?

Rhonda Arvin

Seasons

There are winters of the soul,
  When the hurt goes deep inside;
Tears even refuse to roll,
  And the pain is hard to hide.

Our strength then comes in knowing,
  The winter must fade into spring;
Again a time, for growing,
  Again our hearts will sing.

As from bud to full-blown flower we go,
  Showing forth all God's beauty;
For to blossom and to grow,
  That is out heavenly duty.

And when the leaves that once were green,
  Have turned to autumn's gold;
God's beauty can still be seen,
  'Tis there for all to behold.

So it matters not the season,
  Winter, Summer, Spring or Fall;
I will not wonder or reason,
  Just look for God's hand thru it all.

Ruth Daehler

Love In Still Waters

Why bind our hands without faith,
When the shadows of angels knock upon our door?
Blindly rebuke the hate and discern the fear,
For prevailing love shall divinely endure.

My sanity is not of substance, but of moral,
Leading any doubt into the anguish of confusion,
Behold my love from the debts of my soul,
I fall upon my knees hailed by emotional illusion.

Dimness is a late breeze calmed by her essence,
I dwell in the untold stories of hopeless pain,
Patient deliberate thoughts of a life beyond her,
Seemingly cast from my heart by the thunderous rain.

The sea's endless shore accounts for my ambitious love,
Overtaken is my soul by her passion unbound,
Honor from our God touches each wind,
These dimensions trusted by oceans unwound.

Destiny is our path in bondage with heaven,
Her souls vast landscape flourishes every breath,
The sword of God glorifies our love forever,
Which I shall pursue until my sensual death.

Scott Michael Brignac

Thoughts of You and Me

It does not seem like that long ago
when your eyes met mine and we said hello
I knew it from the start
That you could be the one to break my heart
I did not care, I took the dare
Now look where we are
We've come so far
Through thick and thin good times and bad
You're the best friend I've ever had
I look back and wonder how
Then I just smile and think wow!
Dreams and prayers can come true
Mine did when I met you
How truly great life can be!
The many wonderful times
We've yet to see
I'm sure will become precious
Memories for you and me!

Thomas E. Raines

Where Are You?

When you cry, I'm there to make your tears dry.
When you're sad, I love you more, to make you glad.
When your down, I've been there to pick you up.
You've never had to ask me to care,
You've never had to ask me to love you.
I can look in your eyes, and read you like a book.
I know always what to do,
Because then I can feel only for you.

Can't I cry, and you make my tears dry.
Can't I be sad, and you love me and make me glad.
Can't I be down, just so you can pick me up.
I always have to ask you to care,
I always have to ask you to love me.
Can you look in my eyes, and read me like a book?
I want you to always know what to do.
Because then and only then,
Can you feel for only me!

Tina Turner

The Innocent One

Why was the innocent one born to me, cause
where he is at, he won't ever be free, he
lives in his own world of make believe,
where people have a chance to always deceive

Our innocent ones aren't the ones to blame,
for our everyday foolish adult, its just a game
nor should they be to blame for the games we play
with the passing of each and every day

Why are they blamed sometimes for things they may see,
cause we're all suppose to be adults, you and me,
and as they get older, and you do to, just remember
the innocent one was born to you

Now tell me why the innocent one was born to me,
Cause where he is at, he won't ever be free,
he lives in his own world of make believe,
Where people have a chance to always deceive.

Suzanne B. Patterson

Just Because They Care

My parents really care,
Where I'm going and how I'm getting there.
They buy me clothes and they buy me candy.
And when I'm lonely they're very handy.
My mother is sweet,
Like a candy treat.
My dad is bold,
That's what I've been told.
Sometimes we may fuss and fight,
But in the end things are all right.
They give me hugs anytime and anywhere...
Just because they care...
Just because they care.

Wendelene Nicole Turner

Where Sea Gulls Cry

I love a place where sea gulls cry,
where meets the glistening sea with sky,
where one can search for shells and such,
where one can feel the oceans touch!

To walk upon the whitened sand,
while clinging to a loved ones hand!
To sense the wonder of the place,
where marks of care are soon erased.

Although I know I can't be there,
I go on whispering wings of prayer,
to seashore with it's splendorous view,
which soars my faith and strength renews.

Oh maker of the sand and sea,
May I return in memory,
to where I'll glimpse the oceans foam!
To where such treasured joys I've known.

Stefanie Dawson

Echo

Beneath the cadence
  wings beat mightily.
Silently we open wide our
  arms in grim submission.
We ache for solace but yield
  mere emptiness.

Still the bellows, the golden feathers
  sparkled in the darkness of the secret.

Robyn O. Zwolinski

America - "Land Of The Free"

America is not a Communist Country
Where on else can anyone prevail?
Criminals are free to roam the streets.
Hardworking tax evaders go to jail.

You should be very proud to be working
They think you shouldn't have a care.
I don't know, I really don't like it,
Isn't there a way I could be on welfare?

To make lots of money, Be independent
Use to be the great American Dream
Now it's to sit home, eat all day,
And watch Oprah on the TV screen.

Is there any hope for America?
Do you think it can be saved?
I doubt it, I'd write forever
If I was only getting paid.

Our forefathers came to this country
Plans of hard work as they crossed the sea
200 years later, people still come
With a new meaning of "Land of the Free"

William J. Florio Jr.

Peace

A place where peace is found
Where the earth begins to descend
Under the depths of the earth's reflection
A place of rock and sand

You are able to look on forever
And feel the breeze come in
It greets you with a clap of foam
And a sudden spray to cleanse in

The eye reflects upon the motion of the water
And notices the grace of the sky
The two sending messages of a delightful day
One to share with you and I

As the sunlight whispers a sweet good bye
To visit another land
The colored horizon insures her return
For our face to grin and mind to expand

I found peace!

Timothy A. Mills

Funeral Day

A tear rolls down from another loved one's eye,
while I keep all my pain bottled up inside.
I stand quietly by not knowing what to say or do.
How can I help people so hurt and blue?
Only death comes to mind as time slowly passes by,
with all of the people questioning why.
I guess It's true that the good must go first,
leaving me here with the rest of the worst.
It seems as if I attend one of these a week,
what kind of justice is God trying to seek?
As loved ones gather around to say their last goodbyes,
the casket creeps into the ground as everyone cries.
As bad as everyone dreaded this funeral day,
they know the pain and emptiness will never go away.

Rodney Chappell

Just For You Mom

Mom, how are you feeling
while I'm having trouble dealing
with the thought that you're not here
and all the times that we held dear
shown to me like a play
on a not so glorious day
I once thought you'd be back
to help me fix what I lack
then when all of us kids where gone
You'd still be there forever on
it sounds silly but its true
I never though death could happen to you
But after all is said and done,
We'll go back to having fun.
But every night before I sleep
Your memory, in my mind, I will keep
And one day when I'm old and grey,
I will see you every day.
Cause even when the body dies,
the spirit will always fly!

Shelly Ames

Little One

The first felt utterance of you, new within—
whispering, laughing, fluttering wings
flirt where boundaries begin.

Later, you dance silently, poke out my belly's skin—
pushing, testing limits
with a hand, foot, elbow again.

At last, urged by contractions, molded by design—
forced beyond all barriers
you loudly scream outside.

Freed at last, you're just beginning.
to unlock the chains
embracing your identity
where freedom truly reigns.

Like before, you'll still explore
with whispers, laughs, dances, cries—
I hope you don't stray
too far away, Little One,

To find your happiness
inside.

Tam E. Polzer

Jasmine

An angel in disguise
Who has fallen from the skies
One who has changed me with her innocence and beauty
A love of a father for his child has no boundaries
She makes me laugh when I'm down and shed
tears of joy
Unavailing in my attempt to determine my
life without her
Welcoming fate with this new millennium
With her debut came ever lasting
sunshine
An indelible fixture in my heart
Trying to provide an impervious wall of
protection from the world
Knowing it is an exercise in futility
I have only to pray
For there are answers for some nemesis
I'm sure she'll be strong
And my God will watch over
My daughter, my love, my Jasmine

Ricardo Vaughn

Looking Glass

Into the looking glass I stare.
Who is this lady with the long chestnut hair?
Dark eyes and freckles on her nose. Who is she
do you suppose?
Laugh lines appear when she grins.
She really looks familiar, but then different.
I imagine years of love on this face. A warm
wisdom that comes with time. I guess it's called Grace.
Tranquility, strength, and kindness balanced
perfectly on a face that's blessed.

NOW I KNOW.

Only one person it could be.
It's my mother's face I see, in my looking
glass looking back at me.

Tammy M. Jumpp

Ballad of Josh Cole

Josh Cole was just a kid. Josh Cole was just a kid.
Who lived a real good life, with everything he ever wanted.

15 was his age. 15 was his age. Riding out life wasn't just a phase.
A set of wheels is all he'd need, that took a lot of green.

Best sports player around. Best sports player around.
Always helping his team to succeed,
Heart is what he'd kick in and heart is all he'd need.

Trophy deer is what he got. Trophy deer is what he got.
Scouting around for the right spot sitting on the ground waiting a lot

Camp is where he could go to get away.
Camp is where he could go to get away.
That's where he was heading just the other day.
But he didn't make it all the way.

Death fed on him that day, the only way he would go.
Death fed on him that day, the only way he would go.
On his four wheeler he wiped out about halfway.
His body lay still, now it always will.

God took him away. God took him away.
An older cousin to me, and a friend.
I wish he were around to see me again.

Willy Williams

Teddy, The Tall Oak Tree

There once was a tall oak named Teddy,
Who saw a man approach him one day,
Before Teddy could ask,
What do you want from me?
The man began to cut down,
Teddy, the tall oak tree.

I am strong and still want to grow,
I have been around for hundreds of years,
As most of you know.

Indian boys and others climbed my limbs,
And I have catered to the birds and squirrels whims.
I hold moisture, help prevent floods, and purify the air,
Just the thought of someone cutting me down I just cannot bear.

I will no longer be reaching for the sky,
And if you look close, you can see me cry,
How sad to think that man can destroy me,
For I should be around for your children, too, you see.

Theodore Wyczynski

Pappaw

There is a great man
Who sits in his lazy boy every day
Always telling tales to his grandchildren
Trying to lead them in the right way
He never got mad with them around
He just smiled if they did something wrong
He said not to do it again
And then he went on
He always took them on the four-wheeler,
to play in the yard, in the beautiful
garden his wife and him had fixed up
Because they always work so hard
He always had bubble gum with him just for the kids
It didn't matter when
But he always did, I tell him I love him,
    as much as I can
Because my Pappaw is "THE GREATEST MAN".

Tara Nicole Drake

The Crossroads

Many times in life we face choices to make,
    Whose answer determines the path our life takes
We must choose our path and proceed confidently ahead,
    Debating past decisions only clouds your head.

When you reach middle age and look at your past,
    Did you reach all your goals, are you happy at last
Don't look in the mirror and start doubting,
    Life is to short and the future exciting

Live your life for yourself, not friends or loved ones,
    When you look at your life, you will know that you've won
Always think positive and do your best,
    And you will pass your personal crossroads test.

Robert B. Scearce II

When The Wind Blows My Way

When the wind blows my way,
Will I hear a child crying;
A child that was not born unto me,
Will I hear faint laughter from a child's mouth
    that I lost;
That I lost from the selfishness of myself,
When the wind blows my way,
Will I yearn for a time that could have been mine of watching
    a child grow;
To hear, see, or touch a loving face that could have been
    a special bond with me;
When the wind blows my way,
Will I die a thousand times for someone so small and sweet;
Or sigh of lost warmth that comes from the heart of content;
When the wind blows my way,
Will the rest of the world hear the tear that I shed;
Will they feel the sorrow or the hollowness that's left
    here instead,
For a life, for a life I could have spared!

Sharon Cleghorn

A Grandmother's Lament

Lord, where has she gone?
Why has everything gone wrong?
Alcoholism is such a deadly thing!
Only pain and despair can it bring
Make her see
Just what she means to me.
What has gone wrong?
Why can't my precious Granddaughter be strong?

Rose Klocke

"Christmas"

Gifts from the heart are like thoughts of gold.
Wishes on star dust, create a blanket of snow.
Songs being sung of stories that were told,
Brings together family and friends, both young and old.
Laughter of children, amazed at the sight,
Of Christmas morning, how the presents delight!
Warm, cozy homes, filled with love,
Must be the best present sent from above.
A long day of splendor remembered by the fire,
With hopes and dreams of future desires.
A time to be thankful, with this I agree.
Paul, I'm glad you are a friend to me.
I hope your holiday is filled with great cheer,
and I wish you the very best for the new year!

Susan C. Robak

The Thin, Old Man

The thin, old man walked very slowly
With a badly chipped, wooden cane.

His stiff back was always bent,
And his aged body was trembling as if he was cold,
But he was actually warm.

His thin, white hair was tangled,
And his hands and face were wrinkled and sagging.

The thick glasses that he wore on his face were crooked.
Since he didn't have teeth, he couldn't chew his food.

No doubt about it, the effects of aging
Have consumed his body like an incurable disease.

Sharon D. Person

The Undoing

The moon touched her
-with a soft, lazy caress it slid a ray deftly onto her arm
Then she was no more
On the crisp November twilights
when the trees lift their sore, fading limbs to the sky
A silhouette stands forlorn and tattered on the breadth of
the incoming night wind
It fades slowly to a dark onyx that mingles with the deep
richness of the night sky, and is no more
When the sterile breeze blows down from the farthest corner
of the north
all lies still and sleeping beneath layers of chilled ivory
A thin outline appears on the slumbering land
    Watch as the delicate fingers reach out and grasp for
    what was, and will never be again
    Then melt away to blend into the velvety undergrowth of
    time and space
Transcending the aura of life and serenity
We come to face the reality of the cycle
As it creeps up with bewitching arms flung wide

Rebecca Van De Voort

Seed of Goodness

Buried deep within
    every person's heart
Lies a seed of goodness
    that will awake with a start;
If it is watered and cared for
    with kindness and good deeds
It will spread like ivy
    reaching towards people's needs.

Stephanie Griese

The Year's of Spring

I remember well, our years of spring
With body's strong, and limb's of steel.
That crossed the field's as though on wing's
And down the road, raced spinning wheels

But mortal's change with passing year's
Plaguing some with pain and tears.
While others wince, with muscle's sore.
With slowing pace, to run no more.

No longer do we race the wind.
For us, those years have passed away.
Leaving weak and stiffened limb.
To soon, we too, shall pass away.

Freeing us from earthly harm
No longer body's tormented with pain
Then God shall open wide his arms
And lasting spring shall come again.

Reas Allen

Yesterday Gone

If there's no tomorrow why be a today;
With heartaches and sorrow and hurt all the way;
Why be a tomorrow with sadness of heart;
Why be a tomorrow without any heart;
Tomorrows should be of happiness flow;
Not of loneliness and aching of soul;
But of fulfillment of life and light shining glows;
Of cups runneth over and love's even flow;
Of sharing and giving unselfishly though;
To be given and received from the heart and the soul;
So free and so lovely no money can buy;
From Trinity come my tomorrows of life; and my cup runneth over my
light's even beam; comes from the Heavens of God's golden beam; for
today I am happy for the beauty within; for my heart and my soul are
once free again; the darkness has ended, the sunshine begins; the
beauty of life which never ends; My tomorrows will grow with wisdom
within; that is only given to me by him; my yesterdays gone but the
knowledge lives on; to help conquer my tomorrow and help each day be
won; in the battles of life that is to come; my yesterdays, todays,
and tomorrows will be won; only through God and His only Son.

Sharon J. Agee

Grandmother's Quilts

She measured, Oh, so carefully
With patterns placed just right,
Then snipped and snipped with resolute
The pieces dark and light.
In shapes of diamonds, circles too,
Triangles, hearts and flowers,

All shades of yellow, blue and red,
The process could take hours.
With blocks then placed on background "bed"
The quilting could begin,
With yards and yards of stitching
That took miles and miles of thread.
The final touch, to trim the edge
With straight or scalloped hem.
She heaved a sigh of great relief,
The project now would end.
But with weary back and idle hands,
This Grandmother didn't fret,
But stated positively,
"Next week I'll start the best one yet!"

Ruth N. Jenkins

Confidence

Carelessly his wings breastward fold,
With strength natural, yet light as a zephyr.
His feathered flippancy - hint of temperament bold-
Bright white flashes where once dark
and he cocks his head.

With bright eye he watches-intense.
An experience-wizened critic, he
flutters quickly as if startled or caught.
Felt danger leaves his senses bound taut.
He tosses into the soft-soft wind
His unhurried manner no traitor to him.

From somewhere far off my mockingbird sings,
Can he possibly know the pleasure he brings?

Theresa C. Von Plinsky

So Many

Well you're on your own and you realize you're living
with the sad intention of blood, pain and fear.

A king's on his throne with his heart laced in stitches
for he feels for lives that have been overthrown.

If all your life is cutting to the quick
open your mind and gather your wits.

So with a truth for life may the children learn
feel the full moon's rays cause the tides to turn.

So many faces, so many thoughts, so many heart's beating feeling the cost
So many within, so many without, so many like me without a doubt

If you hurt me again I just might wash up on shore
But I'm dying to see what life has in store

If this is a game I won't play by the rules
And we never keep score that's for loser and fools.

So many faces, so many thoughts, so many hearts beating feeling the cost
So many within, so many without, so many like me without a doubt

Life is not a dream, it's a dream brought to life
So brush off all the dirt and put up a fight

Take my hand, we'll head towards the light
For love and forever, we stand and unite.

Robert Bove

Reflections Of A Bittersweet 1994

As last year began 365 days ago,
With the usual Happy New Year's and Ho-Ho-Ho's;
The year unfolded as one of the most traumatic years
Seasoned well with many pains - many tears.

July and August took the biggest toll.
Oh, how much pain can wrench the soul!
Two dear people - grown close to my heart,
Took leave of this earth, one month apart.

One I called Mom and the other was Dad;
I am so thankful for the last years we had.
As I poured myself out trying to ease their pain,
A place now in Heaven they too can claim.

A sweet memory from down Mexico way;
Came September 10th - our Anniversary Day!
A strolling Mariachi band played a special tune;
As we sat on a veranda out under the moon.

As this hard year comes to an end,
I wonder what next year's weaves will blend!
Just remind me, dear Lord, when the threads come undone,
With your hand in mine, we are not two - but one!

Sara Louise Smith

You Again

I saw you again today, the woman
with you looked at you the way I did on
that warm November day.

You held her hand and you laughed together,
In my heart rain seems to be the weather.

You seem to have forgotten how I used to
hold you, and the way that we kissed when our
love was new.

Did you find in her the woman you were
looking for in me? I've tried to forget, but
somehow I know I can never let it be.

I still hear your voice through every song
on the radio, and your face is imprinted in
the sky every night when the sun is low,

You left saying we needed time to mature,
So tell me, how much have you grown up since
you've been with her?

Vicky Starling

Shadow Of Love

Crying in despair, you know that he is coming
With your fear you run an endless run,
Turning every turn, looking from side to side.
Not being able to escape, but you try,
You can hear his heartbeat;
He can smell fear.

You beg him please, please go away
I have had you once before; I do not want you again
Finally you come to a dead end,
Looking everywhere for some place to hide
Then you listen and there is nothing but silence
You say to yourself I beat him, I finally beat him.

Then you turn to go and he grabs you by surprise
Hopeless no where to go;
You lie there in his arms to die bitterly and slowly.

Vanessa Herrera

"The End"

Slowly but surely time passed us by,
without a word, without a cry.
I took advantage, how could I not see
that sooner or later you'd chose to leave me.

As I watched you turn and walk away,
I knew nothing would make you stay.
The wrong I did, the times I lied,
tragically our love has died.

The tender words I used to greet,
now seem sour, no longer sweet.
Looking back, I was wrong -
to want too much for far too long.

Now we stand so far apart,
words unspoken from the heart.
If only I could change the end,
you would be at least my friend.

Shawna Poole

A Magnificent Woman, In Memory Of

Softly, she touches my heart
    Without warning

Slowly, she begins to fill my heart
    with her love

As I gaze into her eyes, I am not aware
    that she is much more than a woman

Suddenly, she smiles and strokes me
    with her fingertips
Confidently, she knows that with her touch
    her love has entered my life

Unconsciously, I have no fear, but yet
    I am uncertain of who she is

Desperately, I reach out with both arms
    and smile

My mother, she picks me up
    and cradles me in her arms forever

William M. Thomas

Watch What You Say

If walls could speak, what would we hear?
    Would they shed some light on yesteryear?
Would they unleash gossip dating way back in time,
    And tell us some things that will boggle our minds?

Would they tell stories about a scandalous affair?
    Would they give us the names? Would they dare?
What famous people came through the doors?
    Did they see peace? Did they see war?

Happiness! Tragedy! Tales of woe!
    I wonder what depth the stories would go.
Secrets! Surprises! The sharing of wit!
    Would it be complete tales or pieces and bits?

What if the walls should make up lies?
    Not a word of truth, it was all falsified?
What a disaster if that should be the case.
    Maybe it's best that walls just stay in their place!

Always remember to watch what you say,
    You never can tell, just maybe, one day,
Those walls with ears, may learn to speak out,
    And you might be the one they start talking about.

Sandra Stanton Cole

Valentine

Would you love me if I were a tree?
Would you feed me if I were a dog?
Would you hold me if I were a book?
Would you oil me if I were a cog?

Would you sweep the leaves from off the lawn, if that is were I lay?
Would you teach a trick that I could do like sit, or speak, or stay?
Would you turn my pages briskly, or read each one out loud?
Would you recognize the things I do, though hidden in a shroud?

Would you know me in the waters?
Would you see me in a stone?
Would you feel me in the sunshine?
Would you hear me in the drone?
Would you take a drink at moon-rise, to quench an inner thirst?
Would you toss me in the placid, and count the ripples burst?
Would you warm your face upon me, or turn and walk away?
Would you listen to my music, how awkwardly I play?

Randolph A. Jacobsen

Tea with the Pope

I had tea with the Pope last night
Yes, he strolled in my room and flipped on the light
"Hello young woman" he gently coaxed
"Get up out of bed and we'll have a toast"
Well, I scratched my head thinking this is a hoax
'Til he pulled out a tea pot and tray from his coat
We sat and we laughed as he tickled my nose, yes he
tickled and tickled with the hem of his robes
and when we finished every drop of tea,
we both were exhausted from our hour of glee
then, he very gently lifted me back to my bed
and said "Sweet dreams and blessed be"

Vickie Shevde

That Old House

See that old house on yonder hill?
Yes, that one there by that old mill.
I lived there when I was a child.
Played when the days were warm and mild.
Listen to the wind blow through those
old window panes.
And the patter of the soft winter rains.
In the springs my grandma came to stay,
awhile.
I can see her now, her grand old smile.
She would tell us stories of the days of old
Tell of men brave and bold.
Tell of her love for the land.
And the love for her fellow man.
As the day drew to a close.
There was a warm felling in my heart that glowed.
The love that was in that old house, on the hill
Could fill the stream there by the mill.
Oh! To have that feeling in my heart again,
So I could truly love, my fellow man.

Virginia Acklin

Matthew Philip

His room is filled with memories
Yet somehow, something is not there
Toys, trucks, baseball, gloves and bats
The beginning of a fun-filled life.

A little boy doing little boy things
Playing, running, reading and laughing
His grin, his smiles; always a joy
Emanating a wondrous and glorious light.

This young lad had many loves
His family, his friends, his life
The frequent trips to the fire station
Brought him countless pleasures.

Our son, our child, our friend
Is now sharing his life with God
He has bestowed upon us a gift; his legacy
To have shared and been part of his life.

The emptiness and despair that we now feel
May never seem to disappear
We are filled with wonderful memories
And somehow, Matthew Philip is there.

Stephen J. Noonan

Untitled

When loved ones are gone and life goes on
you can look back to the memories
In your mind remembering a true friend
you will always have because you shared so many things
Like talking and goofing and just hanging out
you can look forward into the future
because you will always be together in spirit
and more memories are yet to be made
You can cry all your tears away
because you are sad they are leaving
and because you are happy you got to know them
When loved ones are gone and life goes on
I'll think of you every single day
Wondering what you're doing
and what it would be you'd say
When loved ones are gone and life goes on
I'll see you again someday.

Shonda Blackburn

Nightmare

The madman's breath grew closer.
You felt it, burning on the back of your neck.
Felt his scabby paws reach out near you.
Creeping closer, his hand brushed your back,
In his desperate attempt for conquest.
His teeth glinted brightly in the moonlight, like daggers.
And softly, then loudly, he cackled in his throat,
A gurgle that came from the depths of his rotted soul.
His body, wet with perspiration and rain,
Reeked like the bowels of street alleys,
And smothered you like a pillow. It had seemed like mere seconds
Since you had seen his face, gnarled and disheveled,
With blood trickling forth from those eyes, burning
with fury, ready to pounce and rip you apart with their ferocity.
Then you cried as you tripped and crumpled to the ground.
Writhing in pain, you tried to crawl away.
But he was fast, oh so very fast.
You then turned for one last time, as you saw him leap upon you,
His horrid fangs dripping with hunger and saliva.
And then...oh God, and then... You woke up.

Rachel Wright

Where Is It Written

Tell me where is it written that I have to like what
You like. Tell me where is it written that your
Thoughts have to be mine. Tell me where is it written
That the rules you call laws have to apply to me. Tell
Me where is it written that I have to be judged by
Society. Tell me where is it written that the gifts you
Bring into the universe have to be mine. It is written
That the creator gave to each man the measure of faith
That will unveil the many talents and gifts stored
Inside our hearts to share with others and to add
Meaning to this place we call home.

Sonji Venetta Nettles

For Today

I won't contemplate tomorrow, Lord, for I must face today;
With yesterday behind me, I kneel each dawn to pray.
Let me defeat the liar and make the gossip halt,
Let truth and love prevail Lord, and let no one be at fault.
Let me show your garden, of peace and love for all;
And when my step should falter, will you listen to my call?
Each day I ask for guidance as I face the trials of life;
Each night I kneel to thank you, for soothing this day's strife.
Now, when tomorrow gets here Lord, I will kneel again to say -
I believe in all you goodness, please help me face today.

Sharon L. Brooks

Special Friend

Honesty and loyalty is what a friend should be,
You never underestimated the faith you had in me.

Always there to talk with me and you never pushed me away,
You're the friend I'll always need when my life goes through a change.

I know I can always turn to you for some good advice,
You're the only friend for life to treat me kind and nice.

When my tears are falling, you're there to wipe them away,
Your shoulder you let me cry on, when I want to leave you say stay.

How can I ever thank you for the gratitude you've shown,
For everything you've done for me, so much you've helped me grow.

Whatever can I repay you for the gratefulness I owe,
You're the perfect friend that everyone should know.

With this poem I dedicate all of friendships love,
Never to be mistaken for our power comes from above.

Tina Elise Wokuluk

Because I Love You

Because I love you I will ascend earth's highest peak and sing you songs of love to be echoed in the winds for centuries to come.
Because I love you I will with just the wave of my hand, rearrange the stars in the heavens above into a magnificent painting of two lovers locked in a passionate embrace.
This masterpiece with utmost grandeur will appear in the bowels of the night inspiring generations of lovers unborn.
Because I love you I will simply pluck the sun from the morning sky and place it upon your head to wear as a crown.
This crown of opulent omnipresent light will gloriously shine, melting away all of your sorrows, casting its rays to ensure brighter tomorrows.
However, I am just a man of mere mortal means unable to perform such feats.
So I ask you to accept this simple poem inscribed with divine guidance from the Gods above because I love you.

Reubin E. Burney

Where Did It Go?

When you came into my world,
you turned my life around.
Your everything I'd every wished for,
and so much more.
But tell me?
Where did your love go?
That's something I would like to know!
I used to say I love you!
But you wouldn't say it back.
I wanted to spend time with you.
But you were always occupied.
I made you feel like you were everything,
and you just put me down.
Tell me, where was the loving affection.
Tell me, why did you send me the rain of rejection?
So with these tears I cry,
I can only say good-bye!
But before I go. Please let me know.
Tell me? Where did your loving go?
That's all I want to know!

Sean L. Harper

No Longer There

You were so young when you were taken away,
You were just learning to live and to play.

You disappeared without a trace, she begged and pleaded
With tears running down her face.

She blamed another for the deed she had done.
Said he took her car and children and run.

Eight long days, with each statement she gave,
The lies got longer while a lake was your grave.

You are in heaven now, we know this is true
She gave you life then she took it from you.

The whole world hoped and prayed
Knowing in our hearts you'd always stay.

We came to love you, though we did not know,
Our love for you would grow and grow.

People everywhere came to care for two little boys
That are no longer there.

Rebecca Mallicoat

The Art of Dying

As I hide the moon within my robe and darkness takes the sky,
You'll feel a warmth of unknown death caress you while you die.

At your side your family kneels, their heads upon your chest,
Now that I have stole your soul, they can have the rest.

I've saved you from your daily life, and all routine that you have hated, I've given you what you always wanted - you are finally de-created.

Now you have a brand new body, I'll tear it part by part,
From head to toes and in between - I wonder where I'll start.

I've chained you up inside my mind, I'll never set you free,
I'm the jury on the court ... I'd like you to meet eternity.

I'm the dark side of your soul you wish you could express,
Law and order hold you back, they keep you from success.

All the sick and all the wounded are just a step ahead,
They're just before where you are now - locked within my head.

Take these thoughts and use them well, I was never lying,
Somehow we are all caught up in the perfect art of dying.

Ryan Farmer

Love Unspoken

You feel me with a since of warmth I can't explain,

Your touch is like heaven with so much love directed only to me.
Your eyes they glow like the stars above with dreams that forever come true,
Maybe that's why I Love You.

You make me feel like I'm the only person in the world
and that everything you do or give is for me.
You're sexy in your own kind of way, with so much passion
to fulfill my every need,
Maybe that's why I Love You.

Your lips, the softness of cotton.
Your hands, the touch of fire.
Your body, the touch of fulfillment.
Your love, your passion, your sexiness,
Maybe that's way I Love You, This is my love unspoken to you.

Shadiyah Bey

The Finding

A desolate singular woodsman exploring ancient ruins, amidst
   golden piercing ears.
Desperately he searches for artifacts of bones, char, flint.
Minute jutted rock fruiting through dusted soil.
He stops...hesitantly...Perhaps this could be a find.
Fooled before forces him not to stoop quickly and pluck this rock.
Calmly but soul bearingly he flips this sediment from rows of grain...
Spats it surface with drool...and frictions away moist clinging soil.
Exposed are fluted crafted marking of knowledge passed on and on
   through tribesmen.
Immediate recognition with this artifact draws him deeper and deeper.
He empathizes with their life and wishes his life was such quiet simplicity...
When a man could live only for the survival of his family among the
   sun, soil and wind.
Conflicts of social modern day enhance the hypnotic connection to the numerous
   finds... drawing him silently into earth's moist blanket.
Now the sun, soil and wind jars my apprenticing days.
And I remember the knowledge passed on from the desolate woodsman.

    Sandra R. Berryman

The Legacy

Year after year as the young boy grew he helped his father toil. He
watched his father lose his youth to the worn-out Texas soil. He
could not seem to understand his father's need to stay; His need to
try and coax some life form the worn-out Texas clay. The father
tried to give the boy a feeling for the land, but he refused to love
this dirt that extracted such demand. He swore some day when he was
grown-he'd leave it all behind, all the sweat and work and pain would
vanish from his mind. But in his youth he could not know that time
would change his plan and when his father passed away- the boy became
a man. He put his back against the plow, he stood up straight and
tall. The only son, it fell to him, to take care of it all. And as
the years went slowly by he remained at home. He brought his bride
onto the land and had sons of his own. And as he struggled in the
dirt, working day to day, in his soul he began to form a kinship with
the clay. And when his own sons swore to him they'd never choose the
land, he'd only smile and shake his head- someday they'd understand.
For he had finally figured out what his father had tried to say; That
God formed man from the dust of the earth and their hearts from Texas
clay.

    Shirley Miller

Pop Didn't Take No Mess

I endured my childhood with a certain bother, I wondered if my father
was in fact my real father! I contemplated destiny, and the ambiguity
of fate, seemed to make me, and everything I did so inadequate. This
disturbed me a great deal, and it made my childhood much harder, until
I realized that none of this seemed to bother my father, he was more
concerned with his self image in the face of a friend, than providing
love, and a self image for all his children. I then realized what
separated everyone from me, it was my father's lack of love there was
nothing wrong with me! This is what destroyed a potentially great
family. Yeah Poppa was hard on us, he was so hard in fact that for
years he thought he was respected but it was only an act! So we had a
mother who also was a father, but that wasn't so bad, it was knowing
that we didn't have what normal families had. So all of us each grew
up in a different direction, all caused by a lack of paternal
affection. Don't get me wrong I'm not bitter maybe just sad, because
he never seemed to miss us but we did love our DAD! Like all MOTHER
NATURES things that cease to grow anymore, they just die and wither
into the nothingness they lived for.......

    Stephen New

The Empty House

Through the broken gate unmended
Past the garden long untended
Stands the house, drab and lonely,
Harboring shadows and memories only.

No windows bright with welcoming light
To shine the father home at night.
The door swings open on shuttered gloom,
Silence...fills the empty room.

Stand and listen if you will,
The baby's cry is long since still.
The sounds you strain so hard to hear,
Are only heard in memory's ear.

Nothing stirs the settled dust,
A trace of mice, the smell of must.
The walls are steeped in silent sound,
The phantom family is all around.

Throw open the windows, let in the air
In hopes the family, will soon be there.
And the road that bends, and curves away
Perhaps...will bring them home some day.

    Pat Lamdin

"Sail Boat"

Possessed by the wind
Skimming the water lightly
Moving speedily
Sailboat so graceful and light
Pride of the many oceans

    Ryan Daviduke

Mr. Society!

Oh, Mr. Society,
   you're quite a possessive guy!
You tell people what to do,
   when and where, but not why.

Who gave you the power
   to rule the thoughts and actions of man?
I'm wondering if there's much good in you,
   for you never give man a good chance.

If you were put on trial,
   I wonder what the verdict would be?
For lately your power's been falling,
   for as a man thinketh, so is he!

    Shirley Antoinette Anderson Blakely

Dear Daddy

Dear Daddy,
You've been gone quite sometime now,
Fourteen years, to be exact.
I'd give anything in this world, to talk to you,
Put my arms around you, five minutes to have you back.
The Lord took you away for a good reason,
If nothing else, to ease your pain.
Even after all these years, on days just like today,
I can't hold them back, my tears, they fall like rain.
I love you Daddy, I miss you,
You being gone, it hurts me so much.
Even though I know, your in a better place,
With the Lord, in heaven above.
I hope that the Lord thinks I'm a good boy,
Even though I'm a forty year old man.
So that one day I can walk in Heaven,
Beside you Daddy, holding your hand.

    Your Loving Son

For A Friend, Now Gone

When you died,
Riding in a Matchbox car,
And lay,
Doing the dead man's float,
They stuck you back together
With Elmer's. It stunk.
And so there wouldn't be Mr. Messies
They peeled it dried away from you.
You looked like Barbie Head from
Second grade, made up.
GI Joe Man
Twisted, bent
You held all your
Big boy toys.

Ring around the rosies
I have no more posies
You are ashes
Ashes
And I've fallen
Down.

Mikaela Lidgard

Heal This Land

Keep the wounds of the past from
Reopening
Hear the voices of your children
Let justice roll down like living waters
And compassion flow without persecution
Heal
    This
        Land...

So that our men will have backbone
As our women blossom
Like lilies in the valley
For when we reach from within
We can become Masters of our own house
Heal
    This
        Land...

E. Dwayne Dillard

Loving You Still

A shadow passes before my eyes,
Reminding of love and joy he tries,
My heart is wanton for his touch,
I question. Do I ask to much?

The love I feel pains my heart,
Our joy was sudden to depart,
I know I want and ask too much,
To see his smile and feel his touch.

Will I ever love another as much,
Will I ever again feel as such,
My life now empty, hollow and thin,
Can there ever be such love again?

Today a new the feeling has returned,
My love another has truly earned,
My love of past will never depart,
Now with joy, there are two in heart.

My one, a shadow alive in heart and mind,
His love and joy for eternity are mine,
My other each day I feel his loving touch,
Both will I love together, forever, as much.

Leon E. Earwood

Pioneers

Bluebonnets,
Real pioneers!
Trodden by cattle and buffalo,
Fanned by arrows of Indians,
Scared by scorching furnace blasts,
Flogged with whips of merciless rain,
Spent: speared by molten sun-lead.

Beaten by wheels of oxcarts,
Beaten by wheels of covered wagons,
Beaten by the wheels of cannon,
Sprayed with crimson blood,
Flattened by falling heroes.

Exiled by plow of iron,
Superseded by mercenary cotton-plant.
Bluebonnets,
Field of blue;
Not so many as before,
But blue.
Bluebonnets,
Real pioneers.

Louise Shilling Livingstone

Cybernetics

(A Consensus Of Opinion)

A simple verse wipe off that frown
Read it as it's written down
New age dawn's computer talk
Relax just do the finger walk

Depress the keys observe the screen
A fount of fact that may haven been
Perhaps it's yet a time to come
Electric dreams filed one on one

"Who goes there? The password please!"
Protection form not birds and bees
Boys own dream a work of art
Emotion free no bleeding heart

Decisive action-packed control
Sensorial feedback on a roll
Crack the code fly five alive
Segmented programmed mega drive.

J. Atkinson

Song Of Despair

The lily wilts within me.
Razors slash unceasingly,
'til bone lies bare—
Vanilla white nothing's there.
Hurts of years, a mountain building
naught a hug for me asheilding.
As fiery barbs of spoken sin,
sink deeper, ever deeper in—
Then, voices of memories past
(when hope cooed newborn pink, at last)
splay me with nostalgic haunt
persisting in their wicked taunts.
'Tis now despair's upon the throne,
I glance around, though sink alone.
(wistfully) Is someone there,
as I wither in this state of bare?
Instead, bedecked by the Spartan dress
of unadulterated loneliness,
I pull the cloak of self around
waiting 'til relief is found.

Lisa Marino

"Memories Of The Seasons"

Spring
    Pussy willows
    In the meadows,
        Kites a flyin'
        Birds a chirpin'!

Summer -
    Watermelons and beaches
    Fishing and leeches,
        Humidity and vacations
        Lazy and ambitious.

Fall -
    Orange and yellow
    Brown and red,
        'Tis said
        Life is mellow.

Winter -
    Bare trees
    Crisp air,
        All wear,
            Down and fleece.

Judith A. Haas

Promise Me Tomorrow

Promise me a sunrise,
Promise me a sunset,
Promise me a winter,
Summer, spring and fall
Promise me starry nights
And bright lights.
Promise me a rainbow
Promise me tomorrow.

Millie Katsbulas

Untitled

A picture
pops into my mind;
fragments of him,
his smile, his kiss
him, shouting my name
and me, turning away
and he once turned away from me
in my hour of need.
Him, wondering where I am,
where his child is
and me, running away with her.
As I bore her, and nursed her,
As I struggled through school and
a motherhood come too soon, alone.
What made him so special?
What made him so young?
I was only sixteen, too.

Natalie Ryan

Little By Little

Music notes dot the staff.
Poco un poco
Dynamics crescendo to forte
Tempo allegro plays
Staccato quarter's
Legato sixteenth's
Presto!
Gradual decrescendo piano
Legiaro
Ritardando...
Poco...un...poco...

Michelle Graber

Daddy

Daddy, Daddy why must you go?
Please tell my heart, for I do not know.
Daddy, Daddy I love you so much,
My heart cannot take pain of this such.

Daddy, Daddy make the pain stop,
My heart feels as if it may drop.
Daddy, Daddy I miss you so,
But I will not stop you if you must go.

Daddy, Daddy please never forget me
I will miss you while you are gone,
But you say it must be.

Daddy, Daddy please stop by,
My heart says please do not go,
For I still don't know why.

Daddy, Daddy again I say,
I'll always love you,
Even when you are far away.

Kelli Manning

Goodbye

Goodbye
Please don't cry,
I'll miss you, Mom,
I hope you won't be gone for long.
But even if you are,
There will always be a song,
That you have left in my heart.
Please don't leave me,
Oh, please don't go,
I'll miss you so.
I need you here,
So we will always be near.
Goodbye,
Mom,
Goodbye.

Melanie Palmer

Snapshot

Pages from the past
Placed neatly in an album.
Date, Time, Place.

My daughter -
Proudly clutching
her "pet" frog.

My son -
Face out glowing
his shinny new bike.

My husband -
Beaming proudly,
embracing his new born babe.

Treasured moments
Never repeated.
Memories frozen in time.

Laura M. Chavez

Sleep

I don't think nothing
I just lay there
I just lay there

I don't talk to my brothers
They are usually asleep
I just lay there until
I drift away into nothing.

Tracy Stout

Ashes To Ashes

Conglomerating,
place of worship
Bells ringing,
listening
praying
Mourning death,
loved one
Crying,
Dark veils
long dress black.
Wondering...
door to thereafter?
Dead now at rest,
time goes by
all memories lost
except ashes.

Joe H. Eggers

Midnight Blue Predator Eyes

The menace
    Perched high alone
    Cloaked in a mantle of dark
    A low growl
    Inaudible throb
    Vibrating clamped jaws
    Eyes reflect cold light
    Patience
    Waiting isolated
    Constant scanning
    Unwilling to enter the circle
    Danger radiates
    Silent
    Velvet claws
    Slash swift
    Chill of cold
    Chill of kill
The menace

M. S. Rogers

    She likes to watch
    peel the scabs
    salt the wounds
Walk on broken glass
    f*** on feathered beds
    all nite ecstasy
(private payments in dark alleys)
    stab at answers
    late nite prancer
        needle fix
    The river styx
    son of a b**ch...

    Oh so cold

Matthew Trenka

The Music

The music, so beautiful.
Play me a song.
The music, flitting through the air.
Like a little humming bird.
The music, clear as a bell.
Tolling through the breeze.
The music, so sweet.
Sweet as sugar.
Playing just for you.

Jackie Lonier

Virtue

How I long for perfection raw,
Past the shimmering of paste;
Seeking brilliance among the flaw,
Unwrought charm elegantly awaits;

Restless for the singular find,
Wading though mediocrity;
Without a map or trusted guide,
A solitaire hidden awaits discovery;

Lured by bright and baited glittering,
Too anxious, too bold, too weak;
Too quickly, too crudely shattering,
The one true jewel I seek;

Belongings mark no worthy measure,
To a faithful connoisseur of life;
Perfection's lone uncommon treasure,
Is passion stirred from mortal strife;

My distressed soul patiently yearns,
For a brilliant consuming fire;
My eternal flame despairingly burns,
A flickering hunger of immure desire.

Keith T. Hall

Our Home - God's Dwelling Place

"Behold I stand at the door and knock"
Our Savior's voice doth say.
And so within our humble home,
We ask Him here to stay.

To guide us and to nurture us,
To share with us His grace.
That He might find within these walls,
A blessed dwelling place.

May this home be a lighthouse,
That stands upon the hill.
To be a witness for our Lord,
And do His precious will.

May words of love and wisdom
Ring inside these earthly walls,
And may we ever ready be
To heed Him when He calls.
To serve Him as our Risen Lord,
To share with all His love.
The Love that He so freely gave,
"HIS SON" sent from above.

Kathleen M. Holcomb

In Sight

In Times of grief and trouble
our Lord is ever near
I see Him bent low listening
so attentively to hear

His arm encircles around
holding you ever so near
To bring you love and comfort
and wipe away all tears.

I hear Him gently calling
saying, come unto me
In the sunlight we'll go walking
Together eternally

My heart is lifted up-ward
In heavenly joy and praise
For love triumphs forever
And my peace returns again!

Mary C. Reimers

Age

Is it how we look at people,
Or how we feel about people?
To know someone all our life,
They never change.

When we see someone we don't know,
We may think they are old.
They are just someone,
Time has claimed.

Age is what we have learned,
All our life,
In our minds,
Not our shells.

I am young and know not much,
The next time you really look at me.
You will think, surely she is wise,
For time will have claimed me too.

Mimi Kubos

Untitled

Without dignity
Or an ounce of grace
I fell to my knees
Tears on my face
With sobbing breath
And painful cries
I told you I'd forgive you
For all your lies
You showed little emotion
Small regret
Just a desire to leave
And try to forget
The past twelve years
That we had spent
Vows that you'd broken
Rules that you'd bent
Leaving me shattered
And all alone
You drove off to her
And your new home

Katrina Hunter

Together Young

No dreams of the future
only memories from the past.
The mirror image revealed
her beauty had faded.

The flesh had grown weary,
one more crease added to her brow.
As she looked deeper into the mirror
I looked deeper into her soul.

Her inner beauty, everlasting,
lives in this mortal body;
a mere shell of a house,
where age doesn't exist.

It is in this place of timelessness
where we are as one,
together young;
my grandmother and me.

Janet Brustle

...A Father Without...

Today I bought a toy,
One made for a little boy.
Buying just wasn't the same
for it has been a while since
I've seen him, and
now I am going insane.
My love for him is true,
days gone by,
without him here,
brings a tear to my eye.
If you see him, tell him
I LOVE HIM.
I want to be with him,
play with him, hug him,
care for him.
I miss him, I really do.
But till I see him again,
I'll sit at home feeling blue.
Today I bought a toy,
One made for a little boy.

Pedro Gonzalez III

Man

Birds fly so carefree in the sky, with
    one big fear...man.

The trees blow so freely in breezes with
    anxiety towards...man.

Our food grows large and beautiful with
    one poisoning agent...man.

All animals, especially ones we eat and
    hunt, have a fear of...man.

What a pity to travel and fear theft,
    accidents, and fellow...man.

The most horrible tragedies in life are
    mostly caused by...man.

Our whole earth leans to destruction
    from...man!

Why, if all the earth fears man,
    can't we turn it around and solved it,
        because WE ARE...MAN!!!

Linda D. White

Inevitable Truth

On the edge of the cliff
On the tip of the mountain
In the depth of the cave
There lives your fear

Beyond the plateau
Is where it will go
To stock and remind you it is near
The look in your eyes
The tug at the heart
The racing breath
Why, it is an art

To some it will kill them
To some they will thrive
Afraid of fear
But yet not fear at all
Only the reflection that you see!

Leticia Sandoval

A New Day

This morning I saw the sea,
On the sea sat the sun on a whale
The whale is the king of the sea.
The sun looked like a mellow orange
That touched the darkness of the night
The anticipation of a new day
A new beginning a new start

Life
As the whale swam across the huge ocean
surface he grew tired and pushed the
sun up off its back into the wild
wondrous world.
The day was finally here.
I wonder what happens to the light
at night.

Miriam Litterer

Passage

Top to bottom - riding high
On his father's shoulder,
Stairs are not an obstacle
'Til the child is older.

Walking slowly down those steps
Guided by his mother,
Childish wonder, pure delight!
One foot meets the other.

Running breathless up the stairs,
Coming home from school,
Time has added expertise
To a well learned rule.

Bounding down that stairwell,
Off to conquer worlds,
Taking treads by two's and three's
Life at last unfurls.

Marguerite Melin

Fix-It Man

Each day I see him work with care
On broken things; fix and repair.
His gentle touch with such concern
To make things work adjust and turn.

When relaxing he'll choose to be
With the car, He calls it "she".
He listens closely and sees each mark
Polishing, touching, caressing 'til dark.

So much time and energy,
Oh how I wish it could be me!
Or even to hear your gentle voice,
Must I be a car? Do I have a choice?

When will I finally end my fast?
And be important to you at last.
Must I compete with things and cars
Locked away from you by mental bars.

I don't want much from you each day.
I'll be no burden, but is it wrong to say
I need your time, I need your touch,
I need daily love so very much!

Lisa M. Boring

At One A.M.

One bird sings,
on a night dark and cold.
His song is so pretty,
it lifts a heavy soul.

I wonder how this can be,
knowing he should be asleep-
and, somehow I also understand
that it's a vigil he must keep.

As I lie in bed listening-
I feel nothing could be wrong,
and I fall to sleep knowing-
it's to God he sings his song.

Patrice Wolfe

A Tribute To Jake

Thrown out of a truck
On a highway one day;
Picked up by a youngster
In no shape to play!

Fixed up in time
And given away;
To a brother depressed
In need of a friend!

Loved more than ever
Bringing life to the boy;
Who's days had been numbered
All sickness ... no joy!

The stars always shine now
On the boy and his Jake;
This is more than a tribute
Something much deeper
Two lives, Two loves, one stake!

Peggy Breen

Within Reach

Every child has some vision
   of what he wants to be;
Mostly a dream or goal come true
   is what he wants to see.

His mind is full of thoughts and plans
   of things he hopes to earn;
Throughout his life he works and works
   for much there is to learn.

Life has its share of joyful days
   when birds just sing a song;
Life also has its dreaded days
   when things all seem so wrong.

No matter what the days do bring
   each child must learn to fight;
For without his strength and hard work
   the dreams are lost from sight.

Always striving for what one wants
   is what I hope to teach;
Dreams that are seemingly hopeless
   are always Within Reach.

Lisa G. King

Grace

As Time unfolds a Tattered page
Of Wearied words and Unread meaning
The Heavens howl with Angry rage
And God appears — Redeeming

The Book of Life he holds with grace
A page flaps in the breeze
The hand of God so smoothly tears
The page with fearful ease

I turn my face in tearful horror
As flames consume the ink
The Raging wind — The Restless flames
Destroy the dreadful link

Of Life gone by and soon begotten
Today is forever forgotten
I fall to knees and beg with fear
He lifts my heart and dries a tear

A New Day begins in the Life of Time
A Page of White in the Book of Life
Now my Heart heals in the Hands of
Heaven
And my Soul in the Heart of God

Linda June Wagner

-30 +17 -2 +3 -19 +4 -8 +5

Take the total from the title,
Of this poem you've come to see.
Then you will know the person,
If you start with ninety-three.

Should you think that it's a girl,
You could possibly be right.
But in reality for this pearl,
Think different as day and night.

Just look into those brown eyes,
Or perhaps they're really blue.
If you want the truth not lies,
Then the first one isn't true.

When meeting for the first time,
True love they tried to carry.
However there was a large crime,
For this they could not marry.

If now the name you have not found,
Use five letters here that rhyme,
Then to get the really true sound,
On alpha twelve do spend some time.

Linda DuBose

"Jester's Crown"

On sunlit docks which fade away,
Of moonless nights that time forgets,
By morning light a new foray,
Which dreaming leaves in deep regrets.
The nocturne hopes, of time's release,
Ease living in the tempest's wake.
And with the drone of life's increase,
Reminds the soul what men forsake.
I travel through the plains of dream,
And live there as a sovereign proud.
My realm is only as it seems,
An escape from the mindless crowd.
Though in dreams my peace may abound,
In life I reign with the jester's crown.

John A. Campbell

Morning

Wakes to sound
of birds. In

breeze, chimes
spin in cool elegance.

So, leaving heart
behind, enters,

quietly, knows to
say, and does.

But I am who you
mean.

Mark E. Russell

Spanish Gold

Upon the sandy ocean floor
Of a tropic Southern sea,
   A glittering pile of golden coin
Pours from its casket—free.

   Spanish doubloons, strings of pearls,
Rubies with smoldering fires,
   And all about the sea-weed curls,
Neptune's floral choirs.

   The iron-bound casket molds away,
Eerie in emerald light;
   A grim bleached skull eternally
Presides each day and night.

   And no one but the blanched skull,
And the dwellers of the sea,
   Has ever seen the treasure,
Except for you—and me.

Frederick W. Dunlap

Black

   Black is the sound,
Of a train in the night.
   Black is the story,
Of horror and fright.

   Black is the color,
Of a Halloween cat.
   Black is the picture,
Of Dracula's bat.

   Black is the taste,
Of wrong desire.
   Black is the smell,
Of wood a fire.

   Black is the feeling,
Of quiet despair.
   Black is the knowledge,
That no one is there.

   All of these features,
Wrapped into one.
   Black is the future,
When nothing can be done.

Lehua Chong

Untitled

I saw a winter tree
with leaves,
Then all the leaves fell
rapidly to earth,
Birds!

Daniel J. Murray

Disillusionment

I stood in the aisle
of a city transit bus
the day we decided to
"leave the driving to us".

Standing room only
the seats were all full.
Then a little old man
gave my arm a pull.

"I offer my seat here
to the older lady" said he
I looked all around
and found it was me.

Though I felt insulted
I made no outward fuss
as it got me a seat
on a very crowded bus.

Lee Etta E. Ogorek

Garden Thoughts

Standing in a garden,
O'er which the moon shines,
I found myself a wondering,
Wondering 'bout my life.

My life, my love,
Such terrible things.
Terrible, yet wonderful,
Wonderful things.

My life, so boring,
Yet great in its size,
Compared to that
Of a beast, "civilized."

My love, oh my love!
She's a beautiful thing.
She doesn't know it,
But I love her much.

Standing in the garden,
O'er which the moon shines,
I forget my life,
And my love takes my mind.

Jimmy Hobbs

Ode To A Sheet

Ghostly, stifled stillness floats
O'er billowed, cushioned air,
Amid the silent, sacred blue,
Secured with a prayer.

Scenes of centured living
Are their secrets ever kept;
Unnumbered are the teardrops held
When joy or sorrow wept.

Here in daily ritual,
Revives the whole of man;
Awaking to a new day's dawn
As yesterday began.

LaVonne R. Rients

Burning Trees

Late in the autumn
Trees are like a burning flame
lighting up the sky

Steven Rowe

Teddi

Even if I cried a river
Now no one would dry my tears
Love we think is there forever
But it's only for few years.

You came from the Olympic Mountain
A rainy night in eighty one
When inside we could not catch you
The SPCA was asked to come

Like a bird you flew around
But ended up inside their net
It was midnight when it happened
And looked just like a movie set

My childhood yellow Teddi bear
He looked just like you
That's why I wander you Teddi
And you were cute as few.

Forget you I will never
Hope we will meet again
I know you went to heaven
My dearest little friend

Kerstin Schold

Thoughts Of Freedom

I...had been held captive.
Now I am very tired.
Had I gone to sleep,
Time might have expired.

A blindfold..., brought darkness,
...ropes, got tighter and tighter.
Now I am able to see
I am! a natural born fighter.

I felt, for hunger, of
Freedom, Justice and Love;
It made me angry
Push came to shove.

The time has come,
A last show of a card.
You've called my bluff,
This is ending, NOW! in your backyard

Freedom to,
Shout! Aloud.
Simply - I am an American!
Yes, I am proud.

John W. Minton

Our First Ten Years

Together ten years,
Not without tears
Of joy and of sorrow.

Awe, appreciation,
Love, Anticipation
Of all the tomorrows.

With you as my friend,
My lover, my life,
We are without end
As husband and wife.

Together or apart,
You are always in my heart.
The energy of my dreams

You turn dark into light.
Be with me day and night,
Forever a team.

Mary L. Hepler

Sea Forming Fear

You begin to pursue the sparkling water
not knowing what is to come
your emotions flow together
where the air and water meet

Waves start to invade the shore
forcing to move your body side to side
you're now face to face with death
you're only way to survive is a miracle

You gasp failing to let go of yourself
you create a sudden thrust of life
in defeat you've won a second chance
you feel on the top of the world

Your hand is stretched into the air
A firm object grabs a hold of you
you're rescued you are in a deep shock
your body lays motionless upon the death bed

You begin to cry, your emotions run wild
Flowing into the dreadful sea
What first seemed as just curiosity
is nothing more than the truth of the death
blue sea

Michelle Behrens

Butterflies Are Free

Mink coats cost a fortune,
(Not for folks like me)
Castles are for princes,
But butterflies are free!

Tapestries in palaces
Are royal in their place,
But give me finger paintings
And a child's smeared, painted face.

Diamonds are for lovers,
Orchids for success;
Still, neither brings a feeling
Like my contentedness.

Gardenias for the lovely,
Sweet nectar for the bee,
But just a flaming sunset
Brings joy and peace to me.

So many kinds of treasures
Are found from sea to sea,
But I would roam the meadow
Where butterflies are free!

Marjorie Easter Kemp

The Finish Line

I can run
  not fast but hard
weak and tired
  my legs pull my body down
I catch my breath
  I think of you
I bring myself to my feet
  I feel sore
I start walking
  away from you
forward to the finish line-

Mary Schuh

My So Called Life

Not a soul in sight
  No sign of life
On the dark forbidding
  road I run,
The ROAD of my life.

No trees, no grass, no flowers
  Just tall mountains
That I MUST climb
No birds do here sing
No seasons change
Dark, thunder clouds
Here forever remain

The rain falls, the fire burns
The fire is my anger
My tears are the rain
At the end of the road
All that I have gained is PAIN.

Mohammad H. Yousaf

Omnis

No words define me.
No forms confine me.
I am older than Time.

No rhythm or rhyme
To sing my song.
No meter to measure
The beat of my heart.
My portrait to paint,
No art.

Surrender dear singers, poets and such
Artists who'd dare render me
With pen, chisel or brush.
Useless against the boundless,
This thing you call love.

J. Gerard Ferrara

Help Me

  The colt is weak and very
nimble.
  For when it walks it will often
tremble
  It needs some help from its
loving mother
  To get one leg up and then
the other.

Natali Bennett

Night

Within the after of sunset,
Night, the ebony cloaked,
Wrecked its havoc upon the Earth,
covering it with a blanket of all
consuming darkness.

Shortly after, like a fierce wind,
Stars appeared, hovering in the
Sky and twinkling with delight
Then the moon showed itself,
shining a ghostly light upon the ground.

As dawn, the yellow robed,
laid a golden net of sunshine
upon the ground,
the divinities of night are
relieved of duty,
As a new day had begun once again.

Kathryn Martinez

Dying Darkness

The mist has come and
night is near.

The falling rain is
all I hear.

Darkness comes and
closes in

upon a world that
knows no sin.

Though it is dark there
is no fear,

Only cries you can
not hear.

Because they are
not alone,

For in their hearts
God sits upon
His golden throne.

Katherine Fowler

Promise Of Love

So in love am I with thee
never again alone shall thy be.

My hand shall hold thou's tight
so that thee shall never again
be touched by fright.

My eyes shall watch thee far
and near to comfort and protect
when wounded to tears.

My lips shall quench thy thirst
thy need before mine own shall
always be met first.

My heart shall share thy pain
until time heals and a distant
memory is all that remains.

My arms shall carry thee when
thou tire thy sweet love is all
I shall ever desire.

Pearl E. James

Jewish American Princes

Why aren't you married yet?
My mother hangs on every word
And repeats it all too often
It's becoming quite absurd

A lawyer, an accountant,
A doctor, man of means.
Your cousin Sophie married one,
Their living up in queens.

They've also got three children
Made her mother very proud.
Why can't you find a good man?
She was yelling oh so loud.

So, I followed her advice one day,
Hooked a doctor, with a twist,
Little did I know he was
A door to door Gynecologist!

Linda Everett-Sunstein

Searching

My love, my love, my love;
My love I yet not know?
My love is out there somewhere,
but where to look I've yet to go.
I've looked in so many places;
I've searched in so many faces;
for the one true love of mine -
but she is just too hard to find!
You might give me a whisper,
You might toss me a clue;
and after that I may finally know,
just what I am to do?
But until then she is out there,
may God have pity on her soul
that maybe one day I'll find my love,
before we grow too old!
There is one thing I've thought of too -
my love might be,
the one reading me,
my love, I hope, is you!?

Jay L. Kizziar

Untitled

It's so hard inside my mind,
my love for you is so divine.

And when I think of you each day,
all the pain you have to pay.

I like all the things you like,
I even like to bike and hike.

I love you dad, you're in my heart,
I love you dad, we'll never part.

Kelly Smith

Making A New Start

You've robbed me of the things inside
my heart you've torn apart
so all I can do is cover and hide
until I can make a new start.

Everyone tells me to get over you
but it's easier said than done
the reason why I'm now so blue
is because I wanted to be your only one.

You were number one to me
out of everyone that I knew
what I gave up you didn't see
because it was given to you.

You, my dear, will never know
what my heart will go through
'cause the pain I feel inside
is all the things you do.

Judy Gallagher

Sweet Array

There was a shadow
which covered the meadow.
From this garden came a flower
Which laid upon an ivory tower.
The man took a pot of clay
and into it he put a sweet array
which laid upon the tableside,
for each and every passerby.

Sheryl Lane-Lytle

Disengagement

Prepare me for my virgin bed;
My head displace the eiderdown,
Each strand of glory frame my face,
In place a smile soft fingers press,
Eternal pillow now repose me.
This nose no fragrance will inhale.
My Humpty-Dumpty heart at last
Let's past forget its agony.
I'll sleep until the morrow's light:
Tonight no dreams will tarry here,
No rape of life, no unsung songs,
No stillborn dreams, the dishes done,
The diapers clean, the rain is soft.
The gentle wind is warm.

Margaret A. Ryan

House Of Usher Rock,

Grand Canyon

Looming dark, immense above
my frail tent, a red slate roof

offers no foothold to those
who cannot grasp the sky. Turrets,

towers, above, below. Spies hidden
within deep recesses, unfurled

banners of raven wind. Sidewalks
of brittlebush and tamarisk bid

unwelcome visitors no purchase,
uncaring of our approval. Beneath

twisted cornerstones and roots
of cold ember, doorless dungeons

whisper ancient rumblings.
Shadows shift, growing

at twilight: basaltic eyes and mouth
gape open. In unpainted gables

nest our national heritage. Through
its front porch flows the great

muddy southwest. Across layered
expanses exist no common life.

Mike Day

On Being Alone

Although I love
my fellow man,
There comes a time,
When if I can,
I need to be alone.

Alone to let my mind explore
the depths of me,
And from this deepness,
Comes the essence,
That free and unencumbered soars.

It ascends beyond
the rising sun,
And sets below the seas.
It searches into years gone by,
And into times to be.

This lonely journey that I take
Refreshes my troubled soul.
It quickens my senses,
And quickens my senses,
And I handle my problem with ease.

Lois Studer

Isolation Sweet

Though times in solace
my being soars,
over unclaimed hurdles
thru thrown back doors.
To reach an unforgotten place
where life attains a solid grace.
Moments quite fastened
with one's path design,
only to be forsaken
confidence unkind.
To find engulfed
with undeniable need,
a soulful yearning
of other hearts that bleed.
Having known the face
that my heart has sought,
only to be obscured
by unanswered thought.
I remain entranced by a single thread,
of what is to be and what's left unsaid.

Diana L. Collins

My Son

Watching you grow up brings so
much joy to my heart knowing
I have so much to be thankful for.

Seeing you cry and laugh
watching you become a young man
before its time.

There will be lots of people to
meet and lots of places to go so
live your life one day at a time
and be kind as you go.

Watching you has been a job
to do just remember your
mother loves you.

K. McDaniel

Hours Away

Forward through rain
moving on the highway
I'm on my way back to you

Longing to feel your touch
longing to absorb your smile
held tight in your peaceful arms
I will be

Many miles to go
too many hours
wishing to be with you now
missing you....

Moses Naedele

Memories

Memories are
like the days of
the year. They come,
they go; some are
good, some are bad.
Sometimes you don't
understand them but
they always have
a meaning.

Robin Davis

A Mother's Job

Mothers may daze and
mother's may weep
But mother's can't rest
till every child sleeps
Till every mouths feed
And bed monsters are
   dead
Till every head clean
And every child seen
Through thirteen and
   fourteen and fifteen
   and on
Through grade school
   and high school till
   every child's gone
No handbook is given
no test they must make
For a mother's a mother
And this job you
   honorably take

Michelle Phillips

Eternal Love

A hand to hold
More Precious than gold,
A mountain of memories
Time will mold.

Years of laughter and some cries,
Unconditional Love, Unbreakable ties.
Growing old, weary and worn,
The pages of life quickly being torn.

The hand we hold
will surely slip away,
But the hand that holds us
Will bring us together again someday.

Eternal Love cannot be bought or sold,
It's how we choose which hand to hold.

Kimberly L. Sisk

Bodies

Our bodies tick
mine like a metronome
gliding back and forth
intentionally awaiting
throbbing vigorously
yours like a bomb
filled with explosive material
ready to combust
our bodies are ticking
beating
pulsating
throbbing
we are in motion
releasing kinetic energy
our bodies matrixed
forming a mold
transgressing
our desire
dizzying
an explosion

Heather Brown

Memories

The feel of your arms surrounding
  me at night
Assures me again everything is
  all right.
Your soft whisper against my
  cheek,
"I love you funny face" makes me
  feel weak.
I smell your cologne, I feel your
  touch.
Have I told you lately I love you
  that much?
It's great having a lover even if
  you're out of sight.
Because, God called you home two
  years ago tonight.

LoNetta White

Somehow....

Somehow I'll make a difference
Maybe I'll declare world peace
Or make a war cease.

Somehow, Someday I'll make a difference
Not by TVs or VCRs
But by Mother-Nature as my guide,
Maybe.
Somehow..........

Kerri Zamora

A Son's Thanks

Some few years a man,
Many more yet to live.
I stand now and e'ermore
A reflection of you.

By word and by thought,
By action and deed,
You sculpted my mind,
My heart, and my soul.

Your guidance, your wisdom,
Your caring firm hand,
Without them I ne'er
Would be who I am.

For this and much more,
With pride equaled by none,
And love filling my heart,
I thank you, your son.

Michael O'Shea, Jr.

Heather

I'm so happy you're here,
making a new start.
There's nothing to fear,
we shall never part.

All's I ask,
is you be my friend.
It's really no task,
for all that we can mend.

I believe in you,
and think we can do this.
All games are through,
it's only me and you sis.

Lisa M. Canfield

I Care Enough To Send The Hairy

The long days of winter.
Make us long far spring.
Trees blossom and flowers bloom
And birds start to sing.
Beautiful sights and
  beautiful sounds
Make us appreciate all,
  the nice things around.
If you look all around you
I'm sure you'll find,
There's so much to be
  thankful for —
And happiness isn't far behind
Just keep looking and you'll see!
The beauty God created
Just for you and me.

Gypsy

Untitled

  People who
love kissing,
have secrets so deep
they cannot convey,
the more you kiss
the more you express
without ever having to say,
so can you kiss my lips
so sweet, as though
we cannot speak?
Show me
your hearts desire
as we are lip to lip and
cheek to cheek,
kissing is so pure
and I believe
kissing is so true,
I long for your
kisses so kiss me
because kissing is so you.

Linda Dominique Grosvenor

Love Is

Love is me, love is-you two
Love is all we've been thru
Love is caring, love is sharing
Love is a lot never sparing
Love keeps growing, to all its' showing

Love is giving, keeps us living
Love reaches out, before being asked
Love builds for the future,
Learns from the past

Love is gentle, love is strong
Love is right never wrong
Love has it's source from God above
For that's where we first learn love.

Mary Burns

Birds

Singing to us Sweetly
Always ready to meet thee
Fluttering in the breeze
Flying with ease
Stay and watch and
they'll watch me
filled with curiosity

Stephanie L. Hoskins

Prairie Fire

The texture of your
love
Feels like silk against my
skin
Your touch is like
fire
Sweeping over the
prairie
When its crisp and
brown
We will wait for
spring.

Polly Shelton

A Midnight Contrail

The Milky Way is Bold Tonight
looking like a Midnight Contrail
Breaking the Limits of
Earthbound Flight
A Space Ship taking Humans
Beyond their Daydreams
Surpassing Nightdreams
Breathing Life to Those
Courageous enough to lift
Their eyes to Galaxies Beyond

Pamela Herring

Demon

Searching through the mind
looking for a good line
there is no telling what one may find.

There is not always laughter
nor mushy thoughts of love.

Try as I might
tonight the demon
rules all thought.

I wonder if Goethe and Poe
enjoyed this experience
or merely went with the flow.

A pact with the devil Goethe made
was it for the maiden
or the gift to write a masterpiece.

Originality is damming.
The poet flirts with the devil.
I retire my poison poetry quill
and bid au revoir demon.

C. David Enderle

Untitled

  Many times I look into the
mirror imagining the future me.
I see my self radiant and glowing,
as fresh as the morning dew on a
crisp red rose. I see myself
strong enough to embrace life
firmly, yet meek enough to know
my limitations. I see myself a
teacher to my children, yet a pupil
of life itself. I see myself gracious,
loving and compassionate. For when
I look into the mirror, imagining
the future me, the image I see
is a portrait of my Mother.

Furphy

Mirrorman

Who is the man.
Looking back at me.
Is he the evil,
That all others see?

He lives in world,
That is parallel to mine.
Could I enter it.
Across the reflecting line?

In his world.
There are no pains.
It is always sunny
And it never rains.

I wish I could live
In that perfect place
And leave this world
Without a trace.

Michael J. Fox

"Imagination"

Winged ones in flight
Loathe the laughter
Winged ones at night
Hunt and slaughter

Surviving in the wild
Claws grip the earth
Calling to a child
Calling for rebirth

Clip the wings
Clip the claws
Imagination has flaws

A. N. Walsh

"Life"

Life is short, or so some say.
Live this life, take this day.
This day may bring some laughter.
Or perhaps some pain or sorrow.
Yet surely this day will pass.
And will become tomorrow.
Where one goes, one will be.
Where one looks, one shall see.
What one thinks, one will feel.
Let good thoughts reign, with no repeal.
To have goals in our life.
Is a definite need.
Let all goals be noble.
Not formed-out of greed.
To live is to love, be it bad- or good.
Love's known by all, and-well understood.
Through all the strife, this world has
known.
The single word love, sits high on a throne.
There is always the message, to one and to all.
With love there is life, and it will conquer all.

Lawrence C. Kirkwood

Golden Silk

It blows like the wind
It shines like the sun
It smells like a slice of pie
Soft to the touch
To looks so fine
I love the way it sways
your golden silk hair...

Rochelle Woodson

"The Advent Of The 21st Century"

Some people across our great nation
Live in wonder or frustration
Time so quickly-passing by!
Life questionable-hopes high
Super highway-internet-legal protection
Biochemistry-DNA-genetic selection
Do we walk in the spirit or the soul?
Are alien contacts our future goal?
More than ever eyes search the sky
What are Gods' plans for you and I?
Some things we know-we fear!
As the 21st century-draws near.

Margaret Boyd Horstman

A Mother's Love

Face so Alert
Little hands that Look Big
Mom and Dad rejoice with Love

A son is born
My grandson is here.
Alexander is his name.

I hold him now,
I feel his warmth and now in my heart.

I glance at my son.
I smile.

No words are spoken.
He knows now how much
I love them both.

Pat Parrelle

Vending Machine

Wrappers shining
like soldiers at attention.
All types all colors
there are so many rows.

Chocolate, non-chocolate
chewy, hard, nutty,
caramel, nougat, solid,
dark, light, creamy.

What number to push
one two, one five, one nine?
The digits flash
his number's up
and a soldier falls.

Jeannette Leeds

My Love

Like flush of dawn on snow capped hills
    Like kiss of virgin dew
Like clarion call of larks, aloft
    Against the azure blue,
Like pungent scent of gentle rains
    On sun parched lips of earth
Like dreamy lullaby of winds
    That cradles spring at birth.
Like jocund laugh of children fair
    Who dance upon life's way,
Like crested clouds in crimson cloaks
    That drape the break of day,
Is every tender thought of you
    Your voice, your touch, your love
Transcends all else, and lifts my heart
    To lofty realms above.

Mary E. Clauss

Death and Life

When our life ends, the new begins;
like downy feathers that float on winds.

Then life sets just like the sun,
you know your life has just begun.

It matters not, if you have friends,
the light shines in and never ends.

People live and people die,
just to be taken up on high.

This day will come some day for me,
and I'll be there on bended knee.

I'll wait my turn for judgement day,
and while I live I'll always pray

That Mom and Dad and siblings too,
will go to God with life anew.

To live eternal side by side,
where peace and unity abide.

To God we pledge our grateful thanks,
to be amongst his chosen ranks

Paul R. Schiller

Hang On

Through the pain and sorrow's song,
Life can never be too long.
Flesh will drown in tears unless
There's hope to find some happiness.
Though someday seems so very far,
Remember blessed is what you are.
In the past we've been done wrong,
Be bold and strong and just hang on.
And in the midst of suicide,
In a friend you can confide
To help you rid of death's depress
And straighten out that dreaded mess.
Soon we'll fly like eagles soar,
With nothing to worry about anymore.
When life leaves you barely drawn,
Think of this and just hang on.

Megan C. Weick

A Sad Awakening

We were all together
Laughing and talking real loud
It really did feel wonderful
Being in a crowd.

Once in a while a baby
Would toddle across the floor
Another one would drink his milk
Then he'd ask for more.

Someone would play the piano
We'd all join in and sing
The family being together
Was such a wonderful thing.

Time came for parting
We hugged and kissed goodbye
As we all were leaving
There was a tear in every eye.

All of a sudden I opened my eyes
And felt like I could scream
I realized the family gathering
Had only been a dream.

Pauline Manning Norman

Crisis

Haloes of apathy
    keep us apart.
How long,
    before the shadow
Of the cypress
    will absorb the sunshine.
The street has no leaves
    for the death of the sparrow,
Not a song
    in the algid wind
Under his lifeless wings.
    On the grass of a morning
Drowned in a cloak of brume,
    falls the first light
Dance the snowflakes, and
    vanishes last dream.

Maria Zaccanti

"Life" - Rated R

Viewer's discretion is advised,
Keep away from all those lies.
Keep away from the stories untold,
Stand back and watch the future unfold.
For life is like a dark alley,
You never know what you will find,
So take a flashlight and an open mind,
Explore the challenges and events
in store,
But don't settle for less when you
can have so much more.

Melissa Adams

One More Try

I remember when it used to be,
Just you and me destined to be.
Side by side in the candle light,
We held each other oh so tight!

Was it true love?
Or love at first sight?

Our love was strong but over time.
We lost the bond that made us one.
Broken hearts and shattered dreams,
Left only memories of you and me.

As I sit and silently cry,
Can we give love just one more try?

Misty Bales

God Can Speak To You

God can speak to you —
    Just as He does to me-
He speaks in what we think-
    In what we hear and see.
Then He speaks to others in what
    We say and do-
Demonstrating His love for everyone
    Just as for me and you.

We need to be still—listen
    To what He has to say—
It may take a little time—
    You may not hear Him everyday.
Don't be discouraged—
    Just keep on listening and pray—
Practice living in His Presence-
    His Holy Spirit will lead the way.

Frances J. Creech

The Flowing Spring

Love is the spring of eternal life
Joy, grief, compassion
For all humanity alike
It is the inner freedom of one's heart
Oblivious to what is said or done.
Or the road that lies ahead of us.

It is the happy gleam that lights
The face with radiant beauty.
The animated walk that sets
The frame with glorious grace
The anguished look on a hopeless face
The tender touch on a feverish brow.

Love is the incomprehensible fear
That's in one's heart
That makes one want to know
What's in the other's heart and mind
Love is but the beginning of life itself
The mystery of mankind.
Love is the spring of eternal life
The fountain of mankind.

Maria V. Rosiak

Jealousy

Ruby tresses of trembling rage,
Jade eyes of jagged fury,
Silver lips of iced passion,
An ebony heart smoldering
    with envy,
Smiling maniacally she enters,
Piercing the room with her
    slivers of chilling laughter,
Her conversation, fragments of
    broken dreams.

J. E. Coakley

Because Your Love

When I'm scared inside
I've nowhere to hide,
my soul cries out for
someone to love, your
hand goes out to me,
so I give my heart to
you, then I'm at one with
your soul.

Kerri Stone

The Sunset

A sunset paints the sky
Its radiance so ethereal
The sky reminds me of you
In all its beauty and amazement

I sit here waiting it
Hoping it never leaves
Longing to hold it and not let go
Drinking in all its beauty

Perhaps my sunset will be kind
And stay for an eternity
Or perhaps my sunset will disappear
Wishing only to move on

For now I just enjoy it
Watching its every move
Never leaving my window—

You are my sunset

Monty Youngblood

The Lord's Precious Gift

Snow reminds me of the sacred host
It's pure and white and blesses most
I think of snowfall from above
As expressing our Lord's true love
Snowflakes look like tiny crystals
Falling from the sky
They cover trees and meadows
Gently with a sigh

R. Damian DeCicco

Color Me

When we are not together
it's like a night without a star,
or the sky with no perfect sunset.
As we drift apart,
I feel the trembling with in my heart
if you could paint me as a color
I'd like it a shade of blue,
because that's how I feel
when I'm not with you.
But when we are together
turn the shade to white
because you brighten my life
when you come into sight.

Michael Lane

What Is Love

What is love
Its just a word
Created by man
It is so absurd

Every definition
Its different in kind
There surely is not
One you can find

Everyone thinks
They know for sure
The meaning of love
From broken hearts they cure

There is no dictionary
So smart and true
That could give the definition
Of love through and through

I have found my meaning
In my heart its been filed
The true meaning of love
Is surely a child.

Marti L. Elliott 'Martel'

Book Of Life

In this book of life we live,
It's filled with many joys and sorrow.
Scattered through are hopes and dreams,
Of what might be tomorrow.

Our lives are touched in many ways,
As experiences come our way.
Through family, friends, and co-workers,
As we face each passing day.

It's how we choose to live this life,
That can lead us even more,
To the final chapter waiting,
At the gates of heavens door.

Judie Raymond

If I Could Reach The Sky

If I could reach the sky
  it would be me pushing
  the clouds by
If I could reach the sky
  controlling the winds
  it would be I
From a great gust
  to a gentle breeze
Controlling with my Feelings
  I could do as I please
Making the sunset
  and the sunrise
  I could do this...
If I could reach the sky

Lee Livermore

Untitled

There is a house I hold in my mind,
It took many years to find,
The wood to build this mansion great,
And seal it with an iron gate,
The windows through which I see my soul,
As I think, thunder will roll,
Lightning strikes with the pain,
The windows open, I go insane.
Lock the door, Close it tight!
And hold it closed with all my might!
A pillar falls with a crash,
A window breaks with a smash,
Tear-drop rain falls to the ground,
And far away, I hear a sound——
  Goodbye.

Lisa Kattan

Untitled

The sun shines bright,
  it makes the world light.
It shines during the day,
  except when it's gray.
The sun beats down hard,
  all over the yard.
Then at night,
  the moon comes out,
And the sun is out of sight.

Jessica Waxenberg

Music Is The Master

Music guides our life.
It leads us down our trail.
It hurts us like a knife.
Or cures us when we're pale.
Music is the master.

It's bravery like the bulldog.
Leading to the fight.
Or cower like the groundhog.
Fleeing from the night.
Music is the knight.

As music makes our trail.
In which we follow through the dark.
Our life is so frail.
Like Noah in his ark.
Music is the master!

Jonathan Woolsey

"Endings"

I know the end is coming
It isn't far away
I know nothing last forever
The end gets closer everyday
There's no way to prevent it
Nothing you do or say
Will stop the end from coming
Things end each and every day
There will always be a last time

For everything you do
There will always be a stopping point
Hard to believe, but true
But with each and every ending
There's the start of something new
Something else will be there
Waiting just for you
So even though the road you're on
Is coming to an end
Remember it's not time to stop
Soon a new road will begin

Jessica Gordon

First Love

Your first love,
It is always the best
Until your love
Needs a rest.
Your heart is broken,
Your tears don't stop,
And when the pain keeps coming
You want to drop.
But after you get it together,
You realize
Your life is filled
With more than one
FIRST LOVE....

Janell Dickens

Heart And Soul

Dedicated to Richard Kiefert

My love for you,
  it grows and grows.
How do I explain -
  my heart and soul?

My heaven, my hell,
  and through it all-
  burns the everlasting glow.
Oh how do I explain-
  my heart and soul?!

A jeweler make's a diamond,
  from just a lump of coal;
much like the way,
  you have shined in
  my heart and soul.

When you need me-
  look into your heart.
  I am there.
When you need my love-
  look into your soul. It is always there.

You, my love- are my heart and soul.

Marsha Lungstrom

Dream

He walks to the outer edge of the circle
it gets cold.
He turns his head in disbelief
mumbles a few words to himself
they disagree
he smiles
walks back into
the center of the circle
where it's warm
welcoming conversation
picturesque illustrations
musical tonality
demonstrative thought
here is where the day breaks
before the edge of midnight
falls away half asleep
until tomorrow.

Peter Petino

Broken Dreams

It doesn't seem fair.
It doesn't seem right.
Dreams carefully planned,
and kept in your sight.

With the blink of an eye,
and a turn of the clock;
Dreams turn to dust
with the crash of a rock.

Dreams turn to dust,
and with tears in our eyes;
We pick ourselves up
and ask ourselves why?

Only He knows for sure.
Trust him they say.
But why did He take
your unborn child away?

Trust Him they say.
Trust Him we must.
Ashes to ashes,
and dust to dust.

Lori Kemp

Singing Can Make You Well

Singing can make you well;
It can put you in a spell
Of happiness, contentment, joy.

Singing can cure your ills.
You'll need no more pills;
You'll feel on water-top like a buoy.

So start your singing today
And make it a habit always.
Sing! Sing! Sing! Sing with a lilt!

Then it'll soon be uncovered
What you have just now discovered:
The mys'try of a life fulfilled.

Get out of that hell
By singing yourself well —
A spirit that's filled with "tongues."

Then interpret it back what's spoken
The thoughts you're evoking —
The words coming deep from your lungs.

Mary Helen Boardman

Nigh To Thee

So still life is
it can not be heard
so sweet 'tis
straining cream

Accepting as is
all that advances forth
breathing in scent
from history and current

Past and present
is in my grasp
unclouded crystalline
and vivid

Utterly now
when you are nigh
antiquity and today
the morrow has no edge

I embrace this futile pace
that this age doth require
whereas you retain the essence
within my spirit

Karol Ruding

Autumn Came Today

I saw autumn come today.
It blew across my lawn
And stirred my neighbor's trees.
It bent and twisted the branches
And loosened yellowed leaves.

I heard the sound of autumn today.
It whistled past my window
And moaned against the wall.
It drowned the noise of traffic
And the birds' incessant call.

I felt autumn come today.
It chilled me with its breeze
And made me feel forlorn.
It took the bleakness of the night
And ushered in the morn.

Mary N. Gold

The Unicorn

It seems the noble unicorn
It back from ancient times
Into our homes and offices
In stores and nursery rhymes.

With coat so white and silky
Cascading mane adorn
Flowing tail, a small goatee
Not to mention a fore front horn.

Stuffed to set on a grown-ups bed
Or squeezed by tiny arms
Latched in rugs and pillows
Gold or silver pendants and charms.

A rearing steed on canvas
Figurines in clay or wood
A handle on a dainty bell
In a novelty shop he stood.

Once gracing medieval castles
As a symbol of purity
He entered into our modern world
From oblivion the unicorn's free.

Katherine Green

The Uncertainty Principle

The principle uncertain
Is with us all the while
As hidden truths remain
Its strength is full of guile.

Men add up sums and worry
Subtract in fear and doubt
Multiply them in a hurry
And end up where without

The answer's in the tissue
Somewhere in someone's brain
To take up on the issue
So far it's all in vain.

The wondrous space, so wide
This earth, the moving mass
They haunt us to the graveside
The aeons, silent, pass.

But mankind's lonely culture
To find the truth, at last
Is what makes up the future
Which soon become the past.

Margaret King

Headed for the Twenty-First

The end of a century,
Is upon us so near.
The twentieth is leaving,
And not shedding a tear.

The years have been good,
The years have been bad.
To some they've been happy,
To some they've been sad.

In war and in peace,
We have learned to cope.
We look to the twenty-first,
With spirit and hope.

To the old and the young,
To the rich and to the poor.
The twenty-first century,
Is right at your door.

Mark L. Williams

To Love You Now

To love you now
Is to love you long
A love that has grown
Ever so strong

To love you now
Is to love you with zest
A love that we have
Is love at its best

To love you now
Is to love you so tender
A love that we share
Our hearts never surrender

To love you now
Is to love you so fast
The times we're together
Just don't seem to last

To love you now
Is to love you forever
My goal in love
Is to leave you never

Kenneth Wichoski

Heed

LISTEN! Listen -
Is that a cry,
    for help?

LISTEN! Listen -
Is that a sob,
    for help?

LISTEN! Listen -
Is that a moan,
    for help?

Mary Jane Wilt

Cards Played From Heaven

As a well-planned card
Is played from a deck
We are pushed into light
To take our first breath.

From an imperfect deck
That the dealer has stacked,
He places his kings
And his one-eyed jacks.

We emerge from each task
Triumphant or defeated,
As kings, feeling lucky-
As jacks, feeling cheated.

Cards are placed near us-
To be loves, to be foes,
At times and for reasons
The dealer well knows.

Have peace when things change,
In the lifetime trek,
Perhaps its the dealer
Just shuffling the deck.

Janice M. Estes

My Love For You

My love for you,
is ocean blue.
It runs as high,
as mountains in the sky.
My love for you
is deep from my heart,
But the question
Do you want to start.
To love me forever
As I'll love you true,
But to actually be serious
I would say that I love you.
As time rolls by
Our love will grow,
As high as the heavens
We'll never know.
Forever and ever
Until we shall part,
That's the way I feel
Deep from my heart.

Mark Winters

Regret

Knocking upon the heart
She does not open the door
Becoming afraid of her own
Selfishness
She opens the door to
Nothing
What might have been.

Scott C. Philpot

Life's Philosophy

It seems that life
is like a dog race,
where people spend
their whole lives chasing
after a plastic rabbit.
Eventually, everyone
becomes caught-up
in the race.
Only a fortunate few
come to realize
that what really mattered-
was up in the stands.

Nikki Sullivan

"The Girl I Love"

The girl I love
is kind and sweet
She's more lovely than a dove
And flowers blossom when she speaks.

She's very kind
She's courtesy and polite
She's a girl who can freeze time
She shines brighter than a spotlight.

She's my special someone
She's out there somewhere
When I find her, we will have fun
She has to know that I care.

She's smart and nice
She can walk on air
She's like sugar and spice
She has out of this world hair.

The girl I love
is out there waiting for me
She's a girl I would love to hug
And carve our initials on a tree.

Lawrence B. Lester III

A World Oh, So Refined

What I want to leave behind
Is a world oh, so refined.
Things shall be green
For every adult, child and teen.

The sky will be blue
Oh, we have so much to do!
We have to get started
For so many have parted.

So many are not able
To sit at our master's table.
To change this world, this place
Will bring a smile to everyone's face.

That is what I want to leave behind
Is a world oh, so refined.

Monica L. Ewertz

Children

The child as an infant is
Loving but loud.
The child as a toddler is
demanding but proud.
The child as a teenager
unforgiving and cruel.
Yet the child in adults are
still breaking the rules.

Annalisa Raymond

An Offering

I look up
into the reflection before me.
A mirror,
presenting questions,
probing judgments.
I look first
to my skin,
at its imperfections.
Then I notice
the dancing images upon my chest,
how the candles light
gently
kisses my flesh
caressing my shoulders.
I look
at the white of my eyes,
a thin membrane over an unborn child.

Laurain K. Gray

Untitled

Walking into the darkness
into the black of the night
Unable to see the future
Unable to change the past
Not being able to see a thing
Unknowing
and confused
not sure of what lies ahead
but proceeding anyway
being strong
being brave
but scared
scared of living
scared of dying
but you keep walking forward
trying not to look back
unable to change your pace
unable to see what lies ahead.

Meredith Grossman

Christmas Thoughts

As Christmas time is drawing near,
Into our hearts creeps holiday
    cheer.
Now as we sit with our family
    and friends.
We pray hatred and hunger will
    soon come to an end,
But now be content to bow
    your head,
And be thankful as the good
    Lord said.

Kyra Johnson

Untitled

Look deep
into my eyes
can you see the tears
caused by your lies
all that you wanted
was a second chance
all that I needed
was a little romance
why keep dreaming
why keep taking
you had my heart
and my soul you were taking

Jessica Cahill

Baptism (For Pat)

We crawl/inside ourselves
Inside/each other
Feeling/not touching
living these
parallel lives
Baptize myself
in the/strength/of your river
Wrap myself in your/warm/sun
You left/came back to me
Stand on
    your own shore
Stand on
    my own shore
By this
    ocean
This world
this
    imperfect
        heaven.

Mark Bryson

Funeral Scene

I smiled when I seen you
in your eternal bed
the makeup caked on
your eyes sewn shut
filled with anticipation
will your eyes open?
Will you arms lift again
to plunge the dagger in my heart
death has never looked better
you are sealed
you are lowered
you are buried
I am happy

A. Tapia

Envious

To sympathize with the pain
in which thrashes in the air,
By the anger of being envious
of another one's love affair.
With the restless nights of
visualizing one's romantic regale.
To grieve the misfortune
of knowing that one has failed.
To Desire the chance to surrender
my heart for one to hold.
To share the world of passion
with one heart and the heart
of one's soul.

Juan Diaz Jr.

Untitled

I'm the shunned beast trapped
In the corner of his mind
Needed only in sadness
I'm unchained and beauty
I become
When my job is done
The beast is chained again
And left to wonder will I
Ever be beauty again?

Kari Lynda Soper

Tribute to Our State

We have fifty great states
in the land of the free,

But to me there is none
greater than the state of
Tennessee.

It's mountains and flatlands,
It's rivers and lakes,
Form a picture more beautiful
than any artist can paint.

It's beautiful cities have
a historical past,
And yet modern day progress
that will help them to last.

We have great schools and
Churches of most every kind,
That testify of our faith and a God so divine.

Yes, there are many other
places you might choose to roam,
But you'll find nothing
greater than the place I call home

Rev. Claude Weatherford

The Rose

A red flower that blossoms
in the day and goes back
to sleep at night. That brings
a fragrance so sweet in the
morning and takes it back
at night. A beauty that
shows for a while then
goes back to hiding when
the sun goes down. Then
it gets cut and shall bloom
no more, no more of its fragrance,
no more of its beauty, for
the rose has died and
the beauty lies with it.

Katrina Broderick

Anima of Endymion

I have evolved a moon
in my man-of-Adam's imagery,
to balance a dance
throughout a book of clouds.
In this mist,
a water of mirrors
echoes my shadowed cave....
Upon her entry,
the heart makes
its myriad complexes —
throughout.
I sleep in tales:
in a labyrinth of else....
priested by a moon — on behalf
of next — eversince,
an untoward night ever fell.
This house! This house!
Holding cats, women and mice;
won't let go, get out —
or scream!

C. H. Barry

Kentucky

Fields of kentucky
Smoke veiled haze on fragrant meadows
I long to see you again
Sandra Barker

Military Man

He was a military man,
In his navy blue and white.
He stood so tall and grand,
With his medals and his stripes.

He had a gal in every port,
But no cottage on the land.
He told them of the wars he fought,
As a military man.

He sailed the oceans far and wide,
And always took a stand,
He read the stars and learned the tides,
He was a military man.

But, he's old and gray now,
With a tremor in his hand.
Yet his sailor's heart is marching,
To a military band.

His uniforms are packed away,
He knows the future plan,
He will march with pride and glory,
To a military land.

Lee Allen

Untitled

my father lies cold
in his cold grave
swept by indifferent
winds against December
gray skies
     he lies beneath
a gray stone placed
upon him that he
restless does not rise to
seek me for memories
ungathered and tears unshed
B. Green

Realization

I see you standing there,
In deepest state of mind,
Questioning a reality,
That you'll never find,
Thinking of the things,
That you had hoped to do,
Thinking of your lies,
And knowing they are true,
Different from the others,
Society's laughing stock,
Wish it would go away,
Wish it all would stop,
Hate is on your mind,
Pity's in your soul,
Shotgun's in your hand,
Your finger takes control,
Blackness fills my thoughts,
It wasn't hard to see,
How could I have missed it,
You were really me...
Mona Cavaluzzo

Untitled

A lighted candle
in a window sill...
A long journey
acquired the soul
from the storm
in the night.

From within,
laughter broke out
and silenced the thunder.

Mike Pangrac

A Tree's Lament

A long, long time ago
In a lovely woodland
I did grow.
A haughty woodpecker,
Upon my limb
Drilled for bugs,
And made me slim.

After a decade
To the ground I fell,
No remedy could
Make me well.

Branch after branch
Turned to stone,
In a petrified forest
I laid alone.

Today it's a new home,
In Virginia, with H.E.C.
Where at last my spirit
Is set FREE!

Martha Lindley

"An Act Of God"

It took me years, but I finally realize
I'm not a freak, nor am I odd.
My epilepsy had no known cause.
It's my belief it was an act of God.
God doesn't hate me,
nor was he trying to be cruel.
He wants me to teach,
what they won't teach in school.
Other children in school would
forever tease me and taunt me.
It's a memory, that to this day,
continues to haunt me.

Lisa-Marie Kinsman

Breezy

What's to do
I'm empty
Just drop the bags
And left them
Back at the bus stop
Forgot exact change
So I felt wind
It was lifting
Breezy like a warm release
What happened to self answers
People forgot them
To much for granted just to much

Michael Barditch

"Love Each Other"

What can I tell you
if you are white or black
Oriental or Latin.
I still believe we should
love each other.
No matter if my Mother
or my Father are different.
Don't you think that you and me
we should love each other?
Like you and me and my brother?
Why we fight for something
that could not be more strong.
Than our love
my love I'll give you
today, tomorrow and always
we have to love.
Love each other
like Jesus Christ
and the Father, "Love each other"

Manuel M. Meneses

Mystical Dreamer

I see you in my dreams
If only you were real
You, standing there so perfect,
   yet so real.
You are my dream,
And my creation alone.
For just a moment if only it
   were possible,
To steal one mystical kiss
I would give my greatest possession,
   "My heart," and all the
   love, secrets, and wonders
   my world has to offer.
To only know for just a minute,
   you, my mystical prince,
   would indulge yourself in
   my soul, my dreams.
To just let me know what real
   love is, if only, in a dream.

Molly Belbeck

If I Were An Artist

If I were an artist,
I'd paint the tall pine tree;
It is king of the mountains
As stately as can be.

I'd paint the majestic mountain,
Frame them with the azure sky;
Not forget the billowy clouds
That drift silently on by.

I'd paint all this beauty
So all the world could see.
That's why I love this country
And it means so much to me.

June R. Horrocks

Love

Our love is different
But so dear and great
And can't help myself
It is never too late

To keep our love going
Is trying every day
True love in my heart
In my life to stay.

Virginia Viers

Untitled

In the flame of the candle
   I wonder
Why do you dance so?
Just to.... and fro?

In the light of the candle
   I marvel
Why does your light calm?
Relaxing mind and soul.

In the scent of the candle
   I bask
For it is in the aroma
I am entwined.

In the heat of the candle
   I explode
As the heart boils
The heart believes.

Paul J. Lakis

"Trouble With Snow"

Snow, snow
I wish it would go.
It's up to my head
Which I easily know.
It's bad that I'm stuck
In a five foot drift.
But to top that off
I'm only four foot six!

Michael Moyer

No Answers

While waiting for you,
I watched an albino squirrel
run from tree to tree,
gathering seeds from silver maples,
unaware that our children
were making those macaw-like sounds.
Cool spring air
and Miriah wiped her nose
with her dress.
Zane played on the old cannon
in front of the Law School,
asked about the Civil War
and why was the South grey.
I shook my head,
feeling old because
I had no answer.
He wanted to know why
the cannon's barrel was filled
with cement.

Linda Gentry Thorn

The Setting Sun

As I walk along the beach,
I watch the golden sun set
behind the mountain.
The sea gulls fly away,
As I walk toward them.
Then the sun goes behind
the mountain.
Now it is dark and I
must leave.
But again I will return
tomorrow to see it slip
slowly away.

Jacob Cole

A Memory Of Me

A memory of me
I want to be
A happy second somewhere in time
A tender moment in some mind
Of someone, somewhere in life I've been
And oh to think back
Back to when

A thought of me, yes, as a child
When I was young and free and wild
Of peculiar ways and things I've done
Of times with me when I was fun

Not of the times when sick or sad
Nor of the times when I've been mad
Or of the times when things went wrong
When life seemed like it last too long.

Kathy Tallmage

Love

I didn't want to say good-bye
I thought our love was true,
But on the day you bled and died
I didn't know what to do
I think about you every day
Wishing you were here,
But in my heart I feel you close
Knowing you are near
The thought of being without you
Is harder than it seems
In my mind I see you,
But it's only just a dream
When I gave my heart to you
I thought it would always last,
But now my heart is broken in two
And the pain will never pass
Forget me not my love
For I will never forget you
Cause when we fell in love
I knew it would be true

Mica Belcher

Secret Love

My heart's on fire,
I think I'm in love.
She is so beautiful,
like the stars above.

I wish I could call her,
send her flowers.
Be with her for days,
not just hours.

Whenever I see her,
my heart starts to race.
It's her hair, her eyes, her body,
and oh that gorgeous face.

She makes me dream of life with her,
and how happy we could be.
I think about her all the time,
but I know that's not good for me.

To hold her in my loving arms,
that's the way it ought to be.
I want to give her all I can,
in a world where nothing's free.

Mark A. Hillsburg

Lost

In the midst of the crowd
I stand by myself only to feel
the loneliness of my heart and spirit.
Where has the love gone from my
black people in the midst of my
generation crowded by prejudice
a sleep in religion?
Addicted to life for the lust of
freedom enslaved by money
blinded by drugs.
Where is the love for my black
children, where has it gone?
Help us God almighty.
We are only children, black
children in their eyes only...

Marvin Jenkins

When

When I look into your eyes
   I see warmth.
When I touch your hands
   I feel strength.
When I kiss your lips
   I feel tenderness.
When you put your arms around me
   I feel safe.
When you listen to me
   I know care.
   When you speak
I know there is love.

Nancy S. Johnson

Staring Into Innocent Eyes

 · Staring into innocent eyes
I see no anguish or grievous memories,
just love and simplicity.
   Meaningless confusion circles
round and round inside a child's head.
Their thoughts are their's
alone not programmed or influenced
by society.
   Children are our future most
everyone agrees, but I see it in a
different senses in which children's'
mind should stay innocent forever,
never to be changed to fit our
society's selfish criteria.

Kelly Embry

The Family Urn

When the old site burned, the frost,
I saw it constellated on glass melt
I reached and touched the walls felt
Hot from a fire still enclosed.

Imagine it later in spring you can
See yellow flags spot the dark plains
And grasses cover the corner stones
Newly rent a star-scattered clan.

The wind took the embers out last
Far as the boulevards through lights
Hollow laughter and drunken fights
The sparks pass out unnoticed ash.

   Restless in dreams, no more return
   To ruminate this house my family urn.

M. A. LiBrizzi

Mountain Sadness

It was summer.
I sat on the porch and cried.
The mountains echoed my loneliness;
Uncle Fulton had died.

It was winter.
These mountains are stark, merciless!
He cried.
I didn't think so, but then,
It was not my brother that died.

Jane Capwell Brown

Goodnight Prayer

As I lay me down to sleep,
I pray my soul the Lord will keep.
For without my soul who will I be?
If I shall die before I wake,
I pray my soul the Lord will take.
For with my soul,
Someone, will be me.
And then,
Who shall remember me?

Lisa Pepin

Tomorrows' Rain Is A Sunny Day

When I open my eyes
I ponder the reflection
of your smiling face,
you are so far away
that my tears become
the symbol of tomorrows' rain.
From the depths of my mind
I unconsciously admit
that even with the strength
of my own two hands
I could never grasp
the missing of you!
So when we meet again
my cheerful face
will then represent
tomorrows' sunny day.

Lloyd Clark

The Reason

Would you like to know the reason why
   I picked you for a Mother —
When thousands more I could have chose,
   And yet, I chose no other?

You made me welcome on that day
   I came to you a stranger,
You never let me feel the pangs
   Of hunger, fear or danger.

Your arms, a cradle of the deep,
   Your smile to see me through,
Courage for a thousand tasks
   Was mine — when I chose you!

Louise Williams Porter

Forever

This feeling I feel,
This pain I hold,
This hell I live,
This is my life,
I wish it gone.
I shall Forever be Gone!

Jennifer Brantley

Guilty As Charged

dedicated to Francis Scott Bailey
I often walk in the rain
the coldness around me numbs the pain
of my deep and torturing shame
for they have refused to say my name
no one there to share my fame
only on myself, I put the blame
Iron rails laid out on a plain
on top of them, there is a moving train
heading straight into disaster
'Twere mine, it would go a bit faster
upon me, they put a stain
the same black mark as He put on Cain
I am a victim that they claim
Judged harshly, I'll never be the same
A human they try to tame
Not physically but mentally maim
coldness around me numbs the pain
For I walk in the bitter rain.

Patsy Gervais

All Because Of Me

I loved you,
I never said,
sometimes ... I just sit,
and stare at your bed.

You didn't say goodbye,
but neither did I,
we should have loved each other,
before you died.

The pain I had,
it was so strong,
we didn't say goodbye,
but I didn't cry.

We weren't very close,
I don't know why,
But I guess that's good,
'Cause I hate saying goodbye.

It was because of me,
It's just not fair,
I'm to blame,
Just because I didn't care.

Jill White

The Needs of Love

Hold me close,
I need your warmth.

Ease my anxieties,
I need your patience.

Give me a push,
I need your encouragement.

Make me laugh.
I need your humor.

Dry my tears,
I need your comfort.

Listen to my heart,
I need your understanding.

Trust in my fidelity,
For it is you that I love.

Karen Troccola

The Letter

Dear Daddy,
I miss you very much
I miss our talks, the
    walks.
I hope you are happy
    where you are.
Daddy you gave so much
    to me.
You gave of your time,
    and love.
I'll always remember
    your smile or the
    private joke, to make
    one laugh.
I know you had to go
    away for a while.
You had something to do.
Until the time we meet
    again, you rest peacefully.
    I Love You.

Lillian Jenkins

"Mother"

Mother, Oh dear mother
I love you more each day
God chose you for me
To help me make my way.

You are a special rose
He picked you for me
To lead, guide and direct
Through out eternity.

Mom, you are a chosen one
Your rarity is beyond compare
I knew each time I needed you
That you would always be there.

Although you're weak and feeble
And feel bad too
You had a smile upon your face
That says "I Love You",

Well Mom, This is closing
But I had to let you know
Just how much I love you
With all of my Heart and Soul.

Linda Fee

"My Shining Star"

My dearest Lord
I love you each day
Glorifying your name
Each and every way.

A loving God
Indeed you are
I look to you
As my shining star.

Everywhere I look
You're all around
A true friendship I have
In Jesus, I have found.

Marygrace Esposito

I Am an American

I am an American
I live in this land
Give me my liberty
And I will do the best I can

Give me equal rights
For I was born free
If given the opportunity
I will make you proud of me

Everyone should learn
To love one another
And be thoughtful and caring
Like sisters and brothers

Just being an American
Makes me proud and true
So I will be loyal to my country
And strive to do my best too

If we work together
The banner we can wave
In this land of the free
And the home of the brave

Lois Johnson

The Pinnacle of Heights

As a child I like to play.
I like to move, to melt
to be unconfined,
to express myself all the time
with shouts of joy
and laughter full of life,
and jump, dance and sing,
to talk about anything,
to wear a t-shirt and suspenders
as I engage the splendor of the day,
before the blue skies fade away
and the children cease to play.
I want to know the heights and altitudes
the love has got!
For a pair of souls intertwining
in constant renewal
is the pinnacle of love's rewarding approval.
Thus, in assessing potential relationships,
it's a soul tie for which I cry,
beyond sexual sportsmanship.

Paul "Duke" Davis

The Will To Survive

A child lost in the wilderness,
    I know not where to go
Surrounded by the emptiness,
    of a love that left me cold
I stumble through the darkness,
    of nights that have no sunshine,
    to warm my broken heart.
Like a bird brought down by stones,
    from an unknown jealous sling.

A stranger took you from my arms,
    and I lost everything
In days to come, I nearly ran of
    ways to stay alive
But through it all, I never lost
    the will to survive.

Melanie Lovelady

Without You

Without you by my side
I just want to die.
You're the one who kept me alive.
I still think of you night and day.
My days become really grey
when you're not around.
I can't sleep at night knowing
you're not there when I wake up.
I feel like I'm living a nightmare
and I can't get up.
I always sit and wonder
why I'm having this awful dream.
But, all that comes up makes it seem
that this should have happened.
Everything is blackened
and caving in now that you're gone!
I wish we could have that special bond
between us again.
But will this nightmare ever end?

Kelly Preston

My Friend

Sometimes when I go to sleep,
    I just lay there and cry.
I wonder why my feelings are so deep,
    And why my eyes won't stay dry.

Will I ever find happiness?
Hopefully; I guess!

At times I sit to think about my past,
    The good times and the bad.
I often wonder how long I'll last,
    Since I'm always so sad.

Will I ever love again?
Hopefully; my friend!

Sometimes it's just so hard to trust,
    Not just you but everyone.
But I now know that I must,
    So I can find that special one.

I say I love you;
At least I think I do!

    The only question is:
    "Do you love me, too?"

Monica McNutt

Stolen Heart

You came into my life one night
I didn't plan for you to stay;
But close to you is what I got,
With each new passing day;

I said I wouldn't let you,
But now I can see;
Somehow you have managed,
To steal my heart from me;

I don't know how you did it,
Maybe I never will;
You stole It from me anyway,
And have it with you still;

I want you to keep it,
Please hold It close to you;
Because I truly hope and pray,
I stole yours from you too.

Joseph Schank

A Student Nurse's Dilemma

I know a real nice fellow and,
I hope is always will be.
He's in a wonderful profession,
In fact the same as me.

He's full of fun and humor but,
He knows when to stop.
To me and to others,
He's classed as a wonderful Doc.

Some folks call him doctor.
While others call him Paul
I only wish that some night,
I'd be called to O.R. call.

This way I see him in the halls,
or maybe see him eating,
And, when I stop an gaze at him,
My heart would really start beating.

My love for him is in a whirl,
My thoughts for him is routing,
I hope someday he'd notice me,
I do hope he asks me dating.

Nancy M. Wescott

Heart Breaking Love

Every night,
I hold my necklace tight
Think about you, and what you do,
and us together too.
Wonder where you are,
hope your not very far.
Then I sigh,
and remember why.
I remember,
that we use to be together.

Kristen Liberatore

Solitude

Of these four walls of mine,
I enclose the around me.
I sit here and wait, although -
I know the centuries you'll take,
Just to set eyes upon you again.

I can't hear you - why?
I can't see you - why?

This silence is unbearable,
But I can't go astray.
So I shall sit here and wait, however -
I know, one day, I'll see you again
At a glance from the horizon.

I can hear you - what?
I can see you - what?

What ecstasy you give me.
Finally to set eyes upon you again.
Now hear me -
Forever in time, and all in my mind,
Your soul is my soul -
    everlasting.

Josette Urich

I Dream

I dream all day
I dream all night,
Upon a star that shines so bright
And then that day when I open my eyes,
My dreams will forever fly away.

Where they fly to I will never know,
Could it be to the rain,
Could it be to the snow,
Could it be to my heart where there
Once was no key,
An undesired love,
One that no one can see,
That's one thing I need to find out-
Where my dreams are without a doubt.

Kerri Karles

Alone With Love

I reach but nothing is there
I cry without tears
My heart pounds and breaks
The silent
There is love, but I can not
find it.
How long do I search for
Something just out of my reach.
With a ray of light God
Appears, and I am alone with love.

Mable Garrett

My Handprint Quilt

I took a nap to rest today
I covered myself with the quilt you made
I felt so warm and cozy
I said a prayer of thanks to God
    for you daughter,
The one who made it for me

I know it took a lot of time
    and patience on your part
To do such a lovely thing for anyone
    would have to come from your heart

All of the hands are so different
    and they mean so much to me
They are all so very special
    because they belong to my family

It's nice to have an original one
    because it's like no other
I feel this way about my quilt
    and also about my daughter

Mary Tyler

To the Late '60's

The spinning vinyl put away
I choose to cork the bottle tight
Without concern my sterile day
Spirals silent into night
Another day to say goodbye
Filled with arbitrary space
Another year without a cry
Or laugh upon my eunuch's face
But there were times we sang the songs
United in a single voice
And braved the lines and concert throngs
Content to revel and rejoice
In smiles of light and urgency
Oh, what our music meant to me.

Nicholas Petrone

Mike

There's a look inside your eyes
    I can't quite explain
But it gives me a feeling
    Like running naked in the rain.

Such a warmth about your touch
    Making me feel so weird
Like it chased away the nightmares
    of everything I feared.

Your voice sends me gentle warmth
    As would a cozy fire's flame
Slowly these feelings make me complete
    I'm happy just hearing your name.

I look forward to tomorrow
    Like I never have before
And as long as you are by my side
    I'll enjoy them even more.

Lundi Johnson

Poem For Adam

The life that's before me
I can mold like my own
so helpless and needy
my heart I will loan
to keep my son safe
is all that I ask
to God I've assigned
this wonderful task
I hope that he knows
I love him so much
and I hope that his life
with my heart I will touch
he was given to me
through song and through prayer
to love and to hold
I'll always be there

S. Clary

My Farm Life

My name is Kelsi,
I am nine years old.
I have a cow named Delsi.
She is strong and bold.
That is what I have been told!

But this is what I know.
I'm a little farm girl.
short, but sweet.
I like to hear the birds
sing tweet tweet tweet!!

Out in the open,
I like to play,
and when I do,
I may go jump in the hay!!!

There's nothing like
clean country air
or going to the
County Fair!!!!

Kelsi Wilcox

Untitled

A little red roan
    nibbling on a blade of grass.
    Flies are a buzzing.

Toni J. K. B. Alatan

Untitled

Tattered, ripped and torn
Hurt and bleeding
Lying on the floor
Deep red rivers dry
Staining the tile
Footprints in blood lead to the door.

There's no love left
On the Edge of Death
A heart lies crushed
But finally at Rest.

P. S. Rosemary

Frightened Child

I see a child's face
Huddled in a corner
Who wants to leave without a trace.
She's frightened of her father
Who beats her; her face

Is covered with tears.
She sits and wonders where he is.
She has so many fears -
She's afraid of him coming to her room;
Why must there be tears?

She knows
He's out drinking,
Till it really shows.
She wants to run away,
But there's nowhere to go.

This may be
Hard to believe, but it's true.
So, can't you see
This child's frightened eyes, afraid
Of what's about to be?

Lauren Shown

Reflection Of Me

Do you ever wonder
how you came to be?
As I gaze into the mirror,
I contemplate who I see,
Merely a little girl
playing with all her toys
to a young women
making many ploys.
The time seems to have gone by slowly
from infancy to today,
but my mom has assured me
that time has slipped away.
I hope when God is finished
in perfecting me.
I turn into the person
he most wants me to be.

Melissa Sneed

"Friends, Again"

Since I started talking to God again,
I have discovered a long lost friend.
As silent as he may be,
There is always a sign to see.
I had to wipe my eyes of the devil,
And take myself back to God's
level.
Now I try to talk to him everyday,
Looking for the signs of His way.
Even if life begins to look Him,
I must remember to keep faith in him.

Norma Jean

Awakening

I never knew
 how much?
There is to life
 until -
I started on the trail
 to die.
Now, I hunger for
 "tomorrows"
Trusting each 'today'
understanding wonder
Seconds ticking time -
Make "yesterdays" -

Leif Olson

Meanwhile

Meanwhile, OH! Wonderful You'
How could I ever really be blue?
As always God's love so true
Meanwhile, God's sun is shining
With you I like to be dining
The dross God's is ever refining

Meanwhile, let me walk with Thee
In Thy love so free
So much happiness I ever see
Meanwhile, I'll sing and rejoice ever
Then so happy my days, Because Christ

Olamae Kruger

The Blossoming

A poem. You say:
 "How charming and clever.
  Yet there are plenty of those.
  Not alarming, not ever,"

Millions of words
Jot down in a jumble.
Meaningless, nothingness,
Unless they are humble.

Words of thought, wisdom,
Words of painstaking time.
Words of hurt, sorrow,
Those that are mine.

To grow a flower,
Please now take heed,
Guidance and pampering
Brings forth from the seed.

A flower that's grown,
Not quite what you knew,
Needs praises you sing.
A drop of fresh dew.

Natalie Thompson

Impulses

Never and Forever
Are but words of desires
Sworn to while engulfed in
Those passionate fires
Fires fueled by love and hate
But soon the rage dies out
And the love grows cold
Leaving behind a heart full of doubt
Leaving behind a heart grown old

Robin S. Armitage

My Tennis Shoes Are White

My tennis shoes are white
How can I keep them this way?
Brand new, out of the box
They soon will look worn.

How can I keep them this way?
Shiny and smelling new
They soon will look worn
No matter how hard I try.

Shiny and smelling new?
The feeling will never last
No matter how hard I try
The shoes will get scuffed.

The feeling will never last
Brand new, out of the box
The shoes will get scuffed
My tennis shoes are white.

Marie A. Urquhart

The Kiss

Eyes of fire in my heart,
Hope that it never comes apart.
Silky skin, smooth as lace,
Only beauty claims your face.

Lips of passion, hair that flows,
Everything about you glows.
Thinking of you day and night
Nothing else but you in sight.

Wishing that this love so true,
All these thoughts surrounding you.
Thinking of a love like this,
With this long, hot, passionate kiss.

Jerome A. Fox

Fox And Hound

As trumpets sound on the meadow green.
Hooves fly fast through air, and the
quick red fox slips away, away from
death's black lair. The men in their
coats of red and grey, do ride over
marsh and dale, but the fox runs
fast, very fast, away from the hunter's
tail. A merry chase doth near its end,
but the fox is nowhere to be found.
Would take a wiser and faster
horse, in this chase of fox and hound.

Maggie Marcus

"When Dreams Come True"

I used to dream of a little bog
Holding him was quite a joy
We romped and played
And how I prayed
That it wasn't quite a dream
Then one day, out of the blue
There you were
And it was true
You weren't just a dream.
That little boy
Was quite a man
When I saw you
I took your hand
I won't let you go again.
My little man.

K. De Primo

Somalia

Unkissed children stare
Through windblown savanna sand.
Near, rival clans clash.

Walter A. Schartmann

Penman's Glory

His mind is genius
His heart is loving
His words are passionate
His thoughts are pure

His reason is plenty
His style is original
His place is different
His ink is lasting

He pushes down once
And a song appears
He sinks in chorus
His talent is done

He rests in amazement
Creating a whole new song
An artist of words
But the penman's glory rests in the mid-
night ink.

Bethany Raines

Our Home

I will build a home for you,
High upon a hill and it will be
a happy home where time stands still.
Painted white perhaps with shutters
Trimmed in green and it will have
the greatest flower garden
you have ever seen.
Holly Hocks and morning glories
and Roses or every hue.
Butter cups with piquant little faces
opening up to catch the dew.
It will have a flag stone walk
and a bench nearby where we
can sit and talk.

Yes, I will build a home for you
beneath the age less sky,
and let the rest of the world go by.

H. Fountain

Lights Darken,
Her Presence Known

Lights darken
    her presence known
passion burns
    love pierces deep
Deep
    feelings
    lust becomes
deep within
    into night
as stars glean bright
    her eyes glisten
as I gaze into
    night
between
    two
hearts
    love burns

Mark Evans

Fear of Death

I look, I see, I wish I could feel.
Her pain, her questions.
No one could guess,
No one could answer.
Thoughts running through her
mind, like a train traveling across
the land.
Memories are what she has left.
To tired to think of anything else.
Her love for everything drained
from her soul.
Now tears of hurt fill her body as
she slowly dies.
Rising above everyone else.

Kate Sciacca

Don't You See?

Don't you see them lying there,
Helpless at your feet?
Pains of hunger striking them,
With nothing ever to eat.

Don't you see them sitting there,
Begging for a scrap?
Nothing but a crying child,
Lying in their lap.

Don't you see them sobbing there,
Memories flowing fast?
Of playful years and joyful tears,
Those of a better past.

Don't you see them dying there,
But did you stop to aid?
It might have made a difference then,
But no, you had it made.

Melissa Janet Wenzei

The Fire Blazed

The fire blazed
Heat so cold
Standing there amazed
Feeling so old.

Youth long gone
Now only a dream
Of a life bygone
Gone like steam.

Memories come back
Like hauntings to visit
The furies come - then they attack
Momentarily lifting high my spirit.

My days winding down
Are near the end
My smile now a frown
Painted to my skin.

The sun had set
The iron bells groaned
I have no regrets
None... none I had known.

Maurice C. Mobley Jr.

Crying

Plants grow and days grow longer.
Winds blow and hearts grow fonder.
Lives die and bluebirds fly.
And that's the reason that we cry.

Shelby Nicole George

Drumming Eagle

Rock is sleeping
He sleeps loud

Behind Eagle eyes
Drums are beating
Look at what he sees

How can one ask about his
drum, drum, drum...

Talons scratch the itch
Perched and waiting

The parameter of his field
Yields to his sound

Movement captures the
drum, drum, drum...

Eagle soars rock sleeps loud.

Patricia Anne Taylor

Jack Frost

When old Jack Frost appeared last night
He painted all the birches bright
He sketched upon my window pane
The blossoms of the wild flea-bane.
He kissed the apple's blushing cheek
And trimmed the maple leaves with pink
He caused the great oak trees to blush
Upon the brook he caused a hush.

With pallet board of every hue
He mixed the colors with the dew.
Upon the earth he slashed a chill.
And traced each flowers upon the hill
He trimmed the sugar maples gold
And tatted webs of silvery lace
On every weed of cloistered place.

Orva Lee McCarson Warren

Grandpa's Bicycle Basket

In Grandpa's bicycle basket,
He may carry a rubber gasket,
Or a coil of rope,
And half a box of laundry soap.
Rolls of toilet tissue and paper towels,
Used rusty cement trowels,
Plus lots and lots of other tools,
In Grandpa's basket junk always rules.
He may carry smashed Coke cans,
Chocolate milk and old pans.
A loaf of day-old bread,
Hats to wear upon his head.
A bag of frozen hot dogs,
Matches, sticks, and rotted logs.
Ancient marigold flower seeds,
Other things that he needs.
And when I was only three,
Grandpa's basket carried me.

Micah Mesler

Time

Time has a permanent
hold on us the moment we're born.
It allows us to grow, to get big.
We go to school, we find jobs,
We fall in love, get married
and have children.
Time let 's us do all these things,
But then in the end it kills us,
Time is like a friend, only for a time

Julie DuBois

The Minister

We never knew from whence he came
He just blew in with the wind and rain
Or else God threw a boomerang
   The Minister

He set the Church upon it's ear
They come from far, they come from near
They come to see, they come to hear
   The Minister

Such a heavy cross upon his back
But never stoops nor does he crack
A Might Oak with roots in tact
   The Minister

There's such a glory in his face
A love for all the human race
I think he's from another place
   The Minister

To see an Angel would be such a wow
I don't know why or don't know how
But I think I gaze upon him now!
   The Minister

Joel Coleman

My Better Half

When a fellow talks about his wife,
He calls her "better half."
I use to think that was just a joke
Because we would sit around and laugh.

To me it's not a silly joke.
It's a mighty truth indeed.
For, when my better half's around,
I'm a better me.

She sees in me the little things
That others never see.
She makes our life a beautiful song
Played in rhythmic harmony.

She passes over the foolish things
Which are heaped up in my heart,
And brings to light the radiant glow
That's hidden in the dark.

Without her half, I'm half enough.
Half of what could be.
But with her half, it's just enough
To make the whole of me.

Larry Culbreath

Rancher's Dilemma

The modern day cowboy
Has a gun in each hand,
But his talent he doesn't employ
Against his fellow man.

His cattle aren't worked
With a rope any more,
But their necks are jerked
In a chute by the door.

He longs for his saddle,
As knee deep in mud
He gives shots to his cattle
To temper their blood.

His constant enemy is disease,
And ever present pangs of hunger
He must prepare to ease,
But modern methods keep him younger.

Leonard A. McKnight

My Lover's Name Is Loneliness

My lover's name is loneliness,
He beds with me each night.
He wraps me in his cold, cold arms
And holds me close and tight.

In his embrace, I cannot breathe.
My eyes soon fill with tears.
My lover's name is loneliness;
He's been with me for years.

He's placed a curse upon my soul
To keep me his, I've learned.
For every time I fall in love,
My love is not returned.

I often try to break away,
To leave - ESCAPE - to flee.
It seems no matter where I go
He always follows me.

"I'll never let you go," he says
Each night with frigid breath.
"Your lover's name is loneliness.
You'll be mine till your death."

Marc E. Melvin

Someday

I'm sad, I'm lonely
Have no companionship
I need to love, and be loved
Someday, maybe some day

The days are long, nights longer
No one to hold on to
No one to cuddle
Someday, maybe someday

There's no future
No children
No companionship
Someday, maybe someday

Alone I stay, alone I will be
Maybe someday
They'll be someone for me
Someday

Kimberley A. Reid

Keep Alive

Let the
   Good out of your body
   Before time comes to ruin it
   And live with a rotten breath.

Let the
   Nice out of your body
   Before time comes to destroy it
   And live with an ugly sight.

Let the
   Truth out of your mouth
   Before time comes to lie about it
   And live with the devil in the dark.

Let the
   Stored virtue out of your soul
   Before time comes to punish yourself
   And live with the impact shame.

Let the
   Magic of your body
   Out for the time comes
   To turn it over,
   To live with the peace of mind.

Najat Sukhun

Untitled

Brilliant colors, perfect blends.
God's own creation.
A sight to behold-
Complete elation.

The sun sets over the ocean.
Nature is at its peak.
Its vastness and impact,
the mighty shall feel meek.

When the world and its problems
become too much to bear.
Look to the beauty of a sunset.
See the calm and simplicity there.

As the sun sets and darkness surrounds.
The sky no longer brilliant blue.
Reflect and be convinced,
each day is lived to its fullest in you.

Time passes and lives move on.
Each day ends in a blaze of glory.
Absorb the integrity that nature manifests
and make it your life story.

Michelle R. McLeish

Mirror

Look to my face
Full of sharp angles
Look at my upturned nose
My blank
Blue-eyed gaze
Faded freckles
Sweep of black lashes
Small mouth
It's all an illusion
A pretense
Tell me
When you look at me
Do you see my hurt?
My joys?
My inner struggles
And dreams?
The music in my veins?
I cannot.
So why do they call it
A reflection?

Michelle Williams

Racism

Racism is stupid,
Full of dismay,
You see it all over,
Each and every day.

I don't see why,
There is all this anger
Between colored and white
Even between strangers.

We all need to look,
At the inside of a person.
Not at their history,
Not at their skin.

If we could do this,
We would all soon see,
We can get along,
And not be enemies.

So next time you seem
Someone of a different race,
Look at their inside
And not at their face.

Nathan C. Barrett

Life

Life is like a long dream.
From when you are born
to your death is like a
dream.
Some dreams are shorter
than others.
But in the end the dream
must fade.
Someday we all go to the
World of Peace.

Pleaman A. Shaver

The Return Of The King

The shout will fly up
from those like me,
whose cries have been changed
to shouts.
We will all shout
and the earth will bow to see Him.
All the earth shall see Him
not as the child they remember,
but as He is-
    -wholly God
    -wholly man.
Jesus.
Jesus.
    -And we shall see him-
-Jesus!

Jeremy Thomas

Other Women

Other women get flowers
From their lovers.
You bring me ice
Packs for my swollen,
Ugly face.

I tell them I
Fell down the stairs.
But there are no stairs—
Leading anywhere except
To the abyss where

Love used to live.
You said you wouldn't
Hurt me again. Other
Women would leave; I
Bought a gun.

S. Marie Shuman

"The Moon Light"

If the sun stayed down
And the moon stayed up
How long could we stay in its light?

That light of beauty.
That light of the night.
The cold dark night.

Sleep when the light is a glow.

A sweet sleep, a soft sleep.
The sleep of night!

Rebecca R. Ebert

Love Sleeps In Corners

I've seen ladies falling
    from the sky
wondering why
    I wasn't one

Then I stopped
    and realized
when I close my eyes
    it doesn't matter

I've heard whispers softly
    through the air
floating there
    in color

I've felt the waves of life
    tumble me
'til I could see
    the ocean

Love sleeps in corners
    and dreams
hiding, it seems
    in secret

Kedi Bond

The Pain Of Suffering

Rain made the gloomy view
from her window look distorted.
With the lights off she sat in
the corner. Razor blade in one
hand, suicide note in the other.
She sat crying, thinking, "Will I
do it or suffer some more?"

Khristina Anna Yates

The Pretty Ones Get Away

Fluttering around
From Flower to Flower
They Fill The Air
Like A Fine Misty Shower

As Free as can be
They Fly around me
Pretty and Delicate
As a Ray or sunshine

I reach out my hand
For one with a Gold Band,
around its red eye
And a shade of blue
Like the color of the sky

It left me that day
Now I can say
The prettiest Butterflies
Are The ones that get away

James N. Dean

An Alien Visitor

Time came, a pepper-mill,
grinding-away, eroding.
Touching the heart with a
searing warmth, a feeling
of sadness.
Life, sweet waning life!
Time went, with the
clock ticking on and on.
A coldness entered.
A stranger - Death Watch.

Muriel M. Prahler

Cat Black

My words reflected
    from a window
    of glass
Possible to use
    your phone
    I asked
Blank stare
    strait ahead
Alone their look
And off they sped
Blood run down
    the line of flow
Where does Its soul go
Don't cry passer-by
    and bye
As tears dry
on my face
Stain in the gutter
    Its last trace?

St. Even

My Little Aura

You are as gentle as a smile,
For you're my inner child.
Won't you come and play awhile?
    Oh, don't be shy!
Because you asked me why,
You may come as you are.
Like a morning star
Shining ever so bright,
Like a glowing light.
I want to feel your presence
With all of my essence.
So, won't you come to play,
And, hold my hand and stay?

Loretta Sipes

A Little Word

Think not of what the words may say,
For they can't really care,
They cannot portray the winds' caress
Nor fragrance in the air.
How could you take a group of them
And weave them in a sense,
The feelings that come over you
Or what your heart has spent?

Love is such a small word,
A connotative brand.
It means a thousand thoughts or more,
Some simple and some grand.
With two tiny bands you wed,
And words will have their fare.
But what cannot be said will be
The little word you share.

James C. Boutwell

What Is Happiness?

The colors of a rainbow,
Or just a fallen star.
A worm in an apple,
Or dew on a barn.
A child in a garden.
A fish in a pond.
A tear to say goodbye,
where ever you are...

Crystal Register

Springtime/Disillusion

Fabric of creation leads us to reach
   For the moon and the stars.

The wishes of youth stand
   In awe of material choices.

Seeping maturity reignites a vision
   To regain the celestial.

Springtime in all our lives
   Is the crucible of hopes and dreams.

Yet Winter bodes,
   Though we choose to ignore.

Golden is not age,
   Golden remains as our dreams.

Pleasures of life aside,
   We face the same destination.

Hurts we would love to cure,
   Passions we would desire to claim.

Where is time? What happened to time?
My life is love, my love is life.

What is to happen to my journey of
dreams—-
   And yes - the moon and the stars?

   Michael J. Brooks

To Chris:

Believe in me,
   for I am true.
Believe in me,
   for I believe in you.
Doubt me never,
   for I am always here.
And, even when we are miles apart,
   in our hearts we are always near.
Most important,
   don't ever walk away,
For I need you here with me,
   each and every day!!!

   Kimberly A. Kaltenbach

Reasons

There are reasons for this game,
For him to cry out in the dark,
Loneliness, abuse, and shame
Have torn his soul apart.

The anger has mounted there,
with shadows of the past
Have given away to fear
that always seems to last.

But somewhere in a future time,
Hostile rage will dwindle,
Happiness will emerge as prime,
Successful peace to kindle.

   Kathleen E. Adams

He Will Come

Do not worry,
For he will come
Wipe away your tears,
For he is coming
Fear no more,
He will be here,
Rejoice,
He is here

   Judith Moore

The American Flag

The flag should fly ever so gloriously
   For all mankind to see...
Let us not forget the sacrifice made
   In order to be free...
Let us fly her with dignity and pride
   For all who have served and those
      who have died
Never fly her when she is worn
Don't let her fade or become torn
She flies by the hand of you and me
Please, fly her honorably.

   Natalie Jean M. Kaluza

Inside

A secret wish, a longing prayer,
for a love that is not there.
A sighing breath, a silent cry,
for someone that does not care.

A laughing way, a happy cover,
for a love that shows no affection.
A distant state, a scattered mind,
for a love that moves one direction.

A smiling face, a friendly heart,
for a love that will not see.
A numb feeling, a lonely life,
for a love that will never be.

   Marlene J. Wagner

Only God Knows

People are put on Earth
for a certain reason, but
no one knows why. Everybody
says they know, but they are
just mistaken. They waste their
time trying to figure out why.
But they never come up with
the right answer. There is only
one person who knows the
reason, and that is GOD. The
DEVIL tries to steer you the
wrong way, some do and
some don't. The devil will try
'til he succeeds. So don't follow
him. Follow GOD, and fill your duty
on EARTH.

   Marlayna Moore

Dream

Make a dream for today....
Follow your heart....
Reach for the highest star.
Search for an answer -
Fly with the birds.
There is no time for delay,
for tomorrow may never come.
Live for today.
Sing for today.
Love for today.
Look for the rainbow,
for today may be your last.

   Lisa Moyer

"A Small Gray Mouse"

In my house I saw a
Fluffy gray mouse, and I know it
saw me.

Then I saw it multiplying in
my mind, one, two, and three.

I looked right in its brown
eyes; and I know it looked right
at me. I wanted to kill it;
and I wanted to set it free.

Finally I decided; it was a
small, gray, fluffy creature of God
so I'd just let it be.

   Pamela C. Krystopolski

Indifference

Soft gray apathy
floats
in a spherical pool of stagnant water
quietly whispering
emitting no odor

slick, cool, and yielding to the touch
like a severed pancreas
tasting of dry mutton,
poignant apathy

   Greg Graybill

God Bless My Darling

God bless my Darling, he's somewhere,
Fighting for freedom and right.
And as I kneel here before You,
I wonder where he is tonight.

Give him the courage he needs, Lord
Stay by his side thru the fight.
God bless my Darling, he's somewhere,.
Please God, stay with him tonight.

Our babies keep asking for Daddy,
I tell them he'll soon be home.
Please Father, don't disappoint them,
Don't leave us here all alone.

I know that all power is Yours, Lord
There's nothing that You can not do,
So stay with my Darling tonight, Lord
I know he'll be safe with You.

   Isabelle Van Brocklin

Within

Wishes thought lost,
Feelings dead and gone,
Now come to haunt me
Pushing me along.

For just one moment
To be lost in your charms,
A long burning kiss
Locked in your arms.

Melting in your heat,
Your hand on my face
This would bring life
To an empty place.

   Peggy Bingham

The Motionless "Nerd"

I sit here in the morning Dew
feeling very blue.
When I look up at the sky.
It makes me want to fly.
When I look up at the sun.
Wishing I knew how to have fun.
I wish I was a bird.
I wish I wasn't a Nerd.
I sit here in the morning Dew.
Feeling a lot less blue.

Nikki Walton

A Once Red Rose

The crushed rose colored sands of life
Fall through the glass of time,
Whose life falls first is left unknown
Yet yours has fallen leaving mine.

The months have passed now, day by day
The petals of the rose are gone,
The moon is here, the sun has set
And our memories are now done.

The rose that once was held by you
Has been laid into my hands,
Yet the petals have all fallen now
Through the glass of time as sand.

The memories of that once red rose
Are beginning to turn pale shades,
But the memories of our once love
Will never begin to fade.

For that one red rose holds meaning
In the hourglass of time,
As a past and fading memory
Of happiness that was once mine.

Lacy A. Mills

You Focus

You focus
everything else goes away
except that one thing
that hand coming over you
grabbing you
taking you away forever
but there's still hope
that you might be able
to catch that ship back
to where you started from
you focus
and you think about
that one thing
right now that's the only thing
that matters
that one thing
It's amazing when you
think about how fast
it takes to get back to where
you started from
You focus

Melodie Serrano

Untitled

Surrounded by people, peers
envious, indignant
Can you see my tears?
Are you my friend?
—yes—
But not tomorrow
when you're with others
We're companions today
because I'm here
—in your face—
Don't call me friend
when you'll tell someone else
something else
—truth, no lies—
Don't say it
unless you mean it
—say it to my face—
Surrounded by people, peers
shameless, greedy
Can you see my tears?

Pam Chapman

Valse Triste

The breeze caresses me
Enveloping my reverie.

No more am I with aching bones,
My body's young and full of grace.
I dance with joy, the music flows,
It moves me in its sweet embrace.

My arms are curved like willow trees.
My head is poised in sure perfection.
My feet glide softly, wondrous ease,
A ballerina, art's reflection.

My gown flows round me, chiffon swirls,
My chignon gleaming, ebon, flawless,
And down my cheeks Victorian curls
Flutter and wave in timely chorus.

The music ends. I curtsey deep.
Bouquets of roses, lilies sweet
In fragrant beauty round my feet.
The dance is ended.
Welcome sleep.

Myra Y. Balinson

Thirty-Five Pounds Of Dynamite

You are quietly sitting at home
Enjoying a really good book
When you hear something outside
And turn your head to look.

The windows start to rattle
And the house starts to shake
You wonder if it's a tornado
Or possibly an earthquake.

Fear grips your throat
The chill in your spine is cold
Then the door bursts open
And there stands your three year old!

This thirty-five pound terror walks in
You would like to flee in fright
Because you know her destructive force
Is equal to her weight in dynamite!

Just when you are about to run
You realize what you have to do
You reach out and give her a hug
After all she is a copy of you!

Lonny R. Kipple

Foghorn

In the stillness of the night
    echoes a cry,
So pitiful and lost.
It rings throughout the darkness,
Softly fading.
Again it breaks the quiet calmness,
Cutting through the forest,
Slipping to the sea.
There is no motion in the forest,
While the foghorn rings.
When the lonely calls are through,
The ships sail,
The creatures scurry,
Until the next mournful chime.

Laura English

Love Is A Rose

Love is a rose

Ever so innocent as a bud
Eager to flourish
To its height of beauty

Ever so lovely
As each petal spreads
To attain its flawless goal

Ever so sad
In its quick death
Leaving torturous memories of life

Love is a rose

Lee Whelan

A Wedding Prayer

Oh Lord, as we stand before you
each taking this sacred vow,
May we always look at life
as happily as we do now.

As we go through life may we learn
to trust, to love and to care.
And remember that we have someone
with whom burdens we can share.

May our lives be blessed with children.
And may we help them find
the happiness we found in love.
May they grow to be gentle and kind.

As we grow old together, let us do so
with dignity and grace.
And all the happy days we spend
let not time erase.

And now as we go together, walking
down life's rough way,
may we remember to thank you Lord
for each and every day.

Marilyn Roe

"Reality"

To face the world with
eyes wide open to create a
life of gaiety, to someone sad,
as well as glad.
To nurse the wounds that this
old world has put into our
souls, and flesh, and when life
has put upon us what we do
not wish to hear, nor see,
to me that's what it really
means to know reality.

Nancy L. Schmidt

489

My Friend, The River

Drawn to the waters of the river
during my darkest hour,
I longed for peace and contentment
from my Lord's Holy Power

I was heavy hearted,
and all torn inside
from the pressures of the world
that had served as my guide

So to my friend the river
with all its mysteries and bins,
I extended my hands
in gesture of a friend

And like two minds meeting
we joined together as one,
and I knew nothing on God's Earth
could weaken the bond.

So true to the story
told long, long ago,
I found peace and contentment
with friend river below.

Nancy B. Shepard

The Power

The power is there
Drawing me, pulling me in.
I must resist,
Though not sure why.
It's getting stronger, nearer as
I pull away
But like a magnet
I am forced closer still.
Arms reach out toward me
Almost touching as
Electric waves shock my fingers,
Scorching in their heat.
These waves waft over me,
Envelop me.
I am inside now
The unseen force has taken me,
Though with much resistance.
You come,
Folding your electric arms around me
And I am yours.

Marcia Plante

Talking with God

Reaching up to God when He's reaching
  down to me —
    is prayer.
Thanking Him for food, for shelter
  and clothes —
    is gratefulness.
Praising him for being the almighty,
  Omnipotent force —
    is adulation.
Asking him for care, for guidance,
  And for help —
    is faith.
But just knowing God and knowing
  He knows me —
    is security.

Nell W. Meriwether

Brief Moment

The foolish young must hide themselves
  Down in a dim cafe,
While the old seek out
  A bright and cleanly place.
The young are fools who fling the years,
  The precious years away,
While the old seek out
  Omega face to face.

Jay Garver

The Cold

Cold, ever cold, cold.
Down I fell in hate.
I can still feel it,
The knife against my throat.
Behind me he came,
My purse tossed into a puddle.
I can still feel it
The muddy cold, cold splash
On my leg.

He cut and cut
Into my soul;
My blood still stains that street.
He raped, he raped, he raped.
I can still feel it,
His cruel, angry hate.
I lay there hours
And cried dry and raging tears.
I can still feel it,
Oh the cold, cold, cold
After 19 years.

K. B. Zettlemoyer

An Eye For Beauty

His eyes follow me across the room,
dissect me

into curves,
carve me

into bite-sized bits of flesh.
I am trapped

inside a Picasso,
frozen

inside a Rodin.
If I am Venus,

he wants my arms.
If I am Mona,

he wants my smile.
His eyes

are builders of beauty,
enemies of art.

Lora Passetti

Sort And File

A woman told me to look
for my dreams. I didn't
know that I had lost them.
Only just filed my dreams
away. Until I sort out
what I want to do with my
life. Or weekend. Whichever
comes first.

Corey Slavin

Alienated Life

I try to transpose the ironical
dislike of life.
It's impossible.
I live in an alienated world,
where no one knows reality from pretend,
where lies are considered truth,
and truth considered foretold stories
of generations.
I feel like I'm suspended into the air.
No one is helping me.
Now I'm free.

Kelley Hearn

Untitled

Two wandering souls
destined to find one another
Deceived by the security
we have now
We can only sit back and
let time lead our lives
Only a tear can symbolize
our love for now
Maybe heaven will be
our time and place
And only then will
I be eternally happy

Jeanni Berryman

The Tree

I see the tree standing alone,
I can see its almost grown.

A weeping willow,
A tear filled pillow.

I see the many things the
tree can be.

A friend to mend what life
has broken.

A companion to speak what
needs to be spoken.

The tree is everything I
could ever want it to be.

So when you see the tree,
remember and be the best
friend you can be.

Shannon Kelley

Untitled

I have risen before
I can do it again
As low as I've been
I will overcome it
As long as I don't
Dam the river of my feelings
Doing that will slow my healing
  or prevent it.
Expression will mend my heart
Silence will not
That which does not kill me
Will only make me stronger
And I can sometimes feel the strength
Surge into me
Revitalizing
Reconstructing
Releasing my pain
I will walk on.

Steven James Lubrano

We Used To Be Best Of Friends

We used to be the best of friends.
We would be loving, caring and teasing.
We sent cards and bought the newest trends.
Your touch would be soft and pleasing.

The evenings used to be our highlight.
Your stamina seemed to last forever.
The passion and desire burned bright.
Extinguished, we slept, unable to sever.

Now it seems we have lost our light.
The children constantly scream and wail.
We cannot get free of the endless fight.
It's as though we are destined to fail.

Can't we remember what was shared.
Find the moments of precious time.
Bring back the feelings when we cared.
To scale those heights we used to climb.

Letitia Fredley

Each Of Other's Arms

The time I thought was ours forever
We'd stay in each others arms, we'd always be together.
As time went by I felt slipping away.
Then I realized you were not going to stay.
Then I grasped for you, but you were no longer in reach.
The memories are all I have now,
and in my heart they'll always keep.
It went by so very fast.
The nights we had just didn't seem to last.
I will always repeat the words you said to me.
I will always ask myself why you had to leave.
Deep down I knew time wouldn't be our forever.
But how I wish we could stay in each others
arms, so we always be together,

Keesha Wells

What Are Teddy Bears?

What are teddy bears you ask?
Well for one they don't wear a mask.
You still want some clues?
Well they don't sing the blues.
You still want to know?
But frustrated to show?
I'll make you a list, but that won't help
You need to see one by yourself.
I myself will lend you mine.
But give it back...soon it will be my bed time

Lindsay Barazsu

Welcome To The Cardinals

Welcome to our home, little mother.
We're happy to have you here!
You and your crimson mate could have chosen
Another place to build your nest -
One not quite so near.

But we're honored and we promise
To respect your privacy.
We'll come and go very quietly
And pray there will be no piracy
Of your perfectly constructed residence.

And when those tenderly cared for eggs
Become three brand new babies red -
We hope you'll teach them to always
Come back here—and with us, make their bed.

Lila W. Cashion

Looking For A Home Land

The children cry, and mothers say goodbye
Were loaded down double hull canoes
Full at life, the sea is quiet
We leave under a full moon and rising tide.

The priest gives us his chant of our home land
The ocean like mountains we ride
The young and old dream of islands
In the deep blue sea.

We eat what we catch nothing goes to waste
Its been three months and no land

But today the ewa bird fly by.
Its a good sign we see in the distance clouds
Dancing on mountain tops

We cry with joy Akua, God has been good to us
The old men's tears fall from there eyes
We see our home land

We touch the sand on our beaches
And look at our green valleys
We are home. We are Hawaiian.

Our home land is Hawaii tears fill our eyes.

Kawika David-Cutcher

Untitled

It's excess fat that fills our jeans,
We're not anorexic by any means.

It's kind of hard to be proud of ourselves,
When we eat more food than a thousand elves.

We've got to learn to push back from the table
Get slim, get trim — do it while you're able.

If we wait too long — take to loo to ponder
Next thing we'll know is we're six feet under.

I'm not sure about you but this understand
I want you around 'cause you're my friend.

So, let's work real hard, we've no time to waste
You're my friend on purpose, because I have
good taste.

Patricia Courteau

Homework

Homework, homework
What a bore
I won't do it anymore.
I don't care if I don't pass,
I'll just work for Burgers Fast.
I'll live with my parents all my life,
And then I won't have to be a wife.
I'll ask my parents for extra money.
They'll say, "Sure, let me get it, Honey."
I'll go to the mall and spend it all,
And with my new clothes I'll have a ball.
Then I'll go home to ask for more money...
But what if they say, "There is no more, Honey."
After all of this, I've finally learned.
You can't just have something
You haven't earned.

Jenna Crouch

Untitled

War?
What for?
All it does is kill
For most, against their will
No matter what they say, every soldier is scared
Entering in the military, victory they were dared
In a strange land they continue to fight
A man lies dead, a God awful sight
You can't imagine the hell they've been through
Why was it them and not everybody else too
All you can do is say "it's okay"
But you weren't there when they were away.

Kirk Langlois

"A Friendship Lost"

We once were friends so long ago
What has happened do you know
Although it's been years since I've seen your face
No one could ever take your place
I loved you once for more than a friend
You broke my heart time and again
We've both been to heaven and hell
When will we heal only time will tell
I thought that you'd be here to help me through
I guess I was wrong what should I do
How can I lose you once again
You were my oldest and dearest friend
Maybe someday our paths will cross
Maybe we'll find our friendship lost
I'll never forget you as long as I live
Remember me always I've friendship to give
My arms are always open my ears here to lend
My shoulder to cry on a friendship to mend

LeAnn Leonard

"Hello Mr. Tree"

Hello Mr. Tree! How did you grow so tall?
What have you had to endure to be so beautiful?
What challenges did you meet in summer, winter, fall?

How many birds have nestled on each limb?
How many Squirrel's have found shelter from within?

Your roots are planted deep within Mother earth.
The sky's the limit for your growth after birth.

A Tree is a Tree is a Tree, and is free
to bend, to sway and Be.

I too can bend, sway and Be;
As long as I declare I Am Me, I Am Me!
Free to live, love and grow tall like the Tree.

I too am one with the earth, one with the universe,
one with the tress, I am one with all creation!

Now I clearly see...only God can make a Tree...and me...and thee!

Jaqualyn Hope Fries

Weep

Weep not for me upon my death
Weep for my loved one at the loss of a love
Weep for my children at the loss of a parent
Weep for my parents at the loss of a child
Weep for my friends at the loss of a friend
Weep for the lives that my life will not have a
  chance to touch
Weep not for me upon my death for I will
  always be in your heart!

Jimmie Easter

I See

What is this I see?
What is this that my heart feels?
A perplexed and confused society.
A sad condition of the world to be
Full of violence, hatred and strife
A condition that's taken a toll on the young and old' life
A society where morals and values are barely taught
A society where drugs is a way of life, to be sold and bought
This is a world of destruction
For the length of a life is uncertain
I see a world of stress, where your best is not enough

I see a world of abortion
I see a world of death
I see a world of deception
I see a world of drugs
I see no life, only barriers and uncertainties that man has
placed upon himself
This is What I See!

Mae Reather O'Neal

God Knows Our Need

He measured the waters in the hollow of His hand.
Whatever my fears, I know He will understand.

He made the earth by His power and stretched out
the heaven by His skill.
Jesus said. "Resist the devil for he is out to destroy and to kill".

Call unto me and I will show thee mighty things thou knowest not.
Even before I called He knew my every thought.

Cast all your care upon Him for He cared for you.
The very hairs of our head are numbered, though many or few.
Delight thyself in the Lord and He shall give the
desires of thine heart.
If He knows the sparrow that falls, He knows my
need right from the start.

Mattie Hershey

That Day

It was in the time of "The Me's"
When a reality check brought me to my knees
Job losses, suicide, recession
The heavy, heavy, blanket of Depression
That day we had to sell
Our truck, our boat and trailer
G'ma's Best China as well
The jobs we had were long weeks and hard
No time to care for even our yard.
A sickly child, one that's wild,
The thirds problems seemed most mild
That day my health began to Fail,
My mind began to slip as well.
That day I gave up! I suppose like most,
And came face to face with the Holy Ghost,
We talked awhile, I began to smile,
He showed me that my pains the way,
To be with him again someday
Love is the secret, Love is the way
Oh thank you Lord, For "That Day."

Lora L. Needham

The Sea!

  Out along the sea,
With all the fish, sharks and whales,
Even water snakes with long slimy scales.
In on land with sand between your toes.
It's not like out there where the water
just flows.

Sarah Horn

Addiction

The mystery of trying something unknown.
When concurred you feel as if you're sitting on a throne.
The fulfillment and energy that this provides,
makes your heart start throbbing as if cut by knives.
The people, the laughing, the way things feel;
the uncertainness of walking, nothing feels real.
The lights, the spinning, the way things sound;
the world is moving all around.
The shaking, the flinching, my body won't stop.
You feel as if you're falling off a never ending drop.
Waking up every morning needing this rush.
Your eyes bloodshot and your face is flush.
Through all the excitement and the fear,
comes rolling down your cheek one little tear.
Caused by the feeling of such satisfaction,
the fear of being in never ending traction,
doesn't seem to bother you at all,
because this is like a telephone call.
Calling you to a place that gives many people the creeps;
down with the rest six feet deep.

Natalie McCauley

The Reason for the Season

Well, it's that time of year
When family and friends come together again
In the spirit of love and good cheer
And put aside their worries of the world we're living in

A miracle is drawing near
It's written in the stars
Of all that's peaceful and dear
With a glimmer of hope in our hearts

All through the world
In His holiest light
Prayers of every boy and girl
Echo through this night

A soul so tender and mild
Born in blinding, bitter cold
God's only child
The greatest love I know

So, during this joyous Christmas season
I write these words to you
For a lifelong wish, my only reason
Lord willing may come true.

Laurel Beavers

A True Life Story In Poem

At the age of sixteen, so young and so sweet,
When girls are beginning to date, she married a man
by chance she did met, so begins this story of late.
Gloriously in love, so happy were they,
a child conceived, then two.
A man and a woman are living today, a symbol of love so true.
Eleven years later death opened its doors,
took the husband and father away.
Tears upon tears where shed by the score,
When he left this world to stay.
Seven years alone, with the children she stayed,
Working and planning, and each day she prayed,
That God would watch over her and work out his plan,
She met and married another man, whose occupation was an engineer,
They faced the future without any fear.
Both children got married and have a life of their own.
After seventeen years, God took this man home.
Now, another marriage, to another man, is carrying on
with a happy life span. Be a fighter, and be true,
There are always good things waiting for you!

R. Estelle Wilson

What Does Death Hold For Me?

I wonder what death holds for me
When I die and get to be part of eternity.
Will I have a long, long wait
Before I enter heaven's golden gate?

I'm not afraid to go that way;
For I know I must go someday.
But the saddest thing I know,
Is leaving loved ones when I go.

But I know the Lord will take good care
Of them while I am there.
And bathe them in his light that shone
Until he comes to take them home.

The grace of God I will behold
When to heaven he'll call my soul.

But I will pray through the night,
For God's glorious golden light
To shine in my life a little while,
Until I walk my last mile.

Lorita G. Peterson

Appreciation

You walk with me by the peaceful stream,
When I have fear, you hold my hand.
May I always in the presence of your glory be,
Give me the words to describe thy lands.

The tranquility, the purity, of a snow covered scape,
The sliver of a new moon and a lonely star,
The presence of your power in a great earthquake,
In the mystery of the mist, your face is there.

The song of nature in a waterfall,
The mighty elephant, the graceful swan
The colors in the rock of a sheer cliff wall,
The graceful movement of a fish in a placid pond.

You may have forbidden us Eden,
But you've still shown us your grace,
In the radiant sunset of the evening,
The wind is your breath on my face.

The power and the glory for all is yours,
Yet these things you've shared with me.
I've seen the great beauty of this magnificent earth,
With you, I pray to spend eternity.

Minerva K. O'Malley

In Time

I know the time will come
when racism is at it's end;
and to each other a message of peace
is what we'll send.
A time when humanity will not be judged
by the color of your skin-
but instead of what is within.
A time when language barriers are broken
and what you feel can be spoken.
A time when religious persecution has perished
and the freedom and equality you gain
shall be cherished.
A time when there are no homeless on the street-
and all those in need have shelter and food to eat.
A time when justice is served fairly.

Jynine Haydee Cubillas

Starmaker

Such a long time ago,
When I was but a boy,
By a messenger I was told,
A starmaker you will know.

Throughout my life I have searched.
Years of looking to quench my thirst.
The prisoner of a quest throughout all times,
A starmaker I must find.

A spirit has brought me to this place,
Of silver castles with smoky glass gates.
An astrologer had seen a sign,
Here a starmaker you will find.

Upon a white chariot she will ride,
Said the keeper of the night.
Look for her golden hair and her fiery pride,
With this, no longer will your starmaker hide.

At last I have found what I was told.
But rest not for the quest still burns within my soul.
For she is the starmaker upon this land,
My life, my heart, I put into her hands.

Noel N. Pass Jr.

Why Is It My Time?

Why is my life so wonderful,
    When it should be so miserable.
Why am I now just realizing the meaning of life,
    When I have known it all along.
Why am I so happy and cheerful,
    When I should be in such pain and sorrow.
Why is it time for me to shine,
    When others haven't had a chance.
Why do I get the spotlight,
    When another deserves it more.
Why am I not feeling pain right now,
    When I should be drowning in it.
Why Do I seem so far from the fire,
    When I am so close I could be torched.
Why are my feelings this way,
    When is it going to stop.
Why, why is this happening to me,
    When will it come to an end.
Why do I have to go through this now,
    When will it not be my time.

Jennifer R. Crew

Untitled

Grass is so very green
when the seasons roll around spring
but then comes summer when days get so hot
the green fades away a lot
fall appears and grass is not green at all
winter comes with abound
ice and snow covers the ground
when it seems like you'll never see the green again
seasons bring back the spring
and all the beauty of the color of green
will then slip from under everything
that's like love in the young heart
during the seasons of life, it sometimes seems to part
the innocence seems to fade away
no matter how many layers of darkness may stay
the light of love will show through someday
eventually, the dark, hard, shell of life will fade
and leave only the fresh, spring light to shade.

Micah Wolfe

What Happened

What happened to the world today?
When life was respected in so many ways,
When you felt good just being alive, having friends
    and being able to socialize,
So many neighborhoods are now in decay
Jasmine and Joey can't go out to play,
Their best friend was shot just yesterday
What have we done to our legacy,
We need mutual respect, and the right to be free
to live in peace and harmony,
You must do your part, you know, the one that
You promised before you got in,
You sounded so honest and so sincere
You gave us hope to let go of our fear,
But didn't you hear our plea, to change the tide before it's too
late,
to stop us from drowning and losing our faith.
Let us walk in the streets with our head and up high,
and say hello without blinking an eye,
Give us the hope we so desperately need.
and do what you must,
Don't destroy our trust.

Orlando A. Cavallo

Why Now? My Dream

Why now does it find me?
When most of life's play has been written,
And time has not paused for summer's lengthening,
But has fled into autumn's grasp.

Oh, that the spring of life's race could now begin
And I, with dream in heart, would engage.
The moments would not waste.

And would my dream come seeking,
Then would it find me in the sweetness of its living,
And not in the longing shadows of autumn's eve,
Where now I am.

Why, now, does it find me?

D. L. Robinson

The Field

The field where nothing matters.
When nobody is around.
Except the trees and flowers.
Where nothing can be found.
You can run and play or sit and gaze.
Just waiting for the sun.
It can rain or shine anytime.
Giving the flowers a drink or waiting.
Nobody cares who they are or how they look.
Just knowing that they're all one.
The flowers can see as plainly as tea.
Like the trees who buzz with the bees.
There green luscious leaves and bright
purple petals gleam in the sun
Peoples rosy red cheeks and smiles.
Tell you that they are kind.
They even wave at you when you go by.
No one is mean or hateful they just
like to see you smile.
That shows them that you care.

Meesha Gallichan

Will I Ever See The Day

Will I ever see the day
  when the gray will lift away

When the sun will shine
  and the heart that beats will be mine

Will I ever find a cure
  that can wipe away the blue
   and find a soul that is true

Will I ever see the day
  when I'll look at who I have become
   and admire thing's I have done

Will the sorrows and sighs of today
  ever fade away

When the birds that sing
  will be my spirit set free

Will I ever see the day
  when the poem I write today
   will be a distant faded memory

Will I ever see the day
Natalie L. Yewshenko

DOWN ON THE FARM

"The Model T Ford"

Transportation was slow, and our spirits soared
  When we came to possess a Model T Ford
Then our life took on a very fast pace
  That wagon and team, the Ford could out-race
Of course, it had to be cranked to get it started
  Whereas, a team of mules had it out-smarted
And since the mules' feed was grown on the farm
  To "feed" that Ford, could be cause for alarm
As a gallon of gas cost fifteen cents at the time
  It was during the depression, and scarce was a dime
It was long before Roosevelt offered up his New Deal
  And life in those times, today would not appeal
But we were a farm family, young and happy as could be
  If one thought we were poor, we would not agree - in our Model T
Returning home in the T, after a trip to town
  We had to wait for Caney Creek to run down
After a heavy rain storm had caused it to flood
  We cautiously forged across, then got stuck in the mud
That is when we came to realize
  There would be problems to modernize!
Pauline Neal Dishman

The Plan

Did you ever have a perfect plan
Where everything worked out?
Nothing ever missing, not even room for doubt
This plan so simple, things, people, ways.
Ever so bright the sunshine
Joyful were the days.
Time passed slowly, never a tear shed this plan of
mine so lovely no one hurt or bled.
Then God said to me "Life can't be that way"
You've got to hurt bleed and stumble along life's mysterious way
Without rights, there would be no wrong, no triumphs to help you grow
So personally if life was perfect the hardships I'd rather go.
I thought for a moment and thought some more there would be
no good times if not for bad
That's what imperfect is for.
Kyle DeFrain

To Fly

To get there is the goal, a journey you say
when you set out and depart
for leisure, for work, or simply just play
it's traveling, the ultimate art

You choose to fly to save some time
You select a seat by the aisle
Survival is where you focus your mind
The take of, the significant trial

There's no chance for comfort, your legs keep crampin'
sleeping can never take place
The Pillows a diaper, the blankets a napkin
And a fat lady consumes the next space

Your almost there, buckle up you are told
Stow your items, your seatbacks and trays
Set your watch to the new time, the news paper you fold
After landing all you hear are hoorays!

Welcome to home town, our gate is 6A
Thank you for flying with us
Watch your step as you exit, please enjoy your stay
You say to yourself "I'll return on a bus"
Jeff Sannes

The Seafarer's Enchantress

Romance me, sweet sailor,
When you touch my heart at dawn,
And into your arms I am drawn.

Enchant me, mysterious mariner,
With tales of wondrous chances
Taken among azurine sea life dances.

Guide me, St. Elmo's seaman,
Through salt, sand, sun and sky
To the maritime bed in which you lie.

Teach me, Neptune's captain,
To navigate oceans as you do
Among stormy vessels life leads me through.

Protect me, harbor master,
When distant ports and piers deny
Entrance to the shelters of my mind.

And after you have romanced, enchanted, guided, taught,
and protected me, I will-

Lie beside you, sweet sailor,
And touch the places in your heart
Where oceans and I now share a part.
R. Helene Butler

A Magical Land

I dream of a land, where horses run wild,
Where stallions rule, and where rivers touch the sky.
Where the little foals sleep silently,
While the mothers stand near-by.

The stallion stands high, high on a ridge,
Watching alertly over his pride.
I dream of riding this beautiful horse,
With quivering nostrils and throbbing muscles.
His black coat is soaked in sweat, how I wish this
Wonderful beast was my pet.

I dream of this Magical land, a land of
Peace, joy, happiness, and hope.
Kelly Bunch

Angel's Arrival

In the forest
Where Shakespeare's fairies dance,
I wait for my angel
Lying in the grass.
Voices ring in my ear
Saying that my angel will
Never appear.
Tears roll—my face frowns
Fearing that my angel will never
Come down.
When—out of the darkness comes
A sparkle—the sparkle of
Eyes matching the brightness of a mysterious smile.
Behind the blinding tears—the negative words,
My angel appears, greeting me
With a tender kiss.
We leave the forest where
Shakespeare's fairies dance,
My angel and I walking happily
Across the grass.

Kelli M. Smith

Strive To Be Heard

The infant nation worships a fetish reigning dour,
Where the virtuous are kept silent the blood meets the floor,
What good is a well possessing no rope.

In a world where respect is gained and lost,
Many find carnality the poison to indulge,
There are some who can never redeem.

The strong will change and the weak remain,
As the seasons pass the pain is the same,
regret becomes a game.

When gold glitters a soul, words are only the wind,
Where lies are the truth men settle for scarce freedom,
What good is an anvil with no fire.

Like a strong pong advancing in the killing mist,
My sword is raised, mighty iron fists,
the tool of war punctures hypocritical flesh,
they will never dicker with my right to be heard.

D. Sanger

"The Love You Never Knew"

What happened I don't know.
Where we lost it, I'm not sure.
For me, love still existed, so I grew with that love.

Now you tell me, "you didn't feel it at all,
my life has been a lie". Not I, my love.

Sad to see, you can't see, never did see,
how much I love you.

Sad to realize, you have decided it's over,
without hearing me out, without giving
love (as you say) a try.

Hurts so much, to hear you ask, "if I've
been faithful, if I've ever loved you".

What sacrifices I have made. Because if love
were present in your heart - you would know.

Yes, I admit to neglecting our relationship
at times, weak as a woman. But alone I found the
strength for our love and carried on.

Now, what's left 'til death do us part is a shell
of what used to be a loving, compassionate, patient
woman, eager to love and be loved "you just didn't know how!"

LaSandra Ye Vette Akesson

Forever In A Dream

Soft-soft pillow take me to the peaceful stream
where we never know what the night may bring,
but pleasant, pleasant dreams.

A feeling of what should have been, must never enter in.
For there will always be passions to guide us from with-in.
Feelings that pass in the night
remind us of what love could be.
To carry us in our flight
in search of ecstasy!!!
For I do not wish to awake
  "Forever in a dream"

R. Albertson

Thee Loving Desert Rose Layer

Gentle and caring were his hands,
which laid thee precious Desert Rose stones,
on a heart - felt home.
The touch of each Desert Rose, expresses his love, and warmth,
that he's given to so many.
Each stone of Desert Rose, reminds us, of his love he gave,
to his family, and friends.
Never should we take life for granted,
for like the stones he's laid,
teaches us to follow, the path of love.
When we begin to lay down, our own stones,
we'll start to build our dreams, on endless paths.
Each Desert Rose stone he's laid,
will always stay close to our hearts, and minds,
bringing smiles of hope,to carry us through,
valley's and mountain's, we'll encounter along the way.
Such an honor to see Desert Rose stones,
surrounding a home, so blessed by God.
One shall never forget!
Thee loving Desert Rose layer.

Raynette Vega

Untitled

A single flower
Which stands all alone
Can hold so much power
It doesn't even need a garden to call home
Because alone it represents so much
Be careful, its delicate to the touch
The smell so sweet
Sweeps me off my feet
I have one flower in my life
It takes away all my strife
Its quite like the sunlight
Keeping all my days shining bright
Giving me something to lean on
Something to make me smile when everything else goes wrong
For some people
Their flower is a teddy bear
A deep sleep or a silent prayer
My flower isn't one you'd find in a vase
Its not in a garden or wrapped in lace
Its a real person, a human face.

Kimberly Driggers

"Recognition"

A work of art
Is still a part
Of someone's mind,
So you will find
Acknowledgment is needed
For joy to be seeded
And gloom to be weeded.

Rosemarie Blair

Lost! — In Thought!

A sour old man slouched in his chair
while I passed by and saw him there.
He grasped my eyes, though I thought them dim,
then he beckoned me to come to him.

When I was young, said he to me,
My worries were what was to be.
When you grow old, don't be thus sad.
Remember—What it was you had.

I saw the anguish inside his soul
but not the reasons that formed the whole.

As I sit slouched within my chair,
his words return and haunt me there.

What were their names? How were their faces?
What part of me such thought erases?
What I have known was never bound.
What I have lost cannot be found.

Now I have dreams, and sometimes visions.
Both are forms of my new prisons,
for when I wake, both schemes diminish,
and I cannot the pictures finish.

D. Jacques Little

Bless Our Troops

O God, with our troops ever be,
While on foreign land across the sea;
Keep them as they cross the desert hot and dry,
Help those who find themselves wondering why;
May they place their trust in thee,
As they try to bring others liberty;
Guide their hands upon the gun,
Direct each step of the missions they run;
Bless those who keep watch over the sea,
And should the waters fill with turmoil,
Let them, your guiding hand see,
Till once again they reach American soil;
Bless the families of those who's life has been given,
Keep their honor and memories living;
That when we look upon the flag flying high,
Our heroes, in vain did not die;
Use our troops, O God, to help freedom ring,
That all may, of sweet liberty sing;
Hold in your loving hands, each chosen one,
Till victory in battle is won.

Louise Y. Dean

The Chase

Gems sparkle in her violet eyes,
while she lovingly gazes towards velvet black skies.
At night time her whispers are heard far away,
echoing distant, and faint in the day.
The silvery strands of her hair flow down,
while children hide in the folds of her gown.
She is the guardian of intuition,
while he stands strong for illumination.
He sees everything with clarity of vision,
and his reign in day is her contradiction.
His hair is golden, a spiralling vortex of light
striking fear at the hearts of our demons of night.
Fire and ice streak across each horizon;
hark! See his brazen hail! Sense her silence.
Through day and night they assume a chase
which casts different shades of light on my face.

Mara Barcay

Where We Sleep

The horizon dims with silhouette, on a morbid pirate sea.
While sirens sing, we seal our crypts, with jest and wine and rosary.

We remember to forget the plunder; with time we'll wash the sands.
And the jewels will lure legends, and the rings deny our hands.

We reap some color from the rainbow, to beautify our dreams.
While our banners turn to mud, the faithful offer screams.

We justify our rest, with the secrets that we keep.
And those boasting knowledge, claim to know just where we sleep,
just where we sleep.

The duration of a trinket, resists its end demise.
In hopes to bask again in glory, and tease the wanting eyes.

While we inspire liars, and nourish fond repeat.
We watch our encore staged, and hear the cheers for our defeat.

We do succumb to mire, unlike the trinket with strength to keep.
But the once that was, we will retain, for you wonder where we sleep,
you wonder where we sleep.

Michael Shumway

Through the Eyes of a Child

See the pebbles iridescent in the early morning hours,
White perfection in a beige backdrop
Forgotten amid the search for sunken treasures and
pirate ships,
Gemini twins lost without each other
Lovely enough to grace a lady's ears or to be on
display in the ballerina music box on her night stand.
Opalescence, a clarity to read the future with
Gypsy stones belonging to a caravan complete with exotic creatures,
Drivers with downy cheeks and crystal eyes.
Eyes, the complete set lying at my feet between the sand.
Pick them up to feel the smoothness of a millennium
The trademark of a long, lost race called childhood.
To see through the eyes of a child, any child, is true knowledge.
Even the elderly retain their innocence
It is the loss of insight that brings about extinction.

Kimberly Solomon

Martin Luther King, Jr.

Once there was a man
Who always said, "I can".

He fought for bravery
And against all slavery

He made a choice
To use his voice
So all the people could rejoice!

His words were full of grace
And so they will always embrace.

When he died the world cried
But his memory will always be deep inside.

This man was Martin Luther King, Jr.

Laura Quezadaz

A Human Heart

A human heart is a fragile thing,
when love can wound it with its awful sting.
The pain cuts deep into the quick,
and lingers there, so dense and thick.

Yet, a human heart is strong and tough.
It keeps going on when you think it's had enough.
It springs back ready for love again,
to face the threat of love's sweet pain.

James R. Cook

Red, White and Blough

Oh, pity the plight of the immigrant wight
Who comes to our land to dwell;
He changes his tongue to Americun,
And figures he must learn to spell.

But he learns that what counts, is how to pronounce
This language, with all of it's traits;
An example we'll use on how we confuse
Is the ending "O" "U" and "G" "H".

When you go out to plough use a horse, not a cough,
A marital spat is a rough.
You get sick with the 'flough, your car is brand nough,
And there's always too much work to dough.

Plant a plant, watch it grough, keep your voice 'way down lough,
And when you're not fast then you're slough.
People smoke and dip snough, cotton balls feel like flough,
And you powder your face with a pough.

So, pity the plight of the immigrant wight
Do not laugh at him, snicker or cough;
If once in a while he slips, give a smile,
It's an error, he's not showing ough.

R. Douglas Manning

Mary, Our Mother

Where can you go when you're lonely?
Who is there when you're afraid?
In doubt and despair, is no one out there
To help send all trouble away?

Yes, there is someone to go to
A person as human as I;
But oh so much more, a person so rare
The mother of God's only Son.

Mary is there when you need her.
Her ear is prayer's call away.
So don't be afraid to beseech her
When life sends its troubles your way.

Yes, ask what you will of your mother.
She's waiting for you every day
And whatever she asks of God, our Father,
It's sure to be right on the way.

Paul A. Trouve'

The Healer

Yesterday, I said I'm going to become a healer
who loves and touches and hugs and cares
soothes the pains, relaxes the panic.
a healer who feels others' problems
and they know I care.
Sometimes I think I'm psychic
As bad vibes reach out
and I catch them through a phone wire
or a mere look
As someone passes or waits in a grocery line
good vibes, too. that jump forth with happy energy.
but I haven't learned how to be a healer
Yet, if my wish is granted first to help
would be the children
sick in body or unfocused in mind
who need clear eyes
and knowing laughter-
the invisible veils removed
from their shining souls.

Mary Ellen Quinn

Untitled

How many times have you loved me?
Who's in your dreams at night?
Who's name do you whisper when you're lonely?
Why do you keep your heart bound so tight?
If I should tell you "I love you" will you leave here
With a treasure that's hard to attain
Or will you leave me in silence and solitude
With no hope of your passion ever again?
What do you expect of my kisses?
Will you hide them forever inside?
Are they like roses, beautiful today,
Tomorrow withered and dried?
How long can you keep me a secret?
How long will it take to become
The master of life and destiny
Instead of a slave to love?

K. L. Stackhouse

A Puzzled Friend

Where do you do your shopping? I asked
Why! at the Gift Shoppe - my dear friend,
There are tea pots blue, and tea pots brown
Either plain, or with hand painting on.

Pretty cups in which tea will taste fine
To your special guests when they come to dine
My friend, you need not puzzled be
With such fine and pretty gifts as these.

There are exquisite gifts of fine silverware
Beautiful glass and chinaware
Gifts too innumerable to mention here
The rest I'll leave it to you - my dear.

But if you go in and browse around
First thing you'll know - that you have found
Something that has caught your eye
You can't resist it - and so you buy.

Patricia Marshall

Old Man On The Sea

Old man on the sea,
Why can I not stand on your bow
To see what you see

To gaze at the morning sky as it shows itself so slowly
As the sun lights it up

An endless illusion of blue and green
Melting together on the horizon

To lie mesmerized on the deck watching
As the clouds chase each other across the sky

To witness the sun begin to disappear and the shades of blue
Darken with each passing moment

To attempt to count the galaxy of stars dimly twinkling
Or brightly winking as they capture our full attention

Old man on the sea,
How I envy as I dream of the day
When I, too, can chart my course towards the heavens.

Melissa G. McCoig

My Gift Of Life

Dedicated to Dwayne Anthony Saxton (son)
and Tawanna Nicole Saxton (daughter)

Have you ever wondered why you're here
Why, for me to love and care for my dear
When you were conceived, it was out of love not hate
And it took nine months for you to make
The father that was suppose to be
We never married, let this not be a mystery
I'll feed you, so that you never experience the hunger pains
I'll cloth you, so that your body never feels the frost or rain
I have little money to offer
But will you accept my gift of life my son and daughter
For you were born out of wedlock, which is nothing new
THE MOST IMPORTANT THING IS THAT I'LL ALWAYS
LOVE YOU

    Pamela J. Saxton

Tomorrow Is Another Day

If things seem to go all wrong.
Why not try singing a peppy, happy song.
Maybe things will change, maybe not.
But my friend you haven't loss a lot.

Problems are opportunities turn inside out.
It doesn't do any good to pout.
Let's stop and look at it this way.
Tomorrow is another day.

Things even then may be still...
Just a little bit up hill.
Tho later, who knows, you might be able to say,
You know, my problems have gone away.

So when confronted with problems, don't despair.
Just go ahead and hang in there,
And always remember to say,
Tomorrow's gonna be a better day..

    J. M. Hill

Out Of Chaos

Time is one place where Seekers find
Why, out of chaos, clarity
emerges as the verb TO BE.

Knowing the first commandment is
that "Thou shalt love the Lord thy God
with all thy heart, and soul, and mind,"

Know, down the ages, where the Word,
as Son-of-God, is recognized,
eternal Laws are energized:

As mass accrues from what was His,
the Ah-ha-flash, though primary,
marks what-is-not-thought-through, "deferred"!

Leptons and quarks, the building blocks
for subatomic particles,
reject, in recent articles,
the old earth-air-fire-water quiz.

While Science, for precision timing,
relies upon atomic clocks,
powered by Higgs' pervasive aether-wraith,
Bosons, conveying concepts, re-form faith—

    Phebe Alden Tisdale

Home

"Oh" God, I wonder the mystery,
Why thy hand, has passed over me,
Why, I must live this life of pain,
And others pass, each day the same.
Others seem, the chosen few, that belong to you.
What, must I do?
How can I, find you in my heart,
When, I feel were apart.
Is it my soul, that cries for
love from you Lord above.
Can't you see? - it's me
That needs a' reason
To pass each day and season
To find a moment of peace,
my soul, I would release
For you to have and hold
And when I'm told
That God loves' me, I would happily
Go into thy throne, and find
that place called home.

    Marie L. O'Connor

All Mazed Up

The little mouse is on his own now.
Will he make it through this maze?
He encounters many turns and dead ends,
But the wrong path does not bring any praise.

Will he never taste the cheese
At the exit for which he hunts?
Will he ever reach his goal?
Will he ever get what he wants?

The little mouse explores every turn now.
He refuses to give up on his plight.
He travels in many directions,
But there seems to be no end in sight.

Will he ever choose the right path?
Will he ever find his way?
He may be searching for a while,
But he will find his way out someday.

    Keith E. Savage

Love Wonders

I wonder if there's answer to the questions that I ask.
Will I feel the calm again, or must I wear this mask?
Can I find the smile I lost somewhere in the crowd?
Help me hold my head up high and say that I am proud.
Squeeze my hand and whisper, tell me "it's O.K.".
"Life is just beginning, there's peace in each new day."
Keep me strong, please guide me through
Until I feel the sun
Warm my heart and tell me that
You and I are one.

    Janis V. Smith

One Life's Journey

The days go by slowly and since the last goodbye
which one of us went the wrong way.
We both hid our pain in one destructive way.
Choices. Too many decisions. I was there to help you fight and
soon I became a slave just like you. We made the choice. But how
long did it last? The road to happiness was in the past. We
always fight but no one seems to win. A constant battle in our own
soul. Who knows when we shall meet again. Maybe never. So all
we'll share is memories. But somehow I will find a way to make it
as it was, before my long and strange journey.

    Shannon Chanel Schmidt

Together

If I tell you I love you,
will you care?
If I tell you I need you,
will you be there?

through the days and nights of gentle despair,
Our love has come a long way
And both you and I have brought it there.

You have walked on thick and thin
I have walked on hot and cold
for our love to stay together
and never let it unfold.

Though the days are getting longer
and the wind may blow too cold,
we'll still stand by each other
and walk down loves' twisted road.

Nita Sylvia

Imagine

Imagine if the birds didn't spread their
  wings and fly away,
Imagine if they didn't chirp and sing
  day after day.
Imagine if the bees didn't buzz all around,
  or if the ants didn't crawl on the ground.
Imagine if the sun would no longer
  shine, and what if a cat had
only one life instead of nine?
  Imagine if a dog could not bark,
Imagine Noah, without an Ark.
  These are things we take for granted
everyday throughout the years,
  imagine if one day, the world disappears.

Nicki Hinman

Winter Wonderland

The farmhouse lights are warmly glowing on a starry moon-lit
  winter night.
The barn packed with cattle, milked and bedded to the farmer's
  great delight.
The tractor, plow and hay rake huddled 'neath a snow laden shed;
The farm hands leaping through the snow-drifts to the farmhouse
  to be fed.

The pine forest on the hillside looks like winter Wonderland.
Snow covered weeds and brush were painted by God's hand.
The full moon sends its beams of light across the sparkling snow,
Where laughing children ride their sleds, throwing snowballs
  as they go.

A flock of geese fly overhead, and I marvel how they know;
At the changing of each season, which way that they should go.
I hear the beating of their wings, and the honking that they make.
Gazing up, I almost see God's finger pointing the way that they
  should take.

A silver cloud passes and the moon seems peaking through;
And in that space between moon and cloud, I think God is
  watching too!
I would not exchange these happy memories for any city life;
Thank God that I have chosen to be a country wife.

Marion Schoonbeck

Paradise Cafe

A grease-stained rag
  wipes smile-wrinkled eyes
as long-haired barefoot children
  dodge the broken glass and run their muddy
  chocolate fingers over the rusty iron bars
squinting through dirty windows
at smoke-enveloped turntables of dusty donuts
  stale and forgotten remembering...
the thick calloused fingers of workers, and
the smell of coffee at midnight
now, a faded blue overhang
  torn, sagging with the weight of
  Time and weary raindrops
as the fluorescent light
  flickers, and flies tiptoe
across the cracked plastic booths
And the tired old lady with the
  green-handled broom
sweeps away the cobwebs
  and the memories of paradise.

Kim Burnside

Untitled

When like a tree in the wind you sway
Wistfully to me, as languid with need,
The sweetest words I could dream would not say
What clearer in your reaching arms I read.
And like a tree you awaken to me,
Barn forsaken for skin of an dread
Borne softly here from some old mythology
With limbs alive, so beautifully bodied,
That I would wish to free this world of words,
Grow roots, clap hands in applause of the wind,
Be silent with you but for a few birds
Whose happy speech any can understand.
Girl, when you tilt your arms to me like this,
Your love's more articulate than a kiss.

S. Benado

My Granny's Curls

When I was just a little girl
  with a "hot-dog" curl,
My mom told me never to stare.
I loved to watch my Granny brush her long brown hair.
Her hands were so quick,
  as she brushed it back so slick.
All placed neatly in a ball
  letting me pin the hair as we sit at the dresser in the hall.
I was sad when she got her first perm,
  it made her look a bit stern.
Her hair was all in a curl,
No more brushing while telling stories of when she was a girl.
She did not look like my Granny anymore,
  looking up at her with teary eyes as I sit on the bedroom floor.

Patsy Ann Penny

Untitled

It came as a surprise on that dreadful day,
When I got the call that you'd been taken away,
I couldn't believe what I was told,
My heart that once beat was now stone cold,
I couldn't understand why it had to be you,
I did not know what I was to do,
But now I see why it ended this way,
Why God had taken you on that day,
So when I pray, I pray someday to see,
My special uncle that was taken away from me.

Kaysee Mathis

Love Thy Neighbor As You Love Thyself

What a wonderful world this would be,
with all it's wonder to see;
so much love to give, we could live so peaceful,
so happily, if only we would love our
neighbor as we love ourself.

The splendor of living, loving, sharing and
Oh yes, caring about each other.
The joy of giving, the ability to forgive,
the humbleness that comes only by love,
making understanding not only possible
but easy to, all of this and more can be ours,
if we would love our neighbor as we love ourself.

The true meaning of family, as only God intended,
united as one, bound by love, standing together in harmony,
seeking eternal bliss by way of righteousness,
surely we must all come to realize,
that these things we will understand,
only when we love thy neighbor as we love thyself.

Mary F. Nicholson

"My Only True Love"

I am alone, in the still of the night
With darkness all around,
Thinking of how it could've been with you
The only true love I had found.

All of the time we spent together
All of the fun we had,
My feelings were of happiness
And now my feelings are sad.

You were the only one to understand
My thoughts and my fears,
The only one who was there
To wipe away my tears.

In your eyes I seen my life
And with your words I was swept away,
These things I think to myself,
While here in confusion I lay.

As I look at the sky
And the twinkling stars above,
I ask myself, crying
Did I loose my only true love?

Monica Michelle Price

Seductress

You are in the moment
   with her.
You constantly step outside to be
   with her.

She's intoxicating, captivating,
   stimulating!
You're like a pole wrapped up
by a tetherball, bound-to her.

You can't get enough of her.
You inhale her, smell like her and represent her.

She says, "Spend money on me."
   You do.
She wants you to give her your energy.
   You are.

And she asks that you rest
   in peace with her -
      you will.

She's all yours, and you hers.
   She's your little cigarette,
   she tempted me too.

Nancy Anne Chapin

The Christmas Tree

Beautiful tree, its branches are beaming,
With lights of all colors
Ornaments with special meanings.
The month that it lives
In houses and buildings,
So radiant and pretty,
So full of life, and still breathing.

Yet then comes the day
The tree loses its beaming
Undecorated, left barren,
No special meaning.
The Christmas tree that once was so pretty,
Is now just a tree, not even breathing.

The tree cannot choose to live or to die,
It just shrivels away, no sound, no cry.
The tree is left, to be broken and torn,
Stricken with death, no longer loved and adorned.

Maria R. Kelly

"Campfire"

   Come sit by my fire and talk
with me awhile.
   Let me get to know you
I kinda like your style.

   We seek to warm our bodies by
the fire and hot coals;
   The conversation of kindred spirits
will warm our hearts and souls.
   As we look into the flame see the
burning embers a glow;
   Maybe like the campfire, the warmth
of our friendship will continue to
grow.

   Looking across the campfire through
the flickering fire light, illusions come then
fade away, as reality and truth shine
forth bright as day.

   Long after the campfire's ashes have
grown cold the distant, stirring memories
will burn within our soul.

Paul E. Wilson

Two Grains of Sand

Two grains of sand lay on separate shores
With millions of grains — yet alone.
Then the ocean of love washed them away
On a journey to a new home.

The both saw their share of stormy seas.
They saw the ebb and the flow of the tide.
They felt the salt in the sea that surrounded their lives,
And they remembered the tears they'd seen cried.

At last, they both came to rest on a singular shore —
Held together by one drop of sea.
No longer alone; no longer apart —
The force of nature had answered their plea.

And now two grains of sand become one through their need —
Their long journey home finally done.
And the ocean of love ebbs and flows at their feet
As they bask in the slow-rising sun.

Michael S. Kelley

Unaware, Unforgettable, Yet A Cherished Proposal

Under the moonlight
with my boyfriend for life
hand on hand as we slow dance
looking into each others eyes
with such feeling and pride
sneaking a kiss from time to time.

Music slows down as another song began's
some couples disembark
while others take a spin
leading me off the dance floor
we go back to sit
when my boyfriend bends down on one knee
with a little black box in hand
he says you have been my sunshine and sunset
now it's time for my girlfriend to become
my night, moonlight, and importantly my wife
well you marry me with love in his eyes
My reply is yes with no doubt in my mind.

Shamika Gilkey

Sunset Rising

The southern hills of Tennessee were green
    With pine, and each mound pushed the next until
They left small space for little dells between,
    As roads went either up or down a hill.

The sun that lingered in the western sky
    Looked low to me when I was the dell,
But when I topped the next hill, it was high;
    It seemed to bounce as quickly as it fell.

The western sun, poised large and round and gold,
    Dipped down below the hill top. It had set.
But as I climbed another hill, behold!
    I saw the sunset rise! how strange! and yet - -

As I face now my lowering western skies,
I marvel how you make my sunset rise!

Lois Hervey

Sweet Sympathy

And his whisper was the kindling for her soul;
With that soft light, it was easy to see the emptiness
dancing with the dead.
His kisses were her breath for a new life resuscitated.
Dreams remembered, identities forgotten or left behind.
Convenient clean choices rusted in this bitterly cold clear light.

His touch remembered her passion.
Dulled nerve endings screamed in seeming pain and delight;
Liquid tongues nipping at icicle veins.
Baptized in his flesh and her need,
Her path made more difficult for the seeing of it,
The knowing of it, the choice of it,

Sweet Sympathy, help me to dream, to remember.
Illuminate my journey.
Cleanse me that I may see my direction
And burn me with your eyes
That I may feel the pain of life's joy.
Clutch my memory of you.
Keep me close. Keep me alive.

Lee Anne McCain

In Transition

Fear, a gray amorphous mass, envelopes me
With the viral fever, the headache, the maybe
Hallucinations, "Could he die, Ed?" "Perhaps."
Fear at first, then acceptance, not to struggle.
Recurring each night 'til any struggle is gone—Sleep.
Gone with spirit is goal, focus;
Resolve is gone, limping after awareness.
Potency leaves with sense of self-assertion—Sleep.
Abdication of self leaves the hollow man,
The microcosmic inner self, no longer inner directed—Dream.
The empty inner eye and aging outer together in acuity
No notice or response to danger nor to opportunity—sleep.
Fear cusps in acrophobia; the terror is not in falling.
Cold sweat shows one wishes to fall: fake a life.
Flaccidity follows the pubertal spurt of self-determination
And makes resurrection of potent self a chancy thing—Fear.
Remove the fog; I deadened myself.

Mike Ryan

The Night

You were a moment in my night.
With you my life seemed so bright.
It seemed a never ending song.
Sometimes painful, sometimes happy.
Sometimes weak, sometimes strong.

I dream of you, a friend once true.
We were together, it seemed forever.
But then you turned,
for the old you I did yearn.

What you did, I can not forgive.
You held a knife, you took a part of my life.
There was no blood,
but of pain there was a flood.

You didn't care of the pain you left there.
Now, you pretend we were not friends.
The road we walked, has now an end.

You were a moment in my night.
Now of you I want no sight.

Kim Fadenrecht

The Storm Within Me

Up the coast, this storm did come,
without a warning or prediction of none.

Blowing its fearful winds and fiery temper,
it ripped through me with every strength in her.

Tossing and turning, leaving me lost at sea,
peeling layer upon layer, of all my humanity.

Till and endless sleep of fog, rolled in from sea,
smothering me from all breath, preparing for what's to be.

Then a prism of light, shined through my very core,
a lighthouse above, beckoning me safely ashore.

To the light my storm driven body did follow,
till all was light, and no tomorrow.

God's light of love had set me free,
calming the storm within me.

No more pain nor suffering I will bare,
only God's eternal life I shall share.

Kathy Preston

The Thief

A grown man sitting under a willow tree
wonders how his precious life
could have withered away so suddenly
His childhood, adolescent years
all specks of the past
How could this be?
One day it's here, and the next, it's gone
Gone with the wind as Margaret Mitchell would say
And the man weeps...and weeps some more
Time keeps passing as the day grows old
Noticing weeping won't accomplish anything
the man begins to walk, he walks
as time keeps passing by, and the sun begins to set
Another day here ... and gone
all of the past, and soon will be dawn
so cherish each and every moment of your life
for no moment can happen twice
A great man once said,
"There is only one thief in this world
And that thief we cannot catch - Time"

Kingto Tsai

Importance of Life

If life would lay beyond your dreams,
Would it ever end or fray at the seams.
Should destiny call who could stand proud?
Life goes beyond just following the crowd.

Innocence leads hearts into happiness
this feeling fades for a reason I guess.
When growing older you become aware,
What once were chances are no longer there.

Life seems clearer when you're in charge
If you fall behind problems seem large.
So if life betrays your only dreams,
Always remember the chances it brings.

Michelle Burtner

"Life's Colors"

If we could but choose our color
Would we choose white or black?
Or would we choose red or yellow,
Maybe even another color from life's color stack?
There are browns of many shades
And reds and blacks and white.
No matter what color we might choose,
Does my color make it right?
I do not know Gods reason
That man comes in many colors and hues,
But I do believe He gave us an example
Not only for me but also for you.
Did not God create the beautiful wild flowers,
That grow in yonder field?
Whether they are black or white, brown or yellow,
They grow in harmony—it's Gods will.

Margie Reed Barnwell

Snow

Snow is like feathers falling down,
And flying all around.

When the snow reaches the ground,
It makes a little "tink" sound.

As the snow gets higher and higher,
The weather gets drier and drier.

Snow is a good feeling,
Which shows a sign that fall is leaving.

Sonia Jomaa

The Race

I run to relieve the pains of despair
Yearning for a dream to perceive.
Somewhere in time's lonely bottomless lair
I search for a way to leave.

A fear to allow the gift of the heart to give,
And a trust that desires be built;
Making each day a joy to relive,
A time without sorrow or guilt.

So longs this heart to find its way,
To reach the crest of love's hill,
Sharing and spending life's long day
As if time itself stood still.

Can life be endured and fulfilled to its heights
When one's heart is lonely and stained?
Or is there a dream to be held in sight?
Else all life's emotions be drained.

And so I run to relieve the pains of despair,
Knowing full well this dream is not real.
And I stay in life's lonely bottomless lair
Unable to love or to feel...

P. Gayle McCarthy

A Vase On My Window Sill

There is a vase on my window sill, that has filled this space for years. I placed it there when my children were small. They would come in with wild flowers pulled by the roots, held in their grubby little hands and say, "Mama, I brought you a bouquet." I would take them with my heart full, to know, even in their playing time they took time to remember, Mama.

Then they grow up and move on to more important things. It sets empty for years, but I still keep it handy just in case.

Then life takes a turn and they marry and move away to start homes of their own. They then begin to bring you more important things, one of life's most wonderful gifts, "Grandchildren."

No more wonderful call to receive than to hear, "Mama, it's a boy!" or "it's a girl!".

In a few years the vase begins to be used again.... "Grandma, I brought you some flowers."

I will always keep my vase on the window sill ready. I hope there will always be someone to come along to fill it.

When the lord calls me home, I would request there be a vase on my grave, where my children, grandchildren, and even great grandchildren can come by and say, "Mama, I brought you some flowers...."

Maude F. Truluck

The Beauty Of Nature

I am astounded by the beauty of nature.
Yet, some people let it pass them by.
They never notice the sunset,
Or the way that the birds fly.

They've never gazed at the stars
On a night that is so clear.
They never appreciate the smell of cut grass,
Or the sound of a whip-o-whil.

They've never felt cool water on their feet,
From a fresh mountain stream.
They've never starred at the clouds,
And created a new dream.

They go through life with narrow minds,
And appreciate only material things.
They never realize the beauty of nature,
And all the tranquility it brings.

Julie A. Hawkins

Lost Time

The hands of time are spinning,
yet we always seem to lack
the fact that time is passing
and we may never gain it back.

Living for the moment,
is what we're always told —
to be free in spirit,
to be daring and be bold.

We constantly complain
that there's no time for this or that.
Think of all the time we've wasted
on the chair on which we sat.

Time is our most precious gift,
I truly am sincere.
Do not waste, but cherish it —
there's no telling how long we'll be here.

Kara DeDecker

The Price Of Freedom

Man, clever creature with superior brain
You are chained to the earth by your own selfish gain.
You cry, "We're the masters of all that we see!"
But greed feeds on itself, you will never be free.

I'm the vulture, a scavenger, a scourge of mankind.
Yet, I clean up the spoils that you leave behind.
I fly on the currents, so don't pity me.
Alone in the heavens, I know I am free.

I'm the jackal, repulsive; a feral beast.
Your refuse and carrion make up my feast.
At night as I howl at the sky and I see
The moon in the heavens, I know I am free.

An algae eater, with no real contribution?
I do not waste, but clean up the pollution.
As I purge the rivers, the lakes, and the seas,
In the depths of my heavens, I know I am free.

As you squander our land, and our food, fuel and wood,
Use your power and talents as you know you should.
Be selfless, be caring, protect all you see.
Take a lesson from nature and then you'll be free.

Judith Green

Poem About Fall

The leaves fall like feathers on your face
You can jump in its pile
You can climb the tree
Your hands will touch the beautiful trees
You can even find inchworms
living on the leaves
The colors I see are gold, orange, red
sometimes even purple.
A chill in the wind comes brushing by
and blows you into the pile of colorful leaves
You can find a comfortable spot in a tree
If you look up you can see
the cotton clouds go by
Soon, I will be sad to see
branches covered with snow and ice
The golden colors of fall will be replaced
by the blanket of snow that winter folds
across the world . . .

Nicole DiAlfonso

Traces Of Us

Standing where Penfold road meets Lake Louise
you can see the smoke still hangs
on the cracking trees
from the house fire that ran the cellar
and wrapped Brent's hands forever
with deep purple stains like velvet.
The breeze crawls thick through the fields
on the corner stirring
the solemn hopes and scent of cloves
we draped there trying to find
answers to our misleading youth
hidden in the long grass.
And mornings when the sun pounds hard into the lake,
our frail young spirit shines up through her,
grinning an innocence it holds
from our first nakedness the night
we convinced ourselves we'd sinned well.
These things will not change now.
They're a part of the landscape, as touchable
as the heat, as moveable from there as from us.

Kathryn Flewelling

I Loved You

When I found you, I wasn't looking
    you caught me off guard.
When I fell for you, I did it right,
    fell real hard.
When I let my heart be taken
    I gave it all the way
When my love for you awakened
    you became apart of my every day.
It was the first time, I ever felt so alive
It was my first love, and baby
    I already past 25.
I loved you for your honesty,
    your strength, and your pride.
I loved you for the butterflies,
    you made me feel inside.
I loved you for the way you cared,
    the strength you gave, when I was scared.
    I loved you for, your laughter shared.
I loved you for, your heart that's free.
I loved you just, for loving me.

Patricia Ann Sandoval

Dreams Of Long Ago

Sometimes at night when you're sound asleep
You dream of lying in the grass so sweet
As Indians, people of long, long ago
Found splendor in nature both high and low
But misuse and change have wasted it all
leaving but a trace of what once was so great
The white brought new things
Just drove out the old
Slaughtering the ways
Indian stories untold
And bringing their armies
Their Killers
Their Men
Forced the ending people
to give up their land
The Indians living in concealment
And fear
Afraid we white were stalking
Or near.

Joanna Nelson

My Friend

Goodbye sweet Wylie, I miss you so!
You gave me more pleasure than you'll ever know!
Only God could design such a gorgeous creature,
So cunning and perfect in every feature!
I know you longed to be wild and free,
So selfish to keep you, just for me!
Your yellow eyes outlined in black,
The guard hairs standing on your back,
Your ears aware of the faintest noise,
Standing there in elegant poise.
Gods awesome creature on display.
Mine for awhile, now gone away.
Back to the wild where you belong,
Running free - singing your song.

Merlene S. Watkins

Warriors of God

Oh warriors of God
You guide us with Strength and Wisdom

Your gloves are pure velvet
And are filled with His power

His Word is your sword of righteousness
It cuts to the heart with precision

It illuminates our lives
To guide us out of the darkness
Into which we have cast ourselves into

It holds words of Hope, Glory and Greatness
Of Resurrection, everlasting Life and Love

Adorned with your armor of Grace and Faith
Your souls stay calm but powerful
Able to meet any challenge

Nigel Johnson

Always

You have guided my life with your warm and tender heart
You have helped me see the way through your bright and shiny eyes
You have helped me when I needed you over silly little things
You always make me smile when I hold you in my dreams
I love the way you love me and kiss me tenderly
I love to hear your laughter and see your smiling face
I hold you in my arms and feel your warm embrace
I know I'll always need you you're so much a part of me
We have a perfect love for which I'm proud to say
All the love and all the caring keep growing day by day
I know I'll always love you until death do us part
But even at that moment you'll still be in my heart
For now you see my darling how much you mean to me
For I believe that love for us will always be

Linda Kisovic

Imagine

The wind who cries so loud and clear
Yet whispers softly into my ear
Tells me of a place not very far from here
Where I can go to quench my fears.
It's not very big nor tall nor wide
But inside this place there's no reason to hide.
A warm soothing mist linger sweetly in the air
And inside this place all is calm, all is far
Here the gentle caress of a fairies' touch
Can send you into a dream world of knights and armor and such.
This place beyond your wildest creation
Can only be found in your imagination.

Kate Bergen

Spirit Of Your Mind

Rest, oh child, rest....
You have too much on your mind,
Too many things to do and think about.
Rest, and you shall be rejuvenated
For you have been ill from the poison of your mind.

You need to rest...
I will guide you.
Do not worry...for in time...you will know
You need a change in your life.
It will be hard for you at first — the change.
But you will know why it came about.
Rest and renew yourself now.

Oh spirit of your mind...
Renew yourself now.

Karolyn Bader

The Best In Me

In your eyes and in your voice
    You haven't left me any choice.
Your arms around me, hold me tight
    there's no way I can leave tonight.

I want to tell you how I feel,
    and how your heart I want to steal.
To cherish you and make you smile
    and stay around a long, long while.

To share our lives, our dreams, and hopes
    and run to when it's hard to cope.
Let's fight, let's love, let's laugh and cry
    but please, let's never say goodbye.

I need you in my life you see
For you bring out the best in me.

Laurie Jackson

"For A Friend"

You wiped away my tears,
You heard and knew all my fears.
I knew I could talk to you,
You knew how to act and what to do.
You listened so carefully...
You knew how much it meant to me.
You are a true friend, I won't deny.
You are honest and won't lie.
You care so very much.
To me you have a special touch.
I trust you will all my heart.
Our friendship is a magical piece of art.
So remember me my special friend,
I'll remember you till the end.
I'll know you'll always be there.
To listen, understand, and care.

Leslie Perez

Marriage

There is a time coming,
Where there are no goodbyes.
When the day ends in the arms of one another.
There is a time coming,
When we share our personal struggles.
Hand in hand we learn to support without suffocation.
When necessary a shoulder is available.
There is a time coming.
It seems I have waited so long for,
Where I receive as much love as I give.

Kay Camacho

"Sailing"

You ask me if it's all too much.
You know - the wine, the music, the candle.
And I remember how you dusted the long-stemmed champagne glasses
And how you lit the candle filled with oil for the first time,
Carefully - hoping it would offer just the right amount of light.
And then you kissed me, laying me in your bed,
Joining me with both glasses of Callaway wine,
A discovery if yours from a California vineyard.
With my head on your pillow, close to you, touching.
I watched the images on the ceiling.
A soft, sculptured shadow painting
Emanating from the windows of the lighthouse candle.
And I remembered your love of the wind and the water
And wondered how it feels to sail on a July night like this.
And then you touched my hair,
The softness surrounding my face that has never been touched.
It is then that I learned the gentleness of the waves
And the undulating infinite of my lover of the sea.

Marianne Peel

The Pepper Tree

Pepper tree, you're such a wondrous sight,
you loom up with much strength and might.

Some green, as if to never fade.
Some barren, dry, as if that way made.

As a child, a remembrance of a pepper tree,
held a swing of many moments of glee.
When I dared, I heard my own laughter,
And childhood songs of rhyme.
Feeling free as a child should be
Which was seldom, at the time.

A wonderful memory made from the past from me,
By a grandpa, with a shy love,
And quiet laughter in his heart.
He had comfort in knowing,
This child's memory, his loving hand took part

Marjorie Kosareff

You're The One For Me

You brighten all my days.
You make my life worth living in so many ways.
Your everything my love.
Your the joy to my world.
And your smile brings out the warmth
    in my heart.
My friends say how lucky, how lucky
    I am to have a love like you my Dear.
I remember things you do and remember things
    you say.
And the look on your face takes my breath away.
I knew for long time you were the one
    for me.
And no one can ever take your place
And Darling I hope you'll always be, always
    be in Love with Me.

Nicholas Ranalli

Compromise

If you compromise your integrity —
You make the wrong choice,
If you are deceptive —
You chose the wrong voice,
If you err in your perception —
redirect your eye,
For your soul is far too much to pay —
for the pleasure of a lie.

If you right the wrongs of indiscretion —
peace of mind will follow,
If you right the wrongs of deception —
peace of mind will follow,
For peace lies in the ocean of truth —
where integrity shines bright,
not within any sea of money —
one pays in exchange for what's right.

So never compromise your integrity —
to your ownself forever be true,
For there is one person you could never avoid —
undeniably till death it is you.

S. Jyla Lacy

"My Mother"

You are a woman who's thoughtful, kind, and sweet,
You never minded the dirtiness of my face, hands, and feet.

When I ask you questions, you try your best to reply;
When I just need to talk, you are always close by.

Because I know your advice is true,
What you say, I will do.

You work so hard at work and at home,
You do what's right, even when alone.

No matter what you're doing, or even how bad you're bored
You always try your best and ask for help from the LORD.

Whenever I need to shed a tear
You always seem to be right here.

Sometimes, you cry right along with me
And even let me sit upon your knee.

You laugh with me, you cry with me,
You give your input happily.

The reasons that I love you are far too may to count,
The medals to give you would be far so too many to mount.

I love you, don't you see?
And I know that you love me!

Leslie Richards

Love

Hello
you are laughing; rolling me over
into your arms; holding me;
kissing me; saying how lucky you are
I am content; fulfilled, happy watching you
revel in your Manhood.

Suddenly

you are angry; pushing me away
from you; shoving me ; hitting me;
saying how suffocated you are
I am terrified; wounded, slain watching you revel
in your manhood,
Goodbye.

Patricia A. Stokes

When I Look Upon This Child

When you look at this child
you see ugliness, Black, Scrawny, Loud, dusty woolly hair,
Big lips, Bucktooth, bugged out eyes, Pungent odor.

When I look upon this child, I see, Beauty without comparison.
Smooth ebony skin stretched over a lithe frame.
Elegant in it's movements, no matter how rapid.

When I look upon this child
I listen to the voice that will one day rule as a leader
or in harmonious melody, transfix millions.

The woolly hair, a symbol of what humanity should be,
undivided, intertwined with one another in glorious union.

The full curvaceous lips, which spreads when amused
and pouts when disappointed, encases pearl white bone.

The eyes, as it stares in wonder at a strange world, absorbs the good
and the bad.
Looking into them reveal an ever growing flame, that only negativity
could dampen.

The scent, a product of activity from within combined with exterior
forces untouched by fabricated aromas.
All these elements chant an ancestry of Divinity and Order
of Struggle and Hope, of Love and Conquest, a Oneness with it's
Creator...............

Kenol Lamour

A New Beginning

Just when I feel the pain is too great
you show me a new beginning
As the sun shines down from the heavens above
I realize there is no ending

As I grieve over my painful loss
you are welcoming someone back home
A place I can only dream about going
Where no one is ever alone

A place where sadness and sorrow don't go
where the streets are forever clean
And the fruit on the trees is bountiful there
A place where everyone sings

So let me rejoice on this day of my loss
for the life that is now beginning
Let the sun shine down from the heavens above
I realize there is no ending.

Misty Dawn

Love's First Lesson

You and I met — we thought "God send"
You sought my allegiance — time again.

Marriage you wanted — "yes," I said.
Instead, we confirmed our love in bed..

Trusting in love — my riches, I did lend.
Because of love, a spiritual purse I did spend.

Love me, yes. Your love was only a want!
The Lord parted our way — now, feelings just haunt.

Strangers bestirred with time, no more to gain.
I still love you as my first, but last you became.

Joan E. Simonetti

My Son, My Son

I've been with you from the very moment
you took your first breathe of life.

When I embrace you and hold you ever
so close to my breast, I don't want you to
ever know about hardship and strife.

The beginning years are filled with the
first of this and the first of that, and I try
to instill in you to remember to say please and thank you,
and I wonder what will you be?

As you travel through your wonder years
and find the things that interest you, I
say to myself, those expressions you make
remind me a little of me.

Please let me say I'm sorry for working and working
so long. I'm hurt inside when I look up to see how
tall you've become. Oh God! I cry, am I too late?
When and where has all the time gone?

With a wife in mind at this time,
I know my job is done. I'll say good-bye
to my little boy, but you'll always be my son.

Michelle A. Thomas

"A Birthmother's Prayer"

For all the year's we were apart,
You were always in my heart.
I sent you a kiss into the wind,
Hoping each time, it would reach you then
I kissed the wind so you
Would feel a Mother's love so very real
I ask the heavens to keep you safe,

To hold your hand, to watch you play.
I find you now my dream come
True, I only wish the best for you
A part of me, you will
Always be waiting here for you to see.

Mary H. Hart

"God's Special Gift"

I couldn't wait to hold you in my arm's,
    You were so perfect.
I counted every little finger and toe
    just to make sure they were all there.
I would watch you while you slept.
And there were times when
    I'd just sit and hold you
    just to feel you close to me.
You were my special gift from God.
You taught me to love when I
    thought I couldn't love anymore.
Now that you are getting older, I can't hold
    You on my lap anymore, or watch you
    while you sleep.
But I want you to know that no matter
    how old or how big you get,
    I will always love you.
You will always be my special gift from God.

Joann Britt

Whispers To A Friend

I look up at Heaven and see you standing still.
You will never know the fortunes of what might have
been a good life.
Makes me wonder what really lies above.
Are you happy there riding eternity on a cloud?
Why did no one listen,
When you reached out for help?
Why was no one listening when you heart beat it's last time?
I look up at Heaven and see you standing still;
And I realize nothing in life comes easy.
I whisper your name in the wind hoping I'll
hear an answer, but no one talks back.
Makes me wonder what God has to offer.
I look up at the skies, looking for answers,
But all I see is a calmness...
Your memory standing still in mine,
And I wonder - is there really happy ever after?

Patti Kostiou

The Town Of Don't You Worry

There is a town called don't
you worry in the banks of
river smile, where the cheer up
and be happy blossom sweetly all the while.

Where the never grumble flower
blooms beside the fragrant try,
and the never give up patience
point their faces to the sky.

In the valley of contentment
in the province of I will,
you will find this lovely city
at the foot of no fret hill,

Rustic benches quite enticing
you'll find scattered here and
there, and to such a vine is
clinging call the fragrant earnest prayer.

Every body there is happy
they are singing all the while,
in the town of don't you worry
on the banks of river smile.

Minnie Lee Hope

The Tiny Dancer

Tiny dancer, tonight was your night.
Your dance recital, everything was just right.
As you soared through the air and you twirled and you pranced
You knew they were watching and clapped as you danced.
Your beautiful Mom with her radiant smile
and your famous Daddy all made it worthwhile.
Your family all came, your grandparents, too.
They were all watching, all watching you.
Pretty pictures were taken with your Mom and with Dad
and to a posh restaurant, a fancy meal to be hand.
The night was complete when you sat down to eat
to celebrate your dance and give you a treat.
Then later that evening was a gruesome attack
and your momma lay bleeding and she's not coming back.
You try to be strong as you comfort your brother,
but no one can ever take the place of your mother.
You went to the funeral and you gripped you Dad's hand
You looked up in his face, but you couldn't understand.
Tiny dancer, we're weeping with you
for all that has happened and all you've been through.

Vicki Arnold

Soul Of Eve

Soaring at the speed of light
Your eyes are the portals
Taking my spirit, my essence to another universe, another dimension
Gliding gently aloft on the wings of souls
To that land of vast eternity, of perpetual infinity
A thousand radiant moons, a million brilliant suns
Purple hanging cliffs and deep lavender mountains
Raging oceans of red crashing upon limitless white shore lines
Angry blaze orange seas smashing across sparkling reefs of diamond
Rivers of gold bathing valleys of pearl
Ancient monuments of silver embraced by divine clouds of platinum
This land so rich, so pure
This world so rare, so true
This universe, this dimension
That is your soul

Michael Adam Acevedo

Hard to Say Good-Bye

The day you were born the sun was bright,
your fingers and toes all in perfect sight.
I was only 18 when you came into my life,
I was just a mommy and not a wife.
Our lives were so complete, just you and I,
Five years so fast it just all blew by.
I always expressed how much I loved you,
I wish I could still hear those words too.
Now God has chosen for you to be with him,
I feel like a tree with all dead limbs.
I feel so alone and so scared,
you are my son, the one I barred.
Please send a sign son to the reason why,
you left me alone and made me say good-bye,
though I know you're safe in heaven above
what am I suppose to do, I have no one to love.
Again someday you'll be in my arms and I'll never let go,
we will be together someday I know.
So if you can hear me I just want to say,
I will never forget you for you're in my heart every day.

Melissa Helmick

A Person In Need

Although I wonder in my mind.
Your love my LORD is hard to find.
The streets are bare and taverns full.
No one out but me the fool.
Yet I seek a brand new life.
With joy of riches in grand delight.
So much my mind contest to thee.
Oh! bring me home from this misery.
How late the hour and weak my faith.
Can JESUS CHRIST still save today?
I cry within, my life is doomed.
Can you enter this lonely room?
A door is set before my eyes anew.
The LORD says knock and I will end your gloom.
I knock, the door is open wide.
To receive the Groom to its Bride.
The Groom is JESUS, the Bride the Church.
He awaits repentance, confession, a new birth.
Come my children I have paid the price.
Receive Me in your heart tonight.

Humble Love

Life

To care is important but not everything—we also need to share
Will sharing fill the empty space—only with concern that's fair

Will concern itself stop the hectic pace—no! patience must appear
Will patience cure the daily aches—no! But faith will heal the fear

Will faith make music fill the air—no! Laughter has it's place
Is laughter the answer by itself—no! Empathy shows with grace

Will empathy end it all with peace—no! Religion soothes the soul
Will religion end the futile search-it helps but love becomes the goal

Then love is it, the search is through—think wisely heart for love is you.
Remember all virtues have time and place—and life goes on from case to case

We conquer adversity day by day—we worry, we fret, we stand in dismay
In the end we finally know—the struggle was the thing that made us grow

Love wins the final battle and calms the sea-to love is to be loved
and to love is to be.
    Ralph C. Dix

Captivity

Your eyes cast the shadows of the desires, held captive within.
Your smile, nonchalant in effort to disguise your depravation,
While resting upon your forehead, there is a map to all that is
    and has been foreign to you.
The lines display, the wants you've yearned to possess
    and the needs you've yet to fulfill.
Your hands, they tremble as you eagerly reach to feel me in
    your embrace.
Your lips, they hunger thirstily to feel the closeness of mine.
Your heart, it beats fervently against my back as you become
    imprisoned by the thought of someone loving you,
As you once loved.
The more you touch, the more you want to feel.
The more you taste, the more you hunger.
The closer you get, the more you fear...
Loving again....
So you distance yourself and remain captive to a once broken heart.
    L. Shelton

I Am

I am a colored girl in an uncolored world I wonder if my grandchildren
will be able to play outside without having to worry about what racist
names they'll be called. I hear racist names being called out to my
son as he is walking to school in the mornings. I see myself fighting
so that my kids and I will be treated as equal as an uncolored person.
I want my son to be able to go outside in an uncolored neighborhood
without being harassed. I am a colored girl in an uncolored world.

I pretend not to hear the low names people call me and my son as I
ride my broken down bike down Main Street on my way taking him to the
doctors office. I feel the torment my child
is going through at school, when
he's trying to make a true friend. I try to touch the negative
feeling in people's heart. I worry if the racist name calling will
come to an end. I cry every night when my son comes crying, asking,
"mommy do I have to go to school?" The tears come running down my
face when I look into his eyes and say "yes"!

I don't understand why people show there true feelings toward other
people, but I do understand that people have opinions. I say to my
son don't cry it will all be over one day soon. I dream of the day
when I can ride in the front of the bus without going to jail. I
try to make myself believe that all of this hell I's going through
will soon come to an end.

I hope someday colored and uncolored will get along. I am a colored
girl in an uncolored world.
    Krystin S. Dwight

Mustang

You're fast as the wind!
You're swift as the flight
    of a wild bird
    as it flaps through the night.
Tail streaming behind you,
Hooves pounding the ground
    like thunder claps all around.

You're wild as storm
Fierce but light
    As you blow through the prairie
    With strength and might.

Power surrounds you.
You have no fear
As you frolic on the bluffs, whinny and rear.

Your coat like chestnuts on a forest floor,
Your mane like clouds, before the rain will pour.

Your hide is glossy, you're slim and sleek.
Your reflection dances on a bubbling creek.

Beauty is yours with muscular grace.
For you are a mustang
In an enchanted place.
    Liz MacDonald

Granddaughter

When you were born, angels sang, I know.
You're God's handiwork from your head to your toe.
A bundle of joy from heaven above
Our little angel to cherish and love.
You have made our world a happier place,
Every time we see your beautiful face.
You have filled our lives with so much love,
My wish for the world is the same from above.
Thought we had everything till the day you were born.
Found out we had nothing, then you came along.
God bless you and keep you safe from all harm
Our beautiful Brighid, our angel, our charm.

    Love Grandmom,
        Pat Griffin

"My Pumpkin, My Angel"

Over a year and a half ago
You, my pumpkin, entered my life
Because I had longed for you so long
nearly ten years, I was so very happy
when I learned that you were a part of me.

As I eagerly awaited your arrival, I knew
the void would soon be replaced with bundles
of love, happiness, and joy.

But yet it wasn't meant to be
You see, God knows what's best and he chose to
have you live with me for five months and to spend
an eternity with him.

Now my pumpkin is an angel,
Oh, what sweet peace—to know that she's safe
In the arms of the Lord, and that He, too, has a
rockin' chair—
    "MY PUMPKIN, MY ANGEL"
        Mary L. Davis

Passion

Right from the very start
You've held a piece of my heart.
What are we going to do
Now that I've fallen for you?

I've been searching a lifetime
For someone as passionate as you.
Will we last this time,
Or just for a day or two?

You take me to ecstasy
And make my body sing.
Are you just a fantasy
Or a passionate fling?

Our passion fills a space
That was long overdue.
You put a smile on my face
Just by thinking of you.

Rose M. Stevens

Fallen Star

Hey star!
You're done for but you don't know it.
Because you're cracked,
You're demented and deranged.
You can't believe they want you
Back on the stage.

You are lost.
Drowning in your house
With all your photos,
Seeing what you used to be.
Poor pitiable star.

So what do you do?
You buy a young man's affections.
And when he tries to be rid of you
You blow a hole in him.
For shame.

Psst...a little tip, movie star.
GET YOUR HEAD EXAMINED AND
JUMP INTO THE NOW!!!

Shelley Stevenson

My Last Melody

My lady,
Your love was the most beautiful
Melody of my life.
It was a rock and a rose
Kissing each other with passion
In the immensity of the world.
It was the echo of eternity
Coming like a dream to my sorrows.
It was my love in God forever...
It was my sweet last melody.

Tomorrow
I will go to the square,
I will jump into the world
To be one more ghost on main street,
Or on another street of the world,
But, forever
I will keep the best moments
To remember your love.

Rene Barrios

Untitled

To think and feel the way I do,
You'd have to wear my shoes.
The reasons here, I will describe
To have you see my blues,

My silver streak, in younger days,
My friends, they meant to say-
"You look so good, and smarter too."
Instead, "Oh my God, the GRAY!"

My body has some aches and pains,
The weight it gains and gains.
The stripes that run all down my legs
Are actually my veins!

My children talk of leaving home,
their allowances they've blown.
I know I'll end up paying them
To get out on their own!

The smile you see upon my face
Is truly out of place.
You see, I'm always losing ground
In this big old Human Rat Race!

Sheila Longnecker

Plugged In

When you touch
you will find
it has the power
to blow your mind.
A little hum here, a big zap there,
what its got will curl your hair.

It has within
its core you see
sensations of great intensity.
I tell you this to let you know
that once it grabs you
it won't let go.

You know how they say
oil and water don't mix,
and that opposites attract.
What was said is true
the shock it gives you
will knock you flat on your back.

Shirley Harris

On Being Bombed In Winter

The earth is hard.
You can't dig into it.
Only press into the snow.
Wails and screams
And only black night.
White snow and red flashes
There is no color.
I press against ungiving ground.
Now I understand fear.
And regret for things I did not do
and women I passed up.
I was too shy.

Thomas Redick

Rain

Rain is clear you can see it.
It will get you wet too.
You can see rain on flowers,
Rain falls from the clouds,
After rain falls a rainbow comes,
It is so colorful to me.

Robert Hemphill

Angels

Angels walk on the clouds
yet often assume human form.
The wings as so silky
and dresses so white.
They walk on velvet into the night.

There sent from heaven, that's
for sure and no one knows
who there really here for, flying
through the heavens, looking
down on us all.
Looking for the one they have to call.

We don't know who will go
or which way the wind will blow.
Then back up to heaven
From which they came, for
Which gods gift they have gained.
To bring one back to be the same!

Rosemary Spearnock

Clouds

They rush about on their merry way
yearning to take a friend along
they reach their goal
and say goodbye
Then shed their tears a mile wide
now it starts all over again
they rush about to find the end.

Robert Milton Evans

What I Want To Be

I want to be fun again
Without this shadow hanging over me
Clouding every thought like rain
Blurring and darkening all I see

I want to be whole again
Without ever feeling this brokenness
To be without the grip of pain
To dance without a single step missed

I want to feel beautiful again
To walk tall and proud
Catching the eyes of men
And admirers from the crowd

I want to be home again
Where I am forever loved
Where they understand my pain
And the security feels like a glove

What I want to be
When I looked in the mirror
Once I used to see
Now, lost and not getting nearer.

Rebecca Dugger

Just Do It!

Just let your heart run free.
Let your soul unfold.
Just take a look, feel the pain...
taste the anger... laugh our
tears.
Just take this day; LOVE ME.
Let go of all the anchors.
Just hold on, don't let go,
  hold me tight.
Just say it, say you love me.
JUST DO IT!

Samantha Helfrich

"Goodbye, My Love"

I bid you happiness
  with your new love,
Even though I wish
  It were me that you're thinking of
The days are long
  Without you near,
Especially this cold
  Time of year.

For it was this same month
  So very long ago,
When I first held you tight,
Not wanting to let you go.

But times have changed
  As they days unfold,
Now I'm alone

With no one to hold.

But I will try to be happy
  If his love is true,
Remember, dear sweet Sonia
  I will always love you.

Shannon Lee Bales

Untitled

Cravings that come
With the silence
Lent from a store of promises
That can not be met
And solitude
As solid
As the green moss carpet
Outside the window
In warmer weather
The coolness
Requires toe diggings
And contemplations
Rushed
With decisions
Relished hungers
To fill
Empty pockets

Sarah Cox

The New Baby

(Author - age 7)

A new baby's arrived
with pretty blue eyes.
With hair like the nite
that sparkles with white.
With skin so soft
it feels like soap.
With fingers and feet
so very petite.
I love your new baby...
like an angel without wings.

Shannon Hill

Willows

The willow trees across the road
Keep waving in the wind
Their shadows on Aunt Ella's house
Are constant with no end
And though she is not there now
They never said goodbye
The shadows keep on dancing
They don't know how to die.

Wade Barnes

The Day I Found Out Who Jesus Is

I see a man in a far off distance,
with people all around,
I slowly look up, then again put my
head to the ground,
He walks close to me and puts his
hand in mine,
I look into his eyes and see a
wisdom that is so sublime,
I walk with him and talk with him,
yet I know not who he is,
He tells me things that makes me
feel warm and a bliss,
My life has changed,
and my old life is done,
As I sit with my heart all aglow,
I know now who this man is,
his the one they call Jesus,
Gods son!

Terry Lynn DeVore

To a Lost Love

I think of you a thousand times
with every passing day.
And then I wake up in the night
And in the dark I pray
That God will fill your heart with joy
As He did mine before
When you loved me and every day
I loved you more and more.
I 'spose some day I'll cease to care
With passing months and years
But I shall ne'er forget your face
Seen dimly through the tears.

Raymond F. Mosher

She's Always There

She's always there when you need her,
With cookies, a hug, or a smile.
She loves it when you visit,
If only for a short while.

Her middle name is adventure,
She loves to have some fun.
The Beast, the Racers, and Vortex,
She rode them at age eighty-one.

Who is the person I write about?
There really is no other.
The lady that I love so much,
Is my neat grandmother!

Tommy Stark

Patient Guidance

Through troubled times
When confusion abounds
Let not the heart control the mind
Nor the mind control the heart
Lest we lose sight
Of that which matters most
  ourselves
Ask first for guidance
Then for patience
For change is frightening
And sometimes painfully slow
And it is only through accepting
Patient guidance
That we allow ourselves to grow

Steve Null

Moonlight On Lace

Moonlight on lace
with a passionate sigh
stretching with wanting
silk midnight sky

Contented kisses
heavens look down
satiny caresses
soft velvet ground

Roses on flesh
deep twilight glow
Perfumed magnolias
winds lightly blow

Whispered pleas
words unspoken
pleasure's release
silence unbroken

Victoria Elzey

Will There Always Be an Autumn?

Will there always be an autumn,
Will the forest always bloom?
With the colors in a carpet
Just before the winter resumes.

Watch the leaves spread out and scatter,
Playing hop-scotch on the grass;
Then the wind rounds out the pattern
In Nature's quilt as in the past.

See the applique in the center
Sewn with leaves in red and gold.
Overlaid with crimson maples,
What a carpet to behold!

Rushing in to join the picture
In the forest which neatly holds,
Ash-leaved maple and Box Elders,
What a story to be told!

Yes, there'll always be an autumn,
And the leaves will freely fall,
All in nature will continue—
God is the engineer of it ALL.

Vernese Carter McKoy

Change

Where does time go?
Why do things change?
When you're happy one way,
why can't things stay the same?
When you love someone,
Why does their focus shift elsewhere?
Where does the magic go
that the two of you can no longer share?
How do you move on
from the only thing you know?
How can you cope with it
without having your feelings show?
Where are the answers
to what I should do?
Will I ever be able
to stop feeling so blue?
As life goes on
and things continue to change,
I still have to wonder
why couldn't they have stayed the same?

Terina Brunet

My Cover Girl

I gazed upon a magazine
  Whose cover I had never seen
  And fell in love
With a fairy queen
Although she was not more than four
She was the one that I adored
She seemed to play
So hard to get
You know the one
That little coquette

Thomas Whitaker

Anxiety

THWACK! Shhh! THWACK! Shhh!
"Who's there?" I say.
"Who's There?!"
THWACK! Rrrreeeeh! THWACK!
No answer comes, as the groans
accelerate to a high shrill.
This perpetuates until my heart
beats with rapid succession,
joining this FRIGHTENING
orchestration of sound.

I rise with trepidation from
my chair. This time unable to
inquire as to who is the cause
of this CLATTER. Slowly, I pull
back the curtain of my window
to attain a glimpse of the CULPRIT.
To my relief, it is just the WIND.
With that, I relax to the sounds
I hear.
THWACK! Shhh! THWACK! Shhh!

Suzanne C. Murphy

My Little Boy

You're my precious little baby
Whom I hold so dear and tight
I've loved you since conception
now I love you more than life.

Your smile brings me happiness
your hugs and kisses too
You're the greatest gift of all-
with light brown hair and eyes of blue.

You warm my heart and fill me with pride
you're the center of my world
And the apple of your daddy's eye.

I thank God for you every single day
you're my angel straight from heaven
You're my blessing for which I prayed.

When I'm with you, I'm on cloud nine
but sometimes I cry— big tears of joy
Oh, how I love you, Brock Mikeil,
my precious little boy!

Shawn Marie Smith

"Rocks"

As a child seldom speaking a word-
People saying things,
Throwing rocks that really hurt-
I used to run away, and then to hide,
But one day I grew tired-
And joined them.
Throwing 'rocks' at myself...

Robert E. Ackerson

Death Shall Come

Death shall come to those who wait,
Who wait for life to begin,
Life is not a mortal,
Death is not a sin.

Death killed my brother years ago,
I stand now over his grave,
I wish I got to meet my brother,
He must of been very brave.

I set some flowers on him so,
My mother starts to cry,
I understand the loss she had,
Her son is in the sky.

We put pine cones around his grave,
To show our unity,
Everyone must die someday,
Even you and me.

Death shall come to those who wait,
Who wait for life to begin,
Life is not a mortal,
Death will win again.

Ryan Ross

What Happens

What happens to the young boy
Who lives without his Dad
He'll never know the joy
of the love he should of had

What happens to the young man
Who lives without his father
Will he ever understand
that it was too much of a bother

What happens to the lives affected
what road is there to take
feeling alone and unprotected
Paying for mistakes that we make

What happens to the missing part
of a life that will never be whole
What happens to the lonely heart
of a boy with just half of his soul....
  what happens....

Teresa Morrison

Joey

There is a little guy next door to me,
who is just about to turn three.
He is so cute and quite strong,
He won't be little very long.

The "Why is why?", he asks of me,
Seems to go on endlessly.
It seems no matter how I try,
He ends up always asking me, Why?

The "Why stage seems to have no end,
But his little mind won't bend.
"Why is this and Why is that,
Why oh why is a cat a cat?"

"Why do squirrels climb up trees,
And why do they spit down seeds?
Why do I sweep and clean the walk",
The "why" goes on the more I talk.

I love that little guy of almost three,
And yes, you've guessed, his name is Joey,
He smiles so cute and has sparkling eyes,
He winds you over—doesn't even try.

virginia schelosky

What Is A Friend?

A friend is someone very special,
Who guards over you with pride.
A friend is one who
Will stand by you,
When no one's on your side.

A friend is one who will
share each and every dream,
Although your friend may
Know your dream,
Is not what it may seem.

A friend will make you laugh,
When in your heart your sad,
When someone treated
you like dirt and made
you feel real bad.

A friend will always
be there when you
really need a lift,
And you will always thank the
Lord for giving you this gift!!!

Stefanie Lynn Del Toro

Pat Who

Pat who is my godmother
Who always loved me
Who always had time for me
Who was always there when I needed her
Who was the best person I knew
Who is gone now
Who was a victim of cancer
Who I will always Love and Remember.

Trevor Allen Bartlett

Guardian Angel

My guardian angel appeared to me,
where no one else could see,
he was a gentleman,
so very nice,
he stood there in his divine disguise.

I was afraid and all alone,
I called on him to bring me home,
I felt left out without a doubt,
and there he stood,
he gave a shout,
he said "don't worry, I'm looking out,
for you and everyone about."

So now when things don't work out right,
I'm not afraid,
he's by my side,
he watches over me,
day and night,
that makes everything, alright.

Sara Barker

Untitled

Strive for your dreams,
  reach for the sky.
Don't be afraid,
  of not knowing why.
Believe in yourself,
  be the best you can be
Run with the wind,
  and set your spirit free.

Stephanie Wentzell

Where Is?

Where is a tear God cannot wipe?
Where is a battle, God cannot fight?
Where is a scar, God cannot heal?
Where is a hurt, God cannot feel?

He's Merciful and Mighty
He has everything we need
All He ask is that we have
the faith of a little mustard seed.

Amazing is His grace,
all power is in His hands.
His love is everlasting,
on His word we can stand.

Where is a heart,
God can't live
Where is a sin,
God can't forgive.

Virginia Alder

Haiku Collection

Silence in the wood,
Where have all the birds gone?
Will we follow them?

A butterfly floats
above, to guide us toward
our destiny.

One smell or sweet song
brings memories of the past,
a smile and tear.

A new life began
suddenly one summer eve,
when eyes and souls met.

I was born again
on a hot summer morning.
God is the reason.

Robert McAllister

Where Is He?

Searching, but not finding.
Where could he possibly be?
He asks himself this question
Quite frequently, you see.

Looking, but not seeing
What life may have in store.
He only knows he's tired
And he can't take much more.

Talking, but not hearing
The words he has to say.
He's playing business games
To pass the time away.

Walking, but not moving
There's really no place to go
When he hasn't a destination
Except where the wind may blow.
Crying, but not sobbing
Over what he'll never be.
He thinks about his life and
What he'll not ever see.

Vickie Blasingim

And Beyond

To look at the Land
Where Beauty lies.
To feel the Air
Where Music flies.
And in the Water
Joy floats by.
But look not at the Sun,
There Fire runs free.
There nothing lives
And Joy, Music, and Beauty
Shrivel up to die.
So take a step back
And look aside.
See all that is given
Life by the Sun.
Hold
Your gaze on Earth
And do not look Beyond.

Sarah Bartsch

In My Time

When life gets too fast paced,
When things don't go right,
And there's not a minute to waste,
God gently reminds us "in my time."

When all there's left to life is sorrow,
Wondering if it will ever get better,
Hoping for a better tomorrow,
God gently reminds us "in my time."

No more crying or pain,
No more death,
No more pressures or strain—
That's what heaven will be like.
But, in the meantime,
God gently reminds us "in my time."

Robin Lynn Snyder

Sister's Reunion At Vi's

Time goes fast when having fun
When there are five -
Instead of one -
I've made new friends
Here and there
These little ladies
With their white hair
I loved every minute
With my sis, Vi
But now it's time
To say good bye.

Ruth Deck Cole

"Fine Pate"

Unripe, the apple that you pick,
When attention, you don't pay.
Just as quick, you may get sick...
When with it's worm you play!

Not perfect, nor complete,
An apple and it's worm.
Best leave it for the birds...
To them, it's fine pate!

Robyn L. Murray

Loneliness

The sky was dark this morning
when I raised my head
She stares through my window
and cries to me in bed
She holds me tight every night
with the passion of a flame
She took me as her prisoner
and lonely is her name
She keeps me warm in sorrow
She kisses me good night
She walks me through tomorrow
and tells me it's all right.
Lonely is my lady
the princess I can't see.
Loneliness is my true friend
she's always there for me.

Richard Bloomfield

It Was Not Long Ago

(Written at age 12)

It was not long ago
When he passed away.
I knew that I really
Wanted him to stay.

You can't replace the joy
That he brought to me.
He made me laugh,
He made me so very happy.

I miss him very much
That I hope he knows.
Because I really loved him,
Loved him so.

Sometimes I talk to him
Even though he is not there.
But what I do know is he's
Talking back to me from somewhere.

I knew that God would take someone
To that world above.
But why did he have to take
The man I dearly loved?

Valerie Dillard

Denial

What my eyes do behold
What my mind doth full know
Can I then cover this
With a blanket of snow?

What my soul understands
In both fullness and thirst
Can I make of this naught
As if a bubble in burst?

Can a beast of its kind
Take the form of another?
Can a newborn re-enter
The womb of its mother?

When a path has been taken
And a deed has been done
To deny that it happened
Starts the soul on the run

From the truth and the light
Toward dark gloom and despair
From the bosom of the savior
To the adversary's snare.

William Wedgworth

A Love To Call My Own

When I first met you, you
were just another flirt, yet
I feel in love with you
knowing I'd be hurt.
I thought I could tie you down,
and make you love just me,
but how can I do something
no one else has done.
I know you'll never love me
and I'm trying not to cry
for someday I'll find the
strength to kiss your lips goodbye.
When you come look for me
you'll find I won't be there.
I want a love to call my own not
one I have to share.

Samantha Torres

Weather

Weather is hot
Weather is cold
Just like yesterday
When it snowed

Weather is good
Weather is bad
And sometimes makes people
Very mad

Weather is freezing
Weather is sleet
Then there'll be ice
On the street

Weather is windy
Weather is tornado's
It hit our house
When we were peeling potatoes

Robert G. Taber

Move Ahead and Fall Behind

Daylight fades to black
We walk the streets in fear
The doors are locked tight
Our concerns are clear
Violence is rampant
The footsteps are near
Our children are the sacrifice
For them we shed a tear
What can be done
Our values they jeer
Responsibility and discipline
No longer held dear
Love thy neighbor
We do not hear
Seeds of discontent and discourse
Fill my ear
We think not of others
Our charity is mere
The course is befuddled
From salvation we veer

Stephen H. Frank

Little Feet

A little white cloud dances by
Riding the brilliant blues,
Sun is setting, softly flowing
Rainbows through the trees.
Little feet stepping, stone to stone,
Hurrying ten toes home.

Samuel Wayne Jones

Running With The Herd

We brake o'er the horizon.
We sweep through winding curves.
The dust and stone are flying
I'm running with the herd.

One pulls out to pass me.
I gain on him a bit.
We weave through slow and weak ones.
We're agile and we're quick.

Our passing sounds like thunder.
We're a raging, churning tide.
Our safety is in numbers.
We're running side by side.

A wolf it lunges from the side.
It pulls our leader down.
So we slow down to sixty five,
look in our mirrors and frown.

Driving fast on highways,
is a habit I must curb.
But I can't resist my nature,
when I'm running with the herd.

Steve Detmer

To My Bride

On this day that we wed,
we become one.
To show my love, not enough can be said.
We are greater than the sum.
You become I;
I become you.
With a gleam in my eye,
I am proud to say

I DO!

Scott Matthews

Love, Lies And Pain

Do you remember ... love?
Was it yesterday
You held me in your arm so tight?

Do you remember ... lies?
You said you loved me
or was that just for the night?

Do you remember ... pain?
You made everything better
When you kissed me till dawns
early light.

Love, lies, and pain
that's all you gave to me
hurt, tears, and rain
For one whole year
Was all I could see

I remember warmth
And I want the sun to shine again
You clouded up my life
and only let bad weather in.

Sarah Thompson

Dead End Street

Drugs and Violence, gangs and Girls
Walking tall, walking still

Always looking for someone else
Knowing not where you'll find yourself

Up all night, down the other
Fighting is the way of life

Pain and suffering brothers dead
Life today is a hellish bed

I want out but I don't know
Where I've been, or where to go

The bullet's mine I start to shout
This for me the only way out

Pain so deep inside my chest
Blood's all over my favorite vest
I am gone so carry on
Stop the violence destroy the guns

Shadow Wolf

Unending Walks

Thoughts and feeling upset
Walk a path to relaxation
Wanting solitude, having company
With a cool breeze around
And the full moon above...
Deep conversation is inevitable.
Idle chat to start
Personal feelings arise.
Watch gold dancing above the water
While trying to find the words
Expressing myself as good as possible,
Flames inside subside
Return to calm, normal self
Glad to have company unwanting solitude
Still left with unanswered questions
Seeds for the next companioned walk

Rusty A. Weingard

An Empty Vase

My life is like an empty vase
    waiting to be filled.
Needing to be needed.
Thirsting for the life sustaining liquid
    to quench my parched body.
Let me frolic in the succulence.
Give me leave from the dryness.
See me,
    Use me,
        Fill me.
            Wait. Something is happening!
The dryness disappears.
I can feel the cool, blue liquid
    flowing through me.
Oh! Can it be real? Or is it
    my imagination?
Finally, filled with a single crimson rose
    from that special one and only.
That is what my life is like.

Rebekah Caylor

The Architect

Your body is the landscape
Upon which I build my dreams;
The length of your arm the ruler
By which I measure all happiness.
In your hand the blueprint
That guides my master plan;
One finger to mine, all power diffused,
Something wonderful created.
In your ear I whisper
A sonnet to your soul;
From the lips that speak
A message to the world.

With your eyes
I see,
And through you
I am alive.

Stephanie M. Brown

Emptiness

The full moon shows the inner soul,
upon the black sky an empty hole,
beauty seen yet all alone,
so many times that I have known.
On the waves its sparkles dance,
I feel my body in a trance,
gazing, lost in thought I see,
the truth - what is reality?
I yearn for friendship I don't know,
for someone else that I can show
the full moon; look the inner soul,
upon black sky see it glow.

Sam Andras

The Virgin

Innocent and pure she was
   untouched by man or light
She was raised by loving parents
   of values which were right
Her sheltered childhood
   led her into the unknown
She walked a straight and narrow path
   then ventured on her own
The surprises that awaited her
   were fresh, new, and strange
She put up a guard around her
   to protect her sacred values
But the world kept enduring
   and curiosity pursued
So in man's deceit she fell
   into the depths of sin
Stained and scarred for life
   only wishing she didn't give in
Now the virgin is left with shame
   of the never ever unending pain

Sherry Wickel

Some Thoughts;

If I know
What love is,
It is
Because of you,

Loving you is as natural
As loving sunsets,
Rainbows and April showers
For they are all
Simply beautiful.

Stephen A. Kujawski

The Pain Of Remembering

A weary rose, that budded
unexpectedly late this summer
and blossomed to uncanny beauty,
wielding to the forces of fall.

Chilling winds bend its stalk
and one by one remove the soft
red petals filled with the rose's
intoxicating scent.

Lovingly tending the barren bush
a gardener endures the painful
thorns
sustaining himself on the memories
of the late summer blossom
and the promise of its return.

Ross C. Lord

Comparisons

Rocky meetings of land and sea,
Turning leaves upon a tree,
Brilliant skylines of the city,
Rolling clouds which make one giddy —
All these things alike you see,
But not as pretty as you to me!

Victorious athlete shouts with glee,
Children swinging from a tree,
Girl receives unexpected flower,
Birds singing in the morning hour—
Again alike these things may be,
But not as happy as you make me!

Number of leaves in the largest tree,
Drops of water in the sea,
Sum of links in an endless chain,
Blades of grass upon the plain—
Alike, Alike again you see,
But numbers can't measure my love for
thee!

Timothy D. Phipps

Trees

Leaves grow on trees.
Trees are brown and black.
Palm trees mostly growin'
Arizona,
Trees have trunks.
Paper and tooth picks
are made from trees.
Trees give people shade.
The leaves are red, orange, and
brown in the fall.

Ursula Davis

Untitled

Art is life
Forever wanting,
and fortunate are those
whose life is Art
in whatever form -
your heart, my love,
is fortunate -
and so am I
to share it.

Alfred Cambry

Spot

All around the Chesapeake
transit schools of fish we seek.
Seekers, from a varied lot,
Stand by for a fish called spot.

Two surface spots, small and dark,
are the splotches for their mark.
Fish these next lines for a clue
of what's hidden from purview.

Despite all around we plot,
only luck finds the spot.
Bait when sized to catch a lot
is a coaxing tiny spot.

Expect a vile yucky splot,
the moment you touch a spot.
Even though we sort out tots,
the plate's morsel is a spot.

Nature's simple, wily clue
is sufficient for a few.
But, there are a few who know
What makes the spot apropos.

William R. Gongaware

The Quest

Thus have I come quietly today
To the place I love the best;
The quiet, holy thoughtful hour
When the inner soul resumes its quest.

The quiet hour when all my heart
Has turned, my father, unto thee.
All pain and confusion quite forgot
Only thy Holy Radiance do I see.

So long have I thus turned to thee
My heart again with rapture fast
Beats so swiftly for long, oh God,
Have I found that this love will lot

So I come with joy to this horn
To quietly spend the time with thee,
Strength flows joyously into my soul,
And courage to face what yet must be

Vela Bess Walker

Missing You

I sailed across the ocean,
to see what I could find.
Took the world that I grew in,
and left it all behind.

Thought I'd find a better place
that I could call my home,
but as soon as I went sailing
I found myself alone.

There's not a day that goes on by
that I'm not missing you.
And wish that in my sailboat
I'd built a seat for two.

We could have sailed together.
My dreams with you, I'd share,
cause through my journey I have found
how friendship is too rare.

And when I'm sailing back to you,
I hope that what I find
is just the place I'm looking for,
that world I left behind.

Shelli J. Koontz

Beginners Luck to Vent

In a fishing boat -
To sail away the afternoon
Seas untraveled by me to see
A rod and reel in tow
To cast in the deepest water.

An hour or so from shore
Three lines went out to catch.
A reel began to spin -
With a big one on the end
Gone - not mine!

My line felt a tug
A big catch struggling in the water
The rod anchored tightly in my grip
The reel spinning fast and as fierce
As one could master.

Some twenty minutes or so
To the boat she did show
Fifty six pound, eighty nine inches
A sailfish was spent
Then saved by a taxidermist.

Theresa B. Trapp

The Harvest

The father gives a seed to you,
    to plant and to nurture.
He gives the feel for what to do,
    for the plant to mature.

The soil that you plant it in,
    is love and constant giving.
Mistakes, though made, be not sins,
    when dealing with the living.

The plant then turns to flower proud,
    honest eyes, shed humble tears.
"For not," the farmer says aloud,
    "Did I, with all my fears."

"Take this seed, this baby given,
    and wholly on my own,
Start the life, now that's living,
    in this farmer's home."

"For what I have, this child now,
    and for just a while."
The question asked is, "Only how
    to loose with but a smile."

Teresa Schell

A Death And A Life

A death has occurred he went too soon
to me without a cause or a true purpose.
He left me all alone without someone to
love. He walked this earth for so
long. He spread so much love for a
cause just to do it. He went too soon
and hardly did all he planned, he
wanted to marry, his lady and spread
his love and share all his great
experiences. A life also occurred his
baby was born with his eyes and his
cheeks and a smile of undeniable love
to spread. When I look at him I cry
but my tears are not of pain they're of
joy. The joy which we shared. When I
look at him I cry because of the way he
resembles him but that is not of
disgrace or of torture, they're of love
for there was a death but in the life
of his son, he shall live on.

Tywana Denise Bankhead

The Beach

The beach is a wonderful place
to go when you are bothered by troubles.
There are many things to look at.
There are the many colors on the shells
scattered about and the blue cold
water that seems to go on forever.
You can see and hear the sea gulls
squeaking and the waves shattering
as if glass as they crash into rocks.
You can taste the salty air as the
light breeze blows the scent around.
You can hear the breeze as it blows
through the grass as if it was whistling.
A day at the beach is a great cure
to many of your daily problems.

Randy Hines

Shadowbox

Awakened from the nightmares
To find my fears are true
By a venal kind of onslaught
I'm rendered black and blue

Youthful views once buoyant
Sunk by mocking doubt
No cynics in paradise
The cherubs keep them out

I shadowbox a phantom
That knows my moves so well
The blows connect right through my guard
If I surrender to its spell

Starting early in the morning
Until far into the night
My foe consumes a piece of character
Each time I fail to fight

This apparition that I shadowbox
Employs anger to confuse
Because a battle waged upon emotion
Is a battle I'm sure to lose

Thomas Eldridge

Images Of Autumn

Autumn's cardinal so gaily red!
To cooler climes for refuge fled,
As savage heat of summer's lease,
Scorches and sears, without relief.

Autumn's rye of verdant hue!
Blades refreshed by morning dew.
Bare earth with grassy carpet hide,
Winter grazing for calves provide.

Autumn's hickory in colors bold!
Leaves arrayed in richest gold.
In warmest russet snugly clad;
Fading green, abandoned, sad.

Autumn's images, majestic decoration!
Glorious essence of Divine creation!
Sensuous scenery of sublime delight,
That stirs the soul and indulges sight.

Sandra H. Bounds

Home

There once was a land that was given
To a people bent on forgivin'
It was a wonderful race
In a wonderful place
For nobody there was a sinnin'

It was a far away land
That had way too much sand
Their creed was a cry
An eye for an eye
And that they played in their band

It was another old place
An entire different pace
This tribe we describe
Had a wonderful hide
And didn't have use for mace

It was the land of the might
That had the terrible blight
She had to rule all the lands
And all of their bands
It sure is a horrible sight

William G. Kneen

Dame Nature

Let us stop and give a tribute
    To a lady grand and old
Who has secrets closely hidden
    Many wonders to unfold.

Like a woman so beguiling
    Spreads her colors far and wide
Every season finds her changing
    Putting on some new disguise.

She is kind so gentle, patient
    Waiting for each hour to go
Yet she does not waste a minute
    Causing some new thing to grow.

Then when Autumn comes upon her
    Gingerly she waves her arms
And like an extravagant old lady
    Showers the earth with all her charms.

Ruth Penn

North North-East

Sun dogs stuck
to a grey-sheet sky.
Pale light jabbed
by naked willows.
Tracks. Blotches
staggered to dimness
on a frozen sea.
White, unmoving.

South winds suck
the swirling masses,
cloak in white
the greening bushes.
Winter rime
in the softening air,
sheds tears of welcome
for coming spring.

Roland Soper

Season Of The Soul

Winter has come;
'Tis the season of my heart,
Unseen gelid tears flood
the tundra of my soul.

My brain no longer a;
saving beacon of thought
To guide me through this
wasteland
For mine is the desperate
season of the soul.

Sandy G. Gordon

Monomorphous

God, take me by the hand
  Thru the land I never
  Lived in before.
  Guide my thoughts
  In a clean and clear direction!
Let my message be yours
  To open new doors
  But to remember the old ones,
  Not to forget where I came from
  And what I am capable of!

Ralph Capone

Black Widow

Gunners ran through the synagogue,
through the crowded temple in Istanbul.
When the guns were silent,
when even the children lay
stained in panels of sunlight,
survivors say the killers stopped.
Did they turn back to look?

A black widow spider dropped
into my white kitchen sink.
Its legs lashed —
I smashed it with the meat
tenderizer. I stopped
then, and turned it on its back
to be sure of that blood-red spot.

Valanee Eriksen

Passion From The Heart

The wind breathing
through my soul,
as fire burns in my heart
for we will never be apart.
Like Sunshine in the day,
and Shadows in the night
a warm sweet glow in your eyes
dancing in the light.
Rain showers at mid day
and clouds passing
through the skies,
The thought of your smile
is forever in my eyes.

Victoria A. Hughes

Life

Life is a door that opens every day.
Souls going in and out,
But never does one stay.
You'll go through many hardships,
And other little things,
But when your life is over,
You'll hold the joy it brings.

Shelby Jacob Crisp Smith

"Trail Of Tears"

The campfire has been lit,
they wait with patient eyes,
they salute their gods of war,
with cheers, chants, and cries.
They raise their hands above them,
and the fortress built with pride,
crumbles into little sticks,
that roll the mountain side.
They go out for their enemy,
to win their taken land.
their only means of protection,
is their weapons and their bands.
Some die heroes
some die in defeat.
Their home is taken away,
right from underneath their feet.
The ones who survive the horror,
move with doubt and fears,
leaving their path behind them,
their own "Trail of Tears."

Sharron Dumas

Poor Black

As black as they can be
they sit and stare at me
Are they jealous?
Jealous of us
because we have a home to go to
and they must scrap for food
maybe it's because we live so bold
and they must live in the cold
they are always stealing from the fields
yet they always hang out
in the cities we build
As black as they can be
I wonder if the crow wishes he was me

Reginald L. Williams II

Untitled

The tears I have not wept,
The years that I've held back,
Into my soul have crept,
And turned my spirit black.

My happiness suppressed,
My hatred fed and fueled,
My being was undressed,
Remade with wicked tools.

My love of life was lost,
My fear of death no more,
Compassion turned to frost,
Trust, thrown out the door.

Revenge became my passion,
Violence was my lover,
A rage in every action,
Myself above all others.

To live like this is to slowly die,
To never love,
To never cry.

Vincent Seminara

The Soul Manager

He is long, slender, and lean.
The words he says, he does not mean.

Push, push to the brink of self-distrust.
Only letting the self-image to rust.

The pieces fall, only to be caught.
Molded to an image tired and distraught.

Finding the pieces of my mind.
Only to think, "I must be blind!"

To take a step back to see.
His image of the perfect employee.

Richard D. Frahler

Death at Night

It's a dark summer night
The wind is howling
The rain is pouring.
Death floats in the air,
Like clouds across the sky.
Trees wave in the wind,
Like phantoms in the night.
Fog cloaks death like a veil
over a brides face.
Rain falls like ghosts descending
onto the earth.
Clouds streak the moon
As blood streaks the cloak of an
old man who has died.
His family cries tears of pain
As his life was taken by the insane.

Dawn comes and the darkness flees
The soul of the demon is pleased.
Life was taken by the strong there was no
justice for this wrong.
Legions of dark ones will come someday to
take all life away.

Rhett D. Cropper

Silent Snowflakes

The first day of November
the wind began to blow
Small white specks
suspended in the sky
slowly began to show.
The soft tears of the sky
fell upon our heads
like fairy dust from angels on high.
We watched them slowly fall
out of sight
like a shadow in the night.
The soft white blanket
covered the ground.
We listened carefully
there was no sound.
The first day of November.
The first snow of the year.
So begins another winter,
which nobody can hear.

Randi Sanders

A Promise

To remember Christmas past,
the unchangeable times and memories
we have (nor will we) forget.

There is nothing overly noble or
godly in this Christmas 1994.
No demons under the tree though either!
Truly it will no less be a Christmas
To remember,
this unchangeable promise I give to you;
all of you.

I will remain myself.
I have earned the right
To remember Christmas past,
this one...

Paul Stephens

When Snow Relents

There is a time in winter, when
The snow relents; then
My garden ground
Becomes a study in brown - -
Bald clods jut
Above the rotting rubbish, where
Bare middles butt
Dead debris covering rows once there.
Beaten down, broken-over stems
Strew a bedraggled still life.

There is a day in winter, when
The snow relents; then
My garden stay
Becomes a study in gray.
Withered, matured vines sag
Past usefulness they lag,
Doddering,
Diminished,
Dated,
Fulfilled still life.

Roy N. Byrd

I Hear An Echo

I hear an echo of my sadness
   the rushing of tears,
   the wasted years
   of life searching
   for enlightenment.

I hear an echo of my loneliness
   the sting of ploys,
   the death of joys
   of life waiting
   for acknowledgment.

I hear an echo of my gladness
   for pleasure in the moon
   and dining every noon
   of life savoring
   my contentment.

I hear an echo of my thankfulness
   the glory of seeing
   spring, summer, winter, fall —
   the blessing
   of being on God's earth at all.

Sara Briar Kurtz

Enlightenment

I have searched for my flowers.
The ones that remind me of you.
And perhaps was a little unsettled
When I couldn't find them
Dancing on the side of the road
Absorbing the sun
Looking so brilliant and
Beautiful.
The ones that remind me of you
For their purity and natural love for
Life.
I searched for my flowers
and found them to
Exist in a single moment of
excellence
When you looked at me
and took my hand.
And for one second
I felt perfection.

Rachel Holten

Scars

You brought back the past
The old tortured scars
Scars I had forgotten
Lost some place deep and far

Old love, old love
A sour and corroded phrase,
But it's still in the past
What about the next page?

The page where we were happy
And we all got along,
But alas, it is forgotten
As old lovers forget their song.

I thought we were friends again
What happened to the trust?
It's lost somewhere in time and space
Caught between love and lust.

It's the past,
Can't we forget,
And return to a time
Of true friends and no regrets?

Shanna Kunce

My Love...

My love comes from very deep inside.
The love I show I cannot hide.
My love is always helping me.
I wonder where my love could be?
My love is very bright.
His love for me is just right.
When I'm with my love I feel free.
I wonder when my love will come for me?
My love is like the sun.
My love is the only one.
My love never says "I" it's always "We"
My love I will someday see.
Knock, Knock, Knock at the door.
It's my love forever more.

Tansy K. Hall

"Flight Of The Moonfish"

On a distant highway
the lone traveler
watches random colors
play against the damp night sky —
they glide on celestial wires,
effortlessly pushing.

The fugitive,
seeking and sought,
leaves a miserable cage
where festers a terrible wound —
where steel grows ever higher
and cold stone edifices
harbor unthinking mutants.

A plague has descended upon the city,
and its name is mediocrity.

Ralph Aquila

If I Had A Friend

If I had A friend
The kind I'd keep forever
If I had a friend
One I'd distrust never
If I had a friend
I'd make him just like you
   and how many times.
And how many ways
can I say it again
again and again
   I miss you.

Now the miles separate us
with mountains and seas between
The mailman is the only thing
Left to connect us
So we write faithfully - day after day
And I'll buy me a plain ticket
one of these days
Just so I can see you, and just so I can say-
I Love You - in so many ways.

Rebecca Williams

The Soul

Desire within
the feelings of joy and disaster
commute in one
Life affects the soul
in a way we could never understand
A piece of (clay that could be and)
is molded into what we are today.
It is self-being, self worth
without it we are nothing.
Doesn't it breath as we do
the emotions it brings out
is what we are
for it is our soul that
determines who we are....

Woody Douglas V

Fire And Ice, Night And Day

The night is the fire.
The day is the ice.

I live for the night.
But go through the day.

I love the bright heat of the fire
and to forget
at dawn
the cold hurting pains will return.

Shannon Fitts

Icy, Icy (Cold And Damp)

Icy, icy
the cold, harsh looks of the public
staring down on you like
a wet, dingy dog seeking
shelter in any door step he
can before being booted out
with his tail between his legs.
Don't it make you angry,
they can bleed, but don't ever
let them catch you with an
open wound.
You, the one among them all
that really knows what it
means to bleed, to feel for
and of things
with you there is no icy,
icy but they won't let you bleed.
With you there is no icy,
Icy but they won't let you
bleed.

Scott Masters

The Glory of Today

Have you seen the glory of today?
The clouds have fled our skies,
And left us with a gentle breeze,
And the sun to lead our eyes.

So here's our chance to start anew,
And leave our tempered past behind.
Please take my hand and walk with me.
See what feelings we can find.

Stan Ward

Excellence

Going far beyond
the call of duty, doing
more than others expect...this is
what excellence is all about.
And it comes from striving,
maintaining the highest
standards, looking after the
smallest detail, and going the
extra mile. Excellence means
doing your very best.
In everything. In every way.

...A special thanks to all who
made this evening possible,
a list too long to print.

Robert Palermo

Apache Spirits

The young Indian boy thrives upon
the apache traditions. He crosses the
plain as a steadfast warrior. He lifts
his weathered hands to the spirits
in search of answers from the
sky. As the ancient one, he projects
his wisdom across the flames
to the younger warriors. The war
begins, and he seeks guidance from
his rulers of the above once more.
The white buffalo roams the lands
with him, as he stealthily carries
out his quest of life. The Indian
finally is forced to wait no
more; he dies with the honor
of the apache 'cross his soul.
He rests in the sky with the
spirits forevermore.

Sarah Blake

Sunday

Unsheathed our words finally splinter
the air
rapiers greased with
Last night
scotch and sherman smokes
two wharf gulls squabbling at scraps
tossed into the fog
Her legs tucked
enveloped in white sheets of linen
sitting there glaring like Medusa
chewing my salty heart
remnant of a cruel November storm
my Sunday morning offering bleeding
down her chin and between her breasts
The walls shudder tanks churn
through the gravelstone street
I slink away alongside frightened
buildings
a leprosied armadillo
leaving its curse

Ron DeNicola

Mama's Quilt

There's a quilt upon my closet shelf
That means a lot to me. You see,
'Twas made by special hands and heart:
The Quilt my Mama made for me.

Her scraps were jewels of color bright,
Sorted out with Loving hands.
She cut and matched the pieces then,
To fit into her master-plan.

With trembling hands and dimming sight,
She sewed the pieces, one by one.
She toiled, though she grew weary,
Until her gift of Love was done.

When I lie beneath the quilt she made,
And let my thoughts soar free,
Abundant warmth and love still flows
From the Quilt my Mama made for me.

Ruth Cooper Welton

Much Love

You give me so much love
that I'll never be without
Your heart is so true
in my mind there is no doubt.

Of all the love
I have ever searched for
I've found it here with you.
Of all the dreams
I have ever hoped for
My dreams have all come true.

So much love in this heart of mine
just waiting to be given away
Waited so long for a love like yours
with your love my heart soars.

Of all the love
I've have ever searched for
I found it here with you.
Of all the dreams
I have ever hoped for
My dreams have all come true.

Tina Cormier

"A Terminal Illness"

A disease uninvited,
that helps itself within,
your body cannot fight it,
there is no cure to win.
The pain is so revolting,
the fight goes through and through,
a killer far from halting,
it's merciless on you.
It is not normally seen,
yet can be taken out,
a disease that's fairly mean,
it multiplies and sprouts.
Innocent or guilty,
happy or depressed,
you are not immune you see,
you're just like all the rest.
Don't let it get the best of you,
you've got to fight it strong,
you know what you have got to do,
the struggle will be long.

Renee Wright

Memories of Christmas

Christmas is a time of year
That fills the senses like no other,
With the sights and smells and sounds
Reminiscent of a gentler age.

The bright red berries of the holly
Twined around the newel post,
Such a festive dash of color
Against the deep and noble green.

The fresh, sweet fragrance of the pine
Permeates the air with memories
Of ancient, peaceful forests
In a world still evergreen.

The songs and laughter of the children
Fill the heart with special gladness
For a season filled with wonder
And a touch of innocence.

Sally Deems-Mogyordy

Caring Too Much Too Often

Caring too much too often,
Tends to destroy all hope for peace.
Of Soul and of body
I let others do too much to me
They embed in my heart and eat it away
Mesmerize my mind so that all thoughts
Are of them
Getting off on the most available drug.
The highest high,
Or the lowest low
Never Knowing which will occur
I must stop this carousel
Take people for what they are
Or leave them for what they are not
This trip is too much for me.

Tracey Corwin

Only I Know Me

Tell me how I'm feeling
Tell me what I dream
Tell me I'm just acting
Tell me how I seem
Tell me who I hate
Tell me who I like
Tell me how I rate
Tell me you are right
Tell me how I am
Tell me how I look
Tell me all you can
Read me like a book
Then, I'll tell you something
Although you won't agree
Only I know what I'm thinking
Because only I am me.

Tara McNeely

Alone

Drowning,
Suffocating
In the lake
Of loneliness.
Knowing,
Believing
I can swim.
Wondering,
Waiting
For the ship
Of serenity.
Wanting,
Needing
To feel love.

Rosanne Robinson

My Tifani

Tifani, you are to me
The most beautiful girl I've ever seen.
With eyes so blue,
And hair so fine,
I'm very glad to call you mine,
For eighteen years I'll watch you grow,
And how I'll hate to see you leave home.
But you'll be fine,
And so will I,
Because I know you'll always be mine.

Tina Merritt

Such Love

Such love
Such love
I've never known
Such love
Such love
To call my own
Such love
That one would die for me
Such love
And set my spirit free
Such love
You spoke into my heart
Of words that never will depart
Such love
You spoke into my mind
Of peace and joy that I could find
Such love
Is you inside of me
Such love
You set my spirit free.

Wanda Nixon

An Old Church Asks For Help

The little church among the pines
Stands bravely, on it's hilltop high.
Still radiant with God's holy love
Its steeple pointing to the sky.

Long years ago the pioneers
Eleven strong with brick and stone,
Toiled diligently to build God's house
And now it's standing all alone.

The elements are busy, too,
The wind and rain, the winter's snow
Have brought decay upon its walls
It weakens daily from the foe.

With dignity it faces death,
Unless another chosen few,
Will aid us in our efforts to
Repair its structure, make it new!

Rubye Bradshaw Dowell

Mountains

Mountains are such a beautiful sight
Standing so straight and proud.
Never moved by a gusting wind,
and the tops can reach the clouds.

Snow covering the wooded land
a storm being the source.
Animals rushing to get their food
mother nature takes her course.

Waterfalls, creeks, and rivers
bring water to living things.
Deer, bears, and sly raccoons
relax to the songs birds sing.

Quiet is not the describing word
peaceful is more the thought.
Not a pin drop can be heard there
Heaven is what was caught.

Richard A. James

Why Isn't It Me?

I see love all around me
Springing up so many ways
It radiates on their faces
Their glow they can't contain.

I do share in their happiness
So glad they found "the one"
For I know they both were looking
And now true love has come.

But I cannot help wondering
For in my heart I ache
I want to fill the void I have
But my turn is second rate

For I just seem to miss it
So close within my grasp
But always slips away from me
Why isn't it me, I ask?

For I have waited long
for true love to appear
How come it just keeps missing
Why isn't it me this year?

Rebecca G. Reddig

Spring

For most of the people
Spring
Is the
Most beautiful
Thing, for
Me...too!
For me
Spring is
A Hope,
After cold
Winter.
Spring is
A pleasure, to see
A Sun and
Green grass,
To hear a singing
Birds
And playing
Children.
Spring, is the most beautiful Thing!

Stanley Michonski

Sunrise

Breathtaking landscape hills upon hills
Speckled with tulips and daffodils
Upon the land's first rays of sun
Blades of grass glistening with dew
The birds commence to singing
A sure sign of a day anew
And as eyes fall back on the land
They gaze upon a sight so grand
The trees the skies the shimmering lake
How much of this land we do forsake
The warm summer air
Will take you there
A world far away
Where it's hard to say
What on earth could be more tranquil
More utterly magnificent
More giving of a sense of peace
Than the sun rising in the hills

Scott E. Criswell

Love

Love is wonderful with someone
   special.
Love is great with someone to share
   with.
Love can be hateful with someone
   who doesn't care.
Love is in the world there is someone
   for everyone.
If you're with someone don't let go.
Love can be special with a special
   love one.
Be careful of love it can destroy things.
Love can do a lot of things.
Love can be a lot of things.
Love is confusing.
At least if you love someone it is
   for good not bad.
Robin Snyder

Moonlight

Moonlight shimmers shining
Sparkling on waters still.
Hiding depths of beauty,
Sharp rocks, or bogs that kill.

And hidden in the silent heart
Are treasures far more dear,
But treacheries too may there be hid,
Our motives not be clear.

Yet light breaks on the surface,
And stars shine in the deep,
My life a mirror to show your love,
My heart your love to keep.
Shirley Samarzia

"Hold On"

Everyone needs a hand
Sometimes
   To hold on through the good
and bad times
   You can be black or you can
be white
   As long as you can hold on
tight
   You can be rich or you
can be poor
   Just make sure you can
hold on more
   We all need a hand
till our dying day
   And you can let go in
peace we lay.
Vicki Gajdica

End Of Winter's Chill

Old Man Winter tries
to hold on
Keeping the land cold
ignoring the Sun
The wind blows -
The tip of my nose -
He breathes his last breath
For summertime rest
Richard Livsey

My Cross

In life's love relationships
so many actions
too much responsibility
To love you or anyone
in the face of
judgements eye
only to find I point the
finger
Rather then take in
my grey coat of shame
Grey is its color
for it represents
vague, dim and dulled
desire
Passion uncovered
coated and stored away
Kindling wood
fuel for my rage
which way will the path go
to destruction or divinity
Suzanne Van Johns-Junsch

"Loving Nature"

The water in the sea
So blue and so green
Gives me a feeling of bliss.
The sun reflects off of it
To give a view of the sky.
The sea and its wonders
Are not all to what we think they are
But what we make of them.
As the birds fly overhead
We can only imagine a unity
A unity between the earth and sky
And to what makes them so wonderful.
William D. Laslavich

Season Cycle

Winter is white as paper,
Snow falls in blankets,
People skating on frozen ice,
And the children laughing,
As the time goes.

Spring comes so soon,
Warming the earth,
Snow melts to water,
And the trees start to bud.

Summer is here,
The hot sun blazing,
Everyone is swimming,
Or drinking lemonade.

Then the Fall comes creeping in,
Cooling water and land,
The leaves begin to drop,
And here we go again!
Regina Schaffer

Silhouettes

I love to look at silhouettes,
They seem alive yet then,
No one knows who they are,
Or from where they've been,
These people of shadows we know not of,
And to try to is in vain,
We only know that they've been here,
Far back - to our dawn.
Steven Morrison

Untitled

So define their spirits meet
small cherubs with his guiding
fleet.

While wings unfold, the story told
Soft candle glows from days of old.

Pink sands of time as crystals fell,
like roses in a wishing well.

A golden ring around the moon.
rejoice the hand to wear it soon.

As solemn vow is being said.
The dove of peace upon each head.
Susan Pollina

"Lonely Nights And Lonely Days"

Lonely nights are here to stay,
since you left and went away,

I don't want anyone but you,
tell me now what will I do,
with lonely nights and lonely days.

I keep wishing I could be with you,
I am dreaming of the things we'd do;
return to me your charming ways,
come end my lonely nights and
lonely days.
Vel Ivanetich

Nighttime

A moonbeam,
silvery, pale, gleaming.
Beaming gently from the heavens.
Bathing the world in silent, soft light.
Battling the black emptiness,
Rescuing people from darkness,
And yet,
it's so very,
Shy.
Sarah Skowronski

Thoughts Of My Heart

Thoughts of my heart
   sift through the years
Gliding on rainbows
   born out of tears;
Wreathing the sounds
   of voices and places
Into the scenes
   that memory embraces.
Wafting as fragrance
   they flow through my mind,
Conjuring feelings
   so long left behind.
Thoughts become whispers
   of laughter and dreams,
Bound in the heart
   where love seals it's seams.
Mellowed by years
   of life nearly done,
Sadness and joy
   now meld into one.
Shirley M. Myers

The Sun

The Sun has shone for a million years,
Shone and watched man cry futile tears.
Shone through hunger and love long lost.
Shined on causes, won at great cost.
To shine in war and in peace.
Shining on, though life shall cease.
Shine to warm the tortured land.
Shone to guide man's mortal hand.
Shine it will, when man is gone.
And shine it shall, at man's new dawn.

Steve Pflum

Sunny Days

I am looking at your lovely face
shining through my window
early in the morning.
You will be there, shining through
the Universe with a glow,
giving the earth just enough light
to make each plant and flower grow.
You were there in Hawaii
I remember seeing you
peeking through the mountains,
and when evening came
how beautiful your face was
setting through the Magic
palm trees and in the tropical sea.
Sun You are the Lord of Creation,
the Masterpiece.

Simone Nadeau

Waterfall

Pure,
Shining,
Flowing clean and cold

Bright,
Clear,
From high mountains it has rolled,

Beautiful,
Amazing,
It dazzles with colours bold.

Todd Levine

Untitled

O where is my love?
She's gone from my side
The snow is too deep
And the river too wide.

My love, I can't find you
The night is too cold
My soul begs for freedom
My body grows old.

My God, all around me
I feel you, my love
The fires burn below me
The stars shine above.

My love, now I join you
Who first set you free
My love, please forgive me
I did it for thee.

Tom Drury

To A Modern Ulysses

There's sweet seduction in her voice,
she sings her sentences with poise,
aware of what a man enjoys
and can't endure.
She'll snare her man and then rejoice
upon the shore.

As you sailed by tied to the mast
the ropes that held you could not last
and you, forgetting all your past,
began to hear
her siren song pulsating fast
deep in your ear.

Content you dropped upon the sand
and let this stranger take your hand
to welcome you as others planned
across the sea.
But home fades out from where you stand
too easily.

Vicki Buder

Grandmother's Visit

We sit across a kitchen table
Sharing coffee and family secrets
I notice her hands, strong hands
As if each finger was a paragraph
In the most brilliant of novels
And each wrinkle was a sentence
Telling of turmoil and happiness
And her face, almost childlike
Eyes screaming with innocence
A kiss that would soothe any child
And each and every grey hair
Is a strand of wisdom she's earned
An idol of idol's
For she is a hero, my hero
Staying neutral in a heated debate
Yet you know just how she feel
So loving and so available to us
And answers to the hardest questions
Seem to be second nature to her
She is my grandmother and I love her

Renee Meyers

Fulfillment

How the dark
Seeks the night
Is why the day
Peaks with the light.

Oh when the dark
Has conquered light
The breath of wildness
Comes to life.

When it happens
How or where
You're sure to find it
Stay aware.

It's like no other
Time in the day
For it's when the spirits
Have come to play.

There is no beginning
No end no stop
Till dawn cracks its'
Smile and takes dark back.

Stephanie A. Nemec

The Old Wooden Swing

A meadow
Rolling hills
A tall oak tree
An old wooden swing
Back and forth
Back and forth
Higher and higher I go
Soaring through time
Flying through the sky
No worries
No cares
Free
Free from life

Darkness
Shadows
Walls
Life returns
The sky is black
Time rushes on
The dream has vanished

Tracy N. Castle

Freedom

Orange flow
red glare
of a rolling tear,
silence (let's pretend)
staring at clouds.
Motionless time
taking me down and away
lending nothing
come far.
The present lingers on my brow
counting infinity,
let me be.

William E. Clark

"Empty Nest"

Gone - all gone,
  Reared with pride;
Echoes abound,
  No voices inside.
The nest is empty -
  My job, well done;
The circle closes
  To where it begun.
Oh empty nest,
  My youth you hide!

Shirley A. Knight

"Winter"

Outside I looked
Between the trees
Into the woods
Down the street
Toward the field
On the ground

Outside I saw snow.
In January, winter is here

Jill Coulter

Beige

Fields of clover
raped race over
indian spirit forever lost
political worm pol
media remote control
industrial holocaust!
elusive perception
pugilist redemption
queens of bondage throat
blind arrogant crown
abandon babies drown
death bed of Castles Moat!
frozen leaf wall
ignorant brawl
oh God feel our rage
card tables turn
greed culture burn
world society of Beige!

Robert L. Mouton

Rainbows

I like
rainbows because of the bright
colors and the big shape
of good luck. Rainbows are
things you will find anywhere.
In a puddle, in the sky,
in a cloud up so high.
The colors of a rainbow
reminds me of colors on
people's clothes. At the
end of a rainbow there
is a gold pot waiting for you!

Brian Miller

Memories Awakened

Home alone what a treat
Radio on, no one at my feet
Song comes on, memories awaken
Song of your brother belongs to another
Told of the story at your bedside
My heart felt a little dead inside
Your days were numbered
Your innocence stolen at birth
Your life a tragedy from the first
Your death a sin of life
Good-bye my brother
I've lost you here forever now
I've got you in my heart forever bound
Good-bye my Friend
Good-bye my Brother
I Love You

Robert Flaherty

Untitled

Love is a joyous awakening of
    the heart ...
Let it be lived each day.

Love is an inspiration for dreams
    ... deep does mine grow.

Love has an unending need to be
    fulfilled ...
    I am full.

Therese D. Naughton

"Pride"

How can a person be truly
proud of their country when
we see people using the
streets as a bed to lay
down their weary heads?

How can a person be truly
proud of their country when
racism an hatred eat away
at our hearts and our minds
slowly day by day?

Are we America, land of the
free, home of the brave?
Or are we just repetitious
hypocrites seeking fault in
others and seeking none in
ourselves?

Sonia V. Purcell

Untitled

I let you see the warmth within me.
Power me over with your eyes
that shine so bright.
I let you feel the truth
of how I feel,
Captured in a successful retreat
of caressing appeal.

I adore the moment of time
we share,
The need of each other in a loving,
tender way.
I feel safe and secure knowing your
the one.
That will fulfill my desires of
love making passion.

I lay beside you holding on tight,
breathing and feeling my heart beat.
Flowering of beauty, love fulfilled.
You have shown me through.

Renee Jensen

I See You Grandmother

I see you Sister
playing with us,
listening to the radio,
picking up nicknames.

I see you Mother
telling me the difference
between right and wrong.

I see you Mrs. Putz
working all day in that small office,
never getting mad, even though...
you wanted to!!

I see you Grandmother
holding me up when I was small,
I never did fall.
Taking care of me all the time,
acting as a mother
when I couldn't have mine.

Samantha Van Voorst

Roses And White Lace Curtains

Come stroll with me along the
    path of row houses

White lace curtains inside
    each tiny window.

Breathe in the rose perfumed air.
Beautiful roses are everywhere.
Vibrant red roses proclaiming victory

Pink roses blushing and shy as a maid
    in history

White roses open, angelic and pure,
God is here. His presence is sure.

Espaliers, bushes, sprays of roses

Frame the tiny windows
    with white lace curtains.

Viola M. Young

"Drive"

Pathways grooved
    Out in the rain,
As lines they race
    Throughout my brain.

Entranced in mist,
    My eyes burn red.
One false move
    And all is dead.

Wings that wipe
    The tears away
Victimize all,
    Their fallen prey.

Arms in motion,
    To and fro,
Smoothing all,
    Sedating slow.

Wasted nights
    I cried alone,
For days long gone,
    I'm almost home.

Wilton C. Calderon

It's Your Life

This silent death is overcoming
our nation, from children to adults
it shows in discrimination.

You could be white, black, gay
or straight, but by the time you
get it, it's too late.

Your sentence is life without
an appeal was it really such a
good deal?

To have unprotected sex for
fun or a thrill. How many others
does it have to kill?

So protect yourself or there
will come a day,

When you stand in the mirror
and wished you had listened to
the facts about AIDS and paid
close attention.

Stacy Uden

The Flower of Life

It represents
our friendship and lives

Its center is
the core of our souls.

It binds us together
making us one.

The petals fall off
causing our lives to change,
but the strong core
of friendship makes things "ok."

The stem holds us
tall and upright,
it won't let us
sway into trouble.

Roberta McManus

Miracles

I cannot feed the multitudes,
   Or calm the stormy sea.
I do not even understand
   How such great things can be.

I don't know how to raise the dead,
   Or even heal the blind.
I cannot even comprehend
   Such things within my mind.

I cannot part the great red sea-
   Or cause it to return.
Or understand in the fiery furnace
   How the children did not burn.

My mind can hardly even grasp
   How the sun and moon stood still
Or what exactly happened
   On that Golgotha Hill.

But it doesn't matter, that I don't understand.
   For from the beginning it was already planned.
Miracles still happen both large and small
   And I know the one who does them all.

Roberta Neeper

Questions

I saw a rose
One early spring night
Half covered with snow,
Blood red and white
And wondered
Was it beauty accentuated
Or purity defiled?

Then the morning came
First the dawn,
Then the light,
And then the bright white sun.
What had been snow
Was water,
And questions too, had melted.

Robert J. Whitmore

Just Be

Long drive that lead to nowhere
on roads which have no end
sleepless nights time is fleeting
On the horizon a new day begins
alone with my thoughts in silence
In the wee hours of the night
Memories racing through the cobwebs
keeping inner feelings bottled up tight
What are these walls I hide behind
allowing no one to tread
Tightly holding onto promise
which were better lift unsaid
Many questions gone unanswered
Truth being covered by many a lie
Placing the quilt an blame on myself
without knowing the reason why
time only knows how the story will end
Until then its just wait an see
Take each day as it comes an goes
And remember to just be me

Rosetta Ramsby

"My Valentine"

You got the kind of love
Oh yes, I am really scared
Especially when I think of
All the secrets that we've shared
To think about your nearness
This leaves my mind in awe
As a matter of fact:
You're the best I've ever saw
Like a baseball player needs a glove
My heart needs your love
You were made for me
Of this I am really sure
For if this is a sickness
I know there is no cure
And if this is my very last line
Will you please be my Valentine.

Willie J. Reed

The Struggle To Survive

We go about our daily tasks
Often doing what we are asked.

We toil and toil to get ahead
sometimes needing lots of prompting
just to get out of bed.

There's no promises in the days
that lie in wait.

A steady job, a car that runs,
or food upon the plate.

The bills are a-coming;
times is a-running.
No end in sight;
No wrong or right;
Just trying to stay alive.

The hope for tomorrow is
The struggle to survive.

Ralph T. Williams

Alone At Sea

The dappled shadow
of the setting sun falling
across the limp sails.

White birds in the sky —
billowing sea swells rising
stir up memories . . .

Anchored, she's below
Good smells rise from the galley
She smile up at me.

Coffee in our cups
side by side in the cockpit
we sit together.

A distant bleak shore
my boat at sea, now adrift
without my Sonya Lee.

A star glows brightly
like her smile those shining days.
The sea consoles me.

Robert Tralins

Home

In younger days, I went in search
   of knowledge still untold,
Convinced a man was only worth
   the wisdom he could hold;

As time went by, I thought about
   the home life left behind,
A mother's touch, a father's strength,
   the caressing peace of mind;

So wisened now by age am I,
   so envied by my peers,
So much so, I wish that I could
   turn back all those years;
For of the lessons I have learned
   there's one I should have known,
A builder may construct the house
   but a family makes the home.

Robert Walter Huge

Songbird

The bird it sang its hollow song,
Of False rejoicing on false ground,
The cheery melody of sound,
Sung of desolate burial mounds -

Of emptiness both far and wide,
Of Loneliness right by the side,
Of Desperate People,
   Mocked them round,
A merry, melancholy sound.

It rose and fell as of a tide,
Sweetly singing of a kind,
A siren's singing of men's sorrow,
Of Nature's fate no time to borrow,
And hearing thus the men they sighed.

Shari Kolnicki

"A Poem Of Love"

"Is it the smell
of a rose?
Is it the sound
from the head to the toes?
Is it the man
of spirit?
No wait!
I can hear it,
it is love in
the air,
it's glistening
from your hair,
it's in your heart
and
it is a wonderful art."

Randy Diaz

The Empty Chair

As we gather on this festive
occasion.
The laughter of the children
The yule log a blazing
The blessing of the food
Was done with a prayer.
A toast was raised to the
empty chair.
Though we mourn our lost
in our own way.
Her spirit is with us this
Christmas Day.

Robert G. Neylon

Passion

My Eyes are shining, glazing in the sun
O what have I done?
I am to be cherished
To be loved
To be cared for.

From great Seas, glazing in the sun
I am like a Dove
Floating in the water
Like a star
Glaring in the Sky
What am I
O What am I?

Sophia M. O. Young

Oh, Use Rhyme Up States Award

Use this For Offer do with pride
Now Render as to Note facts dear.
In One To school again mind stride.
This from Mind Offer hope make clear.
Extend Thus as One of entree-
Do Herald our U.S.A. true.

So Inside a Real "down-read" see
That Rhyme For my entree do.
A True Inside give my "by line"
To Enter For me on this day.
Enjoy with Eyes To see "mind dine"
So Now You rate me grade "A".

Ray W. Connor

A Life Of Self Hate

She lived her life,
Not showing her pain.
Her life became thin,
As the blood began to drain.

She took the huge leap,
Into the dark pit of death.
The end came closer,
With every gasping breath.

She was alone in her life,
Alone in the world.
Into the fiery depths of Hell,
Her soul was eternally hurled.

She now lives forever,
Her worst nightmare came true.
She can never end her torture,
She can never begin anew.

She was a faceless victim,
To the cruel game of fate.
Suicide was the only end,
To her life of self hate.

Stephanie Puckett

Heaven's Stairway

Too short, too soon
Not fair to be gone
To feel alone
Unrested inside
Something's not right
Nor complete
An empty space
never to be filled
who's to die!
How and when?
Memories - which are only memories
Sparked by a flash of remembrance
No one can explain the purpose
It's beyond our thought and control
Where does one stand,
When the truth comes about?
A feeling that can't be felt
But a love that will always be loved

Tam Hartman

No One Walks Alone

Although you feel mature and grown,
    None of us walks this world alone.
Many hands help along the way
    Lifting loads to brighten the day.

When you're at the edge of a bluff,
    You want to cry and say enough,
Don't quit, lay down and wait to die,
    Know you can do it, if you try.

Don't give up when your days grow dim,
    Know you can always count on Him.
Reflections in a rainbow's hue.
    Show that Angel Hands will guide you,

Be a friend and lighten your load
    As you travel the time-worn road.
It's a fact, life can be more fun,
    That all your trials can be won.

Be a beacon, a shining ray
    Give love and help along your way.
You can count on your fellowman
    It's according to God's Great Plan.

Shirley Smalley Price

Untitled

Lost in the dark
No where to go
Why did you leave me out in the cold

Lost on the road
No where to run
Can't find my way out give me a gun

Lost in my mind
No where to see
Somebody throw me into the sea

Lost in my world
No where to be
What did I do?
Nobody wants me

Vicky Rodriguez

Alone

No one was there
No one to talk to
You must still care
I needed you

I was so angry
I suppose scared too
I could not see
It was so new

Where were you
It was bad timing
But I needed you
Can't stop crying

Rebecca Longtin

A Simple Donkey

He's a lowly Beast of Burden
No grateful steed is he
With his floppy ears and stubborn way
He's just a simple donkey

We use him now to ride upon
Sometimes he's on T.V.
for miners who go look for gold
He's just a simple donkey.

But his greatest task in life was
When the starring role had he
He carried Christ upon his back
Yet - just a simple donkey
No greater honor could be his
But he'll not change, he'll always be
A humble beast of burden
Just a simple donkey.

Viola Paulus

Untitled

As I travel down the
promenade of tribulation, I glimpse
a sole leaf oscillating favorably to
the ground below.
    Landing as though upon a berth
of cotton.
    I sequesters, my breath to
see such levity toward death, to
see it succumb so pliantly to the
hands of it earth.

Valerie L. Buell

Black

Black is Vietnam in
nineteen sixty-nine.
Black is scorched flesh
after stepping on a mine.

Black is mosquitoes
as big as helicopter rotors.
Black is hiding in the rice
while VC are shooting mortars.

Black is a dungeon
in a castle of old.
Black is the future
when a fortune is told.

Black is a hidden scream
ringing out in the night.
Black is a shadow
that blocks out all the light.

Black is a scaly,
slime-covered snake.
Black is death,
a path we all must take.

Ryan Goss

Unique

As I look into the
    night sky...
Your florescent sparkle
    fill my eyes.
As your radiant glow,
Illuminates the sky...

You fill me with magic
    and wonder, as you fill
    the night with your beauty
    and glow.

I want to touch you
    and hold you.
For in my eyes,
    I will never let you go...

Regina Armstrong

About A Guy

He walks by my window at
night singing a song I
know nothing of.
He shares his love through
the midnight air.
I feel his presence in the room
where he sits watching
over me at night.
I see his shadow lurking far
behind me.
I know he's there, watching me.
Watching me move, breath,
sleep, and live.
He's the guy, the guy that
I love.
A guy I feel for, and live for.
This guy I need to keep me
safe and secure.
About a guy I know nothing of.
About a guy I love.

Stephanie Baxter

Untitled

Loved, just once, maybe more
Never certain of another's feelings
Led on beyond control
Happiness abounding

Sunlight fading, skies darkening
That's how it is with Love
Sun - once beholding happiness
Makes way for sadness

Once the knife has stabbed
And the wound begins to heal
Certain words or certain songs
Only twist the blade and cause remorse

Sleep, peaceful quiet sleep
Peace envelopes my body, finally.
My eyes close, my bones rest
Remorse makes way for slumber.

Valerie Ferrell

Mad

I smash my fist
    Needles in my arm
Frustration-
    I scream like an animal
My most precious possessions
    Grow wings
Shattering noises
    only I can hear
It seems nothing else matters
    except my outrage
at the world
and myself.

Stephanie Anne Sylverne

Everyone Wants To Fit In

The torrid relationship is ripping
my soul to nothing, but bits
and pieces of bloody pulp
left behind by rowing cannibals.
Wear a mask, or build a wall.
As you stand over
the wall looking over everyone.
Trying to rescue the
unloved mutated souls
of the lost journey.
Once in awhile you want
to be noticed or heard.
And not passed by like
a herd of forever lost cows.

Sarah Kahler

I Have Seen The Face Of God

My work is finished
My soul is complete
I have given it my all
I have answered the call
I HAVE SEEN THE FACE OF GOD

My perplexities were many
My temptations were not few
My heart once revered material things
But now, my heart sings
I HAVE BEEN THE FACE OF GOD.

My trials used to irritate me
I become desolate, deceitful
It was my pain, anger for all to see
But now, I see only happiness, joy
I HAVE SEEN THE FACE OF GOD.

Viveca L. Metze

Solid Gold

Girl, I just want you to know,
My love for you, is solid gold.

As I lay asleep in bed,
Thoughts of you drift through my head.
Feelings or pleasure - times of fun,
Moments of past - things to come.

Driving home in the night,
My arms so long, to hold you tight.
To be so close, is so nice,
My hold on you, is like a vice

As I walk through life each day.
You're by my side - needless to say.
My every thought, has you in mind,
You are a "gem," a real "find".

Girl, I just want you to know,
My love for you, is solid gold

Richard Anderson

In Late July

In late July
my husband died

Friends since Fifty One
Married since Fifty Six
After all these years
We shed some tears

Although only Fifty Seven
His soul journeyed
up to heaven

Our precious son
flew far and wide
just to be by his dad's side

To find out nothing could be done
only knew that we had not won.

God told me to let him fly
We shall meet someday
Perhaps in late July.

Shirley A. Dungey

A Beautiful Sunset

When dawns the dusk of eventide,
My heart within me calms.
For all about the meadowland.
The flowers bend their halms.

The forest creatures crawl inside
Their curious, little homes,
And tiny creatures of all kinds,
The fields begin to loam.

For yonder in the eastern sky,
A scene now is painted.
At once, the cool, clear atmosphere,
With color is tainted.

Then glory breaks, and all is still,
To see the matchless sight.
The sun shines bright upon the moon.
And day turns into night.

Rebekah M. Gallagher

My Own Special Butterfly

My own special Butterfly
my daughter made for me
It just consists of thread and wood
And done so beautifully
Hanging on my Kitchen door
Basking in the sun
Little do you know my dear
How Lovely it's become
My Little girl passed away Last year
So very sick and frail
But that butterfly Lives on and on
As though it were really real
The happiness it brought me
The sight to gaze a delight
That butterfly Lies in my heart
Every day and every night
Yes sweet daughter
I know it so true
There lies something special
In that butterfly and you

Shirley Donelan

Flight of Fancy

Behold the stars!
My breath is no more
The planets, they pale
cannot even the score.

How I long to join
that harmonious sphere
where my body would mesh
with the starry frontier.

Surrounding myself
in countless lights
in an ocean of emptiness
in the darkest of nights.

A heavenly body
looking down on the earth
A morning star
illuminating new birth.

Valerie Raab

Teenagers Questions

What in the world, will I wear?
Mother, how will I fix my hair
No! No! That dress won't do!
You wouldn't make me wear it,
now Mother (would you)?
Mother, is my hair nice this way?
Oh! I better change it.
This is a special day.

Mom, do you think my teacher's swell?
Jeepers! I have even got his mail.
Who of the boys do you think is nicer,
Pete, John, Dick or Paul?
I think John is the nicer of all.
On second thought I like Pete.
Golly Gee! I think he is sweet.
Jeepers, How I am talking.
Mother, lets you and I go walking.

Ron Strong

Untitled

Wind blows
minds wonder
to and fro
gentler still
the mind goes
out the door
to wander
to be free
cobwebs unwinding
in the chambers
of my mind
freedom to feel
to think
lulled to sleep
- at peace
with the gentle
cleansing breeze
of my soul.

Susan A. Huber-Huffman

Melodic Truth

To gaze through glass,
Methodically whispering to oneself,
Lyrically awestruck,
As colors dance through light,
Acting with pretentious flight,
The notes that create us,
Imagine the rhapsodist,
In the panicle below,
Bearing light,
None better is an orchid or prairie,
In this realm, there lives no material,
Capable of rendering thought,
As does the songs of our beings.
What if the rhapsodist became mute?
Everything may perish?
Suggests tales of old and new,
Forever rebellious, splendor the key,
Amongst other realms are we.

Stephen Ashley

No Fear

Running away, never to look back.
Memories lost, some we lack.
Look before, look behind.
Not just physically, but in your mind.

Running from what, I seem to forget.
Time is over, the sun is set.
Fears we gain, fears we lose.
Most of us will just have to choose.

No fear of time, in your mind.
No fear of devils of any kind.
No fear of anything, great or small.
No fear of something, big and tall.

I fear no animal with big teeth.
I fear no murderer or a thief.
I fear no words in your mind.
I fear nothing of any kind.

Tim Monday

Untitled

It's a simple message
    meant to reach all teens.
That being the sentence,
    follow your heart.
    Believe in your dreams.
Though others you may meet
    may try to lead you astray.
Follow your insides
    or your dreams will slip away.
Some will say
    do this all others do.
Remember another phrase
    To Thine Own Self One Must Be True.
You are the future.
    You will dictate what life will be.
So follow your heart
    and like the Mighty Eagle Spread Your
Wings
What you wish for all be something
someday
    You will live, love, touch and see!

Steve Horrigan

Mothers

Sparkling eyes that always glow
Love that always seems to show
Sometimes they yell
They even scream
They may even seam
just a little bit mean
Some are happy some are sad
but when you are sick
and feeling blue
They make you better, by just saying
I love you!

Wendy Baker

Adults (Children Speak Out)

Look what they've done,
Look where we're heading,
Look around,
See the faces of the next generation,
Dying for help and renovation.
Looking at our future,
Wondering if we will make it,
And what are they doing about it?
Nothing. They're doing nothing.
Done nothing about it,
Look at how selfish they are,
Caring only about today,
If they would open they're eyes,
They would see that we're dying,
Nothing left for us.
No planet, No future.

Stephanie Schmidt

Places And Faces

In my life there are times...
Those times are my places.
One place is the road...
And those roads are my home.
In my heart are many lives...
And those lives are my faces.
One face is a song,
And that song is my soul.

Susan M. Tonini

Down By The Waste Side Or Not

I go down by the waste side and
look at waster and ask myself do
I want to be a waster or not

I go down by the waste side and
see all the misery and trouble
there and ask myself do
I want this for myself and other

I go down by the waste side and
cry cause I am close to being
in the wasteland

I go down to the waste side to learn,
and to give help, so I can stay out
of the wasteland.

I go down by the waste side to build
a better waste side for tomorrow.

What good today, tomorrow, will be
better as long as we work together
for a better waste side for all
Tom L. Thompson

Ode To The Cat

Drifting clumps of
Long white hair
Show the cats
Are everywhere.

With tail in air
And nose up high
They stalk
The house
In mischief

Fluffy tails,
Warm wet noses,
Loud motors,
And soft ones, too
Show the cats
Have come to you.

Sara L. Friedemann

Eternal Love

Look into my eyes
   Let me drink
From your soul
   Let me fill
     my cup
Let us be one whole

Let our lips
   Touch
Let our Bodies
   Entwine
Let our souls
   Melt together
For all
   Of time
Shirlee Zimmerman

Silhouettes

I love to look at silhouettes,
They seem alive yet then,
No one knows who they are,
Or from where they've been,
These people of shadows we know not of,
And to try to is in vain,
We only know that they've been here,
Far back - to our dawn.
Steven Morrison

Wintercoast

Rainwaves
   Lash
     Rocks.
He rues.

Window spatters
   Poor
     tend
The blues.

Engine heater
   hums,
     drums.
She sues.

Strange rhythms
   Pay
     Days
Free dues.

Colorful
   Kayaker
     Kapsizes
It's news.....on wintercoast.
Stephen E.W. Savage

Forever

If ever there was Joy
I've felt it in your arms

If ever there was Magic
it's hidden in your charms

If ever there was Vision
I've pictured it with you

If ever there was Happiness
it's in the things we do

If ever there was Caring
I've never left like this

If ever there was Breath
it's stolen by your kiss

If ever there was Once
I've spent it by your side
If ever there was Feeling
it's this I can not hide

If ever there was Music
I've heard it sing your song

If ever there was Together
it's where We Do Belong.....
Susan M. Zammikiel

Peace

Peace-Where does a person find it?
It's within one's self.
Peace is like a quiet running brook
Silently.

Peace-Where does one find it?
It is within your heart.
Peace is like a heart beating quietly.

Peace-Where does one find it?
It is in your mind,
Thinking clear as a brook.

Peace-Where does one find it?
Sleep.
Shirley Scott

A Wish For Life Too Short

Life is just a simple thing,
It's wants and needs are few.
Though some would try to complicate;
I give these thoughts to you.

A newborn asks for food and love,
An old man asks the same.
What transpires, in between,
Is mankind's useless game.

We struggle for unending wealth.
We search for things of gold.
But when we draw the bottom line,
We find life's not so bold.

A taste of food, a sip of wine,
We ask for from above.
We want someone to keep us warm.
We want to share our love.

When we're born, and when we die,
is not of great import.
When love is lost, life's much to long,
when found, it's much to short.

Thomas A. Dinkel

My Mother's Love

My mother's love, so soft and sweet
It's the greatest thing
That this old life
Will ever bring

A touch, a kiss
A fond caress
With her love
I've been blessed

All it takes
To make my day
Her sweet voice
Not far away

When I'm in need
Her ear does listen
When I'm sad
With tears, her eyes do glisten

Her loving arms
Never let go
My mother's love
I'll always know.

Tracie L. Beck

My Father's Death

Upon the Sea a Frigate paused -
its distance feigned a toy
whose awesome power undisplayed
to such a little boy.

Upon the Sea the Frigate swelled
batting waves beyond;
in awe I felt in all its strength
the Sea become a pond.

Upon the Sea - despairing I watch
a lighthouse on the Sand -
as brutal waves dissever
the Frigate and a man.
Rick Kachigian

"You"

People say
It will work out
But when they say it
They always shout

Is it true
Could it be
That's we're in love
You and me

I care so much
My heart bleeds for you
I guess that's a hint
That our love is true

Whether skies are grey
Or they are blue
I will always
Always love you

There is not much
I wouldn't do
Because of the love
That I hold for you

Tammie-Sue Hollands

Life's Soul

Your soul is trapped in your body.
It wants to be free.
There's a gap between it being free.
That is life. Life is what is
keeping it from freedom.
You need life so you can glide
though your inner most secrets.
Your soul is clear. It has
no fear! Music glides through
your soul like tides go in and
out. Music is life, when the
song ends your soul is free.

Wellesley W. Baun

Living Room

I like the living room
It sparks and glooms.
I wish I could live there,
But that's where I do my hair.
You can see right out the glass,
The window is bigger than my class!
It is very beautiful-
And it's always musical.
It makes me feel so good,
Cause I do what I should.
This room is secure-not desperate
I hope we never get separate:
I love the living room.

Tiara Perry

"Poem For A Poet"

Poems are of words of a man
One who makes us laugh and love
Or tears us in two with hate and fear
Some are very short
Other's go on for a long time
All in all they tell a story
To fit are deepest feelings
When one reads those words
From the poet in a man.

Shane E. Hensel

Life

Life is full of surprises,
It has its ups and downs,
Life is full of magic,
Its like a merry-go-round.

Life is full of love,
It holds out its arms,
Life is full of jewelry,
But some without its charms.

Life is full of heartaches,
It pours out its soul,
Life is full of food,
That holds an empty bowl.

Life is full of happiness,
It puts smiles upon our faces,
Life is full of mysteries,
That sometimes leaves no traces.

Life is full of questions,
Like what should I do?,
Life is full of answers,
Don't you wish you knew?.

Teresa Reynaud

The Single Sea Gull

The single sea gull flies alone;
It could be you or me.
The sun is bright, the clouds are white,
But darkness looms upon the sea.

Nothing seems to lie ahead,
Yet the sea gull journeys on
To distant unknown places;
To life or death beyond the dawn.

One might wonder about a bird
Drifting up and far away.
Does it fly to distant nest?
Eternal rest? What of today?

Not to know? Oh breathe a sigh,
And feel the emptiness.
Left standing on the shore
Submerged in loneliness.

Robert L. Morris Jr.

Only You

As perfect as the night
Is what you are to me
Your eyes like the stars
Shining above each tree.

Your smile brightens my day
Much more than the sun
A day without hearing your
Laugh could never be done.

Your touch is the reason
For which I exist
Your love is number one on
My "most treasured" list.

You're more important to me
Than a breathe of fresh air
For it seems as though without
You to live I would not dare.

Renee M. Kliebert

The Color Of Life

My life as I see it
is right in front of my eyes.
It's a misty grey color,
it cannot be disguised.

Each day passes,
and I live for the day.
Hoping and praying
that I'll soon find my way,

My life is not white,
where I can see clear.
But my life is not black,
where I have tones of fear.

It is a misty grey color,
where all confusion is held.
Thoughts of where I might be going,
I cannot yet tell.

Rachelle Grosser

Our Bond

The special bond between us,
is always great and strong.
The special bond between us,
is like a boastful song.

We live to dream, to be it,
With us our special bond.
We live to dream, to be it,
And need no special wand.

The special bond between us,
is different than any other.
The special bond between us,
is the bond of sister and brother.

Toby D. Cary

Untitled

A pondered past
Is a lover unearthed
A retreat to many a moonlight
Of ripe bounteous desire
Eyes that touch
Soft, bare shoulders
A search for the soul
Upon my aching breasts.
Stroking black velvet
Long and shiny
An essence of sensuality unexplored
Together
Fingers intwinded
A lattice captivated by a longing
As time gently soothes
An inhibition confessed
Yet mine, alone, is inflamed
To prostitute an old fervent love.
Devastates a passionate heart
Longing still for his remembered touch.

Rachel Morales

Untitled

I looked before me
For the budding rose.
I searched and hunted
Until in defeat,
I turned to weep and
Saw behind me the
Flower had bloomed and
Died unseen.

Zackary Varvel

The Dove Of God

I saw a dove take flight,
Into the bright and starry night.
It was as white as white could be,
What a wonderful sight to see.
A dove is the sign of God's Peace,
And may his wonders never cease.
We all should do our best,
To help the homeless and
All the rest,
Find food, shelter and jobs,
For all the Joe's, Jane's & Bob's
When the dove see's all is well
From the skies,
All the tears will be erased
From God's eyes.

Shanna Ryan

Untitled

I am-slowly deteriorating
  into nothing
For I am- a separatist
  separated from everything
  including my friends
I am distant and far away
  from everything including myself
For all is lost inside of us
  and we are nothing at all
We are gone
We are gone
So long it has been
  since I've been in touch
  with all that has been reality
Beyond the beginning
  there was a trace of pleasure
But now there is nothing.

Stephen O'Hara II

Karmic Carping

My good deeds won't come back to me,
in this lifetime, I fear.
I've cancelled some with slips of tongue
and caused myself arrears.

My good deeds won't come back to me
'til further down the road,
when time is generations hence
to lighten my sin's load.

My good deeds won't come back to me
to balance out the scale.
I've run rough-shot o'er many heads,
and left a bloody trail.

My good deeds won't come back to me,
though that would be my goal.
Where will I seek the answers now,
to what will save my soul?

Sandra Olsen

A Dream

A dream to me is a fantasy.
In your dreams you achieve your destiny.
Your destiny maybe far or it maybe near.
It maybe painful, but do not fear.
In your dreams you achieve your goals.
It comes from deep within your soul.
Your mind knows what you need,
so it plants a little seed.
From this seed your dreams grow.
So that they won't fade or ever go.

Sunshine Hubbard

Untitled

I saw silver cobwebs,
in the sky last night.
Floating in the rain and fog,
listless yet sublime.

They spoke to me in words unheard,
and songs unsung.
Telling me of sights unseen,
and thoughts unknown.

They traveled past me,
with the wind,
then slowly disappeared,
beyond the street light.

It was yet another sign,
that there is more to me than me,
and that I stand in the midst,
of all that is,
of the same.

Robert W. Van Harlingen

Pat

I pray for you my darling,
In the quiet of the night
When all around are sleeping,
And I feel the time is right.

I ask the Lord to be with me
And stand beside your bed
And listen to my inner thoughts,
And every prayer I've said.

It was with deep emotion then,
I felt that he was there,
And I knew inside my heart, my love
God heard each fervent prayer -

I ask the Lord to make you well
And bring you back to me,
So we can live our lives again,
As it was meant to be.

William H. Nuckols Jr.

To Thomas: I Will Be There

I will be there
in the morning when you awake
Lying in your arms
I can feel you shake
What are you thinking?
What do you fear?
is it your past
that sticks you with a spear?
How can it hurt you?
Hurt you this way
You never talk
will I ever hear you say?
I want to know
everything about you
I want to help you live
your whole life through; tell me your secrets
and every thought you hold within
I want to know everything even your
greatest sins
I'm not trying to frustrate you or make you blue
I worry and wonder only because I love you!

Sara Scott

In The Silence

Beyond my eyes
In my soul
Somewhere in between
  I am silenced

Tears burn my eyes
And frustrate my skin
Still I fear
  But my tears are silenced

I open my mouth
From my heart
My spirit's broke
  My words are silenced

Within myself
Down deep were it hurts
My feelings are real,
  But like everything else
    They are there in the silenced.

Shylo Lee

Two Quarters

I held two quarters
In my hand.
One dated 1969,
The other dated 1994.
Two and a half decades.
Twenty-five years.

I had twenty-five years
Of life and death,
Love and hatred,
Peace and war
In my palm.

Now I minutely know
How my God feels.

Seneca Berry

"The Meanest Cowboy"

He was the meanest cowboy
  In all the wild west
When it came to pistol shootin'
  He knew he was the best
His reputation was renown
  No one would give him trouble
And if by chance, someone did
  Well, he would bust his bubble
A better horseman you won't find
  You can search the wide world over
Because he can ride and rope and shoot
  He's more than just a drover
So if it's trouble that you want
  You'll find it in his town
He'll face your smoking six guns
  And leave you in the dirt, face down
But you'll have to wait a little bit
  To face this famous chap
For his mother just gave him a call
  It's time for him to take his nap

Robert P. Cooper

"Reeling Story"

Projections flash against the wall
Images crafted long and tall
Life that lasts hours on end
Until the last frame begins

You can escape in the light
Slip of mind ever so slight
Live the lasting moment now
Imagination now begins

Taking over for what you hate
The world starts to dissipate
It has to be much better there
A new life will it soon begin

But the minds eyes sees through it all
Make flashing images realized small
See what you have isn't so bad
A new life make it now begin

Thad A. Smith

Outcome

I have returned from my journey
I'm home
However now,
I am a witness of facts
That occurred in the past

I had a chance
To see and to learn
From the actual source
And now it's my turn

As a witness
To grow in a world
That made me aware
How fast life could perish

And the meaning of silence
Took a different turn
No more, no more,
Since I am here with 6,000 marchers
To stop the atrocities
That were brought down systematically.

Sabina Tomshinsky

Pain

You give me yours and
I'll give you mine;
supper shared over
an aged oak table stained
to be a circular, muddy sea.
Bread torn from the whole
leaving crumbs we collect
into cupped palms,
one hand each and unobtrusively
hold.

The apple sliced,
the silent seeds shown:
dense,
dark,
tears
between us.

Virginia Barrett

Heaven

Heaven for me would be
if my loved ones acted like a family.
It would mean so much to me -
if my family could be together and
enjoy one another's company.
In heaven I would be if women
never knew the hard, cold world of man
or the hit of their hand.
In heaven I would be -
if children never had to go hungry.
If I never had to cry again
for things I've said, done or been.
In heaven I would be -
if I had a child to love me.
If animals never had to suffer -
If all people could only love each other
regardless of sex, size or color.
If all these prayers came true
it would surely be heaven
not just for me, but also for you.

Suzanne Capko

Who Am I?

I am the one
If given a chance
That could be
Your best friend

I am the one
You could laugh with
In times of joy
Your best friend

I am the one
You could cry with
In times of sorrow
Your best friend

I am the one
You could talk to
Being there when you
Need a best friend

I am what I am
With all my faults
If given a chance
Could be your best friend

Steven R. Bachar

For You

If my mind had the power of God,
I'd create a flower just for you.
Its stem would be made of the
Strength of Truth.
Its roots would drink from the
Power of Love.
Its flower would emanate pure
Life and Light.
Its fragrance
Would sing music to your mind.
And if you ate it,
It would satisfy your deepest hunger
And bring Unity, Goodness and Beauty
To Your Soul Forever.

William J. Berardo

Only If I Could (For Cheryl)

If I could put you on a necklace
I would wear you everyday
You are my special angel
I need you in every way
I've got you on my mind
Morning, noon and night
Since you've come into my life
The future sure looks bright

Only if I could
You know what I'd do
Only if I could
I'd give the world to you

I would wear you close to my heart
You could keep me from harm
If the world had paradise
It would be in your arms
I need you forever more
This I cannot deny
If I miss one day with you
I always start to cry

Richard D. Jackson

My Wife

I loved her in the beginning
I will love her to the end
I would love to send her flowers
I would love to hold her again
I wish she had been my first
I know she will be my last
I want her to always love me
I know of the trouble in the past
She may not understand me
She may not even care
She knows I really love her
She knows I want to be there
She is my only love
She is my only life
She is my only friend
She is the one, my wife
I hope she always loves me
I hope she's in my life
I hope that she will be there
I pray she stay's my wife

Robert F. Pople

A Child's World

Staring up at the sky
I watch the clouds drift by,
Scoops of ice cream
Searching for the Milky Way,
Santas beard
Disguising his sleigh.
Cotton candy, the color of the snow
Wandering a way from a circus show.
A cuddly, white bear
That I won at the fair.
And popcorn popping
While children are stopping
To watch the world go by...

Stacey Kirk

Once Upon A Time

Once upon a time
I was known, and I was loved
The Gods sent me a sign
A sign from far above.

Sometimes long ago
Or maybe it's tomorrow
I wished that it would snow
And wash away my sorrow.

Sometimes life is almost dead
And sometimes it's just pain
Sometimes, just sometimes, in my head
Instead of snow, it's rain.

The rain will pound on me and say
That you don't deserve to live
Then it will take me far away
Where all I do is give.

Maybe, in my hallowed past
Or the future, in a rhyme
I will find myself at last
Once upon a time.

Tessa McIntire

Mother

When you left
I thought
there was no more to say

We'd been lucky.
There was
time to speak our love

And ease the pain
of loss
because we'd said goodbye.

Then why do I
still call your name
when things go wrong

Or when I want
to share
a loaf of new-baked bread?

I need you still.

Roberta Weitzman

I Think.

I Think,
I Think too much.
When I think,
I Think of him.
He Thinks of me too,
I think.
I think I think
of him too much,
Too long, too often.
When I think of him,
I think I see him.
Oh, my God, there he is!!
I think?

Tamara Malumphy

Always On My Mind

In my heart and an my mind
I think about you all the time
I think about you when I sleep
Memories of you are what I keep
Your on my mind throughout the day
Thought of you just seem to stay
Your eyes are loving, lips so sweet
Something I would like to meet
I think about you day and night
Sometimes it just doesn't seem right
I just want you in my life
I would like to be your wife
Hour after hour, day after day
Memories of you just seem stay
Your in my heart and on my mind
Baby I'm just trying to say
I want to be with you every day

Rose Binner

Poetic Notion

Quite often I find
I surge with the notion
To write poetic verse
Putting words into motion.

I line up ideas
That float in my mind,
Arrange all the words
Till suitably rhymed.

Sometimes it's easy
Words fall into verse;
Sometimes I struggle,
And juggle and curse.

With sudden awareness
I capture vague thoughts,
And give to them shapes
Where they had naught.

A pen and my mind,
The only tools I need,
My candle burns brightly,
With words, I am freed!

Valerie Davis-Rineveld

Value Of The Remote

When it comes to T.V.
I shout "Give the remote to me!"
The joy of holding it immense
But do I control it for pleasure
For favorite sitcoms I treasure
Controlling it at my children's expense?
Are you a flicker
Your index finger moving quicker
Or do you pass the remote away
Letting another choose the show today
Don't be so quick to say...
"Nonsense!"

Robin M. Candelario

Crying

Crying
Why are they so sad
Crying
Is it 'cause there mad
Crying
Some people say they have had it
Crying
So bad.

Beth Arena

Winter Solace

Deep in the Winter,
I remember the warm days
Of Summer in the land
Where no-seeums swarm.

Mists in the morning
Shroud the dark waters
Of marshes and lake,
Home to the loons and the otters.

Soon the sun rises,
And burns off the mist.
The blueberries ripen,
Fragrant, sun-kissed.

To stand on the rocks,
To watch as the heron glides
Above the tree line —
Time stops, serenity abides.

Ruth Cleaveland

Without

Give me your ears
  I no longer can listen
Give me your eyes
  I no longer can see
Give me your heart
  For I no longer can feel
Give me your air
  I cannot breathe
Give me your knowledge
  I know not what is real
Give me your strength
  I cannot move
Give me your body
  Mine is no longer trying
Give me your soul
  I shall leave without fear.

Rachel A. Pancheri

The Survivor

I am like an old jalopy;
I make it down the road
but who knows how?
My brain is overheating,
steam spouts out my ears,
and each breath I take
adds more weight to my chest.
I feel my body chug and sputter
but nobody else seems to notice.
Tears overflow internally
and pool upon my soul.
My wheels keep rolling
as I start to break down.
But I make it down the road
and who knows how?
It must be my lost soul mate
giving me a tow.

Tiffany Walter

Sucka Punch

I had a girl you had a man
I had a girl you had no man
I had a girl you had a plan
  that plan was to make me your man.
I had a girl and I had you
I had you and I had a girl
I had you and only you
I had you and you still had a plan.
  that plan was to find another man.

Treva Boone

When I Say

When I say to my boys,
"I love you,"
I'm also saying "Darla I love you."

When I say to my little girl,
"I love you,"
I'm also saying "Darla I love you."

When I say to you, "I love you",
I'm also saying,
Thank you God for bringing
us together.

I love you.

Raymond J. Swinger

"Who Is He?"

He walks by, I stop and stare
I look again, he isn't there
That smiling face that says so much
Is never near for me to touch.

I see him each night in my dreams
The days drag by or so it seems
We've never met, I wish we had
I feel inside, we'd be so glad.

He's tall and dark with rugged looks
The sort we mostly find in books
His voice is deep, his laughter sweet
But only in my dreams we meet.

Rhoda Haas

The Sounds Of A Storm

Once upon a midnight hour,
I heard the church bells ringing.
And as I listened to the chimes,
In the distance I heard soft singing.
It was more like a whistling,
High pitched, yet soft.
Then all of the sudden,
The sound was choked with a cough.
Then I thought silently to myself,
The singing was just the wind.
And the cough.....
Was just the roar of thunder.

Stacey Delzer

My One Love

To the man I love
I give my heart and soul
To the blue sky above
that I call my own

I will never forget
the good times we've had
When we first met
I knew he was the one

The one that I could tell
my deepest thoughts to
the one that fell,
for my love so true.

My love so true
is what I give this man
just like the sky so blue
that I call my own.

Valerie Dimock

The Leaf

The sun is bright today,
I hear the leaves beneath my feet.
The october breeze is blowing,
the fragrance of fall like candy sweet.

I look high into the tree,
a leaf give's up it's hold.
As I watched it flutter,
the day was growing old.

We can not stop the autumn of life,
as darkness turns to day.
Little in life can compare,
to a child when they play.

For in a world of make believe,
with castles in the sky.
A child's hand is reaching out,
as life went fleeting by.

The leaf lit softly upon the ground,
it's journey now complete.
The october breeze is blowing,
the dust of time across my feet.

Raymond Browning

Desperate To Survive

As I sit here in my seat,
I have desperate thoughts running
from my head to feet.
I need a job to support my family,
my dad might be going on strike,
oh how could that be.
It's hard to find a job when you're
fourteen years old, who's going to hire
you through the heat or cold.
I wonder how the three of us will
survive, where are we going to get money
to eat, how will we stay alive?
Are we going to have to sell our
things, our home, I know I'm not but
I feel so alone.
In the black sky I seen a star very
bright, I made a wish for my dad to
keep his job, let the wrong be made right.
To the Lord I make a big pray,
that he will lead us the very best way.

Tiffany A. McMullen

My Gift

All my life
I have been waiting
I got a gift
It is very special to me
I try to spread my gift around
Some people turn it away
That hurts me
But the people who do not turn it away
Return my gift happily
That makes me feel good
For my gift is "Love"
And "Love" should be given to everyone.

Rica Francisco

My Solitary Retreat

On a deserted beach
I have a retreat
I walk there barefoot
In the wet sand

All is still
I watch the waves
Swell, crest, and break
Against the beach

I see the sun sparkling

And dancing on the waves
The sea gulls swoop low
And the sea roars

I hear the song
Of the mighty ocean.

Shirley C. Holman

Grief

In deep despair
I gather
Thoughts of you

A wide eyed grin
A gentle touch
Lines of wisdom
Etched
Upon your face

I find comfort
Knowing
You have not
Yet
Faded
From my mind

Shirley J. Rehn

Obsession

Please forgive me
I followed you home I saw her
She's so pretty
So innocent.

Please forgive me
I love you
Your for no one but me
You know you want me
You desire me
You need for me.

She won't stop me
She's gonna pay
You love her don't you not for long!

I took her, I killed her
Cuts on her face
I put her in the place

Now your mine, but you say no
You don't love me
Sorry wrong answer
Your in this too I killed for you!

Stephanie Jimenez

Untitled

When I think about yesterday,
I feel so alone,
so wrong and don't know
what to do.
When I'm living for today,
I know I hate,
incapable of love and
can't get through.
When I wonder about tomorrow,
I see the desperation,
the need to thrive upon
one so true.
When I see myself,
I'm frightened of all
I know and feel but
it's nothing new.
I hope that someday
my days will be brighter
or else I'll turn in before
my time is due.

Stephanie Satriano

"Want"

I don't want to feel any feeling,
I don't want to see any cheating,
I don't want to do any beating,
I just want to hang from a ceiling.

Like a monkey in my tree,
A tree - Oh a tree,
It shall be good enough for me.

Now there isn't any feeling,
Now there isn't any cheating,
Now there isn't any beating,
And I'm hanging from a ceiling.

Now - I float in the air,
Float to here,
Hover over there.

There isn't any sound from my state,
No enemies - no people to hate,
There isn't any life left from my death,
No more heartbeat - No more breath,
Now that I stare at my body so dead,
I now wish I were alive instead.

Robert Wedge

Breaking The Circle

You're doing it again
I can't understand why
I keep pretending you're not
But I know it's a lie
You say that you love me
Then walk on my heart
You say you'll protect me
Then leave me in the dark
You say you'd never hurt me
Yet here comes the pain
You say you'll never leave
But here you go again
I've had my eyes closed
But now I'm awake
This time is the last
This circle I'll break

Stacey Felice

The Path

Still one more year has slipped away
How quickly, now they go
And time, once slow, now races by
To where, we do not know

We only know our steps are slow
Our eyes are growing dim
We try to stay upon the path
And follow after him

And as we travel down the path
Where flowers bloom and sway
We know that we are headed right
For God has passed this way

Ralph Webb

Aquatic Scene

Little fishy of the sea
How I wish I was with thee,

Under the sea's so calm and blue
Swimming freely me and you,

Suspended in our transparent world
Floating over coral reefs; swirled,

Warm tropical sea
Swimming in silent lucidity,

From coast to coast
Sea to sea

Two little fishy's
Just you and me.

Shannon Mears

I Don't Care

I don't care how you are
I don't care if your blind
or if you can hear
I don't care if your in a
wheelchair. I don't care about
any of these things or anything
you might think I
might think I care about.
What I really care about is you.

Shawna Wilkins

Rest Your Soul

Angel dear
How have you been?
Oh fine
Thank you for all you have
Done
I'm proud and mostly I'm happy
To hear form you.
Lay your head down
Rest your soul
go to sleep now angel
dear
Just rest in peace

Turina Thompson

One Life Only

I wrote a poem today,
Hoping my words a message to convey.
One of lives, loves and sorrows known
And temples made of flesh and bone.

For the philosopher hath said
Unexamined life is better dead.
But if this truth a poem may spin,
The race of life we may yet win.

For when the race the apostle named
Is finished and the trophy claimed,
Will you regret the legacy lost
And wonder at not weighing the cost?

One life only have we to live
So may we risk our love to give
More meaning to our existence here
While yet we may touch those we hold dear.

Thomas Lee McGee

Mistletoe

Christmas is the time of the year for,
Holly, berries, and snow.
Raising our glasses to say "cheers,"
Icicles on the Christmas tree glow.
St. Nick will soon be here,
To bring the presents, I know.
Mistletoe is hung,
And the bells are rung.
Santa rubbing his belly, Ho! Ho! Ho!

Shelly Marie O'Dowd

"Unwanted Tears"

He began to cry,
his tears began to flow,
he sat down,
with his head down low.
He had just gathered up,
his children, his saints,
and took them home with him,
through his heavenly gate.
He began reflecting on,
what had just come to pass.
Tears again filled his eyes,
for his people had rejected him again,
he loved them loved them so-
Giving up his life, what more,
could he do, they didn't believe him,
and didn't won't too!
And now, they can't be with him in,
his heavenly place. Seek him,
before it is to late!
Don't let him shed his tears for you!

Susan Guinn

Untitled

I want to be part
but not your side,
Just to end it all with suicide
When I looked up to you,
I thought you were real.
But now I look on
because you're gone.
Moving on and I don't know why,
I still don't know what made you cry
or gave you the idea that you had to die.

Tara Hills

Chains

They were hauling him away that day,
His face in all its agony.

They took him wrapped him chains
    you see
He could not move, could not get free.

Then I saw her to one side,
His pain reflected in her eyes.

Caught up in his fate
    was she
Wrapped in chains, she could not see.

Now I wonder
Could I be,
Held by the chains
I chanced to see?

Sarah J. Quisenberry

A Love Runs True

They called it puppy love;
High school sweethearts we were,
    Innocent and young at heart.

A love runs true.

Our interest the same
    Yet different as miles apart,
Football games, proms, graduations,
    Just for a start.

A love runs true.

Years came and years went by
    Raised a family, proud
Times we laugh and times we cry.

A love runs true.

Together forever, never to part
We played it safe, we played it smart
    Bound heart to heart.

A love runs true.

Sherry D. Bateman

Peace

Say,
    Hello to God, throughout the day,
    It never hurts to stop and pray
No matter how successful we are.

When our soul's at peace it's
Much better by far.
So keep in touch with the one above,
Surround yourself, with His
Eternal love,
With all life's ups and downs
We need His grace to
Stay on firm ground

Peace.

Richard A. Granholm

Harvest Plenty

In the fields of harvest plenty.
Golden wheat fields sway to and fro.
As the wind seems to make it dance.

Barefoot I run among its fields
free and uninhibited,
against a sun as warm and golden
as the fields where I run.

Wanda Horner

Shadow Dancer

Off in the shadows-
    half in.
        half out.
    Stands the shadow dancer.
    Light illuminates the man we know,
    Darkness hides his lonely soul.
    Who is master-
        dark,
            or light?
        What awaits the coming night?
    Consumed by secrets-
        of guilt
            and pain.
    Life's become an actor's game.
    Yet still he stands-
        alone.
            Afraid.
    Silence is the price he's paid.

Rick Main

Thank You, Dad

In one of life's
greatest moments
I received a kiss from
    my daughter.

For 16 years we had a bond.
A mutual respect and pride
    in each other.

A kiss on the cheek
expressing love and thanks.
So rare, her first kiss,
to be repeated never more.
She left this year
to kiss the cheek of God.

Thank you God
for my memories of her.
They being the warmest,
most cherished moments
    of my life.

Roy A. Parker

Untitled

Grandmother, Grandmother who is so
great, cooks such good things to eat,
makes my belly feel so good when I
eat yummy things to fill my stomach
to feel so good! Grandmother,
Grandmother I love you, wish you
were here today to cook some yummy
things, but now your in heaven cooking
for all above, but I'll remember your
yummy goods that filled my stomach
to make me feel happy, Grandmother,
Grandmother God Bless You!

Stephanie Lee

Morels

Through a window in my mind
Fondly there I see the times
When as a child I would seek
Behind the house along the creek
For the places you were hiding,
And the pleasures there abiding;
For in those places there were pleasures
That were truly double measures.
One measure was to seek and find;
The other came at eating time.

Robert M. Whitfield

For My Dad

Jesus take his soul to thee.
Grant him peace, please let it be.

Though we know he was no saint,
Let him enter heavens gate.

Keep him in thy loving care,
Someday i will see him there.

What can we say about his life
He loved his children and his wife.

No trophies did he leave behind,
but we knew his heart was kind!
He always did all that he could.
In this man there was much good!

So, please Jesus let him know,
That we love; and miss him so!
Be with mama, she's so sad.
Take care of him,
Cause he's my Dad.

Sondra D. Osborn-Hopkins

Grandma

This is a little story about our
Grandma Bob, Oh! She was a feisty
lady, who never took things for granted.
    She stood by us all, in lending a
helping hand. Even though we called
her granny or gramp's from time to time,
she would just laugh and say "I'm
not old."
    She sometimes would even give
advice and be there when we were
down, but we always knew that
somehow she would be around.
    But when the time came to say
Goodbye. We knew in our hearts
that someday on the other side,
where roses never fade, we would all meet again.
    As time fades, and days go
by we just think of happy
times when our Grandma Bob was
here and alive.

Tracy Reed

Black Stallion

Black Stallion run faster,
Gallop into the night.
Let the wind stop my worries,
So everything will be alright.

Black Stallion don't slow down,
The pain is coming back.
Stay on the path of happiness,
Don't ever loose the track.

Black Stallion don't stop now,
The pain, it's just too strong.
Don't stop our freedom yet,
Or everything will go wrong.

Black Stallion don't leave me behind,
You can't leave me here all alone.
I need to know if your still there,
Your shadow is all that is shown.

All is silence now,
As everything suddenly dies.
Only the sound of knowing your not there,
Sounds of my awful moans and shrieking
cries.

Rachel Wolfe

Butterfly Kiss

Butterfly fluttering
Gaily dancing
Wings of velvet
Vibrant, entrancing

Graze flower blossoms
In perpetual flight
Suave, gracious motions
Marveling delight

Brushing petals
Softly lingering
As lovers lips
Senses mingling

Mirrored Vision
Exquisite pools
Delightful thoughts
Sparkling jewels

Eyelashes feathery touch
Fascinating bliss
Suspended time
Whimsical kiss
Renaye Green

Dance of Winter

Silent winds embrace the ground.
Frozen fingers all around.
The dance of madness the faces do.
For each other and for you.

All is numb
As all should be, waiting only
To be set free.
The hand of god,
This must surely be.
For all of us to look and see.

And in his measure
Of thought and time.
This show of his,
Is yours and mine.
Richard LaRue

Stay On Quest

Words close in
from those who oppose
causing sharp pricks
like thorns on a rose
spirited dreams shot down
by arrows
now the path of belief
slowly narrows
once a passion, turned
tainted muddle
left lingering
a wish to be cuddled.
But allow the appetite of dare
to stay on quest
it confirms a way
to find the crest
discouraging words
try to resist
listen to the voice of the dream
that continues to persist.
Sandra L. Parmenter

I've Had Enough

What do you want
from me?
I gave you my love
and my heart.
I tried my best to
please you.
You took my heart
and stepped on it.
Now I don't want to
feel anymore.
Not
lovehatepainsad
nessjoyangeretc.
Leave me alone cruel
world.
I've had enough.
Thurman Jamison

Vision Of Will

At first sight
From heaven
Into my life
She is born

Somewhere in the realm
Of angelic mortality she dwells
With the soul
That bleeds a flow of love

Why hath she flown upon thee?
I can not explain
Though as I gaze into her crystal eyes
'Tis the Lord I see in disguise
Blessing me with one of his own seed

I desire and strive
To keep fire out of her eyes
And pursue life beyond living a thrill

So everyday I pray
That eternity be our destiny
If it be in God's Will
Wilson Afrikano Smith

The System

It's called the system.
Fraud, corruption, deception, lies.
People want what's best for them
what we get is what the money buys.

Money buys anything
in the world today.
Opinions do not mean much
so I will go about as I may.

Start a movement;
you have to know the king.
You have to fight the red tape;
to change something.

We live on
and fight the beast
We live in
What we like the least.
Richard Smart

The Wildflower

I am a wildflower.
Fragile, yet strong of heart.
I am the essence,
of the Power of the Universe.

I glory in the knowledge,
that He covers me with His beauty.
The fragrance of His breath,
flows through my petals.

I am the manifestation of His love.
A windflower to the lonely wanderer.
Outstretched toward heaven,
in His love, I have everything.

My only work is to bloom.
And in the doing,
I give Him praise.
Sandra O. Urbanek

"A Few Minutes"

A few minutes never the time,
for these feelings I leave behind.
Rather an eternity to hold in place,
the warmth and peace to fill the space.
Inside my heart to calm the storm,
uncontrolled with urges borne,
but at the center tranquility lies,
with just one glace into your eyes.
The whole meaning oh my life,
I find with you, my darling wife.
Just a few minutes is all the time,
to hold your hand know your mine.
Robert P. Pieron

My Heart And My Soul

Keep me oh Lord, please do!
For my heart and my soul I
Give to you
And walk with me each step
That I take
Be near me each morning when
I awake
Be the sunshine that warms
My heart
And the light that shines as
My day starts
Give me wisdom to do your
Will
And when I hear gossip hold
My tongue still
And let my love show
As yours long ago
For I give to you my
Heart and my soul
Ruby Andes

Missing

You were and are gone
as quickly as a smile
from a child's face,
Whose sandy turrets
are erased by a
salty sea of tears.

And all we are left
are vague impressions in the sand.
Tom Thompson

Splendor of Flowers

Flowers will bloom by the way
for me,
In meadows, by sidewalks,
On the shores, on high lands.
In sands we'll gather
sea shells
Wonder aimlessly, watch sunsets
of splendor go to evening rest.
Wake up with the sunrise
Starting another day
Where man and creature
Are free to roam the earth
Where flowers of bright colors
grow —
Near trees of green in fields
of daffodils,
Near lake of water crystal clear,
Shimmer like diamonds on a sea.

Velma Pendleton

Rest Assure

Rest assure, my boy, my friend
For kind advice to thee I lend
A word of wisdom that I send,
To stand the test of time

For to no man, you must confess
Fulfill your purpose to progress
A land of hope will be your test
the limits are your mind.

Sammy Aviles

Waiting

Waiting-as time passes by,
   for how much longer, I do not know,
   but I hope for only a short while.
But what is time when you are waiting?
An infinite amount of minutes
Filled with nothing except Waiting-
Minutes that seem like hours,
   you try not to look at the clock,
   but it calls out to you
To look its way with its timely ticks,
   ticking...ticking...ticking...
Louder and louder they echo in you ears,
   how long has it been?
How long will it be?
How long?
Waiting...

Richard T. Le Master

Forgotten Words

My thoughts seem to wander,
For a word I cannot find;
But I know if I wait patiently,
It will come to me in time.

Where once my days were filled with words,
My parchment scrawled with rhyme;
Now the quill often lays still,
While my soul longs to pen one line.

Susan G. Gathings

A Thought Of Spring

Spring time is here and the
Flowers are all in bloom
Song birds are singing their
Most delightful tunes

Warmer weather is coming
Snow and cold will soon be gone
Then the next thing will be
The moving of our lawns.

Heat will soon over take us
We will wish for cooler air to appear
But who in heck is satisfied
With all those things all year?

We're all wishing far perfect weather
But that will never be
So why not be content and live just
happily?

Vera Dahna

Fearsome Nights

Burning cold eyes
Flashing in the dark
Flaring up in lust
Death comes in love
Ringing out the light

Fingers curl like claws
Clenching in the dust
Sound soon disappears
Wind screams agust
Breathing others laments

Sun journey's past horizon
Inhibitions lose all life
Lightning crackles 'tween lost sighs
Evils laughter flies unheeded
Ever shrieking through the night

Fearsome in the darkness
Desire cries out from flight
Revenge of double edge
In life so subtle with evil
Feel love swoop out of sight

Richard Burgeson

On Having Dinner...

Sitting inches from you
Feeling worlds apart
As you look across the flicker
Gently bathing your face

Wondering what you'll say
Whatever could you do
To heal the hurt
And close the gap between us

I used to feel as safe with you
As the bubbles softly cocooned
Slowly rising to the top of
The intoxicating beverage before us

But just as they meet
Their ultimate demise
Ascending to an environment
Where they can not survive

I peer into those windows
That reveal your soul
And without further illumination
Fear I'll meet the same fate

Terri Firebaugh

Horse

I talk
fast and unsure
while you just walk
like a pro

I sing
slowly and softly
while you lead me
where ever we go

I rhyme
we and me, free verse
while you take me
somewhere, anywhere

You listen
quietly and surely
not saying a word

Tara Botero

The Hunt For Life

Like the wind I rush pass the trees
Fast, alert, and alive
I sense the smell of life
It's getting closer, closer, closer
Now I slow down to a halt
I have found life
I have found vitality

It's a pygmy creature
Guarding it's whole treasure
I can't ask for a better gift
It will suppress my desire
At my sight it disappears in panic
But it's not fast enough to escape

Giving me it's whole gift
I enjoy it to it's fullness
Yet I must save some
Toward the other part of me
The part that will not taste it
Now it will accomplish it's purpose

And like the wind I leave

Rodrigo Mansilla

Christmas Memory

It is Christmas and the snow is
falling gently on the ground.

In the corner I see the children
fooling around.

My heart jumps with joy.
When I see them play with a toy

It reminds me of the time long
gone when I was a boy.

And somewhere in the recesses
of my mind, I hear the echo of
Ho, Ho, Ho.

Tony Cuseo

The Wall

Binding are the hands of time;
As "hearts" begin to fall.
A stillness gathers deep within;
Arise again the wall!

Touch me not the blinding pain;
Deep within my soul.
Time must pass, a wound must heal;
To once again make whole.

Virginia C. Barber

Race

Mask upon mask
Face upon face.
So much confusion
about your race.
You could be white
and love only that.
You could be black
what's wrong with that?
You could be alone
and want no one to care.
You could be friendly
and have people there.
You could do anything
you set your mind to.
So what's your decision?
What have you decided to do?
You could do anything
don't let anyone tell you what to do.
It's your decision,
it's up to you.

Tanisha Edwards

The World Today

What' wrong with the world today?
Everything seems so dark and gray.
That's not how things should be.
Are we blind, can't we see?
The world was once so bright.
Now it's faded dark as night,
All of this hatred going on,
What happened to the happy song?
That we once used to sing.
Remember the joy it would bring?
People have become so strong.
My only hope is the world will change.

Robert Miller

Stormy Weather

Our cries of solitude,
Echo through time and space.
Seeking out a destiny,
That will bring us face to face.
We search through the country,
And down every city street.
In hope that our pleas of love,
Will someday finally meet.
We will look forever,
Search till the day arrives.
When our souls will join as one,
For the rest of our lives.
But until that day,
We have much to achieve.
We must constantly strive,
And always believe.
Someday,
We will be together.
Together.
We will survive The Stormy Weather

Robert D. Hedrick

Peace on Earth

P-people all around the earth
E-everyone who is giving birth
A-all of the things that go wrong
C-children from here to Hong Kong
E-enough of the violence

O-ones who are living in silence
N-never ending contributions

E-everyday resolutions
A-anyone awaiting change
R-remember this world is strange
T-the many things that come after birth
H-honor,glory and peace on earth.

Terry Deshawn Long

Two Doves

Early morning
driving to work
alongside the road
two mourning doves lurk
one is moving
one is still
one yearns for the other
the other never will

next morning the sun shines
at the same place and when
but not for two doves
together again

Richard G. Henriet

Dreamer and Believer

I have been a
"Dreamer and Believer"
of so many things
I have chosen
to fulfill,

And even though some of those
dreams will never come true,
I'll continue to believe in
myself strangely at will,

That's one day,
I'll be the best at what I do by
doing the best that I can,

Because I will forever
believe in myself as one
determined kind of man.

Randolph D. Cappe Jr.

Truth

Latter days of truth,
enveloping the hearts of old.
Nor, has the young,
battled the invisible foe.
Etched in the heart,
dormant, stale, waiting.
Endless time it endured,
but alas, I fear,
its silence, its death.

Roger D. Duke

Teardrops

I saw a teardrop fall today,
Down Beneath your eyes.
I saw the sorrow on your face,
That comes when someone dies.

I felt the pain that's in your heart,
Stinging you inside.
It shows upon your every move.
It's something you can't hide.

Though I cannot heal you pain,
Nor dry your tears away.
I'll ask the Lord to comfort you,
And help you through this day.

I saw a teardrop fall today,
Down beneath your eyes,
The pain and sorrow on your face.
Brought teardrops to my eyes.

Randy Cook

Adornment Road

Tracing wonder,
down adornment road;
    where wooded lakes
reflect the Truth...
of those jagged cliffs
    above.

Wind blown and sculptured-
    they recede
    in grace.

...As ancient wisdom
stars to show...
    they crumble and fall
below.

...Making a pathway-
    for those who
    starts to know-
the story about,
    ...adornment road.

Sujata Goetz

Motherhood

In a world where success is measured in
dollars and cents,
business suits,
mergers,
investments and
dividends,
I am a pauper.

In a world where success is measured in
hugs and kisses,
first steps,
dandelion bouquets and
I love yous,
I am a queen.

I am a queen.

Suzanne Kail

"Extinction"

How sad to see such beauty
Disappear one by one
Animals no longer running free
Shot by people with their gun.

Skins and fur used in profit
As the animals fade away
Belts, handbags and clothes are knit
Still hunted each and every day.

Soon the animals will be gone
And our children will no longer see
The beauty and freedom brought upon
What God made to be free.

Yoshiye Kimura

The Cruelty of Love

The cruelty of love
Desire supreme
One wants more
The other nothing.

We pass through this world
Some lucky,
I guess.

But others in love
With ones
Who
Love
Less.

Valecia Veasey

My Grandma's House

My Grandma's house is a special place
Deep within my heart.
I cannot forget the warmth and love
Even though we are apart.

My favorite place was the attic room
To hide in and to play.
I loved to pretend and imagine
In my own little world each day.

And let's not forget the bedtime snack
Each night before going to sleep.
Grandma's love with cookies and milk
Made for sweet dreams to keep.

Memories are for us to cherish
And never give away.
Thank you Grandma, for making mine
So special in every way.

Terri Rene Mena

"The Walk"

I walk in the enduring heat.
Day after day.
Smashing the many
buzzing flies off me
with my large ears.
The walk is peaceful.
Silent.
All heard is the pound
of large feet on the warm dirt.
Then...
    Loud Noise.
My brother suddenly
    becomes one with the Earth.
        Everyone Scatters.

Rebecca Britton

Cry Sea, Cry

Hear the cry of the wind
crying for the children
but they don't hear her
none know of her fear

Feel the pounding of the sea
forcing its way, it has to be
children gaze at the mighty sea
never hearing, her silent plea

Cry sea with your windless face
how is it you can show disgrace
it's not all one and the same place.

All the children run and play
the same things, same time everyday
all of them feeling very gay
never knowing, its just another caraway
it's just a caraway
It's a caraway

Sandy Chavis

Do You Know That God Above

Do you know that God above,
Created you for me to love?
He picked you out from all the rest,
Because he knew I'd love you best.

I had a heart and it was true,
But now it's gone from me to you
Take care of it as I have done,
For you have two and I have none.

If I'm in heaven before you're there
I'll carve your name on a golden stair,
So all the angel's there will see
What you my darling mean to me.

If, you're not there by judgment day,
I'll give the angel's back their wings,
Their golden harp and other things,
And just to show you what I'll do,
I'll even go to hell with you.

Ruth Hites

Infinity

Feeling down feeling blue
Come with me and start anew

Never far neither near
Distance makes no difference here

A place to live, a place to love
A place for us and God above

Love the old as the new
This was wrote for me and you

When I've grown old, my live is through
Look for me as I will you

Don't be sad, don't be blue
Look about full of cheer

For you'll find my presence here.

Toby Looney

The Circle Of Life

Father Sun and Mother Earth
Combined to give us human birth
Human birth turned into a child
With no thoughts being defiled
Innocent children turn into teens
Now knowing what evil means
Teens turn into knowing adults
Each remembering human faults
Adults turn into man and wife
Uniting together, all through life
Man and wife turn into parents
Each one with much forbearance
Parents turn into wise elders
Of all, these are the thinkers
Elders turn into wind blown dust
Returning to Mother Earth as we all must.

Rosena Glant

Untitled

    As I rest in my rocking
chair on Christmas morn,

    I hear the honkers singing on
their southward flight,

    And hear the black labs
working their bovine hooves
to a delight.

The wrestling of paper
As children frantically open
Their surprises.

    Something special is happening
All around, as the cycle of life
Again arises.

Steven K. Hawkins

Untitled

The Heart is a gentle thing,
    Caress it,
    Hold it,
Make it sing!

Life is yours,
So live it well -
How long we have it,
Who can tell?

Love so true,
is hard to find,
and love unreal - is truly Blind -

Passion so real, only comes with love,
'tis truly not lust,
that comes from above -

So, cradle your Heart,
Live long - good Health -
Love strong and well,
For Here is your Wealth!!

Sandra Cronenwett

Retnuh's Folly

Your natural beauty and allure
captivate my every venue;
I am not trusting of myself
when you are near.
You once graced my ear
with the warmth of your breath,
And to my vigilant olfactory -
the honeysuckle aroma of your hair.
My shoulder briefly
cradled my every desire -
An innocent touch watched,
as a passionate embrace escaped.
As my lips tremble away words,
a betraying heart skips cadence.
Do you look my way,
or is this infatuation's folly?

A. C. Rushe'

The Candle Of Love

In the darkness of the night you
Can see a drop of light it's kinda
A sign from above its the candle
Of love. Its hard to hold a candle
In the rain because the memories
Come back and you'll feel the pain.
A tear will fall down from your eye
You'll never know the reason he said
good-bye. The candle of love will burn
out, if its not meant to be, maybe
In his eyes you wasn't meant to see.
He was the wrong one for you, but how
could this be true, cause isn't love
what its all about? The candle of love
just went out.

Rachelle Aughinbaugh

Mending of a Broken Heart

Emotional scars left behind
   by the tears of pain that have
   fallen from my eyes.
Bringing back memories of the good
   and bad.
Wondering when the pain will stop.
Staring up at the starlit sky,
Listening to the sorrow filled
   songs on the radio.
Feeling nothing at all,
   no one there to hold on to.
Still have hope things will go
   back again as they were before.
Crying out for help, but knowing
   only you can put it back together

Starting now!!

Wendy Widhalm

Hide A Smile

I could be feeling sorry
But no one else can tell
I could be feeling worried
I think I hide it well
If I'm feeling lonely
Or have no place to go
If I have been hurt by you
There's no way you can know
If I'm feeling down and out
I think I'll cry awhile
My smile hides my feelings
And my feelings hide a smile

Rebecca Bayuk

The Parting-Au Revoir, Adieu

The passage of my life,
by shame it is marked.

For I have placed a high
value on power and fame.

And to my ever growing shame,
foul mouthed obscenities and
uncontrolled rages have all
been my thing.

As time passes, I see the
folly of the old game.

So I have found a
new, a new coach, a new
idol, a new life
with Jesus Christ.

Tom Graves

Somewhere Summons

My heart is somewhere in the glen
By mossy ponds where clear brooks wend
Where fountains froth and sparrows play
In the sage-incensed woodsy day...

My heart abides within the scene
Of wondrous walks as prospered dreams
Beyond the moon- aloft the dawn
This is where my heart has gone..

My heart is somewhere in the mist
Of emerald meadows- flower-kissed
Of clouds that fly and suns burn—
I will return.

Victoria Beane

No One Knows About Love

It hurts at times
but yet, it is
joyful and glorious.

No one really knows
what Love is
No one ever will
You can only guess
what it is
or what it feels like.

Yes, I know Love exists
I Love You
you Love me
But, do we know
what Love is?

We know we feel
for each other
but know one knows
what Love is.

Steve Hardin

Theresa

Just yesterday or so it seems,
But was it long ago?
While in your swing
Beneath our tree, you sang a song
Of love for me,
As I pushed you to and fro.

The tree still stands,
But the swing has gone with
That sweet time of life
Which hurried on.

But tucked away
In my memories,
The little girl in her swing
I'll always see,
And hear her song of love for me.

Grandpa Robert P. Shepard

Captive In A Free World

The lives seem unimportant,
but the dreams remain unchanged.
For in the eyes of each,
lies the desire for an escape.

They left for honor and peace,
yet, returned to us in shame.
These, our fallen heroes,
so strange...so brave.

The fear was wholly present,
and never seemed to cease.
The pain remained through life,
existing, for all to see.

In the time of strife and woe,
we acknowledged our mistake.
For, through their eyes of pardon,
we grasped our chance for escape.

Shelly Mack

Leaders And Followers

Leaders are those who lead,
But take heed,
Know that they have wisdom
And not greed!

Followers are those who follow,
So let your head be clear,
Know the leaders that you follow
Don't let your head have a hollow!

Leaders should be wise,
So investigate the cause they lead
Know that they are honest
And tell no lies!

Followers one day may be leaders,
And leaders one day my be followers,
Know which one you are
And know why!

Rosemary B. Horn

Untitled

I know that things are sad,
But just remember
That you are the best thing
All of us have.
Your smile, your looks,
Your thoughts,
Just give us the most wonderful
Touch to the heart.
Don't lose faith.
You were always there,
With me through my hard times,
Whether mental, physical, or spiritual.
I know how much you cared.
Your laughter is the best medicine
You can ever have,
Sometimes it is out of happiness,
Sometimes out of fear,
It will always keep you going
and need to always be there.

Rebecca Adams

Mirror

I look into the mirror
But I see to my surprise
A totally different person
looking deep into my eyes.

The carefree little girl I saw
When I was 4 or 5
has now became a young woman
fighting to survive.

It's sort of scary
that time has gone so fast
for what then I called the present
has now become the past.

I look deep into the mirror
and looking back at me
is the face of a young lady
where a little girl used to be!

Shannon Wilkinson

You Hurt Me Again

You hurt me again,
But I can't let you go,
As if it never happened,
But we both know,
You play with my heart,
As if it were a toy.
But all I do is just let it pass by,
Your presence makes me happy,
Your absents makes me sad,
No matter how bad you hurt me,
Or how long I cry,
You know I'll always be here,
Right by your side,
Until the day I open my eyes,
And see how it is,
And that I should just move on,
Then you'll be sorry that I'm finally
gone...

Sheri Staszewski

Forever

I've loved you forever
But how can that be?
When we found each other
Life started for me.
We've had our bad times
But most were good,
If we could do it all again
I know I would.
You and me together
Forever, for life
Our own little family
Husband and wife.
And when it's all over
We'll look back and see
Our love has been great
Let's share eternity.

Ramona Cooke

To Hear The Rain...

She hears the rain
But does not listen
Listen to...
Her heart that cries
The weeping soul
Inside her spirit

For she remembers...
Remembers the day
The sun caressed
Her face and his
Her bare skin shoulders
His pale white skin
And they walked the path
A festival path
Of arts and music
Of literature and poise
And they found themselves
At the market cafe
Where the aroma was strong
Of Hazelnut Au lait...

Viki Jew

A Sapling Of Gold:
A Story To Be Told

Though our friendship is
    but a sapling in a vast grove,
I feel I've found the strongest
    trunk in any hill, forest or cove.
You've helped me turn
    a separation of cone from tree,
Into a sprout of new life
    that, many ages will see.
And if friendship is the
    only fruit this tree bears;
Then gold it will be worth,
    for knowing that someone cares.

Todd D. Varner

Passifloura

Your graceful pedals tenderly
brush my skin
as I inhale your perfumed vapors softly
in the wind.

Passive is my stature
as I hold you in my palm
that finds its joy in the nature
of your inspired calm.

Rejoice! The trumpets sounding
calling all who care to listed
to tear away that bonding
them to their self-interested mission.

I wish all the world and every land
to stop their focused duty,
and stand together hand in hand
to live and breath in beauty.

Wren Greene

The Untouched Room

White
Black
Mixed
Come together to make the ceiling
Grass
Moss
flowers
Come together to make the carpet
Dirt
Mud
Cracks
Come together to make the floor
Rivers
Trees
Animals
Come together to make it alive
At least
One Room
On this Earth is still
Untouched

Shelley Dial

Reach Out

Flowers in spring
Birds that sing
The earth so brown
With help becomes green

The sky so blue
With clouds that fly by
Then turns dark
And the stars light the sky

When all things seem to go wrong
Look, there are happy times to be found
Reach out, extend your hand
It's important to know that you can

For as sure as day is light
And dark is night
There are those who love you
Just look and you will find

Rita Heilman

Golf Scores

Eagles are rare, will cause a smile,
Birdies can come once in a while,
Better than average is par,
Bringing respect, almost a star.

Bogies come often, don't feel bad,
For a double could make you mad,
And a triple could give you shame,
Or resolve to improve your game.

On those others, swallow that cuss,
For it happens to all of us,
Grit your teeth and see the humor,
For success comes out of failure.

The score tells us who won or lost,
The glory, the pain, or the cost,
Did you try? Did you do your best?
The score's the answer to the test.

Count them all, the long and the short,
Be true to yourself and the sport,
One less is better than one more,
For this grand game requires a score.

Robert W. Miller

Persephone

In that lone life-sleep
Between the breasts
In the mother-scent of milk,
In that cradle lies my head

Then, the seeded kiss within my mouth,
Over which my tongue rolls
And years follow,
Indebts me to that portion
Of my seasonal life.

And, now, I sleep,
Imitating needlessness,
One part of the time,
Two parts awake.

Windy Satterlee

Untitled

Curl the toes
Beneath the muck of sand
The water whirls down
Under your feet
Deeper you sink, up to your knees
Now you're stuck
The tide
It's coming in
Arms folded, over one another
Eyes shut into the wind
You sway in the breeze
As a daisy does
Emptying your mind
Of all thoughts
Waves splash against your waist
Coldness runs through your spine
Your legs are numb
Your not there anymore
You've left with a smile
And a wave good-bye

Timothy P. Kelley

Thoughts Of You

Before me lies the seed I've sowed
beneath the earth of days gone past
and even still the roots grow fast
enriched within its shroud

Memories that ebb like waves
crash upon the shoals of time
while the siren sings in rhyme
and through her music saves

And sometimes in the dark of night
there burns the flame of destiny
that whispers words to comfort me
and warm me in its light

Above the clouds divide the blue
unleashing torrents in my path
and with me in the aftermath
there flies the thought of you

You are the seed from which my love stems
You are the song that never ends
You are the passion that burns like fire
You are the object of my desire

Robert Bruce Stewart

Triumphant Heart

Dark night of the soul
behold the rising sun,
The battle is over,
truth has won.

Dark castles in ruins
broken dreams revealed.
False kings defeated,
layers of armor peeled.

In its place
its defenses behold,
a human spirit
a heart of gold.

Humility stood,
the greatest king,
In silent peace
our hearts would sing.

Peace defeated
the terrible war
The wall became
an open door.

Rob Killam

Growing Up

Lost teeth, Skinned knees,
Bed time curfews, Climbing trees.
A fury kitten, A playful pup,
It's all a part of growing up.

Kindergarten, school plays,
Pee Wee football, field days.
Sadie Hawkins, Initiation
High School prom, Graduation.

College dorms, Engagement Rings,
Wedding bells, Baby things.
P.T.A., matching coffee cups
It's all a part of growing up.

Shonda Smith

Shared Sorrow

I felt his pain across the miles,
  awareness stirred within.
His sorrow came and covered me,
  like ash upon the flame.

And when he spoke those words to me,
  I longed to be his comfort.
My need, much more than his,
  for once, I too had suffered.

When youth was strong within my soul,
  I lost one near to me.
I never knew in passing years,
  how deep that loss would be.

It matters not the ways we count,
  one day our life source dims.
I lost the one who gave his name,
  my love, the one who nurtured him.

Rosemary Mackin

I Dream I Dreamed

A Dream I Dreamed

I dreamed I dreamed this dream before,
At life's attempt, an open door.
Across... a cross I had to cross,
Spring at the chance before life's lost.

I stand to stand the stand I chose,
My head held high as I first rose.
A start this start that I must start
The sun comes up, I have the part.

I work the work, work seems like play,
Enjoy the moment, life works that way.
And sweat the sweat to sweat out pay,
To feed the soul, that hungers day.

I rest the rest of evenings rest,
I lay at peace, I've given best.
Thoughts I thank, I want to think...
Life's been a dream in just a wink.

It's close, this close of life's swift close,
To rise and toil and thank and pose.
To end the end of ends that end,
When one dreams over... new life begins.

Seldon R. Estep

Blue

I hold onto you
As you held me once
In the depths of your salty waters
Teeming with life
Raging and rocking the shore
Cradling and crying
Crashing against warm, dry sand
In a beautiful, screaming song
Holding me upwards, connected
My lungs burning from being -
So damn close to you.
But I, with all my levels,
With all my youth and life,
Could never touch bottom.
I haven't the courage or lung capacity.
I turn blue from trying.

Shane Trayers

Friends

Friends are good to have
around.
    They are there when you need
them to give you a hand.
    They make you laugh and
feel good.
    They do things with you and
for you.
    But most of all their fun
to be around.
    Life would be a lonely place
without friends.
            Robin R. Hughes

A Poet's Prayer

If there be any poets in heaven,
anywhere near the likes of me;
who share the feelings that I have
with the same desires to be free;
if I could have just one request
when this life is o'er,
I'd like to sit down with all of them;
on heaven's golden shore.
With pen in hand in the promised land,
we could write out all our feelings,
of the beauties there
in heaven so fair,
with all of God's revelings.
And with a special touch;
if its not asking too much,
maybe write a poem for Jesus,
and show our gratitude and our thanks;
for He's done so much to please us.
            Shirley Dale Caldwell

"The Game"

I look in the mirror
And what do I see?
My happiness and traumas
Flashing before me.

Some petals have fallen
From my blood red rose
It beholds my life
Some things nobody knows.

Sure friends have deserted
I've deserted some too.
The Lightning is striking
Out comes a full moon.

My feelings are neutral
Nothing stands the same
I know there's no winning
Life or "The Game".
            Stephanie Stoudt

Try to See

I have been trying my hardest,
And I am getting nowhere.
I keep trying to love you,
And love you the best that I can.,
But you can't see it...
You only see what you want to see.
You never see the hurt inside of me.
But can you try for me...
Try to see how you're hurting me.
            Terri Downing

Perspective!

I've been to the ocean,
And watched the water roll over
What mysteries lie beneath
That vast wet cover?
The mountains at sunrise,
So quiet and serene
Nature comes to life,
I indulged in the scene.
Standing in the forest,
As the sun goes down.
So tranquil a feeling,
Vastly quiet is its sound.
The desert, so barren and wasted.
Yet, so beautiful at dawn
The colors so magnificent,
With such magnitude, the picture is drawn.
The river, winding its way to somewhere,
So patient it has cut its course.
Dominant in its direction.
Yet so majestic and peaceful a force.
            Robert Schmock

Dream

Dark skies turn bright
And the sun casts shadow
Rivers stand still
And the ground begins to flow

Sands of time go sideways
And the world falls apart
As I finish a race
That I never did start

The outside is within
The inside is without
And when they are quiet
I can hear them shout

The moon rises in the west
And sets in the sea
You are here in my arms
And that's all that matters to me.
            Vinnie Desai

Strangers In Blood

We share the same blood
And the same name

Yet we're strangers
Just the same

Conversation cold
A struggle it seems

I have dreams
You have views
If only you're reality

I ask myself
If your were not my father
And we come to meet

Would you like me
Would you give me
The time of day

Or would I be
Just another stranger
You'd pass on your way

It's funny sometimes
I feel like that today
            Walter S. Blamer III

Brotherhood

The night wind blows
And the full moon rise.
Hear the pack singing their songs
That tells of happiness and sorrows.

Join them in the hunt
As they race after the selected prey.
Rejoice in the kill
That will fill their empty bellies.

Bathe in the blood
As it drains in the ground.
Taste it
And know the pleasure it brings.

Eat the meat
That the pack provides.
Share in the feast
As they savor the moonlight.

Return with them
As they head for their dens.
Go into a deep sleep
And dream about the night.
            Tracye Pelton

Reality

Your leg does not fascinate me
    and that is why, dear girl,
    I cannot love you

I like your mind, it is quick and agile
    I like your sympathetic hand
    when reaching out to mine

I'm afraid I like most all of you
    but, part of all is not enough
    as you and I both know

Therefore, I cannot love you
Your leg does not fascinate me
            Skip Seelman

Do It Yourself

I fixed the sink, but tore my nail
And smashed my finger too;
At least it was to some avail,
The water now drains through.

The chair is scraped, the brush awaits
The next weekend for sure;
I'll ply this hand to a task it hates
Until I've found a cure.

No wonder all those workers speak
And foremen set the pace
To put in thirty hours a week
Then work around their place.

It puzzles me why lawyers plumb
And plumbers make out wills
There must be someone awfully dumb
To think this cuts out bills.

I guess it's time I did what's right
See wife about that shelf—
And hire a carpenter tonight
Or tell her, "Do It Yourself."
            Robert S. Vandiver

A Hole In My Sock

There is a hole in my sock
and my toe is sticking through
Yet nobody notices
Because it's in my shoe
What if it was visible?
I wonder what I'd do?
But thankfully it's hidden
Completely out of view
I'm not sure how it got there
I really have no clue
It seems like only yesterday
These socks were both brand new
Perhaps it was a defect
That slid by the quality crew
Or a rare form of a string disease
That makes them break in two
I'll never know exactly why
They appear out of the blue
But there is a hole in my sock
And my toe is sticking through

Scott Ferguson

Finding You

I seemed so lost, confused by my dreams,
And my mind could only wander.
Then I met you and thought
That my life would just go on.

I found you interesting, so strange,
Alive in a way I never knew.
But my courage way lost,
From a heart not yet healed.

Then we met again passing,
And talked, as one found the other.
But still the fear was with me,
And so I didn't let you know.

Now we're together, though it's new,
And I want to know you better.
Together we'll learn and a friend
Is what we both may find.

For you I write this now to show
That somehow I know our love
Will grow and then we'll see
That we'll last through the end of time.

Richard A. Bender

A Writer Dies

I've written many poems.
And all of them were true,
Some were really painful,
Others a blessing to do.

I've cried days and nights,
And used a lot of paper,
All were worth the effort,
All trial and error.

I think I know its best,
My time has finally come,
I feel the need to quit,
And start all over where I begun.

I'm talking about a life,
I'm talking about a love,
I'm talking about poetry,
I have to give up.

Tessa K. Ray

Our Tranquility

When life is getting you down
and it is hard to look up
You feel a gentle tug on your chin
as the Lord lifts you up

He shines His wisdom
down through your eyes
Lighting them up,like
the starry night skies

Letting His knowledge
transcend upon you
Twirling and whirling
your whole body through

Letting His light shine
brighter and brighter
Until transfixed
your soul can go no higher

And as that tear
trickles out of your eye
He is cleansing your heart
of that human desire

Tamara J. Moss

Cage Without Walls

I'm in a cage without walls
and everybody ignores my calls
I want someone to help out
but I'm filled with so much self-doubt
I'm stuck in this damn cage
while inside I silently rage
about the way I've screwed my life
and about my internal strife
Without courage or esteem one might
as well be dead
you see, my cage can't be touched
the damn thing is in my head.

Sean McGranahan

"I Put You In Jesus' Hands"

When waves of strife
And cares of life
Tear at our "Sunny-Day" plans

When the sky grows dark
And there is no ark
I put you in Jesus' hands

As I feel your pain
Through tears like rain
I can see, there's only one plan

No words will do
No prayer or two
I just put you in Jesus' hands

For my hands, though willing
Are feeble and weak
There's no magic sentence
That my tongue can speak
When my troubled heart
Cannot understand...
I put in Jesus' hands

Ron Spann

Why?

Why do things we care about
always turn out this way

They hurt you and leave you
When you still have so much to say

The time you spent together
will mean so much to you

As the songs and pictures you
shared will leave you sad and blue

The days seem to pass on
more slowly and leave you sad

wanting to be with them and love
them hurts your heart so very bad

with everyday that passes on you wish
you could share your love with them

Even though you know your chances
of that happening are very slim

Your mistakes and heartache
will always be there

But who ever told us
life or love was ever fair

Wyndi Milam

Please Take The Time

I'll take the time to walk with you
along the sandy beaches

If you take the time to gaze with me
at the sky, as far as it reaches

I'll take the time to share with you
each day of life, forever,

If you take the time to give to me
your love, which I will treasure

I'll take the time to age with you
throughout our future years

If you take the time to comfort me
through my deepest, darkest, fears

And when our time is over
and when our days are gone

Through the times we've given
our love will linger on

This will be our special gift
we will leave behind

For others to discover
if they will take the time

Vicki Lynn Tatum

"Love"

A pen that's always busy,
A voice upon the phone,
A letter in the mail,
To prove were not alone,
A voice within the air,
Reassurance of a love done,
To show how much I care,
To prove my love is sacred,
To help you understand.
That my love is always near.
On my tips within my hand!

Sheila Richmond

This Rose

I walk softly
alone in my thoughts
you died so quickly
silently and fast
I miss you today as I think of you.
Walking in the early morning
before the rising sun
the morning dew falls softly
as unknown to you as a silent kiss
as if to share with you its beauty.
A small flower
nestled in a garden
petal so soft
color so vivid
it's as perfect as you in every way.
The dew drops lay
adding to the beauty
of this perfect flower,
memories occupy my thoughts
as I lean to smell the remembrance of you in
this rose.

Shannon Allred

"My Little Grandson Ben"

I came into the world
After knocking at the door
Ever so hard for my tiny fists
Door was closed like steel.

Little pink fists
I pounded till red
Will you fools keep me here
Till I'm completely dead?

What do I care about contractions?
I'm like the mighty wind!
Water, water everywhere!
Let me swim on in.

Here I come, awfully late
Screaming in!
Worn nerves on end
A tiny red bundle
Dark brown tufts awry
A little sad mouth
All screwed up.
Ready to cry!

Theresa Terreson

New Love

I should be, I think,
Afraid of you
But I curl like a cat
Against the warmth of your voice
Purring contentment
For your hand in mine.

Sleepy warm dreamy night
We build igloos of words
Against the cold.

Mystery man with fiery eyes
Touching my secrets
Caressing my dreams
As if you too understand
The bittersweet hunger of memory
As if you too know
The shadowdance of desire and need
As if you too see
The waste of life not lived.

Sharon A. Petronella

"Adorn"

A Rose
adorn with tears of life and death
Graceful
through the passing of the winter

A question to ask... Care?
Accept blessings with understanding
and faith
Become everything you hope for

Even in the blowing rain and
the sun drenched sky
All of you, you for all
Pass the day away, Calmly

Trevor Noakes

Old Shoes

The closet black
Abiding there-in
Old wrinkled shoes
Lopsided dusty
Laces frayed, eyelets gone
Replaced soles worn thin
Miles trod
Sun, mud, fun
Yet shined
Youth but memory.

Much like my old shoes
Am I
Eyes dimming
Soul tired, body worn
Sun, mud, fun, miles trod
Mayhap's a youthful gleam stirs.
Here I be
Senile
A closet black
There-in I abide.

Ralph N. Smiley

Untitled

Love is
a strange thing...
born in the heat
of a
moment,

or...
in plain despair

in the eyes of a total stranger
who says hello...and a few other words
just to fill the
gap...

Ah,
If he only knew how lonely
you have been...

before him...

Taraneh Mira

"Where Live Treasures"

I know a place spectacular
A spot that's nonpareil
A secret, earthy paradise
That speaks, but never tells.

This wondrous place spectacular
Is not an ocean pier
It's not an isle or sandy beach
and yet it's always near.

A haven for the homeless
A secluded, lush retreat
A place where winged dreams dare to soar
Without imminent defeat.

This special little place unique
is filled with homemade love
It's grand as any summit's peak
One ever dared dream of.
This singular location
is but a master's work of art,
A grand divine creation
So called the human "heart".

Sharon Lynette Cole

A Friend

A friend is like a flower,
a rose to be exact.
Or maybe like a new gate,
that never comes unlatched.
A friend is like an owl,
both beautiful and wise.
Or perhaps a friend is like
a ghost,
Whose spirit never dies,
A friend is like a heart that goes
on strong until the end.
Where would we be in this
world,
If we did not have a friend?

Tina Watts

Poem of a Poem

She read the poem,
a million times over;
She grasps the meaning (sort of).
The discussion leads another way
a path not seen, nor thought.

What of the yellow fog, creeping,
and sneaking 'round the house?
a cat, of course!
But not at all.
She saw the hand of death,
Come to invade their daily life.

Yes,
She read the poem
a million times over.
The meaning it held was lost.
Forever gone, forever lost,
in the realms of the abyss.
The cause: A literal point of view.

Sandra Parcher

Lonely Roads

The road to loneliness
a highway to hell
I stumbled many times
before I finally fell

Feelings of sorrow
Tears like acid rain
the burning of hatred
the sting of pain

My hands were scraped
my jeans were torn
I walked for miles in shoes
no one else had worn

I picked myself up
and gathered my pride
only I could tell
that my soul had died

Sheryl Lynn Largent

Untitled

Lord let me be
a child, for awhile.
To discover each day
through a child's eyes,
to be content
as only children are.
Let me build a new world
out of blocks
and knock it down,
sing nonsense songs
and laugh.
Let me cry and be comforted,
let me run for the joy of it
and spin around
'til I'm dizzy.
Let me love and trust
with innocence.

Lord let me be
a child, for awhile.

Shannon M. Boff

Black Ice

You Know
6'3 Black as Coal
Skin as smooth as Ice
Mmmmmm

You Know
When he touches you on a hot
summer night he cools your skin

You Know
He makes you feel like you don't
ever want to let go

You Know
Ice melts if you hold it too tight
and slips right through your fingers.

Loving Black Ice

Susan M. Copeland

The Woman with Fading Tears

There is a woman I know, who tells stories of her childhood. Stories
of sadness that does not reflect, therefore is not easily understood.

She talked of being molested by her father when she was small. And
the same by her step-father when she had grown tall.

She married at fourteen to run away from the pain. Only to find that
she had married a man full of vain.

He abused her and tormented her out of his own anger. Until three
years later, they had a child and soon it was in danger.

Courage finally found her and she divorced, again from the pain she
ran away. Now as I look into her eyes, I see the strength that she
had found came to stay.

She is now a woman, standing on her own two feet. Ready to reach her
goals, and accomplish any challenge she is to meet.

She has supported herself, now for many years. And for so long, she
has had no tears.

She keeps herself on the upward bound. She explores all of life's
adventures that are waiting to be found.

In this woman I have found admiration and devotion. For I am the one
she saved from a lifetime of mixed emotion.

Today, this woman is my mother and stronger than ever. And the day
she will hurt again, is no sooner than never.

Jennifer Waddell

Kiss

Lips meet and out of the shallows of repetition comes something
undefined, something true to its form, but false to everything else.
It swells up from the inside — feeding off the decay and rot of
unspent ambition — growing beyond itself, doubling, tripling, eating,
itself into existence. It grabs, clutches, claws its way free. Now
spreading within its victim, feeding on emotions, some undiscovered
some kept locked up — chewing at them, screaming down their throats,
setting them ablaze. Uncontrollable, flashing, sparking, seeping into
the outer reaches of what used to be an intellect, capturing all
reason, all thought, all senses, it blasts — shoots arrow upon arrow
into every pore, every space no matter the size. The body, alive,
sizzling, scorched to the core, bursts into an internal explosion of
excitement. Lips part and from within comes a calming, releasing all
of that which had been held. Now dying away, longing, reaching, it
smolders — dampened by the space, starved by the memory and put to
rest by the absent lips of a kiss.

Jeff Martinson

What I Was Actually Doing That Whole Time

Behind the hot curtain of wild green wood and wet window at the edge
of summer I turned a face into the pillow, brushed a day out of my
eyes with my palms, drew sleepy pictures with markers and paper from
the bookcase at the end of the bed and spread them on the floor

Sniffed through the sweaters and jackets in the closet, played with
the plastic toy, spider and the swiss army knife on the night table,
climbed back into the heavy comforter

With the rhythm of the rain rocking my head deeper into the pillow
I contemplated the powerful distance from one shoe to the other, and
brushed a whole rainy summer day out of my life by turning in the low
bed and listening to the rain, sitting up to look through the titles
in the bookcase, falling asleep, waking up

Crumpled up the pictures, went into the kitchen and ate some leftover
sausage with rice, smoked a cigarette, went back inside, the room
edged in amber incense and tiger balm and trace marijuana and the
heavy round end of summer

Uncrumpled the pictures, set them before the bed, changed my mind and
threw them back in the trash before laying back and closing my eyes

Then the rain brought me out, the heat and the pillowcase muffling
everything so I went back to sleep for a while before I woke up again
to listen some more.

Jean Olasov

Secrets Of The Aging Heart

O Lord my God, my heart is in much turmoil,
My days are long and lonely and filled with menial toil.

My hands and fingers grow stiff from working each day.
At night my hands tingle and keep my sleep away.

My body grows old and my desires seem to fade.
But to you, O Lord, I come for much needed shade.

Help me find the time to lay my head upon your breast.
There I will also find much needed rest.

I love the mate you have given me with all my heart.
He gives to me without regard to himself and I pray we never part.

I know you see us as one, but at times it seems hard to submit.
To you O Lord, this I must admit.

At times my heart longs for earthly things,
But sometimes they only bring my heart more stings.

Help me desire only what you want for my life,
Then my heart will know no strife.

I will rest on your loving breast,
For my life I know you want the very best.

I will trust and not be afraid,
For my God will keep me in His shade.

Inez Marie Hayford

This Feeling

As long as I'm with you,
My days could never be blue.
For a love like ours was always meant to be,
To live throughout eternity.

To you my love will always belong,
This can't be described by a mere love song.
These feelings come from deep inside me.
How can I make you see how much you mean to me?

When my skies turn gray,
I know that you won't be far away.
For when I love, I love forever,
It's not something one can sever.

For me, love isn't a toy,
You're not just another boy.
This feeling won't simply fade away,
Because you mean a lot to me in a very special way.

Jo Dell Smith

The Best Is Yet Ahead

The journey was long - I stopped to rest -
   My eyes then welled with tears.
My feet were sore - and strength nigh gone -
   I'd fallen through the years...

So satan whispered, "You've always failed -
   A pillar you'll not be!
Throw up your hands and call it quits-
   Forget eternity!"

But God did listen - and saw despair -
   He hates the devil so!
He whispered, "My child, please don't quit -
   A few more steps to go!

When you're weak I'm strong - no need to fret -
   I'll carry you," he said.
"So lift your eyes - look up above -
   The best is yet ahead!"

Jim Aller

I'm Not Going Away

"Do not cry, I'm not going away,"
My father said before he passed away.
"You'll find me always when you need me,
I'll be close to you, you'll see.
Don't spend your time in loneliness,
Live life in earnest with cheerfulness."

Many years have passed since I made that vow
To heed his message of love, somehow.
And, quite truthfully, I'm glad to say
That my dad's still with me today.
For on many a sunny day, far in space,
In the fleeting clouds, I've seen his smiling face.

Emmie H. Shigezawa

The Darkness Of Day

Stumbling; with words and lines.
My grumblings; thoughts in rhyme.
Jumbled thoughts seem through my insanity..
I've forgotten what it was like, to
feel young and free.

The older people listen, and give an
understanding nod.
With age comes a wisdom, as sent by
GOD.
The ignorant people slander, curse
me out loud.
I quickly withdraw, into a deeper shroud.

I laugh to myself, in a demented way;
None of you know;
THE DARKNESS OF DAY.

Bill Fleming

"Hands Across America"

Your world, my world together we stand,
My hands seize your life and we demolish the plan

Your faith, my works can build a foundation
Of strength, my hope, your heart will create a defense

And through it all let us use our minds,
Map out a path that will lead the blind

Encourage our children, and fuel ourselves with
Knowledge, these days it's not enough to just advance to college

We must return and take back from the beginning
of birth, the gentle calm of Mother Earth.

Aydiee' Vaughn

"Lost"

Oh lost one,
My heart cries for you as you wander the streets.
People laugh and stare at you;
They are afraid of you, but they don't understand,
For you are lost, lost and all alone,
But I know where you are,
For I know what it is like to be lost
Lost in the endless depths of one's mind,
Lost as one suffers from the devastating torment of
   mental illness,
Lost from reality,
Lost———
Is there any help?
Will you spend the rest of your life
Lost from that which so many take for granted?
No one really knows.
One must only hope that someday
There will be help for all who suffer,
For all who are lost in the darkness of mental illness.

Ellen C. Huth

To A Runaway

Alone I meet the gray blue dawn, I scarce can greet the day.
My heart is heavy, I am well spent, life seems to ebb away.
Through many long night I've search the memories of my mind
To find a shred of evidence that you have left behind.

Oh where, oh where did I go wrong? I cry out in my grief.
And in sad, sweet memory I sometimes find relief.

You are my little child, and I can hold you close.
I hear your childish lips say, "Mommie, I love you most!"
But as you grew so worldly wise, and oh, the world crept in,
It makes my old heart grieve right now, to see how sin can win.

Then I heard the still small voice, it came deep within:
"Oh, child of mine, you too have grieved, and surely you have sinned.
Forgive, forget, and let it pass." I quickly close life's door.
"For time will come and time will go, and time will be no more.

All must come before my throne, and all must give account.
All who are my very own, I shall surely bring them out."

Golda Moser

No Where To Turn

I feel like there's no where to turn,
  My heart is in a state of burn.

I cry for help,
  Like a dog I yelp.

The tension lingers, I can't carry on,
  Hope and dreams seem to have gone.

The future is blurry, the past is the past,
  Everything seems to be moving so fast.

Like a flower wilting, I fade away.
  Grasping for life, I can't find a way.

Amanda Masters

The Hidden Secret

I walked into the room not knowing what to behold
My heart started pounding, my fingers grew cold
The windows were all shattered, the roof was caving in
I knew all along that this place was full of sin
The whispers in the dark, the coldness in the air
I don't know what it was but it wanted to scare
Me away from here, they must have seen my face
You could tell that I despised, this ugly forbidden place
Broken pieces of glass, cracked boards of wood
They finally figured out, that I understood
The torment and torture that happened years ago
Now I finally realized that I was last to go.

Chrystal L. Kubis

Yesterday, Today And Tomorrow

Yesterday - was filled with sadness and despair.
My heart was empty, my life going nowhere.
The sky was cloudy filled with fog and with haze.
My heart with no laughter, my mind in a daze.

Today - brings new hope, with a day that's calm.
My mind is peaceful, my heart is warm.
My eyes are focused, my soul is free.
Like the birds that fly from tree to tree.

Tomorrows - A new dawn...
  A new start...
  A new day...
I hope the Lord can show me the way.

Ivy A. Cosse

Condemned To Die

You had a choice — should I live or die.
My insignificant body was aborted and
the genesis of my life was terminated — can you tell me why?

In my temporary environment, in limbo I lie.
But, my beating heart was silenced forever.
You had a choice — should I live or die.

Before I felt your warm breast, you said good bye.
My right to be born was not granted and
the genesis of my life was terminated — can you tell me why?

I was flushed out, like a hot tear from your eye.
My five senses were alive and I wanted to live.
You had a choice — should I live or die.

I wished to see the blue of the sky.
This precious chance I was not given and
the genesis of my life was terminated — can you tell me why?

My ears will never channel the aria of song birds.
My tiny nose will never know the scent of gardenias.
You had choice — should I live or die.
I am dead forevermore — mother, can you tell me why?

Jane Athey

The Tree

So says the tree I feel so bare
My leaves have left and people do stare
I was so beautiful, shaped so fine
With beautiful leaves I felt like a shrine
I was home to the birds
And gave much needed shade
To the tired and weary
Through the sunny faraway
So now I am bare, so lonely and blue
Just waiting for Spring to come shining through
The Winter snow so soft, so cold
Falls on my limbs and begin to mold
Beautiful shapes of white soft snow
The blistering wind would begin to freeze
The snow shapes so crystally
Then once more I am beautiful to see
With crystal white limbs
Now a shimmering tree.

Domenica Halvorsen

La Luz Trail

Moving onward up the trail
my legs in rhythm tuned
the mountains see a distant sail
hang gliding in the sky.
Far below the city lies,
oblivious to the deer who browse
along the canyon walls. The bear and cat
are also close, tho rarely are they seen.
The juniper and pine and cedar brush and weed
are there, and color dots the rocky slopes
as flowers wild and random grow.
The mountain shows its mighty weight
as slowly I ascend to leave the city far below
and watch the river flow
along its snaky sluggish path.
The air gets thin as I ascend
and gives its life sustaining air in ever thinner gulps.
I struggle on to reach the crest,
and gaze exultantly upon the scene below,
and stand in awe upon the world.

Jason P. Moore

548

Lost in Love

Moment to moment, day by day,
My life without you is hard to say.

I'm lost in love with so much pain,
I've lost everything with nothing to gain.

Nothings the same without you around,
I guess in me it wasn't true love you found.

It's hard to believe you lied for so long,
But now that it's over you can go on.

You've already moved on as I can see,
I guess that just proves we weren't meant to be.

Christina Rivera

Night-Sky Journey

My travel's course will never give me rest;
My long-sought goal in reach of me won't be.
I rule the dark and ever chase her west,
Although at times a glimpse I see of she.
I shine not from myself but from her light;
We rule the country same but kingdoms not.
I seek the day where I'll be without night
And up to her I fin'ly will be caught.
At times she lies directly in my way,
But much too far ahead for me to greet.
I can but chase away the dying day;
Some remnants of the one I wish to meet.
I take her place and know as I ascend
Our dance of light and night will never end.

Jeremy Higginson

Untitled

My heart weeps, but no tears, from the eyes
My longing, my needs, you had satisfied.
But now, as season's go, so has your love.
I asked for only to continue
Love, and friendships that you have bestow.

But knowing underneath they could not be freely given.
How I am sad, but joyful that it was there.
Only that short spanned of time
But a life long memory
To cherish and keep.
I miss you and can only
Dream of the time we had
And the time we spent.
May the love always be there
To make us strong and wise.

Jane Schrecengost

My Love Lost

My love lost, how can I reply?
My love lost, without you I can't fly.

My love lost my where ever your roam?
My love lost, can I lead you back home.

My love lost, I know you search for cover.
My love lost, I love you like no other.

My love lost, your heart is overdue.
My love lost, can my heart shine through.

My love lost, I wish I could show you every part.
My love last, can I open my heart.

My love lost, can we start again as two.
My love lost, my heart only yearns for you.

James Palmer

God Said

Think positive, my child I never fail
My love is greater than the gates of hell.
Think positive I'll carry you
Through every fear under the blue.
Don't listen to doubt when it does appear
Just remember my promise 'I'm always here'.
Troubles may roll, clouds may look dark,
Just think positive as Noah did on the ark.
You are in a cocoon and I will protect
You are covered and one of my elect.
Men can't harm or touch your soul,
Remember my words and what I've told.
Think positive, put yourself in my hand,
I'm your master and I'll always understand.
Even when doubt tries to crowd your heart,
Remember to think positive right from the start.
I gave my life that you might live,
My child I have so much love to give.
So feel protected thinking positive each day,
Look up my child and hear what I say.

Dorothy Davis

'Tonight'

As I think of you while laying in near darkness
My mind wanders through memories past.

Indecision - revelation - and to religion
You have become... my only one.

Thoughts of you to last a lifetime
Dreams of you yet to come true.

Wanting, needing, and loving
Simple to say - 'I Miss You.'

A summer breeze wisps rose petal scents my way
A reminder of soft kisses comes to stay.

A gentle rain caresses deep my skin
Touches from you spread cautiously again.

While laying in near darkness wrapped up so tight
Holding you close again tonight.

John E. Zasadny

Through Child Like Eyes

Here I am, sitting idly by on a bench in New York City
My business suited people bustle here to there,
    and there to here.

Look at one look at many,
    and see their cold nestled
    furrowed brow.
Look at one look at many,
    and see how we've evolved to
    be your own best friend.
Look at one look at many,
    and see how the real world
    has become cold and ruthless.

How many steps shall I take to change golden walk way of ambition?
How many steps shall we take to be an obvious, overt nation united?

Christine Lee

549

A Chance

Each time I see you, my heart skips a beat
My soul rejoices, each time we meet
I love your total being
If you only knew, what I was feeling
I spend hours a day, dreaming of you
Wondering if you feel the same way too

I know right now, it cannot be
But all I want, is a chance for you and me
And if you give me this chance
I will show you true romance
If you knew the passion inside of me
You could unlock it, for you are the key

I would show you a world of wonder
You desire for love, you would never hunger
For I would give you, all there is for me
Displaying our love for all to see

If you grant this small request
You can put my feelings to the test
And what you will find
Is that I love you with body, soul and mind.

Bart D. Blanchard

Pain

My hands tremble as I write,
My tears so easily accessible,
How I want to scream and cry,
It is not fair my mother must die.

I did not know this man called pain
He knocked on my door and I let him in.
He told me his name and I did not believe him.
He tried to explain and I chose to ignore him.
"You must get to know me, I'm part of your life.
You mustn't ignore me, pretend its alright.
I'll give you strength if you live through me,
If you take my hand, I'll show you what could be.
I will then let you go, and a soft wind will blow."

How I want to scream and cry,
It is not fair my mother must die.

Alison June Parker Benton

When Stillness Of The Night
Makes Way To Sleepless Flight

When stillness of the night makes way to sleepless flight
My thoughts travel back to things long past,
I sigh at remembering the hopes, dreams I sought,
And with sadness realize there is no time to waste.

Then my eyes fill with tears,
For precious family and friends
Who have traveled to the other side to be
Embraced by the light.

I wonder on a love lost
And sigh, pondering what might of been.
There are no regrets, my road is well traveled
What is was meant to be, I am thankful.

Moon beams peer through window pane
To illuminate your sleeping face
My thoughts turn to you, dear friend,
All hope is restored and sadness ends.

Eveline Smith

In Seething Night

Of blackest magic, and purest white,
my tongue has tasted the dark, mine eyes, seen the light;
I breath fire, bleed the blue sky.
Upon paths of phantasmic horror, I travel,
through strange, witch-haunted glades,
whose night noises, my sanity unravels,
onto barren fields, of gloom and mourn,
this tormented soul of mine, does wander,
and following, with such eerie stare,
a thousand, shifting eyes of scorn;
shadows, whose countless bodies, of demon and ghoul,
will be no longer silent, in their larkings far under,
where the grim-god, Beveros, whose mad writhings breed,
murder upon murder,
awaits no more to feed, in seething night, no more shall slumber.

Donrie Paul Boyd

Tuesday

The truth, my only weapon
My words, a precise point
Plunging knives through your hearts with precision
Your wounds have yet to be restored

Gawk at your lacerations with astonished eyes
Swelling detestation often causing me to blink
Not capable of mending the holes in your hearts
So I don't anticipate you shall feel the scares in your souls

My love, a star shining in the day
My anger, a sun burning without lighting its sky
My soul, a lighted bug gleaming through your jar
And the truth, my only weapon

April Hotrum

Love; Found And Lost

Lorn, behold the magic made true thru thine eyes.
Mystical yet always present waiting to be consecrated.
Obvious or oblivious I give into its conjuring.
To be consumed by such pleasure, and baptized in such pain.
As that of life it is born into something pure never to be chaste thereafter.
It breathes life to drain it into the vast hole we call memory.
The sadness it brings forth is all too comforting.
Joy of all joys it infects me with irrationality.
When the madness came it enthralled my soul and made my heart to fly.
Yet each flight is perfect, so perfect by its lack of resilience.
Moments made so vivid you become lost in its splendor.
To capture its essence is non-concerning; to bask in it your lustful
   conviction.
'Twas brought to me on wings of an angel or so I thought.
Idealistic I go blind from it absence, my tears the only witness of
   my journey.
As my pupil pleads for the meaning of life, the only wisdom I offer
   through my smiling lips are:
Lorn, behold the magic made true thru thine eyes.

Allen Saunders

On Reaching Seventy

Of my three score years and ten,
Seventy will not come again.
I've seen the cherry hung with snow
When 'bout the woodland I did prowl.
I saw the hawk and heard the owl.

These years unnumbered left to me,
I'll use in sweet serenity.
In for'st, field and marsh I'll go,
To seek, in spring, the blue-eyed grasses,
And Bryant's Gentian as autumn passes.

Alfred Wolf

A Season's Piece

A moonbeam bent through frosted glass
Nature's blight on blades of grass
Petals drop from roots that drink
Fall is gone . . . for good I think

Come thee far from skies so cool
Sent here swiftly . . . heaven's tool
Weep not for the autumn's gone
Snowflakes do now crowd the lawn

Now the breeze, so soft, so fine
Wood and foam across the brine
Light much longer, forests sing
Would this be, could this be, should this be spring

A scent of rubber, roses, and leather
Children playing in the heather
A sun that yawns . . . stars ashine
Give me, please give me, the best . . . summertime

James Brady Marshall

Dogwood Winter

When month and mercury disagree
Near the merry days of May.
The snowy petals curl in hate
At the final arctic hiss.
Such a rude interruption;
Just when the heat was growing nicely
And my coat was dead and buried.
This raw intruder steals the night
He sprays the dawn with icy dew
He paints my cheeks a bloodless blue
But it's really not so bad.
His stay is brief and he'll be chased away
And summer will be upon us.
But in six month's time he shall return
Quite persistent and more insistent
And sadly then no summer left
To save the days of May.

Barry Moore

Circle Of Strength

Circle of unity standing strong
Neither shaken nor trembling but rejoicing in song
Uniting in hand, spirit, and mind
People from every race, religion, people of every kind
Our strength is our diversity can't you see
Each and everyone of you creates the unity
Our circle is growing linking nation to nation
But we mustn't quit until our final destination
We must always welcome others in and never push away
For friend and foe alike will come ready to stay
We are growing stronger, banding together never to break
Each challenge and obstacle will be ours to overtake
Together we can do it if only we try
If they tell us we can't its nothing but a lie
So stand strong you mighty circle, be as the power of one
And now and forever our battles will be won.

Hope Billingsley

Entangling Love

Love is an entangling of the heart and the soul.
Passion is an entangling of the mind and the body.
Love and passion is the intertwining of two lovers,
entangling them together to live as one.
Loves ribbon holds there heart and soul united.
Passion holds there minds and bodies fast and true.
Passion is the beating of heart and body,
Love is the bond between soul and mind.
And all love's passion keeps lovers forever intertwined.

Abbie M. Levesque

When I Was A Boy

So young and carefree
Never knowing who or what to be
There you were so larger than life
Building a family with your loving wife
Riding my bike or playing in the sand
I reached up to my fathers hand

When I was a teen all dazed and confused
Watching old movies to keep me amused
There you were looking at me
I sometimes thought, do you like what you see
Driving my car tuned in to a band
I wish I had reached out for my fathers hand

Now I am older with a family of three
It took me sometime but now I agree
There you were standing tall and proud
Always a step ahead of the usual crowd
Now we are friends and where ever I stand
I'll be holding on to my fathers hand

Brian Ofstedahl

Wordage

In the act of learning
new shape of a stone, new turn of a road, new
expression on a face
I encounter
in the act of naming
new combination of letters, new sound against the wall, new
image on the tip of tongue
still strange
in the act of taming
when in front of "new" I put "mine"
a bird in hand: feathers, heart, beak, flesh, claws,
and eyes; just hand, but flight
new way of the tamed, new truth of a thought, new
"mine" of the "new"
in the act of amazing

Ela Kotkowska

Anniversary of Time

I saw your face for the first time
No matter what I did, your smile
stayed on my mind. Yes my love
7 years have gone by.
Some time later you asked if
I would become your wife and
for awhile we suffered stiff &
strife for just beginning our new
life my hon does time fly, yes
my love 7 years have gone by.
Sincerely in our world, there are so many
things we're unsure of, we change as
time rushes past our eyes and we really
have to hold on to the only real things
in our lives, but for so many years
we've been on our own. Your love
has been the best thing. I've ever
known. My hon does time fly, yes
Charles my love 7 years have gone by.

Denice Griffin

Brother Of Mine

You're the brother of all brothers,
(No offense to the others)
But your the one whose always around
making me laugh or making me shout!
You have a way of getting to me,
but there is no other way I'd rather it be.
I appreciate all the help that you've offered
(none of the others ever bothered)
You've made donations to my lacking cash flow
and bought me concert tickets when I had no dinero.
You bought food and sweets for Shawn and I,
And I'm Damn proud to have you as a brother of mine!

Denise Colvin

Silence

Silence — the worst kind of noise
No one really listening
No one really talking
The world seems so far away
But people are all around
Trying to keep your chin up
Talking and smiling at others
The more you try the farther away people get
The less you try the farther away you get
The words begin to echo in the silence
Becoming jumbled and so confused
Trying to sort out the words
Trying to understand what is being heard
Fighting to get back to the real life
But only seeming to get farther away
Feeling like no one else is around
The world seems so far away
No one really talking
No one really listening
Silence — The worst kind of noise

Janna Stoner

House of Memories

Upon a hill there stands a house, and it stands all alone.
No one to play upon its steps, no one to call it home.
A few years back there was some life upon its wooden floors.
And you could hear the laughter through the windows and the doors.
The kitchen smelled of fresh baked bread, the parlor smelled of flowers.
Sometimes you could hear the piano playing for hours upon hours.
The bedrooms were on the second floor, they stood side by side.
The sun shone through the windows, that were always open wide.
The beds were dressed in homemade quilts, the curtains made of lace.
Every room throughout the house had nothing out of place.
The family, they loved the house, they looked after it with care.
They kept it neat and tidy, everyone did their share.
Although the house is just a shell now, with nothing left inside.
It still stands upon the hill with dignity and pride.
Thinking of those few years back when it was not alone.
But cherished by a family that called the house their home.

Beth Bazylewicz

In the Fall of the Snowflake

In the fall of the snowflake and flickering flame
Of the fire and candle on frosted white pane,
In the soft silver glow of the tinsel projecting
In myriad points the tree lights reflecting,
In the song of the carollers passing at night
And the thought of the Christchild is swaddling clothes white
Lying there still 'neath the radiant star
Guiding the shepherds and wisemen afar,
Filling each symbol of Thee with the story
Thy peace shall reign, Thy love and Thy glory!

Ivy K. Stott

Why Me?

No-one has promised me skies of blue,
nor that my paths would be straight and true.
If there were no valleys for me to have crossed,
the view from the mountaintops then would be lost.

When I am tempted to hang my head,
I'll square my shoulders and face instead
all challenges that come my way,
for I will be very strong today.

Courage is not measured in metals won,
accolades gained or battles done.
Courage, the ability to face each day,
and smile at the stumbling blocks placed in our way.

If I may sometimes ask, why me?
God grant me the wisdom that I may see,
when things are hard and the going tough,
perhaps it was me who was strong enough.

Dick Highfill

Patriotism

Desert sands in desert lands, the war is coming soon.
Not cold war, but heated war, in store for my platoon.

I sit and stare but nothing's there. Dear Lord, why are we here?
I think I'd cry, (I'm scared to die) but the sun would steal my tears.

I'd like to ask a simple task. Please hear my words, dear Lord!
I'd like the chance for one last glance at what I had before.

Just a dream, is what it seems, has burst into our lives,
As every day we wait and pray for husbands and for wives.

The "spears" I pack upon my back produce a deadly sting.
Do you forgive the men who live who've caused such suffering?

Dear God, I know, as Christians go, I'm faulty as can be.
But with your love and a little shove, you'll set this sinner free!

A little breeze, three soldiers sneeze—we treasure every breath.
Fists are clenched. My shoulder flinched. So far no sign of death.

We can't complain, it never rains. Bad storms are in our past.
My only fear as I wait here—these words may be my last.

Alicia K. Marks

The Last Whisper Of Sunset

I press into the darkening woods,
  not conscious if I ever stood,
among the tall and slender trees,
  while I listen with soul set free,
for the last whisper of sunset.

The place is cool and damp to feel,
  the sun is scarce, the wind is still,
and yet the stirring deep within,
  causes my journeys whim,
to proceed till the last whisper of sunset.
On ward, deeper, my desperate quest,
  flirting with my inner breathlessness,
is the thought that far behind,
  warm lights of home no longer shine,
lost in the last whisper of sunset.

I fight back with fervent zest,
  and run toward home, I've passed the test,
and I rejoice with renewed hope,
  for lights shine bright upon the slope,
and I'll be home before the last whisper of sunset.

David A. Coon

Trapped

Alone in this dark and gloomy place,
Not even the sun to shine on my face,
How much I want to get out of this place,
To run with a happy smile on my face,
Run through a field of flowers,
Look over and see the ocean where waves make
Children run like cowards,
Take a long deep breath of ocean air,
Run along the shore without a care,
But alas, I am locked up in despair,
Nobody will save me, nobody will care,
A free bird's wings flap,
But here I shall forever be trapped.

Jared Schnader

Beauty

BEAUTY is streams and skies that are clear and blue
    not filthy and brown
BEAUTY is trees that are tall and green
    and not charred black and cut down
BEAUTY is fish that do not float but swim
BEAUTY is a religious leader who does not sin
BEAUTY is a bird that flies free and is
    not covered with oil
BEAUTY is an indigenous people who live free on their own soil.
BEAUTY is a world where to be different is not to be wrong
BEAUTY is a John Lennon song
BEAUTY is my girl-friend to me
BEAUTY is not allowing an EXXON tanker in an open sea
BEAUTY is a woman free to choose
BEAUTY is a Boston Red Sox team that does not lose
BEAUTY is an Earth where there is no such word as hate
BEAUTY is that same Earth free of AIDS
BEAUTY is a place where racial harmony is not just a thought
BEAUTY is a place where peace is not just dreamed about
    but sought.

Daniel M. Edwards

Untitled

A child, innocent and sweet
Not knowing what the future holds
Loving parents at her side
    with a bandage for wounded knee
    and encouragement at every milestone

Years of loving and funning in the sun
Fishing, hiking, hunting, camping,
    playing in sprinklers on torrid summer days
First winters in the snow
And the uncontrollable joy of her first snowman
Sculptured by her own imagination

Rough times she would not have gotten
    through without the gentle guiding
    hand of those who love her
Yet not knowing at 13 she would lose
    the influence in her life
Always being there when needed
    now not in flesh but in spirit
Never understanding why or how
But always knowing the love of her Father

Julie Eileen Theiss

Tragedy of Cherry

Sweet little cherry shaken from tree
Not quite ripe, nevertheless set free
Wandering throughout forests of adolescence
No Handsome or Regretel making woods less dense
Lacking patience for time's progression, why
You'd toss up an egg, expect it to fly
Waiting on fate at each clearing
Causes too much pain in the grass
Besides, one who breaks his compass
Dares not sit on the shards of glass

Enduring one full circle of pain, within half a season's time
Not finding some way home soon, might make cherry misplace her mind
Then you and dates will never be in sync
Love surrounding, but poisonous to drink
Still, shed your last shred, dive right out of your skin
Forget testing water before you begin
Now only if pit was left with stem -
At the critical point of delivery
For although you've lost your faith in men
You'll never give up Christianity.

Carl Hines

Travelling

I'm in line on the runway, waiting to take flight.
Not sure where I'll be landing, or what the weather will be like.
Will I reach my destination, will I even get off the ground?
Will I slowly make my way, or will I reach the speed of sound?
Will I fly just above the water, or will I soar among the clouds?
Will I feel like I've been cheated, or be content with what I've found?
Will I render to life's temptations, and contribute to my demise?
Will I believe in what I hear, and not what I see with my own eyes?
Will I always eat with a plastic fork, and be fed by silver spoon?
Will I set my course to reach the stars, or will I settle for the moon?
And what if I change direction and head directly towards the sun?
Will I burn before I enter space, or will my victory have been won?

Jason Klenetsky

Nothing At All

One day there was nothing
Nothing at all
The squirrels weren't climbing
The birds did not call
That's why we should save animals and all

One day there was nothing
Nothing at all
The bees weren't buzzing
The ants did not crawl
That's why we should save insects and all

One day there was nothing
Nothing at all
The grass wasn't growing
The leaves did not fall
That's why we should save plants and all

One day there was nothing
Nothing at all
The people weren't walking
No kids to play ball
That's why we should save this world and all

Gregory Costanzo

Teacher

Make the day brighter with a smile
Nothing can be more helpful to a child.
They travel this same path every day,
You are the one to show them the way.

A guiding hand is what they need,
Always caring and lending an ear.
Guiding their feet - holding their hand
Somehow they know you care and understand.

You were blessed with talent and patience,
Although sometimes tried but true.
You may not see the good you do now
But someday the light will shine through.

After your day of toil and labor is over
And is slowly coming to an end,
Remember you not only taught a child
You made a lifelong friend.

Betty C. Holloway

Downcast

Darkness, is what I see when my eyes open,
Nothing, is what I see when I try scoping,
Pressure, is what I feel now my body's hurting,
Emerge you evil spirit, set my soul free,
Oh father, come in I think I'm ready to accept thee,
Your fee, expensive, don't think that I can hack it,
My bag, full of nothing,
I'm the one who packed it.
Depressed, is what I call this state of mind,
Confused, is what I am can't seem to find, myself,
I'm tired of standing on this island,
So far out, can't even see the mainland.
I'm journeying into a black hole without a way out,
I'm trying to enter the realm but my mind is doing roundabouts,
Ring around the rosie
Pockets full of posies
Confusion is stalking me
I sleep,
Now I'm cozy.

Andria A. Ottley

The Pilot Reborn

Oceans of water and air; the firmament recedes.
Nothing truly matters but the art...
navigation (stars tell all).

The Pilot reborn, conceived in the clouds and streams.
Turbulence engendering spirit.
The soul Glides, adhering only to the waveforms;
troughs and crest, and stretches of peace.

Silently slipstreaming, dreaming in blue.
Sailing endlessly, the Pilot is reborn.

Quietly moving under the eyes of stars;
Shears and eddies breaking confines.
In timeless currents; in comforting swells and broad horizons,
the pilot is reborn.
Wish for Oceans and immortality.

Clayton D. Risher

Light Of Other Days

The limpid notes of the flute
Reduce fatigue, make its nagging mute;
My fingers lift and fall with practiced ease
Until with thoughts of you I cease
my exercise; my silver cylinder once more
I lay aside, its enchanting musical store
left floating in the light of other days,
when you were here to share its lyrical ways.

James R. Bearden

My People

For many years People kept us in the dark.
Now we can see a light and make a brand new start.
People tried to take away something within.
But our hearts were too strong to let them win.

People try to say that we are nothing.
But we all know that we are something.
People try to say that my people are poor.
But we all know that we want more.

People try to say that my people
Caused all this sadness.
But what they don't know is that
We are a small part of this madness.

People try to say that my people
Caused all of this destruction.
But we all know that we "ain't did Nuttin!"
People try to say that my people's music cause violence.

But we all know they're just mad because
We got so much talent.
My people, my people they try to say
It's my people.

Christi Thomas

The House I Live In

The house I live in is not just a
nursing home, but a haven from heaven
The care and support which I receive
   makes me surely believe
that the things I still yearn to do
   will certainly come true
before my time to say adieu!

Administration, Human Resources,
Social Services, Nutrition, Dietary, Doctors,
Nurses, LNA's, Therapists, Housekeeping,
Maintenance, Activities Departments and
Volunteers too
Just to mention a few
Sounds like an army, but that's
what it takes to keep from going balmy.

   How does one say THANKS to people
such as these
   Who give of themselves so unselfishly
without any cease!!

Hattie Mays

Forever Young

F orever young.
O h, the words, they embed -
R ing in my
E ars, and shout in my head.
V ictory doesn't seem fair
E ven though you're now above;
R easons of greed, make me need your love.

Y ou'll never experience the life
O thers had thought you'd lead;
U nderstanding this - makes one's heart bleed.
N o one wants to imagine what you've been through, but
G od protects our Forever Young, and God is holding you.

Emily Kelley

Chasms!

Snowflakes, snowflakes, little snowflakes,
  O so little, dressed in white,
    you are like my childhood visions,
    childhood visions O so bright!

Falling, falling, softly falling,
  falling softly, falling down,
drifting, drifting, slowly drifting,
  drifting slowly to the ground!

    (Every child is a dreamer!
    Dreaming dreams of great renown!
    Slaying dragons by the thousands
    in every village, wick, and town!)

Melting, melting, slowly melting,
  melting slowly in the sun,
    like my mighty dreams of yore
    that evermore remain undone!

Dreaming, dreaming, always dreaming,
  dreaming dreams that cannot last!
thinking, thinking, always thinking
  thinking always of the past!

     John W. Seamster

Perfect Vision

How wonderful to see through the eyes
  of a child.
The imagination and excitement runs wild.
The beauty he sees, the happiness, the smile.
No ugliness, No evil, No doubt all the while.

Admiration, Happiness, Love and Affection.
Through his young eyes he sees a world
  near perfection.
Seeing only the person that lives within,
There is no enemy.

Wrinkled Grandma is no older at sixty-four.
Than his best friend and playmate who
  lives next door.
What a beautiful gift to have on
  this earth.
To be able to see people for their
  true worth.

For soon, too soon, we will take
  this gift away.
With our garbage collected during our days.
Our bitterness, hatred and prejudices, too.
We will cloud this great view quiet
  effectively.

     Bonny Withrow

Asphalt Wars

A veteran recounts stories,
Of ambush, casualties, and loot.
He recalls,
in flashback,
Comrades lost at random.
He cries when he thinks he
Could have saved his brothers. But
instinct commanded retreat.
Taken at the hands of their own,
They are carried off to the land of statistics
Where asphalt wars are tallied tragedies of youth
And the veteran wonders why he never fought,
A soldier not enlisted, but drafted by birth.

     Jorge A. Alday

Suicide And He Died

I didn't really know him, but he was a friend.
Of course all good things just end.
It happened one night and ended one day.
It was like he just flew away.
I saw my brother, it was his friend.
I tried to speak, but I felt too weak, and I just didn't know
what to say.
My brother always had this fear, and it ended in tears.
I still think about him and I don't accuse him of sin.
For I still feel him close to my heart, and I believe he is
still near.
I think he could of worked things out, but I don't think he had
that doubt.
Even though we miss him so.
Our friend thought he needed to go.
He was insane, and it left us in pain.
He didn't know so many people loved him, until he was looking down
from above.
On March 12, 1994.
He had just closed the door, but I do believe he is safe above.
So Wesley D. Blomberg, you'll always have all of our love!

     Crystal N. Oldfather

Don't Give Up

When you have done all in your power to be the true child
  of God and know
You have wrong no one, don't give up.
When family and friends don't seem to care for you because
  you don't see
Things their way pray. And don't give up.
On the job, or traveling, or where ever you may be just
  just let the devil
Know you are a true child of God. And keep your head up and
  don't give up,
The Lord thy God don't wont us burden down with the cares
  of this world.
That's why he tell us in his world "Let not your heart be troubled".
Keep his word. Keep on praying and don't give up.
Because Jesus Christ is the answer. So put your trust in Him
  and not in man
Just keep the faith and he will see you thru. So love ones,
  don't give up
In the name of Jesus don't give up.
  AMEN

     Geraldine Smith

Our Volunteers

A volunteer is one who shares; who gives
of his love and really cares.

Who brings food to the shut-ins with a smile
and a chat. Which brightens their day, we can vouch for that.

Who gives of his time to keep things strait, so that
we all have a place to congregate.

Who entertains us seniors with their joyful cheer,
and for a time we forget all our fears.

For many the parties you worked so hard to create,
we want you to know we appreciate.

God gave us all a free will of our own: to
share or be selfish, its our choice alone.

So our thanks and our love is for everyone
here for being angels of mercy and our volunteers.

     Jean Bulinski

My Dream

I close my eyes, in which to dream,
Of hot summer days and babbling streams,

Of birds singing in the trees,
Of a softly whispering breeze,

Oh how I love to relax and dream
For only then may I be queen.

I can float up to the stars
I am the ruler of Venus and Mars.

Being childish you may say,
But this is my dream, and I'll dream away.

Etta N. Kowalski

How I Think Of The World

The world is a place of seriousum,
of laughter, of happiness, and of sadness.

I like to think of the world
as a never ending series and we are
all born over and over again.
Some people are tiny, some people
are big. It doesn't matter what size
you are, what matters is how big your heart is.
I love the world, it is where I live.

Audra Karp

Forever Flame

The first time I met you, I looked into your eyes, and saw the spark
Of love, that would forever rule our lives.
I knew you felt the same, when I heard you whisper, my name.
Your eyes told me of love, and happiness to come.
When you and I become one.
The spark is burning brightly, and has burst into flame.
To bind us forever, in love and in your name.
We walk this life together, hand in hand. In happiness and sadness.
Still we wear our wedding bands.
Together we have walked this world, and reaped the fruits of life.
To come close to our burning flame.
I loved you then and I love you still,
And I know you feel the same.
And when it comes our time to go, we will reunite in eternity our
  Forever flame

Alice Rose

Ode To Meg

The brewing storm is in the womb
of maternal clouds that peer-
the impending thoughts of darkness and gloom,
so unbearable- my thoughts I must steer.

The genesis of the rumbling cloud
stirs up my fears inside;
I go to the river where I have vowed
to rest by your wearisome side.

I talk to you, and wish you well
and wonder why you died?
The storm moves in, the clouds now swell-
I must seek shelter inside.

I'll abort the thoughts of feeling your touch
and continue on to revive-
your precious memory in which I clutch,
Serenity surpasses the storm now alive.

All I have to do is get through this day,
rain beats down, filling the streams.
Yet I have what only sleep can convey-
the life of you in my dreams.

Avery L. Chappell

Winter Skaters

As tall as I, my shadow never tires. It pricks the rigid edges
of my smile, the one I wear to excuse and circle love's quick days.
Two tied to habits and yens, we're skaters caught on black ice,
our blades new knives, the splintered ice dark glass below
moonrays;

and twice we spin around this rink of tangled pledges, past small, dim
lessons, our skates crackling ice that borders "Should I stay or go?"
We slice through hard hours, pulled to predawn tinting us gray
from blades to hands, from skirts to scarves. If, if I go I'll know

blame when Lover's hand draws down a marigold shade at noon
to banish his wife's plain face and my shadow like blossoms
thrown to
skin and glide and scatter across ice, unless I stride past his fancy
house, the shade up, my shadow close behind me instead of him.

Dee Duffy

For You......

I have written so many poems, stories and letters for you,
  of our time together, but this one stands alone.
I love you... for what we are and for what we hold...
Know in your soul
  that each night when I close my eyes,
  I thank God for the years with you.
I love you... for what you give... for all of the sweet, melancholy
  memories... I love you for your caring and protectiveness...
I love you because you always touch me.
I love you... because of those eyes, because they look
  at me so many, many times... and I love those eyes because
  they cried for me.
I love you...because you share your life with me.
I love you...for your pride, your confidence and
  your inner strength.
I love you...for those words of yours...
Will you promise to love me...
  Tharco, you are my life...my only true love.
I love you...
  because you let me go.

Caroline Anne Kelly

Your Song

Sing to me your song
of places and persons of long gone
of faded dreams erased by time
hopes whisked away by wind and chime.

Sing to me your song
of desire for love and spirit strong
of greed and lust and deadly sin
the thread to where heaven ends and hell begins.

Sing to me your song
of never ending passion born
of a heart which lost to foolish ways
how empty are these endless days.

Sing to me your song
of memories and pictures worn
of regrets of youth, mistakes once made
of acres of granite and shadowed spade.

Sing to me your song
of pleading hands and guilt that's spawned
of shimmering hope at final grasp
spoken at a breath of last.

Annette H. Baldao

A Mother's Endless Love

Night flows and approaches like a stream
of sleepy water.
The air is cool; it brushes and fondles the
skin, a mildness fragrance seeping in with
each breath, I smile, and take in the
sweetened air deep within my lungs.

I think about her, and a glow begins; I
feel the warmth of her. Closeness of her
draws near, she's before me for an instant
then vanishes. Will she return?
Again I see her and now she takes my
hand and holding my hand she speaks:

"My Child, my Child, an endless love I
have, for I am always there in your
thoughts."

David J. Czepiga

Untitled

Of Spirit... he is the gentleness of men.
Of Strength... he is steel being honed for his adult years.
Of Love... he offers purity and wonderment.
Of mind... he is clear... forever searching.
Of masculinity... he is a free-spirited stallion of the fields.
Of trust... he is cautions, not yet knowing why.
Of intellect... he is aware, not knowing his capacity is limitless.
Of demeanor... he is shy, inquisitive, somewhat proper, quick to
     smile.
Of pride... he values himself, though is too judgmental for his age.
Of son... he breathes love into my soul.
... he gives me warmth when my mind is cold.
... he stands for an accomplishment in my life.
... he is reward for a deed, I yet do not understand.
... he is proof that I was here.
... he has tested my selfishness and gently shadowed its existence.
... he has asked me to be nothing more than I am.
... how desolate my life would have been not knowing this man.

Jaire F. Shocket

He's Coming

Our Saviour has promised He's coming again
Of the hour and the day we know not when
But until that day when He does appear
Let us be found working for the time
     draweth near
And there is still lots of work yet to
     be done
Souls that are dying in their sins
     waiting to be won
So awake Christian brethren and on to the
     race
Until at last we shall meet our Master
     face to face
And with arms outstretched He shall welcome
     us home
With a smile on his face as He speaks to us
     these words "Well done".

Dorothy Jones

"The Colors of Winter"

White is the snow that fell to the ground,
Orange is the fox hunting without a sound.
Red are the ornaments hanging from the tree,
Green is the Christmas tree inside safe with me.
Yellow is the fire crackling at my feet.
Blue is the jay outside taking a seat.
Brown is the color of our favorite sleigh,
I just can't wait for Christmas Day!

Christopher Pedersen

My Valentine

I had the image in my heart you see,
Of the Ideal girl just right for me.
I looked high and low and grew weary and faint.
I'll not find the Ideal girl-I know I can't!
Why I believed the Ideal Girl did not exist.
I was so sure I almost missed-
     The charm of your laughter-
     The thrill of your glance
     The way you make my glad heart dance!

I had the image in my heart you see,
Of the Ideal girl just right for me.
I looked high and low and grew weary and faint.
I'll not find the Ideal girl- I know I can't!
Why I believed the Ideal girl did not exist.
I was so sure-But I was wrong as wrong can be.
I looked again and could see!
You're the girl just right for me.
     I love the presence of being with you-
     The thrill of your glance-
     The way you make my glad heart dance!

Calvin Craighead

Conservation

Pressed in the yellow pages
Of the lost souls
One was found
Lying there for me to see
It's history a quandary; a lovers taken; a forgotten art
     Or simply a mistake

The veins so obviously traced
To the stem of ages past
Over decades and still in tact
It has been hidden
Until today, when I found it,
My link to yesterday
I held it in wonder
It's crisp body, flattened, yet strong
Under the tremendous weight of time
I put it back
Put it in it's home, between the words of Chauser and Joyce
Another decade or a few
For another to find anew.

Barb Weber

Revel In The Madness

Come revel in the madness, and bathe in the steam
Of the passion and desires I create,
In my dreams.

Come dance with me, run with me, far far away
To the soul of my being
I have hidden away.

In the closet of shadows where I keep, who I am
Travel, with me now, to be free
From the "scam".

Far from the fears, wrapped by bars covered with rust
Dive into the pool, find joy
You can trust.

Shared never with any, I've kept all, to myself
These creative conclusions I have left,
On a shelf.

Who knows how I'll feel when the shadows meet light
Release them with me, release me
Tonight!

Jill A. Creed

The Wedding Gown

There once was a Love story that should be told,
of two people now, that have become very old.

They are your Grandparents,
Who are special and should be treasured,
For the love they have showered,
Can never be measured.

All through the years they loved and shared,
Always giving to others, showing they cared.

All through the years they loved and shared,
Always giving to others, showing they cared.

So it was, their pledge of love,
That created this gift to be blessed from above.

May all future grandchildren be Christened in this Satin and Lace,
And know that their Grandparents will always be watching,
Through the eyes of an Angel's face.

May you pass along their story, of their love and their family,

To future generations, whose hearts will be touched warmly.

It was Love that began this special tradition,
And may it be Love that passes it to each new generation.

Denise R. Parlovecchio

I Did Not Die

Think not of me with past regrets,
Of words unspoken, or deeds undone; of promises unkept.

Look not for me in misty rains, or dark of night;
Where shadows play on moonlit lanes.

Weep not for me in cloistered keeps,
Or beside the turbulent sea;
Whose murky depths beguile an endless sleep.

Sing not for me a sad refrain,
Or melody of loneliness;
Haunting notes that whisper lullabies of pain.

I am found in the brilliant sunshine
That melts the stark white snow,
Or in the April shower that softly
Awakens the Easter lily from winter's cold.

I am found in the sultry summer dusk,
Dancing on moonbeams that splay across the guilded pond;
Or on the wings of soaring birds
Taking flight among the vivid hues of Autumn's blush.

I did not die.
I am with you always.

Judy A. Wilson

Come, Extol The Refunding Binding Latches

An uncivilized stream before our faces
Often flows in cunning workplace stride.
It is the old selfishness narrow or wide
That pollutes our heart of social graces.

A Mother - Woman Exemplar among us embraces
The in-gathering of our roguish deride
She entreats us to give heart felt confide
With Please, Thanks, Pardon - Me that traces.

O let us ford the stream of greed-branches
To consider others to our far-reaching gain.
We can, the way Mother-Woman Exemplar reaches,
Touches and heals a main the uncaring disdain.
Come, extol the refunding binding latches
Of who and what we are in the work domain.

Andy Anderson

Nature's Way

Far away the wind does blow;
Off in the distance I hear a crow.

The fields of wheat are bowing low;
As the wind wisps by, it echoes "hello".

The eagle looks with a watchful eye;
As a tiny mouse goes scurrying by.

One great swoop is the eagle jest;
And there is food in the eagles nest.

A quiet brook goes trickling by;
And shadows back the blue of the sky.

A lark in the meadow begins to sing;
Reminding all the seasons change.

As the nights grow long and the days grow short;
Nature prepares to follow it's course.

With winter's cold and autumn's falling leaves;
As summer grains dance in the breeze.

Spring will come and with it new life;
Letting us know that all it right.

The cycle of life has never changed;
From the beginning to end, it remains the same.

Betty J. Luther

"Weather"

The wind comes by and pulls the leaves
    off the branches of the trees.

The rain pours and fills the creek,
    so higher ground, the people seek.

The snow falls in the winter time
    as if it were a silent chime.

The sleet makes life harder to bare
    streets are covered with ice everywhere.

Whether it is July or December,
    We cannot control the weather.

But when the weather is just right,
    it satisfies us all tonight.

Carlene Frye

The Sandcastle Princess

A castle not tall, not bold
— on a fragile foundation
    at the edge of a moving world -
is not sure yet whether to stand or fall
The young princess dwelling there
— as if fashioned from the air-
ascends the stairs to sit in the towers
and gaze pass the gates
She grows old in the hours but patiently waits
and fancies her prince across the land
(which in truth is not fields but meadows of sand)

Now after the years she sadly hears
the thunderous roar
threatening the shore the tide rushes in, recedes
— her castle stands no more -
And with her castle
her dreams too washed away
And if you ask her
she'll tell you love is worth the trouble
to make it worth the pain.

James Shuler

Some Sounds In The Night I Find A Delight

The sweet sound of children's laughter
  on a warm summer evening at play
But soon comes the teasing and jostling
  and mom has to call it a day.

Raindrops that fall on my window
  seem to march to a silent beat
Each drop following the other
  till they merge and land in a heap.

The wail of the night train whistle
  moans loud as the train rushes by towns
Lights flashing, bells ringing, gates closing
  what exciting sights and sounds.

Often the call of the nighthawk is heard
  as he flies on a warm, summer night
Watching for any flying insects
  that might be a tasty delight

I am just a lonely old granny
  E'er listening for the sound I like best
Morning, noon or evening time
  a phone call would lead all the rest.

Ethel Reinhold

Hymn To Heimdall

The White Browed God stands watch at night,
On Bifrost Bridge above great heights.
With Gjallerhorn hung at His side,
He wards Nine Worlds with the greatest pride.

Heimdall is His own proper name;
His sharp senses put ours to shame.
He sees and hears from His watch star,
All events on Earth both near and far.

He is the foe of Jotan-Loki,
Who piled Freya with lots of hokey.
When Loki stole Brisingamen,
Heimdall returned it to Her again.

He once appeared on Midgard wide,
To live amongst us side by side.
He taught us our appointed tasks,
And that is all that we dare to ask.

Some dark day full ages hence,
Chaos will assault Valhalla's fence.
And when then crows the Golden Cock
Heimdall will herald the Ragnarok. Heilsa Heimdall!

John William Matson II

Autumn Legacy

When God directed me to earth
On that assigned day of birth
He destined my life in fashion, and course
And life proceeded without evil force
My parents did guide with love and direction
In their eyes I was a source of perfection
Within some years, I also mirrored these joys
When I was gifted with my own girls and boys
As the autumn of life now is near to me
I wonder what God will allow me to see
Before he calls me to rest
With those he loves the best
I pray that life will still continue to be
A pattern of love, as vast as the sea
I hope my heirs find that above all the rest
They were given much love, that's the key to success

Eleanor Burns

A Tribute To The Moon

Moon, moon, I saw you in all your majestic splendor,
  on that eventful day, when Neil touched you ever so
tenderly upon your face; which will forever be known as
  Tranquility base. No longer will you be known as the
  Green cheese thing, Eagle has landed on fiery wings,
While Mike in Columbia circled you round and round
  Neil and Buzz jumped up and down testing your
ground, ancient dust was all they found.
  While far below men watched in awe
As Houston gave the command "two degree yaw."

  Yes, I watched as all your enveloping mystery was
taken away on that fateful day, when three courageous
Earthmen first came your way, and although your
mystery is gone, your romantic enticement lingers on.
  As Cupid's commander you remain despite
Their landing on your terrain, a host of lovers gaze
  upon your domain, on earth the tides still flow, to and fro,
As majestically through the heavens you go.

George E. Couch

Dreams

A human bond is formed
On the deepest level of creation
Tied together by feelings
Of fondness, love and appreciation
Where even the slightest pangs of desire
Form bubbles fanned by cosmic fire
They rise to the top
And set imaginary ripples and waves in motion
Causing the entire ocean
To sway to the rhythm of raucous commotion
And while two bodies are swept by the sea
They brush against each other
Softly and delightfully
The world comes alive
The senses aware
There's music and laughter in the air
Cradled in the bosom of a warm lovely night
They ride back out with the rising tide
The sunset envelops the vanishing shape
And carries them home to where dreams are made

Heather I. Proffer

The Other Side Of The Sun

The shrinking strong-man sits in his trailer
on the edge of the sofa bed (not folded up for days)
As the hot sun beats down
on the tin roof of the porch.

He thinks of his wife
long since gone with his heart
and cries inside, as he does each day
He thinks of his sons, far away
One bitter for the way he used to be.

One out of touch,
his yellowed letters and faded pictures in the drawer
by the sofa bed
He doesn't wonder anymore
Or try to mend or sweeten.

Light filters through the blinds, showing dust
on her clown statue next to the sofa bed
He looks at his watch and remembers
When the bluebirds came and ate out of his hand
And the sun wasn't so hot
And didn't beat so hard on the tin roof of the porch

Carla Henschen

A Penny

What is this I have found, as I walk outside?
On the front is an Indian, a tribal chief
On the back
two olive branches running up the side, converging on a shield,
Below, arrows tied in a bow to the branches,
In the center is printed one cent
It is a penny, that is what it is, But how can that be?
It looks nothing like a penny, Where is Abraham Lincoln
Where is his memorial?
1909
You are an old penny, that explains it to me
Where have you been? Many places in the past seventy-five years
Chicago, Los Angeles, New York
Maybe even another country, Now you sit here before me
What have you seen? Only history can tell
A great depression, industrial revolution, two world wars
The births of many, also many deaths
All the many hands you have passed through
only to end up in mine.
Where will you go after me? Only time will tell

Eric M. Gillins

Memories Of Robert At Christmas

Your Dad and I, we placed a tree,
  On your grave this day;
Then we stood back so quietly,
  Thinking how life's changed since you passed away.

Our darling Robert, it will never be known,
  Why, from this earth, you had to leave;
You were twenty-three when God called you home,
  Leaving your Dad and I here to grieve.

Rows of tinsel, in the air shone,
  While your wedding picture above your name;
That's carved upon your marble tombstone,
  Reminds us of the man you became.

As a husband and father, you worked so hard,
  And as a provider, you tried to be smart;
Seeing Tyler happy was your greatest reward,
  But soon your marriage had fallen apart.

You were finally putting your past behind,
  When the terrible accident did take place;
Yet, there's one fact which comes to mind,
  We'll always see you through Tyler's sweet face.

Carolyn Rebecca Cauthen

Part of Me

What would have been won't be no more,
Once I enter and depart this door.
There was this chance that I might have seen,
  another little part of me.
Clinging to thoughts of what could have been,
  thinking of how I loved him.
Through the passage I entered, into this room
  which was a center, I had a seat facing the door,
  trying not to think of what would be no more.
Strangely I thought as I looked around, all these
  ladies and not a sound.
They too, their minds a wonder, probably
  thinking of their love blunder.
Oh, part of me that was within, someday
  I too will end.

Hershel W. Martin

Our Love

The petals fall gently, my love,
One by one from the roses.
As they fall, each one
Is a moment of my love for you.
Each rose describes a place where we have loved,
Full of peace, warmth, joy and all of the
Beautiful, common, simple things
No one else can see.
The time has come for the two of us to become one,
The dreams we have will fade
From fantasy into reality,
Our love will forever be strong.

Erin L. Southard

Walk Away

Oh pretty one, don't be so sad
One day your eyes will burn a hole in someone's soul
And you can take the place that's rightfully yours.
The future seems sad... when you're afraid
But inner strength will reap its own reward
Your face will shine like a brilliant sunrise.
Somebody let you down
Somebody's done you wrong
Gather the will to simply walk away from it
You can still walk away.

I want to tell you how brilliant you are
But you'd only shoot down my ideas like you do your own
I can't put inside you what's not already there.
You want a savior, you crave an end point
But you don't see all along... the greatest one is you
You stare your rescue in the face every morning.
Glance in the mirror
Your smile is magic
You leave behind a trail of hope if you just walk away
You can still walk away.

David Jesitus

Life On The Farm

Life with my family, life on the farm
One in the same, we're all part of it's charm.
Not a real big farm, not a whole lot of hogs,
We even have enough room for two black lab dogs.
Plenty of help always lending a hand,
My favorite part is working the land.
And a newborn pig just too cute to mention
All of them always get plenty of attention.
So many stories, too many to tell
The only thing that bothers me, is the smell!
Whether we have grain to be hauled, or hogs to be sold
It's one of the few jobs that's government controlled.
Oh the many families the farmers do feed
But because of the big companies, we're no longer in need.
So many good times, so many years
Believe me, it's easy to shed a few tears.
Life with my family, and all of it's charm
Life as we know it, may not be on the farm.

Jody Johnson

Trapped

Trapped in the flood of broken tears
My heart rides the crest of a golden rainbow.
Unable to free itself, it falls in the pit of loneliness
Can the silent cry be heard?
Or will it go unnoticed by the smiles of yesterday?
Or remain trapped in the unspoken words.
My only freedom "Now" is to ascend on the breath of a butterfly's
  wings and wait
"You"

David Wilkerson

Babes

Worth every moment of your life is
one innocent smile of a child. One cry is
worth one million heartaches. One slight little
grin is worth all the money in the world.
The love of a child young and true is
worth everything to me; when it may
mean nothing to you. The only thing left
in the world not corrupt is the heart of the
babe. Fresh from a mothers womb it knows
nothing but love and care if given the
chance to know this. Now in these times it is
getting so rare for love to exist anywhere.
When a new baby is born love should
lead the way to little ones joys. So often
there's little girls and boys being thrown away
for mothers toys. The untrue in heart should
not conceive the love that is given from a
child. Love everyday that little babe
because love now days is not easy to find
since so many hearts are not true and kind.

Jennifer L. Velez

The Last Waltz

Come dance with me my love, across the empty floor
One last dance, to hold my heart
Through eternity and more
The band has not lingered, to play our last waltz
So I will sing in your ear
Words of my loving and longing and wanting
That never again you will hear
For after this I must leave you, never again to appear
For to have this last dance, with you my love
I have left my debts in arrears
My creditors are all waiting, looking through hells open doors
Knowing that soon, I must return
Then I will be theirs and not yours
So, come to me quickly my love, and share in this final embrace
In an empty ballroom at midnight
With a lover who can't show his face
How I wish I could stay with you my love, but satan demands his price
So I must return to my lonely grave and you must return to your life
Think of me sometimes my darling, for I will be thinking too
Of how any price was worth it ... to share that last waltz with you

Geri Powers Lawson

Untitled

Two people
  one so different from the other
  that understanding wasn't even a barrier.
It just simply wasn't there.

And though their hearts were one
  they shed the tears that people do
  when they know that love just isn't enough.
It simply wasn't enough.

Two people
  as close as love could possibly bring them
  but so far apart
  that pretending to understand
  was the best they could do.

And now they're just two people
  but their hearts are still one.
  - love is now the barrier -
  and pretending not to love
  is the hardest thing to do.

Jody L. Smith

"A Forgiving; Good-Natured Heart"

It is wise to have a forgiving Heart,
One's forgiving Heart might say,
For it is always hate that twists the mind,
And places a Heart in dismay,
Yet for one's Heart,
Who is of forgiving nature,
The pain never seems to ease,
For a forgiving Heart is always willing,
And ever so eager to please.

To go with this Heart,
Is a set of misty eyes,
With also a set of ears,
To hear the words that cut like a knife,
And fill them full of tears,
But for each tear that falls,
There also is a smile,
Because each tear the Good-Natured cries,
Brings him one more mile.

Chris Beathard

Younger Innocence

Walk down a hidden path,
  Only remembered by a time long past.

Where trees gently sway,
  As leaves dance lazily to music only nature can create.

The cool breeze brushes by,
  With haunting whispers that take you back,
  To a younger innocence,
    Running, smiling, laughing,
    Sitting by a lonesome tree,
    Rustling around with a furry childhood friend.

How fun it would be to let yourself go free,
  Like it used to be,
  Just for a little while.

Out in nature, you can't help,
  But to remember special memories of your
  younger innocence.

Angela Wright

Troubled Teen

Went to a party at a rivalry school,
Only to clash with the personality fools,
Indulging into the world of alcohol,
Walking around as if I were 7 ft tall,
As the lights slowly went out that night,
I woke into a mirror with a fright,
Broken nose, swollen eyes bloodied lip
crippled pride,
I watch my blood run thin,
I feel this rage growing within,
Taking another look into my nightmarish life again,
Fighting this paranoid beast within,
This battle that rages on in my head,
The battle of a beast who I wish dead,
I feel I can no longer deal with this insanity,
I want no longer to live this life in vanity.

Hervey J. Miller Jr.

My Child

My Child, My Child
My Poor Little Child
You are so small, so big
First you were a little baby
but you will grow into a big strong man
I will shower you with gifts of the word
and you shall be blessed by the Lord Jesus Christ our Saviour

Christopher Scotte Sawyer-Nieves

Verse And Worse By Anon

"Hark! I will, anon, appear,"
Ophelia, to her beloved Hamlet, said.
The lines, aloud, to us from Shakespeare —
Simplified for Sixth Grade were read and read!

("Ophelia, here's a clue; watch what you do.
Five things observe with care:
Of whom you speak, to whom you
Speak, and how, and when, and where.")

"I will come, anon, to bed," Othello,
Filled with black rage, to Desdemona says.
Sixth graders perceived that Anon, just so,
Was in all of Shakespeare's plays.

(Desdemona, I knew, on harsh words must chew:
"Five things observe with care;
Of whom you speak, to whom you
Speak, and how, and when, and where.")

In truth, Anon wrote not poetry but verse.
Each school grade—it got worse and worse.
Anon., not a poet, was a preacher!
His tone was like that of my teacher!

James W. Byrd

The Chess Game

We faced each other
Opponents
Different
Yet alike.

The first move was made
King-pawn to the Fourth Rank
Sometimes giving, sometimes taking
Each decision weighed heavily
On the outcome of the Game.

It was early apparent I was outmatched;
He had played the Game more times than I.
I tried to out-maneuver him with my Knight,
But, his Queen was all over the Board
Whittling away at my uncertain defenses.

He won.
The Conquest having been made,
The Game was over.
"Bon Jour" Boredom.
He'll soon be looking for another challenge.

Dianne Suhara

Why Do I Dream

I dream of my husband and his loving face.

I dream of the days, when my children will always be safe.

As a housewife, with plenty to do; I dream when I'm scared, lonely or blue.

I dream when the stress of people get me down. When their caring is fake, or their presence brings me down. As I whisper to God, with patience at bay; How much Dear Lord must I take?

Why do I dream, I don't know. Sometimes my mind needs a place to go.
Where there is no killing, or hate, or no race; Just a beautiful field full of God's love and grace.

Delores M. Middleton

Marking Time

Others watch the stars make giant arcs
Or count the convulsions of tortured quartz
(The Inquisitor grins as his counters fly),
In other rooms they're watching cobalt die.

My clock flips numbers at irrational intervals,
Pretending to mark the passage of our night,
But I can catch the whirring bastard,
And stop it if I hold on tight.

I've stopped it cold at three-oh-six—
I thinks it has to win and sits red-glowing,
Gathering its springs and gears for when I doze,
To rush and catch time's flowing.

For nothing.

Your heart's beat is all that marks my time.
I won't sleep and make their clocks come true.
What might I miss or fail again to do
If I should sleep before I wake again with you?

James M. Greenland

Tilting With Windmills

Have you tilted with any windmills lately
Or dreamed impossible dreams
Robert Browning tells us
That man's reach should exceed his grasp else what is Heaven for
How easy to be bogged down by the necessary and mundane
To do what's reasonable and expected
But how exhilarating and sublime
To do the unexpected, the irrational act
A special love, an intense relationship
An unexplained reaction a serendipitous event
To lift us from the ordinary
To challenge us, enlarge our vision
Expand our vistas, impel us to reach out
Even to do something that makes no sense at all
How wonderful it is to know that whatever power created us
Vested in us the capacity and the urge
To imagine windmills and to tilt with them
To dream impossible dreams and even to pursue them

Frank E. Marsh

Walking Through Life

I don't care for plush hotels and their crowded bars
Or driving down the freeway in big expensive cars
I would like a plot of land as green as it could be
And someone who would like the same to walk through life with me

I don't care for motor boats and I don't like yachts
Sailing on the seven seas is never in my thoughts
I would like a little house beneath a big shade tree
And someone who would like the same to walk through life with me

I don't care for parties where you have to wear a tux
Women with their furs and jewels and all their talk and such
I would like a great big dog without a pedigree
And someone who would like the same to walk through life with me

Then one day I met her while riding on the trail
A turned up nose big blue eyes and a little pony tail
We talked about the things of life and we both agree
And now I have that someone who will walk through life with me

We have built a little house with a picket fence
Living in a mansion to us just don't make sense
We have a big old shaggy dog who's happy as can be
He wags his tail and walks through life with my wife and me.

June Frandsen

Agnosticism

Is there a heaven or a hell
Or is this earth the end?
The fear of death makes my heart swell,
Yet religion I cannot defend.
I cannot adhere to any one belief
For the exclusion of all others.
But science cannot explain human grief
And the emotional turmoil between each other.

I wonder if God does exist
And how he can persist
To create such a world with hate,
And evil such a frequent state.
Starvation and death occur more
Than love and peace in a quick tour.
In a glorious search for power,
The grenade destroys the beautiful flower.

And you may ponder this poem or toss it aside,
But my convictions are not alone.
Organized religion has its pride,
But I prefer to wander with no such home.

Ari Greenberg

Is It Possible For One To Be Worse...

Reality our teacher to everyday endeavor.
Or memories etched in your mind forever.
Can either be worse when they are one in the same.
The separation of two leaves someone to blame.
Does today's reality hurt more than yesterdays memory.
Or yesterdays memory hurt to face today's reality.
You and I together as one
Not a care in the world
except to have fun
Today you are my friend
With a yesterday memory
holds a place in my heart never to end
I cry a tear as well we slowly let go
because the memory that's left is all we know.

So I ask you again ...

Can we painlessly compare

The pain of reality becoming a memory.

Or the pain of memory which once was reality.

The memories we hold can only mean
Your survival from reality was never a dream.

Debbi Jean Hermanson Watkins

Two Days (Social Work?)

Stepped out the door before music's end
our beers guzzled down
before death's smell surrounded.
Walked to the edge
where a forest hides
a doe and her fawn, dead in time.
Their story was cut short by a car,
ran off the road
she died for a while
as her tender fawn cuddled and watched.

Will step out the door where asphalt is king
and faces hit hard
   Death Surrounds.
I'll walk to the edge
where a jungle hides
a woman and her child
the needle and the virus.
Their story will be short
they'll die for a while, but the mother will not cuddle
   Death Surrounds.

Frank Magazu Jr.

Methinks Something's Bogus In Buffalo

Methinks something's bogus in Buffalo
Or was it rather in Tuppelo?
Give me your name
And I'll tell you the same
Nothing is quite as it seems.

Methinks something's bogus in Buffalo
What's true and what's false, I don't know
I'd heard that love
Had come down from above
But that only happens in dreams.

Methinks something's bogus in Buffalo
With questions like these where do you go?
I've tried different answers
But they all gave me cancers
And I'm coming apart at the seams.

Methinks something's bogus in buffalo
Or was it rather in Tuppelo?
Give me your name
And I'll tell you the same
Nothing is quite as it seems.

Craig Kubias

"The Pleasure Of Being With You"

Makes my day go as wonderful as any
other day I had to share my thoughts
with you and to allow my feelings to
flow through the darkness when I sit
holding you in my arms, tells me that the
pleasure is all mine.

Your sweet gentle body caressing against my
soft body turns my mind around and around. The
touch of your hands when their touching my body
sends me drifting through wonderland. The softness
of your lips makes my body wiggle.

Dancing to soft music on the radio draws
me closer to you and it makes me feel
comfortable. But in this short length of time
it will be time to say good-bye.
until we meet again the pleasure was
still all mine.

Jennifer Crews

To Bee Or Not To Bee

Oh! Bee you shouldn't have ventured inside.
Our garden is full of flowers outside.
This new exploration is dangerous for you
   and for me.
I know we have roses on our table
But backyard roses are better for you
   and for me.
Don't you see?
Bees gilded wings shield sharp stings
I have been sorely bitten
By love when greatly smitten
Far sharper than your needle
Still, don't tempt me to chase and wheedle
Let me spare your tiny, busy, buzzing life.
Too many humans live in strife -
Freedom is your prerogative,
Little Bee, fly free, and LIVE! LIVE! LIVE

Cathy Babcock

Our Sunflower Sentry

Standing so tall out in the field,
Our sunflower sentry with golden shield.
Standing at the edge of the yard,
Like a brave soldier-our fearless guard.

Through harsh summer storms and weeks of drought,
You're the heartiest by far-there was never a doubt.
As we watch through the window from morning to night,
You stand so erect with shield glowing bright.

As summer day turns to a cold fall night,
You begin to fall-you have lost the fight.
Like a worn out soldier you begin to fall,
You have fought the battle-you hear the call.

As you fall to the ground we take up your heed,
No need to explain as we gather the seed.
And when winter becomes spring by the warm new light,
We'll again plant that seed-what a beautiful sight.

As you take up your post armed with power and might,
Your golden shield will shine again-ever so bright.
We'll reverently watch from our window pane,
As you start the whole process all over again.

Gloria M. Newhard

My Meistersinger

This mockingbird, my nightingale,
Outlined the stillness and
Perfumed the night with his solitary song.
Night upon night this meistersinger
Presented his purloined repertoire
Portraying all the roles in his nocturnal operetta.
Not for audience, applause or cheer
His for all or none to hear.

But came a void of voice;
No final act.
No curtain call.
No "Bravo!"
Just discords of emptiness - end of show.

Searching sounds distant unavailed.
Only echoes of stillness prevailed.
The song was gone.
Memories alone to me belong;
Memories and loneliness.

Dorothy A. Franks

Rocking Chair

Nothing is more soothing or comforting than my rocking chair,
Over the years we've been a pair.
I have many memories of the past we've rocked through,
I have the future to think about too.
At times I've rocked away my whimpering blues,
Whatever it took to get me through.
Beyond my window, I enjoy watching the tree branches blow,
At night I'd float off, while staring at the moons glow.
I like to rock-on quietly in my chair,
Peacefully view the colorful leaves dance about in the air.
I take delight in seeing the very first snow fall,
While safely wrapped inside a warm shawl.
I adore watching the sparrows fly,
Listen to the cars drive by.
Nurse my baby while I sway and sing,
Look for any signs of spring.
Sometimes I rock to forget, sometimes I rock to remember,
From the beginning of October to the end of September.
Yes I do treasure rocking in my favorite chair,
To feel the pleasant flow of love there.

Jillian Reis-Matz

The Sea

Sitting here by the sea
Overcoming a feeling of tranquility
Away from all the problems and fears
The sea devours all of my tears

A sense of freedom overwhelms me
I can dream anything I want to be
To fly like a bird — be captain of the sea
The inspiration sweeps me right off my feet.

The sea is unending, such as my dreams
An unsolved mystery — at least that's what it seems
To have something so great locked deep inside of me...
Only to be pulled back to reality

So I take all my dreams and store them away
Only to return to them some other day...

Caterina Pacella-Donohue

A Timeless Landmark

The lighthouse now aging from storms raging
Paint faded and cracking
Sailboats tacking toward the landmark they knew
While sea gulls around her head flew
Nighttime - while others slept, her light was brightly kept
Waves that turned and tossed, vessels at sea - lost
Wooden ships of days gone by, that would give a desperate cry
Through the raging storm they'd see, a sign of hope, alas home free!
Small twinkling white, they followed her light
To a crew at sea, a welcoming sight
She stood there in the still of night, waves crashing at her feet
A beacon light, she would guide the way - each and every fleet
Her crown is cloaked in puffy clouds, thrill the eyes of passing crowds
Look closely at her today-see parts now crumbled and washed away
This historical piece of yesterday
Crewmen past say they'll adore this timeless landmark evermore
Set against an evening sky, she stands proudly, up so high
While years, like ships, keep passing by.

Jodi L. Warner

"Desde El Cielo Azul." "From Out Of The Blue."

From the heart of a child;
Palabras de Amor del corazon de un Nino!
Love is a heart of a child!

"Mom, right, I take care of you,
   and you take care of me.
We don't need dad!"
   "Yes, my son, You take care of me,
   I take care of you.
   I love you!
   Always remember, my son,
   Mom will always be your Best friend!"

From the heart of a child;
Palabras de amor del corazon de un nino!
Love is a heart of a child!

"From out of the blue,"
"Desde el cielo azul."

Betty Watts

A Promise for Life

I (state your name) take you (state his/her name) to be my partner in life, to love, honor, and cherish you till our dying day. In sickness or in health, and for better or for worse. I promise to love you for all eternity. I only wish that each day we spend together our love for each other grows more and more, and if a day should ever come that you doubt my love for you or your love for me... look deep into your heart and remember all the good times we have shared and are going to share. And if there is still some doubt in your mind look deep into my eyes and see the love that I feel for you. My love for you is the purest and truest love to ever occur on this earth. So when you ask me if I'll take your hand in life Yes I Will. It would be the greatest honor to sit by your side and to take your name. I will do my best to live up to your expectations for you are my first true love. A love like ours only comes along once in a million years. I love you with all My Heart and Soul!

Bonnie Louise Smith

Two Souls Touch

Two souls were passing in midair
Pausing a few seconds to commune,
The grandfather on his way to heaven,
The grandson on his way to be born.

The death of one, and the birth of the other,
What a strange turn of fate,
That one life should end, the other begin
At the same time, on the same date.

One soul was weary and ready for home
Though triumphant over pain and strife,
The other was eager and ready to go
To start on his brand new life.

The angels who were taking the one soul home,
And the angels cheering the young one forth,
Stopped a moment to smile when the two souls met
Somewhere between heaven and earth.

And in those brief shining moments,
When the two souls touched in midair,
A lifetime of love and companionship,
An eternity was theirs to share.

Carol K. Dunnagan

Leaves of November

How you glide over the matted, frost-bitten grass
Performing the last dance
A ritual before death
An unseen choreographer guiding your every movement
The wind, your lover, picking you up
Tossing you around in the air
Whirling you about as if on some great dance floor

Sometimes you dance in groups
Thousands of you in constant motion
Moving to your lover's music in no particular direction
Other times you dance alone, gliding through the air
Touching down here and there
Waiting, hoping for your lover's touch

The costumes are beautiful shades of gold and red
Autumn's finest
With only an occasional brown
The shade of impending death

Soon you will be lifeless
Forgotten by your lover
A thing of the past, to dance no more

Barbara M. Thomas

"The Good Old Days"

We use to have all day singing and dinner on the ground.
People would come from miles around.
They would come from near; they would come from far.
That was before they had a car!
They would hitch the mule to the wagon
and sometimes the ox to the cart.
They didn't want to be late; So, they would get an early start.

The preacher would always pray;
And thank the Lord for another beautiful Sabbath day.
They would sing the good old songs of yester year;
the good old songs we old folks hold so dear.
They would sing old"Amazing Grace", how sweet the sound!
Load plant my feet on higher ground!
They would sing and sing until their throat got sore;
then eat dinner and sing some more.

They would spread the tablecloth out on the ground;
Seemed there was always some ants around!
They would have cornbread, turnip greens,
home-made biscuits, and butter beans.
They would have good fried chicken, country hams,
creamed potatoes, and candied yams!
They would have pickles and pies and cakes galore and eat
and eat until they could eat no more!

They would go back into the church and sing again and thank
the Lord that it didn't rain.
Those were the good old days we did adore.
We wish we had them one time more!

Annie Durden

An Unachievable Dream

The starry-eyed child
Picks up the dusty, but still alive, balloon
And when he gazes through it
For behind the dusty, but yet still shiny metallic color,
He sees a world;
A world where all of his worries and fears were gone
A world without poverty, drugs, crime, or pollution
But all of a sudden, the balloon popped.
He stops and looks around him
and his dream is crushed.
He finds himself standing alone, hungry, and cold
In the deadly street under the barely dim light
From the unconfessing lamp post.
He sees the real world.
He is only one of the many,
One of the many that get lost in the same dream
Everyday. These children can only hope and pray
That their dream would might someday become
A reality instead of just an unachievable dream
And a hazy vision in a balloon.

Christy Coonan

Time Passage

Daylight is fading, night is nigh
Pinpoints of light across the sky
Angels sleep and angels wait
For light to stream through heavens gate.

Day has faded, time has stopped
A dark black veil on the earth has dropped
The sky has lost its sheen of blue
Starlight gleams bright and true.

Day is done, night winds are flowing
Stars in the heavens are brightly glowing
Night time is fading daylight is nigh
The hours pass with barely a sigh.

Alice Hill

Bobby

I just love my tabby cat Bobby
Playing with him is more fun than any hobby

I love to squeeze his soft, round tummy
And watch him eat his food so yummy

He tries to sample my food with his paw
while those whiskers jiggle from his jaw

He chases his sister, Coco, around the house
as if he were pursuing a little mouse

Go... Bobby... Go
Seize Coco

Grab her by the neck and pull her down
then get up and get ready for the next round

And when he hears me coming through the door
Bobby jumps from the window to the floor

What I like most is his soft, fluffy fur
And the way he curls up to me and purrs

Although he's just a little cutie
if he's bad, I'll spank his bootie

But Bobby's such a sweet, lovable cat
So I rarely have to do that

Barbara Tyson

"Cry For Life"

Mom?
Please don't throw away my chance at life
You were so fortunate to have,
The chance to feel my baby's breath when I suckle at your breast
Or rock me gently while I sleep, feeling safe upon your keep.
Mom?
Would you not like to see me grow
To toddle toward your arms outstretched
with heart so full of love, and loving trust
To hear my cries of joy, when home you come with gift in hand, a toy.
Mom?
Give me the chance you had, to grow, to run,
to explore the wonders of "His" world.
The right to pain, and sorrow, to all the joys
brought on by all tomorrows.
Oh!
If scream I could, but doubt that you would hear me
Your mind's made up, you think a burden of me
You'll get along as free as ever, and a chance at life?
Never.

Elvera C. Flores

The Wrapped Gift

A day with you is a wrapped gift
Presented with bold eyes smiling.
Gently I take it from your extended hand,
To hold the thought of it a moment
Before I pull away the soft binding of morning.
Then we two fold away each hour,
And with excited surprise
We are in wonder at what we two have found.
When the full gifts of all the hours
Have been laid out before us
We are surprised to find it is so soon evening.
Then it is time to touch each gift,
And to recount it for our treasure house,
Knowing that tomorrow there will be
The wrapped gift of a new day ready for us.

Carroll Thompson

Summers Edge-Winter Nights!

The waning days of summer
Plus the balmy winter nights.
Lead to the thoughts of life sublime.
And to the thoughts of a happy time!

The last warm days of balmy seas
Followed by the coolest of an evening breeze.
Waves rolling in toward Pacific shores.
Warning all lovers "Hold close all he adores!"

Winter night-stay close to the fire inside
Like wild little beasties, searching for and wide,
Searching for their lair, sometimes for food
Longing for warm days of summer when all was well and good!

Summers edge comes all too soon.
"God outside for a walk-gazes at the moon."
Winter nights popcorn and shrimp-eaten inside!
Warm Cider to drink reminders of things by which we must all abide!

Summers edge likened unto winter nights.
Ebb into the thoughts of spring and blights!
Summer edge, likened unto summers heat.
Winter nights-will two lovers never again meet?

Constance C. Keith

The Climb

To revere the soul of a
powerful deed

Sweat poured out from each hole in my skin
and the burning sun singed my skin
I spoke to the mountain, he answered in silence.

My breath was ragged and hard,
I couldn't find strength from my womb
From my indian spirit
my maker
I felt raw
I trembled, I was fragile
I am fragile

I reached for the jagged edge
of that piece of rock
man rock, mean rock that punished me for
daring to conquer, and touch it, to place my woman's body on
its skin.

I was crying and laughing
and when I reached the top
I discovered that I wanted to live.

Elizabeth Gonzalez

A Step from Eternity

A lonely soul settles and sulks on one empty porch,
propped back and dreaming endlessly of a Juliet.
His fate seemed sealed and the light ahead looked nebulous until...
electrified by jolts of life he left his past promising
a future, searching for his partner in passion.
and then....
Unknown to the other their souls clasped as one, like
the moon to the sun — an eternal connection.
This 'ol boy turned gentle and pampered this perfect prize,
only to drop tears at the sound of goodbyes.
He promised his soul to clench this new love and fell
to his knees to gain guidance from above.
However, as a shadow in the night walks unseen,
this mourning man realized retaining his Dulcinea was dubious.
Once again he rests and wonders if dreams can come true...

Brett Bieske

Sanity's Gone Where?

Oh Sanity, you babbling bubble;
Protector from the raving rubble;
Portrayer of a wistful balance;
Defender of the "straight-laced valance!

I'm told you're here, somewhere between
This earthly plane, and heaven's scene;
I've search both in and outside too,
Without success of finding you!

Yet there are those, like Freud and Jung,
Who promised that, I might find some
Of sanity, though not too much,
Somewhere within my eager touch!

But alas, my search is lost
Within a maze of daffy cost;
And as I feared, I search in vain,
For Sanity has gone....insane!

Derryl Rabb Mullican

Little Maestro

Grubby little fingers gently grasp a bow
Pudgy little fingers springing to and fro
Chinned atop the purfling, chubby cherub rests
Primed for patient plunking—pizzicato tests
Vamping with vibrato, valor vacillating
Stamping with staccato, sweetly scintillating
Billowy clouds of rosin o'er the sunbeams rise
Pillowy little pixie, weary, softly sighs
His fingers cramped, the notes seem sour
Been plunking now for most an hour
Laying aside his instrument, he quickly steals a glance
Happy now, his friends arrive, eager to play and prance
Sincerely he's performed his chore, of that he can be proud
Solemn face now breaks with smile, hearing praise, sung aloud
A critic's reproach he'll never know
Discordant tones blend sweet and low
For my heart is tuned to my little maestro.

Alice M. Filbin

Over Vivid Mounds Of Treetops

Over vivid mounds of treetops creep silent ghosts, the clouds
Puffy white blotches contrast expansive blue sky...broad, foaming sea
Globs of mashed potatoes, squirts of shaving cream, small wisps of
clouds fade into pastel sky
Into clouds planes disappear
Into clouds a hot sun hides
From angry gray clouds the rain pours down
From winter day clouds the snow falls
From imagination, clouds form scenes, when children look up and stare
into the distance
In the early evening, clouds change colors, making a puffy rainbow
from the setting sun
Still, they never cease, always spreading out and changing shape in
the air, moving somewhere, getting nowhere
Clouds, the chalky brush strokes on the light blue easel of sky, over
vivid mounds of treetops, they will always fascinate me

Heather Henckler

The Storm

The winter storm drives by and makes the
ocean fume and foam.
The night storm rages and leaves the toadstools
in various stages.
The rainstorm walks by; washes windows and
peoples' faces.
The raindrops patter 'cross the village,
and are gone.

Glen Bruce

The Understanding of a Friendship

The understanding of a friendship is somewhat like a jigsaw
puzzle. Putting the pieces together, and having to want it to
stay in place and not ever want to lose a piece. To have to hold
and cherish the special moments that is shared between two people
can longly be endeavored as a mystical and magical bond that one
longs to hold so close and dearly. The joy, laughter and tears
that has been expressed so beautifully, has yearned to touch so
deeply in one's heart, and reach out to the call of a true friend.
The rivalries, the disappointments, construes to be an awakening
of one's mind on the dark side, a self destruction that one hopes
to be an illusion and not degenerate one's soul and prevails
one's heart.
A friend in need is a friend indeed, to devour all faults and
relinquish all guilt, to call out to a friend to relieve pain
and anguish, is a friend indeed.

Elizabeth Lee

Faun

He stands in shallow water listening,
Quite still, head poised, hands raised to mouth
Cupping... what does he cup so carefully,
The careless one? What does he seek to hear
In winds that rustle through the restless reeds?
Why does he wait so long and now at last
Begin ... begin such melody
As never faun or nymph or river knew,
High, clear and sweet and wistful, echoing
Some cry of pain so close to love itself
That arms reach out to him forgetful of
Goat's feet and budding horns and hairy flanks
And bruising lust? For pity of clear eyes
Puzzled and sad, not knowing how to weep,
And voice soft-calling to the echoes "Nymph?
Where are you, Nymph? Why do you hide from me?"
The arms reach out, but they are broken grass,
Merely reeds now, on which the satyr plays,
And all their touch is one high threnody,
And soon he throws them down and moves away.

Joan Quarm

Don't Weep For Me

Don't weep for me,
Rather, I should weep for you,
Don't weep for me,
It's something wonderful I'm going through,
For I see my Father, master of time and space,
I'm looking at Him face to face,
He's more majestic than an earthly king,
More beautiful than anything.
Where I am I feel no earthly pain,
Now I'm in His eternal domain.
So don't weep for me,
I love it here,
I'll love it even more, when you one day appear.
Please, don't weep for me,
He and I will weep for thee.

Aaron Ludwig

Love Vs. Hate

Laugh with happiness over it.
Often it comes unexpectedly.
Victory comes to those who open their hearts to it.
Equality enhances it.
   vs.
Hope that it happens seldom.
After the thought you think it over.
True hatred is seldom come by.
Everyone tries to dispel it.

Brian Bergner

Franklin Elementary Is A Great School!!!!!

Friends and families pulling together.
Reaching out and touching someone.
Able to stand together through thick and thin.
Notice a smiling face in the hall.
Kind words that have been said.
Leadership of a fine school.
Ideas in children's heads.
Neighborly place to be.

Excellence in the staff.
Learning different things.
Educating the minds of children.
Memories of the past.
Esteem and praise.
Nice principal.
Teachers that care.
Achievement for doing and the opportunity to do more.
Respect of teachers and kids.
Young hearts dreaming.

Judy Jackson

A Vision

I hold this feeling, in the palm of my hand
reaching out to touch the sky
above this land.

I have a vision
longing to be held without
any fears.

Then on moonlight nights when stars fall
an angel shall arise from the sky

Are you here for me - I ask
am I to meet this beauty
from afar
Are you my angel
my life above the clouds
so bright
so here
so now.

Barbara Sanders

Tell Me Why

I looked into her sad, weeping eye,
Recalled the ancient smile of days gone by
And the missing breast which cancer stole;
No hospital bed can be passion's goal.

The room is stark and surgical clean,
Tubes and drains are clearly seen;
The patient like a bride in white
Cannot even stumble toward the light.

Loved ones come to stare and sigh,
Share a glimpse, a prayer, and ask why;
This deadly germ that weaves a path
Multiplies in blood-soaked math.

O' God above who knows no strife;
Did you really need my lovely wife?

Joseph Goldberg

Snowland

Snowland is a place where it always snows.
Snowland is a place where the wind flows.
Snowland is a place where the sky is high.
Snowland is a place where the birds fly.
Snowland is a place where the lake is clean.
Snowland is a place where the birds sing.
Snowland is a place where the clouds are white.
Snowland is a place where people don't fight.

James M. Wroblewski II

Through The Canyon

The sun kisses the earth, and she responds to create the dawn.
Red walls of the canyon beckon me, calling my name ever so softly
    across the great divide.
I descend happily toward the center of the mother.
The rustle of scree and shuffle of feet are my mesmerizing echoes of
    the early morning.
The constant flow of water and wind; the changing, but ever
consistent
    heart of the world.
Temples of rock, cathedrals of rock, the greatest church; the birds
    sing your daily praises! On we march over the river,
she beats to the music of a thousand souls.
Looking down, she courses under our feet. Colors of the rainbow
    light up each crest that dances around the boulders and lightly
brushes the sand. Into the box, slowly squeezed down to size,
praying in my head for relief from the sun.
Hear the waterfall? Is it a mirage? Drawing its prey closer to the
    cooling water that is life.
Put each foot down softer now; have respect for the mother.
She has given us so much.
Gaze up the side and sense how insignificant one life can feel; but
    we are all part of the chain, and even one link gone is a sadness.
Protected by the arms of the mother, we continue to the top.
Earth stretches as we scratch her backbone. She yawns, welcoming the
    rising moon and planets. She cloaks herself in stars, lit at the
    edge by the setting sun.
The moon rules now, amid dark and secrecy, as we sleep to the
moans of
    the universe.

Barbara Hugendubler

Home

Home is where you can take off you mask and shoes,
Relax and be yourself.
It is a place where you speak freely to your family.
Not having to weigh your words.
Although some times we hurt those we love most.
Home is where you forget the day.
Collecting your thoughts and solving your own problems.
One's home is characteristic of the folks
that make this place called home.
Such as Books, pictures, plants, pets, hobbies.
Home is your corner of the world.
Where you climb into bed at night, where peace and love entwine.
You awake in the morning, regenerated to begin
a new day in this old world again.

Grace Porter

"Remember"

When all goes wrong and you've lost your song,
remember I'm your friend.
When the sun doesn't shine, and hurt
is all you can find, remember I'm your friend.
When there's no one to care,
and your load is to hard to bear,
remember I'm your friend.
Remember I'm your friend, not only
when your unhappy and down,
but also when hopes are high.
and rainbows fill your sky.
This is all I ask, no great task,
Just remember, ... I'm your Friend.

Dawna Flatt

A Package Of Memories

A package of memories I'm sending to you.
Revealing the days that I spent here with you.
We laughed, and we cried, we loved and we died!
Those wonderful memories with you by my side.

A package of memories tied up with a string
telling how love was that wonderful spring.
No more sweet words you often would say
No more sweet glances you sent forth my way.

A package of memories to keep by your side
Will always reveal what I did, how I tried!
To love you, to care for you, day after day,
before I was taken from you, that sad day!

I'm home safely now, in the arms of my Lord,
You, too will be here, God's final reward.
A package of memories I left here with thee
When softly I whispered "Come home dear with me!"

Grace Carlin Mitchell

Untitled

'Twas the day after Christmas, oh what a mess
Ribbons, and papers, and boxes, and bows -
It's the joy of Christmas, as everyone knows!
Soon everyone is gone - and I am alone
The house is quiet - this is Home Sweet Home!
We've had food and candies, salads and "goodies"
Music and songs - laughter and tears
Beautiful memories - that will last through the years.
Children, grandchildren, great-grandchildren,
so many I can't count them all
But today, my concern is - will they remember
Jesus = born on Christmas Day - is Lord over all!
Will the gifts they've received remind them, of His love from
above?
Will we daily remember - our blessings and His love?
Lord Jesus - help us all remember
Help our little ones find their way
Through this sinful world each day
And may the blessings of peace and happiness
Fill our hearts with love - today and always.

Hilda Beltz

The Key

Make a promise to forever keep,
Riches and rewards are yours to see.
Plant a seed and watch it grow,
Then you may reap what you sew.

Also beware of what you seek,
Bare no malice to the weak.
Be pure in heart, mind and soul:
And the keys to life you will surely hold.

Like sands through the hour glass,
The present soon becomes the past.
Time will not stand still,
It never has and never will.

But a foolish man just bides his time,
Forever waits and falls behind.
While others pass him by,
A foolish man he'll surely die.

David Tumbleson

Carmine O'Keeffe

The dancers from their pagan catacombs
Rise, celebrating immemorial life;
Gregorian reveries reverberate
As onto lawns and terraces they spring.
And laughing, they transcend the centuries.
And I am standing underneath a hill
In crimson country; harlequins and light
Mingle with golden raindrops.
Someone peers among the images and welling song -
Tiwa and Latin, old cacophonies -
Time is all one with fleeting, other time,
When halcyon hope stood on its own plateau
And bayed the waxing moon.

Through myriad holidays the throbbing song
Crescendos, echoing the yellow light
And wild vermilion strata of the cliffs.

The tumult whispers into memory.
Carmina meets in shadowed corridors
The dancers returning. Tonight they are burning
Forgotten desires in the Indian fires.

Charlotte Schofield

Night Happenings

A fantastic sight
rises from nothing in the land of Nod.

The sky dances with a lake,
Up combines with down.

To make everything obtainable
to even the plebeian,

It is sight from within.
While drifting in the clouds,
things from future or past may speak.
If you listen, the stars will show the way,
or blind the beholder.

In the night hours, ideas are moving,
forming, creating new life.

The day is concluded, black falls,
the curtain down.

My mind seems confused, but once inside
feels free from even thought.

In the sky we walk with silence,
soaring with thought.
I found my ship.

Gregory Haley

My Child

You now are small - we cuddle and play
You make me laugh each and every day
Though you may not know the extent of my love
You're my little princess, my beautiful Dove

The fears I have - you are oh so small
With every little step and every big fall
I'll be there for you - like a hand in a glove
You're my little princess, my beautiful Dove

Stay as sweet as you are - so innocent, so true
And remember your mommy will always love you
You are my life - You are my love
You're my little princess, my beautiful Dove

Kathleen Farrell

No. 5 Subway - New York City

Steelwire snake, glided elides
rollercoaster ride on electric dreams,
over unfurling life's endless streamer.

Fertile soil penetrate clanging girders,
cold metal, blue flame, spark frantic frenzy.
Dark tunnel vision
opens out - houses schools trees were once.

Walls cave in. Shriek close.
You can almost knock a pane, break tile,
touch a face.

Pace quickens, memories blur,
thoughts dart about
like bats in the dark.
Rhythmic thrusts of metal through
columns of oil
will st - sto -stop.
Stop.

And you get off
looking for friends.

Aarti Chandawarkar

Memories

A young boy running across the street
Rushing through the door expecting a treat
Tossing his jacket down on the floor
Eating his cookies and asking for more
Then rushing outside to climb up the trees
Now all of those things are just memories.

After a hard day of school and an evening of play
He creeps in the house at the end of day
Dirt on his face and his clothes in amiss
He gives me a flower and sometimes a kiss
Then lays on the floor to watch some TV
Now all of those things are just memories.

Without warning he grew up and moved away
For now as a man he must live life his way
Filled with pride I held back the tears
As he drove away I remembered those years
Of that dirty faced little boy always in trees
Knowing I will always cherish those precious memories.

Betty J. Hugley

Aria

Sad is a little one,
sad is her soul;
tears of prayer
fall in volumes of gold.
Sleepy little child
upon her pillow weeps,
forgiving nightmares and
dreaming of prettier dreams.
Lonely little flowers
bow upon the bare of your feet,
lying where the grass
and sky begin to meet.
"SHHH"
I can almost see an Angel sing,
and I hear her flying by with dancing clouds of wings.
My child of love,
if ever you shall doubt,
whisper to the Angel above,
keep my tears sacred,
and for Faith, hold my love.

Andrea F. Newburn

They Need You On Earth

Religion is: "The opium of the people,"
said Karl Max. Could he have been right?
There is no more powerful drug in the world!
Wars are fought, people loose their legs,
their arms, their sight.
Cities are bombed, countries are devastated.
Children cry for their moms and their dads...
Taken away from their home lands
by some humanitarian organization
and like young trees they are transplanted
to foreign soil...

Some may have been lucky!
By giving their lives for an ideal
which was never understood,
they encounter death on the way...
They will suffer no more!
And when they will meet
the Almighty God face to face, they will ask:

What are You doing in Heaven
when they need You on Earth?!

Jose M. Raposo

A Kiowa Conversation

The old one, the young one
  Sat side by side.

With innocent eyes
  Wide upon the world,
  The young one asked,
  "Grandmother,"
  What would you be
  If you weren't you?
  A pony?"

"No, my little one, the rider would be too heavy."
  "A butterfly?"

"No, someone would throw a net over me."
  "A bird?"

The old one paused,
Then answered slowly.
  "No, my little one,
  His voice may be beautiful,
  But in all his life
  He has only one song
  To sing."

Doris M. Compton

Untitled

Since the day on the cross, when he died to
save the lost sinful folks have turned
him down by the score.
First because they don't know that
Jesus washed them white as snow,
and prepares for them a place forever more.
Isn't he wonderful, Isn't Jesus my Lord
wonderful?
For he died on the tree for you and me.
That my Savior he might be for you
and for me.
Isn't Jesus my Lord wonderful?

Hazel Hauser

The Honeybee

Heard ya yelpin; d'ya get stung by a bee?
Saw ya jumpin up and away from that tree!
Whatever ya got, ya better throw down,
Cause the bee's gonna chase you all 'round
'til he gets his sugar to make honey in his tree.

Ya still yelpin; d'ya get stung by a bee?
Too late jumpin up and away from that tree!
You the main attraction; he'll leave you cryin,
Leave you with his stinger; he'll die trying
to get all your sugar to make honey in his tree.

Ya still yelpin cause ya got stung by a bee?
Too late jumpin and runnin from that tree!
Shun't give off nectar lessen
ya don't mind suffrin;
Blackberry's sweet and not just for nuthin;
he's gotta have sugar to make honey in his tree.

Delores Elizabeth Harrington

Forever Then

The magic in her touch
Says she loves me so much

I can see it in her eye's
That her love will never die

Her heart is open her love goes so deep
My heart is lost it can't be reached

My love will never sore
For thoughts of love before

I wish I could open and let her come to me
But I hate this world for what it had done to me

She needs to be loved like the love that she gives
My love will never be enough for as long as I live

She needs someone special like her
Who can give her the love she deserves

I must tell her goodbye she will survive
Then go to sleep and never rise

Gerald McWilliams

Don Juan In Drag

Say what you will, you Fool on the hill,
Scratching your head in doubt.
Whatever the word, whatever you heard
"Uncertain" is nothing to flout.

Agreeing with bees, hobnobbing with fleas,
Hopping from one to the next.
You think you're so smart, where is your heart?
It's not the muscle you flex!

Leaving your name, playing your game,
Thinking this time you'll score.
Subtracting the old; adding the bold,
To you, one plus one equals four.

Your logic is cool, leaves room for no rules
To bind or hold you down.
Keep using your tool, you silly old Fool,
There's not enough slaves to go round.

Connie Bennett Davidson

The Boldest Beam

All life suction from all existence, lights turn from green to red,
Seasons may change but never evolve, faces scream by at speed of light
Never to stop to say hello, all victims of a cruel game with no end,
No way of escape, no way of surrender, reality no more consumes,
The clay mass society portrays,
Sculptors mold the world into what is known,
Like the sniper on the tower, I know now what he feels,
The blade cuts, but only the wound bleeds,
Cold steel laughing at your innocence,
Making the past hurt more, throws salt into the wound,
All that we touch, taste, or feels turns away in anguish and disgust,
Even the bravest mortal cringes and hides in the dark,
Turning out the light, helplessly run into the night,
Blood cold with fright, no more second sight,
Born into this world only to be betrayal,
He who spits in the well and damns them to hell,
They can kill the physical from but,
the written will always haunt them

John Bowman

Velvet Solitude

I wore my solitude like a velvet cape, rich and dark in color,
    seductively soft and comforting.
Folds of darkness and softness swirled around me, insulated me,
    protected me.
Sleeves covered my fingertips; the hood shadowed the features of
    my face.
My shoulders ached from the weight; the soft folds around my neck
    tightened ever so slowly, so softly.
My back bent and was unable to straighten; my steps slowed.
As the years passed, the soft velvet began to show wear.
A hard shininess appeared in the lines of its many folds.
The velvet grew brittle; here and there cracks formed, and light
    began to penetrate its heavy folds.
And with the light came a soft breeze, drifting in between the
    cracks.
It began to lift the cloak away from my body giving me strength;
    I was able to stand straighter, to flex my arms and shoulders.
The cloak split and gave way and fell into a hard, brittle heap
    at my feet.
The soft breeze gently moved me, nudged me back into life.

Jamie Cypher

The Rose

It grew in me like a flower, growing from a
seed and stemming through my every thought.
It grew stronger with the shower, quenched by
my tears with a sweetness unlike that which
could ever be bought.

The petals were light but would always keep
their shape even after the greatest of winds.
But the monotony of fights soon weighed heavy
and caused the delicate stem to bend.

It seemed I was slowly dying but wherever
the warmth of light I would lean.
My tears were slowly drying and my thirst
caused the leaves to eventually lose their green.

Love grew in me like a rose with a beauty,
brightness and its color of red.
Love grew in me like a flower but its life
quickly faded until soon it was dead.

Jennifer M. Larson

Untitled

Send me out in a bottle,
send me out to the sea.
I will live on the ocean,
the ocean will live under me.
During the days I will live under
rays of the midday open sun.
During the night there is no light
while storms are brewing a gag.
I'm not in the mood to eat sea food
day after day, today its quite dumb
I'm having no fun, aboard my bottle at sea.
I wish I had time to be a mime.
I would climb a ladder that led to nowhere,
I would surf a board that did not look hard.
I would fall in the water then get in my bottle.
I'm dying out here send a boat to help me.
If I drown, send me down, to the ocean floor,
where I will be safe forever more.

George F. Huber

Conquest

Glorifying war breeds repetition
Senseless acts, not once learned;
Marching on through fields of desperation
Insanity turned sane.

Confusion reigns, here now
Dividing things like game pieces;
Still walking the same path
Exploding at the end.

People keep going, commanded to the front
Leaving all their love behind;
One idea condemns another
All fruits are not universal.

To and fro frustrations are hurled
Cyclical change cannot be found;
Systems ingrained, still rule
Plenty of hate to go round.

Silence draws near for many in the wake
Rulers claim triumph while others fall
Nothing is won, save face
Madness begins again.

James Matthew Boyle

Grandma's Babies

So little are, my newest loves,
    sent to me, from God above.
This grandma thanks the Lord each day,
    for sending these babies her way.

They entered this world on the same day,
    and for their safe birth, I surely did pray.
God answered my prayers, and as they grow,
    so different, yet so alike;
    Alike, because they are mine,
        And I love them so.

Grandpa's proud as he can be,
    for he loves them too, just like me.
I love their laughter,
    their "cooing sounds" like little doves,
So little are, my newest loves.

Delores M. Polonus

Rendered Soul

Thinking of you I see
Shadows dancing across vaulted ceilings,
Skies that grieve over lost luminescence.
What, if anything,
lies at the bowels of the deepest oceanic trench?
Will I be taught the ever eluding myth of contentment?
So many mistakes, such bitter disillusionment,
What is the nature of this Beast that will not be denied?
Hold up my Pisa Tower,
ward off this fiery void with a blanket of emanating love.
As two I am whole again,
and the sounds of my laughter are finally audible to me.
Come fly with me.
Would you like to soar above the trees,
to examine the universe through the eyes of wise men?
And if we must part let me be numbed to the grip of my Enemy
he who would leave me a lone wanderer.
Forever just a lone wolf circling the lives of the blissful.

Brian Elliott

Her Love Resurrected from the Tomb

A lady known to me once erect as a peacock and, full of vigor.
She calmed the troubled waters as her love gleamed across its shores.

Silver-hair lady with slow stepping feet, is now an aged woman and,
    an antique stone.

The hard blows of life have bent her over like the camel's back.
Yet, no hurricanes or tornadoes could keep her from the old
    churchyard.

Creation remembers her gleaming love that crossed its seashore in
    her youthful days.

Lady of love is now purging herself in the ocean waters.
She hears the earthly clock ticking nonstop and the heart beating
    nonstop.

She, stands by the Pine Tree and grasps for the freshness of the air.
The last breaths exhaled and inhaled as her soul took flight to
    paradise.

Mt. Olive holds only her body waiting to become ashes to ashes and
    dust to dust.
The tomb lost the fragrance of her love...it resurrected in
    the hearts of love.

Gayle Bellizan-Johnson

"Our Mom Is Eighty Years Old This Year"

Mom stands real tall today.
She did what was right along the way.
From raising six children with love and care.
To making a home for all to share.

And that's not all I have to say.
'Cause Mom is our sunshine ray.
Beautiful flowers planted so plentiful for all to see.
Classical music played softly as a gentle breeze through a tree.

A big heart for charities, grandchildren and family.
Weekly visits to church and prayers privately.
Mom loves to travel from place to place throughout the year.
And learn all she can from what she can see and what she can hear.

Her home is her castle and open to all.
With treasures, pictures and shelves on each wall.
Mom loves all her children and their families always.
Their birthdays are remembered and Christmas days.
Yes, the Lord Almighty watches over Mom every day.
As she prays for her family in a very special way.

David E. Brown

Vannessa

A pretty girl at the age of ten,
She died one day while asleep in her bed.
   She was pale white and with no main cause,
Her family was confused, lonely and awed.

   The doctors say she died from AIDS,
Her parents now know the price that been paid.
   Her best friend's name was Casey Lee Devons,
She was sure Vannessa went straight to Heaven.

   Her eyes were as crystal as creamy, white pearls,
Her favorite song was the "Duke of Earl".
   She was sweet, sensitive, a great friend to all,
Vannessa was kind when she died this cold fall.

   Her parents feel guilty that they were not by her side,
Her sister was very upset and just cried.
   Her brother was younger and didn't know what was going on,
He just knew that his beloved Vannessa was gone.

   Vannessa was a great role model for all,
Strong and kind is what made her call.
   She was loved by everyone and was one of a kind,
No one knew why Vannessa had died.

   Jessica Adams

A Good Christian Man

She drives the kids to school in a shinny cadillac
She drops them at the door but she doesn't look back
She rabbits back to home just to spend some time alone
Thinking 'bout her good Christian man

He tells them every time just to keep it in their minds
He's the one that puts the food on every plate
He never says goodnight when he's turning out the lights
He just tells them he's a good Christian man

Everything that's going 'round is just about to get him down
He's made his mind to set the record straight
He's finally satisfied he's got to keep the word alive
He says that he's a good Christian man

He puts a twenty-two in the head of Suzy Q
Because she doesn't want to be a mom
He doesn't hesitate doesn't care that she was raped
He tells us he's a good Christian man

   Eddie Slusser

My Angel Works Overtime

My angel works overtime for you see,
she had the misfortune of getting stuck with me!
The poor thing's wings are all tattered and torn,
and I'll bet she regrets the day I was born.

"Don't rush, be good, look out from behind!"
Was that her voice? Oh well, never mind.
I'm off having fun, making sin without thought,
of the love of another whose blood my life bought.

But lately I'm beginning to see
that this fast life has caught up with me.
Things that were important don't matter anymore,
and I understand what my life is really for.

So my pace of life is finally slowing
and for the first time I feel like I'm growing,
for a better life for which one has sought,
of the love of another whose blood my life bought.

So the next time you are rushing around,
slow down, take time, put your feet on the ground.
And if is life crazy and you're feeling blue,
just remember- your angel, may be working overtime too!

   Bethine Daehler

What An Odd Child

"What an odd child," people called out.
She is muttering in some foreign language—
   always isolated.
She comes to one school for two years,
   And she leaves.
Is she ever going to adapt?
She seems to bright;
   yet, she cannot count.
"Leave her alone," her parents shout.
There she stands but she is not there.

Who would today believe that I am no longer the
   quiet little child who could not count?
When old friends come to see me, they ask my
   parents for the pale Belgian girl.
"Oh, she is the one with rosy cheeks in the middle
   of the crowd," my mother answers.

   Hilde Heremans

The Other Half

The space between the lines,
she is my expression when other muscles, other eyes move my face.
She is who I am when "I am not myself today"
Things look new, disconcert me. As I open my eyes, waking,
her face comes to me, blurring my own.

Once we floated beside each other, hairless, swirling unnamed.
Tiniest of fisharms, faceless mer-sisters entwined.
In a lake of lifelines and muffled love, each a half-cell
kissed by potent sperm we prepared to emerge.
Dark heart drums urged us out.

First in line, I accepted the wave and climbed on, riding back and
   forth,
pushed into flesh, fluorescent sounds and shades of green.
At the last moment, she must have heard my cry and
understanding more than I, declined the invitation.

Now named and featured, I reach out, am touched by real things.
The mist comes through my window at dawn.
I hear the echo of her voice before I wake.
A blur of my face is her face.

I enter the day. She remains in the dispersing mist.

   Janice Blacksten Cooper

Storm Of A Summer Night

Night dimmed the moon, and drew her somber shades of black, instead.
She made no sound, but waited — tense, afraid.
And, far behind the restless clouds, the host of stars had fled,
For storm was grimly threatening to invade.

First, came a warning rumble from across the distant hills.
A gust of rising wind flung stinging sand.
And sweeping through the treetops, it ruffed the robin's quills,
And woke the slumbering creatures of the land.

A fiery, jagged finger streaked across the western sky.
Rude thunder answered with a startling crash.
Across the sullen rainclouds, the wind clouds twisted by,
And churned in darkness, save for lightning's flash.

Now thirsty earth was waiting to cool her parching tongue,
And soon, in welcome torrents, came the rain.
Plants lifted high their leaves that the drought had limply hung,
As eager rootlets deeply drank again.

And then, when summer storm had passed, sweet night regained
her calm.
An insect choir's glad music thrilled the air;
While, from majestic pines, arose a clean and fragrant balm -
Incense of nature, and her song of prayer.

   Ferne Eikenberry

Untitled

there's this lady i see everyday
she sits on a stool in front of some apartment
her hair is knotted her face is dirty her clothing is ripped
she looks tired she looks hungry

in her hand is a blue cup
when i walk by she mumbles
"HELP ME PLEASE, A PENNY OR TWO, I WOULD REALLY
APPRECIATE
IT FROM YOU"
i give her a quarter she mumbles

i look down at my self nice new shoes, a nice warm coat
i look back at her see a jacket torn apart
and toes sticking through her shoes

why are some people homeless? i ask
that's just the way it is. she replies
i walked by her spot yesterday she was lying down
I notice she isn't breathing
i felt a tear come down my cheek

since she's been gone i find it hard to walk by that spot
i always think something is missing i miss her a lot
even though i never spoke to her i feel i know her so well

Jaime Lederer

Incognito

The princess at the party, she wasn't really there.
She thought about her languidness, and if she would be care.
The food it seemed alive — so pungent and so tentative.
The guests were only faces, she didn't know their traces.

All sweetness and nostalgia was not the same to her as when in better
    graces, she wore abundant laces.
She only wanted love and this was not the place.
Events they are tumultuous, and may avert the dream,
She wants to scream, and be victorious, but seen astride a tempest
    brew,
Alas gets carried down the slue.

Then heartless on she makes her way, none shall prey upon me, they
    who stringently would try to see the inner workings of my chi.

Jonell B. Nelson

My Dog Princess

There once was a little dog who lived in a pen,
she was sad, she was lonely, and she needed a friend.

Each day she would sit in her pen all alone,
and dream of a friend, a home, and a big bone.

Then one day a young lady came by,
the sad little dog, she said, is the one that I'll buy.

She took the little dog home, with the hungry sad eyes,
but the little dog got sick and she thought it would die.

With the help of the Lord, and the care of the vet.,
the little dog grew into a wonderful pet.

Now this little dog lives in a beautiful home,
with a fenced in yard, and a big rawhide bone.

Although this little dog is only a mutt, she's priceless you see,
because this little dog is a "Princess" to me.

Joseph G. Tizzard

Into The Darkness

On a cold, cold night on the 5th of December,
She went to a nightclub in the golden gate city,
And now, maybe now, is the time to remember....
But no, the goblins crowd around with no pity.

This rock'n roll lady there expected no thunder:
She'd been there before, the door had no warning;
He took his place on the stage, she watched him in wonder,
And when he stared back the sun rose in her morning.

For a few months she tried to shrug him away,
The goblins said, "Come along now, this is a mistake;"
But when she realized he had determined to stay,
The demons dealt vicious to force her to break.

Their love lived on in her heart as months, then years, passed,
While the devil's dogs drowned her in chaos and terror;
She fought on alone waiting to meet him at last:
It seemed the demon king had made a small error.

The fight rages on, but changes have lately occurred:
The white dove who whispered now sings right out loud;
The rock'n roll prisoner wants her word to be heard,
She wants the wall to come down and the fools off her cloud.

Diana Randrup

Untitled

One hundred and thirty feet the fall
She wonders if its worth it all
To give away everything she's got
Her palms are sweaty-its getting hot
Now its time to learn to fly
Hear harps playing in the sky
Her long hair blowing in the breeze
She starts to cry and drops to her knees
One more breath before she dies
She looks down below and says good-bye
One last tear rolls down her cheek
Her future is looking rather bleak
She jumps off the building and sees a light
The moon has bloodstains on it tonight

Giovanna Iacobacci

Need Some Help?

"Need some help?" I turn.
She's 8, tanned, sand clinging to her skin.
Her kite, fluttering high in the air.

In her hands. My kite.
She climbs the bluff, ready to release.
I watch, string let out, ready.

She yells. "GO." I turn.
I'm 50, running, sand flying everywhere.
My kite, flies, then drags behind.

"Let's try again." We try.
She climbs, I run, gasping for air.
My kite, stubborn, refusing to fly.

"It's no use." I turn.
The sun sinks, swallowed by the sea.
Her question, echoing in my ears.

"Need some help?"

Charlotte Cardey

Untitled

My mother loves me and I'm so glad
she's the best little mother a son could ever have.
I was a weak son and she made me strong,
and when I was bad she made right of my wrong.
I LOVE MY MOTHER that's all I know,
she's always been there to help me grow.
We all need a mother and mine is the best,
I LOVE MY MOTHER, she's a step above the rest.
To her lips a smile I shall bring,
and to her heart a song to sing.
I LOVE MY MOTHER this she must know,
and within her love my hope of life can truly grow.
We all need a mother and I love mine,
she loves me and that is just divine.
I LOVE MY MOTHER, oh I love her so,
I LOVE MY MOTHER and this she must know.
    Love,

Kevin D. Kronner

Untitled

In the night sky
shines a pale eye
like flaming fires of the mind
emotions flowing with the tide
distorted figures roaming free
water flooding ancient trees
flowers groping priceless bees
time has changed me
weathered walls closing in
it's time to begin the endless ritual proceeds
life, death, gone without seeds
nothing's left to plant and feed
the sun has gone with the breeze
rain ran away last night
and the moon is not in sight
convulsions rake my empty bones
seaweed clinging to my clothes
sinking to a lower floor
darkness blinds my naive eyes
if only I could cry, at least breath a sigh before I die

Crystal Hartsook

Dead of Alive

Every day the light shines,
Shines on my pathetic life
All hidden behind the curtain
The curtain you never want to touch
The curtain that disgusts you,
Do you want me dead?
Sometimes I think so
I think you don't want to
Put up with me
I never wanted to put up with you
What is the purpose of me living,
To please you?
To please myself?
I am sure not pleasing myself
I really don't care what the hell you think
The closer I get to myself
The more you push me away
I have been dead for years,
Dead ever since you told me I was born.

Aaron Young

"Flames Of Love"

Look at the stars everywhere so bright
Shining so bright in the night
Each flaming star is placed just right

Each one is how much I love you
To how many it is there is not a clue
Each star shines brightly just for you

The ones that are so bright are me
The ones so bright is my love you see
My love set free to you from me

Flames are lighted on every one
To show you there is someone
Someone that loves you when you're lonesome

So when you're lonely and feeling sad
Look of all those stars and be glad
Each one shows all the love we had

Eternal flames of love
Stretched out from heavens alone
Eternal flames of love

How much I love you want to know, well look
at all those stars that glow, my love the stars will show
  Beth Howell

Special Moments

It is very quiet here, the night is stark black, but the stars are
shinning brightly as though a thousand diamonds were scattered
across the heavens.
The moon is full and vibrant, and we can see clearly, for we have
no fear of dark, as the dark doesn't touch us.
We breathe in deeply to smell the country air, the bouquet of trees,
that have grown gnarled and old through the years from holding us,
and those before us tightly within their grasp.
We are standing together, hand in hand, with the stars reflecting
from the sky and into our eyes, as our little faces are lifted
high to pray and sing to the angels above us.
We feel them dancing with us, guiding us in harmony, as our hearts
are innocent and pure.
As we have grown now, years from those special nights, I never
look upon the stars without saying quietly to myself,
"I wish I may, I wish I might, have the wish I wish tonight."
  Cindy Crowell

Oh, Ain't Christmas Fun

Oh, ain't Christmas fun! Always on the run.
Shopping, baking, cookie making, feet aching.
Back feels like its breaking.
Oh, ain't Christmas fun!

Had a little spat with Honey, cause I spent too much money.
Party going, to much celebrating.
Now my head is aching.
Oh, ain't Christmas fun!

The night before Santa comes, everything is almost done.
No more shopping, gift wrapping, tree trimming.
Hope I didn't miss anyone.
Oh, ain't Christmas fun!

Christmas day is finally here, everyone is in good cheer.
Smiles on children faces, Adults embracing.
Wish we could keep this Holiday spirit throughout the year.
After all is said and done...
Yes, Christmas is Fun!!!
  Bea Fisher

L.A Law

Acquitted! The most unjust finding ever!
Should a man be beaten like an animal? Never!
Pictures don't lie, the videotape showed plainly,
That a human being was treated inhumanely.

The jurors might all have been wearing robes.
The ones the Klan wears, you're familiar with those.
They weren't dressed in Klan robes outwardly,
But their judgment was "Klanish," don't you agree?

What a shame in America!!! The universe has seen,
Four white officers acquitted for abusing Rodney King.
We've regressed- gone back to slavery days; you must see
That verdict can only lead to a reign of tyranny.

Oh, if the Nation had only followed Dr. King's plea
For non-violence, freedom, justice and equality.
His name sake Rodney would not have been beaten in L.A.
There would have been no riots; and China would have had
  nothing to say.

He that tells the guilty he is innocent, shall the people curse,
You'll find that in Proverbs 24, the twenty-fourth verse.
It will go well with those who the guilty convict.
It says so in the Bible: we cannot contradict.

Edna Simmons

A Tribute To The Blind

The trite expression— "Blind Leading the Blind"
Should be changed for they often lead mankind.
Have you not observed they seldom complain
Whereas we fret at the least little thing.
They're always pleasant, yet a cross to bear
While we grumble, they walk as if no cares.
Some can sing melodies ever so sweet
And play music with an enchanting beat.
We often say, "Lord, why this thing to me?"
But the blind will say, "My Lord leadeth me,"
And the things they can do, puts us to shame—
But if reversed, how would we play the game?
If for just one day, we covered our eyes
Walking in darkness, could we sympathize.
And as we bathed and dressed, how would we do;
Would colors be right, or have matching shoes?
We'd grope through the day and far into night—
Things left yet to do—a most unpleasant sight!
So wear a smile, be thankful for your lot—
Count your blessings, we truly have a lot!

Dorothy M. Guest

The Light

As I walk forward, the light shines brighter.
Silence comes as the voices grow quieter.
Frightened and scared, I take a step back.
The voices return and the light fades black.
The choice is mine, there's no one to turn to.
Bewildered and confused; what should I do?
"Come back" are the words calling in my ear,
But I'm so curious of the light so near.
The question to me still remains unknown,
The answer exists and is clearly shown.
Entering into the pearly gate,
I no longer know the meaning of hate.
At the end of the walk, one step to bear,
All that is left is my hesitant stare.
My life flashed before me in the light grey sky.
As I listened, I heard voices of goodbye.
God spoke to me as black and white filled the space.
Then He showed me an expression upon my face.
The dark case revealed a profile of me,
As I soon realized where I might be.

Amanda Fuller

Survival

Each day the scarf sits atop her shelf...woven of gentle silver-blue
silk, delicate yet strong...Five hundred and ninety-three
rows complete.... Knit one, pearl two, Knit one, pearl two
Almost done, you would think...but she is not alone

Each day, Hatred, Anger, Anxiety and Fear walk by and they work
to tear her gentle threads apart - Each day they pick and grab
and tug and pull... She fights the strain until her fragile rows
unravel - Until one lonely row remains.

Then Gentle's hands lift her up off the ground
Generosity and Kindness hold her up and begin to weave her back
together... Understanding and Love come and help to knit
Knit one, pearl two, Knit one, pearl two

Her beautiful blue silk threads begin to hold together again and
form a strong bond...Five hundred and ninety-three perfect rows
Not quite complete, but once again a beautiful silver-blue scarf,
Sitting on her shelf.

And she asks if one day Anger and Hatred and Anxiety and Fear will
no longer come...And Hope replies, "I'm sorry, no, but each day
Kindness, Generosity, Love, and Understanding will return with
Gentle's hands to weave you together again to face another day."

Deanna M. Carter

"The God Who Calls Me Wife"

I no longer dispute my insignificance,
Since you've ingrained in me that such is true.
If all Gods exact an emolument, then who am I
To query one so righteous, yet as you?

Accordingly, I prostrate my nether self
Before all trite altars (that) you proudly erect.
(Although earth Gods who rule by leaden hand,
Were never ordained by Heaven, - I suspect.)

I'm prone to ruminate upon matter beyond my ken,
As I genuflect before you, weary, on my knee;
Sometimes wondering if, - forgotten or unknown,
Some quaking creature, somewhere, bends in awe of me.

I know, Master, you deplore my lack of gratitude
Toward you who have, so often, spared my wretched life;
Forgive me, now, my futile attempts to run away
From you, my gracious God, who calls me wife.

I've sacrificed my bleeding soul and now I beg to rise,
So, if I remember to hang my head - ever so low,
While truckling in the shadow of your tall stance:
Oh! Master! Will you grant me leave to go?

Anna Marie Smith

Solace

Sinking
Sinking so fast there isn't sand quick enough to catch me
Standing still but not feeling the earth beneath me
Watching the ball of silky light move through the cluster of cotton
Trying to sing myself from the coffin
But the blues just got black and so did the night.

Sitting in the dark
Singing out my heart
Feeling life ease its bite
Losing sight
Seems to be the reapers night
And then to his delight
The cold black night inhaled
And
Extinguished my flame
I remain only as a memory
To those whose hope burns eternal
And whose flame ignites the earth.

Gael Brown

Sister!!!

Where have you been?
Sister! I have been crying out for you.
I cried a long time.
Sister! I needed someone to help me
Sister! I was in a dark and lonely place.
Sister... I welcomed your light.
But it never came.
Sister! The PAIN! The DARKNESS! The SCREAMS!
My screams bounced of the hollow walls of loneliness
Sister! I screamed to see if any one could hear me
but there was no one to hear my screams.
Did you not hear the screams.
Or was it you only can hear your own screams.
Sister! You abandoned me!
Sister! I never abandoned you.
Do you not remember.
When you screamed I came.
Sister! I needed someone to help me with the pain.
Sister! I am over the pain and living in the light.
Why do you appear now SISTER? SISTER WHY?

Alicia Kong

The Light

She knows not peace who has never known despair.
Sitting at twilight, in a dreary cell of a room.
Evening falls, it's gloom steals away the sun.
Sinister dark shadows mantle the room.
Frightening, Impenetrable.
Will this darkness never pass?
Not even a pale sliver of light pierces this gloom.
Will a new time ever lead to joy?
At the final breath, I sigh. A faint light glimmers
    through a narrow crack.
My soul gladdens.....Witness that the sun never sets
    and soon will rise again.
The light on which I had turned my back, the Lord, has
    brought again His power and glory.
I found His everlasting Kingdom.
He takes my hand: I enter the light.
I've come home.

Denizilye Douglas

My Gift To You

Though times this year have been unfairly rough,
Situations arising with the sole
Purpose of causing pain, we all have lived
Through our dark times, so I pray this enough.
That this small token I have to give you
Will be adequate in all you've given
Back to me. My only regret during
This festive time of rejoicing I knew,
Was all I had to offer as a gift
Were these few petty words which are all I
Know in this existence. So, don't despair
Over things you could have, your mind adrift
To dreams of material possessions.
When what really counts is not the gifts you
Expected of me, not the very depth
Of your desires or your obsessions.
For this season we should not be apart,
But gathered together to celebrate
Not St. Nick but our Savior Jesus Christ,
Resting assure this verse comes from my heart.

Cristina Garcia

This Burning Flame

My love for you was like a candle stick
Slowly burning I never gave up I tried and tried
Never to let go although I always cried
Wishing you would hold me tight
Until the early morning light.

The candle light slowly burning
The full moon barely turning
I wish you would hold me tight
Hold me with all your might

Never letting me go
The candle light is burning low
I can barely see the flame
Who is to take the blame.

I keep trying to light the candle stick
All I can see is the little wick
Please don't stop burning
My heart is still yearning
To hold on tight
To the early morning light.

Irma R. Sanchez

Happiness

When you are sad and alone
Smiles gleam as a light.
From the tears and cry's
Laughter appears as stars of the night.
A caring word, from a cherished friend,
Opens the door, to the gentle side.
The heart is home to the soul,
When broken, the small gate will disappear,
Leaving an opened spirit, to fall prey to fear!
But with laughter, happiness and joy
Your gate will open, and your smile will reappear.
To whom to say, who we are,
Emotions as waves guide us
Both near and far.
A caring thought, is enough, to take us
To the next star!

Jeani Borreggine

Her Last Words

I've been here before,
smiling with your kiss still fresh on my lips,
warm in my stillness
and remembering
how we walked whispering, lost and found,
in the smoldering dusk
walked whispering,
one with the trees, the swaying trees,
dear lonesome leaves
until an old barn, where we rested.
That night the warm winds fled the hills,
and in the pallid morning you left me with a kiss
remembering

Jeff Rainbolt

twenty second christmas

i stood before the christmas tree
and pondered immortality
and wished that it would beat no more
an end to dover's deaf'ning roar
dreaming of a nameless death
blank epitaph forgotten breath
food for worms forever wrought
blinded by the light forth brought
by the camera shot
and caught

Robert Brunelle

Winds Of Time

Children play, and the winds of time, gently flow.
Snug, are they, bathed in the warmth of youthful ignorance.
Of time, The children, do not know.

Teenagers thoughts, never dwell on time, so many things to do.
No chill, for them ever enters, as cooler winds circle past.
Their warmth, a youthful knowledge, time, will ever last.

Never resting, the winds of time, much cooler now, and longer last.
As young adults, begin the march on, warmed, with the knowledge,
tomorrow, their tomorrow's, will forever last.
No thoughts to time, as winters ebb, and flow. Much colder,
and more swiftly now, the incessant winds still blow.

Middle age, slowing them now, thoughts of time, warm memories dwell,
no wrappings seem to warm completely,
as much colder winds now gust, and swell.

Howling now, the winds of time, bringing winter, to so many life's.
They seek the memories, of time's long past, of warmer,
gentler winds, when no thoughts, to time, abound.

Flower's gently laid to ground, some are now at rest.
The winds of time, that have ceased for them, still seeking,
all the rest...

John A. Baird

For You My Love

My eyes, my eyes are like the morning sky.
So bright and blue for the love of you.
My lips, my lips are like dying rose petals.
Always saying how much you mean to me.
My heart, my heart always pounds for you.
Which tells me that my love for you is true.
My soul, my soul so dark and deep.
Tells me that I can not keep my love for you.
Until I know you love me so.
My love, my love will always grow.
Around my heart I can always know.
My life, my life which is telling me.
That my love for you will always be.
For you are the one I'll always keep.
In my heart way down deep.
Always and forever will I love you.
Until the day my soul is gone.
Will my love for you never go.
For right now I love you so.

Amanda C. Hancock

When I Was A Wee Little Lad

The wind, roaring in from the sea
So cruelly edged with a dangerous glee
Laughed itself up to a rapturous whirl
Aiming its strike with a ghastly swirl.
No man on this earth dost wager the worth
Of the wind from the sea the wind happy and free.

When I was a boy and I'd talk to Dad
He'd say, "Listen to me, my little lad.
"The sea is great, but it will destroy
The heart of a man, not just as coy.
He must prove to be Master without disaster."
Then Dad would look sad, when I was a wee little lad.

Geraldine A. Cooke

Time

Time passes by
   so fast, so slow
An hour a minute
   a minute an hour
Now is then,
   But then shall never be now,
   for it has passed onto then to never be now.
Then can be yesterday,
   yesterday then
But yesterday cannot be not
for it has passed onto then to never be now.

Jennie Phillips

For a Minute of Time is but Mine

(Dedicated in honor of President Ronald Reagan)
Memories are the gateway to the past,
So I shall hold onto them,
For as long as they will last.

Things seem to come and go,
And sometimes my thought pattern ceases to flow.

I was on my way somewhere
I was sure I needed to be,
But then I wasn't sure where,
And the desire arose within me to flee.

I was delighted to see this one I loved,
But suddenly it was a stranger,
And I did not know where I was.

It use to be that some days were better than others,
Now I hold onto the minutes,
For even they are beginning to flutter.

I wish I could absorb the cloud within my mind,
And live into tomorrow as if there were no time.

Now as I quietly recede within my mind,
And all those I love and things I know,
Will simply fade away and go......

Carolyn A. Curran

Keep The Faith

As doth the rivers travel to meet the sea,
so is man's yearn for knowledge which makes
him be.
   Destined circumstances govern our course
we morally take; sometimes good, sometimes
bad, giving us no control as we make.
   Far between Heaven and earth we question
why what we do, with answers bestowing us
seldom of any hopeful clue.
   Continue with relentless faith, being
able to falter not, and maybe someday
an answer will teach us of what we ought.
   Accord yourself to generous ways, accepting
every defeat, strive again and calamity
should not be yours to meet!

Alan R. Olson

Killing A Life?

Isn't abortion Killing a life?
People might have one because they're not husband and wife.
That little baby is gift inside.
A life is something it shouldn't be denied.
That poor little baby didn't ask to be born.
Now they're going to make their life all torn.
Adoption is another way to go.
Maybe after this poem, your stomach will start to show.

Joy Manbeck

Friendship

My life revolves around our friendship,
So let me let you in on a little tip.
I hope our friendship you will not sell,
for then will I be but a hollow shell.

Living my life day by day,
As if I were an actor in a play.
Just knowing that you were there,
Would make it seem like you really did care.

Our friendship is like a bond,
And of you I grow quite fond.
But let me give you this little token.
Before our friendship is ever broken.

All the things I ever dreamed of, I saw in you,
And then my dreams finally did come true.
Little did I know how my life would bend,
But you became my one true friend.

Chuck Barron

Transformation

Three years ago we received this child - -
    So light, so thin and sickly beside
With her tiny voice she faintly cried,
    Surely she was our frailest child.

We bathed her with loving care,
    Fed her well the most nutritious fare,
Built her confidence so she can dare
    Develop her varied talents under our care.

She twirled and swayed like a gymnast queen,
    Sang songs of joy, her words so sweet so keen
With skill and grace she looked supreme,
    Surely, Jaymee now is our lovely queen.

Jose U. Lim

A Word of Life

Life will always be what you make it,
So live your's full and don't forsake it.
Live day by day and night by night
And let not death fill you with fright.

We live our lives as we think we should.
Some live their's bad, will you live yours' good?
Be happy, and always make a friend
And you will feel better in the end.

Life and death are one and the same
And, both are parts of God's big game.
Don't be sad, be happy at least,
Enjoy your life and die in peace.

Craig Willeford

Looking Through My Eyes

Looking through my eyes I see
People aren't what they want to be.

Why do they do this I don't understand-
Living at someone else's demand.

Everyone should live in his own domain
And own his own claim to fame.

Everyone is different in his own way
Of course we were all molded from different clay.

Being different isn't the key
Being yourself that's what to be.

Angela McCorkle

Wind, Return Us

We'll catch a breeze and ride the wind,
    soar over life's troubles and rustle through the
    branches of our goodness.

Whirling, to linger around the loving moments in our lives,
    and racing, through the hurting feelings the world throws
    our way, quickly, so as not to get familiar there.

Then, a gusty thrust of air will move us on until, the settling,
    calming breeze once more, sets us gently down, with the
    grace and sweetness of a lover's hand.

And there we wallow, 'til the next breath from heaven comes along.

And without fear, we are carried by the wind once more,
    knowing that soon, we will come to rest again, in our special
    place.

That place that holds the love we share.

There is where we want to stay.

But sometimes, whirlwinds come along, cross our paths and
    whisk us up into flight toward some other direction.

Then, we must ride the wind again, patiently, for we know in our
    hearts, where it is we shall return.........
to each other.

Antonetta Carver

Paul

He was a breeze that lingers in the air,
Softness and sweetness, with scuffled-up hair.

Peaches and cream with sparkling blue eyes,
Laughter and giggles yet clever and wise.

Mischief and charm that tugs at your heart,
Aloof yet enchanting, right from the start.

This was my Paul, my pride and my joy,
My friend, my companion, my sweet little boy.

It's been a while since he went away,
Yet it breaks my heart as it did that day.

Nevermore will I see his smiling face,
Or hear his laughter in any place.

So forever I'll cherish each of his days,
His mischievous deeds and clever ways.

His crooked smile and tapping hand,
And wish I could watch him grow to a man.

But in my heart is where he'll stay,
That's where he's been ever day.

Only in my dreams can he be seen.
Where forever, he's fourteen.

Francine Isom

World Pollution

Can anyone make sense of the world today
Some are cleaning it up, while other's throw
    it away
We're still making machines that pollute the air
While others try to reduce pollution, well,
    at least they care
We keep cutting down trees which help us breath
And in their place we put industries
We disintegrate the ozone with aerosol cans
While those against it are joining hands
You'll probably be dead before the world dies, so you
    don't care and refuse to be kind
But always remember that when you die, your children
    have to live in whatever you leave behind.

April Tucker

To Whoever Wants To Listen

When playing poker I'd always deal
Some people say, I'm not for real
They say that I am great with the ball
But guys don't look at tomboys when they're cruisin' down the
hall I may not be so perfect that I'm worshipped with every
word sometimes I'll even soar... just like a tiny bird
But some people... they're just like a dam
They want to stop you, just cause they can
Guys don't like girls who play football and stuff like that
They walk all over you just like a muddy mat
They don't care about your feelings, they don't care at all
It's like they're the big and your just the small
You say that it's not fair, well, nothing really is
They'll always do much better on the hardest of the quiz
There's really nothing you can do
They do everything better than you
They run, sing, and pick popular friends
You be nice to them, they'll never bend
So if you see a so called "snob" just walk on by
Cause they are sneaky people with more than meets the eye

Elizabeth Anne Palmer

Untitled

Will ever, I, a Romeo, be?
   Some quick delighted fantasy
   an object of a lover's kiss
someone special, someone to miss
with gentle hands of love's desire
   where fingers tips and whispers conspire ...

Will ever, I, a Romeo, be?
   with words of guile and mystery
   a lively heart like sparkling wine
that cherish and flourish in love divine
to share beneath a lovers moon
   a love song sung so soft in tune...

Will ever, a Romeo, be, I?
   without a lonely night to cry
   where pouts and fits of heartache leave
so tears again may not conceive
will ever this, become of me
   will ever, I, a Romeo, be?

Chris Norris

The Dedication

They stood on the grass and the walkways,
some with tears in their eyes.
They stood silently and remembered
as the rifle team raised their guns to the skies.

They remembered the days of fighting,
of loved ones that had gone to war.
They stood — and they silently prayed
that war would be never more!

And as the veil tumbled down from the memorial
a gasp went through the crowd,
there it stood so elegant and stately,
a monument for all to be justly proud!

A monument built by the people
with dollars and dimes and pride,
a monument to those who serve their country,
a memorial to those who had died.

And as the sound of Taps gently faded,
and the people walked away,
on the black marble base lay a rose,
And we knew it had been a meaningful day.

Eileen D. Wilson

"Deliver Me From The Wolves"

I need someone of substance.
Someone I can touch and call them my savior.
Send me to a land where I can rest my soul.
My land of salvation, where I may live in peace.

We'll make the pilgrimage together - be you male or female
- friend or lover, either way, we are eternal.

I am the lamb, you are the dove -
In unity symbolize innocence and love.
I will walk forever on tiny hooves - just deliver me from the wolves.

Walk beside me in life - fly beside me beyond.
for the journey that lies before us is far and great.
Dark and cold, it camouflages the many wolves.

They will watch from the shadows,
sneering and drooling at this succulent lamb.
But our union we have forged will hold them at bay -
Leaving their teeth yellow in the absence of blood.

Cold and grey - love and hate
Two wings - four tiny hooves.
They'll get no life from the throat they drink.
So deliver me from the wolves.

Christopher Dunn

"Substance"

Once
Someone told me I was pretty
And his words brushed pink upon my cheeks and once
I tripped in the hall and dropped all my books
And the laughter got in my eye
So I pushed it back with the rest of my hair and once
Someone said "I love you"
And that catalyst caused by heart to explode.

Words are tangible.
They are soft kisses
And black guns.
We have forgotten the power we have.

Chellee Harris

My Hometown - Only A Memory

I search all the faces hoping to see-
   someone who says "they're glad to see me"
Where I learned, grew, laughed and played-
   where I loved, sang, cried and blundered.
Was it really me, or just a dream? - I wondered.
   "My home"? -Strange folks go inside.
Apartments now I'm told abide.
   Do the authors of "books on my hometown" say
that they as children did run here and play?
   Did they lie on the beach? - Did they swim in the bay?
When the water was clear - the sand clean and white;
   the hill closed for sledding on a crisp winter night
on the sparkling clean snow?
   These things - I remember. These things do they know?
I walked in the footsteps of "my grandparents" you see.
   The best things in life, - I thought they were free.
Could someone tell me just for my sake -
   How many generations should it take
for an "honorary member" make - of "my hometown"

Dan James Austin

Everlasting Glisten

Sometimes I feel the end is near
Sometimes I ask of why I am here
Truth is the words that I speak
And never does my faith ever get weak

Wasting the terrible trials of sin
While the highness of hope is born within
And all my troubles that harshly surround
Start to fade away and are soon broken down

For faith is the ear that will always listen
Then truth is bloomed with an everlasting glisten
And fate is the tree that shall always stand
Due to the growth of hope that tends to expand
Beauty is the rose without doubt
Its thorn is the symbol of what faith is about
And from the harmful weeds it shall defend
As its hope and faith starts to blend

The horizon is filled with the light of happiness
Which brightens the darkness of my emptiness
For faith is the sun that has been risen
As the bloom of life remains an everlasting glisten.

James S. Hodges

The Seed

I am a beggar, but I still have a heart
Sometimes I tire from pushing my cart
Through tired eyes I watch those who succeed
None of them know the basics of need.

I have my place and here it seems I will stay
But I'll keep my place, dream of better days.
One day the world's eyes will recognize need
And one who is able will plant the first seed.

It's been a tough life, I may be set free
Your gift's brought to light the heart of my dream
For this gift you have granted the palm of my hand
I will prove myself worthy, with the strong I will stand.

The seed has been planted and from it I grew
The dreams I have had have finally come true
I now have acquired what I once called a need
From what I was given I chose to succeed.

From the first step, I have climbed many stairs
And now I too can show now I care.
The fruits of the seed are given to you
I offer a dream make it come true.

Dorothy Brannon

Rick

I have a dream, it never ends.
Sometimes it seems it might come true,
then fades away.
How long do you wait for a dream.
How long can one care.
Life keeps moving by, is it worth the chance.
They say chase after your dream,
Mine runs away.
So I wait with hope of a second chance.
Scared of the unknown and putting faith into my dream,
I pray to come true.
I know in my heart its a dream to come true and will be better then
any dream anyone could have.
I may be silly or a fool to wish a dream to come true, but, I have
only one life to find happiness.
I believe in dreams.

Evonne J. Nerat

I'm Really In Here!

I'm really in here!
Somewhere down deep
I'm really in here!
Light bursting, trying to escape
I feel it! I really feel it! There's hope!
Thank you, God, I feel the healing
It's there! It's starting to come.
It's not there yet, but it's a start.
Renewed...what a good word!
I feel the strength building.
I feel the real me sinking back into my body...
Ebbing and flowing
All through me, in and out, over and over.
Did I ever really know who I am?
I don't know. But I'm finding me now!
A better-than-ever, stronger me.
Terrific! Beginnings! Believing feelings!
Capable of strength
For myself, my partner, my children.
Eternal hope...bubbling, flowing, over the edge.

Alice Neaves

Untitled

The moonlight stroked a forest clearing
sparrows and butterflies hummed like streetlights
purple/silver hues and highlights
she sat naked on a piano bench
time was then only musical notes
and they danced on tufts of breeze like feathers

Unlike the dream that was black and white
the only black and white
were those 88 keys, but too shiny and slick
were the ebony holes
warm, inviting the sexy ivories
were the bats dancing?
And the owl's hologram shadowed the right
side of the scene while
she sat naked on a piano bench

Barton Comly Boyce

Forever Lost

Statuesque in form; soft in heart,
Speckled cheeks upon swarthy skin
That cloud my mind and set apart
My lustful thoughts of life and limb,
Eyes filled with rain from swollen skies,
All that was gained had gone awry.

Her charm bewitched and grasped my mettle,
While mindless, I ignored her spell
Through times when pride proclaim and yell
To take that chance; but alas I fail,
Beauty was lost, never to be nigh
Eternal bliss that had surely gone awry.

Besieged by passion; consumed by desire,
I've lost her now, my mind has felt,
I've nothing left, but my soul is afire,
So be not proud for your heart to melt,
And venture hard to chase that sign
Before all is lost and gone awry.

John F. Fitzpatrick

The Butterfly

Floating, flying towards the flowers
Speechless and amazed staring for hours

The glossy wings so colorful and bright
It is the most wonderful sight

Gazing at its beauty for so very long
As it gracefully sings its silent song

Trying to grab it in my hand
But nothing can hold a beauty so grand

Up through the air this creature flies
As it soars up through the clear blue skies

The beautiful creature free as the air
I'm lost in a bewildered stare

Delicate patterns printed on the wings
The world is silent, and the butterfly sings

Clarisa Foncea

Yellow Rose Sonnet

Bright roses trail across the lawn's edge
Spilling color in pleasing disarray
From golden flowers old fashioned as croquet.
Like weeds the eager plants spread to the hedge;
Woody stems with thorns, abundant foliage,
Have open buds and blossoms on display.
Like untidy maidens shedding lingerie
Petals strew the lawn with careless privilege.

Flowers lacking neatness have a certain charm;
Add to human pleasure in springtime hours,
Yellow roses show golden blossoms in mid-May
Offering their treasures when days are warm.
Gaining their prime before more cultured flowers
Emitting fragrance as rural as new hay.

Evalyn Anderson

My Knight

My life seemed like an endless void, an emptiness within
   Sporadic bouts of happiness, then sadness setting in

Daydreaming of a handsome knight to come and to save the day
   To cherish me the one he loves until his dying day.

Walking to reality my dreams a memory
   Longing for my handsome knight to find the real me

You waltzed into my forlorn world, the answer to my prayers
   A man with loving tenderness, the Knight who truly cares.

You understand my grumpy moods and lend a helping hand
   You never judge or criticize, you always understand

If there is one thing I can say to make you understand,
   I tell you all the love I feel and give no other man

I love you with all my heart, and this love is here to stay
   I thank the Lord who is above
For bringing you my way

Elizabeth Patton Thomas

"Seasons Confused"

Crocus blooming
Snows a falling
Dreary skies o'er head

How a palling Autumn leaves not yet fallen
Still clinging to their bough

How can we tell one season from another
fall, winter, spring
How they all become one big season now?

Doris M. Bennett

Sacrifice

Its a cue coming from your side when things start to go wrong.
Standing back I watch us go through the motions, in this
   foolish game we create.
I feel the misunderstanding in your eyes.
But only after the fact, sensitivity builds a wall, I feel
   haunted, wondering if somewhere it all ends in flames.

We tiptoe around it, like walking around glass.
You say good-bye doesn't mean forever.
But all that's coming are two hearts living in separate worlds.

Its cold now, colder as I near your body.
Lovers now, we know no shame.
Time, it does so much.
When the scent of you lingers, and temptations are strong,
   into the boundaries sweet deceit comes calling,
   bringing tears of delight.

The memory returns.
But is it enough to keep it alive?

Beverly S. Ernesti

"Duchess"

There she sat,
staring at me through the glass.
Her big brown eyes fearful but inquisitive
Asking, "Will she come out again?"

I tried twice before, first with kind words
then with some food. I just wanted to help her,
but she was too scared. Someone must have hurt
her...hurt her bad.

Then, on the third try, in my crouched position
I saw, through her big scared eyes, a glimmer of trust.
That encouraged me. I talked to her.
I told her I could help her. Feed her, give her a warm place
to sleep. Hold her.

She took a few steps forward, then one back. Scared...so very scared.
I told her to come to me. Then, I promised her I would take her home.
Finally, giving into her fear because of exhaustion and hunger,
she padded over to me and let me hold her.

I stroked her silky brown fur and scratched behind her big floppy
ears. I whispered to her, "It's okay now, girl. The hurt is over.
I'll give you a home and love you forever, Duchess."

Britta K. Pitocchelli

Untitled

Love is like a rainbow
starting low and growing tall
rounding off
But soon to fall
The colors each a symbol
Red... the lust, the heat
Orange... the taste how sweet
Yellow... the feeling of warmth like the sun
Green... the jealousy has begun
And on the other side
the rainbow is a colorful slide
leading downward to a pot of gold
Perhaps someday....
but most just fade away.

Dawn Kaminsky

Sing Oh South Africa

The storms of memories long past
still reverberate in thick clouds of thunder

Blocking what is known, but not sometimes felt,
the brilliant and warm light of your souls

Know now that the gales were nothing more
than gentle drops of dew for growth

It is time for the tempests to pass,
for there has been enough moisture

The radiance of your higher selves
glow strongly on top of those clouds

And longs to caress the hills and valleys of life
with understanding, acceptance, and Love

Aaron Hoffer

Her Call

He sits quietly, pensive
Stirring the tobacco in his pipe,
  he carefully lights it
The fragrance of cherry encircles the room
The weathered face sees beyond dusty panes
Youth stolen silently by her siren deceit
Stinging salt brine in the wind
Brash, chiding sea gulls
Lilting, creaking decks, straining
Heavy, harsh, twisted ropes
He feels the familiar beckon
but age's response is wiser.

Becky Shaffer

Sins Forgiver

One man of many,
stones cast upon him by all,
screams of wrong against his right,
yet he stood tall.

Convicted for his bravery,
silenced for his beliefs,
betrayed by his people,
yet he stood tall.

Thorns of death placed upon his head,
shouts of hate thundered through the sky,
his blood poured down before them,
yet he stood tall.

His cries could be heard through cities,
the love he had the wounds could not break,
all the pain he suffered because of them,
yet,
      he forgave us all.

Christina Wierschem

Always and Forever

An empty heart, a lonely space, can any one fill this vacant space?
outlining the future, never looking back, keep looking forward
forgetting the past.

crying night and crying day, trying not to remember
you are a part of my heart always and forever.
crystal will always shine, a dime will always be worth a dime
the clouds will always touch the sky, birds will always learn to fly
eagles will always soar, lions will always roar
I will never tear away from you, I hope this is how it will be
always and forever here with me.

Elaine I. Alvarado

Cause Nobody But Nobody Can Make It Out Here Alone

Lying on my bed looking out the window wishing I had a hero that can
stop the violence and stop these crimes because all we ever to do is
die. I wonder what I would do if my mother died too. All the boys
think they're bad to the bone but they need to stop cause nobody but
nobody can make it of here alone. Thinking about all the people
who died I pray to God that I will survive, seeing people die one by
one then-their souls fly up near the sun. No one can walk alone on
the streets; you know what, I'm going to try to make peace. You
should know that guns are not toys- nobody but nobody can make it
here alone. Sometimes I pray to God that people wouldn't die; I
pray and pray that my people would just stay. I wonder what it
would be like without all of this violence and without people
dying but it's not all guns' faults. Most of it has
to do with drugs and AIDS. Where do drugs come from how,
do they make them, what is the plan to kill everyone in our nation?
Listening to gun shots, bullets pop-it's a shame how people have to go
through all that pain. Don't people think before they kill, what's
the deal?

Ebony Shante Gould

Will Work For Food

I was driving by in my car one rainy day
stopped at a stop sign and much to my dismay.

A woman was holding a sign above her head
the big bold letters stated WILL WORK FOR BREAD!

Much to my amazement I couldn't understand all the "whys"
that a hungry American citizen would have to advertise.

I tried to blow off this situation but it haunted me
So I pulled over to the side of the road so I could see.

This woman's face was so distraught and full of pain
so I got out of my car to talk to her in spite of the rain.

I asked her what type of work she would do
and she stated whatever work I wanted her to.

I wanted to know if she would take on the chore
of escorting me to the restaurant next door.

She looked up at me with a surprise on her face
and then down at her dress with the dirty lace.

She took me up on my offer and to the restaurant we went
it was such a pleasure to be a part if this happy event.

She ate a three course meal and gave me a smile -
And so very politely said, "I love you" "God bless you, child."

Alice F. Hill

Pueo (Hawaiian Owl)

On golden, silent wings she flies,
straight out of moonlight, midnight skies,
to destinations that we earth bound
can only dream!
She hovers silently for a closer look,
with eyes that penetrate to your very core.
And with her questions answered,
she'll circle and continue on...
Leaving the earthbound filled
with awe and wonder,
the beauty of it all!

Judith Parsons

Night, Morning and Other Feelings

I drape myself in a cloud watch a
    strange sky turn pink
I go to the kitchen to fix a comfortable drink.
I wave at a squirrel who has stopped to stare, unswayed.
I realize this day.

I would like a piece of the moon
He is shiny and true. "Don't disappear too soon."
I invent pictures that calm or frighten me.
Eyes quiver under soft lids, and I stir like the sea.
I am content tonight.
Morning brings a cheerfully cold light to my dim bedroom.
I have no time to fume.
My mind is drenched, though waking leaves me unquenched.

When my eyes adjust, I can almost see darkness close around
In absence of sound I am ready and waiting for ultimate
    healing.
It is the perfection of an apple on a sunny day,
as feeling comes over me and I yearn to play
I fall to the dirt as I hear the ground screech.
I run to the sky. I am a peach.

Jennifer Lynn Schiffer

The Nursery

In the eternal dismal shadow of the county hospital
stretch the lonely fingers of the nursery,
seeking sunlight in any direction
but the darkness drowns them in its murky sweep.
Here, those whose labors frustrate them from nurturing
those who were their own nourishers
deliver their cherished flora in diffident hope,
expecting torpid hearts to supersede their souls.
Many of those planted take no root,
crawling through the fingers in search of living memories,
grasping only vacant walls, empty eyes, barren wastes.
Those who do anchor in the arid soil
shrivel into ghosts neglected by the gardeners,
hollow images wilting into dust.
One by one, the creeping night gathers them
to its triumphant bosom
as we who passed their sentence
weep.

Harry E. Fitch

"Through Our Windows"

I sit looking at the raindrops
striking the window. Different shapes
and styles made like a spider weaving
his wed. All intricate, all beautiful.
Dissolving at the touch of a finger only
to make another shape even more beautiful
than before. Puddles of water forming on
the cold ground only to part from an unknown
step of a human walking though their own
life. Who knows how many people are
shut up behind closed doors watching
the raindrops as I do? Happy thoughts
intermingle with the sadness, making
life a little more tolerable. Heaviness only
comes now and then. Raindrops will fall
again, one day to be warm against your
skin, instead of bits of ice piercing your
soul into the depths of your heart. Is
that you crying, Jesus, because of the sadness?

Angela McGlothlin

Life's Journey

Bouncing on the bottle's fill.
Sloshing round and up and down,
Torn ever from, but knowing still
Of the serenity when "nectar kissed the cork."
But as the sweet draught begins
To pour from out its bound
A coursing must from Nature's law be formed
And that peace that was
Never more shall be until
All has passed and there be nothing found.

John D. Reynolds

Broken Earth...

So many little crevices
So many scars of journeys long before
All of which waiting to be explored
The answers to which
Remain a mystery
To everyone and
Everything
except...this small piece of the broken earth
Where has time taken this nomadic wonder
Why has it come to me

Gina M. Saracco

Storm

In from the stormy sea skulks a purring fog
slyly casting its ghost-like shadow
while high in the heavens stalks an eerie moon.

As the hungry sea lashes the storm-wearied crags,
an angry sky explodes in bitter wrath
as downward rushes relentless rain.

The savage wind booms irate commands,
as nature wreaks unbridled passion
on an unsuspecting world.

Elizabeth A. Garvin

So Has Our Love

Like the first breath of the newborn
So has your love given me life
And no more shall I languish without purpose
Like the new green of spring
Showering with freshness
So has your love opened my eyes
To see the brilliance of each day
Like the unlimitedness of the heavens
So has my love for you been able to grow
Until the last flicker of light goes from me

Greg C. Antcliff

Untitled

Run, run quickly, run swiftly, run peacefully,
run softly to and through the calm nothing,
and once you reach the edge of where
nothing meets something jump into the
unexplored, unknown dreams of fantasy
images. Then sleep in thoughts of reality
not yet created in the eyes no one sees
through. Because they are shut to the darkness
of the bright light that shines through a
barrier of emotion felt by to many. Blinded
by reasons overpowering, keep running to
the end of the end.

John Murray

Awaking from a Dream

Go and bedevil organ grinder monkeys - needle their gypsy blood
aboiling with rotten bananas - *skedaddle them shrieking* -

Call out the olive drab National Guard rolling down freeways -
Old Glories whipping from radio antennas on faded canvas-covered trucks
to feed the poor in your dreams
who lick milk and honey off their bayonets...

Release white doves
for every prisoner free...

But when the good sense of love
comes knocking at your door -
both barrels blazing gold dust and champagne corks -

You'd better open up -

Let the monkeys swing about
without their leg irons,
the doves dance with their
white silk top hats
tilted back *cooing*...

Otherwise you're just
spinning your wheels in sand,
Honeybones.

Frank Morris

Indecision

YES came before me, dressed in red, and with a smile, sweetly said,
"Brass rings come 'round just once they say,
  by saying yes, it's yours today -
Choose me or you will never guess all the joys of saying yes."

NO came before me with a frown, face was quiet, eyes turned down
-
"Brass rings are not what they should be,
  and nothing's new that comes for free -
Avoid the change of winds that blow -
  keep warm and safe by saying - no."

MAYBE stood between those two, a perfumed beauty, it was true.
Fixed upon me with her eye, and whispered softly,"They both lie -
Take my hand until it's done, wait with me, choose neither one."
So while I tarried all year long, and listened to her siren song,
She took from me what made me whole, cooked my will and ate my
soul.

Gentle reader, stay a bit, what just passed was more than wit -
Remember this on where to go, when choosing either YES or NO -
Wisdom says, "choice matters not,
  what the month or what the day be,
Choose YES or NO and leave that spot,
  'cause you can die from MAYBE".

Charles V. Allen

TRIBUTE TO A DENTIST

How do you pray so God is taken by surprise?
My brother longed for angels to cross him over on wings.
When cancer felled him, I started having mental swings.
I recall the root-canal job he did for me, the wise
Talking heads on TV that annoyed him, the black rap bland
Or giddy, barking distractions loud and loathsome.
His words worth repeating: "A gentle flight to His Kingdom."
I remember his tolerance for things hard to understand.

He clutched my wrist when we were kids crossing the street,
And a pebble dangled from his neck on a yellow string.
Angels, he believed, are the only immortality. Last spring
Before he ceded his breath, "Angels," he said. "Repeat
Los angeles." In my mind I saw a place with no sex in it.
The prayer for angels to fly the dead—how do you say it?

F. D. De Castro

Confess

Confess your belief in Me
By writing the vision I give to thee.
For as you pen the words so true
In others will spring Life anew.

Confess your belief in Me
That they may accept and receive
The freedom that is yours today
They will enjoy when they know The Way.

Confess your belief in Me
That they may know that I Am He.
And if they will confess and stand;
I will uphold them with My Right Hand.

Confess your belief in Me
That through your life others will see
The blessings from struggles you go through,
Then they will <u>know</u> My Words are true.

Confess your belief in Me
And you will truly be
With the Son of Man
When I rule upon this land!

Karen Nikkel

A Gift Called Love

Times that are tough, times that are easy,
This ride called life can make you queasy.
Through all its ups and downs,
Causing many frowns,
There is still a gift you can receive,
But in this gift you must really believe.
Believe that it will help you through life,
With all the joys, heartaches, and fights.
This gift comes from the God above,
It's the special gift called love.
No matter what you encounter,
Love will be there to make things sounder.
When you feel lower than the bottomless pit,
Love is there helping you through your fit.
If you feel higher than the sky,
Love is there enjoying your high.
Love is something quite unique,
It's different for everyone, depending on what they seek.
But to receive this gift called love,
You must *really* believe in the God above.

Rachel Ferguson

Golden Splendor

Silence.
Shhh...
It's a golden sound,
That happens rarely in *the city*.

Golden silence is my best friend,
Silence, allows my brain to solve my daily dilemmas.
Silence, allows my soul to breathe easier.
Silence, provides with my best work.

Shhh...
Please don't interrupt.
Once the silence is broken.
You can never duplicate the golden splendor it delivered.

Ah, I love to let the silence embrace my body.
Only silence can engulf my spirit.
Ring, ring, ring... knock, knock,knock... Tracy, Tracy, Tracy...
My friend *silence* starts to fade away into his shell, as the sounds of life
enter our embrace!

Tracy-Betina Caldwell

Timothy Tyler Thomas Tinsel

Couldn't Remember How to Write With a Pencil

Timothy Tyler Thomas Tinsel
Couldn't remember how to write with a pencil
He tried using his fingers
Even his toes
And why he did that
Nobody knows
He tried writing with one end
Then the other
But all he could make was a sigh
"Oh Brother!"
He decided to shave the colored part off
But got a splinter in his thumb
So he dipped it in ink, tried writing like that
But it dried before he was done
Soon he had a sudden thought
And began to pitch a fit
I went through this, and no one told me
That I forgot to sharpen it!

Kimberly R. Mueller

It's Greedy The Cat

Pouncing on a bit of lint, it throws its *"victim"* into the air.
Tiring of this game, she stops to gracefully lick
her hair, most carefully lick her hair.
Pretty kitty, are you a mamma kitty? Time will tell.
Very fluffy cat, with your fur so soft and fat, you wear your colors
very well. With a white bib, and mask, and paws encased in little
snowy booties, you can't help but naturally be a beauty.
Your eyes of wide yellow-green translucently calm as ice;
yet off on a whimsy they go in a flash at the least change of scene.
Grey ears that stay perked, ever alert to adventure
that's Greedy, our cat. Alert to adventure like the racy stripes
that line you head to tail-stripes of grey against
stripes of dark. You wear your colors well.
Suddenly, she's turning to jump on a fellow cat. How
lively their game of wrestling! How delighted they are in pestering
each one the other in their game of rollicking with
both tails waving to and fro while upside down; both
paws held to the others' neck.
Such things are sure to be as these,
unless the cat is diseased. That's Greedy our cat.

Darlene S. Flores

Love?

What is Love?
Who the hell knows?
Can I look it up?
"a deep and tender feeling of affection or attachment
or devotion to a person or persons" *
What the hell does that mean?
Do I have it?
Does anybody have it?
How do I know?
How do I know if I'm in Love?
Love!
Ahhh LOVE!
How do I find it?
Where does it go?
How do I Know?
Tell me! Tell me!
I want to know!
What is Love?

*David B. Guralnik, ed., Webster's New World Dictionary, Second
College Edition (New York: Prentice-Hall, 1983) love.*

Craig Clark

The Hateful Bind

Love excuses all sin,
Symbiotic proportions take shape when I see his eyes,
Beautiful, powerful eyes, waiting to be
Emasculated by my deviousness.
Careful plans forming,
Shifting, breathing
Real life expectations, as much is done in love's name.

I await as he makes his decision,
Of life-long magnitude and proportion.

Alas, he needs time, time, time.

My sin forgotten, my love overridden
By the powerful entity who meets out the punishments,
Who determines the moment it is to happen.
A moment for which I cannot wait.
But when all is lost, the veneer of evil in sin
Is slowly replaced by the veneer of holiness in love
Enmeshed in one hateful bind.

Michelle Phipps

Dream Reason

Reach,		catch a dream,
	Push	into dream reality
	Be	entwined, embodied, enveloped
	Follow	the plot unfolding
		the play as rehearsed,
	Ride	electric currents, bubbles of energy,
		The paths of your mind's eyes
Imagine		you become the dream
	Push	aside the formulas past the cue cards
	Be	cunning, crazy, creative
	Examine	new pathways, energize new circuits
		Change the rules
Imagine		the dream becomes you
		Ultimate You,
		Enlarging, empowering, entering YOU
		You become Ultimate You
		dream becomes reality, reality becomes dream
	Push	yourself to be who you
		should be, could be, **will be** ?

Wm. D. Ellis

mitigated endearment

were i to drink my blackened caffeine at home
necessity would disallow causality -
sheeped to a place to drink
(social)
and i drive fast for my mother.

pagan rituals tell of snow
wind writes dialogue all its own
i need no place but home
yet fail in the modest attempt of procuring creativity

soo i drive fast for my mother.

knock on the door to escape
wait up late night
for sounds that should have been hours before
but i have a retarded pronunciation of time

still i drive fast for my mother.

graciously glorified for .90 a cup
meticulous in layout
baked and ground in designation
i migrate between the many

and **SHIT** on the way

(a-social)
therefore i drive fast for my mother.

Peter J. Dahlstrand

The Family At Christmas Time;

so far and yet so near

Many times throughout the year but especially at
Christmas time these thoughts appear.

How far apart we all are and yet so very near.

The family, a haven for us all—a cherished place in our
hearts for those we hold dear.

The memories of our youth all brought into view
and the happy Christmas gatherings we all knew.

The happy times, the loving times, the sad times,
the hello times, the good-bye times, the family times;
the Christmas times.

Christmas is a special time to share the love we have
for all the family and yes, with everyone!

It is our resolve this Christmas Season to say a silent
prayer to the "Little One" in thanksgiving and with a
heartfelt prayer; that we will always have our family
near to us, no matter how near or far.

God Bless us every one....Merry Christmas!

Carl & Irene Tinebra

Whatif?

Whatif nobody cares?
Whatif there's a day I'll be attacked by bears?
Whatif I'm stung by a bee?
Whatif I go blind and can't see?
Whatif they've called me dumb in school?
Whatif my teachers all are cruel?

Whatif my dog eats my homework?
Whatif I'm to suddenly go berserk?
Whatif I miss the bus to school?
Whatif they've added a NO SPORTS rule?
Whatif nobody gives back things they borrow?
Whatif there's no tomorrow?

Whatif my mother feeds me peas?
Whatif I weren't allowed to sneeze?
Whatif my money is all spent?
Whatif they've elected Hillary as president?

Kristofor R. Sauer

Living the Past

My life is filled with hopes,
As well as fears.
About the haunting past and future.
And the moment of our time,
Now.
Our lives are living our parent's, parent's mistakes.
The mistakes on the precious earth we live in,
On, and about.
They didn't know.
We look at what they were and are today,
And laugh at their naiveté.
How our world has changed,
Just from day to day.

Erika Jordan

The Artist

His brush stroked that canvas,
the most vivid colors He did use,
with fiery reds and brilliant oranges
and all of the golden hues.
This artist was not inspired
for He does this every fall,
to show a change in the season,
a true wonder to us all.

Ginger Wolfe

Atonement

Forsaken and weary in these Golden Years;
Beseeching a blasé world to allay the fears,
As brazen betrayals merge in a vale of tears.
Bowed down, by this heavy cross, as twilight nears.

Naught heeding the forewarnings from the start;
Blithely pursuing the rainbows of a smitten heart.
An interlude, 'ere the sun its brilliance loses;
Fading are halcyon "the days of wine and roses."

Deceptions and misgivings cloud the storm-laden air.
Solemn vows, dreams and promises vanquished there.
The infinite furloughs of sojourning apart
Channeled yet deeper chasms in a wounded heart.

Flagrant 'amours' churned a seething froth of distrust;
Spurning an always faithful heart and embracing lust.
Reality dawns—to none, would he ever be true!
Alone, ascends the soul to you beckoning blue.

The ominous clouds engulfing the sky above,
Deluge the sodden myth of an enduring love.
Whence, a glimmer of atonement the heavens rend—
Behold! A glorious rainbow beyond the bend!

Lillian Blazek

On Discovering the Poetry of Dresbach

A cold day of strife put me in the mood
For a place of beauty and quietude —
A short drive perhaps, I'd no time for more.
What fortune to have found this old book store.

In a case marked 'Poetry - Bottom Shelf'
I sought verse to lift me out of myself.
Did you once wander by this restful place
To show your heart to a more quiet pace?

Perhaps once, on this very spot you paused
To see desert blooms describe nature's laws.
The wild cactus blooms are no longer here,
Yet it seems as ever, beauty is near.

Forms come and go. The essential remains;
Writing born of frost on different panes,
Wild flowers - be they petals or pages,
Awaiting discovery; one through ages.

Seán McGill

Late Spring Snows

Birches are bending tonight, groaning, cracking under a
mantle of white that caught new leaves in their coming out
to lay in deadly weight where a week before the feathery
symmetric flakes might well have sifted between the branches,
blanketed upon a foot of snow fallen since autumn's
crown of gold and red fluttered to the grass below
in those last days of October warmth.

Yet, like the proverbial spirit
yearning to be free, refusing to bow
forever beneath the weight of years
that threatens with its curvéd scythe
to silence the impassioned, rhythmic beat,
the birches will again reach upward
toward the light, again restirring,
renewing in deep slow motion, new life,
when the goldfinch and the chicadee
return, as they have since the beginning
of bending birches, yearly migrations
and the crushing weight
of late spring snows.

Daniel William O'Connor

Marked Deck

Feelings of love, of hate, of fear,
Shuffled as one would a deck of cards.
Each fragile layer stacked upon another:
One flat, one upright, one flat again,
Built into a very fragile house that
Breathing hard will fell quite easily.
So tenuous the balance of the structure
Is, that I have even tried with glue
To cement conflicting parts together,
And lock up self, safe and tight inside;
Then I can face my highfalutin friends
Without the nauseous, sinking feeling
Haunting me at every moment of the day
That I will end up breaking down,
Collapsing from the inside out,
As if I were that toppled game of chance,
And spilling all my deck of feelings
On the table like some tarot reading
For the world to see my shaky future
From a past transparent to the eye.

Nyuka Anaïs Laurent

The Lone Star

I saw one star in the sky tonight
It was shining just for me
I know it was sent from heaven
For its twinkle was heavenly

I thought that I might make a wish
Hoping for a dream to come true
But decided to admire its beauty
And its special presence too

For it reminded me of a story
Told so long ago
About a savior named Jesus Christ
Someone I've come to know

I thanked God for this gift of light
That brightened up the dark sky
A smile was slow in coming
As my heart began to fly

When I dropped my head to think
The star was soon to disappear — now, it's gone
But my memory of its presence
Shall remain with me throughout the years

Shuntrela Rogers

A Mother's Rainbow

Many colors does my rainbow hold
There's blue and green and even gold
Colors come from many places
But mine are in my children's faces

My children range from big to small
But in my heart I love them all
I love to watch them through the day
And hear the many things they say

Like, mommy Bubby took my book
Or all day long it's "mommy look"
From mommy can I have some juice
To mom I think my tooth is loose

While the small one's pants are likely wet
The big one's French she just can't get
Another's hungry for a snack
It's "TIME" I often find I lack

A rainbow God put in the sky
His promise we would all stay dry
But the rainbow God has given me
Is one that only I can see

Beth Reynolds

To You I Am Nothing

Just a speck on the face of society
Just an insignificant nothing
That your full life doesn't need, or want
But to me you are everything
Your mind intrigues me
Your thoughts penetrate me
Your soul intoxicates me
I want to reach into your body
And pull your memories out
I want to pull them apart and
Remember them like you did
I want to evaluate them to
Understand why that cold shield covers
Your heart
I want to slip
Inside your body and observe as you do
Think what you think
Know what you know
Feel what you feel

Lys Yvette Tourjee

Words

Most come from our emotions
    We throw to the dust,
In all shapes and meanings we
    Talk, talk, talk...
I hear them for a moment and
    Then they're gone!
I can't always grasp each one.
    Some are really keepers,
Some are none, some caress me,
    Some are cold, some warm.
Some I write, some I store, others
    Are just lost in time.
They approach me from others and
    Get mixed up with mine.

Jeanette Holder

After Images

He smiled and joked every time I met him - everything seemed fine.
I wonder if he knew how precious he was to us - or at least to our illusions.
    The rabbit lay writhing in the middle of the road, just hit by the car I'd passed.
    I stopped, not knowing how to help - thank God I hadn't heard it scream.
He bought the gun on Sunday - alone.
    I yelled to scare it away from oncoming cars.
    I writhed in inexorable pain up to the curb, alone in its mute suffering.
    If only I could help it die quickly, but I didn't know how.
Monday, Tuesday he worked, he smiled, he joked with us again.
He said he looked forward to his upcoming vacation - he was content.
    I couldn't stop the rabbit's pain - I got in my car and drove away.
Tuesday he worked, he did his laundry, he cleaned his apartment.
The comforting pleasure of acts performed for the last time.
The poignant touch and feel of things to be nevermore, like a mother's last remembered caress.
    But I had to try to help the rabbit - I drove back
    To see a crow descended upon the not-yet-dead body - its prayed-for relief.
He picked up the gun after work - alone.
    Driving away, I looked back to be sure the crow hadn't been scared off by my car.
Amid the riot of spring flowers, the light dawned on this crisp spring day.
To the sound of a bullet felt, but heard by no one.

    Jeannette Eichholz

Father Time

Day by day, night by night, my youth was vanishing,
though I was lofty, soaring the clouds.
Never close to reflection, my feet seldom touched the ground.
I wish I'd turned around, I would have seen him in pursuit.

Watching my desires fade, year after year,
I was bound and determined, they'd never disappear.
but the years of earth did pass beneath my feet,
I saw nothing and felt little, life was too fast, I was a fury.

Invisibly at war with a creature, as nameless, as he was faceless,
a thing without shape. He was the shadow, moving in and out of view.
Spied him once at my father's door, frightening, but easy to ignore.

He's rumbled about my entire life, picking, choosing carefully his fight.
With pick and chisel squarely in hand, he works as slow as tomorrow,
at times next year. A constant bloodletting, adding to my sorrow.

Under preconceived plan, was every moment of my life,
chased in open ground, stalked in woods deep,
powerless to stop him, nothing precious to keep,
so it is this youth I surrender as my key,
I never dreamed father time could catch me.

    Émile Michael Harry

Rita, the Love of My Life!

This poem is dedicated to Rita, the love of my life!
She is the kind of woman that I want to have as my wife.
When I was lost or strayed too far off the path, she was there to enlighten.
She always gave freely without judging me by her own standards when
She was not emotionally attached to the subject. Otherwise, she often
kept her views inside, allowing the freedom needed for my feelings to guide
My actions, for that was the only way to know what were my true intentions.
She kept it all hidden deep within, without an angry word, without any mention,
Meanwhile giving all of her patience with plenty of time for me to notice and redeem.
But, my head was in a different place and I did not catch on or understand; it seems
That I was like many men, too busy doing things my way to notice her pain.
Too busy to know that I was rejecting her even while her love, I tried to maintain.
Too blind to notice how my decisions, my actions and my idiosyncrasies manifested,
Never realizing that my behavior shut down her spontaneity as it surely limited
Her open display of affection and her eagerness to blossom with me at her center.
I must have inadvertently closed the door to my emotions and she could not enter.
She could not flourish that way, so, she reluctantly cut the stem one Fall day.
Yet, all the while, I know I loved her dearly and I have locked her essence in my heart
And in my mind. I know she will always be the love of my life. We will never be apart.
For I still think about Rita often and want her in my arms forever. The love of my life!
I will always love Rita!

    Billie Parrish

Freedom

I never knew how free I was,
until they put me in these places,
or how many people there were
until I saw all these faces.
I realize life isn't all it seems-
until you want or fear.

People scare you,
People dare you,
But most of all-
People care about you.

You're not alone or by yourself
no matter what you think.
Maybe some day you'll
realize this just by taking a wink.
So, if you feel that you're alone,
just cause you're not at home,
do me a favor and think....
Think about this poem.

    Susan Quigley

A Tree for Nicky

I planted this tree for you to see
some day when you grow old,
in hopes that you will realize
the bliss that you bestowed.
Growing up you will be
as mighty as this tree
in body, mind and soul.
So here my son,
a gift for you,
our journey has just begun.

    Sandi Sites

Joy Ride At Sunset

In the calm of evening
On a quiet harbour bay,
Five little sea birds paddle
   silently into
Sunset's fading flame —
Alone they ride on
   golden glowing ripples,
Into night's shimmering
   vespered moments,
Now amethyst, now gray —
Five little sea bird silhouettes
   glide serenely by,
Into night's velvet darkness
They suddenly disappear;
They're gone in a magic instant,
Gone with the sunset!

    June Allegra Elliott

Autumn Leaves

Autumn leaves are all different colors
on every treetop up above us

falling on the cold hard ground
falling falling earthward bound

cluttering up gutters and spouts
hearing lots of cheerful shouts

piles of leaves here and there
children playing everywhere

sounds of rakes is all you hear
and no more children's happy jeer

    Jason Guinn

Our Strength

As we go down life's rocky road,
Struggling beneath this worldly load,
Put your trust in the Savior, God's only son,
That your race on earth, may be safely run.
So your step never falters, your eye it be clear,
On that goal set, by your savior, so dear.
As we run in the race, keep always in mind,
The Lord is beside us, not lagging behind.
When life slows us down, with just a touch
He renews the strength, that's needed so much.
Fills our bucket of love, up to the rim,
That our caring for others, never grows dim.
Our good deeds to others, a true gift from Him,
Makes their cup also, overflowing the brim.
Frank E. Reeher

Identity

I am the colt
    struggling on my delicate new legs.

I am the duckling
    swimming in a beautiful pond, yet not flying.

I am the joey
    awed by glimpses of the world
    -from my mother's pouch.

I am the newly hatched sea turtle
    trying to reach the security of the sea.

I am the monarch butterfly
    flying toward a destination of which I know nothing.

I am the young bird
    thrown from my nest too early.

I am the kitten
    who has not yet learned to kill.

I am the child
    brought up in a world of chaos and unknowns.
    Elizabeth Clay

Face The Sun

Don't hunt after trouble, but look for
    success,
You'll find what you look for, don't look
    for distress.
If you see but your shadow, remember, I
    pray,
That the sun is still shining, but you're
    in the way.
Don't grumble, don't bluster, don't dream
    and don't shirk,
Don't think of your worries, the work will be
    done,
No man sees his shadow who faces the sun.
    Charley Carr

A Step in the Sand

As each step leaves its mark in the sand,
The water comes to take it away.
Each step has become a memory,
A memory etched forever in three minds.

We are each a step in the sand,
Special and unique in our own way.
Yet we stay only as long as He wants us to,
Then the wave comes to take us away . . .

Just like a step in the sand.
    Glen K. McGraw Jr.

Such A Lady As She

Let us not forget
Such a lady as she
The courageous first lady,
Mrs. Jacqueline Kennedy.

All over the world,
Women emulated her poise, style, and smile.
They too, wanted to see, A Lady such as she,
First lady, Mrs. Jacqueline Kennedy.

The year nineteen sixty-three
With two children, a widow she be
Such a lady as she
Of the late President, John F. Kennedy.

Later in life she became the wife
Of Mr. Aristotle Onassis.
She gave us a smile, and set the style
By wearing large frame sunglasses.

Now at rest is the Lady Such as She,
Left with us much history.
We'll never forget the Kennedy name
As they rest by the eternal flame.
    Arrayyel Radoll

The Morality/Insanity Cocktail

Human tragedies surround us all; world wide,
Such as small wars, starvation, and social decline.
Crime is rampant throughout many nations
As is drug use, and sales of frightening dimensions.
Illegal guns sold to irresponsible juveniles
By unscrupulous dealers with greed as their bibles.

Apparently there are those seeking a "meaning" to their lives
Who now seek causes using "tunnel vision" as a guide.
A fetus is medically aborted safely and legally,
Now mix in "murder" of doctors as a moral incredulity.
Solving socio-economic problems throughout our world
Cannot even be considered as we put "them" all in jail.

Some people go to bars for a drink to un-wind
While others go home to a cocktail, that's fine!
But the mix is healthy and not mis-guided
As they read and listen and perhaps pray for guidance.
With so much in chaos in our world today
Why mix morality with insanity as the course of the day.
    Anthony Torres

Untitled

I am like the wind.
    Supple and fresh,
interweaving through the virgin flowers.
    Deliberate and heated,
taunting sultry bodies under the flaming sun.
I am like the wind.
    Bold and crisp,
arousing the air before I slumber.
    Icy and bleak,
chilling the earth to her very core.
    Raging and savage,
consuming all in my way.
    Then tranquil and sedate - waiting.
I am like the wind.
    Unsettled and never predictable,
blowing everywhere, but nowhere at all.
    Jennifer A. Boatwright

Camelot Lady

Camelot Lady, dining and entertaining kings,
  Surrounded by the riches that this life brings,
Grace, and such charm, shone from your face,
  As you dressed for the ball in satins and lace.

Camelot Lady, your eyes held a story,
  For the price that you paid for your fame and glory.
Troubles and sorrows came your way too,
  All the money of this world could not buy happiness
  for you.

Camelot Lady, are you entertaining Jesus, our King?
  Have you seen the peace and riches that Heaven can
  bring?
Did you accept Jesus as your Savior and Lord?
  Was He the one you loved and adored?

Camelot Lady, have you no more sickness or pain?
  Are you walking with loved ones and smiling again?

Annette Mollura

What You Mean To Me

Take away the clouds from the skies up above
Take away the rays from a sun that's filled with love
Take away the sunsets o'er the oceans so blue
That's the way my life would be if I were without you.

You have brought meaning into this life of mine
And like the rays from the sun you make days shine
All of the sunset's o'er the oceans so blue
They lack the beauty dear I have found in you.

For you are always near me
To comfort me and give me love
I'd never find more peace of mind
In the heavens up above.

Say you'll never leave me, here all alone
Say you'll share my life and I will make for you a home
And I will make you happy and keep the tears away
By giving you my love dear, now, and till my dying day.

David E. Zongker

My Parents

My parents' love is like a golden wall
surrounding me protecting me from harm...
My parents' comfort is like a soft cloud
wrapped around me floating me through
hard times...
My parents' forgiveness is like an unending
river...
My parents' help is like a beautiful pass
through a hot desert that is not like a desert
at all but more like an oasis...
My parents' support is like a beautiful
waterfall holding me...
My parents' proud eyes are like stars shining
down on me...
The kind words my parents whisper are like
a brook of clear, clam, fresh water...
My parents' open arms are like a mother cat
cuddling her young...
But most importantly my parents will love
me no matter what.

Dana Forde

Untitled

The power will completely
Take control of your mind
leaving the normal world and reality behind.
It's there, you need it
just like it needs you,
It's alive and surrounds you
There's nothing you can do!
You can run, but you can't hide
cause the power has got you
And it comes from inside.
It has harbored and festered
In the depths of your soul
You're just a victim in its control.
The power pounds
like the beat of your heart
There's no escaping now
Or you'll fall apart.
The power imbeds itself that you knew,
But you better believe in it
'Cause now it's in you!

Dee Ann Lynn Yocum

Thoughts on New York at Night

Atop the Empire State, stood I
Suspended between earth and sky.
Below, a man made world stretched far.
Above, God's universe, Sky, Moon, and Star.

That man made monster, which below I'd found,
Build on that rocky isle there, water bound,
Seemed lifting up its mighty arms to God.
From depths where feet of millions trod.

Its arteries stretched distant through the night.
Flowing along with ceaseless, nervous light.
Its mighty bowel agrumble deep within,
It swallowed and belched forth a human dim.

That mighty, noisy, brilliant, moving sight
Contrasted above the calm, still, brilliant night.
Below, all seemed a slave; above all free,
I stopped to ponder long, its destiny.

Catherine A. Reinheimer

Blossom Of Time

Cherish the blossom of the day,
take life in just that way.
Soak up the fragrance be it weak or strong,
for tomorrow the blossom may be gone,
Take away without rhythm or reason,
never to return or have a new season.
The garden of life is hard to endure
with each step you take it's very unsure,
but cherish them, remember them and keep them in you heart
for tomorrow they could be torn apart.
Scattered about in the wind's of time,
just memories and dreams of day's gone by;
Never to forget the pain and sorrow,
it's part of the past now look forward to your tomorrows.
Fill them with laughter, sunshine and rain
for we know you will never forget the pain.

Debbie Bolton

591

Atonement

Alone at last, so let it be.
Take off that mask called identity.
Bare feet caressed in warm sand,
I walk by the sea, seeking to understand.
Uninvited sea gulls join in the stroll,
A teardrop falls, but cleanses my soul.
The tide rolls in, waves lap at the shore.
Meditation flows freely as never before,
Turning events have hammered by senses,
blurring my vision and building fences.
Shattered dreams must now be reckoned.
Idols have fallen and turned to ashes.
Love has died while my world crashes.
Life is painful, death unspeakable.
Love is a condition and quite unbelievable.
A necessary affliction, but never fatal.

Diane L. Grabske

A Wife's Prayer

Dear Lord I pray look down from above
Take special care of the one I love.
Help him to see and help him to know
My love for him will only grow.
While he is so far away -
Please God take care of him day after day.
Be with him and help him through each task he must perform.
And hold him always in your strong arms.
While we are so far apart. Keep me always in his heart.
Give him strength to look to Thee. And help him then to come to me.
For I know God, you should always come first,
for knowledge of you we all should thirst.
But please Dear Lord when his day is through
After he has talked to you.
Please let him think of me - his wife
and know that he's the center of my life.

As he goes to sleep each night.
Let him know in my thoughts he'll be held tight.
And till you bring him home to me.
Help both of us to look to thee.

Jan Cox

Ephraim

O Ephraim, my dear son, where art thou?
Taken you were from mine own, my good land;
The land that I gave thee, that which I vow
To Abr'ham, thy father, whose God I am.

Ephraim, you I watched, for you are mine;
Obey and be faithful, to me be true.
You forgot me; my love you did decline.
So you sang to strange Gods; them you pursued.

Yet, Ephraim, I will not forget thee,
E'en though banished were you from Palestine;
Made a slave wretched, a poor refugee
In an evil land with idols enshrined.

I spread thee, Ephraim, o'er the far west
To hide thee in a good, and pleasant land
That flows with honey and milk, this world's best;
And make of thee a people, great and grand.

I know thee, O Ephraim, my dear love,
My hand is held o'er thee, you are my own.
I'll restore thee to the tents of Jacob
In the latter days, and will bring thee home.

Edward J. Sleger Jr.

"The Teacher"

Fly a kite, catch a wave,
teach a child to be brave.
Feet in sand, sky so blue,
These are things that remind me of you.

Show us love, we learn of kindness,
warmth, and friendship, colored blindness.
Memories of a heart so true,
These are things that remind me of you.

Gift of laughter, gift of life,
Gift of kindness, gift of sight.
Frown on you face, not even a few,
These are the things, that made us love you.

Demetria Boulageris-Mercado

I'm Going Sailin'

I'm going sailin'! I'm going sailin'!
Testify! My, oh my! I'm going sailin'.

I'm going alone.
I'll call you on the phone!
'Cuz I'm going sailin'.

Jump in a hole, and take your fishing pole!
I'm going sailin'.

I love the wind.
I love the sea.
I love sea gulls.
Hurrah! Whoopie!

There's no one in sight
When the time's just right
Mom, I'll be home
when it comes to be night.
But right now, I'm doing my deeds —
Me and my boat will race at top speed!
I'm going sailin'!!

Brandon A. Biggs

Father Andy Kitzenberger

He was more Friar Tuck
Than the great Melchizedek,
And he wore his collar unbuttoned
Because it was too tight;
And when his voice laughed, which was often,
The rest of his body laughed within him.

But his laughter ceased
With his heart
(And rarely returned, although the latter did)
And he found himself in a chair,
Decorated with tubes of man-made life;
And it was a different man that sat solemnly there,
With just a hint of a resigned smile
Above a buttoned-up collar that fit loosely.

Connie Weber

My Prayer For You

I'll keep you in my prayers, and speak your name to God each day,
To ask Him to ease your troubles and protect you on life's way.

I'll plea that you stay healthy, that all your problems cease,
That you receive good fortune and your mind is put at peace.

I'll ask for your successes in everything you do
And for many friends to give love and happiness to you.

I'll keep you in my prayers, for, in my life, you play a big part.
So, I'll put you in God's hands, but, I'll keep you in my heart.

Emily M. Harper Cattuna

Tears Of Remembrance

A sadder day I've never known
Than to say goodbye to my buddy and friend;
Life was too cruel for you to endure,
But I know that you're safe in God's loving embrace.
And soon before I know it's time,
We will in eternity unite once more;
In that great beyond where we're whole again,
More perfect than this life by far.
Where we will relive the good times we shared,
Yet the pain of this life is no more.
Time will be swift 'til the day that we meet,
I await with remembrance, heartfelt tears, smiles of joy.
So goodbye my friend — save a place for me,
Your memory will live forever in my heart.

Jane L. Blackburn

Let Me Be Me

You're never going to be any closer to me
Than where you are right now.
And you're never going to find the way to my mind.
You wouldn't like it anyhow.
For can't you see I've got to be me,
Living under no man's authority?
And I know too that you've got to be you.
My life's with good people too.

It's not my way and I'm not gonna say
That you're like all the rest.
"Cause you're different too
It's the one thing that you
And I know is for the best.
I like my stand and I don't need a man
Just good friends will do
So be what you'll be, but don't pressure me.
I need good people like you.

Jill G. Pounders

Certainty Amongst Uncertainty

I find no comfort in the knowing I'm not alone
That alas there are countless albeit to me unknown
Wretched hearts adrift ever searching for home, heavenly home
I find no peace in this tragic truth that trials strengthen
Or 'tis inevitable that night will continually lengthen
Before the dawning light of love rises to challenge its apprehensive
     tension
So, with guarded pessimism I reluctantly admit my silent fears
While with anticipated optimism I pray, that unmasked their end be
     near
Still, it's the journey between this realization and their impending
     end
In which the heart welcomes the elation of finding perhaps that one
     friend
Who though may not always be able those cuts to mend
Will always be one upon whom the heart and soul depends
So with sweet, though overdue, affirmation, I proclaim you are my
     heart
Who amongst this chaotic fray rekindles the lost loving art

Jeffrey L. Schult

Phillip

Phillip is a young boy, who stands by the gate,
waiting for his friends to go by, on a certain date.
Phillip is a young boy, who walks around the lake,
watching for the sun rise, before the sun may wake.
Phillip is a young boy who runs down the lane,
running and running faster, just to keep sane.
Phillip is a young boy, dreaming all the day,
watching as the clouds may form in a million different ways.
Phillip is a young boy.

Brian Johnson

Diversified Musing

Thoughts are based on what we knew
that came then from where we grew.
Sexism, racism and culture shock
were never mentioned on our block.
We were safe and happy in our place,
we didn't need another race.

Then, too soon, we were adults
and recognized all others' faults.
Our lives were filled with total strangers
oh, how we knew the many dangers.
A crook, a lout, a drunk, a thief,
and none could tell his true belief.

Then came the light, we took a stand,
we chanced to shake our neighbor's hand
The danger was only in our minds
and fear was not the tie that binds.
Understanding and care filled the bill,
and it really wasn't a bitter pill.

Glenn Cundiff

Can't They Hear Me?

That feeling I can't explain,
That cold-clammy touch,
The eery and scary, webby musty clutch.
As I walked up the hallway staring,
I noticed the light, and that music blaring.
That music! So unexplainable, so unreal,
It has no meaning, I can't grasp the feel.
My head was spinning, my eyes were blind,
What was happening? Was I losing my mind?
My eyes opened again, what were those noises?
Where was I...I heard strange voices.
They're louder now-I screamed "What happened to me?"
I hear a loud yet solemn voice say, "He's dead—
Overdosed on LSD."
But here I am...listen to me,
I tried to reach out, set me free-set me free!
Oh God, why aren't they listening, why aren't they near?
But I can't be dead...I'm here!!! I'm here!!!
As my own voice slowly faded, my eyes glazed over,
   ... My death certificate was dated.

Amy J. Meyrer

God Help Us

God help us if we fail to see the suffering and the pain,
That drunken drivers do inflict time and time again.

God help our law-makers understand just why, we need to
Change some stupid laws. How many more must die?

God help us when the courts decide on minor punishments,
To those drunk drivers, who cause major accidents.

God help us when their insurance companies who only, count the cost.
Care nothing for the victim's or their family's tragic loss.

God help us if we're blind and deaf, and fail to hear the cry,
Of mother's against drunk driver's who's children should not have
     died.

God help us in our fight against those who kill and maim. Let's
Get them off our highways, before they kill again.

We can not wait much longer, and this is very true.
Because the next victim could possibly be you...

Joseph Endrich

Tranquility

The high blue cliffs look over the salty waters
that fill the air with the sweet smell of
freedom.
The peach, salmon sun hovered by wispy
gray clouds is descending ever so slowly.
Sea gulls are cawing at the rays through
the clouds made by this sun and sky.
While dipping beneath farther mountains
the darkness begins to fill this world with tiny sparkles,
And holding only half the moon
as the other glows a bright
white.
A swift breeze laps over the ocean
rushing the waters toward the beach
and rocks below.
Now the creatures in the sky made by
star connections are out watching over
the ocean like guards
As the night gathers, lovers sleep.

Dyan Spain

Untitled

Sing me a song 'O Father
That fills your heart with sorrow
Yet is peaceful serene
Like rocking a hysterical child
To calm her convulsing breath
Hush..... Feel the rush of Poppa's warmth inside you

Write me a song 'O Father
That tells me how to live
Before the days of family
When the red-tail frolicked in your mind
Playing dance-tag with the sun
Feeling the lake to caress its mirrored winglets

Sing me a song 'O Father
That lets me love you
Yet protects me from
Enough to give me back my childhood and you

Remember the silky feeling of silt between your toes?
The rain?
Your breath with mine as we dreamed on the couch

Charlene Jacobs

Softly He Sleeps

Softly he sleeps and I re-live the Day
That he touched my soul when he touched my hand -
Showing me places through his mind's eye:
A fantastic voyage on an 80-foot schooner
And a special, private spot in the Islands.

His Smile - as bright as the sun when it rises
Radiates freedom, happiness and love of life.
He listens intently and speaks without talking
Of acceptance, sharing and unconditional love.

Softly he sleeps and I re-live the Night when two became one -
The warm glow of a candle and music that moved me.
He lifted and filled me with passion like fire...
Intense, burning, all-consuming desire.

His Eyes - as blue as the sky and the sea
Delve deep through my heart and gently caress me -
Wanting me, needing me, holding me, loving me.

Softly he sleeps and I re-live the Moment
I knew I could spend the rest of my life
Touching him, holding him, loving him Forever.
I will never forget this feeling.

Cristen L. Emley

My Christmas Prayer

The Lord said that He'd never leave us,
That He'd come to us in many ways.
I never knew how true this was,
Until this "Special Christmas Day."
How can one count all that is dear,
That comes to us, in just one year?
He brought us through rough times,
He gave us our health.
Through our love for each other,
We have lots of wealth.
I'd like to take this time to say
To say "Thank You, Lord," for this special day.
My children are all here, and my husband so dear
And my family and friends, to share Christmas Cheer,
Yes, You said You'd never leave us,
And You "have" come in many ways
I'm glad You've come to join us,
On this "Special Christmas Day."

Johannah M. Johnson

No Answers

The end justifies the means,
that is a lie beyond all that is seen
babies dying,
holding tight to their mother's breasts,
while a bomb of devastation is being put to the test

Vietnam, a land of the dead
nothing living,
nothing to tread
areas all around, where trees used to be
here and there,
exactly where, don't ask me

The world takes pride in death
pride in destruction,
this place of so called love, peace and harmony
that in reality, is a land of corruption

You can ask why
maybe there's an answer,
but for now, what needs to be solved,
is the cure for all the ailments,
that are presently unanswered.

Cynthia A. Green

Perfect Vision Zero

Our human minds engage themselves so much with what we see
That many times we miss the joy of virtuality.

Such virtue here involves a sense beyond the five we know,
A sense beyond the physical, but one that steals the show.

Our perfect vision cannot see the love that dwells within
Some other soul and shines on us as if to make us kin.

A kindness we can never see is deep within the soul
But what a joy it is to feel when pressing toward our goal.

Our sight can never see a truth that's hidden in the mind
Of anyone we know who only seeks the truth to find.

The physical can never see the essence of our life,
For kindness, love and truth are spirit-things, without the strife.

Our sight and hearing touch and smell detect no spirit-things.
Yet spirit-things provide escape and give our body wings.

Our perfect sight is zero help in righteousness and love,
While spirit-things revitalize and lift us up above.

Herbert Badger

Our Sympathy

I don't know how to say it, but somehow it seems to me
that maybe we are stationed where God wanted us to be;
That little place we're filling is the reason for our birth,
and just to do the work we do, He put us here on earth.

If God had wanted otherwise, I reckon He'd have made
each one a little different, of a worse or better grade,
and since God knows and understands all things
of land and sea, I think He has placed us here
just where He wanted us to be.

So when our work is ended and He calls to us to come,
we answer very readily
His call we cannot scorn
for it may be the reason God allowed us to be born.

Faye L. Ricci

Ode To Fredric

A heart frozen in time
That never dreamed, never felt, never cried
Unaware of its impending thaw
And to myself, forever lied.

Emblazoned now the new horizon
Slowly but surely the tides have turned
Where there was smoke there is now fire
A heart no longer branded "liar"...

For a being of light has entered my life
So strong, so pure, so free
From God he came, to God he'll go
Yet for now he lays with me.

They say He works in mysterious ways
His wonders to perform
But I know we were meant to be
From the moment we were born!

I Thank You Sweetheart.

Denise Archibald

Our Treasure Chest Of Desires

What a shame to keep under lock and key
That part of you that longs to be
Brought to the surface and in full view
Reveal that never been opened part of you

The part that longs to ski down an icy slope
Or ride as a queen on the winning float
To look just ravishing and be the belle of the ball
Or to sing in an opera at carnegie hall

Or perhaps to dive beneath the waters deep
Or over high hurdles be able to leap
To stalk through jungles behind big game on the run
Or to be out on the golf course making that hole in one

To be the writer of a popular tune
Or walk weightless as an astronaut upon the face of the moon
To ride like the wind in a steeple chase
Or to be the grand winner of the derby race

Yes, there is in all of us, I'd be willing to bet
That treasure chest of desires that has never been opened yet

Juanita L. Stollings

I'm sorry to hear,
  That someone so dear,
    Has passed upon their way.

The time they were here,
  Was especially dear,
    But forever, they could not stay.

And though they are gone,
  It is not all wrong,
    For they lived, many a good day.

I'm sure they would say,
  Were they here today,
    Please continue, to live, work and play.

So shed a few tears,
  Cast out all your fears,
    Have faith, in the Lord above.

For it is God's plan,
  To take this person,
    Their mission on Earth, is done.

D. B. Springer

The Garden Of Magic Dreams

Somewhere, I know that there is a mystical garden,
That takes away one's fears.

It brightens the faces of little children,
And takes away their tears.

A fountain lies in the center,
And roses climb the fences high.

I never could really believe,
That this garden would ever die.

Sparkling streams flow through the land to the valley above,
And lets you feel the garden's tender breeze of love.

Here you can feel as free as the wind, ...the wind beneath your wings,
While you listen to the sounds that the beautiful birds sing.

But, as I grow...,
The garden seems to fade away.

Still, somewhere in my heart, I know,
That this garden will always stay.

Jennifer Wilburn

"Remember When"

Mama made soap from lard and lye
That was in days gone by
She stored the eggs in water glass
But that was when I was just a lass.

The threshers went from farm to farm
For miles around neighbors sent a man
To help their friends and lend on arm
Ladies also come to help put on the meal
To a kid like me that was an exciting deal.

Things such as these you don't forget
Mom sending Sis to take a dollar to market
Ten pounds of pork chops she was to get
This, today, I wouldn't even try
That's why I like those days gone by.

When you could mail a letter for just 3
Now the cost is up to 32
Where in the world is it going to
The future for us seems mighty blue
Guess I'll just remember days gone by.
Sounds a bit like pie in the sky.

Barbara V. Rogers

Saturday Morning

Stab me with a knife and cut my throat as you would cut an apple
that was me Saturday morning after I saw my mother
saw my mother as I did and always do
but it was different this day I felt as I drove out of her drive
my tears could not release, the pain I felt was far too severe
knowing she was living but not alone inside
this intruder she had was destroying her I felt somehow
or was this my perception of this all?
Knowing I can't kill this demon within her
as much as I want to fight it myself
I want to grab it with my soul and hand and pull it out
but there it stays and stays this intruder will not leave
it grows and grows and spreads and spreads all through
my mothers flesh and bone
I see it and it sees me, it seems as though it's laughing somehow
my tears could not release, the pain I felt was far to severe
it was so ugly, when I looked at my mother she knew my pain
I held her hands but the emotions were not there
then she smiled at me and I think in this moment the intruder
was asleep.

Elaine Reyes Kunkleman

"Moments To Remember"

It was five whole years after dad and I were wed
That we worried and wondered what was ahead
Would we have any children that we could raise
And then we heard the doctor say in strong praise
Mr. and Mrs. Cerulli I'm pleased to announce
You have a bundle on the way to cherish and bounce.

We counted ten little fingers and ten little toes
And we could see our daughter had eyes and a nose
You had so much hair we could tie it with a bow
And the face of an angel and we loved you so.

You grew through the stages parents go through with pride
We loved every moment you were by our side
And now you're a mother with children of your own
And you know what joy you brought to your parents alone

You're forty years old now a new plateau of your life
Enjoy it and live it without any strife.
Your family all love you and wish you the best
You're a wonderful daughter, mother and sister
We've all been blest.

Jeanette Cerulli

Untitled

perfect imperfection
that's my self perception
the bird stops it's dance and gracefully flies
sight comes too late for my blind eyes

pure impurity
that's all I see in me
beautiful bird only seen high in trees
only caught traces of her scent in the breeze

secured insecurity
who would want to be with me
so very perfect the bird can climb and dive
hope of catching one keeps me alive

Jacob Frick

Dear Michael

They say when you least expect it, it comes silent as a dove
That's the way you and I tumbled into love

Just when we stopped looking and though it would never come
We felt the magic that is only felt by some

We didn't know we built a foundation that is strong
A foundation that may last a lifetime long

All I know is that I fell without knowing I took a step
And when I wasn't looking into my heart you crept

You were always very sweet and kind down to the core
And as I got to know you I needed you even more

And though I didn't want to I started to depend on you
I guess I loved you longer then even I knew

In you I see the person I've waited my whole life for
And I see how empty my life was before

I want to share my life with you as a lover and a friend
And continue on this circle with no beginning and no end

Christie E. Rogers

A Big Kiss, Maybe Two Or Three

One percent results, the rest just wishing
That's what happens, when one goes fishing

Dreaming and planning, most of the week
For those creatures, you actively seek

The rod of course, certainly must endure
Enabling you, that big catch for sure

Selecting the line, that must be right
Attaching the lure, and hook they might bite

In the event, one percent prevails
Return home, to tell "tall-fish-tales"

Should all your attempts, fail at fishing
Food on your table, you won't be dishing

Be sure to stop, at your favorite store
That offers every, fresh fish galore

Put the "catch", in your trusty old creel
Pretend your fortune, at the end of the reel

Tell your wife, the fishing was GREAT!
Look what we have, on our bountiful plate

Give her a big KISS, maybe two or three
There's always next week, to fish for thee

Clyde Wilson

Growing Old

Wrinkles and crinkles that line the face
That once was a vision of beauty and grace

Memories that come and go
Of people and faces I don't even know

Eyes that no longer behold the light
And ears that no longer hear in the night

Legs so wobbly and weak
They can hardly support my feet

Hair so thin and white as snow
Wonder where the years did go

Justin P. Skaggs

December

Here it comes. Right at the perfect time, right after dark.
The air is still and silent...nothing stirs.

First you smell it so distinct. Vivid, warm memories flash
through your mind.

Then you feel it. So subtle. But sure as anything, it's there.
It gives you a chill. Not a cold or terrified chill. But like
the chill you get when stepping from a wind swept porch into a
wonderful, cozy kitchen.

Still now...don't move...As loud as the silence, you can hear it.

You strain to listen. Like rain, only tiny. A light, soft,
frozen snow. The small silent tinkling of snow flakes chiming
against the windows, on the roof. Even in the grass. Some of
the magical music that winter brings.

By morning, the landscape comes alive with beauty that gives a
vision you can hear.

The world is blanketed with glittering crystals, sparkling in
the frosty sunlight.

Such beauty...such calm...exhilarating serenity. Breathless
wonder. A wonder that makes this life worth living.

David Stinson

Stallion

The wild is his home, his heart and his soul
The black night of which he is formed
Cannot hide the sparkle in his eyes

He is free

Wild horse in his stall
Kicks at the door
Hating the halter than binds him
He throws each captor in turn that dare mount him
For that's what a moment's freedom is worth
But again he is caught,
Tears in his eyes

He is Chained

One morning dreams come true
Door open, he leaps for the wild
Pursued up to the dead man's cliff
A choice between life and death as it seems
Or perhaps between freedom and enslavement
With one look back, he leaps for his doom.
He is free

Elizabeth Walker

Twilight

Moments ago the lights were bright;
The brilliance ebbs away, and its soon twilight.
The day is gone,
The journey comes to an end;
It's time to rest,
There's no going round the bend.

I wished to go on forever.
This world I love;
To part with it - never!
My journey's I made, enthusiastically, to return;
The finale, it comes, and suddenly I see no turn.

This involuntary journey stills my mind.
Of those beauteous glimpses, could you remind?

Anup Pradhan

Ka-Wa-Nee

A cathedral of trees surrounded
The bonfire flames that licked the gentle night.
The tom-toms became her heart beat,
As the sacred dance began.

She made her own music,
Coming from bells, dangling from leather
Strips that hung around her neck.
Stepping...tinkling
Ka-wa-nee motioned the smoke to
Curl around her.

The Moon Dance began.
Drumbeats, stepping, chanting, tinkling,
Breathing in the smoke,
All beckoned her to the circle.
Oh, Mother Moon, guide me,
Let me be strong enough
Not to step into the false steps of others,
But let me step bravely,
Alone, if need be,
To find my own path.

Jackie Brown

Concord

Concord, where liberty was born! Concord, on a frosty april morn!
The British were coming down from boston bay
To sweep anything that would dare stand in their way.
But they didn't know a band of patriots blocked concord's wooden span,
Whose love of country made them the most valiant in the land.

Suddenly in the distance, echoing with a beat,
Reverberating in cadence came a thousand marching feet!
Our boy's dug in to take their stand in front of concord's stream,
To halt the foe from stamping out freedom's cherished dream.

As the redcoat's converged upon them a HUSKY voice rang out:
"Throw down your arms and run away, you ragged rebel louts,
Or we will write your epitaph and make this your final bout."
For his reply a shot rang out—"A shot heard round the world,"
And the battle for liberty was about to be unfurled.

The musket balls from the foreign guns at our lads did fly,
And many of that gallant group fell 'neath the blue new England sky.
Spurred on by the bravery shown in that bloody fight,
Many new Americans began to see the light.
And in the annals of history the books have this to say:
"We owe a debt of gratitude to those who fought and died that day."

Alvin Bachman

Ageless Children

Do we ever really get beyond adolescence?
The calendar keeps check on what ought and what is.
Maturity's illusion prevents not avoidable pain.
Who does the grown soul battle with most consistently?
A collection of mistakes each basket holds.
With enough room left to add the next flawless error.
Gratification, when do you move on
When desires change little over the years.
Adjusted youth, how old are you
If consummation is related to time and measured by experience.
Ever evolving foresight foreshadows forfeiture
To stagnation and then only a search
For truth, if its necessity is acknowledged.
But that search is a lonely voyage that requires
Knowing its need.

That period of life in which the child changes into the adult.
Is there actually enough time to grow?

Eric Houser

Forever... Just Around The Corner

Why so much pain?? It can't be that this is constant and never ending.
The change — the change has always been just around the corner.
It seems I've avoided, missed somehow — the corner just up ahead.
I know it must be there because I couldn't live with the knowledge
   that it isn't. Somewhere ahead — .....
Is it that I'm not really a part of any reality?
An entity that became, somehow, lost in this routine world where
   I can't see the routine, the schedule, the path, the reality??
Am I real? Or have I tried so hard for so long to be real and fit in
   That I have succeeded at fooling myself on a part-time basis?
   When, in reality, I don't belong here at all?
Whoops! I'm sorry sir. I think I got off at the wrong stop —
   When's the next bus? No more busses?? Trapped in the wrong mold!!
It's heavy and dark and ugly and it hurts.
   It's frightening and unsolvable and horrifyingly unknown...
And yet... it seems there must also be, somewhere within my mutated
   and deformed self-universe, ...an answer.
I have wandered the outer corridors so very long that I've lost my
   way back to that central place where the answer is.
       You know... that place... just around the corner...

Adria Skaggs

The Prairie

The long grass waves,
The clouds drift by,
A golden glow,
Lights the sky.

The scent in the air,
Of flowers so wild,
Drifts in the breeze,
Blowing so mild.

The landscape so great,
Is one of peace,
Of tranquility,
And of beauty so rare.

And standing out amongst the grass is a young girl,
A bouquet in her hands.
Her flowing dress flaps,
As her long, golden hair streaks the sky.

Her thoughts are of someone whose love,
Is like that of the open prairie.
Surrounding her, commencing her, and filling her,
With complete and utter content.

Crystal Goltz

Bittersweet

Through the trials of life, their love had died,
The couple, still evolving grew more apart.
For fear of loneliness, he swore, he'd never let her go.
Conjoined, a bound hell, together they stayed,
But living their lives, dangling, like a mobile.
A new love came for him, but her mask cracked,
So he returned, more changed, harsh and distant.

Then He appeared for her.
Just as she had dreamed he would be,
With his kind and gentle ways,
He held his closed hands out to her,
And when he opened them, they held nourishment,
From which she ate hungrily, and it was delicious.
She grew strong, and wrapped a cocoon around her heart,
To protect their love inside,
And there it grows and thrives, like an oak.
She is waiting, for her chance to break free,
All the while, every night she pleads,
"Dear Lord, let him be my destiny"!

Beverly Stanczyk

Solitary Solitude

Night approaches:
The darkness rolls in
Along with the sense of impending doom.
I am alone,

Together with my thoughts
However, I am not scared.
Everything I need and love I have with me;
I do not require anyone or anything else.

Everything is superfluous
And unreliable.
The people are fickle;
Sometimes friends, sometimes enemies.

I am my companion,
Content in solitary solitude.

Elizabeth S. Evans

"The Gargoyle: Guardian Of The Night"

The town is an empty barrel of fruitless night air.
The dim statue compelled for ten decades
by cold stone like a wretched hampering snare
is shaken by roaring renegades.

The creature of the dark is ready to sunder
rock shattered by the sound of thunder.
This stranger in a new age leaps from his stand.
Flapping his wings, he views perilous land.

The beast senses evil he must overpower
as he bids farewell to his tower.
Swooping down, his keen eyes detect the prey he must devour.
The young woman in danger was now safe.

The monster made the outlaw look like a living callow waif.
The mystic creature caught a fearful sight.
He was petrified by the morning bright light
but still is the Gargoyle: Guardian of the Night.

James Tieng

Horizons

Two cages stood side by side
The door to his, open wide.
The door to hers, closed, rusted shut.
"Go fly the world and like Noah's dove return to me."
Embraced by bonds of Love, he spread his wings.
Like Darius he did fly, like Icarus he did soar,
Held by his tether from the Sun,
Above the Aare, the Rhine, the Alpen Sees.
Hearing choruses of a cappella sing,
Soprano bells hung from sheep and goats,
Tenors, altos around cows' throats,
Occasional basses of sour notes
Clanging in atonal cacophony.
Too late, too high to hear the cuckoos' vesper calls
Resound from valley walls.
The snows had come to dust the Alpine slopes
When he returned to tell her all he saw
Beyond her cage's rusted door.

Alfred Owczarzak

Flowers

A flower has petals that shine like the sun.
They glitter and sparkle with a morning hum.
There up in the mountains and close to trees.
Since there so beautiful they sway with the breeze.
Then in the winter there covered with snow
and then spring brings flowers that glow.
They shine so pretty they shine so bright
if you listen close they sing people to sleep at night.

Christy Echols

The Ship

Once upon a time, a man had a dream.
The dream was about a ship.
A ship that all of his friends could sail away on.
    The ship was fashioned of all the craftsman
partaking of different tasks.
One to gather the wood for her hull,
one to seem the cloth sails, one
to build her rudder, and one to navigate
by the stars.
    His crew would be made of many
talents, and with these talents
combining his dream, would one day
become a reality, because he,
believes that if a crew sticks together,
they can lick the world and faith
will build ships.

Jeff B. Becerra

"Our Meme"

She's a very special lady,
The earth has been blessed-
To have known her, now to let her go,
That, my friends, is our test.

"Humble" would be an understatement,
But she's dignified as a queen,
She had her way of doing things the way she wanted-
But ever thoughtful, never mean.

Her sight was long since gone,
But her vision never left,
Telling us much about the future, and life-
In ways we will not forget.

We all love you, Meme
And you'll always be in our hearts,
Our lives you've touched and molded-
From this, we'll never depart.

But if you're wondering where she is-
She can now see EVERYTHING here today,
But she's also in heaven with angels;
Meme, save us a place, we'll be with you there someday.

Becky Murdoch Clay

Untitled

Nothing is the title of this poem to vindicate
The emptiness of the universe beyond the realm of matter.
To think, imagine and exploit the concept can stimulate
Billions of neurons and needless chitter chatter.

The thought of nothing should compel one to converse,
"Was it nothing or something that came first? Without a burst?"
How? How! Does nothing beyond nothing create nothing?
No time, gravity, space, heat or cold, one's mind could burst, first!

There must be two Gods - one God to create one believable God in space
God of nothing, God of something - either one is a possible disgrace
Does nothing begin instantly where something ends unexpectedly?
Only the Gods dictate this floppy trend that flips over expectedly!

This floppy trend makes no sense the Gods give you the day you're born
A death sentence, plus, perhaps a life of pain and continuous scorn.
Of course, always respect the powers of both Gods with foresight,
But, not how the Gods use their powers with thoughtless mind sight.

God is the name of nothing that became something that made
Something out of nothing and that is something.
To believe in one of the Gods, you must also believe in nothing to grade
Your thoughts of pros and cons then to realize you end up with ...O

Carl B. Lordo

The Return

    When we have returned,
The fires under the kettles—
These fires will have burned,
Melted our brains, burned our mettles.

    We'll return with bloody hands, bloody feet,
With one heart, and one eye,
With a life but so fleet,
A life burned to ashes in it's heat!

    Then, with one eye
We sight at the bottom of the lake
The multitudes that yearn and sigh
To the world all too fake!

    We'll sink to the bottom of the lake,
Where the bell is heard to toll.
With a long and rusty rake,
Scrape up for me a riderless horse,
    for you a ragdoll....

Ago Loide

Foodline

They stand sadly in line, the lost souls searching for a savior.
The food, a glint of hope.
They smell like rotten corpses,
forgotten by civilization,
and their clothes are in shambles:
torn, worn, and soiled beyond recognition.

The smell of watery soup and the cheap ground meat
creeps through the air like poison through one's veins.
Drawn faces advance as the skin and bones
move toward redemptive nourishment,
redemption from the sin of poverty
placed on them by the financially wealthy.
The food line is the life blood of the poor.

The stomachs and minds of these unfortunates scream
like cursed banshees asking for the light of another day.
The air tastes of dirt and onions,
the smells combining into a death syrup.

As the daylight fades,
the wandering souls fade away like a diminishing rainbow.

Alexander J. Budney II

Share the Sunshine

Come out to the green fields,
the forests, the streams.
Come out to the free spirit, felt in your dreams.
Come out of the darkness, the den of despair.
Come out and feel free,
come share the sunshine with me.

Come take my hand,
we'll walk for awhile.
Give me half your sorrow,
I'll give you a smile.
Learn how to make living feel good,
learn it's not too late,
if only you could...

Come out to the green fields,
the forests, the streams.
Come out to the free spirit felt in your dreams.
Come out of the darkness, the den of despair.
Come out and feel free,
come share the sunshine with me!!

Frances Howard Tolfa

Brotherly Love

Submit to the world of the mad and macabre
the freedom of choice and life he did rob
Marked by the scar of the nights refrain
Silent tears fell from his heart like rain
For he knew he had lost his battle with power
As his weakness increased in the diminishing hour
With his strength cowering into lands unseen
His deathbed he forsakes, feeling unclean
Then Jesus appeared, bleeding from hand and foot
And asked for forgiveness which he claimed his Lord took
Disappearing into mist his next sight was Mary
All but frail bones he could see her barely
Exploding into fragments of bone and skin
She disappeared and he walked in
Lucifer appeared to watch our Lord die
"Brother you've won" he said, as he closed his eyes.

Adam Wiggins

Ode To Joe

The Joe we all know
The funny guy the happy guy,
All is about to change, ya know!
The blessed vows of marriage, oh my!
All fun is coming to an end.
To sign that document, perilous task!
You have got to be good and conform and bend.
So by all means be good and hide your flask!
So, so many of the blessed vow's
I've seen come and gone
The more I see, the more I like cows
So, by all means, be home by dawn
Just a poem to make you think
For all is lost in the ring.
Be good, be faithful, try not to drink.
Cause if you ain't she'll make you sing.

David Graeber

Gifts

Turn slowly child and you will see
The gifts God made for you and me.
The trees, with leaves, all forms and shapes,
The grass along side countless lakes,
The fertile earth where farmers grow
Food for thought, row by row.
The mountain high with snowy peak,
The valley low with deer and sheep.
The mountain brook so crystal clear,
The cliffs with walls completely sheer.
The sun, its rays so very bright,
The moon, the stars, the birds of night.
The rain that wets the ready soil
Rewarding farmers for their toil.
The wind, feel the wind as it cleans the air
Of dust and smog with special care.
Turn slowly child and you will see
The gifts God made for you and me.

Daniel Goodwin

Blizzard

It was dark and cold outside.
The rain was falling like tears to the ground.
It was blowing and whistled right past the window.
The snow is falling like rain covering the ground
with a soft blanket of cotton.
Inside the bed is like a soft, fluffy cloud.
The covers are like a blanket of cat fur.
The fire seems to be singing a soft lullaby.
The pillow is as soft as a Teddy Bear.
And the dog is sleeping on a rug at the end of your bed.

Dana Park

Forever A Sunset

Now I've seen the rolling hills
The grassy green stretching into infinity
I know the real gold
It lies in the sun
A treasure held there 'til the end of time
Every morning a rebirth of life
Every night it slowly sinks into the land
Its last rays struggle to reach through the trees
But every day it dies a bold and magnificent death
As it glows bright orange, pink, and purple against the cloud
    streaked sky
A strange dignity and peace about it
It leaves another life behind with thousands of others it has seen
    before
To rise up again like a God looking over his land and liking what
    he sees
The treetops ablaze with the dying embers until...it's gone.

The blanket of darkness weights it down
Sadness overflows you as the light seeps out of the sky and your heart
Until you remember another tomorrow.

Brooke Mitchell

The Poet At The Peasant's Door

Come, poet, from the peasant's door, his verse and rhyme must wait
The harvest won't and he is poor, and so he labors late
You must come spend the while with me 'til dusk's dark shadows fall
For my name is Time, you see, so quite well known by all

Some think I'm grand, some misery, but still to all I'm lent
And those who use me foolishly soon wonder where I went
For instance there's the peasant's wife, she scurries me away!
But once she struggled for her life and begged for me to stay

By kings I'm offered crown and throne, treasured above their queens
The wisest trust in me alone, rich, poor and in-betweens
I'm always here, I'm always gone, 'though 'oft my flight seems slow
I'm with you when you're all alone, I follow where you go

Look yonder, poet, watch with care, you may derive a plot
You may see something you can share with all the common lot
Watch closely as the peasant nears his humble cottage door
His life's but labor, sweat and tears, but still there's one thing more

Does he not slow his weary pace? Does not mine now seem less?
Yes, even I am offered grace when used in thankfulness
That silent moment at his gate, did I not too stand still?
When given thanks I gladly wait for each and all who will.

John L. Ferguson

The Home Of Goalie

Under the spreading hockey net,
The hometown goalie squats;
His brow is creased with purple welts
From taking head-high shots
And his battered ears remind us of
A Boy Scouts granny knots.

A row of scars conceal a face that sparkled
Once with youth.
And as he squats he contemplates
The ever-present truth that soon some puck may extricate
His one remaining tooth.

One eye is blue and crossed and glazed,
The other reddish-plaid,
Although his nose is flattened out,
You'll never see him sad;
He knows that for a one-year-man,
He's really not too bad.

James A. Stieb Jr.

Untitled

The ebony darkness of her hair,
The infinite warmth of her heart,
Both I can see each day,
And always it rips me apart.

For she is a fallen angel,
Yet still too high for me.
Far easier than winning her love,
Would be taking a spoon and drinking the sea.

Her crimson lips curve upward in a smile,
But alas, it's not for me.
Never again will I ever see,
Any mortal so beautiful as she.

She gives, it seems, to anyone,
Her smile which gleams like gold.
I would ask for that smile if I dared,
But alas, I am not so bold.

Joshua R. Mills

When The Wind Touches The Heart

May the rest of my earthly journey be like
the invisible wind, soft and warm to cradle
and embrace you from the hard realities of life,
but strong enough to lift and place you above the
horizon.

Here among the clouds your senses will awaken.
Behold! the majesty of God's paintings are revealed
in shades of green, blue, red and gold. Hush!
Be Still! Listen!

Did you hear the message rippling through the trees,
swirling in the streams? It is not new, but buried
and waiting for the wind to touch your heart.
God whispers in the wind—Love, Care, Give and Forgive.
There is peace when the wind touches the heart.

Beverly J. Tomlinson

I Can Just Imagine

I can just imagine
The kiss he lays upon my lips
Like the whisper of a secret so important
It can only be shared by the wind and the trees

I can just imagine
His hands caressing my face, my body!
Like the shaping of time, so precise and careful
It can send only me into pure ecstasy!

So soft and gentle is his kiss
Like a feather falling lightly upon a sleeping baby's cheek
So sacred, that I'd lay it upon a velvet pillow
And place it in a glass casing to be treasured
  Forever and ever
  By me!

Donna Marie Zimmerman

A Funeral

We followed the hearse and stopped at the graveyard.
The leaves crunched as we followed the casket.
It was then laid down and flowers were placed on it.
It was a truly unforgettable feeling.
As the casket went into the ground a tear rolled down my cheek
and a shiver went up my back.
It was a strong feeling of discomfort.
But somehow God will comfort me and take the sorrow away.
Just as he did with the suffering of my friend.
And things will get better.
For as we know all things will pass,
but not the love for the person.

Alyssa M. Andrew

A Sense of Lost Reality

Living a life in poverty wishing someone rescue thee
The life that there living is the only life that they see
could it be? A sense of lost reality?
Or a mere image only seen in the midst of a dream?
Is this all they know? This is all it seems
Seelin' dope to make a livin', only life they know is drug dealin'
Wanting to rise as thigh as the skies
But is only the black man society despise
Livin' life in a community where everyone is judging me
This is all I know if this is all I see
Hustlin' in the streets, trying to make a livin'
All I see around me is prostitutin' gang bangin' and drug dealin'
People puttin' me down on how I live
But they can't understand my struggle if they don't know how it is
How can this be, livin' in society?
Is it me or the sense of lost reality?

Angelique M. Childs

"My New Day"

Quietly, I await the hush of dawn,
The light that tiptoes gently over the land,
Revealing what will be mine
If I but reach out my hand.

Slowly the warmth steals in and brings
A happiness proclaiming a lovely, new day
Promised by God to all of us
To be used in some wonderful way.

A sigh of pleasure escapes my lips,
Freeing my heart to soar and meet the sun.
Joy fills my being to accept His gift
As my precious new day is begun.

I take it in both hands to treasure it well,
Not trade it for gloom or despair,
Not casting aside what He is giving to me;
My days are all beautiful in His care.

Florance Ann Vickers

Swimming To The Moon

Swimming to the moon;
The moonlight glinting silver on the water
Like steel satin.

It slides over my skin;
Smooth, soft,
Liquid whispers.

I swim and swim forever.
The world fades.
It is only me and the moon,
The water and the night.

I am a magical creature, never tiring.
Fish, flash and molten moonlight.

Swimming into other realms
Where all is soothing mystery.

Precious solitude of the magic night.
Ebony silence of the silken light.

Silver and black.
The moon, the night,
The water and me,
          forever... forever... forever...

Carol A. Payne

Leave Me Here

Take me not to the desert sand,
The mountains high or the prairie land.
Just leave me here in these wooded hills,
Chasing wild game over rocks and rills.

Take me not to the ocean's roar,
Where salt winds blow and sea gulls soar.
Just leave me here in this wooded land,
Where grouse abound in the forest stand.

Take me not to the city's throng,
Where asphalt grows and men go wrong.
Just leave me here in this lake sprinkled pew,
Where fish swim free in the waters blue.

Take me not from this land that I love;
Just leave me here till that call from above.

Don C. Carey

A Quiet, Holy, Night

So quiet, so peaceful, so holy it was,
The night when baby Jesus was born.
A bright star was shining,
Three wise men came calling,
With gifts on that first Christmas morn.

His mother and father both knelt by his crib
While shepherds were watching their sheep.
The angels were singing,
And joy bells were ringing,
But baby Jesus lay fast asleep.

Because he was born in a stable forlorn,
The animals were all by his side.
But Joseph and Mary,
Were so very happy,
Their hearts overflowing with pride.

Today we remember as we celebrate,
That wonderful time of his birth.
With people all sharing,
And Christians cheering,
The reason why he came to earth.

Gwen Irwin

Graveside Feelings

The wintery wind blows across the frozen ground.
The old man stands with silvery head bowed.
The tears on his cheeks say he silently weeps
for the lady he held so dear.
Just look at his face, see the tear,
as it slowly falls at his feet.
Then, as if in a trance,
he hangs his head in defeat.
The pain you can see with just a glance,
has broken his once strong soul.
And he wishes in his heart,
that he was beside his wife in that deep, dark hole.
Now he sits dejectedly beside the stone
that marks the time of her passing.
He knows in his heart that love, unlike life,
is everlasting.
So he waits for the time when his name is called
in heaven up above.
Then at last he'll be united again,
with his one and only love.

Brent Cunningham

The Child Within Us

Whatever happened to that little child we all knew,
The one that was there for us through and through?
Did it grow up and move away,
Or did it remain young and decide to stay?

Is it playful, as it used to be,
When it would run with you and me?
Does it still call our name out loud,
To come out and look at every cloud?

Does it still want to run through a field,
To run and play, and never yield?
What ever happened to that little child we all knew,
The child that lives within me and you.

Jessica Dobbs

Remember And Pray

Who are these souls, other than me,
The ones who are broadcast all over T.V.
Statistics who live in some bad, awful place
No person that I've ever seen face to face

I cry for them hoping that I'll never be
Splattered all over national T.V.
Am I awful for feeling relieved when I'm spared
The suffering that all of the victims have shared

I pray for the people who they've left behind
That they will eventually find peace of mind
Maybe one day peace will reign in the land
Maybe one day we will walk hand in hand

Until that day pray for the souls who remain
Pray we can rid earth of this ugly stain

Joyce P. Fields

Untitled

In my room I stay,
The only place I can escape to,
The only place I feel free from everything.
The only place I can be free to do anything.
Otherwise I'm trapped like a bird in a cage,
Where forever I will stay,
Imprisoned because of one mistake,
A mistake that I wish I had never made,
Because this one mistake changed my whole life.
If only I could go back and change everything,
Then I would not have to stay here trapped and alone.

Dawn Van Duzer

God Danced At Christmas

God danced at Christmas - with mirthful abandon
   The ordinary was transformed into a miraculous display
   Of Eternity wrapped in a baby.

'Tis reason enough for joy, if ever reason was needed to express
   Forever the entrance of the Divine in a wee body.

Dance on with God, through the days ahead dance on,
   For life is gentler, filled with Joy and Love because of
God's incredible Act — when heaven and earth touched in
   one brief moment — FOREVER.

Elwyn M. Williams

Down By The Sea

Down by the sea on one long hot summer day...
The passion was so great it took my breath away.

Down by the sea is where it all began...
That is when I knew He was my one and only man.

Down by the sea the waters were so still and calm...
That is when He began to turn on the charms.

Down by the sea, He held me so tight...
I realized it was love at first sight.

Down by the sea is where He asked to marry me...
I said yes, now we have a happy family.

Betty L. Reed

The Shell

While walking down the beach one day, I came across a shell.
The patterns on the side of it, cast a mystic spell.

I stared down in bewilderment, then stooped to pick it up.
It was fragile and filled with water, just like a china cup.

I was simply filled with awe, I wanted it for myself.
I wished to take it to my home, and put it on a shelf.

It all seemed so unfair, it made me very mad,
That this shell could not return the feelings that I had.

How dare it be so selfish to not think I am grand!
It filled me with such anger that I cast it on the sand.

Just then the tide came in, and water engulfed me.
It took away my shell and dragged it out to sea.

How could I be so silly, so stupid and naive.
It's just a simple shell, it couldn't live or breath.

Yet, I expected feelings like those which came from me.
Instead I lost my shell to the pounding of the sea.

But, the same shell came back to me and Lord knows only how.
I'll never be that way again I swear this solemn vow.

"I won't expect feelings in return for those which I dish out"
Isn't that what sharing love is really all about?

John Bozick

The Poet

One day I am going to be a poet
the poet writes songs, sings and knows many things
the poet see's what everyone wants to see,
but most can't look at reality
the poet relates to you and me, after all,
if they didn't who or what would they be?
How do some see what they see?
For more than some, this causes misery.
Maybe that's why people can't see what they see
but many still relate to you and me.
Maybe they could see if they would turn around and look at reality.
If society could look and see, maybe, there
would not be so much strife and misery.
We could see what we need to see the truth and reality
and just maybe we would not have to go through
some of this strife and misery.
For the poet bears the problems of society on themselves sometime.
Look and you will find that some have ended before their time.

Alton Keith Smith

The Cessation Of The Conundrum

The pieces are starting to come together,
the puzzle will soon be complete.
I'm starting to see everything
through new eyes.
What I'm seeing
is traveling to my heart.
My heart knows how to feel now
how to love, and care, and trust.
You've brought these feelings out in me
along with keeping the old—anger, annoyance;
but that's natural.
Sufficient to say the best of me—
you've brought out.
No one has ever done that;
no one has ever cared so much,
that much.
No one has made me happier
than I have been these several weeks
with a permanent smile to last
a lifetime and a half.

Catherine Marie Caputo

Distortion

Opium based lyrics fill the air
The red death is heard with faint footsteps.
Confused dogs that are very aware
find the trace scent of glass.

But wait says one with a pitch-forked tongue.
I must find the light of the setting sun.
Only months remain while I am still young.
Do not despair for I hear the fog horn.

Entendons a les enfants
parce quils sont jeunes et libres.
N'oubliez pas la glace.
Quand elle fond, je lis un livre.

The red scarlet stains the ground.
Admire the spectacle of nature
And what in this world is the most profound?
Why it is the delicacy of the falling leaves.

Bryan Hanysak

Broken Rope

I lay my hands comfortably in yours,
the rope of trust tied around our fingers.

You were the deer. I was still a fawn.
You were the sky I couldn't reach.
That friend that was always there,
the love I never had.

Why?! Why did you do it?
Driven knives through my heart, the lights have changed.
Tears roll painfully down my face, to lie in anguish on my pillow.

You left me filled with endless pain,
to sit by the window sill,
looking out onto my shattered world,
now broken to tiny pieces.

You turn the key slowly, to lock me out of your world.
I don't need a looking glass, now the lies come clear as ice.

The rope is torn, broken to nothing.
Now I can see, that you were misconceived.
The scar you made is here for life.

I can't forget the hurt,
and I will never, ever forgive.

Amber Lanvin

"This Country Boy"

Hands that have known the shovel and the plow.
The same hands know a trade by now -
Eyes that can see what others fail to find,
Little education, but a brilliant mind -
A courage to conquer weaknesses -
Loyalty that has become so rare -
The right words when you feel only despair -
Sometimes gay, sometimes sad -
Surely you have guessed by now -
This country boy is my Dad!

Doris K. Harvell

We Are Products Of Our Past

We are products of our past, and in
the shadows of our minds are the
scars made by our past.

To search and probe the mind is to
become aware of such scars before they
infect the mind itself.

To infect the mind is to become bitter
and hostile, to show hate, to lash
back at others for the hurt and
torment we once encountered.

To accept the scars of our past is to not
be embittered by them, to understand
them, to learn by them, to become a
better and deeper person because of them.

DLC

Falling Apart

My legs are short, my hips are wide, my chest is flat and saggy.
The skin beneath my baby blues is kind of loose and baggy.
Now muscles which I used to have, have somehow turned to flab,
The eloquence I once possessed is now my gift of gab.

The spots which once adorned my face as freckles, went away.
And now I'm getting liver spots—I found one just today.
It seems that I have shrunk in height, and a few pounds I have gained.
I know my waist will never be a twenty four again.

I have arthritis in my hands, can't feel my left big toe,
My tummy aches, my throat is sore, sometimes my brain is slow.
They put me on a diet. That's something that I hate!
I can't have cake and ice cream—I have to watch my weight.

My life is really pretty good despite my pains and aches.
I know I'll have a happy life, no matter what it takes.
I still can laugh and sing and dance and read and write and drive,
But as I read this silly poem, it's a wonder I'm alive!

Arlene Brunton

"Bang-Bang"

Bang-Bang goes off the gun,
that kill another parents daughter or son.
A victim of someone's games,
goes and burst into flames.
This child may have held hopes and dreams.
But now it doesn't matter, so it seems.
So six feet under their put in a hole.
And only God could have save d their soul!!!
Dig this you daughter and sons
don't play with fire.
Cause BANG!! BANG!! GOES THE GUN.

Collette Rhea Gray

Little Babies

Buzz of fluorescent lights too bright overhead
The smell of sickness, death and fear
Glued to her tongue;
She unable to swallow it away.
Bloody tincture smeared across her
Belly and inner thighs
Her body sighs as her strained muscles relax
She feels flush all over
Yet cold inside the pit of her stomach
She tries to remember why she came here
And can not recall leaving her home and its comforts
She hears the gentle woman voice say,
"It's over now."
It's barely audible above the roar inside her ears
She sees the face that belongs to that kind voice,
Her outline blurry through guilt-fed tears
And she turns her face away
From those loving eyes ashamed.

Annette D. Kowalski

The Last Knight

I rise up from the sweltering heat of the battle
The smoke all around me clearing
As I drop my sword I'm suddenly hearing
The calls of my Queen
The bloodied enemy have all fallen
And I bow down kneeling
My heart roaring with its undying feeling
That I shall never fail my Queen
I am the last knight of her guild
And by Heaven I shall see the kingdom rebuilt
Lest I fall to my own vanities
But I shall not allow such profanities
For my Queen has need of me
And it is a proud lion's heart that will gladly see
A new kingdom come to be

Cody Marmon

The Melody of Nature

Once in a field, high in a tree,
The song bird sang a sweet melody.
The grass was green and blue was the sky,
Over the field, an eagle did fly.

Free were the rabbits and the deer to roam,
For this was the place they called their home.
But the change of the seasons brought a new,
And so went the animals forced to move.

Now stands a building, instead of a tree,
And the once green field, is no longer green.
Gone are the eagles, rabbits and deer,
For they have left, out of fear.

The skies are clouded and filled with smog,
The once bright stars, are hidden by fog.
No longer a home, this is no doubt,
Because of the changes man has brought about.

And like the world, the melody has changed,
To the faint cry of nature, shakin' with fear.
To be alive again is her dream,
But its up to man, so it seems.

Carrie Borowski

The Funeral

The coffin is set in the ground.
The soul is laid to rest.
Yet the relatives huddle closer
And talk long into the night.

The next morning has barely arrived
When kin are already groping.
Some are still in nightclothes,
But all are talking, talking.

Remembering past shared times,
Feeling the present pain,
Not ready to look beyond that moment
To their return to the order of their lives.

Though it took a death for this gathering,
A sense of belonging is the result.
Folks must need time to be
With those who are like themselves.

Judy Moffet

"When I Found You I Found Me"

The grass is green the sky is blue
The sun shines bright when I'm with you.

The birds sing sweetly the stars shine above
But not as clearly as you my love.

You brighten my mornings you sweeten my days
You're the love of my life in many ways.

You make my problems seem smaller
You make my bad days seem good
You lift up my spirits like no one else could.

You're the green in the grass
You're the blue in the sky
You're the bright in the sun and I know why.

You're the shine in the stars
You're the sweetness in the song
With you by my side I can never go wrong.

I can't explain in words how much I love you
But each time we're together I feel brand new.
To put it bluntly you're my cup of tea
Because when I found you I found me!!

Janell Longwell

Unknown Glare

A gentle breeze glides through the air.
The sun, warm and inviting, returns again.
The glistening grass, covered with dew.
A new day, common although rare.
Folks arising in a robotic routine.
Ignorant numbers, if only they knew.
Universe of knowledge yet riddles remain.
Unaware of the sun but blinded by it's glare.
They probe from their own mercenary.
Squandered by the fire, few are detained.
Penetrating their hollow souls without a care.
Unleash the dread and come to dusk.
Dawn's phase is only a picture away.
Echoed by the glare with a tolerant fate.

Deborah Leeper

Homecoming

I stood at the window and looked west
The Sun's sleepy gaze met mine
A blanket of crimson and orange had engulfed The Great Knight
 of the Noonday and soon he would sleep.

I listened for a moment, and then I heard it
It was so faint at first I almost missed it
Ever so slowly the night song began to stretch itself through
 the city and across the sky, I looked up and saw the moon
The beautiful soprano of the night sky was in full voice that night
I could feel my heart pounding in my chest as she sang her sad,
 sweet lullaby to the weary inhabitants of the city

I listened more intently as, one by one, the stars added their
 voices to this sweetest of melodies
I stood and listened for a long time as a tear broke free of its
 bonds and danced slowly down my cheek, I had heard this song
 before.
Many years ago in a dream now long forgotten my heart danced to this
 song.
But my heart had not danced in many years, until that night,
 that night my heart danced to this song like never before and I
 knew, Beyond any doubt, I was Finally
Home.

Fernando L. W. Campos

The Pool

I rested in a pool of blackness.
The swirling pain and anger grabbed at my life.
But they can't touch me now.
I sit back and laugh at them.
You have reached in and pulled my soul out.
Through You I have escaped the pain
But I am still dependent on Your strength.
Only your voice keeps me from sinking back in.
I fear returning more than I fear anything.
The pool is lies,
The pool is pain.
The pool is sadness.
The pool is weakness.
I didn't even realize I was in it.
Until I wasn't there anymore I even liked it.
Now my eyes can see through the dark.
Now I fear that you will let me fall back in.
Don't let me fall.
Hold me. Keep me out.
I don't want to go back. Please.

Alex Ramel

Why

After all the times you hurt me
the times you made me cry.
Why do I forgive you with every little sigh?
The times that you betrayed me
and the times of painful good-byes,
Why do I still need you after all those lies?
The times that you ignored me
and the times that my pain has shown
Why do I still care for you,
though you left me all alone?
With the scars you left upon me,
and the tears that fall each day
Why am I still in love with you,
though you treated me this way?

Cindi Renee Box

Journey

The scene has no dialogue.
The traveler hesitates,
unfolding a map of stars.
And somewhere other sunsets blink
like so many scarlet and turquoise lovers,
catching up to find each other.
Pluto is gone.
Persephone is released.
The time-traveler waits
as the galaxy shifts
and is nowhere mentioned.
The course has been set.
He must go in,
into Vulcan's fire,
into Solar Plexus One,
into Mind...
And somewhere
other travelers hesitate
like so many gods,
like so many stars.

Dwight Stevers

Aftermath

There's a wind-loomed hush on the hills tonight.
The trees stand stark in the moon's bright light;
Down in the valley the fog drifts white...
   And the hunter has gone home.

Doe mother nuzzles her soft brown fawn;
Quivers and waits for the frosty dawn.
A watch for her mate .. he's been gone so long.
   And the hunter has gone home.

There's emptiness in the muffled bleat;
Restlessness in the shuffled feet.
Lonely fear as the brown eyes meet
   And the hunter has gone home.

Claryce Casey Grimm

Dominion

In effort winter's coming to appease;
The trees throw leafy jewels at his feet.
Then, starkly shivering stand they ill at ease
Humiliated, barren, incomplete.
And Heaven cries cold tears without cessation
While groundling leaves sound out death rattle
Of summer and lament her short duration.
Bold winter gains the field without a battle.
Then icy-sceptered Merlin casts a spell
Of enchantment with his potent, numbing breath
Enrobing in habiliments dire chill
With rigid robes close fitting as is death.
But life, though now a captive in death's reign,
Will rise in spring to find a new domain.

Evalyn Torrant

Jeff

   The love I feel is so unreal.
The love is burning from deep inside of me.
His body is so strong and warm.
He fills me with joy. His luscious lips
pressed against mine takes me to a world far
beyond. As I think of his body and as close
as we could be, I realize now nothing could ever
stop me. He fills my life with pleasure and
if only we could become best friends and lovers
and unite only as one.

Angie Dutton

Thank You Father

Thank you Father, thank you so much for everything you've done...
The trials and tribulations I've been through...you've brought me
through each one...no one can tell me their isn't a God... for
I've witnessed it myself...my needs aren't plenty and I want
just a few...father all I need and want is you...you were there
when I was born you'll be there when I die...and I know within
my heart that I'll meet you in the sky. They'll never be another
one like you, you're one of a kind and I love you too...
Sometimes I get really down and you seem so far away...
Then I say a little prayer and my frown goes astray...
And I then begin to smile, because I know that it's you...
Sending me your love father like you always do...
Thank you father, thank you so much for everything you've done...
And I want to thank you especially for sending you're only begotten
son.

Annette P. Hillian

Winter Winds And War

I fought for this country; I've killed and killed again.
   The true hell of war, is living in sin.
Broken marriage, and too many broken dreams -
   I live alone with nightmares; alone, I hear the screams.
If you ask, "Why is war?" I do not hold an answer
   It surely seems, just to be another form of cancer.
Men die fast and often times, agonizingly slow -
   And winter winds when they come, fiercely do they blow.
Like winter winds that chill the bone and spring seems far away
   The scars of war are yours alone; you live with them every day.

My name's not etched in that Great Black Wall;
   The names that are have sacrificed it all.
For the names that are, I have shed the tear-
   And winter winds blow back each year.
I pray my son never lives war or dies in it's hands-
   If by fate he leaves our shore to fight in other lands
The price of death our young sons pay for freedom and it's gains-
   Winter winds will go away, but the war inside remains.
Like winter winds that chill the bone and spring seems far away
   The scars of war are yours alone; you live with them every day.

Berman L. Van Buskirk

A Love I Can't Deny

As gentle words fell from his lips,
   the truth was revealed in his finger tips.
   when he touched me and held me tight,
   I knew that it was just another night.
The storm settled and I opened my eyes
   to see our love drowning in lies.
A stronger before me, the man I thought I knew
   broke my heart through and through.
Fooling myself, trying to stay,
   dreams of a lifetime faded into yesterday.
Empty promises, wanting to believe
   and loving arms needing to receive.
I walk away dying inside,
   not looking back, to much pride.
Always in my thoughts, he's a part of me,
   A love I can't deny, wanting him to see.
The way I feel, I can't explain
   but to live without him is living in vain.

Amanda Dawson

The Tune of the Merry Horseman

In the middle of December, when Winter's here once more
The tune of the Merry Horseman swirls around the forest floor.
As dancers to the Horseman's tune sparkle 'neath the crisp new moon
In silence fade, still listening, keeping time with the merry tune.
As the white rose spreads 'cross the darkened sky, anointing the ground with white,
The tune of the Merry Horseman hums a cappella in the night
Washing pure the year's dirt gone with gentle sprinklings of his song
In merry notes his tune is made, it's joy fulfilled that never fades.
The tune the Merry Horseman sings with whirling violent crescendo rings
To lift him high o'er tallest tree on trails the horseman knows
Each step and time is different, unique is each new show.
The tune of the Merry Horseman in sweet harmonic repose
Leaves a lithe waif dancer gently on my nose
With the subtle aromatic whiff of a pure white perfect rose.
And the silent dancers watching weep as winter begins her snowy sleep
And melts away at dawnings keep the tune of the Merry Horseman.

Amanda J. Rutledge

Love

Love is a word many don't understand
The use of it often gets quite out of hand.
Some say they love while they inflict deep pain
In a way that could drive the most innocent insane.

It scares me how easily some say this word
They use it and abuse it till it seems quite absurd.
For how can one love while he's full of deceit
And is constantly looking for someone to cheat.

I feel that love is the most ultimate high
And don't see how it can exist amidst lies.
This feeling is one of the most beautiful ways
For two people to spend happy and joyful days.

Like in all things in this type of beauty so rare
It is long in receiving and needs tender care.
For if it is hurried or misused at all
This bridge among people will crumble and fall.

You will know when you have finally found love
You'll feel like singing to the skies above.
And the person who has opened this feeling in you
Will join you in spirit, becoming one, and not two.

Denise Humke

S S The Wood

An illuminated Star Ship marooned on a cloud of memories;
The voices hum in descents, raise to a crescendo-then stop.
Supper! To break bread together is a sacred rite.
Since man knew man.
A cornucopia of fruits and nuts, Balsam, holy, laurel and oak
  on an altar of mums.
The totem pole from the Fruit Charismatics,
The Minora of the seven sacred lights,
Incense and wild roses and Holy candle burning
The calm hands that gather offer grace in song as
  the Fanner Bees spray jasmine.
The prager flags sway in the whisper of a southern breeze.
The glow on each face in the riche of kin
The wishes of kinship are prayer.
In the strains of Mozart's Magic flute, the choir sings, "Te Deum".
The Lamplighter is here.!

Fannie Fiore

The Big Snow

Who could forget the night of the storm
The warning signs all through the morn.
It was a dreary December day
The wind so bitter and blowing our way.
We stacked the wood against the old stone wall
waiting for the big snowfall.

The snowflakes come down all through the night
We woke up in the morning to see everything white.
A new world of wonders all shiny and bright
All because of the show fall that came in the night.

The rays of the sun that shone down on the snow
Glistened like diamonds with beauty to show.
The world changed in to a beautiful sight
All because of the snowfall that came in the night.

Doris Larson McCay

Treasured Friend

As we travel through life, God gives us dear friends to help us along
    the way.
I've recently lost such a dear friend whom I've treasured each and
    every day.

The good Lord put us together long ago for a reason
and our caring and love continued to grow through many years and
    seasons.

God knew that we would need each other and gave us friendship
    from the start
and a love for each other that was always in our heart.

I must learn to face each day when you're gone and we are apart
but I know you'll always be near and forever in my heart.

But now that you're gone, I know your destination is met and that with
    your dear wife
you'll be in heaven to look down together to watch over me.

Judy Fabrycki

True Love

I never thought that I could feel,
The way I feel about you,
The way you make me feel.
I thought that I could love No more!
Until you came and walked through my door.
And you got me started at a love game once more!
You showed me what true love's about,
Believing in someone without a doubt.
And when they think they can take no more,
You're there to push them a little bit more.
So they can see that they can be,
Who they want if they just believe.
And when things go wrong as they often do,
And we take a bad turn down a wrong road or two.
They're there to guide us which road to take,
And to stand beside us when we make a mistake.
True love's not just saying I Love You,
It's believing in someone and I Believe in You!

Diedre Brunk

All The Races Of Humankind

There are no superior races, there are no inferior races
There are differences, there are similarities
There are perceptions, there are misperceptions
There are experiential cultural learning of races
There are academic cultural learning of races
There are empirical cultural instruction of races
There are academic cultural instruction of races
There are no superior races, there are no inferior races
There is the allness and oneness of humankind

Ida J. Dunson

Sonnet

I hope I never hear you laugh again
The way you laughed when you perceived my start!
I knew you spoke the words in merry vein,
And yet I took them to my foolish heart.
If I had answered, "You had not the need
To ask. "You only want the words from me."...
You may have smiled. Instead, I but agreed
In silence, with a nod. You laughed in glee!

And yet, I said so much without a word;
A nod should please you more than verbal guile.
I gave you answer, though I spoke unheard.
The gulf between your laughter and your smile
Is wide, but nothing wider than the reach
Between a silent nod and gilded speech.

Burl Bredon

God's Window Sill

I see within my heart upon this hill,
the way your love comes to me
across the miles, which brings a thrill
Like a clap of thunder, wild and free
into my soul, my heart in simile.
as I sit by God's window sill.

Your loving face, I see repeatedly
in the blackness of the universe, so still
reflecting back to me, enchanting harmony

A sparkling star, it will remain to be
known alone to me, throughout eternity.
You fill my cup endlessly.

Quaff it now, once more, I will
as I gaze upon your face
next to God's window sill.

Glenda Anne Piearson

"Redwood Forest"

Explosion of light, the ocean's might.
The wind delights me in its gentle caress
While passing over all the rest.

The rocks are massive strongholds,
To me they are dark, forbidding, bold.

While underneath the sea's diamond exterior
As fragile creatures glide underneath,
We stand up here and call Them inferior?

As you sit here, take a moment and pause,
Does nature really have any flaws?

Life is not really what it seems,
But someone in heaven must know what it means.
The good Lord made this giant place.
We owe it to future generations not to lay it to waste.

As you sit here you know nothing is amiss.
Surely, the Garden of Eden still exists!

So, when you leave this place, content,
Take comfort knowing your time was well spent.
And lastly, please listen, Children of Earth,
Remember this place and how much it is worth.

Chag Lowry

Silent Yearning

Standing alone in the distance,
The wind sighing with gentle persistence;
Over the water my attention was drawn,
To something rising above the dawn.
Flying over seas of blue,
A hawk sails, strong and true.
I find myself think and questioning why;
Wondering how something so lonely could fly.
He soars higher, and lets out a wail,
It dances along the silent gale.
I watch as he soars over fields of green,
Reminding me of all I've never been.
I look across the field of dreams,
And find that nothing is as it seems.
I gaze at the hawk and yearn to fly;
Though I don't understand why.
I begin to run, and approach a ledge;
I spread my arms as I walk to the edge.
As I raise up to meet the breeze,
I find myself strangely at ease.

Heather Berube

Rebirth

As I look about me, the trees turning wildly in the turmoil of the wind, the beauty of life maybe enclosed in these trees of rainbow colors. As dusk falls upon these giants, I wonder how they prevail to stand sturdy amongst the wildest wind, shedding leaves like shedding skin, to be reborn in the spring. When darkness falls upon them, do they feel the loneliness against them, in the depth of the night do they fear, or is it there courage that makes them stand so tall. And when the heavens open up to give them drink, do they thrust towards the Gods, to await the sun glistening beneath there glorious colored leaves, is there a lesson to be learned, for every being is a different color, turning wildly in this turmoil of life, to be nurtured with love and courage so they too can stand tall when the trials come, shedding the pain to become all that is, being reborn through truth and when the darkness comes, they too will be sturdy as the trees, and await the birth of a new day dawning, so yes the lesson is learned.

Gail Wilhelm

The Unknown End

You say we've got two broken legs, but together we are strong,
The winds blow cold this New Year's Day, our paths are further along
Moving to the other side, awakening the dawn,
Feel the bliss from this place, with the power of a thunder storm

Know the safety in our hearts, allowing souls to join,
Reaching out into the void, explore the journey home.
Free to feel just who I am, there's no need to hide,
Touched by love forever changed, life's fire glows inside.

Healing as an aloe leaf placed upon the heart
Guided by integrity, our friendship never to part.
You say we've got two broken legs, I think Wings on the Mend,
Like moving birds about to fly, To the Light, the unknown end.

Anita Tavernier

Farewell, Love

May happiness be your lasting reward.
Wandering is mine, of my own accord.

Need of freedom; to live, to love, to be
Transcends my desire for security.

Time is so fleeting, the world is so vast,
I fear if I stop, my time may be past.

Please never regret the passions we dared,
Please never forget the love we have shared.

John W. Hudec

Our Grandchild

There is a seed that grows inside,
The womb is shelter, a place to hide,
I know not when — the time is near,
It's crying and wailing I long to hear.

If it's a boy — it will bring us joy,
If it's a girl — blue-eyed, blonde with curl,
Tiny small hands and small feet,
This grandchild will be so complete.

Our lives will change,
There is no doubt,
With each new inch
Of growth and sprout.

The days will pass to months and years,
Our love undying — quiets the fears,
This gift you hold — serene and dear,
May God Bless and keep you near.

Erma Stephens

Untitled

The sky is as black as evil
The world is silenced, the wind is howling
The air is cold like a dead man's blood
He walks to the graves.

The moon is full covered with clouds
He lowers himself into a grave
He sleeps with the dead.

Shadows and fire encircled him
He is slashed with the claws of devils and stabbed
   with their arrowed tails
His blood-stained clothes lay in mangled rags
   around him
He crawls away, chains binding his ankles
He is tossed into a rat invested cell, strapped
   to the wall, he is bit and slowly eaten alive
Silence except for squeaks of rats and his
   blood curdling screams
The sun rises, he stumbles home with raging
   fire still burning inside
Dare to discover the dark side

Beth Strzempka

Peace

Peace is a pleasant word;
The world may never see.
It helps us love each other;
As it was meant to be.
Like water gently flowing on a warm summers day;
Or the sweet smell in autumn of the golden fresh cut hay.

Sometimes I set and wonder as the years go drifting by;
How can we hate each other as I begin to cry.
So when trouble is a brewing;
Please don't let it start.
It's then you'll begin to realize,
Peace can live within your heart.

Clay Timothy Slash

Searching

It's been too long since that maternal touch;
The touch I burn and yearn for so much.
Remember when last time we met,
When I held you so tight;
That, I'll never forget.
But now your not here
And it's life that I fear -
I'm empty without you, mother!

Gabriel Butrim

Con-Science

Sometimes when clouds come rolling in,
The world seems dark, the sun spreading thin
Pray for the ozone and the stratosphere,
But hold close the things that are near and dear

I'm no doctor or professor of psychology,
We're all unique in our human ability
We're taught to lean on theory and analogy,
Trash all that, we're heaven's human chemistry

Don't always rely on what's logical and smart,
We have the best program within our heart
Not every issue is so complex and long,
There's just a difference between right and wrong

We've created mechanical monsters we faithfully feed,
Forgetting each other, but each other we need
Formulas get longer while microscopes grow taller,
A never ending game as these particles become smaller

So don't worry the future or fret the past,
Unlike these tenses, the present doesn't last
Instead, Con-Science and live for this day,
Follow your conscience and live the human way.

Dane S. Jester

The Wretch's Sonnet

The cruel world could never anticipate,
The wretch within, also outside was thus,
The same as I, looked upon with disgust.
I broke free from my cell and sealed my fate.
My crimes were unholy and full of hate.
I hurt them slowly, as I thought I must,
The "beautiful" ones who betrayed my trust.
They pleaded for forgiveness much too late.

My misery buried in their bodies
With my abhorrence and melancholy,
I ended my reign and breathed my last breath.
Finally free of painful agonies,
my euphoric thoughts in tranquility,
I found final peacefulness in my death.

Christopher Louvet

"Daddy"

One day we're just visiting or playing cards and having fun
Then all that changes and he's gone with the rising of the sun

We adults became babies pleading "Daddy breathe, please don't go
We need you to be here with us, we all love you so"

He fought hard to stay with us, he tried and he tried
But God's plan didn't agree, we lost... and he died

God answered our prayers though for a quiet and peaceful death
We all said "goodbye, I love you" and he took his last breath

We know he's watching over us from heaven above
He'll live in our hearts forever and will always have our love.

Christella M. Nelson

Whispering Sands And Dancing Tumbleweeds

I walk alone in my desert
   to bring back memories of a golden sunset.

The evening is dry and warm
   as I view natures chromo cactus garden.

A perfume is lost in gusty winds
   as blue shadows fall upon dancing tumbleweeds.

Only memories remain of a golden sunset
   as I listen to whispering sands and dancing tumbleweed.

Evelyne Hill

Friends to the Very End

Friends to the very end, we use to say
Then go off to laugh and play
You had said you would be with me forever
Even through the stormy weather.

You said you would never leave me alone
And yet I am sitting here on my very own
You said you'd never go away.
Until death came creeping up one day.

While we were walking to the store one day
A drunk driver got in my way
And then without a clue
You pushed me out of the way and he hit you.

In the hospital there you lay
Every night and every day
I stayed with you the whole night thru
I prayed to God to help you through

Then one dull morning cold you lay
And right then I knew you had been taken away
As I sit here, just a lonely fool
I wonder how life could be so cruel.

Carrie Ann Myers

Children

Children start off as being just infants,
Then you start loving them that very instant.
The months go on as they learn to talk,
Then before you know it they will learn to walk.
As the months fly by their first birthday comes along,
You have cake and ice cream and sing a birthday song.
Won't be long before the first day of school,
And being in kindergarten they think is cool.
Before too long they start to date,
Then soon after that is when they graduate.
Then comes the day when they leave home,
To start a family of their own.
Then you begin to think about the day when,
Someday you will have your own grandchildren.

Debra Simpson

The Wonderful Son

There are times, when the day is blue,
  There are moments, when you don't know, what to do,
But look up, into the sky blue,
  The Son, is there, shinning for you.

This Son, will direct your way,
  Then, there is no reason, to stray,
As this Son, is always, before and beside you,
  To lead, direct and guide you.

Who, is this Son, we are talking about?
  That is wonderful, great and devout,
This name is the Son, Jesus Christ,
  As he will, keep you, in his vice.

So when the road, grows drear,
  You have no fear,
Just look to the Son,
  As he, is always near.

So since, he is near,
  And you, have no fear,
Put your hand, into his hand
  Because, you are in his plan.

Glen Summers

Life Is A Rose Bush

Our family roots are deeply buried in the ground.
There are new rosebuds sprouting up all around.
Our body is the stem and our soul is the rose.
The leaves and thorns are life's happiness and woes.
Our dreams can blossom like soft gentle petals.
Coming in all colors, reds, whites, pinks and yellows.
Smelling so sweet, like nature planned them to be.
Given as a gift they bring so much joy to you and me.
Some are weak, while others grow strong and proud,
With God's sunlight and rain that falls from the clouds.
They grow thicker and thicker with a lot of room for all,
God's children on earth, whether they are big or small.
When God plucks a rose from your bush for his garden of paradise,
Never knowing if today or tomorrow will be the end of our lives,
I pray that God plants me next to my loved ones,
Because Life is a Rose Bush and my pruning is yet to come.

Alexis McCamey

My Mother My Friend

How do I find the words
There are so many
I just close my eyes and open my heart
My feelings come flooding in

How do I tell you... How do I let you know...
I just close my eyes and open my heart
and there you are, my tears come falling

Once a little boy, now a man
Full of love and sorrow
Full of anger and peace
I just close my eyes and open my heart
It's not open-Temporarily Closed

What do I do, I cannot move
Whom do I tell, I am afraid
Once a man, now a little boy
I just close my eyes and open my heart and there you are
Once a mother, once a friend
Still a mother, still a friend

I have opened my eyes and opened my heart
I have found the words, My Mother My Friend I Love You!

John W. Steen Jr.

Cry No More Tears Tonight Leticia

Cry no more tears tonight Leticia
There are too many stars shining bright
Wait for that special one to fall
Then wish for all that you want

Cry no more tears tonight Leticia
It's not how you win but the race
Cry no more tears tonight Leticia
Only you can set the pace

Cry no more tears tonight Leticia
When you put the kids to bed
Let that be the time when you rest your weary head

Cry no more tears tonight Leticia
Set the demon free
He wants to make you think he is the ruler of your destiny

Cry no more tears tonight Leticia
Let me be a friend
A friend who will truly care for you
And love you until the end.

Andrea Griffith Matteo

Poetry So

"Dear Folks" I want you all to know!"
"There certainly is writings of Poetry so!"
"I have read them over and over you know!"
"Words so contenting and soothing they cradle ones musings to and
    fro!"

"When I was young many I did not comprehend though."
"But now that time is seasoning me the reasoning is so."
"Just like the waves of the great blue sea;
    words of life swell high and low."
"Many are strong and stumbling to good words flow!"

"But", "Also there are words over contenting you know!"
"Why is it?" "The reason they write Poetry so?"
"Is it mainly to mellow often to many words of high and low?"
"Is it truly poetry that can even tongues flow?"

"As the water trickles over the rocks singing its own low;"
"The writings of Poetry so; do the same with life's words you know."
"If spoke more as poetry so we would not stir temperaments
    so quickly to go!"
"Maybe too;" "We could walk those more shy into life's learning?"
    "You know!"

"We all ponder words of Praise and Raze to waffle each other to and
    fro!"
"Spoken words to commend and condemn so high and low."
"After reading years of poetry so; Now I know!"
"We all should have spoken more like Poetry so!"

Gary Hendershot

Socio-Evolu-Tuality

Above the ground; beneath the clouds beside a soaring eagle
There I Am

In the wind; through the leaves; beyond the horizon
Where I Have Been

a pioneer - one of many
charting unknown waters; carving new passages
developing innovative ideas
facing dinosaurs of society
understanding borne of experience
scars from battles fought and ceilings of glass
alone
yet, surrounded by millions
fighting for a freedom
rightfully mine

On the ground; above the mountains; on top of the world
Where I Will Be

joan

Remembering

I am standing in the quiet room looking out the open window.
There is a large field, a field full of many beautiful things.
The goldenrod seems taller and more golden this year.
The pond we used to sit by everyday seems sort of lonely,
but peaceful and calm.
We used to play down there, by the pond...
The times we had, sitting by the pond, throwing small stones,
seeing who could throw the farthest.
Then there is that old tree we used to climb, my sister and I.
We'd take a book up there and read, or we'd talk a while.
Then when it got dark, we would climb down from the tree and race
each other across the field to our house.
But we're grown up now, remembering,
remembering all the things we used to do,
the things we're too big for now.
But now we can watch our kids do the same things we did,
and we know,
that they will have memories too.

Emily Larson

Decisions

I have no mind to change my decision.
There is no chance to sway me
And even though you might envision
A plausible solution, there can not be.

The clouds are already so very dark,
The sun will never shine through,
If there were a chance to see a spark,
It would never get through to the blue.

How do you erase or make right what was wrong?
It's not easy to make amends.
When you've made a mistake, do you suffer lifelong?
Or do you come through slowly and re-ascend?

There is only one way that I know it can be done,
That is to go all the way back
And start right from the bottom to reach for the sun
And don't ever let up on the slack.

Dolores De Tolla

A Modern Fairy Tale

Once upon a time in a land no longer here
there lived a Love strong enough to hold
The earth where the stars ran out of sky
as mythic nemeses are often remembered

A lad named Ramo believed his love, Ena
commanded the future in moon phases
Virtues blossomed and they built Love
which permeated every world's soul

Heaving hearts were made light as helium
in an atmosphere of content feeling beings
She gave him more than was herself to give
while he resented her intensity and precision

She became him with foresight
and could make hours from minutes
He grew young with her age
so time stood still when they met

That fatal night armed with each other's
weaknesses, they destroyed their building
The Love in all the world's hearts perished
and they never lived so happily thereafter.

Anne Mackie

Sins Of The Father

The life we lead takes us many directions,
these directions can either bring joy or great pain
and sorrow.

Pain is everlasting it never leaves it never dies.
We ask for forgiveness yet we do not receive it.
Let these that shall be done,
be our court our judge.
Our forgiveness is ours to give not to receive.
Please do not hold my sins up against me.
My mind and heart were of a child's.
Those sins shall not be mine.
They shall be yours dear father.
Your mind was the leader.

Ann E. Schlatz

"Obscured By Clouds"

As I lie dying, I am visited by the ghosts of my past
They appear and fade away stirring vast emotions
   -Emotions I have not felt in years.
Some come to haunt; others come to remind me of my coldness-
   Three remain behind to conquer my fears.

The first supports my soul:
   I gain faith, lose innocence, and find peace in an ending world.

The next supports my body:
   The firm limbs touch me and reaffirm the strength, courage,
   and power I had in my youth.

The third spirit assists my mind:
   Gentle and Christ-like, it gives me purity and moral righteousness.

Although my light is quickly extinguishing and the spirits are
   obscured by clouds
My fears and doubts have dissipated-
I am guided and guarded by a White Cross.

    Erik W. Van Treek

Why I Love You

There's some reasons why I love you, every moment, everyday.
They are reasons much more precious, and the one's that last for years

You are love more than the sunshine that shines down from up above.
And I'll treasure your sweet purpose in my life for years to come.

You are comfort when I need you in the days of darkest storms.
When the earth is fresh with raindrops in the springtime of the year.

You're a friend of deepest caring loving one's you see in need
And I'll thank my heavenly Father for you above all things.

You're a gift of rarest beauty from my Lord God up above
And I pray he'll bless you always with his dear undying love.

You are full of deepest sorrow when you see one trip and fall.
But your face shows glorious radiance when one enters God's safe fold.

You have God's own understanding when one needs strong, sure support
And you take them to the scriptures instead of using your own words.

You're my husband, friend, and lover, and everything I'll ever need
And I know you are truly saved full of God's mercy, love, and truth.

    Charity Renae Willis

Children's Fuss, A Child's Fussing

Children fuss all night long, in the morning,
they are singing a song, Oh what a song, a
joy to hear, "Oh hear, "Oh hear,"
the song so sweet, that restore my faith, upon
day light, and morning dew.
How weary we get, when children fuss, come awake
and feel the bliss, beautiful laughter, sunshine
amidst.
Look at their faces, when yet they fuss, you will
see sorrow within, yet when they sing songs of joy,
you catch the flicking light of time, across the
heart of a once fussing child.
"Let the child fuss, "Let the child sing,"
"Let the child laugh," "Let beautiful glory ring,
For these are all sounds of a once, fussing,
child's love.

    Julia Rivers Marshall-Hayes

The Leaf

This leaf is a whole made up of two equal halves;
They are sustained by the same root system of Love.
The leaf stem separates the two sides,
But the life-giving branches of love sustain both sides.
The sides are different, but the differences do not matter;
The freedom to be different is a gift from the whole.
Neither side says to the other:
"You must change to be like me."
This leaf has been buffeted by winds of adversity;
It has been blessed by rain and sun;
It has seen dark days and bright days—
It is sustained by its strength.
Its strength comes from its wholeness and its separateness.
And its freedom to be what Life meant it to be.

    Donald W. Gordon

Angel

Angels are described in many shapes, and forms
They come in different ways, and styles
There's one angel in a league of her own
That thrills me every time she smiles

She appeared when least expected
Out of the blue in times of need
She's been there from that day on
When needed coming to a heed

She was sent from above
A life saver you could say
A friend to listen, and to talk too
Always there night or day

Very beautiful, special, and bright
Every man's dream come true
A sight seldom seen
With eyes like the sky so blue

So here's to you my heaven sent friend
Whom I came to meet from a place afar
A lady who's been everything to me
An angel to me is what you are

    Favian Padron

The Last Minute

   I heard some one say about the disappointment
they felt, when no one acknowledge her absence
because of ill health.

   The chance to show love, a bit of concern, was
lost in an instant, we turned to ourselves...
   A minute is all it would take, a smile,
a nod "nice to see you back, Kate". But we
turn to ourselves, we are now too late.

   A lesson to learn, a smile in return, to
show we love others in spite of ourselves
   To give the warmth of love unsolicited, to
give a handshake firm in just that instant.

   We can do more if we try, but just a start
in that direction gives heart. So make it a
point, smile at your brothers and sisters.
Realize they are here now, Don't forget the
minute that could hold your love in it.

    Evelyn L. Bock

Stolen Words

Just by chance this certain day, a group of words I saw.
they filled me up with interest, in search, I looked for more.
A phrase or two familiar, a paragraph I knew.
My search I thought was fruitless but I had to see it through.

I searched the valleys and shadows of my mind
an endless journey deep within, these words I had to find
If one must steal or copy, to bring his point to light
I think it quite dishonest, by no means good or right

I found myself surrounded, with dots and numerous dashes
a period, a question mark, a noun, a vowel that flashes
Confused was I words so deep, my head did seem to bust
but carry on this endless trip - these words to find, I must

A last resort did come to me, as if a bolt of light
If I just juggle stolen words, its better not to write
Alas! the answer I have found, and has set me free
as I look back you see, I simply steal from me.

Gerard E. Tillman

Farewell to My Brother

Listen to me brother and to the words I have to say.
They may not mean much to you now,
But I know they will someday.

You must live and learn, and
Learn to burn some bridges to your past.
Because one thing I have learned in life
Is life just doesn't last.

So take the road that you choose,
Not the road that's chosen for you.
With faith you'll never lose.

Say the things you have to say,
Not what you're told is proper.
You'll be happier that way.

So live the way you need to live.
Don't live your life in sorrow.
Always remember, but try to forgive,
And you'll find peace tomorrow.

Jennifer Hope Farner

Stork

Oh Stork, oh, stork
They say they deliver babies,
They did!
Why do they, deliver kids?
Why not a horse, a cow; or even a pig.

They say they come in such a rush!
Why don't parents make a fuss?
They do not know, their kids are
brought home in a bag with a tag.

When the tikes get to their home
The parents put them in a crib, all alone

But when Christmas time finally comes
and all the stockings are already hung.
The stork knows that his job is done!

Jessica-Rose O'Keeffe Patterson

Future Peace

Affordable health care is a big hit!
There is a sound and balanced budget.
Welfare programs are reformed.
Thank you God! A miracle is performed!
Safe and quality housing for all
Dream! Work hard! Strive! or Fall!
Understanding, love, and unity preferred.
Peace... has finally occurred!

Jeanette Dotson

Clinically And Irritancy Tested

Those tender moments, so much like facial creams.
they start by whispering,
cleansing all those unsightly dreams.

They kiss you all over
tone, new dreams of wonderful things.
leaving you refreshed and standing on your own two feet.

They caress and add protection
creamed against harmful, unwanted things encouraging daily
routine.

New foresight you're rediscovering self-within,
alpha hydroxy is now regenerating new being.

You're loved and held, in case you're not intact on self-esteem.
cover-up, it's call and understood, leaving behind old dream.

More love and kisses
powder evenly and lightly, diminishing the shine away
last stage cosmetic play for more whispering increasing time
for more hours of play.

Celia Valenzuela

Whales

They swim across the ocean wide,
They swim in groups side by side.
Sperm, Blue, Bryde, and Minke,
As I think about them I stop and think.
These gentle giants of the deep,
Come up for air, and take a peek,
To see if their worst enemy-man,
Is on the sea, not the land.
If they are upon the sea, they often plot to kill me.
Why my life they wish to take,
Things of my body they want to make.
Oil, make-up, and shoelaces, you see,
Are some of what they make of me.
I truly do not understand,
Why these creatures God called Man do not understand.
Though a whale I may be,
My life is precious, at least to me.
To save a whale is a great cause,
Believe in us not Santa Claus.

Christy Boulier

This One's For The Children

Sometimes kids think their life is so bad.
They want just the best and what is "rad."
When they're told to neaten. They think their folks are mean.
But others would love a room to clean.

The homes of these children are so poor.
Things are in shambles. The couch. The windows, the door.
They have no room to call their own.
And their house hardly feels like a home.

Money is hard to find.
It's been a long time since they're pleasantly dined.
No one likes them. Though they're peaceful as a dove.
The only thing holding them is their love.

But then, on one sad day
One of the children starves and faints away.
There is sadness and tears galore.
And if we don't help, there could be more.

So many people are in need.
So many people that we should feed.
Helping gives you a good feeling inside.
People will laugh that have once cried.

Julia Skowronski

Who And What Are Performers

Performers are a very special kind
They'll keep going even with things on there mind
Up early in the morning, rehearsing their act
Ready to move on, their bags always packed
They will make you laugh or perhaps even weep
And their day usually ends when your fast asleep
Show them courtesy and let them do their part
For what they do really comes from the heart
Applaud them too whether their good or bad,
For one things certain they gave all they had
Their pretty lonely when the show closes at night
But from your laughter they know they did right
Remember any of those people could really be you
So give them the praise you think you are due
Because if you think of what you do each day
You'll see that everyone's a performer in their own little way

Edna E. Cillo

Days Of Love And Life With My Mother

First memories; loving hands,
Thin and shapeless; nothing fit right,
Making me clothes from feed sacks,
There were many alteration,
Upset she'd get; as well she might, sometimes gave little whacks,
To end she'd have a creation.

One memory: on the floor playing;
At the sewing machine, Mother,
Lightening struck, in one window and out the other,
Crashing circles around my mother;
Wouldn't have cared had it been another,
Scared me to death; could have lost my mother.

Sitting at her feet; looking in her sewing basket;
These days, she was my reason for living.
"Don't hurt yourself, Needles, pins, and razor in that wicker basket."
Tools of her creation; for her gift was giving.

Mother has been gone 5 1/2 years by cremation,
She'll live in my heart for the duration.
She was one of God's great Creation,
To have known and loved her; God's Donation.

Barbara Ann Sullivan Baxter

"Maybe Next Time"...

Look at all those things happening
Things I wish I could someday be involved in. "Maybe next time"...

Look at the father playing catch with his son-
That mother pushing her daughter in that swing. "Maybe next time"...

Look at all those children playing in the park-
Eating ice cream - getting dirty in the sand. "Maybe next time"....

Look at all those people enjoying the rays of
The sun on their skin - soon the fall weather will come, the trees will change - winter and Snow - but not for me. "Maybe next time".....

Look I should have waited to be inside you at A different time - a time when I was more important To you, than not protecting yourself better. A time when you cared what you put into your body. I'm sorry I did all the wrong things - it was all My fault you did all those things to me - I should Be down there playing and running, eating ice cream All the things little children do. I'm sorry mommy, I'll get it right.... "Maybe next time"......

Jacqueline Cooper Davis

Fire in the Sky

Looking back on yesterday
Thinkin' it could have been better than it was then
But for better or worse
No matter where we're going
Or who we pass by
We'll never forget yesterday
That Fire in the sky

Always wondered what tomorrow will hold
Never lookin' back before the light we hold
But these truths we hold now and forever
They bring us together today till never
We know the yesterday we shared will always be there
But lets leave it there
Though we'll never forget yesterday
The tears we fought together
Will be with us forever
Remember yesterday
That fire in the sky

Janie Duncan

Isle of Nevermore

Welcome to the isle of nevermore, greetings to my home.
This is no paradise by far.
I live in hope and decay,
Now there's no time to play.
I don't need to listen any more.
I don't need to leave this island called, Nevermore.

This island has become my home.
The surf of blood, sand of tears.
I have no reason to live without love, here on Nevermore.
The cobwebs of time, they wreath through my brain and heart.

This is no paradise by far.
I live in misery and strife,
Now there's no need to live my life on this
Isle called Nevermore.

Geoff Feddersen

"Little Bold Soul"

Cold stone walls so shallow and cold
This little soul so young and bold
No one knew of the terrible shame,
for all those things she suffered the blame
Not a soul to save her, to take her away,
The sad little girl, every moment she prayed
Oh! God please help, find me the way
I have to get over the giant wall of gray.
Huge stones piled up so high
God you know my wish to die,
Nobody likes me cause I'm so bad
Nobody cares if I'm happy or sad
Where I live is terribly black
I must go and never come back
If only I could fly up so high
I mean make it right over the wall to the sky
I know you can help me, just make me die
I'm almost over the stone wall of gray
Oh! God please help me, find me the way.

J. J. Crab

Tired And Confused

Been no-one forever, stolen, misplaced, left scratching this earth,
this piece of nothing, this part of a life.
Can't say what it means, just keep on doing it,
doing it to save me, or so I'm told.

In place, but not part of it, we are,
here where they left us, not our choice.
Been told to get on with it ever since,
been told to stay out of it, for ever.

A hundred years or two, maybe four, that's a long time,
a long time to laugh and wonder whose joke I am.
Whose fear and sadness was I made from, not mine,
for sure, maybe his, I don't know, maybe mine?

Forever's a long time, but I won't live forever,
thank God, damn God, I want to live like you,
not me, you made me, I hate me, I hate you, I think.
And that's where it gets all unhinged and I know I'll leave this earth
as tired and confused as I was, those four hundred years ago.

Christopher Billing

If I Where In Your Pocket

Aye but Miss, I must lament, 'though I appreciate the sentiment,
This restriction I resent, being a rather passionate gent -
There's not room for two in your pocket.

If I must be so small I couldn't reach 'round you at all.
Alas your legs would be so tall to shinney up would earn a fall
Even before I reached your pocket.

Oh, I could travel 'cross your knee if lying horizontally, but
up your tummy 'twould be to me like the Sea to Kon Tiki
If I struggled from your pocket.

When between your breasts I strolled 'twould be as 'twixt two
mountains cold. Alas I would be not bold and hide myself 'neath
Left side fold, while wandering from your pocket.

Your nose, your lips, your toes, your knees, your thighs
And all the goodies love implies would not blend with my size.
Pray please release me from your pocket.

Let me be a full grown man that I can love you as you know I can.
Let me rise up from within your hand and live in the world of man.
'Tis better for both than in your pocket.

Harold J. Hill

Storm Fear

A storm is a'brewing, the air feels strange,
  this sunny day it will soon derange.
Distant thunder roaring it's dangerous intent,
  thunders rumbling,
    this is no subtle hint.
Dark angry clouds rush to cover blue sky,
  winds blowing and gusting,
    to be brave I will try.
The deluge has begun, rains are now smashing,
  down to the ground limbs come crashing.
Lighting flares of intense hostility,
  it's no wonder storms petrify me.
Thunder booming so loud the ground quakes,
  childish fears are not gone,
    I have the shakes.
Lighting splits the darkness, slashing through the night,
  just let me sleep under the bed,
    come tomorrow I'll be alright.

Becky Powers

Untitled

She haunts me
this treacherous heart
never lose this pain
I have nothing to gain
possible peace
Accept this pain? Should I?
she, she is always
hot summer wind
searing, piercing the marrow of my thoughts
time is kind, deceitful
love let me find myself in your light
once again
cannot make it out of this pit
on the spit, turning, burning in these flames
wanting, yet not, this
find I'm at the bottom, one more of innumerable times
she, she is always
cannot shake this demon
the grip had loosened, now tightening ever more
I am hers, she is never mine.

Aaron Baldwin

I Wonder

I wonder if I was really part of this world,
This world of love, hate, and all in between.
I wonder if I really am going to
travel beyond places than my room,
Where I go past in time and into the future.

I wonder if I will ever see dinosaurs lurk the planet,
The sea gulls dancing across the sky,
The birds singing their sweet melody.
I wonder if I will ever be able to see

The president make a speech,
Or my friends make it to thee,
I wonder if I will try different things.
I wonder if I will soar out of this world,

Making the wind flow past my body,
The trees sweeping behind me.
I wonder if I will go out into space..
I wonder what will happen to me.

Judy Cheng

Red, White, Blue, And Jesus Christ

Red, White, and Blue colors ripple in the wind.
Those three colors, our Soldiers Gallantly defend.
Three colors and the Lord our forefathers sought
Our for fathers would weep for those who do not choose Christ.
Red, White, and Blue were planned to be colors for Christ.
Red: As the blood that Christ shed for our sin.
Blue: As the sky that leads to the kingdom of Christ.
White: As the light in your soul when you
Accept Christ as your Savior.
Prayer has been ruled out of education.
God and his word are no longer in schools.
Do not be full of sorrow fellow Christians.
Christ will come for us all.

Joey C. Brown

"Memories"

Music is softly playing
through the caverns of my mind.
Gently it stirs the memories
of yesterday's good times.

The memories are there to linger,
to endure the "Ages of Time"...
Isn't it sad for some to have
No memories such as mine.

Helen L. Downs

What He Was

Never once he spoke with words kind.
Those were the type he'd likely choke upon.
Instead he chose to utter those of brine
And fill his mouth up with a bitter taste.

Never once he cast emotion-glazed eyes.
With those, swear I, he likely couldn't see.
Instead he chose to see in black and white
And dismissed all color for only shades of grey.

Never once his hands were warm to touch.
With those, I think, he couldn't really feel.
Instead he fashioned hands from stone and ice
    and reached for only hardened emptiness.

And never once I wanted what he had.
His bitter tongue. Of ice, his eyes and hands.
And not for long lingered at his side.
I needed love. A heart he did not have.

Erin Elizabeth Eschik

Yet To Know

I hear speak of it by others.
Though I bear not possession myself.
To hear their praise; it be an incredible thing.
Oh, to be touched by it. To savor it.
To surrender my heart and let it encompass me but once in this lifetime.
Surely, it be heaven.

Though I have yet not to experience this marvelous thing.
Surely, it could not be that I am undeserving.
Please, that my time has simply not yet come.
Pray, my chance be soon.
To know such haven. To feel such serenity.
To have someone whose poverty of words not impede their passion.
That they be a zealot in desire to weave their soul with mine.

Oh, to be as fortunate.
With each breath, to innately know that inside my heart -
therein lies a constant.
Its name be love,
Its display be kindness,
and its custom be steadfast regard.

Ann Jacques

Creature of the Night

I live among the creatures of the night.
Though I wish for things to be different,
I can't stand up to fight.
Being thought of as weird things a lot of pain.
Why can't people see that deep inside we are all the same?
Looking down from my second story window,
I have the sudden urge to fly.
Not to soar like a bird,
But to fall from the sky.
Thud cries my fragile body as it greets the Earth,
Now being carried away by the hired hearse.
To late to stand and fight
Because now I truly am a creature of the night.

Abbie J. Ramsey

The Hills

The hills are eternity's children
They were here long before
And will remain long after
I am new to them
but they know me well
As they have known many before
Each came seeking her ownself
And the hills talked to them
As they talk to me now.

Edith M. Bowen-Wilcox

Roses On The Ground

Yesterday when I knocked upon your door
Though I'd been there many times before
I knew I didn't live there anymore
You looked at me as is it were a chore
I asked you for forgiveness, for the things I said and done
I told you, you were my only, only one
I gave you roses that you threw upon the ground
You told me you didn't ever want me to come around
There on the ground the roses lay
The roses I gave you yesterday
To say I'm sorry I hurt you so
How much I love you, you'll never know
I can't sleep
Because I weep
For the roses on the ground
And the love that will never be known

Joyce White

What Is A Woman?

What is a woman? Is there any other question?
Though much remains unanswered,
You are the first of answers
Which are found in wondering so —
The mystery of difference
As well as desires aborning
Which stir in the center of me.
And so it is still
And always will be —
That single beginning
Which is forever a mystery,
And therefore priceless and precious!

George E. Bailey

The Storm

Sailing the emotional seas on a rotting ship
Thoughts shifting from happiness to anger
The storm grows worse

Nursing my broken soul
The darkness of the sea is my black hole
The wrath of the storm beats on me mercilessly
The storm grows worse

I am banished to loneliness
The boards creak on the ancient ship
I am scared
The storm grows worse

Suddenly the pounding rain ends
The angry sea calms
But the dark clouds stay to remind me... of the storm

Chris Ratliff

Hello Again

In the corner of my heart there's a place for you with a thousand yesterdays and a million memories.

And on those lonely nights when my world is filled with the sound on raindrops and lightning shares the sky with thunder.

I turn to one of those yesterdays pull out one of those memories, and share it with the rain.

I'm happy with the life I've made, and though I'm not in love with you. There will always be a place for you.

Along side a thousand yesterdays and a million memories too soothe my soul....

Donna Marie Adams

Artist For A Day

If an artist just for a day I could be
Three pictures I would paint - and only three.
The stars and stripes with all her glory unfurled
A symbol of greatness to the entire world.

A landscape scene of our beautiful land
From the rugged mountains to the restless strand,
The final scene I would like to show
A family at worship, with faces aglow.

The flag gives me pride which no other can.
The landscape shows the touch of the Makers Hand.
The third is what makes a nation great
A family at worship - as before God they wait.
These and only these, again I say
I would paint if I were an artist just for a day.

Carlisle Bagwell

Shadows

Night fills my room
Through a lace curtain covered window whispering
Breezes rustle
    What's left of dying leaves and
    Blow through
My screen giving my curtains
A ghostly image

I walk slowly to the glass and look outside
I see
    Shadows against a harsh street light
    A single star hanging like a tiny spark
I make a wish and shut the window
I lie down on my back
I close my eyes as it starts to rain

Falling drops
    Tap on my roof
    Slide down my pane
They glisten in the pale moonlight
I lie there and wish I wasn't

Alone

Haley Edwards

Heaven Adorns

Heaven whispers her sweet songs to me,
through her winds singing in the trees.
I can almost hear her soothing voice say,
I am here to guide and protect you today.

I send the rains to gently wash away your tears,
to cleanse your soul, chase away your fears.
The massive Sun raises to send its warm rays,
to light the path throughout all your days.

The Dew will gather and sustain Earth's life,
as it gently nourishes every plant in sight.
Like tiny tears sliding down blades of grass,
keeping them green so they will forever last.

Beautiful flowers will adorn the land, to bring
contentment and beauty to man.
Gentle creatures to be your friends,
to bring true happiness and meaning from within.

Dorothy Stone

Not Our Fault

We said our love would always be
Through their bitter and cold accusations
They search to the depths of their bigotry
And only find constant objection

The stars and the moon can always attest
To their words of racial insults
But we keep the good and ignore the rest
We are in love; it's not our fault

Just because we are not the same color
Doesn't mean we can't be in love
And I would never ask for another
For me his love is always enough

Deborah K. Meyer

Stone Mirrors

A little hand of three or four,
throws stones that splash beside the shore.
And the sea is wondrous.

The strong smooth hand within its prime,
throws stones too when there is time.
And the tide rises, and the tide falls.

The wrinkled hand no longer strong,
leaves the stones where they belong.
And the sea is patient.

The stones remain at the tidal crest,
no hand disturbs their silent rest.
And the sea is timeless.

Bruce Back

Rainy Days Bring Clouds of Gray, Thunder and Lightning

Rainy days bring clouds of gray,
thunder and lightning.
Vapors descend upon us with tiny
drops or a heavy deluge.
Torrents that almost flush us away!
Have you ever wondered how this comes to be?

Tons of water suspended in space —
And then turned loose to cover the earth.
Who gives the order when to release
and when to restrain?
Gigantic drops of water or trinkles.
Some Superior Being is definitely in control!
Have you ever tried to hold back a
drop of rain in the sky?
Let alone buckets full at a time —
Before they almost reach the earth!

Joanne J. Saunders

Life's Journey

Take my hand and walk with me
Through fields of green and fields of brown.
Tho life has its up's and downs
We tread the path of good and bad.
We start out one step at a time,
Stumble and fall and try again.
We trudge along to school to church,
With friends we play everyday
Quarreling and yelling at everyone.
Patience we learn and sharing with others.
Disappointments come our way,
Along with rewards for work well done.
We fall in love, marry and have a family.
May God bless us and guide us all the way.

Betty E. Ransom

Seasons

SUMMER is just a memory of days we spent together beside the changing tide; laughing, talking, simply hanging out being best friends. You and I had weathered stormy nights and shared the most excellent adventures. We vowed our friendship would always be.

FALL, as with the colored leaves, changed us forever. You were no longer there and I am here wondering why. Where did my forever friend go? But the stars, though bright, remain silent against the velvet sky and my tears, though many, have no answers to my questions.

WINTER winds have chased my hopes away and still I wonder where you
are. Has the snow chilled your heart or does a fire warm your soul beside another? Like icicles on the dead branches, the bond we once shared has frozen and cracked - lying broken on the ground.

SPRING has found me standing on my own — like the sunflowers growing tall and strong in the bright sunshine. Are you happy my friend? I hope that you are. And as the seasons change and once again you hear laughter floating across the bay, think of me only once and wish me well.

Donna M. Tregear

The Awakening

Days come and go,
time endlessly flows...
I stand on the mountain, alone,
wondering where or when.

Among the rocks and soil
of the earth's crust,
scattered with wild mountain flowers,
I await answers and guidance
to questions that plague my thoughts.

As I peer into the voids amongst the clouds,
and lose myself in the brilliant chasm,
my being is lifted away
in the flight pattern of a majestic eagle.

My emptied shell collapses onto the igneous pinnacle,
minus its heavenly soul,
while I intermingle with a sea of spirits,
freed from my earthly chains.

Oh, to soar through the kingdom of our Lord.
I can now understand...
My questions have vanished, the answers now here.

Brett Lawrence Sposito

Keepers of Thy Souls

How the shadows grow heavy against the walls.
Time for the nightly watch
People passing in the dark,
　enemy or foe?
How hours roll by slowly
　for the Keepers of the night.
Each second, each minute
　as precious as the last.
Oh how Thy enemies beckon thee
　in the hours of the night
Anxiously awaiting for Thy
　careless fate.
To prance gracefully upon thee
　if Thou watches not.
So watch, watch keepers of Thy souls.
Watch for all Thy enemies
　but never let them know.

Barbara Payton

Chaos

I met a goddess one day and on her wings I flew away
To a world of which I have never seen And things I could not believe.
There were oceans of stone And dust for air, Thorns of fruit And I just stood and stared.

And I cried, "Please take me away, away from this god awful place Goddess, please take me away. What has happened to the human race?"

She said, "This world before you is yours With rivers of mud, waterfalls of sand. It can all be blamed on the human races's hand. Don't try to look for love ones or friends because the human race Has come to an End."

She said, "The animals used to live in peace the plants used to grow and breath Before man attacked Mother Nature and treated her like a whore. She tried to survive, but she lives no more."

In disbelief, I wept at the Goddess' feet.

As tears rolled down my face, I dreamed of no human race I dreamed of a world that was Peaceful and clean I could hear the whale's cry, And hear the lion's roar, I listened to the wolves howl And watched the eagles soar.

The Goddess picked me up and wiped the tears from my eyes if only the human race had stopped and realized.

J. Curtis Kolb

To Amy And Reid On Their Wedding Day

My precious Reid got married today,
To Amy a sweet loving gal.
I knew from the moment I met her that day,
That Reid had found a new pal.

A mother never wants to let go.
And let someone else have her son,
But from their faces there was such a glow,
I knew my work was done.

I'm very happy Reid took a wife.
They've found something special I know.
And as they wind down that road of life,
They share more and more as they go.

Charlene Vondersaar

Rows Of Stone

I've come back to this place to rest my weary bones
To be among my many friends, behind these rows of stone
I've hunted these woods and fished these streams
And flown these skies above,
But now the time has come oh Lord
To join the once I've loved.

Here's Mom and Dad the kid and pudge and all the kinfolk too.
Resting on this hillside with the farm in view.
Oh they cleared this land and plowed this ground
And hoed these rows so true
Now from their labors they all rest
To be Oh Lord with you.
Behind these rows of stone, Behind these rows of stone.

As Quakers from the East they came in peace to settle here
A few went West but they've returned to join the others here
Some were teachers, one a preacher, an engineer and now a pilot too.
From life's tests, we'll all rest
On this hill with you.
Behind these rows of stone. Behind these rows of stone.

Darrell R. Larkin

Untitled

What is it like
To be in love with you -
That special yearning
Which needs no cue??

To listen, but not talk,
To hear, but not say
All that's on one's mind
Least you run away.

To give to you willingly
For comfort and joy
To share all that's me -
Like a kid with a new toy!

I watch you sleep And want to lie there
And tightly hold on to you, but I do not dare ...
For then you are awake, your guard, cold, doth burn
And I am lost and alone with no deposit, no return!

For the man I cannot have the hurt runs truly deep ...
For the sharing you guard so well, I cry, silently, not a peep.

And when you leave without me, hard, but I must endure
Whilst my heart snaps apart - as for love, there is no cure ...

Judi Grater

Next To Nil

Unlike others, she got to chose
To be on the winning team, or the one that got to lose
She couldn't stand to be faceless and cool
Putting on make-up and looking like a fool
Nope that's not her thing
Most of her friends are junkies and/or gay
Reading Burroughs, Carrol, and Hemingway
Meeting others from different towns
Instead of staying in a snobby click
Not wanting to be a jocky ne'er - do - well
She paints and goes to shows for kicks
She's straight, but they call her a druggie
So, she tells them to go to hell
Knowing that she'll become something in the long run
and they'll be next to nil

Catherine Kaleel

A Letter To A Friend

I know it must be very hard
To be so far from home,
Even for a little while,
With many - yet alone.

The sun shines by day,
The moon at night.
The world goes on
But why must they fight!

We all want peace and justice,
Except the terrible Suddam Hussein,
Doesn't he see
That all he causes is pain?

It's hard for those who wait at home,
They try hard not to show it,
By putting on a smile or telling a joke-
It seems to help a little bit.

We hope to see you home again soon,
Along with all the others.
This is the continuing prayer of
Friends, fathers, brothers, sisters, wives and mothers!

Betty Wineinger

The Dreaded Day...

The last time to look upon your face
To caress your face with my hands and run them over you shoulders
And down the sides of your arms to meet your hands and finger tips
To surround your hands with mine
To embrace you and hold you close to my bosom and heart
To tenderly kiss your eyes and cheek
To touch your lips with my finger tips
The seasons of our life together flash before me
And then
The final farewell!
My dear, sweet, love I must depart, but don't despair for you will
always remain in my heart and soul and
I will never forget!
Perhaps, we'll meet again??

Edda Duenn Nomikos

You Gave Me A Rose

You were the first man to ever hold me.
To comfort me when I cried.
You watched me grow from a child to a woman
You gave me guidance when I needed it.

Somehow you always knew what to say
You were patient when it counted the most
You supported me in my times of hardship
And showed me love at my lowest points.

You saw me fall and helped me up.
You saw me laugh and laughed with me.
You saw me in pain and just held me.
You saw me happy and shared it with me.

In your own way you gave me the best
And I realized it all the time
When I needed your acceptance most of all
You gave me a rose!!
I LOVE YOU DADDY

Debbie Buckner

Autumn Leaves

To fall straight to earth
To enjoin with the masses
To decay and enrich the soil

Or

To fall . . .and be caught in the wind
To be lifted perhaps, even higher than life
To soar

To catch in a friendly branch
There to remain and observe the forest naked

To insulate a nest by design
To witness a birth therein

To embark on a voyage cross the surface of a lake
To sail downstream to the sea

To yet live in a second life
Before coming to ground

James Bach

Hunger For Knowledge

Hunger for knowledge
Thirst for love
Search for the truth
In the stars above
Cherish your friendships
And hope they last
Live for the future
Try to learn from the past

Charles Tumbleson

For the Moment

To be alive, would be wonderful and great
To feel the warmth of the sun
To be with someone you love
To live in peace and harmony...

But deep in every single soul
Something deep and dark
is always lingering in there
for no human can find total happiness..

Deep and dark, it awaits for the right moment
   to pounce at you
   to put you in a pool of tears
   to swallow you whole
So the clouds would be dark
where not even the brightest sun
can shine through...

That, my friend is a part of us
which we cannot chain.
which we cannot lock away.
But to push it aside to the deepest part of us
where it will be kept in, for the moment.

   Jamie Goh

I Promise

I promise, as long as you will have me
To give all my love, completely to you
To be there for you, as long as you need me
To stand beside you, at whatever you choose to do
I promise my faithfulness, in body and soul
To be creative, so our love never grows old
I promise to kiss, only your lips and each day
and never to wander, or let someone else take me away.
I promise to listen, to always hear you thru
And above all, to be patient
Till you are ready too.
I promise not only to say
But I promise I Will Do
everything and more I promised
because I Love You

   George Sandlin

"I Wish I Were An Angel"

I wish I were an angel
to guide you on your way'
to help you when your lonely
Although your far away
I'd like to be there always
to help you with the fight,
The days, the weeks the months,
That you fight for what is right.
Now that you must leave me
And work for Uncle Sam
I keep wishing and thinking
"I wish I were an angel and not what I am!'
But when this war is over
And you come back to me
I'll know you had that angel
to keep you safe for me.

   Cynthia Belanger

Untitled

A mask is something to hide your face
To hide your fears and your disgrace
When it's off you're sad and blue
If only anybody knew
The pain I feel behind the mask
To take it off would be too much to ask
Behind the mask I am hiding in shame
Afraid to get help
Afraid I am the one to blame
I wear the mask to hide this pain
I smile and act happy but I am going insane
I can't assure myself everything will be okay
Please listen carefully and hear what I can't say
My mask can be removed but it will take a little time
I feel like asking for help
would be committing a crime
My history of pain builds strong walls
Please try to knock them down and make them fall
Who is this person you may ask?
I am right in front of you wearing my mask.

   Jennie Eddlemon

Springtide

The doors of Fall open
To let the cool mornings arouse
My skin to goose flesh.
The fragrance of death and decay lingers
Through the scarlet and amber tinted leaves
As they rustle beneath my feet.
As I walk, I drift
To the green meadows of Springtide,
When mother's ambrosia
Simmers on the stove,
And father's cigar smoke
Haloes his head
As he swings the evening to an end.
It is a time cradled in twilight.
And with each leaf
Tumbling from its existence,
I begin to frost,
Awaiting the onset of Winter.

   Christopher Alan Hempfling

Caroling In The Night

Listen to those words, as they seem
To linger in the air, like a feather
Caught in a breeze. The singing is clean,
With each syllable, echoing near the heather,
Covered with snow. Listen, and think
Of the marvelous event, that took place,
Oh, those many years ago, in a wink
Of God's eye, which inspired these words, with grace
And faith. The rhythm glides peacefully,
As the melodious tones bring tear drops,
Dripping with joy, for that holy,
Baby boy born, who would be King, and the tops,
Of all men. So, listen closely, and hear the height,
Of these words, with the caroling, in the night.

   Eva M. Roy

This Old Farm House

Would you folk bend an ear, while I talk
to my friend? Heavenly father, you know that
old farm house that I live in - I keep it in
pretty good shape don't I?
That old farm house talks to me, just like I
talk to you. Do you know how it talks? When
its roof starts leakin' and its paint starts peelin',
I get really concerned because I have to live in
that old house. I put forth labor plus material,
and that cost me money.
But I read where you just spoke the word
and folk were healed. No labor, no material,
just the word.
You live in this old Tabernacle
of Clay - you walk up and down in it day after day -
Now my roof's not leakin', and my paint's
not peelin' but I know a precious little old
grandmother who could sure use some divine
healin' right this very moment. Heavenly Father,
I feel like we've just touched the hem of your garment.

Al Sweatt

Orchestra

You stepped out of the orchestra
to perform a solo. Play a beautiful
recital. Soothe me, soothe me, for
I am ravaged by my past, baffled,
misunderstood and overstocked. There
is so much music for my soul to play.
Memories recites identity bringing forth
that which is thee. Who shall bring the
notes of courage that will awaken the
cries of residual concerns, that beat the
unspoken rhythm at the key strokes of life.
Put to a ballot the sharp edges and flat
tunes of holding a beautiful instrument and
not playing its music, is finding out you
are who you was pretending to be, just part
of the orchestra.

Diana L. Hardin

Just A Life

i decline
to recline
so i find myself walking home alone

stop at a bar
'cuz home's too far
and the juke's crankin' heartache tonight

sup the last sip
wipe a drop from my lip
it's poison but it gets me where i'm goin'

home too late
to be up by eight
nine-to-five's nowhere anyway

turn on the tube
watch some boob
selling things that nobody needs

crank it up loud
'cuz i'm too proud
to listen to the sound of my heart breaking

Cindy Lipka

The Teacher

The choice long ago he made, to tread where others chose not,
To sculpt the minds of the young, to nourish their yearning to learn,
To guide the destinies of the seas of humanity,
Each one clamoring for his station in life.

Friend to the child needing care, helping the many who know no help,
Beacon of light for the mind lost at sea,
Forging among his disciples, islands all, a common thread,
A road of discovery, leading to the light at the end of their toil.

Each day unique unto itself, different from others before,
Facing new challenges, new shoals to cross, new outcomes to attain,
Teaching one to strive for the best, to settle for nothing less,
Assisting a child to reach the stars, to climb the rainbow of success.

To touch the heart of each child, to transform hostility into
    compassion,
Reaching out to those most in need, affording all opportunity to
    succeed,
To listen to a voice sing, vibrant, dauntless and bold,
To watch an athlete compete in quest of the gold.

To witness children perform magical miracles of endeavor,
To hear a child confess that you made a difference forever,
For these reasons is the teacher born, for these reasons does he subsist,
No mightier calling has man pursued, no nobler profession can ever
    exist.

George Chrissos

Untitled

'Twas in November when I was told
To "sit down first" I was so old
"Another baby is on its way"
And there was nothing I could say

I was not thrilled or even glad
I thought of my Jo and troubles she had
That old stairway I could plainly see
And knew just what was ahead for me

The weeks went slow for Mom and Dad
For Grandma too they were quite bad
She was so concerned for Mother- to- be
God cared for all as you can see.

He arrived July eight in eighty eight
Eight pounds three was his recorded weight
His hair was black and eyes were brown
He truly did deserve a crown.

Jon Robert was the chosen name
I don't ask for the Hall of Fame
For all his life I ask God's will
And may be grow that place to fill.

Daisy Hanson

Untitled

Is it possible for a young child
    to grow too fast?
There by leaving her childhood behind.
    Thus becoming an old woman before her
    time.
    The flesh is corrupt in all its ways.
    The ravage of men through all their days.
A lust is what the eye both see.
    Desire becomes reality.
    All men of you have to concede.
    The spirit is willing;
    But the flesh is weak.

    Corruption.

Henry Murphy

Footprints

It was a cold and stormy night, and I was eager and bold
to take a stroll through the snow, which was as low as the ground
that we walk around on. But I would not let that bother me, for I
am determined to continue my journey.

Although it's a cold and stormy night, I pray to the heavenly Father
that if my eyesight should fail me, would he do the honor of guiding
me through this stormy night.

And as I continued my quest to search for a place to rest, I realized
that I could not see a single tree in sight, so I dropped to my
knees to plea for this night to end.

And as I closed my eyes in fear, I started to cry with a tear
so that my dear heavenly Father can tell me if I am near, but
instead I hear a voice say, open thy eyes my son and follow my
Footprints that will show you the way.

And so I opened my eyes to see His Footprints and said my dear
Father I can not see your Footprints in this stormy night, and so
he shined a bright light, so that I may have sight to see His
Footprints.

And with His Footprints help I have made a safe journey home.

Hector L. Colon

The Looking Glass

Looking through the window,
to the painful memories.
They once brought me laughter,
Now only misery.
Looking in the pictures,
Though they seem to look back.
They bring great sadness,
And lost rememberings.
Lost in my mind for what seems like forever.
Trying to forget the great pain and suffering deep inside.
Within.
The word I utter seem to be forgotten.
They stumble over my tongue,
Mindless and unheard.
They are the words of a dying soul,
Trying to be heard.
Staring into the mirror
Plainly and confused.
Someone stops to listen.
The soul is finally heard.

Heather Miller

Gratitude

When I wake up at the start of each morn
To the sound of a far away train's lonesome horn
Thinking how glad I am to have been born
I am blessed.

Walking through leaves all alone in a park
Watching the sun 'til it's gone and quite dark
Building a fire and watching it spark
I am blessed.

Swimming through waves rolling in on the beach
Wishing on stars so high no one can reach
Speaking good words in the hope they will teach
I am blessed.

Looking for fireflies, seeing their glow
Making an angel in the new fallen snow
Loving my children, watching them grow
I am blessed.

Holding hands, being touched in the night
Knowing I'm loved, loving too when it's right
Laughing, crying, dreaming with all of my might
I am blessed.

Diane M. Henry

The Painting Of A Winter Scene

Her wheelchair rolled so easily guided by the lady's hands
To the window by the table where her painting easel stands.
Brush in hand she painted as the picture did unfold,
To capture, what she saw out of the window, was her goal.

The sky is gray as evening and the wind is howling 'round.
The pond is frozen solid and snow spread upon the ground.
The trees are magnificent in their trim of greens and white.
Suddenly! in a clearing, came a deer fawn into sight.

Colors on the children's clothing, who were skating on the ice,
Their cheeks as red as roses with their shining happy eyes.
wore hats and scarves and gloves of reds,blues, browns and golds,
Pants and coats of blues and yellows kept them from the cold.

Blue smoke lazily curls from the chimney 'cross the way
And gray squirrels go in hasty flight from tree to tree in play.
A cardinal in his dress of red and his wide black design.
Perched upon a snowy branch, found red berries on which to dine.

Bounding in startling contrast, our American flag still flew,
However, in harmony with winter in it's red white and blue.
A snow bird flew upon the flagpole but quickly took it's flight
And the painting was completed, Every brush stroke was just right!

Anne Kline

Silence (So Much Meaning)

To hold you in my arms is a silent way to say stay with me...
To touch your face while looking into your eyes is to say you're
special in my life...
To hold your hand with either a soft or hard grip is to say that
you are my friend and more...
To kiss your lips tenderly is to say I love you...
To send a smile your way is to say I adore you...

The beauty of silence has so many different meanings...
Share them with someone who you care for...
And feel the warmth...

John C. Sison

Time May Change But We Have Our Memories

In 1984, I was eight,
To young to go out and party till late.
Inside my house, I'd sit and play,
The Bangles, from sun up, until the end of day.

I look back on the music from then,
No cussing, no fussing, no political trends.
The music was about fun and having a life,
Not about people who killed with a gun or a knife.

I admired the Bangles,
They had style,
They didn't preach to kids,
Be obnoxious and vile.

But who do kids admire today?
When the music is not about fun and play.
When the music is about sex and killing,
How can kids grow up with feelings.

Time may change,
and what will be will be,
but at least I'll still have,
my fond memories.

Amber D. Gray

As If It Was Yesterday

As if it was yesterday, it was.
Today is a gift, da present, heaven sent,
Minus da madness, plus da fun.
It's not often dat we party without a gun,
Ghetto life projected on a big white screen,
Niggas, bitches, thieves and crackheads,
Death, drugs, deceit, disillusions
Spread all over my television, my magazines, my textbooks,
Yesterday, today, tomorrow,
Then, da same, nothing's changed,
All I see are hieroglyphics on a golden wall,
They see scribbling dat's dirty, nasty, niggalike,
Yesterday, we are all slaves together,
Today, we are all free and divided.
Tomorrow, we cry and wished dis day never came,
As if it was yesterday, it was.

Erick B. Cooper

Together Forever

My love is a calm river, yet a wild sea.
Together and forever, we'll live in harmony.

The peace of God above, will guide us
through the years.
Through the good and bad times, he'll
wash away the tears.

When we finally leave this place, to
rest eternally.
I know that you and I will be,
together... forever... happily.

Gary A. Jones Jr.

Untitled

Let the candles burn and the music play
Together we can drift away

Sharing time, just me and you
Through sun filled skies or clouds so blue

Hold me tight, don't let me stray
Sharing one sweet magic day

I'll caress your body and kiss you gentle
Let the jazz play a soft, smooth instrumental
I'll share my feelings straight from the heart
You'll stay with me, we'll never part

I'm telling you now, you're a special girl
With your deep brown eyes and your hair's slight curl

You give me chills with every touch
You're the one for me. I love you much.

Jesse Radant

Snow

It is crystal white it lays on the ground and in the tree.
The white animals blend in.
The children play, but not me.
They make snowmen and angels.
They shout and dodge the snowballs
The snow is good to play in.
It's very pretty.
I sit inside watching through the window all alone,
   wishing I could play.
But I am to sick.
Though I watch them play.
Though the little glass window.

Julie Haigh

The Rage Within

The power that came from the earth
   torrents of pounding rain
Winds that slice hope and scatter
   them across the fields.
Power filling her being
   with relentless anger
Unlike the winds
   her anger does not disperse,
Rains that could wash away the evils of man
   cannot wash her of her anger
This anger destroys her being
   As the winds and rain of a hurricane
Destroy the earth
   from which it has lived.
Short and powerful it is
   with the strength of millions,
It's wrath, that of an angry world,
A world that like herself
   hold within themselves,
Their own destruction.

Amity Caton

Weeping Willow

Weeping willow is no one there weeping willow no one really cares.
Tossing turning in the wind, frontwards, backwards where do I fit in.
I'm just a weeping willow a weeping willow weed just a little person
   they shouldn't have planted my seed.
I'm just an ordinary little person a little person indeed.
I'm just a wondering weeping willow seed.
A seed can get lost in such a tall forest of trees,
but I'm not a tree, I'm just a weeping willow seed.
I float from place to place not knowing where to land.
Then I try to figure out what I have at hand.
Sometimes I may talk funny or say things I don't mean,
but could I ask for forgiveness or am I still that wondering seed.
I'm not asking for self pity, I'm not asking for a plea,
I'm just asking for some guidance to lead this little seed.
I'm just a weeping willow a weeping willow weed.
Looking for, some guidance to turn this weed into a tree.

Cynthia Belcher

Frozen Desert

Walking through a frozen desert, rings around the starlight-
traveling on, all alone, in a sentimental state of mind,

Tell me can you hear it, the sound is so clear-
the deafening sound of silence broken only by the cold whistling
wind-

With rings around the starlight, travel on, all alone-
in a sentimental state of mind-

Can we meet half way, traveling alone, together,
could we meet half way in a frozen desert,
before time takes our world away-

Guided only by the rings around the stars,
travel on, all alone-

I need to see your face,
when I'm in a sentimental state of mind,
when the world outside seems so unkind,
it seems sometimes like a frozen desert.

Forrest Martin

a love sonnet

a hot summer night under a green sky
trees tower over me and smile brightly
wind tickles my ears and makes me feel high
a coyote treks by, plunging to sea

flashing lights barricade me from my way
as I chase the fat boy throughout the park
unceasing laughter in the sunny day
bright lights encircle me, hidden in dark

driving through time in the butterscotch car
fleeing from the black thing not far behind
I was stoned after the descending star
enlightened and delightful from my find

tripping from star to star in levity
a lapse in time all for insanity

Amanda Briggs

After the War is Over

After this war is over and the world is once more free of men who tried to conquer these lands across the sea.
We'll try and keep these nations in freedom for evermore or let some other dictator start up from the very core.
Will these nations stick together when one gets out of line and stop him from the very start? Which takes such little time.
Or will these nations let him go just like they did before and cause a lot of misery that people have to bore.
I say let's take these tyrants and hang them one by one and stick to the job we started until the task is done.
And then the people in this world until eternity can live fearless day and night.
A world once more set free.

James J. Allen Sr.

Legacy Of Tomorrow

While mothers weep for Mogadishu's dead
Troubles are brewing in the bowels of Kremlin.
There's a ghostly rattling behind the curtain of iron.
And the strip that's Gaza
Has turned blood red with Agony.

Nuclear weapons of Massive destruction,
Instill object fear of mayhem and murder.
While children wail with swollen, empty bellies,
We shut our eyes to their cries of sorrow.

Voices on the wind speak of a new world order.
Laced with hope, justice and visions of peace.
But is peace negotiable, if tempered by hatred?
What a legacy for our children!
And the future of their tomorrow.

There's a glimmer of hope in this Abyss of darkness.
It begins with you, me and the flames of desire.
Desire for truth, peace and above all love.
It's not impossible, if done in the spirit of kindness.
So take his hand, her hand and mine.
And build a bridge of Love that will last for all time.

Felicie A. Drigo

Beware

Beware of guys with eyes of blue,
they kiss you once and then its through.
Beware of guys with eyes of green,
they kiss you once and make you dream.
Beware of guys with eyes of brown,
they kiss you once and make you frown.
Beware of guys with eyes of Hazel,
they kiss you once and make you dazzle.
Beware of guys with eyes of Black,
they kiss you once and throw you back.

Denise K. Flores

With Love Forever More

Here we are just you and me
True lovers we must be.
You just wait and see,
No need to worry follow me,
We've been together for quite sometime now,
Now that I know your love is forever mine,
I'm ready to give you all my love,
You know I promised
That I was worth the wait
Oh please don't hesitate
you make me tremble,
with your warm kisses
I never knew I could feel this way
I never really noticed all the magic in your eyes,
Baby don't let that be a surprise,
I wanna share forever with you baby
And that's no maybe.
That's why I tell you my feelings are so true,
I love you right down to the earth's core
With love forever more.

Billie LeAnn Hicks

Life's Mystic Flow

Enter life's mystic flow,
Try to be worthwhile...we're —you go.
Life's filled with ups ... downs,
Still ... there's beauty abound.
Look to the bright side,
Find logic's ways ... to stem the — bad tide.

Stay with the mystic flow,
Admire the sun's rays ... the — moon's glow.
Make good beds ... sow good seeds,
Keep away from monstrous weeds.
Enjoy the wind...the sun...the rain,
Make-do with what good you've — attain'd.

Continue with the mystic flow,
Life's ... such a marvelous show.
People from near ... far,
Everyone's ... reaching for the stars.
Hold your head up ... high.
Remember your brother . . . try!

Aston Anderson

Memories

Did you know in the fall of an evening;
Under a velvet-star studded sky.
If you listen very quietly you can hear memories walk by?

It may be the hushed step of a loved one,
Or the faint cry of a child in the night.
Or it may be the sound of laughter
Or the feeling of someone holding tight.

It may be the tiny clank of dishes
Being stacked from an afternoon tea.
On the muted bark of a cherished pet,
Sitting quietly at your knee.

It may be the feeling of sadness.
O'er the passing of a being or thing.
On it may be the happiness you still feel
The day you received your first Ming.

But whatever the memory that time let's see.
The sweet and tender moments are there.
And the sorrows and pain, they all fade away.
And we know God is still everywhere.

Ellaree Winn

Sugar Bunny

Father's Day, warm June afternoon...remembering another.
Twelve years earlier, death snatched the grandmother.
June 19th - sadness...today changing.

Nine months of preparation...today small bloody membranes.
Such quick pain...body racking with terror.

Too Fast...Too Fast...

"No way," the doctors yelled, "Hours before happening..."
Body in control, watching in shock.

Too Fast...Too Fast...

Body heaving...passage still not ready.
Hearts stop...unable to take the pounding.
Black tunnel pulling...life interrupted

Too Fast...

"We're loosing them," he yelled...hands thrust deep inside
Trying to save the treasure.

Child dead white...doll limp in suspension.
Two at stake...both drifting toward extinction.

A third soul twelve years departed...smiled down upon them.
"Too soon," she whispered, "You must go back."

Death and birth...mingled, producing my gift...a daughter.
Janis Meade Ritter

Violence

Violence is just a word to some, Violence is a life that's done.
Two parents stand and look up at the sky praying that the Lord
will keep their children alive.

A father stays up all night to wonder where his child has gone. No
ring of the phone at one o'clock, just a real hard knock. He
opens the door praying its not bad. An officer stands in blue, a
tear runs down his face.

A women cooks outside for dinner feeling very happy suddenly
shots fired from everywhere two children hit. Sirens, lights,
fear, and anger two children's lives gone forever.
Violence is just a word to some, Violence is a life that's done.

Two parents stand and look up at the sky praying that the Lord
has their children tonight.
April Willbanks

Echoes of the Woods

Quietly and peacefully I blossomed,
Uncultivated, Unadulterated,
In oneness with Nature
And the beauty of the Creator.
The waters ran peacefully below,
And the birds with joy flew above.
The creatures within me in harmony,
Sang of the beauty of the Creator.
And then came that day; the day of doom,
The tool of destruction, man's civilization
Invaded my bowels for expansion
Plundered and polluted the waters,
And shrouded the beauty of the Creator:
The path of man to self destruction, it is.
Debo Richards Obawole

Fireflies

One balmy night I was running in circles in my backyard
 Underfoot I could feel the c o o l grass
 trying to sneak up between my toes
We did everything together - the grass and I
 jumping and rolling and crawling and hiding
 my treasures and Me...

But on that night
 I chanced to see a light
 A light so dazzling and alluring that I ran to catch it
 And I did
Catch that magnificent Treasure
 The glow on my face eclipsed the One in my hands
 How Wonderful the night
 that I should be so Blessed!

Funny...
 The next day I looked to see my Prize
 and I found a bug...
 It was just a bug!

I've known several Fireflies in my life
 I guess I never learned the lesson from that warm summer's night!
Cathy J. Berenberg

Young Boys' Prayer

Dear God watch over these boys tonight, they may not understand...
Why the gift of life is gone from such a wonderful man...
Find a way to let them know it's natural to shed tears...
As the family joins together to remember one so dear...
Please don't let them place the blame, as this would be wasted time...
The memories of their father should always be fresh in their minds...
Help them recall the fun they had and all the love they shared...
And with your love and guidance, let them know how much you care...
All boys need their fathers in many different ways...
They need to know he'll be watching over them, and in
their hearts he'll stay...
Diane E. Evans

Untitled

The directions in which our lives proceed
Unknown to all
Predictability impossible
Unbelievability in retrospect
Characteristics formed by a series of fortuitous events
Lives touched

Emotions uncontrolled
Throughout time
Individuality results
Sculpting souls
Providing a foundation
Preparing for a future
Analyzing the past
Enduring the present
Absence of regret

Imperative
Education the reality
Fulfillment
Peace
Love...within
Holly Lynn Clark

In The Flower Garden

I am just sitting
up looking out. In the
flower garden: Watching the kitten, to and fro.
While the butter flies flap their wings,

In the flower garden.
gold and blue ma caw, male
yellow throat: Red hen chickens, a garden spider
in the flower garden. I am just

Sitting up looking out.
In the flower garden. Watching
all those beautiful roses shining in my eyes,
it is beauty. I am just sitting

Up looking out, in
the flower garden. Watching the
kitten. To and fro. While the butter flies
flap their wings, in the flower garden.

Gold and blue ma caw,
male yellow throat. Red hen
chickens. A garden spider. In the flower garden.
I am just sitting up looking out.

Clovis Lloyd Johnson

Sadness

Sadness lies like lead
upon a heart weighed down
with centuries of unshed tears

Grey molten weight
burdens and encases
the yearning passion to release
new lyrics in healed whole tones

Still paralysis
flows in veins and arteries
bathed in pained and salty tears of loneliness

Weep my heart!
Shed these millennial oceans of sorrow
that you may wake and sing!

Audrey Doetzel

Stab

I watched my mother bleed one night. Coming
upon her in the kitchen, bent body unforgiving
like Africa and elbows working, working the
dishes before her, the sink a yawning hole. I
saw when her body absorbed the shock - the slow
implosion of her belly as a tear in the uterus
drew downward to splash on the worn linoleum
floor. She fell back, unaccustomed to the force
of pain, though surely having felt its shadow
before, on other nights. I could have reached
to touch the yellow fabric of her dress or
fallen to my knees pressing forehead to skin,
but my ovaries, intact and full, screamed a
choral protest and I recognized myself in that
form across the expanse of tile, knew my body
would fit in the curve of air her's assumed.
I watched until she drew a breath, finally
turning away as she gnawed at grief, blood
flowing like milk over her feet.

Anne-Marie B. Flannery

Reflections

The blinding darkness that you see,
Was here long before you met me.
The loudly deafening sound you hear,
Can only come from what you fear.
Tightening places opened wide,
To the seeded guilt you hide.
Only from the Mirror's light can you
see clear, True Right!
The Wrong's awaiting tomorrow's dawn,
To change your thoughts, to write your song.
But when Today's tomorrow's past,
I hope you find your dreams at last.
And like an arrow shot from a gun,
You stand your ground, refuse to run.
For your reflection is all you see,
There's noon else starring back at thee.
So when your waves top their roll,
And you find nowhere else to go.
Just reach inside for your breath,
And face your truth with your time Left!

James W. Iles

Conflicts Of Life

The birth of a child with beauty arrayed,
victims of murder, a body decayed.

The scent of a rose in the cool of day,
the stench from a landfill, miles away.

The innocence of a child asleep in the night,
screams of people, tormented with fright.

Winter lights in a window, the earth blanketed with snow,
devastation of fires, and storms the seas throw.

The humility of a child, their contentment with life,
adults full of hatred envy and strife.

Cities full of kindness, helping strangers in need,
yet from these same towns, come malice and greed.

The peace of a sea gull soaring the shore,
the outcry of a soldier, wounded in war

Oh when will it end, life's conflicts in man,
where justice claims victory and all evil is banned?

Dennis Hornberger

The Icy Enemy

When a vagrant chill sets on your doorstep
  waiting for your children to come out;
be sure to tell your young ones to be careful
  and that winter's bite is very stout.
    I see anguish, I see grief.
    Icy, is the ground beneath.

Be advised and weary of the dangers
  outside the cozy comfort of your home.
Keep an eye upon your happy children;
  do not ever let them run or roam.
    I see heartache, I see pain.
    Icy, is the freezing rain.

And if winter ever gets one of your children;
  take a lesson from the star of sun-
when you find something that does not suit you
  destroy it and it shan't bother anyone.
    I see sadness, I see fright.
    Icy, is the air tonight.

Brett Leabo

Searching for Foot Prints

I searched and searched
Wandering around like drifting duckweed
I finally discovered
The footprints of my grandfather
In this foreign land
In a corner of the lowest class

I searched and searched
Hovering like floating duckweed
The footprints seemed to be soaked in blood and tears
They impel me to work hard
The footprints seemed like blooming flowers
They inspire me to excel
Hang Ching Yip

My Vagabond Heart

Hush, be still my vagabond heart, My soul
Wandering life's pathway, for love's ecstasies to unfold

Seeking contentment in life's uncharted avenues
Reminiscent of past romantic interludes

Beating to love's tempo of uncertainty
That in some way shapes our destiny

Having mystical thoughts of love's grandeur
Anticipating all of it's splendor

Hoping to satisfy heart's ardent endeavor
Willing to accommodate mere hint's of pleasure

Beckoning the thrill of love to manifest
Beguiling attributes, like the rushing tempest

Like the unchanneled wind that blows
So my vagabond heart roams.....
Barbara F. Spencer

Circles of Fate

Into the darkness we roam the corridors of life.
Wanting, more, we grasp each hand in uncertain bound,
Searching for that one person to guide us to light,
Often failing to see what appears so profound.

We cast off the safety for just expedience,
Through it all we ask ourselves why it happens when,
We're trying to travel through the passage by chance,
Only to find ourselves, in time, reaching again.

Enclosed in circles, our souls are governed by fate
While all along, our freedom lies within ourselves.
The fallow of our mind in falsehood we create
The images we quest for - not knowing our hell.

Our only true love we find, will remain in thought
Regardless of saviors we religiously sought.
Alex Koprivica

Essence

Gaze towards the flicker of light
this candle of brightness
has an essence of companionship,
with it is the scent of a smile.
A pool of tears, melting away,
searching for time to complete its welcome.
A breath of life can end its existence,
yet the swirl and continuance
of its creeping smoke lifts,
and journeys toward the sky;
As to recall the single flame.
Crissy Theiste

Lost Without You

Feeling sad and so alone,
   wanting to call him,
With each glance at the phone

The memories that go threw my heart,
The pain from being so far apart

Knowing when I need him he won't be there,
Somehow, inside it doesn't seem fair

As I wonder through the day,
Does he hurt inside the same way?

Does he even miss what we had,
Do our special times gone make him sad?

I gave him my heart and soul
Where did all our love go?
Darcey Kruisenga

Cuttingly Clear

The plaintive chirping of a tiny bird
Was the only sound I really heard
Echoing still across that blighted wood
Where once a majestic forest stood...

What strange thing here has occurred
As more than hewn stumps we preferred
Finding shady cool haven if we could
A baking yellowed orb we not withstood

Would be back to just spread this word:
Logger's lobbies are grounded on turds
Petition now for future baby birdies good—
Save our only woods please - if U so kindly would...
Alan Hastings Jr.

Success

There was a special pre-school, my daughter
   wasn't accepted
My son weighed too little for the peewee
   football team
My daughter wanted to be the Sugar Plum Fairy,
   she was the Dew drop
My son swam for the gold, he took home the silver.
My daughter wanted a man who thought she hung the moon.
She now has someone who is the sunshine of her life
My son wanted someone he didn't have to train
He's now being trained by a very special woman

Now my children stride resolutely through life,
   creating their own opportunities.
Shaped for success by difficulties and failures?
They were always winners.
Gerri Engles Gessner

My Best Friend And Lover

There are friends, and there are lovers-
   usually it's one, or the other-
      when you find the lover, that is your best friend-
      the joy in your heart, will never end-

      The sparkle in your eyes, reveals the pride-
         the laughter in your voice, rolls out from inside-
         the touch, the looks, the sudden glances-
            make the sparks glow, to all who passes-
            True love, is the hardest thing to find-
               but for those who do, will always shine-
               few ever luck out, and find each other-
               "I'm one", who is my best friends lover-
Bobbi Beasley

Kill The Giant

"Class it's time for a film." The teacher says with a smile. I don't
watch the film though. To me it means my escape out of reality. To
think about other things occupying my mind. To think about my dreams
and nightmares I had the other night. To try to make something of the
scrambled mess of flashbacks playing and replaying in my head. To try
to make something of my life, instead....
It is hard for me to understand what makes us different. If you look
we do things almost the same. How can there be individuality in a
world that promotes us to buy, use, and wear alike.
Materialization has conquered us.
And your God is no longer the same as mine.
We listen to music to which the lyrics make no sense. But the bass is
real good so we resume listening. And hearing the words of the
dominant ones. Those who are supposedly having so much fun. It is
time to stop, to make all silent. Listen to your heads, kill the giant.

Carolyn Farnsworth

A Flash In The Sky

I was watching the sun set over the mountains
Watching all the radiant colors die behind them
Purky pinks, violent violets and radical reds

As the last colors died out, tiny stars awakened
I watched each one awake and twinkle at me
Turning to leave, a flash of white caught my eye

Sitting back down a lady in white hovered above me
The sky around her turned minty green
She danced playfully around the stars

She would disappear and reappear
In a different patch of the sky
I felt like she was calling me to join her

I watched her for hours. But with a twist
of her minty green gown she disappeared

Someone told me I saw the Northern Lights
But I like to think of the majestic beauty I saw
As the Mysterious Lady of the North

Corinne Yonker

Untitled

There has never been a more beautiful creation than a woman
  watching her as she walks, her lithe graceful movements.
Her hair, her eyes, they set my soul on fire.
Her beautiful shape and form entices my eyes and desires

Woman with her cunning and beauty,
  can sometimes be gentle, and sometimes ferocious.
Always alert, always aware you never seem not to care.
Your sense of danger and sense of fear, you are always near
  to lend an ear

You give birth and you raise, now upon you I heap much praise.
You take care of family, job and house, yet still find
  time for your needs.
Living, loving and giving these are all parts of you
Oh woman, how I love you

You give love freely and openly
  on no condition is it based, you look
  life's problems right in the face,
  but you are tough, and you will survive
  oh woman, the most beautiful creature on earth,
  this poem cannot measure your worth.

Dan Iverson

Hope In Question

Our hope in God is easy when the
Waters around us are quiet,
When the trip undertaken finds
Our hope and dreams gratified.

But holding on to God is hard
When fighting with our questions,
And when the storms are fiercest,
And our boat is tossed about.

It's then our hope is shaken,
When the Creator's sound asleep,
Not knowing we are sinking, and
The waters around are deep.

Then we wonder how he, who's Creator
Of all the sea and land,
Could seem to be so unaware
Of our calamity.

Then when our hope seems weakest, God
Will calm the soul and sea,
And when we are most troubled
He'll touch, and make us complete.

Joseph B. Good Jr.

Waves

Waves crashing against a wall of stone
Waves attempting to snuff out the signaling lighthouse
Waves concealing the jagged rock which sits alone

Waves stifling sounds of drowning men's pleas
Waves taunting the ship which dares to sail
Waves rumbling their warning of treacherous seas

Waves gently licking the sandy shore
Waves playfully tickling your barefoot toes
Waves delivering precious shells from the ocean floor

Waves echoing to lovers a uniting hum
Waves enticing the spirit of your soul to soar
Waves whispering, beckoning for you to come

Who then are we to second guess
The waves changing temperament
Nature's power and nature's graciousness.

Jennifer Milsten-Holder

Thanksgiving Dinner

I see the shiny knives, the pat of butter on my potatoes and the
wax melting off the bright candles.

I smell the gravy as it pours over my plate, drowning everything,
on it, the turkey with delicious stuffing, and the puffy smoke
going up the chimney.

I taste the pumpkin pie, with the crust ever so crisp, the golden
yellow corn brushed in butter and shaken with salt and the sweet
cranberry dumplings that are juicy and red inside.

I hear the wind blowing heavily, the water dripping off the roof
because of the melted snow and the forks hitting the plate as we eat.

I touch the piping hot bowl of mashed potatoes, my cup which holds
just a little wine that I'm allowed to have at Thanksgiving and
the cold doorknob as I leave my grandmother and grandfather's house.

Danny Hoelzl

Lovely Song

I live in the country I want you to know,
Way far into the Ozark hills you must go.
My home is on top of the ridge that I love,
And is also home to two beautiful doves.

These two doves are a loving pair,
Dull grey brown with a sophisticated air.
This morning their coo has a lonesome sound,
But for me no lovelier a song can be found.

These two had a nest, with an offspring of one.
A beautiful little fledgling, this little one.
I saw her one morning in a tree,
Looking wide eyed down at me.

To my horror the next morning there she lay,
Dead on the ground killed by a Jay.
This morning two doves coo a lonesome call,
No longer a lovely song at all.

Julie A. Olson

Saying Goodbye

Saying goodbye is such a final deed
We are never ready the goodbye to read
Never knowing how long it will be
Its good the future we can't see

Each day we all walk closer to the grave
We don't really realize, death makes us afraid
Instead of trusting the Lord up above
We cling to earth and things we love

When ole Father time on our shoulder taps
No attention to age is paid a time like that
Some are young, some very old
When we leave this earth and all its gold

Each day of our life we should prepare our way
We know it has to happen, we don't know the day
Keep our eyes on the heavens above
And God will greet us with his love

Danese Wilford

Here

Here we can't have any fun,
We can't even go feel the sun!
Here we are treated like we're little,
And it makes them mad when we only piddle!
Here no staff enjoys any wit,
All we can do is simply sit!
Here there is nothing we can do,
This place reminds me of a zoo!
Here all staff is mostly sour,
They want it to look like they have power!
Here its bad to show any fear,
And they get mad if they see a tear!
Here every door is always locked,
Once we got in trouble as we talked!
Here they have such stupid rules,
They think of us as little fools!
Here I can do only so much art,
That's the only thing they don't chart!
Here real early you get woke up,
But I must go and hush now; Yup!

Angela R. Cooper

Heart Of Gold

From her childhood stories that she often told
We could tell that from birth she had a heart of gold
As her years went by and her family grew
We knew her as grandma we were a lucky few

There was warmth with her presence
She was never cold
We could tell that inside her
Was that heart of gold

But as her days grew many and her mind grew weak
Not often did she smile not often did she speak
It seemed that from us she was drifting away
Even the heart of gold was going astray

But suddenly she smiles upon us
With an old familiar grin
Much happier now
For she knows us all again

No she's no longer with us now
In her flesh that had grown so weak and old
But with us now there will always be an angel
An angel......with a heart of gold

John Hunter

Even As The Years Go By

We don't know what to say to you.
We don't know how we'll make it through.
Tears are on our face, now that you're gone it's such a lonely place.
We will never forget this sad moment in our lives:
   Even as the years go by
With Gods own grace we know you've gone to a much better place.
Your memory will always live on, even now though you are gone.
We know you wouldn't want us to cry, but this is our way of
saying goodbye.
Today we are all gathered together to say goodbye to the one
that's gone. We will cherish you forever.
The most we all fear is the emptiness left inside.
This we will always feel:
   Even as the years go by.

Colleen Laxton

The Love Of My Life

When I was a young man I married my pretty wife.
We have stayed together through sickness and strife.
We have children three, with no more to be.
We have travelled together on land and at sea.
Divorce comes easy for those that don't care.
Loving comes natural to those who will share.
Her bright hair has faded, it is now a pale grey.
I just love her more with each passing day.
Through all of the years, she is the love of my life.

Now we are much older and time has taken it's toll.
We walk close together on our evening stroll.
Her soft warm hand will gently creep into mine.
No words need be spoken to know all is just fine.
There are many marriages, that failed down the line.
We have love for each other and she is just mine.
She is my sweetheart, the love of my life.

Gardner M. Kelley

When We Arrived

When we arrived on earth,
we saw the beauty of the wilderness
A kind of a place that left one speechless
We awoke to the songs sung by the birds in
the mornings and admired the stars, the different
moons, and the calmness of the evenings
But all of that changed through the course of time
The beauty was replaced by smog and pollution and the
happiness had become sadness and confusion
The sounds of the cheerful birds in the mornings
were now the sounds of wars, gunshots and fighting
The evenings were just another time for the coroners
to count the killings and the moon and stars reflected
the damage that shined down on the ashes that were
once buildings...

Joe Wolfe

Family

We are warm on the inside, but our skin is cold.
We see more wrinkles, we are growing old.
So much wiser and not so bold.
So much to offer, so much to unfold.
To sit and stare with pictures in hand,
Thinking of loved ones in different parts of the land.
And all those thoughts constructed like a mold,
Fixed, bonded and can't be sold.
As we hold on to these special times,
Playing them over and over in our mind.
Realizing our days together are priceless,
And that our minutes count too,
We can search our daydreams
And find many "I love you's"
So as the sun starts to fade,
And the day to fold.
We have all those special memories,
And that's worth growing old.

David L. Collier

I Raise My Cup To You, My Love

In the sunset of your days, In the Autumn of your years
We shall drink to our good fortune,
And vanquish all life's tears.

As you recall life's story ... Remember no wrong deeds,
But rather... Envision a Hero, then surmise it must be you.
Yes, recall the struggle and the victory obtained,
But look now more closely, See the true Warrior who remained.

She had such a fragile frame,
Yet; watch her as she slays your Dragon.
Did you stand by her when she was down?
Did you join in the battle,
or leave her there to die, yes...drown?

And as you walk away...
In the Autumn of her years, In the Sunset of your day,
She raised a goblet, your chalice to her lips;
That last day, She drank deeply to your good fortune;
Lest, she may have sacrificed in vain, her own life's blood,
And she is not the fool my friend.

Debra L. Selman

The Madness Of Intolerance

For those who revere peace and the measure of a man,
We should all remember Gandhi who led his oppressed land.
By selfless sacrifice and example he united his nation
Against the bullish colonial rule of another mighty nation.
Yet, two religious factions later dis-unite his country's union
Through religious hate, violence and tragic disillusion.

How repeatedly insane that peace and freedoms price is lost
By nations once united and who are now mired in endless wars.
The savagery of men that claims innocent women and children;
Non comprehensible, in lieu of respect and peaceful co-existence.
Is tolerant behavior beyond the grasp of all men
Thus continuing the madness that leads to civilized descent?

Anthony Torres

Golden Years

When another year has gone on its way
  We thank the Lord for letting us stay
Here on earth among the living
  While our time and talents we are giving
To those who need our assistance
  Accept our giving without resistance
For the joy is in the giving
  While we are here on earth and living
When Heaven is home to many we know
  Life must go on here on earth below
The days come and go so fast
  At our age we would like for them to last
With the dawning of each new day
  We welcome the light as we go on our way
Facing the trials strewn in our path
  With the strength and wisdom from the past
Through living and loving we do learn
  To share with others the compassion they yearn
Blessed are those with days of good health,
  To be blessed in that fashion is their true wealth

Bernice Volesky

That Time of the Year

As the year makes it's mark in history and winds down to a close,
We turn our attention to the birth and the one the Lord chose.
To save this lost world and deliver his people from sin,
By redirecting our fate to heaven, and away from satan's den.

To celebrate this occasion, traditionally we share tokens of love,
Conveniently called gifts, as an earthly symbol of our father - above
Beneath the decorative covered tree, the neatly wrapped gifts lie,
Awaiting the day in which they become the apple of someone's eye.

Needlessly to say, we dare not forget the purpose of this joyous day,
To spread a little Christ-like love in our own unique and special way.
"Tis the season to be Jolly", is America's favorite song,
Which extends far beyond a season, in fact, all year long.

Now, that we have spread a little love, peace and cheer,
Breathlessly we say —— it's just that time of the year.

Eugene Stewart

Salt of the Earth

On this planet in the universe,
we are all mere specks of salt.
Sent to flavor the earth,
and correct those at fault.
As Christians, we are to spread God's Word,
and make sure that it be heard.
If our words fall on deaf ears,
keep talking until someone hears.
We must continue until we lose our savour.
For we are the salt of the earth and of Christ our Saviour.

John Travis Howe

Dreams of a Prison Inmate

Early one morning about the break of day
We were all called out to hear what words
the warden had to say. It wasn't very
clear as the day began, sometimes
during the night a few other prisoner
decided to run.

As time goes by you sit and wonder
why all your friends that you have known
have moved onto another camp to
finish doing their time I often think back
and remember of the days at home, we
all surely miss.

A letter from one or perhaps
a friend can sometimes heal the loneliness
we feel. Knowing that someone is
waiting for your return, knowing all of
this can bring you such relief. Even a lie
unknown will take away some of this grief.

John Henry McCarter

Encore Presentation

Lights! Camera! Action!
Welcome to a production of your life.
How you directed it, how you starred in it,
How I became a part of it.

I miss how you inspired me,
How you taught me so much.
You made me a better person,
I thank you for that.

But why did you turn the lights out.
Why did you stab me in the back.
I'm sorry you felt like you did,
But I'm not the one to blame.

The show is drawing to a close.
Everyone is filing out the doors.
I turn around and I see your face
Resting in the shadows.

I don't mean to be rude, but I must leave.
I have a life to live.
So take it easy my friend—
Someday we will meet again.

Anthony Woody

The Man I Love

The man I love I married him in 1988.
Well I was really happy then and I could hardly wait.
My mom came to my wedding. Her boyfriend, Gene did too.
The wedding it was really nice we had a lot to do.
My Husband wore a suit of Tan I wore a dress of white.
I never will forget the day or our wedding night.

I was happy that they came-It meant so much to me.
They prove a lot of miles so my wedding they could see.

The man I Love-we were together two short years.
Now I miss him, oh, so much! I've cried a lot of tears.

Well its been two years now. And we've become good friends.
I hope we will remain this way 'til our time on this earth ends.

I am really happy now cause we both get along.
We've talked a lot, I've learned so much. It's made me very strong.

The man I love-I'll love him until the day I die,
when God comes here to take me to his mansion in the sky.

Well, I will pray to God each that we can stay good friends
Until my life is over and God says it's the end.

Claudia Schneider

Faces Of The City Streets

The faces of the city streets
were colored but looked so bleak.
It was the middle of the summer heat
yet no one even missed a beat.

Who was that face that looked so sad?
And cried out, "Where is my dad?"
As many laughed at that poor lad,
I wondered, where was his dad?

Who was that face that looked like a pearl?
There was no mistake she was a girl.
Her lips were red and her skirt made a twirl,
And soon she rode off in a mighty swirl.

The faces of the city streets
Go to and fro and never meet.
They only care about the beat
That causes them to feel the heat.

Elizabeth Ann Wilkinson

Destiny

Were we destined to meet
Were we destined to fall in love
I don't know the answer
The power comes from above

It seems our paths were meant to cross
On that warm and sunny day
When you stopped your car and called to me
and beckoned me your way
The feelings inside me came flooding through
Even though I had tried so hard to forget you

But destiny took over, and it's power shone through
Bringing our two hearts together
Oh' if only we knew
That we should one day have to part
and break in two both our hearts

So sad, we couldn't let our love
have the chance to grow
We met at the wrong time, that I know
We could have been so good together
We could have dreamed our dreams forever

I will never forget you
Even though we have had to part
And when you next see a raindrop
It's a tear from my heart.

Georgina Rose Pavitt

Cancer

Cancer the unwanted seed. That grows, just like a
weed. Eating away inside our bodies, destroying all
them precious cells that we need to stay well. We
must fight with everything we have in us to get rid
of them hot cells.

I am going to fight this cancer that is inside my body.
With every ounce of strength that I have. It may take
my life, but not without a fight. I will stand tall
until I fall. Which could be any day. My faith in god
has brought me this far. It will take me the rest of
the way.

Jeanette Stamper Huff

My Team-1993

The ump screams "Play Ball"
We've got everyone we need,
We've got Little Curly with tremendous speed.
With a nasty spitter, as our homerun hitter.
We've got John as our pitcher,
He's our "You know where itcher."
Kurt is kneeling as catcher he likes to pound in his mitt,
Over at third Ryan watches the ball being hit.
Jason and Andy stand at second and shortstop,
Nothing gets by because they're always on top.
Moving to first is big ol' Fletch,
Sorry to say but he can't catch.
Over in left we've got scrawny Joel,
I don't know why but he stands on a knoll.
At center and right we have two brothers,
Over the crowd all you can hear is their mother,
Riding the pine there's big heavy Tommy,
that wimpy kid always cries to his mommy.
When your playing our team let me tell you now,
You'll feel tall as a smurf because you'll be eating the turf.

Andrew S. Trudeau

Deep Inside

Wake up, it's a brand new day
We've got to go through changes, as they come our way
And all the while you'd hold my hand, say it's alright
Together, we'll make it, you and I
Inside I feel so much peace and joy
Because we've weathered each and every storm

You.... have touched my life
You gave me hope and inspired me
You.... touched me deep inside
And I am so thankful to you

Coming to the close of yet another day
What we've been through.. wishing won't make it go away
You kept believing in me. You never let me down
Took me through the little things, that tried to turn me around
The gift of love, I didn't know where to find it
Then you showed me, it was there all the time

You.... have touched my life
You gave me hope and inspired me
You... touched me deep inside
And I am so thankful to you

Barbara Anderson

Fluffy

"Look at Fluffy - isn't he cute? Come to Momma baby"
What a moron. Doesn't she know by now that I'm not budging? And
would I really believe that she's my damn mother?
She and all her fat-ass friends huddle around me during
Tupperware parties, their breath so heinous I have to hide
behind the couch. And when I do finally slink out, they think
I'm being friendly because I want to cuddle.
Damn it, I'm kissing up because I'm starving!

I wish I could live in the days of my ancestors - lazily soaking in
the sun all day, and at night I'd bat around a rodent until
I finally devour him-and no cutesy names like 'Fluffy' or 'Mittens'!
Man, those were the days! Not having to answer to anyone.

Now when Gertrude thinks I've been a 'good boy' she'll let me outside.
But I swear, not more than an hour passes before she opens
the back door, the one with dingy, chipped white paint,
to shriek "Fluffy! Where are you, you naughty boy?"
The neighborhood cats think I'm a schmuck but I'll prove them wrong-
Tonight while Gertrude sleeps I'm going to shred
the furniture and piss on her fuzzy sky blue cashmere sweater!
I'll show them all I'm a cool cat.

Erica Edson

Shadows In The Sky

Look up, look up, what do you see?
What are those strange objects?
Is there anyone who can tell me
Why are we their chosen subjects?
Shadows in the sky, shadows in the sky.

Those strange and bizarre streaks,
Take a look tonight and you shall see;
Are they real or are the nature's freaks
Or are they other intelligence seeking you and me?
Shadows in the sky, shadows in the sky.

How long they will be there I cannot say,
But beware, beware until the crack of day.
Give a smile or a wave, and if you dare
Show them that you understand and care.
After doing that, you won't need to "Beware"
Shadows in the sky, shadows in the sky.

Bob S. Davidovic

A Mother's Lament

Tired little air man, missions o'er.
What dreams were your's that night when war was done?
Do you sleep well beneath the ocean's heaving crest,
my weary son?

Sleep on my son, let dreams be sweet for you,
Purged by the tears the sorrowing angels wept.
Oh gentle sea, was there a lullaby for him
Before he slept?

I will not grieve, lest it disturb the deep
Tranquility of your new mother's breast.
And so I'll say my last farewell to you,
and let you rest.

Catherine Donelan Wirtz

A Crime Done

He thought all was better now-
What he wanted to do was done.
But something tiny yelled in his ear
to tell him he had done wrong.
Throttled and pushed back
by layers of guilt,
he suppressed within a criminal, himself,
to slumber.
Awakening he discovered himself
pondering over a decision blundered;
he realized he never would have envisioned it
if not doused in intoxication.
Something that arouses wonder
the drink of danger
just waiting to kill.

Anisha Raghavan

Deep Thoughts

I often think and wonder,
what if cows could fly.
But what if I thought deeper,
through the endless sky.

Thoughts would surround me,
Drown me in a sea.
Like how would a cow with wings appear,
Funny, awkward, or like a tailed bumble bee.

So if one day your thinking,
what if cows could fly.
Think to yourself this little thought,
who cares and why.

Amy Horvath

Me I Do Not See

I... am not me, this is not who I am.
What is going on I do not understand.
My mind is no more at this point in my life.
My heart and my mind have become hollow because of a knife.
My heart and mind minced into pieces
that cannot work alone. So you see they
will never work, because I am alone and
at night I show it with my tears and moans.

My mind is I thought capable of more,
but it's not happening for me. I wanted to
fly I wanted to sore, but as you see I am
not because this is not me. I am searching,
where am I. Me I do not see.

Angela Thomas

Healing Yourself With Help

Healing
What is in the word?
To heal
It can be done when your hurt
That is what everyone is looking for
At anytime of their lives
You can be healed by a doctor, shaman, or
Any other
But are you truly healed?
You can be healed by a psychiatrist, psychic,
Or any other
But are you truly healed?
We all need help
Help with healing ourselves
The help is God
Our spirits must be healed in the soul
Then the body will be healed.

Christopher Nichols

Black Slave

Black slave black slave
What is it to be a black slave?
The slave is the voice without a name
That is just a crying shame.

A child born without freedom
A person whose heart and soul feels alone
All that is left to do is cry and moan
For the hope and the dream to desire.

The slave, the slave, oh the slave
Taught to obey and behave
To learn the ways to cook and save.
Oh, if only one knows the torture of the slave

The human being not being acknowledged
A human being that had no knowledge
How could this be?
That the black slave wasn't free to be.

I feel so much sadness in my heart
To know that families were apart.
I open my eyes and see that
Those black slaves could easily have been me.

Briana Epps

Stories, Secrets, Treasures

If I could read your mind, what stories would you tell?
What secrets would I figure out?
What treasures would I uncover? Would your
stories be true? Would your secrets be real?
Would your treasures be rich? Would you spin
yarns about fantasy and fairy tales, far away
lands and fanciful kingdoms. The secrets would
hold messages to help a lost child find the
path home, a prince find his princess. And
the treasures would be still the kingdom and
all its citizens with beauty, gold, silver, diamonds,
rubies,a beauty beyond belief.

But these are only stories of imaginary people
and places. The secrets are only in the mind,
and the treasures are only dime store jewels,
if I could read your mind, stories, secrets,
treasures.

Elaine Bird

Dare A Genie

Who upon the deep made a young reflection
What sought in spite to tame this connection
Saying in his thoughts
The boy as thee in my Right
Mine divine yet stings
Save if need be two
Opportunity of defeat
Come this image shall have no name
But the provided for answered Jesus
To which a stung devil said
God looketh down
Would the boy looketh up
Nay, now to celebrate
for as to lift up he would
have to be a Genie
And the boy said
Father I will look up
And by thine hand I might lift up
Father let us go ahead
and make the world

Donnell Winfred Partin

The Thunder

When I was a little girl, I would often wonder,
What would happen to the thunder as I got older.
Some say that it would stay.
Others said it would go away,
But still I would ponder.

As I got older, about nine or ten,
I would ask my mother now and then,
"What is this thunder that I so often hear about."
She said, "In time my dear you'll figure it out."

Now that I am older,
The meaning is so clear.
The thunder is in me and not what I hear.
The thunder is my courageousness,
and my will to carry on.
The thunder is my soul and my heart as it pounds.
The thunder resounds.

Jayme Drumgo

Contemplation

When my skies turn grey, and there is darkness all around.
When castles I have built, all come tumbling down.

When my heart is filled with pain and grief.
When all that's with in me cries out for relief.

Then I think of those who before me have trod.
And the faith that they had in the living God.

Then my skies turn blue, and the sun shines bright.
For my heart and mind is then set aright.

Because I know that no pain, grief, and woe.
Can take me where others haven't been and God can't go.

John Bradford

The Search

There comes a time in a young man's life
When he must choose a loving wife.

Will she be pretty, will she be fair
Like the fragrance of flowers
In the soft, summer's air?

Gentle of word with the sweetness divine
Oh, will she ever, ever be mine?

Radiance, shining, an inner glow
Tenderness emitted as the words of love doth flow.
Today and tomorrow and forever true
Loving you, loving you.
A search that has been of dreams and joy
A special girl for a special boy
Forever and always to be true
Loving you, loving you.

Judy Cottle

If He Were Only Here

I have a dream world, where he is still alive.
When I awake from my dream world,
I must realize, he did not, but I survived.
I loved him so very, very much, but now
he is gone and even his soul I can not touch!
Sometimes I will be talking,
but to who I do not know, for he, my love
is no longer walking, but still, I love him so!
They came to my door and told
me he had died, for days, weeks, and
months, I had cried. Even though they had said:
I'm really very sorry to say:
The pain, always remained.
I had loved him then,
I love him now, I'd give anything to see
him once again, but I truly don't know how.

Danielle Marie Entsminger

Never Got To Say Thanks

I messed up a lot, in the past few years
When I cried, you wiped my tears
You were understanding and always there
You tried to help me, when I didn't care
You gave me love, you filled my sorrow
You brightened up my every tomorrow
You held me tight, when I would bend
As my parents you showed best friends
At the rate I was going, I could have belonged to the court
But THANK YOU for helping me, with all your love and support

Jaimie Lynn Callander

As Friends And As Lovers

You are my better half,
When I feel depressed and sure I can't go on,
You are there to keep me strong and encourage me.

You are my glorious half,
When I feel joyful and need to share my victorious moments.
You are there to share it with me and make me feel even happier.

You are my solid half,
You are there to listen to me even when I sound silly.
You understand me even when I can't explain myself.
You are always there to make me feel good about myself.

Indeed you are my very best friend and I am sure it was
destined in the stars even before we were created.
So I say thank you for being my friend but most of all I thank
God for bringing you into my life and connecting
Us so perfectly together.

Irene A. Asuen

I Wonder

I wonder....
When it's sunny I think of you.
Of course, it's hard not to.
Because when I think of you I always wonder
if you would be afraid of thunder.
There are a lot of things I would like to know about you,
like what kind of toys you would like to play with or if
you would enjoy to sit and mold clay, I wonder if you would be happy
with playing Barbies with your older sister.
When I'm alone I feel like crying because I'm sad that..
you didn't get to listen to music or learn to walk or talk
I wonder what kind of music you would like
I wonder what you would look like
I wonder if you would have blonde hair
with blue eyes or brown hair
with hazel eyes, long hair,
short hair curly hair straight hair,
But I would always love you no matter what.
I wonder if you would love me
I often wonder these things.

Jennifer Tabor

When I Am Gone

Remember me;
When the flowers have wilted,
the days turn to nights,
and the race I began, years ago, has finally ended.
My memory will live on.

Talk about me;
The times we have shared,
the songs I have sung,
and the words I have spoken.
My voice will not fade.

Love me;
Do not feel sorrow, for your heart is a tree,
and when the tree turns green
the birds of happiness will return.
Our love is like an eternal flame.

Have faith in my promise;
By remembering me,
talking about me,
and loving me,
I will always live on.

Jenny Chang

Tearful Eyes

Do not fear the tears as beckoned they've come,
When the hurt is so deeply imbedded that damage is done.
For to hold in the pain, would cause it to swell,
As inward we'd punch, so other's couldn't tell.
But agony has a way of letting go,
Sometimes so quickly, we're the last to know.
So do not fear, if a tear would arise,
Because this blessing will gently wash your eyes.
And as it washes the eyes to see,
It relieves the pain inside, by setting it free.
Remember when tears overflow in surprise,
Do not turn away or try to disguise.
Let the love light shimmer as it falls from your cheek,
For the heart that feels pain, knows the love we all seek.
Donna J. Waugh

"When My Time Comes"

When my time comes to leave this place,
When the Lord shouts down and calls my name.
Please don't weep and feel sad for me,
Because I've lost the living game.

For as I depart this world of ours,
I'll be heading for a much better place.
Where I'll suffer no more from the hardships of life,
Where we'll all be an equal race.

Where there is no one dying of illnesses,
Where there is no wars left to fight.
Where there is peace and harmony,
For this place is a beautiful sight.

A place where I'll find true happiness,
And where I'll find peaceful rest.
And relief from the pain I've endured in life,
And relief from this world of stress.

For the ones, I knew that loved me,
Please don't feel no hurt or pain.
Go on with your lives, and believe in our God,
For someday we'll be together again.
Bernard E. Simmons

Glances in the Dark

Can you feel them, they're out there,
when the wind blows do you hear them.
Late at night when no one is near, and you're all alone dreaming, do
you see their faces or just empty glances hiding back in dark places.
Or maybe you've felt their touch, but thought you were mistaken.
Paranoia starts to set in and you wonder if it shows,
or maybe you think everyone knows.
You're trying so hard not to let your mind blow.
But they're there wherever you go.
Invading your thoughts and bringing you down, a mental haunt!
And all the time they're just the demons in your mind.
You know the ones that you just can't face,
all those past regrets, your secret mistakes
the kind of things you thought time would erase.
It doesn't so confront it or run from it.
After all it's your fate!
Elsa M. Cardenas

Fear

I look up into the night and staring back at me is a glowing,
Yet dim star flashing on and off like a siren.
My eyes are getting heavy, as heavy as an iron.
Everything is loud, but silent to me and when I look to see,
There is nothing, nothing for miles of me.
Yet, by the beat of my heart and the sound of my breathing,
I realize that I'm just afraid...afraid of the night and the silence.
Conan Armijo

My Mother

Mother was always the first Doctor called
When things went wrong she was there for us all
There were words that Mother could say
That would take us safely throughout the day.

Those little special warm and thoughtful things
That Mother does, reminds you of a flower in Spring
She taught us children to love and share
And that it was so wonderful just to care.

She taught us independence and the meaning of success
And that through God we could find true happiness
Mother was so warm hearted and forgiving
She always added enjoyment and courage to living.

It was the little things she would do
To bring such special memories to you
Mother was always so wonderful and sweet
To little children or anyone she meet.

Her friendship and love meant so much
To each and every life she touch
Her love and wisdom will last my whole life through
And Mother, I was lucky to have a mother like you.
Carnell Grant

The Christ Child

This is the season of the year
When we hold the christ child dear.
They named him Jesus, our Christ and King,
Born to die and rise again.

In a stable with cattle and sheep,
In a bed of hay clean and sweet.
The low of cattle, the sheep's soft bleat,
The wise men placed gifts at his feet.

Gifts of myrrh, frankincense an gold,
They had followed a star, their king to behold.
These men who kept sheep in their fold,
Were to have Christ as their shepherd the story is told.

The babe that lay there on the hay,
Born to take out sins away.
Born to know the souls of men,
Born to make us whole again.

This is the season of the year,
We honor the birth of the Christ child dear.
We lift our voices in loud proclaim,
To cherish and honor his holy name.
Ethel Berger Pack

"The Mind's Boundaries"

I view a world where love has no boundaries.
Where the persistent chattering of jealous people,
hold no sway to true and natural feeling.
To a world where beauty has no boundaries,
people would walk oblivious to the pressure of others.
What feelings have we lost to a world held by beauty.
What thoughts escape us as we focus on that beauty.
I view a world where beauty has no boundaries.
Where hurtful words are long since forgotten.
Where blissful happiness takes hold of your soul.
I view this world where love is forever.
Where a tender kiss and loving embrace,
chases away all the heartache inside.
So I sit and watch and wonder,
if this world could actually exists?
If is does, where is it?
I guess we just haven't found it yet.
Brian James Hatrick

Thoughts

In the silence of the night,
When your thoughts take on flight,
Every memory is like new,
And any wish comes out true, in your thoughts:

There exist no hurries, no deadlines,
No "I'm sorry"; no bills nor fines,

Everyday a vacation place,
You're in Europe: Paris, Rome,
There's no time to be alone,

There's no need for cemeteries,
No more illnesses, no ones buried,
No type of problem to cause wary,

Your actions do not need explanations,
Wars are non-existent, it's a peaceful and friendly nation,

It's Christmas day all year long,
Family dinners; children playing,
Silent nights and Santa Claus,

No one argues, no one cries, there's no need to say good-bye,

In the silence of the night when your thoughts take on flight,
Every memory is like new, and any wish comes out true.

Anna Reynoso

The City

The city is a place where people hurry;
Where animals have no room to scurry;
Where the birds have hardly any trees,
And there's not many flowers to feed the bees.

The city is a place where buildings stand tall,
And there's never any room for the kids to play ball;
Where the cars and buses and trucks and trains,
All drive the people close to insane.

The city is a place where the noise stands out;
Where fathers and mothers always shout;
Where cranes and bulldozers knock out walls,
And restore them with gigantic malls.

The city is a place where the skies are gray;
Where the fog and the smog stay all day;
Where the children play in a dirty lot,
and old used cars stand and rot.

The city is a place where nature is not.

John Kazlauskas

Black Man

Black Man
Where are you?
Black Man
Will you help me?
Black Man
Why do you put me down?
Black Man
What has taken you from me?

Maybe it's the absence of my father
Maybe it's my intelligence
Maybe it's my strong will

I just can't seem to find a good
Black Man to stand by me

I need someone to lean on and share my problems with
I need someone to cherish, who cherishes me
I need someone to treat me the way I deserve to be treated

Can you do that Black Man?
Will you try Black Man?
Are you Man enough Black Man?

Eboney K. Mitchell

Where Was Love?

When there was slavery in the world,
    Where as love?

When the holocaust was taking place,
    Where was love?

When we made laws against illegal aliens,
    Where was love?

When the homeless were left out in the cold,
    Where was love?

When the world health organization refused to
Give free vaccines offered by the army to combat
Cholera,
    Where was love?

When thousands of babies are aborted every year,
    Where was love?

When Sister Theresa went to work in Calcutta to
Help the poor sick,
    There was true love

When Jesus died on the cross,
    There was eternal love

Al Brozowski

Giggles

What makes them,
    where do they come from?
Seems as though
    Something is hidden.

Through THEM, energy is released
    To repress what one wishes to express.
I wander what it is,
    'Cause I know it's a burning quander.

Maybe it has something
    To do with courage.
The fear hiding behind
    the ever desire to express the forbidden.

She stares with a giggle of mischief
    And wonders where the attention will be directed.
For a brief moment I feel her thoughts
    Close to understanding; still falling short.

One day when her giggles
    Descend into meaningful and understanding words
She will express
    What is truly in her heart.

Earl Patterson

My Small Town

I hate this big city, cold and remote,
where people exchange quick nervous glances
and never meet one another eye to eye.
I can't find any peace in this place.

Give me that quiet burg where a quaint
old courthouse is the center of town,
and old men sit on rusty iron benches
and swap gossip and spit tobacco.
The whole town and shuts down at five o'clock.

I'll find some white frame house with a
gray concrete porch and orchards and a garden.
There's room for sweet corn and mellon planting
and neighbors dropping by
Blue bonnets along highways in the spring time
Wild grapes down country roads in summer
I've been away too long - goodbye!
I'm going home today.

Janette E. Hernandez

A Snow Bird Returns

I'm back in town from sunny Florida
Where humid days grew hot and horrider,
Back to the glowing resplendent azaleas
Back for the fragrantly pungent vidalias,
Where people smile and smile, and smile
And friends with gifts stop by awhile
Where every store sells plants galore

And flowers adorn the hardware store,
Where drivers zip through every street
And keep me nimble on my feet,
Where I can buy a junk food treat
And no one frowns at what I eat,
And no one stares at how I dress
In pants or skirt or crazy vest,
Where freedom reigns, midst nature's scenes;
Though prices soar, they buy my dreams,
So gladly do I pay my bills
And gaze with joy upon these hills.

Charlotte Himber

Two Beauties

One deep within the soul
   where peace and love rules your attitude
Their's yet another beauty
   where many fall into distress
You must look within one's simple covering
   for the heart beats within those thoughts
The true character of a person
   comes out of them thoughts
Your true beauty
   is hidden within your looks
Just as your heart pumps your livelihood
   so must we seek heart felt vision
From within that vision
   your character is born
As you spread that vision of character
   others are attracted or shut off
We are all dynamic in purpose
   if that purpose is life
Indeed, should not that vision be love
True Love has no remembrance of evil.

Henry J. Parson Jr "Hank"

Jilted Lady

Stone walls surrounded a secret garden
Where wild flowers perfumed the air,
And on a summer's night when the moon was bright
You could see her walking there.
Yes, she travelled down that garden path
In a long white gown and a veil of lace
Waving to her guests as she passed
A smile for all upon her face.

Up to the arbor where she knelt
As she would have one that special day
Had fate not come to intervene
And take her precious dream away.
They never stood before a man of God,
Their friends and family
Nor vowed to love each other
Throughout eternity.
For on that fateful morn, so long ago,
As the sun came up to greet the day
A young man left his father's house
And simply rode away.

Becki Dodson

A True Friend

Two doors alike I stood before one looking rich, the other poor
Which door to chose, but whose is whose?

One covered in gold; a dazzling display
The other familiar and worn away.
One a bright, illuminating door,
But was it fake or was it more?

The other one was harder to see, but it was the one best suiting me.
Inside I found someone dear, seeing him brought me a tear.

But had I taken the other door was it worse or was it more?
Alas, I would begin to see a demon loose, a demon free.

Had it come from me inside, or had my eyes told me a lie?
She was a person I knew to be, a friend once close, now far from me.

She betrayed my innocent soul, in my heart she drilled a hole.
I chose the one who showed me love, a friendship as pure as a dove.

Erin Schroeter

Open House

Make empty again this house
   which was never shared.
Leave nothing behind.
Watch the landlord in the yard,
   his arm around the shoulder of another young man.
Let him have this home
   in this nice neighborhood.

Measure the importance of your possessions.
Take half.
Give what you can to his relatives.
See if they can find him.
Sell the rest or donate it
   in black plastic bags on the curb.

Keep what remains.
Wrap it in newspaper.
Stuff it tight in cardboard boxes
   taken from the grocery store dump.
Stack the boxes in the hallway.
Wait for the rented van to arrive.
Move on.

Joe Carrithers

The Coming Of Spring

My cat chased a bird up in the tree,
While bees bussed right beside me,
Hummingbirds fluttering their wings,
The noise of the cricket as he sings,
The crock of a frog,
The bark of a dog,
The smell of a flower, sweet like honey,
The hop of an easter bunny,
Look at the mountains, the snow is all gone,
See the cute little baby fawn,
Feel the warmth of the sun, see its red glow,
The roses are all planted in a neat little row,
Feel the wind in the air,
As it ruffles your hair,
The clang of the church bell as it rings,
All these things remind me its spring.

Cindy Ward

A Butterfly Is Born

The soothing warmth of sunlight spreads and chases Autumn's chill,
While it wraps a cloak of amber 'round an oak tree on the hill.
Encased within thick branches, lies a tiny woven shell.
A safe cocoon of silken threads - a place for life to dwell.

The soft glow soon caresses the gentle soul within.
It stirs - as it awakens; soon freedom will begin.
The resting stage has ended; the protective shell is torn.
Emerging from the silk cocoon - "A butterfly is born!"

On wings outstretched and lifted, a free new life takes flight,
And communicates with nature, in a graceful dance of light,
A kaleidoscope of color brightly decorates the day.
Each small prism dyed by nature; tints the hillside with soft rays.

Fragile wings beat out soft rhythms that propel it through the air.
On a search for fragrant blossoms, where it settles with great care.
Taking sips of thick, sweet nectar; it now flits and darts about.
Perfumed scents, and brilliant colors, greet the butterfly en route.

Now embracing all of nature, in a frenzy of pure glee;
It drinks of life, to celebrate - "The butterfly is free!"

E. Carol Walker

"Get A Cause In Life"

Articulate I am, I analytically think;
While some sit at home and academically sink;
Never finished school, can't read a book;
And don't want a another chance to take a second look;
Brains on drugs and drugs on brains;
What's wrong with you kids, are you going insane;
You don't need the gun, put down the knife;
Build up your self-esteem, get a cause in life;

You can't push play, if you're on pause;
You can't move in life, is you have no cause;
Preoccupied with money, don't be a fool;
Keep yourself away from drugs, keep your but in school;
You want to sell drugs, read a book instead;
Get your life together friend, screw on your head;
Women with the babies, they suffer the most;
Gun shots claiming' fathers from coast to coast;
Die before your 30, the life of dope;
Why beat around the bush, hang yourself with a rope;
Support your kids, take care of your wife;
Build up your self-esteem, get a cause in life;

Eric Blaine Thomason

Untitled

Breathe softly fresh breezes, the name of my love
Whisper his message to me
Bring me warm kisses, caresses divine
From wheresoever he be
Tell me he loves me, and thinks of me still
Tell me he'll always be mine
Tell him that this world that I'm living in
Is only a moment in time
Take him my kisses fresh breezes tonight
Take him my dreams and my sighs
Across all the worlds that keep us apart
Whisper, true love never dies
And when thou art gone, sweet breezes of love
I shall pause in the soft evening air
For one thing I never shall let thee take
My tears of despair

Barbara Ruth Fitzpatrick

The Parting

The heaving and sighing of the autumn days,
whispering goodbye to summer along the way
The lands are ablaze, a Van Gogh's palette.

Leaves, gracefully departing from trees
swishing, swaying around our feet as we walk
through the park
Scampering chipmunks, a lone red fox darts out
Birds that stay home of various colors flying about.

As sunlight comes creeping through,
I pluck a crimson leaf as I go
and a shower breaks anew.

Near the path a white birch grows,
a silent drop of rain trickles down its' trunk
like a tear
Perhaps for the parting, the summer truce.

Diana Dolhancyk

False Love

Thief of my heart, you played the part with kindness, wit and charm.
White lies and fake smiles were my alarm.
Disguised as a gentleman, you slowly broke into my life.

A crazed culprit of jealous love, you bludgeoned my heart and
  murdered my dreams.
Obsessed with my life, you raped me of precious hours, luring me with
  sweets and flowers.
Possessed with lust, a false love, I cannot trust.

I awaken during the cold night to hear my soul silently scream.
I would rather serve time in hell than live in your prison cell,
  the final death blow...

Gail Ann Seiffert

The World As A Piano

Dr. Martin Luther King was a determined man,
who desired that all people have equal rights.
Unfortunately, there's still work remaining.
Perhaps, Dr. King thought of the world as a piano.
  that had billions of keys,
  both black and white.
The keys were close together and touched,
they didn't appreciate each other,
as some people do.
  Nobody played the piano
  because the sounds were discordant.
  The discordant sound were
  the keys arguing,
  as sometimes people do.
Dr. King helped make the piano play harmonious notes.
However, Dr. King's work was never finished.
  We should work together
  so that his dream will come true
  and the piano keys will play
  harmonious notes forever on.

Glenda L. Richardson

Mine Eyes

Mine eyes will ne'er behold
Which my heart doth seek so clearly,
Inward stirs this passion,
Deep, yet benighting,
Leading my path away from all, and to my love.

I reach out for thee,
And pray thy hand be there to welcome mine.
Thine light to illume where mine light be spent,
And allow my soul to soar.

Amanda Falcone

"Don't Light My Dark"

Why does this light intrude upon my dark?
Who gave it permission to break into my night?
I close my eyes trying to hold onto my dark,
but the light refuses to surrender.
My night brings me comfort,
the comfort I cannot find in the light.
My dark is calm like the sea at night.
My night is a soothing dark sky,
yet it is still adulterated by flecks of light.
The light shows all of the anger and hate.
The night contains the peace and love
that I always seek.
The light unleashes danger in every corner.
The dark bathes me in safety at every turn.
Stay away light... I need my night... I need my dark.

Hendrix S. Boags

Lost Souls

How many lost souls walk the earth,
Who live the death before the birth.
Confused, afraid, filled with despair,
Cursing fate for that which is not fair.
Plodding through forbidden lands
With the weight of burdens held by their hands.
And desperate, alone they've cried,
Searching for all they've been denied.
Turning round they cannot keep
What they have had, what they will reap
From all the soil the earth can give—
Alas, a nightmare in which to live.
But stumbling, they hurry on
For something which they know is gone—
Condemned to roam the roads of scorn
Through valleys which have long been torn.
And yet they manage to survive,
Though through all darkness they must strive.
Yes, how many lost souls walk the earth
Who live the death before the birth.

Janice Veramay

Life's Sweet Dreams

There is a man named Walter
Who took me to the alter
We took our wedding vows
A few years later, we were so proud
Baby, babies, babies, three
The miracle of birth __ a mystery.

The years go by, things fall into place
Everything moving at a steady pace
Nursery school, kindergarten, high school
College and careers
Now the world has new nurses, computer
operators and engineers.

Mom and Dad's mirror shows snow on the mountain
"Shall we grow old gracefully or "search
  for a youthful fountain?"
Seeing the family enjoying life,
Makes it worth all the strife,
Then, the sweet voices of grandchildren
Their laughter, smiles and pitter pat.

Janet F. Lattimer

Love This Child

Why take this child of mine?
Who waits to cry for life,
Listen to the sounds that he makes,
With his first deep breath for life.

Many take and take before that cry,
So small, so gentle and unfolded,
No choice this child has, but to die,
Now the weight is put upon your shoulders.

Who really knows the way you feel,
Thou shalt not take another's life,
Confused and unsure of what to do,
Only give this child a right to life.

There is another who will keep,
Love and care for this child,
So open your heart and soul to another,
Because Jesus Christ once was that child.

Debra Marie Kenney

You're Special, Helen

I'm happy to pause for a moment. And send you this message, Helen.
Who you are in this world. Is special and wonderful.

You are forever kind and, deserving of admiration.
I notice your special qualities. You are always helpful quick to
lend a hand.
Because of you the office is brighter.

You never would settle for less, than being exceptional.
You're not just good. You're the best.
An example to which many aspire.

You've learned there's fulfillment in lending a hand.
You are a helper, giving your support to others.
As they do what they must do.

I wish I could tell you, so that you know
Deep in your heart, how very special
You are to me.

May God be with you always, through the storms of life.
May you bend gracefully with the wind, supported by God's firm
    foundation.
His blessings be with you today and always.
May your retirement be filled with cheer,
Like the joy that you have given everyone.

Duane E. Lee

A Gift From God

I look at you and smile, for love is what I see.
Whoever thought one glance could make my heart leap?
Feelings fill my head: joy ... trust ... peace ... love!
How can I think ... where do I go from here?

Gently I take your hand, so soft .. so precious.
With warm brown eyes, so full of trust, you look at me.
Do you see love?
So long have I waited to feel so warm inside,
You lay your head against my breast ... such trust you find in me.

Looking into the starless night, my tears I try to hide.
For the Lord has blessed my soul with a precious baby boy.
This love is sure to be sincere ... yet so much do I fear.
Is this not a dream ... are you truly here?

I always thought love could not be found within a single moment.
But this is love I feel for you.
It is not a whim, a lost dream....this love is fresh and everlasting,
A gift given from God.

Heather M. Weeks

A Daughter's Gift

How fortunate to have a mom so dear,
Who's happy face outshines her birthday year.

How lucky to know that she is mine,
For she has taught me in song to take,
   One day at a time.

Her care and love have given me a strong base,
When life's hardships I have had to face.
The prayers she taught have kept my spirit
In God is very light,
Even in the desolate winter of night.

Like a thief, Alzehiemers her mind has robbed,
Though through science, Cognex has bought us time,
Allowing her some dignity and quality time.

My love I give which is her due,
In the form of a poem, written, dear Mother,
Just for you.

Elizabeth L. Flores

Metamorphosis

I was the young monarch of all those great solitudes
whose kingdom was trees, sand, sea and wind.
I had no dreams but to reign over space, the chaste kiss of salt,
the fragrance of the forest living and decaying,
and to give obeisance only to the howling buffets of the biting wind.

What overpowering malignancy transmogrified my realm?
Why am I exiled to a hostile clime of cemented sand
where the sea surges into gigantic waves of glass,
the frozen trees enmesh in a copper web,
and the pliant wind ducts through fiery cylinders?

From this cruel banishment
ultimately I am freed to obedient slavery
in that pure realm of charred memories
where transparent waves forever rise and dissipate
in their eternal battle with the drifting sand.

James Kohfeld

Death

Here I stand wondering,
Why am I here on this earth.
I go to the top of cliff and look over it,
And see a sea of blood, I think about jumping

Then I go to jump and fall into a trance.
I think about me dying.
I see a tree and it makes me think of being
 6 feet under,
While my skin is falling off green & blue.

I slowly awake, wondering why am I still here
I say "so." I walk over to the cliff again,
I look down, a tear rolls down my cheek,
I think its a night thing. I place my
 ring & glasses beside my feet

I take one look back
I jump!
Just as I'm falling, I think.
"Why me!?"

Heather Cummings

Why?

Why did you have to leave me?
Why did you have to go away?
Why couldn't it only be for a few minutes?
But instead it was to stay.

Why did you leave me all alone?
In this big world to sit and cry.
Why didn't you let me get to know you?
Instead of a hug, a kiss, and a good-bye.

I wish you could have stayed,
And only God knows how I prayed,
To have you here with me,
The way it should be.

But yet, I wonder why?
Why did you have to die?
Sometimes, my heart feels empty.
And yet, I still sit, wonder, and cry.

Barbara Jean Akins

Someday Grandma, Someday

Daddy, where's Grandpa
Why didn't he come with Grandma?

Grandma, I'm glad you are staying with us.
Will you teach me to cook and sew like you do?
Will you read me a story?
And tuck me into bed?
Please, Grandma, tell me about Grandpa.
Where did he go?

Daddy, why can't Grandma stay with us anymore?
Please, Daddy, I love Grandma!
I don't want to say goodbye!

One day Jesus will lead me to a little cottage.
There will be flowers all around.
The air will smell of home made bread and apple pie.
Grandpa will sit rocking just outside the door.
And Grandma will come running out to welcome me.
Someday Grandma, Someday.

Cheri R. Moser

Song Of The Unborn Baby

Why do they have to die,
why do the abortionists have to lie,
to tell you that I do not know why,
all I know is that they die.

Some believe the reason to be a woman's right to choose,
but in regard to abortion women, children, and society lose,
for women the cost is the knowledge, that their
beloved children are forever lost.

Children lose their right to be,
to live, to love, to be free,
to imagine, to play
and to lead our society to a better day.

Therefore, our society loses too, you see,
for in the future there may be
a song to be sung,
and a dream to be won,
but this song and dream shall never be fulfilled
for today we have allowed it's achievers to be killed.

Carol Areus

Dare To Discover Love

What do you do when you dare to discover love?
Why do you dare to discover love?
Everyone has dared to discover love!
What? Why? Everyone!
Have you dared to discover love?

What is love?
What is love leaving you with?
What does love do to the world?
What? What? What?
What does love do to you?

Why is love so confusing?
Why is love such a mystery?
Why does love lead you into a blind alley?
Why? Why? Why?
Why is love do this to you?

Everyone has different answers about love!
Everyone has different questions about love!
Everyone has been or is going to be deceived by love!
Everyone! Everyone! Everyone!
Everyone has been loved before and still is by God!

Jamie Branan

Why?

Why are the skies so bright and blue?
Why in math does one plus one equal two?

Why do we have ten fingers and toes?
Why is a point on our face called a nose?

Why do the leaves only change in the fall?
Why do we all like to shop at a mall?

Why is a kilometer shorter than a mile?
Why can we tell time with a sundial?

Why do adjectives modify nouns?
Why does everything that goes up must come down?

Why on our head do we wear a hat?
Why do we hit a baseball with a bat?

Why must we live, and why must we die?
I guess only God knows all the answers to why!

Deanna J. Mantoni

Why Is It...?

Why is it that people say one thing and do another?
Why is it people ask you to do something then say you asked them?
Why is it people promise things then don't keep them?
Why is it that life isn't fair?
Why is it people can't ask somebody if they said something instead of assuming what's being said is true?
Why is it people take advantage of other people?
Why is it love has to hurt?
Why is it that we live in a one sided world?
Why is it that people who love each other so much have to be apart so long?
Why is it that I can't hate anyone no matter how mean they are to me?
Why is it life is easier for one person and not another?
Why is it people always sugar coat what they say instead of just coming out and saying the truth?
Why is it I can't stay mad at the one I love for more than a second then I have to say "I'm sorry love please forgive me"?

Amelia Ann Peridore

The Stories of the Sycamores

Leaves dancing in the air, images on the streams,
Why is it that life and love, are much more than they seems?
Like the simple things, like traffic sounds,
Days gone by, nights, quieted by the dark,
The glistening sounds of pebbled brooks, and yes,
The age old Stories of the Sycamores.
These are pleasures chosen but by a few,
Ones that refuse to see the same,
scenes of life, the early morning dew,
They look and perceive, there are many names.
You see, only those that seek the path of
Love and joy, harmony and peace,
Relish the rhymes of love and life, and
The age old Stories of the Sycamores.
Nature beckons to us all!, but only a few truly perceive,
That when you see, there's much you can miss,....
To some, is life but a dream?
Of fantasies, and memories, of love lost days gone by,
And so, you stop ..., reach out for more ..., like
THE AGE OLD STORIES ..., OF THE SYCAMORES.

Al B. Darn

To The World

To the World I say,
Will we have another day?
Not money, not power will stop the push.
I fear our world will soon decay.

A child is born, whose heart is pure,
Adding to it's parents' woe.
Though life is precious, as we know,
In what world will it grow?

In times of plenty, we give thanks,
While others die a living death.
To the World I say,
Help us find another way.

If man's (mankind) words were true as gold,
Might we have less fear?
A new life, our future's life,
Would truly be most dear.

Elizabeth L. Mayeux

House Built Of Love

Upon a hillside sits an old story house.
Windows and doors are locked,
  all is quiet as a mouse.
Let's take a step inside, visit the old place again.
The worn out curtains still there,
  hanging across the window panes.
The pictures on the wall, tell us a tale.
Of the happiness this beautiful house had, still prevails.
Dirty little fingerprints left here and there.
We had lots of children, the fingerprints are in pairs.

This tattered old furniture has seen it's last days.
We don't want to move it, let's hope it stays.
As a never ending reminder of the happy times we had.
For changing it about would make us so sad.
Over the fireplace sits mother's old clock, still
  covered with dust.
That old timepiece, we all learned to trust.
We should close the door now, leaving memories behind.
The love we had then abounds now,
  with vivid pictures in our minds.

Ailene Braden

"I Will Live Just Because"

In the almost seven thousand six hundred days I've lived,
Winds have blown unforgettably, but, I chose to forgive.
I can't control the weather, no matter how slight it is,
Loneliness was the result of the paradise I missed.
Love was often obstructed by the problems of others,
Life goes on regardless of what the harsh winds may utter.
I really can't stop the things they say, I can't help to listen,
Volume varies from time to time, so do my decisions.
Each problem that arises, I try to make the right choice,
Just sometimes the wrong decision has the audible voice.
Unless another's doesn't interfere, my life gets worse,
So then my situation becomes worse than the first.
Through the continuing trouble, I've gain understanding,
Because of tribulations, my patience keeps expanding.
Every problem seems to have different solutions,
Come to think about it, I'm often left in confusion.
Almost every occurrence, my mind starts drifting to sin,
Uncontrollable thoughts start flying off with the wind.
So I'm on bended knees, asking for forgiveness for my flaws,
Endlessly living in my faith, "I will live just because."

Andres Dominguez

Only Half Of My Heart Remains

Darling I'm thinking of you today my love.
Wishing for one more day.
With all the nice thing we had in life,
now is all fading away. I know you had to
leave my love. It was so sad to see you go.
But when it's my turn to leave this world,
darling you made it so much easier for me to go.
You meant so much to me my love.
Only my heart does no.
I must have meant the same to you,
only half of my heart remains.
It will never be the same without you,
because my heart tell me so.
We will only have a half of a heart,
until it's my time to go.

Genevia Beard

God's Love

Autumn is a beautiful time of the year
With a briskness around that you can breathe
And as the leaves change color upon the trees
I think of what God has given me to see
The tree, strength in my Lord to withstand
What comes my way, because of his love for me so dear
The colors remind me of my Lord
The yellow is like his sunlight
The orange like a setting sun
The light brown is like the sand Jesus walked
Upon and sheltered me in his arms
And the russet red is the blood His son Jesus shed
A reminder of God's love, so great for you and me
The tree gives shelter in the storm, like my Lord
His power is mighty, His love is great
His wisdom beyond imagining, and a love that can't be beat!
My Lord the creator of all things, who has redeemed
Me by His son Jesus's blood
And who sustains me in my storms of life
My Lord, my Savior, my friend, my counselor
My Father in heaven, who speaks to me in nature
showing the beauty of Him.

Edith Mohan

The Littlest Angel

There was a little Angel with shiny golden hair
With big blue eyes and rosy cheeks
She was so gentle and so fair.

The littlest Angel's name was Faith for her faith was beyond compare
She was happy and contented and always willing to share.
Now the littlest Angel worked very hard to be what she should be,
But one day she looked so troubled, as she sat on the Masters' knee.

Why do you look so troubled? she heard the Master say
And the littlest Angel looked at him and shed a tear that day.
The Master took his hand and brushed the tear away.
As he heard the littlest Angel say, I must learn to fly today.

Be not afraid my little Faith for I'll be with you all the way,
For my precious little Angel cannot fail on such a beautiful day.
And Faith did learn to fly for the Master she could see,
He never left her sight as she soared high and free.

The littlest Angel may have let a cloud of doubt slip in,
But she was never once afraid when she kept her eyes on him.

Judy Stephenson

Until He Came

The children played in the street,
With dusty hands and bare feet.
They went about their daily chores,
And their schoolwork - their 2 x's 4s. Until he came.

Parents chatted about Sara's new tooth,
And when they would get a visit from Aunt Ruth
They talked about the new neighbor,
And the growing loss of labor. Until he came.

Fathers talked about working hard,
As they watched their children have fun in the yard.
Mothers sewed and sometimes baked,
As reluctantly the leaves got raked. Until he came.

Carefree voices of children at play,
From early winter to the month of May.
All these meant much more than fame,
All these, that is, until he came.

He came like a vulture swooping down, the span of his wings
overshadowed the town. Then, with an eagle eye, he picked his prey,
not the guilty-only the innocent had to pay. When he came.
Only the innocent had to pay. When he came.

Jessica Lamphier

Seed-Like Faith

There shall nothing be impossible to you
  With faith even as a mustard seed.
You have the ability to touch your dreams,
  Though with the eye they can't be seen.

Faith of this size seems of no effect,
  But Jesus said it's all you need.
Mountains will move and be cast in the sea,
  If only you can believe!

This seed-like faith can conquer all things—
  And bringing victory over your problems.
With faith in action and doubt aside,
  The answers are there to solve them.

There is much power in any faith;
  Whether it be great or small.
As long as you genuinely trust in God,
  You have power to conquer all!

Dianna M. Franklin

The Long Walk

I walked through life without a care,
With friends and family around me,
Over mountains and through tunnels
We stuck together always,
One day we walked a path,
Through the greatest of the mighty forest,
I took the lead,
And began to think,
Of all the things I had missed,
I turned to consult.
With these friends of mine,
But they had all disappeared,
I looked around,
And my path was gone too,
So here I have been,
And here I shall stay,
Alone.

Julie Mack

"In The Arms Of God"

So many hearts touched by this one
With gifts, love, and caring, she shared the Son
Still faced with trials from evil we run
While united with Christ this race she's won.

Through memories bright we see her clear
Each precious moment in love held dear
Shared by those her love did see and hear
With Christ, soon again we'll hold her near.

Please God, we cried as she left our home
Don't take her now she is our own
A gift she was from God a loan
We're the travelers, she's now home.

Her body a temple created by God
Past evil and danger she trod
Though her body is held by earth's heavy sod
Peaceful she sleeps in the arms of God.

Dale Brakenhoff

"Pass Me By Lord"

Lord, as I stand here on your fertile land,
with head bowed and hat in hand,
asking You to pass me by, I know You will wonder why.

You have given me so very much,
the senses of sight, sound and touch,
the ability to work, with good health,
amongst all of natures wealth.

Allowed me to be born in this land of the free,
I feel you are looking after me,
letting me worship in the church where I please,
in all things, giving me a life of ease.

You gave me a place here among men,
and a good name to carry on till when,
I shall pass it on to my sons,
when my place in glory has been won.

So Lord, with your bounty, pass me by,
give to those who are not as fortunate as I,
take care of the sick and down-trodden,
I'll manage Lord, look after the forgotten.

Lord, pass me by!

Joe N. Brown

Immigrants' Dawn

The glow to their backs in the sun drenched dawn,
With hope of new life driving them on;
Pink gray strata fired with near eternal light,
Eyes cast o'er shoulders pooled from umbilical bite.

Look over behind you and remember the sight,
Soft pastel glow and then dazzling light!
Breathe deep excitement, stow away fear,
Behold as the flames in her hand appear!

Panoramic the vision, lustrous the sky,
White cumulus clouds aglow with fire from on high.
An ocean between them, but still the same sun,
Draw strength from the past for the new life begun.

Hal D. Crenshaw

"Your Beauty"

Each day the sun Rises
With it's light shine through
Yours is A Beauty equal to that First Ray of light.
Yet unlike the Suns Beauty
Your's does not Fade At night.
You are perfect in every way
And worth far more than any worldly possession.
This is why you are the object of my obsession.
Each time that I see you.
You take my Breath Away.
Just the mere mention of your name.
Brings joy to my dreariest of days.
You are like a dream, from which I do not
Wish to wake and find not true,
I want to touch caress, and express my love to you.
I don't know what I would do if you were ever taken away.
This is why each night I thank God for such a
    heavenly gift as I pray.

Dylan Keenan

The Girl That I Call Dear

Young was she, with beauty so fine,
With lines graceful as a deer.
With a radiant smile, and laughing eyes,
Was the girl that I called "Dear."

She caused me to fall in love with her,
With her charms so sweet and clear,
And she has graced my life through all the years
This girl that I call "Dear."

Her lines have grown some deeper now,
As she's passed from year to year.
But her beauty remains as it was back then,
This girl that I call "Dear."

Her life has blessed this home of ours,
With her love from year to year.
She has filled me with love, and she always will
This girl that I call "Dear."

Now time has passed so rapidly,
Filled with her joy as well as tears.
And she still remains my lovely "Bride,"
This girl that I call "Dear."

Harold L. Boggs

On the Banks of Village Creek

I remember when I used to tag along
With my Granddaddy

He was not beside me this day
He has not stood beside me on Village Creek
For the past two years now

I stood on the sandy bank of Village Creek
With tears swelling up in my bespeckled eyes
Missing those long afternoons I had with him

I wondered why he left me
Before he finished teaching me
Everything he knew about this world

I heard the thunder clamor
In the Heavens above the clouds

Suddenly I knew
Deep down in my searching soul
Everything was okay
I knew
Positively knew —

Gregory Ellis McLaughlin

"Mansions In Heaven"

Once I was walking one of life's roughest roads,
With no one beside me, afraid and alone.
Hopelessly wandering with an ache in my soul,
A traveling fool with no place to call home.

Then Jesus reached down and took me by the hand.
He said: Build on the rock son, not on the sand.
Make sure the foundation is solid and true.
Then a mansion in Heaven will be waiting for you.

I fell to my knees as the tears filled my eyes.
I had uttered no words, yet the Lord heard my cries.
My blessed saviour looked on me from above,
And lifted me up with his unending love.

Jesus reach down, take us all by the hand,
Lead our wandering spirits into your promised land.
You're our salvation, dear Lord that is true.
And our mansion in Heaven are built only by you.

Yes, Jesus reached down and took me by my hand
He promised to lead me into his promised land,
He is my salvation, now I know that is true.
But ...will a mansion in Heaven be waiting for you?

Jon Eric Baucom

Wishful Thinking

Do you ever sometimes wish you could start over
with parents, friends, or a lover
Doing things that should have been done
but never were
Saying things that shouldn't have been said
until you knew for sure
Do you ever sometimes wish you could do it all again
Only this time, don't treat it like a sin
Do all the things you ever wanted to do
Give all the things they ever needed from you
Do you ever sometimes wish you didn't have to say goodbye
That there'd never be a time you had to cry
Do you ever sometimes wish
you could have everything you ever dreamed
That love really could be everything it ever seemed
Do you even sometimes wish
you could take back the things you didn't mean
That there was someway you could have made your love seen
Do you ever just sometimes wish...

Gabrielle Whitehurst

Mommy

Born forty years ago
with not much on his mind,
except the face above the crib
it always seemed to shine.

And just one call
it took that's all and I knew right then
she'd be there to take me from night
and hold me till light.

Sometimes when the nights were so long
and the care of her eyes
God makes mothers wise
though the worry she never could hide.

And she loved me with pride, saw something inside
I guess only mothers can see
and you played it right through
hope it would come true.

From a boy to a man you've been there
and it doesn't seem funny when I call you honey
'cause you know Mom I'll always be there.

I Love You, Mommy.

Douglas A. Scribner

The Fortified Heart

Who dare step upon my slab and rap against my door?
With rhythmic pounding resounding — leaving me breathless for more...
You will lack the help from me to see your way inside and through
Please...if this visit is momentary, dare not further as something
    to prove
Take chivalrous pity, a cavity is better than a ruin of such a
    cathedral
True, it stands lonely and inviting, but at least it stands tall
I hide behind these walls of simultaneous protection and captivity
Shielded by vines restricting my steps — locked in sentinel misery
Venture toward the guarded tear-stained-glass window of memories past
And feel me wriggle in the pain of this naked vulnerability at last
Persevere beyond this appendage and into the cold marble entrance
To endure this frigid foyer, hold tight to your patience
Once through, securely lock yourself inside to feel love's radiance
And if your "pounds" become my feeble heartbeat by chance,
Never leave, lest all should crumble in your wake
Leaving echoed footsteps behind to console my heartache

Heather Davis

To Live and Die and Live Again

You walk toward me briskly as you used to way back when,
With that smile upon your face — that smile of my old friend.
You take me by the hands and tell me what it's like
To live and die and live again.

You tell me of your life — the way it used to be,
Of the pain you suffered and the moments filled with glee.
And how it felt to die! And then you tell me what it's like
To live and die and live again.

You tell me that the step to death is quicker than the eye.
That suddenly you see a glorious light way up high
And music — and the voice that you hear
When death is so very near.

You tell me of the One who leads you to the light
and how your body is transformed and pain takes flight.
Your eyes are all aglow as you tell it all to me —-
How wonderful you felt to finally be set free.

You say that you had to come to let me know you care
And thank me for my many words of prayer. But wait, don't leave,
I'm the one who should be thanking you for showing it all to me and
helping me understand what it's like to live and die and live again.

Jean Leistra Wilkinson

As I Sit...

As I sit and look at the world with open eyes, I see a cloudless sky with the blazing, lustrous sun creeping up over the beautiful mountains, but when my eyes are closed I see is a furious raging storm brewing within.

As I sit with my eyes closed I hear, nature's soft whispers blowing in the wind, telling me she needs help in saving her precious trees and animals from the chain saws, matches, guns, pollution and toxic fumes.

As I sit with my eyes closed I see families destroyed by adultery, abuse, alcohol, or drugs. I see brutal and vicious wars, famines, hatred, hostility, bitterness, malice, and sadness in everyone's eyes.

When my eyes are open I see the world with, happiness, joy, laughter, prosperity, cheer, intrigue, confidence, opportunities for everyone.

As I sit and look at the world children are sitting on park benches resting after playing on the playground.

As I sit and look at the world trees are swaying in the wind, birds are flying high above, cows are grazing in the fields, pigs are rolling in the mud, little puppies are resting on rugs, and elephants are wondering the land for peanuts.

As I sit and look at this world promise, assurance and hope is what I see.

As I sit and look at the world I never want to close my eyes again.

Jill Pettit

Touching The Decades

The nights are long and lonely
With the kids all grown and gone
And I'm left with thoughts of times gone by
When my days began at dawn.

I stroll into the darkened den
And see the albums all in line
As they fill the shelves of yesteryear
With memories lost in time.

What's happened to those years, I ask
How can they all be spent...
I reach to touch the decades
To determine where time went.

And there it lay before me
A binder of events that drew tears
Contagious smiles of my daughter and son
Recalling memories so precious, so dear.

So my evening alone with the albums
Brought an end to the nights by myself
As I relived my past in those pages
And I discovered my wealth on that shelf.

Bonnie Rae Peterson

Where Does Love Lie?

Why can't we all just get along?
Why can't we see that hate is wrong?
If we all could just join together,
Then we would have enough love to last forever.

If we could get people to step from darkness to light,
Then so many more things would be right.
If everyone could learn to love one another,
Then maybe we wouldn't try to kill each other.

Why can't we see what's happening here?
If we don't our end might be near.
Where does true love lie?
Because we don't know many people die.

Julie Swinson

"A Golden Black Knight"

Like magic you appeared—a golden Black Knight in the hue of darkness.
With the stature of royalty in your veins you shown like a star
    in the sky;
Enveloping the strength of a redwood you stood tall and wise and sure;
And your eyes reflected a glow opaqued that comes only from the
    knowledge of caring.

Like magic you appeared—a golden Black Knight in the hue of darkness.
And as our lost Black Unicorn once strode, your step was precise and
    eloquent;
Your word spoken was as soft and gentle as a morning's dew upon a rose,
Yet delivered with the impact of waters rising from Neptune's wrath.

Like magic you appeared—a golden Black Knight in the hue of darkness.
A sparkling treasure within the realm of those who try to strip you of
    your sword;
But you endure—and do so strongly, royally, knowingly and so
    eloquent and gently.
And, as never-ending as magic, so too your magnificence will
    manifest itself.

Like magic you appeared—a golden Black Knight in the hue of darkness.

Amala S. Ilahi

For One In Heaven

I went down a golden road today
With the sunshine shining so brightly...
I knew God had lifted an angel up
As the cottony clouds blew so lightly.
The budding spring trees, like sparkling glass,
With crystalline coats of glistening ice,
Made me feel, momentarily, that I'd
Somehow passed into Heavenly Paradise.
A place so fair and bright and clear,
Where God can keep and hold her near.
In loving arms, she rests her head,
We know, for sure, she is not dead.
She's a fair, young angel in His Heavenly throng,
And her voice is raised in a sweet, angelic song.
We surely know that, when our Earthly life is done,
We, too, shall join our angel in the Kingdom of the Son.

Bonnie Seeley

"Have Trash, Will Travel"

Once there was a floating barge.
With trash that was filled high and large!.
Every where he went, there,
had followed a terrible scent!.
He went from port to port,
with all that trash!.
But, nowhere could it be stashed!.
He's still sailing that smelling barge,
with trash filled up,
high and large.

If you should see him, just wave him by,
with his smelly barge of,
now, compose, And,
make sure You're wearing a mask,
or at least, HOLD YOUR NOSE!!!!.

As he sails on by,
the shores of gravel,
he's well known, as, "HAVE TRASH,
WILL TRAVEL!!!."

JoAnn Deisinger

Untitled

Flowers bloom in colorful arrays until they
    Wither, brown, and are gone.
Spring melds into Summer and into Fall, until all
    Succumb to Winter's cold deep sleep.
     All rivers flow until they are dry.
     The four winds blow until they die.
Man and woman, they live, they share their lives
Together, but they too fall forever asleep.
      All lives. All dies.
Mountains laugh at the ages and taunt eons until
     They finally relent and crumble.
     Even the shining stars above fade, fade
      Until they shine no more.
All in the universe diminishes, dwindles, and soon
     Must bow to infinity-all but one.
     Only one stands side by side with eternity
      And is forever anew.
       Endless...
       Timeless...
       It is my love for you.
Janice E. Kiehl

Callous Devotion

The wind blows through the trees; ruffles the leaves to the ground without regard;
Then divulges itself freely through space. So, also, is this
  impenetrable master.

His surface is overabundant; his core, destitute and removed.
His heart gives, but his soul conforms to his mind, and yields.

His breath is quiet and his body still, while his eyes are fixed
on the convictions of his heart.
He questions his circumscribed mind; he questions his heart; and
  again, he questions his mind.

His mind justifies his reasons and produces excuses, while his
  heart constantly observes the absolute
  hope it feels under the influence of love.

How mysterious is love's conception in this master's core.

And yet his exterior does not deceive, but conceals itself while his
  mind abandons his heart.
Is faith or hope to be obtained by this confound master?

I am persuaded that love is manifest. Therefore, his convictions
  will be revealed to him.
Only then will this master's heart secure it's rightful place in
  his mind and conquer it.

Then his love will prosper and will be desired by all.
His eyes will no longer be fixed on his convictions, but they will
  be seeing love through love's eyes.
Brenda J. Shields

My Daughter, My Friend

A spirit of beauty, innocent and bold,
With scented love, hot candy and treasures untold.
An aura of monopoly filled with Broadwalk and glee,
Winsome child, this angel is she

Iridescent eyes; that captivates your soul,
Mesmerizing smile; from days of old.
Embraced by her mystery, her all power knowing,
An eternal flame that's luminous and glowing.

Forever an angel in all of her glory,
Kissed by the universe of her "neverending" story.
Jennifer Kaaihue

The Little Man!

An empire never could have been
Without the help of "little men,"
Nor would "Britannia" e'er been seen
Without the faithful "Gunga Din."

The simple faith of a common heart
Has broken mighty states apart.
Through home bred steady, faithful will.
They shed their blood. Their lives fulfill

In God enlightened common sense,
A course with little recompense.
In stink of sweat, in endless pain,
Their lives seem to have been in vain,

A pawn of kings long dead. But how will
Kings to be, their dreams fulfill,
And how will travel to the moon
Yet be, sans "little man's" kind boon

Of self to lend a willing hand?
In spite of snub and reprimand,
They'll keep their faith as best they can
We honor you, the "little man."
Arthur James Webb

Black Haze

Every day at this time of year I wonder
Wonder why this reoccurring black haze falls over my eyes
The evil pulsates within
Along with thoughts of forever loneliness
Thoughts disturb me, while everyone else rejoices
In this eternal black hole that I live
I search for the smallest glimpse of a threshold of light
For at this bleak time of year
My ocean is ever so deep and drowning with waves of blackness
Barely buoyant is the ship that I sail
For each tear that is wept from my uncontrollable eyes
I pray that it's forever banished from the scorned face it runs off
Confiding the tears within one's self is detrimental to the health
But finding ways to seduce the pain is unthinkable
Hardened like a warrior's heart is
So now is bestowed upon my own
Wretched is this time of year, for I do not celebrate
Hoping it passes through like the sudden change of the weather
Entwined and misplaced are my feelings for now
I live a mere death, to one it might seem
Erin Bertrand

Life

Your life is yours live it with love live it
With peace and live it now
So many things are waiting to be realized
You can't make your heart feel something
I can't feel
Friend is a word that I don't throw around
Although its used and abused I still like the sound
If you don't find it in your heart to forgive
The flaws of others you'll find yourself isolated
And missing out on friendship with excellent people.
Love is about having no doubts loving with
No selfishness accepting the person for
Themselves standing by the person through rough times and good
You can't live for anyone and no one can live for you
Only your opinion matters
If everyone lived to please everyone
Than no one would be happy I was lost but now I am found
I was blind but now I can see
Sometimes life can be funny and it always
Brings you back to the end of the tunnel.
When you are able to forgive
You can love, laugh, and celebrate.
Amy Reid

Cruel Love

I sit alone in the dark of the night
wondering why this has happened to me

There were no excuses for the things he has done,
the pain, the sorrow, the emptiness inside.

All of my hopes and dreams fade away
the longer I make excuses.

But now it's time to say good-bye,
for I could not take the pain anymore.

He was, I thought, the love of my life
but I was young and living a life.

I gave him all the love I had.
He took that from me and gave me pain.

Will my life ever come together?
Will I ever be able to trust another man with my heart?
Or will the answers be just as painful?

I am afraid that the fear he has given me will ruin my life forever.

Where did all the happiness go?
I want all this sadness to go away.
Dawn Wyrick

Going Back To Shadows

She sweeps the corners of the seldom home,
working the straw into a worry.
Her children gather in meaningless moments,
and then disperse like autumn leaves.
And still she sweeps 'til the next time,
pushing the years in like dresser drawers,
going back to shadows for respite.

They'll come again, they always do,
and move from room to room,
pulling out drawers and wondering
where the years went
that make a home,
and raising dust,
always dust.
Carol Robertshaw

To Rob (Rags)

  Shabby clothes and ragged hose,
Worn with pride, adorned in style,
  Guitar in hand, song in mind,
His day began in quarter time.

  He stood alone his head erect,
A heart of gold, I have been told,
  Throughout his life, cut short by fate,
A love emerged, but why so late.

  I can't explain his wondrous gift,
He touched the hearts of all he met,
  Fear of life, but not of death,
He was at peace as we all wept.

  He took his life one dreadful morn,
I know not why, I can't convey,
  But do know, I'll miss-it's true,
Hair of blond and eyes so blue.

  I do believe with all my heart,
That angels sang when he did part,
  Rejoiced for him, who was alone,
For he was home where he belonged.
Doug Kane

If Today's TV Covered The Gettysburg Address

Today's TV crew at Gettysburg
Would be a motley lot -
Especially as they put Poor Abe
Square on the spot.

First thing they'd ask the leader of the nation,
"Why aren't there more Blacks in your administration?"
Abe would get around this in a sly decree-
"I wouldn't want to debate that on TV."

Then just before the speech 'neath an old shade tree
One reporter would blare out -
"Abe, you ever committed adultery?"
Abe would shrug his shoulder and say in tone
"Let the one without sin cast the first stone."

Then after the address and the last beat of the drum
A reporter would query "Who did you copy that material from?"
On the air immediately after, a group of experts would
rehash and say-
"The world will little note or long remember anyway."
John G. Maycox

Imagine

Imagine if the world was square instead of round
Would the earth rotate evenly on it's axis?

Imagine if there was only one race of people.
What race would it be and would we all look alike?
Imagine if we all spoke the same language.
How boring it would be - - we could never whisper secrets,
Because everyone would understand.

There could never be another war
What would be fight about?
We're all alike-same race-same language
and we would all think alike.

If the world were really square instead of round
Imagine what would happen if the world had four corners.
What would we do with these corners?
Oh well, good thing I just like to imagine. Imagine!
Estelle Walton

Kathryn

Where are you Kathryn?
Yes, we see you here in this place for
  the sick and the old.
But is it really you?
You smile a strange smile not the one we know.
Your eyes look but you do not see.
You look the same but somehow different,
The spark of life is gone.

You are existing only in a world we do not know.
We miss you Kathryn, we are sorry life has to be this way.
We want to see you again as you were before
An elegant, warm and wonderful lady.
But that's not the way it will be.
You told me once that you've had a good life
Not much you could ever want for.
I'm glad!
For now that you are lost in that world of your own,
We can hope you are there in the past reliving your
  good life.
Diane Herzog

The Specks of Sand

Life goes on, day by day
　　yet another reflection of the sun's final ray
The dark emerges before we can prepare
　　As a blind search through the tarred night we dare.

Before we know it, our vision restored
　　the night forgotten, we surrender the sword
It all happens so fast, each moment at hand
　　As through the hourglass fall the fleeting specks of sand.

Time flies, traveling at the speed of light
it doesn't really exist, just a fragment of the mind's sight
One second comes before we realize the other is gone
The eyes close at night, mysterious opening at dawn.

The truth is clear, not a moment should be wasted
Every precious breath of air felt, every split second tasted
All feeling expressed while the chance is still here
The risk to be taken while loved ones still near
　　and living not under leadership of the concept of fear.

Angella Charnot

Life

Life is full as a rose in bloom.
Yet death conquers life as quickly as water dampers
a raging fire.
Life is love and laughter sometimes pain and sadness.
Yet with life so full no one can really take it away....
for even as we die yet we live.
For everyone has left a part of themselves in someone
else and as the years go by we are passed on down the
generations.
Life is forever...
As our thoughts and our memories live on in our family
and friends, we still are alive in another form....
For we don't die just our bodies die our souls live
on and on....

Debbie Koehn

Living Small

We lived in a dwelling plenty large for two
Yet I tried to live small.
Things transpired.
Morning glories spilled blossoms all over
Monarchs paid visits while on their way to Natural Bridge
Mockingbirds talked and I spoke their prose.
They teased me with their unrestrained existence.
Slowly I spread out, bit by bit, just to enhance my soul.
"O No! Not to be," said he.
I gathered myself and became small once more.
Then...the rains leaked through clouds of black
Mother Earth became green and fragrant
Poppies and cosmos nodded and bid me come.
I'm lured and gently ramble throughout.
"O No! Not to be," said he.
Then...a honeybee tattooed me with her wings.
Like a newly-born butterfly
I emerged, hung my wings to dry and took flight
Not once glancing back.

Faye Anglin

"Beauty Is My Darling Baby Girl"

Beauty is an everlasting thing
beauty is love for everything.
Beauty is the wind that whines,
beauty is the grapes and vines.
Beauty can be anything,
even the joys of a song you sing.
One of the beauties in my world,
is you my Darling Baby Girl.

Linda Harrell

"Alone, Yet Not Alone"

Alone in life, alone in death to be.
Yet not alone for one is in my heart -
The Lord of all, who never shall me part
from His own self, though devil blacken me
through trickery, or things I cannot see.
Though doubt may form from reading of some chart,
some book that scientists have made an art,
I'll follow Him, and find true ecstasy
On life's stumbling highway He gives me grace.
Each morn I wake with His renewing strength.
At night He's nearer me than during day,
for through my prayers He gives me hope and faith and charity.
My depth, and width and length of life shall end upon His holy bay.

Dolores V. Posatiere

Bear

Bear, you haven't even been with me for a year,
Yet you are extremely special.
The way you look with that flannel shirt covering
your white teddy bear body.

You used to smell of Liz Claiborne, now you have
acquired your own smell of
dust and wear, from being held and cuddled by an auto mechanic.

You symbolize a very special relationship between
two people who have learned to love
each other, but to also love you.

I want so much to wash the dust and dirt away from you,
but at the same time I never
want to wash the fond memories from you and I.

Amy Kathleen Honchar

Best of Friends

I only showed you fear,
Yet you wipe away my tear.

You cherished my heart
And I know now and forever we'll never part.

You shared my dreams
Together you and me were a team.

You change and bloom before my eyes
You make new friends, but our friendship never dies.

As we grow we find our differences,
And choose different sides
Finding our selves separated.

We have different classes, friends, and interests.
We may have disagreements,
But I remain a loyal friend you could trust and depend.

This poems ends but has no beginning.
This may crumble or burn.
Not strong as a stone,
But made of love alone.

Jasmin Roberson

He Speaks

God speaks to us, every night and day
With His cool breezes, and soft rain.
His songbirds, rainbows and stars.
Sometimes with thunder, lightning, and surf.
His Gifts are numerous and Great.
But His greatest Gift is a Precious Child
Who can copy these Gifts?
He who gives so readily to many
Who do not want to accept or see
His glorious Gifts!

Eula D. Foret

Recognition

How can I know me, when all my life I have tried to reflect you,
Lest I be uncaring?

How can I love my body, when it was always forced to obey
another's idea of beauty,
Lest I be immodest?

How can I feel my spirit when it has always been whipped
into submission,
Lest I be arrogant?

How can I trust my heart when it always has to be bleeding for others,
Lest I be selfish?

Today, I will listen to my inner voice until I recognize my name.

Today, I will believe in my body until I can see the beauty
that is my birthright.

Today, I will touch my spirit as it sings it's authentic song to me.

Today, I will trust my heart to know the love this child deserves.
        Janis Reynolds

A Friend Through It All

Even with all of your beauty
You always go beyond the call of duty.
I know you are a gift from above
And yet with me you share your love.

If you ever left me it would tear my heart
For with you I never want to part.
You always know how to make me feel better
Even if it is in a letter.

As the guys come and go
You'll never leave me I know.
To me you have never told a lie
Which gives me no reason to ever sigh.

You always share your thoughts
So many things I've been taught.
After all we've been through
I know when asked about my best friend my thoughts always turn
to you.
        Jennifer McCarthy

Love Garden

    I am the dirt that lays in the ground
You are the seeds that make the flowers in a garden
Love is but a garden that beautiful flowers may grow
We are the flowers that grow and live in the garden
Our children are the seedlings trying to stand tall and proud
Your smile and joy is the sun that helps us grow
Your care is the water that feeds our roots
Anger is the weeds that choke out our garden's life
Sleep is the winter that put our flowers to rest
Hope is the spring that brings us back to life
Truth is the fertilizer that makes us strong
Dreams are the way we want our garden to look
Don't take away the good parts of the garden
For all that would be left is weeds and dirt
Once the winter comes and the weeds die
springtime winds would simply blow the dirt into the sky.
        Brent Bartlett

Lord

You are the way, the truth, the life.
You are there for me
In all my pain and strife.

You keep me warm when it's cold.
When I'm scared, you make me bold.

You make me happy when I'm blue.
All my anger, pain and sorrow I shall give to you.

When I feel alone you let me know you're there,
With kindness and mercy I know that you care.

You are my Lord,
I love you so very much.
I love you and your gentle touch.

I love you for all that you do.
Most of all, I love you
For just being you.
        Chris Ezit

Why Must Life Be So Cruel?

Sometimes life is just great,
You can be floating on cloud nine,
But suddenly it turns - a twist of fate,
You feel like an icy hand has gripped your spine.
So, why must life be so cruel?

Why does life grant something that can't be replaced?
Why does life allow you to get to know and cherish it?
But then rips it away, making your heart beat high paced,
And when it happens you can't believe it.
Then you must ask yourself, "Why must life be so cruel?"

But after all this happens and you have time to reflect,
You'll think about it over and over,
And you'll realize that life isn't as cruel as you might expect,
And what has just happened is once in a lifetime, like finding a four
    leaf clover.
So, is life really that cruel?
        Christopher Kelley

Hidden Predator

It spreads everywhere,
You can't see it,
But it's there,
Everyone feels its presence.

It's horrible, ugly and vicious,
Throughout time it has been here,
Causing death and hate
Everyone feels its presence

Prejudice is the predator,
Now, in the present, it is bigger than ever
Wars, killing and violence are the results
Everyone feels its presence.

Every race, color and religion are affected
Everywhere around the world
Everyday of our lives someone becomes a victim
Everyone feels its presence.

No one person can stop it,
But, if we learn how to prevent it
In the future there will be a better tomorrow
Everyone will not feel its presence.
        Jeffrey J. Ong

The Pushover

"The best revenge is to be happy,"
You counsel me.
"He left you to hurt you,
Can't you see?"
You offer, "He's miserable
With her now anyway."
But I don't relate to the things
You say.

Revenge is not the medicine I seek
For the grave injustice I endure.
To think of him as miserable now
Does not provide my soul a cure.
You say I'm a pushover because I forgive
And try to forget and go on without bitterness.
"Why?" you ask in awe.
Simply because I must to live.

Charlotte Pace

"It's Still Your Day"

It's Father's Day - but you are not left out
You don't have children that run and shout!
But Fathers Day rolls come in many a form
I've heard you have an animal dorm
When home from work you do retreat
To watch TV and rest your feet
Upon your lap your cat will creep
To rest or play or even sleep.
And when the storm above will rumble
Into your bed - a dog will tumble
No greater joy - they won't go away
For all year long - to them its "Master Fathers Day."

Delores Marlow Tramontana

Teeming Liquid

Your eyes are distinct
you eat out my flesh
Chewing and knawing
straight down to the bone
Mine scream in agony
as I bow to your thrown
tears scorch a path
beautifully down my throat
Veins extend
with the pulse of my still, slow-beating heart
Threatening the breath
seething down my throat to my breast
Bloodshot eyes bleeding tears of remorse crying out
with jagged nails teeming, gouging down my arm
liquid seeping, flooding onto the floor
pooling next to me in a mocking rain to my despair
where my lungs no longer have a breath
where you see me lying on the floor
with liquid pooling next to me teeming over the bottles
into the grave

Julia Barbee

Image

I look into the shattered mirror.
To see the broken pieces of a life I once remember.
A broken home, a broken heart.
Like my whole world it was torn apart.
I see the image of a broken dream.
Keep hoping its not as bad as it seems.
I Look into a piece of glass and wonder is this all my past.
To see the pieces on the floor.
To loose the dreams I had before
I look into a shattered mirror to see the image of a life I once
remember.

Diane Nix

Ode To Madeline, My Mentor

You smiled at me when no one else would
You gave me laughter when nobody else could
You were there for me when I was feeling down
You helped me get rid of my frown
You listened when I needed someone to talk to
You spoke kind words to help me not feel so blue
You make me have cloudy days when you're not here
You give me rays of sunshine when you are near
You took the time to ask how I was doing
You give me so much but you never ask for anything
You touched my heart with your smile and kindness
You have given me so much happiness
Thank you for everything you've done for me
Thank you for filling my life with your beauty

Estela S. Serna

Daddy

Leaning against the neighbor's '85 Ford,
You hide your tan, weathered face in the shadow of your Co-op cap.

I only see your back, but I imagine
    Your glasses
      Speckled with iron, paint, and dirt.
    Your bristles always reminding me of
      Corn stubble during silage season.
    Your huge, calloused hands with fingers thick as sidewalk chalk,
      Often picking wildflowers for Mom and me.

I remember
    Sitting beside you during meals,
    Watching your biceps bulge.
    You lifted a single fork.

I remember
    Unlacing your boots at night,
    Polishing your shoes for church,
    Removing slivers from your fingers and
    Admiring your golden wedding band.

I used to think you were the tallest man alive.
Now, I've grown up and know you are.

Bridgette Blomster

Lonely Bus Ride

...so turn your head and look at me
you just might like who you see.
If your heart beats too fast,
I'll know I have a small chance.
If you smile will I know what to say?
If our eyes meet will I look away?
We're at a red light now but soon it'll be green,
and maybe that's just what I need.
But it's almost time for me to go.
Strangers meet often with people they don't know.
And will I see you again around here?
For some unknown eyes it looks real clear.
Still a familiar mouth doesn't know what to say.
And one chair apart seems so far away.
So don't pull that string or walk out that door,
'Cause when it closes it could open a sore,
And when I ride away that sore might become infected.
But I'd rather bleed alone than be rejected.

Harry MacLacklin

The Wake

Why did you come here, without any remorse or sympathy
You make your way through the line, no tears, no empathy
My son lies behind me, so still in his blue casket
Your contempt for me so obvious, you don't try to mask it.

Everyone said this tragedy would make you
Do the right thing
Surely when you saw the departed and heard
The death bell ring

But you approach me and can't even shake my hand
Hug me, whisper sorry in my ear
I am bleeding, crying out for my child
And you compound, extend my grief year upon year.

James Sferrazza

The Thanksgiving Turkey

Oh, I'm the bird you purchased at the butcher store;
    You took me home and plucked my feathers by the score.
You put me in the oven and you shut the door —
    Remember me?

You took me out and showed me to your company;
    And, bit by bit they plucked a little piece from me.
And now a plate of bones is all that's left of me —
    Remember me?

Make me wish (they're pulling me apart again).
    Make a wish - I wish your wish comes true again - AMEN.

Now I am not the same old bird I used to be;
    For I was led into a big catastrophe.
A little burp — and that's the very end of me —
    Remember me?

Hank Glittenberg

You

Call me if you need to, love me if
You want to, like me if you can,
Because I will be there to give you
A helping hand, cause I love you so.

There ain't nothin' in this world
That I wouldn't do for you,
You made my dreams come true.
When I am away from you I feel so blue,
All I need is you.

You came into my life and I will never set you free,
Cause you make me feel like a queen,
I know it no dream boy,
because I had a dream and oh what a dream!
I dream of so many things,
some of the things that I dream will never come true,
But as long as I have you boy I will never be blue.

Carolyn Thompson

Fighter

Forced into this world far too early
    You fought to live with a passionate fury.
Each gasping breath bought you one minute more, but
    Breath by breath, you drew nearer the closing door.

We all gathered closed to help if we could;
    But all our technology could do you no good.

Ten fingers; ten toes; a sweet innocent face;
    A product of love, of God's giving grace.
A fighter to the end; we all cheered you on.

But to no avail—God took this baby home.

Cheryl Kelley

America

My country, my land, my freedom, my friend,
You were once so innocent, but now you are so indecent
Where have you gone, what did I do wrong.

Our sky, our land, our waters are spoiled,
With the filth of greed our hands we have soiled
Children crying, children dying and who knows for how long.

My friend died last year by his own hand,
Not in America, my country, my land
It was once in my heart but now I've forgotten the words to the song
America who are you, who am I
Give me an ear and look me straight in the eye,
Is GOD's love still here or is it long gone.

How much time do we have left,
My mind, my heart, my body is all part of the theft
America needs you needs me to live to love is to get along
Should we, will we once again sing the song.

Gilbert Rocamontes

Untitled

My words could never express my feelings toward you
You will always be my first love, yes, that's true
I will never forget that special time
When you were in these arms of mine.

You were always there for me, bad times and good
Always caring for me, like a dear boyfriend should
The happiest times in my life were spent with you
You made me laugh when I was feeling blue

I loved the way you turned me on
But then one day, you were gone
You disappeared without a trace
I cried and cried, remembering your face

I thought the whole world had turned black
But then you came crawling back
I was filled with extreme joy
I screamed and screamed, on boy, oh boy

I opened the door for you again
I should have known better than to let you in
You hurt me till I could take it no more
That's when I decided to close my door

Amanda Lamberth

You're Some Dad, Dad

You play with the kids,
    You yell and you scream.
Then you give them a hug,
    when they awake from a dream.
You're stern when it's needed,
    you tickle and tease.
You love with a passion,
    and try hard to please.
And tho I get angry,
    and try to protect.
I can't stay mad long,
    with the love you project.
I sit and watch with awe and wonder,
    at the spell you put our children under.
A kind word, a smile, a hug so sweet,
    and their faces light up with a joy so complete.
A mothers love is special, it's true.
    but the rare special gift is a father like you.

Adrienne Garcia

You'd Need To Wear A Space Suit

You'd need to wear a space suit to travel up in space
You'd be bouncing up and down going to and fro
No air friction there would be

You'd need to wear a space suit
with a helmet that had a strobe light
You'd see the moon a whole different way
going round and round
No light you would see

You'd need to wear a space suit with air tanks attached
You'd be making funny noises beep, beep when you talked
No air there would be

You'd need to wear a space suit to float all around
You'd weigh nothing on the moon so diet no more
No gravity there would be
You'd need to wear a space suit....

Jessica Ray Huffman

Butterfly From Hell

She's pretty as a picture, she seems to be the best.
You'll think that she is grand, but she's different from the rest.
She'll take you to a place where you've never been,
And give you message that you'd never send.
She'll look your eyes while she steals your heart,
Then when your lost in love she'll tear you apart.
So pack up your heart and run while you can, take what you have
while still a man. Don't let her colors lead you astray,
Cause you'll never have her, she'll never stay. She'll find a new
flower on which to feed, looking for someone to furnish her need.
And when it's all over and you sit and moan,
With only the sound of a heart that's a lone,
You'll wonder just how she caused you to fall.
Wonder just why you loved her at all.
And you'll search forever for what you have lost,
For loving her you've paid the cost .
She'll fill up your cup with all her charm,
While deep in her heart she's planning you harm.
Cause while on the surface everything's well,
Way deep inside she's a Butterfly from Hell.

Jamie Toland

A Passing Star

You were such a pretty girl
Your cute smile, your curly hair
You sent New England in a twirl
You had style, what flair

You were picked to go in space
You were the first female civilian to go
Who knew, that we see the last of your face
Who knew, that the shuttle would blow

The launch looked so right
Less than two minutes of the flight
We heard an explosion at the height
We saw a big ball of bright light

You left us on that January day
You left your family behind
Life can be cruel, unkind
There is not much we can do but ask God, and pray

God bless, so you can rest:

Donald A. McDermott

God's Little Child

Your God's little child you precious little thing
Your God's little child joy and happiness you'll bring
Your heart is pure, your mind is free
Your God's little child, and you belong to me.

My life is filled with love and laughter because it's filled with you.
Your hands, your arms, your touch is tender,
Your kiss will make my heart surrender.

Your eyes are sparkling and bright
Your hair is soft as the evening night.
Your smile will make my heart fill with joy,
You were sent by God above to be my little boy.

Your God's little child you precious little thing
Your God's little child joy and happiness you'll bring
Your heart is pure, your mind is free
Your a gift from God and you belong to me.

Johnny Lee Arrowood

Dream Lover

In my dreams, I see you dancing above my head with
your hands held high and your head moving back an forth.
you come towards me with your arms held in front of you,
wanting me to come forward.
But all I can see of my lover is his naked body
for my lover has no face.
He is of many men who walk through my dreams late at night,
wanting me to come forth to join them in a love match.

But my body does not move from the bed that it lays upon.
For you see, I'm waiting for my lover who's face I can see.
Who's dreams are real and not make believe.
So I wait
One night....two nights and then on the third, he comes to me.

His body is that of many men but his face is of but one man.
And that one man belongs to me.

For he has made all my dreams come true.
For that one man is you

Carol Glisson Wurts

You're a song.
Your harmony excites me.
Your melody invites me
  To a world I've never known,
  A side I've never shown to anyone.

You're a dream.
You drift into my mind.
My cares are left behind
  For thoughts of happiness,
  Completely in access of your control.

You're my life.
Your love makes me exist.
The first time that we kissed,
  We found the rainbow's end,
  We formed the perfect blend of two souls.

Bonnie J. Greenawald

Children Of Yesterday

Traveling for days
To reach tomorrow,
Forgotten by day
Hidden by night,
We are the children of yesterday.
Be a reader of riddles
Be a singer of echoes,
Yes,
We are the children of yesterday.

Christina Klien

Chess!

The battle rages!
Your head pounds with the pain of failed plans.
Knights stand frozen,
Trapped in a face off.
Castles destroyed.
Armies advance and a King retreats.
He has lost his hope as well as his Queen.
Troops surround, none of them yours.
No place to hide.
No place to run.
Isn't this fun?
CHECKMATE!

John William Blessing

Party

You're invited to a party, I'd like you all to come
Your host is Dr. Feel Good, remember you are number one!

Who will be there? Well I'll tell you,
The guest list is awesome,
The heroin witch, and LSD rabbit,
The can, glass and bottle; Shh!, don't tell anyone!

Guess who called and will be making an appearance?!
It's cocaine and crack, want to test your endurance?
It should be lots of fun!

Yes, I knew you'd ask!
They will all be there, tobacco, pills and grass.

Now the party has begun!
Sniff and huff and snort,
Scramble up your brain waves,
Come on feel good - You are number one!

Oh, the party's now over, what a shame, what a shame!
He's dead? Well what's his name?
She remembers nothing, will never be the same -

Well, this was a party, they knew when they came,
I can't be responsible, as they play the devil's game.

Joy Campbell

Test Of Time

My heart is entangled with pain, cause you left me in doubt.
Your lips were mine, you're passion I live with out.
You're heart is no longer here.
But my heart is still waiting.
I hope you'd revere what my heart is anticipating.

Although you're gone I take this in stride.
I prolong so much pain. But hoping we won't subside.
I can't endure this pain that's deep within.
It disturbs my heart, and inhibits me to win.

I need you to hold me so I won't cry.
Give me a kiss, show me love won't die. As long as we persist.
I miss you're eyes, and everything they used to show.
Give us a chance to grow .
So our love can enhance, never let me go.

I'll always keep us inside, if you're love has strayed
My love will always abide. Don't forget my heart.
It won't exist without you're touch.
Without you there's no start, and the pain would be too much.

Without you, I would die, but my love will still subsist.
Without you, I would cry cause my heart won't be with bliss.

Anthony Crespo

Island

An island within an island across the bay
Your rolling hills and towers, stand
majestically against the blue skies

The bridge that gaps, us a sweet sensation
of temptation

Upon our arrival at your port, we stand
in awe and don't know what to say

Breathing in your fresh air and digesting
all beauty, we long to stay

Pitched against the sky you are a large
silhouette of crimson

Resting our feet upon this island, is like a
soft velvet touch

I may never get to embrace you again
Thank you for your beauty

Dorothy R. Wade

In This Moment With You

In this moment
your small personal self,
warm
alert
alive
skin softer than cashmere
smell newer than the newest puppy
the toasty warmth of you fills my nostrils and expands in my lungs
mesmerized by the blueness of your eyes
transformed by a seamless moment
times unmoving window on the day you first lay crying on my stomach
the first time you smiled at me
a window
on all the firsts in the tomorrows to come
words, steps
school, friends
dates, college
marry....
All in this cozy, quiet, intimate, jointless moment enraptured by you
and missing you already

Catherine G. Bratton

Be Gentle With My Heart

Your eyes so pure and gentle,
Your smile a pleasant glow.
I see a handsome, dapper man,
Someone I'd like to know.

From the moment that our eyes met,
Till the time we said 'Hello,'
I found myself so lost for words,
And prayed it would not show.

Sometimes, I dream "In Love With You,"
Or falling way too fast.
Or is it fascination?
Something that cannot last?

I want to hold you close to me,
Yet want to take it slow.
Let's walk and talk — Share all our dreams —
Together we may grow.

Growing is a precious need,
Together or apart.
If the latter be my fate,
Be gentle with my heart.

Donald Bacon

Ocean Enigma

Tumultuous Ocean, relentless and cruel
Your swashbuckling capers wreck driftwood or jewel
You belch with distaste and hurtle your spray
On richer or poorer, on all in your way
You're seeking no favor, no fame and no wealth
Yet splash onward in splendor, or creep toward in stealth
Your course is unaltered by pleadings of men
Your actions repeated — repeated — again

Yet you are the home of creatures that play
Of creatures that love you and laugh at your spray
Of fishes that flicker their eyelids at men
That spurn them and fear them and dart from their ken
Of creatures that trust you and cling to your shores
Knowing only protection in your swashbuckling floors.

Ethel Dodson

Hello, Goodbye...

Hello, goodbye... it was over that fast
your visit here was just too swift.
You were not expected... and quite a surprise
but then we waited and hoped and prayed.

Hello, goodbye... were you ever here?
I don't recall meeting, but yearn for your eyes.
why did you visit... but not let us see
what was your purpose, why were you here?

Hello, goodbye... what is your name?
did I ever know it, just the same.
I feel that it's written into my heart
but my lips are silent, no name comes to mind.

Hello, goodbye... I wanted to see you
to hold you and smile, will you wait there before me
will you wait... for a while?

Hello, goodbye...I had such grand plans before we had met.
Your visit would change them, I wish that I might.

Hello, goodbye... I'm glad for your visit,
though brief, you'll stay with me
hello,... goodbye.

Joseph L. Clupp Jr.

Sitting on the Beach

Sitting on the beach watching the tide roll in takes all
your worries away.
What a wonderful way to spend a summer day.
When we sit and stare its like the ocean has feelings and it cares.
It seems to solve everything; just like to write poetry, dance,
    or sing.
The ocean is a wonderful thing, pick up a shell and hear it ring.
The ocean can be fierce, calm or rough, the sand through your toes can
    be soft or tough,
There're sea gulls and sail boats and an undertow; and small little
    cracks where hermit crabs stow.
The rocks are covered with seaweed and slime, it will soon be high tide
    in a short period of time,
When you want to relax or get away, the beach is a perfect place
    for you and your worries to drift away.
Your heart is as warm as the sun, and just as the sun gets taken over
    by the rain, you'll have no pain tomorrow because with the tide
    went your pain and sorrow.

Julie Scaife

You're Always Blind

When the night is dark and unilluminated...
You're blind.
When love is thought of as wasted time...
You're blind.
When a jubilant smile is greeted with a scornful snarl...
You're blind.
When unlimited potential is referred to as limited talent...
You're blind.
When a warm summer day is wasted on thoughts of winter
blizzards...
You're blind.
When you can't appreciate the beauty of simple things,
When you can't help build hope in the lives of the hopeless,
When you can't reach out and comfort a hurting child,
When you can't simply take time out to relax
and enjoy a moment in a day in your life,
that is not always promised to you,
Then you are blind in your mind,
and in your heart...

Daryl Thomas

Seasons Of Love

As spring brings the green grass to grow,
You're my lover and my best friend you know,

When we spend time together you and I,
The quiet times and the noisy ones,
Learning how to fly.

As winter brings the crisp white snow,
You're my lover and my best friend you know.

Snowmobiling high on the mountain tops,
Enjoying Gods beauty at each every stop.
As summer brings many bright sunny days in a row,
You're my lover and my best friend you know.

Camping, fishing, reaching for the bright stars at night,
Striving hard to always do what we think is right.

As fall brings down the leaves and in the cold.
You're my lover and my best friend, even as we grow old.

With all the busy times ahead,
our love has stood the test,
It's with you and only you,
I want to spend the rest.

For you're my lover and my best friend you know.

Cheryl Thorpe Allbee

My Best Friends

You've paved the roads for me to drive
You've built bridges for me to cross
Bumpy roads you've made smooth.

You've helped me when times were tough
You've helped me when life was rough
When I'm sick you make me well
When I fall you pick me up.

You've helped me through the thick and thin
And I hope I'll be there when...you need me

I put my thoughts down on paper
For if I said them it would take forever
I love you Mom and Ray
And I hope that you will stay
MY BEST FRIENDS.

Dion Miller

This Quiet Place

Amid the distant roar of the highway and the hushing of the rushing
wind, speckled by the sunlight peaking through the trees and
surrounded by the peeping of the birds,
   I stop.
   I listen.
I open myself up to hear God's word - to feel the universe's touch.
To be ... and become — fully part of this creation miracle. The
colors of early spring surrounds me, as at once, I understand my
minuscule place in the beautiful circle of life. I am taken away
into the very fiber being of this scene. At once, I am the blade of
grass sweet and new, or the hot orange-red tulip petal about to fall
to the ground, complete in the knowledge that I will come again yet
next year. I am the brittle decaying leaves still left in the corners
of the walk. I am inside the cold, hard, sandstone of the prayer
monument. I am a new leaf bursting with energy as I stretch to grow to my full potential.
   I am Life!
The Life within and the Life without. The Life force flows in me,
through me, until every part of the universe is... at oneness,
   whole, at peace.
And I am freed of my pain. I glow with the Christ light, a new
creation. A creation of love embodied and peace portrayed.
My soul dances with this joyful knowledge.
   I am a godling — perfectly me, and I blessed by and a blessing to this world

    Cathy Goevert

No More Pain

God gave you to me one cold day, we didn't know how long you'd stay.
The doctors said about two years, you proved them wrong when time was here.
I tried to care for you at home, but could not do it all alone.
So sick you stayed at home my love, I prayed to God, the one above.
God sent a place to care for you, they knew exactly what to do.
From such a tiny seven pounds, they got more weight on you, I found.
To leave you there was hard to do, it only shows that I love you.
A little angel in disguise, I could see that in your eyes.

You should have left when you were five, but fought so hard to stay alive.
Your body here was crippled dear, to lose you was my biggest fear.
I knew one day you'd have to go, but when that was I did not know.
For three more years you stayed with us, never one time did you fuss.
When Jesus came to take you home, I knew you would not be alone.
With Uncle Wallace waiting there, I know he'll give you so much care.
He knew you'd come to him one day, to laugh, to sing, to run and play.

A little girl he said he'd take, at Heaven's gate he said he'd wait.
He finally got his little girl, it must have set his heart a whirl.
With no more pain you two shall bare, a place in heaven you both now share.
No longer are you in disguise, you fly up high above the skies.
Dear Uncle Wallace now you see, it was always meant to be Kristi.

    Charlotte Risner

Untitled

As I was traveling down a country road in East Texas, I came
upon a massive pine tree that had died. All that was left of the once
full branches was two large limbs that appeared to reach toward
heaven.

Why me Lord?
Why me Lord? What did I do to deserve this desolate death.
I have done nothing to harm a living soul.
My branches have swept about me, nourishing the needles and the seeds
to give life to others like me.
My deep green needles have not only given pleasure to the eye of the
persons around me, but have provided them shade in the hot summers,
and clean air for them to breathe.

The deer and the cattle have sought shelter beneath my arms,
the rabbit, and the lowly mouse have found warmth in the needles at my
base, as squirrels and red birds danced about my limbs.

My cones have floated to the ground and sprouted young seedlings to
grow in my likeness. And so the cycle goes on. Others will grow in my
place, and their time will come. It is thy will.
It will be done.

    Jean Tully

Don't Promise Your Love

Don't promise me forever, don't promise me
your love, for promises are broken - they're
just things that are spoken of;

Don't promise me forever, as forever may
not be, as time has no limit but love's
eternity

So don't promise me forever, don't promise
me your love, just give it full and free as it
was given from above.....unconditionally
I love you....

    Dave A. Ward

A True Friend

If you go through life with one true friend,
You've had something most people never have!
A friend is there when you're in a rut, and
Not just when you're glad.
The ones who are there when you're riding high,
And then leave you when you're down...
They really aren't friends at all,
If they're never REALLY around!
Everything I'm saying,
It's really quite all true!
The very best friend you'll ever have
Is one that would die for you!

    Joletta Cook

In Memory of Cyndie Gracey

12/31/63-10/13/94

I see you in the sunrise,
   your beauty shines forth.
I see you in the sunset,
   your beauty shines truth.

My heart aches to hold you,
   but you're no longer here.
My fingers long to touch your face,
   to wipe away the tears.

Words no longer do justice,
   to describe your precious soul,
And everything you meant to me,
   the memories that I hold.

    Ellen L. Stanfill

Jeanne

I searched the world over to find only you-
Your beauty, your charm, and your heart so true.

I though at my age, true love I had missed-
But I knew it was you the moment we kissed.

For many a month you've shown your resistance-
So all I can offer is love and persistence.

My love will be yours if you will be mine-
my devotion I offer till the end of time!

You brighten my smile, You're the light of my life-
And my only desire is to make you my wife!

I'm a prisoner of love that only you can set free-
So, Jeanne my darling, please marry me!

    Bruce St. Amour

Seasons

In spring, the bird sings
Of love and warmth, and all the things,
That make the world
A wondrous thing.

Then summer, comes with its
Wondrous glow of trees of green.
And sky's of blue, that only God
Could make so true.

The fall is upon us once again,
It turns the land to red and tan.
And breezes blow the leaves on high,
And covers all country side,
With colors that just can't hide.

Then winter's here with sky's so clear.
You know the holiday's are near,
With sparkling snow and mistletoe,
And fireplace all aglow, and happy people
Everywhere, proclaim the coming of the
New Year,
With peace and love and good cheer,
And we thank the Lord for another year.

Jack Sheehan

The Core

In the deep still serenity
of my soul's reflection
I'm alone with truth
of life's direction

The past seems to vanish
like bubbles in champagne
Won't contemplate the future
it's my "now" that remains

It's now I'm attuned
to my center of being
And sense all there is
without ever seeing

I sense that my core
is no different than others
Can that be the reason
we're sisters and brothers

I sense God is there
in the center...the core
Entwined with our souls
Yes, mine and yours

Glory Strauss

Snooky

In a little wooded section
of the Great Miami shore
Lived a hunter - Andrew Shepherd
with a dozen hounds or more.
My dad, he loved his liquor
and also his maple shade.
We'd often go to visit
and they'd tell their yarns and trade.
One day we paid a visit
and much to my surprise
He had a possum and five babies
with shining beady eyes.
I asked if he would give me one
and he smiled through eyes of blue.
Said "child just pick your favorite
and take it home with you.
I lost my little pet one night,
It almost made me cry.
From a tiny hole that was in his cage
He escaped to the forest nearby.

Freda Spencer Thomas

Pictures

Staring at the pictures
Of my sweet family
I close my eyes and remember
All the happy memories
The time we were together
As we ran through the Park
All the times together
From daylight 'till dark
Pictures to remind me
Of all the times we've had
Some of them good
Some of them bad
Pictures to remind me
Of times past and gone
Pictures to remind me
That I have to carry on
Pictures to remind me
Of times I don't want to forget
The pictures must be working
I haven't forgotten yet...

Charles K. Hickey

My Imagination

Sometimes I imagine a world
of my very own

Just me and my imagination
taking over this world.

I want to reach for the
Stars and go places I've never
gone before.

I want to walk across a rainbow
and jump into my own colorful
world.

I want to sore like the eagles
and be set free.

I love my imagination, because
it's my very own.

Cristy Cawthon

Dearest Dear Dear Daddy

I'm sending you a box
Of new all white hankies
And white matching magic socks

Put a pair on right away
They will keep your toes toasty
Even on a cold January day
When its blustery mostly

Matching magic socks will
Always keep you very neat
Because they match when
You put them on your feet

Love your silly daughter from Texas
Carolyn

P.S.

If you should cough or
You should sneeze
Use one of your new
White hankies fully
Guaranteed to please.

Carolyn Sue Smith Spears

The Candle

As the Candle burns, the scent
of peach fills the air giving
the atmosphere a touch of romance
and magic.

The soft glow of the flame casts a
silhouette of bodies on the walls.
and as it flickers and waves, they
appear to be as one.

The only sounds are the whispers
of two lovers making promises of
Love, heartfelt desires and future
plans.

As the candle burns to its end,
daylight has begun to filter through
the window and these two people
come awake, still wrapped in each
others arms, renewed, refreshed,
Eager for the night to come and
light another candle.

Joya Lynn Bruce

River Of Love

Over the edge
of the mountain of sin;
The river will rise,
from this rage within.

The water is deep
on this side of the river;
Mine eyes cast a shadow,
and my lips begin to quiver:

Moments of terror;
Lost and afraid;
Stricken by heartache;
Will these feelings ever fade?

Oh,...losing a father,
never seen nor heard;
For hearts not yet broken;
flows the "River of Love."

Joyce L. Edwards

Touch Of Love

You lifted me from the sea
of weakness,
planted my feet on solid ground,
refused to let me drown.

You lifted me from the street
of loneliness,
guided me where I could be
so blessed,
forgave me of sins confessed.

You lifted me from the prison
of blindness,
gave me sight beyond my years,
assured me of your undying love,
and dried my tears.

You lifted me from the valley
of darkness,
placed in me the light.
For your touch of love
I thank thee, O God, tonight.

Janie M. Durham

Sun's Child

Adorned with her golden mane
Oh, of the sun
And in lofty heavens
What's left but none.

High upon the skyline
A floating light
That shines into tomorrow
Remaining ever bright.

Child-like faith, my love
I have in you
To remain mine and up above
To be forever true.

In fields of honey and tulips
Barefoot and purely sweet
With the sun upon your beauteous face
I cross the rails to meet.

A flowered dress and whispering breeze
Her voice this soothing call
Which holds me in her celestial soul
And never lets me fall.

Joel Hartmann

Celebrate The Now

We viewed ourselves and family
On homemade films of yesterday
When we were smaller, slimmer, healthier
All sharing love on Christmas day

We guess of future festive days
With the growths and changes of tomorrow
Births and illness, weddings, joy
In a picture show of fun and sorrow

We take in the present Christmas time
Its warmth and joyful, living today
Our cinema of celebration
A loving, peaceful holiday

Jack Merewether

Mom

I cry when I think of Mom.
On that awful day in December
when news of a parent that's gone
on a day I don't want to remember.

The sadness of its come unknowing
with tears and a hole in my heart.
I remember her love overflowing,
to God's house I know she's a part.

There are things I would like to share,
I pick up the phone and then....
I know that no one is there.
And the sadness is here again.

It seems worse in bed as I lay,
thinking of things that are gone.
I wish for one hour to say
things I should have said all along.

For now I will say my good byes,
I hope to see you again one day.
Please watch over me and my family,
I love you now and will always.

Debbie Lima

"I Shall Sail"

I shall sail the sea
  on the rippling waves,
  follow the sunset;
  as each day will pass

I shall sail the world
  if that's what it takes,
  to seek the love
  I once lost.

I shall sail not by temptation;
  but inspiration,
  for the loneliness I have inside;
  once my love took to sea.

Carol Marino

At Empire Lake

I come here to find you, Goddess,
on this day of the sun
Too long lost and wandering,
dwellings impinge on
my spirit.
I come,
lady of the lake,
to be one with your music;
to heal my soul in
the quiet of your deep pools,
tranquil shallows.
I will be one with your
rippling calm, gentle breezes.
I drift, I cease to be -
here and now
diffuses
into
then, now,
and will be.

Julie Post

Souler Coaster

I spill the pain
On to the floor of my life,
The smell of my agony
Stabs my heart like a knife.
So I ponder great questions
And spin my way around the truth,
Should I hold my confessions
I give my heart to you.
Please come to my door
And close the dark past,
We will dance with the devil
Yes, I'll break my molded cast.
I'll never forget the smile
Now, push away the tears,
Lets go run through the moonlight
Lets go run from our fears.
My blood flows in a rage
While our souls are driven,
Won't you take my hand
This is my heart I have given.

David W. Bunch

Politicking

It's the oldest game in town,
one day you're up,
the next day you're down,
but it's in your blood,
even though it can cover
you with mud,
you can't quite contain,
but there's a measure at which you
must remain,
for when the chips are low,
and you take a blow,
you get on your feet,
and beat back a defeat,
you win triumphantly,
support for you is abundantly,
and there you are on the Hill,
which for you is a big thrill,
for although you take a licking,
there's nothing quite like politicking.

Celine Rose Mariotti

There's Only One .....

There's only
One moment.
There's only one day.
There's only one place,

Where we can
Run away.
There's only
One lifetime,
Where I am to
Live. There's
Only one love

Who I think of
There's only one day
Where I can stay.
There's

Only One Song
I can sing
And I am singing
It for you,
Cause you mean everything ....

Angelina Meadows

Michigan Winter

This year it froze hard
  one night after a rain,
The snow falling
  froze into a thick glaze
  on all the branches.

We woke up to a white land -
  all covered with white
  on every outside thing.
Cars had a hard covering so thick
  under inches of snow
That doors had to be cracked open.
Everything outdoors had to be
  broken into because of the hard ice
Under the snow.

Wires fell.
Electricity went out.
Some left their homes and
  stayed overnight in motels.

But the beauty was incomparable!
A gift.

Jean Tillinghast

Determinism

My life is all written
One second before.
It's etched into glass
and then
Thrown on the floor.

The future will sparkle
If it catches the light.
The past lies
in splinters of
What's wrong or right.

There's one bit of glass
I can hold in my hand.
It was given
to me,
But, I don't understand.

If I hold it too tight
Will it cut in my flesh?
If it's dropped
will it break,
Or just fall into place?

Gladys Ashenfelter

The Edge of the Night

When the sun hangs low
Orange, yellow and bright
Flaming through the night tide
Like a candle light
Dancing on a draft

In the corner of a room
Lacing shadows across the night
Across this prairie
Screaming with distance
From the sound of the crickets chorus
The music of the night

Take my hand, well walk the night
Well leave this sight over the edge
The edge of the night where all is light.

And though our shadows have passed on
The music of the night plays on to the edge
Of the night, where curtains have bloomed
Open wings of a new Dawn.

Greg D. Prinzing

Mind

Conscious, unconscious processor
Originating in the brain,
Intellectual power
To direct or to refrain.

What you think is what you are
And what you will become.
It is the path that you will choose,
The path that you will run.

Think not for self alone.
With others you must deal,
Come to see their point of view
And know the way they feel.

Make for your mind the law of right,
Take in knowledge that you may know
That your perception is not dulled
And in a righteous way you go.

There is a law that is unchanging.
To get the very best of living,
Train your heart and mind together
In the happiness of giving.

Dale Stanley

Love Scene

We walk the path
Our hands together
Our souls aglow
Ignoring weather

We lay together
In love entwined
Two bodies merged
In heart and mind

Our passions spent
But for a time
We joy in touch
The feel sublime

The shadows move
Across the room
The hush of sleep
Unweaves the loom

Our web of fate
Has now been spun
We pledge our love
The scene is done

Harley R. Ferguson

The Firefly Waltz

With shadows from the trees as
our stage

Beneath a crescent moon's glowing
light

A rhythmic waltz glows against a
darkening night ·

Led by a maestro unseen, we
dance to his silent tune

We follow melodic notes ears will
never hear

As this melody plays on for eyes to see,
the fireflies waltz with me

Esther S. Shirley

A Vision

When they pulled the car up
out of that lake
It was more than the people
or lawmen could take.

For there in the back seat
Still strapped in their chair
Were two little boys
Holding hands with great care.

The whole world cried
when they heard this you see
And I cried too
Till a vision I did see.

An angel in white
Smiling down from above
Saying hold hands tight now
Let me take you to love.

Then the greatest of visions
was shown unto me
Two little children in heaven
Smiling down tenderly.

Donna Wolfe

Sleepless Sorrow

Through my dreams it chases me
Over a stony sea
Ruthlessly it tackles me
Then leaves me there to bleed
A sleepless sorrow sinking in,
    deeper every day
An agony that never ends, and
    never go's away
My heart cries out
The pain runs much too deep
A secret that possesses me, and
    is much too hard to keep
I try to explain the torment
It's like a leach upon my soul
Once upon a time there was a
    childhood that leach unfairly stole
My life's been led by tears and pain
So many questions unanswered
So many tears remain
I search for a sign
To let me know
My questions will be answered...
I'll have revenge upon ny foe.

Rebecca Ann Anderson

La Guardia At Night

Gray leaden blanket
Over flickering red lights,
Cold.
Child cries softly
At an officer's side,
Frightened.
Footsteps echo down
concrete canyons,
Hollow.
Hawker of heaven stands
With homemade sign,
Hoping.
Life streams unsteadily
Cold, frightened, hollow,
Hoping, hoping, hoping.
La Guardia at night!

George T. Tade

Wrongfully Reduced

Fearful eyes
Paralleling blank skies
Tearful cries,...
Elongated she lies
Emaciated in size...
Sounds off to self,
A rhetorical repertoire
Of never ending, "whys"...
Consumed by cancer
In quest of answer

Donna Marie Vessini

"Ecstasy"

I was consumed by your sacred devotion
Only to behold blemished promises and
deranged trinkets of evasion
Tear me from this spiralling exile of
diminishing attachments
Pour my liquid essence onto this shallow
terrain, for I
feel no feelings
sense no senses
live no lives.

Forrest D. Jordan Jr.

The Wait

Life is a blurred vision
passing us by
    day
       by
          day
displaying a created motion
bending
    twisting
spiraling across the sky
its source forever unknown

The ultimate realization
is what will be waited for
but never will it arrive
So the waiting goes on...
    an eternity...

Jill Clark

Poise

Just when some
Pegasus thought of mine
Soars to the Heights
To dwell there
With the Gods
And I am filled
With the yeast
Of self-satisfaction,
Then do I hear
From the thickets
Of my heart
A bird sing sweetly.
"Pewee."

Helen M. Rambow

Contemplations Of Life

A million light reflections
piercing from within
like shards of broken crystal
scattered in the wind.

They cast a mirror image
of the soul down deep inside
to reveal unspoken mysteries
of the fearful place we hide.

Lo, arising through the silvery mist
a rainbow's glimmer melds
the spectrum of the universe
onto the captives held.

Their fortress built of shattered dreams
bound tightly with past sins
silently waiting to break free
like the crystal in the wind.

Ann Cole

"Peace"

People kill one another because
  of ones skin color,
Each day millions steal just
  to have another meal
And each night children cry as they
  watch there parents die.
Can't we help those in need yes
  but instead we watch them bleed,
Each night I lie down and close my eyes
  and ask one question WHY!

Brandy Trusler

Weathered Pages

The story of a commoner,
Plain as it may be,
Is the heart, the roots, the origin
Of persons much like me.

Its existence is but history,
A sequence of events,
That passed from father to son
As the years came and went.

Thank God for the quiet man
Who took the occasion to write
About his ordinary days
By the dim candlelight.

His hardships and joys,
Expressed on weathered pages,
Reveal a host of occurrences
Passed down through the ages.

Through the leaves of a journal,
We walk his steps a mile;
Feel his heartbeat, touch his hand,
Spend time with him awhile.

Janet Lux

I Am No Poet

Oh come all yo
poetry lovers
and think positive

If you think you are beaten.
  You are.
If you think you dare not.
  You don't
success begins with your
  own will...
It's all in your state
  of mind.
Life's battles are not
  ..always won
By those who are stronger.
  or faster.
sooner or later the person
  who wins
is the person who thinks
  he can.

Casmer Cihone

Let the Wolf Live

There is a wolf inside of me
  powerful and strong,
There is a wolf inside of me
  shy and very quiet.

The wolf inside of me
  is afraid of nothing,
  and will stand by me at will.
But the wolf will not come to me
  when I'm scared of fright.

For the wolf himself is scared
  of something I know not,
And that is why I'm scared
  to open up to the world,
For I am scared that he
  will not return to me in time
To save our lives.

Brandon Wahlen

My Boyhood Niche

Youth have their own genetic choir.
Pre-hominid had trees to climb.
I climbed for Kites or views afar.
The best of worlds that far off time.

My boyhood niche to me seemed large,
Yet, mile from home, I saw no one.
Each small arroyo seemed a gorge.
I magnified my happy home.

From vantage points I saw blue hills.
They seemed a few miles further west.
I learned they were 100 miles.
Nevada range. I saw the crest.

Near nine decades have rolled along
Since I enjoyed what I call best,
Panoramic view across the plain,
Longing to scale Nevada's crest.

We have spent trillions to destroy
All bio life, should we decide.
Why not a mite to send a boy
To mountain lake with horse to ride?

John W. Adams

My Homies

The final joint is one
Puff after another.
Then it leads me into a gang.
This gang leads me to see the death
of my homies it leads me
in the cemetery to say
goodbye to all my dead homies
who has left me for good.
I break down in tears for
the love of my Homies
as I walk through my
barrio like a Valley of
Memories leads me to
confusion to think about
all the Homies that are gone.
I shall never rest in peace
till I kill the one that
killed the homies of my barrio.

Esmeralda Tristan

Our Lady Queen of the Angels

Our Lady
Queen of the angels.

Our Lady
Queen of Heaven and Earth.

Our Lady
Queen of the Saints.

Our Lady
Queen of Peace

Our Lady
Queen of the Holy Rosary.

Our Lady
Queen of all
miracles large and small.

Joe Miller

Medals

Medals of Kings
   Queens and such
Will likely possess
   your soul.

As images in
   great escape,
will find a
   place so cold.

One will seek
   of fortune
One will seek
   for fame.

One will worship.
   way's of the world
one will master
   the game.

Claudia Scarbrough

Untitled

Morning —
   quiet stillness
   like no other
   time of day.
Just before the dawn
   when the world
   is still asleep
   and peace seems
   abundant.
Wouldn't it be sweet
   to have such peace
   and harmony
   throughout
   the rest
   of the day?

Debra Higgason

Pathway Of Dreams

The pathway corks into a spiral,
Ranging far and deep within
Lean inside and slide along
One begins to swerve and spin
Entering a land of dreams,
Too good to be true it seems
Swirl across the winded path
Dreams come true of the past
Close the eyes and slide along
One may hear a sacred song
Dream and dream of a cause
Round and round, there'll be no pause

Josh Adam

Painted Pictures

We are merely painted pictures
on life's canvas
Made by the light
that reflects from God's being
His aura is all around us
A rainbow of emotions
We are scattered as the light changes to
darkness,
as night is transposed by day
We are colors on God's canvas
No black
No white
But merely shades of gray

Hermenegildo Santiago Jr.

The Raven's Rape

The blackened raven
Ravagely circles the grave
Newly birthed corpses
Fresh prey obstructed from feast
Soured by their innocence.

The grieving raven
Tenderly weeps tears of pain
On tombs of sorrow
The loss of humanity
Kills the appetite of lust.

The hardened raven
Gorges fiercely on the feast.
Compassionate touch
Destroyed by indifference
The benign rape of passion.

Angela M. Olsen

Seasons

Spring
Reaching for the blue
Yellow-green in misty rain
Tender blades of grass.

Summer
Magical seahorse
Mystery of the ocean
Rocks in tidal flow.

Fall
Gold finch spiralling
Milkweed fluff dusting the wind
Summer passing by.

Winter
Sculptured beauty
Against star-lit indigo
Elm arms etch designs.

Carolyn D. Kulp

Wind

Can you hear the eerie whistle?
Reckless, furious, destroyer,
Branches fighting frantically, battle,
Raised havoc, desolate, barren,
Unremorseful as it ruins,
Mocking as it passes.

Can you hear the soft whistle?
Delicate, swift, peaceful,
Branches swaying gently, tapping,
Joyful giving, sweet shiver,
Calmness as it lays to rest
Harmony as it passes.

Dina DuBois

Three Pecans

There they are
Three pecans
Lying in my hand
They have been there for sometime now
I often wonder, should I eat them
And become a part of them
Or should I just lose them
Like I found them.
After all they're only nuts.

Calvin Leroy Bonner

Piano

Plinkedy plank PLANK
release my emotions
outlet my pain
soothe my wounded me
tappedy tap on the ivories
Ivory is illegal
must stow it
PUSH down falling feelings
Ride on the brain waves of a freak
maybe you'll find something deep
who knows???
follow the keys keep on beat
metronome
take me home

Debra Heitmann

Remember

Remember all that we shared
Remember how much I cared
Remember that I love you
Remember that you loved me too
But you left for someone new
I just don't know what to do
Should I cry or should I die
Remember when you're with a guy
Remember that you're just fine
Remember that you were mine
Remember me on sleepless nights
Remember to call and write
Remember that you hold the key
I pray to God you remember me

Craig Piagari

'Nam Dreams '66

For those of us who cherish life,
Remember those who pay the price.

They hear a cry and try to give,
Of what they have in hopes to live.

But, he who hesitates is lost,
And they alone understand the cost.

Yet, on they strive and dare not sleep,
But only dream of lasting peace.

Edward J. Mescall

Mom

Mom what do these letters
   represent?
Moments of mercy
A wonderful woman - God has
   sent!
Mom was there to erase my
   fear and doubt
She was always there for me
Mom; I look at you and see a
   woman so stout
It's sad your time was cut short
I felt so much pain and so hurt
Mom, I won't grieve for now -
You were a victorious sport
But, I do grieve - you were the
   greatest person I ever knew
Mom - I Love You!

Dennis Anders

Your Stockings You Hang

The letters you wrote two weeks ago
Requesting this and that
On Christmas Eve Santa will come
Will he leave you a bike or a bat?

Just before you go off to bed
You make sure your stockings are hung
He always fills them overflowing
Especially if you are young.

The next morning when you awaken
You'll dress and go to see
What lies for you by the fire place
Will make you jump with glee!

Albert Canales

Bells Of The New Year

Ring out, Oh bell of liberty
Ring louder than before
Ring out to every man on earth
Your message, O'er and O'er.

Ring out the false, ring in the true
Wherever men are found,
That those in darkness and in doubt
May see the light and higher ground.

Ring out your bells, ye child of God,
With all the force you can,
For now's the time when God and man
Must labor, Hand-in-hand.

Ring out, Oh Bell of Liberty
Your echoes from the past,
That free from tyrants we may be
As long as earth shall last.

Allie G. Thomas

Only

Only, I can feel the sun's heat
   run through my blood to my heart.

Only, I can see a fire's glow
   standing bright and tall.

Only, I can see and feel the love
   in my heart for you.

Only, I can see a rose and
   feel its fragrance and silk
   against my skin.

   And only I shall be enchanted
   and in love with thee.

Bonnie Cawley

Never Lost

If you love,
Set it free.
Was once told me.
Anyone whose loved
Knows how hard
Not to guard.
I've set it free
Never to return to me.
Was it for the best?
I believe it to be
For now I know
It was never gone from
me.

Donna L. Lansberry

The Light

   I look outside and
see the light,
   The flower pedals and
sun so bright.
   I see the moon and
all the stars,
   Oh big dipper there
you are.
   I see the rain and
rainbow too.
   Oh God, Oh God where
are you?
   Through the clouds and
into the night,
   I find you God in the
light.

Jasmin Vitale

A Soul Rescue

The four winds- hungry,
seek the truth.
Ever persistent,
the winds do not die;
they move inward
to search the void.

A lone rider tossed,
a rocky stream leaped.
One soul lost,
the truth, the winds to keep.
A child starves amid splendor,
and has no father.
An angel looks down on man
to see his past.
A tear unfelt by flesh,
can it sting no less?

A breeze finds a child hungry,
and the winds, empty,
whisper to the child's heart.

David J. McCarthy

Innocence

Whispering winds and babbling brooks
Send songs near and far
Carrying them to those who listen
To the wishes of a star

Heeding not the big worlds rules
Laughing as they cheat
Ignoring those who care not
For those whom they meet

Whispering winds and babbling brooks
Sing to me each day
Taking me to places they have seen
That are so far away

Deanne Burgess

Like

Like a watch that has no hands
or a calendar with no dates
Like a song with no notes
or an expression without a face

Like a map with no direction
or a star with no light
Like a hunter with no prey
Like death that never had life.

Christopher Luby

The River Wide

Oh wonderful winding river wide,
Settled between the mountains high,
Flowing free like the birds in the sky.
Shimmers of light coat you with beauty,
Welcoming the weary as they pass by,
To rest from their tired journey,
And drink of your healing force.

Your gift gives them strength,
An emotional breath,
To continue on their journey's length.
Leaving you to help,
The next poor traveling man,
Oh wonderful winding river wide.

Barry J. Weaver

To Believing

She believes him with her eyes,
She believes him with her heart,
She believes him with her body and
soul, and never wants to part.
He believes nothing,
He believes in only himself,
He believes he comes first
I don't care about any one else.
She wants him, but he don't want her.
She needs him, but he don't need her.
There's a thin line between what
she believes, and what he believes,
Between these two,
Believing is just a word.
To Believing

Jennie Boyd

Ode To Mother Nature

Mother nature has many talents
She is a work of art
To help out Father Time
She really does her part
She brings the snow in winter
To cover up the ground
Then just as quickly, wipes it clean
Not a trace to be found
She colors the flowers in springtime
A bouquet for us to behold
Then makes them turn brown in Autumn
From the rain, the wind and the cold
In summer her work is harder
She brings storms, hail and heat
But she also brings things of enjoyment
To make the cycle complete
A painter, destroyer, builder and bore
Exciting, creative, all these and more
A busy lady who is Heaven sent
Constantly changing our environment

Betty Zimmerman

Day Moon

Was it strange
Or was it different
This moon now seen
In the sky of day

Two souls bond
As they debate
This curious occurrence
On such a sunny day

Diane Ferguson

Homeless

Strikes the clock-
Shifts the sun-
and mountainous metro
sends shadows over a
cardboard tribe.
Gathered shanties huddle
for purpose of mismatched
misery;
like quilted patchwork
sewn on soil with
newsprint thread.
Ever migrating
employees of the elements
Once victors, now victims.
Cities silent sons,
the new American-
    Indian.

Calvin R. Pollard II

November Fifteen

Intense calm, after
    shrieking winds.
Terrors of the night
    lie down softly
    and flow away.

Flowers have faded,
    leaves shriveled,
Revealing lucidity of sky
    and empty field.

There is no time.
There are no seasons.
Only a white bird floating
    on blue air.

Joanne Gellerman

Spanish House

Somewhere there is a
Shuttered
Spanish house waiting-
Its dark rooms dusty-
Its fireplaces yawning;
Sleepily waiting
Just for me.

I shall live there
Sometime-
Somewhere-
I shall dream there
Upstairs in the
Balconied bedroom;

I shall grow old there
Happily,
Snugly,
And never leave there
Alive.

Dorothy H. Welker

On Wings of Silver

On wings of silver,
The beautiful bird flew.
Over beaches made of sand,
And up into the Holy Land.

It flew in silence,
    It flew in grace.
My one true wish...
    To take its place.

Brandi Moon

Where Has The Romance Gone?

It's been so long
    since I've had
    a compliment from you.

Where has the romance gone?
    Am I wrong in wanting to
    hear you
    say "I love you."

Where has the romance gone?
Can we get it back?
Can we attack the lethargy
    that has corroded
    our marriage?

Where has the romance gone?

I could write a song—
    but I don't know
    what went
    wrong.

Ginny O'Neil

Alone

Darkness...flashes...deadly...quiet
Sit as one on your bed beside it.
Shiver....Whisper....glance around
Never sure of what you've found.
Darkness peering frightened sigh
Bury your head with a pillow....cry.
Shiver...wonder...scary dreams
Life is Never what it seems.
Darkness opens... darker sounds
Trapped inside the prison grounds.
Shiver....cover...rest...sleep
Close your eyes....begin to weep.
Of all the tortures, make it known,
The worst of all is to Be alone.

Jessica Hope Germann

It Doesn't Ring Anymore

The phone
Sits alone
Lost its voice
But not by choice.
It's old
And cold
And longs so much
To reach and touch.

Ninety years old
She's cold
And alone
Watching phone
Someone will call
But one and all
To heaven they've gone
And left her only a song
And modern day
Advanced in every way
Cannot connect from here to there
Yet she sits and waits for someone to care.

Alice G. Dow

Unwanted

Young and old people everywhere,
sitting here and there,
reaching out for your hand.

Children staring at you,
with their longing eyes,
to belong.

Reaching out with their hands,
crying out, help me, help me.
No one sees me, no one cares.
Reach out, reach out
As I sit here and there.
No one's hand to hold me tight.
Look at me, look at me,
people everywhere.
You have no shame
As I sit here and there;
No one to hold me tight.

Jane Roberts

Do I Have To Die?

When I've been laid
Six feet under
Then will you care?
Then will you cry?
Then will you remember
The days we spent together?
Do I have to die
Before you'll take my hand?
Do I have to die?
Do I have to cry?
When worms eat my flesh
Will memories eat your brain?
Do I have to die
Before you can love me?

David E. Miller

Cycles

The tree looks elderly in late October.
Slender leaves like dying thoughts.
Bare limbs - wrinkles, thin and
weak, against the autumn sky.

But the aging does not last.
The tree is reborn with another Spring
Young dancing leaves and branches
Supple and laughing in the breeze.
Ah, could it be that such a cycle
holds for another of Nature's
creatures - the human?
That there is an inner spirit
that survives the dissolution
of the body and returns to life?

Dorothy Harbin

Skating

Sharp, steel blades
slicing the slippery ice,
spinning, swirling
scratching the smooth surface,
sliding across a sheet of glass.
Silvery ice shining,
slush circling,
searing,
stinging the skin,
glistening in the sunshine.

Ann Marie Hoppel

Alone

In the bayou,
Slowly guiding my pirogue.
I am alone.

The overhead cry of a hawk,
startles my thoughts.
I am alone.

Honeybees in an ageless cypress,
humming their own tune.
I am alone.

A breeze stirs the spanish moss,
it makes no sound.
I am alone.

A gator wakes from his nap
to watch me pass...

In the bayou,
Slowly guiding my pirogue.
I am alone.

Anita Horn

Sleep And You

The cares of each and every day,
Slowly seem to slip away,
As lightly into bed I slide,
My favorite place, with you 'longside.

I feel your love reach out to me,
And wrap me in its luxury,
And then I feel the warmth of you,
Your gentle breathing, as you do.

Arms enfold and hold me fast,
The long day's gone; it's here at last—
The peaceful sleep of lovers past.

Barbara Smith Elward

Untitled

The gentleness of a falling
  snowflake
The beauty of the sun as we
  wake
The softness of a flowers
  pedal
The hero that proudly wears
  his medal
A child's laughter on a day
  in spring
A returning bird who softly
  sings
An evening of watching the
  brightest stars
Promises to bring a brighter
  day by far.

Edith Muro

A Place

The sky so blue, the grass so green.
The birds soar high, the cats prowl low.
But where, where shall I go?
Someday I'll know, a place of peace,
A place of no harm, a dream or
A nightmare, maybe not in this life, but
someday I'll know where I belong.
Heaven or Hell.

Carolyn McCort

Song Of The Bride

Jesus, fill my heart so poor,
So barren, dull and cold,
With ardent bridal love for you,
Fiery, sweet and bold.

Inflame my heart with passion fierce,
To love against all odds,
Every moment of each day
My heart entranced with God.

What sweet romance the Father wrote
When You, His only Son,
Came down to earth and by Your Cross
Your Bride forever won.

My eyes upturned into Your Face
Enraptured by Your gaze,
Look longingly towards the end
Of life; O happy days!

When I shall "See Thee as Thou Art,"
My Bridegroom, God and King,
And You will take me to Your side,
Your Queen, with You, to reign.

Fiona Rodriguez

Oh Merciful Tree

I see you standing there,
So beautiful, yet so lonely.

I want to climb on your branches,
And feel your strong support.

To master all your mazes,
And make my way to the top.

To look down on the Earth,
And see everyone below,
Still struggling to conquer,
All the secrets that you hold.

Beth Kristin Strausbaugh

A Silver Lining

As seasons change,
So do the lives,

Of sons and daughters,
Of husbands and wives.

Lives once perfectly balanced,
Can change more than slightly,

As new challenges arise daily,
And new fears appear nightly.

Yesterday is no longer
within our control,

But today can be filled,
with new hope for us all.

As you wait for tomorrow,
Keep an open heart and mind,

So you don't miss the cloud, with
A silver lining that shines from behind.

Debra McCluskey

Untitled

Why is life
So hard.
When you have a friend,
Who's in need
Of love,
but won't accept.
You try to help,
but it never fades,
away.
if love is so cheap,
why don't people
accept?
In life there's two choices,
to live
or
to die.
hopefully they will
choose to live...
forever!

Amber Witt

Untitled

So many tears fall away —
So many days go by;
So many walls strengthen and hold
Over time.

So many storms swirl and fade,
So many clouds pass by;
So many sun rays shine —
For a fleeting time.

So many minutes make their mark
As the hours fall;
So many days well and fade,
So many years pass on.

And through the shadows —
The twisted strands of fate —
I struggle; so alone.
As the tears fall.

As the sun shines for so short a time —
As the minutes bleed the hour away;
As the days gather through the years —
I stand lonely.

Christina J. Lewis

To My Dying Love

This night has left me
Sodden with sorrow!
Depleted!
My love given
Unendless thru time.
Each hour burning!
With minutes left
To live, I give thee
Hope. In this lifetime
Precious moments remain.
Come to me! Grasp
My hand! Share my sorrow.
There is time
To pray together.

John F. Naz

Who Am I To Her

I'm not just someone
  Some are cold
  Some are gold
  Mine is crystal
  Delicate and brittle
  Beautiful and shimmering
  It must be handled with care
  For it may be shattered
  When asked who

I'm not just someone
Christopher P. Krotche

Friends Are Friends Forever

Friends are friends forever,
Some go thru so much.
Some come single, one by one,
And some come in a bunch.

Some may grow up spoiled,
And not know how to act.
Some are just real faithful,
They will watch your back.

There are many people
Who are really great.
Some are real winners,
And some are just 1st rate.

Some are only followers,
Some friends, they shall lead.
You are the type who will help out,
The type who does good deeds.

There are times we will not write
Or even lift the phone.
But still I know that in my heart,
Your friendship has a home.
Brian K. Higginbotham

The Way We Care

Some of us care, but not enough
Some of us love, much too much
Some of us care, only to the cusp
Some of us love, beyond life, as such

Some of us never seem to open up
Some of us go all the way
Some of us never fill our cup
Some of us, the love will never stray

Some of us share love, but only part
Some of us give it all we got
Some of us hold feelings, from the start
Some of us love no matter what

This poem is difficult to finish
Because it really has no end
True love can never ever diminish
That love need not ever mend.
James M. Pinelli

Shadows

Dual figures in unison walk
One is silent while the other one talks.
Constant companions in light of the sun
Nowhere to be seen when day is done.
One alone to the naked eye
'Til dawning sun cast shadows in the sky.
Gina Dette

Love Sonnet

Once in a lifetime
someone comes along,
who makes your heart rhyme
like words in a song.

When you do find her
treat her fair and kind,
be a gallant sir
better you'll not find.

It's real uplift
when you fall in love,
a wonderful gift
from the lord above.

  Let your true love show,
  never let her go.
Gregory E. Hensley

Untitled

I open my eyes and I see,
  someone watches over me.
When things go wrong and there's no hope,
I cross my fingers and try to cope.
  Someone watches over me.

When I see no reason to go on,
And I wish I wasn't born.
  Someone watches over me.

When life sends me an unexpected
surprise, I don't give up....I rise.
  Now I know that's the key,
  I won't give up now I see.
  Someone watches over me.
Darlene Rhodes

A Sign Of Age

I'm often chided,
  sometimes derided,
for the romantic novels I shun;

"They're sordid and hot,
  and likely as not,
you'd learn to really have fun!"

But it seems to me,
  though the lesson is free,
I'm wasting my time to peruse it.

For when I climb into bed,
  touching pillow to head,
I'm fast asleep before I could use it!
John Turnbull

"Sound Could Be"

Sound could be crying
Sound could be someone dying
Sound could be a moonbeam
Sound could be a shattered dream
Sound could be quiet
Sound could be loud
Sound could be someone in a death shroud
Sound could be a midnight dark
Sound could be a singing lark
Sound could be a heavy metal dance.
But my favorite kind of sound is silence.
Allen Wolf

Raindrops

The gentle fall of heaven's tears
  sparked by God's emotion,
caresses a fevered earth below
  with thunder-clad devotion

Absorbent of a loving touch
  relieving burning thirst,
in flowering appreciation
  fragrant buds do burst

Crusts of drought are softened
  far-reaching fields retilled,
a blessing bestowed on Mother Earth
  land's prayer to God fulfilled...
Evelyn M. Cole

Untitled

People see me as nice
Speaking words never cold as ice
They say I have a heart of gold
That within me will never grow old

In other people's minds
I always seem kind
Without a doubt
Inside and out

Polite to everyone I know
Never make them feel low
Giving good wishes and luck
Never saying they suck

Feeling sorry for the ill
Hoping that they will
Get better soon
And singing for them a lovely tune

People see me as nice
Speaking words never cold as ice
They say I have a heart of gold
That within me will never grow old
Jeanette Adams

Now You Must Go

Spread your wings, great bird
Spread your wings and fly
Keep your dreams close to heart
And your goals soaring high.

Spread your wings, great bird
Take that final step
Soar high, fly free with pride
Over the ground once carefully crept.

Fly great bird,
I will not bind you
For when I look within my heart
I know I'll always find you.
Jenn Gallo

Obstacles To Overcome

A cripple walked with me,
to a high mountain top.
I saw all things,
just as the blind man said I would.
I listened to the world below,
as per the deaf girl's instructions.
A mute called up to me from below,
"How do you perceive the world?"
"Handicapped" I responded "but hopeful"
David Hamilton

Dusk

The rolling hills at eventide
Stand dark against the sky.
Gone are their brown and emerald gowns,
Their crystal streams laid by.

While far below the earth's dark rim,
The sun still flings its light
In flaming red and burnished gold
Reflected 'gainst the night.

Now mists begin to float between
The valleys dark and deep
And all grows could and earthy still
On rolling hills asleep.

Edith P. Crabbe

Untitled

I see her
    Standing,
Hands worn
    With work.
Surrounded
    By noise and people.

I wonder if she felt
    Isolated, alone, even then;
Did she look within or without
    To find contentment.

Or is it just my perception:
    Things now known,
Placed on a memory,
    Colorizing the past.

Betty L. Deemer

Snow

In the dead of winter
stillness prevails,
snow falling softly, silently.
White, pure
crystals sparkling,
Moon illuminating little stars
on the snow's surface,
Twinkling, gleaming,
winking their brightness.
Happy tears from the heavens
melting gently
on upturned faces,
caressing hardened souls
with snowflakes featherlike.

G. Harvey-Lucero

Untitled

Dark leathery skin
    Stretched tight
    over the bone of skull
Withered lips pulled back
    In a grimace/smile
    to reveal
    bleached white gravestone
    nubs of teeth
Eyeballs dried into
    leftover grape skins
    In their sockets
Body splayed in the deserted street
The photographer stoops down
    to get a better angle

Alan Choi

Sally Forth Illusions

Lighted fragrant joss sticks
Stuck in a dark bark niche

Destiny can be had ad-nauseam
Forbearance with all its malum

Pondering with sleight Old Nick
Hoping somehow for no b**ch

Job's comforter will interpelled
A taskmaster in its hell

To see Miracles in the light
Life upside down in day of night

Replace the image of body
Mind now not so haughty

Shifted shadow Oh so flighty
Known to trek of stars delightly

Some distant time prior Kantian
Abort aloft yore clay Pre-Cambrian

United with strength in all its thoughts
Too late remembered set fob naught

Soul all malcontent breakthrough anew
Judgment cloud portends a Thanatos view

John F. Schwei

Our Love

Our love is like a crisp Fall Day

clearly defined in every way.

We've known each other for
    such a short time,

Yet we fit together like
    rhythm and rhyme.

We were both in need of
    someone who'd share.

Someone who'd love and
    help and care.

Someone we could depend on
    each day.

Someone to talk to, chase the
    cares away.

Someone with whom to laugh and to cry.
Someone on whom we could always rely.

To give support, to lend an ear.
To love and chase away the fear.

Someone to share the good and the bad.
Someone to laugh with when we felt sad.

Darlene T. Dunn

"Jeffie"

Hardly had a chance for living.
Taken long before your time.
Child of my blessed child
There's no reason, and no rhyme.
You were loved from the beginning.
Little "king" around the house.
Curly locks, and vim and vigor.
Running back and forth, and in and out.
Memories are always with us.
They will have to do for now.
Someday in some bright tomorrow.
We will sort it out somehow.

Deloris Reimers

Forsaken

Spring brought romance amidst tulips.
Summer blossomed as a lovely lark.
Fall left reflections of happiness.
Winter set thoughts that are dark.

Lights flash, eyes see rainbows,
remembering beauty of life gone by.
Of summer greens and winter snows,
with romance clear as a cloudless sky.

Face a past gone with future blank,
as summer is over and leaves fall.
Winter darkened while hopes sank.
Thoughts turned to spring, of recall.

Mound of dirt exerts energy to past,
waiting for notice to eclipse the end.
Memories engraved to view the last.
Energy lingers for lover and friend.

Tears welled up like a raging storm
twisting the rose as petals form.
Sadness stirred the darkest cloud.
The winter wind forced the cries aloud.

Annie L. McClure

Untitled

rising over the peaks
sun tan hair
shining
as she walked
    hair whipped her back
each strike
gained a gold aura

under the shade
grape vines overhead
can't reach
and can't remember what the fox
    did in the children's fable

red leaves all around her toes
and brown ones a couple feet away
breeze dances with her hair
and the segregated leaves
become one non-discriminant swirl

Cariann Colman

Haiku On Solitude

Solitude is peace,
sweet silence-inspired thinking,
joy to be alone.

Not forlorn, but glad,
no one else—just you and God,
meditation time.

Leisure hour for prayer,
solitude is warm and deep;
draws you nearer heaven.

Lie quiet at night,
hear the still sounds of darkness;
feel God's tranquil touch.

Solitude makes real
study of God's word in depth,
restoring the soul.

Elma Clark Norwood

October

October is a dancer
swirling her skirts
of brown and red and orange.
She can give you Beauty, Love,
excitement, and Hurt.

October is a butterfly
of brilliantly colored hue.
She will nod for all
To come and play with her.
But wants no one but you.

Here today — off tomorrow!
Enjoy her lifting laugh;
Her riot of color;
The fun in the sun.
But beware — you'll only have chaff!

Elizabeth D. Mossey

My Love

Recycle my love,
Take what I give to you
And return it to me.
I'll do the same,
And we'll both be free.

We shall stand on common ground,
I'm with you, you with me.
Build an alliance, safe and sound.

On all things, we'll not agree.
Like a limb that branches
To be free,
It cannot breathe,
Without the tree.

James N. Nicholson

Lonely

Old Woman
Tattered rags
Huddled

Atop
Cold city street
Clutching life
In paper bag
Begging warmth
From iron vent

To kind her feet
Munching
Molded bread
Of days spent

Wanting
Hoping

Needing

Friend

Elsie M. Hall

"Sadness"

Sometimes I feel I have no face
That it's just an empty space
no one cares, no one stares
As
    tears
        stream
            down,
down like a babbling brook
in spring
What will this sadness bring?

Cassie Lee Page

Alone

The little boy feared alone
tears fall, turn to ice.
Haunted by the martians faces blank
locked in his mind.

They resented his creative differences,
thought him only a meaningless child
Left him alone to his quiet day dreaming,
escaping the fright.

He drew his own wild conclusions,
surely they were all aliens but him.
Reaching over for the king's ray gun,
he escaped.

Annie Tucker

"Eyes"

Life is full of obstacles,
Temptation, lust and greed,
Everyone out to beat the rest
A byway I just don't need.

But, now and then, it comes to pass - -
The search comes to an end,
When someone special looks your way
And you know to call him "Friend".

At a glance, he can but understand - -
It's something that's not heard,
For eyes can talk and tell it all,
Without speaking a single word.

I believe I've found a happiness,
Though I thought I never would,
With someone who takes the time to care,
And his eyes tell me that it's good.

My days are a whole lot easier now,
No longer searching for the rainbow's end,
Cause I've found my little pot of gold,
In the eyes of my special friend.

Cheryl J. Vercillo

My Father

You were my earthly father-
Tender and warm and loving.
And then one day you left me.
Suddenly, there was nothing.

My hand reached out to hold yours
But you had gone away.
Your choices took you from me
And I could only stay.

I built my life without you
But the emptiness was there.
I had no "Dad" to hold me,
There was no man to care.

In the midst of all the sorrow
There was one who felt my pain,
One who reached down to me
And brought sunshine through my rain.

I have a Heavenly father
And He will always be there!
He filled the emptiness in my heart
With His tender, loving care.

Debra K. Main

"Love"

Love is a touch,
    Tender with care,
A meaningful look,
    Secrets to share...

Love is a mood,
    Laughter and tears,
Shared by two hearts
    Which grow close
Through the years...

Love is faith,
    That dreams will come true,
Love is wonderful,
    Love is you...

Faye Bromley

Me

There is always more to me
than you can ever see
no matter how long you look
I'm bigger than your book.

I am more than meets the eye
more than can be described.
As you start to zero in,
I'm something else again.

No universe can hold me
I invent more all the time.
A lunatic once told me,
best playgrounds in the mind.

Key to understanding me
I'm simple as can be
surprise as I am molded
delight at what I see.

As this process never ends
it's clear for all to see
I'm always inventing me
and what I want to be.

David Sweezea

The Tree

Oh can't you see,
That big old tree.

That gives us lumber,
for places we slumber.

It gives us shade,
for places we've laid.

It replenishes our air,
so better we fare.

It gives us wood,
warming places we've stood.

So why shouldn't we,
each plant one tree.

So our future will be,
much better you see.

Don McCrea

Life Is Death

Friends are like sunshine,
  that can easily fade away.
Sunshine is like peace,
  which brings a brighter day.
Peace is a flower,
  that opens wide.
A flower is like a child,
  who has never lied.
A child is star,
  which shines so brightly.
A star is like the breeze,
  which blows slightly.
The breeze is like a laugh,
  which makes the heart feel gay.
A laugh is a gift,
  that can never go away.
A gift is life,
  which slowly fades away.
Life is Death,
  the promise of a new day.

Angelika Klien

Trapped

The world is a demon
that clutches without fear.
It trembles and roars,
but it won't let go.

The world cuts through me
like a thick razor.
I scream. I scream,
but it only cuts deeper.

Hatred. Hatred. Hatred. Hatred.
It spews forth, dark
as a river of blood.
The world simply waits.

The world grasps me,
as a cult grasps its members.
I am seized, trapped.
Left with nothing to feel.

Christine Brakke

On Winter's Trees

On Winter's trees, a ridge of snows
That coalesced on branches, froze
  Like glassine serpents lying there
  With captured moonbeams in a lair
Of opal until winter's close.

The beauty of the landscape grows
In depth around the trees who doze
  And pay no heed to what lies where
  on winters trees.

For crystal beauty comes and goes
With thaw- but life, awakened, flows
  Unseen until small buds declare
  A winter gone, though earth is bare.

It's gossips truth — a new wind blows
  on winter's trees!

Dorothy Chapman

My Room

This is my room I'd like to share,
That I'll only go in if you dare.
There is so much stuff on the floor,
So you can't even open the door.
There is so much junk all over,
You'll maybe even find a clover.
You can not even find my bed,
My mom came to clean it but she fled.
I decided to clean my room,
So I swept it all up with a broom.
I put it all in the trash can,
And when I was done I said "Oh Man."
I threw all of my clothes away,
So I have nothing to wear today.

Brooke Kreikemeier

Love

I find it hard to believe,
That just one look,
Into your soft eyes,
Can make me feel perfectly at ease.
I feel so revitalized,
Just being near you.
Now even the simple things,
Amaze me.
The grass is greener,
And even the sky is a deeper blue.
I feel your heart beating,
So close to mine.
I know my future is with you.
With my hand on my heart,
I promise,
To love you forever.

Christopher Bernier

Snowman

The night can hide the silent soul,
That makes his way through haunting cold;
Alone he simply pays his toll,
And never tells those tales untold.

Snowflakes will be his meal this night,
And perhaps his blanket as well;
The darkness sees this lonely sight,
But who can darkness ever tell .

He alone can suffer the gale,
That carries his tired breathe away;
And with it comes the snowy pale,
That cuts on those found astray.

None discover this passerby,
As they are turning out the lights;
There is no place for him to lie,
So he wanders these frozen nights.

As you arise from your warm bed,
His steps will be growing slow;
And as you brace the cold with dread,
He takes his rest in soft white snow.

Gary D. Mitchell

Coffee Time

It's not the coffee in the cup,
That makes me want to take a sup.
It's not smelling the aroma,
Nor the flavor made with care.

Then why do I have such a craving?
When my body shows signs of aging.
Why must I sit and sip
With fine china to my lips?

I must say the price I pay,
To have this pleasure day by day,
Jittery nerves and sleepless nights,
Splitting headache and upset stomach.

The time has come to refrain
Since there's naught to be gained.
This I owe to myself,
Put the coffee back on the shelf.

Helen Bellinger

Hidden Feelings

I've been hurt so many times
that my feelings seem to run away
day by day.

If you could only see how much I care,
you would see it's just not fair.

I look at you and wonder why I
even seem to try.
I know it's wrong,
but why do these feelings seem
as if they are so strong?

Although I know we could never be,
couldn't you once, just think of me?

I know you can't see the tears,
for behind my smile lies the fears.
Some days it hurts to bad to think
about tomorrow,
when there is so much sorrow
behind the wall that just once
would like to fall.

Carrie L. Sanders

Always Trust Your Mother

You say there's no true women
That they are all untrue
But that is where you're very wrong
There's one who'll stand by you

There is one woman you can trust
Who is always true and just
You should know it is no other
But your own darling MOTHER

You never write when you are gone
You don't care if she is alone
Please write her a line wherever you go
And if you love her tell her so

Don't say things that you'll regret
She can forgive but can't forget
You make her awful sad and blue
But she will never be untrue

Eythel Williams

Blaming God

Sometimes things go wrong in life,
  that we don't understand.
Some blame themselves and others.
  Some even blame God.
Sometimes it's no one's fault,
  but God gets the blame.
So if your sick, or hurting,
  instead of blaming God,
Reach out, He's reaching out to you!
  Your friend, He wants to be!

Sometimes things go wrong in life,
  that we don't understand.
Some blame themselves and others.
  Some even blame God.
So when you are hurting deep within,
  sadness fill your heart.
Reach out, He's reaching out to you.
  Your friend, your helper,
He wants be!
  God cares about you!

Annette Rodriguez

Never Mislead Yourself

Into thinking a phrase existed
That would have forced
My ears and mind
To open.

You set a task for yourself, mother
That could not
Be done.

You did not fail.

I know you watched
In painful concealment
As I struggled and cried
With why
Ever on my tongue.

We share genes and gestures
But I was keeping treasures
Of hatred - and sans ego
All for myself.
Until the day I chose
To give them all up

To greet me.

Erin K. Heppner

"I'm Blue For You"

I want you back
That's the only fact
I'm blue for you
I wasn't smart
Now were apart

You found someone new
You said we were through
My blues are for you
When you were here
You leaving was my fear
I'm blue for you
If ever there were a day
That you would come my way
I'll be true to YOU!

Chrissy Hoover

The Miracle of Love

The miracle of love,
That's what I feel,
A kiss and a hug,
It's all that is real.

The miracle of love,
I'm searching around,
A touch, a feel,
An embrace in your arms.

The miracle of love,
I'm thankful to God,
For letting you be,
Part of my life.

The miracle of love,
I'm thankful to God
For putting your love
Inside of my ...
  ... heart.

Carolyn Irizarry

Future's Past

Look ahead look ahead,
  that's what we have to do.

Never look behind you,
  on what you say or do.

The roads we take are winding,
  they're really never true,

That's why we sometimes get off track,
  on what were suppose to do.

If we had all the answers,
  it would be so sublime.

To know we made the right decision,
  over the brief period of time.

But life isn't always easy,
  we must do the best we can.

So do your best with what you have,
and leave the rest behind.

Donald J. Heimbaugh

The New Things

How we dislike the new things
The changes bound to come;
Our hearts rebel at loss of friends,
We think it is the end of fun.

And when we move to new lands
We think we've lost indeed;
We feel so all alone and sad-
'Tis cheering up we need.

But then 'fore long a neighbor smiles
Or sends a friendly word or two;
The neighbors here are just the same-
'It's really up to you.

For folks are just the same all 'round
They'll all meet you halfway
It's not so hard to face the change
If you smile and greet those new each day.

Isabel Helbig

Life

The sun comes up
The coffin is closed
The birds fly high
The daisies posed

The crowd is silent
The wind blows
The sermon is over
Everyone goes

The box is lowered
The wind is still
One soul left alone
Crying at will

One life dies
Another begins
A new baby cries
And the cycle
Starts again.

Cindy Ciotola

I Am Dead

In my coffin, it is bare and old
The coffin is leaking, it smells of mold
I am dead. I am dead.
My black velvet dress is soft yet rough
against my cold clammy skin
The roses are withering
My mother laid them in my hands,
As a single tear rolled down her cheek.
My invisible soul was watching from afar.
I am dead. I am dead.
My soul is reborn, to begin life again
Humans die, souls are reborn
Again and again. It never ends
The silence is deafening
Join me.

Jessi Thwaites

Sunsets, Sunrises

The hues,
The Colors,
The texture,
The sky,
emotions evoked.
There I lie,
Facing the above.
The sun sets.
The moon rises.
Stars twinkle;
Bright is their gleam.
There I lie,
Facing the above.
Sun rises, moon sets.
I am still watching.
There I lie,
The grass surrounding me.
Heaven envelopes me.
In the sky is the key,
to life.

Florence Juillard

Sweet In Our Memory

Oh, Mother dear if you were here,
The day would brighter be;
But, we shall meet you some day
In that land so far away,
On God's chosen pathway.

It has been many many years since
You went away,
But, the love that you gave us,
Has indeed saved us from those
Who would betray us.

The love that you gave us
Has sustained us,
In the good old American way.
Mother, you remain ever
"Sweet in our memory".

Ernest E. Gragson

Happy Thoughts

I lie awake and dream my dream,
the dream of happy thoughts.
The thoughts that make Peter Pan fly,
to Never-never Land.
If our world were happy thoughts,
there would be no pain.
If our world was filled with joy,
there would be no sadness.
But our world is not free,
from crime and hate,
of the things that separate us
from Never-never Land.
Our world is filled with crying,
tears that overflow the human heart,
the human soul.
But tears move us to help,
unlike happy thoughts.

Amie Street

Don't Wait Too Long

Don't wait too long to satisfy
The dream that is a luxury,
For dreams are ever passing on.
Those satisfied are shortly gone.
Those lingering on lose hope and die.

So suffer no uncertainty.
Build on the lot with the rare red tree,
For which the road is named—Madrone.
Don't wait too long.

Cross over the river. By and by
Take the valley road that rises high
And stops where darkness settles down.
Look back and see the lighted town,
The orange tower in the sky.
Don't wait too long.

Helen Burton

Untitled

The brown earth beneath
the bedroom window lies -
Waiting for a day so fair
For the seed to be sprinkled there.
Can it be that the summer will go
With ne'er a single blade to mow?
I am sure this will not be true
For come September God's dome of blue
Will look down upon a carpet of green
The beauty of which has never been seen.

Dorothy B. Way

Untitled

I am no longer in control
The escalator propels my body vertically
I turn my head to see the ground
Bam, I am playing on a jungle gym
Bam, my first date what a disaster
Bam, graduated high-school
What a time in my life
Bam, college years
Nothing like it
Bam, my first love
Wedding bells jingle
Bam, our first born
Let's call him Eric
Bam, gray hair is showing
It's just you and me
Bam, I feel dizzy
The light is blinding
Stop, I can't take it any longer
Bam, rise and shine sweetheart
It's time for your medicine

Eric Bernstein

Fall

The wavering trees
the falling leaves
lie dying on the
ground.
Fall is here again,
The cooling breeze
brings the wandering
clouds.
And rain like tears
comes showering down.
As if mourning the
trees' loss.
Fall is here again.

Juan Cantu

Time to Think

I'm riding fence to check the herd,
    The gate, the fence, the tank;
I see the grass has grown so tall.
    This ride, a time to think.

I think of life, of death, and when
    I'm scared by thoughts of it,
I think of God, of Mom, and Dad.
    Old "Paint" moves with the bit.

I think of what controls me so—
    The rule, the hope, the time.
I think of man, the large and small.
    My work is for a dime.

I think of rain, of clouds, and crops;
    My mind is full of play.
I think of rich, of poor, and wise;
    Their love, and hate, and pay.

My home is open to the land.
    My thoughts are wide and free.
My kind is rare and full of life.
    This trade, my life to me.

Cade Shepard

In The Eyes of Tombstones

Water in the sky
The graveyard smiles
It engulfs us
As we set our bodies free
Falling into one another
Over and over again
Lips searching
Touching as flesh quivers
On cold, hard stone
Oblivious to the world
In the eyes of tombstones
Making love in the night
Soft raindrops on the ground

Fred B. Amos II

Upon Leaving Fall '93

How do you leave
the house you grew up in?
The stairs that you climbed,
every night before bed?

And how can you wave,
to the people who changed you?
The people that raised you,
taught you to behave.

How can you smile,
as you walk out the door?
Knowing that now,
you're no longer a child.

And when you return,
will it still be as easy?
As it was as a girl,
to settle in rest.

Cara Kokolski

My Life

You were my life
The joys, the tears
The laughter, the hopes
Though all our years

Now where do we turn
To replace our years?
Will it be that easy
Are we both to burn
In eternal erosion?

When did the sparkle in your eyes leave
when you looked at me..
When did my heart stop pounding
at the joy of your touch...

Could we have stop the lose
On was it in the stars
Only to share a portion of our time
To go on without for all eternally...

    Yes, I was your wife and
    Yes, you were life

Dona Jourdan

Tea For Two

It was the warmest of days,
The kind we both love -
Berries and buttercups in bloom,
A blue sky all above.

A moment then softly embraced us,
With teacups and old lace -
And we sat together smiling,
Wrapped in this time and place.

Sunshine curls and eyes full of wonder,
Before me I could see glow -
So perfect this tiny treasure,
So dear and precious to know.

Would you care for more cookies,
Or another cup of tea -
I want to stay here forever she said,
Always my sister and me.

Dawna MacDougall

"The Memories We Shared"

Looking over the memories we had,
The love, the life, the sadness she shared.
The happy gatherings on holidays,
The sadness of lost loved ones.
Life's ways we live on earth we may regret
And also may hurt.
But the love, the life,
The sadness we had
Will never be forgotten
When looking over
The memories we shared.

Amanda Petska

Colors

Pink for love,
   the love we feel inside.
Blue for sadness,
   the tears we often hide.
Purple for uniqueness,
   our differences from the world.
Yellow for happiness,
   the flower petals curled.
Red for anger,
   the hatred we fell.
White for the afterlife,
   when all our wounds begin to heal.
Green for life,
   the eyes of a baby.
Black for death,
   the end? maybe ...

April L. Becker

Halls

Listen to the sound of the bells.
The bells are hollow they say.
Listen to the people running by.
No time, money, or attention to pay.

The halls are empty again.
   No people shall attend.
The halls are hollow again.
   As if it were the end.

Listen to the halls, they are empty.
Listen to the halls, they are hollow.

Gregory S. Morrison

Fort Smith I Love

Fort Smith I like
The moon in the sky
When sunset and sunrise
I begin my new life

Fort Smith I love
The mountain and flowers
With my friends good heart
I don't forget ever

I hope in the future
Come back Fort Smith I love
To meet my good neighbors
And my old house very poor

We will tell some stories
Some souvenirs when we leave
Together at Wirsing Ave
With some cups of coffee.

Arthur Pham

Imagine

I want to dance and wile away
the morning;
I long to ride the wind
and visit God;
to flaunt the same
for every new tomorrow,
and purse my pockets full
the past again.

   To sift and sort
   all wonderment allowed me,
   embracing the growing phases
   row by row,
   to clutch upon my breast
   the moon's desire
   with You, my Lord,
   in sprinklings of snow.

Carol Chevchuc

The Owls

The trees are shimmering.
The night is cold.
I'm sitting in my rocking chair
that is all so old.
I see the night owls,
as they fly through the night.
Their eyes glow like headlights,
as they are in flight.
They see their prey,
and off they go.
Flying ever so swiftly
swaying to and fro.
With one fail swoop
the pray is all but gone
and the night owls night
continues on.

Edward E. Finch Jr.

Changing Of The Seasons

The winter air is setting in
The nights are getting colder
She's sitting by the fire
With her head upon his shoulder
The nights are now becoming long
As the leaves blow from the trees
And love will warm the shivering -
And knocking of the knees
People will come together
No one knows the reason
For love will only last as long
Till the changing of the seasons.

Cindy Musarra

The Ocean

The ocean is beautiful.
The ocean is sand.
The smell smells like
The water.

The sight stretches
Off into the distance.
The ocean, the
Ocean, The ocean is
Beautiful to me.

Joseph Giovanini

The Pain

The Pain of a lost soul.
The pain of a deceased mother.
The pain of sickness.
The pain of not knowing yourself.
The pain of being mislead.
The pain of being falsely accused.
The pain of being incarcerated.
The pain of being hungry.
The pain of being poor.
The pain of being lonely.
The pain of being laid off work.
The pain of being blind.
The pain of being speechless.
The pain of being homeless.
The pain of being on the bottom.
The pain of so called remedies.
The pain of a lost relationship.
The pain of lost desire.
The pain of lost child.
The pain of lost love.
The pain of death.

Artis C. Lampkin

To See You Now

The bonds have been severed
the pain of the past is left to the past
we were kids
half developed
we sought each other's strengths
to complete our growth.
it's on to a new world
to be ourselves
to revel in our individuality
to seek what we want from life.
But to see you now
the tears
it's not fair
the years. Are they over?
But remember the pain.
Yes, they're over.

Edward J. Benoit

Gather Your Children

Ha ha haaa... You bastards. Born on
The plains of oz I stretch
My column finger then writhing
Alive I breathe. Northeast I —
Hunt you. My jortex of madness
Gather the children. Ha Ha
No place to hide. A city
Block wide. Cyclonic demonic.
A siren of blood and
Bone in screaming progression.
Eating a church.
Ha Ha Haaa.. The preadlers
Fist waving, skulls
Cellars and dwellers.
I'm born on the
Plains of oz
And
Then
I'm
Gone.

Gerald Harris

career women winds

i cried for you and me today
    the plane soared after the thrust
        gave it wind beneath its wings.

who is the wind
    beneath our wings?
        like a sodden feather we flutter.

regardless of race or gender
    successes share two traits:
        a simple, focused life;
            or permanent gusts of wind.

our-age society cannot cope
    with multiple trade-offs.
        our hope is younger-age society.

we are the front line
    and cannot fly as far.
        but we can explain the change
            clearly to those who follow.

we are their wind.
    we must not fail to lead.

faye l. smith

Nowhere Is Far Away

Nowhere is far away, way and away beyond
The Purple Land
And homeless lily pond. The trees
In tripled soldier rank must stand
And scrape against the sky to move
The pity of the gate there, chained
To love the lighter things which fly
And flit above the ground.
The poor ones are the good ones,
Those who paint a sight, a sob,
A glance, a word, to earn
Whole civilizations in a poem.
So soon so much is sad that better
We who scamper in the air past
Years of tears of history. No time
Behind us, shabby-skinned, whole-hearted
Sons, to dig among the iron earth
With warm and human hands.
A life-span in the air is our only dare
To spark the eye.

Erwin E. Bach

Lauren

A rainbow fades
The raindrops end
How could you say good-bye to a friend
The wind will blow
You will know
I will always love you so
You were so young
You had to leave
God took you away
And you were only seventeen
And days to come
I will close my eyes
And see...
You
Standing there
Looking at me!!...

Gillian Hoffman

vodka jazz

with fingertips i trace
the rim of the glass and
the notes follow my seductive
caresses before slipping with the
sound with the trumpet's slide
disappearing, drunk with the vodka
and one fingertip swirls in
the intoxicating liquid
relinquishing in the ripples
dissolving and as i am
seduced in my sedation i
believe i am watching the
chaotic semblance of notes
spill from the trumpet and
i coax them to join me
in taking one more shot from the glass.

Heather Miller

The Rooster Struts

The rooster struts
The rooster crows,
And everywhere the rooster goes
The shy little hens side steps and bows
Make way for the rooster!
He's coming now
With his wonderful tail
And his golden eyes
Make room for the rooster
He's passing by!
The rooster flaps,
The rooster blinks,
And it is very clear the rooster thinks
Each shy little hen wishes she were he,
But each little hen
Clucks happily
As she settles down
On her brooding nest
For being a hen is what she likes best!

Berna Coots

The Thread Of Life

How fragile is mortality,
The silken thread of life.
The gossamer of a spider web
In the dewy morning light.
We tend to take for granted
The life we lead each day.
We don't realize in seconds
Life can be snatched away.
When we come face to face with death
And feel the cold hand of fear
How tenaciously we hold on
To the thread of life so dear.
I know our days are numbered
From the time our life's begun.
But we fail to see the miracles
With each rising of the sun.
Live life to the fullest,
Make the best of it you can
For life is but a silken thread
And you are just a man.

Donna Merrill

Figure Unknown

Early in the morning I look up at
the sky; I see a figure. I shut my
eyes quickly because I'm blinded
by the sun's ray's. As I close my
eyes I hear the cries of the wind
nearby.
Now it's late a afternoon; the suns
going down. I look up in the sky once
more; the figure whispers a soft
phrase, "I'm watching you, I'm watching
you I say." Then it vanished, now, I
hear the voice again it is louder and
closer. I say "I'm here in front of
you are you afraid?" I reply "Me afraid
of a figure, never, you are merely a
zigzagity line made in the image of
a person, I am not afraid." He cries,
"So be it, I shall begone but not for
long." I reply, "I hear your cry, but
I am still unafraid of your unbearing lies."

Jessica Almaguer

Beautiful Sunrise

Beautiful, beautiful sunrise!
The sky is on display.
Beautiful, beautiful sunrise
That turns the night into day!

Beautiful, beautiful sunrise!
God's gift to man I say.
Beautiful, beautiful sunrise
That drives the clouds away.

Beautiful, beautiful sunrise!
The sky's golden hue.
Beautiful, beautiful sunrise!
That melts the black into blue.

Beautiful, beautiful Sunrise:
God's gift to man I say.
Beautiful, beautiful sunrise!
The sky is on display!

George G. Ezzard

December, Christmas, And Winter

The twinkle of a star,
The soft blowing of the wind,
The falling of the first snow,
And December is here.

The laughter of the children,
The happy tears of the newborn,
The talks and hugs of love ones together,
And at last Christmas is here.

The bundles of clothes,
The hats, coats, and scarfs,
The icy streets and the closed schools,
And surely this means winter is here.

The sun comes out,
The trees blossom new,
The snow and winter both are gone,
And the children want to know why winter
had to go.

The baby is growing older,
The children are back in school,
The parents are off to work,
And they all look forward to next December, Christmas, and winter.

Amanda Le Ann Rice

The Way Of The Sea

Upon the beach and near the shore
  The Southern breezes blow,
Where death is found and joy is around
  Upon the sandy ground.

What stories of treasures our oceans hold
  As our forefathers have often told,
Within its depths we attempt to grasp
  But our dreams far exceed our cast.

What life it has it draws within
  What death it has it sweeps ashore,
The drawing tide and the sweeping wave
  Beating together throughout a day.

We watch our children as they play
  Trusting the wave overlooks its prey,
When among the tide you hear a cry
  The ferocious sea has dimmed a light.

The cruel tide so often hails
  While once again setting it's sails,
We continue to learn...regardless of plea,
  Independence...is THE WAY OF THE
SEA.

Ernie M. Flores

In Terra Non Pax

Nostradamus! Dost thou hear
The stupid battles, rampant fear?
Remember thee thine ancient dreams
Of conquered worlds, inhuman screams?
Thy warnings fell on deafened ears,
For mankind's labored years
Fail all. We grope in vain
Still tolerant to war and pain.

Prophet great, who spelled our fate,
If living above, will thou in love
Gain favor for this maddened earth,
Entreat for it a second birth?

Betty Phillips

Destiny

With the first ray of sunlight
the stained glass window
awakens and becomes
the treasure of rare beauty
it was destined to be.

The bits and pieces of my life
although gaily colored
and molded together in
    balance
    symmetry
    design
are nothing
until the light of Christ
shines through each tiny facet.
Then and only then
does my life
transcend the commonplace
and become
radiantly beautiful.

Elma N. Forshey

Whisper

Whisper- beautiful, ebony, proud.
The stature of the mysterious Sphinx.
The tenderness of a young lover.
Walking as if acknowledging his eventual
fate, with no trepidation.
Brilliant staring eyes of green.
Staring as if he is aware of your thought.
Sleek, independent, carefree-
Yet loyalty and honor are his highest
priorities.
Sitting with him gives a sense
of peace and safety.
His luscious purr brings a tranquil
drowsiness over my quiet being.
Friends may come and go- Except
for Whisper who will stay
to the very end.

Jan Cotton

Discovery

Little boy leans out a window.
The sun warms, glows.
Stares down at the pavement so far below.
Something invisible whips
With dry harsh tugs.
Where does it come from?
Why can't he see?
It encircles.
Oh to fly.
To fly.
If only he could try.
Trains and teddies are the experiment.
They whip and twirl.
What carries them?
Held by the breeze,
They crash and fall through the trees.
He leans, gripping the window sill tightly.
Looking down below-where he belongs.
Unsteady
Wishing he could reach the clouds instead.

Elizabeth Conter

The I'll Fated Aviators

It was a beautiful day in March,
  The sun was shining bright;
People were thoughtless of the news,
  That would come to them that night.

Two men were flying in a plane,
  Their names will be told soon;
When they lost control of the plane
  It was in the afternoon.

The pilot, Walley M. Goldsberry,
  The student, Everette R. Depew;
They who saw the tragedy,
  Were only just a few.

They saw a flash of lightning speed,
  "A plane gone down" they said;
And whoever is in that plane
  They certainly must be dead.

Many people gathered quickly,
  For the news spread far and near;
They gathered fragments of the plane,
  To keep as souvenirs.

Dorothy M. Fannon

Waiting

I waited for a friend to die,
The time uncertain drawing nigh,
I say a prayer, or two or three,
But words don't seem to solace me.
Confusing memories flood my mind
Of times gone by, but times is kind
and thoughts are loving, even sweet
For only good things now repeat.
A remembering of the years long past
Inside my mind I know they'll last.
Now I can hold all memory dear
and sometimes even bring them near.
Thinking of a smiling face,
A happy laugh, another place
The yesterdays seem closer still
As I dream on and on until
the understanding comes at last.
That which I thought was ever past
Is only parting for a moment or two
In God's space of time, when this life is
thru.

Bonnie Jean Lance

Candle Broke

The fire starts,
the candle flames.
I love the fire and,
everyone around me.
Then the hate is seen.
The flames fails.
The love withers.
Everything breaks down.
The pain is ignited,
everything is gone.
The candle is starved of love,
and it brakes.

Dana Ashton

"The Trees"

Walking through the forest,
The trees have phantom leaves.
They tap you on the shoulder
To see how fast you'll leave.

Some trees weep to show their pain
Some stand tall and show their vain.

Some shed their leaves
As a sign of fall.
Some do not lose
Their leaves at all.

Some bear fruit for you to eat.
Some lay low and give you a seat.

Some are homes for
Animals and things.
Some are a perch
For birds that sing.

The trees all have different names,
But all are beautiful just the same.

Jenny Williamson

Who's The One To Blame

Who's the one to blame
the victim or the accuser?
Is it the child or
child abuser?
Does the child have to
pay for the mistakes an
adult made?
The child isn't the one
who made the mistake
But they both end up serving time
But the child serves more
because they're younger.

Debby Winkos

Homestead Light

Oh what a welcoming sight,
The warm glow of my homestead light.

Through the field and up the rise,
Awaits rest for my weary eyes.

The day was long, so long,
To be from my homestead gone.

Greets me my faithful hound,
Who loyally awaits my footsteps sound.

Close the gate and enter home,
Contentedly, I to sit alone.

View the pasture, horse and pond,
Homestead of which I am so fond.

In my heart, homestead I keep
My hound, my home, I fall asleep.

Dana L. Tensfeldt

Valentine

Between two pages
That smelled of time,
I found a faded flower
And a valentine;
Put there lovingly I know.
The valentine said -
"I love you so!"
A bit of lace,
and a line of prose
Memories in a pressed wild rose.

Esther L. Doran

Dreams

I still have dreams of him
the way he held me just right
or the way he kissed me just right

I dream of all he did,
of all we did together

He promised he'd love,
keep, and
hold me forever

Where are you now?
Then I wonder does he dream
of me as much as I dream
of him?

Angela Lueck

The Difference

The voice I speak you do not hear
The way I look you do not see
The food I eat you do not taste
The scent I have you do not smell
The hand I hold you do not touch
All of this is because ....
I speak with the voice of the Lord,
Look the way of Mary,
Taste the food of Christ,
Smell the scent of Glory,
And hold the hand of Jesus.

Brandi L. Clayborn

Untitled

Life is like
the weather
Feel the beauty of it

Feel the calm when it flows thru you...
leaving a clarity and a sense of freedom
that seems to purify your soul

Feel the storm which rushes in...
throwing you about
roaring uncontrollably
lashing out in all directions
then scurrying away
with no concern for
the destruction left behind

Feel the rain...
Oh yes! God's tears
some of joy, some of pain

We know not the difference
Nor do we care
We just expect

Carol Sorenson

Signs of the Times

Doves on wing,
the red birds sing.
Robins hopping by.
There's starlings and the meadowlark.
Can you guess? It's spring.
There are nests to build
and food supplies.
Oh! How busy they all seem.
Their needs, like ours, will all be met.
Cause God is still supreme.

Evelyn Ledgerwood

"A Touch Of Genesis"

My very essence cannot cope
The works of man discourage hope
For me the world by God designed
My every fiber so inclined
The high country, the mountain meadow
Here by my joy, here be my credo
Regal Redwoods heaven bound
Virgin forests new snow crowned
The smell of pine on crisp clean air
Fox and mink and sleeping Bear
Hawk and Eagle on the wing
A drinking Cougar at the spring
the Grand Creator's works abound
I sense Almighty God around
My soul his work replenishes
For here...."A Touch Of Genesis"

Bob Strauss

The Seasons

The days of summer have now gone past,
The year will meet its end,
For winter is setting in.
Spring is a time of love.
Summer a big holiday.
Fall is back to school.
Winter has no end.
The seasons that go year round.
Never seem to last
They just go like dust on
A piece of grass.

Jessica Herrin

Butterflies

God made the pretty Butterflies
their harmless as can be
they fly around God's green earth
and never bothers me

I wish I was a butterfly
so I could spread my wings
and fly to every flower
to hear the Birds that sing.

Their Blessed with many colors
so bright and so fair
they fly around all over
and they never have a care.

We're much like the Butterfly
Someday we'll fly away
When Jesus calls our number
We'll be going home to stay.

Jessie Gamble

On The Eve Of Greatness

On the eve of greatness
their young feet whisper

Chanting secrets in the
halls of our minds

We seek to find a reason
for what could have been

The hopes and dreams of our future
fall with a crashing boom

Laughter ceases in a crimson dawn

Elisa Alvarado

Clouds

Look closely at the clouds, child
Then tell me what you see.
No, not pictures that you conjure
Or the weather soon to be.

See - shifting mounds of cotton
Piled higher than the skies?
Now, watch the colors underneath
It's the Heavens without disguise.

See the angels busy painting
with their brushes full of fire.
They race between the horizons
And there - one went a little higher!

Did you see the flash of lightening?
Hear low thunder as it spoke?
Or was it the pleasure of some deity,
Just laughing at a joke?

Soon the rain will begin, child.
No, the angels will be fine.
Then, all the colors they've painted
Will make a rainbow shine.

Alice Lankford

No One Alive

I'm loving you, I know you're
there. (In my heart.) I want to tell
You that: I Love You! I'm not sure,
If I know just how.

In every star I watch
twinkling in the sky, it reminds
me of that wonderful sparkle in
Your eyes. I can feel you,
wiping my tears,
and asking, Please, not to cry.
But no one alive can feel this
love we have inside. No one alive
can touch our hearts like we touch
each others. I can feel you,
as you grasp my hand.

People stare, and we wonder
Why? Why, because,
no one alive can
feel this love we have inside.

Jeannie Saunders

Christmas 1994

If in a corner of your heart,
There is a smile for me,
Then let me see it while I can,
While still my eyes can see,
If kind words wait within your soul,
Those words so soft and dear,
Then let them fall upon my ears,
While still my ears can hear,
Do the things that mean so much,
Sing all the happy songs,
Show your gladness to the world,
Bring joy where it belongs,
Send no flowers when I'm gone,
Shed no tears for me,
Let us share our happy times,
For one and all to see,
At this most precious time of year,
Our hearts should be in peace,
Not steeped in all the wordily cares,
Enjoying sweet release.

Anthony F. Conte

A World That Would Never Be

A long, long time ago,
There was a world of peace.
Where animals were tame,
And people were wiser.

It was a world where people didn't pollute
But were more caring.
A world where people shared their joys with others.

It was a world where animals
weren't mistreated but respected.

A world where there was no wars
but freedom and equality.
And people weren't greedy but giving.

A world of love and happiness
that we could never see.

Jojo Lee

The Standoff

Two convicts escaped jail
   There was chaos in the town;
They're in the house on the hill
   Now the cops are all around.

The convicts won't come out
   So, what's it all about?
They don't want to go back
   No matter what the attack.

Officers go in the door
   Shots rang in the air;
One officer was shot in the arm
   Another was shot to the floor

Fire broke out in the home
   The swat team ran in the door;
The officer was removed
   His limp body carried out the door.

The house went up in flames
   The convicts burned; that were to blame;
Now the families are all sad
   And a small girl has lost her dad

Janice Kelley

Pains

There's no moon tonight
There's no stars in the sky
No one says goodnight
And no one says good-bye

The sun's disappeared
And there's no sign of light
But I never feared
Being alone through the night

My body is aching
With memories I feel
And I'm not mistaken
'Cause these pains are real

The times aren't dreary
But some things are missing
I slowly grow weary
As fate starts her kissing

I bask in contentment
Throughout summer rains
Yet I wonder what's meant
As I'm feeling these pains

Amy L. Curry

Winter Time

It's cold and the northwind is blowing
There's snow and ice on the lakes
The ducks and geese have left them
To move to a warmer place.

The bear have gone deep in the hillside
To sleep in their warm cozy den
The deer have gone deep in the forest
To escape the cold north wind

It's cold and the north wind is blowing
There's snow and ice on the ground
The turkey and deer are hungry
For food is hard to be found

George E. Basham

Untitled

They fall so easily now,
   these tears from my eyes.
In any emotion I project,
   they tend to find their ties.

Sadness is usually what they portray,
   but lately that's not all.
Stress, frustration, anger, joy,
   all give me cause to bawl.

Tears are our outward signs
   of what's going on inside.
Tears will always know the truth,
   and in them you can confide.

I used to be ashamed to cry,
   "that's not what big girls do."
But now I welcome my tiny friends,
   as many, or as few.

Claudine Jaboro

Thank God For Sisters

Thank God for sisters,
They are the salt of the earth.
They are friends you grew up with,
You have known them since birth.

I only have one sister,
Where once I had three,
But, the only sister she has,
Is some one I call "me"

We are friends by choice,
And sisters by birth,
So, thank God for sisters
They are the salt of the earth.

Betty Corbett

Pictures

Memories untold
They sit and gather dust
Locked up
Only one day will they be admired
Once again
As they had their day in the sun
Aging, nobody cares
Molding, nobody hears
One day they will be looked upon
If they are not already gone
Brought out and shown
Stories retold
Their remembered memories
Held close to the heart
In the hands of the old
Made by the young

Elizabeth M. Baker

River Of Tears

As I lay down
They start to fall
Cascading down my cheeks
Like roaring water, screaming
As it hurls itself over a cliffs edge.
And now I am drowning.
Drowning in a river of my own tears.
Being sucked into the dark, insane
Abyss of my mind,
Where I die in solitude.
With all the world's worries,
On my shoulders.

Jami Cole

Summer's End

A country road
Thick with dust,
A plow in a field
Left there to rust
Grasshoppers hoppin'
Through the weeds
What a good day
For doin' good deeds,
Birds flyin' south
Day by day
We'll miss their songs
While they're away,
Grass is brown
Trees are bare
Summer's gone
Winter's here.

Flossie Springer

The Substitute

Candlelight against
thin crystal
a joyous wine
a leaping fire
and tranquillity -
you didn't want
to be here —
I know that and accept.
But I didn't mind
being another time —
another place —
another person —
for you —
for my being was starved
for warmth,
tenderness,
and minds touching.

Honey Whiting

Untitled

  Memories, like chains, tie us to
things we'd like to forget.
  I walked the lane tonight beside
crystal waters, hearing the wind
paying court to the firs. The moon,
cold and blue, gazes down from
velvet skies, watching my progress.
Questions not my motives, nor
making fun of silvery tears.
  The shadow on the path is
loneliness, lagging one step
behind.

Georgia Abbuhl

Please Consider...

Softly whisper to me
  things I want to hear
All the things it will take
  just to bring you near
I care for you so deeply
  I know its hard to comprehend
Won't you come unto me
  My heart is yours to spend
You say we are so different
  and your heart you close and latch
But I swear unto you Renee',
  We are a perfect match....
Consider all of this I've said
  and right before you do
I haven't said all I could
  Renee' I love you...

John Dermott

Faith

A man must carry in his head
Things that really matter;
Like truth and faith, and even love,
though people laugh and chatter.

It takes real guts to chart a course
Through rocks and pounding reef,
Although you lose some fickle friends
Or cause them angry grief.

For every man must take his stand
Whatever he thinks best,
And try to hold his head up high,
Though he differs from the rest.

For man is not the final judge,
Nor does he rule the fates,
For there is just one who knows,
When you knock on heaven's gate.

So, if you've tried to live your life,
While sands of time run faster,
You answer not, to man at all,
But only to your Master.

George E. Roush

Be Pretty For Me

Be pretty for me
  this Christmas,
pretty baby?
  If you be pretty
for me
  this Christmas,
pretty baby,
  I'll have a
Merry Christmas
  and a
Happy New Year, for the
  rest of my life.
If you be pretty
  for me,
this Christmas
  pretty baby...

Elwood Isaiah Ogilvie

The Creature

With one large, purple eye
This guy is very shy
Seven fingers on each hand
On six feet it does stand

With one mouth on each side
Behind a tree it tries to hide
All three arms were sticking out
His presence was felt without a doubt

With two feet large and three feet small
It would be easy to kick a ball
A nose on it I did not see
I hope he is not after me

Clothes on him I could not find
I did not see him from behind
Where he is from I do not know
I just wish that I could go

A ship appears in the sky
In gets the alien and they fly
I will not mind if they come back
As long as they do not attack

Clinton Matsler

The Colonel

How long have we really known him?
This person we call friend.
When did we first meet the man?
This leader among men.
It doesn't seem like long ago,
Yet, time goes by so fast:
For we all develop friendships;
But, sometimes they don't last.
This friendship based on mutual trust
Has endured for many years:
We smiled thru the happy times,
While tragedies brought tears.
The colonel now has passed away
And we'll miss him one and all;
For compared to other leaders
This gentleman stood tall.
The colonel wasn't with us long,
And that was our biggest regret.
He was an inspiration to all of us,
A legacy we shall never forget.

Edward F. Davis

Affection Is Forever

Sing of faith!
This world is callous enough.
Even with rancor and cynicism,
No falsehood is invincible.
Faith is a miracle!
It strengthens the frailties of a soul.

Speak of hope!
This world is unfeeling enough.
Even with frivolity and indifferentism,
No trouble is infinite.
Hope is a potion!
It pierces the darkness of oblivion.

Think of love!
This world is complicated enough.
Even with impiety and materialism,
No hardship is insurmountable.
Love is a fragrance!
It presents joy to the lonely and forgotten.

Carmelita Ledesma Agnas

Mirandy!
  ...thou dusky one in the corner,
  face tilted up to tempt the sun,
  red lips pursed and kissable!

Mirandy!
  first rose to greet the season!
A rose by every name is still a rose!
  But...
your blushes speed my pensive blood,
  your sultry fragrance -
    fire in my heart;
  your velvet cheeks -
    soft in my caressing hands.
Mirandy!

John D. Craig

Thoughts Of You

To thee I ask,
Though thoughts have told;
To be my lover,
Someone to hold.
I need you now,
I want you forever;
To love and cherish,
To leave me never.
The thought of your kiss
On a cold winter's night;
The thought of a fire,
You holding me tight.
These words that I say
Are real and true;
And the love that I feel
Is all for you!

Brenda L. Callahan

My First Day Of Pre-School

With school bag and lunch box,
Though three I only was,
I proudly walked along with Mom,
She said, "It's fun because ...

They know that you are special.
They'll love you up and down.
Smiles are their daily dress,
And kindness is their crown!

They sing to you most precious songs,
You'll learn so much each day.
They always give you time to talk,
It's important what you say."

And so I kissed my mom good-bye,
And sat down on their rug.
I watched her go, I stayed at school,
And gave myself a hug!

I knew that I would love it there.
I had know doubt at all!
Calvary Pre-school is the place,
That I loved most of all!

Ellen Ingelli

My Visit

I had a visit with my children today
Though we are many miles apart,
As I looked through snapshots of the past
They were there within my heart.

The expression on each precious face
As I looked through them one by one,
Brought back many pleasant memories
Of the things that we have done.

So, when I want to visit those
That are closest to my heart,
I get the snapshots out and bridge
Those many miles we are apart.

Gael Morris

Friends Forever

Friends are forever
Through joy and in pain,
If they should ever leave you,
Them shall live their lives in vain.

Friends are forever
As most people would say
Friends stick together
Forever day by day.

I want to be a friend of yours
And share fun filled memories
I want to be friends forever
For however long
Forever maybe.

Danielle V. Sanderson

Standing On The Beach

The boats stagger in
Through the channel
After a rough day at sea.

I stand on the beach
Looking at them.
I am humbled.

For these bits of board
Have survived the fists of Nature
And the name-calling of the Wind.

Although these boats
Have been through Hell,
They came through it boldly.

And now they return
To the harbor and prepare
To do it all again tomorrow.

I stand on the beach
Looking at them.
I wish I had their strength.

Dianna Lee Shepard

Innocence Of Change

I put down my drink and began to
  think, and think and think.
Next thing I knew I began to feel
  "real feelings" and they didn't
  come from the drink, they came
  from the "think".
It cost me some meditation time
  but the feeling is "just fine".
I took off my mask with the help
  of a friend and a friend and a
  friend.
Thank you for being, That friend.

Anna Show

Untitled

I struggle to see the clear picture
Through the clouded glass.
Frustrated, ear piercing screams
Crack the fragile sheet.
Pieces fall quickly around me.
I gently glide over the sharp edges
To see the beautiful flood of red
glisten resolutely.
A perfect lake with perfect pieces of
Salvation
The Red Sea parts not,
It is steadfast.
Surrounded by such strength
I am untouchable —
My struggle subsides and I am
The picture.

Angela Raye Brown

Ghetto Life

I walk slowly
through the ruins of time.

Wind blows through
the doorways and windows of life.

I can hear them
playing in the light—

Ghetto life...

Rodents biting,
roaches siding the cake;

Pastors breeding
making money from hope;

Spare the promises,
give them all some sight—

Ghetto life...

Who can laugh here?
All they know is how to fight.

Smell of ashes,
senseless patches of joy.

Who will help them?
Who will give them some life? Ghetto
life...

John P. Del Valle

My Love

Soaring
Through those naive early years
Somewhere
(I'm not sure where)
I shed my delicate wings
Trading them
For two sturdy legs
That would carry me
Over the hills of life
Until I met you
At first you left me
Stumbling over my new feet
Like a child
As time went on
However
You helped me find my wings again
A glorious accompaniment to my freshly
polished gait.

Amy Melissa Polster

Memories

I gaze into a misted window,
through which I cannot see,
and missing that sky is indigo,
reminds me of how it used to be.

The golden fields of years ago,
are still so dear to me,
these thoughts I sow,
into my dreary days of memory.

But yet I must say,
I will be sad to go,
and go soon, I may,
to become part of the past,
a memory forgotten long ago.
Alissa Moyer

What Do Eyes Really See

Evil solemn dark blue eyes
Thunder crashing in the skies
Lightning shining in your eyes
A sight you see that never dies

Fire on the lake that steams
Snow capped mountains as it seems
Ice glitters on the daylight beams
Like a jewel the rainbow gleams

A river flowing to the sea
Starlight blinds and amazes me
Who are you who could you be
Dark bestowing eyes that see
Christine Kingsbury

Today

In such a day as this,
Time is slow,
The hours are long, the
pressure is on.

On a day such as this, you
want to be home

A day like today, just
Reminds you of, the next
four days to come.

As you might have known
Today is Monday.
Bernice Dozie

Blackbird

Dark wings unfold,
tinged with violet
by a brush of sunlight,
rising to their full upstroke

as the legs beneath
break their delicate link
to the solid branch,
and the eyes,

specks of brilliant blackness,
look up to the sky,
perceiving beneath the shadow of a cloud
the reds, greens, and grays

that swirl violently there
on a painter's palette,
waiting for a brush
to give them form.
Gregory S. Hickman

"Rosebuds"

Rosebuds are like
  tiny eyes
Waiting to open with
  sweet surprise
Bits of happiness ever
  so small
Here in spring, gone
  in fall.
The scents will carry
  you away
To the pleasures of
  another day
They give friendship
  forever more
For love is what rosebuds
  truly stand for
Emily Heintz

PXL

Change from the state quiet shadow
to a real confident voice,
then the strainer of life will let
the liquid like friends stream through,
keeping only those with solid souls.

My eyes once swelled with tears of
disappointment, but now they see
the hard to swallow truth,
but as I would once spit the truth
out, it goes down now.

Every sharp, painful, medicine tasting
bit of reality slips off my tongue
towards my heart.

I now digest only the honesty
around me.
As I am truly purified of those
toxin-like people.
Cathy Karmilowicz

Journey To Freedom

My soul longs for freedom!
To be AS free as a river
that flows, floats, rises, and falls
My soul longs for freedom.
My soul longs for Jesus.

My soul thirsts for eternal life.
It longs to leave this painful world,
To find fulfillment
In my heavenly home.
If I can but be free,
Be free to see my Master's face,
Be free to praise Him in
  the fullness of His Glory!

I am God's child in a suffering,
  sorrowing, confusing world.
In a world that will not, cannot,
  let me be free
Oh, how I long for my freedom!
Oh, how I long to shed this
  physical body!
Carolyn H. Chatman

Untitled

The greatest gift from God is life
To enjoy together as man and wife,
Another great gift is health
Worth more than any amount of wealth,
Live life with a clear mind
Be peaceful, helpful, and kind.
Place love in your heart every way
Think of nice things to say,
Be generous to your fellow man
Help him all you can.
To all the young and old
You'll be rewarded ten fold,
Rewards, can be even more
Your life richer than before,
Sounds like sugar and spice?
Then take it, its good advice.
Frank Pellegrino

Aspire

Young man and woman aspire.
To go higher.
Then those before you.
For they have retired.
Never lose your desire.
When they say you can't.
Prove them a liar.
For it is you they will soon admire.
Keep your eyes on the prize.
Forsake the foolish.
And aspire to be wise.
Forever seek knowledge.
Even beyond and after college.
Keep high self esteem.
Aspire to bring forth reality.
From a dream.
Aspire to move mountains.
Let the vision in your eyes flow like a
fountain.
Of water to the sea.
For what you in your heart aspire. You
soon will be.
David Preston

Pose

Good for spring to me
To heal winter wounds
Good, for baby's birth
Escape Mothers womb

Choice of life and death not given to me
Belongs to one who lets spring be

Stare down the laboratory tubes of death
And accept the gloom
Remember, In your bosom a flower Blooms

Could've been a Dandelion or a Rose
Or a Tulip to pose, In some great artist
Masterpiece

Forget Not, No, Not the least
The seed or the deceased
Give it a chance to grow to bloom
In the garden in my room

Forsake Not, the sunlight or the rain
That nourishes & washes away pain

Remember, could've been a
Dandelion or a rose or a Tulip, to pose....
Joey Lowe

New Beginnings

How often we wish for another chance
To make a fresh Beginning
A chance to blot out our mistakes
and change failure into winning -
those who have such fear
that it does not take a new year

And the time with hearts of fine
it only takes the deep desire
to make a brand new start
to try with all our heart
to write a little letter
so we could live better

To the world in which we are living
and always be forgiving
and to add a little light
when the sun shine is bright
always be aware some times things are not fair
so never give up in despair
and think that you are through
and a chance to start a new.

George Fernandez

it's important
to me
that I see you
in the morning
before
a mirror does.
So you might know
that Revlon complexions
and carefully-combed
hair
are not the important things
that I see in you.
Portraits

should be left
to the artists
of the world;
and you

Un-retouched

to me
John J. Quirk

Lament Of An Immigrant Lawyer

He came from a faraway city
To sit in the halls of great men
Their wisdom and justice he trusted
The truth was their goal to defend.

How sadly he faced disappointment
The honor of those who stood tall
Let greed and ambition overcome them
Their values by the wayside did fall.

This story of man is repeated
As the pages of history unfold
Men never stop reaching for power
'Til an almighty hand wax them cold.

United in love, they can prosper
Divided in hate, they will fall
If each did his share to show kindness
This world could be happy for all.

Deloris Portillo

Death

Death; Oh! How I would welcome thee
to sleep the deep and dreamless
sleep of peace; for this I yearn.

To know no more pain or sorrow
This I crave, for I am not brave.
I cannot face the life before me.

Coward that I am, I cannot take
my own life.
Even though I know It would end my plight.
I see headline's of death everywhere
But yet you do not take me.
Oh! Death, I would welcome thee.

Angelic Hollander

War Clouds

The bugle sounds the call to arms
To soldiers all across the land
They leave their cities and their farms
To man the line drawn in the sand
The diplomats still talk and think
And though the deadline's drawing near
They neither budge nor do they blink
When trading currency of fear
The war machine now rumbles north
As sands slip through the hourglass
Soon the horde will sally forth
To meet the Tyrant's pawns at last
The new-age blacksmiths stand prepared
To forge a new world order
With swords unsheathed and talons bared
They stare across the border
The families wave from the gate
Smiling bravely through their tears
They pray for strength to help them wait
And not take counsel of their fears.

Chuck Burrows

Sensing Transformation

In life it is strength we need
    to strive in our journey on earth.
We search for ways to grow
    and be someone indeed of worth.

Learning from each experience
    we come our "Self" to know.
Only then the old is shed
    and the gifts of newness show.

As a tree becomes barren
    and some must even die,
Just beyond it can be seen
    a live tree catching the eye.

Slowly and surely the blossoms
    will appear,
Just as our old self must die
    and we're transformed year by year.

It is a matter of awakening;
    it is a matter of re-creation.
And as Self-Knowledge takes its hold,
    it is a sensing transformation.

Eugene Gizzi

Return Unto Me

I waited for you patiently
To trust and have faith in me
Your patience was short
You journeyed alone

I wanted you to look unto the hills
From whence cometh your help
You looked to man
And have nothing left

I wanted you to pick up your cross
And follow me
You laid it down
To follow instinct

I waited for you to hear
My beckon and call
You dialed the phone
To talk with someone else

Now your are in the valley
Full of despair
Waiting anxiously
Return, return unto me!

Gayle Y. Tunkara

Sunday Morning Lottery Blues

I broke my date to stay up late
To watch the balls a-popping
Again-bad luck has sealed my fate
Again my hopes are dropping.

Well, I sold my old car
And stayed home from the bar.
Said "I'll walk up to the corner
Hey, It's not very far."

My electric was turned off
And the telephone was too.
Mortgage man is on my tail
I don't know what to do.

Sold pictures off the wall
And my new T.V.
Is this the end of all?
What is wrong with me!

There goes the waterbed!
Lotto fever! Get out'ta my head!
Ticket money, ticket money. It's not funny
(No Sireee) Sunday morning lottery blues.

Dorcela Iagulli

Mother Nature's Revenge

I stood upon the mountain top,
to watch the suns light rise and sunder.
Before me rose a great black cloud,
lightning flashed and roared thunder.
A creature rose before me tall,
reaching well into the blackened sky.
It thrust its fists up overhead,
and with a shriek began to cry.
You arrogant mortals oh why,
have you desecrated me so?
How could you have forgotten me,
the very thing that let you be and grow.
I have watched while my waters died,
and I have seen the rape of my land.
Your insolence I can not bear,
so the end of you must be at hand.
Now with all my earthly powers,
I will remind you of your true place.
I am sorry I could not teach you,
to dust again and so ends your race.

Jennifer L. Cloud

If Only You Were Here

If only you were here,
To wipe away every tear;
Every tear I cry in pain,
Every tear I cry in vain;
Every tear I cry in sorrow,
Every tear 'til the morrow;
Every day a little older,
Every year a little bolder;
Sometimes I just sit and cry,
Now I even wonder why;
A little older, a little wiser,
Or so they say a great advisor;
Every time I see you near,
If only you were here.

Jennifer McClanahan

"Why Are We Here?"

  Alpha
Today is the day,
The beginning,
Not promised;
Yet has come. Why?
Not we ourselves know,
For are we not on borrowed time?
It is here,
  Armageddon.
  In front us,
   Behind us,
    Beside us,
      Today is the end.
Omega

Joan A. Windsor

Untitled

How lucky can us parents be
to have a girl like you
Who is not only a good looker
but a wonderful daughter too
So as I said before I don't want
you to ever forget you'll always
be our precious child no matter
How old you get.

My daughter who just turned 48
really appreciated this little poem
I included it on her birthday Card

Charles Accisano

To The Mother Of My Children

I realize how lucky I am
  To have someone like you
    So caring
    So understanding
    So special
I don't tell you this very often
  But it's easier on a day like
    Mothers day
A day so special that's made for
  saying you mean everything to me
And thank you for being the mother
  Of our children

James P. Meola

Fountain Of Joy

Joy begins bubbling
  deep inside
    where no one can see

Joy rises
  gurgle by gurgle
    to the surface

Then suddenly joy appears
  in one great gush
    and flows

Running freely
  swiftly
    in rippling waves

Joy sprays droplets
  onto the lives
    of others

Then overflows
  spreading smiles
    everywhere.

Linda Darlene Evans

A Wish for a Peaceful World

I walk among the
  dead
    wounded and dying
on a blood spotted field.
I hear their cries of anguish to go
unheard and smother the sky.
Their mudcaked and blood stained
faces search the sky, hands reaching
for the mighty yellow burst of flame
above the smoky atmosphere.
As they breathe their final warm
breath, their hand falters and it
lies still in a placid state of peace.
I wish I could help them in their
pain so that I may comfort those
who suffer in never ending despair.
I can only wish for serene peace
where war and grief would not grasp
the world like withered hands to the
sky asking, pleading for forgiveness.

Melissa Moysan

Joan of Arc

Cry long, Cry hard
Cry for your personal Joan of Arc
Martyr in your heart
Keep her there
And beware
The times will try to steal her away.

When courage dies,
And the only things you hear are lies,
Beware
Of the Martyr in your heart
Keep her there
Or nowhere
Can you find solace.

Oh, Joan of Arc,
Don't cry.
When you were burned
We saw the fire in the sky
Keep the Martyr in your heart
Keep her there
And beware.

Kathleen Elmore

Stereotype

I never met a woman who's
Cruel to her jewelry,
Unkind to a diamond,
Or crude with a ruby.

She won't disparage sapphires,
Seldom belittles a pearl.
Her respect for gold's developed
Since she was just a girl.

So men get wise - keep your eyes
On what sparkles and realize,
That DeBeers is to women
What trucks are to guys.

James J. Dulong

Ode to a Telephone Pole

Tall gaunt messenger
Crucifix of wood and metal
embodying hope, joy and despair,
linking ancient lands to new
with sinewy arms of copper and steel
What secrets flow through your
veins of cable - what are the
songs you hum with lips
of wire and glass -
you are new, but old,
doomed to extinction by
satellites in heaven

J. Winston Slinn

Mujer-Woman

Creature of wonder.
Creature of light.
Creature of terror.
Creature of love.
Mujer-woman
Complex and confusing,
So many facets,
As the wondrous diamond.
Mujer-woman
Tears and laughter.
Stern and forgiving.
Sanity and insanity.
Strength and fragility.
A kaleidoscope in action.
Mujer-woman.

M. S.

A Dim Star

Its cell walls,
  covered with skin.
Dumping my pride,
  hiding within.
It's violent rages,
  boils its back.
He's lived for ages,
  covered in Black.

And I looked through this tunnel,
  saw the other side.
With eyes lurking behind.
  The feeling
    the sinking,
      he's Breathing
        and thinking,
My surprise has come to life.

Michael J. Garcia

The Source

The darkness will soon fade to light,
Cool breezes turn to warm,
The touch of understanding,
The peace after the storm.

To some it seems like stormy nights,
Tossed upon the sea,
The search in vain for sheltered ports,
Brings no tranquillity.

When darkness comes,
You'll have the stars,
To guide you on your way,
You've found the source-it's Jesus...
He'll turn your darkness into day.

Jamie Jennifer Sharbak

"The Destruction Of Love"

The pain is fierce
    consuming the heart like a vulture,
The forgotten strength hides deep
    in the dark of the conscience,
The life is no longer
    yet it still draws breath,
To feel is a memory, no longer alive
To love is a lie
    the heart has surrendered
    The life is no more

K. Adamo

Confused

Confused child, why do you cry
Come with me, and get high
Out in the cold, all on your own
Getting old, looking for a home
Is reality to much for you
Didn't they tell you, its a zoo
Come with me, I will make you see
How reality wants you to be
So confused that's what I am
Lord doesn't know were just men
For we're on earth, are we not
Or is it hell, I forgot
Death and war, in my brain
Make it stop, on the pain
Am I dead or am I alive
No one cares, why should I
This is how reality wants me
But for you, you must see.

Patrick A. McGill

Memories of Home

Ken's farm in April—
Colts in greening fields
    stamp the stubble-sheltered land,
    baring fertile beds.

Main Street in August—
Children, sprinkler-soaked,
    crowd around the ice cream cart
    on sun scorched pavement.

Campus in October—
Sumac, red-plumed, flares,
    and ebon shelled cricket chirps;
    gold sweater girl cheers.

The park in December—
Knuckles of oak bend
    to reach boggy-gray clouds through
    needles of chilled wind.

Mary G. Walters

Spring

Dead
Cold, Stiff
Sleeping, buried, nothing
Dark, black, sun, bright
Moving, jumping, walking
Warm, awake
Alive

Joshua Kuelper

Speak Jesus' Name

Let's think for a moment,
    close your eyes.
Did you know that goodby's
    can become hi's?
Just remember satan tries
    to tell us lies,
    because he wants to hear our cries.
But speak Jesus' name and
    satan flies.
Now feel the Hand of Jesus
    as our tears he dries.
Thank you Jesus, and once again
    our heart sighs.

Patricia M. Absher

Untitled

Hovering around the right words
clinging to an idea
without any real reason to hold on
yet still zeroing in on the target
steadying my sights
and squeezing the trigger
tight
slowly
effortlessly
releasing all of my pent up
emotion with the bullet.

Joanna Lynn Sprtel

Untitled

Dawn crept in,
changing noise into silence,
as the morning sky swirled
into a tye-dyed spectrum
of lights and colours.
Effervescent opal-like droplets
of dew clung to the grass.

The beauty of it all over-whelmed me.

Then it was gone.
Lost forever in a secret place
that awaits for dreams
to become a reality.

Kimberly K. Robinson

The Prize Fight

My brown challenger is muscular
    dark demonic eyes
    broad nose with flaring nostrils
    flat deformed ears
    anvil chin
Flaying fists everywhere
    so too blood and spittle
After round three he yet stands tall
    but in round nine I stand alone
    any my brown arm is raised

Lee Kontur

Untitled

Rocking alone in my old rocking
chair rocking alone I have
no one to care if I live to
he eighty I'll still be there
rocking alone in my old
rocking chair.

Its better to rock then lay
in the bed, if I had to choose
I'd take the rocker instead
so old people get up out
of bed, as long as you
are rocking you'll know you
are not dead.

Margaret Bechtel

My Golden Meadow

Like waves of grain
Caught by the wind,
My golden meadow stood.

Where sunrise brings
It's glistening rays,
My golden meadow stood.

Where birds have fun
And pheasants run,
My golden meadow stood.

Where tadpoles splash
And rabbits dash,
My golden meadow stood.

Then one day to my dismay
Where once my meadow stood,
No golden glow at break of day.
Instead, structures of wood.

For these must pass
And then at last
My golden meadow will rise again,
To frolic once more in the summer rain.

Michael J. Jay

Patterns

Patterns in the sand
Carved away gracefully by water
Leaving its mark on the beach ...

A beautiful sculpture ...
But nothing to compare ...
    with the patterns
You've carved on my heart and mind.

Mary Jo Sisson

Beginnings

When Spring picks up the mantle
    carefully laid by Winter's snows,
And buds leaf out with luscious
    greens
And everything that grows
    begins anew —
So must I too; forget the errors
    that are mine
Or of those who pass my way —
And lift my heart and spirit up
For this a newer day —
    begin anew!

Metta J. Moughon

Up There

Hey, hey you up there
Can't you here me,
Don't you care?
Please come down
From way up there.

Take away my fears
Take away my tears
Take away the sorrow
That I will leave down here.

My pain is deep inside;
I shouldn't be waiting
For you to make me fly.

For my loved ones to mourn
Is far beyond death;
So save me from this awful time
If you hear me, give me a sign.

I shall be a flawless thing in the sky
Way up there, way up high
So God, please take me up now.

Way up there, in the sky.
Kim Ogden

"One Final Goodbye"

How much more pain can I take
Can I handle this heartbreak
Only one more, a final pain
From this, no more will I remain
Some say to think about it isn't cool
But no longer can I remain the fool
Each day I contemplate
Will I go at a steady rate?
Is it time for it all to end
Will I be remembered as "just friend"
Was I a good lover?
Or was I like a mother?
All in all, I'll be gone
Leaving only memories to live on.
Misty Michelle Yarbrough

Elemental

Dew, rain and waterfalls
Camouflage and try to disguise
The emotion that killed my ego.

Heartbreak in waves of sea breezes
Fall unsuspectingly to erode the rock
Of my trust, so I disregard my shadows.

Miles of shoreline as it dries
The clear blue water fades
Water to create my tears
Water to calm my fears
Has left again tonight.

Water is elemental.
Kai R. Johnson

Mental Anguish

Desire to compose-pose to think.
A quill scribbles simple phrases-
Draft ushers in writer's downfall
Upon an eve indicating a new born
Untamed creative imagination.
Defeated and trod under by words,
As effort exacts damp dew drops.
Simplicity or project deceives.
A tragedy, yet not a tragedy.
R. F. Bob Caldwell

A Pause in the Void

Refinish your unballad suite
    By rose pollen dances
    In wind swirl. Complete
Trances to ward off echoes. Then,
    Look inside to where sea meets
    Shore as the currents
Caress the coupling of body and soul.
    Make peace with earth
    The mind's optical glow
Coming from down below, fire kissing
    Flame as the darkness
    Blinds the heat like
Silence's shadow - (the deadly elf)!
Peter Andrew Mohacsy

Untitled

Lines drawn
By a wandering soul
Free and lucid
Ecstatic thoughts
Travel the virgin mind
In hopes of finding something new
Fresh and cold
It clings in terror
As if loves first thoughts
Were meant only to harm.
Corey Baird

Sleeping Mountains

A blanket of fog is on us
  But yet, we are not warm
We sit among the mountains now
  That have no color, shape or form.

Trees cry out their existence
  The wind shakes every stem
They shiver as if naked
  But, this blanket covers them.

Misty rain floats like smoke
  It swirls and circles 'round
The crackle of this fire is silent
  For dampness makes no sound.

I guess the mountains have to sleep
  So Mother Nature tucks them in
She puts on this foggy blanket
  And pulls it tightly to their chin.
Katie Maxwell Brand

Untitled

Brought me from my homeland
To a land I did not know;
Told me I was nothing,
And said I'd never grow.
But now I am alive
And now my eyes can see
Now I'm proud
Proud, just to be me.
Me — a young, gifted and black female.
Now I am not afraid of power
The power to succeed.
Angela Renee' Boseman

King Of Hearts

He is the King of hearts,
but this she didn't know
He's charmed with kind
words and a smile, so his
motive wouldn't show.

He showered her with gifts
and flowers, but what he
really wanted,
was to steal a kiss from
her sweet lips that would
always leave her haunted.

Oh yes, she fell in love with
that notorious King of Hearts.
From just one kiss he
didn't miss the breaking
of her heart.

He left as quick as he came
Leaving behind only his name
The King of Hearts.
Mollie J. Ison

Democracy

Democracy should not be demanded
But should be taken
When or wherever it is demanded
And has been given
It is no longer a democracy
That leads its believers to freedom
But it is rather a policy
That drives them to the bottom
Of the sea like a sinking boat
Far away from hope
It is time to wear a coat
Of faith and courage to cope
With the lack of freedom and democracy
Although we are in pain
Let's not have a love deficiency
Our suffering will not be in vain
May God be our leader
For he owns the ladder
That will take us there
And please, be there
Marie J. Latortue

A Smile

I've always wanted to heal the world
But she belongs to God

He may allow me though
To bring a smile to you

A prayer
A touch
A word or call
A note
A gift of love

But if I can bring you a smile
It surely is
A gift from God
Through me
To you
Marilyn Jean Lally

Bittersweet Tears

Last night a memory was made,
but sadly, for some memories hold
no promise of tomorrow.
Yet I smile, tasting bittersweet tears
as I carefully wrap this memory
in tissue paper
and store it
in the attic of my mind where,
on some tomorrow's lonely eve
I can take it out, dust it off
and try it on again.
And smile, tasting bittersweet tears.

Lydia C. Nussbaum

A Love Poem..A Challenge:

Oh my
But I love him.
Oh dear
But I care
My love fills..spills over
My desire..that he was here.

He left..its only been a minute?
A secret I will tell
I missed him before he left
Now it seems that cliche'..a year.

I am but only one of
Those silly women who
Fall in love with love..with love..
With love..am I a FOOL?..

If so..surely not alone am I
The world is full
All ages past..and now..tomorrow..
With all my sisters of the heart.

Josefa Von Bondenhaven

Fading In The Distance

I feel it fading in the distance;
    but I don't know what it is.
Something or someone very special to me;
    and when it is gone I will be too.
Not in body, but in soul,
    what is it.
Why don't I see it.
If I knew I could help;
    is it my fault,
    am I the problem,
    I feel it fading away from me;
    but I don't know what it is.
I try to reach out and grab it;
    but I can't seem to get it.
I feel it fading in the distance;
    but don't know what it is.

Michelle Wawersich

The Unbreakable Barrier

A clear wall, as thin as glass
but as strong as steel.
It can never be broken.
We can see them,
They can see us,
but we can never touch.
We can breathe the same air,
but it will always taste different.
We can feel each other's heat,
but it is covered by the ice
of that clear wall.

Lisa A. Kramer

A Poem

A poem is like the wind,
brushing against your cheek.
A song in the breeze,
which is so unique.

A poem is,
a feeling inside.
Something you know,
you cannot hide.

Now you know,
you love to write.
It feels just like,
you're flying a kite.

Katie Gordon

Gentle Rain

The rain fell softly, gently,
Brushing against my cheeks,
Engulfing my mind and soul
In a gentle, soothing caress.

The rhythm of the rain
Soothed my troubled soul.
It eased the pent up tensions,
Restored my strength anew.

The slow, steady beat
Gave wings to my soul.
It soared like an eagle
While the thunder gently rolled.

Oh, the smell of freshness
That cloaks the earth once more.
The gentle rain revives Her,
And gives me hope once more.

Lois G. Ophoven

The Art Of Love

Time, in all relationships,
Bring emotions that can bear
The rituals in the art of love,
Made manifest when we care.

We meet, at first, as strangers
And ponder what to say,
Yet time moves on and fears succumb
To kinship day by day.

But love, like springtime, blossoms
Transcending lengths of time,
Rescinding winter's solitude
From decadence to sublime.

The art of love seems simple
When friends can reminisce
A chance encounter, that happenstance
Which ended in a kiss.

A kiss that says, I love you,
Like sunshine from above,
Warms to heart those blissful woes
Within the art of love.

Kevin G. Rattliff

On Raising A Child

Raising a child
both brave and bold,
Weak or mild?
On NO!

Fashioning a mold,
unfinished clay,
approaching its Zenith,
A man's progeny.

Echoes of laughter
- a crying tear,
Heart felt rapture
- hold me dear.

Duties performed - unbidden,
 a lifetime spent
fearing to stumble
- the sculpture sent.

A father am I
this is certain,
betrothed to my child
To serve and to hold.

Mark Rebello

Hope

Oh child from my womb, were you
born to break my heart?

So many seasons have past our way,
each leaving with no delay.
When was it that winter decided to stay,
to not let us share any more spring
or summer days?

The time has come now for winter to
thaw, as there is new life coming to
us all.

Oh child of mine, your babies first
cry of life will bring us spring with
more seasons to pass, windows of hope
beginning for us at last.

Mary Ruth Barrett

Boo

Boo! said the ghost
Boo! I said back
through my sheet, which was colored
eternal
black.

He raised his hand
so I raised mine
our fingers touched
in an unconscious
sign.

The blood on my fingers
intermingled with his
both red, both dying
at least we had
this.

Far off, we could hear them
engrossed in their war
all of us dying
beneath black sky
and white stars.

Lani Brezina

Infinite Eyes

I dreamed of ——
Blue upon blue eyes.
They were the color ——
of the sky.
I dreamed of tear drops —-
Falling together — ending never.
I told no-one, and now ——
My dream unfolds.
I heard only two ——
Of six chimes.
I was looking high ——
Where the hawk flies.
Blue upon blue eyes.
I went my lips with your sighs!
I heard no cries!
There were only tear drops ——
Falling together — ending never.
Blue upon blue eyes.

Jeanette Holder

Alaska

Cold winds through mountains.
Blue skies in autumn.
Rocky land forgotten.

Running streams half frozen.
Great land still open.
Lovely pristine grandeur.

Snowy isolation.
Peaceful place of patience.
Land of winters nature.

Cold winds through flora.
Land of natural order.
Crystal running water.

Living land half frozen.
Living land still open.
Place of pristine splendor.

Jeffrey Levine

Racing The Wind

I feel the wind
blowing through my mane and tail.
I feel the power and swiftness
of my legs beneath me.
I feel my hooves, kissing the ground,
ever so lightly as I fly across it.

I feel the warm and friendly sun
shine down upon my sleek coat,
woven from the black night itself.
I feel as if I am flying so high,
nothing can touch me;
Nothing but the singing stars,
to keep me company.

I feel so free,
as free as I could ever be,
just me,
here,
now,
racing the wind.

Lone Wolf

The Snow Flower

The snow flower
    blooming as the dream durates.
Rising alone
    on a hillside of many,
        complacent in its splendor,
Yet in all
    it strives to exist,
It survives
    in a world
        of vases.

Michael R. Parsell

How

You just ignored us
Blocked us out of your mind
We tried to be friendly with you
But you just couldn't be kind.
Your mother babied you
She showered you with gifts
A present always put you
Right up in the lifts.
You never understood me
Like what I like to do
And I never knew with you
It was always something new,
How can I ever tell
What you want right now
How can we stay as friends.
How? How? How?

Melissa Calhoun

A Twilight Reverie Of Nathan

As the April wind
blew in the Novembered trees
I was running through
what was once their finest
leaves, now dead
and flaky, ground under
soles of rubber
and with moonlight sneaking
through lonely cracks in the barn
you became slightly visible
though I pretended not to see you
hiding behind a stiff soldier of hay
waiting for the snow

Megan McCarbery

My Porch

The summer breeze
Blew in from the sea
And rustled the magnolia tree.
It made it shudder,
Shimmer in the sun,
And cast its stripes
On everyone.
The summer chairs
Of green and white
Made such a restful sight.
The carpet was a sea of green,
Sparkling with diamonds.
On its sneer,
It seemed to beckon,
Come and rest.
Of all the places
In my house,
I like my porch the best.

Marguerite Goddard

The Starling

By the side of Gravel Hill Road
beneath the naked trees—
the ground a brown wasteland
of winter's passing,

I found a starling
scattering leaves with its wings
vibrating in suspended flight
unable to escape the bond of earth,

Held captive. I glimpse the reason—
a mate clutched in relentless claws.
Dead.
But not yet unyielding.

A plaintive whir of wings
above the whispers of leaves,
the starling struggles alone
to lift its burden from earth.

Lola Biuckians

Cry of the Angel

The world
beckons to the outside -
planes of humanity
cease to exist.

Hopes,
with dreams
of futures long lost
never to beckon again.

We hear their fears -
and their tears fall
upon their warn hands,
at the loss.

The children cry
as their world
begins to die
but we never hear...

The land weeps,
but we never hear
the cry of the angel
long lost in the past forgotten.

Michael Johnson

The Garden

In a garden far away,
Beautiful children laugh and play,
And love fills my heart.
My heart,
My heart is filled with love,
And my spirits soar,
Soar to the highest mountains,
Soar past the heavens,
Farther, Farther.
My ears fill with the laughs of the
children,
Fill with their happy cries as they
Frolic in the marigolds.
The sun shines down on us,
Shines with glory,
Shines with feeling.
The skies are a clear blue,
There is not a cloud to be seen,
And the beautiful children still play,
In a garden far, far away.

Leah A. Wren

One Wet Dream

To hold you once more would
be too much.
I dream every night about
your tender touch.
Now I have you only in
my dreams.
Waking up in the middle of the
night crying, in between screams.
Indeed your one of the most
beautiful woman I've ever seen.
Life is not fair nor easy, but
why does dejection always happen to me.
Even though rejection hurts, I will
never be bitter, nor hate you.
Nor will it be easy for me,
that's who.
But I can neither fool myself any longer nor
hold on to the past.
I must let our memories go
because they won't last.

E. S. L.

The Gift of Love

Love is like a friendship, it cannot
be bought nor sold.
It is such a priceless gift, more
precious than silver and gold.
We cannot keep love hidden nor
trodden under our feet, for our love
will radiate to everyone we meet.
It causes us to love the unlovely,
As God loves us you know.
We pass that love on to others as
On our daily rounds we go.
God gives us the will to love in
each thought and action we do.
And now dear friends as God loves
me, I give my love to you.

Mildred Ray

The Spider Web

A strand - a gossamer
Band of dreams - wafer thin
Stretched beyond my sight.
It held the world - so fragile,
Just a breath could send
Us flying straight to
Hell.
Did it hold us - or we
   hold it?
Would the sparkling beam
Remain untouched or brushed
Aside with nature's swift
   decay?
Beyond it all, do we fear
Life as much as silent
   Death?
The endless strand stands
Mute - a timeless entity!

Kathy Kuzma

Truth

I speak, my words of Truth unheard;
A deaf ear lent by those unstirred.
As prophesies the mutes profess-
The ignorant can only guess
What wonders blind men do behold,
As needy beggars count their gold.

Ibti Vincent

"Muffin"

She greets me in the morning.
At the top of the stairs,
Coaxing me to come on down,
So I can feed her there.

She is a fussy eater,
Only wants the best,
Likes the warm sunshine,
Where she can take a rest.

She climbs in the windows,
Scratches on the couch,
Eats the leaves on my flowers
Runs through the house.

She is very temperamental,
A lively little pest,
We love her very much,
Our "Muffin" cats the best.

Isabell Entsminger

Striving of a Dream

They found a foundling
   at the edge of the shore
wrapped in seaweed.

The human child rested
   unaware seaweed, as a
blanket, was not usually there.

Vast authorities came,
public media, legal aid,
pestilence of every kind,
descended, unafraid.

How long can a gentle
   newborn last,
who had no warmth
   of family?
no ties to any past?

Should they be allowed
to achieve personal modesty?
Or, how to cough and sneeze
if their mentors and they do not please?

Marilyn Higham

Love

I sat
At my desk
Pieces of you
Laid out
Before me
There's your
hand
There's your
Mind
Here's your
Heart
I ripped it up
And threw it
away
"Oh"
I said
Picking up the pieces
again
I guess this is
recyclable

Lisa Lazar

Diamond And Glass

Whispering
as though what we speak of
is Glass.
Ever so carefully
paying attention
to the delicate situation.
Whispering
in reckless abandon
through passionate kisses,
hasty plans.

Four years is a lifetime.

But what we speak of
can't be glass!
Glass is too weak, too fragile
What we have is strong.
Diamond.
hard enough to cut glass
pure and beautiful
Diamonds last forever.
What is four years in the span of Eternity?

Karen Kyles

Imagine

I can Imagine the joy
As Mary birthed her baby boy
   Jesus!
I imagine she forgot the pain
As she repeated her baby's name
   Jesus!

I know Joseph was proud
As he shouted to the crowd
I have a son - Jesus!

The inn was full
there was a lull
When Jesus was born

Three kings came
Bearing gifts of silver and gold
Diamonds and pearls

The crowd grew thick
As the word passed quick
That a king was born
   Jesus!

Mazie B. McDuffie

Friends

Friends are as good,
   as good as can be.
And they are,
   very special to me.

There are many games,
   we like to play.
Softball and swimming,
   and rolling in the hay.

I love my friends,
   all through the year.
And when I'm sad,
   they fill me with cheer.

Krystal Boothe

Untitled

Snarling, she clung to the tree
As Dad, in happy recognition
Lifted her off.

It's Boots, gone wild! He said.
The restless cat endured the trip
Through darkened woods.

At length
The lamp-lit kitchen reached,
The family gathered round.
His face transformed,
Dad showed his prize.

That night, belly full
Of cream and dinner scraps,
She slept upon the porch.
An owl called.

Mary E. Garzone

Our Love

As lovely as the sun that shines
As beautiful as the stars
This describes our love

Like a flower in a meadow
Sticking with you like a shadow
This describes our love

As strong as we want it to be
Long-lasting as it should be
This is our love.

Lee Ann Martin

Rejoice

Rejoice mankind this Easter morn
Arise in consciousness
Christ resurrected lives through you
Your life to bless
Look deep into your soul and see
The way you travel is eternity
Drink from the chalice of his love
And let it through you flow
Ever to surround you as you go
Christ rolled the stone of doubt
And human error away
The father and I are one
Did he not say?
You too a child of God
Can christened be
You too can demonstrate the truth
That sets you free
Rejoice mankind this Easter morn
And at heart's alter pray
Rejoice in resurrection day by day.

Pearl N. Sorrels

"Before"

We loved before in another life,
As Marduk and Ishtar we roamed the
    cooling desert sands at night.
In hand, we walked the blue and gold
    processional way, our sandled
    feet on smooth worn stone.
We enter the Ishtar gate on New Years
    Eve and see our Babylon in golden
    splendor.
Linger with me awhile in love
    and endless time.

Penny Pesta

My Sister Brandy

Little brothers and little sisters -
Are born each day of the year;
And I wish that everyone could have -
A sister like my Brandy dear.

Her personality and character -
Combine to make her be,
A person of strength and understanding,
And I love her don't you see.

She has style, she has charisma,
Her charm and love never end.
And She's the one I turn to -
When an ear I want to bend.

When my life builds up with problems,
That I myself can't bare -
I always turn to Brandy,
For her strength I know she'll share.

She's always understanding -
She never turns you away.
A sister like my Brandy -
You won't find every day.

Margaret Alexander

To Suzy Far Away

I know that I with ease could find
Another lover to treat me kind
One to hold me as you do so dear
Then all your faults would disappear

But this the truth is known to me
No one woman could there be
But ten or more it would require
To equal all your loving fire.

The quick and crazy roads you fly
They often cause my eyes to cry
But many good things that you are
They outweigh these faults by far

Now dreams will carry me along
Trusting in our love so strong
You see the truth is known to me
Together we were meant to be.

Peter J. Buchmann

Walking With God

May your dreams be many
and your worries few, may you
find comfort from God all
around you, he will walk with
you daily and show you the
way, and give you more strength
with each passing day. Just
trust in the Lord with all of
your heart and he will be with
you and never depart. He is
faithful, kind, loving, and
true and he is always ready
to hear from you. So remember
your prayers each and every
day, for he loves to hear
what you have to say.

Patsy Kaiser

Chronology

Tell me from your heart,
    and your soul.

If your blood is cold,
    like that of a deceased?

For no more will I be deceived
    by your lies or broken promises.

Out of hate,
    you love nothing.

Out of love,
    you love only yourself.

You are never content.

For you, what you lose
    will always be replaced

Replaced with value and looks,
    but you are losing something,
    something you can never replace.

Something that is here today,
    but gone tomorrow.

You are losing time.

Michelle Taylor

Wishes For You

May your days be filled with sunshine
and your nights be free of tears.
May loving arms surround you
as you go through the coming years.

May life's doors be opened for you
and your friends stay by your side.
May inner peace go with you
and may happiness be your guide.

May rainbows hover overhead
and no object block your view.
For God made many people
but he made only one of you.

Kenneth L. Crouch

When We Were

When we were twenty I was fat
and you were skinny.
And as the years went by
I thought of you and you though of I.
And when we were, and when
we wasn't, I swear we were
and you'd swear we wasn't.
But ones things for sure
I love you girl, you're the
most important thing to me
in this world, and all I
ask of you in turn, is to
remember me and when we were.

Jerry Austin

Untitled

Goose, gull, goose, gull, come
and mind your geese. They
are making such a cackling
we don't have any peace.
Lead them to the water
where they ought to be
I'll sit you down to
watch them beneath
the widow tree.

Lillian Outten

Dust

When she was dry as the desert
and walked with a sideways gait
like an old land crab,
seeking the shadows from which
it had been disturbed,
she still sang.
Some called it keening
but those who listened
heard the sensuality,
no lamentation in the song,
and her sinewy old arms would be bent
as if to hold a long lost lover
or a child.

Phyllis Kasler

Forgetful

I see them if I close my eyes
and try and reach for bygone times.
To capture some few whispered sighs
like half remembered nursery rhymes.

My darling girls with shining smiles.
My handsome sons with quiet ways.
Each had their own distinctive styles
but I have failed to seize those days

A few old pictures help unfold
still images of long ago.
It pains me that I cannot hold
those million moments I should know

I wish there was some way to mend
forgetful holes within the mind.
Like sand through fingers in the wind.
my memories swirl and fall behind.

Paul D. Nees

Love

As the leaves of passion fall
And the trees are standing naked
One can hear the mating calls
And the branches being forsaken

The fruits are all too ripe
Oh how everything flows with time
And now the lovers of the night
Change their fate with a drink of wine

If I show you my branches tonight
Will you bear fruit with me tomorrow
Or is this just another night
That will leave me filled with sorrow?

Monika Thompson

Untitled

In a winter wonderland of snow
Another day comes to a close
As the sun slowly slips away,
The moon glides up to stay
Bringing shimmering beans of light
To dance on the snow at night
Where hand in hand young lovers go
Frolicking through the sparkling snow
With a song in their hearts
They promise to never, ever part
With their futures looking bright,
They bid each other a good night.

Marie L. Sides

Grandpa

How I long for yesterday,
And the times that we would play.
How I miss our nice long walks,
And our quiet little talks.
We would sit upon those stairs,
And you would ask me there,
"How big are you today?"
"This big," I would say.
My arms stretched open wide,
My heart so full of pride.

I know that you must leave,
It is not time to grieve
Although, I will be sad,
My grandma will be glad.
A long time she did wait,
Just to meet you at those gates.
It's time to say good-bye,
A tear falls from my eye.
My arms stretched open wide,
My heart so full of pride.

Pamela K. Stanley

'Neath The Silver Sycamore

Where the willow meets the water
And the moon flows on the shore
A breeze beguiles the leaves
Of a silver sycamore

And whispers of the passion
And a promise to be true
It overheard the night
I pledged my love to you

It echoes your sweet laughter
Caresses my worn face
And comforts me recalling
The warmth of your embrace

For I died there of the longing
For the solace of your love
Now my heart and soul lay haunting
The moon and stars above

Where the willow meets the water
And the moon flows on the shore
I keep a silent vigil
'Neath the silver sycamore

Marcia C. Smith

One True Friend

Friend, greet me with a friendly smile,
And talk with me a little while;
Please send me on the road ahead,
Much better off, for what you've said!

Uplift me with a pleasant thought,
Help find the answer I have sought,
A better world with hope anew,
Make it that way because of you!

Please search until at last you see,
A thing or two worthwhile in me,
Restore my faith in God and man,
And courage to fulfill life's plan!

Then as I travel on my way,
Let all the things I do and say...
Help others as their ways they wend;
That I may also be a friend!

Keith R. Frost

Thoughts of You

My thoughts of you fill every hour
and stir my blood with such a power
That only you can turn the tide
with which they flood my troubled mind

Your beauty surely is not real
For from the sight of you I feel
A pounding yearning deep desire
to kiss your lips and build the fire
that burns so high it can't go higher
and makes my need for you entire

But all of this that I've been saying
is said more simply by displaying
the feeling which is so sincere
the reason why I call you dear
I love you.

Mary Curl

God Can

Who can take a lump of clay
And roll it around in his hands,
And breathe into it the breath of life
And it becomes a man?
God can.

Who can take a mustard seed
Which is almost too small to see,
And cause it to germinate
And it becomes a tree?
God can.

Who can take a dry tree
And set it on fire,
And the tree fails to burn up
Right before your eyes?
God can.

Who can emerge from nowhere,
Organize somewhere,
And get in the center of somewhere
And establish everywhere?
God Can.

T. D. Walker

Temporary Love

As I lay here
and recap our day,
I feel an unexplainable
difference of heart.

It is as though, my heart is sore-
injured- in a hatred way...

Scary, this emotion-but
I'm trying to remain calm-
to not give in and cry...

because that is what I
want to do...

It seems that my happiness
is always temporary!

Lorraine Pitre

Untitled

I looked at you today
And realized
You're only a man
Not a hero
If shocked me
As nothing else could
I believed so much
In you
That I turned a blind eye
To your faults
Forgetting all you lies
Only remembering
Something from long ago
When you kissed me
And I knew
I belonged to you
Always.

Jennifer M. Cino

Untitled

Dawn is inauguration
And passing is a destination.
And existence is a voyage;
From infancy to seasoned
And juvenile to mature;
From purity to learned;
From folly to caution
And then conceivably to erudition;
From vigor to ailment
And then, we beseech, to vitality anew;
From infraction to pardon,
From secluded to attachment,
From exhilaration to appreciation,
From distress to compassion,
And sorrow to comprehension.

Michael Levine

Where Shall I Go

The sky was dark
And oh so dreary
Lord, where shall I go.

I closed my eyes
And hung my head
Lord, where shall I go.

A beam of light broke
through the clouds
And I saw the face of God.

He said "Come home my Child"
and with me you will be,
For this is where you are going.

Louise Brunson

Reality

They spoke of their love
  as something brand new -
These feelings they felt,
  these passions held true.
Forever was stated
  and death us do part,
But tomorrow brought hard times
  the penny turned dull,
And the love that was boundless
  fell prey to the cold.

Patricia Lee Eidson

Bittersweet Melange

Then all the seas did blow
And more than souls let go
Among the lost were many things
Paltry treasures least of these

For when the fine line snapped
The cursed waters ate our young
And belched us out fighting
To stare down two score burning suns

Harder decisions at every hand
Would test our metals tempered ends
I would not say we held our tongues
And make my own a forked one

Among us love was ever lost
For all those days we turned and tossed
The salt soon sealed our lips
So that not a word could cross

And our small boat so scant
Grew larger as the days were spent
Till only seven souls disheartened
Would ever taste lands sweet melange.

John S. Harper

Baby Love Unaware

I thought I would be so very loved
And longed to meet my little brother
But then I was violently aborted
And never got to know my mother

The pain was so unbearable
My tiny body ripped apart
How could a baby be so terrible
And how could they break my tiny heart

In heaven I still love my mom and dad
And I guess I'll never understand
Why they made me so sad
And never gave me a chance

I can still forgive them away
The pain in my heart hurts no more
And I long to meet them one day
Hoping I will be loved and loved forevermore

Patricia Cox Napoli

See, My Child

See, my child, thru my eyes
and let me get used to yours.
Help me to see the world
with growing pains of stubbornness.
You've your whole life ahead of you
I have not mine anymore.
See...
Laugh at the clown
  Delight in a kitten
    Grow thru knowledge
  contained in your books
    Attest to the wondrousness
  of the stars
Gain admittance to adulthood
with laughter and pain
So you can one day
say to your own child
  Look...
And see the world in my eyes
while I get used to yours.

Karen Bernardy

Candle Lights

I looked into your shining eyes
and knew that you where mine,
I found a flicker in our hearts
that lit the flame to shine.
I saw the way we had that
Certain spark together.
That lit up our lives
and kept it burning
Forever
For even if our
Flame had it's
Flickering ways.
Never did it get snuffed out.
It stayed shining everyday.
For in fact it got
much Brighter, and
it flamed within our hearts.
For like a lighted candle it has
An eternal flame to spark.

Mindy Haukos

Quiet Man

In your strength
  and in your caring...
I grow
In my silence
  and in my dreams...
It is peaceful
In the gentle tide of your wisdom
  you fill my emptiness...
In the quiet promise of your touch
  you give ne strength...
    And my heart...
      And soul...
        Are...
          Free.

Jennifer Adams

Memories

We shared a lot together
and I thought it was going to last
forever. I told you things that I
haven't told my best friend, that's
why we mend. You told me secrets
about you, that nobody else knew.
So then I knew I wasn't going to
be used. You were special to me,
why don't you see? I still love you,
but it will be hard not to feel
blue. I tried to cover my sadness
up with lies, but it didn't work,
all I did was sigh. I'll never
let go of the memories of you
and I. When I go back and reminisce,
I will cry.

Molly Keezer

You To Me

A light shines through
A dark forest -
Giving all that is
A chance to grow
And making it beautiful
When otherwise it
Would be not.
I am the forest
And you are the light
That touches me deep inside.

Jennifer L. Souza

Untitled

I walked up to the river
and I thought about jumping
in and it looks like that's
what I'll have to do if I ever
get a bad hand again, it doesn't
make since to try and can't
win, so if I get a bad hand
I'm going to cash all my troubles in
I know the Lord will take
a liken to listing to all my
prizes, it ain't that I hated
living but boy it was cold
down there

Kennard Gregg

Swing Time

When my burdens get heavy
And I tend to despair,
There's nothing that soothes me
Like swinging in air.
Then, letting my thoughts
Fly carefree and far,
They sail out in space
To some distance star.
First one, then another
Sends back its bright rays,
To say I've imagined
My burdens for days.
My spirits are lifted,
My heart is made glad,
And then I forget
All the troubles I had.
So when I feel low
With no song to sing,
I go out and spend
Some time in a swing.

Olaf Dahle

My Child In My Heart Forever

You departed dear daughter
And I still cannot believe it;
Your absence has made me suffer,
My crying has had no limit.

But there is consolation
In knowing you went to Eden;
Of that there is no question
In my heart, my soul, my feeling.

During all your life pretty dove,
So short, and yet, so beautiful,
You went to extremes spreading love
And sweetness too, so plentiful.

May The Lord bless you forever
For all the things that you gave us:
Gallantry and happiness ever
And behavior so courageous.

So long, my very dear child;
I hope to put aside my pain
In order not to become wild,
Till in heaven we meet again.

Carlos O. Contreras

Be My Friend

No, I'm not crazy.
And I am not mad.
I'm not being silly,
I'm just feeling sad

Indulge me now,
Just let me cry.
Allow my self pity,
For me, please try.

Tomorrow I'll be happy.
I promise. You see,
I always did manage
To land on my feet.

For now let me linger,
A moment or two,
In a bout of self pity.

It will be over quite soon,
For the cure, my dear friend,
Is just talking to you.

Miriam Dankberg

A Prayer For A Friend

I said a prayer just yesterday
And hoped it would come true
I asked the Lord for help and love.
But first I asked for you.

I prayed that I would be to you,
A loving, loyal friend.
I prayed for fun and lots of laughs,
And friendship that won't end.

I prayed that you and I might bring.
New life to every day,
I prayed that both of us as friends
Would learn to work and play.

I prayed for guidance down the road,
A prayer I would repeat.
To help us smile through good and bad,
At everyone we meet.

And in the darkness of the night
In sleep I was to see,
Dreams of us years down the road,
Living true and free.

Kimberly A. Allen

Trop d'Amour

She came to me at midnight,
And her heart was in her eyes;
I took her gently in my arms
And whispered foolish lies,
I petted and caressed her,
Gave her promises galore;
I pledged her my undying love,
And still she begged for more!

At last I wearied of her,
Feared my love would turn to hate;
"Get out, you stupid cat!" I cried,
"Your breakfast comes at eight!"

D. I. Treece

Limbwork

You were born hot against cold
and for me there's no place
cold enough there's no breath
cool enough to rest me in palms

Still though the timid jacana holds
dripping lilies to balm your face
dripping lilies her trembling earth
an exhalation of intuitive psalms
Still even the common penguin waddles
the cowardly world of his surethick ice
and works me a comic crystal wreath
nothing more due me it calms

The warmth's then yours yes?
in ten years we share charms yes?

Michael Hines

Why?

I slept on the grass
and felt thistles of pain
in the nape of my neck.
I looked up at the sky
and asked of it
a wide open question.
I turned and felt
warm, damp earth on my face.
And I wept
on the wide open plains.
Go. Go look for the wind.
And if you should find,
in the wind's labyrinthine ways,
a whisper of reason,
come, come and tell me.
I will be here
by the sunset;
a crumpled foetus
drowning in rain-

M. A. Malik

Baseball

Baseball is my favorite sport to play
and even watch.
Some major league teams are the
Rockies, the Braves, and the Sox.

My favorite teams are the Rockies
and the Braves.
The pitcher Greg Maddox makes a lot
of good saves.

My favorite teams played against each
other the last game of the
season.
I rooted for both teams for some
reason.

Michael Van De Wyngaerde

From One American To Another

You are black
and
I am white
Can we be friends today?
I am white and you are black
We can
If we don't listen
to what
"they" say

Penny Johnson

Dad

Oh, how you left us on that dark,
and dreary night
As we all stroked your head,
told you we loved you,
and held your hand so tight.
You left us all to quickly,
With many things left to say.
Your pain and suffering was over,
but our emptiness is here to stay.
no one could have prepared us for
What we were about to go through.
no one knew what to expect or
What the changes in our lives would do.
We miss you each and every day,
like some share never know,
And until we meet in heaven again
Our love will always grow

Mary Laughlin

Untitled

Sometimes he acts so friendly,
and at times knows not my name.
What is this power he has over me?
On my mind he plays some game.

Sometimes he is so loving,
and at times I'm a deadly disease
What does he want to happen?
For him I'd fall down to my knees.

I wish we were together,
so I'd know he would be true.
But, now I feel he's done with me,
and wanting someone new.

I feel so strongly for him,
He's forever on my mind,
I wish he'd see my feelings,
But, he seems to be so blind.

It lingers inside of you forever,
the feeling of getting hurt.
And you never get used to
being treated just like dirt.

Karen Guerrieri

The Dream

I knelt at the sage's feet
And asked for one great truth
To stand me firm on common's ground
And set my life as proof.

He pondered, then he made a field
Of arid desert sand,
And in its midst, suff'ring from thirst,
There stood a blindered man.

He sought the image of a pond
So far along his track;
Had he but simply loosed his blinds,
A lake lay at his back.

He died upon that endless path,
Ne'er thought to turn around;
With water so within his grasp,
It was in sand he drowned.
From troubled sleep I then awoke,
To ponder o'er this plan,
But greater wonder vexed me still;
Where did I get this sand?

D. A. Neiburg

A Day

Sprinkle of lights,
and a ball of glow;
the night is so bright
better turn it down low.

Twisted heated nuclear glow,
makes the day so bright;
must see it now flow,
in time for twilight.

First came the dawn,
and second came dusk;
Day came in like a fawn,
but ended like the husk.

Now I just want a dish,
serve a new day bright;
now let me have my wish,
end this one's hard plight.

Mike Licht

"Friends Forever"

A shoulder to cry on,
An ear to bend,
Money to borrow,
Clothes to lend.

Friday night fun,
Afternoon walks,
Bring together,
Our "private" talks.

Mending those hearts,
Crying those tears,
Planning our futures,
Screaming our fears.

Our memories together,
May they never end,
Always together,
Forever friends

Lisa A. White

That Boy

Hide N Seek?
An abandoned toy.
Leap off the couch.
Where's that boy
Where is that boy?
Two mischievous eyes
   in a crouch.

OO OOO La La...
In Unison Sing
Bouncing butterflies
   take wing.

Cackles and smiles
They could run miles
A little man and her
In arms of love
   and gossamer.

Bounce Sing and Shake
Joining in Harmony. . .
   the lake.

John Christopher Morris

Green Grow The Grasses

I think of you, my love, my love,
Although you're far away-
Because you're part of day and night,
And part of me always.

Because of you, my love, my love,
The sun does ever shine
And grass is green, and rivers flow,
And always skies are fine.

If life should pass me by, my love,
With you not by my side-
I'd sense that I had lost my way,
But know that I had tried

To make a place for you, my love,
Away from grief and woe-
With home, and love and little ones,
Where greener grasses grow.

Henry Lyndon Despard

Green

Yellow chair
alone in room nothing else
but a broken cup and
a red spool of thread
under the chair in the room that's bare
The walls are white with specks
of grey and fingerprints
small, like a child's
They're paint, yellow and blue
but they don't make green
and there's a picture, purple crayon,
of a man and a cat
The man is holding a bottle but
it's not purple, it's black and empty,
like the room with the chair and
the cup that's broken-no handle
and one spool of red thread

Lauren Creamer

Homeless

They wander the streets
alone and scared
but people laugh
and say they're hopeless

They stand on street corners
begging for help
but still people look at them
but do not lend a hand

They scavenge through trash cans
hoping there's food for the next meal
for some might have families
or some just might be alone

They're hungry and cold
and it seems no one cares
they wear shaggy clothes
and have no sense of belonging

They're seen sleeping in cardboard boxes
or huddled in groups in alleys
but people call them bums
and walk on by

Patti Burget

It Fell On The World

A brown cocker spaniel
All turned white.
A blue Oldsmobile
All turned white.
When it fell on the world
All through the night.

The wood covered roof
All turned white.
Santa and his sleigh
All turned white.
When it fell on the world
All through the night.

My long, blonde hair
All turned white.
My purple and red coat
All turned white.
When it fell on the world
All through the night.

Michelle Zickel

Recipe For An Ice Cube

We're sixteen little ice cubes
All in a line
And we'll get into your glass
Without costing you a dime.

Everyone always wants us
When they've got a drink that's hot
But no one wants to fill us
Which really doesn't take a lot.

The solution is quite simple
To this problem of all time
Just follow the instructions
In the balance of this rhyme.

After we are empty
Simply take us to the sink
And fill us with tap water
In the time it takes to blink.

Now hold us very steady
Trying not to spill a drop
A little while in the freezer
And we'll be ready with a plop.

Linda Gayle Chilcoat

Black River

Surrounded by people,
all alone.
Music and laughter all around
a dead silence encloses my soul.
Helping hands reaching out,
falling though darkness,
no one to hold.
Sinking down,
seeing horrors,
my worst fears real,
my prided dream mocked.
Pulled down into a darkness,
of silent thought.
Down, into the depths of my soul,
demons sleep,
angels sing,
where the black river of my tears runs by,
gurgling your name,
it drowns me in my own sorrows.

Meghan Bourke

Untitled

And at last,
Alas
This day will pass
Into the neither realms of yesterday,
Clouded
but ne'er forgotten.
How might I forget?
for today
you are radiant as the sun.

Kay L. Anderson-Gomez

The Drunken Ecstasy

I want us naked
again...
parked in that hayfield
with the rain
softly cascading the window
serenading the lovers
within...
I want to recapture
the rapture of then...
bodies blended
like fine Tennessee tea...
please tell me
it has not ended...
the drunken Ecstasy!...

Joni Brown

Impressions

I cast a pebble into the lake,
A thoughtless act, but telling,
For, as that pebble sank from sight,
There came a thought compelling.
Upon each perfect crystal crest
Of waves so gently shifting,
I seemed to see in symmetry
A simple act, but lifting;
An impact strong, or imperceptible,
But impact none-the-less,
Upon the shoreline of the lake
The waters did caress.
Perhaps it moved some grain of sand,
Or undercut some sod,
Some splash upon the igneous mass,
Unmarked except by God.

Merrill B. Tew

Fountain Of Youth

There is a fountain of youth,
  a power that keeps us young.
It guides us through or life,
  and all we have done.
To obtain this youthful power,
  some sacrifices we will make.
This power plays games with us
  emotions it will give and take.
In order to harness this power,
  all you have to do
Is find that special person in life
  who makes Love feel so new.
For the person which you Love
  is your fountain of youth
And as long as you Love each other
  you'll have everlasting truth.

Michael A. Bodnar

Human Nature

Oh, how I missed the point.
A mistaken reaction
to an innocent request.
I asked for a kiss,
and she said no.
A question she asks
I know no answer,
just only what my heart says.
I am confused,
for truly she wanted a kiss.
What is the point I could have missed?
I go on night and day
to think of a solution.
The dilemma I am in
asking for a kiss.
Then one day, aha
I have an answer
for my spontaneous rapture:
My dear it is pure and simple,
it is called human nature...

Jerry D. Abuan

Fear

Another accident
A mindless right
Another statistic
A killer's delight
A dreaded disease
Takes the pleasure of love
A terrorist's bomb
Rains debris from above
A lightning bolt strikes
In the blink of an eye
A pusher's drug
Takes another to high
A gangster's stray bullet
Brings a mother to tears
It seems the end of life
Is always near
To fear it is understandable
To live in fear of it
Means the end has already come

Paul Geller

Polyphemus

Adrift, amid a summer's breeze
A massive moth flew from the trees

And landed 'side my pale porch light
As softly as an elfin sprite.

He nestled near the window pane;
Polyphemus was this name.

Two shiny eyes shone back at me
While I wondered how it could be

Named for a monster with one eye;
A son of Neptune in the sky?

With sullen beauty and floating grace,
This doesn't have a cyclops' face.

And so he looms and looks my way,
Glaring, staring as if it could say,

"If I'm a monster of myth and lore,
Are you demon from Styx's shore?"

Mark Smith

The Perfect Gift

All my life I've longed for
 a man who wants just me.
I would be his one and only
 for all the world to see.

All my life I've wanted
 the respect that would be there.
From all who got to know us
 they would see the love we'd share.

To me that would be the ultimate,
 the very best gift there is.
I'd give him all my trust and love
 and he would give me his.

Pamela Bruner

A Wedding Wish

On the day that you are wed
A lit candle and a prayer
That the Lord will keep you happy
And safe within His care.

May you both always be as happy,
May all your dreams come true,
May all the world smile with you,
In whatever you both should do.

So, take the leap; say those vows
You've already come so far.
There's so much love to build upon
That no other can unbar.

Michelle K. Rohde

Despair

A darkened gloom so bleak with pity.
A heavy haze over such a city.
Its walls,
So hard ... of steel and stone.
So many people ... so all alone.

It jagged facets give no love,
As people hurry, push and shove.
A scream...
In silence of darkened night,
As one stumbles and others fight.

It's a sadness that breaks my heart,
To see another fall apart.
To look,
Not at the jagged skies,
But deep within my brother's eyes.

What once was light now falls with rain.
Love replaced with twisted pain.
There is no hope residing there ...
Only anger, frustration and
Despair.

Jonathan M. Sallo

"Overcome, Peace, And Unity"

Have we really overcome?
All the hatred and anger is still there.
Peace!
Is peace the answer?
Or is the answer unity?
How can one be in unity with
others and can't find peace
within himself?
Have we really overcome?

Ni-Kisha Moore

Caged Bird

Trapped in body,
a free spirit ready to soar.
Trapped in the cage,
ready to fly away
soaring above treetops,
everything below
small, insignificant.
Freebird gliding
through the blue sky!
Reach the sun,
through the light,
the energy burning,
nothing is left.
The body vanished,
the spirit in a resting place,
a peaceful universe, stands.
Reality strikes hard,
the body, the cage,
a home but nowhere to go!
Caged bird, alive but dead.

Marisa S. Volpe Bolton

A Dog Named Sheeba

I had a dog named Sheeba
a feisty dog was she
Sheeba would run after anybody
who even came near me.

I've had her now for eight years,
her health is diminishing
and you can see the tears
from the pain from within.

How do you tell the kids of your own
that the time has come
That God needs to take your dog
to heaven, his home.

We have one dog left
Katy is her name
She was Sheeba's best friend
and always willing to play a game.

Sheeba may have been just a dog
but to us - she was part of the family
She is gone, but not forgotten
Her memory still lives with us.

Patricia Ann Sulcs

Hosannas for H-E and R H_ _ _ _

Fifty years wed!
 A feat for how few!
1938 when dewy intent
 Helen-Ed and Robert vowed.
Two then though one in much
 began the strains of the yoked:
earlier understandings in question,
 assumptions, bared, in conflict
fluxes embroiled as the rest of us
 all managed tamed meshed.
What forbearances! courtesies!
 What silences of the blessed sort!
The solo blind drives bowed
 the paired strengths won
both staunch at the trials
 holding under the blows
to reach at last a serenity
 different for each.
Awed, we salute you!

Mary Arbiter

"Transparent"

Dark, cloudy, gray wet,
A death in every drop,
That glistens on the glass.

Transparent, shapes and sizes vary,
A past in every drop.

Running, sliding aimlessly
To a destiny unknown.
They touch and become one
Millions touch and become one.

Nourishing the earth,
Life comes out of each death.

Some run faster than others
Many wait to be touched,
Before falling hopelessly, endlessly,
And they all become one.

Jill Marie Thompsett

The Conceited Female

She is said to be;
a contrary egocentrical person.
She is, very eager to unfold what's
(meaning) gift wrap...

She is a ballroom singer.
She is perpetual.
She is perfecting because
She is design to
She is fashion.
She is classy.
She takes notice-
She grabs fastly.
The conceited female,
Is mostly likely....
Like I said
She is female-
Conceited.
Like me.

Kathleen Wight

Cut Short

A yard of cloth,
A cloth for the yard,
For the cloth is being cut short;

A minute a mile,
A mile a minute,
For the mile is being cut short;

A board from the tree,
A tree for the board,
For the tree is being cut short;

A blade of grass,
Of grass a blade,
For the grass is being cut short;

A rose from a plant,
A plant for a rose,
For the plant is being cut short;

A minute in a life,
A life in a minute,
For lives are being cut short.

Melinda Scribner

"Me"

The sad face in the mirror
a bewildered look I see.

Not knowing the future
or what to believe.

Loving the present
that I am so scared to leave.

Yet knowing to advance
I must depart not retrieve.

Hesitant to take the first step
I wearily proceed.

With only one step forward
I feel the vines that cling.

Strip and tear at my soul
as I struggle to leave.

For the next step taken
is toward my very being.

I linger at each stride
so I can truly see

The progress I've made
and who is really me.

Nicky Stockton

The Genetic I

There I dangle
A bead at the end of DNA.
Ordered,
In life's tangle.

Microscopically speaking,
I am elaborately cross linked.
Fixed, for a generation.

Destiny's spiral
Is a germinal helix.
Mutated, for my child's chance.

The essence of passion
Is a unique chromosomal matching.
Fused, your only heritage.

Nature's gamble
This wondrously random combination
Governs our biologic future.

There I dangle
A bead at the end of DNA
Re-ordered,
In life's tangle.

Murray R. Blair

"If"

If one hath intelligence, wealth,
And knowledge, but they hath not
love,
    They are but am empty shell.
    If one hath pride, but lacks
humility,
    They are lost in self esteem
If one gives nothing of himself.
But takes all, they
leave nothing to posterity.
    If one loves God and
helps his fellowmen
His is an image to follow!

Mrs. J. R. Pelles

the mask

A piece of invaluable material
used as a shield for protection
a wall to hide behind
a strong and powerful weapon
strong enough to shelter the
deepest emotions
powerful enough to shun the
softest touch
deadly enough to ruin the
most reputable character.
The smallest flaw can be tragic;
just big enough for a ray of light
just small enough to go undetected
only to be conquered by
the unstoppable hand of time
the unforgettable touch of love
the undeniable presence of truth.

Kerrie Ann Tinelli

The Always Diet

Just a dab of this and a dab of that
Too much you know will make you fat
There's one person I just hate
The one who says, "You're gaining weight"

Six months have passed
I'm off my diet at last
I step on the scale
Then let out a wail

Every day I've pained
But five pounds I've gained
I'm still big and round
That fat keeps rolling around

Bill Horewitch

"Maze"

The maze of life I have walked through
Traveling roads in the sky and ships that
have sailed the tides...

Remembering paths I have taken wondering
when? I'd awaken...

Going through valleys, hills, and streams
Life to me is still a dream...

But when I awake in a land beyond I'll
Remember the ball of earth I was on...

And in the silence of my thoughts I'll
Remember the maze I had walked...

Diana Mitchell

Humble Pay

Smile and smile and light the way
Turn someone's night back into day

Do these things of simple truth
And love shall be your humble pay

Hold the hand of someone falling
Soothe the cry of someone calling
Grasp their fear and hold it tight
Bring some sun to light their night

Listen close to what you hear
Touch a face and dry a tear
Spread some hope along the way
and love shall be your humble pay.

Judy C. Komula

Interlude

Hush!
Trespass not the current PEACE
Do not breathe your thoughts
Let not a single word escape
while the water
lies placidly like this.

Let your mind manifest,
And within meditate
That the soul of the sea
No doubt is the Lord
No ripples — no stirring discord.

Imagine with me
That the globe has stalled
The silence prevails for miles and miles.

Unseal your since long
Concealed secrecy
And share utterly
Your soul's diary
This moment with me — This NOW...

Annemarie Viglione

The Two Of Us

Here we are, the two of us,
Trying to make it through each day
With all the trials and tribulations,
The debts we all must pay.

But someday we'll rise above all this;
Forget this dreary summer night.
We'll rise to greatness and in our wake
They'll cower from our might.

We'll escape this horrid world,
And linger in the mist.
And cry for those who stayed to die
Beneath the clenching fist

Of conformity and material rule.
We'll pity those too blind to see
They only played the fool.

But for now,
Here we are, the two of us,
Just trying to make it through.
And we'll succeed someday, somehow.
Together, we'll make it through.

Julie Wheeler

That Little Boy Of Mine

A tiny turned up nose,
Two cheeks just like a rose,
He's sweet from head to toe's,
That little boy of mine.

Two eyes that shine so bright,
Two arm's that hold me tight,
Two lip's that kiss good night,
That little boy of mine.

No one will ever know,
Just what his coming has meant,
Because I love him so,
He's something heaven has sent.

He's all the world to me,
He climbs upon my knee,
To me he'll always be.
That little boy of mine.

Ethel D. Hardin

Choices

Left or right,
Two different ways.
            One is here.
One is there.

If there is a fork
in the road,
Which way should I go?

When I am writing,
with a pen or pencil
What hand should I use?

Left or right

So many choices in life.

    What should I do?
    Left or right.
        Christina Posch

Two Hands

I looked down and saw my two hands,
Two hands that no one could understand.
Why had I been given this fate?
That no one could appreciate,
Not even the owner of these two limbs.
Life wasn't fair, future looked grim.
Inconveniences filled my waking days,
And made me feel like a castaway.
I was shunned to another place,
And left, alone, to live in disgrace.
If I could tell, I would tell all.
But only these hands will ever recall,
The things I think, the things I say.
But I will continue on this way,
For I have been dealt hands of fate.
A fate I've learned to appreciate.
        Jamie Childs

Fear

In the dark silence U are alone.
U are afraid of what isn't and what was.
Unsure of what will be,
and what could've been.
U become insane from not knowing
what to think.
U hide, but from what U do not know.
U runaway afraid to look back,
afraid of what U might see.
What U cannot face is a fear in
which U created, one that does not exist.
But one U believe to be true.
        Brenda Jhon Stone

Day Dreams

Day dreams of you and me
Under the tall pine trees
Wishing you were here, and
Wanting to hold you near
The way you hold me, and
the way you kiss,
The special way you love me
Is truly what I miss
Though our time together
Is far and few between
Nothing can take away
My precious day dreams
        Ellen Merrick

Don't Wait

Don't wait until tomorrow or
until I'm gone to say sweet
things about me, I would
rather hear one kind word
said today, than have a
book full read when I'm dead.

Don't wait until I'm gone
and give me a truck load
of flowers, or showers of love
that I cannot see or feel,
I would rather have one
little rose while my nose
can smell it, and once
Kind word while I can hear it.

How much sweeter would life be,
How much more would one give, or
How much longer would one live if only
some love, some kindness, and
Some appreciation were shown today.
Don't wait until tomorrow it may be too late.
        Annie K. Ross Perry

Die

Die, die makes you fly
up in heaven in the sky.
People who die, just like me
All you can do is pray for thee
People who die make us sad.
When we hurt it feels so bad.
God helps them every day
If you know one, just pray
If someone close has died
Please go ahead and cry
Dry your eyes
It will be alright
Pray is all you can do
If you do, they'll be happy like you.
        Jacob Schofield

Clouds

As I lie upon the grass and gaze
up into the soft snowy haze

Pictures there are to me revealed
that before today have been concealed

A large white vessel floats leisurely by
upon the waters of the deep blue sky

Alas, the sun comes peeking 'round
and spoils the wonders I have found

But I shall plan to come each day
and watch new wonders on display.
        Charlotte G. Ianni

About Being a Doctor

I asked him, then,
what appealed to him
about being a doctor. He said,
"It's good, sometimes,
to confront the reality of death."
"Really," I said. "And,
do you do that? Do you
confront the reality of death?"
"No," he said,
"no, I don't."
        Di Starr

"I'll Miss"...

So many sunsets I shall miss,
    upon the town in which I dwell.
No more starry skies at night,
    for which my eyes have fell.

The sweet aroma of the spring,
    which I shall smell no more.
The rosy cheeks of a paper santa,
    at christmas, hanging on my door.

All these things I will miss,
    when my life is through.
But most of all my love.
    the thing I'll miss is you.

Will anyone really miss me,
    when I'm finally gone?
If only one person remembers me,
    my memory will live on and on.
        Dorothy Barnwell

Untitled

Decisions
Values to choose
Dreams to lose
Opinions you hear
Your own not clear
The one you love
God above
What would they choose
To win or to lose
So hard you have fought
But in the madness you are caught
Choose good or bad
To be happy or sad
What will you do
Just to make it through
In a world full of decisions
Not easily made...
        Denyel O'Brien

If You Believe

The time has come to choose your path
Walk straight ahead with guard and staff
Do not stop to look behind
For stumbling blocks is all you'll find.
Push aside your envious thoughts
Love who you are, not who you're not
Grasp your dreams and make them real
Let no one change them, shrink, or steal
For God has given to us all
A heart and mind to stand up tall.
Look in the mirror and you'll see
The greatest miracle, if you believe.
        Jamey Wood

My Baby's Gone

In a cradle rock a bye
walking, talking, by my side
Gone to school.
That's the rule,
Carrying books in her hand
No more playing in the sand
Met a boy what a joy
Getting married
His name is Ron
My Baby's Gone
        John Guadagna

Here Then Gone

Life with you here
Was filled with many dreams
There was never any trouble
Or hate it seems

Tender, loving words
It was you who spoke them
Your caring, sharing, and kindness
Was strong as a stem

You brought out the sun
And tears in every way
Your gentle hands touched the sad
Each and every day

Your memory stays
In each and every heart
When you gave us hugs goodbye
We knew to depart.

Bob Randl (10/18/78 - 9/19/93)
Adam Buechel (3/31/79 - 9/19/93)
Heather Hahn

Untitled

Some of that sweet joy
    was very beautiful
The love of girl and boy
    The pure of life's flow.
The song of the Robin in spring
    The mournful cry of the love
Called life to return again
    With the joy of love.
Its like the soaring eagle
    Over mountains and trees
I feel it where I go
    It is enshrined in these:

Music and beauty and tears
Rapture and laughter and fears!
Eunice M. Shoops

When My Heart Cries

Sitting at the beach watching the
waves come ashore, thinking of you and
All the time we shared the excitement
and the love that we shared together
When my heart cries

I recall just the sound of your
voice brought chills over my body so
I'll linger at home watching the phone
When my heart cries

Remembering our exotic love making
brings tears to my eyes as I look
over my shoulder and you're not there
When my heart cries

The day you walked into my life
you brought me joy, happiness, love and
fulfilled my every most fantasies

The night you walked out of my life
you took a part of my heart that
will never be replaced
When my heart cries
Elizabeth Hopper

"Life's Way"

Timing is life's way.
Way of life is timing
Decisions, futures based on time.
Time to make mine

Dollar drafts, plenty of laughs
Buffet blaring, not really hearing
Thinking of those who past by me.
And of those past to me.

Life can be changed in an instance
Keep your thoughts today
Don't let your present wander away.
Act now! Don't live for the distance.

Remember the words I say
Do what you want, today.
Timing is life's way.
Way of life is timing's way.
Eric Kiggen Hill

Birds

See the birds how smooth they fly
Way up in the sky on high,
Isn't it a blessed thing
To see them with an open wing
Soaring up and down and round
Looking for food upon the ground
The Lord he makes such wonderful things
No wonder a bird just flies and sings
They're glad they're here upon this earth
Where everything's a sacred birth
We all are here this is his will
And yet there is unrest here still
If ever this old world should end
I'm sure it would be heaven sent
So live each day love one another
As you would love a sister or brother
No matter how many years are left
Be glad they all are heaven blessed
Alton L. Blose

Rust, Wrinkles, Pains

Hardened love is home to our likes
we all have some, pain.
Crusty for more reasons than lines
of age we gather some, rust.
Worn specks to glitter the uneven
Edges of, good wrinkles.
Raised bumps for diversion of a
Pulled face, added pains.
Extended cycles of late darkened
Moons, crumbled rust.
Deepened lines of anguish and
Stress, wasteful wrinkles.
Fearful that life is wilting in
fretful ways, evil pain.
More courage is needed, the
Heart has endless chambers of
Rust.., wrinkles..., and..., pains.
John McDowell

The Master's Poet

We are at one, who are we
We are thee
Who speaks, thy Master
Who listens, thy servant
I ask of thee that I may be whole
In my heart and in my soul
And filled with the holy spirit
That I may be as one with thee

And with this gift
I shall use wisely for now
I am a poet that has been filled

With peace in my heart
God in my soul
and Strength in my mind

"With thou I am pleased."
I thank thee for wisdom,
and knowledge, and the strength of peace.

For this I say
That he is me, and I am him
Thy Master's poet
Eric Pruitt

Twilight Swimming

On that early morning we conversed.
We brightened the path for tie's passage
with brief, yet saturated phrases.
Words flowered like silver fish bellies
slipping over stones. Occasionally
one wedged between two rocks until
the pressure built and pushed it through.
Always, they conquered and traveled
to the delta of a soul, lodging
deep in fertile warmth. Seven seasons
passed and still, there were fish left
to sojourn. The fathoms between us
tired them and slowly, beautifully,
the sea filled with silver fish bellies
turned to the brilliance of the sun.
Soon only two were left, and so we
named them freedom and growth. We cast
them, preserving a time when small silver fish
danced gracefully between
two deltas.
Angela Beauchamp

On the Road We Travel On

On the road we travel on.
We must continue though it's long.
There may be dips and bumps and cracks,
and strenuous things that break our backs.
But we must continue on and on.
Down the road we travel on.

Through the years we keep from falling,
but no one is listening to our calling,
and as we walk we hold our head up high,
trying to reach the great blue sky.

And though we may age and age and age,
we still feel locked up in a cage,
And when you die,
you touch the sky,
and you look behind you,
and see what you've been through,
and it doesn't look bad,
in fact you're sad,
that you are gone,
from the road you've traveled on.
Diana Manriquez

The Seasons

As the summer sun shines upon us.
We suffer from its heat:
We enjoy a nice sun tan.
And walk in our bare feet:
To wish that winter comes again.
to feel its cool breeze:
We walk around with nothing on:
and then we start to sneeze:
Does Man know what he really wants:
Or his life just that way:
Did mother nature give us seasons.
just to make man pay.
To pay for all that man has taken.
from this beautiful earth:
for all the sins stored upon it:
From the beginning of its birth.

Andrew Malato

The Edge

On the brink of humanity
We teeter
As if on a see-saw of decision
Not acknowledging that we're scared
And scared
Of what we refuse to comprehend
And as focus and command
Leave our grasp
We strive to find
Our true selves

Dawn Haeneit

Untitled

What is a sign, for who is to judge

I just don't understand
We think that we know everything
but we are all just man.

We know not when the time will be
yet many do proclaim
Year in, year out "Our Saviors Come,
Christ has come again!"

But through His eyes He beckons us,
"please don't be afraid.
And do not try to rule the world
that I alone have made
Beware that one day I shall return,
but you shall not fore See.
For I alone know the time
my children will be free."

Juanita Marie Strickler

Words

Most come from our emotions
we throw to the dust,
In all shapes and meanings we
talk, talk, talk...
I hear them for a moment and
then they're gone!
I can't always grasp each one.
some are really keepers,
some are none, some caresome,
some are cold, some warm.
Some I write, some I store, others
are just lost in time.
They approach me from others and
get mixed up with mine.

J. Holder

Untitled

If, throughout the year
We would show
The "LOVE" of CHRISTMAS
As we go.

Instead of Waiting
Until now
To show each other
The "WHY" the "HOW"

We really CARE
Not just in this SEASON
We truly show
JESUS is the REASON!

Let's try to show it
DAY by DAY
At WORK, at HOME
And at PLAY

For those at HOME
And those 'round HERE
Let's make CHRISTMAS
Last all the YEAR!!!

Erma J. Brumley

Moment In Time

For just us
We wouldn't notice
What is happening
May never again
We are alone
Two of us
Taking the time
Doing with it
What we can
For a moment

Donald M. Spangler

"Weaving Baskets"

Meandering through life is like
weaving baskets.
Your life is of your own creation.
What you make of it shall be.

It's true that not all lives
can be woven perfectly,
but no one's life is perfect.

For what it's worth - and how
rare life is to you alone - carry
the fibers and threads of your
existence in one hand, while
holding on to me with the other.

You're important to me, and
weaving through life is only
complicated when you have to do it
alone.

Brenda Lee Coons

Pulsations

Can you feel your heart a beatin'!?
What from?
Stroke of genius,
feeling under the gun?
More Y-T-D per EKG
pointed-finger palpitation?
Or just the sudden realization,
that the plastic heart meld,
held?

Daniel P. Hill

Beware!

In the morning,
Well after ten.
At the office,
Surrounded by friends.
I'm not very social,
Instead rather lofty;
Until I've consumed -
My eighth cup of coffee.
I know it's been said,
By others not me:
That I'm not human,
During those hours, you see.
So wait if you can,
Say hello at eleven -
It's hellish before,
But then, it's heaven!

Don Means

He Was A Simple Man

He was a simple man,
Well mannered and bred.
To all who dared to be his friend.
And loved ones, he shared his all to
them.

The race he just ran is not lost.
But was just won
His reward was sleep. A never ending
sleep.
Oh what a rejoicing there will be
if ever his awake.

Georgia Pern

What Happened To The Dinosaurs?

Dinosaurs, Dinosaurs!
What happened to the dinosaurs?
Did they go
Because of the snow?
Did they die
Because the sun made them fry?

Dinosaurs, Dinosaurs!
What happened to the dinosaurs?
Did they disappear
Because of their fear?
Have they vanished
Because they were banished?

Dinosaurs, Dinosaurs!
What happened to the dinosaurs?

Dorothy Hughlett Ethridge

Untitled

Love is...
What is love
so wonderful and true
What is love
does it interest you?

Love is much more
than either I or you will know
Love is a thing
you will learn as you grow.

Love is a lesson
you will have to learn
Love is a blessing
just wait for your turn.

Chrissy Cobb

"Emotions"

In this world so full of confusion,
What is this emotion we call love?
Is it merely an illusion,
Like the magician's dove?
Maybe its life's delusion,
Or a gift from above.
In this world so full of confusion,
What is this emotion we call hate?
Is it merely an illusion,
Like the sorcerer's weight.
Maybe its life's conclusion,
Or simply one's fate.

Bridget Delehanty Lucia

Hurt

When I am feeling alone or blue,
what might you ask do I do?
My emotions can be all mixed up.
I may not cry
And I don't write my good-byes.
Sometimes I get extremely mad,
but I might also get incredible sad.
Though I may shed a tear,
while in pain.
At least it keeps me from
going insane.

Cheryl Patton

This Old House

If this old house could talk
What stories there would be
Of a family filled with love
This family belonged to me

A Dad who labored by the day
A Mother who worked hard and long
But with children gathered round
Their hearts were filled with song.

They were not blessed with worldly goods
Yet they were rich beyond compare
As the children filled with laughter
Gathered round the table there

Now this old house is gone
Both Mother and Dad laid to rest
But the family still gathers together
And the Lord has surely blessed

Annie Smithson

A Fond Farewell

You pushed me away
When I should have been
There. You left me behind,
Not knowing I cared.

You pushed me away
When I wanted to be
A part of your life...
Just like family.

You pushed me away
When I thought I belonged
But as each day passed by,
I found out, I was wrong.

You pushed me away,
And I still know not why
So I guess it be best
If I just say, goodbye

Cathy Bingham

Overdose

I can't think, I can't see,
what the hell is wrong
with me?

I look around with my head
spinning,
Oh my God, this is only
the beginning.
What was I thinking
What have I done?
My only problems have just begun.

I can't sleep, I can't eat,
my hands go numb
now my feet.

I can't see, I can't walk,
sometimes its a pain
to just even talk.

Now it feels like a bomb in my
head.
It explodes, I think I'm dead....

Christopher Zarek

Small And Humble

Small and humble is
what the Lord is all about.
He told the tale of the
mustard seed and the
cleansing of the soul from
the inside out.
Small and humble is
what the Lord is all about.
First we're wrapped
with the Baby in a stable,
drinking milk.
Then we graduate with
God and wear white robes
of silk.

Betty A. Karnstedt Fisher

Words - The Way

Words are to say
What you want
What is the way
I found the way - I found my want

She was eighteen - so was I
Now I am eighty
Where is she now - the one I love

She was my wife
She is my life
She is waiting for me
Soon I will again - find the way

August Metzenheim

"Creator"

Humans.
We are motley characters
Lost in a snow globe
Nativity scene.

The rumble,
shaken too many times
at His celebration.
The powerful
grip of the overzealous child ...
I hear him laughing.

Joel Marinan

Goals

I have uncertainty
When climbing a tree
I am afraid I will fall to the ground
Closing my eyes
Here I go-my best try
Just remember not to look down
Step by step
I go higher and higher
Branch by branch
I'm almost beaming with pride.
The top is so near
Only a few flights away
Looking back there's no fear
I know I can succeed any day.

Erin Domorski-Jones

Sue's Poem

When I feel scared or sad at heart
When I feel sick or torn apart
All around me, in the air,
Close at hand, everywhere
Are angels at my beck and call
To catch me if I slip and fall
I ask for them and they are there
To tend to me with loving care

Some have huge and feathery wings,
And some go 'round in human skin
Some angels can't be seen with eyes,
And some are those I've sat beside
Some angels can't be heard with ears
And some speak the words I need to hear

Truly, I have known the bliss
Of having an angel in my midst
So often words I needed to hear
Came from a voice so sweet in my far
More often than just a time or two
The sweet voice I heard was the voice of Sue.

Brenda L. Kern

Nasturtiums

Nasturtiums were my favorite flower
When I was only five
My Grandma said to keep them picked
To keep new buds alive.

When new blooms burst among the leaves
In colors orange and red
I always kept a small bouquet
Placed close beside my bed.

I'd nibble on the pale green stems
And smell their sharp perfume
But never eat the leaf or flower
I thought that'd lead to doom.

The whole plant now I know is safe
In salads bright and bold
With lettuces and vinegars
And celery, crisp and cold.

But, best of all, I love the scent
They scatter on the breeze.
Nasturtiums, still my favorite,
They never make me sneeze!

Joanne Phipps

Pitt

I met him early in the morning
When it was cool
But bright, and you could see the day.
He helped me see it clearly.
We danced together
And had no trouble enjoying.
Warm, comfortable, happy Light.
But morning passes quickly,

And then...

And now,
He pulls the night up over us
Like a great quilted blanket
Made of the memories of the day
To keep us warm at night.

Harrison Rutter

The Telephone

In the stillness of the evening...
When the birds have ceased to sing,
I sit patiently awaiting... for
the telephone to ring.

Ever conscious of the moment...
When first he held me tight,
I watch the stars ascending...
For their rein throughout the night.
In the hush, long after midnight...
When the city's fast asleep,
I sit with tear-stained eyes now...
My constant vigil keep.

I'm remembering the promise...
He made the night before,
That he would surely phone me...
Upon the strike of four.

In the coolness of the morning...
When the birds begin to sing,
Yet I wait, Yet I listen... for
the telephone to ring!

Bernice M. Winston

Lady

How shall I count my tomorrow's,
When your inestimable blessings are
Rapturous tones of love,
That hold me spellbound in your arms.

My soul, has conceived what my heart
Knew all alone.
And that is! you will never be
Faithful to just one man,

How splendidly beautiful you are,
You move with the grace and agility
of a God!

Your array of beauty render to all
Races, on no terms do you discriminate,

Oh how! Phidias or Michael Angelo
Would have been delighted to chisel
In diamond or marble your noble form.

It is from these thoughts that I find
You most profound, for you are
The most beautiful lady I've ever known,
I shall call you Life..

Joseph Biggs

Dreaming

Dreaming is something to do
when your up in a tree.
Be careful what your dreaming,
just dream about me.

When you fall asleep,
your eyes go round and round.
But when you are dreaming,
your dreams have out-of-bounds.

When you become sleepy,
and your eyes begin to weigh,
Just think about what you have done,
all the time that day.

Dreaming is something pleasant,
when your in a good mood,
Just don't fall asleep,
when your not good.

Aaron A. Webster

When My Tears Fall

My tears fall
When you're away
Knowing you'll call
Still wishing you could of stayed

Remembering how it used to be
Makes me smile
Only wishing you were here with me
Just for a little while

As time goes on
My heart aches
Knowing that you're gone
Makes my heart break

The love we have
Will never die
Remembering what we could of had
When I look into your eyes

Darryl Lemke

Letting You In On A Feeling

Thanks for being there
Whenever I need you.
I know you must really care
To want to pull me through.

When I get depressed
And don't think things are fair.
You help me to express
The feelings I need to share.

You listen at your best
And seem to understand.
You show all your interest
And lend a helping hand.

I have to say thank-you
For being such a friend.
And what I say is true,
We both gained in the end.

Jacquie Spier

It's in the quiet
where all things wait...
Hopes and dreams
one's future, fate

Voices stilled
a solemn hush
No forced hand
to pull or push.

It's in the quiet
where life begins
What we are
and where we've been

Sights unseen
by human eyes
Show themselves
without disguise.

It's in the quiet
where vision clears...
Let's one see
beyond the fears.

James F. Banar

The Dry Falls Of The Cullasaja River

I stood beneath your mighty falls,
where Indians once had stood,
I listened to your mighty roar,
what tales if you just could!

I felt your mist of waters fresh,
I tasted as I paused;
I heard your guests from distant lands,
and watched them as they paused.

The air was sweet beneath the falls,
your waters purified,
The rocks were slick, I watched my step,
and I felt sanctified,

No man can estimate your price
to mankind now or then,
A priceless gift from God above
no question why or when.

Cathedral of my God art thou,
O Cullasaja! Could
I pray as my forefathers did?
One God! One Brotherhood!

Esther C. Cunningham

Upon A Butte

Tall trees loom
where no man
stood
nor grasped a better
sight of thee,
and tonight
I lay beneath this mighty tree
four-hundred and reaching,
wrapped in a quilt
that befriended me,
I stare up belittled
by your enormity
and wish that my
mortality
could only see
deep into thy history.

Jamie Flolid

Untitled

We'd play across the moonlit waters,
    Where reflections are so clear,
    We'd dance the fairies dance
The one which is so dear
    We'd long for the dream
    To ever end,

To last throughout our nights
    To keep and never lend

We'd ask the sky's to join in
    With an open hand

To race across the world
    Yet never touch the land

Our minds how they wonder
    And sometimes make us fear
    That all may be forgotten
    In the passing years

So in these days I let you know
    The feelings are deep and constantly flow

The heart and mind they seem
To conspire - to let me know It has been you
I desire.

Hadidjah Holland

Birdland Place

I have a place
Where the birds call home
There they fly high or low
Options to nest or roam

A natural setting -
My house with yard
Arboretum midst open fields
Back away from the street and guard

Sights and sounds are varied
Bright colors and dark
Just the caw or sweet melody
Almost like government park

Their ways are so winsome:
Friendly and quick to respond
Birdbath - feeders - houses
Of each one I really am fond

Every bird has its name,
Its song, and special ID
Watch and listen -
Learn personality!

Bernadette Sievers Gannon

Mother

She always came a-running
    when we cried out in the night.

Her gentle hand and tireless love
    would soothe us 'til the light.

She taught us pride and courage
    and to care for one another.

We loved her then,
We cherish her now,
This woman we call
Mother.

Gary A. Adams

Untitled

I found your eyes on the horizon,
where the sky met the ocean
when the mists lifted;
in the faintest cirrus,
the highest wisps of the heavens;
in my memory of still mornings . . .

I have found your eyes reflected
as the skies in the water:
I look beneath the surface
to see myriads of fish swarming
in the midst of clouds . . .

Trying to remember their color
I find it meandering through my past,
informing me, noting as marked pages
mystic images that remain
of walking and times alone,
when not even a breath of wind
ruffled the surface of my inland lake.

James Thatcher

Our Christmas Adventure

Let's take an adventure, just you and me.
    Where watchful eyes might fail to see.

We'll upon our favorite chair,
    and open our book to everywhere.

Now close your eyes....let's drift away,
    off to the North Pole, we'll go today.

Hear the jingle of Christmas bells?
    And the chatter of the elves?

They're all busy making toys
    for good little girls and boys.

Look at the reindeer resting in the hay.
    They're getting ready for the big day
When Rudolph will lead Santa's sleigh.

Over the roof tops they will go;
    traveling through the wind and snow.

Then down the chimney Santa will come.
    Leaving gifts of love for everyone.

Close up the book, it's time to go.
    Aren't you getting chilly out here in the
snow?

Joan Ulam

So Close, So Near

The suspense is building
While my heart is pounding
What did I do with it?
Where did I put it?
I know I had it
I know it's here
My trouble is finding it
So close, so near
I open my book
For one more time to look
And ...
Phew, I found it
So close, so near
Now that I found it
So close, so near
I won't have to use my excuse
That it was eaten by a bear.

Heather Little

Waiting for the Magic

I'm waiting for snow to come
whirling past the window
jitterbugging while smoking
and drinking whiskey from the
wild turkey bottle, with the label
peeling off from the moisture.
A fire place burns
filling the room with warmth
I drift into slumber
on the tan, red, and gray rug.

The bony kitten wakes me
with mews of hunger
ribs a slinky under
his dirty yellow coat.
Coffee steams
in the cold kitchen
with its large dark table
outside the snow is falling.

John L. Opskar

With; in the Living Trees

Something in the living trees
Whispers to me deeply
Standing there so all alone
locked within a space.

Something in the living trees
Pleads to me desperate
Swaying in the gentle breeze
dancing on a limb.

Something in the living trees
Questions to my soul
Why does man disrespect us
burn and trample me.

Oh something in the living trees
Somewhere deep inside
A living purpose a fragile thing
in the living trees.

Something in the living trees
Staring thru my window
Seeing all my darkest fears
within the living trees.

Clarence E. Lippard

Autumn Leaves

Twisting and turning, earthward bound
Whistling and churning, spinning round
A gentle breeze to whisk them on
And then, again, they're earthward drawn.

Oaken brown and chestnut red
Scarlet and garnet, maples bled
Curled and dried and laid aground
Beauty, peace and sleep abound.

Sullen still and quiet creeps
Where this earthly beauty sleeps
From out the hills, a breeze's call
And sleepers quickly rouse and fall
In dance and merriment.

Ann S. Gray

Journalism

Who comes first?
Who comes last?
Who comes between
That goes so fast?

What is the moon?
What is the star?
What is the come?
That sails way afar?

Where comes the rain?
Where comes the snow?
Where comes the wind
That makes it blow?

When is the beginning?
When is the end?
When is the middle
That causes the blend?

Why comes the Spring?
Why comes the Fall?
Why comes the Winter
That ends it all?

Heidi M. Fisher

Two Ends Together

You are the sun
  who rises each day
To bring new light
  upon the land, so they say.

I am the moon
  who guides thee through the night
To let one see
  evil they must fight.

As you rise,
  I fall.
I come the skies,
  you with draw.

At separated ends we sit
  connected only by reason.
We go as we must
  day by day each season.

Only so often
  will we ever cross paths.
This, where we meet,
  we will finally share a laugh.

Jaime Atherbery

Rescue Mission Man

A multitude of faces,
Whose names I do not know...
All walks of life before me,
younger than before.
Reconciliation,
is in the Father's plan,
for the last, the lost...
the rescue mission man.
A mission of mercy
to bar the gates of Hell
A light in the darkness:
"Jesus Never Fails"
Reconciliation
is in His father's plan,
for the least, the last, the lost...
the rescue mission man.

Donald K. Lefevra

My Mother, My Friend

You are not just someone
Who will love me till the end
You are not just anyone
You are my best friend.

A friend who stood close by me
And tried to guide me through
A friend who tried to make me smile
When I was feeling blue.

Sometimes I often wondered
Why you stuck around
And why you always picked me up
Every time that I fell down.

The hurting that I caused you
The sorrow and the shame
It's to late to say I'm sorry
But I'm sorry just the same.

I Thank you for believing in me
I thank you for all you do
But most of all, I thank God
For a mother and friend like you!

Gerri Lynne Galo

Day Dreaming

If I were not me,
Who would I be?
Would things be different
Than what I now see?

Would the sky be more blue
Through other eyes?
Or the sun feel different,
In some other guise?

Would I be wiser?
Kinder deeds done
If I changed my form
From this to that one?

The world will be better
I know you'll agree,
When I find the way
To be happy, as me.

Elva R. Jones

Solitude

What is life
Why are we put through strife
Must keep spirits up
Never to fall down

Move thoughts inward
Look at yourself
But through another set of eyes
See yourself in a new light

See things a whole new way
What else can you say
We are put here for a reason
How do you see yourself

I see pain and solitude
Deep within myself
For reasons unknown
I am alone

A thing that can be changed
Loneliness is not prearranged
It is not chosen
One lives it for lack of another way.

Christopher Beaumont

Why?

Sometimes I sit and wonder
why fish swim - or why birds fly?
I haven't found the answer.
Sometimes I sit and wonder
how I could have friends -
or how the ocean roars?
I haven't found the answer.
Sometimes I sit and wonder why?
Why do I wonder
When I never find the answer?
When I never search hard enough,
Or just... enough?
Then I found the answer.
I wonder too much.

Amber Atchley

"Riot"

Happy shoppers, chatting tourists
Window talks as well
Crash
Says window
As rock hurls self through

Shoppers shouting, tourists crying
Excited in my head
Guilt
For excitement
Just as anger causes fear
Riot

Dean Simakis

Man Who Had No Face

There once was a parade
With a man who had no face
It was his funeral march
Many laughed. Spit and scorned
At the man who had no face
He had been hurt more than most
His very soul was torn by them
He was a man of great love
But they killed his will his body
They could never kill his spirit
Of the man who had no face
He shed many tears not for himself
But for the poor and sick
They needed love and peace
But the others did not
So they killed the man who had no face
His body they broke
His mind they tortured his will they stole
But his soul they could. Could not take
From the man who had no face

John E. Thompson

Friend

A friend is someone
  with whom you share
    someone there,
    someone to care.
A kind word they always bring
good love, good times
  they always sing.
In good and bad
  they are there
for it's someone to hold
  and someone to care

Jennifer Dodson

Diamonds of Love

Please don't shower me
with diamonds for show,
Emeralds and rubies
that may lose their glow.

Rather give me the things
of which you're a part,
Love and understanding
from the depth of your heart.

Let me always enjoy
the smile on your face,
Be my karat of happiness
that no gem can replace.

May our lives be jeweled
in peace of a dove,
As we walk together
in Diamonds of Love.

Gloria C. Sutton

Air War

Jungle boots in alien juxtaposition
With impotent riveted shields.
Rushing spear seeking.

Flight suit soaked in realization:
White strobes, urgent peals,
Rattling pulse portending.

Desperate counters, maneuver calls
To no avail. Imploding shards,
Shattering, taking, rending.

Leagues of air winging, red mist walls
Prevail. Scythe-tipped guards
Of shrouding pall demanding.

Plunging, toppling, footless honor lost.
Inexorable thicket nears.
Refusing, denying, accepting.

Impact. Crushing, meaningless cost.
Sojourning in silence; fears
For those remaining, keening.

Frank Harden

I Wish I Could - I Know I Should

This love I have for you is real
With it I cannot part
I wish I could - I know I should
Take you from my heart

I know my love for you is wrong
But what am I to do
I wish I could - I know I should
Get over loving you

I guess I've loved you all my life
Or that's the way it seems
I wish I could - I know I should
Keep you from my dreams

This love of mine I'll try to hide
But I can't make it go away
I wish I could - I know I should
But I think its here to stay

Jewel Darlene Virden

Uncle Jerry

He Smiles the room lights up.
With knowing me he welcomed
me in his life.
The lost of someone so special
brought us together.
At times when I felt low his
voice alone manage to lift me up.
No matter how much unnecessary
distance I put between us he's always
happy to see me when I regain
my senses.
If I was thinking clearly I would
ask for help instead I choose
to deal with painful things silently
and alone. So please don't give up
on me because I do love you. After
all you are the wind beneath my wings.

Christi Ross

From My Bed Room Window

I saw God wash the world last night
With showers from on high,
And then, when early morning came, I saw
him hang it out to dry.

He wash each tiny blade of grass
And every trembling tree;
He flung his showers against the rocks,
And swept the billowing sea.

There's not a bird, there's not a bee.
That wings along the way,
But is a cleaner bird and bee,
Than it was yesterday.

The white rose is a cleaner white,
The red rose is more red,
Since God washed every fragrant face
And put then all to bed.

Catherine Gurley Godfrey

The Dawn

Another day dawns
With the glow of the sun -
Bright and warm -
Shining its rays down upon us.
The earth awakens from its slumber.

The grass sparkles with dew,
The flowers open their eyes -
Hungry for the light -
Leaning toward the rays around us.
Nature awakens from its slumber.

A chill wind blows
Making music through the trees -
Nature's melody -
It wraps its rays around us.
Wild life awakens from its slumber.

The glory of Nature
As it awakens in the morning -
Reaching out towards the sun -
Eager for the new day.
All awakening from their slumber.

Teri L. Massey

Autumn Regrets

How many times at eventide
With the lamps turned low
  and the windows wide
To catch the last lingering scent
  of the Jasmine tree
Ere summer's spent
Have I thought of thee?

As many times
As the leaves fall slow
  with a graceful flutter
Like scarlet snow
  in the wan, bright sun
A golden day ere winter's begun
Have I thought of thee.

Howard Hinckley

Untitled

Under the huge sprawling trees
with their bright, shiny leaves.
Where the quiet is broken
only when the birds have spoken.
The squirrels in a hurry
their winter nuts to bury
and the little rabbits play
until something scares them away.
This is the home of peace,
to which we must all return
when God has deemed
we have learned all we can learn.

Cecelia Claybrook

Could?

Should I never think to shed a tear,
With thoughts that you might not be near?
To close my eyes of blue, I will
With memories of you and I does fill.
Never could I imagine life not with you,
Though God is the one who knows it true
Cause you and I will make it last,
Like players in a theater's cast.
Drawn, not needing it to find,
The Love, we share, doesn't seem to mind,
The lingering task it looks to hold,
From that time then, until we grow old.

David James Dello Russo

Wrinkles In The Counterpane

A little boy made up his bed
  Without an ugly frown or pout,
It was a rather ragged job
  Till Mother smoothed the wrinkles out.

The rumpled sheets and counterpane
  Are petty things to write about;
One look at them made Father smile
  But Mother smoothed the wrinkles out.

The world is full of rumpled sheets
  And rocky roads, without a doubt
It's good to know there's always one
  Who's glad to smooth the wrinkles out.

David P. Dean

Dream, You're Not

Your impression left,
Without face or form.
Cool emerald eyes,
Hair dark as night.
In my dreams you come,
Yet I wait for you.
My heart aches for your touch.
Remembering sweet, your taste.
I walk the world in search of you.
Close my eyes,
Only to find you there.
Don't let it be a dream.
But, my reality.
Unlock the door, to my insanity,
With heaven near, are you there?
It's hell for me, chained to this dream.
In a crowd I look for you.
Hoping I'll find you there.
To turn only in despair.
Like mist, your gone when the sun comes out.

Edward Holtz

Friendship

How close can friendship be
Without invading privacy?

To want to know one
So deeply
To touch the soul but tenderly.

To freely give and freely take
Confidences, moods, and pleasures.
But not to touch
Nor steal one's treasures.

How to stop an overwhelming need
To know, to know, to know.
Is it wrong to have this need?
Can friendship smother
From a drive that pries?

One seeks fulfillment—
One drinks when thirsty
One eats when hungry
One asks when questions
One needs an answer
How close can friendship be?

Joan K. Smith

Good Little Cupid Valentine

Good Little Cupid Valentine
Wonder all the night
Seeking out young lovers
And urging them to write:
With bags full of sugar-plums
Rose and violet bowers,
Heart, doves, true loves knots,
And lace paper flowers.
Good Little Cupid Valentine,
By the moon's beam
Went seeking out young maidens
And urging them to dream:
With ribbons for their ringlets;
Love silken strings
Orange - blossom posies
And gold wedding - rings.

Diem Nguyen

"The Answer"

My loneliness was like a veil
Worn during a period of mourning.
I wondered if I could ever prevail
And come into the light of morning.

One day the answer sought me
through the pages of a book.
I found the power to break free.
One prayer was all it took.

My life was instantly transformed.
In that moment all became clear.
My mind and heart reborn,
In the Lord's arms I know no fear.

Chasity Brown

Paintings

If I were young, like once I was,
  Would I still play the fool?
  Could I command
  Or understand
The things I learnt in school?

If I could love, like once I loved,
  Would loving now mean less?
  Would I concede
  Or have no need
  For softness and caress?

If I could live, like once I lived,
  Would life now be the same?
  Could I stay young
  Like paintings hung?
  I've only me to blame.

Edward M. Ducko

My Life

To dwell in a cell;
wouldn't be so bad;

But to think of my life;
the way it was then;
is very sad;

He'd call, he'd harass, hunt, and grab;
and then you scream dad;

But it is not the same;
your not playing his game;

Rape!

But what about defend;
I don't want to die;
I don't want it to end,

All that's left is the knife in my neck;
I'm thinking hard I have to deck;

I did what I said;
and now he's dead;

Self defence from the innocent
girl that didn't want it to end.

Donna Falter

Remember

Remember, I am a letter you can
  write, when you feel alone
  and lost in the world that
  surrounds you.
Remember, I am someone you can
  softly turn to when you need
  a friend in the middle of
  the night.
Remember, I am your light when
  you lose your way in the
  darkness.
Remember me, even though we
  drifted a part, I'll always love
  you until the very breath is taken
  from my chest.
Remember me, as I once was not what
  I become for I filled your life
  with sunshine and laughter.

Debra Smith

"Never Forgetting You Dad"

Dad its me, your youngest son,
  Writing you to say
With my heart, I Love you so
  Each and every day.
You made my life worth living.
  And brought me up with pride,
A lot of times I didn't hear
  But you were on my side.
I don't know if you knew it
  But you weren't just my dad.
You were more than that to me
  The best friend that I had.
Now your gone, no longer here
  And though we are apart,
Never once have I forgot
  Your always in my heart.
Even though it's once a year I know that on
this day,
You return for just awhile to read what I
will say.
  I must go and close for now
And thought I shed a tear,
  I love you more than you will know
I'll write again next year, I promise.

Darrell Ward

The Realm

There is a realm with no volume,
Yet is as thick as you and I.

It has no mass,
Yet is filled to the sky.

It has no space,
That we can touch,
But feel,
Deep inside.

This realm is love,
And it fills us all.
No matter how big,
Or how small.

Christopher Austin Galle

Echoes

Some times I hear a voice
Yet it's origin I can not find
Seems to weaken, and slowly fade
Like an echo
In the chambers, of my mind

To fade into a whisper
Like a child's breath
As in sleep
Only to recur, when my thoughts
are aimless, long and deep

And at times when I'm at rest
My mind is quiet and still
The whisper becomes an echo
Some times against my will

As yet my will, has not the strength
For it always yields the way
To a voice that keep coming back
With echoes of yesterday.

Don Richards

Grandmother

Quiet words,
yet powerful.
Spoken with utter love and care.
But none can ever compare
to that word of
"grandmother."
Her summertimes of playful cheer.
Her love, a most powerful perfection.
Starry eyes of tenderness.
Smile of sunny skies.
Broken hearts were always mended
with needles threaded with love.
Her magic could heal a cut
with a single kiss to make it better.
Her warm hugs.
My endless childhood,
with my grandmother.
My memories I shall keep with me.
Lasting forever...

Christy Duhon

Morning

The day begins innocently enough.
You and I linger blissfully
over our morning fare,
stretching the moments before us
as if the very air was in
concordance with some furtive
contract to gainsay advancement.

Unreal city—in lieu of brown fog,
we watch lonely faces
as they stick faster and
faster to the web.

My thoughts swirl beyond
my facile grasp—
but not far enough for
any real satisfaction.
Your eyes betray their
luster lost to daily sadness.
The moment gone, we rise to depart.

Do not ask me why, or even how.
For I can show you only what.

John P. Shields

Haunted Words

"Forgive me",
You asked with such hunger,
Shaming me to give my wheel of scars
A quick turn.

"I forgive you",
I offered all in the same
  soft key.
Your lottery winner gushing
Thanked forgive for the
  painless removal of all scars.

But a dull pang told me
It had only been painted over.

Dorothy Randle Clinton

Mom

You mean more than words can say
You fill our hearts everyday
Words of wisdom you do know
Strength and courage you do show
Always moving without doubt
Always giving and going without
This is what you always say
Where there's a will, there's a way
Your words will always be with us
Even when we make a fuss
And even when we're apart
We'll always love you with all our heart!

Alice K. Monahan

Life

Life, oh how unfair can you be.
You give so much, but take even more.
You give love, joy, and
happiness then
take them all away
precisely when
life would be unbearable
without them.
So, what is left to take?
Nothing, but life
itself and you take that too.

Iris Prieto

A Grandchild

A newborn baby, in your arms,
You keep him safe, from all harm.
Then he bestows a smile on you,
The bond is there, forever true.

He reaches for your hand to walk,
His eyes light up, as he talks.
He comes to you to cure his ills,
A loving grandparent, always will.

A grandchild is a special love,
A cherished gift, from above.

Elaine K. Wyckoff

Untitled

What's an oar without a boat;
What's a song without a note?
What's a wave without the sea;
What's a leaf without a tree?
What's a bird without a wing;
What's a bell if it can't ring?
They are nothing - this is true —
That's how I am without you!

Dorothy Reisig

She Gave, You Took

She gave you all you asked and more,
You led her heart astray,
All she asked of you was love,
But you took her love away.

More honest hearts were never found;
And though her love shone through
Her only dream was to be loved,
But it never came true.

Now she lay, oh blessed heart,
Beneath six feet of earth
She never knew, or did receive
All that she as worth.

She gave all she had and more,
Losing more each day,
Never knowing that you
Were taking her love, her life away.

Jennifer Johnson

You Wait And See

One of these days,
you wait and see,
The time will come for
you and me.
We will be together
once again-laughing
and playing-like we first began.
The time you spent
here on earth wasn't very long
But I know within my heart-
There is a reason that you're gone.
My nights are so long
and my days are too
But I know within
my heart-one of these
days I will be holding you.
So one of these days
you wait and see-
The time will come
for you and me!

Brandi Ramsey

A Magical Land

  Come with me, into the door.
You won't have any troubles anymore;
because we'll be in a magical
land!!! Where lions roar, and birds
go about! In the river you'll find
a trout! There is peace all around!
There's shiny grass on the ground
On, Oh! A magical land! Where
baby deer are being born! On
a rhinoceros, you'll find a horn!
In the magical land!!! If you want,
you can fly! You can even touch
the sky! I never knew you could
do that you'll also find a cat!!! It's
a sparkling place, with everything
you want! In the magical land!

Brittany Stalsburg

My Love

My love for you will never die.
You'll always be in my heart.
We were meant for one another.
Just you and I.

With out you my heart will break.
Nothing or no one could put
the pieces together again.

For I will always love you.
With all my heart.
So all I ask is please
don't break my heart.

So again I say, "I love you."
With all my heart.
For you and I will never part.

Cora T. Padilla

A Song To John

'John Lennon' he said evenly,
you'll be dead
    in five minutes...'
the vicious murder
the broken december
    vortex night
the tired death of a God.
The "ad-campaign for peace"
    done away with
dear, dear John lost
lost, lost once again
"mother, you had me..."
John Lennon was pronounced
dead
on December 8, 1980

Alex Smith

Generations

Mom, can we trade?
Your Beatles
for my
Guns and Roses
Your Volkswagen Bus
for my
4X4 Blazer
Your Marijuana
for my
Crack
Your Pregnancy
for my AIDS
Your Mom and Dad
for my
Father his New Wife and my Half Sister
Your Generation
In exchange
For Mine
What do you Say Mom!
CAN WE TRADE?

Hilary Jeavons

Laney

Giving love is what you do.
Your heart is full,
And you are true.

A true friend to me you've always been—
Sharing, caring again and again.

You love me
And I love you,
But my question is:
Do you love you?
True happiness lies within self.

Keep on loving,
Laney, but please,
Love yourself.

Andrea Cadenhead

I'll Be There

You mean so much to me,
Your love is all I need,
Your friend is what I'll be,
You need help then look for me.

I'll always be your friend,
from the beginning to the end,
I'll stand beside you through it all,
I'm here to break your fall,
My love is what you've got,
and I'm giving it nonstop.

A lie you'll never hear,
because to me you are so dear,
I hope we're friends forever,
to loose you I hope never.

A friend will always listen,
a friend will always try,
you look around and you will see,
that my friendship you will find!

Juliane Milota

The Wolf

It is called the Wolf
your sixth sense
entwined into your soul
as a defense

Confronted by people
you are kind to strangers
and can even sense
the slightest hint of danger

Your whole attitude
reflects this animal
with the survival sense
You're the Being untameable

And for you the Wolf,
there can be no clone
and you stand, live, and die
by instinct alone

T.R.

What Lies In The Future?

What lies in the future?
You're not a kid anymore
You have choices to make now
No one can make them for you
Will you make the right decisions?
And what happens if you don't?

I'm not a kid anymore
My future is looking me in the eyes
Except the eyes of my future
Are shaded, I can not see them
This means I still have decisions to make
Until I make them I will never
See the eyes of my future
What lies in the future for me?

Anita Diniz

My Dearest Son - Tony

I'm proud to be your Mother
You've fulfilled my every dream
From infancy to adulthood
You've made my life Supreme

I felt pain when you were teething
I felt sad when you started school
I felt empty when you married
But from all there came good

Now that you are thirty
And are striving for success
I know you'll have a life fulfilled
And truly Godly Blessed!

Angie Demar

The Ride

Oh what a thrill to pedal my bike,
You'll never know what a thrill it's like,
I go along, swift as a breeze,
I feel it from my toes to my knees,
I never tire pumping along,
Swiftly as I sing a song.
It's a past time full of fun,
Pedaling along under the sun.
Then when it's time to go home,
I'll wait for the next ride,
So again I can roam.

Edith Grosso

Reality

I sat, looking up at the sky;
At first, it seemed so very high,
Untouchable to such a one
Whose weary life was
    almost done.

Suddenly, though, it came
    to me
That there was more than
    I could see,

For vision often misses
    much,
And there is something
    beyond touch
To make Eternity quite real.
God gave the heart power
    to "feel."

Betty Crilley

Prelude to Canvas

Shades of the flower
Reflect the color of her eyes
Long blond hair
Held by a scarf she ties.

Beauty captured by an artist
Enlightens a memory so true
As she gazes upon the mist
Settled on the blue.

A vision of one kneeling in prayer
He blends the heavenly hue
Out of hope and despair
He discovers a talent anew.

The age of innocence
A butterfly in flight
Soft clouds expire
Perfections in the light

A long awaited ambition
Came out on canvas that day
A portrait of his reflection
Displayed in the Spa city gallery.

Harriet J. Warmack

Untitled

Live each day as if
    It were to be your last.
Live, so that those around you
    Will feel touched by your presence.
Live each day individually,
    Do not get caught in traps
        Be your best self each day.
Live each day gloriously, so that
    It will be a happy memory.
Live for the future, not for the past
    For in looking forward
        You grow a little wiser about the past.
Live for yourself, not for others
    So that when you look back in future days
        You can smile, and say:
"I did my best, and accomplished something."

Willie F. Jackson Jr.

I Mean it

*(Dedicated to Sean Dallmeyer, Sarah Haegele
and Mark Polite - my inspirations)*
It's hard to say "I Love you" and mean it.
Knowing that God is up there and seen it.
But I do it anyway because its true.
Because in my Heart is my love for you.
From ashes to ashes, From dust to dust.
through all the pain Heart break & Lust
My love will be here forever for you, Loving
You the way I do.

Amanda Crawford

Spring Memories

    A spring flower sweet as honey,
brings smiles to everyone.
    Helpless as a baby it sways in
the wind.
    It brings a fragrance of a spring
day into the air.
    Bright as a red summer sun
setting, it gives me a small burst
of life, with petals soft as a velvet
pillow.

Rebecca Miller

My Plate Is Full

Food for thought at the brake of day,
A plateful of accomplishments to pave the way

A particular zeal demanded by each task,
Sometimes heralding thoughts of rebellion so vast.

Yet, rejoicing continually with a song in my heart,
Just enough zest to give me a start.

Running smoothly with utmost precision,
Striving to exact perfection in every decision.

Never untimely in any way,
But, just how many hours can you cram in a single day?

Aye, but victory forever to proclaim,
The strength to cope is not mine but in the Victor's name.

So, I praise God for a plate that is more than ample,
And that He has placed me in a family so loved, an example.

Arnold E. Gillespie

A Sparrow Fell to the Ground

One day while I was sitting on the porch just looking all around,
A tiny sparrow fell from somewhere and fluttered to the ground.

I watched to see if it would fly again,
But all its efforts seemed in vain.
Because cruelty of man, its little head was bleeding,
And as I bent to pick it up, his eyes seemed to be pleading.
I gently wiped the blood away, but more just took its place,
Oh, what I felt for this little creature as I looked into its face.
God knew what had happened to that tiny bird,
And its cries of pain, I knew He heard.

So I held his little body and stroked his little chest,
His little heart beat wildly within his tiny breast.
He looked at me, then gaped his last breath,
His little heart stopped beating as he quietly found death.

Rosie L. Buckland

Possibilities

Insecurity on my part delays our initial meet.
To see you after all these months of imagining will be no
easy feat...

Will I measure up to your standards of perfection or become
just another number?
Will you disturb my conjured fantasies or be realized as
my knight in shining armor?

Linda M. Knock

Thanksgiving

Everyday I think and rethink about why I am.
I have chosen to live at Peace.

To be my only one, to live on my own thoughts.
We survive in a world of hypocrisy.

One day we're all WHITE,
the next day we're all black.

One day we give thanks,
the next day we hate what we are thankful for.

So I choose to live my life
with my own created knowledge.
Knowledge that is fabricated from there and here-
Bits and pieces from what good,
Man has done.
And I shall survive on that knowledge
and use it to keep my mortal self strong
until the day I become
One with God
and One with my true Peace.

Joel Cruzada

Death Lives On

Midnight moon shadows outside my door linger,
As silence beckons with a long withered finger.
Such words of death whispered are slowly injected
Alone in a segment of time; my heart so infected.

Run! Run! To the Ocean! I stumble; I kiss his wet lips.
Faint images of him fade with the passing of ships.
My soul melts on his body of silky black sands
I cry out for my love with clenched heart and hands.

A prayer surges through the pores of my skin
My vision is tearing my veins from within;
Blood viciously boils, emotions like lava erupt;
I inhale my surroundings and exhale the corrupt.

When at last I have not a tear left to weep
My pulse beats to the cloud and down to the deep.
Waves whisper secrets with the shy blushing shore
Where fears were emerging only moments before.

My desecrated existence can not be God's will;
Years past the torture this dream haunts me still.
Standing breathless in time, I breathe the air of tomorrow,
Revived by my prayer, I let go of my sorrow.

Lydia Akin

And For That....

Patience is a virtue I have mastered.
I want more than a solitary glance,
And for that, my love, I will wait.
I want more than a lone touch,
And for that, my love, I will wait.
I want more than just one kiss,
And for that, my love, I will wait.
I want more than a single night of passion,
And for that, my love, I will wait.
I want more than simple feelings,
And for that, my love, I will wait.
I will wait my entire life for you.
Even as I draw my dying breath,
I will wait for you to say that you love me, too,
And for that, my love, I will wait.
Patience is a virtue I have mastered.

Larissa L. Simmons

In Memory Of Samuel Evans Sr.

As I heard the news my throat tightened and I prayed
"Let it not be true" as I fell to my knees - I heard a quiet inner
voice say ever so sweetly "Be still"

Pain seething through my soul like a molten rod of steel - all joy in
my heart overcome by the shadow of death - my thoughts raced of past
memories and happier times as the tears trailed down my face.
Again the inner voice "Be still"

I thought "What manner of God has removed this man is his prime when
so many people cherished the essence of his life. Is it the same God
who changed him from a wild-spirited troubled youth into a gentle
loving man. The same Lord that brought him safely home from Desert Storm.

Would I choose that Samuel had never breathed life that I could escape
the agony of his death. Can I elect to praise God for the sweet and
not be willing to praise him for the bitter. I choose to be thankful
that by the death of one man others are wiser, more compassionate and
closer to the will of God.

Thankful that the colors of spring appear more vibrant knowing that
they too shall fade. Thankful that melodies are sweeter as they
release the buried emotions. And thankful that the aroma of life is
more precious, because I will never forget the taste of death.

A new joy and peace has entered my heart knowing that death has no
dominion over Samuel. He now rests in the house of the Lord. Again,
louder and clearer I heard the inner voice "Be still and know that
I am GOD!"

Michelle E. McKinney

Heartache of a Child

Daddy why did you leave me
    without a trace
I tried looking for you but I
    never had the right place.
I was just a little girl daddy
    not even a year old.
I was always there waiting for
    you to hold.
You should've come back daddy
    now it's too late
The emptiness in my heart has
    filled with hate.
I don't love you no more daddy
    you're out of my life.
Does it hurt in your heart
    like the edge of a knife.
It will for a while daddy but
    it goes away.
Just like you did on that cold
    summer day.

Amanda Hughes

Slow Down, Time

Slow down, time. You go too fast
Your yearning for some far-off day
Has seen my milestones slip away
They now lie in the distant past
Where I was young
And life was gay

Your future holds no joy for me
I'd gladly trade it all away
If I could re-live just one day
And know the joy that used to be
When I was young
And life was gay

Barbara Lee Guard

When I Cheat the Devil

When I cheat the devil, there will be laughter
but I will have the last laugh
the devil will be mad as hell
and I will be homeward bound
it's wonderful when all that evil can be outsmarted
and so sad when someone loses
but the devil will be a better person to learn my lesson
and I a little wiser

Richard R. West

Live For Today

Life is too short to live in the past,
The weeks and years go by too fast.
It's said by many to live just for today,
Yesterday's gone, tomorrow may never come your way.

For if you dwell in the past for too very long,
Today's beauty you'll miss and that would be wrong,
Each day is so precious, exciting and new,
New places to go, and new things to do.

But if you keep yourself shut in yesterday,
These new experiences surely won't come your way.
So live each day to it's fullest as if it's your last,
Because life's much too short to live in the past.

Deanna L. O'Rourke

ABBUHL, GEORGIA F.
[pen.] Georgia Abbuhl; [b.] April 18, 1941, Utica, NY; [p.] Gerald and Julia Foster; [m.] Howard Abbuhl, October 17, 1959; [ch.] Dave, Dan and Dale; [ed.] High School Graduate, 2 years Asco Degree Comm Art.; [occ.] Senior Teller and Commercial Loans Person at Local Banking Institution for last 19 years.; [memb.] National Honor Soc. - 2 yrs. President Ordained elder - Presbyterian Church Farm Bureau.; [hon.] Editor's Choice Award - 1994; [oth. writ.] Many poems but none published until 1994; [pers.] My writings are emotion on paper, windows thrown wide on my heart and mind.; [a.] Ava, NY

ABDALLAH, FAREED B.
[pen.] Fareed/"The Nuyorican Morrocan"; [b.] October 24, 1967, Hell's Kitchen, NY; [p.] Abdelkrim Abdallah, Ramona Abdallah; [ed.] Julia Richman H.S., La Guardia College (Cuny) Associates Degree in Liberal Arts.; [occ.] Singer, song writer, I also work for viacom/MGS services, and sony theatres.; [memb.] A.S.C.A.P., Dead End Pub., Nuyorican Poets Cafe, and First Avenue Records.; [hon.] Award for a benefit performance from the muscular dystrophy association.; [oth. writ.] "Crimes of Passion", "Betrayal" the two songs in which I co-wrote and sang with spirit matter on midnight son records.; [pers.] Don't be afraid to follow your dreams because your dreams are a reflection of your self. I have been influenced by the poet/rock star Jim Morrison, and my spiritual brother Andrew Welsh.; [a.] New York, NY

ABED, SADIE ALHANDY
[pen.] Sandy; [b.] February 23, 1912, Michigan; [p.] Abraham and Mary Alhandy; [m.] Joseph, 1936; [ch.] One; [ed.] Three years college; [occ.] Oil painting; [memb.] APOA Member, Detroit Round Table of the National Conference of all faiths.; [hon.] Spelling Champion; [oth. writ.] Poetry; [a.] Dearborn, MI

ABRAHAMS, MITCHELL ROSS
[b.] January 16, 1958, Miami, FL; [p.] Stanley and Bernice; [m.] Never married; [ed.] Art Institute of Fort Lauderdale ASAD - Asso. Science Advertising Design; [occ.] Commercial Artist, Advertising Art Director: Community newspapers; [oth. writ.] I've had 2 of my poems published with the paper I work for.; [pers.] My poetry is me... my feelings and desires... no matter how unconventional. My influences are EE Comings, Shel Silverstein, Rod McKuer, Dr. Suess, Frost and Shakespere. Hope you enjoyed it!; [a.] Miami, FL

ABSHER, PATRICIA M.
[b.] March 5, 1948, Millsboro, DE; [p.] Mr. and Mrs. Clifford Messick, Sr.; [m.] J. L. Absher, September 13, 1992; [ch.] C. Jennifer Jacobs, William John and Kevin Jay Absher; [pers.] As you read my writing, may God bless you.; [a.] Mill Spring, NC

ABUAN, JERRY D.
[pen.] Kazia, Kerasia, Chance Indigo; [b.] October 1, 1970, Philippines; [p.] Rodolfo Abuan, Esper Abuan; [ed.] Kearny High, Mesa College; [occ.] Artist, Musician, Floor Lead at Sea World; [hon.] Honorable mention - Clarement Art Guild 1992, 2nd prize - Symphony Towers Art Competition 1995; [oth. writ.] Chance Indigo Series, Short Stories from Poland, my untitled book of poems; [pers.] You will never know happiness unless you experience sorrow. I am but a simple man who strives for none other than pure happiness. So what I write about most is that human condition called sorrow.; [a.] San Diego, CA

ACKLIN, VIRGINIA LEE
[b.] November 12, 1927, Texas; [p.] Roy Skipper, Margarett; [m.] C. F. Acklin, May 9, 1947; [ch.] Iris Straitt, Dean Acklin; [ed.] Beaumont High, Weatherford College Cloud Croft Art School, 3 yrs. New Mexico; [occ.] Artist - Teacher Antique Dealer and Poet; [memb.] Church of Christ Evans Ron Art Assoc., Morgan Art

Council West Virginia, International Song Writers Union, Nashville, TN.; [hon.] (3) Poems published World of Poetry, (2) Sparrow Grass Poetry forum. Book - Personalities of the South, National Library of Poetry - Outstanding Poets 1994; [oth. writ.] (1) Song Published Record and Tape "Must I Bear this Hurt Alone".; [pers.] I love poetry, it helps me to bring out what's in my heart.; [a.] Berkley Springs, WV

ACOSTA, ANGELO
[pen.] Nero; [b.] April 27, 1979, Mexico City; [p.] Arturo F. Acosta, Virginia Acosta; [ed.] I'm a sophomore in Morton East High School; [occ.] Student; [memb.] YMCA [hon.] Silver Honor citizenship award, student of the month; [pers.] Stay alive don't do Drugs!!; [a.] Cicero, IL

ADAM, JOHN N.
[pen.] Anonymous to all but me; [b.] February 6, 1946, Baltimore, MD; [p.] Lawrence and Jean Adam; [m.] Bernadette A. Adam, May 26, 1968; [ed.] University of Baltimore Class of '68; [occ.] Stock Broker, V.P. Investments Dean Writer Reynolds Inc.; [memb.] NRA Life Member; [hon.] My wife, family and friends; [oth. writ.] Plebe Prayer submitted to the U.S. Naval Academy, May 1994; [pers.] Be true unto one self; [a.] Sykesville, MD

ADAMO, KATHY
[pen.] Kathy Collins; [b.] November 2, 1955, Queens, NY; [p.] Edward and Eileen; [m.] Divorced; [ch.] Eileen and Chrissy; [ed.] The Assium H. S., Plaza Business College; [occ.] Consumer Banker; [hon.] President's List for 4.0 G.P.A.; [oth. writ.] Several poems and a children's story; [pers.] A pen is a tool that can speak for my heart!!!; [a.] Rego Park, NY

ADAMS, DONNA MARIE
[pen.] Mouse Marie; [b.] October 8, 1966, Saint Louis; [p.] Everett A., Joan Marie Hopper; [m.] Mikel Adams, May 27, 1989; [ed.] Meramed Community College, Creative Writing.; [occ.] Mig Welder; [oth. writ.] Town papers, Reader's Digest (QQ); [pers.] Set, Mom and Dad I finally get the last word. I do love you more!; [a.] High Ridge, MO

ADAMS, CHRIS
[b.] March 29, 1968, Boston, MA; [p.] Joseph N. Adams, Jr., Mary B. Adams; [ed.] B.A. in English, Suffolk University, Boston, MA.; [occ.] Writer; [memb.] Sigma Tau Delta; [hon.] Runner-up for "Best Rock Critic", The Noise, 1992, speaker at Sigma Tau Delta National Convention, San Jose, 1990; [oth. writ.] Have been published regularly in several Boston-based music/pop culture magazines and contributed to independent English publications. Have also written several papers on Kerovac and the Beats.; [pers.] A good poem is a yardstick by which we measure our proximity to God, or our distance from it. A great poem is one that closes that gap, at least temporarily.; [a.] Boston, MA

ADAMS, GARY A.
[b.] August 1, 1949, Altus, OK; [p.] W. L. and Ednad Adams; [m.] Karen Adams, July 9, 1994; [ch.] Jana, John, Jason, Jeff and Alana; [ed.] Altus High School, Altus Junior College, Midwestern University, Wichita Falls, TX; [occ.] Owner/Manager of the Sonic Drive In restaurant; [oth. writ.] I keep a personal collection of thoughts, philosophies, emotions and humorous poems.; [pers.] I write for personal enjoyment and emotional release as clearly, completely, correctly and concisely as I can.; [a.] Alva, OK

ADAMS, CRYSTAL D.
[pen.] Crystal Boyd; [b.] May 5, 1971, Nashville, TN; [p.] David N. Boyd, Sheila K. Boyd; [m.] William L. Adams, April 30, 1993; [ch.] Roy A. White Jr., Austin Adams; [ed.] Cheatam Co. High Gwinnett Tech; [hon.] I won 2nd place trophy in a contest of Trevecca Nazarene College for the TNT program; [oth. writ.] I have several

poems collected that I wrote and shared with others; [pers.] Poetry, to me should be stated simply and to the point - there is not a poem I've written, that doesn't have a true, simple meaning to it!; [a.] Suwanee, GA

ADAMS, JACLYN FREEHAUF
[pen.] Jaclyn Freehouf Adams; [b.] March 20, 1983, San Antonio, TX; [p.] Kathleen Adams and Dan Adams; [ed.] Kindergarten through sixth grade; [occ.] Student; [memb.] Blessed Trinity Catholic Church - B. T. Basketball team - B. T. Volleyball team - B. T. Track team.; [hon.] A-B Honor Roll Straight A Honor Roll, Second and Third place High Jump, 1st in the 440 relay; [a.] Ocala, FL

ADAMS, KATHLEEN E.
[b.] August 31, 1942, New Zealand; [p.] Alan and Joan Lowe; [m.] Ralph E. Adams, November 1, 1974; [ed.] T.T.C. (New Zealand) B.A. (Iowa Wesleyan College) M.A. (West Virginia University) Post graduate work; [occ.] 6th Grade Teacher (Ashland City Schools), Golf Course Worker; [memb.] Loudonville Lions, Perrysville Presbyterian Church, Ashland City Teachers, Ohio, Education Assoc., N.E.A., Ohio Conservations and Outdoor Educ. Assoc.; [hon.] Magna Cum Laude (Iowa Wesleyan). Woman of Achievement, 1993 (Ashland Country, Ohio); [oth. writ.] Local poems curriculum education material.; [pers.] I believe in the grandeur of nature and the worth of every person.; [a.] Perrysville, OH

ADAMS, SHEILA
[b.] November 7, 1955, New York City; [p.] Mr. Shelley-Louis Dupont, Mrs. Ruby Dupont; [ch.] Michael R. Dupont, Kenyatta E. Graham; [ed.] Central Commercial High School N.Y.C.; [occ.] Child Care-provider; [memb.] Neighborhood Help Center - N.H.H.C. N.Y.C.; [oth. writ.] 3 other poems written in leisure time at home.; [pers.] Put God first, in all your thoughts and actions and all good things shall come to you! Thank you God!; [a.] Bronx, NY

ADAMS, MELISSA ANN
[pen.] Melissa Adams; [b.] September 18, 1979, Gainesville, GA; [p.] David and Joyce Adams; [ed.] North Hall High School still in school - 9th grade; [memb.] VOCA - School Vocational Club; [hon.] 4th place trophy for vocational mathematics; [oth. writ.] I have many very personal poems no one reads.; [pers.] Poetry is like the human body. You mold and shape it until it's what you like. Put everything you've got into what you believe in.; [a.] Gainesville, GA

AGNAS, CARMELITA LEDESMA
[pen.] C. L. Agnas; [b.] December 28, 1939, Roxas City, Philippines; [p.] Ricardo Agnas Sr., Cristita Ledesma; [ed.] Bachelor of Science in Education, University of San Agustin, Iloilo City, Master of Arts in Teaching, Marikina Institute of Science and Technology, Metro Manila, Philippines; [occ.] Teacher; [memb.] Filipino American Movement in Education; [hon.] Certificate of Merit for Mathematics Instruction, Certificate of Recognition on Teachers' Assessment, U.S.A., Certificate of Merit, Scholarship, Department of Education, Philippines.; [oth. writ.] "This Heart! This Heart" and other poems, "Search for an Identity and People's Power"; [pers.] "Let my teaching drop as the rain, my speech distill as the dew, as the droplets on, on the fresh grass, and as the shower on the herb." Deut., 32:2; [a.] San Jose, CA

AIKAT, ASHA B.
[b.] September 19, 1945, Calcutta, India; [ed.] B.Sc. with Distinction Bachelor of Science degree from Calcutta University of India, with distinction; [occ.] Auditor for Busch Gardens and Tax work for H&R Block; [memb.] Volunteer for (1.) American Heart Assoc., (2.) American Red Cross, (3.) Dogwood Garden Club of Williamsburg.; [pers.] "Each day, Take one step forward, to make this world beautiful in someway"

influenced by 2 great poets: Helen Steiner Rice and Rabindranath Tagore (India); [a.] Williamsburg, VA

AIKINS, ROBERT T.
[pen.] A. K.; [b.] April 19, 1976, Parsons, KS; [p.] Pale and Vickie Aikins; [ed.] Parsons High School, G.E.D.; [occ.] Incarcerated in one of Americas Concentrations Camps.; [pers.] Someone will always be affected because of somebody else's ideas. Being around society's "outcasts" has helped create my bond with writing. Because no one is truly free.; [a.] Parsons, KS

AIMONE SR., WILLIAM F.
[b.] November 6, 1918, Paterson, NJ; [p.] William and Ruth Aimone; [m.] Sabrina Skala, September 19, 1943; [ch.] Patricia S. Critelli, William F. Aimone Jr.; [ed.] B.S. New York University - graduate, Management at Princeton Univ. B.M. University of NC at Chapril Hill; [occ.] Retired - insurance consultant and agency owner; [memb.] Chartered property casualty underwriter (1953 C.P.S.U.) - Fellow Insurance Institute of America (1941 F.I.I.A.), National Assn. of Counter/Intelligence Corps (C.I.C. - Army); [hon.] Captain Army C.I.C. World War II and Korea (1941-51); [oth. writ.] Presently writing family history of Tilton/Antonides/Aimone Sime John Ann William Tilson Lammen with pilarms at Lynn, MA in 1625-30. Including service at battle of Mormouth, NJ in Revolutionary War (1778), No published writings (so far) but have been writing for business pleasure since age 10.; [pers.] From High School French, this idiom: "Ou Bieu - Ou Rien." (Do it well or not at all) this has carried me through successful army and insurance agency business.; [a.] Alpharetta, GA

AKESSON, LA SANDRA YE
[pen.] "Vettie" or "Vettita"; [b.] September 15, 1957, Cleveland, OH; [p.] Marvin and Treavie Wimbush; [m.] John "Frederik" Akesson, December 31, 1994; [ch.] Akia La Saundra Morales and Alexander Simone Morales II; [ed.] John Hay/John Adams High, L.A.B.C., L.A.C.C., Metro C.C., L.A.D.W.P. sponsored training and programs.; [occ.] Assistant District Clerk with Los Angeles Dept. of Water and Power; [memb.] Founder and Director, of dream quest enterprises, Inc./NAACP's San Gabriel Valley - Education Committee Member/Family and Education Affirmation Action Council Member and Founder; [hon.] Merit thru the City of Los Angeles' Productivity Commission/NAACP's Executive Committee/National Teen Patient Winner", Miss Right on" of 1973/I.I.E. Facilitator; [oth. writ.] Several poems published in other books (such as Quill Books 94-95); [pers.] Remember: "Without Dreams, there would be no fulfillment". My soul of ancient is one of romance, love and spirituality. I express these aspects thru music, art work and poetry. I have found my inner self, and she is now happy and complete.; [a.] Walnut, CA

AKINS, BARBARA JEAN
[pen.] Bobbie Wiseman; [b.] February 3, 1963, Memphis, TN; [p.] William Akins, Ophelia Akins; [m.] David Lewis Wiseman, September 6, 1980; [ch.] David Lewis Wiseman Jr.; [ed.] Olive Branch High School, Rutledgo College; [occ.] Train employee Trune Service Parts, Memphis, TN.; [memb.] Church of Jesus Christ of Catter Day saints, womens relief society American Cancer Society, American Heart Association; [hon.] Dean's List, (4) Award of Merit Certificates, one Golden Poet Award from the World of Poetry.; [oth. writ.] Written several poems for the World of Poetry Contest.; [pers.] I feel that if you sincerely and truly love a person, you should tell them while they are alive and well. Don't wait until they get sick and die. This poem is dedicated in memory of my baby David Lewis Jr.; [a.] Memphis, TN

ALATAN, TONI J. K. B.
[b.] March 29, 1952, Hono, HI; [p.] James W. Bradley Jr., La Verne Jean Johnston; [m.] Ernest Alatan, April 5, 1989; [occ.] Pa'u Rider, Pupukea, Hawaii.

ALBERT, JACQUELINE
[pen.] Shanty; [b.] August 2, 1931, Morgantown, WV; [p.] Bryan and Ethel Devsenberry; [m.] Tony Albert Jr, July 3, 1947; [ch.] Robert David, Grandchildren - Jason, Brady, Theana; [ed.] Brevard Jr. College Cocoa, FL, Primary Education Morgantown, WV; [occ.] L.P.N. Charge Nurse Madison Manor Nursing Home Madison, AL; [hon.] A.S. degree; [oth. writ.] Ouill Books, (a) A time to be Free, (b) Going Home, E. Coles, (c) Anthology - Today's Best Poems; [pers.] I strive to maintain an awareness of the post-depression era - not only spiritually but, the family bond that enabled these Americans to survive.; [a.] Harvest, AL

ALBERT, THOMAS WILLIAM
[pen.] TWA; [b.] November 28, 1950, Richland, WA; [p.] William G. Albert, Beatrice M. Albert; [ed.] Downers Grove North High School, Richland High School, J.M. Perry Institute, Columbia Basin College; [occ.] Maintenance Manager Nuclear Power Plant; [memb.] National Management Association.; [oth. writ.] Local newspaper article, several poems, several song lyrics (not shared or submitted for consideration); [pers.] Poetry gives me peace. It's a way of expressing the small part of living that I have so far been able to embrace. There is so much out there that I haven't begun to touch on.; [a.] Richland, WA

ALDAY, JORGE A.
[b.] June 15, 1975, Washington, DC; [p.] Jose Alday, Genoveva Alday; [ed.] St. Ann's Academy, Gonzaga College High School, Boston University; [occ.] Student; [pers.] Thank you God for your blessings, thanks Mom, Dad, and Javi for being everything to me. Thanks to Sean Pete, Fitz, Rob, James, Christina, Sleeper, Matt. "Till the Judgement that yourself arise, you live in this, and dwell in lover's eyes." - Shakespeare; [a.] Boston, MA

ALDRIDGE, CHRISTIAN
[b.] October 4, 1968; [p.] Dr. John William Aldridge, Elizabeth Anderson Aldridge; [ed.] Carnegie-Mellon University, New York University-Tisch School for the Arts, Sarah Lawrence College; [occ.] Actor; [pers.] "Blood should sprinkle me to make me grow" Richard II; [a.] San Francisco, CA

ALEXANDER, MARGARET
[pen.] Peggy Alexander; [b.] January 6, 1944, Dover, DE; [p.] Edward and Virgie Alexander; [m.] Divorced; [ch.] Edward Savin and Fred Savin, Jr.; [ed.] John Bassett Moore High, Delaware State College, Del. Tech and Comm. College - Dover, DE; [occ.] Order Picker for Playtex of Dover, DE; [hon.] Retired from the State of Delaware after 30 years service.; [oth. writ.] Many poems for family and co-workers regarding birthdays, retirement, their life's accomplishments, but nothing ever published. However, I've seen many happy faces filled with delight from my poems; [pers.] In my poems I try to bring out that person's character and how important they are to those around them, just for being themselves. It's my way of rewarding them for being who they are.; [a.] Smyrna, DE

ALLEN, HILLIARD
[b.] 1897, Brooksville, FL; [p.] Joseph Edward and Martha Ann; [m.] Jessie Mae, 1921; [ch.] 8; [ed.] 10th Grade; [hon.] Purple Heart (1918), wounded in action at The Second Battle of The Marne (Chateau Thiery in 1918); [oth. writ.] 20 Poems; [pers.] My father wrote this poem in 1923. I'm putting his name in the space above; [a.] Brooksville, FL

ALLEN, KIMBERLY
[pen.] Thee Gracious Poet; [ed.] LaFayette High - Brooklyn, NY; Center for Media Arts - New York City, NY; [occ.] Singer, songwriter, Kultural Designer-Tailor, New Afrikan Writer; [memb.] Caribbean - Afrikan Unity Org.; [hon.] Allah School in Mecca Award, Capt. Brooklyn, NY Division, Harlem, NY Division; Fruit of

Allah 1989-90; [oth. writ.] Prose poetry published in "Urban Scientists - CA," local newsletters, essays - "The Word" - Brooklyn, NY, short stories and seeking publication for three books of prose, poetry, essays, and songs book.; [pers.] The reward of a real poet/writer is to "touch" the soul. This is all I strive for, to open the sacred immortality of love [of knowledge].; [a.] Brooklyn, NY

ALLEN, MELISSA
[b.] January 15, 1981, Winnipeg, Canada; [p.] Robert Allen, Shaiba Allen; [occ.] Student 8th Grade Madison #1 School, Phoenix, AZ.; [hon.] Principal's List, Madison #1 School; [a.] Phoenix, AZ

ALLER, JAMES S.
[pen.] Jim Aller; [b.] December 31, 1950, Royal Oak, MI; [p.] Harry Aller, Ruth Aller; [m.] Caroline Aller, November 21, 1972; [ch.] Emily Aller, Jenimae Aller; [ed.] Galesburg High School, Lincoln Barber College, Dept. of Corrections Training Academy; [occ.] Correctional Officer, Western IL. Correctional Center, Mt. Sterling, IL.; [memb.] Non-Denominational Christian Convention Grounds; [oth. writ.] One poem published in a small town newspaper. Have recited my poems at two funeral services. Have written some spiritual hymns.; [pers.] I try to reflect in my poems the proper way the Bible teaches us to walk as Jesus did on our journey towards eternity.; [a.] Mount Sterling, IL

ALLISON, EURIE L.
[b.] July 21, 1919, MS; [ch.] Carlene ("Susie") Brunt; [ed.] High School grad., one year college; [occ.] L.P.N. until retirement; [memb.] Ladies Aux. of VFW W.O.M. - Eastern Star. Member Lake Harbor Baptist Church.; [oth. writ.] Enjoy cartoon drawings - limericks. Song writing, for my own amusement and personal satisfaction.; [pers.] Seventy five years old, Retired - past time writing poems, Easy way to express my thoughts, feelings.; [a.] Brandon, MS

ALVI, WASIMA ENVER
[pen.] Gul; [b.] July 20, 1961, Lahore, Pakistan; [p.] Mian Enver Saeed Alvi, Surraya Alvi; [m.] Major Agha Ali Imam Naqvi, January 28, 1993; [ch.] Nader Ali; [ed.] Indiana University, IN - MS in Special Education. Punjab University, Pakistan - MA Secondary Education. Kinnard College, Pakistan - BA. Cathedral High School, Pakistan - Metric Certification. CA. Community College Credentials for Instructor and Service for develop. Disabled.; [occ.] Consumer Service Coordinator and Qualified Mental Retardation Professional.; [memb.] Islamic World; [hon.] 1984-85 Scholarship award for studies. 1993 Program Director/QMRP for 91 bed facility for develop. Disabled, 1986 IU Grad. Student Senator, IU Pakistan, Student Assoc. Vice President, 1980 Pakistan National Women Guard - Platoon Commander.; [oth. writ.] Several poems in English, Urdu.; [pers.] Be what you can be and not less and let be the next generation what they can be and more.; [a.] Ontario, CA

AMES, MICHELLE
[pen.] Shelly Ames; [b.] October 17, 1978, Salem, OR; [p.] James Ames and Sandy Bilbery; [ed.] Sophomore at Billings West High School; [occ.] Student; [memb.] Billings West High's Chanteurs, former member of the Laurel High School Debate Team; [hon.] Honor role student, United States Achievement Academy National Awards; [oth. writ.] Other poems and short stories none published; [pers.] I believe that life's too short to sit and wait for thing to happen. I've been very influence by my God friend Helen Todd, she rest in peace.; [a.] Billings, MT

AMISTADE, SHIRLEY P.
[b.] July 16, 1938, New Brighton, PA; [p.] Elsa and Carl Philipp; [m.] Gerald, May 26, 1973; [ed.] Graduate of New Brighton High School class of 1956 - attended Geneva College; [occ.] Clerk for a Utility Co. for 39 yrs.; [oth. writ.] I am trying my hand at writing my first children's book I have written many poems but this is the first time I have submitted one for publication.; [pers.] I am an avid reader. I love to cook, play the piano and organ and I love to draw. I feel poetry is a melody of words that expresses our thoughts and feelings.; [a.] Rochester, PA

AMSTEAD, KEVIN S.
[b.] January 6, 1961, Austin, TX; [p.] Mr. and Mrs. C. R. Amstead, Sr.; [ed.] Bachelors of Music Education from Southwest Texas State University, School of Fine Arts and Communication; [occ.] Teacher-Band, Director in Texas Public Schools; [memb.] Texas Music Educators Association, Association of Texas Small School Bands, Texas Band Masters Association, Southwest Texas Band Alumni, Del Valle H. S. Alumni.; [oth. writ.] "Solitary Sound" - American Anthology of Poetry, American Poetry Society, "Stay With Me Awhile" - Hollywood Gold, Sons, I'm a writer of poetry, essays and songs.; [pers.] As stated above, I write in several different areas. I like to submerge myself in music and thought, I guess I often attempt to rationalize all the havoc and chaos we see in our lives today.; [a.] Batson, TX

ANDERSON, REBECCA
[b.] May 10, 1962, Philadelphia; [p.] Rebecca and Milton Anderson; [ch.] Nicole and Christopher Crosby; [ed.] High School West Philadelphia; [occ.] College Student at Community College Philadelphia

ANDERSON, ROXANNE M.
[b.] September, 16, 1964, Glen Falls, NY; [p.] Donald C. and Frances M. Anderson; [m.] Paul J. Sandidge, May 4, 1992; [ed.] Art Institute of Fort Lauderdale, A.S. - Fashion Design, Fort Lauderdale College B.S., International Business; [occ.] Flight Attendant, Fashion Designer, Image Consultant; [pers.] This poem is dedicated to Holly M. Grandlund and family (May 21, 1964 - June 29, 1987). The burden of societal normality sometimes can kill the spirit: May You Rest in Peace!; [a.] Orlando, FL

ANDERSON, BARBARA
[b.] Philadelphia, PA; [ch.] James, Everett and Curtis; [ed.] Simon Gretz High School, College of Performing Arts, Freedom Theatre.; [occ.] Songwriter; [memb.] ASCAP (American Society of Authors, Composers and Publishers.); [hon.] Several trophies for singing, certified honorary member of the Border Legion for singing in West Germany for American troops. Certificate Esteem for singing in Iceland, Germany and Portugal and the U.S. Biosdone in local newspaper; [oth. writ.] Give Me A Little, It Should Be Enough, Without Question, Shining Star, I Searched For You, My Inspiration; [pers.] Began writing poems in 1967 and was in creative writing classes thru high school when I also began my singing career. It is a blessing I love to share with my family and the world.; [a.] Philadelphia, PA

ANDREW, ALYSSA MARIE
[pen.] Felicity; [b.] June 20, 1982, Allentown, PA; [p.] Thomas and Mary Ann Andrew; [ed.] 7th Grade St. Ann School, in Emmaus, PA. I've always been in Catholic School.; [occ.] Student; [hon.] I have never gotten any awards for my poems but I am an honor student and I also have gotten 3 medals for my ice skating.; [oth. writ.] Yes, I do have many writings, I hope to have them published someday.; [pers.] If you really want to do something, just put your mind to it and you can do it. I've always wanted to be a poet.; [a.] Emmaus, PA

ANDREWS, SUSAN J.
[pen.] Susan; [b.] January 7, 1962, Fort Monmouth, NJ; [p.] Fred C. and Emiko Scxhoenagel Jr.; [ed.] B.S. Recreation and Parks, Penn State University (1984), A.S. Physical Therapist Assistant (1991) also Penn State University; [occ.] Physical Therapist's Assistant Rehabilitation of traumatic brain injured clients, DuBois Regional Medical Center; [memb.] Water safety instructor, lifeguard training instructor of American Red Cross since 1985, Penn State Alumni Association, lifetime member (1984); [hon.] Voice of Democracy 2nd place (1979), Who's Who Among American High School Students (1980); [oth.writ.] Personal writings of my thoughts and dreams; [pers.] My feelings and thoughts form into rhymes and I write them down, some are better than others. [a.] DuBois, PA.

ANGEL, BETTY BOYER
[b.] October 20, 1922, Stearns, KY; [p.] Mr. and Mrs. A. G. Boyer; [m.] M. B. Angel, December 30, 1939; [ch.] Bernard Andrew Angel, Bernice Leigh Angel; [ed.] High School; [memb.] Church; [oth. writ.] Book of other poems one child's story; [pers.] I love to try writing poetry and drawing on my stationery also love to read and write letters.; [a.] Winston Salem, NC

ANGLIN, FAYE
[b.] Coal Fork, WV; [p.] Russell Anglin, Pauline Anglin; [ch.] Donald Ray, Mark Eric, and Tammy Leigh Curfman; [ed.] Nitro High School, University of Kentucky; [occ.] Officer Manager, Social Science Dept., San Jose State University, San Jose, CA.; [hon.] I have been invited to do various readings of my work.; [oth. writ.] My prose and poetry emerged from personal journal writing which began 10 years ago while I traveled through Russia and Scotland.; [pers.] I write mostly from direct personal experience. Usually some profound transformational experience will inspire me. I write as a made of expression and self exploration. I also have a background in music — violin and piano.; [a.] Santa Cruz, CA

ANNA, JAMES E.
[pen.] Jym Anna; [b.] November 21, 1967, Troy, NY; [p.] Arthur and Helen Anna; [ed.] Graduated from Walnut Ridge High School - Columbus, OH, Graduated from Ohio State University; [occ.] Financial Planner Tampa, FL

ANSCHUTZ, CURTIS L.
[b.] November 17, 1981, Overland Park, KS; [p.] Wendall and Nita Anschutz; [ed.] Cure of Arzizona 7th grade; [occ.] Student

ANTELIS, ROSE
[b.] Brooklyn; [p.] Salvatore and Frances D'Amato; [m.] Dr. Eugene Antelis, May 8, 1980; [ch.] Robert, Frances and Lisa; [ed.] Prospect Heights H.S. Kingsboro College; [occ.] Office Manager; [memb.] MADD Assoc.; [pers.] I try to express my love for my children and grandchildren; [a.] Brooklyn, NY

ANTLE, EVELYN
[b.] November 14, 1916, Terlton, OK; [p.] Joe and Selma Hicks; [m.] Joe Antle Sr., November 26, 1936; [ch.] Joe Charles, Caren Jean, Wm. John, Joan Kathleen, Jackie Ray, Rex Robbie; [ed.] Lemon High School, Lemon, MO., attended Skiatook, OK schools previously.; [occ.] Housewife and Home maker; [hon.] Grandmother to 11 grandchildren, 10 greats; [oth. writ.] This is my first poem to be published, we're all excited.

APPEL JR., ROBERT C.
[b.] December 18, 1940, Urbana, OH; [p.] Robert C. and Catherine S. Appel; [ch.] Jennifer Lynn Appel, Eric Allen Appel; [ed.] BSBA in Accounting from Baruch College of City Univ. of New York graduate of the BAI Graduate School of Banking at the Univ. of Wisconsin, Madison; [occ.] Certified Public Accountant; [memb.] American Institute of Certified Public Accountants,

Texas Society of CPA's and Houston Chapter TSCPA; [hon.] Beta Alpha Psi; [oth. writ.] Regular contributing writer for the Philippine Observer, article published in the Urbana Daily Citizen, Urbana, Ohio; [pers.] Constantly striving to improve myself as a human being and to leave the world a better place than I found it.; [a.] Houston, TX

APPELL, SHARON ANNETTE
[pen.] Sam; [b.] October 15, 1965, Columbus, OH; [p.] Ruth Yocum and Robert; [m.] Tommy Appell, June 9, 1990; [ch.] Christopher McCarty, Patrick McCarty, Kimberly Appell; [ed.] I went to 10th grade but I am currently trying for my G.E.D.; [occ.] Mother and Housewife; [memb.] First Pentecostal Church at 421 Dakota Avenue; [hon.] I got an Editor's Award for the poem Friends and Flowers published in Journeys of the Mind in spring of 1995.; [oth. writ.] Yes I wrote a poem called Friends and Flowers and I had one published in a Catholic book when I was in 7th grade and in Jack and Jill in eighth grade.; [pers.] With God in my life I've been able to forget my dreadful past and, write about them in poems. It helps ease the anxiety I've been through. It also helps having a loving, trusting husband.; [a.] Columbus, OH

AQUILA, RALPH
[b.] July 31, 1962, Brooklyn, NY; [p.] Sam and Phyllis Aquila; [ed.] Suny at Stony Brook, Iowa State University, Syracuse University, Tulane University; [occ.] Philosophy Instructor, Tulane University, New Orleans, LA; [pers.] My poem, "Flight of the Moonfish," is about the tension between a sensitive person and his brutish social environment. The "Moonfish" is a delicate creature of tropical waters.; [a.] New Orleans, LA

ARANA, MS. PATRICIA
[b.] December 15, 1957, New York City; [ch.] Luis Jr., Patricia Jr., Joseph, Stacey, Jonathan; [ed.] Currently attending Mercy College for B.S. in Behavioral Science - graduation date May '96; [occ.] College Student - and mother; [hon.] Soroptimist Award for outstanding school grades and community service, Member of Psi Chi Honer Society; [pers.] I feel that if everyone tried to help at least one other person there would be no one left without help.

ARELLANO JR., RODOLFO S.
[b.] June 26, 1964, Odessa, TX; [p.] Rodolfo Arellano Sr., and Irene Salinas; [ed.] Clinical Psychology B.A. - Eastern Washington University Cheney, WA, Clinical Psychology M.S. Degree - Eastern Washington University Cheney, WA; [occ.] Councilor; [memb.] M.E.Ch.A, NACS; [pers.] "I can do all things through, Christ who strengthens me." Phil. 3:14; [a.] Othello, WA

ARENS, CAROL
[pen.] Carol Arens; [b.] February 9, 1991; [p.] Lyndia Arens and Robert Arens; [m.] Single; [ed.] Currently I am a student at Lansing Community College; [occ.] Burger King Employee; [pers.] It is important to remember, who wrote the poem is not important, but rather what is important is the message it sends to those living now and in the future!; [a.] Lansing, MI

ARMINGTON, ELSIE
[pen.] Elsie Armington; [b.] September 17, 1931, Millville, NJ; [p.] Henrietta and Furman Biggs; [m.] Lincoln Armington, Sr.; [ch.] Lincoln Jr. - Stephen; [occ.] Homemaker; [memb.] West Side Meth Church, Millville Woman's Club, Poet's Club (6 Women involved); [pers.] I have several hobbies one is dole collecting - another is photography - Also I love all animals especially cats presently have seek. I enjoy writing poetry; [a.] Millville, NJ

ARMSTRONG, SANDRA L.
[b.] November 9, 1935, Boston, MA; [p.] Rose J. Perpall; [m.] George O. Armstrong, August 9, 1953; [ch.] George, Randel, Timothy, Patrick; [ed.] Santa

Clara High, O'Conner's School of Nurses - L.V.N. Program (Licensed - Vocational Nurse); [occ.] In-Home Health Care; [oth. writ.] I have written many other pieces of poetry. I started writing at age 7 and for most of my adult life.; [pers.] I would like to think that my poetry reflects the goodness of mankind. I am greatly influenced by all living creatures.; [a.] San Jose, CA

ARROWOOD, KELLIE D.
[b.] November 14, 1968, Morganton, NC; [p.] Glenn Thomas and Shirley Creech Thomas; [m.] Tony Wayne Arrowood (deceased 1990), September 23, 1988; [ch.] Heather Diane Arrowood; [ed.] McDowell High, McDowell Technical Community College; [occ.] Student at MTCC; [memb.] Calvary Temple Church; [hon.] Dean's List at MTCC; [oth. writ.] Various personal writings this will be my first major publication; [pers.] I thank God for my talent, my parents for having me and Dr. Jim Robinson and Freddy bradburn for helping me to believe in me.; [a.] Nebo, NC

ARROWOOD, JOHNNY LEE
[b.] August 19, 1946, Joplin, MO; [p.] Elmer M. (Ben) and Jean L. Bennett; [m.] Jim E. Arrowood, October 9, 1968; [ch.] Christian Arrowood-Siler Tabitha Jean and (Jimmy) James Jr.; [ed.] Carterville High 3 1/2 yrs Grad. Western High Last Vegas NV, Insurance School, Sign Language School; [occ.] Entertainment full service - agent, mngr, audio, video; [memb.] Calvery Community Church former member HXO Ham Radio Club; [hon.] Red Cross Work With Ham Club on flood watches in Las Vegas; [oth. writ.] Cook Book on Dehydrated foods; [pers.] I believe we choose to be happy, sad, angry, whatever the emotion... Life is too short to hold hatefulness, anger and violence in our hearts. We need to choose to be happy and helpful...; [a.] Carterville, MO

ARTERBERRY, GEORGE FRANKLIN
[b.] April 14, 1956, Atlanta, GA; [p.] Mr. and Mrs. Melvin Arterberry; [ed.] B.S. Morehouse College - Atlanta, GA. 1978, USC School of Medicine 1978-1982, Crenshaw High School - Los Angeles, CA. 1974; [occ.] Own my own business, African-American Art Production and Distribution; [memb.] National Association of Securities Dealers, 101 Foundation for Disadvantaged Youth, Beta Kappa Chi-National Science Humor Society; [hon.] Motipational Speaker, Outstanding Young Men of America; [pers.] All limitations are self-imposed. I don't have to build a better mousetrap — just my own!! My legacy should be that I didn't just exist — but that I made a difference.; [a.] Palo Alto, CA

ARVIN, RHONDA
[b.] January 13, 1962, Winchester, KY; [p.] Robert and Mary Parker; [m.] Gary W. Arvin, September 4, 1993; [ch.] Teri Lynn; [ed.] George Rogers Clark H.S.; [occ.] Office at Kroger - Nicholasville, Kentucky; [pers.] My grandmother, Grace P. Miller, integrated my wild imagination and great love of books. Humanity in general command my thoughts. If everyone would let their light of goodness thru the world would shine. Some shine brighter than others, and still more are knowingly extinguished.; [a.] Nicholasville, KY

ASANTE, JOSEPH E. BOAKYE
[pen.] Odasani Dadwene; [b.] January 12, 1960, Accra, Ghana; [p.] Mrs. Comfort Yeboah and Fred Asante; [m.] Marion Boakye-Asante, May 31, 1994; [ch.] Inez Asante; [ed.] Valco International School, Seton Hall University; [occ.] Entrepreneur, Accountant; [memb.] Akim Abuakwa Association, Presbyterian Church and NABA.; [hon.] Dean's List; [oth. writ.] All personal poems to wife and self.; [pers.] Pray to God for the ability to perceive and understand. Lead with honor and purpose for prosterity to account for your deeds in the balance sheet of life.; [a.] Plainsboro, NJ

ASHLEY, DOROTHY
[pen.] Shorty; [b.] April 2, 1947, Brooklyn, NY; [p.] Murry Gooding, Mary Gooding; [ch.] Andrea Ashley, Maebert Ashley, Jerry Ashley IV; [ed.] Nyack High, Clara Barton, Hofstra University, District 65 (UAW) Education Program; [occ.] Bookkeeper, Seta-Soie Int'l Ltd.; [memb.] Special Olympics NY, Vice President-Student Government Choir leader, Recreation Instructor Black Affairs, Girl Scout Leader; [hon.] Dean's List, World of Poetry - Merit Award Student Award of Achievement, District 65 Distributive News/Hefston News, Captain, Service Squad; [oth. writ.] Poems for all school occasions/holidays and people who inspire me.; [pers.] Inspirations, Timothy Bryant, Toby Emmer, Minerva Pirilla I love to write poems about people's accomplishment, Poems to lift people's spirit.; [a.] Brooklyn, NY

ASUEN, IRENE
[b.] August 1, 1970, New York; [p.] Micheal Asuen, Florence Asuen; [ed.] Federal Government Girl's College, Nigeria, City College of New York, New York (CCNY), Manhattan College, Riverdale, New York; [occ.] Graduate Student (MBA Finance); [memb.] International Honor Society of Economics. City College Alumni.; [hon.] Cum Laude degree (BA Economics and Finance), Chirron Delta Epsilon, Dean's List. Role Model Program, March 1993; [oth. writ.] Several unpublished poems, unpublished manuscript.; [pers.] I strive to inspire people with my writings. Writing to me is the medicine to all emotional pain and discomfort for misunderstood people.; [a.] Bronx, NY

ATHEY, JANE M.
[pen.] Johannes Green; [b.] September 22, 1939, Cumberland, MD; [p.] Arnold and Mary De Pollo; [m.] Ronald Athey, May 2, 1959; [ch.] Crystal and Laura, Grandchildren - Corinne, Christopher and Gina; [ed.] Fort Hill High School, Catherman's Business School; [occ.] Executive Receptionist at Black and Decker's Corporate Headquarters; [pers.] The poems of St. Francis of Assisi and Langston Hughes have inspired me to love God and respect life. Everyone writes, directs and stars in their life story - so, select your supporting cast carefully.; [a.] Towson, MD

AUFRICHTIG, JANETTE
[pen.] Dax De Aurora, Jayanti; [b.] April 30, 1944, New York City; [p.] Cora Lee Brown, Henry Brown; [m.] Burton Aufrichtig, December 24, 1984; [ed.] B.A. Long Island University, Master of Science (Guidance Counselling) Lohman College; [occ.] Retired H.S. Guidance Councilor (Sleepy Hollow H.S. in North Tarry Town, NY).; [memb.] NYS Retired Teacher's Association; [hon.] Had a New York state grant to study anthropology in India.; [oth. writ.] Book of poems published called "Black Empress", wrote newspaper articles; [pers.] Avid traveler, visited 35 countries, poems reflect yours of living, feeling, observing experiences, loving, hurting, in short 20 years of me.; [a.] Glen Oaks, NY

AWKWARD, DAN
[pen.] Raven Wolfe; [b.] March 10, 1958, Rockville, MD; [p.] Daniel and Margaret Awkward; [ed.] Col. Zadok Magruder High University of MD (College Park); [memb.] DC Blues Society, Montgomery Players, Amnesty International, The National Arbor Day Foundation, Montgomery Community Television Inc., Fraudulent Productions; [oth. writ.] Another Macbeth; [pers.] My life in the arts is part of a greater journey. I wonder in the realm of myth and vision to bring a dream into the waking world.; [a.] Brookeville, MD

AYERS, BARBARA G.
[b.] February 20, 1960, San Diego, CA; [ed.] A.A. Grossmont College, named 1980, "Women of Distinction", B.A. in Art at San Diego State University; [occ.] Public Relations, San Diego Zoo; [memb.] Board of Directors, CHAD (Combined Health Agencies Drive),

Board member, Ocean Beach Town Council, National Assn. of TV Arts and Sciences (NATAS), Surfrider Foundation; [hon.] 5 times Emmy Award Winner for Feature Segment, Children's Program, Art Director, Animator, Promotional Announcement and other nominations; [oth. writ.] "Howdy's Adventure" Children's Book Series submitted for publication; [a.] San Diego, CA

AZEVEDO, TONY
[b.] April 30, 1927, Escalon, CA; [p.] John Azevedo, Mary Azevedo; [m.] Ibet Azevedo; [ch.] Ronald Azevedo, Anthony Azevedo, Loribet Aponte, Benjamin Aponte; [ed.] 8 years; [occ.] Loan officer; [memb.] 2 years on Board of Directors Academy of Country Music; [oth. writ.] Songwriter with B.M.I. Grapes of San Joaquin, Hill Billy Gypsy Man, Simple Way of Life, Nine Times Out of Ten, Asphalt Cowboy; [pers.] All good things are worth waiting for.; [a.] Rialto, CA

BACHMAN, ALVIN L.
[pen.] AL. Bachman; [b.] June 29, 1920, White Plains, NY; [p.] Frank and Rae Bachman; [m.] Florence, November 14, 1957; [ch.] Robert, Barbara; [ed.] Graduated - White Plains (NY) High School, Attended University of Idaho at Moscow, Idaho; [occ.] Retired - Boxing Mgr. But Split Wood Part Time; [memb.] Chappaqua Chamber Orchestra - Trustee - Hillside Church (Armons, NY American Ass'n Boxing V.P. New Castle Seniors Church and Senior Choirs (Tenor); [hon.] Won "Song for Sale" Song C.B.S. contest 1950 at N.Y. City Honored as boxing trainer - A. Ass'n improve boxing a senior olympic softball hitting champ; [oth. writ.] Poems - Buckskin Bill Idaho, Three Songs Published Ghost writer for Rocket Marciano - Book on Boxing Instruction; [pers.] Volunteer For Chappaqua, N.Y. organizations; [a.] Chappaqua, NY

BADILLO, KEVIN
[b.] March 24, 1968, Queens, NY; [p.] Manuel and Rose Badillo; [ed.] Assoc. Degree from Suffolk Community College 3.3. 6PA Regents Diploma from Brentwood High School, Top 10%; [hon.] Talent Roster Minority Award - College, Academic Awards: Soc. Studies, AFJ ROTC - High School; [pers.] As man approaches the new millennia, it is time for us to help preserve the race by cleaning the planet and ourselves of bigotry and racism.; [a.] Brentwood, NY

BAGWELL, CARLISLE
[b.] January 5, 1910, Clyde, NC; [p.] Jerusha and Will Bagwell; [m.] Helen, August 20, 1938; [ch.] Melinda, James Lee, Lewis B. Bagwell; [ed.] A.B. Degree in Education Wofford College Spartanburg, SC; [occ.] Retired from Mgr. of 3 Social Security Officers. These offices were in upper S.C.; [memb.] Church, American Legion. Disabled American Veterans; [hon.] Every honor that social Security offices gives.; [pers.] There is no such thing as something for nothing, someone pays for it.; [a.] Greenwood, SC

BAILEY, STEPHEN JAMES
[b.] December 26, 1991, Alma, MI; [p.] Stanley Allen Bailey, Anne Louise Bailey; [m.] Shelly Ann Bailey, March 6, 1989; [ch.] Meghan, Andrew, Christian, James; [ed.] Eshpeming High School BS, Mercy College of Detroit Surgical Residency Yale University/Norwalk Hospital; [occ.] Physician Assistant in Cardiac Vascular and Thoraic surgery; [memb.] Michigan Association of Physician Assistants, America Association of Physician Assistants, Michigan Waterfowl Association, Duck's Unlimited, Mitchell United Methodist Church Finance Committee, Marquette Community Theatre; [hon.] Magna Cum Laude Who's who in American Colleges and Universities 1983; [oth. writ.] Bear (novella), Many short stories, many poems; [pers.] My writings attempt to express the inner working of life, stress, conflict, joy, peace etc.; [a.] Negaunee, MI

BAKER, HERBERT
[b.] October 20, 1949, Mississippi; [p.] Hattie and Rufus Baker; [ed.] B.A. the city college of N.Y. (philosophy) 1973 M Div. Andover - Newton Theological School, Newton, Mass, 1979; [occ.] Ordained Minister, and Mental Health Counselor; [oth. writ.] Poems (unpublished); [pers.] I am an Afro-American who believes poetry transcend ethnic boundaries, and speaks from the heart to the Human experience. There is a common ground which all people can relate to in poetry. Words have power to bring all people together.

BAKER, PETER
[b.] November 5, 1976, Phoenix, AZ; [p.] Peter and Janice Baker; [ed.] Greenway High School; [occ.] Full Time Student; [memb.] National Honor Society; [hon.] DECA Nationlist, Boy's State Senator, 3rd place in school poetry contest Junior and Senior year, voted Most likely to become a Cartoon Character; [oth. writ.] Poem entitled "Why" published in a church newsletter; [pers.] I attribute any and all talent and inspiration to my divine creator. I try to glorify him through all of my writings and endeavors. My favorite poet is Walt Whitman.; [a.] Glendale, AZ

BALAREZO, OSCAR FUXA
[b.] February 23, 1932, Peru; [p.] Antero Balarezo, L. Grocida Fuxa; [m.] Kolene Uhre Balarezo, April 24, 1977; [ch.] Ronald Robert Donald, Dennis, Katherine; [ed.] Graduated from L. A. Valley College plus 12 units, Nebraska University 24 units, Northridge University 3 units; [occ.] Waiter at Musso Frank Grill Hollywood; [memb.] Republican Party Santa Anita Enter, Stock Holder; [oth. writ.] Wrote 25-30 Poems.; [pers.] I write and recite poetry english, spanish since I was 12 years old.; [a.] North Hollywood, CA

BALDI, CINDI
[pen.] Sea; [b.] February 18, 1973, Laconia; [p.] Lawrence and Patricia Baldi; [ed.] UNCW (University North Carolina Wilmington) Business Administration Major; [occ.] Student

BALL, DAWN LEE
[b.] March 9, 1947, Chester, PA; [p.] Gustave and Gladys Ball; [m.] Darryl Roy Heckman (Divorced), April 1, 1967; [ch.] Daniel Christopher, Darren Jon, Dona Marie; [ed.] Ridley High, Delaware County Community College; [occ.] Retired; [memb.] Staff of Pegasus at DCCC in 1978-1979, Staff of Archive at Ridley High, Smithsonian, American Red Cross, Eagles Nest Church; [hon.] Past President of Jr. Red Cross, Diamond certificate key jewelry, Jean Gayle Modeling, Crozer Hospital Volunteer; [oth. writ.] In Pegasus at DCCC 1978 titled "the Lovers", poems published east gate Presbyterian Church and Eagles Nest Church. A book of poems called "Reflections of dawn" and "Inspirations"; [pers.] I was first inspired to write when I was 16 after I fell in love with Darryl. Then I was just inspired by life itself. I enjoy the works of Elizabeth Barrett Browning and Ben Berrows.; [a.] Millsboro, DE

BALLARD, VICTOR C.
[pen.] Cristerfer Brint; [b.] January 17, 1952, Detroit, MI; [p.] James Ballard and Alberta Ballard; [m.] Lisa J. Ballard, January 20, 1984; [ch.] Chantail, Dawn, Chretha, Victor Jr., Cristal; [ed.] Mumford High, Wayne Com. College; [occ.] Computer Tech.; [hon.] Received High Achievement Award US Army 1974; [oth. writ.] Several poems publish in local newspapers.; [pers.] I believe the best things in life are not free, we just feel good about paying the price for them.; [a.] Detroit, MI

BALLARD, DAVID A.
[b.] September 26, 1961, SD, CA; [p.] Wallace Ballard, Joanne Gregory; [ed.] Graduated Groton High School; [occ.] Bartender, Comic; [memb.] ACA, Family Fitness, WKKA; [hon.] Most improved final year in H.S.; [oth. writ.] On my wall; [pers.] Somewhere in the transition from childhood to adulthood we forget how to

just be, therefore, as a result, we lose God and our integrity; [a.] Temecula, CA

BALLBACH, PHILIP T.
[pen.] Phil Ballbach; [b.] May 22, 1939, Lansing, MI; [p.] Nathan and Thelma Bowes Ballbach; [ed.] B.A. and M.A., Social Science, Michigan State University; [occ.] Political and social research analyst, current events media consultant; [hon.] Elected seven times to Ingham County Board of Commissioners, listed who's who in America - 1995; [oth. writ.] California Train Ramble On, Midwestern Days and Utopian Nights; [pers.] In my poetry and other writing I often try to relate the endurance of the human spirit to the prevailing social hypocrisies of our times.; [a.] Lansing, MI

BALOG, MARGE HOWARTH
[pen.] "Gypsy" "Silly Rabbit"; [b.] November 3, Coalwood, WV; [p.] Julia and Louis Howarth; [m.] Michael Balog-deceased 1972, Sept 1, 1945; [ch.] Michael and Marjorie; [ed.] S.R. High School some home Study-College, Art instructions also home study-learned to sew from Mom and working at it.; [occ.] Retired, Sewing, Drawing at home and writing and volunteer work; [memb.] A.A.R.P. St Marys Church, S.R. The Club New Brunswick, NJ. Horizons, Lawrence Harbor NJ. C.O.M.H.C.D. Coalition of Mental Health Consumer Organization and American Heart Association; [hon.] My poem being published is my first Award and Honor and I've had a few covers that I've drawn for the club Newsletter who also has had several poems in the New St. News I also draw for my friends.; [oth. writ.] I like to write short stories, especially children's stories, and stories about small animals. I hope to be published one day.; [pers.] My philosophy or my personal note would be for all of us, keep busy and do the best in whatever you choose to do. Keep close ties with family and enjoy life, love and trust in "God".; [a.] South River, NJ

BALUNSAT, ALEXIS
[b.] January 16, 1939, Manila, Philippines; [p.] Antonio and Maria Balunsat; [m.] Maria Carillo Balunsat, 1988; [ch.] Audrey Biddle, Craig Balunsat and Zandra Balunsat; [ed.] B.A. World Business, San Francisco State Univ, Graduate Studies, George Washington University, Graduate Studies, Bowie State University.; [occ.] In transition, former auditor, Usgao, Ustreas, US Army; [memb.] Former memberships in AGA, Assoc of US Mil Comptrollers, Municipal Finance Off Association, Amer. Society for Public Admin.; [hon.] Senator O'Reilly Scholarship Bowie State University, Honors list - Dean, Tribuvan University. Scholarship (not taken) Far Eastern University (Manila) Honors List, Gold Medalist (High School); [oth. writ.] Closed Windows - Screenplay, unpublished, James Woman - Novellette (unpublished Phil. Free Press) Mt. Parnassus - Short Story, Various poems published in school and local papers.; [pers.] Business for humanity. The true and ultimate objective of big business/and government is the preservation of mankind without which they would not exist; [a.] Broken Arrow, OK

BANAR, JAMES F.
[b.] Akron, OH; [ed.] B.S., M.S. University of Akron; [hon.] 5 - Star Award Winner, DPC: 1991, 1993; [oth. writ.] Composer of over 150 poems; [pers.] "When I write I may be that which I truly and" JB 51692; [a.] Newtown, PA

BARCAY, MARA
[pen.] Mara Barcay; [b.] March 20, 1972, Great Falls, MT; [p.] Russell Cykoski, Judith Powers; [m.] Robert Barcay, September 25, 1994; [ed.] High School and Junior College level (Poudre High School, Fr. Collins, Co.) Front Range Community (Fort Collins.); [occ.] Waitress - Sunset Jazz Club.; [hon.] Dean's List; [oth. writ.] I have never been published, but have always had a unique talent for writing, fictional prose is my first love, and now I'm working on a novel, that will be the

first of a series; [pers.] I have seen the world through cautious eyes, while asleep in the walls of my cocoon. Now I hear the knock of springtime, inviting me to spread my wings and fly!; [a.] Fort Collins, CO

BARCOMB, BARBARA
[b.] June 24 1939, Utica, NY; [p.] Gladys and Stanley Penc; [m.] Ronald Barcomb, August 16, 1958; [ch.] Lyle, Kyle, Cherry, Timothy, Kathy, Marriane, Frank Carzo, Eric; [ed.] Graduate in High School, H&R Block Tax School; [occ.] Secretary Auto Damage Appraisers; [memb.] I am a grandmother 8 times over. They and my husband are my memberships.; [pers.] Remember the grass only looks greener on the other side.; [a.] Utica, NY

BARD, MICHAEL
[b.] July 14, 1963, Louisville, KY; [p.] Margaret Bard; [ed.] High School Graduate; [occ.] Bank Security; [oth. writ.] I have written hundreds of poems, since the age of 14, that I believe would serve well for poetry or lyric publication; [pers.] If you can find a beautiful thought that rhymes, or learn something new why not file it in your mind and heart; [a.] Louisville, KY

BARNES, MARTINE SHERI
[b.] October 1, 1982, Tampa, Fl; [p.] William D. and Marilyn B. Barnes; [ed.] Just 6th grade center; [occ.] Student; [memb.] AIIAC (American Indian Issues and Action Committee), Baby Sitters Club, Spanish Club; [hon.] Yellow belt - Taek Won Do, President's National Physical Fitness Award 1993-4, Tropicana/University of Florida Public speaking Award, Science Achievement Honor, Music Award, 1st Runner-up Little Miss Sunburst USA, Tampa Florida, October 1990, First Runner-up, Miss Tampa Bay Sunshine - September 1985, Dance Dynamics, Palms Court, Tampa, FL, Third Runner-up, Florida State Baby Pageant - 1984 - Evelyn Stewart, Tampa, FL, Second Runner-up, Evelyn Stewart Baby Contest - 1984 - Tampa, FL, Best Model - Evelyn Stewart's Florida Model School and Agency Modeling Class, Tampa, FL; [oth. writ.] Poem: "Feelings", published in: "Just Great" School Newspaper; [pers.] I have just one plea to all man (and women) kind —— "Be good to our mother, mother Earth".; [a.] Tampa, FL

BARNES, SHEILA M.
[b.] May 17, 1945, Jamaica, West Indies; [p.] Dr. Edgar and Anita Angell; [m.] William, 1968 (Divorced-1982); [ch.] Michelle (24), Reginad (19), Anita (13); [ed.] Tuskegee University BS. 1968 Cleveland State University Masters Degree - 1989; [occ.] Teacher - Certified in Specific Learning Disability Health Education, Phy Ed and Drivers Education; [memb.] Cleveland Tuskegee Alumni Club American Federation of Teachers Council for Exceptional Children Alpha Kappa Alpha Sorority Gamma Sigma Sigma Sorority Olivet Institutional Baptist Church and Eta Phi Beta Sorority; [pers.] As a dog returneth to his vomit, so a fool returneth to his folly. Proverbs 26:11, We must use our mistakes to improve our lives and not make repeated mistakes. Let God be your daily guide. Most of my poems are on real situations. This poem is dedicated to my son, Reginald. I enjoy swimming, doing writing poems, Calligraphy and travelling. I would like to have my own private school for the Learning disabled grades 1-6; [a.] Solon, OH

BARNETT, SUE
[pen.] Mattie; [b.] July 18, 1950, Leake, CO; [p.] James D and Velma Moore; [m.] Unmarried; [ch.] Sonya-25, Rachael-21, Lauren-8; [ed.] Carthage High School, Walnut Grove High School; [occ.] Sales Representative for mobile home marketing, Inc.; [pers.] This poem written by inspiration from God, was given to me at a time when I was going thru tremendous hardships, and I hope it will be inspiration to someone else!; [a.] Brandon, MS

BARNETT, ERIC
[pen.] Charles Long; [b.] July 12, 1972, Rimini, Italy; [p.] Terry Barnett, Patricia Barnett; [ed.] Sky View High; [occ.] United States Marine; [pers.] My writing is a view of mankind, which holds the beauty and complexities of life.; [a.] Camp Lejeune, NC

BARNWELL, MARGIE R.
[pen.] Marge; [b.] May 5, 1933, Hendersonville, NC; [p.] A.E. Reed, Marie King Reed; [m.] Edgar Barnwell (deceased), November 22, 1953; [ch.] Gary, Julia, James and Joan; [ed.] Dana High, N.C.; [occ.] Retired, Now part time toll collector FL Turnpike; [memb.] Treasure Coast Art Assoc.; [hon.] First Place "Art"; [oth. writ.] Poem in newspaper N.C., Article in FL. Newspaper; [pers.] I plan to publish a book of my poetry with my art to reflect upon the beauty of God, creations; [a.] Fort Pierce, FL

BARRETT, SHARON M.
[b.] May 2, 1944, Cadillac, MI; [p.] John R and Zona McVety; [m.] Joseph Wm. Barrett, September 9, 1966; [ch.] Cynthia Dianne 26 yrs, Joseph Wm. Jr. 23 yrs. old; [ed.] High School LPN Graduate of Medical Ctr. School of Practical Nursing; [occ.] House-wife and Day Care for grandchildren; [memb.] Member of Alexander Chapter #328 Order of the Eastern Star; [oth. writ.] Private writing none published.; [pers.] To receive true honors and awards/reward, I must extend myself to others in need with the compassion my Lord has instilled in me.; [a.] Waverly Hall, GA

BARRETT, VIRGINIA
[b.] June 7, 1963, NY, NY; [ed.] B.A. English University of Virginia, M.A.T. Rhode Island School of Design; [occ.] Writer/Artist; [oth. writ.] Artist's books: Into An Earlier World, Sometimes Feeling Like Eve; [a.] San Francisco, CA

BARRIOS, RENE
[b.] January 6, 1955, El Salvador; [p.] Rene Barrios and Gloria Avelar; [m.] Ana Leonor Cortes Andrino, March 24, 1983; [ch.] Rene, Ana Leonor and Liza Natalie; [ed.] Colegio Fu Hsing Kang (Taiwan), Political War, Los Angeles City College, Psychology, Small Business Courses; [occ.] Notary Public, Translator; [memb.] National Notary Association; [hon.] Editor in the Poetry weekly page "Taller Literario De Los Angeles", interviews in channel 34 and 52, and K Fox, Editor in "La Gaceta De Los Angeles"; [oth. writ.] Several poems and short stories published in differents newspapers and magazines, and a lot of writings no published yet.; [pers.] Life is eternal, so writing poetry is to leave a path to find ourselves in the future.; [a.] Los Angeles, CA

BARTLETT, TREVOR
[b.] August 21, 1981, Riverdale, GA; [p.] Sue Fuller, Larry Bartlett; [m.] Brandi (Girl Friend); [ed.] Flat Rock Middle School; [occ.] Student; [hon.] Computer Award; [pers.] I wrote this poem a year after my aunt died. I was twelve years old. My aunt was very special to me. She was a great person and a great humanitarian. People loved her and she loved them too. She was very Christian and she believed in the word of God.; [a.] Tyrone, GA

BARTON, CAROLYN M.
[b.] June 30, 1939, Tennessee; [p.] Charles and Mable Brown; [m.] Jimmy Y. Barton, June 8, 1990; [ch.] Carol Johnson, Nancy Butler, Sam Butler, Tina Baran; [ed.] Springville High; [occ.] Consultant For China and Steam Ware.; [pers.] To make one be in more contact with their "deep" personal feelings. And have a better out look on life!; [a.] Springville, AL

BASHAM JR., GEORGE E.
[pen.] George Edward; [b.] December 21, 1931, San Antonio, TX; [p.] George E. and Myrtle Mae Basham; [m.] Martha Lee Frazer, August 28, 1952; [ch.] Sharon,

Larry, Karen, Kathy, Diana, Anna, Susan, Theresa, James; [ed.] Hot wells high. San Antonio, TX, Del Mar College. Corpus Christi, TX; [occ.] Retired; [memb.] V.F.W American Legion Post 0571, Sweethome, Texas; [pers.] The world is beautiful; [a.] Hallettsville, TX

BATEMAN, SHERRY D.
[b.] November 22, 1948, Alabama, NY; [p.] Louise and C. P. Daily; [m.] John Bateman, February 12, 1970; [ch.] Two; [ed.] One year college; [occ.] Homemaker, Wife and Mother; [memb.] Baptist Church; [oth. writ.] Gluten-Free Cookbook published in 1991, Other poem published; [pers.] I write for myself and hope others will enjoy it. When I write from my heart I know it is given to me from God.; [a.] Fairburn, GA

BATISTA, MARIA SAMANTHA
[b.] November 14, 1967, Bronx, NY; [p.] Carmen Rivera, Peter Jimenez; [m.] Amado Batista Jr., April 7, 1989; [ed.] Grace Dodge Vocational H.S., Kansas State University, La Guardia Community College; [occ.] Administrative Asst. for Chase Manhattan Bank; [memb.] United Way Association; [hon.] Grace Dodge Honor Society, Special Achievement Awards in Orchestra and Chorus; [pers.] Dedicated to my husband, Amado. Always try to be a step ahead and prepared to meet the next day's trial of life.; [a.] Astoria, NY

BATT, MRS. ALVIN
[pen.] Nellie Crabb Batt; [b.] August 1, 1916, Weir, KS; [p.] Charles and Della (French) Crabb; [m.] Alvin Batt, July 22, 1942; [ch.] Cynthia and Candace; [ed.] Weir High School, Pittsburg State Teacher's College, Tabor College Graduate Study Tours; [occ.] House wife - I am a retired 30 years teacher; [memb.] United Methodist Church - State and National Retired Teachers Assoc. City Library Board - Community V.W.C.A.; [hon.] Valedictorian - High School, Dean's Honor Rolls-College, Delta Kappa Gamma, First Place in Oratory; [oth. writ.] Articles in newspapers, Church papers, short story contest. I wrote and published a Family History after 20 years of research.; [pers.] Practice the Golden Rule. Faith, prayer, hope and love are life's greatest needs in shopping one's life. God is the Father of us all. Life is a glorious adventure with Christ at the Center.; [a.] Florence, KS

BAUN, WELLESLEY W.
[b.] September 15, 1984, Grosse Pointe, MI; [p.] Mark A. and Caprice W. Baun; [ed.] Fourth Grade - University Liggett School, Grosse Pointe, Michigan; [occ.] Student; [a.] Grosse Pointe Farms, MI

BAXTER, BARBARA ANN SULLIVAN
[pen.] Jean Elane; [b.] September 17, 1932, Alabama, NY; [p.] Mary Grace Grabb Michael, Charles Eugene Sullivan; [m.] Willard Thoms Baxter, May 18, 1983; [ch.] Charmain Dee Whitman, Jonathan Claire, Cynthia Ann, Mark Ethan, and Timothy Allegu Dunn; [ed.] Grade School, Jr High, Elmira Free Academy, Miami Dade Community College, and Florida International University.; [occ.] R.N. Home Health Supervisor, Previously Director Of Nurses of Homestead Manor, FL; [memb.] Toners on wheels, Family Motor Coach, R Ving Women, Good Sam, September Days, Moose, Resort Properties Inc, Outdoor Adventure Resorts, and Club and Coast to Coast; [hon.] Dean's list, Registered Nurse Baccalaureate; [oth. writ.] My top 10 Vocation Spot Bear Tooth Mountain, Montana and Hobo Convention, Britt Iowa, '95 Annual in 1995.; [pers.] I try to tell the way things were, and tell of my mother. I am also writing my life story as it happened, in the good old days.; [a.] Okeechobee, Fl

BAYSE, DONNA L.
[b.] November 21, 1937, Newton, IA; [p.] John and Marguerite Bayse; [ed.] Master's Degree from 1970 University of Missouri at Kansas City in Education, 1964 B.A. William Jewell College, Liberty MO; [occ.] Teacher/Coordinator Zoo-Option, Southeast Middle

Magnet School, Kansas City, Missouri; [memb.] Assoc. of Supervision and Curriculum Development, American Federation of Teachers; [hon.] Outstanding teacher of the year award 1972 Honorary Mention, long poem contest, christian topics.; [oth. writ.] Editor of 15 in service workshops on human relations, UMKC 1971 writer and co editor of the capsule published for 11 years and distributed in all 50 states and 24 foreign countries grants; [pers.] They would not read if we did not write. Poetry reflects the inner man's interaction with life.; [a.] Cameron, MO

BAZYLEWICZ, BETH A.
[b.] July 22, 1965, Detriot, MI; [p.] Sherman and Elizabeth Watkins; [m.] James M. Bazylewicz, October 14, 1989; [ch.] Jeremy Michael; [ed.] Western High, Detriot, MI, Henry Ford Comm. Coll., Dearborn, MI; [occ.] Housewife; [memb.] FAITH TABERNACLE Church of God (Substitute teacher, preschool class.) For Sunday School; [oth. writ.] I have several other poems written. Also, several children's stories with illustrations, which are unpublished at this time.; [pers.] I want my poems to reflect my love for writing. It is my hope that publishers will see my creative ability, and want to review some of my work.; [a.] Southgate, MI

BEARD, SHIRLEY
[b.] June 4, 1931, Bellingham, WA; [ch.] Donna Charlotte Butler, Arthur Beard Jr.; [ed.] North Kitsap High, College Courses Holmes Jr. College, East Central College, Canton Vo Tech Edison Tech; [occ.] Medical Secretary; [memb.] Saint Matthews Methodist Church, Woodmen of the World; [hon.] Torch Honor Society MS Congeniality; [oth. writ.] Training Manual - Garmet Plant - Job descriptions High School Essay - Winner Creative Writing Class; [pers.] To my fellow writers, free the creative talents within you. Express them as only you can.; [a.] Ridgeland, MS

BEARDEN, JANIE N.
[pen.] Jane Bearden; [b.] October 29, 1904, Noble, IL; [p.] George Diey Miller; [m.] James S. Bearden, June 23, 1940; [ch.] Marjorie Ann Bearden; [ed.] Nine - others - Seminar, Business English, Art, Music, Sewing, Roberts Law.; [occ.] Fabricare - specialist, retired.; [memb.] Mothers Club, B. P. Women's Club, Chamber of Commerce.; [hon.] Volunteer work. President Dwight Eisenhaber, Red Cross, Civil Defence. Honorary life Membership, US Air Defence; [oth. writ.] Lakeland Ledger "where people have their say."; [pers.] Love of life, God and country, be happy, keep busy, keep interested in life, stay young.; [a.] Lakeland, FL

BEARDEN, JAMES R.
[b.] December 26, 1938, Holcomb, MO; [p.] James C. and Verla Bearden; [m.] Barbara P. Bearden, August 15, 1959; [ch.] Timothy J. and Scott A. Bearden; [ed.] Utley High School, University of Michigan-Flint, University of Michigan, University of Colorado, A.B., M.A. - University of Michigan; [occ.] Humanities and German Instructor, Central High School, Flint, MI, Adjunct Professor of German, Mott College, Flint; [memb.] National Education Association, Michigan Education Association, United Teachers of Flint, National Audubon Society, Genesee Wind Symphony; [hon.] Valedictorian, Dean's List, Various Photographic Awards: Photographic Society of America, Southwestern Michigan Council of Camera Clubs; [oth. writ.] German and English Curriculum, Humanities Curriculum, Flint Public Schools, Assorted poetry, Editorial for Flint Lensman and SWMCC publications; [pers.] Matthew Arnold's famous poem "Ulysses" sums up my own attitude toward life: "To strive, to seek, to find, and not to yield."; [a.] Flint, MI

BEASLEY BILLIE LEANN HICKS
[b.] August 2, 1978, Gainsville, GA; [p.] Martha L. Hicks and William Douglas Hicks; [m.] Michael Lee Beasley, February 12, 1995; [ed.] Lumpkin Co. High School; [occ.] Housewife; [memb.] Columbia House Music.; [hon.] Scholastic Award in 1st Grade.; [oth. writ.] I have written many poems, but never published them.; [pers.] I really enjoy writing poems, it brings joy unto my life. I hope you enjoyed this one as much as I did.; [a.] Dahlonega, GA

BEATTIE, SHERRY LYNN
[b.] June 9, 1981, Wilmington, DE; [p.] Sarah Rushing and Jim Beattie; [ed.] 8th Grade at Our Lady of Fatima School; [occ.] Student; [hon.] 2nd Place in Fire Prevention Essay Contest; [oth. writ.] Poem published in school yearbook; [pers.] I feel age should not be a limit to what you can achieve. At age 13, I like to write about emotions.; [a.] Newark, DE

BEAUMONT, CHRISTOPHER
[b.] May 23, 1975, Falls Church, VA; [p.] Wayne, Nancy Beaumont; [m.] Single; [ed.] Our Lady of Lourdes High School, Dutchess Community College; [occ.] Student; [hon.] Grand prize M.A.D.D. writing contest, Academic Citation; [oth. writ.] Articles for high school paper, Poems in College paper; [pers.] I use my writing as a release of my emotions. I am mostly influenced by music.; [a.] Wappingers Falls, NY

BEAVERS, LAUREL
[b.] September 14, 1967, Louiseville, KY; [p.] Faye Lancaster and Henry Voyles; [m.] Jerry Beavers, November 30, 1990; [ch.] Corey Adam, Caitlin Ann; [ed.] Marion C. Moore School and Watterson College.; [occ.] Homemaker; [hon.] President's List and Dean's List at Watterson College and Graduated Cum Laude; [oth. writ.] Several poems but none of which has been published. However, I did win an honorable mention in a poetry contest in 1985!; [pers.] To my best friend, Cheryl Beair Odle. If not for a promise that I made, and her Love and belief in my talent, this poem would still be nothing more than an echo of the heart!; [a.] Louiseville, KY

BECKER, JOY A.
[b.] July 18, 1977, Denver, CO; [p.] Robert and Linda Becker; [ed.] Graduate of Weld Central High School, currently a freshman at Brigham Young University Hawaii; [occ.] Full-time college student; [oth. writ.] Can I trust you? To whomever, to my brother, a sudden death, him, who will care? My fear; [pers.] Laughter is the way to happiness. Happiness is the key to life life is obtained on earth laugh, smile and save the planet.; [a.] Brighton, CO

BEDNARSKI, ALLEN GREGORY
[pen.] Big Al; [b.] September 16, 1974, Cleveland; [p.] James and Joanne Bednarski; [ed.] Two years of art at North High School 88 to 90, two years at Willoughby Technical Center Commercial Art 91 to 92; [occ.] Heat Treater for Linderme Tube Company; [hon.] Editor's Choice Award from National Library of Poetry; [oth. writ.] Why? Twilight of Night, Thanks Friend, A Summers Eve Stroll, No Stopping my Love for You, Missing You, My World, Please Never Leave Me, Together Forever; [pers.] You must believe in yourself before you can believe in others, when black clouds appear its best to prepare for a hurricane rather than light rain, good friends are hard to find; [a.] Eastlake, OH

BEETS, CHRIS
[pen.] Christian Beats; [b.] January 15, 1974, Knoxville, TN; [ed.] Attended Atlanta Institute of Music, Art institute of Fort Lauderdale, Attending Pellissippi State College; [occ.] Student, Musician; [pers.] Plays bass and guitar, write songs, poetry. Plans to make a career in the music and entertainment field; [a.] Knoxville, TN

BEGAN, BLAKE CARL ANDRE
[b.] December 21, 1976, Warren; [p.] Dennis and Marilyn; [ed.] North Farmington High school - 95 senior; [occ.] Dietary Aide - Botsford Hospital; [pers.] I try to get what's in my heart onto the paper.; [a.] Farmington Hills, MI

BELIZAIRE, GARRY
[b.] January 11, 1966, Port-au-Prince, Haiti; [p.] Jean and Annette Belizaire; [pers.] My poems are from the Lord for the glorification of his name and the edification of his Saints.; [a.] Miami, FL

BELK, CLOTHILDE
[pen.] C. Joy; [ed.] Howard University, P-G. Community College; [occ.] Publisher and Writer; [memb.] Tutor For The Foundation For Exceptional Children, Board of Directors of Serenity Players, The Nuturing Network; [hon.] Featured in several newspapers, many awards for volunteer service; [oth. writ.] "You Are A Star", "You Can", "Variety Premiera Magazine", "Listen Dad", "Metro Exchange Newsletter", "Look A Little closer", "My Soul", "Conscious Directional Recipes For The 90's" There must be an answer and many editorials and short essays.; [pers.] I fell "GOD" has given me something to say and I'm going to say it. (Don't use the lead in a gun, but the lead in a pencil) your mind and my mind can influence other minds; [a.] Temple Hill, MD

BELTZ, LUELLA E.
[pen.] Lou Beltz; [b.] February 23, 1908, Irving, KS; [p.] Mr. and Mrs. Albert Strader (Both deceased); [m.] Ernest A. Beltz, July 30, 1927 (Deceased); [ch.] Margery Fair, Ernie Beltz; [ed.] High School, Omaha Nebraska; [occ.] Retired; [memb.] Corpus Christi, Bowlers Hall of Fame Abiding Savior Lutheran Church; [hon.] I was awarded a Certificate of Achievement Award for successfully completing (6 mo.) The Cardiac Rehabilitation Program, Inducted into Corpus Christi, Bowlers Hall of Fame, won two (2) Texas State Bowling Tournaments - Doubles with my daughter Margery Fair.; [oth. writ.] I started writing poems in November 1994. It was something I always wanted to do, but didn't get around to doing it.; [pers.] Both my parents and my husband are deceased.; [a.] Corpus Christi, TX

BEMBENEK, EMILY-JO
[b.] February 19, 1982, Cudahay, WI; [p.] Mike and Gina Bembenek; [ed.] 7th grade; [occ.] Student; [hon.] Honor Student, Honor roll; [oth. writ.] Nothing published, though I write a lot of poetry; [pers.] I enjoy playing the clarinet, I enjoy school, I enjoy reading, I also enjoy life; [a.] Mukwonago, WI

BENNETT, TRYSTAN
[b.] January 22, 1985, New York City; [p.] Jerre and Catherine Bennett; [ed.] Student Ridgewood Public Schools Ridgewood, NJ, Accepted to fall term at Tuxedo Park School, Tuxedo Park, NY.; [memb.] Allendale Horse Dressage Riding Club. YMCA Rocket Club. Saint Elizabeth Episcopal Choir, Saint Elizabeth Episcopal Acolyte; [hon.] '92 Huntington Learning Center Merit Trophy, '92 NJ Certificate of Recognition, '94 NJ Certificate of Recognition

BENNETT, MRS. DORIS
[b.] October 31, 1922, Palestine, TX; [p.] Rev Alfred, Ella Holiday; [m.] Tom Bennett, November 26, 1953; [ch.] Alvis, Margaret and Billie; [ed.] BA., Degree, Languages and Literature - Bishop College, 1944 Graduate Studies, Univ. New Mexico, National Univ. Mexico City; [occ.] Retired Teacher Graduated: Central High Sch. Galveston, Texas Taught at Central High Sch. 1940-1944-47 Spanish; [hon.] Alpha Theta Sigma Ch. Sigma Gamma Rho, Sorority; [pers.] I embrace the ideals of the colonial period; [a.] Galveston, TX

BENNY, JASON R.
[b.] October 16, 1974, Poughkeepsie, NY; [p.] Robert and Sandra Benny; [ed.] Spackenkill High School Dutchess Community College; [occ.] Student; [hon.] Phi Theta Kappa, Who's Who among American High School Students, Dean's list, Dean's Scholarship; [pers.] When time dies we shall fly into pureness, inside and outside all, the realization of success.; [a.] Austin, TX

BENOIT, EDWARD J.
[b.] August 17, 1959, Ocean, NJ; [p.] Paul and Marian Sue Benoit; [ed.] B.S. Chem. Eng'g, Rutgers University 1981; [occ.] Project Management Consultant, Stull and Benoit Associates, Inc., Jersey City, NJ; [oth. writ.] Various poems written over the past few years; [a.] Jersey City, NJ

BERARDO, WILLIAM J.
[b.] December 21, 1944, Bay City, MI; [p.] James and Margaret; [m.] Mary M., April 28, 1973; [ch.] Justine, William Jr. and Rosemary; [ed.] St. Marys H. S. Lansing Michigan State University, BA University of Detroit, I. D; [occ.] Attorney; [memb.] Ancient order of Hibernians, Incorporated Society of Irish American Lawyers, Michigan Connections Association and Business Network International.; [oth. writ.] Numerous unpublished poems.; [pers.] I work to bring truth goodness and Beauty into my Heart and Actions.; [a.] Berkley, MI

BERGEN, KATIE
[b.] February 7, 1981, North Tarrytown, NY; [p.] Kathy Bergen, Michael Bergen; [ed.] Pocantico Hills School, Grade 8; [occ.] Student; [memb.] Yearbook Committee Student Newspaper; [hon.] 7th grade honor role; [oth. writ.] Poetry published in TYWN, unpublished Sci-Fi Novel; [pers.] "Destiny is being born to do something but not knowing what it is." (Quote from "Forest Gump") (Favorite Quote); [a.] North Tarrytown, NY

BERRY, KENNETH REA
[b.] November, 15, 1944, Ashland, OR; [p.] Fern Berry (Deceased); [m.] Vera Irene Berry, October 31, 1993; [ch.] Megan Rea Berry; [ed.] Masters Degree in Psychology - Auburn University; [occ.] Computer Specialist, Gunter Air Force Base, Montgomery, AL; [hon.] Psi Chi, Phi Kappa Phi, Deans List, Eagle Scout, BS Degree in Psychology with High Honors, Auburn University at Montgomery.; [oth. writ.] A book "whispers', 1992, published by University Editions, Inc. (poetry); [pers.] Big believer in life after life/life between lives...that our soul goes on forever: that the purpose of life is gaining knowledge, experience, and - above all - LOVE!; [a.] Montgomery, AL

BERRYMAN, SANDRA R.
[b.] December 25, 1946, Dubuque, IA; [p.] Wm. C. and Violet W. Brady; [m.] Thomas H. Berryman and the late Dennis E. Brenkle; [ch.] Flint, Patrick, Deborah, Jade and Mason; [ed.] Dubuque Sr. High, Clarke College, Mesa College; [occ.] Caterer of Cuisines; [memb.] "The Last Word" Writer's group. "Professional Womens Network"; [hon.] Former and First City Council Woman of East Dubuque.; [oth. writ.] Commissioned by Sisters of Charity, B.V.M. for Hysterical Production with the poem, Passage. Gramercy Park Promotional Video for fund raising with several selections.; [pers.] My poetry leads me from the simple to the eccentric. Imagination is great. Thanks Mom and Dad.; [a.] East Dubuque, IL

BERRYMAN, JEANNI
[b.] December 21, 1974, Oklahoma, OK; [p.] John and Shauna Berryman; [ed.] Graduated from Edmond Memorial High School in 1993; [pers.] Inspirations for my writing: Loves, friendships, bad and good memories, rainstorms, dreams, and The Lizard King. [a.] Edmond, OK

BERUBE, HEATHER
[b.] July 6, 1981, Concord, MA; [p.] Katherine Berube and James Berube; [ed.] Anchor Bay Junior High.; [occ.] Student; [pers.] I enjoy writing greatly, and sometimes when I write, I play the major role, for all that I write comes from the heart.; [a.] New Baltimore, MI

BESHEARS, RACHEL ANN RICHARD
[b.] April 19, 1965, Lafayette, LA; [p.] Melvin and Ruby Richard; [m.] Divorced; [ch.] Khrishandalyn Beshears, Tiffany Beshears, Soleil Richard, Angelle Dotch; [ed.] Central High, L.S.U.; [occ.] Self employed; [memb.] P.T.A. - St. Paul Catholic Church Choir, African-American Diocesan Mass Choir; [oth. writ.] None published; [pers.] I thank God for giving me the talent and the courage, and "Nuchock" for giving me the inspiration.; [a.] Baton Rouge, LA

BEST, PATRICIA
[pers.] We all subsist on illusions.; [a.] Detroit, MI

BETHKE, TAMI
[pen.] Jem; [b.] March 23, Springfield, MO; [p.] Dorothy Deahr; [ed.] Western Towa Tech Comm. College Iowa City High School; [occ.] LPN; [oth. writ.] Several poems in local newspapers. 1st novel written in high school - collected rejection letters for it.; [pers.] I'm half comanche on my father's side and my writings usually reflect the duality of my background. I wish I had room to thank all the people who have encouraged me, especially in high school; [a.] Iowa City, IA

BIANCHI, EUGENE V.
[b.] July 27, 1938, Oil City, PA; [p.] Anthony and Carmela Bianchi; [m.] Lynne M. Bianchi, August 13, 1984; [ch.] Timothy A. and Pamela A.; [ed.] Edinboro College (B.S.) Buffalo State College (M.S.); [occ.] Retired English Teacher; [oth. writ.] Several Sports columns in local newspapers; [pers.] I strive to inject an element of humor in my writing; [a.] Peekskill, NY

BIDWELL, JON
[b.] July 26, 72, Kansas City, MO; [ed.] Very Little; [occ.] Starving Artist; [memb.] NORML, NPCA; [oth. writ.] A few published poems in local papers; [pers.] I have a dog and his name is Lennon.; [a.] Lawrence, KS

BIESKE, BRETT
[b.] October 28, 1974, Waukesha, WI; [p.] Donald Bieske, Bonnie Bieske; [ed.] Oconomowoc High School, presently attending Ferris State University; [occ.] College Student; [memb.] Professional Golf Management Student Association; [oth. writ.] First Writing Submitted; [pers.] "Life's many corridors are only opened by the fantasy of ideas."; [a.] Oconomowoc, WI

BILLICK, SHAWN-MARIE
[pen.] Shawn Conrey, Carolyn, 'C'; [b.] December 15, Mount Holly, NJ; [p.] John and Shirley Conrey Billick; [occ.] Customer Administration - Management; [oth. writ.] A private collection of yet unpublished poems; [pers.] "My poems reflect the mirror of life, the heart of the matter, memories from the past and future dreams of a lifetime to last!!"; [a.] Florence, NJ

BINCAROUSKY, JOSEPH A.
[pen.] Josef Alexander; [b.] July 30, 1981, Meadowbrook, PA; [p.] Alfred Bincarousky, Karen Bincarousky; [ed.] Cedar Grove High School; [occ.] Student; [hon.] Four Academics Plus Awards, Principle's Honor Roll, Middle School Writing Awards; [oth. writ.] Personal portfolio; [pers.] A great number of my poems are based on special people in my life. The main reason why I'm a writer is because of one of my Elementary School Teachers, Marilyn Wittenstein, She taught me to Appreciate the language of poetry.; [a.] Philadelphia, PA

BINES, TAMEKA
[b.] July 30, 1978, Queens, NY; [p.] Mrs. A. Bines and Mr. H. Bines; [ed.] 11th grade (Currently); [pers.] Enjoy life while you have the time because it is too short to dwell on problems only.; [a.] New York, NY

BINNER, ROSE A.
[pen.] Sis; [b.] June 2, 1981, Tampa, FL; [p.] Donald R. and Mary D. Binner; [occ.] Student; [pers.] Would like to dedicate this poem to my family and friends; [a.] Reading, PA

BIRD, LINDA KAY
[b.] February 21, 1957, New Castle, IN; [p.] Darrell and Dovie Henderson; [m.] Divorced; [ch.] David Harold Lawrence Jr. - 17; [ed.] Richmond Senior High School Graduated 1976; [occ.] 6 1/2 years/Certified Nursing Assistant (CNA) at Heritage Regency Nursing Home.; [hon.] Honored locally (Richmond Indiana) for essay, I care, I work in a Nursing Home in Home Town Paper.; [pers.] I enjoy writing inspirational poems. If I can make someone smile, it makes my day.; [a.] Richmond, IN

BIRD, ELAINE
[pen.] Elaine S. Manley-Bird; [b.] October 1, 1964, Massachusetts; [p.] David Sr. and Anita Manley; [m.] James Bird, Ground Hog's Day - February 2, 1985; [ch.] Sara Bethany, Matthan Daniel, Jesse Aaron, Rebekah Lauren-Rose; [ed.] Newburgh Free Academy, Dutchess Comm. College; [occ.] Day care, provider; [memb.] Point of Grace Ministries; [hon.] Quassaick Chapter, Daughters of the American revolution and the NFA Home Economics Award; [oth. writ.] The Colonade - 1982 - high school publication of poem and short stories; [pers.] My writings are dedicated to those who believe in the world of dreams, magic and mystery for that is where the treasures of life are from.; [a.] Schenectady, NY

BISHOP, JENEECE
[b.] November 23, 1949, Illinois; [p.] J. C. and Jeneece Kirk; [m.] Dennis DeCoursey, March 18, 1994; [ch.] Daniel Lee Bishop, Julie Cherie Johanson; [ed.] B.A. - Southern Illinois Univ., M.S.E. - Southern Illinois Univ; [occ.] Associate Professor of English - John A. Logan College Carterville, Illinois; [memb.] Phi Delta Kappa, National Council Teachers of English, I.E.A./N.E.A S.I.U. Alumni Association Beta Sigma Phi Eagles Auxiliary #1549, A Brotherhood Aimed Toward Education; [hon.] Who's Who Among America's Teachers - 1994; [oth. writ.] 1. A road map to successful research on the Information Super highway. 2. Implementing the initiation theme into the teaching of Adolescent Literature. 3. Black English; [pers.] I attempt through my writings to, not only give a reflection of my personal experiences but to also provide glimpses and insights into the human condition.; [a.] Herrin, IL

BITHELL, IDA
[b.] December 22, 1923, Ohio; [ch.] 4 children, 10 grandchildren and 3 great grandchildren; [occ.] Special Education Assistant, Buchser Middle School and pianist, silicon gulch jazz band; [memb.] American Federal of Musicians local 153, San Jose, CA, California School Employee Assoc.; [oth. writ.] I write a column called "Jazz reminiscence" in the "South Bay Beat".; [pers.] Music and poetry express a full range of emotions. We may all dance to a different drummer but are brought together by that mysterious force called "Love"; [a.] Santa Clara, CA

BLACK, TINA LOUISE
[pen.] Tina L. Black; [b.] April 25, 1965, Los Angeles, CA; [p.] Clyde Thomas Black, Linda LouVan Sayoe; [ch.] Amy Lynn Black, Brandon Andrew Black, Hayley Nicole Black, Timothy Edwar Black, Devon Marie Black; [ed.] Santanna Continuation High School; [occ.] I'm currently laid off and looking for another job; [oth. writ.] I write other poems, I enjoy writing poems. But

happiness is my 1st. poem to be published; [pers.] I write my poems from things happening in my own life. I love to read poetry. The 1st poem I ever took notice to was "Tokens". I says: Most of what's said is for the birds, actions speak louder than your words. I was 18 yrs. and I applied that poem to my life; [a.] San Bernardino, CA

BLACK, HEATHER R.
[b.] August 20, 1970, Plattsburgh, NY; [p.] Linda Black; [m.] Charles P. Montbriand, January 12, 1995; [ed.] Graduated from Plattsburgh High School - 1989, Graduated from Clinton Community College 1994 - Associates in Criminal Justice; [pers.] Youngest of eight children. Personal thought 'of all the things you can teach a child, reading is the most fundamental'.; [a.] Fairfield, CA

BLACKBURN, SHONDA
[b.] March 20, 1979, Westminster, CO; [p.] James and Sharli Blackburn; [ed.] Lakewood High Sophomore; [occ.] Student; [pers.] I write from my heart and from the hearts of those around me.; [a.] Lakewood, CO

BLACKWELL, VIOLA
[b.] December 1, 1908, Richmond, VA; [p.] Lula and Joseph Suitt; [m.] Thomas Blackwell, December 25, 1969 (2nd time); [ch.] 4 boys, 3 girls, (1 marriage); [ed.] High School Graduate; [occ.] Housewife; [pers.] I have not even had any poems or books publish before I only started writing 2 years ago and I read you ad in a book and sent in two I have forgot title.

BLAKE, ROSE-ANNE
[b.] March 15, 1938, Hermon, ME; [p.] Martell and Frances McPheters; [m.] Duane E. Blake, August 27, 1962; [ch.] Denise Memmelaar/Debra Burke/ David Blake; [ed.] Bangor High School/U.S. Navy Reserves; [occ.] Accounts Payable Clerk/Tech. for Neurology Associates of Eastern ME, PA

BLAKELY, SHIRLEY ANTOINETTE ANDERSON
[pen.] Shirley Antoinette Anderson Blakely; [b.] January 22, 1946, NC; [p.] Alexander Sr. and Hattye Anderson; [m.] Lindorf Scipio Blakely, August 18, 1968; [ch.] Lindorf Steven Blakely; [ed.] B.S. Tuskegee University High School - Ala. State Lab High; [occ.] Director Child Care Management Services - The Child Care Group, Inc.; [memb.] President Collin County Association for the Education of Young children, Delta Sigma Theta, Dallas Tuskegee Alumni Club; [hon.] Dean's List, who's who among college or univ., student, Miss Tuskegee University '68, Distinguished Service Award and TCC group; [pers.] Poetry allows me to escape into a private world of renown.; [a.] Garland, TX

BLAMER III, WALTER SCOTT
[pen.] Walter Scott Blamer III; [b.] October 23, 1956, Hart, MI; [p.] Mr. and Mrs. Walter Blamer; [m.] Single; [ch.] Sara Tice; [ed.] Graduated Montaque High 75 Michigan; [occ.] Chef; [memb.] Member of ASAI; [oth. writ.] Large volume of both poetry and lyrics, member of NASI, currently pursuing writing career.; [pers.] Writing is a God given gift and therapy for the soul. My dream is to be a free lance lyricist and poet.; [a.] Montague, MI

BLASIE, MICHELLE RENEE
[b.] July 5, 1977, New Rochelle, NY; [p.] Ronald and Carol Blasie; [ed.] New Rochelle High School Freshman at Iona College New Rochelle NY; [occ.] Attending Iona College; [pers.] Do not look back but look ahead, the future is yet to come but the past is dead I have been encouraged to pursue my poetry writing by my ninth and 12th grade English teacher Mrs. Forte; [a.] New Rochelle, NY

BLASINGIM, VICKIE
[pen.] Jewel; [b.] March 15, Amarillo, TX; [oth. writ.] Poems written over the years for various personal events, gatherings, occasions, etc.; [pers.] My poems reflect my emotion of the moment; [a.] Houston, TX

BLAYNEY, DON F.
[b.] March 24, 1929, Fresno, CA; [p.] (Deceased); [ed.] San Francisco State University, B.A., MA; [occ.] Retired Teacher, Educational Software Consultant; [memb.] Society of Children's book writers, Calif. Retired teacher's Assoc, Phi Delta Kappa Education fraternity; [oth. writ.] Numerous articles and poems, college newspaper, feature articles, local newsletters and community publications, two unpublished children's novel's, poetry collection (in progress); [pers.] My poetry is a reflection of the true inner core of my human experience. All my work, often symbolic, is an attempt to explore the heart and soul of my emotions, a spiritual journey through life.; [a.] Petaluma, CA

BLOOMFIELD, RICHARD
[b.] September 23, 1966, Macomb, IL; [p.] Conrad and Patricia Bloomfield; [ed.] Colchester High School, Colchester, IL; [occ.] S.I.A. Production Associate, free lance photographer and writer.; [memb.] United Methodist Church; [oth. writ.] A poem written for and read as part of an obituary deliverance for Melissa and her mother. Also articles in the Macomb daily journal and the Colchester Chronicle.; [pers.] Reflections of my past and the reality of the present tend to influence my thoughts and flow through my pen. All emotions are important to me.; [a.] Lafayette, IN

BOAGS, HENDRIX S.
[b.] March 22, 1972, Charleston, SC; [p.] Isadore Boags Jr, Carol Boags; [ed.] James Island High, University of South Carolina; [occ.] Student; [hon.] Dean's List, Achievement in Math and Science; [oth. writ.] Various poems and short stories; [a.] Charleston, SC

BOATWRIGHT, JENNIFER
[pen.] Jennifer Boatwright; [b.] September 14, 1970, Michigan; [p.] Joseph and Ann Vella; [m.] James, November 13, 1993; [ed.] Schoolcraft College; [occ.] Office manager in a dental office; [oth. writ.] None published several short stories and poems; [pers.] I feel writing is the greatest form of self-expression that anyone can do. I enjoy it greatly and hope those who read my work are touched by it in some way; [a.] Canton, MI

BOAYUE, JULIEN KAU
[pen.] Kau, JB; [b.] September 17, 1962, Liberia, West Africa; [p.] Mrs. Jenneh Dunbar and Mr. Joseph Boayue; [m.] Divorced; [ch.] Kau-Rosa, Winston Aloysius, Preston Tuku; [ed.] Monrovia College and Industrial Training School, Klinifred Jr Hartey United Methodist School of Nursing; [occ.] Registered Nurse; [hon.] First place in class of Eight (Nursing) and achieve highest cumulative average in Liberian Nursing State Board Examination; [oth. writ.] Unpublished; [pers.] The quilt of life we sew for ourselves does not always. Seem to go according to our expectation but no matter what the situation always remember that you can do better. Don't defeat yourself.; [a.] Brooklyn Park, MN

BOCHAIN JR., NICHOLAS
[b.] November 5, 1953, New London, CT; [p.] Grace and Nicholas Bochain Sr.; [ed.] 4 years college no diploma, I write alot. Poems, songs, editor, short stories.; [occ.] Entrepreneur; [oth. writ.] I enjoy writing so political humor, humor, letters too; [pers.] Think about other things beside money, but don't cross it off your list, keep trying and trying etc... Question authority, and than question the answer.; [a.] Moosup, CT

BODNAR, MICHAEL A.
[b.] June 29, 1954, Lynchburg, VA; [p.] Al and Donna Bodnar; [m.] Sharon Key Bodnar, October 1, 1994; [ed.] Graduated Lynchburg College Lynchburg, VA;

[occ.] Construction Manager Realty One Property Mgmt; [memb.] (K) Fraternity, Northern Ohio Chapter of Apartment Managers Assoc.; [oth. writ.] A bachelors book of love, Poetry and prose (unpublished); [pers.] I have been influence by many people whom I've had the pleasure to meet. My work is inspired by love, and Emotions.; [a.] Westlake, OH

BOGGESS, SABINA C.
[b.] March 30, 1978, Fort Collins, CO; [p.] Jerry and Josephine McClure; [ed.] Goodnight Elementary School, Pitts Middle School, Pueblo West Middle School, Rye High School; [occ.] Full time student at Rye High School.; [memb.] Young Life Youth Group, Rye Colorado City Saddle Club, Rye High School Band; [hon.] Riverside Saddle Club Princess, Received a lettermen's jacket for band.; [oth. writ.] Article for Greenhorn Valley Newspaper; [pers.] After I graduate from high school I would like to go to college and become an english teacher so that I may reach out to students and influence them the way that my teachers have influenced me.; [a.] Rye, CO

BOHANNON, JOHN C.
[pen.] John Clarence; [b.] August 31, 1961, Chattanooga, TN; [p.] William Bohannon, Carolyn Bohannon; [ed.] University of TN at Chattanooga (B.S.), '84, University of Minnesota (Ph. D.) '90; [occ.] Finance Consultant/Professor; [memb.] American Finance Association, Financial Management Association; [hon.] John W. Herrick Fellowships, several teaching awards (Tulane); [oth. writ.] Poet's Guild - Best New Poems 1994; [pers.] I write to organize my thoughts; [a.] Metairie, LA

BOIVIN, LONNY L.
[pen.] Doc; [b.] July 15, 1958, Plattsburgh, NY; [p.] Betty J. Terry (Maiden); [m.] Valerie J. Benson, Common Law Only; [ch.] Patrick James, Matthew Robert.; [ed.] High School ('76) Graduated, U.S. Navy Vet (12/76-7/78).; [occ.] Disabled Vet, 55 DI Benefits.; [memb.] Alcoholics and Narcotis Anonymous, Clean date June 27, 1991.; [hon.] Licensed for Small Gas Engine Mechanics ('74-'76).; [oth. writ.] "Docs Log" (O manuscript).; [pers.] "Docs Log" is a poetic or essay account of my first year of recovery from Alcohol and Narcotics abuse. More directly the emotions I felt during this time period.; [a.] Westminster, CO

BOLENDER, KATE D.
[pen.] Kate D. Bolender; [b.] January 10, 1949, Davenport, IA; [p.] Jeanne Marie Schwab; [m.] Darrell L. Bolender, February 18, 1990; [ch.] 5 Boys, 2 Grandchildren; [ed.] 2 years at Kirkwood Communication College; [occ.] Day-care provider; [memb.] 4-C's Child-Care Association; [hon.] "Blended Family Matriarch"; [oth. writ.] Currently working on a book of Poetry entitled 40 something? Also writing a series of children's stories entitled the Cow Folks; [pers.] Life can be an adventure. We are born with our courage and we must maintain our sense of humor; [a.] Iowa City, IA

BOLLOM, ZANE R.
[pen.] Z. R. Bollom; [b.] March 16, 1954, Oak Park, IL; [p.] Richard F. and Joyce L. Bollom; [m.] Deborah L. Bollom, April 6, 1974; [ch.] Jared Z. Bollom, Kendra D. Bollom; [ed.] High School Graduate, Hudson 1972, Have attended many Business Seminars and have accumulated credits toward a business degree at WI, Indianhead Tech College, New Richmond WI; [occ.] Quality Assurance Coordinator Andersen Corp. Bayport MN. 55003; [memb.] Trinity Lutheran Church - Hudson. American Diabetes Assoc. American Society for Quality Control National Rifle Association; [oth. writ.] None Published or sought to be published. Perhaps that will change.; [pers.] Life and living are sacred and precious. To make the most of them you have to share and give yourself to others. I have loved poetry since elementary school and the two Browning and Longfellow are among my favorites.; [a.] Hudson, WI

BOLON, LEIGH ANN
[b.] May 20, 1975, Salem, OH; [p.] Thomas and Linda Bolon; [ed.] East Palestine City Schools K-12, The University of Akron.; [occ.] Student, Food Hostess.; [memb.] Several University Bands.; [hon.] John Philip Sousa Band Award, Solo and Ensemble Awards.; [oth. writ.] My love, Jackass City, Several untitled poems.; [pers.] "Fate will lend a hand to those who believe." "I write poems to express my many moods, and in the end, I always felt better."; [a.] East Palestine, OH

BOLTON, MARISA VOLPE
[pen.] Marisa; [b.] June 23, 1954, Italy; [p.] Quintino and Bina Fabrizi; [m.] (Ex.) Mario Volpe/(present) Antonier Bolton, January 27, 1995; [ch.] Geoffrey, Michael, Jonathan (First Marriage); [ed.] 2 years at Lorain County Community College; [occ.] Artist, poet, writer, model, actress; [memb.] National Honor Society in High School. Phi Beta Kappa in College. Amherst Soccer. PTO in St. Peter School.; [hon.] Writing Award in Italy (National) in the 60s. Poetry semi-finalist in College two years in a row.; [oth. writ.] Mostly wrote for self.; [pers.] Life is an adventure. Each day we embark on a boat of new experiences which enrich our souls until we are one with our creator.; [a.] Lorain, OH

BOLTON, VIRGINIA C.
[b.] June 22, 1931, Russellville, AL; [p.] John W. And Lillie M. Henry; [m.] Clovis J. Bolton, January 13, 1950; [ch.] Glenda Carol, Donna Elaine, Judy Lynn, Deborah Ann.; [ed.] Cherokee High School; [occ.] Retired, love to cook and garden, write poems; [memb.] Church of Christ; [oth. writ.] Clovis and Virginia were married January 13, 1950 in Tuscumbia, AL, moved to Chicago IL. Lived there 42 yrs. retired Sept. 1990 and moved back to AL.

BONNER, CALVIN LEROY
[pen.] Calvin; [b.] March 16, 1958, Marietta, LA; [p.] Helen and Frank Bonner; [m.] Sharon Delouis Bonner, May 7, 1992; [ch.] Guineviere, Calvin Jr., Michael (Deon); [ed.] Marietta High, Reinhardt College Southern Technical Institute of Technology; [occ.] Illustrator, Lockheed Aeronautical Systems Co., Marietta, GA.; [memb.] Local 709 IAMAW union life time and there after membership with "God"; [hon.] NAACP Artist Award, Commendation of work performance (LASC), 1st place best artist Reinhardt College (1978); [oth. writ.] I have own personal book of writings but never published them. Always just let friends read them.; [pers.] I strongly believe in God and Jesus. I try to tell others of their (God and Jesus) kindness, good fortunes and blessings that's been sent to me. How faith is the key to happiness; [a.] Powder Springs, CA

BOOKER, VERNON SEMBLEY
[pen.] Vernon S. Booker; [b.] August 8, 1960, Richmond, VA; [p.] Virginia G. Boisseau; [ch.] Michelle Renee, Matthew Vernon; [ed.] Varina High School, Rich VA, Computer Learning Network; [occ.] Waiter; [pers.] What you think you think is not what you thought you would think, because what you thought you would think has already been thought; [a.] Mechanicsburg, PA

BOONE, TREVA D.
[b.] October 23, 1971, Brooklyn, NY; [p.] Gerald Best and Shirley Boone; [ed.] Lafayette H.S, Brooklyn, NY Livingstone College, Salisbury, NC; [occ.] Math Tutor, Livingstone College and Poet; [memb.] Omega PSI PHI Fraternity; [oth. writ.] Several poems published in local newspapers, poems in the following books: Reflections of Light, Seasons to Come, and Songs on the Wind; [pers.] I love to write just to promote thought, I believe if you can get a person to think, their heart and mind will guide them towards their fate; [a.] Salisbury, NC

BOONE, KERRY ALAN
[b.] January 16, 1963, Vicksburgh, MI; [p.] Orville and Rayletta Boone; [ed.] Graduated High School Vicksburg, Michigan; [oth. writ.] Writes songs and is currently writing a book. Recently had one of his poems published in local news letter (common thread); [pers.] Accomplished self-taught musician. Versatile on piano and guitar. Struggling with manic depression

BORING, LISA M.
[pen.] Lisa Williams Boring; [b.] March 4, 1963, Baytown, TX; [p.] Roland and Kathy Williams; [m.] Donald E. Boring, September 12, 1986; [ch.] Rachael Marie 7 years old, Megan Kathleen 5 years old; [ed.] Ross S. Sterling High School, Florida College; [occ.] Owner of the radio shop; [memb.] Westside church of Christ; [pers.] I had many struggles in my life at the time of this writing. I believe this poem was inspired by God in the early morning hours.; [a.] Arvada, CO

BORKOSKI JR., EDWARD A.
[b.] January 18, 1916, Short Hills, NJ; [p.] Edward and Elizabeth Borkoski; [m.] Pearl Borkoski, October 26, 1947; [ch.] Donald - Son; [ed.] Architect zyrarts class Engineer, Newark College.; [occ.] Retired

BORREL, ANITA
[b.] July 8, 1964, Lake Charles, LA; [p.] Deloris Turner and Charles Turner; [ch.] Justin Borrel, Lacey Borrel, Channing Borrel; [ed.] Sam Houston High, Moss bluff, LA; [occ.] Hostess "Evening Manager", Paw Paw's Stk House Lake Charles, LA; [memb.] Westwood Baptist Church "Choir"; [oth. writ.] I have several other poems "not published yet" but I share with family and friends also with my church; [pers.] I dedicated this poem to my mother. She has shared a lot of love with us but has never showed the pain. She's passed this on to me and one day I'll give it to my children "keep" smiling; [a.] Moss Bluff, LA

BOSEMAN, ANGELA
[b.] February 23, 1982, Pittsburgh, PA; [p.] Alvin and Jacki Boseman; [ed.] Currently a Junior High student; [occ.] Student; [hon.] Highest honor student; [oth. writ.] Christmas Poem read on local television station; [pers.] I like to read black poetry, especially by poets like Gwendolyn Brooks, Phillis Wheatley, and Maya Angelou. I enjoy writing my thoughts down on paper.; [a.] Verona, PA

BOULIER, ANNA CHRISTINE
[pen.] Christy Boulier; [b.] June 14, 1982, GA; [p.] John W. and Anne L. Boulier; [ed.] Attending Excel Christian Academy; [occ.] Student; [pers.] I write to express my feelings about life and its wonders.; [a.] Cassville, GA

BOURET, MS. V. G.
[pen.] Gabriella Bouret; [b.] July 3, 1930, Tulsa, OK; [p.] Deceased; [m.] Deceased; [ch.] 2 Daughters both married; [ed.] College - Nurse; [occ.] Retired; [memb.] In Light Operas in School and City. (School) - In The Past!; [hon.] Award - Volunteering many hours in V. A. Hosp. here in California, near San Jose, GA. 1st Runner up - Beauty Contest Miss Semper Fidelis - 1948.; [oth. writ.] Too many to put down here.; [pers.] I have been writing since in High School I also had the lead in school plays. I always was interested in being a "Nurse."; [a.] Campbell, CA

BOUTWELL, JAMES CONNETT
[pen.] James C. Boutwell; [b.] January 11, 1957, Mississippi; [p.] W.C. and Lula Mae Boutwell; [m.] Carollyn Faye Boutwell, July 28, 1989; [ch.] Sarah Marie, Stepchildren Ronald Dwayne, Michael Paul, and Jade Nicole Harper.; [ed.] Kosciusko High, Holmes Jr. College; [occ.] Musician, Painter; [memb.] Methodist church, The Syndicate (a group of friends I grew up with), and The Musicians; [hon.] Encouragement from family and friends.; [oth. writ.] Poems published in a local paper, wrote for the Holmes Jr. College "Growl". Short stories and poems in abundance, just never had the nerve to send them off.; [pers.] Influences range from Poe to Sandberg. I feel that words are tools forged in the heart, to be used to grasp attention, shake it, and set it free.; [a.] Kosciusko, MS

BOWENS SR., DEWANE C.
[b.] November 3, 1966, Seattle, WA; [m.] Erika L. Bowens, August 9, 1987; [ch.] DeWane C. Bowens Jr., DaQuan J. P. Bowens; [ed.] Degree in Electrician, Lic. Barber, Graduated from Rainier Beach High School; [occ.] Hair Designer, Poet, Artist, Electrician; [hon.] Award in high school for a painting. Honorable discharge from the U.S. Navy; [pers.] I just would like to thank God for all the talents He gave me.; [a.] Seattle, WA

BOWLES, JEAN
[b.] March 3, 1927, Cherokee, AL; [p.] O.L. Quillen, Nannie Quillen; [m.] Henry D. Bowles, November 9, 1946; [ch.] Joanne Hargett, Sandra Bowles, 2 grandsons; [ed.] High School, The Institute of Children's Literature; [occ.] Retired; [memb.] Woodmont Baptist Church Ala. Ladies Golf Assoc.; [pers.] Through my writings, I attempt to convey to generations growing up under changing technology, morals, and mores, the knowledge of a gentler, sweeter time.; [a.] Florence, AL

BOWMAN, JOHN
[b.] November 8, 1976, Sterling, IL; [p.] Tom and Judy Bowman; [ed.] Sterling High School, Sauk Valley Community College; [occ.] Factory Worker; [memb.] The National Writers Association, Richard Petty Fan Club; [hon.] Diploma Endorsement; [oth. writ.] The stage is set, in the cold of December, selfishness, Non-violent Crime, The Lovers that Never Were, River of Sorrow, Wasted Time, The Sucking Wound, Take a Number, Love is Mightier then the Sword, Emotions, The Meaning of Life. Anger and Love, The Souvenir, Society, Shattering the Mirror of Reality, Remembrance, Holiday Interlude, Misty, Falling Down, Deception, Death of Another Day: Another Light. Past Afflictions, Love of a Lady, Longing to be Loved. Blood Lines, Karen Paige, A New Horizon, Rebecca, Home Isn't Where the Heart Is, Like Leaves in a breeze, What is Love. The Quest, Locked in the Closet, Slaves to the Grind, Numb, Cold, So Many Songs, Not as Many Matches, The Tolling, Failure of Time, Dismantled, 4 more Untitled (none of these published or copyrighted at this time).; [pers.] I want to show the darker side of mankind to make readers try to make sense of their troubled times in their lifetimes. Inspirations and influences come from my soul and personal experiences.; [a.] Sterling, IL

BOX, CINDI
[b.] December 15, 1979, Colorado Springs; [p.] Cathi Bearden, Gregory Box; [ed.] I'm in the 9th grade right now and my schools' name is North Hardin High; [occ.] I'm a baby sitter to earn an extra money; [hon.] When I was 7th grade I got on award for being the best story writer in the 7th grade.; [oth. writ.] I've got 58 more poems and about 6 or 7 stories.; [pers.] I started writing poems or stories since I was ten or eleven years old. I thank it all to my 7th grade literature teacher Mrs. Joanna Balmos; [a.] Rodcliffe, KY

BOYD, SHELLEY
[b.] September 6, 1957, Vancouver, WA; [p.] Eva Becker, Ray Becker; [m.] Kirk Boyd, March 21, 1990; [ch.] Adam J. Williams; [ed.] Evergreen High School, Vanc, WA.; [occ.] Orthodontist Assistant, Dr. Gary G. Miller, D.M.D.; [oth. writ.] Several Other Poems; [pers.] Poetry to me is a gift to be cherished from God above to be able to reach within one's soul and to share message with all mankind.; [a.] Woodland, WA

BOYD, SHARON J.
[pen.] Suzan Jamez; [b.] November 8, 1942, Colorado Spring, CO; [p.] Austin and Fern Clampitt; [m.] John W. Boyd, August 3, 1978; [ch.] Suzan and James; [ed.] Quincy Sr High - Quincy Illinois, 1 yr College - Quincy College, Institute of Children's Literature Writer's Digest School, Currently in ICS - Journalism; [occ.] Office Manager for A Construction Co.; [hon.] Award from Illinois for volunteer work.; [pers.] I hope to touch others through my writing, as other writers have touched me.; [a.] Lawrenceville, GA

BOYER, KALANI CHUN
[pen.] KC Boyer; [b.] May 15, 1975, Honolulu, HI; [p.] Douglas Boyer and Donna Keopuhiwa-Emfinger; [ed.] North Pole High School United States Marine Corps Reserve; [occ.] Currently a Latter-Day Saint Missionary for two years; [hon.] A couple local poetry awards in the Fairbanks North Star Borough.; [pers.] Of the few poems I've written, each one resembles a testimony of my values and beliefs or a journal entry in a time of sacred inspiration. I owe it all to Joseph Jensen, my greatest friend and poet.; [a.] North Pole, AK

BOYER, SHARRON
[pen.] Sharron Grinder Boyer; [b.] March 23, 1953, Raton, NM; [p.] John and Julia Grinder; [m.] Joe Melonzon, October 6, 1994; [ch.] Jason Shawn and Justin; [ed.] Globe Elementary and Globe High School, Globe AZ. Mesa Community College, Apollo College, Mesa AZ; [occ.] Cardio-Pulmonary Tech, EMT; [memb.] American Heart Assoc. AART, American Assoc. Office Nurses; [hon.] Apollo College graduate honor roll, Apollo College Award for perfect attendance; [oth. writ.] Children stories several poems, published in local papers; [pers.] I love life and try to live each day as if it were my last; [a.] Globe, AZ

BOZICK, JOHN
[b.] March 31, 1965, Detroit; [p.] Charles Buzick, Frances Buzick; [m.] Joanne Buzick, June 24, 1995; [ed.] Lakeshore High School, Lake Superior State College; [occ.] Environmental Engineer; [pers.] The key to solving problems is communication. The key to communication is an open mind.; [a.] Warren, MI

BRADDOCK, MARGARET JEAN
[pen.] Peggy Braddock; [b.] January 29, 1947, Cleveland, OH; [p.] Marie and Lester Saben; [m.] Gary L. Braddock, February 1, 1964; [ch.] Cathi, Gary Jr. and Anna; [ed.] West Geauga High School, Lakeland College; [occ.] Designing Window Treatments. My workshop is in my home; [memb.] Unity Church; [hon.] Rather than honors or awards, I volunteer, helping children with Learning disabilities, I receive many rewards from their accomplishments; [oth. writ.] I write mostly for my own pleasure. My family and the woods that surround our home are my inspiration; [pers.] Families are our most valuable resource. We most not let them be destroyed. Families take a lot of work; [a.] Chardon, OH

BRADEN, AILENE
[pen.] Ailene B; [b.] April 11, 1941, Harlan, KY; [p.] Enoch Shell and Opal Shell; [m.] Richard M. Braden, October 31, 1959; [ch.] Larry Wayne Braden, Jereld Scott Braden; [ed.] Hall High School completed grade 12 Harlan County Kentucky; [occ.] Former Bell Telephone Operator/Telecommunications Supervisor; [memb.] Church Organizations and Charitable Organizations; [oth. writ.] Never before published looking for publisher of book of poetry already written.; [pers.] I have been influenced by many great poets since childhood. My writings, I hope will convey my wish for hope, peace, love and tranquility in this great world we live in.; [a.] Dearborn Heights, MI

BRADFIELD, GEORGIA ATKINSON
[b.] October 13, 1895; [p.] William Yates Atkinson; [m.] Lieutenant Loyd Bradfield, 1918; [ed.] Salem College in Winston-Salem, North Carolina, and holds a degree in dramatic-arts from Cox College in Atlanta, degree in contract bridge from Ely Culbertson and Charles Goren, Enrolled in a senior citizen's art class sponsored by Daytona Beach Community College. Before long she was taking private lessons, studying oils with the late Virginia Curry, then watercolors with California artist, Joy Simon, and master-artist, Irene Ceraldi.; [hon.] In August, 1980, Georgia has a one-woman show of her painting at the Ormond Memorial Art Gallery, where the late Ormond Beach mayor, Charles Bailey, proclaimed Georgia Atkinson Bradfield Day, in her honor. Former Governor, Ellis Arnall, and his daughter, came to honor her.; [a.] Ormond Beach, FL

BRADISH, REBECCA
[b.] June 18, 1959, Dearborn, MI; [p.] James and Alfreda Boatright; [ch.] Jessica Mae, Corry James and Terry Lee; [ed.] Addison High School, Michigan State University; [occ.] Production Control Assistant, Randall Textron.; [memb.] APICS (American Production and Inventory Control Society), PTA; [oth. writ.] Mr. Piano Man, The Funeral, (Poems Published in Local Publications); [pers.] Writing is my way of expressing deep emotions about life's realities.; [a.] Honover, MI

BRADLEY, JUNE STOUT
[b.] September 2, 1929, Buckhannon, WV; [p.] John and Alma Davis; [m.] Forrest W. Bradley, June 9, 1989; [ch.] Glenda Hain, Sandra Vogel; [ed.] Washington Irving H.S. Clarksburgh, WV, Famous writers school westport, Conn. Writing workshops; [occ.] Retired Secretary; [memb.] First Christian Church Springfield, OH, Charles I. Lathrem Center Rosewood Arts, Kettering, OH; [oth. writ.] Two books in my processor; [pers.] I always wanted to be a writer. It's time to get busy. It's a joy to watch a poem come out of my pen!; [a.] New Carlisle, OH

BRANATH, JOHN
[b.] November 24, 1957, Nyack, NY; [p.] Herman Branath, Lillian Bobb; [ed.] Attending College (Rockland Community College) Nyack High School; [occ.] Cable TV Technician TKR Cable Co., West Nyack, NY.; [memb.] Shore Guard, Orange County Militia, Rank Corporal, this is an American Revolutionary War Reenactment Group. Member Empire H and L Co. #1, Nyack fire Dept.; [pers.] I am a veteran and I support the POW/MIA issue as well as veteran recognition; [a.] Spring Valley, NY

BRANCH, JAMES E.
[b.] July 27, 1970, Holyoke, MA; [p.] Walter J. Branch, Dorothy J. Branch; [ed.] Associates in Computers Bachelors in Business Mgmt.; [occ.] Sales Coordinator; [hon.] Dean's List, President's List; [oth. writ.] Love Is The Witch; [pers.] I always put myself into my work; [a.] Claremont, NH

BRAND, KATHLEEN
[pen.] Katie Brand; [b.] October 18, 1952, West Palm Beach, FL; [p.] Bobbie Maxwell, Edgar Maxwell; [ch.] John Panozzo; [ed.] Forest Hill High, Palm Beach Community College; [occ.] Building Evaluator Palm Beach County Property Appraiser; [memb.] United Methodist Church of the Palm Beaches, Florida Flywheelers Antique Engine Club, yesteryear antique power assoc, Florida trail Assoc.; [hon.] Outstanding service award - Palm Beach County Parks, outstanding service award - Fla. Trail Assoc.; [pers.] Writing poetry is a wonderful gift from God being able to share it is an added blessing; [a.] West Palm Beach, FL

BRANDON, MICHAEL L.
[b.] September 29, 1958, Spokane, WA; [p.] Barbara and Carr L. Brandon; [ed.] Oak Park High School

Keimo, Maplewoods College K.C. MO. The degree of Associate in Arts; [occ.] Disabled; [hon.] Phi Theta Kappa; [oth. writ.] Poetry and Short Stories; [pers.] I wish we could become more truly self aware and realize the power to change ourselves because their's is not only to do or die their's also to reason why.; [a.] Kansas City, MO

BRANNON, DOROTHY C.
[b.] October 30, 1965, Fort Hood, TX; [p.] Henrietta and Ray Brannon; [hon.] Some of my art work was showcased in LBJ Library in Texas 1979 (Lyndon B. Johnson), and we took a trip and got to see his house. (Our art class); [pers.] I've always enjoyed writing and drawing it's a special place that my heart takes me.; [a.] Albuquerque, NM

BRASSEUR, R. GARNER
[b.] May 11, 1933, Hazen, ND; [p.] Joseph O. and Emelia Brasseur; [m.] 1955; [ch.] Pierre, Jauhn, Real and Miette; [ed.] 1952 graduate of C.C.H.S., Miles City, Mont. Colleges: Concordia College Moorhead, Minn/Northern Montana College - Havre, Mont./ Univ. of Mont. Missoula Mont/Univ. of N.D. - Grand Forks, ND. (B.S)/ University of Wash. School of Medicine (M.D.) - Seattle, Wash. 1962.; [occ.] Physician; [memb.] Germans from Russia Heritage Society; [oth. writ.] None published, other than 2 previous poems in The National Library of Poetry Publications; [pers.] Continuing of strive, under the influence of my 4 brothers, Eugene, Duane, Victor and Philip.; [a.] Las Vegas, NM

BRAULT, VIOLA M.
[b.] May 30, 1909, Hamburg, IA; [p.] John and Sara C. Edwards; [m.] Deceased, August 10, 1926; [ch.] Raymond Brault, Orlena Childs, Mildred Angel; [ed.] Freshman year High School - Selden, KS; [occ.] Homemaker; [memb.] St. Helena Cathedral Parish; [hon.] 5 County honors, cooking, canning, sewing and penmanship. 16 State poetry prizes - 1 world prize in poetry Pres. of Missoula, MT Poetry club - 3 yrs - Vice Pres. 2 yrs., Belonged to St. Ann's sodality, Altar Society, Farm Bureau. Several poems published in News Papers. Awards 5 times at Montana Gov. Convention on poetry. Awards was Golden poet in 1991 in "Our World's Most Treasured from Magazine "Montana 89r." on poem. Have entertained with my poems at schools and Sr. Centers. 7 yrs. as a Sr. Companion.; [pers.] I always try to write about what I see in nature and include God who made it all. I also use History or History in the making as my poem "The Flight of Apollo II."; [a.] Helena, MT

BRAZIL, LAUREN
[b.] February 1, 1978, Alabama, NM; [p.] Doug and Mia Brazil; [ed.] 3 yrs. High School at Highland High School, Albuquerque, N. M.; [occ.] Student; [memb.] Creative writing club, French Club, Yearbook staff, Varsity softball volleyball; [hon.] 3 yrs. letterman's letters in both volleyball and softball, Editor of the yearbook; [oth. writ.] Several poems published in California newsletters, published own paperback poetry book, poems and short stories printed in school paper; [pers.] My goal is just that the reader might leave with either a smile or something to think about. My inspirations are my best friend, Christina Parrych, and the early romantic poets. Both have helped to shape who I am.; [a.] Albuquerque, NM

BRECKEL, KATIE M.
[b.] August 4, 1983, Adrian, MI; [p.] Allen and Kathryn; [ed.] YMCA Preschool, Sutton Elem., Herrick Park Elem., Tecumseh Jr. High. Or you can say Tecumseh Public Schools.; [occ.] Student; [memb.] Cottonwood Cloggers; [hon.] Nominated for Tecumseh Rotary, Good Citizen Award (reports not posted yet) by Mrs. Lois Fleming, Elementary Principal - Tecumseh Public Schools.; [a.] Adrian, MI

BREEN, MARGARET
[b.] November 26, 1940, Huntington, NY; [m.] Michael, February 17, 1990; [ch.] Eight; [ed.] High School and Beauty Culture; [occ.] Manager in Sales; [pers.] Treat everyone the very way you like to be treated and strive to make my children all that they can be! Then hope it happens.; [a.] Northport, NY

BRENNAN, SUZANNE R.
[b.] August 1, 1965, Rochester, NY; [ed.] Fairport High, Monroe Community College, Hudson Valley Community College; [occ.] Customer Service Rep.; [memb.] Long Ridge Writer's Group, Conn.; [hon.] Dean's list, President's list for X-Ray Technology; [oth. writ.] I am a fledgling free lance writer embarking on a new career.; [pers.] I want to show the angst of my generation, the generation with no name, in my poetry.; [a.] Rochester, NY

BREWER, TEXEE
[b.] March 30, 1978, McRae, GA; [p.] Tex and Margaret Brewer; [ed.] I am currently a junior at Telfair County High School in McRae, Georgia. (But shall be a senior in the fall when the anthology is published.); [oth. writ.] Fourteen poems, two essays, and I'm working on a short story. This poem will be the first work of mine published.; [pers.] The wilted rose is perfect to one who will not see.; [a.] Lumber City, GA

BREZINA, LANI M.
[b.] April 17, 1970, Philadelphia; [p.] B.J. and Michael Brezina; [ed.] B.A., Temple University 1993; [occ.] Assistant Manager; [pers.] I began writing poetry when my grandfather passed away in 1985. My emotion and love for him, and my grief at his passing were the original force which compelled me to write

BRILLMAN, ROBYN
[b.] December 1, 1972, Milwaukee, WI; [p.] Carol and Michael Brillman; [ed.] Homestead High School, currently a student at Arizona State University majoring in Theatre Education; [occ.] Student; [memb.] International Thespian Society; [hon.] Dean's list fall 1991 and fall 1994.: [oth. writ.] Poems published in! of Diamonds and Rust (I Love you), and Amenean Poetry Anthology 1989 (friendship).: [pers.] I write about things happening in my life at the time. It is the only way I can express my feelings. This poem is about a guy I like, but I can't gather up the courage to let him know.; [a.] Scottsdale, AZ

BRINE, KELLEY MARIE
[pen.] S. K. H.; [b.] July 19, 1978, Maplewood, NJ; [p.] Sara and Ron Brine; [ed.] Currently attending Northern Valley Regional High School at Old Tappan NJ 11th grade; [occ.] Student; [memb.] Creative Writing Club reporter for the Lance.; [pers.] "Never walk blindly through the dark, for there are always things to be seen" S.K.H.; [a.] Norwood, NJ

BRITT, DONNELL ARTHUR
[pen.] D. A. Sharp; [b.] October 20, 1984, Denver, CO; [p.] Donald and Lynnell Britt; [ed.] Gilpin Elementary School; [occ.] 4th Grade Student; [memb.] King Baptist Church Denver Lightning Track Team, Aurora Youth League (Baseball, Football) Young Men of Gilpin; [hon.] Honor Roll and attendance creative Writing, Certificate Awards Gilpin Spelling Bee Winner - 2nd Grade Gilpin Show/Poetry ontest winner, Aurora Youth League Trophies; [pers.] To fail is not to be a failure, it just proves one is human.; [a.] Denver, CO

BROCK, JASON
[pen.] Dennis Trantham; [b.] March 1, 1970, Charlotte, NC; [m.] Susan Brock; [ed.] West Charlotte and Myers Park Sr. High, Central Piedmont Community College; [occ.] Photo Lab Manager; [memb.] Photo Marketing Association's (PMA) Society of Photofinishing Engineers and Certified Photographic Counselors (Also PMA); [hon.] Extensive training and certifications from

Fuji, Kodak, CPI/Fox and Wolf Camera; [oth. writ.] Publication in local newspapers and magazines in Charlotte, NC; [pers.] Self reliance is the key to self - actualization. I am also a musician, artist and photographer.; [a.] Winston-Salem, NC

BRODERICK, KATRINA ANN
[b.] March 4, 1981, Phoenix, AZ; [p.] Edward and Sheila Thompson; [ed.] Westland School; [occ.] Student; [oth. writ.] I have written other poems for school.; [a.] Phoenix, AZ

BROOKS, SHARON L.
[b.] August 7, 1940, Cortland, NY; [p.] Clair and Monnie Bingham; [ch.] Eleven; [ed.] RN from Sister's Hospital Buffalo NY; [occ.] Registered Nurse; [pers.] Poetry - my first love, my answer, my philosophy. Poetry extends my thoughts and my heart to help others.

BROOKS, STEVE
[pen.] Paradox; [b.] March 3, 1966, Philadelphia, PA; [p.] Kevin Brooks and Theresa Brooks; [ed.] Cardinal Dougherty High School; [occ.] Supervising Cook Gettysburg College; [pers.] The simplest way, I have found to communicate my feelings, is through my poetry, I try to have my poems reflect the true feelings I have deep in my soul; [a.] Gettysburg, PA

BROOKS, ROBERT J.
[b.] September 3, 1950, St Petersburg, FL; [m.] Brenda Brooks, February 22, 1969; [ch.] Charlotte Frances, Lora Suzan; [ed.] Northeast High School, FL. BS-Rollins College, FL; [occ.] Retired Major, USAF; [hon.] I several USAF awards during 21 year career, Achievement, Commendation and Meritorious Service; [oth. writ.] Yes not published; [pers.] My limited writings have primarily been influenced by three people, my wife, my daughters and my father (deceased).; [a.] Palm Bay, FL

BROTZMAN, AUGUSTA DAWN GOOLEY
[pen.] Augusta Dawn Brotzman; [b.] August 30, 1974; [p.] Richard and Irma Gooley; [m.] Christopher Brotzman; [ed.] Graduated from Menchville High in Virginia in 1992; [pers.] I live with Cystic Fibrosis and have lost my brother, Brent Gooley, to CF, and I dedicate my poem "Journey My Heaven" to him.; [a.] Peru, NY

BROUSELL, HEATHER
[b.] November 17, 1979, NJ; [p.] Marilu Brousell, Ronald Brousell; [ed.] Shore Regional High School; [pers.] I write to express my feelings. My idol is Maya Angelou and hope that one day my writing can be as good as her poetry.; [a.] West Long Branch, NJ

BROWN, AMY
[b.] August 15, 1980, Tahlequah, OK; [p.] Kim and Larry Brown; [ed.] Cleveland Middle School, 8th grade, currently; [occ.] Student (teen ager); [hon.] Citizenship Awards, Student of the Month, Honor Roll; [pers.] I try to write what I feel. I have found that many people share the same feelings. My greatest influence is the late-great lead singer of Nirvana, Kurt Cobain.; [a.] Tulsa, OK

BROWN, BETTY HAZEN
[b.] December 22, 1928, San Diego, CA; [p.] Norman and Belle Hazen; [m.] Lofton C. Brown; [ch.] Bobette Brooks Lamb, Lacey Lamb Dailey, Jeremy Brooks Lamb (Grand Children); [ed.] A.A. Pensacola Junior College A.S. in Nursing. Pensacola Junior College B.S. Elem. Ed. University of West Florida, Pensacola, FL; [occ.] Retired Teacher; [hon.] Honors PJC. Phi Theta Kappa Dean's List; [oth. writ.] Poems on various subjects used in my teaching others for my family and friends.; [pers.] My father taught his children certain basic values - honesty. Fairness, responsibility for one's actions, etc. He also stressed the absolute necessity of the 3 R's. All of these became part of who I became as a person; [a.] Pensacola, FL

BROWN, DAVID E.
[pen.] David E. Brown; [b.] August 8, 1938, Christopher, IL; [p.] Ellen and Theorn Brown; [m.] Carol M. Brown, April 16, 1982; [ch.] Stacie, Lisa and Jeffrey; [ed.] Master's Degree in Education, Bachelor of Science; [occ.] Elementary School Teacher and High School Supervisor; [memb.] Macomb Humane Society, Salvation Army Volunteer Program, Utica Education Association, Macomb Center for the Performing Arts, Wayne State University Alumni, Association of Supervision and Curriculum Development.; [hon.] Outstanding Young Educator, Teacher of the Year, Citizen of the Year, Apple Award for Law Education, Y.M.C.A Appreciation Award, Distinguished Citizen President Award for Volunteerism - President Award for Union Activities; [oth. writ.] "Read It, Sign It, Pass It" a reading program to motivate young readers.; [pers.] I believe in Jesus Christ as my personal savior and following the American Dream.; [a.] Sterling Heights, MI

BROWN, HEATHER
[b.] January 7, 1976, PA; [p.] Frances Brown, Barbara Brown; [ed.] Stella Maris Elementary School, Girard Academic Music Program, Community College of Philadelphia; [occ.] Student; [memb.] American Red Cross Donor National Honor Society; [hon.] Phi Theta Kappa, Drama Award, Alto Award, Presidential Academic Fitness; [oth. writ.] This is my first publication.; [pers.] Keep away from people who belittle your ambitions. Small people always do that. But the really great make you feel that you, too, can become great.; [a.] Philadelphia, PA

BROWN, JODY C.
[b.] October 25, 1974, Hamberg, IA; [p.] Steven and Michele Brown; [m.] Single; [ed.] Potomac High School, attended Nova Briefly. Nova is a local College.; [occ.] Department Manager for Walmart; [memb.] 1st Baptist Church of Woodbridge. A Conservatives Republican Constituent. I discovered the National Library of Poetry from a conservative newspaper.; [hon.] Having Jesus Christ as my personal savior!; [oth. writ.] Two other publications for the Sparrow Grass Poetry forum: Awaken Angel from Heaven, and Raven Headed Mistress; [pers.] I am not a scholar or a philosopher. I simply write what I think and pray that people enjoy it!; [a.] Woodbridge, VA

BROWN, JONI
[pen.] Miss 'T' Music; [b.] February 19, 1046, Everett, WA; [p.] Dan and Lucille Martin; [m.] Robert Brown, August 4, 1989; [ch.] Billy, Jorja, Jeffrey and Thomas; [ed.] Recently completed a screen-writing class from producer/director Merlin Miller.; [occ.] Free-Lance Writer; [hon.] Semi-Finalist in Billboard song writing contest.; [oth. writ.] Several poems published in local anthology...short story in newspaper and news letter; [pers.] My private motto...if you do but one good thing in this life, do it for a child!; [a.] Trenton, MO

BROWN, KATHERINE S.
[pen.] Katherine S. Brown; [b.] September 23, 1977, Lebanon, PA; [p.] Teri Brown; [ed.] 11th grade. Still in School, but I am taught at home; [occ.] Student; [memb.] United Methodist Church in the Church of my baptism (in Jonestown, Pennsylvania); [pers.] I give my many blessings and eternal thanks to Our Father in Heaven, and to His Son Lord Jesus Christ. For bestowing upon me the ability to write poetry to all, knowing that my talent is being shared by others.; [a.] Coopers Mills, ME

BROWN, LINDA HURT
[pen.] Linda Hurt Brown; [b.] February 11, 1951, Ashland, KY; [p.] Corbett and Nahdeen Hurt; [m.] Ronald J. Brown, May 8, 1970; [ch.] Casey Rene Brown, Dawn Nicole Brown, Natalie J. Brown; [ed.] Mullins High School, Pikeville, KY Eastern Kentucky University, Martin's School of Business, Winchester KY. Honor graduate; [occ.] Customer Relations Manager; [pers.] If a mother enters into motherhood with an open mind, open heart and open arms, it can be one of the most rewarding journeys she will ever take; [a.] Tequesta, FL

BROWN, MARGARET
[pen.] Little Head; [b.] November 27, 1944, Dillon, SC; [p.] John and Evelyn McClellan; [m.] Bernard Brown, September 20, 1962; [ch.] Lisa Tirena Brown; [ed.] James City E. School, J.T. Barbara Junior High; [occ.] Britthaven Nursing Home N.B., housekeeping; [memb.] St. Matthew's Church of Christ, Disciples of Christ Usher Board; [hon.] Britthaven Nursing Home N.B. 55 years service; [oth.writ.] Many poems written for church groups; [pers.] I enjoy reading and became inspired to write. It give me a feeling of confidence. [a.] New Bern, NC.

BROWN, PEARL A. SHARP
[b.] September 1, 1955, Clearfield; [p.] David A. Sharp, Nellie V. Coutter Sharp; [m.] Lynn A. Brown, October 12, 1991; [ch.] Vickie L. Goodrow, Dorsey E. Goodrow II; [ed.] Graduated from Clearfield Area High School certificate in food service, Candy Striper earned 3 stripes Clearfield, Jefferson Mental Health/Mental Retarded. Caring for handicapped persons.; [occ.] Home Health Aide Private duty Care Nurse; [memb.] Sabula Fire Company; [oth. writ.] A precious gift, A tribute to you.; [pers.] I strive to make others happy weather in my writings or in my work as a care giver to others.; [a.] DuBois, PA

BROWN, ROSEMARY J.
[pen.] Rosemary Cacolice Brown; [b.] Pittsburgh, PA; [p.] Joseph and Mary Cacolice; [m.] George Brown; [ch.] Matthew John, David Joseph, Pamela Maria and Paul Christopher; [ed.] High School; [occ.] Secretarial; [oth. writ.] I now have a short essay published in Sunshine Magazine, two fiction stories published in St Joseph's Messenger, and one fiction story soon to come out in the 95/96 season of Clubhouse, a magazine for children. I now have several poems in my collection. However, I've been reticent about submitting any of it and your contest is the first I've ever entered. I am grateful that you found "Children Are the Weavers" worthy enough to put in your upcoming book "Tomorrow Never Knows."; [pers.] I enjoy writing poetry of universal appeal - the kind that is easily understood and (hopefully), enjoyed by those with a stream of "credits" in life experience.; [a.] Lincoln Park, MI

BROWN, STUART L.
[b.] August 30, 1968, Dalton, GA; [p.] Jack Brown, Zeta Brown; [m.] Lisa Brown, November 20, 1993; [ed.] Embry-Riddle Aeronautical University, B.S. 1994 - Professional Aeronautics, Community College of the Air Force A.A.S 1993 - Aircraft Maintenance Technology; [occ.] United States Air Force Tactical Aircraft Maintenance Technician; [pers.] In my writing I reflect thoughts, dreams, and emotions for the reader to see, feel and hear. This is what makes writing such an Art.; [a.] Calhoun, GA

BROWN, THERESA
[pen.] Courtney Nichol; [b.] January 12, 1971, Columbus; [p.] William and Pamela Bornhauser; [m.] Timothy Brown, July 17, 1993; [ch.] Peter Anthony Caranci, Neil Ryan; [ed.] Riverside High School, Lakeland Community College; [occ.] College Student; [hon.] Dean's List; [pers.] By using my own life as a basis for my poetry I feel I can bring a stronger emotionally feeling to the readers.; [a.] Geneva, OH

BROWNE, MAXINE ANNE
[b.] Akron, OH; [p.] Frank and Elizabeth Browne; [m.] Single; [ch.] Michael Alan and Angela Lynn; [ed.] Leggett Elementary, Central High in Akron, OH, Chicago-Wilson Community College - A.A. with honors; University of Illinois at Chicago - B.A. with honors, Chicago State University - M.S. Ed., Georgia State University, Educational Supervision courses, Atlanta,

Georgia; [occ.] College Professor, specialty area - reading; [memb.] International Reading Association, National Council of Teachers of English, Association for Supervision and Curriculum Development, American Federation of Television and Radio Artists; [hon.] Phi Theta Kappa National Honor Society, Distinction in Sociology - University of Illinois at Chicago; [oth. writ.] Cover stories: "Going Home Again," "Past Perfect, The Way We Were"; poetry: "Akron, Ohio-Circa 1940"; [pers.] My writings explore the everyday occurrences that evoke feelings of nostalgia, commonality and love. My favorite poets include James Wright, Theodore Roethke, Elizabeth Bishop, Naomi Shihab Nye and Mary Oliver. [a.] Stone Mountain, GA.

BROWNING, RAYMOND C.
[b.] August 24, 1950, Virginia; [p.] Grace L. Shannon; [ch.] Clinton Keith and Jason Shane; [occ.] Environmental Director; [oth. writ.] I have written many story poems. Some being published in our company news letter.; [pers.] If I can touch someone's emotions with my poetry, if one tear falls upon the page. My time upon the earth will then have meaning.; [a.] Fairfield, OH

BROZOWSKI, AL
[pen.] Al Brozowski; [b.] June 21, 1923, Chicago, IL; [p.] Michael and Lucille; [m.] Trudy, November 3, 1951; [ch.] Maria, Michael, Alan; [ed.] Univ. of Illinois Loyola of Chicago San Diego State; [occ.] Retired Police Lt. Real Estate Bruker; [memb.] San Diego Illinois Club Porae Loyda Alumni; [hon.] Marriage to my wife; [oth. writ.] To write a book on police stories; [pers.] Be true to yourself; [a.] El Cajon, CA

BRUCE, JOYA LYNN
[b.] November 23, 1959, Bathesda, MD; [p.] Sus'Ann Jones, Otis Bruce; [ch.] Stephanie Sus'Ann, Julius Ray, Dominique Nicole; [ed.] High School of Commerce Springfield, MA; [occ.] Correctional Officer, Osborn Correction Institute Somers, CT; [pers.] My writings are a reflection of my life, loves, disappointments and dreams. I am truly honored for this opportunity to share this part of myself with others.; [a.] Indian Orchard, MA

BRUNELLE, ROBERT N. J.
[b.] July 3, 1972, New Bedford, MA; [p.] Normand and Pauline Brunelle; [ed.] Fairhaven High School, University of Massachusetts Dartmouth; [occ.] Student; [pers.] "The quest for knowledge is itself the tragic action."; [a.] Fairhaven, MA

BRUNER, PAMELA G.
[b.] June 4, 1952, Sidney, NE; [p.] Ralph and Dorothy Bruner; [ch.] Thaddeus Richard Kosse, Tobias Orion Kosse; [ed.] Central High School, Aurora Co.; [occ.] U.S. West Direct - Office Administrator; [pers.] I was inspired by my grandmother Mina Richardson Bruner who has written two books of poetry, 1. My poetry pail - copyright 1941, 2. The purple Tree and Waysine Grasses - copyright 1963; [a.] Aurora, CO

BRUNK, DIEDRE
[pen.] Me; [b.] April 21, 1970, Detroit, MI; [p.] Mr. and Mrs. Walter Hays; [m.] David Brunk, July 18, 1992; [ed.] I have a Bachelors in Science and Nursing and am starting on a masters degree in science and nursing; [occ.] Nurse; [memb.] I am a member of PRCUA; [pers.] I have a truly wonderful husband who was my inspiration for this and many other poems I've written I believe the world would be a much brighter place to live five all gave a little bit of hope, faith and love; [a.] Madison Heights, MI

BRYAN, CHRISTOPHER
[b.] January 11, 1948, Denver, CO; [p.] Herbert and Veva Bryan; [m.] Divorce/Single; [ch.] Carrie Colleen and Michael William; [ed.] Comm. College of Denver, 1 yr Criminal Justice, 2 yrs Photography; [occ.] Certified Nurse Assistant, Photographer, Landscape and Property Maint.; [memb.] I am a Vietnam Veteran

United States Army 1966-69; [hon.] My Photography has been exhibited at the State Capital Building in Denver, National Center of Atmospheric Research in Boulder, Co., Dallas City Hall, Texas, and I've been published in several small publications.; [pers.] Love has no boundaries; [a.] Fruita, CO

BRYSON, MARK
[b.] February 15, 1959, Abilene, TX; [p.] Dan and Joyce Bryson; [ed.] Cooper High School, Abilene, TX; [occ.] Dispatcher for a freight company; [pers.] Our relationships with others often leads us down paths of bliss and despair. It is the emotional serenity and turmoil of this journey that drives my pen.; [a.] Houston, TX

BUCHMANN, PETER JAMES P. E.
[b.] October 15, 1935, Northern, Ontario, Canada; [p.] Karl and Astrid Buchmann; [m.] Sue Parsley Buchmann, September 11, 1989; [ch.] Kurt, Suzanne, Karl; [ed.] B.S.M.E. 1960, Michigan Tech. Sports Hall of Fame (Hockey/Football); [occ.] Engineer: Paper Industry (Consultant) Limited to Support (Have Epilepsy) cannot drive; [memb.] Professional Engineer; [hon.] U.S. National Hockey Team 1969, Stockholm World Games.

BUCK, WILLIAM BRET
[b.] August 11, 1967, AZ; [p.] Robert and Bertha Buck; [ed.] Sunny Slope High School and Wisdom of Elders; [occ.] Parts Manager.; [hon.] Various athletic awards in cross country and track, Jeff Gentleman award.; [oth. writ.] Many but not published.; [pers.] Be yourself, don't be your own enemy by forgetting your own convictions. If anyone says you can't, do whatever it takes to prove them wrong. Believe in yourself.; [a.] Phoenix, AZ

BUCKNER, DEBORAH C.
[pen.] Deb; [b.] August 25, 1960, Sacramento, CA; [p.] Don and Donna Hendrinks; [m.] Mark Buckner, December 31, 1992; [ch.] Rene Lyn - Daughter, Kyle Mark - Stepson; [ed.] Graduate of T.C. Roberson High; [occ.] Receptionist of Wilsonart International; [memb.] Racking House Association; [pers.] When you inspect others hearts and not their minds, it is amazing what breathtaking things can be revealed.; [a.] Fletcher, NC

BUDER, VICTORIA
[pen.] Victoria Landesman; [b.] January 3, 1959, New York; [p.] Susan Coan and Bill Landesman; [m.] Wayne Buder, June 27, 1993; [ed.] BA Northwestern University; [occ.] Development, Marin (Fundraising) Country Day School; [memb.] Vice-President, Development for Little Brothers-Friends of the Elderly; [oth. writ.] Published in The Poet, Peu a Peu and Great Contemporary Poems, 1978; [a.] Mill Valley, CA

BUDNEY II, ALEXANDER J.
[b.] October 3, 1977, Chicago; [p.] Albert Budney, Karen Budney; [ed.] Noble and Greenough School Pembroke Hill School; [occ.] Student; [oth. writ.] Poems and short stories published in school publications.; [a.] Kansas City, MO

BUERMANN, JOSHUA
[pen.] Manson's Wall; [b.] April 1, 1977, Detroit Lakes, MN; [p.] Sharon and Dennis Buermann; [m.] Erica Berning; [ed.] Detroit Lakes High School, attending Northwestern University Fall of '95; [occ.] Student; [memb.] A lot of organizations that in the greater extemporal view of the cosmos mean nothing.; [oth. writ.] A recently started compilation of about 250 poems, as well as a short screenplay; [pers.] The poem in question is a Manson Wall dirty of a more-or-less surrealistic nature and origin, seeking to turn big words into poetry. I've been influenced by W.C. Williams, Sim Morrison, and M.J. Wamsach. I like Pith too.; [a.] Ogema, MN

BURKDORF, REBECCA
[b.] December 16, 1971, Little Falls, NY; [p.] Mr. & Mrs. William Brinski; [m.] Peter Burkdorf, August 8, 1992; [ed.] Dolgeville Central High School Elmira College - Associates Degree Utica College of Syracuse University - B.A. in English and Sunt Cortland candidate for master's in reading December 1995; [occ.] Full-time graduate student and certified high school English teacher.; [oth. writ.] Poem published in Mohawk Valley Review Spring 1990, articles in local newspapers and currently trying to print my personal collection of poetry. I have also written many short stories.; [pers.] I have been writing poetry and short stories since junior high school. My poems and stories represent my emotions and thoughts of serious and light hearted topics. For me, writing has been and will continue to be an emotional release, often proving its therapeutic powers.; [a.] Little Falls, NY

BURKE, MICHAEL T.
[b.] July 22, 1967, Philadelphia, PA; [p.] Thomas and Bridget Burke; [m.] Single; [ed.] Duxbury High School (Duxbury, MA), 1985, Stonehill College, (N-Easton, MA), 1990- B.A. in Communications.; [occ.] Benefit Plans Representative for State Street Bank and Trust Co.; [memb.] American Diabetes Association, Linda M. Burke Memorial Scholarship Committee, Federal Communications Commission (FCC) Licence.; [hon.] Eagle of the Cross Award - 1987.; [oth. writ.] Currently working on two book projects, which will include a collection of my short stories and poems.; [pers.] With my writing, I try to bring a page to life, in hopes of creating something that will not be soon forgotten.; [a.] Duxbury, MA

BURNS, MARY ANN
[pen.] Mary Anne; [b.] Portland, Maine; [p.] Eveline Modes, Bill Modes; [ch.] Peter Miner, Jennifer Miner, Bubby Burns, Toby Burnse; [ed.] Portland High School, also home studying; [occ.] Home maker; [memb.] Alliance for the mentally ill of Maine, (Doing much research to help adults and children) also a member of the Autism society); [hon.] I won in a talent contest at the Auburn Mall in Auburn Maine, I wrote the words and music (a song for you) I sang with my guitar (I played) it was on a local radio station. I passed a writers attributes test and was excepted to study for writing childrens stories; [oth. writ.] I write childrens stories, for children I work with, I write jokes for personal friends, I have "many" songs and poems written over the years. I write my diary in poetry to capture the most sensitive parts of my life. To look back and see where I've grown; [pers.] My mind thinks poetry, I like to find simple words to reach the unreachable prejudices of the world. To speak for the children who can't speak for themselves, the handicap, the poor, the abused, to draw with words that reach the hearts of it's readers; [a.] Auburn, ME

BURNS, RUFUS J.
[pen.] Jim; [b.] August 8, 1922, Holly Hill; [p.] Alice Burns (Mother); [m.] Evelyn Burns, January 18, 1943; [ch.] Gordon, James and Alicia; [occ.] (Retired) Tile Contractor; [pers.] This poem was written in remembrance of my mother who passed away when I was 15. It made me feel sad and lonely, so I put my feelings in this poem.; [a.] Holly Hill, FL

BURRIS, VADELLA
[pen.] VaDella Burris; [b.] March 10, 1927, Sapulpa, OK; [p.] Ellis H. and Nelle Rider; [m.] E. John Burris, December 11, 1945; [ch.] Cheryl, David, Janna and Dawne; [ed.] Graduate of Wewoka, OK High - Oral Roberts University (Some Credits); [occ.] Co-owner of the Victorian Rose Inn, Eureka Springs, AR; [memb.] Eureka Springs B&B Asso. - First Assembly of God, Rainbow Girls (1940's); [hon.] First place award in dramatic reading (poetry) in High school worthy advisor of Rainbow Girls Student council SEC'S; [oth. writ.] Three Victorian Novelettes - (unpublished) sev-

eral poems I have written through the years - and also a few songs.; [pers.] I write about different subjects - especially Spiritual and patriotic inspirations.; [a.] Springfield, MO

BURROWS, CHUCK
[occ.] Captain, Infantry, U.S. Army; [pers.] This is the first poem of a trilogy written in 1991 in southwest Asia. While dedicated to all who were there and those who died, Marine Captain Jonathan Edwards and his family are especially remembered.; [a.] Killeen, TX

BURTON, KENNETH
[pen.] Ken; [b.] July 10, 1963, Bogalusa, LA; [p.] Milton and Jerry Burton; [m.] Paula Burton, November 14, 1992; [ch.] Chandler Mikhail Burton; [ed.] Graduated from Dillard University, New Orleans LA. 1986 Enlisted in the Navy December '86 - July '94; [occ.] Medical Assistant Naval Reserve; [hon.] To have one of my writings published; [oth. writ.] Published poems in High School Paper in 1982; [pers.] Writing is the Less Emphasized key to Communication, if you can't say it, write it!; [a.] Washougal, WA

BURTON, HELEN V.
[b.] December 31, 1932, Virginia; [p.] Mary and John Dudley (Deceased); [m.] Edward Burton, June 25, 1955; [ch.] Ann Y. Burton, M. D. Resident of Internal Medicine Cook County Hospital, Chicago, IL.; [ed.] Bachelor of Science, Eastern Michigan University, Ypsilanti, MI., Master of Social Work, Wayne State University, Detroit, MI.; [occ.] Director, State of Michigan, Child and Family Services Center, Taylor, MI.; [memb.] Literacy Volunteers of America, Council of Catholic Women, United Community Services - Advisory Board Taylor Teens Advisory Council; [hon.] Catholic Woman of the Year - 1993, Spirit of Detroit - 1990; [oth. writ.] 35 poems published at this time.; [pers.] Through poetry I endeavor to express my life experiences and reflections and observations about the world around me.; [a.] Detroit, MI

BUTLER, MARTHA PENNEY
[b.] June 28, 1923, Alabama; [p.] Fannie and Henry Penney; [m.] November 5, 1949; [ch.] Cindy and Scott Butler; [ed.] Hokes Bluff High School in Alabama Athens College in Alabama BA Degree Department of Agriculture Graduate School in D.C. (3 yrs); [occ.] Secretary for ALTSHU Corp. in Accokeek.; [memb.] Calvert Manor Garden Club Accokeek Lioness Club; [hon.] Meritorious and suggestions received several awards in National Park Service. 1994 Editors Choice Award from the National Library of Poetry; [pers.] My writings reflect my love of nature and my appreciation for our Supreme Artist.; [a.] Accokeek, MD

BUTLER, JULIE ILKANIC
[b.] June 9, 1956, Cleveland, OH; [p.] Angela Parisi Ilkanic, John Ilkanic; [ed.] Regina High School, Notre Dame College; [occ.] Copywriter; [memb.] Cleveland Society of Communicating Arts; [hon.] Phi Beta Kappa The one show national advertising award national ADDY awards art director's club of New York ANDY award, best-of-show Honors Three Times in Cleveland Advertising Shows; [oth. writ.] Children's Short Stories, Both Lyrics and Music for over 50 songs, working on two novels, ads for print, TV and Radio, Promotional PR Writing and Proposals.; [pers.] I believe that if my writing can make someone feel an emotion or gain an insight that really touches them, then I have done my job. I love writing so much. There aren't enough hours in the day to write all I want to write.; [a.] Cleveland, OH

BUTLER, SUSAN
[b.] Nov 23, 1970, Nyack, NY; [p.] Harriet Hale, Robert Butler; [pers.] We need to change our futures. We need to start with the children. Feed their minds and all will fall into place; [a.] Orange City, FL

BUTLER, EFFIE L.
[b.] November 6, 1961, Columbia, SC; [m.] Terry L. Butler, March 25, 1988; [ch.] Marguerite E. Germany, Michael C. W. Butler; [occ.] Housewife; [pers.] I believe in and have a strong faith in God, I love my family, my friends, my church and in my fellow humankind.; [a.] Chandler, AZ

BYRD, ROY N.
[b.] Ada, OK; [p.] Roy and Camilla Byrd; [m.] Katy Byrd; [pers.] Before I myself end in the deep compost heap, I have some poem writing time to keep.; [a.] Toyanvale, TX

BYRNE, MICHELLE DIANE
[b.] February 24, 1963, Colorado; [p.] Pennie and Garry Smith; [m.] Christopher Michael Byrne, May 22, 1982; [ch.] Meagan Diane Byrne - 11, Sean Michael Byrne - 10; [ed.] Del Campo High School Fair Oaks California Graduated 1981; [occ.] Bookkeeper, Trepke's Tire Town; [memb.] Catholic Charities and Community Services March of Dimes; [pers.] The poem I wrote was influenced by my now deceased grandfather and my family. It was my first attempt at writing and reflected feelings and thoughts a the time. I believe I did it as a project in high school. My mother, bless her heart, had the faith in me to submit the poem to the National Library of Poetry.; [a.] Golden, CO

CAHILL, JESSICA
[b.] March 11, 1981, Norristown, PA; [p.] Barbara Harvey and James Cahill; [ed.] Presently a student at Pottsgrove Middle School.; [occ.] Student; [memb.] JV and Varsity Field Hockey; [hon.] Seventh grade Perfect Attendance Award,; [oth. writ.] I write on a regular basis, this is my first publication (I am only 13 years old); [pers.] I express all of my feelings, good or bad, through my writing. It helps me through alot.; [a.] Pottstown, PA

CAHILL, THOMAS
[b.] November 22, 1951, Utica, NY; [ed.] Marquette University (B.A.), George Mason University Law School (J.D.), University of Brussels (LL.M.); [memb.] Team New York Aquatics (Swim Team).; [oth. writ.] "The Swimmer", "The Pool", "He Swims-She Swims", "The Wall", (all poems).; [pers.] Poetry is all about using your imagination; [a.] New York, NY

CAIN, CHRISTINA L.
[pen.] ME, Tika; [b.] June 28, 1965, Arizona; [ch.] 5 children, 1 boy Damien, 4 girls Reyna, Mandi, Ninja and Doudat; [occ.] Housewife; [pers.] Poem was written and put in a Christmas card made by myself my kids for Earl. While he is away!; [a.] Globe, AZ

CALDWELL, TRACY-BETINA
[b.] February 19, Detroit, MI; [p.] Al and Nell Caldwell; [ed.] MBA - Penn State Univ., BBA - Western Michigan Univ.; [occ.] Employee Relations - Ford Motor Company; [memb.] National Black MBA Assoc. - Detroit Chp., Secretary, Delta Sigma Theta Sorority - Detroit Alumnae Chp., Jim Dandy Ski Club; [pers.] "Golden Silence" is my writing debut to the world. Today, I share my unclothed jargon.; [a.] Detroit, MI

CALLAHAN, BREANDA
[pen.] B. B. Blue; [b.] November 3, 1972, Neptune, NJ; [p.] Bart Callahan and Nancy Howle; [ed.] Freehold Boro High School, Brookdale Community College, Performance Training Institute; [occ.] Legal Secretary; [memb.] National Arbor Day Foundation, Who's Who Among American High School Students; [hon.] Most creative - Annual sandcastle contest.; [oth. writ.] Articles in High School newspaper.; [pers.] I was born a dreamer, I may live as a fool, but you can bet... I will die happy.; [a.] Englishton, NJ

CALVIRD, GAYNEL L.
[pen.] Gaynel; [b.] March 30, 1937, Wyandote, MI;

[p.] Robert and Hermine Calvird; [m.] Carol Calvird, April 2, 1966; [ch.] Gregg; [ed.] Associates Degree in Metallurgy - other related technical courses.; [occ.] Retired - now doing volunteer church work and working on a manuscript from previously written poems.; [hon.] Chosen by God to be one of his children. Summa Cum Laude; [oth. writ.] Three poems published in Sparrowgrass Poetry Forum - early 90's anthologies - Approx. 200 poems written - 35/40 published in church newsletter in past 15 years.; [pers.] Some works are light, nonsensical, or philosophical. Most are done with specific reason and tend to express the importance of Christ in our lives and his tremendous impact in mine.; [a.] Allen Park, MI

CAMACHO, KAY
[pen.] Kay Camacho; [b.] June 27, 1956, Charlotte, NC; [p.] Don and Bernice Seymour; [m.] Edward McNamara, September 17, 1995; [ch.] Jason Thomas Camacho, Kaitlin Jo McNamara; [occ.] Owner Writer and poet, New moon: Words spoken from the heart; [memb.] Poetry in the Woods Ft. Lauderdale, FL.; [oth. writ.] Pieces of Me, a collection of thoughts and expressions.; [pers.] Words written from the heart are felt by the heart, and remembered. Words Written from the Intellect are pondered upon, and most often forgotten. My wish is to touch the heart.; [a.] Pompano Beach, FL

CAMARILLO, JESSICA A.
[pen.] Jess; [b.] November 22, 1971, Port Hueneme, CA; [p.] Jess Camarillo, Victoria Camarillo; [occ.] Student; [oth. writ.] Several poems published in Anthologies by National Library of Poetry.; [pers.] I feel expression is God's greatest gift. It keeps us sane!; [a.] Hacienda Height, CA

CAMPANOZZI, CHRIS
[pen.] Chris Campanozzi; [b.] October 8, 1973, Wayne, NJ; [p.] Ralph and Gerri; [ed.] Ocean County College; [occ.] Student - want to be an actor; [oth. writ.] Several poems and short stories; [pers.] Never let any one tell you your no good. I am influenced by John Lennon, Edger Allen Poe and William Blake; [a.] Bayville, NJ

CAMPBELL, TODD ALLEN
[pen.] Todd A. Campbell; [b.] April 23, 1967, Omaha, NE; [p.] Eugene Campbell, Mardelle Campbell; [m.] Single; [ed.] Glendale and Fort Collins High Schools, DADC. Any class I find that interests me.; [occ.] Property Management. Singer/songwriter/poet.; [memb.] American Red Cross, Green Mountain Poetry Group.; [oth. writ.] Listen for music written or performed by "Allen Todd".; [pers.] My writings are of my life lessons, observations, and events.; [a.] Denver, CO

CAMPBELL, JOHN ANDREW
[b.] April 12, 1973, Omaha, NE; [p.] Richard and Judith Campbell; [ed.] Midway High School, Texas A and M University McLennan Community College; [occ.] Student at Texas A and M; [memb.] Corps of Cadets at Texas A and MU, Texas A and M Anthropological Society, Walo sailing club; [hon.] Commander NROTC color guard Texas A and MU.; [oth. writ.] One poem published in the poetry shell (a literary magazine for Monterey, CA in 1981), two poems published in a high school literary magazine.; [pers.] Bryon and Shelly are my greatest inspirations for poetry, as well as Shakespeare and Burns. Sailing and cooking are my favorite hobbies.; [a.] Hewitt, TX

CANGUREL, DR. SUSAN
[b.] September 11, 1946, Madison, WI; [p.] John Mather Murray and Lois Wiessinger; [m.] Mel Cangurel, April 8, 1985; [ch.] Lora Quezada, Julie Colarusso; [ed.] PhD in Business Administration with Human Resource Management Option - with honors from century University Albuquerque, NM; [occ.] Human Resources Director at R.M. Personnel; [memb.] 1. Society for Human Resources Management, 2. National Assoc. of Female Executives, 3. American Assoc. of University

Women; [hon.] 1. Doctorate, Masters, and Bachelor Science Degrees with honors, 2. Listed in Who's Who in America and American Women; [oth. writ.] Numerous poems and short stories; [a.] El Paso, TX

CANO, PAUL E.
[b.] September 6, 1973, New York; [p.] Antonio and Ines Cano; [ed.] Holy Name Elementary, Cardinal Hayes High School, Sacred Heart University; [occ.] Student of Life; [oth. writ.] Several poems published in local newspaper, Latino Village Press.; [pers.] Racism is a nightmare that we may never wake up from unless we educate the ignorant masses of people who wonder around with false hatred. Learn to love and understand people of all races before you condemn a race to prejudices and stereotypes that may not be true. Think with your heart as well as your mind.; [a.] New York, NY

CANSLER, ALFREIDA KAY
[pen.] Kay Jones; [b.] January 19, 1966, Shelby, AL; [p.] Geraldine Cansler, Alfonso Jones; [ed.] Graduated May 30, 1984, Memphis Technical High School, Graduated June 30, 1988 Memphis Institute of Technology, Office Automation, Medical Terminology.; [occ.] Medical Assistant, Family Practice Associates; [memb.] Annual Staff, Quill and Scroll, Deca Club Newspaper Staff, Class Reporter, College, News Paper Staff, Year Book Staff.; [hon.] Perfect attendance, 10,11,12, American History Award Honor Roll, Basketball Princess most intellectual girl, BA0-Beta Alpha Phi, BA0-Articulating on one's mind to be careful of one's behavior, self discipline; [oth. writ.] Newspaper staff "The Yellow Jackets", newspaper staff "The Output" The mystified inspiration of poems and poetry, written in 1983 by Alfreida Kay Cansler; [pers.] Know something, know it well do something, do it well to create the highest element of perfection in order to precede predominate leadership.; [a.] Memphis, TN

CANTU, JUAN
[b.] January 10, 1967, Oakland; [p.] Refugio and Patsy Cantu; [occ.] Auto worker; [memb.] NRA; [oth. writ.] Several poems and a short story all unpublished.; [a.] Hayward, CA

CAPLES, MICHELLE
[b.] April 5, 1968, Milwaukee, WI; [p.] Wiley Caples Jr., Jo Ann Roundtree; [m.] TBA; [ed.] Milwaukee H.S. of the Arts, University of Wisconsin - Milwaukee; [pers.] Writing keeps my soul honest and it never ceases to amaze me how poetry acts as the kaleidoscope of human nature, the colors stay the same, but the picture is ever changing; [a.] Milwaukee, WI

CAPONE JR., RALPH
[b.] May 11, 1948, Queens; [p.] Ralph and Norma; [ch.] Andrew Capone, Staci Capone; [ed.] East Rockaway HS attending Farmingdale Univ.; [occ.] Assistant Manager in Car dealer ship; [oth. writ.] A collection of short stories unpublished at this time.; [pers.] My writings are inspired by all the mirrors that walk the planet. They are the reflections for my pen. Let it flow forever!; [a.] East Rockaway, NY

CAPUTO, MICHAEL
[b.] April 21, 1925, New York, NY; [p.] Morris and Josephine Caputo; [m.] Mary Caputo, December 3, 1960; [ch.] Christine, Danielle (grandchild); [occ.] Retired School Bus Driver; [pers.] The innocence and trueness in the hearts of children have always been my biggest inspiration.; [a.] Brooklyn, NY

CAPUTO, CATHERINE MARIE
[b.] December 12, 1976, Brooklyn, NY; [p.] Marie Caputo; [ed.] John Dewey High School, (Regents Diploma); [occ.] Student at Brooklyn College; [hon.] Poetry Awards in High School; [oth. writ.] A poem published in "Seasons to Come".; [pers.] I tend to put all of my bottled up feelings and emotions into my poetry. I can express myself much more clearly and comfort-

ably on paper.; [a.] Brooklyn, NY

CARALLO, ORLANDO
[pen.] Tony; [b.] June 23, 1945, Bronx Parkcheska, NY; [p.] Orlando and Madeline; [m.] Donna; [ch.] Jennifer, Kelly; [ed.] BA Saint Johns Ms. CCNY JD Touro Law; [occ.] Reading Teacher; [pers.] Change must take place to safeguard our youth and pressure our world.; [a.] Bronx, NY

CARLSON JR., PHILIP C.
[b.] August 2, 1960, Harvey, IL; [p.] Philip C. Carlson, Phyllis A. Carlson; [ch.] Laura Catherine Carlson; [ed.] Griffith High, Purdue University, West Lafayette, B.A.; [memb.] Griffith Lion's Club; [hon.] Eagle Scout, B.S.A.; [oth. writ.] Was a sports correspondent for the Times newspaper in NW Indiana; [a.] Griffith, IN

CARLYLE, SUSAN
[b.] May 26, 1961, Ft. Worth, TX; [m.] John Carlyle, November 27, 1980; [ch.] Cortney Carlyle, Christina Carlyle; [occ.] Mom and Housewife; [memb.] Stonebriar Country Club, United States Tennis Assoc., Tennis Competitors of Dallas.; [oth. writ.] Only personal writings about life experiences, I began doing this as a part of therapy, writing about feelings or memories of childhood experiences.; [pers.] I speak freely today for all the years I felt I could not and for all abused children who are afraid to speak or the children who speak but go unheard; [a.] Dallas, TX

CARNRIGHT, J. M.
[pen.] Jack Caravaggio; [b.] July 21, 1945, U.S.A.; [p.] William E. Carnright and Helen L. O'Brien; [m.] Margaret E. Carnright; [ch.] William-Christopher Carnright; [ed.] University of Colorado, BFA degree; [hon.] University of Colorado, Best of year Award - Painting and Sculpture. Palmer-Hoyt Scholar, Denver Univ., Bogardus Scholar - Pratt Institute; [oth. writ.] "Aria Hahn" (Futuristic Novel), Poetry Books: 1. "The Nuclear Amusement Park" 2. A File On Barflys" 3. "Beat street" Short stories: 1. "50,000 Grandis" 2. "Turnstiles" and writings published in newspapers, magazines and small poetry books. Teleplay: "No Laughing Matier" and others.; [a.] Westport, CT

CARPENTER, ROSIE LENE
[b.] May 21, 1939, Alabama; [m.] H. Claytoa Carpenter, July 16, 1960; [ch.] One; [ed.] BS-Business Administration University of North Alabama Florence, Alabama; [occ.] Tennessee Valley Authority; [oth. writ.] Unpublished poems; [pers.] My writings are heart felt and inspired by God.; [a.] Town Creek, AL

CARR, TRISH
[pen.] Trish Luv; [b.] February 25, Philadelphia, PA; [p.] Cheryl Little, Harvey Carr; [ed.] Central High School, attending California Univ. of PA.; [occ.] Student; [memb.] Holy Temple, Triple AAA, Black Student Union, Gospel Choir (Young and Gifted); [hon.] Dean's List; [pers.] I would like to thank Mom and Dad, God, sister, friends, grandmom, and my boyfriend J.D., all have supported me. If you believe it, you can achieve it.; [a.] Philadelphia, PA

CARR, CHARLES
[pen.] Charley Carr; [b.] November 30, 1922, Knoxville; [p.] Luther and Lassie Mae Carr (D); [m.] Goldie (deceased), July 7, 1945; [ch.] E. Sue, Charles E., Gary W., 5 grandchildren, 1 greatgrand child; [ed.] Rule High, Indiana Extension BA., Journalism; [occ.] Retired after years of double-career as Postal Services employee and a freelance outdoor columnist/editor. My work has been published in National, Regional, State and local publications.; [memb.] Retired - Southeastern Outdoor Press Association.; [hon.] 3 times columnist of the year., 2 times photographer of the year.; [oth. writ.] My columns and photographs have been published in national, regional state, and local publications for outdoor sports and conservation.; [pers.] Since

poetry is the purest form of writing, I reach deep inside me to find the purest and simplest of words to form my "inspirational verses" so that everyone can read, understand, and enjoy my work.; [a.] Knoxville, TN

CARROLL, ROBIN
[b.] December 24, 1968, Chester, PA; [p.] Jane Carroll; [ed.] Graduated from Chester High School in 1986. Graduated from Penn State University in 1991 with a Degree in Communications.; [occ.] Assistant Service Manager for Corestates Bank.; [memb.] New Jerusalem C.O.G.I.C. Public Relations Dept., Choir Secretary, Youth Dept, and Drama Dept.; [hon.] Young Publisher's Award; [oth. writ.] A short story and essay published in a local magazine, a play currently being put into production.; [pers.] I am grateful for the gift that God has bestowed upon me and for allowing me to share that gift with the world through my writing.; [a.] Parkside, PA

CARROLL, DIANA
[b.] September 11, 1974, Boston, GA; [p.] Linda and Donald Carroll; [ed.] Cardinal Cushing H.S. 1992 graduated, currently going to school nights for Criminal Justice-Bunker Hill CC; [occ.] Pitney Bowes, site representative; [oth. writ.] Many other unpublished poems.; [pers.] Poetry helps me express my feelings best.; [a.] Braintree, MA

CARRUTHERS, ROSIE LEE
[b.] December 8, 1943, Jackson, MS; [p.] Tom B. and Lucille Davis; [m.] Rosevelt Carruthers, November 14, 1993; [ch.] Teresa, Anthony, Pvon, Rosslyn Arvetta, Shiron; [ed.] Completed 12th grade went to Rockhurst College, majored in Office Skills also went back to college took up Law Enforcement.; [occ.] Bus Driver, Vancom; [memb.] Sisterhood, Apostolic Church of Jesus Christ; [hon.] Honor roll in high school, citizenship awards. Principal good standing list.; [oth. writ.] Church Bulletin Schools special Occasion, such as Holidays, Black History.; [pers.] I am thrilled at writing poetry to be able to share my dreams with and thoughts with the world. I been enthused to write every since the age of 12, by my mother.; [a.] Kansas City, MO

CARTER, B. J.
[b.] June 6, 1932, Munford, AL; [p.] Joseph and Jimmie Carter; [m.] Marie White Carter, September 29, 1957; [ch.] Kathryn, Karen, Kellie; [ed.] B.A. Birmingham, Southern College, M. Div. Emory University.; [occ.] Pastor First United Methodist Church Sylacauga; [oth. writ.] A shout from Mt Zion published 1991; [a.] Sylacauga, AL

CARTER, E. VERNESE MCKOY
[pen.] Vernese McKoy; [p.] Henry, and Ethel J. McKoy; [m.] Divorced; [ch.] Orestes J. Carter; [ed.] B.A. in English from Brooklyn College, Masters in Education - Hunter College of the City University.; [occ.] Retired Teacher Rush Henrietta Schools; [memb.] International Women's Writing Guild; [oth. writ.] Why the Crow only says caw, caw, caw. (a fable), On City Streets (short story), and other poems published in Pathways, voice of educators in Western New York region and Arcadia Poetry 1993; [pers.] The autumn of our lives is that time when we have reached the full bloom of our accomplishments which we feel makes us worthy of enjoying all that life has brought, beauty of the forest in autumn.; [a.] Fishkill, NY

CARTER, HOLLY
[b.] June 18, 1981, Kendallville, IN; [p.] Carole Frye and Gordon Carter; [ed.] Central Noble Middle; [hon.] Creative Writing Essay (1st), United Woodsman of America; [a.] Albion, IN

CARTER, OPAL R.
[pen.] Opal Carter; [b.] July 10, 1922, Carter Nine, OK; [p.] Grover and Pearl Rhoton; [m.] Bobbie Jack Carter, August 9, 1941; [ch.] Renae; [ed.] Carter Nine H.S.,

Shidler Jr. College, Northern Oklahoma College; [occ.] Retired High School Secretary; [memb.] Oak Grove Baptist Church, Kaw City, OK, Poetry Society of Oklahoma; [hon.] Colleges - Dean's Lists Poetry Society of OK, 1st place award for poem in National Poetry Day Contest. Poem winner in Annual Awards Contest.; [oth. writ.] Poetry entries in state contest. Poems concerning family, friends, nature, school, devotionals, church, and humorous ones.; [pers.] Any inspiration for poetry that I have written - I owe to my Creator, my Lord, and my Saviour.; [a.] Shidler, OK

CARTER, THELMA J.
[b.] Virginia; [p.] Cornelius and Elsie Smith; [m.] Walter J. Carter Sr., July 29, 1972; [ch.] Walt, Cherita and Bernadette; [ed.] I C Norcom High School, Norfolk State University; [memb.] Public Relations Committee (church); [oth. writ.] Old Man Time, How Much Shall I Give, Fantastic Lady; [pers.] Thank God for giving me the gift, knowledge and ambition to share my thoughts with others as I write.; [a.] Portsmouth, VA.

CARUANA, JEFFREY
[b.] March 24, 1966, Detroit, MI; [p.] George and Patricia Caruana; [ed.] University of Michigan; [occ.] Sales Representative (Manufacturing); [memb.] Detroit Area film and television, Greater Detroit and Windsor Japan-American Society; [hon.] Awards from the University of Michigan and the Chicago International Film Festival for film making; [pers.] Must influenced by 20th century American poets; [a.] Beverly Hills, MI

CASTLEBERRY, HEATHER B.
[b.] March 13, 1964, Weston, Ontario, Canada; [p.] Audrey and Robert Linn; [m.] Grant Castleberry, October 21, 1989; [ed.] Churchill High School, School Craft College, Michigan Paraprofessional Institute Middleton Real Estate School; [occ.] Realtor; [memb.] Wayne Oakland County Board of Realtors; [pers.] Since a child, I've had the ability to turn my thoughts and emotions into poetry. It's a cleansing act for me and I thank God for blessing me with this gift. I can only hope that others will be as moved while reading my work, as I have been while writing it.; [a.] Redford, MI

CATON, AMITY L.
[pen.] Amity L. Caton; [b.] October 19, 1979, Saint Mary's County, MD; [p.] Lucy and Jerry Caton; [ed.] Sophomore at Chopticon High Graduated from Mother Catherine Spalding in Helen Maryland School; [hon.] 8th grade Citizenship Award Catholic Daughters (Poetry 3rd place Art Poster 1st place); [oth. writ.] "Silent Cry" published in church bulletins, "Mountain", "You and I" published in 2 other anthologies.; [pers.] My writing stems from the emotions surrounding me everyday.; [a.] Chaptico, MD

CAUDLE, KAREN E.
[b.] December 2, 1961, Miami, FL; [p.] Charles P. Caudle, Patricia Caudle; [ed.] B.S. in Psychology - Florida International Univ. Miami, FL.; [occ.] Manager in Retail Operations, Miami, FL.; [memb.] World Wildlife Fund, Indian Relief Council, S.P.I.N. PBA.; [oth. writ.] Abundance of other songs and poems ready to be published; [pers.] My songs and poems have been greatly influenced by my own personal experiences and love of music.; [a.] Miami, FL

CAUTHEN, CAROLYN REBECCA
[pen.] Poetry Lady; [b.] February 27, 1945, Kingston Springs, TN; [p.] Cheatham and Ruth (Judd) McElroy; [m.] David Franklin Cauthen; [ch.] Bradley Cheathan (stepchildren, Dee, Kenny, and Robert) Anita (Blalock) Steen; [ed.] Grades 1-9 Kingston Springs Elementary, Grades 10-12 Bellavue High, 1 year Middle Tennessee State College; [occ.] Custadian: Brantwood High School, Cooks Bethany Hills Campgrounds; [memb.] Kingston Springs Church of Christ, the Highlander Club, Harpeth High Band Boosters; [hon.] The only

honor I've ever had bestowed on me is the faith placed in me by 2 Brentwood High teachers - Glen Burton and Joan Harrah.; [oth. writ.] "In Loving Memory." (After Mom's death, I had to express my feelings on paper. This poem was the beginning. Also wrote "A Merry, White Christmas Day."; [pers.] I'll be 50 tomorrow (2-27) and at last I've done something I can be proud of. It's the best birthday present (especially, if I win a prize!); [a.] Kingston Springs, TN

CAWLEY, BONNIE
[pen.] Bonsee; [b.] August 25, 1964, Philadelphia, PA; [ch.] John, Steven (2 boys); [ed.] High School Business School Banking; [occ.] Banking, Public Speaking; [memb.] Gyms, National Association of Female Executives.; [hon.] Sports, Communizations, Sales.; [pers.] Write for the heart and feel what you write.; [a.] Philadelphia, PA

CAYLOR, ALBERT
[pen.] Al B. Darn; [b.] August 26, 1951, Dalton, GA; [p.] Justin and Polly Caylor; [m.] Divorced "Babe", March 20, 1977; [ch.] Pookie, Nikque, Coryman; [ed.] B.S. Ed Georgia Southern 1975, Masters Music MD.U. 1987; [occ.] Sales, Songwriter, Poet; [memb.] "Life"; [hon.] 7th Annual St. Louis Music Contest - "Turn out the lights one more time"; [oth. writ.] 40 songs 10 bits of prose, an autobiography in process.; [pers.] "Be Good to Yourself" and "Let Happiness Happen"; [a.] Columbia, MO

CAYLOR, REBEKAH ANNE
[pen.] Rebekah Anne Caylor; [b.] September 1, 1970, Holyoke, MA; [p.] Dan and Susan Nix; [m.] Jeffrey Allen Caylor; [ed.] Granite Hills H.S. in El Cajon, Ca. class of 1988 Grossmont J.C., general education. Continuing education thru Duni Bradstreet home study courses; [occ.] Management and Sales for Gold's Gym, East Bridgewater; [hon.] Granite Hills H.S. Honor Roll, Distant cousin to Emily Dickinson on my grandfather's side of family. I think that's an honor.; [oth. writ.] None published - yet!?; [pers.] Thank you Mr. Sebastian for believing in my talents and getting me started and interested in poetry. And Jeffrey, my love, your support means everything; [a.] East Bridgewater, MA

CHAMBERS, MARJORIE HARVEY
[b.] September 10, 1949, New Orleans, LA.; [p.] James C. Harvey, Sr., Grace Goodrich Harvey; [m.] Gilbert L. Chambers, November 22, 1986; [ch.] Tyrone, Angele Renee, Lance Trent; [ed.] North High School, University Nebraska At Omaha; [occ.] English teacher, Gateway College, Omaha, NE.; [pers.] I believe the traits of honesty, dedication, discipline, resilience, love, hardwork, courage, faith and my firm belief in God will prevail against any injustices I will encounter.; [a.] Omaha, NE

CHAMBERS, NORMA K. JONES
[pen.] Camron Jones; [b.] June 1948, Sandusky, OH; [p.] Frank and Louise Jones; [m.] Mark A. Chambers, June 1985; [ch.] William C. and Robert C. Griffin; [ed.] Sandusky High School - 1966, Dayton University: Driver's Education Instructors Certification; [occ.] Homemaker; [memb.] Unity School of Christianity - Unity Village, MO; [pers.] Love is all we need and we all need to love, and be loved, on our life's journey as we are passing through.; [a.] Huron, OH

CHAMBERS, RUTH
[pen.] Ruth Chambers; [b.] February 19, 1941, San Diego, CA; [p.] Ralph and Helen Chambers; [ed.] San Diego State University, B.A. U.C.L.A., M.F.A. Santa Monica College, Photography Certification; [occ.] Photographer and Volunteer at the California Raptor Center; [memb.] National Press Photographers Assoc. Calif. Press Photographers Assoc. Press Photographers Assoc. of Greater Los Angeles, Sierra Club, Sacramento Area Regional Theatre Alliance, California Rap-

tor Center, Volunteer; [hon.] For Photography Wave Finalist, Excellence in Local Programming, 1993 1st place, Best of Show, S.M.C., 1987 2nd Place, Features, on the Spot, J.A.C.C. - State Competition, 1988 2nd Place, National Canon Contest, 1985 being selected by the National Library of Poetry for their next published collection.; [oth. writ.] Sierra Club, Mother Lode Chapter, Bonanza, March 1995 California Raptor Center, Talon, Spring 1995; [pers.] Being known is not the point of my work, being effective is. Should someone read my poems and find encouragement in their own growth and efforts, then we can add another warrior in a good fight we may not completely understand, but know in our hearts is just.; [a.] Davis, CA

CHANG, JENNY
[b.] November 4, 1979, Toronto, Ontario; [p.] Mike and Su-Lam Chang; [ed.] Courtice Secondary School, Courtice, ON, Canada (9-10th grade), West Ottawa High School (11th), Holland, MI.; [occ.] Student (Junior); [memb.] High School Symphonic and Jazz Bands, S.A.D.D., National Honor Society, Student Senate, German Club (treasurer), Fall Musical; [hon.] 9th Grade - Honor Roll, Top Mark in Science (9th), 10th Grade-Honor Roll, 11th Grade-National Honor Society.; [oth. writ.] Poems and short stories - unpublished, several poems published in school publications; [pers.] This poem is dedicated to my best friend, Pauline Clarke. You have taught me so much, thank you.; [a.] Holland, MI

CHAPIN, NANCY ANNE
[b.] July 10, 1951, Seattle; [p.] Wilmer Larsen, Inger Larsen; [m.] Jeff Traynor Chapin, May 28, 1988; [ch.] Rondalee Ravicchio; [ed.] S. Eugene High, Foothill Jr. College, W. Valley College, and Sand Jose State; [occ.] Outside Sales.; [memb.] Christian Women's Club; [hon.] Dean's list and an Awarding Daughter!; [oth. writ.] I am an actress, this is my first submitted poem, and I'm leaving towards play writing.; [pers.] Trust in God's word and follow your heart.; [a.] Temecula, CA

CHAPLIN, CLARIN M.
[pen.] Clarin Chaplin; [b.] August 5, 1940, Baltimore, MD; [p.] Clarence and Isabelle Wilder; [m.] William R. Chaplin, March 28, 1981; [ch.] Karen, Denise, Debra, Kim, Scott, Donna, Karen, Glenn, Sharon and Shawn; [ed.] Glen Burnie Senior High School.; [occ.] Auditor - Home Depot Inc.; [hon.] Nat'l Honor Society, National Thespian Asso.; [oth. writ.] There such a good girl. (Short Story). Inspirational Verses; [pers.] Life is real and must be faced head-on. Fairy tales can only be imagined; [a.] Greenwood, DE

CHAPPELL, RODNEY WELDON
[b.] September 30, 1973, Mount Airy, NC; [p.] Roger Chappell, Delight Conner; [ed.] High School Diploma from New Life Christian Academy; [occ.] Employed by Cross Creek Apparel; [hon.] National Defense Ribbon and a AAM both of which I received while in the United States Army.; [oth. writ.] I've wrote several other poems and a few songs. None of which have ever been published.; [pers.] I was seventeen when I wrote the poem Funeral Day. I had just lost someone close to me for the fifth time in under two years. It's a shame it takes such pain to being out such beauty.; [a.] Cana, VA

CHARNOT, ANGELLA
[b.] November 28, 1976, Chicago, IL; [p.] Robert James Charnot and Marianna Charnot; [ed.] Queen of Peace High School, University of Chicago; [occ.] Student; [pers.] Always love and live every day as if were the last. This is the only way to achieve true happiness.; [a.] Orland Park, IL

CHATMAN, CAROLYN H.
[p.] Eula M. Hardy; [ch.] Dionne Lynetta, Michelle Dateria [grnch.] RaQuan T. Chatman-Kluttz; [ed.] Carver High, Benedict College, Converse College, University of S.C., National Baptist Congress of Chris-

tian Education; [occ.] English Reading Teacher, Carver Jr. High, Spartanburg, SC; Hospice Volunteer, SRMC; 2nd Year Short-term Volunteer Missionary to Kenya, Africa; [memb.] Mt. Moriah Baptist Chruch (Evangelism Committee, Missionary Society), NEA, SCEA, Alpha Kappa Alpha Sorority; [hon.] Dean's List; Honor Graduate; [oth. writ.] Biographical sketch published in college anthology; several poems published for church bulletins, cards; unpublished poems; [pers.] My writings reflect on issues related to God, African-Americans, and humankind.; [a.] Spartanburg, SC.

CHENIER, AMY
[b.] April 27, 1972, Escanaba, MI; [p.] Don and Paula Chenier; [ed.] Lincoln Park High School, Wayne County Community College, Middle Tennessee State University; [occ.] Fine Artist/Painter; [hon.] Numerous awards for artwork and academics.; [pers.] The Word of God is my biggest influence in all that I do.; [a.] Lincoln Park, MI

CHO, BOWEN SANG WOO
[p.] Ji Min Cho; [a.] Dix Hills, NY

CHRISSOS, GEORGE
[b.] September 4, 1925, Union City, NJ; [p.] Deceased; [m.] Patricia Chrissos, June 10, 1951; [ch.] Mrs. Joan Chrissos Roberts, Mrs. Laurie Foster; [ed.] B.A. City College of New York, M.A. Teachers Coll., Columbian Univ.; [occ.] Retired; [hon.] Arista Society; [oth. writ.] (Poem) A Time for Planting Appeared in Quill and Scroll Literary journal. (Poem) River of Life. Appeared in The Silver Quill literary journal.; [pers.] My writings deal with a myriad of topics. Life, social commentary, nature, humor, tragedy. My favorite is Walt Whitman.; [a.] Winter Springs, FL

CHRYSSIS, GEORGE C.
[b.] May 21, 1947, Crete, Greece; [p.] Christopher, Ourania (Kamisakis); [m.] Margo (Sayegh), May 21; [ch.] Rania, Lilian, Alexander; [ed.] Second Lyceum, Chania-Crete Wentworth Institute, Boston-MA Northeastern University, Boston-MA; [occ.] Businessman/Entrepreneur; [memb.] Massachusettes High Technology Council, American Hellenic Institute, AHI Network, Friends of the University of Crete, Northeastern University Huntington Society, Alpha-Omega Council, Friends of Maliotis Cultural Center, Phi-Kappa-Tau Fraternity, PanCretan Association of America; [hon.] Board of Overseers and Corporator Northeastern University, Corporator and Director of National Council Wentworth Institute, Trustee and House of Stewards Hellenic College/Holly Cross, received SBANE "New Englander Award" 1989, Wentworth Institute "Golden Leopard Award" 1991, Boston Diocese "Laity Award" 1993 listed "Who's Who in America", "Who's Who in the World" and ten other Who's Who titles; [oth. writ.] "Echoes and Re-Echoes" poetry book published by the Greek Institute 1993. "High Frequency Switching Power Supplies" published by McGraw-Hill 1984 and 1989. Several technical and literary articles, essays and poems published in various magazines, journals and newspapers; [pers.] In my writings I project the human ability to achieve, through kindness, love and self respect. I especially try to project positive ideas and traditional values. I am optimistic for the future and I believe that values will prevail over materialism.; [a.] Weston, MA

CIHONE, CASMER
[b.] March 3, 1912, Detroit; [occ.] Retired; [oth. writ.] Casmer Cihone 331912 - 84 I am tired of being retired? No noise no confusion. Nothing to do but just sit and enjoy the solitude. How did I ever stand it?

CILLO, EDNA
[pen.] Becky or Edna Cillo; [b.] October 13, 1925, NJ; [p.] Mr. William and Mrs. Lillian Becker; [m.] Anthony Cillo, July 1, 1972; [ed.] Graduated from Snyder High in Jersey City in New Jersey, times were not to good and

college could not be afforded; [occ.] I am retired now which gives me more time to write; [oth. writ.] I enjoy writing poetry, and also write books of fictional status, and do wood burning paintings along with creating things on looms. I have my own book of many poems and really enjoy every minute writing them; [pers.] Poetry to me has a meaning of a sort which could be of life, beliefs, comedy, happiness and love and much more having those who write it hoping that people realize all that is put into a poem.

CIMINO, DONNA LASORDA
[pen.] DLC; [b.] August 28, 1942, Norristown, PA; [p.] Dominick and Esther Lasorda; [m.] November 1962; [ch.] Edward and Donna; [occ.] Founder, Director, R.A.P. Inc - State Licensed Home for Abused Girls ages 11 thru 18.; [pers.] My motivation in writing comes from all the abused young ladies who have deeply touched my life with their courage to heal.

CIORA, ANDREA J.
[b.] February 12, 1963, Cleveland, OH; [ed.] Lakewood High School Cuyahoga Community College, Associate of Science Meridia Huron School of Nursing; [occ.] Registered Nurse - Meridia Huron Hospital, East Cleveland, OH; [memb.] Alumni Assoc. of Huron Rd./Meridian Huron School of Nursing, Ohio League for Nursing, Church of God.; [hon.] Dean's List, graduated Magna Cum Laude; [oth. writ.] Poems, skits, Bible devotions written for local use, one poem published in a National Religious magazine for women.; [pers.] My poetry reflects my innermost feelings and beliefs. Christ is a very important part of those beliefs, and I strive to honor him through my writings.; [a.] Cleveland, OH

CIRRILO, TONY
[pen.] Tony Cirrilo; [b.] December 2, 1960, Marion, VA; [m.] Helga Cirillo, September 3, 1994; [ch.] Richard (Stepson); [ed.] Graduate of Mid-America College of Funeral Service; [occ.] Embalmer; [oth. writ.] Several other short poems; [pers.] Thanks be to my wonderful wife Helga Cirillo, to who I owe everything. She is the inspiration of all poems I've done; [a.] Charlotte, NC

CITIZEN, ROBYN
[b.] December 21, 1979, Houston, TX; [p.] Pat Citizen, John Citizen; [ed.] Owens Elementary, Truitt Jr High, Cy-Falls High School; [occ.] Student and did volunteer work; [memb.] Note - through children Int. I sponsor a child from Ecudor; [hon.] Distinguished newspaper student; [oth. writ.] Several poems and short stories; [pers.] I write about the things that haunt me and keep me up at night, I've been influenced mostly by Edgar Allan Poe.; [a.] Flouston, TX

CLAPHAM, KATHARINE ROSE
[b.] May 29, 1986, Boston, MA; [p.] Susan and David Clapham; [ed.] Bamber Valley Elementary School, Rochester, MN; [occ.] Student; [memb.] Girl scouts, SE MN Suzuki Music Association.; [pers.] Writing is like a flower: it grows and grows and grows. I hope my knowledge of writing will continue to grow, too.; [a.] Rochester, MN

CLARK, JAMES
[b.] March 5, 1952, Waltham, MA; [p.] James A. Clark and Helen C. Henninger; [ed.] Fairport Harbor Harding High, Lakeland College; [occ.] Electrical Contractor Professional Soldier, Freelance Ballet Dancer; [memb.] National Guard Association of Colorado, County Sheriffs of Colorado; [hon.] Various military awards, currently at work on a book of 50 poems; [pers.] I write to express my convictions of love, of God, and how people treat other people. A study of one's beliefs and actions evaluates his integrity.; [a.] Bailey, CO.

CLARK, JILL
[b.] May 29, 1973, Chicago, IL; [p.] Robert and Sandra Clark; [ed.] Shenendehowa High, Ithara College; [occ.]

College student, Prospective Secondary English Teacher; [memb.] Sigma Tau Delta; [hon.] Dean's List; [oth. writ.] Numerous unpublished works in various genies; [pers.] I strive to reflect the complex and universal truths of the human spirit in my writing, I am greatly indebted to my family and friends for their neverending support and inspiration.; [a.] Leawood, KS

CLARK, LLOYD EUGENE
[pen.] L. Eugene Clark, N. Love; [b.] February 3, 1963, Watsonville, CA; [p.] Melvin and Judie Clark; [m.] Pamela Sue Casada-Clark, August 25, 1995; [ed.] Watsonville - Renaissance High, Cabrillo College; [occ.] State Strawberry Inspector; [memb.] Red Cross Volunteer, Watsonville City League Flag, Football Coach, Youth Group Home Volunteer.; [hon.] Graduated with honors at Cabrillo College; [oth. writ.] None published; [pers.] Through the creative reflection of writing poetry, I can express sentiments of love and happiness for our world to share. Poetry is speaking via the soul.; [a.] Watsonville, CA

CLARK, WILLIAM EMMETT
[pen.] William E. Clark; [b.] October 7, 1976, Worcester, MA; [p.] Richard and Mary Clark; [ed.] High School for the Performing and Visual Arts in Houston, TX.; [occ.] Student and Jazz Musician; [oth. writ.] Several other poems and short stories and recently started a novel; [pers.] I believe the subconscious is the most powerful aspect of human intelligence and in my writing I explore the concept of memories and emotions.; [a.] Houston, TX

CLAYBORN, BRANDI
[pen.] "B"; [b.] November 13, 1980, Montgomery, AL; [p.] Jerilyn Clayborn, Fredrick Williams; [ed.] I attended Vaughn Rd Elem grades K-4, Davis Elem grades 5-6, and now I am attending Bellingrath Jr. High 8th; [occ.] Attending School; [oth. writ.] I write for my grandparents, parents, and friends. I write when I'm sad, down, or just have nothing else to do. I love writing.; [pers.] I've always enjoyed writing poetry. I didn't ever think that a poem by me would ever be published. Keeping my faith in "God" and it happened.; [a.] Montgomery, AL

CLEWLEY, MARY COLEEN
[b.] July 4, 1963, Redford, MI; [p.] Albert Craig and Mary Craig; [m.] Russell J. Clewley, October 18, 1986; [ch.] Ashley Lynn and Daniel Joseph; [ed.] Howell High, Ferris State Univ.; [occ.] Executive Secretary; [memb.] National Assn Female Executives, Coach Odyssey of the Minds; [hon.] Deans list, FSU accomplished flutist; [oth. writ.] Collection of over 100 poems and a "family epic" titled: Generations - currently seeking publisher.; [pers.] Writing is my way of capturing experiences on paper so as to put life into perspective in terms of what things are genuinely important.

CLIFTON, BREANNE LEAH
[b.] December 7, 1980, Steubenville, OH; [p.] Deborah and Clyde; [ed.] McKinley School 'til 5th grade, currently attending harding middle school as an 8th grade student.; [occ.] Student; [memb.] Power of the pen, yearbook staff, honor roll; [hon.] Power of the pen.; [oth. writ.] Poetry forum, power of the pen, speak your mind.; [pers.] "Follow your heart to fulfill your dreams, knowing that someday it will lead you to everlasting love and happiness."; [a.] Steubenville, OH

CLINGAN, MELISSA JEAN
[pen.] Melissa Clingan, M.J.; [b.] October 25, 1978, Seattle; [p.] Bill and Deb Clingan; [ed.] Shorewood Elementary K-2 Ocosta Elementary 3-6 Ocosta Jr and Sr School, which I currently attend; [occ.] Baby sitter; [memb.] FBLA, (Future business leaders of America), softball, First Presbyterian Church, Pep Club, Cheerleader; [hon.] Honor Society; [pers.] I just write what comes to me. I write on now I feel inside not what shows or the outside.; [a.] Westport, WA

CLINTON, ELVERA YVONNE
[pen.] Yvonne Clinton; [b.] April 3, 1919, Everett, WA; [p.] Olaf and Julia Bruseth; [m.] Capt. Daniel J. Clinton U.S.N. (Deceased), August 31, 1984; [ch.] Ronald and Michael Pitts (Deceased); [ed.] Graduate of Auburn Academy, Washington and forever student of Life's Drama; [occ.] Retired Librarian; [memb.] Santa Barbara Seventh Day Adventist Church, TROA (the retired Officers Assn - auxiliary member, the citizens Planning Assn. Santa Barbara, CA; [hon.] To receive the love of family and friends and the respect of the community are my greatest honors.; [oth. writ.] A collection of unpublished poems and a yet to be published novel, "The Ear Of Malchus" - the story of the almost forgotten man who arrested Jesus in Garden of Gethsemane.; [pers.] I am a collector of perfect moments; [a.] Santa Barbara, CA

CLOUD, JENNIFER L.
[b.] October 27, 1772, Asheville, NC; [p.] Jon and Linda Owen; [m.] Richard Cloud, July 2, 1994; [ed.] Reynolds High, A.B. Tech. Community College; [occ.] Textile worker; [oth. writ.] Several short stories, poems, and two published fiction novels; [pers.] Each moment in time has its own story to tell and I capture it with my pen.; [a.] Ashevile, NC

COBB, CHRISTINA MARIE
[pen.] Chrissy Cobb; [b.] March 17, 1980, Stephens County, GA; [p.] Deborah Rhodes, Roddy Cobb, Wayne Rhodes - step father; [ed.] I'm currently in Belton - Honea Path High School, where I'm a freshman.; [memb.] Grades 6-8 I was in Beta Club, as of this year I'm in a program called Renaissance.; [hon.] Have won lots of awards, but none that are major; [oth. writ.] I have written several other poems, but haven't sent any others out, until this one. I think maybe I'll send out more.; [pers.] I write how I feel.; [a.] Belton, SC

COFFIN, MARVIN
[b.] January 22, 1945, Detroit; [p.] Carson Coffin, Helen Coffin; [ch.] Kimerbly Gradow, Donna Saroli; [ed.] Wilbrur Wright High; [occ.] Die Setter; [pers.] Human has four element of it own see, hear, feel and think; [a.] Taylor, MI

COFFMAN, CHRIS
[b.] June 3, 1960, North Hollywood, CA; [p.] Bill Coffman, Thelma Coffman; [m.] Amy Coffman, October 7, 1989; [ch.] Valerie and Andrea Coffman; [ed.] Ged, 1978; [occ.] Cook; [hon.] USMC Honorable discharge, 100 mile club USMC; [oth. writ.] None ever published. Just writings to my wife; [a.] Taos, NM

COGGINS, LINDA SMITH
[b.] June 9, 1947, Plainfield, NJ; [p.] Dorothy and Angelo Fusco; [m.] Ralph Jones Coggins, September 28, 1984; [ch.] 4 - Lisa Elizabeth, Christopher Anthony, Jason Michael, Lindsey Elizabeth; [ed.] Plainfield High, Taylor Business Institute, Union College, Thomas Nelson Com. College; [occ.] Asst. Gen. Manager of WMBG and WPTG Radio Williamsburg, VA; [memb.] St. Bede's Catholic Church, Wmsbg. PTA, American Cancer Assoc., Leukemia Society, Sigma Alpha Pi, Nu Tau Sigma; [hon.] Dean's List TNCC, Jaycee's Award, 1/4 Finalist Lyricist Contest, Golden Poet Award 4 years World of Poetry; [oth. writ.] Lyricyst finalist, Hollywood California, several Poems Published through "The World of Poetry." [pers.] My poetry tends to reflect many of the personal experiences I have faced in life and the knowledge I have gained along the way.; [a.] Williamsburg, VA

COHEN, MATTHEW JOSEPH
[b.] October 10, 1982, Long Beach, CA; [p.] Paul and Terri Cohen; [ed.] Attending Carden Hall in Newport Beach, CA.; [occ.] Student in sixth grade at Carden Hall.; [memb.] Pony League Baseball. I also enjoy chess and writing and computers.; [oth. writ.] Working on a children's book; [pers.] I thank my parents and

teachers for their encouragement.; [a.] Newport Beach, CA

COHEN, ARLENE
[pen.] Arlene Botkelen or Arlene Botkelen Cohen; [b.] March 15, 1936, Brooklyn, NY; [p.] Rose and Ben Betkonen; [m.] Howard Cohen, August 1, 1977; [ed.] Brooklyn College, S.J. Tilden High School; [occ.] Retired; [memb.] National Assoc. of Women Artists; [pers.] My poetry celebrates those moments in our lives when we have a revelation that moves us closer to the reality and glory of our true selves and as spiritual beings.; [a.] Valley Stream, NY

COHEN, STEVEN J.
[b.] December 31, 1959, Newark, NJ; [p.] Jerome Cohen, Lillian Cohen; [m.] Susan Cohen, January 8, 1982; [ch.] Jennifer Leigh, Michelle, Renee, Lulu; [ed.] Cedar Ridge High School, Matawan, NJ, Associates Degree Applied Science, Aircraft Avionics Systems Technology, Community College of the Air Force; [occ.] Msgt 1E-7 USAF, F-15 Avionics System Specialist; [memb.] North American Fishing Club, North American Hunting Club, Florida Police Athletic League; [pers.] No man is too much a man to enjoy reading or writing poetry.

COLE, ANN
[b.] April 1, Hattiesburg, MS; [ed.] Hattiesburg Public Schools, Hattiesburg High School, Creative Writing Courses, Univ. of Southern, MS; [memb.] Women in the church, First Presbyterian Church, Rainbow Garden Club, The Garden Guild; [oth. writ.] Several short stories, and numerous poems (most of these for the enjoyment of family and friends); [pers.] Coming from an artistic; family, I have always enjoyed writing as a hobby. Now I am looking forward to writing in more of a professional capacity. Having my poem published is my dream reward!; [a.] Hattiesburg, MS

COLE, EVELYN M.
[b.] January 18, 1924, Lincoln, NE; [p.] Floyd H. and Marie A. Zerbel (Deceased); [m.] Orven S. Cole, April 9, 1944; [ed.] Havelock High (class of '41) Lincoln NE; [occ.] Housewife; [hon.] I have been recently published in the anthology River of Dreams and the forthcoming best poems of 1995 ... receiving an 'Editor's Choice Award' therefrom.; [oth. writ.] Many poems - all types and subjects; [pers.] Our family moved to California in my post-graduate year of '42. I had several occupations before I married. I have been the sole office help for my husband, a Heating and Air Conditioning Cont'r for 49 years. We celebrated our 50th Golden Wedding Anniversary in April '94. In an effort to learn to play the piano in '54 I began writing poetry for my own pleasure and still do. The Lord has been very kind...; [a.] Los Angeles, CA

COLE, JACOB A.
[b.] January 22, 1983, Muskogee, OK; [p.] Becky L. Cole, Jerry Cole; [ed.] 6th grade - Pawhuska Indian Camp School; [occ.] Student - 6th grade Indian Camp School; [a.] Pawhuska, OK

COLE, SANDRA S.
[b.] October 15, 1958, Greenville, SC; [p.] Billy Stanton (deceased), Evelyn Segee; [m.] Mark A. Cole, October 30, 1976; [ch.] Nathan Randolph Cole; [ed.] Parker High, 1975 Honor graduate Greenville Technical College, 1976; [occ.] Telecommunications Analyst; [hon.] English Award - 1975, and Shorthand Award - 1975 (PHS, who's, who, among, Distinguished American High School Students, Beta Club; [oth. writ.] Poem published in High School Year book - 1975; [a.] Travelers Rest, SC

COLEMAN, JENNIFER D.
[b.] July 1, 1961, Zachary, LA; [p.] Tom and Deloris Deemer; [m.] David L. Coleman II, July 28, 1984; [ch.] David III and Julien; [ed.] St. Joseph Academy, Univer-

sity of New Orleans (BS in Accounting-82); [occ.] Systems Accountant; [memb.] Blacks in Government; [pers.] Writing is sweet music to the mind. Behind the lyrics, through the years, I've written all my hopes and fears.; [a.] New Orleans, LA

COLLIER, JUDITH A.
[b.] November 4, 1946, Stockbridge, MI; [p.] Harry and Carolyn Collier; [m.] Divorced; [ed.] High School; [occ.] Factory Worker; [hon.] "2nd Place" - Song Writer Talent Show Hastings, MI; [oth. writ.] Several Country songs and poems; [pers.] Songs and poems are just another way of expressing feelings you may not be able to sometimes say.; [a.] Otsego, MI

COLLIGNON JR., JAMES R.
[b.] December, 1938, San Antonio, TX; [p.] Agent John H. Collignon and Jeannine C. Naquin (my brother and sister); [m.] Mary Ann Brockhoeft, November, 1958; [ch.] Shea John, Dirk James, Jill C. Jeffers; [ed.] Louisiana State, University at New Orleans, 1967, BS, University of South California, 1977, MCJ; [occ.] Private Investigator, retired SA/FBI; [memb.] Society of former special agents of the Federal Bureau of Investigation American Legion Holy Name Society; [hon.] Medallion of St. Louis, Archdiocese of New Orleans; [pers.] This poem of praise was given to me by my Angel Guardian and through it, we both give praise to God; [a.] Covington, LA

COLLINS, EDWARD LEE
[pen.] "Abel" Lee Collins; [b.] October 16, 1934, San Diego, CA; [p.] George and Addie Collins; [ch.] Coleen Mattison, Sharon Garcia, Deanna Collins (adp. daughter), Nicole Letourneau, Andria Paul; [ed.] Biola University 1 1/2 yrs Los Angeles, CA, Butte Junior College 1 1/2 Oroville, CA.; [occ.] Janitor, Church Maintenance man, Retired city of Chico, California Firefighter.; [memb.] Pleasant Valley Baptist Church, Community Grace Church, St. John Catholic, Chico, CA.; [hon.] Gold Poetry Award, Sparrowgrass Poet; [oth. writ.] "Angels And Stars", Redwood Trees, The Flames of Love; [pers.] I think "God Alone", give each person many talents - it is up to each one to develop poetry is a spiritual reals for me - which I'm thankful; [a.] Fort Bragg, CA

COLLINS, ERIC D.
[pen.] Eric Collins; [b.] May 2, 1982, Detroit, MI; [p.] Cordell Collins, Tracey Collins; [ed.] Gesu Catholic School; [occ.] Student; [hon.] Citizenship Award, Reading Award, Honor Roll Award, 3 on 3 Tournament Basketball Award, City Wide Champs 13 and under Baseball Award, C.Y.O. Basketball Champs Award; [pers.] My writings explore my inner feelings about life, my surroundings, experiences as I grow up and my spiritual awareness.; [a.] Detroit, MI

COLLINS, JUDITH D.
[pen.] Judy Collins; [b.] May 12, 1940, Muncie, IN; [p.] Leonard Allen, Dorothy Allen; [m.] Albert Lee Collins, December 11, 1987; [ch.] Ellen, Shannon, Michael, Lora (Moody) (previous marriage); [ed.] Claremont High School in California, some college chaffey JC and Butler University Indianapolis, IN; [occ.] Disabled; [memb.] Bartlettsville Christian Church; [oth. writ.] I have written several poems. I have never submitted any for publication before this one.; [pers.] My inspiration for writing came from my father. My love for writing came from all my thoughts and all my feelings about the paradise among us.; [a.] Heltonville, IN

COLLINS, LINDA M.
[b.] Michigan; [p.] William Neal and Ova Marie Hayes; [m.] John A. Collins, July 29, 1972

COLLINS, MARY
[pen.] Louise Collins; [b.] Tuscumbia, AL; [p.] Robert and Margaret Beckwith; [m.] Robert Lee Collins (Deceased), May 31, 1973; [ch.] Robert LeBron and Kesha LaMargaret; [ed.] Trenholm High Western Kentucky State Tech; [occ.] Retired, TVA, Env. Tech. Muscle Shoals, AL; [pers.] I am an aspiring new writer. I love to write and I write what I feel. This poem is dedicated to a friend (Jerry) because he was there when I needed someone to talk to.; [a.] Muscle Shoals, AL

COLLINS, SARAH DIANNE
[b.] January 24, 1955, McKenzie, TN; [p.] Cecil and Mable Johnson; [m.] James E. Collins, March 28, 1985; [ch.] Stephanie Dianne, Dennis James; [ed.] Gleason High School; [occ.] House wife; [memb.] Jolly Springs Baptist Church.; [hon.] Top ten in High School, 1973 Trotter spirit and pride; [pers.] Write from your heart feel it in your soul. I pray that God guides my pen to success.; [a.] McKenzie, TN

COLLINS, SHIRLEY
[b.] Lake Providence, LA; [p.] Nathan and Mattie Collins; [ch.] Kennedy Rochelle; [ed.] Graduate of Southern University in Baton Rouge, LA, B.S. Degree in Business Education, other teaching areas: Math, English, Special Ed.; [occ.] Business Teacher; [memb.] Shared Decision-Making Committee at place of employment Graduation Committee, Youth Sponsor at Riceville Baptist Church; [oth. writ.] Inspirational Religious Writings, Curriculum Writing, Freelance Poetry, Poetry for children; [pers.] I write because I must. It's a means of sharing a comfort zone. My writings are inspirational, motivating, captivating, and most of all thought-provoking, often with a twist of humor. Inspired by Maya Angelou; [a.] Houston, TX

COMPTON, DORIS M.
[b.] July 9, 1927, Kansas; [m.] Dale K. Compton; [ch.] Christine; [ed.] A.B. Fort Hays State Kansas, M.A. Univ. of Arkansas, Post Grad, Fort Hays, Emporia State Kansas; [memb.] A.A.U.W., A.P.C.E.; [hon.] Sang a full opera in Cairo, Egypt, 1992, at age 65, International poetry reading. Honored by General Assembly of Presbyterian Church, June 1994, upon my retirement; [oth. writ.] Whisper in the Pines, published 1972, Cairo, Egypt completing anthology of poetry, Gigli y Los Santos; [pers.] I have just retired after 44 years of teaching in Kansas, Egypt, Venezuela, Puerto Rico, since 1921, I have lived overseas 20 years working with Presbyterian Church.

CONGDON, MARION A.
[pen.] Marion A. Congdon; [b.] November 28, 1917, Newfield, NY; [p.] David E. and Marion Starr Miller; [m.] J. Lyman Anderson Congdon, July 20, 1940; [ch.] Mariel J. Wallin, David R. Congdon, John L. Congdon; [ed.] Ithaca High School '34 Williams Business College Ithaca, NY; [occ.] Retired (was legal Secretary); [oth. writ.] None published prose and poetry; [pers.] To be twenty- going on twenty one is such agony. The shell has been broken, the raw, nasty, fragrant, awesome brilliance of truth, of time, of life, convolves me... All the ballast of parent's teachings and the lessons of the church, are shorn - shattered - debris at my feet. And I must choose. I must chose. I must choose! Oh, the urgency..! Conformity and mediocrity or I must blaze a frontier through my mind to sustain my hunger, to appease my thirst, to bring fulfillment to the I'd that is the fire within me and must consume, must prostrate, must purify... And one day I will be sixty, going on sixty-one... and only time has won..? - this poems, my philosophy all through the years, was not titled in 1938. At "sixty-going on sixty-one (1978) the appropriate title - in retrospect, should be, it seems.; [a.] Chatham, NY

CONIGLIO, MARY ANN
[b.] August 4, 1956, Buffalo, NY; [p.] Lillian Pagliei, Pat Pagliei (Deceased); [m.] Samuel Coniglio, Septem-

ber 9, 1977; [ch.] Steven Frank, Rachel Lynn, Daniel Patrick; [ed.] Immaculate Academy, Erie Community College; [occ.] Dental Hygienist; [memb.] Right to Life Association; [pers.] Faith in Christ and deeply seated principles are the basis for my writing. "Nature's Empathy" expresses how God's creation helped me deal with the loss of my father

CONLEY JR., MILAS B.
[pen.] M. B. Conley; [b.] February 1, 1940, Colbert Co., AL; [p.] Willie Sybil and Milas Conley; [m.] Regina Posey Conley, February 18, 1979; [ch.] (By 1st) Sharon M., Micheal Ray, Jo Ann; [ed.] Changed schools 17 times. Graduated Sheffield High 1958, Northwest Junior College: AA-BA 1986, AA-FS 1988 Campbell, AL 35581, Alabama State Fire College: Fire officer I, 1990 Instructor I, 1988; [occ.] Firefighter (24 yrs), Muscle Shoals Fire Department; [memb.] Nitrate City Baptist Church, Mason, American Heart Association Affiliate Faculty and Instructor, Basic EMT State of Alabama (20 yrs); [hon.] Deans List: National Registry 1986, "Who's Who".; [pers.] "I Came." "I Saw." "I Wept," Offered Help, We Refused, Man's Life - How Empty.; [a.] Muscle Shoals, AL

CONTE, ANTHONY F.
[pen.] Tony; [b.] September 9, 1930, Italy; [p.] Natale Conte, Helen Conte; [ed.] New Utrecht H.S. N.Y.C; [occ.] Retired; [memb.] Natl. Comm. to preserve Soc. Sec. and Medicare; [hon.] Honor Society, French Medal, Jr. Arista.; [oth. writ.] Inspirational poetry since 1967 (unpublished), Editor Community Newsletter, articles for local newspaper; [pers.] At Christmas and Easter especially, I am inspired to write and send my poems to family and close friends.; [a.] Gaithersburg, MD

CONTER, ELIZABETH R.
[b.] April 22, 1972, Milwaukee, WI; [p.] C. Michael and Karen Conter; [ed.] University of Missouri-Columbia Bachelor's in Journalism; [occ.] Television News Producer; [oth. writ.] First time I've ever entered a poem for publication.; [pers.] This poem is dedicated to Dan... the little boy I never met, yet know so well.; [a.] Overland Park, KS

CONWAY, HIRAM W.
[pen.] Hiram W. Conway; [b.] January 1, 1952, Forth Worth, TX; [p.] Hiarm and Maxine Conway; [m.] Diana Conway, June 20, 1992; [ed.] North Side High, University of Texas at Arlington.; [occ.] Artist, Writer; [memb.] Texas Pottery and Sculptures Guild; [hon.] Rio Chi Honor Society, Dean's List; [pers.] With a positive outlook on life and a wonderful wife, all things are possible. Be good. Be creative.; [a.] Arlington, TX

CONYERS, CASSANDRA
[b.] December 22, 1961, Miami, FL; [p.] George and Irolla Conyers; [ch.] Juan Smith Jr.; [ed.] Evander Childs H.S. Herbert H. Whiman College BSN; [occ.] Asst Head Nurse Bronx Municipal Hospital Center - Home Care; [memb.] New York State Nursing Association, Eastern Stars; [hon.] Dean's List; [pers.] Life is to be lived! Not to be endured. We all have the capacity to make the world a more beautiful place.; [a.] Bronx, NY

COOK, JAMES R.
[pen.] JRC; [b.] June 5, 1954, Independence, MO; [p.] Rex C. and Ruby P. Cook; [ed.] Van Horn High; [occ.] Shipping Clerk; [oth. writ.] 3 Poems published by "World of Poetry" press; [pers.] Yesterday's future is tomorrow's past; [a.] Independence, MO

COOK, LESLIE MAXWELL
[pen.] Blue Gums; [b.] May 9, 1958, Detroit, MI; [p.] Carrie B. Maxwell, Melvin L. Maxwell; [m.] Tim Cook, April 30, 1994; [ed.] 1. Mumford High, Univ. of Michigan, 2. Laney Cosmetology School, 3. Computer Learning Center, 4. Diablo Valley College/Environmental Engineering Dept.; [occ.] Environmental Field Technician, Uribet Associates; [memb.] 1. Member of

Glide Methodist Episcopal Church, San Francisco, CA, 2. National Cosmetology Association/Platinum Member (since 1989), 3. Look Good...Feel Better, Program (1991) (since) Cancer Make over Program.; [hon.] 1. Burgandy and Blue Honors Club (Mumford High School) (1976) [oth. writ.] Extensive Collection of poems focusing on: joy, peace, life, suffering of mankind and woman kind and humanity and also poems from personal experience and survival through illressest adversity from (1970) to present; [pers.] 1. I pray for continued grace and mercy from God, while living a life filled with passions that create, "A boil that cannot be stirred down."

COOK, KEVIN BRANDT
[pen.] Kevin B. Cook; [b.] August 26, 1961, Denver CO; [p.] SGM Walter C. Cook, Rose Hildebrandt Cook; [m.] Single; [ed.] Leavenworth High School, Vincennes University Vincennes Indiana, Leavenworth Kansas; [hon.] Religions petty officer, US Navy, Basic Training Orlando Florida; [pers.] Always remember that love is the heartbeat "Heartbeat" of your life... "Pain" Heaven...; [a.] Lansing, KS

COOK, JOLETTA
[b.] October 12, 1978, Batesville, AR; [p.] Ronald and Carol Cook; [ed.] I am in tenth grade at Evening Shade High School.; [oth. writ.] I also write short stories as well as poems. At the moment I am working on a novel.; [pers.] I enjoy writing about reality and love. I enjoy all kinds of literature. My philosophy for life is look to your inner self for personal strength.; [a.] Evening Shade, AR

COOKE, RAMONA
[pen.] Ramona Roth; [b.] December 22, 1958, McKinleyville, CA; [p.] William Roth, Nell Roth; [m.] Robert Cooke, December 31, 1977; [ed.] McKinleyville High School; [occ.] Freelance Writer; [pers.] My writings are very personal, they are usually to or about my husband or a family member. That is where I get my inspiration.; [a.] Corning, CA

COONAN, CHRISTY
[b.] April 23, 1977, Saginaw, MI; [p.] Micki Coonan; [ed.] Graduated Central High School, Delta College, attended Nasa Space Academy; [occ.] Student; [memb.] Vice President French Club, Cheerleader; [hon.] Graduated with honors, National Honor Society, English Honor Society, Citizenship Club.; [a.] Bay City, MI

COOPER, ROBERT PAUL
[pen.] Robert Paul Cooper; [b.] May 9, 1928, Watertown, NY; [p.] Fred and Elizabeth Cooper; [m.] Norma Freda Cooper, July 7, 1986; [ch.] Robert Searles Cooper; [ed.] Adams Center High School, NY., Remington Institute Watertown, NY; [occ.] Retired; [memb.] Live oak golf and C.C. AARP Farm Bureau former member of Poetry Society of Texas, member US Army 1950-52 Korean War Trinity Episcopal Church; [hon.] 1987 1st place prize in Ft. Worth Poetry Contest '89 Golden Poet Award '90 Golden and Silver Poet Awards World of Poetry, Poem "Forever Love" on 912 of vol. II of "Great Poems of Western World "John Campbell Pub. '95; [oth. writ.] All state ins. faxed one poem to their main office to be put in a newsletter '94. Weatherford Nat'l Bank had my poem in their newsletter. Kips Restaurant had my poem in newsletter 1983; [pers.] Through my poetry, I can see myself as a better, more caring and thoughtful person than what I may think I am.; [a.] Weatherford, TX

COOPER, SAMANTHA
[pen.] Samantha Cooper; [b.] March 25, 1969, Defiance, OH; [p.] Jerry L. Bush and Bonnie L. Bush; [m.] Richard L. Cooper Jr., April 28, 1990; [ch.] Laven Cooper III, Nicholas Cooper; [ed.] Bryan High School, Four County J.V.S.; [occ.] Individual ready reserve, housewife; [memb.] Paulding Worship Center; [hon.] Honors and dietitian in Army Reserves, F.H.A.; [oth.

writ.] Several poems yet not published.; [pers.] I credit my talent and strife for excellence to God.; [a.] Hicksville, OH

COOTS, BERNA
[pen.] Berna Coots; [b.] September 1, 1984, Waynaka, OK; [p.] Patty Coots; [ed.] 4th grade, 1994-95 Erick Grade School Erick, OK; [occ.] Student I am 10 years old and in the 4th grade; [memb.] 4-H of Erick, OK; [hon.] Principal's Honor Row 2 times this year awards for reading. Awards for 4-H club; [oth. writ.] Poems published in local newspaper, Erick Democrat.; [pers.] I like to write poems. I hope other's enjoy reading my poems.; [a.] Erick, OK

CORBETT, ANDREW T.
[pen.] Randy Corbett; [b.] August 28, 1972, MA; [p.] Lois J. and Niall P. Corbett; [ed.] Minuteman Tech - High School Installers Institute, Electrical Wiring; [occ.] Operation Management Bohemis, NY; [pers.] In the hopes of being discovered by a musician and or recording company, I continue to write poems and songs. I, myself, am a musician, playing guitar and drums, but enjoyment also comes from writing. The National Library of Poetry is another way for me to be discovered. Wish me luck.; [a.]Lake Ronkonkoma, NY

CORMIER, TINA
[b.] July 29, 1970, Crowley, LA; [p.] Durphy Cormier Sr., Lydia L. Cormier; [ed.] Crowley High; [oth. writ.] A poem published by Famous Poets Society; [pers.] With my poetry, I hope to make the world a little brighter.; [a.] Crowley, LA\

CORTEZ, NICOLETTE R.
[pen.] Nicolette R. Cortez; [b.] January 26, 1963, Denver; [p.] Rita H. Garcia; [ch.] Ruchonna, Rudy (Garza), Amber, Roman, Mariah (Cortez); [ed.] G.E.D., West High School; [occ.] Admission Representative Ceniror Foundation Inc.; [oth. writ.] Many other unpublished at this time, but will continue to seek publication.; [pers.] I have an AIDS Diagnosis, founded in 1993. Am inspired by my new positive outlook of living am also a recovering cocaine and crack addict in currently Cenikor Rehab.; [a.] Denver, CO

CORTHELL, JUDITH K.
[pen.] Catherine Cortney; [b.] November 28, 1938, Fremont, OH; [p.] Richard and Olive Stucky; [ch.] Tara Hartke, Todd Corthell, Irissa Carter; [ed.] Port Clinton HS, St. Luke's Hospital School of Nursing, Western Reserve University, University of Calif. Santa Barbara, Wright State University.; [occ.] Realtor; [memb.] National of Realtors, Ohio Association of Realtors, Dayton area Board of Realtors.; [pers.] I wish to express situation of duress. Mixing cadence and mirth for what its worth.; [a.] Kettering, OH

COSTELLO, HAROLD THOMAS
[pen.] Harry "C"; [b.] September 15, 1932, New York, NY; [p.] Harold Costello, Mildred Costello; [m.] Janet E. Costello, September 18, 1977; [ch.] Colleen Regina, Suzanne, Theresa Marie, Timothy Edward, Michelle, Kathaleen Ann, Patricia-Ann; [ed.] Forest Hills High; [occ.] Retired Lic. Electrician currently Pen and Ink Artist and Calligrapher; [memb.] Honor member local #3 I.B.E.W., Woodhaven Historical Society; [hon.] First and second place Ribbons I.B.E.W art show 1993; [oth. writ.] Have written other poems, none published, also short stories, none published; [pers.] I try to express my feelings in poems and my art work. I draw life, and I write about life as I have lived it...; [a.] New York City, NY

COTTLE, JUDY CHRISTMAN
[b.] July 12, 1943, Hagerstown, MD; [p.] William John and Mildred Rose Christman; [m.] Elwood "Woody" Cottle, May 26, 1961; [ch.] Celia Dawn and Wendy Lyn; [ed.] Gaithersburg High School, Gaithersburg, Maryland; [occ.] Homemaker; [memb.] National Mul-

tiple Sclerosis Society, Human Society of the United States; [pers.] My world has been filled with great love and prosperity. Living each wondrous day in amazement, I am unable to keep in within the confines of my mind. My release is in the printed word and to be able to share my joy with others.; [a.] Wilmington, NC

COUCH, GEORGE EUGENE
[pen.] Gene Couch; [b.] April 5, 1923, Turin, GA; [p.] Eddie C and Mae W. Couch; [m.] Gladys V. Stull Couch, May 3, 1962; [ch.] Georgene, Linda, Kenneth, Carl, Angela, John, David, Violet.; [ed.] AA Degree, Fresno City College, Fresno, CA; [occ.] Retired US Army; [memb.] Lifetime disabled American Veterans.; [hon.] Four times Dean's List, Fresno, City College.; [oth. writ.] Several poems never published.; [pers.] Always give your best at whatever you do, one should strive to always do that which is right.; [a.] Newnan, GA.

COULBY, MARY A.
[b.] October 14, 1963, LaPlata, MD; [p.] Shirley Coulby and Adrian Coulby; [m.] Jacob L. Johnson III, June 16, 1990; [ed.] B.A. Psychology St. Mary's College of MD; [memb.] Psi Chi, Maryland League of Foster Parents, Foster Parents Association of Washington County.; [hon.] St. Mary's Scholar Award, 1988 Human Development Division Award, 1988, National Dean's List, 1987, 1988, 1989; [pers.] The poem "Jenny Wren" was written in honor of my sister for the strength and courage she demonstrated while battling cancer.; [a.] Smithsburg, MD

COULTER, JILL
[b.] September 7, Beacon, NY; [p.] Joan and Michael Coulter; [ed.] Saint Joachim/Saint John Middle School Grace 6; [occ.] Student; [memb.] Saint Joachims Church CYO Bastketball Team; [hon.] Cheerleading and basketball trophies. Report card 1st honors; [a.] Beacon, NY

COURTNEY, CHERIE LYNN
[b.] June 17, 1958, Harriman, TN; [pers.] My passion came from inspiration when two souls touched each other in a very unique way, which brought forth this beautiful poem. Dedicated to Bill Thomas with all my love; [a.] Burns Harbor, IN

COUSINS, IVAN E.
[b.] November 26, 1929, Baileyville, ME; [p.] Omar and Stella (Gower) Cousins; [m.] Dorothy Ellen Stetson, June 25, 1954; [ch.] Ellen Julig, Brenda Schenck, Mark Cousins, Karen Miller; [ed.] U.S. Army 1947-1950, Eastern Nazarene College, non-graduate - 3 years; [occ.] Retired, Industrial Engineering; [memb.] Church of the Nazarene 48 years; [oth. writ.] Leading the way Library of Congress ISBN-1-56167, 264-5 in Reflections of Light for July 1995

COX, SARAH
[b.] January 30, 1945, Wilson NC; [p.] Jennie L. and Sim A. Wooten; [ch.] Chance D. Cox; [ed.] Limeston College Gaffrey SC U.N.C. Chapel Hill NC. Meredith College Raleigh, NC.; [occ.] Education; [pers.] I did not know what else to do in this life - all I have ever known has been in the arts.

COX, JAN
[b.] April 24, 1955, Fort Payne, AB; [p.] Raymoth Goodwin Kirby, Ross Kirby; [m.] DeWitt Cox, April 21, 1979; [ed.] Sand Rock High School; [occ.] Unemployed; [hon.] Beta Club; [pers.] I only write about people or things about which I feel very deeply, such as my native American heritage, family, etc. When an idea comes to me the poem usually writes its self.; [a.] Leesburg, AB

COZMYK, PETER
[b.] February 20, 1975, Lorain, OH; [p.] Jon and Dorothy Cozmyk; [ed.] High School Diploma, Avon

High School currently going to Cleveland State University to get a degree in Physics; [occ.] Ford Motor Co. Assembly line; [a.] Sheffield Village, OH

CRABBE, EDITH P.
[b.] August 2, 1910, Chicago, IL; [p.] Morris and Mary Kennedy Prescott; [m.] Kenneth Crabbe (Dee), September 12, 1933; [ed.] Oak Park - River Forest High School, Knox College, Galesburg, IL., University of Chicago, Chicago IL; [occ.] Retired - Social Worker (1933-1973), Public Relations, writer; [memb.] Zonta International, Nineteenth Century Woman's Club (past Pres.), First United Church of Oak Park (IL); [hon.] Knox College Alumnae Achievement Award 1988 "in recognition of her outstanding career as a social worker and volunteer extraordinaire", elected to 1988 Senior Citizens Hall of Fame, City of Chicago, Dept of Aging and Disability May 26, 1988, Eugene Sawyer, Acting Mayor; [oth. writ.] Columns and articles in social work publications, newsletters, poems, music program and publicity notes; [a.] Maywood, IL

CRAIG, MARY LOUISE
[pen.] M.L.C., Lou-Lou; [b.] September 3, 1962, Detroit, MI; [p.] Naomi Lewis and Willie Walker; [m.] Michael Anthony Craig, August 9, 1985; [ed.] Pershing High, Ross Buss. Inst. Lewis College of Business; [occ.] Striving Poet; [memb.] Detroit Center Seventh Day Adventist Church; [hon.] High School Diploma, Business Clerk Certificate; [oth. writ.] Forever you'll stay in my heart sonet, and currently working on poems for Mrs. Barbara S.; [pers.] My goal is to share the gift God has given me, with all who will given me, with all who will open there hearts to listen! I have been influenced by family members, and also by my roll models Maya Angelo, and Lankston Hughs; [a.] Detroit, MI

CRANDLE, VIRGINIA LEE
[pen.] Williams; [b.] April 20, 1912, Dexter, MO; [p.] James B. Williams, Maude Asler France; [m.] Dr. Ellis Roland Crandle, November 24, 1923; [ch.] 3 Daughters; [ed.] St. Louis High School - 4 years, Washington University 3 years, Nursing Registered Nurse, Night School Rec. Public Health Degree; [occ.] East Class Work - RPH Maternity Hosp. Deliver Baby Home etc.; [memb.] Various Clubs! Presbyterian-Faithful A.A.R.P, Garden Church Faculty group. Antique Study Club; [hon.] Church group for Flora Arrangements Judging, Chicago Honors Rural Judging Arrangements, X-ray Class Worker with Nutrition, Gardening Landscape Flora Arrangements Judging 1992-1994.; [oth. writ.] "Small writing to Readers Digest" poetry enjoyment at parties!; [a.] Carbondale, IL

CREECH, FRANCES J.
[pen.] Frances J. Creech; [b.] September 15, 1913, Saint Pauls, NC; [p.] Charlie and Katye Byrd Jones; [m.] Wilbur L. Creech, March 31, 1934; [ch.] Wilbur Lewis Creech, Jr., Frances Jones Creech, James Edward Creech, Alice Byrd Creech, Foster Children, Charles L. Creech, Janice Simmons, Betty Bradley Crabb.; [ed.] 71st H.S. Fayettesville, N.C. Pineland College, Bond Byrd School of Music, Mendenhall School of Speach Wayne Community College.; [occ.] Home teaching, tutoring, counseling.; [memb.] St. Paul U. Methodist Church Order of Eastern State, WCTU, US Chamber of Commerce.; [oth. writ.] Poems, letters, short stories, prayers published in news papers, books.; [pers.] Lord, love through me each soul I see hungering - searching Lord for thee. Grant me wisdom - courage to do my part to lead them to you, mind, soul, heart! [a.] Goldsboro, NC

CREWS, JENNIFER
[pen.] Jinn; [b.] January 1, 1967, Centreville, AL; [p.] Lula and Willie Crews; [ch.] Crystal Marie Crews; [ed.] Cody High School, Ross Business Institute, Crokett Vocational School for Nursing.; [occ.] Care Provider; [memb.] I'm a member of Greater Heaven of Rest

Church of God in Christ; [hon.] Typing Award in College, in honor roll while in college and high school.; [oth. writ.] Several poems I've written for my church and my mom.; [pers.] God has given me knowledge to write poetry that captures ones attention, I pray that God continues to give me wisdom to succeed. Thank You!!; [a.] Detroit, MI

CROCKETT, MICHAEL W.
[pen.] Ward Crockett; [b.] October 28, 1976, Denver, CO; [ed.] George Washington High School; [occ.] Student; [memb.] Thespian Society, Tragic House of IB; [oth. writ.] One other poem published in an anthology, currently working on a novel.; [pers.] I always strive to be original and as different as I can. Be strange!; [a.] Denver, CO

CROOK, HEATHER M.
[pen.] Adriana Marie; [b.] December 15, 1973, Cleveland, OH; [p.] Ken and Shelley Crook; [ed.] Mentor High School and Lakeland Community College; [occ.] Guest Service Rep., Fairfield Inn, Willoughby, OH.; [oth. writ.] Various unpublished poems and novels.; [pers.] My writing reflects the many aspects of my personality.; [a.] Mentor, OH

CROUTHER, VANESSA
[b.] July 12, 1958, Ft. Campbell, KY; [p.] Elvin F. Crouther and Florine Crouther; [ed.] Loyola University of Chicago; [occ.] Library associate, Loyola University of Chicago - Lewis Library, and writer; [hon.] Honorable Mention - 1990 IsFic (Illinois Science Fiction in Chicago) Contest, First Place - 1991 IsFic Contest; [oth. writ.] Short story, "Soul to Take" was published in Journeys to the Twilight Zone (DAW, 1993).; [a.] Chicago, IL

CROWLEY, JANEY JENINE
[pen.] Janey Jenine; [b.] August 28, 1942, Detroit, MI; [p.] Albert and Flora Mendelsohn; [m.] James Crowley; [ch.] Debbi Lynn Kessler and Dan Jay Fielding; [ed.] Seven years training in counseling bio energies, meditation, positive thinking, bio feedback, selt expression, group training.; [occ.] Owned and operated several businesses including antique stores, retail store Phoenix, AZ. Para-Psychologist in Semi Valley CA. and author unique poetry. Was also Vice President of Tower Plaza Mall in Phoenix, AZ.; [hon.] Hawaiian Dancing including being the first to ever Hawaiian dance on TWA Airplane with my group. Several awards and honors for Hawaiian dancing honors and awards for porcelain dolls I made, ceramic chess set and statues. Honors for oil painting and needle point. My best honor is my grandchildren Michael Justin November 15, 1991 and Sean Mathew August 19, 1993.; [oth. writ.] The collectors limited edition poems first edition and second edition by Janey Jenine Crowley. "Hello Lord" published in "Today's Great Poems." "Grandma's Delight" in east of the sunrise. And mesmerized published in "Songs on the Wind" also picked for cassette; [pers.] I point out the happy things in life I believe in happiness and cheerfulness and I let love be the end of all my thoughts, words, and actions. I want my poetry to give others cherished moments!!!; [a.] Three Rivers, CA

CRUZ, REV. DR. EDGARDO RIVERA
[pen.] Prince; [b.] March 23, 1958, NY; [p.] Ramos Rivera, Carmen Cruz; [ch.] Richard and Sheila; [ed.] Doctor in Philosophy, Theology, Religion, Biblical Studies Divinity, Medicine, Law Student.; [occ.] Archbishop - Cathedral St. Martin de Porres.; [memb.] Universal Life Church, American fellowship. Church, Cathedral St. Martin De Porres, Bishop of all Church Abene, journalist and writer Dominica Republic.; [hon.] God Conduct Medal U.S. Memorial Corps, Overall coordinator., Prince of the Patriarchate of Antioch.; [oth. writ.] At Days End - National Library of Poetry, Re - The Flower of Our Own Country the Rose. The Flower of Our Own Country - The Rose Treasured.

Poems of America writen 1995; [pers.] The lady's of the world are of the heart of their wish and I am your wish, love me eternally.; [a.] Miami, FL

CRUZADA, JOEL
[b.] 10/29/70; Manila/Phil.; [p.] Juan Cruzada and Erlinda; [m] Dina Cruzada, July 30, 1993; [ch.] Lauressa Tiana; [ed.] Lane Technical H.S., Chicago; School of the Art Institute of Chicago; [occ.] Senior Art Director; [memb.] Internal Order of Foresters; World Wildlife Federation; [pers.] God the creator, made us in His own image. Thus, we too are creators. Live you life by creating - from a garden to a painting masterpiece. Whatever it may be don't stop creating!; [a.] Orlando, FL.

CRUZAN, PATRICIA
[pen.] Pat Cruzan; [b.] November 15, 1945, Jacksonville, FL; [p.] Clarence Cannon, Ruth Agnes Cannon; [m.] Charles Cruzan, November 4, 1977; [ch.] Christopher Cruzan; [ed.] A.L. Miller High, Tift College, Georgia State University; [occ.] Reading And Math Teacher; [memb.] Fayetteville First Baptist Sunday School, Choir and Ensemble, International Reading Association, SCBWI, International Society of Poets; [hon.] Dedication page in Dictionary of International Biography 1995, Life Member of International Biography Association, Tri-Beta Music in College [oth. writ.] Several poems published by the National Library of Poetry, two pieces in church publications, Honorable Mention in Byline for "The Grand Old House on Oak Haven"; [pers.] God gives us poetry and music to help us enjoy the glimpses of sunshine that come from a loving relationship with him.; [a.] Fayetteville, GA

CUMMINGS, KENNETH L.
[pen.] Ken Cummings; [b.] February 27, 1916, Washington, CT; [p.] Estelle and Ernest Cummings (deceased); [m.] E. Jeanne Cummings (deceased), August 31, 1942; [ch.] Pam, Lynne and Kim; [ed.] Nichols Grammar School 1929, Nichols, CT 1933- Warren Harding High School, Bridgeport, CT, 1937-Marietta College, Marietta, OH, 1941-U of Louisville, School of Medicine, Louisville, KY; [occ.] M.D. (Neurosurgeon); [memb.] American Ass'n of Neurological Surgeons Congress of Neurological Surgeons Fellow, American College of Surgeons (FACS) Pan American Medical Association Screen Actors Guild (SAG); [hon.] Diplomat, American Board of Neurological Surgery; [pers.] Lucky Lindy was written by me in 1928, as student in Nichols Grammar School Nichols, CT, Age 12.; [a.] Las Vegas, NV

CUMMINGS, HEATHER
[pen.] Sweet Pea.; [b.] January 17, 1981, Edina, MN; [p.] Jenean and Richard Cummings; [ed.] I am in the 8th grade.; [pers.] "Keep your head up, stand tall and believe in yourself and everything will be alright."; [a.] Hastings, MN

CUNNINGHAM, ESTHER C.
[b.] May 22, 1918, Macon Co., NC; [p.] Zeb and Nellie Clouse; [m.] James P. Cunningham, Sr., January 22, 1939; [ch.] Brenda Elliott, Suzanne Williams, James P. Cunningham, Jr.; [ed.] Franklin High, Western Carolina University, Cullowhee, N.C. Also, Artistic Beauty Institute, Atlanta, GA.; [occ.] Retired Teacher (K-9) Macon Co. Public Schools; [memb.] Save Our Rivers, Inc., Western N.C. Alliance, Inc. (protects environment), Memorial United Methodist Church.; [hon.] The Western N.C. Alliance, Inc. presents, the Esther Cunningham Award annually to the person in the western part of N.C. who has done the most to protect our environment.; [oth. writ.] Several poems published in local newspapers and in environmental publications and church newsletters et al. Also, National Library of Poetry. Published in '92 and '93. "Dray Falls of the Cullasaja River" was the first poem I ever wrote.; [pers.] I believe that we shall die of our own waste if we continue to pollute the earth. We must learn and reduce,

reuse, and recycle.; [a.] Franklin, NC

CUNNINGHAM, BECKIE
[b.] December 23, 1948, Bledsoe Country, KY; [p.] George and Viola Hale; [m.] George Washington Cunningham, March 20, 1969; [ch.] Martha, North, Sarah, West; [ed.] 10th Grade; [pers.] I used my own names I don't know were the poem came from I wrote the poem used my brother names; [a.] Mansfield, OH

CUPPETT, CATHLEEN G.
[b.] September 30, 1966, Odenton, MD; [p.] Joyce and Alex Cuppett; [ed.] Bowie High School Wheaton College B.A. University of Virginia M.A.; [occ.] Graduate Student; [memb.] Modern Language Association, Sigma Delta Pi, ACTFL, AATSP, NAACFLLF; [oth. writ.] Article for Romance Notes; [pers.] I want my works to be authentic and accessible; [a.] Charlottesville, VA

CUTCHER, KAWIKA DAVID
[pen.] Kawika Cutcher; [b.] January 30, 1958, Honolulu, HI; [p.] David and Ruth Cutcher; [m.] Yolanda Cutcher; [ch.] Kawika Cutcher, Kavi Cutcher, Liana Cutcher; [ed.] Kailua High School, Windward Community College Army Intelligence Law Enforcement; [occ.] Construction, Mason; [memb.] Kalahui Hawaii Anahola Youth Association Kapaa Assembly of God member; [hon.] Honorable Discharge U.S Army Guard 1989 Employee of Year Amfac Resorts - 1985, Life Saving Award 1985, Employee of Months 1983-84.; [oth. writ.] 1,000 Tears of Aloha, Articles in the Garden Island newspaper and Kauai Times concerning my people; [pers.] I write about my culture and my peoples struggle to get back our lands and rights. And how it is being a native Hawaiian in the 1990's; [a.] Anahola Kauai, HI

DAEHLER, RUTH
[pen.] Ruth Daehler; [b.] July 12, 1919, Rockford, IL; [p.] Deceased; [m.] Quintin Daehler, July 1, 1945; [ed.] High School, Business College and Continuing Education Courses; [occ.] Retired; [memb.] Business and Professional Women Past District Director, Past Pres. - Lexington, Past Pres. - Odessa.; [hon.] Lexington B.P.W. Woman of the Year; [oth. writ.] The Teddy Bear Story, The Teddy Bear Song, lots of poetry, several other songs!; [pers.] My writings are done mainly by inspiration and I pass it on!; [a.] Mayview, MO

DAEHLER, BETHINE L.
[b.] October 1, 1954, Richland Center, WI; [p.] Robert Neefe, Darlene Neefe; [m.] Charles Daehler, October 28, 1989; [ch.] Andrew Kapellusch, Ethan Daehler; [ed.] Salem Central High, Gateway Technical Institute, U. W. Parkside; [occ.] Licensed Practical Nurse, substitute teacher, farmer; [memb.] United Methodist Women; [oth. writ.] Monthly column in Lexington, United Methodist Circuit Rider. Write children's stories, poetry, short stories yet to published.; [pers.] Faith in God allows us endless possibilities. We limit only ourselves without Him.; [a.] Lexington, MO

DAELEY, NANCY
[b.] August 16, 1951, NY; [m.] Kirk Daeley; [ch.] Daniel, Jennifer, Matthew; [occ.] In transition; [pers.] My writing is done as a two step healing process. First for myself and then to help others. This particular poem was written to help children and adults come to terms with depression and loss. To realize there are people who care and there is always hope.; [a.] Laguna Beach, CA

DAHLEN, LLEWELYN ELLSWORTH
[pen.] Lew Dahlen; [b.] August 13, 1921, Cambridge, MN; [p.] Deceased; [m.] Dorothy M. Dahlen, August 28, 1948; [ch.] Pamela Ann, Craig James, Gary Bernard; [ed.] Central H.S., St. Paul, MN (Grad) Sev. Night Courses - Var. Subj. Dale Carnegie/Toast Masters; [occ.] Retired; [memb.] Tennessee Songwriters Country Musoic Society of Amer., Ass'n, Pro Ball

players Amer., Cloisters Home Owners Ass'n, Resort Condominiums Int'l, AARP; [hon.] Veteran W.W. II, past Pres. (sev. yrs) Cloisters BD., current V.P. BD-Gov.-Tuckaway Condos, past Founder Pres - Milw Chapter, Delta NU Alpha Transp Society, past Reg. V.P. Delta NU Alpha, Editor - Cloisters Newsletter; [oth. writ.] Catalog of songs - Country, Gospel, Tex-Mex etc. 30 in no - lyrics and demos, poems - various subjects personal autobiography 20 chapters; [pers.] The ability to write songs and poetry came to me under very mysterious circumstances that involved a very crucial time of my life in 1980. I have to be a true believer; [a.] Greenfield, WI

DALY, GAIL MARIA
[pen.] Robbie Daly; [b.] April 17, 1950, Camden, NJ; [p.] Richard M. and Jessie M. Condon; [m.] David D. Daly, July 16, 1994; [ed.] High School; [occ.] Real Estate Agent with Legal assistant/secretary background; [memb.] NRA and Eagles; [oth. writ.] Numerous unpublished poems and short stories; [pers.] To my Mom for her continued encouragement of my poetry. My Dad taught me you could do anything you put your mind too.

DALY, LINDA
[b.] September 20, 1937, Long Island, NY; [p.] Arther Welch, Helen Riley; [ch.] Brian Wesnofske, Jerelyn Daly, Erin Daly, Jeremiah Daly.; [ed.] Glen Cove, High School; [occ.] Mother, grandmother; [oth. writ.] Blind at Christmas, Small Whip, Upon a Sea of Silence; [pers.] For my children, and thank you David Gault

DALY, JAMES
[b.] January 1, 1937, Bellingham, WA; [occ.] Artist; [oth. writ.] One and 3/4 novels (unpublished), numerous short stories (unpublished) and a handful of poems (unpublished).; [pers.] I try to reintegrate the disowned parts of my personality into my conscious self. My painting helps. But when frustrated in my painting, I sometimes turn to prose or poetry.; [a.] Laguna Beach, CA

DANIEL, JEAN GILBERT
[pen.] John or Danny; [b.] September 29, 1925, RI; [p.] John and Anita Daniel; [m.] Simonne V. (Tancrede) Daniel, August 19, 1946; [ch.] John, James, Jeanne, Jo Ann, Joan; [occ.] Retired Home Builder and General Contractor; [memb.] Retired member of: LIONS - H.N.S. - C.B.A. - B.S. of A. - S. Master. Life Membership: U.B.C. of A. - V.F.W. A.L. - 80th Div. Asso.-S.P.W.W. - N.C.W. Coord. (active) - editor of a monthly advisory letter. (2600 copie).; [hon.] 100 days of continues combat, (rifleman). C.I.B. - 1 Silver and 3 Bronze Stars. Pass Presi. of several Inc. and Assoc.; [oth. writ.] A (20) Chapter Combat Novel, 100 poems by J.G.D., several short stories. In progress: (2) Novels, (200) Poems by J.G.D. and several short stories.; [pers.] I found, early in life, that only through poetry and writing can one visualize and sense the true values of general human virtues. And through the general application, find a wealth of heeling, both mental and physical.; [a.] St. Petersburg, FL

DANIELS, DEBRA ANN
[b.] JulY 16, 1961, Pine Bluff, AR; [p.] Henry and Hallie Walters; [m.] Donald, September 18, 1990; [ch.] Derrell, Gwone, Corlena, Donald (Stepson); [ed.] 1 1/2 yr. college University Maryland, City College of Chicago; [occ.] Factory Worker; [memb.] International Society of Poets, Tabernacle Church of God and Christ; [hon.] Poet of Merit Award, Editors Choice Award, Certificate of Appreciation for Achievement in poetry, from U.S. Army Pine Bluff, Arsenal wrote them song for local Radio Station.; [oth. writ.] Poetry published in anthology, dark-side-of-moon, anthology, Best poems of '95, Anthology East of the sunrise reflections magazine. Poem published in Military newspaper; [pers.] With God nothing shall be impossible. Luke 1:37; [a.] Pine Bluff, AR

DANLEY, LELA PEDEN
[pen.] Lela Danley; [b.] July 9, 1933, Tularosa, NM; [p.] Claude and Maggie Belle Danley; [m.] Raymond Peden, October 6, 1951; [ch.] Terri Lela 1954, Ray Jr. '56, Rynell '58, Bobby Gene '63, and Jim W. '65, Rodney '60; [ed.] G.E.D.; [occ.] Retired Nurses Aide; [hon.] 1st mention in over Hoo jingles (local event); [oth. writ.] Songs - sung in schools, dances, churches and performing arts - the Oregon Walts I wrote in 1958 is being considered for the official Ore. State Waltz.; [pers.] I've been on TV and Radio, had my own TV song writer show, performed at Salem, Ore. State Cap Bldg, Show cased in Nash. Published "Comfort Cards". Self taught guitar at 12 years, song writer at 15, Country Gospel, Country Love Songs, Country Ballads. Dad was stroke by lightening at the White Sands when I was 7 and lived 8 more years.; [a.] Spokane, WA

DARRELL, LEANNE M.
[b.] April 7, 1980, Connellsville, PA; [p.] Rosemary and Terry Darrell; [ed.] Student, Connellsville Jr High East 8th grade; [oth. writ.] Lots, I love to write.; [pers.] Do the best you can, and dream big.; [a.] Connellsville, PA

DAUGHERTY, ROBERT E.
[b.] November 17, 1937, Warren, OH; [p.] Audrey and Grace Daugherty; [m.] Donna, April 16, 1956; [ch.] Michael, David, Ronald; [occ.] Retired from U.S. Navy as well as Federal Service; [memb.] Fleet Reserve Association, NARFE, AARP; [hon.] Vietnam Veteran; [oth. writ.] Several poems in local newspaper; [pers.] Extensive overseas travel, 12 grandchildren and a dairy farm boyhood has provided me a wealth of personal experiences on which to draw. I enjoy the 18th and 19th century poets. Rhyme is my crime.; [a.] Napa, CA

DAVIDOVIC, BOB (SLOBODAN)
[b.] February 20, 1960, Serbia, Yugoslavia; [p.] Dusan and Linda Davidovic; [m.] Radojka Davidovic, May 16, 1992; [ch.] Alexsandra; [ed.] B.A., B.B.A., M.B.A. M.B.A. Wayne State University 1987 Detroit, Michigan; [occ.] Management Consultant, Marketing Consultant; [memb.] Variars social and professional organizations. Amer. Assoc of Individual Investors Assoc. of MBA executives; [hon.] Ethnic Broadcasting Award, Professional Achievement Award, Soccer Awards; [oth. writ.] Film scrips and ideas, short stories. Managerial and marketing articles.; [pers.] "Life is a interesting journey of self discovery and not merely a destination towards some certainty. Growth and creativity are its major catalysts leading to a wise maturity"

DAVIDSON, AMY J.
[b.] June 15, 1965; [ed.] Battle Creek Central High, currently working on a B.A. in English; [oth. writ.] Various pieces of poetry and short stories; [a.] Charlotte, MI

DAVIDSON, CHRISTINE
[b.] March 19, 1966, Ainsworth, NE; [p.] Paul Davidson, Ruth Davidson; [ed.] Holland Patent High, Wheaton College, Elms College; [occ.] Elementary Teacher; [memb.] Albany Rock and Mineral Club; [hon.] Alpha Kappa Delta National Honor Society, Regents Scholarship, Eleanor Kowalsky Voice Scholarship, Utica Chorale Voice Scholarship; [pers.] I enjoy writing poetry that will instill an appreciation and a deeper understanding of the wonders of nature.; [a.] Barneveld, NY

DAVIES, NICOLA J.A.
[pen.] Nicola Darcy; [b.] 01.05.64, Crumpsall UK; [.] Vera and Alan Ball; Peter Davies, 30.4.94; [ed.] Bolton School, University of Surrey, Sorbonne, Paris; [occ.] Personnel Officer; [hon.] BA(hons.) French; [oth. writ.] Collaborated on article published in "Madame Figaro" -- 100 years of Coca-Cola.; [pers.] I adore reading, and have a very catholic taste in books. I greatly admire the works of e.e. cummings and Elizabeth Barrett-Browning.; [a.] Manchester, UK.

DAVIES, WILLIAM
[pen.] Scouse; [b.] March 26, 1938, Liverpool; [ch.] Michael Alexander; [ed.] Our Lady's Eldon St. Liverpool England; [occ.] Tile Setter; [pers.] I laugh, I cry, I live, I die, Why?; [a.] Midvale, UT.

DAVIS, BETTINA
[b.] March 2, 1978, Pinebluff, AR; [p.] Billy and Diana Davis; [occ.] A High School Junior will be a senior this fall.; [a.] Dumas, AR

DAVIS, BRENDA
[b.] February 23, 1972, Cedar Falls, IA; [p.] Ted Davis, Jane Davis; [ed.] Student, currently studying at Eastern MI, University for Elem. Ed.; [occ.] Waitress, Bartender, Cake Decorator; [memb.] St. Michael's Luthern Church; [hon.] Working with people, making new friends; [pers.] My ultimate goal in life is to make people feel good about themselves. I believe the best way to do this is through words of those who care.; [a.] Canton, MI

DAVIS, HEATHER
[b.] October 23, 1976, Atlanta, GA; [p.] Gerald B. and Donna C. Davis; [ed.] Senior at Eisenhower High School; [occ.] Student; [memb.] JV/Varsity Track, National Honors Society, UIL Calculator Team, Habitat for Humanity, St. Ambrose Church (Assist Children's Liturgy and Usher), and PETA; [hon.] Who's Who Among H.S. Students, Chemistry Student of the Yr., English II Student of the Yr., U.S., Achievement Academy Nat'l Award for Outstanding Achievement in Math, USAA Nat'l Award for All-Am. Scholar at large, USAA Nat'l Award for Leadership and Service; [pers.] All aspects of life serve a purpose. In order to lead a good, happy life, you must find the best inside or from those chronicles.; [a.] Houston, TX

DAVIS, JOYCE PRESLEY
[pen.] Ellen Thompson; [b.] February 8, 1930, Tennessee; [p.] Charles William Presley, Kathleen Thompson Presley; [m.] A. E., June 18, 1948; [ch.] Kathleen, Judy, Beth; [ed.] Nurse; [occ.] Retired; [pers.] Always wanted to write poetry and short stories, that would help others. Too unsure of myself. Had one poem published almost fifty years ago.

DAVIS, LENA ELIZABETH
[pen.] Alexandria Michelle Chanlor; [b.] July 29, 1962, Shelby, NC; [p.] Clyde William and Elizabeth Ann Davis; [ch.] Michael Antonio RaShaun, Chanlor JaMaal McArthur, Kevin James Alexander Davis; [ed.] Certified Welder 1 yr. Cleveland Community College Shelby, N.C.; [occ.] Cook and welder; [hon.] My welded art work was put on display at Cleveland Community College. At age 12 received an academic excellence award from English Teacher. Creative writing.; [oth. writ.] The author of over 300 poems unpublished. Writes children stories for home class through the Institute of Children Literature.; [pers.] Follow your heart and you will find true happiness.; [a.] Shelby, NC

DAVIS, PAUL
[pen.] Duke; [b.] November 28, 1969, Orlando, FL; [p.] Paul and Paulette Davis; [m.] Single; [ed.] B.S. - U Central Florida, M - Divinity (Spirit Life Bible C), CA Brooklyn Law student presently, NY; [occ.] Student (law); [memb.] Songwriters, Hall of Fame, AFAA - personal trainer, Gold's Gym member licensed real estate salesman, Fl, Law student - U of Hong Kong, summer '95; [hon.] Missionary to Russia, Africa, lifeguard competitor, body builder; [oth. writ.] Lyrics for songs; [pers.] I seek women to correspond with in romantic poetry; [a.] Brooklyn Heights, NY

DAVIS, SCOTT LYNWOOD
[b.] July 17, 1983, Newport News, VA; [p.] Bill and Barbara Davis; [ed.] Attends Hines Middle School is in the 6th grade; [hon.] Received 1st place in the PTA Reflections contest for Literature in the 1991-1992

school year. Also received Honorable Mention for some contest the next 2 years.; [oth. writ.] Short story "Aribus, Son of Nix" and "Fight for the Americas"

DAVIS, TIM
[pen.] David T. Wayne; [b.] April 16, 1957, Tulsa, OK; [p.] Robert and Wanda Davis; [m.] Gloria Gay Davis, October 18, 1991; [ch.] Lacey 10, Matthew 9 months; [ed.] Charles Page HS, Neo A&M Junior College, University of Central Oklahoma degrees include A.A.E., B.M.E. + 6; [occ.] Marketing Manager; [memb.] Omea Retired, Baptist Church; [hon.] Top Trainee Sales Class 1994, 15 Year Music Educator Award.; [oth. writ.] Currently 5 Fiction/Sci-Fi, Adventure/Suspense Novel yet unpublished; [pers.] My deepest desire is to some-day be a full time professional writer. I want to write stories which entertain the mind.

DAVIS, URSULA DAMARA
[b.] July 5, 1984, Phoenix, AZ; [p.] Karen Becketts, Lewis Davis; [ed.] 4th grade student at Sierra Vista Elementary School; [hon.] Superintendent Math Achievement Club Award, City Worker Award, Principal's Award for Academic Scholarship, Certificate of Achievement in Reading, Perfect Attendance; [a.] Phoenix, AZ

DAVIS, ZOLLIE
[pen.] The Crow; [b.] March 1, 1978, Newport News, VA; [p.] Shirley A. Davis; [ed.] Student 11 grade; [hon.] Reading trophy, poetry contest winner before in school poetry contest. Got an A in school on a poem I gave to the teacher.; [oth. writ.] Spring Mornings; [a.] Newport News, VA

DAWSON, DANNI STARR
[pen.] Danni Starr; [b.] November 28, 1950, Louisville, KY; [p.] Mr. and Mrs. Paul and Veronica Guest; [m.] Divorced; [ch.] Todd Murphy and Raven Dawson; [ed.] Graduated from Southern High School, Louisville, KY in 1968; [occ.] Facilities Administrator; [oth. writ.] Tender Branches, Hit and Run, Just Passing Through and Reflections; [pers.] To have a lasting relationship it takes commitment, but to have a meaningful relationship it takes devotion.; [a.] Laguna Niguel, CA

DAY, MARY JANE THOMAS
[b.] October 12, 1927, Connors, NB, CANADA; [p.] Angus and Delina (Michaud) Thomas; [m.] Howard M. Day, July 1, 1949; [ch.] Laurie Anne Day Greene, Angus H. Day; [ed.] B.S. in Geography U of MD., 1974, B.S. in Bus & MGT U of MD., 1977; [occ.] retired - Aide Hanger 8, Eastern Airlines, N.Y.C., 1946-47, U.S. Weather Bur., Washington, 1948-50, Cartographic Aide U.S., Navy Hydrographic Office, Suitland, Md., 1950-57, cartographer, 1957-63, cartographer U.S. Navy Oceanographic Office, Suitland, 1962-72, Def. Mapping Agy., Suitland/Brookmont, 1972-93, cartographer USNS Harkness, 1978, Indonesian Naval Personnel, Jakartak, Indonesia, 1981-82.; [memb.] Nat. Aeronautic Ass., Am. Soc. Photogrammetry and Remote Sensing. Club: Andrews Officers (Md.).; [oth. writ.] Compiled, wrote and published "The Descendants of John Thomas of Connors, N.B., 1988"; [pers.] Avocations: ice skating, sky diving, traveling, genealogy, foreign languages.

DEAN, DAVID R.
[pen.] Cyclone Millsap; [b.] July 23, 1898, Detroit, TX; [p.] W. A. and Minnie Lee Dean (Both Dead); [m.] Ruby Dean, March 12, 1953; [ed.] Okla., University, BA; [occ.] Retired, now 96 yrs. of age.; [memb.] Too many to mention; [oth. writ.] Smackover Rose (Oil Field Novel) and several other novels.; [pers.] I hope to live at least to be 125. My twin brother (recently deceased) and I have made big gifts including several huge buildings to several universities including many scholarships. When I see your book in the Fall, I may want to get a dozen more for my friends.

DEAN, MANDY
[pen.] Mandy; [b.] August 14, 1979, Jackson, MS; [p.] Sherry Dean and Sonny Dean; [ed.] Newton County High School; [oth. writ.] Several poems, which I have never sent in anywhere.; [pers.] My poems are to express my own feelings about experiences which I go through. I write to let other people, who read them, know how I feel about that subject.; [a.] Chunky, MS

DECILLO, R. DAMIAN
[b.] February 16, 1954, New Brunswick, NJ; [p.] Frank DeCillo, Mary Ardolino; [m.] Roxanna DeCillo, October 5, 1975; [ch.] Ricci Damian, Nicole Lisa; [pers.] Reflecting on..... love, the will to extend one's self for the purpose of nurturing one's own or another's spiritual growth; [a.] East Brunswick, NJ

DECKER, MARK
[b.] December 12, 1948, Woodfield, OH; [p.] Miles Burris Decker, Eloise Romaine Kremer; [m.] Maureen McEwan, February 3, 1973; [ch.] Mark Jr. born 11-8-75, Susan born 6-10-81, Kelly born 4-20-90; [ed.] BS, Kent State University 1972, Juris Doctor, George Mason University; [occ.] President and Chief Executive Officer - National Association of Real Estate Investment Trusts, Inc.; [memb.] The Metropolitan Club of Washington

DEEMS-MOGYORDY, SALLY
[b.] March 3, 1953, Dennison, OH; [ed.] BA in Psychology, Kent State University Summa Cum Laude; [occ.] Freelance Writer; [hon.] I wrote the copy for one "Louie" award, winning greeting card and another that was nominated. The "Louie" awards are held annually to acknowledge excellence in the greeting card industry.; [oth. writ.] Many greeting cards and several posters.; [pers.] My writing reflects both my humorous and serious sides. My profound love of nature is reflected in much that I write.; [a.] Sheffield Lake, OH

DELZER, STACEY
[b.] August 10, 1982, Waukesha, WI; [p.] John and Brenda Wysocki; [ed.] Saratoga Elementary School, Central Middle School; [occ.] Student; [hon.] Delta Kappa Gamma, Young Author Award - 1st place, district winner; [oth. writ.] Party frights, poem published in Waukesha Freeman; [pers.] My writing is greatly influenced by lifestyle and world affairs, also by inspirational authors, both fiction and non-fiction.; [a.] Waukesha, WI

DENNISON, ERIC
[b.] February 5, 1972, Philadelphia; [p.] Patricia Dennison; [ed.] North Penn High School Montgomery County Community College; [pers.] Favorite authors include Edgar Allen Poe, Ray Bradbury, favorite novel is "Something Wicked This Way Comes" by Ray Bradbury; [a.] Hatfield, PA

DENUNZIO, MARY KOLAR
[b.] September 12, 1962, Youngstown, OH; [p.] Joseph and Agnes Kolar; [m.] Robert P. Denunzio, April 23, 1988; [ed.] B.A. in Psychology Youngstown State University; [occ.] Career Services Director, New Castle School of Trades; [memb.] Junior League of Youngstown, Mahoning Valley Home Builders Assoc., Scholarship Committee - Active in the Youngstown Playhouse.; [hon.] Dean's List; [pers.] The poem "And When I Think About Him..." was written in the memory of Eric Cowen who was killed in a traffic accident December 18, 1994; [a.] Youngstown, OH

DEPRIMO, KATHERINE
[pen.] Katie; [b.] April 23, 1914, PA; [m.] October 28, 1931; [ch.] 2 Boys; [ed.] Gone up to 8th grade; [occ.] Housewife; [oth. writ.] In the process of writing a book - of my personal life; [pers.] Meeting my son after 50 years, gave me the inspiration to write the poem

DERMOTT, JOHN STEFAN
[b.] May 3, 1966, Cape May Courthouse, NJ; [p.] Elizabeth Dermott and Anthony Verdi; [m.] Renee Anne Dermott, December 30, 1994; [ch.] Robyn Marie Dermott, Madalyn Paige Dermott and Baby Dermott (due July 95); [ed.] Lower Cape May Regional; [occ.] Construction and Sales; [oth. writ.] "Renee", "Forever A While...", "Rainy Day", "Silent", "Ode to Tammy", "While You Can..." and others; [pers.] The masses of skeptics see little in the minute effort of the single individual. However, it's the collection of individual efforts, usually led by an individual that moves mountains.; [a.] New Port Richey, FL

DERSHEM, AMANDA
[b.] May 10, 1956, San Francisco, CA; [p.] Barbara Smith, Lowell Smith; [m.] Stephen M. Dershem, Ph.D, April 19, 1980; [ed.] California High, De Anza College, Mississippi, State University; [occ.] Claims Reinspector and Trainer, State Farm Insurance; [memb.] National Assoc. of Female Executives, Calif., Conference of Arson Investigators, San Diego County Archaeological Assoc.; [hon.] Lifetime member of the National Forensic League; [pers.] With faith, with joy in God, with the support of my husband and friends, I survive and conquer.; [a.] San Diego, CA

DESPARD, HENRY LYNDON
[b.] March 21, 1912, Detroit, MI; [p.] Henry L. and Elizabeth B. Despard; [m.] Marjorie Despard, February 12, 1944; [ch.] Jorilyn Niedzielski, Jeffrey Despard; [ed.] B.A. Lafayette College Easton, PA.; [occ.] President - Despard & Co., Advertising Agency; [memb.] Boy Scout of America - Eagle Scout; [hon.] U.S. Army - Bronze Star WW II; [oth. writ.] "The Times and Tides of Simon Metcalfe", "Simon Metcalfe's Notebook"; [pers.] "It's a wonderful world!"; [a.] Birmingham, MI

DESTEFANO, JAMES MICHAEL
[pen.] Paul; [b.] December 25, 1963, NY; [p.] Marion and Sam Aliberti; [m.] Faith Allison, December 31, 1981; [ch.] Steven Tyler and James Michael; [ed.] College Graduate, Thomas Edison State Univ.; [oth. writ.] "POEMS from the Heart" in the near future on life and spirituality; [pers.] To spread the message of Medjugorie that our lady brings from her son to us. Through verse.; [a.] East Brunswick, NJ

DETOLLA, DOLORES R.
[pen.] Dolores R. DeTolla; [b.] April 3, 1929, Dunkirk, NY; [p.] Frank and Jessie Scarlata; [m.] James A. DeTolla, September 16, 1950; [ch.] James A. DeTolla, Robert G. DeTolla, Susan Badgley, Carol Horrigan, Janice Best; [ed.] High School - Bryant and Stratton Buffalo, NY, College - SUC at Fredonia, Fredonia NY; [occ.] District Clerk - Board of Education - Silver Creek Central School; [memb.] Chautauqua County Secretaries, New York State Education Office, Personnel National Education Office Personnel; [hon.] Professional Standards Program - National Education of Office Personnel; [oth. writ.] Have written a short story, not published yet.; [pers.] I count my blessings when I wake up.; [a.] Silver Creek, NY

DEWOLFE, PHILLIP
[pen.] Wolfman, Bird man; [b.] October 12, 1979, Oklahoma City, OK; [p.] Christy D. DeWolfe; [ed.] Currently attending Smithson Valley Middle School; [hon.] Track, Basketball, Football, Soccer, Baseball Student of the month award.

DIAZ, DELIA M.
[pen.] Del Diaz; [b.] May 30, 1954, Puerto Rico; [p.] Arcadio and Inocencia Diaz; [m.] Single; [ed.] B.A. Degree in English Literature (expect to receive it Fall 1995); [occ.] Exec. Staff Assistant Cornell University Cooperative Extension; [memb.] I am a member of The Puerto Rican Travelling Theatre, Museum of Natural History, Institute of Puerto Rico; [oth. writ.] Currently working on writing a book (fiction) "My Family";

[pers.] My poetry is a reflection of life experiences.; [a.] Bronx, NY

DIAZ, RANDOLPH RAY
[pen.] Ren, Mr. Meerkat; [b.] October 19, 1977, Austin, TX; [p.] Raymond Diaz, Mary Diaz; [ed.] James Bowie High School; [occ.] Student, James Bowie H.S.; [memb.] World Wildlife Fund, National Parks and Conservation Association, National Wildlife Federation, Books Nippon Japanese Animation Fan Club.; [oth. writ.] Several poems but never published. Currently working on stories.; [pers.] Patience and knowledge is some thing to strive for Martial Arts is a great way to find the essence of life.; [a.] Austin, TX

DICKENS, MARJORIE
[b.] November 11, 1940, Crystal, WV; [m.] Charles Dickens, May 2, 1970; [ed.] Bluestone Jr High, Newton High, Bluefield State College, City College of N.Y.; [occ.] Retired from Nynex (New York Telephone Co.); [memb.] Telephone Pioneers of America. Allen A.M.E. Church; [oth. writ.] Several writings and poems published in college newspaper and family reunion bulletins.; [pers.] Be optimistic, wear a smile and the world will look brighter and so will you.; [a.] Hempstead, NY

DICKERSON, LAVOYCE
[b.] June 25, 1938, NC; [p.] Ray and Arabella Wyatt; [m.] Raymond Dickerson, January 27, 1974; [ch.] Robert Shaffer, Toya Walbrecher; [ed.] 4 yrs College; [occ.] Retired; [hon.] Dean's List; [oth. writ.] Poetry, short stories, none published, never attempted publication; [pers.] I have written since I was a small child. I express myself better in written words than in spoken words; [a.] Kingsville, MD

DILLARD, ELWYN DWAYNE
[pen.] E. Dwayne Dillard; [p.] Mr. and Mrs. Preston Dillard Sr.; [m.] Single; [ch.] Degray, Elwyn Jr, Joshua and Leon Dillard; [ed.] B.A. Prairie View, A&M University - M.A. Houston Graduate School of Theology Computer; [occ.] Teacher, Writer; [hon.] Poem's have been published in Scoeral New's papers throughout the Houston's Dallas Texas areas.; [oth. writ.] Published first book "The Lord Is My Light And My Salvation."; [pers.] This Nation which symbolizes Democracy, must rise up and live out the true meaning of its creed. "We hold these truth to be self evident that all people are created equal", and should be treated equally.

DINKINS, JOSEPH DEE
[pen.] True-Poet Lil. Jody; [b.] December 21, 1970, Washington, D.C.; [p.] Candy Ethel Katz; [ed.] G.E.D. Edison Job Corps., Telecommunications Diploma, TransWestern Inst. Long Beach, CA, Commo Specialist U.S. Army; [occ.] Dining Room Attendant. Old Country Buffet.; [memb.] Macedonia Baptist Church, Augusta, GA. The G.Q. Loc Crew, Compton, CA., for which I am the president; [oth. writ.] Over 100 poems, most unpublished. Also several songs R&B, Gospel, and rap. Also unpublished.; [pers.] Always stay true to your self, make the best of your life. I write from my heart, because I enjoy it. Don't let your talent go to waste. Peace.; [a.] Augusta, GA

DITIZIO, PAULETTE SENIFF
[b.] October 13, 1956, Elmer, NJ; [p.] George C. Seniff, Estelle Robinson; [m.] Anthony DiTizio, June 15, 1985; [ch.] Jacqueline Marie, Anthony Jr.; [ed.] Gloucester City High School, Gloucester County Technical Institute; [occ.] Data Entry Clerk; [hon.] Editors Choice Award Nation Library of Poetry; [oth. writ.] "The Miracle of the Ocean" Dusting Off Dreams, Quill Books; [pers.] We should always be aware of and appreciate the beauty and goodness in life, but we should also be aware of the bad and ugly, and strive to eliminate it. Dream the dream, dare to make it come true, and delight in the rewards it will bring you.; [a.] Westville Grove, NJ

DIXON, LLOYD T.
[b.] September 29, 1928, Westmoreland, NY; [p.] Harold Dixon, Lena Dixon; [m.] Constance Dixon, October 1, 1955; [ch.] Laurie Ann Dixon, Douglas Mark Dixon; [ed.] Westmore Laud Central High, American Management Association; [occ.] Retired Tinsmith; [memb.] USGA, Oneida Community Golf Club, Oneida Silversmith Retiree Club; [pers.] My writings are heartfelt and spur of a the moment; [a.] Sherrill, NY

DOBSON, KAREN
[pen.] Karen Dobson; [b.] October 30, 1946, Coldwater, MI; [p.] Kenneth and Cora Dobson; [ed.] Quincy High School Quincy, Michigan Class of 1965; [occ.] Houseperson at a hotel-Detroit; [hon.] Hotel Employee of the month December 1993, 25 year service award at the hotel; [oth. writ.] Song lyrics and other poems.; [pers.] I also create my own cartoon characters. I have in a 1993 copyright on my cartoon Martian - Michael John Marston. I love Robert Frost poems.; [a.] Detroit, MI

DODSON, ETHEL M.
[b.] April 22, 1900, Ringgold, VA; [p.] Mr. and Mrs. H. J. Dodson; [ed.] M.S. in Journalism from Northwestern University, B.S. from Longwood College in Virginia, Major, English and Literature, Minor in Math; [occ.] Retired; [memb.] First Baptist Church, AAUW, Historical Society, Danville Art League - I have done more painting than writing since retirement.; [hon.] Have received ten ribbons on paintings. School publication I have sponsored received awards. My school year book that I sponsored and school newspaper received awards.; [oth. writ.] My work dealt largely with sponsoring high school publications. Have written many poems for special occasions. Not many published.; [pers.] I have had a rich full life, am now 94 years old, living in a lovely retirement home. My hobby is painting and playing bridge, also reading. I write many poems for special occasions here.; [a.] Danville, VA

DOETZEL, AUDREY
[b.] January 9, 1939, Saskatchewan, Canada; [p.] Jacob Doetzel, Justina Stang; [ed.] B.A., B.Ed., University of Saskatchewan, Teacher Certification, Saskatchewan, Teachers College, Master of Divinity (M.Div.) and Doctor of Ministry (D. Min.) - Toronto School of Theology, University of Toronto.; [occ.] Coordination of "Relation and Encounter", Education Consultant and Adult Religious Educator; [memb.] A sister of the Congregation of Our Lady of Sion.; [pers.] Active in interfaith relations, especially among people of the Christian and Jewish traditions - to help faster mutual understanding and to bring our faith values to combat injustices related to religion, race and ethnicity.; [a.] Brooklyn, NY

DOLE, JANET
[b.] September 11, 1906, Somerville, MA; [m.] William L. Dole, April 1930; [ch.] Barbara 1931, Richard 1935, Linda 1943; [ed.] Framingham State Teacher's College; [occ.] Taught third grade in the Boston area; [memb.] Immanuel Congregational Church; [hon.] During the 50's and 60's Janet's paintings won a number of prizes at both the Hartford and West Hartford Women's club art shows.; [pers.] "What do I want to do next?" she asks. "I want to write a book for young people and I'm working on it. I've enjoyed 84 years, blessed by a family I cherish. And I'll always love to paint!"

DOLLISON, THERESA M.
[pen.] Teri Doll; [b.] December 4, 1970, Dallas, TX; [p.] Jerry Dollison and Belinda Ruff; [ch.] Franklin V. Lepgold; [ed.] Van High School, Van, TX., Delta College, University Center, MI; [occ.] Cashier/Clerk (Convinient store); [memb.] MCCPC (Midland County Child Protection Council), (Volunteer) Red Cross; [hon.] College Honors Program, on College Vice President's List for outstanding academic performance.; [oth. writ.]

I have many writings but I have never attempted to have any published.; [pers.] At age ten I wrote my first song which brought tears to my mother's eyes. Since then, writing has been to me, like the comforting embrace of her arms.; [a.] Midland, MI

DOMANSKI, PAUL EDWARD
[b.] September 20, 1972, Brookhaven, NY; [p.] Barbarann Conte, Paul Steven Domanski; [ed.] Connetquot High School; [occ.] Tax Adjustment Clerk, Internal Revenue Service, Holtsville, NY; [memb.] NASCAR - National Association for Stock Car Automobile Racing, Blood Donor of America; [hon.] Creative Writings both short stories and poems; [pers.] To help those who are less fortunate and help give them something to believe in; [a.] Bohemia, NY

DOMINGUEZ, ANDRES
[pen.] Addman; [b.] November 16, 1973, Los Angeles; [hon.] First place in pastel and charcoal drawing at creativity conference. April 26, 1991; [pers.] Dedicated to the National Library of Poetry, my Mom, Juanita, Carmen, Gloria Ray, Albaro, Grandma, Tom McCrery and family and above all Jesus. Thank you all for your support in my dream to become a successful singer/song writer/comic artist.; [a.] Fontana, CA

DOMINGUEZ, JOY LYNN
[b.] October 9, 1959, Perryton, TX; [p.] Vida Mae and the late Floyd C.; [m.] Coffin; [ch.] Amanda Brianne; [ed.] Amarillo Community College; [oth. writ.] Poems published in "Texas Association of Vietnam Veterans" newsletters.; [pers.] I have found poetry to be the choice of expression when simple statements cannot do the emotion justice.; [a.] Austin, TX

DONG, NGO
[pen.] Ngo Dong; [b.] October 4, 1937, Hanoi, Vietnam; [p.] Deceased; [m.] Deceased; [ch.] 3 sons and one daughter, all graduated from Colleges; [ed.] Ph.D., retired after 20 years teaching at University of Florida; [occ.] Master and founder of Cuong Nhu Oriental Martial Arts since 1965 with over 2,000 in USA, Scotland, France and Australia. 68 schools in USA; [hon.] From Vietnamese Government. The most decorated civilian in Vietnam. August 31 was named "DOCTOR NGO DONG DAY in city of Gainesville and Alachua County, Florida, Mental Health Association, Alachua County Florida; [oth. writ.] Cuong Nhu Oriental Martial Arts Training Manual 4th edition American Heart Association; [pers.] Condensed in three Open Philosophy: OPEN MIND (oneness) to learn, OPEN HEART (togetherness) to love, OPEN ARMS (forgiveness) friendship; [a.] LaMesa, CA

DOW, ALICE G.
[ed.] M.A. English/Journalism Marquette Univ. Further study Ireland and Italy; [occ.] Ohio State Employee, Ohio Exposition Center

DOWELL, RUBYE BRADSHAW
[b.] Beaconsfield, IA; [p.] Milton and Charlotte Bradshaw; [m.] Pherrin Charles Dowell, May 29, 1942; [ed.] Three degrees. University of Northern Iowa, Cedar Falls Iowa - 1 degree, Drake University, Des Moines Iowa - 2 degrees; [occ.] Retired Teacher, Volunteer for AARP Vote; [memb.] Delta Kappa Gamma International, An Honorary Society for Women Teachers. Daughters of Union Veterans, Iowa Rose O'Neill Ass'n International; [hon.] Pres. of Delta Kappa Gamma, State Pres. of Rose O'Neill Chapter, Demonstrations relative to teaching "Lots of Talks" to organizations. Just made a video 3/7/95 to be used in meetings relative to "stroke" patients.; [oth. writ.] Educational articles book - A Handbook to Assist Parents and Teachers in Counseling Pre-school and Primary children; [pers.] I teach adults to read, and tutor and counsel children who are having behavior and educational problems. This service is free. I believe in helping others relative to their individual needs.; [a.] Des Moines, IA

DOZIE, BERNICE
[b.] Chicago; [p.] Virgie Dozie; [m.] Single; [ed.] St. Marys Campus, College of St. Catherine; [occ.] Full time RN student, part time writer; [memb.] Community social services and candy striper.; [oth. writ.] Children's book (unpublished); [pers.] Being a simple person I am inspired by day to day living, depending on the moon for that day, and what goes on in it. If the day goes well, I am happy and have a happy message to share. If the day goes bad, my message is melancholy. I try to write everyday things that everyday people can relate to simply put, reflections on daily life.; [a.] Saint Paul, MN

DRAKE, NICOLE
[b.] August 28, 1979, Little Rock, AR; [p.] Wanda Huckaby; [ed.] Woodlawn High School, 10th grade; [memb.] Beta Club, FHA, Library Club; [hon.] Class Favorite 10th, Cheer Captain 8th, Cheerleader (8 yrs.), Most School Spirit 10th, Best All Around 9th, National Geography Olympiad Award, Woodlawn High School Honor Student, Homecoming Court (10th), Class President 8th, Class Secretary 10th, Sensational Spirit, 8th; [oth. writ.] "Friends", written to my best friend, Dana Hamilton, "Without A Sound, Without A Peep"; [pers.] I write poetry because it relaxes me and I enjoy it and my mother always told me I could do it, she influenced me and encourage me. I couldn't have done it without her, She is my inspiration. Since the poem was written my Pappaw, J.E. Rauls, passed away on February 24th, my poem was read at the funeral in memory of him. Before he passed away he got to read it and I know he would have been proud of me for the honor that has been given to me.; [a.] Rison, AR

DRICK, LISA
[pen.] Lyssa Aja; [b.] May 28, 1962, Joliet, IL; [p.] Jacky and Tony Drick; [ed.] Enrolled at Kennesaw College; [occ.] Medical Transcriptionist, writer, poet; [memb.] Rainforest Action Network, supporter of Leonard Peltier (Defense Committee), Atlanta Songwriter's Association; [oth. writ.] Published in "Seasons To Come", pending poetry at this time; [pers.] "Anything is possible if you believe!"; [a.] Woodstock, GA

DRIGO, FELICIE A.
[b.] June 8, 1963, Dominica, West Indies; [p.] Elezabeth and Perry Alcide; [m.] John Drigo; [ch.] Jawara Drigo; [ed.] High School, Dominica West Indies; [occ.] Housewife; [pers.] Everyone regardless of race color of creed has something of importance to impart, I always listen and hear. Inspired by Terry McMillan, Maya Angelou.; [a.] Bronx, NY

DROZDEK, MR. JOSIP
[b.] September 5, 1963, Yugoslavia; [p.] Mr. Ludvik and Mrs. Mischelle Drozdek; [m.] Single; [ed.] James Madison High; [occ.] Computer Chip Maker at AVX; [oth. writ.] First time poetry writing in National Library of Poetry; [pers.] I thank my parents and God for supporting my talented poem. No one is alone with diabetes. I too have type 1, Juvenile diabetes. I would love to become a poet, so please read my poem. Also I thank my younger brother Ivica and the people were I work at AVX. Thank you all for reading my poem. It has a meaningful message, to those with diabetes.; [a.] Portland, OR

DRUCHNIAK, GREGORY G.
[b.] March 14, 1958, Detroit, MI; [p.] Robert and Catherine Druchniak; [m.] Susan M. Druchniak, June 24, 1978; [ch.] James Gregory, Jackie Lynn, Susan Margaret; [ed.] Aquinas High School; [occ.] Master Plumber; [memb.] Knights of Columbus, St. Albert the Great Ushers; [hon.] This is my very first entry.; [oth. writ.] Personal writings and poems not yet released.; [pers.] I believe identifying your emotional feelings, introduces the person you truly are, and creates a harmony among people you touch, all through life.; [a.]

Dearborn Heights, MI

DRUMGO, JAYME
[b.] January 8, 1977, Annapolis, MD; [p.] Cora B. Drumgo, John W. Drumgo; [ed.] Northern High School; [occ.] Student; [memb.] National Honors Society, St. Edmonds United Methodist Church Youth Choir; [hon.] Superindent's Award in 9th Grade, Honor Roll 9-12 grade, Perfect Attendance 6-12 grade, Honor Roll; [oth. writ.] Several unpublished poems.; [pers.] I like to express my thoughts and feelings in my work. I tend to use nature a lot. The study of human behavior's and feelings are most influential to me.; [a.] Huntingtown, MD

DRZEWIECKI, ELLEN
[b.] November 15, 1977; [p.] Patricia Drzewiecki; [ed.] Seneca Valley High School, will attend Mount St. Mary's College in fall '95; [occ.] Student; [memb.] Red Cross Baby sitter, American heart Association Mother Seton Parish; [hon.] Outstanding student in English; [oth. writ.] Several poems published in High School Literary magazine, article for Our Parish Times; [a.] Germantown, MD

DUBE, MOLLY ANN
[b.] August 16, 1973, Holyoke, MA; [p.] Wayne and Teresa Bushey; [m.] Peter David Dube, September 19, 1992; [ch.] Cody Ian Dube; [ed.] Holyoke Catholic High School, Chicopee Comprehensive High School; [occ.] Homemaker; [pers.] I strive to reflect the beauty of love in my writing. I have been greatly influenced by my husband.; [a.] Goldsboro, NC

DUCKETT, BERNICE ARCHIE
[b.] May 16, 1923, Clinchco, VA; [p.] Mr. and Mrs. William A. Archie; [m.] Divorced; [ed.] BS State Univ., Ms A and T State University, additional studies Atlanta University, S.C. State Univ. and Univ. of South Carolina.; [occ.] Retired teacher and Guidance counselor 40 years; [memb.] Morris Chapel Bapt. Church, American Red Cross, American Cancer Soc. Voc. Rehab, Delta Sigma Theta, Greenwood Museum, Greenwood Mental Health Ass'n, Past Member: NEA, SCEA, SCPGA, ASCA, GCTA; [hon.] Nominated to the 1969 Edition of personalities of the South, 1968 OEO Rural Service Award, Member of Gov. McNair's Task Committee, for the blind and Visually impaired; [oth. writ.] I have written more than one hundred poems and songs. I have just written and filed them.; [pers.] I have laborated in this human laboratory for many years aiding in the growth and development of young people man of whom have been an inspiration for many of my songs and poems.; [a.] Greenwood, SC

DUDLEY, DAVID A.
[b.] May 2, 1981, Allegan; [p.] Mary Cousins, Dave Dudley; [ed.] Fennville High School 8th grade; [occ.] Pompered Pet Motel; [hon.] Band awards, Baseball, Spelling Bee

DUFFY, DELIGHTE J.
[pen.] Dee Duffy; [b.] February 8, 1930, Hobart, IN; [p.] Frank and Beatrice Simmons; [ch.] Gordon Roberts, Glenn Roberts, Karen Roberts-Pitts; [ed.] BA, English, St. Joseph's Colg, IN; [occ.] Writer in various genres; [memb.] San Diego Center for Children (abused children); [hon.] Head of Eng. Dept. in a junior high school, Gary, IN.; [oth. writ.] Poem published in Orbis mag., in England; [pers.] I like a realistic viewpoint that contains hope.; [a.] San Diego, CA

DUFFY JR., ROBERT T.
[pen.] Rob Duffy Jr.; [b.] November 10, 1967, New York; [p.] Robert and Elaine Duffy; [ed.] West Milford High, Ramapo College; [hon.] Bachelors of Fine Arts and Music; [oth. writ.] Musical compositions, various musical recordings. Which include music and lyrics; [pers.] Believe in yourself, believe in your dreams, and follow your heart, it will always steer you in the right

direction.; [a.] Hewitt, NJ

DUGGINS, SHERRIE
[b.] April 8, 1976, West Plains, MO; [p.] Gary and Janice Duggins; [ed.] West Plains High School, University of Missouri - Columbia; [occ.] College Student, Child Life Specialist (Pre-Med); [memb.] First United Methodist Church; [hon.] Dean's List, Honors College, Curators Scholar, Numerous Drama and Music Ratings and Awards; [oth. writ.] Mostly just for myself and those around me.; [pers.] Sometimes our deepest thoughts are also our most terrifying. Life is not about covering those moments up, but exploring them.; [a.] West Plains, MO

DUHON, CHRISTY
[b.] March 22, 1975, Lake Charles, LA; [p.] Clarice and David Duhun; [ed.] A.M. Barbe High Currently enrolled at McNeese State Univ. majoring in visual arts.; [occ.] Student; [oth. writ.] Several unpublished poems and plays including short stories; [pers.] In writing whatever that I'm writing, my main goal is make my audience feel the feelings that I have placed in that piece. If they achieve those emotions, then my Goal in writing is truly complete.; [a.] Lake Charles, LA

DUKE, JEREMIAH DAVID
[pen.] Jeremiah Duke; [b.] August 15, 1976, Denton, TX; [p.] Rusty Duke, Cheryl Duke; [ed.] Newman Smith High School; [occ.] Student, Stephen F. Austin State University; [memb.] Varsity Cheerleader, Delta Tau Delta Fraternity; [hon.] Dean's Lest, President's List; [pers.] I believe we accomplish in proportion to what we attempt.; [a.] Carrollton, TX

DUMAS, SHARRON GRACE
[b.] August 1, 1973; [ed.] Graduate from Mary G. Montgomery with the class of 93. I now attend Faulkner State Community College, where I serve as Editor of the School Newspaper.; [occ.] Part time Disc Jockey for 96.1 WMYC Young Country. A local radio station.; [memb.] Drumbeat Staff, and International Society of Poets.; [hon.] Presidential Scholarship, first place winner of Prom Promise essay contest, second place winner of F.B.L.A. talent search. I have a poem published in the Anthology of Poetry called River of Dreams.; [oth. writ.] I am working on a book for possible Publication sometimes in 1995.; [pers.] Writing is my life, it is what I live, breath, and sleep. There is nothing more that I enjoy. I hope that my writings can be just as inspirational to others just as some have been to me. I hope that my writings can be just as inspirational to others just as some have been to me. I hope that I can make a difference in this violent world, with just my words and imagination.; [a.] Mobile, AL

DUNNAGAN, CAROL K.
[b.] March 28, 1933, Salisbury, NC; [p.] Deceased; [m.] William B. Dunnagan (Deceased 5-22-94), September 7, 1957; [ch.] William B. Dunnagan Jr., David N. Dunnagan; [ed.] Catawba College BA 1955; [occ.] School Social Worker, Nassau County School Board; [memb.] United Methodist Church, Fernandina Beach Women's Club; [pers.] Writing poetry is therapeutic in dealing with the stresses of life. The poem submitted was written following the death of my husband and the birth of my grandchild on the same day (May 22, 1994).; [a.] Fernandina Beach, FL

DUNSON, AYDIEE VAUGHN
[pen.] Aydiee Vaughn; [b.] January 2, Los Angeles, CA; [p.] Henry and Jacquelyn Ruth Dunson; [ed.] Attended: San Diego School of Create and Performing Arts, United States International University, and Educational Cultural Complex.; [occ.] Entertaining relations emphasis: Choreography, Talent Exec Coordinator and Artist Development; [memb.] (SAG) Screen Actors Guild, (AFTRA) American Federation of Television Radio Arts. Former member of Girls Clubs of America, (USGF) United State Gymnastics Federation;

[hon.] Readers Diegest Career Key Award, Essay Writing Regional Winner. Kensington Optimist Club. Business and Professional Women's Club, Southland Professional Women, Various Pageant and Talent Titles. Credits in Television, Video, Theater, Film and Commercial.; [oth. writ.] Have been writing actively lyrical, creative writing, children short stories, literary, poetry and various creative projects. Newspaper journalist in college. Poems selected for High School magazine. Writing have been performed in pageants. First National Publication.; [pers.] Poetry and Music will forever have a Universal existence, long after the people have gone who created them.; [a.] Woodland Hills, CA

DUPLANTIS, KRISTY L.
[b.] November 20, 1979, Houma, LA; [p.] Mr. and Mrs. Erich Duplantis; [ed.] A sophomore in high school - Ellender Memorial High School.; [memb.] I have a Key Club Membership, The National Library of Poetry Membership; [hon.] 1 poem published in the Journey of the Mind. 92-93 award for dance team, 88-89 award for citizenship; [oth. writ.] 1 poem published in Journey of the Mind. Also other poems in sweepstakes. These poems were inspired by my 21 yr. old brother, who was severely injured in an auto accident in 9/93.; [pers.] This is the second poem that is being published. I will continue to strive for excellence in my work, and hope to influence others as others inspired me.; [a.] Houma, LA

DURDEN, MRS. ANNIE
[b.] August 13, 1901, Newton County, GA; [p.] Hugh and Harriet Portwood, Montgomery; [m.] Harvey Lee Durden, August 27, 1916; [ch.] Lottie Louise, Parham - deceased, Evelyn Grace Story; [ed.] Mixon County - Flint Hill - and Cornish Hill, Walton County; [memb.] Mt. Gilead Baptist Church, Home Makers Club, Happy Timers; [hon.] Home Maker of the Year in 1971, over 100 1st and 2nd place ribbons in Fair for Cake Baking and Quilts.; [oth. writ.] Other poems (never published). Quote: "Never give up - just keep plugging on."; [pers.] Raised on farm, Retired from Textile Plant, Cake decorator for twenty years (until eye sight failed), Read Bible than 13 times before eye sight failed.; [a.] Zebulon, GA

DURKEE, ERIN
[b.] March 5, 1980, Ann Arbor, MI; [p.] Scott and Lora Durkee; [ed.] Tecumseh High School; [hon.] 1992: Received: Presidential Academic Fitness Award Tecumseh Public Schools Honor Roll: 1st - 9th grade; [pers.] Ricky Casteller was a very close friend of mine who died unexpectedly on April 5, 1994. We were only 14 years old. And no one close to me had ever died. I wrote "About Ricky" because it was easier to put my feelings on paper than to talk about them. This poem is dedicated to Ricky, his family, and anyone whoever knew him.; [a.] Tecumseh, MI

DWIGHT, KRYSTIN S.
[b.] August 11, 1980, Kansas City, KS; [p.] Harold C. and Peggy J. Dwight; [ed.] Harmon High School - 9th Grade; [occ.] Student (9th Grade); [memb.] Marching Band, Symphonic Orchestra, Church Youth Choir, Jazz Band, Drill Team, Cheerleader, Pep Club; [hon.] Honor Student, All American Scholar

EAGAN, JILL L.
[b.] June 4, 1982, Baltimore, MD; [p.] Frederick M. and June E. Eagan; [ed.] 7th grade-currently in Junior High School Ridgely Middle School; [hon.] Won 1 other state/county award for poetry (came in 3rd place); [a.] Baltimore, MD

EARWOOD JR., LEON E.
[pen.] Leon E. Earwood Jr.; [b.] October 09, 1979, WV; [p.] Mary Blake, Leon Earwood Sr.; [ed.] 3 years college 25 years continuous education retail business/ human relations; [occ.] Telecommunicator 911 - Police Dept; [memb.] Associations chamber of commerce law enforcement association national retail association; [hon.] National Retail Association - P.H.D. Certificate State Bureau of Investigation - Certificate Volunteer work in hospital emergency rooms; [oth. writ.] Twenty and other Non-published poems. Consumers Book "Let the Buyer Buy Smart."; [pers.] Poetry comes from my life's experiences, Hopes, and observations of people, nature and the events created by all of them.; [a.] Farmville, NC

EASTER, JIMMIE D.
[b.] August 6, 1956, Cario, IL; [p.] George L. and Clara J. Easter; [ch.] Sara Lyn Easter, age 14, James Eric Easter, age 9; [ed.] Manteno High School - Manteno Il.; [occ.] Mental Health Worker, Shapiro Developmental Center Kankakee, IL; [pers.] This is my first poem. It came to me at a low point of my life. I hope my poem will give comfort to any one who has lost a loved one; [a.] Bourbonnais, IL

EASTER, CLARENCE
[b.] May 5, 1974, Emporia, VA; [p.] Deloris Easter Russell; [ed.] Park View Senior High School, North Carolina Central University; [occ.] Student, North Carolina Central University, Durham, NC; [memb.] North Carolina Central University Dance Group; [hon.] Editor's Choice Award, Dean's List, and various scholastic achievement awards.; [oth. writ.] "This Woman", published in Reflections of Light and on the tape Sound of Poetry, "Inspiring African-American Women" and "This Man" (Dedication to Martin Luther King, Jr.) were published in the school newspaper, Campus Echo, "Christ Baby", published in South Hill Enterprise during Christmas 1994.; [pers.] I am a person who stands for positiveness and success. God and Jesus Christ are the reason for my strength, blessings, leadership, and achievements. I strive to touch hearts, to reach souls, and to inspire through all of my writings.; [a.] South Hill, VA

ECHOLS, CHRISTY
[b.] April 3, 1981, Hot Springs, AR; [p.] Renee Ellis and Jack Echols; [ed.] 8th grade at Lake Hamilton Junior High School.; [hon.] Last year while I was in 7th grade I was one of the four people chosen to be on the 9th grade tract team. Every track meet I went to I one 2 ribbon so a awards for being in girls track.; [oth. writ.] No. this is my first one.; [pers.] I love writing poetry, it's one of my favorite hobbies. Besides running track, poetry is number one!; [a.] Hot Springs, AR

ECKHART, CRYSTAL
[b.] April 21, 1981, Fontana, CA; [p.] Marc and Debbie Eckhart; [ed.] Troth St. School and Jurupa Middle School; [occ.] Student; [memb.] Jurupa Valley Middle School Band.; [hon.] Band Awards and Science Trophies; [oth. writ.] Other poems are Brandon, Feelings About Opinions, and, Wait; [pers.] I fit in where there is room.; [a.] Mira Loma, CA

EDDLEMON, JENNIE LEE
[b.] June 8, 1977, Jackson, IN; [p.] Mary Willis and Perry Eddlemon; [ed.] I will be graduating from Sevier County High School in June of 1995; [occ.] I am a volunteer at Lakeshore Mental Health Institute; [hon.] My poem Beneath the Surface was published in the Walters State Community College Competitive Writing Competition; [pers.] If you want something bad enough keep trying and you will eventually get it; [a.] Pigeon Forge, TN

EDMUNDS JR., MERLE
[pen.] Merle Edmunds Jr.; [b.] March 9, 1919, Bloomington, IL; [p.] Merle Clara Edmunds (deceased); [m.] Florence A. Edmunds, August 16, 1963; [ch.] Terry and Stan Edmunds, Liza Cooper, Jennifer Joyce; [ed.] College Ill. State University; [occ.] Insurance - Music; [memb.] 32nd mason shriner - eyes - club VGW AM Legion - DAV 2nd presentation Church; [hon.] Lifetime VFW. Wrote songs; [oth. writ.] Other poem in magazines, newspapers I strive for reflections for children; [a.] Bloomington, IL

EDWARDS, HALEY
[b.] May 3, 1979, Kalamazoo, MI; [p.] Linda Finn and Robert Edwards; [ed.] I'm a sophomore at Kimball High School; [oth. writ.] School newspapers and publications; [pers.] I write from the heart, and sometimes it's my only way of expressing myself. It's how I deal with my feelings.; [a.] Royal Oak, MI

EICHHOLZ, JEANNETTE
[b.] November 8, 1953, Milwaukee, WI; [p.] Orma and Lester Eichholz; [m.] Ronald Rogers, November 7, 1987; [ch.] Goeffrey Rogers; [ed.] MA English Literature; [occ.] Senior Staff Analyst; [memb.] Society for Technical Communications, Greenpeace, Andubon, National Parks

EILERS, KIMBERLY D.
[b.] November 4, 1966, Ainsworth, NE; [p.] Dudley Broughton, Carla Broughton; [m.] William Eilers, December 28, 1990; [ch.] Dusten Burke, Destiny Eilers, Dakota Eilers; [ed.] Wood River High School; [occ.] Housewife, mother; [oth. writ.] Poem "Lost", given certificate of merit, by world of poetry.; [pers.] Poetry with meaning, comes from within. They express feelings and emotions that come from the heart.; [a.] Utica, NE

EISENHAUER, CHRIS
[b.] June 7, 1976, North Platte, NE; [p.] Ron and Shirley Adkissor; [ed.] Medicine Valley High School, University of Nebraska - Kearney; [occ.] Student; [hon.] National Honors Society, Dean's List; [pers.] A lot of our greatest inspirations come from our deepest sorrows.; [a.] Curtis, NE

ELANDT, REUBEN H.
[b.] September 12, 1931, Weyauwega, WI; [m.] Marian L. Stouffer, July 18, 1957; [ch.] 6 children, 6 grandchildren; [ed.] Maple Grove Elementary School, Waupaca High School - 2 1/2 years; [occ.] Now semi-retired construction worker of 40 years; [oth. writ.] Enjoys writing prose and poetry especially about nature and ecology.; [a.] New London, WI

ELGIN, DIANNE
[pen.] Blue Bird Lady; [b.] May 30, 1950, Kewanee, IL; [p.] Bill and Eva Wright; [ed.] Woodruff High, Riverland Technical College; [occ.] Homemaker; [memb.] Calvary Baptist Church, Peoria Poetry Club, United Amateur Press; [hon.] Golden Poet Award, Silver Poet Award, Honorable mention Award copy writed my first song in 1977, first poem 1987, first children's story in 1989; [oth. writ.] Published in Church paper, Several newspaper wrote my own paper and published monthly with united Amateur Press. Published in five states. (After brain surgery) Design cover for booklet of my own poems and recorded 1st tape of poems and songs to sell; [pers.] Writing is a gift and a joy to be able to share feelings that may not other wise be expressed. After brain surgery in 1990 I still am able to have my love for writing. I want to encourage others to write too!; [a.] Rochester, MN

ELLINGTON, MICHAEL EARL
[pen.] Michael Earl Ellington; [b.] October 4, 1963, Livermore, CA; [p.] William and Evangeline Hurst; [m.] Charlotte Ranee Ellington, Common Law (July 30, 1992); [ch.] Jeniffer, Shandy, Stacy, Bubba, Justin and Casey; [ed.] South Birdville Elementary, Haltom Jr. High, GED from Windham Schools, Huntsville Texas.; [occ.] Unemployed; [memb.] International Society Of Poets.; [hon.] Induction into the International Society of Poets. Poet of Merit Plaque. Editors Choice Award. Professionally Recorded Cassette Album.; [oth. writ.] "Devoted To You", The National Library of Poetry's "Dark Side Of The Moon" Anthology.; [pers.] The constructive critics, our friends. Never fail to give them a careful listening.; [a.] Navasota, TX

ELLIOTT, EDWARD M.
[b.] December 29, 1931, Rome, Ca; [p.] Edward M. (Sr.) and Minnie Lee Elliott; [m.] Lois Massey Elliott, February 23, 1951; [ch.] Edward III, Walter, Linda, Frances, Rebekah, Carolyn; [ed.] Rockmart High (GA), Jones College, Bible Baptist Seminary, Baptist Theological Schools (Texas); [occ.] Pastor Alvation Baptist Church, Georgia; [memb.] Arlington Baptist College Alumni Association Western Baptist Association Missions Committee; [hon.] Th.D.; [oth. writ.] Several books of poems for family and for Church members, poems published in local newspaper.; [pers.] It is my desire to honor the Lord, Jesus Christ and His relationship with man in drawing upon my own personal experiences.; [a.] Alvaton, GA

EMBRY, KELLY ANN
[pen.] Kelly Ann Embry; [b.] July 17, 1982, Denver, CO; [p.] William and Sandy Embry; [ed.] 7th Grade, Smiley Middle School; [occ.] Student; [hon.] (1) Highly Gifted and Talented Program, (2) Denver All City Band (3) Alter Server Cure D'ars, Catholic Church; [oth. writ.] None published; [pers.] Strive to become a well known author, symphony player, photographer, and veterinarian. I am the youngest of 14 siblings.; [a.] Denver, CO

EMERY, WILLAMAE LORA
[pen.] Lora Emery; [b.] August 2, 1930, Los Banos, CA; [p.] Lucile and Edward Parsley; [m.] Paul R. Emery, April 18, 1980; [ch.] Judy, Richa, Marla, Terry, Tina, Charles, Sandee, Deana; [ed.] Graduated 1948 - Los Banos, High School; [occ.] At this time housewife - retired education; [memb.] First Nozarene Church Order of the Moose - C.S.D. Child Care Division Special Olympics Ass.; [hon.] Illeod Press Honorable Mention.; [oth. writ.] Poems to be published in Musings, Verses - Reflections, Voices - best poems of 1995; [pers.] I can inspired by my children and grandchildren and base my works on life, love, and spiritual awareness; [a.] Shady Cove, OR

EMLEY, CRISTEN L.
[b.] March 28, 1970, Cleveland, OH; [p.] William and Wynette Emley; [m.] Skeeter Harris (significant other); [ed.] The Ohio State University (B.S.) and The University of Miami (MS Ed.); [occ.] Sports Nutritionist and Exercise Physiologist; [memb.] American, Florida, and Broward Country Dietetic Associations, The American College of Sports Medicine; [hon.] Golden Key and Mortar Board National Honor Societies, graduated "Cum Laude with distinction in Medical Dietetics" from OSU, received "Achiever's Scholarship Fund Award" from ADA in 1993.; [oth. writ.] Columnist for a monthly newsletter, "Energy", published by BCDA, research abstract published in ACSM journal in May 1994; [pers.] The greatest gift in life is true, unconditional love. It is a bond between two people that allows them to remain independent yet inseparable. It is this gift I have received that I will cherish for the rest of my life and is reflected in my poetry.; [a.] Fort Laudervale, FL

ENDERLY, BILL
[b.] November 5, 1960, Bronx, NY; [p.] William H. and Marie Enderly; [ed.] Montclair State College; [occ.] President of Wild Bill's Enterprises, Inc; [memb.] A.B.A.T.E., Belleview Chamber of Commerce, Harley Owners Group, N.R.A., Independent Businessmen's Association, Gainsville Jazz and Blues Club; [hon.] Cum Laude degree, MSC member of "Who's Who" in American Universities and Colleges; [oth. writ.] Several poems published in magazines; [pers.] I write about the reflections of my life usually with a touch of optimism. Greatly influenced by Kahlil Gibran and Rock Lyricists. Poems dedicated to those that see no boundaries. "Home is a place in your heart you can never leave"; [a.] Belleview, FL

ERNESTI, BEVERLY
[pen.] Shea; [b.] February 14, 1972, OH; [p.] Larry and Doris Wood; [m.] Alan Ernesti, May 27, 1994; [ed.] Lebanon, High Skagib Valley College; [occ.] Accountant; [hon.] FBLA Awards from College, Highest Exam Grade last semester; [pers.] I believe the best way to express myself is through my writing. It gives me personal satisfaction to find someone who can relate; [a.] West Point, NE

ERNST, LAUREN ASHLEY
[b.] January 3, 1986, TX; [p.] Jo Ann Smith Ernst, MD; [ed.] Woodcrest Elementary School - grade 3; [occ.] Student; [memb.] Little Indian Singers, Class Senior; [hon.] First prizes in literature (poetry) and music 1993-1994 and 1994-1995 in PTA Reflections Competition; [oth. writ.] "My Gift" published in Dark side of the moon by the National Library of Poetry; [pers.] We can all do something to help the world; [a.] Port Neches, TX

ESCHIK, ERIN ELIZABETH
[b.] March 30, 1976, Detroit, MI; [p.] Peggy A. and Ernest G. Eschik; [ed.] High School Graduate. I am currently attending Saint Mary's College, Orchard Lake MI, Studying English and Biology - Double Major.; [memb.] Students Against Driving Drunk (secretary), student Judiciary Board Member; [hon.] High School Awards: Numerous awards for singing in state and local competitions, attendance, academics, athletics.; [oth. writ.] Published poetry in my High School Newspaper, numerous articles written for that as well.; [pers.] Writing poetry is deeply personal for me. Everything I write about stems from an experience I've had and what I've felt while going through it. Many of my poems may have an element of bitterness, but life is often bitter. And beauty often stems from sadness.; [a.] Oxford, MI

ESPINO JR., RAYMOND
[b.] March 29, 1958, Kauai; [p.] Raymond and Carol Espino; [m.] Linda Espino, January 31, 1987; [ch.] Carlina, Victoria, Alana Espino; [ed.] Waimea High School; [occ.] Equipment Operator; [pers.] To suffers all over the world. Surfing is not just a sport but away of life, to express your feelings, have peace of mind to be one with mother nature and God I wrote this poem 20 years ago in high school, surfing was my first love to all my surfing buddies on Kauai keep on surfing!; [a.] Hanapepe, HI

ESPOSITO, MARYGRACE
[pen.] Marygrace Esposito; [b.] May 15, 1956, Hollis, Queens, NY; [p.] Marilyn Foutz Phillips, Ralph Esposito; [ed.] West Babylon High School, Long Island NY, no college; [occ.] Art Model University of South Florida, Live Art place, Tampa Museum of Art; [memb.] Sacred Heart Church, Tampa, Fla.; [oth. writ.] Other religious poems at where I live, The Methodist Place; [pers.] The Lord helps those who helps themselves and what you give, you'll get back.; [a.] Tampa, FL

ESSICK, ALONZO
[b.] May 6, 1918, Indianola, IA; [p.] Mr. and Mrs. A. J. Essick; [m.] Frances Essick, July 4, 1942; [ch.] 7; [ed.] High School; [occ.] Retired; [hon.] Purple Heart from World War - Two

ESTEP, SELDON R.
[b.] September 12, 1946, Hamilton; [p.] Seldon and Mary Estep; [m.] Tammy S. Estep, April 23, 1988; [ch.] Tara Nicole Estep, Angela Diane Estep, Steven Wayne Birchfield; [ed.] Univ. Cincy, Univ. of Saigon, Toledo Tech.; [occ.] Technical writer, consultant; [memb.] K.O.A., Veterans of Foreign Wars, Precious Memories, American Kenner Club Associate.; [hon.] Stars and Stripes Contributor, Yearbook Achievement, Journal News and Hazard Herald Guest Writer; [oth. writ.] Several Appalachain poems, Christmas poems, Jaquar pamphlet, Cadillac Tech Manuals, Sugar Industry Manuals, Sugar Industry Manuals.; [pers.] I don't write with feeling, I feel by writing. I bring precious memories to the hearts of past thoughts; [a.] Hamilton, OH

ESTRELLA, CRISTINA
[b.] January 23, 1995; [p.] Maria Estrella; [ed.] St. Bernadette's Springfield VA ('94-'95) ('95-'96) West Springfield High School; [pers.] I try to tell people to be thankful of what they have right now.; [a.] Springfield, VA

ETHRIDGE, DOROTHY HUGHLETT
[b.] December 30, 1933, Minga Congo Belge, Africa; [p.] Dr. William S. Hughlett, Violet Packard Hughlett; [m.] Ralph Gates Ethridge, March 29, 1975; [ed.] College - Ashbury College, High School - Central School for Missionaries Children, Lubordai Belgian Congo, Africa; [occ.] Retired Elementary School Teacher - Florida Schools, Tampa Bay Area; [memb.] St. Lukes United Methodist Church, Suncoast Cathedral - Silver Saints; [oth. writ.] A poem published in the Asbury Collegian, (ABC Tongue Twisters, Various Phonics Based Poems and Story Poems, Multiple Meaning Words in Sentences to be matched with pictures (all of these as yet unpublished); [pers.] My parents instilled in me a profound faith in God, coupled with my own personal experience of coming to know Jesus as my Lord, and Savior. I am endeavoring to use the talent He gave me.; [a.] Saint Petersburg, FL

EVANS, DIANE
[b.] January 11, 1959, Columbus, OH; [p.] Wilbert and Shirley Mills; [m.] Steven W. Evans, October 14, 1978; [ch.] Gene - 13 years old, Clay - 10 years old; [ed.] 1977 Graduated of Westland High School; [occ.] Cashier/Clerk; [memb.] A member of the football mothers club of Grove City High School where my son will be a freshman in 1995-1996.; [oth. writ.] I have done some acrostic poems for some local businesses and family and friends.; [pers.] With the support of my family and friends it makes the words come from my heart and onto the paper with ease, no words go down on paper till first myself, I please...; [a.] Grove City, OH

EVANS, ROBERT
[pen.] Milton Evans; [b.] June 30, 1972, Grangeville, ID; [p.] Robert and Jolynn Evans; [m.] Desiree Lara Evans, December 26, 1994; [ed.] Accounting Degree - University of South Florida, Business Degree Univ. of South Florida. Seeking M.B.A. from Franciscam Univ. of Stebenville; [occ.] Sales; [pers.] I strive to reflect the joy and pain that a yours man of this time feels. All the while, learning to cling to Jesus.; [a.] Fort Myers, FL

EVANS, HAZEL N.
[b.] Neptune, NJ; [p.] Jesse and Bernice Evans; [ch.] Mary Ellen and Mark Evans; [ed.] Masters in Education, Graduate of the Monmouth Bilde Institute (MBI) and Career and Technical Institute of Ocean Country.; [occ.] Elementary School Teacher - Lakewood NJ; [memb.] N.J. Ed. Assoc., Lakewood Ed. Assoc., Board of Cosmetology and Hairstyling,; [hon.] Dean's List, Several Community Service Awards - Honors Awards from MBI and career and career and Techni. Institute; [oth. writ.] Several poems published in school and college newspaper; [pers.] Poetry is your heart talking to anyone who wants to listen. I enjoy reading it, listening to it and writing it.; [a.] Farmingdale, NJ

EVANS, LORETTA MAE
[b.] October 7, 1976, Marshall, MO; [p.] Earl and Judy Evans; [ed.] A junior at Marshall High School.; [occ.] A student and employee at Pizza Hut delivery as a cook.; [memb.] FFA; [oth. writ.] I write poems for friends, and I write poems for a hobby.; [pers.] Writing poems I like to do, rather I'm happy or sad it really tells how I feel, or who I am. I continue to write.; [a.] Marshall, MO

EVANS, DIANE
[pen.] Deanna Darby; [b.] December 28, 1950, San Gabriel, CA; [p.] M. Ray Evans, Maguerite Evans; [ed.] Monrovia High School, Pasadena City College, Mira Costa College, Chaffley College - I.C.S.; [occ.] Student of Fine Arts and Desktop Publishing; [memb.] Alpha Gamma Sigma, Book Publicists of San Diego.; [hon.] "Alpha Gamma Sigma." Award of Merit Certificate from "Famous Poet" Society - "The writer's Convention", The National Library of Congress.; [oth. writ.] A few poems published in Poetry Anthologies and unfinished poetry and songs.; [pers.] "No one can make you feel (inferior) except yourself"; [a.] Carlsbad, CA

EVANS, LINDA DARLENE
[b.] January 3, 1957, Fort Smith, AR; [p.] Charles E. Evans, Lois Welch Evans; [ed.] Northside Senior High School, Fort Smith Ark., Westark Community College, Fort Smith Ark., Arkansas Tech University, Russellville AR.; [occ.] Medical Transcriptionist; [memb.] Arkansas Association for Medical Transcriptionists Society of Collegiate Journalists, 1979-1980.; [hon.] Dean's List for Outstanding Scholarship, Arkansas Tech University. Soprano with Westark Community College Choir that sang in Washington, D.C. for the Arkansas Day Celebration, 1976.; [oth. writ.] Human interest stories and lifestyles features for the Southwest Times Record Newspaper, Fort Smith, AR. Poetry in the "Pentecostal Evangel." Poetry in "The Five Cent Cigar," ATU Literary Magazine. Feature stories "Arka-Tech" newspaper.; [pers.] I was deeply influenced by my English teacher, Polly Oliver, and by the "Naggin' Wagon" friends and family who believed in me and in my writing when I did not believe in myself.; [a.] Van Buren, AR

EZIT, CHRISTOPHER
[b.] May 5, 1973, Denver, CO; [p.] Debra Ezit; [ed.] Rangeview High School (9th) grade GED; [occ.] Roofer; [memb.] Heritage Christian Center; [oth. writ.] I have many other poems not yet published. Wings To Fly, Blind Love, Time Will Mend I Feel For You, Slipping Away, Sorry, Come Back, Gift From Above, and others that are untitled; [pers.] In my writing, I try to show the emotions of relationships, love, loss, joy, pain, etc... I personally experience a lot of joy in my life thanks to the Lord Jesus Christ; [a.] Aurora, CO

EZZARD, GEORGE G.
[b.] July 31, 1913, Lawrenceville, GA; [p.] Mr. and Mrs. H. H. Ezzard; [m.] Mrs. Betty B. Ezzard, September 12, 1941; [ch.] 3 Boys - ages 50, 44, 41 and 1 adopted girl 41.; [ed.] BA and MA.; [occ.] Retired - Was Elementary School Principal (29 years); [pers.] The only safe way to live is in the present. Yesterday we cannot reach except we can repent of our sins and be forgiven. The future has not yet come, but it will be sufficient unto itself upon its arrival. Today is our own. The duty of life with us is now, to live humbly toward God, to live courageously and generously reaching out our hands in a brotherly and doing what good. We can today is our privilege. Each day lived right makes it better for us tomorrow.; [a.] Cooleemee, NC

FABRYCKI, JUDY ANN
[b.] March 6, 1946, North Carolina; [p.] Virginia and Adrian Morris; [m.] Daniel Fabrycki, November 1, 1980; [ed.] Madison District Schools, Madison Heights, MI; [occ.] Employed by an educational supplies company, Sterling Heights, MI; [memb.] Great Lakes Lighthouse Keepers Assoc. (I currently share my love for lighthouses by reading stories about them to Elem. School Classes.); [pers.] The pleasure I receive from my writing goes hand in hand with my life long love of books. The inspiration for my poem, "As we travel through life" was my dear friend William A. Schmidlin who died in November 1994 at the age of 94 years. His life's example has taught me so very many things, most especially that there truly need not be such a thing as a "generation gap." He enriched my life greatly and I

shall treasure his teachings and our friendship forever.; [a.] Sterling Heights, MI

FAIRFIELD, KELLY B.
[b.] May 5, 1962, Albany, NY; [p.] Arlene Sill, Harold Fairfield Jr.; [m.] William R. Hilton, August 29, 1994; [ch.] Joshua Fairfield - son, Tiffany Fairfield - daughter; [ed.] 1. 1984 The Stratford Business College Intro to Computer College Programming/Business Administration), 2. 1994, Mildred Elley Business College / Medical Assistants; [occ.] Case Investigator/System Administrator - Empire Blue Cross; [memb.] 1. American Association of Medical Assistants, 2. National Association for 3. Female Executives, 4. American Heart Association Green Cross National 1 Safety Council; [hon.] 1. Empire Blue Cross Blue Shield - Circle of Stars Team Award - 1993 - for going above and beyond. 2. Dean's List, Mildred Elley Business College; [oth. writ.] Expectations, questions of the heart, honesty, stand by me, dreams of a future believe, dreams of the past, always, when should I speak of love lonely thoughts, imagine, what is a friend.; [pers.] I write on the feelings generated and absorbed from those around me, I write of truth; [a.] Watervliet, NY

FAIRGRIEVE, IDA MAE
[pen.] Ida Mae; [b.] September 10, 1942, MD; [p.] James and Mabel Rankin; [m.] Raymond M. Fairgrieve (deceased), December 19, 1969; [ch.] Robin Louise, Raymond Allen, and Rhonda Sue; [ed.] Beall High School, Frostburg, MD; [occ.] Marriott Services, Frost. St. Univ. (FSU); [oth. writ.] Poems and short stories, this poem was written after the sudden death of my husband. It tells my fears and feelings and how I over came them.; [pers.] I try to write what other people can relate to with a message of help or hope attached.; [a.] Cumberland, MD

FANCETT, CLAIRE
[b.] July 9, 1979, Trenton, MI; [ed.] Attending Baton Rouge Magnet High School; [memb.] Key Club; [hon.] The Bravery Award at Camp Ruth Lee; [oth. writ.] Same poem published in treasured poems of America; [pers.] When there is nothing to look forward to you'll end up looking back, your thoughts will run hysterics and you'll reminisce of thoughts you lack.; [a.] Baton, LA

FARLOW, SANDRA
[b.] April 16, 1953, Keyser, WV; [p.] Vernon and Bernice Giffin; [m.] Gary Farlow, June 22, 1973; [ch.] Claire Elizabeth, Bryan Giffin; [ed.] B.S. Salisbury State University, Salisbury MD., Masters from University of Tennessee; [occ.] Middle School Teacher, Knox County, TN; [memb.] St. Andrew's Episcopal Church; [pers.] This poem is dedicated to my dad who instilled the love of nature and poetry in me. Thanks, Dad.; [a.] Maryville, TN

FARMER, JESSICA D. CLIFFORD
[b.] January 9, 1964, San Antonio, TX; [p.] Don and Carol Johnson; [m.] Craig Farmer, May 14, 1988; [ch.] Chandler Craig, and Jenna Sioux; [ed.] Labette County High School, University of Oklahoma, Oklahoma State University; [occ.] Emergency Medical Technician-Intermediate; [memb.] American Heart Association, Instructor, Oklahoma EMT Associations, Oklahoma Farm Bureau Young Farmers and Ranchers; [pers.] I believe all good writing comes from the heart and lets us understand a part of someone's else's world. I've enjoyed sharing my world with you.; [a.] Buffalo, OK

FARNER, JENNIFER HOPE
[pen.] Jennifer Stough; [b.] August 7, 1974, Gastonia, NC; [p.] Martha Jane Stone and Richard Farner; [ed.] Tellico Plains High; [occ.] United States Navy; [memb.] Overhill Band of Indian Descendents; [hon.] Tennessee High School Press Association (THSPA) Awards for editorials and critical review. Features and opinions editor for the "Sequoyhan."; [pers.] No matter how

fiery your troubles and strife, remember to keep God first in your life.; [a.] Tellico Plains, TN

FARRELL, ASKIA A.
[b.] December 30, 1969, New York, NY; [p.] Norma Farrell; [ch.] Evan Justin; [ed.] School of Visual Arts - New York, NY; [occ.] Advertising Executive; [memb.] Black Film makers Foundation; [oth. writ.] Currently writing a screenplay; [pers.] Never accept mediocrity from anyone - especially from yourself. You can do and observe better - Always, special thanks to best friend Grace N. Campbell to whom this poem is dedicated.; [a.] Bronx, NY

FARRELL, KATHLEEN
[b.] July 11, 1963, Mineola, NY; [p.] Charles and Elizabeth Lace; [m.] James E. Farrell III, October 14, 1989; [ch.] Kelly Elizabeth; [ed.] West Babylon Senior High; [pers.] My daughter is my inspiration, she is my world!; [a.] Farmingdale, NY

FAUBERT, DIANNE
[b.] October 12, 1942, Detroit, MI; [p.] Gerald and Frances Faubert (Deceased); [ch.] Brothers: Richard, Michael, Gregory Sister: Bernadette Burkhardt; [ed.] Immaculate High School, Detroit Business Institute, Macomb Comm. College; [occ.] Administrative and Legal Secretary and starting my own company; [oth. writ.] Have written several poems and am in the process of writing a book.; [pers.] I write from my heart. - At the moment, that is, at the present time, a broken heart. - Yet, I have faith - prayer alone, however will not not do it, only action will get you through it, so you must pursue it!!; [a.] Rochester Hills, MI

FAUBERT, DIANNE
[b.] October 12, 1942, Detroit, MI; [p.] Gerald and Frances Faubert (Deceased); [ch.] Richard, Michael, Gregory, Bernadette Burkhardt; [ed.] Immaculata High School Detroit Business Institute Macomb Community College; [occ.] Administrative and Legal Secretary and Starting my own company; [oth. writ.] Have written several poems and I am in the process of writing a book.; [pers.] I write from my heart. At the present time, a broken heart. Yet, I have faith. I believe that:, [a.] Rochester Hills, MI

FAULKNER, PATIENCE
[b.] August 25, 1967, San Francisco, CA; [p.] Terry and Judy Hedgecock; [m.] Jeff Faulkner, November 19, 1988; [ch.] Jacob Robert and Morgan Kaylee; [ed.] Tracy High School, Cert CNA course, Tracy Convalescent Hospital Tracy, CA; [occ.] Homemaker; [oth. writ.] Other poems, all pertaining to real life and emotional events (never entered for publication); [pers.] I started writing my inner emotions on paper approx. 1 year ago after the passing of our 10 year old relative. It helped somehow to give myself and other some sense of peace in life.; [a.] Manteca, CA

FEDDELSON, GEOFFREY HALU
[pen.] Halu Gosard; [b.] April 29, 1979, Okla City; [p.] Lonnie and Tania Muse; [ed.] Alvin High School; [memb.] Generation 13: an acting troupe for teenagers and young adults that deal with our problems faved film; [hon.] Alvin I.S.D. Merit Award for Drama; [oth. writ.] Two other poems in a Junior High School creation writing publication entitled The Wild Hued; [pers.] My writing to flocks all I am, all I live for. Its also collects my imagination. I am highly inflamed by my classic writers teacher Shakespeare, Poe, and R. Browning.; [a.] Alvin, TX

FELDER, JESSICA RENEE
[pen.] Mia Richards; [b.] December 30, 1979, Marietta, GA; [p.] Sherry Felder, William Felder; [ed.] Currently attending high school; [occ.] Student; [memb.] Cobb Hospital Volunteer Program, Hollydale United Methodist Church; [pers.] Always look beneath the surface. Never accept anything at face value.; [a.] Marietta, GA

FELLA, MATTHEW T.
[b.] May 16, 1977, Bethpage, NY; [p.] Eileen Fella, Angelo Fella; [ed.] Senior at North Babylon High School; [occ.] Student; [a.] North Babylon, NY

FELT, LAWRENCE L.
[pen.] Larry Felt; [b.] March 21, 1920, Whitefield, ME; [p.] Lester Felt and Flossie Moody; [ed.] Gradi Gardiner H.S., Gardiner ME, 1937, Gradi Kennebec School of Commerce, Gardiner ME, 1939, attended: Colby College, Waterville ME; [occ.] Retired, Employment Counselor and living on hard owned by grandparents over 100 years ago.; [memb.] Society for Protection of Cruelty to Animals, Past President and Life Member of The Maine Horse Association, Inc., One of the founder, and past President and Honorary Life Member of The Maine Trail Riders Ass'n Inc.; [hon.] Numerous medals and awards with horses shown and Trail Riding Competitions.; [oth. writ.] Articles written on equine topics in various horse oriented magazines and papers.; [pers.] I have always tried to produce my work in a folksy, easy to read manner. To present a picture that comes straight from the heart.; [a.] Whitefield, ME

FENNELL, MARK
[b.] September 29, 1970; [ed.] B.S. Chemistry, USF; [occ.] Graduate student, Materials Science UNT; [memb.] International Society of poets, Charter Lifetime Member; [hon.] Featured on latest six editions of "The Sound of Poetry", four editors choice Awards; [oth. writ.] Lonely Roads (1994) Poems published in anthologies include: "Aztec in a Limo", "Lonely Roads and Barbed Wire Fences", "When Will I Win?" and, "A Quiet Evening With Poe."; [pers.] I enjoy the sound of words and try to convey principles in a way that pleases the ear. My poems cover everything in life, but are always written with realistic optimism.; [a.] San Francisco, CA

FERGUSON, DIANE
[b.] June 24, 1956, Fairfield, CA; [p.] Gertrude Scanlon and James Wallace; [m.] Jeffrey Ferguson, February 29, 1980; [ed.] Armijo High School, Solano Community College; [occ.] Personnel Specialist Dept. of Defense, USAF; [pers.] My inspiration is my love of nature, and the beauty I see there. I try to reflect this in my writing. Day moon is my first attempt at poetry.; [a.] Fairfield, CA

FERNANDEZ, GEORGE
[b.] March 4, 1948, Bronx; [p.] Nicolas Fernandez Father; [m.] Carmen Fernandez Mother, August 26, 1943; [ch.] They have five sons George, Felix, Michael, Charles, Nick; [ed.] Cambridge Academy Stuart Florida graduated in December 1980 course correspondence; [occ.] I am with a company called International Buying System 259 West 30th Street between 7 Avenue and 8th Avenue in Manhattan N.Y phone 1-212-269-3839; [memb.] Enrollments; [oth. writ.] I wrote a song in the year 1984 on the country creations and Royal Master Records Inc., the one who believes in magic.

FERNANDEZ, KRISTY J.
[b.] November 22, 1971, E. Stroudsburg, PA; [p.] Roger and Jeanne Kostenbader; [m.] Mark A. Fernandez, November 24, 1989; [ch.] Kristina Marie - 5, Scott Anthony - 6 1/2 mons.; [ed.] Graduate Equivalency Degree, Completion of a Competency Evaluated Nursing Assistant (C.E.N.A.) course.; [occ.] C.E.N.A. (Previously) knows as C.N.A.; [memb.] I am a member of the Lenawee County Conservation League; [oth. writ.] My Dad in process of being published your first day of school (being published currently) in memory of a father (published); [pers.] I would like to thank Kelly Zimmerman, my parents, and my husband for all their support they've given me. Also, I'd like to thank my friends for doing the same; [a.] Manchester, MI

FERRARA, JOSEPH GERARD
[pen.] Kalle; [b.] February 7, 1955, New York City, NY; [p.] Marie Emanuel and Cosmo Ferrara; [m.] Sandra Ferrara, April 28, 1978; [ch.] Joseph; [ed.] J.D. University of Houston, Bates College of Law; [oth. writ.] Songs of an Exiled Lover - a collection of love poems and epigrams; [a.] Washington Crossing, PA

FERRIS, KENNETH T.
[b.] January 24, 1954; [m.] Kimberly Ferris; [ch.] Nicole Ferris; [pers.] I strive to correlate the metaphysical, the physical and the spiritual in my thoughts and writings.; [a.] Henderson, NV

FERRITO, SHELLEY
[b.] February 1, 1954, Milwaukee, WI; [p.] Robert and Conni Unger; [m.] Sal Ferrito, December 15, 1973; [ch.] Danielle Margo and Jaymie Heather, granddaughter: Kaylee Rae; [ed.] Muskego High School; [occ.] Corporate Secretary, Treasurer, Safeway Pest Control Co., Inc.; [memb.] Norwegian Elkhound Assn. of America Greater Milwaukee, Norwegian Elkhound Assn. Northeastern Illinois Norwegian Elkhound Association, St. Leonard Congregation; [hon.] Treasurer, Wisconsin Pest, Control Association, 22 years.; [oth. writ.] Large Collection of poetry; [pers.] The joy and suffering we experience in life are not ours alone. The wisdom they bring to us is our responsibility to share. The written word is the most powerful tool we have to communicate this gift of wisdom.; [a.] Muskego, WI

FIELDS, BARBARA P.
[pen.] Fox; [b.] January 29, 1950, Brooklyn, AL; [p.] Doris (Wander) and Philip Goldin; [m.] Nolan I. Fields, October 3, 1980; [ch.] Brihany Leigh Fields, Adam Wayne Linder, Stephanie Jill Fields, Brent Clifford Fields; [ed.] American Musical and Dramatic Arts (NYC); [occ.] Director of Corporate Affairs - Hart to Hart Entertainment; [memb.] Founding President CHADD (Children With Attention Deficit and Hyperactivity Disorder) Nassau County; [hon.] Professional Singer - many awards, Leadership Award for Volunteerism on Long Island, Who's Who in American Women, Who's Who in Contemporary Achievements, Who's Who in the World, Platform Association, Speakers Bureau; [oth. writ.] Many newsletters and local papers; [pers.] To make a difference in the world around me by sharing my life's journey thru my poetry.; [a.] Holbrook, NY

FIORE, LANNIE
[pen.] Castanza Thorne; [b.] May 9, 1911, Millbrook, NY; [p.] Giuseppe and Maria Tirante; [m.] Giuseppe Fiore, January 11, 1931; [ch.] Theresa Brown Constance, Kirwin Sue Massarella; [ed.] High School, 1930, M.N.Y., 1970 Bonnett College, five years taught creative writing U.B Dutches Comm - short stories, children's books and taught Italian to 5 and 6 grade, Sylva; [occ.] Seminar at Vassar College, writing, oil and water painting; [memb.] St. Joseph Church, Millbrook, NY, St. Mary's and Sylva NC, Garden Club, Coop ext, environment courses, Conyers, Mary's helpers, Georgia; [hon.] My Rosary has turned gold. Is that an honor.; [oth. writ.] Children and books, gothic short stories art of painting with a needle "How to" the singing leaves poetry and thoughts, "The Power Of The World"; [pers.] When I was young and foolish, I dreamed of how, Waltzes, the English Yew Garden where I grew up "Thorndale", then I'd say, but in the 90 - man will have evolved into a spiritual being and the world would beautiful and clean technology"

FIORVANTE, FLORENCE
[b.] December 22, 1930, Queens, NY; [p.] Joseph-Stella, Vasta; [ch.] Joseph and Anthony Fiorvante; [sib.] 2 yrs. Literature, 2 yrs. Journalism, Stony Brook University, Long Island, NY.; [ed.] Homemaker - Retired; [pers.] I love those six grandkids of mine "that's all it takes," for the sweetest topping on my banana split; [a.] Jackson Heights, NY

FIRMIN, DALE E.
[b.] April 28, 1963, Franklin, CT; [p.] Charles Albert and Sally Kingsley; [m.] Todd Firmin, August 9, 1986; [ch.] Justin Kingsley; [ed.] Norwich Free Academy; [occ.] Service Representative Southern New England Telephone Company; [memb.] Lions Club International G Union of Telephone Workers; [pers.] It brings great joy in knowing what I write impacts the lives of many. Because of the Lord, this is so.; [a.] North Franklin, CT

FISHER, BETTY A. KARNSTEDT
[pen.] Betty A. Karnstedt Fisher; [b.] July 25, 1942, Saint Louis, MO; [p.] Mrs. Frieda Warmann (nee Neibling) and Mr. Martin E. Warmann (Both deceased); [m.] Twice Married, Vern C. Karnstedt (August 30, 1963), Thomas Fisher (July 25, 1990); [ch.] Laena Marie, Curt Alvin Karnstedt, Paul Thomas Karnstedt, George Kokoris (son-in-law); [ed.] St. Louis Ebeneger Lutheran, Lutheran, High School, South Carolina: Greenville Tech - Child Development, Nursing, Spec Education - Wofford - Park Hill (Dr. Jenkins); [occ.] Unemployed - In the past I have worked for Head. Start (1978-1983) and Montessori (past time) 1986-1991; [memb.] St Louis: St Louis Lutheran Children's Choir, Luth. HS Gleeclub, the St. Louis. Back Concert Chorale. Greenville SC: abiding Peace Evangel. Lutheran Church. I am an organist and evangelist, the Cancer Annovation, the World of Poetry, the Institute of Children Literature (1983-84 Corresp. Student) Certified Nursing Assist. October 16, 1991, 8840E, AARP.; [hon.] Head Start plague most volunteer hours in 1978, the Golden and Silver Poet's Certificate awards for honorable mention from the world of poetry society.; [oth. writ.] Bonds of Difference, God is my Coffee, (I'm that Little Sparrow, If You Have The Faith of A Mustard Seed., Thick or Treat for Samuel Griddly written for my teacher guide at the Institute of the Literature.; [pers.] I can always distinguish the consequences of my behaviour what influences others have made and what God has allowed. The only thing I know for sure is that God has been waiting with open arms whether I've been good or bad. He daily and faithfully will continue to forgive my penitent heart and save me from myself.; [a.] Greenville, SC

FISHER, HEIDI M.
[b.] March 24, 1964, Concord, NH; [p.] Constance and Arthur Thurber; [m.] Jonathan Fisher, February 24, 1990; [ch.] Thomas, Mark, Jesse, Benjamin, Rebekah and Kurt; [ed.] Coe-Brown Northwood Academy, Coastal Carolina Community College; [occ.] Mother; [memb.] AWANA Leader, attend Epsom Baptist Church; [hon.] 1981 Miss New Hampshire's Miss United Teenager essay winner; [pers.] I enjoy writing poetry, especially several children's books that I hope to have published some time in the future. Thanks be to God.; [a.] Pittsfield, NH.

FISHER, KELLY LEIGH
[pen.] Kiki; [b.] March 13, 1979, Oklahoma City; [p.] Jim and Debra Fisher; [ed.] Currently in 10th grade; [hon.] Honor roll student 3.97 gpa for 3 years; [a.] Oklahoma City, OK

FITCH, HARRY E.
[pen.] Thornton Fitch; [b.] April 6, 1945, Neward, OH; [p.] Robert Fitch and Jean Fitch; [m.] Liz Fitch, June 14, 1969; [ch.] Brian Emmette, Jessica Lynne; [ed.] Newark (OH) High, Kent State University; [occ.] Language Arts Teacher, Fayette County (GA) High School; [memb.] National Wildlife Federation, The Nature Conservancy; [oth. writ.] Two Chapbooks - Mirrors and Street Scenes; [pers.] All writers reflect life, but each does so with a unique mirror.; [a.] Peachtree City, GA

FITZPATRICK, BARBARA R.
[b.] February 28, 1946, England, UK; [p.] Edna and Jack Beckley; [m.] Divorced, March 26, 1967; [ch.]

Felicity R. Fitzpatrick, my daughter is currently earning her PhD at Claremont, CA; [ed.] Sale Grammar School for Girls; [occ.] Owner, Sandra's Secretarial Service (didn't change name!); [oth. writ.] Numerous poems; [pers.] I wrote most of my poems, including Breathe Softly Fresh Breezes, during my teen years in England.; [a.] Wailuku Maui, HI

FLANNERY, ANNE-MARIE B.
[b.] March 1, 1972, Milwaukee, WI; [ed.] Double Major in Psychology and English to be completed in May of 1995 from UW-Milwaukee.; [memb.] 1. Assistant Poetry Editor of UW-Milwaukee's Literary Magazine The Cream City Review. 2. Member of Sigma Tau Delta (English Honor Society); [a.] Port Washington, WI

FLESHER, JOYCE LEA
[pen.] Lindsay Cheveley; [b.] June 30, 1980, Sallisaw, OK; [p.] Shirley and Leon Flesher; [ed.] Lindwood Academy of Home Schooling; [occ.] High School Freshman; [memb.] Children International Sponsorship; [pers.] Of all I've ever wrote, I've found my work is better when it comes from God, so I'd like to tell Him thank's and that He's all the inspiration I need because without Him this would of never been published.; [a.] Gore, OK

FLOLID, JAMES EVERETT
[pen.] Jamie; [b.] March 30, 1950, Minnesota; [p.] Dr and Mrs E. M. Flolid; [ch.] 1 son; [ed.] AA Commercial Art, AA Soc. Sci., Near BA (in progress); [occ.] Pres. RJ Investment Group of UTAH; [hon.] Dean's List SJSU, Golden Poet, Great American Poet; [oth. writ.] 502 published poems, 7 short stories; [pers.] My first published poem was in 8th grade, I've lived many lives in one, my poetry is my soul, I collect baseball cards for fun, I am only a human in search of love.; [a.] Ogden, UT

FLORES, DARLENE S.
[pen.] Darlene S. Flores, Darlene S. Groce, Darlene S. Floyd; [b.] June 6, 1950, Indianapolis, IN; [p.] Thurle Clifton Floyd, Mary Armina (Messina) Thornton; [m.] Federico Corona Flores, May 6, 1985; [ch.] 7 plus 7 step-children, 7 sons, 7 daughters (age 6, 3, to 8, two deceased); [ed.] George Washington High School, Science and Math - Home Economics majors Business and English minors; [occ.] Housewife and Mom, Laundry attendant or any kind of cleaning; [memb.] Jehovah's Witness Institution of Holy Matrimony. High School Sorority - The 'K.P.'s.'; [hon.] Some from the 60's volunteer work: Singing group, medical work, social work with children, patients, and school.; [oth. writ.] Many unfinished ideas, stories, poems and some songs cartoons, inventions (improvements on inventions). Some art work. Much 'work' was thrown away or given away.; [pers.] 'Read God's' Word Daily at all costs - endeavor to use it to improve your life and that of others in these special times. It is the oldest of all 'Holy' writings - the most fiercely disputed to be translated and most accurate even to this day!; [a.] Indianapolis, IN

FLORES, ELIZABETH L.
[b.] Sanderson, TX; [p.] Simon and Gloria Lopez; [m.] Adolfo S. Flores, November 22, 1959; [ch.] Kathryn Marie Iverson, Michael Anthony Flores; [ed.] BA - Early Childhood/Sp. Ed. Arizona State University, MA - Education, Arizona State University Doctoral Program - 1981 - Univ. of Co. Boulder; [occ.] Adjunct Professor at Univ. of Texas at El Paso. Co-owner of two businesses - Tiny Gowns and Postal Annex; [memb.] El Paso Del Norte, Chapter of Kappa Delta Pi, Teaching English to Students of Other Languages (TESOL), The Hispanic Business Membership Club Texas Association for Bilingual Education; [hon.] Graduated "Cum Laude" Arizona State Univ. 1975, Award of Scholastic Excellence by the faculty, of the Dept. of Education, Arizona State Univ., 1975. Selected by TEA (Texas Education Agency) and the Departamento de Educa-

tion y Ciencia de Madrid to participate in the III Summer Institute on Children's Literature at the Universidad Complutense in Madrid, Spain.; [oth. writ.] "La Tortilla Huida" (The Runaway Tortilla", children's book published by Donor's Production. Poem of love for Dad, (Spanish) Father's Day 1988, Today's Catholic. "From Civil War Archives", a story of Hispanic Valor, Vista Magazine, 1990; [pers.] When something or someone touches that inner core in my very being, there is this urgency to write a poem. The words just seem to flow.; [a.] El Paso, TX

FLORES, DENISE
[b.] August 26, 1982, Los Angeles, CA; [p.] Carlos and Giville Flores; [ed.] Grade 7th, Waite Middle School; [occ.] Student; [hon.] Behavior and Attendance; [a.] Norwalk, CA

FLORES, ERNESTO M.
[pen.] Ernie; [b.] September 24, 1928, San Antonio, TX; [p.] Carlos Flores and Rafaela Flores; [m.] Bernice C. Flores, ("Bonnie" Nick-name) February 18, 1950; [ch.] Dennis Ray, Larry Anthony, Gene Allen, Thomas Wayne, Ernest Francis, Bonnie Sue, David Bernard; [ed.] San Antonio Vocational and Technical High School; [occ.] Retired; [memb.] Bellaire United Methodist Church, Bible Study Group "Seekers", and AARP.; [hon.] U.S.M.C. World War II, SN 597284 (USMC Reserves, recalled during Korean Conflict) sergeant USMC, Expert Rifleman, (Member of USMC Rifle Team), (Rifle Range Instructor Camp Pendleton, CA) (Honorable Discharge Quamico, VA); [oth. writ.] "In 3rd Grade" I wrote: "I love to go out in the meadow, and see the trees all green, to seethe pretty flowers and hear the little birds sing". (Eleanor Brackenridge Elementary School) San Antonio, Texas (1936); [pers.] "The way of the sea", was written by me in the eleventh grade of High School and my teacher would not accept it as mine. That happened forty-five years ago, and now I have the opportunity to write it again. (Forty-five years ago it really hurt me); [a.] Houston, TX

FLOYD, LYNNETTA
[b.] December 14, 1965, Tulsa, OK; [p.] Dorothy and Jerry J. Bradley; [m.] Ronnie L. Floyd, June 9, 1984; [ch.] 2 sons, De'Marco Anthony (9 yrs) and Cameron Sayvon (16 mos.); [ed.] Graduated from HG Spruce H.S., Dallas Tx. 1984, Great Plains VoTech Lawton OK 1987, Fayetteville Tech. Fayetteville NC 1989 and California Coll. of Health Sciences 1994; [occ.] Cardiopulmonary Technician and Certified Resp. Ther. Tech.; [oth. writ.] Numerous writings that have not been published over 300 personal poems.; [pers.] Poetry is in everyone, our manners of expression may vary from one person to the next, but the talents are there. My greatest poetic inspiration is Ms. Maya Angelous - "I know why the caged bird sing."; [a.] Dallas, TX

FORDE, DANA
[b.] July 6, 1982; [p.] Christine and Andrew Forde; [ed.] Dover Elm. Lee Burneson Middle; [occ.] Student; [memb.] Drama Club; [hon.] Honor Roll, High Honors; [oth. writ.] Several published poems; [pers.] We are all human, no one is perfect strive to reflect the good in all.; [a.] Westlake, OH

FORET, EULA D.
[b.] Raceland, LA; [p.] Deceased; [m.] Deceased, December 23, 1938; [ch.] 5, 4 grandchildren; [ed.] High School, B.A. College Degree, N.S.U. Thibodaux, LA; [occ.] Retired (special ed.) Teacher taught severe and profoundly retarded; [memb.] Teacher's retirement, Council of Catholic Women; [hon.] "Teacher of the year", (Developmental Training Center) 1990, Page dedicated in College (N.S.U. Annul. Degree at age 66 (1986); [oth. writ.] 2 books in progress; [pers.] God sent me the opportunity to teach and train a hundred plus special children who in turn taught me life's values.; [a.] Raceland, LA

FORREST, DONNA MARIE
[b.] June 4, 1957, Chattanoga, TN; [p.] William Asbury and Helen (Sisk) Smith; [m.] Kenneth Forrest, September 27, 1985; [ch.] Sabrina Marie, Cinnamon, and Benjamin Cody; [ed.] TN. Temple Univ. Chattanooga, TN 1978 THCo, and 1992 B.S. in Pyschology (Magna Cum Laude): LAEL Graduate Studies, Masters Degree: family counselling - 1996; [occ.] Substitute teacher: homemaker, home schooling parent: World Learning Coordinator; [memb.] Women on Mission, 1985, Mirray Co., Associational Missions, (1994-95) Murray Co. Homeschoolers Fellowship, (1994-), Phi Psi Sigma, 1992, Concerned Women of America (1988-), Christian Writers Guild (1985-), Moms in Touch Prayer Fellowship; [hon.] National Dean's List (1981-1992) (Vol 1): Phi Psi Sigma, (Husband Beloved Wife and Children Super Mom) this is the greatest honor she has!!; [oth. writ.] Many letters on social issues, community events - Chatsworth Times: Poetry Contest - college - divisional winner currently writing two different books; [pers.] I believe that the importance of my life is based on my personal relationship with the Lord Jesus Christ. And that relationship enriches my every endeavor.; [a.] Chatsworth, GA

FORSHEE, DANIELLE
[b.] July 27, 1982, New Jersey; [p.] Sharon and Robert Forshee; [ed.] St. Dominic's School in Bricktown, NJ. 7th grade.; [hon.] I was in "Publish s book contest", and I only made in through 2 judging processes. I got a merit award. This was March 5, 1994.; [oth. writ.] In the "Anthology of poetry by Young Americans", I wrote a poem titled "Frogson Lilly Pads"! I was 10 years, 1993 edition.; [pers.] In my poems, I write about nature, and the beauty within it. Nature and beauties fantasies inspire me, and makes my writing come to life. I owe great dedication to my sixth grade English teacher, Mrs. Coll, who helped my talent to grow.; [a.] Lanoka Harbor, NJ

FOSSO, JASON M.
[b.] September 27, 1971, Cincinnati, OH; [p.] Kart and Ann Fosso; [ed.] Magdalena High School, University of New Mexico.; [occ.] Sales; [memb.] I have been inducted into the "Who's Who Among Students In American University and Colleges", and was a member of the ROTC Army Ranger Challenge Team, Golden Bear Brigade, Lobo Battalion (U.N.M.), as well as the Army ROTC Color Guard.; [hon.] I have received the following, while in Army ROTC at UNM, the Sgt. York Award, Outstanding Academic Achievement Award, and the Silver ROTC Medal from the National Society of the Sons of the American Revolution.; [oth. writ.] None published.; [pers.] I have found that hope can be a great inconvenience. This is especially true when there is not enough to give us unquestioning faith, but just enough to keep us from giving up and moving on.; [a.] Albuquerque, NM

FOURNIER, SHIRLIE
[b.] February 1, 1950, Boston, MA; [p.] Patrick and Annie Sark; [m.] Norman Fournier; [memb.] Family of Christ; [oth. writ.] Various feelings in poetry, however this is the first published; [pers.] Trust in the Lord, for everything.

FOX III, MICHAEL J.
[b.] February 11, 1976, Philadelphia; [p.] Michael J. Fox Sr., Kathleen E. Fox; [ed.] Central High School, Community College of Philadelphia; [occ.] Student; [hon.] Honor Roll at Community College of Philadelphia; [pers.] I have been influenced by the music of Nirvana, Pearl Jam, Nine Inch Nails, and Smashing Pumpkins.; [a.] Philadelphia, PA

FOX, GRACE MARIE
[pen.] Marie Jacob; [b.] February 2, 1927, Wichita, KS; [p.] Walter Jacob and Olive Jacob; [m.] Vernon Fox; [ch.] Colleen, LeAnn, David, Glenn; [occ.] Secretary, Ark Valley Christian Church, Wichita, KS; [memb.]

Ark Valley Christian Church; [oth. writ.] Editorial published in The Wichita Eagle, several short articles published in The Ark Builder; [pers.] My writing style depicts the values I received from my parents in my formative years. I am currently working on a book centered around my early life during and following the Depression years.; [a.] Wichita, KS

FOX, JEROME A.
[b.] May 12, 1975, Willmor, MN; [p.] Alan and Carolyn Fox; [ed.] Waverly High, Jr. at Acusa in OKC, OK, Oklahoma Christian University; [occ.] Full time student; [memb.] Member of the Memorial Church of Christ, Member of Chorale, and Symphonic and Jazz bands.; [hon.] Dean's List, National Honor Society, NCNSA; [oth. writ.] I have written other poems that are unpublished; [pers.] I write most of my poetry to honor a very good friend, Lori Ann Peek. She is the soul inspiration and example I try to preserve when writing poetry. Thank you, Lori.; [a.] Waverly, KS

FOXE, JERRY RUNNING
[b.] June 4, 1927, Bandon, OR; [m.] Jean Running Foxe, March 12, 1971; [ch.] One; [ed.] Myrtle Point Univ High; [occ.] Retired Cross Country Truck Driver; [memb.] Vice Chairman Coquille Indian Tribal Council, Center for study of first Americans; [hon.] Indian of the year "1976" represented all Indians of Southwest OR. at B. Centennial in Washington, DC; [oth. writ.] Many of my poems have appeared in Tribal Newsletter, Bandon Historical Museum displays one.; [pers.] In mot of my poetry, I try to reflect the life and legends of my ancestors, although, some of writings are about travel on the road; [a.] Cottage Grove, OR

FRALEY, DEBRA S.
[pen.] Debra Sue Martindale; [b.] July 29, 1954, Erie, PA; [p.] Marie Martindale - Wheater disabled Vietnam Veteran; [m.] Bernie Fraley - Marine Corp., Force Recon, 1985; [ch.] Tobias Parker, Chris Austin/granddaughter - Jessica Parker; [ed.] Jamestown Community College University South Carolina and Union Liberty University, Lynchburgh VA. B.S. Psychology, 6 credits - masters in counselling; [occ.] While in grad School multiple sclerosis snuck upon me which left me disabled and be fuddled.; [memb.] Disabled American Veterans Aux. chapter #25 Apitherapy Society, MS Society, USC-U Alumni, Liberty Alumni 7 yrs. of battle with the veterans Administration for husbands entitled benefits - awarded 100% service connected condition (PTSD) won with Aagent Orange Settlement in 1991, Dean's List - JCC, Jamestown, NY (accomplishments); [oth. writ.] Unpublished research paper on credit card Fraud kept by professor of Criminal Investigation Class. Research papers on agent orange exposure in South Vietnam from Washington Briefs; [pers.] The question is, are we our brothers keeper? Yes, when called to do so, I've sheltered the homeless, fed the hungry, gave refuge to woman and children, raised my girlfriends son, seen miracles happen. But most of all we cannot stop believing in self and the light within must never go out.; [a.] Buffalo, SC

FRANK, STEPHEN H.
[pen.] Harbinger; [b.] August 16, 1963, Hot Springs, VA; [m.] Jeanette Ruminer Frank, December 27, 1986; [ch.] Daniel Chase, Amy Eileen, Christy Lea, Jeffrey Ryan; [ed.] BA, Virginia Tech University MBA, Strayer College; [occ.] Political Consultant; [memb.] City of Manassas Park Planning Commission, Virginia Tech Alumni Association; [pers.] My mission is to create a social awareness of the times in which we live and a revelation of things to come.; [a.] Manassas Park, VA

FRANKLIN, DIANNA MERCEDES
[b.] April 21, 1957, Stringtown, OK; [p.] Cleveland and Gracie Neal; [m.] Leon Franklin, July 2, 1977; [ch.] Katrina and DeJuan; [ed.] Bachelors in Business Administration, Central State University, Edmond, OK in 1980; [hon.] Who's Who Among Students in Jr. Col-

leges - 1977 - Eastern OK. State College - Wilburton, OK; [oth. writ.] Unpublished collection entitled, down but not out; [a.] Oklahoma City, OK

FRANSON, SUNNY
[pers.] We, that is, everything and everyone, are part of a whole. So when we are thoughtless, we hurt ourselves. It is time to respect all living things, to nurture the earth.; [a.] Lake County, CA

FRANTZ, JOANNA
[b.] June 10, 1974, Thailand; [p.] Larry and Rojana Catlin; [m.] David Spencer Frantz, April 30, 1994; [ch.] Spender Alan Frantz; [ed.] McEachern High, Concorde School of Hair Design; [occ.] Student at Concorde School of Hair Design; [pers.] This poem was inspired from the moment I held my son. I owe everything I am today to my family, and the person I will become to my husband.; [a.] Longbranch, NJ

FRAZIER, PANSY MERRICK
[pen.] Pansy Merrick Frazier; [b.] January 22, 1915, Clinton, LA; [m.] Ogden Andrew Frazier (Deceased), June 9, 1940; [ch.] Sandra, Ogden II, Ralph George, Terri Ann; [ed.] McKinley High Baston Rouge, LA Various correspondence courses; [occ.] Retired and enjoying the beauty of the earth.; [memb.] Church Women United Afro American Historical Committee; [hon.] The poem "The Lady Lex" was published by the Corpus Christi Caller (TX) Prime Time magazine with as layout of the U.S.S. Lexington; [oth. writ.] Many other poems and various other writings I hope to put in book form.; [pers.] I don't have any special talents or skills, but I hope my poetry has appeal because I just take my pen in hand and write the way I feel. Poets that I admire: Long Fellow. Stevenson, Tennyson and Paul L. Dunbar.; [a.] Kingsville, TX

FREEMAN, GWENDOLYN SESSION
[b.] August 27, 1950, Houston, TX; [p.] Mary Martin, Ardis Session; [m.] Lawrence L. Freeman, August 7, 1971; [ch.] Keisha Eval Freeman, Barbetta Laurice Freeman; [ed.] Charles R. Drew High School, Texas Woman's University (TWU); [occ.] RN - Francis S. Key, Middle School, Houston Texas; [memb.] Greater Christian Fellowship Bapt. Church and Choir, M.B. Smiley High School PTA and Band Booster Club.; [hon.] Teacher of the Year '89-'90 - Francis S. Key Middle School, Mother of the Year '83 (Learning Tree Academy); [pers.] I strive to live a Christian life so that others may see the Bible thru me.; [a.] Houston, TX

FREEMAN, MICHAEL TODD
[pen.] Mike Freeman; [b.] April 30, 1978, Plainview, NY; [p.] Ellen Freeman, Stephen Freeman; [ed.] Amityville Memorial High School; [occ.] Student; [memb.] Key Club, Tri-M Honor Music Society, National Honor Society.; [hon.] National High School Honor Society; [oth. writ.] Poem published is "Poetry In Motion" magazine, poems published on America on line.; [pers.] You can't avoid the inevitable and there is no such thing as a real choice. We all follow our own "yellow brick road".; [a.] Massapeque, NY

FREEMAN, CYNTHIA D.
[pen.] Cynthia Deleveaux; [b.] September 29, 1956, Hollywood, FL; [p.] Hosea and Dorothy Delevoe; [m.] Divorced; [ch.] Justin A. Freeman; [ed.] Hollywood Hills High, Norfolk State University, Clark/Atlanta University (MBA); [occ.] Staff Manager; [memb.] Delta Sigma Theta, Gresham Park Civic and Athletic Association Board of Directors; [hon.] Phi Beta Gamma, Who's Who Among Students at American Colleges and Universities; [oth. writ.] Several poems published in anthologies compiled by Poetry Press, Pittsburg Texas; [pers.] I strive to reflect simplicity, coupled with my strong morale background in my writing. I have been greatly influenced by my father, who was a minister and a writer.; [a.] Decatur, GA

FREEMAN, NATALIE ROSE
[pen.] Natalie Freeman and Thrailkill; [b.] February 27, 1970, Cheyenne, WY; [p.] Gary Freeman, Amy M. Libbey Freeman; [m.] Darin Thrailkill, June 9, 1990; [ch.] Step-son: Darin Levi Thrailkill; [ed.] Northglenn High School, Academy of Beauty Culture; [occ.] Nail Technician; [oth. writ.] Many poems of varied themes, and short stories; [pers.] My writing comes straight from my heart! My family members, both near and far away, are my source of inspiration, words full of love and dreams!; [a.] Grand Junction, CO

FREIRICH, SHELLY
[b.] July 7, 1968, Michigan City, IN; [p.] Jim and Sandy Reed; [m.] Mike Freirich, July 23, 1994; [ed.] Williamette University BA, Masters of Teaching; [occ.] Sixth grade teacher; [hon.] All American Swimmer, Asthmatic Athlete of the year, graduated Cum Laude; [oth. writ.] A personal collection of poetry; [pers.] Writing is both a release and a means for me to contemplate and evaluate things that I don't understand.; [a.] Boise, ID

FRICK, JACOB
[b.] January 27, 1976, Carbondale, IL; [p.] James Frick and Nancy Frick; [pers.] If only we all saw through the eyes of the poet.; [a.] Iowa Falls, IA

FRIEDEMANN, SARA L.
[b.] April 22, 1982, Menomonee Falls, WI; [p.] Scott Friedemann and Carolyn Friedemann; [occ.] Home-schooled in 8th grade; [occ.] Student; [memb.] Junior Philatelists of America, Earth Friends, Faith Baptist Church, and Friends of the Marshfield Public Library; [hon.] 1st Place in National Essay Contest, many awards for Ballet, Tap, and Jazz.; [oth. writ.] Poem "Moonlight Shadows" published in Echoes of Yesterday, National Library of Poetry, poem "Kairos's Song" published in "Best Poems of 1995", National Library of Poetry, essay for "Stamps" magazine and other unpublished works.; [pers.] I must write. It's a part of me.; [a.] Marshfield, WI

FRIES, JAQUALYN HOPE
[pen.] Jaqua-Lynn, Lynn Taylor, Benna Bard, Jackie Lynn Taylor, Hope Frees; [b.] June 29, 1925, Compton, CA; [p.] Chester and Ethel Taylor; [m.] Jack Fries, August 6, 1966; [ch.] Six beloved step children by two previous marriages: Brandi Bryan and Bartley Bard, Cheryl Valencia Icard and Jerry, and Anthony Valencia.; [ed.] Film Studies and Private Schools (1-12), Child Actress, Began Films in Legendary Little Rascals of Our Gang; [occ.] Spokeswoman for "Ultra Life" Natural Health Products. Motivational Speaker-Teacher.; [memb.] Screen Actors Guild (SAG), American Fed. Television, Radio Artists (AFTRA), Sacramento Assoc. for the retarded (SAR); [hon.] San Francisco TV Woman of the Year (1954), Honored 1991 for Pioneer Broadcasting since 1951 by Nat'l Academy of TV Arts and Sciences, and San Diego Nat'l Press Club.; [oth. writ.] Co-authored book with husband "Jackie Remembers Our Gang" currently updating book in verse and writing "Cat Tails" in verse; [pers.] In America all things are possible to achieve, I have lived the American dream - it's never too young to begin and you are never too young to begin. Mary Baker Ebby, Religious Pioneer and Elizabeth Barrett Browning have been my inspiration to write. I portrayed E.B. Browning as a young actress at the Ben Bard Playhouse in Hollywood; [a.] Citrus Heights, CA

FROST, KEITH R.
[b.] March 25, 1918, Stillwater, MN; [p.] Roland M. and Ruth E. Frost; [m.] Margaret H. Frost, February 11, 1942; [ch.] Sheila Kay and Jack R.; [occ.] Retired Personnel V-Pres.; [memb.] Toastmasters International (Dan Patch and P.R.O.S. TM Clubs) Institute of Certified Professional Managers.; [hon.] Accredited Toastmaster (1982), Certified Administrative Manager (1977), District VI Toastmaster of the Year 1970; [oth.

writ.] Started writing poetry while in the teens, still writing at present. Have never submitted poetry for publishing before. Article on Eulogies published in Toastmaster Magazine.; [pers.] I believe that we are on earth to learn and to grow until our final breath. It is our duty to help others through this process whether recognized or not. That is the meaning of life and human existence. Favorite poetry collection: "Rubaiyat of Omar Khayyam"; [a.] Minneapolis, MN

FRYE, MYRON
[b.] July 29, 1961, Kansas City, MO; [p.] Marjorie and Homer Frye; [ed.] Northeast High; [occ.] YMCA Program Director Youthnet Outreach Coordinator; [pers.] My poems are an extension of how I feel inside. I endeavor to radiate a message of happiness in my writing; [a.] Kansas City, MO

FULLER, DERRICE LENAY
[pen.] "Little Indian"; [b.] May 21, 1967, Houston, TX; [p.] Penny and Glen Powell; [occ.] Purchasing Agent; [hon.] To be a child of God. (My awards) simply the gifts of life itself.; [oth. writ.] Grandma's strength, family tree, gossip, fork in the road, mental daze, creative medication, dream spirit, passion song, eternal valentine, a prayer for Brenda, New Life, Cupids Arrow, Christmas Time.; [pers.] A thought to live by: When someone tells you "Life just isn't fair" It's important to prove them wrong by setting a new standard for the game of life. Always Play Fair!; [a.] Austin, TX

FUNK, ROBERT JACKSON
[pen.] Jack; [b.] March 2, 1959, Winchester, VA; [p.] Otis and Margret Funk; [m.] Mary Elizabeth Funk, February 24, 1981; [ch.] Jeremy, Larry, April; [ed.] High School; [occ.] Supervisor; [pers.] Never say can't; [a.] Old Fields, WV

FUSINSK, KEITH
[b.] August 3, 1970, Garden City, MI; [p.] Robert Fusinski and Betty Beagan; [m.] Kelly Fusinski, October 4, 1993; [ch.] One on the way; [occ.] Home improvements; [oth. writ.] Sadistic interlude (soon to be published); [pers.] Follow your dreams, they are the key to the future!; [a.] Hamtramok, MI

GABRIEL, TRENTON
[b.] September 5, 1969, Quezon City, Philippines; [p.] Lilian and Rudolfo Gabriel; [ed.] B.S. in Sociology 92' Old Dominion University Norfolk, VA; [occ.] School Community Trainer, Mt Hermon Elementary School, and Residential Counselor, Pines Residential Treatment Center, Portsmouth VA.; [memb.] In support of children O.D.U.; [pers.] The purpose of life is not to procreate or to gain material wealth, but to find a soulmate to share a life full of love, understanding and compassion; [a.] Norfolk, VA

GAJDICA, VICKI
[b.] July 13, 1982, Dallas, TX; [p.] Gary and Debbie Gajdica; [ed.] 7th Grade (now); [occ.] Student; [memb.] ROJH Drill Team Project Success

GALBREATH, JANICE
[pen.] Silence Reapplear; [b.] May 12, 1963, Sacramenta, CA; [p.] Kenneth and Marge Sullivan; [m.] Samuel A. Thomas I. (Fiance) May 26, 1995; [ch.] 3 - Ashley Rae, Stephanie, Sam II; [ed.] Completed Comm. College (GCC) Secondary Ed. (Area of Specialization - English attending ASU-West. Preparing for entry into the Teaching Program; [occ.] Dog Groomer; [pers.] The key to success is education. A dreamer fantasizes about a better life, one who continues to pursue knowledge - achieves it.; [a.] Phoenix, AZ

GALE, DAVID
[pen.] Kuf Sak Nup; [b.] July 06, 1980, Fairfield, CA; [p.] Matthew Gale and Sandra Grevard; [ed.] Still in high School, 9th Grade, Will C Wood High, Vacaville, CA.; [memb.] Transworld Skateboarding, International Jet Sports and Boating Asso (IJSBA); [oth. writ.] The Lenning, What I Do, Me, My Feathers, God Who? Sorry, Valentine Loves None; [pers.] M.I.A.D.A.I.M. (me is as Dorky as is me); [a.] Vacaville, CA

GALFORD, PATRICIA
[pen.] Pat Galford; [b.] June 11, 1948, Detroit, MI; [p.] Frank E. Clowes and Leoca B. Clowes; [m.] Stanley W. Galford Sr., June 22, 1965; [ch.] Tammy L. Privette, Mary F. Galford, and Stanley W. Galford Jr.; [occ.] Church Secretary for Sr. Pastor; [oth. writ.] A collection of my thoughts, visions and verses. I've got other stories, poems, and personal writings, but haven't pursued publishing yet.; [pers.] I have been an admirer of Helen Steirer Rice for many, many years. I write what is in my heart and the things I see through my heart, for without the heart, for without the heart there is no life.; [a.] Rochester, MI

GALLE, CHRISTOPHER A.
[b.] December 17, 1981, Chicago Heights, IL; [p.] William K. and Linda L. Galle; [ed.] I presently attend Junior High School in Kennedale, TX, where my family moved in 1988.; [memb.] I am a member of the National Jr. Honor Society; [pers.] Love Science (especially Astronomy), and play soccer for recreation. My poetry is inspired by the occurrences, actions, and events of my every day life.

GALLICHAN, MEESHA
[b.] January 10, 1982, Bellvue, WA; [p.] Michael and Jo Gallichan; [ed.] I am in the seventh grade.; [pers.] I write according to my feelings, and what mood I'm in. I think writing is a fun hobby, anyone can write if they have an imagination.; [a.] Puyallup, WA

GALVAN, ALFONSO J.
[b.] July 30, 1973, Houston; [p.] Candelario H. Galvan Jr. Antonia Sendra Palma Galvan; [occ.] Medical Transcriptionist; [pers.] 1. You can only do that which you don't doubt. 2. The only true limitations are those influenced upon you lay others. 3. The pain endured from accomplishments is temporary, the pride earned from it is forever; [a.] Houston, TX

GAMBLE, MICHAEL
[b.] June 24, 1939, Merced, CA; [p.] Chester and Stella; [m.] Betty Jo, September 18, 1973; [ed.] Hayward High UG Miss, 2 years of Coll. 24 years other schools while in A.R; [occ.] Network analyst and programmer; [oth. writ.] Mostly poems

GANIME, KATHRYN J.
[b.] February 18, 1979, Gulph Mills, PA; [p.] Dr. Peter and Regina Ganime; [ed.] 2nd yr. Archbishop John Carroll High School, Radnor, PA; [occ.] Student; [memb.] Carroll Drama Club, Nakord Karate System, Ashford Farms Riding School; [hon.] Equestrian ribbons, A gold and silver medal won in Karate tournaments; [oth. writ.] Poems and essays published in school papers.; [pers.] I want to study composition and English literature in college, as well as theater.; [a.] Gulph Mills, PA

GARCIA, MATT
[b.] December 22, 1976, Oconomowoc, WI; [p.] Alfred and Rosemary Garcia; [ed.] Currently a Senior at Anchor Bay High School in New Baltimore, MI; [memb.] Student Council, the A.B.H.S. Christian Youth Club, Student Congress, and the School Beautification Committee.; [hon.] 1995 Voice of Democracy Essay Contest 2nd place winner.; [oth. writ.] Has written for his school for plays, Academic Awards night Graduation Ceremonies, has performed at a bookstore on numerous occasions and has had poem Contemporary Chivalry published in 1993; [pers.] Friends are the easiest to find, yet most valuable treasure on Earth. Thank you Tamie Coyer, Carrie Proctor, Tonia Stabryla, Cristan Lentine, and Jason Davidson for all of your support in my writings.; [a.] New Baltimore, MI

GARCIA, CRISTINA
[b.] August 20, 1976, Sweetwater, TX; [p.] Erlinda Garcia; [ed.] Sweetwater High, Baylor University, Freshman year; [occ.] Student; [hon.] National Honors Society; [pers.] I try to express emotions I have experienced or thoughts that I have in all the poetry that I write. It is my way of showing the world how I truly feel.; [a.] Sweetwater, TX

GARCIA, INGRID ELIZABETH
[pen.] Liz, Iggy; [b.] July 30, 1975, Santa Clara, CA; [p.] Gilbert and Guadulina Garcia; [ed.] Paulding County High School, West Georgia College,; [occ.] Full time student and part hairstlist; [hon.] A Golden Award For Poetry; [oth. writ.] Other poems, the face in the mirror, rain storm, A love never there, haunting me, Inner fire, the mask, life and death, unknown soldier, endless highway and dreams; [pers.] Poetry is my Life! When I write poetry I can express all my feelings of anger, frustration, depression, love and and happiness in one poem. This is one of many reasonably I love to write poetry.; [a.] Dallas, GA

GARNER, GAIL
[b.] December 12, 1938, Southgate, MI; [p.] James and Carmen Ammons; [ch.] Jody, Roy, Marcia and 7 grandchildren; [ed.] Eastern Michigan Univ.; [occ.] Freelance Technical Writer; [memb.] Faith Presbyterian Church, National Writers Association Society for Technical Communication; [hon.] Graduated Magna Cum Laude from Eastern MI.; [oth. writ.] Technical Writing for Mechanical Engineers. Lyrics for songs, not yet published.; [pers.] Sometimes life is wonderful, sometimes horrid. A little faith and a little humor gets us through it all. Sometimes a thing is so lovely, or so poignant, or so funny, that I simply have to write about it.; [a.] Aurora, CO

GARNET, JENNIFER
[b.] December 10, 1976, Philadelphia, PA; [p.] Dr. Richard and Mrs. Beverly Garnet; [ed.] Currently a 12th grader at Richmond High School, Richmond, IN; [occ.] Work as a tutor (4 days a week-part time); [memb.] First English Lutheran Church; [hon.] Ball State University Journalism Camp: Best Copy, Award of Excellence in Copy Writing; [pers.] While most writers stress life's goodness or cruelty, I try to incorporate the aspects of life's challenges in the hopes of someday overcoming them.; [a.] Richmond, IN

GARRUES, LUIS A.
[pen.] Scorpio; [b.] November 3, 1974, Lima-Peru; [p.] Luis Garrues and Patricia Insua; [ed.] San Antonio De Padua High School, Phoenix College; [occ.] Proof Operator; [memb.] Phi Theta Kappa; [hon.] Finalist in an essay writing contest sponsored by The Prudential. Second place on Accounting competition (ASU Business Skills Day); [oth. writ.] Several short stories still unpublished. The earth chronicles (part I published in a local magazine, part II and III still unpublished). Other poems still unpublished.; [pers.] There must be someone up there laughing. It'd be mean from us to let him laugh alone, but when we cannot laugh anymore we must cry with heart and soul and decide if we want to go on.; [a.] Phoenix, AZ

GARVIN, PEGGY ANN
[b.] July 6, 1947, Kansas City, MO; [p.] Charles Leon Wade Sr. and Nelle Chris Wade; [m.] W Franklin Garbin, September 6, 1980; [ch.] Robert Thomas Blackburn, Michelle Blackburn Scott; [ed.] Lord De La Warr High Castle, Delaware Goldey - Beacom Jr. College Wilmington, Delaware Aiken Technical College Aiken, SC; [occ.] Graphic Artist, Graphics and Illustration Savannah River Site, Aiken, SC; [hon.] My first romance novel was nominated for 4 awards at the TunnelCon III convention in July, 1994.; [oth. writ.] Fanzine Romance Novels Published by Dream Weavers, Montmorenci, SC Parallel Worlds Within The City and I shall But Love Thee Better... Various poems

published in other fanzines; [pers.] I've always written poetry to express my deepest feelings. My first book was written during a particularly. Dark time in my life - escaping into the lives of my characters enabled me to survive the harshness of reality. Writing enhances the quality of life!; [a.] Aiken, SC

GASKAMP, ALISON LANHAM
[b.] July 31, 1958, Pasadena, TX; [p.] Jack and Ada Lanham; [m.] Curtis Gaskamp, January 2, 1982; [ch.] Brian Jacob Gaskamp (9), Brett James Gaskamp (7); [ed.] Pasadena Evening Community School (GED), Blinn Jr. College (Sophomore); [occ.] Currently I am a Student at Blinn; [memb.] Phi Theta Kappa, Sigma Thi Delta (Spanish Club); [hon.] I received a special award on another poem titled "Mistaken Love" through the American Collegiate Poets.; [oth. writ.] I have written many poems and am currently writing a book.; [pers.] I like to write about events which reflect feelings from my own personal accounts (or friends) political, even famous people, although some are purely fictional. My English professor (Dr Dietrich) gave me great encouragement to keep writing.; [a.] Brenham, TX

GASPAR, MARY C.
[b.] July 25, 1919, Cheyenne, WY; [p.] Mark H. Nelson, Agnes Nelson; [m.] Nicholas J. Gaspar, August 30, 1941; [ch.] Sharon Marie, Barbara Ellen; [ed.] Burley Grammar School, Lakeview High School, Chicago, Il.; [occ.] Part Time Secretary; [memb.] W.T.T.W - Public Television Antique Comb Collectors Club, Smith-Sonian Museum; [pers.] Most of my poetry has been written for and in memory of my late husband.; [a.] Chicago, IL

GATHINGS, SUSAN
[b.] January 30, 1945, San Antonio, TX; [p.] Dorothy Murphy, Paul Ervin Gathings; [ed.] Tivy High University of Texas; [occ.] Retired Controller of Hotel Indus.; [memb.] International Accountants Society American Cancer Society; [hon.] Won Boss of the year in our community of 17,000; [oth. writ.] Father is in the International Blue Book of Poets I have been writing since 5 yrs. old but never submitted anything for publication. This honor is especially meaningful to Susan as she was diagnosed with a pseudo tumor in Nov. '93 and is now on disability due to pre-mental dementia. This has left her not able to write anymore but one morning she got up and wrote two poems. These were her first in over a year and she hasn't written since but if you knew here you'd know she expects to.; [pers.] Dedicated to my beloved family, friends and soul mate Dessie Marsh without whom I could not have made it through a recent illness.; [a.] Kerrville, TX

GEHRLING, ALYCE LISA
[b.] New York City; [p.] Kenneth K. Linson, M.D., Alyce Coine Hobbs; [ch.] Gerald K. and Paul E.; [ed.] B.A, Orchestra; [occ.] Writer, Artist, Poet; [memb.] Long Island Poetry Collective, Lifetime member International Society of Poetry, Resident Poet Myasthenia Gravis NY Chapter; [hon.] 18 Anthologies, 28 Honorable Mentions, 5 Gold Awards, 2 First Place for "Susan" and "Barby"; [oth. writ.] St. Jude's Journal, many school publications and newsletters. First published at age 7 of drawing and poem age 7, High school orchestra, Pres. and Editor of Science New Hunters, Teen Model.; [pers.] Remember the power of words to heal or harm.; [a.] Seaford, Long Island

GELDMEIER, LEE R.
[pen.] (L.R.) Les Readem; [b.] July 18, 1915, Riesel, TX; [p.] Henry and Alma Geldmeier (deceased); [m.] Gloria Lee Geldmeier, June 2, 1943; [ch.] Gana Marie Crenshaw, Gina Lee Wilkinson, Lee R. (Robbie) Gelmeier, John Mark Geldmeier and Laura Leigh Geldmeier; [ed.] B.A. degree (4 yrs.) Baylor U., M.A. degree Theology Perkins S.M.V. (3 yrs.); [occ.] Retired United Methodist Minister; [memb.] Masonic Lodge Kiwanis Waco Seniors Central U.M.C. Reisel histori-

cal Society; [hon.] 50 yrs, as active methodist Minister haven't kept Up! In who's who of methodism, in international Biography, etc.; [oth. writ.] Many poems some 250 last 3 yrs. no books; [pers.] "United we stand divided we fall" "We see what we are prepared to see" "One universe not a duplex"; [a.] Waco, TX

GELFOUND, MAX L.
[b.] April 12, 1908, Massachusetts; [p.] Not living; [m.] Sarah M., June 22, 1929; [ch.] Son, Daughter-in-law 3 grandchildren 3 great grands; [occ.] Retired; [oth. writ.] 2 Short story's (Credit Union National Magazine)

GELLER, PAUL
[b.] September 30, 1965, Ellenville, NJ; [p.] Don and Natalie Geller; [ed.] Clarkstown South Rider University; [memb.] Thai Boxing Association Toastmasters club (Princeton Chapter); [hon.] Associate Instructor in Thai Boxing Dean's List; [oth. writ.] This is my first poem to be published; [pers.] I thank God for each day to try and improve myself and help others.; [a.] Plainsboro, NJ

GEMES, MASON DOROTHY
[b.] September 28, 1910; [p.] Mr. and Mrs. E.E. Mason; [m.] Charles J. Gemes (deceased); [ch.] Theresa Gemes Mathis; [occ.] I worked as a bookkeeper until I retired.; [oth. writ.] I have written several other poems. My poem "Living" is in the National Library of Poetry's Book "The Dark Side of the Moon", on page 160. I had no biography in that book.; [pers.] I want to dedicate this poem "Simple Happiness" to all my family, both alive and deceased. God and family are the most important part of our lives. I enjoy writing poetry. I hope to win the prize money in the National Library of Poetry Contest.; [a.] Stone Mountain, GA

GEORGE, PETER
[b.] August 3, 1953, Chicago; [p.] Nicolas George, Rita George; [m.] Rita Marie George, March 20, 1983; [ch.] Nicolas, Donovan, Ryan, and Cora; [ed.] TAFT H.S. DePaul University; [occ.] Police Office Lincolnwood Police Department, Lincolnwood Ill; [memb.] Fraternal Order of Police Moose Lodge; [oth. writ.] Currently working on a hard-boiled crime fiction novel.; [pers.] Don't give up in whatever you choose to do.; [a.] Niles, IL

GEORGE, PATTY E.
[b.] August 21, 1957, Texas City, TX; [p.] Charles and Barbara Risch; [m.] Gary L. George, July 30, 1994; [ch.] Dustin Taylor; [ed.] Alvin High School, 1975; [occ.] Purchasing Assistant.; [memb.] Tri-City Corvette club; [pers.] The love of my family and may belief in God inspire me to write poems. The "Babies are fun"...was written for my newest nephew Charles Alexander who tried to come 12 weeks early, but waited til Feb. 22nd to come into this world at 5lbs. 2oz.; [a.] Lumberton, TX

GIBSON, HEATHER
[b.] July 1, 1983, Monmouth; [p.] Terri and David Gibson; [ed.] 6th Grade; [occ.] Roller blading and ice skating.; [memb.] Modern Woodmen of America.; [hon.] I won some spelling bees. I also won a division one on my vocal solo.; [oth. writ.] I just started writing.; [pers.] I dedicate this poem to my family and Birgeetta Van Auken my Best friend.; [a.] Keighsburg, IL

GIDDENS, MICHELE JACQUELINE
[pen.] Mickey; [b.] December 27, 1976, Petersburg, VA; [p.] Paul and Barbara Giddens; [ed.] I will be graduating from McIntosh H.S. in June 1995 and have completed a Summer Scholar Program at the George Washington University; [occ.] Student; [memb.] President of Church youth group, on city organization called The Youth Advisory Board, student council, member of local political organization; [hon.] Graduated Local citizens Police Academy, German III Award; [pers.] "Nothing great was ever achieved without enthusiasm". Ralph Waldo Emerson; [a.] Peachtree City, GA

GIFFARD, SHARON LOUISE
[pen.] Sharon L. Giffard; [b.] March 17, 1975, St. Lucia; [p.] Camilla Bell; [ed.] John Jay College of Criminal Justice; [memb.] World scholar athlete game participant 1993 as well as an alumni; [hon.] Athlete of the year 1994; [oth. writ.] Several poems in my school note books and others on pieces, of paper.; [pers.] I have great expectations and falling short of them is my greatest fear. When my expectations are getting the best of me, I fight back by waiting poetry to propel me. Also, I write poetry to remember who I am.; [a.] Brooklyn, NY

GILL, PAULA MARIOLA
[b.] December 20, 1960, Denver; [p.] Roger and Marge Mariola; [m.] Larry Gill, June 11, 1994; [ch.] Goldie and Maggie; [ed.] Jefferson Co High, University of Wyoming B.A. Lesley College M.A.; [occ.] 3rd grade teacher Brown Elementary in Denver; [memb.] Greenpeace; [hon.] Sharing life with Larry; [oth. writ.] Hundreds of unpublished writings in any journal titled "Scratch paper poems"; [pers.] My husband suffered from manic and depression. He is the spark in many of my previous writings. I miss him very much. I've been frozen for awhile but poetry is helping me cope. Thank you all. Write on...; [a.] Golden, CO

GILLEY, PEGGY
[b.] January 14, 1958, Altoona, PA; [p.] Paul E. Kough, SR., Ruth L. Kough; [m.] Walter R. Gilley, May 16, 1987; [ch.] Jeremy Kough Gilley, Erik Kough Gilley, Sarah Kough Gilley; [ed.] Penn Cambria High School, Cresson, PA and Mount Aloysius Jr. College, Cresson, PA; [occ.] Legal Secretary now housewife; [oth. writ.] I write poems only at special times in my life. I wrote each of my children a poem to read when they are grown up.; [pers.] I strive to be the best person and mother I can be and to keep a very optimistic outlook on life. Being a loving wife and mother is very important to me.; [a.] Havre de Grace, MD

GILLINS, ERIC
[b.] October 2, 1974, IN; [p.] Gerald and Jackie Gillins; [ed.] Purdue University (North Central) N.C. (current student); [memb.] Karate Achievement School; [hon.] Dean's List, All-conference Tract High School; [a.] Valparaiso, IN

GILMAN, LORI D.
[pen.] Lori M. Dinnella; [b.] June 19, 1968, Upper Darby, PA; [p.] John Dinnella, Louise Kabalan; [m.] George R. Gilman, Jr., August 12, 1989; [ed.] Middle Township High School currently attending Arizona State University; [occ.] Accounting clerk, student; [pers.] My first published work!!; [a.] Mesa, AZ

GIOVACCHINI, MICHAEL GINO
[pen.] Michael G. Giovacchini; [b.] November 10, 1950, Sacramento, CA; [p.] Gino Gulio and Pauline Mary Giovacchini; [m.] Vicky "Chea" Giovacchini, November 22,; [ch.] Jeonae Vechea, Chella Luchea; [ed.] Princeton High, Delta College, University of Utah, Surgery - Recovery CPR, ACZS Languages, ORTHO casting- splinting techniques Pedi-Adult.; [occ.] Retired Surgical Nurse, Short Stay Consultant, and Lecturer Delta College Neuro Trauma Nursing Students; [memb.] Chairman of Charity Golf Tournaments for the children of need. Honorary Member Order of the Arrow and Eagle Scout, Porsche Club of America; [hon.] Eagle Scout with all bronze, silver, and gold clubs, Order of the Arrow, Dean's List, Multi Lingual Volunteer for the needy, Leadership Pyramid Award, past Presidents Cap Champion Golf, X-3 Amateur Qualifier to Spyglass Golf.; [oth. writ.] Non-published on my request till now! I've written a total of two book of poetry often I tasted death in 1983...and since then I look at life totally different. My books were private hat now I'm ready to reveal my truths of man and woman that have been kept a secret since 1983.; [pers.] 1. Never say never, 2. Never go through life and state you

wish you would have done it...do it! 3. Treat others as you would want to be treated, 4. Never consider any question as a dumb questions but of intellect.; [a.] Valley Springs, CA

GLANT, ROSENA J.
[pen.] Serena W. Wolf; [b.] November 19, 1976, Williamsport, PA; [p.] Alice and Russell Glant; [ed.] Hughesville Jr/Sr High School; [occ.] Student; [hon.] National Honor Society; [oth. writ.] Other poems, songs, stories, and wise sayings; [pers.] Pride keeps us from saying things that need to be said. Words will last forever if they are shared, kept locked up inside us words will die when our bodies turn to dust.; [a.] Montoursville, PA

GLINS, MARGARET L.
[b.] June 10, 1917, Cincinnati, OH; [p.] Clarence and Willa Cleaver; [m.] John J. Glins (deceased 1988), August 16, 1941; [ch.] Judith Clare and Brovage, Nancy Ellen Leeds; [ed.] Norwood High School, Bethesda Hospital School of Nursing; [occ.] Retired; [memb.] Indian river United of Cheboygan County; [hon.] 2nd Century Woman a united methodist women honor; [oth. writ.] I have written numerous other poems for family, friends, church meetings and programs. None are published; [pers.] I feel that my poems are definitely little messages from God which I love to share with others.; [a.] Indian River, MI

GLODDEN, THOM
[pen.] Giggles; [b.] November 22, 1974, Southfield, MI; [p.] Thomas and Bernadette Gladden; [m.] Single; [ed.] Rochester High, Central Michigan University; [occ.] Theatre Major (Student) at Central Michigan University; [pers.] Why do people park on drive ways and drive on parkways? I write honestly, compassionately, and I allow the idea from my mind to transpose itself magically, effortlessly down unto the withered paper before me.; [a.] Rochester Hills, MI

GODDARD, MARGUERITE
[pen.] Maggie Patrick; [b.] June 4, 1910, Colorado, OH; [p.] Franklin and Charlotte Patrick; [m.] John Marvin Goddard, April 4, 1932; [ch.] Sally, John, Sandra-Holly; [ed.] Central High School; [occ.] God's waiting room; [pers.] We lived on our yacht-oso-moso 20 yrs. - clearwater beach Fla. was much influenced by the sea hurricanes - travel - sunsets; [a.] Saint Petersburg, FL

GODFREY, CHRISTINA LEE
[b.] December 14, 1979, Charlotte, NC; [p.] Charles and Scarlett; [oth. writ.] Poems published in Echoes of Yesterday and the best poems of 1995, Anthology of Poetry by young Americans 1994 and 1995 editions; [pers.] Poetry is an escape from reality for me. Everyone needs an escape.; [a.] Charlotte, NC

GODFREY, CATHERINE G.
[pen.] Catherine Gudley Godfrey; [b.] December 27, 1946, Marion, SC; [p.] Mildred Gurley - Walter Gulrey; [m.] Alphonso Godfrey (Deceased, January 6, 1963); [ed.] Johnakin High, Marion SC, Vocational School for Nursing CHA; [occ.] CHA with DHEC; [memb.] State of South Carolina Bureau of Home Health and Lung Term Care. St John AME Church, Choir, and Usher board.; [hon.] Certificate of Completion and requirements of caring for the alcohol, other drug abusing client with HIV and AIDS, and for Adult Assessment Council, "Facing the Challenges of the Nineties.; [oth. writ.] Yes.; [pers.] After this contest is over, where do I go from here? How, or what must I do to continue my writings.; [a.] Marion, SC

GOETZ, LINDA MARIE
[pen.] Sujata; [b.] May 1, 1957, Westchester, NY; [p.] Bill and Evelyn Goetz; [m.] Richie Cercena; [ed.] Traditional Schools and "life" itself; [occ.] Published photographer Gardener - landscape designer; [memb.]

Osho's Mystery School.; [oth. writ.] Published several poets with the National Library of Poetry under old Pen name "Raleigh"... Published book of 200 Poems: The book is called: "The Goddess is the Grail" by Sujata.; [pers.] Poetry seems to be my number 1 art form in this lifetime ... the last lifetime? ... would you believe: Screwball "Carole Lombard!"

GOEVERT, CATHY
[pen.] Catrina; [b.] October 24, 1962, Wichita; [p.] Willy and Mary Goevert; [ed.] Bachelor of Arts from Baker University Masters in Process University of NE - Omaha; [occ.] Public Relations, Poet, writer; [memb.] Public Relations, Society of America, America Mktg Association, Shins Academy - Martial Arts, Omaha Modern Dance collective, Journal writers of NE; [hon.] Blue belt - Hapiko 1986, Addy Awards - Topeka KS, Ad Club; [oth. writ.] Article for Form Magazine "Are You Leaving Money On The Table" November '89, numerous other poems.'; [pers.] I use my poetry to heal the wounds of my past and to express the divines light through me. I hope you enjoy it.; [a.] Omaha, NE

GOFF, VICTORIA
[b.] August 10, 1980, Salem, OR; [p.] Victor and Sylvia Goff; [ed.] Home schooled 8th grade; [occ.] Modeling; [hon.] 1st Place - Clatskanie Arts Poetry Contest for "Rainy Nights" while in 5th grade.; [oth. writ.] "How it Hurts to Love" published in hardback book musings.; [pers.] As a teenager, I enjoy writing poetry about life from a teen's point of view and feel it's a good way to find out what's happening around us in today's society.; [a.] Clatskanie, OR

GOINS, BOB J.
[b.] February 18, 1940, Sweetwater, TN; [ch.] Six; [ed.] B.A. from Bob Jonet University in Music and Bible; [occ.] Ministry and Weaving Contractor; [memb.] Taberwords baptist Church; [hon.] World of poetry Inc. Silver poet 1990, Golden poet 1991, Who's Who in Poetry 1992, poems published by world of poetry Inc; [oth. writ.] Numerous Poems, and gospel songs book being written prose and praise; [pers.] I love to write religious poems and songs. Many of my poems reflect my humor God said "A Merry Heart Is Like Medicine"; [a.] Greenville, SE

GOLABDAREI, MAHMOOD GHADERI
[pen.] Mammo Golli; [b.] January 18, 1940, Tehran Persia, Iran; [ed.] 1962-1967 Study of literature, London College, England; [occ.] 1992-Present Hitchhiking through the United States, writing about my observations and experiences. 1991 Anaheim, CA. Had my own show on the "24 Hours Radio Show" a Persian language station. 1988-1991 Worked for the Swedish Cultural Ministry as an advisor on Persian Literature. 1979-1980 Worked as a writer for the Persian National radio and television, reading poems and novels. 1970-1979 Worked as an editor of literature for children and young adults in Persia.; [oth. writ.] Had many articles and short stories published in major Persian magazines and newspapers in California. 1990 Had a short story published in Swedish, while living in Sweden. 1961-1988 Had 14 novels published in Persia. "Ishmael Ishmael" was translated into Arabic and sold over one million copies. It was later made into a major Persian motion picture for which I wrote the screen. The other thirteen novels have also sold over one million copies. Also wrote short stories and essays for major Persian publications.; [a.] St Petersburg, FL

GOLDBERG, JOSEPH
[b.] March 25, 1921, Kiev, Russia; [p.] Kalman Abraham and Ita; [m.] Judith, August 27, 1944; [ch.] Barbara, Miriam, Robin; [ed.] Brooklyn College, Wayne University, New York University; [occ.] English Teacher High School Principal; [memb.] Phi Delta Kappa Americans and Canadians in Israel Agudath Israel of America; [hon.] Phi Delta Kappa Freedom Foundation Award Dean's List; [oth. writ.] Junior Code of Law Adminis-

tration and Supervision of Summer High Schools New York City Teacher's Guide; [pers.] The poem in this publication etches my grief over the death and pain of my beloved wife, Judith, whom I treasured for 50 years; [a.] Staten Island, NY

GONGAWARE, WILLIAM R.
[b.] October 30, 1940, Fort Wayne, IN; [p.] Francis and Anna Gongaware; [m.] Betty, June 29, 1962; [ch.] Christopher, Gregory, and Stacey; [ed.] Miami Technical High School, North Carolina State University, United states Naval Postgraduate School; [occ.] Associate Professor, J. Sergeant Reynolds Community College; [memb.] ASEE; [oth. writ.] Co-authored an ISA Journal Article.; [pers.] One who understands their subjects, circumvents paradigms, employs persistence, and maintains humility can accomplish.; [a.] Richmond, VA

GONZALEZ III, PEDRO
[pen.] Pete Gonzalez; [b.] December 1, 1965, Alice, TX; [p.] Pedro Jr. and Benilde M. Gonzalez; [ch.] Brandon Lee Gonzalez; [ed.] Alice High School, Military Training, Bee Country College; [occ.] Student of Bee Country College, Alice, TX; [hon.] Phi Theta Kappa, Dean's List, Air Traffic Controller of the Year 1992, Persian Gulf War Veteran; [pers.] Thank's to God who gave me my experiences and love ones to write from. My influences are family, son, Fiancee Venessa J. R., Teachers and College Instructors.; [a.] Alice, TX

GOOD, MARGARET
[b.] February, 1933, NM; [p.] C. and B. Brown; [m.] Paul W. Good, March, 1962; [ch.] Three; [ed.] Estancia High School Harding College; [occ.] Retired; [memb.] Church of Christ ISP; [hon.] Salutatorian High School; [oth. writ.] Several poems published in High School and College Poetry Anthologies, a couple in NLP Anthology's; [pers.] Credit to my 6,7,8th grade teacher, Eulah Watson, now deceased, who started me writing.; [a.] Griffith, IN

GOSS, RYAN
[b.] September 25, 1978, Lapeer, MI; [p.] Dollie Boyne; [ed.] North Branch High; [occ.] Student; [pers.] I also enjoy writing horror stories. My influence to do so has been by Stephen King; [a.] Silverwood, MI

GOSTLIN, TIMOTHY JOHN
[b.] January 7, 1957, Detroit, MI; [p.] Edmund and Eilleen Gostlin; [m.] Julie Ann Gostlin, February 12, 1983; [ch.] Barrie, Zachary, Jessica, Joshua; [ed.] Euart High School; [occ.] Machinist; [memb.] U.A.W. Labor Union; [oth. writ.] Several poems and songs yet to be published.; [pers.] More understanding and less conflict is the only way we shall have peace with ourselves, and in the world.; [a.] Leroy, MI.

GOTAY, JEANNETTE E.
[pen.] Jeannette E. Gotay; [b.] September 1, 1934, Ohio; [p.] Carmelo and Mildred Cheraso 3rd; [m.] Erasmo Gotay, September 11, 1989; [ch.] Duane Matthew Danchuk, Wendy Rae Bourdeaux; [ed.] Fenn College, Kent State Univ., Alabama State - Special Ed. and Rec. Therapy; [occ.] Unemployed now, was Activity Director 5 yrs, at Duvall home for Retarded as Dir. of Special Serv.; [memb.] Wesley players in college snow queen - KSY chairman of "Pork-barrel" of my dormitory - KSY; [hon.] Received citizenship awards, honor roll, 3rd place in county-wide speech contest in Ohio "Joan of Lorraine" receiving award at duvall home "For going that extra mile"; [oth. writ.] I used to write all my own plays, poems for programs we performed for the public duvall home choir. I used to do all the art work as well; [pers.] Though, born of deaf though poor, we were rich in love God has been good to me, gave me 3 beautiful children, one of whom God "loaned" me for 14 yrs, my son "Scotty Danchuk" born with cyto-megallic inclusion disease due to the Rubella Virus. He was my inspiration - He was beautiful despite his afflictions; [a.] Brooksville, FL

GOULD, EBONY
[b.] December 29, 1982, Newark, NJ; [p.] Lutrecia Gould, Walter Brown; [ed.] St. Bridgets, Harriet Tubman, Academy of St. Benedicts and the Chad School; [hon.] Athletic Award, School Safety Award, Merit, Participation, Academic Achievement, Attendance, Science Club, Cooking class, Citizenship, Charm Club, Honor Roll, Student Council, Pre-school Diploma, and 4th grade diploma.; [oth. writ.] I did other writings, but never published them before.; [pers.] I have been influenced by Maya Angelou and my best friend. I'm happy that my poem is being published because when I grow up and have children I can tell them that had my first poem published in 7th grade.; [a.] Newark, NJ

GRAEBER, DAVID
[pen.] D. Dean Graeber; [b.] July 17, 1963, Cheyenne; [p.] Daisy June and Robert "Bob" Graeber; [ch.] Chelsea Lyn Graeber; [ed.] East High School, Laramie County Community College; [occ.] Laboratory Tech., WYO DOT; [hon.] National DECA Champion (Petroleum Engineering); [oth. writ.] Many poems and prose one short novel (the journey); [pers.] Most of my writings have been inspired by an extremely ugly divorce however through deep insight into yourself things do workout. My 7 year old daughter has been an extremely important person in my life; [a.] Cheyenne, WY

GRAMOLINI, DANTE
[pen.] Dan; [b.] January 28, 1924, Brighton, MA; [p.] Deceased; [ed.] Graduate from Evening Classes High School; [hon.] Received two "Editor's Choice Award" Certificates out of four poems submitted to "The National Library of Poetry"; [oth. writ.] At the present time I am writing on a book titled "Humor is contagious lets start an Epidemic." From remembering humorous jokes I've heard throughout my lifetime; [pers.] Don't try to push destiny it's been pushing us around all our lives. "Try" and endure with patience (My Own Original Statement); [a.] Billerica, MA

GRANHOLM, RICHARD ALFRED
[b.] July 5, 1940, Bronx, NY; [p.] Henry and Catherine Granholm; [ed.] Jamaica High School Marine Corp. GED, Beaufort SC; [occ.] Retired Postal Worker; [pers.] Live and let live; [a.] Jamaica, NY

GRANSBERRY, SHEENA CAREY
[pen.] Sheena Carey Gransberry; [b.] August 1, 1956, Montclair, NJ; [p.] Ruby Patterson Carey, Norman Dugger; [m.] Everett Gransberry, January 1, 1993; [ch.] Kami Jamila Carey Mahdi Atif Gransberry; [ed.] McKinley Technical H.S. Marquette University (BA in Journalism, MA in Speech Communication); [occ.] Communication Consultant, Freelance Writer, Adjunct Professor; [pers.] I can confidently and with pride say when asked what I do for a lining that I am a writer. When asked what it is that defines me, completes me, I say with quiet assurance that it is my writing that makes me who I am.; [a.] Milwaukee, WI

GRANT, CARNELL
[pen.] Connie; [b.] July 17, 1928, Aberdeen, MS; [p.] Pirt Lee and Elizabeth McClendon; [m.] Lloyd Grant, August 9, 1952; [ch.] Lenise Norris, Marilyn Hudson, Elise Taylor, Lloyd Grant Jr, Phil Grant, Sabrina Grant, Darlene Grant and Linda Grant; [ed.] High School; [occ.] Retired (Self-employed dry Cleaner); [memb.] New Covenant Missionary Baptist Church, Lavarnway Boys and Girls Club, Church women unity of Milwaukee, Juneau fidelity Temple #247, Illinois, Wisconsin State Association, and Elco's Bowling League.; [hon.] 1988 Distinguish service award, 1989 Volunteer service Bronze award by the Boys and girls club, 1990 service award Juneau fidelity Temple, (Sect.) of the Year Award from Badger Council and 1989 the Jefferson Award.; [oth. writ.] None that has been published.; [pers.] I enjoy writing poems, doing volunteering service at schools, volunteer service for the boys club, visit the sick and shut in members of my church, and I enjoy reading poems.; [a.] Milwaukee, MI

GRAY, STEPHANIE COLLETTE RHEA
[pen.] Collette Rhea Gray; [b.] July 21, 1958, Cininnati, OH; [p.] Ulysses and Bennie Rhea; [m.] Glenn A. Gray Sr., July 28, 1979; [ch.] Shalonda Renee Gray (15) Glenn A. Gray Jr. (13); [ed.] Graduated Woodward High Cincinnati, OH 1776 Graduated in 1978 Jefferson Tech College Degree in Law Enforcement, Attended Univ. of Steubenville, studied early childhood Development and Psychology classes; [occ.] Self employed homemaker, Poet and write poetry for all occasions for others; [memb.] Petra Ministries (Pitts., PA), singing group, (Christian Journey); [hon.] Dean's List, Citizenship Awards, Black ensemble, Black theater; [oth. writ.] The poem "The Pied Piper". Time, ma-te-al things. I have taken things that I feel I have felt from my life and put them into poetry that's all I know; [pers.] "Life is very difficult with the struggles of this race, but give it to God and seek only after this face; [a.] Wenton, VA

GRAY, RAQUEL
[pen.] Jerry Gray; [b.] October 17, 1971, Salt Lake City, UT; [p.] Jerry Gray, Gayle Gray; [m.] Ray Alba, October 1, 1994; [ed.] Tracy High, Delta College; [occ.] Realtor Associate; [memb.] American Heart Association, American Diabetes Association; [hon.] Delta Honor Society; [oth. writ.] Several unpublished poems and short stories.; [pers.] My true inspiration is my father, poetry is a love we share. He taught me to write about life the way we live it.; [a.] Tracy, CA

GREEGOR, DIANA LYNN
[pen.] Susy Greegor; [b.] October 15, 1952, Shreve; [p.] Mr. Newton Greegor, Mrs. Edna Steele; [ch.] 1 boy or son; [ed.] Chester Elem., Smithville Jr High, Ohriville High School; [occ.] Cleaner or Janitorial Serve; [oth. writ.] Song and poem, and Recipes Award; [pers.] I started writing poems and songs in the second grade in Chester Twp.; [a.] Wooster, OH

GREEN, MS. DOREEN CHARLOTTE
[pen.] Reenie; [b.] June 9, 1956, Fort Leavenworth, KS; [p.] Christine C. Bolton; [m.] Divorced; [ch.] Anthony L. Green (18), Christopher S. Green (13); [ed.] High School: Morrison Academy in Taichung, Taiwan, Franklin University College, Columbus, OH; [occ.] U.S. Government Contract Specialist; [memb.] Hospice Foundation for the Terminally Ill, National Contract Management Association; [hon.] NCMA Scholarships (2), Sustained Superior Performance Awards, Gov't. Suggestion Awards, Dean's List.; [oth. writ.] Article for the Columbus Dispatch, Several articles published in various magazines; [pers.] I am constantly inspired through my poetry and writings by the victorian aspect of romance.; [a.] Reynoldsburg, OH

GREEN, JOY
[pen.] Joy Pursifull Green; [b.] October 20, 1931, Tampa, FL; [p.] Dorothy and William W. Efird; [m.] Twice Widowed, April 6, 1950 and December 10, 1966; [ch.] (Grown) Michael and Kimball, Pursifull - Melissa Green Akerman (three grandchildren); [ed.] No formal education, graduate of St. Petersburg High School and some Art and Modeling Schools; [occ.] Health Care State, Agency - Mentally and Physically Disabled Adults - employed 8 yrs; [oth. writ.] Numerous lifetime collection of unpublished poems and manuscripts. Most, quite lengthy; [pers.] I'm probably what could be called "A closet writer." Since everything I write is secretly written and withheld. My writings come in an uncontrollable, compulsive force without plan, form, study or direction. Almost as if it's "a purge of my inner self." Whatever inspiration I have, seems to come from life experiences, humor, fantasy and reflections.; [a.] Saint Petersburg, FL

GREEN, RENAYE VANESSA
[b.] May 9, 1968, Leadville, CO; [p.] Rudy and Annabelle Mascarenas; [m.] James Buck Green, May 21, 1994; [ch.] Jorel Donae Green, Adrienne Aleris Green; [ed.] Penaso High, Northern New Mexico Community College; [pers.] If everyone would perceive all and everything around them, they would observe as I do that you can't escape poetry, we live it every day, it's in the beauty of life itself.; [a.] Leadville, CO

GREEN, SHERRY LYNN
[b.] January 23, 1978, Georgetown, OH; [p.] Brenda Green, James Green; [ed.] 10th grade; [oth. writ.] Other poem's; [pers.] I try to reflect the grief of my grandfather who died a week before thanksgiving day in this particular poem; [a.] Ripley, OH

GREEN, CYNTHIA ANN
[pen.] Justice Ward; [b.] June 13, 1970, Houston TX; [p.] Betty J. Edwards and Colonel Catholice Green; [ed.] S.P Waltrip Senior High School Houston Community College; [occ.] Medical Record Analyst At Martin Luther King Clinic (The Harris County Hospital) District; [memb.] Txhima, Ahima; [hon.] Houston Community College - Dean's List and Honor Roll; [pers.] There are many obstacles in life. The greatest is the fear within us all the searches for an inspirational light.; [a.] Houston, TX

GREEN, BERNARD A.
[b.] January 2, 1938, New York City; [p.] Jacob Green, Sadie Green; [m.] Mary K. Green, April 25, 1975; [ch.] Jacob, Katherine; [ed.] B.S., CC NY, Ph. D, Univ of Michigan; [occ.] Psychologist; [memb.] Michigan Psychol Assn., American Psychol Assn., M.S.P.P.; [hon.] Amer. Board of Prof. Psychol., Phi Beta Cappa; [oth. writ.] Innumerable poems, many short stories; [pers.] I like to explore the infinity of the moment; [a.] Southfield, MI

GREENAWALD, BONNIE
[m.] Thomas Greenawald, May 18, 1990; [ch.] Deborah, David, Laura and Scott; [occ.] Corporate Loan Administrator; [pers.] My writing is a reflection of the extreme love that I share with my husband, my four children and my faith in God.

GREENAWAY, ELVA JEAN
[pen.] Elva Jean King; [b.] March 15, 1925, Pennsylvania; [p.] Allen and Oneta King; [ch.] Allen Fleming, Linda Fleming, Minnie Pearce; [ed.] Commodore High Penna Green Twp.; [occ.] Retired from Spaulding Fibre; [memb.] Past Matron Eastern Star American Legion Am Vets Charter Member Church of Nazarene at Lookport New York, Member of IAM-AFOLCIO past union steward; [hon.] Miss Senior Citizen of NW Fla. 1985 Walton County; [oth. writ.] I have published several poems in my union paper the Fibre Sheet also treasured poems of American Fall 95 have also submitted to Rural New York and Pennsylvania Grit Magazine; [pers.] My poems are written by divine inspiration coming to me at most unusual times I strive always to be an uplifting influence to those who read my work. Hoping always to trust God.; [a.] DeFuniak Springs, FL

GREENBERG, ARI
[b.] September 25, 1973, Washington, DC; [p.] Harrey and Ellie Greenberg; [ed.] Now in senior year at the University of Denver. I am graduating in June, 1995 with a B.A. in psychology and teaching license; [occ.] Student teaching elementary school for a teaching position next year; [memb.] Psi Chi, Community Action Program (CAP), student Environmental Action Coalition (SEAC); [hon.] Honors scholarship, Dean's List, Graduation from high school in top 10; [oth. writ.] Articles for the Clarion (DU), many unpublished poems; [pers.] My poetry is an outlet to express the issues facing "generation X" and hope for a better tomorrow.; [a.] Denver, CO

GREENE, LEWIS D.
[b.] September 30, 1933, Cambridge, MA; [p.] Darcy Greene, Marjorie Greene; [m.] Frances Greene, April

1976; [ch.] Lisa Maria, Laura Anne, Lynne Ellen; [ed.] Rindge Tech High NYCC College; [occ.] Medical Technologist (Ret.); [hon.] Two Community Awards by Police Dept.; [oth. writ.] Penalty death, in the morning, little girls, little boys, fly, what you didn't see, (unpublished)

GREENE, TONIA
[b.] March 10, 1959, Kingstree, SC; [p.] Ellis Fulton, Rhodelle Fulton; [m.] John M. Greene, separated, January 5, 1981; [ch.] Kiera Laron; [ed.] Chicora High, University of South Carolina Webster University, St. Louis Missouri; [occ.] Jr. High School Counselor; [memb.] North Carolina Education Association Dollar for Scholars Board, Licensed Associate Counselor, SC; [hon.] National Dean's List; [oth. writ.] Poetry performed at the dock street theater, poetry read in the park in Charleston, SC; [pers.] I am an inspired writer who receives inspiration from viewing the meaning of life, love and oneness with the universe. I believe in listening to the voice of nature (GOD), relating my interpretation to uplift: Offer hope and faith!; [a.] Gastonia, NC

GREENE, WALT
[pen.] Walt Greene; [b.] July 8, 1923, Kiowa, CO; [p.] William Green, Beatrice Green; [m.] Ethyl M. Green, November 20, 1948; [ch.] Shari Yvonne, Bradley Colin; [ed.] Kiowa High, B.A. CO. College, M.A. Denver Univ., 103 Graduate hours beyond masters.; [occ.] Retired from teaching Denver Public Schools; [memb.] Life member retired officers Assoc., Educational Organizations; [hon.] 4-H Leadership Awards; [oth. writ.] Two copy writed WWII songs, winning article Denver Post, personnel collection of stories and poems.; [pers.] I try to reflect in words the emotions displayed as I see them in people and in nature.; [a.] Indian Hills, CO

GREGG, KENNARD DARYL JOHN
[pen.] Kennard D. Gregg; [b.] January 7, 1955, Philadelphia, PA; [p.] Simon and Sarah Gregg; [ed.] Overbrook High Shormaker Jr High in Philadelphia, PA; [occ.] Vendor; [hon.] I think it was my going into the army or playing baseball for my school or be able to write poem; [oth. writ.] I took some time, dreams, just enough to make it, I called you this morning you just want it because you see it, and I sat and wrote; [pers.] I hope to be able to write a book or finish the one I have I am now living in Atlantic City; [a.] Atlantic City, NJ

GREGORY, LINDA
[b.] April 3, 1959, Baltimore; [p.] Eva Jane Brooks; [ch.] Tiffany Nicole, Megan Renee; [pers.] I wrote this poem, for my mother, as a Mother's Day gift in 1979. This was my way of expressing my love and thanks to her for being such a wonderful mother.; [a.] Baltimore, MD

GRIECO, ELIZABETH
[pen.] Elizabeth Fontaine-Grieco; [b.] August 14, 1957, Montreal; [p.] John and Denise Fontaine; [m.] John A. Grieco, August 21, 1976; [ch.] John, Michelle, Rose-Marie, Francis, Richard, Elizabeth; [ed.] High School, College majored in Humanities; [occ.] Mother, homemaker writer and artist; [hon.] From Kiwanis club; [oth. writ.] Essay on the hazards of drugs and its effects on young children of today.; [pers.] Writing for me is one of the sincerest forms of self-expression. It keeps us in touch with ourselves and our surroundings.; [a.] Saylorsburg, PA

GRIFFIN, DENIECE
[pen.] Baby D-C; [b.] August 27, 1966, Seattle, WA; [p.] James Rashid and Lee Kinzy; [m.] Charles Griffin, July 4, 1987; [ed.] Renton High, National Broadcasting and Telecommunication School, (grad) Apartment Management School Grad; [occ.] Property Managers and Park Ranger Mt. Rainer; [memb.] Worthy Matron O.E.S. American Lupus Foundation. Temple Kung-fu Apartment Manager's Congress. A group I formed in City of Des Moines; [hon.] Expert Grenaduer, Expert

Marksman, U.S. Army.; [oth. writ.] Winds Of Time, Friends Programmed for Love, The Sun, That's the Way of the world. I am Black.; [pers.] I hope to bring out the love of one for all. My influences are the many words of music I love of a lifetime.; [a.] Kent, WA

GRIFFIN, PATRICIA
[b.] December 18, 1934, Philadelphia; [p.] Joseph and Regina O'Mara; [m.] Edward Griffin, October 10, 1959; [ch.] Regina Griffin-Kelly and Patricia Griffin, 1 grandchild: Brighid Griffin Kelly; [ed.] John W. Hallahan Catholic High School for Girls Graduated 1953; [occ.] Waitress in the Officer's Dining Room of the Federal Reserve Bank; [pers.] Throughout my life, I have found it much easier to express myself through the written word rather than the spoken word. In my writing, I try to paint a picture of the feelings in my heart.; [a.] Philadelphia, PA

GRIFFITH, KATHY E.
[b.] March 6, 1952, Oakland, CA; [p.] Elmer and Beeky George; [m.] Michael Griffith, August 29, 1981; [ch.] Melissa; [ed.] High School Business College; [occ.] Housewife; [hon.] In high school I did a lot of creative story, writing; [oth. writ.] I just recently wrote a children's book called My friend Eddie it's about our family cat, that we have owned for 11 years. Carlton Press in New York are going to publish this book; [pers.] I love to write I can be very creative with my poems and story writing. My favorite author is Danielle Steele.; [a.] El Dorado, CA

GRIFFITHS, SHANE ERIC
[pen.] Eric Shane; [b.] December 27, 1959, Orlando, FL; [p.] Dr. William Shane Griffiths and Connie Griffiths; [ed.] Colonial High Valencia Community College Rollins College; [pers.] God grooms me in my impatience; [a.] Orlando, FL

GRIMES, ULYSSES
[b.] August, 18, 1941, Alcua County, FL; [p.] Angie Grimes and William Grimes; [m.] Divorced; [ch.] Rosetta A. Grimes, Jason T. Shannon S. Marcus Jonathan; [ed.] Graduate Camden High School 1960; [memb.] Thomas H. Kean NJ State Aquarium TV 12 WHYY; [oth. writ.] Several poems this is first ever submitted for publication.; [a.] Camden, NJ

GRIMM, PAMELA
[pen.] Pam G.; [b.] February 25, 1958, Nashville, TN; [p.] Maurice Grimm, Marjorie Grimm; [ed.] Castlemont High School, Oakland, CA, USC, Los Angeles, CA, College of Alameda, Alameda, CA, Nashville Technical State College, Nashville, TN; [occ.] Student Records Asst, Vanderbilt University, Nashville, TN; [memb.] Metropolitan Interdenominational Church, Volunteer in AIDS Vaccine study at Vanderbilt University, Nashville, TN Member 12-step Program (I have been drug-free for a little over 2 yrs.); [hon.] California State Scholarship, National Honor Society, Who's Who Among Junior College students; [oth. writ.] Small piece published in "The Vac Scene" Newsletter (newsletter of AIDS Vaccine Unit), Nashville, TN; [pers.] My primary objective, by writing about my real-life feelings and experiences, is to in some way touch the hearts of those who have had similar feelings and experiences. I am inspired by life itself. I would like to one day, open a halfway house for women with nowhere to go; [a.] Nashville, TN

GRIMM, CLARYCE CASEY
[pen.] Claryce Casey Grimm; [b.] May 15, 1925, Stockton, KS; [p.] Harold V. and Irma Lyon-Casey; [m.] Melvin F. Grimm (deceased), April 19, 1945; [ch.] Gloria Beth, Kenneth, Scott, Melinda and Alan; [ed.] Washburn High, Topeka, KS/Washburn Univ., Topeka, KS/Spokane Falls Comm. College, Spokane, WA; [occ.] Retired - (gallery owner and picture framer - writer); [memb.] CAAA, Spokane, WA/Poetry Scribes (past pres), Spokane, WA Zeta Tau Alpha (Washburn

Univ) PPFA, OES #274; [hon.] Lilac Poet-city of Spokane - 1975 Poet of month - Spokesman - Review, Spokane, WA 4 times; [oth. writ.] Turquoise Lanterns (anthology of Poetry Scribes) Spokesman - Review, Spokane, WA; [pers.] "It isn't your face they'll remember no - likely not even your name - but small deeds of kindness and love left behind will reward you for better than fame!"; [a.] Spokane, WA

GROVES, HEIDEROSE
[pen.] H. R. Groves; [b.] September 13, 1945, Germany; [p.] Marianne Ott; [ch.] Lisa Katherine, Rober Marion, John Adrian; [ed.] Kensington High School; [occ.] Human Services; [pers.] I wish that I could write a poem for peace, so profound that all people would stop briefly to drink in the words and know the destruction we are headed for.; [a.] Philadelphia, PA

GUERRA, ADRIANNE J.
[b.] February 5, 1982, Miami, FL; [p.] Armando Guerra and Maria C. Guerra; [ed.] Currently enrolled at Carrollton, school of the Sacred Heart in Coconut grove, Fl; [a.] Miami, FL

GUISEPPE, NICHOLE RENE
[pen.] Nikki Guiseppe; [b.] August 07, 1979, PA; [p.] Steve and Lanita Guiseppe; [m.] Single; [ed.] Scott Intermediate High School. Also Center for Arts and Technology for Culinary Arts.; [occ.] School Student, Veterinarian's Helper.; [hon.] Good citizenship award's were given to me in: 1987, 1988, 1989, 1990.; [oth. writ.] Several poems not submitted at present time.; [pers.] Creating poetry is my most favorite positive someday, I feel my lyrics will be put to music.; [a.] Coatesville, PA

GUNDERSON, WALLACE JOHN
[pen.] Wallace John Gunderson; [b.] December 8, 1932, Oklee, MN; [p.] Gunny and Alice; [m.] Patricia, April 26, 1991; [ch.] Scott, Lon, Lisa, Kelly, Shon, Robert; [ed.] H.S. College; [occ.] Unemployed because of my age no one will hire me (retired) on S.S.; [hon.] Several in public broadcast of sales; [oth. writ.] Currently writing a novel entitled "Love me forever"; [pers.] I was recently diagnosed with adenocarcinoma cancer at the V.A. Hosp. My life span is approx 1 yr with this part of life left - my wife and I are moving to old Mexico, so I can finish my novel before my life's over.; [a.] Wichita, KS

GURNEY, GEORGE ROBERT
[pen.] George Gurney; [b.] October 23, 1933, Seneca, KS; [p.] Datha Alice and Charles Marion Gurney Sr.; [m.] Shirley Joyce Gurney, June 21, 1953; [ed.] 12th Grade National School of Aeronautics Numerous Training Classes by "TWA"; [occ.] "TWA" medically retired; [memb.] Immanuel Lutheran Church Faternal Communicator at Church Cancer Support Group "Make Today Count" International Society of Poets; [hon.] Numerous Awards by Employer Cancer Bike-A-Thon two years three Editor's Choice Awards from National Poets Society Semifinalist awards at International Society of Poets 1994; [oth. writ.] Numerous poems in local newspaper, Many poems for "Cancer Support Group" and friends. Poem published in Hospice Shareletter. (hospital news letter) Copyright on book of poems ("Thought Of A Daydreamer").; [pers.] Motto "Expect A Miracle - Miracle Do Happen"; [a.] Wentzville, MO

GUTWIN, SHARON
[b.] April 10, 1957; [p.] Bill and Jean Barlow; [m.] Paul; [ch.] Karl, Rebecca, Anna; [occ.] Physical Therapy; [pers.] My friend - Bruce; [a.] Williston, VT

HAAS, JUDITH ANN
[b.] January 27, 1949, New Rockford, ND; [p.] Norman and Audrey Braaten; [m.] Duane Haas, October 7, 1988; [ed.] B.S. Elementary Education and English Taught School 17 years; [occ.] Housewife; [memb.] North Dakota Education Association, Democratic Party,

Catholic Liturgy Group and reader in church; [hon.] Honor student in High School; [oth. writ.] Wrote stories and poetry as a child as a pastime.; [pers.] I enjoy writing about the wonders in the world the seasons and concrete and abstract wonders; [a.] St. John, ND

HAGEN, KENNETH J.
[b.] December 7, 1964, AL; [p.] Duane and Lucille Hagen; [m.] Divorced; [ch.] Elizabeth Sarah Hagen; [ed.] Daleville High School, Aviation College, George C Wallace College, Auburn; [occ.] Supervisor, Industrial maintenance; [oth. writ.] Many personal writings none published.; [pers.] I am a weekend father now. I pay child support. I will always love my daughter Elizabeth with all of my heart.; [a.] Daleville, AL

HAGOOD, REBECCA
[pen.] Rebecca Mallicoat; [b.] April 1, 1971, Bristol, PA; [p.] Ralph Mallicoat and Barbara Mallicoat; [m.] Scott Hagood, February 11, 1995; [ch.] Tyler Alexander Scott, Tiara Nicole Hunter; [ed.] Fulton High School Diploma; [occ.] Homemaker; [memb.] Hoitt Ave. Baptist Church; [hon.] National Vocational Honor Society in High School. Deca Pres. in High School.; [oth. writ.] many other writings none have ever been submitted for publication until now.; [pers.] I write what I see and feel and how it effects myself and others.; [a.] Knoxville, TN

HAHN, HEATHER ANN
[b.] November 13, 1978, Fond du lac, WI; [p.] Ronald and Debra Stahman, Donald and Peggy Hahn; [ed.] Holy Rosary, New Holstein Elementary School, New Holstein High School; [oth. writ.] A poem published in River of Dreams; [pers.] I enjoy writing about the sadness and happiness of life ... love and death.; [a.] New Holstein, WI

HAILE, LILLIAN Y.
[b.] November 24, 1933, Alachua, FL; [p.] Rev. and Mrs. George Haile (both deceased); [ed.] College Degree - Elem. Ed., Special Ed., High School, Physical Education, Fiction Writing, Nursing, Police Science, (some Spanish); [memb.] County and State Teachers Unions, Federal Employee Unions, International Association of Investigators and Special Police Organization, Alpha Kappa Alpha Sorority; [hon.] Miss S.C.T., Miss Florida Normal College, Alternative Services - Employee of the Year - working with special children. Plaques and trophies in the field of publishing.; [oth. writ.] Articles in the Orlando Sentinel (FL), College Newspapers, Southern Dawn Publishing Company - Articles and Poetry, accepted submission to Exposition Press.; [pers.] In my writings, I strive to present the facts but remembering reality. I use humor to smooth the sadness. Presently, I am working on a book, "Living Beyond Poverty." The material is from my real life experiences.

HAKY, HELEN E.
[pen.] Mary George; [b.] February 8, 1928, Bradenville, PA; [p.] John and Susan Haky; [ed.] Jane Addams Vocational High, St. John College, Cleveland Ohio, Ursuline College, Cleveland, University of Illinois, Kent State University; [occ.] Retired Teacher (after 41 years); [pers.] All through my years of teaching on the elementary, secondary and college levels I felt that what student looked for most in a teacher was kindness, patience and justice. Hopefully, these characteristics which I tried to exemplify to them are still a part of my life as a semi-retired Ursuline.; [a.] Pepper Pike, OH

HALEY, GREGORY JACKSON
[pen.] Greg Haley; [b.] September 15, 1973, Dallas, TX; [p.] Margie Jackson Haley and John Marshall Haley, Md; [ed.] The Episcopal School of Dallas, Southern Methodist University; [occ.] Student Adventurer; [memb.] Eagle Assn., Boy Scouts of American Texas Rugby Union; [hon.] Few intellectual honors so far, but numerous athletic recognitions and awards; [oth. writ.] Poetry published in school and Dallas Area newspa-

pers; [pers.] I enjoy challenges of all kings — intellectual as well as athletic. Working hard and playing hard is fun and keeps life interesting.; [a.] Dallas, TX

HALK, PATRICIA A.
[b.] April 30, 1944, New York; [p.] Frank Deco and Rose Lyons; [m.] Charles, July 20, 1968; [ch.] Christine Anne, Stephen Charles; [ed.] Santa Monica H.S. (Calif) College of Staten Island for Paralegal certificate; [occ.] Paralegal and Legal Assistant; [oth. writ.] None published - any poems I have written were just for my own personal satisfaction.; [pers.] My poems reflect how I feel at the time they are written.; [a.] Staten Island, NY

HALL, TANSY KAY
[b.] June 30, 1983, New Albany, MS; [p.] Joseph Luther Hall and Tracy Knox Golden; [ed.] Pre-school Blue Mountain College, Mattie Thompson Elementary School, BF Ford Elementary School, New Albany Middle School; [occ.] Student 6th grade, New Albany Middle School; [memb.] Girl Scouts of America, Tae Kwon-Do Club, New Albany Middle School Band; [hon.] National Honor Student; [oth. writ.] I wrote a poem titled "I Wonder Why" when I was in the fourth (4) grade.; [pers.] I base my writings on what I think about every day.; [a.] Blue Mountain, MS

HALL, KEITH T.
[b.] April 29, 1966, Honolulu, HI; [p.] Robert and Berna Hall; [pers.] Lapidary? Of course not. Patience.

HALL, CINDI
[b.] September 14, 1955, Detroit, MI; [p.] Ted and Helen Anderson; [m.] Steve Hall, November 24, 1980; [ch.] Daughter - "Courtney Amber", Sons - "Jordan Randall" and "Branden Kyle"; [ed.] High School Diploma; [occ.] House Goddess; [oth. writ.] Several stories published in local newspapers... poem published in an anthology of poems through the Mile High Poetry Society; [pers.] My poetry reflects what I feel in the depths of my soul; [a.] Show Low, AZ

HALSNE, GRANT L.
[b.] August 10, 1937, Webster City, IA; [m.] Janice, 1963; [ch.] Three; [ed.] B.S. Iowa State University 1961; [occ.] Telecommunications Sales Representative; [memb.] Luren Singers - A Norwegian based Chorus of 60 men here in Decorah, IA, Museum Guide - Vesterheim Museum, (a Norwegian folk museum in Decorah); [hon.] All big 8 Baseball played Professional 2 years, Cincinnati Reds Farm System; [oth. writ.] Lyrical of Iowa Asso. Trapeze Magazine (a quarterly publ), have been writing poems for just 2 years; [pers.] The poems I write have been based on fact or personal experience. I try to tell a story. Previously, most poems I have written have been about the game of baseball, from Little League to Major Leagues; [a.] Decorah, IA

HAMILTON, DAVID M.
[pen.] Story Teller; [b.] October 2, 1970, Indianapolis, IN; [p.] Stephen and Barbara Hamilton; [ed.] University of Missouri - Rolla; [memb.] Proud alumnus of the Alpha Lota Chapter of Sigma Pi Fraternity. "The Greatest Fraternity of all time."; [oth. writ.] Currently unpublished novel.; [pers.] Nothing in life is impossible, its just not possible the way you're trying to do it.; [a.] Ypsilanti, MI

HAMPTON, SHAWN A.
[pen.] Alan Hampton; [b.] November 11, 1975, Lincoln, NE; [p.] Sandy and Greg Anderson; [ed.] Southeast High School Lincoln, NE; [occ.] Night stocker, waiter/dishwasher; [memb.] The International Thespian Society, Stephen King Library; [hon.] International Thespian Society, Drama letter, Best Technician 1993-1994 High School drama, etc...; [oth. writ.] Surrender to Truth: Published in Darsive of the Moon - The Nat'l. Library of Poetry/About A Girl: Published in The Best of 1995 - The Nat'l. Library of Poetry, and a

writing book of mine that keeps getting thicker!!; [pers.] To scare, or torment, other people, I only wish to make you feel, laugh, cry, and say what truth is in your Heart!!; [a.] Lincoln, NE

HAMPTON, RUTH LUCILE
[pen.] Lucy Hampton; [b.] February 7, 1955, Denver, CO; [p.] J. E. Kemper, Velda Kemper; [m.] Divorced; [ch.] Stephanie F. Hampton; [ed.] Pratt High School May '73 some early college training including certification as Nurse Aide; [occ.] Self employed thru STRUCCO; [memb.] The family of God - The First Assembly of God Church, Pratt, KS, 1 of 6 children in loving Christian Family; [hon.] Record for sales of Rainbow Rexair Carpet Cleavers - 3 state are 1982.; [oth. writ.] Since September 26, 1994 to date the Holly Spirit has given me over 80 songs (lyrics and melody) and an additional 8 or 9 poems too. As yet unpublished I've been known to receive as many as 5 in one 24 hour period. Recipe - "Life of Pleasure"; [pers.] I strive to all ways let the Sonshine thru the window of my life that all may see the light! This is my business motto. Business name STRUCCO (Stephanie, Ruth, Christ and Co.) daughter, self, Saviour and Lord, friends; [a.] Pratt, KS

HANDY, DARLENE GIRROIR
[b.] June 30, 1953, Westfield, MA; [p.] Russell and Marlene Handy; [m.] Michael Girroir, December 23, 1983; [ch.] Richard, Randy, Rusti-Lin, and Raymond; [ed.] Suffield High School, Morse Business College; [occ.] Photographer, Fine Focus Photography, Owner; [oth. writ.] Short articles for local newspapers; [pers.] I've always wanted to leave behind something permanent on this earth, a true part of me, in my writing you will find me forever, here. Greatly influenced by my children and their live's.; [a.] Southwick, MA

HANKINS, THOMAS V.
[b.] May 19, 1912, Veedersburg, IN; [p.] Thomas E. and Lury L. Hankins; [m.] Doris Hankins (deceased); [ch.] Sharon K. Driscol, Nancy E. Craft, David H. Little; [ed.] 8th grade graduate Raab Elementary School; [occ.] Coal miner, retired operating engineer; [memb.] Masonic order, Eastern Star, IUOE local 841; [hon.] Past Master Masonic Lodge AF and M, 60 years loyal custom celebration day; [pers.] This poem was written about the day named in my honor for having been a loyal customer of the Veedersburg State Bank for 60 years.; [a.] Veedersburg, IN

HANSON, DAISY PINKERTON
[b.] February 20, 1914,; [p.] Robert and Clara Pinkerton; [m.] James Edward Hanson; [ch.] Jerry Wayne - Deceased, Nita Mae, and Mary Jo; [ed.] High School graduate - Booker, Texas, Lippert's Bus. College Grad. - Plainview, Texas.; [occ.] Homemaker, grandma and great grandma; [memb.] Plainview first church of the Nazarene, Pink Lady Volunteer for Methodist Hospital Plainview; [oth. writ.] Poems for many occasions all my life including, dedication of mountain cabin, anniversaries, birthdays, story type poems,; [a.] Plainview, TX

HARBIN III, JAMES L.
[pen.] Van Drake; [b.] April 26, 1971, Greenville, SC; [p.] Jean B. Harbin, James L. Harbin Jr.; [ed.] Faith Christian High; [occ.] Electronic Technician, Fruit of the Loom; [memb.] United State Navy 90-93.; [oth. writ.] Various unpublished works; [pers.] I believe it best to experience everything in life. Good as well as bad. That way choices are made by experience not ignorance. That is the true nature of wisdom. I try to reflect this experience in my work.; [a.] Whitmire, SC

HARDEN, DIXIE
[b.] June 10, 1957, Marengo, IA; [p.] Calvin and Beverly Davis; [m.] Jack Harden Jr., November 28, 1974; [ch.] Shawn Michael Harden; [pers.] Adopted children should never feel that they were unloved. A lost child is not a forgotten child, they remain a part of your life forever,

whether or not you're ever to meet again. We did meet my husband's daughter, once she was grown and it meant more than words could ever express. [a.] Ladora, IA.

HARDEN, FRANK
[b.] October 9, 1936, Macon, GA; [p.] Oscar and Marie Lee Harden; [m.] Karen Harden; [ed.] BA - History, MA - Education, Inter-American University of Puerto Rico; [occ.] Retired; [hon.] Magna Cum Laude, Distinguished Flying Cross, Air Force Commendation Medal, Air Medal; [oth. writ.] Dire Necessity: A short story; [pers.] Poet of greatest influence: Edgar Allan Poe; [a.] Luray, VA

HARDY, M. MICHELE
[b.] August 6, 1967, La Plata, MD; [p.] Don and Elizabeth Hardy; [ed.] La Plata High School, University of MD - Theatre 2nd English John Hopkins - creative writing; [occ.] Bartender; [hon.] Numerous acting awards Dean's List; [pers.] To capture a moment, feeling, or experience and be completely honest is the poet's greatest challenge, I also strive to take the English language and "make it new."; [a.] Laurel, MD

HARE, CHAR M.
[pen.] Char Hare; [b.] July 15, 1948, Shelbyville IN; [p.] Dorothy (Marks), James Hare; [m.] Divorced, February 20, 1967; [ch.] Candace Michelle Kohler, Gregory Alan Hare; [ed.] Howe High School Indpls, IN; [memb.] Jennings Co Genealogy Society - Iteration of Poets Society, Lifetime member - Indiana Genealogy Society - Eagles Club; [hon.] Editors Choice Award (ISP) Agoraphobia (published journey of the minds); [oth. writ.] Snyder Cemetery (1993) Snyder Cemetery Indexed 1993 Story of my life (1989) Happiness Through the Tears (1995); [pers.] My poetry writing has been my voice for most of my Life. I could say on paper feelings I could never share with anyone verbally. My poems are my inspiration therapy for Life.; [a.] Greenwood, IN

HARLESS, LANDON C.
[b.] June 24, 1971, Bristol, TN; [p.] Gene and Ruth Harless; [ed.] B.A. in English, minor in Business, University of Tennessee.; [occ.] Teleservices representative, Whirlpool Corporation.; [memb.] Metropolitan Community Church; [hon.] Estes Kefarer Scholarship recipient, Univ. of Tennessee Alumni Scholarship recipient; [pers.] I write mostly about the moments in life that reveal something about relationships people have with the universe, the environment, and each other.; [a.] Knoxville, TN

HARPER, VERBIE J.
[pen.] Verbie J. Harper; [b.] January 19, 1924, Senath, MO; [p.] Lige Norris, Sarah Norris; [m.] Earl W. Harper, July 1, 1978; [ch.] Dwight Goodin, Leslie Goodin, Robert Harper, Sharon Van Orman; [ed.] High School Graduate (Senath High School) 1942; [occ.] (Retired) House-wife; [memb.] Trinity Wesleyan Church; [oth. writ.] (Poems - that were copyrighted - but not published) down home paper, love letters publications - Women's Circle Magazine, Church Publications; [pers.] My poems were written at different seasons of my life. I hope they relay the message of hope and blessings. The humorous ones hopefully will lighten, the hearts - bring joy for those who need a boast.; [a.] Southgate, MI

HARPER, VALERIE
[b.] August 18, 1980, Hoboken, NJ; [p.] Marietta Cutillo, Gerald Harper; [ed.] Huber Street Elementary School, Secaucus High School; [occ.] Student; [memb.] ICC Youth Group Secaucus Sign Language Club, Key Club; [hon.] Honor Roll Student; [oth. writ.] Several poems published in the Secaucus School "Middle Pages"; [pers.] I feel through my writing I have an opportunity to express my views and feelings about life, society and the world in which I live.; [a.] Secaucus, NJ

HARRELL, LINDA B.
[b.] August 6, 1945, Cairo, GA; [p.] R. A. Bynum (deceased), Irene Rich Bynum Exum (deceased); [m.] Deceased, December, 1979; [ch.] Johnny Harrell Jr, Debra Harrell Mixon; [ed.] GED after 10th grade; [occ.] Part time waitress; [oth. writ.] (1). "The Man I Love" (2) "My Little Boy You're like a little Racoon"; [pers.] This poem "Beauty Is" is dedicated to my beautiful daughter Debra Irene Mixon whom was my first pride and joy I love her beyond words.; [a.] Orlando, FL

HARRINGTON, DELORES E.
[pen.] Delores E. Harrington; [b.] August 31, 1929, Cincinnati, OH; [p.] Helen Marr, Harvey Green; [m.] deceased; [ch.] Robert G. Reed Jr. 45 yrs, Joel J. Harrington 22 yrs; [ed.] High School, Business School 1 yr. of College; [occ.] Retired Secretary for Penn State University; [memb.] Covenant Church of Pittsburgh; [oth. writ.] Collection of poetry, short stories and essays titled, "And So She Wrote History....Her Own"; [pers.] When Dee met Jesus Christ, through personal experience in 1978, her whole life changed. She wrote an eight page book describing how the Lord brought her through many life experiences, funny and sad as she raised her youngest son alone without her husband. Now she faces cancer.; [a.] Pittsburgh, PA

HARRIS, COURTNEY
[b.] March 16, 1978; [p.] Robin Smith and Ron Harris; [ed.] High School River Ridge High; [occ.] School; [hon.] Track and Field Awards and Honor Roll; [oth. writ.] Several other poems; [a.] Newport Richey, FL

HARRIS, SHIRLEY ANN
[b.] September 18, 1953, Detroit; [p.] Lillian and Stephen Harris; [ch.] Son Keller A. Saunders 10 yrs old; [occ.] Teacher's Aide; [pers.] When you share the gift God gives you, you plant your seed in the soil of the universe.; [a.] Detroit, MI

HARRIS, CHRISTOPHER M.
[pers.] Wrote this shortly after seeing Tim Burton's Edward Scissorhands.; [a.] Aurora, CO

HARRIS, PAUL EDWARD
[pen.] Paul Edward Harris; [b.] May 4, 1946, New London, CT; [p.] Marion Madalin Sabastian; [m.] Cheryl Adamec; [ch.] Paul Harris IV, Christina Harris; [ed.] Mohegan Community College, West Hartford School of Music, Albano School of Ballet; [occ.] Full-time Student, Artist, Jass Musician.; [memb.] Mashantucket Tribal Member and Mashantucket Pequot Indian. Connecticut Society of Genealogist, American Legion Member Post 200; [hon.] Connecticut Jaycee (Man of The Month 1982), holder of every Jaycee Award during that year. U.S. Navy 1963-1967, Connecticut Health System Agency.; [oth. writ.] New London Day Newspaper (Family History); [pers.] To find balance and harmony in life is my goal.; [a.] New London, CT

HARSON, MARIAN K.
[b.] December 26, 1927, Akron, OH; [p.] Walter and Mary Harson; [ed.] Garfield High School; [occ.] Retired from Goodyear Tire and Rubber Co.; [memb.] Cuyahoga Valley Art Center in Cuyahoga Falls, OH; [hon.] Honorable mention for pastel painting entitled "Monterey Cove" September 7, 1970 (entered in Golden Years Exhibition); [oth. writ.] Several published poems; [pers.] Prayer has been the staff of my life. My belief in Christ has made all my requests a reality.; [a.] Cuyahoga Falls, OH

HART, RENNIE
[pen.] Rennie; [b.] July 24, 1953, Denver, CO; [p.] Merrill Hart, Rita Hart; [ch.] Christopher Ryan Hart; [ed.] Englewood High School, San Diego Evening College, Arapahoe Community College, Metropolitan State College; [occ.] Accident Victim, but am active as volunteer (handicap groups) and Photographer; [memb.] Colorado Head Injury Foundation (CHIF); [hon.] Honorable mention in 4 photography contests; [oth. writ.] Poems published in CHIF newsletter (Had column entitled: Rennie's Room); [pers.] This poem was inspired by an accident I was in that caused a brain injury that changed my life completely. My eyes are open in my new life and I see the world and its inhabitants in a new and significant way.; [a.] Englewood, CO

HART, MARY K.
[pen.] Mary K. Hart; [b.] June 10, 1966, Fort Worth, TX; [p.] C. D. Hart Jr. Roselynn F. Hart; [ed.] BBA - General Business - TCU Masters of Architecture - UT Arlington (in process); [occ.] Student; [memb.] TX Army National Guard - CPT, 249th Signal BN.; [hon.] Superior Cadet, TCU, Certificate of Achievement, SOBC; [pers.] Translating feelings into words, though often inadequate, is a great accomplishment of man. Beautiful articulation of these words is the accomplishment of the poet.; [a.] Fort Worth, TX

HARTMAN, TAM
[b.] March 24, 1966, Harrisburg; [p.] John and Margaret Hartman; [m.] Darren M. Motter, June 24, 1995 (to be); [ed.] B.S. in Therapeutic Recreation from York College of PA; [occ.] Certified Therapeutic Recreation Specialist; [memb.] American Red Cross (Waters Safety Instructor), American Therapeutic Recreation Association, National Council for Therapeutic Recreation Certification; [hon.] 1993 Direct Service Staff, Recognition Award for Dauphin Retardation Program.; [pers.] This poem I submitted is a reflection of my thoughts and emotions on my my dearly beloved brother, Jack, and his unexpected death.; [a.] Harrisburgh, PA

HARTZELL, JOHN
[pen.] John Hartzell; [b.] January 23, 1945, Hardtner, KS; [p.] Freda Hartzell, Kenneth Hartzell; [m.] Never married; [ed.] Medicine Lodge Schools, Pratt Jr College, Southwestern College; [occ.] Service Tech; [memb.] Presbyterian Church AM Legion, VFW, Northern OK Word Smiths, Kansas Author's Club, Kiwanis International; [hon.] Many poems published in books, newspapers, etc. several awards, Kansas award winning poet; [oth. writ.] I've filled one book of my poem's now on second.; [pers.] "Poetry made simple so all may understand"; [a.] Winfield, KS

HATEM, CHRISTOPHER
[b.] December 17, 1974, Methuen, MA; [p.] Robert Hatem, Maureen Hatem; [ed.] Salem High, Keene State College; [pers.] To my grandmother, you will never walk alone. I am influenced most by life, pain, the distant wars and the rain; [a.] Salem, NH

HATTON, LAURA J.
[b.] February 21, 1979, Arlington, TX; [p.] Stephen and Gwynne Hatton; [ed.] I am a Soph. at Mansfield High School.; [occ.] Student; [memb.] National Honor Society, Student Council, TAFE, Youth Choir, and Methodist Youth Group.; [hon.] Language Arts Award, Honors Biology Award, Who's Who In American High School Students, Top ten of class, Honor Roll United States Achievement Academy Award for French language, and all American Scholar.; [a.] Mansfield, TX

HAUKOS, MINDY ALEXIA
[b.] August 7, 1973, Willmar, MN; [p.] Mel and Judy Haukos; [ed.] I graduated from Willmar in 1992; [occ.] Sales; [memb.] Active member in church groups, member of S.A.D.D. and key club in 1992, now an active member with children's clubs.; [hon.] 4th in gymnastic competition, Student of the week award; [oth. writ.] Article published in local newspaper, have written a book of poems and working on a book.; [pers.] Never dwell on mistakes in life, use them as a learning advice for new accomplishments.; [a.] Waite Park, MN

HAUSE, MELODY ROSE
[b.] November 20, 1953, Cleveland, OH; [p.] Frank and Ameila Hula; [m.] Jerry, June 2, 1972; [ch.] Stephanie Marie and Dale Allen; [ed.] Barkwill Elementary, Myron T. Herrick, South High; [pers.] To all of the young men who serve in my neighborhood of Hamm Avenue, Barkwill Avenue, Broadway, Dolloff, E 48 St., E 49 St., of Cleveland, Ohio and to all of the young men who serve in this war.; [a.] Newburgh Heights, OH.

HAWKS, SCOTT
[pen.] Pete; [b.] April 3, 1962, Battle Creek, MI; [p.] Gordon L. Hawks and Nancy C. Hawks; [ed.] B.S. Food Science Michigan State University 1985; [occ.] Research support specialist; [memb.] United States Kali Association, United States Grappling Association; [hon.] Patent 1994 "Making stable foams from where protects", Phi Tau Sigma Honor Society Instructor Martial Arts; [oth. writ.] None other than scientific papers; [pers.] Work had at playing because you will always work hard at work. Bills must be paid. Therefore, enjoy life at all times.; [a.] Ithaca, NY

HAWLEY, ADWELL
[pen.] Sequoyah Saponi; [b.] August 30, 1955, Oxford, NC; [p.] Hubert Hawley, Ada Hawley; [m.] Bachelor; [ed.] Vance Senior High, U.S. School of Music; [occ.] Unemployed; [hon.] Humanitarian Award; [oth. writ.] Real Power, Forgiveness, According to the Bible, unpublished; [pers.] A problem is only a prelude to the solution. Dreams are an echo of the subconscious. Real Power is self-control. Love is essential.; [a.] Henderson, NC

HAYES, DAVID
[b.] May 9, 1963, Saint Joseph, MI; [p.] Beverly, Lawrence; [ed.] Bettendorf High, University of Iowa; [occ.] Engineer; [oth. writ.] To be published book titled: Interpretations of Observation. 100 poems written by same author.; [pers.] Interpretations of observation overwhelm my subconscious; [a.] Phoenix, AZ

HAYES, JULIA R. MARSHALL
[pen.] Julia Rivers M-Hayes; [b.] July 23, 1943, South Ca.; [p.] Abraham and Jannie Rivers; [m.] Roland Chester Hayes, (widow) Remarried September 23, 1995; [ch.] Cliff, Carla, Janice, Shawn, Robyn, Stevie; [ed.] High School, Manhattan Comm. College for 2 yrs. Liberal Arts, Manhattan Bible Inst. also am now in the Evangelist class, objective is to become an evangelist.; [occ.] Word Processor III; [memb.] Greater Central Baptist Church, member of Cathedral Choir, and Usher Board, Sickle Cell foundation of Harlem, NY; [hon.] Graduate of Christian Workers class, with all honors, in June 1994 to which I am very proud of, as I have learned so much more about the bible. I was given an award for fund rising for the Sickle Cell Anemia foundation.; [oth. writ.] Have written poems for personal enjoyment, funeral services, essay for sociology class, poem for home town paper once long ago. I am also a Cosmetologist, I have a US Gov. Patent in a fingernail device that I design. I am also a minister of healing of God praying band.; [pers.] I would like to bring understanding and beauty to everyone in all walks of life, the expecting mother and baby to the old and in firm, most of all to bring love to ones life through my writings.; [a.] Jersey City, NJ

HAYNES, LAURA
[b.] November 22, 1979, Gainesville, GA; [p.] Glenn Haynes, Rhonda Haynes; [ed.] Currently in the 9th grade at East Hall High School; [hon.] Young writers award, 1st place in cosmetology competition in the vocational opportunities clubs of America; [pers.] I started writing in the 8th grade about nature but now I am beginning to write about the greater aspects of life; [a.] Gainesville, GA

HEARN, KELLEY
[b.] March 2, 1977, Nashville, TN; [p.] Gwen Hearn, Joe Hearn; [ed.] East Robertson High School Cross Plains, TN; [occ.] Student; [oth. writ.] I have written many poems, but have never had any published.; [pers.] I would like to have all of my poems published one day.; [a.] Orlinda, TN

HEARNE, KALOA
[pen.] Kaloa Illana; [b.] December 6, 1967, Los Angeles; [p.] Mary Clanton, Robert Hearne; [ed.] Northwestern High, Detroit, MI, University of Maryland; [occ.] Administrative Specialist U.S. Army; [pers.] Each one reach one, each one teach one.; [a.] Detroit, MI

HEDLUND, PAUL P.
[b.] June 16, 1925, Duluth, MN; [p.] Agnar and Ellen Hedlund; [m.] Marcella (deceased), September 9, 1950; [ch.] Paula and Laurie; [ed.] Duluth Denfeld High, Duluth Jr. College, Duluth, MN, Univ. of MN (MPLS) (Engineering) (Institute of Technology); [occ.] Retired from MN Dept. of Natural Resources; [memb.] Life member of the U.S. Chess Federation, while at the U of MN; member of Delta Kappa Phi Fraternity; [hon.] 18 years of service as a graphic arts specialist with the Dept. of Natural Resources (MN State); [pers.] As an artist, I have painted over 400 original paintings in all mediums. Taught art and chess and fly tying over 6 years in the St. Paul and Roseville Adult Evening School Programs. While painting it inspired me to write poetry.; [a.] Saint Paul, MN

HEGEDUS, TAMARA
[b.] June 12, 1979, Ohio; [p.] Robert and Deborah Hegedus; [ed.] St. Adalbert, Berea Ohio Berea High School, Berea Ohio; [occ.] Student; [memb.] Honor roll, Student Council Board, RSVP, Cheer leading squad, Track and Field team, St. Adalbert Church; [hon.] Blessed Mary Angela Award, Citizenship Awards, Attendance Award, Sports Awards, Freshman Award, Student of the Quarter, Honor Roll; [oth. writ.] Numerous poems and short stories.; [pers.] I have my family to thank for my encouragement, I do it for them, and a special thanks to my mom.; [a.] Brook Park, OH

HEILER, TODD
[b.] May 29, 1963, Springville, NY; [p.] Lavern and Judy Heiler; [ed.] Graduate Springville Griffith High school, BS in Criminal Justice Suny College at Brockport NY; [occ.] Security officer Naples Beach Hotel Naples, FL; [oth. writ.] Several other poems as yet unpublished; [pers.] I believed in being open and honest about my emotions and I hold sacred all that is beautiful within ourselves and all around us. Though my writing I seek to share myself and the beauty that I see in life; [a.] Naples, FL

HEINS, HAZEL
[pen.] Hazel Heins; [b.] May 10, 1921, Youngstown, OH; [p.] Swan and Maude Pearson; [m.] Thomas Heins, February 9, 1942; [ch.] Thomas Jr., David, Robert, Connie and Bonnie, Vickie, Gregory; [ed.] Completed 11th grade; [occ.] Housewife; [memb.] Church Trinity Lutheran; [hon.] Small beauty contest, small chili contest; [oth. writ.] Poems and songs never sent to publishers; [pers.] Wish we could all live in peace and harmony help one another everyone drawn closer to God.

HEINTZ, LINDSAY
[pen.] Stacy Marie; [b.] January 1, 1987, Detroit; [p.] Mary Jane and Kenyon A. Heintz; [ed.] 2nd grade; [memb.] Monky Club, Burger King Kid's Club, Sickle's Dance Gallery; [hon.] (March of Dimes) Reading Champion-Gold Medal, Dance Trophies, Two 1st place, Learning Fair; [oth. writ.] Sharing non-published; [pers.] I am very happy that you have chosen my poem as a semi-finalist, and to be published.; [a.] Redford, MI

HEINTZ, EMILY
[b.] April 21, 1981, Springfield, OH; [p.] Kurt and Christine Heintz; [ed.] Currently in 8th grade; [hon.] Excellence in writing 1995 honor roll top 10% of class left to write contest

HEITMANN, DEBRA
[b.] April 18, 1973, Brooklyn, NY; [p.] Elsbeth and Richard Heitmann; [ed.] Freehold Boro High School, Rowan College of NJ; [occ.] Actress/student; [memb.] Campus players, vice president of Bureau of Theater Dance Activities, Lab. Theater; [hon.] Dean's list, Alpha Psi Omega; [oth. writ.] Still in a box under my bed, performed at coffee houses; [pers.] With God by your side, you can do anything. I love the works of Alice Walker, Alfred Lord Tennyson, and Emily Dickinson.; [a.] Madison, MS

HELBIG, ISABEL GOODWILLIE
[b.] May 19, 1915, Detroit, MI; [p.] William and Elizabeth Goodwillie; [m.] Edward Helbig, July 30, 1940; [ch.] William, Nancy, James; [ed.] 2 yrs - College; [occ.] Housewife; [memb.] Four Octave Club of Detroit and Tuesday Musicale of Michigan; [hon.] High school Valedictorian - 1932; [oth. writ.] Many poems.; [pers.] Have written many poems but always too shy to show them. I am overwhelmed at your compliments and delighted beyond belief. I thank my granddaughter Karen - whom submitted the poem.; [a.] Harper Woods, MI

HELGESEN, CHAR
[b.] July 9, 1929, Portland, OR; [ed.] BA - Education, Advanced studies in speech pathology - university in Washington, Seattle, VA; [occ.] Semi-retired speech pathologist seattle public schools; [memb.] Washington Speech and hearing assn., national education assn; [pers.] I have been greatly influenced by my catholic faith and strive to accent the need for world peace in my poetry, as well as a return of civilization to moral values, for the sake of children.; [a.] Seattle, WA

HELMICK, MELISSA MARIE MELCHER
[b.] December 26, 1969, Adams County; [p.] William and Roberta Melcher; [m.] Rick Brent Helmick Jr., January 1, 1994; [ch.] Kirk M. Melcher deceased, Karrissa R. Helmick; [ed.] Bellmont High School Indiana, Purdue University of Ft. Wayne, Lutheran College Health Professions; [occ.] Mgr. Womans Retail Store (Sycamore) Ft. Wayne, IN; [memb.] St. Paul (Preble) Lutheran Church; [oth. writ.] Many personable poems relating to my deceased son and my deceased son and my life together alone for 3 years to which I have made a scrap book of.; [pers.] All my poetry reflects on my deceased son and my life together. By writing my thoughts it helps to release anger and sorrow. Kirk (my deceased son) greatly influenced my life 2 years ago and still does. He will always be my hero and inspiration on life.; [a.] Garrett, IN

HELTON, SHERRY
[pen.] Sherry Love; [b.] March 28, 1961, Columbus, OH; [p.] Janice Lee; [m.] Dwayne Helton, August 7, 1983; [ch.] Johnathan Dwayne Neal Helton; [ed.] Lake Brantley High; [occ.] Homemaker, author; [oth. writ.] Adventures of Scruffy the Squirrel, poems "Ode to a Fishermans Wife", Troubled Teen, Unwanted Love, Love for the Holidays, Hearts and Souls, all unpublished copyrighted recently; [pers.] Beautiful words on paper can brighten the dreariest day and can often soothe a troubled soul. I write because I enjoy it. I hope others may enjoy reading what I've wrote.; [a.] Orlando, FL

HEMPHILL, ROBERT WILLIAM
[b.] July 7, 1986, Phoenix, AZ; [p.] Yvette Hemphill/Robert Hemphill; [ed.] 3rd grade student at Sierra Vista Elementary School; [hon.] Certificate of Achievement in reading, perfect attendance award; [a.] Phoenix, AZ

HENDERSHOT, GARY LEE
[b.] March 21, 1952, Waterford, OH; [p.] John and Irene Hendershot; [m.] Divorced, September 3, 1977; [ch.] Traci Marie Hendershot, Tina Lee Hendershot; [ed.] 12th Grade GED, Waterford High School, Waterford, OH, Vice President Senior Class of 1970; [occ.] 22 years Concrete Construction; [memb.] United Methodist Church; [hon.] 2nd Place tie in state of Ohio S.A.T. 10th grade Geometry: moved toward personal trust after moving from rural area of country. Never directly aligned with political factions or power factions of Metropolitan areas. Respect open mindedness and all people until they become of trespass.; [oth. writ.] Many proverbs (quotes) "Oh Time of Life" 69 lines poem of Time and Life's Dual Journey of Love of life and time. Part of "Oh Time of Life" will be published in the Detroit Free Press March 10th 1995. "Me" a nice personal poem, "Peons" a poem pleading better education for the children of all, "I See Dad" a satirical poem turned serious in respect of a good disciplining father, "Writings" a good poem "Dear Father and Mother, in Memory of Your Labor I Love" a high character questioning poem that ends in great respect.; [pers.] More defined leadership for the entire country its people and the stability of their jobs. A nationally inspired self-survival program to alert the young how vulnerable they really are comparing graphically to our young how people in a country like Rwanda cannot exist without education especially education of Agriculture. Thirdly, a national program to teach the male and female sexes to understand each other better and to educate them of the dangers of trying to dominate or control each other.; [a.] Holly, MI

HENDERSON, DILLARD W.
[b.] May 3, 1929, East Saint Louis, IL; [p.] Frank and Irene Henderson; [m.] Marilyn A. Henderson, August 11, 1957; [ch.] Lisa A. Maznio, Tami R. Kauffman; [ed.] Bachelor of Science Degree from Indiana University; [occ.] Retired; [memb.] Life Member of "The Freedom from Religion Foundation, Inc." Madison, WI 53703; [hon.] Deans List two years at Indiana University. Board of Directors member of "The Freedom Religion Foundation, Inc." Madison, WI. 53703; [oth. writ.] Various Free-Thought Articles, some of which have been published. There is not a great demand for Atheist Material.; [pers.] I am an avowed free thinker, an atheist. My poem "Omnipotent One, How Can It Be" clearly demonstrates this. I can only write from the heart.; [a.] Royal Oak, MI

HENDERSON, WENDY N.
[pen.] Wendy N. Henderson; [b.] March 15, 1968, El Paso, TX; [p.] J. D. Scoggins, Karen Jo Winters; [m.] Bob Henderson, December 31, 1992; [ed.] Sierra High, Colorado Spgs., Co. Modesto Jr. College, Modesto, CA.; [hon.] Marketing Dvlpmtl Awards at City and State levels, Who's Who among American High School Students 1985-86,; [pers.] I give glory and honor to God my Father, for the gift of writing, and for this opportunity to share with mankind His awesome grace, love, and salvation! (John 3:16, Eph. 2:8-10); [a.] Covington, GA

HENDRICK, OTELIA CRAWLEY
[b.] March 15, 1943, Newport News, VA; [p.] James Collins Crawley, Annie Bell White Crawley; [m.] Frank Delino Hendrick Sr., May 9, 1964; [ch.] Frank Delino Jr., Cedric Damon, Julian Collins; [ed.] Isle of Wight High School, Smithfield VA, Norfolk State University, Norfolk VA, Hampton University, Hampton VA; [occ.] Registered Nurse Veterans Affairs Medical Center, Hampton, VA; [memb.] American Nurses Association, Virginia Nurses Association, Rehabilitation Nurses Association, Gerontological Nurses Association; [hon.] Salutatorian of High School Class, Who's Who Among Students in American Universities and Colleges, Hampton University Nursing Honors Award, Distinguished Registry of Certified Gerontological Nurses; [oth. writ.] Poem published in a Local newspaper; [pers.] "A new

beginning is offered each day through persistence and determination". My writing reflect the physical, psychosocial and spiritual aspects of Nursing to help mankind.; [a.] Hampton, VA

HENDRICKSON, JEAN MCLEOD
[pen.] Alexis McLeod; [b.] December 27, 1942, Portland, ME; [p.] Lt. Col. Murray and Mrs. Addie L. McLeod; [m.] Widowed (George M. Hendrickson), September 25, 1992; [ch.] Susan McLeod Hall, Timothy Leland Hall, Kerry Jean Hall, Greca, Rachel Leah Hendrickson; [ed.] UTEP-1964 BA's in Psychology and English, U of North Florida, performing Arts, Advanced studies in Clown Performing Arts; [occ.] Social worker, professional clown; [memb.] World clown association, clowns of America, International, Toastmaster's International lapsed member of MENSA; [oth. writ.] Short story Reader's Digest September 9, 1994, Myriad articles in daily press of VA Peninsula, Lifenet, Laugh Makers, recently finished a novel looking for a publisher; [pers.] Live, love, laugh and be happy!; [a.] Hampton, VA

HENDRIX, TRAVIS LEE
[b.] September 3, 1971, Hannibal, MO; [p.] Ronald and Teresa Hendrix; [m.] Single; [ed.] Van-Far R-I, Vanoalia MO. CMSU Warrensburg, MO. Hannibal LaGrange College, Hannibal, MO; [occ.] Student; [memb.] FBLA 1 yr. Track Team 3 yrs.; [hon.] Dean's List majoring in Data-processing-computer information system and criminal justice; [pers.] I would like to dedicate my poem to my cousin Chris Lovelace, who was killed January 14, 1994. I returned to college in 1994 after being out for 2 year, I had cancer and lost my eye sight because of it, therefore my poem is about that.; [a.] Vandalia, MO

HENKE, ANITA
[b.] September 20, 1958, Pontiac, MI; [p.] Shirley Brinkley, Charles Henke; [ed.] David Starr Jordan High School Long Beach, California; [occ.] Child care; [memb.] U.S. Lighthouse Society San Francisco, California; [pers.] I like lighthouse, the victorian era, New England Coast, Ireland and St. Patrick's Day!; [a.] Bloomfield Hills, MI

HENKEL, DONALD G.
[pen.] Donald G. Henkel; [b.] December 5, 1930, Middlebranch, OH; [p.] Hilda Fry Henkel - Herbert Henker; [ch.] Denise Barnhart, Mark B. Henkel, Donald B. Henkel; [ed.] Greentown High School, Greentown Ohio, Journey-man carpenter, Journey-man Machinist; [occ.] Architectual Brick Sales, Detroit, Michigan Arga; [memb.] Flat Rock First United Methodist Church - Part of Mission Team to Costa Rica; [oth. writ.] Poem's "Promise to Ed Dolan" "Where's our little goldilocks?" "A visit in the Orchard".; [pers.] Live one day at a time and fill it with faith, hope, and charity along with the Golden rule.; [a.] Trenton, MI

HENNING, DOUGLAS P.
[pen.] Doug Henning; [b.] September 19, 1937, Chicago; [p.] Charles and Lola Henning; [m.] Elizabeth A. Henning, December 22, 1990; [ch.] Douglas and Veronica, Marie and Raymond; [ed.] Harvard grade school Parker High School; [occ.] Experidtor; [oth. writ.] I have other writing unpublished.; [pers.] Because of my believes and great desire to put on paper, some of my thoughts, and feelings, to share with others that might care to read some of my writings.; [a.] Justice, IL

HENRIET, RICHARD G.
[b.] November 12, 1950, Detroit, MI; [p.] Marcel and Georgette Henriet; [m.] Mary Ann Garner (girlfriend); [ed.] B, Ph Thomas Jefferson College, Grand Valley State; [occ.] Manufacturing Technician, Ford Motor Company; [memb.] Whitefish Point Bird Observatory (Life Member), Nature Conservancy, Green peace, National Audubon Society, Sierra Club, NRA, Plan-

etary Society; [oth. writ.] Poetry, short stories. Nothing published worth writing about.; [pers.] "People are all different, humans are all the same, all people are human." Science has yet to make that subtle distinction.; [a.] Fenton, MI

HENRY, ANGELA L.
[b.] February 3, 1964, Tacona, WA; [p.] Reiko and Late Larry Henry; [ed.] John F. Kennedy Memorial High University of Washington; [occ.] Staff Supervisor - key Bank of Washington, Seattle, WA; [memb.] Diversity Committee (Key Bank of WA); [hon.] High School, Nat'l Honor Society Nat'l Spanish Honor Society, Who's Who High School Students; [pers.] Inspiration for my poems are dramatic experiences in my everyday life. It happens at any emotional peak moment at night or day. Whatever touches my heart. I've loved poems since I who 8 years old and now I try to write them more often.; [a.] Seattle, WA

HENRY, ELLA MAE
[b.] July 11, 1967, Gallup, NM; [p.] Mary Dayea; [m.] Keith Henry, March 15, 1988; [ch.] Vonerick Henry, Shantel Henry; [ed.] Ft. Wingate High School; [occ.] Certified Nursing Asst.; [hon.] National Honor Society; [a.] Mesa, AZ

HENRY, DIANE M.
[b.] May 4, 1936, Chicago, IL; [p.] Paul D. and Charlotte M. Henry; [ch.] Pamela Rae Ewing, Steven Reid Burdick, Kristen Rene Burdick, Joel Daniel Burdick; [ed.] Hirsch High School, Chicago, IL., St. Joachim Grammer School, Chicago, IL.; [occ.] Administrative Assistant for Engineering Consultants; [memb.] Austin Visual Arts Association Bat Conservation International, PBS Stations KUT-FM, KMFA-FM, and KLRU-TV National Wildflower Research Center O'Henry Museum, Xeriscape Garden Club; [hon.] I have an honor for coordinating an in-house art exhibit called "On My Own Time" sponsored by the Chamber of Commerce. I was awarded first prize for an oil painting and third prize for a face I sculptured from clay.; [pers.] I work up one morning to a train whistle. I started the poem a few minutes later and finished it before getting out of bed. This is my first poem. I also love to draw and paint and hope to have a showing one day.; [a.] Austin, TX

HENSLEY, GREGORY E.
[b.] February 4, 1964, Middletown, OH; [p.] James and Clara Hensley; [m.] Tracey Lynn Hensley, March 18, 1995; [ch.] Dustin Alexander - step son; [ed.] Deland High School, Seminole Community College; [occ.] Parts Manager, City of Sanford Fla.; [pers.] I dedicate this and all my poetry to my beautiful wife Tracy.; [a.] DeBary, FL

HENSON, RUBY G.
[b.] February 14, 1912, Gastonia, NC; [p.] Sarah Jane Boyles, Melvin A. Grigg; [m.] Deceased; [ch.] 3 (one is deceased); [occ.] Retired; [memb.] Silver Striders Walking Club Raleigh, NC, Fitzgerald Church of God Young at Heart Club; [oth. writ.] Poems in newspapers, Church bulletins, senior citizens papers (poems published in Fitzgerald Herald Leader and Gaston Observer.; [pers.] My desire as to share my talents with others hoping to help and inspire someone along the way God has given me a talent and I feel that it's important to use it for His glory; [a.] Fitzgerald, GA

HEREMANS, HILDE ANNE
[b.] June 1, 1979, Sint-Lambrechts-Woluwe, Belgium; [p.] Joseph P. Heremans, Claire Mali; [ed.] Detroit Country Day School; [occ.] Student (10th grade); [memb.] Metropolitan Youth Symphony; [hon.] Science and Engineering Fair of Metropolitan Detroit, First place in 1992, 1993, 1994, 1995., National Junior Honor Society in 1992, 1993.; [a.] Troy, MI

HERGET, LINDA M.
[b.] July 20, 1963, Cincinnati, OH; [p.] John R. and Mary A. Herget; [ch.] Crystal M. Herget; [ed.] Mt. Healthy High, Great Oaks Vocational, Southwestern College of Business; [occ.] Medical Assistant; [memb.] American Medical Association; [hon.] Deans List; [oth. writ.] My first poem; [pers.] I just wanted to give something to my daughter, that she could keep for years to come.; [a.] Cincinnati, OH

HERNANDEZ, ESTRELLA
[pen.] Black Widow; [b.] January 10, 1972, Guayama, PR; [p.] Carmen O. Quinones; [ed.] Graduated High School Miami Jackson '90, Navy Schools - currently involved with H-46 Air Crew Training; [occ.] US Navy (4 years) currently stationed in Norfolk, VA; [hon.] 5 awards for service with the US Navy; [pers.] I write my poems due to poet experiences in my life anything I accomplish in life is because of my loving mother that taught ne to write what I always felt. Love you always

HERNANDEZ, YIANICE
[b.] July 26, 1979, New York, NY; [p.] Lucy and Eladio Hernandez; [ed.] Dodge Vocational High School; [occ.] School; [oth. writ.] Many more non-published; [pers.] I am 15 years old. I can honestly tell you I have no influence for other poets I get my inspiration from what I see in the world around me and what effects me and the life around me that's it.; [a.] Bronx, NY

HERVEY, LOIS GOBLE
[b.] December 30, 1910, Artesia, NM; [p.] Oscar R. and Virginia D, Goble; [m.] Hubert C. Hervey (deceased) June 2, 1930; [ch.] Hubert C. Hervey Jr., Donald G. Hervey, Sylvia Hervey Barham, Richard Lee Hervey; [ed.] B.A. Texas Tech University 1930 (English major), creative writing courses, Centenary College, Shreveport, La.; [occ.] Volunteering; [memb.] St. Luke's United Methodist Church, Houston, TX, Pres., Ecuminical Older Adult main Streamers; [hon.] Mayor's Award, Outstanding Volunteer, Houston, TX, Distinguished Life Award, St. Luke's United Methodist Church, Houston, TX, Stonewall Student Council Citizen of the Year Award; [oth. writ.] I have been writing poetry and prose since I was five years old. A booklet of childhood writings was published, and individual poems have seen print from time to time. I write for, and have been editor of the Mainstreamer News.; [pers.] I feel always an underlying sense of gratitude for the many blessings that life has brought me.; [a.] Houston, TX

HESS, CAROL J.
[b.] December 24, 1943, Pontiac, MI; [p.] David N. Hewitt, Naomi H. Hewitt; [m.] Ellery M., April 2, 1966; [ch.] Ellery M II, Amy Kristin; [ed.] Pontiac Central High, Pontiac General Hospital - School of Radiologic Technology, Oakland Community College, University of California Health Sciences; [occ.] Radiation Therapist Technologist; [memb.] A.R.R.T., A.S.R.T., M.R.S.T.; [hon.] Coach - Webster Indian Cheerleaders; [oth. writ.] Family Poetry, In Loving Memory Mother, Forever Love,; [pers.] Deep feelings no matter how they manifest themselves are still deep feelings.; [a.] Pontiac, MI

HEWES, SHIRLEY M.
[b.] March 29, 1967, Chestertown, MD; [p.] Samuel F. and Linda D. Hewes; [ed.] 1985 Graduate of Middletown High School, Middletown Delaware; [occ.] NAPA Distribution Center; [hon.] Having three poems published by The National Library of Poetry; [oth. writ.] Wrote poems for friends and place of employment; [pers.] It's a thrill and a pleasure to have everyone read my poems. Your poem comes from the warmth and love of your heart and soul from within.; [a.] Middletown, DE

HEWLETT, HOLLY DAWN
[b.] December 31, 1963, Biloxi, MS; [p.] Patricia Anne, William Norman; [ed.] The entire universe and everyday life; [occ.] Professional truck driver; [pers.] To leave more than I take. To help stop hate. We are all connected we need to work together to help each other reach our greatest potential; [a.] Mission, TX

HICKEY, MARTHA BOOKOUT
[b.] 1953, Charlotte, NC; [p.] Martha and Conrad Bookout; [m.] Joseph; [ed.] B.A. Queens College M.S. George Peabody College (of Vanderbilt University), PhD Univ. Aberdeen, Scotland; [occ.] Rehabilitation Counseling Psychologist - U.S. Dept. Veterans Affairs; [pers.] My favorite poems are "Do Not Go Gentle Into That Goodnight", "Life For Me Ain't Been No Crystal Stair" and "Life Is The Most Beautiful Place." My inspiration is my mother.; [a.] Atkinson, NC

HIGGINS, RUTH E.
[b.] February 8, 1980, Chicago, IL; [p.] Harry and Dorothea Higgins; [ed.] Home schooled presently in ninth grade; [occ.] Assist. Water Safely Instructor, Red Cross; [memb.] Arlington Sting Rays Competitive USS Swim team, Arlington, Park Baptist Church Nursery Helper and Youth Group Worker - Fundraiser; [hon.] Arlington Sting Rays swimmer of the month for Feb. '95 and Mar. '95, National Physical Fitness Award 1994; [oth. writ.] Portfolio of Poetry with illustrations; [pers.] To write more poetry and to stand by my convictions: Life is short pray hard! Eternity is long - don't be wrong!; [a.] Arlington, TX

HIGGINSON, JEREMY
[pen.] Geronimo; [b.] January 9, 1976, Mountainview, CA; [p.] Larry and Karen Higginson; [ed.] El Camino High School, Gonzaga University (sophomore); [occ.] Student; [hon.] High school Salutatorian, Dean's list of G.U., honor roll; [oth. writ.] Poems published in high school literary magazine, produced a book of poems in high school to graduate with honors; [pers.] I try to write universally, so no one poem can be tied down to a specific time, place, race, creed, or religion.; [a.] Spokane, WA

HIGHAM, MARILYN S.
[pen.] Sybil Brown; [b.] September 14, 1941, Rockville, CT; [p.] James Brown; [m.] Dorothea Gertrude Brothers; [ch.] Marvin Irwin Brown, Phyllis Linda Brown; [ed.] Early childhood preparation; [pers.] Poetry, for excellence and communication of thought, insight and a way of sharing with the fellow traveler.; [a.] Seymour, CT

HIGHFILL, DICK
[b.] January 2, 1947, Buffalo, MO; [p.] Leo and Juanita Highfill; [m.] Kelly D. Highfill, March 14, 1986; [ch.] Amy M, Elizabeth D. (step) Hillcrest High, Drury College; [ed.] Hillcrest High, Drury College; [occ.] Insurance Agent - Farmers Insurance Group; [memb.] Past member, President of local Sertoma Club, Kiwanis, Rotary; [oth. writ.] Humor columnist since August 1994 for the Lawrence County Record Mt. Vernon, MO.; [pers.] I try to have my writings reflect my belief that we sometimes take ourselves too seriously.; [a.] Mt. Vernon, MO

HILL, REBEKAH
[pen.] Becky; [b.] February 1, 1979, Cleveland, OH; [p.] Michael and Elizabeth Hill; [ed.] Right not I'm attending Normandy High School in Parma, OH. I'm involved in girls choir and taking college preparatory classes. I'm a sophomore and working towards a honors diploma; [occ.] Student; [hon.] Currently on the Honor roll and have since 7th grade. Involved in the Cleveland orchestra youth chorus. Love to sing act, and model. Have been in numerous plays including "The sound of music" with the Cleveland opera; [pers.] My great, great, great, great grandmother was a full-blooded cherokee Indian. Seeing how much the Indians have been used and abused, moved me to write this.; [a.] Parma, OH

HILL, SHERRIE
[pen.] Shades; [b.] March 19, 1978, Hutzel Hos.; [p.] Jenesta Smith; [ed.] 11th grade, GPA: 3.0, Pershing High School, Honor Roll and etc.; [occ.] Working at little Caesar, Singing, Writing; [hon.] Certificate of excellence for Marketing Class, Two Gold Medals for Running, Spelling Contest; [oth. writ.] Books: The little girl who has nothing, The Different Kinds of Love, lots of more poems, (variety choices), songs, raps, letters; [pers.] I love to write no matter what it maybe. I really appreciate your company accepting my poems.; [a.] Detroit, MI

HILL, HEATHER MCMUNN
[pen.] Camelle; [b.] October 22, 1976, San Francisco, CA; [p.] Fred Hill, Jeannie Hill; [ed.] Pleasant View Christian School, University of Tennessee, Knoxville; [occ.] Student; [memb.] Youth Choir, Volunteers for Christ, the Tennessee Health Enhancers, Alpha Epsilon Delta; [hon.] Phi Eta Sigma, Valedictorian (of high school class of 1994), 1st in district and state in the category of Original Persuasive Oratory (Tennessee Association of Christian Schools); [oth. writ.] Song writing and poetry composition featured in Middle Tennessee Fall Festival and annual Women's Convention, original song performed in country wide Sycamore Valley Days music showcase; [pers.] But by the grace of God I am what I am, and His grace toward me was not in vain....I corinthians 15:10; [a.] Pleasant View, TN

HODGES, JAMES S.
[pen.] Eagle Swanson; [b.] May 8, 1975, Reidsville, NC; [p.] Donald and Rachel Hodges; [ed.] Graduated with Class of '93 from RCSHS.; [occ.] Machine operator; [memb.] Member of The Association of Research and Enlightenment (A.R.E.); [hon.] Honored with a Journalism award in high school. Awarded the Editor's Choice from the National Library of Poetry.; [oth. writ.] "Blood" published in Echoes of Yesterday. "Stone Gathering" published in Best Poems of 1995; [pers.] Be true to your heart mountain will crumble river will part.; [a.] Reidsville, NC

HOEFT, JAMES
[b.] February 5, 1972; [p.] Allen and Linda; [ed.] Bachelors degree in Business Administration Specific Poetry, writing; [occ.] Sales Rep. for Discount Office Supply, Inc. in Michigan; [memb.] Plan on joining Poets House in New York.; [hon.] Had a manuscript with Carlton House in New York, but they wanted a large sum to publish. This is the 1st company that I have really tried to work with.; [oth. writ.] Currently working on a copyrighting a song writing company called Divine Right Music Ltd. over 375 pages of poetry and songs.; [pers.] In the future would like to be a full time writer and lyricist.; [a.] Howell, MI

HOFFMAN, GILLIAN L.
[b.] April 27, 1977, Stamford, CT; [p.] Jo-Anna Fleming, Richard Fleming; [ed.] St. Lukes, Wilton High School; [occ.] Student; [hon.] Honor Roll, Photography awards, Journalism, sports, drama, writing; [oth. writ.] Different poems that relate to how I feel short stories and stories, plus articles in school paper and newspaper 2 poems printed in the WHS 94-95 Literary Magazine published by NLP in Dark Side of the Moon; [pers.] I live life day by day taking baby steps up the ladder of life. I write my feelings, thoughts and dreams in words. People can only see the "real me" through my writings.; [a.] Wilton, CT

HOFFMANN, LEAH
[b.] August 14, 1978, West Lafayette, IN; [p.] Christoph and Karen; [ed.] Student at West Lafayatte High School; [occ.] High School student; [memb.] Student's Against Drunk Driving, Actirists for a Healthier future, World Affairs Discussion Group, Sierra Student Coalition, National Forensic League; [hon.] Editor's Choice Award 1994 National Library of Poetry, 1st of division in 1993 Local Science Fair, Outstanding Scholar for ICIM Al-

gebra I and II tests, Music Honor award 1993-94, Local Site Award for ICIM Geometry test; [oth. writ.] Poem published in Echoes of Yesterday, poem published in The Best Poems of 1995; [a.] West Lafayette, IN

HOLCOMB, KATHLEEN M.
[pen.] Kathleen M. Holcomb; [b.] June 7, 1949, Rock Island, IL; [p.] Walter and Blanche Allen; [m.] James R. Holcomb, October 12, 1968; [ch.] William Russell and Daniel James; [ed.] Moline Sr. High; [occ.] Homemaker; [oth. writ.] I have written many other poems and would like to put them together in a book form.; [pers.] Each poem written has a special person or circumstances in mind. I believe this is a gift from God to be used as His tool to comfort and bring joy to those He has brought into my life.; [a.] Warren, MI

HOLDEN, MARIA
[pen.] Maria (roadrunner); [b.] April 15, 1955, Baltimore, MD; [p.] Guse Nora Magnotta; [m.] Joel Henry Holden, April 27, 1991; [ch.] Gina Maria Holden, Analisa Veda Holden; [ed.] B.A. Music - Theatre, Dance Loretto Heights College, Denver, CO; [occ.] Raising kids, making dollar, golf and music, I'm changing my mind; [memb.] Natural World, the zoo! Channel 6 - 12 Public TV Underground Joke Network; [hon.] Smiliest Italian, one who never stops making noise, life loving lady; [oth. writ.] Various musical arrangements, original score and verse; [pers.] Our hope is in our children. Love is in our skies! Don't get too serious about yourself!; [a.] Littleton, CO

HOLDER, JEANETTE
[pen.] J. Holder; [b.] March 31, 1958, San Jose, CA; [p.] Lavern and Lucille Gist; [m.] Steve Holder, March 25, 1986; [occ.] Optometrist Asst. Waco, TX; [memb.] Astara; [oth. writ.] Love me now, shadows, and swing set day published by Poetry press. Ten of hearts pub by the Amherst Society and Iliad Press. Relics pub by Iliad Press and Sparrowgrass Poetry Forum. Reckon published by Iliad Press co-writer of March on Crystal Caves Doorway published by Sparrow grass Poetry Forum.; [pers.] The mission had become retreiving intercepted letters of love. So if one be found still in bound. There's a heart in search of letters of old, letters of love.; [a.] Mt. Calm, TX

HOLLAND, ALBERT JACOB
[pen.] Yakubu Gabas; [b.] April 17, 1933, Dayton, OH; [p.] Richard Holland, Marian Holland; [ed.] MA, Georgetown University MA, University of Northern Colorado; [occ.] Sociology Instructor, Bowie State University; [memb.] District of Columbia Sociological Society, USA Hockey; [pers.] There is only one success...to spend your life in your own way.; [a.] Washington, DC

HOLLAWAY SR., ERIC H.
[b.] March 17, 1966, Saint Petersburg, FL; [p.] Horace and Eula Hollaway; [m.] Traci Lynne; [ch.] Eric Horace II, Lorielle Joy, Brooke Michelle; [ed.] Osceola High, St. Petersburg Junior College; [occ.] Student, musician, songwriter; [memb.] First Baptist Church of Sun City; [hon.] Army Commendation Medals, Certificate of Meritorious Academic Achievement, Honor Roll, Fine Arts Scholarship Recipient for Voice/Vocal Performance; [oth. writ.] Several poems, songs, and short stories (never published); [pers.] An open mind and a realistic point of view will take you as far in life as you desire... with God at the stern.; [a.] Saint Petersburg, FL

HOLLIDAY, GARY ALLEN
[pen.] Zhan; [b.] November 18, 1949, Greenville, SC; [p.] Charles D. and Floree E. Holliday; [m.] Mercedes Julia Chopo Claramente, November 14, 1975; [ch.] David G. and Alexandra M. Holliday; [ed.] B.S. Business Administration, University College, University of Maryland; [occ.] Computer Specialist, GS-13; [memb.] Commonwealth Avenue Pottery Cooperative; [hon.] BETA Club, 1968; [oth. writ.] "On The Other Side"

1988; [pers.] Poetry is an expression of man's universe and is to be shared with everyone.; [a.] Alexandria, VA

HOLLINGSWORTH, GLORIA M.
[pen.] G. M. Hollingsworth; [b.] April 29, 1954, Forrest County Hattiesburg, MS; [p.] D. B. Cooley Sr. and Marie; [m.] E. L. Hollingsworth, July 3, 1988; [ch.] Nicholas Bridges; [ed.] Forrest County AHS - 1972, University of Southern MS-degree in Merchandising - 1976, Social Work Degree pending - August 1995.; [occ.] Student - USM; [memb.] Truelight Baptist Church Merione of Jericho Court #236; [hon.] Christian Valley Baptist Church, Greater Mt Zion Baptist Church, Peace and Goodwill Baptist Church, (Singing and playing music at community civic and churches); [oth. writ.] I write poetry whenever I am happy, sad or experiencing difficulties in my life. I have never publish anything I have written.; [pers.] I write poetry for those who are overcome by grief or overwhelmed with joy. As a social worker I am inspired by the rapentic nature of poetry and music; [a.] Hattiesburg, MS

HOLLINGSWORTH, RYAN DAVID
[b.] March 29, 1982, Spokane, WA; [p.] Terri and Joel Stenson; [ed.] 7th grade, Greenacres Jr High; [memb.] School ASB, Basketball; [hon.] 2nd place in School Writing contest 6th Grade, Honor Roll 7th; [oth. writ.] Poem titled "If I Could Give The World A Gift" other poems written in school.; [a.] Greenacres, WA

HOLLOWAY, WILLIAM ALLEN
[pen.] Al Soloman; [b.] August 8, 1952, Batesville, AR; [p.] Valmon Holloway, Eva Holloway; [ch.] Allison Kay Holloway and Ashly Brooke Holloway; [ed.] Leachville High - G.E.D. Georgia Tech "A recent graduate from the school of hard knocks"; [occ.] (Shipping Dept.) Traffic Coordinator - Sunbeam Outdoor Products Paragould, AR; [memb.] Songwriter - BMI affiliated, member of the National Geographic Society; [hon.] Musician: Singer, performer, guitarist, nightclub circuit for 25 years; [oth. writ.] Billboard Top Single Pick February 1978. Title "River Flow" (song) B-side; [pers.] My faith lies within the "Circle of Life" and the "Cross of Death" I was born on the 8th month, the 8th day, I weighed 8 lbs and 8 oz and I am the 8th child of my family.; [a.] Paragould, AR

HOLT, KALAN JAY
[pen.] K. J.; [b.] October 28, 1971, Omaha, NE; [p.] George and Mary Holt; [ed.] High School diploma and GED.; [occ.] Hospital Janitor; [memb.] Harambee Afrikan Cultural Organization. PO Box 2500 Lincoln, NE 68542 471-3161 ext (3380) c/o Shaheed K. Hanza Dixon; [hon.] One 2nd place award for rap contest.; [oth. writ.] "Excitement", "Sunshine", "Afrikan", "Beauty", "No be Sweet", "Unexperienced", "How, When, What, Where, Why?" "Unpublished Poetry"; [pers.] I'm deeply determined to have other writing published. I'd also like to be an assistant writer for positive rap artists. In influenced by Aaron Hall, Phil Collins, Toni Braxton, Queen Latifah, Elton John and Marvin Gaye.

HOLT, VIOLET M.
[b.] May 30, 1940, Cheboygan, MI; [p.] Charles W. Burns (deceased), Caroline (Clear) Burns; [m.] Rotha Holt, October 15, 1960; [ch.] David, Dale, Donald, Charles, Steve (deceased at age 23 yrs.); [ed.] High School Graduate I'm Free Lance writer beginner. I'm writing childrens books, also some articles on a number of Important Issues like, sexual abuse, teen problems, abortions, welfare reforms, etc.; [occ.] Retired Nurses' Aide due to a stroke and deafness I'm forced into retirement.; [memb.] Was member and then Mother for Cub Scouts, Counselor in Drug and Sexual Abuse Programs. Teacher at YMCA and Boys Clubs. Nurses Aide (12 yrs.) Very active in Church Youth Program.; [hon.] Song writers Award for New Commers. 1961 from Nashville, Tennessee, New Songwriters Award for music city song crafters March 24, 1961; [oth. writ.]

Poetry and songs mostly; [pers.] I am a descendant of the late Robert Burns of Scotland. My poetry is #2 in my Life. My family is first. After death of my son Steve 5 yrs ago. I've decided to take up writing which I've always dreamed about.; [a.] Concord, AR

HOLTMANN, KENDRA
[pen.] Katylyn T. Hope; [b.] January 7, 1980, Denver, CO; [p.] Ken and Cori Holtmann; [ed.] Rangeview High School Freshman (9th grade); [occ.] Student; [hon.] Honor Roll; [pers.] Because I tend to be a non-verbal person, I find I can express my feelings and emotions through my poetry. I like to write about real issues.; [a.] Aurora, CO

HOLTON-MULLER, REGINA
[b.] Rex Lee Tomlinson, Jeanne La Verne Tomlinson; [m.] Paul-Albert Miller; [m.] October 26, 1991; [ed.] Slaton High, South Plains College, Acute Cardiac Life Support, CPR Instructor; [occ.] Registered Nurse - Operating Room, The Surgery Center of the Woodlands; [memb.] Association of Operating Room Nurses, Texas Nurses Association, American Nurse Assoc.; [hon.] Who's Who in American Nursing '93-'94, South Plains College Outstanding Achievement in Maternal-child Nursing, Certified Nurse of the Operating Room; [oth. writ.] Poems published in The Coming of Dawn - The National Library of Poetry, All My Tomorrows - Quill Books, Dusting Off Dreams - Quill Books, focus on Animals Vol. 1, Num. 1, Summer '94 - Humane, Society of Montgomery County; [pers.] My poetry allows me to express my inner-most thoughts on the emotional events and social interactions that occur in my life. I write from the heart - good or bad.; [a.] The Woodlands, TX.

HOOGLAND, JAMES
[pen.] By James; [b.] December 31, 1938, Lyon County, IA; [p.] Vernon and Sophie Hoogland; [m.] Judy Hoogland, June 30, 1959; [ch.] Jerrold, Joel, John (deceased); [ed.] Adrian High School Adrian, Minnesota; [occ.] Disabled; [memb.] St Pauls Luthern Church; [hon.] Merit award for thirty five years as a DHIA test supervisor; [oth. writ.] I've written for Banquets, Anniversaries, Birthdays, Funerals, the Church news letter and our Christmas cards.; [pers.] I strive to make the reader feel they know personally who the poem's written about or feel they are at the place written of. My favorite poet is Edgar Allen Poe. His poem 'The Raven'; [a.] Watertown, MN

HOPPEL, ANN MARIE
[b.] April 13, 1978, Denville, NJ; [p.] Mike Hoppel, Audrey Hoppel; [ed.] Bishop George Ahr High School; [memb.] Sisters in Crime, NJ Devils (hockey team) Fan Club (active member); [hon.] First Honors (grammar and high school); [oth. writ.] Poem published in Merlyn's Pen; [pers.] Many thanks to Mrs. Pat Bilby at B.G.A. for all her help and encouragement; [a.] Piscataway, NJ

HOPPER, ELIZABETH
[b.] May 12, 1966, Ft Lauderdale, FL; [p.] George Hopper, Annie Hopper; [ch.] Jasmine Janen' Lewis; [ed.] Boyd Anderson High Career City College (Business); [occ.] Senior Rep. for the Debits/Credit dept. Caremack Prescription Serv.; [pers.] I enjoy writing, by letting people know anyone can have a creative mind and if my writing can make a statement I'm all for it.; [a.] Fort Lauderdale, FL

HORN, DANIEL
[pen.] Redemption Omega; [b.] August 13, 1969, Brooklyn, NY; [p.] Gail and Wilford Horn; [ch.] Brandon Horn; [ed.] High School; [occ.] Song writing and producer of "Baby Paw" Management; [hon.] 1989 Spanish Gloves Champion of New York State, and 1990 Golden Glove semi-finalist of New York State.; [pers.] I would like to be remembered for exactly what my name stands for, "Redemption Omega", which means: Restore until the end. So have no misconception, we

must always try to uplift and help the younger generation although my life is filled with pain and sorry my mind often wonders, and hopes for the children of tomorrow. Remember: "Redemption Omega".

HORNER, WANDA
[pen.] Wanie; [b.] January 23, 1948, Scioto County; [p.] Clyde and Alice Horner; [ed.] Graduated from Green Twp. High School; [occ.] Cook; [memb.] International Poetry Society; [hon.] Editors Choice Award from National Library of Poetry; [oth. writ.] Have poem published in Anthology famous poems of today in the, famous Poets Society, 2 other poems published in anthology of National Library of Poetry Journeys of the mind and A Moment in Time; [pers.] I enjoy all types of poetry but mostly I write free verse I hope to soon have my own book of poetry published; [a.] Franklin Furnace, OH

HORNUNG, TONYA LYNN
[b.] October 26, 1964, Ferndale, MI; [p.] Barbara and Jerry Hornung; [m.] single; [ed.] Milford High School, Oakland Community College. Photography and Camping were hobbies along with reading and writing; [occ.] Secretary Chrysler Corp; [memb.] Gift of Life. Organ Donor Organization - Ann Arbor, MI; [hon.] National Honor Society (High School) Leader Pompon Squad; [oth. writ.] Once published in Local Newspaper; [pers.] She was a giving person during her short life - she gave even in death to help four other people live a fuller life!; [a.] Highland, MI

HORTENSTINE, FAYE S.
[b.] April 11, 1921, Ontario, Canada; [p.] J. Franklin Stoness, MD, Edna Turnbull Stoness; [m.] Clarence B. Hortenstine, MD, June 26, 1947; [ch.] Anne H. Rosin, MD, Jill H. Iglehart, Martha H. Silver, MD, Jay S. Hortenstine, MD; [ed.] Flushing H.S., L.I., N.Y., Queen's Univ., Canada, Barnard College, N.Y. English Lit. major B.A. degree; [occ.] Housewife, grandmother and retiree; [memb.] Westminsters Presby. Church, Lauderdale County Medical Alliance; [hon.] Freshman English prize Queen's U.; [oth. writ.] Publicity articles for various organizations, article for Barnard alum. mag., articles for church monthly, skits and intros for a women's choral group, Christmas poems used for med. aux. sharing card and also by church.; [pers.] I write poetry to and for my husband, children and thirteen grandchildren, but mostly for me. Sometimes I write to cope, sometimes for fun.; [a.] Killen, AL

HORTON, ELIZABETH YVONNE
[pen.] Damia Knight; [b.] May 28, 1978, Marietta; [p.] J. C. and Janice Horton; [ed.] Junior in High School, studying to be a music teacher; [occ.] Student; [memb.] Interact, band; [pers.] No matter where you go, there is always someone to turn to. All you have to do is look.; [a.] Canton, GA

HOVATTER, BEN
[b.] February 9, 1983, Morgantown; [p.] Donna Rae Hovatter; [ed.] Westwood Middle School Completing 6th Grade; [occ.] Student; [memb.] 1. Member: West and Middle Sch. Band 2. Member: Riverside Apostolic Church 3. Participated: W.V. University, Summerfest Programs, 1992-1994. 4. Soccon Tem: Family Med. Fliers 5. Basketball Team: Vikings.; [hon.] 1. Bible Quiz tournament awards, 2. Soccon Trophy 3. Basketball Trophy 4. Mongolia Creative writing contest, 4th place 1993, 5. Honor roll - Westwood Middle Sch.; [oth. writ.] None published. Placed in Mon. CT. Creative writing contest Essex: A Day in the woods.; [pers.] My writing tries to reflect the experiences of my life.; [a.] Morgantown, WV

HOWARD, WANDA
[b.] December 27, 1960, Charlotte, NC; [p.] Arthur and Gerry Moss; [m.] Marty Howard, September 1, 1984; [ch.] Christy, Jeremy, Kimberly; [occ.] Office support, Advertising, Carolina Controls Co.; [a.] Charlotte, NC

HOWARD, BERLENE
[pen.] Berlene Howard; [b.] September 24, 1934, Emerson, GA; [p.] Thomas Fowler, Lula Fowler; [m.] Joe W. Howard, October 13, 1957; [ch.] Joe C. Howard, Aulexia C. Howard; [ed.] Austin Higer and Knoxville Tenne. control data business school; [occ.] Retired; [memb.] Community beautiful and local health club; [hon.] Award of Merit certificate for poem titled - the only gift March 22, 1990 served as librarian at Jones St Library Cartersville GA 1985; [oth. writ.] Was guest columnist for cartersville tribune news, Newspaper; [pers.] I strive to do my best at all times and to be a good influence to children and to be kind and helpful to the elderly.; [a.] Cartersville, GA

HOWARD, FLORENCE
[b.] August 27, 1985, TX; [p.] Elizabeth Howard; [ed.] I am in the 3rd grade I go to Meadow Creek School.; [memb.] I am a member of Dance of America Dance Club for girls 5 and 14; [pers.] I love poetry. I want to be like my grandmother she writes poetry to. This poem was written for my Papa his name is Bert Swift. I love you Papa. And I want to thank my nanny for helping me.; [a.] Bedford, TX

HOWELL, KATHRYN ANNE
[b.] March 4, 1955, Ottawa, Ontario, Canada; [p.] Carl and Ruth Schmelzle; [m.] Roger W. Howell, June 12, 1987; [ch.] William Tyler Howell; [ed.] Bellevue University, NE. Currently pursuing a Bachelor of Arts in English; [occ.] Writing tutor, Bellevue University; [oth. writ.] Bellevue University newspaper article published in The Vue.; [pers.] God remains the only constant in the universe, and His truth the only reality.; [a.] Bellevue, NE

HUEY, STEPHEN P.
[pen.] Paul Stephens; [b.] September 26, 1945, Sparta, IL; [ed.] University of Missouri at St. Louis; [occ.] Program Manager; [oth. writ.] "Time Splices" a collection (in work); [pers.] If I cannot be stated in one page - the thought was too long in the first place; [a.] Florissant, MO

HUFF, JEANETTE STAMPER
[b.] May 2, 1934, May King, KY; [p.] Bill and Manda Stamper; [m.] William Huff, April 6, 1957; [ch.] Kenneth and Tommy; [ed.] Graduated from High School Whitesburg High School, Whitesburg, KY 1953; [occ.] Disabled cancer patient.; [hon.] My first poem will be published in the Anthology. A Moment in Time summer 1995. A proud semi-finalist for my 2nd poem cancer.; [oth. writ.] many other's I started writing in 1992. By writing, the story of my three grandchilren's lifes. Then my two boys, nine brothers and sisters story from there to poems and short stories.; [pers.] My writings and grandchildren have been my inspiration to live. As long as I can move my fingers in going to write. I feel I have been blessed and I want to share it.; [a.] Maple Heights, OH

HUFFMAN, MARK
[b.] August 19, 1974, Phoenix, AZ; [p.] Karen Wood, Richard Huffman; [pers.] Dedicated to: Aubrey Phillips and Sherry Gardner; [a.] Phoenix, AZ

HUGENROTH, PHILIP
[pen.] Philip Hugenroth; [b.] May 31, 1918, Door County, WI; [p.] Aloyisous and Eva Hugenroth; [m.] Audrey Mae Nelsen, November 5, 1943; [ch.] Jim, Rita, Jennifer, Joe, John; [ed.] High School; [memb.] Veterans of Foreign war, Elks Lodge, Moose Lodge, Lions Club - AARP Former City Councilman, Clovis, CA; [hon.] Lions Club Pres. elected city councilman Elks Lodge Trustee; [oth. writ.] Wrote the song "The San Joaquin"; [pers.] This poem was written after the death of Phil's wife, Audrey in 1988. They were married 42 years and he felt so alone without her.; [a.] Page, AZ

HUGHES, SUSAN LEE
[pen.] Suzzi Lee; [b.] December 16, 1946, Saint Paul, MN; [p.] Edward M. Lee and Eleanor Trudeau Lee; [m.] Divorced, October 1, 1966 - October 22,1992; [ch.] Randall Eric, Corey Garrett, Tanya Suzann, Nichole Lee; [ed.] White Bear High School - Class of '64, Student of Lakewood College; [occ.] Writer, Single Mom; [memb.] CFS Association of Minnesota, Sister Kenny Institute, Courage Center of St. Croix, Open "U" (University of Minnesota); [oth. writ.] My poetry is being used in the school curriculum, at White Bear High School. Articles for local newspaper.; [pers.] Much of my writing mirrors the "unique" path I've been called to travel. My heart's conviction is to share the intrepid, faithful, and resolute love of my living savior, and very closet friend - Jesus Christ.; [a.] White Bear Lake, MN

HUGHES, VICTORIA A.
[b.] August 15, 1969, Wichita, KS; [p.] Betty Hughes, Ralph Hughes; [ed.] Wichita West High; [occ.] Silk Screen Printer; [oth. writ.] Other poems, not yet seen by any other. Trying to write children's books.; [pers.] Nothing means more to me than the natural state of God's great Earth, and love; [a.] Wichita, KS

HUGLEY, BETTY JEAN
[b.] July 21, 1933, Sherrill, AR; [p.] Sue Owens and Johnny Parker; [ch.] John Davis, Michael Davis, Kennett Davis and Glen Davis; [ed.] Miller High, Wayne County Community College; [occ.] Retired; [memb.] Emma V. Kelley Temple #650 IBPOE of W. Miller Alumni, Inc. International Society of Poets.; [oth. writ.] Self published book of poems titled "Solace-Past and Present".; [a.] Detroit, MI

HULSEY, CHRISTINA MARIE
[pen.] Chris-Christine; [b.] October 30, 1967, Tocoma, WA; [p.] Linda and Roger Bodde, Linda and Carm Modestino; [m.] Phillip Hulsey, November 5, 1987; [ch.] Zachary G. Hulsey; [ed.] Bonner Springs High, Johnson County Community College; [occ.] Pre-school Teacher; [oth. writ.] Children's book Joining Together; [pers.] I only have moments in which I like to write but feel that all my writing comes from personal experiences. I enjoy children and my family and I've found I can be a romantic when I want to be.; [a.] Kansas City, KS

HUNT, GRACE DUPUIS
[pen.] Grace Dupuis Hunt; [b.] February 21, 1938, Breaux Bridge, LA; [p.] Mr. and Mrs. E. V. Dupuis; [m.] Bill Ray Hunt, October 26, 1959; [ch.] Carl, David, Carole and Claire (twins); [ed.] St. Joseph Academy (New Orleans), Univ. of Southwestern Louisiana, B.S. in Institutional Mgt. (Lafayette, LA.); [occ.] Homemaker; [memb.] American Dietetics Assn., St. Paul Catholic Church (Ahar, Soc., Education, Library, Bldg. Committee), Huntsville Museum of Art,; [oth. writ.] Several poems published in Newspaper, (many unpublished), Essays, Booklet "Christendom."; [pers.] My "French Acadian Parents" - (Father began education at age 18 and became a French/Eng. teacher and Mother was partially blind, 3rd grade Ed.) taught me about responsibility to develop God given talents to serve others.; [a.] Athens, AL

HUNTER, CATHERINE E.
[b.] May 17, 1982, Harvey, LA; [p.] Cheryl F. Hunter, Rick Hunter; [ed.] Bebee Elementary, Ellsworth Elementary, Thunder Ridge Middle School; [occ.] Full time student; [memb.] Thunder Ridge Basketball and wrestling team, Rebels football; [hon.] For play writing, "100% heart award" Honor Roll, Class President; [oth. writ.] "Snowflakes" in a local paper, "The Too Long Season" a play performed by Child's Play Touring Theater; [pers.] I enjoy writing about the little things that happen everyday that we take for granted. If people look they see that the world is filled with emotion.; [a.] Aurora, CO

HURD, TIM R.
[pen.] The Dragon and The Dove; [b.] March 13, 1960, Indiana; [p.] Elfriede Schuell; [m.] Sharon; [ch.] Ryan; [ed.] All of life's mysteries, good and bad; [occ.] Maintenance Tech. Craftsman, Builder, Grounds keeper; [memb.] AMA, NRA, NAHC, HOG, Bro's Club; [hon.] (Have been Acknowledged by my peers); [oth. writ.] Short stories, poetry; [pers.] I am fulfilled in life to have known many emotions and peace of mind. And hope these words offer something to someone in need, to understand your center and beyond.; [a.] South Bend, IN

HURLEY, WYNONA
[b.] January 15, 1935, Shawnee, OK; [p.] Mr. and Mrs. Charles Mein; [m.] Bill Hurley, December 28, 1950; [ch.] Debra - Billy - Charlotte, Deana - Gerald; [ed.] Capitol Hill OKC; [occ.] Cook Luken Manor Rest Home; [hon.] Local paper; [oth. writ.] Someone said a prayer for me

HUSSAIN, QUADIR
[pen.] "Shorty" for being a short kid.; [b.] October 17, 1978, Hedrabad, India; [p.] M. Zakir Hussain and Arif P. Hussain; [ed.] Spring Shadows Elementary, Pennbrook Middle School, Bearden High School; [occ.] Student at Bearden High School, 11th grade junior; [memb.] The Spring Shadows Elementary Poetry Contest (SSEPC) and Pennbrook Middle School Poetry Contest (PMSPC); [hon.] Third place in (SSEPC). Second place in (PMSPC).; [oth. writ.] There are two poems that I wrote in Middle and Elementary School which I don't recall.; [pers.] I all ways strive for the apex. I was so astonished when I reached the semi-finals for the first time in my life. I read other peoples poems to get ideas for my poem. It took me two to three weeks to think of what to write in my poem "Summer venturing around." Like I said, "I always strive for the apex, or highest possible." I am so astonished, shocked and bewildered. Please do not release my poem until May 30, 1995 for very important reasons.; [a.] Knoxville, TN

HUTCHISON, JAMES W.
[b.] October 22, 1918, Milwaukee, WI; [p.] Samuel and Laura Farr Hutchison; [m.] Single; [ed.] Riverside High (Milwaukee) Wisconsin, Conservatory Music, Northwestern University (B.M. and M.M.); [occ.] Prof. Emeritus, St. Lawrence University , Cantor, NY; [memb.] Phi Mu Alpha, American Musilogical Society; [hon.] Fulbright Scholar Austria, 62-63; [oth.writ.] Essays, short stories, piano music, songs; [pers.] The creative process of any level is a God given privilege (trust) and should never be debased.

HUTH, ELLEN C.
[m.] Alan C. Huth; [ch.] 3; [ed.] University of GA, B.S. Degree; [memb.] Mental Health Assoc. of the N. GA Mtns. MHAG, Toccoa Alliance for the Mentally Ill, GAMI, GA Mental Health Consumer Network; [hon.] Dean's List, Magna Cum Laude, Phi Beta Kappa, Phi Kappa Phi, Alpha Lambda Delta Honorary Sorority; [oth. writ.] Several poems published in local and state mental health newsletters; [pers.] One of my goals in life is to educate people and help them understand as much as possible about mental illness.; [a.] Toccoa, GA

IAGULLI, DORCELA
[pen.] Ginger; [b.] March 12, 1935, Nelson, OH; [p.] Thelma and Harland Hurd; [m.] Joe Iagulli, December 1, 1958; [ch.] John, Brenda, and Dennis; [ed.] High school graduate, Garfield High - in Garrettsville, OH; [occ.] Housewife; [memb.] A.A.K.P. (Kidney Patients Organization); [oth. writ.] None since High School - But I am self taught artist using shells collected exclusively on Hollywood Beach. Jewelry (Mermaid Gems) and Art objects - (Treasures from the Mermaids Den) Displayed in local Gallery; [pers.] 16 years dialysis patient working hard to stay strong and praise God for the beauty of the earth and sea through my art.; [a.] Hollywood, FL

IALONGO, MARISA
[b.] March 29, 1979, Rochester, PA; [p.] David and Lydia Ialongo; [ed.] Sophomore at Lincoln High School in Ellwood City, PA; [memb.] School Clubs, Y-Teens, Ski Club, Spanish Club, SADD (Students Against Drunk Driving), Concert Choir, Choral Copers, Christian Assembly Church; [hon.] Top Five in Class Academically ranked, MAC, WPIAL, and State Cross Country Champions, Y-Teen Court; [oth. writ.] This is my first poem; [pers.] Sports - Cross Country, Track, Varsity Fast Pitch, Youth Softball, Piano Student

IGNACIO, LAWRIE ANN
[b.] June 2, 1965, Honokaa, HI; [p.] Larry and Carol Ignacio; [ed.] St. Joseph High School, Gonzaga University (B.A.), Bowling Green State University (M.A.); [occ.] Student - graduate in Clinical Psychology; [pers.] The makings of great things by great people move me to capture their spirits in poems.; [a.] Honolulu, HI

ILAHI, AMALA
[pen.] Amala; [b.] August, 15, 1949, Cleveland, OH; [p.] Dominic Farris, Virginia Farris (deceased); [m.] Happily divorced; [ch.] Sunnah Ilahi, Muhyi Ilahi, and Ftimah Ilahi; [ed.] Cleveland Public Schools, Cuyahoga Community College; [occ.] Law Office Administrator; [memb.] American Management Association, National Businesswomen's Leadership Association, Cleveland Magic Club, International Brotherhood of Magicians; [oth. writ.] In progress: The Black Unicorn, a children's fantasy, and lyrics being set to music from songs included in The Black Unicorn.; [a.] Shaker Heights, OH

INGLEDUE, JACQUELYNE L.
[b.] July 31, 1934, Orangeburg, SC; [p.] Lucille Hunt Bowles, (the late) Russell Bowles; [m.] Thomas Charles Ingledue, August 31, 1957; [ch.] Thomas Charles III, Steven Russell and Michael Dean; [ed.] Cope High School, Winthrop College (B.S.), Stanford University (M.A.), Now Winthrop University; [occ.] Fine Arts Photographer; [hon.] I have had a one woman show and have participated in many juried photography exhibits. I have won awards for theme work as well as for individual subjects. The Foundation on Culture and the Arts (State of HI) has purchased a photograph for its collection.; [pers.] I enjoy embedding in all the wonders of visual beauty... looking then, ultimately, seeing. Writing poetry is a new experience for me.; [a.] Kaneohe, HI

INGOLD, KAREN
[b.] June, 1950, MA; [m.] Robert, summer 1982; [ch.] Two daughters; [ed.] Wsfld State College, Wsfld, Mass - Bach. of Science in Elem. Ed., Attending WSC Graduate studies, Masters in Consulting Teacher of Reading; [occ.] Substitute Elem. Ed. Teacher; [memb.] Mass. Teacher's Assoc., National Educational Assoc.; [hon.] Graduated from WSC 1994 with honors; [oth. writ.] I am in the process of writing a children's book.; [pers.] Our house is a mini-library. I read to my children before they were even born. They love to read and write as much as I do, and they have found that writing is a wonderful way to express themselves. It's nice to know I'm to blame for something so positive. I hope this poem and future writings will make readers think and/or put a smile on their faces.; [a.] West Springfield, MA

INGRAM, JAIME
[b.] September 11, 1976, Wyandotte, MI; [p.] Gary and Marie Ingram; [ed.] Southgate Anderson High School, Wayne County Community College; [occ.] Day Care Worker; [hon.] Who's Who Among American High School Students 1991-1994; [oth. writ.] Short story: "The Piano Princess"; [a.] Southgate, MI

IRIZARRY, CAROLYN
[b.] November 9, 1963, Manhattan, NY; [p.] Vidal Collado, Carmen Collado; [m.] Edgar Irizarry, November 12, 1988; [ch.] Jordan Emmanuel Irizarry; [pers.] Before writing anything I search for spiritual inspiration and this helps me put into words, my feelings of love towards my husband, child and family. And I thank God for providing me with this talent from time to time.; [a.] Killeen, TX

ISGUR, DAVID C.
[b.] September 17, 1957, Boston; [p.] Irving Isgur, Arlene Noodell Isgur; [ed.] Boston University Framingham North High School; [occ.] Newspaper Editor; [memb.] American Civil Liberties Union, American Indian Relief Assoc.; [oth. writ.] Other poems have been converted into songs and have been performed locally.; [pers.] I am influenced by my studies of Native American Shamanism and the belief that we must all speak from the heart. Thanks to all the special women who have taught me and been part of my journey.; [a.] West Hardford, CT

ISOLA, MARIA LIGONS
[b.] January 10, 1953, Oakland, CA; [p.] Doretha Thompson-Adams, S. L. R. Ligons; [m.] Darrel Guido Isola, July 31, 1983; [ch.] Daughter Asia Jovan Isola, Daughter Ylina Raee Isola; [ed.] High School Graduate St Elizabeth Oakland, CA, College American River J.C. Sacto, CA. A.A.; [occ.] Operating Engineer, Boarding Home operator/owner for mentally ill adults; [memb.] The Human Race member in good standing; [hon.] My husband is my only Honor. My children my Awards. (A poem of mine) Asia, Ylina Raee, Darrel; [oth. writ.] Heaven Bound, There's no paper or blood, she called my child a zebra! Papa, My tear are prayers, My Blessings, There ain't enough love in this world.; [pers.] All of my poems come from my feelings, they are either happy, sad, or prayers, I hope to write the story of my life someday in poetry and prose.; [a.] Concord, CA

ISOM, FRANCINE E.
[pen.] Francine Ford; [b.] March 31, 1952, Oakland, CA; [p.] Frances Ford and Robert Ford; [m.] Larry D. Isom, August 10, 1970; [ch.] Karri M. Isom, Paul D. Isom, Robert D. Isom; [ed.] Associate Arts from LeVerne University, Pacific Coast University of Law; [occ.] Volunteer for Association for Retarded Citizens; [memb.] Parents and Advocates for the Developmentally Disabled, Association for Retarded Citizens - Riverside, Association for Retarded Citizens - California; [hon.] Outstanding Service Award - SR9 Review Select Committee - 1990 PADD - Founder President 1988-1993 ARC - California Outstanding Service Award - Residential Committee 1992-1993, ARC-Riverside - Grieshammer Award for Outstanding Service - 1994; [oth. writ.] Short stories, poems and Editorial Articles published in specialty publications; [pers.] Inspired by the love of my special child, I struggle to capture in words only what the heart can truly know.; [a.] Redlands, CA

IVERSON, DANIEL LEE
[b.] November 25, 1975, Chicago, IL; [p.] Gerald and Mary Lou Iverson; [ed.] Oak Park-River Forest High School, currently a student at Triton College; [occ.] Part time computer aide at the Oak Park Public Library; [memb.] St. Matthew Lutheran Church Choir; [hon.] Dean's List (H.S.) Honor roll (H.S.); [pers.] Woman is the greatest gift God gave to this earth. I look all they have to endure and see the strength that carries them through and I am totally left in awe; [a.] River Forest, IL

IWAZAKI, RYUJI
[b.] December 21, 1965, Japan; [occ.] Screenwriter; [oth. writ.] Several poems unpublished, Several movie scripts unpublished.; [pers.] I am an aspiring screen writer, and have written a variety of sections, i.e., romance, mystery, science fiction, comedy, and action. My motto is "Do not be afraid to challenge and do not give up on my dreams." I believe in possibilities of an "Overnight Success."; [a.] Syracuse, NY

JABBOUR, DIANA J.
[b.] January 18, 1966, Fall River, MA; [ed.] Southeastern Massachusetts University (UMASS - Dartmouth) B.S. in Marketing; [occ.] Creative Marketing Associate, Henry Schein Inc. - New York

JABORO, CLAUDINE
[b.] February 3, 1974, Detroit, MI; [p.] Najy and Catherine; [ed.] Our Lady Star of the Sea Elementary and High School Macomb Community College.; [occ.] Student of Science at Macomb Community College; [pers.] Be strong, stand up for what you believe in an take on the world!

JACKSON, DIANE E.
[pen.] Sister Diane B. Jackson; [b.] April 4, 1944, Teaneck, NJ; [p.] George S. Cooper (deceased), Katherine Cooper Brinson; [m.] Rev. James C. Jackson Sr., August 4, 1964; [ch.] Diane Denise, James C., George S., Evelyn L., Jerome K.; [ed.] Completed 12, Scotts College of Beauty Culture 1962, Newark, NJ; [occ.] Housewife, Minister's Wife, Evangelist; [memb.] Poetry Society of America-1993, Greater Israelite Christian Center, C.O.G.I.C.- 1971-1994; [hon.] Golden poet award 1985, 1986, 1991, 1992, Silver Poet Award 1989, 1990, Awards of Merit 1986, 1991, 1991, Echoes of Yesterday, National Library of Poetry - 1994, Editor's Choice Award - National Library of Poetry 1994 East of the sunrise - National Library of Poetry 1995; [oth. writ.] Echoes Of Life by A Preacher's Wife 1981, Hope's in life by a preacher's wife 1992, Poems published in local Newspapers, Newsletters, etc.; [pers.] Most of my poems and other writings are of an inspirational nature, designed to inform, encourage, and comfort.; [a.] San Diego, CA

JACKSON, JUDY C.
[b.] July 30, 1957, Franklin; [p.] Joe Crouch, Jean Crouch; [m.] Charlie Jackson, August 8, 1975; [ch.] Deborah Jean (11), Tiffany Denise (7); [ed.] Franklin High School til 11th Grade. I went back, Sept. '94 passed my GED.; [occ.] Five Points Drug Store Soda Fountain; [memb.] Cool Springs Primitive Baptist Church; [pers.] When you want something bad enough, go for it. Don't put it off. Life don't come easy, unless you make it. Have faith in yourself!; [a.] Franklin, TN

JACKSON, SHERRIE
[pen.] Sherrie Tackett; [b.] April 30, 1957, Ports Mouth, OH; [p.] Clarence and Paula Tackett; [ch.] Aimee Jackson, Mishel Jackson; [occ.] Alliedsignal Aerospace Co.; [memb.] Toast Masters International Word of Grace Church; [pers.] I wish to share my emotional healing with others who are hurting. I write about my own pain and the peace and joy that only God can bring.; [a.] Chandler, AZ

JACKSON, JACQUELINE D.
[pen.] Jaqui; [b.] May 18, 1960, Sardis, AL; [p.] Theodore and Emma Towns; [m.] Charles F. Jackson, Jr., September 14, 1984; [ch.] Whitney Monet and Shayna Chanise; [ed.] Henry Ford High School, University of Detroit Mercy College; [occ.] Legal Clerk, Law Office of Mark Teicher, Southfield, Michigan; [hon.] Presidential Scholarship, University of Detroit Mercy College; [oth. writ.] "Do not be concerned as much about what others expect of you, only what you expect of yourself, for only then will you achieve your ultimate goal"; [a.] Detroit, MI

JACKSON SR., JAMES
[pen.] James Bigsmoke; [b.] February 16, 1948; [m.] Elvira Jackson; [ch.] Deborah, James, Jasmine, Jacob, Jesse, William, Samuel; [ed.] Coulee Dam High, Columbia Basin, Big Bend, and Berean (Bible) Colleges, Powerplant Operator apprentice, Electrician (ICS) Course (Home study); [occ.] Power Operations specialist; [pers.] My goal is to bring as many people to our Lord and Savior Jesus Christ before I die, so that they may dwell in heaven with Jesus after death.; [a.] Coulee Dam, WA

JACKSON, COLLEEN CAPES
[b.] December 4, 1951, Covington, GA; [p.] Marshall I. Capes, Corris Slaughter Capes; [m.] Steven Dwayne Jackson, December 5, 1969; [ch.] Heath Marshall Jackson, Whitney Laine Jackson; [ed.] Newton County High, Dekalb Community College; [occ.] Bookkeeper, Truss Systems and GED Chief Examiner, Dekalb Tech; [memb.] First Church Of Nazarene; [oth. writ.] Several poems published in Creative Licence, 1993, Treasured Poems of America, 1992.; [pers.] This poem is dedicated to my great nephew, Timothy David Case, for whom it is written. Timothy will celebrate his first birthday in eternity September 15, 1995.; [a.] Covington, GA

JACOBS, PAMELA
[b.] February 4, 1954, Harrison, MI; [p.] Anthony Dietz, Ida Dietz; [m.] Augustus Jacobs, July 2, 1972; [ch.] Brandon Kevin Jacobs; [ed.] Seventy-First Senior High Pembroke State University, BS Pembroke State University, MA Ed.; [memb.] NEA, NAEYC, Alpha Chi, National Honor Society; [hon.] Alpha Chi, Chancellor's List, National Honor Society; [pers.] Life is full of surprises. Isn't it fun to get a present almost everyday.; [a.] Fayetteville, NC

JACOBY, MICHELLE L.
[b.] January 14, 1955, Kokomo, IN; [p.] Donnabelle Hayes, Richard R. Hayes; [ed.] Mid Florida Technical Institution; [occ.] Disabled; [memb.] Science of Spirituality; [oth. writ.] Several poems, some published in newsletters; [pers.] My poetry is always an expression of, or reflection on, my feelings about circumstances which directly or indirectly affect my life, or the lives of those who are dear to me.; [a.] Haines City, FL

JACQUES, ANN
[b.] May 26, 1958, Atlantic City; [p.] Lillian and Vernon Spinney; [m.] Leon Jacques, May 17, 1986; [ch.] Robert, and Charlotte, (step children) Donna, Alan and Lynn; [ed.] Associate of Science; [occ.] Medical Transcriber with plans to enter Nursing school; [oth. writ.] Articles in local newspaper; [pers.] I was born an idealist, and live to appreciate the simple things I'm blessed with around me. I'm a dreamer in life, and a dreamer in my writing. I have a special fondness toward writing of motherhood, and of the humor that can be found in raising children.; [a.] Sierra Vista, AZ

JACQUES, JESSICA
[b.] May 10, 1982; [p.] Michael and Lisa Jacques; [ed.] I attend 7th grade at Coventry Middle School Coventry Rhode Island; [oth. writ.] "Life" Published in "Todays Great Poems" 1994.; [pers.] I would like to graduate Coventry High School and attend College on a scholarship program. I want to become a physical therapist and help handicap children.; [a.] Coventry, RI

JACQUES, VALERIE F.
[pen.] Fang and Starlight; [b.] October 31, 1973, Trenton, MI; [ch.] Raven M. Jacques (Ambrose); [ed.] O.A. Carlson High School (Gibraltar) then to John Glenn High School (Westland); [occ.] Full-time single parent; [memb.] American Red Cross Volunteer Blood Donor.; [hon.] Editor's Choice Award 1994 - National Library of Poetry. I am greatly honored to have my 3rd poem published by National Library of Poetry; [oth. writ.] In 1994 "Frozen In Time Without A Chance" was published in: Echoes Of Yesterday, 1995 "In Existence With The Moon" published in: The Best Poems of 1995 - National Library of Poetry.; [pers.] My poems are filled with every emotional twist known to humanity past, present and future. I can only hope more pieces of my dream come true...; [a.] Westland, MI

JAMES, RICHARD A.
[pen.] Richard A. James; [b.] September 22, 1965, Liberty, SC; [p.] Gerald and Roberta James; [m.] Jody James, June 27, 1987; [ch.] Ethan Richard, Emily Diane; [ed.] Liberty High School; [occ.] Polymerization B.A.S.F. Corporation; [memb.] B.A.S.F. Bass Fishing Club Eastside Baptist Church; [pers.] To my family, after all these years, they finally talked me into submitting my poems.; [a.] Liberty, SC

JAMES, KATIE DALYN
[b.] December 15, 1979, Tacoma; [p.] Rebecca Adams and John D. James; [ed.] Currently attending High School in South Kitsap.; [occ.] Student; [oth. writ.] My first out of many to be published.; [pers.] The beauty of God's creations and the love of my brothers is what keeps my spirit strong.; [a.] Colville, WA

JAMES, PEARL E.
[pen.] Lori Maze; [b.] September 7, 1970, Richmond, VA; [p.] Henry and Betty James; [ed.] Currently working on Degree in Journalism; [occ.] Freelance writer/student; [oth. writ.] "Poems to Ponder" and "The Promise", published poem in the anthology, "Echoes n the Silence" by Quill Books; [pers.] I gather some of my ideas for my poems and books from my own experiences and often from things and people that surround me.; [a.] Richmond, VA

JAMES, GLADYS
[b.] June 12, 1917, Gonzales County, TX; [p.] Christian and Nora Spellmann; [m.] William James, February 7, 1941; [ch.] Francine Wright, Billy James and Randy James; [ed.] Bachelor of Arts Degree Texas State Teacher's College, San Marcos, TX; [occ.] Retired High School English Teacher, Somerset, TX; [memb.] Methodist Church Texas State Teacher's Association, Somerset City Council Republican Party; [oth. writ.] My grandson, Trey James, had a book of my poems printed and copies made as Christmas gifts for the family.; [pers.] Writing poetry allows me to express my feelings better than dancing. And I can sit down to do it. I love doing both.; [a.] Somerset, TX

JAMES, MARY D.
[b.] April 2, 1966, Springfield, TN; [p.] Betty J. James and G. Harold James; [ed.] Arsenal Tech High School, Indiana University, Columbia School of Broadcasting; [occ.] Marketing Assistant; [memb.] Trinity C.M.E. Church; [hon.] Dean's List; [oth. writ.] These Eyes, Uneven Score Epitome of a Woman, Deirdra; [pers.] My goal is to tell the story of life through the delicate words of poetry.; [a.] Indianapolis, IN

JAMES, VAUGHN EDWIN
[pen.] Ed James; [b.] December 21, 1931, Crestline, OH; [p.] Coy James, Elsie James; [m.] Betty Alexander James, February 13, 1987; [ch.] Bertrand Russell James, Robert Michael James; [ed.] B.S. from Bowling Green State University, with major in chemistry, M.B.A. from United States International University, with major in economics and finance. Certificate from University of Minnesota, in Information Systems Analysis and Design; [occ.] Computer Consultant; [memb.] Institute for Certification of Computer Professionals, Toastmasters; [hon.] Awarded Competent Toastmaster by International Toastmasters, Awarded $500 by Business Department, St. Cloud State University for publication of "User Functional Procedures", in Journal of Systems Management; [oth. writ.] "Encouraging Use of Reference Documentation" in October 1975, Journal of Systems Management, "Userfunctional Procedures" in September 1982, Journal of Systems Management, numerous other articles on computer technology; [pers.] While I recognize the ever present dangers associated with technological advances, I believe that creation of a kinder and gentler world depends on such technological advances along with advances in population control, animal including human rights, and welfare provision for ourselves and our environment.; [a.] Minneapolis, MN

JAMESON, FRANK JOHN
[pen.] John Jameson; [b.] July 2, 1918, Rupert, VT; [p.] William and Philena Jameson; [m.] Anna Margret Price, July 2. 1945; [ch.] Phylys, Ralph, Nancy, Jacqueline Frank Jr., Donna, Carol, Ginger; [ed.] 8th grade; [occ.] Retired; [memb.] V.F.M., American Legion, D.A.V.; [oth. writ.] Poems for Local School and Realtor; [pers.] I write about love and beauty, that God gave to you and me, also for the good of my fellow man.; [a.] Golden Valley, AZ

JAMISON, THORMAN E. W.
[b.] February 19, 1975, Yonkers, NY; [p.] Ruth Jamison and Daniel Jamison; [ed.] Calhoun Conty High School, St Matthews, SC, Claflin College, Orange Burg, SC, Pace University, White Plains, NY; [occ.] Accounts payable Clerk, Health and Hospitals Corp., Goldwater Memorial Hospital New York, New York; [hon.] Editor on both College newspapers, Editor-in-Chief from 1990-1993 on High School Yearbook, Who's Who Among American High School Students twice.; [oth. writ.] Wrote on the editorial page for the Pace Press, incorporating my poetry. Wrote several poems about people and my everyday life.; [pers.] I thank my College English Teacher for introducing me to poetry and for encouraging me to write. I have been greatly influenced by e. e. cummings, Langston Huges, James Baldwin and Mia Angelu.; [a.] New York, NY

JAY, MICHAEL J.
[b.] December 3, 1930, Bayonne, NJ; [p.] Deceased; [m.] Alice Ann, December 26, 1964; [ch.] Maureen, Kathleen, Jennifer; [ed.] Bachelor of Science Degree - Seton Hall University, South Orange, New Jersey; [occ.] Chemist; [oth. writ.] Published: "Introspection", "The Goodness Of Music", "Dancing Leaves." Many that are yet unpublished.; [pers.] I must truly say my writings are of a romantic nature, and of nature itself and spiritualistic in a sense that humbly gives meaning to life.; [a.] Chatham, NJ

JENKINS, MARVIN
[pen.] Blue; [b.] August 15, 1961, Harrisburg, PA; [p.] Virgina Jenkins, Author J.; [ch.] Daughter - Taylor C.; [ed.] 9th Grd, Harrisburg High, one year Milled School, 2 yrs Doweny Elem.; [occ.] Tantor Labor Harrisburg Housing Authority 5 yrs; [memb.] Poetry group; [oth. writ.] I have a few more, I write for enjoyment; [pers.] I am a recovering addict and a single father. From the time I knew of the struggle I was black as my father so as his before him and than came death as a man; [a.] Harrisburg, PA

JENKINS, TENNYSON
[pen.] Tink and Katinka; [b.] March 4, 1922, Eugene, MO; [p.] Ingram Dwight Jenkins, Lettie Hollaway Jenkins; [m.] Kathryn (Kati) Adcock Jenkins, January 28, 1945; [ch.] James Lee Jenkins, JD Jeans Louise Jenkins Toll; [ed.] Florida State Christian College, Ed. D, University of Missouri, Columbia, ME, James Millikin University, BS.; [occ.] Teacher Emeritus, Fullerton College, writer; [memb.] PHSA, Inc-Life, American Legion-Life, AARP; [hon.] Magna Cum Laude, Florida State Christian College, Phi Kappa Phi, Millikin University, FBLA, Honorary Life Membership, Chapter 140, Anaheim High, CA.; [oth. writ.] Published poetry. Projected: Katinka Land: The story that couldn't wait.; [pers.] Every person is either a teacher or student or both - either teaching by word or deed or learning either directly or indirectly. Katinka is the 'Ti' that binds Kati and Tink together, 50 years of married life. I am a christian.; [a.] Wildomar, CA

JENSEN, ESTHER
[b.] April 10, 1922, Wellsville, NY; [p.] Martha and Rolland Ketchner; [m.] Frank E. Jensen; [ch.] James, Marilyn, Karen, Kirby, Anne and 5 grandchildren.; [ed.] Graduate at Wellsville High School; [occ.] Homemaker; [memb.] Christian Women's Club, AARP, Garden Club, Friendship Club; [oth. writ.] Poems pub-

lished in school newspaper during high school, Articles in local newspaper, other unpublished poems and songs, plus children poems.; [pers.] I try to maintain a positive mental attitude, a sense of humor, a strong faith in God and gratitude to Him, a desire to bring joy to others.; [a.] Ocala, FL

JENSEN, DIANE KAY
[b.] December 1, 1959, Brookings, SD; [p.] Clifford and Lois Sorenson; [ch.] Keith Alan, Stacey Nicole; [ed.] Brookings High School; [occ.] Clerk/Counter help; [memb.] South Dakota Emergency Medical Tech. Association; [oth. writ.] I have wrote many poems but this is the only one I have ever sent in, to this date.; [pers.] I use my poems at away to express my feelings as I am no a very talkative or expressive person. My poems are who I am.; [a.] Brookings, SD

JESITUS, DAVID A.
[b.] October 14, 1966, Ohio; [p.] Elayne Malloy and Robert Jesitus; [ed.] B.S. in Pharmacy, Ohio Northern University, 1990; [occ.] Hospital Pharmacist and part time musician; [memb.] OSHP; [hon.] Dean's list, Outstanding student - Ethics - Ohio Northern University; [oth. writ.] Music Lyrics - several of which appear on self titled "Still Life" release; [a.] Cleveland, OH

JESTER, DANE STEVEN
[pen.] Dane S. Jester; [b.] February 23, 1959, Bastrop, LA; [p.] Claudette N. Smith; [ed.] East Elementary, Prairie View Academy, Ouachita Vo-Tech-Electronic Engineering, Northwest La, University General Studies/Biology; [occ.] Electronics, Compositions, Poems, Songs, Stories; [memb.] Private Groups: Assembly of God, Book Club, Religious Clubs, Science Clubs; [hon.] Literary Rally Compositions; [oth. writ.] Working on two books. Prefer not to list titles, at this point, other than those submitted.; [pers.] Writing is freedom: I feel it should be straight from the thought to the page. Science is great as a tool, but don't allow it to replace your own ideas or sway your convictions.; [a.] Bastrop, LA

JOHNSON, LOIS
[pen.] Lois Johnson; [b.] May 3, 1929, SC; [p.] Ernest and Minnie Brown; [m.] James W. Johnson, August 26, 1949; [ch.] Herbert, James, Lansen, Pamela; [ed.] High School and some College Courses; [occ.] Housewife; [oth. writ.] Two books of poems, bouquet of poems, speakin in poems; [pers.] Received correspondents from - Pres. Clinton, Rev. Jessie Jackson, and Maye Angelou, for personal poem, write for Odessa still Gospel time on NABQ in Cleveland Ohio

JOHNSON, JODY
[b.] February 13, 1959, Osage, IA; [p.] Al and Louise Halbach; [m.] James Johnson, April 24, 1976; [ch.] I have 3 children, Jenisha, Jaython, Jeramie; [ed.] I am a high school graduate. I went to Osage Community Schools.; [occ.] Dietary aide at Faith Lutheran Home in Osage. Also a farm wife.; [memb.] Our Saviors Lutheran Church, Farm Bureau, Osage Booster Club; [oth. writ.] I have written a few other poems; [pers.] I was first inspired to write poetry 7 years ago, after the death of my Dad. My first poem was about him. It actually took me 7 years to complete it. I enjoy writing about events in my life. "Life On The Farm" came from my feelings about my family and the farm. I have since been forced to find a job away from our farm.; [a.] Osage, IA

JOHNSON, CLOVIS
[pen.] Clovis; [b.] April 12, 1961, Jamaica; [p.] Azarine, Mother, Vincent T. Johnson; [ed.] 4th Grade; [occ.] Unemploy; [pers.] Human Being is unpredictable; [a.] Suffield, CT

JOHNSON, JENNIFER R.
[pen.] Jenny Johnson; [b.] April 5, 1983, Port Huron, MI; [p.] Frank and Joyce Johnson; [ed.] Cros-Lex Middle School; [occ.] Student; [memb.] 6th grade Stu-

dent Council; [hon.] Presidential Academic Fitness Award, Honor Roll Student; [pers.] My writings is based on my opinion about different topics.; [a.] Croswell, MI

JOHNSON, GAYLE BELLIZAN
[b.] April 14, 1950, New Orleans; [p.] Mr. Paul Bellizan Sr., Mother, the late Myrtle Vivian Brooks Bellizan; [m.] Oscar Johnson Jr., October 28, 1981; [ch.] Lyntrell Catrice; [ed.] Assoc. Degree/Business, High School: Walter Louis Cohen Junior High: Samuel James Green Elementary: Paul Lawrence Dunbar; [occ.] Administrative Secretary Orleans Parish School Board; [memb.] New Orleans Public Schools (NOPS) Assoc. Educ Office Personnel (AEOP); [hon.] New Orleans Public Schools Certification Program for Secretaries (CEOE), Certified Secretary; [oth. writ.] Lovebirds, Nature Loving at Sunset, Tribute to Fathers, A courageous Woman, The Man Who Moves Me and Creation, And Life is Like a Clock that ticks and A heart that beats (all published); [pers.] My desire thru my prose, poetry and writings is to touch the saddest heart and bring sunshine to the inner soul. I want my readers to know that, I see them as "A Precious Pearl.".; [a.] New Orleans, LA

JOHNSON, PATRICIA IRENE
[pen.] Irene Gothard; [b.] February 8, 1941, Miami, AZ; [p.] Herman George and EdDith Gothard; [m.] L. L. Johnson (deceased); [ch.] Michelle Christine; [ed.] Miami High Arizona Western Jr. College; [occ.] Retired; [memb.] Veteran - US Army, Natl Honor Society, D.E.S. Ruby Chapter #3; [pers.] I'm happiest when I can make someone else smile.; [a.] Tucson, AZ

JOHNSON, NANCY S.
[pen.] Nancy Johnson; [b.] May 22, 1955, Belvidere, IL; [p.] Elmer Frank, Della Mae Audley; [m.] Russell E. Johnson, July 30, 1983; [ed.] Belvidere High, Rock Valley College; [occ.] Research Reader Bacon's Information, Rockford, IL; [memb.] Salem Lutheran Church; [hon.] Dean's List Rock Valley College, Going beyond Barriers Award; [oth. writ.] Other poems not seen, but cherished by me.; [pers.] I wrote this poem for my husband to let him know how I feel, and feel about him.; [a.] Rockford, IL

JOHNSON, MICHAEL
[b.] July 14, 1975, Allentown, PA; [p.] Marlene Johnson, Robert Johnson (deceased); [ed.] High School, Emmaus; [occ.] PC/Lan Specialist; [oth. writ.] Future Specs - Multimedia J.E.D.; [pers.] Do not let the past dictate the future - for the future is yours alone. Success is what you earn and not what you've given.; [a.] Macungie, PA

JOHNSON, NIGEL LAMAR
[pen.] Nosnohu Legin; [b.] May 10, 1959, Oakland; [p.] Cleve and Betty Johnson; [m.] Sharon Dian Johnson, July 1, 1995; [ch.] Ryan, Cameron, Trevor, Vaughn; [ed.] Graduated - Monte Vista High School in 1977 - 2 yrs Diablo Valley College; [occ.] Inventory Control Consultant - TIFCO Industries; [memb.] San Francisco Christian Center, Carpenters Union Local 152 Martinez California; [pers.] My writings are solely influenced by God. I am but a vehicle for his glory.; [a.] Oakland, CA

JOHNSON, PENNY
[pen.] Penny Johnson; [b.] July 1, 1940, Danville, KY; [p.] Irene Sebastian, Bufuro Carr; [m.] William Evan Johnson, July 15, 1958; [ch.] William E. Johnson Jr., Robert Anthony Johnson; [ed.] Graduate Famous Writers School - Westport, Conn. - Newspaper Institute of America - N.Y. U.S.A.; [occ.] Free-lance, Writer-poet; [memb.] International Society of Poets - International Order of Merit - National Writer's Club - American Biographical Institute - International Biography Center - England; [hon.] Golden - Ruby - Emerald Poet-Editors Choice Award, National Library of Poetry - Semifinalist North American Poetry open - 4 Awards of Merit - I.S.P.; [oth. writ.] "Awesome" - "The Balance of Nature" - "Light in the Night" - "Fall's Fabulous Gifts"

- "A Poem for Peace" sent to the United Nations - "A Magic Moment"; [pers.] Poetry expresses feelings in a special way - The Poet and the reader have a bond that can never be broken - "It is a spiritual thing"; [a.] Lexington, KY

JOHNSON, BREE LYNN
[pen.] Bree Lynn; [b.] March 9, 1977, Boise, ID; [ed.] I am a student at Highland High School, Craigmont.; [oth. writ.] Short stories, other poems and a single play that I performed at Drama Districts and got 3rd; [pers.] No matter what never quit. If someone says that you can't prove to them that you can.; [a.] Reubens, ID

JOHNSON, LUNDI LEE
[pen.] Lundi; [b.] June 9, 1974, Winterset; [p.] Dale Johnson; [ed.] Winterset High School, Hamilton Business College.; [occ.] Secretary; [hon.] Dean's List; [pers.] I have loved poetry since I was a child, I think enjoying it inspired me to write it. You learn about me and my life through my poems.; [a.] Winterset, IA

JOHNSTON, JULIE KATHRYN
[b.] April 14, 1982, Grafton, ND; [p.] Linda and Jim Johnston Jr.; [ed.] I am in the 7th grade at Nash School, Nash, North Dakota. I take piano lessons and band lessons. I have also been trained in baby sitting at a clinic in Grafton at the Vocational Center.; [memb.] Zion Lutheran Church, Youth Group, and Conformation Class, rural Hoople, ND, Girls basketball in Grafton, ND; [hon.] I was the 1994 State winner of the Michael Jordan Foundation Education Club. I was awarded a weekend trip to Chicago to meet Michael Jordan. They gave me many wonderful prizes. I was a member of the North Dakota State Prairie Rose Games Championship Basketball Team in 1994.; [oth. writ.] I won a jingle contest for Raney's Recycling Center in Drayton, ND. I was given a t-shirt.; [pers.] Never stop trying because someday you might succeed.; [a.] Grafton, ND

JOHNSTON, NICHOLE DIANE
[pen.] Niki, Love (favorite name); [b.] March 17, 1977, Mesquite, TX; [p.] William and Alice Johnston; [ed.] West Mesquite High School; [hon.] Who's Who Among American High School Students; [oth. writ.] Hundreds of other poems that I would like to have published someday so that others can enjoy them as much as I do.; [pers.] I believe in love and friendship, and that is the bottom line behind everything I write. My inspirations are simply the people that love me... nothing more, nothing less!!; [a.] Mesquite, TX

JOLLY, TRICIA
[b.] December 16, 1976, Kansas City, MO; [p.] Bill Jolly, Ken and Kathleen McDonald; [m.] Adam Haas, March 10, 1995; [ed.] High School - Shawnee Mission Northwest in Shawnee, Kansas. I'm currently enrolled there and also at our local Community College.; [occ.] Student; [memb.] Youth Group at Emmanuel Baptist Church in Overland Park, Kansas; [hon.] Honor Roll at Shawnee Mission Northwest High School; [oth. writ.] This is my first piece of published poetry, but I have been writing for many years now.; [a.] Lenexa, KS

JONES, ANDREW L.
[b.] March 19, 1935, Detroit; [p.] Hubert Jones and Carrie; [m.] Rosa L. Jones; [ch.] Jeffrey, Adrian, April Jones; [ed.] Graduate of Highland Park High; [occ.] Retiree of Chrysler Corp.; [oth. writ.] As a hobby, I have written several poems as a non-professional during 1959-1962.; [a.] Detroit, MI

JONES, ELVA R.
[pen.] Elva Jones; [b.] September 13, 1930, Halley, AR; [p.] Richard and Ruth Bullock; [m.] Stuart Jones, July 30, 1986; [ch.] Carol L. Froysland, Lynn M. Force; [ed.] Dermott High School, various college extension courses. U.S. Air Force, Control Tower Operator School; [occ.] Retired - Editor and writer of "Valle Verde Voice" Newsletter.; [memb.] Women in Military Ser-

vice for America Memorial Foundation; [oth. writ.] Ex-editor and writer for "Inside the Reef", Midway Island Newspaper. "A Pacific Island Fable" and "The Adventures of Winner the albatross", Children's Stories Awaiting Publishers.; [pers.] It is the rhythm, as well as the rhyme of poetry that I find satisfying. I like trying to communicate emotion, whether by poetry or prose. It's a way of sharing.; [a.] San Marcos, CA

JONES, ERIN BREE
[b.] May 23, 1975, Tampa, FL; [p.] Thomas and Susan Domorski; [m.] James Michael Jones; [ch.] Rachel Virginia; [pers.] This poem was written for encouragement before my first job interview. I dedicate it to every child with a dream. Go for it and don't look down!

JONES, FRANCES FLETCHER
[b.] August 4, 1929, Springfield, OH; [p.] Brindley and Mary Carter; [m.] Orland Jones, June 6, 1981; [ch.] 3 by previous marriage are Deceased - 5 step children; [ed.] High School graduate Chaple Hill Studying Childcare Supervision; [occ.] Retired; [a.] Springfield, OH

JONES, LESLIE RENEE STINEHELFER
[b.] July 22, 1966, Atlanta, GA; [p.] James D. Nancy C. Stinehelfer; [m.] Kenneth Carroll Jones, October 5, 1984; [ch.] Jamie Denise Stinehelfer, Jesse Garrett Jones; [ed.] Elm. School, some High School; [occ.] Homemaker; [oth. writ.] Various poems not yet submitted to anyone.; [pers.] Treat your fellow man with respect. Strive to do your best always. Honor God in everything you do.; [a.] Norcross, GA

JONES, PAGET
[pen.] Paget Mohammed; [b.] March 18, 1957, Wichita, KS; [ed.] B.A. English Literature, M.A. in English - Columbia University, New York; [occ.] Teacher, Educator; [memb.] Active member of Humane Society of the U.S., Active member of PETA; [hon.] Kappa Delta Pi; [oth. writ.] Author "Making of a World." Editorials published in various newspapers.; [a.] New York, NY

JONES, PATRICIA ANN
[b.] February 27, 1960, Cleveland, OH; [p.] Ethel and David Jones; [ed.] Jane Addams Vocational High School, Cuyahoga Community College - Metro Cleveland State University; [occ.] Office Assistant I Cleveland Board of Education; [memb.] First United Methodist Church; [hon.] The Martha Holden Jennings Award, Golden Book Award; [oth. writ.] My Father My Tree, Freedom, Abiding Citizen, Love is Kind, Who Dare Dream America, not published; [pers.] Peace is not something to be won in a fight it lives deep in our souls empowers us to do what is right — Peace unto mankind for God He is love; [a.] Cleveland, OH

JONES, TANYCE
[pen.] Tanyce Jones; [b.] June 25, 1972, Chicago; [p.] Marshell Austin and Charlie McCray; [m.] Daryl Jones, February 14, 1991; [ch.] Beunca Jones; [ed.] Southeast College, Kansas Voc. School, Southside High, Lincoln Jr. High; [occ.] Computer Operator (lead); [oth. writ.] Book (To Lovers Everywhere) which contains 40 poems due to be published by Dorrance Publishing Company.; [pers.] My writings are often the inspiration of people in love. I am greatly influenced by the sadness of the earth.; [a.] Memphis, TN

JONES, VICKIE RENEE
[b.] October 22, 1961, Hattiesburgh, MS; [p.] Roosevelt and Bertha Lewis; [m.] Rev. Robert C. Jones Jr., May 17, 1980; [ch.] Robert C. Jones III, Tonia Trinette Jones and Roosevelt Cortez Jones; [ed.] 1979 Graduate - East St. Louis Sr. High, East St. Louis, IL 1985 Graduate - Hickey Business School, St. Louis, MO.; [occ.] Customer Service Clerk - Union Electric Co., St. Louis, MO; [memb.] I.B.E.W. Local 1455, Interdenominational Pastors and Ministers Wives, East St. Louis, IL, St. John Missionary Baptist Church,

Centreville IL; [pers.] Writing for me is an inspiration from God and it is to Him I give all Glory and Praise.; [a.] East St. Louis, IL

JONES, WILLIAM Q.
[pen.] Hasaah; [b.] August 29, 1968, Baltimore, MD; [p.] Rosa and William Jones; [ch.] Quinlena Jones; [ed.] Fredrick Douglas High School, Baltimore, MD, Wake Tech Community College; [memb.] Brother-Hood in Islam!!; [hon.] Being a semi-finalist in the 1995 North American Open Poetry Contest; [oth. writ.] 2 unpublished books entitled, "Shadows of my Soul," and "No One to Hear Me Cry"; [pers.] I write what my heart and soul feel and see. I believe that as a man in this day and time, we as humans have to search for the truth that will allow our "Leaders of Tomorrow" to be secure in a world that at times, will fail them.; [a.] Raleigh, NC.

JONES JR., EARL
[pen.] Earl Jones Jr.; [b.] May 27, 1948, Philadelphia, PA; [p.] Earl Jones Sr. and Doris Jones; [m.] Brenda Taylor, February 24, 1968; [ch.] Brenda and Rashaun Jones; [ed.] South Philadelphia High School and Community College of Philadelphia; [occ.] Contractor, Singer, Songwriter, poet; [memb.] Mt. Airey Church of God in Christ, Mt. Airey Drama Guild, Gospel Singing Group "New Image"; [hon.] High School Graduate; [oth. writ.] A variety of songs and several poems published in vocal newspapers; [pers.] My ambition is to be an established songwriter and poet. My philosophy "Dream and Pursue that dream, because dreams do come true, God is in control"; [a.] Philadelphia, PA

JONES JR., GARY A.
[pen.] E. Nigma; [b.] July 24, 1979, Cleveland, OH; [p.] Gary A. Jones Sr., Marcella Jones; [ed.] Home Schooling; [occ.] Student, Sales-person; [memb.] LYO, (at Church); [hon.] Honor and Merit Roll, Student of the Quarter; [oth. writ.] Several poems being kept in a notebook, waiting to be read by all the world; [pers.] I got my inspiration to write my poetry from my girlfriend Jamie. She means the world to me. I love you Jamie; [a.] Cleveland, OH

JONES SR., BOBBY J.
[b.] March 24, 1951, Jackson, MS; [p.] Ruth and Robert Jones; [m.] Divorced; [ch.] Bobby Jr. and Jennifer; [ed.] Jeff Davis Jr. College, Gulfport, MS; [occ.] Sales Consultant; [memb.] Nativity Lutheran Church and Choir.; [pers.] My writings have been based generally on life and my travels, but also on the people that have shared my existence on God's Earth.; [a.] Florence, MS

JORDAN JR., FORREST D.
[b.] September 3, 1953, N. N., VA; [p.] Forrest D. (Bill) Sr. and Dorothy H. Jordan; [ch.] Pebbles; [ed.] Frank W. Cox High, Tidewater College, Famous Arts Schools; [occ.] Professional Musician, Computer Designer, Writer; [memb.] American Cancer Society, Star Light Foundation; [hon.] Dean's List; [oth. writ.] "Forrest: The collective works of", "Bill and Me"; [pers.] Any and all my works are hereby dedicated to my beloved father who recently went into the presence of our Lord, January 26, 1995. Thanks for always being there for me, Dad...; [a.] Virginia Beach, VA

JOSEPH, MICHELE
[b.] April 7, 1978, Columbus, OH; [p.] Tony Joseph, Linda Joseph; [ed.] Ft. Hayes Metropolitan Education Center; [occ.] Student; [memb.] Columbus Museum of Art; [hon.] Honor roll, Athletic Awards, Certificate of merit for Art, Certificate of Scholarship for American History, Academic Awards (Page, Knight), Citizenship Awards, Yearbook Award.; [oth. writ.] Several poems one of which is published as a greeting card.; [pers.] I am highly interested in writing and learning more about poetry; [a.] Dublin, OH

JOSEPHSON, GRETCHEN L.
[pen.] Gretchen; [b.] August 25, 1954, Denver CO; [p.] Carl J. Josephson M.D. (deceased), Lula O. Lubchenco M.D.; [ed.] Denver Public School - Special Education (Gretchen has down syndrome); [occ.] Stock Floater at Foley's Department Store; [memb.] Country Music Association Warren United Methodist Church Jewish Community Center, Arc of Denver, Mile High Down Syndrome Assoc., Smithsonian Institution; [hon.] Mile High Down Syndrome Associations, Presidents Award; [oth. writ.] Peace and other poems, Bus Girl, Love for Always. (Selected ones published in the National Down Syndrome News); [pers.] I dream of having my poems purr to music by country music artists; [a.] Denver, CO

JUNG, VICKI
[b.] May 28, 1947, Charlottesville, VA; [p.] Doris and Joe Vicars; [m.] Brian Jung, December 30, 1988; [ch.] Stewart Grossman, Kimberly Grossman; [ed.] M.A. in Psychology; [occ.] Certified Mental Health Counselor at Jung, Jung and Associates; [memb.] American Association of Suicidology, Allied Health Professionals, Washington State Youth Suicide Prevention Committee; [hon.] "Giraffe" Award—for "sticking my neck out" as Co-founder of the Youth Suicide Prevention Center; [oth. writ.] Articles of youth suicide prevention published in "The Eastside Mother's Helper", 1990 Resource Directory and in "Bothell Police Officers Guild 1993 Business Directory and Safety Journal", several articles published in Seattle newspapers.; [pers.] "I Love You Because..." in memory to my husband, Brian, who died November 4, 1994.; [a.] Bothell, WA

KACHIGIAN, RICK
[b.] January 22, 1955; [p.] Jack and Nancy Kachigian; [m.] Susan Kachigian, December 18, 1976; [ch.] Nikki Sue, Lauren Brooke, Courtney Marie; [ed.] Garden City High School, Tennessee Temple University; [occ.] Retail Management - Damman Hardware

KAHN, JEROME
[b.] June 9, 1943, Philadelphia; [p.] Edward and Shirley Kahn; [m.] Victoria Hopkins Khan, May 1, 1988; [ed.] BA Temple U., Philadelphia, PA, 2 yrs. graduate studies, Philosophy U. of Manitoba, Manitoba, British Columbia; [occ.] Federal Prisoner; [oth. writ.] University and local newspaper, Outlaw-Biker Mag (article on Prison Life), Autumn Meditations (book of poetry); [pers.] Utilitarian-Skeptic scientific Weltans Chauung "Through my writing I attempt to stimulate thought."; [a.] Glendale, AZ

KAIL, SUZANNE
[ed.] Capital University, Ohio State University; [occ.] English Teacher, Gahanna-Lincoln High School, Gahanna Ohio

KAISER, PATSY
[b.] March 24, 1955, San Bernardino, CA; [p.] Dolores Douglas, Arthur Douglas; [m.] Wally Kaiser, February 4, 1989; [ed.] 1-12 and 1st year of college.; [occ.] Office Assistant Patton State Hospital; [oth. writ.] I've been writing poems since I was in Junior High. I haven't written much in years, until I came to the Lord recently this last year in 1994.; [pers.] I hope this poem would reach people and help them give their lives to the Lord. So they could see how much better their lives could be with the Lord helping them, and loving them like he does. God can change your life.

KAMINSKY, DAWN
[b.] February 18, 1970, Chestnut Ridge, NY; [p.] Howard and Karen Kaminsky; [ed.] Spring Valley High, State University of New York at Delhi, State University College at Oneonta; [occ.] Teacher (Elementary) Cobleskill-Richmondville Central School; [hon.] 1990 National Dean's List; [a.] Schoharie, NY

KAMMERER, MARK JUSTIN
[pen.] Mark Kammerer; [b.] September 27, 1972, Denver CO; [p.] Mary and Carlyle Kammerer; [ed.] Community College of Aurora. Aurora, Colorado; [occ.] Apprentice Electrician

KANE JR., DOUGLAS
[pen.] Doug Kane; [b.] October 20, 1941, Brooklyn, NY; [p.] Douglas Kane, Margaret Kane; [m.] Divorced; [ch.] Michael Kane and Robert Kane who is now deceased; [ed.] Midwood High School Brooklyn, NY - presently attending Broward Community College for A.S. degree in Paralegal Studies; [occ.] Legal Reorder-clerk for legal aid services of Broward County Inc.; [oth. writ.] Collections of poems; [pers.] To Rob (Rags), was penned in loving memory of my son Robert, who took his life at the age of sixteen; [a.] Margate, FL

KAPHAN, ADAM J.
[b.] January 31, 1984, Bronx, NY; [p.] Robin F. and Mitchell L. Kaphan; [ed.] I am a 5th grade student at William B. Ward Elementary School, New Rochelle, NY; [occ.] Student; [memb.] U.S.T.A. Beth El Synagogue Youth Group; [hon.] William B. Ward School Student Service Award; [pers.] I feel that all people should be encouraged to respect and care for the earth. It will not be around forever if we don't take care of it.; [a.] New Rochelle, NY

KARLES, KERRI
[b.] April 21, 1980, Mesa, AZ; [p.] Louis and Susan Sesate; [ed.] I'm a freshman at Gilbert High School.; [occ.] Student; [hon.] National Junior Honors Society. I'm also being honored to be in an Advanced Women's Choral group; [oth. writ.] About five poems in my school newspapers.; [pers.] "When I write my poems I'm usually writing my feelings and it's much easier to write my feelings down than just talk about them." [a.] Gilbert, AZ

KARPER, AMY R.
[b.] February 18, 1968, Harrisburg, PA; [p.] Mona Nailor/Bill Nailor and Ray Getz/Linda Getz; [m.] Robert S. Karper, October 18, 1992; [ed.] Cumberland Valley H.S. 1986; [memb.] VFW Ladies Aux Newville Post 6070; [pers.] My writings are my deepest feelings. My grandfather and nana were my greatest influence. Nana always said patience is a virtue.; [a.] Aspers, PA

KASTNER, TAYLOR
[b.] May 2, 1978, Ida Grove, IA; [occ.] Working on BSN Degree; [pers.] Why are we fighting ourselves my friend? Can't you see that we are all brothers. First fight the struggle inside yourself before you fight the struggle of our world.; [a.] Castana, IA

KATZ, PETER H.
[pen.] Michael Orogo (previous); [b.] May 2, 1916, Vienna, Austria; [p.] Leo Katz, Hedwig Korngold Katz; [m.] Evelyn Borkovec Katz, February 14, 1982; [ch.] Robert Borkovec, George Borkovec, Rick Borkovec, Thomas Borkovec, Michael Steven Katz, David Katz; [ed.] Vrye School, Yale University, Westminster College, So. Cal. School of Music and Arts; [occ.] Arts and arts instruction Parnassus Academy of the arts; [memb.] Augustana Lutheran Church US Air Force, Music Teachers Assn., Eagle Country Club, Opera West, Catharsis, US Fencing Assn. Cheyenne Fencing Assn. Tech Writers and various little Theater Groups and Art Groups; [hon.] Prizes for Art Contests Musical Compositions Performed, Directed Opera and plays, paintings, Hon. Mention, Writings, and Acting Nominated for Anthony Award in Cyrano; [oth. writ.] Poems, stories, plays, articles and sermons, in German, Dutch and English Technical documents; [pers.] I refuse to limit myself to my knowledge of the obvious. Life is not "This or that" but "this and that"; [a.] Denver, CO

KECK, JAY ELDON
[pen.] The Vietnam Boogie Man; [b.] January 20, 1947, Kendallvile, IN; [p.] Ralph Sr. and Ruth Keck; [m.] Linda Lou Keck, March 3, 1971; [ch.] Carrie - 12, Aaron - 11; [ed.] Lakeland High School, LaGrance IN Class of '65; [occ.] VA Disability; [memb.] DAV VVA; [hon.] Purple Heart; [oth. writ.] The Vietnam Boogie Man - Book of poems about Vietnam; [pers.] Helping to heal other Vietnam and survivors of PTSD; [a.] Wolcottville, IN

KEELING, RODGER HAROLD
[pen.] Rodger Harold Keeling; [b.] June 29, 1959, Chicago, IL; [p.] Harold Keeling, Ramona Keeling; [m.] Single; [ed.] College 2 years; [occ.] Construction-musician carpenter; [memb.] Civil defense, Martial Arts; [oth. writ.] Bomb Sadam, The Seek, Trouble Music is my Wife, etc.; [pers.] Rodger is a unique song writer musician and poet. Rodger's dream is to be recognized as a rock and roll performer. He would love to hear from anyone interested in his talents.; [a.] Tarpon Springs, FL

KEHRER, MELVIN RAY
[pen.] Melvin R. Kehrer; [b.] January 12, 1941, Ypslante, MI; [p.] Joseph L. and Dorothy May Kehrer; [m.] Evelyn Jenkins, 1981; [ch.] two daughters and one son; [ed.] Milan, Mich. and graduated from Milan High School in 1959.; [occ.] Greenup Farmer's Supply as a certified small engine tech for the last four years.; [memb.] In High School I was in speech, one year band-as color guard, and Jr. and Sr. plays.; [oth. writ.] I wrote a lot at Fo. Mo. Co. but have taken it serious the last few years.; [a.] Southshore, KY

KEIGLEY, MARGARET
[b.] May 9, 1915, Minneapolis, MN; [m.] October 23, 1954; [ed.] Central High School, Minneapolis, Minneapolis School of Fine Arts Univ. of Minnesota; [occ.] Retired; [memb.] United Church of Christ. United Federation of Doll Clubs Boone County and Madrid Historical Society, Senior Assoc. of Madrid, Anna Dalander Questers Chp. 912; [hon.] Ribbons and Awards at various state and county ceramic shows and fairs.; [oth. writ.] Prose and poetry published in regional convention publication.; [pers.] I enjoy writing and hope that I will leave a useful message. Whittier and Longfellow are two of my favorite authors. My grandmother was a very wonderful poet.; [a.] Madrid, IA

KEITH, DARLENE BROWN
[b.] October 3, 1960, Bristol, TN; [p.] Jerry L. Brown, June A. Damron (deceased); [m.] Kanta Leon Keith, January 31, 1991; [ch.] Branden L. Keith, Wykisha D. Keith; [ed.] Gibbs High, Corryton, TN.; [occ.] Disabled-Housewife; [memb.] American Diabetes Association; [hon.] Certificate of Excellence choral whittle springs Jr. High Knox., TN; [oth. writ.] I have written numerous poems and songs never published; [pers.] "There are numerous family members I wish to thank for my special talents. Because each and everyone of them lives in me, one way or another. "God bless us everyone."; [a.] Knoxville, TN

KELLAHER JR., WILLIAM J.
[b.] November 12, 1931, Brooklyn, NY; [p.] Alice and William (Deceased); [m.] Elaine (Deceased); [ch.] William III; [ed.] Law School; [occ.] Senior Appeals Rep. Paralyzed Veterans of America; [oth. writ.] Book of poetry entitled "He Never Asked Why" Franklin Publishing Co., Philadelphia, PA, Library of Congress Catalog Card #76-22289 ISBN #0-87133-070-9 Copyright 1976; [pers.] The poet is (normally) the non-biased observer of human nature and universal life. Poetry should enrich and touch people. Pretty words without power cannot uplift or reach out or affect change.

KELLER, DIANA
[b.] January 25, 1982, Elkhart, IN; [p.] Vance and Laura Keller; [occ.] Student; [memb.] Westside Middle School Volleyball, Basketball, American Volleyball Assoc. player, AAU Basketball player, Little League, Teen NYI Drama Group; [hon.] MVP Softball 116th grade principal's honor roll 94-95, Community Service Award 94, Optimist Club Speech Award 94, Best Attitude Award 6th grade basketball.; [oth. writ.] Many poems; [a.] Elkhart, IN

KELLEY, TIMOTHY P.
[b.] September 20, 1970, Lowell, MA; [ed.] U Mass at Lowell American Studies Grad: 1993; [occ.] Carpenter; [oth. writ.] Lots and more; [pers.] I had spent the Summer of "94", traveling in my pick up truck across the country and have settled in Boulder Co, for the time being.; [a.] Boulder, CO

KELLEY, CHERYL
[b.] August 12, 1947, Waterloo, IA; [p.] M. D. and Eula Kelley; [m.] Jimmy Key, February 14, 1988; [ed.] ADN - McLennan Community College, Waco, TX, BSN-University of Texas, Arlington; [occ.] Registered Nurse (Psychiatric); [pers.] As a student nurse, I stayed with a premature baby (just born by C-section) until it died. I then met the mother after the surgery and talked with her about her baby boy.; [a.] Fort Worth, TX

KELLEY, CAPT. GARDNER M.
[b.] January 20, Jonesport, ME; [m.] Vera, October 27, 1931; [ed.] High School and College of Hard Knocks, Self taught Navigator; [occ.] Retired; [memb.] AFAL Seamans Union, Maritime Union, AF and AM Masons, ELKS Lodge, Two Writers Groups; [hon.] 82 years of Membership of Life; [oth. writ.] 5 unpublished books; [pers.] I write fiction only of things that happen or could happen; [a.] Zephyrhills, FL

KELLOGG, PATIENCE JOYCE
[pen.] Mardi Treadwell; [b.] April 9, 1937, Claremont, NH; [p.] Ernest and Rachael Kangas; [m.] Gerald L. Kellogg, January 27, 1968; [ch.] Abe 21, Alan 23, Andy 25 Kellog's-Idaho; [ed.] Spokane Comm College, Springfield High School, Waterbury High School, Rockpoint School for Girls; [occ.] C.P.R. certified volunteer 2/95 Loundry Aide, Practical Nurse, Vegetarian Cook; [memb.] YWCA for 10 years, Women's Club Toastmaster's Adventist Church, 12 more Spo. St. Andrew's Episc.. Church Spo. Denver's Park Dept. Seniors 50+.; [hon.] Being a mother to 2 smart - wonderful children. Springfield, VA, published a poem for me. 1st, 2nd, 3rd prize in 50+ Joggers Medals.; [oth. writ.] "Gratitude" - "Interview Me" - "Father's Day"; [a.] Lincoln, NE

KELLY, JOEY MERIS
[b.] April 25, 1951, Windber, PA; [p.] George and Nancy Merisko; [m.] Joseph J. Kelly, currently separated; [ch.] Nancy, 18 yrs., and Shawn 10 yrs.; [ed.] B.S. Penn State MBA and Ph.D. Columbia Pacific University, Flight Schools - Rcud Helicopter Commercial, instructor, instrument, instructor ratings; [occ.] Helicopter Pilot Instructor; [memb.] Whirley Girls #762 Ninety-Nines, Nat'l Council of Women in Aviation and Aeronautics, Nat'l Aeronautics Association, American Helicopter Society, Seaplane Pilots Assoc. Aircraft owners and pilots Assoc.; [hon.] Mu Alpha Theta (Nat'l Math honor society), Scroll's (university women's honor society), H-H Merit award - Leadership (as county agent) 4-H State Award (as youth); [oth. writ.] Training Manuals on Youth employment programs and career development, articles on flight training; [pers.] This poem "The measure of a man" was written in memory of William R. Kelly, Sr., my late father-in-law. I wrote it at his funeral mass as a way of dealing with my grief.; [a.] Orlando, FL

KELLY, MARIA R.
[b.] March 20, 1975, Orlando, FL; [p.] Michael J. and Rose M. Kelly; [hon.] Dean's List; [pers.] My poetry is a personal glimpse into the exciting life which I lead.; [a.] Orlando, FL

KELLY, TERESA BAKER
[b.] January 10, 1949, Tallassee, AL; [p.] Henry; [m.] John Kelly, August 19, 1972; [ch.] Ryan 14, Wisley 20; [ed.] BS Univ. of Ala. MA Livingston, Additional study Trinity College, Cambridge, Greek Hellenic Union, Athens; [occ.] English Teacher Selma Middle School and Concordia College; [memb.] Mississippi Writers Association Mississippi Philological Assoc. College Language Assoc.; [oth. writ.] Article of Faulkner published in PMPA, author entry in Guide to Alabama Literature, "My Concerns" in Alabama English

KELSCH, CHLOE J.
[pen.] Victoria Marie; [b.] December 2, 1981, Piedmonth, GA; [p.] Penelope Kelsch, Edward Kelsch; [ed.] 7th Grade at Avondale Elem., Howard Hughes Summer, Science Inst. Graduation; [occ.] Baby-Sitter; [hon.] Writers Tea Beta Club Award Citizenship Award - 7 Honor Awards, Howie - Best Characters, Social science fairworld first place; [oth. writ.] The Rose-May, My Baby life-Genral Lee April-Spring - Summer-Winter; [pers.] I believe in myself and that if you try hard enough at anything you'll be able to do it! And don't ever let anybody tell you that you can't do something.; [a.] Avondale Estates, GA

KEMP, LORI
[b.] September 3, 1968, Phoenix, AZ; [p.] Jack and Anita Riehm; [m.] Lewis A. Kemp Jr., February 24, 1990; [ch.] Erika Tara; [ed.] Shadow Mountain H.S., Rio Salado Community College; [occ.] Service Deli Bakery, Assistant Manager; [oth. writ.] Other poems published in church bulletins and high school anthology; [pers.] To have my poetry help others through emotional hardships as writing it has helped me through mine; [a.] Phoenix, AZ

KEMP, MARJORIE EASTER
[b.] April 16, 1922, Rochester, NY; [p.] Howard H. and Ruth Brown Kemp; [ed.] Graduate (1945) of University of Miami, Florida Music School, studied with fine 'cello teachers at Eastman School of Music, Rochester, NY, further education, Fredonia State Teachers College, NY, Music Therapist, Cedar Grove, NY; [occ.] Retired, but actively engaged musician; [memb.] Sigma Alpha Jota, National Honorary Music Fraternity, Daughters of American Revolution, Downtown United Presbyterian Church in Rochester, NY (3rd generation member); [hon.] Sigma Alpha Jota, Sword of Honor for 18 years of Brailing books for the blind for Des Moines, Iowa library (volunteer); [oth. writ.] (10 books of poetry) "From the Ridiculous to the Sublime," "Keep Time to the Drum," "Can't Help Singing," "Rainbow Before Seven," "Yet Another Summer," "Pick O'the Poet," "Even Song," "Bootprints in the Snow," "The Empty Cross," "Poetic Postline"; [pers.] Received more recognition in my hobby, writing than in my profession (music). Avid oil painter, taught ten years, violin, 'cello, piano and autoharp at Hochstein Memorial Music School in Rochester, NY. Taught public school music at Bainbridge, NJ. Composer of 8 anthems and various other musical compositions.; [a.] Rochester, NY.

KENNEALLY, MARY L.
[pen.] Mary L. Kenneally; [b.] May 9, 1918, Boston; [p.] Tajshan; [m.] John, September 21, 1946; [ch.] Theresa, Patrick, Vincent; [ed.] Mt. St. Mary College Hooksett, New Hampshire; [occ.] Retired, in process of Writing; [memb.] My life history many people requested it made influence in Maine Ocean Park National Library of Poetry; [hon.] Life Stanier written in many papers. Many awards poetry, readings - each year at Univ. of New England poetry readiness, had many "honan" are gate for my drawings illustrations and poetry; [oth. writ.] Promote for many local newspapers on Women's League of Voters, Eldenhaste, local community news; [pers.] Poetry should be an honest expression on what one believes faith and morale also it should inspires other people to wish to write?

KENNER, JOSEPH R.
[pen.] Joe; [b.] April 27, 1975, Grosse Point Farms, MI; [p.] Mr. Jerry Kenner and Mrs. Brenda Kenner; [ed.] Lincoln High School Macomb Park Adult Education; [occ.] Owner of Nation Transmission; [pers.] My girlfriend sent this in and I thought I had no possible chance to get in. I guess I was wrong and I love her for sending it in. I just want to thank her for everything.; [a.] Warren, MI

KENNEY, MARAMA D.
[pen.] Ramie; [b.] July 4, 1919, Chester, IL; [p.] Otto and Dora Durkee; [m.] Bernard L. Kenney; [ch.] Bernard R. Kenney III; [ed.] High School; [occ.] Retired; [memb.] D.A.V. Auxiliary A.A.R.P.; [pers.] Love all sorts of animals, and the wonders of nature, which I write about, in the evenings, when I'm home alone, with my cat.; [a.] Utica, NY

KERR, NANCY
[b.] March 17, 1953, Houston; [p.] Sharman and Vicki Glass; [m.] Jay Kerr, June 11, 1977; [ch.] Mary, Matthew; [ed.] Robert E. Lee High Houston, Southwestern University Georgetown, TX, U.T. Austin, B.S. Elementary Ed., U.T. El Paso, Masters of Arts; [occ.] First Presbyterian, Pre-school Teacher - Computers; [memb.] Zeta Tau Alpha Sorority, Junior League of El Paso, El Paso Bar Aux., First Presbyterian Church; [hon.] Who's Who in American Colleges and Univ. '93.; [a.] El Paso, TX

KESTER, DELLA
[pen.] Dee Frances; [b.] August 10, 1950, Saint Louis, MO; [m.] Harry, May 2, 1975; [ch.] Five; [ed.] High School; [occ.] Writer; [oth. writ.] Profile of Abuse, Thirteen Blessings of 12 Steps, How to Stay in Love, Poems and Growth, In The Mid O Mid, Reflection of a Time; [pers.] Healing through use of the arts gives to us the self esteem of our own creations.; [a.] Saint Louis, MO

KESTER, JENNIFER
[b.] November 26, 1978, Lebanon, PA; [p.] Gaile and Jessie Kester; [ed.] Tulpehocken High School; [occ.] Student; [pers.] I wrote this poem in memory of my father, who passed away when I was 9 yrs. old.; [a.] Myerstown, PA

KEYS, MARY ALLENE
[b.] January 23, 1977, Childress, TX; [p.] Sharlynn and Larry Keys; [ed.] Bowie High School, Bowie, Texas. Graduate in May of 1995.; [occ.] Waitress at Sketti's and Student; [memb.] Peer Assistance and Leadership (PAL), North Texas High School Rodeo Association; [oth. writ.] Poems including: Burning Love, Seniors, Heart and Soul, Aaron and Together We stand.; [pers.] I've always been taught to believe in myself. Therefore I know that if I believe it I will achieve it.; [a.] Sunset, TX

KIDD, JULIA A. BRIGGS
[pen.] Julia Briggs Kidd; [b.] January 12, 1959, Montgomery, AL; [p.] Adam and Betty Briggs; [m.] Divorced; [ch.] Andre' Duane and Kiondra Jeanel; [ed.] Eastern Michigan University, BBA., Management. Madonna University, Education. Michigan College of Beauty, Cosmetology; [occ.] Banker; [memb.] Phi Gamma Nu sorority; [hon.] High School Homecoming queen, board of regents scholarship; [oth. writ.] Unpublished: My Journey, How did we get here, people, into my life you have come.; [pers.] My writings have always been inspired from personal experience. I have a deep appreciation for the work of Maya Angelou and Langston Hughes.; [a.] Oak Park, MI

KIGHT, TABATHA L.
[b.] March 9, 1966, Charleston, SC; [p.] W. T. Huff and Carolyn Sanders; [m.] Soon to be ... David Lockridge; [ch.] Brian Christopher, Lisa Elaine Lockridge (Step daughter); [ed.] Sea Island Academy, St. John's High School; [occ.] Filling supply operator, Clinton Mills, Inc.; [hon.] For Brian Christopher Kight, Lisa Elaine Lockridge, David S. Lockridge; [oth. writ.] The masterpiece, Seasons In Limbo, Mama's Little Man, One of our Special Times, Father, Forever Remembered, Just Between Us, and a few more, but none of these published as of yet, with the exception of Spring Morning.; [pers.] I only wish to share with the world, some of the beauty I see in life, and hopefully bring a smile to someone's day!; [a.] Clinton, SC

KILLAM, ROB
[pen.] Rob Killam; [b.] December 11, 1960, Denver, CO; [p.] John Killam and Ann Killam; [ed.] Life! Columbine High, Boulder School of Massage; [occ.] Massage Therapist; [memb.] American Massage Therapy Association; [hon.] Certificate of Birth,; [oth. writ.] Poems written for graduation speeches and friends (graduation); [pers.] Life is a spiritual journey. And when one looks inward to the "Kingdom of Heaven" one's life becomes an adventure. My poetry reflects that adventure of life.; [a.] Denver, CO

KILLEN, JUDY L.
[pen.] Judy Griffith; [b.] July 30, 1953, WV; [p.] Dallas Griffith, Ruby Griffith; [m.] Curtis M. Killen, August 15, 1975; [ch.] Dawn Marie Killen; [ed.] Lorrain High School, Night school at Admiral King High Lorain Ohio.; [occ.] Knitter Battcher Inds.; [oth. writ.] Poems of "Love" company in the Graybeards, Korean War Veterans papers.; [pers.] I try to touch reality and caress all that is here and now, for it will too soon be gone.; [a.] Collins, OH

KIM, CONNIE
[b.] October 31, 1983, Garden Grove, CA; [p.] Sun Kim and Kyung Kim; [ed.] Imperial Elementary School, 6 Grade; [occ.] Student; [hon.] Academic, Eagle of the Month; [oth. writ.] One poem published in the Korean Central Daily Newspaper; [pers.] Ever since I was in 1 Grade, I wrote short poems. Few years later I continued to write them. Soon I knew God gave me the gift of writing. Now I want to be a poet as well as other things.; [a.] Anahein Hills, CA

KING, NATHAN DELMONT
[b.] November 19, 1979, Strawberry Plains, TN; [p.] Eulis Delmont and Kathleen R. King; [ed.] 9th Grade Jefferson County High School. Plan to go through College: Become a teacher.; [occ.] Student; [memb.] Interact Club Voices and Visions; [hon.] Honor Student; [oth. writ.] Have written many songs and poems. Plan to published someday; [pers.] God created all men in his image. My goal is truing to make all people realize this, no matter the skin color. We need peace and love in our world.; [a.] Strawberry Plains, TN

KING, B. CARLTON
[pen.] BC King; [b.] January 3, OK; [pers.] I hope to stimulate deep thinking to replace in place of easy acceptance

KING, ZACHARY
[b.] January 23, 1978, Baton Rouge, LA; [p.] Richard A. King and James H. Batchelor; [ed.] Currently a junior at McKinley High School in Baton Rouge, LA; [pers.] Teach your heart well, then follow its wisdom; [a.] Baton Rouge, LA

KING, GERALDINE W.
[pen.] Miss Perrin Winkle and Cheryl Lee Headley; [b.] June 25, Fort Wayne, IN; [m.] Divorced; [ch.] Bridgette Denise and Danielle Christine; [ed.] College and Life; [occ.] Artist for a Book Publisher and a Sculptor on the week-ends; [memb.] Writing Center, A Great Place;

[oth. writ.] 8 childrens books, 38 poems, 3 fiction and 1 non-fiction and counting; [pers.] I love my children, life and God, so I write about it and enjoy it.; [a.] San Diego, CA

KIPPLE, LONNY
[b.] January 24, 1963, Alma, NE; [p.] James and Mary Kipple; [m.] Wendy Kipple, August 29, 1987; [ch.] Christi Kipple; [ed.] Northern Valley High School, Northwest Kansas Vo-Tech School. Oklahoma Horseshoeing School; [occ.] Horseshoer/Blacksmith; [pers.] I was raised on a farm and many of my poems are inspired by life as a farmer and rancher. I have been influenced by the great cowboy poet Baxter Black.; [a.] Fairplay, CO

KIRBY, SHANNON MORGAN
[b.] January 2, 1966, Albertville, AL; [p.] Ronald and Barbara Kirby; [occ.] Freelance Writer; [memb.] Crohn's and Colitis Foundation of America.; [hon.] Thousands of Poems: (Conceptual and other) - various newspaper articles - one Novel (to date unpublished) - Comics and Comic scripts for various companies.; [oth. writ.] Sometimes I find myself wondering, "Is the 'Tunnel of Light,' often experienced after death, merely a vague remembrance of 'Birth?'"; [pers.] Albertville, AL

KIRKWOOD, LAWRENCE C.
[pen.] Lawrence Kirkwood; [b.] May 27, 1947, MN; [p.] Frank J. and Ethel R.; [m.] Deceased; [ch.] Laura Lynn; [ed.] High School (G.E.D.), City College - San Diego, Auto Mechanics - English Writing; [occ.] Automotive Electrical Technician; [memb.] V.F.W. - A.M. Legion; [hon.] Many - Military and Civil, none in the literary field, U.S.M.C. Hon. Disc. 1970 - 4 yrs. serv., 19 mos. Vietnam Service; [oth. writ.] Personal poems; [pers.] I hope that my poems or writings will find in enough of mankind to make a difference....In how mankind treats itself. We have been tough. On ourselves.; [a.] San Diego, CA

KISER, DAVID
[b.] September 7, 1968, Roanoke, VA; [p.] Steve and Vicki Kiser; [hon.] Life itself.; [a.] Charleston, SC

KIZZIAR, J. L.
[pen.] Jay Loren; [b.] July 7, 1975, Euless, TX; [p.] Wayne Kizziar, Loretta Kizziar; [ed.] Boswell High School; [occ.] Assistant Parts Manager; [hon.] Three first place ribbons and a best of show in a welding course in High School; [pers.] I live my life day by day in hope to see the entire big picture.; [a.] Saginaw, TX

KLEMSER, BILLIE
[pen.] BK; [b.] October 12, 1951, New Jersey; [p.] Stewart and Martha Cummings; [m.] Richard Klemser, December 9, 1967, widowed July 30, 1977; [ch.] Kimberly and Robert Klemser, Grandchildren: Richard C. Montanye and Brandon J. Young; [oth. writ.] "Just watching you", "What was she before, that now she remembers", raised by my father and grandmother, Emma for whom I wrote the poem, "Take the time", "Love you very much"; [pers.] For all the people whose lifes have crossed with mine, my knowledge of the human race has been enlarged and my life enriched for having met you and I thank you; [a.] Dunellen, NJ

KLINE, BILLY JOE
[pen.] Bill Kline; [b.] March 28, 1964, Quonset Point, RI; [p.] Robert H. and Anna L. Kline; [m.] Shirley Kline, December 3, 1993; [ch.] Dennis and Rachel; [ed.] High School Equivalency Welding Technical College, Lexington, Kentucky; [occ.] Welding; [hon.] Graduated from Welding College with honors for grades of 4.0; [pers.] Victory and defeat are both good, or bad, depending on what you do with them.; [a.] Lexington, KY

KLINKHAMMER, TINA
[b.] May 17, 1966, Rockford, IL; [p.] Marilyn Forrester (Grandmother); [m.] Shawn Klinkhammer, July 8, 1994; [ed.] Sierra High School; [occ.] Housewife, Aspiring writer and Security Officer Training; [oth. writ.] I'm currently working on a novel and have written several other poems.; [pers.] With everything I write I work very hard to reach and touch other people's lives in a way to improve and leave an impression. I hope that this poem is enjoyed by all. I also want to give thanks to God for giving me the talent, and to my grandmother for everything she does and for giving me the inner strength, inspiration and fortitude to try to write poetry.; [a.] Rockford, IL

KNIEP, JOANNA M.
[b.] January 26, 1969, Elkhorn, WI; [p.] Norma Kniep and the late Gerald Kniep; [ed.] Lakewood High School, currently enrolled at St. Petersburg Junior College, St. Petersburg, FL.; [occ.] Apheresis Specialist and Phlebotomist, Florida Blood Services, St. Petersburg, FL; [pers.] No matter what doors a person comes up against, there is always a way to break through. Thank you to my family and friends, I have finally broken through. My inspiration was my comp. professor at SPJC.; [a.] Saint Petersburg, FL

KNIGHT, SHIRLEY ANN
[pen.] Shirley M. Knight; [b.] March 6, 1936, Medford, MA; [p.] Walter and Pearl Giannone; [m.] Robert Allen Knight, November 20, 1955; [ch.] Kenneth Joseph, Cheryl Jean and Steven Michael; [ed.] Somerville High and Various College Courses; [occ.] Retired; [memb.] Past Volunteer throughout the School Systems and at the Local Health Center; [hon.] Honor Roll High School - 6 year Perfect Attendance Award - Penmanship Certificate; [oth. writ.] Poetry for local school projects; [pers.] If eyes are the windows to the soul than words are windows to the brain!; [a.] Wilmington, MA

KNIGHT, DEBBIE
[pen.] Debbie Austin; [b.] October 6, 1961, Anderson, IN; [p.] Frank and Barbara Austin; [m.] Charles E. Knight Sr., May 17, 1980; [ch.] Charles Jr., Keith and Holly; [ed.] Working on getting high school education; [occ.] Housewife; [memb.] Redmen Lodge; [pers.] To get as much education as a person can get. Learn as much as a person can.; [a.] Fort Wayne, IN

KNUTSON, JEWEL D.
[b.] September 20, 1952, Springville, AL; [p.] Ray and Willie Holmes; [m.] Alec W. Knutson, March 9, 1984; [ch.] Tammie Pearson and Kenneth M. Smith Jr.; [ed.] West End High; [occ.] Housewife; [memb.] Samuel's Chapel United Methodist Church; [oth. writ.] Some more poems I have never published, I am not able to work, I have a lots of medical problems.; [pers.] I hope and pray that my poem may be a blessing to anyone who may read it. I know God, is my greatest influence in life.; [a.] Altoon, AL

KOCH, ALICE
[b.] 1907, Colorado; [m.] Paul Koch, June 24, 1928; [ch.] Paul, Desmond, Clayton, Evelyn; [ed.] High School of poems written, hope to have a book printed soon; [occ.] Retired; [oth. writ.] I have lots.; [pers.] I am 87 yrs. old in good health. Do my own work, live alone. I still write and make and quiet hand mode quilts

KOEHN, DEBORAH
[pen.] Debbie Scott, Debbie Koehn; [b.] December 13, 1960, Austin, TX; [p.] William A. Scott, Charlene Scott; [m.] Perry K. Koehn, November 23, 1984; [ch.] Joshua Caleb and Jacob William; [ed.] McCallum High School; [occ.] Housewife and mother; [memb.] Church of Christ at Hyde Park; [oth. writ.] Poems written to family and various friends.; [pers.] I write for the joy it gives me to create. It also gives me release of pent up feelings of everyday life and experiences.; [a.] Pflugerville, TX

KOGEN, LEAH
[pen.] Leah Kogen; [b.] July 14, 1978, Moscow, Russia; [p.] Boris Kogen, Shanna Kogen; [ed.] Yeshiva Rabbi Samson, Raphael Hirsch High School, student; [memb.] (N.C.S.Y.) National Council of Synogogue Youth, United Synogogue Youth (U.S.Y.); [hon.] An Achievement Award, an Alliance for health, physical education, recreation, and dance.; [pers.] Through my poetry I try to express my feelings, thoughts, and imagination that I hope would turn into reality.; [a.] New York, NY

KOHLER, MARY J.
[pen.] Mary Kohler; [b.] September 22, 1926, Muskogee, OK; [p.] Pauline and Charles Stroup; [m.] Kenneth L. Kohler, March 5, 1950; [ch.] Patricia, Paul, Ruth Ann, David; [ed.] Okmulgee High, Tulsa Jr. College, Manteca Adult School; [occ.] Housewife; [oth. writ.] Religious poems and songs

KOLF, STEVEN J.
[b.] August 30, 1959, Green Bay; [p.] Joyce (deceased) and David (living); [ed.] 2 years college equiv. attended Northeast WI Technical Institute, St. Thomas College, St. Paul MN, St. Norbert College De Pere WI; [occ.] Recreation Supervisor City of Green Bay; [memb.] Highland Crest Baptist Church Green Bay, WI; [pers.] Any talent I have feel is God given. I am inspired by people and events around me; [a.] Green Bay, WI

KOLNICKI, SHARI
[p.] Sue and Frederick Yeh; [m.] Gary; [occ.] Evaluator, United States General Accounting Office; [a.] Westlake, OH

KOLPACKI, BERNADETTE
[b.] August 5, Dearborn, MI; [m.] Widowed; [ch.] Michael and Tina; [occ.] Retired; [memb.] Numerous church activities; [hon.] "Toastmaster's Club"; [oth. writ.] Book of Poetry, "Passages From Within" and a Grief support booklet "Journey Onward..."; [pers.] I love working with children in all matters of grief and divorce. My ambition is to work with abused children and also to write a book on auto accidents and how a person's whole life is changed as a result of auto insurance failure to stand behind their auto insurance policy.; [a.] New Port Richey, FL

KOMULA, JUDY C.
[b.] August 8, 1949, Louisa, KY; [p.] Clarence Cook, Bettie Cook; [m.] Steven L. Komula, July 12, 1985; [ch.] Michael, Randy and Robert Joner; [ed.] Superior High, Apollo College; [hon.] Academic Achievement Award, Apollo College; [oth. writ.] Several poems published in local newspapers. Numerous unpublished poems, song lyrics, and inspirational thoughts; [pers.] One of the greatest rewards we can attain in our lives is the knowledge that in helping others, we help ourselves. The reasons "Why" I write, doesn't matter, the heart my writing touches, does. I write what I feel, I feel what I experience; [a.] Tonto Basin, AZ

KONTUR, LEONARD PAUL JOSEPH
[pen.] Lee Kontur; [b.] November 13, 1928, Chicago, IL; [p.] Joseph and Margaret Kontur; [ed.] L.T.H.S., La Grange, IL., Kalamazoo College (BA '53), Western Michigan College, Michigan State University.; [occ.] Retired but not.; [memb.] American Legion Post 0016; [hon.] International Society of Poets, Homer Honor Society of International Poets; [oth. writ.] Of Yesteryear, Cops Cry Hard, The Platform, Nineteen Forty Nine, Fools Never Learn, Red Snow Of Minnesota.; [pers.] "Though my lance be broken, yet the ends of justice do I serve" is where I'm at.; [a.] Bagley, MN

KOPRIVICA, ALEX
[b.] December 15, 1967, Detroit, MI; [p.] Milan and Ellen Koprivica; [ed.] Finney High School, Wayne State University; [occ.] Sales Manager, Joe Ricci Dodge, Inc.; [memb.] The Ludwig von Mises Institute, The Heritage Foundation, St. Lazarus Serbian Orthodox Church; [hon.] Volkswagen's Wolfsberg Crest Club, Mercedes Benz Star Sales Guild; [pers.] If you make one person smile a day - eventually the whole world will be happy.; [a.] Detroit, MI

KORNAHRENS, WALDEMAR
[pen.] Walt; [b.] January 20, 1978, Clinton, SC; [p.] Mary Kornahrens, Byrle Kornaherns (Deceased); [ed.] I am a senior in high school.; [memb.] Marching band, symphony in school, Charleston Youth Symphony Orchestra, Honor band at University of South Carolina clinics, All-County and All-Region bands, Honor bands of CSU.; [hon.] I have been ranked as one of the best percussionists of high school in the state of South Carolina several years in a row.; [oth. writ.] I have written many poems, but this is the only one I have sent into a contest of any type or have had published.); [pers.] Many people write from the mind. The heart is the place where you find feeling. It's the mind that interprets these emotions.; [a.] North Charleston, SC

KORNING, JESSICA L.
[b.] October 18, 1979, Spearfish, SD; [p.] Tim and Kathy Koenig; [ed.] Freshman at Sundance High School - Sundance, Wyoming went 6 years to 4 - Oaks a country school in rural Wyoming.; [occ.] Student and life guard at Belle Rec Center; [memb.] FHA and F-H Club, ARBA (American Rabbit Breeders Association); [hon.] President of 4-H Club, Bearlodge Wranglers.

KOSTIOU, PATTI ANN
[pen.] Babe; [b.] April 12, 1964, Beaver County, PA; [p.] Mr. and Mrs. Richard D. Scarsellone; [m.] Nicholas S. Kostiou, May 16, 1989; [ch.] Thomas White, Amber Kostiou, Melissa Kostiou; [ed.] Aliquippa High School graduated Top 20 of class.; [occ.] Housewife, mother; [memb.] Queen of Peace Catholic Church, Saint Joseph Catholic Church; [hon.] Who's Who Among American High School Students 1981-1982 16th Edition Vol. II feature Editor of the High School Newspaper "The Quippan."; [oth. writ.] Articles: "Dying For No Good Reason, published: "Priority should be to help our own", published in Great Lakes, IL Chicago Sun Times newspaper, "Turn to Children" published in Hampton Daily Press Newspaper, Articles published, "Just Say No" published in Great Lakes, IL Sun Times newspaper, "School Costs Challenged" published in Great Lakes, IL Sun Times, "Good Jobs End Welfare" published in Daily Press newspaper Hampton, VA, "Don't Label Poor" published in Daily Press Newspaper, Hampton VA., "Ringless Marriage Has Defender" published in Beaver County Times Beaver, PA, "There Are Concerns Greater Than Lyrics" published in Beaver County Times Beaver, PA.; [pers.] To Quote my mentor Jackie Kennedy, on a personal level, "I believe that if you fail at raising your children, nothing else in life you do really matters." On a writers note: If you write from the Heart you can not fail in obtaining your dream.; [a.] Hampton, VA

KOUF, DAWN D.
[pen.] Dawn D.; [b.] July 18, 1974, Phoenix, AZ; [p.] Pamela Kouf, Ron Kouf; [ed.] Phoenix Christian High School, 2 years Phoenix College, Currently at Grand Canyon University (graduation date, December '96); [occ.] Accounting Clerk (at ABC Nissan); [memb.] Valley View Bible Church, The Q Sports Club; [hon.] Academic Scholarship to any Maricopa Community College (for 2 years); [oth. writ.] This is my first published work.; [pers.] I enjoy writing as a hobby. I believe anyone who experiences life can be a great writer, it's whether or not they choose to try to be one.; [a.] Phoenix, AZ

KRANYS, SHERRY
[b.] June 4, 1942, Wilkes-Barre, PA; [m.] Rudy; [ch.] Kelly, Kim, Molly, Megan; [a.] Coconut Grove, FL

KREJNUS, JOHN
[b.] May 8, 1971, Spangler, PA; [p.] Steve Krejnus Jr., Nancy Krejnus; [m.] Single; [ed.] Cambria Heights High School Patton PA - Admiral Peary Vo Tech Ebensburg PA - Triangle Tech DuBois PA.; [occ.] Electrician at Steve Umstead Electric Altoona PA; [memb.] Veterans of Foreign wars Bakerton PA - Bakerton Athletic Association, American Legion Barnesboro, PA; [oth. writ.] Many poems in a personal collection that I hope to perhaps have published in the future.; [pers.] I like writing poetry because its not only gives me a way to express myself but it also provides a way to relate with other people and their thoughts and feelings about life.; [a.] Bakerton, PA

KROGER, SHANE W.
[pen.] Kroger or William; [b.] August 18, 1973, Granite Falls, MN; [p.] Bill and Joyce Kroger; [ed.] Cottonwood Elementary Lake View High School Southwest State Univ.; [occ.] Bus boy at Olive Garden; [memb.] Promise Keeper, Green DonKey's, Fellowship of Christian Athletes, Gospel for Asia; [hon.] Being alive, having a family to love me and friends to fellowship with... spending every waking moment with my eternal lover!; [oth. writ.] Sunshine, Deer, Moon Song, Eternal Lover, Salt Pillar, The Funeral Ball, Forgiven, And Then There Was You.; [pers.] To knew Jesus is to know the Father. To know the Fathers is to now and feel the very essence of love, for He is love!; [a.] Orlando, FL

KROLL, STEVEN J.
[b.] September 7, 1950, Saint Paul, MN; [p.] Roman and Euphemia Kroll; [m.] Mary Jean, July 8, 1972; [ch.] Ann, Michelle, Melissa; [ed.] Johnson High School; [occ.] Furnace Operator Northern Iron Corp.; [oth. writ.] I have written several poems about Love, Death and War. During the Gulf War I wrote those papers and mailed them to over 100 of my friends, just to share my thoughts!; [pers.] If you ever have a thought or a rhyme in your heed take a minute to write it down or something very special may be left forever.; [a.] Saint Paul, MN

KROLL, TIFFANIE
[pen.] Tiff Kroll; [b.] May 4, 1980, MO; [p.] Jerry Kroll, Denise Kroll; [ed.] Jana Elementary School, St. Angela Merici School, Rosary High School; [occ.] (9) Ninth Grade student at Rosary High School; [memb.] National Junior Honor Society Rosary High School Drama Club; [hon.] St. Angela Merici Service Award, St. Angela Merici Honor Roll; [pers.] The poem, Jennifer is written about my best friend, Jennifer 1993.; [a.] Florissant, MO

KROMER, DELLA HARRISON
[b.] April 10, 1925, Whitewater, KS; [p.] Raymond and Mabel Miller Harrison; [m.] Kermit K. Kromer, June 17, 1945; [ch.] Nona Joelene-Alderfer-Loreda-Dianne-Horutz; [ed.] Newton Kansas, and Valley Center Kansas High School, Cake Wilson Decorating School; [occ.] Retired - Cake Decorating Teacher-crafts; [memb.] Polk township fire co-ladies auxiliary Kreskeville, Pa, Schwenkfder Church Warcester, PA; [hon.] Cake decorating Potstown - PA and Crafts West end fair.; [oth. writ.] Time and you and me, Big sister,-to-Nona-my sister, Evelyn, to Loreda-Autumn Lee-the dream goes on to Virginia all published; [pers.] I would like to dedicate this to my husband Kermit Kromer - my love and best friend to whom I will be married fifty years. June 17, 1995; [a.] Kunkletown, PA

KRONNER, KEVIN DAVID MICHAEL
[pen.] Kevin Kronner; [b.] September 10, 1961, Detroit, MI; [p.] William and June (Nolie) Kronner; [ed.] St. Athanasius grade school, Eisenhower Elementary, John F. Kennedy Jr. High School, Fraser High School, Graduated June, 1980; [memb.] Altar Boy, St Athanasius Chief Squire 1977-79', R.F. Kennedy #2438 Fraser Jaycees, Catechist Teacher, St. Athanasius, Chairman Pro-Life Committee, Knights of Columbus, 1st Degree Staff JFK Knights of Columbus, Principal Ora-

tor Pioneer Major Degree Staff of Knights of Columbus, Warden John F. Kennedy #5460 K of C; [hon.] 1976 Certificate of Merit, Squires of Robert F. Kennedy, 1977-79 Chief Squire Plaque of Robert F. Kennedy Circle #2438, 1981 Certificate of Appreciation, Mental Retardation Drive, 1983 Achievement Certificate, Religious Education Teacher, St. Athanasius, 1983 Achievement Certificate, Christian Service Commission, St. Athanasius, 1984 Achievement Certificate U.S. Jaycess, 1985 Knight of the Month Plaque, John F. Kennedy Knights Of Columbus; [oth. writ.] A collection of poetry written to special people for special occasions. Several poems published in the Knights of Columbus Newsletter; [pers.] Kevin passed away at the age of 23 on February 28, 1985. During his life he was a positive influence on many young people, particularly through his church and as a member of the Knights of Columbus. His work as a volunteer in the community gained him the respect from all who well privileged to know him. He continues to inspire us through his poetry.; [a.] Fraser, MI

KROVONTKA, MINDY
[b.] November 30, 1980, Mesa, AZ; [p.] Ruth Ann and Patrick Krovontka; [ed.] Fay Galloway Elem., John A. Dooley Elem., B. Mahlon Brown Jr. High; [occ.] Student at B. Mahlon Brown Jr. High; [memb.] National Jr. Honor Society, Honor Band, Nevadans, Science Club, and Art Club.; [hon.] 3rd place T-shirt design from the State Fair/1st place and ceramics from State Fair - 1st place for Bookmark Contest; [oth. writ.] The Unicorn/ Love, Money and Success published by the National Library of Poetry; [pers.] Poetry is a way of expressing yourself to others. Don't ever say you can't do it, everyone can write poetry; [a.] Henderon, NV

KRUEGET, OLAMAE
[pen.] Olamae Krueger; [b.] April 19, 1914, India Homa, OK; [p.] John Greenhaw and Myrtle Greenhaw; [m.] Ernest G. Krueger, November 7, 1940; [ch.] Patrician E. Jacobsen, 1 son Richard Jacobsen Jr.; [ed.] College Graduate; [occ.] Retired; [memb.] Maranatha C. Fellowship Church; [hon.] I was on honor roll in Hobart, Okla High School in 1933; [pers.] You do not have to use this if you don't care too. It makes no difference to me.; [a.] Modesto, CA

KUBIAS, CRAIG
[pen.] Craig Owen; [b.] April 6, 1955, St. Louis, MO; [ed.] Ph.D. Philosophy of Religion, University of Denver; [occ.] Adjunct Prof. of Philosophy, Red Rocks Community College, Denver; [oth. writ.] Several poems published in anthologies, love and other neat stuff unpublished book, songwriter, mostly folk music.; [a.] Denver, CO

KURTZ, MARK D.
[b.] November 14, 1967, Billings, MT; [ed.] AAS in Police Science, BS in Criminal Justice; [occ.] Seeking Police Work; [memb.] National Rifle Association; [a.] Bedford, TX

KUZMITZ, MICHAEL
[b.] November 27, 1961, Detroit; [ed.] Schoolcraft College (Currently); [occ.] Craftsman; [memb.] Associate Member of International Society of Poets; [hon.] Rosalyn Bryant Foundation for Aid To Abused Children, Editor's Choice Award - National Library of Poetry 1994, 3rd prize, 1994 North American Open Poetry Comp.; [oth. writ.] 3 poetry volumes: "Neon Tombstones", "Searching A Phrase", "Lock and Key", 1 Non-fiction book: "Sociological Impulse", 1 Fiction Novel: "Spectral Wrath", several short stories - all currently unpublished

KYRIACOU, STEPHANIE
[pen.] Frenchie; [b.] April 1, 1961, Long Island, NY; [p.] Harold Dobbins, Marvy Dobbins; [m.] Alexander Kyriacou, February 3, 1980; [ch.] Erik, Alex Jr., Adam; [ed.] North Babylon Senior High School; [occ.] Medi-

cal Asst.; [pers.] This poem was greatly influenced by my husband Alex. His constant encouragement and positive reinforcement enable me to push forth in life. Thank you Alex, you're always there for me.; [a.] North Babylon, NY

LACK, JEDEDIAH
[pen.] Jed Lack; [b.] July 22, 1977, Redding, CA; [p.] Matthew Lack, Katey Lack; [ed.] Foothill High; [occ.] Dishwasher, Marriott Foodservice; [oth. writ.] I have never before been published, but have written poetry and songs since the age of 13; [pers.] Like so many before me, I am a dreamer. I find writing to be the best way to express my aspirations.; [a.] Spokane, WA

LAMARRE, CHIP
[b.] March 20, 1948, Brooklyn, NY; [p.] Charles and Victoria LaMarre; [ch.] David Charles; [ed.] Bishop Chatard H.S., Indianapolis Indiana 1996 - Western Michigan University Kalamazoo, Michigan 1976; [occ.] Professional Golf Instructor; [oth. writ.] 3 Songs Published - two Inspirational Childrens Book (one self published, other in manuscript form) - A Reading For A Wedding; [pers.] My purpose in being here is to teach through my words and my actions, I can set an example for my son and help others to find peace.; [a.] St. Clair Shores, MI

LAMBERT, MIKE
[pen.] Hobbit; [b.] January 21, 1981, Wiltoughby; [p.] Dave and Patricia Lambert; [ed.] I am currently in 8th grade attending madison middle school; [occ.] Student and paper deliver; [oth. writ.] None other published; [pers.] I usually write poems to or about certain individuals. "The Line" was written about a friendship and is dedicated to Tami Ashba.; [a.] Madison, OH

LAMBERT, PAMELA J.
[b.] April 6, 1964, Yuma, AZ; [p.] Corbett and Eileen Combest; [ch.] Krysten Eileen, Thomas Jack; [ed.] Kofa High (1 yr.), Salome High (3 yrs.); [occ.] Correctional Deputy, Riverside Co. Sheriff's Dept.; [hon.] Who's who among American High School Students (2 consecutive years); [oth. writ.] Poems published in local newspaper; [pers.] This poem is dedicated in memory of Zachary Lambert. He was 22 months old when he was taken from us. It was a short time, but we have a lifetime of memories. Inherited this talent from my Mother.; [a.] Blythe, CA

LAMOTHE JR., MARC ARTHUR
[pen.] Mocombha; [b.] July 14, 1962, P-au-Pce; [p.] Odette and Marc Lamothe; [m.] Yvrose P. Lamothe, January 1988; [ch.] Marcuse Jennifer Lamothe, Marc Arthur Phillip Lamothe III; [ed.] Ecole Dominique Savio (Elem School), College St. Pierre (Baccalaureate), Institut Sup des Sces Economiques et Politiques (University). SCS (D.T.T); [occ.] Console Operator, Journalism; [memb.] Grand Council, VP: Resp Lodge: "St Jean de Jerusalem #6". Orator: Resp Lodge: "Grand Rosaire #1." Grand Orator: "Grande Loge Haitien ne de St Jean Des Orients d'Aitreller Inc" Editor, speaker. "Radio Konbit".; [hon.] "Meritarious Award Aug 1990, Resp Lodge: "Grand Rosaire #1." Orator of the Year, (Dec. 1991). Mason of the year, (May 1993): Resp Lodge: St Jean de Jerusalem", Most wise and Perfect Master. (T.S.A) of the 18 chapter. "Mont des Oliviers #1"; [oth. writ.] Elise/French collection of poems, 1982). Philosophical, Metaphysical and Theosophical Essays. Various articles in "Renaissance" (Newsletter). Pawol Granmoune (Radio Show); [pers.] May the innerlight of pure love be the expression of art that will place together, in harmony, all men of any races, sexes, ideologies and creeds.; [a.] Brooklyn, NY

LAMOUR, KENOL
[pen.] Kenol Lamour; [b.] November 10, 1956, Brooklyn, NY; [p.] Kiss Lamour, Anne A. Lamour; [ed.] H.S. of Art and Design, The College of Staten Island, A.A.,

Fashion Institute of Technology, B.F.A.; [occ.] Designer - The Very Vest Collection; [hon.] PPF International Award Beefeater's GIN Fashion and Jazz Award, I Loved New York Fashion Award; [oth. writ.] 'Crossroads', Alicia in Wonder-Land; [pers.] It is wise to keep in mind that no success or failure is necessarily final.; [a.] Brooklyn, NY

LAMPKIN, ARTIS C.
[pen.] Mr. Outstanding; [b.] September 19, 1953, Richmond, VA; [p.] Mr. Artis, J. Lampkin; [m.] Mrs. Jean E. Lee; [ed.] Andrew Jackson H.S. New York City Community College And City College; [occ.] Protection Officer For U.S. Trust Co. Of N.Y.; [memb.] Genesis II B.O.R. of N.Y.C. (Vice President); [hon.] Bethel Bible Institute Course in Evangelism (Diploma) Ordained Evangelist From Bethel Gospel Tabernacle; [pers.] Serve time most high God always in Love, Fait, and purity and you will never go wrong.; [a.] New York, NY

LANCE, BONNIE JEAN
[b.] October 7, 1926, Ashland, OH; [m.] Divorced, February 1, 1947; [ch.] Linda, Barbara, Bobbie and Stephen; [ed.] Hayesville School-Ashland High School - Ashland College (Only nite classes); [occ.] Retired and nite clerk for funeral home; [oth. writ.] Unpublished poems - short stories.; [pers.] Try to accept people for their inner self and not what they pretend to be. If a person is a friend its not because of what they have but what they have become.; [a.] Ashland, OH

LANDES, CAROL
[pen.] Carol Neufeld; [b.] December 17, 1950, Brooklyn; [p.] Sidney Neufeld, Marion Neufeld; [m.] Stuart Winter, October 7, 1988; [ch.] Daniel Kaufman, Lauren Landes and Lexis Winter; [ed.] Lafayette High School, Brooklyn College; [occ.] Pre-School Teacher; [oth. writ.] I submitted a poem to a local community newspaper, the Flushing Tribune, and I submitted a poem to you about a year and half ago, entitled: Christopher Columbus.; [pers.] Today's society needs something to bring the goodness back into their lives, and if can do that by just writing a single poem, then I know I have accomplished a great task. I have been inspired by the great Classic writings of Edgar Allen Poe, Charles Dickens and many others.; [a.] Flushing, NY

LANDIS, MARIE
[pen.] Marie Landis; [b.] March 17, 1948, Philadelphia; [p.] Mr. and Mrs. Philip Fusco; [m.] Divorced; [ch.] Paul (26), Michael (24), Christina (16); [ed.] High School Diploma; [occ.] Vocalist, Musician, Owner of Marie Landis Orchestra (Big Band Leader); [memb.] American Federation of Musicians, Local - 77 - Phila, PA, Local - 62 Trenton, NJ, Local - 21 - Delaware, (Also on executive board of local 21); [oth. writ.] I have written songs and other poetry, however, this is my first attempt to publish.; [pers.] I feel my performance whether in music or poetry is an ability and opportunity to reach out, touch and become one spiritually with others.; [a.] Philadelphia, PA

LANE-LYTLE, SHERYL
[pen.] Sher; [b.] April 11, 1958, Kittery, ME; [p.] Dewitt C. Lane, Elizabeth Wilson; [m.] Bruce Edward Lytle, December 18, 1992; [occ.] Artist; [hon.] 1992 Golden Poet Award; [oth. writ.] History of Portland, ME 350th Anniversary publication. MADAS - Salt Magazine How To Build A Friendship Sloap - Salt Magazine; [a.] Cape Neddic, ME

LANGSDORF, LEAH E.
[b.] November 28, 1971, Melbourne, FL; [p.] Raymond Hall, Brenda Hall; [m.] John Langsdorf, June 18, 1994; [ed.] Martin High School, Arlington, TX, University of Texas at Austin— Bachelor of Arts in English; [occ.] Financial Assistant at an Institutional Brokerage Firm; [hon.] Who's Who Among American High School Students, 1986-1989, Outstanding Student of the Year,

1986, Outstanding French Student at UT, 1990, Gamma Phi Alpha Honor Sorority, 1990.; [pers.] My greatest influence in poetry is Rogert Frost. His ability to unite readers through the universality of his work is what I strive to achieve in my writings.; [a.] Austin, TX

LANIER, JEANNE H.
[pen.] Jeanne H. Lanier; [b.] July 29, 1944, Belefonte, PA; [p.] Ben and Nilah Hausdorf; [ch.] Heather Hurt, Emily Hamilton, Laura Crabtree; [ed.] Chazy Central Rural School, Dekalb Community College, State University of N.Y. at Plattsburgh, (B.A.), Southern Ill. University (M.S.), University of South Florida (Teaching Certificate); [occ.] Exceptional Education, Teacher of Severely Emotionally, Disturbed at Hamilton Disston School, Gulfport, FL; [hon.] First Prize in poetry two years in a row - National League of American Pen Women's Arts and letters Contest' Phi Kappa Phi Honor Society; [oth. writ.] Poem published in the Georgia Poet's Anthology, articles published in local newspaper. Poems published in National League of American Pen Women's Arts and letters Booklets.; [pers.] Beyond the veneer, I strive to illuminate aspects of the grain that celebrate human dignity. My joy is found in feeling spiritually connected to others through the creative process.; [a.] Gulfport, FL

LANSBERRY, DONNA L.
[b.] March 21, 1972, Spangler, PA; [p.] Harold E. and Martha J. Lansberry; [ed.] Bishop Carroll High School And Cambria Height High School; [occ.] Certified Nurses Aide at Haida Manor; [memb.] Saint Boniface, Church; [oth. writ.] Published 1 poem have 2 being published this year other poems written yet to be submitted or published; [pers.] My poetry is inspired by people I meet and family. I hope my works speak for others. Poetry doesn't always need to be a published word.; [a.] Patton, PA

LARAMIE, K. J.
[occ.] I am a painter; [oth. writ.] I am listed in the Fine Art Index, North American Edition 1993, published by International Art Reference, Chicago.; [pers.] The "biography of limitless space and all-knowing divinity within each one of us is not easily put in words. My poertry comes to me in a meditative state so it would be presumptuous to claim authorship.; [a.] Daphne, AL

LARGENT, SHERYL LYNN
[b.] September 10, 1972, Orlando, FL; [p.] Brenda and Art Henning; [m.] Divorced February 14, 1992; [ed.] High School and a course through writer's digest Novel and Short, Story Writing; [occ.] Senior Fulfillment Asst. for Conde Nast Publications; [memb.] YMCA - Young Men's Christian Association, (Still looking for a good writers group Association to join); [hon.] I have received many written responses with positive remarks - whether it be certificates from courses or simple sticky notes - that's my honor; [oth. writ.] These too shall be heard Arcandia Poetry Anthology Vol IV poetic voices of America out of the blue National Creative Arts magazine; [pers.] I owe the expressions of my life to those that pass through it. Those who let me express love and the knowledge I've gained from those who suppress it.; [a.] Dacono, CO

LARIONI, ROY
[pen.] Roy Larioni; [b.] March 31, 1949, Jessup, PA; [p.] Valentino G. Larioni, Anne Filip Larioni; [occ.] Artist; [pers.] Let it be know that the money flavors of life, have seasoned my soul. And the love of Jesus has lifted my spirit.

LARKIN, DARRELL R.
[b.] May 11, 1921, Dayton, OH; [p.] George R. and Florence A. Larkin; [m.] Janet I. Larkin, December 13, 1976; [ed.] Vandalia Butler High School, Sinelair College Dayton Ohio, DEG. Bus. Eng. Mgmt.; [occ.] Retired Lt. Col. USAF/OHANG.; [memb.] Order of Oaepalians, in Sept. '83 GEO, larkin, our Father, was

laid to rest in a small hillside cemetery, in South Western Ohio, Overlooking the farm on which was born. Following the services my brother and I circled the cemetery in our airplane and looking down the expression rows of stone was made by one of us. In the out that followed these word came to me. Mother joined him in Nov. 1994.; [hon.] Legion of Merit.; [oth. writ.] One poem for the High School Newspaper 1939; [a.] Hillsboro, OH

LATCHEM, KELLI K.
[pen.] Belle; [b.] March 5, 1984, Fort Wayne, IN; [p.] Thomas W. and Sandy Strawbridge Latchem; [ed.] 5th Grade Student at Woodland Elementary School in Perrysburg, Ohio.; [occ.] Full-time student; [memb.] Laurel Hill Swim and Tennis Club, Perrysburg Youth Soccer Association, St. Timothy's Episcopal Church; [hon.] Perrysburg Youth Soccer Association Certificate(s), Fort Wayne Historical Society Art Contest, Youth Ballet Awards; [oth. writ.] Numerous other writings (poetry and prose) in school. Many poems about nature, its beauty, and its ferociousness.; [pers.] I wrote this poem while in third grade. It was my first attempt at poetry but I have since written numerous poems and short stories. I especially enjoy describing my subjects and my characters in descriptive detail.; [a.] Perrysburg, OH

LATHAM, MANDY
[b.] December 12, 1979, Greenville, KY; [p.] Tammy and Greg Latham; [ed.] Central City Elem - Grad. 1992, Muhlenberg North, Middle School Grad - 1994, Present, Muhlenberg North High School - Freshman; [occ.] Student; [memb.] Richardsons Chapel General Baptist Church; [hon.] Solos and ensembles 1992 scored superior rating on flute solo; [oth. writ.] "The Idea Man", "Look My Way", "Love is Crue", Missing Grandma"; [pers.] If someday I don't succeed in being a famous author, my goal is to go an orthadontic assistant.; [a.] Central City, KY

LATHAM, MICHAEL ALVIN
[b.] November 10, 1933, Sevier Co, TN; [p.] Michael and Mary Jane Hembree Latham; [m.] Ruth Elaine Craven Latham, May 2, 1957; [ch.] Letha Clarice Latham Driver Jonathan Michael Latham, Michelle Elaine Latham; [ed.] BA - High Point University 1962, Master of Divinity - Candler School of Theology, Emory University 1969.; [occ.] United Methodist Minister; [memb.] Member of Western N.C. Conference of the United Methodist Church, member of BD. Of Directors of John Wesley Camp, Member of Bd. of Directors of Randolph Prison Chaplaincy Program; [hon.] Special award for serving as president of the Bd. of Directors of Randolph Prison Chaphincy program; [oth. writ.] One verse of another song, extra verse to a hymn; [pers.] "Jesus is the answer to the problems of our society, world"; [a.] Asheboro, NC

LAU, PAOLA N.
[pen.] Paola Lau; [b.] November 23, 1979, Guatemala; [p.] Lidia V. Lau; [ed.] Ambassador Christian High School in Fontana; [occ.] Student - 10th grade Ambassador Christian High School; [memb.] Martial Arts America - blue belt in Tae-Kwon-do.; [hon.] "Who's who among American High School Students" 1994 and 1995, honor roll 4.0 GPA at Ambassador Christian High School. Miss Jr. South Rialto Teen 1995.; [oth. writ.] Several Poems, I've been writing since I was 12 yrs. old.; [pers.] I tend to think that one needs to search for the meaning of the poem, not just read it. (I enjoy the writing of Robert Frost.); [a.] Rialto, CA

LAUGHLIN, MARY
[b.] December 19, 1963, Burdette, Tonlin; [p.] Dominick and Ruth Caprioni; [m.] Frank M. Laughlin, May 19, 1984; [ch.] 3 Frank M. Laughlin 2nd Samantha M. Laughlin, Richard A. Laughlin; [ed.] Middle Township H.S.; [occ.] Homemaker - Waitress, Doc's Too - Ocean View; [memb.] American Cancer Society, MADD - St

Casimir - Roman Catholic Church; [hon.] Silver Poet Award 1986; [oth. writ.] I have over 70 poems that I have written within the years; [pers.] My dream is to some day publish a book with all my poems

LAURENT, NYUKA
[pen.] Nyuka Anais Laurent; [b.] October 6, 1945, Springfield, MA; [p.] Frances Ellen Hayes and Larry Lawrence; [m.] Divorced; [ch.] Sonny (Lise), Sebastien and Thierry Laurent; [ed.] Graduate of Univ. of Paris, Paris, France with Maitrise d' Enseignement (Med) cum laude 1969; [occ.] Writer/Illustrator and commercial artist/designer; [memb.] Chamber of Commerce, Lenox MA National Assoc. of Female Executives Green peace Union des Francois de L'Etranger Amnesty International Now and ACLU; [hon.] Who's who among students, Who's who world wide; [oth. writ.] An International Journal, Translations of letters to Anais nin from Antonin Artaud and "The Street Where I lived - on the trail of Henry Miller" by Beatrice Commange. Also, volume of poetry entitled pleasure boat and other poems in collections; [pers.] Presently at work on 2 fantasy novels a volume of poetry and collection of short stories, no matter how many other fields I have pursued (art, real estate brokerage, professor of English, Esland French, sales in hospital industry) I always come back to writing. It gives me (and others, I hope) joy and fulfillment.; [a.] Chester, MA

LAVOIE, CHATERINE E.
[pen.] Caiti Lavoie; [b.] March 14, 1982, Fall River, MA; [p.] Raymund B. Lavoie, Elsie Lavoie; [ed.] C.V Carroll Elementary School, James M. Morton Middle School.; [hon.] Presidential academic award, Honor roll; [pers.] I write about things that I have experienced in my life. These experiences have influenced me to write my poetry.; [a.] Fall River, MA

LAWS, ANTHONY PAUL
[pen.] Anthony P. Laws; [b.] September 1, 1958, Augsburg, Germany; [p.] William and Christine Laws; [m.] Jennifer M. Hamilton-Laws, September 30, 1988; [ch.] Anthony Paul Junior, Brandon Tyrea Floyd Hugh Stewart; [ed.] AAS - Eastfield College, Dallas WH Adamson High School Dallas; [occ.] Research Assistant Mars Promotional Services Dallas TX; [hon.] Honor Graduate - AII. US Army, Honor Graduate ASI US Army, Commandant's List PLDS. U.S. Army; [oth. writ.] Several poems and short stories; [pers.] Many have said it before luck is simply preparation meeting opportunity; [a.] Garland, TX

LAWSON, BRIAN JOHN
[b.] April 2, 1976, Worcester, MA; [p.] Dawn M. Lawson and David Ford; [ed.] Francis J McGrath Elementary, Forest Grove Middle School, Wachusett Regional High, Quinsigamond Community College; [occ.] Full time student cemetery sales telecommunication; [hon.] Recognition by the national library of poetry; [oth. writ.] Numerous, unpublished works of literary art in a "little black diary"; [pers.] Double oops! It has to be perfect! Please don't shorten this. I don't have alot of other info before this! Seems to me, as the world turns.. The world dies and the worst has yet to be perceived, as we engrave ever deeper scars on the face of the earth. Poetry is my chance of will, brimmed with the nectar of the Gods, shedding light on shadows to describe this world I cannot change. It'll be a cold day in hell when we all love at first sight... But it'll be cold in heaven til then.; [a.] Rutland, MA

LAWSON, GERI POWERS
[b.] November 28, 1966, Ft Lauderdale, FL; [p.] Joan R. Lindsey; [m.] Warren Lawson, August 29, 1993; [memb.] Tampa Bay Poetry Council; [oth. writ.] Numerous, as of yet, unpublished poems; [pers.] With my poetry I endeavor to look into the shadows found in the mirror of self reflection. One of the strongest influences on my work has been the writings of Edgar Allen Poe.; [a.] St Petersburg, FL

LAWSON, JAMIE RENA
[pen.] Jamie R. Lawson; [b.] January 7, 1978, Frankfort, IN; [p.] Rosie and James Lawson; [ed.] Currently enrolled as a Junior at Whitley County High School.; [memb.] S.A.DD. Students Against Drunk Driving 4-W Club.; [hon.] Who's What Among American High School Students (1993-1994) Presidential Academic Fitness Award, 2nd Place District Conservation Essay Contest.; [oth. writ.] "Unreality" Echoes of Yesterday published by the National Library of Poetry (Editors Choice Award), "Pain" Today's Great Poems published by famous poets society, several poems published in school literary magazine, Colonel Creations; [pers.] "Alone holding emptiness, my words, crush, tear, soothe, and love. Between them I am mostly pain. I still sometimes smile at brief moments of truth and in life isn't this accomplishment enough when blinded by more than the sun."; [a.] Williamsburg, KY

LAZAR
[pen.] Maria; [b.] July 15, 1935, Romania; [p.] Dihel Gheorghe and Dihel Nicolita; [m.] Lazar Eugeniu, October 25, 1955; [ch.] Lazar, Lili, Eugenia; [ed.] H.S. Bacallaureate Diploma Accounting Major, 2 years faculty of general econ. "Industrial" (University) expelled medequate politic, Certificate-project Design Water Supply and Allen School N.Y. Nursing assist.; [occ.] Health Care - Hospital St Vincent's N.Y.; [memb.] L.I.R.S., Feed the children, is a member in good standing - International Society of Poets - Lifetime - and Hutt River Province - Australia from - Royal Patronage Status; [hon.] Hereby award - the International Poet of Merits Award - U.S. Holocaust Memorial Mas-Name Of Donor. For benefits of Scholars, Journalists and other visitors, Hutt River Province Royal Patronage Certificate Honor-from- Australia - Royal Patronage Australia? "Hutt River Province"; [oth. writ.] U.S. and Canada Newspapers, "Micro Magazine" Anthology- A Break in the clouds wind in the nightly, and in the desert sun repeat: USA and Canada news paper Micro Magazine -Wind in the night sky - anthology USA - A break in the clouds - anthology USA, - In the desert sun - anthology USA; [pers.] The juncture politic of abolish socialite and protector of a Universal Dedar. Rights people for life, freedom and security - Peace and science and culture of people - and "In God We Trust"; [a.] New York - Hateu Island, NY

LAZAR, OPAL H.
[b.] November 17, 1919, Lapaz, IN; [p.] Ralph Huff and Sadie Heckaman; [m.] Nick Lazar, January 24, 1948; [ch.] Cathy, Anne, Reynolds, Linda, Sue Hauer; [ed.] Lapaz Ind. High Indiana University Purdue U. - 6 months after 4 yrs at IU.; [occ.] Retired; [memb.] Central College Presbyterian Church, NARFE-Nat'l Assn. Fed. Retired Employees, DAR - Daughters AM. Revolution, AARP - AM. Assn. Retired People; [hon.] H. S. Salutatorian; [pers.] I like to convey my philosophies of obtaining a happier and better outlook on life to all plus ways to add strength and courage to living.; [a.] Columbus, OH

LAZAR, LISA
[pen.] Lisa; [b.] April 7, 1979, New York; [p.] Renee and Steve Lazar; [ed.] I am currently in 9th grade at Lawrence Woodmere Academy.; [memb.] I am very active in Amnesty International, and I am in an environmental club in school, and the Art club.; [hon.] 7th Grade most improve in academy 8th Grade Most improved in English. In basketball the coaches award and 4 sport participation; [pers.] Don't let anyone tell you "You Can't" because you can. Many people told me I could not. I heard it so much that I started to believe them. Believe in your self and you will go far.; [a.] Bellmore, NY

LEAIRD, CATHERINE ELOISE MANGUM
[pen.] Mimi Elizabeth Leigh; [b.] April 7, 1950, Union Co., NC; [p.] Byrone Lee and Eloise Richardson Mangum; [m.] Robert M. Leaird, December 7, 1968;

[ch.] Robert, "Mitch, Jr. Age 25, John Ryan, age 22; [ed.] High School Graduate, Pageland High School 1968, Attended Chesterfield Marlboro Technical College, Southeastern College of Beauty Culture First year student of Christian Writer's Guild; [occ.] Retail Store Clerk, Part-time nail technician, Freelance Writer; [memb.] Member, First Baptist Church of Pageland, SC, Member - Arthritis Foundation, Member - SC SHARE, Volunteer for American Cancer Society, Member Disabled American Veterans; [hon.] Favorite writers are Elizabeth Barrett Browning, Helen Steiner Rice, Marjorie Holmes and Virginia H. Ruehlmann.; [oth. writ.] A Matter of God's Goodness A Collection of Faith Writings, I'll Bear the Thorns The Way Back; [pers.] My poetry and freelance writing reflects thoughts of deep with in a loving God. I strive to portray to my readers a portrait of how wisdom and peace may be obtained through the pursuance of God's will for our lives.; [a.] Pageland, SC

LEANEN, BETTY JANE
[b.] July 30, 1928, Batavia, NY; [p.] William and Alice Selhorst; [m.] Harry Leanen, April 8, 1972; [ch.] Ross Baglio, Gus Baglio; [ed.] Perry High School, Perry, NY; [occ.] Homemaker - Retired, Do Volunteer Work; [memb.] First Baptist Church - Choir Little Theatre of Palm Coast (Florida), Sharps and Flats Club, Flagler County Council for the Arts, Flagler County Art League; [hon.] Certificate for outstanding performance in tap dancing in Palm Coast; [oth. writ.] Several poems published in Daily News Paper - Batavia, NY, Short Stories; [pers.] I enjoy keeping active; [a.] Palm Coast, FL

LEE, JENNIFER A.
[b.] April 14, 1971, Van Nuy; [p.] Mr. and Mrs. John and Linda Lee; [ed.] Self-Studied graduate L.A.C.H.S.A; [memb.] International Society Of Poets; [hon.] Top, first seeded merit in competition the International Society of Poets, and recorded artist Sound of Poetry; [oth. writ.] Dance on the Horizons Best Poems of 1995, National Library of Poetry; [pers.] Voice behind the curtain of resonance, To simplify, at the seat of Comprehension; [a.] Camarillo, CA

LEE, DUANE
[pen.] Blessed Poet, Dangerous D.; [b.] May 5, 1968, Fayetteville, NC; [p.] SonSeahrey Howe, Robert E. Lee Jr.; [ed.] Spingarn Senior High, University of the District of Columbia; [occ.] Occupation support, Department of Education; [memb.] Mount Sinai Baptist Church; [hon.] Army Achievement Medal, Battalion Awards, Honor Roll Certificates; [oth. writ.] Retirement poems, mother's day poems, religious poems; [pers.] A good poem can touch many people. I thank God that he blessed and guided me to compose poetry; [a.] Fayetteville, NC

LEE, CHRISTINE
[pen.] Chris; [b.] December 3, 1978, Queens Minto, NB; [p.] Theo Lee, Salina Lee; [ed.] West Windsor Plainsboro High School; [memb.] American Red Cross Club, Amnesty International, Ministry Team; [hon.] PTA Awards.; [pers.] See now the world turns and write now to ease it's pain. Knowledge is only restricted by it's imagination.; [a.] Cranbury, NJ

LEE, CALDWELL J.
[pen.] Caldwell Lee; [b.] March 31; [occ.] Dorrance Publishing Co., Inc. :NLP :ISP; [memb.] International Society of Poets; [hon.] International Society of Poets, Poet of Merit Awards: (1993/1994). The National Library of Poetry: Editor's Choice Awards (1993/1994); [oth. writ.] Caldwell Lee: The poet to be. The Forthright Omnipotence Era. $7.95 :ISBN #0805935266 Dorrance Publishing. Whispers in the Wind: The National Library of Poetry.; [pers.] Gary Postrech and Noreen Doloughty for a superb work of art. Handcrafted and molded for the love of both you and me, Tailored and Precisioned is the Poet to Be.; [a.] Port Tobacco, MD

LEEDBERG, MICHAEL D.
[b.] September 9, 1971, Chelmsford, MA; [p.] David A. Della E. Wickens; [ed.] UMASS Lowell, BA of Science in criminal Justice, minor in political science; [occ.] Legal Intern; [hon.] Editor's choice award 1994 from the national library of poetry, magna cumlaude from UMASS Lowell; [oth. writ.] Various poems and comedy routines; [pers.] To me poetry is the most efficient tool one can utilize in expressing one's feelings, thoughts and desires.; [a.] Westford, MA

LEEPER, DEBORAH
[b.] June 29, 1967, TX; [p.] John and Nancy Barnett; [m.] Bryan Leeper, October 16, 1982; [ch.] Gregory Martin, Timothy Bryan, Trevor John; [ed.] Clarendon College, West Texas A and M State Univ; [occ.] Student; [memb.] National Multiple Sclerosis Society Clarendon Volunteer Ambulance Authority Clarendon Firebelles Phi Theta Kappa; [hon.] Dean's List; [pers.] God gives us insight via obstacles throughout the coarse of life.; [a.] Clarendon, TX

LEFEVRA, DONALD K.
[pen.] Feebe; [b.] November 9, 1946, Lowell, MA; [p.] Donald, Hazel; [m.] Donna, September 24, 1988; [ch.] Natalie, Donnie, Troy, (Amy, Scott-Step Children); [ed.] Graduate of Ft. Wayne South Side. Attended FT Wayne Art School. Chaplain and pastoral training; [occ.] Gage Control At Zollner Corp Ltd.; [memb.] North American Hunting Club, National Rifle Asso. U.A.W. #2357 Word of Liberty Church; [hon.] 1st Place National Poetry Anthology Contest 1965. Frost Illustrated Magazine 1969 produced a record for radio 1971-Tapes 1993; [oth. writ.] Song writer and composer and musician. Currently active and performing. In concert and ministerial duties. Have small recording studio; [pers.] In spite of all my failures and weaknesses I know the everlasting love of the God of all creation, through Jesus Christ, My Lord and Savior; [a.] Fort Wayne, IN

LEGGETT, STEPHANIE B.
[pen.] Angeline Bender; [b.] June 29, 1940, Houston, TX; [p.] John C. and Gretchen L. Bender; [m.] Toby J. Leggett, October 1, 1979; [ch.] Clinton Bender Gough; [ed.] Lamar High School-Houston Texas Tech University Southwestern Business University Houston Bible Institute; [occ.] Housewife/Write; [oth. writ.] "Integrity and Humility" "The Desert Soul" "A Helping Hand" "Christmas Celebration" "The Balloon" "Of Hats and Halos"; [pers.] Our words and thoughts are of little value if we do not share them.; [a.] Houston, TX

LEMAITRE, LIZZETTE
[b.] October 8, 1967, Brooklyn, NY; [p.] Alida and Emilio Miranda; [m.] Pablo F. Lemaitre, December 31, 1991; [ch.] Thina-Marie, Gilberth, Junior, Roy.; [ed.] I have a G.Ed Through home study I would like to encourage other mother's who want to further there education, to do the same; [occ.] Student/Housewife; [oth. writ.] This poem of mine is the first to be published. I have many other poems on all subjects that deal with our lives, and I will continue to write many more. I am very proud of myself.; [pers.] I am a very sentimental person, threw my poems I can express myself, I in specially enjoy to write love poems.

LEMKE, DARRYL
[b.] July 21, 1973, Mercy Community Hosp.; [p.] Joseph and Margaret Lemke; [ed.] Delaware Valley High School Graduated - G.E.D.; [occ.] Maintenance; [oth. writ.] Several other writings that are unpublished; [pers.] Would like to be recognized as a writer, and someday will hope to find a career in it. Influenced by certain people in life who greatly inspire my work.; [a.] Matamoras, PA

LENOIR, CHRIS
[b.] July 12, 1974, Birmingham, AL; [p.] F. Wyne Lenoir, M-Cynthia Lenoir; [ed.] Vestavia Hills High School Samford University, Sophomore; [occ.] Student

LENTS, STACIE
[b.] December 12, 1977, St Louis, MO; [p.] Don G. Lents, Peggy I. Lents; [ed.] John Burroughs High School, Idyllwild School of Music and the Arts (now a Junior), Interlochen and Bennington summer programs; [occ.] Student, part time drama, dance counselor; [memb.] Alpha Players Theatre Co, St. Louis, MO, International Society of Poets, Idyllwild School of Music and the Arts Theatre company, Model United Nations; [hon.] Editor's Choice Award for "Release" as published in the National Library of Poetry's In the Desert Sun, Best Actress nomination for portrayal of Anne in "The Diary of Anne Frank"; [oth. writ.] "Minority" in the National Library of Poetry's The Best Poets of 1995.; [pers.] My goal is to express the discoveries of my personal experience in the poetic language which describes and provokes the emotions of all. My love and thanks to Kelsey Lec and Carissa Beth and to my Parents.; [a.] St Louis, MO

LEONARD, CHRISTINE
[pen.] Jo Moore; [b.] October 30, 1943, Rutland, VT; [p.] Edward and Mary Canney; [m.] Raymond Leonard, February 27, 1965; [ch.] Brett Raymond, and Deanna Christine; [ed.] Mt. St. Joseph Academy Trinity College, VT St. Michaels College, VT; [occ.] Homemaker; [a.] So. Burlington, VT

LEONARD, PHILBERT
[pen.] Philbert Anderson; [b.] March 9, 1955, Albany, GA; [p.] Esco and Julia D. Anderson; [m.] Jerome Leonard, March 15, 1979; [ch.] Deirdra Nicole and Vashon Damond; [ed.] Monroe High and Essex County; [occ.] Customer Service Repr Chemical Bank NJ; [hon.] All - Star Award for a superior job performance. The prize was $5000.00.; [pers.] Through my poetry I hope to bring about peace, love and harmony through out the world. I hope my poems let the world know that Jesus still lives.; [a.] Sicklerville, NJ

LESS, JOANNE G.
[b.] November 9, 1928, Toledo, OH; [p.] David Less, Sophia Less; [ed.] Bachelor of Education, Master of Education from University of Toledo; [occ.] Retired; [memb.] Order of time Eastern/Star, National Educ. Association (Life Member); [hon.] Phi Kapp Pi (National Honor Society). Kappa Delta Pi (National Honor Society for Teachers); [oth. writ.] My poem "Yellow Mums" has been published in Darkside Of The Moon several poems published in Local News Papers; [pers.] My poems deal mainly with such subjects as the transiency of Human Experience and the beauty of nature as therapy for man's struggles. The English Romantic Poets have had an important influence on my writing,; [a.] Royal Oak, MI

LESTER III, LAWRENCE
[pen.] La Joy; [b.] January 8, 1974, Memphis, TN; [p.] Lawrence Lester II, Ida Mae Lester; [ed.] High School Graduate from Fairley High School; [occ.] Part time work at a private clinic; [memb.] French club, Ursher Club, Runners Club, Student Correll and V.P. of Production in a High School Economic class.; [hon.] Most Friendliest, Best Supporting Actor, Most Writers Actor, Top English Student; [oth. writ.] I've entered your 1993 poetry contest. I didn't include my biographical data or oder In the Desert Sun. Other than that I write poems for a hobby.; [pers.] I haven't won a contest of any kind before. I try to make most of my poetry rhyme so people can remember it better. In High School, The poems we had to recite from memory was hard. They didn't rhyme.; [a.] Memphis, TN

LEVESQUE, ABBIE M.
[pen.] Abbs; [b.] January 15, 1969, Valporaise, IN; [p.] Priscilla Ponader; [m.] Kevin S. Levesque, July 25, 1987; [ch.] Jason 8, Justin 5, Alex 2; [ed.] Merrimack High in NH, 1 year at Coastal Community College in Jacksonville, NC and still continuing. Education is never ending; [occ.] Mother and Wife and Hopeless Dreamer; [memb.] Poet's Guild, and the Chapter 1 parent advisory board.; [oth. writ.] I am closet poet just opening the door. Most of my work is in journals. Also published in Best New poems from the poet's guild; [pers.] Never stop dreaming, it is the spice to all lives, loves and happiness

LEVINE, BETTE V.
[b.] July 18, 1913, New Jersey; [p.] George Y. and Marcella C. Van Fleet; [m.] Hermon M. Levine (Deceased), February 11, 1938; [ch.] Michael V. Levine (Dec) Hugh Anthony Levine; [ed.] N.J. and Guadalajara, Jalisco, Mexico Various Adult Ed. Courses here and there.; [occ.] Retired; [memb.] American Women's Voluntary Services, National Geographic Society, American Assoc. of Retired People, Rossmoor Library Assn. American Society of Jalisco; [oth. writ.] Local newspaper features and articles in N.J. poems published in The Vermonter, and other small mags. Wrote and published small monthly local newsletter, The Millstone Paper, in Clarksburg, N.J.; [pers.] "The Scattering" was written in memory of my husband, (who died of Alzheimer's) after my son scattered his ashes in the Pacific; [a.] Walnut Creek, CA

LEVY, RONALD P.
[pen.] Ronald P. Levy; [b.] December 25, 1950, Rockford, IL; [p.] Staley Levy, Edith Levy; [m.] Barbara Anne Murphy Levy, August 17, 1974; [ch.] Jennifer Lauren, James Daniel; [ed.] CCSF, SFSU; [occ.] Advertising/Sales; [hon.] The National Library of Poetry Comes to mind.; [oth. writ.] 'A Fire In Heaven', 'Rice Paper', a book of aphorisms and a book of songs, unpublished but still in existence. S.F. Newspaper Agency; [pers.] I'm not a writer because I say I am, I'm only a writer because someone else says I am.; [a.] Petaluma, CA

LEWIS, SHARON G.
[b.] June 10, 1937, Twin Falls, ID; [p.] Louise Morse and James A. Kellar; [ch.] Susan L. Lewis-Hoffmeister; [ed.] Eureka High; [occ.] Retired; [memb.] Several Wildlife Organizations. Statue of Liberty Foundation; [oth. writ.] Childrens Stories and songs, lyrics only; [pers.] Your quality of life is up to you. I have multiple sclerosis, and writing is a wonderful diversion, I enjoy poetry on real life, Humorous and sentimental. I seem to be a gifted writer.; [a.] Palo Alto, CA

LEWIS, PAUL B.
[b.] May 18, 1987, Boston; [p.] Alfred Lewis and Daine Sherlock; [ed.] Currently a second grade student at the chestnut hill School, Newton, MA; [occ.] Student; [oth. writ.] "The dog who drooled too much," a children's mystery, now being reviewed by publishers. Also, I'm editor of "The Kid's Record," our class newspaper; [pers.] I wrote this poem for school and I love Halloween poetry.; [a.] Weston, MA

LEWIS, CONNIE L.
[pen.] Connie Lynne Menges; [b.] October 25, 1951, Norton, KS; [p.] Mr and Mrs Jay Gallentine, WJ Menges; [m.] Divorced; [ch.] Jennifer Renee, Amy Marie; [occ.] Accountant/Comptroller, The Boese Hilburn Co., Merriam, KS 66203; [memb.] Eckankar, Kansas Prochoice Alliance.; [oth. writ.] First publication. Currently compiling 20 years poetry, prose, and journals to seek publication.; [pers.] When I write, there is no barrier between the flow of my words and the feelings of my heart. I try to express the love and the truth of my soul, and occasionally, to taste of a flight of fancy...; [a.] Olathe, KS

LEWIS, LAILONI M.
[pen.] Loni; [b.] March 31, 1981, Omaha, NE; [p.] Lorri A. Lewis, Lawrence E. Rose; [ed.] Franklin Learning Center Columbian Elementary; [occ.] Student; [memb.] Girls Club Inc. Compass Ministries; [pers.] Loni Lewis, March 31, 1982, Omaha, NE. Parents: Lorri A. Lewis and Lawrence Rose, Education: Franklin Learning Center, Columbian Ele, I enjoy writing poems

LEWIS JR., FELIX
[b.] November 2, 1944; [p.] Felix and Margaree Lewis; [m.] Opal Lewis; [ch.] Nikita Rene Lewis, Jonathan Mychael Lewis; [ed.] BA in Sociology, 42 credits Toward MAT; [occ.] Graphic Artist, Writer; [memb.] African American Fellow Univ. Pittsburgh; [hon.] Deans List SVSU (Saginaw Valley State Univ.); [oth. writ.] The Gospels of Matthew, Mark, Luke and John is now a "Poem". It tells the story of Jesus from birth thru the resurrection in poem.; [pers.] The only way to save America is to return our trust to him who empowered America in the first place.; [a.] Library, PA

LI, JENNIFER H.
[b.] January 26, 1978, Johnson City, NY; [p.] Dr. H. Harry Li and Mrs. M. Frances Li; [ed.] Thomas J. Watson Elementary School, Jennie F. Snapp Middle School, Westlake High School, Carnegie Mellon University; [pers.] I want to experience so many things to travel the world, the seas, and the stars, but no matter which path I choose to take, I hope to share my experiences with others and create happiness. After all, happiness is at the very heart of living.; [a.] Austin, TX

LIDGARD, MIKAELA
[pen.] Daphne Wynn; [b.] April 3, 1975, Edinburgh; [p.] Carol and Graham Lidgard; [ed.] Currently Attending The George Washington University, Wellesley High; [occ.] Student; [hon.] Dean's List, Coppell Junior Leadership Award; [oth. writ.] Features Editor of IT magazine; [a.] Washington, DC

LIGHTFOOT, DORIS MARIE
[b.] December 29, 1927, Rogers, TX; [p.] Dovie Alldredge, George W. Cooksey; [m.] Richard E. Lightfoot, September 29, 1945; [ch.] Darlene, Glinda, Dixie, and tommy E. Lightfoot; [ed.] Polytechnic High, Texas Women's University B.S. Med; [occ.] Retired Science and Math Teacher Meadowbrook Middle School Ft. Worth TX; [memb.] TOPSTX 162, Wed. Sen. Bridge Club, The Gideons International; [hon.] At 10 yrs old one of my poems-won and was read on the Radio, I won a wrist watch, Another of my poems won a trip for the whole family and was read on T.V., I was one of the top 20 winners in a writer's contest; [oth. writ.] In 1968 and my short story was printed in the Daedalian - A TWU publication.; [pers.] I have realized my dreams of being a wife, mother, School Teacher, and a writer-poet of sorts. It has been a charge head-don't let anything stand in your way wonderful life; [a.] Arlington, TX

LINDLEY, MARTHA
[pen.] Meglin; [b.] April 23, 1923, Hamilton, OH; [ed.] Ross High, Ross, Ohio; [occ.] Retired; [memb.] Charter member and field Representative WIMSA (Women in Military Service for America) also shipmate U.S. Navy, Memorial; [oth. writ.] None published; [pers.] My paths lead to many locales and interesting people. Wonderful childhood in Ohio, two years with U.S. Coast Guard during WWII in Florida, 30 yrs marriage in California writing and copy and designing layouts, currently happy trails in Arizona with sojourns to the eastern shore line and Virginia. Most Influential Writers: Ralph Waldo Emerson, Henry Wadsworth Longfellow; [a.] Sun City, AZ

LIPA, TAMMY R.
[pen.] Bunny Rose; [b.] September 4, 1975, Canton IL; [p.] Patricia and Joseph W. Lipa; [ed.] Liberty Union High School Brad 3.2, Freshman at MSCD; [occ.] Food

Handler And full time student; [pers.] The poem One Rose was inspired by my mother Patricia and Lipa's marriage to Peter John Sonner in 1993. The poem was read at the exchanging of rose. A symbol of everlasting love; [a.] Denver, CO

LIPAROTE, DEBORAH ELAINE
[pen.] Debbie Liparote; [b.] October 7, 1953, Longbeach, CA; [p.] Estel Beller, Theora Stroup; [m.] Divorced; [ch.] Mealine, Debralee, Tony Jr. Liparote; [ed.] Canyon High College of the Canyons A.V. College (Nursing School); [occ.] Nursing; [memb.] Heart Association, Little League; [hon.] Girls Glee, Girls volleyball team Certified Nurses Aid, The State of California; [oth. writ.] Just writing poems at home this was my daughters idea (Debralee) to place these poems in a magazine she was reading.; [pers.] These poems I write is out of the free time I have. I've been writing for about 5 years. Off and On. I started a little book of my own called Debbie's poems Forever and Always. Just something to pass on to my children. Little did I know my children thought they were good enough to win a contest, I'm so proud.; [a.] Pueblo, CO

LIPPI, MICHAEL
[b.] December 30, 1953, Weehawken, NJ; [p.] Mario Lippi, Yolanda C. Lippi; [m.] Single; [ed.] U.S. Armed Forces Institute (GED), Newspaper Institute of America (2-Courses) Current student, Writer's Digest School, Institute of Children's Literature; [occ.] Machine Operator; [memb.] Tennessee Writer's Alliance (Since 1991); [hon.] The National Library of Poetry Editor's Choice Award 1994; [oth. writ.] Apple Pie, published in echoes of yesterday, Broken Dreams, published in Best Poets of 1995, various unpublished short stories; [pers.] All ideas are good that are good or serve a good purpose; [a.] Cowan, TN

LITTLE, MAUDE
[b.] July 16, 1935, Washington, CO; [p.] Charlie and Myrtle Grindstaff; [m.] Dewey Little, September 14, 1957; [ch.] Gregory, Susan, Danny, Grandchildren - Josh, Matthew; [ed.] High School Jonesborough High school, Jonesborough, Tennessee, 1954; [occ.] Housewife; [oth. writ.] Poems - operation Divine shield - So All Alone Love - The Little Hat The Old Man and The New; [pers.] I claim Jesus as Lord and I give Him all the glory, for His poems.; [a.] Johnson, TN

LITTLETON, ATONIO PIERRE
[b.] December 3, 1973, Detroit, MI; [p.] Pierre Beauford, Shirley Littleton; [ed.] Murray_Wright High, University of Michigan; [occ.] Full-time college student (senior).; [memb.] National Honor Society, Big Brothers/Big Sisters of Washtenaw County.; [hon.] Wade McCree Scholarship, Class Honors (University of Michigan) Wade McCree Scholar; [oth. writ.] A poem published in a student magazine, poem for Church competition (won trophy).; [pers.] Never dwell on what could have been in the past, but look forward to what can be in the future.; [a.] Detroit, MI

LIVSEY, RICHARD
[b.] January 26, 1970, NY; [p.] Ron and Pat Livsey; [ch.] Amanda and Clelsie; [ed.] Currently studying at Borough of Manhattan Community College; [memb.] Green peace, Rain forest Action Network; [oth. writ.] Currently working on a short story collection.; [pers.] "Help the ones who want to be helped, teach those who want to be taught, love the ones, that need to be loved, and find the souls that are lost."; [a.] New York City, NY

LIZARRAGA, CARLOS
[b.] April 16, 1951, Mexicali, Mexico; [p.] Francisco Lizarraga, Maria Franco; [ed.] Imperial Valley College; [occ.] Delivery Driver CS North Hollywood California PX Drugstore; [pers.] Pleasurable flourishing moments of inspiration that blossom into a joyful song, are the priceless gifts of an enchanting women.; [a.]

Tujunga, CA

LOCEY, ANGELINE
[b.] July 30, 1928, Honolulu, HI; [p.] Gordon Hopkins, Myrtle Hopkins; [m.] Richard Locey, June 5, 1948; [ch.] Leslie, Michael, Patrick, Stephen; [ed.] Roosevelt High School Hon. HI.; [occ.] Hawaiian Homestead Farmer and Hawaiian Healing practitioner and facilitator; [memb.] Kupuna Council of the Independent Nation of Hawaii; [hon.] Kauai Island Po'o for the independent Nation of Hawaii; [pers.] May this unique and magical experience contribute to the perpetuation of Queen Lili'uokalani's heart's desire for her people, Aloha Aina, where the budding and the blossoming continues to reign.; [a.] Anahola Kauai, HI

LOCKER, GARY E.
[pen.] Mr. Hidden Narrator; [b.] July 24, 1940, Dayton, OH; [p.] Richard, Rosella Locker; [m.] Nan E. Eisenberg; [ch.] Kerry Evan, Garth, Sean David, Torri, Christopher A,; [ed.] Fairview High Dayton Eastman School of Music; [occ.] Salvation Army; [memb.] International Musicians Union, Green Peace, Cleveland Museum of Art; [hon.] Fleur de Gurre, Haiti 94, (In Rosentia), N.A.R.D. National Drum Contest runner up '56, Parachuting License; [oth. writ.] "Gronk The Christmas Dragon", "Parque Me Las Palomas", "Magoi (The Sand Kings)", "Haitian Dance", "Cities Asleep Series", "Rainbow In The Eye Of A Tear"; [pers.] "You're in Good Hands with Shiva"; [a.] Cleveland, OH

LOGAN, ADAM J.
[b.] November 22, 1974, Fairview Park; [p.] James R. Logan and Anne Ruehlman; [ed.] Graduated from Avon Lake High School and currently attending Lorain County Community College.; [occ.] Student; [pers.] I dedicate my work to Tricia Sedar, whom I love very much.; [a.] Avon Lake, OH

LOGAN, LYNDA
[b.] December 14, 1947, Albany, KY; [p.] Clara and Jack Ferguson; [ed.] Clinton County High School, Albany, KY, Western Kentucky University, Bowling Green, KY; [occ.] National Account Manager, U.S. Paging Corp.; [hon.] Graduate Assistant, Dean's List, Western KY University; [oth. writ.] This is the first poem that I have submitted for a contest or publication.; [pers.] My writing is directly from the heart. I have been greatly influenced by Mother, My Father and a beautiful little dog, Kacey.; [a.] Sunnyvale, CA

LOMAX, JAN
[b.] February 9, 1956, Knoxville, TN; [p.] John and Bettye Lomax; [ch.] Nikisha, Jaianna, Jumucho Lomax; [ed.] Graduate - B.S. University of Tennessee - Communications; [occ.] Musician - Producer, Song Writer; [hon.] Publish Records For distribution; [oth. writ.] Feature Stories for U.T's Beacon News Paper Author of unpublished book (titled) Small Town Political Regime; [pers.] Glory be to God for his inspiration; [a.] Knoxville, TN

LONG, TERRY DESHAWN
[pen.] Terry Long; [b.] May 6, 1978, Cleveland, AL; [p.] Carolyn Long, James Dixon; [ch.] 1 Brother, James Andrew Long; [ed.] Attending Southview High School 2270 E42 Loraine Oh.; [occ.] Employee of Rax Restaurant's and Morning Journal Carrier; [memb.] SouthView's 94-96, Vocational Welding Class, Attends Victory Baptist temple of Elyria Ohio; [hon.] Academic Achievement presented by Lorain County Alliance of Black School Educators.; [oth. writ.] Martin Luther King Jr. which was never published.; [pers.] I am an aspiring poetry writer, and will look for further contest's involving poetry, and some day will be a well known person from coast to cost!; [a.] Lorain, OH

LONG, CHRISTOPHER JAMES
[b.] November 15, 1977, McKees Rock, PA; [p.] William and Josephine Long; [ch.] Christopher James

Modes-Long Jr.; [ed.] 1995 Graduate of South Eastern Reg. Vo - Tech High School; [occ.] Breakfast Chef, Brother's Restaurant in Brockton MA; [memb.] Vocational Industrial Clubs of America; [hon.] Gold Metal Winner at District Level VICA; [oth. writ.] Published in High School Literary magazine. Novel entitled "The Dream". Other writing includes poems, a song, and honoring biographies; [pers.] Inspired Deeply by the Love of my life, Lorelei Modes; [a.] Brockton, MA

LONGO, DOMENICO
[pen.] Emmanuele Dibene; [b.] December 4, 1965, Italy, Sicily; [p.] Giuseppe Longo and Maria Cacciatore; [ed.] Reseda High, Los Angeles Valley College.; [occ.] Poet; [hon.] In Recognition For outstanding performance in: Team Work and Staff of the Month.; [oth. writ.] I did publish a book of poetry on my own.; [pers.] I have so much love in my heart that I would like to share it with those who understand the art of love.; [a.] Palmdale, CA

LONON, KEITH ALLAN
[b.] March 31, 1971, Morganton, NC; [ed.] Graduated McDowell High School in 1989.; [oth. writ.] I am currently trying to be a published writer either from a novel or short stories, and also a book of poems I am working on. Nothing else has been published, but I have never sent a poem before. I am currently working on a sci-fi fiction short story, that I hope will be published one day. I would like to write for a living.; [pers.] I like Edgar Allan Poe's work and other poems that Rhyme. I write from the heart, but all of the outdoors is really the inspiration.; [a.] Marion, NC

LOONEY, TOBY
[b.] July 31, 1938, SC; [m.] Joanna Pittman Looney; [occ.] Body Shop Owner; [pers.] The poem I submitted came to me in a dream in its entirety, before this I had never wrote any poetry what so ever. The only thing I can take credit for I gave it a name infinity; [a.] Piedmont, SC

LOPES, O. A.
[b.] March 10, 1921, New Bedford, MA; [m.] Lois C. (Smith) Lopes, August 14, 1943; [ch.] Carolyn L. Barkley, Head of Central Library, Virginia Beach, VA.; [ed.] Bridgewater (MA) State, BS Ed, Bread Loaf School of English at Middlebury College, MA, John Hay Fellow in Humanities at Harvard U.; [occ.] Retired Head of English Dept, Long meadow High School. Spending 6 months each year in Fulbrook, Oxfordshire, England.; [hon.] Appointed John Hay Fellow at Harvard 1960-61; [oth. writ.] "Pastoral" (poem) appeared in The Countryman Magazine (Oxfordshire) in the 1989 autumn issue, Norwich Hill (poems), 1993, For the Duration (poems), 1994, privately published in Britain.; [pers.] My poems attempt to render time's experience less elusive through shape and form. Mine is no "lover's quarrel" but is an enduring affair with the variety with which the past informs the present.; [a.] Donamor Ln, MA

LORDO, CARL B.
[pen.] Del Castle; [oth. writ.] Teaches ways to bypass learning disabilities, damaged cells, dyslexia, etc. "How to Implant Implosive seeds of survival knowledge." Seeds Stimulate Synapses' Receptors to "think".) $15. "Survival Knowledge, talent, skills and IQ tests." $15. (Pupils may look for answers. Develop Comprehension. Standard tests develop cheaters, dropouts, illiterates.) $15. "Guide for tutors, educators." (Quickly teach with authority.) $35. "How to quickly qualify, join del's tutoring service." (Franchises available coast to coast. Free rent! Tutor pt/f time.) $5. "Promoting softwares, Tv documentaries, games.) $5. "De's new sayings, proverbs," $5.; [a.] Miami, FL

LOVE, JOHNETTA E.
[pen.] Johnetta Love; [b.] August 21, 1945, Chatt, TN; [p.] Johnny and Dorothy Tucker; [m.] Roger Love, June 22, 1972; [ch.] Valencia, Edward, Darlene, Tracey, Destiny; [ed.] Mercy College-Bachelor Degree; [occ.] Mary Kay Cosmetics, Primerica Financial Services-Martin and Associates; [oth. writ.] Fifteen Other Poems; [pers.] I strive to reflect the things that I love and appreciate.; [a.] Oak Park, IL

LOVY, MICHAEL FRANCIS
[b.] July 3, 1951, Bronx, NY; [p.] Mavis Rodriguez, Frank Lovy; [m.] Abby Lovy, June 13, 1976; [ch.] Eric, Rachel and Rebecca; [ed.] James Monroe and Chaffey H.S. College L.A. Valley College and UCLA; [occ.] Door to door salesman Vacuum cleaners and shoes NY to California; [memb.] Screen actors guild associated actors and artists of America - AFL - CIO. (Church on the way, choir); [oth. writ.] School poems and song writing published and copy rights. All of my writings come from life my life and the life of others. Feelings of truth is my goal. Influenced by life truth is my goal. Influenced by life from all walks of life all!!; [pers.] Making God the important part of my daily walk is my strength. To fall to fail, fumble, forget and forgive. Is the love Christ Jesus has given me. Love kills hate. Thanks to mavis for a good start in song and poetry.; [a.] Bronx, NY

LOVY, MICHAEL F.
[b.] July 3, 1951, Bronx, NY; [p.] Mavis Rodriguez, Frank Lovy; [m.] Abby Lovy, June 13, 1976; [ch.] Rachel, Rebecca and Son Eric; [ed.] High School (Chaffey H.S.), 3 years of College (Nights), Major English Drama Theater History (L.A. Valley College U.C.L.A.); [occ.] Sales-Vacuums, Shoe Sales, Part time Actor; [memb.] Screen Actors Guild, S. A. G. Church On The Way; [hon.] From my children Rachel and Rebecca as the greatest daddy in the world!!; [oth. writ.] Song writing - Winner of School poems. High School And College; [pers.] Thanks to my Mother (Mavis) Love God, and you will learn to love! Love will always kill hate. "You can be anything you wait to be my love". Read-write and learn (God is love Jesus Is Lord); [a.] Sherman Oaks, CA

LOWE, TONY
[b.] May 29, 1968, Louisville, KY; [p.] Sam and Pauline Lowe; [m.] Jodi Lowe, June 26, 1993; [ch.] First child expected in June; [ed.] Iroquois High Spalding University; [occ.] Capital Goods specialists; [memb.] Alpha PSI Omega National Theatre Fraternity; [hon.] Dean's List; [oth. writ.] Recently completed works entitled attic salt; [pers.] Making time for reflection in our society seems almost lost. Just like an elephant, there's one in a lions cage but no one will call it one.; [a.] Louisville, KY

LOWE, JESSICA SHANNON
[b.] July 5, 1978, Fontana, CA; [p.] R. Steve And Jan L. Lowe; [ed.] Currently a Junior San Gorgonio High School San Bernardino, CA; [occ.] Student; [memb.] Member French Club, San Gorgonio High School, Member, Crestview Baptist Church, San Bernardino, CA; [hon.] Earned sports letter for tennis, Aquinas High School, San Bernardino, CA 1993; [oth. writ.] In my everyday life I try to remain focused on truth, and it is my deepest desire to keep in perspective what most people have a tendency to ignore.; [a.] San Bernardino, CA

LOWRY, CHAG
[b.] November 15, 1974, Susanville, CA; [p.] Ike and Sandra Lowry; [ed.] Second year at Lassen Community College; [occ.] Tutor at Susanville Indian Education Center; [memb.] Senator in Associated student body at lassen College, Member of lassen county American Indian Organization; [hon.] Dean's list for 2 years at Lassen College, selected to be in Who's who in Junior Colleges in America; [oth. writ.] I have written various

articles for the Cougar, the newspaper for the campus at Lassen College.; [pers.] The greatest influence in my writing has been, and always will be, my Native American ancestry.; [a.] Susanville, CA

LUBBEN, TWYLA M.
[b.] March 6, 1912, Forsythe, MT; [m.] Henry Lubben, December 31, 1943; [ch.] Legally adopted: Maria E., Timothy S. Joel M., Jonathan L., Elizabeth J., Tresa R., Nancy L., Christina L., Annalyn S. M. Patricia G.; [hon.] Service to mankind Award Good Samaritan Award, 1984 Senior Citizen Award, Dept. of Health and Human Service Award, Golden Acorn Award, First Citizens Award Spokane WA; [oth. writ.] Personal Column two newspapers several years, many articles and poems in magazines and papers, Book "Christina's World" printed by Zondervan Publishing House.; [pers.] Nurtured and rocked over 100 babies, one-third have been cocaine affected. Spoken in seven states on "Faith and Children" remembering the words of Christ "Inasmuch as ye have done it unto the least of these may bretheran, ye have done it unto ME."; [a.] Maple Spokane, WA

LUCAS, ERNESTINE
[b.] June 18, 1975; [p.] Verlee and Dorothy Lucas; [ed.] Forrest City High, Currently enrolled at Arkansas State University; [memb.] National Geographic Society, National Wildlife Federation, People for the Ethical Treatment of Animals; [oth. writ.] Several published in High School Newspaper, article for "Youth 94"; [pers.] There's no such thing as writer's block. When your mind goes blank, just speak through your heart.; [a.] Colt, AR

LUCAS, MEGAN RAE
[b.] October 28, 1983, Price, UT; [p.] Jimmy L. and Paula Q. Lucas; [ed.] Ferron Elementary 5th Grade; [memb.] L.D.S. Church Girl Scouts of America; [hon.] First place in reflections contest in our district first place in invent America in our district and several awards on art work.; [pers.] This poem won the reflections contest in the literature category and was inspired by a 12 yr. old boy that died waiting for a heart and lung transplant. I have won sweepstakes for tole painting and several coloring contests.; [a.] Ferron, UT

LUCIANO, NORMA ACEVEDO
[pen.] Norma Acevedo; [b.] November 16, 1962, Vtuado, PR; [p.] Armando and Maria Luisa; [m.] Miguel Gonzalez, May 23, 1981; [ch.] Shesly Gonzalez and Dalyvette Gonzalez; [ed.] Graduated from H.S. in Puerto Rico, Computer Training in Philadelphia; [occ.] Tax Examiner and Part time Retail Sales; [memb.] Member of Mentoring Program on job, Vita Programs and Outreach; [hon.] Medals in literature, science, and first places won on poetry contests and essays.; [oth. writ.] Essays, Spanish poems, others.; [pers.] All my verses to the love of my life, Shesly and Daly.; [a.] Philadelphia, PA

LUDWIG, AARON
[b.] April 17, 1976, Green Bay, WI; [p.] Eugene and Mary Ludwig; [ed.] Pilgrim Lutheran School, N.F.W. Lutheran High, Concordia U. Wisconsin, UW-Green Bay.; [occ.] College Student; [memb.] National Honor Society, Tri-M Music Honor Society.; [hon.] National Choral Award, Tri-M Master Musician Award, 1st at Regional for solo and Ensemble comp, and 1st at State Comp.; [oth. writ.] This is first time I've ever submitted a piece of my work to some comp.; [a.] Green Bay, WI

LUECK, ANGELA
[b.] October 18, 1979, Hutchinson, MN; [p.] Bill and Peggy Lueck; [ed.] Hutchinson High School, K-9; [occ.] Independen' Studies; [memb.] Tiger's Eye Newspaper, Leader Shopper Inc.; [hon.] Honor roll, third place in Hutchinson Science fair; [oth. writ.] I walked in tomorrow never knows; [pers.] "Life may kick you when you're down, but you've go to learn to kick back."; [a.] Hutchinson, MN

LUNA, LEILANI
[pen.] Lani Starr; [b.] May 5, 1944, Springfield, MA; [p.] George and Edna Roberge; [ed.] Commerce High; [occ.] Homemaker; [memb.] Third order dominican lay sister (person).; [hon.] Runner up for Miss Riverside; [pers.] Life is what we make it.; [a.] Chicopee Falls, MA

LUNGSTROM, MARSHA
[b.] December 7, 1956, Belvidere, IL; [p.] Audrey Lungstrom, Melvin and Joann Lungstrom; [ch.] Zechari James Philbrick, Trevor Dillon Philbrick; [ed.] Belvidere High School, Belvidere, IL, HSED in Green Bay WI; [occ.] Housewife/Mother; [hon.] Graduated with honor's from HSED Class; [oth. writ.] Several Short Stories and poems published 1973 School Paper; [pers.] Currently living in Green Bay Wisconsin with Richard L. Kiefert and her two son's Zechari and Trevor.

LUSTER, WILMA RAY
[b.] February 10, 1927, Imboden, AR; [p.] Mr. and Mrs. Brneat A. Ray; [m.] Joe Luster, January 28, 1957; [ch.] Condita Luster; [ed.] Sloan Hendrix Academy, and St Imboden Arkansas. Bernards Hospital Janenberg, Ark; [occ.] Nurse; [pers.] My sister Wilma Ray Lusted died November 26, 1987 was comotosted for 5 1/2 years from a heart attack. She left a stack of beautiful poems having never published any of them.

LYNN, KATIE
[pen.] Caitlinne Tash; [b.] March 3, 1979, Gainseville, FL; [p.] John and Elizabeth Andracki; [m.] single; [ed.] High School Student Class of '97; [occ.] Student; [hon.] "Spirit of Ocala" Creativity Contest (Poem) 1st place; [oth. writ.] Compilation of poetry, not published (yet); [pers.] Life is what you make it, if you think that it is hard it will be. That's from personal experience.; [a.] Ocala, FL

MACDONALD, HEATHER
[b.] November 29, 1977, Falls Church, VA; [p.] Barbara and Joel MacDonald; [ed.] Currently a junior at Georgetown Middle/High School, Georgetown, MA; [occ.] Student; [memb.] High School drama and community service leaders clubs.; [hon.] Member of National Honor Society, 3rd place in 94-95, Voice of Democracy contest (sponsored by V.F.W.); [oth. writ.] Poems, short story and novelette - all unpublished at present; [pers.] To find the words, to express the thought, to capture the emotions, and to conceive the story is to write.; [a.] Georgetown, MA

MACKEY, CHRISTA
[b.] December 25, 1977, Harrisburg, PA; [p.] Alex and Gloria Mackey; [ed.] Emmanuel Baptist Christian Academy, Mechanicsburg PA; [hon.] Who's Who Among American High School Students, National Young Leaders Conference participant; [oth. writ.] Many short stories - none published.; [pers.] I like to be different, but not eccentric. "Fun is one of the main words in my Vocabulary - but so is "responsibility".; [a.] Harrisburg, PA

MACLACKLIN, HARRY
[b.] July 23, 1976, Philadelphia, PA; [p.] Harry and Cathy MacLacklin; [m.] Andrea Davis (Fiance), November 21, 1994 (First Kiss); [ed.] Roman Catholic High School, Freshman at King's College.; [memb.] Campion Society Poetry Association; [hon.] Summa Cum Laude, Dean's List; [pers.] I am a spokesperson for life in the city. I use my writing to reflect the feelings and struggles of people who are forgotten in the dirty neighborhoods of Philadelphia. I am highly influenced by Bruce Springsteen.; [a.] Philadelphia, PA

MACMONAGLE, AMY
[b.] February 4, 1975, Tioga, ND; [p.] Dwight and Ruth Mac Monagle; [ed.] Tioga High School, University of North Dakota, UND-Williston; [occ.] Student;

[hon.] President's List, National Honor Society, National Merit Scholar - Honorable Mention, Presidential Academic, Fitness Award; [a.] Williston, ND

MADEJEK JR., EDWARD
[b.] June 2, 1959, Norwich, CT; [p.] Edward and Stella Madejek; [m.] Barbara Madejek, May 19, 1990; [ch.] Stephen Madejek; [ed.] Norwich Regional Vocational Technical School; [occ.] Machinest Kaman Aerospace Corp.; [memb.] Connecticut Zoological Society, Wolf Education and Research Cntr, Earth Island Institute; [hon.] Five Certificates of Achievement for advancement of machining practice ideas.; [oth. writ.] Poetry not currently published.; [pers.] There can be no greater gift in poetry, love or life then to have something come from the heart and that's where my feelings come from.; [a.] Voluntown, CT

MAGAZU JR., FRANK
[b.] September 30, 1968, Stony Point, NY; [p.] Yolanda and Frank Magazu; [m.] Single; [ed.] Bachelor of Science Saint Thomas Aquinas College - Sparkill NY; [occ.] Social Worker/Adoptions Counselor - U-21; [oth. writ.] Published in College many more waiting to be published or sung my works vary.; [pers.] My dream is to put my poems to music. "The rainbow is my road where life is lost and found."; [a.] Palm Harbor, FL

MAHATO, ANDREW
[b.] September 3, 1952, Jersey City; [p.] Adele and Charles Malato; [m.] Susan, August 7, 1971; [ch.] Andrew, Nicholas, Daniel, and Jill; [ed.] High School grad. 1970; [occ.] Butcher; [memb.] North Bergen Chamber of Commerce. National Federation of Independent Business; [oth. writ.] Several, but they are not published.; [pers.] A person who is sensitive to the sensitivity of other persons, truly has a rare gift.; [a.] North Bergen, NJ

MAHER, NICCI
[b.] March 27, 1980, Brookings, SD; [ed.] In high school; [oth. writ.] I have written many other poems which have not been published, mostly, about life and death.; [pers.] The main reason I have gotten started with writing poems is because of my brother. My brother was killed in a motorcycle accident when he was 18. I started writing in May of 1994.; [a.] Brookings, SD

MAIN, RICK
[b.] March 7, 1958, Tacoma, WA; [p.] Charles D. and Vetra A. Main; [ed.] B.A. Elementary Education, Washington State University; [occ.] Multi-aged Early Childhood Educator, John Campbell Primary Seluh, WA; [hon.] 1994 District Teacher of Year, President's List, Deans List, Cum Laude; [oth. writ.] Created 5 inspirational pamplets for people suffering from eating disorders; [pers.] My poetry reflects the personal struggle of the individual in modern society. I've used poetry as an emotional outlet in my own struggles in my own struggle and recovery process.; [a.] Yakoma, WA

MALCOLM, CHRIS
[b.] May 14, 1964, Flagstaff, AZ; [p.] James and Susie Malcolm; [m.] Lorraine Shobe-Malcolm, June 29, 1991; [ch.] Andrea L. Malcolm - 3, Sara Malcolm - 9, Melissa Malcolm - 8; [ed.] Idaho Christrin College, U.S. Army - Computer Programmer; [occ.] Loose Prevention Officers for Meijer's Corp., Computer Electronic Tech. for Champaign Unit and Schools; [hon.] U.S. Army, Defense Service Medal - I, Army Achievement Award - 7, Soldier of the Quarter, NCOIC Soldier of the Year Award; [oth. writ.] This is my first; [pers.] My wife wrote this to me when we got married and I loved it so much, and I'd never read any poems that expressed her feelings like this one and I asked her if it was OK to enter it in this contest so that others could read and share it.; [a.] Champaign, IL

MALIK, MOHAMMED ABDUL
[pen.] Malik; [b.] October 13, 1967, Hyderabad, India; [p.] MA Hafiz, SA Mannan; [ed.] BE (Mechanical Eng'g) Osmania Univ., India MS. (Eng'g Science) University of Mississippi, MS.; [occ.] Software Engineer; [oth. writ.] Advertising copy in India; [pers.] To find in the words that we use, an understanding of our inner selves. I have been greatly influenced by T.S. Eliot and the urdu poets, Ghalib and Faiz.; [a.] Detroit, MI

MALIMATH, MANJULA V.
[b.] August 25, 1965, Bangalore, India; [p.] Vijayakumar S. Malimath and Premadevi; [m.] Shanmukhaswami S. Salimath, December 24, 1993; [ed.] Sophia High School: I.C.S.E., Mount Carmel College: BA, Bangalore University: MA, M. Phil., Ph.D. in Organizational Psychology; [memb.] Indian Society of Organizational Behaviour, Senate of Bangalore University; [hon.] National Merit Scholarship (Govt of India), Junior Research Scholarship (University Grants Commission), First Rankin BA and MA, Two Time Gold Medal Recipient, Two State Awards, Merit Certificate, Numberous Prizes and Awards for Academic Excellence Conferred by State Government and University; [oth. writ.] Research Publication in 'Journal of the Indian Academy of Applied Psychology,' article published in 'Carmelian', Dissertation and Thesis in Organizational Psychology, several poems (unpublished).; [pers.] Writing poetry is an expression and outlet for intense experiences in my world. My Philosophy is: Always strive to be on a higher level of existence than where you are.; [a.] Ardmore, OK

MALLIK, AMRITA
[b.] October 16, 1981, Poughkeepsie, NY; [p.] Chandan Mallik, Dr. Aparna Mallik; [ed.] 8th grade, Montclair Kimberley Academy; [occ.] Student; [oth. writ.] Several poems published in Montclair Kimberley Academy's Literary Review; [pers.] In my works, I hope to make people realize that they can make a difference to help change the world. We all are one.; [a.] Montclair, NJ

MALONE, LYNDA S.
[b.] September 22, 1945, Oklahoma City; [p.] John Rowden and Kathryn Whitford; [m.] John Edwards; [ch.] Murrel Leon Malone, William Lee Malone; [ed.] 12 grade Noble High School, Noble Okla; [occ.] Housewife; [hon.] 1988 Golden poet award, 1989 silver poet award; [oth. writ.] The wind blew cold black are the roses hello Mr. Sunshine thoughts and dreams several other poems one published in on guard magazines, the Guardsmen's wife; [pers.] Be the best you can be with what you have and above all love yourself.

MALONEY, ALICIA SUZAN
[b.] January 18, 1973, Fort Worth, TX; [p.] Robert E. and Alice K. Maloney; [m.] Kevin Knandel, November 25, 1995; [ch.] Joshua Knandel; [ed.] B.A. from Texas Woman's University Major, English, Minor, Government/History Endorsement, English as a second Language and certification.; [memb.] Sigma Tau Delta, Minter's Chapel Methodist Church, American Cancer Association, Texas Narcotics Association, War on Drugs.; [hon.] Dean's list, National Dean's List, Sigma Tau Delta; [a.] North Richland Hills, TX

MANESIS, JOHN
[b.] 1936, Eau Claire, WI; [occ.] Physician; [oth. writ.] My poems have been recently published in mediphors, Wisconsin Review, Midwest Poetry review, and Opus Literary Review; [a.] Fargo, ND

MANN, CHRISTINE H.
[pen.] C. Mann; [b.] February 4, 1947, Washington, DC; [p.] Helen and Tredwell Bailey; [m.] Earl K. Mann, October 23, 1989; [ch.] Maureen, Lisa, Kim and Heather; [ed.] N. VA. Community, Art, Classes, excelled in English Various Seminars; [occ.] Owner Em-

pire Plbg and Southwest Connection, Inc. and Eaglestone Emer Ranch; [hon.] None as yet. Just beginning to write for publication; [oth. writ.] Personal journals kept for 20 years. Letters to White House, correspondence to politician, known firms, wrote policies and procedures in the Charles E. Smith Corp. Arlington, VA.; [pers.] Your Struggles and Personal difficulties are the basis for inner growth. Four children and failed marriages have attributed to my personal growth. At last, 'I am a success, in this life'; [a.] The Plains, VA

MANN, KATHRYN A.
[pen.] Kalexandra Mann; [b.] February 19, 1950, Hudson, NY; [p.] Henry and Jane Wagner; [m.] Burton (Bud) Mann, January 20, 1981; [ch.] Ronald, Amy, Jason and Jamie, daughter-in-law - Heather, grandchildren - Danielle, and Jonathan; [ed.] Hudson High School, Albany Medical Nursing School; [occ.] Home Maker and Aspiring; [oth. writ.] Numerous poems and short manuscripts published in local papers; [pers.] My writing has always been a catharsis for the adversities I've dealt with most of my life. Sharing my pain, hopes and dreams, through my writing, has not only helped me accept them as a part of my life, but overcome and rise to un level of my being.; [a.] Hudson, NY

MANNEH, MABINTY
[b.] June 18, 1978, Washington, DC; [p.] Ibrahim and JoAnne Manneh; [ed.] Currently Junior in High School; [occ.] High School Student; [memb.] DC Youth Ensemble (dance, drama, voice girls service club - Community Service Organization, Saint Augustine Young Historian thru Acting History of Church, Community); [pers.] To be a role model to younger kids just as my mom and grand mother, and aunts are to be. I'm influenced by people such as Maya Angelu.; [a.] Washington, DC

MANNING, MARTHA S.
[b.] February 11, 1945, Chatt, TN; [p.] Fred and Margie Schlosshan; [m.] David; [ch.] Sheri, Toni, David, Richard, Robert; [occ.] Customer Service Mgr.; [pers.] I write from the heart and soul of reality.; [a.] Chattanooga, TN

MANNING, R. D.
[b.] October 5, 1925, Ingersoll, Ontario, Canada; [p.] R. L. and E. O. Manning; [m.] M. Eilleen Manning, June 19, 1952; [ch.] Margaret Poeppel, Bob Manning, John Manning, Dorothy Manning; [ed.] M. D. U. Western Ontario London, Ontario, Canada; [occ.] Retired; [hon.] Past Choir Director (25 yrs.) past school board member, past mayor, past industrialist; [oth. writ.] Poetry, music and lyrics, working on autobiography. "One Liners."; [pers.] "Teachers are not to teach, they are to inspire. Teaching is imposed, true education comes from disruption by the yearning heart" "Too bad regret comes after rather than before the event"; [a.] Prairie Grove, AR

MANSILLA, RODRIGO
[pen.] Rodrigo Mansilla; [b.] September 8, 1978, Buenos Aires, Argentina; [p.] Edgar and Dora Mansilla; [ed.] High School Student; [occ.] Student; [memb.] Highland Baptist Church, Public Library; [hon.] "Central High School all A's Honor Roll 1993-1994". "Central High School Perfect Attendance - first semester."; [a.] Louisville, KY

MANTONI, DEANNA JOY
[b.] February 11, 1981, Putnam, CT; [p.] Ronald and Cassandra Mantoni; [ed.] Eighth grade student at St. James School, 120 Water St, Danielson, CT 06239; [occ.] Student - 8th grade; [memb.] Drama Club, Dottie's School of Dance, 8th Grade class President, SJS Varsity Basketball Team, Student Council, Senior Soccer League Member.; [hon.] National Junior Honor Society, Lion's Club Academic Award of Excellence, Highest Honors Grades 4th through 8th., CT State Winner for Invention Convention, Civic Oration Finalist; [pers.]

I strive to be the best I can be in all that I do. I believe through hand work and determination all my dreams can come true.; [a.] Dayville, CT

MANWILLER, SARA N.
[b.] July 24, 1980, Pottstown, PA; [p.] Donald Manwiller, Ann Marie Stonesifer; [ed.] Freshman, St Pius X High School, Pottstown; [occ.] Student; [pers.] Pain lingers long after the wound has healed. I strive daily to make the scar vanish.; [a.] Pottstown, PA

MARCIAL, KEVIN JAMES
[b.] November 10, 1977, Arlington Heights, IL; [p.] Tom and Diane Marcial; [ed.] A Junior at Mattawan High School; [hon.] High Honors at Mattawan High; [oth. writ.] This is all of my writing that has ever been published, but I have an extensive collection of poetry and prose which I have been adding onto for the past four years.; [pers.] My poetry's intentions to induce a unique feeling in each human being who reads it. Every poem I write has a particular aura implanted in it, but the reader should have a special feeling about it which he/she shares with no one. Poetry should simply display possibilities, the reader can decide which one suits him/her best.; [a.] Kalamazoo, MI

MARCKS, LACEY LOUISE
[b.] November 17, 1975, Detroit, MI; [p.] Judith and Louis Marcks; [ed.] Henry Ford II High School; [pers.] I have been greatly influenced by Christina Rossetti. I hope to become a writer myself one day and open the worlds eyes to the beauty of love!; [a.] Sterling Heights, MI

MARINO, LISA
[pen.] Liliana Alexander; [b.] October 16, 1960, New York City; [p.] Attilio and Diana Capponi; [m.] Philip A. Marino Jr., November 11, 1989; [ch.] Gabriella Angelise, Philip Alexander and Adriana Giselle; [ed.] Cortland University, Duke University School of Medicine; [occ.] Full time mother; [memb.] American Academy of Physician Assistants, Myasthenia Gravis Foundation; [hon.] Cum Laude graduate, Tri Beta Honor Society, American Academy of Distinguished High School Students; [oth. writ.] Poem published September 1, 1994; [pers.] Spiritually in my life is the directing force for my writing and the poetry will often reflect the extremes of these experiences.; [a.] Paradise Valley, AZ.

MARMON, CODY
[b.] April 12, 1968, San Diego, CA; [p.] Robin and Linda Marmon; [m.] Tammy Lynn Miller-Marmon, August 10th 1995; [ed.] Graduated from Westburg Central High School in Morgan Country, TN., in 1987; [occ.] Night-stock worker at Bi-La Grocery Store; [oth. writ.] I have a book of poetry I'm hoping to have published soon, but "The Last Knight" is my first published work of any kind.; [pers.] This is what I do, it's not a job, description, or a requirement, this is my life. If I didn't have this beautiful outlet, I'd be dead already. It's that simple. Period.; [a.] Lancing, TN

MARSDEN, EMILY CARAKER
[b.] April 3, 1960, Boston; [p.] Ed and Marjory Caraker; [m.] Steve Marsden, June 14, 1980; [ch.] T. J. 1985, Alissa Chere 1987, Mike 1992; [ed.] Wayland High School Bridgewater State College; [occ.] Business Manager, Mom!; [oth. writ.] Personal journal of various poetry.; [pers.] I hope my poetry brings thoughtful mindful reflection to those who read it. I thank my best editor, Steve, for all his loving encouragement.; [a.] Lunenburg, MA

MARSH, FRANK E.
[b.] November 27, 1919, Worcester, MA; [p.] F. Eugene and Selma Marsh; [m.] Virginia Horns-Marsh, December 14, 1986; [ch.] 3 stepchildren, 7 step-grand-children; [ed.] A.B. Clark University, M. Ed. Univer-

sity of N.H., Ed. D. Boston University; [occ.] Retired - Dean and Professor of Education Emeritus Northeastern University, Supervisor - student Teachers UAB; [memb.] Kappa Delta Pi, Phi Delta Kappa, Riverchase United Methodist; [hon.] Kappa Delta Pi, Phi Delta Kappa, Honor Key-Kappa Delta Pi, National President-Kappa Delta Pi; [oth. writ.] Chair-KDP Educational Foundation Numerous Journal Articles; [pers.] Education should assist us to discover who we are-motivate us to express our thoughts-feelings-hopes-and concerns. Art, poetry, music offer a way to engage in the exciting process of seeking, discovering and expressing who we are. Each day we should do something physical, something mental, and something for someone else.; [a.] Birmingham, AL

MARSHALL, VICKI R.
[pen.] Vicki R. Marshall; [b.] November 19, 1955, San Diego; [p.] Ronald and Nadine Hendee; [m.] Thurman E. Marshall, January 2, 1988; [ch.] Shannon Bussey, Charles Bussey Jr., Paul Marshall, granddaughter-Victoria; [ed.] Currently obtaining a degree in business.; [occ.] Document control, Representative Valor Elec. San Diego; [hon.] Dean's List, 1993-94 yr.; [oth. writ.] Children's stories and a journal, this will be the first time published.; [pers.] I've learned that life is actually very short, savor everyday.; [a.] Escondido, CA

MARSHALL, PATRICIA NANCY
[b.] Richmond Hill, Ontario, Canada; [p.] Jeremiah Smith, and Effie Smith; [m.] Brian Marshall, July 21, 1961; [occ.] Homemaker; [oth. writ.] "The Master Artist", "Awake O Joyous Spring", "Thanksgiving" (2 writings), "Love's Garden", "Gertrude's 75th Birthday" "Scamp's Farewell"; [pers.] I am grateful for my many talents, pursuing them regularly in many ways bringing me happiness, and much admiration from friends and strangers.; [a.] Wyevale Ontario, Canada

MARSTON, WENDY
[pen.] Ace; [b.] August 27, 1972; [p.] Walter E. Marston; [ed.] Midland Park High, Bergan Community College; [occ.] Receptionist at a their and nail salon.; [memb.] The church of religious science; [hon.] High School Athlete Awards for Softball and Volleyball; [pers.] Action speaks louder then words. So act as thou you are happy and free. Then and only then you shall be.; [a.] Fairlawn, NJ

MARTENS, BRADLEY
[pen.] Bradley Coyote Martens; [b.] January 27, 1956, Toledo, OH; [p.] Bob and Eva Martens; [m.] Divorced; [ch.] Son Eric who died before he could learn to fly; [ed.] 10th grade did not graduate high School; [oth. writ.] Eight poems published from 1987 - on - by - American Poetry Association; [pers.] Live each day as if it was your last and die with a sense of humurer (influenced by Bob Dylan and Arlo Guthrey) I am a recluse.; [a.] Maumee, OH

MARTIN, AMANDA GREY
[pen.] Amanda Grey Martin; [b.] May 29, 1987, San Antonio; [p.] Randy Martin; [ed.] In the 2nd grade; [occ.] School Student; [hon.] Good Citizen Award; [pers.] She thinks people should be nice to each other.; [a.] San Rafael, CA

MARTIN, DOM
[b.] August 4, 1950, Moshi, Tanzania [p.] Vincent Xavier Verediano and Teodora Effrezina; [m.] Patricia A. Maier, June 4, 1982; [ed.] Saint Anthony's College; [occ.] Poet, Writer, Artist, Foundation - Director; [hon.] Six Honorary Doctorates, Knighthood of the Royal Order of Piast "International Man of the Year" (IBA Award) 1992-93.; [oth. writ.] The Day Before and Day After, 1986, The Principles of Zerometrics, 1989, A Thousand Eyes for an Eye.; [pers.] Existence is afflicted by reality, and reality incites my creativity.; [a.] Mill Valley, CA

MARTIN, BRAD
[b.] September 21, 1978, Jacksonville, FL; [p.] Larry Martin, Janice Martin; [ed.] Saint John Lutheran High School; [occ.] Student; [memb.] National Junior Honor Society, Students Against Drunk Drivers, Fellowship of Christian Athletes; [hon.] Honor Roll, United States National Football Award Winner; [pers.] The goodness and the support of the Lord are with me always in everything I do.; [a.] Ocala, FL

MARTIN, JENNIEVY
[pen.] Jennievy; [b.] September 24, 1981, San Diego, CA; [p.] Jeannette and Eduardo Dizon (Mother and Stepfather); [m.] March 25, 1989; [ch.] Chanelle and Ian; [ed.] 7th grade at Orville Wright Middle School; [hon.] I won 1st place in an Art Contest throughout the San Diego District in the third grade against an eight grader. I won Two First Class Tickets to Paris. I have another painting in the Museum of Art in San Diego; [oth. writ.] I wrote other poems which I haven't yet entered but I'm planning to.; [pers.] I dedicate this poem to all my friends that inspired me to enter the contest, Karina Juarez, Cris Auggier, Katherine Alvaraog, Larry Hoecklemen; [a.] Los Angeles, CA

MARTIN, SANDRA B.
[b.] January 3, 1949, Pulaski, VA; [p.] Geneva Siler and James A. Brumfield -deceased; [m.] Divorced; [ch.] Sharon L. Martin; [ed.] Graduated from Andrew Lewis High School, Salem, Va., Took Computer course Salem High School, attended R.C.E.C. and completed V.O.T Program; [occ.] Housewife/Working on my poetry and other writing; [memb.] Faculty at Salem High School, Regional Science Fair, Secretary of Sunday School class Bethel Baptist Church; [oth. writ.] I wrote a poem entitled "Homeless" which was published in a newspaper in Arizona. I have written numerous works never submitter; [pers.] I like to make poetry have rhythm so its interesting to read. I like for the poem to get a point across also. (To say something); [a.] Phoenix, AZ

MARTIN, JUDY MARIE HERMAN
[pen.] Judy Marie; [b.] May 27, 1963, Evergreen Park, IL; [p.] Walter C. Herman, Kathleen L. Leone; [ch.] Marie Louise, Niki Ann, Judy Marlene, Charles Eugene, Jenny Lee; [ed.] I had dropped out of school in 10th grade. I passed my GED, went to school to be Certified Nurses Aide and am enrolled in St. Pete Junior College.; [occ.] CNA and Asst. Housekeeping Supervisor; [pers.] I dedicate this poem to my children without them I would not have wrote it, also Dr. Reese for inspiring me to mail my poem and Victor Sanitate for his time.; [a.] St. Petersburg, FL

MASHAK, WILLIAM JASON
[b.] September 9, 1973, St. Joseph, MI; [p.] Bill Mashak, Tonda Cooper; [ed.] Currently attending Chattanooga State College; [occ.] Self employed, also a part time musician; [memb.] U.S. Taxpayer Club (fun, fun, fun); [hon.] High School Honor Roll; [oth. writ.] Poems published in High School Publication, Sunlight and Shadows; [pers.] Search...Learn...reflect....teach... and all things will become clear as....Mud; [a.] Ooltewah, TN

MASHBURN, PAM
[b.] March 14, 1953, Atlanta, GA; [p.] Walter and Margie Mashburn; [ed.] Columbia High School, DeKalb College, Georgia State Univ. and Mercer University; [occ.] First Grade Teacher, Locust Grove Elementary, Locust Grove, Georgia; [memb.] First Methodist Church in McDonough, GA, Delta Kappa Gamma, Phi Delta Kappa; [pers.] Through my poetry, I write my inner most thoughts and feelings. My hope is that through my poetry others will be touched and find meaning too.; [a.] McDonough, GA

MASIAK, PAIGE
[b.] April 18, 1959, Pomona, CA; [p.] Beverly Smith; [m.] Single; [oth. writ.] No others published yet.; [pers.] My experiences and perceptions influence my emotions. To write them in a poetic form has moved me, and others I've been able to share them with. I want to make a difference.; [a.] Copperas Cove, TX

MASON, KEN
[b.] October 13, 1957, Cornelia, GA; [p.] Swayne and Lucille Mason; [ed.] BA in Psychology and Social Studies - Piedmont College; [occ.] Former High School, Teacher and Coach; [hon.] Two time Teacher of the Month, three time Assistant Coach of the Year in Girl's Track, Assistant Director of GA. State Wrestling Tournament 1990-1995.; [oth. writ.] Two children's book manuscripts; [pers.] This poem: "Ever Growing Flowers", was written for my fiance Susan Castleberry who makes every day seem like a poem!; [a.] Oakwood, GA

MASON, BRENDA D.
[b.] November 6, 1947, Paris, TX; [p.] James Mason and Flora Mason; [ch.] Orren Chaucey Webber; [ed.] Western High School, University of Nevada, Las Vegas Western State University Law School; [occ.] Staff Assistant United States Attorney's Office; [hon.] Who's Who Among American University and College Students Who's who Among black Americans National Scholarship Finalist, Dale Carnegie Effective Speaking Award; [oth. writ.] Collection of Poems and short stories; [pers.] I strive to emulate the inner feelings of women in my writing.; [a.] San Diego, CA

MASSEY, ELIZABETH DUFFIE
[pen.] Elizabeth Duffie Massey; [b.] March 16, 1912, Malvern, AR; [p.] Judge and Mrs. William Reuben Duffie; [m.] Ronald Lee Massey, January 3, 1942; [ch.] Hannah Elizabeth Massey, William Lloyd Massey; [ed.] BSE, MSE in Art, MSE in Eng. Lit. Henderson University Arkadelphia, AR, Studied art Univ. of A Fayetteville, Memphis Academy of Art - Ark Art Center; [occ.] Private Art Teacher, Retired, First grade teacher (32 years); [memb.] First Baptist Church - Malvern Teacher, WMU member and Leader - FBC Malvern, Chapter BC, PEO, Malvern, Womans Club of Malvern, Malvern Musical Arts Club, DAR, Onachitor Chapter, G Alpha, DKG - Malvern Book Club; [hon.] Boyle House Museum, Volunteer of yr '91 - HOnored for 77 yrs in 1st Baptist Church '93, Honored by Malvern Nat'l Bank with reception after completing 48x8 ft Mural Tail Painting, Defeating Malvern and Hot Spring Co. History. They bought the mural and installed it across front of bank.; [oth. writ.] I have notebooks full of little poems written in last 40 yrs. "October" is the only one ever submitted.; [pers.] Micah big is my philosophy ... "What does the Lord require of thee? Act justly, love mercy and walk humbly with thy God."; [a.] Malvern, AR

MASTERS, ERIC
[pen.] Stone Masters; [b.] January 23, 1978, Tennessee; [p.] Sloan and Richard Miles and Steve Masters; [ed.] Denham Springs High; [occ.] Utility and hot cook at Golden Corral; [memb.] Drama Club; [oth. writ.] Many non-published poems and philosophies.; [pers.] True poetry comes from the inner depths of your soul with a little mind, body, and spirit intermingled. I am influenced by spirituality based poems; [a.] Denham Springs, LA

MATA, RICHARD
[pen.] Santowns; [b.] November 28, 1969, Kinshasa, Zaire; [p.] Mata Kilolo Victorine and Mbamu Francois; [ed.] Official School of Limete (Zaire) - Elementary School (Kinshasa/Zaire) Secondary school of Lumumba (Kinshasa), Industrial Technic Institute of Gombe-Sainte Marie (Kinshasa/Zaire), Winding Electric Motor College (Zollikofoen-Bern/Switzerland); [occ.] Carton art Drawing; [memb.] Jordan Brant Membership, Mont Carmel Church of God; [oth. writ.] Songwriting and

movie writing

MATHIS, VERDI
[b.] April 18, 1963, Beckley, WV; [p.] Joline M. Bloxson; [m.] Joseph E. Mathis, Sr., June 20, 1987; [ch.] Joseph Jr., and Jonathan; [ed.] Spingarn Senior High School, University of the District of Columbia; [occ.] Personnel Management Specialist, IRS; [oth. writ.] Several poems published in High School bulletins, currently working on first novel.; [a.] Washington, DC

MATHIS, EVA MAE
[pen.] Lady 99; [b.] January 20, 1951, Lamont, FL; [p.] Joseph Mathis Sr. and Eva Mathis; [m.] Single; [ch.] V.E.B., T.R.M., G.R.M., and T.S.M.; [ed.] Greenville Training School in Greenville, FL, Principal Mr. Merritt; [occ.] Director at T.I. Inc.; [memb.] (Churches) B.M.B.C. in Cairo, GA, G.W.C.F.B.C. in Homestead, FL; [hon.] Headstart Volunteering, Volunteering in different school events. Missionary work; [oth. writ.] I write books, songs, other poems, all types or sorts of cards (greeting, sympathy, birthdays, holiday greetings, riddles, jokes, etc.; [pers.] In my writing, I tries to reach out to others, to help them not to make the some mistakes I've made in life, why? Because many trials are in life. My writing come natural straight from the brain and heart. My father Joseph Mathis Sr. was also a creative writer as I am myself. I love music, I love to sing gospel songs.; [a.] Cairo, GA

MATSON II, JOHN WILLIAM
[pen.] Bragi Odinnsson; [b.] September 15, 1944, Nashville Tennesse, MD; [p.] John William Matson and Janet Reese Matson; [ed.] Diploma Glendale High School (1962), AB William Penn College (1968) AM Creighton University (1971); [occ.] Security, Supervisor for Pinherton; [memb.] PHI Alpha Theta International Historical Fraternity, American National Historical Society, Liberty Lobby Board of Policy, Asatru Folk Assembly of North America, American Scandinavian Federation; [hon.] Honors Award in history William Penn College (1986) Certificates of appreciation National Police Officials Association (1972) and 2nd Amendment Foundation (1983); [oth. writ.] Editor of "How To Make Gas Hole On Your Kitchen Counter" and "Some Songs About Asatru"; [pers.] To my parents who taught me about my own ancestral heritages. And to heimdall as the ancestral teacher of European man.; [a.] Glendale, CA

MATSUSHIMA, GREGG
[b.] January 3, 1953, Honolulu, HI; [p.] Dick and Helen; [m.] Charlene Matsushima; [ch.] Calvil and Katie; [ed.] Kalani High School, University of Hawaii - Manoa; [occ.] Planner, Hawaii Dept. of Transportation, Honolulu, HI; [pers.] I we must be stranded in time, let it be among the rocks, the trees and clouds. Share rainbows and thunderstorms with all the animals in the world and with those you truly love.; [a.] Honolulu, HI

MATUNAS, JOSEPH
[pen.] Black-Sheep; [b.] August 23, 1909, Elizabeth, NJ; [p.] Lithvania-Europe; [m.] Deceased-Olga-Matunas; [ed.] 8th grade, went tonight school, self education by reading and writing poems 60 years.; [occ.] Retired as Chief specialist in machine; [memb.] National Guard Lieut-Junior Police in NJ Marksman Shatter.; [hon.] I was a Consultant on Tolling and Machinery for G.M. Diehl M. Co. made special took Son Boon B. Site; [oth. writ.] I was a member of local #3 for 29 yrs and retired about 40 yrs International Brotherhood of Electrical Workers Local #3 New York City; [pers.] I love writing have quite poems made up all these years some and good and some good for music; [a.] Linden, NJ

MAUNEY, ADRIENNE R.
[b.] February 17, 1980, Hampton, VA; [p.] Melville and Brenda C. Mauney; [ed.] Freshman at Kecoughtan High School; [memb.] St. James United Methodist Church, Chrome; [hon.] Winner of Oratorical Expo, John Hopkins Talent Search Recipient; [pers.] "I feel that poetry is the best form of entertainment. No matter how you interpret, your interpretation can never be wrong."; [a.] Hampton, VA

MAURO, JOSEPH SCOTT
[pen.] Kris Will; [b.] February 6, 1962, New Rochelle, NY; [m.] Marianne Joan Mauro, October 1, 1982; [ch.] Kristen Patricia, William Scott, and Meaghen Emily; [ed.] University at Albany B.A. in Political Science/Economics; [occ.] Operations Manager for Prudential Securities, Inc.; [memb.] National Youth Sports Coaches Association; [pers.] I love to work——it keeps me out of trouble....; [a.] West Nyack, NY

MAW, JOHN THOMPSON
[pen.] Jack Maw; [b.] December 10, 1912, Toronto; [p.] Vohnt Maw - Caroline Maw; [m.] Vera Bernice Maw, July 11, 1957; [ed.] 1938 Graduate University of Toronto BCS. mining Engineering; [occ.] Retired

MAY, CHANDA
[b.] April 18, 1971, Mosow, ID; [p.] Bill and Bonnie Barhett; [m.] Jerry May, March 17, 1993; [ch.] Jessica May, Monty May, Brookelyn May; [ed.] Graduated Pullman High after attending Potlatch High completed a home study course in paralegal studies; [occ.] Housewife and full time mother; [pers.] This poem was written in memory of my first born child who died of AIDS on September 1, 1992. He will forever be the joy of my life and deeply missed.; [a.] Princeton, ID

MAYNARD, SHANDYLINN KELLY
[b.] May 4, 1979, Independence, MO; [p.] Michael J. and Leanne E. Maynard; [ed.] Plans to graduate in 1997 at Blue Springs South High School; [hon.] Honor Roll average GPA 3.571, 1994 Judo Champion of AAU in Missouri, American Red Cross Lifeguard, A Volunteer Lifeguard for Youth for Christ Summer Camp at Circle-C, 1995 mission trip with youth for Christ in Jamaica, Counselor for choices (Kids with problems, drugs, etc.), Light board operator for school dramas, including, "Annie" and "Our Town".; [a.] Blue Springs, MO

MAYS, FREDA MAE
[b.] March 24, 1936, Kansas City, MO; [p.] Ferdinand and Ruth Brockington; [ch.] Donald Birdwell, Brenda Smotherman (two eldest of 9 children); [ed.] 2 years of college, Majored in Business, and Administrative justice classes; [occ.] Retired Government employee, formerly Jr. Accountant; [memb.] Members of Eastern Star (not active); [hon.] I have had many job related through the years; [oth. writ.] I have several unpublished writing, and working on more writing is a healing process for me for some of the situations and good situations that I have had during the years; [Pers.] My writings are true experience, with hopes of inspiring others. These experiences are mine, and of my family.; [a.] El Cajon, CA

MAYS, HATTIE
[b.] April 17, 1920, NYC; [p.] Joseph Friedson, Sarah; [m.] Charles Mays, December 14, 1941; [ch.] Michele Lee, Howard Marshall; [ed.] Center Commercial High School in New York City; [occ.] Retired; [memb.] Greater New York Girl Scout Council, PTA for PS 75, Lenton Ladies, Hadassha, ORT, Officer of the Sunshine Park Co-op, V.P. of Mgc Resident Council, Officer in Dania Antique Dealers Assoc., Bellevue Hospital Candy Stripers; [hon.] Bronze Statue for outstanding Service to community. Many testimonials for Public Performed before and after stroke.; [oth. writ.] Started writing at age 11 - first writing done in 6th grade about "What Easter Mean To Me" won $50.00 at the height of the depression; [pers.] To be kind to each other and to teach

your children values because it truly rubs off on them.

MCCABE, KELLY J.
[pen.] Dylan Kincaid; [b.] May 7, 1968, Cincinnati, OH; [p.] John McCabe, Shirley McCabe; [m.] Karen McCabe, February 19, 1994; [ed.] Springstead High; [memb.] Children's Last Wish Foundation; [pers.] All my poetry comes from my heart and many good memories of days gone past.; [a.] Spring Hill, FL

MCCAIN, LEE ANNE
[b.] December 29, 1964, San Antonio, TX; [p.] Coriene and Chester Huskey; [ed.] Thomas Jefferson H.S., University of Texas at San Antonio and Arlington.; [occ.] Student: Psychology and Biology Major.; [memb.] Fund raiser for love for kids and the Dallas Mayor's Committee for the Emptiness of People with Disabilities.; [pers.] Reach for the stars.; [a.] Bedford, TX

MCCAMEY, ALEXIS
[pen.] Alexis McCamey; [b.] January 15, 1957, Germany; [p.] Mr. and Mrs Alex McCamey; [ch.] Willie, Cory, and Justine.; [ed.] Forest Park Senior High School; [occ.] Office Secretary II, State Retirement Agency, Division of Investments.; [memb.] State Center Toastmaster Club #4597, The Fulton Baptist Church, and Personal Poems Society (PPP).; [hon.] Ten Years Service for State of Maryland, Humor Speech Contest 1993, Award and Competent Toastmaster Honor (1995).; [oth. writ.] I have written over 80 personalized poems for birthdays, weddings, anniversaries, etc. "What Is Your Claim to Fame" was published in a local newspaper, the Black Poet Magazine.; [pers.] I began to write poems in memory of my baby sister, Sallie McCamey. My poetry genuinely touched the hearts of people. I dedicate all my work to the love I have for her and the love she gave my family during her precious life here on earth. I have always admired Maya Angelo and Nikki Giovanni.; [a.] Baltimore, MD

MCCANN, DANIELLE
[b.] August 23, 1978, Morristown, NJ; [p.] Diana Tardine, Edward McCann; [ed.] Empire Beauty School; [occ.] Student; [memb.] FFA; [oth. writ.] Though I have compiled over 110 poems in the last 2 years this is my first publication, except for an editorial in the Express-Times.; [pers.] This poem "Last Good-Byes", is dedicated in memory of Colleen Bortscheller, August 10, 1977-December 5, 1994. Also, I would like to show my appreciation to the following: Robert Nichols, Michael Chanda, Courtney Morrow, Mathew Petrick and Angel McNeel, for allowing me to fulfill my need to write and encouraging me.; [a.] Easton, PA

MCCANN, SHIRLEY A.
[pen.] Shirley A. McCann; [b.] November 10, 1925, Detroit, MI; [p.] Charles K. and Dorothy L. Schippel; [m.] William W. McCann (Divorced), September 14, 1946; [ch.] Richard Wayne, Patricia Gail, Sally Ann, Jan Shelley; [ed.] Edwin Denby High; [occ.] Retired, housewife; [memb.] Advent Lutheran Church; [hon.] The National Library of Poetry, to be picked as a semi-finalist and to have my poem published. My first poem in a contest.; [oth. writ.] Several poems on different topics. Started writings at age of ten years old.; [pers.] I would like to be 25 good a poet in my time as Percy Bysshe Shelley was in his time or even better. Whom, I am a descendant of.; [a.] Harder Woods, MI

MCCARTHY, ELIZABETH T.
[b.] December 3, 1927, Brooklyn, NY; [p.] Modesto and Agnes Cappelluti; [m.] Thomas Edward, September 17, 1949; [ch.] Thomas Edward Jr., Tara Anne Mary; [ed.] St. Elizabeth's School Midwood High; [occ.] Housewife; [memb.] Country Knolls Womens Club; [a.] Ballston Lake, NY

MCCLAIN, COLLEEN J.
[b.] 1951; [p.] John and Delores White,; [m.] Jerry McClain; [ch.] Matt and John; [ed.] Graduate at

Donovan High School in IL, and two correspondent writing courses, one on writing short stories and one on poetry; [occ.] I am employed at Saving 1 Heart Enterprises in Watseka, Illinois, Singer, Songwriter, signed with "Heart-Throb", in Watseka.; [oth. writ.] My poetry has been published in newspapers in Illinois and an anthology in 1985; [pers.] I believe that writing is as essential to the poet, as water is to a man dying of thirst. It is not a hobby, or taken lightly. Rather, it is a driving force, a creative need that must be fulfilled.

MCCLANAHAN, JENNIFER
[pen.] Kristen Lane; [b.] March 24, 1980, Kankakee, IL; [p.] Jack and Linda Mc Clanahan; [ed.] Currently a Freshman in High School; [occ.] Student; [memb.] FFA, Speech Club, Central High School Flag Corps, Central High School Math Team, School Play Crew; [hon.] 9 yrs. on Honor Roll, FFA Green Hand Pin, multiple chorus and math team awards; [oth. writ.] Several poems and short stories - not published; [pers.] Poetry requires the courage to expose your innermost feelings. One must be willing to be vulnerable to achieve personal growth.; [a.] Chebonse, IL

MCCLELLAN, MRS. EDNA
[b.] November 1, 1962, San Diego; [p.] Riley/Antonia Cummings; [m.] Mr. Aldin E. McClellan, June 7, 1985; [ch.] Monique, Aldin II, Edward; [ed.] High School; [occ.] Writer/Homemaker; [oth. writ.] The Rope: The wheel.; [a.] San Diego, CA

MCCLURE, ANNIE
[b.] April 28, 1925, Navarro Co., TX; [p.] Ida Rivers Williams and Jesse Rivers (deceased); [m.] E. Dean McClure (deceased), June 4, 1943; [ch.] Renee' Anne McClure; [ed.] Associates Degree Arts and Sciences, Mountain View College, Dallas, Texas; [occ.] Retired; [hon.] Dean's list. Outstanding Academic Achievement Award; [oth. writ.] Several poems published book of poetry "Memories in Flight" Essay "Family History of World War II"; [pers.] Dedication to each endeavor. Words hold a special magic to stir the imagination and cleanse the soul.; [a.] Duncanville, TX

MCCORT, CAROLYN
[pen.] Carrie; [b.] July 6, 1983, Wheeling, WV; [p.] Hubert and Regina McCort; [ed.] Barnesville Junior High, I plan to graduate and go to college.; [occ.] Student; [memb.] Band; [hon.] Science Award, Basketball Tournament Winner 1st place; [pers.] I wrote my poem for my grandfather George B. Clark, who passed away April 8, 1994, I dedicate this poem for or to my "Pap Pap" George B. Clark.; [a.] Barnesville, OH

MCCOY, JUSTIN K.
[b.] March 18, 1984, Elizabeth, NJ; [p.] Michael L. and Sheilah F. McCoy; [ed.] St Elizabeth School, Linden NJ; [occ.] Student; [memb.] Communicant at St. Elizabeth Church Linden, NJ; [hon.] Justin just obtained the highest award in Cub Scouts, The Arrow of Light and is going on to Boy Scouts, in pursuit of Eagle Scout.

MCCOY, MAUREEN
[b.] October 25, 1963, Akron, OH; [p.] Patrick and Catherine Cassidy; [m.] Richard McCoy, August 15, 1992; [ch.] Nichole, Kari Ann, Tyler; [ed.] Barberton High School, Akron University; [occ.] Homemaker; [hon.] Editor's Choice Award; [oth. writ.] A few poems published in a magazine and pamphlet.; [pers.] Most of my poetry is on a personal note. I like to write about everyday life and the special joys and sometimes sorrows we find.; [a.] Barberton, OH

MCDERMOTT, DONALD A.
[b.] March 7, 1961, Winthrop, MA; [p.] Donald J, Mary McDermott; [ed.] Malden High School; [occ.] Lykes Pasco Inc.; [memb.] Moose - Eagles IACC of Malden, MA.; [oth. writ.] Several poems not published; [pers.] Keep the faith in God, no matter what happens and take one day at a time, for that is what we really only have!;

[a.] Zephyr Hills, FL

MCDONALD, MICHAEL
[b.] February 7, 1960, Rockville Centre, NY; [p.] James A. McDonald, and Helen McDonald; [m.] Mary McDonald, February 6, 1993; [ch.] Danielle Kathleen, Kelley Elise; [ed.] St. Agnes Cathedral High School Villanova University; [occ.] Letter Carrier - USPS; [memb.] Men's Senior Baseball League; [a.] Baldwin, NY

MCDOWELL, HATTIE
[pen.] Big-Big; [b.] April 19, 1923, Spartanburg, SC; [p.] Beulah and Calvin Parks; [m.] Claude McDowell, September 7, 1946; [ch.] Brenda, J.C., Edward, and Furman; [ed.] Fairforest High School; [occ.] Housewife; [memb.] Mount Monah Baptist Church, Mother Board, and Progressive Club; [hon.] Piedmount, Interstate Fair (1935-1993); [oth. writ.] Several gospels put to music, which I song at church and other poem I have written for different occasions.; [pers.] I am blind, I have always written poetry before I became blind, just couldn't get any published until now. May I purchase the book later.; [a.] Spartanburg, SC

MCFALL, IAN
[b.] March 17, 1940, United Kingdom; [p.] Peter and Nan; [m.] Glenys, June 8, 1961; [ch.] Andrew, Corran (Twins); [ed.] BS Mathematics (UK), MS Operations Research U. of Hull (UK); [occ.] Self employed software developer.; [memb.] Pacific Area Soaring Association (PASCO); [oth. writ.] Several articles on Soaring in Natural and local gliding magazines and newsletters. "Assessing risk in major capital investments" February, 1967 Manager (UK).; [a.] San Francisco, CA

MCGHEE, TONI KATHLEEN
[b.] June 15, 1965, Chattonooga, TN; [p.] David and Martha Manning; [m.] Staff Sgt. Tim McGhee U.S. Army, June 9, 1983; [ed.] Tyner High School; [occ.] Bank Teller; [pers.] I would like to dedicate this poem to be members of our Armed Forces and their families. I pray that the people of the United States and the world know the sacrifices that are made. 3/23/94 - The crash at Pope AFB; [a.] Trenton, GA

MCGHIN, JAMES O.
[b.] September 28, 1964, Baltimore, MD; [p.] Patricia Moffitt, Otis J. McGhin, Esq (Deceased); [ed.] Loyola College, Bachelor of Arts, Political Science Univ. of Baltimore - Master of Arts Legal Studies '95; [occ.] Home improvement contractor; [memb.] Columbia Ski Club; [hon.] Senatorial Scholarship '86, Academic Honors - Loyola '86, Academic Honors - Univ. of Dayton '83, WHo's Who Among Student at Universities and College 1993-94, First Place Essay '94, Hoffberger Center for Professional Ethics; [oth. writ.] "Professional Ethics in the Legal System" $200 cash award; [pers.] True success lies not in reaching expectations but in surpassing the limits of one's own mind; [a.] Baltimore, MD

MCGRAW JR., GLEN K.
[b.] February 8, 1975, Cleveland, OH; [p.] Glen and Carol McGraw; [ed.] Brunswick High School; [occ.] US Air Force Security Policeman; [memb.] Civil Air Patrol, Air Force Security Police Association; [hon.] Honor Graduate for Air Force Basic Training, Air Force Achievement Medal, Southwest Asia Service Award; [oth. writ.] GKM other unpublished poems.; [pers.] To live life completely you must not be afraid to try new experience. Otherwise you will have missed so much. Carpe Diem.; [a.] Brusnwick, OH

MCGRAW, CHARLOTTE
[pen.] Charlie Stout; [b.] June 28, 1931, Detroit, MI; [p.] Henrietta and Norman Stout; [m.] Donald McGraw, August 13, 1966; [ch.] Jadie, Janie and Joanie; [ed.] High School - Mt. Clemens, Mich.; [occ.] Retired - after 34 years - switchboard operator.; [memb.] AARP Se-

nior Club of Oak Park, IL.; [hon.] 13 medals from local, state and nationals senior olympics - in billiards, shuffle-board, horse shoes basketball throw and mile fast walk race; [oth. writ.] Laura Jean, Judie, Janie, Joanie. Shuffle Board Club. Krista and Halloween; [pers.] Be satisfied, there is always someone, worse off than you.; [a.] Oak Park, IL

MCGUIRE, THOMAS G.
[b.] March 5, 1918, Burlingame, CA; [p.] Michael and Cecelia; [m.] Patricia McGuire, 1946; [ch.] Helen, Anne, and Gregory; [ed.] Master of Arts, English, at UCLA, Los Angeles.; [occ.] Retired from Valley College, LA.; [memb.] UCLA was president of Poetry Club. I spent 4 years of WWII I was an Air Force fighter pilot and a trainer in P-38s.; [hon.] Graduated with highest honors. I was Faculty President for two elections. 4 years as Chairman of English Dept.; [oth. writ.] With another professor we wrote an English book - Design, which was popular with 4 editions.; [pers.] As faculty president I arranged to present poets: Randall Jarrell, Robert Lowell, Dylan Thomas, Karl Shapiro; [a.] Los Angeles Van Nuys, CA

MCINTYRE, RENEE
[pen.] Renee Frank; [b.] December 3, 1960, Mattoon, IL; [ch.] Jennifer Marie, Ashley Nicole; [ed.] Arlington Court Reporting Colleg, Arlington, TX, Office Careers Centre Accounting, Forthworth, TX; [occ.] Inventory Control CEO, General Bargains Aerospace, Industrial and Government Surplus; [memb.] Volunteer for "Womens Haven of Fort Worth", which is a shelter for abused women and children. A member of "Kenneth Copeland Ministries - Eagle Mountain Church"; [hon.] Arlington Court Reporting College - G.P.A. 4.0 received the achievement Award for having the highest grade point average in the field of "Law and Legal Terminology." Office careers centre - Accounting graduated a "A" average,; [pers.] This poem is dedicated in beloved memory of my Dad - Bob Frank.; [a.] Benbrook, TX

MCKENZIE, BETTY ANN FURMAN
[pen.] Christian Garrett; [b.] November 28, 1933, Ft. Worth, TX; [p.] Frank Hays, and Helena Pond Furman; [ch.] Jeffrey, Christopher, and Garrett McKenzie, and five above average Grandchildren.; [ed.] Class of 1952, Landon High School, Jacksonville, Florida, Class of 1956, Florida State University.; [occ.] Private Duty Home Health Care; [memb.] Coral Ridge Presbyterian Church, St. Lauderdale, Fl., Tiderwater Kennel Club, Scottish Terrier Club of America, Mariner Ship Duntless, G.S.A.; [oth. writ.] Past editor of Paws and Patter, Tidewater Kennel Club, Editor of Circle The Wagons, "protect us from our kids", a quarterly news letter. Hardtimes Hannah, a column written for Circle the Wagons. Poetry: Midwife Chivalry, The Kid In Grandma, My Momma's Hairbrush, Carl Andrew Hutchins, The Writer/ The Actor, Spondee? The Sugar Maple, Soaps, The Nudge. Non-Fiction: 1995 Artical: Leap of Faith, 1995 Artical: Hardtimes Hannah, "Ode to caregivers and who the deuce will take care of them?"; [pers.] Burn-out is an undeniable part of care giving. Shakespearean Actor, Charles Keating, and actresses, Victoria Wyndham resurrected my interest in the Arts: Plays, concerts, and writing. To say they saved my life is not hyperbole. I will be forever grateful.; [a.] Swansea, SC

MCLAUGHLIN, SHARI
[b.] June 22, 1970, Allentown, PA; [p.] Richard McLaughlin, Ann McLaughlin; [ed.] California State University, Chico, BA Psychology; [occ.] Pre-School Teacher YMCA Encinitas, CA; [memb.] PACS - Psychology Association of Chico State; [hon.] Dean's List; [a.] Carlsbad, CA

MCLAUGHLIN, GREGORY ELLIS
[pen.] G. E. McLaughlin; [b.] Beaumont, TX; [p.] Gerald and Sharon McLaughlin; [ed.] Tivy High School,

Schreiner College, Kerrville Texas; [occ.] U.S. Department of Transportation Office of Inspector General Auditor; [memb.] Texas Heritage Music Foundation; [hon.] Garland H. Lang Academic Scholarship, Honor's list; [oth. writ.] 1988 and 1989 The Muse - Schreiner College, Music reviews in Kerrville Daily Times; [pers.] I write from reality, not dreams, I try to see the good in all things around me.; [a.] Fort Worth, TX

MCLENDON, KEITH O.
[b.] November 22, 1970, Wadesboro, NC; [p.] Gladys B. McLendon; [ed.] Anson Senior High, Fayetteville State University; [occ.] English Teacher; [memb.] Phi Beta Sigma Fraternity Inc.; [hon.] Dean's List, National Deans List; [oth. writ.] A few unpublished poems and short stories.; [pers.] I write about my feelings and the things going on around me. I have been greatly influenced by the Harlem Renaissance Writers.; [a.] Lilesville, NC

MCMICHENS, KIM
[b.] March 5, 1079, Birmingham, AL; [ed.] Corner High School, Warrior, AL; [occ.] Student; [hon.] U.S. National Mathematics Award 1994, U.A.B./Jefferson Co. Bd. of Ed. Junior Academy of Math 1990-92, BETA Club, Cheerleader

MCNAMARA, THOM
[b.] April 18, 1981, Detroit, MI; [p.] Edward and Debra McNamara; [ed.] Lindbergh Elementary Bryant Middle School; [occ.] Student; [memb.] Dearborn Hockey Association; [oth. writ.] Anthology of Poetry by Young Americans 1994 Edition; [a.] Dearborn, MI

MCNAMARA, EDWARD D.
[pen.] Eddie Mac; [b.] March 26, 1958, Hollywood, FL; [p.] Leonard McNamara and Margaret Ruffert; [m.] Kay L. Camacho-McNamara, March 15, 1995; [ch.] Kaitlin Jo McNamara, Jason Thomas Camacho; [occ.] Audio/video Engineer; [pers.] 1. Going through life being misunderstood, is one of life's greatest misunderstandings, 2. The Tone of your voice will determine how to other person will react to what you just said.; [a.] Pompano Beach, FL

MCNEELY, TARA
[b.] August 6, 1980, Dorchester, MA; [p.] Estelle and James McNeely; [ed.] Ninth grade at Newman Preparatory School, Boston, MA; [occ.] Student; [memb.] C.Y.O., Cheering Team, Mass Bay Skating Club; [hon.] Certificate of Poetic Achievement by the Amherst Society for the poem "Race"; [oth. writ.] Several poems and stories. One poem "Race" published in the American Poetry Annual; [pers.] If you don't think you're good at something, try it anyway. Because you never know what could happen.; [a.] Saugus, MA

MCNEIL, JOHNATHAN
[b.] December 27, 1924, Boston, MA; [p.] Lillian P. Gill-Hugh J. McNeil; [m.] Carol Ann (Liversidge) McNeil; [ch.] Christine, Derek, Debbie, Frankie, grandchild: "P.J.", Michelle, Jacqueline, Christopher, Jillian and Derek Jr.; [ed.] So. Boston High Grad., Federal Police Acad, FBI and Mass Criminal Justice sponsored Seminars; [occ.] Retired Federal Law Enforcement Officer; [memb.] Life Member-Rep. Presidential Task Force, Rep National Committee Area 6 Rep. Platform Planning Comm. Legion of Merit.; [hon.] Certified Bomb Search, Bom Scene Officer, Terror Hostage Negotiator and N.C.I.C. teacher. Immigration Officer and Special U.S. Deputy Marshal, Regional (R1) S.O.R.T. Team Commander, Veteran of World War II and Korean Conflict; [oth. writ.] Columnist for two local Newspaper, (Social and Philosophical topics), A Cabinet of unpublished writings under the heading: "Words And Empressions Of Johnathan"; [pers.] I have been told, I have a "Gift" but I see it as the God given ability to translate the impressions that come from a Higher Power into the Language of Human Understanding. I endeavor to paint "Word Pictures" as a

method of sharing my experiences.

MCNEILL, DANIEL
[b.] September 8, 1930, Brooklyn, NY; [p.] Daniel and Elizabeth McNeill; [m.] Marlene McNeill, November 30, 1963; [ch.] Elizabeth Ann, Robert Daniel, Kenneth James, dauther is retarded; [ed.] Went to PS31 for Kids - Jansen City, PS 28 - Dickinson High School, PS 28 - Dickinson High School.; [occ.] Retired from Post Office; [memb.] AARP; [pers.] In my writing this poem I tried to tell how people have trouble going to sleep and what goes through their minds when they do.

MCPHERSON, KATRINA
[pen.] Katrina Cox; [b.] November 24, 1973, Phoenix, AZ; [p.] Larry and Susan Cox; [ed.] Marcos de Niza High School, Phoenix College; [occ.] Accounting Secretary, US Home; [pers.] Follow your heart, and always be true to yourself.; [a.] Phoenix, AZ

MEADER, KATHLEEN
[pen.] Katie or Kate; [b.] April 29, 1969, Oklahoma City, OK; [p.] Sharon Meader and Herb Meader (divorced); [ed.] I attended 1 1/2 years of MSU in Kentucky and graduated from Peducah Tilghman High School in May of '87.; [occ.] Aspiring writer of songs and poetry; [memb.] Jaycees; [hon.] I was mentioned in my year book as wanting to be a writer mainly because I spent most of my time writing humorous short stories and some poems that made several issues of the school paper in my junior and senior year; [pers.] I hope to make a difference in peoples lives making them aware of the needs of special children and to bring hope to those who have none Helen Stiener Rice and Robert Frost have been my inspiration for years I also enjoy seeing the humor of situations and enjoy writing short stories.; [a.] Denver, CO

MEADOWS, DANIEL SKIS
[pen.] Ruthless Scrivener; [b.] November 7, 1968; [ch.] Kathleen Louise Hart, Beth Evelyn and "R.J." Sansarico; [ed.] B.S. Degree in R.S. from University of H.K.; [occ.] Ass. Mng. of B.S. at R.S. Inc.; [memb.] Church of What's Happin' - Now, Worshipper of O2; [oth. writ.] "On the verge of value" "The Lil' Hood that Could," "How to Marry a Manic Depressive"; [pers.] Abound! When you wield a sword — dully procure in the face that you're in.; [a.] Riverside, CA

MEADOWS, ANGELINA
[pen.] Angel; [b.] December 25, 1982, Warren, MI; [p.] Mark and Victoria Meadows; [ed.] 6th grade student; [occ.] Student; [memb.] Girl Scout of America; [hon.] Won Reflections Program 2 yrs. in a row. Won young Author's Contest March of Dimes Reading Winner.; [pers.] More children should be able to express more of their feeling - go on paper. Because, they have a lot to say.; [a.] Sterling Heights, MI

MEARS, SHANNON
[b.] June 1, 1970, Austin, TX; [p.] Cherylann Mears and Dale Mears; [ed.] Lake Travis High Austin Community College; [occ.] Business Administrator; [hon.] Won 3rd place in essay contest in high School, Sophomore year, 3rd place essay contest on women in Texas, sophomore year in High School; [pers.] Love and peace and earth is a better place to be.; [a.] Irving, TX

MEDINA, CYNTHIA
[pen.] C. J. Hollerman; [b.] June 13, 1974, Pasadena, CA; [p.] Carlos Medina, Noemi Yonts; [ed.] Bonita High, Citrus College, Cal Poly Pomona Univ.; [occ.] Piano Instructor; [memb.] Society for Advancement in Management, Grace Bretheran Church and College Group.; [hon.] Presidential Academic Fitness Awards and Piano Festival awards; [oth. writ.] I include poetry publications in the Bonita, Litrus and Esprit Magazines.; [pers.] I am in love with the human heart, mind and spirit and their blend of colors. Their picture reflects life's complexity and simplicity, the beauty of

God's hands.; [a.] La Verne, CA

MENA, TERRI
[b.] May 22, 1958, Frankfort, Germany; [p.] Cliff and Lavelle Wagner; [m.] Ricky Mena, June 17, 1983; [ch.] Nicklas Joseph, Leanne Nicole; [ed.] Burges High School, University of Texas, at EL Paso (UTEP); [occ.] Kindergarten Teacher, Clint ISD; [memb.] International Reading Association, Saint Raphael Parish, PTA; [oth. writ.] Several poems written to use in my classroom (unpublished); [pers.] Children are our most precious treasures. When loved and respected, they will blossom into productive adults deserving of lifes greatest gifts.; [a.] El Paso, TX

MENDEZ, MARINA R.
[pen.] Al-Mari; [b.] January 18, 1957, Hispaniola; [p.] Ramona Jimenez-Mitchel; [m.] Genaro R. Mendez; [ch.] Maria Trinidad Sanchez; [ed.] Hostos High School N.Y.C. ASS at Hostos Comm. College, B.A. in Psychology Lehman College City College of New York, Doctor Degree in Divinity Vision University NY; [memb.] Shmitsonion Association, New York Museum of Art, Bronx Museum of Art, CUNY Disable Student Assoc., Christian Coaliton, American Bible Ass./World Vision; [hon.] Puerto Rican Council Multi-Service N.Y.C., 1981 - best design place student, 1986 - March - student of the Month-Hostos College, 1986 - The March ESL Student in writing 1st and 2nd place, Boytown, North Shone, Animal League, Americans Society for prevention of cruelty of animals.; [oth. writ.] 1986, Hostos Comm. College City of N.Y.C. essay of the month, 1992, ESL student illustration Lenhan College of N.Y.C; [pers.] It doesn't matter how people appear. I love them because I see God in each human being. Without God's love, peace and freedom we are nothing.; [a.] Bronx, NY

MENESES, MANUEL
[b.] May 26, 1928, Chile, South Africa; [m.] Margarita Meneses, September 17, 1953; [ch.] 3 sons (5 grandchildren); [ed.] H.S. Molloy College L.I. 2 Violin (Orquestra); [occ.] Retired; [oth. writ.] I have been writing music, for long time but I have been not (like lucky (so far) classical in pop. Is my forte, also in violin playing.; [pers.] We come to America, myself and wife, and my 3 children 1965, my wife is a nurse, 2 of my sons, went to college. And we love America, America is our country and all of us love this country (God Bless America)

MERCADO, DEMETRIA BOULAGERIS
[pen.] Demetria Boulageris Mercado; [b.] September 2, 1963, Philadelphia; [p.] Michael and Evelyn Boulageris; [m.] Luis G. Mercado, October 22, 1983; [ch.] Rina L. Mercado, Michael J. Mercado; [ed.] Wildwood High School, St Demetrios Greek School; [occ.] Food Service; [memb.] St. Demetrios P.T.O. Member. Active in childrens recreational sports. Sunday School Teacher. Active in Girl Scouting.; [oth. writ.] Several unpublished poems; [pers.] Human kindness is the most important thing in life, if everyone had my teacher Efstathia Kaloudis - there would be no hate. So I dedicate this to her eternal memory, and to my parents, who instilled goodness in all their children.; [a.] North Wildwood, NJ

MEREWETHER, JACK
[b.] May 3, 1919, Detroit, MI; [p.] Edward and Winnifred; [m.] Lindy Sryder Merewether, September 9, 1943; [ch.] Bruce and Jean M. Coverdill; [ed.] BA and MA and Ph. D. in English MA in Guidance and Counselling MSW in Social Work; [occ.] Retired college instructor, presently part-time psychotherapist; [memb.] Nat'l Assoc. social workers' AM Assoc. professional hyprotherapists; [oth. writ.] Two poetry books: Songs of a Detroiter and A Green Bough, one family history book: The Searching Family; [pers.] I write from a strong, positive, moral viewpoint and seek to promote a rich, positive, healthy life in my readers and

in my clients in therapy.; [a.] Southfield, MI

MERILA, RICHARD C.
[b.] May 15, 1947, Washburn, WI; [p.] Toivo and Geneva Merila; [m.] Kristin Lindberg Merila, October 8, 1993; [ed.] Washburn High School Ashland County Teachers College, Instructor: Boyceville Community Schools; [occ.] Childrens Pastor, worship leader; [memb.] Disabled American Veterans, American Legion, Post 86; [hon.] Honor Student, Honorable Discharge - USAF; [pers.] Every person needs love. Every person can given love. God is love.; [a.] Ashland, WI

MERILA, RICHARD L.
[pen.] Bud; [b.] May 15, 1947, Washburn, WI; [p.] Toivo and Geneva Merita; [m.] Kristin Lindberg Merita, October 8, 1993; [ed.] Washburn High School, Ashland Country Teachers College, Eau Claire State University (night classes); [occ.] Former Instructor Boyceville Comm. Schs., Retired - USAF Work as Children's Pastor/Worship leader; [memb.] Disabled American Veterans American Legion; [hon.] Salutatorian/Social Suc Award, Latin Award/Honorable Discharge US Air Force; [oth. writ.] Poems - 1. An Act of Kindness, 2. Don't Ever Let Go; [pers.] People are in need of love. Everyone can give love. God is love.

MERIWETHER, FRANK HENNING
[pen.] Zack Lee Toll; [b.] May 6, 1921, Jackson, TN; [p.] William P. Meriwether and Eloise Henning Meriwether; [m.] Mildred Brittain; [ch.] Marnie Caini, Michael Meriwether, Frank H. Meriwether II; [ed.] Huntersville High School, St. Martin College, (4 year) Graduated Magna Cum Laude, other Military School,; [occ.] Retired Military, and Correction Officer; [memb.] American Legrin (39 years) VFW. Methodist Church; [hon.] EAME Theatre Ribbon with 3 bronze stars, air medal with 4 oak leaf cluster, distinguished unit citation AAF Crew MBR Badge (wings) WWII, European Theatre, AF.; [oth. writ.] Several poems, local paper, Lungshingt, Presently have submitted a litenzy work, "South of my village", to be copy righted. (Very recent). (Incorporates my submitted poem); [pers.] I like my work to reflect the mystery of our lives and times seasoned by serindipper traits and the sanctim of our loving Lord...; [a.] Jackson, TN

MERIWETHER, NELL W.
[b.] June 17, 1931, Taylorsville, MS; [p.] Henry and Ora Wood; [m.] Carl L. Meriwether, Jr., August 22, 1952; [ch.] Lester, Lindy, Anita, Lauren; [ed.] BA Mississippi College Clinton, MS, Med Louisiana State University, Baton Rouge, LA; [occ.] Teacher, English Tara High School, Baton Rouge; [memb.] Delta Kappa Gamma, Louisiana Writers Guild, East Baton Rouge Parish Teachers of English and Louisiana State Teachers of English Association, First Baptist Church, Baton Rouge, LA; [hon.] Finalist Teacher of the Year, East Baton Rouge Parish, Won several grants for English classes.; [oth. writ.] Other poems published locally, two children's books Lauren and Papillion and Camping with Timmy, essay and poem in different editions of Louisiana Anthology, Twelve easy steps to writing the research paper for High School Students to be published by NTC publishing in Chicago, 1996.; [pers.] Besides teaching, my love is writings, through it I share myself with others.; [a.] Baton Rouge, LA

MERRICK, ELLEN
[b.] September 24, 1967, Passaic, NJ; [p.] Robert Herberger and Mary Boatwright; [m.] Aaron, April 6, 1988; [ch.] James, Amanda, Melody; [ed.] Graduated Seminale High School, Sanford, FL - 1985; [oth. writ.] Several unpublished poems; [pers.] Many of my poem originate from happenings in my life, and each one hold a special place in my heart.; [a.] Fitzgerald, GA

MERRIGAN, TINA
[b.] June 4, 1980, Stockton; [p.] Ida and Don Merrigan; [ed.] Middle 9th grade; [occ.] Student; [hon.] 2nd place

in a short contest; [oth. writ.] Lost of different poems and a couple of short stories and a 2 songs; [pers.] Poetry is nothing but a feeling of the soul, a memory of the mind, and the lost loving beat of a heart.; [a.] Klamath Falls, OR

MEYERKORTH, LILA
[b.] November 18, 1933, Shubert, NB; [p.] Glen and Gladys Vice; [m.] Deceased; [ch.] Pam Ganger, Mike Meyerkorth, Greg Meyerkorth, Judith Meyerkorth; [ed.] Shubert High School, Peru State College, NB; [occ.] Secretary for IN - HOME, Health Care, Inc. Auburn, NB; [memb.] Mt. Zion Brick Church, Shubert American Legion Auxiliary; [hon.] 4 year award for outstanding sportsmanship (high school) Honored as teacher of best students article Submitted on, my Community and me. National Library Award for top 3% poets.; [oth. writ.] Book - Memories of Indian Cave State Park, Book - Historical Mount Zion Brick Church, To my Valentine - Using titles of Songs; [pers.] I have been greatly influenced by the honesty and hard work of my parents. My motto is "Prefer One Another."; [a.] Shubert, NB

MEYERS, RENEE MARIE
[b.] February 25, 1973, Hazleton, PA; [p.] Nancy Ciotda and Ray Meyers; [ed.] Hazleton High School, East Stroudsburg University; [oth. writ.] Several unpublished poems, currently working on short stories for children. [pers.] I dedicate this poem to everyone who has the pleasure of having life's most treasured gift, a grandmother. [a.] Hazelton, PA.

MICHAUD, MELISSA L.
[b.] December 13, 1951, York, ME; [p.] Kenneth and Diane Card; [m.] Kenneth Naughton and Catarina Michaud; [ed.] Graduated from Kennebunk High School with Honors.; [occ.] Homemaker/Craft maker; [pers.] Live each day to the fullest and appreciate your loved ones; [a.] Kennebunkport, ME

MICHIELI, MITCHELL BRIAN
[pen.] Kick - Michell; [b.] August 11, 1968, Sterling CO; [p.] Ronald and Barbara Michieli; [ch.] Darby Lane Michieli - Welch; [ed.] Yorktown High, Various Courses in the Arts; [occ.] Musician and Free lance insanist; [hon.] Reviews by various musical publications; [oth. writ.] Several articles and reviews of music and writings in local papers across the east and west coasts; [pers.] There is a whirlpool of personal experience that collects itself at the end, of a page, through my favorite black pen; [a.] Denver, CO

MICHONSKI, STANLEY JOSEPH
[b.] April 1, 1950, Poland; [p.] Weronika, Josef Michonski; [m.] Sofia Michonski, August 27, 1977; [ch.] Anna Teresa, Adam Krzysztof; [ed.] Vocational High, Poland; [occ.] CNC Automatic Lathe Set-up Operator; [a.] Atkinson, NH

MIDDLETON, DELORES MARIE
[b.] October 9, 1962, Patuxent River, MD; [p.] Katie (Williams) Taylor, Isaac Taylor; [m.] Cecil L. Middleton, August 7, 1993; [ch.] Francis Ernest, Briana Nicole, stepdaughters: Cecilia, I'yeesha Shayla; [occ.] Housewife; [pers.] My husband was my inspiration to do this poem. He has shown me that love has no bounds, with the support of God, and your family behind you. All things are possible!; [a.] Fort Riley, KS

MIDYETT, BETTY JEAN
[b.] December 16, 1931, Nuyaka, OK; [p.] Wm. Floyd and Pauline Beasley (Revs); [ch.] Donnie Dean Midyett, Jr. Ricky Dean Midyett, Roddy Gene Midyett; [ed.] High School, 1 year in college; [occ.] Was employ of Bank for twenty years, now unemployed due to disability. Love to the Lord's Work!; [memb.] Attend Grandview Assembly of God Church Elk City, OK; [hon.] Lots of Love from Sunday School Children; [oth. writ.] Have written quite a number of letters to the editor

to local newspaper for political reasons and many for profile, for life of the unborn child and against abortion.; [pers.] I am a Christian, and pleasing Jesus is my deepest desire. My poem was actually give to me by the inspiration of the Holy Spirit. I love to teach (share, pray, love, listen to) the word of God.; [a.] Elk City, OK

MIHALIC, SUSAN
[b.] August 5, 1961, Jackson, MS; [p.] Mike and Pauline Henley Mihalic; [ed.] BA in journalism from University of Southern Mississippi, Hattiesburg, Mississippi. Graduated with highest honors.; [occ.] Writer and editor, Jostens Learning Corporation, therapeutic horseback riding instructor, Helen Woodward Animal Center; [hon.] Helen Woodward Animal Center Volunteer of the Year in 1991, California Network for Equestrian Therapy Top Volunteer in 1993, Omicron Delta Kappa Scholastic and Leadership Honorary Society.; [pers.] "Sophia the Cat" is based on my observation that cats are true to themselves, which makes them very wise indeed. The real Sophia is a gusty, independent creature who listens to herself. We should all be so evolved.; [a.] San Diego, CA

MILLER, DANA
[pen.] Dana Miller; [b.] September 5, 1983; [p.] Tina and Ray Miller; [ed.] I attend Benjamin Franklin Middle School and I'm in the 6th grade.; [hon.] I was on the honor roll for four years in a row.; [a.] Teaneck, NI

MILLER, ELVA LENORE
[pen.] Lenore Miller; [b.] March 12, 1931, Chester, PA; [p.] Lewis and Elizabeth Ponte fract, Kline Jr.; [m.] Bruce A. Miller, September 22, 1951 (1st), June 4, 1965 (2nd); [ch.] Kenneth L. Stoudt Jr., LuAnn Stoudt, Kerry R. Stoudt, Kevin W. Stoudt, Arnold F. Miller; [ed.] 12 Grades - Liberty Joint High School Southern Tioga District; [occ.] Caring for Elderly in his Home; [memb.] East District Menmnite Church, Tops Club, Inc. Sebring Grange, Senior Citizens Huntersville, Penna, Salem Ladies Aid, Lathern Church; [oth. writ.] One poem published in 1988 American Anthology of Contemporary Poetry; [pers.] I strive to reflect the goodness and ways to achieve in my writing. I'm inspired by speakers and take notes in poetry.; [a.] Turbotville, PA

MILLER, LYNN FRANKLIN
[b.] March 23, 1935, Potosi, MO; [p.] Arthur and Myrtle Miller; [m.] Marcella Miller, April 3, 1954; [ch.] Pamala Jane Miller, Barbeau Gordon Lynn Miller; [ed.] Advanced Vocational Training; [occ.] Maintenance Manager; [memb.] Jefferson Country Chamber of Commerce; [pers.] I am primarily a self-educated man. My poetry is the reflection of my emotions, my daily experiences, and the love of my family.; [a.] Fenton, MO

MILLER, CRAIG A.
[pen.] Miller, Craig A.; [b.] November 26, 1958, Kellogg, IA; [p.] Ivan Miller, Donna Miller; [m.] Lori Miller-Eklund; [ch.] Shannon and Ivan; [ed.] Sandstone H.S., S.W. Minn. St; [occ.] Electro-Chemical Grinding Master, Delavan Inc. DSM IA; [memb.] National Heart Council, Chairperson for C.F.S.L. and Associates, Local Y.M.C.A. Volunteer.; [pers.] I feel that it is very important to write from your heart. Your feeling are one of the few things that will always come back too you.; [a.] Des Moines, IA

MILLER, DAVID
[pen.] David Paul Miller; [b.] July 8, 1981, Royal Oak, MI; [p.] Dan and Joy Miller; [m.] Not married; [ed.] 8th Grade Student. (I was 11 years, 10 months old and in the 6th grade when I wrote the poem.); [occ.] 8th grade student - Our Shepherd Lutheran School; [memb.] Troy Youth Soccer League - Premier Team School Soccer Team - Captain School Basket Ball Team; [hon.] President, 8th Grade Class; [pers.] I wrote this poem about one month after my grandmother's death. This poem is

about my grandmother going to heaven, because I know she did.; [a.] Troy, MI

MILLS, TIMOTHY A.
[b.] August 9, 1966, Mountainview, CA; [p.] Edward and Mary Mills; [m.] Jennifer Mills, August 11, 1990; [ch.] Zachary Daniel; [ed.] Archbishop Mitty High, Arizona State University; [hon.] 1984, Bank of America Music Award, 1988 MBNA Outstanding Young Man of America; [pers.] Make someone else happy!

MILLS, JOSH
[b.] August 27, 1977; [ed.] High School Senior; [a.] Lebanon, TN

MILOTA, JULIANE
[pen.] Julie Milota; [b.] March 18, 1980, Tarzana, CA; [p.] Donna Milota; [ed.] Freshman in High School at Saugus High; [occ.] Student/Acting; [oth. writ.] Goodbye and something missing published in voices; [pers.] When your mind is full, and you can't talk to anyone, writing is the best alternative. It's a good way for anyone to get their feelings out, and also understand them better.; [a.] Saugus, CA

MINES, ROSETTE
[b.] April 1, 1929, Brooklyn; [p.] Samuel Esther; [ed.] Erasmus High School Brooklyn College; [occ.] Own Bus. Customer Service, McPrinters; [hon.] Editors Choice National Library Artist League/honorable mention Artist League of poetry honorable mention. Artist League of Brooklyn Poetic Eloquence, Honorable Mention Feelings; [oth. writ.] National Library of Poetry Editors Choice Creating through painting and writing is my lose. Writing bring me close to nature, animal people and love.; [pers.] See previous unto biographies for information; [a.] Brooklyn, NY

MINTON, KIMBERLY ANN
[pen.] Kimberly; [b.] July 5, 1976, Kileen, TX; [p.] Larry Minton, Sunyop Sain; [m.] F. J. Frazier, December 29, 1995; [ed.] Currently a freshman at Northeast State Community College in Jackson County Alabama.; [occ.] Work for KFC. I hope to be an Occupational Therapist.; [memb.] I was a member of several groups in High School, but now I am only a Member of First Baptist Church of Scottsboro; [hon.] Most dedicated in students for Christ 3 years in a row. Who's who of American High School Students for two years.; [pers.] I write for personal reasons, basically to describe A hope, a tear, a love. My two inspirations are God and My fiance Phillip Jason Frazier; [a.] Scottsboro, AL

MINTON, JOHN W.
[b.] May 8, 1953, Indianapolis, IN; [p.] David J. and Eloise Claire Minton; [m.] Divorced; [ch.] William D. B. Minton; [ed.] Indiana Purdue Univ. at Indianapolis, University of Oriental Philosophy USA Okinawa Japan, Cardinal Ritter HS, Indianapolis, IN; [occ.] Martial Arts Instructor, Youth Coaching; [memb.] Juko-Kai USA Int'l, Int'l Okinawan Martial Arts Union, Okinawa Japan, Nat'l Assoc. for self employed.; [hon.] Meritorious promotions and awards for military service.; [oth. writ.] Several (over ten) letters to the editor in the San Francisco Bay Area Newspapers concerning government fraud, waste and abuse.; [pers.] Young people today need positive role models from their local communities.; [a.] Whitmore, CA

MIRA, TARANEH
[b.] November 24, 1957; [m.] Single; [ed.] 1. Masters in Management, Golden Gate University, 2. Bachelor in Business, University of San Francisco; [occ.] Artist/Writer; [memb.] 1. Amnesty International, 2. Diable Road Runners Club.; [oth. writ.] Greeting Cards, Cartoon Writing, Illustrator; [pers.] I live for love, freedom, laughter and running.; [a.] Walnut Creek, CA

MIRACLE, JOAN MAYNETTE
[b.] May 1, 1942, Stock Dale, TX; [p.] Joseph Murray, Violet Parks; [m.] Robert L. Miracle, December 4, 1965; [ch.] Debbie, Brenda, Tammie, Doug, Michelle; [ed.] Thomas Edison High School, San Antonio, TX; [occ.] Retired; [oth. writ.] Auto Biography, many other poems and profound statements, "Tuna"; [pers.] Congratulations on getting published Mom! I love you! Douglas.; [a.] Westminster, CO

MITCHELL, EBONEY K.
[b.] January 27, 1979, Detroit, MI; [p.] Denise A. Mitchell; [ed.] Martin Luther King Jr., Sr. High School Detroit, MI; [occ.] Student; [memb.] Business Club, Ski Club, Role Playing Club, Explorers is Law Outpost; [oth. writ.] Several poems published in school anthologists.; [pers.] I believe that love can conquer all evil. Good relations between the races as well as sexes is not impossible if we but try hard enough.; [a.] Detroit, MI

MITCHELL, GARY DEAN
[b.] July 12, 1955, Carson City, MI; [p.] Avis Barnes and Robert Mitchell; [ed.] Grad. Saint Louis (Michigan) High School June 7, 1973, 2 yrs Lake City Comm. College, FL. Continuing Ed. at Central Mich. Univ. Mount Pleasant, MI.; [occ.] Student, Architectural Designer; [oth. writ.] I have written many, many poems, but have not tried to publish any, until now.; [pers.] I travel in my grandfathers footsteps, and find great joy in the precise forms of rhyme, line, and measure.; [a.] Saint Louis, MI

MITCHELL IV HENRY LEE
[b.] September 20, 1981, Saint Louis, MO; [p.] Henry and Alice L. Mitchell; [ed.] St Louis Jr. Academy Cross Road School St Louis, MO; [occ.] Student; [hon.] 3.1 grade point average

MITCHELL, MARY ANN
[pen.] Mary Miller; [b.] August 1, 1937, Louisville, KY; [p.] Bernard and Catherine S. Carrico; [m.] Wm. R. Mitchell, August 25, 1962; [ch.] Mike, Anne, Kate; [ed.] 1. B.S.N. - Iniv. Colo., 1962, 2. St. Joseph's Infirm School Nursing, 1958, 3. Sacred Heart Acad. Louisville, NY, 1955.; [occ.] Retired R.N.; [memb.] AAUW (American Association University Women); [pers.] I frequently write from compelling sense of dejavu. Kind of an "I've Been Here Before?" feeling.; [a.] Littleton, CO

MITCHELL, BROOKE E.
[pen.] Lost N. A. Dream; [b.] September 19, 1980, Winston-Salem, NC; [p.] John and Lesley Mitchell; [ed.] I'm in 8th grade at Laurens Junior High School (LJHS), Laurens, SC; [occ.] Jr. High Student; [memb.] I'm a member of the National Junior Honor society and of the first Presbyterian Church I'm a clarinetist in the Laurens Junior High Tiger Band; [hon.] Award for highest grad point average in sixth grade, award for highest number of accelerated reader points in 6th grade; [oth. writ.] Had several writings published in school newspapers.; [pers.] Watch a sunset.; [a.] Laurens, SC

MITCHELL, DIANA
[b.] September 1, 1957, San Joaquin, CA; [p.] Gene, Reda Engles; [m.] Doyle Mitchell; [ch.] Gypsy Jolene Dallas, Jason Lee Mitchell; [occ.] Domestic Engineer; [pers.] I truly feel we are all walking a maze in life.; [a.] Tipton, CA

MIZE, REBECCA LYNN
[b.] January, 1981, Wayne, MI; [p.] Gerald and Kathleen Mize; [ed.] Ninth Grade Plymouth-Canton High School; [hon.] Honor Roll Student through Middle School. MVP and All-Star for three years in softball.; [pers.] In my writing I try to express the importance of life.; [a.] Canton, MI

MJS-HELD, BRI
[b.] June 9, 1964, Sharon, PA; [ed.] Amityville High School, United States Air Force (1981-1985); [occ.] Writer-Director/Actor; [memb.] Women Make Movies, AIVP, Film Video Arts; [oth. writ.] "References Required", a one-act play produced in NYC in 1993, "Lost People Who Sell Maps", A short film produced and directed by the author, several pull-length screenplays.; [pers.] Mahatma Gandhi stated, in part, "There is an art which kills, and an art which gives life..." Let my art always be that which gives life!; [a.] New York, NY

MOGYORDY, PAUL L.
[b.] December 25, 1921, Cleveland, OH; [m.] Maria K.; [ed.] Western Reserve University Northern Illinois College of Optometry; [occ.] Optometrist; [memb.] Optometric Association Kiwanis; [oth. writ.] For many years editor for weekly Kiwanis Bulletin; [pers.] Best achievement: Raising 7 wonderful bright children!; [a.] West Lake, OH

MOHACSY, PETER ANDREW
[pen.] Anonymous, Alice; [b.] June 15, 1962, Philadelphia, PA; [p.] Emil and Ilma Mohacsy; [m.] Single; [ed.] High School Diploma from Salzburg Int'l Prep School Salzburg, Austria. Bachelor's Degree in Chemistry, Stoction State College, Pomona, NJ.; [occ.] Tutoring Math and Science; [memb.] Spiritual Army; [hon.] A year varsity letter man in wrestling, 2 yr. varsity track and field, 4 yrs. Junior Varsity Football, 1 yr. honor roll, 4 yrs. Merit Roll. Straight A's in organic chem.; [oth. writ.] "Elimination of Distorted Sounds in Music" Stockton Journal of Physics. Poem "To You" published in Calif. Treasury Classics. I have own personal collections of poems and short stories from Aspan of 14 yrs.; [pers.] "Poetry cannot exist without science and science cannot exist without poetry" Goethe, To me mythology is science of the soul and alchemy in my theological chemistry. Pertaining to pause in the void. Adonis is wind flower.; [a.] Destin, FL

MOHL, COURTNEY RED-HORSE
[b.] February 7, 1985, CA; [p.] Valerie Red-Horse Mohl and Curt Mohl; [ed.] Woodcrest Elementary Honors Student; [occ.] Student and Actress; [memb.] Screen Actors Guild, American Federation of Television and Radio Artists

MOLINO, MARGARET MAGEE
[pen.] Maggie Magee Molino; [b.] October 23, 1935, Philadelphia, PA; [p.] John J. Magee and Ruth Blackall Magee; [m.] Don F. Molino; [ch.] Susan Johnson, Laura Wallace, Patty Tobin, Jack Tobin, and Jennifer Tobin, Grandchildren: Tommy and Matthew Johnson, (Son Jack and his wife, Mary are expecting their first child July 1995.); [memb.] President, Ridgewood Camera Club.; [hon.] Photography Best of Show, New England Camera Conference - Honorable Mention and many acceptances in PSA International Salons 1995 First Place Pictorial, Competition Ridgewood Camera Club.; [pers.] One's family is everything in this life. They are the ones who love and stand by you. They are both your life jacket and your anchor. I have been blessed with mine.; [a.] North Haledon, NJ

MOLLURAI, ANNETTE
[b.] June 18, 1946, England; [p.] Fred and Queenie Wright; [m.] Andrew Mollura, October 2, 1968; [ch.] Paul and Arron; [ed.] St Louis Convent School Newmarket England St. Mary's Hospital, Kings Lynn, for nursing I didn't finish; [occ.] Sales Clerk; [hon.] Daily Mirrow life saving gold medal; [oth. writ.] Inspirational many more inspirational poems, that have also been dedicated to family and friends; [pers.] I feel my poetry is a God given gift the honor goes to my God. Praise him.; [a.] Prestview, FL

MONDAY, TIMOTHY
[b.] April 9, 1978, Indianapolis, IN; [p.] Jeanne Monday, Robert Monday; [ed.] Current Sophomore student at Cascade High School; [memb.] Cascade High School Football Team; [pers.] All it takes is one thing your good at, to be talented.; [a.] Clayton, IN

MONTANARO, JOSHUA
[b.] November 23, 1982, Norristown, PA; [p.] William and Roseanne Montanaro; [ed.] 6th grade, Pine Forge Elementary School; [occ.] Student; [memb.] Boyertown Optimist, Basketball team, Pine forge Baseball Team, Pottstown church of the Nazarene; [a.] Boyertown, PA

MOORE, RYAN
[b.] May 3, 1979, Lancaster, CA; [p.] Carol and Gary Thompson; [ed.] Currently High School Sophomore - Emphasis in Science, Math and Computer-Aided Design; [occ.] Student; [memb.] Society for Creative Anachronism West Omaha Soccer Ass'n Univ. of NE at Omaha, Fencing Club; [hon.] National Jr. Honor Society Duke University Talent Search, Designee; [oth. writ.] Assorted poetry and short stories published in school publications and other publications featuring student's work.; [a.] Omaha, NE

MOORE, LAVERNE
[pen.] Blondy; [b.] November 7, 1918, Gibson, TN; [p.] Mr. and Mrs. A. M. Pillow; [m.] J. H. Moore (deceased), February 19, 1943; [ch.] 1 son, Billy W. Moore; [ed.] High School - some College work - U.T. at Martin - TN, a member of Art - Council, Draughon's Busnish College, Memphis - TN Cosmotomergy (Mellanera) College (Memphis) TN - ('94); [memb.] A member of first Baptist church, since 1941 an a big heart to do good things. Lots of church work. A donner of cancer and heart.; [hon.] Awards of disabled-american veterans. 94 and 95 USPE Offica Cert. 1993; [a.] Memphis, TN

MOORE, CHRISTINE E.
[b.] December 24, 1947, Green Bay, WI; [p.] Ray Hussin, June Hogan; [m.] George Ray Moore, June 25, 1993; [ch.] Joseph Vanvonderen, James Vanvonderen, Monica Vanvonderen; [ed.] East High, Northeast Wisconsin Technical College, Carolina Vocational Center; [occ.] Journeyman Carpenter, Certified Nursing Assistant (CNA); [memb.] Piedmont Wood Carvers Association; [hon.] Horsemanship, reining and girls barrel racing - 1st place; [pers.] This poem was written from the depths of my heart, in less than 45 seconds, to my best friend and partner, my husband, George Ray.; [a.] Marietta, SC

MOORE, KARAC CHANTELL
[pen.] Karac Chantell; [b.] July 8, 1964, Chicago, CA; [p.] Robert and Patricia Moore; [ed.] Osseo Sr High School, North Hennipen Community College, Brown Institute for A degree in Broadcasting; [occ.] Customer Service Representative; [hon.] Was selected to perform a broadcast show from school - received 5 awards for taking #1 in sales, for home improvements.; [oth. writ.] I have many poems. Currently I've turned my writings into songs and am working on a singing project for which I wrote the lyrics to 4 songs. This poem is going to be a song and recorded a metro studios in Minneapolis.; [pers.] My inspiration to write comes from music and a famous Performer and lyricist in the music industry. Love is always an inspiration in writing during times when it is painful; [a.] Maple Grove, MN

MOORE, NIKISHA
[pen.] Ni-Ni (Dimples); [b.] December 23, 1973, Fort Dix, NJ; [p.] Karen Cook McLean and Marvin G. Moore Jr.; [ch.] Two, Tequoine Wright, and K'ron Moore; [ed.] Graduate of Bayside High School VA. Beach, VA.; [occ.] Cashier, Farm Fresh, Writer, Mother; [memb.] Black Culture, Club, YPWW, Epiphany Songbirds; [hon.] English, Math, Science, Spanish honor, Dance, Modern Dance, Cheer Leading, Student Coun-

cil.; [oth. writ.] Wrote a christian play "Will You Be Ready" when Jesus Comes? For Tarik Tabari, has not yet been published.; [pers.] Writing is something that I take alot of pride, and time in. It is very important to me, because it makes me feel good. That's how I want to make others feel too.; [a.] Virginia Beach, VA

MOORE, JASON PRIOR
[pen.] Jason Moore; [b.] January 22, 1915, Bell Co, TX; [p.] Lawrence and Dessie Moore; [m.] Virginia B. Moore, August 28, 1940; [ch.] Marjorie Shrefer, Jon L. Moore, Elizabeth Moore, Jason H. Moore; [ed.] Denton High School (Tex), B. Architecture, the University of TX., Austin, 1939; [occ.] Retired Architect; [memb.] The American Institute of Architects, Master Runners UNLTD, Duke City Marathon Committee; [hon.] AIA Senior Architect, various Awards for older runners since 1978; [pers.] I would like to become known as a wise man who expresses the imprint of the experiences of a long lifetime in rhythm and beauty.; [a.] Albuquerque, NM

MOORE, KEVIN GLEEN
[pen.] Kevin Moore; [b.] August 27, 1965, Longview; [p.] Jeanette Moore, Charels Moore; [ed.] Hallsville High Kilgor College - One sem; [occ.] Auto Mechanic; [hon.] Outstanding percussionist, SFA Band Camp 1978; [oth. writ.] Lots of poems but none published - also several songs not yet published.; [pers.] I base my poetry and song lyrics on real life experience's and feelings the way I see things and the effect they have on me; [a.] Hallsville, TX

MOORE, KAY
[pen.] Kay Moore; [b.] February 11, 1945, TX; [p.] Ada Richardson; [m.] David Moore, May 1, 1971; [ed.] High School - Dalhart Texas various banking schools; [occ.] Vice President - Banking Houston Texas; [memb.] Professional Associations; [hon.] Numerous banking honors; [oth. writ.] Published 1995 "Seasons To Come"; [pers.] Due to my sisters "Doctor Donna Hall - TCU and Joy Johnson, Dalhart Texas I have expressed my personal beliefs into writing since 1968 and have just started to submit for publication. I have collected my poems into a book and have seen my growth as an individual expressed over the past twenty years. Writing is the best relief when taking doesn't work. I have read many poems through the National Poet Society and feel close to the writers.

MOORE, MADELINE R.
[pen.] Madeline Moore; [b.] December 23, 1934, Lake Charles, LA; [p.] Clare N. Moore and George H. Moore; [m.] Jack Ritter, John Hummel (Divorced), June 10, 1955; [ch.] Diane Ritter Whipple, Susan Clare Cade, Rebecca Hummel Moore; [ed.] The University of Texas: 1970 Ph. D, (English Literature) 1962 B.S. Education; [occ.] Free Lance Writer, Novelist Professor of english literature, University of California Santa Cruz; [memb.] The Virgin Woolf Society The Modern Language Association San Francisco Museum of Modern Art; [hon.] A. 1994: Discussion/order following Claire blooms performance of Virginia Woolf's Mrs. Dalloway Cowell Theatre, San Francisco , October 1, 1994, B. 1993: Invited by virginia Woolf society of Japan of lecture at 4 Universities on Virginia Woolf's Orland. Japanese tour took place in October, 1993, C. 1992: Winner of Second Annual Fiction Contest sponsor by Spintors Ink Book Company; [oth. writ.] 1. The Short season between two silences - George Allne and Unwin, 1984. 2. As you desire, spintors Ink, May 1993, 3. Poetry published in R.S.V.P, Highwashburg Literary Journal, Kingfisher, and Porter Gulch Review 1986-1994.; [pers.] In both poetry and fiction, I know that the initial rhythm in language determine the resulting the of entire work, my work involves a willingness to be vulnerable, while simultaneously maintaining the highest standards of craftsmanship. I am influences by Virginia Woolf's Style and her permission and by James Joyce's style.; [a.] San Francisco, CA

MORAN, TOBITHA R.
[b.] October 19, 1942, Americus, GA; [p.] Tom and Irene Reddick Moran; [ch.] Solita and Sol Moran; [ed.] Booker T. Washington High School and Keith Bible Institute, Chattanooga, Tennessee and City College, New York, New York; [occ.] Account Manager The Bank of New York; [memb.] The Gallon Club, Greater New York Blood Bank; [oth. writ.] Contributor short story to III Spring, an English class publication at City College, published a book of poetry "My Poetry, My Heart and Me" - Vantage Press, New York, NY, October 1987, contributed poems to two of The National Library of Poetry anthologies: "Blue Me" to Dance on the Horizon and "An African Connection" to Echoes of Yesterday.; [pers.] No one takes the sojourn through life without adversity, but with determination and perseverance anyone can overcome anything.; [a.] New York, NY

MORELLI, JOSEPH P.
[b.] June 14, 1968, Dearborn, MI; [p.] Frank and Mary Morelli; [m.] Lisa Ann Morelli, August 29, 1992; [ch.] Ashley Sarah Morelli; [ed.] Melvindale High School, Michigan State University (B.S.N.), Central Michigan University (completing masters Degree in administration); [occ.] Registered Nurse in CCU, Oakwood Hospital, Dearborn, MI; [memb.] American Heart Association (AHA), MSU Alumni Association, AACN - American Association of Critical Care Nurses, American Diabetes Association,; [hon.] CPR instructor VIA AHA, Research Assistant for "Family Matters Storyboard Project" in CCU and Oakwood Hospital, Permanent member of National Honor Society, including a scholarship winner, Member of "Who's Who among Students", Maintains nursing license in State of Michigan, Maintains Advanced Cardiac life Support Certification through AHA; [pers.] I continually strive to be the best I can be, and... to make everyone around me better.; [a.] Westland, MI

MORRIS, MICHAEL P.
[pen.] Michael P. Morris; [b.] August 11, 1956, Bennington, VT; [p.] Wilma Dennis, William Morris; [m.] Divorced; [ch.] Jeremy Cooper Morris; [ed.] G.E.D. Diploma and some College (Schenectady Country Community College) Student at Burnt Hills Music Academy; [occ.] Highway Maintenance Supervisor for New York State; [memb.] Guam - Ho - Ha Fish and Game Club, Fish Creek Boot Scooters Country Dance club, Singles Out Reach Services, Newtonville United Methodist Church; [hon.] Certificates of Appreciation from US, Army Fort Dix, Achievement Award Department of the Army Fort Lee Virginia, Honorable Discharge; [oth. writ.] Essays: Changes in the weather, my garden within, things that Annoy me and stepping in the puddles and various poetry and songs; [pers.] Writing, to me, is a reflection of the Soul turned out wards. The words I use and the stories I tell gives validity to my beliefs.; [a.] Mechanicville, NY

MORRIS JR., ROBERT L.
[b.] January 22, 1934, Norfolk, VA; [p.] Robert and Ruth Morris; [m.] Jacqueline Wright Morris, July 28, 1956; [ch.] Robert III, Vernon D. Beverly McConnell, Samuel A.; [ed.] Maury HS, Univ of Richmond BA Southeastern Baptist Theo Sem MDiv. Wesley Theological Sem D Min.; [occ.] United Methodist Pastor, Va. Annual Conf. Ret. U.S. Army Ch.; [memb.] VA. Nat'l GD Assoc, 82D Abn Assoc., tidewater, Cassia Masonic Ldge AF and AM, Middlesex Clergy, Lower United Methodist Church; [hon.] Doctor of Ministry, Wesley Seminary, Brigadier General, Virginia Militia (Un-organized) Legion of Merit, Bronze Star, Army Commendation Medal (2) all stated Band (VA) (2); [oth. writ.] Many unpublished poems and sermons. Doctrinal Dissertation: Job Descriptions in the local church.; [pers.] Poetry is a creative art form that conveys a message both in content and in appearance.; [a.] Hartfield, VA

MORRIS III, FRANK (CONWAY)
[pen.] Frank Morris; [b.] February 14, 1947, Pocatello, ID; [p.] Dr. Frank Morris, Lesley Morris RN.; [m.] Divorced; [ch.] Alyssa Morris, Shaun Morris; [ed.] Corvallis High, OSU (Oregon State) U of O (Oregon), Naropa Institute.; [occ.] Factotum; [memb.] Like Ground! I'd never belong to any organization that'd have me as a member.; [hon.] Jim Morrison said I was the only one who never up on him. Investigated by Secret Service for a poem about rush Jim Baugh.; [oth. writ.] Letter in Psychology today, poems, letters and editorials in Colorado Daily, poem in Denver's Red Wheel borrow.; [pers.] Strive to be the best darned chimneys sweep proctologist I can be. Being "an actor out on loan," drinking with and stopping few fights between Charles Bukowski and others while in coast guard got me ready for the upcoming darkness and rapturous union with the other.; [a.] Gunbarrel, CO

MORRIS, MCGUFFY ANN WISDOM
[b.] May 26, 1959, Chicago, IL; [p.] Max and Joyce Anne George-Parnell; [m.] William H. Morris, June 6, 1981; [ch.] Gwendolyn Teresa Morris; [ed.] High School Graduate. However I'm also a student of the "School of Hard Knocks."; [occ.] Wife, Mother; [memb.] Affiliations - Saint Peter Church, Animal Protection, Pow-Mia's (Vietnam) AKC (Shelties); [hon.] (NJROTC in high School); [oth. writ.] I have had several poems published, in various anthologies. I have written nearly 3,000 poems, since adolescence, but, my best is yet to come, as I'm still growing, as a person and poet.; [pers.] I am a wife and mother of one. I have several cats, and a blue merle Sheltie. Family is my anchor. I feel there is poetry in all of us, and therefore should not be limited in form or style, it is individual, yet universal.; [a.] Antioch, IL

MORRIS, JOHN C.
[pen.] John C. Morris; [b.] May 5, 1954, Lincoln, NB; [p.] Wilbur L. Morris, Martha Morris; [m.] Gail, April 1, 1994; [ch.] Paul Kenneth, Derick Raymond; [ed.] Truman High School, Electronics Institute, Missouri Western State College.; [occ.] Broadcast Engineer Student.; [hon.] Consistent honor roll when I now attend school (Electronics Institute of K.C.); [oth. writ.] Several poems and writings published in a church periodical.; [pers.] Walk .... Watch..... Hear.... Ask... Pray.... Play.... Contribute... Eat.... Give Thanks .... and Wipe your feet.; [a.] Grandview, Missouri

MORROW, JOHN ROBERT
[pen.] John Leslie Ross; [b.] October 31, 1955, Mooresville, NC; [p.] Ross and Pearl Morrow; [occ.] Owner-Contracting Firm; [oth. writ.] Several Song, Poems novel in progress.; [a.] Mooresville, NC

MORSE, SANDRA M.
[pen.] Sandra M. Morse; [b.] May 8, 1938, Batavia, NY; [p.] Charles and Marquerite Morse; [ed.] Alexander Central High School; [occ.] Factory Worker; [memb.] St. Vincent de Paul Church C.D.A. Ct 1012, Attica, NY, National Honor Society; [hon.] National Honor Society Award. Manke Home Economics Award Editor's Choice Award for the poem Look to the Rainbow, Editor's Choice Award for the poem a sad farewell.; [oth. writ.] Poems for C.D.A. Share Magazine, local newspapers, also writings and poems for P.W. Minor and Son, Inc. Shoe Factory Newspaper, the poem, A Sad Farewell, published in River of Dreams; [pers.] I like to bring out the Love of God, the beauty of nature and deep feelings in my poems.; [a.] Alexander, NY

MORSE, BRIAN ALLAN
[b.] February 15, 1957, Long Beach, CA; [p.] Seabert W. and Barbara J. Morse; [occ.] Furniture Maker/Artist; [a.] Temecula, CA

MORTON, JOSEPH
[b.] December 31, 1957, Bronx, NY; [p.] Joseph Morton and Eileen Morton; [m.] Elizabeth Morton, March 31, 1979; [ch.] Joseph Jr., Tracy, Michael, Kristen; [ed.] Brooklyn Technical High School; [occ.] Highway Construction Engineering Inspector of N.J. Dept. of Transportation.; [oth. writ.] Sunday, The Can Man, A Dad's Christmas Day. Soon to be published.; [pers.] I have always been inspired by other people's stories and feelings. I stop and talk with them all, Rich or Poor, I learn from them all.; [a.] Easton, PA

MOSELEY, JENNIFER
[b.] September 25, 1969, Houston, TX; [p.] Myron and Jessie Silcox; [m.] James Moseley, June 6, 1987; [ch.] Krysten Anna, Sophie Nicole, and Benjamin Scott; [ed.] Dropped out in 11th grade, but went back to get my GED.; [occ.] Mother, wife, homemaker; [hon.] I am honored to live the life I have. May awards are all the wonderful people who love me, especially my husband and children.; [oth. writ.] I have a journal in which I keep many other poems I've written, however none have been published or printed yet.; [pers.] All of my poems are written from my heart. My children are my world and influence me greatly. Children are what make the world worth while.; [a.] Corpus Christi, TX

MOSELLE, KYLE M.
[b.] December 18, 1974, Seattle, WA; [p.] Robert Moselle and Debra Knudson; [ed.] Graduated Thomas Jefferson High, Attending Pikes Peak Community College; [occ.] Working for a happier world; [memb.] American Poet's Guild, Life, Love, and the Joys of each.; [oth. writ.] "Wind through my heart," Amherst Society - American Poetry Annual "Your Special Night," Poet's Guild - Best New Poems; [pers.] Life is the most beautiful poem, yet very few people choose to read it completely. Some never open the book. Thank you to my Lord, my family, and my love, which have all allowed me to write a sentence in that back of life.; [a.] Colorado Springs, CO

MOSIEN, CARL B.
[pen.] Silver Fox; [b.] April 11, 1927, Chicago, IL; [p.] Blanch Henry Mosier (deceased) and Irene Mosier; [m.] Veola D. Mosier, June 11, 1950; [ch.] Irene and Carl Jr.; [ed.] Lindbloom High (Chicago) Wilson Jr. College (Chicago), Cortez Peters Business College (Chicago); [occ.] Retired Internal Revenue (Management Analysts); [memb.] Bethel A.M.E. church Vice President Men of Bethel Commission on Social and Political Action, Commission on Membership and Evangelism, Stewart Board and 1 Bethel A.M.E. church; [hon.] Chairman of Men's Day 1994-95 Bethel AME church Los Angeles, CA; [oth. writ.] Several poems published in the local News Express of Bethel A.M.E. church, Los Angeles, CA; [pers.] If my writing on poems will make someone smile than I will be smiling; [a.] Los Angeles, CA

MOSLEY, ANDREA N.
[b.] August 5, 1974, New Haven; [p.] Clarence and Doreatha Mosley; [ed.] Eli Whitney R.V.T.S. - High School Southern Ct. State University. A second semester Junior majoring in public health at the present time.; [memb.] Literary volunteers of greater new haven; [oth. writ.] Many unpublished poems, books and short stories.; [pers.] I want my words to anger, inspire, motivate and give hope to my people; [a.] New Haven, CT

MOTTOLA, DONNA MARIE
[pen.] Donna Marie Mottola; [b.] January 24, 1968, Newark, NJ; [p.] Frank and Frances Marchesano; [m.] Alfred Scott Mottola, November 11, 1989; [ch.] John Victor Mottola, Alfred Scott Mottola, Jr.; [ed.] Queen of Peace H.S., Occupational Training Courses; [occ.] Reservationist, Certified Vacations, Ft. Laud., FL; [a.] Plantation, FL

MOZINGO, CYNTHIA
[pen.] Cynthia Mozingo; [b.] December 2, 1963, Newark, NJ; [p.] Jessie Cedric Mozingo, Salli Ruth Mozingo; [ed.] Cittone Institute, Seton Hall University; [occ.] Systems Analyst, Solomon Brothers, Rutherford NJ; [memb.] Christ Church of Montclair, Solomons Womens Softball League; [hon.] AT and T Bell Laboratories outstanding accomplishment, two-time solomon Brothers BTO communications award recipient; [oth. writ.] Beyond the stone; [pers.] To deny the existence of God is to deny oneself the most precious gems life has to offer. The wisdom of his word, hope for tomorrow, joy unspeakable; [a.] Cedar Grove, NJ

MUDGE, STEVEN K.
[b.] December 12, 1971, Manchester, NH; [p.] Doris Lamarche; [ed.] Memorial High, Keene State College; [occ.] U.S. Army, Military Intelligence.; [oth. writ.] I have been influenced only by those individuals who are able to see, feel, and hear, with an aura, which is unseen, unfelt, and unheard of.; [pers.] Fort Meade, MD

MUHAMEDHAN, DEENA
[pen.] Deena Muhamedhan; [b.] April 27, 1956, Kazakhstan; [p.] Kayum, Farhinur; [ed.] Leningrad Adult Education Institute, Doctor of Education degree, Boston University, I'm graduating this May with Ed. M. in Education Administration.; [occ.] Participant of the program "Freedom Support Act" launched by US Congress in former Soviet Union and sponsored by US Information Agency; [memb.] Member of Kazakhstan, 1) Educator's trade union, 2) Environmental Defense Fund (here); [hon.] I was selected and awarded grant for gaining Ed. Administration degree; [oth. writ.] More than 40 works published in Kazakhstan, Russia and USA a result of the research and presentations at international conferences (Stanford, Harvard, St. Petersburg) on professional culture of educator, teacher trinity. Articles in newspaper (Kazakhstan) different topics.; [pers.] 1. Wise poetry speaks to hearts and minds of people of different cultures, languages and believes, 2. Overcoming of stereotypes is one of the ways out for building a better world to live in, for bridging countries and nations.; [a.] Boston, MA

MULLICAN, DERRLY RABB
[b.] December 14, 1937, New Orleans, LA; [p.] Isaac Alonzo Rabb and Catherine Smith Rabb; [m.] Thomas E. Mullican (deceased), November 20, 1965; [ch.] Kerrie Catherine 29, Kelli Anne 27, Kay Elizabeth 25, Kimberly Klare 22; [ed.] Graduated 1955 St. Mary's Dominican High N.D. LA, Attended Charity Hospital Sch. of Ngs., and UNO in New Orleans,; [occ.] Semi-Retired; [pers.] Widowed at age 38, and left to raise four young children alone I began to pour my joys, sorrow, as well as grieves into poetic expression. Thus this poetic art form became a constructive, as well as cathartie outlet for me, and remains that even to this day!

MUNDTH, BRIDGET
[pen.] Bridget Emily; [b.] August 31, 1957, Reedsburg, WI; [p.] Andrew Schyvinch, LaVonne Schyvinch; [m.] Larry Mundth; [ch.] Jeremy, Miranda, Justin Special friend David; [ed.] Webb High, MATC, Reedsburg; [occ.] Agricultural Engineer; [oth. writ.] I am currently writing a book of Inspirational Thoughts and have written other poems.; [pers.] There is good and positive in everyone and everything if you look deep enough. Believe in yourself. Follow your dreams. Listen to your heart. Success; [a.] Reedsburg, WI

MUNOZ, AURORA
[b.] April 23, 1943, Havana, Cuba; [p.] Javier Labrador and Hilda Hernandez; [m.] Jacinto Munox, July 16, 1960; [ch.] Juan C. Munoz, Maria E. Munoz, Beatrice Munoz Reina, Erika Munoz; [ed.] Montclair State College; [occ.] History teacher, Memorial High School, West New York, NJ; [hon.] Dean's List; [oth. writ.] Several poems in Spanish as well as in English. Encounter published by the National Library of Poetry in

the book seasons to come.; [pers.] Poetry is the open door to the caged soul, and the source of inspiration is the key to eternal freedom, that should be thanked forever.; [a.] Lodi, NJ

MURFF, DONNA L.
[pen.] Donna L.; [b.] September 10, 1952, Little Rock, AR; [p.] Floyd and Laura Pennington; [m.] Duane Van Murff, July 11, 1970; [ch.] 2 sons — Duane Van Jr., Casie Damont; [ed.] Associate degree Liberal Arts, Penn Valley Community College, Central High School; [occ.] Health Insurance Specialist; [memb.] Board of Directors of Eastwood Hills Association; [pers.] I love to express my experiences and feelings in my writing. I am a lover of life.; [a.] Kansas City, MO

MURPHY, LENA LATIMER
[b.] May 21, 1914, Cross Plains Carroll Country, GA; [p.] Bernice Latimer and Charlie Latimer (deceased); [m.] Hewlette Carter Murphy (deceased November 5, 1978), June 20, 1937; [ch.] Bernice Murphy Humphreys; [ed.] West GA College (Carrolton GA) business Math (a) accounting (a -) Kept books for 3 O.K. Vaughn; [occ.] 1 Furniture Stores (Retired) Newna GA from Post Office July 1980; [memb.] Mt. Carmel methodist church - member since August 1926 member of AARP; [hon.] (Gold medal 1924) Countywide 5th and 6th grade story writing (the automobile) I was 10 and in 5th grade (county wide - no previous knowledge of subject) Gold medal (1928) analysis of sentence contest county wide 8th and 9th grades - I was in 8th grade I was 14; [oth. writ.] Poem "After You've Said You Were Rob't Brennen - copyright 1933 soldiers returning from battle. Vol. V impressions copyright 1941 outstanding song poems and lyricists page 371. "There was an old covered bridge contentment" Recompensed" the exposition press on Spruce St. New York, NY; [pers.] Am thankful for christian parents - father played Banjo could play organ and piano, but left these instruments for my mother and younger sister - father a Stewart in Mt. Carmel Church until death in 1950; [a.] Newnan, GA

MURPHY, LANEA NAYLOR
[b.] April 20, 1981, Portland, OR; [p.] Malea Naylor; [ed.] 8th grader at Sellwood M.S. Grades 1-5 Lewis Elementary School; [occ.] Student; [memb.] Portland Park Swim Team, 1989-1992, Mt. Scott Swim Team 1988-1994, Boys and Girls Club Basketball 1992-1995; [hon.] PAL Scholarship 1992, Top Reader in March of Dimes 5 years 1988-1992; [oth. writ.] Several poems and stories creating literature windows for peaceable Kingdom Bookstore 1992-1995; [a.] Portland, OR

MURPHY, THOMAS JOHN
[b.] March 15, 1962; [ch.] Thomas J. Murphy Jr.; [occ.] Up and Coming Actor, Comedian, Singer; [pers.] I have been truly blessed with many talents. My hopes are to achieve my goal, and bring joy and happiness to everyone who has the chance to encounter me at my very best...; [a.] Rockaway Beach, NY

MURPHY, KRYSTAL
[b.] October 7, 1981, Philadelphia; [p.] Dorothy O. and Mike J. Murphy; [ed.] Holicong Middle School, Buckingham, PA; [occ.] Student; [memb.] Manager, Wrestling Team Member, Volleyball Team; [hon.] Got honor before 3 out of 4 times 1 year.; [oth. writ.] Nothing published, but, I do write stories and poetry.; [pers.] I learned how to put feeling and effort into my writing, because of past experiences. And, I would like to thank my Mom, for all of her support.; [a.] Plumsteadville, PA

MURRAY, ROBYN
[b.] July 27, 1971, Teaneck, NY; [p.] Melva and Cortland Murray; [ed.] Associate: Science Nursing. Associate: Liberal Arts Humanities. Passaic County Community College.; [occ.] Nurse; [memb.] Phi Theta

Kappa, Alpha Eta Chi - National Honor Society. National League of Nursing Member.; [hon.] "National Dean's List" Multiple Year Award.; [oth. writ.] Song writer. Two published songs, "Been hit by the backlash of love", "You're fizzin' to the top."; [pers.] "If you never get around to facing tomorrow, today means nothing!"; [a.] Paterson, NJ

MURRAY, DANIEL J.
[pen.] Frescyn Oland; [b.] September 28, 1937, Indiana; [m.] Nancy O'Farrel Rich-Murray, January 1979; [ch.] Bridget Murray; [ed.] Associate of Arts - drama Pasadena City College; [occ.] Historical Artist; [hon.] Superior Achievement in Telecommunications - 1967.; [oth. writ.] Friends - sung by Judith Collins 1971, Just a romantic notion - song - new 50's love ballad style; [pers.] Psalm 51, 2 Samuel 23:1-7, Zechariah 13:6,7, Deuteronomy 6:4,5.; [a.] South Bend, IN

MURRAY, DONALD W.
[pen.] Sonny Murro (Sometimes); [b.] April 30, 1924, Bolivar, MO; [p.] John A. and Effie P. Murray; [m.] Gloria, September 17, 1964; [ch.] Four; [ed.] 1 yr. College; [occ.] Retired from LA. State Police and Corrections; [memb.] American Legion - Texas Sheriffs Assoc. Louisiana Sheriffs Assoc. 'National Timberwolf Association, 104th Infantry Division.'; [hon.] Bronze Star, W.W. II; [oth. writ.] "Earth Up Above," song recorded by Jerry Lee and Linda Lewis.; [pers.] I have composed, approx. 200 poems and songs primarily as a hobby, hoping to some day getting them published. I was inspired to write "the trip" in hopes it would have an impact on our future generations.; [a.] Denham Springs, LA

MURRAY, JOE
[b.] April 26, 1973, San Pedro, CA; [p.] Tom and Rose Strye; [m.] Leah Murray, July 8, 1995; [ed.] North Douglas High School, Lane Community College; [occ.] Student at Lane Community College; [hon.] I have many awards from high school including student of the month for Language Arts, Music, computers as well as Douglas Co. skills contest certificates.; [oth. writ.] Other poems that have not yet been published. I am working on a short story at this time.; [pers.] Life is too short. Live each day to the fullest.; [a.] Curtin, OR

MURRER, LAURA
[pen.] Jetro; [b.] September 11, 1979, Rochester, NY; [p.] James Murrer, Kathy Murrer; [ed.] Gates Chili Middle School, Gates Chili High School; [oth. writ.] I wrote other poems, but I never entered them in any contests.; [pers.] I try to say how I feel inside when I write my poems. I also try to express what the real life around us is like in my poems.; [a.] Rochester, NY

MURRY JR., WILLIE
[b.] August 31, 1958, Isola, MS; [p.] Willie Sr., Ethel Murry; [m.] Gabrielle Maria Murry, October 20, 1988; [ch.] Daniel Alexander Murry, Amy Ruth Murry; [ed.] Allied Health Science Associate's Degree; [occ.] Don US air Force Medical Technician; [oth. writ.] Very much poetry

MUSARRA, CYNTHIA M.
[b.] April 14, 1964, Cleveland, OH; [p.] Sam and Frances Musarra; [m.] James D. Adam, June 2, 1984; [ch.] Amber and Kara Adam; [ed.] Strongville Senior High School; [occ.] VP of S.F. &C. Electric, Inc.; [memb.] National Multiple Sclerosis Society; [oth. writ.] I've written many poems as a teenager but never pursued publication.; [pers.] Live in "Today" not yesterday or tomorrow.; [a.] Medina, OH.

MUSE, CHARLES
[pen.] Charles Muse; [b.] August 18, 1966, Detroit, MI; [p.] John and Lenora Muse; [m.] Single; [ed.] High School Graduate, Robichaud High School; [occ.] Maintenance Tech.; [oth. writ.] Unpublished Book's - 1. Unknown Poem's, 2. Book of Lost Poem's, 3. Book of

Poemless Poem's, 4. Book of endless Poem's, 5. Name-less Poem's, 6. Hidden Poem's, 7. Timeless Poem's, 8. Forbidden Poem's, 9. Us and them, 10. Remembered poem's , 11. Book of Confusion, 12. Book of Reality, 13. Lost Feelings, 14. Book of Freedom, 15. Emptiness, 16. The Cold Room Experience, 17. Book of Stone, 18. Book of Fate, 19. Ride the Lightning, 20. Book of Serenity, 21. Book of the Aftermath, 22. Book of Mood's, 23. Book of Struggle, 24. Book of Change, 25. Useless Timespand, 26. Forgotten Poem's, 27. Missing Poem's; [pers.] The ink from my pen flows with life just as the blood flows through my vains.; [a.] Dearborn Heights, MI

MYERS, DELORES A.
[pen.] Dee Myers; [b.] April 14, 1929, Remer, MN; [p.] Sid and Millie Myers; [m.] Raymond Myers, August 21, 1949; [ch.] Keith, Cheryl, Judy, Marcia, Steven Randall-Bryan; [ed.] High School - L.P.N. Training; [occ.] (Now Retired) After 25 years of Nursing.; [memb.] Saint Joseph Hospice Volunteers, Our Saviors Lutheran Church M.R.S.E.A. (Minnesota Retired Senior Employee Association), R.S.V.P. (Retired Senior Volunteer Program); [hon.] Previous entries submitted approved for publication, by National Library of Poetry; [oth. writ.] Several poems printed in newspapers, magazines and bulletins.; [pers.] My writings reflect conscientious and religious through, with touches of caring and compassion. These are based on my life experiences, through its living.; [a.] Pequot Lakes, MN

NAEDELE, MOSES EDWARD
[pen.] Moses Naedele; [b.] October 26, 1967, Johnson City, TN; [p.] Carol Naedele; [ed.] Currently enrolled at Lexington Community College in Lexington, Kentucky; [occ.] Mail Clerk; [oth. writ.] I've written the lyrics to twenty-five songs for my rock band named GNARLY LOVE. I'm also the singer in the band. "Soup of life" and "collect a memory" are two songs I'm very proud of.; [pers.] Good poetry is a form of positive power. The power of poetry enables the human mind to shine and grow.; [a.] Lexington, KY

NANCE, LESLEE
[b.] December 12, 1969, Pomona, CA; [p.] Walt and Rochelle Hoylman, Ed and LuCrecia Nance; [ed.] H.S. Diploma - Covina High A.A. Degree in Psychology - Citrus College Life!!!; [occ.] Residential Aid; [memb.] Miracle Sunday Fund Organization - Secretary; [hon.] Dean's List High School, CSF Lifetime Member Covina High; [oth. writ.] Several unpublished poems. Newsletter for adult survivors of sexual abuse.; [pers.] I think it's an automatic giver that mothers and daughters have love/hate relationships. But it is through the power of growth and acceptance that can keep the bond strong forever. It takes less energy to love than to hate! I love you Mom.; [a.] Astoria, OR

NANCE, LESLEE R.
[b.] December 12, 1969, Pomona, CA; [ed.] Covina High - 1987, Citrus College 1993; [occ.] Residential Aid with people who have development disabilities; [memb.] Secretary of miracle sunday fun with leisure quest dance studio; [hon.] Deans List - CSF lifetime member Individual athletic awards - H.S.; [oth. writ.] I've written several poems approximately 15-20, however this poem marks the beginning of more to come.; [pers.] Life is never easy especially relationships. My writings are almost always influenced by my childhood - which I know reflects similar characteristics of others. Life isn't about winning - it's about the preparation; [a.] Astoria, OR

NAPOLI, PATRICIA
[pen.] Patricia Cox Napoli; [b.] February 27, 1938, Pittsburgh, PA; [p.] Geo and Agnes Cox; [m.] Joseph Napoli, November 12, 1966; [ch.] Angelo - 27, Mariak - 24, Joseph - 18; [ed.] Annunciation Grade School, Annunciation High School; [occ.] Homemaker, former Legal Secretary and Notary; [memb.] Nat'l Authors

Registry, Children's Book, Writers Society, Int'l Society of Poets, Poets' Guild, Int'l Society of Authors and Artists; [hon.] Poet of Merit Int'l Society of Poets, Honorable mention, Iliad Press, Three Editor's Choice Awards, Nat'l Library of Poetry. Certificate of Poetic Achievement, Poet's Guild, Certificate Artistic Merit Amherst Society; [oth. writ.] Reflection for Peace Minus War, Musings, Amer Poetry Anthology, Poetic Voices of America, The Best of Feelings, Westbury Anthology, Best Poems, 1994, and 1995; [pers.] Poetry is one of the most expressive ways to tell how you feel on any given subject and is a pleasure to read.; [a.] Springfield, PA

NASH, RUSSELL W.
[b.] February 25, 1921, Minneapolis, MN; [p.] Maurice W. L., Elsie E. Nash; [m.] Ruth L. Nash, February 1, 1944; [ch.] Andrew, Pamela; [ed.] BA. V. of MN 1943, MA Columbia U '49, graduate studies, New School for Social Research; [occ.] Retired College Teacher of Sociology; [memb.] AARP, NAACP, Dub. Co. Democratic Central Committee, "Question Box", Community Access Cable, TV show producer, Smith soniar Institution; [hon.] Associate Prof. of Sociology, Emerity, University of Dubuque; [oth. writ.] "Picasso News" (poems), Lyric Iowa poems, Dubuque fell Writers Guild Annual poems; [a.] Dubuque, IA

NAUGHTON, THENESE D. SPANIER
[b.] November 3, 1952, Minneapolis, MN; [p.] Oscar Spanier, Dolores P. Satiner; [m.] Kevin F. Naughton, May 26, 1990; [ch.] (step) Conor, Megan, Ryan, Monica; [ed.] Graduate Irondale H.S. 1970, AA degree in Nursing 1976, Metropolitan Community College, critical care speciality Parish Nurse program, Concordia College, Moorhead, MN, at Luther - Northwestern Seminary Feb-May 1995; [occ.] R.N. Cardiac Cathlob, Abbott - Northwestern Hospital Mpls, MN.; [memb.] Previous - Alfred Adler Institute, Minnesota Astronomical Society. Presents - The Left (A Literary Guild), Minnesota Nurses Association, Co-chair Professional Practice Council (ANW Hsp.); [hon.] Dean's List - 1 quarter Nursing School; [oth. writ.] Poetry and creative writing in high school and through the left in past; [pers.] I love people and am inspired to pursue professional writing for publication in future. My creative writing is primary of poetic nature with strong emphasis on love themes.; [a.] Saint Paul, MN

NAVARRETE, MARIE
[b.] April 28, 1964, Big Spring, TX; [p.] Al and Edia Hernandez; [ch.] Alicia Crystal; [ed.] Midland College, Baylor University Medical Center; [occ.] Radiation Therapist; [memb.] A.S.R.T.; [pers.] My poetry captures the essence of many experiences reflecting emotions, dreams and memories that will always linger.; [a.] Tucson, AZ

NAVARRO, ALBERTO S.
[pen.] Alberto S. Navarro; [b.] November 21, 1925, Tanauan Leyte, Philippines; [p.] Mr. and Mrs. Lucio Y. Navarro; [m.] Catalina Osit Navarro, September 22, 1951; [ch.] Alberto Faro, Ma. Bernardita, Ma. Gracia, Ma. Charito, Romeo Lope, Walden Leo, Ma. Evelyn, Rey Prospero, Twins - Thomas Edwin, Thomas Erwin, Twins - Joel Wilfred, Noel Winfred; [ed.] Elementary Teachers Certificate, Bachelor of Science in Education, Master of Arts (22 Units); [occ.] EXCEL Representatives, Executive II, NU-Concepts in Travel; [memb.] Philippine Public School Teachers Association - 1956 to 1985, Knights of Columbus SHJ Council No. 6325, American Association of Retired Persons, Philippine Scouts Heritage Society, Christian Concern for Filipino Veterans of World War II; [hon.] Meritorious and Outstanding Services Award by the Moncayo Public School Teachers Association (2 years); [oth. writ.] "The Dream of Veterans", Published by Famous Poets Society, 1994; [pers.] "A plant takes time and needs a fertile soil in order to bear fruit.; [a.] Los Angeles, CA

NAYLOR, MARK A.
[pen.] Mark A. Naylor; [b.] June 26, 1961, Marion, OH; [p.] Darlene and Keneth E. Kirby; [ch.] Tai Eugene, Justin Andrew, Cody Allen; [ed.] 12th Education with High School Diploma, Harding High School; [occ.] Restoration Tech; [oth. writ.] Many poems plus other real little poems; [pers.] Hoping everyone with enjoy my poems. Which mostly reflect upon real life, and maybe they will help people become more aware!; [a.] Newark, OH

NEAVES, ALICE
[pen.] Alice Neaves; [b.] April 26, 1959, Greer, SC; [p.] Mary Phillips and Joe Phillips (deceased); [m.] Marshall P. Neaves, February 24, 1981; [ch.] Brand Neaves, Adam Neaves; [ed.] Eastside High School, Greenville Technical College; [occ.] Housewife, Mother; [memb.] PTA, Pelham Road Elementary Volunteer, School Room Mother for EHP self-contained class. Pleasant Grove Baptist Church, Fountain Inn, SC; [hon.] Outstanding Young Women of America, Vice President of Student body Greenville Technical College; [oth. writ.] Poem published in School Literary Magazine; [pers.] I have post traumatic stress disorder due to childhood abuse. Currently I continue to write poetry and I am working on a book. My writings are healing for me and I hope they may reach out and help others with similar experiences to realize they are not alone.; [a.] Simpsonville, SC

NEDILKO, ANDREY G.
[b.] December 10, 1972, Stanitsa Kalnibolotskaya, Russia; [p.] Grigoriy M. Nedilko, Raisa A. Nedilko; [ed.] Kalnibolotskaya High School (Krasnodar region, Russia), Krasnodar State University (majoring in the English Language); [occ.] Exchange student at Texas Tech University September 94 - May 95, September 95 - June 96, student at Krasnodar State University; [hon.] High School Golden Medal, President Honor Roll (Texas Tech University); [pers.] The more one lives, the less he believes people, and the more he wants to believe them.; [a.] Stanitsa Kalnibolotskaya Krasnodar Region, Russia

NEEDHAM, LORA C.
[pen.] Lora C. Needham; [b.] December 18, 1952, Renton, WA; [p.] Floyd and Mona Wilson; [m.] Michael A. Needham, August 3, 1983; [ch.] Serena, Diana, Rebecca, Greg Brian and Echo; [ed.] Kentridge High BCIR Business College; [occ.] Flagger; [memb.] Mothers against drunk driving united we stand America St. Barbara's Church Blk. Diamond Ravensdale walter supply co. Volunteer; [pers.] The older I get, the more time I take to count my blessings. I wish peace to all mankind thru introspection.; [a.] Ravensdale, WA

NEES, PAUL D.
[b.] February 7, 1941, Hydro, OK; [p.] James Nees, Leta Nees; [m.] Dyan Nees, April 3, 1978; [ch.] Jennifer, Jeffrey, Jeremy, Jill, Juliet, Joni, Jonathan; [ed.] Putnam City High Yale University (U.S.A.F.); [occ.] Retired, 26 years - Southwestern Bell; [memb.] Telephone Pioneers of America American Association of Retired Persons; [hon.] 1964 United States Air Force - Air Medal -; [oth. writ.] Numerous other poems as yet unpublished.; [pers.] I enjoy writing all kinds of rhyming poetry. I am working on a childrens book at present.; [a.] Moore, OK

NEGRON, EUNICE
[b.] October 22, 1961, New York City, NY; [p.] Maria Cartagena Negron Nicholas Negron; [ed.] One Year Of College. Marymount Manhattan College (Liberal Arts).; [oth. writ.] Two children stories that were recently sent to the library of congress to be copyrighted. Hopefully they will be published one day.; [pers.] I love children and animals. I write about them and convey to youngsters the importance of loving and caring for animals of all different species.; [a.] New York City, NY

NEGRON, EUNIC
[b.] October 22, 1961, New York; [p.] Maria J. Cartagena Negron, Nicholas Negron; [ed.] Marymount Manhattan College 1 year of Liberal Arts; [hon.] Editor's Choice Awards; [pers.] My aspiration is to become a writer of children's books. I recently submitted a copy of a short story I wrote to the Library of Congress to be copyrighted, hopefully to be published. I love animals and I use them as characters in my stories. Through my stories I convey to children to love and care for all animals.; [a.] New York City, NY

NEIBURG, DAVID A.
[pen.] D. A. Neiburg; [b.] October 5, 1951, Derby, CT; [p.] Robert 1 and Thelma A. Neiburg; [m.] Sally Sue Crawford Neiburg, July 10, 1993; [ch.] Tamara Michelle Neiburg; [ed.] Willmar State Junior College University of Minnesota (Minneapolis); [occ.] Truck driver, firefighter; [memb.] Co A, 7th Ga Vol Inf (Civil War Reenactor), MENSA; [oth. writ.] Quest For The Unicorn, "When I'm Elected Dictator of the World", Surviving Chaos, various short stories, tales, and articles; [a.] Senoia, GA

NEITZEL, ERIKA L.
[b.] April 3, 1980, Cleveland, OH; [p.] Sally and Robert Neitzel; [ed.] Attending Orange Christian Academy in Orange, Ohio - High School; [pers.] Don't try to be something you aren't, if you give your natural ability a chance to grow, you could find a beautiful talent. And if people don't like it then they're not worth being around.; [a.] Macedonia, OH

NELSON, CARLA D.
[b.] May 10, 1969, Hanford, CA; [p.] Carl and Pat Nelson; [ed.] Bachelor of Science degree in Microbiology at CSU - Fresno, Hanford High School; [occ.] Medical Technologist El Camino Hospital, Mt. View, CA; [hon.] National Honor Society Dean's List - CSU - Fresno; [oth. writ.] I am proud to say that this is my first contest and publication. I'm ecstatic!; [pers.] I enjoy writing as a form of expression. There is much to be said about the lessons I have learned about myself and from those who have touched my life. I hope for continued growth and discovery.; [a.] San Jose, CA

NELSON, JONELL BOLANDER
[pen.] Jacqueline Dubois; [b.] April 17, 1950, San Antonio, TX; [p.] Magnus Bolander, Willie Bolander; [ch.] Christopher Bolander Nelson; [ed.] Stephan F. Austin, High School, University of Texas, B.A. Spanish '81. S.W.T.S.U. Lawyer's Assistant Program Certificated '87.; [occ.] Legal Assistant; [memb.] S.A.I. Music Fraternity, AATIA, Translators Association.; [hon.] Music Scholarships (2) in High School. SAI Rookie of the year. Elected Ethics Committed Chairman, member at large, CAPA.; [oth. writ.] Submitted story to Children's Writer's Magazine contest. Submitted poems for poetry review. Wrote column for CAPA. Unpublished poems to be published in future. Taking Children's Writing Course.; [pers.] The soul is the spirit by which we are creative.; [a.] Austin, TX

NEMEC, STEPHANIE
[b.] October 16, 1961, Cleveland, OH; [p.] James and Mary Nemec; [ed.] Orange High, Ohio University, Gonzaga University in Florence, Italy; [occ.] Director of Materials Management, CSA Health System; [memb.] American Hospital Association, Zeta Tau Alpha; [hon.] Poetry award in High School; [oth. writ.] Continue to create poems and songs. Songs used by several local musicians.; [pers.] I love the classical poets like Walk Whitman and his poem entitled "House on the Hill".; [a.] Lyndhurst Cleveland, OH

NESS, STEPHANIE JEANELLE
[pen.] Amy Michelle; [b.] October 21, 1979, Jamestown, ND; [p.] Mike and Trud Ness; [ed.] 9th grade, Sumner Jr. High; [memb.] Columbia House; [hon.] Lettered in Varsity Cross County, Basketball, Gymnastics and

Track. Ran The Sound To Narrows (7 miles run).; [oth. writ.] nothing published; [pers.] I write to think of my sister. I'm influenced by my father. I think that no one has a perfect life. If it seems perfect they have to be hiding something. I thank my parents for there support. I would rather give to a thousand people who don't know my name than have a thousand people give to me because of my name.; [a.] Sumner, WA

NEW, STEPHEN
[pen.] The New Guy!; [b.] February 16, 1958, Brooklyn; [p.] David and Catherine; [m.] Joanne, March 22, 1979; [ch.] James, Simone, Brandon; [ed.] 1 1/2 yr College, dropped out; [occ.] Direct Sales Mgr. I sell books business to business; [memb.] Sports Illustrated, Llama Pai Kung Fu School; [hon.] Stage plays - Lead role in 5 on the Black Hand Side, lead in Music Man Leading Pearly Victorious, lead in Ceremonies of Dark Old Men, Outstanding Sales Mgr., of the year 1985-1992 etc.; [oth. writ.] Screen Plays - "The Nuttiest Ninja", "Laughter and Tears", "Cold Blooded", "The Preacher that Never Showed Up", "Past Beyond". I have never been published or recognized. To say I'm honored would be a masterpiece of under statement. Bless you!; [pers.] Always follow your dreams!! God gave them to you. You must always listen to your inner voice. Self is everything! You can conquer yourself or be conquered by yourself. You would not dream dream if you didn't have what it takes to make it true.; [a.] Roosevelt, NY

NEWBURN, ANDREA
[pen.] Andrea Francelle; [b.] December 17, 1974; [a.] Bullard, TX

NEWMAN, RAY E.
[pen.] Joshua Light; [b.] April 27, 1953, Akron, OH; [p.] Ray B. and Dorothy I. Newman; [m.] Pamela Newman, September 26, 1982; [ch.] Brian, Laura, Michael Ray, Bobbie Jean.; [ed.] A.A. in Optics, cert. and lic. optician; [occ.] Supv. Customer Services and EI/QWL District Facilitator/USPS; [memb.] VFW, DAV, NALC, NAPS, Church of the Nazarene; [pers.] Perceptions are everything and nothing because so much of life escapes us. Truth is the key to wisdom, and wisdom is a gift to cherish.; [a.] Gallipolis Ferry, WV

NEWMAN, MARA LYSOVA
[pen.] M.E.L. Newman; [b.] Berlin, Germany; [ch.] Leslie M. Newman, Ronald P. Newman; [ed.] Educated in Europe and U.S.A. Lifetime Credential in Theatre Arts from CLC (California); [hon.] 1986 - Mayor's Award for the performing arts. October 14, 1986- The Ventura County Supervisor's Award for her contribution of the performing Arts in the county. Twice judge for santa barbara chapter of the National Society of arts and letters.; [oth. writ.] Currently working on a book, "Stories of the winter years." Compilation of 5 short stories, (fiction) also a book of selected poems.; [a.] Ventura, CA

NGUYEN, VINCENT
[b.] October 3, 1981, Chicago, IL; [p.] Hung Nguyen, Van Nguyen; [ed.] Hubble Middle School, Wheaton Warrenville South High School; [occ.] Student, Wheaton Warrenville South High School; [memb.] Royal Midwest Cruz Azul Soccer Club; [hon.] Five Tournament Soccer Championship; [oth. writ.] None. "Eyes of the Deer" is my first piece; [pers.] I have always been motivated by my dad. He taught me never give up in life. Always follow the sign of your heart.; [a.] Warrenville, IL

NGUYEN, DIEM T. N.
[b.] November 1, 1979, Vietnam; [p.] Le Huynh and Thanh Nguyen (Separate); [ed.] Richfield Junior High School (grade 8); [occ.] Baby sitting for a friend. (Every days); [hon.] Well, I'm on B's Honor Roll in school.

NICHOLSON, JAMES
[pen.] James N. Nicholson; [b.] November 5, 1965, Greenville, SC; [p.] Aaron Nicholson, Mary Nicholson; [m.] Gina B. Nicholson, August 8, 1988; [ed.] Mauldin High, Greenville Technical College Management Courses.; [occ.] Research and Development Technician; [memb.] Greenville Sniffs Association, Free Masons, most important membership is my family.; [hon.] This is my first; [oth. writ.] None published as of yet.; [pers.] I have written things on and off all my life, but only now am I starting to take it seriously. I like to write about how to make the world a letter place, peace, love, motivation, inspirational, etc. I would love to write my way out of life corporate jungle. I would like to try to work with a song writer. Country/rock.; [a.] Greenville, SC

NICOL, DANIELLE
[pen.] Danielle Nicol; [b.] August 7, 1946, Bulgaria, Europe; [p.] An-Marie Chan and Jordan Disney; [ed.] Philosophy and Sociology; [occ.] Restaurant Owner; [memb.] Business Community Association, Eagle Point, Oregon, Oregon Poetry Association; [hon.] Gold Medal Poetry at Sofia Bulgaria - 1984, PhD Philosophy, PhD Sociology; [oth. writ.] Novels, Poetry Books, Numerous of articles, essays, short stories, recitals Talk shows at Sofia, Bulgaria, Eastern Europe; [pers.] Poetry for me is a sanctuary, a way to let my soul fly free and undisturbed. It is a holy world where everyone and everything obeys to Her Highness's BEAUTY and His Majesty LIFE.; [a.] Eagle Point, OR

NIKKEL, KAREN
[pen.] Karen Nikkel; [b.] October 16, 1942, Newton, KS; [p.] Tillman Rodgers and Dorothy Hoffman Talbert; [m.] Leon Nikkel, January 31, 1960; [ch.] Vincent Nikkel, April 14, 1961; [ed.] Newton High School, LaSalle Extension University, continuing education at Emporia State Univ., and Butler County Community College, Victory Fellowship Bible College.; [occ.] Home Engineer; [memb.] Alexanderwohl Mennonite Church (33 yrs), American Quarter Horse Assn (Lifetime member), Australian Shepherd Club of America (23 yrs.); [oth. writ.] "The Master" in "Dark Side of the Moon", "Jesus' Smile" in "Echoes of Yesterday", and "Jesus' Love' in "Best Poems of 1995."; [pers.] Currently pursuing education through more Biblical training. All thanks, glory and honor for my poems, must be given to my precious Father, my Savior and Lord, Jesus and my loving Holy Spirit, without them I could do nothing. Praise God! Thank you my Elohim!; [a.] Lehigh, KS

NILLEN, JEANNIE
[pen.] Regina Marie; [b.] July 10, 1951, Houston, TX; [p.] Frank Usrey, Evelyn Borden Usrey; [m.] Ronald, July 15, 1972; [ch.] Kristin Marie, Rhonda Michelle; [ed.] University of Texas Medical Branch - Galveston. Degree in Biology Medical Technology; [occ.] Research Analyst, KRUG Life Sciences; [memb.] KRUG National Management Council, Galveston County 4-H Clubs, Arcadia Christian Church; [oth. writ.] Many other poems I have not attempted to publish.; [pers.] I have used my poems to express my feelings when I am unable to express them in any other way. Poetry is truly the mirror of my soul; [a.] Santa Fe, TX

NIXON, GRAHAM
[b.] March 16, 1982, Detroit, MI; [p.] Denise Graham, Md, and William Nixon; [ed.] S.U. Laboratory School (Middle School); [memb.] Young Astronauts Club, Quizbowl, Teens In Action; [hon.] Honor Roll; [pers.] I write whatever comes to my mind, because my mind and my pen flow together.; [a.] Jackson, LA

NIXON, KELLI
[pen.] M. K. Drew; [b.] October 7, 1978; [p.] Jeanne Nixon, Charles Nixon Jr.; [ed.] Dondero High School, Junior (currently); [occ.] Transportation Specialist; [hon.] Presidential Academic Fitness Award, Principal's List; [oth. writ.] Brainbows and Wordfalls (Junior High

Publication); [pers.] Don't keep your feelings bottled up. Take a stand, or you'll always be walked on or left behind.; [a.] Royal Oak, MI

NIXON, RICHARD PAUL
[b.] September 1, 1964, Tripoli, Libya; [p.] John W. Nixon, Helene W. Nixon; [m.] Wanda Louise Nixon, July 25, 1992; [ed.] Sligo Grammar School, Ireland Portora Royal School, N. Ireland Pierrepont School, England; [occ.] Systems Administrator; [oth. writ.] Working on personal novel; [pers.] "Open your eyes before old age robs you of your sight."; [a.] Melbourne, FL

NOAKES, TREVOR
[b.] March 8, 1974, Roseville, CA; [p.] Bob and Nancy Noakes; [oth. writ.] Currently composing folk-based songs with guitar; [pers.] "Keep the Magic"; [a.] Boring, OR

NOAKES, TREVOR
[b.] March 8, 1974, Roseville, CA; [p.] Bob and Nancy Noakes; [oth. writ.] Currently composing folk-based songs with guitar; [pers.] "Keep the Magic"; [a.] Boring, OR

NOHR, STEVE
[pen.] Steven Elliott; [b.] March 2, 1970, West Allis, WI; [p.] Marilyn Nohr, William Nohr; [ed.] Home Stead High; [occ.] Health Care; [oth. writ.] Short stories, currently working on a novel; [pers.] I always hope my writings reflect the bittersweet drama of life.; [a.] Thiensville, WI

NOLAN, BRUCE D.
[b.] September 4, 1929, Ft. William, Ontario, CA; [p.] Henry and Gladys Nolan; [ed.] Sir Adam Beck Collegiate, University of Western Ontario, London Teachers' College; [occ.] Retired; [memb.] Optimist Club - Life Member; [hon.] Life Membership in Optimist International (1986). London Teachers' College Student, Parliament's Honorary List; [oth. writ.] Articles for Uplands Times, (Ottawa), Canadian Press (1956); [pers.] I wish to break down barriers and build bridges between all people! I was greatly influenced by Philip Wylie's book "Generation of Vipers", and the writings of Kahil Gibran, in particular 'The Prophet'.; [a.] London Ontario, Canada

NORDSTROM, JANET M.
[b.] June 12, 1944, Texas; [p.] Ruth and Arthur Nordstrom; [m.] Divorced; [ch.] 5 Tony, Bobby, Jeffy, Lori, Tommy; [ed.] Basic and 2 years CVTC; [occ.] Exe. HSKP. International Franchised Hotel; [oth. writ.] Nothing but personal poems to children and grandchildren and friends

NORMAN, KENNETH L.
[b.] August 8, 1972, Orlando, FL; [p.] Agnes D. and James L. Norman; [ed.] Lake Howell High, University of Central Florida; [occ.] Walt Disney World Host; [oth. writ.] Personal writings; [pers.] Life is not a problem to solve or a race to win, it's a reality to experience.; [a.] Orlando, FL

NORRIS, CHRISTOPHER B.
[pen.] Chris Norris; [b.] October 12, 1966, San Antonio, TX; [p.] James Norris, Margaret Norris; [m.] Jessica Norris; [ed.] Lee High, San Antonio TX; [pers.] I try to instill the feelings of heart in my poems.; [a.] San Antonio, TX

NORRIS, MARK
[pers.] I am inspired by the writings of Thomas Jefferson, George Washington and Thomas Paine. I believe it is time to get back to the principles on which this country was founded.; [a.] Converse, TX

NORWOOD, ELMA CLARK
[p.] Dulie Elmos Clark and Willie Louise (Morris) Clark; [m.] Richard D. Norwood (dec.); [ch.] Daniel Richard Norwood, Jane Louise (Norwood) Williams; [ed.] Durant High Moody Bible College; [memb.] K Street Baptist Church; [hon.] The Salvation Army's Distinguished Service Award; [oth. writ.] Several poems and articles published in local newspapers. And church bulletins. Manuscripts: two books of poetry; [pers.] "Trust in the Lord with all your heart and lean not to your own understanding. In all your ways acknowledge Him and He shall direct your paths." Proverbs 3:5,6, Bible - "Others, Lord, yes others let this my motto be, help me to live for others that I may live like Thee." C. D. Meigs; [a.] Ardmore, OK

NOVEMBER, JEFF
[pen.] Porcupine; [b.] March 30, 1965, Anaheim, CA; [p.] Murray and Teri November; [ed.] Fullerton College, University of New Mexico; [occ.] Social Worker; [memb.] The Band "MUDFROG", Ickywood Lethargy Institute, Secret Luncheon Society; [oth. writ.] I am currently unpublished. Until now, I haven't attempted to be published. Maybe someday more of this will happen!; [pers.] Some make music out of Mayhem, others make Mayhem out of music. Follow a snails trail at least once a week.; [a.] Santa Cruz, CA

NOWITZKE, MICHELE
[b.] January 26, 1964, Detroit, MI; [p.] Richard and Margaret Manenty; [m.] Paul Nowitzke, November 22, 1986; [ch.] Neil Anthony and Catherine Theresa; [ed.] Edsel Ford High School, Henry Ford Community College; [occ.] Accounts Receivable Specialist, William Beaumont Hospital, Royal Oak MI; [pers.] If you're unhappy, pursue a dream, the more dreams you pursue, the more reason of why you are here.; [a.] Dearborn Heights, MI

NULL, STEVEN E.
[b.] May 3, 1958, East Saint Louis, IL; [p.] Henry Null, Carolyn Pezzini; [ed.] High School Grad., Stephen W. Kearny High, San Diego CA. 1 year College, Hartnell College Salinas CA.; [occ.] Gen. Manager Salinas Alano Club, Salinas CA.; [memb.] Salinas Alano Club, Salinas Chamber of Commerce; [oth. writ.] Numerous poems (unpublished); [pers.] Most of my writings are about personal experiences and trials coping with everyday life; [a.] Salinas, CA

NUNN JR., K. DAVID
[b.] July 9, 1978, Burlington, NC; [p.] Keith and Helen Nunn; [ed.] In High School; [memb.] Rocky River Bapt. Church; [hon.] District Band, Directors Award for band, Duke's Talent Identification program.; [oth. writ.] Many kept in notebooks none published.; [pers.] What I write doesn't have much meanings, I just write what I see and don't think others notice.; [a.] Siler City, NC

O'BRIEN, MELISSA
[b.] August 5, 1975, Cleburne, TX; [p.] Maryann and Tim O'Brien; [ed.] Conway High; [occ.] Dance Instructor; [memb.] U.S.G.F Member, Founder of E.D.C.A (Everyone Deserves Clean Air).; [hon.] 1988 State gymnastics champion, 1993-94 dance teacher of the year award, 3rd place winner of the library author award, and so on.; [oth. writ.] I've written other poems such as: sounds of silence, down the deepest depths, a distance apart, etc.; [pers.] Let the power of creativity rule your mind and guide your soul...; [a.] East Northport, NY

O'CONNOR, DANILE WARD
[b.] March 17, 1925, NJ; [p.] Daniel, Emma; [m.] Carolyn, June 26, 1954; [ch.] Kathlyn, Danile III; [ed.] Dartmouth: AB: 1945, Union: M.DIV: 1950, Columbia Univ.: MA: 1956, Columbia Univ.: Phd: 1960.; [occ.] Charles A. Dana Professor of Religious Studies and Classical Languages, Emeritus; [memb.] Rotary International; [hon.] Fellowships: Melon - 1969-70, Charles A. Dana - 1979. Charles A. Dana choir of religious studies and classical languages, St. Lawrence Univ., Canton, NY; [oth. writ.] "Peter in Rome: An Acheological, Liturgical, Historical study" Columbia Univ. Press, 1969. "Peter", Encyclopedia Britannica articles and reviews in numerous journals, Ex: JBU, JR. etc.; [a.] Canton, NY

O'CONNOR, MARY ELLA
[b.] June 5, 1978, Towson, MD; [p.] Herbert and Kathlee; [ed.] Maryvale Preparatory school currently a junior; [memb.] French and national honor society, field hockey basketball and lacrosse teams, treasurer of the student council, public relations club, literary magazine cast member of sounds of music; [hon.] First honors, university of Maryland leadership Conference Maryvale representative; [oth. writ.] Literary magazine contribute; [pers.] Three candles that illumine, every darkness: Truth, Nature, Knowledge, "An Irish Wisdom"; [a.] Towson, MD

O'HANLON, BETTY M. BOWERS
[b.] January 27, 1928, Hocking County Logan, OH; [p.] Florence Mauk Bowers and Washington Bowers, Sr.; [m.] Richard M. O'Hanlon, August 26, 1950; [ch.] Deborah Marie and James Richard; [ed.] Lofan High School, Bliss Business College, Columbus, OH (Diploma 4.) Credits from SUNY, Bridge Instructor Brenau College,; [occ.] Self employed typist....computer operator.; [memb.] United Metho. Church, D.U.V., MADD, NDTF, USS Constitution Museum, Nat'l Parks and Conservation Assoc., UMW.; [hon.] Humanitarian award in 1993 from the United Methodist Women's Club McEver U.M. Church, Pres. BPW, Eta Upsilon Gamma,; [oth. writ.] Editor: Chief Logan, Author is James Heinlein, Logan Daily News: By Line for High School News Column; [pers.] The poem, TREES made on everlasting impression on me and has influenced my feelings for God's world.... I see the beauty in it.; [a.] Oakwood, GA

O'HARA II, STEPHEN
[b.] April 8, 1978, Las Vegas, NV; [ed.] High School Student; [hon.] National Library of Poetry's Editors Choice award; [oth. writ.] Two other poems published in Darkside of the moon and Best of 1994 by The National Library of Poetry; [pers.] Are you lost with out your leader or are you the leader which is lost; [a.] Las Vegas, NV

O'NEAL, RAY W.
[b.] January 1, 1932, Trussville, AL; [p.] James and Pearl O'Neal; [m.] Divorced; [ch.] Teresa, Winifred, Peggy and Fred; [ed.] City College San Diego, CA; [occ.] Retired; [memb.] Christian Faith and the International Society of poets.; [hon.] Dean's List; [oth. writ.] Published in the "River of Dreams", the "Best Poems of 1995", the "East of Sunrise" and recorded in the "Sound of Poetry" and "Visions", also other poems in contests pending.; [pers.] Listen to the song of life and share discreetly.; [a.] San Diego, CA

O'NEAL, MAE REATHER
[b.] September 12, 1951, FL; [p.] Benny O'Neal Sr., Doretha Speed O'Neal (Deceased); [m.] Divorced; [ch.] Wendy Nicole Lawrence, Krystle Doretha Lawrence; [ed.] S.E. Business College - Job Corp Interlachen High School - Santa Fe Community College.; [occ.] Senior Word Processor; [memb.] Johnson Chapel Baptist Church; [oth. writ.] Few non-published poems; [pers.] For I pass this road of life only once - let me do a kind deed - say a kind word or just be of some service to someone in need; [a.] Gainesville, FL

OBAWOLE, DEBO
[pen.] Debo Obawole, Debor Richards; [b.] October 13, 1957, Lagos-Nigeria; [p.] S.A. Richards and A.N. Richards; [m.] A.B. Obawole, April 2, 1983; [ch.] Jimi and Emmanuel Obawole; [ed.] BA & MA Philosophy;

[occ.] Studying to become a nurse; [oth. writ.] Many unpublished poems and short stories; [pers.] I wish this earth would go back to its original state of purity in nature and man to live purity of mind.; [a.] Austin, TX.

ODEGAARD, ROBERT W.
[b.] October 26, 1959, Columbus, MS; [p.] Arthur Odegaard, Arline Sande; [m.] Sandy Odegaard, December 17, 1978; [ch.] Laura Lee, Kristen Leigh; [ed.] Wahpeton senior high school, North Dakota State University; [occ.] Seventeen Years in U.S. Coast Guard, Substance Abuse Counselor; [memb.] Chief Petty Officer Association, Girl Scouts of America; [hon.] Coast Guard Achievement medal, Navy Achievement medal; [oth. writ.] Several poems awaiting review; [pers.] I strive to write poems that are spontaneous, and generally based on spirituality, soulfulness and nature.; [a.] Honolulu, HI

OENNING, BRENT JAMES
[b.] March 8, 1974, Davenport, WA; [p.] Richard and Jeanette Oenning; [ed.] Ferris High School - Class of 1992, Washington State University - Majoring in Accounting/Finance; [memb.] Tau Kappa Epsilon Fraternity; [a.] Spokane, WA

OGILVIE, ELWOOD
[b.] April 14, 1920; [p.] Both deceased; [ed.] B.S. in English, A Master's in Gerontological subjects, topics, essays etc news articles senior citizens; [occ.] None, writing new books from biblical inspirations, compilings etc.; [memb.] Church, Schools is civics; [hon.] WW II Badges, stars overseas strips. Honors for pre-war-donation of war and post served the longest war services-town of duty in WW II; [oth. writ.] A prophet's Rosewall, Power of the New World personality, and spiriotherapy: Great inspirations as compiled from the Holy Scriptures - some of the greatest spiritual topics ever published - (Now being completed soon); [pers.] Poetry is the music of the soul, a theme of life and light. It is the highest form of prose. Healing power prevail, inspired by faith, hope, and love, poetic ideals become scriptural; [a.] Atlanta, GA

OLSEN, ANGELA MARIE
[pen.] A.M.O.; [b.] December 6, 1968, Iron Mountain, MI; [p.] Patricia S. Olsen, Jerry E. Olsen; [ed.] Hamilton College - B.A. Georgetown University, Catholic University of America - M.S.; [memb.] International Society of Poets; [hon.] Editor's Choice Award, Journey of the Mind - 1994; [oth. writ.] "The Rosebud" published in Journey of the Mind; [pers.] I have been strongly influenced by the Asian styles of writing and by my analytical studies of Shakesperian symbolism. I thank my professors at Hamilton College for their encouragement and support.

OLSEN, MARY JO
[b.] March 5, 1939, Los Angeles, CA; [p.] Sarah Jane Bolger, Jim Bolger; [m.] G. P. Olsen, July 2, 1980; [ch.] Ann Capp, Chuck Capp, Jennifer Capp, Tom Capp; [ed.] Immaculate Heart High School - Santa Monica City College U.C. LA.; [occ.] Artist; [memb.] Houston Art League - Water Color Society of Houston; [hon.] Many Juried Art Shows through out country; [pers.] Let the words speak.; [a.] Houston, TX

ONG, JEFFREY
[pen.] Jeff, Jeffrey Ong; [b.] January 12, 1989, Phoenix, AZ; [p.] Jim and Gloria Ong; [ed.] Freshman at Thunderbird High School, Attended Mountain Sky and Catalina Ventura middle schools, and Sevilla Elementary School, Phoenix, Arizona.; [occ.] Freshman at Thunderbird High School; [memb.] Writer for Thunderbird High School Newspaper (challenge) staff, Organization for Multi National Interests (OMNI), Publications Club; [hon.] National Junior Honor Society, Principal's list, Vice-President of Sevilla Student council, Superior ratings at ASMTA (Arizona State Music Teacher's Association) Piano recital at Arizona State University ASMTA piano ensemble, secretary of OMNI, student of the month; [oth. writ.] Published in Jr. High poetry book, story written for young author's week book sale, staff writer for school paper; [pers.] My family's love and support have given me the desire to enjoy doing the best I can, whether it be in school or in day to day activities.; [a.] Phoenix, AZ

ONOFRE, DALMY
[b.] February 15, 1962, Brasilia, Brazil; [p.] Divino Onofre Gomes and Maria Abreu Onofre; [ed.] Henry Ford Community College - English Major, in Detroit.; [occ.] English Teacher at the University of Detroit Mercy, Detroit; [hon.] Certificate of Proficiency in English from the University of Michigan, MI; [oth. writ.] Several poems published in local newspapers. Won two poetry contest at Henry Ford Community College.; [pers.] I strive to reflect the goodness of mankind in my writing. I have been greatly influenced by my own experienced.; [a.] Detroit, MI

ONYENYEONWU, LETICIA HEANYI
[pen.] Leticia Heanyie Onyenyeonwu; [b.] May 9, 1967, Onitsha; [p.] Mr. and Mrs. P. O. Onyenyeonwu; [ed.] 1. B.A. (Hons) English University of Ibadan, Nigeria 2. MBA: Fayetteville state university, North Carolina (ongoing); [occ.] M.B.A. Student; [hon.] NBMBAA Scholarship award, NYSC Director's Award for excellence, FSU chancellor's Honor Roll. High School Debate award for excellence.; [oth. writ.] 'Black American reality'- 1988 'Dynamics of leadership, moving principles into action' - 1994. 'Career mobility of African Americans' - 1995; [pers.] Artistic creativity is a soothing balm to the Enigma of life.; [a.] Fayetteville, NC

OPSKAR, JOHN L.
[b.] December 4, 1972, Duluth, MN; [p.] Jane and Paul; [ed.] High-School, Western Michigan University; [occ.] Student at Westein; [pers.] This is the first piece of work I have published. For anyone who is trying to get publish for the first time, keep trying. It will happen.; [a.] Belmont, MI

ORLANDI, CAROLINE M.
[b.] May 6, 1925, Philadelphia, PA; [p.] Agatha and Joseph Negro; [m.] Albert, August 30, 1940; [ch.] Carole Barr, John Orlandi; [ed.] Hallahan Catholic H. Berlitz School; [occ.] (Retired) Teach Italian Lessons - Interpret and translate Italian; [memb.] Italian Americans of Del. Co. Sons of Italy Lodge - Literary Club NY, Lion's Club, OISA Wash. DC. community club-PHLA. PA.; [hon.] Amer. Legion Medal Poetry Awards-World of Poetry Honors in Italo-American Drama Honors in Teaching Italian language Honors in Playing for Day Care Group Chaplain of four chaplains; [oth. writ.] Short Stories, Genealogy of Family Roots; [pers.] I enjoy writing poems for birthdays, weddings, babies, also the sick and those in sorrow. I am a retired librarian in Phila PA and make calls for friends; [a.] Philadelphia, PA

OSBOURN, CIELLE LORD
[b.] December 29, Northern England; [p.] William Lord, Lillian A. Lord; [m.] Lt./Col. USAF Albert W. Osbourn (Deceased); [ch.] Gayle; [ed.] Private School Stand Grammar School, England Burroughs and Greenwood Business Colleges. An Inst. of Banking.; [memb.] Am. boucer Soc., U.S., Humane Societe, The Okaloosa, Symphony League, USAF Open Mess.; [oth. writ.] Short stories and poems for children.; [pers.] During my role as "co-pilot" in an Air Force marriage, we were stationed at Lackland A.F.B. Texas. Due to the distance between the Base ad San Antonio, the availability of recreational facilities for children and teenagers was practically NIL, so, I started a "Children's Theater" comprising Ballet and Music Appreciation and also a "Modelling and Finishing" course for teenagers. The poem "Dancing Class" was inspired by the beloved children who attended with such dedication and devotion. If my words can touch and illuminate the soul of one single person - I to shall not have lived in vain.

OSBURN, NICHOLAS G.
[b.] April 8, 1977, ID; [p.] Terry Osburn, Margaret Osburn; [ed.] Currently enrolled as High School Senior; [occ.] Student; [memb.] Pres. German Club, V.P. Math Club, Key Club, German American Partnership Program, National Honor Society, Marching Band, Pep Band, Concert Band, Boy Scout Troop 455, Washington Cultural Exchange with China; [hon.] Eagle Scout, B.S.A., United States Achievement Academy All American Scholar, 1992, 93, 94, Distinguished Scholar, Washington Interscholastic Activities Association, 1993, 94, Who's Who among American High School Students, 94, 95 National Science Merit Award Recipient; [a.] Renton, WA

OSTROFF, CHRISTINA
[b.] April 4, 1978; [p.] Vickie and Kevin Ostroff; [ed.] Present student at the Colony High School; [oth. writ.] Unpublished poems, short stories; [a.] The Colony, TX

OTOSHI, YOSHIYUKI
[b.] July 23, 1920, Hiroshima, Japan; [p.] Asazo Otoshi, Tamano Otoshi; [m.] Betty Kiyoko Otoshi; [ch.] Grant Yukio and Beverly Yukino; [ed.] McKinley High School (Honolulu), American Institute of Banking (Standard Certificate); [occ.] Retired since 1985, after working 43 years with the First Hawaiian Bank as an Accountant.; [memb.] Honolulu Japanese Chamber of Commerce, Hawaii Economic Study Club, Honpa Hongwanji Mission of Hawaii, Japanese Cultural Center of Hawaii.; [oth. writ.] My poem, "Of Tassels in the Wind" was selected for printing in the anthology, JOURNEY OF THE MIND (Library of Congress ISBN 1-56167-263-7), "Bits of Beauty" was also A MOMENT IN TIME (Library of Congress ISBN 1-56167-266-1). And, current selection, "A place on Earth I love to be" in forthcoming anthology EAST OF THE SUNRISE (Library of Congress ISBN 1-56167-268-8).; [pers.] I became a naturalized citizen of the United States of America on February 26, 1953—it was a proud and happy moment of my life. To my Senior Class (1938) Core Studies teacher, Mrs. Mary Robey Harris, I am deeply grateful for first opening my eyes and mind into literature and poetry. With thoughts and deeds, however puny they may be, I strive to make our world a bit more beautiful.; [a.] Honolulu, HI

OTTLEY, ANDRIA A.
[pen.] Shorty Roc; [b.] July 7, 1975, Brooklyn, NY; [p.] Ursula Ottley, Ulrick Ottley; [ed.] High School (Brooklyn Technical High School) College St. John's University) 2nd year biology major; [pers.] This poem reflects a stage in my life that I had to get through. Although this was a very stressful and depressing time for me I was able to overcome it with the help of God, my family and dear friend's. I would especially like t thank my cousin Cameron and dear friend Deirda for always listening and lending support.; [a.] Brooklyn, NY

OUELLETTE, MIRIAM
[b.] August 25, 1979, La Paz Bolivia, South America; [p.] Jim and Joan Ouellette; [ed.] Northeast Regional Catholic School (K-8 grade), presently I am attending Unity High School. I plan on going to college.; [memb.] I am presently on the year book committee, the French Club, the Drama Club, and I like to be a manager for various sports like volleyball, wrestling, girls basketball, softball.; [hon.] Many Honor Roll Awards, Civic Oration Award (speech) French Award.; [oth. writ.] Speech/Biography on Anne Frank, Another poem "I love my parents", published in Anthology of Poetry by Young Americans, which tells of how and why my parent adopted me.; [pers.] I only want people to enjoy rending my poems. My poems are usually loosed on my past experiences. I believe I have to express my thoughts and experiences in words. This is how I do that.; [a.]

Milltown, WI

OUTLAW, MICHAEL TOD
[pen.] Tod Outlaw; [b.] May 22, 1958, Clifton, TX; [p.] Clyde Outlaw, Katie Outlaw; [ed.] Clifton High School (Valedictorian), Baylor University (BBA-1979), Tarleton State University (MBA-1982), East Texas State University (MS-1994), East Texas State University (E.J.D. Candidate-19945); [occ.] Instructor; [memb.] Who's Who, Kappa Delta Pi; [pers.] Take an adventure by read Robert Frost's collection of poetry.; [a.] Clifton, TX

OUTLAW, TAHLMA
[b.] May 11, 1911, Norility, TX; [p.] Burby B. and Ida May Golden; [ch.] Nancy Jane Wible Fike; [ed.] Graduated from high school at East Texas State Teacher's College, now ESTu TOOR, several classes at LA City Colleges; [occ.] Retired from Pacific Bell; [memb.] Telephone Pioneers of America, AARP, Chruch Missionary Council; [hon.] Excerpt from my essay printed in the new book, "In the Spirit of Service," won second prize on senior mobile home living poem contest put on by three large mobile home parks.; [pers.] I like to write about beautiful things, no trash.; [a.] Riverside, CA.

OUTTEN, LILLIAN AUGUSTA
[pen.] Lillian Outten; [b.] November 15, 1953, Free Port, Bahamas; [p.] Louise Cecilia Outten; [ed.] Owens Town High School Androes Bahamas.; [occ.] C.N.A. Certified Nursing Assistant. At home nursing Miami FL

OVERSTREET, BARBARA WRIGHT
[b.] October 19, 1957, Sanford, NC; [m.] Tillman G. Overstreet (3rd); [ch.] Tia and Tillman J. Overstreet; [ed.] (New York) P.S. 123, Shimer JHS, Richmond Hill HS, Hunter College-BA and MS; [occ.] NYS Division of Parole; [memb.] Mt. Morris Ascension Presbyterian Church and choir, Mt. Morris Park Community Improvement Assoc., 100 Black Women; [oth. writ.] Gospel song "Still I Rise"; [pers.] Singer and songwriter (gospel, rhythm and blues). Guest soloist performer at NY Cotton Club Gospel Brunches. Motto: "With God All Things Are Possible"; [a.] New York, NY

OWEN, JACKIE
[b.] July 30, 1972, Fort Benning, GA; [p.] Joe James and Debra Palmer; [m.] Don Owen, August 20 1993; [ch.] Brittany Ashden Troxtell; [ed.] Gallup High N.M. OKC Barber College; [occ.] Student, mother and housewife; [oth. writ.] I've wrote several poems. I wrote one on the behalf of my great grandmother, Grace McGee. Thoughts of her will always be with me.; [pers.] I can always look back at the past, and look forward to the future. Every poem has it's own meaning. Mine comes straight from the heart.; [a.] Davenport, OK

OWENS, REGINALD R.
[pen.] "El Cid"; [b.] August 26, 1938, Philadelphia, PA; [p.] Reginald and Clare Owens; [m.] Barbara K. Leroux Owens, July 6, 1970; [ch.] Reginald, Andreas, Julie, Lisa, Gregory, Janette, Anastasia; [ed.] North East High, Upper Iowa Univ (BA), Central Michigan (MA), and Columbia Pacific (Ph.D.); [occ.] President, International Management Enterprises, Inc; [hon.] Outstanding Young Man of America (1972), Military: Meritorious Service Medal, Bronze Star Medal, Two Commendation Medals, Vietnam Service Medal and Nine (9) others.; [oth. writ.] Poems printed in various publications and magazines both here and abroad.; [pers.] My work as a business person, painter, poet, composer and writer is deisgned to reflect the human spirit and experience as seen through my eyes.; [a.] Downingtown, PA

PACE, CHARLOTTE
[b.] November 14, 1943, New Orleans, LA; [p.] John Q. and Sarah Adams; [m.] James Mark Pace, November 6, 1976; [ch.] John, Guy, Anneli; [ed.] B.S. - Florida

State University, M.Ed. - Southeastern La University; [occ.] Retired from Federal Civil Service - former Army Officer and School teacher (english and language Arts in Florida and Louisiana) for 10 years each.; [hon.] Numerous Awards for performance excellence in the Army and in Federal Civil Service. Summa Cum Laude graduate (4.0 average) in Masters Degree program.; [oth. writ.] Published two previous professional articles on information (automation and communications) support in Army peace time environment, and to Operation Desert Storm.; [pers.] Concentration on the positive - they joy of life, the beauty of love, the power of the human spirit; [a.] Sierra Vista, AZ

PACHECO, WENDY
[b.] March 11, 1961, New York City, NY; [p.] Antonio Pacheco, Gloria Pacheco; [m.] Lawrence A. De Joseph; [ch.] Fernando, Jose, Damaris Isabel, John Anthony; [ed.] Evander Child's H.S., Hunter College; [occ.] Sales Assistant; [hon.] Gladys Rapp Award, Bronx District Attorney Award, Bronx Borough President Award for Participation in Bronx Week, Honor Roll; [oth. writ.] Several poems in High School yearbooks; [pers.] I am inspired by those I love and the moments we share.; [a.] New York, NY

PACQUING, SHAMMA
[b.] September 11, 1977, Salinas, CA; [p.] Sandra Bacon and Mario Pacquing; [pers.] In this particular poem, I create love as a person. A person that can destruct, cause pain, and give life. Many are not spared by love and only a few are blessed.; [a.] Eureka, CA

PADILLA, TAMI
[pen.] Tami Lynch; [b.] July 14, 1973, Arcadia, CA; [p.] Alexander and Lynn Padilla; [ed.] Fountain Valley High School, graduate, A.A. degree, working on BA in Education at CSULB with minor in language arts.; [occ.] Teacher's Aide; [hon.] Star Certificate in Performing Arts; [pers.] I believe that time is valuable and must be used wisely in order to not repeat mistakes of the past. I like to write poetry to make my readers think about mankind and both its positive and negative aspects.; [a.] Fountain Valley, CA

PADILLA, CORA T.
[b.] October 31, 1966, Walsenburg, CO; [p.] Pete and JoAnn Martinez; [m.] Adam C. Padilla, February 8, 1986; [ch.] Bianca, Briana, Brittany; [ed.] West Las Vegas High School Las Vegas N Mix; [occ.] Housewife and Mother; [pers.] First time I ever wrote a poem. Was written for my husband.; [a.] Greeley, CO

PAGE, CASSIE L.
[pen.] Casandra Tee; [b.] August 27, 1981, Worcester, MA; [p.] Joseph R. and Debra J. Page; [ed.] Trinity Catholic Academy, Paxton Center School.; [occ.] Student, future artist and writer; [memb.] Drama School Club; [hon.] Honorable mention for my first water color. First prizes in different Craft items at local fairs, first prize in book marker contest; [oth. writ.] First book written in childhood "win your wings" and many other unpublished stories and novels not knowned yet.; [pers.] I want to thank my closest inspiration, nature and imaginary things that help me create all I do.; [a.] Paxton, MA

PALMER II, JAMES WHITCOMB RILEY
[pen.] Jim Palmer; [b.] July 26, 1964, Fort Worth, TX; [p.] Kora Lea Palmer; [m.] Kellie Ann Palmer, April 2, 1987; [occ.] Shop foreman of Ford Dealership.; [pers.] Write to release feelings inside me. This poem was written after my wife left me in search of herself. Still separated as of now.; [a.] Burleson, TX

PALMER, FRANCES P.
[b.] December 20, 1909, Rockport, IL; [p.] William Hoskins, Maude Hoskins; [m.] Edmund R. Palmer, April 18, 1930; [ch.] Dr. Russell G. Palmer; [ed.] New Canton Ill. Community High, Western College,

Macomb, Ill., Elementary School Teacher; [occ.] Retired; [memb.] 55 yrs. Arch St. United M.E. Church, Mark Lwain Senior Citizen, Center R.S.V.P.; [pers.] Love is the most important possession on earth. Being kind to everyone, and having an attitude of caring, will lead to love, and enhance the civility of mankind.; [a.] Hannibal, MO

PAMIN, DIANA DOLHANCYK
[pen.] Diana Dolhancyk; [b.] December 13, Cleveland, OH; [p.] Peter Dolhancyk, Diana Dribus Dolhancyk; [m.] Leonard Pamin; [ch.] Diana Anne, Louis Peter; [ed.] West Tech High, Titus College of Cosmetology; [occ.] Hobbies Interior Decorating, Art, Music, Books,; [memb.] Arthritis Foundation, I've sponsored a young girl in India for the past 15 years. My roots begin in Europe (Russia); [hon.] Editor's Choice Award for "The Parting" published in "Journey of the Mind"; [oth. writ.] "Stormy" published by National Library of Poetry in "Songs on the Wind"; [pers.] Always give someone a smile, you'll never know whose heart you might lighten. I strive to see beauty in all things. I wrote my first poem at age 12. I wanted to be a singer, dancer, writer, in the arts, anything creative.; [a.] North Royalton, OH

PANCOAST, MICHELE
[pen.] Michele; [b.] April 7, 1969, Farmington Hills; [p.] Lorraine Hipkins, Michael Pancoast; [ed.] Going to college at Detroit College of Business, my major is Legal Secretary. Graduate in 1998 with Bachelor's Degree.; [occ.] Liquor Coordinator; [hon.] Scholarship to attend Detroit College of Business for 2 years. And that my poem (bless me) will be published.; [oth. writ.] Wrote other poems but haven't been published.; [pers.] I really like to write poems, they inspire me. All I need is just a title and I go from there. Which is a rare talent.; [a.] Westland, MI

PANNELL, JULIE A.
[b.] September 3, 1970, Virginia; [p.] Ray and Nina Ashley; [m.] E. G. Pannell, June 13, 1992; [ch.] Ashley Danielle Pannell; [ed.] Nelson Country High School, Piedmont Virginia Community College, MJH - CATEC School of Practical Nursing, USNY; [occ.] Nurse; [memb.] Rockfish Valley Volunteer Fire Department and Rescue Squad, Blueridge Chapter Multiple Scelerosis Society; [oth. writ.] Unpublished poems and short stories; [pers.] I suffer with multiple schlerosis and my poetry and writings are just another way I use to express my feelings and thoughts.; [a.] Faber, VA

PAPACCIO, PHIL
[b.] October 6, 1934, Bayonne, NJ; [p.] Lucia and Biagio Papaccio; [m.] Jonna Lee Papaccio, October 6, 1959; [ch.] Patrick, Joseph, Lisa, Susan; [ed.] St. Peter's Prep High School, U.S. Naval Academy - Bachelor, Univ. Southern California - Masters; [occ.] Retired, former Vice President TRW Inc.; [hon.] Beta, Gamma Sigma, Meritenious Service U.S. Air Force; [oth. writ.] The Cultivation Of Creativity Paper for U.S. Air Force, Software Productivity, several papers and articles on the Management of High-Tech Organizations; [pers.] In my writing I try to reflect the inner journey. I have been greatly influenced by the great spiritual teachers, founders of religions and thought past and present.; [a.] Rolling Hills Estates, CA

PARDOE, ROBERT C.
[b.] September 4, 1934, Franklin, PA; [p.] Mr. and Mrs. Benjamin H. Pardoe; [ed.] Academy of Psychiatry - Warren, PA/Norristown, PA US Air Force Medical and Surgical Academy, Washington, D.C.; [occ.] Retired - Psychiatric Technician; [memb.] The Veterans of Foreign Wars, The American Legion, The Loyal Order of Moose; [hon.] Two Academy Awards - World of Poetry; [oth. writ.] Fifty-six poems; [pers.] A life, is but a moment in time. May a poem make someone happy in that moment.; [a.] Grove City, PA.

PARHAM, ALISON N.
[b.] September 8, 1981, Richmond, VA; [p.] Annette R. and Keith L. Parham; [ed.] King and Queen Elementary School, Central High School, King and Queen County; [memb.] Future Business Leaders of America, Future Homemakers of America, First Baptist Church, Hockley, Junior Usher Board and Junior Choir, Eighth Grade Class Treasurer; [a.] Shacklefords, VA

PARK, KELLY
[pen.] Kyungwha; [b.] January 27, 1985, Barberton, OH; [p.] Youn W. Park, Kay Park; [ed.] Our Lady of the Elms Elementary School; [memb.] Mini Maestros; [hon.] Scholarship, Silver Trophy for Korean Chicago Times Book Review Contest; [oth. writ.] Several unpublished stories, books, and poems; [pers.] I am encouraged to write about the world around me and what I experience; [a.] Akron, OH

PARKER, MAX GREGORY
[b.] May 23, 1959, Wurzberg, Germany; [p.] Clay Parker, Ann Parker; [ed.] Madison East High University of Wisconsin; [occ.] RCT- State of Wisconsin, and Security Officer; [memb.] American Red Cross First Aid; [hon.] State and Regional Pop-a-shot Champion, employee of the month, RC Cola Grand Prize Winner; [oth. writ.] Employee Quote of the Month: There's No Motion Like In Motion.; [pers.] I strive to have a positive attitude, winning is my natural habitat, I must win again, and I will win again.; [a.] Madison, WI

PARKS, LOU HENSLEY
[pen.] Lou Hensley Parks; [b.] April 29, 1938, Mexia, TX; [p.] Lucy L. Denmon and William H. Hensley; [m.] Joe P. Parks, April 8, 1993; [ch.] Dan McNabb, Bart McNabb, Tim McNabb, Lance McNabb, Tamera M. Day; [ed.] High School and College various courses, Houston, TX.; [occ.] Retired from legal work I was a legal assistant for years.; [memb.] Hill of God Church, Joshua, TX, Former Member National NLA, State TNLA and Houston HNLA and Fort Worth Assn. of Legal Secretaries Assts.; [hon.] Several awards connected with my work.; [oth. writ.] Various connected with memberships in former organizations, some in religious papers and bulletins, etc. nothing widely acclaimed.; [pers.] I wrote my first song at age 12. It was about my mother. Never written professionally, although I've been urged over lover to try to break into it especially for greeting cards, etc. Poetry comes from my heart, so does my religious writings also from what I know of Christ, God, Love and Life.; [a.] Alvarado, TX

PARRISH, RAJONDA E.
[pen.] Jonnie; [b.] November 15, 1962, Dundee, FL; [p.] Wanda and James Fenley; [ch.] Steven and Erik; [ed.] Haines City High School; [occ.] Homes of Merit; [oth. writ.] Personal Journal, Songs and many poems.; [pers.] I have been writing poems since the age of 12. My friends encouraged me to send this one in. It's my first time. I have many other poems. I'm a romantic!; [a.] Winter Haven, FL

PATE, LEI ANN
[b.] November 19, 1968, Knoxville, IN; [p.] Nancy Pater and Jerry Pate; [ch.] William Christopher Pate; [ed.] Nova High, Ft. Lauderdale Fla., Knoxville College; [occ.] Service Representative, Social Security Admin.; [hon.] Dean's List, Who's Who Among Students in American Colleges and Universities, 1992; [pers.] Childbirth is poetry. Death is poetry. Poetry is the facade of life. Every living thing is a stanza in the poem of creation.; [a.] Knoxville, TN

PATTERSON, JESSICA-ROSE O'KEEFFE
[b.] July 27, 1983, Lakewood, NJ; [p.] Patricia Anne Patterson and Alan James O'Keeffe; [ed.] Student 5th Grade Elementary #II Middle Township Cape May Court House, NJ; [occ.] Student; [oth. writ.] This was my very 1st poem. I wrote it in about 45 min. After I saw the Add for your contest.; [pers.] I am 11 years old. A survivor of a Rare Brain Cancer, for which at the age of 1 year, I underwent a 17 hour operation and then 18 months Chemotherapy. I love poetry, writing stories and drawing. My Father, Alan James O'Keeffe, is a Journalist with The Irish Independent Newspaper in Dublin Ireland, Patricia, My Mother writes stories but I like poetry and I surprising family doing it,; [a.] Cape May Court House, NJ

PATTERSON JR., EARL F.
[b.] May 13, 1968, Birmingham, AL; [p.] Earl and Phyllis Patterson; [ch.] Michael Taylor Patterson; [ed.] 1 yr. College at Thomas Nelson Community College, Naval Nuclear Power School and Electrician School Leans High School; [occ.] Naval Electrician; [memb.] Phi Theta Kappa, First Baptist Church; [hon.] Phi Theta Kappa Member for International Junior College Honor Society.; [oth. writ.] "Pondering Heart", A poem published in Tomorrow Never Knows (a poetry book).; [pers.] Experience what you are doing, not what you hope to do.; [a.] Leeds, AL

PATTON, RICKI
[pen.] Reshae; [b.] April 15, 1978, Mobile, AL; [p.] Richard and Janice Patton; [ed.] Grade 10, Kankakee Valley High School; [memb.] FCA, Sunshine, Environmental; [oth. writ.] Lots of other poems; [pers.] I would like the poem to be dedicated to "Brett Waistra" I want to thank my family for everything and all their support. I love you guys; [a.] Fair Oaks, IN

PAYNE, CAROL A.
[b.] October 25, 1948, Oakland, CA; [p.] High M. Gallaher and Elna W. Gallaher; [m.] Robert A. Payne Sr., August 5, 1972; [ch.] Robert A. Payne Jr.; [ed.] Riverside Poly H.S., Riverside City College, B.A., Theatre Arts, University of Calif. Irvine, Juris Doctorate, University of Denver, K-12 and Teaching Credentials; [occ.] Attorney, Carol Payne and Associates, P.C.; [memb.] Delta Psi Omega, Am. Bar Assoc., Colo Bar Assoc., Arapahoe Bar Assoc., S.E. Metro Law Club, S. Metro Denver Chamber of Commerce, Denver Business Women's Network, East Coalition of Senior Services, Senior Referrals, Alumni Associations: U.C. Irvine, U. of Denver.; [hon.] Order of St. Ives, Six American Jurisprudence Awards in various legal subjects, Honors - Legal Research and Writing, Editor Univ. of Denver Law Review, D.U. Merit Scholarship, U.C. Dean's List, R.C.C. Woman of Distinction Theatre Arts, C. Ness Memorial Scholarship Award, Who's Who International, Who's Who Business and Professions; [oth. writ.] Numerous produced plays and puppet plays, Published: "Carrots for Charlie", short story, "April", poem in H.S. Bear Tracks. Early 4th Place, Nat'l Winner of Nameframe Essay Contest. Several unpublished works, including juvenile novel Code Breaker, poems and stories, currently working on poetry book, Hostage Butterfly, for submission.; [pers.] In my early years, I wrote because of school assignments. Later, I wrote plays because I was a director and needed plays, I liked appropriate for my cast. Then, as a puppeteer, I wrote puppet plays for various occasions. In my 30's, I wrote what I thought editors wanted. Now I write because I have to - it just comes.; [a.] Parker, CO

PAYNE, ROBINLEE
[pen.] Robinlee; [b.] December 13, 1967, Ann Arbor, MI; [p.] Sandra M. Payne, Robert L. Payne; [m.] Single; [ed.] Carlson High, Rockwood, MI; [pers.] I feel harmony is the key to peace and happiness. I try hard to live my life in harmony with nature.; [a.] Flat Rock, MI

PAYTON, BARBARA
[pen.] Barbara Meyers, Delores Chavez Ariel, Barbara Kennedy; [b.] December 25, 1962, Portales, NM; [p.] Joe Meyers, Eudean Meyers; [m.] David Kennedy; [ch.] Joshua; [ed.] At present working toward Bachelors of Arts in Education, possible minor in Linguistics.; [occ.] Assistant to speech and drama professor,

grade school crossing guard; [memb.] Phi Theta Kappa, have been associated with SPWO and horror writers of America; [hon.] Error President's List, worked 4 1/2 years with Battered Women Shelter; [oth. writ.] Articles and letters in several local newspapers error; [pers.] We must do the best we can, each of us, to make this a better world now and for the future.; [a.] Gainesville, TX

PEACH, RUBYE D.
[b.] November 15, 1933, Tuscumbia, AL; [p.] Reverend and Mrs. John A. Doss; [m.] Matthew H. Peach, June 15, 1984; [ch.] Clifford O. Davis; [ed.] Trenholm High-Tuscumbia, AL., Lane College - B.A. Degree - Jackson, TN., Wayne State University - MA Degree - Detroit, MI; [occ.] Retired Classroom Teacher; [memb.] AFT-Retired Teachers, Pi Lambda Theta-National Honor Society, Bethel A.M.E. Church Senior Choir, Lesley Temple C.M.E. Church; [hon.] 1986 Outstanding Young Women of America, 30 Years Public Education 1963-1993, E.F. Swinney-Real Woman of the Year Award; [oth. writ.] Sacred songs - copyrighted and recorded in an album entitled" A Touch From Jesus"; [pers.] I believe life is the most important gift man has been given. Therefore, it is the responsibility of each man to be the best human being he/she can be. I further believe that the positive or negative signals we send out in terms of (love, hate, biases, scorn, etc.) tend to multiply and spread to impact the life of others.; [a.] Kansas City, MO

PEARSON, REBEKAH V.
[b.] February 24, 1953, East Tennessee; [p.] Harry and Alfreda Lorraine Collins; [m.] John R. Pearson; [ed.] Sullivan Central High School, elective courses: ETSU, UT, Continuing Education: Northern Virginia Community College, USDA, Georgetown University; [occ.] Management Analyst, Bureau of Alcohol, Tobacco and Firearms, Washington, DC; [memb.] National Association of Female Executives, NAA, American Red Cross, Architectural Designer and Space Planners, Grace Presbyterian Church.; [hon.] Water Safety Instructor for 6 months to 85 years of age. Interior Designer.; [oth. writ.] Personal Journals. Creative Writing, Georgetown University; [pers.] "Give me any word - and I will make up a poem or song"!; [a.] Springfield, VA

PEASE, CHRISTINE R.
[b.] September 21, 1939, Sarasota, FL; [p.] Edna J. Carr (father deceased); [ch.] 1 Daughter, Wendy Dufon, 2 Grandchildren, Justin - 9 and Christina - 8.; [ed.] High School and Business College in the "Governor's Highway Safety" newsletter in 1972.; [occ.] Administrative Secretary, Florida Highway Patrol, employed since 01/18/71 (24 years); [memb.] Former NSA (National Secretaries Association) member.; [hon.] 1977 - NSA - Secretary, I also received a plaque from the FSA (Future Secretaries Assn.), Southeast High School Chapter, Bradenton, FL for work I did with the students. 1975/76; [oth. writ.] I had one poem published; [pers.] My job has influenced my poems. Highway safety, etc. is a big factor and I would like to see people more aware of the serious responsibility they accept when they drive. I also have two (2) wonderful grandchildren who influence my life and my poems. I like to express what they mean to me by writing about them in poetry.; [a.] Bradenton, FL

PECK JR., HARRY G.
[pen.] H. Gwinn Peck; [b.] April 19, 1960, Montgomery, WV; [p.] Betty Newton Peck and Harry Peck Sr.; [ed.] Concord College, Athens, WV, studied Art. WV University, studied Psychology and Public Health.; [occ.] Asst. Coordinator, W.V.U. Wellness Prog.; [memb.] W.V.U. Students with Disabilities Org., National Honors Society. Harry begin losing his eyesight in 1990 and returned to college in 1991. Still writes and paints.; [hon.] Phi Kappa Phi, National Honor Society. Master of Science Degree, Sch. Med., W.V.U.; [oth. writ.] I've been writing for 20 years and just storing my

poems, prose and short stories away in an old boot box.; [pers.] Everything I write is heart and soul felt...dealing with persons, places, times and events in my life and the feelings they've brought forth. If someone else enjoys what I've written, and it causes them to pause and reflect, then the effort was worth it.

PECKHAM, ELLEN
[b.] September 28, 1938, Rochester, NY; [m.] Anson Peckham, 1976; [oth. writ.] Poetry and prints published in literary magazines in the USA and in Great Britain.; [pers.] As a print maker and assemblagiste works under the none E. Stoepel Peckham. Co-Founder of Atelieraye a private gallery in N.Y.; [a.] New York, NY

PELLAND, JANET
[b.] November 27, 1955, Japan; [p.] Frank Funk, Eugenia Funk; [m.] Divorced; [ch.] Danna Lee Pelland, Lindsay Grace Pelland; [ed.] Castleberry H.S. Tarrant Co. Jr. College; [occ.] Confinement officer; [pers.] The works of Shelly, browning, and shakespeare helped open up my soul to an inner talent. When I suffer, or when I'm happy I try to capture those feeling on paper which helps me let go and go on with my life.; [a.] Arlington, TX

PELLEGRINO FRANK
[b.] June 10, 1922, Niagara Falls; [p.] Michael and Frances; [m.] Theresa (deceased), June 1, 1958; [ed.] 11th Grade, Trott Vocational High School, St. Joseph R.C. Church School; [occ.] Retired from: N.Y.S Park Commission; [memb.] D.A.V., St Joseph's Church; [pers.] My pen is sharper than any sword, take my hand and guide me, dear Lord.; [a.] Niagara Falls, NY

PELTZ, TAMMI A.
[b.] May 30, 1961, Brighton, CO; [p.] Floyd - Katherine Gallegos; [m.] Kirk Peltz, April 19, 1987; [ch.] 1 Katherine Mariah Peltz, 9 1/2; [ed.] Graduate 1979, Brighton High School, and Various Trade Schools and Community Colleges.; [occ.] Travel Agent (Outside T.A. (Independent Contractor.); [oth. writ.] I've written several poems about people who have tugged at my heart-strings at my most susceptible moments.; [pers.] I've always looked at life thru rose colored glasses, love is what makes the world go round sometimes we need to keep one eye open as so not to miss.; [a.] Brighton, CO

PENNER, DIANA C.
[b.] August 5, 1963, Kansas, USA; [p.] Larry, G. Penner and Karen Suderman Penner; [ed.] B.S. Education from Kansas State University; [occ.] Language Arts Teacher at Ball High School in Galveston, Texas; [oth. writ.] Poems "Rain, A Request", "Caribbean Phenomena", "Beyond Belief," "Sasha," "The Man," "The Mosquito Bites But only once," "His Current", "Behind Blue Eyes"; [a.] Galveston, TX

PERALES, REGINA KATHRYN
[pen.] Jeannie Kay; [b.] March 9, 1961, Frankfort, IN; [p.] Adopted; [ch.] One boy William Louis and Tonya Lynn, one girl; [ed.] GED, Somerset Community College (now attending); [occ.] Mother, College Student; [oth. writ.] Several other poems, I'd like to enter another one called "Our Knights, Nightmares", copy enclosed. Also included: Gods "Greatest Gift"; [pers.] All my writing is from personal experience, from the heart of those close to me and myself. Comment! The leaves are changing has been shorten from the original copy I wrote; [a.] Monticello, KY

PERCY, LYDIA
[pen.] Adah; [b.] August 27, 1960, Flushing Queens, NY; [p.] William H. and Hardelio M. Percy, Sr.; [m.] Divorce/Sadig Jones; [ch.] Yasmine Hagar Jones, August 5, 1985; [ed.] Queens College City University of New York, 79-82; [occ.] Administrative Assistant/ writer; [memb.] Poetry Project/Writer's Center Queens Women/NOW; [hon.] McDonald's Literary Award 1987; [oth. writ.] Volumes of poetry and one act plays,

short stories; [pers.] I am living when I write, for art is the key to sustaining life, without it there is nothing.; [a.] Queens Village, NY

PERKINS, JUDITH M.
[b.] August 15, 1947, South Bend, IN; [p.] Richard Pitts and Patricia Jordan Pitts; [m.] Kenneth P. Perkins, December 27, 1969; [ch.] Kelly Renee', Carrie Ann; [ed.] Brown County High School, Nashville, IN, Indiana University - 1 year; [occ.] Homemaker; [oth. writ.] "A Baby Boy" published in the Family Treasury of Great Holiday Ideas 1993. Several poem booklets self-published.; [pers.] I believe writing poetry is a gift from God. My goal is to bring Him glory and to bless the reader. If I do this, I too, am blessed.; [a.] Marietta, GA

PERRETTA, MARY
[b.] July 11, 1938, St. Mary's Hoboken, NJ; [p.] Michael and Frances Marra; [m.] John Anthony Perretta, May 28, 1961; [ch.] (5) Francine Angela Lisboa (Nurse), Roseanna Solamen (College Student Dentistry), Mary Elizabeth (Current Student Architect), Anthony Perretta (Mason), John Anthony Perretta (Student of Univ. of Florida); [ed.] Napolitan School of Music, High School Graduate, 1 year Nursing, (Certified Medical Lab Tech. Graduate), Certified Cardiology Tech.; [memb.] World of Potery, Animal and Forest Preservation, American Association of Doctor's Medical Assistants, Washington, DC; [hon.] Received the Golden Potery Award and Silver Potery Award and Honorable Mention Award from Potery World, California, one poem was published in our city new's. Invited to Annual T.V. Potery Award could not attend.; [oth. writ.] I have written forty-one poems of which three were submitted and awarded and one poem (The Poet) recently sent to N.L.O.P., I wish to publish a book of Potery in the near future.; [pers.] I write with hopes to inspire the spirit of man, woman and child.; [a.] New Milford, NJ

PERRIN, AIMEE M.
[b.] December 18, 1976, Desmoines, IA; [p.] Jac and Bonnie Perrin; [ed.] Will graduate from Central High School (In St. Paul) in June of '95.; [occ.] Student; [memb.] National Right To Life Committee; [hon.] Enrolled in second year of the post secondary enrollment options program allowing me to complete two years of college (Bethel College, St. Paul) during my final two years of high school. I sang at the ordway music theatre in St. Paul with an all City Honors Choir in 1991.; [pers.] My grandfather, Richard N. Kinney, a published author, is my role model and inspiration. I attribute all my blessings and gifts to my Lord and Savior, Jesus Christ.; [a.] St. Paul, MN

PERRY, MARIE
[b.] April 2, 1942, Hindman, KY; [p.] Gabe Ritchie and Norsia; [m.] Robert L. Perry, April 1, 1959; [ch.] Robert, Jr., Johnny, Norman, Bobbie Jo; [ed.] Jenning Co, High School; [occ.] Regal - Rugs Taper; [memb.] Church of God Grayford Road; [oth. writ.] Memories - Norsia Ritchie, Enclosed copy; [a.] North Vernon, IN

PESICKA, BERNADINE J.
[pen.] BJ Pesicka, Bernie Pesicka; [b.] January 17, 1939, Belle Fouche, SD; [p.] Adopted Reinhold and Emma Fiechtney, Real parents Pete L. Helen Wilson; [m.] divorced; [ed.] I went through 12th grade no college or other type; [occ.] I am a certified nurses aide at a nursing home in Aberdeen, S.D.; [memb.] I am a member of Praise Family Bible Church in Aberdeen also Women Embracing The World - this has to do with women and couples has missionaries in Russia, Haiti, Japan and so on; [hon.] I sent a poem to Great American Poetry, contest in 1987 on April 28 for the poem Golden of Gestlemane on honorable mention on April 12, 1990 the poem Molter and through the Day Aug 31, 1990 World of Poetry Honorable Mention.; [oth. writ.] I have a poem put in a booth called treasured poems of American - none of poem in (Life) in the winter of 1990 they claims it as being Inspirational; [pers.] I love writing

poetry, and it is my own thoughts and really mostly, the help of God and prayer that my poems come forth; [a.] Aberdeen, SD

PETE, LAWRENCE ROY YOUNGE
[b.] May 24, 1976, Rochester, MI; [p.] Lawrence and Mary Pete; [ed.] Avondale High, Oakland University; [occ.] Student, Freelance Artist, Cook, Aspiring Musician; [memb.] National Eagle Scott Association, Oakland University, Global Preservation Society, Order Of The Arrow - Boy Scouts Of America; [hon.] Avondale Drama Department, Player Of The Year 1994, National Honor Society, Scholastic Art Awards, Presidential Academic, Fitness Awards, Who's Who Among American High School Students 1994; [oth. writ.] Poems published in local literary magazines, many unpublished poems, songs, short stories, and monologues.; [pers.] It is my belief that fine arts of all kinds help to nurture human emotion and spirituality. I strive for a better understanding of all people and the world in which we live.; [a.] Rochester Hills, MI

PETERS, KIM
[b.] March 17, 1963; [p.] James and Dolores Holloway; [m.] Jeff Peters, November 26, 1994; [ch.] Deziree Bollinger, Alissa Bollinger; [oth. writ.] Many other poems; [pers.] I feel writing is one of the best forms of expression and a way to get in touch with your own feelings.

PETERSON, CONNIE
[pen.] Connie Peterson; [b.] April 11, 1940, Bessemer, MI; [p.] Toivo and Helga Taivalmaa; [m.] Richard Peterson, April 8, 1961; [ch.] John, Bryan and Kristen; [ed.] A.P. Johnston High School, Bessemer R, Mich.; [occ.] Legal Secretary; [hon.] Received 9th Honor Scholarship in High School out of 100 Students.; [oth. writ.] Local Newspaper, my poetry; [pers.] My mom died in 1984 in one week of 3 strokes, and I have written poetry since. Also, I'm a recovering woman alcoholic.; [a.] Niles, IL

PETERSON, LORITA G.
[m.] Michael A. Peterson; [ch.] Miguel Antonio, Stacy, Nicole, Christopher Andre' and Kelley Simone; [ed.] BA Degree Early Childhood and Elementary Education, from McNeese State University in Lake Charles, La.; [occ.] Teacher - St John the Baptist Parish in Louisiana.; [pers.] Through my poetry I hope to touch and enrich the lives of others as I hope I have touched enriched the lives of my students by showing them through example that it's ok to show patience, compassion, respect and most of all love for others as well as oneself.; [a.] LaPlace, LA

PETRICK, SHANNON
[b.] December 6, 1977, Dallas, TX; [p.] John and Kristin Petrick; [ed.] South Forsyth High School; [occ.] Job in used Bookstore; [hon.] Was chosen to star in rock music video for "New Age Girl" by Deadeye Dick, numerous superior ratings in musical competitions; [oth. writ.] Published poems in High School Literary Magazine; [a.] Cumming, GA

PETRONE, NICHOLAS
[pen.] Howard Roark Jr., Hyman Ripps; [b.] December 3, 1956, New York, NY; [p.] Nick J. and Vivian Petrone; [ed.] John Adams H.S., Cuny System English, Literature - Major, Music - Minor.; [occ.] Writer, Lyricist, Keyboardist; [memb.] Member MENSA, B.B.M. member., I.B.T.C., pres.; [oth. writ.] Soon to be published the volume of poetry entitled "Beached Wails and Pig Whistles", and the rock and roll epic called "Periscope Man." Lyricist for the musical group "Baby Bunny Mounds"; [pers.] Firm believer in karma and have come to know that "Time wounds all Hells."; [a.] Ozone Park, NY

PETRONELLA, SHARON ANN
[b.] February 23, 1959, Galveston, TX; [p.] E. Earl and Jo Llewellyn; [m.] Frank P. Petronella, Jr. August 3, 1992; [ch.] Frankie B. Petronella and one on the way!; [ed.] BA with major in English, graduated magna cum laude from the University of Houston-Clear Lake, currently completing M.S. from the University of Texas Medical Branch at Galveston, graduation summer '95.; [occ.] Coordinator of Special Programs, the University of Texas Medical Branch School of Nursing at Galveston; [memb.] Tau Sigma Delta Literary Honor Society, Phi Kappa Phi Honor Society, Alpha Chi Honor Society, Alpha Phi Sorority; [hon.] Outstanding Young Women of America, 1989, Outstanding College Students of America, 1987-1990, National Dean's List, 1987-1989, Who's Who Among Students in American Universities and Colleges, 1995, UH-CL Dean's List, 1987-90.; [oth. writ.] I have published one short story in a local publication.; [pers.] I believe the written word to be mankind's greatest tool. Our ability to craft the language is our ability to share our dreams, and in doing so, to define our future.; [a.] Galveston, TX

PETTIT, JILL M.
[b.] February 28, 1977, Alaska; [p.] Jeff and Sharon Pettit; [ed.] Graduated on 24 of May 1995 from High School; [occ.] Work for Safeway Inc.; [memb.] American Heart Association, American Red Cross, Peace Lutheran Church Youth Group Treasurer; [hon.] Honor Society, 4 year athletic letter for track and field.; [pers.] All your life you are told the things you cannot do. All your life they will say you're not good enough or strong enough or talented enough, they'll say you're the wrong height or the wrong weight or the wrong type to play this or be this or achieve this. Thru will tell you no a thousand times no until the no's a become meaningless. All your life then will tell you no, quite firmly and very quickly. They will tell you no. And you will tell them Yes. Magazine Article.; [a.] Eagle River, AK

PHAM, ARTHUR
[pen.] Pham-Nghe; [b.] October 28, 1930, Vietnam; [p.] Pham-V-Le, Do Thi Luat; [m.] Le-Tuyet-Hong, November 5, 1955; [ch.] Quan, Viet, Pham Trinh Pham, Trang Pham, Tuyet Pham; [ed.] Graduate from "Ecole Normale De Musique De Paris" France as Violinist; [occ.] Professor of Music; [oth. writ.] Several poems published in the Vietnamese Magazine; [pers.] I have been greatly influenced by the TAOISM and confucianism

PHELPS, LYNN Y.
[b.] February 28, 1963, Honolulu, HI; [p.] Fay J. Kawagoe, Leslie Okasaki; [m.] Dock Phelps III, June 19, 1982; [ch.] Dock IV, Shawnalyn S., Gene M.; [ed.] McKinley High School; [occ.] Homemaker; [memb.] D. Co. 3rd AA Bn. Key Wives Program; [pers.] Be hopeful and happiness will meet you along the way.; [a.] Twentynine Palms, CA

PHILLIPS, CRAIG
[b.] September 28, 1978, Columbia, MO; [p.] Steven Phillips and Dianna Eimlinger; [occ.] High School Junior; [hon.] Competition at State for Poetry in 1995.; [pers.] I am not a poet, I am a servant only doing the bidding of my Lord, Jesus Christ.; [a.] Sedalia, MO

PHILLIPS, ROBIN L.
[b.] February 3, 1950, Coatesville, PA; [ch.] Terrence Pattis, Ryan Phillips, Shay, Phillips'; [ed.] High School; [occ.] Unemployed - currently writing a book; [hon.] I won an Award for a picture I entered into the "Let Freedom Ring" contest put on by parade magazine. My picture was published in their book.; [oth. writ.] I have written many songs and poems that I keep to myself.; [pers.] I love to write and do so whenever the mood strikes. I have a very strong creative sense and I express it in every facet of my life - My home, my style of dress, etc.; [a.] Ft. Worth, TX

PHILLIPS, PLEASURE MICHELLE
[pen.] Mic Phillips; [b.] September 28, 1978, Jacksonville, FL; [p.] Mary and Ed Thomas; [ed.] Junior at Zephyrhills Senior High School; [memb.] F.B.L.A. (Future Business Leaders of America) 9th and 11th grade.; [hon.] Who's Who of America High School Students (9th) Honor Role; [oth. writ.] If There Were Never Sight, Living in the Past, and many others unnamed.; [pers.] "Knowledge can only be learned if taught. Always listen you never know what you haven't listened to yet." "If you don't try someone else will"; [a.] Zephyrhills, FL

PHILLIPS, BLANCHE TIPTON
[b.] July 22, 1934, Ponta, TX; [p.] A.G. and Mildred Tipton; [m.] Donald T. Phillips, November 25, 1991; [ch.] Lonny Keith Wells, Andria L. Stewart and Carrie L. Stirling; [ed.] Graduate of Bullard, TX, Grammar and High School and Graduate of Tyler Commercial College; [occ.] Homemaker; [memb.] Bullard, TX, Church of Christ; [hon.] Perfect Attendance Awards, Grades 1 thru 12, "B" Merit for Attendance Award, Bullard, TX, Tex A and M Fire Protection Training Division, Clute, TX, Brazoria Co. Fireman's Ass'n. Fire Training Course, Scholarship to Baker's Business College; [oth. writ.] All retained - none sent in for publication; [pers.] All my writings are of a personal nature and would make a moving statement if one could read them with explanation and especially if they were simulated and video taped - having been a victim of child abuse, losing two husbands by death, married for 3rd time, having gone thru chemo with a daughter, etc. I'm 60 yrs. old; [a.] Bullard, TX

PHILLIPS, GEORGE C.
[pen.] George Phillips; [b.] September 30, 1951, Windber, PA; [p.] David Phillips, Ruth Phillips; [ch.] Stephanie Lee - daughter; [ed.] Trimble Technical High School Tarrant Country Junior College; [occ.] Marketing Representative; [memb.] Pastel Society of the Southwest; [pers.] My writing and my artwork are influenced by the colors and sounds of life.; [a.] Bedford, TX

PHILO, JASON
[b.] August 16, 1975, Phoenix, AZ; [p.] Kris and Nancy Philo; [ed.] Milton High; [occ.] United States Navy; [oth. writ.] Many unpublished poems for my own personal satisfaction and enjoyment; [pers.] Writing has always been a good outlet for frustrations, problems, etc., it helped me through many difficult times.; [a.] Milton, FL

PHILPOT, SCOTT CHARLES
[b.] December 11, 1970, Irvington, NJ; [ed.] University of Hawaii, DeVry Technical Institute and various Naval School and Pleasant Valley High School.; [occ.] Digital Electronics Technician; [memb.] Department of Veteran Affairs; [hon.] Many US Naval Award and decorations Deans lists; [pers.] My inspirations and influences come from all the women who broke my heart and helped me to lose my smile; [a.] Scylorsburg, PA

PHIPPS, TIMOTHY D.
[pen.] Douglas Timms; [b.] September 1, 1968, Baxter Springs, KS; [p.] Timothy R. and Linda L. Phipps; [ed.] Galena High School, Galena KS, BS - Pittsburg State Univ. Pittsburg, KS PO - Univ. of Health Sciences - College of Osteopathic Medicine; [occ.] Physician; [memb.] American Osteopathic Assoc.; [hon.] I have the distinct honor, along with my brother Matthew, of being the sons of the Greatest Parents on Earth!; [oth. writ.] Many poems, none of which have I ever attempted to have published before.; [pers.] The making of a poem: It's the merging of every emotion into a solution which is then extruded through the tip of a pen. Only a poet can know the pleasure of making one.; [a.] Galena, KS

PIAGARI, CRAIG
[b.] March 13, 1978, New Jersey; [p.] Mary Hegyi, Richard Piagari; [ed.] Currently in Bordentown Regional High School hopes to attend college.; [occ.] Student; [oth. writ.] Published in Anthology of Poetry by Young Americans 1994 Edition

PIANO, PAULINE ROBIN
[b.] October 17, 1957, Fond Du Lac, WI; [p.] Irene Kounelis Goyer, Clayton Goyer; [m.] Dr. Theodore J. Piano, December 14, 1977; [ch.] Troy Austin Piano; [ed.] Wauwatosa West High School, Wisconsin, Stockton State College, New Jersey, Midwest School of Dog Grooming, Chicago-IL.; [occ.] Self-employed, Medical Business Manager.; [memb.] PETA, National Wildlife Federation, American Arthritis Foundation.; [oth. writ.] Published poem "Self-Reliance" in Polumathian, Wauwatosa West, Vol. XLV; [pers.] Writing poetry for myself has been an act of love. I truly enjoy sharing it with others.; [a.] Navarre, FL

PICARD, LILLIAN N.
[pen.] Lilly; [b.] July 22, 1951, Albuquerque, NM; [p.] Ted and Olivia Padilla; [m.] Robert J. Picard, October 30, 1982; [ch.] Robert C. "Joey" Picard, Tina R. Giraudo; [pers.] Own and operate business- substitute teacher and am a certified instructor coach for youth bowling

PIQUE, ROGER OLIVER
[pen.] Roget Pigue; [b.] February 1, 1941, Detroit, MI; [p.] Oliver and Eleanor Pique; [m.] Mary Edith Wilson Pique, August 26, 1973; [ch.] Roger Oliver II, Robert Rossini, Kipp Gregory; [ed.] Fulton High, Fulton KY, Colorado State University, Fort Collins, Colorado, Dale Carnegie Course; [occ.] Retired Insurance Executive; [memb.] Honorary Mason, 3rd Degree, FEAM 1211, 1st United Methodist Church, Welcome Wagon Sponsor, WPSD TV Cripple Children's Telethon Association; [hon.] Quill and Scroll Society President High School, Alpa Tau Omega, Dean's List College, Salesman of Year 1973-1977 Combined Insurance Company of America; [oth. writ.] Several poems published in local newspapers and magazines throughout the United States. Help religious clergy with ideas about sermons. From my poems - critical acclaim, romanticist poems "Blood and Honor", "Life's River and Beyond"; [pers.] I express my personal writing to reflex guidance, comfort and protection emphasized by justice, freedom and honor through God Almighty! (Good Orderly Direction); [a.] Fulton, KY

PISHEH-EHSAN, PARVIZ M. H.
[pen.] Varenawich; [b.] December 12, 1953, Rasht, Iran; [p.] M. Taghi Pisheh Ehsan (Father) Marmar Paguman (Mother); [m.] Gerlinde Pisheh-Ehsan (Separated), May 9, 1983; [ch.] Baran Pisheh-Ehsan; Ph.D. (Linguistics), Former University Professor; [occ.] Poet And Writer; [memb.] I.P.S. (Iranian Professional Association); [hon.] Two Literary Awards in Spain and Turkey one for a short story in Spain and one for a poem in Turkey and letters of appreciation from leaders of political parties in Europe for my writings in their papers; [oth. writ.] Two Books In Spain, Two Books in Turkey, Articles and poems in various Iranian and none Iranian Newspapers. Presently I am working on four books of literary and poem.; [pers.] Through my writing, I have always strived to teach people what I have learned, and by composing poetry I have endeavored to reflect human's pain and agony. My heart beats with love for "The Children Of Abyss", and although I am nothing but a glow worm, 'til the moment of sunrise, I try to dispel the bitter darkness in my periphery.; [a.] Montreal Province of Quebec, Canada

PITOCCHELLI, BRITTA K.
[pen.] Britta; [b.] December 26, 1972, Methuen, MA; [p.] Frank (deceased) and Kathie Pitocchelli; [ed.] High School - Methuen High, BA English Minor Communications - Complete- May 1995, University of North

Carolina Charlotte; [occ.] Fitness Consultant at the Kings Gym and Full-time UNCC student; [pers.] I try to let my true feelings show in my writings so that my voice is heard by my audience; [a.] Charlotte, NC

PITRE, SHILDA
[pen.] "Shadow"; [p.] Ethel B. Newsom Jackson; [m.] Sherman E. Neal; [ch.] Donald, Printice, Gavin and Avram; [occ.] Child Management; [oth. writ.] Article in Forward Times and a series of poems presented in a WICOGIC (Church) play.; [pers.] I would attempt to awaken the spirit while touching the soul, and to feel the heart while provoking passion.; [a.] Houston, TX

PLANT, MARY
[b.] February 22, 1918, Massachusettes; [p.] Margret and Dominic Olivo; [m.] David Plant, November 1935; [ch.] John, Lorrie, Dominic and Mary Lou; [ed.] Gramar School, St. Mary; [occ.] Retired; [memb.] Catholic Women Club, Grand Pass. Writers, Workshop, Senior Citizens Organization; [oth. writ.] Writing Book on Poetry also my Autobiography; [pers.] My poetry reaches out. Communicate with life.; [a.] Rogue River, OR

PLANTE, MARCIA
[pen.] Marcia Plante; [b.] February 16, 1947, Worcester, MA; [p.] Myron and Lucille Plante; [ed.] D'Youville College Bachelor of Science in Elementary Education, 30 hours graduate credit; [occ.] Former elementary school teacher, current: artist, craftsman, song writer and poet; [memb.] D'Youville College Alumni Association; [hon.] National Merit Scholarship, Diocesan Teaching Scholarship; [oth. writ.] Short stories, song lyrics and poems.; [pers.] Having recently begun writing poems and songs, I am pleased that one of my first poems was chosen for publication. I enjoy writing about my personal experiences and the people who have touched my soul.; [a.] Lackawanna, NY

POINDEXTER, VINCENT
[pen.] Vee; [b.] April 19, 1966, Paterson NJ; [p.] Melvin Poindexter, Patricia Robertson; [ch.] Ravon Pondexter, Kadijah; [ed.] John S. Kennedy High Barclay and CLC College; [occ.] Splicer the Okonite Cable Co.; [memb.] ABC Bowling Local 637 Committee; [pers.] I like to thank all who came in my life who influence me to write.; [a.] Paterson, NJ

POLLARD, FRANK
[pen.] Frank Pollard; [b.] February 25, 1934, Olney, TX; [m.] Jane Shepard; [ch.] Brent and Suzanne; [ed.] Bachelor of Business Administration degree from Texas A and M, Bachelor of Divinity degree from Southwestern Baptist Theological Seminary, D. Min. degree from New Orleans Baptist Theological Seminary, L.H.D. degree from CA Baptist College and doctor of divinity from Mississippi College.; [occ.] Pastor, First Baptist Church, Jackson, MS; [hon.] In 1979 elected by TIME magazine as one of the "seven most outstanding Protestant preachers City in America." Received the "Distinguished Alumnus" award from Southwestern Seminary in 1987. In 1993 received the Golden Gate Baptist Theological Seminary Alumni Assn.'s "Distinguished Service Award."; [oth. writ.] 1. How to know when you're a success, reprinted as The Bible In Your Life, 2. After you've said I'm sorry, 3. Keeping free, and 4. You can be a champion.

POLLARD II, CALVIN L.
[pen.] C. P. Cardigan; [b.] November 17, 1969, Langley, VA; [p.] Calvin and Carolyn Pollard; [ed.] Widefield High School, Colorado Springs, CO, attending University of Houston (Sophomore) for B of Arts Degree in Communications; [occ.] Work at a Major Radio Station in Houston (KILT); [memb.] Delta Upsilon Men's Fraternity, University of Houston; [hon.] Honorable Discharge from U.S. Navy.; [pers.] My writing describes the different aspects of my life. The things that I've seen or been a part of. My writing is dedicated to those who understand me and to those that

are still trying to. Stay green.; [a.] Houston, TX

POLONUS, DELORES M.
[pen.] Dee; [b.] December 4, 1931, Minnesota; [p.] Ludvig and Louise Olson; [m.] Jack, April 14, 1951; [ch.] Michael, Marshal, Cheryl, Robert and Steven; [ed.] High School plus Countless classes to further my job skills as an associate Administrator.; [occ.] Retired - Housewife; [memb.] Eastern star fraternity and Lutheran Church; [hon.] A Honor Roll 8th grade graduation. B Honor Roll - Hi School Grad. Senior Class Queen; [oth. writ.] I have written approximately 10 other poems (all truth) about my children grand children, brother and husband; [pers.] This Grandma wrote this poem, "So Little Are," soon after her first two grandchildren were born (on the same day) 1200 miles apart. Jennifer and Stephanie are their names.; [a.] Shingletown, CA

POLZIN, LINDY MELINDA
[pen.] Lindy; [b.] May 8, 1961, San Francisco; [m.] David Polzin; [ch.] Three children; [ed.] Cal Poly Pomona, Drama, Cal Poly San Luis Obispo, Speech, Cal St. Long Beach, Interpersonal and Organizational Communication; [occ.] Children's Theater Teacher, Grand Traverse Children's Theater Unity Church; [oth. writ.] Manuscript in progress, it is a collection of short stories and poems.; [pers.] My goal is to touch others hearts and feelings, to let them know, then are not alone through my writing.; [a.] Traverse City, MI

POOLE, JANIE
[b.] September 10, 1952, Braddock, PA; [p.] James E. Briggs and Mary L. Byrd; [m.] Larry L. Poole Sr., June 27, 1970; [ch.] Larry L. Poole Jr., Timothy R. Poole; [ed.] Hempfield Senior High, Pittsburgh Academy Beauty; [occ.] Hairdresser; [memb.] Kingdom Hall of Jehovah's Witness.; [oth. writ.] Several poems written through the years, currently writing. A biography of my life that begins way back from my mother and fathers childhood through move and down to my children.; [pers.] I truly love the beauty of heartfelt poetry. I strive to take my poetry from my heart to tell a story of how I really feel inside. If it brings a tear to the eyes, then I know I've reached the readers heart also.; [a.] Greensburg, PA

POOLE, DONNA R.
[pen.] Donna Poole; [b.] June 3, 1953, Greenville, SC; [p.] Mr. and Mrs. Russell Roper; [m.] Reger D. Poole, May 9, 1973; [ch.] Daniel Ryan Poole, Amy Elizabeth Poole; [ed.] Blue Ridge High School, Greenville Technical College; [occ.] R.N. - St. Francis Hospital - Greenville, SC; [memb.] Anna, Bonnet; [oth. writ.] Presently working on short stories.; [pers.] When you have an idea, it's an error glorious gift. Act upon it. I have been encouraged by great friends and supportive family; [a.] Marietta, SC

PORTER, LOUISE WILLIAMS
[b.] August 16, 1907, Birmingham, AL; [m.] Deceased; [ch.] Mary Anne Stroud, J. Grant Porter Jr.; [ed.] High School, one year college, Howard College, Birmingham, AL, (now Samford University); [occ.] Retired from The United Methodist Children's Home, Selma, AL; [oth. writ.] A book published of my collections of poems over the years titled, "Hate Off To Mother", the book also includes one short story. It can be found in Selma's Sturdavant Hall Gift Shop, Prince Edward Library, Framville VA., and The Dallas County Library, Selma, AL.; [pers.] Along the way I've entered contests most of which I've won, poems published by The Birmingham News, I love life, people in general, the outdoors, just living, and putting a few words into poetry helps me release these great feelings.; [a.] Selma, AL

PORTILLO, DELORIS
[pen.] Adriane Cole; [b.] October 9, 1939, Speedwell, TN; [p.] Jesse James and Mossie Elizabeth Heck; [m.]

Enrique Lopez Portillo, April 4, 1964; [ch.] Miguel Enrique Portillo, Leslie Ellen Portillo (Brooks); [ed.] Powell Valley Ele. (TN, Speedwell), Monroe High, Monroe Michigan; [occ.] Semi retired, caring for 98 yr. old father; [oth. writ.] Readers Digest, currently working on autobiography of my father, have published short stories; [pers.] I endeavor to write based on familiar surroundings or personal experiences from friends or family members leaving character anonymous; [a.] Speedwell, TN

POSCH, CHRISTINA
[b.] April 5, 1985, Detroit; [p.] Joseph and Margaret Posch; [ed.] Ferry Elementary School, Fourth Grade; [occ.] Student; [memb.] Grosse Pointe Academy of Tae Kwon Do; [hon.] Newspaper publication, 7th place, NASTAR State Ski Competition, Tae Kwon Do Senior Blue Belt; [pers.] I believe that self-confidence is important for achieving one's goals and that we should respect all living things and our environment. Robert Frost has inspired my writing.; [a.] Grosse Pointe Shores, MI

POTTER, CORA LYNN
[pen.] Cory Potter; [b.] March 2, 1964, Eureka, CA; [p.] Timothy F. Potter and Diane Ruth Potter; [m.] Cindy Baker, December 19, 1985; [occ.] I am a journeyman, painter - 10 years in the field.; [pers.] I decided to pursue writing due to the children who suffer at the mistake of society and the need to expand our social vision of family. The passing of amendment 2 in Colorado in '92, necessitated my speaking out.; [a.] Denver, CO

POULSON, JENNIFER
[pen.] Jenn Poulson; [b.] March 10, 1975, Pueblo; [p.] Carmen Poulson, Errol Poulson; [ed.] Northglenn High Mesa State College (Grand Junction); [occ.] Full-time Student; [memb.] Church of Jesus Christ of Latter Saints, Votech Honor Society, Drama Club, French Club; [hon.] Presidential Academic Award, Honor roll, Votech Honor Society, Drama Award, Perfect Attendance, Science Student Month Award, Seminary Graduate; [oth. writ.] A few poems published in Northglenn's Syllran; [pers.] Life is deep small wonders, that are constantly overlooked by glamourous ideals of society.; [a.] Grand Junction, CO

POWELL, KEVIN ELVIS
[b.] August 16, 1961, Capeville; [p.] Bennie and Evelyn Powell; [a.] Capeville, VA

POWERS, REBEKAH
[pen.] Becky Powers; [b.] February 28, 1958, Cottage Grove, OR; [p.] H. H. and Frances Madewell; [m.] Chuck Powers, August 10, 1974; [ch.] Kimberly, Danika, and Charlie; [ed.] Santa Fe High C.O.M. Junior College; [occ.] Homemaker; [a.] Arcadia, TX

PRATICO, NATALIE
[b.] April 25, 1978, Trenton, NJ; [p.] Edna Pratico, Nate Pratico; [ed.] Yardville Elementary School Reynolds Middle School Steinert High School; [occ.] Student; [memb.] Steinert High School Marching Unit, Jazz Band, Track Team; [hon.] Art work has been put in art shows, a letter in track, awards for marching unit and jazz band; [oth. writ.] A poem was published in the school's issue of "Parallax"; [pers.] I put the emotional moments of my life into the form of a poem.; [a.] Allentown, NJ

PRATT, ROBERTA
[b.] December 11, 1949, Chicago, IL; [p.] Robert Drews and Cloie Drews; [m.] Charles J. Pratt, April 17, 1982; [ch.] Richard Jay, Anthony Robert, Brian Joseph, Granddaughter: Jazmine Lalena; [ed.] Oak Lawn High, Illinois, Mesa Community College, Arizona; [occ.] Housewife; [pers.] I am just beginning to express my feelings on paper. I hope my poems will open peoples eyes not only to the bad, but also the good in this life.;

[a.] Scottsdale, AZ

PRATTE, LOIS A.
[b.] February 3, 1933, Calais, VT; [p.] J. Earle and Addie Pike; [ed.] Graduated - Cabot High, Attended: Mid-Western UN, Witchita Fall, Tex., B.S. Degree in Human Services from N.H. College Human Services; [occ.] Homehealth Aide at Branford VNA; [oth. writ.] Summer was published In Dance On The Horizon, The Piano Is Silent is published in Dark Side Of The Moon; [pers.] I write about the beauty of nature. My christian faith and compassion for others is reflected in my writing.

PRAVDA, MRS. MURIEL
[b.] Brooklyn, NY; [m.] Arthur; [ch.] Amy and Don, son-in-law, Jay and grandchildren Deena and Gregg; [ed.] 3 yrs. Credited Attn. Brooklyn College, Traphagen School, Accrd. Atterbury School of Sculpture, Accredited So. Florida Art Inst., Bruno Lucchese Seminars; [occ.] Artist - Sculptor, was student in So. FL. Art Inst. and taught 14 years in same school; [memb.] Charter Member Nat'l Museum of Women Arts, Nat'l Sculpture Soc., Int. Sculpture Society, Community Art Alliance, Miami Art League; [hon.] (Many awards in poetry and sculpture), Listed Who's Who In American Art, 93-94, Who's Who In American Woman, 95-96; [oth. writ.] Poem published in The Miami Herald also local news. Many articles published regarding sculpture.; [pers.] Bringing happiness to others has taken precidence to my creativity.; [a.] Miami, FL

PRENTIS, EDNA ZIMMERMAN
[b.] November 15, 1915, Welcome, NC; [p.] E. J. and Beatrice Zimmerman; [m.] Rev. Robert B. Prentis, October 23, 1934; [ch.] Linda Prentis Cecil; [ed.] Graduated from Welcome High School, attended Duke University, 2 yrs., studied Music for 2 yrs. and also Art (Painting); [occ.] Artist, Music Teacher, Write Column for County Paper; [memb.] Davidson County Museum of Art, Welcome Home and Garden Club, "Friend of County Store", (non profit organization) that promotes Arts and Crafts at the Country Store at Welcome (Senior Citizen Outlet). Also Festivals.; [hon.] Welcome Civitan Club's Citizen of the Year Award twice and Honorary Mention of the Jefferson Award, 1 year, (Winston-Salem NC); [oth. writ.] Besides poetry I have written music and lyrics to songs.; [pers.] My philosophy is to make: The world better and more beautiful. That encompasses environment, road safety (have worked for safer, better streets in my town), and beautification of surroundings.; [a.] Welcome, NC

PRESSLEY, CYNTHIA
[pen.] Cindy; [b.] July 2, 1946, Florida; [p.] Mr. and Mrs. W. F. Martin; [m.] Ted W. Pressley, December 21, 1986; [ch.] Shawn, Stacy and Shari, 2 step daughters, 3 granddaughters, 3 step grandchildren; [ed.] High School Graduate, 1965, when I was in school, Literature was still is my favorite subject. Poetry gives me up and lift.; [occ.] Chapter I Tutor, Reading/Math, 10 yrs. working in School System.; [memb.] Member of Emmanuel Pentecostal Church.; [hon.] As a child Writing Award; [pers.] I wrote this in memory of my Dad. I've always enjoyed writing poems and short stories for my family. When I saw your advertisement I decided to enter so I sat down and wrote my poem immediately. My Dad just passed away, May "94"; [a.] Ocala, FL

PRESTON, MARY KAY
[pen.] Mary Kay Preston; [b.] June 18, 1961, Denver, CO; [p.] Gerald D. and Mary T. Preston; [ch.] Jeremiah Carl Danielson, Jacob Wayne Danielson; [ed.] G.E.D., Big Sandy School, Simla, Colorado 80835; [occ.] Unpublished Writer; [memb.] Roman Catholic Church; [hon.] Honorary Award for Playing Scrooge. Three First Place Bowling Trophies for Junior League; [oth. writ.] Several more poems. Including my unpublished book entitled Poems from the Heart. Or Poetic Thoughts by: Mary Kay!; [pers.] The joy of the moment is like a

lifetime, neither can ever be replaced. My poem entitled "There's A Feeling I Have Growing." Was inspired by the man I love. Larry J. Russom Sr.; [a.] Aurora, CO

PRESTON, KELLY
[b.] August 10, 1979, Cumberland, MD; [p.] Dale Preston Jr and Terry Preston; [ed.] Westmar High School; [pers.] I am greatly influenced by all my friends; [a.] Barton, MD

PRICE, SHIRLEY SMALLEY
[b.] August 15, 1929, San Bernardino, CA; [p.] Arthur Denemark and Janette Elizabeth Smalley; [m.] Robert Eugene Price, June 9, 1951; [ch.] Lee E. Price, 40, Craig R. Price, 39, Kristine L. Louviere, 34; [ed.] San Bernardino High, San Bernardino Valley College, Degree AA and 80 hrs.; [occ.] Owner - Odd Jobs, Exclusive Volunteer, Secretary - Wilford Hall, Preventive Med., Lackland Air Force Base - 1000 hrs.; [memb.] (Calif.) Native Daughters of the Golden West, Austin Writers League, Kelly AFB Officers Wives, Kelly AFB Wives Bowling (WIBC), Red Cross Volunteers, Wilford Hall Volunteers, Calliope Talent and Modeling Agency, The Creative Edge - The Way of the Ants; [oth. writ.] Approx 500-600 poems, also write stories of articles - but none have been published, this is the first contest I ever entered - actually did enter another contest several years ago with a different poem and it got honorable mention, but not sure if it was a legitimate contest, just recently published in the Creative Edge - Monterey, CA; [pers.] I write poems for the enjoyment of others and to make them feel better. It is better to have a happy, positive outlook and to say something nice to each person you meet - in this way the world will be a better place in which to live.; [a.] San Antonio, TX

PRIETO, IRIS
[b.] December 23, 1973, Los Angeles, CA; [p.] Juan Prieto, Mirta Prieto; [ed.] West High S.W. Longview Private School, El Camino College.; [occ.] Teacher Assistant; [hon.] California Association for Bilingual Education Award for Outstanding Paraprofessional.; [pers.] Life can be very unfair and the future seems uncertain, but if we have faith in Jehovah God's promises for the future, living life will be worth the efforts.; [a.] Gardena, CA

PRIKRYL, MISTY D.
[pen.] Mist; [b.] July 1, 1968, New Mexico; [p.] Larry Connelly and Adonna Robinett; [m.] Bill Prikryl; [ch.] Christopher Wayne, Amanda Gabrielle, Amy Morgan; [ed.] Cooper High School, Abilene Texas; [occ.] Housewife and Mother; [pers.] All my poetry is written from the heart but inspired by my Grandmother, Catherine connelly. Without her my poetry would not be possible.; [a.] Cedar Park, TX

PRUITT, ERIC
[pen.] The Master's Poet; [b.] March 5, 1972, Centerville, IL; [p.] Dianne Pruitt; [m.] Marvel (Coranberry) Pruitt, February 14, 1993; [ch.] Dwight Granberry, Arvell Pruitt; [ed.] I am currently in school for my G.E.D. and I would like to thank my teacher Pat. Gamp and my wife.; [occ.] Building Maintenance; [memb.] I am a member of Bethesda Temple Church of the Apostolic Faith; [hon.] I have received an award for creative writing from my school; [oth. writ.] I have written over 40 different poems and I am still writing more. One of my poems have been published in my school's paper.; [pers.] I strive to bring poetry back to it's roots. It began with God and I feel there is no better person to write about, for He is the circle in my life, and I enjoy doing the Lords work through my poetry; [a.] Saint Louis, MO

PURTLE, KACI MARIE
[b.] October 21, 1981, Kansa City, MO; [p.] Gene and Susan Purtle; [ed.] Currently attending middle School; [occ.] Student; [hon.] Talents noted in several writing contest locally.; [pers.] I write to reflect my inner emo-

tions, to express the way I feel openly. I was to make my readers understand what I'm feeling.; [a.] Independence, MO

PURVIS, LINDA K.
[pen.] Linda K. Glenn; [b.] Oklahoma; [p.] Steven Glenn, Sarah Hanes; [ch.] Melissa Lynn, Crystal Aline; [occ.] Paralegal; [oth. writ.] Several poems and short stories for all ages; [pers.] Being one of a family of ten children, with a professor for a father and an exceptionally talented mother who possessed a 100% photographic memory was the training ground for my love of people and my great delight in the art of writing.

PUTZ, JAMES CHARLES
[b.] June 17, 1947, Philadelphia; [p.] Charles, Catherine Putz; [m.] Renee A., June 11, 1970; [ch.] Christina Lynn, Douglas James; [ed.] Cardinal Dougherty High, Temple University; [occ.] Unemployed; [memb.] Sir John Barbirolli Society, Muscular Dystrophy Assoc., Widemen Memorial Home, And School Association. Vietnam Veterans of America; [oth. writ.] Other than various editorial comments to local newspaper and musical journals, this is my first effort in the genre; [pers.] Great music, Beethoven, Brahms and Mozart never lets you down. Always listen for the sweet sounds of encouragement. Believe in yourself and trust your judgement. Listen to the music of Leonard Cohen.; [a.] Philadelphia, PA

QUEZADAZ, LAURA
[b.] December 11, 1980, Stanford, CA; [p.] Francisco Quezadaz, Deborah Quezadaz; [ed.] Garfield Elementary, Castilleja Middle School; [occ.] Student; [hon.] Honor roll student, 1993 Achievement Award - Garfield Elementary; [oth. writ.] Several poems and short stories published in school newspapers.; [pers.] Though writing is currently not my first priority, I would like to later pursue a career as a writer. I encourage those with dreams to do their best and realize that they can make a difference.; [a.] Redwood City, CA

QUIGLEY, SUSAN A.
[pen.] Star; [b.] February 1, 1980, Vineland, NJ; [p.] Rose Quigley and Lewis Dutton; [m.] Keith Van Scoy (Fiancee), September 26, 1998; [ed.] Millville High, plan to go to nursing school to become a nurse.; [occ.] Student; [memb.] Student Council, Assembly Committee.; [hon.] Student of the month in Science (February 1995); [oth. writ.] Several other poems about love life and Death and Hurt.; [pers.] Whatever goals you have in life, don't ever give up. Follow them with all determination, and you will achieve it. My goals are to become a nurse, and marry a wonderful man. I'm already half way there.; [a.] Millville, NJ

QUIRK, JOHN J.
[b.] Kansas City, MO; [ed.] Bishop Hogan High School, Kansas City, MO Rockhurst College, Kansas City, MO; [occ.] Emergency Medical Technician; [oth. writ.] A Gathering of Dust, Dorrance and Company, Philadelphia 1975; [pers.] The poems started, when I was seven or fight years old, as "Thank - you I love you notes" to my mother. They have evolved since then, have become, thank - you words to others I have loved: Tributes to the importance of love. Whether it was walking into the front doors of my life for a very first time, or leaving for a last time. They have always been a celebration of love; [a.] Kansas City, MO

RACE, LOIS JUNE "PUDDIN"
[pen.] pr; [b.] October 27, 1945, Birmingham, AL; [p.] Red and Lila Houston; [ch.] Roger Houston Race, Ben Charles Race; [ed.] 12 years of school in Orlando, FL, Indian River Community College; [occ.] Public Education Specialist-St. Lucie County -Ft. Pierce Fire District; [memb.] St. Andrews Episcopal Church; [pers.] The world is happier when people laugh together...gentler when they share their understanding.

RADIGAN, BRANDIE
[pen.] Brandie Radigan; [b.] October 27, 1973, Alaska; [p.] Ann Holm and Randy Radigan; [ed.] High School Diploma Start College in Fall of '95; [occ.] Receptionists; [memb.] Sunny Shae Model, growing up in the woods save me an opportunity to experience things most people can't I would like to help then see these things through my poetry.; [oth. writ.] "Tribute to my Father." A Vietnam Vet Hero in Local Paper; [pers.] I would love to share the goodness of the earth through my writings.; [a.] Lynnwood, WA

RAFFAELE, JOSEPH
[b.] September 18, 1975, Cape May, NJ; [p.] Joseph Raffaele Jr. and Barbara Boyce; [ed.] Palm Beach Community College; [oth. writ.] Poem published in Poet's Guild's Best New Poems; [pers.] I love to embrace the unknown to reveal the foolish side of human nature. Influences are Jack Kerovac, Jim Morrison, Woody Allen; [a.] Boca Raton, FL

RAGHAVAN, ANISHA
[b.] August 25, 1979, Cleveland, OH; [p.] Prakash and Parvla Raghavan; [ed.] Student at Wichita Collegiate High School. (Sophomore) [occ.] Student; [memb.] Pro-Humanitatae Community service group), save the whales club, save the Trees club, environmental group, literary club, youth group; [hon.] High Honor Roll Volunteers Award, Headmaster's Scholarship Cup,; [oth. writ.] 2 poem published in "poetic Justice (local magazine) and 2 poems published in "write of passage" (national literary magazine).; [pers.] Writing poetry is a talent that fulfills the need to express oneself and achieve personal satisfaction.; [a.] Wichita, KS

RAGHUNATH, NATALIE SHANDA
[b.] April 1, 1978, Jamaica, NY; [p.] Krisha and Esther Raghunath; [ed.] Hillcrest High School (2 yrs) (NY) Coconut Creek High School (2 yrs) (FL); [hon.] Winner of the 1989 district 29 spelling bee (word-assassinate)... Due ti this, all winners had a ceremony (please make this sound worthwhile and good), to receive plaque from the Queensborough President Claire Schulman. Picture was taken in the New York Daily Newspapers; [oth. writ.] Several other poems kept for personal safety; [pers.] I would like to thank those special people in my life, for giving me that benefit of the doubt. You have a place in my heart that I will carry with me always!! I love you!; [a.] North Lauderdale, FL

RAHAM, LORRAINE PITRE
[pen.] Amittai; [b.] August 1, 1951, New York; [p.] Felix Pitre and Rosa Iglesias; [m.] Abraham Raham, May 21, 1972; [ch.] Jermaine Xavier Raham, Rene' Michael Raham; [ed.] Roosevelt Hosp. School of Nurse Bronx Community College Lehman College; [occ.] Registered Nurse; [memb.] Red Cross Heart Assoc. Gay Men Health Crisis; [hon.] American Red Cross Volunteer Service New York University Hosp. Certificate for Health Career Counseling; [oth. writ.] Escape into Reality Shifting to High Gear Perceptions, Needle Tracks/Life Tracks In Essence Last Kiss; [pers.] My writings reflect the voices of my soul that will sing, beyond the horizon of my Existence.; [a.] New York, NY

RAINES II, THOMAS E.
[b.] October 29, 1964, Pensacola, FL; [p.] Col. and Mrs. Thomas E. Raines, Sr.; [ed.] J.M. Tate High School Pensacola Jr. College A.S., E.M.T Troy State University B.A.S., M.P.A.; [occ.] Law Enforcement Officer; [memb.] American Red Cross American Society of Public Admin. (ASPA) Alpha Sigma Lambda World Bow hunters; [hon.] Eagle Scout President List (numerous) Deans List (multiple); [oth. writ.] Seeds of greetings in inside kung fu magazine, several other a poems and uncompleted works.; [a.] Pensacola, FL

RAMMING, JENNIFER
[b.] January 2, 1977, Pauls Valley, OK; [p.] Luann Elmore and Lyle Elmore; [ed.] Quanah High School; [hon.] U.I.L One act play all star cast, senior class favorite who's who among American High School Students, United States Achievement Academy History and Government Award; [pers.] I want my writings to reflect youthful views and insights in a constructive, peaceful way. There is enough violence in the world, I wish to show that emotions can be expressed in much more beautiful manner; [a.] Quanah, TX

RAMSEY, ABBIE JOLENE
[b.] December 2, 1979, Fernley, NV; [p.] Connie Craig and Randall Craig; [ed.] Fernley High School; [occ.] Student; [hon.] Honor Roll, Freshmen Homecoming Princess; [pers.] Though I like writing on controversial topics, I do not support suicide.; [a.] Fernley, NV

RANDRUP, DIANA
[b.] May 14, 1945, California; [ed.] Tamalpais High School, Diablo Valley College; [pers.] My poem was inspired by Jim Carroll. I also honor the work of Roger Waters, Bob Dylan, Joni Mitchell, Stevie Nicks, Robbie Robertson, and other friends unmet.; [a.] Concord, CA

RANNEY, CAROLE A.
[b.] February 4, 1940, Pawhallska, OK; [p.] Ira Barkman and Pauline Barkman; [m.] Donald E. Ranney, June 28, 1958; [ch.] Christine, Julie, Jeff, Nancy, Scott, Jennifer, Steven; [ed.] Saint Marys High School Wichita State Univ. Continuing Education.; [occ.] Owner Artistic Endeavors Art Studio/Art Teacher for Children and Adults.; [memb.] Wichita Artist Guild Wichita Women Artist Kansas Watercolor Society Ministry with Persons with Disabilities (advisory board); [hon.] Numerous awards in Art - including published art for the national academy of science - poetry published in "The Silver Quill." Chairperson - "Art From The Heart"; [oth. writ.] Writing and Public appearances for 20 years about art working with the disabled and writing recipient state journalism award in high school; [pers.] I share my feelings and thoughts, through words and paintings, about my world and my life; [a.] Wichita, KS

RANSOM, BETTY E.
[b.] October 23, 1919, Elm Grove, VA; [p.] Lewis D. and Otie Bell Simms; [m.] Glenn I. Ransom, July 26, 1941; [ch.] Drea, Kathy, Linda and Glenn L.; [ed.] High School and 2 years College; [occ.] Retired former Real Estate Sales Person; [memb.] Pres. Senior Citizens AARP, Farmers Union; [oth. writ.] Articles in local newspaper; [pers.] Hate to see this great country of ours destroyed by great leaders.; [a.] Butler, OH

RAPOSO, JOSE M.
[pen.] Michael Miguel; [b.] October 1, 1950, Sao Miguel, Azores; [p.] Joao Jorge Raposo and Maria Da Conceicao Vicente; [m.] Maria Isilda Raposo, July 29, 1973; [ch.] Michael Vincent Nunes Raposo; [ed.] Bachelor of Science; [occ.] Self Employed Dry Cleaners/ Bookkeeping and Income Taxes; [memb.] Member of several Portuguese - American organizations; [oth. writ.] One Book Published in 1994 in Portuguese, title (Alma Repartida) (divided Soul) Several poems published in the Portuguese Times of New Bedford Several articles focusing the portuguese way of life integrated in the American system.; [pers.] We are travellers in a confined space of imagination and transcendentalism, where th empirical will meet the spirit on the material road of self destruction.

RASSON, HEATHER KRISTINE
[b.] June 12, 1974, Houston, TX; [p.] Morag Baillie and James Rosson; [ed.] Writing and art come from within.; [occ.] Artist; [memb.] I affiliate myself with no organizations S.; [hon.] I received an honorable mention for the 1994 writer's dehist competition and first prize for an art exhibition at my college.; [oth. writ.] I have four books of poetry written by the are of 20. They

all exemplify truth and pain. I try to speak as simply and brutally as I can.; [pers.] To make people listen to you, you must make them feel what you have felt. I write about my grief and anger mainly for it can be identified by all.; [a.] Houston, TX

RAY, TESSA KAYE
[pen.] T. K. Ray; [b.] June 11, 1974, Beaumont, TX; [p.] Doyle and Bety Ray; [ed.] Nacogdoches High, Tyler Junior College, Angelina College, Stephen F. Austin State University; [occ.] Secretary, College student; [memb.] Stephen F. Austin Diabetic Support Group; [hon.] Drama, Poetry, Reading in High School.; [oth. writ.] I have written hundreds of poems, but I felt that none of them were good enough to publish, not until now.; [pers.] To me success is knowing that in some way my writing has helped someone. I thank God for my talent, and my parents for urging me to pursue it.; [a.] Nacogdoches, TX

RAYMOND, JUDIE
[b.] June 11, 1955, Iowa; [p.] Ervin and Ruth Farmer; [m.] James Raymond, August 3, 1974; [ch.] Jeanne Ann Raymond, Joanie Lea Raymond; [ed.] Charles City Comm. High; [occ.] Dental Assistant Free Lance Writer; [memb.] United Methodist Church; [oth. writ.] Several poems for local magazines and newspaper, also a book of poetry published for friends and family. Luthern Digest; [pers.] My writing reflects the spiritual view of every day life.; [a.] Dike, IA

REBELLO, MARK STEVEN
[pen.] Lord Sterling; [b.] March 18, 1965, Fall River; [p.] Edward Rebello and Claudette Sirois; [m.] Brenda Rainey-Rebello, July 9, 1994; [ch.] Morgan Judith Rainey Rebello; [ed.] Sophomore in College; [oth. writ.] MYTH, pub. 1994 Prevailing Winds/ College Literary Magazine; [pers.] All the hardships of life (homelessness) include mean so much less when my daughter looks with her sparkling eyes and says, daddy best friends, I Love You.; [a.] Fall River, MA

REDDIG, REBECCA GOTWALD
[b.] March 21, 1957, Carlisle, PA; [p.] James and Helen Gotwald; [ed.] 1977 Graduate Temple University Carlisle High School; [occ.] Dental Hygienist; [a.] New Cumberland, PA

REDICK, THOMAS F.
[pen.] Thomas F. Redick; [b.] October 20, 1923, Lowelville, OH; [m.] Wini Redick, July 6, 1990; [ch.] Samuel Redick; [ed.] Miami University, BA University of Pittsburgh, PA, Philadelphia; [occ.] College Teacher Frostburg State University; [hon.] Honorary Professor of Research - Univ. of La Laguna - Tenerife - Spain

REDWINE, BERTHA
[b.] March 7, 1952, Leavenworth, KS; [p.] Susie and Jim Stone; [m.] Henry Redwine, October 18, 1992; [ed.] High School; [occ.] Line server/dishwasher in cafeteria; [memb.] Member of church of Christ penecostal church. Member of the Missionary board.; [hon.] Missionary license; [oth. writ.] I have others, but this is the first I have ever sent in to any where; [pers.] As a christian I feel it is our duty and obligation to help every one all over the land know and prayers God as their savior and live together in peace and love; [a.] Kansas City, MO

REEHER, FRANK E.
[pen.] Frank E. Reeher; [b.] April 11, 1920, Transfer, PA; [p.] John and Elizabeth Reeher; [m.] Lida Rowe Reeher (deceased), July 5, 1946; [ch.] 1 Step - Daughter; [ed.] High school several service schools during military service; [occ.] Retired; [memb.] Member Holy Trinity Lutheran Church Grove City, PA, life member V.F.W.; [hon.] Publication in previous poetry volume of echoes of yesterday, monthly publication in church paper "The Quill"; [oth. writ.] None other than poetry writing off and on for over 50 years.; [pers.] All my

works are by inspiration of God in response to different situations and circumstances. Trusting that my poems will bring strength and increased faith to reader; [a.] Mercer, PA

REGAN, LEONORA M.
[pen.] Leonora M. Regan; [b.] November 12, 1980, Staten Island, NY; [p.] Mr. and Mrs. James and Barbara Regan; [ed.] Student of high school; [occ.] Student of Saint John Villa High School; [pers.] I wish to convey feelings through the art of poetry. Inspirations can come from even the worst of events.; [a.] Staten Island, NY

REICH, MILTON
[b.] October 13, 1914, Cleveland, OH; [p.] Louis and Dora; [ed.] High School Graduate Evening Colleges; [occ.] Retired; [memb.] Scout and Cub Master Boy Scouts of America Bnai Brith Charter Member North Hollywood Ca. Toast Masters, Jewish War Veterans Cleveland, OH, 31 years financial planner; [hon.] Boy scouts of America Committee Chairman. Vice President Jewish War veterans, Charter Member Cleveland, OH, Educational Vice President Toastmaster various clubs; [oth. writ.] Personal experiences, plays I monologue, many poems, writing since age 13.; [pers.] If we do not learn to live together, we will surely die together. I believe in man's basic goodness.; [a.] Chula Vista, CA

REID, RODNEY
[b.] October 16, 1958, Lawton, MI; [p.] Barbara Leonard; [ch.] Geoffrey Reid; [ed.] Graduate Lawton High School; [occ.] Label Press Operator; [oth. writ.] Many poems and lyrics on a wide range of topics. Have also written comedy material, plus a screen play that friends and I made a homemade fill, from; [pers.] I have been writings as a hobby for a couple of years. This is my first published pieces. I enjoy writing on many subjects.; [a.] Lawton, MI

REISEDGE, SHARON L.
[b.] March 12, 1948, Howell, MI; [p.] Helen F. Lewis and Ernest C. Bennett; [m.] William Reisedge, June 22, 1968; [ch.] Kortney Lynn Dailey, Kevin J. Dailey; [ed.] Howell High School, Lansing Community College; [occ.] Secretary, General Motors Corp.; [pers.] Though I have experienced tragedy, I try to remain hopeful. Poetry is a glimpse of the inner person in all of us.

REISIG, DOROTHY
[pen.] Dotty Ditty Mouse; [b.] April 29, 1922, Cleveland, OH; [p.] Hilda and Augustus Ditmars; [m.] Tony - deceased, May 30, 1947; [ch.] Kathy Patricia, Tony Lee; [ed.] High School and 1 Year College; [occ.] Widow-housewife; [memb.] Historical Society Democratic Club; [oth. writ.] Elected To School Board of Maple Hts. in 1970's Served as Recreational Director of City of Maple Hts in late 60's organized, written plays, and directed play for Maple Hts, little Theatre; [pers.] I've written poems and stories since grade school; [a.] Maple Heights, OH

REISSMAN, MARSHALL G.
[b.] April 6, 1955, New York, NY; [p.] Nathaniel (Dec.) and Diana Reissman (Dec.); [m.] Shannon Boyce, April 22, 1995; [ch.] Jake A. Allen; [ed.] Florida State University, B.A. (1976), J.D. (1980); [occ.] Attorney, Pritchard and Reissman, P.A.; [memb.] The Florida Bar; [hon.] Phi Beta Kappa; [oth. writ.] Florida Boundary Law and Adjoining Landowner Disputes, P.E.S.I. 1988, 1989,1990.; [pers.] "Be what you is, 'cause if you be what you ain't, you ain't what you is." (Recent bumper sticker sighting.); [a.] Treasure Island, FL

RENZ, CASEY
[b.] September 22, 1979, Edison; [p.] Robert and Linda Renz; [ed.] Monroe Township High School 1986; [memb.] Footlights Dance Co.; [hon.] National Honor Society, National Art Award, 1st Place Starlight Productions National Dance Competition, Star express Talent Competition 1st place; [a.] Jamesburg, NJ

REYNOLDS, ELIZABETH RENFROW
[pen.] Beth Reynolds; [b.] March 17, 1961, Kentucky; [p.] Owen and Nella Renfrow; [m.] Harry Reynolds, July 5, 1991; [ch.] Bethanie Cronin, Stephanie Cronin, William Reynolds, Rebecca Reynolds; [ed.] Dariess County High School; [pers.] Events surrounding my family and friends are where my poems come from. God give me my words, I merely put them on paper.; [a.] Richland, IN

REYNOLDS, JANIS
[pen.] Janis Roark Reynolds; [b.] July 31, 1937, Cincinnati, OH; [p.] Lola and Byron Roark; [m.] Floyd, August 20, 1955; [ch.] Four; [ed.] Indian Hills High School, University of Cincinnati, Batavia Branch, studied as Fine Artist (painting in oils and watercolor); [occ.] Artist, Writer, Photographer, Homemaker; [memb.] Grand Marais, (MN) at Colony, WOI Public Radio, W.A.R.M, Minneapolis, MN. (Women's Artist Registry); [oth. writ.] Have written quite a bit of poetry dealing either with my life on the Canadian Border in N. MN. (15 yrs.), or my emotional response to life events.; [pers.] As with my painting, I often use writing poetry to help chart a successful journey through a particular scenario in life, or sometimes to clarify the lesson learned after the fact.; [a.] West Des Moines, IA

REYNOLDS, JOHN D.
[pen.] John D. Reynolds; [b.] June 1, 1923, Havre De Grace, MD; [m.] Mary J. Reynolds, December 28, 1923; [ed.] Havre De Grace High School University of Maryland; [occ.] Retired; [memb.] Lions Club, AARP, Narfe (National Association of retired Federal Employees), American Legion, VFW, Military Order of purple heart, Archaeology Society of MD, Planetary Society; [hon.] Graduated University of Maryland with High Honors. Numerous Awards from Department of Defense; [oth. writ.] Monthly column of 503rd parachute regiment activities in the static line, a publication for airborne units. Editors of monthly lions club newsletter; [pers.] "You never know what is going to happen to you." Slings and arrows will be sweetened with kisses and caresses. You must be prepared to absorb and embrace them all.; [a.] Joppa, MD

REYNOLDS, ROY E.
[pen.] Roy E. Reynolds; [b.] August 26, 1950, Indianapolis, IN; [p.] Roy H. Reynolds and Marjorie H.; [m.] Julia L. Reynolds, January 21, 1972; [ch.] Julie R., Natasha D., Travis C., Marjorie M., Roy A.; [ed.] High School Graduate and 5 year apprenticeship Grad.; [occ.] Steam fitter; [memb.] Steam fitters Local Union #440; [hon.] 3rd place medal Elvis Impersonator contest Portage IN. Oct 1993.; [oth. writ.] "It ain't over"/ "Angel" recorded in Nashville TN. November 1985. "Past Beginnings - Tribute to Jim Rogers" printed in local Union #440 newsletter.; [pers.] For this poem, Dear Daddy", to be published in this book, only substantiates the old cliche,' "keep the faith and never give up'. This poem is dedicated to all of those who knew my father, Roy H. Reynolds; [a.] Indianapolis, IN

REYNOLDS, STEVE
[b.] January 10, 1960; [p.] Robert and Dolores Reynolds; [m.] Divorced in 1988; [ed.] Bay View H.S., life; [occ.] Full time truck driver, part time photographer; [hon.] To be in this book; [pers.] I'll try anything at least once, and I want to go out of life with the regrets of things I did, and not the things I wish I did; [a.] Greenfield, WI

RHODES, EDWARD R.
[b.] August 28, 1954, PA; [p.] Herman R. Rhodes, Florence A.; [ch.] Steven Ross; [ed.] Highland Regional High Glendale Community College Arizona State University; [occ.] Retired; [memb.] Mended Hearts, Franklin Institute of History Smithsonian Institute of space and science and history; [pers.] My writings come from the magic of children and love of life.; [a.] Phoenix, AZ

RHODES, ERIC J.
[b.] December 29, 1968, Atlanta, GA; [p.] James and Pat Rhodes; [m.] Jodi M. Rhodes, September 25, 1993; [ch.] Shyanne, Christopher; [ed.] College Student; [occ.] Student; [pers.] Be honest in life and it will show in your writing.; [a.] Albuquerque, NM

RHODES, DARLENE
[b.] January 30, 1967, Washington, DC; [p.] Velma Colson; [m.] Victor Parker; [ch.] Donnel, Runeeki, Quanisha; [ed.] Highlands High; [occ.] Cosmetology Student; [pers.] Thanks Mom for believing in me. I always write from the heart and that's always been the best way.; [a.] Wichita, KS

RICE III, WILLIAM
[pen.] Prince William III; [b.] December 6, 1967, Huntsville, AL; [m.] Dawn L. Rice, December 15, 1993; [ch.] Steven and Carl; [occ.] Meat Operations Managers - Ryan's Steak House; [oth. writ.] Assorted Poems and Songs; [pers.] Feelings that "can't be put into words," I put into words.; [a.] Austin, TX

RICE, AMANDA LEANN
[b.] December 9, 1979, Knoxville, TN; [p.] Jim and Karen Rice; [ed.] Central High School of Knoxville, TN; [a.] Knoxville, TN

RICHARDS, DON
[b.] August 31, 1935, Newark, OH; [p.] Walter and Mary Richards; [ch.] Four sons, One daughter; [ed.] Graduate High School; [occ.] Custodian Newark City Schools; [memb.] Life Time Member I.S.P. President T. Licking County Golden Writers. Eagles; [hon.] Editors Choice Award 1994-95, I.S.P. Poet Merit Award Hon. Men. Magazine I.S.P ask to Coordinate and teach a creative writing class for licking Co. aging program.; [oth. writ.] Published in local newspapers, newsletter. Mental health association, Newsletter, Licking Co. Aging Program Five time world published poems; [pers.] I try to touch. People with poetry. To share the beauty that some would otherwise never know.; [a.] Heath, OH

RICHARDSON, WANNA EUGENIA
[b.] November 23, 1945, Camden, NJ; [p.] Thomas and Iona Richardson; [m.] Divorced; [ch.] Tyrone Wesley; [ed.] Woodrow Wilson High School - Camden N.J. Rutgers University - Camden NJ; [occ.] Project Coordinator Namibia, Southern Africa; [hon.] Ford Foundation Fellowship; [oth. writ.] Several poems and musical compositions. Article published in the courier post (Camden NJ); [pers.] I write from my heart. I seek to articulate man's deepest and most profound emotions; [a.] Palm Bay, FL

RICHARDSON, FRANCES K.
[pen.] Frankie K. Richardson; [b.] April 29, 1936, Hartsville, SC; [p.] Mr. and Mrs. Robert K. Kea; [m.] Bobby Richardson, December 1, 1962; [ed.] High School- Hartsville; [occ.] Homemaker, Church worker; [memb.] St. Pauls United Methodist Church Chesterfield, S.C; [oth. writ.] I got other writing God has given me. I've shared with friends church and Poetry reading at my home.; [pers.] God has blessed me with all of my poems. It is God I praise and thanked. I have many hobbies, and go fishing. I've done book keeping, Mgr., Food (counter) store early in life.; [a.] Chesterfield, SC

RICHIE, GORDON D.
[pen.] Gordon Richie; [b.] July 2, 1964, Long Beach, CA; [p.] Jeannette Haigy; [m.] Karen Richie, August 13, 1989; [ch.] Anthony D. Richie, Tyna M. Richie; [occ.] U.S. Navy USS California CGN 36; [a.] Bremerton, WA

RICKER, CY W.
[b.] May 18, 1974, Greensburg, KS; [p.] John, Cindy Ricker; [m.] Mellissa Ricker, July 31, 1993; [ch.] Sierra Irene; [ed.] Medicine Lodge High; [occ.] Rancher; [pers.] I wish to express through my poetry, The life and

times of a working cowboy. Hobbies I enjoy roping, hunting, the outdoors altogether.; [a.] Utica, KS

RINEVELD, VALERIE LYNNE
[b.] December 5, 1951, Battle Creek, MI; [p.] James and Doris Davis; [m.] Dan Harper Rineveld, July 21, 1973; [ch.] Dan Matthew, Wendy Kathleen, Marie Lynne; [ed.] Bronson Methodist Hospital school of Nursing - registered Nurse, Western Mich. University - BS in Health Studies; [occ.] Registered Nurse; [memb.] Michigan Nurses Association Celery City Cloggers, Portage United Methodist Church Committees, Portage Central High School Band Boosters, Famous Poets Society; [hon.] Deans list at Western Mich University, Academic Scholarships; [oth. writ.] Footprints of a Passing Soul, published in Famous Poems of Today, several publications in local papers; [pers.] I write to try to capture the everyday moments of despair, joy, and everything between's them - to leave footprints of my passing soul for those yet to come.; [a.] Portage, MI

RISHER, CLAYTON DAVID
[b.] August 30, 1966, Austin, TX; [p.] James and Joann Risher; [m.] Tammi S. Risher, February 25, 1995; [ed.] B.A. Boston University; [occ.] International Sales Exide Electronics, Realign, NC; [oth. writ.] Winner - American Fiction Great Stream Review, Boston Daily Free Press Weston Town Crier. Boston Universities Reporter; [pers.] "Where did all the good literature go?"; [a.] Raleigh, NC

RISK, NAKLEY A.
[pen.] Nakley A. Risk; [b.] October 10, 1936, Lebanon; [p.] Dead; [m.] Rita J. Risk, October 23, 1969; [ch.] (1) Antonio N. Risk; [ed.] Coll. B.A. Hotel Management Academie Libanaise Des Beaux-Arts, (Lebanese Academy of Fine Arts); [occ.] Beauty Salons owner. Apts. owner; [oth. writ.] 4 screen plays on the market and 1 novel (unpublished); [pers.] Earn your living the good old fashioned way: Work for it. And never bite the hand that fed you!; [a.] Hampton, VA

RISNER, CHARLOTTE
[b.] July 14, 1965, Florence, AL; [p.] Fred and Shirley Smith; [m.] Jeff Risner, February 14, 1990; [ch.] Christopher, Kristi (deceased) and Jeffery; [pers.] I just want to thank God, my angel Kristi, and Uncle Wallace for my inspiration.; [a.] Florence, AL

RITCHIE, J. M.
[b.] December 23, 1967, Columbia, SC; [p.] George and Elina Ritchie; [m.] Jacqueline Heiter Ritchie, August 5, 1995; [ed.] McGill-Toolen H.S. Bachelor of Science in Psychology, masters of education in counseling and guidance (both U. of Monetvallo); [occ.] School Counselor, Hoover, Public Schools, Hoover, AL; [memb.] Lambda Chi Alpha International Fraternity; [oth. writ.] I have been published in local anthologies, but nothing yet on the national level. I have written extensively since I was 13 years old.; [pers.] Robert Frost is my main philosophical influence and has taught me much about my writing. I believe in life's easier, freer, down to earth aspect.; [a.] Mobile, AL

RITTER, JANIS MEADE
[b.] January 22, 1945, Washington, DC; [p.] Josephine B. and Seibert D. Meade; [ch.] Kelly Lynn Moore married to Raeford Moore.; [ed.] Graduate of Timestone College Gaffney S.C. December 16th 1995; [occ.] Furniture Sales Consultant, Brown Furniture, Gaffney, SC; [memb.] American Business Woman's Assoc., High Point, N.C. Green Bethal Baptist Church, Boiling Springs, NC; [hon.] Graduated with honors from Linestone College with a double major in English and Business two days after becoming a grandmother for the first time.; [oth. writ.] Several poems published in the Guilford College Newspaper for adult students called the Seeker. Published a short story called, "Long Hollow," in the Scott Country News out of Nickolsville, VA. Wrote "Scooter Pie Cookies" in honor of my new grandson Titus Anthony Moore. Published "The Magic" in several publications which include the Shelby Star, the Christian Leader, and hope to publish a complete book of my poetry in 1996.; [pers.] For many years, I have admired the following passage from Rainer Maria Rilke which says: "Be patient toward all that is unsolved in your heart and try to love the questions themselves...DO NOT...seek the answers, which cannot be given you because you would not be able to live them. And the point is to live everything. Live the question now. Perhaps you will...gradually, without noticing it, live along some distant day without noticing it, into the answer."; [a.] Boiling Springs, NC

ROBBINS, JO ANNE R.
[b.] June 21, 1938, Toledo, OH; [p.] Elizabeth and Robert Rahm; [m.] Zebulon S. Robbins Jr., July 1, 1961; [ch.] Zebulon S. Robbins III, Geoffrey Mills Robbins; [ed.] B. S. University of Toledo, M. S. State University of New York at Albany; [occ.] Special Education Administrator of Federal Project and Instructional Support; [memb.] Delta Delta Delta St George's Episcopal Church Junior League of Schenectady, NY capital Region BOCES Professional Associates Group, Special Education Administrators of New York State; [hon.] Outstanding Performance Award 1988 - Capital Region BOCES Alpha Phi Gamma Who's Who in American Colleges/Universities; [oth. writ.] Several poems, most motivated by a variety of memorable family event or activities. My goal is to publish a book of poetry in the next year.; [pers.] As a musician, poetry in the form of hymns and the words to anthems has always inspired me and has been the root of my growing interest in poetic expression.; [a.] Clifton Park, NY

ROBBLEY, PHYLLIS
[b.] June 17, Chicago; [ch.] Four children and three grown grandchildren; [ed.] Bachelor and Master Degrees; [occ.] Retired teacher, but still very busy with Condo Assoc.; [memb.] Literacy volunteer-reading-English, Literacy volunteer-DuPage Retired Teachers, Raising a family and teaching kept me too busy to continue some membership.; [hon.] Graduated with honors from University of college. Won grade school award for best story. (I was nine often years old). There were no Jr. Highs then.; [oth. writ.] Poems and "other stuff" written for special occasions and for special people.; [pers.] Nothing is static. Different circumstances force us to make changes in how we go on, especially in my case, when children grow up and grandchildren appear. We remain a loving family. Unusual happenings from childhood on have forced me to constantly be alert to what goes on about me.; [a.] Glen Ellyn, IL

ROBERSON, JASMIN
[b.] October, 21, 1981, Philippines; [p.] Marion and Nelly Roberson; [ed.] Orville Wright Middle School, 8th Grade; [pers.] The best poems are felt in the heart. It sends hints of messages of hope and joy.; [a.] Los Angeles, CA

ROBERTSON, LAURA J.
[b.] April 5, 1965, Highland Park, MI; [p.] Harold and Rose Cope; [m.] Daniel S. Robertson, July 16, 1988; [ed.] Waterford Mott High School Class of 1983; [occ.] Owner of Razzle Dazzle Pet Grooming; [memb.] National Arbor Day Foundation, Michigan Humane Society (contributor to); [oth. writ.] Many personal poems, journals, and greeting cards. All unpublished written from my heart to those I know.; [pers.] I am an honest person with old-fashioned values and a deep moral commitment to love, faith and the caring for others. I believe all is possible through love and selflessness.; [a.] Waterford, MI

ROBERTSON, RICHARD
[pen.] Rick-man (only occasionally); [b.] July 20, 1971, Baton Rouge, LA; [p.] Alfred and Myrtle Robertson; [ed.] B.A. degree in History from Dillard University, Fall '94; [occ.] Qualmy Assurance/Documentation at IOCAD Services Inc.; [memb.] Golden Square Lodge #24, Prince Hall Masons; [hon.] Dillard University Academic Scholarship '89; Dillard University Alumni; Perpetual Scholarship '93; [oth. writ.] None published, but I have a host of other material in my personal library.; [pers.] Just living is not enough; one must find the catalyst that drives him to make life worth living.; [a.] Baton Rouge, LA

ROBERTSON, THOMAS W.
[b.] December 25, 1913, Charleston, WV; [p.] Judge Thomas D. Ors Lee, Robertson; [m.] Nona L., March 8, 1935; [ch.] Donna Krafick; [ed.] Charleston High School LaSalle Uni. Chicago Orlando School Real Estate Law attended Seminolu College; [occ.] Retired; [memb.] All masonic organization former 'Elks Club' Greater Orlando Board of realty; [hon.] Numerous Sales Awards Pres. Orlando, Down Town Sertoma Club Served - Pres. J Chairman of the Board Goodwill Industries Central Flurid. Outstanding Home Builder - 50 year Master Mason - 50 "Masonic Shrine"; [oth. writ.] 56 plus poems - Commenemorate writings, event in a placer; [pers.] The mind, as someone has sad is a terrible thing to waste writings every day keeps the mind active - the soul alive- extend life adds pleasure to life encourages others

ROBINSON, KERIM
[b.] April 16, 1957, Miami, FL; [p.] Barbara Ririus, Ronald J. Robinson; [m.] Karol A. Ruding, December 24, 1994; [ed.] Currently pursuing a masters' degree in Psychical Therapy with a minor in English; [occ.] Student and Fitness Trainer and a Health SPA; [memb.] Phi Theta Cappa, honor society and Nova, (N.YA comm. College) Dean's List; [hon.] Poems published in one other competition in LA. Honorable mention for painting in N. VA Art show Governor's Honors in Poetry 1975 in Georgia, 3rd place in Nat. Libr. of Poetry '94; [oth. writ.] Short stories, essays and about a million letters; [pers.] To endeavor to paint, sculpt, and create with the medium of words for the pleasure of others is more than satisfying, it's as intoxicating in it's infancy as it is on completion, yet as humbling as a first step on a new world. Thanks Karol! Love ya!; [a.] Arlington, VA

ROBINSON JR., FRANK
[b.] November 2, 1952, NY; [p.] Frank and Janie Robinson; [ed.] John Bowne H.S., Queens College; [occ.] Vocalist/Lyricist/Voice-Over Spokesperson/ Computer Opr.; [oth. writ.] 3 unpublished collections of poetry, prose, short stories, and lyrics; [pers.] Reality is but a reflection of that which we hold dear; [a.] Jamaica, NY

ROBINSON, SUSAN LEIGH
[b.] June 11, 1981, South Carolina; [p.] Patti and Sam Robinson; [ed.] I am currently in the 8th grade.; [pers.] I love animals, especially dogs and horses. I enjoy reading and writing. I enjoy singing and going to symphony concerts.; [a.] Duncan, SC

ROBINSON, NANCY
[b.] July 20, 1969, Great Bend, KS; [p.] Blanche and Donald Robinson; [ch.] Kashina Jones; [a.] Great Bend, KS

ROBINSON, KIMBERLY
[b.] December 9, 1972, Jacksonville, FL; [p.] Robert and Thelma Ayers; [m.] John H. Robinson IV, May 12, 1994; [ed.] Art Institute of Philadelphia; [occ.] Artist; [memb.] People for the ethical treatment of animals, aid's foundation, American cancer, society, wildlife preservation society.; [oth. writ.] Poems published in local newspapers; [a.] Newport News, VA

ROCAMONTES, GILBERT
[pen.] S. W. Rocket; [b.] August 8, 1953, San Antonio, TX; [p.] Gilbert Rocamontes Sr., Josephine Rosas; [m.] Margaret A. Rocamontes, February 18, 1983; [ch.] Gilbert III, Israel, Larry James; [ed.] So. San Antonio High School, St. Philips College, Toledo Bible College; [occ.] Equip. Oper. Street Dept. (City of Bucyrus); [oth. writ.] Never Published; [pers.] Live, don't lie, live, don't steal, and you'll live; [a.] Bucyrus, OH

RODDEY, CYNTHIA P.
[b.] April 6, 1940, York County; [p.] Isaiah Burris and Ruth Jordan Plair; [m.] James Eddie Roddey, Sr., December 23, 1961; [ch.] James E. (Yoland P.) Roddey, Jr., Thomas G. Roddey, Oresa R. (Samuel, IV) Wallace, (Grandchildren) Eric M. Roddey, Gavan J. Roddey, Samuel Wallace, V; [ed.] 1990 Mid-Atlanta Theology Seminary - DM, 1967 Winthrop University - MAT Library Science, English, 1960 J. C. Smith University BA English, Religious Education 1957 Immanuel Lutheran High School Diploma, 1945-54 Public Schools of Charlotte, SC and Rock Hill, SC certificate, 1994 Clinton Junior College - Librarian, 1969 Winthrop U. - summer school instructor, 1967 - 1968 Carolina Community Action - Head Start teacher, center director, 1964-67, 68-94 Charlotte-Mecklenburg Schools - teaching assistant principal, teacher, media coordinator, 1963-64 York, SC School District 1 - elementary teacher/assistant librarian, 1962-1985 Liberty Hill Baptist, Foundation and Red Oak Methodist.musician, 1961-63 Rock Hill School District 3 - high school english teacher, 1960-61 Johnson C. Smith University - library assistant; [occ.] College Librarian; [memb.] 1994 Southern Eastern Library Association - media utilization committee, 1993-95 Metrolina Library Association - local conference committee director for public schools, 1992 NC Educational Media Assoc. - conference hostess National Council of Negro Women, Order of Eastern Star - district choir director Heroines of Jericho, Templer's Crusaders, Delta Sigma Theta Sorority, Inc., - life member, membership trainer, undergraduate advisor, SAR council member, historian and journalist, chapter officer and committee member, conference worship leader, national and regional protocol committee, NC Forum Scholarship Selection Committee and Fellow, SC Commission on Women, Advisory Council of the Recruitment and Retension Project, USC - Lancaster, Black Alumni Advisory Committee, Winthrop Committee The Herald Diversity Committee, Prince of Peace Lutheran Church, Charlotte, NC - member Grace Lutheran Church, Rock Hill, SC - member of Campus Ministry Committee, guest soloist, Liberty Hill Baptist Church, Catawba, SC- deaconess, guest organist; [hon.] National Honor Society Phi Kappa Alpha Humanities Honor Society Alpha Kappa Mu Honor Society NAACP Education Award Olympic/ South Teacher of the Year - Charlotte - Mecklenburg Schools, Alumnae, Teaching Scholar, - NC Center for the Advancement of Teachers, Winthrop U. - RODLEY-MCMILLIAN NEWSLETTER, Convocation Speaker, Greek Advisor of the Year Award, Black Alumni recognition Delta Sigma Theta Sorority, Inc. - Regional Great Teacher Award, Women Who Are Making A Difference Award, 25 Year Membership Award, 30 Year Membership Award, Seed Grant Winner, two-time regional project winner, Chester Alumnae Chapter, DST Sorority, Inc. - Great Teacher Award, Sisterhood Award, 10 Year Service Pin Xi Beta Chapter, DST Sorority, Inc. - Cynthia P. Roddey Scholarship, Visible Woman Award, Founders Day Recognition, Convocation Recognition, C.T. Roddey Family - Service Award, National Gallery of Art Proposal Winner NASA Orbiter - Naming Program participant, Steele Creek Elem. School - Civil Rights/Education Award Vision Cable - Cable in the Classroom Programming Winner Who's Who Worldwide Registry, Inc., listing National Library of Poetry - semi-finalist; [oth. writ.] "Thus Far By Faith" teaching the Dewey Decimal System Through Poetry"; [pers.] God is the source of my being and faith in Him makes the impossible, pos-

sible.; [a.] Catawba, SC

RODRIGUEZ, VICKY
[b.] October 28, 1978, Long Beach, CA; [p.] Vicente Rodriguez, Editha Rodriguez; [ed.] Mar Vista Middle School, Chula Vista High School; [memb.] Yearbook photographer, editor and juniors section, A.F.O. Co-Comm. of cultural dance, CVHS marching spartan alliance and pit percussionists, California Scholarship federation, peer counselor; [hon.] Participant of California, Teen leadership program at UCSB, Finalist of the art instruction school contest; [oth. writ.] Freelance write for newspaper staff at CVHS; [pers.] I believe that ones writing reflects ones own personal thoughts from ones mind and heart; [a.] San Diego, CA

RODRIGUEZ, FIONA
[b.] November 25, 1953; [pers.] I wrote this poem after I saw your poetry contest ad. It's the first poem I have ever written. It was an unexpected delight to have written it: "wow! Where did this come from!?" It's now both a pleasure and a passion for me to write songs of love to Jesus. Thank you!!; [a.] Hebbronville, TX

RODRIGUEZ, MELANIE
[b.] May 24, 1995, North Carolina; [p.] Ismael Rodriguez, Norma Herrera; [m.] Paul Jansen, September 9, 1993; [ch.] Ryan and Miranda Jansen; [occ.] Student; [oth. writ.] I've written poems for years as an outlet for strong emotions. I've never before attempted to have and published; [pers.] The subject of the poem is my husband Paul.; [a.] Denver, CO

ROE, MARILYN
[b.] July 31, 1950, Fort Worth, TX; [p.] Bill H. Roe, And Ida Mae Roe; [ch.] 2 daughters - Coy Yon Hamilton, Misti Dawn Ashmall; [ed.] Brewer High School Fort Worth Christian College; [occ.] National Parks Volunteer; [hon.] National Honor Society; [oth. writ.] Several poems 15 songs,one short story; [pers.] I live each day to it's fullest, taking time to observe the nature around me. It is from nature that I draw my strength and receive peace of mind.; [a.] Grandbury, TX

ROGERS, DIANA LYNN
[pen.] Diana Rogers; [b.] May 7, 1947, Kokomo, IN; [ch.] Michelle Renee', Jarrett Wade; [ed.] Western High School; [occ.] Territory Mgr, Carole Fabrics; [memb.] Family Worship Center; [oth. writ.] Personal Writings of Poetry and Songs; [pers.] Because of God's faithfulness of me, my greatest desire is to glorify God as during the most tragic period of my life the holy spirit has brought me through it all.; [a.] Kokomo, IN

ROGERS, BARBARA V.
[pen.] Barbara V. Rogers; [b.] March 26, 1921, Current Add.; [p.] Leo and Eva Hall Volk; [m.] Robert C. Rogers (2nd Husband), September 24, 1977; [ch.] 0 of my own 1 step son; [ed.] High school Grad; [occ.] Retired and Physically challenge by stroke; [memb.] None at present, I did belong to score prior to my illness; [hon.] 1 third place ribbon for an, acryillic painting "Spring Flowers" in 1992 Senior Comp WCCU; [oth. writ.] Several others poems and all the verses for my greeting card; [pers.] It's difficult for me to get around so I point and write poetry and make my own greeting cards from "scratch" as a hobby; [a.] Belle Vernon, PA

ROGERS, CHRISTIE E.
[b.] October 8, 1971, New Bedford, MA; [p.] Mr. and Ms. Ronald J. Rogers; [m.] Fiancee Michael J. Larke; [ed.] Bishop Stang H.S., Converse College, BA Webster University, MA; [occ.] Counsellor for the deaf; [oth. writ.] Several poems and articles in newspapers; [pers.] "Dear Michael" is for my best friend who shares my hopes and dreams. This poem is for you M.L.

ROGERS, ROBBIN L.
[b.] September 22, 1961, California; [p.] James and Geraldine Rogers; [ch.] Todd Alan Goss; [ed.] Sierra

High, San Bernardino, Valley College, Rio Hondo College; [memb.] Immanuel Baptist Church P.T.A., Highland Y.M.C.A.; [oth. writ.] Several poems not yet published. One published in journey of the mind, National Library of Poetry.; [pers.] My poems are inspired by the people in my life, but mostly by God.; [a.] Highland, CA

ROGERS, SHUNTRELA DENISE
[b.] July 8, 1974, Ft. Laud., FL; [p.] Janice and David Rogers; [ed.] Ely High School, Nova Southeastern University; [occ.] Teller, First Union National Bank of FL; [memb.] Nova Score Program, New Beginning Christian Center (Deerfield Beach); [hon.] Dean's List, Who's Who, Principal's Award, Outstanding Tutorial Service Award, Home EC Student of the Year '91, Honor Roll; [oth. writ.] Spiritual Poetry of Encouragement for Youth Sundays at church and personal enhancement; [pers.] You can do anything with nothing when God is your everything.; [a.] Deerfield Beach, FL

ROGOSKI, SHARON
[b.] December 8, 1977, Mineral Wells, TX; [p.] Mr. and Mrs. A. H. Rogoski; [ed.] Millsap High School; [pers.] I use poetry as a catalyst for my frustration in an effort to leave my turmoil and leave me with hope.; [a.] Millsap, TX

ROJAS, PATRICK
[pen.] Patricio Rojas; [b.] January 24, 1933, Santa Maria, CA; [p.] Patrick and Helen Rojas; [m.] Joanne Morrow Rojas, August 15, 1954; [ch.] Patrick Rojas, Anne Ewing, Ellie Long; [ed.] Graduate UCSB, Graduate School UCLA; [occ.] Retired; [pers.] Interested in Calif History - Great, great, great grandfather, Jose Manuel Boronda came to Monterey Ca. in late 170 is established 1st boys school.

ROLLINS, SELISA FASHA
[b.] August 22, 1986, Phoenix, AZ; [p.] Karen Becketts and Willie Rollins; [ed.] 2nd Grade Student at Martin Luther King Elementary School - Gifted Program; [hon.] Outstanding Artwork, Running Start Challenge, Certificate of Achievement in Reading, Achievement in Art, Perfect Attendance, Student of the Month; [a.] Phoenix, AZ

ROMANOV, SVETLANA
[b.] February 4, 1977, Russia; [p.] Svetlana Romanov and Nicholas Romanov; [ed.] Specialized English High School in Russia, music school (Russia), Miami Dale Community College.; [occ.] Student at the Miami - Dade CC.; [oth. writ.] Actually I'm a songwriter. I have over 70 songs. And this poem is one of my favorite songs. Few of my other songs were successfully performed in different bands,; [pers.] I write about what I see, I write what I think, and I keep it in a very simple style, so that it would be easy for anyone to read it and understand it. Sometimes people say that's exactly what I wanted to say I just didn't know how to put in words.; [a.] Fort Lauderdale, FL

ROOK, PAUL M.
[pen.] Yosemite Paul; [b.] September 9, 1955, Kennett, MO; [p.] Miles P. Rook, Emma J. Rook; [ed.] Orange High, Orange CO., I.C.S. - International Correspondence School of Photography; [occ.] Welder H and H Industries, Riverside; [pers.] Their are several other poems I've written. Which I hope to publish in the near future. All my poems and especially this one are true event that really happen in my life, or I've seen happening.; [a.] Riverside, CA

ROSE, ALICE MARIE
[pen.] A. Rose; [b.] January 30, 1937, Taylor, TX; [p.] Lymon and Mary Rinderknecht; [m.] Charles H. Rose, January 7, 1957; [ch.] Debra Lyn Rose Aulin, Dale Ray Rose; [ed.] Eight months College; [occ.] Disabled Housewife (Heart); [memb.] Grace Luthern Church U.S. Army (1955 to 1957); [oth. writ.] Two poems in progress

I finished (old glory) four poems total.; [pers.] To put into words what I cant say; [a.] Mart, TX

ROSE, MICHAEL
[b.] January 16, 1974, Florida; [p.] Ron and Sherry Rose; [m.] Dana Rose, June 5, 1993; [ed.] Jacksonville High; [occ.] Flexographics Printer; [pers.] I've written only one poem. Thanks to my mom it was noticed.; [a.] Hope, AR

ROSENBLATT, MYRTLE
[b.] October 5, 1931, Newark, NJ; [p.] Ethel and Benjamin Emmer; [m.] Jack Rosenblatt, June 28, 1952; [ch.] Jerry Rosenblatt, Debra M. Montagna; [ed.] Graduated South Side High School in Newark with honors. Took up a college course but was unable to attend due to financial difficulty.; [occ.] Executive Secretary to Chairman John Urban (worked for him over 20 years) for Edwards and Kelcey, 299 Madison Ave. Morristown, NJ; [memb.] Unfortunately, do not belong to any organizations.; [pers.] I enjoy writing poetry and get easily inspired when things happen to me. It is my release and I can express my feelings through poetry. Perhaps this is a new "beginning" for me. I enjoy my job and my family and actually enjoy life, although sometimes I do find that "Life is not Fair"; [a.] Edison, NJ

ROSS, RYAN
[pen.] Raven; [b.] December 23, 1977, Albuquerque, NM; [p.] Larry Ross, And Darla Ross; [ed.] Del Norte High School, Junior Year; [occ.] Student; [memb.] Del Norte DECA, Del Norte MESA, Tennis, and Del Norte Phantom Knight Marching Band.; [hon.] Deca State Qualifier, Tennis District Qualifier, PKMB Drumline "2nd in State" Member, 5th and 9th place MESA UNM competition, etc.; [oth. writ.] Uncharted Waters, Drowning Sorrows, Tears of Sorrow, Noble soldier, mourning. (All are poems), The Michigan Cheerleader Massacre (play); [pers.] "Every person must be themselves and not follow others, for follows at most end second best."; [a.] Albuquerque, NM

ROSS, CHRISTLE
[b.] September 29, 1971, Detroit, MI; [p.] Gerald and Connie Grady; [m.] Noah Ross, May 11, 1990; [ch.] Noah Baine, Jessica Lynn; [ed.] Plymouth - Canton High School 1989. Dorsey Business School; [pers.] We only get one chance in life, but we have two roads to choose from. We can either work hard and try to make the world better. Or, we can stand on the sidelines and complain.; [a.] Wayne, MI

ROSSI JR., TONY
[b.] September 22, 1935, New Jersey; [p.] Mary and Tony Rossi; [m.] Donna Rossi, April 10, 1060; [ch.] William Rossie, Laural Rossi; [ed.] High School Northeast High; [occ.] Executive Chef; [memb.] Chef De Cuisin of San Diego; [hon.] Chef of the year 1993; [oth. writ.] A lot but never sent any in till now. I wrote the poems for my wife only

ROTHSTEIN, SHARI LYNN
[b.] July 17, 1966, Plainview, NY; [p.] Frederick and Andrea; [ed.] Syracuse University St. Newhouse School of Communications; [occ.] Writer; [memb.] Sigma Delta Tau; [oth. writ.] Articles for various entertainment magazines domestic and international. Staff writer for gifts and decorative accessories.; [pers.] Never give up. You're only a failure if you don't try. Everyone has a special talent and it will surface when and where you least expect it.; [a.] New York, NY

ROUSE, PRIMA MORANDA
[pen.] Pep Pep, Randa, Gradma; [b.] May 25, 1975, Pittsburg; [p.] Mary L. Rouse; [ed.] Woodland Hills High School Eastern Mennonite University Community College; [occ.] Student At EMU; [hon.] Graduated from High School with Honors, choice award from the National Library of Poetry in 1994, and my biography in Americans most honor student in U.S.; [oth. writ.]

"Having Hope", "Fluxuate", Dreams", "Lonely Thoughts", "A man I love", ect.; [pers.] "People in this world have a great mind. They just have to find the right way to use it."; [a.] Turtle Creek, PA

ROY, EVA M.
[b.] October 31, 1932, Owosso, MI; [p.] Frank Austin and Viola (Sanders) Austin; [m.] Gordon D. Roy, June 27, 1959; [ch.] Brian, Lisa; [sib.] High School; [occ.] Home-Maker and Writer; [memb.] International Society of Famous Poets Society National Library of Poetry; [hon.] Nine Golden Poet Awards Forty Awards of Merit Awards Fourth Place in Poetry Contest, Twenty nine poems published in poetry books.; [oth. writ.] Newspapers School and Church Bulletins; [pers.] I write poetry for enjoyment and to relax. I love putting words together in story form and letting the words rhyme.; [a.] Lakeview, MI

RUBINOSS, DAME DARLENE
[pen.] Dame Darlene Rubinoss; [b.] May 12, 1927, Ohio; [p.] Ethel and Charles Conrad; [m.] December 23, 1972, Deceased; [ch.] Eight Children; [ed.] Ohio State University Rice University St. Thomas University of Houston; [occ.] Writer - Inventor; [memb.] Director Houston World Literature Center, Phi Beta Fraternity for the Arts, Director of Friends of Music University of Houston member Toastmaster, International; [hon.] Best Speaker - Toastmaster Outstanding Artist Phi Beta for Dance of the Russian Peasant", V.S. Patents; [oth. writ.] Dance of the Russian Peasant Day after Tomorrow what happened to Monday the Deadly Cure Love Sonnets - Poetry Book; [pers.] As window of the Great Violinist composer and Conductors and mother to eight children 7 grand children I have much to draw upon for my writing; [a.] Houston, TX

RUDASILL, NANCY BALTHAZAR
[b.] April 30, 1953, Rego Park, NY; [p.] Robert and Norma E. Balthazar; [ch.] Robert Thomas Rudasill; [ed.] Henderson High, Dekalb Jr. College; [occ.] Director of Sales and Marketing - Seasons, A Classic Residence by Hyatt; [memb.] Sponsor - Nat'l Stroke Association Women in Health care Chamber of Commerce; [hon.] Outstanding Services Award IREM Institute of R.E. Mgmt., Atlanta Chapter 67 - 1985, IREM ARM of the Year 1986 and 1987 - Atlanta chapter 67, IREM National ARM of the Year 1986; [oth. writ.] Several poems currently unpublished.; [pers.] I strive to see the good in all people and about our life issues that I feel strongly about. I am greatly influenced by my lifelong love of music and by specific musicians and songwriters.; [a.] Boca Raton, FL

RUDING, KAROL
[b.] February, 21, 1959, Washington, DC; [m.] Kevin Robinson, December 24, 1994; [ed.] University of South Carolina; [occ.] Financial Analyst; [memb.] NRA; [pers.] A poem sometimes pleases a few and sometimes many. Who it touches is the mystery and the poet's pleasure. Night to Thee was written to my loving man.; [a.] Arlington, VA

RUSSELL, MATTHEW
[pen.] Jason A. Roland; [b.] November 15, 1959, Council Bluffs, IA.; [ed.] B.A Degrees in Theology and theatre arts.; [oth. writ.] Novels: His God was horror, the testimony which is not called, the Psalm of sin, in the place of askings, currently, come forth by day. Also, numerous screen plays.; [pers.] Mr. Roland is as dedicated to writing for others as he is for himself, He will consider all offers. He can be through his legal reference: Matthew Russell, contacted V1405 McPherson Ave., Council Bluffs, Iowa, 51503; [a.] Council Bluffs, IA

RYAN, MARGARET A.
[pen.] Peggy Ryan; [b.] November 28, 1923, Philadelphia, PA; [p.] James and Betty McGovern; [m.] William J. Ryan Jr., August 1, 1943; [ch.] William 44,

Nancy 46, Robert 48, James 53, Margaret 58, Joanne 60, Regina 65; [ed.] Presently a Junior, Monmouth College, West Long Branch, NJ 07764; [occ.] Part time tutor in English skills, also dressmaking.; [memb.] St. Mary's Church, deal, NJ, Rosary Altar Society Church Choir, Cantor,; [hon.] National Honor Society Of Psychology, Dean's List Spring, Fall, 1994, Spring 1995 LAMBDA Sigma Tau the honor society of Monmouth University; [oth. writ.] Many short, philosophical poems, all unpublished. Extensive research and essay papers related to science in the humanities; [pers.] In my struggle for personal identity, self-esteem and the meaning of life, many changes have occurred. One thing remains, my humpty dumpty heart lands upright.; [a.] West Long Branch, NJ

RYAN, MIKE
[b.] April 27, 1939, Cleveland, OH; [ed.] BA, MA (Eng. Lit.); [occ.] Writer; [memb.] Southwest Writers Groups Albuquerque, NM; [pers.] Joseph Campbell, Listen to someone speaking, not to the words, but to what is talking; [a.] Albuquerque, NM

RYAN, SHANNA MARIE
[b.] May 12, 1978, Johnstown, PA; [p.] Robert J. and Karen M. Ryan; [ed.] 11th Grade Student at North Star High School Boswell, PA; [occ.] Student; [memb.] Student Council at my School.; [a.] Jennerstown, PA

RYNO, JEANNETTE B.
[pen.] Owner J. D. Data Service; [b.] May 22, 1924, USA; [p.] Herman and Leta Linn Baver; [m.] Charles E. Ryno, Sr., September 23, 1944; [ch.] Charles Jr., Diane, Gretchen, Nina, Michael; [ed.] High School; [occ.] I do a number of things, some more skillfully than others.; [memb.] United Methodist Church of Andover Democratic Party the Concord Coalition; [oth. writ.] Clerical techniques for quality information management, lyrics, commentaries, a novel (Sammy); [pers.] I believe that the invasion of a personality beyond the invitation to the invader, generates a poverty of creative ability. I try to encourage the development of personal strength; [a.] Espyville, PA

SADLER, RACHEL DEIRDRE
[b.] April 25, 1979, Springfield, OH; [p.] Kathy S. Sadler; [ed.] Sophomore at Kingman High, North, Kingman, Arizona.; [occ.] Student and Waitress, would like to become an architect; [memb.] Slick Snooty Racing; [hon.] Poem published by The National Library of Poetry, Darkside Of The Moon.; [oth. writ.] Several other poems, three short stories and one novel; [pers.] The way you feel can't say anything but can mean a lot. What you say can mean so little, and at the same time, mean a lot. To those who care and those who don't, say what you feel and not what you don't.; [a.] Kingman, AZ

SAIKUS, CHRISTOPHER ANDREW
[b.] November 30, 1979, Cleveland, OH; [p.] Rimantas (Ray) and Sylvia J.; [ch.] Sister Christina; [ed.] University School - currently in the 9th grade; [occ.] Student - University School in Shaker Heights, Ohio; [pers.] Poem written in the sixth grade.; [a.] Euclid, OH

SALES, LEONIDES S.
[pen.] Leo Sales; [b.] April 22, 1936, Bacarra, Ilocos Norte, Philippines; [p.] Gregorio Albano Sales and Maria Sales; [m.] Erlinda V. Sales (divorce), March 3, 1955; [ch.] Victor Sales, Glenda Sales, Anthony Sales, Ferdinand Sales, Geraldine Shimos, Christopher Sales, Lilibeth Sales and Ronald-Reagan Sales.; [ed.] Kabankalan Academy, Negros Occidental, Bachelor of Science in Commerce, University of the East, Manila, Philippines.; [occ.] Philippine Air Force, Armed Forces of the Philippines, Leutenant Retired, 23 years of service. Former Security Aide of President Ferdinand Eralin Marcos of the Philippines.; [memb.] American Association of Retired Persons - May 1986. Filipino American Community of Los Angeles Inc. - 1989-

1990. United Bacarreneous of Hawaii Inc. 1992. Kiss AM Fun Club, Hawaii 1992, Filipino-Californians Senior Citizens Society, Inc. 1993, International Circle Incorporated 1993 to date.; [oth. writ.] Several articles published "The Youth Grinder", Bacarra Provincial High School newspaper.; [pers.] Strive hard to be a successful writer and poet. What you can do today must not be your work tomorrow.; [a.] San Francisco, CA

SALTER, SANDRA
[p.] Robert and Nadine Russell; [m.] Tom Salter; [ch.] Eric, Chris, Charra, Aaron, Candice; [ed.] High School Diploma; [occ.] United States Post Office; [memb.] Shekinah Church; [pers.] The Lord has supplied a lifetime of needs, and the privilege of the pen brings joy to those who create and receive. Special thanks to Mom.; [a.] Whitmore Lake, MI

SANBORN, HELEN MANN
[b.] February 23, 1928, Sterling, MA; [p.] Walter Mann and Ethel Mann; [m.] Homer C. Sanborn, August 18, 1946; [ch.] Ford, Karen, Donald, David, Valerie, Dale, Holly, Glenn; [sib.] Leominster, MA High School, also several archaeology courses at Fitchburg Art Museum; [occ.] Retired news writer (now at home mother and grandmother); [memb.] Woman's Club, Patrons of Husbandry (Grange), Assabet Valley Master singers, Milford Community Chorus, United Parish Church and choir, Upton Historical Society, UCC Conference Delegate; [hon.] First prize, Mass Federation of Woman's Clubs poetry contest, (High school: Latin, French, English prizes.); [oth. writ.] Numerous feature articles for Worcester Telegram and Gazette, poems in a "personal collection" often given as gifts, special report for National Women's Conference (UCC), poem for rededication of Upton Town Hall ceremony; [pers.] Life seems to me a wondrous adventure. When experiencing its emotional highs and lows or absorbing nature's beauty, poetry seems the only adequate way to express the feelings which come from deep inside.; [a.] Upton, MA

SANBORN, THOMAS P.
[pen.] Sandy; [b.] August 25, 1955, Darby, PA; [p.] John and Dorothy Sanborn; [m.] Frida Q. Sanborn, June 4, 1984; [ch.] Dorothy C. Sanborn, daughter; [ed.] Business Management Assoc. Degree; [occ.] Counselor, Fairmont Memorial Park; [hon.] Granada Decorated, Veteran USAF SSgt 10 yrs. of service; [pers.] To live is to write, to write is to live.; [a.] Spokane, WA

SANCHEZ, ERIK LEDESMA
[pen.] E.S.L.; [b.] March 30, 1966, Cuba; [p.] Bengina Perez Ledesma, Orlando Oliva Sanchez; [ed.] Life and A.A. in History and Psychology; [occ.] United Parcel Driver; [memb.] Homosapien Male; [hon.] Many nomination, but refuse to conform society's stereotype; [oth. writ.] Many personal expressions non published but hopeful.; [pers.] Insatiable appetite for knowledge; [a.] Tampa, FL

SANCHEZ, IRMA R.
[pen.] Sanchez; [b.] May 23, 1957, Clayton, NM; [p.] Sadie Castillo and Jimmy Sanchez; [ch.] Jessica, Rachael, Toby; [ed.] Clayton High School; [occ.] Teacher Aide; [oth. writ.] Several poems, one song has been published; [pers.] Never give up today, what you wish to accomplish tomorrow.

SANDERFORD, MARTHA JEAN
[b.] December 5, 1977, Corpus Christi, TX; [p.] Matthew and Margarita Sanderford; [ed.] San Marcos Baptist Academy; [occ.] Student; [memb.] National Honor Society, Daughter of American Revolution; [oth. writ.] Several other poems; [pers.] Everything I write, I dedicate to the honor and glory of my Father God, who has blessed me with this talent.; [a.] Fort Worth, TX

SANDERS, BRENT W.
[b.] September 23, 1978, Alexandria, LA; [p.] George Sanders Jr. and Linda Sanders; [ed.] Jr. at Holy Savoir Menard Central High School; [memb.] Who's Who in American High Schools, American Scholars; [hon.] American Scholar, Honor Roll; [oth. writ.] Poems in Untouched Horizons; [pers.] Thoughts are to be shared.; [a.] St. Landry, LA

SANDOVAL, PATRICIA ANN
[pen.] Patricia Ann Sandoval; [b.] December 8, 1963, Fort Wainwrite, AK; [p.] Jo Mitchell and Tristan Huat; [ch.] Jessica Gamboa, Jesse Gamboa, Brian Henderson; [ed.] Adamson High, Gary Job Corps. "Carpentry" Lindsay Cooper A/C Heating Repairs" Mans field Business School "I.W.P."; [occ.] Freelance Painter Carpentry Contractor; [memb.] American Poetry Association World of Poetry; [hon.] Merit award published world of Poetry Worlds best loved Poems "Break Down" 1983, Anthology of Poetry title "Love"; [oth. writ.] Private unpublished books entitled poetry emotion hook I and II children's book title: Oh Halloween Night 28 pgs.; [pers.] Upon the reconciliation of my beloved, nothing of value could express how much I cherish and learned to respect the delicacy of a relationship. This is my recital to the world in dedication to Ronnie Henderson.; [a.] Dallas, TX

SANGER, DONALD
[pen.] A. Hardcoret, D. Sanger Jr.; [b.] July 16, 1975, Buffalo, NY; [p.] Donald K. Sanger Sr., M. Ward; [m.] Single status; [ed.] Lancaster Central Sr., High School; [occ.] Laborer; [memb.] Book Club by Mail; [oth. writ.] Novel "Revenge"; [pers.] In my writings, the efforts are observations of my soul, and the goal is to express them. Ancient poems that conjour the flame within make poetry all the more captivating.; [a.] Depew, NY

SANNES, JEFFREY W.
[pen.] Jeff Sannes; [b.] July 2, 1958, Royal Oak, MI; [p.] Loren and Alice Sannes; [m.] Rache, July 19, 1980; [ch.] 4, Emily, Lindsay, Nancy, Julie; [oth. writ.] Numerous personal writings, nothing previously published.; [pers.] Life is about experiences and sharing them with others. I write to capture lite, experience by experience!; [a.] Brighton, MI

SANTOS JR., MANUEL
[b.] May 31, 1973, Houston, TX; [p.] Manuel Santos Sr. and Virginia Santos; [ed.] Phillis Wheatley High; [oth. writ.] A few poems published during my senior year in high school, in the school anthology.; [pers.] I continuously strengthen my mental and spiritual outlook on life through my poems, with some small hope to spark beauty within the hearts of us all.; [a.] Houston, TX

SARACCO, GINA MARIE
[pen.] Gina Marie; [b.] October 16, 1967, Arcadia, CA; [p.] John Darryl Vickery and Karin Elaine Charles; [ed.] Westchester High School, Los Angeles, California, Santa Monica College, Santa Monica, California; [occ.] Bookkeeper, Precision Automotive, Los Angeles, California; [oth. writ.] Currently working on a screenplay and trying to publish one of my short stories for children.; [pers.] SRM, Thanks for helping me believe in myself. I did it! Look out world, Gina Marie is here.; [a.] Culver City, CA

SATRIANO, STEPHANIE
[b.] May 3, 1975, Jamaica, NY; [p.] Josephine and Thomas Satriano; [ch.] Jasmine Amanda Gonzalez; [ed.] New Utrecht High School; [occ.] Freshman at Kingsborough Community College, CUNY, Brooklyn, NY; [memb.] American Museum of Natural History, Smithsonian Institution; [oth. writ.] A poem printed in my elementary school yearbook and a personal collection of poems and essays.; [pers.] I mainly write about what I feel and what I experience in life. I believe that

readers can get a better understanding of me this way.; [a.] Brooklyn, NY

SAUNDERS, ALLEN DAVID
[b.] December 24, 1965, Detroit, MI; [p.] Albert Saunders and Joan Lucia; [m.] Julie Ann Saunders, October 16, 1993; [ch.] soon expecting - Kristen Joan or Eric Anthony; [ed.] Fordson High School, Henry Ford Community College; [occ.] Machine Repairman (Journeyman) for Rouge Steel.; [hon.] Honor society in both high school and college.; [oth. writ.] Currently delving into script writing.; [pers.] Life is like a whisper. It doesn't matter if it is loud or soft. Only that it exists!!!; [a.] Dearborn Heights, MI

SAVILLE JR., JOHN K.
[b.] December 3, 1916, Evanston, IL; [p.] John M. Saville and Lydia M. Saville; [m.] Nellie Anne Saville, August 19, 1942; [ch.] Susan, Deborah, Mary, John III; [ed.] Occidental College - B.A. 1938, Church Divinity School of the Pacific B.A. 1942.; [occ.] Retired Pastoral Assistant, Trinity Church, Redlands, CA; [memb.] Rotary Club - District Chairman, Chairman - Meals on Wheels, Chairman - Clergy Commission on Alcoholism; [hon.] Honorary Canon Episcopal Diocese of Los Angeles 1973, Rector Emeritus St. Michael's Church, Anaheim CA 1945-1980: Doctor of Divinity 1989, Phi Beta Kappa, 1989; [oth. writ.] Susan Lay Ministry on the Frontier 1985. Western National Parks in Poetry. Christian Saints in Poetry; [pers.] I want to try to share God's love in nature's beauty and in the caring lives of the saints; [a.] Redlands, CA

SAVRTKA, DEBRA
[pen.] Debra Paulk Savrtka; [b.] January 29, 1969, Ft. Worth, TX; [p.] Lewis and Patty Paulk Sr.; [m.] Douglas Savrtka, August 22, 1987; [ed.] Castleberry Baptist Christian School, Baptist Bible College, Tarrant County Junior College; [occ.] Veterinary Technician; [memb.] Faith Baptist Fellowship Church; [hon.] National Honor Roll Society, 6th Place, Nationals - Short Story, 3rd Place, Nationals - Female Solo in Voice; [pers.] Each life we touch, we leave heart-prints, may they be filled with truth and kindness. Jesus is my soul inspiration. From God's heart to my pen, may His message always send. Hurting, yet, healing hearts write poetry.; [a.] Ft. Worth, TX

SAWAYDA, JENNIFER
[b.] July 25, 1985, Clearwater, FL; [p.] David and Judith Sawayda; [ed.] Student at Largo Central Elementary, Largo, FL; [hon.] Honor roll and Principal's List; [pers.] My hobby is reading.; [a.] Largo, FL

SAXENA, SHIV
[pen.] Shiv; [b.] January, 1934, India; [p.] Mr. Ladli Parshad Seth and Mrs. Ishro Devi Seth; [m.] Swaran Lal Saxena, July, 1956; [ch.] Gunita Saxena, Ursula Hust, Meenakshi Saxena; [ed.] Bachelor of Arts, JBT (Teaching Diploma); [occ.] Vice President and Corporate Secretary; [memb.] Hindu Temple, Mahatma Gandhi Center, Sikh Study Circle and Jain Center; [pers.] Give more them you want to receive from others. Respect the authorities and law. Be parents is then friends to your children. Have faith in God.; [a.] Saint Louis, MO

SCAIFE, JULIE ANN JESSICA
[pen.] Jewel; [b.] December 21, 1980, Fortuna, CA; [p.] Jo Shamblim and Jim Scaife; [ed.] Student - 8th grade; [occ.] Student; [hon.] 1995 president: Toddy Thomas School, Miss Pre-Teen, (First Place Scholastics) "A" Honor Roll (4 yrs), 1994 Treasurer

SCANLAN, JOPAT
[b.] March 14, 1957, California; [p.] Bill Woodson, Pat Schuermann; [m.] Noel Scanlan, November 24, 1989; [ch.] Sean, Pat, Arin, Eric, Bridget, Sarah; [ed.] Homemaker; [pers.] I have been writing for 23 years and now I have realized my dream. Thank you, my dearest

husband.; [a.] Kansas City, MO

SCEARCE II, ROBERT
[b.] February 19, 1965, Danville, VA; [p.] Robert and Anette Scearce; [ed.] 1. B.S. Business Admin - Univ of S Carolina, 2. Attending Naval Postgraduate School - Monterey, CA; [occ.] US Navy Lt; [memb.] American Legion, Surface Navy Association; [hon.] 2 Navy Achievement medals, 2 Navy Commendation medals; [a.] Monterey, CA

SCHAFFER, REGINA
[pen.] Ann Schaffer; [b.] August 23, 1982, Kansas City, MO; [p.] Roswitha and Kenneth Schaffer; [ed.] Plaza Middle School; [oth. writ.] I have never written anything else that was published; [pers.] All the poems I write have to do with nature.; [a.] Kansas City, MO

SCHARTMANN, WALTER A.
[b.] August 16, 1950, Munich, Germany; [p.] Walter and Elizabeth Schartmann; [m.] Judith M. Schartmann, June 12, 1970; [ch.] Allan, Daniel Schartmann; [ed.] State University of New York at Oswego NY; [occ.] United States Marine Corps Officer; [pers.] Haikus rise from chaos and bring order out of struggle and hope.; [a.] Oceanside, CA

SCHAU, DONALD WARD
[pen.] Don Schau; [b.] December 27, 1922, Kalamazoo; [p.] Anna and Harvey Schau; [m.] Colleen J. Schau, November 3, 1944; [ch.] 5 - Richard, Randell, Scot, Steve, Jordan; [ed.] High school - Kalamazoo Central High; [hon.] Being a grandfather with 13 grandchildren; [pers.] I always liked poetry because it taught you a lot about life.; [a.] Kalamazoo, MI

SCHELOSKY, VIRGINIA
[pen.] Virginia Schelosky; [b.] April 24, 1921, Detroit; [p.] William and Marie Scurlock; [m.] Edgar L. Schelosky, September 9, 1943; [ch.] David A. Schelosky; [ed.] High School Graduate, Course in Business at D.R.I.; [occ.] Retired Housewife; [hon.] None, other than being honored by your publishing "Depression" in your book "Tomorrow Never Knows"; [oth. writ.] Poems that I have kept over the years.; [pers.] "Joey" in this book was inspired by the little boy next door. A lovable three year old. Most of my poems were inspired by my son.; [a.] Allen Park, MI

SCHLEGEL, SANDI Y.
[pen.] Sandi Y. Schlegel; [b.] July 12, 1975, Reading, PA; [p.] Jeffrey Himmelberger and Karen N. Manley; [m.] Theodore Schlegel, June 27, 1992; [ch.] Tiffany Y. Schlegel; [ed.] Reading High School aspiring on going to College within a few months; [occ.] Bindery Collator (Collating reading materials for use in schools); [oth. writ.] I have written many other poems that I would like to have published someday soon.; [pers.] When something can be read with little effort great effort has gone into its writing.; [a.] Reading, PA

SCHMIDT, NANCY
[pen.] E. J. McClure; [b.] October 11, 1936, Pennsylvania; [p.] James and Edna McCalmont; [m.] Robert Schmidt, June 5, 1953; [ch.] Cheryl, Timothy, Sandra and Robin; [pers.] When I write I try to convey my feelings of life as it unfolds with all of its infinite realism.; [a.] Surprise, AZ

SCHMIDT, VICTORIA
[b.] July 19, 1908, Saint Louis, MO; [p.] Gottfried Schmidt, Christina Juenger Schmidt; [ed.] A.B. Harris Teachers College, St. Louis, M.A. Teachers College, Columbia U., N.Y., Ed.D. U. Colorado, Boulder CO, Ran for Congress to learn politics; [occ.] Taught 50 years, all levels, last 30 years, Prof, Harris Teachers College, retired as teacher, 1978. Traveling and writing.; [memb.] Retired School Employees of St. Louis — Parlimentarian, Library of Congress Associates, Smithsonian Institution, American Museum of Natural

History World Wildlife Fund, Environmental Defense Fund, Polo Club, Explorers Club, Crow Canyon Archaeological Center; [oth. writ.] Victoria's Story, Reincarnation, God's Love Returned, Vantage Press 1992. Matrix of Our Lives used in Introduction. Bible Stories From Heaven, MS copywriter 1979. More Victoria's Story now in MS.; [pers.] Have traveled all over the world, including both polar regions, all five continents. Survived plane crash, two train crashes. Still traveling, writing. Each day is a precious gift to be fully lived. My writings carry a message to the world.; [a.] Saint Louis, MO

SCHNEIDER, SARAH
[pen.] Sarah Schneider; [b.] January 8, 1916, Winnipeg, Manitoba, Canada; [p.] Samuel and Golda Dorfman; [m.] Benjamin, April 7, 1935; [ch.] 4 sons, Dr. Jerry, Dr. Paul, Lawrence, Mark; [ed.] Mt. Clemens High School - Creative Writing Class in Southfield.; [occ.] Housewife; [memb.] Many help giving organizations; [hon.] Valedictorian, National Honor Society; [oth. writ.] Short Stories and Poetry in Creative Writing Class; [pers.] Put your heart and soul in everything you hope to accomplish.; [a.] Southfield, MI

SCHNEIDER, JOHN
[b.] January 14, 1962, Akron, OH; [m.] Julia Paisley-Schneider; [ed.] BSEE University of Akron; [occ.] Electrical Engineer; [a.] Avondale, AZ

SCHOEDINGER, TRACY
[b.] August 21, 1980, Florida; [p.] Debbie Schoedinger and Don Schoedinger; [ed.] Attending Middle School; [occ.] Student, Tequesta Trace Middle School; [a.] Davie, FL

SCHOESSEL, HAROLD C.
[pen.] HcSch; [b.] September 15, 1914, Imperial, MO; [p.] Hugo R. and Rose Ann Schoessel (nee Schwebel); [m.] Lora Virona Schoessel (nee Richards), May 31, 1956; [ed.] Grade school, one year Business school; [occ.] Military service WWII 4 1/2 years Army Engrs., Personnel Div. (Paragraph Trooper in the Chairborne Command), Retired since September 9, 1979; [hon.] None to date, but still anticipating; [oth. writ.] Poems only, but many; [pers.] I enjoy a serious effort to control my balance with physical and mental discipline. We all become old, but only when we loss control of our balance. I strive to rest when I work and work while resting. THANKS! For the opportunity to edit my poem in a classic, quality hardbound volume. I was always very reluctant to have it published in a magazine or newspaper, that would be tossed in the trash the next day. SINCERE SENIOR CITIZEN; [a.] Manchester, MO

SCHOFIELD, CHARLOTTE
[pen.] Charlotte Schofield; [b.] June 8, 1930, Fort Worth, TX; [p.] David and Carrie Schofield; [ch.] Aaron B. age 31, Carolyn Gray age 29; [ed.] M.A. - University of Texas City and Regional Planning, 1958 Fashion Design - College of Alameda, California, 1985; [occ.] Freelance Designer, Artist, unpublished poet; [oth. writ.] Poetry, essays, short stories all unpublished to date. Published: The Fashion Portfolio UNM/TI 1991; [pers.] Carmina O'Keeffe recalls the haunting, sacrilegious sounds of Carl Orff's and Carmina Burana juxtaposed against the shrubbed desert, "yellow light" and "wild vermilion strata" of that corner of New Mexico immortalized in the canvasses of Georgia O'Keeffe.; [a.] Austin, TX

SCHOFIELD, JACOB
[pen.] Jake, Jacoby; [b.] March, 84, Townsend, MA; [p.] Tom and Tammy; [sib.] 5th grade - Squanacook Elementary School, Teacher: Mrs. Norma King; [memb.] Very active in TYSA soccer, PAT Ice Hockey, TAP Basketball and the The Townsend Little League; [oth. writ.] Will have my poem "My Life's A Mess" published in the Anthology of Poetry by Young Ameri-

cans in 1995.; [pers.] Many of my recent writings have been greatly influenced by my Uncle David's recent illness and subsequent death. I miss you David!; [a.] Townsend, MA

SCHROCK, ROE
[b.] July 25, 1947, Philadelphia; [p.] Joe Walters, Josie Walters; [m.] Joe Schrock (deceased), February 18, 1967; [ch.] Dawn, Joey, Jake; [ed.] St. Maria Goretti High, now attending Community College of Phila; [occ.] Bookkeeper, Management Mulberry Deli; [memb.] Hockey Mom - St. John Neuman H.S.; [hon.] Dean's List; [oth. writ.] Poems published in local newspaper; [pers.] I strive to awaken the deepest human feelings and emotions in all mankind through my writings; [a.] Philadelphia, PA

SCHWEI, JOHN
[b.] January 20, 1922, Iron Mountain, MI; [p.] Elizabeth and John Schwei; [m.] Anne Bray (deceased), May 18, 1946; [ch.] Greg, James, Mark, Mary Anne, Robert, Laurene; [ed.] Iron Mountain High, MI, Mira Costa College, CA; [occ.] Medical Service Corps, U.S. Navy; [memb.] U.S. Navy, Distinguished Flying Cross Society; [hon.] Distinguished Flying Cross by 1st Sec. of Defense James V. Forrestal, Air Medal and Two (2) Leaf Clusters, Presidential Unit Citation, WW II; [oth. writ.] 'The Last Patrol' (Twilight Zone), May You Koan Shee; [pers.] I endeavor for complete independence from perilous encludes which entangle the soul of influences upon life in the realm of perceiving oneselve as unjustly treated. Being aware of the temptation to satisfy self forces responsibility. Thou I sometimes stumble, I'm still balanced, free and worthy.; [a.] Carlsbad, CA

SCHWETER, CAROLINE K.
[pen.] Caroline Anne Kelly; [b.] July 28, 1962, Cleveland, OH; [p.] Mary Louise Meyer and James Kelly; [m.] Marco Polo, August 20, 1994; [ch.] Grace Bernadette, age three (3) months; [ed.] Holy Name High School; [occ.] Paralegal - Irwin M. Frank and Thomas Longo; [memb.] National Shrine of St. Jude, Church of St. Michael; [oth. writ.] Cleveland State University Magazine - 1979, Contemporary Poets of Britain and America, published 1994.; [pers.] My poetry reflects past lives, and learning experiences. Through those in my past, I have become the person I am today. My husband, Marco, has brought such joy to my life. My daughter Grace Bernadette, means more to me than life itself. They are my true heroes.; [a.] Euclid, OH

SCOTT, IVORY LESHEA
[b.] September 24, 1964, Monroe, LA; [p.] Ms. Mary E. Scott; [m.] Single; [ed.] Wossman High School (Monroe, LA) - Class of '82, Louisiana State University - AA degree in Business, National Education Center - Small Business Management degree and Personal Fitness and Nutrition Trainer; [occ.] Law Enforcement; [memb.] Read America, Read Program! (Tutor Program); [hon.] National Honor Society and Who's Who Among American High School Students (3.88gpa), Coach's Award for Outstanding Service and Coaching at Wossman High School, Leadership Award, outstanding service, Desert Storm Award and Outstanding Athlete Award all while in the U.S. Air Force; [oth. writ.] Currently trying to get three book published. A 50 poem book called Life's Everchanging Journey, and two fiction books called Strength Through Pain and Notice Me. With the help of God and the right publisher it will happen!; [pers.] Always believe in yourself and never let anyone else control your actions, ideas, and thoughts. Stay strong toward your goals in life and make sure God is number one in your goals and life.; [a.] Las Vegas, NV

SCOTT, JEAN
[b.] December 23, 1914, Adrian, MI; [p.] T. Fred and Leah Y. Older; [m.] Cornelius W. Scott (Deceased), 1938; [ch.] 3 children, 6 grandchildren, 5 great-grandchildren; [ed.] B.A., M.A. - Eastern Michigan University, Postgraduate - Wayne State; [occ.] Retired from Eastern Michigan University; [pers.] To sift from our beleaguered lives each fragment that can make us glad to use the immutable freedom that lets us choose the Beautiful and not the Bad; [a.] Ypsilanti, MI

SEAVEY, GEORGE BARTLETT
[pen.] GB; [b.] March 20, 1936, Newbury Port, MA; [p.] Ralph Seavey and Esther Seavey; [m.] Betty Ann Davis (Div), August 24, 1957; [ch.] Kari, Scott; [ed.] Dover High School; [occ.] Mechanical Sales and Guidance; [oth. writ.] Angels of Unity, the Spirit EED Titus (Special occasion) within his work; [pers.] Some may think the thing I do, lack good sense and timing. But life ain't easy, when all your thoughts continually are rhyming.; [a.] Kissimmee, FL

SEAY, RAMONO M.
[b.] July 24, 1929, Clarksville; [p.] Hugh E. and Martha E. Martin; [m.] Floyd R. Seay, November 21, 1951; [ch.] Deborah J. Bumpus, Michael R. Seay and Linda K. Zitek; [ed.] Clarksville High graduate attended Austin Peay State; [occ.] Housewife; [memb.] First United Methodist Church, Children's Ministeries 1987-89, Worship Coordinator 1989-1992, Sunday School Teacher's Assistant 1993-1995; [hon.] 1983 Our Western Worlds Greatest Poems - John Campbell, Editor and Publisher, 1985 American Poetry Anthology - John Frost, Editor, Spring Addition, 1992 Yarn Spinner - The Southern Poetry Association; [oth. writ.] Several poem's published in local newspaper, and the Methodist Reporter; [pers.] I was inspired by my father, who was an unknown poet, who taught me to love my fellow man and to put my trust in God and thank Him for my talent.; [a.] Clarksville, TN

SECKEL, SHARON
[b.] January 21, 1950, Michigan; [p.] Walter C. and June L. Beveridge; [m.] Arthur J. Seckel, May 30, 1980; [ch.] Brian Allen, Bradley Arthur; [ed.] South Lake High; [pers.] I'd like to thank my sister, Barbara Collins, for submitting my poem and for thinking it was worth submitting, thanks Barb!

SEDITA, CHARLES
[b.] October 11, 1943, New York City; [p.] Grace and Charles Sr.; [ch.] Sandra and Gabrielle; [ed.] BA English - Queens College (en route), with minors in Secondary Education and French.; [occ.] Freelance writer and Clerk with NYS Attorney General's Office.; [hon.] 1994 Sandra Schorr Award for Excellence in Literature for a first novel, "The Learning Place." Formerly fiction editor of "New Press Literary Quarterly."; [oth. writ.] Several short stories and essays published internationally, including Reader's Digest Special Book Edition, France.; [pers.] Bilingual (French/English), I hope to teach in the very near future, and pass on my passion for literature to my students, as I have done with my children, who inspire most of my poetry.; [a.] New York, NY

SEELEY, BONNIE M. CHABOT
[b.] May 2, 1949, Bath, NY; [p.] Bruce M. and Bessie M. Reynolds Chabot; [m.] Floyd Martin Seeley, June 19, 1971; [ch.] Aaron Christopher Seeley, Nathaniel Peter Seeley, Benjamin Andrew Seeley; [ed.] Bachelor of Science in Elementary Education from Elmira College (1971), Master of Arts in Education from Elmira College (1975).; [occ.] Freelance Journalist and Retired Elementary Teacher from Odessa-Montour Central School after 22 years of teaching; [memb.] Odessa-Montour Fine Arts Booster's Club, Odessa-Montour Sports Booster's Club, Co-coordinator of Friends of the (Dutton S. Peterson Memorial) Library, Editor of the Village Messenger (Odessa Baptist Church News-Let-

ter) and The Peterson Post (DSPML Newsletter); [hon.] Who's Who in American Education, 1985-'86 and 1987-'88.; [oth. writ.] Arbor Day Story - "Advice from a Wise Old Oak", weekly neighborhood article in local newspaper (the Watkins Review and Express) coverage of local government (for WR and E), lyrics for songs to be sung in school productions.; [pers.] My goal in writing is to always look for the best, most positive aspects in any situation. I especially enjoy writing prose and poetry about the wonders of Nature.; [a.] Odessa, NY

SEELING, PAUL J.
[pen.] Paul James; [b.] July 23, 1951, Minneapolis, MN; [p.] James and Paula Seeling; [m.] Gina A. Seeling, July 4, 1986; [ch.] Benjamin Joshua, Luke Weston, and Paula Jayne; [ed.] Minnehaha Academy, Outward Bound, U. of M, Dale Carnegie; [occ.] President, Apex Eco Resources - Design and Contract Landscapes; [memb.] St. Andrew Lutheran Church, Minnesota Nursery Landscape Assoc. (MNLA). National Ski Patrol - Quadna Mountain, Chairman Public Relations Committee, Minnesota Nursery Landscape Assoc., Sons of American Legion, Youth Soccer Coah, Eden Frairie; [hon.] 20 Years of Service Award - National Ski Patrol, 17 Years Service Award, Minnesota Valley Landscape, Project Manager for MNLA Award of Excellence Recipient Project .3M/275, 1993.; [oth. writ.] Business and Technical, several unpublished poems and short stories. Lots of ad copy.; [pers.] Finding the time is so hard sometimes but, writing like skiing is a wonderful creative outpouring that releases positive and negative energy - when the right conditions come together there is exhilaration! Some days it just isn't worth the effort - but a fresh snow shower and ideas will come again. Inspired by Robert W. Service.; [a.] Eden Prairie, MN

SELLEN, ANGELA
[b.] October 28, 1975, Grove City, MN; [p.] Richard and Jeanne Sellen; [ed.] Atwater - Cosmos - Grove City High School, Willmar Community College; [occ.] Student; [hon.] Dean's List; [a.] Grove City, MN

SELLERS, ERICA ELLEN
[b.] January 12, 1977, Springfield; [p.] Tom and Sharon Berthiaume; [ed.] Holy Name School K-8, Chiropee Comprehensive HS 9-12; [occ.] Manager McDonalds, Secretary - A Shopper's Dream; [memb.] Tennis team, Drama Club; [hon.] Who's Who among American Students - 2 years '93-'94, Outstanding Achievement Tennis, Silver Cast Award Drama; [oth. writ.] Published poem in school newspaper and literary magazine; [pers.] Writing is a state of mind. It's a place where I lose myself and I find myself; [a.] Chicopee, MA

SELLINGSLOH, HULDA KNIPLING
[pen.] Hulda Sellingsloh; [b.] November 29, 1912, Port Lavaca, TX; [p.] Henry J. Knipling and Hulda Knipling; [m.] August Sellingsloh, May 1, 1943; [ch.] Susan Louise, Marian Kay, Ellen Agnes, and John August; [ed.] Port Lavaca High School, Draughan's Business College, Texas Lutheran College, Houston Law School, and various courses in Journalism and Art.; [occ.] Homemaker and Semi-retired Professional Artist; [memb.] Texas and Tarrant County Bar Associations, Eastside Creative Arts, Templeton Art Center, Secular Franciscan Fraternity, and various community and religious organizations.; [hon.] Law School Debating, First Prize College Poetry Contest, College Oratory, President Women's Bar Assoc., President College Students Council, in Professional Art, numerous Blue Ribbons including Best of Shows in landscapes and portraits. Listing in "Who's Who in the West," "Who's Who in Texas," and "American Artists of Renown," honored to be sister of Renowed Scientist Dr. Edward F. Knipling; [oth. writ.] Wrote poems and commentaries in college papers, poetry in newspapers, publicity for numerous organizations and edited newsletters for various clubs, etc.; [pers.] I have always tried to live a Christian life, to be a force for good in whatever I do. This influenced

my efforts in legal work for justice - in being a professional visual artist interpreting the beauties of nature and characters in portraits - and being a good influence in published writings. I consider my best efforts thus far has been my (portrait) production in color of a martyred priest during the Holocaust with prayers and scripture quotes sent to over 10,000 prisoners and other interested individuals. Ideal: To be a force for good.; [a.] Crowley, TX

SELMAN, DEBRA
[pen.] Deb; [b.] July 17, 1959, Gasaway, WV; [p.] Mark McAllister, Bonnie McAllister; [ed.] Doherty Memorial High, (Mass), Armstrong State College, BS in Medical Technology, Internship from Candler General Hospital; [occ.] Medical Technologist, Consultant to Dept. Rehabilitation Services; [memb.] Life Inc., (Board of Directors), ISCLT (International Society of Clinical Laboratory Technologist), Circle of Friends (persons with disabilities, activist and support group).; [hon.] I feel honored to sit or stand side by side with other persons with disabilities, fighting for the rights of persons with disabilities; [pers.] "They that wait upon the Lord shall renew their strength, they shall mount up with wings as eagles, they shall run, and not be weary, and they shall walk, and not faint." Isaiah 40: 31 KJV; [a.] Savannah, GA

SELVI, NORMA M.
[pen.] Norma Selvi; [b.] February 9, 1910; [p.] Louis H. Mark, Josephine Sell; [m.] Arthur M. Selvi, September 1, 1940; [ch.] Peggy Cunningham; [ed.] James Madison HS, Brooklyn, N.Y., Columbia University; [occ.] Retired; [memb.] Several writers' groups, Faculty Wives, CCSU, First Church of Christ, Congregational, N.B. Museum of American Art; [hon.] First prize for essay in New England Homestead; [oth. writ.] CROSSROADS - Stories and Poems (1984), Crystal Madonna, A Song in my Heart, Romantic novels, published short stories and poems in Kosmos, The Villager, Bristol Poetry Magazine, Hartford Courant, etc.; [pers.] Volunteer work at Middlesex Hospital, Red Cross, Blood Bank. Philosophy: "There are no strangers in the world, only friends waiting to be met."; [a.] New Britain, CT

SEMINARA, VINCENT J.
[b.] July 20, 1978, Brooklyn, NY; [p.] Greg and Roseanne Seminara; [occ.] Student; [memb.] W.D.S.; [oth. writ.] Some other poems; [pers.] "The Revolutionary reaches beyond dissent to nihilism and anarchy," Mayor John V. Lindsay.; [a.] Brooklyn, NY.

SEPRISH, EUGENE L.
[pen.] Sierra Seabring; [b.] February 14, 1995, Phillisburg, PA; [p.] Andy Seprish, Lenore Poorman; [m.] Sandra Seprish, July 8, 1970; [ch.] Michael, Jesse, Rebecca and Samuel; [ed.] State College High School, State College, PA, also 3 years of Police Science while in the Marine Corps; [occ.] Operating Engineer; [memb.] I belong to the IUOE - International Union of Operating Engineer; [hon.] Decorated War, Vietnam Veteran; [pers.] At the age of 7 or 8 when I heard the Berlin Wall was completed I realized what this wall meant. I felt as if there was a line drawn straight thru humanity. I was oppressed when the wall was dismantled, I got goose bumps, my knee got weak. I felt as if a giant weight was lifted off my shoulders, we still have along way to go; [a.] Waukesha, WI

SERRANO, MELODIE BURKE
[pen.] Venus Brooks; [b.] May 23, 1982, Manhattan, NY; [p.] Jacquelene Burke, Wilfred Serrano; [ed.] PS 105, David A. Stein, MS 141, Bronx; [occ.] Student M.S. 141; [memb.] Greanday Fan Club; [hon.] Band Award, Monitorial Service, General Excellence; [oth. writ.] Several children's books published; [pers.] Music has helped me a lot. Most of my poems were originally songs, composed for the guitar. My grandpa and uncle have inspired me to write about life and love.;

[a.] Bronx, NY

SESSOMS, BARRY EDWARD
[b.] May 6, 1958, Greensboro, NC; [p.] Bill and Betty Sessoms; [m.] Karen Lynn Sessoms, March 19, 1994; [ed.] Grimsley High, Wingate College; [occ.] Travel Consultant; [oth. writ.] Forthcoming; [pers.] I write what I feel, sometimes more, my heart goes out to those that dare to believe in the impossible; [a.] Bedford, TX

SESTER, KENDRA ELAINE
[b.] February 9, 1976, Somerset, KY; [p.] Kenneth and Paulene Sester; [ed.] Laurel Creek Elementary, Clay County High School, Eastern Kentucky University; [occ.] Student and Deputy Clerk at the Clay Circuit Court Clerk's Office; [memb.] International Society of Poets; [hon.] National Merit Scholar; Who's Who Among American High School Students Dean's List; Editor's Choice Award (1994) National Library of Poetry; Graduated with honors (9th out of 216) at Clay County High School; [oth. writ.] Poetry published in local & school newspaper, poetry published in "Journey of the Mind" National Library of Poetry - Various poems not published; [pers.] If you are going to walk on thin ice, you might as well dance. Be young - have fun - live life to the fullest.; [a.] Manchester, KY.

SETZER, JOYCE
[b.] May 5, 1922, Mexia, TX; [p.] Clifford, Mabel Miller; [m.] Delbert Setzer, September 6, 1941; [ch.] Delbert Jr., Ralph; [ed.] Carnegie, Okla (H.S.), Biela University, La Miranda, CA, Journalism, La Pantes Beauty College, La Miranda CA; [occ.] Home maker, artist, writer; [memb.] Rescue Mission, Feed the Hunger, SK Care Center Christian Church; [hon.] Bowling, Beauty College, Writing (Awards); [oth. writ.] Many poetry in newspapers, radio, 2 books written, fillers for short subjects, foreign countries, occasional cards, tapes in Canada, and America, lyrics by request (songs); [pers.] Personal joy that's received by me. I've given hundreds of poems away to others. My inner feelings on paper; [a.] Arroyo Grande, CA

SHACKLEFORD, RUBY P.
[b.] December 17, 1913, Wilson, NC; [p.] Sallie and Joshua Paschall; [m.] Richard W. Shackleford; [ed.] UTOC Grunsboro NC, AB UNC Chapel Hill NC, MA Graduate Study, Duke Uni, Durham, NC; [occ.] Teaching English Lit and Biber at Wilson Technical Community College; [memb.] DKG (Past Pres. of American Chap., AARP, Lay Speaker of Mich. Church; [hon.] "Citizen of the Month" local newspaper Daily Times, Art Awards, local contest, Phys. Educ Award in NC State Sr. Games. Prizes in Poetry, Awards in Walking (Senior Games); [oth. writ.] Short Story in NCAE, Articles in Current English, Seven Columns of Poetry, Editor of Goldminds, Poetry of Wilson Technical Community College, Alumni and Student Body.; [pers.] 61 years of teaching to help young people expand their horizons. To foster creativity, to keep my own mind open and receptive; [a.] Wilson, NC

SHANNON, DAVID B.
[b.] September 14, 1974, California; [p.] Robert and Carol Shannon; [ed.] Escalon High School, Universal Technical Institute; [occ.] "After Hours" - Custom Car Club - Freitont, CA.; [memb.] Writer of the month - Escalon High School; [pers.] David wrote this poem almost 1 month before a drunk driver took his life on May 21, 1994. Written to Leslie Due, Manteca, to whom he was planning engagement.; [a.] Escalon, CA

SHARMA, PUNEET
[pen.] Clark Brown; [b.] March 27, 1969, Chandigarh, India; [p.] Balkrishan Sharma and Saroj Sharma; [m.] Single; [ed.] D.A.V. College, Christian Medical College; [occ.] Doctor; [oth. writ.] Poem 'The Blizzard' published in 'Songs on the Wind'; [pers.] Follow your instincts and do what you love.; [a.] Boston, MA

SHAUL, AMANDA
[b.] October 11, 1982, Detroit, AL; [p.] Bill and Sherry Shaul; [ed.] Attend Jefferson middle school - Saint Clair Shores; [hon.] Publication: Anthology of poetry by young Americans

SHAVER, CHIP
[pen.] Chip Shaver; [b.] May 10, 1981, Portsmouth, VA; [p.] Pleaman and Marci Shaver; [ed.] 8th grade; [occ.] Student - ASSETS School, Honolulu, HI; [memb.] HUGS (Help, Understanding, and Group Support for Hawaii's seriously ill children and their families).; [hon.] 1991 GI Joe Search for Real American Heroes, June 14, 1991 recognized as Hawaii's State Real American Hero and received medal and certificate from Gov. John Waihee; [pers.] Diagnosed in Feb. '88 with a highly anaplastic astrocytoma (brain tumor) with 1 to 2 years life expectancy. Chip is now a long-term survivor. Many of his friends, however, have been taken by their illnesses. He feels their loss and was inspired by them.; [a.] Kaneohe, HI

SHEEHAN, JOHN A.
[pen.] Jack Sheehan; [b.] February 13, 1932, Paterson, NJ; [p.] Frank and Grace Sheehan; [m.] Jessie N. Sheehan, February 11, 1956; [ch.] Joh and Debbie; [ed.] Butler H.S.; [occ.] Truck Driver.

SHEFFIELD, DENICE
[b.] October 28, 1970, Houston, TX; [p.] Mary Wheeler Hayes; [m.] Frederick J. Sheffield, May 8, 1993; [ch.] Tifanny Cy-Reen Sheffield June 30, 1989; [ed.] Caddo-Kiowa Votech Practical Nursing Program 1991-1992; [occ.] Licensed Practical Nurse; [memb.] Member of the Church of Jesus Christ of Latter Day Saints; [oth. writ.] I have other writings that have never been submitted for publication; [a.] Mountain View, OK

SHELTON, TONY DALE
[pen.] Tony; [b.] May 31, 1955, Surry CO; [p.] John Q. and Jackie Shelton, Jr.; [m.] Deborah Raines Shelton, June 9, 1973; [ch.] Adam 14, and Matthew 10; [ed.] Flat Rock Elem., North Surry High School, Surry Comm. College; [occ.] disable police officer and mechanic; [memb.] Boy Scouts of America, Flat Rock Ruritan Club; [hon.] Numerous Scouting awards and District Award of Merit.; [oth. writ.] Numerous poems, and currently working on book, "On His Way to A Man" by the father of an Eagle Scout.; [pers.] There are far too many people trying to succeed and far too few. Willing to proceed. Failing to look at our beautiful surroundings a long life's path toward fortunes hunt.; [a.] Mt. Airy, NC

SHEPARD, NANCY BAYLIS
[pen.] Nancy Baylis Shepard; [b.] April 13, 1942, Farmerville, LA; [p.] Elizabeth and Otha Baylis; [m.] Wilbert M. Shepard, November 26, 1966; [ch.] Sabrina Faye Shepard; [ed.] B.S. Grambling State Univ. Master's - McNeese State Univ. specialist - McNeese State Univ.; [occ.] Executive Director of Calcasieu Community Detox Center; [memb.] Zeta Phi Beta Sorority, Top Ladies of Distinction, Inc., Caleasieu Arts and Humanities Council Panel, Louisiana Minority Arts and Humanities council, SWAB'M, Nic - Acorn, Grambling Alumni, McNeese Alumni.; [hon.] World Pavillion fair 1884-1984, Honorary Governor of Louisiana, National Service Award for Zeta Phi Beta Sorority Inc., Honorary Treasure of Louisiana Grambling State Univ. Dance Award, Who's Who in the South, Hall of Fame Louisiana; [oth. writ.] Novels - my sister, my friend I and II, Birds Gotta Fly, Shared Gifts, with Love, Moments, Thoughts and Deeds, Rhythmic Alphabets, Part Dance, Part Black, First Step Arithmetic; [pers.] I believe a person can achieve any goal in life if he or she desires to do so, because no task is too difficult for God.; [a.] Lake Charles, LA

SHEPHERD, JO ANN
[b.] July 12, 1956, Oklahoma; [p.] Steve and Rosemary Ricetti; [ch.] Jason Vern, Drew William, Jenna Rosemary; [ed.] High school - Oklahoma, HI; [occ.] Homemaker; [pers.] When you get a new release on life, you see things you never noticed before in God's creation. Somehow everything is beautiful - things we take for granted.

SHERRY, BERNICE
[b.] May 1, 1900, Hartford City, IN; [p.] Earl and Grace Griffith; [m.] Raymond E. Sherry, February 12, 1990; [ch.] Gwendolyn Sherry Johnson (deceased); [ed.] Business College and Correspondence Courses; [occ.] Retired; [memb.] Forscore Sunshine Society, Indoorables; [hon.] Various Awards for Poetry and Writing; [oth. writ.] "Ain't It The Truth", editorials for local papers. Various writings and poetry printed in "Grit", "Living Magazine" and others; [pers.] A most interesting life as well as extremely difficult and traumatic - yet somehow able to surmount it all - as I relied on the thought "This too will pass"... as it inevitably did!; [a.] Lubbock, TX

SHERWIN, HELEN
[pen.] Illeanna Lazar; [b.] March 10, 1924, Aurora, IL

SHIELDS, BRENDA J.
[b.] May 31, 1964, Baltimore, MD; [m.] Curtis W. Shields; [ch.] Sarah Elizabeth, Amanda Lae, Alexandra Rosa Marie, and Victoria Aron; [ed.] Old Mill High School; [occ.] Foster Parent for Saint Mary's Country.; [memb.] Maryland League of Foster and adoptive Parent's, Lexington Park Church of God.; [hon.] Executive Citation for Adoption; [oth. writ.] I've been writing poetry since I was 14 years old and am currently working on a book relating to foster care.; [pers.] My writings always reflect my life. My hope is that others can learn from my life and realize that all can be turned into good, even when things don't seem so good for a time.; [a.] Leonardtown, MD

SHIERS, JOHN R.
[b.] September 7, 1945, Bentonia, MS; [p.] Fred Shiers, Ida Shiers; [ch.] John Palmer, Aaron Floyd; [ed.] Redwood High; [occ.] Railroad carman; [hon.] Beta Club, Who's Who; [pers.] I enjoy telling the story of the common man.; [a.] Vicksburg, MS

SHIGEZAWA, EMMIE
[b.] Honolulu, HI; [ed.] University of Hawaii, BA (Psy); [memb.] National Writers Club; [hon.] University of Hawaii - Dean's list, Phi Kappa Phi; [oth. writ.] 1st prize Charles Eugene Banks Memorial Prize, University of Hawaii.; [a.] Honolulu, Hawaii

SHIRLEY, ESTHER S.
[pen.] Lou Simmons; [b.] August 23, 1943, Greenville, SC; [p.] Woodrow C. and Margaret Simmons; [m.] William L. Shirley, August 16, 1957 (div. 1994); [ch.] William L. Jr., Christopher A. and Weston L. Shirley; [ed.] High School, Waldreps ACD., Greenville, Tec., WYATT Real Estate Inst.; [occ.] Realtor R, and Business Owner, Retail Store; [memb.] S.C. Writer's Workshop, "Kituwah" (Native AM, Arts Group, Ashville, NC).; [oth. writ.] News Article's (pub) working on novel. Early 1700's with NATWE American Focus; [pers.] Poems are written from personal experiences, often from a philosophical mood, "Ornaments From The Tree", was from experiences over 7 years followed by notes - currently working on a novel; [a.] Pelzer, SC

SHIRLEY, PATRICIA
[pen.] Patricia Shirley; [b.] Oklahoma City, OK; [m.] Ray Shirley, Sr.; [ed.] Alumus, The University of Tennessee, Knoxville (Journalism and Creative Writing); [occ.] Freelance writer; [memb.] Natn'l League American Pen Women, Appalachian Writers Assoc., Appal. Studies Assoc., Thomas Wolfe Society, East Tenn. Historical Soc.; [hon.] Margaret Artley Woodruff, Captain Robert A. Burke Prize, Appalachian Writers Assoc.,

Green River Writers, Appalachian Woman Grant; [oth. writ.] Books: Pearl, Mary Pearl Kline, and Dear Flora Mae and other stories. Included in 8 anthologies and several magazines, including Modern Maturity.; [pers.] Although I write about a number of themes, my primary writing interest is rural Southern Appalachia. I hope to always depict this area and its people in an honest and truthful manner.; [a.] Knoxville, TN

SHRIVER, MONICA
[b.] November 20, 1977, Denver, Co; [p.] John and Kathy Shriver; [ed.] Sinagua High School; [occ.] Student; [oth. writ.] Many writings for my own enjoyment.; [pers.] Playing the tenor saxophone has and always will be the best way for me to express myself. My emotions are felt through my music. However, sometimes words are needed and that's where poetry comes in for me. Words add a new dimension to creativity and to understanding.; [a.] Flagstaff, AZ

SHULER, JAMES
[b.] November 23, 1963, Bryson City, NC; [p.] Grover and Fannie Shuler; [ed.] Swain County High, Southwestern Community College; [occ.] Freelance ("starving") artist/Factory worker; [hon.] Several awards throughout high school, college, and after-in achievement in art.; [pers.] I am primarily an illustrator. My poetry is an offshoot of my song writing efforts - an expression almost always personal. I am pleased at having this piece published, and am inspired and encouraged to write more.; [a.] Bryson City, NC

SHUMAN, S. MARIE
[b.] November 10, 1959, Evanston, IL; [p.] Bruno Mazur, Vivian Mazur; [m.] Robert E. Shuman, July 27, 1991; [ed.] Arvada West HS, Highline Community College; [a.] Frederick, MD

SIBLEY, JODY
[pen.] Sibley O'Bhraorain; [b.] February 1, 1975, Houston, TX; [m.] Not Married; [ed.] Klein Oak High School; [occ.] Musical Group, H2O; [oth. writ.] Write many songs, currently working on personal anthology entitled "Beyond the Darkness"; [pers.] After spending 2 years in the U.S. Army, I became horrified by the injustice and inhumanity of the government. My poetry embraces man's ability to dream and envision in the midst of oppression.; [a.] Spring, TX

SIDES, MARIE L.
[b.] April 25, 1953, Cape Girardeau, MO; [p.] Cora L. Howard and Henry Howard; [m.] Ronald Lee Sides, May 24, 1993; [ed.] 12th Grade; [occ.] Housewife; [oth. writ.] I write poems for birthdays—on cards when I give gifts to people; [pers.] I enjoy gardening and quilting.

SIMAKIS, DEAN
[b.] January 3, 1980, Columbus, OH; [p.] George and Efty Simakis; [ed.] K-8th, I'm working on the rest; [occ.] Freshman at Hawken High, Reviewer of Music; [memb.] Greek Orthodox Youth Association, Student Forum and Comic/Animation Forum on Compu Serve, Burger King Kids Club; [oth. writ.] Various music reviews for the Cleveland Plain Dealer and the Hawken Aff No, a Plethora of Unpublished poetry and songs; [pers.] "I can't believe it's not butter!!"; [a.] Cleveland, OH

SIMBECK, BRONWYN
[b.] November 16, 1982, Lawrenceburg, TN; [p.] Michael Simbeck and Linda Prince; [ed.] Home School and Ethridge Elementary School, presently in the sixth grade.; [occ.] Sixth Grade Student; [hon.] Honor Roll and local recognition for art work.; [oth. writ.] Over twenty poems and several short stories.; [pers.] I enjoy writing, music, and art. In my spare time, besides writing, I draw, paint, work in leather crafts, and practice on the guitar.; [a.] Ethridge, TN

SIMIC, VISESLAV
[pen.] Sima Simic; [b.] February 2, 1965, Serbia; [p.] Ljubisa and Dobrila Simic; [ed.] B.A. - University of Colorado at Boulder; [occ.] Writer and Translator; [hon.] 3 Prizes for Best Short Stories in the Serbian Language. Awarded by the Serbian Community in Exile, in Germany, in 1991 and 1992. Literary award "Milan Lalic" for a novel "Serbian Parchments." Awarded in Belgrade, Serbia.; [oth. writ.] Numerous poems and short stories published in various publication in the USA, Canada, UK, France, Australia and Serbia. Active political Essay Contribution to Serbian Exile Publications.; [pers.] Studying the past and passions, I try to understand and describe the present and the decision making process. It might bring better future and greater inner satisfaction.

SIMON, LAURA
[pen.] Allison Simoncic; [b.] March 23, 1975, Cleveland; [p.] Yvonne and Geoff Simon; [ed.] Olmsted Falls High School, Cuyahoga Community College; [occ.] Malley's Chocolates; [hon.] Editor's Choice Award for Poetry in 1994 from The National Library of Poetry; [oth. writ.] Published in Echoes of Yesterday and Best Poets of 1995; [pers.] "Love should be felt not forgotten, then broken hearts would never exists."; [a.] Olmstead Falls, OH

SIMPSON, JOEL P.
[b.] April 2, 1982, Philadelphia, PA; [p.] Virginia Simpson and Richard Daniel; [ed.] Ethel Allen Elementary, E. Washington, Rhodes Middle School; [occ.] Volunteer Work Student; [memb.] Swimming Club, Martial Arts School; [hon.] Honor Roll; [oth. writ.] Love poems, poems about peace; [pers.] I have been greatly influence by Longston Hueghe; [a.] Philadelphia, PA

SINDYLA, LISA R.
[b.] February 20, 1970, Cleveland, OH; [p.] Raymond and Donnal Sindyla; [ed.] St. Augustine Academy, Cuyahoga Community College; [occ.] Commercial Artist, Photographer and Executive Administrator; [memb.] P.E.T.A., National Humane Society, Greenpeace, A.P.L.; [hon.] Honor Roll, Merit Roll, Dean's List; [oth. writ.] Several poems published in school papers and my own private library of written material currently unpublished; [pers.] When I write, it's from my inner soul. I cannot force a poem, song or story. It just flows out and I write it from the heart with expressive emotion.; [a.] Cleveland, OH

SISON, JOHN C.
[pen.] John C. Sison; [b.] March 23, 1970, Ogden, UT; [p.] Antonio and Abella Sison; [ed.] Francis Polytechnic HS, College: Los Angeles Valley College; [occ.] Legal Clerk, Z.G.&T Law Offices; [oth. writ.] Several poems (not published), other: Some poems printed in HS paper; [pers.] My words reflect on what is in my heart. If anyone reads my work and is affected in a positive way. I need not ask more.

SIWEK, PAUL
[b.] April 23, 1972, Philadelphia; [p.] Marion and Krystyna; [m.] Colleen Svitak-Siwek, July 21, 1994; [ch.] Cyal Jacob; [pers.] My wife Colleen and my son Cyal are my inspiration.; [a.] Philadelphia, PA

SKAGGS, ADRIA
[b.] June 1, 1949, Salt Lake City, UT; [p.] George and Beth Eason; [m.] James C. Skaggs, April 1, 1988; [ch.] Sterling Retzko Chavis, Anthony Sebastias Chavis (also six children by 2nd marriage - step children); [ed.] Olympus High, Eastern New Mexico University (Theater), International School of Broadcasting; [occ.] Teach vocal lessons and piano lessons.; [memb.] National Assoc. for Family and Community Education; [hon.] 1 - "Most promising actress" in school, 2 - Top student in class - Broadcasting, 3 - Numerous awards for different aspects of writing and directing stage plays.; [oth. writ.]

Many other poems and stories in my computer files! This is the first I have submitted for publication or in any contest.; [pers.] Between deep despair and ultimate joy is LIFE. I try to live it all and that's what I write about.; [a.] Thermopolis, WY

SKELLEY, SHEILA J.
[b.] February 13, 1938, Elmira, NY; [p.] Margaret and Paul Skelley; [ed.] Southside High, Elmira N.Y., Military - US Army School's; [occ.] Security Monitor; [memb.] Fund Raiser - Amer. Cancer Society - Amer. Heart Assoc., Arthritis Foundation; [oth. writ.] Large number of poems - none published; [pers.] Enjoys reading Mark Twain and Robert Frost; [a.] Berwyn Heights, MD

SKELTON, NICOLE JENNIFER
[b.] 1983, Fort Wayne, IN; [p.] Dean and Maxine Skelton; [ed.] I am presently in the sixth grade.; [hon.] Last year in the fifth grade, I won a blue first-place ribbon in the Young Authors' Contest for my book of cinquains at Perry Hill School.; [oth. writ.] Space, Plants, Christmas Tree, Geography; [pers.] I write stories and poems for fun.; [a.] Fort Wayne, IN

SKOLNIK, DR. NANCY
[b.] December 29, 1945, Chicago, IL; [p.] Milton and Lee Hudak; [ch.] Ramdi Michelle and Ronald Alan; [ed.] University of Illinois BA State University of New York MS United States International Univ Ph. D; [occ.] National Univ-Teacher of English, High School Teacher of English and ESL at Mar Vista High School; [memb.] Mensa San Diego Association for Teachers of the Gifted PBS; [hon.] Outstanding Young Women of America Dean's List; [oth. writ.] Poetry, fiction and college materials related to the teaching of writing and grammar; [pers.] I go through life with a smile on my face and my fingers crossed! My children light up my life.; [a.] San Diego, CA

SLASH, CLAY TIMOTHY
[b.] August 30, 1957, Huntington, WV; [p.] Clayborne and Alice Slash; [ch.] Timothy J., Jason, Jessica Slash; [ed.] Bussiness degree, management; [hon.] Honor graduate from U.S. Army cook school, I finished 3rd in class out of 36; [oth. writ.] I also wright songs, and play lead guitar.; [pers.] I think people should work together instead of against each other, to make the world a better place to live; [a.] Huntington, WV

SLASKI, DUANE D.
[pen.] Duane D. Slaski; [b.] January 1, 1968; [p.] Linda Slaski, Ed Slaski; [ed.] Saucon Valley High, Bethlehem Area VO-Tech; [occ.] Mechanic, Lehigh University; [oth. writ.] First published poem; [pers.] I enjoy writing material that opens the reader up to different points of view.; [a.] Hellertown, PA

SLAVIN, COREY
[b.] February 19, 1964, Los Angeles, CA; [p.] Judy and Herb Slavin; [ed.] B.A., UCSD; [occ.] Campaign Association, Jewish Federation Council of Los Angeles; [hon.] Published in Journal of Chiver Studies, Provost's Honor list, Dean's list; [oth. writ.] Published in on the bus: A New Literary Journal, Spillway, A New Direction in Writing, News from Inside, Betray Anthology; [pers.] To me writing is a current that connects my physical being with my spirituality.; [a.] Los Angeles, CA

SLUDER, JOAN
[pen.] Jo; [b.] November 5, 1946, Fontana Village, NC; [p.] John and Helen Sluder; [ch.] Peggy Icenhower and Janet Crisp, 3 grandchildren; [ed.] Robbinsville High School; [pers.] I have been influenced by my grandfather Spurgeon Hall and by my mother, Helen Sluder. My two granddaughters also writes poems. Living in the smoky mountains of Western NC inspires my work.; [a.] Robbinsville, NC

SMALLS, UNA
[b.] Jamaica, WI; [p.] Edith Smith, John Smith; [m.] Biggie Smalls, February 14, 1993; [ed.] Jose Marti High School - Spanish Town, Jamaica WI, Dental Auxiliary School - Kingston, Jamaica WI; [occ.] Dental Hygienist; [pers.] If at first you don't succeed try and try and try again.; [a.] Bronx, NY

SMART, RICHARD
[pen.] L. T. (Little Tokyo); [b.] July 11, 1968, Killeen, TX; [p.] Matsuko Landa; [ed.] Senior at Southeast Texas State University, Majoring in Exercise and Sport Science, Grad. Dec. '95; [occ.] Bus Driver for Southeast Texas/Self-employed; [memb.] Fellowship of Christian Athletes 9/93 - 5/94 Southwest Texas State University; [hon.] Dean's List fall - 1994; [oth. writ.] Several other poems as Myself, L.T., T. Stewart, Frant Stewart; [pers.] Live simply and enjoy life! Remember everyone has feelings! Appreciate little things in life!; [a.] Killeen, TX

SMINK, JENNIFER
[b.] December 12, 1975; [p.] Richard and Sandra; [ed.] William Tennent High School; [pers.] This poem was written after my very 1st boyfriend broke up with me. To all people out there with broken hearts write poetry - it helps get your feelings out. I also want to say thanks to all my friends!; [a.] Warminster, PA

SMITH, SANDRA L.
[b.] February 6, 1940, Union, MS; [p.] Eleanor and William Buckwalter; [m.] Divorced; [ch.] Kevin S. Smith, Melinda L. Stinson; [ed.] University High School (Los Angeles), B.A. from University of Colorado, M.S.S.W. from University of TN; [occ.] Social Worker; [memb.] National Association of Social Workers; [hon.] Phi Kappa Phi; [oth. writ.] Letters to the editor of The Commercial Appeal (local newspaper); [pers.] I feel that my poetry is an extension of my spirituality and my universal spiritual connection. It is my way of expressing this special link to others so that they too may share in this infinite "soul to soul" connection.; [a.] Germantown, TN

SMITH, ALTON KEITH
[b.] November 2, 1967, Decatur, GA; [p.] Alton Smith and Marcia Smith; [ed.] Statesboro High, Swainsboro Technical Institute; [occ.] Electronic Technician; [memb.] Fletcher Baptist Church; [hon.] All State Baseball, 1984; [a.] Statesboro, GA

SMITH, BONNIE LOUISE
[b.] February 26, 1977; [ed.] Capac High School; [oth. writ.] I have written 5 other poems. They range from hatred to love. I have also written 9 short stories. That I wish to turn into movies.; [pers.] The poem that I submitted was truly written from the heart. I wrote it for my first love. He was (is) my one and only true love. The only inspiration I had for the poem was our undying love for each other.; [a.] Capac, MI

SMITH, DONNA A.
[b.] February 15, 1941; [p.] Anna Pearl Kelleher (deceased); [m.] Divorced; [ch.] Richard, Maria, Carla, John, James Jeffery, Jody, Michael; [ed.] Norton High, went to Massasoihi College in Brockton for pre-school teacher; [occ.] At home; [oth. writ.] I have written several poems none have been published, I'm also interested in writing children books; [a.] Brockton, MA

SMITH, EVELINE
[b.] June 28, 1953, Germany; [p.] Anna DePalma, Ralph Lates Jr.; [m.] Wayne R. Smith, April 14, 1973; [ch.] Heidi Marie Smith and Heather Ann Smith; [ed.] Southbury High School and Missoula Vo-Tech; [occ.] My husband and I are self-employed I do the Secretarial/Bookkeeping; [memb.] Lifetime member of the International Society of Poets and member of the National Writers Association; [hon.] I received honorable mention awards through World of Poetry. I've been published in Complete Woman magazine, New Voices and the Best Poems of 1995; [pers.] We are all poets. Poetry is a reflection of one's life, spirit and soul. I strive to make my writing an extension of myself reflecting both positive and hopeful energy.; [a.] Lolo, MT

SMITH, FAYE L.
[ed.] BBS, MBA, Ph.D.; [occ.] Assistant Professor; [memb.] American Association of University Women, The Central Exchange, Academy of Management, Toastmasters International; [pers.] E.E. Cummings inspired me. I have no need for capital letters.; [a.] Kansas City, MO

SMITH, H. JAMES
[b.] September 18, 1963, Hawaii; [p.] Tony and Betty Smith; [m.] Pauline Smith, September 16, 1989; [ch.] Franchon Ann and James Kenneth; [ed.] Chanute High School; [occ.] P.C. Boards Inc. Chanute, KS; [oth. writ.] Several poems; [a.] Chanute, KS

SMITH, JAMES E.
[pen.] Ariyah Miykaal (M.Y.E.Y); [b.] November 17, 1965, Milford, DE; [p.] Samuel and Rose Smith; [oth. writ.] Woman Is Special, Can You, Truth, Still Worth My Time.; [pers.] Humans can behave like honeybees or flies. One always seeks out and thrives on the refuse of others' mistakes thus infecting society with diseases such as hopelessness and unforgiveness. But thank heaven for those who seeks out the flowers of other's positive potential, refining the nectar of talent into the sweet honey of success that spreads hope to everyone.; [a.] Fort Lauderdale, FL

SMITH, JO DELL
[pen.] Jo Smith, Jodi Hill; [b.] April 3, 1970, Medina, OH; [p.] Linda Anderson, Steve Hill and Step-father Andy Anderson; [ed.] Graduated 1988 from Highland High School. Currently working towards Associates Degree in Science at Cuyahoga Community College; [occ.] Laboratory Tech.; [memb.] Rainforest Rescue, International Society of Poets; [hon.] Editor's Choice Award for Outstanding Achievement in Poetry.; [oth. writ.] Other works can be found in Poetry Anthologies entitled The Garden of Life and The Journey of the Mind, published by the National Library of Poetry; [pers.] I write poetry as a way to express emotion and give attention to the small things in life. I have been greatly influence by Robert Frost and John Keats.; [a.] Medina, OH

SMITH, MALISSA
[b.] September 25, 1979, Loveland; [p.] Alice Proctor and Dan Smith; [ed.] I am in 9th grade at Thompson Valley High School; [occ.] Student; [pers.] I like to be with my friends and read and write poetry. Sometimes I like to go to quiet places to think. I love animals. I want to be a pre-school teacher, writing teacher or a model.; [a.] Loveland, CO

SMITH, MARK DANIEL
[b.] February 15, 1975, Saigon; [p.] Jim and Judy Smith; [ed.] Sterling Heights High School, Class of '93, Macomb Community College; [pers.] May we live the lives dreams are made of, and still have the desire to dream.; [a.] Sterling Heights, MI

SMITH, MICHELLE
[b.] September 3, 1978; [p.] Venessa Smith; [ed.] South Gate HS; [occ.] Student; [memb.] Vice President of the Key Club of South Gate. Member of J.S.A. and a program aid at Skylake Yosemite Camp; [hon.] Optimist Club Award for Academic Achievement and also for running a 5K dare run and not quitting.; [pers.] Personal morbid poems are my favorite. Emily Dickenson is a favorite write of mine. She make death seem so easy, like a walk in the park. I take my hat off for her.; [a.] South Gate, CA

SMITH, SHELBY JACOB CRISP
[pen.] J.C.; [b.] January 22, 1982, Williamsburg, VA; [p.] Georgette and Jesse Smith; [ed.] 7th grade; [occ.] Student; [pers.] 11 years old when I wrote this poem (Life); [a.] Williamsburg, VA

SMITH JR., ROOSEVELT
[b.] May 11, 1952, Tuskegee, AL; [sib.] Associates of Arts, Tric Cleveland, OH.; [memb.] Poets League of Greater Cleveland; [oth. writ.] A book of poetry I plan to publish.; [pers.] Poetry is an art and it's meaning is in the ear of the beholder; [a.] Cleveland, OH

SNAUFFER, WILLIAM C.
[pen.] William C. Snauffer; [b.] July 15, 1940, Sunbury, PA; [p.] William H. and Edna M.; [m.] Divorced; [ed.] Masters - Psychology, West Virginia University, Morgantown; [occ.] Facility Director Psychologist; [memb.] American Psychological Association, American Asso. on Mental Retandation, American Management Asso.; [oth. writ.] Professional Papers, Psychology and Management; [pers.] Automatic writing; [a.] Coatesville, PA

SNEIDERMAN, JOE RICHARD
[b.] September 1, 1954, Springfield, MO; [p.] Herman and Lou Sneiderman; [ed.] Graduate of Montgomery Blair High School Silver Spring Maryland, Maryland College of Art and Design, Cosmetology, licensed instructor in Virginia.; [occ.] Artist; [memb.] (1) Masonic Lodge, (2) Trinity Methodist Church, (3) Various Artist Groups; [hon.] (1) Swimming and Diving - YMCA, (2) Red and Blue Ribbons for Art work in contests.; [pers.] 11th generation descendant of French Huguenot Protestant family - Jean and Mary Salle CA 1650, from Isle of Re, Saint Martin, France.; [a.] Mountain Grove, MO

SNOOK, DAN
[b.] October 30, 1957, St. Louis, MO; [p.] Charles Snook, Emma Snook; [ch.] Jason Michael, Ceselie Marie; [ed.] Aledo High School, Weatherford College; [occ.] Production Control Lockheed; [memb.] St. Peter's Catholic Church Assn., International Assn. of Machinist; [hon.] National Honor Society, St. Louis Post Dispatch Science Fair Award; [pers.] My writing derives from diverse life experiences and friendships.; [a.] Fort Worth, TX

SNOW, HELEN I.
[pen.] "Blondie" (Za-Za); [b.] September 28, 1929, Huntley, WY; [p.] Alex and Christina Keller; [m.] Marvin K. Snow, April 26, 1985; [ch.] Judy, Randy, Deb, Marsha, Monte; [ed.] I have a degree in Food and Restaurant Mgmt.; [occ.] I've owned 3 restaurants. Have 45 years of food exp. Retired as a journeyman - meat-cutter. Retired housewife at present. Have 8 grandchildren; [memb.] Ladies Auxiliary American Legion, First Congregation Church.; [hon.] Degrees in restaurant, cooking and specialty foods; [oth. writ.] I have written probably 50 songs and several poems. I have sent into many publishers. Have sent my songs into publishers and recording companies; [pers.] I strive to be a senior Entertainer. My husband and I play the guitar and sing Country Western for Senior Citizen Centers. We enjoy. I truly much, between the two of us we have written 225 songs.; [a.] Wheatland, WY

SNOW, HILDEGARDE M.
[b.] August 27, 1913, What Cheer, IA; [p.] Rev. and Mrs. Otto E. Mueller; [m.] Samuel H. Snow, August 19, 1945; [ch.] Stephen, David and Paul Snow; [ed.] Waupun H.S., Waupun, Wisc., 1 yr at Valparaiso Univ., various writing courses at Clark Univ., Worcester, Ma.; [occ.] Retired - Housewife; [memb.] Formerly member of Worcester County Poetry Assoc.; [hon.] Several articles published in Worcester Sunday Telegram about "My Best Vacation"; [oth. writ.] Numerous articles in Worcester Sunday Telegram, My Best Vacation.; [a.] Shrewsbury, MA

SNYDER, ROBIN

[b.] January 29, 1971, Lakewood, NJ; [p.] Roberta and Richard Moody; [m.] Glenn Snyder, October 26, 1991; [ch.] Amber Marie Snyder, Ashley Lynn Snyder; [ed.] Buena Reg. H.S., Atlantic County Vo-Tech; [occ.] Housewife; [oth. writ.] Unpublished poems; [a.] Hammonton, NJ

SOLOCINSKI, MICHELLE MIENTEK

[pen.] Michelle Mientek Solocinski; [b.] October 4, 1967, Warren, MI; [p.] Michael and Rene Mientek; [m.] Alan H. Solocinski II, August 1, 1988; [ch.] Jeremy Mientek (10), Matthew Solocinski (6), Daniel Solocinski (3).; [ed.] Graduated from Hazel Park High School in Hazel Park, Michigan.; [occ.] Housewife.; [oth. writ.] Night sky to be published in Poetic Voices of America, fall 1995.; [pers.] I would like to thank my husband and my family for their support and encouragement.; [a.] Jacksonville, FL

SOLON, LORETTA

[pen.] Lady in Black and Paxy; [b.] April 29, 1956, Flint, MI; [p.] Ollie and Juainta Joseph; [m.] Robert J. Solon, August 18, 1992; [ch.] Chris, Will, Mike, Julia, Zack, Gaberelle; [ed.] 11th Grade; [memb.] Former Member, Michigan Gospel Music Association; [hon.] Certificate of Excellence, Stardom and Associates; [pers.] I strive to display in my writing, everyday emotions and the things in life, most taken for granted!; [a.] Clifford, MI

SOOHOO, JOHN

[b.] August 27, 1953, Bronx, NY; [p.] George Soohoo and Chin King Choy; [ed.] Bronx Community College, Associate in Science, City College of New York (Bachelors in Computer Science); [occ.] Computer Operations; [memb.] Smithsonian Institute; [hon.] Dean's list; [pers.] I believe that people are what makes the believable and continues to make it worth while to write about.; [a.] Flushing, NY

SOPER, WILLIAM WAYNE

[b.] May 8, 1941, Macomb, IL; [p.] Bob and Rose Lee Soper; [m.] Anne (Odle) Soper, November 17, 1962; [ch.] Nicole Ann; [ed.] Valley High School (Vikings) Fairview, Fulton Country, IL; [occ.] Retired from Western Union After 34 years - Now a care giver for Senior Services Unlimited; [pers.] To express into words and the feelings in my heart for human kind, for the goodness of life and the beauty of God's creations; [a.] Saint Peters, MO

SOWER, IRWIN B.

[b.] December 26, 1920, Wilder, ID; [p.] Forrest L. and Lillian K. Sower; [m.] Widowed (Cleone), June 17, 1968; [ch.] Marilyn L. Sower; [ed.] Nampa High School, 1 1/2 yr. College of Idaho at Caldwell Broadway - Edison Technical School (Seattle) Texas Astrologers Assn., Three in One Concepts; [occ.] Jack of all trades and master of most.; [memb.] The Aquarian Foundation, Masonic Lodge, Musicians Union; [hon.] Master disignated, Spiritual Healer and Medium.; [pers.] As we understand the true nature of the Universe, and our relationship to it we are free to express our special brand of Creativity.; [a.] Coppell, TX

SPANN, RON

[b.] April 8, 1962, Nashville, TN; [p.] Oscar and Betty Spann; [occ.] At present I am Song Leader and Organist at a Church in California; [oth. writ.] I enjoy very much writing gospel songs and have had the privilege of sharing them with my gospel fans at singing's across the country.; [pers.] Some folks say, I have been blessed with a special talent as a musician, with a love for the piano and organ since a small boy. Gospel music has played a big part in my life.; [a.] Nashville, TN

SPEAKES, SUSAN

[b.] October 6, 1961, Elgin, IL; [p.] William and Judy Crawford; [m.] Dennis W. Speakes, January 17, 1981; [ch.] Erin, Emily, Jacob and Denny; [ed.] Elgin High School, and Elgin Community College; [occ.] Certified Pharmacy Technician at Delnor Community Hospital; [memb.] Food Shepherd Lutheran Church, Asthma Explorers; [hon.] I'm on the Dean's List at Elgin Community College; [oth. writ.] None yet.; [pers.] This poem was written at a time of great sorrow over the loss of my son Dennis W. Speakes II. It is meant as a tribute to him. Sleep with the angels my love.; [a.] Elgin, IL

SPEIR, DIANE WRIGHT

[b.] May 3, 1957, NJ; [p.] Mr. and Mrs. Nels B. Larsen; [m.] Mr. Emory M. Speir Jr., January 3, 1995; [ch.] James M. Wright (10); [ed.] High school graduate; [occ.] Teacher Asst. - Boston Ave. School; [memb.] Woodmen of the World Lord 625, member of Good Shepherd Evangelical Lutheran Church; [pers.] Writing poetry has always been comforting to me.; [a.] Deltona, FL

SPENCER, PAUL

[b.] April 15, 1966, London, England; [p.] Molly and Malcolm Spencer; [ed.] Bachelor of Science, University of Western Australia; [occ.] Computer Consultant; [oth. writ.] Short stories and music reviews published in Australian magazines.; [pers.] I try to approach everything with my eyes and mind open, and never let others do my thinking for me. Freedom comes from within.; [a.] Sacramento, CA

SPENCER, BARBARA F.

[pen.] Allyson Faye; [b.] Jamaica, WI; [p.] Ulysses and Daphne; [ch.] Gina La Sean and Laurence; [ed.] Manual Arts L.A. City Coll. Calif. Coll. of Dental Training So. Bay College of Business Business Industry School.; [occ.] C.N.A.; [memb.] World Vision Paralyzed Vets of America.; [oth. writ.] Poems published in local newspaper (Los Angeles Sentinel), my autobiography, two fictional and one true stories. Currently in process of getting a book of poems published.; [pers.] I love writing poetry. I am also taking a writing course to write children's literature at the institute of children's literature west redding C.T.; [a.] Los Angeles, CA

SPICKERMAN, KAREN SUE

[pen.] Karen Holt-Spickerman; [b.] January 10, 1958, Hudson, NY; [p.] Franklin D. ("Mickey") Holt and Alice N. Holt; [ed.] Chatham Central High School; [occ.] Plastics Injection Molding, Chatham, NY; [hon.] Have one - various awards (locally) for poetry written.; [oth. writ.] Have had several poems published in local newspapers, a few short stories, a poem published in a (local) book of poetry, occasional song lyrics.; [pers.] I would love nothing more than to share the world, as I see it, with others. I pray that I can accomplish this through my poetry. If I can cause a tear to fall, or leave a smile on someone's lips, then I have achieved my dream.; [a.] Chatham, NY

SPIDLE, MATTHEW D.

[pen.] Matt Spidle; [b.] October 18, 1974, Des Moines, IA; [p.] Danny Spidle and Patricia Spidle; [ed.] Abraham Lincoln High School; [occ.] Major Insurance Company Law Department Personnel; [pers.] Live your life to the fullest, but live it for yourself. My writings come from personal experiences.; [a.] Des Moines, IA

SPIREY, MARY J.

[b.] December 11, 1929, New York, NY; [p.] Rose A. and Thomas F. Hyland, [m.] Major William D. Spirey (Deaceased), June 1960; [ch.] Noreen R. Thames (Divorced), June 1960; [ed.] St. Jean Baptist High School, New York, Pace Univ, New York, N.Y. Brevand Comm College, Cocoa, Florida, Rollins College, Winter Park, Florida, Fort Valley State College, Fort Valley, Georgia; [occ.] Semi-retired, Retired Robins AFB, May 28, 1993, Journalist, Creative writer, poet, artist (oil painting); [memb.] Peach Valley Artist, Fort Valley, Georgia, Writers Club, Fort Valley State College, Fort Valley, Georgia; [hon.] While in St. Jean Baptist, High School, New York, N.Y. Won 2 essay contests, had 2 paintings recognized by Young America points, and on display at Metropolitan Museum of Art in 1940's.; [oth. writ.] There are so many I stopped counting over the years.; [pers.] The current poem is on a plaque in McEvoy Middle School, Macon, Georgia in remembrance of Ethel Thomas who was shot and killed by her son, who was later sentenced to life. Ethel Thomas was a teacher at McEvoy,; [a.] Warner Robins, GA

SPITZIG, FRANK

[b.] October 27, 1918, Cleveland, OH; [p.] Joseph A. Spitzig Jr. and Mary Loretta Spitzig (nee O'Reilly); [m.] Among the Departed; [ch.] 14 (4 Deceased); [ed.] B. Arch. '41, The Catholic University of America, Washington DC, after graduating from Cathedral Latin High School, Cleveland, OH., '36. The day I received my college degree was the day I started to learn, a process that has continued ever since, thank goodness, because understanding human nature is essential to success in all walks of life.; [occ.] Nobody wants an ancient architect-planner-developer, even one so skilled as I am. Therefore, I'm enjoying a second career in marketing, having been a moonlighter therein for many years to support my family.; [memb.] None any more. It's less hectic without them. I do my good deeds now minus the limelight. It's just as satisfying and far more peaceful.; [hon.] 10 surviving children, all adults educated in private schools and colleges, are my highest honors. My awards are the sizable chunks of those institutions I now own according to bills winning second place in the 1937 NATIONAL Collegiate Oratorical Contest in Constitution Hall compares thereto, though I did it as a Freshman, making me ineligible for that competition in subsequent years. Neither does my most recent honor, meaning the certificate of Royal Patronage awarded by the Principality of Hutt River Province, Australia, where I'm known now as "The Honorable ES".; [oth. writ.] I've been writing music (with lyrics) since I was only 16, none published (a loss to the world). I became hooked on narration in 1963 (fiction and nonfiction) and have completed (or nearly completed), some of them quite good (another loss to the world). This proves that I could do other things, not just make babies.; [pers.] What life has taught me is that most people have a distorted idea of what "Love" is. Real love is NOT sex, despite what most writers, producers, and advertisers say. Love is a mental decision - and HARD WORK! A selfish person is incapable of real love. The lack of real love causes I our of every 2 USA marriages to fail. While my first marriage was annulled, the second fell apart due to selfishness and introduced me to the dreadful pain of "Unrequited Love." If you love, you please another gladly ahead of yourself without expecting a pay back UNLESS it requires acceptance of an intrinsic evil!; [a.] Cleveland, OH

SPRIGGS, WANDA

[pen.] Miranda Mayberry; [b.] April 15, 1957, Atlanta, GA; [p.] Mother: Susie Marie, Father (deceased); [m.] Steve Spriggs, April 12, 1986; [ch.] Wayne, Everitt and Charles R. Spriggs; [ed.] Towers High, Southwest Community College, Real Estate Training Institute; [occ.] Real Estate Agent; [hon.] High School Art Award in Drawing, Painting. Medal of Merit 1984, Ronald Reagan President for Presidential Task Force.; [oth. writ.] Many unpublished poems, and working on a family personal life book and hope to have it published in the future.; [pers.] I write from the heart, and my inspirations come from every day surroundings and happenings. The truest feelings within.; [a.] Fort Worth, TX

STAATS, SHYLO L.

[pen.] Shylo Lee; [b.] June 2, 1979; [p.] Anthony and Felicea Catapano and Thomas Staats; [ed.] Islip High School, Brentwood Schooling; [pers.] I never believe my poems meant anything to anybody but me. I guess

I was wrong, thanks to these people, L.S., J.D., A.R., and my beloved family.; [a.] Brentwood, NY

STAGG, VERNA
[b.] September 12, 1914, Agra, KS; [p.] Leslie and Harriet Powell; [ch.] Marcia McClain; [ed.] Kirwin Kansas High School, Fort Hays College, KS, B.A., Denver University - School of Social Work M.S.W.; [occ.] Retired; [memb.] N.A.S.W., Methodist Church, Phi Kappa Phi; [hon.] Scholarship to Denver University. Deans List Fort Hayes. Service Recognition Award from Indian Health Service - USPHS.; [oth. writ.] Poems for friends and relatives enjoyment.; [pers.] I worked with Native Americans for most of my working years. Their love of life is a joy to behold after the many years of deprivation they have endured.; [a.] Phoenix, AZ

STANCZYK, BEVERLY
[b.] March 13, 1946, Chicago, IL; [p.] Marguerite and Robert Forrow; [m.] Theodore Stanczyk, July 23, 1975; [ed.] Crane High, Northwest School of Real Estate; [occ.] Janitorial Supervisor, Amoco Building, Chicago, Illinois; [hon.] Baldwin Certificate of Achievement, Scholastic Arts Certificate, Real Estate License; [oth. writ.] Poems: Nighttime In My Town, Bittersweet, and forthcoming Shadow Man, by The National Library of Poetry; [pers.] I write my poetry to appeal to most people. If it wasn't for my friends, Yvonne Austin and Charles Fairman, who have encouraged me to do the things I love. I wouldn't have returned to my writing. Our motto is "If it doesn't hurt anybody, go for it"!; [a.] Country Club Hills, IL

STANLEY, DALE
[b.] April 13, 1927, Fairfield, IL; [p.] Ben Stanley and Lola Stanley; [m.] Nancy Stanley, September 5, 1993; [ch.] John Dale; [ed.] Certified Master Graphoanalyst, Licensed Nurse and Paralegal; [occ.] Nurse and Physical Therapy Technician; [memb.] International Graphoanalysis Society; [hon.] Pediatric Nursing Award; [oth. writ.] "Woman - Earth's Most Beautiful Creation", a collection of romantic poems, and several children's stories in rhyme; [pers.] In my writings, I attempt to promote the spirituality of man and the understanding of human nature with the hope that the reader will genuinely experience the feelings expressed.; [a.] Warwick, RI

STANTON, JACQUELINE V.
[b.] June 7, 1981, Fort Sill, OK; [p.] Leonard and Elizabeth; [ed.] Pottstown Middle School, 8th Grade; [hon.] Honor Roll and High Honors; [a.] Pottstown, PA

STARK, THOMAS C.
[b.] March 14, 1978, Cincinnati, OH; [p.] Thomas and Marilyn Stark; [ed.] Junior - Western Hills High School, Cincinnati, OH; [occ.] Student; [hon.] Student of the Year 1992-93, National Honor Society, Spanish National Honor Society; [pers.] This poem was written in honor of my grandmother's birthday for all the special times we share together.; [a.] Cincinnati, OH

STARR, DI
[b.] February 23, 1953, Boston, GA; [p.] Harold and Rita Starr; [ed.] Marlboro College, University of Mass.; [occ.] Artist, Writer, Illustrator; [memb.] San Francisco Women Artists; [hon.] 1995-6 Who's Who of American Women, 1993 Art of California Discovery Award; [oth. writ.] A nationally exhibiting fine artist. Currently writing and illustrating a children's story book.; [pers.] When words and rhythms start to flow, I copy them down: Feelings and colors, thoughts and images, rhythms and sometimes rhymes.. just a few lines can tell secrets.; [a.] El Sobrante, CA

STEAD, KATE
[b.] November 28, 1957, Monticello, IA; [p.] Vance and Roody Stead; [ed.] University of Northern Iowa, BA - Education; [occ.] Writer, Health Care, Head Injury Rehabilitation, Student of Life; [hon.] Certificate of Merit in Saving A Life, music voice; [oth. writ.] As a beginning writer, I have many poems, inspired by music and life's experiences.; [pers.] I give heart felt thanks and gratitude to SPIRIT, for the guidance and strength I find through my words and feelings. I am grateful for my special friend, Kat, to whom this poem is dedicated, and who inspired me to write. And to my friend, Yame, for her support and love in my journey in this lifetime... thank you...; [a.] Fairview, NC

STEEN JR., JOHN W.
[pen.] John W. Steen Jr.; [b.] April 23, 1967, Weymouth, MA; [p.] John Steen and Joann Burice; [ed.] High School; [occ.] Registration Technician with DEA - also an actor; [memb.] California Miracle Center, Study in a course in Miracles; [oth. writ.] First Writing; [pers.] This poem was a gift to my mother in Christmas of '93. It was framed for her. I was inspired by seeing Maya Angelou at a lecture. I dedicate this to my mother and my love for her.; [a.] San Francisco, CA

STEINER JR., FRED
[b.] March 10, 1927, Prescott, AZ; [p.] F. K. Steiner and Ruth M. Steiner; [m.] Jacque Steiner (Yelland), July 20, 1952; [ch.] Rick, Kathi, Ann; [ed.] Stanford University (B.A., 1950), Stanford (J.D., 1952), Norwich Univ. (Vermont College) (M.F.A., 1982); [occ.] Attorney; [memb.] Law related memberships and activities: American Law Institute, Council - Indian Law Section- Arizona State Bar, Arizona Industrial Relations Association, Arbitrator for American Arbitration Association, American Bar Association, Arizona Bar Association, Maricopa County Bar Association, Arizona Bar Foundation, Delta Theta Phi, Cons. on state law - Boston College Industrial and Commercial Law Review, Advisory Committee - University of Arizona Annual Labor-Management Conference, Civic activities and memberships: Friends of ASU Libraries - board member, Arizona Humanities Council - board member, Listed, Who's Who in America", Phoenix Arts Commission - member, Aid to Adoption of Special Kids ("AASK Arizona") - Board of Directors, Phoenix Rotary Club 100, Delta Theta Phi, Board of Directors for Arizona Foundation for Children, Crisis Nursery, Executive Committee of Phoenix Mountains Preservation Committee, Phoenix Solicitations Board, Phoenix Growth Committee, Phoenix Citizens Bond Advisory Committee, Trustee - Barrow Neurological Foundation, EPI-HAB Phoenix Inc - Board member, Arizona Ballet Theater, Board member, Arizona Tuberculosis and Respiratory Disease Association - Board member, Greater Maricopa Tuberculosis and Respiratory Disease Association - Board member, Phoenix Little Theater - Board member, President - Lafayette School Men's Club, Clubs: University Club of Phoenix, Paradise Valley Country Club, Stanford Alumnae; [oth. writ.] Publications: "State Law on Indian Reservations Efficacy of State Lien Recordation and Filing Laws", presented to State Bar of Arizona, Indian Law Section, 1994. "Bargained For Group Legal Services: Aid for the Average Vage Earner," Arizona Law Review, 1969 "Foreclosure and Repossession," National Business Institute, 1987, "Financing the Modern Indian," National Business Institute, 1987, "So You Thought Space was the Last Frontier - An Introduction to Doing Business with the Indians." Arizona Bar Association, 1991 "Take Me to Your Level Playing Field," Arizona Tribal Economic Development Conference, 1993; [a.] Phoenix, AZ

STEPHENS, PATRICIA
[b.] January 17, 1947, Marshall Co., AL; [p.] Mr. and Mrs. G. W. Cofield; [m.] Phillip G. Stephens, February 11, 1969; [ch.] Kristin Leigh (12), Mary Elizabeth (deceased); [ed.] 1. Boaz High School, 2. BS Degree - Jacksonville Univ., 3. University of Alabama - Master's Degree; [occ.] English teacher - Boaz High School, Boaz, AL; [memb.] Kappa Kappa Iota, Delta Kappa Gamma, AEA, NEA, former March of Dimes County Walk-a-Thon Chairman; [hon.] 1994 Boaz High School Teacher of Year, 1994 Marshall County nominee for Jacksonville State Univ. Teacher Hall of Fame; [oth. writ.] Poems published in School Literary Journals. Poem published in The Poet 1978 "For How Long"; [pers.] Influenced by Thoreau's philosophy: "You can never do anything good aesthetically ... unless it has at one time meant something important to you."; [a.] Boaz, AL

STEPHENSON, JUDY A.
[b.] February 1, 1948, Charleston, WV; [p.] William J. Blankenship; [m.] Hilda Blankenship, (divorced); [ch.] Charles L. Stephenson, Kimberly D. Stephenson; [ed.] East Bank High School, Garnet Career Center; [occ.] Secretary; [hon.] Editors Choice Award - National Library of Poetry; [oth. writ.] "The Light", published by Quill Books, "Alone", published by National Library of Poetry, "Under The Willow Tree", published by National Library of Poetry.; [pers.] I dedicate this poem, "The Littlest Angel" to my granddaughter - Catherine Elizabeth Stephenson, born March 7, 1994.; [a.] Marmet, WV

STEVENS, ROSE M.
[b.] May 6, 1952, OK; [m.] Deceased, July 27, 1994; [ch.] 2 - Karen, Johnny, 3 grandchildren; [ed.] Northern Oklahoma College; [occ.] Office Manager and a Notary; [hon.] President/Phi Beta Lamda, during College; [a.] Blackwell, OK

STEVERS, DWIGHT
[b.] November 10, 1954, OH; [p.] Dwight Stevers Sr. and Hope Harris; [ed.] Gallia Academy High School, Ohio State University; [occ.] Hairstylist; [memb.] Multimedia Studies Program at San Francisco State University; [hon.] High School Valedictorian, Class of 1972; [oth. writ.] Two unpublished collections of poetry: Pieces of Self ... And Others; [a.] San Francisco, CA

STEWART, LUCIOUS G.
[pen.] Lucian; [b.] July 17, 1958, Houston, TX; [p.] Rayfield and Autrey Stewart; [m.] Deborah J., August 23, 1980; [ch.] M.C. Williams Jr., Sr. High (1976), Univ. of Texas, Omega Training; [occ.] Public Speaker/ Lecturer; [memb.] Toastmaster's Intl., National Forensic League; [hon.] CTM - (Toastmst.), Degree of Distinction (NFL), Qualified Submarines, Pres. Expeditionary, Medal, Various Competitive Speaking Awards (TMI); [oth. writ.] "The Shadow's Edge"; [pers.] Life is communication. My desire is find connection with others and ultimately, myself.; [a.] Lecanto, FL

STEWART, MICHAEL DAVID
[b.] August 22, 1978, Annapolis, MD; [p.] John H. and Geraldine F. Stewart; [ed.] Present Junior at St. John Vianney High School, Holmdel, New Jersey; [occ.] Full time student; [memb.] People to people International, United States Golf Association; [hon.] Monmouth County Community Service Award; [a.] Matawan, NJ

STEWART, JEFF
[pen.] Venus Church; [b.] May 16, 1966, Fremont, CA; [p.] Danny and Sharon Stewart; [ed.] Far beyond the sun; [occ.] Musician - Songwriter; [memb.] Cader Publishing, Poet's Guild, Tin Pan Alley; [hon.] The spirit of life within each soul.; [oth. writ.] Pyramid Dreams, Kingdom, The Gift, Instant of Eternity, Honest Deceiver, Where's Everybody Going?; [pers.] Beyond my existence, I thrive without, broken glass of endless distance, pages of life disconnect. Reason or rhyme investigate your fate.; [a.] Reno, Nevada

STEWART, CAITLIN
[pen.] Caitlin; [ed.] St. John the Evangelist School in Morrisville; [occ.] Student; [pers.] I am an Irish dancer I play the piano and I like to do gymnastics and girl scouts, my favorite food is smoked salmon.; [a.] Yardley, PA

STIEB JR., JAMES A.
[b.] August, 24, 1979, St. Louis, MO; [p.] Jim and Roberta Stieb; [ed.] Presently attending Cleveland Jr. Naval Academy as a Sophomore; [occ.] Currently working with a group of Published Canternistana project to develop a serious documentary comic on HIV with documenting and helping with story line. Wants to be in Naval Intelligence, Seals, when he finishes getting college degree in "The Sciences" (Chemistry, atomic, etc.); [hon.] Blue Belt Tae Kon Doe, Hunters Safety, Drives Bull Dozen (cat), "Loger", fisherman, Nitendo, Tractors, Computer, Drawing, Chess, very analytical and find solutions to problems; [oth. writ.] Numerous other poetry, stories; [pers.] Enjoys being out in the country on ur 23 acres farm, lot working with month, conservation to improve our land; [a.] Ballwin, MO

STIER, ALYSON
[b.] May 11, 1982, Austin, MN; [p.] Sylvia M. and Greg E. Stier; [ed.] Pacelli Junior High, grade 7, Austin, MN; [occ.] Student; [memb.] 4-H, Violin/Orchestra, Track, Ice Skating, United States Figure Skating Club; [hon.] I got a blue ribbon at the Minnesota state fair for my cat project, I made the high honor roll with a score of 3.8333.; [oth. writ.] I also like to write stories.; [pers.] The rule I go by is: I like to try as many different activities as I can to discover what I may have a talent for. I really enjoy writing.; [a.] Austin, MN

STINSON, DAVID
[pen.] D. S. Stinson; [b.] February 28, 1957, Greeley, CO; [ch.] Randi Kay Stinson; [occ.] Carpenter; [memb.] Green Mountain United Methodist Church; [pers.] I'll surely miss the information super highway while I sit and watch the ducky on their morning trek to the pond. Or sit and listen to a noisy den of cyote pups yipping goodnight to one another. But I've noticed that as I sit and experience these things, between sips of coffee, and conversation with my dog, I smile.; [a.] Evergreen, CO

STOCKARD, JOHN
[b.] July 4, 1969, Fort Worth, TX; [pers.] This was written as a reflection on the condition of Ulster and its proud but neglected history.

STOCKTON, NICKY
[pen.] Nan; [b.] October 4, 1956, Little Rock, AR; [p.] Tip and Peggy Eubanks; [m.] Divorced; [ch.] Jason (16), Kendra (10); [ed.] Currently enrolled in a Respiratory Care Program, Completed First Steps Program, Marks System, Freshman Year, Customer Service Seminars; [occ.] Respiratory Therapist, Student; [memb.] First-steps Volunteer, Army Community Service Volunteer during Saudi-Arabia Deployment, N.Y.S.L. (National Youth Sports League) Coach 1994; [hon.] Dean's Honor Roll December 1994 at Eastern Oklahoma State College, Wilbarton, 1974, Draftsman of the year Harrah, OK., 1974 2nd place Scholastic Meet in Drafting, Central State University Edmond OK.; [oth. writ.] "None Published" Books "Married to an Outlaw" and "With a Dream"; [pers.] I write about what I know and have lived. If someone can learn from my mistakes, then I welcome their new found knowledge for their own personal gain.; [a.] Checotah, OK

STOKES, PATRICIA ANN KEITH
[b.] August 5, 1963, Fort Meade, MD; [p.] Elsie R. and Alton L.; [ch.] Dustin, Laurissa and Travis, (Nephews) Andrew Ray, Jarad Lee; [ed.] Oklahoma City Community College, Francis Tuttle Vo Tech, University of Central Oklahoma, Thomas Nelson Community College; [hon.] Phi Theta Kappa, National Vocational Honor Society, National Dean's List; [pers.] The only way to have peace is to learn tolerance and understanding especially of those ideas we find most offensive.; [a.] Hampton, VA

STOLLINGS, JUANITA L.
[pen.] JLS; [b.] August 12, Huntington, WV; [p.] Harry L. and Helen Harris (Deceased); [ch.] Edward L.

Stallinorth, Jr., Anita Jean Taylor, Sherrie L. Hall (deceased), Andre' Alan and Stallworth; [occ.] Retired; [hon.] Selected as one of the "Ten Top Women" of The Miami Valley in 1988; [pers.] I believe that my talent for writing is a God given talent and I am grateful for the opportunity to share my gift of poetry writing with the reader.; [a.] Dayton, OH

STONE, LEE HARVEY
[pen.] Yabach or Lee Stone; [b.] March 15, 1969, Astoria, NY; [p.] Harvey Lee Stone and Trumilla Stone; [ed.] State University of New York - Old Westbury, Forest Hills High School; [occ.] Self Employed, RECO; [memb.] Omega Phi Alpha Fraternity, Inc., American Society of Composers, Authors and Publishers, Audio Engineering Society.; [hon.] None as of yet. One day somebody will feel me.; [oth. writ.] Edited and published "Underground" magazine. Numerous songs and poems.; [pers.] You can find a peace of mind!; [a.] Jamaica, NY

STONE, KERRI
[b.] January 27, 1976, Fall River, MA; [p.] Joan Stone; [pers.] I always try to touch my readers hearts, for them to understand my feelings.; [a.] Fall River, MA

STOTT, IVY K.
[b.] February 8, 1921, South Wales, Great Britain; [p.] Hugh and Eva Stott (both parents deceased); [ed.] High school graduate, 2 years college; [occ.] Retired legal secretary - studying medical transcription; [memb.] St. Christopher's Church (Episcopal) Choir member, Chicago Park District Outing Club, The Prarie Club, YMCA Women's Health Center, YMCA Prime Time Class (Aerobics); [hon.] Dean's List, Oak Park Twp. Lunch Program volunteer, Senior Companion Program, two one year awards; [oth. writ.] Poems previously published in church newspaper in Elmhurst, IL. (First Baptist) article published in Chicago Daily News at age 9; [pers.] Very much like poems of John Keats, etc. and Elizabeth Barrett Browning; also enjoyed books by Elizabeth Goudge. Enjoy hiking in woods and hiking for hunger (crop) 6.2 miles.; [a.] Oak Park, IL.

STOUFER, PATRICIA J.
[pen.] Pat Stoufer; [b.] February 25, 1934, Macks Creek, MO; [p.] Leonard and Hazel (Allen) Lynch; [m.] Johnnie J. Stoufer (Deceased), February 26, 1955; [ch.] Son, Lewis C. Sr., Carla, Grandson, Lewis C. Jr.; [ed.] Macks Creek, High; [occ.] Garage owner, Vehicle Inspector and Bookkeeper.; [memb.] Pleasant Grove Baptist Church, Pres. Ladies Aux. and Dispatcher for Macks, Creek Volunteer Fire Protection Inc., started a Support Group called "The Good Grief Bunch". For anyone who has lost their Mate due to Death three years or less.; [hon.] For my involvement in my City and Community. Started Park Funds, raised the first monies.; [oth. writ.] I have a note book full of poems, I read lots of poems in church but I have never published a poem. I have given copies to friends and family and signed them. This one was printed in our Church paper and in our City paper.; [pers.] President John F. Kennedy said Country. I say Community. "Ask not what your Community can for you, but ask what you can do for your community."; [a.] Macks Creek, MO

STOUT, REANNA C.
[pen.] 'Christian'; [b.] May 7, 1979, Florida; [p.] Richard and Janet Stout; [ed.] Sophomore-Edgewater High School Orlando, Florida; [occ.] Student and volunteer (C.I.T.E.); [memb.] EHS Crew Team, Marine Corps. Junior Reserve Officers Training Corp. Staff Sgt.- ROTC, 1995 Youth Volunteer Award-Orange County's Citizens Commission for Children; [hon.] Staff Sgt.- ROTC, 1995 Youth Volunteer Award-Orange County's Citizens Commission for Children, poetry awards from school; [oth. writ.] Soon to be famous works; [pers.] I have always been inspired to write about the 'unspoken'. The love that no one would admit, secrets that are never openly shared, the emotions that are never thought

to be expressed, and the fear that is trapped deep inside the soul-alone. It is not morbid or suicidal that I seek, it is the understanding of what no one wants to acknowledge. Emily Dickenson and Edgar Allen Poe were great inspirations for my work.; [a.] Orlando, FL

STOVALL, MRS. FRANCES
[pen.] Fran; [b.] June 1, 1961, Indianapolis, IN; [p.] Robert Ferguson and Nancy Myers; [m.] Anthony Lee Stovall Sr., January 30, 1979; [ch.] Anthony Lee Stovall Jr., Christina Michelle, Vanessa Lynn; [ed.] Allen Co., High Scottsville KY.; [occ.] Housewife; [pers.] Thank you to God above for the words. My husband and children for standing behind me, and their influence.; [a.] Firtgerald, GA

STRANGE, CHRISTINE
[pen.] Christine; [b.] February 17, 1959, CA; [p.] Lincoln and Patsy Smith; [ch.] Martin and Bobby Strange; [occ.] Glove Packer at Tillotson's Health Care; [pers.] No child should pay for Adult mistakes!; [a.] North Stratford, NH

STRAUSS, GLORY
[pen.] Glory; [ch.] Jimmy, Linda, Vicki, Cyd; [ed.] Miami Dade Jr. College - Life Lab; [occ.] Writer - Artist Illustrator; [memb.] International Society of Poets - Amnesty International, American Indian Relief Council; [oth. writ.] There is a space inside of me Poetry Book, "Silly Dilly Children's Books", "Silently I Speak", Whispers and Thoughts, and a Mini-series, I Am A Star, etc. - Journals since 1975.; [pers.] The writings in my books were created while in pursuit of the essence of Life's meaning. I am compelled to share what meaning I have found with the Lovers. The Searchers and the Dreamers; [a.] Gainesville, FL

STRAYER, MARILYN
[b.] November 17, 1952, Honover, PA; [p.] Bernard Warner and Mary Warner; [m.] Lance Strayer, September 14, 1991; [ed.] South Western High School, Millesville University York College of PA; [occ.] Systems Manager, O'Shea Lumber Company; [memb.] YWCA; [hon.] Dean's List, Cum Laude Graduate; [pers.] In the fast-paced society of the 90's, I enjoy the calming effect of creating poetry and also of capturing one heartbeat of time through photography. It is my intention to allow others to pause for a moment of reflection as a result of my efforts.; [a.] Mount Wolf, PA

STREET, AMIE
[b.] October 13, 1980, Bartlesville, OK; [p.] John Street and Pam Street; [ed.] Currently in 8th grade; [occ.] Student; [hon.] Finalist in Dickens on the strand essay contest, honor society, solo flute and piccolo, superior plus ratings for 6 years in Gold Cup Piano Competition, 8th place in Top Region Band for Flute, 1st Division for UIL Contest, National Junior Honor Society; [oth. writ.] Illegal immigration essay for Dickens on the Strant Contest; [pers.] I try to use my talents to demonstrate my feelings, either on paper through literary works or through music.; [a.] League City, TX

STREUR, CINDY
[b.] October 20, 1948, Spencer, IA; [ch.] Caleb, Rachel, Taber; [ed.] a. BA - Arizona State University, b. MA - Central Michigan University (BA-Education)(MA Art History); [occ.] a. 6th grade Teacher (Evergreen Schools, Vancouver, WA), b. Adjunct Professor of Writing (Portland State University, Portland, OR); [memb.] NEA (National Education Ass.), Oregon Road Runner's Club; [hon.] 2nd place in Black and White in National Photography Contest; [oth. writ.] Published: a. An article titled "Yoga with Children" in Teaching K-8 Magazine and b. An article "Italic Puts Art into Penmanship" in Teacher Magazine.; [pers.] Teaching writing to children and engaging them in the process of writing is rewarding and instills long-term benefits in organization, building of self esteem and appreciation of good

literature.; [a.] Vancouver, WA

STRICKLAND, CHARLES MARTIN
[pen.] Shawn Wesley; [b.] March 9, 1951, Columbus, OH; [p.] Charles and Cleo Strickland; [m.] Patricia Strickland, October 29, 1976; [ch.] Monica Strickland; [ed.] Centerbury High School, Diploma in Computer Programming for Business - Devry Institute of Technology; [occ.] Computer Programmer; [hon.] National Honor Society - Centerburg High School, Presidential Honor Society - Devry Institute of Technology; [oth. writ.] Poem "Give Up Your Guns", published in "Echoes Of Yesterday". Poem "When I See", to be published in "Songs On The Wind", poem "I Am Not Born Today" to be published in "Best Poems Of 1995".; [pers.] I love to write poetry and I hope that somehow my poems will make a difference in someone's life.; [a.] Centerburg, OH

STRONG, RON
[pen.] Ron Strong; [b.] November 20, 1960, Indiana, PA; [p.] Clarence and Verla Strong; [ch.] Ron and Roger Strong; [ed.] Saltsburg High; [memb.] American Legion; [oth. writ.] Several poems written but not published at this time; [pers.] I venture to bring one's true self out. I have been greatly inspired by my maternal grandmother, a writer herself.; [a.] Daytona Beach, FL

STUDER, LOIS EZELL
[b.] December 30, 1916, St. Louis, MO; [p.] Chas A. Ezell, Leota Marie Goss; [m.] Lester L. Studer, August 17, 1934; [ch.] Two, Sara Jane died at age of twenty-four; [occ.] Retired now; [hon.] I can't think of any awards etc., but I attend a Unity Church that asks me to read my poetry to them on Sunday - which I consider to be an honor, they all enjoy it!; [oth. writ.] I am getting into writing short stories - maybe they will be children stories - I hope so. My poetry gives me ideas I can use to weave into children books; [pers.] Because of the fact that I have reached the age of Seventy-eight, I find myself writing more material about ageing. I am so pleased that I have been able to write something that can make others feel comfortable "about old age".; [a.] Sedalia, MO

SUDA, WILLIAM R.
[pen.] Rocky Suda; [b.] September 4, 1946, Columbia, MO; [p.] Bill Suda and Marcelle Suda; [m.] Carol Reinholdt Suda, November 14, 1981; [ed.] B.A. University of Houston, History 1970; [occ.] Real Estate; [memb.] Screen Actor's Guild, Actor's Equity Assoc., Sigma Chi Fraternity; [hon.] None Grand enough to mention.; [oth. writ.] Poetry, Editorials, Musings.; [pers.] Communication extends individuality and personal growth - and I don't mean the media.; [a.] Round Rock, TX

SUMMERS SR., GLEN E.
[b.] October 4, 1931, Ardeola, MO; [p.] Earl Summers, Dovie Summers; [m.] Nancy Summers, June 17, 1988; [ch.] Glen Edwin, Krystal Renea; [ed.] Bell City, Mo. High, Porterville, Calif. J. C., Sacramento, Calif. J. C.; [occ.] Retired; [memb.] Odd Fellows, D. A. V., American River College Personnel Committee, President, 1965.; [hon.] U. S. Air Force, Airman of the month, 25 year outstanding service, from my previous job.; [oth. writ.] Several poems, highly rated from community residents and leaders: Also, currently, starting, to write fiction.; [pers.] Since retiring, I love to write, for a hobby and pleasure, hoping, as I, get my writings out, they will be an enjoyment, to people, who read them.; [a.] Sacramento, CA

SUMRAH, JAGNARINE
[b.] January 15, 1972, Guyana, South Africa; [p.] Jhagatt and Nelamattee Sumrah; [occ.] Account Representative; [pers.] I live by the word "opportunity", if you're looking for it, it's out there. You just have to look until you find it. Never ever give up.; [a.] Brooklyn, NY

SUNSTEIN, LINDA EVERETT
[b.] June 15, 1950, San Diego; [m.] Michael Sunstein, December 3; [ch.] 8 Children; [ed.] Gen Ed High School, Kent St., Mesa, College - S.D.; [occ.] Owner - MRI Center, Medical Facility; [memb.] National Association of Female Executives. YMCA Staff Assoc.; [hon.] Nat'l Video Arts Award. (Corp.); [oth. writ.] Biography - many poems; [a.] San Diego, CA

SUSIENE, LINDA L.
[b.] November 22, 1944, Seattle, WA; [p.] Simon Hoffarth, mother deceased; [m.] William T. Susiene, December 16, 1967; [ch.] Carina Lynn Susiene, William H. Susiene, Sabrina Louise Halverson; [ed.] Kennewick Sr. High, Modern Business College; [occ.] Housewife; [memb.] International Society of Poets, Franklin County Historical Society, (Membership chairman), Richland Players, Juvinile Justice Center Diversion Program; [hon.] Poet of Merit 1989 - American Poetry Assoc., Golden Poet 1992 - World of Poetry, Promenader of the Year, Honorable Mention - 1991 - World of Poetry; [oth. writ.] Play - "Sarah's Visitor", for visions and voices teen theater, children's stories, "Peril On The Raft, The Hiding Place, The Silent Boy," whimsical poems for fun with children; [pers.] My goal is to up lift mankind's thinking. Strength comes from finding goodness and beauty. Adding brightness to even one soul gives meaning to my writing.; [a.] Pasco, WA

SWANSON, ASTRID A.
[b.] March 13, 1918, Finland; [p.] Bruno And Emilia Anderson, [m.] Wilbert Sandvik, June 2, 1946, Bertel Swanson, June 14, 1980 (Both Deceased); [ch.] Carl and William Sandvik; [ed.] Grade School in Mt Vernon, N.Y. and A.B. Davis (High School) One of my classmates was Art Carney who later became "Ed Norton" of the Honeymooners" TV series.; [occ.] Was a secretary before raising my sons, Now I've been caring for my grandson since he was a baby while parents work.; [memb.] Caledonia Sr. Citizens, Avon Wesleyan Church (both south of Rochester, N.Y.); [oth. writ.] Lyrics for a recorded hymn "A Morning Meditation". Have written articles in Swedish that were published in Sweden and in New York. I also write letters to relatives in Scandinavia, as well as the English ones here. Reading is my other special hobby.; [pers.] I have been fortunate in experiencing some fantastic travelling in my later years—Bermuda, the Pacific Northwest, Hawaii, the Grand Alpine Tour to Germany, Austria and Switzerland, St. Petersburgh, and also several trips to Scandinavia to see my relatives. Returning from my first trip overseas in 1976 we circled over Manhattan which was a thrilling sight and tremendously moving. I have been blessed with seeing some of God's wonderful world, and the beloved hymn "How Great Thou Art" Says it all! As my name means "to the stars" I identify with "Ad astra per aspera (to the stars through difficulties.; [a.] Caledonia, NY

SWEATT, AL
[b.] June 3, 1920, Lula, OK; [p.] Harg and Allean Sweatt; [m.] Opal Jean, January 7, 1944; [ch.] Seven; [ed.] High School - Lula High; [occ.] Retired Home Builder; [memb.] Broadcast Music (B.M.I); [hon.] To have one of my songs recorded on M.G.M. label (Stealin Sugar) many more on smaller labels.; [oth. writ.] "Grandkids Think I'm Cool" sent to Barbara Bush, and she sent back a praise of this song with his signature; [pers.] In the 50's I was known as "Al Your Radio Pal". On a radio station in Tuba. I received 347 cards and letters in one single day. Which represented 76 towns in Oklahoma and Kansas.; [a.] Hollett, OK

SWEENEY, LISA
[b.] October 1, 1979, Denver, CO; [p.] Bill Sweeney and Judi Dressler; [ed.] Sophomore at Boulder High School; [occ.] Student; [memb.] Youth Opportunities, Advisory Board (City Council, Sub-Committee), Young Adult Advisory Board (Library Board Sub-Committee), International Thespian Society; [hon.] Rocky Mountain Talent Search, Thespian, Colorado Library Association Outreach Award.; [oth. writ.] Essay in Boulder Daily Camera: Several poems published in various school newspapers, I have only just begun to attempt publishing my work.; [pers.] I write about my life and the experiences of living, of being young and growing. "Maddest of all is to see life, not as it should be, but as it is." - Don Quixote.; [a.] Boulder, CO

SWEGER, JESSICA L.
[b.] October 6, 1980, Harrisburg, PA; [p.] Rober L. and Wendy L.; [ed.] 8th grade student Greenwood High School - Millerstown, PA; [memb.] Students Against Drunk Driving Club, Student Council, Art Club; [hon.] Honor Roll Student; [a.] Millerstown, PA

SWINNEY, PANSIE
[b.] June 14, 1938, Collins, MS; [p.] Hiram and Alice Cruise; [m.] Robert Lee Swinney, September 24, 1955; [ch.] Beth, Bobby, Robin, Alicia; [ed.] Calhoun High School; [occ.] Housewife; [memb.] Salem Heights Baptist Church, Mission Friends Teacher, TOPS "Take Off Pounds Sensibly", President of my Sunday School Class; [hon.] My greatest honor is to honor my Lord Jesus Christ; [oth. writ.] I have other poems some written for my own personal readings. Some have been published in the magazine Poet Forum Hattiesburg, MS; [pers.] I enjoy writing poetry especially religious poems and my poems are simple, but inspiring words to others.; [a.] Laurel, MS

SZYMANSKI, PAUL
[b.] March 20, 1968, Glendale, NY; [p.] Mr. Stanley Szymanski, Mrs. Barbara Szymanski; [ed.] 3 1/2 yrs. of College Associates in Accounting; [occ.] Clerk; [hon.] Editor's Choice Award for (M)(O)(N)(O)C. Eastgood poems in The National Library of Poetry's anthology, Dark Side of the Moon. Poem, an Ocean is Life is published in the World of Poetry; [pers.] "Follow your bliss", Joseph Campbell - a poem doesn't necessarily reflect the poet's personal opinion. In most cases I wholeheartedly believe in our educational system's efforts. But, there are cases when it miserably fails. Ex. who taught the builders of the nuclear bombs. A better example is the movie, Dead Poets Society.; [a.] Bay Shore, NY

TALLEY, SHARON H.
[b.] June 7, 1949, Georgia; [p.] Inez-Earl Hulsey; [m.] Joe; [ch.] 5; [ed.] High School; [occ.] Housewife; [pers.] I have been writing since I was a teen. I love poetry and hope to have more published.; [a.] Murrayville, GA

TANNER, TAMI LEE
[b.] May 10, 1977, Waco, TX; [p.] Ronnie and Charlotte Tanner; [ed.] Hewitt Elementary, Midway Junior High, Waco Midway High School; [memb.] First Baptist Church of Hewitt Youth Council, Business Professionals of America, PALs, Student Council; [hon.] Thespian Society Member Member, National Honor Society, who's Who Among American High School Students, Rotary Youth Leadership Award, All-Academic Award, UIL State One-Act Play Honor Crew; [pers.] The Lord Jesus Christ is my inspiration and I do all things in honor and love of him.; [a.] Hewitt, TX

TAYLOR JR., JAMES KENT
[pen.] Jim and Big Daddy; [b.] July 5, 1960, Pasadean, CA; [p.] Charlotte W. Taylor; [m.] Karen June Taylor; [ch.] James C. Taylor, Crystal Taylor, Joshua Taylor and Joey Taylor; [ed.] High School; [occ.] Plumber Apprentice

TAYLOR, MICHELLE
[b.] November 15, 1979, Phoenix, AZ; [p.] Coy Taylor, Joanna Taylor; [ed.] High School Student; [occ.] Student; [memb.] JGAA; [hon.] Various Music Awards. School Sporting event awards. Junior Golf awards.; [pers.] I can do all things through Christ Who gives me

strength.; [a.] Glendale, AZ

TAYLOR, JEREMY
[pen.] James Eric Cleray Vaogue; [b.] February 1, 1974, Ogden, UT; [p.] James B and Penny P. Taylor; [ed.] High School; [occ.] Stock Clerk; [memb.] Currently Transition Council; [hon.] Best choice editors award for last written the script; [oth. writ.] Street, Souls, Electric, Drop'n, Rebel, Dream, Forbiden, Child, World, Death's and others.; [per.] Through the story thought of belief the dream can became reality"

TEACHNOR, MARK S.
[pen.] Scot Marte; [b.] September 25, 1942, Indianapolis, IN; [p.] Forrest and Margaret Teachnor; [m.] Linda M. Technor, February 16, 1984; [ch.] Destiny, Scott and Craig; [ed.] 10th grade drop out; [occ.] Self-employed, i.e., Office Supply and Copier Company; [memb.] First United Methodist Church; [oth. writ.] "Love Is What You Make It", i.e. a book of poetry chronicling the days spent in prison over 6 years. Currently writing a biography entitled, "The End of Abuse"; [pers.] If you don't do it today it's too late. There's no guarantee of tomorrow's sunrise.; [a.] Blissfield, MI

TENCH, AUREY
[pen.] Annie; [b.] March 20, 1979, Cleveland; [p.] Jim Tench, Sandy Tench; [ed.] Trinity High School; [pers.] Time flows like sand through an hour glass, if you don't live each grain of sand to the fullest you'll spend the rest of your life living on a beach as a grain in the ocean.; [a.] Cleveland, OH

TENSFELDT, DANA LYNNE
[b.] October 15, 1959, Sacramento, CA; [p.] George Chuck Morton, Anna Lee Marton; [ed.] Elk Grove Jr and Sr. High, Consumes River College, Sierra College Studied Art, English and Music; [occ.] Horse Trainer and Riding Instructor; [memb.] Milo Riding Club of Arkansas; [hon.] First woman hired to the sacramento County Transportation Division as a Traffic Signs Maintenance Worker.; [oth. writ.] My own personal book of poetry. I especially like writing lengthy letters to family members and close friends.; [pers.] Having grown up on several ranches and currently living on one, my writings are based mostly on a country setting, I would hope that those who have not experienced country life will gain some insight to its serenity through my poems.; [a.] Crossett, AR

THEIS, REANN LORRAINE
[b.] May 16, 1990, Santa Cruz; [p.] Teresa Theis and Toby Rappolt; [ed.] Soquel High School 9th Grade Drama at Cabrillo College. Dance Class for 5 years. I have been painting for ten years.; [occ.] Student and Entertainer.; [memb.] North Shore Animal league. The National Arbor Day Foundation.; [hon.] 1985 Calif. State special Award. 1985 Universal Pageant First Place 1986. Miss Le Petire First place, 1987 Best Free and Easy Child. 1994 I had the lead in "Alice In-Wonderland: My favorite story.; [oth. writ.] A few poem's and some short story's; [pers.] I would like to be a Photo Journalist, Model and Actress. My "God Mother", Julie Reed, introduced me to the Joy's of Living, she always has creative and artistic thing's for us to do. I love the Theatre Painting and Traveling. But Dancing is my first love. It is my way of Praying.; [pers.] Santa Cruz, CA

THOM, NEVA G.
[pen.] Neva Thom; [b.] May 13, 1921, Memphist, TN; [p.] David George Greenroos; [m.] Minnie Penny Lutts; [ch.] Carol Ann Griffin and James Arthur Griffin; [hon.] A gold record from Electra Records, memphis 1st Oscar for co-writing the song. For all we know" for the movie " Lovers and other stranger" in 1971 this was BMI's citation of achievement in recognition of the great National Popularity as measured by Broadcast performances attained by the song - "For all we know."; [oth. writ.] My son found and produced and wrote 1/2

of the songs and music and was the lead vocal and arranger and musician and he now plays several instruments well including the piano and guitar while he sings he has a beautiful voice range and he writes beautiful songs; [a.] Memphis, TN

THOMAS, JUNE D.
[b.] June 9, 1921, Washington, DC; [m.] Randal L. Thomas, April 22, 1955; [ch.] Patricia Ann Bennett (daughter), Kevin Lee Thomas (Son); [ed.] McKinley High School, Wash. DC.; [occ.] Retired; [pers.] To God be the Glory! He gave me the words in their poem to let it be known that "friends" are truly a gift from him.; [a.] Alexandrin, VA

THOMAS, BARBARA M.
[pen.] Ann Thomas; [b.] Lula, GA; [p.] Wm. Coil Maney (deceased), Lola Mae Moss Maney (Mother); [m.] John William Thomas, August 9, 1963; [ch.] (son) William Blake Thomas; [ed.] High School, A.S. Degree, working on Bachelor Degree (Banks County High School) (A.S. degree from Gainesville College); [occ.] Admn. Secretary Continuing Education Division Gainesville College, Gainesville, GA; [memb.] Banks County Farm Bureau Women's Committee, Banks County Chamber of Commerce, Longstreet Society; [oth. writ.] I have, so far, only written poetry. This is the first time to submit a poem for publication.; [pers.] To me, poetry is the window to one's soul; [a.] Lula, GA

THOMAS, BRENNAN
[b.] July 26, 1978, Dayton, OH; [p.] Jim and Cele Thomas; [memb.] National Honor Society; [hon.] State finalist creative writing 1993 - 4H VFW "Voice of Democracy" winner; [pers.] I have but one wish in this lifetime: to be heard. And...remembered.; [a.] Eaton, OH

THOMAS, WILLIAM
[b.] September 12, 1968, Ann Arbor, MI; [p.] Helen and Carl Thomas; [ed.] G.E.D. 1 1/2 years College 28 credit hours Trade - Basic Electricity; [pers.] Write from your heart and everyone will know the truth, for ones heart never lies...; [a.] Brethren, MI

THOMAS, TRACY L.
[b.] August 19, 1965, Highland Park, MI; [p.] Jack Thomas, Kitty Thomas; [ed.] Troy Athens High School, Oakland Community College; [occ.] Information Receptionist, Crittenton Hospital in Rochester, MI.; [memb.] Member of ASPCA (The American Society for the prevention of cruelty to Animals); [hon.] American guild of Music Lakes Regional Competition - First Place Solo (Vocal); [pers.] Every facet of my life is an inspiration to my writing. I wish to thank all of the people I love so dearly for their support, encouragement and love.; [a.] Madison Heights, MI

THOMAS, ELIZABETH PATTON
[b.] December 13, 1959, Providence, Rhode Island; [p.] Leslie Patton Sr, Joyce Patton; [m.] David Lawrence Thomas Jr, December 31, 1994; [ch.] Lesley Elizabeth De Santis, John Edmund De Santis; [ed.] AGUA Fria High School; [occ.] Marketing and Sales Support, MPI Business Systems, Inc.; [pers.] Being true to one's self allows you to be the person you truly are and not the person others want you to be; [a.] Waldorf, MD

THOMAS, ODESSA
[b.] April 4, 1960, Mobile, AL; [p.] Mr. James Noelie Thomas, Mrs. Leotha Collins Thomas; [ed.] General Studies, Word Processing and Business Clerical.; [occ.] Employee of Colorado RMBCS Operator, National Bank located in Denver Colorado.; [memb.] Odessa is a member of Zion Temple Pentecostal Church Pentecostal Church, located in Denver Colorado Pastor: Bishop Roland Martin 1st Lady: Evang Arlee Martin; [oth. writ.] The Gift of the Holy Spirit. Given to me by God himself May 24th 1981. Include a book of poetry that dates back to May 1981 including such topics is:

The Night In Eternity, It's Almost Midnight, In The Beginning, I Must Be Like Jesus, Heal Me, Hush Love one's, The Thought Of God etc...; [pers.] No philosophical statement. Only a personal note, every man, woman, Girl and Boy was created for a purpose and a reason which can be found in God word. Until we each fulfill our purpose for creation, we have not embraced life.; [a.] Denver, CO

THOMAS, ANGELA NICOLE
[pen.] Nue Nue; [b.] August 27, 1979, Frederick, MD; [p.] Eddie Thomas, Vonda Thomas; [ed.] 9th grade now; [oth. writ.] I have written many poems, but this is the first one to be sent away.; [pers.] My dream is to be a writer. This is all I think about 24-7 This is the happiest thing to have happen to me in yrs. My whole life has been only filled with pain. My happiness; [a.] Frederick, MD

THOMASON, ERIC BLAINE
[pen.] "PSYC 101" the true Prince; [b.] November 16, 1967, Philadelphia, PA; [p.] Edward Thomason, Marlene Holmes; [ed.] West Catholic Philadelphia High for Boys, BS in Psychology from Campbell University, N.C.; [memb.] Rhyme Scholar Society; [hon.] Mayna Cum Laude, President's List; [oth. writ.] Married Men (a warning to cheating husbands); [pers.] We rule men only words, everything we write and say changes the words around us; [a.] Philadelphia, PA

THOMASON, KELI
[b.] June 21, 1980, Warren, MI; [p.] Suzi B. Robert Thomason; [ed.] Sophomore at Uncoln High School; [oth. writ.] Many other poems and short stories that are unpublished.; [pers.] I try to stress my personal thoughts and life in all of my writings. I was very inspired by Lisa Binkley and Debra Kulesza.; [a.] Warren, MI

THOMPSETT, JILL MARIE
[b.] February 21, 1971, Islip, NY; [p.] Lloyd Thompsett, Candace Thompsett; [ed.] Islip High School, Suny Brockport, Suny Old Westbury. Certified Elementary teacher, American Studies major, English minor.; [hon.] Dean's List and semester honors 1993-1995. GPA and semester honors 1993-1995. GPA of 3.5 or better four successive semester.; [oth. writ.] Status pending on many poems. Many short stories for compilation in a fiction novel in progress at this time.; [pers.] People are born with the capacity to Formulate their own opinions and conclusions, to exercise free will. Don't blindly follow what those before you have proclaimed. I strive to bring forth views not yet examined.; [a.] Islip, NY

THOMPSON, DIANE C.
[b.] August 27, 1967, Hempstead, NY; [p.] Geneva B. Thompson; [ed.] Hempstead High School, Nassau Community College, Vassar College, University of Iowa, Emerson College, Boston, MA, Graduated Student,; [a.] Quincy, MA

THOMPSON, FARROLL
[b.] May 2, 1927, Augusta; [p.] Bert and Bertha, Deceased; [m.] Elizabeth, December 28, 1991; [ch.] 4 by precious marriage, Bart, Allen, Delta, Phyllis; [B.] B.A and M.A.; [occ.] Entrepreneur; [oth. writ.] Many poems. A men newspapers at time publish so one of my poem.; [pers.] Poetry is the international language of mankind...it is more expansive those bring one language. It speaks to the heart of mankind

THORNTON, CINDI A.
[b.] September 10, 1956, Oregon; [p.] Pat and Betty Briley; [m.] Stan D. Thornton, August 21, 1989; [ch.] Ivan Scott Thornton; [ed.] Oregon City High School, Clackamas Nursing Program, Concordia College; [occ.] Registered Nurse; [oth. writ.] I've written several poems, but have not submitted for publication.; [pers.] I have much personal cor. tragedy in my life, with the love and support of my parents and the writing of my poems I was able to rise above it.; [a.] Portland, OR

TIENG, JAMES FRANCIS
[b.] August 15, 1982, Ridgewood, NJ; [p.] Joseph V. Tieng, Fortunata T. Tieng Siblings: Joseph John, Arlene; [ed.] St. Anne School, 7th Grade, Fair Lawn, NJ; [memb.] Unlimited Martial Arts, Inc. (Black Belt), Student Council (Treasurer), Fair Lawn Bantam Bowling 1992-1994; [hon.] Outstanding Citation (1992-1995), Student of the Month (1992-193), 1st Place 1992 Bowling Team Sec. B Fair Lawn Rec., Silver Medal in 1st PA TaeKwonDo Governor's Cup, 2nd Place Columbus Day essay contest; [oth. writ.] "The Monkey and the Banana Tree" (poem) published in Filipino Reporter, "Our Earth" (poem) published in Anthology of Poetry by Young Americans, and Columbus Day essay.; [pers.] If a person believes in oneself, that person can make a difference. The diversity in the world is overshadowed by one man's dream of equality.; [a.] Fair Lawn, NJ

TOMS, MRS. LINDA G.
[b.] September 30, 1958, Valdosta, GA; [p.] Joe L. Cooper Sr. and Evelyn Cooper; [m.] Ralph J. Tomas Jr., August 30, 1984; [ch.] Sha-Nel Toms, Tyisha Sharay Toms and Ralph J. Toms III; [ed.] Thomas Jefferson H.S. Bklyn N.Y., Bullard Haven Voc/Tech.; [occ.] LP Nurse; [memb.] Charge of: Rehoboth COGIC Purity Group with missionary Martha Everson - Pastor: Augustus D. Pullen.; [oth. writ.] I write letters of "encouragement" for my church bulletin board and to pass out in the community. I've also written several poems one day would like to have published in my own book.; [pers.] I strive to encourage those that are without faith, and those with faith to keep that faith alive. I have been greatly influenced and inspired by the greatest book ever written - the Holy Bible; [a.] Stratford, CT

TORO, STEFANIE LYNN DEL
[b.] November 9, 1981, Seguin, TX; [p.] Raul and Rebecca Del Toro; [ed.] 7th Grade; [occ.] Student; [hon.] Honor Student Corbett Jr., High School

TORRES, SAMANTHA
[pen.] Samantha; [b.] October 7, 1979, San Antonio; [p.] Maria B. Torres; [ed.] High School; [occ.] Student; [a.] San Antonio, TX

TOURAY, KAWSU S.
[pen.] Kei Esstee, Mjei Keitee; [b.] 1962, Salikenni; [p.] (Alhagi) Abu Touray and Fatumat Fotana; [ch.] Muhammad Mustapha Touray, Fatou Ceesay Ida.; [ed.] High School, Diploma in Correspondence - writing and Journalism; [occ.] Poet, Journalism, hunter nursing assistant (Registered).; [memb.] North American Hunting Club, writer's Digest Book club, Gambian writer's and artists' Association; [hon.] Nigeria High Commission Award (1975/76), center for Foreign Journalists in Virginia (1989) (child survival issues), Gambia Red Cross Award on Poetry (1990) Published in National Library of Poetry's Coming of the Dawn with the poem prisoners (1992/93).; [oth. writ.] Short Stories for Radio Gambia West Africa include: Academic Passport, Retributive Vengeance. Environmental Writings, Language Scripts for Gambia (in pipeline), Science, Astronomy and Religion. Novel in Pipeline. Writer for daily observer (Gambia); [pers.] The births of Adam, Eve, and Jesus were the most miraculous in the order of Adam's being out of neither of father nor a mother, and Eve's being out of a father only, and Jesus being out of a mother only. However, they like any of us are the creatives of Allah.; [a.] Minneapolis, MN

TOWE, CARMINA AMEZCUA
[b.] December 29, 1970, Grosse Pointe, MI; [p.] Alan and Paula D'Augustine; [m.] Eric Samuel Towe, November 13, 1993; [ch.] One on the way (20 June 95); [ed.] Lutheran High North (1 yr) (3 yr) Grosse Pointe South High School United States Naval Academy; [occ.] Naval Officer; [oth. writ.] Personal Journal And Poetry; [pers.] Writing, To me, is a stream of Consciousness

TRAMONTANA, DELORES MARLOW
[pen.] Dee Tramontana; [b.] November 11, 1929, South Bend, IN; [p.] Adeline and B.A. Marlow; [m.] Widow; [ch.] Debra Nepote, Michael Barrett; [ed.] North Liberty High; [occ.] Retired; [memb.] American Diabetic Association; [oth. writ.] I'm writing a book of "The life of my sister and I".; [pers.] I love reflecting my Feelings to others through my poems.; [a.] Brooksville, FL

TRUMBLE, HAROLD V.
[pen.] Harold V. Trumble; [b.] March 16, 1949, Adams, MA; [p.] Harold V. and Ella C. Trumble (both deceased); [m.] Norma Jean Trumble, April 17, 1992; [occ.] Wallpaper Artist; [oth. writ.] Numerous poems, none of which are published to date.; [a.] Raleigh, NC

TRYON, LYLE W.
[pen.] Lyle Wade Tryon; [b.] September 22, 1973, Syracuse, NY; [p.] Lyle (dad), M. Tryon (mom); [m.] Mary Ann E. Tryon, Februay 25, 1995; [ch.] (daughter) Brittany Rose Tryon; [ed.] High School; [occ.] Maintenance at McDonalds and Janitorial Downtown Syracuse; [memb.] Music Clubs; [hon.] Sports award-football, pop warner; [oth. writ.] Several; [pers.] You must help your self before helping others; [a.] Syracuse, NY

TSAMBO, SUSAN LINDIWE
[b.] June 28, 1951, South Africa; [p.] Sidwell and Maus Ncala; [m.] Moses Mihuthuzeu Tsambo, January 13, 1973.; [ch.] Linda Auralia, Tshepo Claude, Ntando; [ed.] Seminary Student. Currently at the Southern Baptist Theological Seminary. Lou., KY; [occ.] Student. Seminary Student Ambassador; [memb.] Bates Memorial Baptist Church.; [oth. writ.] Article for "Bona" and Tswelelopele, South African National Magazines.; [pers.] I am Fascinated and attempt to Explore Broad Sociological Concepts that seem to have Universal Application.; [a.] Louisville, KY

TUNKARA, GAYLE Y.
[b.] August 7, 1956, Cleve., OH; [p.] Wilbert and Elsie Mae Jackson; [m.] Divorced; [ch.] KaTrina Evonne, Johnny Edward, Isaiah Kaye; [ed.] Glenville High, Dyke College, Cuyahoga Community College; [occ.] Payroll Administrator; [hon.] Dean's List; [oth. writ.] Copy written collection of over 50 Spiritual Poems all inspired by Biblical Scripture/Verse, Retirements, Anniversaries, Birthdays and Greeting Cards.; [pers.] I would like to write has World Of God in poetry to minister Faith, Hope and Love.; [a.] Shaker Heights, OH

TURNER, ANDREA
[b.] October 30, 1978, Savannah, GA; [p.] Marlene Woleslagle; [ed.] Still a high school student at Effingham County High School (10th Grade); [occ.] Student; [pers.] I truly enjoy writing. It relaxes me.; [a.] Springfield, GA

TURNER, WILLIAM B.
[b.] August 13, 1939, Roselle Park, NJ; [p.] Luther Turner, Lyda Catherine Turner; [ch.] Traci Cassilly, William Turner Jr.; [ed.] Cranford High, University of Kentucky, M.S.; [occ.] Geologist Tribow Oil and Gas Corp.; [memb.] Creative Life Church Bd. of Trustees, Exi, EVE; [pers.] My poetry is an attempt to reflect on the abstract in the concrete, my search for soul.; [a.] Spring, TX

TURNER, MARJORIE L.
[pen.] Marjorie L. Turner; [b.] February 18, 1919, Wilkes Barre, PA; [p.] William H. List and Nellie Light; [m.] Eugene A. Turner, June 6, 1947; [ch.] Paul B. Turner and Nancy Parlette; [ed.] High School and Green Mt. Jr. College and: I have studied poetry and creative writing at Trenton State College, and Rider College, and have audited at Princeton University under such poets as Maxine Kumin, Stanley Plumly and Jared Carter as well as Denise Levertof.; [memb.] I have been a member of the Pennsylvania Poetry Society, the National Federation of State Poetry Societies, New Jersey Poetry Society, St. Davids Christian Writer's Assn., Nat'l League of American Pen Women, Louisiana State Poetry Society, and Delaware; [hon.] Valley Poets, Inc. and have received honors from many of these societies.; [oth. writ.] Self Published: Water, Fire and Wings and Roots and Reasons, Truth That Is Never Loud published by Golden Quill Press, Francestown, New Hampshire.; [pers.] I have been influenced by Wm. Cullen Bryant, Edna St. Vincent Millay, Emily Dickinson, Robert Frost and Richard Wilbur.; [a.] Blue Bell, PA

TUSTIN, GLEN
[b.] February 4, 1936, Tyler Co, WV; [p.] Carl Tustin, Day Tustin; [m.] Elizabeth Tustin, June 1, 1963; [ch.] Michael Glen, Gregory Harold, Leigh Ann, Stephen Robert, Ryan Andrew; [ed.] Washington Irving High School, Salem College Harrison County WV; [occ.] Teacher - Football Coach Burkhannon Upshur Middle School, Buck Hannon, WV; [memb.] WV Coaches Assoc.; [oth. writ.] Yesterday's Girl, Solitude, Is He The Same Lonely Boy?, The Girl Who Thinks Too Much, Autumn's Child, Walk The Hunter's Moon, Remember, The Cabin, An Early Morning Mood, Uttering's Night Walk, Silence of Thought.; [pers.] Enjoy the attitudes of Nature, for in Her we find happiness.; [a.] Clarksburg, WV

TUZZAINO, PAULA
[b.] June 8, 1956, Cleveland, OH; [p.] John and Rose Marie Perl; [m.] Michael Tuzziano, May 5, 1984; [ed.] Lumen Cordum High School, University of Akron; [occ.] Self-Employed; [memb.] American Dietetic association Ohio Dietetic Association, International Food Service Executive Association, Cleveland Dietetic Association, American Society of Hospital Food service Administrators; [a.] Maple Heights, OH

TYSON, BARBARA
[pen.] Barbara Tyson; [b.] September 29, 1956, Natchez, LA; [p.] Thedogia and Dorothy Tyson; [ed.] St. Petersburg Catholic High School, attended St. Petersburg Jr. College; [occ.] Secretary; [memb.] The Nathori Writers Guild; [hon.] National Honor Society; [pers.] I strive to reflect the emotions of life in my poetry and writing; [a.] St. Petersburg, FL

TYSON, WYCLIFFE E.
[pen.] Wycliffe E. Tyson; [b.] January 12, 1953, Nevis, WI; [p.] Samuel Tyson, Margery Tyson; [ed.] Trinity International University, Florida, B. Sci Human Resources Mgmt. Biblical Studies, Miami Dade College Fl. A. Sci. Dietetic National Care Cleyton School of National Heeling, Alabama; [occ.] Student, pursuing Dr. Naturopathy; [memb.] First United Methodist Church, Miami, FL, International Ministerial Fellowship Minneapolis, Minnesota; [hon.] All respect to my lady friend Miss Cassie Lewis, a great woman. My greatest respect for my mother, brother and sisters, friends with love honor; [oth. writ.] Author of book entitled "Messages, Prayers, and Poetry."; [pers.] "The Splendor of pave love is from God", Preach, Teach, and Beach".; [a.] Miami Beach, FL

UDALL, RASHELLE
[b.] January 4, 1971, Mesa, AZ; [p.] Richard and Pamela Harris; [m.] Daniel S. Udall, September 1, 1990; [ch.] Scott Ryan Udall; [ed.] Westwood High School; [occ.] Housewife and mother; [pers.] My inspiration comes from my family and the beautiful Utah mountains. I am truly blessed each day to be part of both.; [a.] Saint George, UT

ULUS, FUAT
[b.] January 1, 1943, Istanbul, Turkey; [p.] Turhan and Zehra Ulus; [m.] Fusun Tunca, November 27, 1975; [ch.] Eda Ulus, Ece Ulus; [ed.] 1. Medical College, Istanbul University, Istanbul, Turkey, 2. Psychiatric Residency Training, Warren, PA., 16635; [occ.] Psy-

chiatrist (MD); [memb.] American Psychiatric Association; [oth. writ.] Few articles and one book, "The Young, Healthy and ... Depressed"; [pers.] A leaf which goes with the flow in the creek, my stuck to the branch of a bush ... no problem! Just be patient as the rain increases the level or draught my decrease it, our leaf goes either over or under the branch, be free again; [a.] Hollidaysburg, PA

UNGARI, WENDY
[b.] January 18, 1968, Edmonds, WA; [p.] Paul Austin, Edith (Kitty) Whitley; [m.] Joseph Ungari, July 28, 1990; [ch.] Paulina Ungari; [ed.] Meadowdale High, Seattle Art Institute; [pers.] The reward you get for loving a child is the ability to discover the deepest and richest emotions imaginable. Paulina you are as beautiful as the poem you inspired. Mommy loves you.; [a.] Everett, WA

URICH, JOSETTE I.
[b.] December 28, 1967, Dallas, TX; [p.] Joe I. Pino decease, Goldie Pinod; [m.] Divorced; [ch.] Joshlin Lynn, Tara Polarr, Dakota Westin - Pino; [ed.] (GED) Olathe Beauty Academy, Haskell Indian Nations University; [occ.] F.T. Student at HINU, in Liberal Arts.; [memb.] Tesuque Pueblo, P.T.A.; [hon.] Haskell Football's, Trainer - Video Tech., Dean's List; [oth. writ.] Several poems - unpublished; [pers.] Most of my poems come from my inner self, retrospect of the deceased. "Life's gilded, hour, devoured by destiny."; [a.] Lawrence, KS

URICK, GWENDOLYN ROBERTSON
[pen.] Gwen Urick; [b.] Fort Bragg, NC; [p.] Ann J. and Allan B. Robertson Sr.; [m.] Jerry Urick; [ch.] Jennifer A. Carey, Shaun M. Carey, Vanessa R. Urick, Trisha D. Urick; [ed.] South Mtn. High School, Phoenix, Az., Glendale Community College, Glendale, Az.; [occ.] Purchasing Agent, Food Service Equipment; [pers.] I believe we are all spiritual beings experiencing a physical existence. Life is simply a learning experience; [a.] Phoenix, AZ

URQUHART, MARIE A.
[b.] April 17, 1959, Detroit; [p.] John and Theresa Urquhart; [ch.] Kyle James, Amanda Marie; [ed.] Grosse Pointe North H.S., Macomb Community College, Oakland University; [occ.] Computer Programmer; [oth. writ.] Several poems, short stories and screen plays.; [pers.] "If you believe in yourself, anything is possible."

USHER, CYNTHIA G. WILLIAMS
[pen.] Pandora; [b.] November 18, 1953, Savannah, GA; [p.] Marshall and Lillie Williams; [m.] Elijah E. Usher, September 2, 1975; [ch.] Eugenia S. Usher, Sean A. Usher; [ed.] MS - Troy State University, BS - Cameron University, attended Oberin College; [occ.] U.S. Military (Army) Veterinary services; [memb.] Human Resources Society, Veterans of Foreign Wars, Transportation Corps. Museum Foundation; [hon.] Numerous Military Awards, highest being the Meritorious Service Medal with Oak Leaf Cluster; [oth. writ.] 6th Prize, National Library Poetry contest, 1974 "Some Day" various unpublished poems, prose, and essays.; [pers.] I believe we exist to nurture one another. Convergence is my favorite word. I seek the lowest common denominator, to reach what I call the absolute of goodness, beauty, and truth. Herman, Hesse, is my favorite author.; [a.] Lawton, OK

VALENTINE JR., THOMAS EARL
[pen.] Tommy; [b.] May 22, 1964, Detroit; [p.] Thomas Sr. and Geraldine; [m.] Sylvia Williams, January 12, 1994; [ch.] Thomas III, Alicia Nicole Valentine; [ed.] Osborn High (Det., Mich.), Fort Valley State College; [occ.] Truck driver for the City of Detroit; [memb.] Wyoming Ave Church of Christ. American Legion member.; [hon.] Several Military Awards for rescue missions during the Desert Shield - desert storm war. Music writing honors; [oth. writ.] Several per-

sonal poems none ever published; [pers.] When I write I want people to read as if their souls were taking a journey.; [a.] Detroit, MI

VALLE, JOHN P. DEL
[b.] October 4, 1950, New York City, NY; [p.] Juan Del Valle, Carmen Durecut; [m.] Danita Del Valle, April 30, 1983; [ch.] John Dominique, Janean Jasmine, Paul Del Valle; [ed.] Samuel Gompers, H.S.; [occ.] Unrecognized Rhythm and Blues Artist; [pers.] Truth, in its pure form, is too painful, to the eye, so we look away hoping no one will notice — but our spirit never lies..; [a.] Orlando, FL

VAN DORPE, ROGER L.
[pen.] Van; [b.] June 4, 1913, Ghent, Belgium; [p.] Albert and Cesarina Van Dorpe; [m.] Betty Jean Linn, August 2, 1941; [ch.] Paul Emerson Van Dorpe and 3 grandchildren, all living in Iowa City, Iowa; [ed.] St. Catherine High School, Detroit, Michigan 1931; [occ.] Retired from J.L. Hudson Company, Detroit, Michigan 1975, after 46 years employment; [memb.] Life member, Knights of Columbus. Our Lady of Sorrows Church, Farmington, Michigan. 58 years of singing in area Catholic church choirs.; [hon.] Received Papal dispensation from church law of abstinence through paternal grandfather, who was a papal soldier under Popes Pius IX and Leo XIII.; [oth. writ.] About 150 poems, many appearing in The Hudsonian, J.L. Hudson Company house organ. "Ben Aly's Folly", I'm Whispers in the Wind. An article in the Detroit Frss Press, A poem in the Boston Globe.; [pers.] We are not on this earth of our own volition. There is an all-pervading Intelligence which directs our destiny.; [a.] Farmington, MI

VANDEVORDE, CURT
[b.] November 13, 1955, Kalamazoo, MI; [p.] Richard and Beverly VandeVorde; [ch.] Eric Scott, Bethany Lynne, Brad Michael; [ed.] Parchment High School, Parchment, MI, B.A. Alma College, Alma MI, M.B.A. Wayne State University, Detroit, MI; [occ.] President, Cynosure Financial Inc. - Insurance Brokerage; [memb.] Christ the King Lutheran Church Grosse Pointe Woods, MI; [oth. writ.] Several poems currently being published as children's books.; [pers.] I have always enjoyed writing and find that through poetry I am able to touch peoples' lives.; [a.] St. Clair Shores, MI

VANDIVER, ROBERT S.
[pen.] Bob; [b.] December 11, 1917, Florence, AL; [p.] Robert S. and Birdie Lee Vandiver; [m.] Bess B. (deceased) and Jennie B. Vandiver, March 8, 1964; [ch.] Carol Lark, June E. Burton, Robert D., Cynthia Bean, Samuel B., Andrew C.; [ed.] BA, Florida Southern College. USAF Pilot Training, Command and General Staff Schl., Army Language Schl. (Russian); [occ.] Colonel, USAF, Retiree; [memb.] Order Daedaliens, Retired Officers, Assn. 8th Air Force Historical Foundation, Military Order of the World Wars. 2nd Schweinfurt Memorial Assn., 385th Bomb Group Memorial Assn. Air Force Assn.; [hon.] President, Art Gallery and Gardens Ormond Beach, Florida Chairman, (10) years Airport Advisory Committee, Ormond Beach, FL, Military - Legion of Merit, Distinguished Flying Cross, Bronze Star, Air Medal with four Oak Leaves, Air Force Commendation and numeriys Campaign, Air Power Historian - "Power Politics: Old or New?" "Deterrence: Fact or Fancy?"; [pers.] Completed combat tour over Germany during World War II (1943-44) Participated in seven major engagements in Korean War (1950-52) Served at Bases in Alabama, Texas, England, Florida, California, Japan, Arizona, Alaska, Nebraska, Washington DC; [a.] Ormond Beach, FL

VASQUEZ, JOSE R.
[b.] January 9, 1973, Brooklyn, NY; [p.] Marilyn Gennis and Jose Vasquez Sr.; [ed.] F.D. Roosevelt High School, Brooklyn College; [pers.] Just trying to represent and show that I'm Puerto-Rican and proud of it.; [a.] Brooklyn, NY

VASQUEZ, JEFFREY ARMANDO
[pen.] The Lost Poet; [b.] February 14, 1979, New York; [p.] Scarlett, Armando Vasquez; [ed.] Manhattan Christian Academy; [occ.] Student (high school junior); [hon.] Honor roll; [oth. writ.] Many unpublished works hungry to be seen; [pers.] For one to find, one must first be lost.; [a.] Woodside, NY

VAUGHN, TERRY
[b.] June 11, 1957, Hamilton, OH; [m.] Dianne Vaughn, June 11, 1976; [ch.] 1 son - Terry Vaughn; [ed.] High School Daytona, Beach Fla. 15 years dance study - Music including black at Jordon College of Music Top and Jazz Indianapolis.; [occ.] Power Company Technician Substation and Relay; [oth. writ.] Include assorted poetry, greeting cards etc.; [pers.] I pew the door to the world with every present love. Not letting one beautiful thing go unnoticed as you pass. My work is inspired by life.; [a.] New Smyrva Beach, FL

VAUGHN, LYNN
[b.] December 23, 1935, Ava, MO; [p.] Raymond and Dora Vaughn; [m.] Patricia Vaughn, October 20, 1993; [ch.] Kim Springsteud; [occ.] Retired; [memb.] American Legion; [oth. writ.] Poems - non published, Novel - non published; [pers.] I started writing poetry to free my soul of anger and hatred that I felt after my first wife's death 24 yrs. ago. This is the only way that I got rid of it. Now I can write more kind and loving things.; [a.] Olathe, KS

VAVER, KAREN M.
[b.] January 27, 1946, Menomonie, WI; [p.] Harold and Helen Weaver; [m.] James W. Vaver, May 20, 1972; [ch.] Scot W. Vaver, Brian M. Vaver; [ed.] Menomonie H.S., P.B.I. Minneapolis, MN (Lab Tech), CVTC, Eau Claire, WI (CNA); [occ.] Disabled; [memb.] VFW, St. Pauls Evangilical Church; [a.] Menomonie, WI

VAZQUEZTELL, CARMEN A.
[b.] February 25, 1952, Cabo Rojo, PR; [ch.] A 12 year old daughter named Lizette who is a constant source of joy and inspiration; [ed.] B.S. in secondary education and foreign languages and an M.A. in Educational Administration from New York University, a professional diploma in reading from Hofstra University, currently pursuing a doctorate in reading, language, and cognition from Hofstra; [occ.] Principal-Adult Services Western Suffolk BOCES; [memb.] Member of International Reading Association, NYS Association for Bilingual Education, NYS Teachers of English to Speakers of Other Languages, National Association for Biligual Education, American Vocational Education Association, Association for Supervision and Curriculum Development, Supervisors and Administrators Association of New York State, Council of Administrators and Supervisors; [hon.] Recipient of the Dr. Martin Luther King Scholarship Award, US Office of Education Title VII Fellowship, John Dwyer Citizenship Award, Outstanding Achievement Award in the Study of Foreign Languages and International Education; [oth. writ.] Poem titled, Stolen Moments, published in the National Library of Poetry anthology EDGE OF TWILIGHT, an unpublished collection of poems on discovering the "me within" written during 1993-94; [pers.] Discovering the "me within" is a long and arduous process. Through life's challenges and adversity we find the power, strength and courage to boldly and defiantly define ourselves. I am grateful for all life's challenges and obstacles—and for the inner strength and peace they have allowed me to discover.; [a.] Jackson Heights, NY

VERAMAY, JANICE
[b.] September 27, 1969, Detroit, MI; [p.] Donald Veramay, Louise Veramay; [ed.] B.M.A., Music Theory, University of Michigan, Ann Arbor; [occ.] Student; [hon.] First Place, Agora writing competitions, Poetry Division, 87, semifinalist, essay competition on The

Fountainhead sponsored by The Ayn Rand Institute, 87; [oth. writ.] "The Heroic in Man," "The Dawn," "A Point There Is," "The Image in the Looking Glass," 'Horizons," "The Past"; [a.] Northville, MI

VERGILIO, JOSEPH ALAN
[b.] September 5, 1958, Los Angeles, CA; [p.] Ione and Anthony Vergilio; [m.] Jamie Vergilio, January 27, 1994; [ch.] We have 6 children; [occ.] Carpenter; [memb.] National Rifle Ass.; [oth. writ.] Joe has written 500 poems for his wife over a 2 year period. This is his first publication; [pers.] I was inspired by the love and beauty of my wife.; [a.] Palm Desert, CA

VERNETTI, MICHAEL
[pen.] Mark Chase; [b.] September 23, 1971, Canon City, CO; [p.] John W., Katherine C. Vernetti; [ed.] Canon City High, Ohlone College; [pers.] The greatest desires of the heart can be attained solely by the grace of God. Embrace your dreams! Peace.; [a.] Las Vegas, NV

VESSINI, DONNA MARIE
[b.] June 17, 1963, Chicago, IL; [p.] Ernest and Dorothy Vessini; [ed.] Mother Theodore Guerin H.S., Rosary College, River Forest, IL; [occ.] Freelance Artist Visual Merchandiser Commercial/Community Events; [pers.] I view my writings as independent endeavors, aesthetically encouraging each, as individual, to embrace spirituality which in turn will credit the connection of "Art and Soul". Art, as life, in general is most richly glorified when reduced to simplicities, if we choose to live life as an art form, we will indeed see, "Less is More"; [a.] Elmwood Park, IL

VEST, BEVERLY LYNN
[pen.] Bev; [b.] June 7, 1950, Philadelphia; [p.] John and Ida Vest; [m.] Single; [ed.] Neshaming High School; [memb.] DAV - Commanders Club American Legion, Church Methodist Church; [oth. writ.] Several poems not published (My Valley) (Only You) grandmother; [pers.] I write poems to express my life and deepest feelings

VETERE, MARK F.
[b.] October 21, 1951, Ankara, Turkey; [p.] Francis P. and Margaret W. Vetere; [m.] Vanessa Louise, November 26, 1994; [ch.] Nicole Alexandra Vetere, Nicole Christine Kimball (step daughter); [ed.] Clifton High School Clifton, New Jersey William Paterson College of N.J. Wayne, New Jersey; [occ.] Self employed; [oth. writ.] Several poems published in local N.J. newspapers; [pers.] Take one day at a time; [a.] Hollywood, FL

VIERS, VIRGINIA
[pen.] Cinny; [b.] January 13, 1937, Baltimore, MD; [p.] Deceased; [m.] Divorced; [ch.] Joanne, Bob, Lynne Ryan; [ed.] Lowell High School; [occ.] Matron at Tri-Creek School Corp. 15 yrs; [oth. writ.] A friend a brighter day. Poem in the National Library of Poetry - Owing Mills, MD. at day end; [pers.] Just write how I feel and thoughts of sentences

VIGLIONE, ANNEMARIE
[pen.] Anne-Marie Cederlund; [b.] December 25, 1923, Sweden; [p.] Sven Alfred and Anna Ronell of Sweden; [m.] Carlo D. Viglione, January 28, 1968; [ch.] Lenah Christina Cederlund - Margard; [ed.] Stockholms Ensk. Handelsgymnasium, Sweden; [occ.] Self employed - Designer and Artist; [memb.] SWEA, Swedish Women's Educational Association Inc., The International Society of Poets.; [hon.] Editors Choice Award The National Library of Poetry "A Far Off Place" 1993. Several of my poems selected for reading on tapes; [oth. writ.] Editor's Column SWEA Int., San Francisco Chapter and Editor's Column SWEA Forum International, members 5,500. Voluntary work. Editor. Translation of poetry. Swedish-English-Italian. Poetry Workshop V.C. Berkeley Spring of 1995; [pers.] I want to believe that goodness shall prevail over the evil of the times. As

a writer I wish to join the forces striving to repair the damages done to our world by mankind against mankind. Many finally have begun to realize that we must take better care of our natural resources and our children's education. I want to believe that there is still hope for future generations.; [a.] San Francisco, CA

VILLARREAL, SYLVIA
[b.] June 28, 1939, San Antonio, TX; [p.] Joseph and Maria von Wernich; [m.] Oscar Villarreal, January 24, 1959; [ch.] Denise Branna, Deanne White; [ed.] Brackenridge High School, San Antonio College; [occ.] Housewife; [memb.] 1. Revival Temple Church, 2. Women's Aglow Fellowship International; [hon.] Past president of Sand Antonio Day Chapter Women's Aglow Fellowship (WAF); [pers.] I wrote "The Mask" as a cry of my heart. Many lives have been touched as I have spoken at different places and I have had to uncover "The Mask".; [a.] San Antonio, TX

VON BOUDENHOVEN, JOSEFA
[b.] November 5, 1933, Iowa; [m.] Unmarried - divorced; [ch.] With their peers - adults; [ed.] High School, 1 year of Tech., College.; [occ.] Unemployed - SSI disabled; [memb.] Naturalized American Citizen - Blue Birds, Girl Scouts, FFA, Iowa, Ex-Air Force dependent; [hon.] High School diploma, Employment History, Citizenship; [oth. writ.] 'Europe' newspapers, 'Europe' religion denomination pamphlets, newspaper items prior to the Nazi takeover also same before communist takeover; [pers.] As a war victim, displaced - as an American citizen - saying goodbye to those currently entering the field is a way of life.; [a.] Estherville, IA

VORBACH, JAMES
[b.] July 27, 1956, Mineola, NY; [p.] Joan and Lawrence Vorbach; [m.] Linda Graceffo-Vorbach, April 17, 1994; [ed.] Ph.D. Applied Mathematical Sciences, University of Rhode Island; [occ.] Professor, St. John's University Jamaica, NY; [memb.] Fulbright Association, Association for Computing Machinery.; [hon.] Fulbright Scholar, Poland, 1992; [oth. writ.] Many wait patiently in paper files, jealous of the one herein, while I search for that which is most sought after—time.; [pers.] Don't let constraints at work constrain the soul, imagination should know no bounds. I have been deeply affected by "The Miracle of 34th Street", and "It's a Wonderful Life."; [a.] Port Washington, NY

WADDELL, LAURA WOODWARD
[b.] March 16, 1995, Tampa, FL; [p.] Charles and Mary Woodward; [m.] Dewey A. Waddell, May 21, 1968; [ch.] Tim and Deann Coop, Dal and Darcey Waddell; [ed.] Graduate from Leesburg High School, Attended Lake-Sumter Community College and Florida State University; [occ.] Owner-bookkeeper M&C Supply, Inc., Leesburg, FL; [a.] Leesburg, FL

WADLEY, DAMON E.
[b.] September 27, 1976, Detroit; [p.] Lolita Wadley; [ed.] Grade School: Peace Lutheran, HS: Lutheran East College: Indiana Institute of Technology.; [occ.] Librarian Assistant; [memb.] Was in United States Naval Sea Cadets for 3 yrs. Currently a brother of Sigma Phi Epsilon (Indiana Eta Chapter); [hon.] Letter in Track and Cross Country. Made Dean's List at Indian Tech. Nominated to receive the All-American Scholar Collegiate Award; [oth. writ.] "A Story of Love. "He Can't Love you Like I Can." "True Feelings." And others none of which were published.; [pers.] Love the one you with because the feeling of being alone really hurts.; [a.] Detroit, MI

WAGNER, MARLENE J.
[pen.] M. J. Wagner; [b.] December 5, 1949, Harrisonville, MO; [p.] Wm. M. and Carol Carroll; [m.] Michael E. Wagner I, May 26, 1978; [ch.] Shelly Lea Hasbrouck USAF, Mike E. II, Matt E., and Grandson Curt Hasbrouck; [ed.] BS Graphic Arts Technology and Management, Minor-Art; [hon.] Support staff

member of the year 1992 - Griffith - Ferguson - Florissant - MO; [oth. writ.] (Book) "In the Right Mind, of The Write Woman", (poem) ADD Me used to open conferences and workshops on attention deficit disorder. Poems: "What is Sky! and "Inside"; [pers.] Life is too short to be unhappy.; [a.] Florissant, MO

WAGNER, JACQUELINE
[b.] January 12, 1937, Newark, NJ; [p.] Evelyn and Robert Larson; [m.] Joachim J. Wagner, November 21, 1959; [ch.] Michele, Elise, Therese, Robert, Mary, and Julia; [ed.] Drake Secretarial School; [occ.] Homemaker; [oth. writ.] Currently working on a novel with my sister, Susan Griffin; [pers.] As children my sisters and I liked to read stories and poetry to each other. Often I would put my younger sisters to bed by promising them that I would make up a story for them.; [a.] Cazenovia, NY

WAGNER, LINDA JUNE
[b.] March 6, 1960, Cleveland; [p.] Phyllis and Terrence Grospitch; [m.] John F. Wagner III; [ed.] BA Liberal Arts, MA Education, University of Akron; [occ.] Theatre Arts and English, Teacher of; [memb.] Ohio Assn Health, Phys ED, Rec, and dance, and National Council Teachers of English; [hon.] Malone Player of the year '92 theatre award; [pers.] I wish to express spiritual and philosophical beliefs through the beauty of poetry. I am inspired by the writings of Elizabeth Barrett Browning and Emily Dickinson.; [a.] West Salem, OH

WAHLQUIST, CHRISTINE D.
[b.] January 6, 1950, Saint Louis, MO; [p.] Marian Gough and Harold Dorn; [m.] Reed P. Wahlquist, November 23, 1976; [ch.] Brian Reed, Eric David, and Chad Michael; [ed.] BA Brigham Young University, Provo, UT, MA University of Utah, Salt Lake City, UT, Ph. D. University of Utah. Theodore Roosevelt High School, St. Louis, MO; [occ.] Educational Administrator; [memb.] Association for supervision and curriculum development, Phi Kappa Phi, Phi Delta Kappa, Cooperative Learning for Utah Educators, National Education Association; [hon.] Davis County School District Teacher of the Year, Phi Kappa Phi; [oth. writ.] Unpublished dissertation-Teacher Assessment: Thought and Practice in Cooperative Learning Grouping Decisions. University of Utah, 1994.; [pers.] Of all the things that matter in this world it is our association with others that matters most. We must build each other's hope and support all because we care.; [a.] Salt Lake City, UT

WALKER, NATASHA
[pen.] Tasha; [b.] December 31, 1979, Brooklyn, NY; [p.] Cerece Walker, Larry Lewis; [ed.] Washington Irving HS 10th grade, New York, NY; [occ.] Summer Job computer programer apprentice BMCC; [memb.] The Museum of Natural History; [hon.] Jr High School Spanish Award, High School Volley Ball, Kick Ball Soft. Ball awards for outstanding player; [pers.] I wrote the poem "We So Cool" when I was 10 years old. I gave it to my mother as a gift. Needles to say she was pleased. So she kept it and 5 yrs later submitted it to a publishing company.; [a.] Brooklyn, NY

WALKER SR., REV. THEODORE
[pen.] Theodore Walker Sr.; [b.] January 8, 1915, Rick Hill, SC; [p.] William Walker and Ora Walker; [m.] Mary Edna Walker, August 30, 1952; [ch.] Theodore Walker Jr. Minister, Kenneth Edison Walker Minister; [ed.] Doctor of Divinity or DD from Universal Bible Institute Birmingham Alabama. April 10, 1977, Studied Art in Detroit at School of Arts Crafts-learned to paint Scentry people still life and Absirnet; [occ.] Preaching weekly owner the radio. Sen. afternoons at 4:00 PM. Also associate minister of Shiloh Bapt Church in Greensboro, NC Pasturemeritis of first calvary Baptist Church Salisbury, NC; [memb.] Shicoh Baptist Church of the City of Greensboro, NE, Ph. In space time I recycle caps ever other day retired from the ministry as

pastor of a church, but I'm yet preach at conductor wedding cere malts and reformira Weddings; [hon.] A plaque from first Calvary Baptist Church for being a devoted pastor for 18 years rain-snow-or fair weather July 10, 1983, 1. Certificate of distinction from lottery foreign missions connection 1988, 2. Certificate of merit from High Punt, NC 1988, Roman Baptist Asso.; [oth. writ.] Poems orations-sermons songs plays - dialogues, books of jokes or guides, books of art drawings, essays. Religious true stories and case histories. Books of recipes certificates of merit from USA 1965 in Jacksonville, NC.; [pers.] God helps those who helps themselves it's better to make a life then to make a living. Is a person can't help you be can't harm God. I believe in helping people in every way I can. If a matter is worth saying once its worth repeating. Fun I laughter help us forget our troubles.; [a.] Greensboro, NC

WALKER, MYRON
[b.] October 19, 1971, Cleveland, OH; [p.] Robin M. Walker; [ed.] John Hay High School Currently attending, Cuyahoga Community College majoring in Business Management; [occ.] Student; [memb.] North East Ohio Jazz Society, Cuyahoga Community Jazz Fest; [hon.] Top Twenty Grade Point Average Award in High School, Second Place Black History Oratorical Contest, National Honor Society, Who's Who Among American High School Students, Scholarship In Escrow; [oth. writ.] Unpublished Book Of Poetry; [pers.] I strive to relay a message of inspiration for others in the poems that I write. My hope is that my poems will influence others to achieve their goals.; [a.] Cleveland, OH

WALKER, NANCY K.
[pen.] Skidunki; [b.] October 30, 1947, Tulsa, OK; [p.] Charlie Delbert Hatfield and Patricia Sue Ann Margaret (Richmond) and Jim Lewis; [m.] Albert E. Walker (divorced 1979), May 2, 1970; [ch.] Richard Henry, Angela Pauline, Margaret Heather; [ed.] Catoosa High School, Hillcrest Medical Center, Radiology Program, Northeastern State University, Tahlequah, Oklahoma; [occ.] Radiology Technologist, WW Hastings Hospital, Tahlequah, Oklahoma; [memb.] American Registry of Radiologic Technologists, United Pentecostal Church Ladies Auxiliary Secretary, past member Bacone College Admissions Committee and Executive Committee, Muskoge, Oklahoma; [hon.] Most Valuable Technologist from Bacone College Radiology Class, 1988, Dean's Honor Roll, Northeastern State University, Tahlequah, Oklahoma; [oth. writ.] Weekly Church News, Daily Press Tahlequah, Oklahoma, several short stories, poems unpublished; [pers.] I attempt to bring feelings to life in my writings. Everyday happenings, tragedies and joys give me a basis for what I write. I enjoy giving ordinary life extraordinary depth and poignancy.; [a.] Park Hill, OK

WALKER, VELA BESS HOLMES
[pen.] Vela Bess Holmes Walker; [b.] May 5, 1917, Valley Mills, TX; [p.] Peyton and Lexie Holmes; [m.] Oscar L. Walker, November 3, 1943; [ch.] Ralph Oneal Walker, Anne, Bartlett, Tommy Walker, Shanon; [ed.] High School - Fabens, TX, BA - New Mexico State Masters - Sul Ross State Teachers College; [occ.] Retired teacher; [memb.] Delta Kappa Gamma, Retired Teacher, Trinity First United Methodist Church; [hon.] Essay Contest 1931 again 1933; [oth. writ.] A simple poem in a teacher's edition 1945 short essay in a book 1972.; [pers.] I taught school 32 years, we raised 4 children, have 9 grandchildren, 2 great grandchildren.; [a.] El Paso, TX

WALKER, BENFORD MIFFLIN
[b.] January 17, 1915, Des Moines, IA; [p.] Charles B. and Florence E. Walker; [ed.] Johnston High (Johnston, Iowa) and Drake University (Des Moises, Iowa); [occ.] Farmer; [oth. writ.] Short stories and poems; [a.] Ankeny, IA

WALL, MIKE
[b.] February 16, 1956, Queens; [p.] Marjorie and Fred Wall; [hon.] Has had several poems published in National anthologies. Accepted into International Society of Poetry; [oth. writ.] "Poems Inspired by You" A collection of 47 poems.; [pers.] We all have dreams far too often, for whatever reasons, our dreams go unfulfilled to be published by this National Library of poetry is very fulfilling, and a dream come true.; [a.] Lindenhurst, NY

WALLACE, RODNEY CHEVALLE
[b.] July 21, 1972, Fort Riley, KS; [p.] James and Bessie Wallace; [m.] Loleta Feagins-Wallace, October 14, 1994; [ch.] Leilani Sade Wallace born January 24, 1995; [ed.] Longview High School 1990 graduate, Southern Methodist University, BA Sociology, 1994 graduate.; [occ.] Child Care Specialist with Dallas Country's Youth Village; [memb.] Union Church of Christ (F.C.A.) Fellowship of Christian Athletes; [pers.] I strive to live every day of my life like my grandfather, Marcellous Johnson. He is a very dedicated and hard working farmer, rancher, and family man. I too want to be remembered as such. I have been greatly influenced by Langston Hughes.; [a.] Dallas, TX

WALLER, AUDREY R.
[b.] May 20, 1982, Gannison, CO; [p.] Kay Galon and Leon Waller; [ed.] I'm a twelve year old girl, that attends Mission Hill Jr. High; [oth. writ.] Nothing published but I have a collection of poems and short stories.; [pers.] I reveal my heart and my soul in my poetry.; [a.] Santa Cruz, CA

WALSER, JAMES P.
[pen.] J. P.; [b.] July 25, 1957, Owosso, MI; [p.] Bernard and Sophie Walser; [m.] Michelle R. Walser, August 21, 1982; [ch.] Kyle James (9), Tiffany Renee (6); [ed.] Chesaning High (Chesaning, MI), Lansing Community College (Lansing, MI); [occ.] Student, Kennel Owned (Networker); [oth. writ.] To on going writings put into a book (Lyrics of the Heart) Take my hand, I cry, One Sons Love, Remembering, You, Spirit Free; [pers.] The poem (Look For Me) was written for and is being dedicated to the memory of-Sophie Walser Born December 16, 1916 passed away November 2, 1994. You are loved and will be missed; [a.] Oakley, MI

WALTER, TIFFANY
[b.] October 8, 1966, Modesto, CA; [p.] Don and Judy Riise; [m.] Widow to Christopher Walter; [ch.] Thomas Henry (Hank); [ed.] BA Political Science, University of California at Santa Barbara; [occ.] Graduate Student; [pers.] I dedicate my writing to my sweet husband, best friend, and love of my life who died tragically at the age of 30.

WALTERS, MARY
[b.] September 27, 1936, Boston, MA; [p.] Milan and Florence Ivanoff; [m.] Miles Walters (deceased), May 7, 1956; [ch.] Max and Melanie; [ed.] Duxbury HS, Duxbury, MA, Rock Valley College, IL, Rockford College, IL; [occ.] Between Jobs (former HS teacher); [memb.] Phi Beta Kappa; [hon.] Graduated summacumlaude from Rockford College; [oth. writ.] Short stories and poems, some published in local publications; [pers.] I enjoy watching people interact, and then I create "Beyond The Obvious" stories about their relationships.; [a.] Loves Park, IL

WALTHALL, MELVIN CURTIS
[pen.] Walt Hall; [b.] July 30, 1920, Mingo, TX; [p.] James Harrison Walthall and Bessie Viola (Weaver) Walthall; [m.] Emma Shoemaker Walthall, December 19, 1949; [ch.] Joanne K. Wisby, Diana C. Place, Steven L. Walthall; [ed.] Two Year College Cert. TCU, Univ of Texas, Univ of Washington, Univ of Wisc., Univ. of MD Officers Advance Course, Ft. Benning, GA Officer's Information School, Ft. Slocum, NY Infrequent speaker about WWII and Korea.; [occ.] Ret.

US Army, Maj. and Free Lance Writer. Military Historian.; [memb.] 144th Inf. Assoc., 36th Inf. Div. Assoc. 25th Inf Div. Assoc. Association of the US Army, The Retired Officer's Assoc. and the reserve Officer's Assoc.; [hon.] Honorary member First Va. Regt, Honorary Citizen Ft. Worth, TX, Honorary Col. WV Nat'l Guard, Lifetime member 25th Div Assoc.; [oth. writ.] "We Can't All Be Heroes." "Lightning Forward" Books Publ 1975 and 1979. Approx 25 poems publ, and approx 40 articles. Working on "Orange Four" my third book.; [pers.] To be a writer the only person one has to convince is their self. But one then must Scribble, Scribble, Scribble like Charles Dickens and try to get their little gems published, and don't worry about a reject. Just keep trying and maybe you will eventually meet an Editor that knows something about writing. Many editors are not writers and they let many gems get away from them.; [a.] Wichita, KS

WANGLUND, CHRISTIAN ARIELLE
[pen.] Christian Wanglund; [b.] April 3, 1980, Ithaca, NY; [p.] Maureen Wanglund, Stanley Wanglund Jr.; [ed.] Went through Maine-Endwell school systems from kindergarten to present, am currently a freshman at Maine-Endwell Senior High School; [occ.] High School Student; [memb.] School clubs including the Future Teachers of America and the Writer's Club; [hon.] First place in an oratorical contest, first in school wide American Mathematics contest, first in physics, environmental problems and grade in science fair; [oth. writ.] Several poems published in school paper and district calendar; [pers.] I strive to be a person who has the ability to envision the truth when others cannot. Truth is the road to wisdom. I credit my family and my teacher and mentor, Mr. William Smith, as my greatest influences.; [a.] Endwell, NY

WARCZAK, GLORIA OTT
[b.] December 28, 1936, Butler, WI; [p.] Madelen And Armin Ott; [m.] Patrick T. Warczak, January 16, 1960; [ch.] (3 sons) special Sister Carol Schmidt, Special Nieces - Liz Johnson, Cathy Schmidt, Mary Wendricks; [ed.] No. Div. High-Milw., some College Milw. Area Tech. College, 20 yrs. piano Wisconsin Conservatory of Music; [occ.] Working on ful length mystery novel, and poetry collection, non-field Editor Taste of Home Magazine,; [memb.] Homemaker St. Francis Borgia Catholic Church - Cedarburg, Wisconsin piano student Wisconsin Conservatory; [hon.] Editor's Choice Award, National Library of Poetry, Nominated Poet of year '95, International Society of Poets.; [oth. writ.] Numerous unpublished poems and short stories, one recipe, one recipe with layout, one full page with color spread, including photos, article and recipes, taste of home mag. One unfinished novel and poetry collection one poem published in seasons to come.; [pers.] I hope that, through all my creative endeavors, i.e., music, art, writing, and creative cookery, I will be able to leave a lasting cultural legacy to all those who follow me.; [a.] Cedarburg, WI

WARD, SURETTA K.
[pen.] C.R.E.A.M.; [b.] November 28, 1980, Cleveland, TN; [p.] Sylvia Ward and Howard Ward II; [ed.] 8th grade; [occ.] Junior High Student; [oth. writ.] Visions, Love is..., Why? If Only People Knew, Tears, She Holds, When? As She Climb, I'll Never Forget Him, Sometimes I feel, The World, Friends, All Wishes, All She Wants; [pers.] I am sending $20.00 for the nominal fee.; [a.] Spring Valley, NY

WARD, CYNTHIA
[pen.] Cindy Ward; [b.] August 8, 1951, Nucla, CO; [p.] Gene Closser - father, Rosalie Closser - mother (deceased); [m.] Dean Ward, December 26, 1974; [ch.] Willis Doan Ward, Melissa Lavone Ward; [ed.] Pasco High School, Pasco, Washington; [occ.] Secretary; [pers.] I write my poems for enjoyment and the feeling of accomplishment.; [a.] Clifton, CO

WARKANS, GERALD M.
[b.] December 30, 1940, Hollywood, CA; [p.] Leonard and Sally Warkans; [ed.] Memorial High School West New York, NJ, Fairleigh Dickinson University Rutherford, NJ, Thomas Edison State College Trenton, NJ; [occ.] Airline Executive and Real Estate Investor; [memb.] Center for the Arts, Pepperdine University, Malibu, CA, Crest Associates, Pepperdine University Malibu, CA., International Facilities Management Assn., Make a wish Foundation; [hon.] The poem herein published, "Through His Eyes" was written in 1950 when the author was 17 years of age and a High School Senior this poem was selected by the National High School Poetry Association for Publication in the Annum, Anthology of High School Poetry (1958); [oth. writ.] Several Essays published in various publications, both domestically and Internationally; [pers.] The joy of life, to a great degree, can be substantially augmented by giving of yourself to others - freely and without expectations. Poetry is but one means of such giving.; [a.] Los Angeles, CA

WARMICK, MARY ALICE
[pen.] Mary Alive; [b.] September 25, 1914, Spangle, WA; [p.] Hazel and Joe Schieche (deceased); [m.] Donivan Warmick (deceased), February 17, 1936; [ch.] Karla Novotney, Donald Warwick Karyn Lee and Rusty Warwick; [ed.] High School and some College Beauty School; [occ.] Retired City Clerk and presently City Treasurer; [memb.] Eastern Star; [oth. writ.] "A Salute to Fathers" "Harrington" "A Smile or Two" "Autumn" and various other poems.; [pers.] I have written many poems for Eastern Star and do this as a hobby. "A salute to fathers" was published in a local newspaper by the Eastern Star as I've never sent any of my work in before. My philosophy is to enjoy each day as much as possible and try to help others.; [a.] Harrington, WA

WARNER, JASON
[b.] September 20, 1978, Olean, NY; [p.] Dennis Warner, Amy Warner; [m.] Kris Jokinen, December 26, 1994; [ed.] Friendship Central School; [occ.] Student (High School Junior); [memb.] Gay and Lesbian Youth Services (GLYS) of Western New York, International Pen Pal Program Sponsored by Youth Outreach and project 10; [hon.] National Honor society; [oth. writ.] Various writings for close friends and school; [pers.] I try to use my writings to reflect and embody the passions and positive aspects of the homosexual lifestyle; [a.] Friendship, NY

WARSAW, LADE M.
[pen.] Fanta L. Carter; [b.] Monrovia, Liberia; [p.] Fred and Louise Warsaw; [ed.] Tubman High, Liberia, Biloa University, California; [occ.] Medical Office, Manager; [memb.] Local Christian Youth Organizations; [hon.] Torphy - 1st runner up, Miss Liberia Beauty Pageant 1972, several trophies, certificates, and other awards in track and field competitions, BA, in Sociology, B.A. in Bible, and Fashion model; [oth. writ.] A couple of poems published in overseas newspapers.; [pers.] I strive to reflect the realities of life in my writing. I have been greatly influenced by both the early and contemporary poets; [a.] Norfalk, CA

WASYLYK, ALEXSANDRA MARIA
[pen.] Unek Angelwuf; [b.] October 24, 1953, Chicago, IL; [p.] Eva and Wasyl Wasylyk; [ed.] BA Education/University of IL, Chicago - continuing education in the healing arts.; [occ.] Educator/transformational counselor/astrological counselling; [memb.] NCEA, American Society of Alternative therapist, NAPT; [hon.] Hero of the Natural Law Party; [oth. writ.] Article on TM Meditation published in thresholds. Processing a book on astrology, color, and sound.; [pers.] To assist and be of service. To teach others identity fulfillment, and reveal to them their true potential.; [a.] Chicago, IL

WATERMAN, STACI
[b.] August 20, 1981, California; [p.] Patti and John Waterman; [ed.] In 8th grade now; [occ.] student; [hon.] I won 1st place in a contest at my school 2 years on 2 different poems 7th and 8th grade; [oth. writ.] I have my own book of poems that I made; [pers.] I express my feelings in my poems - about life - earth - animals and death; [a.] Vista, CA

WATERS, STEPHAN FRANKLIN
[pen.] Steve Waters; [b.] December 9, 1944, Hemingway, SC; [p.] Louis and Dorothy Waters; [m.] Kate Waters (Kathryn), July 26, 1980; [ch.] Michael Stephan Waters (my son from a previous marriage) of Florida Southern College; [ed.] High School Graduate, Wakefield High, Arlington, VA, US Navy Electronics Technician, "A" School, Associate of Electronics chemoketa Com. College,; [occ.] Television Repairman for sears Service Department, Salem OR; [memb.] Ex-President, Ex-Salem Chess Club, Amnesty International, History Book Club, Science Book Club, and all-too-human race.; [hon.] National Honor Society of secondary schools, Qualified US Navy Submarine Service, Certified Diver, Licensed Oregon Electronics Technician, Qualified Nuclear Reactor Operator.; [oth. writ.] Various piles of poetry, several clipboards full of scribbled insight in the beat of inspiration, cartoons, musical lyrics, and pithy notes to anyone showing the least interest in my work.; [pers.] Life is a fractal algorithm of Fourier series coalesced into substantially from poly field relativity, coordinated by the Free will of mankind, and subordinated to the will of God.; [a.] Lyons, OR

WATERS, MITZI MARIE
[b.] June 5, 1964, Upland, CA; [p.] Charles and Patricia Pfister; [m.] Jon William Waters, November 6, 1982; [ch.] Dereu, Larly, Wendy, and Jared Waters; [ed.] Working on a political science degree of Calstate University, Bakersfield; [occ.] Farmer and Homemaker; [memb.] California Certified Organic farmers Assoc. - Western Growers Assoc. Church of Latter - day Saints, concerned Citizens Coalition (watchdog grove); [hon.] Having a husband and four children; [pers.] Work hard, love life, live true... and blessings will come to you.; [a.] Keene, CA

WATKINS, DARYL
[b.] January 14, 1979, Hampton, VA; [p.] Dr. James and Hardenia Watkins; [ed.] Bethel High School; [memb.] First Baptist Church Morrison, Chrome, FBLA, Bethal High Football team, Bethel High Football team, Bethel High Indoor Track team, Model United Nations; [oth. writ.] So Fine, Loss of Luscious Love, "N", Love in a Mix; [pers.] I believe that love is truly powerful. Therefore through my poetry, people can experience just how powerful it is.; [a.] Hampton, VA

WATLAND, KRISTEN MAE
[b.] June 7, 1978, Redding, CA; [p.] Ken Watland, Susan Santilena; [ed.] Currently a High School Junior; [occ.] Student; [memb.] Shasta County Arts Council, High School year book staff.; [oth. writ.] A few short stories, poems; [pers.] Always think happy thoughts.; [a.] Redding, CA

WATSON, TINA
[pen.] Tina Turner; [b.] April 21, 1964, Turlock, CA; [ch.] Tasha, Ene and Aliena (Boo) Turner; [pers.] All the poems I have written have all have inspired by the man of my dreams, Jeff R. Phillips. The only man ever, who will never let me give up, what I love to do the most write poetry. I will love you for eternity.; [a.] Waterford, CA

WATTS, MURIEL TRACEY
[pen.] Muriel Watts or Tracey Watts; [b.] November 26, 1967, New Orleans; [p.] G. Patricia Watts; [ed.] Walter L. Cohen Sr. High, Southern University at New Orleans - BS Business Administration; [occ.] Federal Employee; [memb.] Toastmasters International, United Scleroderma Foundation; [hon.] "Best Speaker" and "Best Table Topics" Toastmasters Int'l, Dean's List and Honor Roll - Southern Univ. at New Orleans; [oth. writ.] Several poems and speeches delivered at special functions; [pers.] In life we face many obstacles, how you overcome them depends largely on your attitude!; [a.] New Orleans, LA

WEATHERFORD, REV. CLAUDE
[pen.] Rev. Claude Weatherford; [b.] January 28, 1928, Stewart, CO; [p.] Lester and Allie Weatherford; [ed.] No formal education; [occ.] Retired Minister; [memb.] Mt. Herman Baptist Church; [hon.] License in Ministry (5-4-60), Ordained October 8, 1978, Proclamation by Mayor, Naming Claude Weatherford Day. 1969 Handicapped Citizen of Year. Poem accepted in Kennedy Library. Tennessee Colonel.; [oth. writ.] Greatest Miracle, My Life Ambition, Life Story Included, Numerous Others; [pers.] I can do all things through Christ, which strengthen me (Phillipians, 4:13).; [a.] Clarksville, IN

WEATHERS, JEAN
[b.] November 30, 1946, Chicago, IL; [p.] Arthur James and Claudia Hillery; [m.] James H. Weathers, February 21, 1969; [ch.] Katrina (daughter), and Ramen (grandson); [ed.] Attended Proviso East High School, and Freeman's Business College; [occ.] Contract Specialist for the Department of Veterans Affairs Pharmaceutical Division; [memb.] I am Founder of the "You Go Girl" "African American Book Club", established in 1993. Very active in Church Community Affairs.; [oth. writ.] Saturdays' Past is the only serious writing I did and thought good enough to submit, I think the ice has been broken and I feel confident to try again.; [pers.] My philosophy in life is to allow the higher power to engulf my very being that I may tap into that inner strength which allow me to do anything and be all I want to be, for nothing is impossible, especially for me.; [a.] Broadview, IL

WEATHERS, ARTHUR
[b.] October 5, 1970, Newport News, VA; [p.] Julie Dargan, Arthur Sanford; [m.] Divorced; [ed.] Ferguson High School; [occ.] U.S. Army Sergant; [memb.] SPA Fitness Center; [oth. writ.] Several Poems in Army Newspaper; [pers.] When writing a poem, just remember to put your mind at ease and love everybody. I look forward to making a book one day. So, keep your head high and be all you can be.; [a.] Newport News, VA

WEATHERSPOON JR., SAMUEL I.
[pen.] Spran; [b.] June 26, 1954, Fort Pierre; [p.] Samuel I. Weatherspoon, Ruby Maye Weatherspoon; [ed.] Masters Art Degree, Gourmet Cooking Degree; [occ.] Commercial Art; [hon.] Local, Courier New Paper, 2 awards; [oth. writ.] Avenue, Of Life, (Hollywood Calif) The Phantom, called, Racism, (North Carolina).

WEAVER, JOHN
[b.] March 16, 1948; [p.] Fredrick and Anne Weaver; [occ.] Accountant; [hon.] Honorable Mention for poem "A Shadow of Yesterday"; [oth. writ.] Novel Starcrossed: Beyond The Dream and Memories! When Our Hearts Were Young and Free, Also Book of Poems "Poems of Prosperity and Peace"; [pers.] I am an advocate of world peace and personal growth; [a.] Berkeley, CA

WEAVER, BARRY
[b.] April 6, 1974, Paris, TX; [p.] Dean Weaver, Jane Weaver; [ed.] Forth Worth Boswell H.S., Sam Houston State University; [occ.] Student-athlete (football); [memb.] Sigma Nu Fraternity, Officer; [oth. writ.] Several poems; [pers.] I do not restrict my writing, but allow myself to freely express my true feelings; [a.] Forth Worth, TX

WEBBER, AMY ELIZABETH
[b.] August 1, 1972, Providence, RI; [p.] John and Kathryn; [ed.] Barrington High School, Siena College; [occ.] Receptionist, Secretary; [pers.] Stay gold.; [a.] Troy, NY

WEBER, DIANA
[b.] July 31, 1954; [p.] Joseph H. Martin, Mary Ann Martin; [ch.] Scott Thomas Weber, Kimberly Dawn Weber; [ed.] Lawrence High School, Trenton State College; [occ.] Art Teacher, Hamilton Township, NJ; [hon.] Dean's List Governor's Teacher Award of NJ; [pers.] I believe in living life on a wing and a prayer. In searching my heart, poetry has become a way to express my love for God.; [a.] Lawrenceville, NJ

WEBER, CONNIE D.
[b.] April 3, 1969, Wichita, KS; [p.] Kenneth Weber, Carmen Weber; [ed.] Goddard High School, Kansas State University; [occ.] News reporter, KTOK News Radio, Oklahoma City, OK; [hon.] 1st place, Kansas Association of Broadcasters - In-Depth News Reporting in a Series: The Trouble Guns (1994); [pers.] I try to find the human element in its rawest form in my writing. Sometimes it's beautiful, sometimes it's not - demonstrative of life itself.; [a.] Oklahoma City, OK

WEDEKIND, GEORGIA BROWN
[pen.] Georgie Girl; [b.] December 20, 1949, Newark, NJ; [p.] George H. Brown and Grace Romona Davis; [ch.] Maralynn Beth (23), Donald Edward II (20); [ed.] County College of Morris, Randolph, N.J., William Paterson College, Wayne, NJ; [occ.] Marketing Secretary for ASCO; [pers.] My strong beliefs and feelings are the bread and butter of my poetry sugar coated by God. My late Mom's integrity will always be my inspiration.; [a.] Dover, NJ

WELCH, MAXWELL MILLARD
[b.] January 11, 1913, Strong, ME; [p.] Roscoe Benjamin Welch, Maude Blossom Ranger; [m.] Elizabeth Lincoln Dorr, May 29, 1943; [ch.] Kenneth Albert, Thomas Dorr, Susan Cassova Maude, Patricia Elizabeth; [ed.] Strong Elementary, Strong High, Bowdoin College, Brunswick ME, Bangor Theological Seminary, Bangor ME courses at the University of Lisbon, Portugal; [occ.] Clergy (retired) United church of Christ; [memb.] Connecticut Conference of the United Church of Christ, (from 1947-1958 a member of the American Board of Commissioners for Foreign Missions serving in Angola, Portuguese West Africa.) (No fraternity connection in college, or seminary).; [hon.] Dean's List 1943, Bowdoin; [oth. writ.] None for public consumption. To date my principal interest has been for family consumption, or occasionally in a parish setting.; [pers.] My teacher and mentor in college days was Robert Peter Tristam Coffin (1892-1955). The other poet and influence was Robert Lee Frost (1874-1963). My interests lie in the areas of religion and nature - the divine creatorship of the natural world about me, and reflecting upon humanity's relationship to it.; [a.] Walpole, ME

WELLS, LINDA
[b.] October 7, 1947, Detroit, MI; [p.] Howard and Joyce Klaasser; [m.] Richard E. Wells, March 26, 1983; [ch.] Michelle Blaszczyk, James C. Blaszczyk

WENZEL, STERLING
[b.] November 17, 1915, Langdon, ND; [p.] Jake and Anne Wenzel; [m.] Esther Wenzel, May 10, 1942; [ch.] Lee Wenzel, Shirley Beine, Mary Baltzer, and Mark Wenzel; [ed.] North Central College Evangelical Theological Seminary at Naperville, IL; [occ.] Died April 23, 1991; [memb.] United Methodist Dakota Conference. Church World Service (CROP), Lions, Ministerial; [hon.] Trustee of Westmar College for 12 yrs.; [oth. writ.] Sermons for 40 years; [pers.] The Lord has been our Shepherd.; [a.] Olivet, SD

WENZEL, MELISSA
[b.] October 4, 1980, Tempe, AZ; [p.] Yvonne and Paul Purvis; [ed.] Mountain Pointe HS; [occ.] Student; [memb.] National Wildlife Fed. School Activities. (Clubs) including the environmental and ceramics.; [hon.] Academic Awards; [oth. writ.] Several unpublished poems; [pers.] I would like to dedicate my poem to my family and friends for their support.; [a.] Phoenix, AZ

WEST, JOHN L.
[pen.] Mickey; [b.] June 25, 1952, Cleveland, OH; [p.] John and Ruth West; [m.] Single; [ed.] John F. Kennedy High School - Class of 1970; [memb.] Minority AIDS project, CARA-A-CARA Aids Latino Project Volunteer; [hon.] Merit of Achievement 1991 for fund raisers and volunteer with cara-a-cara and for 1994 also.; [oth. writ.] Everything You Need Is Within You 8-1-94. This Time It's For Me 8-7-94, Whenever You Need Me 8-19-94, Let Me In 8-20-94, Created From Love 12-9-94, Safe And Sound (In A Field Of Love) 1-20-95; [pers.] If everything you do in life is simply from the heart, no matter how tough it may get. You can never go wrong. Trust, respect and believe in yourself; [a.] Los Angeles, CA

WEST, JOETTE RAE FISH
[pen.] Rae Fish; [b.] November 25, 1960, Great Falls, MT; [p.] Dermith J. Fish, Shirley M. Matney; [ch.] Nicole Colette, Jesse Allen, Cory Lynn, Krista Rae; [ed.] Leileihua High School, Hawaii; [occ.] Full time Mother of 4, starting a small in home business.; [memb.] Hallelujah Christian Fellowship, The International Society of Poets, P.T.A. at Twin Lakes Elementary School, Democratic Party of Clark County; [hon.] Editor's Choice Award for "Strength In The Valley's", published in Edge of Twilight, and for "Being A Mother," published in Echoes of Yesterday.; [oth. writ.] I continue to write and revise poems (prayers) of praise to the Lord, to strengthen and encourage myself and others. Several have now been accepted and/or published by The National Library of Poetry, and others have been printed and/or recited at Church's.; [pers.] The glory for these words has to go to God, for He's my inspiration, and my only hope is that a Seed for the Lord may be planted in someone's heart as they read these poems.; [a.] Las Vegas, NV

WHALEY, JACQUELINE
[b.] October 26, 1960, Detroit, MI; [p.] Rev. and Mrs. Clarence and Lillie Taylor; [m.] Frederick Darnell Whaley, June 11, 1983; [ch.] Frederick Darnell Jr., Terrell, Vonzell, Sedric Whaley; [ed.] Completed 12-years of school. A graduate of Southeastern High School. Detroit, Michigan 1979.; [occ.] A housewife, and mother.; [pers.] I have always been inspired by other poets, and have always wanted to pursue a career in poetry writing. I hope that someday to become a great and poetic writer as I continue to write.; [a.] Detroit, MI

WHEELER, SYLVIA M.
[b.] July 31, 1965, Cleveland, OH; [p.] Richard and Hattie Wheeler; [ed.] Bachelor of Science in Accounting, June 1987; [occ.] Sale Representative; [memb.] Delta Sigma Theta Sorority Inc., Karamu House Theater; [hon.] Who's Who Among American Universities and Colleges, First Place Winner of Creative Writing Contest, Dean's List (Seven semesters); [oth. writ.] Poems published in local newspaper; [pers.] To exist is to change, to change is to mature, to mature is to create oneself endlessly (unknown); [a.] Cleveland, OH

WHEELER, MARDY
[b.] May 9, 1938, Easton, MD; [p.] Robert B. Harrison, Elizabeth F. Harrison; [m.] David W. Wheeler, May 9, 1962; [ch.] Paul, Marjory; [ed.] BA U of ME 1968, (English), MS (HRD), The American Univ. 1982; [occ.] Consultant - training and Development; [memb.] ASTD, SITE, ODN; [hon.] Who's Who - American Women, Who's Who in the East; [oth. writ.] Published in numerous magazines co-author - Communication Skills for Managers AMA 1982, Quality Customer Service, HRD Press 1995; [pers.] Poetry is my personal stress - reliever and the medium in which I am truly honest.; [a.] Natick, MA

WHITAKER, JEFFERY
[pen.] Jeffery Whitaker; [b.] April 13, 1980, Florence, AL; [p.] Jeff and Anita Whitaker; [ed.] 4th grade student; [memb.] Colbert County 4-H Club, Allsboro Presbyterian Church, Cherokee Dixie Youth Baseball, Football and Basketball.; [hon.] 2nd place in watercolor art contest for Kindergarten, 1st place in pencil art in 1st grade class A-B honor student for past 5 years; [pers.] My goal in life is to be an accomplished man of many things. I want to be a rancher and architect and have a pretty wife and children; [a.] Cherokee, AL

WHITCHER, KEVIN
[b.] August 27, 1957, Bridgeport, CT; [p.] Lois and Cliff Whitcher; [m.] Lisa, February 27, 1982; [ch.] Heather Laura, Bradley Methew; [ed.] Lyman High; [occ.] Carpenter; [oth. writ.] Several poems and song for country Western Artists. Have a children book in the process of being published; [pers.] There is no greater language than the language of love.; [a.] DeLand, FL

WHITE, BARBARA A. HUDSON
[pen.] Star-Lin; [b.] February 4, 1940, Franklin, IN; [p.] Mr. and Mrs. Paul L. Starlin (deceased); [m.] Micheal L. White, February 14, 1995 (2nd marriage); [ch.] Scott (deceased), Renee and Andrea Hudson; [ed.] Portland High school, Portland, IN, Toledo Art Museum School of Design, Toledo, Oh., Art Studies in Europe 1978, Also studied Classical piano, dance and modeling.; [occ.] Artist, self employed, I paint in oils, acrylics, watercolor, and pastels. People are my favorite subjects.; [hon.] Art Awards and 'one-women' art show by invitation: Hoosier Salon Indianapolis, IN. Received Scholarship Grant for continued study from Art Interest Inc., Toledo, OH. 1974-1977.; [oth. writ.] My writing has always been a love of mine, but it has been on private level. This contest was my 'coming out', my first exposure.; [pers.] I write from the heart. I write about feelings and life experiences, my feelings and experiences, knowing that we all at some time in lifetime live with love, pain, loneliness, happiness and loss. If I can bravely spill the words onto the paper, maybe sometime, somewhere the words will reach someone who cannot verbalize the feelings and they will be consoled. I believe our only lesson to be learned here on earth is, How to give Love and Receive Love.; [a.] Fremont, OH

WHITE, GWYNNETH
[b.] October 11, 1947, Elyria; [m.] Charles R. White; [occ.] Homemaker; [memb.] I'm a member of Mt. Zion Baptist Church of Oberlin, Ohio. (30 yrs) Rev. Fred L. Steer is my pastor. I'm also on the teaching staff of our Sunday School, plus I am the Assistant Superintendent, of which I've received certificates of appreciation of devoted services. I'm also a member of our sanctuary choir. I'm very active in my church.; [oth. writ.] I wrote a poem for my pastor on his 42nd anniversary which will be put in a book of other tributes.

WHITE, JILI KRISTEN
[b.] September 23, 1981, Whiteville, NC; [p.] Doug and Anita White; [ed.] Myrtle Beach Middle School; [occ.] Student (7th grade); [memb.] Club Volleyball, Middle School Band; [hon.] Honor roll student, superior band soloist, band officer, outstanding leadership award; [oth. writ.] I'm just a poor woman, Ludwig Van Beethoven; [pers.] Don't take anything for granted.... ever; [a.] Myrtle Beach, SC

WHITE, LANCE
[b.] September 27, 1961, El Paso, TX; [ed.] No thanks I know too much already; [occ.] Lump; [memb.] "Me against the world" Club. (President and only member);

[hon.] First place in the tattoo contest at the "crusty cup cafe"; [oth. writ.] Grocery lists, checks and signatures on speeding tickets; [pers.] Lighten up. Laugh a little. Life is too important to be taken seriously.; [a.] Riverside, CA

WHITE, LEAH
[b.] May 10, 1977, Soldotna, AK; [p.] E. James and Judith White; [occ.] Currently preparing to graduate from High School; [memb.] Student; [pers.] I consider the Israeli Fighter and poet Hannah Senesh as one of my greater influences, both in terms of her art and her life.; [a.] Goshen, OH

WHITE, LINDA D.
[b.] September 30, 1945, Baltimore; [p.] Howard and Mildred Lynch; [m.] James D. White Jr., May 22, 1971; [ch.] Heather Dawn, Colleen Danielle, Melissa Denise White; [ed.] Eastern High School, Harford Community College; [occ.] Administrative Assistant Baltimore, MD; [memb.] Churchville Presbyterian Church, Committees, PTO, Amer. Lung Assoc. Harce Forest Cedarette, Stephanie Roper Committee WF Youth Group; [hon.] For Volunteer Work; [oth. writ.] Local organizations, poems for advertisement, newsletters gifts, church, school, local newspapers; [pers.] I try to offer encouragement and positive messages in my work. My best works come from within just about word perfect. Others I choose to write and work hard at them. I thank God for my gift.; [a.] Churchville, MD

WHITE, TERESA
[b.] March 27, 1947, Seattle, WA; [p.] James H. Blake, Molly Blake; [m.] Robert E. White, October 26, 1972; [ed.] Roosevelt High University of Washington; [occ.] Sweater-Pattern Consultant for U.S. Yarn Distributor; [memb.] Tend to be a loner; [oth. writ.] One novel, one novella (prepublication) over 500 poems titled "In what Furnace" in progress, over 90 songs - lyrics and music; [pers.] I have always felt that because writing poetry comes so effortlessly to me that my ability is, indeed, a gift bestowed by my creator. My poems come thru me more than by me.; [a.] Seattle, WA

WHITING, HONEY W.
[pen.] Honey W. Whiting; [b.] December 3, 1935, Whiting, IA; [p.] Norman and Mary Whiting; [m.] Divorced; [ch.] Jeffrey Clayton and Norman R. Clayton (both of California); [ed.] Bachelors in Education from St Cloud State Teachers College, St Cloud, Minors. Attended Whiting, IN, Public Schools, Stephens College, Columbia, MO, Univ. of AZ, Tuczon, AZ, and Bobson College - Lake Wales, FL; [occ.] Retired from S.B.U.S.D. Special Education Dept. San Bernardino, CA; [oth. writ.] This is my second (lifetime) entry in any contest. Won 2nd place in an Iowa (Poetry) school competition (state wide) when in 8th or 9th grade.; [pers.] Taught in California for 29 years, then retired to the beautiful Ozarks. I now have time to pursue my writing, gardening and craft interests. Am currently remodelling an old Arkansas from house.; [a.] Calico Rock, AR

WHITMIRE, BONITA D.
[pen.] Pulaski D. Ethridge; [b.] August 8, 1959, Baltimore, MD; [p.] John and Eva Lee Whitmire; [ed.] Southside High, Greenville Technical College, University of South Carolina; [occ.] Day Care Director and Lead Teacher - Twinkle Kiddie College; [memb.] Pleasantburg Lions Club - 1st female member, 1st female president 94-95. Member of Chancel Choir of Edwards Rd. Bapt Church, Greenville, SC.; [hon.] Melvin Jones Fellowship 1992 highest award that can be received from the lions.; [oth. writ.] 2 poems, published in the Reedy River Review, poem published in the Palmetto Lion.; [pers.] My writing reflects the core of my being. Often, when I write, what I write pours out of me, as if I have no control over it.; [a.] Greenville, SC

WHITSETT, AMANDA CAMILLE
[pen.] Mandy; [b.] October 30, 1983, Ohio; [p.] Lula Anako and Perry Williams III; [ed.] 6 Grade Central Middle School; [occ.] Student; [memb.] Greater Prayertown CDGIC "BABES" Prevention Program Central Middle School Choir Catholic Big Brother, Sisters Cuyahoga County Southern Baptist Assoc. Children's Church; [hon.] Perfect Attendance student of the month; [oth. writ.] Short stories and poems used at school; [pers.] I like to write because it is fun and it helps me when I am sad or in trouble. I am in the 6th grade. I hope to be a Vet. because I love animals. I also believe in animals rights.; [a.] Cleveland, OH

WICKERSHAM, ELIZABETH C.
[b.] November 20, 1925, TN; [p.] Tom and Elvie, McGee; [m.] John A. Wickersham; [ch.] Barbara, Roger, Peter and Earl; [ed.] TCHS, Hartsville, TN; [occ.] Homemaker; [oth. writ.] Slogan For Union Pacific R.R. Caboose; [pers.] Give the Devil or never take from anyone what they have coming; [a.] Logandale, NV

WIERSCHEM, CHRISTINA SUSAN
[b.] September 9, 1977, Japan; [p.] Charles And Kazumi Wierschem; [ed.] 1995 graduate of Paradise Valley High School; [occ.] Student, Writer; [memb.] Asian American Journalists Association, Quill and Scroll; [hon.] Dow Jones Newspaper Fund Student Writing Award, Editor-in-Chief of High School newspaper, Layout Manager of Wisteria - a paper produced at NAU, high school recognition of stories.; [oth. writ.] Poems and a short story published in Jasper's song - a literary magazine, articles published in local newspaper, story published on the front cover of the Phoenix youth commission, articles in high school paper.; [pers.] Hold onto every experience and learn from them for the knowledge you gain and emotions you feel will bring you a lifetime of wisdom and growth.; [a.] Phoenix, AZ

WIKOFF, SHAWON ROSE
[pen.] Sharon Rose; [b.] April 11, 1951, Massillon, OH; [p.] Rev. Lloyd and Edna Hostetler; [ch.] 2 adult sons: Jason Lee Wikoff, Travis James Wikoff; [ed.] Claymont High School, Uhrichsville, OH, Computer Class, Buckeye Joint Vocational School New Philadelphia, Oh.; [occ.] Public Relations Dept. Office-Clerical at County Club Retirement Center - Dover, Ohio; [memb.] Christian Temple, Uhrichsville, Ohio; [hon.] National Honor Soc. in High School, Represented Claymont High School in the 1968 "All Ohio State Fair Choir" in Columbus, Ohio, Recorded one album "Feeling At Home" by the "Proclamation Singers" Urrichsville, OH, Organized and toured briefly in Gospel Group; [oth. writ.] Early, unpublished works of skits, plays, songs used at local church.; [pers.] If life has handed you a tragedy, and you feel shattered, find a way to pick up the pieces and make a Mosaic. It's quite possible that it will be more beautiful than your original dreams.; [a.] New Philadelphia, OH

WILCE, JOHN R.
[b.] February 18, 1970, West Frankfort, IL; [m.] Jamie Wilce, October 15, 1991; [ch.] Shayly Wilce; [ed.] High School Graduate, Frankfort Community High School; [occ.] Plant Manager; [oth. writ.] Stive For Perfection; [pers.] I've never really been influenced by other poetry. My writings come from feeling the struggles, joys and sadness of others. The emotions they show, and sometimes don't, are then expressed on paper; [a.] West Frankfort, IL

WILCOX, KELSI
[pen.] Kelsi Wilcox; [b.] July 12, 1985, Jamestown, NY; [p.] Craig and Carol Wilcox; [ed.] Lander Elementary, Theater Workshop, Chautauqua Institution; [memb.] Boys and Girls Club, Eastern Dairy 4-H Club, Junior Holstein Club, Junior Dairy Bowl Team, Sunday School; [hon.] Piano, Showmanship award, 4-H Jump for Heart been in Several Plays, Waren Players Club, A pay called "She Loves Me" with, summer

playhouse, the Struthers Library Theater; [oth. writ.] Essay, Sugar Grove American Legion, Poem My Farm Life in 1995, Addition by Young Americans Farm Safety Poster Contest Winner, Library Radio Announcement, Wrote Advertisement myself; [pers.] When something is done and over don't worry about it you can't do anything about it anyway. Just go on and be happy and do the best you possibly can.; [a.] Russell, PA

WILEY, LEAH KAREN
[pen.] Leah; [b.] April 11, 1959, Atlanta; [p.] Ronald and Jean Johnson; [ch.] Tony, 21 and Kevin, 17; [oth. writ.] Hundred's since 15 yrs. old, never anything published, or submitted.; [pers.] May we all look to the creations and see: "Only pure poetry"!!!

WILKERSON, DAVID
[pen.] Oba-Bede-Kuumba-Kyquiba-Simbila; [b.] April 15, 1941, Baltimore; [p.] George Watson and Clara Wilkerson; [ed.] Dunbar High School Essex Community (Essex, MO); [occ.] US Postal-Worker; [memb.] African Heritage Dancers and Drummers (Washington, D.C.); [hon.] Certificate of appreciation mayor's office. Honorary Discharge MS Air Force; [oth. writ.] And If I Cry, I Must Stop Running, Blur Dolphin, How Long Will You Wait, I Have Seen The Joy, But Yet To Taste It's Sweetness; [pers.] Look into the mirror not just to see but view the beauty of your soul there in (my influence the arts); [a.] Baltimore, MI

WILKERSON, RICHARD J.
[b.] March 31, 1954, Orlando, FL; [p.] L. H. Wilkerson and Gail Trubey Baer; [ed.] Received G.E.D. in June 1980 at Seminole Community College in Sanford, FL.; [occ.] Retired Bankers Helper - Charlies Gourmet Bakery; [memb.] Central FL. Blood Bank - Blood Donor; [hon.] New Life Center Laurel Perez, Director.; [oth. writ.] I have written other poems based on my experience as a child and my adult life.; [pers.] Alma, Arthur, Mae and Floyd, Trubey, Frances C., Carter and Alice Napoli have all helped me thru out my life, thank you!; [a.] Orlando, FL

WILKOVICH, GREG
[b.] May 7, 1975, Pittsburgh, PA; [p.] Dan Wilkovich, Sandra Fleischer; [ed.] Arundez High, Anne Arundez Community College; [occ.] Student; [hon.] Phi Theta Kappa, Dean's List; [oth. writ.] School literary magazines, Essay in Ohio Association for Gifted Children, several underground publications; [pers.] Aw Yeah!; [a.] Crofton, MD

WILLIAMS, BROOXIE
[b.] April 4, 1920, Trenton, TN; [p.] Irby and Linnie Arnold; [m.] James B. Williams, July 8, 1939; [ch.] Beverly, Linda, Craig; [ed.] High School, Nursing; [occ.] Retired Nurse; [oth. writ.] Have many poems written through the years and in time of stress, mostly, but none were even published; [pers.] "Do Unto Others" and help where I am needed. My life has been devoted to nursing since age 16 and it still is.; [a.] Hendersonville, NC

WILLIAMS, CHRISTINE
[b.] December 8, 1981, Maryland; [p.] Mark and Barbara Williams; [ed.] 8th grade; [occ.] School; [memb.] Creative writing, Drama club; [hon.] Writer of the month 3rd grade, San Bernadino, CA, 3rd place Science Award 1989; [pers.] Anything is possible if you just apply yourself.; [a.] Oklahoma City, OK

WILLIAMS, REV. ELWYN M.
[b.] December 21, 1922, Ilion, NY; [p.] Thomas J. Williams and Minnie C. Williams; [m.] Annette Smith Williams, May 29, 1949; [ch.] Gail A. Bloom, Mark F. Williams, Thomas A. Williams, Robert C. Williams; [ed.] High School - Camden, NY 1940, Syracuse University, AB 1948, Boston University M. Div 1951; [occ.] Retired - part time Syracuse University, Development Associate; [memb.] Oregon - Idaho conference -

The United Methodist Church, AARP, Masonic Order, Acacia Fraternity, Former President, Welsh Singing Society of Columbus, Ohio; [hon.] Otterbein College - Distinguished Service honorary Alumnus - Otterbein College Southern Poetry Association - Honorable Mention, WW II Veteran - 10th Weather Squadron, Burma; [oth. writ.] Poems published by Southern Poetry Association, Weekly Devotions - Methodist disciplines, 1989, Numerous Sermons and poems; [pers.] Ordained United Methodist minister, served Otterbein College Pacific University, Willamette University. University of Florida, Syracuse University Interboard Council of Methodist Church in Indiana, Several pastorates.; [a.] Palm Coast, FL

WILLIAMS, ERICA A.
[b.] October 25, 1974, Philadelphia; [p.] Pete and Antoinette Williams; [ed.] Bodine HSIA PC Textiles and Science Craft Institute Community College of Philadelphia; [occ.] Designer and Dressmaker; [oth. writ.] Was I rocking? Daddy's not crying... is first and only; [pers.] My grandmother has been everything to me, my family, friend, nurture, provider, teacher, idol, inspiration, fears, joys, tears, and laughter. She has given me life and death, despite her departure from me physically in 1987 she has and will always be with me spiritually. I love you grandma.

WILLIAMS, KEVIN
[pen.] George Kansas; [b.] February 8, 1976, Naperville, IL; [p.] Darrell and Ann Carol Williams; [ed.] University of Central Florida; [occ.] Elementary Education Major; [hon.] Congressional Award for Excellence, National Honor Society; [oth. writ.] Several short stories published at state and local levels.; [pers.] I have found myself through my writings and I am here to stay.; [a.] Sarasota, FL

WILLIAMS, MARK L.
[b.] July 9, 1959, Rantoul, IL; [p.] Richard O. and Doris Williams; [ed.] Garfield High School Garfield, NJ, Bergen Community College; [occ.] Police Officer Garfield, NJ; [memb.] PBA Local #46, NJ Police Honor Legion; [oth. writ.] This is "Hopefully the first of many."; [pers.] You must take advantage of a situation, before that situation takes advantages of you.; [a.] Garfield, NJ

WILLIAMS, SCOTT ALAN
[pen.] S. A. Williams or S. A. Hood; [b.] June 18, 1970, Fort Wayne, IN; [p.] Jimmy and Diann Williams; [ed.] Bachelor of Arts in Communication from Bowling Green State University. Bowling Green, OH; [occ.] Supervisor Photo processing lab for Meijer, Inc.; [hon.] Member of the First Families of Allen County Indiana; [pers.] My writings are a reflection of my whole self, they include every ounce of energy, emotion and fortitude that my body can give.; [a.] Albany, IN

WILLIAMS, TANGENICKA BRITANNICA
[b.] June 20, 1977, Green Ville County; [p.] Lillie Bell Williams; [ed.] Laurences Dist. 55 High School; [memb.] Pleasant View Baptist Church, Gray Court SC.; [hon.] Junior Honor Society - Solo Ensemble Festival for South Carolina Band Directions Associations; [oth. writ.] I have wrote over as poems since December of '94! I also have wrote poem for funeral; [a.] Gray Court, SC

WILLIAMS, VELMA TAYLOR
[pen.] Velma Taylor Williams; [b.] December 2, 1955, Essex, MO; [p.] Hosic L. and Bertha M. Taylor; [m.] Divorced; [ch.] Kenya R. Williams; [ed.] Oran High School, Three Rivers Community College, Currently enrolled. Working toward nursing degree (BSN); [occ.] Central Service Technician, Missouri Delta Medical Center, Sikeston, MO.; [oth. writ.] Mysterious Tree for the National Library of Poetry and House Organ at place of employment, famous poets society.; [pers.] I enjoy writing poetry of all types, but Christ and spiritu-

ality seem to influence me most.; [a.] Sikeston, MO

WILLIAMS, VIRGINIA HOLDEN
[pen.] Vicki Stuart; [b.] October 22, 1920, Michigan; [p.] Rev. and Mrs. Charles Wesley Holden; [m.] Earl Jefferson Williams, June 1, 1968; [ch.] Four stepchildren—Earl Jr., David, Linda, Julie; [ed.] BA, Albion College, MA Northwestern Univ of Michigan, MA Middlebury, Vt. Post graduate USC, U. Chicago, U. Ill. Univ. of Denver, Northern Ill. Univ.; [occ.] Retired — but active in community and church endeavors; [memb.] AZ retired Teachers, AAUW, DKG, BPW, PEO, Methodist Church, Kappa Delta, Gideons, Albion Alumni, AZ Historical Assoc., Arizona Preservation Assoc., AAUP NATE, Ill. Education Assoc.; [hon.] On Univ. Ill. Coordinating Staff for teaching of English in Secondary Schools... other recognition as English Curriculum head in Eisenhower HS, District 218, Ellinois Awarded local minister—IL conference college scholarships, Original musical produced by WIU orchestra special honors in church leaderships awarded HS Master Teacher Recognition; [oth. writ.] Professional article in English Journal, articles in religious magazines... Several hundred poems, dramatic skits, talks, sermonettes, articles local in newspapers, booklets; [pers.] Greatly influenced by my minister father and teacher-mother, I have strived to instill a love for learning (in my 40 years of HS and college teaching)... And an appreciation of literature. I have been encouraged by the poet Robert Frost who was a near resident at Bread Loaf post graduate college of English, Middlebury, VT. My life and writing has been focused in sharing the positive in life and the goodness of God; [a.] Prescott, AZ

WILLIAMSON, DEWEY
[pen.] Dew; [b.] April 3, 1928, LA; [p.] Dewey and Mary Williamson; [m.] Mary B, February 12, 1949; [ch.] Terry, Mark, Mary C. Avalon; [occ.] Retired; [memb.] Ocean Shores Baptist Church; [hon.] USAF Air Defense Command Commendation; [oth. writ.] AIDS - The answer God is, You Need Jesus Christ, Hypocritical Pledge, Ocean, In God's Time, Beauty Is, Only a two foot window - only a house God is Good, Lover of my Soul; [pers.] To Bring Honor and Glory, To my Lord Jesus Christ; [a.] Ocean Shores, WA

WILLIS, CHARITY R.
[b.] January 26, 1961, Bremerton, WA; [m.] Craig N. Willis, February 16, 1980; [ch.] Ezekiel Daniel, Jonathan Isaiah, Wendall Patrick, Bradley Wayne.; [ed.] BA Interdisciplinary Studies (English and Elementary Education) at University of Texas at Arlington; [occ.] Substitute Teacher; [memb.] Rutherford Institute; [hon.] Salutatorian of High School Class; [oth. writ.] Blue Roan of Kentucky, Jonathan Junebug, Cartoons: High way Jet and Marty Sparrow, The Lineman Series.; [pers.] In my experience I am first a Christian, then a Southern Baptist. I love the Lord Jesus Christ with all my heart, soul, and mind. I thank him greatly for his gift of salvation.; [a.] Fort Worth, TX

WILLIS, SUSAN
[pen.] Susan Pastorius; [b.] February 28, 1954, Akron, OH; [p.] Charles and Geraldine Pastorius; [m.] Michael Willis, May 17, 1975; [ch.] Steven, Mary, Charles; [ed.] Manchester High School current - student Kentstate English Major, writing program minor; [occ.] Factory worker; [pers.] I'm an observer in a rapidly changing world, I wish to present reality and the spirituality just within my grasp.; [a.] Randolph, OH

WILOWSKI JR., E. J.
[b.] November 21, 1957, Manhasset, NY; [p.] Judge and Mrs. Edmund J. Wilowski; [m.] Heidi M. Wilowski, June 3, 1990; [ch.] Hedy-Helene and Marc; [ed.] Holy Cross High School Flushing NY, St. John's University Jamaica, NY; [occ.] Songwriter and musician; [oth. writ.] Numerous songs and music scores, as well as several short stories.; [a.] Locust Valley, NY

WILSON, CLYDE
[b.] November 8, 1920, Alameda, CA; [p.] Clyde Sr. and Melva; [m.] Barbara, June 23, 1943; [ch.] Karna, Clyde III, Dean, Janinne; [ed.] Alameda High School; [occ.] Retired; [hon.] Reflections of light, Library of Congress - ISBN 1-56167-264-5 US Patent #3752766; [pers.] May your Mettle surpass the crucible of challenge and change; [a.] Moraga, CA

WILSON, DIANA
[b.] March 11, 1978, Peru, IN; [p.] Jack Wilson, Miriam Wilson; [ed.] I am attending River Forest High School and graduate in 1996.; [pers.] I have been greatly influenced by my English teacher at River Forest High School, Mrs. Sandra Mihalik. She helped me remember how good it felt to write from the heart. I hope to become a great writer someday.; [a.] Lake Station, IN

WILSON, KELLIE R.
[b.] May 4, 1979, Longview, WA; [p.] Carolyn and Clarence Wilson; [ed.] Completed 10th Grade at Mark Morris High School in Longview, Washington June, 1995; [occ.] Kentucky Fried Chicken Counter Girl; [memb.] Faith Temple Church and Emannuel Lutheran Church; [hon.] Editor Choice Award '94-The National Library of Poetry; [oth. writ.] Poem Published in Local Newspaper in 3rd Grade and winter of 94 The National Library of Poetry Published my Poem Entitled "Beware" in Darkside of the Moon.; [pers.] The spirit itself beareth witness with our spirit, that we are the children of God: Romans 8:16; [a.] Longview, WA

WILSON, KERRY
[b.] July 16, 1968, New Castle, IN; [p.] Perry Wilson, Jereen Wilson; [m.] Randall Smith, (fiance); [ed.] Wayne Memorial High, Western Michigan University, Academy of Court Reporting; [occ.] Legal Assistant; [a.] Livonia, MI

WILSON, NANCY GRADY
[b.] December 27, 1939, Wayne County, NC; [p.] The late Needham B. Grady, Henrietta S. Grady; [m.] Snodie Bond Wilson, December 30, 1962; [ch.] Steven Bryan, Carolyn, and Gerald; [ed.] BF Grady High School, East Carolina College, Duke University; [occ.] Third Grade Teacher, Pink Hill Elem. School, Pink Hill, NC; [memb.] Wesley Chapel United Methodist Church, Beta Eta Chapter of ADK, NC Education Association, Eastern NC Council of the International Reading Association; [hon.] Valedictorian of High School Class, Alpha Delta Kappa, Served 4 years on NC Textbook Commission, Graduated Magna Cum Laude from East Carolina College, Received M. Ed. Degree from Duke University.; [oth. writ.] Poetry published in American Poetry Anthology, Great Poems of the Western World, Vol. II, New Dimensions, Cornucopia, Beta Eta Scroll; [pers.] I strive to reflect the love of God and his marvelous creation in my writing. I am grateful for the inspiration and wisdom of many writers, past and present, who have had a tremendous impact on my life.; [a.] Kenansville, NC

WILSON, PAUL E.
[pen.] Paul E. Wilson; [b.] August 5, 1939, Chesterville, ME; [p.] Herbert G. Wilson, Florence Alberta Wilson; [m.] Eda Harris Wilson, October 18, 1955; [ch.] Julie Ann Sienkiewicz, Mark Andrew Wilson and Paula Faith Wilson; [ed.] New Sharon School, New Sharon, ME; [occ.] Van Dorn Demag Plastic Mach. Div., (Load Person) Duncan, S.C.; [hon.] Over the years I have received several salesmanship awards from employers.; [oth. writ.] I have written a number of other poems, which I hope to have published in a book sometime soon.; [pers.] I feel I have a God given talent and feel inspired to cypress it in my poems about God, nature and mankind. Some of the poets whose works that I admire are Robert Frost, Carl Sandburg and Henry Reevs, Edgar Allan Poe; [a.] Grover, NC

WILSON, WILMA L.
[b.] May 14, 1920, Taunton, MA; [m.] Harvey W. Wilson Jr., April 24, 1948; [ch.] William, Patricia, Joanne, Margaret (deceased), Bonnie, Terri, James; [occ.] Housewife; [memb.] N Taunton Baptist Church, MADD (Mothers against Drunk Driving) Charity Donations, Special Olympics (disabled children) charity donations; [hon.] Honorable mention, Award of Merit Certificate for Poem - Washday Observations from World of Poetry Contest, Sacramento California; [oth. writ.] Several poems published in my local newspaper, The Taunton Daily Gazzette Awarded 1st prize for 1992, Valentine poem by my local Newspaper; [pers.] My poems reflect on my personal life, growing up on a country farm and the pleasure of leaving these precious memories to my family and future generations; [a.] Taunton, MA

WILSON JR., BOB
[b.] October 12, 1978, Schenectady, NY; [p.] Bob and Kim Wilson; [ed.] Christian Brothers Academy; [occ.] Student; [memb.] New Life Academy Youth Movement; [oth. writ.] Several, but have not been seen or submitted; [pers.] In my poems I strive to show the beauty and perfection of women. And I would like to dedicate my poem in this book to Christie Anne Wey.; [a.] Schenectady, NY

WILT, MARY JANA
[b.] November 30, 1918, Pennsylvania; [p.] Matthew Calvin and Helen Schmidt Calvin; [m.] William Wilt; [ch.] Four sons and daughter, seven grandsons; [ed.] High School - Lewis Hotel School, different writing and philosophy courses offered at close by colleges; [occ.] Retired; [memb.] Charles Town Presbyterian Church, Smithson van, Community Ministries, A.C.B.L.; [hon.] The great reward is life itself.; [oth. writ.] I've been writing poetry for 60 years. First I ever submitted any.; [pers.] I love life and God's beautiful world I want to be kind to all I write because I can not write.; [a.] Charles Town, WV

WINDHAM, MILDRED DEAN
[pen.] Denna; [b.] November 3, 1944, Laurel, MS; [p.] Robert and Mary Truett; [m.] Bill Windham (deceased in 1992) September 19, 1960; [ch.] 5 children, 4 grandsons; [ed.] Quit in the 6th grade, went back after 27 years and received my G-E-D; [occ.] Floral and Gift Shop; [memb.] SPA Chapbook, pass Christian, MS I had a small book, published, by "Spa Chopbook, and sold several copies. I hope to have another publication.; [hon.] Have won several awards through SPA chapbook. Also having a poem published in their anthology book. I have written over 100 poems.; [oth. writ.] Have written articles that appeared in our Laurel Leader call... and the impact which is a newspaper.; [pers.] If I have any talent I owe it to the Lord, he gives us the gifts he wants us to have.; [a.] Laurel, MS

WINDSOR, JOAN A.
[pen.] Ariel Jones; [b.] May 19, 1975, Brooklyn; [p.] Ms. Patricia Windsor; [ed.] Bishop Loughlin Memorial H.S., Long Island University - Brooklyn; [occ.] Student; [memb.] Long Island University Honors Program, University Honors Spectrum Magazine, Student Activities, Student Mentor Group.; [hon.] Recipient of Emigrant Savings Bank Scholarship Award; [oth. writ.] Proposal written and accepted for National Honors Collegiate Council.; [pers.] Never settling for less than what I put out is my goal of striving towards excellence. Putting my best foot forward allows me to keep reaching higher because the sky is my limit.; [a.] Brooklyn, NY

WINN, ELLAREE
[pen.] Ree Winn; [b.] January 17, 1925, Ben Hill, CO; [p.] Henry and Gertie Smith; [m.] Divorced, December 10, 1941; [ch.] 3 living, 1 deceased; [ed.] GED; [occ.] Retired Nurse; [hon.] Several Honorary Awards and Written Several eugoties of friends.; [pers.] I love to write poetry. But I usually write about life, memories,

love and the funny side of life; [a.] Fitzgerald, GA

WINSTON, BERNICE M.
[pen.] Denise Davis; [b.] November 22, 1933, Yazoo City, MS; [p.] Benny Winston, Margaret Winston-Harris; [ch.] Cheryl Excellent, Kim Owens, Two grandson's Sean Owens and Christopher; [ed.] Du Sable High School, Chicago, IL; [occ.] Retired; [memb.] Chatham Park Village, Co-op member and antioch Baptist Church.; [hon.] Awarded Monetary Award for one writing. Outstanding Secretarial Award during employment with U.S. Postal Service.; [oth. writ.] Several poems written, one of which was published in local newspaper at age 18.; [pers.] Life offers some happiness and oft times many disappointments. Reflections of both are within each poem I write. Personal Note: I write from the heart and experiences as opposed to the mind only.; [a.] Chicago, IL

WOKULUK, TINA ELISE
[b.] August 28, 1975; [p.] Anna and Harry Wokuluk; [ed.] Roseville High School; [pers.] I specially thank my friend Destalee for being a true friend.; [a.] Roseville, MI

WOLF, ANNE
[b.] January 16, 1951, Witchita, KS; [p.] Dennis and Jane Dullea; [m.] Michael E. Wolf, July 15, 1978; [ch.] Christopher, Brian, Allison; [ed.] B.S., Kansas Newman College, 1973, M.A. Psychology, Wichita State University, 1976; [occ.] Homemaker, Community Volunteer; [hon.] 1993 Volunteer of the year for VITAS Innovative Hospice Care, Dallas; [oth. writ.] Prose and poetry for personal interest and enjoyment; [a.] Carrollton, TX

WOLFE, MICAH L.
[b.] February 21, 1982, Ben Hill County; [p.] Larry and Rita Wolfe; [ed.] My mom home school me. I am in the seventh grade.; [memb.] I am a member of Westside Baptist Church. A member of the Royal Ambassadors and 4-H.; [oth. writ.] I have my own collections of poems in a book that I have.; [pers.] I want people to feel, and visualize my writing. My second grade teacher Eleasha Daniels inspired me to start writing and my Mom encouraged me to continue; [a.] Fitzgerald, GA

WOLFE, RACHAEL LEANN
[b.] December 29, 1979, England; [p.] Barbara and John Wolfe; [ed.] 9th grade; [hon.] Academic honor role; [oth. writ.] Together Forever, Never Say Never, One Day, A Single Tear, Yesterday... Today... and Tomorrow; [pers.] I wanted to say thank you to my mother and father and my best friend, Melissa, for supporting me all through my writing.; [a.] Waldorf, MD

WOOD, KATHLEEN
[pen.] Kathleen Wood; [b.] June 27, 1946, Morristown, NJ; [p.] Arthur F. and Blanche Ringwood; [ch.] Peter Shawn "Rocky" Doran; [ed.] Hatborn-Horsham H.S., B.S. West Chester State Univ., M.A. - U.H. Post Graduate at U.H., Doctoral Candidacy; [occ.] College Instructor, Communication Specialist; [memb.] International Society of Poets, Texas Junior College Teachers' Ass'n, Pasadena Little Theatre, Texas Gulf Coast Consortium Literary Arts Rep.; [hon.] Spirit of San Jacinto Award, 1990-1994, Honorary Sheriff's Deputy-Harris County, Letter of Commendation from various charities.; [oth. writ.] Poem: "Nicole Remembered", Poem in Journey of the Mind, Songs: "Renegade", "Avenger", "Ballad For Billy", Newsletters: Access, Vocare, and Cub Reporter.; [pers.] The Fine Arts must be protected and perpetuated for future generations. The freedom of self-expression artistically must be allowed and preserved.; [a.] Houston, TX

WOODARD, NICOLE
[b.] January 16, 1979, Trenton, NJ; [p.] Martha and David Woodard; [ed.] Sophomore at Sullivan High

School; [occ.] Student; [hon.] Academic Awards, TIP program, National Book of Who's Who, Music Awards, Young Authors Awards; [oth. writ.] 123 other unpublished poems, 24 unpublished song, and 2 unpublished short stories.; [pers.] "Feelings written on paper, jotted down in rhyme, To try to sort through the confusion from time to time. - from the poem poetry by me.; [a.] Shelburn, IN

WOODS, BEATRICE H.
[pen.] Bea Woods; [b.] July 31, 1919, Gassaway, WV; [p.] Mr. and Mrs. Cochie R. Stout; [m.] Paul N. Woods, February 5, 1938; [ch.] Kay, Jack and Shirley, Grandchildren 9; [ed.] High School, Gassaway, WV; [occ.] Retired; [memb.] Brimfield Church of God Kent Ohio; [hon.] My books are in several book stores - in "The Gift Shop-In" the WV State Capitol at Charleston WV my home state; [oth. writ.] A book "Roses and Thorns" published 1982 at McClain Printing Company Parsons, WV 2nd printing 1991 Books Available $6.00 EW.; [pers.] I write poems and short stories I plan to publish another book soon. Some poems and writings published in church papers - also in my home town - weekly news paper in Sutton WV and other's.

WOODS, KAREN L.
[b.] February 1, 1961, VA; [m.] Billy J. Woods; [ch.] 1 son Wakie Woods; [pers.] I write what I feel in my heart. About life and love.; [a.] Asheboro, NC

WOODSEN, RACHELLE MERIA
[pen.] Roach, Punkin; [b.] October 23, 1963, St. Louis; [p.] Barbara, Joesph Woodsen; [ed.] High School, GED Diploma; [occ.] Private Aid; [memb.] Bally Health Club, Sam's Club; [hon.] R.O.T.C., Perfect Attend., Honor Roll Student, C.P.R. Letter of commendation for helping to save a man's life in his 70's.; [pers.] I like to be myself in my poems. My poems are about some of my feelings and my life.; I feel very proud I almost gave up hope in ever writing a poem again. I just don't believe it. Thank God! Thank you!; [a.] Kansas, MO

WOOLARD, OLGA
[b.] August 2, 1955, Saint Joseph, MO; [p.] Gregory and Anna Kalamon; [m.] Stevey J. Woolard, November 17, 1989; [ch.] Shane A. Smith, Justin M. Smith; [ed.] 12 yrs. at Benton High School; [occ.] Mead Products going on 21 yrs.; [memb.] WIBC - Women International Bowling Congress; [hon.] 3rd place Ribbon in model car show.; [oth. writ.] Wrote poem's for family members in school for certain subjects. And they ace'd there poem's.; [pers.] I have always wanted a poem published. If this is possible that would be the greatest gift ever.; [a.] Saint Joseph, MO

WOOLSEY, ED H.
[ed.] B.A. University of Arizona; [occ.] Entrepreneur songwriter and poet; [hon.] Who's Who in California 1986 Department of U.S. Navy letter of appreciation "Desert Storm Poems"; [oth. writ.] 1995 Rainbow Records "There's a song in my heart, about Jesus" 1994 Hilltop Records, "When we celebrate at Christmas", CBS X'mas Special (TV) 1995, "Merry X'mas, Merry X'mas", and "We Know it's Xmas"; [pers.] Everything I see, hear, eat, love, etc., is a song or poem to me.; [a.] Sa Diego, CA

WRIGHT, ANGELA
[b.] July 9, 1972, Arkansas; [p.] Albert and July Wright; [ed.] Broken Arrow High School currently working on associate degree in accounting.; [occ.] Senior Group Coordinator Denticare of Oklahoma - Tulsa OK; [oth. writ.] Personal collection of poems and short stories. This is my first writing to be recognized and published.; [pers.] Reading poetry is a release from reality. Writing poetry is a form of personal growth to be shared with a reader.; [a.] Broken Arrow, OK

WRIGHT, RACHEL
[b.] January 3, 1981, Arlington, TX; [p.] Ron Wright, Lori Wright; [ed.] Student, 8th grade Worley Middle School; [occ.] Student; [memb.] Daughters of the Confederacy, Daughters of Union Veterans, Daughters of the American Revolution, National Junior Honor Society; [hon.] President's Award, member of Gifted and Talented Program, U.S. History Award, National; [oth. writ.] None published or submitted; [pers.] Poetry for me is one of the best relievers of stress. In losing myself in my writings, I am able to release my worries and tensions.; [a.] Arlington, TX

WURTS, CAROL G.
[pen.] Karol Maxwell; [b.] November 24, 1952, Raeford, NC; [p.] Dolores Mitchell - Mac and Nancy Glisson; [m.] Ted L. Wurts, August 7, 1993; [ch.] Angela and Michael Johnson; [ed.] Sonoma High, California, 5 Mos. College; [occ.] Housewife; [oth. writ.] Award of Merit 1990 Golden Poet 1991 - Plus a few others published.; [pers.] To always believe in something - no matter what it is.; [a.] Hendersonville, NC

WYCKOFF, NIKKI
[b.] September 9, 1978, Kendallville, IN; [p.] Don and Cheryl Wyckoff; [ed.] East Noble High School; [occ.] Student; [memb.] Dance Academy, School Dance Squad, Thespians, Drama Club; [hon.] Articles about poetry in local paper; [oth. writ.] Unpublished poems; [a.] Kendallville, IN

YABASH, KATRINA
[b.] September 15, 1954, Hilite, WI; [p.] Jo Ann Thomas and Bob Killick; [m.] Spinster; [ed.] High School diploma, Extensive Readings of EE Cummings and Roget's Thesaurus; [occ.] Retired Foreign Correspondent; [memb.] Lone wolf; [hon.] Journalism Award; [oth. writ.] Gossip Column; [pers.] I thank you E. E. for most this amazing work, for the thrumming charted squirts of verse and the kodacolor of imagery, and for every line which is oh my which is encore which is amen.; [a.] Overland Park, KS

YEBRA, CARRIE E.
[b.] August 21, 1981, Austin, TX; [p.] Wendy Smeltzer; [ed.] Now attending Marmaton Valley Jr. High - Moran, KS 7th grade; [pers.] I write what I feel.; [a.] Savonburg, KS

YERRO, TEODULFO T.
[b.] September 16, 1913, Philippines; [p.] Prudencio T. Yerro; [m.] Antonina M. Taluyo, November 29, 1935; [ch.] Teodulfo Jr., Jose, Lusviminda, Vicenta, Emily, Florence, Josephine, Franklin, Claire, Lynn, Faith, Gladys Hope; [ed.] P.N.S. Grad (E.T.C.), B.S.E., M.A minus thesis; [occ.] Retired; [memb.] Aklan Pub. Schools Teachers Asso., Phil. Pub. Schools Teas. Asso., Light of Agcawilan - Phil., East Val. Sr. Cit., International Society of Poets Golden Years Society; [hon.] 1. Graduated from the 7-year elementary grades in just five years, with one-half year in Grade IV, one-half year in Grade V, and 19 days in Grade VI. 2. Was dubbed "Poet Laureate" of the 4th year High School Class for having the first poem published in the school Journal. The same poem - "If Eyes, Then... "was included in an anthology which was published in Manila before WW II. 3. Awarded a Plaque as an outstanding school administrator upon retiring in 1976. While a District Supervisor, I was instrumental in making Kalibo Pilot Elementary School No. 1 in the whole Philippines. The school was a UNESCO AID recipient. 4. Received an Outstanding Aklanon Plaque for Arts (Poetry) in 1993. Aklan is my province of birth. 5. Received Golden Poet of The Year Trophies for seven consecutive years - 1986 to 1992 from the World of Poetry of Sacramento, CA. 6. Received two Plaques as an International Poet of Merit from the International Society of Poets for 1993 and 1994. 7. 14 poems earned 14 Award of Merit Certificates Honorable Rank from the World Of Poetry. 8. 5 poems earned 5 Editor's Choice Certificates from

The National Library of Poetry. 9. 1 poem earned one Gold Medallion from the Poetry Academy of Beverly Hills, CA in 1994. 10. Won a fifty-dollar award/prize at the Poet's Convention and Symposium in Washington, DC. in August 1994. 11. Included in Who's Who in Poetry Vols. II, III and IV.; [oth. writ.] 1. 6 short stories for children were published in Teacher's Magazines in Manila, Philippines. 2. Two articles were published with some poems in both English and Pilipino in Teacher's Magazines, Manila, Phil. 3. Numerous poems had been published by The Aklan Reporter, Aklan, Philippines. 4. Numerous poems had been published by the California Examiner, World Reporter, TM Weekly Herald of Los Angeles, California and of the Bernardi Multipurpose Center for Senior Citizens of Van Nuys, CA. 5. 5 poems were included in five anthologies published by Quill Books of Texas. 6. 8 poems are included in 8 anthologies published by the World of Poetry of Sacramento, CA. 7. 7 poems included in 7 anthologies published by the National Library of Poetry of Maryland. 8. 2 poems are included in 2 anthologies published by the Sparrowgrass Poetry Forum of WV. 9. Had a column for two years in The Aklan Reporter, a weekly Newspaper of Aklan, Philippines, entitled - As I See It.; [pers.] Poring over the pages of my life, I have come to deduce two conclusions: One is, whatever you do, the result is determined by the diligence and dedication you put into it. The second is, always assert your right and stand for whatever you think is the right thing, for right will always triumph. When I started teaching in the public schools, the first day I reported for duty to the District's Supervisor, I had some "hot" words with him. In later years, I clashed verbally with 3 of my school principals, with one more District Supervisor, and with two Division Superintendent of Schools, the highest official in the province. In two occasions, I had also exchanged some words with the famous politician in the province. But unbelievably, in spite of the prevailing ugly wind in the government system, I kept on climbing the ladder, so to say, so that from a classroom teacher I ended up as a Division or General Education Supervisor before I retired to prepare to come to this great country. I have always believed that one must only fear right and the Almighty!; [a.] North Hollywood, CA

YEWSHENKO, NATALIE L.
[b.] November 21, 1968, Somerville, NJ; [ed.] Marymount College Palos Verdes. Harvard University Summer Program.; [occ.] Jeweler; [hon.] Awarded a three year Summer Scholarship, Harvard University Awarded the Frances Lusardi, Scholarship for outstanding performance in Art.; [oth. writ.] Greeting cards sold at local stores.; [pers.] I have learned that so many of us are afraid to express our feelings. In the past five years I have had dreams, I have heard songs, I have read and I have written. I have come to understand that its ok to express, to share, to care, and to love. My writing is inspired by all who have left an impression on my life. Thank you Christy, Joe, Uncle Ady, Nicky, Karen and Bill, Mr. and Mrs. McCarthy, David and Andrew, and my best friend, my Mom.; [a.] Neshanic Station, NJ

YOGGERST, KAREN K.
[pen.] Karen Kaye; [b.] June 28, 1939, Concordia, KS; [p.] Olan and Mabel Salmon; [m.] David Yoggerst, February 13, 1960; [ch.] Donald L., Kenneth M., Scott D.; [ed.] Agenda High School - Agenda, KS, Brown-Macke School of Business Selina, KS; [occ.] Homemaker; [oth. writ.] I have written several poems. This is the first one I have sent away to be published.; [pers.] I try to put a story behind each one of my poems, some happy, some sad, but all with a special meaning.; [a.] Rockaway Beach, MO

YOUNG, ACE C.
[pen.] Ace Young/Lingual Bard; [b.] April 5, 1922, Reno, NV; [p.] Acy C. Young and Lillian B. Farrell; [m.] Olga Marie Reginato, May 8, 1942; [ch.] Brian, Forrest, Loa Lynn; [ed.] 12th Grade plus courses in

Aircraft Template, Electronics, Telephony, and Air conditioning; [occ.] Retired Telephone Supervisor and Instructor; [memb.] Elks Lodge and Masonic Lodge; [hon.] Previous work read on Kolo-Reno T.V. and published in 1994 Echoes of yesterday; [pers.] I have been writing poetry since age 12 and have a personal collection of 75 that I consider worthy of reading. Many of my works are in story form and are 6 to 10 pages in length.; [a.] Sacramento, CA

YOUNG, MARK E.
[b.] December 22, 1956, Plainview, TX; [p.] Raymond and Betty Young; [ch.] Evan Mark Young and Kellen Ray Young; [ed.] San Marcos High, Palomar Junior College; [occ.] Welding Contractor; [memb.] AMA; [pers.] To know and accept yourself for who you are is a great accomplishment. For everyday is a challenge dealing with our own minds and emotions, much less having to go out into society and be a part of all the other lives we touch and come in contact with. God be with us.; [a.] Temecula, CA

YOUNG, SOPHIA M. O.
[pen.] Melissa; [b.] December 14, 1982, Guyana, South Africa; [p.] Denise Miller and Christopher Young; [ed.] Grade School and Junior High, Museum School - P.S. 25, John Borroughs Jr. High; [occ.] Student; [memb.] Christian Organization (Church); [hon.] School Awards for outstanding performance in writing, hockey, basketball, art, etc. Outstanding Academic Awards received from school for reading, etc.; [oth. writ.] My Heart, The Night, Valentine, Non-Violence, Weapons, Equal; [pers.] I feel that poetry is a gift that few are blessed with and if you are one of the few that is blessed with this talent you should share it among others.

YOUNG, VIOLA M. SMITH
[pen.] Viola M. Young; [b.] December 3, 1913, Patterson, MO; [p.] Charles and Helen Kukal Wachal; [m.] Fowler A. Young (deceased), September 2, 1979; [ch.] F. A. Young, Martha Young Miller (step children); [ed.] B.S. Ed Southwest Missouri State University, graduate courses Univ. of Missouri; [occ.] Retired Home Economist Univ. Of Missouri; [memb.] First Baptist Church Twin City Garden Club - California, MO. Epsilon Sigma Phi - life member Cole Co Mo Historical Society Moniteau Co. Mo. Historical Society, Nat'l Audubon Society, Nat'l Assn Ret Fed Employees, Missouri Conservation Federation AARP, Missouri 4-H Alumni Assn, Missouri Univ. Alumni Assn.; [hon.] Univ. of MU Ext Assn Distinguished Ser 1970, Univ. of MU Ext Assn Meritorious Ser 1972, Certificate Senior Series MU 1991, Certificate of Appreciation MU 1979 for 33 years, Nat'l Assn Ext H.E. 1971; [oth. writ.] Monthly publication to 1000 Senior Citizens in 8 counties in Missouri for 3 years - news column "Violas Vittles"; [pers.] The world is so full of so many things, it's a shame to miss any of them. Young people are so exciting - senior people have so much to share, I love them all.; [a.] Columbia, MO

YOUNGBLOOD, MONTY L.
[ed.] Tarrant County Junior College, Assoc. of Arts - Psychology, Assoc. of Applied Science - Office Systems Technology.; [occ.] Federal Aviation Administration - SW Region; [pers.] Kepp writing and, sooner or later, you will get noticed.; [a.] Ft. Worth, TX

ZACAPA, EDWARD
[pen.] E. M. Zacapa; [b.] March 4, 1973, Santa Clara, CA; [p.] Maximiliano/Lavinia Zacapa; [ed.] Attending San Jose State University, attended Santa Clara High School, Journalism Major; [occ.] Journalist; [pers.] Follow the zeal in your heart and it will carry you aflight.; [a.] San Jose, CA

ZAMMIKIEL, SUSAN M.
[b.] 1970; [memb.] International Society of Poets; [hon.] Published In Spring "95" Anthology Journey of the Mind. Have been requested and read at Weddings,

Anniversaries, Funerals. Published in local newspaper (Memorial).; [oth. writ.] Types of Poetry: Christian - Christ centered, Love, Friendship, Inspirational, Wedding, Bereavement/Funeral Nature, etc. Styles of Poetry: Several. Constantly filling requests for Family and friends.; [pers.] Psalm 18:2 The Lord is my rock, and my fortress, and my deliverer, my God, my strength, in whom I will trust, my buckler, and the horn of my salvation, and my high tower. "Poetry is a Silent Song, every word is an instrument...S.M.Z."; [a.] White Plains, NY

ZAWALSKI, ROBERT C.
[b.] December 18, 1947, Herkimer, NY; [p.] Chester and Eleanor Zawalski; [m.] Mary Kelly Smith Zawalski, August, 1976; [ch.] Mary Jo; [ed.] HerKimer High School, Clarkson College of Technology -BS, University of Georgia - Ph.D Physical Organic Chemistry; [occ.] Industrial Research and Development Chemist; [memb.] American Chemical Society, former Peace Corps Volunteer, India (Science Teachers Workshop); [hon.] Several patents is "ozone friendly" Freon technology, awarded visiting Professional (Chemistry), at College of the Virgin Islands U.S.V.I. (1978); [oth. writ.] Recently published in local writer's league monthly, poetry performed for adult and children audiences (light verse read in local schools); [pers.] Much of my writing is in a humerus, whimsical style. I enjoy making people laugh, or at least smile involuntarily. Although life has its frustrating side, humor and beauty are never completely shadowed. Ogden Nash is one of my heroes.; [a.] Houston, TX

ZICKEL, MICHELLE LAUREN
[pen.] Michelle Zickel; [b.] November 27, 1982, Chicago, IL; [p.] Cynthia and Lawrence Zickel; [ed.] Briggs Elementary/Maquoketa, IA, MAQUOKETA MIDDLE SCHOOL/Maquoketa, IA, (1995 - 6th grade); [occ.] Student; [memb.] T.A.G. - Talented and Gifted 1991-1995, Student Council 1995, School Newspaper 1995; [hon.] 1994 - Presidential Academic Achievement Award, 1994 - Briggs Academic Excellence Award, 1995 - Honor Roll (Maquoketa Middle School); [oth. writ.] School Newspaper, Poetry - Local Newspaper; [pers.] I would like to say a "Special Thanks" to: Mom, Dad, Jacquelyn, Katlin, Grand Dad and Grandma, Thanks also to C.G. and A.B.; [a.] Maquoketa, IA

ZIEGLER, ELLEN
[b.] March 25, 1939, New City, NY; [ch.] Jordan, age 24, (medical student, won naval "Congressional Medal of Honor"), Wayne, age 32; [ed.] Jamaica High School, City University of NY., Ramapo College at New Jersey, Workshops with various well-known authors and editors.; [occ.] Writer/Artist; [memb.] IWWG (International Women's Writing Guild); [hon.] 1. 3rd prize nationally for "Family Circle's" "Christmas Poem of Year" 2. Honor and award for completion of "Writer's Digest" Fiction writing course 3. Honorable Mention - "Writer's Digest annual Short Story Contest. 4. 6 awards for lyrics in "Music City Song Festival" competition. 5. Top prize in FLA. State international short, short story contest.; [oth. writ.] Poetry, fiction, essays, articles, lyrics in top magazines and literary journals.; [pers.] "I wrote to strike a common, universal cord and to make sense of the world. I write because I can't picture not writing"; [a.] New City, NY

ZIMMER, JULIE ANN
[pen.] Julie A. Zimmer; [b.] May 01, 1980, Royal Oak, MI; [p.] David Rodney and Donna Bell; [ed.] Currently in High School, Marian High School, Seaholm High School; [occ.] Full time student; [memb.] USTA - Tennis; [hon.] Honor Roll at school 100% Science Meap Scores '94; [oth. writ.] Poetry: Waves "In Dusting off Dreams" "To My Friend" in; [pers.] Every decision you make is a step into the road of your life. Each little aspect in your lifetime may put you in a different direction. Choose wisely where you decide to step.; [a.] Birmingham, MI

ZIMMERER, JOSEPH
[b.] January 22, 1979, San Jose, CA; [p.] Druama and Phillip Childs; [ed.] Fred C. Beyer High School; [occ.] Student; [pers.] I see many people who try to obtain other peoples traits. Find yourself and when you do look beyond the norm!; [a.] Modesto, CA

ZIMMERMAN, GLENN A.
[b.] August 21, 1964, Chicago, IL; [p.] John and Elizabeth Zimmerman; [m.] Janice Zimmerman, February 22, 1992; [ed.] Gordon Technical High School; [occ.] HVAC-R Technician; [oth. writ.] Several poems yet to be submitted.; [pers.] Our destiny is inside of us. It is in our minds. All we have to do is search and find it.; [a.] Park Ridge, IL

ZIMMERMAN, LARRY H.
[pen.] Lzim; [b.] July 8, 1940, Allentown, PA; [p.] Alma Culp; [m.] Divorced; [ch.] Son: Bryan, (Grandson): Julian; [ed.] Allentown High School; [occ.] Salesman, W.S. Reichenbach and Son Inc. Allentown, PA; [oth. writ.] My heart lies in composing instrumental music in my home studio, where I find peace and happiness and a dash of inspiration.; [pers.] "Shining Eyes" was inspired by my aging golden retriever. My dream in life is to someday release my music to the world.; [a.] Allentown, PA

ZOE, THOMAS
[b.] July 18, 1957, Victoria, TX; [p.] Eugene Zoe and Margaret Powell; [ed.] 2 yrs Degree Mechanical Eng. Tech.; [occ.] Student at Davenport College of Business, As of Sept. 95; [memb.] International Society of Poets; [oth. writ.] Whispering spiders friendship and love both published with the N.L.P.; [pers.] My philosophy in life is patience, prayer and persistence; [a.] Grand Rapids, MI

ZONGKER, DAVID E.
[b.] October 17, 1949, Kingman, KS; [p.] Mother: Ruby E. Kee; [m.] Juana (Jaye) E. Zongker, December 15, 1979; [ch.] Elizabeth Anne, Thomas Esse, and David Esse Jr.; [ed.] Corona High, Palo Alto College; [occ.] Unit Steno for the state of Texas, San Antonio, Texas; [hon.] Several Military Awards, Dean's List; [oth. writ.] Several poems

ZOSSETT, SOPHIA A.
[pen.] Sophia A. Zossett; [b.] February 27, 1971, Detroit, MI; [pers.] Walk by faith and not by sight and you will crush your enemies while looking up to the heavens. And remember "Love is what love does."

ZUBIA, COREY
[pen.] CC Gemini; [b.] May 21, 1971, NM; [p.] Jesus and Rosetta; [ed.] Business Management Interest in Psychology; [occ.] Craftsman, Colorado; [oth. writ.] In process; [pers.] I long to pursue the love of my own life, never yet been released Only a reflection of my love's eye in fantasy. God Bless!; [a.] Loveland, CO

ZWOLINSKI, ROBYN
[b.] September 25, 1953, Providence, RI; [p.] Frank and Patricia McGuinn; [ch.] Kira and Frank Zwolinski; [ed.] B.A. Providence College; [occ.] Insurance adjuster; [a.] North Kingstown, RI

Brown, Donald W. 186
Brown, Gael 576
Brown, Heather 472
Brown, Jackie 597
Brown, James W. 20
Brown, Jane Capwell 481
Brown, Jennifer N. 155
Brown, Joe N. 643
Brown, Joey C. 615
Brown, Joni 690
Brown, Judy 404
Brown, Julia P. 43
Brown, Katherine 106
Brown, Linda Hurt 173
Brown, Margaret 100
Brown, Pauline Mixon 140
Brown, Pearl A. 90
Brown, Phyllis M. 104
Brown, Robert Jackson 427
Brown, Sabrina 231
Brown, Stephanie M. 515
Brown, Stuart L. 233
Brown, Theresa A. 220
Brown, Velma Lipe 393
Brown-Keith, Darlene 189
Browne, Maxine A. 284
Browning, Raymond 533
Browning, Robert M. 221
Brownstein, S. 103
Brozman, John Vincent 195
Brozowski, Al 636
Bruce, Glen 567
Bruce, Joya Lynn 656
Brumley, Erma J. 695
Brunelle, Robert 577
Bruner, Pamela 691
Brunet, Terina 511
Brunk, Diedre 607
Brunk, Jennifer L. 18
Brunson, Louise 687
Brunton, Arlene 604
Brustle, Janet 468
Bryan, Christopher 31
Bryl, Dolores 78
Bryson, Jennifer 204
Bryson, Mark 478
Buchanan, Kenrick 283
Buchmann, Peter J. 685
Buck, William Bret 236
Buckland, Rosie L. 704
Buckley, Ilena 348
Buckner, Debbie 619
Buder, Vicki 522
Budney, Alexander J. II 599
Buell, Valerie L. 525
Buendia, Gretchen 68
Buffington, Ginger J. 184
Buffington, Jan 169
Bulinski, Jean 555
Bull, Preston 209
Bullock, Joie L. 303
Bumgarner, Jacinda 343
Bunch, David W. 657
Bunch, Eldred E. 348
Bunch, Kelly 495
Bundrage, Linda 172
Bunk, Marilyn 93
Burch, Marti L. 309
Burgeson, Richard 537
Burgess, Deanne 661
Burget, Patti 689
Burkdorf, Rebecca 223

Burke, Michael 322
Burleson, Ruth 245
Burnett, Anita 352
Burnett, Mary A. 146
Burnette, Bill 329
Burney, Reubin E. 464
Burns, Eleanor 559
Burns, Mary 473
Burns, Rufus J. 391
Burnside, Kim 500
Burris, VaDella 241
Burrows, Chuck 678
Burtner, Michelle 503
Burton, H. T. 108
Burton, Hallie 200
Burton, Helen 669
Burton, Helen V. 221
Burton, Kenneth 323
Burton, Marilyn 294
Bushek, Teresa 389
Buss, Ron 215
Butler, Christine E. 188
Butler, Effie 338
Butler, Jason D. 121
Butler, Jennifer 195
Butler, Martha Penney 100
Butler, R. Helene 495
Butler, Susan 418
Butrim, Gabriel 609
Butterworth, Daniel Drew 209
Byerly, Dicy Hall 147
Byers, Krista Nicole 174
Byrd, Christy 337
Byrd, James W. 562
Byrd, Roy N. 518
Byrne, Henry 182
Byrne, Michelle Diane 263
Cada, Heather 371
Cadenhead, Andrea 703
Cady, Trendle 438
Cahill, Jessica 478
Cahill, Karen M. 94
Cahill, Tom 455
Cain, Christina 14
Cala, Santo Joseph 226
Calderon, Wilton C. 523
Caldwell, R. F. Bob 681
Caldwell, Shirley Dale 543
Caldwell, Tracy-Betina 585
Calhoun, Lynadese 82
Calhoun, Melissa 683
Calhoun-Medlock, Nancy 130
Cali, Beth 188
Caliri, Janice A. 371
Callahan, Brenda L. 676
Callander, Jaimie Lynn 634
Calvird, Gaynel 373
Camacho, Kay 505
Camarillo, Jessica A. 274
Cambry, Alfred 515
Cameron, Lisa 98
Camino, Jessica 384
Camp, Amone 355
Campanozzi, Chris 188
Campbell, John A. 469
Campbell, Joy 653
Campbell, Sally Douglass 438
Campbell, Steve 412
Campbell, Todd A. 225
Campello, Jason M. 102
Camper, Mark K. 96
Campoli, Robert A. 446

Campos, Fernando L. W. 605
Canales, Albert 661
Candelario, Robin M. 532
Canedy, Charlotte 10
Canfield, Lisa M. 473
Cangurel, Susan 211
Cano, Paul E. 163
Cansler, Alfreida Kay 204
Cantu, Juan 669
Capka, Jerry 89
Capko, Suzanne 531
Caples, Michelle 180
Caplin, Elliott 186
Capone, Ralph 517
Cappe Jr., Randolph D. 538
Capps, Jonathan 48
Caputo, Catherine Marie 603
Caputo, Michael 267
Card, Misti Devlin 310
Carden, Amy 332
Cardenas, Elsa M. 635
Cardey, Charlotte 574
Carey, Don C. 602
Carlo, Jana 193
Carlson, Carol 12
Carlson Jr., Philip C. 107
Carlyle, Susan 237
Carnright, Jack 269
Carpenter, Catherine P. 365
Carpenter, Elaine 373
Carpenter, Karen R. 277
Carpenter, Rosie Lene 420
Carpenter, Tomi 399
Carr, Charley 590
Carr, Trish L. 241
Carriger, Clarissa 15
Carrillo, Beatriz V. 55
Carrithers, Joe 637
Carroll, Crista S. 348
Carroll, Diana 76
Carroll, Emily Jane 206
Carroll, Robin M. 221
Carruthers, Rosie Lee 243
Carter, Allen Claude 21
Carter, B. J. 319
Carter, Deanna M. 576
Carter, Holly 350
Carter, L. Bernadette 315
Carter, Opal 120
Carter, Thelma J. 224
Cartwright, Beth 62
Caruana, Jeff 136
Carver, Antonetta 579
Cary, Toby D. 529
Cashion, Lila W. 491
Cassady, Mary Lou 304
Castellano, Rebecca 443
Castile, Marlena R. 299
Castillo, Jes 366
Castle, Tracy N. 522
Castleberry, Heather 143
Catania, Lee 300
Caton, Amity 623
Cattuna, Emily M. Harper 592
Caudle, Karen E. 153
Cauthen, Carolyn Rebecca 560
Cavallo, Orlando A. 494
Cavaluzzo, Mona 479
Cavoto, Caryn Anne 57
Cawley, Bonnie 661
Cawthon, Cristy 656
Cayless, F. Anthony 138

Caylor, Rebekah 514
Cerritelli, Jennifer 24
Cerulli, Jeanette 596
Chacon, Genny 31
Chaffey, Christine 342
Chagois, Cynthia C. 184
Chambers, Marjorie Harvey 172
Chambers, Norma Jones 94
Chambers, Ruth 442
Chancey, Velva M. 400
Chandawarkar, Aarti 570
Chang, Jenny 634
Chapin, Nancy Anne 501
Chaplin, Clair 377
Chapman, Dorothy 667
Chapman, Pam 489
Chappell, Avery L. 556
Chappell, Rodney 458
Chaput, Ethel M. 47
Charlson, Eric 9
Charnot, Angella 648
Chatman, Carolyn H. 677
Chavez, Laura M. 467
Chavez, Trudi 404
Chavis, Sandy 539
Cheek, Bria 370
Cheek, Bridget Lynn 196
Cheng, Judy 615
Chenier, Amy 328
Chevchuc, Carol 670
Chew, Jonathan 28
Chilcoat, Linda Gayle 690
Childs, Angelique M. 601
Childs, Jamie 693
Chiren, Christine 185
Chisholm, Ethel Marie 365
Chismark, Sandy 401
Chollet, Eileen Emily 197
Chong, Lehua 469
Chopdekar, Rajesh 403
Chrissos, George 621
Christensen, Colleen 196
Christie, Marlon 250
Christle, Marjorie L. 133
Christofferson, Virginia T. 213
Christopherson, Marie 160
Chryssis, George C. 329
Church, Jeannette 330
Churchill, Max W. 159
Cialkowski, Jo Santoro 22
Cihone, Casmer 659
Cillo, Edna E. 614
Cino, Jennifer M. 687
Ciora, Andrea J. 208
Ciotola, Cindy 668
Cirillo, Tony 453
Citizen, Robyn 448
Clapham, Katharine Rose 259
Clark, Cindy 328
Clark, Craig 586
Clark, Holly Lynn 625
Clark, James 208
Clark, Jill 659
Clark, Lin 153
Clark, Lloyd 481
Clark, Maria 163
Clark, Michelle D. 299
Clark, Patricia 295
Clark, Patricia L. 272
Clark, William E. 522
Clary, S. 483
Clauss, Mary E. 474

Heilman, Rita 541
Heim, David J. 34
Heim Sr., Tyrone 443
Heimbaugh, Donald J. 668
Heins, Hazel 330
Heintz, Emily 677
Heintz, Lindsay 191
Heinz, Cassie 393
Heitmann, Debra 660
Helbig, Isabel 668
Heldreth, Ruth 395
Helfrich, Bernice M. 366
Helfrich, Samantha 510
Helgesen, Charlene 343
Helmick, Melissa 508
Helms, Rebecca D. 240
Helton, Cynthia Dawn 11
Helton, Sherry A. 454
Hempfling, Christopher Alan 620
Hemphill, Robert 510
Hemphill, Robert F. 453
Henckler, Heather 567
Hendershot, Gary 611
Hendershot, Leroy-James 95
Henderson, D. L. 93
Henderson, Dillard (Dill) 328
Henderson, Teresa 439
Henderson, Wendy N. 422
Hendrick, Otelia Crawley 307
Hendrickson, Jean M. 184
Hendrix, Travis Lee 212
Henke, Anita 367
Henkel, Donald G. 64
Henley, Caroline 335
Henley, Elizabeth M. 170
Henning, Doug 73
Henriet, Richard G. 538
Henry, Angela L. 198
Henry, Diane M. 622
Henry, Douglas Duane Ware 328
Henry, Ella Mae 76
Henry, Kelly 147
Henry, Nina 160
Henry, Stephanie 457
Henschen, Carla 559
Hensel, Shane E. 529
Hensley, Gregory E. 664
Hensley-Parks, Lou 99
Henson, Ruby 222
Hepler, Mary L. 470
Heppner, Erin K. 668
Heremans, Hilde 573
Herget, Linda M. 256
Herman, Lena 319
Hernandez, Janette E. 636
Hernandez, Melinda Joleen 102
Hernandez, Rob 454
Hernandez, Star 227
Hernandez, Yianice 215
Herrera, Vanessa 462
Herrin, Jessica 673
Herring, Pamela 473
Herron, Kayci 121
Hershey, Mattie 492
Hertz, Julia T. 406
Hervey, Lois 502
Herzog, Diane 647
Hess, Carol J. 333
Hetfleisch, Cathy 33
Hetman, Ellie 386
Hettinger, Paul 264
Hewes, Shirley M. 232

Hewlett, Holly Dawn 311
Hickey, Charles K. 656
Hickey, Martha B. 161
Hickman, Gregory S. 677
Hicks, Billie LeAnn 624
Hicks, Vincent 219
Higgason, Debra 660
Higginbotham, Brian K. 664
Higgins, Jared 270
Higgins, Jeff 294
Higgins, John Tate 12
Higgins, Ruth 427
Higginson, Jeremy 549
Higham, Marilyn 684
Highfill, Dick 552
Higley, Carrie Louise 201
Hild, Loryn 164
Hileman, Alexis 381
Hill, Alice 565
Hill, Alice F. 583
Hill, Becky 339
Hill, Daniel P. 695
Hill, Eric Kiggen 694
Hill, Evelyne 609
Hill, Harold J. 615
Hill, Heather McMunn 293
Hill, J. M. 499
Hill, Lillian 133
Hill, Rufus S. 409
Hill, Shannon 511
Hill, Sherrie 216
Hill, Steve 419
Hill, Tara 398
Hillian, Annette P. 606
Hills, Tara 534
Hillsburg, Mark A. 480
Himber, Charlotte 637
Hinckley, Howard 700
Hines, Carl 553
Hines, Coletta M. 189
Hines, Michael 688
Hines, Randy 516
Hinman, Nicki 500
Hiscock, Patricia W. 95
Hitchings, Phillip Brian 300
Hites, Ruth 539
Hobbs, Gwen 202
Hobbs, Jimmy 470
Hobbs, Stephanie 448
Hodgdon, Kelly 102
Hodge, Jody Raelene 384
Hodge, Neisa 92
Hodges, James S. 581
Hodson, Glenda 359
Hoeft, James 136
Hoelzl, Danny 628
Hoffer, Aaron 583
Hoffman, Gillian 671
Hoffman, Kurt 166
Hoffmann, Leah 285
Hogberg, Lee 95
Holbrook, Eva K. 43
Holcomb, Kathleen M. 467
Holden, Maria 210
Holder, Catherine L. 30
Holder, J. 695
Holder, Jeanette 588, 683
Holder, William F. 226
Holladay, Courtney Lane 66
Holland, Carol 365
Holland, Hadidjah 698
Hollander, Angelic 678

Hollands, Tammie-Sue 529
Hollaway Sr., Eric H. 194
Holley, Christina 367
Holliday, Kimberly A. 157
Hollingsworth, Gloria M. 372
Hollingsworth, Ryan D. 210
Hollis, Kelley 142
Holloway, Allen 360
Holloway, Betty C. 554
Holm, Joel 73
Holmack, Larry 94
Holman, Shirley C. 533
Holmblad, Loretta 255
Holmes, Stella Princess 433
Holobowski, Beth 190
Holt, Kalan Jay 178
Holt, Violet 233
Holt-Spickerman, Karen 97
Holten, Rachel 518
Holton-Muller, Regina 444
Holtz, Edward 701
Honchar, Amy Kathleen 648
Honeycutt, Paul E. 324
Hoogland, James 20
Hooper, Mildred E. 108
Hoover, Chrissy 668
Hope, Katylyn T. 299
Hope, Minnie Lee 508
Hopfe, Lavinia R. 107
Hopkins, Jennifer 25
Hoppel, Ann Marie 662
Hopper, Elizabeth 694
Horewitch, Bill 692
Horn, Anita 663
Horn, Daniel 26
Horn, Rosemary B. 540
Horn, Sarah 492
Hornberger, Dennis 626
Horne, Delbert E. 385
Horner, Wanda 535
Hornung, Tonya 244
Horrigan, Steve 527
Horrocks, June R. 480
Horstman, Margaret Boyd 474
Hortenstine, Faye S. 347
Horton, Elizabeth 200
Horton, Hilda 86
Horton, Pam 86
Horvath, Amy 632
Hoskins, Patricia 164
Hoskins, Stephanie L. 473
Hotrum, April 550
Hotsinpiller, Judi 144
Houser, Adrienne 46
Houser, Eric 597
Houston, Linda R. 269
Hovatter, Benjamin A. 426
Howard, Berlene 21
Howard, Florence 71
Howard, Wanda 432
Howe, John Travis 630
Howe, Noelle 273
Howell, Beth 575
Howell, Kathryn Anne 172
Howell, Laura 104
Howell, William V. 434
Howes, Brian 72
Hradil Jr., John A. 359
Huang, Paul 162
Hubbard, Peg 269
Hubbard, Sunshine 530
Huber, George F. 572

Huber, Tonya 433
Huber-Huffman, Susan A. 527
Huckestein, Jon 67
Hudec, John W. 608
Huff, Jeanette Stamper 631
Huffman, Jessica Ray 652
Huffman, Margaret 162
Huffman, Mark 167
Huge, Robert Walter 524
Hugendubler, Barbara 568
Hugenroth, Phil 260
Hugger, Wanda 423
Hughes, Amanda 705
Hughes, Robin R. 543
Hughes, Stephanie 230
Hughes, Susan Lee 323
Hughes, Victoria A. 517
Hugley, Betty J. 570
Hulber, Jill 12
Hulsey, Christine 379
Human, T. 174
Humke, Denise 607
Humphrey, Jeanne M. 96
Hunley, Troy L. 394
Hunt, A. J. 268
Hunt, Grace Dupuis 197
Hunt, Gregory Alan 24
Hunter, Catherine 9
Hunter, John 629
Hunter, Katrina 468
Hurley, Nina A. 304
Hurley, Wynona 242
Hurtado, Angelica 190
Hussain, Quadir 261
Hutchison, James W. 364
Huth, Ellen C. 547
Hyde, Barbara 58
Hysell, Janet L. 5
Iacobacci, Giovanna 574
Iacona, Karla 250
Iagulli, Dorcela 678
Ialongo, Marisa 274
Iannarino, Timothy Jason 451
Ianni, Charlotte G. 693
Ignacio, Lawrie Ann 93
Ilahi, Amala S. 645
Iles, James W. 626
Iley, John R. 187
Ilkanic-Butler, Julie 328
Ingelli, Ellen 676
Ingledue, Jacquelyne 348
Inglesby III, Gerald A. 65
Inglett, Kate 114
Ingold, Karen 273
Ingram, Jaime L. 203
Inman, C. M. 320
Inman, Yvonne D. 245
Ioerger, Lindsay 319
Iovino, Annette 338
Ireland, Evelyn 370
Irizarry, Carolyn 668
Irwin, Gwen 602
Isaiah, Elwood Ogilvie 675
Isgur, David C. 202
Isola, Maria Ligons 147
Isom, Francine 579
Ison, Mollie J. 681
Israel, Jennifer 6
Ivanetich, Vel 521
Iverson, Dan 628
Ivey, Walter 237
Ivy, D. Granville 168

McGarry, Frances C. 108
McGee, Dorothea 195
McGee, Thomas Lee 534
McGhee, Toni 389
McGill, Patrick A. 680
McGill, Seán 587
McGinn, Janet L. 313
McGlothlin, Angela 584
McGlothlin, Pennie 138
McGranahan, Sean 544
McGrath, Courtney 49
McGraw, Charlotte A. 46
McGraw Jr., Glen K. 590
McGrew, Patrick 248
McGuffey, Jean 205
McGuigan III, Leo J. 141
McGuire, Tom 437
McIntire, Tessa 532
McIntyre, Renee S. 244
McKee, Beulah 370
McKee, Elaine 385
McKenna, Mathew Karl 317
McKenzie, Betty Ann 337
McKenzie, Bud 334
McKenzie, Mary Burton 288
McKinney, Edwin, Jr. 187
McKinney, Michelle E. 705
McKnight, Leonard A. 486
McKoy, Vernese Carter 511
McLain, Lonnie H. 115
McLauchlin, Delta 327
McLaughlin, Gregory Ellis 644
McLaughlin, Shari 216
McLeish, Michelle R. 486
McLendon, Keith 112
McMahan, Gloria 327
McMahon, Arleen 330
McManus, Roberta 524
McMichens, Kim 261
McMillan, Jean 82
McMullen, Tiffany A. 533
McMurtry, Leoda Maye 156
McNamara, Edward 107
McNamara, Thomas 419
McNeely, Tara 520
McNeil, Johnathan 358
McNeill, Daniel 195
McNish, Frances 19
McNutt, Monica 482
McVeigh, Jon 22
McWain Jr., Dorian Dale 352
McWilliams, Gerald 571
Meader, Kathleen 278
Meadows, Angelina 657
Meadows, Daniel C. 198
Mealey, Nichole 176
Means, Don 695
Mears, Shannon 534
Medford, John Allen 283
Medina, Cynthia 327
Medley, Sarah E. 240
Mefferd, Paige 307
Megrail, Beth 57
Meinhardt, Laura 185
Melin, Marguerite 468
Melton, Melissa 110
Melton, Mercedes 95
Melvin, Marc E. 486
Mena, Terri Rene 539
Mendez, Marina R. 274
Menefee, Sunshine 256
Meneses, Manuel M. 480

Mentzer, Denise 189
Meola, James P. 679
Merewether, Jack 657
Merila, Richard L. 406
Meriwether, Henning 101
Meriwether, Nell W. 490
Merrick, Ellen 693
Merrigan, Tina E. 222
Merrill, Donna 671
Merritt, Bertice Lee 3
Merritt, Tina 520
Mescall, Edward J. 660
Mesler, Marilane 151
Mesler, Micah 485
Messenger, May 295
Messina, Nicole 291
Metoxen, Sarah 446
Metz, Karen 214
Metze, Viveca L. 526
Metzenheim, August 696
Meyer, Deborah K. 617
Meyer, Jaymie 73
Meyerkorth, Lila 272
Meyers, Renee 522
Meyrer, Amy J. 593
Michaud, Melissa 94
Michelena, Rosa 394
Michieli, Mitchell 139
Michonski, Stanley 520
Midcap, David A. 41
Middlebrook, Bryan 12
Middleton, Delores M. 562
Midyett, Betty Jean 344
Mihailin, Tara 222
Mihalic, Catherine 70
Mihalic, Susan 420
Milam, Wyndi 544
Milavec, Rose 219
Miller, Aaron 337
Miller, Anne Whiting 104
Miller, Argie Jay 70
Miller, Betty 353
Miller, Brian 523
Miller, Chester H. 29
Miller, Craig A. 401
Miller, David E. 662
Miller, David Paul 3
Miller, Dion 654
Miller, E. Lenore 129
Miller, E. W. 294
Miller, Grace B. 137
Miller, Heather 622, 671
Miller, Joe 659
Miller Jr., Hervey J. 561
Miller, Lynn F. 273
Miller, O. Jeanne 174
Miller, Rebecca 704
Miller, Rebecca L. 396
Miller, Robert 538
Miller, Robert L. 227
Miller, Robert W. 542
Miller, Shirley 465
Miller, Tiffany 389
Millhouse, Dan 58
Mills, Joshua R. 601
Mills, Lacy A. 489
Mills, Robert A. 443
Milner, Joshua P. 105
Milota, Juliane 703
Milsten-Holder, Jennifer 628
Milton, Laura 88
Mines, Rosette 249

Minnis, Michelle 158
Minter, Kim 116
Minton, John W. 470
Minton, Kimberly 146
Mira, Taraneh 545
Miracle, Joan M. 113
Mirza, Sarah 224
Miska, William F. 438
Mitchell, Brooke 600
Mitchell, Diana 692
Mitchell, Eboney K. 636
Mitchell, Gary D. 667
Mitchell, Grace Carlin 569
Mitchell, Ingrid 163
Mitchell IV, Henry Lee 307
Mitchell, Ivory Jazz 204
Mitchell, K.E. 259
Mitchell, Mary Ann 146
Mittig, Patrick John 105
Mize, Rebecca L. 331
MJS-Held, Bri 22
Mobley Jr., Maurice C. 485
Mock, Dorothy J. 53
Moeckel, Emma K. 54
Moffet, Judy 605
Mogelson, Luke 150
Mogyordy, Paul L. 152
Mohacsy, Peter Andrew 681
Mohan, Edith 642
Mohl, Courtney Red-Horse 337
Mohr, Jerri J. 15
Molino, Maggie Magee 175
Mollura, Annette 591
Momcilovich, Kathryn 126
Monahan, Alice K. 702
Monday, Tim 527
Mondragon, Darcy L. 382
Money, Jo 355
Montanaro, Josh 328
Montpas, Andrea 49
Moody, Kelly 97
Moody, Lindsay 144
Moody, Lula V. 124
Moon, Brandi 662
Moore, Aimee R. 71
Moore, Barry 551
Moore, Christine 331
Moore, Donna B. 344
Moore, Hazel S. 379
Moore, Janice 300
Moore, Jason P. 548
Moore, Jo 348
Moore, John J. 47
Moore, Judith 488
Moore, Karac Chantell 150
Moore, Kay 135
Moore, Kevin 142
Moore, Laverne 88
Moore, Madeline 319
Moore, Marlayna 488
Moore, Ni-Kisha 691
Moore, Phyllis G. 285
Moore, Ryan 395
Moorshead, Amanda 20
Morales, Rachel 529
Moran, Tobitha R. 230
Morelli, Joseph Paul 95
Morgan, Carole 333
Morgan, Catherine 318
Morgan, Kelly 168
Moritzky, Andrea 206
Morrill, Niki 296

Morris, Dorothy 25
Morris, Frank 1, 585
Morris, Gael 676
Morris, John Christopher 689
Morris Jr., Robert L. 529
Morris, Marcia 289
Morris, McGuffy Ann 87
Morris, Michael P. 284
Morris, Robert 449
Morrison, Gregory S. 670
Morrison, Steven 521, 528
Morrison, Teresa 512
Morrison, Valerie 406
Morrissette, Amy 347
Morrow, John R. 377
Morse, Brian Allan 193
Morse, Mary A. A. 177
Morse, Sandra M. 222
Morton, Joseph 150
Moseley, Jennifer 329
Moselle, Kyle W. 260
Moser, Cheri R. 640
Moser, Golda 548
Moser, Katherine 127
Moser, Terri 228
Mosher, Raymond F. 511
Mosier, Carl B. 77
Moskoff, Miriam 146
Mosley, Andrea N. 338
Moss, Tamara J. 544
Mossey, Elizabeth D. 666
Mottola, Donna 15
Moughon, Metta L. 680
Mouton, Robert L. 523
Moya, Linda 101
Moyer, Alissa 677
Moyer, Lisa 488
Moyer, Michael 480
Moyo (Chimbumu), Ruth J. 232
Moysan, Melissa 679
Mozingo, Cynthia L. 338
Mudge, Steven Kubpatrick 444
Mueller, Kimberly R. 586
Mueller, Violet L. 246
Muhamedhan, Deena 32
Mullen, Millie 111
Mullens, Ella 74
Mullican, Derryl Rabb 567
Mullican, Loveta 117
Mundth, Bridget 66
Muñoz, Aurora 350
Munson, Rondalee 217
Murff, Donna 193
Muro, Edith 663
Murphy, Henry 621
Murphy, Kathleen Ann 129
Murphy, Krystal 118
Murphy, Lena L. 312
Murphy, Nancy 104
Murphy, Suzanne C. 512
Murphy, Thomas 246
Murray, Daniel J. 469
Murray, Donald W. 376
Murray, Joe 352
Murray, John 584
Murray, Mae 176
Murray, Robyn L. 513
Murrer, Laura 94
Murry Jr., Willie 432
Musarra, Cindy 670
Muse, Charles 47
Myers, Carrie Ann 610

White, LoNetta 473
White, Rosaland 428
White, Teresa 441
Whitehurst, Gabrielle 644
Whitehurst, Regina C. 448
Whitfield, Robert M. 535
Whiting, Honey 675
Whiting, Tracey L. 415
Whitmire, Bonita D. 344
Whitmore, Mark Cristopher 120
Whitmore, Robert J. 524
Whitsett, Amanda 340
Whitten, Brenda 79
Wichoski, Kenneth 477
Wickel, Sherry 515
Wickersham, Elizabeth C. 357
Wickham, Allan Gerard 343
Wictor, Mary R. 333
Widhalm, Wendy 540
Widner, Ayanna 201
Wieder, Nikki 109
Wiener, Rick 390
Wierschem, Christina 583
Wiesenmayer, Raymond 242
Wiggins, Adam 600
Wight, F. V. 170
Wight, Kathleen 691
Wikoff, Marian Brown 133
Wilburn, Jennifer 595
Wilce, John R. 343
Wilcox, Helen G. 36
Wilcox, Kelsi 483
Wiley, Arlene 327
Wiley, Leah K. 164
Wilford, Danese 629
Wilhelm, Gail 608
Wilkerson, David 560
Wilkerson, Richard J. 239
Wilkins, Christopher 368
Wilkins, Shawna 534
Wilkinson, Elizabeth Ann 631
Wilkinson, Jean Leistra 644
Wilkinson, Lori 311
Wilkinson, Shannon 541
Wilkovich, Greg 342
Willbanks, April 625
Willeford, Craig 579
Willhite, Roberta M. 228
Williams, B. Marie D. P. 281
Williams, Brooxie 48
Williams, Christine 335
Williams, Earle N. 68
Williams, Elwyn M. 602
Williams, Erica 203
Williams, Eythel 667
Williams II, Reginald L. 517
Williams, Iris 199
Williams, June Vanleer 341
Williams, Kevin 287
Williams, Laurie 106
Williams, M. Anthony 153
Williams, Margaret 128
Williams, Marie S. 102
Williams, Mark L. 477
Williams, Matthew 168
Williams, Meghan 290
Williams, Melody 101
Williams, Michelle 486
Williams, Ralph T. 524
Williams, Rebecca 518
Williams, Tangenicka 231
Williams, Velma Taylor 402

Williams, Virginia Holden 219
Williams, Willy 459
Williamson, Dewey E. 346
Williamson, James 380
Williamson, Jenny 673
Willingham, Daniel E. 45
Willingham, Linda H. 81
Willis, Charity Renae 612
Willis, Eliott C. 208
Wilowski, E. J., Jr. 96
Wilson, Berniece I. 372
Wilson, Clyde 596
Wilson, Diana 359
Wilson, Eileen D. 580
Wilson II, Herman 32
Wilson, Janice 349
Wilson Jr., Bob 364
Wilson, Judy A. 558
Wilson, Kellie R. 106
Wilson, Kerry 317
Wilson, Nancy Grady 111
Wilson, Paul E. 501
Wilson, R. Estelle 493
Wilson, Shawn 425
Wilson, Wanda J. 407
Wilson, William E. 229
Wilson, Wilma L. 400
Wilt, Mary Jane 477
Windham, Glenda J. 4
Windham, Jordan 297
Windham, Mildred D. 265
Windsor, Joan A. 679
Wineinger, Betty 619
Winkley, Cynthia Sue 365
Winkos, Debby 673
Winn, Ellaree 624
Winston, Bernice M. 697
Winters, Mark 477
Wire, Catie 333
Wirtz, Catherine Donelan 632
Wirtz, Peggy 93
Wise, Florence M. 24
Witek, Marsha 118
Withrow, Bonny 555
Witt, Amber 663
Witt, Mary Ann 179
Wittenberg, Paul 89
Wokuluk, Tina Elise 464
Wolf, Alfred 550
Wolf, Allen 664
Wolf, Lone 683
Wolf, Matthew F. 289
Wolf, Shadow 514
Wolfe, Donna 658
Wolfe, Ginger 587
Wolfe, Joe 630
Wolfe, Kelly 181
Wolfe, Micah 494
Wolfe, Patrice 469
Wolfe, Rachel 535
Wolford, Catherine Mary 197
Wolkenberg, Theresa 418
Won, Charles 327
Wood, Jamey 693
Woodard, John H. 115
Woodard, Nicole 132
Wooddell, Lisa 132
Woodley, Rebekka 406
Woods, Bea 326
Woods, Karen 113
Woods, Kelvin E. 170
Woodson, Rochelle 474

Woodward, Kevin 127
Woody, Anthony 631
Woolard, Olga 279
Woolsey, Ed H. 341
Woolsey, Jonathan 476
Workman, Linda L. 83
Wren, Leah A. 683
Wright, Angela 561
Wright, Charles D. 112
Wright, Diane 72
Wright, Dwanda 183
Wright, Margaret 126
Wright, Rachel 463
Wright, Renee 519
Wright-Overstreet, Barbara 327
Wroblewski II, James M. 568
Wurm, Virginia 212
Wurts, Carol Glisson 652
Wyckoff, Elaine K. 702
Wyckoff, Nikki 296
Wyczynski, Theodore 459
Wyrick, Dawn 647
Wysocki, Melissa 308
Wysocki, Yolanda 236
Yabash, Katrina 140
Yager Jr., Edwin H. 378
Yang, Kidd 254
Yanick, Karie 138
Yannayon, Margaret L. 255
Yarbrough, Misty Michelle 681
Yarnell, Rosie 434
Yates, Allen Louis 47
Yates, Everett Charles 366
Yates, Khristina Anna 487
Yeager, Diane E. 382
Yeager, Kristy 137
Yearby, LaShonda 298
Yell, Donna B. 61
Yelra, Carrie 344
Yerro, Teodulfo T. 429
Yewshenko, Natalie L. 495
Yip, Hang Ching 627
Yocum, Dee Ann Lynn 591
Yoder, Amy 368
Yoder, Rick J. 440
Yoggerst, Karen K. 119
Yonker, Corinne 628
York, Shirley 408
Yost, Rebecca 288
Young, Aaron 575
Young, Ace C. 16
Young, Darin 350
Young, Florence 75
Young, Gwendolyn 193
Young, Kara 169
Young, Louise E. 300
Young, Mark E. 96
Young, Mary Beth 131
Young, Robert Patrick 420
Young, Shannon 422
Young, Sophia M. O. 525
Young, Viola M. 523
Youngblood, Monty 475
Your Loving Son 465
Yousaf, Mohammad H. 471
Youtz, Angela 20
Yurek, Thomas E. 437
Zacapa, E. M. 324
Zaccanti, Maria 475
Zahra, Martin 157
Zalewski, Jared 131
Zammikiel, Susan M. 528

Zamora, Kerri 473
Zarek, Christopher 696
Zaremba, Elizabeth 27
Zasadny, John E. 549
Zastrow, Vickie L. 430
Zawalski, Robert C. 434
Zearing, Michelle 83
Zelman, Marvin 259
Zettlemoyer, K. B. 490
Zhan 45
Zickel, Michelle 690
Ziegler, Ellen 191
Zimmer, Julie A. 190
Zimmerer, Joseph 129
Zimmerly, Edith 20
Zimmerman, Betty 661
Zimmerman, Donna Marie 601
Zimmerman, Glenn 332
Zimmerman, Larry H. 283
Zimmerman, Shirlee 528
Zindulis, Holly 27
Zoe, Thomas 416
Zongker, David E. 591
Zubia, Corey 206
Zwolinski, Robyn O. 458